T H E
ESSENTIAL
EVERYDAY
BIBLE
COMMENTARY

THE
ESSENTIAL
EVERYDAY
BIBLE
COMMENTARY

with the complete text of the
New King James Version

Notes by
Warren W. Wiersbe

THOMAS NELSON PUBLISHERS

Nashville

Library of Congress Cataloging-in-Publication Data

Bible. English. New King James. 1993.
    The essential everyday Bible commentary : with the complete text of the New King James Version / notes by Warren W. Wiersbe.
    p. cm.
    "Also published under the title: With the word Bible commentary"— T.p. verso.
    ISBN 0-8407-3439-5 : $24.99
    1. Bible—Commentaries. I. Wiersbe, Warren W. II. Thomas Nelson Publishers. III. Title. IV. Title: With the word Bible commentary.
BS195.N38 1993
220.5'2037—dc20
               92–39931
               CIP

1 2 3 4 5 6 7 8 9 10 11 12 13 14 15—98 97 96 95 94 93

CONTENTS

CONTENTS

PREFACE

Purpose

In the preface to the 1611 edition, the translators of the Authorized Version, known popularly as the King James Bible, state that it was not their purpose "to make a new translation . . . but to make a good one better." Indebted to the earlier work of William Tyndale and others, they saw their best contribution to consist in revising and enhancing the excellence of the English versions which had sprung from the Reformation of the sixteenth century. In harmony with the purpose of the King James scholars, the translators and editors of the present work have not pursued a goal of innovation. They have perceived the Holy Bible, New King James Version, as a continuation of the labors of the earlier translators, thus unlocking for today's readers the spiritual treasures found especially in the Authorized Version of the Holy Scriptures.

A Living Legacy

For nearly four hundred years, and throughout several revisions of its English form, the King James Bible has been deeply revered among the English-speaking peoples of the world. The precision of translation for which it is historically renowned, and its majesty of style, have enabled that monumental version of the word of God to become the mainspring of the religion, language, and legal foundations of our civilization.

Although the Elizabethan period and our own era share in zeal for technical advance, the former period was more aggressively devoted to classical learning. Along with this awakened concern for the classics came a flourishing companion interest in the Scriptures, an interest that was enlivened by the conviction that the manuscripts were providentially handed down and were a trustworthy record of the inspired Word of God. The King James translators were committed to producing an English Bible that would be a precise translation, and by no means a paraphrase or a broadly approximate rendering. On the one hand, the scholars were almost as familiar with the original languages of the Bible as with their native English. On the other hand, their reverence for the divine Author and His Word assured a translation of the Scriptures in which only a principle of utmost accuracy could be accepted.

In 1786 Catholic scholar Alexander Geddes said of the King James Bible, "If accuracy and strictest attention to the letter of the text be supposed to constitute an excellent version, this is of all versions the most excellent." George Bernard Shaw became a literary legend in our century because of his severe and often humorous criticisms of our most cherished values. Surprisingly, however, Shaw pays the following tribute to the scholars commissioned by King James: "The translation was extraordinarily well done because to the translators what they were translating was not merely a curious collection of ancient books written by different authors in different stages of culture, but the Word of God divinely revealed through His chosen and expressly inspired scribes. In this conviction they carried out their work with boundless reverence and care and achieved a beautifully artistic result." History agrees with these estimates. Therefore, while seeking to unveil the excellent form of the traditional English Bible, special care has also been taken in the present edition to preserve the work of precision which is the legacy of the 1611 translators.

Complete Equivalence in Translation

Where new translation has been necessary in the New King James Version, the most complete representation of the original has been rendered by considering the history of usage and etymology of words in their contexts. This principle of complete equivalence seeks to preserve all of the information in the text, while presenting it in good literary form. Dynamic equivalence, a recent procedure in Bible translation, commonly results in paraphrasing where a more literal rendering is needed to reflect a specific and vital sense. For example, complete equivalence truly renders the original text in expressions such as "lifted her voice and wept" (Gen. 21:16); "I gave you cleanness of teeth" (Amos 4:6); "Jesus met them, saying, 'Rejoice!' " (Matt. 28:9); and " 'Woman, what does your concern have to do with Me?' " (John 2:4). Complete equivalence translates fully, in order to provide an English text that is both accurate and readable.

In keeping with the principle of complete equivalence, it is the policy to translate interjections which are commonly omitted in modern language renderings of the Bible. As an example, the interjection *behold*, in the older King James editions, continues to have a place in English usage, especially in dramatically calling attention to a spectacular scene, or an event of profound importance such as the Immanuel prophecy of Isaiah 7:14. Consequently, *behold* is retained for these occasions in the present edition. However, the Hebrew and Greek originals for this word can be translated variously, depending on the circumstances in the passage. Therefore, in addition to *behold*, words such as *indeed, look, see,* and *surely* are also rendered to convey the appropriate sense suggested by the context in each case.

In faithfulness to God and to our readers, it was deemed appropriate that all participating scholars sign a statement affirming their belief in the verbal and plenary inspiration of Scripture, and in the inerrancy of the original autographs.

Devotional Quality

The King James scholars readily appreciated the intrinsic beauty of divine revelation. They accordingly disciplined their talents to render well-chosen English words of their time, as well as a graceful, often musical arrangement of language, which has stirred the hearts of Bible readers through the years. The translators, the committees, and the editors of the present edition, while sensitive to the late-twentieth-century English idiom, and while adhering faithfully to the Hebrew, Aramaic, and Greek texts, have sought to maintain those lyrical and devotional qualities that are so highly regarded in the Authorized Version. This devotional quality is especially apparent in the poetic and prophetic books, although even the relatively plain style of the Gospels and Epistles cannot strictly be likened, as sometimes suggested, to modern newspaper style. The Koine Greek of the New Testament is influenced by the Hebrew background of the writers, for whom even the gospel narratives were not merely flat utterance, but often sung in various degrees of rhythm.

The Style

Students of the Bible applaud the timeless devotional character of our historic Bible. Yet it is also universally understood that our language, like all living languages, has undergone profound change since 1611. Subsequent revisions of the King James Bible have sought to keep abreast of changes in English speech. The present work is a further step toward this objective. Where obsolescence and other reading difficulties exist, present-day vocabulary, punctuation, and grammar have been carefully integrated. Words representing ancient objects, such as *chariot* and *phylactery*, have no modern substitutes and are therefore retained.

A special feature of the New King James Version is its conformity to the thought flow of the 1611 Bible. The reader discovers that the sequence and selection of words, phrases, and clauses of the new edition, while much clearer, are so close to the traditional that there is remarkable ease in listening to the reading of either edition while following with the other.

In the discipline of translating biblical and other ancient languages, a standard method of transliteration, that is, the English spelling of untranslated words, such as names of persons and places, has never been commonly adopted. In keeping with the design of the present work, the King James spelling of untranslated words is retained, although made uniform throughout. For example, instead of the spellings *Isaiah* and *Elijah* in the Old Testament, and *Esaias* and *Elias* in the New Testament, *Isaiah* and *Elijah* now appear in both Testaments.

King James doctrinal and theological terms, for example, *propitiation, justification,* and *sanctification,* are generally familiar to English-speaking peoples. Such terms have been retained except where the original language indicates need for a more precise translation.

Readers of the Authorized Version will immediately be struck by the absence of several pronouns: *thee, thou,* and *ye* are replaced by the simple *you,* while *your* and *yours* are substituted for *thy* and *thine* as applicable. *Thee, thou, thy* and *thine* were once forms of address to express a special relationship to human as well as divine persons. These pronouns are no longer part of our language. However, reverence for God in the present work is preserved by capitalizing pronouns, including *You, Your,* and *Yours,* which refer to Him. Additionally, capitalization of these pronouns benefits the reader by clearly distinguishing divine and human persons referred to in a passage. Without such capitalization the distinction is often obscure, because the antecedent of a pronoun is not always clear in the English translation.

In addition to the pronoun usages of the seventeenth century, the *-eth* and *-est* verb endings, so familiar in the earlier King James editions, are now obsolete. Unless a speaker is schooled in these verb endings, there is common difficulty in selecting the correct form to be used with a given subject of the verb in vocal prayer. That is, should we use *love, loveth,* or *lovest? do, doeth, doest,* or *dost? have, hath,* or *hast?* Because these forms are obsolete, contemporary English usage has been substituted for the previous verb endings.

In older editions of the King James Version, the frequency of the connective and far exceeded the limits of present English usage. Also, biblical linguists agree that the Hebrew and Greek original words for this conjunction may commonly be translated otherwise, depending on the immediate context. Therefore, instead of *and,* alternatives such as *also, but, however, now, so, then,* and *thus* are accordingly rendered in the present edition, when the original language permits.

The real character of the Authorized Version does not reside in its archaic pronouns or verbs or other grammatical forms of the seventeenth century, but rather in the care taken by its scholars to impart the letter and spirit of the original text in a majestic and reverent style.

The Format

The format of the New King James Version is designed to enhance the vividness and devotional quality of the Holy Scriptures:

- Words or phrases in italics indicate expressions in the original language which require clarification by additional English words, as also done throughout the history of the King James Bible.

- Oblique type in the New Testament indicates a quotation from the Old Testament.

- Prose is divided into paragraphs to indicate the structure of thought.

- Poetry is structured as contemporary verse to reflect the poetic form and beauty of the passage in the original language.

- The covenant name of God was usually translated from the Hebrew as "LORD" or "GOD" (using capital letters as shown) in the King James Old Testament. This tradition is maintained. In the present edition the name is so capitalized whenever the covenant name is quoted in the New Testament from a passage in the Old Testament.

The Old Testament Text

The Hebrew Bible has come down to us through the scrupulous care of ancient scribes who copied the original text in successive generations. By the sixth century A.D. the scribes were succeeded by a group known as the Masoretes, who continued to preserve the sacred Scriptures for another five hundred years in a form known as the Masoretic Text. Babylonia, Palestine, and Tiberias were the main centers of Masoretic activity; but by the tenth century A.D. the Masoretes of Tiberias, led by the family of ben Asher, gained the ascendancy. Through subsequent editions, the ben Asher text became in the twelfth century the only recognized form of the Hebrew Scriptures.

Daniel Bomberg printed the first Rabbinic Bible in 1516–17; that work was followed in 1524–25 by a second edition prepared by Jacob ben Chayyim and also published by Bomberg. The text of ben Chayyim was adopted in most subsequent Hebrew Bibles, including those used by the King James translators. The ben Chayyim text was also used for the first two editions of Rudolph Kittel's *Biblia Hebraica* of 1906 and 1912. In 1937 Paul Kahle published a third edition of *Biblia Hebraica*. This edition was based on the oldest dated manuscript of the ben Asher text, the Leningrad Manuscript B19a (A.D. 1008), which Kahle regarded as superior to that used by ben Chayyim.

For the New King James Version the text used was the 1967/1977 Stuttgart edition of the *Biblia Hebraica*, with frequent comparisons being made with the Bomberg edition of 1524–25. The Septuagint (Greek) Version of the Old Testament and the Latin Vulgate also were consulted. In addition to referring to a variety of ancient versions of the Hebrew Scriptures, the New King James Version draws on the resources of relevant manuscripts from the Dead Sea caves. In the few places where the Hebrew was so obscure that the 1611 King James was compelled to follow one of the versions, but where information is now available to resolve the problems, the New King James Version follows the Hebrew text.

The New Testament Text

There is more manuscript support for the New Testament than for any other body of ancient literature. Over five thousand Greek, eight thousand Latin, and many more manuscripts in other languages attest the integrity of the New Testament. There is only one basic New Testament used by Protestants, Roman Catholics, and Orthodox, by conservatives and liberals. Minor variations in hand copying have appeared through the centuries, before mechanical printing began about A.D. 1450.

Some variations exist in the spelling of Greek words, in word order, and in similar details. These ordinarily do not show up in translation and do not affect the sense of the text in any way.

Other manuscript differences such as omission or inclusion of a word or a clause, and two paragraphs in the Gospels, should not overshadow the overwhelming degree of agreement which exists among the ancient records. Bible readers may be assured that the most important differences in English New Testaments of today are due, not to manuscript divergence, but to the way in which translators view the task of translation: How literally should the text be rendered? How does the translator view the matter of biblical inspiration? Does the translator adopt a paraphrase when a literal rendering would be quite clear and more to the point? The New King James Version follows the historic precedent of the Authorized Version in maintaining a literal approach to translation, except where the idiom of the original language cannot be translated directly into our tongue.

The King James New Testament was based on the traditional text of the Greek-speaking churches, first published in 1516, and later called the Textus Receptus or Received Text. Although based on the relatively few available manuscripts, these were representative of many more which existed at the time but only became known later. In the late nineteenth century, B. Wescott and F. Hort taught that this text had been officially edited by the fourth-century church, but a total lack of historical evidence for this event has forced a revision of the theory. It is now widely held that the Byzantine Text that largely supports the Textus Receptus has as much right as the Alexandrian or any other tradition to be weighed in determining the text of the New Testament.

Since the 1880s most contemporary translations of the New Testament have relied upon a relatively few manuscripts discovered chiefly in the late nineteenth and early twentieth centuries. Such translations depend primarily on two manuscripts, Codex Vaticanus and Codex Sinaiticus, because of their greater age. The Greek text obtained by using these sources and the related papyri (our most ancient manuscripts) is known as the Alexandrian Text. However, some scholars have grounds for doubting the faithfulness of Vaticanus and Sinaiticus, since they often disagree with one another, and Sinaiticus exhibits excessive omission.

A third viewpoint of New Testament scholarship holds that the best text is based on the consensus of the majority of existing Greek manuscripts. This text is called the Majority Text. Most of these manuscripts are in substantial agreement. Even though many are late, and none is earlier than the fifth century, usually their readings are verified by papyri, ancient versions, quotations from the early church fathers, or a combination of these. The Majority Text is similar to the Textus Receptus, but it corrects those readings which have little or no support in the Greek manuscript tradition.

Today, scholars agree that the science of New Testament textual criticism is in a state of flux. Very few scholars still favor the Textus Receptus as such, and then often for its historical prestige as the text of Luther, Calvin, Tyndale, and the King James Version. For about a century most have followed a Critical Text (so called because it is edited according to specific principles of textual criticism) which depends heavily upon the Alexandrian type of text. More recently many have abandoned this Critical Text (which is quite similar to the one edited by Westcott and Hort) for one that is more eclectic. Finally, a small but growing number of scholars prefer the Majority Text, which is close to the traditional text except in the Revelation.

In light of these facts, and also because the New King James Version is the fifth revision of a historic document translated from specific Greek texts, the editors decided to retain the traditional text in the body of the New Testament and to indicate major Critical and Majority Text variant readings in the references. It is most important to emphasize that fully eighty-five percent of the New Testament text is the same in the Textus Receptus, the Alexandrian Text, and the Majority Text.

Textual Notes

Significant explanatory notes, alternate translations, and cross-references, as well as New Testament citations of Old Testament passages, are supplied in the textual notes listed at the bottom of the text column on each page.

Important textual variants in the Old Testament are identified in a standard form.

The textual notes in this edition make no evaluation of readings, but do clearly indicate the manuscript sources of readings. They objectively present the facts without such tendentious remarks as "the best manuscripts omit" or "the most reliable manuscripts read." Such notes are value judgments that differ according to varying viewpoints on the text. By giving a clearly defined set of variants, the New King James Version benefits readers of all textual persuasions.

Where significant variations occur in the New Testament Greek manuscripts, textual notes are classified as follows:

1. NU-Text

   These variations from the traditional text generally represent the Alexandrian or Egyptian type of text described previously in "The New Testament Text." They are found in the Critical Text published in the twenty-sixth edition of the Nestle-Aland Greek New Testament (N) and in the United Bible Societies' third edition (U), hence the acronym, "NU-Text."

2. M-Text

   This symbol indicates points of variation in the Majority Text from the traditional text, as also previously discussed in "The New Testament Text." It should be noted that M stands for whatever reading is printed in the published *Greek New Testament According to the Majority Text,* whether supported by overwhelming, strong, or only a divided majority textual tradition.

The textual notes reflect the scholarship of the past 150 years and will assist the reader to observe the variations between the different manuscript traditions of the New Testament. Such information is generally not available in English translations of the New Testament.

FOREWORD

The main purpose of this book is to assist you in discovering and applying some of the basic spiritual lessons found in Scripture. Where needed, explanations of difficult texts are given, but this is intended as more of a devotional commentary than an explanatory one.

The Bible is God's truth (John 17:17), and that truth is given on several "levels." The foundation is *historical truth*, the record of facts and words that involve real people and real events. From these facts we learn *doctrinal truth* concerning God, man, sin, salvation, and a host of other subjects. Of course, the end result must be *practical truth*, for we get God's blessing by *doing* His Word and not simply by *learning* it (James 1:22–25). Learning must lead to living.

The Bible was written for the heart as well as for the mind and the will, which is where *devotional truth* comes in. We use the Bible devotionally when we allow it to speak to us personally as we are taught by the Spirit of God (John 14:26; 15:26; 16:13–15). All Scripture was not written *to* us, but it was written *for* us (2 Tim. 3:16–17); and it can enlighten, enable, enrich, and encourage us if we will only let it.

Charles Haddon Spurgeon, the famous British preacher, said, "No Scripture is of private interpretation: no text has spent itself upon the person who first received it. God's comforts are like wells, which no one man or set of men can drain dry, however mightily may be their thirst."

When we read the Bible devotionally, we focus on the spiritual essentials, not the historical or geographical accidentals. God has often encouraged me from the first chapter of Joshua, but this does not mean I can walk into the Jordan River and expect it to open up before me. However, I have seen Him "open up" difficult situations in ministry as I have trusted Him.

The Word of God is given to warn us (1 Cor. 10:1–12) and to offer hope to us (Rom. 15:4). It can do these things for us only if we receive the Word personally and let it work in our lives (1 Thess. 2:13).

Christian biography is filled with examples of God's "speaking" to His servants from the Word and giving them just the truth they needed for making hard decisions or facing difficult challenges. My wife and I have experienced this in our ministry. God has revealed His mind to us at just the right time through a portion of Scripture that was part of our regular daily reading. People who "just open the Bible anywhere" and ask for help are turning God's Word into a magic book and are tempting God, not trusting Him.

A word of caution here: we must be very careful of saying, "God told me to do this." God does not address us today as He did Moses and Joshua and Paul. It is far better to say, "This is what the Spirit revealed to me from the Word, and I'm praying about what God wants me to do." After all, Satan also knows how to use the Bible (Matt. 4:5–7). "It is written" must be balanced by "*Again* it is written."

If you want to get the most out of this book, I suggest that you do the following:

1. Have a program for reading the Bible, a definite time and place and a schedule to follow. Random Bible reading is better than no reading at all, but it is rarely edifying.
2. Read the Bible passage first, asking the Spirit to instruct you. Think about it and seek the truths God has for you.
3. Read the devotional comments. Think about them, and assimilate whatever truths God impresses on your heart.
4. Trace the cross-references. Compare Scripture with Scripture, and see how one passage sheds light on another.
5. Pray the truth into your inner being, and ask the Spirit to help you put it into practice. True Bible knowledge, properly assimilated, will lead to a "burning heart" that wants to obey (Luke 24:32) and not to a "big head" that wants to show off (1 Cor. 8:1).

In addition to my cross references and comments, some of the Bible verses which contain important biblical truths or which have been discussed in the notes have been highlighted. This should make them easier to find, and is intended to help you in your study and meditation on God's Word.

To benefit from this book, you do not have to agree with everything I have written. My comments on the Word are not the meal; they are the menu that describes the meal. They are not the road but signal lights that help point the way. If any devotional material ever takes the place of your own meditation on the Bible, you will cease to grow. Bible knowledge alone is not spiritual nutrition.

I have been reading the Bible faithfully ever since I became a Christian in 1945. Many of my comments have come from the material that I wrote in notebooks I have kept for the past twenty years. When my good friend Dr. Victor Oliver suggested that I write a devotional commentary, I had the opportunity to examine those notebooks again and "mine" from them the truths that I thought would help fellow pilgrims on the path of life. At least they have helped me, and for this, I am grateful to the Lord.

—Warren W. Wiersbe

THE
OLD TESTAMENT

GENESIS

Genesis is a book of *beginnings:* creation (chap. 1); human history, including marriage (chap. 2); sin and death (chap. 3); the promise of the Redeemer (3:15); human civilization (4:16ff.); Babylon (chap. 11); and the Jewish nation (chap. 12). Things that start in Genesis are carried through the Bible narrative and are fulfilled in the book of Revelation.

It is a book of *begetting,* describing the family tree from Adam to the founding of the nation of Israel. Ten different genealogies are recorded in Genesis. The account focuses on six persons and their families: Adam (chaps. 1—5); Noah (chaps. 6—10); Abraham (chaps. 11:1—25:18); Isaac (chaps. 25:19—27:46); Jacob (chaps. 28—36); and Joseph (chaps. 37—50). These genealogies may be boring to us, but they are important for tracing the Redeemer's ancestry.

It is a book of *believing.* Noah believed God and built an ark. Abraham believed God and left home for the Promised Land. Abraham and Sarah believed God, and He gave them a son. God gave His promises and then acted on behalf of those who trusted Him, just as He does today. (See Heb. 11:1–22.)

It is a book of *becoming.* God patiently worked with His people to make them what He wanted them to be. They failed Him often, but God did not give up on them. He is still the God of Abraham, Isaac, and Jacob, and He can accomplish in your life all that He has planned for you.

1 In* the beginning God created the heavens and the earth. ²The earth was without form, and void; and darkness *was*ᵃ on the face of the deep. And the Spirit of God was hovering over the face of the waters.

³*Then God said, "Let there be light"; and there was light. ⁴And God saw the light, that *it was* good; and God divided the light from the darkness. ⁵*God called the light Day, and the darkness He called Night. So the evening and the morning were the first day.

⁶Then God said, "Let there be a firmament in the midst of the waters, and let it divide the waters from the waters." ⁷*Thus God made the firmament, and divided the waters which *were* under the firmament from the waters which *were* above the firmament; and it was so. ⁸And God called the firmament Heaven. So the evening and the morning were the second day.

⁹Then God said, "Let the waters under the heavens be gathered together into one place, and let the dry *land* appear"; and it was so. ¹⁰And God called the dry *land* Earth, and the gathering together of the waters He called Seas. And God saw that *it was* good.

¹¹Then God said, "Let the earth bring forth grass, the herb *that* yields seed, *and* the fruit tree *that* yields fruit according to its kind, whose seed *is* in itself, on the earth"; and it was so. ¹²And the earth brought forth grass, the herb *that* yields seed according to its kind, and the tree *that* yields fruit, whose seed *is* in itself according to its kind. And God saw that *it was* good. ¹³So the evening and the morning were the third day.

1:2 ᵃWords in italic type have been added for clarity. They are not found in the original Hebrew or Aramaic.

CHAPTER 1

1:1ff We are conscious every day of the visible world around us. We need to remember that this world speaks to us of God, His existence, His wisdom, and His power (Rom. 1:20; Ps. 19:1–3).

1:3 *God creates.* Everything begins with God and fulfills His purposes for His glory (Col. 1:16–17; Rev. 4:11). He works by the power of His Word (Ps. 33:6–9), the same Word that can work in our lives (1 Thess. 2:13). He works according to a plan: first He forms, then He fills. He formed the earth and filled it with plants and animals. He formed the firmament and filled it with stars and planets. He formed the seas and filled them with living creatures. He can form and fill our lives today if we will yield to Him. Persons who have trusted Jesus Christ are a part of the new creation (2 Cor. 4:6; 5:17; Eph. 2:8–10).

1:5 *God names.* He named what He made, and we have no right to make changes: "Woe to those who call evil good, and good evil; who put darkness for light, and light for darkness" (Isa. 5:20). God calls things by their right names; if we use His vocabulary, we must also use His dictionary. (See Prov. 17:15.)

1:7 *God divides.* He separated the light from the darkness, the dry land from the waters, and the waters above from the waters beneath. This principle of separation

(continued)

(continued from previous page)
is basic in all the Bible: He separated Abraham from Ur, the nation of Israel from the Gentiles, His church from the world (John 17:14–16). He wants His people today to be separated from all that defiles (2 Cor. 6:14—7:1).

1:28 *God blesses.* The first man and woman were the only part of creation especially blessed by God. Because we are created in the image of God, we are different from the other creatures God has made, and we must be careful how we treat one another (Gen. 9:6; James 3:9). Sin has marred that divine image, but one day all true believers will bear the image of Christ (Rom. 8:29). The more we are like Christ, the more we will enjoy His blessing (2 Cor. 3:18).

CHAPTER 2

2:1ff Now we are given the details concerning the creation of man and woman and their place in God's plan. The account does not contradict chapter 1; it complements it. We see the man involved in several activities.

2:2, 3 *Resting.* God's rest was the rest of completion, not the rest of exhaustion, for God never gets weary (Ps. 121:4). Adam must have rested also, fellowshiped with the Lord, and worshiped Him. The seventh day, the Sabbath, became a sign to Israel that they were God's special people (Exod. 31:13–17). It is also a symbol of the eternal rest God's people will have with Him (Heb. 4:9–11).

¹⁴Then God said, "Let there be lights in the firmament of the heavens to divide the day from the night; and let them be for signs and seasons, and for days and years; ¹⁵and let them be for lights in the firmament of the heavens to give light on the earth"; and it was so. ¹⁶Then God made two great lights: the greater light to rule the day, and the lesser light to rule the night. *He made* the stars also. ¹⁷God set them in the firmament of the heavens to give light on the earth, ¹⁸and to rule over the day and over the night, and to divide the light from the darkness. And God saw that *it was* good. ¹⁹So the evening and the morning were the fourth day.

²⁰Then God said, "Let the waters abound with an abundance of living creatures, and let birds fly above the earth across the face of the firmament of the heavens." ²¹So God created great sea creatures and every living thing that moves, with which the waters abounded, according to their kind, and every winged bird according to its kind. And God saw that *it was* good. ²²And God blessed them, saying, "Be fruitful and multiply, and fill the waters in the seas, and let birds multiply on the earth." ²³So the evening and the morning were the fifth day.

²⁴Then God said, "Let the earth bring forth the living creature according to its kind: cattle and creeping thing and beast of the earth, *each* according to its kind"; and it was so. ²⁵And God made the beast of the earth according to its kind, cattle according to its kind, and everything that creeps on the earth according to its kind. And God saw that *it was* good.

²⁶Then God said, "Let Us make man in Our image, according to Our likeness; let them have dominion over the fish of the sea, over the birds of the air, and over the cattle, over all*ᵇ* the earth and over every creeping thing that creeps on the earth." ²⁷So God created man in His *own* image; in the image of God He created him; male and female He created them. ²⁸*Then God blessed them, and God said to them, "Be fruitful and multiply; fill the earth and subdue it; have dominion over the fish of the sea, over the birds of the air, and over every living thing that moves on the earth."

²⁹And God said, "See, I have given you every herb *that* yields seed which *is* on the face of all the earth, and every tree whose fruit yields seed; to you it shall be for food. ³⁰Also, to every beast of the earth, to every bird of the air, and to everything that creeps on the earth, in which *there is* life, *I have given* every green herb for food"; and it was so. ³¹Then God saw everything that He had made, and indeed *it was* very good. So the evening and the morning were the sixth day.

2 Thus* the heavens and the earth, and all the host of them, were finished. ²*And on the seventh day God ended His work which He had done, and He rested on the seventh day from all His work which He had done. ³Then God blessed the seventh day and sanctified it, because in it He rested from all His work which God had created and made.

1:26 *ᵇ*Syriac reads *all the wild animals of.* 2:4 *ᶜ*Hebrew *toledoth,* literally *generations*

4*This *is* the history^c of the heavens and the earth when they were created, in the day that the LORD God made the earth and the heavens, 5before any plant of the field was in the earth and before any herb of the field had grown. For the LORD God had not caused it to rain on the earth, and *there was* no man to till the ground; 6but a mist went up from the earth and watered the whole face of the ground.

7And the LORD God formed man *of* the dust of the ground, and breathed into his nostrils the breath of life; and man became a living being.

8The LORD God planted a garden eastward in Eden, and there He put the man whom He had formed. 9And out of the ground the LORD God made every tree grow that is pleasant to the sight and good for food. The tree of life *was* also in the midst of the garden, and the tree of the knowledge of good and evil.

10Now a river went out of Eden to water the garden, and from there it parted and became four riverheads. 11The name of the first *is* Pishon; it *is* the one which skirts the whole land of Havilah, where *there is* gold. 12And the gold of that land *is* good. Bdellium and the onyx stone *are* there. 13The name of the second river *is* Gihon; it *is* the one which goes around the whole land of Cush. 14The name of the third river *is* Hiddekel;^d it *is* the one which goes toward the east of Assyria. The fourth river *is* the Euphrates.

15*Then the LORD God took the man and put him in the garden of Eden to tend and keep it. 16*And the LORD God commanded the man, saying, "Of every tree of the garden you may freely eat; 17but of the tree of the knowledge of good and evil you shall not eat, for in the day that you eat of it you shall surely die."

18*And the LORD God said, "*It is* not good that man should be alone; I will make him a helper comparable to him." 19Out of the ground the LORD God formed every beast of the field and every bird of the air, and brought *them* to Adam to see what he would call them. And whatever Adam called each living creature, that *was* its name. 20So Adam gave names to all cattle, to the birds of the air, and to every beast of the field. But for Adam there was not found a helper comparable to him.

21And the LORD God caused a deep sleep to fall on Adam, and he slept; and He took one of his ribs, and closed up the flesh in its place. 22Then the rib which the LORD God had taken from man He made into a woman, and He brought her to the man.

23*And Adam said:

"This *is* now bone of my bones
And flesh of my flesh;
She shall be called Woman,
Because she was taken out of Man."

24Therefore a man shall leave his father and mother and be joined to his wife, and they shall become one flesh. 25And they were both naked, the man and his wife, and were not ashamed.

2:4, 8 Working. Rest and work must be in balance. Human history involves three gardens: the Garden of Eden, where man took of the tree and sinned; the Garden of Gethsemane, where the Savior took the cup and went to the tree to die for our sins; and the "garden city" of glory where God will take all His children to live forever (Rev. 21—22).

2:15 Work is not a curse. God gave Adam the task of guarding the Garden and tilling it. It was a fulfilling ministry for him. Man and God must work together to produce the harvest. St. Augustine said, "Pray as though everything depended on God, and work as though everything depended on you."

2:16, 17 Submitting. The Creator has the right to govern His creatures. Love sets limits for the good of man. God calls us to obey Him because we want to, not because we have to. He wants children, not machines. Note especially the word *freely* in verse 16.

2:18, 20 Naming. Man's naming the animals was a part of his "dominion" as the head of creation (1:26–28). He lost this dominion because of sin (Ps. 8), but we have regained it through Christ (Heb. 2:5ff.).

2:23 Adam also named his mate; he called her "Woman." Later, he would call her "Eve." God established marriage to meet man's need for companionship (2:18) and to provide for the rearing of children (1:28). In addition it served as a picture of Christ and His church (Eph. 5:25–32). Adam gave of himself for his bride, and Jesus gave of Himself for His bride (John 19:31–37).

2:14 ^dOr *Tigris*

CHAPTER 3

3:1–6 *The voice of deception.* Up to this point, God's word is the only word that has been at work, creating and commanding. Now another "word" enters the scene, the word of Satan, the deceiver. He is a serpent that deceives (2 Cor. 11:1–3), a liar, and a murderer (John 8:44). He questioned God's word and God's goodness (v. 1), denied God's warning (v. 4), and then substituted a lie for God's truth (v. 5). "You will be like God" is his master lie (Isa. 14:12–14; Rom. 1:21–25), and people still believe it.

3:6 Eve was deceived when she ate, but Adam was not; he sinned with his eyes wide open (1 Tim. 2:14). He would rather forfeit his dominion than be separated from his wife.

3:8 *The voice of love.* Guilt produces fear, and fear makes us want to run and hide. Ordinarily, Adam and Eve would have run to meet God, but they had become sinners (Rom. 3:10–12). Sinners cannot cover their sins by their own works, nor can they hide from God.

3:9 The Father sought the lost sinners, as Jesus did when He was on earth (Luke 19:10), and as the Holy Spirit does today through His people (Acts 8:29ff.). God wants to use *us* to call men and women to salvation (Acts 1:8).

3:14–19 *The voice of judgment.* God cursed the serpent and the ground, but He did not curse Adam and Eve. The consequences of man's fall are all around us, and we suffer because of them. The ultimate judgment is death. Man can overcome a difficult environment to some extent, but he can do nothing about "the last enemy," death (1 Cor. 15:26). His only victory over death is through faith in Jesus Christ (John 11:25–26; 1 Cor. 15:57–58).

3:15 *The voice of grace.* In verse 15, God declared war on Satan and gave the first promise of the Redeemer. Satan would bruise Christ's heel, but Christ would bruise Satan's head and defeat him (John 12:31; Col. 2:15).

3 Now* the serpent was more cunning than any beast of the field which the LORD God had made. And he said to the woman, "Has God indeed said, 'You shall not eat of every tree of the garden'?"

2And the woman said to the serpent, "We may eat the fruit of the trees of the garden; 3but of the fruit of the tree which *is* in the midst of the garden, God has said, 'You shall not eat it, nor shall you touch it, lest you die.' "

4Then the serpent said to the woman, "You will not surely die. 5For God knows that in the day you eat of it your eyes will be opened, and you will be like God, knowing good and evil."

6*So when the woman saw that the tree *was* good for food, that it *was* pleasant to the eyes, and a tree desirable to make *one* wise, she took of its fruit and ate. She also gave to her husband with her, and he ate. 7Then the eyes of both of them were opened, and they knew that they *were* naked; and they sewed fig leaves together and made themselves coverings.

8*And they heard the sound of the LORD God walking in the garden in the cool of the day, and Adam and his wife hid themselves from the presence of the LORD God among the trees of the garden.

9*Then the LORD God called to Adam and said to him, "Where *are* you?"

10So he said, "I heard Your voice in the garden, and I was afraid because I was naked; and I hid myself."

11And He said, "Who told you that you *were* naked? Have you eaten from the tree of which I commanded you that you should not eat?"

12Then the man said, "The woman whom You gave *to be* with me, she gave me of the tree, and I ate."

13And the LORD God said to the woman, "What *is* this you have done?"

The woman said, "The serpent deceived me, and I ate."

14*So the LORD God said to the serpent:

"Because you have done this,
You *are* cursed more than all cattle,
And more than every beast of the field;
On your belly you shall go,
And you shall eat dust
All the days of your life.
15 *And I will put enmity
Between you and the woman,
And between your seed and her Seed;
He shall bruise your head,
And you shall bruise His heel."

16To the woman He said:

"I will greatly multiply your sorrow and your conception;
In pain you shall bring forth children;
Your desire *shall be* for your husband,
And he shall rule over you."

17Then to Adam He said, "Because you have heeded the voice of your wife, and have eaten

Overcoming Temptation—God tests us to bring out the best in us, but Satan tempts us to bring out the worst in us (James 1:1–15). Satan "baits the hook" with what seems good, and we take the bait and end up doing something bad. We can overcome the tempter by having faith and putting on the armor God provides (Eph. 6:10–18), by using the Word of God, by praying, by trusting God for the way of escape (1 Cor. 10:13), and by depending on the power of the Spirit.

from the tree of which I commanded you, saying,
'You shall not eat of it':

> "Cursed *is* the ground for your sake;
> In toil you shall eat *of* it
> All the days of your life.
> 18 Both thorns and thistles it shall bring forth
>   for you,
> And you shall eat the herb of the field.
> 19 In the sweat of your face you shall eat bread
>   Till you return to the ground,
>   For out of it you were taken;
>   For dust you *are*,
>   And to dust you shall return.' "

20*And Adam called his wife's name Eve, because she was the mother of all living.

21Also for Adam and his wife the Lord God made tunics of skin, and clothed them.

22Then the Lord God said, "Behold, the man has become like one of Us, to know good and evil. And now, lest he put out his hand and take also of the tree of life, and eat, and live forever"—23therefore the Lord God sent him out of the garden of Eden to till the ground from which he was taken. 24So He drove out the man; and He placed cherubim at the east of the garden of Eden, and a flaming sword which turned every way, to guard the way to the tree of life.

4 Now* Adam knew Eve his wife, and she conceived and bore Cain, and said, "I have acquired a man from the Lord." 2Then she bore again, this time his brother Abel. Now Abel was a keeper of sheep, but Cain was a tiller of the ground. 3*And in the process of time it came to pass that Cain brought an offering of the fruit of the ground to the Lord. 4Abel also brought of the firstborn of his flock and of their fat. And the Lord respected Abel and his offering, 5*but He did not respect Cain and his offering. And Cain was very angry, and his countenance fell.

6So the Lord said to Cain, "Why are you angry? And why has your countenance fallen? 7If you do well, will you not be accepted? And if you do not do well, sin lies at the door. And its desire *is* for you, but you should rule over it."

8Now Cain talked with Abel his brother;e and it came to pass, when they were in the field, that Cain rose up against Abel his brother and killed him.

9*Then the Lord said to Cain, "Where *is* Abel your brother?"

He said, "I do not know. *Am* I my brother's keeper?"

10And He said, "What have you done? The voice of your brother's blood cries out to Me from the ground. 11*So now you *are* cursed from the earth, which has opened its mouth to receive your brother's blood from your hand. 12When you till the ground, it shall no longer yield its strength

---

4:8 eSamaritan Pentateuch, Septuagint, Syriac, and Vulgate add *"Let us go out to the field."*

3:20 Adam believed the promise that his wife would bear children, and his faith saved him. He called her *Eve*, which means "life-giver." In response to their faith, God shed innocent blood and clothed them. The only way sinners can be saved is by faith in the shed blood of Christ (Heb. 9:22; see also Isa. 61:10; Eph. 2:8–9).

Jesus Christ is "the last Adam" (1 Cor. 15:45–49). The first Adam's disobedience plunged us into sin, but the Last Adam's obedience brought salvation (Rom. 5:12–21). The first Adam was a thief and was cast out of Paradise. The Last Adam told a thief he would enter paradise (Luke 23:43). In Adam we die; in Christ we have eternal life.

CHAPTER 4

4:1 Satan is a serpent that deceives and a lion that devours (1 Pet. 5:8–9). He used Eve to tempt Adam and Cain to destroy Abel. The two "seeds" of Genesis 3:15 came into conflict, for Cain was a child of the devil (1 John 3:10–12), while Abel was a child of God (Matt. 23:35). Like his father, the devil, Cain was a liar and a murderer (John 8:44).

The marks of God's children are faith, hope, and love (1 Cor. 13:13; 1 Thess. 1:3–4). The marks of the devil's seed are unbelief, despair, and hatred, and they are evident in Cain.

4:3 *Unbelief.* When God killed animals and clothed Adam and Eve (3:21), He taught the significance of blood sacrifice (Heb. 9:22). Cain brought the wrong sacrifice in his hands and had the wrong attitude in his heart. His was not a sacrifice of faith, and God rejected it. God also warned Cain that sin was lying at his door, waiting to pounce on him.

4:5–8 *Hatred.* Cain's anger slowly became envy and hatred, and then it led to murder (Matt. 5:21–26). When you start to play with temptation, you will soon be caught (James 1:13–16). Cain was guilty of every sin that God hates (Prov. 6:16–19).

4:9 *Despair.* God's question to Adam and Eve was, "Where are you?" His question to Cain was, "Where is Abel your brother?" Do we know where our brothers and sisters are? Do we care? Or are we making excuses, as Cain did?

4:11–14 Now God curses a man! But Cain was not convicted about his sin; he was concerned only about his punishment. Cain's unbelief, hatred, and deceit destroyed
(continued)

Controlling Anger—We may have righteous anger against sin (Mark 3:5; Eph. 4:26), but too often our anger is itself sinful. Jesus warned that anger could be the first step toward murder (Matt. 5:21–26). We must ask the Holy Spirit to help us control anger (Prov. 15:18; 16:32), manifest love to those who offend us (Matt. 5:43–48), and learn to practice forgiveness (Eph. 4:26–32).

(continued from previous page)
every relationship in his life: his relationship with his brother, God, himself, and the world around him. All of us are pilgrims on this earth, but Cain became a fugitive, a wanderer. "Thou hast made us for Thyself," said St. Augustine, "and our hearts are restless until they rest in Thee."

4:25 Hope. Cain tried to compensate for his despair by building a "civilization" in the land of Nod ("wandering"). Since Adam and Eve had many children, Cain must have married a relative. He had many fine things in his city, but God rejected the whole thing and gave Adam another son, Seth ("appointed"), to carry on the godly line.

CHAPTER 5

5:1ff The Old Testament is "the book of the genealogy of Adam" (v. 1). It tells us about Adam's descendants, and the story is not a happy one. In fact, the Old Testament closes with "lest I come and strike the earth with a curse" (Mal. 4:6). The New Testament is "the book of the genealogy of Jesus Christ" (Matt. 1:1); before it ends, it declares, "And there shall be no more curse" (Rev. 22:3). The first Adam brought the curse; the Last Adam bore the curse (Gal. 3:13). Adam's sin caused thorns to grow (Gen. 3:18), but Jesus wore those thorns as a crown (Matt. 27:29).

5:3 God made man in His likeness, but sinful man now begets children in his likeness (v.3). We are all born sinners (Ps. 51:5). But when a sinner is born again through faith in Christ, he or she begins to grow into the likeness of the Last Adam (Rom. 8:29; 2 Cor. 3:18).

5:5 Eight times in chapter 5 you find the sobering phrase "and he died." Death is an appointment, not an accident. Because sin was reigning, death was also reigning (Rom. 5:14, 17), but in the life of Enoch, *God's grace was reigning* (Rom. 5:20–21). He believed God (Heb. 11:5–6), walked with God in the midst of a godless society, and witnessed for God (Jude 14–15). Enoch did not die; God raptured him away to heaven. This is the "blessed hope" of all Christians (Titus 2:11–14; see also 1 Thess. 4:13–18).

to you. A fugitive and a vagabond you shall be on the earth."

[13]And Cain said to the LORD, "My punishment *is* greater than I can bear! [14]Surely You have driven me out this day from the face of the ground; I shall be hidden from Your face; I shall be a fugitive and a vagabond on the earth, and it will happen *that* anyone who finds me will kill me."

[15]And the LORD said to him, "Therefore,[f] whoever kills Cain, vengeance shall be taken on him sevenfold." And the LORD set a mark on Cain, lest anyone finding him should kill him.

[16]Then Cain went out from the presence of the LORD and dwelt in the land of Nod on the east of Eden. [17]And Cain knew his wife, and she conceived and bore Enoch. And he built a city, and called the name of the city after the name of his son—Enoch. [18]To Enoch was born Irad; and Irad begot Mehujael, and Mehujael begot Methushael, and Methushael begot Lamech.

[19]Then Lamech took for himself two wives: the name of one *was* Adah, and the name of the second *was* Zillah. [20]And Adah bore Jabal. He was the father of those who dwell in tents and have livestock. [21]His brother's name *was* Jubal. He was the father of all those who play the harp and flute. [22]And as for Zillah, she also bore Tubal-Cain, an instructor of every craftsman in bronze and iron. And the sister of Tubal-Cain *was* Naamah.

[23]Then Lamech said to his wives:

> "Adah and Zillah, hear my voice;
> Wives of Lamech, listen to my speech!
> For I have killed a man for wounding me,
> Even a young man for hurting me.
> [24] If Cain shall be avenged sevenfold,
> Then Lamech seventy-sevenfold."

[25]*And Adam knew his wife again, and she bore a son and named him Seth, "For God has appointed another seed for me instead of Abel, whom Cain killed." [26]And as for Seth, to him also a son was born; and he named him Enosh.[g] Then *men* began to call on the name of the LORD.

5 This* is the book of the genealogy of Adam. In the day that God created man, He made him in the likeness of God. [2]He created them male and female, and blessed them and called them Mankind in the day they were created. [3]*And Adam lived one hundred and thirty years, and begot *a son* in his own likeness, after his image, and named him Seth. [4]After he begot Seth, the days of Adam were eight hundred years; and he had sons and daughters. [5]*So all the days that Adam lived were nine hundred and thirty years; and he died.

[6]Seth lived one hundred and five years, and begot Enosh. [7]After he begot Enosh, Seth lived eight hundred and seven years, and had sons and daughters. [8]So all the days of Seth were nine hundred and twelve years; and he died.

[9]Enosh lived ninety years, and begot Cainan.[h] [10]After he begot Cainan, Enosh lived eight hundred and fifteen years, and had sons and daugh-

---

4:15 [f]Following Masoretic Text and Targum; Septuagint, Syriac, and Vulgate read *Not so.*   4:26 [g]Greek *Enos*
5:9 [h]Hebrew *Qenan*

ters. 11So all the days of Enosh were nine hundred and five years; and he died.

12Cainan lived seventy years, and begot Mahalalel. 13After he begot Mahalalel, Cainan lived eight hundred and forty years, and had sons and daughters. 14So all the days of Cainan were nine hundred and ten years; and he died.

15Mahalalel lived sixty-five years, and begot Jared. 16After he begot Jared, Mahalalel lived eight hundred and thirty years, and had sons and daughters. 17So all the days of Mahalalel were eight hundred and ninety-five years; and he died.

18Jared lived one hundred and sixty-two years, and begot Enoch. 19After he begot Enoch, Jared lived eight hundred years, and had sons and daughters. 20So all the days of Jared were nine hundred and sixty-two years; and he died.

21Enoch lived sixty-five years, and begot Methuselah. 22After he begot Methuselah, Enoch walked with God three hundred years, and had sons and daughters. 23So all the days of Enoch were three hundred and sixty-five years. 24And Enoch walked with God; and he *was* not, for God took him.

25Methuselah lived one hundred and eighty-seven years, and begot Lamech. 26After he begot Lamech, Methuselah lived seven hundred and eighty-two years, and had sons and daughters. 27So all the days of Methuselah were nine hundred and sixty-nine years; and he died.

28Lamech lived one hundred and eighty-two years, and had a son. 29*And he called his name Noah, saying, "This *one* will comfort us concerning our work and the toil of our hands, because of the ground which the LORD has cursed." 30After he begot Noah, Lamech lived five hundred and ninety-five years, and had sons and daughters. 31So all the days of Lamech were seven hundred and seventy-seven years; and he died.

32And Noah was five hundred years old, and Noah begot Shem, Ham, and Japheth.

6 Now* it came to pass, when men began to multiply on the face of the earth, and daughters were born to them, 2that the sons of God saw the daughters of men, that they *were* beautiful; and they took wives for themselves of all whom they chose.

3And the LORD said, "My Spirit shall not strive^f with man forever, for he *is* indeed flesh; yet his days shall be one hundred and twenty years." 4There were giants on the earth in those days, and also afterward, when the sons of God came in to the daughters of men and they bore *children* to them. Those *were* the mighty men who *were* of old, men of renown.

5*Then the LORD^f saw that the wickedness of man *was* great in the earth, and *that* every intent of the thoughts of his heart *was* only evil continually. 6And the LORD was sorry that He had made man on the earth, and He was grieved in His heart. 7So the LORD said, "I will destroy man whom I have created from the face of the earth, both man and beast, creeping thing and birds of the air, for I am sorry that I have made them." 8*But Noah found grace in the eyes of the LORD.

9This is the genealogy of Noah. Noah was a just

6:3 ᶠSeptuagint, Syriac, Targum, and Vulgate read *abide*.
6:5 ᶠFollowing Masoretic Text and Targum; Vulgate reads *God*; Septuagint reads LORD *God*.

5:29 *Noah* means "rest." Mankind was in misery and longed for the promised Redeemer to come. He *has* come, and we can come to Him and find true rest (Matt. 11:28–30).

CHAPTERS 6—8

6:1ff The account of a flood is written into the history of many ancient peoples, and the results of a flood are seen in many places on the earth. Jesus believed in the Flood (Matt. 24:37–39), and so did Peter (1 Pet. 3:20) and the author of Hebrews (11:7).

6:5–7 *The holiness of God.* God saw a world of people who were inwardly corrupt, outwardly violent, and upwardly rebellious. Noah was the tenth generation from Adam. It didn't take long for sin to spread in the human race. When the world is again as it was in Noah's day, watch for the return of the Lord (Matt. 24:37–39).

6:8–21 *The grace of God.* Noah was saved just as any sinner is saved, by grace (Gen. 6:8), through faith (Heb. 11:7). (See Eph. 2:8–9.) He heard God's Word, believed God's promise of protection, and proved his faith by his works. There was only one way to be saved from destruction, and that was by entering the ark; and the ark had only one door. It is a picture of the salvation we have in Christ.

man, perfect in his generations. Noah walked with God. 10And Noah begot three sons: Shem, Ham, and Japheth.

11The earth also was corrupt before God, and the earth was filled with violence. 12So God looked upon the earth, and indeed it was corrupt; for all flesh had corrupted their way on the earth. 13And God said to Noah, "The end of all flesh has come before Me, for the earth is filled with violence through them; and behold, I will destroy them with the earth. 14Make yourself an ark of gopherwood; make rooms in the ark, and cover it inside and outside with pitch. 15And this is how you shall make it: The length of the ark *shall be* three hundred cubits, its width fifty cubits, and its height thirty cubits. 16You shall make a window for the ark, and you shall finish it to a cubit from above; and set the door of the ark in its side. You shall make it *with* lower, second, and third *decks.* 17And behold, I Myself am bringing floodwaters on the earth, to destroy from under heaven all flesh in which *is* the breath of life; everything that *is* on the earth shall die. 18But I will establish My covenant with you; and you shall go into the ark—you, your sons, your wife, and your sons' wives with you. 19And of every living thing of all flesh you shall bring two of every *sort* into the ark, to keep *them* alive with you; they shall be male and female. 20Of the birds after their kind, of animals after their kind, and of every creeping thing of the earth after its kind, two of every *kind* will come to you to keep *them* alive. 21And you shall take for yourself of all food that is eaten, and you shall gather *it* to yourself; and it shall be food for you and for them."

22Thus Noah did; according to all that God commanded him, so he did.

7 Then the LORD said to Noah, "Come into the ark, you and all your household, because I have seen *that* you *are* righteous before Me in this generation. 2You shall take with you seven each of every clean animal, a male and his female; two each of animals that *are* unclean, a male and his female; 3also seven each of birds of the air, male and female, to keep the species alive on the face of all the earth. 4For after seven more days I will cause it to rain on the earth forty days and forty nights, and I will destroy from the face of the earth all living things that I have made." 5And Noah did according to all that the LORD commanded him. 6Noah *was* six hundred years old when the floodwaters were on the earth.

7So Noah, with his sons, his wife, and his sons' wives, went into the ark because of the waters of the flood. 8Of clean animals, of animals that *are* unclean, of birds, and of everything that creeps on the earth, 9two by two they went into the ark to Noah, male and female, as God had commanded Noah. 10*And it came to pass after seven days that the waters of the flood were on the earth. 11In the six hundredth year of Noah's life, in the second month, the seventeenth day of the month, on that day all the fountains of the great deep were broken up, and the windows of heaven were opened. 12And the rain was on the earth forty days and forty nights.

13On the very same day Noah and Noah's sons, Shem, Ham, and Japheth, and Noah's wife and the three wives of his sons with them, entered the ark— 14they and every beast after its kind, all cattle after their kind, every creeping thing that

7:10–24 The wrath of God. God was very patient and gave the world at least 120 years of opportunity to be saved (Gen. 6:3; 1 Pet. 3:20; 2 Pet. 2:5). The world refused Noah's witness and rejected God's grace up to the very day Noah and his family went into the ark. God waited another week (how the neighbors must have laughed at Noah!), but then the judgment came. As David proclaimed, "The LORD sat enthroned at the Flood" (Ps. 29:10). He is sovereign in all things! The next worldwide judgment will be with fire, not water (2 Pet. 3:1–12).

creeps on the earth after its kind, and every bird after its kind, every bird of every sort. 15And they went into the ark to Noah, two by two, of all flesh in which *is* the breath of life. 16So those that entered, male and female of all flesh, went in as God had commanded him; and the LORD shut him in.

17Now the flood was on the earth forty days. The waters increased and lifted up the ark, and it rose high above the earth. 18The waters prevailed and greatly increased on the earth, and the ark moved about on the surface of the waters. 19And the waters prevailed exceedingly on the earth, and all the high hills under the whole heaven were covered. 20The waters prevailed fifteen cubits upward, and the mountains were covered. 21And all flesh died that moved on the earth: birds and cattle and beasts and every creeping thing that creeps on the earth, and every man. 22All in whose nostrils *was* the breath of the spirit*k* of life, all that *was* on the dry *land,* died. 23So He destroyed all living things which were on the face of the ground: both man and cattle, creeping thing and bird of the air. They were destroyed from the earth. Only Noah and those who *were* with him in the ark remained *alive.* 24And the waters prevailed on the earth one hundred and fifty days.

8 Then* God remembered Noah, and every living thing, and all the animals that *were* with him in the ark. And God made a wind to pass over the earth, and the waters subsided. 2The fountains of the deep and the windows of heaven were also stopped, and the rain from heaven was restrained. 3And the waters receded continually from the earth. At the end of the hundred and fifty days the waters decreased. 4Then the ark rested in the seventh month, the seventeenth day of the month, on the mountains of Ararat. 5And the waters decreased continually until the tenth month. In the tenth *month,* on the first *day* of the month, the tops of the mountains were seen.

6So it came to pass, at the end of forty days, that Noah opened the window of the ark which he had made. 7Then he sent out a raven, which kept going to and fro until the waters had dried up from the earth. 8He also sent out from himself a dove, to see if the waters had receded from the face of the ground. 9But the dove found no resting place for the sole of her foot, and she returned into the ark to him, for the waters *were* on the face of the whole earth. So he put out his hand and took her, and drew her into the ark to himself. 10And he waited yet another seven days, and again he sent the dove out from the ark. 11Then the dove came to him in the evening, and behold, a freshly plucked olive leaf *was* in her mouth; and Noah knew that the waters had receded from the earth. 12So he waited yet another seven days and sent out the dove, which did not return again to him anymore.

13And it came to pass in the six hundred and

8:1–22 *The faithfulness of God.* Noah had faith in God's promises, and God did not disappoint him. (See 1 Kings 8:56.) True faith does not get in a hurry (Isa. 28:16); Noah waited until the word of God told him what to do. The first thing Noah and his family did on the cleansed earth was to worship the God who had faithfully cared for them (Ps. 116:12–19; Rom. 12:1–2). God gave them a covenant that assured them of the continuity of creation despite man's evil heart. This covenant makes possible the sustaining of life on earth. God has been faithful to His covenant, but man has not been faithful in his stewardship of the earth. (See Rev. 11:18.)

7:22 *k*Septuagint and Vulgate omit *of the spirit.*

Faithfulness to God—Noah and his family were the only believers on earth, yet they witnessed courageously for God and against the evil of their day. They were faithful to God when everything seemed to be against them. God still calls His people to stand alone if needs be, and He promises never to forsake us (Heb. 13:5–6). God will judge us not on the basis of our popularity but on our faithfulness to Him (1 Cor. 4:2). God needs courageous witnesses today.

first year, in the first *month*, the first *day* of the month, that the waters were dried up from the earth; and Noah removed the covering of the ark and looked, and indeed the surface of the ground was dry. 14And in the second month, on the twenty-seventh day of the month, the earth was dried.

15Then God spoke to Noah, saying, 16"Go out of the ark, you and your wife, and your sons and your sons' wives with you. 17Bring out with you every living thing of all flesh that *is* with you: birds and cattle and every creeping thing that creeps on the earth, so that they may abound on the earth, and be fruitful and multiply on the earth." 18So Noah went out, and his sons and his wife and his sons' wives with him. 19Every animal, every creeping thing, every bird, *and* whatever creeps on the earth, according to their families, went out of the ark.

20Then Noah built an altar to the LORD, and took of every clean animal and of every clean bird, and offered burnt offerings on the altar. 21And the LORD smelled a soothing aroma. Then the LORD said in His heart, "I will never again curse the ground for man's sake, although the imagination of man's heart *is* evil from his youth; nor will I again destroy every living thing as I have done.

> 22 "While the earth remains,
> Seedtime and harvest,
> Cold and heat,
> Winter and summer,
> And day and night
> Shall not cease."

9 So* God blessed Noah and his sons, and said to them: "Be fruitful and multiply, and fill the earth.*l* 2And the fear of you and the dread of you shall be on every beast of the earth, on every bird of the air, on all that move *on* the earth, and on all the fish of the sea. They are given into your hand. 3Every moving thing that lives shall be food for you. I have given you all things, even as the green herbs. 4But you shall not eat flesh with its life, *that is*, its blood. 5Surely for your lifeblood I will demand *a reckoning;* from the hand of every beast I will require it, and from the hand of man. From the hand of every man's brother I will require the life of man.

> 6 "Whoever sheds man's blood,
>   By man his blood shall be shed;
>   For in the image of God
>   He made man.
> 7 And as for you, be fruitful and multiply;
>   Bring forth abundantly in the earth
>   And multiply in it."

8Then God spoke to Noah and to his sons with him, saying: 9*"And as for Me, behold, I establish My covenant with you and with your descendants*m* after you, 10and with every living creature that *is* with you: the birds, the cattle, and every beast of the earth with you, of all that go out of the ark, every beast of the earth. 11Thus I establish My covenant with you: Never again shall all flesh be cut off by the waters of the flood; never again shall there be a flood to destroy the earth."

12And God said: "This *is* the sign of the cov-

CHAPTER 9

9:1–7 Government. God gave some new rules for life on the cleansed earth. He always guides His redeemed and shows them His will. Noah and his family could now eat animal flesh (Gen. 1:29), *but they were forbidden to eat the blood* (Lev. 17:11–14). The sanctity of human life was affirmed in the ordaining of human government (Rom. 13). God established government because man is basically a sinner and must be kept under control. Murder is a terrible crime because man is made in the image of God, and to kill a human being is to attack God's image. All people are not children of God, but all belong to one human family because God made us of one blood (Acts 17:26).

9:9–17 Grace. God gave assurance that He would never send another flood to destroy life on the earth. The covenant included not only man but also birds, cattle, and the beasts of the field (Ezek. 1:10; Rev. 4:7). The sign of the covenant was the rainbow, a bridge of beauty that joins heaven and earth. Whether we look at the rainbow or not, *God* looks upon it and remembers His promises. Noah saw the rainbow *after* the storm; Ezekiel saw it *in the midst* of the storm (Ezek. 1:4ff.); and John saw it *before* the storm of judgment (Rev. 4:1–3).

9:1 *l*Compare Genesis 1:28   9:9 *m*Literally *seed*

enant which I make between Me and you, and every living creature that *is* with you, for perpetual generations: ¹³I set My rainbow in the cloud, and it shall be for the sign of the covenant between Me and the earth. ¹⁴It shall be, when I bring a cloud over the earth, that the rainbow shall be seen in the cloud; ¹⁵and I will remember My covenant which *is* between Me and you and every living creature of all flesh; the waters shall never again become a flood to destroy all flesh. ¹⁶The rainbow shall be in the cloud, and I will look on it to remember the everlasting covenant between God and every living creature of all flesh that *is* on the earth." ¹⁷And God said to Noah, "This *is* the sign of the covenant which I have established between Me and all flesh that *is* on the earth."

¹⁸Now the sons of Noah who went out of the ark were Shem, Ham, and Japheth. And Ham *was* the father of Canaan. ¹⁹These three *were* the sons of Noah, and from these the whole earth was populated.

²⁰*And Noah began *to be* a farmer, and he planted a vineyard. ²¹Then he drank of the wine and was drunk, and became uncovered in his tent. ²²And Ham, the father of Canaan, saw the nakedness of his father, and told his two brothers outside. ²³But Shem and Japheth took a garment, laid *it* on both their shoulders, and went backward and covered the nakedness of their father. Their faces *were* turned away, and they did not see their father's nakedness.

²⁴So Noah awoke from his wine, and knew what his younger son had done to him. ²⁵*Then he said:

"Cursed *be* Canaan;
A servant of servants
He shall be to his brethren."

²⁶And he said:

"Blessed *be* the Lᴏʀᴅ,
The God of Shem,
And may Canaan be his servant.
27 May God enlarge Japheth,
And may he dwell in the tents of Shem;
And may Canaan be his servant."

²⁸And Noah lived after the flood three hundred and fifty years. ²⁹So all the days of Noah were nine hundred and fifty years; and he died.

10 Now* this *is* the genealogy of the sons of Noah: Shem, Ham, and Japheth. And sons were born to them after the flood. ²The sons of Japheth *were* Gomer, Magog, Madai, Javan, Tubal, Meshech, and Tiras. ³The sons of Gomer *were* Ashkenaz, Riphath,ⁿ and Togarmah. ⁴The sons of Javan *were* Elishah, Tarshish, Kittim, and Dodanim.ᵒ ⁵From these the coastland *peoples* of the Gentiles were separated into their lands, everyone according to his language, according to their families, into their nations.

⁶The sons of Ham *were* Cush, Mizraim, Put,ᵖ and Canaan. ⁷The sons of Cush *were* Seba, Havilah, Sabtah, Raamah, and Sabtechah; and the sons of Raamah *were* Sheba and Dedan.

9:20–23 Guilt. Imagine, a "preacher of righteousness" (2 Pet. 2:5), who was over six hundred years old, *getting drunk!* (See Gen. 6:5; 8:21; 1 Cor. 10:12.) Ham should have grieved over his father's sins, not gloated over them (Prov. 14:9). His brothers did what love always does: "covers all sins" (Prov. 10:12; 12:16; 17:9; 1 Pet. 4:8).

9:25–27 Noah's words must not be interpreted to mean that certain races are inferior and destined to be enslaved. In fact, history shows that some of Canaan's descendants were mighty nations with great empires. For that matter, even the Jews, the descendants of Shem, have had their share of captivity. His words were a prophecy: the sin of Ham would be visited on his son Canaan, who must have been involved in some way; Shem would have God's blessing (Rom. 9:1–5); Japheth (the Gentiles) would multiply and would worship the God of Shem. John wrote, "Salvation is of the Jews" (John 4:22). People who trust Christ for salvation are all one in Him (Gal. 3:28; Col. 3:11).

CHAPTERS 10—11
10:1ff From Noah's three sons, God made a new beginning in human history. He set apart Shem to be His special channel of blessing, and it was through Shem that Abraham, the father of the Jewish nation, was born (11:10ff.).

Sin always separates: man from God (chap. 3); brother from brother (chap. 4); family from family (chap. 9); and now nation from nation.

10:3 ⁿSpelled *Diphath* in 1 Chronicles 1:6 10:4 ᵒSpelled *Rodanim* in Samaritan Pentateuch and 1 Chronicles 1:7 10:6 ᵖOr *Phut*

10:8–11 Note the name of Nimrod (10:8–10). The phrase "mighty hunter" implies that he was a rebel against God and a tyrant against his fellowman. He founded two cities important in Bible history: Babylon and Nineveh.

11:4 Man seeks unity and notoriety, and he tries to accomplish these things by his own wisdom and strength. Lucifer wanted to be like God (Isa. 14:14), and man wanted to make a name for himself. But only God can make a person's name truly great (Gen. 12:2; Josh. 3:7).

11:7–9 *Babel* means "confusion," and "God is not the author of confusion" (1 Cor. 14:33; see also James 3:16). Babylon will appear often in the biblical record as the enemy of God's people. Wherever there is confusion, the spirit of Babylon—the world and the flesh—is at work. Ultimately, the whole "Babylonian system" will be destroyed (Rev. 17—18).

The confusion of tongues that began at Babel was reversed at Pentecost (Acts 2:7–8). A descendant of Ham, an Ethiopian, was saved in Acts 8; a descendant of Shem, Paul, was saved in Acts 9; and the gentile descendants of Japheth were saved in Acts 10. Unity is not worked up by man; it is sent down by God (Ps. 133; Eph. 4:1–6). As we share the gospel with others, we are helping to unite what sin has torn apart (Eph. 1:10–11). Christians are indeed the peacemakers of the world.

8*Cush begot Nimrod; he began to be a mighty one on the earth. 9He was a mighty hunter before the LORD; therefore it is said, "Like Nimrod the mighty hunter before the LORD." 10And the beginning of his kingdom was Babel, Erech, Accad, and Calneh, in the land of Shinar. 11From that land he went to Assyria and built Nineveh, Rehoboth Ir, Calah, 12and Resen between Nineveh and Calah (that *is* the principal city).

13Mizraim begot Ludim, Anamim, Lehabim, Naphtuhim, 14Pathrusim, and Casluhim (from whom came the Philistines and Caphtorim).

15Canaan begot Sidon his firstborn, and Heth; 16the Jebusite, the Amorite, and the Girgashite; 17the Hivite, the Arkite, and the Sinite; 18the Arvadite, the Zemarite, and the Hamathite. Afterward the families of the Canaanites were dispersed. 19And the border of the Canaanites was from Sidon as you go toward Gerar, as far as Gaza; then as you go toward Sodom, Gomorrah, Admah, and Zeboiim, as far as Lasha. 20These *were* the sons of Ham, according to their families, according to their languages, in their lands *and* in their nations.

21And *children* were born also to Shem, the father of all the children of Eber, the brother of Japheth the elder. 22The sons of Shem *were* Elam, Asshur, Arphaxad, Lud, and Aram. 23The sons of Aram *were* Uz, Hul, Gether, and Mash.q 24Arphaxad begot Salah,r and Salah begot Eber. 25To Eber were born two sons: the name of one *was* Peleg, for in his days the earth was divided; and his brother's name *was* Joktan. 26Joktan begot Almodad, Sheleph, Hazarmaveth, Jerah, 27Hadoram, Uzal, Diklah, 28Obal,s Abimael, Sheba, 29Ophir, Havilah, and Jobab. All these *were* the sons of Joktan. 30And their dwelling place was from Mesha as you go toward Sephar, the mountain of the east. 31These *were* the sons of Shem, according to their families, according to their languages, in their lands, according to their nations.

32These *were* the families of the sons of Noah, according to their generations, in their nations; and from these the nations were divided on the earth after the flood.

11 Now the whole earth had one language and one speech. 2And it came to pass, as they journeyed from the east, that they found a plain in the land of Shinar, and they dwelt there. 3Then they said to one another, "Come, let us make bricks and bake *them* thoroughly." They had brick for stone, and they had asphalt for mortar. 4*And they said, "Come, let us build ourselves a city, and a tower whose top *is* in the heavens; let us make a name for ourselves, lest we be scattered abroad over the face of the whole earth."

5But the LORD came down to see the city and the tower which the sons of men had built. 6And the LORD said, "Indeed the people *are* one and they all have one language, and this is what they begin to do; now nothing that they propose to do will be withheld from them. 7*Come, let Us go down and there confuse their language, that

10:23 qCalled *Meshech* in Septuagint and 1 Chronicles 1:17 10:24 rFollowing Masoretic Text, Vulgate, and Targum; Septuagint reads *Arphaxad begot Cainan, and Cainan begot Salah* (compare Luke 3:35, 36). 10:28 sSpelled *Ebal* in 1 Chronicles 1:22

they may not understand one another's speech."
8So the LORD scattered them abroad from there
over the face of all the earth, and they ceased
building the city. 9Therefore its name is called
Babel, because there the LORD confused the language of all the earth; and from there the LORD
scattered them abroad over the face of all the
earth.

10This *is* the genealogy of Shem: Shem *was* one
hundred years old, and begot Arphaxad two years
after the flood. 11After he begot Arphaxad, Shem
lived five hundred years, and begot sons and
daughters.

12Arphaxad lived thirty-five years, and begot
Salah. 13After he begot Salah, Arphaxad lived
four hundred and three years, and begot sons and
daughters.

14Salah lived thirty years, and begot Eber.
15After he begot Eber, Salah lived four hundred
and three years, and begot sons and daughters.

16Eber lived thirty-four years, and begot Peleg.
17After he begot Peleg, Eber lived four hundred
and thirty years, and begot sons and daughters.

18Peleg lived thirty years, and begot Reu.
19After he begot Reu, Peleg lived two hundred and
nine years, and begot sons and daughters.

20Reu lived thirty-two years, and begot Serug.
21After he begot Serug, Reu lived two hundred
and seven years, and begot sons and daughters.

22Serug lived thirty years, and begot Nahor.
23After he begot Nahor, Serug lived two hundred
years, and begot sons and daughters.

24Nahor lived twenty-nine years, and begot
Terah. 25After he begot Terah, Nahor lived one
hundred and nineteen years, and begot sons and
daughters.

26Now Terah lived seventy years, and begot
Abram, Nahor, and Haran.

27This *is* the genealogy of Terah: Terah begot
Abram, Nahor, and Haran. Haran begot Lot.
28And Haran died before his father Terah in his
native land, in Ur of the Chaldeans. 29Then Abram
and Nahor took wives: the name of Abram's wife
was Sarai, and the name of Nahor's wife, Milcah,
the daughter of Haran the father of Milcah and
the father of Iscah. 30But Sarai was barren; she
had no child.

31And Terah took his son Abram and his grandson Lot, the son of Haran, and his daughter-
in-law Sarai, his son Abram's wife, and they
went out with them from Ur of the Chaldeans to
go to the land of Canaan; and they came to Haran and dwelt there. 32So the days of Terah were
two hundred and five years, and Terah died in
Haran.

12

Now* the LORD had said to Abram:

"Get out of your country,
From your family
And from your father's house,
To a land that I will show you.
2 I will make you a great nation;
I will bless you
And make your name great;
And you shall be a blessing.

CHAPTER 12

12:1ff God's Word leads to faith. Abram
was an idolater when God called him (Josh.
24:2), revealed His glory to him (Acts 7:2),
and spoke to him. Abram turned from vain
idols to walk with the Lord, and all of this
was by God's grace. The hearing of the
Word creates faith (John 5:24; Rom. 10:17).
Again God's creative Word is at work.

Am I Living by Faith?—When you live by faith, you make your decisions on the basis of the
Word of God (Rom. 10:17), and you seek to glorify God alone (Rom. 4:19–20). True faith is not in a
hurry; it is willing to wait (Isa. 28:16; Heb. 6:12).

Faith obeys God in spite of circumstances or consequences, and it is not afraid of what others
may say or do (Heb. 11:29–30).

12:4 *Faith leads to obedience.* The New Testament states, "By faith Abraham obeyed" (Heb. 11:8). "I will show you, I will make you, I will bless you!" were God's promises, and Abram believed. It has well been said that faith is not believing in spite of evidence; it is obeying in spite of consequences. The proof of faith is obedience, for true faith always leads to works (James 2:14ff.). Hearing leads to heeding.

12:7–9 *Obedience leads to blessing.* We are told nothing about the journey, which must have been very difficult; but we are told that God met Abram when he arrived and gave him a new promise. God always goes before us and has His Word ready to encourage us. From now on, Abram's life will be marked by the presence of the *tent* (a pilgrim on earth) and the *altar* (a citizen of heaven).

12:10–13 *Blessing leads to testing.* Faith is always tested for at least three reasons: to prove whether our faith is real; to help our faith grow; and to bring glory to the Lord (1 Pet. 1:6–9; James 1:1–8). Imagine a famine in the very land where God led him! We can be in the will of God and still suffer trials. It has been said that "faith is living without scheming," but Abram began to scheme. He was walking by sight and not by faith, and it cost him his testimony—and almost his wife! Note that Abram had neither a tent nor an altar in Egypt. "Going down to Egypt" is Bible language for getting out of the will of God.

God blessed Abram *that he might be a blessing.* Through Abram and his descendants, the whole world has been blessed. Whenever God gives you a blessing, it's so that you might be a blessing to others. God's blessings are not luxuries; they are opportunities.

CHAPTER 13

13:1–4 *A new beginning.* God chastened Abram in Egypt, and Abram returned to the land he never should have left. He was a very wealthy man, but his tent and altar were the most valuable things he possessed. When we fail, the Lord is ready to forgive and restore (1 John 1:5—2:2). "The victorious Christian life is a series of new beginnings," said Alexander Whyte.

13:5 *A new burden.* While in Egypt, Lot acquired wealth and a taste for the world, and his temporal interests were partly Abram's fault. God forgave Abram's sin, but He did not prevent the sad consequences. We reap what we sow, even after we are forgiven. Abram's first test of faith came from a famine; his second test came from his own family. Family tests are the hardest tests of all.

3   I will bless those who bless you,
     And I will curse him who curses you;
     And in you all the families of the earth shall be blessed."

[4]*So Abram departed as the Lord had spoken to him, and Lot went with him. And Abram *was* seventy-five years old when he departed from Haran. [5]Then Abram took Sarai his wife and Lot his brother's son, and all their possessions that they had gathered, and the people whom they had acquired in Haran, and they departed to go to the land of Canaan. So they came to the land of Canaan. [6]Abram passed through the land to the place of Shechem, as far as the terebinth tree of Moreh.[t] And the Canaanites *were* then in the land. [7]*Then the Lord appeared to Abram and said, "To your descendants I will give this land." And there he built an altar to the Lord, who had appeared to him. [8]And he moved from there to the mountain east of Bethel, and he pitched his tent *with* Bethel on the west and Ai on the east; there he built an altar to the Lord and called on the name of the Lord. [9]So Abram journeyed, going on still toward the South.[u]

[10]*Now there was a famine in the land, and Abram went down to Egypt to dwell there, for the famine *was* severe in the land. [11]And it came to pass, when he was close to entering Egypt, that he said to Sarai his wife, "Indeed I know that you *are* a woman of beautiful countenance. [12]Therefore it will happen, when the Egyptians see you, that they will say, 'This *is* his wife'; and they will kill me, but they will let you live. [13]Please say you *are* my sister, that it may be well with me for your sake, and that I[v] may live because of you."

[14]So it was, when Abram came into Egypt, that the Egyptians saw the woman, that she *was* very beautiful. [15]The princes of Pharaoh also saw her and commended her to Pharaoh. And the woman was taken to Pharaoh's house. [16]He treated Abram well for her sake. He had sheep, oxen, male donkeys, male and female servants, female donkeys, and camels.

[17]But the Lord plagued Pharaoh and his house with great plagues because of Sarai, Abram's wife. [18]And Pharaoh called Abram and said, "What *is* this you have done to me? Why did you not tell me that she *was* your wife? [19]Why did you say, 'She *is* my sister'? I might have taken her as my wife. Now therefore, here is your wife; take *her* and go your way." [20]So Pharaoh commanded *his* men concerning him; and they sent him away, with his wife and all that he had.

13 Then* Abram went up from Egypt, he and his wife and all that he had, and Lot with him, to the South.[w] [2]Abram *was* very rich in livestock, in silver, and in gold. [3]And he went on his journey from the South as far as Bethel, to the place where his tent had been at the beginning, between Bethel and Ai, [4]to the place of the altar which he had made there at first. And there Abram called on the name of the Lord. [5]*Lot also, who went with Abram, had flocks and herds and tents. [6]Now the land was not able to support them, that they might dwell together,

---

12:6 [t]Hebrew *Alon Moreh*   12:9 [u]Hebrew *Negev*
12:13 [v]Literally *my soul*   13:1 [w]Hebrew *Negev*

for their possessions were so great that they could not dwell together. 7And there was strife between the herdsmen of Abram's livestock and the herdsmen of Lot's livestock. The Canaanites and the Perizzites then dwelt in the land.

8*So Abram said to Lot, "Please let there be no strife between you and me, and between my herdsmen and your herdsmen; for we *are* brethren. 9*Is* not the whole land before you? Please separate from me. If *you take* the left, then I will go to the right; or, if *you go* to the right, then I will go to the left."

10And Lot lifted his eyes and saw all the plain of Jordan, that it *was* well watered everywhere (before the LORD destroyed Sodom and Gomorrah) like the garden of the LORD, like the land of Egypt as you go toward Zoar. 11Then Lot chose for himself all the plain of Jordan, and Lot journeyed east. And they separated from each other. 12Abram dwelt in the land of Canaan, and Lot dwelt in the cities of the plain and pitched *his* tent even as far as Sodom. 13But the men of Sodom *were* exceedingly wicked and sinful against the LORD.

14*And the LORD said to Abram, after Lot had separated from him: "Lift your eyes now and look from the place where you are—northward, southward, eastward, and westward; 15for all the land which you see I give to you and your descendantsx forever. 16And I will make your descendants as the dust of the earth; so that if a man could number the dust of the earth, *then* your descendants also could be numbered. 17Arise, walk in the land through its length and its width, for I give it to you."

18Then Abram moved *his* tent, and went and dwelt by the terebinth trees of Mamre,y which *are* in Hebron, and built an altar there to the LORD.

14 And it came to pass in the days of Amraphel king of Shinar, Arioch king of Ellasar, Chedorlaomer king of Elam, and Tidal king of nations,z 2that they made war with Bera king of Sodom, Birsha king of Gomorrah, Shinab king of Admah, Shemeber king of Zeboiim, and the king of Bela (that is, Zoar). 3All these joined together in the Valley of Siddim (that is, the Salt Sea). 4Twelve years they served Chedorlaomer, and in the thirteenth year they rebelled.

5In the fourteenth year Chedorlaomer and the kings that *were* with him came and attacked the Rephaim in Ashteroth Karnaim, the Zuzim in Ham, the Emim in Shaveh Kiriathaim, 6and the Horites in their mountain of Seir, as far as El Paran, which *is* by the wilderness. 7Then they turned back and came to En Mishpat (that *is,* Kadesh), and attacked all the country of the Amalekites, and also the Amorites who dwelt in Hazezon Tamar.

8And the king of Sodom, the king of Gomorrah, the king of Admah, the king of Zeboiim, and the king of Bela (that *is,* Zoar) went out and joined together in battle in the Valley of Siddim 9against Chedorlaomer king of Elam, Tidal king of nations,a Amraphel king of Shinar, and Arioch king of Ellasar—four kings against five. 10Now the Valley of Siddim *was full of* asphalt pits; and the

13:8–11 Abram was a peacemaker because he lived by faith; Lot was a troublemaker because he lived by sight. Abram chose a heavenly city (Heb. 11:13–16); Lot chose an earthly city, and a wicked one at that. The city appeared to be ideal, but it was headed for destruction. You can move your tent nearer and nearer to sin, *but you cannot take your altar with you.* Lot left God behind and destroyed his home.

13:14–17 *A new blessing.* The man of faith always receives a special word from God after a time of testing. Let others take what they want; our God gives us far more than they can ever imagine (Pss. 16:5; 33:12). Abram lifted up his eyes and saw the land. He lifted up his feet and claimed it by faith (Josh. 1:3). Then he lifted up his heart and worshiped God. Lot had broken Abram's heart, but God blessed Abram's heart—and made him a blessing.

13:15 xLiterally *seed,* and so throughout the book
13:18 yHebrew *Alon Mamre*   14:1 zHebrew *goyim*
14:9 aHebrew *goyim*

CHAPTER 14
Abram won three victories.

14:14 *A victory over Lot.* It would have been easy for Abram to let Lot suffer the sad consequences of his own foolish decision. But a man of faith is called "to be a blessing," so Abram went to the rescue. Lot was not a very dedicated believer, but he was still a brother and needed help. When a brother or a sister creates problems for you, remember Abram and the words of Romans 12:21. Lot went right back into Sodom, but Abram did what he did for the Lord; and that's what really counts.

14:15 *A victory over the kings.* Abram the pilgrim would never have gotten involved in the war except to rescue Lot. Abram did not have a large army, but he battled by faith; that is what gave him the victory (1 Sam. 14:6; 1 John 5:4–5).

14:22, 23 *A victory over himself.* "Let us be as watchful after the victory as before the battle," said Andrew Bonar. Abram was tempted to use God's victory for personal gain, but he refused the offer. The king of Sodom came with a bargain, but the king of Salem (a picture of our Lord Jesus Christ [Heb. 7:1–3]) came with a blessing. Even a shoelace from Sodom would have defiled Abram's godly walk! After every battle, give God the glory; and beware the devil's bargains. If you aren't careful, you may win the war and lose the victory.

CHAPTER 15

15:1ff Abram's reward was not the applause of the people he rescued but the approval of the God he served. This is the first of many "fear nots" in the Bible. Fear after a battle is not unusual, but fear and faith cannot live very long in the same heart (Matt. 8:26). Abram's fears were quieted by three revelations from God.

15:1 *What God is.* God is our protection and provision, so we need not fear the enemy without or our feelings within. God is the great I AM, and He can meet every need. With Him, we have everything; without Him, nothing we have is sufficient.

15:4, 5 *What God says.* Abram looked at himself and realized how old he was getting. Then he looked at his steward, Eliezer, and thought perhaps God could use him. But God told him to stop looking at himself and at others and to start looking up to God. This is the second time he lifted up his eyes *(continued)*

kings of Sodom and Gomorrah fled; *some* fell there, and the remainder fled to the mountains. ¹¹Then they took all the goods of Sodom and Gomorrah, and all their provisions, and went their way. ¹²They also took Lot, Abram's brother's son who dwelt in Sodom, and his goods, and departed.

¹³Then one who had escaped came and told Abram the Hebrew, for he dwelt by the terebinth trees of Mamre*b* the Amorite, brother of Eshcol and brother of Aner; and they *were* allies with Abram. ¹⁴*Now when Abram heard that his brother was taken captive, he armed his three hundred and eighteen trained *servants* who were born in his own house, and went in pursuit as far as Dan. ¹⁵*He divided his forces against them by night, and he and his servants attacked them and pursued them as far as Hobah, which *is* north of Damascus. ¹⁶So he brought back all the goods, and also brought back his brother Lot and his goods, as well as the women and the people.

¹⁷And the king of Sodom went out to meet him at the Valley of Shaveh (that *is*, the King's Valley), after his return from the defeat of Chedorlaomer and the kings who *were* with him.

¹⁸Then Melchizedek king of Salem brought out bread and wine; he *was* the priest of God Most High. ¹⁹And he blessed him and said:

> "Blessed be Abram of God Most High,
> Possessor of heaven and earth;
> 20 And blessed be God Most High,
> Who has delivered your enemies into your hand."

And he gave him a tithe of all. ²¹Now the king of Sodom said to Abram, "Give me the persons, and take the goods for yourself." ²²*But Abram said to the king of Sodom, "I have raised my hand to the LORD, God Most High, the Possessor of heaven and earth, ²³that I *will take* nothing, from a thread to a sandal strap, and that I will not take anything that *is* yours, lest you should say, 'I have made Abram rich'— ²⁴except only what the young men have eaten, and the portion of the men who went with me: Aner, Eshcol, and Mamre; let them take their portion."

15 After* these things the word of the LORD came to Abram in a vision, saying, "Do not be afraid, Abram. I *am* your shield, your exceedingly great reward."

²But Abram said, "Lord GOD, what will You give me, seeing I go childless, and the heir of my house *is* Eliezer of Damascus?" ³Then Abram said, "Look, You have given me no offspring; indeed one born in my house is my heir!"

⁴*And behold, the word of the LORD *came* to him, saying, "This one shall not be your heir, but one who will come from your own body shall be your heir." ⁵Then He brought him outside and said, "Look now toward heaven, and count the stars if you are able to number them." And He said to him, "So shall your descendants be."

14:13 *b*Hebrew *Alon Mamre*

Fear—There is a godly fear, a reverence for the Lord, that must be in every heart (1 Pet. 1:17; 2:17). If we fear God, we need not fear anyone or anything else (Ps. 112; Isa. 8:13). The fear of man trips us up (Prov. 29:25), but if we fear God, we need not fear the words or threats of men (Matt. 10:26–33).

6And he believed in the LORD, and He accounted it to him for righteousness.

7Then He said to him, "I *am* the LORD, who brought you out of Ur of the Chaldeans, to give you this land to inherit it."

8*And he said, "Lord GOD, how shall I know that I will inherit it?"

9So He said to him, "Bring Me a three-year-old heifer, a three-year-old female goat, a three-year-old ram, a turtledove, and a young pigeon." 10Then he brought all these to Him and cut them in two, down the middle, and placed each piece opposite the other; but he did not cut the birds in two. 11And when the vultures came down on the carcasses, Abram drove them away.

12Now when the sun was going down, a deep sleep fell upon Abram; and behold, horror *and* great darkness fell upon him. 13Then He said to Abram: "Know certainly that your descendants will be strangers in a land *that is* not theirs, and will serve them, and they will afflict them four hundred years. 14And also the nation whom they serve I will judge; afterward they shall come out with great possessions. 15Now as for you, you shall go to your fathers in peace; you shall be buried at a good old age. 16But in the fourth generation they shall return here, for the iniquity of the Amorites *is* not yet complete."

17And it came to pass, when the sun went down and it was dark, that behold, there appeared a smoking oven and a burning torch that passed between those pieces. 18On the same day the LORD made a covenant with Abram, saying:

"To your descendants I have given this land, from the river of Egypt to the great river, the River Euphrates— 19the Kenites, the Kenezzites, the Kadmonites, 20the Hittites, the Perizzites, the Rephaim, 21the Amorites, the Canaanites, the Girgashites, and the Jebusites."

16 Now* Sarai, Abram's wife, had borne him no *children*. And she had an Egyptian maidservant whose name was Hagar. 2*So Sarai said to Abram, "See now, the LORD has restrained me from bearing *children*. Please, go in to my maid; perhaps I shall obtain children by her." And Abram heeded the voice of Sarai. 3Then Sarai, Abram's wife, took Hagar her maid, the Egyptian, and gave her to her husband Abram to be his wife, after Abram had dwelt ten years in the land of Canaan. 4So he went in to Hagar, and she conceived. And when she saw that she had conceived, her mistress became despised in her eyes.

5Then Sarai said to Abram, "My wrong *be* upon you! I gave my maid into your embrace; and when she saw that she had conceived, I became despised in her eyes. The LORD judge between you and me."

6*So Abram said to Sarai, "Indeed your maid *is* in your hand; do to her as you please." And when Sarai dealt harshly with her, she fled from her presence.

7Now the Angel of the LORD found her by a spring of water in the wilderness, by the spring on the way to Shur. 8And He said, "Hagar, Sarai's maid, where have you come from, and where are you going?"

She said, "I am fleeing from the presence of my mistress Sarai."

9The Angel of the LORD said to her, "Return to your mistress, and submit yourself under her hand." 10Then the Angel of the LORD said to her,

(continued from previous page)
to see what God had for him (Gen. 13:14; see also 13:10). Verse 6 makes it clear that Abram was saved by faith in God's word (Rom. 4:3; Gal. 3:6; James 2:23), and that is the *only* way to be saved.

15:8–21 *What God does.* God sealed His promise with a covenant. In those days, to walk between the divided parts of an animal was one way to seal an agreement. *But God was the only One who passed between the pieces!* Abram was asleep! God's covenants are all of grace (Eph. 2:8–9), and our works are but evidence of our faith.

When you find yourself afraid or impatient with God's will, look toward heaven and remember His covenant and His promises. When you bring your offering to God, be sure the enemy doesn't steal it. When you can do nothing, rest assured God is at work.

CHAPTER 16

16:1ff Faith and patience always go together (Heb. 6:12; James 1:1–5). Isaiah declared, "Whoever believes will not act hastily" (Isa. 28:16). We must trust God not only for His plan but also for His timing. Before He could send the promised son, God had to wait until Abram and Sarai were as good as dead (Rom. 4:19–21; Heb. 11:11–12). Sarai leaned on human understanding instead of God's promises (Prov. 3:5–6). She trusted a woman from Egypt instead of the God of heaven.

16:2, 5 Sarai was not a strong *believer*, but she was a capable *blamer*. She blamed God for her barrenness, then blamed Abram when Hagar created problems in the home. The wisdom from God is pure and peaceable, but the wisdom of the flesh is always divisive (James 3:13–18). Abram abdicated his spiritual leadership in the home, and the result was confusion.

16:6–9 When we walk by sight and not by faith, we get impatient; we scheme and blame others. Then when things go wrong, we try to get rid of our mistakes. God sent Hagar and Ishmael back to Abram and Sarai, and they had to live with their mistake for at least another seventeen years.

"I will multiply your descendants exceedingly, so that they shall not be counted for multitude." 11And the Angel of the LORD said to her:

"Behold, you *are* with child,
And you shall bear a son.
You shall call his name Ishmael,
Because the LORD has heard your affliction.
12   He shall be a wild man;
His hand *shall be* against every man,
And every man's hand against him.
And he shall dwell in the presence of all
his brethren."

13Then she called the name of the LORD who spoke to her, You-Are-the-God-Who-Sees; for she said, "Have I also here seen Him who sees me?" 14Therefore the well was called Beer Lahai Roi;c observe, *it is* between Kadesh and Bered. 15*So Hagar bore Abram a son; and Abram named his son, whom Hagar bore, Ishmael. 16Abram *was* eighty-six years old when Hagar bore Ishmael to Abram.

16:15 Abram and Sarai greatly wronged Hagar, and they suffered for it; but God stepped in and cared for her and her son. Abram obeyed God and gave the appointed name to his son: "Ishmael—God shall hear." Had Abram and Sarai waited on God instead of running ahead of God, they would have avoided all that pain.

CHAPTER 17

17:1ff New revelations. As far as the record is concerned, God waited thirteen years before He revealed Himself again to Abram. During those quiet intervening years, Abram continued to walk with God and serve Him. He did not need constant special revelations to do God's will, nor do we. God reaffirmed His covenant and then gave Abram the sign of circumcision as the mark of that covenant. How unfortunate that many of the Jews trusted in the sign rather than in the Lord (Acts 15:5; Rom. 4:10; Gal. 5:6)! God wanted an inward change of the heart, not just surgery on the body (Deut. 10:16; Jer. 4:4).

17:5, 15 New names. In Bible history, a new name means a new beginning, a step forward in faith. (See Gen. 32:28; John 1:40–42.) *Abram* means "exalted father"; it became *Abraham,* "father of a multitude." *Sarai* ("contentious") became *Sarah,* "a princess." God even revealed a new name for Himself: God Almighty. The only name that did not change was Ishmael, for what is born of the flesh remains flesh and cannot be changed (John 3:6).

17 When* Abram was ninety-nine years old, the LORD appeared to Abram and said to him, "I *am* Almighty God; walk before Me and be blameless. 2And I will make My covenant between Me and you, and will multiply you exceedingly." 3Then Abram fell on his face, and God talked with him, saying: 4"As for Me, behold, My covenant is with you, and you shall be a father of many nations. 5*No longer shall your name be called Abram, but your name shall be Abraham; for I have made you a father of many nations. 6I will make you exceedingly fruitful; and I will make nations of you, and kings shall come from you. 7And I will establish My covenant between Me and you and your descendants after you in their generations, for an everlasting covenant, to be God to you and your descendants after you. 8Also I give to you and your descendants after you the land in which you are a stranger, all the land of Canaan, as an everlasting possession; and I will be their God."

9And God said to Abraham: "As for you, you shall keep My covenant, you and your descendants after you throughout their generations. 10This *is* My covenant which you shall keep, between Me and you and your descendants after you: Every male child among you shall be circumcised; 11and you shall be circumcised in the flesh of your foreskins, and it shall be a sign of the covenant between Me and you. 12He who is eight days old among you shall be circumcised, every male child in your generations, he who is born in your house or bought with money from any foreigner who is not your descendant. 13He who is born in your house and he who is bought with your money must be circumcised, and My covenant shall be in your flesh for an everlasting covenant. 14And the uncircumcised male child, who

---

16:14 cLiterally *Well of the One Who Lives and Sees Me*

God Almighty!—The Bible affirms our need to rely on God, for whom nothing is impossible (Luke 1:37): "Is anything too hard for the LORD?" (Gen. 18:14). "There is nothing too hard for You" (Jer. 32:17); God is "able to do exceedingly abundantly above all that we ask or think" (Eph. 3:20). So, we may say, "I can do all things through Christ who strengthens me" (Phil. 4:13). Lay hold of God's power!

is not circumcised in the flesh of his foreskin, that person shall be cut off from his people; he has broken My covenant."

15Then God said to Abraham, "As for Sarai your wife, you shall not call her name Sarai, but Sarah *shall be* her name. 16And I will bless her and also give you a son by her; then I will bless her, and she shall be *a mother of* nations; kings of peoples shall be from her."

17Then Abraham fell on his face and laughed, and said in his heart, "Shall *a child* be born to a man who is one hundred years old? And shall Sarah, who is ninety years old, bear *a child?*" 18And Abraham said to God, "Oh, that Ishmael might live before You!"

19*Then God said: "No, Sarah your wife shall bear you a son, and you shall call his name Isaac; I will establish My covenant with him for an everlasting covenant, *and* with his descendants after him. 20And as for Ishmael, I have heard you. Behold, I have blessed him, and will make him fruitful, and will multiply him exceedingly. He shall beget twelve princes, and I will make him a great nation. 21But My covenant I will establish with Isaac, whom Sarah shall bear to you at this set time next year." 22Then He finished talking with him, and God went up from Abraham.

23So Abraham took Ishmael his son, all who were born in his house and all who were bought with his money, every male among the men of Abraham's house, and circumcised the flesh of their foreskins that very same day, as God had said to him. 24Abraham *was* ninety-nine years old when he was circumcised in the flesh of his foreskin. 25And Ishmael his son *was* thirteen years old when he was circumcised in the flesh of his foreskin. 26That very same day Abraham was circumcised, and his son Ishmael; 27and all the men of his house, born in the house or bought with money from a foreigner, were circumcised with him.

18 Then* the LORD appeared to him by the terebinth trees of Mamre,*d* as he was sitting in the tent door in the heat of the day. 2*So he lifted his eyes and looked, and behold, three men were standing by him; and when he saw *them,* he ran from the tent door to meet them, and bowed himself to the ground, 3and said, "My Lord, if I have now found favor in Your sight, do not pass on by Your servant. 4Please let a little water be brought, and wash your feet, and rest yourselves under the tree. 5And I will bring a morsel of bread, that you may refresh your hearts. After that you may pass by, inasmuch as you have come to your servant."

They said, "Do as you have said."

6So Abraham hurried into the tent to Sarah and said, "Quickly, make ready three measures of fine meal; knead *it* and make cakes." 7And Abraham ran to the herd, took a tender and good calf, gave *it* to a young man, and he hastened to prepare it. 8So he took butter and milk and the calf which he had prepared, and set *it* before them; and he stood by them under the tree as they ate.

9*Then they said to him, "Where *is* Sarah your wife?"

So he said, "Here, in the tent."

10And He said, "I will certainly return to you

17:19–22 *New joy.* At last, the long-awaited son would be born, and his name would be Isaac—"laughter." No wonder Abraham laughed (John 8:56). Abraham wanted to cling to his past mistake (v. 18) instead of looking to the future miracle that God would perform. Abraham and Sarah's impatient act of unbelief had brought sorrow and division into the home, but God's miracle of faith brought joy and peace (Rom. 15:13). It pays to trust God's way and wait for God's time.

CHAPTER 18

18:1 *Resting.* Resting in the afternoon is a normal practice in the East, and don't forget that Abraham was nearly a hundred years old. Sometimes the most spiritual thing we can do is take a nap! The believer's body is God's temple and must be cared for (1 Cor. 6:19–20). (See Mark 6:31.)

18:2–8 *Serving.* Abraham had no trouble noticing the pilgrims because it was unusual for people to travel in the heat of the day. The visitors were two angels and the Lord Jesus Christ, in one of His preincarnation appearances. Even though he had 318 servants, Abraham served Him personally, and called Him "Lord." Abraham ran from place to place to make certain the meal they were preparing was the very best.

18:9–14 *Listening.* Abraham stood nearby as the visitors ate, ready to serve them whatever they wanted. But the Lord gave Abraham something better than food: He announced that the promised son would be born within the year. "Where is Sarah your wife?" is the last of three key questions in Genesis (3:9; 4:9; 18:9). The question "Is anything too hard for the LORD?" has been answered by Job (Job 42:2), Jeremiah (Jer. 32:17), and Gabriel (Luke 1:37).

according to the time of life, and behold, Sarah your wife shall have a son."

(Sarah was listening in the tent door which *was* behind him.) 11Now Abraham and Sarah were old, well advanced in age; *and* Sarah had passed the age of childbearing.*e* 12Therefore Sarah laughed within herself, saying, "After I have grown old, shall I have pleasure, my lord being old also?"

13And the LORD said to Abraham, "Why did Sarah laugh, saying, 'Shall I surely bear *a child,* since I am old?' 14Is anything too hard for the LORD? At the appointed time I will return to you, according to the time of life, and Sarah shall have a son."

15But Sarah denied *it,* saying, "I did not laugh," for she was afraid.

And He said, "No, but you did laugh!"

16Then the men rose from there and looked toward Sodom, and Abraham went with them to send them on the way. 17And the LORD said, "Shall I hide from Abraham what I am doing, 18since Abraham shall surely become a great and mighty nation, and all the nations of the earth shall be blessed in him? 19For I have known him, in order that he may command his children and his household after him, that they keep the way of the LORD, to do righteousness and justice, that the LORD may bring to Abraham what He has spoken to him." 20And the LORD said, "Because the outcry against Sodom and Gomorrah is great, and because their sin is very grave, 21I will go down now and see whether they have done altogether according to the outcry against it that has come to Me; and if not, I will know."

22Then the men turned away from there and went toward Sodom, but Abraham still stood before the LORD. 23And Abraham came near and said, "Would You also destroy the righteous with the wicked? 24Suppose there were fifty righteous within the city; would You also destroy the place and not spare *it* for the fifty righteous that were in it? 25Far be it from You to do such a thing as this, to slay the righteous with the wicked, so that the righteous should be as the wicked; far be it from You! Shall not the Judge of all the earth do right?"

26So the LORD said, "If I find in Sodom fifty righteous within the city, then I will spare all the place for their sakes."

27Then Abraham answered and said, "Indeed now, I who *am but* dust and ashes have taken it upon myself to speak to the Lord: 28Suppose there were five less than the fifty righteous; would You destroy all of the city for *lack of* five?"

So He said, "If I find there forty-five, I will not destroy *it.*"

29*And he spoke to Him yet again and said, "Suppose there should be forty found there?"

So He said, "I will not do *it* for the sake of forty."

30Then he said, "Let not the Lord be angry, and I will speak: Suppose thirty should be found there?"

So He said, "I will not do *it* if I find thirty there."

31And he said, "Indeed now, I have taken it upon myself to speak to the Lord: Suppose twenty should be found there?"

So He said, "I will not destroy *it* for the sake of twenty."

18:29–32 *Interceding.* Because Abraham was both the friend of God and the servant of God, he shared God's secrets. (See Ps. 25:14; John 15:15; James 2:23.) Lot had been rescued by Abraham's intervention (chap. 14); now he would be rescued by Abraham's intercession. Abraham prayed for the city on the basis of the justice of God, but God saved Lot on the basis of His mercy and grace (19:16, 19). Interceding for the lost and for needy saints is a high and holy privilege that we must not neglect.

18:11 *c*Literally *the manner of women had ceased to be with Sarah*

32Then he said, "Let not the Lord be angry, and I will speak but once more: Suppose ten should be found there?"

And He said, "I will not destroy *it* for the sake of ten." 33So the LORD went His way as soon as He had finished speaking with Abraham; and Abraham returned to his place.

19 Now* the two angels came to Sodom in the evening, and Lot was sitting in the gate of Sodom. When Lot saw *them,* he rose to meet them, and he bowed himself with his face toward the ground. 2And he said, "Here now, my lords, please turn in to your servant's house and spend the night, and wash your feet; then you may rise early and go on your way."

And they said, "No, but we will spend the night in the open square."

3But he insisted strongly; so they turned in to him and entered his house. Then he made them a feast, and baked unleavened bread, and they ate.

4Now before they lay down, the men of the city, the men of Sodom, both old and young, all the people from every quarter, surrounded the house. 5And they called to Lot and said to him, "Where are the men who came to you tonight? Bring them out to us that we may know them *carnally.*"

6*So Lot went out to them through the doorway, shut the door behind him, 7and said, "Please, my brethren, do not do so wickedly! 8See now, I have two daughters who have not known a man; please, let me bring them out to you, and you may do to them as you wish; only do nothing to these men, since this is the reason they have come under the shadow of my roof."

9And they said, "Stand back!" Then they said, "This one came in to stay *here,* and he keeps acting as a judge; now we will deal worse with you than with them." So they pressed hard against the man Lot, and came near to break down the door. 10But the men reached out their hands and pulled Lot into the house with them, and shut the door. 11And they struck the men who *were* at the doorway of the house with blindness, both small and great, so that they became weary *trying* to find the door.

12*Then the men said to Lot, "Have you anyone else here? Son-in-law, your sons, your daughters, and whomever you have in the city—take *them* out of this place! 13For we will destroy this place, because the outcry against them has grown great before the face of the LORD, and the LORD has sent us to destroy it."

14So Lot went out and spoke to his sons-in-law, who had married his daughters, and said, "Get up, get out of this place; for the LORD will destroy this city!" But to his sons-in-law he seemed to be joking.

15When the morning dawned, the angels urged Lot to hurry, saying, "Arise, take your wife and your two daughters who are here, lest you be consumed in the punishment of the city." 16And while he lingered, the men took hold of his hand, his wife's hand, and the hands of his two daughters, the LORD being merciful to him, and they brought him out and set him outside the city. 17So it came to pass, when they had brought them outside, that he*f* said, "Escape for your life! Do not look behind

CHAPTER 19

19:1–5 Because Jesus did not "feel at home" with Lot in Sodom, He sent the two angels to look into the situation for Him. The angels didn't walk the streets or visit the public places of amusement. *They visited a professed believer to see what his home was like.* Lot's wife and family were far from the Lord. The salt had lost its flavor (Matt. 5:13), so what hope was there for the city?

Abraham was visited when it was light, but Lot received the angels at evening (1 John 1:5–10). Abraham's household obeyed his word as he served the Lord, but Lot's family only laughed at Lot's words. Abraham hastened, but Lot lingered and had to be dragged out of the city. Abraham, who lived outside Sodom, had more influence than Lot, who lived in the city.

19:6–8 Lot tried first to plead with the men at the door, and then to bargain with them. God's approach was to judge them. They loved darkness rather than light (John 3:19).

19:12 God did not find ten righteous people, but He spared Lot and his wife and daughters for the sake of Abraham. While we may hate the sins of Sodom, keep in mind that all those people went to eternal judgment. (See Jude 23.)

19:17 *f*Septuagint, Syriac, and Vulgate read *they.*

you nor stay anywhere in the plain. Escape to the mountains, lest you be destroyed."

18Then Lot said to them, "Please, no, my lords! 19Indeed now, your servant has found favor in your sight, and you have increased your mercy which you have shown me by saving my life; but I cannot escape to the mountains, lest some evil overtake me and I die. 20See now, this city *is* near *enough* to flee to, and it *is* a little one; please let me escape there (*is* it not a little one?) and my soul shall live."

21And he said to him, "See, I have favored you concerning this thing also, in that I will not overthrow this city for which you have spoken. 22Hurry, escape there. For I cannot do anything until you arrive there."

Therefore the name of the city was called Zoar. 23The sun had risen upon the earth when Lot entered Zoar. 24Then the LORD rained brimstone and fire on Sodom and Gomorrah, from the LORD out of the heavens. 25So He overthrew those cities, all the plain, all the inhabitants of the cities, and what grew on the ground.

26But his wife looked back behind him, and she became a pillar of salt.

27And Abraham went early in the morning to the place where he had stood before the LORD. 28Then he looked toward Sodom and Gomorrah, and toward all the land of the plain; and he saw, and behold, the smoke of the land which went up like the smoke of a furnace. 29And it came to pass, when God destroyed the cities of the plain, that God remembered Abraham, and sent Lot out of the midst of the overthrow, when He overthrew the cities in which Lot had dwelt.

30*Then Lot went up out of Zoar and dwelt in the mountains, and his two daughters were with him; for he was afraid to dwell in Zoar. And he and his two daughters dwelt in a cave. 31Now the firstborn said to the younger, "Our father *is* old, and *there is* no man on the earth to come in to us as is the custom of all the earth. 32Come, let us make our father drink wine, and we will lie with him, that we may preserve the lineage of our father." 33So they made their father drink wine that night. And the firstborn went in and lay with her father, and he did not know when she lay down or when she arose.

34It happened on the next day that the firstborn said to the younger, "Indeed I lay with my father last night; let us make him drink wine tonight also, and you go in *and* lie with him, that we may preserve the lineage of our father." 35Then they made their father drink wine that night also. And the younger arose and lay with him, and he did not know when she lay down or when she arose.

36Thus both the daughters of Lot were with child by their father. 37The firstborn bore a son and called his name Moab; he *is* the father of the Moabites to this day. 38And the younger, she also bore a son and called his name Ben-Ammi; he *is* the father of the people of Ammon to this day.

19:30–38 Lot had no tent or altar, and he ended up in a cave committing terrible sins. Were it not for 2 Peter 2:7–8, we might doubt that he was a believer at all. (See Ps. 1:1.)

CHAPTER 20

20:1ff *Relapse.* The man of faith started walking by sight (v. 11), became frightened (Prov. 29:25), and began scheming (Gen. 12:10ff.). This time, even Sarah lied (v. 5)! Whatever we carry with us from the old life (v. 13) will create problems in the new life. It is one thing to *confess* our sins but another thing to *judge* them before God and forsake them (Prov. 28:13). When a marriage must be protected by a lie, the home is in danger.

20:3 *Revelation.* God spoke to the heathen king but not to His own friend, Abraham! Although God kept the king from sinning, He allowed Abraham to lie! God called Abraham to be a blessing, but now he had become a curse in the land. God was protecting Sarah, Isaac, and His great plan of salvation.

20 And* Abraham journeyed from there to the South, and dwelt between Kadesh and Shur, and stayed in Gerar. 2Now Abraham said of Sarah his wife, "She *is* my sister." And Abimelech king of Gerar sent and took Sarah.

3*But God came to Abimelech in a dream by night, and said to him, "Indeed you *are* a dead man because of the woman whom you have taken, for she *is* a man's wife."

4But Abimelech had not come near her; and he said, "Lord, will You slay a righteous nation also? 5Did he not say to me, 'She *is* my sister'? And she, even she herself said, 'He *is* my brother.' In the integrity of my heart and innocence of my hands I have done this."

6And God said to him in a dream, "Yes, I know that you did this in the integrity of your heart. For I also withheld you from sinning against Me; therefore I did not let you touch her. 7Now therefore, restore the man's wife; for he *is* a prophet, and he will pray for you and you shall live. But if you do not restore *her,* know that you shall surely die, you and all who *are* yours."

8So Abimelech rose early in the morning, called all his servants, and told all these things in their hearing; and the men were very much afraid. 9*And Abimelech called Abraham and said to him, "What have you done to us? How have I offended you, that you have brought on me and on my kingdom a great sin? You have done deeds to me that ought not to be done." 10Then Abimelech said to Abraham, "What did you have in view, that you have done this thing?"

11And Abraham said, "Because I thought, surely the fear of God *is* not in this place; and they will kill me on account of my wife. 12But indeed *she is* truly my sister. She *is* the daughter of my father, but not the daughter of my mother; and she became my wife. 13And it came to pass, when God caused me to wander from my father's house, that I said to her, 'This *is* your kindness that you should do for me: in every place, wherever we go, say of me, "He *is* my brother."' "

14Then Abimelech took sheep, oxen, and male and female servants, and gave *them* to Abraham; and he restored Sarah his wife to him. 15And Abimelech said, "See, my land *is* before you; dwell where it pleases you." 16*Then to Sarah he said, "Behold, I have given your brother a thousand *pieces* of silver; indeed this vindicates you*g* before all who *are* with you and before everybody." Thus she was rebuked.

17So Abraham prayed to God; and God healed Abimelech, his wife, and his female servants. Then they bore *children;* 18for the LORD had closed up all the wombs of the house of Abimelech because of Sarah, Abraham's wife.

21 And* the LORD visited Sarah as He had said, and the LORD did for Sarah as He had spoken. 2For Sarah conceived and bore Abraham a son in his old age, at the set time of which God had spoken to him. 3And Abraham called the name of his son who was born to him—whom Sarah bore to him—Isaac. 4Then Abraham circumcised his son Isaac when he was eight days old, as God had commanded him. 5Now Abraham was one hundred years old when his son Isaac was born to him. 6And Sarah said, "God has made me laugh, *and* all who hear will laugh with me." 7She also said, "Who would have said to Abraham that Sarah would nurse children? For I have borne *him* a son in his old age."

8So the child grew and was weaned. And Abraham made a great feast on the same day that Isaac was weaned.

9And Sarah saw the son of Hagar the Egyptian, whom she had borne to Abraham, scoffing.

20:9 Rebuke. What a humiliating thing to be openly rebuked by a pagan king. God sometimes uses the unsaved to chasten the saved. The fact that Abraham was a believer did not give him license to sin. Unfortunately, years later, Abraham's son Isaac would imitate his father's sin (Gen. 26).

20:16–18 Restoration. In those days, the paying of a large sum of money was public "atonement" for guilt; however, sin is never profitable. God did not forsake His friend (Ps. 105:15; 2 Tim. 2:12–13) but honored him in the end and answered his prayer. Financially, Abraham was richer; spiritually, he was poorer. He lost character as well as opportunity to witness and glorify God.

CHAPTER 21

21:1–7 Family joys. God kept His promises, followed His schedule, and did not fail. This time, Sarah's laughter was open and sincere, not hidden and skeptical (Gen. 18:12). The name *Isaac* means "laughter," and the boy brought much joy to the aged couple. Through him, joy has come to the world. God makes "everything beautiful in its time" (Eccles. 3:11).

20:16 9Literally *it is a covering of the eyes for you*

21:12–14 Family sorrows. Abraham reaped the sad consequences of forgiven sin. He had lived with Ishmael for perhaps seventeen years, and he loved the lad, so the parting was painful. There comes a time when we must "cut off" the past and make a new beginning. The apostle Paul saw this as a picture of law and grace (Gal. 4:21–31). For Abraham's sake, God blessed the lad and made him a great nation.

21:22–34 Family testimony. Abraham's unsaved neighbors could tell that he was a man whom God had blessed. Abraham didn't try to lie his way out of this problem; he boldly told the truth and trusted God to work. The possession of water is an important thing in the East, and people will fight over wells. God's people must be careful in their relationships with "those who are outside" the faith (Col. 4:5; 1 Thess. 4:12).

Life is a balance of joys and sorrows, problems and blessings. We must learn to accept what God gives us and walk by faith.

10Therefore she said to Abraham, "Cast out this bondwoman and her son; for the son of this bondwoman shall not be heir with my son, *namely* with Isaac." 11And the matter was very displeasing in Abraham's sight because of his son.

12*But God said to Abraham, "Do not let it be displeasing in your sight because of the lad or because of your bondwoman. Whatever Sarah has said to you, listen to her voice; for in Isaac your seed shall be called. 13Yet I will also make a nation of the son of the bondwoman, because he *is* your seed."

14So Abraham rose early in the morning, and took bread and a skin of water; and putting *it* on her shoulder, he gave *it* and the boy to Hagar, and sent her away. Then she departed and wandered in the Wilderness of Beersheba. 15And the water in the skin was used up, and she placed the boy under one of the shrubs. 16Then she went and sat down across from *him* at a distance of about a bowshot; for she said to herself, "Let me not see the death of the boy." So she sat opposite *him,* and lifted her voice and wept.

17And God heard the voice of the lad. Then the angel of God called to Hagar out of heaven, and said to her, "What ails you, Hagar? Fear not, for God has heard the voice of the lad where he *is.* 18Arise, lift up the lad and hold him with your hand, for I will make him a great nation."

19Then God opened her eyes, and she saw a well of water. And she went and filled the skin with water, and gave the lad a drink. 20So God was with the lad; and he grew and dwelt in the wilderness, and became an archer. 21He dwelt in the Wilderness of Paran; and his mother took a wife for him from the land of Egypt.

22*And it came to pass at that time that Abimelech and Phichol, the commander of his army, spoke to Abraham, saying, "God *is* with you in all that you do. 23Now therefore, swear to me by God that you will not deal falsely with me, with my offspring, or with my posterity; but that according to the kindness that I have done to you, you will do to me and to the land in which you have dwelt."

24And Abraham said, "I will swear."

25Then Abraham rebuked Abimelech because of a well of water which Abimelech's servants had seized. 26And Abimelech said, "I do not know who has done this thing; you did not tell me, nor had I heard *of it* until today." 27So Abraham took sheep and oxen and gave them to Abimelech, and the two of them made a covenant. 28And Abraham set seven ewe lambs of the flock by themselves.

29Then Abimelech asked Abraham, "What *is the meaning of* these seven ewe lambs which you have set by themselves?"

30And he said, "You will take *these* seven ewe lambs from my hand, that they may be my witness that I have dug this well." 31Therefore he called that place Beersheba,*h* because the two of them swore an oath there.

32Thus they made a covenant at Beersheba. So Abimelech rose with Phichol, the commander of his army, and they returned to the land of the Philistines. 33Then *Abraham* planted a tamarisk tree in Beersheba, and there called on the name of the LORD, the Everlasting God. 34And Abraham stayed in the land of the Philistines many days.

21:31 *h*Literally *Well of the Oath* or *Well of the Seven*

22 Now* it came to pass after these things that God tested Abraham, and said to him, "Abraham!"

And he said, "Here I am."

2*Then He said, "Take now your son, your only *son* Isaac, whom you love, and go to the land of Moriah, and offer him there as a burnt offering on one of the mountains of which I shall tell you."

3So Abraham rose early in the morning and saddled his donkey, and took two of his young men with him, and Isaac his son; and he split the wood for the burnt offering, and arose and went to the place of which God had told him. 4Then on the third day Abraham lifted his eyes and saw the place afar off. 5And Abraham said to his young men, "Stay here with the donkey; the lad*ᴵ* and I will go yonder and worship, and we will come back to you."

6So Abraham took the wood of the burnt offering and laid *it* on Isaac his son; and he took the fire in his hand, and a knife, and the two of them went together. 7But Isaac spoke to Abraham his father and said, "My father!"

And he said, "Here I am, my son."

Then he said, "Look, the fire and the wood, but where *is* the lamb for a burnt offering?"

8And Abraham said, "My son, God will provide for Himself the lamb for a burnt offering." So the two of them went together.

9Then they came to the place of which God had told him. And Abraham built an altar there and placed the wood in order; and he bound Isaac his son and laid him on the altar, upon the wood. 10And Abraham stretched out his hand and took the knife to slay his son.

11But the Angel of the LORD called to him from heaven and said, "Abraham, Abraham!"

So he said, "Here I am."

12And He said, "Do not lay your hand on the lad, or do anything to him; for now I know that you fear God, since you have not withheld your son, your only *son,* from Me."

13Then Abraham lifted his eyes and looked, and there behind *him was* a ram caught in a thicket by its horns. So Abraham went and took the ram, and offered it up for a burnt offering instead of his son. 14*And Abraham called the name of the place, The-LORD-Will-Provide;*ᴶ* as it is said *to* this day, "In the Mount of the LORD it shall be provided."

15Then the Angel of the LORD called to Abraham a second time out of heaven, 16and said: "By Myself I have sworn, says the LORD, because you have done this thing, and have not withheld your son, your only *son*— 17blessing I will bless you, and multiplying I will multiply your descendants as the stars of the heaven and as the sand which *is* on the seashore; and your descendants shall possess the gate of their enemies. 18In your seed all the nations of the earth shall be blessed, because you have obeyed My voice." 19So Abraham returned to his young men, and they rose and went together to Beersheba; and Abraham dwelt at Beersheba.

20*Now it came to pass after these things that it was told Abraham, saying, "Indeed Milcah also has borne children to your brother Nahor: 21Huz his firstborn, Buz his brother, Kemuel the father of Aram, 22Chesed, Hazo, Pildash, Jidlaph,

CHAPTER 22

22:1ff Offering Isaac on the altar was the hardest test Abraham ever faced, but he came through victoriously because he trusted God (Heb. 11:17–19). He had experienced resurrection power in his own body (Rom. 4:19–21), so he knew what God could do. It was a test of *faith,* far more difficult than the previous tests involving Lot and Ishmael.

It was also a test of *hope,* for God's plan of salvation for the world was wrapped up in Isaac. If Isaac died, how could the Jewish nation be built and the Savior be born? But Abraham had a living hope because he trusted in the living God (1 Pet. 1:3).

22:2 Certainly it was a test of *love.* In verse 2, you find the first use of the word *love* in the Bible. Abraham loved his son, but he loved God more. Isaac was God's gift to Abraham, but the gift had to become a sacrifice to God. If the gift becomes more important than the Giver, it becomes an idol.

22:14 After He tests us, God reveals Himself to us in a new way (John 14:21–23). The name *Jehovah-Yireh* means "the Lord will see to it" or "the Lord will provide." The ram was God's provision for Isaac, and Jesus Christ is God's provision for the whole world. In this experience, Abraham saw Christ by faith and rejoiced (John 8:56).

22:20–24 Why this "family news" in verses 20–24? To introduce us to Rebekah who will become the bride of Isaac (chap. 24). Isaac was a "living sacrifice" (Rom. 12:1–2), and God was working out His perfect will for him.

22:5 *Or young man*   22:14 *Hebrew YHWH Yireh*

and Bethuel." ²³And Bethuel begot Rebekah.ᵏ These eight Milcah bore to Nahor, Abraham's brother. ²⁴His concubine, whose name was Reumah, also bore Tebah, Gaham, Thahash, and Maachah.

23 Sarah* lived one hundred and twenty-seven years; *these were* the years of the life of Sarah. ²So Sarah died in Kirjath Arba (that *is,* Hebron) in the land of Canaan, and Abraham came to mourn for Sarah and to weep for her.

³*Then Abraham stood up from before his dead, and spoke to the sons of Heth, saying, ⁴"I *am* a foreigner and a visitor among you. Give me property for a burial place among you, that I may bury my dead out of my sight."

⁵And the sons of Heth answered Abraham, saying to him, ⁶"Hear us, my lord: You *are* a mighty prince among us; bury your dead in the choicest of our burial places. None of us will withhold from you his burial place, that you may bury your dead."

⁷Then Abraham stood up and bowed himself to the people of the land, the sons of Heth. ⁸And he spoke with them, saying, "If it is your wish that I bury my dead out of my sight, hear me, and meet with Ephron the son of Zohar for me, ⁹that he may give me the cave of Machpelah which he has, which *is* at the end of his field. Let him give it to me at the full price, as property for a burial place among you."

¹⁰Now Ephron dwelt among the sons of Heth; and Ephron the Hittite answered Abraham in the presence of the sons of Heth, all who entered at the gate of his city, saying, ¹¹"No, my lord, hear me: I give you the field and the cave that *is* in it; I give it to you in the presence of the sons of my people. I give it to you. Bury your dead!"

¹²Then Abraham bowed himself down before the people of the land; ¹³and he spoke to Ephron in the hearing of the people of the land, saying, "If you *will give it,* please hear me. I will give you money for the field; take *it* from me and I will bury my dead there."

¹⁴And Ephron answered Abraham, saying to him, ¹⁵"My lord, listen to me; the land *is worth* four hundred shekels of silver. What *is* that between you and me? So bury your dead." ¹⁶And Abraham listened to Ephron; and Abraham weighed out the silver for Ephron which he had named in the hearing of the sons of Heth, four hundred shekels of silver, currency of the merchants.

¹⁷So the field of Ephron which *was* in Machpelah, which *was* before Mamre, the field and the cave which *was* in it, and all the trees that *were* in the field, which *were* within all the surrounding borders, were deeded ¹⁸to Abraham as a possession in the presence of the sons of Heth, before all who went in at the gate of his city. ¹⁹*And after this, Abraham buried Sarah his wife in the cave of the field of Machpelah, before Mamre (that *is,* Hebron) in the land of Canaan. ²⁰So the field and the cave that *is* in it were deeded to Abraham by the sons of Heth as property for a burial place.

24 Now* Abraham was old, well advanced in age; and the LORD had blessed Abraham in

CHAPTER 23

23:1, 2 *Abraham the mourner.* Sarah is the only woman named in the Bible whose age is given and burial described. It was the death of a princess, a woman of faith (Heb. 11:11–13; 1 Pet. 3:6). Abraham felt the pain of his loss and openly expressed his grief. Faith is not the enemy of tears, for we sorrow as those who have hope (1 Thess. 4:13–18). Jesus wept (John 11:35) even though He knew He would raise His friend from the dead.

23:3–16 *Abraham the sojourner.* Ephron did not plan to *give* Abraham a valuable piece of land, but that is how typical Eastern bargaining always begins. The land already belonged to Abraham (15:7), but he could never explain that to his unbelieving neighbors. He was a pilgrim and did not claim any of it for himself.

23:19, 20 *Abraham the owner.* He paid a high price for what became one of the most famous tombs in Bible history, and eventually six people were buried there (49:31–32). Abraham owned only one thing on earth: a grave. Genesis ends with a full tomb, but the gospel story ends with an empty tomb! And because Jesus Christ lives, we who trust in Him never need fear death.

CHAPTER 24

24:1ff This is the longest chapter in Genesis, and it focuses on faith, hope, and love.

22:23 ᵏSpelled *Rebecca* in Romans 9:10

all things. 2*So Abraham said to the oldest servant of his house, who ruled over all that he had, "Please, put your hand under my thigh, 3and I will make you swear by the LORD, the God of heaven and the God of the earth, that you will not take a wife for my son from the daughters of the Canaanites, among whom I dwell; 4but you shall go to my country and to my family, and take a wife for my son Isaac."

5And the servant said to him, "Perhaps the woman will not be willing to follow me to this land. Must I take your son back to the land from which you came?"

6But Abraham said to him, "Beware that you do not take my son back there. 7The LORD God of heaven, who took me from my father's house and from the land of my family, and who spoke to me and swore to me, saying, 'To your descendants^l I give this land,' He will send His angel before you, and you shall take a wife for my son from there. 8And if the woman is not willing to follow you, then you will be released from this oath; only do not take my son back there." 9So the servant put his hand under the thigh of Abraham his master, and swore to him concerning this matter.

10*Then the servant took ten of his master's camels and departed, for all his master's goods *were in* his hand. And he arose and went to Mesopotamia, to the city of Nahor. 11And he made his camels kneel down outside the city by a well of water at evening time, the time when women go out to draw *water.* 12Then he said, "O LORD God of my master Abraham, please give me success this day, and show kindness to my master Abraham. 13Behold, *here* I stand by the well of water, and the daughters of the men of the city are coming out to draw water. 14Now let it be that the young woman to whom I say, 'Please let down your pitcher that I may drink,' and she says, 'Drink, and I will also give your camels a drink'— *let* her *be the one* You have appointed for Your servant Isaac. And by this I will know that You have shown kindness to my master."

15And it happened, before he had finished speaking, that behold, Rebekah, who was born to Bethuel, son of Milcah, the wife of Nahor, Abraham's brother, came out with her pitcher on her shoulder. 16Now the young woman *was* very beautiful to behold, a virgin; no man had known her. And she went down to the well, filled her pitcher, and came up. 17And the servant ran to meet her and said, "Please let me drink a little water from your pitcher."

18So she said, "Drink, my lord." Then she quickly let her pitcher down to her hand, and gave him a drink. 19And when she had finished giving him a drink, she said, "I will draw *water* for your camels also, until they have finished drinking." 20Then she quickly emptied her pitcher into the trough, ran back to the well to draw *water,* and drew for all his camels. 21And the man, wondering at her, remained silent so as to know whether the LORD had made his journey prosperous or not.

22So it was, when the camels had finished drinking, that the man took a golden nose ring weighing half a shekel, and two bracelets for her wrists weighing ten *shekels* of gold, 23and said, "Whose

24:2–9 *The father* loved his son and wanted a bride for him. He had faith that God would keep His promise (Gen. 12:2) and provide the bride. Note that the bride could not be an outsider (1 Cor. 7:39). Is this whole event not a picture of the heavenly Father getting a bride for His Son?

24:10–49 *The servant* loved his master's son and asked for God's guidance. He knew how to "watch and pray" and discern God's leading. He was not disappointed, for God rewarded his faith. Little did Rebekah realize that a small act of kindness would open up an exciting new life for her. "Make every occasion a great occasion, for you can never tell when someone may be taking your measure for a larger place," advised Marsden. The servant talked about his master and not about himself, and he would not eat until he had given his message (John 4:31–32).

24:7 ^{l}Literally *seed*

daughter *are* you? Tell me, please, is there room *in* your father's house for us to lodge?''

24So she said to him, "I *am* the daughter of Bethuel, Milcah's son, whom she bore to Nahor.'' 25Moreover she said to him, "We have both straw and feed enough, and room to lodge.''

26Then the man bowed down his head and worshiped the LORD. 27And he said, "Blessed *be* the LORD God of my master Abraham, who has not forsaken His mercy and His truth toward my master. As for me, being on the way, the LORD led me to the house of my master's brethren.'' 28So the young woman ran and told her mother's household these things.

29Now Rebekah had a brother whose name *was* Laban, and Laban ran out to the man by the well. 30So it came to pass, when he saw the nose ring, and the bracelets on his sister's wrists, and when he heard the words of his sister Rebekah, saying, "Thus the man spoke to me,'' that he went to the man. And there he stood by the camels at the well. 31And he said, "Come in, O blessed of the LORD! Why do you stand outside? For I have prepared the house, and a place for the camels.''

32Then the man came to the house. And he unloaded the camels, and provided straw and feed for the camels, and water to wash his feet and the feet of the men who *were* with him. 33Food was set before him to eat, but he said, "I will not eat until I have told about my errand.''

And he said, "Speak on.''

34So he said, "I *am* Abraham's servant. 35The LORD has blessed my master greatly, and he has become great; and He has given him flocks and herds, silver and gold, male and female servants, and camels and donkeys. 36And Sarah my master's wife bore a son to my master when she was old; and to him he has given all that he has. 37Now my master made me swear, saying, 'You shall not take a wife for my son from the daughters of the Canaanites, in whose land I dwell; 38but you shall go to my father's house and to my family, and take a wife for my son.' 39And I said to my master, 'Perhaps the woman will not follow me.' 40But he said to me, 'The LORD, before whom I walk, will send His angel with you and prosper your way; and you shall take a wife for my son from my family and from my father's house. 41You will be clear from this oath when you arrive among my family; for if they will not give *her* to you, then you will be released from my oath.'

42"And this day I came to the well and said, 'O LORD God of my master Abraham, if You will now prosper the way in which I go, 43behold, I stand by the well of water; and it shall come to pass that when the virgin comes out to draw *water,* and I say to her, "Please give me a little water from your pitcher to drink,'' 44and she says to me, "Drink, and I will draw for your camels also,''— let her *be* the woman whom the LORD has appointed for my master's son.'

45"But before I had finished speaking in my heart, there was Rebekah, coming out with her pitcher on her shoulder; and she went down to the well and drew *water.* And I said to her, 'Please let me drink.' 46And she made haste and let her pitcher down from her *shoulder,* and said, 'Drink, and I will give your camels a drink also.' So I drank, and she gave the camels a drink also. 47Then I asked her, and said, 'Whose daughter *are* you?' And she said, 'The daughter of Bethuel,

Nahor's son, whom Milcah bore to him.' So I put the nose ring on her nose and the bracelets on her wrists. 48And I bowed my head and worshiped the LORD, and blessed the LORD God of my master Abraham, who had led me in the way of truth to take the daughter of my master's brother for his son. 49Now if you will deal kindly and truly with my master, tell me. And if not, tell me, that I may turn to the right hand or to the left."

50Then Laban and Bethuel answered and said, "The thing comes from the LORD; we cannot speak to you either bad or good. 51Here is Rebekah before you; take her and go, and let her be your master's son's wife, as the LORD has spoken."

52And it came to pass, when Abraham's servant heard their words, that he worshiped the LORD, bowing himself to the earth. 53Then the servant brought out jewelry of silver, jewelry of gold, and clothing, and gave them to Rebekah. He also gave precious things to her brother and to her mother.

54And he and the men who were with him ate and drank and stayed all night. Then they arose in the morning, and he said, "Send me away to my master."

55But her brother and her mother said, "Let the young woman stay with us a few days, at least ten; after that she may go."

56And he said to them, "Do not hinder me, since the LORD has prospered my way; send me away so that I may go to my master."

57So they said, "We will call the young woman and ask her personally." 58*Then they called Rebekah and said to her, "Will you go with this man?"

And she said, "I will go."

59So they sent away Rebekah their sister and her nurse, and Abraham's servant and his men. 60And they blessed Rebekah and said to her:

"Our sister, may you become
The mother of thousands of ten thousands;
And may your descendants possess
The gates of those who hate them."

61Then Rebekah and her maids arose, and they rode on the camels and followed the man. So the servant took Rebekah and departed.

62*Now Isaac came from the way of Beer Lahai Roi, for he dwelt in the South. 63And Isaac went out to meditate in the field in the evening; and he lifted his eyes and looked, and there, the camels were coming. 64Then Rebekah lifted her eyes, and when she saw Isaac she dismounted from her camel; 65for she had said to the servant, "Who is this man walking in the field to meet us?"

The servant said, "It is my master." So she took a veil and covered herself.

66And the servant told Isaac all the things that he had done. 67Then Isaac brought her into his mother Sarah's tent; and he took Rebekah and she became his wife, and he loved her. So Isaac was comforted after his mother's death.

25 Abraham* again took a wife, and her name was Keturah. 2And she bore him Zimran, Jokshan, Medan, Midian, Ishbak, and Shuah. 3Jokshan begot Sheba and Dedan. And the sons of Dedan were Asshurim, Letushim, and Leummim. 4And the sons of Midian were Ephah, Epher, Hanoch, Abidah, and Eldaah. All these were the children of Keturah.

5And Abraham gave all that he had to Isaac.

24:58 The bride had nothing to go on but the treasures she saw and the words she heard from the servant. In spite of those who urged her to delay, she made a decision of faith and said, "I will go!" This is an illustration of personal salvation. The Spirit speaks to us about Christ and shows us His treasures, and we trust Christ even though we have never seen Him (1 Pet. 1:8).

24:62 The bridegroom was last seen on the mountain with his father (chap. 22), but now he comes to meet his bride at eventide. That is what Jesus Christ will do when He returns for His church. Then we shall see Him and be like Him (1 John 3:1–2).

CHAPTER 25
The center of attention now shifts from Abraham to Isaac.

25:1–6 Isaac the heir. God's resurrection power continued to work in Abraham; he married again and begat six more sons. God is not likely to do this for people today, but the spiritual lesson is clear: we should be fruitful even in old age (Ps. 92:14). Abraham distinguished Isaac from his other sons: he gave them generous gifts, but he made Isaac his heir (v. 5; 24:35). God gives good things to unsaved people (Matt. 5:45; Acts 14:17; 17:25), but only those who are His children, through faith in Christ, can claim their inheritance. (See Rom. 8:17; Eph. 3:6; Heb. 1:2.)

25:7–11 Isaac the orphan. Abraham lived by faith and died by faith (Heb. 11:13), and God kept His word (Gen. 15:15). Isaac and Ishmael together mourned their father's death, for death is a human experience that binds all men together. Unsaved relatives share in times of sorrow, but their grief is hopeless without Jesus Christ. Compare Ishmael's death (v. 17) with that of Abraham.

25:19–21 Isaac the intercessor. Isaac was forty years old when he married Rebekah. For twenty years, they waited for a family that did not come. God blessed Isaac in everything but the thing he wanted most.

He and Rebekah knew that God had promised descendants (Gen. 15:5), so Isaac laid hold of the promise and prayed. True prayer lays hold of God's Word (John 15:7) and seeks to accomplish God's purposes.

25:24–28 Isaac the father. God gave them twin boys who were opposite each other in every way. He also gave them a revelation that the younger one, Jacob, would carry on the messianic line. For that reason, you would think that Isaac would have favored Jacob, but the physical won over the spiritual. Esau pictures the man of the world who despises the eternal and lives for the temporal.

6But Abraham gave gifts to the sons of the concubines which Abraham had; and while he was still living he sent them eastward, away from Isaac his son, to the country of the east. 7*This is the sum of the years of Abraham's life which he lived: one hundred and seventy-five years. 8Then Abraham breathed his last and died in a good old age, an old man and full of years, and was gathered to his people. 9And his sons Isaac and Ishmael buried him in the cave of Machpelah, which is before Mamre, in the field of Ephron the son of Zohar the Hittite, 10the field which Abraham purchased from the sons of Heth. There Abraham was buried, and Sarah his wife. 11And it came to pass, after the death of Abraham, that God blessed his son Isaac. And Isaac dwelt at Beer Lahai Roi.

12Now this is the genealogy of Ishmael, Abraham's son, whom Hagar the Egyptian, Sarah's maidservant, bore to Abraham. 13And these were the names of the sons of Ishmael, by their names, according to their generations: The firstborn of Ishmael, Nebajoth; then Kedar, Adbeel, Mibsam, 14Mishma, Dumah, Massa, 15Hadar,m Tema, Jetur, Naphish, and Kedemah. 16These were the sons of Ishmael and these were their names, by their towns and their settlements, twelve princes according to their nations. 17These were the years of the life of Ishmael: one hundred and thirty-seven years; and he breathed his last and died, and was gathered to his people. 18(They dwelt from Havilah as far as Shur, which is east of Egypt as you go toward Assyria.) He died in the presence of all his brethren.

19*This is the genealogy of Isaac, Abraham's son. Abraham begot Isaac. 20Isaac was forty years old when he took Rebekah as wife, the daughter of Bethuel the Syrian of Padan Aram, the sister of Laban the Syrian. 21Now Isaac pleaded with the LORD for his wife, because she was barren; and the LORD granted his plea, and Rebekah his wife conceived. 22But the children struggled together within her; and she said, "If all is well, why am I like this?" So she went to inquire of the LORD.

23And the LORD said to her:

"Two nations are in your womb,
Two peoples shall be separated from your
        body;
One people shall be stronger than the other,
And the older shall serve the younger."

24*So when her days were fulfilled for her to give birth, indeed there were twins in her womb. 25And the first came out red. He was like a hairy garment all over; so they called his name Esau.n 26Afterward his brother came out, and his hand took hold of Esau's heel; so his name was called Jacob.o Isaac was sixty years old when she bore them.

27So the boys grew. And Esau was a skillful hunter, a man of the field; but Jacob was a mild man, dwelling in tents. 28And Isaac loved Esau because he ate of his game, but Rebekah loved Jacob.

29Now Jacob cooked a stew; and Esau came in from the field, and he was weary. 30And Esau said

---

25:15 mMasoretic Text reads Hadad.   25:25 nLiterally Hairy
25:26 oLiterally Supplanter

to Jacob, "Please feed me with that same red *stew*, for I *am* weary." Therefore his name was called Edom.ᵖ

31But Jacob said, "Sell me your birthright as of this day."

32And Esau said, "Look, I *am* about to die; so what *is* this birthright to me?"

33Then Jacob said, "Swear to me as of this day."

So he swore to him, and sold his birthright to Jacob. 34And Jacob gave Esau bread and stew of lentils; then he ate and drank, arose, and went his way. Thus Esau despised *his* birthright.

26 There* was a famine in the land, besides the first famine that was in the days of Abraham. And Isaac went to Abimelech king of the Philistines, in Gerar. 2Then the LORD appeared to him and said: "Do not go down to Egypt; live in the land of which I shall tell you. 3Dwell in this land, and I will be with you and bless you; for to you and your descendants I give all these lands, and I will perform the oath which I swore to Abraham your father. 4And I will make your descendants multiply as the stars of heaven; I will give to your descendants all these lands; and in your seed all the nations of the earth shall be blessed; 5because Abraham obeyed My voice and kept My charge, My commandments, My statutes, and My laws."

6So Isaac dwelt in Gerar. 7*And the men of the place asked about his wife. And he said, "She *is* my sister"; for he was afraid to say, "*She is* my wife," *because he thought*, "lest the men of the place kill me for Rebekah, because she *is* beautiful to behold." 8Now it came to pass, when he had been there a long time, that Abimelech king of the Philistines looked through a window, and saw, and there was Isaac, showing endearment to Rebekah his wife. 9Then Abimelech called Isaac and said, "Quite obviously she *is* your wife; so how could you say, 'She *is* my sister'?"

Isaac said to him, "Because I said, 'Lest I die on account of her.'"

10And Abimelech said, "What *is* this you have done to us? One of the people might soon have lain with your wife, and you would have brought guilt on us." 11So Abimelech charged all *his* people, saying, "He who touches this man or his wife shall surely be put to death."

12Then Isaac sowed in that land, and reaped in the same year a hundredfold; and the LORD blessed him. 13The man began to prosper, and continued prospering until he became very prosperous; 14for he had possessions of flocks and possessions of herds and a great number of servants. So the Philistines envied him. 15*Now the Philistines had stopped up all the wells which his father's servants had dug in the days of Abraham his father, and they had filled them with earth. 16And Abimelech said to Isaac, "Go away from us, for you are much mightier than we." 17Then Isaac departed from there and pitched his tent in the Valley of Gerar, and dwelt there. 18And Isaac dug again the wells of water which they had dug in the days of Abraham his father, for the Philistines had stopped them up after the death of Abraham. He called them by the names which his father had called them.

CHAPTER 26

Faith cannot grow apart from trials, and this chapter records several trials that Isaac endured and shows how he responded to them.

26:1–6 Escape. Like Abraham, Isaac started for Egypt (12:10ff.); but God stopped him at the border (10:19) and reassured him. Isaac was blessed because of Abraham (vv. 5, 24). We must never forget our debt to spiritual leaders (and relatives) who have gone before us.

26:7–14 Deception. While in enemy territory, Isaac resorted to the "family lie" that twice got Abraham into trouble (12:10ff.; 20:1ff.). It is sad when the new generation imitates the sins of the old generation. God blessed Isaac in a material way, but we wonder what his spiritual life was like. Did his neighbors trust him after hearing about his lie?

26:15–25 Surrender. Water is a very precious commodity in desert country, and possessing a well is almost the same as having a deed to the land. Instead of defending what his men had done, Isaac moved to new locations. He may have been practicing Romans 12:18.

_____

25:30 ᵖLiterally *Red*

26:26–31 Confrontation. In contrast to his father Abraham, who dared to declare war, Isaac was a quiet, meditative man who tried to avoid trouble. He boldly faced his neighbors with their bad conduct—and he won! Note that he went the extra mile and entertained the men at a feast. (See Rom. 12:18–21.)

CHAPTER 27

27:1–4 A wrong decision. It was only a matter of time before the divided home would start to self-destruct, and it all began with Isaac. He knew that God had chosen Jacob, the younger son, to receive the blessing (Gen. 25:23–26); but he announced that he would give it to Esau. It seems that Isaac was more interested in his physical appetite than in spiritual things. He was not the spiritual person he once had been.

27:5–29 A wrong solution. Rebekah knew what God's promise was to Jacob, and she should have let God work it out in His own way. "Faith is living without scheming," and who can hinder the Lord from accomplishing His purposes (Dan. 4:35)? Instead, she made her son a liar and deceived her husband. If Isaac had trusted the Lord instead of his physical senses (vv. 21, 22, 25, 27), he would not have been fooled.

19Also Isaac's servants dug in the valley, and found a well of running water there. 20But the herdsmen of Gerar quarreled with Isaac's herdsmen, saying, "The water is ours." So he called the name of the well Esek,*q* because they quarreled with him. 21Then they dug another well, and they quarreled over that one also. So he called its name Sitnah.*r* 22And he moved from there and dug another well, and they did not quarrel over it. So he called its name Rehoboth,*s* because he said, "For now the LORD has made room for us, and we shall be fruitful in the land."

23Then he went up from there to Beersheba. 24And the LORD appeared to him the same night and said, "I am the God of your father Abraham; do not fear, for I am with you. I will bless you and multiply your descendants for My servant Abraham's sake." 25So he built an altar there and called on the name of the LORD, and he pitched his tent there; and there Isaac's servants dug a well.

26*Then Abimelech came to him from Gerar with Ahuzzath, one of his friends, and Phichol the commander of his army. 27And Isaac said to them, "Why have you come to me, since you hate me and have sent me away from you?"

28But they said, "We have certainly seen that the LORD is with you. So we said, 'Let there now be an oath between us, between you and us; and let us make a covenant with you, 29that you will do us no harm, since we have not touched you, and since we have done nothing to you but good and have sent you away in peace. You are now the blessed of the LORD.' "

30So he made them a feast, and they ate and drank. 31Then they arose early in the morning and swore an oath with one another; and Isaac sent them away, and they departed from him in peace.

32It came to pass the same day that Isaac's servants came and told him about the well which they had dug, and said to him, "We have found water." 33So he called it Shebah.*t* Therefore the name of the city is Beersheba*u* to this day.

34When Esau was forty years old, he took as wives Judith the daughter of Beeri the Hittite, and Basemath the daughter of Elon the Hittite. 35And they were a grief of mind to Isaac and Rebekah.

27 Now* it came to pass, when Isaac was old and his eyes were so dim that he could not see, that he called Esau his older son and said to him, "My son."

And he answered him, "Here I am."

2Then he said, "Behold now, I am old. I do not know the day of my death. 3Now therefore, please take your weapons, your quiver and your bow, and go out to the field and hunt game for me. 4And make me savory food, such as I love, and bring it to me that I may eat, that my soul may bless you before I die."

5*Now Rebekah was listening when Isaac spoke to Esau his son. And Esau went to the field to hunt game and to bring it. 6So Rebekah spoke to Jacob her son, saying, "Indeed I heard your father speak to Esau your brother, saying, 7'Bring me

---

26:20 *q*Literally *Quarrel*   26:21 *r*Literally *Enmity*
26:22 *s*Literally *Spaciousness*   26:33 *t*Literally *Oath* or *Seven*
*u*Literally *Well of the Oath* or *Well of the Seven*

game and make savory food for me, that I may eat it and bless you in the presence of the LORD before my death.' 8Now therefore, my son, obey my voice according to what I command you. 9Go now to the flock and bring me from there two choice kids of the goats, and I will make savory food from them for your father, such as he loves. 10Then you shall take *it* to your father, that he may eat *it,* and that he may bless you before his death."

11And Jacob said to Rebekah his mother, "Look, Esau my brother *is* a hairy man, and I *am* a smooth-*skinned* man. 12Perhaps my father will feel me, and I shall seem to be a deceiver to him; and I shall bring a curse on myself and not a blessing."

13But his mother said to him, "*Let* your curse *be* on me, my son; only obey my voice, and go, get *them* for me." 14And he went and got *them* and brought *them* to his mother, and his mother made savory food, such as his father loved. 15Then Rebekah took the choice clothes of her elder son Esau, which *were* with her in the house, and put them on Jacob her younger son. 16And she put the skins of the kids of the goats on his hands and on the smooth part of his neck. 17Then she gave the savory food and the bread, which she had prepared, into the hand of her son Jacob.

18So he went to his father and said, "My father." And he said, "Here I am. Who *are* you, my son?"

19Jacob said to his father, "I *am* Esau your firstborn; I have done just as you told me; please arise, sit and eat of my game, that your soul may bless me."

20But Isaac said to his son, "How *is it* that you have found *it* so quickly, my son?"

And he said, "Because the LORD your God brought *it* to me."

21Isaac said to Jacob, "Please come near, that I may feel you, my son, whether you *are* really my son Esau or not." 22So Jacob went near to Isaac his father, and he felt him and said, "The voice *is* Jacob's voice, but the hands *are* the hands of Esau." 23And he did not recognize him, because his hands were hairy like his brother Esau's hands; so he blessed him.

24Then he said, "*Are* you really my son Esau?" He said, "I *am.*"

25He said, "Bring *it* near to me, and I will eat of my son's game, so that my soul may bless you." So he brought *it* near to him, and he ate; and he brought him wine, and he drank. 26Then his father Isaac said to him, "Come near now and kiss me, my son." 27And he came near and kissed him; and he smelled the smell of his clothing, and blessed him and said:

"Surely, the smell of my son
Is like the smell of a field
Which the LORD has blessed.
28 Therefore may God give you
Of the dew of heaven,
Of the fatness of the earth,
And plenty of grain and wine.
29 Let peoples serve you,
And nations bow down to you.
Be master over your brethren,
And let your mother's sons bow down to
you.
Cursed *be* everyone who curses you,
And blessed *be* those who bless you!"

27:30–42 *A wrong attitude.* Esau had made it clear years before that he was not interested in spiritual things (Gen. 25:29–34), and certainly he knew God's word about the blessing. He wept (Heb. 12:17) and begged for a blessing, and then he plotted to kill his brother! His heart was not right with God or man. We are reminded of Cain (Gen. 4).

30*Now it happened, as soon as Isaac had finished blessing Jacob, and Jacob had scarcely gone out from the presence of Isaac his father, that Esau his brother came in from his hunting. 31He also had made savory food, and brought it to his father, and said to his father, "Let my father arise and eat of his son's game, that your soul may bless me."

32And his father Isaac said to him, "Who *are* you?"

So he said, "I *am* your son, your firstborn, Esau."

33Then Isaac trembled exceedingly, and said, "Who? Where *is* the one who hunted game and brought *it* to me? I ate all *of it* before you came, and I have blessed him—*and* indeed he shall be blessed."

34When Esau heard the words of his father, he cried with an exceedingly great and bitter cry, and said to his father, "Bless me—me also, O my father!"

35But he said, "Your brother came with deceit and has taken away your blessing."

36And *Esau* said, "Is he not rightly named Jacob? For he has supplanted me these two times. He took away my birthright, and now look, he has taken away my blessing!" And he said, "Have you not reserved a blessing for me?"

37Then Isaac answered and said to Esau, "Indeed I have made him your master, and all his brethren I have given to him as servants; with grain and wine I have sustained him. What shall I do now for you, my son?"

38And Esau said to his father, "Have you only one blessing, my father? Bless me—me also, O my father!" And Esau lifted up his voice and wept.

39Then Isaac his father answered and said to him:

> "Behold, your dwelling shall be of the fatness of the earth,
> And of the dew of heaven from above.
> 40 By your sword you shall live,
> And you shall serve your brother;
> And it shall come to pass, when you become restless,
> That you shall break his yoke from your neck."

41So Esau hated Jacob because of the blessing with which his father blessed him, and Esau said in his heart, "The days of mourning for my father are at hand; then I will kill my brother Jacob."

42And the words of Esau her older son were told to Rebekah. So she sent and called Jacob her younger son, and said to him, "Surely your brother Esau comforts himself concerning you *by intending* to kill you. 43*Now therefore, my son, obey my voice: arise, flee to my brother Laban in Haran. 44And stay with him a few days, until your brother's fury turns away, 45until your brother's anger turns away from you, and he forgets what you have done to him; then I will send and bring you from there. Why should I be bereaved also of you both in one day?"

46And Rebekah said to Isaac, "I am weary of my life because of the daughters of Heth; if Jacob takes a wife of the daughters of Heth, like these *who are* the daughters of the land, what good will my life be to me?"

27:43 Rebekah's "a few days" (v. 44) became over twenty years! Despite all her scheming, she never saw her son on earth again.

28 Then* Isaac called Jacob and blessed him, and charged him, and said to him: "You shall not take a wife from the daughters of Canaan. ²Arise, go to Padan Aram, to the house of Bethuel your mother's father; and take yourself a wife from there of the daughters of Laban your mother's brother.

3 "May God Almighty bless you,
   And make you fruitful and multiply you,
   That you may be an assembly of peoples;
4 And give you the blessing of Abraham,
   To you and your descendants with you,
   That you may inherit the land
   In which you are a stranger,
   Which God gave to Abraham."

⁵So Isaac sent Jacob away, and he went to Padan Aram, to Laban the son of Bethuel the Syrian, the brother of Rebekah, the mother of Jacob and Esau.

⁶Esau saw that Isaac had blessed Jacob and sent him away to Padan Aram to take himself a wife from there, *and that* as he blessed him he gave him a charge, saying, "You shall not take a wife from the daughters of Canaan," ⁷and that Jacob had obeyed his father and his mother and had gone to Padan Aram. ⁸Also Esau saw that the daughters of Canaan did not please his father Isaac. ⁹So Esau went to Ishmael and took Mahalath the daughter of Ishmael, Abraham's son, the sister of Nebajoth, to be his wife in addition to the wives he had.

¹⁰Now Jacob went out from Beersheba and went toward Haran. ¹¹*So he came to a certain place and stayed there all night, because the sun had set. And he took one of the stones of that place and put it at his head, and he lay down in that place to sleep. ¹²Then he dreamed, and behold, a ladder *was* set up on the earth, and its top reached to heaven; and there the angels of God were ascending and descending on it. ¹³And behold, the Lord stood above it and said: "I *am* the Lord God of Abraham your father and the God of Isaac; the land on which you lie I will give to you and your descendants. ¹⁴Also your descendants shall be as the dust of the earth; you shall spread abroad to the west and the east, to the north and the south; and in you and in your seed all the families of the earth shall be blessed. ¹⁵Behold, I *am* with you and will keep you wherever you go, and will bring you back to this land; for I will not leave you until I have done what I have spoken to you."

¹⁶*Then Jacob awoke from his sleep and said, "Surely the Lord is in this place, and I did not know *it*." ¹⁷And he was afraid and said, "How awesome *is* this place! This *is* none other than the house of God, and this *is* the gate of heaven!"

¹⁸Then Jacob rose early in the morning, and took the stone that he had put at his head, set it up as a pillar, and poured oil on top of it. ¹⁹And he called the name of that place Bethel;ᵛ but the name of that city had been Luz previously. ²⁰Then Jacob made a vow, saying, "If God will be with me, and keep me in this way that I am going, and give me bread to eat and clothing to put on, ²¹so that I come back to my father's house in peace, then the Lord shall be my God. ²²And

CHAPTER 28

28:1–5 *A day of disappointment.* Jacob was a lonely fugitive, forced to flee from home. Even though he left with his father's blessing (and Isaac knew what he was doing), Jacob faced an unknown future, and his brother still wanted to kill him. Not an encouraging beginning for a new chapter in his life! But God was still in control (Rom. 8:28).

28:11–15 *A night of discovery.* Jacob was literally between a rock and a hard place. But that night, Jacob made several discoveries that helped to change his life. He discovered that God was with him and working for him and had a perfect plan for his life. Jacob may have been separated from home, but he was not separated from heaven. (See John 1:51.) The very angels of God were caring for him (Heb. 1:13–14). "When the night is the darkest, you see the stars the brightest."

28:16–20 *A morning of dedication.* Jacob began his day worshiping God and turning his hard pillow into a holy altar. He gave the place a new name: "house of God." Wherever God meets us, that place becomes a holy sanctuary. Jacob's faith as yet was weak, but he did lay hold of God's promises, even if there is a bit of "the bargainer" in his vow to give God the tithe. Jacob was making a new beginning, and twenty years later he would return to Bethel a more mature believer.

28:19 ᵛLiterally *House of God*

CHAPTER 29

Abraham's faithful servant had found a wife for Isaac, but Jacob had to find his own wife. God's plans are different for each of us, and we must accept His will (Phil. 2:12–13).

29:1–14 The guest. God's providence brought Jacob to the well just as Rachel was arriving. (See Gen. 24:27.) True to his scheming nature, Jacob tried to get rid of the shepherds so he could have her all to himself! It was love at first sight. That first month in Uncle Laban's home must have been heaven on earth to Jacob, but it didn't take long for things to change.

29:15–30 The worker. Jacob was not wealthy as Isaac was when he got his wife (Gen. 24:36, 53), so he had to work for his uncle to have the woman he loved. But love takes the burden out of work and makes time pass quickly. Jacob the schemer met his match in Laban and soon began to reap what he had sown. Jacob had deceived his father, and his father-in-law deceived him.

this stone which I have set as a pillar shall be God's house, and of all that You give me I will surely give a tenth to You."

29 So* Jacob went on his journey and came to the land of the people of the East. ²And he looked, and saw a well in the field; and behold, there *were* three flocks of sheep lying by it; for out of that well they watered the flocks. A large stone *was* on the well's mouth. ³Now all the flocks would be gathered there; and they would roll the stone from the well's mouth, water the sheep, and put the stone back in its place on the well's mouth.

⁴And Jacob said to them, "My brethren, where *are* you from?"

And they said, "We *are* from Haran."

⁵Then he said to them, "Do you know Laban the son of Nahor?"

And they said, "We know him."

⁶So he said to them, "Is he well?"

And they said, "*He is* well. And look, his daughter Rachel is coming with the sheep."

⁷Then he said, "Look, *it is* still high day; *it is* not time for the cattle to be gathered together. Water the sheep, and go and feed *them*."

⁸But they said, "We cannot until all the flocks are gathered together, and they have rolled the stone from the well's mouth; then we water the sheep."

⁹Now while he was still speaking with them, Rachel came with her father's sheep, for she was a shepherdess. ¹⁰And it came to pass, when Jacob saw Rachel the daughter of Laban his mother's brother, and the sheep of Laban his mother's brother, that Jacob went near and rolled the stone from the well's mouth, and watered the flock of Laban his mother's brother. ¹¹Then Jacob kissed Rachel, and lifted up his voice and wept. ¹²And Jacob told Rachel that he *was* her father's relative and that he *was* Rebekah's son. So she ran and told her father.

¹³Then it came to pass, when Laban heard the report about Jacob his sister's son, that he ran to meet him, and embraced him and kissed him, and brought him to his house. So he told Laban all these things. ¹⁴And Laban said to him, "Surely you *are* my bone and my flesh." And he stayed with him for a month.

¹⁵*Then Laban said to Jacob, "Because you *are* my relative, should you therefore serve me for nothing? Tell me, what *should* your wages *be?*" ¹⁶Now Laban had two daughters: the name of the elder *was* Leah, and the name of the younger *was* Rachel. ¹⁷Leah's eyes *were* delicate, but Rachel was beautiful of form and appearance.

¹⁸Now Jacob loved Rachel; so he said, "I will serve you seven years for Rachel your younger daughter."

¹⁹And Laban said, "*It is* better that I give her to you than that I should give her to another man. Stay with me." ²⁰So Jacob served seven years for Rachel, and they seemed *only* a few days to him because of the love he had for her.

²¹Then Jacob said to Laban, "Give *me* my wife, for my days are fulfilled, that I may go in to her." ²²And Laban gathered together all the men of the place and made a feast. ²³Now it came to pass in the evening, that he took Leah his daughter and brought her to Jacob; and he went in to her. ²⁴And Laban gave his maid Zilpah to his daughter Leah *as* a maid. ²⁵So it came to pass in the morn-

ing, that behold, it *was* Leah. And he said to Laban, "What is this you have done to me? Was it not for Rachel that I served you? Why then have you deceived me?"

26And Laban said, "It must not be done so in our country, to give the younger before the firstborn. 27Fulfill her week, and we will give you this one also for the service which you will serve with me still another seven years."

28Then Jacob did so and fulfilled her week. So he gave him his daughter Rachel as wife also. 29And Laban gave his maid Bilhah to his daughter Rachel as a maid. 30Then *Jacob* also went in to Rachel, and he also loved Rachel more than Leah. And he served with Laban still another seven years.

31*When the LORD saw that Leah *was* unloved, He opened her womb; but Rachel *was* barren. 32So Leah conceived and bore a son, and she called his name Reuben;w for she said, "The LORD has surely looked on my affliction. Now therefore, my husband will love me." 33Then she conceived again and bore a son, and said, "Because the LORD has heard that I *am* unloved, He has therefore given me this *son* also." And she called his name Simeon.x 34She conceived again and bore a son, and said, "Now this time my husband will become attached to me, because I have borne him three sons." Therefore his name was called Levi.y 35And she conceived again and bore a son, and said, "Now I will praise the LORD." Therefore she called his name Judah.z Then she stopped bearing.

30 Now* when Rachel saw that she bore Jacob no children, Rachel envied her sister, and said to Jacob, "Give me children, or else I die!" 2And Jacob's anger was aroused against Rachel, and he said, "Am I in the place of God, who has withheld from you the fruit of the womb?" 3*So she said, "Here is my maid Bilhah; go in to her, and she will bear *a child* on my knees, that I also may have children by her." 4Then she gave him Bilhah her maid as wife, and Jacob went in to her. 5And Bilhah conceived and bore Jacob a son. 6Then Rachel said, "God has judged my case; and He has also heard my voice and given me a son." Therefore she called his name Dan.a 7And Rachel's maid Bilhah conceived again and bore Jacob a second son. 8Then Rachel said, "With great wrestlings I have wrestled with my sister, *and* indeed I have prevailed." So she called his name Naphtali.b

9When Leah saw that she had stopped bearing, she took Zilpah her maid and gave her to Jacob as wife. 10And Leah's maid Zilpah bore Jacob a son. 11Then Leah said, "A troop comes!"c So she called his name Gad.d 12And Leah's maid Zilpah bore Jacob a second son. 13Then Leah said, "I am happy, for the daughters will call me blessed." So she called his name Asher.e

14Now Reuben went in the days of wheat harvest and found mandrakes in the field, and brought them to his mother Leah. Then Rachel

29:31–35 The father. The building of Jacob's family was vitally important to God's plan of salvation, for God would use the nation of Israel to give the world the Bible and the Redeemer. Although Rachel had great beauty, she was unable to conceive, while Leah gave birth to four sons: Reuben ("see, a son!"), Simeon ("hearing"), Levi ("joined"), and Judah ("praise"). The Lord was in control and had a special purpose for each son (Ps. 139:14–16; Eccles. 3:2).

CHAPTER 30

30:1ff There are two major themes in this chapter: the building of Jacob's family (vv. 1–24), and the building of Jacob's fortune (vv. 25–43). Various people (including Jacob) thought they were in control of the situation, but all of it was in the hands of God.

30:3–21 Having grown up his mother's favored son (25:28), Jacob was accustomed to a woman telling him what to do. But now he had *four* different women involved in his life! When he came home from the fields, he never knew which one he would be living with! The schemer discovered the pain that people feel when their lives are selfishly manipulated by others.

29:32 wLiterally *See, a Son*   29:33 xLiterally *Heard*
29:34 yLiterally *Attached*   29:35 zLiterally *Praise*
30:6 aLiterally *Judge*   30:8 bLiterally *My Wrestling*
30:11 cFollowing Qere, Syriac, and Targum; Kethib, Septuagint, and Vulgate read *in fortune.* dLiterally *Troop* or *Fortune*   30:13 eLiterally *Happy*

said to Leah, "Please give me *some* of your son's mandrakes."

15But she said to her, "*Is it* a small matter that you have taken away my husband? Would you take away my son's mandrakes also?"

And Rachel said, "Therefore he will lie with you tonight for your son's mandrakes."

16When Jacob came out of the field in the evening, Leah went out to meet him and said, "You must come in to me, for I have surely hired you with my son's mandrakes." And he lay with her that night.

17And God listened to Leah, and she conceived and bore Jacob a fifth son. 18Leah said, "God has given me my wages, because I have given my maid to my husband." So she called his name Issachar.*f* 19Then Leah conceived again and bore Jacob a sixth son. 20And Leah said, "God has endowed me *with* a good endowment; now my husband will dwell with me, because I have borne him six sons." So she called his name Zebulun.*g* 21Afterward she bore a daughter, and called her name Dinah.

22*Then God remembered Rachel, and God listened to her and opened her womb. 23And she conceived and bore a son, and said, "God has taken away my reproach." 24So she called his name Joseph,*h* and said, "The LORD shall add to me another son."

25And it came to pass, when Rachel had borne Joseph, that Jacob said to Laban, "Send me away, that I may go to my own place and to my country. 26Give *me* my wives and my children for whom I have served you, and let me go; for you know my service which I have done for you."

27And Laban said to him, "Please *stay*, if I have found favor in your eyes, *for* I have learned by experience that the LORD has blessed me for your sake." 28Then he said, "Name me your wages, and I will give *it*."

29So *Jacob* said to him, "You know how I have served you and how your livestock has been with me. 30For what you had before I *came was* little, and it has increased to a great amount; the LORD has blessed you since my coming. And now, when shall I also provide for my own house?"

31*So he said, "What shall I give you?"

And Jacob said, "You shall not give me anything. If you will do this thing for me, I will again feed and keep your flocks: 32Let me pass through all your flock today, removing from there all the speckled and spotted sheep, and all the brown ones among the lambs, and the spotted and speckled among the goats; and *these* shall be my wages. 33So my righteousness will answer for me in time to come, when the subject of my wages comes before you: every one that *is* not speckled and spotted among the goats, and brown among the lambs, will be considered stolen, if *it is* with me."

34And Laban said, "Oh, that it were according to your word!" 35So he removed that day the male goats that were speckled and spotted, all the female goats that were speckled and spotted, every one that had *some* white in it, and all the brown ones among the lambs, and gave *them* into the hand of his sons. 36Then he put three days' journey between himself and Jacob, and Jacob fed the rest of Laban's flocks.

30:22–24 Rachel will have only two sons, Joseph and Benjamin, and Joseph will save the whole family from destruction.

30:31–43 Laban tried to trick Jacob and make him poor, but God overruled and made Jacob a very wealthy man. In fact, God even blessed Laban because of Jacob, and the old trickster admitted it (v. 27)! It was God's blessing and not Jacob's schemes that increased the flocks. God was keeping the promises He had made at Bethel (28:13–15). When we are in difficult situations, we can trust God to care for us.

30:18 *f*Literally *Wages*   30:20 *g*Literally *Dwelling*
30:24 *h*Literally *He Will Add*

37Now Jacob took for himself rods of green poplar and of the almond and chestnut trees, peeled white strips in them, and exposed the white which *was* in the rods. 38And the rods which he had peeled, he set before the flocks in the gutters, in the watering troughs where the flocks came to drink, so that they should conceive when they came to drink. 39So the flocks conceived before the rods, and the flocks brought forth streaked, speckled, and spotted. 40Then Jacob separated the lambs, and made the flocks face toward the streaked and all the brown in the flock of Laban; but he put his own flocks by themselves and did not put them with Laban's flock.

41And it came to pass, whenever the stronger livestock conceived, that Jacob placed the rods before the eyes of the livestock in the gutters, that they might conceive among the rods. 42But when the flocks were feeble, he did not put *them* in; so the feebler were Laban's and the stronger Jacob's. 43Thus the man became exceedingly prosperous, and had large flocks, female and male servants, and camels and donkeys.

31 Now* Jacob heard the words of Laban's sons, saying, "Jacob has taken away all that was our father's, and from what was our father's he has acquired all this wealth." 2And Jacob saw the countenance of Laban, and indeed it *was* not *favorable* toward him as before. 3Then the LORD said to Jacob, "Return to the land of your fathers and to your family, and I will be with you."

4So Jacob sent and called Rachel and Leah to the field, to his flock, 5and said to them, "I see your father's countenance, that it *is* not *favorable* toward me as before; but the God of my father has been with me. 6And you know that with all my might I have served your father. 7Yet your father has deceived me and changed my wages ten times, but God did not allow him to hurt me. 8If he said thus: 'The speckled shall be your wages,' then all the flocks bore speckled. And if he said thus: 'The streaked shall be your wages,' then all the flocks bore streaked. 9So God has taken away the livestock of your father and given *them* to me.

10"And it happened, at the time when the flocks conceived, that I lifted my eyes and saw in a dream, and behold, the rams which leaped upon the flocks *were* streaked, speckled, and gray-spotted. 11Then the Angel of God spoke to me in a dream, saying, 'Jacob.' And I said, 'Here I am.' 12And He said, 'Lift your eyes now and see, all the rams which leap on the flocks *are* streaked, speckled, and gray-spotted; for I have seen all that Laban is doing to you. 13I *am* the God of Bethel, where you anointed the pillar *and* where you made a vow to Me. Now arise, get out of this land, and return to the land of your family.' "

14Then Rachel and Leah answered and said to him, "Is there still any portion or inheritance for us in our father's house? 15Are we not considered strangers by him? For he has sold us, and also completely consumed our money. 16For all these riches which God has taken from our father are *really* ours and our children's; now then, whatever God has said to you, do it."

17Then Jacob rose and set his sons and his wives on camels. 18And he carried away all his livestock and all his possessions which he had gained, his acquired livestock which he had gained in Padan Aram, to go to his father Isaac in the land of

CHAPTER 31

31:1–21 *Escape.* The family situation was not at all comfortable for Jacob or his wives, but he patiently waited for God's instructions before making a move. The seeking heart will always get a word from God when decisions have to be made. Read Psalm 25 in the light of Jacob's situation. Like his mother before him, Jacob did a right thing in a wrong way, and God had to intervene to protect him (v. 24).

31:22 Encounter. Jacob had a three-day lead on Laban, but his father-in-law finally caught up with him. No one can successfully run away from problems. Laban accused Jacob of a breach of social custom, while Jacob accused Laban of breaking his promises for twenty years. There was also the matter of the household gods, for whoever had them could claim possession of Laban's property.

Canaan. 19Now Laban had gone to shear his sheep, and Rachel had stolen the household idols that were her father's. 20And Jacob stole away, unknown to Laban the Syrian, in that he did not tell him that he intended to flee. 21So he fled with all that he had. He arose and crossed the river, and headed toward the mountains of Gilead.

22*And Laban was told on the third day that Jacob had fled. 23Then he took his brethren with him and pursued him for seven days' journey, and he overtook him in the mountains of Gilead. 24But God had come to Laban the Syrian in a dream by night, and said to him, "Be careful that you speak to Jacob neither good nor bad."

25So Laban overtook Jacob. Now Jacob had pitched his tent in the mountains, and Laban with his brethren pitched in the mountains of Gilead. 26And Laban said to Jacob: "What have you done, that you have stolen away unknown to me, and carried away my daughters like captives *taken* with the sword? 27Why did you flee away secretly, and steal away from me, and not tell me; for I might have sent you away with joy and songs, with timbrel and harp? 28And you did not allow me to kiss my sons and my daughters. Now you have done foolishly in *so* doing. 29It is in my power to do you harm, but the God of your father spoke to me last night, saying, 'Be careful that you speak to Jacob neither good nor bad.' 30And now you have surely gone because you greatly long for your father's house, *but* why did you steal my gods?"

31Then Jacob answered and said to Laban, "Because I was afraid, for I said, 'Perhaps you would take your daughters from me by force.' 32With whomever you find your gods, do not let him live. In the presence of our brethren, identify what I have of yours and take *it* with you." For Jacob did not know that Rachel had stolen them.

33And Laban went into Jacob's tent, into Leah's tent, and into the two maids' tents, but he did not find *them.* Then he went out of Leah's tent and entered Rachel's tent. 34Now Rachel had taken the household idols, put them in the camel's saddle, and sat on them. And Laban searched all about the tent but did not find *them.* 35And she said to her father, "Let it not displease my lord that I cannot rise before you, for the manner of women *is* with me." And he searched but did not find the household idols.

36Then Jacob was angry and rebuked Laban, and Jacob answered and said to Laban: "What *is* my trespass? What *is* my sin, that you have so hotly pursued me? 37Although you have searched all my things, what part of your household things have you found? Set *it* here before my brethren and your brethren, that they may judge between us both! 38These twenty years I *have been* with you; your ewes and your female goats have not miscarried their young, and I have not eaten the rams of your flock. 39That which was torn *by beasts* I did not bring to you; I bore the loss of it. You required it from my hand, *whether* stolen by day or stolen by night. 40*There* I was! In the day the drought consumed me, and the frost by night, and my sleep departed from my eyes. 41Thus I have been in your house twenty years; I served you fourteen years for your two daughters, and six years for your flock, and you have changed my wages ten times. 42Unless the God of my father, the God of Abraham and the Fear of Isaac, had been with me, surely now you would have sent me away empty-handed. God has seen my affliction and the labor of my hands, and rebuked *you* last night."

⁴³And Laban answered and said to Jacob, "*These* daughters *are* my daughters, and *these* children *are* my children, and *this* flock *is* my flock; all that you see *is* mine. But what can I do this day to these my daughters or to their children whom they have borne? ⁴⁴Now therefore, come, let us make a covenant, you and I, and let it be a witness between you and me."

⁴⁵*So Jacob took a stone and set it up *as* a pillar. ⁴⁶Then Jacob said to his brethren, "Gather stones." And they took stones and made a heap, and they ate there on the heap. ⁴⁷Laban called it Jegar Sahadutha,ⁱ but Jacob called it Galeed.ʲ ⁴⁸And Laban said, "This heap *is* a witness between you and me this day." Therefore its name was called Galeed, ⁴⁹also Mizpah,ᵏ because he said, "May the LORD watch between you and me when we are absent one from another. ⁵⁰If you afflict my daughters, or if you take *other* wives besides my daughters, *although* no man *is* with us—see, God *is* witness between you and me!"

⁵¹Then Laban said to Jacob, "Here is this heap and here is *this* pillar, which I have placed between you and me. ⁵²This heap *is* a witness, and *this* pillar *is* a witness, that I will not pass beyond this heap to you, and you will not pass beyond this heap and this pillar to me, for harm. ⁵³The God of Abraham, the God of Nahor, and the God of their father judge between us." And Jacob swore by the Fear of his father Isaac. ⁵⁴Then Jacob offered a sacrifice on the mountain, and called his brethren to eat bread. And they ate bread and stayed all night on the mountain. ⁵⁵And early in the morning Laban arose, and kissed his sons and daughters and blessed them. Then Laban departed and returned to his place.

32 So* Jacob went on his way, and the angels of God met him. ²When Jacob saw them, he said, "This *is* God's camp." And he called the name of that place Mahanaim.ˡ

³*Then Jacob sent messengers before him to Esau his brother in the land of Seir, the country of Edom. ⁴And he commanded them, saying, "Speak thus to my lord Esau, 'Thus your servant Jacob says: "I have dwelt with Laban and stayed there until now. ⁵I have oxen, donkeys, flocks, and male and female servants; and I have sent to tell my lord, that I may find favor in your sight." ' "

⁶Then the messengers returned to Jacob, saying, "We came to your brother Esau, and he also is coming to meet you, and four hundred men *are* with him." ⁷So Jacob was greatly afraid and distressed; and he divided the people that *were* with him, and the flocks and herds and camels, into two companies. ⁸And he said, "If Esau comes to the one company and attacks it, then the other company which is left will escape."

⁹Then Jacob said, "O God of my father Abraham and God of my father Isaac, the LORD who said to me, 'Return to your country and to your family, and I will deal well with you': ¹⁰I am not worthy of the least of all the mercies and of all

31:45–55 Expedience. The two men never did agree, and their problems were not solved. Instead, they declared a truce and made a pile of stones the boundary beyond which neither would pass. It was called "the heap of witness" to remind Jacob and Laban that God was watching both of them. (The word *Mizpah* means "watchtower.") The so-called Mizpah benediction is not a correct interpretation or application of this passage.

It is better to declare a truce than to wage a war, but the best decision of all is for brethren to "dwell together in unity" (Ps. 133:1). See Ephesians 4:25–32 for directions.

CHAPTER 32

32:1–2 Jacob expected a battle and his concern was escape, not reconciliation (v. 8). He saw the army of angels protecting him, but even that didn't encourage his faith. *Mahanaim* means "double camp"—his camp and the camp of God's angels. Had Jacob recalled his experience with God at Bethel, he would not have been afraid of Esau (28:13–15).

32:3–28 One minute Jacob prayed for God's help, and the next minute he devised some new way to appease his angry brother. He reminded God of His great promises and then acted as though God had never spoken. This is the conduct of a believer who needed to be broken before God. He prayed to be delivered from Esau (v. 11), but his greatest need was to be delivered from himself.

31:47 ⁱLiterally, in Aramaic, *Heap of Witness* ʲLiterally, in Hebrew, *Heap of Witness*   31:49 ᵏLiterally *Watch* 32:2 ˡLiterally *Double Camp*

the truth which You have shown Your servant; for I crossed over this Jordan with my staff, and now I have become two companies. [11]Deliver me, I pray, from the hand of my brother, from the hand of Esau; for I fear him, lest he come and attack me *and* the mother with the children. [12]For You said, 'I will surely treat you well, and make your descendants as the sand of the sea, which cannot be numbered for multitude.' "

[13]So he lodged there that same night, and took what came to his hand as a present for Esau his brother: [14]two hundred female goats and twenty male goats, two hundred ewes and twenty rams, [15]thirty milk camels with their colts, forty cows and ten bulls, twenty female donkeys and ten foals. [16]Then he delivered *them* to the hand of his servants, every drove by itself, and said to his servants, "Pass over before me, and put some distance between successive droves." [17]And he commanded the first one, saying, "When Esau my brother meets you and asks you, saying, 'To whom do you belong, and where are you going? Whose *are* these in front of you?' [18]then you shall say, 'They *are* your servant Jacob's. It *is* a present sent to my lord Esau; and behold, he also *is* behind us.' " [19]So he commanded the second, the third, and all who followed the droves, saying, "In this manner you shall speak to Esau when you find him; [20]and also say, 'Behold, your servant Jacob *is* behind us.' " For he said, "I will appease him with the present that goes before me, and afterward I will see his face; perhaps he will accept me." [21]So the present went on over before him, but he himself lodged that night in the camp.

[22]And he arose that night and took his two wives, his two female servants, and his eleven sons, and crossed over the ford of Jabbok. [23]He took them, sent them over the brook, and sent over what he had. [24]Then Jacob was left alone; and a Man wrestled with him until the breaking of day. [25]Now when He saw that He did not prevail against him, He touched the socket of his hip; and the socket of Jacob's hip was out of joint as He wrestled with him. [26]And He said, "Let Me go, for the day breaks."

But he said, "I will not let You go unless You bless me!"

[27]So He said to him, "What *is* your name?"

He said, "Jacob."

[28]And He said, "Your name shall no longer be called Jacob, but Israel;[m] for you have struggled with God and with men, and have prevailed."

[29]*Then Jacob asked, saying, "Tell *me* Your name, I pray."

And He said, "Why *is* it *that* you ask about My name?" And He blessed him there.

[30]So Jacob called the name of the place Peniel:[n] "For I have seen God face to face, and my life is preserved." [31]Just as he crossed over Penuel[o] the sun rose on him, and he limped on his hip. [32]Therefore to this day the children of Israel do not eat the muscle that shrank, which *is* on the hip socket, because He touched the socket of Jacob's hip in the muscle that shrank.

33 Now* Jacob lifted his eyes and looked, and there, Esau was coming, and with him were four hundred men. So he divided the children

32:29–32 Jacob was broken to be healed and weakened to be strengthened. When he surrendered, he won and became a "prince with God." His limp would be a constant reminder that God would be in control of his life. "God fights *against* us with His left hand and *for* us with His right hand," wrote John Calvin. When we let God have His way, it is the dawning of a new day (v. 31).

CHAPTER 33

33:1ff Jacob had seen God and been given a new name, but the benefits of his experience didn't appear immediately. Sometimes he acted like Jacob ("the heel-catcher") and sometimes like Israel ("the prince with God"). Many of God's people fail to live up to their new life in Christ because they don't claim what they have by faith. God had to give Jacob a limp to encourage him to walk by faith.

32:28 [m]Literally *Prince with God*   32:30 [n]Literally *Face of God*
32:31 [o]Same as *Peniel*, verse 30

among Leah, Rachel, and the two maidservants. ²And he put the maidservants and their children in front, Leah and her children behind, and Rachel and Joseph last. ³Then he crossed over before them and bowed himself to the ground seven times, until he came near to his brother.

⁴But Esau ran to meet him, and embraced him, and fell on his neck and kissed him, and they wept. ⁵And he lifted his eyes and saw the women and children, and said, "Who *are* these with you?"

So he said, "The children whom God has graciously given your servant." ⁶*Then the maidservants came near, they and their children, and bowed down. ⁷And Leah also came near with her children, and they bowed down. Afterward Joseph and Rachel came near, and they bowed down.

⁸Then Esau said, "What *do* you *mean by* all this company which I met?"

And he said, "*These are* to find favor in the sight of my lord."

⁹But Esau said, "I have enough, my brother; keep what you have for yourself."

¹⁰And Jacob said, "No, please, if I have now found favor in your sight, then receive my present from my hand, inasmuch as I have seen your face as though I had seen the face of God, and you were pleased with me. ¹¹Please, take my blessing that is brought to you, because God has dealt graciously with me, and because I have enough." So he urged him, and he took *it*.

¹²Then Esau said, "Let us take our journey; let us go, and I will go before you."

¹³But Jacob said to him, "My lord knows that the children *are* weak, and the flocks and herds which are nursing *are* with me. And if the men should drive them hard one day, all the flock will die. ¹⁴Please let my lord go on ahead before his servant. I will lead on slowly at a pace which the livestock that go before me, and the children, are able to endure, until I come to my lord in Seir."

¹⁵And Esau said, "Now let me leave with you *some* of the people who *are* with me."

But he said, "What need is there? Let me find favor in the sight of my lord." ¹⁶So Esau returned that day on his way to Seir. ¹⁷And Jacob journeyed to Succoth, built himself a house, and made booths for his livestock. Therefore the name of the place is called Succoth.ᵖ

¹⁸*Then Jacob came safely to the city of Shechem, which *is* in the land of Canaan, when he came from Padan Aram; and he pitched his tent before the city. ¹⁹And he bought the parcel of land, where he had pitched his tent, from the children of Hamor, Shechem's father, for one hundred pieces of money. ²⁰Then he erected an altar there and called it El Elohe Israel.�q

34 Now* Dinah the daughter of Leah, whom she had borne to Jacob, went out to see the daughters of the land. ²And when Shechem the son of Hamor the Hivite, prince of the country, saw her, he took her and lay with her, and violated her. ³His soul was strongly attracted to Dinah the daughter of Jacob, and he loved the young woman and spoke kindly to the young woman. ⁴So Shechem spoke to his father Hamor, saying, "Get me this young woman as a wife."

33:17 ᵖLiterally *Booths*   33:20 qLiterally *God, the God of Israel*

33:6–17 In his attempt to appease Esau, the old schemer used several devices: bowing (vv. 1–7), bribery (vv. 8–11), outright lying (vv. 12–16), and then moving off in another direction (vv. 17–20). Esau went south and Jacob went east! Princes are not supposed to bow, and what about God's promise in Genesis 25:23 and 27:29?

33:18–20 One mistake often leads to another. Jacob ceased to be a pilgrim, purchased the land he was already given by God, built a house, and settled down. He built an altar and called on "God, the God of Israel" (note the new name); but that didn't prevent him from getting into trouble with the neighbors. Far better had he pressed on to Bethel.

CHAPTER 34

34:1–4 *Defilement.* Lot pitched his tent toward Sodom and lost his daughters (19:30ff.), and Jacob moved too close to Shechem and lost Dinah. She was the daughter of Leah (30:21), which explains why Simeon and Levi became so angry (35:23). Had nobody warned her? Was she out looking for opportunities to sin? Or was she completely overpowered by the prince? It may have been love at first sight, but that didn't lessen the guilt or tragedy of the sin.

34:13–24 *Deception.* Note the twofold attempt at deception: Simeon and Levi deceived Hamor, and Hamor thought he deceived them. Jacob's sons had learned much from watching their father. Dinah's two brothers were preparing for war while the men of Shechem were preparing for wealth. When the men of the city were unable to fight, Simeon and Levi killed all the men and took the spoils. It was another case of promoting a holy cause in an unholy way and being motivated by hatred of the enemy instead of love for the truth.

34:30–31 *Disgrace.* Jacob was more concerned about his safety and his reputation than he was the character and conduct of his ruthless sons. Although Jacob was not to blame for their deed, had he not settled near Shechem, this tragedy would not have occurred. On his deathbed, Jacob brought the matter up again (49:5–7). How gracious of God to make the tribe of Levi the priestly tribe! (See Romans 5:20.)

5And Jacob heard that he had defiled Dinah his daughter. Now his sons were with his livestock in the field; so Jacob held his peace until they came. 6Then Hamor the father of Shechem went out to Jacob to speak with him. 7And the sons of Jacob came in from the field when they heard *it;* and the men were grieved and very angry, because he had done a disgraceful thing in Israel by lying with Jacob's daughter, a thing which ought not to be done. 8But Hamor spoke with them, saying, "The soul of my son Shechem longs for your daughter. Please give her to him as a wife. 9And make marriages with us; give your daughters to us, and take our daughters to yourselves. 10So you shall dwell with us, and the land shall be before you. Dwell and trade in it, and acquire possessions for yourselves in it."

11Then Shechem said to her father and her brothers, "Let me find favor in your eyes, and whatever you say to me I will give. 12Ask me ever so much dowry and gift, and I will give according to what you say to me; but give me the young woman as a wife."

13*But the sons of Jacob answered Shechem and Hamor his father, and spoke deceitfully, because he had defiled Dinah their sister. 14And they said to them, "We cannot do this thing, to give our sister to one who is uncircumcised, for that *would be* a reproach to us. 15But on this *condition* we will consent to you: If you will become as we *are,* if every male of you is circumcised, 16then we will give our daughters to you, and we will take your daughters to us; and we will dwell with you, and we will become one people. 17But if you will not heed us and be circumcised, then we will take our daughter and be gone."

18And their words pleased Hamor and Shechem, Hamor's son. 19So the young man did not delay to do the thing, because he delighted in Jacob's daughter. He *was* more honorable than all the household of his father.

20And Hamor and Shechem his son came to the gate of their city, and spoke with the men of their city, saying: 21"These men *are* at peace with us. Therefore let them dwell in the land and trade in it. For indeed the land *is* large enough for them. Let us take their daughters to us as wives, and let us give them our daughters. 22Only on this *condition* will the men consent to dwell with us, to be one people: if every male among us is circumcised as they *are* circumcised. 23*Will* not their livestock, their property, and every animal of theirs *be* ours? Only let us consent to them, and they will dwell with us." 24And all who went out of the gate of his city heeded Hamor and Shechem his son; every male was circumcised, all who went out of the gate of his city.

25Now it came to pass on the third day, when they were in pain, that two of the sons of Jacob, Simeon and Levi, Dinah's brothers, each took his sword and came boldly upon the city and killed all the males. 26And they killed Hamor and Shechem his son with the edge of the sword, and took Dinah from Shechem's house, and went out. 27The sons of Jacob came upon the slain, and plundered the city, because their sister had been defiled. 28They took their sheep, their oxen, and their donkeys, what *was* in the city and what *was* in the field, 29and all their wealth. All their little ones and their wives they took captive; and they plundered even all that *was* in the houses.

30*Then Jacob said to Simeon and Levi, "You

have troubled me by making me obnoxious among the inhabitants of the land, among the Canaanites and the Perizzites; and since I *am* few in number, they will gather themselves together against me and kill me. I shall be destroyed, my household and I."

31But they said, "Should he treat our sister like a harlot?"

35 Then* God said to Jacob, "Arise, go up to Bethel and dwell there; and make an altar there to God, who appeared to you when you fled from the face of Esau your brother."

2And Jacob said to his household and to all who *were* with him, "Put away the foreign gods that *are* among you, purify yourselves, and change your garments. 3Then let us arise and go up to Bethel; and I will make an altar there to God, who answered me in the day of my distress and has been with me in the way which I have gone." 4So they gave Jacob all the foreign gods which *were* in their hands, and the earrings which *were* in their ears; and Jacob hid them under the terebinth tree which *was* by Shechem.

5And they journeyed, and the terror of God was upon the cities that *were* all around them, and they did not pursue the sons of Jacob. 6So Jacob came to Luz (that *is,* Bethel), which *is* in the land of Canaan, he and all the people who *were* with him. 7And he built an altar there and called the place El Bethel,r because there God appeared to him when he fled from the face of his brother.

8*Now Deborah, Rebekah's nurse, died, and she was buried below Bethel under the terebinth tree. So the name of it was called Allon Bachuth.s

9Then God appeared to Jacob again, when he came from Padan Aram, and blessed him. 10And God said to him, "Your name *is* Jacob; your name shall not be called Jacob anymore, but Israel shall be your name." So He called his name Israel. 11Also God said to him: "I *am* God Almighty. Be fruitful and multiply; a nation and a company of nations shall proceed from you, and kings shall come from your body. 12The land which I gave Abraham and Isaac I give to you; and to your descendants after you I give this land." 13Then God went up from him in the place where He talked with him. 14So Jacob set up a pillar in the place where He talked with him, a pillar of stone; and he poured a drink offering on it, and he poured oil on it. 15And Jacob called the name of the place where God spoke with him, Bethel.

16Then they journeyed from Bethel. And when there was but a little distance to go to Ephrath, Rachel labored *in childbirth,* and she had hard labor. 17Now it came to pass, when she was in hard labor, that the midwife said to her, "Do not fear; you will have this son also." 18*And so it was, as her soul was departing (for she died), that she called his name Ben-Oni;t but his father called him Benjamin.u 19So Rachel died and was buried on the way to Ephrath (that *is,* Bethlehem). 20And Jacob set a pillar on her grave, which *is* the pillar of Rachel's grave to this day.

21Then Israel journeyed and pitched his tent beyond the tower of Eder. 22And it happened, when Israel dwelt in that land, that Reuben went and

---

35:7 rLiterally *God of the House of God*   35:8 sLiterally *Terebinth of Weeping*   35:18 tLiterally *Son of My Sorrow* uLiterally *Son of the Right Hand*

CHAPTERS 35—36

35:1–7 *New beginnings.* God once more appeared and told Jacob what to do. This was a part of the Bethel promise (28:13–15). We walk by faith when we obey God in spite of circumstances or consequences. But a change in geography does not guarantee a change in life, so Jacob told the whole family to bury the past and get rid of their heathen charms and idols. At Bethel, Jacob built a new altar and worshiped "the God of the house of God."

35:8, 18, 27 *New sorrows.* Three deaths are recorded in chapter 35, for death is one of the facts of life. Jacob's obedience to God did not prevent him from experiencing trials. He lost a friend, Deborah; a favorite wife, Rachel; and then his beloved father. (In spite of what he said in 27:2, Isaac lived for forty-three years after that!) Perhaps the greatest sorrow of all was the sin of his firstborn son Reuben. Sin is expensive, and this one cost Reuben the birthright (49:3–4; 1 Chron. 5:1).

35:18 *New joys.* The birth of Benjamin cost Rachel her life (30:1). Jacob wisely changed the name from "son of my sorrow" to "son of my right hand" (the place of honor). It was an act of faith at a time when Jacob's heart was broken. Like Benjamin, our Lord Jesus is a Son of sorrow (Isa. 53:3) and a Son of the right hand (Ps. 110:1; Mark 16:19). The tribe of Benjamin gave us the apostle Paul (Phil. 3:5), so the mother's sacrifice bore a rich harvest for the whole world (John 12:24–25).

lay with Bilhah his father's concubine; and Israel heard *about it*.

Now the sons of Jacob were twelve: 23the sons of Leah *were* Reuben, Jacob's firstborn, and Simeon, Levi, Judah, Issachar, and Zebulun; 24the sons of Rachel *were* Joseph and Benjamin; 25the sons of Bilhah, Rachel's maidservant, *were* Dan and Naphtali; 26and the sons of Zilpah, Leah's maidservant, *were* Gad and Asher. These *were* the sons of Jacob who were born to him in Padan Aram.

27Then Jacob came to his father Isaac at Mamre, or Kirjath Arbaᵛ (that *is*, Hebron), where Abraham and Isaac had dwelt. 28Now the days of Isaac were one hundred and eighty years. 29So Isaac breathed his last and died, and was gathered to his people, *being* old and full of days. And his sons Esau and Jacob buried him.

36 Now* this *is* the genealogy of Esau, who is Edom. 2Esau took his wives from the daughters of Canaan: Adah the daughter of Elon the Hittite; Aholibamah the daughter of Anah, the daughter of Zibeon the Hivite; 3and Basemath, Ishmael's daughter, sister of Nebajoth. 4Now Adah bore Eliphaz to Esau, and Basemath bore Reuel. 5And Aholibamah bore Jeush, Jaalam, and Korah. These *were* the sons of Esau who were born to him in the land of Canaan.

6Then Esau took his wives, his sons, his daughters, and all the persons of his household, his cattle and all his animals, and all his goods which he had gained in the land of Canaan, and went to a country away from the presence of his brother Jacob. 7For their possessions were too great for them to dwell together, and the land where they were strangers could not support them because of their livestock. 8So Esau dwelt in Mount Seir. Esau *is* Edom.

9And this *is* the genealogy of Esau the father of the Edomites in Mount Seir. 10These *were* the names of Esau's sons: Eliphaz the son of Adah the wife of Esau, and Reuel the son of Basemath the wife of Esau. 11And the sons of Eliphaz were Teman, Omar, Zepho,ʷ Gatam, and Kenaz.

12Now Timna was the concubine of Eliphaz, Esau's son, and she bore Amalek to Eliphaz. These *were* the sons of Adah, Esau's wife.

13These *were* the sons of Reuel: Nahath, Zerah, Shammah, and Mizzah. These were the sons of Basemath, Esau's wife.

14These were the sons of Aholibamah, Esau's wife, the daughter of Anah, the daughter of Zibeon. And she bore to Esau: Jeush, Jaalam, and Korah.

15These *were* the chiefs of the sons of Esau. The sons of Eliphaz, the firstborn *son* of Esau, were Chief Teman, Chief Omar, Chief Zepho, Chief Kenaz, 16Chief Korah,ˣ Chief Gatam, *and* Chief Amalek. These *were* the chiefs of Eliphaz in the land of Edom. They *were* the sons of Adah.

17These *were* the sons of Reuel, Esau's son: Chief Nahath, Chief Zerah, Chief Shammah, and Chief Mizzah. These *were* the chiefs of Reuel in the land of Edom. These *were* the sons of Basemath, Esau's wife.

18And these *were* the sons of Aholibamah,

36:1ff Since the family was complete, the sons and mothers were listed. Esau's family tree is much more imposing than Jacob's, but this is the last we hear of it. Despite their failures, the sons of Israel are the chosen instruments to accomplish God's will on earth.

35:27 ᵛLiterally *Town of Arba* 36:11 ʷSpelled *Zephi* in 1 Chronicles 1:36 36:16 ˣSamaritan Pentateuch omits *Chief Korah*.

Esau's wife: Chief Jeush, Chief Jaalam, and Chief Korah. These *were* the chiefs *who descended* from Aholibamah, Esau's wife, the daughter of Anah. [19]These *were* the sons of Esau, who is Edom, and these *were* their chiefs.

[20]These *were* the sons of Seir the Horite who inhabited the land: Lotan, Shobal, Zibeon, Anah, [21]Dishon, Ezer, and Dishan. These *were* the chiefs of the Horites, the sons of Seir, in the land of Edom.

[22]And the sons of Lotan were Hori and He-mam.[y] Lotan's sister *was* Timna.

[23]These *were* the sons of Shobal: Alvan,[z] Mana-hath, Ebal, Shepho,[a] and Onam.

[24]These *were* the sons of Zibeon: both Ajah and Anah. This *was the* Anah who found the water[b] in the wilderness as he pastured the donkeys of his father Zibeon. [25]These *were* the children of Anah: Dishon and Aholibamah the daughter of Anah.

[26]These *were* the sons of Dishon:[c] Hemdan,[d] Eshban, Ithran, and Cheran. [27]These *were* the sons of Ezer: Bilhan, Zaavan, and Akan.[e] [28]These *were* the sons of Dishan: Uz and Aran.

[29]These *were* the chiefs of the Horites: Chief Lotan, Chief Shobal, Chief Zibeon, Chief Anah, [30]Chief Dishon, Chief Ezer, and Chief Dishan. These *were* the chiefs of the Horites, according to their chiefs in the land of Seir.

[31]Now these *were* the kings who reigned in the land of Edom before any king reigned over the children of Israel: [32]Bela the son of Beor reigned in Edom, and the name of his city *was* Dinhabah. [33]And when Bela died, Jobab the son of Zerah of Bozrah reigned in his place. [34]When Jobab died, Husham of the land of the Temanites reigned in his place. [35]And when Husham died, Hadad the son of Bedad, who attacked Midian in the field of Moab, reigned in his place. And the name of his city *was* Avith. [36]When Hadad died, Samlah of Masrekah reigned in his place. [37]And when Samlah died, Saul of Rehoboth-*by*-the-River reigned in his place. [38]When Saul died, Baal-Hanan the son of Achbor reigned in his place. [39]And when Baal-Hanan the son of Achbor died, Hadar[f] reigned in his place; and the name of his city *was* Pau.[g] His wife's name *was* Mehetabel, the daughter of Matred, the daughter of Mezahab.

[40]And these *were* the names of the chiefs of Esau, according to their families and their places, by their names: Chief Timnah, Chief Alvah,[h] Chief Jetheth, [41]Chief Aholibamah, Chief Elah, Chief Pi-non, [42]Chief Kenaz, Chief Teman, Chief Mibzar, [43]Chief Magdiel, and Chief Iram. These *were* the chiefs of Edom, according to their dwelling places in the land of their possession. Esau *was* the fa-ther of the Edomites.

37 Now* Jacob dwelt in the land where his fa-ther was a stranger, in the land of Canaan. [2]This *is* the history of Jacob.

36:22 [y]Spelled *Homam* in 1 Chronicles 1:39   36:23 [z]Spelled *Alian* in 1 Chronicles 1:40   [a]Spelled *Shephi* in 1 Chronicles 1:40   36:24 [b]Following Masoretic Text and Vulgate (*hot springs*); Septuagint reads *Jamin;* Targum reads *mighty men;* Talmud interprets as *mules.*   36:26 [c]Hebrew *Dishan* [d]Spelled *Hamran* in 1 Chronicles 1:41   36:27 [e]Spelled *Jaakan* in 1 Chronicles 1:42   36:39 [f]Spelled *Hadad* in Samaritan Pentateuch, Syriac, and 1 Chronicles 1:50   [g]Spelled *Pai* in 1 Chronicles 1:50   36:40 [h]Spelled *Aliah* in 1 Chronicles 1:51

CHAPTER 37

37:1ff As you read the life of Joseph, you see in him a picture of the Lord Jesus Christ. Joseph was greatly loved by his father (v. 3; Matt. 3:17), hated and envied by his brothers (John 15:25; Mark 15:10), plotted against, sold as a slave, arrested unjustly, and made to suffer. But he went from suffering to glory and became the savior of the people who had rejected him.

God's goal for all His children is that we become like His Son (Rom. 8:29). The goal is glorious, but the process is painful. Both Jesus and Joseph had to suffer before they could enter into their glory (Luke 24:26; 1 Pet. 5:10). Had Joseph remained at home, his father probably would have pampered him and ruined his character. God knew what was best.

Joseph, *being* seventeen years old, was feeding the flock with his brothers. And the lad *was* with the sons of Bilhah and the sons of Zilpah, his father's wives; and Joseph brought a bad report of them to his father.

3Now Israel loved Joseph more than all his children, because he *was* the son of his old age. Also he made him a tunic of *many* colors. 4But when his brothers saw that their father loved him more than all his brothers, they hated him and could not speak peaceably to him.

5*Now Joseph had a dream, and he told *it* to his brothers; and they hated him even more. 6So he said to them, "Please hear this dream which I have dreamed: 7There we were, binding sheaves in the field. Then behold, my sheaf arose and also stood upright; and indeed your sheaves stood all around and bowed down to my sheaf."

8And his brothers said to him, "Shall you indeed reign over us? Or shall you indeed have dominion over us?" So they hated him even more for his dreams and for his words.

9Then he dreamed still another dream and told it to his brothers, and said, "Look, I have dreamed another dream. And this time, the sun, the moon, and the eleven stars bowed down to me."

10So he told *it* to his father and his brothers; and his father rebuked him and said to him, "What *is* this dream that you have dreamed? Shall your mother and I and your brothers indeed come to bow down to the earth before you?" 11And his brothers envied him, but his father kept the matter *in mind.*

12Then his brothers went to feed their father's flock in Shechem. 13And Israel said to Joseph, "Are not your brothers feeding *the flock* in Shechem? Come, I will send you to them."

So he said to him, "Here I am."

14Then he said to him, "Please go and see if it is well with your brothers and well with the flocks, and bring back word to me." So he sent him out of the Valley of Hebron, and he went to Shechem.

15Now a certain man found him, and there he was, wandering in the field. And the man asked him, saying, "What are you seeking?"

16So he said, "I am seeking my brothers. Please tell me where they are feeding *their flocks.*"

17And the man said, "They have departed from here, for I heard them say, 'Let us go to Dothan.' " So Joseph went after his brothers and found them in Dothan.

18Now when they saw him afar off, even before he came near them, they conspired against him to kill him. 19Then they said to one another, "Look, this dreamer is coming! 20Come therefore, let us now kill him and cast him into some pit; and we shall say, 'Some wild beast has devoured him.' We shall see what will become of his dreams!"

21But Reuben heard *it,* and he delivered him out of their hands, and said, "Let us not kill him." 22And Reuben said to them, "Shed no blood, *but* cast him into this pit which *is* in the wilderness, and do not lay a hand on him"—that he might deliver him out of their hands, and bring him back to his father.

23So it came to pass, when Joseph had come to his brothers, that they stripped Joseph *of* his tunic, the tunic of *many* colors that *was* on him. 24Then they took him and cast him into a pit. And the pit *was* empty; *there was* no water in it.

25And they sat down to eat a meal. Then they

37:5–11 Joseph's dreams were to him what God's Word is to us today: they gave him the assurance he needed when the going was hard.

lifted their eyes and looked, and there was a company of Ishmaelites, coming from Gilead with their camels, bearing spices, balm, and myrrh, on their way to carry *them* down to Egypt. 26So Judah said to his brothers, "What profit *is there* if we kill our brother and conceal his blood? 27Come and let us sell him to the Ishmaelites, and let not our hand be upon him, for he *is* our brother *and* our flesh." And his brothers listened. 28Then Midianite traders passed by; so *the brothers* pulled Joseph up and lifted him out of the pit, and sold him to the Ishmaelites for twenty *shekels* of silver. And they took Joseph to Egypt.

29Then Reuben returned to the pit, and indeed Joseph *was* not in the pit; and he tore his clothes. 30And he returned to his brothers and said, "The lad *is* no *more;* and I, where shall I go?"

31*So they took Joseph's tunic, killed a kid of the goats, and dipped the tunic in the blood. 32Then they sent the tunic of *many* colors, and they brought *it* to their father and said, "We have found this. Do you know whether it *is* your son's tunic or not?"

33And he recognized it and said, "*It is* my son's tunic. A wild beast has devoured him. Without doubt Joseph is torn to pieces." 34Then Jacob tore his clothes, put sackcloth on his waist, and mourned for his son many days. 35And all his sons and all his daughters arose to comfort him; but he refused to be comforted, and he said, "For I shall go down into the grave to my son in mourning." Thus his father wept for him.

36Now the Midianites[i] had sold him in Egypt to Potiphar, an officer of Pharaoh *and* captain of the guard.

38 It* came to pass at that time that Judah departed from his brothers, and visited a certain Adullamite whose name *was* Hirah. 2And Judah saw there a daughter of a certain Canaanite whose name *was* Shua, and he married her and went in to her. 3So she conceived and bore a son, and he called his name Er. 4She conceived again and bore a son, and she called his name Onan. 5And she conceived yet again and bore a son, and called his name Shelah. He was at Chezib when she bore him.

6Then Judah took a wife for Er his firstborn, and her name *was* Tamar. 7But Er, Judah's firstborn, was wicked in the sight of the LORD, and the LORD killed him. 8And Judah said to Onan, "Go in to your brother's wife and marry her, and raise up an heir to your brother." 9But Onan knew that the heir would not be his; and it came to pass, when he went in to his brother's wife, that he emitted on the ground, lest he should give an heir to his brother. 10And the thing which he did displeased the LORD; therefore He killed him also.

11Then Judah said to Tamar his daughter-in-law, "Remain a widow in your father's house till my son Shelah is grown." For he said, "Lest he also die like his brothers." And Tamar went and dwelt in her father's house.

12Now in the process of time the daughter of Shua, Judah's wife, died; and Judah was comforted, and went up to his sheepshearers at Timnah, he and his friend Hirah the Adullamite. 13*And it was told Tamar, saying, "Look, your father-in-law is going up to Timnah to shear his

37:31–35 Again, Jacob reaped what he had sown. He had killed a beast and lied to his father (27:9ff.), and his own sons lied to him.

CHAPTER 38
38:1–12 Marrying a Canaanite woman was disobedience on Judah's part (24:3; 2 Cor. 6:14—7:1). When one gets away from the family of God, it is easy to fall into temptation and sin (Ps. 1:1). Two of his sons were slain by God, and then his wife died. What tragedy!

38:13–26 It was expected that the next son would marry the widow and thus preserve the family, but Judah probably did not intend to keep his promise (v. 11). Tamar's purpose was good, but her plan was wicked. Leaving the signet and staff was like leaving fingerprints, because each man's was distinctive. Judah was quick to condemn Tamar for sinning, but what about his own sins toward Joseph and Tamar?

37:36 [i]Masoretic Text reads *Medanites.*

sheep." 14So she took off her widow's garments, covered *herself* with a veil and wrapped herself, and sat in an open place which *was* on the way to Timnah; for she saw that Shelah was grown, and she was not given to him as a wife. 15When Judah saw her, he thought she *was* a harlot, because she had covered her face. 16Then he turned to her by the way, and said, "Please let me come in to you"; for he did not know that she *was* his daughter-in-law.

So she said, "What will you give me, that you may come in to me?"

17And he said, "I will send a young goat from the flock."

So she said, "Will you give *me* a pledge till you send *it?*"

18Then he said, "What pledge shall I give you?"

So she said, "Your signet and cord, and your staff that *is* in your hand." Then he gave *them* to her, and went in to her, and she conceived by him. 19So she arose and went away, and laid aside her veil and put on the garments of her widowhood.

20And Judah sent the young goat by the hand of his friend the Adullamite, to receive *his* pledge from the woman's hand, but he did not find her. 21Then he asked the men of that place, saying, "Where is the harlot who *was* openly by the roadside?"

And they said, "There was no harlot in this *place.*"

22So he returned to Judah and said, "I cannot find her. Also, the men of the place said there was no harlot in this *place.*"

23Then Judah said, "Let her take *them* for herself, lest we be shamed; for I sent this young goat and you have not found her."

24And it came to pass, about three months after, that Judah was told, saying, "Tamar your daughter-in-law has played the harlot; furthermore she *is* with child by harlotry."

So Judah said, "Bring her out and let her be burned!"

25When she *was* brought out, she sent to her father-in-law, saying, "By the man to whom these belong, I *am* with child." And she said, "Please determine whose these *are*—the signet and cord, and staff."

26So Judah acknowledged *them* and said, "She has been more righteous than I, because I did not give her to Shelah my son." And he never knew her again.

27*Now it came to pass, at the time for giving birth, that behold, twins *were* in her womb. 28And so it was, when she was giving birth, that *the one* put out *his* hand; and the midwife took a scarlet *thread* and bound it on his hand, saying, "This one came out first." 29Then it happened, as he drew back his hand, that his brother came out unexpectedly; and she said, "How did you break through? *This* breach *be* upon you!" Therefore his name was called Perez.*j* 30Afterward his brother came out who had the scarlet *thread* on his hand. And his name was called Zerah.

38:27–30 Why is this sordid chapter in the Bible? For one thing, we see the contrast between Judah's sin and Joseph's victory (chap. 39), and we realize the importance of purity. But the main reason is to add another link in the Redeemer's family tree (v. 29; Ruth 4:18–22; Matt. 1:3). How gracious God is to mention a prostitute like Tamar in the genealogy of the Savior!

CHAPTERS 39—40

39:1ff The key to Joseph's conduct was his godly character, and the basis for that character was his recognition that he belonged to God and served Him (39:9). "The LORD was with Joseph" is often repeated (39:2, 3, 21, 23).

39 Now* Joseph had been taken down to Egypt. And Potiphar, an officer of Pharaoh, captain of the guard, an Egyptian, bought him from the Ishmaelites who had taken him down

38:29 *l*Literally *Breach* or *Breakthrough*

there. ²The LORD was with Joseph, and he was a successful man; and he was in the house of his master the Egyptian. ³And his master saw that the LORD *was* with him and that the LORD made all he did to prosper in his hand. ⁴So Joseph found favor in his sight, and served him. Then he made him overseer of his house, and all *that* he had he put under his authority. ⁵So it was, from the time *that* he had made him overseer of his house and all that he had, that the LORD blessed the Egyptian's house for Joseph's sake; and the blessing of the LORD was on all that he had in the house and in the field. ⁶Thus he left all that he had in Joseph's hand, and he did not know what he had except for the bread which he ate.

Now Joseph was handsome in form and appearance.

⁷*And it came to pass after these things that his master's wife cast longing eyes on Joseph, and she said, "Lie with me."

⁸But he refused and said to his master's wife, "Look, my master does not know what *is* with me in the house, and he has committed all that he has to my hand. ⁹*There is* no one greater in this house than I, nor has he kept back anything from me but you, because you *are* his wife. How then can I do this great wickedness, and sin against God?"

¹⁰So it was, as she spoke to Joseph day by day, that he did not heed her, to lie with her *or* to be with her.

¹¹But it happened about this time, when Joseph went into the house to do his work, and none of the men of the house *was* inside, ¹²that she caught him by his garment, saying, "Lie with me." But he left his garment in her hand, and fled and ran outside. ¹³And so it was, when she saw that he had left his garment in her hand and fled outside, ¹⁴that she called to the men of her house and spoke to them, saying, "See, he has brought in to us a Hebrew to mock us. He came in to me to lie with me, and I cried out with a loud voice. ¹⁵And it happened, when he heard that I lifted my voice and cried out, that he left his garment with me, and fled and went outside."

¹⁶So she kept his garment with her until his master came home. ¹⁷Then she spoke to him with words like these, saying, "The Hebrew servant whom you brought to us came in to me to mock me; ¹⁸so it happened, as I lifted my voice and cried out, that he left his garment with me and fled outside."

¹⁹So it was, when his master heard the words which his wife spoke to him, saying, "Your servant did to me after this manner," that his anger was aroused. ²⁰*Then Joseph's master took him and put him into the prison, a place where the king's prisoners *were* confined. And he was there in the prison. ²¹But the LORD was with Joseph and showed him mercy, and He gave him favor in the sight of the keeper of the prison. ²²And the keeper of the prison committed to Joseph's hand all the prisoners who *were* in the prison; whatever they did there, it was his doing. ²³The keeper of the prison did not look into anything *that was* under Joseph's authority,ᵏ because the LORD was with him; and whatever he did, the LORD made *it* prosper.

39:7–13 The Lord is with us as we work, and we should do our work as unto Him (Eph. 6:5–8). He is with us when we are tempted and will show us the way to escape (1 Cor. 10:13). We must keep away from temptation (Rom. 13:14); and if it gets too close, we must run away (2 Tim. 2:22). It is better to flee and lose your garment than fall and lose your character.

39:20–23 God is with us as we wait. Joseph spent two difficult years working in the prison, but he held to his faith and did what he could to serve others. The experience helped to "put iron into his soul" (Ps. 105:17–22). If the Lord controls us, it makes little difference who commands us.

39:23 ᵏLiterally *his hand*

40:1–23 The fact that Joseph could interpret the dreams of the baker and butler indicates that he understood the meaning of his own dreams. He knew that one day his eleven brothers would have to bow before him. What an encouragement that was to his faith!

40 It* came to pass after these things *that* the butler and the baker of the king of Egypt offended their lord, the king of Egypt. 2And Pharaoh was angry with his two officers, the chief butler and the chief baker. 3So he put them in custody in the house of the captain of the guard, in the prison, the place where Joseph *was* confined. 4And the captain of the guard charged Joseph with them, and he served them; so they were in custody for a while.

5Then the butler and the baker of the king of Egypt, who *were* confined in the prison, had a dream, both of them, each man's dream in one night *and* each man's dream with its *own* interpretation. 6And Joseph came in to them in the morning and looked at them, and saw that they *were* sad. 7So he asked Pharaoh's officers who *were* with him in the custody of his lord's house, saying, "Why do you look *so* sad today?"

8And they said to him, "We each have had a dream, and *there is* no interpreter of it."

So Joseph said to them, "Do not interpretations belong to God? Tell *them* to me, please."

9Then the chief butler told his dream to Joseph, and said to him, "Behold, in my dream a vine *was* before me, 10and in the vine *were* three branches; it *was* as though it budded, its blossoms shot forth, and its clusters brought forth ripe grapes. 11Then Pharaoh's cup *was* in my hand; and I took the grapes and pressed them into Pharaoh's cup, and placed the cup in Pharaoh's hand."

12And Joseph said to him, "This *is* the interpretation of it: The three branches *are* three days. 13Now within three days Pharaoh will lift up your head and restore you to your place, and you will put Pharaoh's cup in his hand according to the former manner, when you were his butler. 14But remember me when it is well with you, and please show kindness to me; make mention of me to Pharaoh, and get me out of this house. 15For indeed I was stolen away from the land of the Hebrews; and also I have done nothing here that they should put me into the dungeon."

16When the chief baker saw that the interpretation was good, he said to Joseph, "I also *was* in my dream, and there *were* three white baskets on my head. 17In the uppermost basket *were* all kinds of baked goods for Pharaoh, and the birds ate them out of the basket on my head."

18So Joseph answered and said, "This *is* the interpretation of it: The three baskets *are* three days. 19Within three days Pharaoh will lift off your head from you and hang you on a tree; and the birds will eat your flesh from you."

20Now it came to pass on the third day, *which was* Pharaoh's birthday, that he made a feast for all his servants; and he lifted up the head of the chief butler and of the chief baker among his servants. 21Then he restored the chief butler to his butlership again, and he placed the cup in Pharaoh's hand. 22But he hanged the chief baker, as Joseph had interpreted to them. 23Yet the chief butler did not remember Joseph, but forgot him.

CHAPTER 41

41:1–38 Explanation. For two years, Joseph was forgotten by the chief butler, but he was not forgotten by the Lord. It is disappointing to depend on people, for often their help never comes (Pss. 60:11; 146:3). Speaking to the world's greatest ruler, Joseph was careful to give all the glory to God (vv. 16, 25, 28, 32).

41 Then* it came to pass, at the end of two full years, that Pharaoh had a dream; and behold, he stood by the river. 2Suddenly there came up out of the river seven cows, fine looking and fat; and they fed in the meadow. 3Then behold, seven other cows came up after them out of the river, ugly and gaunt, and stood by the *other* cows on the bank of the river. 4And the ugly

and gaunt cows ate up the seven fine looking and fat cows. So Pharaoh awoke. 5He slept and dreamed a second time; and suddenly seven heads of grain came up on one stalk, plump and good. 6Then behold, seven thin heads, blighted by the east wind, sprang up after them. 7And the seven thin heads devoured the seven plump and full heads. So Pharaoh awoke, and indeed, *it was* a dream. 8Now it came to pass in the morning that his spirit was troubled, and he sent and called for all the magicians of Egypt and all its wise men. And Pharaoh told them his dreams, but *there was* no one who could interpret them for Pharaoh.

9Then the chief butler spoke to Pharaoh, saying: "I remember my faults this day. 10When Pharaoh was angry with his servants, and put me in custody in the house of the captain of the guard, *both* me and the chief baker, 11we each had a dream in one night, he and I. Each of us dreamed according to the interpretation of his *own* dream. 12Now there *was* a young Hebrew man with us there, a servant of the captain of the guard. And we told him, and he interpreted our dreams for us; to each man he interpreted according to his *own* dream. 13And it came to pass, just as he interpreted for us, so it happened. He restored me to my office, and he hanged him."

14Then Pharaoh sent and called Joseph, and they brought him quickly out of the dungeon; and he shaved, changed his clothing, and came to Pharaoh. 15And Pharaoh said to Joseph, "I have had a dream, and *there is* no one who can interpret it. But I have heard it said of you *that* you can understand a dream, to interpret it."

16So Joseph answered Pharaoh, saying, "*It is* not in me; God will give Pharaoh an answer of peace."

17Then Pharaoh said to Joseph: "Behold, in my dream I stood on the bank of the river. 18Suddenly seven cows came up out of the river, fine looking and fat; and they fed in the meadow. 19Then behold, seven other cows came up after them, poor and very ugly and gaunt, such ugliness as I have never seen in all the land of Egypt. 20And the gaunt and ugly cows ate up the first seven, the fat cows. 21When they had eaten them up, no one would have known that they had eaten them, for they *were* just as ugly as at the beginning. So I awoke. 22Also I saw in my dream, and suddenly seven heads came up on one stalk, full and good. 23Then behold, seven heads, withered, thin, *and* blighted by the east wind, sprang up after them. 24And the thin heads devoured the seven good heads. So I told *this* to the magicians, but *there was* no one who could explain *it* to me."

25Then Joseph said to Pharaoh, "The dreams of Pharaoh *are* one; God has shown Pharaoh what He *is* about to do: 26The seven good cows *are* seven years, and the seven good heads *are* seven years; the dreams *are* one. 27And the seven thin and ugly cows which came up after them *are* seven years, and the seven empty heads blighted by the east wind are seven years of famine. 28This *is* the thing which I have spoken to Pharaoh. God has shown Pharaoh what He *is* about to do. 29Indeed seven years of great plenty will come throughout all the land of Egypt; 30but after them seven years of famine will arise, and all the plenty will be forgotten in the land of Egypt; and the famine will deplete the land. 31So the plenty will not be known in the land because of the famine following, for it *will be* very severe. 32And the dream was repeated to Pharaoh twice because the thing *is* established by God, and God will shortly bring it to pass.

33"Now therefore, let Pharaoh select a discerning and wise man, and set him over the land of Egypt. 34Let Pharaoh do *this*, and let him appoint officers over the land, to collect one-fifth *of the produce* of the land of Egypt in the seven plentiful years. 35And let them gather all the food of those good years that are coming, and store up grain under the authority of Pharaoh, and let them keep food in the cities. 36Then that food shall be as a reserve for the land for the seven years of famine which shall be in the land of Egypt, that the land may not perish during the famine."

37So the advice was good in the eyes of Pharaoh and in the eyes of all his servants. 38And Pharaoh said to his servants, "Can we find *such a one* as this, a man in whom *is* the Spirit of God?"

39*Then Pharaoh said to Joseph, "Inasmuch as God has shown you all this, *there is* no one as discerning and wise as you. 40You shall be over my house, and all my people shall be ruled according to your word; only in regard to the throne will I be greater than you." 41And Pharaoh said to Joseph, "See, I have set you over all the land of Egypt."

41:39–44 Exaltation. God always exalts the humble "in due time" (1 Pet. 5:6). Joseph started as a servant, but then God made him a ruler (Matt. 25:21). He experienced suffering before God gave him glory (1 Pet. 5:10). God invested thirteen years in making a man out of Joseph; when it comes to building character, God is never in a hurry.

42Then Pharaoh took his signet ring off his hand and put it on Joseph's hand; and he clothed him in garments of fine linen and put a gold chain around his neck. 43And he had him ride in the second chariot which he had; and they cried out before him, "Bow the knee!" So he set him over all the land of Egypt. 44Pharaoh also said to Joseph, "I *am* Pharaoh, and without your consent no man may lift his hand or foot in all the land of Egypt." 45*And Pharaoh called Joseph's name Zaphnath-Paaneah. And he gave him as a wife Asenath, the daughter of Poti-Pherah priest of On. So Joseph went out over *all* the land of Egypt.

46Joseph was thirty years old when he stood before Pharaoh king of Egypt. And Joseph went out from the presence of Pharaoh, and went throughout all the land of Egypt. 47Now in the seven plentiful years the ground brought forth abundantly. 48So he gathered up all the food of the seven years which were in the land of Egypt, and laid up the food in the cities; he laid up in every city the food of the fields which surrounded them. 49Joseph gathered very much grain, as the sand of the sea, until he stopped counting, for *it was* immeasurable.

41:45–57 Expectation. Joseph's new name probably means "the one who furnishes nourishment to the land." He married an Egyptian wife, and she bore him two sons who were given significant names: Manasseh ("one who forgets") and Ephraim ("double fruit"). Joseph determined to forget the past and live for the future. In the Bible, *forgetting* means "not holding it against another." Joseph certainly did not forget what his brothers did, but he did not hold it against them. Instead, he concentrated on living a fruitful life to the glory of God.

50And to Joseph were born two sons before the years of famine came, whom Asenath, the daughter of Poti-Pherah priest of On, bore to him. 51Joseph called the name of the firstborn Manasseh:*l* "For God has made me forget all my toil and all my father's house." 52And the name of the second he called Ephraim:*m* "For God has caused me to be fruitful in the land of my affliction."

53Then the seven years of plenty which were in the land of Egypt ended, 54and the seven years of famine began to come, as Joseph had said. The famine was in all lands, but in all the land of Egypt there was bread. 55So when all the land of Egypt was famished, the people cried to Pharaoh for bread. Then Pharaoh said to all the Egyptians,

41:51 *l*Literally *Making Forgetful*   41:52 *m*Literally *Fruitfulness*

"Go to Joseph; whatever he says to you, do."
56The famine was over all the face of the earth,
and Joseph opened all the storehouses*n* and sold
to the Egyptians. And the famine became severe
in the land of Egypt. 57So all countries came to
Joseph in Egypt to buy *grain,* because the famine
was severe in all lands.

42 When* Jacob saw that there was grain in
Egypt, Jacob said to his sons, "Why do you
look at one another?" 2And he said, "Indeed I
have heard that there is grain in Egypt; go down
to that place and buy for us there, that we may
live and not die."

3So Joseph's ten brothers went down to buy
grain in Egypt. 4But Jacob did not send Joseph's
brother Benjamin with his brothers, for he said,
"Lest some calamity befall him." 5And the sons
of Israel went to buy *grain* among those who journeyed, for the famine was in the land of Canaan.

6Now Joseph *was* governor over the land; and
it was he who sold to all the people of the land.
And Joseph's brothers came and bowed down before him with *their* faces to the earth. 7Joseph saw
his brothers and recognized them, but he acted
as a stranger to them and spoke roughly to them.
Then he said to them, "Where do you come
from?"

And they said, "From the land of Canaan to
buy food."

8So Joseph recognized his brothers, but they
did not recognize him. 9Then Joseph remembered
the dreams which he had dreamed about them,
and said to them, "You *are* spies! You have come
to see the nakedness of the land!"

10And they said to him, "No, my lord, but your
servants have come to buy food. 11We *are* all one
man's sons; we *are* honest *men;* your servants are
not spies."

12But he said to them, "No, but you have come
to see the nakedness of the land."

13And they said, "Your servants *are* twelve
brothers, the sons of one man in the land of Canaan; and in fact, the youngest *is* with our father
today, and one *is* no more."

14*But Joseph said to them, "It *is* as I spoke to
you, saying, 'You *are* spies!' 15In this *manner* you
shall be tested: By the life of Pharaoh, you shall
not leave this place unless your youngest brother
comes here. 16Send one of you, and let him bring
your brother; and you shall be kept in prison, that
your words may be tested to see whether *there
is* any truth in you; or else, by the life of Pharaoh,
surely you *are* spies!" 17So he put them all together in prison three days.

18Then Joseph said to them the third day, "Do
this and live, *for* I fear God: 19If you *are* honest
men, let one of your brothers be confined to your
prison house; but you, go and carry grain for the
famine of your houses. 20And bring your youngest
brother to me; so your words will be verified, and
you shall not die."

And they did so. 21Then they said to one another, "We *are* truly guilty concerning our
brother, for we saw the anguish of his soul when
he pleaded with us, and we would not hear; therefore this distress has come upon us."

22And Reuben answered them, saying, "Did I
not speak to you, saying, 'Do not sin against the

CHAPTERS 42—44
42:1ff These chapters describe Joseph's
dealings with his brothers and the brothers'
consequent confrontations with their father.
The ten brothers had sinned against both
Jacob and Joseph, but they thought that
Joseph was dead and their sin was safely
hidden. Joseph had to deal with them
patiently, honestly, and decisively, just the
way the Lord works with us when we have
tried to cover our sins.

42:14—43:28 Joseph's immediate goal was
to get all eleven brothers to Egypt so they
could bow before him and fulfill the dream
God had given him more than twenty years
before. His ultimate goal was to get them
to confess their sins and be reconciled to
him and Jacob. The men had to come to
the place where their mouths were stopped
(44:16; Rom. 3:19).

41:56 *n*Literally *all that was in them*

boy'; and you would not listen? Therefore behold, his blood is now required of us." 23But they did not know that Joseph understood *them*, for he spoke to them through an interpreter. 24And he turned himself away from them and wept. Then he returned to them again, and talked with them. And he took Simeon from them and bound him before their eyes.

25Then Joseph gave a command to fill their sacks with grain, to restore every man's money to his sack, and to give them provisions for the journey. Thus he did for them. 26So they loaded their donkeys with the grain and departed from there. 27But as one *of them* opened his sack to give his donkey feed at the encampment, he saw his money; and there it was, in the mouth of his sack. 28So he said to his brothers, "My money has been restored, and there it is, in my sack!" Then their hearts failed *them* and they were afraid, saying to one another, "What *is* this *that* God has done to us?"

29Then they went to Jacob their father in the land of Canaan and told him all that had happened to them, saying: 30"The man *who is* lord of the land spoke roughly to us, and took us for spies of the country. 31But we said to him, 'We *are* honest *men;* we are not spies. 32We *are* twelve brothers, sons of our father; one *is* no *more,* and the youngest *is* with our father this day in the land of Canaan.' 33Then the man, the lord of the country, said to us, 'By this I will know that you *are* honest *men:* Leave one of your brothers *here* with me, take *food for* the famine of your households, and be gone. 34And bring your youngest brother to me; so I shall know that you *are* not spies, but *that* you *are* honest *men.* I will grant your brother to you, and you may trade in the land.' "

35Then it happened as they emptied their sacks, that surprisingly each man's bundle of money *was* in his sack; and when they and their father saw the bundles of money, they were afraid. 36And Jacob their father said to them, "You have bereaved me: Joseph is no *more,* Simeon is no *more,* and you want to take Benjamin. All these things are against me."

37Then Reuben spoke to his father, saying, "Kill my two sons if I do not bring him *back* to you; put him in my hands, and I will bring him back to you."

38But he said, "My son shall not go down with you, for his brother is dead, and he is left alone. If any calamity should befall him along the way in which you go, then you would bring down my gray hair with sorrow to the grave."

43 Now the famine *was* severe in the land. 2And it came to pass, when they had eaten up the grain which they had brought from Egypt, that their father said to them, "Go back, buy us a little food."

3But Judah spoke to him, saying, "The man solemnly warned us, saying, 'You shall not see my face unless your brother *is* with you.' 4If you send our brother with us, we will go down and buy you food. 5But if you will not send *him,* we will not go down; for the man said to us, 'You shall not see my face unless your brother *is* with you.' "

6And Israel said, "Why did you deal *so* wrongfully with me *as* to tell the man whether you had still *another* brother?"

7But they said, "The man asked us pointedly

about ourselves and our family, saying, 'Is your father still alive? Have you *another* brother?' And we told him according to these words. Could we possibly have known that he would say, 'Bring your brother down'?"

8Then Judah said to Israel his father, "Send the lad with me, and we will arise and go, that we may live and not die, both we and you *and* also our little ones. 9I myself will be surety for him; from my hand you shall require him. If I do not bring him *back* to you and set him before you, then let me bear the blame forever. 10For if we had not lingered, surely by now we would have returned this second time."

11And their father Israel said to them, "If *it must be* so, then do this: Take some of the best fruits of the land in your vessels and carry down a present for the man—a little balm and a little honey, spices and myrrh, pistachio nuts and almonds. 12Take double money in your hand, and take back in your hand the money that was returned in the mouth of your sacks; perhaps it was an oversight. 13Take your brother also, and arise, go back to the man. 14And may God Almighty give you mercy before the man, that he may release your other brother and Benjamin. If I am bereaved, I am bereaved!"

15So the men took that present and Benjamin, and they took double money in their hand, and arose and went down to Egypt; and they stood before Joseph. 16When Joseph saw Benjamin with them, he said to the steward of his house, "Take *these* men to my home, and slaughter an animal and make ready; for *these* men will dine with me at noon." 17Then the man did as Joseph ordered, and the man brought the men into Joseph's house.

18Now the men were afraid because they were brought into Joseph's house; and they said, "It *is* because of the money, which was returned in our sacks the first time, that we are brought in, so that he may make a case against us and seize us, to take us as slaves with our donkeys."

19When they drew near to the steward of Joseph's house, they talked with him at the door of the house, 20and said, "O sir, we indeed came down the first time to buy food; 21but it happened, when we came to the encampment, that we opened our sacks, and there, *each* man's money *was* in the mouth of his sack, our money in full weight; so we have brought it back in our hand. 22And we have brought down other money in our hands to buy food. We do not know who put our money in our sacks."

23But he said, "Peace *be* with you, do not be afraid. Your God and the God of your father has given you treasure in your sacks; I had your money." Then he brought Simeon out to them.

24So the man brought the men into Joseph's house and gave *them* water, and they washed their feet; and he gave their donkeys feed. 25Then they made the present ready for Joseph's coming at noon, for they heard that they would eat bread there.

26And when Joseph came home, they brought him the present which *was* in their hand into the house, and bowed down before him to the earth. 27Then he asked them about *their* well-being, and said, "Is your father well, the old man of whom you spoke? *Is* he still alive?"

28And they answered, "Your servant our father *is* in good health; he *is* still alive." And they bowed their heads down and prostrated themselves.

44:1, 2 In a masterful way, Joseph wove these two purposes together as he spoke roughly to them, accused them of crimes, and insisted on their bringing Benjamin to Egypt. Outwardly, he was a stern ruler; but behind the scenes, he was a weeping brother.

29Then he lifted his eyes and saw his brother Benjamin, his mother's son, and said, "*Is* this your younger brother of whom you spoke to me?" And he said, "God be gracious to you, my son." 30Now his heart yearned for his brother; so Joseph made haste and sought *somewhere* to weep. And he went into *his* chamber and wept there. 31Then he washed his face and came out; and he restrained himself, and said, "Serve the bread."

32So they set him a place by himself, and them by themselves, and the Egyptians who ate with him by themselves; because the Egyptians could not eat food with the Hebrews, for that *is* an abomination to the Egyptians. 33And they sat before him, the firstborn according to his birthright and the youngest according to his youth; and the men looked in astonishment at one another. 34Then he took servings to them from before him, but Benjamin's serving was five times as much as any of theirs. So they drank and were merry with him.

44

And* he commanded the steward of his house, saying, "Fill the men's sacks with food, as much as they can carry, and put each man's money in the mouth of his sack. 2Also put my cup, the silver cup, in the mouth of the sack of the youngest, and his grain money." So he did according to the word that Joseph had spoken. 3As soon as the morning dawned, the men were sent away, they and their donkeys. 4When they had gone out of the city, *and* were not *yet* far off, Joseph said to his steward, "Get up, follow the men; and when you overtake them, say to them, 'Why have you repaid evil for good? 5Is not this *the one* from which my lord drinks, and with which he indeed practices divination? You have done evil in so doing.'"

6So he overtook them, and he spoke to them these same words. 7And they said to him, "Why does my lord say these words? Far be it from us that your servants should do such a thing. 8Look, we brought back to you from the land of Canaan the money which we found in the mouth of our sacks. How then could we steal silver or gold from your lord's house? 9With whomever of your servants it is found, let him die, and we also will be my lord's slaves."

10And he said, "Now also *let* it *be* according to your words; he with whom it is found shall be my slave, and you shall be blameless." 11Then each man speedily let down his sack to the ground, and each opened his sack. 12So he searched. He began with the oldest and left off with the youngest; and the cup was found in Benjamin's sack. 13Then they tore their clothes, and each man loaded his donkey and returned to the city.

14So Judah and his brothers came to Joseph's house, and he *was* still there; and they fell before him on the ground. 15And Joseph said to them, "What deed *is* this you have done? Did you not know that such a man as I can certainly practice divination?"

16Then Judah said, "What shall we say to my lord? What shall we speak? Or how shall we clear ourselves? God has found out the iniquity of your servants; here we are, my lord's slaves, both we and *he* also with whom the cup was found."

17But he said, "Far be it from me that I should do so; the man in whose hand the cup was found, he shall be my slave. And as for you, go up in peace to your father."

18Then Judah came near to him and said: "O my lord, please let your servant speak a word in my lord's hearing, and do not let your anger burn against your servant; for you *are* even like Pharaoh. 19My lord asked his servants, saying, 'Have you a father or a brother?' 20And we said to my lord, 'We have a father, an old man, and a child of *his* old age, *who is* young; his brother is dead, and he alone is left of his mother's children, and his father loves him.' 21Then you said to your servants, 'Bring him down to me, that I may set my eyes on him.' 22And we said to my lord, 'The lad cannot leave his father, for *if* he should leave his father, *his father* would die.' 23But you said to your servants, 'Unless your youngest brother comes down with you, you shall see my face no more.'

24"So it was, when we went up to your servant my father, that we told him the words of my lord. 25And our father said, 'Go back *and* buy us a little food.' 26But we said, 'We cannot go down; if our youngest brother is with us, then we will go down; for we may not see the man's face unless our youngest brother *is* with us.' 27*Then your servant my father said to us, 'You know that my wife bore me two sons; 28and the one went out from me, and I said, "Surely he is torn to pieces"; and I have not seen him since. 29But if you take this one also from me, and calamity befalls him, you shall bring down my gray hair with sorrow to the grave.'

30"Now therefore, when I come to your servant my father, and the lad *is* not with us, since his life is bound up in the lad's life, 31it will happen, when he sees that the lad *is* not *with us,* that he will die. So your servants will bring down the gray hair of your servant our father with sorrow to the grave. 32For your servant became surety for the lad to my father, saying, 'If I do not bring him *back* to you, then I shall bear the blame before my father forever.' 33Now therefore, please let your servant remain instead of the lad as a slave to my lord, and let the lad go up with his brothers. 34For how shall I go up to my father if the lad *is* not with me, lest perhaps I see the evil that would come upon my father?"

45 Then* Joseph could not restrain himself before all those who stood by him, and he cried out, "Make everyone go out from me!" So no one stood with him while Joseph made himself known to his brothers. 2And he wept aloud, and the Egyptians and the house of Pharaoh heard it.

3Then Joseph said to his brothers, "I *am* Joseph; does my father still live?" But his brothers could not answer him, for they were dismayed in his presence. 4*And Joseph said to his brothers, "Please come near to me." So they came near. Then he said: "I *am* Joseph your brother, whom you sold into Egypt. 5But now, do not therefore be grieved or angry with yourselves because you sold me here; for God sent me before you to preserve life. 6For these two years the famine *has been* in the land, and *there are* still five years in which *there will be* neither plowing nor harvesting. 7*And God sent me before you to preserve a posterity for you in the earth, and to save your lives by a great deliverance. 8So now *it was* not you *who* sent me here, but God; and He has made

44:27 Jacob's responses mirror our responses to God's providential disciplines: "Everything is against me!" (42:36); "Why didn't you do it differently?" (43:6); "Take a gift along" (43:11 [always the schemer!]); "If it has to be, it has to be!" (43:14). From pessimism to fatalism, and very little faith.

CHAPTER 45

45:1–3 *Recognition.* When Joseph saw that his brothers' hearts were humble, and when he heard them confess their sins, he knew it was safe to reveal his identity to them. Had he done it earlier, they would not have been ready for the blessings he had for them; and had he waited longer, the men might have been in total despair. Our Lord knows just how to work in our lives to bring us to submission. Joseph could have fed them and their father without going through this lengthy procedure, but it would only have further ruined their character.

45:4–6 *Reconciliation.* Joseph said, "Please come near to me" (v. 4). He had forgiven them, but they were still afraid. In fact, they would still be afraid seventeen years later (50:15–21). In Jesus Christ, we have been reconciled to God, and we need not fear judgment (Rom. 8:1; 2 Cor. 5:18; Col. 1:20). God wants us to draw near to Him (Heb. 10:19–25; James 4:8).

45:7, 8 *Reassurance.* Joseph explained to them that God had sent him before them to preserve the nation so that Israel could be a blessing to all the earth (12:1–3). God's providential purpose did not minimize their sins or negate their responsibility (Acts 2:23; 3:13–18), but it did help to ease their fear and sorrow. Joseph further reassured them by giving them rich gifts and promising to care for the whole family. The gifts he sent home helped to give Jacob the assurance he needed that Joseph indeed was alive.

Joseph knew his brothers, so he admonished them: "Don't be angry with yourselves!" (v. 5), and "Don't quarrel on the journey!" (v. 24). We quickly lose the blessing when we fail to accept Christ's forgiveness and then love one another. (See 1 John 4:7ff.)

me a father to Pharaoh, and lord of all his house, and a ruler throughout all the land of Egypt.

9"Hurry and go up to my father, and say to him, 'Thus says your son Joseph: "God has made me lord of all Egypt; come down to me, do not tarry. 10You shall dwell in the land of Goshen, and you shall be near to me, you and your children, your children's children, your flocks and your herds, and all that you have. 11There I will provide for you, lest you and your household, and all that you have, come to poverty; for *there are* still five years of famine."'

12"And behold, your eyes and the eyes of my brother Benjamin see that *it is* my mouth that speaks to you. 13So you shall tell my father of all my glory in Egypt, and of all that you have seen; and you shall hurry and bring my father down here."

14Then he fell on his brother Benjamin's neck and wept, and Benjamin wept on his neck. 15Moreover he kissed all his brothers and wept over them, and after that his brothers talked with him.

16Now the report of it was heard in Pharaoh's house, saying, "Joseph's brothers have come." So it pleased Pharaoh and his servants well. 17And Pharaoh said to Joseph, "Say to your brothers, 'Do this: Load your animals and depart; go to the land of Canaan. 18Bring your father and your households and come to me; I will give you the best of the land of Egypt, and you will eat the fat of the land. 19Now you are commanded—do this: Take carts out of the land of Egypt for your little ones and your wives; bring your father and come. 20Also do not be concerned about your goods, for the best of all the land of Egypt *is* yours.'"

21Then the sons of Israel did so; and Joseph gave them carts, according to the command of Pharaoh, and he gave them provisions for the journey. 22He gave to all of them, to each man, changes of garments; but to Benjamin he gave three hundred *pieces* of silver and five changes of garments. 23And he sent to his father these *things*: ten donkeys loaded with the good things of Egypt, and ten female donkeys loaded with grain, bread, and food for his father for the journey. 24So he sent his brothers away, and they departed; and he said to them, "See that you do not become troubled along the way."

25Then they went up out of Egypt, and came to the land of Canaan to Jacob their father. 26And they told him, saying, "Joseph *is* still alive, and he *is* governor over all the land of Egypt." And Jacob's heart stood still, because he did not believe them. 27But when they told him all the words which Joseph had said to them, and when he saw the carts which Joseph had sent to carry him, the spirit of Jacob their father revived. 28Then Israel said, "*It is* enough. Joseph my son *is* still alive. I will go and see him before I die."

CHAPTERS 46—47

46:1–4 It would not be easy for Jacob, now 130 years old, to leave the land God gave him and go to Egypt. Moving to a new home is usually a difficult experience, and the older we are, the more difficult it is. Furthermore, Abraham got into trouble in Egypt (12:10ff.), and God had stopped Isaac from going there (26:2ff.).

But Jacob was able to go with confidence and peace because he was sure of God's promise and presence (46:1–4). In the crisis hours of life, God speaks to us and assures us when we take time to worship.

Furthermore, Jacob knew that God had gone before him and that Joseph was there making everything ready for him. The future is your friend when Jesus is your Lord and you follow Him.

46 So* Israel took his journey with all that he had, and came to Beersheba, and offered sacrifices to the God of his father Isaac. 2Then God spoke to Israel in the visions of the night, and said, "Jacob, Jacob!"

And he said, "Here I am."

3So He said, "I *am* God, the God of your father; do not fear to go down to Egypt, for I will make of you a great nation there. 4I will go down with you to Egypt, and I will also surely bring you up *again;* and Joseph will put his hand on your eyes."

5Then Jacob arose from Beersheba; and the sons of Israel carried their father Jacob, their little ones, and their wives, in the carts which Pharaoh had sent to carry him. 6So they took their livestock and their goods, which they had acquired in the land of Canaan, and went to Egypt, Jacob and all his descendants with him. 7His sons and his sons' sons, his daughters and his sons' daughters, and all his descendants he brought with him to Egypt.

8Now these *were* the names of the children of Israel, Jacob and his sons, who went to Egypt: Reuben *was* Jacob's firstborn. 9The sons of Reuben *were* Hanoch, Pallu, Hezron, and Carmi. 10The sons of Simeon *were* Jemuel,*o* Jamin, Ohad, Jachin,*p* Zohar,*q* and Shaul, the son of a Canaanite woman. 11The sons of Levi *were* Gershon, Kohath, and Merari. 12The sons of Judah *were* Er, Onan, Shelah, Perez, and Zerah (but Er and Onan died in the land of Canaan). The sons of Perez were Hezron and Hamul. 13The sons of Issachar *were* Tola, Puvah,*r* Job,*s* and Shimron. 14The sons of Zebulun *were* Sered, Elon, and Jahleel. 15These *were* the sons of Leah, whom she bore to Jacob in Padan Aram, with his daughter Dinah. All the persons, his sons and his daughters, *were* thirty-three.

16The sons of Gad *were* Ziphion,*t* Haggi, Shuni, Ezbon,*u* Eri, Arodi,*v* and Areli. 17The sons of Asher *were* Jimnah, Ishuah, Isui, Beriah, and Serah, their sister. And the sons of Beriah *were* Heber and Malchiel. 18These *were* the sons of Zilpah, whom Laban gave to Leah his daughter; and these she bore to Jacob: sixteen persons.

19The sons of Rachel, Jacob's wife, *were* Joseph and Benjamin. 20And to Joseph in the land of Egypt were born Manasseh and Ephraim, whom Asenath, the daughter of Poti-Pherah priest of On, bore to him. 21The sons of Benjamin *were* Belah, Becher, Ashbel, Gera, Naaman, Ehi, Rosh, Muppim, Huppim,*w* and Ard. 22These *were* the sons of Rachel, who were born to Jacob: fourteen persons in all.

23The son of Dan *was* Hushim.*x* 24The sons of Naphtali *were* Jahzeel,*y* Guni, Jezer, and Shillem.*z* 25These *were* the sons of Bilhah, whom Laban gave to Rachel his daughter, and she bore these to Jacob: seven persons in all.

26All the persons who went with Jacob to Egypt, who came from his body, besides Jacob's sons' wives, *were* sixty-six persons in all. 27And the sons of Joseph who were born to him in Egypt *were* two persons. All the persons of the house of Jacob who went to Egypt were seventy.

28Then he sent Judah before him to Joseph, to point out before him *the way* to Goshen. And they came to the land of Goshen. 29So Joseph made ready his chariot and went up to Goshen to meet his father Israel; and he presented himself to him,

46:10 *o*Spelled *Nemuel* in 1 Chronicles 4:24 *p*Called *Jarib* in 1 Chronicles 4:24 *q*Called *Zerah* in 1 Chronicles 4:24
46:13 *r*Spelled *Puah* in 1 Chronicles 7:1 *s*Same as *Jashub* in Numbers 26:24 and 1 Chronicles 7:1 46:16 *t*Spelled *Zephon* in Samaritan Pentateuch, Septuagint, and Numbers 26:15 *u*Called *Ozni* in Numbers 26:16 *v*Spelled *Arod* in Numbers 26:17 46:21 *w*Called *Hupham* in Numbers 26:39
46:23 *x*Called *Shuham* in Numbers 26:42 46:24 *y*Spelled *Jahziel* in 1 Chronicles 7:13 *z*Spelled *Shallum* in 1 Chronicles 7:13

and fell on his neck and wept on his neck a good while.

30And Israel said to Joseph, "Now let me die, since I have seen your face, because you *are* still alive."

31Then Joseph said to his brothers and to his father's household, "I will go up and tell Pharaoh, and say to him, 'My brothers and those of my father's house, who *were* in the land of Canaan, have come to me. 32And the men *are* shepherds, for their occupation has been to feed livestock; and they have brought their flocks, their herds, and all that they have.' 33So it shall be, when Pharaoh calls you and says, 'What is your occupation?' 34that you shall say, 'Your servants' occupation has been with livestock from our youth even till now, both we *and* also our fathers,' that you may dwell in the land of Goshen; for every shepherd *is* an abomination to the Egyptians."

47 Then Joseph went and told Pharaoh, and said, "My father and my brothers, their flocks and their herds and all that they possess, have come from the land of Canaan; and indeed they *are* in the land of Goshen." 2And he took five men from among his brothers and presented them to Pharaoh. 3Then Pharaoh said to his brothers, "What *is* your occupation?"

And they said to Pharaoh, "Your servants *are* shepherds, both we *and* also our fathers." 4And they said to Pharaoh, "We have come to dwell in the land, because your servants have no pasture for their flocks, for the famine *is* severe in the land of Canaan. Now therefore, please let your servants dwell in the land of Goshen."

5Then Pharaoh spoke to Joseph, saying, "Your father and your brothers have come to you. 6The land of Egypt *is* before you. Have your father and brothers dwell in the best of the land; let them dwell in the land of Goshen. And if you know *any* competent men among them, then make them chief herdsmen over my livestock."

7*Then Joseph brought in his father Jacob and set him before Pharaoh; and Jacob blessed Pharaoh. 8Pharaoh said to Jacob, "How old *are* you?"

9And Jacob said to Pharaoh, "The days of the years of my pilgrimage *are* one hundred and thirty years; few and evil have been the days of the years of my life, and they have not attained to the days of the years of the life of my fathers in the days of their pilgrimage." 10So Jacob blessed Pharaoh, and went out from before Pharaoh.

11*And Joseph situated his father and his brothers, and gave them a possession in the land of Egypt, in the best of the land, in the land of Rameses, as Pharaoh had commanded. 12Then Joseph provided his father, his brothers, and all his father's household with bread, according to the number in *their* families.

13Now *there was* no bread in all the land; for the famine *was* very severe, so that the land of Egypt and the land of Canaan languished because of the famine. 14And Joseph gathered up all the money that was found in the land of Egypt and in the land of Canaan, for the grain which they bought; and Joseph brought the money into Pharaoh's house.

15So when the money failed in the land of Egypt and in the land of Canaan, all the Egyptians came to Joseph and said, "Give us bread, for why should we die in your presence? For the money has failed."

47:7 Jacob was a blessing in Egypt. He blessed Pharaoh (47:7, 10), Joseph and Joseph's sons (48:15, 20), and all twelve of the sons of Israel (49:1ff.). God blesses us that we might be a blessing. Circumstances change, but God never changes.

47:11, 12 Egypt was a haven for Jacob and his family, and there God protected them and built of them a great people. But Jacob knew that Egypt was not his home, Canaan was; and he wanted to be buried there with the others who had made the same pilgrimage of faith. He was a testimony in life, and he wanted to be a testimony in death. Despite his mistakes and failures in life, Jacob ended well.

¹⁶Then Joseph said, "Give your livestock, and I will give you *bread* for your livestock, if the money is gone." ¹⁷So they brought their livestock to Joseph, and Joseph gave them bread *in exchange* for the horses, the flocks, the cattle of the herds, and for the donkeys. Thus he fed them with bread *in exchange* for all their livestock that year.

¹⁸When that year had ended, they came to him the next year and said to him, "We will not hide from my lord that our money is gone; my lord also has our herds of livestock. There is nothing left in the sight of my lord but our bodies and our lands. ¹⁹Why should we die before your eyes, both we and our land? Buy us and our land for bread, and we and our land will be servants of Pharaoh; give *us* seed, that we may live and not die, that the land may not be desolate."

²⁰Then Joseph bought all the land of Egypt for Pharaoh; for every man of the Egyptians sold his field, because the famine was severe upon them. So the land became Pharaoh's. ²¹And as for the people, he moved them into the cities,ᵃ from *one* end of the borders of Egypt to the *other* end. ²²Only the land of the priests he did not buy; for the priests had rations *allotted to them* by Pharaoh, and they ate their rations which Pharaoh gave them; therefore they did not sell their lands.

²³Then Joseph said to the people, "Indeed I have bought you and your land this day for Pharaoh. Look, *here is* seed for you, and you shall sow the land. ²⁴And it shall come to pass in the harvest that you shall give one-fifth to Pharaoh. Four-fifths shall be your own, as seed for the field and for your food, for those of your households and as food for your little ones."

²⁵So they said, "You have saved our lives; let us find favor in the sight of my lord, and we will be Pharaoh's servants." ²⁶And Joseph made it a law over the land of Egypt to this day, *that* Pharaoh should have one-fifth, except for the land of the priests only, *which* did not become Pharaoh's.

²⁷So Israel dwelt in the land of Egypt, in the country of Goshen; and they had possessions there and grew and multiplied exceedingly. ²⁸And Jacob lived in the land of Egypt seventeen years. So the length of Jacob's life was one hundred and forty-seven years. ²⁹When the time drew near that Israel must die, he called his son Joseph and said to him, "Now if I have found favor in your sight, please put your hand under my thigh, and deal kindly and truly with me. Please do not bury me in Egypt, ³⁰but let me lie with my fathers; you shall carry me out of Egypt and bury me in their burial place."

And he said, "I will do as you have said."

³¹Then he said, "Swear to me." And he swore to him. So Israel bowed himself on the head of the bed.

48 Now it came to pass after these things that Joseph was told, "Indeed your father *is* sick"; and he took with him his two sons, Manasseh and Ephraim. ²And Jacob was told, "Look, your son Joseph is coming to you"; and Israel strengthened himself and sat up on the bed. ³Then Jacob said to Joseph: "God Almighty appeared to me at Luz in the land of Canaan and

CHAPTERS 48—49

What should believers do for their family before God takes them in death? Just what Jacob did.

47:21 ᵃFollowing Masoretic Text and Targum; Samaritan Pentateuch, Septuagint, and Vulgate read *made the people virtual slaves*.

blessed me, [4]and said to me, 'Behold, I will make you fruitful and multiply you, and I will make of you a multitude of people, and give this land to your descendants after you *as* an everlasting possession.' [5]And now your two sons, Ephraim and Manasseh, who were born to you in the land of Egypt before I came to you in Egypt, *are* mine; as Reuben and Simeon, they shall be mine. [6]Your offspring whom you beget after them shall be yours; they will be called by the name of their brothers in their inheritance. [7]But as for me, when I came from Padan, Rachel died beside me in the land of Canaan on the way, when *there was* but a little distance to go to Ephrath; and I buried her there on the way to Ephrath (that is, Bethlehem)."

[8]Then Israel saw Joseph's sons, and said, "Who *are* these?"

[9]Joseph said to his father, "They *are* my sons, whom God has given me in this *place*."

And he said, "Please bring them to me, and I will bless them." [10]Now the eyes of Israel were dim with age, *so that* he could not see. Then Joseph brought them near him, and he kissed them and embraced them. [11]And Israel said to Joseph, "I had not thought to see your face; but in fact, God has also shown me your offspring!"

[12]So Joseph brought them from beside his knees, and he bowed down with his face to the earth. [13]And Joseph took them both, Ephraim with his right hand toward Israel's left hand, and Manasseh with his left hand toward Israel's right hand, and brought *them* near him. [14]Then Israel stretched out his right hand and laid *it* on Ephraim's head, who *was* the younger, and his left hand on Manasseh's head, guiding his hands knowingly, for Manasseh *was* the firstborn. [15]*And he blessed Joseph, and said:

"God, before whom my fathers Abraham and
   Isaac walked,
The God who has fed me all my life long
   to this day,
[16] The Angel who has redeemed me from all
   evil,
Bless the lads;
Let my name be named upon them,
And the name of my fathers Abraham and
   Isaac;
And let them grow into a multitude in the
   midst of the earth."

[17]*Now when Joseph saw that his father laid his right hand on the head of Ephraim, it displeased him; so he took hold of his father's hand to remove it from Ephraim's head to Manasseh's head. [18]And Joseph said to his father, "Not so, my father, for this *one is* the firstborn; put your right hand on his head."

[19]But his father refused and said, "I know, my son, I know. He also shall become a people, and he also shall be great; but truly his younger brother shall be greater than he, and his descendants shall become a multitude of nations."

[20]So he blessed them that day, saying, "By you Israel will bless, saying, 'May God make you as Ephraim and as Manasseh!'" And thus he set Ephraim before Manasseh.

[21]Then Israel said to Joseph, "Behold, I am dying, but God will be with you and bring you back to the land of your fathers. [22]Moreover I have given to you one portion above your brothers,

48:15, 16 *He praised God for the past.* He told his family what God had done for him and how God had blessed him. God had redeemed him and shepherded him all his life (48:15–16). Jacob had been in some hard places, but the "Stone of Israel" had been his refuge and defense (49:24). At the end of life, may we be able to say, "Come, you children, listen to me; I will teach you the fear of the LORD" (Ps. 34:11).

48:17–22 *He gave a blessing while he could.* Reuben's sin cost him the blessing of the firstborn, which went to Joseph's sons. (See Gen. 35:22; 1 Chron. 5:1–2.) Again, God changed the birth order as Jacob put Ephraim ahead of Manasseh. Joseph was disturbed by the move, but Jacob was right. We must never try to tell God how to bless other people. Note that Jacob crossed his arms. Is this perhaps a picture of the Cross that sets aside the first birth and gives us a second birth?

which I took from the hand of the Amorite with
my sword and my bow."

49 And* Jacob called his sons and said,
"Gather together, that I may tell you what
shall befall you in the last days:

2 "Gather together and hear, you sons of
      Jacob,
   And listen to Israel your father.

3 "Reuben, you are my firstborn,
   My might and the beginning of my strength,
   The excellency of dignity and the excellency
      of power.
4 Unstable as water, you shall not excel,
   Because you went up to your father's bed;
   Then you defiled it—
   He went up to my couch.

5 "Simeon and Levi are brothers;
   Instruments of cruelty are in their dwelling
      place.
6 Let not my soul enter their council;
   Let not my honor be united to their
      assembly;
   For in their anger they slew a man,
   And in their self-will they hamstrung an ox.
7 Cursed be their anger, for it is fierce;
   And their wrath, for it is cruel!
   I will divide them in Jacob
   And scatter them in Israel.

8 "Judah, you are he whom your brothers shall
      praise;
   Your hand shall be on the neck of your
      enemies;
   Your father's children shall bow down
      before you.
9 Judah is a lion's whelp;
   From the prey, my son, you have gone up.
   He bows down, he lies down as a lion;
   And as a lion, who shall rouse him?
10 The scepter shall not depart from Judah,
   Nor a lawgiver from between his feet,
   Until Shiloh comes;
   And to Him shall be the obedience of the
      people.
11 Binding his donkey to the vine,
   And his donkey's colt to the choice vine,
   He washed his garments in wine,
   And his clothes in the blood of grapes.
12 His eyes are darker than wine,
   And his teeth whiter than milk.

13 "Zebulun shall dwell by the haven of the sea;
   He shall become a haven for ships,
   And his border shall adjoin Sidon.

14 "Issachar is a strong donkey,
   Lying down between two burdens;
15 He saw that rest was good,
   And that the land was pleasant;
   He bowed his shoulder to bear a burden,
   And became a band of slaves.

16 "Dan shall judge his people
   As one of the tribes of Israel.
17 Dan shall be a serpent by the way,
   A viper by the path,
   That bites the horse's heels

49:1–33 *He warned about the future.*
Chapter 49 is not a father's blessing on his
sons. Rather, it is a prophecy of what the
sons could expect in the future because of
their individual characters and the decisions
they had made. Reuben was the lustful
prodigal son, but Levi and Simeon were
angry elder brothers. Judah would be the
royal tribe, for the Messiah (Shiloh, "the
peace-bringer") would come from Judah.
Joseph was the vine that went over the wall
separating Jews and Gentiles. He was shot
at by his brethren, which often happens to
those who are especially blessed of God.
But the Lord was with him, strengthened
him, and extended his boundaries of
blessing (v. 26). Joseph suffered, and his
sons were blessed by God. Reuben sinned,
and his sons lost the blessing of God.

So that its rider shall fall backward.
18 I have waited for your salvation, O LORD!

19 "Gad, a troop shall tramp upon him,
But he shall triumph at last.

20 "Bread from Asher *shall be* rich,
And he shall yield royal dainties.

21 "Naphtali *is* a deer let loose;
He uses beautiful words.

22 "Joseph *is* a fruitful bough,
A fruitful bough by a well;
His branches run over the wall.
23 The archers have bitterly grieved him,
Shot *at him* and hated him.
24 But his bow remained in strength,
And the arms of his hands were made
strong
By the hands of the Mighty *God* of Jacob
(From there *is* the Shepherd, the Stone of
Israel),
25 By the God of your father who will help you,
And by the Almighty who will bless you
With blessings of heaven above,
Blessings of the deep that lies beneath,
Blessings of the breasts and of the womb.
26 The blessings of your father
Have excelled the blessings of my ancestors,
Up to the utmost bound of the everlasting
hills.
They shall be on the head of Joseph,
And on the crown of the head of him who
was separate from his brothers.

27 "Benjamin is a ravenous wolf;
In the morning he shall devour the prey,
And at night he shall divide the spoil."

28All these *are* the twelve tribes of Israel, and this *is* what their father spoke to them. And he blessed them; he blessed each one according to his own blessing.
29Then he charged them and said to them: "I am to be gathered to my people; bury me with my fathers in the cave that *is* in the field of Ephron the Hittite, 30in the cave that *is* in the field of Machpelah, which *is* before Mamre in the land of Canaan, which Abraham bought with the field of Ephron the Hittite as a possession for a burial place. 31There they buried Abraham and Sarah his wife, there they buried Isaac and Rebekah his wife, and there I buried Leah. 32The field and the cave that *is* there *were* purchased from the sons of Heth." 33And when Jacob had finished commanding his sons, he drew his feet up into the bed and breathed his last, and was gathered to his people.

CHAPTER 50

Three burials are mentioned in this final chapter of Genesis, and each is significant.

50:1–14 *Burying a beloved father.* It is instructive to contrast the simple Jewish funerals with the elaborate burial customs of the Egyptians. There is certainly nothing wrong with caring for the body and expressing grief, so long as we keep things in perspective. Jacob died in faith and was a pilgrim to the very end (Heb. 11:21). He started with his staff and ended with his staff (32:10; 1 Tim. 6:7).

50 Then* Joseph fell on his father's face and wept over him, and kissed him. 2And Joseph commanded his servants the physicians to embalm his father. So the physicians embalmed Israel. 3Forty days were required for him, for such are the days required for those who are embalmed; and the Egyptians mourned for him seventy days.
4Now when the days of his mourning were past, Joseph spoke to the household of Pharaoh, saying, "If now I have found favor in your eyes, please speak in the hearing of Pharaoh, saying,

5'My father made me swear, saying, "Behold, I am dying; in my grave which I dug for myself in the land of Canaan, there you shall bury me." Now therefore, please let me go up and bury my father, and I will come back.' "

6And Pharaoh said, "Go up and bury your father, as he made you swear."

7So Joseph went up to bury his father; and with him went up all the servants of Pharaoh, the elders of his house, and all the elders of the land of Egypt, 8as well as all the house of Joseph, his brothers, and his father's house. Only their little ones, their flocks, and their herds they left in the land of Goshen. 9And there went up with him both chariots and horsemen, and it was a very great gathering.

10Then they came to the threshing floor of Atad, which is beyond the Jordan, and they mourned there with a great and very solemn lamentation. He observed seven days of mourning for his father. 11And when the inhabitants of the land, the Canaanites, saw the mourning at the threshing floor of Atad, they said, "This is a deep mourning of the Egyptians." Therefore its name was called Abel Mizraim,b which is beyond the Jordan.

12So his sons did for him just as he had commanded them. 13For his sons carried him to the land of Canaan, and buried him in the cave of the field of Machpelah, before Mamre, which Abraham bought with the field from Ephron the Hittite as property for a burial place. 14And after he had buried his father, Joseph returned to Egypt, he and his brothers and all who went up with him to bury his father.

15*When Joseph's brothers saw that their father was dead, they said, "Perhaps Joseph will hate us, and may actually repay us for all the evil which we did to him." 16So they sent messengers to Joseph, saying, "Before your father died he commanded, saying, 17'Thus you shall say to Joseph: "I beg you, please forgive the trespass of your brothers and their sin; for they did evil to you."' Now, please, forgive the trespass of the servants of the God of your father." And Joseph wept when they spoke to him.

18Then his brothers also went and fell down before his face, and they said, "Behold, we are your servants."

19Joseph said to them, "Do not be afraid, for am I in the place of God? 20But as for you, you meant evil against me; but God meant it for good, in order to bring it about as it is this day, to save many people alive. 21Now therefore, do not be afraid; I will provide for you and your little ones." And he comforted them and spoke kindly to them.

22So Joseph dwelt in Egypt, he and his father's household. And Joseph lived one hundred and ten years. 23Joseph saw Ephraim's children to the third generation. The children of Machir, the son of Manasseh, were also brought up on Joseph's knees.

24*And Joseph said to his brethren, "I am dying; but God will surely visit you, and bring you out of this land to the land of which He swore to Abraham, to Isaac, and to Jacob." 25Then Joseph took an oath from the children of Israel, saying, "God will surely visit you, and you shall carry up my bones from here." 26So Joseph died, being one hundred and ten years old; and they embalmed him, and he was put in a coffin in Egypt.

50:11 bLiterally Mourning of Egypt

50:15–21 Burying the past. Joseph's brothers did not really believe that Joseph had forgiven them, even though they had heard his words, seen his tears, felt his kisses, and received his gifts (45:1–15). Like the prodigal son, they offered to work their way into his favor (Luke 15:19). Their attitude grieved Joseph, who had endured so much for them, just as we grieve our Lord when we doubt His forgiveness and love (Rom. 8:31–39).

50:24–26 Burying a devoted brother. Like his father, Joseph knew what he believed and where he belonged. If we consider all the difficulties he had experienced in life, it is remarkable that Joseph had any faith at all. He knew God's promise to Abraham that the nation would be delivered from Egypt (15:12–16), and he reiterated that promise to his family. Joseph had brought them to Egypt and cared for them in Egypt. His coffin reminded them that God would bring them out of Egypt. What an encouragement that was during the dark days of their bondage. Our encouragement today is not a coffin but an empty tomb (1 Pet. 1:3ff.).

EXODUS

Exodus means "going out." The book has three main themes.

Liberation (1—18). This section describes Jehovah's victory over the gods of Egypt and the deliverance of His people from bondage. The emphasis is on *the hand of God.* (See 3:20; 7:4–5; 9:3, 15; 13:3, 9, 14, 16.) The Exodus is a picture of the redemption we have through faith in Jesus Christ, the Lamb of God (John 1:29; 1 Cor. 5:7; 1 Pet. 1:18–21).

Separation (19—24). God and Israel entered into covenant relationship at Sinai. God gave them His law that they might be separated from the other nations and devoted wholly to Him. The emphasis is on *the holiness of God.* While God's people today are not obligated to obey all these precepts, the basic principles are timeless and apply to holy living today.

Habitation (25—40). God had walked with His people in Genesis, but now He wanted to dwell with them. The emphasis is on *the house of God* and the priests who ministered there. The book of Hebrews in the New Testament explains how the tabernacle ministry foreshadowed the work of Jesus Christ and His present ministry in heaven as High Priest. Today, God's people are His temple (1 Cor. 6:19–20; Eph. 2:20–22).

CHAPTER 1

1:7–10 The nation growing. God promised that the descendants of Abraham would multiply greatly, and they did (Gen. 13:16; 15:5). God keeps His word and accomplishes His purposes in His time. Over the centuries, nations have tried to destroy Israel but have not succeeded. God gave Israel a special promise in Genesis 12:3, and He is keeping it. God's children today should pray for Israel (Ps. 122:6), share the gospel with them (Rom. 1:16), and minister to them in practical ways (Rom. 15:25–27).

1:11–22 The nation groaning. God told Abraham that his people would experience suffering (Gen. 15:13–14). It is easy for nations and local churches to forget the heroes of yesterday (Heb. 13:7–8). Although we must not "embalm" the past, we certainly must not forget those who helped to make our future possible.

The new Pharaoh was more concerned about national security than human decency. When people become a means to an end instead of an end in themselves, we are not treating them as God wants us to. Enslaving the men and killing the baby boys were Egypt's solution to "the Jewish problem."

1 Now these *are* the names of the children of Israel who came to Egypt; each man and his household came with Jacob: 2Reuben, Simeon, Levi, and Judah; 3Issachar, Zebulun, and Benjamin; 4Dan, Naphtali, Gad, and Asher. 5All those who were descendants*a* of Jacob were seventy*b* persons (for Joseph was in Egypt *already*). 6And Joseph died, all his brothers, and all that generation. 7*But the children of Israel were fruitful and increased abundantly, multiplied and grew exceedingly mighty; and the land was filled with them.

8Now there arose a new king over Egypt, who did not know Joseph. 9And he said to his people, "Look, the people of the children of Israel *are* more and mightier than we; 10come, let us deal shrewdly with them, lest they multiply, and it happen, in the event of war, that they also join our enemies and fight against us, and *so* go up out of the land." 11*Therefore they set taskmasters over them to afflict them with their burdens. And they built for Pharaoh supply cities, Pithom and Raamses. 12But the more they afflicted them, the more they multiplied and grew. And they were in dread of the children of Israel. 13So the Egyptians made the children of Israel serve with rigor. 14And they made their lives bitter with hard bondage—in mortar, in brick, and in all manner of service in the field. All their service in which they made them serve *was* with rigor.

15Then the king of Egypt spoke to the Hebrew midwives, of whom the name of one *was* Shiphrah and the name of the other Puah; 16and he said, "When you do the duties of a midwife for the He-

---

1:5 *a*Literally *who came from the loins of* *b*Dead Sea Scrolls and Septuagint read *seventy-five* (compare Acts 7:14).

Obeying God—Moses' parents and the Jewish midwives are not the only ones in Bible history who had the courage to put God's will ahead of man's law. Daniel and his friends (Dan. 1), the three Hebrew men (Dan. 3), and the apostles (Acts 4:19–20; 5:29) are other examples. Their aim was not to oppose a bad law but to uphold the glory and truth of God.

brew women, and see *them* on the birthstools, if it *is* a son, then you shall kill him; but if it *is* a daughter, then she shall live." [17]But the midwives feared God, and did not do as the king of Egypt commanded them, but saved the male children alive. [18]So the king of Egypt called for the midwives and said to them, "Why have you done this thing, and saved the male children alive?"

[19]*And the midwives said to Pharaoh, "Because the Hebrew women *are* not like the Egyptian women; for they *are* lively and give birth before the midwives come to them."

[20]Therefore God dealt well with the midwives, and the people multiplied and grew very mighty. [21]And so it was, because the midwives feared God, that He provided households for them.

[22]So Pharaoh commanded all his people, saying, "Every son who is born[c] you shall cast into the river, and every daughter you shall save alive."

2 And* a man of the house of Levi went and took *as wife* a daughter of Levi. [2]So the woman conceived and bore a son. And when she saw that he *was* a beautiful *child,* she hid him three months. [3]*But when she could no longer hide him, she took an ark of bulrushes for him, daubed it with asphalt and pitch, put the child in it, and laid *it* in the reeds by the river's bank. [4]And his sister stood afar off, to know what would be done to him.

[5]Then the daughter of Pharaoh came down to bathe at the river. And her maidens walked along the riverside; and when she saw the ark among the reeds, she sent her maid to get it. [6]And when she opened *it,* she saw the child, and behold, the baby wept. So she had compassion on him, and said, "This is one of the Hebrews' children."

[7]Then his sister said to Pharaoh's daughter, "Shall I go and call a nurse for you from the Hebrew women, that she may nurse the child for you?"

[8]And Pharaoh's daughter said to her, "Go." So the maiden went and called the child's mother. [9]Then Pharaoh's daughter said to her, "Take this child away and nurse him for me, and I will give you your wages." So the woman took the child and nursed him. [10]And the child grew, and she brought him to Pharaoh's daughter, and he became her son. So she called his name Moses,[d] saying, "Because I drew him out of the water."

[11]*Now it came to pass in those days, when Moses was grown, that he went out to his brethren and looked at their burdens. And he saw an Egyptian beating a Hebrew, one of his brethren.

1:22 [c]Samaritan Pentateuch, Septuagint, and Targum add *to the Hebrews.*   2:10 [d]Literally *Drawn Out*

1:19–21 The midwives believed in obeying God rather than men (Acts 5:29). Thank God for concerned people who will courageously defend the little ones! God rewarded the women, not by making them sterile (which would have been safer), but by *giving them families!* This shows how valuable children are in the sight of God (Ps. 127:3–5). Ponder the words of our Lord in Matthew 18:1–6.

CHAPTER 2

2:1, 2 Moses' parents, Amram and Jochebed (Exod. 6:20), knew that the times were difficult, but they had faith to get married and have a family (Acts 7:20; Heb. 11:23). Aaron and Miriam were already in the home when Moses was born. It was not easy to provide for another child, but God enabled them, as He still does parents today.

2:3–9 It also took faith for the parents to put their son into the river, obeying at least the spirit of the Egyptian law. God rewarded their faith. Jochebed not only got her son back, but she was paid to take care of him!

2:11–25 Moses had a splendid education (Acts 7:22), but he was lacking in faith. He fought the wrong enemy at the wrong time with the wrong weapon. When you start to look around and ask yourself "Is it safe?" and not "Is it right?" you have stopped living by faith. Sometimes God has to "set us aside" to teach us what we need to know—and to help us forget the way the world does things. Moses' impulsive deed sent him to the back of the desert for forty years, just as his impulsive words would keep him out of the Promised Land (Num. 20:9–13). An impatient spirit is a dangerous thing.

Impulsive People—Prov. 19:2

Moses	Exodus 2:11–14; Numbers 20:9–13
David	1 Samuel 25:1–13
Elijah	1 Kings 19:1–3
Peter	John 18:10
Mary Magdalene	John 20:1–2

12So he looked this way and that way, and when he saw no one, he killed the Egyptian and hid him in the sand. 13And when he went out the second day, behold, two Hebrew men were fighting, and he said to the one who did the wrong, "Why are you striking your companion?"

14Then he said, "Who made you a prince and a judge over us? Do you intend to kill me as you killed the Egyptian?"

So Moses feared and said, "Surely this thing is known!" 15When Pharaoh heard of this matter, he sought to kill Moses. But Moses fled from the face of Pharaoh and dwelt in the land of Midian; and he sat down by a well.

16Now the priest of Midian had seven daughters. And they came and drew water, and they filled the troughs to water their father's flock. 17Then the shepherds came and drove them away; but Moses stood up and helped them, and watered their flock.

18When they came to Reuel their father, he said, "How *is it that* you have come so soon today?"

19And they said, "An Egyptian delivered us from the hand of the shepherds, and he also drew enough water for us and watered the flock."

20So he said to his daughters, "And where *is* he? Why *is it that* you have left the man? Call him, that he may eat bread."

21Then Moses was content to live with the man, and he gave Zipporah his daughter to Moses. 22And she bore *him* a son. He called his name Gershom,*e* for he said, "I have been a stranger in a foreign land."

23Now it happened in the process of time that the king of Egypt died. Then the children of Israel groaned because of the bondage, and they cried out; and their cry came up to God because of the bondage. 24So God heard their groaning, and God remembered His covenant with Abraham, with Isaac, and with Jacob. 25And God looked upon the children of Israel, and God acknowledged *them.*

3 Now* Moses was tending the flock of Jethro his father-in-law, the priest of Midian. And he led the flock to the back of the desert, and came to Horeb, the mountain of God. 2And the Angel of the LORD appeared to him in a flame of fire from the midst of a bush. So he looked, and behold, the bush was burning with fire, but the bush *was* not consumed. 3Then Moses said, "I will now turn aside and see this great sight, why the bush does not burn."

4So when the LORD saw that he turned aside to look, God called to him from the midst of the bush and said, "Moses, Moses!"

And he said, "Here I am."

5Then He said, "Do not draw near this place. Take your sandals off your feet, for the place where you stand *is* holy ground." 6Moreover He said, "I *am* the God of your father—the God of Abraham, the God of Isaac, and the God of Jacob." And Moses hid his face, for he was afraid to look upon God.

7*And the LORD said: "I have surely seen the oppression of My people who *are* in Egypt, and have heard their cry because of their taskmasters, for I know their sorrows. 8So I have come down to deliver them out of the hand of the Egyptians,

CHAPTER 3

3:1ff You never know what a day may bring, so keep your eyes and ears open to the leading of the Lord. Childlike curiosity completely changed Moses' life. God calls busy people to serve Him, and He reveals Himself to them.

God is faithful. He called Abraham, cared for Isaac, guided and protected Jacob, and He would be with Moses. He is the God of the individual as well as the nation, and He does not change from generation to generation.

3:7–10 *God is concerned and compassionate.* He saw the affliction of His people, and He heard their cries. Then why didn't He act sooner? Because He was following a perfect timetable (Gen. 15:13–16). You must learn to wait on the Lord. (See Ps. 37.)

2:22 *e*Literally *Stranger There*

and to bring them up from that land to a good and large land, to a land flowing with milk and honey, to the place of the Canaanites and the Hittites and the Amorites and the Perizzites and the Hivites and the Jebusites. 9Now therefore, behold, the cry of the children of Israel has come to Me, and I have also seen the oppression with which the Egyptians oppress them. 10Come now, therefore, and I will send you to Pharaoh that you may bring My people, the children of Israel, out of Egypt."

11*But Moses said to God, "Who *am* I that I should go to Pharaoh, and that I should bring the children of Israel out of Egypt?"

12So He said, "I will certainly be with you. And this *shall be* a sign to you that I have sent you: When you have brought the people out of Egypt, you shall serve God on this mountain."

13Then Moses said to God, "Indeed, *when* I come to the children of Israel and say to them, 'The God of your fathers has sent me to you,' and they say to me, 'What *is* His name?' what shall I say to them?"

14And God said to Moses, "I AM WHO I AM." And He said, "Thus you shall say to the children of Israel, 'I AM has sent me to you.' " 15Moreover God said to Moses, "Thus you shall say to the children of Israel: 'The LORD God of your fathers, the God of Abraham, the God of Isaac, and the God of Jacob, has sent me to you. This *is* My name forever, and this *is* My memorial to all generations.' 16Go and gather the elders of Israel together, and say to them, 'The LORD God of your fathers, the God of Abraham, of Isaac, and of Jacob, appeared to me, saying, "I have surely visited you and *seen* what is done to you in Egypt; 17and I have said I will bring you up out of the affliction of Egypt to the land of the Canaanites and the Hittites and the Amorites and the Perizzites and the Hivites and the Jebusites, to a land flowing with milk and honey." ' 18Then they will heed your voice; and you shall come, you and the elders of Israel, to the king of Egypt; and you shall say to him, 'The LORD God of the Hebrews has met with us; and now, please, let us go three days' journey into the wilderness, that we may sacrifice to the LORD our God.' 19But I am sure that the king of Egypt will not let you go, no, not even by a mighty hand. 20So I will stretch out My hand and strike Egypt with all My wonders which I will do in its midst; and after that he will let you go. 21And I will give this people favor in the sight of the Egyptians; and it shall be, when you go, that you shall not go empty-handed. 22But every woman shall ask of her neighbor, namely, of her who dwells near her house, articles of silver, articles of gold, and clothing; and you shall put *them* on your sons and on your daughters. So you shall plunder the Egyptians."

4 Then* Moses answered and said, "But suppose they will not believe me or listen to my voice; suppose they say, 'The LORD has not appeared to you.' "

2*So the LORD said to him, "What *is* that in your hand?"

He said, "A rod."

3And He said, "Cast it on the ground." So he cast it on the ground, and it became a serpent; and Moses fled from it. 4Then the LORD said to Moses, "Reach out your hand and take *it* by the tail" (and he reached out his hand and caught it,

3:11–22 *God is long-suffering.* The Lord answered all of Moses' objections and gave one assurance after another to encourage him. Moses said, "I am not!" and God replied, "I AM!" Faith lays hold of what God is and obeys what God says. Faith sees the opportunities while unbelief sees the obstacles. Are you arguing with God about something He wants you to do?

CHAPTER 4

4:1ff Forty years before, Moses was sure he could solve his people's problems; but now that God had called him, he was sure he would fail. He could give no reasons for disobeying God, but he certainly had plenty of excuses. "An excuse is the skin of a reason stuffed with a lie," observed Billy Sunday. But God gave Moses everything he needed for success. All he had to do was trust the great I AM.

4:2 *Credentials.* If we give God what we have, He can use it for His glory: a rod, a sling (1 Sam. 17:40), a net (Luke 5:1–11), or a little lunch (John 6:9). He can even use the hand if *nothing* is in it!

and it became a rod in his hand), 5"that they may believe that the LORD God of their fathers, the God of Abraham, the God of Isaac, and the God of Jacob, has appeared to you."

6Furthermore the LORD said to him, "Now put your hand in your bosom." And he put his hand in his bosom, and when he took it out, behold, his hand *was* leprous, like snow. 7And He said, "Put your hand in your bosom again." So he put his hand in his bosom again, and drew it out of his bosom, and behold, it was restored like his *other* flesh. 8"Then it will be, if they do not believe you, nor heed the message of the first sign, that they may believe the message of the latter sign. 9And it shall be, if they do not believe even these two signs, or listen to your voice, that you shall take water from the river*f* and pour *it* on the dry land. The water which you take from the river will become blood on the dry *land*."

10Then Moses said to the LORD, "O my Lord, I *am* not eloquent, neither before nor since You have spoken to Your servant; but I *am* slow of speech and slow of tongue."

11So the LORD said to him, "Who has made man's mouth? Or who makes the mute, the deaf, the seeing, or the blind? *Have* not I, the LORD? 12Now therefore, go, and I will be with your mouth and teach you what you shall say."

13But he said, "O my Lord, please send by the hand of whomever *else* You may send."

14*So the anger of the LORD was kindled against Moses, and He said: "Is not Aaron the Levite your brother? I know that he can speak well. And look, he is also coming out to meet you. When he sees you, he will be glad in his heart. 15Now you shall speak to him and put the words in his mouth. And I will be with your mouth and with his mouth, and I will teach you what you shall do. 16So he shall be your spokesman to the people. And he himself shall be as a mouth for you, and you shall be to him as God. 17And you shall take this rod in your hand, with which you shall do the signs."

18So Moses went and returned to Jethro his father-in-law, and said to him, "Please let me go and return to my brethren who *are* in Egypt, and see whether they are still alive."

And Jethro said to Moses, "Go in peace."

19*Now the LORD said to Moses in Midian, "Go, return to Egypt; for all the men who sought your life are dead." 20Then Moses took his wife and his sons and set them on a donkey, and he returned to the land of Egypt. And Moses took the rod of God in his hand.

21And the LORD said to Moses, "When you go back to Egypt, see that you do all those wonders before Pharaoh which I have put in your hand. But I will harden his heart, so that he will not let the people go. 22Then you shall say to Pharaoh, 'Thus says the LORD: "Israel *is* My son, My first-born. 23So I say to you, let My son go that he may serve Me. But if you refuse to let him go, indeed I will kill your son, your firstborn." ' "

24*And it came to pass on the way, at the en-campment, that the LORD met him and sought to kill him. 25Then Zipporah took a sharp stone and cut off the foreskin of her son and cast *it* at Mo-ses'*g* feet, and said, "Surely you *are* a husband of blood to me!" 26So He let him go. Then she

4:14, 27 Companion. God already had Aaron prepared and on his way to meet Moses. While Aaron at times created some problems for Moses, he was still a valued helper in the work. He was the speaker, and Moses was the doer. But in time, Moses himself became a great orator.

4:19–23 Commission. God spoke to Moses and gave him the instructions and encouragement he needed. Before he arrived in Egypt, Moses knew that his work would be difficult and that Pharaoh would oppose him.

4:24–26 Chastening. Moses was chastened by God and almost died because he had failed to make his child a son of the covenant (Gen. 17:10). How could Moses lead Israel if his own family was not dedicated to God? (See 1 Tim. 3:5.)

4:9 *f*That is, the Nile   4:25 *g*Literally *his*

said, "*You are* a husband of blood!"—because of the circumcision.

27And the LORD said to Aaron, "Go into the wilderness to meet Moses." So he went and met him on the mountain of God, and kissed him. 28So Moses told Aaron all the words of the LORD who had sent him, and all the signs which He had commanded him. 29*Then Moses and Aaron went and gathered together all the elders of the children of Israel. 30And Aaron spoke all the words which the LORD had spoken to Moses. Then he did the signs in the sight of the people. 31So the people believed; and when they heard that the LORD had visited the children of Israel and that He had looked on their affliction, then they bowed their heads and worshiped.

5 Afterward* Moses and Aaron went in and told Pharaoh, "Thus says the LORD God of Israel: 'Let My people go, that they may hold a feast to Me in the wilderness.'"

2And Pharaoh said, "Who *is* the LORD, that I should obey His voice to let Israel go? I do not know the LORD, nor will I let Israel go."

3So they said, "The God of the Hebrews has met with us. Please, let us go three days' journey into the desert and sacrifice to the LORD our God, lest He fall upon us with pestilence or with the sword."

4Then the king of Egypt said to them, "Moses and Aaron, why do you take the people from their work? Get *back* to your labor." 5And Pharaoh said, "Look, the people of the land *are* many now, and you make them rest from their labor!"

6So the same day Pharaoh commanded the taskmasters of the people and their officers, saying, 7"You shall no longer give the people straw to make brick as before. Let them go and gather straw for themselves. 8And you shall lay on them the quota of bricks which they made before. You shall not reduce it. For they are idle; therefore they cry out, saying, 'Let us go *and* sacrifice to our God.' 9Let more work be laid on the men, that they may labor in it, and let them not regard false words."

10And the taskmasters of the people and their officers went out and spoke to the people, saying, "Thus says Pharaoh: 'I will not give you straw. 11Go, get yourselves straw where you can find it; yet none of your work will be reduced.'" 12So the people were scattered abroad throughout all the land of Egypt to gather stubble instead of straw. 13And the taskmasters forced *them* to hurry, saying, "Fulfill your work, *your* daily quota, as when there was straw." 14Also the officers of the children of Israel, whom Pharaoh's taskmasters had set over them, were beaten *and* were asked, "Why have you not fulfilled your task in making brick both yesterday and today, as before?"

15Then the officers of the children of Israel came and cried out to Pharaoh, saying, "Why are you dealing thus with your servants? 16There is no straw given to your servants, and they say to us, 'Make brick!' And indeed your servants *are* beaten, but the fault *is* in your *own* people."

17But he said, "You *are* idle! Idle! Therefore you say, 'Let us go *and* sacrifice to the LORD.' 18Therefore go now *and* work; for no straw shall be given you, yet you shall deliver the quota of bricks." 19And the officers of the children of Israel saw *that* they *were* in trouble after it was said,

4:29–31 *Conviction*. Moses was sure nobody would believe him; however, when the elders saw the signs and heard the message, they believed and bowed to worship God.

When you face a tough job and you are afraid that you will fail, remember Moses. God keeps His promises, no matter how you feel or how people respond.

CHAPTERS 5—6

5:1–20 When Moses and Aaron began their work in Egypt, their first problem was with Pharaoh (5:1–9). Not only did Pharaoh refuse to let the people leave Egypt, but he made their work more difficult. That gave Moses a second problem—his own people, who blamed him for their plight (5:20–21). He had a foretaste of the criticism and rebellion he would experience for the next forty years. Often the people you help the most appreciate you the least.

5:22, 23 Moses' third problem was with the Lord Himself (5:22–23)! God had promised success but Moses had failed. Even the Jews didn't believe him! Madame Guyon spoke of these kinds of difficulties: "In the commencement of the spiritual life, our hardest task is to bear with our neighbor; in its progress, with ourselves; and in its end, with God."

6:1–13 But God gave Moses the assurance that He needed (6:1–8) and told him to return to his job and stay with it. God doesn't solve every problem immediately, nor does He follow your schedule. When you think you have failed, even when you have obeyed God's will, ponder Isaiah 55:8–9 and Jeremiah 29:11.

"You shall not reduce *any* bricks from your daily quota."

20Then, as they came out from Pharaoh, they met Moses and Aaron who stood there to meet them. 21And they said to them, "Let the LORD look on you and judge, because you have made us abhorrent in the sight of Pharaoh and in the sight of his servants, to put a sword in their hand to kill us."

22*So Moses returned to the LORD and said, "Lord, why have You brought trouble on this people? Why *is* it You have sent me? 23For since I came to Pharaoh to speak in Your name, he has done evil to this people; neither have You delivered Your people at all."

6 Then* the LORD said to Moses, "Now you shall see what I will do to Pharaoh. For with a strong hand he will let them go, and with a strong hand he will drive them out of his land."

2And God spoke to Moses and said to him: "I *am* the LORD. 3I appeared to Abraham, to Isaac, and to Jacob, as God Almighty, but *by* My name LORD*h* I was not known to them. 4I have also established My covenant with them, to give them the land of Canaan, the land of their pilgrimage, in which they were strangers. 5And I have also heard the groaning of the children of Israel whom the Egyptians keep in bondage, and I have remembered My covenant. 6Therefore say to the children of Israel: 'I *am* the LORD; I will bring you out from under the burdens of the Egyptians, I will rescue you from their bondage, and I will redeem you with an outstretched arm and with great judgments. 7I will take you as My people, and I will be your God. Then you shall know that I *am* the LORD your God who brings you out from under the burdens of the Egyptians. 8And I will bring you into the land which I swore to give to Abraham, Isaac, and Jacob; and I will give it to you *as* a heritage: I *am* the LORD.' " 9So Moses spoke thus to the children of Israel; but they did not heed Moses, because of anguish of spirit and cruel bondage.

10And the LORD spoke to Moses, saying, 11"Go in, tell Pharaoh king of Egypt to let the children of Israel go out of his land."

12And Moses spoke before the LORD, saying, "The children of Israel have not heeded me. How then shall Pharaoh heed me, for I *am* of uncircumcised lips?"

13Then the LORD spoke to Moses and Aaron, and gave them a command for the children of Israel and for Pharaoh king of Egypt, to bring the children of Israel out of the land of Egypt.

14These *are* the heads of their fathers' houses: The sons of Reuben, the firstborn of Israel, *were* Hanoch, Pallu, Hezron, and Carmi. These are the families of Reuben. 15And the sons of Simeon *were* Jemuel,*i* Jamin, Ohad, Jachin, Zohar, and Shaul the son of a Canaanite woman. These *are* the families of Simeon. 16These *are* the names of the sons of Levi according to their generations: Gershon, Kohath, and Merari. And the years of the life of Levi *were* one hundred and thirty-seven. 17The sons of Gershon *were* Libni and Shimi according to their families. 18And the sons of Kohath *were* Amram, Izhar, Hebron, and Uzziel. And the

---

6:3 *h*Hebrew *YHWH*, traditionally *Jehovah*   6:15 *i*Spelled *Nemuel* in Numbers 26:12

years of the life of Kohath *were* one hundred and thirty-three. ¹⁹The sons of Merari *were* Mahli and Mushi. These *are* the families of Levi according to their generations.

²⁰Now Amram took for himself Jochebed, his father's sister, as wife; and she bore him Aaron and Moses. And the years of the life of Amram *were* one hundred and thirty-seven. ²¹The sons of Izhar *were* Korah, Nepheg, and Zichri. ²²And the sons of Uzziel *were* Mishael, Elzaphan, and Zithri. ²³Aaron took to himself Elisheba, daughter of Amminadab, sister of Nahshon, as wife; and she bore him Nadab, Abihu, Eleazar, and Ithamar. ²⁴And the sons of Korah *were* Assir, Elkanah, and Abiasaph. These are the families of the Korahites. ²⁵Eleazar, Aaron's son, took for himself one of the daughters of Putiel as wife; and she bore him Phinehas. These *are* the heads of the fathers' houses of the Levites according to their families.

²⁶These *are the same* Aaron and Moses to whom the LORD said, "Bring out the children of Israel from the land of Egypt according to their armies." ²⁷These *are* the ones who spoke to Pharaoh king of Egypt, to bring out the children of Israel from Egypt. These *are the same* Moses and Aaron.

²⁸And it came to pass, on the day the LORD spoke to Moses in the land of Egypt, ²⁹that the LORD spoke to Moses, saying, "I *am* the LORD. Speak to Pharaoh king of Egypt all that I say to you."

³⁰But Moses said before the LORD, "Behold, I *am* of uncircumcised lips, and how shall Pharaoh heed me?"

7 So* the LORD said to Moses: "See, I have made you *as* God to Pharaoh, and Aaron your brother shall be your prophet. ²You shall speak all that I command you. And Aaron your brother shall tell Pharaoh to send the children of Israel out of his land. ³And I will harden Pharaoh's heart, and multiply My signs and My wonders in the land of Egypt. ⁴But Pharaoh will not heed you, so that I may lay My hand on Egypt and bring My armies *and* My people, the children of Israel, out of the land of Egypt by great judgments. ⁵And the Egyptians shall know that I *am* the LORD, when I stretch out My hand on Egypt and bring out the children of Israel from among them."

⁶Then Moses and Aaron did *so;* just as the LORD commanded them, so they did. ⁷And Moses *was* eighty years old and Aaron eighty-three years old when they spoke to Pharaoh.

⁸Then the LORD spoke to Moses and Aaron, saying, ⁹"When Pharaoh speaks to you, saying, 'Show a miracle for yourselves,' then you shall say to Aaron, 'Take your rod and cast *it* before Pharaoh, *and* let it become a serpent.'" ¹⁰So Moses and Aaron went in to Pharaoh, and they did so, just as the LORD commanded. And Aaron cast down his rod before Pharaoh and before his servants, and it became a serpent.

¹¹*But Pharaoh also called the wise men and the sorcerers; so the magicians of Egypt, they also did in like manner with their enchantments. ¹²For every man threw down his rod, and they became serpents. But Aaron's rod swallowed up their rods. ¹³And Pharaoh's heart grew hard, and he did not heed them, as the LORD had said.

¹⁴So the LORD said to Moses: "Pharaoh's heart *is* hard; he refuses to let the people go. ¹⁵Go to Pharaoh in the morning, when he goes out to the

CHAPTERS 7—8

7:1–10 If men will not obey His words of warning, God must speak by His works of judgment. When God speaks, people either obey and submit their hearts or disobey and harden their hearts (Heb. 3:7–13). From the human point of view, Pharaoh resisted God's will and thus hardened his own heart. From the divine point of view, God sent the judgments and therefore caused his heart to harden. The same sun that melts the ice also hardens the clay.

7:11–25 The court magicians were able to imitate Aaron's miracle. Satan is a counterfeiter, and that is one way he opposes God's work today (2 Tim. 3:8–9). Some miracles are lying wonders (2 Thess. 2:9–10). Be sure you can tell the difference (1 John 2:18–27; 4:1–6).

water, and you shall stand by the river's bank to meet him; and the rod which was turned to a serpent you shall take in your hand. 16And you shall say to him, 'The LORD God of the Hebrews has sent me to you, saying, "Let My people go, that they may serve Me in the wilderness"; but indeed, until now you would not hear! 17Thus says the LORD: "By this you shall know that I *am* the LORD. Behold, I will strike the waters which *are* in the river with the rod that *is* in my hand, and they shall be turned to blood. 18And the fish that *are* in the river shall die, the river shall stink, and the Egyptians will loathe to drink the water of the river."' "

19Then the LORD spoke to Moses, "Say to Aaron, 'Take your rod and stretch out your hand over the waters of Egypt, over their streams, over their rivers, over their ponds, and over all their pools of water, that they may become blood. And there shall be blood throughout all the land of Egypt, both in *buckets of* wood and *pitchers of* stone.' "

20And Moses and Aaron did so, just as the LORD commanded. So he lifted up the rod and struck the waters that *were* in the river, in the sight of Pharaoh and in the sight of his servants. And all the waters that *were* in the river were turned to blood. 21The fish that *were* in the river died, the river stank, and the Egyptians could not drink the water of the river. So there was blood throughout all the land of Egypt.

22Then the magicians of Egypt did so with their enchantments; and Pharaoh's heart grew hard, and he did not heed them, as the LORD had said. 23And Pharaoh turned and went into his house. Neither was his heart moved by this. 24So all the Egyptians dug all around the river for water to drink, because they could not drink the water of the river. 25And seven days passed after the LORD had struck the river.

8:1–32 The plagues were God's declaration of war against the false gods of Egypt (12:12). He proclaimed, "I am the LORD" (7:5). They were also a declaration that God had put a difference between the Jews and the Egyptians (8:23).

How sad that Israel saw God's wonders in Egypt and yet did not trust Him (Ps. 106:6–7). They even wanted to return to Egypt after they had been delivered! Great experiences are no guarantee that one has grown spiritually. It all depends on what happens to your heart.

8 And* the LORD spoke to Moses, "Go to Pharaoh and say to him, 'Thus says the LORD: "Let My people go, that they may serve Me. 2But if you refuse to let *them* go, behold, I will smite all your territory with frogs. 3So the river shall bring forth frogs abundantly, which shall go up and come into your house, into your bedroom, on your bed, into the houses of your servants, on your people, into your ovens, and into your kneading bowls. 4And the frogs shall come up on you, on your people, and on all your servants."' "

5Then the LORD spoke to Moses, "Say to Aaron, 'Stretch out your hand with your rod over the streams, over the rivers, and over the ponds, and cause frogs to come up on the land of Egypt.' " 6So Aaron stretched out his hand over the waters of Egypt, and the frogs came up and covered the land of Egypt. 7And the magicians did so with their enchantments, and brought up frogs on the land of Egypt.

8Then Pharaoh called for Moses and Aaron, and said, "Entreat the LORD that He may take away the frogs from me and from my people; and I will let the people go, that they may sacrifice to the LORD."

9And Moses said to Pharaoh, "Accept the honor of saying when I shall intercede for you, for your servants, and for your people, to destroy the frogs from you and your houses, *that* they may remain in the river only."

10So he said, "Tomorrow." And he said, "*Let it be* according to your word, that you may know

that *there is* no one like the LORD our God.
[11]And the frogs shall depart from you, from your
houses, from your servants, and from your people.
They shall remain in the river only."

[12]Then Moses and Aaron went out from Pharaoh. And Moses cried out to the LORD concerning
the frogs which He had brought against Pharaoh.
[13]So the LORD did according to the word of Moses.
And the frogs died out of the houses, out of the
courtyards, and out of the fields. [14]They gathered
them together in heaps, and the land stank.
[15]But when Pharaoh saw that there was relief, he
hardened his heart and did not heed them, as the
LORD had said.

[16]So the LORD said to Moses, "Say to Aaron,
'Stretch out your rod, and strike the dust of the
land, so that it may become lice throughout all
the land of Egypt.'" [17]And they did so. For Aaron
stretched out his hand with his rod and struck
the dust of the earth, and it became lice on man
and beast. All the dust of the land became lice
throughout all the land of Egypt.

[18]Now the magicians so worked with their enchantments to bring forth lice, but they could not.
So there were lice on man and beast. [19]Then the
magicians said to Pharaoh, "This *is* the finger of
God." But Pharaoh's heart grew hard, and he did
not heed them, just as the LORD had said.

[20]And the LORD said to Moses, "Rise early in
the morning and stand before Pharaoh as he
comes out to the water. Then say to him, 'Thus
says the LORD: "Let My people go, that they may
serve Me. [21]Or else, if you will not let My people
go, behold, I will send swarms *of flies* on you and
your servants, on your people and into your
houses. The houses of the Egyptians shall be full
of swarms *of flies,* and also the ground on which
they *stand.* [22]And in that day I will set apart the
land of Goshen, in which My people dwell, that
no swarms *of flies* shall be there, in order that
you may know that I *am* the LORD in the midst
of the land. [23]I will make a difference[j] between
My people and your people. Tomorrow this sign
shall be."'" [24]And the LORD did so. Thick swarms
of flies came into the house of Pharaoh, *into* his
servants' houses, and into all the land of Egypt.
The land was corrupted because of the swarms
of flies.

[25]Then Pharaoh called for Moses and Aaron,
and said, "Go, sacrifice to your God in the land."

[26]And Moses said, "It is not right to do so, for
we would be sacrificing the abomination of the
Egyptians to the LORD our God. If we sacrifice
the abomination of the Egyptians before their
eyes, then will they not stone us? [27]We will go
three days' journey into the wilderness and sacrifice to the LORD our God as He will command us."

[28]So Pharaoh said, "I will let you go, that you
may sacrifice to the LORD your God in the wilderness; only you shall not go very far away. Intercede for me."

[29]Then Moses said, "Indeed I am going out from
you, and I will entreat the LORD, that the swarms
of flies may depart tomorrow from Pharaoh, from
his servants, and from his people. But let Pharaoh
not deal deceitfully anymore in not letting the people go to sacrifice to the LORD."

[30]So Moses went out from Pharaoh and

8:23 [j]Literally *set a ransom* (compare Exodus 9:4 and 11:7)

entreated the LORD. 31And the LORD did according to the word of Moses; He removed the swarms *of flies* from Pharaoh, from his servants, and from his people. Not one remained. 32But Pharaoh hardened his heart at this time also; neither would he let the people go.

CHAPTERS 9—10

9:1ff All Moses wanted was Pharaoh's permission to take the people on a three-days' journey to a place where they could worship God. God had put a difference between His people and the people of Egypt, just as today He has put a difference between the people of God and the people of the world (2 Cor. 6:14–18).
But the world doesn't want believers to be too radical, so it offers various compromises: "Sacrifice in the land" (8:25); "Don't go too far away" (8:28); "Don't take your children" (10:8–11); and "Don't take your possessions to serve God" (10:24–26). Have you been tempted by any of these compromises lately?

9 Then* the LORD said to Moses, "Go in to Pharaoh and tell him, 'Thus says the LORD God of the Hebrews: "Let My people go, that they may serve Me. 2For if you refuse to let *them* go, and still hold them, 3behold, the hand of the LORD will be on your cattle in the field, on the horses, on the donkeys, on the camels, on the oxen, and on the sheep—a very severe pestilence. 4And the LORD will make a difference between the livestock of Israel and the livestock of Egypt. So nothing shall die of all *that* belongs to the children of Israel." ' " 5Then the LORD appointed a set time, saying, "Tomorrow the LORD will do this thing in the land."

6So the LORD did this thing on the next day, and all the livestock of Egypt died; but of the livestock of the children of Israel, not one died. 7Then Pharaoh sent, and indeed, not even one of the livestock of the Israelites was dead. But the heart of Pharaoh became hard, and he did not let the people go.

8So the LORD said to Moses and Aaron, "Take for yourselves handfuls of ashes from a furnace, and let Moses scatter it toward the heavens in the sight of Pharaoh. 9And it will become fine dust in all the land of Egypt, and it will cause boils that break out in sores on man and beast throughout all the land of Egypt." 10Then they took ashes from the furnace and stood before Pharaoh, and Moses scattered *them* toward heaven. And *they* caused boils that break out in sores on man and beast. 11And the magicians could not stand before Moses because of the boils, for the boils were on the magicians and on all the Egyptians. 12But the LORD hardened the heart of Pharaoh; and he did not heed them, just as the LORD had spoken to Moses.

13Then the LORD said to Moses, "Rise early in the morning and stand before Pharaoh, and say to him, 'Thus says the LORD God of the Hebrews: "Let My people go, that they may serve Me, 14for at this time I will send all My plagues to your very heart, and on your servants and on your people, that you may know that *there is* none like Me in all the earth. 15Now if I had stretched out My hand and struck you and your people with pestilence, then you would have been cut off from the earth. 16*But indeed for this *purpose* I have raised you up, that I may show My power *in* you, and that My name may be declared in all the earth. 17As yet you exalt yourself against My people in that you will not let them go. 18Behold, tomorrow about this time I will cause very heavy hail to rain down, such as has not been in Egypt since its founding until now. 19Therefore send now *and* gather your livestock and all that you have in the field, for the hail shall come down on every man and every animal which is found in the field and is not brought home; and they shall die." ' "

9:16, 17 God's judgments had practically ruined the land, yet Pharaoh would not give in. In so doing, Pharaoh thought he was showing great strength; actually, God was using him to display His own sovereignty (9:16; see also Rom. 9:17–18). God is greater than any ruler, so we need never fear (Dan. 4:34–37).

20He who feared the word of the LORD among the servants of Pharaoh made his servants and his livestock flee to the houses. 21But he who did not regard the word of the LORD left his servants and his livestock in the field.

22Then the LORD said to Moses, "Stretch out your hand toward heaven, that there may be hail in all the land of Egypt—on man, on beast, and on every herb of the field, throughout the land of Egypt." 23And Moses stretched out his rod toward heaven; and the LORD sent thunder and hail, and fire darted to the ground. And the LORD rained hail on the land of Egypt. 24So there was hail, and fire mingled with the hail, so very heavy that there was none like it in all the land of Egypt since it became a nation. 25And the hail struck throughout the whole land of Egypt, all that *was* in the field, both man and beast; and the hail struck every herb of the field and broke every tree of the field. 26Only in the land of Goshen, where the children of Israel *were*, there was no hail.

27*And Pharaoh sent and called for Moses and Aaron, and said to them, "I have sinned this time. The LORD *is* righteous, and my people and I *are* wicked. 28Entreat the LORD, that there may be no *more* mighty thundering and hail, for *it is* enough. I will let you go, and you shall stay no longer." 29So Moses said to him, "As soon as I have gone out of the city, I will spread out my hands to the LORD; the thunder will cease, and there will be no more hail, that you may know that the earth *is* the LORD's. 30But as for you and your servants, I know that you will not yet fear the LORD God."

31Now the flax and the barley were struck, for the barley *was* in the head and the flax *was* in bud. 32But the wheat and the spelt were not struck, for they *are* late crops.

33So Moses went out of the city from Pharaoh and spread out his hands to the LORD; then the thunder and the hail ceased, and the rain was not poured on the earth. 34And when Pharaoh saw that the rain, the hail, and the thunder had ceased, he sinned yet more; and he hardened his heart, he and his servants. 35So the heart of Pharaoh was hard; neither would he let the children of Israel go, as the LORD had spoken by Moses.

10 Now the LORD said to Moses, "Go in to Pharaoh; for I have hardened his heart and the hearts of his servants, that I may show these signs of Mine before him, 2and that you may tell in the hearing of your son and your son's son the mighty things I have done in Egypt, and My signs which I have done among them, that you may know that I *am* the LORD."

3So Moses and Aaron came in to Pharaoh and said to him, "Thus says the LORD God of the Hebrews: 'How long will you refuse to humble yourself before Me? Let My people go, that they may serve Me. 4Or else, if you refuse to let My people go, behold, tomorrow I will bring locusts into your territory. 5And they shall cover the face of the earth, so that no one will be able to see the earth; and they shall eat the residue of what is left, which remains to you from the hail, and they shall eat every tree which grows up for you out of the field. 6They shall fill your houses, the houses of all your servants, and the houses of all the Egyptians— which neither your fathers nor your fathers' fathers have seen, since the day that they were on the earth to this day.' " And he turned and went out from Pharaoh.

7Then Pharaoh's servants said to him, "How long shall this man be a snare to us? Let the men go, that they may serve the LORD their God. Do you not yet know that Egypt is destroyed?"

9:27 Pharaoh's "confession of sin" was not sincere; he only wanted Moses to stop the plagues. True repentance involves a change of mind that leads to a change of life. Balaam (Num. 22:34), Saul (1 Sam. 15:24), and Judas (Matt. 27:4) were all guilty of insincere confession of sin.

⁸So Moses and Aaron were brought again to Pharaoh, and he said to them, "Go, serve the LORD your God. Who *are* the ones that are going?"

⁹And Moses said, "We will go with our young and our old; with our sons and our daughters, with our flocks and our herds we will go, for we must hold a feast to the LORD."

¹⁰Then he said to them, "The LORD had better be with you when I let you and your little ones go! Beware, for evil is ahead of you. ¹¹Not so! Go now, you *who are* men, and serve the LORD, for that is what you desired." And they were driven out from Pharaoh's presence.

¹²Then the LORD said to Moses, "Stretch out your hand over the land of Egypt for the locusts, that they may come upon the land of Egypt, and eat every herb of the land—all that the hail has left." ¹³So Moses stretched out his rod over the land of Egypt, and the LORD brought an east wind on the land all that day and all *that* night. When it was morning, the east wind brought the locusts. ¹⁴And the locusts went up over all the land of Egypt and rested on all the territory of Egypt. *They were* very severe; previously there had been no such locusts as they, nor shall there be such after them. ¹⁵For they covered the face of the whole earth, so that the land was darkened; and they ate every herb of the land and all the fruit of the trees which the hail had left. So there remained nothing green on the trees or on the plants of the field throughout all the land of Egypt.

¹⁶Then Pharaoh called for Moses and Aaron in haste, and said, "I have sinned against the LORD your God and against you. ¹⁷Now therefore, please forgive my sin only this once, and entreat the LORD your God, that He may take away from me this death only." ¹⁸So he went out from Pharaoh and entreated the LORD. ¹⁹And the LORD turned a very strong west wind, which took the locusts away and blew them into the Red Sea. There remained not one locust in all the territory of Egypt. ²⁰But the LORD hardened Pharaoh's heart, and he did not let the children of Israel go.

²¹Then the LORD said to Moses, "Stretch out your hand toward heaven, that there may be darkness over the land of Egypt, darkness *which* may even be felt." ²²So Moses stretched out his hand toward heaven, and there was thick darkness in all the land of Egypt three days. ²³They did not see one another; nor did anyone rise from his place for three days. But all the children of Israel had light in their dwellings.

²⁴Then Pharaoh called to Moses and said, "Go, serve the LORD; only let your flocks and your herds be kept back. Let your little ones also go with you."

²⁵But Moses said, "You must also give us sacrifices and burnt offerings, that we may sacrifice to the LORD our God. ²⁶Our livestock also shall go with us; not a hoof shall be left behind. For we must take some of them to serve the LORD our God, and even we do not know with what we must serve the LORD until we arrive there."

²⁷But the LORD hardened Pharaoh's heart, and he would not let them go. ²⁸Then Pharaoh said to him, "Get away from me! Take heed to yourself and see my face no more! For in the day you see my face you shall die!"

²⁹So Moses said, "You have spoken well. I will never see your face again."

11 And* the LORD said to Moses, "I will bring one more plague on Pharaoh and on Egypt. Afterward he will let you go from here. When he lets *you* go, he will surely drive you out of here altogether. ²Speak now in the hearing of the people, and let every man ask from his neighbor and every woman from her neighbor, articles of silver and articles of gold." ³And the LORD gave the people favor in the sight of the Egyptians. Moreover the man Moses *was* very great in the land of Egypt, in the sight of Pharaoh's servants and in the sight of the people.

⁴Then Moses said, "Thus says the LORD: 'About midnight I will go out into the midst of Egypt; ⁵and all the firstborn in the land of Egypt shall die, from the firstborn of Pharaoh who sits on his throne, even to the firstborn of the female servant who *is* behind the handmill, and all the firstborn of the animals. ⁶Then there shall be a great cry throughout all the land of Egypt, such as was not like it *before*, nor shall be like it again. ⁷But against none of the children of Israel shall a dog move its tongue, against man or beast, that you may know that the LORD does make a difference between the Egyptians and Israel.' ⁸And all these your servants shall come down to me and bow down to me, saying, 'Get out, and all the people who follow you!' After that I will go out." Then he went out from Pharaoh in great anger.

⁹But the LORD said to Moses, "Pharaoh will not heed you, so that My wonders may be multiplied in the land of Egypt." ¹⁰So Moses and Aaron did all these wonders before Pharaoh; and the LORD hardened Pharaoh's heart, and he did not let the children of Israel go out of his land.

12 Now the LORD spoke to Moses and Aaron in the land of Egypt, saying, ²"This month *shall be* your beginning of months; it *shall be* the first month of the year to you. ³*Speak to all the congregation of Israel, saying: 'On the tenth of this month every man shall take for himself a lamb, according to the house of *his* father, a lamb for a household. ⁴And if the household is too small for the lamb, let him and his neighbor next to his house take *it* according to the number of the persons; according to each man's need you shall make your count for the lamb. ⁵Your lamb shall be without blemish, a male of the first year. You may take *it* from the sheep or from the goats. ⁶Now you shall keep it until the fourteenth day of the same month. Then the whole assembly of the congregation of Israel shall kill it at twilight. ⁷And they shall take *some* of the blood and put *it* on the two doorposts and on the lintel of the houses where they eat it. ⁸Then they shall eat the flesh on that night; roasted in fire, with unleavened bread *and* with bitter *herbs* they shall eat it. ⁹Do not eat it raw, nor boiled at all with water, but roasted in fire—its head with its legs and its entrails. ¹⁰You shall let none of it remain until morning, and what remains of it until morning you shall burn with fire. ¹¹And thus you shall eat it: *with* a belt on your waist, your sandals on your feet, and your staff in your hand. So you shall eat it in haste. It *is* the LORD's Passover.

¹²'For I will pass through the land of Egypt on that night, and will strike all the firstborn in the land of Egypt, both man and beast; and against all the gods of Egypt I will execute judgment: I *am* the LORD. ¹³Now the blood shall be a sign for

CHAPTERS 11—12

11:1 Life. "One more plague!" The words sounded ominous, and they were, for the last plague was death to the firstborn. When you trust in the Lord, it means the difference between light and darkness (10:21–23) and life and death. God made this difference (11:7), and His people must maintain it (Rom. 12:1–2).

12:3–11 Lamb. Observe the sequence: "*a* lamb" (12:3), "*the* lamb" (12:4), "*your* lamb" (12:5). The Passover lamb is a picture of Jesus Christ who died for the sins of the world (John 1:29; 1 Cor. 5:6–7). Do you call Him "*a* Savior," "*the* Savior," or "*my* Savior" (Luke 1:47)?

Jesus is the perfect Lamb (1 Pet. 1:18–19) who had to die to save us. We are saved not by admiring His example or by studying His teaching, but by applying His blood to our own hearts by faith. The lamb saved the Jews and it also sustained them for their journey. You "feed" on Jesus Christ when you meditate on His Word and make its truths a part of your inner person.

12:15–20 *Leaven.* Yeast is a picture of sin: it begins small but spreads quickly; it puffs up; and it works secretly. When you are saved by the blood of Christ, you want to have a life that is pure and free from known sin. The Jews were not saved by getting rid of the leaven; they got rid of the leaven because God had saved them (2 Cor. 7:1; 2 Tim. 2:19). Note how Paul applied these truths in 1 Corinthians 5.

you on the houses where you *are.* And when I see the blood, I will pass over you; and the plague shall not be on you to destroy *you* when I strike the land of Egypt.

14'So this day shall be to you a memorial; and you shall keep it as a feast to the LORD throughout your generations. You shall keep it as a feast by an everlasting ordinance. 15*Seven days you shall eat unleavened bread. On the first day you shall remove leaven from your houses. For whoever eats leavened bread from the first day until the seventh day, that person shall be cut off from Israel. 16On the first day *there shall be* a holy convocation, and on the seventh day there shall be a holy convocation for you. No manner of work shall be done on them; but *that* which everyone must eat—that only may be prepared by you. 17So you shall observe *the Feast of* Unleavened Bread, for on this same day I will have brought your armies out of the land of Egypt. Therefore you shall observe this day throughout your generations as an everlasting ordinance. 18In the first *month,* on the fourteenth day of the month at evening, you shall eat unleavened bread, until the twenty-first day of the month at evening. 19For seven days no leaven shall be found in your houses, since whoever eats what is leavened, that same person shall be cut off from the congregation of Israel, whether *he is* a stranger or a native of the land. 20You shall eat nothing leavened; in all your dwellings you shall eat unleavened bread.' "

21Then Moses called for all the elders of Israel and said to them, "Pick out and take lambs for yourselves according to your families, and kill the Passover *lamb.* 22And you shall take a bunch of hyssop, dip *it* in the blood that *is* in the basin, and strike the lintel and the two doorposts with the blood that *is* in the basin. And none of you shall go out of the door of his house until morning. 23For the LORD will pass through to strike the Egyptians; and when He sees the blood on the lintel and on the two doorposts, the LORD will pass over the door and not allow the destroyer to come into your houses to strike *you.* 24And you shall observe this thing as an ordinance for you and your sons forever. 25It will come to pass when you come to the land which the LORD will give you, just as He promised, that you shall keep this service. 26And it shall be, when your children say to you, 'What do you mean by this service?' 27that you shall say, 'It *is* the Passover sacrifice of the LORD, who passed over the houses of the children of Israel in Egypt when He struck the Egyptians and delivered our households.' " So the people bowed their heads and worshiped. 28Then the children of Israel went away and did *so;* just as the LORD had commanded Moses and Aaron, so they did.

29And it came to pass at midnight that the LORD struck all the firstborn in the land of Egypt, from the firstborn of Pharaoh who sat on his throne to the firstborn of the captive who *was* in the dungeon, and all the firstborn of livestock. 30So Pharaoh rose in the night, he, all his servants, and all the Egyptians; and there was a great cry in Egypt, for *there was* not a house where *there was* not one dead.

31Then he called for Moses and Aaron by night, and said, "Rise, go out from among my people, both you and the children of Israel. And go, serve the LORD as you have said. 32Also take your flocks and your herds, as you have said, and be gone; and bless me also."

³³And the Egyptians urged the people, that they might send them out of the land in haste. For they said, "We *shall* all *be* dead." ³⁴So the people took their dough before it was leavened, having their kneading bowls bound up in their clothes on their shoulders. ³⁵Now the children of Israel had done according to the word of Moses, and they had asked from the Egyptians articles of silver, articles of gold, and clothing. ³⁶And the LORD had given the people favor in the sight of the Egyptians, so that they granted them *what they requested.* Thus they plundered the Egyptians.

³⁷Then the children of Israel journeyed from Rameses to Succoth, about six hundred thousand men on foot, besides children. ³⁸A mixed multitude went up with them also, and flocks and herds—a great deal of livestock. ³⁹And they baked unleavened cakes of the dough which they had brought out of Egypt; for it was not leavened, because they were driven out of Egypt and could not wait, nor had they prepared provisions for themselves.

⁴⁰Now the sojourn of the children of Israel who lived in Egypt^k *was* four hundred and thirty years. ⁴¹And it came to pass at the end of the four hundred and thirty years—on that very same day—it came to pass that all the armies of the LORD went out from the land of Egypt. ⁴²It *is* a night of solemn observance to the LORD for bringing them out of the land of Egypt. This *is* that night of the LORD, a solemn observance for all the children of Israel throughout their generations.

⁴³And the LORD said to Moses and Aaron, "This *is* the ordinance of the Passover: No foreigner shall eat it. ⁴⁴But every man's servant who is bought for money, when you have circumcised him, then he may eat it. ⁴⁵A sojourner and a hired servant shall not eat it. ⁴⁶In one house it shall be eaten; you shall not carry any of the flesh outside the house, nor shall you break one of its bones. ⁴⁷All the congregation of Israel shall keep it. ⁴⁸And when a stranger dwells with you *and wants* to keep the Passover to the LORD, let all his males be circumcised, and then let him come near and keep it; and he shall be as a native of the land. For no uncircumcised person shall eat it. ⁴⁹One law shall be for the native-born and for the stranger who dwells among you."

⁵⁰Thus all the children of Israel did; as the LORD commanded Moses and Aaron, so they did. ⁵¹And it came to pass, on that very same day, that the LORD brought the children of Israel out of the land of Egypt according to their armies.

13 Then the LORD spoke to Moses, saying, ²"Consecrate to Me all the firstborn, whatever opens the womb among the children of Israel, *both* of man and beast; it is Mine."

³*And Moses said to the people: "Remember this day in which you went out of Egypt, out of the house of bondage; for by strength of hand the LORD brought you out of this *place.* No leavened bread shall be eaten. ⁴On this day you are going out, in the month Abib. ⁵And it shall be, when the LORD brings you into the land of the Canaanites and the Hittites and the Amorites and

---

12:40 ^kSamaritan Pentateuch and Septuagint read *Egypt and Canaan.*

CHAPTER 13

13:3–7 Remembering. God wanted Israel to remember what His hand had done for them (vv. 3, 9, 14, 16), lest in the future they forget to trust Him and serve Him. The setting apart of the firstborn would remind them that the firstborn sons of Israel had been redeemed by the Lord. The annual Passover would remind them to keep their lives pure. When you consider that Jesus Christ has redeemed us by His blood, surely we should give ourselves to Him and obey His Word.

13:8–10 *Instructing.* The younger generation cannot know the works of the Lord unless the older generation tells them.

The Word of God must control our lips (v. 9), our eyes, and our hands (v. 16), and we must share it with others. The Jews took this literally and wore portions of the Law on the forehead and hand, but the Lord was surely speaking in a metaphorical way.

the Hivites and the Jebusites, which He swore to your fathers to give you, a land flowing with milk and honey, that you shall keep this service in this month. 6Seven days you shall eat unleavened bread, and on the seventh day *there shall be* a feast to the LORD. 7Unleavened bread shall be eaten seven days. And no leavened bread shall be seen among you, nor shall leaven be seen among you in all your quarters. 8*And you shall tell your son in that day, saying, '*This is done* because of what the LORD did for me when I came up from Egypt.' 9It shall be as a sign to you on your hand and as a memorial between your eyes, that the LORD's law may be in your mouth; for with a strong hand the LORD has brought you out of Egypt. 10You shall therefore keep this ordinance in its season from year to year.

11"And it shall be, when the LORD brings you into the land of the Canaanites, as He swore to you and your fathers, and gives it to you, 12that you shall set apart to the LORD all that open the womb, that is, every firstborn that comes from an animal which you have; the males *shall be* the LORD's. 13But every firstborn of a donkey you shall redeem with a lamb; and if you will not redeem *it,* then you shall break its neck. And all the firstborn of man among your sons you shall redeem. 14So it shall be, when your son asks you in time to come, saying, 'What *is* this?' that you shall say to him, 'By strength of hand the LORD brought us out of Egypt, out of the house of bondage. 15And it came to pass, when Pharaoh was stubborn about letting us go, that the LORD killed all the firstborn in the land of Egypt, both the firstborn of man and the firstborn of beast. Therefore I sacrifice to the LORD all males that open the womb, but all the firstborn of my sons I redeem.' 16It shall be as a sign on your hand and as frontlets between your eyes, for by strength of hand the LORD brought us out of Egypt."

17Then it came to pass, when Pharaoh had let the people go, that God did not lead them *by* way of the land of the Philistines, although that *was* near; for God said, "Lest perhaps the people change their minds when they see war, and return to Egypt." 18So God led the people around *by* way of the wilderness of the Red Sea. And the children of Israel went up in orderly ranks out of the land of Egypt.

19And Moses took the bones of Joseph with him, for he had placed the children of Israel under solemn oath, saying, "God will surely visit you, and you shall carry up my bones from here with you."*l*

20So they took their journey from Succoth and camped in Etham at the edge of the wilderness. 21*And the LORD went before them by day in a pillar of cloud to lead the way, and by night in a pillar of fire to give them light, so as to go by day and night. 22He did not take away the pillar of cloud by day or the pillar of fire by night *from* before the people.

13:21, 22 *Following.* God frees us from bondage, and He also guides us to the inheritance He has prepared for us. His Word is like that pillar of cloud and fire, and He will show us the way if we will trust Him.

CHAPTER 14

14:1–14 *God sees before.* God knew Pharaoh's plans and saw to it that Israel was cared for. This is *providence,* which means "to see before." He is Jehovah-Jireh (Gen. 22:14), "the Lord will see to it." No matter what the enemy plans to do to you, God has already taken care of it and will tell you what to do.

14 Now* the LORD spoke to Moses, saying: 2"Speak to the children of Israel, that they turn and camp before Pi Hahiroth, between Migdol and the sea, opposite Baal Zephon; you shall camp before it by the sea. 3For Pharaoh will say of the children of Israel, 'They *are* bewildered by the land; the wilderness has closed them in.'

13:19 *l* Genesis 50:25

4Then I will harden Pharaoh's heart, so that he will pursue them; and I will gain honor over Pharaoh and over all his army, that the Egyptians may know that I *am* the LORD." And they did so.

5Now it was told the king of Egypt that the people had fled, and the heart of Pharaoh and his servants was turned against the people; and they said, "Why have we done this, that we have let Israel go from serving us?" 6So he made ready his chariot and took his people with him. 7Also, he took six hundred choice chariots, and all the chariots of Egypt with captains over every one of them. 8And the LORD hardened the heart of Pharaoh king of Egypt, and he pursued the children of Israel; and the children of Israel went out with boldness. 9So the Egyptians pursued them, all the horses *and* chariots of Pharaoh, his horsemen and his army, and overtook them camping by the sea beside Pi Hahiroth, before Baal Zephon.

10And when Pharaoh drew near, the children of Israel lifted their eyes, and behold, the Egyptians marched after them. So they were very afraid, and the children of Israel cried out to the LORD. 11Then they said to Moses, "Because *there were* no graves in Egypt, have you taken us away to die in the wilderness? Why have you so dealt with us, to bring us up out of Egypt? 12*Is* this not the word that we told you in Egypt, saying, 'Let us alone that we may serve the Egyptians'? For *it would have been* better for us to serve the Egyptians than that we should die in the wilderness."

13And Moses said to the people, "Do not be afraid. Stand still, and see the salvation of the LORD, which He will accomplish for you today. For the Egyptians whom you see today, you shall see again no more forever. 14The LORD will fight for you, and you shall hold your peace."

15And the LORD said to Moses, "Why do you cry to Me? Tell the children of Israel to go forward. 16"But lift up your rod, and stretch out your hand over the sea and divide it. And the children of Israel shall go on dry *ground* through the midst of the sea. 17And I indeed will harden the hearts of the Egyptians, and they shall follow them. So I will gain honor over Pharaoh and over all his army, his chariots, and his horsemen. 18Then the Egyptians shall know that I *am* the LORD, when I have gained honor for Myself over Pharaoh, his chariots, and his horsemen."

19*And the Angel of God, who went before the camp of Israel, moved and went behind them; and the pillar of cloud went from before them and stood behind them. 20So it came between the camp of the Egyptians and the camp of Israel. Thus it was a cloud and darkness *to the one,* and it gave light by night *to the other,* so that the one did not come near the other all that night.

21*Then Moses stretched out his hand over the sea; and the LORD caused the sea to go *back* by a strong east wind all that night, and made the sea into dry *land,* and the waters were divided. 22So the children of Israel went into the midst of the sea on the dry *ground,* and the waters *were* a wall to them on their right hand and on their left. 23And the Egyptians pursued and went after them into the midst of the sea, all Pharaoh's horses, his chariots, and his horsemen.

24Now it came to pass, in the morning watch, that the LORD looked down upon the army of the Egyptians through the pillar of fire and cloud, and He troubled the army of the Egyptians. 25And He

14:19, 20 God comes between. The pillar that brought light to Israel brought darkness to the enemy. The people of the world are walking in darkness, but God's people have "the light of life" (John 8:12). The enemy cannot touch you without first encountering God.

14:21–23 God goes ahead. He opens the way and does the impossible. The next time you are in a seemingly impossible situation, remember what God did for Israel at the Red Sea. The people of Israel never forgot this victory (Pss. 66:6; 106:9; 136:13–14). Recalling God's past help can encourage you as you face future challenges to your faith.

14:26–31 *God comes behind.* Isaiah stated, "And the God of Israel will be your rear guard" (Isa. 52:12). The defeat was complete; the Egyptian army was no more. There is much truth in these words: "And this is the victory that has overcome the world—our faith" (1 John 5:4).

took off[m] their chariot wheels, so that they drove them with difficulty; and the Egyptians said, "Let us flee from the face of Israel, for the LORD fights for them against the Egyptians."

26*Then the LORD said to Moses, "Stretch out your hand over the sea, that the waters may come back upon the Egyptians, on their chariots, and on their horsemen." 27And Moses stretched out his hand over the sea; and when the morning appeared, the sea returned to its full depth, while the Egyptians were fleeing into it. So the LORD overthrew the Egyptians in the midst of the sea. 28Then the waters returned and covered the chariots, the horsemen, *and* all the army of Pharaoh that came into the sea after them. Not so much as one of them remained. 29But the children of Israel had walked on dry *land* in the midst of the sea, and the waters *were* a wall to them on their right hand and on their left.

30So the LORD saved Israel that day out of the hand of the Egyptians, and Israel saw the Egyptians dead on the seashore. 31Thus Israel saw the great work which the LORD had done in Egypt; so the people feared the LORD, and believed the LORD and His servant Moses.

CHAPTER 15

15:1ff *The Lord who triumphs.* When they walked by sight, Israel complained (14:10–12); but when they believed God and saw His mighty hand at work, they praised Him. Redemption should lead to rejoicing (Luke 15:1–24).

This first recorded song in Scripture is a pattern for true worship, for it emphasizes the Lord, who He is, and what He has done for His people. He saves His people (vv. 1–10), guides them to their inheritance (vv. 11–13), glorifies His name (vv. 14–17), and reigns forever (v. 18). Today, let God be your strength, your song, and your salvation (v. 2; see also Ps. 118:14; Isa. 12:2).

15 Then* Moses and the children of Israel sang this song to the LORD, and spoke, saying:

"I will sing to the LORD,
　For He has triumphed gloriously!
　The horse and its rider
　He has thrown into the sea!
2　The LORD *is* my strength and song,
　And He has become my salvation;
　He *is* my God, and I will praise Him;
　My father's God, and I will exalt Him.
3　The LORD *is* a man of war;
　The LORD *is* His name.
4　Pharaoh's chariots and his army He has cast
　　into the sea;
　His chosen captains also are drowned in the
　　Red Sea.
5　The depths have covered them;
　They sank to the bottom like a stone.

6　"Your right hand, O LORD, has become
　　glorious in power;
　Your right hand, O LORD, has dashed the
　　enemy in pieces.
7　And in the greatness of Your excellence
　You have overthrown those who rose
　　against You;
　You sent forth Your wrath;
　It consumed them like stubble.
8　And with the blast of Your nostrils
　The waters were gathered together;
　The floods stood upright like a heap;
　The depths congealed in the heart of the sea.
9　The enemy said, 'I will pursue,
　I will overtake,
　I will divide the spoil;

14:25 [m]Samaritan Pentateuch, Septuagint, and Syriac read *bound.*

Praise Him with Song—Singing is an important part of the Christian life, for it enables us to praise God and bear witness to others. Our praise should come from the Holy Spirit within (Eph. 5:18–20) and be based on Scripture (Col. 3:16). In this way, we worship Him "in spirit and truth" (John 4:24).

My desire shall be satisfied on them.
I will draw my sword,
My hand shall destroy them.'
10   You blew with Your wind,
The sea covered them;
They sank like lead in the mighty waters.

11   "Who *is* like You, O LORD, among the gods?
Who *is* like You, glorious in holiness,
Fearful in praises, doing wonders?
12   You stretched out Your right hand;
The earth swallowed them.
13   You in Your mercy have led forth
The people whom You have redeemed;
You have guided *them* in Your strength
To Your holy habitation.

14   "The people will hear *and* be afraid;
Sorrow will take hold of the inhabitants of
Philistia.
15   Then the chiefs of Edom will be dismayed;
The mighty men of Moab,
Trembling will take hold of them;
All the inhabitants of Canaan will melt
away.
16   Fear and dread will fall on them;
By the greatness of Your arm
They will be *as* still as a stone,
Till Your people pass over, O LORD,
Till the people pass over
Whom You have purchased.
17   You will bring them in and plant them
In the mountain of Your inheritance,
In the place, O LORD, *which* You have made
For Your own dwelling,
The sanctuary, O LORD, *which* Your hands
have established.

18   "The LORD shall reign forever and ever."

19For the horses of Pharaoh went with his chariots and his horsemen into the sea, and the LORD
brought back the waters of the sea upon them.
But the children of Israel went on dry *land* in the
midst of the sea. 20Then Miriam the prophetess, the sister of
Aaron, took the timbrel in her hand; and all the
women went out after her with timbrels and with
dances. 21And Miriam answered them:

"Sing to the LORD,
For He has triumphed gloriously!
The horse and its rider
He has thrown into the sea!"

22So Moses brought Israel from the Red Sea;
then they went out into the Wilderness of Shur.
And they went three days in the wilderness and
found no water. 23*Now when they came to
Marah, they could not drink the waters of Marah,
for they *were* bitter. Therefore the name of it was
called Marah.n 24And the people complained
against Moses, saying, "What shall we drink?"
25So he cried out to the LORD, and the LORD
showed him a tree. When he cast *it* into the waters, the waters were made sweet.

There He made a statute and an ordinance for
them, and there He tested them, 26and said, "If
you diligently heed the voice of the LORD your

15:23–26 *The Lord who heals.* The people
went from rejoicing to complaining! It is easy
to sing when the circumstances are
comfortable, but it takes faith to sing when
you are suffering. God tests us in the
everyday experiences of life to see whether
we will obey Him. He is able to change our
circumstances, but He would rather change
us (Phil. 4:10–13).

15:23 nLiterally *Bitter*

15:27 *The Lord who refreshes.* Life is not always battles and bitter waters. God brings us to the refreshing oases from time to time, and for this we should praise Him. However, we can never claim our inheritance if we linger at Elim. We are pilgrims, not residents.

CHAPTER 16

16:1–3 The redeemed Jews were acting like unsaved Gentiles, for they asked, "What shall we eat? What shall we drink?" (Matt. 6:25–34). God did not rescue them from bondage in order to kill them with hunger! (See Rom. 8:31–32.) Their real problem was that they still had the old appetite and needed to learn to enjoy the new food God had for them.

16:14–16 The manna is a picture of Jesus Christ (John 6:30ff.). The manna came only to Israel, and all it could do was sustain physical life. But the Savior came for the whole world, and He gives spiritual life. If the Jews did not appropriate the manna, they died. Sinners must believe on Jesus Christ to receive life.

Feeding on the manna is also a picture of your daily appropriation of Christ through the Word of God. Just as your food becomes a part of your very being, so the Word strengthens your inner person when you read it, meditate on it, and obey it. Just as the Jews could not live on yesterday's manna, so you cannot live on yesterday's spiritual diet. Begin each day with the Lord, and He will give you what you need for facing the burdens and battles ahead.

God and do what is right in His sight, give ear to His commandments and keep all His statutes, I will put none of the diseases on you which I have brought on the Egyptians. For I *am* the LORD who heals you."

27*Then they came to Elim, where there *were* twelve wells of water and seventy palm trees; so they camped there by the waters.

16 And* they journeyed from Elim, and all the congregation of the children of Israel came to the Wilderness of Sin, which is between Elim and Sinai, on the fifteenth day of the second month after they departed from the land of Egypt. 2Then the whole congregation of the children of Israel complained against Moses and Aaron in the wilderness. 3And the children of Israel said to them, "Oh, that we had died by the hand of the LORD in the land of Egypt, when we sat by the pots of meat *and* when we ate bread to the full! For you have brought us out into this wilderness to kill this whole assembly with hunger."

4Then the LORD said to Moses, "Behold, I will rain bread from heaven for you. And the people shall go out and gather a certain quota every day, that I may test them, whether they will walk in My law or not. 5And it shall be on the sixth day that they shall prepare what they bring in, and it shall be twice as much as they gather daily."

6Then Moses and Aaron said to all the children of Israel, "At evening you shall know that the LORD has brought you out of the land of Egypt. 7And in the morning you shall see the glory of the LORD; for He hears your complaints against the LORD. But what *are* we, that you complain against us?" 8Also Moses said, "*This shall be seen* when the LORD gives you meat to eat in the evening, and in the morning bread to the full; for the LORD hears your complaints which you make against Him. And what *are* we? Your complaints *are* not against us but against the LORD."

9Then Moses spoke to Aaron, "Say to all the congregation of the children of Israel, 'Come near before the LORD, for He has heard your complaints.'" 10Now it came to pass, as Aaron spoke to the whole congregation of the children of Israel, that they looked toward the wilderness, and behold, the glory of the LORD appeared in the cloud.

11And the LORD spoke to Moses, saying, 12"I have heard the complaints of the children of Israel. Speak to them, saying, 'At twilight you shall eat meat, and in the morning you shall be filled with bread. And you shall know that I *am* the LORD your God.'"

13So it was that quails came up at evening and covered the camp, and in the morning the dew lay all around the camp. 14*And when the layer of dew lifted, there, on the surface of the wilderness, was a small round substance, *as* fine as frost on the ground. 15So when the children of Israel saw *it*, they said to one another, "What is it?" For they did not know what it *was*.

And Moses said to them, "This *is* the bread which the LORD has given you to eat. 16This is the thing which the LORD has commanded: 'Let every man gather it according to each one's need,

---

Spiritual Food—God's Word is food for the inner person. It is milk (1 Pet. 2:2), bread (Matt. 4:4), meat (1 Cor. 3:1–2; Heb. 5:11–14), and honey (Ps. 119:103). Feeding on the Word should bring joy to our hearts (Jer. 15:16), and we should desire spiritual food more than physical food (Job 23:12; Luke 10:38–42).

one omer for each person, *according to the* number of persons; let every man take for *those* who *are* in his tent.' "

17Then the children of Israel did so and gathered, some more, some less. 18So when they measured *it* by omers, he who gathered much had nothing left over, and he who gathered little had no lack. Every man had gathered according to each one's need. 19And Moses said, "Let no one leave any of it till morning." 20Notwithstanding they did not heed Moses. But some of them left part of it until morning, and it bred worms and stank. And Moses was angry with them. 21So they gathered it every morning, every man according to his need. And when the sun became hot, it melted.

22And so it was, on the sixth day, *that* they gathered twice as much bread, two omers for each one. And all the rulers of the congregation came and told Moses. 23Then he said to them, "This *is what* the LORD has said: 'Tomorrow *is* a Sabbath rest, a holy Sabbath to the LORD. Bake what you will bake *today,* and boil what you will boil; and lay up for yourselves all that remains, to be kept until morning.' " 24So they laid it up till morning, as Moses commanded; and it did not stink, nor were there any worms in it. 25Then Moses said, "Eat that today, for today *is* a Sabbath to the LORD; today you will not find it in the field. 26Six days you shall gather it, but on the seventh day, the Sabbath, there will be none."

27Now it happened *that some* of the people went out on the seventh day to gather, but they found none. 28And the LORD said to Moses, "How long do you refuse to keep My commandments and My laws? 29See! For the LORD has given you the Sabbath; therefore He gives you on the sixth day bread for two days. Let every man remain in his place; let no man go out of his place on the seventh day." 30So the people rested on the seventh day.

31And the house of Israel called its name Manna.º And it *was* like white coriander seed, and the taste of it *was* like wafers *made* with honey.

32Then Moses said, "This *is* the thing which the LORD has commanded: 'Fill an omer with it, to be kept for your generations, that they may see the bread with which I fed you in the wilderness, when I brought you out of the land of Egypt.' " 33And Moses said to Aaron, "Take a pot and put an omer of manna in it, and lay it up before the LORD, to be kept for your generations." 34As the LORD commanded Moses, so Aaron laid it up before the Testimony, to be kept. 35And the children of Israel ate manna forty years, until they came to an inhabited land; they ate manna until they came to the border of the land of Canaan. 36Now an omer *is* one-tenth of an ephah.

17 Then* all the congregation of the children of Israel set out on their journey from the Wilderness of Sin, according to the commandment of the LORD, and camped in Rephidim; but *there was* no water for the people to drink. 2Therefore the people contended with Moses, and said, "Give us water, that we may drink."

So Moses said to them, "Why do you contend with me? Why do you tempt the LORD?"

16:31 ºLiterally *What?* (compare Exodus 16:15)

CHAPTER 17

17:1–6 *Another test.* You never solve your problems by blaming other people. Israel's real problem was unbelief and a desire to go back to the old life. Every difficulty you meet is an opportunity for testing yourself and trusting your Lord, for going forward or going backward. The rock pictures Jesus Christ who was smitten for us (1 Cor. 10:4) that we might have the living water of the Holy Spirit within (John 7:37–39).

17:8–13 ***Another enemy.*** The Egyptian army had been drowned, but the Amalekites were very much alive and did not want Israel in their territory. It was Esau fighting Jacob again (Gen. 36:12). It takes intercession on the mountain as well as intervention in the valley for God's people to win the victory. Israel watched God defeat Egypt, but now they had to enter the battle themselves and trust God for victory. Our High Priest intercedes in heaven for us (Heb. 4:14–16). This is the first mention of Joshua in Scripture. Little did he know that one day he would take Moses' place as leader of God's people.

17:14–16 ***Another assurance.*** Each test can tell you something new about yourself and about the Lord (Gen. 22:14; Exod. 15:26). When you face the battles of life, remember that He is your banner and can give you victory (John 16:33; 1 John 5:4–5).

CHAPTER 18

18:1–12 ***Balance.*** Moses experienced some exciting things after leaving Egypt, but now he returns to the everyday duties of life. God balances our lives and gives us enough burdens to keep us humble and enough blessings to keep us happy. Moses returned to his family, told them all that God had done, and then worshiped the Lord with them.

3And the people thirsted there for water, and
the people complained against Moses, and said,
"Why *is* it you have brought us up out of Egypt,
to kill us and our children and our livestock with
thirst?"
4So Moses cried out to the LORD, saying, "What
shall I do with this people? They are almost ready
to stone me!"
5And the LORD said to Moses, "Go on before
the people, and take with you some of the elders
of Israel. Also take in your hand your rod with
which you struck the river, and go. 6Behold, I will
stand before you there on the rock in Horeb; and
you shall strike the rock, and water will come out
of it, that the people may drink."
And Moses did so in the sight of the elders of
Israel. 7So he called the name of the place Massah[p] and Meribah,[q] because of the contention of
the children of Israel, and because they tempted
the LORD, saying, "Is the LORD among us or
not?"
8*Now Amalek came and fought with Israel in
Rephidim. 9And Moses said to Joshua, "Choose
us some men and go out, fight with Amalek. Tomorrow I will stand on the top of the hill with
the rod of God in my hand." 10So Joshua did as
Moses said to him, and fought with Amalek. And
Moses, Aaron, and Hur went up to the top of the
hill. 11And so it was, when Moses held up his
hand, that Israel prevailed; and when he let down
his hand, Amalek prevailed. 12But Moses' hands
became heavy; so they took a stone and put *it*
under him, and he sat on it. And Aaron and Hur
supported his hands, one on one side, and the
other on the other side; and his hands were steady
until the going down of the sun. 13So Joshua defeated Amalek and his people with the edge of
the sword.
14*Then the LORD said to Moses, "Write this
for a memorial in the book and recount *it* in the
hearing of Joshua, that I will utterly blot out
the remembrance of Amalek from under
heaven." 15And Moses built an altar and called
its name, The-LORD-Is-My-Banner;[r] 16for he said,
"Because the LORD has sworn: the LORD *will
have* war with Amalek from generation to generation."

18 And* Jethro, the priest of Midian, Moses'
father-in-law, heard of all that God had
done for Moses and for Israel His people—that
the LORD had brought Israel out of Egypt. 2Then
Jethro, Moses' father-in-law, took Zipporah, Moses' wife, after he had sent her back, 3with her
two sons, of whom the name of one *was* Gershom
(for he said, "I have been a stranger in a foreign
land")[s] 4and the name of the other *was* Eliezer[t]
(for *he said,* "The God of my father *was* my help,
and delivered me from the sword of Pharaoh");
5and Jethro, Moses' father-in-law, came with his
sons and his wife to Moses in the wilderness,
where he was encamped at the mountain of God.
6Now he had said to Moses, "I, your father-in-law
Jethro, am coming to you with your wife and her
two sons with her."
7So Moses went out to meet his father-in-law,
bowed down, and kissed him. And they asked

17:7 [p]Literally *Tempted* [q]Literally *Contention* 17:15 [r]Hebrew *YHWH Nissi* 18:3 [s]Compare Exodus 2:22 18:4 [t]Literally *My God Is Help*

each other about *their* well-being, and they went into the tent. 8And Moses told his father-in-law all that the LORD had done to Pharaoh and to the Egyptians for Israel's sake, all the hardship that had come upon them on the way, and *how* the LORD had delivered them. 9Then Jethro rejoiced for all the good which the LORD had done for Israel, whom He had delivered out of the hand of the Egyptians. 10And Jethro said, "Blessed *be* the LORD, who has delivered you out of the hand of the Egyptians and out of the hand of Pharaoh, *and* who has delivered the people from under the hand of the Egyptians. 11Now I know that the LORD *is* greater than all the gods; for in the very thing in which they behaved proudly, *He was* above them." 12Then Jethro, Moses' father-in-law, took*u* a burnt offering and *other* sacrifices *to offer* to God. And Aaron came with all the elders of Israel to eat bread with Moses' father-in-law before God.

13And so it was, on the next day, that Moses sat to judge the people; and the people stood before Moses from morning until evening. 14So when Moses' father-in-law saw all that he did for the people, he said, "What *is* this thing that you are doing for the people? Why do you alone sit, and all the people stand before you from morning until evening?"

15And Moses said to his father-in-law, "Because the people come to me to inquire of God. 16When they have a difficulty, they come to me, and I judge between one and another; and I make known the statutes of God and His laws."

17*So Moses' father-in-law said to him, "The thing that you do *is* not good. 18Both you and these people who *are* with you will surely wear yourselves out. For this thing *is* too much for you; you are not able to perform it by yourself. 19Listen now to my voice; I will give you counsel, and God will be with you: Stand before God for the people, so that you may bring the difficulties to God. 20And you shall teach them the statutes and the laws, and show them the way in which they must walk and the work they must do. 21*Moreover you shall select from all the people able men, such as fear God, men of truth, hating covetousness; and place *such* over them *to be* rulers of thousands, rulers of hundreds, rulers of fifties, and rulers of tens. 22And let them judge the people at all times. Then it will be *that* every great matter they shall bring to you, but every small matter they themselves shall judge. So it will be easier for you, for they will bear *the burden* with you. 23If you do this thing, and God *so* commands you, then you will be able to endure, and all this people will also go to their place in peace."

24So Moses heeded the voice of his father-in-law and did all that he had said. 25And Moses chose able men out of all Israel, and made them heads over the people: rulers of thousands, rulers of hundreds, rulers of fifties, and rulers of tens. 26So they judged the people at all times; the hard cases they brought to Moses, but they judged every small case themselves.

27Then Moses let his father-in-law depart, and he went his way to his own land.

18:17–20 *Counsel.* Sometimes an outsider can see things more clearly than those who are doing the work, and we must always be open to counsel (Prov. 12:15; 13:10). Moses was trying to do all the work himself, and he was not making a distinction between major matters and minor problems. He needed assistants, and he needed priorities. Note that Jethro expected Moses to seek God's will in the matter (v. 23). What seems like good counsel from men might be bad counsel in God's sight, so we must always ask for God's directions (Acts 27:9–14).

18:21 *Leadership.* Verse 21 describes the kind of leaders God needs, people characterized by ability, the fear of God, honesty, and a hatred for covetousness. (See Acts 6:3 for additional leadership qualities.) Moses was a great man, but he could not do the job alone. God may not call you to be a leader, but He may want you to help a leader do a better job.

18:12 *u*Following Masoretic Text and Septuagint; Syriac, Targum, and Vulgate read *offered.*

CHAPTER 19

19:3–6 *A special people.* At the Red Sea, God separated His people from their old life; at Sinai, He brought them into a new life, a covenant relationship with Himself. It was like a wedding ceremony, with God as the Husband and Israel as the wife. Whenever the nation turned from God to idols, God accused them of committing adultery (Isa. 1:21; Jer. 3:1–5). Believers today must also beware this sin (James 4:4). The church is a nation of kings and priests (1 Pet. 2:5, 9) called to glorify God.

19:14 *A sanctified people.* Because we belong to God, we must be separated from sin (vv. 10, 14, 22). God's people are set apart from the world and unto the Lord.

19:16–25 *A submissive people.* To impress the people with the fear of the Lord, God demonstrated His power at Sinai and warned them not to come near. It was the childhood of the nation, and the people, like children, learned from rewards and punishments. Hebrews 12:18–29 contrasts this experience with that of the New Testament believer today. We must still fear the Lord and respect the boundaries He establishes, but we are invited to "draw near" (Heb. 10:19–25). The Israelites were not saved from Egypt by obeying the Law, but their obedience enabled them to enjoy all the blessings God had for them.

19 In the third month after the children of Israel had gone out of the land of Egypt, on the same day, they came to the Wilderness of Sinai. ²For they had departed from Rephidim, had come to the Wilderness of Sinai, and camped in the wilderness. So Israel camped there before the mountain.

³*And Moses went up to God, and the Lord called to him from the mountain, saying, "Thus you shall say to the house of Jacob, and tell the children of Israel: ⁴'You have seen what I did to the Egyptians, and *how* I bore you on eagles' wings and brought you to Myself. ⁵Now therefore, if you will indeed obey My voice and keep My covenant, then you shall be a special treasure to Me above all people; for all the earth *is* Mine. ⁶And you shall be to Me a kingdom of priests and a holy nation.' These *are* the words which you shall speak to the children of Israel."

⁷So Moses came and called for the elders of the people, and laid before them all these words which the Lord commanded him. ⁸Then all the people answered together and said, "All that the Lord has spoken we will do." So Moses brought back the words of the people to the Lord. ⁹And the Lord said to Moses, "Behold, I come to you in the thick cloud, that the people may hear when I speak with you, and believe you forever."

So Moses told the words of the people to the Lord.

¹⁰Then the Lord said to Moses, "Go to the people and consecrate them today and tomorrow, and let them wash their clothes. ¹¹And let them be ready for the third day. For on the third day the Lord will come down upon Mount Sinai in the sight of all the people. ¹²You shall set bounds for the people all around, saying, 'Take heed to yourselves *that* you do *not* go up to the mountain or touch its base. Whoever touches the mountain shall surely be put to death. ¹³Not a hand shall touch him, but he shall surely be stoned or shot *with an arrow;* whether man or beast, he shall not live.' When the trumpet sounds long, they shall come near the mountain."

¹⁴*So Moses went down from the mountain to the people and sanctified the people, and they washed their clothes. ¹⁵And he said to the people, "Be ready for the third day; do not come near your wives."

¹⁶*Then it came to pass on the third day, in the morning, that there were thunderings and lightnings, and a thick cloud on the mountain; and the sound of the trumpet was very loud, so that all the people who *were* in the camp trembled. ¹⁷And Moses brought the people out of the camp to meet with God, and they stood at the foot of the mountain. ¹⁸Now Mount Sinai *was* completely in smoke, because the Lord descended upon it in fire. Its smoke ascended like the smoke of a furnace, and the whole mountainᵛ quaked greatly. ¹⁹And when the blast of the trumpet sounded long and became louder and louder, Moses spoke, and God answered him by voice. ²⁰Then the Lord came down upon Mount Sinai, on the top of the

19:18 ᵛSeptuagint reads *all the people.*

We Are Set Apart—To be sanctified means to be set apart for God's exclusive use and pleasure. Christians are set apart by the death of Christ (Heb. 10:10), the indwelling Spirit (Rom. 15:16), and the Word of God (John 17:17; Eph. 5:26).

mountain. And the LORD called Moses to the top of the mountain, and Moses went up.

21And the LORD said to Moses, "Go down and warn the people, lest they break through to gaze at the LORD, and many of them perish. 22Also let the priests who come near the LORD consecrate themselves, lest the LORD break out against them."

23But Moses said to the LORD, "The people cannot come up to Mount Sinai; for You warned us, saying, 'Set bounds around the mountain and consecrate it.'"

24Then the LORD said to him, "Away! Get down and then come up, you and Aaron with you. But do not let the priests and the people break through to come up to the LORD, lest He break out against them." 25So Moses went down to the people and spoke to them.

20 And* God spoke all these words, saying:
2 *"I am the LORD your God, who brought you out of the land of Egypt, out of the house of bondage.
3 "You shall have no other gods before Me.
4 "You shall not make for yourself a carved image—any likeness of anything that is in heaven above, or that is in the earth beneath, or that is in the water under the earth; 5you shall not bow down to them nor serve them. For I, the LORD your God, am a jealous God, visiting the iniquity of the fathers upon the children to the third and fourth generations of those who hate Me, 6but showing mercy to thousands, to those who love Me and keep My commandments.
7 "You shall not take the name of the LORD your God in vain, for the LORD will not hold him guiltless who takes His name in vain.
8 "Remember the Sabbath day, to keep it holy. 9Six days you shall labor and do all your work, 10but the seventh day is the Sabbath of the LORD your God. In it you shall do no work: you, nor your son, nor your daughter, nor your male servant, nor your female servant, nor your cattle, nor your stranger who is within your gates. 11For in six days the LORD made the heavens and the earth, the sea, and all that is in them, and rested the seventh day. Therefore the LORD blessed the Sabbath day and hallowed it.
12 "Honor your father and your mother, that your days may be long upon the land which the LORD your God is giving you.
13 "You shall not murder.
14 "You shall not commit adultery.
15 "You shall not steal.
16 "You shall not bear false witness against your neighbor.
17 "You shall not covet your neighbor's house; you shall not covet your neighbor's wife, nor his male servant, nor his female servant, nor his ox, nor his donkey, nor anything that is your neighbor's."

18Now all the people witnessed the thunderings, the lightning flashes, the sound of the trumpet, and the mountain smoking; and when the people saw it, they trembled and stood afar off. 19Then they said to Moses, "You speak with us, and we

CHAPTER 20

20:1ff The Law does not save sinners (Gal. 2:21; 3:21); it reveals God's holiness and man's need for salvation (Rom. 3:20). It is a mirror that shows us how dirty we are (James 1:22—23), but it does not provide the cleansing we need. Only Christ can do that.

Under the old covenant, God's law was written on tables of stone (Exod. 24:12), but under the new covenant, God writes His word on our hearts (2 Cor. 3:1–3). As you meditate on the Word, the Spirit makes it a part of your inner being, and you become more like the Lord Jesus Christ (2 Cor. 3:18). The Holy Spirit enables us to fulfill the righteous demands of God's law (Rom. 8:1–4).

20:2–11 The first four commandments deal with our relationship with God, while the last six deal with our relationship with others. If we love God and obey Him, we will also love others and serve them. (See Matt. 22:34–40.)

Some people obey God because of fear (vv. 18–21). Others obey only because they want His blessing. The highest motive for obedience is our love for the Lord. But what if we disobey the Lord? God made provision for Israel in the prescribed sacrifices (vv. 22–26). He has made provision for believers today through the work of Christ (1 John 1:9—2:2). Believers are not under law but under grace. This is not an excuse for sin but an encouragement for loving obedience to His will. Ponder Romans 6.

will hear; but let not God speak with us, lest we die."

20And Moses said to the people, "Do not fear; for God has come to test you, and that His fear may be before you, so that you may not sin." 21So the people stood afar off, but Moses drew near the thick darkness where God *was*.

22Then the LORD said to Moses, "Thus you shall say to the children of Israel: 'You have seen that I have talked with you from heaven. 23You shall not make *anything to be* with Me—gods of silver or gods of gold you shall not make for yourselves. 24An altar of earth you shall make for Me, and you shall sacrifice on it your burnt offerings and your peace offerings, your sheep and your oxen. In every place where I record My name I will come to you, and I will bless you. 25And if you make Me an altar of stone, you shall not build it of hewn stone; for if you use your tool on it, you have profaned it. 26Nor shall you go up by steps to My altar, that your nakedness may not be exposed on it.'

CHAPTER 21

21:1–36 Having stated His basic law, God then told Moses how to apply it to specific situations so that everybody would receive equal justice, which is the principle in verses 22–25. No person was to take the law into his or her own hands. When it comes to *personal* retaliation, we must obey Matthew 5:38–48.

God's law shows that He is concerned about everything: men, women, children, the unborn, property, and even animals. This is His creation, and He has the right to tell us how to manage it. The Law did not change people's hearts, but it did help to control their conduct and give order to the nation. Laws and government have been instituted by God, and we should respect them (Rom. 13).

Some penalties given here may seem harsh to us; but keep in mind that the nation was in its "childhood" (Gal. 4:1–7), and children learn best through rewards and punishments. Forty years later, when the new generation was on the scene, Moses emphasized love when he repeated the Law (Deut. 4:37; 6:4–6; 7:6–13). Love is the fulfilling of the Law (Rom. 13:8–10).

21 "Now* these *are* the judgments which you shall set before them: 2If you buy a Hebrew servant, he shall serve six years; and in the seventh he shall go out free and pay nothing. 3If he comes in by himself, he shall go out by himself; if he *comes in* married, then his wife shall go out with him. 4If his master has given him a wife, and she has borne him sons or daughters, the wife and her children shall be her master's, and he shall go out by himself. 5But if the servant plainly says, 'I love my master, my wife, and my children; I will not go out free,' 6then his master shall bring him to the judges. He shall also bring him to the door, or to the doorpost, and his master shall pierce his ear with an awl; and he shall serve him forever.

7"And if a man sells his daughter to be a female slave, she shall not go out as the male slaves do. 8If she does not please her master, who has betrothed her to himself, then he shall let her be redeemed. He shall have no right to sell her to a foreign people, since he has dealt deceitfully with her. 9And if he has betrothed her to his son, he shall deal with her according to the custom of daughters. 10If he takes another *wife,* he shall not diminish her food, her clothing, and her marriage rights. 11And if he does not do these three for her, then she shall go out free, without *paying* money.

12"He who strikes a man so that he dies shall surely be put to death. 13However, if he did not lie in wait, but God delivered *him* into his hand, then I will appoint for you a place where he may flee.

14"But if a man acts with premeditation against his neighbor, to kill him by treachery, you shall take him from My altar, that he may die.

15"And he who strikes his father or his mother shall surely be put to death.

16"He who kidnaps a man and sells him, or if he is found in his hand, shall surely be put to death.

17"And he who curses his father or his mother shall surely be put to death.

18"If men contend with each other, and one strikes the other with a stone or with *his* fist, and he does not die but is confined to *his* bed, 19if he rises again and walks about outside with his staff, then he who struck *him* shall be acquitted. He shall only pay *for* the loss of his time, and shall provide *for him* to be thoroughly healed.

20"And if a man beats his male or female servant with a rod, so that he dies under his hand, he shall surely be punished. 21Notwithstanding, if he remains alive a day or two, he shall not be punished; for he *is* his property.

22"If men fight, and hurt a woman with child, so that she gives birth prematurely, yet no harm follows, he shall surely be punished accordingly as the woman's husband imposes on him; and he shall pay as the judges *determine.* 23But if *any* harm follows, then you shall give life for life, 24eye for eye, tooth for tooth, hand for hand, foot for foot, 25burn for burn, wound for wound, stripe for stripe.

26"If a man strikes the eye of his male or female servant, and destroys it, he shall let him go free for the sake of his eye. 27And if he knocks out the tooth of his male or female servant, he shall let him go free for the sake of his tooth.

28"If an ox gores a man or a woman to death, then the ox shall surely be stoned, and its flesh shall not be eaten; but the owner of the ox *shall be* acquitted. 29But if the ox tended to thrust with its horn in times past, and it has been made known to his owner, and he has not kept it confined, so that it has killed a man or a woman, the ox shall be stoned and its owner also shall be put to death. 30If there is imposed on him a sum of money, then he shall pay to redeem his life, whatever is imposed on him. 31Whether it has gored a son or gored a daughter, according to this judgment it shall be done to him. 32If the ox gores a male or female servant, he shall give to their master thirty shekels of silver, and the ox shall be stoned.

33"And if a man opens a pit, or if a man digs a pit and does not cover it, and an ox or a donkey falls in it, 34the owner of the pit shall make *it* good; he shall give money to their owner, but the dead *animal* shall be his.

35"If one man's ox hurts another's, so that it dies, then they shall sell the live ox and divide the money from it; and the dead ox they shall also divide. 36Or if it was known that the ox tended to thrust in time past, and its owner has not kept it confined, he shall surely pay ox for ox, and the dead animal shall be his own.

22 "If* a man steals an ox or a sheep, and slaughters it or sells it, he shall restore five oxen for an ox and four sheep for a sheep. 2If the thief is found breaking in, and he is struck so that he dies, *there shall be* no guilt for his bloodshed. 3If the sun has risen on him, *there shall be* guilt for his bloodshed. He should make full restitution; if he has nothing, then he shall be sold for his theft. 4If the theft is certainly found alive in his hand, whether it is an ox or donkey or sheep, he shall restore double.

5"If a man causes a field or vineyard to be grazed, and lets loose his animal, and it feeds in another man's field, he shall make restitution from the best of his own field and the best of his own vineyard.

6"If fire breaks out and catches in thorns, so that stacked grain, standing grain, or the field is consumed, he who kindled the fire shall surely make restitution.

7"If a man delivers to his neighbor money or articles to keep, and it is stolen out of the man's house, if the thief is found, he shall pay double.

CHAPTER 22

22:1–15 *Property.* God wants us to respect personal property, and the key idea here is *restitution* (vv. 3, 5, 6, 12). It is not enough to admit the crime and show sorrow over it. There must also be a readiness to make things right with those who have been hurt (Prov. 6:30–31; Luke 19:8). David knew verse 1 and could apply it to others (2 Sam. 12:1–6), but he did not apply Exodus 20:13–14 to himself.

8If the thief is not found, then the master of the house shall be brought to the judges *to see* whether he has put his hand into his neighbor's goods.

9"For any kind of trespass, *whether it concerns* an ox, a donkey, a sheep, or clothing, *or* for any kind of lost thing which *another* claims to be his, the cause of both parties shall come before the judges; *and* whomever the judges condemn shall pay double to his neighbor. 10If a man delivers to his neighbor a donkey, an ox, a sheep, or any animal to keep, and it dies, is hurt, or driven away, no one seeing *it*, 11then an oath of the LORD shall be between them both, that he has not put his hand into his neighbor's goods; and the owner of it shall accept *that*, and he shall not make *it* good. 12But if, in fact, it is stolen from him, he shall make restitution to the owner of it. 13If it is torn to pieces *by a beast, then* he shall bring it as evidence, *and* he shall not make good what was torn.

14"And if a man borrows *anything* from his neighbor, and it becomes injured or dies, the owner of it not *being* with it, he shall surely make *it* good. 15If its owner *was* with it, he shall not make *it* good; if it *was* hired, it came for its hire.

16*"If a man entices a virgin who is not betrothed, and lies with her, he shall surely pay the bride-price for her *to be* his wife. 17If her father utterly refuses to give her to him, he shall pay money according to the bride-price of virgins.

18"You shall not permit a sorceress to live.

19"Whoever lies with an animal shall surely be put to death.

20"He who sacrifices to *any* god, except to the LORD only, he shall be utterly destroyed.

21"You shall neither mistreat a stranger nor oppress him, for you were strangers in the land of Egypt.

22"You shall not afflict any widow or fatherless child. 23If you afflict them in any way, *and* they cry at all to Me, I will surely hear their cry; 24and My wrath will become hot, and I will kill you with the sword; your wives shall be widows, and your children fatherless.

25"If you lend money to *any of* My people *who are* poor among you, you shall not be like a moneylender to him; you shall not charge him interest. 26If you ever take your neighbor's garment as a pledge, you shall return it to him before the sun goes down. 27For that *is* his only covering, it *is* his garment for his skin. What will he sleep in? And it will be that when he cries to Me, I will hear, for I *am* gracious.

28*"You shall not revile God, nor curse a ruler of your people.

29"You shall not delay *to offer* the first of your ripe produce and your juices. The firstborn of your sons you shall give to Me. 30Likewise you shall do with your oxen *and* your sheep. It shall be with its mother seven days; on the eighth day you shall give it to Me.

31"And you shall be holy men to Me: you shall not eat meat torn *by beasts* in the field; you shall throw it to the dogs.

23 "You* shall not circulate a false report. Do not put your hand with the wicked to be an unrighteous witness. 2You shall not follow a crowd to do evil; nor shall you testify in a dispute so as to turn aside after many to pervert *justice*.

22:16–27 *Persons.* These many laws reveal the holiness of God and His desire that we be a holy people (v. 31). When obeyed, these laws protected the people from violence, extortion, oppression, and affliction. God has compassion on widows and orphans, poor workers (James 5:1–4), and strangers. Do we?

22:28–31 *Principles.* Respect God and put Him first in everything. Jesus summarized it in Matthew 6:33. If we truly love God with all our hearts, we will have no desire to hurt others. But if God is not first, we will start exploiting people to get what we want.

CHAPTER 23

23:1–9 *Consideration.* Treating people justly would seem to be an easy thing to do, but the sinful human heart can lead us astray with rumors (2 Cor. 13:1), false witnesses, crowds, and money. The fact that a person is rich or poor, a friend or an enemy, must not blind us to the truth. Integrity must not be for sale.

3You shall not show partiality to a poor man in his dispute.

4"If you meet your enemy's ox or his donkey going astray, you shall surely bring it back to him again. 5If you see the donkey of one who hates you lying under its burden, and you would refrain from helping it, you shall surely help him with it.

6"You shall not pervert the judgment of your poor in his dispute. 7Keep yourself far from a false matter; do not kill the innocent and righteous. For I will not justify the wicked. 8And you shall take no bribe, for a bribe blinds the discerning and perverts the words of the righteous.

9"Also you shall not oppress a stranger, for you know the heart of a stranger, because you were strangers in the land of Egypt.

10"Six years you shall sow your land and gather in its produce, 11but the seventh year you shall let it rest and lie fallow, that the poor of your people may eat; and what they leave, the beasts of the field may eat. In like manner you shall do with your vineyard and your olive grove. 12Six days you shall do your work, and on the seventh day you shall rest, that your ox and your donkey may rest, and the son of your female servant and the stranger may be refreshed.

13"And in all that I have said to you, be circumspect and make no mention of the name of other gods, nor let it be heard from your mouth.

14*"Three times you shall keep a feast to Me in the year: 15You shall keep the Feast of Unleavened Bread (you shall eat unleavened bread seven days, as I commanded you, at the time appointed in the month of Abib, for in it you came out of Egypt; none shall appear before Me empty); 16and the Feast of Harvest, the firstfruits of your labors which you have sown in the field; and the Feast of Ingathering at the end of the year, when you have gathered in the fruit of your labors from the field.

17"Three times in the year all your males shall appear before the Lord GOD.w

18"You shall not offer the blood of My sacrifice with leavened bread; nor shall the fat of My sacrifice remain until morning. 19The first of the firstfruits of your land you shall bring into the house of the LORD your God. You shall not boil a young goat in its mother's milk.

20*"Behold, I send an Angel before you to keep you in the way and to bring you into the place which I have prepared. 21Beware of Him and obey His voice; do not provoke Him, for He will not pardon your transgressions; for My name is in Him. 22But if you indeed obey His voice and do all that I speak, then I will be an enemy to your enemies and an adversary to your adversaries. 23For My Angel will go before you and bring you in to the Amorites and the Hittites and the Perizzites and the Canaanites and the Hivites and the Jebusites; and I will cut them off. 24You shall not bow down to their gods, nor serve them, nor do according to their works; but you shall utterly overthrow them and completely break down their sacred pillars.

25"So you shall serve the LORD your God, and He will bless your bread and your water. And I will take sickness away from the midst of you. 26No one shall suffer miscarriage or be barren in

23:10–13 Conservation. The Sabbath was God's special gift to Israel to mark the nation as His holy people (Exod. 31:13–17). It was also His gift to man and beast to provide needed rest. The Sabbatical Year showed His concern for the land and the poor. It is unfortunate that people today have forgotten these lessons and are destroying creation by their exploitation of resources.

23:14–17 Celebration. God wants His people to celebrate and rejoice in His goodness. If our celebration ignores the Lord, we are guilty of idolatry. (See 1 Tim. 6:17.)

23:20 Consecration. The nation would be entering enemy territory and would be tempted to compromise with the wicked people of the land. They must not even speak about the false gods (v. 13) lest they would be led to bow down and serve those gods (v. 24) and make covenants with them (v. 32). Do not talk yourself into disobeying God!

23:17 wHebrew YHWH, usually translated LORD

your land; I will fulfill the number of your days.
²⁷"I will send My fear before you, I will cause confusion among all the people to whom you come, and will make all your enemies turn *their* backs to you. ²⁸And I will send hornets before you, which shall drive out the Hivite, the Canaanite, and the Hittite from before you. ²⁹I will not drive them out from before you in one year, lest the land become desolate and the beasts of the field become too numerous for you. ³⁰Little by little I will drive them out from before you, until you have increased, and you inherit the land. ³¹And I will set your bounds from the Red Sea to the sea, Philistia, and from the desert to the River.ˣ For I will deliver the inhabitants of the land into your hand, and you shall drive them out before you. ³²You shall make no covenant with them, nor with their gods. ³³They shall not dwell in your land, lest they make you sin against Me. For *if* you serve their gods, it will surely be a snare to you."

CHAPTER 24

24:1–18 There are degrees of nearness to God. The people remained at a distance because of their fear of the Lord. Moses, Joshua, Nadab, Abihu, Aaron, and seventy of the elders went up the mountain to meet God. Then Moses and Joshua went further, and finally Moses went into the glory cloud alone.

J. Oswald Sanders wisely commented, "We are at this moment *as close to God as we really choose to be.*" God invites us to draw near (James 4:8), but often we are unwilling to do what is necessary to meet Him. The people below had the Book and the blood, and they made promises to obey God; but they did not have the vision of the glory of the Lord that Moses had on the mount.

24:10, 11 You would think verse 11 would read, "So they saw God, and they fell down and prayed." But it says, "They ate and drank." The vision of God's glory should not make us careless or impractical. We can eat and drink to His glory (1 Cor. 10:31). But beware lest nearness to God lead to careless familiarity, for "our God is a consuming fire" (Heb. 12:28–29). Nadab and Abihu would find that out (Lev. 10:1ff.).

24 Now* He said to Moses, "Come up to the LORD, you and Aaron, Nadab and Abihu, and seventy of the elders of Israel, and worship from afar. ²And Moses alone shall come near the LORD, but they shall not come near; nor shall the people go up with him."

³So Moses came and told the people all the words of the LORD and all the judgments. And all the people answered with one voice and said, "All the words which the LORD has said we will do." ⁴And Moses wrote all the words of the LORD. And he rose early in the morning, and built an altar at the foot of the mountain, and twelve pillars according to the twelve tribes of Israel. ⁵Then he sent young men of the children of Israel, who offered burnt offerings and sacrificed peace offerings of oxen to the LORD. ⁶And Moses took half the blood and put *it* in basins, and half the blood he sprinkled on the altar. ⁷Then he took the Book of the Covenant and read in the hearing of the people. And they said, "All that the LORD has said we will do, and be obedient." ⁸And Moses took the blood, sprinkled *it* on the people, and said, "This is the blood of the covenant which the LORD has made with you according to all these words."

⁹Then Moses went up, also Aaron, Nadab, and Abihu, and seventy of the elders of Israel, ¹⁰*and they saw the God of Israel. And *there was* under His feet as it were a paved work of sapphire stone, and it was like the very heavens in *its* clarity. ¹¹But on the nobles of the children of Israel He did not lay His hand. So they saw God, and they ate and drank.

¹²Then the LORD said to Moses, "Come up to Me on the mountain and be there; and I will give you tablets of stone, and the law and commandments which I have written, that you may teach them."

¹³So Moses arose with his assistant Joshua, and Moses went up to the mountain of God. ¹⁴And he said to the elders, "Wait here for us until we come back to you. Indeed, Aaron and Hur *are* with you. If any man has a difficulty, let him go to them." ¹⁵Then Moses went up into the mountain, and a cloud covered the mountain.

¹⁶Now the glory of the LORD rested on Mount

23:31 ˣHebrew *Nahar,* the Euphrates

Sinai, and the cloud covered it six days. And on the seventh day He called to Moses out of the midst of the cloud. 17The sight of the glory of the LORD *was* like a consuming fire on the top of the mountain in the eyes of the children of Israel. 18So Moses went into the midst of the cloud and went up into the mountain. And Moses was on the mountain forty days and forty nights.

25 Then* the LORD spoke to Moses, saying: 2"Speak to the children of Israel, that they bring Me an offering. From everyone who gives it willingly with his heart you shall take My offering. 3And this *is* the offering which you shall take from them: gold, silver, and bronze; 4blue, purple, and scarlet *thread,* fine linen, and goats' *hair;* 5ram skins dyed red, badger skins, and acacia wood; 6oil for the light, and spices for the anointing oil and for the sweet incense; 7onyx stones, and stones to be set in the ephod and in the breastplate. 8And let them make Me a sanctuary, that I may dwell among them. 9*According to all that I show you, *that is,* the pattern of the tabernacle and the pattern of all its furnishings, just so you shall make *it.*

10*"And they shall make an ark of acacia wood; two and a half cubits *shall be* its length, a cubit and a half its width, and a cubit and a half its height. 11And you shall overlay it with pure gold, inside and out you shall overlay it, and shall make on it a molding of gold all around. 12You shall cast four rings of gold for it, and put *them* in its four corners; two rings *shall be* on one side, and two rings on the other side. 13And you shall make poles *of* acacia wood, and overlay them with gold. 14You shall put the poles into the rings on the sides of the ark, that the ark may be carried by them. 15The poles shall be in the rings of the ark; they shall not be taken from it. 16And you shall put into the ark the Testimony which I will give you.

17"You shall make a mercy seat of pure gold; two and a half cubits *shall be* its length and a cubit and a half its width. 18And you shall make two cherubim of gold; of hammered work you shall make them at the two ends of the mercy seat. 19Make one cherub at one end, and the other cherub at the other end; you shall make the cherubim at the two ends of it *of one piece* with the mercy seat. 20And the cherubim shall stretch out *their* wings above, covering the mercy seat with their wings, and they shall face one another; the faces of the cherubim *shall be* toward the mercy seat. 21You shall put the mercy seat on top of the ark, and in the ark you shall put the Testimony that I will give you. 22And there I will meet with you, and I will speak with you from above the mercy seat, from between the two cherubim which *are* on the ark of the Testimony, about everything which I will give you in commandment to the children of Israel.

23*"You shall also make a table of acacia wood; two cubits *shall be* its length, a cubit its width, and a cubit and a half its height. 24And you shall overlay it with pure gold, and make a molding of gold all around. 25You shall make for it a frame of a handbreadth all around, and you shall make a gold molding for the frame all around. 26And you shall make for it four rings of gold, and put the rings on the four corners that *are* at its four legs. 27The rings shall be close to the frame, as holders for the poles to bear the table. 28And you

CHAPTER 25

25:1–8 *An offering.* God could have made the whole tabernacle in an instant of creative power, but instead He asked the people to bring Him their offerings. They were privileged to make a sanctuary for God. Today, we are helping to build His church, and we must use only the best materials (1 Cor. 3:9–23). Are you giving willingly to God what He has given to you?

25:9 *A pattern.* God gave Moses the pattern for the tabernacle just as He later gave David the pattern for the temple (1 Chron. 28:19). When God wants a work done on earth, He has a plan for His people to follow. It is dangerous to turn from God's plan and follow the wisdom of this world (1 Cor. 3:18–20).

25:10–16 The ark was the throne of God in the Holy of Holies, and God's glory dwelt between the cherubim on the mercy seat (Ps. 99:1). Our mercy seat is in heaven (Heb. 4:11–16), and the way is always open to God.

25:23–30 The table reminds us that God is the source of our sustenance (Matt. 6:11). The bread also speaks of the spiritual nourishment we have in His Word (Deut. 8:3; Matt. 4:4). The golden candlestick tells us that "God is light" (1 John 1:5) and that we are to be lights in this dark world (Matt. 5:14–16). Just as the lamps were fed by the oil, so we must have the power of the Spirit to be effective witnesses for the Lord (Acts 1:8).

shall make the poles of acacia wood, and overlay them with gold, that the table may be carried with them. ²⁹You shall make its dishes, its pans, its pitchers, and its bowls for pouring. You shall make them of pure gold. ³⁰And you shall set the showbread on the table before Me always.

³¹"You shall also make a lampstand of pure gold; the lampstand shall be of hammered work. Its shaft, its branches, its bowls, its *ornamental* knobs, and flowers shall be *of one piece.* ³²And six branches shall come out of its sides: three branches of the lampstand out of one side, and three branches of the lampstand out of the other side. ³³Three bowls *shall be* made like almond *blossoms* on one branch, *with* an *ornamental* knob and a flower, and three bowls made like almond *blossoms* on the other branch, *with* an *ornamental* knob and a flower—and so for the six branches that come out of the lampstand. ³⁴On the lampstand itself four bowls *shall be* made like almond *blossoms, each with* its *ornamental* knob and flower. ³⁵And *there shall be* a knob under the *first* two branches of the same, a knob under the *second* two branches of the same, and a knob under the *third* two branches of the same, according to the six branches that extend from the lampstand. ³⁶Their knobs and their branches *shall be of one piece;* all of it *shall be* one hammered piece of pure gold. ³⁷You shall make seven lamps for it, and they shall arrange its lamps so that they give light in front of it. ³⁸And its wick-trimmers and their trays *shall be* of pure gold. ³⁹It shall be made of a talent of pure gold, with all these utensils. ⁴⁰And see to it that you make *them* according to the pattern which was shown you on the mountain.

CHAPTER 26

26:1–14 Ten curtains, fifty loops, fifty clasps, forty sockets, twenty boards, two veils—yet it was one sanctuary: "That it may be one tabernacle" (v. 6); "That it may be one" (v. 11). Diversity, yes; but unity in diversity.

There was only *one plan* for the tabernacle, and it came from God (v. 30). Man's cleverness and wisdom may bring success in the things of the world (Luke 16:8), but they will destroy the work of the Lord (1 Cor. 3:16–23). Be sure you get your plans from heaven and not from the world.

26 "Moreover* you shall make the tabernacle *with* ten curtains *of* fine woven linen and blue, purple, and scarlet *thread;* with artistic designs of cherubim you shall weave them. ²The length of each curtain *shall be* twenty-eight cubits, and the width of each curtain four cubits. And every one of the curtains shall have the same measurements. ³Five curtains shall be coupled to one another, and *the other* five curtains *shall be* coupled to one another. ⁴And you shall make loops of blue *yarn* on the edge of the curtain on the selvedge of *one* set, and likewise you shall do on the outer edge of *the other* curtain of the second set. ⁵Fifty loops you shall make in the one curtain, and fifty loops you shall make on the edge of the curtain that *is* on the end of the second set, that the loops may be clasped to one another. ⁶And you shall make fifty clasps of gold, and couple the curtains together with the clasps, so that it may be one tabernacle.

⁷"You shall also make curtains of goats' *hair,* to be a tent over the tabernacle. You shall make eleven curtains. ⁸The length of each curtain *shall be* thirty cubits, and the width of each curtain four cubits; and the eleven curtains shall all have the same measurements. ⁹And you shall couple five curtains by themselves and six curtains by themselves, and you shall double over the sixth curtain at the forefront of the tent. ¹⁰You shall make fifty loops on the edge of the curtain that is outermost in *one* set, and fifty loops on the edge of the curtain of the second set. ¹¹And you shall make fifty bronze clasps, put the clasps into the loops, and couple the tent together, that it may be one. ¹²The remnant that remains of the curtains of the

tent, the half curtain that remains, shall hang over the back of the tabernacle. 13And a cubit on one side and a cubit on the other side, of what remains of the length of the curtains of the tent, shall hang over the sides of the tabernacle, on this side and on that side, to cover it.

14"You shall also make a covering of ram skins dyed red for the tent, and a covering of badger skins above that.

15"And for the tabernacle you shall make the boards of acacia wood, standing upright. 16*Ten cubits *shall be* the length of a board, and a cubit and a half *shall be* the width of each board. 17Two tenons *shall be* in each board for binding one to another. Thus you shall make for all the boards of the tabernacle. 18And you shall make the boards for the tabernacle, twenty boards for the south side. 19You shall make forty sockets of silver under the twenty boards: two sockets under each of the boards for its two tenons. 20And for the second side of the tabernacle, on the north side, *there shall be* twenty boards 21and their forty sockets of silver: two sockets under each of the boards. 22For the far side of the tabernacle, westward, you shall make six boards. 23And you shall also make two boards for the two back corners of the tabernacle. 24They shall be coupled together at the bottom and they shall be coupled together at the top by one ring. Thus it shall be for both of them. They shall be for the two corners. 25So there shall be eight boards with their sockets of silver—sixteen sockets—two sockets under each of the boards.

26"And you shall make bars of acacia wood: five for the boards on one side of the tabernacle, 27five bars for the boards on the other side of the tabernacle, and five bars for the boards of the side of the tabernacle, for the far side westward. 28The middle bar shall pass through the midst of the boards from end to end. 29You shall overlay the boards with gold, make their rings of gold *as* holders for the bars, and overlay the bars with gold. 30And you shall raise up the tabernacle according to its pattern which you were shown on the mountain.

31*"You shall make a veil woven of blue, purple, and scarlet *thread,* and fine woven linen. It shall be woven with an artistic design of cherubim. 32You shall hang it upon the four pillars of acacia *wood* overlaid with gold. Their hooks *shall be* gold, upon four sockets of silver. 33And you shall hang the veil from the clasps. Then you shall bring the ark of the Testimony in there, behind the veil. The veil shall be a divider for you between the holy *place* and the Most Holy. 34You shall put the mercy seat upon the ark of the Testimony in the Most Holy. 35You shall set the table outside the veil, and the lampstand across from the table on the side of the tabernacle toward the south; and you shall put the table on the north side.

36"You shall make a screen for the door of the tabernacle, *woven of* blue, purple, and scarlet *thread,* and fine woven linen, made by a weaver. 37And you shall make for the screen five pillars of acacia *wood,* and overlay them with gold; their hooks *shall be* gold, and you shall cast five sockets of bronze for them.

27 "You* shall make an altar of acacia wood, five cubits long and five cubits wide—the altar shall be square—and its height *shall be* three cubits. 2You shall make its horns on its four

26:16 There was *one set of measurements* for the building (v. 2). When we measure ministry by God's standards, we will have unity, but if we use our own standards, there will be division.

26:31, 32 They used only *the materials* that God told them to use. In 1 Corinthians 3:10–16, read about building with the proper materials that will endure. Note the emphasis on gold in chapter 37, silver in chapter 38, and precious stones in chapter 39.

The sanctuary was indwelt by *one glory,* the glory of God. When man brings in his glory, there is division.

Jesus prayed that His people might be one (John 17:20–23). Are you helping to answer that prayer?

CHAPTER 27

The tabernacle was not a gathering place for worship but a place for sacrifice and holy service.

27:1–8 Sacrifice. The first thing one saw was the brazen altar, for no one can come into the presence of God until sin has been dealt with (Lev. 17:11).

corners; its horns shall be of one piece with it. And you shall overlay it with bronze. ³Also you shall make its pans to receive its ashes, and its shovels and its basins and its forks and its fire-pans; you shall make all its utensils of bronze. ⁴You shall make a grate for it, a network of bronze; and on the network you shall make four bronze rings at its four corners. ⁵You shall put it under the rim of the altar beneath, that the net-work may be midway up the altar. ⁶And you shall make poles for the altar, poles of acacia wood, and overlay them with bronze. ⁷The poles shall be put in the rings, and the poles shall be on the two sides of the altar to bear it. ⁸You shall make it hollow with boards; as it was shown you on the mountain, so shall they make *it*.

⁹*"You shall also make the court of the tabernacle. For the south side *there shall be* hangings for the court *made of* fine woven linen, one hundred cubits long for one side. ¹⁰And its twenty pillars and their twenty sockets *shall be* bronze. The hooks of the pillars and their bands *shall be* silver. ¹¹Likewise along the length of the north side *there shall be* hangings one hundred *cubits* long, with its twenty pillars and their twenty sockets of bronze, and the hooks of the pillars and their bands of silver.

¹²"And along the width of the court on the west side *shall be* hangings of fifty cubits, with their ten pillars and their ten sockets. ¹³The width of the court on the east side *shall be* fifty cubits. ¹⁴The hangings on *one* side *of the gate shall be* fifteen cubits, *with* their three pillars and their three sockets. ¹⁵And on the other side *shall be* hangings of fifteen *cubits, with* their three pillars and their three sockets.

¹⁶"For the gate of the court *there shall be* a screen twenty cubits long, *woven of* blue, purple, and scarlet *thread*, and fine woven linen, made by a weaver. It *shall have* four pillars and four sockets. ¹⁷All the pillars around the court shall have bands of silver; their hooks *shall be* of silver and their sockets of bronze. ¹⁸The length of the court *shall be* one hundred cubits, the width fifty throughout, and the height five cubits, *made of* fine woven linen, and its sockets of bronze. ¹⁹All the utensils of the tabernacle for all its service, all its pegs, and all the pegs of the court, *shall be* of bronze.

²⁰*"And you shall command the children of Israel that they bring you pure oil of pressed olives for the light, to cause the lamp to burn continually. ²¹In the tabernacle of meeting, outside the veil which *is* before the Testimony, Aaron and his sons shall tend it from evening until morning before the LORD. *It shall be* a statute forever to their generations on behalf of the children of Israel.

27:9–19 *Separation.* The tent was surrounded by a fence of linen hangings, for only the priests and Levites could enter the sacred courts. The common people were kept out of the courts and the priests out of the Holy of Holies. God wanted *all* His people to be priests (Exod. 19:5–6), but that would not happen until the finished work of Christ on the cross (1 Pet. 2:5, 9). We today have open access to the presence of God through Jesus Christ (Heb. 10:19–25).

27:20, 21 *Shining.* The lampstand stood in the holy place and helped the priests to see as they served. It did not illumine the camp; the glory of God did that (Exod. 40:38). God's people (Phil. 2:15) and His churches (Rev. 1:12, 20) are lights in this dark world. Be sure you keep your lamp trimmed and your light shining (Matt. 5:16).

CHAPTER 28

The priesthood was both a privilege and a responsibility. It was wonderful to wear the glorious garments and be in the holy courts, but being a priest also brought serious obligations.

28:1–4 *They ministered first to the Lord.* Four times in this chapter, God emphasized this point (vv. 1, 3, 4, 41). God's servants must seek to please Him alone (1 Cor. 4:1–7). We must be "bondservants for Jesus' sake" (2 Cor. 4:5).

28 "Now* take Aaron your brother, and his sons with him, from among the children of Israel, that he may minister to Me as priest, Aaron *and* Aaron's sons: Nadab, Abihu, Eleazar, and Ithamar. ²And you shall make holy garments for Aaron your brother, for glory and for beauty. ³So you shall speak to all *who are* gifted artisans, whom I have filled with the spirit of wisdom, that they may make Aaron's garments, to consecrate him, that he may minister to Me as priest. ⁴And these *are* the garments which they shall make: a breastplate, an ephod,ʸ a robe, a skillfully woven

28:4 ʸThat is, an ornamented vest

tunic, a turban, and a sash. So they shall make holy garments for Aaron your brother and his sons, that he may minister to Me as priest.

5"They shall take the gold, blue, purple, and scarlet *thread,* and the fine linen, 6and they shall make the ephod of gold, blue, purple, *and* scarlet *thread,* and fine woven linen, artistically worked. 7It shall have two shoulder straps joined at its two edges, and *so* it shall be joined together. 8And the intricately woven band of the ephod, which *is* on it, shall be of the same workmanship, *made of* gold, blue, purple, and scarlet *thread,* and fine woven linen.

9*"Then you shall take two onyx stones and engrave on them the names of the sons of Israel: 10six of their names on one stone and six names on the other stone, in order of their birth. 11With the work of an engraver in stone, *like* the engravings of a signet, you shall engrave the two stones with the names of the sons of Israel. You shall set them in settings of gold. 12And you shall put the two stones on the shoulders of the ephod *as* memorial stones for the sons of Israel. So Aaron shall bear their names before the LORD on his two shoulders as a memorial. 13You shall also make settings of gold, 14and you shall make two chains of pure gold like braided cords, and fasten the braided chains to the settings.

15"You shall make the breastplate of judgment. Artistically woven according to the workmanship of the ephod you shall make it: of gold, blue, purple, and scarlet *thread,* and fine woven linen, you shall make it. 16It shall be doubled into a square: a span *shall be* its length, and a span *shall be* its width. 17And you shall put settings of stones in it, four rows of stones: *The first* row *shall be* a sardius, a topaz, and an emerald; *this shall be* the first row; 18the second row *shall be* a turquoise, a sapphire, and a diamond; 19the third row, a jacinth, an agate, and an amethyst; 20and the fourth row, a beryl, an onyx, and a jasper. They shall be set in gold settings. 21And the stones shall have the names of the sons of Israel, twelve according to their names, *like* the engravings of a signet, each one with its own name; they shall be according to the twelve tribes.

22"You shall make chains for the breastplate at the end, like braided cords of pure gold. 23And you shall make two rings of gold for the breastplate, and put the two rings on the two ends of the breastplate. 24Then you shall put the two braided *chains* of gold in the two rings which are on the ends of the breastplate; 25and the *other* two ends of the two braided *chains* you shall fasten to the two settings, and put *them* on the shoulder straps of the ephod in the front.

26"You shall make two rings of gold, and put them on the two ends of the breastplate, on the edge of it, which is on the inner side of the ephod. 27And two *other* rings of gold you shall make, and put them on the two shoulder straps, underneath the ephod toward its front, right at the seam above the intricately woven band of the ephod. 28They shall bind the breastplate by means of its rings to the rings of the ephod, using a blue cord, so that it is above the intricately woven band of the ephod, and so that the breastplate does not come loose from the ephod.

29"So Aaron shall bear the names of the sons of Israel on the breastplate of judgment over his heart, when he goes into the holy *place,* as a memorial before the LORD continually. 30And you

28:9–14 *They ministered to the people.* God's people are like jewels to Him (Mal. 3:17). Our great High Priest carries us over His heart and on His shoulders. He represents us before the throne of God so that we are "accepted in the Beloved" (Eph. 1:6).

shall put in the breastplate of judgment the Urim and the Thummim,z and they shall be over Aaron's heart when he goes in before the LORD. So Aaron shall bear the judgment of the children of Israel over his heart before the LORD continually. 31"You shall make the robe of the ephod all of blue. 32There shall be an opening for his head in the middle of it; it shall have a woven binding all around its opening, like the opening in a coat of mail, so that it does not tear. 33And upon its hem you shall make pomegranates of blue, purple, and scarlet, all around its hem, and bells of gold between them all around: 34a golden bell and a pomegranate, a golden bell and a pomegranate, upon the hem of the robe all around. 35And it shall be upon Aaron when he ministers, and its sound will be heard when he goes into the holy *place* before the LORD and when he comes out, that he may not die.

36"You shall also make a plate of pure gold and engrave on it, *like* the engraving of a signet:

HOLINESS TO THE LORD.

37And you shall put it on a blue cord, that it may be on the turban; it shall be on the front of the turban. 38So it shall be on Aaron's forehead, that Aaron may bear the iniquity of the holy things which the children of Israel hallow in all their holy gifts; and it shall always be on his forehead, that they may be accepted before the LORD. 39"You shall skillfully weave the tunic of fine linen *thread,* you shall make the turban of fine linen, and you shall make the sash of woven work. 40*"For Aaron's sons you shall make tunics, and you shall make sashes for them. And you shall make hats for them, for glory and beauty. 41So you shall put them on Aaron your brother and on his sons with him. You shall anoint them, consecrate them, and sanctify them, that they may minister to Me as priests. 42And you shall make for them linen trousers to cover their nakedness; they shall reach from the waist to the thighs. 43They shall be on Aaron and on his sons when they come into the tabernacle of meeting, or when they come near the altar to minister in the holy *place,* that they do not incur iniquity and die. *It shall be* a statute forever to him and his descendants after him.

28:40–43 They ministered together. God supplied their needs as they served the people. There was no competition or confusion in the holy tabernacle because they served the same Lord and obeyed the same Word. God has a ministry for each of us, and He will equip us to do it.

CHAPTER 29

29:1 We dedicate, but God consecrates. We surrender, but He sanctifies and sets us apart for His exclusive use. As God's priesthood, His people have experienced *spiritually* what Aaron and his sons experienced physically.

29:4 We have been washed. The blood of Christ has cleansed us (Rev. 1:5–6), and our past is gone (1 Cor. 6:9–11). Sinful hearts are purified not by religious rites but by faith in Jesus Christ (Acts 15:9; Titus 3:5).

29:5, 6 We have been clothed. We stand in the very righteousness of Christ (Isa. 61:10; 2 Cor. 5:21) and wear the garments of God's grace (Col. 3:1ff.).

29:7 We have been anointed. We have the Holy Spirit living within (2 Cor. 1:21; 1 John 2:27), and He enables us to minister.

29 "And* this is what you shall do to them to hallow them for ministering to Me as priests: Take one young bull and two rams without blemish, 2and unleavened bread, unleavened cakes mixed with oil, and unleavened wafers anointed with oil (you shall make them of wheat flour). 3You shall put them in one basket and bring them in the basket, with the bull and the two rams. 4*"And Aaron and his sons you shall bring to the door of the tabernacle of meeting, and you shall wash them with water. 5*Then you shall take the garments, put the tunic on Aaron, and the robe of the ephod, the ephod, and the breastplate, and gird him with the intricately woven band of the ephod. 6You shall put the turban on his head, and put the holy crown on the turban. 7*And you shall take the anointing oil, pour *it* on his head, and anoint him. 8Then you shall bring his sons and put tunics on them. 9And you shall gird them with

---

28:30 zLiterally *the Lights and the Perfections* (compare Leviticus 8:8)

sashes, Aaron and his sons, and put the hats on them. The priesthood shall be theirs for a perpetual statute. So you shall consecrate Aaron and his sons.

10"You shall also have the bull brought before the tabernacle of meeting, and Aaron and his sons shall put their hands on the head of the bull. 11Then you shall kill the bull before the LORD, by the door of the tabernacle of meeting. 12You shall take *some* of the blood of the bull and put *it* on the horns of the altar with your finger, and pour all the blood beside the base of the altar. 13And you shall take all the fat that covers the entrails, the fatty lobe *attached* to the liver, and the two kidneys and the fat that *is* on them, and burn *them* on the altar. 14But the flesh of the bull, with its skin and its offal, you shall burn with fire outside the camp. It *is* a sin offering.

15"You shall also take one ram, and Aaron and his sons shall put their hands on the head of the ram; 16and you shall kill the ram, and you shall take its blood and sprinkle *it* all around on the altar. 17Then you shall cut the ram in pieces, wash its entrails and its legs, and put *them* with its pieces and with its head. 18And you shall burn the whole ram on the altar. It *is* a burnt offering to the LORD; it *is* a sweet aroma, an offering made by fire to the LORD.

19"You shall also take the other ram, and Aaron and his sons shall put their hands on the head of the ram. 20*Then you shall kill the ram, and take some of its blood and put *it* on the tip of the right ear of Aaron and on the tip of the right ear of his sons, on the thumb of their right hand and on the big toe of their right foot, and sprinkle the blood all around on the altar. 21And you shall take some of the blood that is on the altar, and some of the anointing oil, and sprinkle *it* on Aaron and on his garments, on his sons and on the garments of his sons with him; and he and his garments shall be hallowed, and his sons and his sons' garments with him.

22"Also you shall take the fat of the ram, the fat tail, the fat that covers the entrails, the fatty lobe *attached to* the liver, the two kidneys and the fat on them, the right thigh (for it *is* a ram of consecration), 23one loaf of bread, one cake *made with* oil, and one wafer from the basket of the unleavened bread that *is* before the LORD; 24and you shall put all these in the hands of Aaron and in the hands of his sons, and you shall wave them *as* a wave offering before the LORD. 25You shall receive them back from their hands and burn *them* on the altar as a burnt offering, as a sweet aroma before the LORD. It *is* an offering made by fire to the LORD.

26"Then you shall take the breast of the ram of Aaron's consecration and wave it *as* a wave offering before the LORD; and it shall be your portion. 27And from the ram of the consecration you shall consecrate the breast of the wave offering which is waved, and the thigh of the heave offering which is raised, of *that* which *is* for Aaron and of *that* which is for his sons. 28It shall be from the children of Israel *for* Aaron and his sons by a statute forever. For it is a heave offering; it shall be a heave offering from the children of Israel from the sacrifices of their peace offerings, *that is,* their heave offering to the LORD.

29"And the holy garments of Aaron shall be his sons' after him, to be anointed in them and to be consecrated in them. 30That son who becomes

29:20 *We belong to God.* The priests were "marked" by the blood on the ear (hear God), the hand (serve God), and the foot (walk with God). The "continual burnt offering" morning and evening was a reminder of their complete and constant devotion to God. Don't forget your daily presentation of yourself to God (Rom. 12:1–2).

priest in his place shall put them on for seven days, when he enters the tabernacle of meeting to minister in the holy *place.*

31"And you shall take the ram of the consecration and boil its flesh in the holy place. 32Then Aaron and his sons shall eat the flesh of the ram, and the bread that *is* in the basket, *by* the door of the tabernacle of meeting. 33They shall eat those things with which the atonement was made, to consecrate *and* to sanctify them; but an outsider shall not eat *them,* because they *are* holy. 34And if any of the flesh of the consecration offerings, or of the bread, remains until the morning, then you shall burn the remainder with fire. It shall not be eaten, because it *is* holy.

35"Thus you shall do to Aaron and his sons, according to all that I have commanded you. Seven days you shall consecrate them. 36And you shall offer a bull every day *as* a sin offering for atonement. You shall cleanse the altar when you make atonement for it, and you shall anoint it to sanctify it. 37Seven days you shall make atonement for the altar and sanctify it. And the altar shall be most holy. Whatever touches the altar must be holy.*ᵃ*

38"Now this *is* what you shall offer on the altar: two lambs of the first year, day by day continually. 39One lamb you shall offer in the morning, and the other lamb you shall offer at twilight. 40With the one lamb shall be one-tenth *of an ephah* of flour mixed with one-fourth of a hin of pressed oil, and one-fourth of a hin of wine *as* a drink offering. 41And the other lamb you shall offer at twilight; and you shall offer with it the grain offering and the drink offering, as in the morning, for a sweet aroma, an offering made by fire to the LORD. 42*This shall be* a continual burnt offering throughout your generations *at* the door of the tabernacle of meeting before the LORD, where I will meet you to speak with you. 43And there I will meet with the children of Israel, and *the tabernacle* shall be sanctified by My glory. 44So I will consecrate the tabernacle of meeting and the altar. I will also consecrate both Aaron and his sons to minister to Me as priests. 45I will dwell among the children of Israel and will be their God. 46And they shall know that I *am* the LORD their God, who brought them up out of the land of Egypt, that I may dwell among them. I *am* the LORD their God.

CHAPTER 30

30:1–10 Remember to pray. The golden altar before the veil symbolized the ministry of prayer (Ps. 141:1–3; Rev. 5:8). God's people today don't stand before the veil: they enter the very presence of God. We need the "fire" of the Holy Spirit or our prayers are heartless (Rom. 8:23–27). Prayer is special, and we must not treat it as common (vv. 34–38).

30 "You* shall make an altar to burn incense on; you shall make it of acacia wood. 2A cubit *shall be* its length and a cubit its width— it shall be square—and two cubits *shall be* its height. Its horns *shall be* of one piece with it. 3And you shall overlay its top, its sides all around, and its horns with pure gold; and you shall make for it a molding of gold all around. 4Two gold rings you shall make for it, under the molding on both its sides. You shall place *them* on its two sides, and they will be holders for the poles with which to bear it. 5You shall make the poles of acacia wood, and overlay them with gold. 6And you shall put it before the veil that *is* before the ark of the Testimony, before the mercy seat that *is* over the Testimony, where I will meet with you.

7"Aaron shall burn on it sweet incense every morning; when he tends the lamps, he shall burn incense on it. 8And when Aaron lights the lamps

---

29:37 ᵃCompare Numbers 4:15 and Haggai 2:11–13

at twilight, he shall burn incense on it, a perpetual incense before the LORD throughout your generations. 9You shall not offer strange incense on it, or a burnt offering, or a grain offering; nor shall you pour a drink offering on it. 10And Aaron shall make atonement upon its horns once a year with the blood of the sin offering of atonement; once a year he shall make atonement upon it throughout your generations. It is most holy to the LORD."

11*Then the LORD spoke to Moses, saying: 12"When you take the census of the children of Israel for their number, then every man shall give a ransom for himself to the LORD, when you number them, that there may be no plague among them when you number them. 13This is what everyone among those who are numbered shall give: half a shekel according to the shekel of the sanctuary (a shekel is twenty gerahs). The half-shekel shall be an offering to the LORD. 14Everyone included among those who are numbered, from twenty years old and above, shall give an offering to the LORD. 15The rich shall not give more and the poor shall not give less than half a shekel, when you give an offering to the LORD, to make atonement for yourselves. 16And you shall take the atonement money of the children of Israel, and shall appoint it for the service of the tabernacle of meeting, that it may be a memorial for the children of Israel before the LORD, to make atonement for yourselves."

17*Then the LORD spoke to Moses, saying: 18"You shall also make a laver of bronze, with its base also of bronze, for washing. You shall put it between the tabernacle of meeting and the altar. And you shall put water in it, 19for Aaron and his sons shall wash their hands and their feet in water from it. 20When they go into the tabernacle of meeting, or when they come near the altar to minister, to burn an offering made by fire to the LORD, they shall wash with water, lest they die. 21So they shall wash their hands and their feet, lest they die. And it shall be a statute forever to them—to him and his descendants throughout their generations."

22Moreover the LORD spoke to Moses, saying: 23"Also take for yourself quality spices—five hundred shekels of liquid myrrh, half as much sweet-smelling cinnamon (two hundred and fifty shekels), two hundred and fifty shekels of sweet-smelling cane, 24five hundred shekels of cassia, according to the shekel of the sanctuary, and a hin of olive oil. 25And you shall make from these a holy anointing oil, an ointment compounded according to the art of the perfumer. It shall be a holy anointing oil. 26With it you shall anoint the tabernacle of meeting and the ark of the Testimony; 27the table and all its utensils, the lampstand and its utensils, and the altar of incense; 28the altar of burnt offering with all its utensils, and the laver and its base. 29You shall consecrate them, that they may be most holy; whatever touches them must be holy.b 30And you shall anoint Aaron and his sons, and consecrate them, that they may minister to Me as priests. 31*"And you shall speak to the children of Israel, saying: 'This shall be a holy anointing oil to Me throughout your generations. 32It shall not be poured on man's flesh; nor shall you make any other like it, according to its composition. It is

30:11–16 *Remember you are ransomed.* They were not redeemed by paying money, nor are we (1 Pet. 1:18ff.); but paying the annual half-shekel reminded them of what God had done for them. The silver was used to make the sockets for the posts of the tabernacle (38:25–37). The foundation for everything is redemption.

30:17–21 *Remember to keep clean.* Like the priests, we are washed once at redemption, but we must keep clean in our daily walk. If they became defiled even while serving the Lord in the holy tabernacle, what must happen to us as we serve in an evil world!

30:31–33 *Remember to honor the Holy Spirit.* The holy anointing oil symbolizes the Spirit of God. We must beware trying to duplicate His work by human effort or treating Him in a common way (vv. 32–33). (See Eph. 4:30–32.)

30:29 bCompare Numbers 4:15 and Haggai 2:11–13

holy, *and* it shall be holy to you. 33Whoever compounds *any* like it, or whoever puts *any* of it on an outsider, shall be cut off from his people.' "

34And the LORD said to Moses: "Take sweet spices, stacte and onycha and galbanum, and pure frankincense with *these* sweet spices; there shall be equal amounts of each. 35You shall make of these an incense, a compound according to the art of the perfumer, salted, pure, *and* holy. 36And you shall beat *some* of it very fine, and put some of it before the Testimony in the tabernacle of meeting where I will meet with you. It shall be most holy to you. 37But *as for* the incense which you shall make, you shall not make any for yourselves, according to its composition. It shall be to you holy for the LORD. 38Whoever makes *any* like it, to smell it, he shall be cut off from his people."

CHAPTER 31

31:1–11 Work. When God wants to get a job done, He calls workers, equips them, and gives them the plan for the task. He also calls people to help them and to provide the needed resources. Bezalel and Aholiab were gifted artisans, but they needed God's calling and enabling before they could do the work to please Him.

31 Then* the LORD spoke to Moses, saying: 2"See, I have called by name Bezalel the son of Uri, the son of Hur, of the tribe of Judah. 3And I have filled him with the Spirit of God, in wisdom, in understanding, in knowledge, and in all *manner of* workmanship, 4to design artistic works, to work in gold, in silver, in bronze, 5in cutting jewels for setting, in carving wood, and to work in all *manner of* workmanship.

6"And I, indeed I, have appointed with him Aholiab the son of Ahisamach, of the tribe of Dan; and I have put wisdom in the hearts of all the gifted artisans, that they may make all that I have commanded you: 7the tabernacle of meeting, the ark of the Testimony and the mercy seat that *is* on it, and all the furniture of the tabernacle— 8the table and its utensils, the pure *gold* lampstand with all its utensils, the altar of incense, 9the altar of burnt offering with all its utensils, and the laver and its base— 10the garments of ministry,c the holy garments for Aaron the priest and the garments of his sons, to minister as priests, 11and the anointing oil and sweet incense for the holy *place*. According to all that I have commanded you they shall do."

31:12–17 Rest. Why did God mention the Sabbath at this point? Perhaps He wanted to remind His people that even the building of the sacred tabernacle was not a reason for breaking the Sabbath law. They needed a day of rest, and since the Sabbath was a sign between God and His people, they needed to honor Him. God wants us to be balanced: work, rest, worship.

12*And the LORD spoke to Moses, saying, 13"Speak also to the children of Israel, saying: 'Surely My Sabbaths you shall keep, for it *is* a sign between Me and you throughout your generations, that *you* may know that I *am* the LORD who sanctifies you. 14You shall keep the Sabbath, therefore, for *it is* holy to you. Everyone who profanes it shall surely be put to death; for whoever does *any* work on it, that person shall be cut off from among his people. 15Work shall be done for six days, but the seventh *is* the Sabbath of rest, holy to the LORD. Whoever does *any* work on the Sabbath day, he shall surely be put to death. 16Therefore the children of Israel shall keep the Sabbath, to observe the Sabbath throughout their generations *as* a perpetual covenant. 17It *is* a sign between Me and the children of Israel forever; for *in* six days the LORD made the heavens and the earth, and on the seventh day He rested and was refreshed.' "

31:18 Law. Luke 11:20 suggests that "the finger of God" signifies the Holy Spirit, who wrote the Word of God (2 Tim. 3:16; 2 Pet. 1:21). He now writes it on the hearts of those who trust Christ and worship Him (2 Cor. 3:1ff.).

18*And when He had made an end of speaking with him on Mount Sinai, He gave Moses two tablets of the Testimony, tablets of stone, written with the finger of God.

31:10 cOr *woven garments*

32 Now* when the people saw that Moses delayed coming down from the mountain, the people gathered together to Aaron, and said to him, "Come, make us gods that shall go before us; for *as for* this Moses, the man who brought us up out of the land of Egypt, we do not know what has become of him."

²*And Aaron said to them, "Break off the golden earrings which *are* in the ears of your wives, your sons, and your daughters, and bring *them* to me." ³So all the people broke off the golden earrings which *were* in their ears, and brought *them* to Aaron. ⁴And he received *the* gold from their hand, and he fashioned it with an engraving tool, and made a molded calf.

Then they said, "This *is* your god, O Israel, that brought you out of the land of Egypt!"

⁵So when Aaron saw *it,* he built an altar before it. And Aaron made a proclamation and said, "Tomorrow *is* a feast to the LORD." ⁶Then they rose early on the next day, offered burnt offerings, and brought peace offerings; and the people sat down to eat and drink, and rose up to play.

⁷And the LORD said to Moses, "Go, get down! For your people whom you brought out of the land of Egypt have corrupted *themselves.* ⁸They have turned aside quickly out of the way which I commanded them. They have made themselves a molded calf, and worshiped it and sacrificed to it, and said, 'This *is* your god, O Israel, that brought you out of the land of Egypt!' " ⁹And the LORD said to Moses, "I have seen this people, and indeed it *is* a stiff-necked people! ¹⁰Now therefore, let Me alone, that My wrath may burn hot against them and I may consume them. And I will make of you a great nation."

¹¹Then Moses pleaded with the LORD his God, and said: "LORD, why does Your wrath burn hot against Your people whom You have brought out of the land of Egypt with great power and with a mighty hand? ¹²Why should the Egyptians speak, and say, 'He brought them out to harm them, to kill them in the mountains, and to consume them from the face of the earth'? Turn from Your fierce wrath, and relent from this harm to Your people. ¹³Remember Abraham, Isaac, and Israel, Your servants, to whom You swore by Your own self, and said to them, 'I will multiply your descendants as the stars of heaven; and all this land that I have spoken of I give to your descendants, and they shall inherit *it* forever.' "ᵈ ¹⁴So the LORD relented from the harm which He said He would do to His people.

¹⁵And Moses turned and went down from the mountain, and the two tablets of the Testimony *were* in his hand. The tablets *were* written on both sides; on the one *side* and on the other they were written. ¹⁶Now the tablets *were* the work of God, and the writing *was* the writing of God engraved on the tablets.

¹⁷And when Joshua heard the noise of the people as they shouted, he said to Moses, "*There is* a noise of war in the camp."

¹⁸But he said:

"*It is* not the noise of the shout of victory,
  Nor the noise of the cry of defeat,
  But the sound of singing I hear."

CHAPTER 32

32:1 *Unbelief.* Despite all that God had said and done, and all that Israel had promised to do (19:8), the nation did not know how to live by faith. Moses had been gone forty days (Deut. 9:11ff.), and the people had become impatient. They still had the fire and cloud to assure them of God's presence, but that was not enough. They wanted another visible representation of Jehovah to encourage them. It was unbelief: "Whoever believes will not act hastily" (Isa. 28:16).

32:2–6 *Compromise.* Aaron was supposed to be the spiritual leader in the absence of Moses, but instead he gave in and let the people have their way. When confronted with his sin, Aaron blamed the people, Moses, and the furnace (vv. 22–24), but he did not blame himself.

32:13 ᵈGenesis 13:15 and 22:17

19So it was, as soon as he came near the camp, that he saw the calf *and* the dancing. So Moses' anger became hot, and he cast the tablets out of his hands and broke them at the foot of the mountain. 20Then he took the calf which they had made, burned *it* in the fire, and ground *it* to powder; and he scattered *it* on the water and made the children of Israel drink *it*. 21And Moses said to Aaron, "What did this people do to you that you have brought so great a sin upon them?"

22So Aaron said, "Do not let the anger of my lord become hot. You know the people, that they *are set* on evil. 23For they said to me, 'Make us gods that shall go before us; *as for* this Moses, the man who brought us out of the land of Egypt, we do not know what has become of him.' 24And I said to them, 'Whoever has any gold, let them break *it* off.' So they gave *it* to me, and I cast it into the fire, and this calf came out."

25Now when Moses saw that the people *were* unrestrained (for Aaron had not restrained them, to *their* shame among their enemies), 26then Moses stood in the entrance of the camp, and said, "Whoever *is* on the LORD's side—*come* to me!" And all the sons of Levi gathered themselves together to him. 27And he said to them, "Thus says the LORD God of Israel: 'Let every man put his sword on his side, and go in and out from entrance to entrance throughout the camp, and let every man kill his brother, every man his companion, and every man his neighbor.' " 28So the sons of Levi did according to the word of Moses. And about three thousand men of the people fell that day. 29Then Moses said, "Consecrate yourselves today to the LORD, that He may bestow on you a blessing this day, for every man has opposed his son and his brother."

30Now it came to pass on the next day that Moses said to the people, "You have committed a great sin. So now I will go up to the LORD; perhaps I can make atonement for your sin." 31*Then Moses returned to the LORD and said, "Oh, these people have committed a great sin, and have made for themselves a god of gold! 32Yet now, if You will forgive their sin—but if not, I pray, blot me out of Your book which You have written."

33And the LORD said to Moses, "Whoever has sinned against Me, I will blot him out of My book. 34*Now therefore, go, lead the people to *the place* of which I have spoken to you. Behold, My Angel shall go before you. Nevertheless, in the day when I visit for punishment, I will visit punishment upon them for their sin."

35So the LORD plagued the people because of what they did with the calf which Aaron made.

33 Then the LORD said to Moses, "Depart *and* go up from here, you and the people whom you have brought out of the land of Egypt, to the land of which I swore to Abraham, Isaac, and Jacob, saying, 'To your descendants I will give it.' 2And I will send *My* Angel before you, and I will drive out the Canaanite and the Amorite and the Hittite and the Perizzite and the Hivite and the Jebusite. 3*Go up* to a land flowing with milk and

32:31, 32 *Intercession.* Had Moses been a selfish man, he could have become the founder of a new nation, but he loved the people and prayed for their forgiveness. (See Luke 23:34; Rom. 9:1–3.) He reminded God of His covenant and of the glory He would lose if the nation were destroyed. When you pray, remind God of His promises and seek to magnify His glory.

32:34, 35 *Discipline.* We all should heed the psalmist's wise words: "You who love the LORD, hate evil" (Ps. 97:10). God in His grace forgives the sinner, but in His government, He must punish the sin. This judgment may seem cruel to us, but the people had been warned against idolatry and had willfully disobeyed God. God had to teach them early not to act like the heathen nations around them. Israel had to remain a separated people, or God could not work out His great purposes through them.

God's Glory—The glory of God is the manifestation of all His attributes and character, all that He is and says and does. Everything about God is glorious, and the highest activity of man is to glorify God (Matt. 5:16; 1 Cor. 10:31). All who trust Christ share His glory today and will see His glory in heaven (John 17:22–24).

honey; for I will not go up in your midst, lest I consume you on the way, for you *are* a stiff-necked people."

4And when the people heard this bad news, they mourned, and no one put on his ornaments. 5For the LORD had said to Moses, "Say to the children of Israel, 'You *are* a stiff-necked people. I could come up into your midst in one moment and consume you. Now therefore, take off your ornaments, that I may know what to do to you.'" 6So the children of Israel stripped themselves of their ornaments by Mount Horeb.

7*Moses took his tent and pitched it outside the camp, far from the camp, and called it the tabernacle of meeting. And it came to pass *that* everyone who sought the LORD went out to the tabernacle of meeting which *was* outside the camp. 8So it was, whenever Moses went out to the tabernacle, *that* all the people rose, and each man stood *at* his tent door and watched Moses until he had gone into the tabernacle. 9And it came to pass, when Moses entered the tabernacle, that the pillar of cloud descended and stood *at* the door of the tabernacle, and *the* LORD talked with Moses. 10All the people saw the pillar of cloud standing *at* the tabernacle door, and all the people rose and worshiped, each man *in* his tent door. 11So the LORD spoke to Moses face to face, as a man speaks to his friend. And he would return to the camp, but his servant Joshua the son of Nun, a young man, did not depart from the tabernacle.

12Then Moses said to the LORD, "See, You say to me, 'Bring up this people.' But You have not let me know whom You will send with me. Yet You have said, 'I know you by name, and you have also found grace in My sight.' 13*Now therefore, I pray, if I have found grace in Your sight, show me now Your way, that I may know You and that I may find grace in Your sight. And consider that this nation *is* Your people."

14And He said, "My Presence will go *with you,* and I will give you rest."

15Then he said to Him, "If Your Presence does not go *with us,* do not bring us up from here. 16For how then will it be known that Your people and I have found grace in Your sight, except You go with us? So we shall be separate, Your people and I, from all the people who *are* upon the face of the earth."

17So the LORD said to Moses, "I will also do this thing that you have spoken; for you have found grace in My sight, and I know you by name."

18*And he said, "Please, show me Your glory."

19Then He said, "I will make all My goodness pass before you, and I will proclaim the name of the LORD before you. I will be gracious to whom I will be gracious, and I will have compassion on whom I will have compassion." 20But He said, "You cannot see My face; for no man shall see Me, and live." 21And the LORD said, "Here is a place by Me, and you shall stand on the rock. 22So it shall be, while My glory passes by, that I will put you in the cleft of the rock, and will cover you with My hand while I pass by. 23Then I will take away My hand, and you shall see My back; but My face shall not be seen."

34 And* the LORD said to Moses, "Cut two tablets of stone like the first *ones,* and I will write on *these* tablets the words that were on the first tablets which you broke. 2So be ready in the morning, and come up in the morning to Mount

---

CHAPTER 33

33:7–11 God's friendship. The tabernacle had not yet been built, so the structure referred to here was probably a tent where Moses met with God and over which the cloud rested. God spoke to Moses as with a friend because Moses obeyed God (Deut. 34:10; John 15:14–16). God could not dwell with a rebellious people, but He could fellowship with Moses (2 Cor. 6:14–18).

33:13, 14 God's presence. The Jews *watched* things happen, but Moses *made* things happen. He knew God's ways (Ps. 103:7) and prayed for God's presence to go with them. Moses could not pray on the basis of Israel's obedience to the Law, but he could plead the grace of God. Believers today are sure of God's presence because He has promised to stay with us (Heb. 13:5–6).

33:18–23 God's glory. Many believers pray, "Show me Your way," but not many pray, "Show me Your glory." No man can see God in His fullness and live, but God can reveal some of His glory. He did that for Moses "in the secret place of the Most High" (Ps. 91:1–4). Our experience of glory today is explained in 2 Corinthians 3:18.

CHAPTER 34

34:1–7 A gracious God. Because He is gracious and long-suffering, God gave His people another opportunity, just as He does with us today (1 John 2:1–2). He gave a "second chance" to Abraham (Gen. 13:1ff.), Jonah (Jon. 3:1), and Peter (John 21:15ff.). The enemy accuses us and wants us to quit, but God is ready to forgive when we turn to Him (Pss. 103:10–14; 130:3–4).

Sinai, and present yourself to Me there on the top of the mountain. ³And no man shall come up with you, and let no man be seen throughout all the mountain; let neither flocks nor herds feed before that mountain."

⁴So he cut two tablets of stone like the first *ones*. Then Moses rose early in the morning and went up Mount Sinai, as the Lᴏʀᴅ had commanded him; and he took in his hand the two tablets of stone.

⁵Now the Lᴏʀᴅ descended in the cloud and stood with him there, and proclaimed the name of the Lᴏʀᴅ. ⁶And the Lᴏʀᴅ passed before him and proclaimed, "The Lᴏʀᴅ, the Lᴏʀᴅ God, merciful and gracious, longsuffering, and abounding in goodness and truth, ⁷keeping mercy for thousands, forgiving iniquity and transgression and sin, by no means clearing *the guilty*, visiting the iniquity of the fathers upon the children and the children's children to the third and the fourth generation."

⁸So Moses made haste and bowed his head toward the earth, and worshiped. ⁹Then he said: "If now I have found grace in Your sight, O Lord, let my Lord, I pray, go among us, even though we *are* a stiff-necked people; and pardon our iniquity and our sin, and take us as Your inheritance."

¹⁰And He said: "Behold, I make a covenant. Before all your people I will do marvels such as have not been done in all the earth, nor in any nation; and all the people among whom you *are* shall see the work of the Lᴏʀᴅ. For it *is* an awesome thing that I will do with you. ¹¹Observe what I command you this day. Behold, I am driving out from before you the Amorite and the Canaanite and the Hittite and the Perizzite and the Hivite and the Jebusite. ¹²Take heed to yourself, lest you make a covenant with the inhabitants of the land where you are going, lest it be a snare in your midst. ¹³But you shall destroy their altars, break their *sacred* pillars, and cut down their wooden images ¹⁴*(for you shall worship no other god, for the Lᴏʀᴅ, whose name *is* Jealous, *is* a jealous God), ¹⁵lest you make a covenant with the inhabitants of the land, and they play the harlot with their gods and make sacrifice to their gods, and *one of them* invites you and you eat of his sacrifice, ¹⁶and you take of his daughters for your sons, and his daughters play the harlot with their gods and make your sons play the harlot with their gods.

¹⁷"You shall make no molded gods for yourselves.

¹⁸"The Feast of Unleavened Bread you shall keep. Seven days you shall eat unleavened bread, as I commanded you, in the appointed time of the month of Abib; for in the month of Abib you came out from Egypt.

¹⁹"All that open the womb *are* Mine, and every male firstborn among your livestock, *whether* ox or sheep. ²⁰But the firstborn of a donkey you shall redeem with a lamb. And if you will not redeem *him*, then you shall break his neck. All the firstborn of your sons you shall redeem.

"And none shall appear before Me empty-handed.

²¹"Six days you shall work, but on the seventh day you shall rest; in plowing time and in harvest you shall rest.

²²"And you shall observe the Feast of Weeks, of the firstfruits of wheat harvest, and the Feast of Ingathering at the year's end.

²³"Three times in the year all your men shall

34:14 *A jealous God.* God works for us, but He expects us to walk with Him. He will keep His covenant, but we must beware not to compromise with evil. It is easy to get into sin gradually. First there is agreement in worship (vv. 12–13), then sacrifice (v. 15), then marriage (v. 16); and the result is the loss of our children to false gods. Note the emphasis on putting God first (vv. 19–22, 26).

appear before the Lord, the LORD God of Israel. 24For I will cast out the nations before you and enlarge your borders; neither will any man covet your land when you go up to appear before the LORD your God three times in the year.

25"You shall not offer the blood of My sacrifice with leaven, nor shall the sacrifice of the Feast of the Passover be left until morning.

26"The first of the firstfruits of your land you shall bring to the house of the LORD your God. You shall not boil a young goat in its mother's milk."

27Then the LORD said to Moses, "Write these words, for according to the tenor of these words I have made a covenant with you and with Israel." 28So he was there with the LORD forty days and forty nights; he neither ate bread nor drank water. And He wrote on the tablets the words of the covenant, the Ten Commandments.e

29*Now it was so, when Moses came down from Mount Sinai (and the two tablets of the Testimony were in Moses' hand when he came down from the mountain), that Moses did not know that the skin of his face shone while he talked with Him. 30So when Aaron and all the children of Israel saw Moses, behold, the skin of his face shone, and they were afraid to come near him. 31Then Moses called to them, and Aaron and all the rulers of the congregation returned to him; and Moses talked with them. 32Afterward all the children of Israel came near, and he gave them as commandments all that the LORD had spoken with him on Mount Sinai. 33And when Moses had finished speaking with them, he put a veil on his face. 34But whenever Moses went in before the LORD to speak with Him, he would take the veil off until he came out; and he would come out and speak to the children of Israel whatever he had been commanded. 35And whenever the children of Israel saw the face of Moses, that the skin of Moses' face shone, then Moses would put the veil on his face again, until he went in to speak with Him.

35

Then* Moses gathered all the congregation of the children of Israel together, and said to them, "These are the words which the LORD has commanded you to do: 2Work shall be done for six days, but the seventh day shall be a holy day for you, a Sabbath of rest to the LORD. Whoever does any work on it shall be put to death. 3You shall kindle no fire throughout your dwellings on the Sabbath day."

4And Moses spoke to all the congregation of the children of Israel, saying, "This is the thing which the LORD commanded, saying: 5'Take from among you an offering to the LORD. Whoever is of a willing heart, let him bring it as an offering to the LORD: gold, silver, and bronze; 6blue, purple, and scarlet thread, fine linen, and goats' hair; 7ram skins dyed red, badger skins, and acacia wood; 8oil for the light, and spices for the anointing oil and for the sweet incense; 9onyx stones, and stones to be set in the ephod and in the breastplate.

10'All who are gifted artisans among you shall come and make all that the LORD has commanded: 11the tabernacle, its tent, its covering, its clasps, its boards, its bars, its pillars, and its sockets; 12the ark and its poles, with the mercy seat, and

34:29–35 A glorious God. Moses not only sought God's glory and saw it on the mount, but he shared it as it reflected from his own face. However, this glory faded away, just like the glory of the Law. As we see Christ in the Word, and the Spirit makes us more like Him, we go "from glory to glory" (2 Cor. 3:12–18; see also Prov. 4:18; Matt. 17:1–8; Acts 6:15).

CHAPTERS 35—39

35:1ff Each aspect of the making of the tabernacle is mentioned in detail because each part was important to God. The smallest wooden peg had to conform to the pattern God gave Moses on the mount. If we expect God to be concerned about the details of our lives, we must pay attention to the details of His instructions.

The construction of the tabernacle involved God's pattern and man's provision. The people had plundered the Egyptians (12:35–36), and they willingly brought that wealth to the Lord. It was an act of spontaneous generosity and not something that was forced from them (35:5, 21–22, 26, 29). Christians today should give in the same way (2 Cor. 8:1–12).

34:28 eLiterally Ten Words

the veil of the covering; 13the table and its poles, all its utensils, and the showbread; 14also the lampstand for the light, its utensils, its lamps, and the oil for the light; 15the incense altar, its poles, the anointing oil, the sweet incense, and the screen for the door at the entrance of the tabernacle; 16the altar of burnt offering with its bronze grating, its poles, all its utensils, *and* the laver and its base; 17the hangings of the court, its pillars, their sockets, and the screen for the gate of the court; 18the pegs of the tabernacle, the pegs of the court, and their cords; 19the garments of ministry,*f* for ministering in the holy *place*—the holy garments for Aaron the priest and the garments of his sons, to minister as priests.' "

20And all the congregation of the children of Israel departed from the presence of Moses. 21Then everyone came whose heart was stirred, and everyone whose spirit was willing, *and* they brought the LORD's offering for the work of the tabernacle of meeting, for all its service, and for the holy garments. 22They came, both men and women, as many as had a willing heart, *and* brought earrings and nose rings, rings and necklaces, all jewelry of gold, that is, every man who *made* an offering of gold to the LORD. 23And every man, with whom was found blue, purple, and scarlet *thread,* fine linen, goats' *hair,* red skins of rams, and badger skins, brought *them.* 24Everyone who offered an offering of silver or bronze brought the LORD's offering. And everyone with whom was found acacia wood for any work of the service, brought *it.* 25All the women *who were* gifted artisans spun yarn with their hands, and brought what they had spun, of blue, purple, *and* scarlet, and fine linen. 26And all the women whose hearts stirred with wisdom spun yarn of goats' *hair.* 27The rulers brought onyx stones, and the stones to be set in the ephod and in the breastplate, 28and spices and oil for the light, for the anointing oil, and for the sweet incense. 29The children of Israel brought a freewill offering to the LORD, all the men and women whose hearts were willing to bring *material* for all kinds of work which the LORD, by the hand of Moses, had commanded to be done.

30And Moses said to the children of Israel, "See, the LORD has called by name Bezalel the son of Uri, the son of Hur, of the tribe of Judah; 31and He has filled him with the Spirit of God, in wisdom and understanding, in knowledge and all manner of workmanship, 32to design artistic works, to work in gold and silver and bronze, 33in cutting jewels for setting, in carving wood, and to work in all manner of artistic workmanship.

34"And He has put in his heart the ability to teach, *in* him and Aholiab the son of Ahisamach, of the tribe of Dan. 35He has filled them with skill to do all manner of work of the engraver and the designer and the tapestry maker, in blue, purple, and scarlet *thread,* and fine linen, and of the weaver—those who do every work and those who design artistic works.

36 "And Bezalel and Aholiab, and every gifted artisan in whom the LORD has put wisdom and understanding, to know how to do all manner of work for the service of the sanctuary, shall do according to all that the LORD has commanded."

35:19 *f*Or *woven garments*

2Then Moses called Bezalel and Aholiab, and every gifted artisan in whose heart the LORD had put wisdom, everyone whose heart was stirred, to come and do the work. 3And they received from Moses all the offering which the children of Israel had brought for the work of the service of making the sanctuary. So they continued bringing to him freewill offerings every morning. 4Then all the craftsmen who were doing all the work of the sanctuary came, each from the work he was doing, 5and they spoke to Moses, saying, "The people bring much more than enough for the service of the work which the LORD commanded *us* to do."

6So Moses gave a commandment, and they caused it to be proclaimed throughout the camp, saying, "Let neither man nor woman do any more work for the offering of the sanctuary." And the people were restrained from bringing, 7for the material they had was sufficient for all the work to be done—indeed too much.

8Then all the gifted artisans among them who worked on the tabernacle made ten curtains woven of fine linen, and of blue, purple, and scarlet thread; *with* artistic designs of cherubim they made them. 9The length of each curtain *was* twenty-eight cubits, and the width of each curtain four cubits; the curtains *were* all the same size. 10And he coupled five curtains to one another, and *the other* five curtains he coupled to one another. 11He made loops of blue *yarn* on the edge of the curtain on the selvedge of one set; likewise he did on the outer edge of *the other* curtain of the second set. 12Fifty loops he made on one curtain, and fifty loops he made on the edge of the curtain on the end of the second set; the loops held one *curtain* to another. 13And he made fifty clasps of gold, and coupled the curtains to one another with the clasps, that it might be one tabernacle.

14He made curtains of goats' *hair* for the tent over the tabernacle; he made eleven curtains. 15The length of each curtain *was* thirty cubits, and the width of each curtain four cubits; the eleven curtains *were* the same size. 16He coupled five curtains by themselves and six curtains by themselves. 17And he made fifty loops on the edge of the curtain that is outermost in one set, and fifty loops he made on the edge of the curtain of the second set. 18He also made fifty bronze clasps to couple the tent together, that it might be one. 19Then he made a covering for the tent of ram skins dyed red, and a covering of badger skins above *that*.

20For the tabernacle he made boards of acacia wood, standing upright. 21The length of each board *was* ten cubits, and the width of each board a cubit and a half. 22Each board had two tenons for binding one to another. Thus he made for all the boards of the tabernacle. 23And he made boards for the tabernacle, twenty boards for the south side. 24Forty sockets of silver he made to go under the twenty boards: two sockets under each of the boards for its two tenons. 25And for the other side of the tabernacle, the north side, he made twenty boards 26and their forty sockets of silver: two sockets under each of the boards. 27For the west side of the tabernacle he made six boards. 28He also made two boards for the two back corners of the tabernacle. 29And they were coupled at the bottom and coupled together at the top by one ring. Thus he made both of them for the two corners. 30So there were eight boards and their sockets—sixteen sockets of silver—two sockets under each of the boards.

31And he made bars of acacia wood: five for the boards on one side of the tabernacle, 32five bars for the boards on the other side of the tabernacle, and five bars for the boards of the tabernacle on the far side westward. 33And he made the middle bar to pass through the boards from one end to the other. 34He overlaid the boards with gold, made their rings of gold *to be* holders for the bars, and overlaid the bars with gold.

35And he made a veil of blue, purple, and scarlet *thread,* and fine woven linen; it was worked *with* an artistic design of cherubim. 36He made for it four pillars of acacia *wood,* and overlaid them with gold, with their hooks of gold; and he cast four sockets of silver for them.

37He also made a screen for the tabernacle door, of blue, purple, and scarlet *thread,* and fine woven linen, made by a weaver, 38and its five pillars with their hooks. And he overlaid their capitals and their rings with gold, but their five sockets *were* bronze.

37 Then Bezalel made the ark of acacia wood; two and a half cubits *was* its length, a cubit and a half its width, and a cubit and a half its height. 2He overlaid it with pure gold inside and outside, and made a molding of gold all around it. 3And he cast for it four rings of gold *to be set* in its four corners: two rings on one side, and two rings on the other side of it. 4He made poles of acacia wood, and overlaid them with gold. 5And he put the poles into the rings at the sides of the ark, to bear the ark. 6He also made the mercy seat of pure gold; two and a half cubits *was* its length and a cubit and a half its width. 7He made two cherubim of beaten gold; he made them of one piece at the two ends of the mercy seat: 8one cherub at one end on this side, and the other cherub at the *other* end on that side. He made the cherubim at the two ends *of one piece* with the mercy seat. 9The cherubim spread out *their* wings above, *and* covered the mercy seat with their wings. They faced one another; the faces of the cherubim were toward the mercy seat.

10He made the table of acacia wood; two cubits *was* its length, a cubit its width, and a cubit and a half its height. 11And he overlaid it with pure gold, and made a molding of gold all around it. 12Also he made a frame of a handbreadth all around it, and made a molding of gold for the frame all around it. 13And he cast for it four rings of gold, and put the rings on the four corners that *were* at its four legs. 14The rings were close to the frame, as holders for the poles to bear the table. 15And he made the poles of acacia wood to bear the table, and overlaid them with gold. 16He made of pure gold the utensils which were on the table: its dishes, its cups, its bowls, and its pitchers for pouring.

17He also made the lampstand of pure gold; of hammered work he made the lampstand. Its shaft, its branches, its bowls, its *ornamental* knobs, and its flowers were of the same piece. 18And six branches came out of its sides: three branches of the lampstand out of one side, and three branches of the lampstand out of the other side. 19There were three bowls made like almond *blossoms* on one branch, with an *ornamental* knob and a flower, and three bowls made like almond *blossoms* on the other branch, with an *ornamental* knob and a flower—and so for the six branches coming out of the lampstand. [20]And on the lampstand itself *were* four bowls made like almond blossoms, *each with* its *ornamental* knob and flower. [21]*There was* a knob under the *first* two branches of the same, a knob under the *second* two branches of the same, and a knob under the *third* two branches of the same, according to the six branches extending from it. [22]Their knobs and their branches were of one piece; all of it *was* one hammered piece of pure gold. [23]And he made its seven lamps, its wick-trimmers, and its trays of pure gold. [24]Of a talent of pure gold he made it, with all its utensils.

[25]He made the incense altar of acacia wood. Its length *was* a cubit and its width a cubit—*it was* square—and two cubits *was* its height. Its horns were *of one piece* with it. [26]And he overlaid it with pure gold: its top, its sides all around, and its horns. He also made for it a molding of gold all around it. [27]He made two rings of gold for it under its molding, by its two corners on both sides, as holders for the poles with which to bear it. [28]And he made the poles of acacia wood, and overlaid them with gold.

[29]He also made the holy anointing oil and the pure incense of sweet spices, according to the work of the perfumer.

38 He made the altar of burnt offering of acacia wood; five cubits *was* its length and five cubits its width—*it was* square—and its height *was* three cubits. [2]He made its horns on its four corners; the horns were *of one piece* with it. And he overlaid it with bronze. [3]He made all the utensils for the altar: the pans, the shovels, the basins, the forks, and the firepans; all its utensils he made of bronze. [4]And he made a grate of bronze network for the altar, under its rim, midway from the bottom. [5]He cast four rings for the four corners of the bronze grating, *as* holders for the poles. [6]And he made the poles of acacia wood, and overlaid them with bronze. [7]Then he put the poles into the rings on the sides of the altar, with which to bear it. He made the altar hollow with boards.

[8]He made the laver of bronze and its base of bronze, from the bronze mirrors of the serving women who assembled at the door of the tabernacle of meeting.

[9]Then he made the court on the south side; the hangings of the court *were of* fine woven linen, one hundred cubits long. [10]There *were* twenty pillars for them, with twenty bronze sockets. The hooks of the pillars and their bands *were* silver. [11]On the north side *the hangings were* one hundred cubits *long*, with twenty pillars and their twenty bronze sockets. The hooks of the pillars and their bands *were* silver. [12]And on the west side *there were* hangings of fifty cubits, with ten pillars and their ten sockets. The hooks of the pillars and their bands *were* silver. [13]For the east side *the hangings were* fifty cubits. [14]The hangings of one side *of the gate were* fifteen cubits *long*, with their three pillars and their three sockets, [15]and the same for the other side of the court gate; on this side and that *were* hangings of fifteen cubits, *with* their three pillars and their three sockets. [16]All the hangings of the court all around *were of* fine woven linen. [17]The sockets for the pillars *were* bronze, the hooks of the pillars and their bands *were* silver, and the overlay of their

capitals *was* silver; and all the pillars of the court had bands of silver. [18]The screen for the gate of the court *was* woven of blue, purple, and scarlet *thread,* and of fine woven linen. The length *was* twenty cubits, and the height along its width *was* five cubits, corresponding to the hangings of the court. [19]And *there were* four pillars *with* their four sockets of bronze; their hooks *were* silver, and the overlay of their capitals and their bands *was* silver. [20]All the pegs of the tabernacle, and of the court all around, *were* bronze.

[21]This is the inventory of the tabernacle, the tabernacle of the Testimony, which was counted according to the commandment of Moses, for the service of the Levites, by the hand of Ithamar, son of Aaron the priest. [22]*Bezalel the son of Uri, the son of Hur, of the tribe of Judah, made all that the LORD had commanded Moses. [23]And with him *was* Aholiab the son of Ahisamach, of the tribe of Dan, an engraver and designer, a weaver of blue, purple, and scarlet *thread,* and of fine linen.

[24]All the gold that was used in all the work of the holy *place,* that is, the gold of the offering, was twenty-nine talents and seven hundred and thirty shekels, according to the shekel of the sanctuary. [25]And the silver from those who were numbered of the congregation *was* one hundred talents and one thousand seven hundred and seventy-five shekels, according to the shekel of the sanctuary: [26]a bekah for each man (*that is,* half a shekel, according to the shekel of the sanctuary), for everyone included in the numbering from twenty years old and above, for six hundred and three thousand, five hundred and fifty *men.* [27]And from the hundred talents of silver were cast the sockets of the sanctuary and the bases of the veil: one hundred sockets from the hundred talents, one talent for each socket. [28]Then from the one thousand seven hundred and seventy-five *shekels* he made hooks for the pillars, overlaid their capitals, and made bands for them.

[29]The offering of bronze *was* seventy talents and two thousand four hundred shekels. [30]And with it he made the sockets for the door of the tabernacle of meeting, the bronze altar, the bronze grating for it, and all the utensils for the altar, [31]the sockets for the court all around, the bases for the court gate, all the pegs for the tabernacle, and all the pegs for the court all around.

39 Of the blue, purple, and scarlet *thread* they made garments of ministry,[g] for ministering in the holy *place,* and made the holy garments for Aaron, as the LORD had commanded Moses.

[2]He made the ephod of gold, blue, purple, and scarlet *thread,* and of fine woven linen. [3]And they beat the gold into thin sheets and cut *it into* threads, to work *it* in *with* the blue, purple, and scarlet *thread,* and the fine linen, *into* artistic designs. [4]They made shoulder straps for it to couple *it* together; it was coupled together at its two edges. [5]And the intricately woven band of his ephod that *was* on it *was* of the same workmanship, *woven of* gold, blue, purple, and scarlet *thread,* and of fine woven linen, as the LORD had commanded Moses.

[6]And they set onyx stones, enclosed in settings

38:22, 23 God gave the plan, and He also gave the workers the wisdom needed to do the job right (35:10, 25, 34–35). There is nothing wrong with dedicated artistry, for God built beauty into His tabernacle. God wants skillful hands as well as dedicated hearts (Ps. 78:72).

39:1 [g]Or *woven garments*

of gold; they were engraved, as signets are engraved, with the names of the sons of Israel. [7]He put them on the shoulders of the ephod *as* memorial stones for the sons of Israel, as the LORD had commanded Moses.

[8]And he made the breastplate, artistically woven like the workmanship of the ephod, of gold, blue, purple, and scarlet *thread,* and of fine woven linen. [9]They made the breastplate square by doubling it; a span *was* its length and a span its width when doubled. [10]And they set in it four rows of stones: a row with a sardius, a topaz, and an emerald *was* the first row; [11]the second row, a turquoise, a sapphire, and a diamond; [12]the third row, a jacinth, an agate, and an amethyst; [13]the fourth row, a beryl, an onyx, and a jasper. *They were* enclosed in settings of gold in their mountings. [14]*There were* twelve stones according to the names of the sons of Israel: according to their names, *engraved like* a signet, each one with its own name according to the twelve tribes. [15]And they made chains for the breastplate at the ends, like braided cords of pure gold. [16]They also made two settings of gold and two gold rings, and put the two rings on the two ends of the breastplate. [17]And they put the two braided *chains* of gold in the two rings on the ends of the breastplate. [18]The two ends of the two braided *chains* they fastened in the two settings, and put them on the shoulder straps of the ephod in the front. [19]And they made two rings of gold and put *them* on the two ends of the breastplate, on the edge of it, which *was* on the inward side of the ephod. [20]They made two *other* gold rings and put them on the two shoulder straps, underneath the ephod toward its front, right at the seam above the intricately woven band of the ephod. [21]And they bound the breastplate by means of its rings to the rings of the ephod with a blue cord, so that it would be above the intricately woven band of the ephod, and that the breastplate would not come loose from the ephod, as the LORD had commanded Moses.

[22]He made the robe of the ephod of woven work, all of blue. [23]And *there was* an opening in the middle of the robe, like the opening in a coat of mail, *with* a woven binding all around the opening, so that it would not tear. [24]They made on the hem of the robe pomegranates of blue, purple, and scarlet, and of fine woven *linen.* [25]And they made bells of pure gold, and put the bells between the pomegranates on the hem of the robe all around between the pomegranates: [26]a bell and a pomegranate, a bell and a pomegranate, all around the hem of the robe to minister in, as the LORD had commanded Moses.

[27]They made tunics, artistically woven of fine linen, for Aaron and his sons, [28]a turban of fine linen, exquisite hats of fine linen, short trousers of fine woven linen, [29]and a sash of fine woven linen with blue, purple, and scarlet *thread,* made by a weaver, as the LORD had commanded Moses.

[30]Then they made the plate of the holy crown of pure gold, and wrote on it an inscription *like* the engraving of a signet:

HOLINESS TO THE LORD.

[31]And they tied to it a blue cord, to fasten *it* above on the turban, as the LORD had commanded Moses.

[32]Thus all the work of the tabernacle of the tent of meeting was finished. And the children of Israel

did according to all that the LORD had commanded Moses; so they did. 33And they brought the tabernacle to Moses, the tent and all its furnishings: its clasps, its boards, its bars, its pillars, and its sockets; 34the covering of ram skins dyed red, the covering of badger skins, and the veil of the covering; 35the ark of the Testimony with its poles, and the mercy seat; 36the table, all its utensils, and the showbread; 37the pure *gold* lampstand with its lamps (the lamps set in order), all its utensils, and the oil for light; 38the gold altar, the anointing oil, and the sweet incense; the screen for the tabernacle door; 39the bronze altar, its grate of bronze, its poles, and all its utensils; the laver with its base; 40the hangings of the court, its pillars and its sockets, the screen for the court gate, its cords, and its pegs; all the utensils for the service of the tabernacle, for the tent of meeting; 41and the garments of ministry,*h* to minister in the holy *place:* the holy garments for Aaron the priest, and his sons' garments, to minister as priests.

42According to all that the LORD had commanded Moses, so the children of Israel did all the work. 43Then Moses looked over all the work, and indeed they had done it; as the LORD had commanded, just so they had done it. And Moses blessed them.

40 Then* the LORD spoke to Moses, saying: 2"On the first day of the first month you shall set up the tabernacle of the tent of meeting. 3*You shall put in it the ark of the Testimony, and partition off the ark with the veil. 4You shall bring in the table and arrange the things that are to be set in order on it; and you shall bring in the lampstand and light its lamps. 5You shall also set the altar of gold for the incense before the ark of the Testimony, and put up the screen for the door of the tabernacle. 6Then you shall set the altar of the burnt offering before the door of the tabernacle of the tent of meeting. 7And you shall set the laver between the tabernacle of meeting and the altar, and put water in it. 8You shall set up the court all around, and hang up the screen at the court gate.

9*"And you shall take the anointing oil, and anoint the tabernacle and all that *is* in it; and you shall hallow it and all its utensils, and it shall be holy. 10You shall anoint the altar of the burnt offering and all its utensils, and consecrate the altar. The altar shall be most holy. 11And you shall anoint the laver and its base, and consecrate it.

12"Then you shall bring Aaron and his sons to the door of the tabernacle of meeting and wash them with water. 13You shall put the holy garments on Aaron, and anoint him and consecrate him, that he may minister to Me as priest. 14And you shall bring his sons and clothe them with tunics. 15You shall anoint them, as you anointed their father, that they may minister to Me as

39:43 Moses was careful to inspect the work to see that it was just what God had commanded. (The word *commanded* is found seventeen times in these chapters.) Moses was faithful as the servant of God to do what God told him to do (Heb. 3:5). Chapter 39 ends by saying, "And Moses blessed them" (v. 43). Have you taken time lately to bless those who have done the will of God in serving you? (See Ruth 2:4.)

CHAPTER 40

40:1, 2 Finished. All the framework, hangings, and pieces of furniture were completed, along with the priests' garments; but Moses waited for the Lord to tell him what to do next. Wise is the leader who gets his orders from God.

40:3–8 Furnished. God told Moses what to do and when to do it. First they were to set up the tent and then put in the six special pieces of furniture, starting with the ark in the Holy of Holies. The right order was as significant as the right furnishings. When he finished with the tent and the furniture, he put up the court around it and set it apart from the rest of the camp.

40:9–11 Fragrant. Everything in the tabernacle was anointed with the holy oil, which set it all apart for God's use. Is there a fragrance about our lives that makes people think of heaven?

39:41 *h*Or *woven garments*

God's Dwelling Places—First, God walked with man (Gen. 5:24; 6:9); then He desired to dwell with him (Exod. 25:8). His glory came to the tabernacle (Exod. 40:34), but when Israel sinned, the glory departed (1 Sam. 4:21–22). The glory dwelt in the temple (1 Kings 8:10–11), but then departed again because of the sins of the people (Ezek. 11:22–23). The glory came in the person of Jesus Christ (John 1:14) and dwells now in believers individually (1 Cor. 6:19–20) and the church collectively (Eph. 2:20–22). One day God's glory will be revealed in a new heaven and earth and a perfect city where His people will dwell forever (Rev. 21—22).

priests; for their anointing shall surely be an ever-lasting priesthood throughout their generations."

16Thus Moses did; according to all that the LORD had commanded him, so he did.

17And it came to pass in the first month of the second year, on the first *day* of the month, *that* the tabernacle was raised up. 18So Moses raised up the tabernacle, fastened its sockets, set up its boards, put in its bars, and raised up its pillars. 19And he spread out the tent over the tabernacle and put the covering of the tent on top of it, as the LORD had commanded Moses. 20He took the Testimony and put *it* into the ark, inserted the poles through the rings of the ark, and put the mercy seat on top of the ark. 21And he brought the ark into the tabernacle, hung up the veil of the covering, and partitioned off the ark of the Testimony, as the LORD had commanded Moses.

22He put the table in the tabernacle of meeting, on the north side of the tabernacle, outside the veil; 23and he set the bread in order upon it before the LORD, as the LORD had commanded Moses. 24He put the lampstand in the tabernacle of meeting, across from the table, on the south side of the tabernacle; 25and he lit the lamps before the LORD, as the LORD had commanded Moses. 26He put the gold altar in the tabernacle of meeting in front of the veil; 27and he burned sweet incense on it, as the LORD had commanded Moses. 28He hung up the screen *at* the door of the tabernacle. 29And he put the altar of burnt offering *before* the door of the tabernacle of the tent of meeting, and offered upon it the burnt offering and the grain offering, as the LORD had commanded Moses. 30He set the laver between the tabernacle of meeting and the altar, and put water there for washing; 31and Moses, Aaron, and his sons would wash their hands and their feet *with water* from it. 32Whenever they went into the tabernacle of meeting, and when they came near the altar, they washed, as the LORD had commanded Moses. 33And he raised up the court all around the tabernacle and the altar, and hung up the screen of the court gate. So Moses finished the work.

34*Then the cloud covered the tabernacle of meeting, and the glory of the LORD filled the tabernacle. 35And Moses was not able to enter the tabernacle of meeting, because the cloud rested above it, and the glory of the LORD filled the tabernacle. 36Whenever the cloud was taken up from above the tabernacle, the children of Israel would go onward in all their journeys. 37But if the cloud was not taken up, then they did not journey till the day that it was taken up. 38For the cloud of the LORD *was* above the tabernacle by day, and fire was over it by night, in the sight of all the house of Israel, throughout all their journeys.

40:34–38 *Filled.* Two things made the tabernacle a special building: the pattern was given by God, and God's glorious presence filled it when He came to dwell with His people. What a gracious God that He should consent to dwell with such a rebellious people!

LEVITICUS

The name of this book means "pertaining to the Levites." Exodus and Leviticus were guidebooks for the priests in their ministry. Israel today has neither priesthood nor temple, so the nation cannot obey these laws (Hos. 3:4), but Leviticus has great value to the Christian. It illustrates the sacrificial work of Jesus Christ and stresses the importance of a life of separation and obedience.

The book emphasizes *sacrifice* (chaps. 1—10), for man must deal with his sins if he expects to have fellowship with a holy God. These five sacrifices are fulfilled in Jesus Christ and picture His perfect life and atoning work on the Cross (Heb. 10:1–14).

Leviticus also emphasizes *separation* (chaps. 11—24), for a redeemed people should walk in God's holy will. These various laws touch on many aspects of everyday life and illustrate principles of holy living that God's children should follow today.

Finally, since God anticipated the nation's entrance into the Promised Land, He gave them some rules for *success* (chaps. 25—27). The land was theirs because of God's covenant, but they could enjoy it only if they obeyed God's will. Obedience by faith always brings blessing.

1 Now the LORD called to Moses, and spoke to him from the tabernacle of meeting, saying, 2"Speak to the children of Israel, and say to them: 'When any one of you brings an offering to the LORD, you shall bring your offering of the livestock—of the herd and of the flock.

3'If his offering *is* a burnt sacrifice of the herd, let him offer a male without blemish; he shall offer it of his own free will at the door of the tabernacle of meeting before the LORD. 4Then he shall put his hand on the head of the burnt offering, and it will be accepted on his behalf to make atonement for him. 5He shall kill the bull before the LORD; and the priests, Aaron's sons, shall bring the blood and sprinkle the blood all around on the altar that *is* by the door of the tabernacle of meeting. 6And he shall skin the burnt offering and cut it into its pieces. 7The sons of Aaron the priest shall put fire on the altar, and lay the wood in

Jesus Christ in the Sacrifices

1. Burnt offering	He showed perfect dedication to God.	John 10:17; Rom. 5:19; Heb. 10:10
2. Grain offering	He had a perfect character, a fragrance to God.	Eph. 5:2
3. Peace offering	He made peace between God and man and between Jew and Gentile.	Rom. 5:1; Eph. 2:14, 17; Col. 1:20
4. Sin offering	He was made sin for us on the cross.	2 Cor. 5:17; 1 Pet. 2:24
5. Trespass offering	He assumed the debt for our sins and paid it.	Luke 7:36–50

order on the fire. ⁸Then the priests, Aaron's sons, shall lay the parts, the head, and the fat in order on the wood that *is* on the fire upon the altar; ⁹*but he shall wash its entrails and its legs with water. And the priest shall burn all on the altar as a burnt sacrifice, an offering made by fire, a sweet aroma to the LORD.

¹⁰'If his offering *is* of the flocks—of the sheep or of the goats—as a burnt sacrifice, he shall bring a male without blemish. ¹¹He shall kill it on the north side of the altar before the LORD; and the priests, Aaron's sons, shall sprinkle its blood all around on the altar. ¹²And he shall cut it into its pieces, with its head and its fat; and the priest shall lay them in order on the wood that *is* on the fire upon the altar; ¹³*but he shall wash the entrails and the legs with water. Then the priest shall bring *it* all and burn *it* on the altar; it *is* a burnt sacrifice, an offering made by fire, a sweet aroma to the LORD.

¹⁴*'And if the burnt sacrifice of his offering to the LORD *is* of birds, then he shall bring his offering of turtledoves or young pigeons. ¹⁵The priest shall bring it to the altar, wring off its head, and burn *it* on the altar; its blood shall be drained out at the side of the altar. ¹⁶And he shall remove its crop with its feathers and cast it beside the altar on the east side, into the place for ashes. ¹⁷Then he shall split it at its wings, *but* shall not divide *it* completely; and the priest shall burn it on the altar, on the wood that *is* on the fire. It *is* a burnt sacrifice, an offering made by fire, a sweet aroma to the LORD.

2 'When* anyone offers a grain offering to the LORD, his offering shall be *of* fine flour. And he shall pour oil on it, and put frankincense on it. ²*He shall bring it to Aaron's sons, the priests, one of whom shall take from it his handful of fine flour and oil with all the frankincense. And the priest shall burn *it as* a memorial on the altar, an offering made by fire, a sweet aroma to the LORD. ³The rest of the grain offering *shall be* Aaron's and his sons'. *It is* most holy of the offerings to the LORD made by fire.

⁴'And if you bring as an offering a grain offering baked in the oven, *it shall be* unleavened cakes of fine flour mixed with oil, or unleavened wafers anointed with oil. ⁵But if your offering *is* a grain offering *baked* in a pan, *it shall be of* fine flour, unleavened, mixed with oil. ⁶You shall break it in pieces and pour oil on it; it *is* a grain offering.

⁷'If your offering *is* a grain offering *baked* in a covered pan, it shall be made *of* fine flour with oil. ⁸You shall bring the grain offering that is made of these things to the LORD. And when it is presented to the priest, he shall bring it to the altar. ⁹Then the priest shall take from the grain offering a memorial portion, and burn *it* on the altar. *It is* an offering made by fire, a sweet aroma to the LORD. ¹⁰And what is left of the grain offering *shall be* Aaron's and his sons'. *It is* most holy of the offerings to the LORD made by fire.

¹¹*'No grain offering which you bring to the LORD shall be made with leaven, for you shall burn no leaven nor any honey in any offering to the LORD made by fire. ¹²As for the offering of the firstfruits, you shall offer them to the LORD, but they shall not be burned on the altar for a sweet aroma. ¹³And every offering of your grain offering you shall season with salt; you shall not allow the salt of the covenant of your God to be lacking

CHAPTER 1

1:9 "All on the altar" is the key to this sacrifice, for it speaks of complete dedication to the Lord. The animal was an involuntary sacrifice that died, but God's people are to be willing *living* sacrifices (Rom. 12:1–2). Do you put *your* "all on the altar" at the beginning of each day (Lev. 6:8–13)?

1:13 The offering must be brought to the Lord, and its purpose must be to please the Lord as a "sweet aroma" (vv. 9, 13, 17). People may not understand you, but if you seek to please Him, He will accept it (1 Pet. 2:5).

1:14–17 No matter how poor we may feel, or how little we think we have to give Him, He will receive what we have and bless it. The important thing is that we give our all to Him each day.

The priest started each day by sacrificing a burnt offering. It became the foundation for all the other offerings put on the altar (Exod. 29:38–42; Lev. 3:5). Unless we have our "all on the altar," our other sacrifices will not mean much to the Lord.

CHAPTER 2

2:1, 4, 7 There was no shedding of blood involved in the grain offering, for it focused on the life and character of our Lord Jesus Christ rather than on His death. In Him was perfect balance; nothing was ever in excess. His life on earth pleased God (Matt. 17:5). As we become more like Him, we shall become more and more balanced in character.

2:2 The oil symbolizes the Holy Spirit who has anointed each believer (2 Cor. 1:21–22). The oil *mixed* with the offering (v. 4) reminds us that our Lord was born of the Spirit with a perfect nature (Luke 1:35). The oil *poured* on the offering (v. 6) speaks of the power of the Spirit given to the Savior (Acts 10:38). We need the fruit of the Spirit (Gal. 5:22–23) and the power of the Spirit (Acts 1:8) if we are to please God in character and service.

2:11 Note that God never wants leaven (a picture of sin [1 Cor. 5:6–8]) or honey (man's glory and not God's [Prov. 25:27]). But He does want salt, which speaks of purity (Col. 4:6), and frankincense, which is praise to God. What a privilege it is to build a Christian life that brings glory to God!

from your grain offering. With all your offerings you shall offer salt.

14'If you offer a grain offering of your firstfruits to the LORD, you shall offer for the grain offering of your firstfruits green heads of grain roasted on the fire, grain beaten from full heads. 15And you shall put oil on it, and lay frankincense on it. It *is* a grain offering. 16Then the priest shall burn the memorial portion: *part* of its beaten grain and *part* of its oil, with all the frankincense, as an offering made by fire to the LORD.

3 'When* his offering *is* a sacrifice of a peace offering, if he offers *it* of the herd, whether male or female, he shall offer it without blemish before the LORD. 2And he shall lay his hand on the head of his offering, and kill it *at* the door of the tabernacle of meeting; and Aaron's sons, the priests, shall sprinkle the blood all around on the altar. 3Then he shall offer from the sacrifice of the peace offering an offering made by fire to the LORD. The fat that covers the entrails and all the fat that *is* on the entrails, 4the two kidneys and the fat that *is* on them by the flanks, and the fatty lobe *attached* to the liver above the kidneys, he shall remove; 5and Aaron's sons shall burn it on the altar upon the burnt sacrifice, which *is* on the wood that *is* on the fire, *as* an offering made by fire, a sweet aroma to the LORD.

6'If his offering as a sacrifice of a peace offering to the LORD *is* of the flock, *whether* male or female, he shall offer it without blemish. 7If he offers a lamb as his offering, then he shall offer it before the LORD. 8And he shall lay his hand on the head of his offering, and kill it before the tabernacle of meeting; and Aaron's sons shall sprinkle its blood all around on the altar.

9'Then he shall offer from the sacrifice of the peace offering, as an offering made by fire to the LORD, its fat *and* the whole fat tail which he shall remove close to the backbone. And the fat that covers the entrails and all the fat that *is* on the entrails, 10the two kidneys and the fat that *is* on them by the flanks, and the fatty lobe *attached* to the liver above the kidneys, he shall remove; 11and the priest shall burn *them* on the altar *as* food, an offering made by fire to the LORD.

12'And if his offering *is* a goat, then he shall offer it before the LORD. 13He shall lay his hand on its head and kill it before the tabernacle of meeting; and the sons of Aaron shall sprinkle its blood all around on the altar. 14Then he shall offer from it his offering, as an offering made by fire to the LORD. The fat that covers the entrails and all the fat that *is* on the entrails, 15the two kidneys and the fat that *is* on them by the flanks, and the fatty lobe *attached* to the liver above the kidneys, he shall remove; 16and the priest shall burn them on the altar *as* food, an offering made by fire for a sweet aroma; all the fat *is* the LORD's.

17'This shall be a perpetual statute throughout your generations in all your dwellings: you shall eat neither fat nor blood.' "

4 Now the LORD spoke to Moses, saying, 2*"Speak to the children of Israel, saying: 'If a person sins unintentionally against any of the commandments of the LORD *in anything* which ought not to be done, and does any of them, 3if the anointed priest sins, bringing guilt on the people, then let him offer to the LORD for his sin which he has sinned a young bull without blemish

CHAPTER 3

3:1–5 Religion is man's attempt to make peace with God on his own terms. Redemption is God's offer of peace through Jesus Christ. But this is "peace through the blood of His cross" (Col. 1:20). The animal sacrifice had to die and the blood had to be sprinkled on the altar before God could declare peace.

Peace with God is a precious blessing that we must never take for granted: "Therefore, having been justified by faith, we have peace with God through our Lord Jesus Christ" (Rom. 5:1).

After the sacrifice, the worshiper and his family would eat what remained once the priest had taken his rightful share (7:11–18). It was to be a joyful feast of fellowship. In fact, the Jews were to consider it a peace offering whenever they slaughtered an animal for food (17:1–9). Do you strive to make each meal an occasion of fellowship and praise to God? If we would present ourselves and the food to Him as an act of worship, our meals might become much happier occasions.

CHAPTER 4

4:2 The sin offering was for unintentional sins of ignorance and not for deliberate sins of disobedience. For deliberate sins, God made no provision for a sacrifice (Num. 15:30–31). All the offender could do was plead the mercy of God (Ps. 51:16–17). But ignorance is no excuse in God's sight! Once we know that we have sinned, we must come to God for forgiveness. Jesus Christ was the sin offering for the whole world, including ignorant Israel (Luke 23:34; Acts 3:17). Our Lord's prayer on Calvary did not automatically forgive their sins, because the people did not repent; but it did postpone the outpouring of God's wrath for nearly forty years.

as a sin offering. 4He shall bring the bull to the door of the tabernacle of meeting before the LORD, lay his hand on the bull's head, and kill the bull before the LORD. 5Then the anointed priest shall take some of the bull's blood and bring it to the tabernacle of meeting. 6The priest shall dip his finger in the blood and sprinkle some of the blood seven times before the LORD, in front of the veil of the sanctuary. 7And the priest shall put some of the blood on the horns of the altar of sweet incense before the LORD, which is in the tabernacle of meeting; and he shall pour the remaining blood of the bull at the base of the altar of the burnt offering, which is at the door of the tabernacle of meeting. 8He shall take from it all the fat of the bull as the sin offering. The fat that covers the entrails and all the fat which *is* on the entrails, 9the two kidneys and the fat that *is* on them by the flanks, and the fatty lobe *attached* to the liver above the kidneys, he shall remove, 10as it was taken from the bull of the sacrifice of the peace offering; and the priest shall burn them on the altar of the burnt offering. 11But the bull's hide and all its flesh, with its head and legs, its entrails and offal— 12the whole bull he shall carry outside the camp to a clean place, where the ashes are poured out, and burn it on wood with fire; where the ashes are poured out it shall be burned.

13*'Now if the whole congregation of Israel sins unintentionally, and the thing is hidden from the eyes of the assembly, and they have done *something against* any of the commandments of the LORD *in anything* which should not be done, and are guilty; 14when the sin which they have committed becomes known, then the assembly shall offer a young bull for the sin, and bring it before the tabernacle of meeting. 15And the elders of the congregation shall lay their hands on the head of the bull before the LORD. Then the bull shall be killed before the LORD. 16The anointed priest shall bring some of the bull's blood to the tabernacle of meeting. 17Then the priest shall dip his finger in the blood and sprinkle *it* seven times before the LORD, in front of the veil. 18And he shall put *some* of the blood on the horns of the altar which *is* before the LORD, which *is* in the tabernacle of meeting; and he shall pour the remaining blood at the base of the altar of burnt offering, which is at the door of the tabernacle of meeting. 19He shall take all the fat from it and burn *it* on the altar. 20And he shall do with the bull as he did with the bull as a sin offering; thus he shall do with it. So the priest shall make atonement for them, and it shall be forgiven them. 21Then he shall carry the bull outside the camp, and burn it as he burned the first bull. It *is* a sin offering for the assembly.

22'When a ruler has sinned, and done *something* unintentionally *against* any of the commandments of the LORD his God *in anything* which should not be done, and is guilty, 23or if his sin which he has committed comes to his knowledge, he shall bring as his offering a kid of the goats, a male without blemish. 24And he shall lay his hand on the head of the goat, and kill it at the place where they kill the burnt offering before the LORD. It *is* a sin offering. 25The priest shall take some of the blood of the sin offering with his finger, put *it* on the horns of the altar of burnt offering, and pour its blood at the base of the altar of burnt offering. 26And he shall burn all its fat on the altar, like the fat of the sacrifice of the peace

4:13 The priest's sacrifice was the same as that of the whole congregation (vv. 3, 14), for the higher the privilege, the greater the responsibility (Luke 12:48). But when the offerings were brought by faith, God promised to forgive (vv. 20, 26, 31, 35). Of course, the final and complete atonement was wrought by Jesus Christ on the cross (Heb. 10:1–14).

When we sin, it affects our prayer life. This is why the priest had to cleanse the golden altar (v. 7). (See Ps. 66:18.)

offering. So the priest shall make atonement for him concerning his sin, and it shall be forgiven him.

27'If anyone of the common people sins unintentionally by doing *something against* any of the commandments of the LORD *in anything* which ought not to be done, and is guilty, 28or if his sin which he has committed comes to his knowledge, then he shall bring as his offering a kid of the goats, a female without blemish, for his sin which he has committed. 29And he shall lay his hand on the head of the sin offering, and kill the sin offering at the place of the burnt offering. 30Then the priest shall take *some* of its blood with his finger, put *it* on the horns of the altar of burnt offering, and pour all *the remaining* blood at the base of the altar. 31He shall remove all its fat, as fat is removed from the sacrifice of the peace offering; and the priest shall burn it on the altar for a sweet aroma to the LORD. So the priest shall make atonement for him, and it shall be forgiven him.

32'If he brings a lamb as his sin offering, he shall bring a female without blemish. 33Then he shall lay his hand on the head of the sin offering, and kill it as a sin offering at the place where they kill the burnt offering. 34The priest shall take *some* of the blood of the sin offering with his finger, put *it* on the horns of the altar of burnt offering, and pour all *the remaining* blood at the base of the altar. 35He shall remove all its fat, as the fat of the lamb is removed from the sacrifice of the peace offering. Then the priest shall burn it on the altar, according to the offerings made by fire to the LORD. So the priest shall make atonement for his sin that he has committed, and it shall be forgiven him.

CHAPTER 5

5:1ff The trespass offering could involve both sacrifice and restitution. It reminds us that sin harms others (v. 16) and that true repentance ought to result in our making right the things we have done wrong.
The sin offering deals with the fact that we are sinners by nature, while the trespass offering deals with individual acts of sin. We must be honest with God about both what we are and what we do (1 John 1:8, 10).
Sometimes we commit sin by keeping quiet (v. 1), or we may cover up (vv. 2–3) or speak out (v. 4). Our sins may be unintentional, and we may be ignorant of them; but once we know about them, we must come to God for cleansing. Sin is *not* "deliberate disobedience to a *known* law." If we disobey God, we are guilty whether we realize it or not.
Have you claimed 1 John 1:9 lately?

5 'If* a person sins in hearing the utterance of an oath, and *is* a witness, whether he has seen or known *of the matter*—if he does not tell *it*, he bears guilt.

2'Or if a person touches any unclean thing, whether *it is* the carcass of an unclean beast, or the carcass of unclean livestock, or the carcass of unclean creeping things, and he is unaware of it, he also shall be unclean and guilty. 3Or if he touches human uncleanness—whatever uncleanness with which a man may be defiled, and he is unaware of it—when he realizes *it*, then he shall be guilty.

4'Or if a person swears, speaking thoughtlessly with *his* lips to do evil or to do good, whatever *it is* that a man may pronounce by an oath, and he is unaware of it—when he realizes *it*, then he shall be guilty in any of these *matters*.

5'And it shall be, when he is guilty in any of these *matters*, that he shall confess that he has sinned in that *thing*; 6and he shall bring his trespass offering to the LORD for his sin which he has committed, a female from the flock, a lamb or a kid of the goats as a sin offering. So the priest shall make atonement for him concerning his sin.

7'If he is not able to bring a lamb, then he shall bring to the LORD, for his trespass which he has committed, two turtledoves or two young pigeons: one as a sin offering and the other as a burnt offering. 8And he shall bring them to the priest, who shall offer *that* which *is* for the sin offering first, and wring off its head from its neck, but shall not divide *it* completely. 9Then he shall sprinkle *some* of the blood of the sin offering on the side of the altar, and the rest of the blood shall be drained out at the base of the altar. It *is* a sin offering. ¹⁰And he shall offer the second *as* a burnt offering according to the prescribed manner. So the priest shall make atonement on his behalf for his sin which he has committed, and it shall be forgiven him.

¹¹'But if he is not able to bring two turtledoves or two young pigeons, then he who sinned shall bring for his offering one-tenth of an ephah of fine flour as a sin offering. He shall put no oil on it, nor shall he put frankincense on it, for it *is* a sin offering. ¹²Then he shall bring it to the priest, and the priest shall take his handful of it as a memorial portion, and burn *it* on the altar according to the offerings made by fire to the LORD. It *is* a sin offering. ¹³The priest shall make atonement for him, for his sin that he has committed in any of these matters; and it shall be forgiven him. *The rest* shall be the priest's as a grain offering.' "

¹⁴Then the LORD spoke to Moses, saying: ¹⁵"If a person commits a trespass, and sins unintentionally in regard to the holy things of the LORD, then he shall bring to the LORD as his trespass offering a ram without blemish from the flocks, with your valuation in shekels of silver according to the shekel of the sanctuary, as a trespass offering. ¹⁶And he shall make restitution for the harm that he has done in regard to the holy thing, and shall add one-fifth to it and give it to the priest. So the priest shall make atonement for him with the ram of the trespass offering, and it shall be forgiven him.

¹⁷"If a person sins, and commits any of these things which are forbidden to be done by the commandments of the LORD, though he does not know *it,* yet he is guilty and shall bear his iniquity. ¹⁸And he shall bring to the priest a ram without blemish from the flock, with your valuation, as a trespass offering. So the priest shall make atonement for him regarding his ignorance in which he erred and did not know *it,* and it shall be forgiven him. ¹⁹It is a trespass offering; he has certainly trespassed against the LORD."

6 And the LORD spoke to Moses, saying: ²"If a person sins and commits a trespass against the LORD by lying to his neighbor about what was delivered to him for safekeeping, or about a pledge, or about a robbery, or if he has extorted from his neighbor, ³or if he has found what was lost and lies concerning it, and swears falsely— in any one of these things that a man may do in which he sins: ⁴then it shall be, because he has sinned and is guilty, that he shall restore what he has stolen, or the thing which he has extorted, or what was delivered to him for safekeeping, or the lost thing which he found, ⁵or all that about which he has sworn falsely. He shall restore its full value, add one-fifth more to it, *and* give it to whomever it belongs, on the day of his trespass offering. ⁶And he shall bring his trespass offering to the LORD, a ram without blemish from the flock, with your valuation, as a trespass offering, to the priest. ⁷So the priest shall make atonement for him before the LORD, and he shall be forgiven for any one of these things that he may have done in which he trespasses."

⁸*Then the LORD spoke to Moses, saying, ⁹"Command Aaron and his sons, saying, 'This *is* the law of the burnt offering: The burnt offering

CHAPTERS 6—7

6:8–12 Let's follow the example of the priest and each morning get rid of the old ashes, stir up the fire, and offer a burnt offering to the Lord (Rom. 12:1–2). The phrase "stir up" in 2 Timothy 1:6 means "stir up the flame into life again." Is the flame burning high on the altar of your heart (Luke 24:32), or are you getting lukewarm (Rev. 3:15–16) or cold (Matt. 24:12)?

shall be on the hearth upon the altar all night until morning, and the fire of the altar shall be kept burning on it. ¹⁰And the priest shall put on his linen garment, and his linen trousers he shall put on his body, and take up the ashes of the burnt offering which the fire has consumed on the altar, and he shall put them beside the altar. ¹¹Then he shall take off his garments, put on other garments, and carry the ashes outside the camp to a clean place. ¹²And the fire on the altar shall be kept burning on it; it shall not be put out. And the priest shall burn wood on it every morning, and lay the burnt offering in order on it; and he shall burn on it the fat of the peace offerings. ¹³A fire shall always be burning on the altar; it shall never go out.

¹⁴*This is the law of the grain offering: The sons of Aaron shall offer it on the altar before the Lord. ¹⁵He shall take from it his handful of the fine flour of the grain offering, with its oil, and all the frankincense which *is* on the grain offering, and shall burn *it* on the altar *for* a sweet aroma, as a memorial to the Lord. ¹⁶And the remainder of it Aaron and his sons shall eat; with unleavened bread it shall be eaten in a holy place; in the court of the tabernacle of meeting they shall eat it. ¹⁷It shall not be baked with leaven. I have given it *as* their portion of My offerings made by fire; it *is* most holy, like the sin offering and the trespass offering. ¹⁸All the males among the children of Aaron may eat it. *It shall be* a statute forever in your generations concerning the offerings made by fire to the Lord. Everyone who touches them must be holy.' "ᵃ

¹⁹And the Lord spoke to Moses, saying, ²⁰"This *is* the offering of Aaron and his sons, which they shall offer to the Lord, *beginning* on the day when he is anointed: one-tenth of an ephah of fine flour as a daily grain offering, half of it in the morning and half of it at night. ²¹It shall be made in a pan with oil. *When it is* mixed, you shall bring it in. The baked pieces of the grain offering you shall offer *for* a sweet aroma to the Lord. ²²The priest from among his sons, who is anointed in his place, shall offer it. *It is* a statute forever to the Lord. It shall be wholly burned. ²³For every grain offering for the priest shall be wholly burned. It shall not be eaten."

²⁴Also the Lord spoke to Moses, saying, ²⁵"Speak to Aaron and to his sons, saying, 'This *is* the law of the sin offering: In the place where the burnt offering is killed, the sin offering shall be killed before the Lord. It *is* most holy. ²⁶The priest who offers it for sin shall eat it. In a holy place it shall be eaten, in the court of the tabernacle of meeting. ²⁷Everyone who touches its flesh must be holy.ᵇ And when its blood is sprinkled on any garment, you shall wash that on which it was sprinkled, in a holy place. ²⁸But the earthen vessel in which it is boiled shall be broken. And if it is boiled in a bronze pot, it shall be both scoured and rinsed in water. ²⁹All the males among the priests may eat it. It *is* most holy. ³⁰But no sin offering from which *any* of the blood is brought into the tabernacle of meeting, to make atonement in the holy place,ᶜ shall be eaten. It shall be burned in the fire.

6:14 Let's also keep the leaven out of our lives (6:14–18), which includes hypocrisy (Luke 12:1), false doctrine (Gal. 5:8–9), and corrupt living (1 Cor. 5:6ff.).

6:18 ᵃCompare Numbers 4:15 and Haggai 2:11–13
6:27 ᵇCompare Numbers 4:15 and Haggai 2:11–13
6:30 ᶜThe Most Holy Place when capitalized

7 ¹Likewise this *is* the law of the trespass offering (it *is* most holy): ²In the place where they kill the burnt offering they shall kill the trespass offering. And its blood he shall sprinkle all around on the altar. ³And he shall offer from it all its fat. The fat tail and the fat that covers the entrails, ⁴the two kidneys and the fat that *is* on them by the flanks, and the fatty lobe *attached* to the liver above the kidneys, he shall remove; ⁵and the priest shall burn them on the altar *as* an offering made by fire to the Lord. It *is* a trespass offering. ⁶Every male among the priests may eat it. It shall be eaten in a holy place. It *is* most holy. ⁷The trespass offering *is* like the sin offering; *there is* one law for them both: the priest who makes atonement with it shall have *it*. ⁸And the priest who offers anyone's burnt offering, that priest shall have for himself the skin of the burnt offering which he has offered. ⁹Also every grain offering that is baked in the oven and all that is prepared in the covered pan, or in a pan, shall be the priest's who offers it. ¹⁰Every grain offering, *whether* mixed with oil or dry, shall belong to all the sons of Aaron, to one *as much* as the other.

¹¹'This *is* the law of the sacrifice of peace offerings which he shall offer to the Lord: ¹²If he offers it for a thanksgiving, then he shall offer, with the sacrifice of thanksgiving, unleavened cakes mixed with oil, unleavened wafers anointed with oil, or cakes of blended flour mixed with oil. ¹³Besides the cakes, *as* his offering he shall offer leavened bread with the sacrifice of thanksgiving of his peace offering. ¹⁴And from it he shall offer one cake from each offering *as* a heave offering to the Lord. It shall belong to the priest who sprinkles the blood of the peace offering.

¹⁵'The flesh of the sacrifice of his peace offering for thanksgiving shall be eaten the same day it is offered. He shall not leave any of it until morning. ¹⁶But if the sacrifice of his offering *is* a vow or a voluntary offering, it shall be eaten the same day that he offers his sacrifice; but on the next day the remainder of it also may be eaten; ¹⁷the remainder of the flesh of the sacrifice on the third day must be burned with fire. ¹⁸And if *any* of the flesh of the sacrifice of his peace offering is eaten at all on the third day, it shall not be accepted, nor shall it be imputed to him; it shall be an abomination *to* him who offers it, and the person who eats of it shall bear guilt.

¹⁹*'The flesh that touches any unclean thing shall not be eaten. It shall be burned with fire. And as for the *clean* flesh, all who are clean may eat of it. ²⁰But the person who eats the flesh of the sacrifice of the peace offering that *belongs* to the Lord, while he is unclean, that person shall be cut off from his people. ²¹Moreover the person who touches any unclean thing, *such as* human uncleanness, *an* unclean animal, or any abominable unclean thing,ᵈ and who eats the flesh of the sacrifice of the peace offering that *belongs* to the Lord, that person shall be cut off from his people.' "

²²And the Lord spoke to Moses, saying, ²³"Speak to the children of Israel, saying: 'You shall not eat any fat, of ox or sheep or goat.

7:19–21 The sin offering was so holy that it could not remain in the defiled camp; it had to be taken outside the camp (5:11–12; see also Heb. 13:10–13). The priests were permitted to eat their share, but only in the holy court of the tabernacle because whatever the offering touched was made holy. Fellowship with God and one another depends on purity (7:19–21).

7:21 ᵈFollowing Masoretic Text, Septuagint, and Vulgate; Samaritan Pentateuch, Syriac, and Targum read *swarming thing* (compare 5:2).

24And the fat of an animal that dies *naturally*, and the fat of what is torn by wild beasts, may be used in any other way; but you shall by no means eat it. 25For whoever eats the fat of the animal of which men offer an offering made by fire to the LORD, the person who eats *it* shall be cut off from his people. 26Moreover you shall not eat any blood in any of your dwellings, *whether* of bird or beast. 27Whoever eats any blood, that person shall be cut off from his people.' "

28Then the LORD spoke to Moses, saying, 29"Speak to the children of Israel, saying: 'He who offers the sacrifice of his peace offering to the LORD shall bring his offering to the LORD from the sacrifice of his peace offering. 30His own hands shall bring the offerings made by fire to the LORD. The fat with the breast he shall bring, that the breast may be waved *as* a wave offering before the LORD. 31And the priest shall burn the fat on the altar, but the breast shall be Aaron's and his sons'. 32Also the right thigh you shall give to the priest *as* a heave offering from the sacrifices of your peace offerings. 33He among the sons of Aaron, who offers the blood of the peace offering and the fat, shall have the right thigh for *his* part. 34For the breast of the wave offering and the thigh of the heave offering I have taken from the children of Israel, from the sacrifices of their peace offerings, and I have given them to Aaron the priest and to his sons from the children of Israel by a statute forever.' "

35This *is* the consecrated portion for Aaron and his sons, from the offerings made by fire to the LORD, on the day when *Moses* presented them to minister to the LORD as priests. 36The LORD commanded this to be given to them by the children of Israel, on the day that He anointed them, *by* a statute forever throughout their generations.

37This *is* the law of the burnt offering, the grain offering, the sin offering, the trespass offering, the consecrations, and the sacrifice of the peace offering, 38which the LORD commanded Moses on Mount Sinai, on the day when He commanded the children of Israel to offer their offerings to the LORD in the Wilderness of Sinai.

CHAPTERS 8—9

8:1ff *Altar* is a key word in these chapters; it is used twenty-three times. Without an altar, there can be no acceptable sacrifice; without a sacrifice, man cannot approach a holy God. But there must also be a priesthood to serve at the altar. In the Old Testament, God's people *had* a priesthood, but in the New Testament, God's people *are* a priesthood (1 Pet. 2:5, 9).

8:6–9 What made the priests acceptable to God? Water (8:6), oil (8:10–12), blood (8:14–29), and garments (8:7–9). We have been washed (1 Cor. 6:11), anointed by the Spirit (1 John 2:20, 27), redeemed by Christ's blood (1 Pet. 1:18ff.), and dressed in His righteousness (Isa. 61:10).

8 And* the LORD spoke to Moses, saying: 2"Take Aaron and his sons with him, and the garments, the anointing oil, a bull as the sin offering, two rams, and a basket of unleavened bread; 3and gather all the congregation together at the door of the tabernacle of meeting."

4So Moses did as the LORD commanded him. And the congregation was gathered together at the door of the tabernacle of meeting. 5And Moses said to the congregation, "This *is* what the LORD commanded to be done."

6*Then Moses brought Aaron and his sons and washed them with water. 7And he put the tunic on him, girded him with the sash, clothed him with the robe, and put the ephod on him; and he girded him with the intricately woven band of the ephod, and with it tied *the ephod* on him. 8Then he put the breastplate on him, and he put the Urim and the Thummime in the breastplate. 9And he put the turban on his head. Also on the turban, on its front, he put the golden plate, the holy crown, as the LORD had commanded Moses.

8:8 eLiterally *the Lights and the Perfections* (compare Exodus 28:30)

10Also Moses took the anointing oil, and anointed the tabernacle and all that *was* in it, and consecrated them. 11He sprinkled some of it on the altar seven times, anointed the altar and all its utensils, and the laver and its base, to consecrate them. 12And he poured some of the anointing oil on Aaron's head and anointed him, to consecrate him.

13Then Moses brought Aaron's sons and put tunics on them, girded them with sashes, and put hats on them, as the LORD had commanded Moses.

14And he brought the bull for the sin offering. Then Aaron and his sons laid their hands on the head of the bull for the sin offering, 15and Moses killed *it*. Then he took the blood, and put *some* on the horns of the altar all around with his finger, and purified the altar. And he poured the blood at the base of the altar, and consecrated it, to make atonement for it. 16Then he took all the fat that *was* on the entrails, the fatty lobe *attached to* the liver, and the two kidneys with their fat, and Moses burned *them* on the altar. 17But the bull, its hide, its flesh, and its offal, he burned with fire outside the camp, as the LORD had commanded Moses.

18Then he brought the ram as the burnt offering. And Aaron and his sons laid their hands on the head of the ram, 19and Moses killed *it*. Then he sprinkled the blood all around on the altar. 20And he cut the ram into pieces; and Moses burned the head, the pieces, and the fat. 21Then he washed the entrails and the legs in water. And Moses burned the whole ram on the altar. It *was* a burnt sacrifice for a sweet aroma, an offering made by fire to the LORD, as the LORD had commanded Moses.

22And he brought the second ram, the ram of consecration. Then Aaron and his sons laid their hands on the head of the ram, 23and Moses killed *it*. Also he took *some* of its blood and put it on the tip of Aaron's right ear, on the thumb of his right hand, and on the big toe of his right foot. 24Then he brought Aaron's sons. And Moses put *some* of the blood on the tips of their right ears, on the thumbs of their right hands, and on the big toes of their right feet. And Moses sprinkled the blood all around on the altar. 25Then he took the fat and the fat tail, all the fat that *was* on the entrails, the fatty lobe *attached to* the liver, the two kidneys and their fat, and the right thigh; 26and from the basket of unleavened bread that was before the LORD he took one unleavened cake, a cake of bread *anointed with* oil, and one wafer, and put *them* on the fat and on the right thigh; 27and he put all *these* in Aaron's hands and in his sons' hands, and waved them *as* a wave offering before the LORD. 28Then Moses took them from their hands and burned *them* on the altar, on the burnt offering. They *were* consecration offerings for a sweet aroma. That *was* an offering made by fire to the LORD. 29And Moses took the breast and waved it *as* a wave offering before the LORD. It was Moses' part of the ram of consecration, as the LORD had commanded Moses.

30Then Moses took some of the anointing oil and some of the blood which *was* on the altar, and sprinkled *it* on Aaron, on his garments, on his sons, and on the garments of his sons with him; and he consecrated Aaron, his garments, his sons, and the garments of his sons with him.

31And Moses said to Aaron and his sons, "Boil the flesh *at* the door of the tabernacle of meeting, and eat it there with the bread that *is* in the basket of consecration offerings, as I commanded, saying, 'Aaron and his sons shall eat it.' 32What remains of the flesh and of the bread you shall burn with fire. 33And you shall not go outside the door of the tabernacle of meeting *for* seven days, until the days of your consecration are ended. For seven days he shall consecrate you. 34As he has done this day, *so* the LORD has commanded to do, to make atonement for you. 35*Therefore you shall stay *at* the door of the tabernacle of meeting day and night for seven days, and keep the charge of the LORD, so that you may not die; for so I have been commanded." 36So Aaron and his sons did all the things that the LORD had commanded by the hand of Moses.

8:35—9:24 The day of dedication began a week of consecration (8:31–36), and the week ended with Aaron blessing the people and the Lord accepting the sacrifices (9:22–24). The glory of the Lord appeared (9:6, 23), which is the purpose of sacrifice and service. Can people say of our worship, "God is truly among you" (1 Cor. 14:25)?

9 It came to pass on the eighth day that Moses called Aaron and his sons and the elders of Israel. 2And he said to Aaron, "Take for yourself a young bull as a sin offering and a ram as a burnt offering, without blemish, and offer *them* before the LORD. 3And to the children of Israel you shall speak, saying, 'Take a kid of the goats as a sin offering, and a calf and a lamb, *both* of the first year, without blemish, as a burnt offering, 4also a bull and a ram as peace offerings, to sacrifice before the LORD, and a grain offering mixed with oil; for today the LORD will appear to you.' "

5So they brought what Moses commanded before the tabernacle of meeting. And all the congregation drew near and stood before the LORD. 6Then Moses said, "This *is* the thing which the LORD commanded you to do, and the glory of the LORD will appear to you." 7And Moses said to Aaron, "Go to the altar, offer your sin offering and your burnt offering, and make atonement for yourself and for the people. Offer the offering of the people, and make atonement for them, as the LORD commanded."

8Aaron therefore went to the altar and killed the calf of the sin offering, which *was* for himself. 9Then the sons of Aaron brought the blood to him. And he dipped his finger in the blood, put *it* on the horns of the altar, and poured the blood at the base of the altar. 10But the fat, the kidneys, and the fatty lobe from the liver of the sin offering he burned on the altar, as the LORD had commanded Moses. 11The flesh and the hide he burned with fire outside the camp.

12And he killed the burnt offering; and Aaron's sons presented to him the blood, which he sprinkled all around on the altar. 13Then they presented the burnt offering to him, with its pieces and head, and he burned *them* on the altar. 14And he washed the entrails and the legs, and burned *them* with the burnt offering on the altar.

15Then he brought the people's offering, and took the goat, which *was* the sin offering for the people, and killed it and offered it for sin, like the first one. 16And he brought the burnt offering and offered it according to the prescribed manner. 17Then he brought the grain offering, took a handful of it, and burned *it* on the altar, besides the burnt sacrifice of the morning.

18He also killed the bull and the ram *as* sacrifices of peace offerings, which *were* for the people. And Aaron's sons presented to him the blood, which he sprinkled all around on the altar, 19and the fat from the bull and the ram—the fatty tail, what covers *the entrails* and the kidneys, and the fatty lobe *attached to* the liver; 20and they put the fat on the breasts. Then he burned the fat on the altar; [21]but the breasts and the right thigh Aaron waved *as* a wave offering before the LORD, as Moses had commanded.

[22]Then Aaron lifted his hand toward the people, blessed them, and came down from offering the sin offering, the burnt offering, and peace offerings. [23]And Moses and Aaron went into the tabernacle of meeting, and came out and blessed the people. Then the glory of the LORD appeared to all the people, [24]and fire came out from before the LORD and consumed the burnt offering and the fat on the altar. When all the people saw *it*, they shouted and fell on their faces.

10 Then* Nadab and Abihu, the sons of Aaron, each took his censer and put fire in it, put incense on it, and offered profane fire before the LORD, which He had not commanded them. [2]So fire went out from the LORD and devoured them, and they died before the LORD. [3]And Moses said to Aaron, "This is what the LORD spoke, saying:

'By those who come near Me
I must be regarded as holy;
And before all the people
I must be glorified.' "

So Aaron held his peace.

[4]Then Moses called Mishael and Elzaphan, the sons of Uzziel the uncle of Aaron, and said to them, "Come near, carry your brethren from before the sanctuary out of the camp." [5]So they went near and carried them by their tunics out of the camp, as Moses had said.

[6]And Moses said to Aaron, and to Eleazar and Ithamar, his sons, "Do not uncover your heads nor tear your clothes, lest you die, and wrath come upon all the people. But let your brethren, the whole house of Israel, bewail the burning which the LORD has kindled. [7]You shall not go out from the door of the tabernacle of meeting, lest you die, for the anointing oil of the LORD *is* upon you." And they did according to the word of Moses.

[8]*Then the LORD spoke to Aaron, saying: [9]"Do not drink wine or intoxicating drink, you, nor your sons with you, when you go into the tabernacle of meeting, lest you die. *It shall be a statute forever throughout your generations, [10]that you may distinguish between holy and unholy, and between unclean and clean, [11]and that you may teach the children of Israel all the statutes which the LORD has spoken to them by the hand of Moses."

[12]And Moses spoke to Aaron, and to Eleazar and Ithamar, his sons who were left: "Take the grain offering that remains of the offerings made by fire to the LORD, and eat it without leaven beside the altar; for it *is* most holy. [13]You shall eat it in a holy place, because it *is* your due and your sons' due, of the sacrifices made by fire to the LORD; for so I have been commanded. [14]The breast of the wave offering and the thigh of the heave offering you shall eat in a clean place, you, your sons, and your daughters with you; for *they are* your due and your sons' due, *which* are given from the sacrifices of peace offerings of the children of Israel. [15]The thigh of the heave offering and the breast of the wave offering they shall bring with the offerings of fat made by fire, to offer *as* a wave offering before the LORD. And it shall be

CHAPTER 10

10:1, 2 It did not take long for sin to enter the priestly family. After a great experience with the Lord, beware the enemy's attack. Elijah ran away after the great victory at Mount Carmel (1 Kings 19), and Jesus was tempted after His baptism at the Jordan (Matt. 3:13—4:11). Great blessings sometimes mean great temptations.

Eleven times in chapters 8—9 you find the phrase "the LORD commanded." Nadab and Abihu did what the Lord had *not* commanded, and the fire of God killed them (Heb. 12:29). At the beginning of new periods in redemptive history, God judged sin in a dramatic way so that the people would learn to fear Him (Josh. 7; Acts 5:1–11).

10:8–10 Did their sin have something to do with strong drink (vv. 8–11)? Paul's admonition in Ephesians 5:18ff. is appropriate here, for there is no acceptable substitute in ministry for the power of the Holy Spirit.

10:19, 20 Aaron obeyed the spirit of the commandment but not the letter. Had he obeyed the letter, he would have been insincere before God, and God would have known that his heart was not in it. Moses looked at the outward appearance, but God looked on the heart (1 Sam. 16:7). God knows your heart and understands you, even when others are critical (1 John 3:20–21).

CHAPTER 11

11:1ff *Defilement.* Chapters 11—15 focus on the concept of "clean" and "unclean" in the areas of food (11), birth (12), disease (13—14), and normal bodily functions (15). Although the laws certainly served a practical hygienic purpose, there was also a spiritual principle involved. As God's people, Israel had to be separated from everything that God called unclean. Other nations might be able to do those things, but the Jews could not (vv. 44–45). Defilement spreads, and one person's carelessness could affect many people.

yours and your sons' with you, by a statute forever, as the LORD has commanded."

16Then Moses made careful inquiry about the goat of the sin offering, and there it was—burned up. And he was angry with Eleazar and Ithamar, the sons of Aaron *who were* left, saying, 17"Why have you not eaten the sin offering in a holy place, since it *is* most holy, and God has given it to you to bear the guilt of the congregation, to make atonement for them before the LORD? 18See! Its blood was not brought inside the holy *place;ʲ* indeed you should have eaten it in a holy *place,* as I commanded."

19*And Aaron said to Moses, "Look, this day they have offered their sin offering and their burnt offering before the LORD, and such things have befallen me! *If* I had eaten the sin offering today, would it have been accepted in the sight of the LORD?" 20So when Moses heard *that,* he was content.

11 Now* the LORD spoke to Moses and Aaron, saying to them, 2"Speak to the children of Israel, saying, 'These *are* the animals which you may eat among all the animals that *are* on the earth: 3Among the animals, whatever divides the hoof, having cloven hooves *and* chewing the cud—that you may eat. 4Nevertheless these you shall not eat among those that chew the cud or those that have cloven hooves: the camel, because it chews the cud but does not have cloven hooves, is unclean to you; 5the rock hyrax, because it chews the cud but does not have cloven hooves, *is* unclean to you; 6the hare, because it chews the cud but does not have cloven hooves, *is* unclean to you; 7and the swine, though it divides the hoof, having cloven hooves, yet does not chew the cud, *is* unclean to you. 8Their flesh you shall not eat, and their carcasses you shall not touch. They *are* unclean to you.

9'These you may eat of all that *are* in the water: whatever in the water has fins and scales, whether in the seas or in the rivers—that you may eat. 10But all in the seas or in the rivers that do not have fins and scales, all that move in the water or any living thing which *is* in the water, they *are* an abomination to you. 11They shall be an abomination to you; you shall not eat their flesh, but you shall regard their carcasses as an abomination. 12Whatever in the water does not have fins or scales—that *shall be* an abomination to you.

13'And these you shall regard as an abomination among the birds; they shall not be eaten, they *are* an abomination: the eagle, the vulture, the buzzard, 14the kite, and the falcon after its kind; 15every raven after its kind, 16the ostrich, the short-eared owl, the sea gull, and the hawk after its kind; 17the little owl, the fisher owl, and the screech owl; 18the white owl, the jackdaw, and the carrion vulture; 19the stork, the heron after its kind, the hoopoe, and the bat.

20'All flying insects that creep on *all* fours *shall be* an abomination to you. 21Yet these you may eat of every flying insect that creeps on *all* fours: those which have jointed legs above their feet with which to leap on the earth. 22These you may eat: the locust after its kind, the destroying locust after its kind, the cricket after its kind, and the grasshopper after its kind. 23But all *other* flying insects which have four feet *shall be* an abomination to you.

24'By these you shall become unclean; whoever touches the carcass of any of them shall be unclean until evening; 25whoever carries part of the carcass of any of them shall wash his clothes and be unclean until evening: 26*The carcass* of any animal which divides the foot, but is not cloven-hoofed or does not chew the cud, *is* unclean to you. Everyone who touches it shall be unclean. 27And whatever goes on its paws, among all kinds of animals that go on *all* fours, those *are* unclean to you. Whoever touches any such carcass shall be unclean until evening. 28Whoever carries *any such* carcass shall wash his clothes and be unclean until evening. It *is* unclean to you.

29'These also *shall be* unclean to you among the creeping things that creep on the earth: the mole, the mouse, and the large lizard after its kind; 30the gecko, the monitor lizard, the sand reptile, the sand lizard, and the chameleon. 31These *are* unclean to you among all that creep. Whoever touches them when they are dead shall be unclean until evening. 32Anything on which *any* of them falls, when they *are* dead shall be unclean, whether *it is* any item of wood or clothing or skin or sack, whatever item *it is,* in which *any* work is done, it must be put in water. And it shall be unclean until evening; then it shall be clean. 33Any earthen vessel into which *any* of them falls you shall break; and whatever *is* in it shall be unclean: 34in such a vessel, any edible food upon which water falls becomes unclean, and any drink that may be drunk from it becomes unclean. 35And everything on which *a part* of *any such* carcass falls shall be unclean; *whether it is* an oven or cooking stove, it shall be broken down; *for* they *are* unclean, and shall be unclean to you. 36Nevertheless a spring or a cistern, *in which there is* plenty of water, shall be clean, but whatever touches any such carcass becomes unclean. 37And if a part of *any such* carcass falls on any planting seed which is to be sown, it *remains* clean. 38But if water is put on the seed, and if *a part* of *any such* carcass falls on it, it *becomes* unclean to you.

39'And if any animal which you may eat dies, he who touches its carcass shall be unclean until evening. 40He who eats of its carcass shall wash his clothes and be unclean until evening. He also who carries its carcass shall wash his clothes and be unclean until evening.

41'And every creeping thing that creeps on the earth *shall be* an abomination. It shall not be eaten. 42Whatever crawls on its belly, whatever goes on *all* fours, or whatever has many feet among all creeping things that creep on the earth—these you shall not eat, for they *are* an abomination. 43You shall not make yourselves abominable with any creeping thing that creeps; nor shall you make yourselves unclean with them, lest you be defiled by them. 44For I *am* the Lord your God. You shall therefore consecrate yourselves, and you shall be holy; for I *am* holy. Neither shall you defile yourselves with any creeping thing that creeps on the earth. 45For I *am* the Lord who brings you up out of the land of Egypt, to be your God. You shall therefore be holy, for I *am* holy.

46*'This *is* the law of the animals and the birds and every living creature that moves in the waters, and of every creature that creeps on the

11:46, 47 Discernment. If they wanted to be pleasing to God, the people had to exercise discernment (vv. 46–47); the priests were supposed to teach them God's will (Ezek. 44:23). The dietary laws were temporary (Mark 7:14–23; Acts 10:9–18; 1 Tim. 4:1–5), but the principle is permanent: believers must have discernment and avoid what is unclean (2 Cor. 7:1; Phil. 1:9–11; Heb. 5:14).

CHAPTER 12

12:1–8 Birth. There is no suggestion here that either conception or birth is an act of sin. After all, God created sex and told us to be fruitful and multiply (Gen. 1:28). God reminds us that we are conceived sinners (Pss. 51:5; 58:3) and therefore need His grace.

12:5 Compassion. Is a female child twice as unclean as a male child? Of course not, for there were no degrees of uncleanness. God was giving the mother extra time to care for a daughter in a masculine society that preferred sons. He was also giving her time to recuperate before the next pregnancy. A husband to whom she bore a daughter might be anxious to try again for a son.

12:8 Grace. Even the poorest could bring an acceptable sacrifice, and God would receive it. This is the sacrifice that Joseph and Mary brought when they dedicated Jesus (Luke 2:22–24). Truly, He became poor that we might be rich (2 Cor. 8:9).

CHAPTER 13

13:1ff Concern. Leprosy was a feared disease for which there was no known cure. God had concern for the leper and made certain he or she was treated with dignity. God gave the priest all the information needed to detect the disease and make sure it did not spread. How tragic it would be to isolate someone who was not really infected or to declare clean somebody who was unclean.

13:3 Characteristics. There is more to this law than a lesson in symptoms; in the Bible, leprosy is a picture of sin (Isa. 1:4–6). The disease was not on the surface; like sin, it was "deeper than the skin." (The phrase is used ten times.) Leprosy spreads in the system and makes the person unclean, so much so that he or she had to be isolated: "He shall dwell alone" (v. 46). How like sin!

earth, 47to distinguish between the unclean and the clean, and between the animal that may be eaten and the animal that may not be eaten.' "

12 Then* the LORD spoke to Moses, saying, 2"Speak to the children of Israel, saying: 'If a woman has conceived, and borne a male child, then she shall be unclean seven days; as in the days of her customary impurity she shall be unclean. 3And on the eighth day the flesh of his foreskin shall be circumcised. 4She shall then continue in the blood of *her* purification thirty-three days. She shall not touch any hallowed thing, nor come into the sanctuary until the days of her purification are fulfilled.

5*'But if she bears a female child, then she shall be unclean two weeks, as in her customary impurity, and she shall continue in the blood of *her* purification sixty-six days.

6'When the days of her purification are fulfilled, whether for a son or a daughter, she shall bring to the priest a lamb of the first year as a burnt offering, and a young pigeon or a turtledove as a sin offering, to the door of the tabernacle of meeting. 7Then he shall offer it before the LORD, and make atonement for her. And she shall be clean from the flow of her blood. This *is* the law for her who has borne a male or a female.

8*'And if she is not able to bring a lamb, then she may bring two turtledoves or two young pigeons—one as a burnt offering and the other as a sin offering. So the priest shall make atonement for her, and she will be clean.' "

13 And* the LORD spoke to Moses and Aaron, saying: 2"When a man has on the skin of his body a swelling, a scab, or a bright spot, and it becomes on the skin of his body *like* a leprousᵍ sore, then he shall be brought to Aaron the priest or to one of his sons the priests. 3*The priest shall examine the sore on the skin of the body; and if the hair on the sore has turned white, and the sore appears *to be* deeper than the skin of his body, it *is* a leprous sore. Then the priest shall examine him, and pronounce him unclean. 4But if the bright spot *is* white on the skin of his body, and does not appear *to be* deeper than the skin, and its hair has not turned white, then the priest shall isolate *the one who has* the sore seven days. 5And the priest shall examine him on the seventh day; and indeed *if* the sore appears to be as it was, *and* the sore has not spread on the skin, then the priest shall isolate him another seven days. 6Then the priest shall examine him again on the seventh day; and indeed *if* the sore has faded, *and* the sore has not spread on the skin, then the priest shall pronounce him clean; it *is* only a scab, and he shall wash his clothes and be clean. 7But if the scab should at all spread over the skin, after he has been seen by the priest for his cleansing, he shall be seen by the priest again. 8And *if* the priest sees that the scab has indeed spread on the skin, then the priest shall pronounce him unclean. It *is* leprosy.

9"When the leprous sore is on a person, then he shall be brought to the priest. 10And the priest shall examine *him;* and indeed *if* the swelling on the skin *is* white, and it has turned the hair white,

---

13:2 ᵍHebrew *saraath,* disfiguring skin diseases, including leprosy, and so in verses 2–46 and 14:1–32

and *there is* a spot of raw flesh in the swelling, [11]it *is* an old leprosy on the skin of his body. The priest shall pronounce him unclean, and shall not isolate him, for he *is* unclean.

[12]"And if leprosy breaks out all over the skin, and the leprosy covers all the skin of *the one who has* the sore, from his head to his foot, wherever the priest looks, [13]then the priest shall consider; and indeed *if* the leprosy has covered all his body, he shall pronounce *him* clean *who has* the sore. It has all turned white. He *is* clean. [14]But when raw flesh appears on him, he shall be unclean. [15]And the priest shall examine the raw flesh and pronounce him to be unclean; *for* the raw flesh *is* unclean. It *is* leprosy. [16]Or if the raw flesh changes and turns white again, he shall come to the priest. [17]And the priest shall examine him; and indeed *if* the sore has turned white, then the priest shall pronounce *him* clean *who has* the sore. He *is* clean.

[18]"If the body develops a boil in the skin, and it is healed, [19]and in the place of the boil there comes a white swelling or a bright spot, reddish-white, then it shall be shown to the priest; [20]and *if,* when the priest sees it, it indeed *appears* deeper than the skin, and its hair has turned white, the priest shall pronounce him unclean. It *is* a leprous sore which has broken out of the boil. [21]But if the priest examines it, and indeed *there are* no white hairs in it, and it *is* not deeper than the skin, but has faded, then the priest shall isolate him seven days; [22]and if it should at all spread over the skin, then the priest shall pronounce him unclean. It *is* a leprous sore. [23]But if the bright spot stays in one place, *and* has not spread, it *is* the scar of the boil; and the priest shall pronounce him clean.

[24]"Or if the body receives a burn on its skin by fire, and the raw *flesh* of the burn becomes a bright spot, reddish-white or white, [25]then the priest shall examine it; and indeed *if* the hair of the bright spot has turned white, and it appears deeper than the skin, it *is* leprosy broken out in the burn. Therefore the priest shall pronounce him unclean. It *is* a leprous sore. [26]But if the priest examines it, and indeed *there are* no white hairs in the bright spot, and it *is* not deeper than the skin, but has faded, then the priest shall isolate him seven days. [27]And the priest shall examine him on the seventh day. If it has at all spread over the skin, then the priest shall pronounce him unclean. It *is* a leprous sore. [28]But if the bright spot stays in one place, *and* has not spread on the skin, but has faded, it *is* a swelling from the burn. The priest shall pronounce him clean, for it *is* the scar from the burn.

[29]"If a man or woman has a sore on the head or the beard, [30]then the priest shall examine the sore; and indeed if it appears deeper than the skin, *and there is* in it thin yellow hair, then the priest shall pronounce him unclean. It *is* a scaly leprosy of the head or beard. [31]But if the priest examines the scaly sore, and indeed it does not appear deeper than the skin, and *there is* no black hair in it, then the priest shall isolate *the one who has* the scale seven days. [32]And on the seventh day the priest shall examine the sore; and indeed *if* the scale has not spread, and there is no yellow hair in it, and the scale does not appear deeper than the skin, [33]he shall shave himself, but the scale he shall not shave. And the priest shall isolate *the one who has* the scale another seven days.

34On the seventh day the priest shall examine the scale; and indeed *if* the scale has not spread over the skin, and does not appear deeper than the skin, then the priest shall pronounce him clean. He shall wash his clothes and be clean. 35But if the scale should at all spread over the skin after his cleansing, 36then the priest shall examine him; and indeed *if* the scale has spread over the skin, the priest need not seek for yellow hair. He *is* unclean. 37But if the scale appears to be at a standstill, and there is black hair grown up in it, the scale has healed. He *is* clean, and the priest shall pronounce him clean.

38"If a man or a woman has bright spots on the skin of the body, *specifically* white bright spots, 39then the priest shall look; and indeed *if* the bright spots on the skin of the body *are* dull white, it *is* a white spot *that* grows on the skin. He *is* clean.

40"As for the man whose hair has fallen from his head, he *is* bald, *but* he *is* clean. 41He whose hair has fallen from his forehead, he *is* bald on the forehead, *but* he *is* clean. 42And if there is on the bald head or bald forehead a reddish-white sore, it *is* leprosy breaking out on his bald head or his bald forehead. 43Then the priest shall examine it; and indeed *if* the swelling of the sore *is* reddish-white on his bald head or on his bald forehead, as the appearance of leprosy on the skin of the body, 44he is a leprous man. He *is* unclean. The priest shall surely pronounce him unclean; his sore *is* on his head.

45"Now the leper on whom the sore *is,* his clothes shall be torn and his head bare; and he shall cover his mustache, and cry, 'Unclean! Unclean!' 46He shall be unclean. All the days he has the sore he shall be unclean. He *is* unclean, and he shall dwell alone; his dwelling *shall be* outside the camp.

47"Also, if a garment has a leprous plague[h] in it, *whether it is* a woolen garment or a linen garment, 48whether *it is* in the warp or woof of linen or wool, whether in leather or in anything made of leather, 49and if the plague is greenish or reddish in the garment or in the leather, whether in the warp or in the woof, or in anything made of leather, it *is* a leprous plague and shall be shown to the priest. 50The priest shall examine the plague and isolate *that which has* the plague seven days. 51And he shall examine the plague on the seventh day. If the plague has spread in the garment, either in the warp or in the woof, in the leather *or* in anything made of leather, the plague *is* an active leprosy. It *is* unclean. 52He shall therefore burn that garment in which is the plague, whether warp or woof, in wool or in linen, or anything of leather, for it *is* an active leprosy; *the garment* shall be burned in the fire.

53"But if the priest examines *it,* and indeed the plague has not spread in the garment, either in the warp or in the woof, or in anything made of leather, 54then the priest shall command that they wash *the thing* in which *is* the plague; and he shall isolate it another seven days. 55Then the priest shall examine the plague after it has been washed; and indeed *if* the plague has not changed its color, though the plague has not spread, it *is* unclean, and you shall burn it in the fire; it contin-

---

13:47 [h]A mold, fungus, or similar infestation, and so in verses 47–59

ues eating away, *whether* the damage *is* outside or inside. ⁵⁶If the priest examines *it,* and indeed the plague has faded after washing it, then he shall tear it out of the garment, whether out of the warp or out of the woof, or out of the leather. ⁵⁷But if it appears again in the garment, either in the warp or in the woof, or in anything made of leather, it *is* a spreading *plague;* you shall burn with fire that in which is the plague. ⁵⁸And if you wash the garment, either warp or woof, or whatever is made of leather, if the plague has disappeared from it, then it shall be washed a second time, and shall be clean.

⁵⁹*"This *is* the law of the leprous plague in a garment of wool or linen, either in the warp or woof, or in anything made of leather, to pronounce it clean or to pronounce it unclean."

14 Then* the LORD spoke to Moses, saying, ²"This shall be the law of the leper for the day of his cleansing: He shall be brought to the priest. ³And the priest shall go out of the camp, and the priest shall examine *him;* and indeed, *if* the leprosy is healed in the leper, ⁴then the priest shall command to take for him who is to be cleansed two living *and* clean birds, cedar wood, scarlet, and hyssop. ⁵*And the priest shall command that one of the birds be killed in an earthen vessel over running water. ⁶As for the living bird, he shall take it, the cedar wood and the scarlet and the hyssop, and dip them and the living bird in the blood of the bird *that was* killed over the running water. ⁷And he shall sprinkle it seven times on him who is to be cleansed from the leprosy, and shall pronounce him clean, and shall let the living bird loose in the open field. ⁸He who is to be cleansed shall wash his clothes, shave off all his hair, and wash himself in water, that he may be clean. After that he shall come into the camp, and shall stay outside his tent seven days. ⁹But on the seventh day he shall shave all the hair off his head and his beard and his eyebrows—all his hair he shall shave off. He shall wash his clothes and wash his body in water, and he shall be clean.

¹⁰"And on the eighth day he shall take two male lambs without blemish, one ewe lamb of the first year without blemish, three-tenths *of an ephah* of fine flour mixed with oil as a grain offering, and one log of oil. ¹¹Then the priest who makes *him* clean shall present the man who is to be made clean, and those things, before the LORD, *at* the door of the tabernacle of meeting. ¹²And the priest shall take one male lamb and offer it as a trespass offering, and the log of oil, and wave them *as* a wave offering before the LORD. ¹³Then he shall kill the lamb in the place where he kills the sin offering and the burnt offering, in a holy place; for as the sin offering *is* the priest's, so *is* the trespass offering. It *is* most holy. ¹⁴The priest shall take *some* of the blood of the trespass offering, and the priest shall put *it* on the tip of the right ear of him who is to be cleansed, on the thumb of his right hand, and on the big toe of his right foot. ¹⁵And the priest shall take *some* of the log of oil, and pour *it* into the palm of his own left hand. ¹⁶Then the priest shall dip his right finger in the oil that *is* in his left hand, and shall sprinkle some of the oil with his finger seven times before the LORD. ¹⁷And of the rest of the oil in his hand, the priest shall put *some* on the tip of the right ear of him who is to be cleansed, on the thumb

13:59 *Compassion.* Our Lord had compassion on the lepers, touched them, and made them clean (Mark 1:40–45); and He gave His disciples power to cleanse the lepers (Matt. 10:8). What Jesus did for all of us is beautifully pictured in the next chapter.

CHAPTER 14

14:1 This ceremony of restoration for the healed leper pictures our Lord's work of redemption. Jesus went outside the camp to meet us and to die for us (Luke 19:10; Heb. 13:10–13). He identified Himself with the outcasts (Matt. 9:10–13)! Whatever is infected with leprosy is fit for the fire (13:52), but He rescued us.

14:5 Birds don't belong in clay jars; they ought to be flying in the heavens. This is a picture of our Lord's incarnation, when He took upon Himself a human body that He might die for our sins. Their turning the living bird loose pictured His resurrection from the dead. The former leper was treated like a priest! (Compare vv. 14–20 with Lev. 8:22–24.) God has made us "kings and priests" through the blood of Christ (Rev. 1:6). Hallelujah, what a Savior!

of his right hand, and on the big toe of his right foot, on the blood of the trespass offering. 18The rest of the oil that *is* in the priest's hand he shall put on the head of him who is to be cleansed. So the priest shall make atonement for him before the LORD.

19"Then the priest shall offer the sin offering, and make atonement for him who is to be cleansed from his uncleanness. Afterward he shall kill the burnt offering. 20And the priest shall offer the burnt offering and the grain offering on the altar. So the priest shall make atonement for him, and he shall be clean.

21"But if he *is* poor and cannot afford it, then he shall take one male lamb *as* a trespass offering to be waved, to make atonement for him, one-tenth *of an ephah* of fine flour mixed with oil as a grain offering, a log of oil, 22and two turtledoves or two young pigeons, such as he is able to afford: one shall be a sin offering and the other a burnt offering. 23He shall bring them to the priest on the eighth day for his cleansing, to the door of the tabernacle of meeting, before the LORD. 24And the priest shall take the lamb of the trespass offering and the log of oil, and the priest shall wave them *as* a wave offering before the LORD. 25Then he shall kill the lamb of the trespass offering, and the priest shall take *some* of the blood of the trespass offering and put *it* on the tip of the right ear of him who is to be cleansed, on the thumb of his right hand, and on the big toe of his right foot. 26And the priest shall pour some of the oil into the palm of his own left hand. 27Then the priest shall sprinkle with his right finger *some* of the oil that *is* in his left hand seven times before the LORD. 28And the priest shall put *some* of the oil that *is* in his hand on the tip of the right ear of him who is to be cleansed, on the thumb of the right hand, and on the big toe of his right foot, on the place of the blood of the trespass offering. 29The rest of the oil that *is* in the priest's hand he shall put on the head of him who is to be cleansed, to make atonement for him before the LORD. 30And he shall offer one of the turtledoves or young pigeons, such as he can afford— 31such as he is able to afford, the one *as* a sin offering and the other *as* a burnt offering, with the grain offering. So the priest shall make atonement for him who is to be cleansed before the LORD. 32This *is* the law *for one* who had a leprous sore, who cannot afford the usual cleansing."

33And the LORD spoke to Moses and Aaron, saying: 34"When you have come into the land of Canaan, which I give you as a possession, and I put the leprous plague[i] in a house in the land of your possession, 35and he who owns the house comes and tells the priest, saying, 'It seems to me that *there is* some plague in the house,' 36then the priest shall command that they empty the house, before the priest goes *into it* to examine the plague, that all that *is* in the house may not be made unclean; and afterward the priest shall go in to examine the house. 37And he shall examine the plague; and indeed if the plague *is* on the walls of the house with ingrained streaks, greenish or reddish, which appear to be deep in the wall, 38then the priest shall go out of the house, to the door of the house, and shut up the house seven

14:34 [i]Decomposition by mildew, mold, dry rot, etc., and so in verses 34–53

days. 39And the priest shall come again on the seventh day and look; and indeed *if* the plague has spread on the walls of the house, 40then the priest shall command that they take away the stones in which *is* the plague, and they shall cast them into an unclean place outside the city. 41And he shall cause the house to be scraped inside, all around, and the dust that they scrape off they shall pour out in an unclean place outside the city. 42Then they shall take other stones and put *them* in the place of *those* stones, and he shall take other mortar and plaster the house.

43"Now if the plague comes back and breaks out in the house, after he has taken away the stones, after he has scraped the house, and after it is plastered, 44then the priest shall come and look; and indeed *if* the plague has spread in the house, it *is* an active leprosy in the house. It *is* unclean. 45And he shall break down the house, its stones, its timber, and all the plaster of the house, and he shall carry *them* outside the city to an unclean place. 46Moreover he who goes into the house at all while it is shut up shall be unclean until evening. 47And he who lies down in the house shall wash his clothes, and he who eats in the house shall wash his clothes.

48"But if the priest comes in and examines *it*, and indeed the plague has not spread in the house after the house was plastered, then the priest shall pronounce the house clean, because the plague is healed. 49And he shall take, to cleanse the house, two birds, cedar wood, scarlet, and hyssop. 50Then he shall kill one of the birds in an earthen vessel over running water; 51and he shall take the cedar wood, the hyssop, the scarlet, and the living bird, and dip them in the blood of the slain bird and in the running water, and sprinkle the house seven times. 52And he shall cleanse the house with the blood of the bird and the running water and the living bird, with the cedar wood, the hyssop, and the scarlet. 53Then he shall let the living bird loose outside the city in the open field, and make atonement for the house, and it shall be clean.

54"This *is* the law for any leprous sore and scale, 55for the leprosy of a garment and of a house, 56for a swelling and a scab and a bright spot, 57to teach when *it is* unclean and when *it is* clean. This *is* the law of leprosy."

15 And* the LORD spoke to Moses and Aaron, saying, 2"Speak to the children of Israel, and say to them: 'When any man has a discharge from his body, his discharge *is* unclean. 3And this shall be his uncleanness in regard to his discharge—whether his body runs with his discharge, or his body is stopped up by his discharge, it *is* his uncleanness. 4Every bed is unclean on which he who has the discharge lies, and everything on which he sits shall be unclean. 5And whoever touches his bed shall wash his clothes and bathe in water, and be unclean until evening. 6He who sits on anything on which he who has the discharge sat shall wash his clothes and bathe in water, and be unclean until evening. 7And he who touches the body of him who has the discharge shall wash his clothes and bathe in water, and be unclean until evening. 8If he who has the discharge spits on him who is clean, then he shall wash his clothes and bathe in water, and be unclean until evening. 9Any saddle on which he who has the discharge rides shall be unclean. 10Whoever touches anything that was under him

CHAPTER 15

15:1ff The key words in this chapter are *discharge* (twenty-four times), *unclean* (twenty-nine times) and *bathe in water* (eleven times). Verses 1–15 refer to discharges from infections, while verses 16–30 refer to the discharges from the normal functions of the body. No doubt sanitation and health were parts of these laws, but fundamentally God was teaching His people how to live separate from defilement (vv. 31–33).

The body is not sinful, and bodily functions are not morally defiling. But man's nature (what the Bible calls "the flesh") is sinful and produces what is sinful and defiling (Mark 7:20–23; Gal. 5:19–21). If we are not careful, what we say and do, and what we are, will touch others and defile them as well (vv. 5–12; Matt. 23:25–28).

shall be unclean until evening. He who carries *any of* those things shall wash his clothes and bathe in water, and be unclean until evening. 11And whomever the one who has the discharge touches, and has not rinsed his hands in water, he shall wash his clothes and bathe in water, and be unclean until evening. 12The vessel of earth that he who has the discharge touches shall be broken, and every vessel of wood shall be rinsed in water.

13'And when he who has a discharge is cleansed of his discharge, then he shall count for himself seven days for his cleansing, wash his clothes, and bathe his body in running water; then he shall be clean. 14On the eighth day he shall take for himself two turtledoves or two young pigeons, and come before the LORD, to the door of the tabernacle of meeting, and give them to the priest. 15Then the priest shall offer them, the one *as* a sin offering and the other *as* a burnt offering. So the priest shall make atonement for him before the LORD because of his discharge.

16'If any man has an emission of semen, then he shall wash all his body in water, and be unclean until evening. 17And any garment and any leather on which there is semen, it shall be washed with water, and be unclean until evening. 18Also, when a woman lies with a man, and *there is* an emission of semen, they shall bathe in water, and be unclean until evening.

19'If a woman has a discharge, *and* the discharge from her body is blood, she shall be set apart seven days; and whoever touches her shall be unclean until evening. 20Everything that she lies on during her impurity shall be unclean; also everything that she sits on shall be unclean. 21Whoever touches her bed shall wash his clothes and bathe in water, and be unclean until evening. 22And whoever touches anything that she sat on shall wash his clothes and bathe in water, and be unclean until evening. 23If *anything* is on *her* bed or on anything on which she sits, when he touches it, he shall be unclean until evening. 24And if any man lies with her at all, so that her impurity is on him, he shall be unclean seven days; and every bed on which he lies shall be unclean.

25'If a woman has a discharge of blood for many days, other than at the time of her *customary* impurity, or if it runs beyond her *usual time of* impurity, all the days of her unclean discharge shall be as the days of her *customary* impurity. She *shall be* unclean. 26Every bed on which she lies all the days of her discharge shall be to her as the bed of her impurity; and whatever she sits on shall be unclean, as the uncleanness of her impurity. 27Whoever touches those things shall be unclean; he shall wash his clothes and bathe in water, and be unclean until evening.

28'But if she is cleansed of her discharge, then she shall count for herself seven days, and after that she shall be clean. 29And on the eighth day she shall take for herself two turtledoves or two young pigeons, and bring them to the priest, to the door of the tabernacle of meeting. 30Then the priest shall offer the one *as* a sin offering and the other *as* a burnt offering, and the priest shall make atonement for her before the LORD for the discharge of her uncleanness.

31*'Thus you shall separate the children of Israel from their uncleanness, lest they die in their uncleanness when they defile My tabernacle that *is*

15:31–33 God made provision for Israel's ceremonial uncleanness, and He has made provision for us. Our heavenly Advocate cleanses us when we come in contrition and confession (1 John 1:5—2:2; see also John 13:1–11). He keeps us clean through His blood (1 John 1:7) and through the cleansing power of His Word (John 15:3; Eph. 5:25–27).

among them. 32This *is* the law for one who has a discharge, and *for him* who emits semen and is unclean thereby, 33and for her who is indisposed because of her *customary* impurity, and for one who has a discharge, either man or woman, and for him who lies with her who is unclean.' "

16 Now* the LORD spoke to Moses after the death of the two sons of Aaron, when they offered *profane fire* before the LORD, and died; 2*and the LORD said to Moses: "Tell Aaron your brother not to come at *just* any time into the Holy *Place* inside the veil, before the mercy seat which *is* on the ark, lest he die; for I will appear in the cloud above the mercy seat.

3*"Thus Aaron shall come into the Holy *Place:* with *the blood of* a young bull as a sin offering, and *of* a ram as a burnt offering. 4He shall put the holy linen tunic and the linen trousers on his body; he shall be girded with a linen sash, and with the linen turban he shall be attired. These *are* holy garments. Therefore he shall wash his body in water, and put them on. 5And he shall take from the congregation of the children of Israel two kids of the goats as a sin offering, and one ram as a burnt offering.

6"Aaron shall offer the bull as a sin offering, which *is* for himself, and make atonement for himself and for his house. 7He shall take the two goats and present them before the LORD *at* the door of the tabernacle of meeting. 8*Then Aaron shall cast lots for the two goats: one lot for the LORD and the other lot for the scapegoat. 9And Aaron shall bring the goat on which the LORD's lot fell, and offer it *as* a sin offering. 10But the goat on which the lot fell to be the scapegoat shall be presented alive before the LORD, to make atonement upon it, *and* to let it go as the scapegoat into the wilderness.

11"And Aaron shall bring the bull of the sin offering, which is for himself, and make atonement for himself and for his house, and shall kill the bull as the sin offering which *is* for himself. 12Then he shall take a censer full of burning coals of fire from the altar before the LORD, with his hands full of sweet incense beaten fine, and bring *it* inside the veil. 13And he shall put the incense on the fire before the LORD, that the cloud of incense may cover the mercy seat that *is* on the Testimony, lest he die. 14He shall take some of the blood of the bull and sprinkle *it* with his finger on the mercy seat on the east *side;* and before the mercy seat he shall sprinkle some of the blood with his finger seven times.

15"Then he shall kill the goat of the sin offering, which *is* for the people, bring its blood inside the veil, do with that blood as he did with the blood of the bull, and sprinkle it on the mercy seat and before the mercy seat. 16So he shall make atonement for the Holy *Place,* because of the uncleanness of the children of Israel, and because of their transgressions, for all their sins; and so he shall do for the tabernacle of meeting which remains among them in the midst of their uncleanness. 17There shall be no man in the tabernacle of meeting when he goes in to make atonement in the Holy *Place,* until he comes out, that he may make atonement for himself, for his household, and for all the assembly of Israel. 18And he shall go out to the altar that *is* before the LORD, and make atonement for it, and shall take some of the blood of the bull and some of the blood of the goat, and

CHAPTER 16

16:1 *The most important day.* The annual Day of Atonement was the most significant of Israel's special days because on it their sins were atoned for. It was the only time the high priest was allowed to enter the Holy of Holies. Nadab and Abihu tried to do it their own way and were judged (Lev. 10), so this ceremony was a matter of life and death.

16:2 *The most important person.* You can see the Lord Jesus illustrated in the high priest. He did the work alone. He laid aside His garments of glory (Phil. 2:5–8), and He sanctified Himself for us (John 17:19). The difference is that Jesus did not offer any sacrifices for Himself because He is sinless. He Himself *is* the perfect and final sacrifice for the sins of the world (Heb. 7:23–28).

16:3 *The most important reason.* The high priest entered the Holy of Holies three times: (1) with the incense (vv. 12–14), (2) with blood for his sins, and (3) with blood for the sins of the people. The cloud of incense speaks of the glory of God, which is the whole purpose of redemption (John 17:1; Eph. 1:6, 12, 14).

16:8–10 *Scapegoat* may come from an Aramaic word that means "to remove." The setting free of the live goat pictured God's forgiveness of their sins (Ps. 103:10–13), but this required the death of the other goat. Salvation is free, but it is not cheap.

put it on the horns of the altar all around. 19Then he shall sprinkle some of the blood on it with his finger seven times, cleanse it, and consecrate it from the uncleanness of the children of Israel.

20"And when he has made an end of atoning for the Holy *Place*, the tabernacle of meeting, and the altar, he shall bring the live goat. 21Aaron shall lay both his hands on the head of the live goat, confess over it all the iniquities of the children of Israel, and all their transgressions, concerning all their sins, putting them on the head of the goat, and shall send *it* away into the wilderness by the hand of a suitable man. 22The goat shall bear on itself all their iniquities to an uninhabited land; and he shall release the goat in the wilderness.

23"Then Aaron shall come into the tabernacle of meeting, shall take off the linen garments which he put on when he went into the Holy *Place*, and shall leave them there. 24And he shall wash his body with water in a holy place, put on his garments, come out and offer his burnt offering and the burnt offering of the people, and make atonement for himself and for the people. 25The fat of the sin offering he shall burn on the altar. 26And he who released the goat as the scapegoat shall wash his clothes and bathe his body in water, and afterward he may come into the camp. 27The bull *for* the sin offering and the goat *for* the sin offering, whose blood was brought in to make atonement in the Holy *Place*, shall be carried outside the camp. And they shall burn in the fire their skins, their flesh, and their offal. 28Then he who burns them shall wash his clothes and bathe his body in water, and afterward he may come into the camp.

29"*This* shall be a statute forever for you: In the seventh month, on the tenth *day* of the month, you shall afflict your souls, and do no work at all, *whether* a native of your own country or a stranger who dwells among you. 30For on that day the priest shall make atonement for you, to cleanse you, *that* you may be clean from all your sins before the LORD. 31It *is* a sabbath of solemn rest for you, and you shall afflict your souls. *It is* a statute forever. 32And the priest, who is anointed and consecrated to minister as priest in his father's place, shall make atonement, and put on the linen clothes, the holy garments; 33then he shall make atonement for the Holy Sanctuary,*j* and he shall make atonement for the tabernacle of meeting and for the altar, and he shall make atonement for the priests and for all the people of the assembly. 34This shall be an everlasting statute for you, to make atonement for the children of Israel, for all their sins, once a year." And he did as the LORD commanded Moses.

CHAPTER 17

17:4–11 *One price.* The only price for sin that God will accept is blood, for the blood is the life of the creature. The sacrifice of blood means one life given for another. We should respect all life and not treat the blood as something common. The Jews were not to bring sacrifices of game (v. 13), because those cost them nothing. (See 2 Sam. 24:24.) The animals shed their blood involuntarily, but Jesus gave His life willingly for the sins of the world.

17 And the LORD spoke to Moses, saying, 2"Speak to Aaron, to his sons, and to all the children of Israel, and say to them, 'This *is* the thing which the LORD has commanded, saying: 3"Whatever man of the house of Israel who kills an ox or lamb or goat in the camp, or who kills *it* outside the camp, 4*and does not bring it to the door of the tabernacle of meeting to offer an offering to the LORD before the tabernacle of the LORD, the guilt of bloodshed shall be imputed to that man. He has shed blood; and that man shall

16:33 *j*That is, the Most Holy Place

be cut off from among his people, 5to the end that the children of Israel may bring their sacrifices which they offer in the open field, that they may bring them to the LORD at the door of the tabernacle of meeting, to the priest, and offer them *as* peace offerings to the LORD. 6*And the priest shall sprinkle the blood on the altar of the LORD *at* the door of the tabernacle of meeting, and burn the fat for a sweet aroma to the LORD. 7They shall no more offer their sacrifices to demons, after whom they have played the harlot. This shall be a statute forever for them throughout their generations." '

8"Also you shall say to them: 'Whatever man of the house of Israel, or of the strangers who dwell among you, who offers a burnt offering or sacrifice, 9and does not bring it to the door of the tabernacle of meeting, to offer it to the LORD, that man shall be cut off from among his people.

10'And whatever man of the house of Israel, or of the strangers who dwell among you, who eats any blood, I will set My face against that person who eats blood, and will cut him off from among his people. 11For the life of the flesh *is* in the blood, and I have given it to you upon the altar to make atonement for your souls; for it *is* the blood *that* makes atonement for the soul.' 12Therefore I said to the children of Israel, 'No one among you shall eat blood, nor shall any stranger who dwells among you eat blood.'

13"Whatever man of the children of Israel, or of the strangers who dwell among you, who hunts and catches any animal or bird that may be eaten, he shall pour out its blood and cover it with dust; 14for *it is* the life of all flesh. Its blood sustains its life. Therefore I said to the children of Israel, 'You shall not eat the blood of any flesh, for the life of all flesh is its blood. Whoever eats it shall be cut off.'

15"And every person who eats what died *naturally* or what was torn *by beasts, whether he is* a native of your own country or a stranger, he shall both wash his clothes and bathe in water, and be unclean until evening. Then he shall be clean. 16But if he does not wash *them* or bathe his body, then he shall bear his guilt."

18 Then the LORD spoke to Moses, saying, 2"Speak to the children of Israel, and say to them: 'I am the LORD your God. 3*According to the doings of the land of Egypt, where you dwelt, you shall not do; and according to the doings of the land of Canaan, where I am bringing you, you shall not do; nor shall you walk in their ordinances. 4You shall observe My judgments and keep My ordinances, to walk in them: I *am* the LORD your God. 5You shall therefore keep My statutes and My judgments, which if a man does, he shall live by them: I *am* the LORD.

6'None of you shall approach anyone who is near of kin to him, to uncover his nakedness: I *am* the LORD. 7The nakedness of your father or the nakedness of your mother you shall not uncover. She *is* your mother; you shall not uncover her nakedness. 8The nakedness of your father's wife you shall not uncover; it *is* your father's nakedness. 9The nakedness of your sister, the daughter of your father, or the daughter of your mother, *whether* born at home or elsewhere, their nakedness you shall not uncover. 10The nakedness of your son's daughter or your daughter's daughter, their nakedness you shall not uncover;

17:6 *One place.* While in the wilderness, the Jews had to do all their slaughtering at the brazen altar and make each animal a peace offering to the Lord. (This law was modified when they entered the land [Deut. 12:20–28].) No other place was acceptable to God. The blood of Jesus Christ, shed at Calvary, is the only acceptable sacrifice for sin in God's sight.

Do you look upon each meal as an offering to the Lord, and do you eat and drink to His glory (1 Cor. 10:31)?

CHAPTER 18

18:3–5 *Standards.* God could not accept the moral standards of either Egypt or Canaan, and the Jews were not to follow them. Instead, they were to obey the laws of God. "I am the LORD" appears twenty-one times in chapters 18 and 19, and the statement reminds us that we are under His authority. (See Rom. 12:2.)

for theirs *is* your own nakedness. ¹¹The nakedness of your father's wife's daughter, begotten by your father—she *is* your sister—you shall not uncover her nakedness. ¹²You shall not uncover the nakedness of your father's sister; she *is* near of kin to your father. ¹³You shall not uncover the nakedness of your mother's sister, for she *is* near of kin to your mother. ¹⁴You shall not uncover the nakedness of your father's brother. You shall not approach his wife; she *is* your aunt. ¹⁵You shall not uncover the nakedness of your daughter-in-law—she *is* your son's wife—you shall not uncover her nakedness. ¹⁶You shall not uncover the nakedness of your brother's wife; it *is* your brother's nakedness. ¹⁷You shall not uncover the nakedness of a woman and her daughter, nor shall you take her son's daughter or her daughter's daughter, to uncover her nakedness. They *are* near of kin to her. It *is* wickedness. ¹⁸Nor shall you take a woman as a rival to her sister, to uncover her nakedness while the other is alive.

¹⁹'Also you shall not approach a woman to uncover her nakedness as long as she is in her *customary* impurity. ²⁰*Moreover you shall not lie carnally with your neighbor's wife, to defile yourself with her. ²¹And you shall not let any of your descendants pass through *the fire* to Molech, nor shall you profane the name of your God: I *am* the LORD. ²²You shall not lie with a male as with a woman. It *is* an abomination. ²³Nor shall you mate with any animal, to defile yourself with it. Nor shall any woman stand before an animal to mate with it. It *is* perversion.

²⁴*'Do not defile yourselves with any of these things; for by all these the nations are defiled, which I am casting out before you. ²⁵For the land is defiled; therefore I visit the punishment of its iniquity upon it, and the land vomits out its inhabitants. ²⁶You shall therefore keep My statutes and My judgments, and shall not commit *any* of these abominations, *either* any of your own nation or any stranger who dwells among you ²⁷(for all these abominations the men of the land have done, who *were* before you, and thus the land is defiled), ²⁸lest the land vomit you out also when you defile it, as it vomited out the nations that *were* before you. ²⁹For whoever commits any of these abominations, the persons who commit *them* shall be cut off from among their people.

³⁰'Therefore you shall keep My ordinance, so that *you* do not commit *any* of these abominable customs which were committed before you, and that you do not defile yourselves by them: I *am* the LORD your God.' "

19 And* the LORD spoke to Moses, saying, ²"Speak to all the congregation of the children of Israel, and say to them: 'You shall be holy, for I the LORD your God *am* holy.

³*'Every one of you shall revere his mother and his father, and keep My Sabbaths: I *am* the LORD your God.

⁴'Do not turn to idols, nor make for yourselves molded gods: I *am* the LORD your God.

⁵*'And if you offer a sacrifice of a peace offering to the LORD, you shall offer it of your own free will. ⁶It shall be eaten the same day you offer *it*, and on the next day. And if any remains until the third day, it shall be burned in the fire. ⁷And if it is eaten at all on the third day, it *is* an abomination. It shall not be accepted. ⁸Therefore *everyone* who eats it shall bear his iniquity, be-

---

18:20–27 Sexuality. Sex is a wonderful gift of God to the human family. When it is used according to His will, it is creative and brings rich blessing. Used apart from His will, sex is destructive and brings tragic consequences. Illicit sex defiles the persons involved (vv. 20–30), whole nations (v. 24) and the land itself (vv. 25, 27).

18:24–30 Sickness. Sexual perversions are abominable to God and make a nation sick. The nations in Canaan were devoted to such practices, and the land "vomited them out" to make room for God's people. God can forgive sexual sins (1 Cor. 6:9–11), but God warns His people not to practice them (1 Thess. 4:1–8; Heb. 13:4).

CHAPTER 19

19:1 God's command for His people to be holy applies to us today (1 Pet. 1:16). The declaration "I am the LORD," found fifteen times in this chapter, reminds us that He must control every area of life.

19:3 The home. Holiness should start in the home as we show respect for our parents (Eph. 6:1–3).
Time. All of our time belongs to God, and we must not waste it (Eph. 5:15–17). But we must also take care to devote special times to Him in worship and service.

19:5–8 Food. Yes, we must eat and drink to the glory of God (1 Cor. 10:31). Our table should be an altar for peace offerings, but too often it is a field for battles!

cause he has profaned the hallowed *offering* of the LORD; and that person shall be cut off from his people.

9*'When you reap the harvest of your land, you shall not wholly reap the corners of your field, nor shall you gather the gleanings of your harvest. 10And you shall not glean your vineyard, nor shall you gather *every* grape of your vineyard; you shall leave them for the poor and the stranger: I *am* the LORD your God.

11*'You shall not steal, nor deal falsely, nor lie to one another. 12And you shall not swear by My name falsely, nor shall you profane the name of your God: I *am* the LORD.

13'You shall not cheat your neighbor, nor rob *him*. The wages of him who is hired shall not remain with you all night until morning. 14*'You shall not curse the deaf, nor put a stumbling block before the blind, but shall fear your God: I *am* the LORD.

15'You shall do no injustice in judgment. You shall not be partial to the poor, nor honor the person of the mighty. In righteousness you shall judge your neighbor. 16You shall not go about *as* a talebearer among your people; nor shall you take a stand against the life of your neighbor: I *am* the LORD.

17'You shall not hate your brother in your heart. You shall surely rebuke your neighbor, and not bear sin because of him. 18You shall not take vengeance, nor bear any grudge against the children of your people, but you shall love your neighbor as yourself: I *am* the LORD.

19'You shall keep My statutes. You shall not let your livestock breed with another kind. You shall not sow your field with mixed seed. Nor shall a garment of mixed linen and wool come upon you.

20'Whoever lies carnally with a woman who *is* betrothed to a man as a concubine, and who has not at all been redeemed nor given her freedom, for this there shall be scourging; *but* they shall not be put to death, because she was not free. 21And he shall bring his trespass offering to the LORD, to the door of the tabernacle of meeting, a ram as a trespass offering. 22The priest shall make atonement for him with the ram of the trespass offering before the LORD for his sin which he has committed. And the sin which he has committed shall be forgiven him.

23'When you come into the land, and have planted all kinds of trees for food, then you shall count their fruit as uncircumcised. Three years it shall be as uncircumcised to you. *It* shall not be eaten. 24But in the fourth year all its fruit shall be holy, a praise to the LORD. 25And in the fifth year you may eat its fruit, that it may yield to you its increase: I *am* the LORD your God.

26'You shall not eat *anything* with the blood, nor shall you practice divination or soothsaying. 27You shall not shave around the sides of your head, nor shall you disfigure the edges of your beard. 28You shall not make any cuttings in your flesh for the dead, nor tattoo any marks on you: I *am* the LORD.

29'Do not prostitute your daughter, to cause her to be a harlot, lest the land fall into harlotry, and the land become full of wickedness.

30'You shall keep My Sabbaths and reverence My sanctuary: I *am* the LORD.

31'Give no regard to mediums and familiar spirits; do not seek after them, to be defiled by them: I *am* the LORD your God.

19:9, 10 *Labor.* We should think of others as we enjoy what God has given to us. If He is Lord in our work, we cannot be selfish.

19:11–13 *Business.* Making dishonest deals, telling lies, holding back money, and using God's name to cover frauds are all out of the question when He is Lord.

19:14–17 *Neighbors.* Unkindness, injustice, gossip, grudges, and hatred (note the sequence) are evil. "Love your neighbor as yourself" is the second greatest commandment (Mark 12:31).

Read the entire chapter carefully and find other areas of practical application.

32'You shall rise before the gray headed and honor the presence of an old man, and fear your God: I *am* the LORD.

33'And if a stranger dwells with you in your land, you shall not mistreat him. 34The stranger who dwells among you shall be to you as one born among you, and you shall love him as yourself; for you were strangers in the land of Egypt: I *am* the LORD your God.

35'You shall do no injustice in judgment, in measurement of length, weight, or volume. 36You shall have honest scales, honest weights, an honest ephah, and an honest hin: I *am* the LORD your God, who brought you out of the land of Egypt.

37'Therefore you shall observe all My statutes and all My judgments, and perform them: I *am* the LORD.' "

CHAPTER 20

The ominous phrase "put to death" is found nine times in this chapter, for "the wages of sin is death" (Rom. 6:23). But fear of death is not the highest motive for holy living. "I am the LORD who sanctifies you" (v. 8) ought to be motivation enough (Phil. 2:12–13).

20:1–5 Idolatry. Molech was the Ammonite god whom the people worshiped by sacrificing their children on the altar or presenting them as temple prostitutes. The modern idols of money, possessions, success, and position have cost many parents their children.

20:6–8 Spiritism. Idolatry and spiritism go together (1 Cor. 10:19–22). The increasing interest in satanism in our own day is frightening, and no Christian ought to joke about Satan or have anything to do with satanic practices.

20:9 Dishonoring parents. This verse emphasizes the fifth commandment (Exod. 20:12) and repeats the law given in Exodus 21:17. (See Prov. 20:20; 30:11, 17; 2 Tim. 3:1–4.)

20:10–21 Immorality. Adultery, incest, homosexuality, and bestiality are condemned, for these things are contrary to nature (Rom. 1:24–27). God created sex and marriage, and we should abide by His laws regarding them.
If Israel allowed these sins, the nation would forfeit its inheritance. (See Eph. 5:5.)

20 Then* the LORD spoke to Moses, saying, 2"Again, you shall say to the children of Israel: 'Whoever of the children of Israel, or of the strangers who dwell in Israel, who gives *any* of his descendants to Molech, he shall surely be put to death. The people of the land shall stone him with stones. 3I will set My face against that man, and will cut him off from his people, because he has given *some* of his descendants to Molech, to defile My sanctuary and profane My holy name. 4And if the people of the land should in any way hide their eyes from the man, when he gives *some* of his descendants to Molech, and they do not kill him, 5then I will set My face against that man and against his family; and I will cut him off from his people, and all who prostitute themselves with him to commit harlotry with Molech.

6*'And the person who turns to mediums and familiar spirits, to prostitute himself with them, I will set My face against that person and cut him off from his people. 7Consecrate yourselves therefore, and be holy, for I *am* the LORD your God. 8And you shall keep My statutes, and perform them: I *am* the LORD who sanctifies you.

9*'For everyone who curses his father or his mother shall surely be put to death. He has cursed his father or his mother. His blood *shall be* upon him.

10*'The man who commits adultery with *another* man's wife, *he* who commits adultery with his neighbor's wife, the adulterer and the adulteress, shall surely be put to death. 11The man who lies with his father's wife has uncovered his father's nakedness; both of them shall surely be put to death. Their blood *shall be* upon them. 12If a man lies with his daughter-in-law, both of them shall surely be put to death. They have committed perversion. Their blood *shall be* upon them. 13If a man lies with a male as he lies with a woman, both of them have committed an abomination. They shall surely be put to death. Their blood *shall be* upon them. 14If a man marries a woman and her mother, it *is* wickedness. They shall be burned with fire, both he and they, that there may be no wickedness among you. 15If a man mates with an animal, he shall surely be put to death, and you shall kill the animal. 16If a woman approaches any animal and mates with it, you shall kill the woman and the animal. They shall surely be put to death. Their blood *is* upon them.

17'If a man takes his sister, his father's daughter or his mother's daughter, and sees her nakedness and she sees his nakedness, it *is* a wicked thing.

And they shall be cut off in the sight of their people. He has uncovered his sister's nakedness. He shall bear his guilt. [18]If a man lies with a woman during her sickness and uncovers her nakedness, he has exposed her flow, and she has uncovered the flow of her blood. Both of them shall be cut off from their people.

[19]'You shall not uncover the nakedness of your mother's sister nor of your father's sister, for that would uncover his near of kin. They shall bear their guilt. [20]If a man lies with his uncle's wife, he has uncovered his uncle's nakedness. They shall bear their sin; they shall die childless. [21]If a man takes his brother's wife, it *is* an unclean thing. He has uncovered his brother's nakedness. They shall be childless.

[22]'You shall therefore keep all My statutes and all My judgments, and perform them, that the land where I am bringing you to dwell may not vomit you out. [23]And you shall not walk in the statutes of the nation which I am casting out before you; for they commit all these things, and therefore I abhor them. [24]But I have said to you, "You shall inherit their land, and I will give it to you to possess, a land flowing with milk and honey." I *am* the LORD your God, who has separated you from the peoples. [25]You shall therefore distinguish between clean animals and unclean, between unclean birds and clean, and you shall not make yourselves abominable by beast or by bird, or by any kind of living thing that creeps on the ground, which I have separated from you as unclean. [26]And you shall be holy to Me, for I the LORD *am* holy, and have separated you from the peoples, that you should be Mine.

[27]'A man or a woman who is a medium, or who has familiar spirits, shall surely be put to death; they shall stone them with stones. Their blood *shall be* upon them.' "

21 And* the LORD said to Moses, "Speak to the priests, the sons of Aaron, and say to them: 'None shall defile himself for the dead among his people, [2]except for his relatives who are nearest to him: his mother, his father, his son, his daughter, and his brother; [3]also his virgin sister who is near to him, who has had no husband, for her he may defile himself. [4]*Otherwise* he shall not defile himself, *being* a chief man among his people, to profane himself.

[5]'They shall not make any bald *place* on their heads, nor shall they shave the edges of their beards nor make any cuttings in their flesh. [6]*They shall be holy to their God and not profane the name of their God, for they offer the offerings of the LORD made by fire, *and* the bread of their God; therefore they shall be holy. [7]They shall not take a wife *who is* a harlot or a defiled woman, nor shall they take a woman divorced from her husband; for *the priest*[k] is holy to his God. [8]Therefore you shall consecrate him, for he offers the bread of your God. He shall be holy to you, for I the LORD, who sanctify you, *am* holy. [9]The daughter of any priest, if she profanes herself by playing the harlot, she profanes her father. She shall be burned with fire.

[10]*He who is* the high priest among his brethren, on whose head the anointing oil was poured and who is consecrated to wear the garments, shall

---

CHAPTER 21

Privilege always brings responsibility. If the nation was to be sanctified, the spiritual leaders had to set the example. God had a word for the priests (1–9), the high priest (10–15), and those who could not be priests (16–24). Note the admonitions in this chapter.

21:1 *"Don't defile yourself!"* Anyone who touched a dead body was ceremonially unclean, so the priests had to be extra careful. They were expected to mourn, but not like the hopeless pagans (v. 5; see also 1 Thess. 4:13–18).

21:6 *"Don't profane God's name!"* If we adopt pagan practices, people think we are worshiping pagan gods, and we dishonor the name of the Lord. "Hallowed be Your name" is the first petition in the Lord's Prayer (Matt. 6:9).

21:7 [k]Literally *he*

21:12 *"Don't profane My sanctuary!"* A defiled or disqualified priest would profane God's holy sanctuary, and God would have to judge. Holy men must minister in holy courts.

21:15 *"Don't profane your posterity!"* So special was the high priest that he could not take anyone but a virgin for a wife to assure the nation that his firstborn was truly a descendant of Aaron. Any sons born with physical defects could not serve, but they received their share of the offerings. The priest who offers a faultless sacrifice (Lev. 22:20–25) must himself be faultless. God wants servants today to be blameless (1 Tim. 3:2, 10).

CHAPTER 22

The chapter begins and ends with the solemn admonition, "You shall not profane My holy name" (vv. 1, 32). In chapter 21, God warned the priests not to be defiled by the unclean things; now He warns them not to defile the clean things.

22:1–9 *Defective serving.* It was dangerous for the priests to serve God if they knew they were unclean. They were insulting God, who knows all things, and deceiving the people who depended on them to present their offerings. The prophet Isaiah advised, "Be clean, you who bear the vessels of the LORD" (Isa. 52:11).

22:10–16 *Defective sharing.* The priests fed their families from the sacrifices the people brought, and that holy food could not be given to outsiders, not even a houseguest. It is good to be generous, but not if our generosity dishonors God's gifts (Matt. 7:6).

not uncover his head nor tear his clothes; 11nor shall he go near any dead body, nor defile himself for his father or his mother; 12*nor shall he go out of the sanctuary, nor profane the sanctuary of his God; for the consecration of the anointing oil of his God *is* upon him: I *am* the LORD. 13And he shall take a wife in her virginity. 14A widow or a divorced woman or a defiled woman *or* a harlot—these he shall not marry; but he shall take a virgin of his own people as wife. 15*Nor shall he profane his posterity among his people, for I the LORD sanctify him.' "

16And the LORD spoke to Moses, saying, 17"Speak to Aaron, saying: 'No man of your descendants in *succeeding* generations, who has *any* defect, may approach to offer the bread of his God. 18For any man who has a defect shall not approach: a man blind or lame, who has a marred *face* or any *limb* too long, 19a man who has a broken foot or broken hand, 20or is a hunchback or a dwarf, or *a man* who has a defect in his eye, or eczema or scab, or is a eunuch. 21No man of the descendants of Aaron the priest, who has a defect, shall come near to offer the offerings made by fire to the LORD. He has a defect; he shall not come near to offer the bread of his God. 22He may eat the bread of his God, *both* the most holy and the holy; 23only he shall not go near the veil or approach the altar, because he has a defect, lest he profane My sanctuaries; for I the LORD sanctify them.' "

24And Moses told *it* to Aaron and his sons, and to all the children of Israel.

22 Then* the LORD spoke to Moses, saying, 2"Speak to Aaron and his sons, that they separate themselves from the holy things of the children of Israel, and that they do not profane My holy name *by* what they dedicate to Me: I *am* the LORD. 3Say to them: 'Whoever of all your descendants throughout your generations, who goes near the holy things which the children of Israel dedicate to the LORD, while he has uncleanness upon him, that person shall be cut off from My presence: I *am* the LORD.

4'Whatever man of the descendants of Aaron, who *is* a leper or has a discharge, shall not eat the holy offerings until he is clean. And whoever touches anything made unclean *by* a corpse, or a man who has had an emission of semen, 5or whoever touches any creeping thing by which he would be made unclean, or any person by whom he would become unclean, whatever his uncleanness may be— 6the person who has touched any such thing shall be unclean until evening, and shall not eat the holy *offerings* unless he washes his body with water. 7And when the sun goes down he shall be clean; and afterward he may eat the holy *offerings,* because it *is* his food. 8Whatever dies *naturally* or is torn *by beasts* he shall not eat, to defile himself with it: I *am* the LORD.

9'They shall therefore keep My ordinance, lest they bear sin for it and die thereby, if they profane it: I the LORD sanctify them.

10*'No outsider shall eat the holy *offering;* one who dwells with the priest, or a hired servant, shall not eat the holy thing. 11But if the priest buys a person with his money, he may eat it; and one who is born in his house may eat his food. 12If the priest's daughter is married to an outsider, she may not eat of the holy offerings. 13But if the priest's daughter is a widow or divorced, and has no child, and has returned to her father's house as in her youth, she may eat her father's food; but no outsider shall eat it.

14'And if a man eats the holy *offering* unintentionally, then he shall restore a holy *offering* to the priest, and add one-fifth to it. 15They shall not profane the holy *offerings* of the children of Israel, which they offer to the Lord, 16or allow them to bear the guilt of trespass when they eat their holy *offerings;* for I the Lord sanctify them.' "

17*And the Lord spoke to Moses, saying, 18"Speak to Aaron and his sons, and to all the children of Israel, and say to them: 'Whatever man of the house of Israel, or of the strangers in Israel, who offers his sacrifice for any of his vows or for any of his freewill offerings, which they offer to the Lord as a burnt offering— 19*you shall offer* of your own free will a male without blemish from the cattle, from the sheep, or from the goats. 20Whatever has a defect, you shall not offer, for it shall not be acceptable on your behalf. 21And whoever offers a sacrifice of a peace offering to the Lord, to fulfill *his* vow, or a freewill offering from the cattle or the sheep, it must be perfect to be accepted; there shall be no defect in it. 22Those *that are* blind or broken or maimed, or have an ulcer or eczema or scabs, you shall not offer to the Lord, nor make an offering by fire of them on the altar to the Lord. 23Either a bull or a lamb that has any limb too long or too short you may offer *as* a freewill offering, but for a vow it shall not be accepted.

24'You shall not offer to the Lord what is bruised or crushed, or torn or cut; nor shall you make *any offering of them* in your land. 25Nor from a foreigner's hand shall you offer any of these as the bread of your God, because their corruption *is* in them, *and* defects *are* in them. They shall not be accepted on your behalf.' "

26And the Lord spoke to Moses, saying: 27"When a bull or a sheep or a goat is born, it shall be seven days with its mother; and from the eighth day and thereafter it shall be accepted as an offering made by fire to the Lord. 28*Whether it is* a cow or ewe, do not kill both her and her young on the same day. 29And when you offer a sacrifice of thanksgiving to the Lord, offer *it* of your own free will. 30On the same day it shall be eaten; you shall leave none of it until morning: I *am* the Lord.

31"Therefore you shall keep My commandments, and perform them: I *am* the Lord. 32You shall not profane My holy name, but I will be hallowed among the children of Israel. I *am* the Lord who sanctifies you, 33who brought you out of the land of Egypt, to be your God: I *am* the Lord."

23 And* the Lord spoke to Moses, saying, 2"Speak to the children of Israel, and say to them: 'The feasts of the Lord, which you shall proclaim *to be* holy convocations, these *are* My feasts.

3'Six days shall work be done, but the seventh day *is* a Sabbath of solemn rest, a holy convocation. You shall do no work *on it; it is* the Sabbath of the Lord in all your dwellings.

4'These *are* the feasts of the Lord, holy convocations which you shall proclaim at their appointed times. 5On the fourteenth *day* of the first month at twilight *is* the Lord's Passover. 6And on the fifteenth day of the same month *is* the Feast

22:17–33 Defective sacrificing. We must give God the best, for that is what He deserves. Since they pictured the coming Savior, the sacrifices had to be perfect. How easy it is to give to the Lord something we don't want anymore! Ponder Malachi 1:6–8.

CHAPTER 23

The Hebrew calendar was organized around a series of sevens. The seventh day of the week was the Sabbath. They celebrated seven annual feasts, three of which occurred in the seventh month. The seventh year was their Sabbatical Year, and after forty-nine years (seven times seven), they celebrated the Year of Jubilee.

23:1–8 God invites us to remember. Passover and the Feast of Unleavened Bread reminded them of their miraculous deliverance from Egypt by the mighty hand of God. The Feast of Tabernacles reminded the people that their ancestors had lived in booths during their wanderings. Each new generation must be taught what God has done for His people; otherwise, they may take their blessings for granted. Specific times of remembering can be good for all of us.

of Unleavened Bread to the LORD; seven days you must eat unleavened bread. 7On the first day you shall have a holy convocation; you shall do no customary work on it. 8But you shall offer an offering made by fire to the LORD for seven days. The seventh day *shall be* a holy convocation; you shall do no customary work *on it.'* "

9And the LORD spoke to Moses, saying, 10"Speak to the children of Israel, and say to them: 'When you come into the land which I give to you, and reap its harvest, then you shall bring a sheaf of the firstfruits of your harvest to the priest. 11He shall wave the sheaf before the LORD, to be accepted on your behalf; on the day after the Sabbath the priest shall wave it. 12And you shall offer on that day, when you wave the sheaf, a male lamb of the first year, without blemish, as a burnt offering to the LORD. 13Its grain offering *shall be* two-tenths *of an ephah* of fine flour mixed with oil, an offering made by fire to the LORD, for a sweet aroma; and its drink offering *shall be* of wine, one-fourth of a hin. 14You shall eat neither bread nor parched grain nor fresh grain until the same day that you have brought an offering to your God; *it shall be* a statute forever throughout your generations in all your dwellings.

15'And you shall count for yourselves from the day after the Sabbath, from the day that you brought the sheaf of the wave offering: seven Sabbaths shall be completed. 16*Count fifty days to the day after the seventh Sabbath; then you shall offer a new grain offering to the LORD. 17You shall bring from your dwellings two wave *loaves* of two-tenths *of an ephah.* They shall be of fine flour; they shall be baked with leaven. *They are* the first-fruits to the LORD. 18And you shall offer with the bread seven lambs of the first year, without blemish, one young bull, and two rams. They shall be

23:16 God invites us to rejoice. At least three of the seven feasts (Firstfruits, Pentecost, and Tabernacles) were tied to the agricultural life of the people, reminders that God was the Giver of all that they needed and enjoyed.

The Seven Feasts Picture Salvation History

Passover	Christ, the Lamb, who died for us	John 1:29; 1 Cor. 5:7
Unleavened Bread	The Christian life of fellowship, separation from sin, and feeding on Christ	1 Cor. 5:6–8
Firstfruits	The resurrection of Christ	1 Cor. 15:20–23
Pentecost	The coming of the Holy Spirit	Acts 2:1ff.
Trumpets	The gathering together of God's people	Isa. 27:12–13; Matt. 24:29–31; 1 Thess. 4:13–18
Day of Atonement	The future cleansing of God's people	Zech. 13:1–2; Rom. 14:10
Tabernacles	The future joy of God's people in His kingdom	Zech. 14:16–21

as a burnt offering to the LORD, with their grain offering and their drink offerings, an offering made by fire for a sweet aroma to the LORD. ¹⁹Then you shall sacrifice one kid of the goats as a sin offering, and two male lambs of the first year as a sacrifice of a peace offering. ²⁰The priest shall wave them with the bread of the firstfruits *as* a wave offering before the LORD, with the two lambs. They shall be holy to the LORD for the priest. ²¹And you shall proclaim on the same day *that* it is a holy convocation to you. You shall do no customary work *on it. It shall be* a statute forever in all your dwellings throughout your generations.

²²'When you reap the harvest of your land, you shall not wholly reap the corners of your field when you reap, nor shall you gather any gleaning from your harvest. You shall leave them for the poor and for the stranger: I *am* the LORD your God.'"

²³Then the LORD spoke to Moses, saying, ²⁴"Speak to the children of Israel, saying: 'In the seventh month, on the first *day* of the month, you shall have a sabbath-*rest,* a memorial of blowing of trumpets, a holy convocation. ²⁵*You shall do no customary work *on it;* and you shall offer an offering made by fire to the LORD.'"

²⁶And the LORD spoke to Moses, saying: ²⁷"Also the tenth *day* of this seventh month *shall be* the Day of Atonement. It shall be a holy convocation for you; you shall afflict your souls, and offer an offering made by fire to the LORD. ²⁸And you shall do no work on that same day, for it *is* the Day of Atonement, to make atonement for you before the LORD your God. ²⁹For any person who is not afflicted *in soul* on that same day shall be cut off from his people. ³⁰And any person who does any work on that same day, that person I will destroy from among his people. ³¹You shall do no manner of work; *it shall be* a statute forever throughout your generations in all your dwellings. ³²It *shall be* to you a sabbath of *solemn* rest, and you shall afflict your souls; on the ninth *day* of the month at evening, from evening to evening, you shall celebrate your sabbath."

³³Then the LORD spoke to Moses, saying, ³⁴"Speak to the children of Israel, saying: 'The fifteenth day of this seventh month *shall be* the Feast of Tabernacles *for* seven days to the LORD. ³⁵On the first day *there shall be* a holy convocation. You shall do no customary work *on it.* ³⁶*For* seven days you shall offer an offering made by fire to the LORD. On the eighth day you shall have a holy convocation, and you shall offer an offering made by fire to the LORD. It *is* a sacred assembly, *and* you shall do no customary work *on it.*

³⁷'These *are* the feasts of the LORD which you shall proclaim *to be* holy convocations, to offer an offering made by fire to the LORD, a burnt offering and a grain offering, a sacrifice and drink offerings, everything on its day— ³⁸besides the Sabbaths of the LORD, besides your gifts, besides all your vows, and besides all your freewill offerings which you give to the LORD.

³⁹'Also on the fifteenth day of the seventh month, when you have gathered in the fruit of the land, you shall keep the feast of the LORD *for* seven days; on the first day *there shall be* a sabbath-*rest,* and on the eighth day a sabbath-*rest.* ⁴⁰And you shall take for yourselves on the first day the fruit of beautiful trees, branches of

23:25 *God invites us to repent.* The great Day of Atonement (chap. 16) required the people to confess their sin and trust God for cleansing. It was followed by Tabernacles, a week of joy and feasting. True joy comes only when we know we are right with God (Ps. 51:8, 12).

palm trees, the boughs of leafy trees, and willows of the brook; and you shall rejoice before the LORD your God for seven days. 41You shall keep it as a feast to the LORD for seven days in the year. *It shall be* a statute forever in your generations. You shall celebrate it in the seventh month. 42You shall dwell in booths for seven days. All who are native Israelites shall dwell in booths, 43that your generations may know that I made the children of Israel dwell in booths when I brought them out of the land of Egypt: I *am* the LORD your God.' "

44So Moses declared to the children of Israel the feasts of the LORD.

CHAPTER 24

Three important responsibilities "before the LORD" (vv. 3, 6, 8) are given in this chapter.

24:1–4 *Providing the oil.* Only God and the priests saw the light, but the lamps had to be kept shining, for there was no other source of light in the Holy of Holies. The purest olive oil had to be used, supplied by the people themselves. Do we today, as God's people, help the light of the church to keep shining continually (Rev. 1:20)?

24:5–9 *Presenting the bread.* Twelve loaves were put on the table each Sabbath, and then the old loaves were given to the priests to eat. They were a reminder that God fed the twelve tribes both physically and spiritually, and that they in turn were to feed the world the truth about the Lord.

24:10–16 *Protecting the name.* The man could not be blamed for his parentage, but he could be blamed for blaspheming. Would someone with Egyptian ancestry glorify Israel's God? (See Exod. 5:2.) Like Moses, we should wait on God for direction (James 1:5). It was a capital offense, and the man was stoned to death. God emphasized again the basic principle that He stated in Exodus 21: equal justice and not personal vengeance.

24 Then* the LORD spoke to Moses, saying: 2"Command the children of Israel that they bring to you pure oil of pressed olives for the light, to make the lamps burn continually. 3Outside the veil of the Testimony, in the tabernacle of meeting, Aaron shall be in charge of it from evening until morning before the LORD continually; *it shall be* a statute forever in your generations. 4He shall be in charge of the lamps on the pure *gold* lampstand before the LORD continually.

5*"And you shall take fine flour and bake twelve cakes with it. Two-tenths *of an ephah* shall be in each cake. 6You shall set them in two rows, six in a row, on the pure *gold* table before the LORD. 7And you shall put pure frankincense on *each* row, that it may be on the bread for a memorial, an offering made by fire to the LORD. 8Every Sabbath he shall set it in order before the LORD continually, *being taken* from the children of Israel by an everlasting covenant. 9And it shall be for Aaron and his sons, and they shall eat it in a holy place; for it *is* most holy to him from the offerings of the LORD made by fire, by a perpetual statute."

10*Now the son of an Israelite woman, whose father *was* an Egyptian, went out among the children of Israel; and this Israelite *woman's* son and a man of Israel fought each other in the camp. 11And the Israelite woman's son blasphemed the name *of the* LORD and cursed; and so they brought him to Moses. (His mother's name *was* Shelomith the daughter of Dibri, of the tribe of Dan.) 12Then they put him in custody, that the mind of the LORD might be shown to them.

13And the LORD spoke to Moses, saying, 14"Take outside the camp him who has cursed; then let all who heard *him* lay their hands on his head, and let all the congregation stone him.

15"Then you shall speak to the children of Israel, saying: 'Whoever curses his God shall bear his sin. 16And whoever blasphemes the name of the LORD shall surely be put to death. All the congregation shall certainly stone him, the stranger as well as him who is born in the land. When he blasphemes the name *of the* LORD, he shall be put to death.

17'Whoever kills any man shall surely be put to death. 18Whoever kills an animal shall make it good, animal for animal.

19'If a man causes disfigurement of his neighbor, as he has done, so shall it be done to him— 20fracture for fracture, eye for eye, tooth for tooth; as he has caused disfigurement of a man, so shall it be done to him. 21And whoever kills an animal shall restore it; but whoever kills a man shall be put to death. 22You shall have the same law for the stranger and for one from your own country; for I *am* the LORD your God.' "

23Then Moses spoke to the children of Israel;

and they took outside the camp him who had cursed, and stoned him with stones. So the children of Israel did as the LORD commanded Moses.

25 And* the LORD spoke to Moses on Mount Sinai, saying, 2"Speak to the children of Israel, and say to them: 'When you come into the land which I give you, then the land shall keep a sabbath to the LORD. 3Six years you shall sow your field, and six years you shall prune your vineyard, and gather its fruit; 4but in the seventh year there shall be a sabbath of solemn rest for the land, a sabbath to the LORD. You shall neither sow your field nor prune your vineyard. 5What grows of its own accord of your harvest you shall not reap, nor gather the grapes of your untended vine, *for* it is a year of rest for the land. 6And the sabbath *produce* of the land shall be food for you: for you, your male and female servants, your hired man, and the stranger who dwells with you, 7for your livestock and the beasts that *are* in your land— all its produce shall be for food.

8'And you shall count seven sabbaths of years for yourself, seven times seven years; and the time of the seven sabbaths of years shall be to you forty-nine years. 9Then you shall cause the trumpet of the Jubilee to sound on the tenth *day* of the seventh month; on the Day of Atonement you shall make the trumpet to sound throughout all your land. 10And you shall consecrate the fiftieth year, and proclaim liberty throughout *all* the land to all its inhabitants. It shall be a Jubilee for you; and each of you shall return to his possession, and each of you shall return to his family. 11*That fiftieth year shall be a Jubilee to you; in it you shall neither sow nor reap what grows of its own accord, nor gather *the grapes* of your untended vine. 12For it *is* the Jubilee; it shall be holy to you; you shall eat its produce from the field.

13'In this Year of Jubilee, each of you shall return to his possession. 14And if you sell anything to your neighbor or buy from your neighbor's hand, you shall not oppress one another. 15According to the number of years after the Jubilee you shall buy from your neighbor, and according to the number of years of crops he shall sell to you. 16*According to the multitude of years you shall increase its price, and according to the fewer number of years you shall diminish its price; for he sells to you *according* to the number *of the years* of the crops. 17Therefore you shall not oppress one another, but you shall fear your God; for I *am* the LORD your God.

18'So you shall observe My statutes and keep My judgments, and perform them; and you will dwell in the land in safety. 19Then the land will yield its fruit, and you will eat your fill, and dwell there in safety.

20*And if you say, "What shall we eat in the seventh year, since we shall not sow nor gather in our produce?" 21Then I will command My blessing on you in the sixth year, and it will bring forth produce enough for three years. 22And you shall sow in the eighth year, and eat old produce until the ninth year; until its produce comes in, you shall eat *of* the old *harvest.*

23'The land shall not be sold permanently, for the land *is* Mine; for you *are* strangers and sojourners with Me. 24And in all the land of your possession you shall grant redemption of the land.

25'If one of your brethren becomes poor, and has sold *some* of his possession, and if his

CHAPTER 25

25:1–7 Resources. The Sabbatical Year (vv. 1–7) and the Year of Jubilee (vv. 8– 55; *jubal* means "to blow a trumpet") were based on two propositions: "The land is Mine" (v. 23), and "The children of Israel are My servants" (vv. 42, 55). God owns the land; we are stewards of what He has shared with us. We must use His resources wisely for His glory, for one day we must give an account of our stewardship (Luke 16:1ff.).

25:11 Rest. There was also an ecological purpose behind these laws, for obedience to them would grant rest to the land, to the beasts who helped work the land, and to the people. Along with the weekly Sabbath, the two events reminded Israel that rest and work go together and that people and God- given resources must not be exploited.

25:16, 17 Riches. There was an economic purpose, for God had a concern for the poor and afflicted (vv. 25, 35, 39, 47). Had Israel obeyed the law of the Year of Jubilee, it would have helped to balance the economy, and the rich would have had difficulty exploiting the poor.

25:20–22 Responsibility. But the overriding purpose was spiritual, a reminder that Jehovah was Lord of both the land and the people, and that Israel had the responsibility to trust Him for everything. They could not sow during either the forty- ninth or fiftieth year but had to wait for the harvest of the fifty-first year. That would take faith (vv. 18–22)!

redeeming relative comes to redeem it, then he may redeem what his brother sold. 26Or if the man has no one to redeem it, but he himself becomes able to redeem it, 27then let him count the years since its sale, and restore the remainder to the man to whom he sold it, that he may return to his possession. 28But if he is not able to have *it* restored to himself, then what was sold shall remain in the hand of him who bought it until the Year of Jubilee; and in the Jubilee it shall be released, and he shall return to his possession.

29'If a man sells a house in a walled city, then he may redeem it within a whole year after it is sold; *within* a full year he may redeem it. 30But if it is not redeemed within the space of a full year, then the house in the walled city shall belong permanently to him who bought it, throughout his generations. It shall not be released in the Jubilee. 31However the houses of villages which have no wall around them shall be counted as the fields of the country. They may be redeemed, and they shall be released in the Jubilee. 32Nevertheless the cities of the Levites, *and* the houses in the cities of their possession, the Levites may redeem at any time. 33And if a man purchases a house from the Levites, then the house that was sold in the city of his possession shall be released in the Jubilee; for the houses in the cities of the Levites *are* their possession among the children of Israel. 34But the field of the common-land of their cities may not be sold, for it *is* their perpetual possession.

35'If one of your brethren becomes poor, and falls into poverty among you, then you shall help him, like a stranger or a sojourner, that he may live with you. 36Take no usury or interest from him; but fear your God, that your brother may live with you. 37You shall not lend him your money for usury, nor lend him your food at a profit. 38I *am* the LORD your God, who brought you out of the land of Egypt, to give you the land of Canaan *and* to be your God.

39*'And if *one of* your brethren *who dwells* by you becomes poor, and sells himself to you, you shall not compel him to serve as a slave. 40As a hired servant *and* a sojourner he shall be with you, *and* shall serve you until the Year of Jubilee. 41And *then* he shall depart from you—he and his children with him—and shall return to his own family. He shall return to the possession of his fathers. 42For they *are* My servants, whom I brought out of the land of Egypt; they shall not be sold as slaves. 43You shall not rule over him with rigor, but you shall fear your God. 44And as for your male and female slaves whom you may have—from the nations that are around you, from them you may buy male and female slaves. 45Moreover you may buy the children of the strangers who dwell among you, and their families who are with you, which they beget in your land; and they shall become your property. 46And you may take them as an inheritance for your children after you, to inherit *them as* a possession; they shall be your permanent slaves. But regarding your brethren, the children of Israel, you shall not rule over one another with rigor.

47'Now if a sojourner or stranger close to you becomes rich, and *one of* your brethren *who dwells* by him becomes poor, and sells himself to the stranger *or* sojourner close to you, or to a member of the stranger's family, 48after he is sold he may be redeemed again. One of his brothers

25:39, 40 Redemption. Jesus used the Year of Jubilee to picture salvation (Luke 4:16–21). Today He offers rest and freedom to all who will trust Him. We are living now in the Year of Jubilee!

may redeem him; 49or his uncle or his uncle's son may redeem him; or *anyone* who is near of kin to him in his family may redeem him; or if he is able he may redeem himself. 50Thus he shall reckon with him who bought him: The price of his release shall be according to the number of years, from the year that he was sold to him until the Year of Jubilee; *it shall be* according to the time of a hired servant for him. 51If *there are* still many years *remaining,* according to them he shall repay the price of his redemption from the money with which he was bought. 52And if there remain but a few years until the Year of Jubilee, then he shall reckon with him, *and* according to his years he shall repay him the price of his redemption. 53He shall be with him as a yearly hired servant, and he shall not rule with rigor over him in your sight. 54And if he is not redeemed in these *years,* then he shall be released in the Year of Jubilee— he and his children with him. 55For the children of Israel *are* servants to Me; they *are* My servants whom I brought out of the land of Egypt: I *am* the LORD your God.

26 "You* shall not make idols for yourselves; neither a carved image nor a *sacred* pillar
shall you rear up for yourselves;
nor shall you set up an engraved stone in your land, to bow down to it;
for I *am* the LORD your God.

2   You shall keep My Sabbaths and reverence My sanctuary:
I *am* the LORD.

3   'If you walk in My statutes and keep My commandments, and perform them,
4   then I will give you rain in its season, the land shall yield its produce, and the trees of the field shall yield their fruit.
5   Your threshing shall last till the time of vintage, and the vintage shall last till the time of sowing;
you shall eat your bread to the full, and dwell in your land safely.
6   I will give peace in the land, and you shall lie down, and none will make you afraid;
I will rid the land of evil beasts,
and the sword will not go through your land.
7   You will chase your enemies, and they shall fall by the sword before you.
8   Five of you shall chase a hundred, and a hundred of you shall put ten thousand to flight;
your enemies shall fall by the sword before you.

9   'For I will look on you favorably and make you fruitful, multiply you and confirm My covenant with you.
10   You shall eat the old harvest, and clear out the old because of the new.
11   I will set My tabernacle among you, and My soul shall not abhor you.
12   I will walk among you and be your God, and you shall be My people.
13   I *am* the LORD your God, who brought you out of the land of Egypt, that you should not be their slaves;
I have broken the bands of your yoke and made you walk upright.

14 *'But if you do not obey Me, and do not observe all these commandments,

CHAPTER 26

26:1–13 Covenant. God used the word *covenant* eight times in this chapter. It reminded the people of their special relationship with Him and the responsibilities belonging to that relationship. If they obeyed the terms of the covenant, they would remain in the Promised Land and enjoy His blessings. God does not promise material success to His new covenant people today, but He does promise to be with us and meet our every need.

26:14–36 Chastening. God's covenant included both blessing and chastening, for God will not share His goodness with rebellious children. Enjoying the gifts while insulting the Giver is both selfish and idolatrous. We should obey God, not to "deserve" His blessings or even to avoid His chastenings, but to show our love to Him and our desire to please His heart.

15 and if you despise My statutes, or if your
　　soul abhors My judgments, so that you do
　　not perform all My commandments, *but*
　　break My covenant,
16 I also will do this to you:
　　I will even appoint terror over you, wasting
　　disease and fever which shall consume
　　the eyes and cause sorrow of heart.
　　And you shall sow your seed in vain, for
　　your enemies shall eat it.
17 I will set My face against you, and you shall
　　be defeated by your enemies.
　　Those who hate you shall reign over you,
　　and you shall flee when no one pursues
　　you.

18 'And after all this, if you do not obey Me,
　　then I will punish you seven times more
　　for your sins.
19 I will break the pride of your power;
　　I will make your heavens like iron and your
　　earth like bronze.
20 And your strength shall be spent in vain;
　　for your land shall not yield its produce, nor
　　shall the trees of the land yield their fruit.

21 'Then, if you walk contrary to Me, and are
　　not willing to obey Me, I will bring on you
　　seven times more plagues, according to
　　your sins.
22 I will also send wild beasts among you,
　　which shall rob you of your children, de-
　　stroy your livestock, and make you few
　　in number;
　　and your highways shall be desolate.

23 'And if by these things you are not reformed
　　by Me, but walk contrary to Me,
24 then I also will walk contrary to you, and I
　　will punish you yet seven times for your
　　sins.
25 And I will bring a sword against you that
　　will execute the vengeance of the cov-
　　enant;
　　when you are gathered together within your
　　cities I will send pestilence among you;
　　and you shall be delivered into the hand of
　　the enemy.
26 When I have cut off your supply of bread,
　　ten women shall bake your bread in one
　　oven, and they shall bring back your
　　bread by weight, and you shall eat and
　　not be satisfied.

27 'And after all this, if you do not obey Me,
　　but walk contrary to Me,
28 then I also will walk contrary to you in fury;
　　and I, even I, will chastise you seven times
　　for your sins.
29 You shall eat the flesh of your sons, and
　　you shall eat the flesh of your daughters.
30 I will destroy your high places, cut down
　　your incense altars, and cast your car-
　　casses on the lifeless forms of your idols;
　　and My soul shall abhor you.
31 I will lay your cities waste and bring your
　　sanctuaries to desolation, and I will not
　　smell the fragrance of your sweet aromas.
32 I will bring the land to desolation, and your
　　enemies who dwell in it shall be aston-
　　ished at it.

33 I will scatter you among the nations and
      draw out a sword after you;
    your land shall be desolate and your cities
      waste.
34 Then the land shall enjoy its sabbaths as
      long as it lies desolate and you *are* in your
      enemies' land;
    then the land shall rest and enjoy its sab-
      baths.
35 As long as *it* lies desolate it shall rest—
    for the time it did not rest on your sabbaths
      when you dwelt in it.

36 'And as for those of you who are left, I will
      send faintness into their hearts in the
      lands of their enemies;
    the sound of a shaken leaf shall cause them
      to flee;
    they shall flee as though fleeing from a
      sword, and they shall fall when no one
      pursues.
37 They shall stumble over one another, as it
      were before a sword, when no one pur-
      sues;
    and you shall have no *power* to stand before
      your enemies.
38 You shall perish among the nations, and
      the land of your enemies shall eat you
      up.
39 And those of you who are left shall waste
      away in their iniquity in your enemies'
      lands;
    also in their fathers' iniquities, which are
      with them, they shall waste away.

40 *'But if they confess their iniquity and the
      iniquity of their fathers, with their un-
      faithfulness in which they were unfaithful
      to Me, and that they also have walked
      contrary to Me,
41 and *that* I also have walked contrary to
      them and have brought them into the land
      of their enemies;
    if their uncircumcised hearts are humbled,
      and they accept their guilt—
42 then I will remember My covenant with Ja-
      cob, and My covenant with Isaac and My
      covenant with Abraham I will remember;
    I will remember the land.
43 The land also shall be left empty by them,
      and will enjoy its sabbaths while it lies
      desolate without them;
    they will accept their guilt, because they de-
      spised My judgments and because their
      soul abhorred My statutes.
44 Yet for all that, when they are in the land
      of their enemies, I will not cast them
      away, nor shall I abhor them, to utterly
      destroy them and break My covenant with
      them;
    for I *am* the LORD their God.
45 But for their sake I will remember the cov-
      enant of their ancestors, whom I brought
      out of the land of Egypt in the sight of
      the nations, that I might be their God:
    I *am* the LORD.'"

46 These *are* the statutes and judgments and laws
which the LORD made between Himself and the
children of Israel on Mount Sinai by the hand of
Moses.

26:40–46 Confession. A gracious God
always leaves the door open for restoration.
That is one loving purpose of His chastening
hand (Heb. 12:1–13). The people may break
their promises to God (v. 15), but God will
never break His promises to His people (v.
44). God forgets our sins but remembers
His covenant! This is not an excuse for sin,
but it is an encouragement for sinners to
repent and return to the Lord.

CHAPTER 27

27:1ff If you have ever found it difficult or impossible to fulfill a promise, the message of this chapter is for you.

In a moment of extreme joy or trial, a Jew might make a vow to God, offering to give Him something valuable in return for His blessing. (See Judg. 11:29–40; Jon. 2:9.)

The vow might involve people (vv. 1–8), animals (vv. 9–13, 26–27), property (vv. 14–25), or produce (vv. 30–33).

27:6 If the person could not fulfill the vow, he was not permitted to back out, nor could he offer a cheaper substitute. He had to give the priest the equivalent in money, plus one-fifth more. This chapter tells the priest how to evaluate the gift so that the Lord would receive the right amount, for the money was used for the work of the sanctuary. The word *valuation* is used nineteen times.

27 Now* the LORD spoke to Moses, saying, 2"Speak to the children of Israel, and say to them: 'When a man consecrates by a vow certain persons to the LORD, according to your valuation, 3if your valuation is of a male from twenty years old up to sixty years old, then your valuation shall be fifty shekels of silver, according to the shekel of the sanctuary. 4If it *is* a female, then your valuation shall be thirty shekels; 5and if from five years old up to twenty years old, then your valuation for a male shall be twenty shekels, and for a female ten shekels; 6*and if from a month old up to five years old, then your valuation for a male shall be five shekels of silver, and for a female your valuation shall be three shekels of silver; 7and if from sixty years old and above, if *it is* a male, then your valuation shall be fifteen shekels, and for a female ten shekels.

8'But if he is too poor to pay your valuation, then he shall present himself before the priest, and the priest shall set a value for him; according to the ability of him who vowed, the priest shall value him.

9'If *it is* an animal that men may bring as an offering to the LORD, all that *anyone* gives to the LORD shall be holy. 10He shall not substitute it or exchange it, good for bad or bad for good; and if he at all exchanges animal for animal, then both it and the one exchanged for it shall be holy. 11If *it is* an unclean animal which they do not offer as a sacrifice to the LORD, then he shall present the animal before the priest; 12and the priest shall set a value for it, whether it is good or bad; as you, the priest, value it, so it shall be. 13But if he *wants* at all *to* redeem it, then he must add one-fifth to your valuation.

14'And when a man dedicates his house *to be* holy to the LORD, then the priest shall set a value for it, whether it is good or bad; as the priest values it, so it shall stand. 15If he who dedicated it *wants to* redeem his house, then he must add one-fifth of the money of your valuation to it, and it shall be his.

16'If a man dedicates to the LORD *part* of a field of his possession, then your valuation shall be according to the seed for it. A homer of barley seed *shall be valued* at fifty shekels of silver. 17If he dedicates his field from the Year of Jubilee, according to your valuation it shall stand. 18But if he dedicates his field after the Jubilee, then the priest shall reckon to him the money due according to the years that remain till the Year of Jubilee, and it shall be deducted from your valuation. 19And if he who dedicates the field ever wishes to redeem it, then he must add one-fifth of the money of your valuation to it, and it shall belong to him. 20But if he does not want to redeem the field, or if he has sold the field to another man, it shall not be redeemed anymore; 21but the field, when it is released in the Jubilee, shall be holy to the LORD, as a devoted field; it shall be the possession of the priest.

22'And if a man dedicates to the LORD a field which he has bought, which is not the field of his possession, 23then the priest shall reckon to him the worth of your valuation, up to the Year of Jubilee, and he shall give your valuation on that day *as* a holy *offering* to the LORD. 24In the Year of Jubilee the field shall return to him from whom it was bought, to the one who *owned* the land as a possession. 25And all your valuations shall be according to the shekel of the sanctuary: twenty gerahs to the shekel.

26'But the firstborn of the animals, which should be the LORD's firstborn, no man shall dedicate; whether *it is* an ox or sheep, it *is* the LORD's. 27And if *it is* an unclean animal, then he shall redeem *it* according to your valuation, and shall add one-fifth to it; or if it is not redeemed, then it shall be sold according to your valuation.

28*'Nevertheless no devoted *offering* that a man may devote to the LORD of all that he has, *both* man and beast, or the field of his possession, shall be sold or redeemed; every devoted *offering is* most holy to the LORD. 29No person under the ban, who may become doomed to destruction among men, shall be redeemed, *but* shall surely be put to death. 30And all the tithe of the land, *whether* of the seed of the land *or* of the fruit of the tree, *is* the LORD's. It *is* holy to the LORD. 31If a man wants at all to redeem *any* of his tithes, he shall add one-fifth to it. 32And concerning the tithe of the herd or the flock, of whatever passes under the rod, the tenth one shall be holy to the LORD. 33He shall not inquire whether it is good or bad, nor shall he exchange it; and if he exchanges it at all, then both it and the one exchanged for it shall be holy; it shall not be redeemed.' "

34These *are* the commandments which the LORD commanded Moses for the children of Israel on Mount Sinai.

27:28–34 Talk is not "cheap"; rash promises can be very expensive. It behooves us to be careful when we experience great joy or great sorrow, lest we make promises to God that we cannot keep. (See Prov. 20:25; Eccles. 5:4–5.) Yes, you can give God something else, but be sure it is equivalent to the original offer—and let Him do the evaluating.

NUMBERS

Numbers gets its name from the numberings of Israel's men of war. The old generation was numbered at Mount Sinai (chaps. 1—4) and the new in the plains of Moab (chaps. 26—27). This is a book of *transition*. God set aside the old generation because of their unbelief (chaps. 1—20) and then prepared a new generation to inherit the Promised Land (chaps. 21—36).

It is a book of *wanderings*, for God made His people wander in the wilderness for forty years until the old generation, twenty years and older, died off. They did not believe God, and their unbelief cost them the inheritance. The New Testament commentary on this event is the book of Hebrews. Unless by faith you enter into your spiritual inheritance in Christ (Eph. 1:3), you will "wander" in unbelief and rob yourself of the blessings God has planned for you (Eph. 2:10).

Bible geography is instructive. Israel in Egypt pictures our lost condition of bondage to the world. Israel in Canaan illustrates our claiming our inheritance by faith and enjoying the fullness of God's provision. Israel in the wilderness pictures carnal Christians whose unbelief and disobedience prevent them from entering into all that God has for them.

CHAPTERS 1—2

1:1–3 Genesis pictures God's people as pilgrims and strangers, looking for their inheritance. Exodus and Leviticus depict Israel as a holy nation of priests, worshiping the Lord. The book of Numbers emphasizes God's people as warriors, overcoming the enemy and claiming the promised inheritance.

1:3–54 They counted the men, twenty years and older, who were able to go to war. They did not ask for volunteers. When you enter the family of God by faith in Jesus Christ, you automatically become one of His soldiers (2 Tim. 2:3–4). Every believer is a soldier, either a good one or a bad one.

1 Now* the LORD spoke to Moses in the Wilderness of Sinai, in the tabernacle of meeting, on the first *day* of the second month, in the second year after they had come out of the land of Egypt, saying: 2"Take a census of all the congregation of the children of Israel, by their families, by their fathers' houses, according to the number of names, every male individually, 3*from twenty years old and above—all who *are able to* go to war in Israel. You and Aaron shall number them by their armies. 4And with you there shall be a man from every tribe, each one the head of his father's house.

5"These are the names of the men who shall stand with you: from Reuben, Elizur the son of Shedeur; 6from Simeon, Shelumiel the son of Zurishaddai; 7from Judah, Nahshon the son of Amminadab; 8from Issachar, Nethanel the son of Zuar; 9from Zebulun, Eliab the son of Helon; 10from the sons of Joseph: from Ephraim, Elishama the son of Ammihud; from Manasseh, Gamaliel the son of Pedahzur; 11from Benjamin, Abidan the son of Gideoni; 12from Dan, Ahiezer the son of Ammishaddai; 13from Asher, Pagiel the son of Ocran; 14from Gad, Eliasaph the son of Deuel;*a* 15from Naphtali, Ahira the son of Enan."
16These *were* chosen from the congregation, leaders of their fathers' tribes, heads of the divisions in Israel.

17Then Moses and Aaron took these men who had been mentioned by name, 18and they assembled all the congregation together on the first *day* of the second month; and they recited their ancestry by families, by their fathers' houses, according to the number of names, from twenty years old and above, each one individually. 19As the LORD commanded Moses, so he numbered them in the Wilderness of Sinai.

20Now the children of Reuben, Israel's oldest

1:14 *a*Spelled *Reuel* in 2:14

son, their genealogies by their families, by their fathers' house, according to the number of names, every male individually, from twenty years old and above, all who *were able to* go to war: 21those who were numbered of the tribe of Reuben *were* forty-six thousand five hundred.

22From the children of Simeon, their genealogies by their families, by their fathers' house, of those who were numbered, according to the number of names, every male individually, from twenty years old and above, all who *were able to* go to war: 23those who were numbered of the tribe of Simeon *were* fifty-nine thousand three hundred.

24From the children of Gad, their genealogies by their families, by their fathers' house, according to the number of names, from twenty years old and above, all who *were able to* go to war: 25those who were numbered of the tribe of Gad *were* forty-five thousand six hundred and fifty.

26From the children of Judah, their genealogies by their families, by their fathers' house, according to the number of names, from twenty years old and above, all who *were able to* go to war: 27those who were numbered of the tribe of Judah *were* seventy-four thousand six hundred.

28From the children of Issachar, their genealogies by their families, by their fathers' house, according to the number of names, from twenty years old and above, all who *were able to* go to war: 29those who were numbered of the tribe of Issachar *were* fifty-four thousand four hundred.

30From the children of Zebulun, their genealogies by their families, by their fathers' house, according to the number of names, from twenty years old and above, all who *were able to* go to war: 31those who were numbered of the tribe of Zebulun *were* fifty-seven thousand four hundred.

32From the sons of Joseph, the children of Ephraim, their genealogies by their families, by their fathers' house, according to the number of names, from twenty years old and above, all who *were able to* go to war: 33those who were numbered of the tribe of Ephraim *were* forty thousand five hundred.

34From the children of Manasseh, their genealogies by their families, by their fathers' house, according to the number of names, from twenty years old and above, all who *were able to* go to war: 35those who were numbered of the tribe of Manasseh *were* thirty-two thousand two hundred.

36From the children of Benjamin, their genealogies by their families, by their fathers' house, according to the number of names, from twenty years old and above, all who *were able to* go to war: 37those who were numbered of the tribe of Benjamin *were* thirty-five thousand four hundred.

38From the children of Dan, their genealogies by their families, by their fathers' house, according to the number of names, from twenty years old and above, all who *were able to* go to war: 39those who were numbered of the tribe of Dan *were* sixty-two thousand seven hundred.

40From the children of Asher, their genealogies by their families, by their fathers' house, according to the number of names, from twenty years old and above, all who *were able to* go to war: 41those who were numbered of the tribe of Asher *were* forty-one thousand five hundred.

42From the children of Naphtali, their genealogies by their families, by their fathers' house, according to the number of names, from twenty years old and above, all who *were able to* go to war: [43]those who were numbered of the tribe of Naphtali *were* fifty-three thousand four hundred.

[44]These are the ones who were numbered, whom Moses and Aaron numbered, with the leaders of Israel, twelve men, each one representing his father's house. [45]So all who were numbered of the children of Israel, by their fathers' houses, from twenty years old and above, all who *were able to* go to war in Israel— [46]all who were numbered were six hundred and three thousand five hundred and fifty.

[47]But the Levites were not numbered among them by their fathers' tribe; [48]for the LORD had spoken to Moses, saying: [49]"Only the tribe of Levi you shall not number, nor take a census of them among the children of Israel; [50]but you shall appoint the Levites over the tabernacle of the Testimony, over all its furnishings, and over all things that belong to it; they shall carry the tabernacle and all its furnishings; they shall attend to it and camp around the tabernacle. [51]And when the tabernacle is to go forward, the Levites shall take it down; and when the tabernacle is to be set up, the Levites shall set it up. The outsider who comes near shall be put to death. [52]The children of Israel shall pitch their tents, everyone by his own camp, everyone by his own standard, according to their armies; [53]but the Levites shall camp around the tabernacle of the Testimony, that there may be no wrath on the congregation of the children of Israel; and the Levites shall keep charge of the tabernacle of the Testimony."

[54]Thus the children of Israel did; according to all that the LORD commanded Moses, so they did.

2:1–34 The army was organized, each tribe with its leaders and its standard. There was unity in diversity. Perhaps the camp of Israel pictures the church. There are different "tribes" and standards, with their different leaders, but it is one army, following one Commander and fighting one enemy: "And this is the victory that has overcome the world—our faith" (1 John 5:4).

2 And* the LORD spoke to Moses and Aaron, saying: [2]"Everyone of the children of Israel shall camp by his own standard, beside the emblems of his father's house; they shall camp some distance from the tabernacle of meeting. [3]On the east side, toward the rising of the sun, those of the standard of the forces with Judah shall camp according to their armies; and Nahshon the son of Amminadab *shall be* the leader of the children of Judah." [4]And his army was numbered at seventy-four thousand six hundred.

[5]"Those who camp next to him *shall be* the tribe of Issachar, and Nethanel the son of Zuar *shall be* the leader of the children of Issachar." [6]And his army was numbered at fifty-four thousand four hundred.

[7]"Then *comes* the tribe of Zebulun, and Eliab the son of Helon *shall be* the leader of the children of Zebulun." [8]And his army was numbered at fifty-seven thousand four hundred. [9]"All who were numbered according to their armies of the forces with Judah, one hundred and eighty-six thousand four hundred—these shall break camp first.

[10]"On the south side *shall be* the standard of the forces with Reuben according to their armies, and the leader of the children of Reuben *shall be* Elizur the son of Shedeur." [11]And his army was numbered at forty-six thousand five hundred.

[12]"Those who camp next to him *shall be* the tribe of Simeon, and the leader of the children of Simeon *shall be* Shelumiel the son of Zurishaddai." [13]And his army was numbered at fifty-nine thousand three hundred.

[14]"Then *comes* the tribe of Gad, and the leader of the children of Gad *shall be* Eliasaph the son

of Reuel."[b] [15]And his army was numbered at forty-five thousand six hundred and fifty. [16]"All who were numbered according to their armies of the forces with Reuben, one hundred and fifty-one thousand four hundred and fifty—they shall be the second to break camp.

[17]"And the tabernacle of meeting shall move out with the camp of the Levites in the middle of the camps; as they camp, so they shall move out, everyone in his place, by their standards.

[18]"On the west side *shall be* the standard of the forces with Ephraim according to their armies, and the leader of the children of Ephraim *shall be* Elishama the son of Ammihud." [19]And his army was numbered at forty thousand five hundred.

[20]"Next to him *comes* the tribe of Manasseh, and the leader of the children of Manasseh *shall be* Gamaliel the son of Pedahzur." [21]And his army was numbered at thirty-two thousand two hundred.

[22]"Then *comes* the tribe of Benjamin, and the leader of the children of Benjamin *shall be* Abidan the son of Gideoni." [23]And his army was numbered at thirty-five thousand four hundred. [24]"All who were numbered according to their armies of the forces with Ephraim, one hundred and eight thousand one hundred—they shall be the third to break camp.

[25]"The standard of the forces with Dan *shall be* on the north side according to their armies, and the leader of the children of Dan *shall be* Ahiezer the son of Ammishaddai." [26]And his army was numbered at sixty-two thousand seven hundred.

[27]"Those who camp next to him *shall be* the tribe of Asher, and the leader of the children of Asher *shall be* Pagiel the son of Ocran." [28]And his army was numbered at forty-one thousand five hundred.

[29]"Then *comes* the tribe of Naphtali, and the leader of the children of Naphtali *shall be* Ahira the son of Enan." [30]And his army was numbered at fifty-three thousand four hundred. [31]"All who were numbered of the forces with Dan, one hundred and fifty-seven thousand six hundred—they shall break camp last, with their standards."

[32]These *are* the ones who were numbered of the children of Israel by their fathers' houses. All who were numbered according to their armies of the forces *were* six hundred and three thousand five hundred and fifty. [33]But the Levites were not numbered among the children of Israel, just as the LORD commanded Moses.

[34]Thus the children of Israel did according to all that the LORD commanded Moses; so they camped by their standards and so they broke camp, each one by his family, according to their fathers' houses.

3 Now* these *are* the records of Aaron and Moses when the LORD spoke with Moses on Mount Sinai. [2]And these *are* the names of the sons of Aaron: Nadab, the firstborn, and Abihu, Eleazar, and Ithamar. [3]These *are* the names of the sons of Aaron, the anointed priests, whom he consecrated to minister as priests. [4]Nadab and Abihu had died before the LORD when they offered profane fire before the LORD in the Wilderness of

CHAPTERS 3—4

3:1–51 The priests were also a part of the battle, for without the blessing of the Lord, there could be no victory. Some of God's people are in the front lines of the battle, while others are behind the lines, interceding to the Lord.

2:14 [b]Spelled *Deuel* in 1:14 and 7:42

Sinai; and they had no children. So Eleazar and Ithamar ministered as priests in the presence of Aaron their father.

5And the LORD spoke to Moses, saying: 6"Bring the tribe of Levi near, and present them before Aaron the priest, that they may serve him. 7And they shall attend to his needs and the needs of the whole congregation before the tabernacle of meeting, to do the work of the tabernacle. 8Also they shall attend to all the furnishings of the tabernacle of meeting, and to the needs of the children of Israel, to do the work of the tabernacle. 9And you shall give the Levites to Aaron and his sons; they *are* given entirely to himc from among the children of Israel. 10So you shall appoint Aaron and his sons, and they shall attend to their priesthood; but the outsider who comes near shall be put to death."

11Then the LORD spoke to Moses, saying: 12"Now behold, I Myself have taken the Levites from among the children of Israel instead of every firstborn who opens the womb among the children of Israel. Therefore the Levites shall be Mine, 13because all the firstborn *are* Mine. On the day that I struck all the firstborn in the land of Egypt, I sanctified to Myself all the firstborn in Israel, both man and beast. They shall be Mine: I *am* the LORD."

14Then the LORD spoke to Moses in the Wilderness of Sinai, saying: 15"Number the children of Levi by their fathers' houses, by their families; you shall number every male from a month old and above."

16So Moses numbered them according to the word of the LORD, as he was commanded. 17These were the sons of Levi by their names: Gershon, Kohath, and Merari. 18And these *are* the names of the sons of Gershon by their families: Libni and Shimei. 19And the sons of Kohath by their families: Amram, Izehar, Hebron, and Uzziel. 20And the sons of Merari by their families: Mahli and Mushi. These *are* the families of the Levites by their fathers' houses.

21From Gershon *came* the family of the Libnites and the family of the Shimites; these *were* the families of the Gershonites. 22Those who were numbered, according to the number of all the males from a month old and above—of those who were numbered *there were* seven thousand five hundred. 23The families of the Gershonites were to camp behind the tabernacle westward. 24And the leader of the father's house of the Gershonites *was* Eliasaph the son of Lael. 25The duties of the children of Gershon in the tabernacle of meeting *included* the tabernacle, the tent with its covering, the screen for the door of the tabernacle of meeting, 26the screen for the door of the court, the hangings of the court which *are* around the tabernacle and the altar, and their cords, according to all the work relating to them.

27From Kohath *came* the family of the Amramites, the family of the Izharites, the family of the Hebronites, and the family of the Uzzielites; these *were* the families of the Kohathites. 28According to the number of all the males, from a month old and above, *there were* eight thousand sixd hundred keeping charge of the sanctuary. 29The families of the children of Kohath were to camp on

3:9 cSamaritan Pentateuch and Septuagint read *Me*.
3:28 dSome manuscripts of the Septuagint read *three*.

the south side of the tabernacle. ³⁰And the leader of the fathers' house of the families of the Kohathites *was* Elizaphan the son of Uzziel. ³¹Their duty *included* the ark, the table, the lampstand, the altars, the utensils of the sanctuary with which they ministered, the screen, and all the work relating to them.

³²And Eleazar the son of Aaron the priest *was to be* chief over the leaders of the Levites, *with* oversight of those who kept charge of the sanctuary.

³³From Merari *came* the family of the Mahlites and the family of the Mushites; these *were* the families of Merari. ³⁴And those who were numbered, according to the number of all the males from a month old and above, *were* six thousand two hundred. ³⁵The leader of the fathers' house of the families of Merari *was* Zuriel the son of Abihail. These *were* to camp on the north side of the tabernacle. ³⁶And the appointed duty of the children of Merari *included* the boards of the tabernacle, its bars, its pillars, its sockets, its utensils, all the work relating to them, ³⁷and the pillars of the court all around, with their sockets, their pegs, and their cords.

³⁸Moreover those who were to camp before the tabernacle on the east, before the tabernacle of meeting, *were* Moses, Aaron, and his sons, keeping charge of the sanctuary, to meet the needs of the children of Israel; but the outsider who came near was to be put to death. ³⁹All who were numbered of the Levites, whom Moses and Aaron numbered at the commandment of the LORD, by their families, all the males from a month old and above, *were* twenty-two thousand.

⁴⁰Then the LORD said to Moses: "Number all the firstborn males of the children of Israel from a month old and above, and take the number of their names. ⁴¹And you shall take the Levites for Me—I *am* the LORD—instead of all the firstborn among the children of Israel, and the livestock of the Levites instead of all the firstborn among the livestock of the children of Israel." ⁴²So Moses numbered all the firstborn among the children of Israel, as the LORD commanded him. ⁴³And all the firstborn males, according to the number of names from a month old and above, of those who were numbered of them, were twenty-two thousand two hundred and seventy-three.

⁴⁴Then the LORD spoke to Moses, saying: ⁴⁵"Take the Levites instead of all the firstborn among the children of Israel, and the livestock of the Levites instead of their livestock. The Levites shall be Mine: I *am* the LORD. ⁴⁶And for the redemption of the two hundred and seventy-three of the firstborn of the children of Israel, who are more than the number of the Levites, ⁴⁷you shall take five shekels for each one individually; you shall take *them* in the currency of the shekel of the sanctuary, the shekel of twenty gerahs. ⁴⁸And you shall give the money, with which the excess number of them is redeemed, to Aaron and his sons."

⁴⁹So Moses took the redemption money from those who were over and above those who were redeemed by the Levites. ⁵⁰From the firstborn of the children of Israel he took the money, one thousand three hundred and sixty-five *shekels*, according to the shekel of the sanctuary. ⁵¹And Moses gave their redemption money to Aaron and his sons, according to the word of the LORD, as the LORD commanded Moses.

4:1–49 It was important that the tabernacle of the Lord go with the people, so God instructed the priests and Levites exactly how to dismantle it and carry it. Each detail about the Lord's work is significant and must not be left to mere human wisdom.

And each person is vital to the work of the Lord, no matter what task God assigns. No task is trivial, not even taking care of the pegs (3:37). Some Levites had heavier burdens than others, but God had given them the assignments and He would enable them.

The putting up and taking down of the tabernacle were tasks as essential as the offering of the sacrifices or the burning of the incense. Spiritual ministry is no place for idle spectators or careless workers, for it is a matter of life and death (4:17–20).

4 Then* the LORD spoke to Moses and Aaron, saying: 2"Take a census of the sons of Kohath from among the children of Levi, by their families, by their fathers' house, 3from thirty years old and above, even to fifty years old, all who enter the service to do the work in the tabernacle of meeting.

4"This *is* the service of the sons of Kohath in the tabernacle of meeting, *relating to* the most holy things: 5When the camp prepares to journey, Aaron and his sons shall come, and they shall take down the covering veil and cover the ark of the Testimony with it. 6Then they shall put on it a covering of badger skins, and spread over *that* a cloth entirely of blue; and they shall insert its poles.

7"On the table of showbread they shall spread a blue cloth, and put on it the dishes, the pans, the bowls, and the pitchers for pouring; and the showbread*e* shall be on it. 8They shall spread over them a scarlet cloth, and cover the same with a covering of badger skins; and they shall insert its poles. 9And they shall take a blue cloth and cover the lampstand of the light, with its lamps, its wick-trimmers, its trays, and all its oil vessels, with which they service it. 10Then they shall put it with all its utensils in a covering of badger skins, and put *it* on a carrying beam.

11"Over the golden altar they shall spread a blue cloth, and cover it with a covering of badger skins; and they shall insert its poles. 12Then they shall take all the utensils of service with which they minister in the sanctuary, put *them* in a blue cloth, cover them with a covering of badger skins, and put *them* on a carrying beam. 13Also they shall take away the ashes from the altar, and spread a purple cloth over it. 14They shall put on it all its implements with which they minister there—the firepans, the forks, the shovels, the basins, and all the utensils of the altar—and they shall spread on it a covering of badger skins, and insert its poles. 15And when Aaron and his sons have finished covering the sanctuary and all the furnishings of the sanctuary, when the camp is set to go, then the sons of Kohath shall come to carry *them;* but they shall not touch any holy thing, lest they die.

"These *are* the things in the tabernacle of meeting which the sons of Kohath are to carry.

16"The appointed duty of Eleazar the son of Aaron the priest *is* the oil for the light, the sweet incense, the daily grain offering, the anointing oil, the oversight of all the tabernacle, of all that *is* in it, with the sanctuary and its furnishings."

17Then the LORD spoke to Moses and Aaron, saying: 18"Do not cut off the tribe of the families of the Kohathites from among the Levites; 19but do this in regard to them, that they may live and not die when they approach the most holy things: Aaron and his sons shall go in and appoint each of them to his service and his task. 20But they shall not go in to watch while the holy things are being covered, lest they die."

21Then the LORD spoke to Moses, saying: 22"Also take a census of the sons of Gershon, by their fathers' house, by their families. 23From thirty years old and above, even to fifty years old, you shall number them, all who enter to perform the service, to do the work in the tabernacle of

4:7 *e*Literally *the continual bread*

meeting. 24This *is* the service of the families of the Gershonites, in serving and carrying: 25They shall carry the curtains of the tabernacle and the tabernacle of meeting *with* its covering, the covering of badger skins that *is* on it, the screen for the door of the tabernacle of meeting, 26the screen for the door of the gate of the court, the hangings of the court which *are* around the tabernacle and altar, and their cords, all the furnishings for their service and all that is made for these things: so shall they serve.

27"Aaron and his sons shall assign all the service of the sons of the Gershonites, all their tasks and all their service. And you shall appoint to them all their tasks as their duty. 28This *is* the service of the families of the sons of Gershon in the tabernacle of meeting. And their duties *shall be* under the authority*f* of Ithamar the son of Aaron the priest.

29"As *for* the sons of Merari, you shall number them by their families and by their fathers' house. 30From thirty years old and above, even to fifty years old, you shall number them, everyone who enters the service to do the work of the tabernacle of meeting. 31And this *is* what they must carry as all their service for the tabernacle of meeting: the boards of the tabernacle, its bars, its pillars, its sockets, 32and the pillars around the court with their sockets, pegs, and cords, with all their furnishings and all their service; and you shall assign *to each man* by name the items he must carry. 33This *is* the service of the families of the sons of Merari, as all their service for the tabernacle of meeting, under the authority*g* of Ithamar the son of Aaron the priest."

34And Moses, Aaron, and the leaders of the congregation numbered the sons of the Kohathites by their families and by their fathers' house, 35from thirty years old and above, even to fifty years old, everyone who entered the service for work in the tabernacle of meeting; 36and those who were numbered by their families were two thousand seven hundred and fifty. 37These *were* the ones who were numbered of the families of the Kohathites, all who might serve in the tabernacle of meeting, whom Moses and Aaron numbered according to the commandment of the LORD by the hand of Moses.

38And those who were numbered of the sons of Gershon, by their families and by their fathers' house, 39from thirty years old and above, even to fifty years old, everyone who entered the service for work in the tabernacle of meeting— 40those who were numbered by their families, by their fathers' house, were two thousand six hundred and thirty. 41These *are* the ones who were numbered of the families of the sons of Gershon, of all who might serve in the tabernacle of meeting, whom Moses and Aaron numbered according to the commandment of the LORD.

42Those of the families of the sons of Merari who were numbered, by their families, by their fathers' house, 43from thirty years old and above, even to fifty years old, everyone who entered the service for work in the tabernacle of meeting— 44those who were numbered by their families were three thousand two hundred. 45These *are* the ones who were numbered of the families of the sons of Merari, whom Moses and Aaron

---

4:28 *f* Literally *hand*   4:33 *g* Literally *hand*

numbered according to the word of the LORD by the hand of Moses.

46All who were numbered of the Levites, whom Moses, Aaron, and the leaders of Israel numbered, by their families and by their fathers' houses, 47from thirty years old and above, even to fifty years old, everyone who came to do the work of service and the work of bearing burdens in the tabernacle of meeting— 48those who were numbered were eight thousand five hundred and eighty.

49According to the commandment of the LORD they were numbered by the hand of Moses, each according to his service and according to his task; thus were they numbered by him, as the LORD commanded Moses.

CHAPTER 5

5:1–4 Defiling. Not everybody in Israel was a soldier or a priest, but each individual was responsible to please the Lord and keep from defilement. Israel was to be holy to the Lord; otherwise He could not bless the nation with victory. You may not think you are important to the spiritual battles going on in today's world, but you are; and you must keep clean.

5:5–10 Defrauding. If the soldiers are not loyal to one another, how can they defeat the enemy? It was not enough to confess the sin; there had to be restitution as well. The people were also reminded to care for the priests because their ministry was important to the victory. Again, each individual had to be sure he or she was obedient to the Lord.

5:11–31 Discovering. This unusual law protected the woman as well as sanctified the marriage relationship. Husbands and wives must be faithful to each other. Marriage is an intimate relationship, and even *hidden* unfaithfulness can create a spirit of jealousy and doubt. If the wife was guilty, the truth would come out; if not, the husband could trust her, and they could live together and have a family. We have no such laws today, but we have an all-seeing God to whom we will answer one day.

5 And* the LORD spoke to Moses, saying: 2"Command the children of Israel that they put out of the camp every leper, everyone who has a discharge, and whoever becomes defiled by a corpse. 3You shall put out both male and female; you shall put them outside the camp, that they may not defile their camps in the midst of which I dwell." 4And the children of Israel did so, and put them outside the camp; as the LORD spoke to Moses, so the children of Israel did.

5*Then the LORD spoke to Moses, saying, 6"Speak to the children of Israel: 'When a man or woman commits any sin that men commit in unfaithfulness against the LORD, and that person is guilty, 7then he shall confess the sin which he has committed. He shall make restitution for his trespass in full, plus one-fifth of it, and give *it* to the one he has wronged. 8But if the man has no relative to whom restitution may be made for the wrong, the restitution for the wrong *must go* to the LORD for the priest, in addition to the ram of the atonement with which atonement is made for him. 9Every offering of all the holy things of the children of Israel, which they bring to the priest, shall be his. 10And every man's holy things shall be his; whatever any man gives the priest shall be his.' "

11*And the LORD spoke to Moses, saying, 12"Speak to the children of Israel, and say to them: 'If any man's wife goes astray and behaves unfaithfully toward him, 13and a man lies with her carnally, and it is hidden from the eyes of her husband, and it is concealed that she has defiled herself, and *there was* no witness against her, nor was she caught— 14if the spirit of jealousy comes upon him and he becomes jealous of his wife, who has defiled herself; or if the spirit of jealousy comes upon him and he becomes jealous of his wife, although she has not defiled herself— 15then the man shall bring his wife to the priest. He shall bring the offering required for her, one-tenth of an ephah of barley meal; he shall pour no oil on it and put no frankincense on it, because it *is* a grain offering of jealousy, an offering for remembering, for bringing iniquity to remembrance.

16'And the priest shall bring her near, and set her before the LORD. 17The priest shall take holy water in an earthen vessel, and take some of the dust that is on the floor of the tabernacle and put *it* into the water. 18Then the priest shall stand the woman before the LORD, uncover the woman's head, and put the offering for remembering in her hands, which *is* the grain offering of jealousy. And the priest shall have in his hand the bitter water that brings a curse. 19And the priest shall put her under oath, and say to the woman, "If no man has lain with you, and if you have not gone astray to uncleanness *while* under your husband's *authority,* be free from this bitter water that brings a curse. 20But if you have gone astray *while* under your husband's *authority,* and if you have defiled yourself and some man other than your husband has lain with you"— 21then the priest shall put the woman under the oath of the curse, and he shall say to the woman—"the LORD make you a curse and an oath among your people, when the LORD makes your thigh rot and your belly swell; 22and may this water that causes the curse go into your stomach, and make *your* belly swell and *your* thigh rot."

'Then the woman shall say, "Amen, so be it."

23'Then the priest shall write these curses in a book, and he shall scrape *them* off into the bitter water. 24And he shall make the woman drink the bitter water that brings a curse, and the water that brings the curse shall enter her *to become* bitter. 25Then the priest shall take the grain offering of jealousy from the woman's hand, shall wave the offering before the LORD, and bring it to the altar; 26and the priest shall take a handful of the offering, as its memorial portion, burn *it* on the altar, and afterward make the woman drink the water. 27When he has made her drink the water, then it shall be, if she has defiled herself and behaved unfaithfully toward her husband, that the water that brings a curse will enter her *and become* bitter, and her belly will swell, her thigh will rot, and the woman will become a curse among her people. 28But if the woman has not defiled herself, and is clean, then she shall be free and may conceive children.

29'This *is* the law of jealousy, when a wife, *while* under her husband's *authority,* goes astray and defiles herself, 30or when the spirit of jealousy comes upon a man, and he becomes jealous of his wife; then he shall stand the woman before the LORD, and the priest shall execute all this law upon her. 31Then the man shall be free from iniquity, but that woman shall bear her guilt.' "

6 Then* the LORD spoke to Moses, saying, 2"Speak to the children of Israel, and say to them: 'When either a man or woman consecrates an offering to take the vow of a Nazirite, to separate himself to the LORD, 3he shall separate himself from wine and *similar* drink; he shall drink neither vinegar made from wine nor vinegar made from *similar* drink; neither shall he drink any grape juice, nor eat fresh grapes or raisins. 4All the days of his separation he shall eat nothing that is produced by the grapevine, from seed to skin.

5'All the days of the vow of his separation no razor shall come upon his head; until the days are fulfilled for which he separated himself to the LORD, he shall be holy. *Then* he shall let the locks of the hair of his head grow. 6All the days that he separates himself to the LORD he shall not go near a dead body. 7He shall not make himself unclean even for his father or his mother, for his brother or his sister, when they die, because his separation to God *is* on his head. 8All the days of his separation he shall be holy to the LORD.

9'And if anyone dies very suddenly beside him, and he defiles his consecrated head, then he shall shave his head on the day of his cleansing; on

CHAPTER 6

6:1–12 *Separation. Nazirite* comes from a word that means "to dedicate." Nazirites were men and women dedicated to the Lord, either for a brief period or for a lifetime (Judg. 13:1–5). Their separation was twofold: *to* the Lord (v. 2) and *from* what defiled (vv. 3–8). Even little things could defile, like the seeds and skins of grapes! When God says something is wrong, it is wrong, no matter how small a thing it may seem to be.

6:13–21 Termination. The Nazirite stated at the beginning how long the vow would last, but our separation to the Lord must be for life. However, it is not wrong occasionally to set aside periods of time for special devotion to the Lord, just as the Nazirites did. If the Nazirite became defiled, all the days of the dedication were lost (v. 12). It is a costly thing to disobey the Lord. Even though the Nazirite had lived in dedication, it was still necessary to bring sacrifices to the Lord, for nobody is perfect before Him.

6:22–27 Benediction. What a privilege it was for the priests to bless the people, and what a privilege it is for us to share God's blessing with others. He blesses us so that we may be a blessing (Gen. 12:1–3). The people were about to enter into war, yet God told them how to have peace. No matter how trying your circumstances may be, you can have God's peace as you live under the blessing of His smile.

CHAPTER 7

7:1–89 The longest chapter in Numbers deals with a generous offering brought by the leaders of the tribes just after the tabernacle was set up. Leaders certainly ought to set the example in giving, and those men did.

The gifts were identical, presented on twelve successive days; and yet in God's eyes, the gifts were individual. If what we give is from the heart, presented for God's glory, He sees it, and He will reward in His own time. Each of those twelve leaders was precious to God. He received their gifts individually.

the seventh day he shall shave it. 10Then on the eighth day he shall bring two turtledoves or two young pigeons to the priest, to the door of the tabernacle of meeting; 11and the priest shall offer one as a sin offering and *the* other as a burnt offering, and make atonement for him, because he sinned in regard to the corpse; and he shall sanctify his head that same day. 12He shall consecrate to the LORD the days of his separation, and bring a male lamb in its first year as a trespass offering; but the former days shall be lost, because his separation was defiled.

13*'Now this *is* the law of the Nazirite: When the days of his separation are fulfilled, he shall be brought to the door of the tabernacle of meeting. 14And he shall present his offering to the LORD: one male lamb in its first year without blemish as a burnt offering, one ewe lamb in its first year without blemish as a sin offering, one ram without blemish as a peace offering, 15a basket of unleavened bread, cakes of fine flour mixed with oil, unleavened wafers anointed with oil, and their grain offering with their drink offerings.

16'Then the priest shall bring *them* before the LORD and offer his sin offering and his burnt offering; 17and he shall offer the ram as a sacrifice of a peace offering to the LORD, with the basket of unleavened bread; the priest shall also offer its grain offering and its drink offering. 18Then the Nazirite shall shave his consecrated head *at* the door of the tabernacle of meeting, and shall take the hair from his consecrated head and put *it* on the fire which is under the sacrifice of the peace offering.

19'And the priest shall take the boiled shoulder of the ram, one unleavened cake from the basket, and one unleavened wafer, and put *them* upon the hands of the Nazirite after he has shaved his consecrated *hair,* 20and the priest shall wave them as a wave offering before the LORD; they *are* holy for the priest, together with the breast of the wave offering and the thigh of the heave offering. After that the Nazirite may drink wine.'

21"This is the law of the Nazirite who vows to the LORD the offering for his separation, and besides that, whatever else his hand is able to provide; according to the vow which he takes, so he must do according to the law of his separation."

22*And the LORD spoke to Moses, saying: 23"Speak to Aaron and his sons, saying, 'This is the way you shall bless the children of Israel. Say to them:

24 "The LORD bless you and keep you;
25 The LORD make His face shine upon you,
   And be gracious to you;
26 The LORD lift up His countenance upon you,
   And give you peace." '

27"So they shall put My name on the children of Israel, and I will bless them."

7 Now* it came to pass, when Moses had finished setting up the tabernacle, that he anointed it and consecrated it and all its furnishings, and the altar and all its utensils; so he anointed them and consecrated them. 2Then the leaders of Israel, the heads of their fathers' houses, who *were* the leaders of the tribes and over those who were numbered, made an offering. 3And they brought their offering before the LORD, six covered carts and twelve oxen, a cart for *every*

two of the leaders, and for each one an ox; and they presented them before the tabernacle.

4*Then the LORD spoke to Moses, saying, 5"Accept *these* from them, that they may be used in doing the work of the tabernacle of meeting; and you shall give them to the Levites, *to* every man according to his service." 6So Moses took the carts and the oxen, and gave them to the Levites. 7*Two carts and four oxen he gave to the sons of Gershon, according to their service; 8and four carts and eight oxen he gave to the sons of Merari, according to their service, under the authority^h of Ithamar the son of Aaron the priest. 9But to the sons of Kohath he gave none, because theirs *was* the service of the holy things, *which* they carried on their shoulders.

10Now the leaders offered the dedication *offering* for the altar when it was anointed; so the leaders offered their offering before the altar. 11For the LORD said to Moses, "They shall offer their offering, one leader each day, for the dedication of the altar."

12And the one who offered his offering on the first day *was* Nahshon the son of Amminadab, from the tribe of Judah. 13His offering *was* one silver platter, the weight of which *was* one hundred and thirty *shekels,* and one silver bowl of seventy shekels, according to the shekel of the sanctuary, both of them full of fine flour mixed with oil as a grain offering; 14one gold pan of ten *shekels,* full of incense; 15one young bull, one ram, and one male lamb in its first year, as a burnt offering; 16one kid of the goats as a sin offering; 17and for the sacrifice of peace offerings: two oxen, five rams, five male goats, and five male lambs in their first year. This *was* the offering of Nahshon the son of Amminadab.

18On the second day Nethanel the son of Zuar, leader of Issachar, presented *an offering.* 19*For* his offering he offered one silver platter, the weight of which *was* one hundred and thirty *shekels,* and one silver bowl of seventy shekels, according to the shekel of the sanctuary, both of them full of fine flour mixed with oil as a grain offering; 20one gold pan of ten *shekels,* full of incense; 21one young bull, one ram, and one male lamb in its first year, as a burnt offering; 22one kid of the goats as a sin offering; 23and as the sacrifice of peace offerings: two oxen, five rams, five male goats, and five male lambs in their first year. This *was* the offering of Nethanel the son of Zuar.

24On the third day Eliab the son of Helon, leader of the children of Zebulun, *presented an offering.* 25His offering *was* one silver platter, the weight of which *was* one hundred and thirty *shekels,* and one silver bowl of seventy shekels, according to the shekel of the sanctuary, both of them full of fine flour mixed with oil as a grain offering; 26one gold pan of ten *shekels,* full of incense; 27one young bull, one ram, and one male lamb in its first year, as a burnt offering; 28one kid of the goats as a sin offering; 29and for the sacrifice of peace offerings: two oxen, five rams, five male goats, and five male lambs in their first year. This *was* the offering of Eliab the son of Helon.

30On the fourth day Elizur the son of Shedeur, leader of the children of Reuben, *presented an offering.* 31His offering *was* one silver platter, the weight of which *was* one hundred and thirty

7:4–6 The gifts were practical, to be used for the service of the tabernacle. When we supply ministry tools for God's servants, we also bring gifts to the Lord.

7:7–9 Everybody but the Kohathites could use the carts for their work. The sons of Kohath had to carry the tabernacle furniture on their shoulders (3:30–31; 4:15). Although there are some burdens others can help us bear, "each one shall bear his own load" (Gal. 6:1–5). David disobeyed this law and brought judgment from God (2 Sam. 6:1–15). Don't refuse the burdens; God will enable you to carry them.

7:8 ^h Literally *hand*

shekels, and one silver bowl of seventy shekels, according to the shekel of the sanctuary, both of them full of fine flour mixed with oil as a grain offering; 32one gold pan of ten *shekels,* full of incense; 33one young bull, one ram, and one male lamb in its first year, as a burnt offering; 34one kid of the goats as a sin offering; 35and as the sacrifice of peace offerings: two oxen, five rams, five male goats, and five male lambs in their first year. This *was* the offering of Elizur the son of Shedeur.

36On the fifth day Shelumiel the son of Zurishaddai, leader of the children of Simeon, *presented an offering.* 37His offering *was* one silver platter, the weight of which *was* one hundred and thirty *shekels,* and one silver bowl of seventy shekels, according to the shekel of the sanctuary, both of them full of fine flour mixed with oil as a grain offering; 38one gold pan of ten *shekels,* full of incense; 39one young bull, one ram, and one male lamb in its first year, as a burnt offering; 40one kid of the goats as a sin offering; 41and as the sacrifice of peace offerings: two oxen, five rams, five male goats, and five male lambs in their first year. This *was* the offering of Shelumiel the son of Zurishaddai.

42On the sixth day Eliasaph the son of Deuel,[i] leader of the children of Gad, *presented an offering.* 43His offering *was* one silver platter, the weight of which *was* one hundred and thirty *shekels,* and one silver bowl of seventy shekels, according to the shekel of the sanctuary, both of them full of fine flour mixed with oil as a grain offering; 44one gold pan of ten *shekels,* full of incense; 45one young bull, one ram, and one male lamb in its first year, as a burnt offering; 46one kid of the goats as a sin offering; 47and as the sacrifice of peace offerings: two oxen, five rams, five male goats, and five male lambs in their first year. This *was* the offering of Eliasaph the son of Deuel.

48On the seventh day Elishama the son of Ammihud, leader of the children of Ephraim, *presented an offering.* 49His offering *was* one silver platter, the weight of which *was* one hundred and thirty *shekels,* and one silver bowl of seventy shekels, according to the shekel of the sanctuary, both of them full of fine flour mixed with oil as a grain offering; 50one gold pan of ten *shekels,* full of incense; 51one young bull, one ram, and one male lamb in its first year, as a burnt offering; 52one kid of the goats as a sin offering; 53and as the sacrifice of peace offerings: two oxen, five rams, five male goats, and five male lambs in their first year. This *was* the offering of Elishama the son of Ammihud.

54On the eighth day Gamaliel the son of Pedahzur, leader of the children of Manasseh, *presented an offering.* 55His offering *was* one silver platter, the weight of which *was* one hundred and thirty *shekels,* and one silver bowl of seventy shekels, according to the shekel of the sanctuary, both of them full of fine flour mixed with oil as a grain offering; 56one gold pan of ten *shekels,* full of incense; 57one young bull, one ram, and one male lamb in its first year, as a burnt offering; 58one kid of the goats as a sin offering; 59and as the sacrifice of peace offerings: two oxen, five rams, five male goats, and five male lambs in their first

7:42 'Spelled *Reuel* in 2:14

year. This *was* the offering of Gamaliel the son of Pedahzur.

60On the ninth day Abidan the son of Gideoni, leader of the children of Benjamin, *presented an offering.* 61His offering *was* one silver platter, the weight of which *was* one hundred and thirty *shekels,* and one silver bowl of seventy shekels, according to the shekel of the sanctuary, both of them full of fine flour mixed with oil as a grain offering; 62one gold pan of ten *shekels,* full of incense; 63one young bull, one ram, and one male lamb in its first year, as a burnt offering; 64one kid of the goats as a sin offering; 65and as the sacrifice of peace offerings: two oxen, five rams, five male goats, and five male lambs in their first year. This *was* the offering of Abidan the son of Gideoni.

66On the tenth day Ahiezer the son of Ammishaddai, leader of the children of Dan, *presented an offering.* 67His offering *was* one silver platter, the weight of which *was* one hundred and thirty *shekels,* and one silver bowl of seventy shekels, according to the shekel of the sanctuary, both of them full of fine flour mixed with oil as a grain offering; 68one gold pan of ten *shekels,* full of incense; 69one young bull, one ram, and one male lamb in its first year, as a burnt offering; 70one kid of the goats as a sin offering; 71and as the sacrifice of peace offerings: two oxen, five rams, five male goats, and five male lambs in their first year. This *was* the offering of Ahiezer the son of Ammishaddai.

72On the eleventh day Pagiel the son of Ocran, leader of the children of Asher, *presented an offering.* 73His offering *was* one silver platter, the weight of which *was* one hundred and thirty *shekels,* and one silver bowl of seventy shekels, according to the shekel of the sanctuary, both of them full of fine flour mixed with oil as a grain offering; 74one gold pan of ten *shekels,* full of incense; 75one young bull, one ram, and one male lamb in its first year, as a burnt offering; 76one kid of the goats as a sin offering; 77and as the sacrifice of peace offerings: two oxen, five rams, five male goats, and five male lambs in their first year. This *was* the offering of Pagiel the son of Ocran.

78On the twelfth day Ahira the son of Enan, leader of the children of Naphtali, *presented an offering.* 79His offering *was* one silver platter, the weight of which *was* one hundred and thirty *shekels,* and one silver bowl of seventy shekels, according to the shekel of the sanctuary, both of them full of fine flour mixed with oil as a grain offering; 80one gold pan of ten *shekels,* full of incense; 81one young bull, one ram, and one male lamb in its first year, as a burnt offering; 82one kid of the goats as a sin offering; 83and as the sacrifice of peace offerings: two oxen, five rams, five male goats, and five male lambs in their first year. This *was* the offering of Ahira the son of Enan.

84This *was* the dedication *offering* for the altar from the leaders of Israel, when it was anointed: twelve silver platters, twelve silver bowls, and twelve gold pans. 85Each silver platter *weighed* one hundred and thirty *shekels* and each bowl seventy *shekels.* All the silver of the vessels *weighed* two thousand four hundred *shekels,* according to the shekel of the sanctuary. 86The twelve gold pans full of incense *weighed* ten *shekels* apiece, according to the shekel of the sanctuary;

all the gold of the pans *weighed* one hundred and twenty *shekels.* [87]All the oxen for the burnt offering *were* twelve young bulls, the rams twelve, the male lambs in their first year twelve, with their grain offering, and the kids of the goats as a sin offering twelve. [88]And all the oxen for the sacrifice of peace offerings were twenty-four bulls, the rams sixty, the male goats sixty, and the lambs in their first year sixty. This *was* the dedication *offering* for the altar after it was anointed.

[89]Now when Moses went into the tabernacle of meeting to speak with Him, he heard the voice of One speaking to him from above the mercy seat that *was* on the ark of the Testimony, from between the two cherubim; thus He spoke to him.

8 And the LORD spoke to Moses, saying: [2]"Speak to Aaron, and say to him, 'When you arrange the lamps, the seven lamps shall give light in front of the lampstand.'" [3]And Aaron did so; he arranged the lamps to face toward the front of the lampstand, as the LORD commanded Moses. [4]Now this workmanship of the lampstand *was* hammered gold; from its shaft to its flowers it *was* hammered work. According to the pattern which the LORD had shown Moses, so he made the lampstand.

[5]Then the LORD spoke to Moses, saying: [6]"Take the Levites from among the children of Israel and cleanse them *ceremonially.* [7]Thus you shall do to them to cleanse them: Sprinkle water of purification on them, and let them shave all their body, and let them wash their clothes, and *so* make themselves clean. [8]Then let them take a young bull with its grain offering of fine flour mixed with oil, and you shall take another young bull as a sin offering. [9]And you shall bring the Levites before the tabernacle of meeting, and you shall gather together the whole congregation of the children of Israel. [10]So you shall bring the Levites before the LORD, and the children of Israel shall lay their hands on the Levites; [11]and Aaron shall offer the Levites before the LORD *like* a wave offering from the children of Israel, that they may perform the work of the LORD. [12]Then the Levites shall lay their hands on the heads of the young bulls, and you shall offer one as a sin offering and the other as a burnt offering to the LORD, to make atonement for the Levites.

[13]"And you shall stand the Levites before Aaron and his sons, and then offer them *like* a wave offering to the LORD. [14]Thus you shall separate the Levites from among the children of Israel, and the Levites shall be Mine. [15]After that the Levites shall go in to service the tabernacle of meeting. So you shall cleanse them and offer them *like* a wave offering. [16]For they *are* wholly given to Me from among the children of Israel; I have taken them for Myself instead of all who open the womb, the firstborn of all the children of Israel. [17]*For all the firstborn among the children of Israel *are* Mine, *both* man and beast; on the day that I struck all the firstborn in the land of Egypt I sanctified them to Myself. [18]I have taken the Levites instead of all the firstborn of the children of Israel. [19]*And I have given the Levites as a gift to Aaron and his sons from among the children of Israel, to do the work for the children of Israel in the tabernacle of meeting, and to make atonement for the children of Israel, that there be no plague among the children of Israel when the children of Israel come near the sanctuary."

CHAPTER 8

Not everybody is called to be a priest or a leader. Some are called to be helpers, such as the Levites. The gift of helps (1 Cor. 12:28) is important in God's work and must never be despised. God considered the Levites as His gift to Aaron (v. 19). We should be thankful for those God gives to help us in our work.

8:17, 18 Substitutes. The Levites were first of all given to the Lord as substitutes for all the firstborn in Israel (vv. 16–18; 3:11–13).

The firstborn belonged to God, but He allowed them to be redeemed (Exod. 13:1, 11–13). You have your work to do for Christ, but don't forget those who represent you as they serve the Lord in different places.

8:19 Servants. The Levites were given to Aaron as workers (vv. 11, 19). They could not do all that the priests did, but they had their tasks and were expected to fulfill them faithfully.

20Thus Moses and Aaron and all the congregation of the children of Israel did to the Levites; according to all that the LORD commanded Moses concerning the Levites, so the children of Israel did to them. 21*And the Levites purified themselves and washed their clothes; then Aaron presented them *like* a wave offering before the LORD, and Aaron made atonement for them to cleanse them. 22After that the Levites went in to do their work in the tabernacle of meeting before Aaron and his sons; as the LORD commanded Moses concerning the Levites, so they did to them.

23Then the LORD spoke to Moses, saying, 24"This *is* what *pertains* to the Levites: From twenty-five years old and above one may enter to perform service in the work of the tabernacle of meeting; 25and at the age of fifty years they must cease performing this work, and shall work no more. 26They may minister with their brethren in the tabernacle of meeting, to attend to needs, but they *themselves* shall do no work. Thus you shall do to the Levites regarding their duties."

9 Now* the LORD spoke to Moses in the Wilderness of Sinai, in the first month of the second year after they had come out of the land of Egypt, saying: 2"Let the children of Israel keep the Passover at its appointed time. 3On the fourteenth day of this month, at twilight, you shall keep it at its appointed time. According to all its rites and ceremonies you shall keep it." 4So Moses told the children of Israel that they should keep the Passover. 5And they kept the Passover on the fourteenth day of the first month, at twilight, in the Wilderness of Sinai; according to all that the LORD commanded Moses, so the children of Israel did.

6*Now there were *certain* men who were defiled by a human corpse, so that they could not keep the Passover on that day; and they came before Moses and Aaron that day. 7And those men said to him, "We *became* defiled by a human corpse. Why are we kept from presenting the offering of the LORD at its appointed time among the children of Israel?"

8And Moses said to them, "Stand still, that I may hear what the LORD will command concerning you."

9Then the LORD spoke to Moses, saying, 10"Speak to the children of Israel, saying: 'If anyone of you or your posterity is unclean because of a corpse, or *is* far away on a journey, he may still keep the LORD's Passover. 11On the fourteenth day of the second month, at twilight, they may keep it. They shall eat it with unleavened bread and bitter herbs. 12They shall leave none of it until morning, nor break one of its bones. According to all the ordinances of the Passover they shall keep it. 13But the man who *is* clean and is not on a journey, and ceases to keep the Passover, that same person shall be cut off from among his people, because he did not bring the offering of the LORD at its appointed time; that man shall bear his sin.

14'And if a stranger dwells among you, and would keep the LORD's Passover, he must do so

8:21 Sacrifices. They were presented to God as "living sacrifices," wave offerings to the Lord (vv. 11, 13, 15, 21). No matter what work you do for the Lord, it should be like offering up a sacrifice of worship to Him (Phil. 4:10–20).

CHAPTER 9

9:1–5 God teaches us in different ways. There are *commandments to obey* (vv. 1–5), and we must know them and do them. Passover was the annual reminder that God had redeemed Israel from bondage and they belonged to Him. Think of the thousands of lambs that were slain so that the people might obey God! Think of the Lamb of God who died for the whole world (John 1:29)!

9:6–14 There are also *exceptions to consider.* The legalist makes no exceptions, and the anarchist makes everything an exception; but the child of God waits on the Lord for His orders. Each problem in life is an opportunity to learn how to wait on God and discover His will. Let's not fear exceptions. Our job is to be obedient even if what we do does not always appear to be consistent.

The Will of God—Never be afraid of the will of God; God's will is the expression of God's love, and it comes from His heart (Ps. 33:11). It is food, not medicine (John 4:31–34), and nourishes us as we obey. Oswald Chambers was correct when he said, "Doing God's will is never hard. The only thing that is hard is *not* doing His will." Are you doing His will now?

9:15–23 There are *leadings to follow*. Note the sequence: obeying the Lord, waiting on the Lord, following the Lord. God has His times and His routes, and we must watch for His leading. Perhaps the most difficult time for us is when God tarries and we have to wait (v. 19). It is also the most dangerous time, for human nature wants to rush ahead. We must "rest in the LORD, and wait patiently for Him" (Ps. 37:7).

CHAPTER 10

The people of Israel were to set out for their God-appointed inheritance. They would go through an unknown land that was dangerous, but God gave them the help they needed.

10:1–13 *His command.* The priests used the two silver trumpets to communicate God's will to the people. The blowing of the silver trumpets would gather them together, move them forward, summon them to battle, or call them to enjoy the feasts of the Lord. They heard the trumpets and watched the cloud, and they were safe.

according to the rite of the Passover and according to its ceremony; you shall have one ordinance, both for the stranger and the native of the land.' "

15*Now on the day that the tabernacle was raised up, the cloud covered the tabernacle, the tent of the Testimony; from evening until morning it was above the tabernacle like the appearance of fire. 16So it was always: the cloud covered it *by day*, and the appearance of fire by night. 17Whenever the cloud was taken up from above the tabernacle, after that the children of Israel would journey; and in the place where the cloud settled, there the children of Israel would pitch their tents. 18At the command of the LORD the children of Israel would journey, and at the command of the LORD they would camp; as long as the cloud stayed above the tabernacle they remained encamped. 19Even when the cloud continued long, many days above the tabernacle, the children of Israel kept the charge of the LORD and did not journey. 20So it was, when the cloud was above the tabernacle a few days: according to the command of the LORD they would remain encamped, and according to the command of the LORD they would journey. 21So it was, when the cloud remained only from evening until morning: when the cloud was taken up in the morning, then they would journey; whether by day or by night, whenever the cloud was taken up, they would journey. 22*Whether it was* two days, a month, or a year that the cloud remained above the tabernacle, the children of Israel would remain encamped and not journey; but when it was taken up, they would journey. 23At the command of the LORD they remained encamped, and at the command of the LORD they journeyed; they kept the charge of the LORD, at the command of the LORD by the hand of Moses.

10 And* the LORD spoke to Moses, saying: 2"Make two silver trumpets for yourself; you shall make them of hammered work; you shall use them for calling the congregation and for directing the movement of the camps. 3When they blow both of them, all the congregation shall gather before you at the door of the tabernacle of meeting. 4But if they blow *only* one, then the leaders, the heads of the divisions of Israel, shall gather to you. 5When you sound the advance, the camps that lie on the east side shall then begin their journey. 6When you sound the advance the second time, then the camps that lie on the south side shall begin their journey; they shall sound the call for them to begin their journeys. 7And when the assembly is to be gathered together, you shall blow, but not sound the advance. 8The sons of Aaron, the priests, shall blow the trumpets; and these shall be to you as an ordinance forever throughout your generations.

9"When you go to war in your land against the enemy who oppresses you, then you shall sound an alarm with the trumpets, and you will be remembered before the LORD your God, and you will be saved from your enemies. 10Also in the day of your gladness, in your appointed feasts, and at the beginning of your months, you shall blow the trumpets over your burnt offerings and over the sacrifices of your peace offerings; and they shall be a memorial for you before your God: I *am* the LORD your God."

11Now it came to pass on the twentieth *day* of the second month, in the second year, that the cloud was taken up from above the tabernacle of the Testimony. 12And the children of Israel set out from the Wilderness of Sinai on their journeys; then the cloud settled down in the Wilderness of Paran. 13So they started out for the first time according to the command of the LORD by the hand of Moses.

14*The standard of the camp of the children of Judah set out first according to their armies; over their army was Nahshon the son of Amminadab. 15Over the army of the tribe of the children of Issachar was Nethanel the son of Zuar. 16And over the army of the tribe of the children of Zebulun was Eliab the son of Helon.

17Then the tabernacle was taken down; and the sons of Gershon and the sons of Merari set out, carrying the tabernacle.

18And the standard of the camp of Reuben set out according to their armies; over their army was Elizur the son of Shedeur. 19Over the army of the tribe of the children of Simeon was Shelumiel the son of Zurishaddai. 20And over the army of the tribe of the children of Gad was Eliasaph the son of Deuel.

21Then the Kohathites set out, carrying the holy things. (The tabernacle would be prepared for their arrival.)

22And the standard of the camp of the children of Ephraim set out according to their armies; over their army was Elishama the son of Ammihud. 23Over the army of the tribe of the children of Manasseh was Gamaliel the son of Pedahzur. 24And over the army of the tribe of the children of Benjamin was Abidan the son of Gideoni.

25Then the standard of the camp of the children of Dan (the rear guard of all the camps) set out according to their armies; over their army was Ahiezer the son of Ammishaddai. 26Over the army of the tribe of the children of Asher was Pagiel the son of Ocran. 27And over the army of the tribe of the children of Naphtali was Ahira the son of Enan.

28Thus was the order of march of the children of Israel, according to their armies, when they began their journey.

29*Now Moses said to Hobab the son of Reuelʲ the Midianite, Moses' father-in-law, "We are setting out for the place of which the LORD said, 'I will give it to you.' Come with us, and we will treat you well; for the LORD has promised good things to Israel."

30And he said to him, "I will not go, but I will depart to my own land and to my relatives."

31So Moses said, "Please do not leave, inasmuch as you know how we are to camp in the wilderness, and you can be our eyes. 32And it shall be, if you go with us—indeed it shall be—that whatever good the LORD will do to us, the same we will do to you."

33*So they departed from the mountain of the LORD on a journey of three days; and the ark of the covenant of the LORD went before them for the three days' journey, to search out a resting place for them. 34And the cloud of the LORD was above them by day when they went out from the camp.

35So it was, whenever the ark set out, that Moses said:

10:14–28 His word. God had already told them how to organize the march, and all they had to do was obey. If we don't obey in the things God has told us, He will not reveal anything new to us (John 7:17).

10:29–32 Experience. Hobab was a brother of Zipporah, Moses' wife; and Moses asked him to come with Israel and share his "wilderness wisdom." Hobab's wisdom did not take the place of God's leading. Rather, Hobab assisted in the everyday problems of a people who were not accustomed to wilderness life. God promises to guide us, but that doesn't mean we should be deaf to the wisdom of experienced people. Hobab did Israel good, and Israel brought good to him (Judg. 1:16; 4:11).

10:33–36 Prayer. The ark represented God's presence and His throne. Moses prayed to God when the people marched forward and when God told them to stop. That's a good example for us to follow as we move through each day.

10:29 ʲSeptuagint reads *Raguel* (compare Exodus 2:18).

"Rise up, O LORD!
Let Your enemies be scattered,
And let those who hate You flee before
You."

36And when it rested, he said:

"Return, O LORD,
To the many thousands of Israel."

CHAPTER 11
This is a chapter of complaining!

11:1–9 *Complaining about bread.* God was leading them, so the people had all they needed; yet they complained again. (See Phil. 2:14–15.) Their grumbling was evidence of the unbelief that would keep them out of the Promised Land. Had they been grateful for God's goodness and obedient to God's guidance, they would have saved themselves a great deal of misery. Let's remember that the next time we are tempted to complain about the providence of God. "The slaves of sin rarely grumble at that slavery; it is their slavery to God they grumble at," said George MacDonald.

11:10–25 *Complaining about burdens.* Moses was grieved when they criticized both him and God. Could they improve upon the manna that came from heaven? Why did they crave food from Egypt? Had they forgotten their bondage in that land? Moses did what you must do when people disappoint you: he took it to God in prayer and told God just how he felt. God met the need, encouraged His servant, and punished the rebels.

11 Now* *when* the people complained, it displeased the LORD; for the LORD heard *it,* and His anger was aroused. So the fire of the LORD burned among them, and consumed *some* in the outskirts of the camp. 2Then the people cried out to Moses, and when Moses prayed to the LORD, the fire was quenched. 3So he called the name of the place Taberah,*k* because the fire of the LORD had burned among them.

4Now the mixed multitude who were among them yielded to intense craving; so the children of Israel also wept again and said: "Who will give us meat to eat? 5We remember the fish which we ate freely in Egypt, the cucumbers, the melons, the leeks, the onions, and the garlic; 6but now our whole being *is* dried up; *there is* nothing at all except this manna *before* our eyes!"

7Now the manna *was* like coriander seed, and its color like the color of bdellium. 8The people went about and gathered *it,* ground *it* on millstones or beat *it* in the mortar, cooked *it* in pans, and made cakes of it; and its taste was like the taste of pastry prepared with oil. 9And when the dew fell on the camp in the night, the manna fell on it.

10*Then Moses heard the people weeping throughout their families, everyone at the door of his tent; and the anger of the LORD was greatly aroused; Moses also was displeased. 11So Moses said to the LORD, "Why have You afflicted Your servant? And why have I not found favor in Your sight, that You have laid the burden of all these people on me? 12Did I conceive all these people? Did I beget them, that You should say to me, 'Carry them in your bosom, as a guardian carries a nursing child,' to the land which You swore to their fathers? 13Where am I to get meat to give to all these people? For they weep all over me, saying, 'Give us meat, that we may eat.' 14I am not able to bear all these people alone, because the burden *is* too heavy for me. 15If You treat me like this, please kill me here and now—if I have found favor in Your sight—and do not let me see my wretchedness!"

16So the LORD said to Moses: "Gather to Me seventy men of the elders of Israel, whom you know to be the elders of the people and officers over them; bring them to the tabernacle of meeting, that they may stand there with you. 17Then I will come down and talk with you there. I will take of the Spirit that *is* upon you and will put *the same* upon them; and they shall bear the burden of the people with you, that you may not bear *it* yourself alone. 18Then you shall say to the people, 'Consecrate yourselves for tomorrow, and you shall eat meat; for you have wept in the hearing of the LORD, saying, "Who will give us meat to eat? For *it was* well with us in Egypt." Therefore the LORD will give you meat, and you shall eat. 19You shall eat, not one day, nor two days, nor

---

11:3 *k*Literally *Burning*

five days, nor ten days, nor twenty days, 20but *for* a whole month, until it comes out of your nostrils and becomes loathsome to you, because you have despised the LORD who is among you, and have wept before Him, saying, "Why did we ever come up out of Egypt?" ' "

21And Moses said, "The people whom I *am* among *are* six hundred thousand men on foot; yet You have said, 'I will give them meat, that they may eat *for* a whole month.' 22Shall flocks and herds be slaughtered for them, to provide enough for them? Or shall all the fish of the sea be gathered together for them, to provide enough for them?"

23And the LORD said to Moses, "Has the LORD's arm been shortened? Now you shall see whether what I say will happen to you or not."

24So Moses went out and told the people the words of the LORD, and he gathered the seventy men of the elders of the people and placed them around the tabernacle. 25Then the LORD came down in the cloud, and spoke to him, and took of the Spirit that *was* upon him, and placed *the same* upon the seventy elders; and it happened, when the Spirit rested upon them, that they prophesied, although they never did *so* again.[l]

26*But two men had remained in the camp: the name of one *was* Eldad, and the name of the other Medad. And the Spirit rested upon them. Now they *were* among those listed, but who had not gone out to the tabernacle; yet they prophesied in the camp. 27And a young man ran and told Moses, and said, "Eldad and Medad are prophesying in the camp."

28So Joshua the son of Nun, Moses' assistant, *one* of his choice men, answered and said, "Moses my lord, forbid them!"

29Then Moses said to him, "Are you zealous for my sake? Oh, that all the LORD's people were prophets *and* that the LORD would put His Spirit upon them!" 30And Moses returned to the camp, he and the elders of Israel.

31Now a wind went out from the LORD, and it brought quail from the sea and left *them* fluttering near the camp, about a day's journey on this side and about a day's journey on the other side, all around the camp, and about two cubits above the surface of the ground. 32And the people stayed up all that day, all night, and all the next day, and gathered the quail (he who gathered least gathered ten homers); and they spread *them* out for themselves all around the camp. 33But while the meat *was* still between their teeth, before it was chewed, the wrath of the LORD was aroused against the people, and the LORD struck the people with a very great plague. 34So he called the name of that place Kibroth Hattaavah,[m] because there they buried the people who had yielded to craving.

35From Kibroth Hattaavah the people moved to Hazeroth, and camped at Hazeroth.

12 Then* Miriam and Aaron spoke against Moses because of the Ethiopian woman whom he had married; for he had married an Ethiopian woman. 2So they said, "Has the LORD indeed spoken only through Moses? Has He not spoken through us also?" And the LORD heard *it*. 3(Now

---

11:25 [l]Targum and Vulgate read *did not cease.*
11:34 [m]Literally *Graves of Craving*

11:26–35 *Complaining about blessing.* Zealous for Moses and his position, Joshua told him to stop the two men from prophesying. James and John made a similar mistake, and Jesus had to rebuke them (Luke 9:49–50). If all of God's people were praising God by the Spirit, they would not be complaining! The Jews got what they asked for, but they lost the spiritual enrichment that comes when people walk by faith (Ps. 106:15). Have you learned to be grateful for *unanswered* prayer?

CHAPTER 12

12:1–3 *The leader denounced.* If you are in a place of leadership, expect criticism, even from members of your family. It happened to Moses, David (2 Sam. 6:20–23), and the Lord Jesus (Mark 3:20–21). Moses' wife was not the real reason for their criticism. Aaron and his sister were jealous of the authority God had given Moses, and they wanted him to share it. Perhaps they were reacting to what God did for the seventy elders (chap. 11).

12:4–10 *The Lord displeased.* Moses did not defend himself; he waited for God to act. If we defend ourselves, we may hinder the Lord from defending us. Next to death, becoming a leper was the worst thing that could have happened to Miriam.

12:11–16 *The nation delayed.* How often people turn for help to the very ones they have criticized! In his meekness, Moses did not rejoice at his sister's punishment; instead, he prayed for her (Matt. 5:43–48). Because of their sin, Aaron and Miriam delayed the march of the nation for a whole week. The sin of criticism is far more serious than most people realize (Matt. 7:1–5; James 4:12).

CHAPTER 13

13:1–25 *Seeing the opportunities.* The people thought they should spy out the land before conquering it, and Moses let them do it (Deut. 1:19–25). God had already told them what the Promised Land was like, so why did they have to investigate? Faith takes God at His word and needs no other evidence (Heb. 11:1). The spies discovered that the land was indeed all that God had promised it to be.

the man Moses *was* very humble, more than all men who *were* on the face of the earth.)

4*Suddenly the LORD said to Moses, Aaron, and Miriam, "Come out, you three, to the tabernacle of meeting!" So the three came out. 5Then the LORD came down in the pillar of cloud and stood *in* the door of the tabernacle, and called Aaron and Miriam. And they both went forward. 6Then He said,

"Hear now My words:
If there is a prophet among you,
I, the LORD, make Myself known to him in
a vision;
I speak to him in a dream.
7   Not so with My servant Moses;
He *is* faithful in all My house.
8   I speak with him face to face,
Even plainly, and not in dark sayings;
And he sees the form of the LORD.
Why then were you not afraid
To speak against My servant Moses?"

9So the anger of the LORD was aroused against them, and He departed. 10And when the cloud departed from above the tabernacle, suddenly Miriam *became* leprous, as *white as* snow. Then Aaron turned toward Miriam, and there she was, a leper. 11*So Aaron said to Moses, "Oh, my lord! Please do not lay *this* sin on us, in which we have done foolishly and in which we have sinned. 12Please do not let her be as one dead, whose flesh is half consumed when he comes out of his mother's womb!"

13So Moses cried out to the LORD, saying, "Please heal her, O God, I pray!"

14Then the LORD said to Moses, "If her father had but spit in her face, would she not be shamed seven days? Let her be shut out of the camp seven days, and afterward she may be received *again*." 15So Miriam was shut out of the camp seven days, and the people did not journey till Miriam was brought in *again*. 16And afterward the people moved from Hazeroth and camped in the Wilderness of Paran.

13 And* the LORD spoke to Moses, saying, 2"Send men to spy out the land of Canaan, which I am giving to the children of Israel; from each tribe of their fathers you shall send a man, every one a leader among them."

3So Moses sent them from the Wilderness of Paran according to the command of the LORD, all of them men who *were* heads of the children of Israel. 4Now these *were* their names: from the tribe of Reuben, Shammua the son of Zaccur; 5from the tribe of Simeon, Shaphat the son of Hori; 6from the tribe of Judah, Caleb the son of Jephunneh; 7from the tribe of Issachar, Igal the son of Joseph; 8from the tribe of Ephraim, Hoshea[n] the son of Nun; 9from the tribe of Benjamin, Palti the son of Raphu; 10from the tribe of Zebulun, Gaddiel the son of Sodi; 11from the tribe of Joseph, *that is,* from the tribe of Manasseh, Gaddi the son of Susi; 12from the tribe of Dan, Ammiel the son of Gemalli; 13from the tribe of Asher, Sethur the son of Michael; 14from the tribe of Naphtali, Nahbi the son of Vophsi; 15from the tribe of Gad, Geuel the son of Machi.

16These *are* the names of the men whom Moses

13:8 [n]Septuagint and Vulgate read *Oshea.*

sent to spy out the land. And Moses called Ho-
shea° the son of Nun, Joshua.

17Then Moses sent them to spy out the land of
Canaan, and said to them, "Go up this *way* into
the South, and go up to the mountains, 18and see
what the land is like: whether the people who
dwell in it *are* strong or weak, few or many;
19whether the land they dwell in *is* good or bad;
whether the cities they inhabit *are* like camps or
strongholds; 20whether the land *is* rich or poor;
and whether there are forests there or not. Be of
good courage. And bring some of the fruit of the
land." Now the time *was* the season of the first
ripe grapes.

21So they went up and spied out the land from
the Wilderness of Zin as far as Rehob, near the
entrance of Hamath. 22And they went up through
the South and came to Hebron; Ahiman, Sheshai,
and Talmai, the descendants of Anak, *were* there.
(Now Hebron was built seven years before Zoan
in Egypt.) 23Then they came to the Valley of Eshcol, and there cut down a branch with one cluster
of grapes; they carried it between two of them
on a pole. *They* also *brought* some of the pomegranates and figs. 24The place was called the Valley of Eshcol,*p* because of the cluster which the
men of Israel cut down there. 25And they returned
from spying out the land after forty days.

26*Now they departed and came back to Moses
and Aaron and all the congregation of the children of Israel in the Wilderness of Paran, at Kadesh; they brought back word to them and to all
the congregation, and showed them the fruit of
the land. 27Then they told him, and said: "We
went to the land where you sent us. It truly flows
with milk and honey, and this *is* its fruit.
28Nevertheless the people who dwell in the land
are strong; the cities *are* fortified *and* very large;
moreover we saw the descendants of Anak there.
29The Amalekites dwell in the land of the South;
the Hittites, the Jebusites, and the Amorites dwell
in the mountains; and the Canaanites dwell by
the sea and along the banks of the Jordan."

30*Then Caleb quieted the people before Moses,
and said, "Let us go up at once and take possession, for we are well able to overcome it."

31But the men who had gone up with him said,
"We are not able to go up against the people, for
they *are* stronger than we." 32And they gave the
children of Israel a bad report of the land which
they had spied out, saying, "The land through
which we have gone as spies *is* a land that devours
its inhabitants, and all the people whom we saw
in it *are* men of *great* stature. 33There we saw
the giants*q* (the descendants of Anak came from
the giants); and we were like grasshoppers in our
own sight, and so we were in their sight."

14 So* all the congregation lifted up their
voices and cried, and the people wept that
night. 2And all the children of Israel complained

13:16 °Septuagint and Vulgate read *Oshea.*   13:24 *p*Literally
Cluster   13:33 *q*Hebrew *nephilim*

13:26–33 *Seeing the obstacles.* Ten spies
emphasized the obstacles instead of the
opportunities and concluded that Israel was
too weak to conquer the enemy. They
walked by sight and not by faith. The people
of the land were giants, the city walls were
high, and the men felt like grasshoppers!
Unbelief blinds you to God's greatness and
magnifies your own weakness.

13:30 *Seeing the Lord.* Caleb was a man
of faith who didn't worry about the size of
the problem because he trusted a great God.
The important question in life is not, "How
big is the problem?" or "How big am I?"
The major question is, "How big is my God?"
The Lord saw the Canaanites as
grasshoppers (Isa. 40:22), but the
unbelieving spies were not looking at the
situation from God's point of view. When you
walk by faith, the future is your friend, and
every enemy is defeated.

CHAPTER 14
    The report of the majority of the spies
brought about a destructive chain reaction
in the camp of Israel.

14:1–10 *Unbelief led to rebellion.* The
people wept, complained, looked back to
Egypt, wanted a new leader, and even
threatened to stone Caleb and Joshua. Such
are the evidences of unbelief. Faith looks
ahead with courage; unbelief looks back with
complaint. Faith unites the people of God;
unbelief looks for somebody to blame. There
was still time to repent and seek God's face,
but the people refused to listen to Caleb and
Joshua.

When You Are Outnumbered—Caleb and Joshua were a minority on the Search Committee
and yet they did not give in, even when the nation turned against them and their lives were in
danger. They had faith in God, they knew God's will for the people, and they stood their ground. It
is not important that we please others, but it is important that we please God. Like Caleb and Joshua,
sometimes we must suffer because of the sins of others; but in the end, God will vindicate those
who trust Him. (See Acts 20:24; 1 Cor. 15:58.)

against Moses and Aaron, and the whole congregation said to them, "If only we had died in the land of Egypt! Or if only we had died in this wilderness! 3Why has the LORD brought us to this land to fall by the sword, that our wives and children should become victims? Would it not be better for us to return to Egypt?" 4So they said to one another, "Let us select a leader and return to Egypt."

5Then Moses and Aaron fell on their faces before all the assembly of the congregation of the children of Israel.

6But Joshua the son of Nun and Caleb the son of Jephunneh, *who were* among those who had spied out the land, tore their clothes; 7and they spoke to all the congregation of the children of Israel, saying: "The land we passed through to spy out *is* an exceedingly good land. 8If the LORD delights in us, then He will bring us into this land and give it to us, 'a land which flows with milk and honey.'ʳ 9Only do not rebel against the LORD, nor fear the people of the land, for they *are* our bread; their protection has departed from them, and the LORD *is* with us. Do not fear them."

10And all the congregation said to stone them with stones. Now the glory of the LORD appeared in the tabernacle of meeting before all the children of Israel.

11*Then the LORD said to Moses: "How long will these people reject Me? And how long will they not believe Me, with all the signs which I have performed among them? 12I will strike them with the pestilence and disinherit them, and I will make of you a nation greater and mightier than they."

13And Moses said to the LORD: "Then the Egyptians will hear *it,* for by Your might You brought these people up from among them, 14and they will tell *it* to the inhabitants of this land. They have heard that You, LORD, *are* among these people; that You, LORD, are seen face to face and Your cloud stands above them, and You go before them in a pillar of cloud by day and in a pillar of fire by night. 15Now *if* You kill these people as one man, then the nations which have heard of Your fame will speak, saying, 16'Because the LORD was not able to bring this people to the land which He swore to give them, therefore He killed them in the wilderness.' 17And now, I pray, let the power of my Lord be great, just as You have spoken, saying, 18'The LORD is longsuffering and abundant in mercy, forgiving iniquity and transgression; but He by no means clears *the guilty,* visiting the iniquity of the fathers on the children to the third and fourth *generation.*'ˢ 19Pardon the iniquity of this people, I pray, according to the greatness of Your mercy, just as You have forgiven this people, from Egypt even until now."

20*Then the LORD said: "I have pardoned, according to your word; 21but truly, *as* I live, all the earth shall be filled with the glory of the LORD— 22because all these men who have seen My glory and the signs which I did in Egypt and in the wilderness, and have put Me to the test now these ten times, and have not heeded My voice, 23they certainly shall not see the land of which I swore to their fathers, nor shall any of those who rejected Me see it. 24But My servant Caleb, because he has a different spirit in him and has followed Me fully, I will bring into the

14:11–19 Rebellion led to intercession. Moses once again stood between God's people and God's judgment and turned down God's offer to make him the founder of a new nation (Exod. 32). Moses interceded for the people on the basis of the character and glory of God.

14:20–38 Intercession led to pardon. God pardoned the people, but at the same time He judged their sins (Gal. 6:7–8). The ten spies died in a plague, and the nation was consigned to forty years of wandering until the people who were twenty years old or older died. Faith brings life, but unbelief brings defeat and death.

14:8 ʳExodus 3:8   14:18 ˢExodus 34:6, 7

land where he went, and his descendants shall inherit it. 25Now the Amalekites and the Canaanites dwell in the valley; tomorrow turn and move out into the wilderness by the Way of the Red Sea."

26And the LORD spoke to Moses and Aaron, saying, 27"How long *shall I bear with* this evil congregation who complain against Me? I have heard the complaints which the children of Israel make against Me. 28Say to them, 'As I live,' says the LORD, 'just as you have spoken in My hearing, so I will do to you: 29The carcasses of you who have complained against Me shall fall in this wilderness, all of you who were numbered, according to your entire number, from twenty years old and above. 30Except for Caleb the son of Jephunneh and Joshua the son of Nun, you shall by no means enter the land which I swore I would make you dwell in. 31But your little ones, whom you said would be victims, I will bring in, and they shall know the land which you have despised. 32But *as for* you, your carcasses shall fall in this wilderness. 33And your sons shall be shepherds in the wilderness forty years, and bear the brunt of your infidelity, until your carcasses are consumed in the wilderness. 34According to the number of the days in which you spied out the land, forty days, for each day you shall bear your guilt one year, *namely* forty years, and you shall know My rejection. 35I the LORD have spoken this. I will surely do so to all this evil congregation who are gathered together against Me. In this wilderness they shall be consumed, and there they shall die.' "

36Now the men whom Moses sent to spy out the land, who returned and made all the congregation complain against him by bringing a bad report of the land, 37those very men who brought the evil report about the land, died by the plague before the LORD. 38But Joshua the son of Nun and Caleb the son of Jephunneh remained alive, of the men who went to spy out the land.

39*Then Moses told these words to all the children of Israel, and the people mourned greatly. 40And they rose early in the morning and went up to the top of the mountain, saying, "Here we are, and we will go up to the place which the LORD has promised, for we have sinned!"

41And Moses said, "Now why do you transgress the command of the LORD? For this will not succeed. 42Do not go up, lest you be defeated by your enemies, for the LORD *is* not among you. 43For the Amalekites and the Canaanites *are* there before you, and you shall fall by the sword; because you have turned away from the LORD, the LORD will not be with you."

44But they presumed to go up to the mountaintop. Nevertheless, neither the ark of the covenant of the LORD nor Moses departed from the camp. 45Then the Amalekites and the Canaanites who dwelt in that mountain came down and attacked them, and drove them back as far as Hormah.

15 And* the LORD spoke to Moses, saying, 2"Speak to the children of Israel, and say to them: 'When you have come into the land you are to inhabit, which I am giving to you, 3and you make an offering by fire to the LORD, a burnt offering or a sacrifice, to fulfill a vow or as a freewill offering or in your appointed feasts, to make a sweet aroma to the LORD, from the herd or the flock, 4then he who presents his offering to the LORD shall bring a grain offering of one-tenth *of*

14:39–45 *Pardon led to presumption.* The people had acted stubbornly like the mule, and now they acted impetuously like the horse (Ps. 32:9). God forgives us that we might fear Him (Ps. 130:4), not that we might tempt Him. The flesh can never accomplish what only faith can do. (See Deut. 1:41–44.)

CHAPTER 15

15:1–21 *Assurance.* God gave the people a word of assurance when He said, *"When you have come into the land"* (italics added). In spite of the nation's sins, the new generation would make it to Canaan and possess the land. (See 2 Tim. 2:11–13.) When they did, they were expected to take time to thank God and worship Him. Do you pause to thank God for sharing His blessings with you?

an ephah of fine flour mixed with one-fourth of a hin of oil; 5and one-fourth of a hin of wine as a drink offering you shall prepare with the burnt offering or the sacrifice, for each lamb. 6Or for a ram you shall prepare as a grain offering two-tenths *of an ephah* of fine flour mixed with one-third of a hin of oil; 7and as a drink offering you shall offer one-third of a hin of wine as a sweet aroma to the LORD. 8And when you prepare a young bull as a burnt offering, or as a sacrifice to fulfill a vow, or as a peace offering to the LORD, 9then shall be offered with the young bull a grain offering of three-tenths *of an ephah* of fine flour mixed with half a hin of oil; 10and you shall bring as the drink offering half a hin of wine as an offering made by fire, a sweet aroma to the LORD.

11Thus it shall be done for each young bull, for each ram, or for each lamb or young goat. 12According to the number that you prepare, so you shall do with everyone according to their number. 13All who are native-born shall do these things in this manner, in presenting an offering made by fire, a sweet aroma to the LORD. 14And if a stranger dwells with you, or whoever *is* among you throughout your generations, and would present an offering made by fire, a sweet aroma to the LORD, just as you do, so shall he do. 15One ordinance *shall be* for you of the assembly and for the stranger who dwells *with you,* an ordinance forever throughout your generations; as you are, so shall the stranger be before the LORD. 16One law and one custom shall be for you and for the stranger who dwells with you.' "*t*

17Again the LORD spoke to Moses, saying, 18"Speak to the children of Israel, and say to them: 'When you come into the land to which I bring you, 19then it will be, when you eat of the bread of the land, that you shall offer up a heave offering to the LORD. 20You shall offer up a cake of the first of your ground meal *as* a heave offering; as a heave offering of the threshing floor, so shall you offer it up. 21Of the first of your ground meal you shall give to the LORD a heave offering throughout your generations.

22*'If you sin unintentionally, and do not observe all these commandments which the LORD has spoken to Moses— 23all that the LORD has commanded you by the hand of Moses, from the day the LORD gave commandment and onward throughout your generations— 24then it will be, if it is unintentionally committed, without the knowledge of the congregation, that the whole congregation shall offer one young bull as a burnt offering, as a sweet aroma to the LORD, with its grain offering and its drink offering, according to the ordinance, and one kid of the goats as a sin offering. 25So the priest shall make atonement for the whole congregation of the children of Israel, and it shall be forgiven them, for it was unintentional; they shall bring their offering, an offering made by fire to the LORD, and their sin offering before the LORD, for their unintended sin. 26It shall be forgiven the whole congregation of the children of Israel and the stranger who dwells among them, because all the people *did it* unintentionally.

27'And if a person sins unintentionally, then he shall bring a female goat in its first year as a sin offering. 28So the priest shall make atonement for the person who sins unintentionally, when he sins

15:22–29 Obedience. God made provision for the forgiveness of unintentional sins. Of course, innocent animals had to die to provide forgiveness, just as Jesus had to die to make our cleansing possible.

15:16 *Compare Exodus 12:49

unintentionally before the LORD, to make atonement for him; and it shall be forgiven him.
29You shall have one law for him who sins unintentionally, *for* him who is native-born among the
children of Israel and for the stranger who dwells
among them.

30*'But the person who does *anything* presumptuously, *whether he is* native-born or a stranger,
that one brings reproach on the LORD, and he shall
be cut off from among his people. 31Because he
has despised the word of the LORD, and has broken His commandment, that person shall be completely cut off; his guilt *shall be* upon him.' "

32Now while the children of Israel were in the
wilderness, they found a man gathering sticks on
the Sabbath day. 33And those who found him
gathering sticks brought him to Moses and Aaron,
and to all the congregation. 34They put him under
guard, because it had not been explained what
should be done to him.

35Then the LORD said to Moses, "The man must
surely be put to death; all the congregation shall
stone him with stones outside the camp." 36So,
as the LORD commanded Moses, all the congregation brought him outside the camp and stoned him
with stones, and he died.

37*Again the LORD spoke to Moses, saying,
38"Speak to the children of Israel: Tell them to
make tassels on the corners of their garments
throughout their generations, and to put a blue
thread in the tassels of the corners. 39And you
shall have the tassel, that you may look upon it
and remember all the commandments of the LORD
and do them, and that you *may* not follow the
harlotry to which your own heart and your own
eyes are inclined, 40and that you may remember
and do all My commandments, and be holy for
your God. 41I *am* the LORD your God, who brought
you out of the land of Egypt, to be your God: I
am the LORD your God."

16 Now* Korah the son of Izhar, the son of
Kohath, the son of Levi, with Dathan and
Abiram the sons of Eliab, and On the son of Peleth, sons of Reuben, took *men;* 2and they rose
up before Moses with some of the children of Israel, two hundred and fifty leaders of the congregation, representatives of the congregation, men
of renown. 3They gathered together against Moses and Aaron, and said to them, "*You take* too
much upon yourselves, for all the congregation
is holy, every one of them, and the LORD *is* among
them. Why then do you exalt yourselves above
the assembly of the LORD?"

4So when Moses heard *it,* he fell on his face;
5and he spoke to Korah and all his company, saying, "Tomorrow morning the LORD will show who
is His and *who is* holy, and will cause *him* to come
near to Him. That one whom He chooses He will
cause to come near to Him. 6Do this: Take censers,
Korah and all your company; 7put fire in them
and put incense in them before the LORD tomorrow, and it shall be *that* the man whom the LORD
chooses *is* the holy one. *You take* too much upon
yourselves, you sons of Levi!"

8Then Moses said to Korah, "Hear now, you
sons of Levi: 9*Is it* a small thing to you that the
God of Israel has separated you from the congregation of Israel, to bring you near to Himself, to
do the work of the tabernacle of the LORD, and
to stand before the congregation to serve them;
10and that He has brought you near *to Himself,*

15:30–36 *Arrogance.* In His law, God made
no provision for presumptuous sin, for such
sinners were despising God's Word and
defying His authority. God in His mercy
could forgive such sins, as He did with David
(2 Sam. 12), but He did not put Himself
under obligation. The man who deliberately
violated the Sabbath discovered that God
is not mocked.

15:37–41 *Remembrance.* The tassels
were small things, yet they carried a big
message: Israel belonged to God and must
respect and obey His commandments. It is
not wrong to have reminders that point us
to God, provided they don't replace God or
His Word. We are to "seek those things
which are above" (Col. 3:1).

CHAPTER 16

16:1–3 A successful leader is often accused
of exalting himself, especially by those who
are jealous of him and want to take his place.
It is true that all of God's people are set
apart by Him and for Him, but it is also true
that God calls some of His people to be
leaders in special places of service. Without
leadership, we would have chaos.

16:12–14 Leaders often get blamed for things they did not do (vv. 12–14). Moses wanted to lead the nation into their inheritance, but the unbelief of the people kept them out. It is easier for rebels to find a scapegoat than to confess their own sins. They said that *Egypt* was a "land flowing with milk and honey." Their statement showed where their hearts really were.

16:15–22 The opposition was impressive: 250 leaders, all united against Moses. But Moses was not intimidated; he took the matter to the Lord and let Him be the judge. God will vindicate His servants better than they can vindicate themselves. Once again, the love and intercession of Moses saved the very people who had created problems for him. (See Rom. 12:14–21.)

you and all your brethren, the sons of Levi, with you? And are you seeking the priesthood also? 11Therefore you and all your company *are* gathered together against the LORD. And what *is* Aaron that you complain against him?"

12*And Moses sent to call Dathan and Abiram the sons of Eliab, but they said, "We will not come up! 13*Is it* a small thing that you have brought us up out of a land flowing with milk and honey, to kill us in the wilderness, that you should keep acting like a prince over us? 14Moreover you have not brought us into a land flowing with milk and honey, nor given us inheritance of fields and vineyards. Will you put out the eyes of these men? We will not come up!"

15*Then Moses was very angry, and said to the LORD, "Do not respect their offering. I have not taken one donkey from them, nor have I hurt one of them."

16And Moses said to Korah, "Tomorrow, you and all your company be present before the LORD—you and they, as well as Aaron. 17Let each take his censer and put incense in it, and each of you bring his censer before the LORD, two hundred and fifty censers; both you and Aaron, each *with* his censer." 18So every man took his censer, put fire in it, laid incense on it, and stood at the door of the tabernacle of meeting with Moses and Aaron. 19And Korah gathered all the congregation against them at the door of the tabernacle of meeting. Then the glory of the LORD appeared to all the congregation.

20And the LORD spoke to Moses and Aaron, saying, 21"Separate yourselves from among this congregation, that I may consume them in a moment."

22Then they fell on their faces, and said, "O God, the God of the spirits of all flesh, shall one man sin, and You be angry with all the congregation?"

23So the LORD spoke to Moses, saying, 24"Speak to the congregation, saying, 'Get away from the tents of Korah, Dathan, and Abiram.'"

25Then Moses rose and went to Dathan and Abiram, and the elders of Israel followed him. 26And he spoke to the congregation, saying, "Depart now from the tents of these wicked men! Touch nothing of theirs, lest you be consumed in all their sins." 27So they got away from around the tents of Korah, Dathan, and Abiram; and Dathan and Abiram came out and stood at the door of their tents, with their wives, their sons, and their little children.

28And Moses said: "By this you shall know that the LORD has sent me to do all these works, for *I* have not *done them* of my own will. 29If these men die naturally like all men, or if they are visited by the common fate of all men, *then* the LORD has not sent me. 30But if the LORD creates a new thing, and the earth opens its mouth and swallows them up with all that belongs to them, and they go down alive into the pit, then you will understand that these men have rejected the LORD."

31Now it came to pass, as he finished speaking all these words, that the ground split apart under them, 32and the earth opened its mouth and swallowed them up, with their households and all the men with Korah, with all *their* goods. 33So they and all those with them went down alive into the pit; the earth closed over them, and they perished from among the assembly. 34Then all Israel who *were* around them fled at their cry, for they said, "Lest the earth swallow us up *also!*"

³⁵And a fire came out from the LORD and consumed the two hundred and fifty men who were offering incense. ³⁶Then the LORD spoke to Moses, saying: ³⁷"Tell Eleazar, the son of Aaron the priest, to pick up the censers out of the blaze, for they are holy, and scatter the fire some distance away. ³⁸The censers of these men who sinned against their own souls, let them be made into hammered plates as a covering for the altar. Because they presented them before the LORD, therefore they are holy; and they shall be a sign to the children of Israel." ³⁹So Eleazar the priest took the bronze censers, which those who were burned up had presented, and they were hammered out as a covering on the altar, ⁴⁰to be a memorial to the children of Israel that no outsider, who is not a descendant of Aaron, should come near to offer incense before the LORD, that he might not become like Korah and his companions, just as the LORD had said to him through Moses.

⁴¹On the next day all the congregation of the children of Israel complained against Moses and Aaron, saying, "You have killed the people of the LORD." ⁴²Now it happened, when the congregation had gathered against Moses and Aaron, that they turned toward the tabernacle of meeting; and suddenly the cloud covered it, and the glory of the LORD appeared. ⁴³Then Moses and Aaron came before the tabernacle of meeting.

⁴⁴And the LORD spoke to Moses, saying, ⁴⁵"Get away from among this congregation, that I may consume them in a moment."

And they fell on their faces.

⁴⁶So Moses said to Aaron, "Take a censer and put fire in it from the altar, put incense on it, and take it quickly to the congregation and make atonement for them; for wrath has gone out from the LORD. The plague has begun." ⁴⁷Then Aaron took it as Moses commanded, and ran into the midst of the assembly; and already the plague had begun among the people. So he put in the incense and made atonement for the people. ⁴⁸And he stood between the dead and the living; so the plague was stopped. ⁴⁹*Now those who died in the plague were fourteen thousand seven hundred, besides those who died in the Korah incident. ⁵⁰So Aaron returned to Moses at the door of the tabernacle of meeting, for the plague had stopped.

17 And* the LORD spoke to Moses, saying: ²"Speak to the children of Israel, and get from them a rod from each father's house, all their leaders according to their fathers' houses—twelve rods. Write each man's name on his rod. ³And you shall write Aaron's name on the rod of Levi. For there shall be one rod for the head of each father's house. ⁴Then you shall place them in the tabernacle of meeting before the Testimony, where I meet with you. ⁵And it shall be that the rod of the man whom I choose will blossom; thus I will rid Myself of the complaints of the children of Israel, which they make against you."

⁶So Moses spoke to the children of Israel, and

16:49, 50 Nearly fifteen thousand people died because of four men who wanted to promote themselves. That danger is still with us, and we must heed Proverbs 16:18; 18:12; and 1 Peter 5:5–6.

CHAPTER 17

17:1–7 God had disciplined the people because of their murmuring and rebelling, but the problem was not yet solved. One of Israel's besetting sins was *murmuring* (1 Cor. 10:10), a sin that we must avoid today (Phil. 2:14).

Korah, a Levite, was not satisfied to serve in the tabernacle according to God's will; he wanted a "promotion" so he could enjoy all the privileges of the priests. It is good to desire spiritual growth and progress, but we must beware selfish ambition that glorifies the servant and not the Master (Phil. 2:3–4). "Selfish ambition" is one of the works of the flesh (Gal. 5:20), and it brings destruction.

Complaining—God's people are commanded not to complain (Phil. 2:14); therefore, complaining is a sin. When we complain, we give evidence of unbelief in our hearts and lack of gratitude toward God. If we were truly "giving thanks always for all things" (Eph. 5:20), we would not be complaining. The best way to overcome a complaining spirit is to accept God's will by faith and thank Him for His goodness, even if we don't see anything good happening. Romans 8:28 is still there for us to claim!

each of their leaders gave him a rod apiece, for each leader according to their fathers' houses, twelve rods; and the rod of Aaron *was* among their rods. 7And Moses placed the rods before the LORD in the tabernacle of witness.

8*Now it came to pass on the next day that Moses went into the tabernacle of witness, and behold, the rod of Aaron, of the house of Levi, had sprouted and put forth buds, had produced blossoms and yielded ripe almonds. 9Then Moses brought out all the rods from before the LORD to all the children of Israel; and they looked, and each man took his rod.

10And the LORD said to Moses, "Bring Aaron's rod before the Testimony, to be kept as a sign against the rebels, that you may put their complaints away from Me, lest they die." 11*Thus did Moses; just as the LORD had commanded him, so he did.

12So the children of Israel spoke to Moses, saying, "Surely we die, we perish, we all perish! 13Whoever even comes near the tabernacle of the LORD must die. Shall we all utterly die?"

17:8–10 God vindicated His servants by bringing *death* to some of their opponents and by giving *life* to Aaron's rod. By the power of God, the dead rod produced beauty and fruit. Spiritual leadership will be recognized by its life and fruitfulness, which come from being in the Holy of Holies with God.

17:11–13 How unpredictable is human nature! One day, the people wanted to serve in the tabernacle; the next day, they were afraid to get near it! They did not sincerely fear God; they feared only His judgment. They *needed* leadership far more than they realized.

CHAPTER 18

18:1–6 The emphasis in this chapter is on *gifts.* God gives *helpers* (v. 6) to assist us in our work, and we must accept them and be grateful for them. Some of the Levites had rebelled against Moses and Aaron, but God still gave them the privilege of serving Him and helping the priests.

18 Then* the LORD said to Aaron: "You and your sons and your father's house with you shall bear the iniquity *related to* the sanctuary, and you and your sons with you shall bear the iniquity *associated with* your priesthood. 2Also bring with you your brethren of the tribe of Levi, the tribe of your father, that they may be joined with you and serve you while you and your sons *are* with you before the tabernacle of witness. 3They shall attend to your needs and all the needs of the tabernacle; but they shall not come near the articles of the sanctuary and the altar, lest they die—they and you also. 4They shall be joined with you and attend to the needs of the tabernacle of meeting, for all the work of the tabernacle; but an outsider shall not come near you. 5And you shall attend to the duties of the sanctuary and the duties of the altar, that there *may* be no more wrath on the children of Israel. 6Behold, I Myself have taken your brethren the Levites from among the children of Israel; *they are* a gift to you, given by the LORD, to do the work of the tabernacle of meeting. 7*Therefore you and your sons with you shall attend to your priesthood for everything at the altar and behind the veil; and you shall serve. I give your priesthood *to you* as a gift for service, but the outsider who comes near shall be put to death."

8*And the LORD spoke to Aaron: "Here, I Myself have also given you charge of My heave offerings, all the holy gifts of the children of Israel; I have given them as a portion to you and your sons, as an ordinance forever. 9This shall be yours of the most holy things *reserved* from the fire: every offering of theirs, every grain offering and every sin offering and every trespass offering which they render to Me, *shall be* most holy for you and your sons. 10In a most holy *place* you shall eat it; every male shall eat it. It shall be holy to you.

11"This also *is* yours: the heave offering of their gift, with all the wave offerings of the children of Israel; I have given them to you, and your sons and daughters with you, as an ordinance forever. Everyone who is clean in your house may eat it.

12"All the best of the oil, all the best of the new wine and the grain, their firstfruits which they offer to the LORD, I have given them to you. 13Whatever first ripe fruit is in their land, which

18:7 God gives us *work to do.* If we are in the will of God, our work is a divine vocation, and we must do it for His glory.

18:8–19 God gives us *what we need.* He fed the priests from the sacrifices brought to the altar and also from the tithes (v. 21). His action reminds us that "the laborer is worthy of his wages" (Luke 10:7; 1 Cor. 9:14; 1 Tim. 5:18).

they bring to the LORD, shall be yours. Everyone who is clean in your house may eat it.

14"Every devoted thing in Israel shall be yours. 15"Everything that first opens the womb of all flesh, which they bring to the LORD, whether man or beast, shall be yours; nevertheless the firstborn of man you shall surely redeem, and the firstborn of unclean animals you shall redeem. 16And those redeemed of the devoted things you shall redeem when one month old, according to your valuation, for five shekels of silver, according to the shekel of the sanctuary, which is twenty gerahs. 17But the firstborn of a cow, the firstborn of a sheep, or the firstborn of a goat you shall not redeem; they are holy. You shall sprinkle their blood on the altar, and burn their fat as an offering made by fire for a sweet aroma to the LORD. 18And their flesh shall be yours, just as the wave breast and the right thigh are yours.

19"All the heave offerings of the holy things, which the children of Israel offer to the LORD, I have given to you and your sons and daughters with you as an ordinance forever; it is a covenant of salt forever before the LORD with you and your descendants with you."

20*Then the LORD said to Aaron: "You shall have no inheritance in their land, nor shall you have any portion among them; I am your portion and your inheritance among the children of Israel.

21"Behold, I have given the children of Levi all the tithes in Israel as an inheritance in return for the work which they perform, the work of the tabernacle of meeting. 22Hereafter the children of Israel shall not come near the tabernacle of meeting, lest they bear sin and die. 23But the Levites shall perform the work of the tabernacle of meeting, and they shall bear their iniquity; it shall be a statute forever, throughout your generations, that among the children of Israel they shall have no inheritance. 24For the tithes of the children of Israel, which they offer up as a heave offering to the LORD, I have given to the Levites as an inheritance; therefore I have said to them, 'Among the children of Israel they shall have no inheritance.' "

25Then the LORD spoke to Moses, saying, 26"Speak thus to the Levites, and say to them: 'When you take from the children of Israel the tithes which I have given you from them as your inheritance, then you shall offer up a heave offering of it to the LORD, a tenth of the tithe. 27And your heave offering shall be reckoned to you as though it were the grain of the threshing floor and as the fullness of the winepress. 28Thus you shall also offer a heave offering to the LORD from all your tithes which you receive from the children of Israel, and you shall give the LORD's heave offering from it to Aaron the priest. 29Of all your gifts you shall offer up every heave offering due to the LORD, from all the best of them, the consecrated part of them.' 30Therefore you shall say to them: 'When you have lifted up the best of it, then the rest shall be accounted to the Levites as the produce of the threshing floor and as the produce of the winepress. 31You may eat it in any place, you and your households, for it is your reward for your work in the tabernacle of meeting. 32And you shall bear no sin because of it, when you have lifted up the best of it. But you shall not profane the holy gifts of the children of Israel, lest you die.' "

18:20 God gives us *Himself.* The priests and Levites were assigned places to live in Israel, but they did not have property from which they could get income (Josh. 13:14). They had to trust God to meet their needs. But when God is your inheritance, what more do you need? (See Ps. 16:5–6.)

CHAPTER 19

19:1 As a holy and separated people, the Jews had to avoid ritual uncleanness of all kinds, especially contamination from dead bodies. No doubt there were hygienic purposes behind this law, but it also reminded the people to avoid sin because of the defilement it brings. God dwelt in the camp and no one was to defile it. The application for today is found in 2 Corinthians 6:14—7:1.

19:17–20 God made provision for restoring persons who became defiled. Blood had to be shed, for the heifer was a sin offering (v. 9). The ashes from the sacrifice were ceremonially clean and were used to make "water of purification." The defiled person could be ceremonially cleansed by obeying God's instructions and using the water of purification.

19:21–22 Water for washing is a picture of the Word of God (John 15:3; Eph. 5:25–27). The Word promises us cleansing because the blood of God's Son was shed for us on the cross (1 John 1:5—2:2). The Word also provides cleansing for the inner person as we read it, meditate on it, and apply it to our lives.

Why should we be defiled and defile others when God's gracious cleansing is available?

19 Now* the LORD spoke to Moses and Aaron, saying, 2"This *is* the ordinance of the law which the LORD has commanded: 'Speak to the children of Israel, that they bring you a red heifer without blemish, in which there *is* no defect *and* on which a yoke has never come. 3You shall give it to Eleazar the priest, that he may take it outside the camp, and it shall be slaughtered before him; 4and Eleazar the priest shall take some of its blood with his finger, and sprinkle some of its blood seven times directly in front of the tabernacle of meeting. 5Then the heifer shall be burned in his sight: its hide, its flesh, its blood, and its offal shall be burned. 6And the priest shall take cedar wood and hyssop and scarlet, and cast *them* into the midst of the fire burning the heifer. 7Then the priest shall wash his clothes, he shall bathe in water, and afterward he shall come into the camp; the priest shall be unclean until evening. 8And the one who burns it shall wash his clothes in water, bathe in water, and shall be unclean until evening. 9Then a man who *is* clean shall gather up the ashes of the heifer, and store *them* outside the camp in a clean place; and they shall be kept for the congregation of the children of Israel for the water of purification;ᵘ it *is* for purifying from sin. 10And the one who gathers the ashes of the heifer shall wash his clothes, and be unclean until evening. It shall be a statute forever to the children of Israel and to the stranger who dwells among them.

11'He who touches the dead body of anyone shall be unclean seven days. 12He shall purify himself with the water on the third day and on the seventh day; *then* he will be clean. But if he does not purify himself on the third day and on the seventh day, he will not be clean. 13Whoever touches the body of anyone who has died, and does not purify himself, defiles the tabernacle of the LORD. That person shall be cut off from Israel. He shall be unclean, because the water of purification was not sprinkled on him; his uncleanness *is* still on him.

14'This *is* the law when a man dies in a tent: All who come into the tent and all who *are* in the tent shall be unclean seven days; 15and every open vessel, which has no cover fastened on it, *is* unclean. 16Whoever in the open field touches one who is slain by a sword or who has died, or a bone of a man, or a grave, shall be unclean seven days.

17*'And for an unclean *person* they shall take some of the ashes of the heifer burnt for purification from sin, and running water shall be put on them in a vessel. 18A clean person shall take hyssop and dip *it* in the water, sprinkle *it* on the tent, on all the vessels, on the persons who were there, or on the one who touched a bone, the slain, the dead, or a grave. 19The clean *person* shall sprinkle the unclean on the third day and on the seventh day; and on the seventh day he shall purify himself, wash his clothes, and bathe in water; and at evening he shall be clean.

20'But the man who is unclean and does not purify himself, that person shall be cut off from among the assembly, because he has defiled the sanctuary of the LORD. The water of purification has not been sprinkled on him; he *is* unclean. 21*It shall be a perpetual statute for them. He who

19:9 ᵘLiterally *impurity*

sprinkles the water of purification shall wash his clothes; and he who touches the water of purification shall be unclean until evening. ²²Whatever the unclean *person* touches shall be unclean; and the person who touches *it* shall be unclean until evening.' "

20 Then* the children of Israel, the whole congregation, came into the Wilderness of Zin in the first month, and the people stayed in Kadesh; and Miriam died there and was buried there. ²Now there was no water for the congregation; so they gathered together against Moses and Aaron. ³And the people contended with Moses and spoke, saying: "If only we had died when our brethren died before the LORD! ⁴Why have you brought up the assembly of the LORD into this wilderness, that we and our animals should die here? ⁵And why have you made us come up out of Egypt, to bring us to this evil place? It *is* not a place of grain or figs or vines or pomegranates; nor *is* there any water to drink." ⁶So Moses and Aaron went from the presence of the assembly to the door of the tabernacle of meeting, and they fell on their faces. And the glory of the LORD appeared to them.

⁷Then the LORD spoke to Moses, saying, ⁸"Take the rod; you and your brother Aaron gather the congregation together. Speak to the rock before their eyes, and it will yield its water; thus you shall bring water for them out of the rock, and give drink to the congregation and their animals." ⁹*So Moses took the rod from before the LORD as He commanded him.

¹⁰And Moses and Aaron gathered the assembly together before the rock; and he said to them, "Hear now, you rebels! Must we bring water for you out of this rock?" ¹¹Then Moses lifted his hand and struck the rock twice with his rod; and water came out abundantly, and the congregation and their animals drank.

¹²*Then the LORD spoke to Moses and Aaron, "Because you did not believe Me, to hallow Me in the eyes of the children of Israel, therefore you shall not bring this assembly into the land which I have given them."

¹³This *was* the water of Meribah,ᵛ because the children of Israel contended with the LORD, and He was hallowed among them.

¹⁴Now Moses sent messengers from Kadesh to the king of Edom. "Thus says your brother Israel: 'You know all the hardship that has befallen us, ¹⁵how our fathers went down to Egypt, and we dwelt in Egypt a long time, and the Egyptians afflicted us and our fathers. ¹⁶When we cried out to the LORD, He heard our voice and sent the Angel and brought us up out of Egypt; now here we are in Kadesh, a city on the edge of your border. ¹⁷Please let us pass through your country. We will not pass through fields or vineyards, nor will we drink water from wells; we will go along the King's Highway; we will not turn aside to the right hand or to the left until we have passed through your territory.' "

¹⁸*Then Edom said to him, "You shall not pass through my *land*, lest I come out against you with the sword."

¹⁹So the children of Israel said to him, "We will go by the Highway, and if I or my livestock drink

CHAPTER 20

20:1-5 Leaders are often discouraged as they go through one trial after another. First, Miriam died, and Moses and Aaron mourned their only sister. Then the people began to complain again, for Egypt was still in their hearts. In the will of God, no place is an "evil place"; but when your inner desires are not spiritual, no place is a good place—except Egypt!

20:9-12 Leaders sometimes disobey God, as Moses did when he was angered by the people (Ps. 106:32–33). Water for drinking is a picture of the Holy Spirit (John 7:37–39), and the rock is a symbol of Christ (1 Cor. 10:4). Christ was smitten on the cross for us that we might receive the gift of the Spirit. He died but once, so Moses should not have smitten the rock again. Instead, he should have spoken to the rock.

20:12 Leaders are disciplined by God, for with privilege goes responsibility. Neither Moses nor Aaron was permitted to enter the Promised Land, although Moses was allowed to see the land from afar (Deut. 3:21–29).

20:18-20 Leaders are sometimes disappointed. Edom would not permit Israel to pass through the land despite the promises Moses gave. The Edomites were the descendants of Esau, Jacob's brother, and were therefore blood relatives to Israel; but they did not act like brethren.

It is not easy to be a leader, and we must pray for those whom God has made leaders in His service.

20:13 ᵛLiterally *Contention*

any of your water, then I will pay for it; let me only pass through on foot, nothing *more*."

20Then he said, "You shall not pass through." So Edom came out against them with many men and with a strong hand. 21Thus Edom refused to give Israel passage through his territory; so Israel turned away from him.

22Now the children of Israel, the whole congregation, journeyed from Kadesh and came to Mount Hor. 23And the LORD spoke to Moses and Aaron in Mount Hor by the border of the land of Edom, saying: 24"Aaron shall be gathered to his people, for he shall not enter the land which I have given to the children of Israel, because you rebelled against My word at the water of Meribah. 25Take Aaron and Eleazar his son, and bring them up to Mount Hor; 26and strip Aaron of his garments and put them on Eleazar his son; for Aaron shall be gathered *to his people* and die there." 27So Moses did just as the LORD commanded, and they went up to Mount Hor in the sight of all the congregation. 28Moses stripped Aaron of his garments and put them on Eleazar his son; and Aaron died there on the top of the mountain. Then Moses and Eleazar came down from the mountain. 29Now when all the congregation saw that Aaron was dead, all the house of Israel mourned for Aaron thirty days.

21 The* king of Arad, the Canaanite, who dwelt in the South, heard that Israel was coming on the road to Atharim. Then he fought against Israel and took *some* of them prisoners. 2So Israel made a vow to the LORD, and said, "If You will indeed deliver this people into my hand, then I will utterly destroy their cities." 3And the LORD listened to the voice of Israel and delivered up the Canaanites, and they utterly destroyed them and their cities. So the name of that place was called Hormah.ʷ

4Then they journeyed from Mount Hor by the Way of the Red Sea, to go around the land of Edom; and the soul of the people became very discouraged on the way. 5And the people spoke against God and against Moses: "Why have you brought us up out of Egypt to die in the wilderness? For *there is* no food and no water, and our soul loathes this worthless bread." 6*So the LORD sent fiery serpents among the people, and they bit the people; and many of the people of Israel died.

7Therefore the people came to Moses, and said, "We have sinned, for we have spoken against the LORD and against you; pray to the LORD that He take away the serpents from us." So Moses prayed for the people.

8Then the LORD said to Moses, "Make a fiery *serpent*, and set it on a pole; and it shall be that everyone who is bitten, when he looks at it, shall live." 9So Moses made a bronze serpent, and put it on a pole; and so it was, if a serpent had bitten anyone, when he looked at the bronze serpent, he lived.

10Now the children of Israel moved on and camped in Oboth. 11And they journeyed from Oboth and camped at Ije Abarim, in the wilderness which *is* east of Moab, toward the sunrise. 12From there they moved and camped in the Valley of Zered. 13From there they moved and

CHAPTER 21

In the journeys of life, God can meet every need.

21:1–5 God gives victory. The nation of Israel was on the move as God gave the people one victory after another over strong kings and armies. Israel could have had this experience *in Canaan* had they trusted God and entered the land. These battles helped to train the younger men for the time when they would conquer Canaan.

21:6–9 God gives healing. Israel murmured not about the battles but about their lack of food and water in the wilderness. It was the old "Egyptian appetite" asserting itself again. Instead of meeting the need immediately, God first disciplined the people until they cried out for help. Jesus used the uplifted brazen serpent to picture His own death on the cross (John 3:14–16). He became the very thing that was killing us—*sin* (2 Cor. 5:21). And the only way to be saved is to look to Christ by faith.

21:3 ʷLiterally *Utter Destruction*

camped on the other side of the Arnon, which *is* in the wilderness that extends from the border of the Amorites; for the Arnon *is* the border of Moab, between Moab and the Amorites. 14Therefore it is said in the Book of the Wars of the LORD:

"Waheb in Suphah,ˣ
   The brooks of the Arnon,
15 And the slope of the brooks
   That reaches to the dwelling of Ar,
   And lies on the border of Moab."

16*From there *they went* to Beer, which *is* the well where the LORD said to Moses, "Gather the people together, and I will give them water." 17Then Israel sang this song:

"Spring up, O well!
   All of you sing to it—
18 The well the leaders sank,
   Dug by the nation's nobles,
   By the lawgiver, with their staves."

And from the wilderness *they went* to Mattanah, 19from Mattanah to Nahaliel, from Nahaliel to Bamoth, 20and from Bamoth, *in* the valley that *is* in the country of Moab, to the top of Pisgah which looks down on the wasteland.ʸ
21Then Israel sent messengers to Sihon king of the Amorites, saying, 22"Let me pass through your land. We will not turn aside into fields or vineyards; we will not drink water from wells. We will go by the King's Highway until we have passed through your territory." 23But Sihon would not allow Israel to pass through his territory. So Sihon gathered all his people together and went out against Israel in the wilderness, and he came to Jahaz and fought against Israel. 24Then Israel defeated him with the edge of the sword, and took possession of his land from the Arnon to the Jabbok, as far as the people of Ammon; for the border of the people of Ammon *was* fortified. 25So Israel took all these cities, and Israel dwelt in all the cities of the Amorites, in Heshbon and in all its villages. 26For Heshbon *was* the city of Sihon king of the Amorites, who had fought against the former king of Moab, and had taken all his land from his hand as far as the Arnon. 27Therefore those who speak in proverbs say:

"Come to Heshbon, let it be built;
   Let the city of Sihon be repaired.

28 "For fire went out from Heshbon,
   A flame from the city of Sihon;
   It consumed Ar of Moab,
   The lords of the heights of the Arnon.
29 Woe to you, Moab!
   You have perished, O people of Chemosh!
   He has given his sons as fugitives,
   And his daughters into captivity,
   To Sihon king of the Amorites.

30 "But we have shot at them;
   Heshbon has perished as far as Dibon.
   Then we laid waste as far as Nophah,
   Which *reaches* to Medeba."

21:16–18 God gives water. This time the water did not come from a rock, for God is not limited to one way of meeting our needs. He provided a well for them in a miraculous way. This shows the grace and goodness of the Lord, for just a short time before, the people had complained about the way He was leading them. Give thanks for Psalm 103:10 and Philippians 4:19!

21:14 ˣAncient unknown places; Vulgate reads *What He did in the Red Sea.*   21:20 ʸHebrew *Jeshimon*

³¹Thus Israel dwelt in the land of the Amorites. ³²Then Moses sent to spy out Jazer; and they took its villages and drove out the Amorites who *were* there.

³³And they turned and went up by the way to Bashan. So Og king of Bashan went out against them, he and all his people, to battle at Edrei. ³⁴Then the LORD said to Moses, "Do not fear him, for I have delivered him into your hand, with all his people and his land; and you shall do to him as you did to Sihon king of the Amorites, who dwelt at Heshbon." ³⁵So they defeated him, his sons, and all his people, until there was no survivor left him; and they took possession of his land.

22 Then* the children of Israel moved, and camped in the plains of Moab on the side of the Jordan *across from* Jericho.

²Now Balak the son of Zippor saw all that Israel had done to the Amorites. ³And Moab was exceedingly afraid of the people because they *were* many, and Moab was sick with dread because of the children of Israel. ⁴So Moab said to the elders of Midian, "Now this company will lick up everything around us, as an ox licks up the grass of the field." And Balak the son of Zippor *was* king of the Moabites at that time. ⁵Then he sent messengers to Balaam the son of Beor at Pethor, which *is* near the River^z in the land of the sons of his people,^a to call him, saying: "Look, a people has come from Egypt. See, they cover the face of the earth, and are settling next to me! ⁶Therefore please come at once, curse this people for me, for they *are* too mighty for me. Perhaps I shall be able to defeat them and drive them out of the land, for I know that he whom you bless *is* blessed, and he whom you curse is cursed."

⁷So the elders of Moab and the elders of Midian departed with the diviner's fee in their hand, and they came to Balaam and spoke to him the words of Balak. ⁸And he said to them, "Lodge here tonight, and I will bring back word to you, as the LORD speaks to me." So the princes of Moab stayed with Balaam.

⁹Then God came to Balaam and said, "Who *are* these men with you?"

¹⁰So Balaam said to God, "Balak the son of Zippor, king of Moab, has sent to me, *saying*, ¹¹'Look, a people has come out of Egypt, and they cover the face of the earth. Come now, curse them for me; perhaps I shall be able to overpower them and drive them out.' "

¹²And God said to Balaam, "You shall not go with them; you shall not curse the people, for they *are* blessed."

¹³So Balaam rose in the morning and said to the princes of Balak, "Go back to your land, for the LORD has refused to give me permission to go with you."

¹⁴And the princes of Moab rose and went to Balak, and said, "Balaam refuses to come with us."

¹⁵*Then Balak again sent princes, more numerous and more honorable than they. ¹⁶And they came to Balaam and said to him, "Thus says Balak the son of Zippor: 'Please let nothing hinder you from coming to me; ¹⁷for I will certainly honor you greatly, and I will do whatever you say to

---

CHAPTER 22

22:1–6 The reports of Israel's victories brought fear to Balak. He knew that the army of Israel could never be defeated by human means because the Jews were *God's* people and the battle was a spiritual one. That is why he asked Balaam to curse the nation. Our battle today is not against flesh and blood but against spiritual wickedness, and we will win the victory only if we use spiritual weapons (Eph. 6:10–18; 2 Cor. 10:3–6).

22:15–21 Balaam was a hireling prophet who finally succumbed to the pressure of greater honor and more money. He was willing to look at things "from another viewpoint" in hopes he could find a loophole in the revealed will of God. It is a dangerous thing to bargain over the will of God. Using one's gifts to make money is "the way of Balaam" (2 Pet. 2:15–16), a sin that God condemns.

Thomas Merton has said that "the greatest evil is found where the greatest good has been corrupted." And Paul warned, "For the love of money is a root of all kinds of evil" (1 Tim. 6:10). Balaam and Judas Iscariot know how true this is!

22:5 ᶻThat is, the Euphrates ªOr *the people of Amau*

me. Therefore please come, curse this people for me.' "

18Then Balaam answered and said to the servants of Balak, "Though Balak were to give me his house full of silver and gold, I could not go beyond the word of the LORD my God, to do less or more. 19Now therefore, please, you also stay here tonight, that I may know what more the LORD will say to me."

20And God came to Balaam at night and said to him, "If the men come to call you, rise *and* go with them; but only the word which I speak to you—that you shall do." 21So Balaam rose in the morning, saddled his donkey, and went with the princes of Moab.

22Then God's anger was aroused because he went, and the Angel of the LORD took His stand in the way as an adversary against him. And he was riding on his donkey, and his two servants *were* with him. 23Now the donkey saw the Angel of the LORD standing in the way with His drawn sword in His hand, and the donkey turned aside out of the way and went into the field. So Balaam struck the donkey to turn her back onto the road. 24Then the Angel of the LORD stood in a narrow path between the vineyards, *with* a wall on this side and a wall on that side. 25And when the donkey saw the Angel of the LORD, she pushed herself against the wall and crushed Balaam's foot against the wall; so he struck her again. 26Then the Angel of the LORD went further, and stood in a narrow place where there *was* no way to turn either to the right hand or to the left. 27And when the donkey saw the Angel of the LORD, she lay down under Balaam; so Balaam's anger was aroused, and he struck the donkey with his staff.

28Then the LORD opened the mouth of the donkey, and she said to Balaam, "What have I done to you, that you have struck me these three times?"

29And Balaam said to the donkey, "Because you have abused me. I wish there were a sword in my hand, for now I would kill you!"

30So the donkey said to Balaam, "*Am* I not your donkey on which you have ridden, ever since *I became* yours, to this day? Was I ever disposed to do this to you?"

And he said, "No."

31Then the LORD opened Balaam's eyes, and he saw the Angel of the LORD standing in the way with His drawn sword in His hand; and he bowed his head and fell flat on his face. 32And the Angel of the LORD said to him, "Why have you struck your donkey these three times? Behold, I have come out to stand against you, because *your* way is perverse before Me. 33The donkey saw Me and turned aside from Me these three times. If she had not turned aside from Me, surely I would also have killed you by now, and let her live."

34And Balaam said to the Angel of the LORD, "I have sinned, for I did not know You stood in the way against me. Now therefore, if it displeases You, I will turn back."

35Then the Angel of the LORD said to Balaam, "Go with the men, but only the word that I speak to you, that you shall speak." So Balaam went with the princes of Balak.

36Now when Balak heard that Balaam was coming, he went out to meet him at the city of Moab, which *is* on the border at the Arnon, the boundary of the territory. 37Then Balak said to Balaam, "Did I not earnestly send to you, calling for you? Why did you not come to me? Am I not able to honor you?"

38And Balaam said to Balak, "Look, I have come to you! Now, have I any power at all to say anything? The word that God puts in my mouth, that I must speak." 39So Balaam went with Balak, and they came to Kirjath Huzoth. 40Then Balak offered oxen and sheep, and he sent *some* to Balaam and to the princes who *were* with him.

41So it was, the next day, that Balak took Balaam and brought him up to the high places of Baal, that from there he might observe the extent of the people.

23 Then Balaam said to Balak, "Build seven altars for me here, and prepare for me here seven bulls and seven rams."

2And Balak did just as Balaam had spoken, and Balak and Balaam offered a bull and a ram on *each* altar. 3Then Balaam said to Balak, "Stand by your burnt offering, and I will go; perhaps the LORD will come to meet me, and whatever He shows me I will tell you." So he went to a desolate height. 4And God met Balaam, and he said to Him, "I have prepared the seven altars, and I have offered on *each* altar a bull and a ram."

5*Then the LORD put a word in Balaam's mouth, and said, "Return to Balak, and thus you shall speak." 6So he returned to him, and there he was, standing by his burnt offering, he and all the princes of Moab.

7And he took up his oracle and said:

> "Balak the king of Moab has brought me
>   from Aram,
>   From the mountains of the east.
> 'Come, curse Jacob for me,
>   And come, denounce Israel!'
>
> 8 "How shall I curse whom God has not
>   cursed?
>   And how shall I denounce *whom* the LORD
>   has not denounced?
> 9 For from the top of the rocks I see him,
>   And from the hills I behold him;
>   There! A people dwelling alone,
>   Not reckoning itself among the nations.
>
> 10*"Who can count the dustᵇ of Jacob,
>   Or number one-fourth of Israel?
>   Let me die the death of the righteous,
>   And let my end be like his!"

11Then Balak said to Balaam, "What have you done to me? I took you to curse my enemies, and look, you have blessed *them* bountifully!"

12So he answered and said, "Must I not take heed to speak what the LORD has put in my mouth?"

13Then Balak said to him, "Please come with me to another place from which you may see them; you shall see only the outer part of them, and shall not see them all; curse them for me from there." 14So he brought him to the field of Zophim, to the top of Pisgah, and built seven altars, and offered a bull and a ram on *each* altar.

15And he said to Balak, "Stand here by your burnt offering while I meetᶜ *the* LORD over there."

CHAPTER 23

23:5–8 God did not shut Balaam's mouth. He let him speak, *but He turned the curse into a blessing* (Neh. 13:2). Whenever you feel that people and circumstances are cursing you, remember what God did for Israel, and trust Him (Rom. 8:28).

23:10 Balaam's descriptions of Israel remind us of the privileges we have as the children of God. We are *safe* (v. 8; Rom. 8:31–39) because we are *separated from the world* (v. 9; John 17:14–16) and belong to the Lord who never lies (v. 19). We have *strength* like an ox (v. 22) and a lioness (v. 24).

Balaam wanted very much to die the death of the righteous (v. 10), but he did not want to live the life of the righteous. Read Psalm 37:37, Proverbs 14:32, and Revelation 14:13, and contrast Paul's testimony in Philippians 1:19–23.

23:10 ᵇOr *dust cloud*   23:15 ᶜFollowing Masoretic Text, Targum, and Vulgate; Syriac reads *call;* Septuagint reads *go and ask God.*

¹⁶Then the LORD met Balaam, and put a word in his mouth, and said, "Go back to Balak, and thus you shall speak." ¹⁷So he came to him, and there he was, standing by his burnt offering, and the princes of Moab were with him. And Balak said to him, "What has the LORD spoken?"

¹⁸Then he took up his oracle and said:

> "Rise up, Balak, and hear!
> Listen to me, son of Zippor!

> 19 "God *is* not a man, that He should lie,
>   Nor a son of man, that He should repent.
>   Has He said, and will He not do?
>   Or has He spoken, and will He not make it
>   good?
> 20 Behold, I have received *a command* to bless;
>   He has blessed, and I cannot reverse it.

> 21 "He has not observed iniquity in Jacob,
>   Nor has He seen wickedness in Israel.
>   The LORD his God *is* with him,
>   And the shout of a King *is* among them.
> 22 God brings them out of Egypt;
>   He has strength like a wild ox.

> 23 "For *there is* no sorcery against Jacob,
>   Nor any divination against Israel.
>   It now must be said of Jacob
>   And of Israel, 'Oh, what God has done!'
> 24 Look, a people rises like a lioness,
>   And lifts itself up like a lion;
>   It shall not lie down until it devours the prey,
>   And drinks the blood of the slain."

²⁵Then Balak said to Balaam, "Neither curse them at all, nor bless them at all!"

²⁶So Balaam answered and said to Balak, "Did I not tell you, saying, 'All that the LORD speaks, that I must do'?"

²⁷Then Balak said to Balaam, "Please come, I will take you to another place; perhaps it will please God that you may curse them for me from there." ²⁸So Balak took Balaam to the top of Peor, that overlooks the wasteland.^d ²⁹Then Balaam said to Balak, "Build for me here seven altars, and prepare for me here seven bulls and seven rams." ³⁰And Balak did as Balaam had said, and offered a bull and a ram on *every* altar.

24 Now* when Balaam saw that it pleased the LORD to bless Israel, he did not go as at other times, to seek to use sorcery, but he set his face toward the wilderness. ²And Balaam raised his eyes, and saw Israel encamped according to their tribes; and the Spirit of God came upon him.

³Then he took up his oracle and said:

> "The utterance of Balaam the son of Beor,
>   The utterance of the man whose eyes are
>   opened,
> 4 The utterance of him who hears the words
>   of God,
>   Who sees the vision of the Almighty,
>   Who falls down, with eyes wide open:

> 5 "How lovely are your tents, O Jacob!
>   Your dwellings, O Israel!

CHAPTER 24

24:1–9 Balak could not silence Balaam no matter how he tried. In his third oracle (vv. 1–9), Balaam saw Israel in Canaan, conquering their enemies and enjoying their inheritance. His statement in verse 9 about blessing and cursing reminds us of God's covenant with Abraham (Gen. 12:3). Balaam was actually condemning himself when he spoke. God does not defend His people's sins, but He always defends His people, for they are dear to Him.

23:28 ^dHebrew *Jeshimon*

6   Like valleys that stretch out,
     Like gardens by the riverside,
     Like aloes planted by the LORD,
     Like cedars beside the waters.
7   He shall pour water from his buckets,
     And his seed *shall be* in many waters.

     "His king shall be higher than Agag,
     And his kingdom shall be exalted.

8   "God brings him out of Egypt;
     He has strength like a wild ox;
     He shall consume the nations, his enemies;
     He shall break their bones
     And pierce *them* with his arrows.
9   'He bows down, he lies down as a lion;
     And as a lion, who shall rouse him?'*e*

     "Blessed *is* he who blesses you,
     And cursed *is* he who curses you."

10Then Balak's anger was aroused against Balaam, and he struck his hands together; and Balak said to Balaam, "I called you to curse my enemies, and look, you have bountifully blessed *them* these three times! 11Now therefore, flee to your place. I said I would greatly honor you, but in fact, the LORD has kept you back from honor."

12So Balaam said to Balak, "Did I not also speak to your messengers whom you sent to me, saying, 13'If Balak were to give me his house full of silver and gold, I could not go beyond the word of the LORD, to do good or bad of my own will. What the LORD says, that I must speak'? 14And now, indeed, I am going to my people. Come, I will advise you what this people will do to your people in the latter days."

15*So he took up his oracle and said:

     "The utterance of Balaam the son of Beor,
     And the utterance of the man whose eyes
          are opened;
16   The utterance of him who hears the words
          of God,
     And has the knowledge of the Most High,
     Who sees the vision of the Almighty,
     Who falls down, with eyes wide open:

17   "I see Him, but not now;
     I behold Him, but not near;
     A Star shall come out of Jacob;
     A Scepter shall rise out of Israel,
     And batter the brow of Moab,
     And destroy all the sons of tumult.*f*

18   "And Edom shall be a possession;
     Seir also, his enemies, shall be a possession,
     While Israel does valiantly.
19   Out of Jacob One shall have dominion,
     And destroy the remains of the city."

20Then he looked on Amalek, and he took up his oracle and said:

     "Amalek *was* first among the nations,
     But *shall be* last until he perishes."

24:15–24 In his fourth oracle, Balaam saw Israel's future glory in the coming of the Messiah (v. 17). God used a covetous prophet to give a beautiful picture of the Savior and the victories He would win. Satan and his followers do their best to curse God's people today. However, through it all, God's grace still works, God's people are still blessed, and God's name is glorified, for God can turn the curse into a blessing.

24:9 *e*Genesis 49:9   24:17 *f*Hebrew *Sheth* (compare Jeremiah 48:45)

²¹Then he looked on the Kenites, and he took up his oracle and said:

"Firm is your dwelling place,
    And your nest is set in the rock;
22 Nevertheless Kain shall be burned.
    How long until Asshur carries you away
        captive?"

²³Then he took up his oracle and said:

"Alas! Who shall live when God does this?
24 But ships *shall come* from the coasts of
        Cyprus,ᵍ
    And they shall afflict Asshur and afflict
        Eber,
    And so shall *Amalek*,ʰ until he perishes."

²⁵So Balaam rose and departed and returned to his place; Balak also went his way.

25

Now* Israel remained in Acacia Grove,ⁱ and the people began to commit harlotry with the women of Moab. ²They invited the people to the sacrifices of their gods, and the people ate and bowed down to their gods. ³So Israel was joined to Baal of Peor, and the anger of the LORD was aroused against Israel.

⁴Then the LORD said to Moses, "Take all the leaders of the people and hang the offenders before the LORD, out in the sun, that the fierce anger of the LORD may turn away from Israel."

⁵So Moses said to the judges of Israel, "Every one of you kill his men who were joined to Baal of Peor."

⁶And indeed, one of the children of Israel came and presented to his brethren a Midianite woman in the sight of Moses and in the sight of all the congregation of the children of Israel, who *were* weeping at the door of the tabernacle of meeting. ⁷*Now when Phinehas the son of Eleazar, the son of Aaron the priest, saw *it*, he rose from among the congregation and took a javelin in his hand; ⁸and he went after the man of Israel into the tent and thrust both of them through, the man of Israel, and the woman through her body. So the plague was stopped among the children of Israel. ⁹And those who died in the plague were twenty-four thousand.

¹⁰Then the LORD spoke to Moses, saying: ¹¹"Phinehas the son of Eleazar, the son of Aaron the priest, has turned back My wrath from the children of Israel, because he was zealous with My zeal among them, so that I did not consume the children of Israel in My zeal. ¹²Therefore say, 'Behold, I give to him My covenant of peace; ¹³and it shall be to him and his descendants after him a covenant of an everlasting priesthood, because he was zealous for his God, and made atonement for the children of Israel.' "

¹⁴Now the name of the Israelite who was killed, who was killed with the Midianite woman, *was* Zimri the son of Salu, a leader of a father's house among the Simeonites. ¹⁵And the name of the Midianite woman who was killed *was* Cozbi the daughter of Zur; he *was* head of the people of a father's house in Midian.

¹⁶Then the LORD spoke to Moses, saying:

CHAPTERS 25—26

25:1–3 Balaam could not destroy Israel with his curses, but he could defile Israel with his counsel. He seduced the Jews into disobeying God by suggesting that Balak invite Israel to the religious feasts of the Moabites (31:16). There the Jews quickly fell into sin.

Moses had commanded the people to separate themselves from the nations around them and to avoid their abominable religious practices (Exod. 34:10–17). Israel abandoned its special position (Num. 23:9) and compromised with sin. The result? Twenty-four thousand Jews died from a plague God sent to the camp.

25:7–9, 12 It was not Moses, the leader, or Eleazar, the high priest, who stopped the plague, but Phinehas, the son of Eleazar. His devotion to the Lord brought him a special commendation and reward from the Lord. (See Ps. 106:28–31.)

God's people must beware compromising with the enemy (2 Cor. 6:14–18). If Satan does not succeed as the devouring lion (1 Pet. 5:8), he will come as the deceiving serpent (2 Cor. 11:3).

24:24 ᵍHebrew *Kittim* ʰLiterally *he* or *that one*   25:1 ⁱHebrew *Shittim*

17"Harass the Midianites, and attack them; 18for they harassed you with their schemes by which they seduced you in the matter of Peor and in the matter of Cozbi, the daughter of a leader of Midian, their sister, who was killed in the day of the plague because of Peor."

26 And it came to pass, after the plague, that the LORD spoke to Moses and Eleazar the son of Aaron the priest, saying: 2*"Take a census of all the congregation of the children of Israel from twenty years old and above, by their fathers' houses, all who are able to go to war in Israel." 3So Moses and Eleazar the priest spoke with them in the plains of Moab by the Jordan, *across from Jericho,* saying: 4*"Take a census of the people* from twenty years old and above, just as the LORD commanded Moses and the children of Israel who came out of the land of Egypt."

5Reuben *was* the firstborn of Israel. The children of Reuben *were: of* Hanoch, the family of the Hanochites; *of* Pallu, the family of the Palluites; 6*of* Hezron, the family of the Hezronites; *of* Carmi, the family of the Carmites. 7These *are* the families of the Reubenites: those who were numbered of them were forty-three thousand seven hundred and thirty. 8And the son of Pallu *was* Eliab. 9The sons of Eliab *were* Nemuel, Dathan, and Abiram. These *are* the Dathan and Abiram, representatives of the congregation, who contended against Moses and Aaron in the company of Korah, when they contended against the LORD; 10and the earth opened its mouth and swallowed them up together with Korah when that company died, when the fire devoured two hundred and fifty men; and they became a sign. 11Nevertheless the children of Korah did not die.

12The sons of Simeon according to their families *were: of* Nemuel,[j] the family of the Nemuelites; *of* Jamin, the family of the Jaminites; *of* Jachin,[k] the family of the Jachinites; 13*of* Zerah,[l] the family of the Zarhites; *of* Shaul, the family of the Shaulites. 14These *are* the families of the Simeonites: twenty-two thousand two hundred.

15The sons of Gad according to their families *were: of* Zephon,[m] the family of the Zephonites; *of* Haggi, the family of the Haggites; *of* Shuni, the family of the Shunites; 16*of* Ozni,[n] the family of the Oznites; *of* Eri, the family of the Erites; 17*of* Arod,[o] the family of the Arodites; *of* Areli, the family of the Arelites. 18These *are* the families of the sons of Gad according to those who were numbered of them: forty thousand five hundred.

19The sons of Judah *were* Er and Onan; and Er and Onan died in the land of Canaan. 20And the sons of Judah according to their families were: *of* Shelah, the family of the Shelanites; *of* Perez, the family of the Parzites; *of* Zerah, the family of the Zarhites. 21And the sons of Perez were: *of* Hezron, the family of the Hezronites; *of* Hamul, the family of the Hamulites. 22These *are* the families of Judah according to those who were numbered of them: seventy-six thousand five hundred.

23The sons of Issachar according to their fami-

26:2–65 The taking of the second census was a sign that the nation's wanderings were soon to end. Note the people in this list who are given special attention: Dathan and Abiram, who rebelled against the Lord (26:9–11); Nadab and Abihu, who defied the Lord (26:61); and Joshua and Caleb, who believed the Lord (26:65).

26:12 [j]Spelled *Jemuel* in Genesis 46:10 and Exodus 6:15 [k]Called *Jarib* in 1 Chronicles 4:24   26:13 [l]Called *Zohar* in Genesis 46:10   26:15 [m]Called *Ziphion* in Genesis 46:16 26:16 [n]Called *Ezbon* in Genesis 46:16   26:17 [o]Spelled *Arodi* in Samaritan Pentateuch, Syriac, and Genesis 46:16

lies *were:* of Tola, the family of the Tolaites; of Puah,[p] the family of the Punites;[q] 24of Jashub, the family of the Jashubites; of Shimron, the family of the Shimronites. 25These *are* the families of Issachar according to those who were numbered of them: sixty-four thousand three hundred.

26The sons of Zebulun according to their families *were:* of Sered, the family of the Sardites; of Elon, the family of the Elonites; of Jahleel, the family of the Jahleelites. 27These *are* the families of the Zebulunites according to those who were numbered of them: sixty thousand five hundred.

28The sons of Joseph according to their families, by Manasseh and Ephraim, *were:* 29The sons of Manasseh: of Machir, the family of the Machirites; and Machir begot Gilead; of Gilead, the family of the Gileadites. 30These *are* the sons of Gilead: *of* Jeezer,[r] the family of the Jeezerites; of Helek, the family of the Helekites; 31*of* Asriel, the family of the Asrielites; *of* Shechem, the family of the Shechemites; 32*of* Shemida, the family of the Shemidaites; *of* Hepher, the family of the Hepherites. 33Now Zelophehad the son of Hepher had no sons, but daughters; and the names of the daughters of Zelophehad *were* Mahlah, Noah, Hoglah, Milcah, and Tirzah. 34These *are* the families of Manasseh; and those who were numbered of them *were* fifty-two thousand seven hundred.

35These *are* the sons of Ephraim according to their families: of Shuthelah, the family of the Shuthalhites; of Becher,[s] the family of the Bachrites; of Tahan, the family of the Tahanites. 36And these *are* the sons of Shuthelah: of Eran, the family of the Eranites. 37These *are* the families of the sons of Ephraim according to those who were numbered of them: thirty-two thousand five hundred.

These *are* the sons of Joseph according to their families.

38The sons of Benjamin according to their families were: of Bela, the family of the Belaites; of Ashbel, the family of the Ashbelites; of Ahiram, the family of the Ahiramites; 39of Shupham,[t] the family of the Shuphamites; of Hupham,[u] the family of the Huphamites. 40And the sons of Bela were Ard[v] and Naaman: *of Ard,* the family of the Ardites; of Naaman, the family of the Naamites. 41These *are* the sons of Benjamin according to their families; and those who were numbered of them *were* forty-five thousand six hundred.

42These *are* the sons of Dan according to their families: of Shuham,[w] the family of the Shuhamites. These *are* the families of Dan according to their families. 43All the families of the Shuhamites, according to those who were numbered of them, *were* sixty-four thousand four hundred.

44The sons of Asher according to their families *were:* of Jimna, the family of the Jimnites; of Jesui, the family of the Jesuites; of Beriah, the family of the Beriites. 45Of the sons of Beriah: of Heber, the family of the Heberites; of Malchiel, the family of the Malchielites. 46And the name of

---

26:23 [p]Hebrew *Puvah* (compare Genesis 46:13 and 1 Chronicles 7:1); Samaritan Pentateuch, Septuagint, Syriac, and Vulgate read *Puah.* [q]Samaritan Pentateuch, Septuagint, Syriac, and Vulgate read *Puaites.*   26:30 [r]Called *Abiezer* in Joshua 17:2   26:35 [s]Called *Bered* in 1 Chronicles 7:20   26:39 [t]Masoretic Text reads *Shephupham,* spelled *Shephuphan* in 1 Chronicles 8:5. [u]Called *Huppim* in Genesis 46:21   26:40 [v]Called *Addar* in 1 Chronicles 8:3   26:42 [w]Called *Hushim* in Genesis 46:23

the daughter of Asher *was* Serah. 47These *are* the families of the sons of Asher according to those who were numbered of them: fifty-three thousand four hundred.

48The sons of Naphtali according to their families *were*: of Jahzeel,ˣ the family of the Jahzeelites; of Guni, the family of the Gunites; 49of Jezer, the family of the Jezerites; of Shillem, the family of the Shillemites. 50These *are* the families of Naphtali according to their families; and those who were numbered of them *were* forty-five thousand four hundred.

51These *are* those who were numbered of the children of Israel: six hundred and one thousand seven hundred and thirty.

52Then the LORD spoke to Moses, saying: 53"To these the land shall be divided as an inheritance, according to the number of names. 54To a large *tribe* you shall give a larger inheritance, and to a small *tribe* you shall give a smaller inheritance. Each shall be given its inheritance according to those who were numbered of them. 55But the land shall be divided by lot; they shall inherit according to the names of the tribes of their fathers. 56According to the lot their inheritance shall be divided between the larger and the smaller."

57And these *are* those who were numbered of the Levites according to their families: of Gershon, the family of the Gershonites; of Kohath, the family of the Kohathites; of Merari, the family of the Merarites. 58These *are* the families of the Levites: the family of the Libnites, the family of the Hebronites, the family of the Mahlites, the family of the Mushites, and the family of the Korahites. And Kohath begot Amram. 59The name of Amram's wife *was* Jochebed the daughter of Levi, who was born to Levi in Egypt; and to Amram she bore Aaron and Moses and their sister Miriam. 60To Aaron were born Nadab and Abihu, Eleazar and Ithamar. 61And Nadab and Abihu died when they offered profane fire before the LORD.

62Now those who were numbered of them were twenty-three thousand, every male from a month old and above; for they were not numbered among the other children of Israel, because there was no inheritance given to them among the children of Israel.

63These *are* those who were numbered by Moses and Eleazar the priest, who numbered the children of Israel in the plains of Moab by the Jordan, *across from* Jericho. 64But among these there was not a man of those who were numbered by Moses and Aaron the priest when they numbered the children of Israel in the Wilderness of Sinai. 65For the LORD had said of them, "They shall surely die in the wilderness." So there was not left a man of them, except Caleb the son of Jephunneh and Joshua the son of Nun.

CHAPTER 27

27:1–11 *Claiming the land.* New problems give us new opportunities to seek God's wisdom and learn new truths: "Yet you do not have because you do not ask" (James 4:2). The five daughters had the courage and faith to ask for their inheritance, and they got it. They also had a part in establishing a law that helped other families in Israel get their inheritance.

27 Then* came the daughters of Zelophehad the son of Hepher, the son of Gilead, the son of Machir, the son of Manasseh, from the families of Manasseh the son of Joseph; and these *were* the names of his daughters: Mahlah, Noah, Hoglah, Milcah, and Tirzah. 2And they stood before Moses, before Eleazar the priest, and before the leaders and all the congregation, *by* the doorway of the tabernacle of meeting, saying: 3"Our

26:48 ˣSpelled *Jahziel* in 1 Chronicles 7:13

father died in the wilderness; but he was not in the company of those who gathered together against the LORD, in company with Korah, but he died in his own sin; and he had no sons. 4Why should the name of our father be removed from among his family because he had no son? Give us a possession among our father's brothers."

5So Moses brought their case before the LORD.

6And the LORD spoke to Moses, saying: 7"The daughters of Zelophehad speak *what is* right; you shall surely give them a possession of inheritance among their father's brothers, and cause the inheritance of their father to pass to them. 8And you shall speak to the children of Israel, saying: 'If a man dies and has no son, then you shall cause his inheritance to pass to his daughter. 9If he has no daughter, then you shall give his inheritance to his brothers. 10If he has no brothers, then you shall give his inheritance to his father's brothers. 11And if his father has no brothers, then you shall give his inheritance to the relative closest to him in his family, and he shall possess it.' " And it shall be to the children of Israel a statute of judgment, just as the LORD commanded Moses.

12*Now the LORD said to Moses: "Go up into this Mount Abarim, and see the land which I have given to the children of Israel. 13And when you have seen it, you also shall be gathered to your people, as Aaron your brother was gathered. 14For in the Wilderness of Zin, during the strife of the congregation, you rebelled against My command to hallow Me at the waters before their eyes." (These *are* the waters of Meribah, at Kadesh in the Wilderness of Zin.)

15*Then Moses spoke to the LORD, saying: 16"Let the LORD, the God of the spirits of all flesh, set a man over the congregation, 17who may go out before them and go in before them, who may lead them out and bring them in, that the congregation of the LORD may not be like sheep which have no shepherd."

18And the LORD said to Moses: "Take Joshua the son of Nun with you, a man in whom *is* the Spirit, and lay your hand on him; 19set him before Eleazar the priest and before all the congregation, and inaugurate him in their sight. 20And you shall give *some* of your authority to him, that all the congregation of the children of Israel may be obedient. 21He shall stand before Eleazar the priest, who shall inquire before the LORD for him by the judgment of the Urim. At his word they shall go out, and at his word they shall come in, he and all the children of Israel with him—all the congregation."

22So Moses did as the LORD commanded him. He took Joshua and set him before Eleazar the priest and before all the congregation. 23And he laid his hands on him and inaugurated him, just as the LORD commanded by the hand of Moses.

28 Now* the LORD spoke to Moses, saying, 2"Command the children of Israel, and say to them, 'My offering, My food for My offerings made by fire as a sweet aroma to Me, you shall be careful to offer to Me at their appointed time.'

3"And you shall say to them, 'This *is* the offering made by fire which you shall offer to the LORD: two male lambs in their first year without blemish, day by day, as a regular burnt offering. 4The one lamb you shall offer in the morning, the other lamb you shall offer in the evening, 5and one-tenth

27:12–14 Seeing the land. Moses saw the Promised Land but (as far as we know) did not enter it until he appeared with Elijah on the Mount of Transfiguration (Matt. 17:1–8). The land of Canaan is a picture, not of heaven but of the believer's inheritance in Christ in the heavenlies (Eph. 1:3). A whole generation died and never saw the land. Ten of the spies saw the land for forty days and then died in their unbelief. Moses saw the land but could not enter it. The new generation, along with Caleb and Joshua, entered the land and claimed their promised inheritance. To which group do you belong?

27:15–23 Conquering the land. As always, Moses' greatest concern was the people and not himself, and God gave him his assistant Joshua to be his successor (Matt. 25:21). Joshua was God's general who would conquer the land and give the people their inheritance. He is a type of Jesus Christ (*Joshua* means "Jehovah is salvation") who conquered our enemies for us and opened the way for us to claim all the blessings God has for us.

CHAPTERS 28—29

28:1–31 The new generation had to be taught the "religious calendar," which would govern their lives after they entered the land. The older generation should see to it that those coming after understand the traditions. They were instructed about the regular offerings and also about the annual feasts. (See Lev. 23.)

All time belongs to God, but it is good for us to set aside special times to remind us of what He has done for us. The Jews presented their worship at the the beginning of each day (28:1–8), at the end of the week (28:9–10), and on the first of the month (28:11–15). We do not bring animal sacrifices. Instead, we present our bodies to the Lord as "living sacrifices" (Rom. 12:1–2).

of an ephah of fine flour as a grain offering mixed with one-fourth of a hin of pressed oil. 6*It is* a regular burnt offering which was ordained at Mount Sinai for a sweet aroma, an offering made by fire to the Lord. 7And its drink offering *shall be* one-fourth of a hin for each lamb; in a holy *place* you shall pour out the drink to the Lord as an offering. 8The other lamb you shall offer in the evening; as the morning grain offering and its drink offering, you shall offer *it* as an offering made by fire, a sweet aroma to the Lord.

9'And on the Sabbath day two lambs in their first year, without blemish, and two-tenths *of an ephah* of fine flour as a grain offering, mixed with oil, with its drink offering— 10*this is* the burnt offering for every Sabbath, besides the regular burnt offering with its drink offering.

11'At the beginnings of your months you shall present a burnt offering to the Lord: two young bulls, one ram, and seven lambs in their first year, without blemish; 12three-tenths *of an ephah* of fine flour as a grain offering, mixed with oil, for each bull; two-tenths *of an ephah* of fine flour as a grain offering, mixed with oil, for the one ram; 13and one-tenth *of an ephah* of fine flour, mixed with oil, as a grain offering for each lamb, as a burnt offering of sweet aroma, an offering made by fire to the Lord. 14Their drink offering shall be half a hin of wine for a bull, one-third of a hin for a ram, and one-fourth of a hin for a lamb; this *is* the burnt offering for each month throughout the months of the year. 15Also one kid of the goats as a sin offering to the Lord shall be offered, besides the regular burnt offering and its drink offering.

16'On the fourteenth day of the first month *is* the Passover of the Lord. 17And on the fifteenth day of this month *is* the feast; unleavened bread shall be eaten for seven days. 18On the first day *you shall have* a holy convocation. You shall do no customary work. 19And you shall present an offering made by fire as a burnt offering to the Lord: two young bulls, one ram, and seven lambs in their first year. Be sure they are without blemish. 20Their grain offering shall be of fine flour mixed with oil: three-tenths *of an ephah* you shall offer for a bull, and two-tenths for a ram; 21you shall offer one-tenth *of an ephah* for each of the seven lambs; 22also one goat *as* a sin offering, to make atonement for you. 23You shall offer these besides the burnt offering of the morning, which *is* for a regular burnt offering. 24In this manner you shall offer the food of the offering made by fire daily for seven days, as a sweet aroma to the Lord; it shall be offered besides the regular burnt offering and its drink offering. 25And on the seventh day you shall have a holy convocation. You shall do no customary work.

26'Also on the day of the firstfruits, when you bring a new grain offering to the Lord at your *Feast of* Weeks, you shall have a holy convocation. You shall do no customary work. 27You shall present a burnt offering as a sweet aroma to the Lord: two young bulls, one ram, and seven lambs in their first year, 28with their grain offering of fine flour mixed with oil: three-tenths *of an ephah* for each bull, two-tenths for the one ram, 29and one-tenth for each of the seven lambs; 30also one kid of the goats, to make atonement for you. 31Be sure they are without blemish. You shall present *them* with their drink offerings, besides the regular burnt offering with its grain offering.

29 ¹'And* in the seventh month, on the first *day* of the month, you shall have a holy convocation. You shall do no customary work. For you it is a day of blowing the trumpets. ²You shall offer a burnt offering as a sweet aroma to the LORD: one young bull, one ram, *and* seven lambs in their first year, without blemish. ³Their grain offering *shall be* fine flour mixed with oil: three-tenths *of an ephah* for the bull, two-tenths for the ram, ⁴and one-tenth for each of the seven lambs; ⁵also one kid of the goats *as* a sin offering, to make atonement for you; ⁶besides the burnt offering with its grain offering for the New Moon, the regular burnt offering with its grain offering, and their drink offerings, according to their ordinance, as a sweet aroma, an offering made by fire to the LORD.

⁷'On the tenth *day* of this seventh month you shall have a holy convocation. You shall afflict your souls; you shall not do any work. ⁸You shall present a burnt offering to the LORD *as* a sweet aroma: one young bull, one ram, *and* seven lambs in their first year. Be sure they are without blemish. ⁹Their grain offering *shall be of* fine flour mixed with oil: three-tenths *of an ephah* for the bull, two-tenths for the one ram, ¹⁰and one-tenth for each of the seven lambs; ¹¹also one kid of the goats *as* a sin offering, besides the sin offering for atonement, the regular burnt offering with its grain offering, and their drink offerings.

¹²'On the fifteenth day of the seventh month you shall have a holy convocation. You shall do no customary work, and you shall keep a feast to the LORD seven days. ¹³You shall present a burnt offering, an offering made by fire as a sweet aroma to the LORD: thirteen young bulls, two rams, *and* fourteen lambs in their first year. They shall be without blemish. ¹⁴Their grain offering *shall be of* fine flour mixed with oil: three-tenths *of an ephah* for each of the thirteen bulls, two-tenths for each of the two rams, ¹⁵and one-tenth for each of the fourteen lambs; ¹⁶also one kid of the goats *as* a sin offering, besides the regular burnt offering, its grain offering, and its drink offering.

¹⁷'On the second day *present* twelve young bulls, two rams, fourteen lambs in their first year without blemish, ¹⁸and their grain offering and their drink offerings for the bulls, for the rams, and for the lambs, by their number, according to the ordinance; ¹⁹also one kid of the goats *as* a sin offering, besides the regular burnt offering with its grain offering, and their drink offerings.

²⁰'On the third day *present* eleven bulls, two rams, fourteen lambs in their first year without blemish, ²¹and their grain offering and their drink offerings for the bulls, for the rams, and for the lambs, by their number, according to the ordinance; ²²also one goat *as* a sin offering, besides the regular burnt offering, its grain offering, and its drink offering.

²³'On the fourth day *present* ten bulls, two rams, *and* fourteen lambs in their first year, without blemish, ²⁴and their grain offering and their drink offerings for the bulls, for the rams, and for the lambs, by their number, according to the ordinance; ²⁵also one kid of the goats *as* a sin offering, besides the regular burnt offering, its grain offering, and its drink offering.

²⁶'On the fifth day *present* nine bulls, two rams, *and* fourteen lambs in their first year without blemish, ²⁷and their grain offering and their drink

29:1–40 The special annual feasts could not take the place of the regular offerings. The way to become more spiritual is to strengthen the regular worship day after day, and then the special times of worship will do us more good. Never neglect the "regular burnt offering" (28:3). The word *regular* is used seventeen times in Numbers 28—29, a reminder that the daily routine is important to God and to us.

offerings for the bulls, for the rams, and for the lambs, by their number, according to the ordinance; 28also one goat *as* a sin offering, besides the regular burnt offering, its grain offering, and its drink offering.

29'On the sixth day *present* eight bulls, two rams, *and* fourteen lambs in their first year without blemish, 30and their grain offering and their drink offerings for the bulls, for the rams, and for the lambs, by their number, according to the ordinance; 31also one goat *as* a sin offering, besides the regular burnt offering, its grain offering, and its drink offering.

32'On the seventh day *present* seven bulls, two rams, *and* fourteen lambs in their first year without blemish, 33and their grain offering and their drink offerings for the bulls, for the rams, and for the lambs, by their number, according to the ordinance; 34also one goat *as* a sin offering, besides the regular burnt offering, its grain offering, and its drink offering.

35'On the eighth day you shall have a sacred assembly. You shall do no customary work. 36You shall present a burnt offering, an offering made by fire as a sweet aroma to the LORD: one bull, one ram, seven lambs in their first year without blemish, 37and their grain offering and their drink offerings for the bull, for the ram, and for the lambs, by their number, according to the ordinance; 38also one goat *as* a sin offering, besides the regular burnt offering, its grain offering, and its drink offering.

39'These you shall present to the LORD at your appointed feasts (besides your vowed offerings and your freewill offerings) as your burnt offerings and your grain offerings, as your drink offerings and your peace offerings.' "

40So Moses told the children of Israel everything, just as the LORD commanded Moses.

CHAPTER 30

30:1, 2 *The power of words.* God takes our promises and pledges seriously, and so should we (Ps. 50:14; Eccles. 5:4–5). If we promise God that we will do something, or not do something, we must keep our word. We must also recognize that *willing* and *doing* are two different things (Rom. 7:18–25). We need the wisdom of God in making our promises and the power of God in keeping them (Phil. 2:12–13). Words are powerful things and must be used carefully. The Quakers say, "Of your unspoken words, you are the master; of your spoken words, the servant; of your written words, the slave."

30:3–8 *The power of authority.* God acknowledges the presence of authority. A wife's vow may be canceled by her husband and a daughter's vow by her father. The wife and the daughter should consider this before making promises to God. Although Moses does not instruct the man of the house this way, certainly the husband and father would want to consider the whole family before making any promises to God.

30 Then* Moses spoke to the heads of the tribes concerning the children of Israel, saying, "This *is* the thing which the LORD has commanded: 2If a man makes a vow to the LORD, or swears an oath to bind himself by some agreement, he shall not break his word; he shall do according to all that proceeds out of his mouth.

3*"Or if a woman makes a vow to the LORD, and binds *herself* by some agreement while in her father's house in her youth, 4and her father hears her vow and the agreement by which she has bound herself, and her father holds his peace, then all her vows shall stand, and every agreement with which she has bound herself shall stand. 5But if her father overrules her on the day that he hears, then none of her vows nor her agreements by which she has bound herself shall stand; and the LORD will release her, because her father overruled her.

6"If indeed she takes a husband, while bound by her vows or by a rash utterance from her lips by which she bound herself, 7and her husband hears *it,* and makes no response to her on the day that he hears, then her vows shall stand, and her agreements by which she bound herself shall stand. 8But if her husband overrules her on the day that he hears *it,* he shall make void her vow which she took and what she uttered with her lips, by which she bound herself, and the LORD will release her.

9"Also any vow of a widow or a divorced

woman, by which she has bound herself, shall stand against her. 10"If she vowed in her husband's house, or bound herself by an agreement with an oath, 11and her husband heard *it*, and made no response to her *and* did not overrule her, then all her vows shall stand, and every agreement by which she bound herself shall stand. 12But if her husband truly made them void on the day he heard *them*, then whatever proceeded from her lips concerning her vows or concerning the agreement binding her, it shall not stand; her husband has made them void, and the LORD will release her. 13Every vow and every binding oath to afflict her soul, her husband may confirm it, or her husband may make it void. 14*Now if her husband makes no response whatever to her from day to day, then he confirms all her vows or all the agreements that bind her; he confirms them, because he made no response to her on the day that he heard *them*. 15But if he does make them void after he has heard *them*, then he shall bear her guilt."

16These *are* the statutes which the LORD commanded Moses, between a man and his wife, and between a father and his daughter in her youth in her father's house.

31 And* the LORD spoke to Moses, saying: 2"Take vengeance on the Midianites for the children of Israel. Afterward you shall be gathered to your people."

3So Moses spoke to the people, saying, "Arm some of yourselves for war, and let them go against the Midianites to take vengeance for the LORD on Midian. 4A thousand from each tribe of all the tribes of Israel you shall send to the war." 5So there were recruited from the divisions of Israel one thousand from *each* tribe, twelve thousand armed for war. 6Then Moses sent them to the war, one thousand from *each* tribe; he sent them to the war with Phinehas the son of Eleazar the priest, with the holy articles and the signal trumpets in his hand. 7*And they warred against the Midianites, just as the LORD commanded Moses, and they killed all the males. 8They killed the kings of Midian with *the rest of* those who were killed—Evi, Rekem, Zur, Hur, and Reba, the five kings of Midian. Balaam the son of Beor they also killed with the sword.

9And the children of Israel took the women of Midian captive, with their little ones, and took as spoil all their cattle, all their flocks, and all their goods. 10They also burned with fire all the cities where they dwelt, and all their forts. 11And they took all the spoil and all the booty—of man and beast. 12Then they brought the captives, the booty, and the spoil to Moses, to Eleazar the priest, and to the congregation of the children of Israel, to the camp in the plains of Moab by the Jordan, *across from* Jericho. 13*And Moses, Eleazar the priest, and all the leaders of the congregation, went to meet them outside the camp. 14But Moses was angry with the officers of the army, *with* the captains over thousands and captains over hundreds, who had come from the battle.

15And Moses said to them: "Have you kept all the women alive? 16Look, these *women* caused the children of Israel, through the counsel of Balaam, to trespass against the LORD in the incident of Peor, and there was a plague among the congregation of the LORD. 17Now therefore, kill every

30:14, 15 *The power of silence.* If the father or the husband says nothing, this is considered to be approval of the vow. Silence can sometimes be more powerful than words and have much greater consequences. (See Ps. 141:3.)

CHAPTER 31

31:1–6 The last battle Moses directed was against the Midianites who, at Balaam's suggestion, had seduced Israel into both idolatry and immorality (chap. 25). Each tribe sent one thousand soldiers, and the high priest went before the army with the ark of the covenant. It was God's battle, and He would give victory.

31:7–9 Balaam did not have long to enjoy whatever rewards Balak gave him because he was killed in the battle (v. 8). Alas, he did not "die the death of the righteous" (23:10)! As Mark wrote, "For what will it profit a man if he gains the whole world, and loses his own soul?" (Mark 8:36).

31:13–18 Israel won the war but almost lost the victory, for the leaders brought some Midianite women into the camp along with the spoils. Incomplete obedience always leads to further temptation. (See 1 Sam. 15.) If we do not defeat the enemy, the enemy will defeat us.

31:19, 20 They had fought a "holy war," but the army was defiled in the slaying of the Midianites. They had to purify themselves and the spoils to be clean before God (chap. 19). Some of the spoils were cleansed by fire. The Lord wants clean soldiers as well as conquering soldiers.

male among the little ones, and kill every woman who has known a man intimately. 18But keep alive for yourselves all the young girls who have not known a man intimately. 19*And as for you, remain outside the camp seven days; whoever has killed any person, and whoever has touched any slain, purify yourselves and your captives on the third day and on the seventh day. 20Purify every garment, everything made of leather, everything woven of goats' *hair*, and everything made of wood."

21Then Eleazar the priest said to the men of war who had gone to the battle, "This *is* the ordinance of the law which the LORD commanded Moses: 22"Only the gold, the silver, the bronze, the iron, the tin, and the lead, 23everything that can endure fire, you shall put through the fire, and it shall be clean; and it shall be purified with the water of purification. But all that cannot endure fire you shall put through water. 24And you shall wash your clothes on the seventh day and be clean, and afterward you may come into the camp."

25Now the LORD spoke to Moses, saying: 26"Count up the plunder that was taken—of man and beast—you and Eleazar the priest and the chief fathers of the congregation; 27and divide the plunder into two parts, between those who took part in the war, who went out to battle, and all the congregation. 28And levy a tribute for the LORD on the men of war who went out to battle: one of every five hundred of the persons, the cattle, the donkeys, and the sheep; 29take *it* from their half, and give *it* to Eleazar the priest as a heave offering to the LORD. 30And from the children of Israel's half you shall take one of every fifty, drawn from the persons, the cattle, the donkeys, and the sheep, from all the livestock, and give them to the Levites who keep charge of the tabernacle of the LORD." 31So Moses and Eleazar the priest did as the LORD commanded Moses.

32The booty remaining from the plunder, which the men of war had taken, was six hundred and seventy-five thousand sheep, 33seventy-two thousand cattle, 34sixty-one thousand donkeys, 35and thirty-two thousand persons in all, of women who had not known a man intimately. 36And the half, the portion for those who had gone out to war, was in number three hundred and thirty-seven thousand five hundred sheep; 37and the LORD's tribute of the sheep was six hundred and seventy-five. 38The cattle *were* thirty-six thousand, of which the LORD's tribute *was* seventy-two. 39The donkeys *were* thirty thousand five hundred, of which the LORD's tribute *was* sixty-one. 40The persons *were* sixteen thousand, of which the LORD's tribute *was* thirty-two persons. 41So Moses gave the tribute *which was* the LORD's heave offering to Eleazar the priest, as the LORD commanded Moses.

42And from the children of Israel's half, which Moses separated from the men who fought— 43now the half belonging to the congregation was three hundred and thirty-seven thousand five hundred sheep, 44thirty-six thousand cattle, 45thirty thousand five hundred donkeys, 46and sixteen thousand persons— 47and from the children of Israel's half Moses took one of every fifty, drawn from man and beast, and gave them to the Levites, who kept charge of the tabernacle of the LORD, as the LORD commanded Moses.

48Then the officers who *were* over thousands of the army, the captains of thousands and captains of hundreds, came near to Moses; 49and they said to Moses, "Your servants have taken a count of the men of war who *are* under our command, and not a man of us is missing. 50Therefore we have brought an offering for the LORD, what every man found of ornaments of gold: armlets and bracelets and signet rings and earrings and necklaces, to make atonement for ourselves before the LORD." 51So Moses and Eleazar the priest received the gold from them, all the fashioned ornaments. 52And all the gold of the offering that they offered to the LORD, from the captains of thousands and captains of hundreds, was sixteen thousand seven hundred and fifty shekels. 53(The men of war had taken spoil, every man for himself.) 54And Moses and Eleazar the priest received the gold from the captains of thousands and of hundreds, and brought it into the tabernacle of meeting as a memorial for the children of Israel before the LORD.

32 Now the children of Reuben and the children of Gad had a very great multitude of livestock; and when they saw the land of Jazer and the land of Gilead, that indeed the region *was* a place for livestock, 2the children of Gad and the children of Reuben came and spoke to Moses, to Eleazar the priest, and to the leaders of the congregation, saying, 3"Ataroth, Dibon, Jazer, Nimrah, Heshbon, Elealeh, Shebam, Nebo, and Beon, 4the country which the LORD defeated before the congregation of Israel, *is* a land for livestock, and your servants have livestock." 5*Therefore they said, "If we have found favor in your sight, let this land be given to your servants as a possession. Do not take us over the Jordan."

6And Moses said to the children of Gad and to the children of Reuben: "Shall your brethren go to war while you sit here? 7Now why will you discourage the heart of the children of Israel from going over into the land which the LORD has given them? 8Thus your fathers did when I sent them away from Kadesh Barnea to see the land. 9For when they went up to the Valley of Eshcol and saw the land, they discouraged the heart of the children of Israel, so that they did not go into the land which the LORD had given them. 10So the LORD's anger was aroused on that day, and He swore an oath, saying, 11'Surely none of the men who came up from Egypt, from twenty years old and above, shall see the land of which I swore to Abraham, Isaac, and Jacob, because they have not wholly followed Me, 12except Caleb the son of Jephunneh, the Kenizzite, and Joshua the son of Nun, for they have wholly followed the LORD.' 13So the LORD's anger was aroused against Israel, and He made them wander in the wilderness forty years, until all the generation that had done evil in the sight of the LORD was gone. 14And look! You have risen in your fathers' place, a brood of sinful men, to increase still more the fierce anger of the LORD against Israel. 15For if you turn away from following Him, He will once again leave them in the wilderness, and you will destroy all these people."

16Then they came near to him and said: "We will build sheepfolds here for our livestock, and cities for our little ones, 17*but we ourselves will be armed, ready *to* go before the children of Israel until we have brought them to their place; and our little ones will dwell in the fortified cities because of the inhabitants of the land. 18We will not

CHAPTER 32

32:5 Some people choose to live on the border of God's blessing. They make their decisions on the basis of material gain and not spiritual blessing. The two and a half tribes did not claim their inheritance in Canaan, though they were very close to it.

32:17, 18 They assured Moses that they would help conquer the land, but the tribes still brought division to Israel. In fact, when the land was fully conquered, the two and a half tribes had to put up an altar to let people know, "We belong to Israel!" (See Josh. 22.) Had they gone over the Jordan and claimed their inheritance, everybody would have known their citizenship.

return to our homes until every one of the children of Israel has received his inheritance. 19For we will not inherit with them on the other side of the Jordan and beyond, because our inheritance has fallen to us on this eastern side of the Jordan."

20Then Moses said to them: "If you do this thing, if you arm yourselves before the LORD for the war, 21and all your armed men cross over the Jordan before the LORD until He has driven out His enemies from before Him, 22and the land is subdued before the LORD, then afterward you may return and be blameless before the LORD and before Israel; and this land shall be your possession before the LORD. 23But if you do not do so, then take note, you have sinned against the LORD; and be sure your sin will find you out. 24Build cities for your little ones and folds for your sheep, and do what has proceeded out of your mouth."

25And the children of Gad and the children of Reuben spoke to Moses, saying: "Your servants will do as my lord commands. 26Our little ones, our wives, our flocks, and all our livestock will be there in the cities of Gilead; 27but your servants will cross over, every man armed for war, before the LORD to battle, just as my lord says."

28So Moses gave command concerning them to Eleazar the priest, to Joshua the son of Nun, and to the chief fathers of the tribes of the children of Israel. 29And Moses said to them: "If the children of Gad and the children of Reuben cross over the Jordan with you, every man armed for battle before the LORD, and the land is subdued before you, then you shall give them the land of Gilead as a possession. 30But if they do not cross over armed with you, they shall have possessions among you in the land of Canaan."

31*Then the children of Gad and the children of Reuben answered, saying: "As the LORD has said to your servants, so we will do. 32We will cross over armed before the LORD into the land of Canaan, but the possession of our inheritance *shall remain* with us on this side of the Jordan."

33So Moses gave to the children of Gad, to the children of Reuben, and to half the tribe of Manasseh the son of Joseph, the kingdom of Sihon king of the Amorites and the kingdom of Og king of Bashan, the land with its cities within the borders, the cities of the surrounding country. 34And the children of Gad built Dibon and Ataroth and Aroer, 35Atroth and Shophan and Jazer and Jogbehah, 36Beth Nimrah and Beth Haran, fortified cities, and folds for sheep. 37And the children of Reuben built Heshbon and Elealeh and Kirjathaim, 38Nebo and Baal Meon (*their* names being changed) and Shibmah; and they gave *other* names to the cities which they built.

39And the children of Machir the son of Manasseh went to Gilead and took it, and dispossessed the Amorites who *were* in it. 40So Moses gave Gilead to Machir the son of Manasseh, and he dwelt in it. 41Also Jair the son of Manasseh went and took its small towns, and called them Havoth Jair.y 42Then Nobah went and took Kenath and its villages, and he called it Nobah, after his own name.

CHAPTER 33

33 These* *are* the journeys of the children of Israel, who went out of the land of Egypt by their armies under the hand of Moses and

32:41 yLiterally *Towns of Jair*

32:31, 32 "Do not take us over the Jordan!" (v. 5) is as much an expression of failure as "Take us back to the land of Egypt!" or "Let us die in the wilderness!" When material gain, not the glory of God, governs our decisions, we will make the wrong decisions. (See Ps. 47:4.)

CHAPTER 33

33:1–49 *Reviewing the past.* Dr. A. T. Pierson said, "History is His story." It is good to review the past and discern the hand of the Lord at work. God delivered them from Egypt and brought them to Sinai, where they entered into a covenant with Him (vv. 1–15). Then He brought them to the border of the Promised Land, where they refused to go in (vv. 16–36). They wandered for forty years and then ended up on the plains of Moab (vv. 37–49). Unbelief means wasted time, wasted lives, and wasted opportunities, but God is gracious and longsuffering with His people.

Aaron. 2Now Moses wrote down the starting points of their journeys at the command of the LORD. And these *are* their journeys according to their starting points:

3They departed from Rameses in the first month, on the fifteenth day of the first month; on the day after the Passover the children of Israel went out with boldness in the sight of all the Egyptians. 4For the Egyptians were burying all *their* firstborn, whom the LORD had killed among them. Also on their gods the LORD had executed judgments.

5Then the children of Israel moved from Rameses and camped at Succoth. 6They departed from Succoth and camped at Etham, which *is* on the edge of the wilderness. 7They moved from Etham and turned back to Pi Hahiroth, which *is* east of Baal Zephon; and they camped near Migdol. 8They departed from before Hahiroth[z] and passed through the midst of the sea into the wilderness, went three days' journey in the Wilderness of Etham, and camped at Marah. 9They moved from Marah and came to Elim. At Elim *were* twelve springs of water and seventy palm trees; so they camped there.

10They moved from Elim and camped by the Red Sea. 11They moved from the Red Sea and camped in the Wilderness of Sin. 12They journeyed from the Wilderness of Sin and camped at Dophkah. 13They departed from Dophkah and camped at Alush. 14They moved from Alush and camped at Rephidim, where there was no water for the people to drink.

15They departed from Rephidim and camped in the Wilderness of Sinai. 16They moved from the Wilderness of Sinai and camped at Kibroth Hattaavah. 17They departed from Kibroth Hattaavah and camped at Hazeroth. 18They departed from Hazeroth and camped at Rithmah. 19They departed from Rithmah and camped at Rimmon Perez. 20They departed from Rimmon Perez and camped at Libnah. 21They moved from Libnah and camped at Rissah. 22They journeyed from Rissah and camped at Kehelathah. 23They went from Kehelathah and camped at Mount Shepher. 24They moved from Mount Shepher and camped at Haradah. 25They moved from Haradah and camped at Makheloth. 26They moved from Makheloth and camped at Tahath. 27They departed from Tahath and camped at Terah. 28They moved from Terah and camped at Mithkah. 29They went from Mithkah and camped at Hashmonah. 30They departed from Hashmonah and camped at Moseroth. 31They departed from Moseroth and camped at Bene Jaakan. 32They moved from Bene Jaakan and camped at Hor Hagidgad. 33They went from Hor Hagidgad and camped at Jotbathah. 34They moved from Jotbathah and camped at Abronah. 35They departed from Abronah and camped at Ezion Geber. 36They moved from Ezion Geber and camped in the Wilderness of Zin, which *is* Kadesh. 37They moved from Kadesh and camped at Mount Hor, on the boundary of the land of Edom.

38Then Aaron the priest went up to Mount Hor at the command of the LORD, and died there in the fortieth year after the children of Israel had

33:8 [z]Many Hebrew manuscripts, Samaritan Pentateuch, Syriac, Targum, and Vulgate read *from Pi Hahiroth* (compare verse 7).

come out of the land of Egypt, on the first *day* of the fifth month. 39Aaron *was* one hundred and twenty-three years old when he died on Mount Hor.

40Now the king of Arad, the Canaanite, who dwelt in the South in the land of Canaan, heard of the coming of the children of Israel.

41So they departed from Mount Hor and camped at Zalmonah. 42They departed from Zalmonah and camped at Punon. 43They departed from Punon and camped at Oboth. 44They departed from Oboth and camped at Ije Abarim, at the border of Moab. 45They departed from Ijim*a* and camped at Dibon Gad. 46They moved from Dibon Gad and camped at Almon Diblathaim. 47They moved from Almon Diblathaim and camped in the mountains of Abarim, before Nebo. 48They departed from the mountains of Abarim and camped in the plains of Moab by the Jordan, *across from* Jericho. 49They camped by the Jordan, from Beth Jesimoth as far as the Abel Acacia Grove*b* in the plains of Moab.

50*Now the LORD spoke to Moses in the plains of Moab by the Jordan, *across from* Jericho, saying, 51"Speak to the children of Israel, and say to them: 'When you have crossed the Jordan into the land of Canaan, 52then you shall drive out all the inhabitants of the land from before you, destroy all their engraved stones, destroy all their molded images, and demolish all their high places; 53you shall dispossess *the inhabitants of* the land and dwell in it, for I have given you the land to possess. 54And you shall divide the land by lot as an inheritance among your families; to the larger you shall give a larger inheritance, and to the smaller you shall give a smaller inheritance; there everyone's *inheritance* shall be whatever falls to him by lot. You shall inherit according to the tribes of your fathers. 55But if you do not drive out the inhabitants of the land from before you, then it shall be that those whom you let remain *shall be* irritants in your eyes and thorns in your sides, and they shall harass you in the land where you dwell. 56Moreover it shall be *that* I will do to you as I thought to do to them.' "

33:50–56 *Anticipating the future.* "When you have crossed the Jordan into the land of Canaan" was a word of promise and assurance that would encourage the nation in their new venture of faith. What a privilege to claim their God-given inheritance! But God also gave some responsibilities: drive out the enemy, destroy their idols, dispossess the people, and then divide the land. First you conquer, then you claim. First the obedience, then the blessing.

CHAPTER 34

34:1–29 God assigned the tribes their inheritance and set their boundaries, but He used human leaders to do it. What a privilege it is to help people claim their inheritance from God!
We must accept what God assigns to us and not complain or covet what others possess. Some land fronted on wilderness (v. 3), and other portions faced the Great Sea (v. 6). Some tribes had mountains in their territory. Like Canaan, the Christian life is "a land of hills and valleys" (Deut. 11:11), and our God is a God of both the hills and the valleys (1 Kings 20:23ff.). He knows what is best for us, and He is always with us.
When you are tempted to complain about what God has assigned to you, ponder John 3:27 and 1 Corinthians 4:7; 12:4–7, 11. Through faith in Christ, we can be content with our lot (Phil. 4:11–13).

34 Then* the LORD spoke to Moses, saying, 2"Command the children of Israel, and say to them: 'When you come into the land of Canaan, this *is* the land that shall fall to you as an inheritance—the land of Canaan to its boundaries. 3Your southern border shall be from the Wilderness of Zin along the border of Edom; then your southern border shall extend eastward to the end of the Salt Sea; 4your border shall turn from the southern side of the Ascent of Akrabbim, continue to Zin, and be on the south of Kadesh Barnea; then it shall go on to Hazar Addar, and continue to Azmon; 5the border shall turn from Azmon to the Brook of Egypt, and it shall end at the Sea.

6'As for the western border, you shall have the Great Sea for a border; this shall be your western border.

7'And this shall be your northern border: From the Great Sea you shall mark out your *border* line to Mount Hor; 8from Mount Hor you shall mark out *your border* to the entrance of Hamath; then the direction of the border shall be toward Zedad; 9the border shall proceed to Ziphron, and it shall

33:45 *a*Same as *Ije Abarim,* verse 44   33:49 *b*Hebrew *Abel Shittim*

end at Hazar Enan. This shall be your northern border.

10'You shall mark out your eastern border from Hazar Enan to Shepham; 11the border shall go down from Shepham to Riblah on the east side of Ain; the border shall go down and reach to the eastern side of the Sea of Chinnereth; 12the border shall go down along the Jordan, and it shall end at the Salt Sea. This shall be your land with its surrounding boundaries.'"

13Then Moses commanded the children of Israel, saying: "This *is* the land which you shall inherit by lot, which the LORD has commanded to give to the nine tribes and to the half-tribe. 14For the tribe of the children of Reuben according to the house of their fathers, and the tribe of the children of Gad according to the house of their fathers, have received *their inheritance;* and the half-tribe of Manasseh has received its inheritance. 15The two tribes and the half-tribe have received their inheritance on this side of the Jordan, *across from* Jericho eastward, toward the sunrise."

16And the LORD spoke to Moses, saying, 17"These *are* the names of the men who shall divide the land among you as an inheritance: Eleazar the priest and Joshua the son of Nun. 18And you shall take one leader of every tribe to divide the land for the inheritance. 19These *are* the names of the men: from the tribe of Judah, Caleb the son of Jephunneh; 20from the tribe of the children of Simeon, Shemuel the son of Ammihud; 21from the tribe of Benjamin, Elidad the son of Chislon; 22a leader from the tribe of the children of Dan, Bukki the son of Jogli; 23from the sons of Joseph: a leader from the tribe of the children of Manasseh, Hanniel the son of Ephod, 24and a leader from the tribe of the children of Ephraim, Kemuel the son of Shiphtan; 25a leader from the tribe of the children of Zebulun, Elizaphan the son of Parnach; 26a leader from the tribe of the children of Issachar, Paltiel the son of Azzan; 27a leader from the tribe of the children of Asher, Ahihud the son of Shelomi; 28and a leader from the tribe of the children of Naphtali, Pedahel the son of Ammihud."

29These *are* the ones the LORD commanded to divide the inheritance among the children of Israel in the land of Canaan.

35 And* the LORD spoke to Moses in the plains of Moab by the Jordan *across from* Jericho, saying: 2"Command the children of Israel that they give the Levites cities to dwell in from the inheritance of their possession, and you shall *also* give the Levites common-land around the cities. 3They shall have the cities to dwell in; and their common-land shall be for their cattle, for their herds, and for all their animals. 4The common-land of the cities which you will give the Levites *shall extend* from the wall of the city outward a thousand cubits all around. 5And you shall measure outside the city on the east side two thousand cubits, on the south side two thousand cubits, on the west side two thousand cubits, and on the north side two thousand cubits. The city *shall be* in the middle. This shall belong to them as common-land for the cities.

6"Now among the cities which you will give to the Levites *you shall appoint* six cities of refuge, to which a manslayer may flee. And to these you shall add forty-two cities. 7So all the cities you

CHAPTER 35

35:1–5 Residence. The fact that the Levites were servants of God did not make them any less citizens of the land. They needed places to live and care for their families when they were not ministering at the tabernacle. The tribes' provision of forty-eight cities for them was done in a fair way (v. 8). God's people should care for God's work and should share as God has provided for them (2 Cor. 8:1–15).

will give to the Levites *shall be* forty-eight; these *you shall give* with their common-land. [8]And the cities which you will give *shall be* from the possession of the children of Israel; from the larger *tribe* you shall give many, from the smaller you shall give few. Each shall give some of its cities to the Levites, in proportion to the inheritance that each receives."

[9]*Then the LORD spoke to Moses, saying, [10]"Speak to the children of Israel, and say to them: 'When you cross the Jordan into the land of Canaan, [11]then you shall appoint cities to be cities of refuge for you, that the manslayer who kills any person accidentally may flee there. [12]They shall be cities of refuge for you from the avenger, that the manslayer may not die until he stands before the congregation in judgment. [13]And of the cities which you give, you shall have six cities of refuge. [14]You shall appoint three cities on this side of the Jordan, and three cities you shall appoint in the land of Canaan, *which* will be cities of refuge. [15]These six cities shall be for refuge for the children of Israel, for the stranger, and for the sojourner among them, that anyone who kills a person accidentally may flee there.

[16]*'But if he strikes him with an iron implement, so that he dies, he *is* a murderer; the murderer shall surely be put to death. [17]And if he strikes him with a stone in the hand, by which one could die, and he does die, he *is* a murderer; the murderer shall surely be put to death. [18]Or *if* he strikes him with a wooden hand weapon, by which one could die, and he does die, he *is* a murderer; the murderer shall surely be put to death. [19]The avenger of blood himself shall put the murderer to death; when he meets him, he shall put him to death. [20]If he pushes him out of hatred or, while lying in wait, hurls something at him so that he dies, [21]or in enmity he strikes him with his hand so that he dies, the one who struck *him* shall surely be put to death. He *is* a murderer. The avenger of blood shall put the murderer to death when he meets him.

[22]'However, if he pushes him suddenly without enmity, or throws anything at him without lying in wait, [23]or uses a stone, by which a man could die, throwing *it* at him without seeing *him*, so that he dies, while he was not his enemy or seeking his harm, [24]then the congregation shall judge between the manslayer and the avenger of blood according to these judgments. [25]So the congregation shall deliver the manslayer from the hand of the avenger of blood, and the congregation shall return him to the city of refuge where he had fled, and he shall remain there until the death of the high priest who was anointed with the holy oil. [26]But if the manslayer at any time goes outside the limits of the city of refuge where he fled, [27]and the avenger of blood finds him outside the limits of his city of refuge, and the avenger of blood kills the manslayer, he shall not be guilty of blood, [28]because he should have remained in his city of refuge until the death of the high priest. But after the death of the high priest the manslayer may return to the land of his possession.

[29]'And these *things* shall be a statute of judgment to you throughout your generations in all your dwellings. [30]Whoever kills a person, the murderer shall be put to death on the testimony of witnesses; but one witness is not *sufficient* testimony against a person for the death *penalty*. [31]Moreover you shall take no ransom for the life

35:9–15 *Refuge.* Six of the Levitical cities were designated cities of refuge. God makes a distinction between murder and manslaughter, the intentional and the accidental. In that day, the nation had no police force to investigate crimes and prosecute criminals, so the innocent had to be protected from angry family members who might want to take justice into their own hands. In the city of refuge, the fugitive was safe until the congregation decided whether he was guilty of murder or not (Deut. 19:11–13).

35:16–27 *Redemption.* Jesus Christ is our "city of refuge" (Heb. 6:18). When we trust Him, our sins are all forgiven and judgment is past (Rom. 8:1). Salvation is not probation. If the fugitive left the city, he was in danger of death. In Jesus Christ, we have eternal life (John 5:24). Our High Priest will never die; therefore, we are saved eternally (Heb. 7:23–28).

of a murderer who *is* guilty of death, but he shall surely be put to death. 32And you shall take no ransom for him who has fled to his city of refuge, that he may return to dwell in the land before the death of the priest. 33So you shall not pollute the land where you *are;* for blood defiles the land, and no atonement can be made for the land, for the blood that is shed on it, except by the blood of him who shed it. 34Therefore do not defile the land which you inhabit, in the midst of which I dwell; for I the LORD dwell among the children of Israel.' "

36 Now the chief fathers of the families of the children of Gilead the son of Machir, the son of Manasseh, of the families of the sons of Joseph, came near and spoke before Moses and before the leaders, the chief fathers of the children of Israel. 2*And they said: "The LORD commanded my lord *Moses* to give the land as an inheritance by lot to the children of Israel, and my lord was commanded by the LORD to give the inheritance of our brother Zelophehad to his daughters. 3Now if they are married to any of the sons of the *other* tribes of the children of Israel, then their inheritance will be taken from the inheritance of our fathers, and it will be added to the inheritance of the tribe into which they marry; so it will be taken from the lot of our inheritance. 4And when the Jubilee of the children of Israel comes, then their inheritance will be added to the inheritance of the tribe into which they marry; so their inheritance will be taken away from the inheritance of the tribe of our fathers."

5*Then Moses commanded the children of Israel according to the word of the LORD, saying: "What the tribe of the sons of Joseph speaks is right. 6This *is* what the LORD commands concerning the daughters of Zelophehad, saying, 'Let them marry whom they think best, but they may marry only within the family of their father's tribe.' 7So the inheritance of the children of Israel shall not change hands from tribe to tribe, for every one of the children of Israel shall keep the inheritance of the tribe of his fathers. 8And every daughter who possesses an inheritance in any tribe of the children of Israel shall be the wife of one of the family of her father's tribe, so that the children of Israel each may possess the inheritance of his fathers. 9Thus no inheritance shall change hands from *one* tribe to another, but every tribe of the children of Israel shall keep its own inheritance."

10Just as the LORD commanded Moses, so did the daughters of Zelophehad; 11for Mahlah, Tirzah, Hoglah, Milcah, and Noah, the daughters of Zelophehad, were married to the sons of their father's brothers. 12They were married into the families of the children of Manasseh the son of Joseph, and their inheritance remained in the tribe of their father's family.

13These *are* the commandments and the judgments which the LORD commanded the children of Israel by the hand of Moses in the plains of Moab by the Jordan, *across from* Jericho.

CHAPTER 36

36:2–4 Moses had already decreed that a man's inheritance must go to his daughters if he had no sons (27:1–11), but that did not completely solve the problem. Some men of the tribe of Manasseh (Zelophehad's tribe) had discussed and pondered the matter and were concerned about the distribution of their tribal land. What if their daughters married into other tribes? Would the inheritance eventually be confused or even lost?

It is good to think about decisions and see their practical ramifications in everyday life. It is good to think about the future and ask, "What may happen?"

36:5–9 The simple solution was to require the women who inherit property to marry only within their own family clan. It is good to inherit wealth, but with the inheritance may come restrictions and responsibilities. If we want the one, we must accept the other. The daughters of Zelophehad married their cousins, so the inheritance remained intact.

DEUTERONOMY

Deuteronomy means "second law." It records the second giving of the Law by Moses as he prepared the nation to enter their promised inheritance. But Moses did more than simply repeat the Law to a new generation. He applied it to their new life in the land and stressed the importance of their loving God and obeying Him from the heart.

Some key words in Deuteronomy are *land* (190 times), *hear* (54 times), *possess* and *possession* (57 times), *heart* (53 times), and *love* (25 times).

The nation *owned* the land by God's grace and *possessed* the land by God's power, but they could not *enjoy* the land unless they obeyed God's Word. When the nation disobeyed, God chastened them *in the land* (book of Judges) and then took them *from the land* into Babylonian captivity.

In the addresses, Moses first reminded the people of God's past leading (chaps. 1—4). The word *remember* is used 14 times in the book. Then he restated and applied the Law (chaps. 5—26), and closed his message with words of warning and blessing (chaps. 27—33). In chapter 34, we read how Moses passed from the scene and Joshua took over.

CHAPTER 1

1:1ff The Kadesh Barnea event is recorded in Numbers 14, and the New Testament commentary is in Hebrews 3—4. God warns against "an evil heart of unbelief" (Heb. 3:12). An *evil* heart! Why is the sin of unbelief so evil?

1 These* *are* the words which Moses spoke to all Israel on this side of the Jordan in the wilderness, in the plain*a* opposite Suph,*b* between Paran, Tophel, Laban, Hazeroth, and Dizahab. 2*It is* eleven days' *journey* from Horeb by way of Mount Seir to Kadesh Barnea. 3Now it came to pass in the fortieth year, in the eleventh month, on the first *day* of the month, *that* Moses spoke to the children of Israel according to all that the LORD had given him as commandments to them, 4after he had killed Sihon king of the Amorites, who dwelt in Heshbon, and Og king of Bashan, who dwelt at Ashtaroth in*c* Edrei.

5On this side of the Jordan in the land of Moab, Moses began to explain this law, saying, 6"The LORD our God spoke to us in Horeb, saying: 'You have dwelt long enough at this mountain. 7Turn and take your journey, and go to the mountains of the Amorites, to all the neighboring *places* in the plain,*d* in the mountains and in the lowland, in the South and on the seacoast, to the land of the Canaanites and to Lebanon, as far as the great river, the River Euphrates. 8See, I have set the land before you; go in and possess the land which the LORD swore to your fathers—to Abraham, Isaac, and Jacob—to give to them and their descendants after them.'

9"And I spoke to you at that time, saying: 'I alone am not able to bear you. 10The LORD your God has multiplied you, and here you *are* today, as the stars of heaven in multitude. 11May the LORD God of your fathers make you a thousand times more numerous than you are, and bless you as He has promised you! 12How can I alone bear your problems and your burdens and your complaints? 13Choose wise, understanding, and knowledgeable men from among your tribes, and I will make them heads over you.' 14And you answered me and said, 'The thing which you have

1:1 *a*Hebrew *arabah* *b*One manuscript of the Septuagint, also Targum and Vulgate, read *Red Sea.* 1:4 *c*Septuagint, Syriac, and Vulgate read *and* (compare Joshua 12:4). 1:7 *d*Hebrew *arabah*

told *us* to do *is* good.' 15So I took the heads of your tribes, wise and knowledgeable men, and made them heads over you, leaders of thousands, leaders of hundreds, leaders of fifties, leaders of tens, and officers for your tribes.

16"Then I commanded your judges at that time, saying, 'Hear *the cases* between your brethren, and judge righteously between a man and his brother or the stranger who is with him. 17You shall not show partiality in judgment; you shall hear the small as well as the great; you shall not be afraid in any man's presence, for the judgment *is* God's. The case that is too hard for you, bring to me, and I will hear it.' 18And I commanded you at that time all the things which you should do.

19"So we departed from Horeb, and went through all that great and terrible wilderness which you saw on the way to the mountains of the Amorites, as the LORD our God had commanded us. Then we came to Kadesh Barnea. 20And I said to you, 'You have come to the mountains of the Amorites, which the LORD our God is giving us. 21Look, the LORD your God has set the land before you; go up *and* possess *it,* as the LORD God of your fathers has spoken to you; do not fear or be discouraged.'

22"And every one of you came near to me and said, 'Let us send men before us, and let them search out the land for us, and bring back word to us of the way by which we should go up, and of the cities into which we shall come.'

23"The plan pleased me well; so I took twelve of your men, one man from *each* tribe. 24And they departed and went up into the mountains, and came to the Valley of Eshcol, and spied it out. 25They also took *some* of the fruit of the land in their hands and brought *it* down to us; and they brought back word to us, saying, '*It is* a good land which the LORD our God is giving us.'

26"Nevertheless you would not go up, but rebelled against the command of the LORD your God; 27and you complained in your tents, and said, 'Because the LORD hates us, He has brought us out of the land of Egypt to deliver us into the hand of the Amorites, to destroy us. 28Where can we go up? Our brethren have discouraged our hearts, saying, "The people *are* greater and taller than we; the cities *are* great and fortified up to heaven; moreover we have seen the sons of the Anakim there." '

29"Then I said to you, 'Do not be terrified, or afraid of them. 30The LORD your God, who goes before you, He will fight for you, according to all He did for you in Egypt before your eyes, 31and in the wilderness where you saw how the LORD your God carried you, as a man carries his son, in all the way that you went until you came to this place.' 32*Yet, for all that, you did not believe the LORD your God, 33who went in the way before you to search out a place for you to pitch your tents, to show you the way you should go, in the fire by night and in the cloud by day.

34"And the LORD heard the sound of your words, and was angry, and took an oath, saying, 35'Surely not one of these men of this evil generation shall see that good land of which I swore to give to your fathers, 36except Caleb the son of Jephunneh; he shall see it, and to him and his children I am giving the land on which he walked, because he wholly followed the LORD.' 37The LORD was also angry with me for your sakes, saying, 'Even you shall not go in there. 38Joshua the son of Nun,

1:32–35 To begin with, unbelief makes God a liar and questions the dependability of His Word. Our responsibility is not to question God but to believe God and do what He commands.

Unbelief wastes time. An eleven-day journey turned into forty years of wandering and death! Unbelief robs us of God's best blessings. God cared for His people those forty years, but how much more He would have done had they claimed their inheritance.

When you come to those Kadesh Barnea places in your pilgrimage, don't look around at the problems and dangers. Look up to the God who is leading you, and walk by faith.

who stands before you, he shall go in there. Encourage him, for he shall cause Israel to inherit it.

39"Moreover your little ones and your children, who you say will be victims, who today have no knowledge of good and evil, they shall go in there; to them I will give it, and they shall possess it. 40But *as for* you, turn and take your journey into the wilderness by the Way of the Red Sea.'

41"Then you answered and said to me, 'We have sinned against the LORD; we will go up and fight, just as the LORD our God commanded us.' And when everyone of you had girded on his weapons of war, you were ready to go up into the mountain. 42"And the LORD said to me, 'Tell them, "Do not go up nor fight, for I *am* not among you; lest you be defeated before your enemies." ' 43So I spoke to you; yet you would not listen, but rebelled against the command of the LORD, and presumptuously went up into the mountain. 44And the Amorites who dwelt in that mountain came out against you and chased you as bees do, and drove you back from Seir to Hormah. 45Then you returned and wept before the LORD, but the LORD would not listen to your voice nor give ear to you.

46"So you remained in Kadesh many days, according to the days that you spent *there*.

CHAPTER 2

2:1ff *God assigns our battles.* He instructed the nation not to meddle with the Edomites, the Moabites, or the Ammonites. The people were to behave themselves as godly pilgrims and avoid creating trouble. For a nation that enjoyed great victory in war, His instructions were probably hard to take, but God had better things for His people than the spoils of those nations. (See Rom. 12:18; Col. 4:5.) It is unwise to meddle in things that God commands us to avoid.

2 "Then* we turned and journeyed into the wilderness of the Way of the Red Sea, as the LORD spoke to me, and we skirted Mount Seir for many days.

2"And the LORD spoke to me, saying: 3'You have skirted this mountain long enough; turn northward. 4And command the people, saying, "You *are about to* pass through the territory of your brethren, the descendants of Esau, who live in Seir; and they will be afraid of you. Therefore watch yourselves carefully. 5Do not meddle with them, for I will not give you *any* of their land, no, not so much as one footstep, because I have given Mount Seir to Esau *as* a possession. 6You shall buy food from them with money, that you may eat; and you shall also buy water from them with money, that you may drink.

7"For the LORD your God has blessed you in all the work of your hand. He knows your trudging through this great wilderness. These forty years the LORD your God *has been* with you; you have lacked nothing." '

8"And when we passed beyond our brethren, the descendants of Esau who dwell in Seir, away from the road of the plain, away from Elath and Ezion Geber, we turned and passed by way of the Wilderness of Moab. 9Then the LORD said to me, 'Do not harass Moab, nor contend with them in battle, for I will not give you *any* of their land *as* a possession, because I have given Ar to the descendants of Lot *as* a possession.' "

10(The Emim had dwelt there in times past, a people as great and numerous and tall as the Anakim. 11They were also regarded as giants,e like the Anakim, but the Moabites call them Emim. 12The Horites formerly dwelt in Seir, but the descendants of Esau dispossessed them and destroyed them from before them, and dwelt in their place, just as Israel did to the land of their possession which the LORD gave them.)

13" 'Now rise and cross over the Valley of the Zered.' So we crossed over the Valley of the

---

2:11 *e*Hebrew *rephaim*

Zered. 14And the time we took to come from Kadesh Barnea until we crossed over the Valley of the Zered *was* thirty-eight years, until all the generation of the men of war was consumed from the midst of the camp, just as the LORD had sworn to them. 15For indeed the hand of the LORD was against them, to destroy them from the midst of the camp until they were consumed.

16"So it was, when all the men of war had finally perished from among the people, 17that the LORD spoke to me, saying: 18'This day you are to cross over at Ar, the boundary of Moab. 19And *when* you come near the people of Ammon, do not harass them or meddle with them, for I will not give you *any* of the land of the people of Ammon *as* a possession, because I have given it to the descendants of Lot *as* a possession.' "

20(That was also regarded as a land of giants;*f* giants formerly dwelt there. But the Ammonites call them Zamzummim, 21a people as great and numerous and tall as the Anakim. But the LORD destroyed them before them, and they dispossessed them and dwelt in their place, 22just as He had done for the descendants of Esau, who dwelt in Seir, when He destroyed the Horites from before them. They dispossessed them and dwelt in their place, even to this day. 23And the Avim, who dwelt in villages as far as Gaza—the Caphtorim, who came from Caphtor, destroyed them and dwelt in their place.)

24" 'Rise, take your journey, and cross over the River Arnon. Look, I have given into your hand Sihon the Amorite, king of Heshbon, and his land. Begin to possess *it,* and engage him in battle. 25This day I will begin to put the dread and fear of you upon the nations under the whole heaven, who shall hear the report of you, and shall tremble and be in anguish because of you.'

26"And I sent messengers from the Wilderness of Kedemoth to Sihon king of Heshbon, with words of peace, saying, 27'Let me pass through your land; I will keep strictly to the road, and I will turn neither to the right nor to the left. 28You shall sell me food for money, that I may eat, and give me water for money, that I may drink; only let me pass through on foot, 29just as the descendants of Esau who dwell in Seir and the Moabites who dwell in Ar did for me, until I cross the Jordan to the land which the LORD our God is giving us.'

30"But Sihon king of Heshbon would not let us pass through, for the LORD your God hardened his spirit and made his heart obstinate, that He might deliver him into your hand, as *it is* this day.

31*"And the LORD said to me, 'See, I have begun to give Sihon and his land over to you. Begin to possess *it,* that you may inherit his land.' 32Then Sihon and all his people came out against us to fight at Jahaz. 33And the LORD our God delivered him over to us; so we defeated him, his sons, and all his people. 34We took all his cities at that time, and we utterly destroyed the men, women, and little ones of every city; we left none remaining. 35We took only the livestock as plunder for ourselves, with the spoil of the cities which we took. 36*From Aroer, which *is* on the bank of the River Arnon, and *from* the city that *is* in the ravine, as far as Gilead, there was not one city too strong for us; the LORD our God delivered all to us.

2:20 *f* Hebrew *rephaim*

2:31–35 *God assures our victory.* When the Lord leads us into battle, we need not fear, for His commandment is His enablement. Israel defeated Sihon, and "there was not one city too strong" (v. 36) for God's people. (See 1 John 5:1–4.)

2:36 *God assigns our inheritance.* God promised to give the Trans-Jordan territory to the tribes of Reuben and Gad (Num. 32), and He kept His promise. (See Ps. 47:4; Acts 20:32; 1 Pet. 1:3–5.) God promises— we possess by faith!

CHAPTER 3

3:1–11 *A possession to claim.* Guided by God's will and fortified by God's promises, the people marched from victory to victory.

Were it not for their unbelief, the former generation could have won the victories in Canaan forty years earlier. The high walls and gates were no problem to God (Num. 13:26–33). He is limited only by our unbelief.

3:12–22 *A promise to keep.* The tribes to be settled east of the Jordan had promised to cross the river and help conquer Canaan (Num. 32:16–23). Now that their land was subdued, Reuben and Gad might have settled down and avoided a lot of danger, but they kept their word. God hears our promises and takes them seriously (Num. 30:2; Eccles. 5:1–5).

37Only you did not go near the land of the people of Ammon—anywhere along the River Jabbok, or to the cities of the mountains, or wherever the LORD our God had forbidden us.

3 "Then* we turned and went up the road to Bashan; and Og king of Bashan came out against us, he and all his people, to battle at Edrei. 2And the LORD said to me, 'Do not fear him, for I have delivered him and all his people and his land into your hand; you shall do to him as you did to Sihon king of the Amorites, who dwelt at Heshbon.'

3"So the LORD our God also delivered into our hands Og king of Bashan, with all his people, and we attacked him until he had no survivors remaining. 4And we took all his cities at that time; there was not a city which we did not take from them: sixty cities, all the region of Argob, the kingdom of Og in Bashan. 5All these cities *were* fortified with high walls, gates, and bars, besides a great many rural towns. 6And we utterly destroyed them, as we did to Sihon king of Heshbon, utterly destroying the men, women, and children of every city. 7But all the livestock and the spoil of the cities we took as booty for ourselves.

8"And at that time we took the land from the hand of the two kings of the Amorites who *were* on this side of the Jordan, from the River Arnon to Mount Hermon 9(the Sidonians call Hermon Sirion, and the Amorites call it Senir), 10all the cities of the plain, all Gilead, and all Bashan, as far as Salcah and Edrei, cities of the kingdom of Og in Bashan.

11"For only Og king of Bashan remained of the remnant of the giants.*g* Indeed his bedstead *was* an iron bedstead. (*Is* it not in Rabbah of the people of Amon?) Nine cubits *is* its length and four cubits its width, according to the standard cubit.

12*"And this land, *which* we possessed at that time, from Aroer, which *is* by the River Arnon, and half the mountains of Gilead and its cities, I gave to the Reubenites and the Gadites. 13The rest of Gilead, and all Bashan, the kingdom of Og, I gave to half the tribe of Manasseh. (All the region of Argob, with all Bashan, was called the land of the giants.*h* 14Jair the son of Manasseh took all the region of Argob, as far as the border of the Geshurites and the Maachathites, and called Bashan after his own name, Havoth Jair,*i* to this day.)

15"Also I gave Gilead to Machir. 16And to the Reubenites and the Gadites I gave from Gilead as far as the River Arnon, the middle of the river as *the* border, as far as the River Jabbok, the border of the people of Ammon; 17the plain also, with the Jordan as *the* border, from Chinnereth as far as the east side of the Sea of the Arabah (the Salt Sea), below the slopes of Pisgah.

18"Then I commanded you at that time, saying: 'The LORD your God has given you this land to possess. All you men of valor shall cross over armed before your brethren, the children of Israel. 19But your wives, your little ones, and your livestock (I know that you have much livestock) shall stay in your cities which I have given you, 20until the LORD has given rest to your brethren as to you, and they also possess the land which

3:11 *g*Hebrew *rephaim*   3:13 *h*Hebrew *rephaim*
3:14 *i*Literally *Towns of Jair*

the LORD your God is giving them beyond the Jordan. Then each of you may return to his possession which I have given you.'

21"And I commanded Joshua at that time, saying, 'Your eyes have seen all that the LORD your God has done to these two kings; so will the LORD do to all the kingdoms through which you pass. 22You must not fear them, for the LORD your God Himself fights for you.'

23"Then I pleaded with the LORD at that time, saying: 24'O Lord GOD, You have begun to show Your servant Your greatness and Your mighty hand, for what god *is there* in heaven or on earth who can do *anything* like Your works and Your mighty *deeds?* 25*I pray, let me cross over and see the good land beyond the Jordan, those pleasant mountains, and Lebanon.'

26"But the LORD was angry with me on your account, and would not listen to me. So the LORD said to me: 'Enough of that! Speak no more to Me of this matter. 27Go up to the top of Pisgah, and lift your eyes toward the west, the north, the south, and the east; behold *it* with your eyes, for you shall not cross over this Jordan. 28But command Joshua, and encourage him and strengthen him; for he shall go over before this people, and he shall cause them to inherit the land which you will see.'

29"So we stayed in the valley opposite Beth Peor.

4 "Now, O Israel, listen to the statutes and the judgments which I teach you to observe, that you may live, and go in and possess the land which the LORD God of your fathers is giving you. 2You shall not add to the word which I command you, nor take from it, that you may keep the commandments of the LORD your God which I command you. 3Your eyes have seen what the LORD did at Baal Peor; for the LORD your God has destroyed from among you all the men who followed Baal of Peor. 4But you who held fast to the LORD your God *are* alive today, every one of you.

5"Surely I have taught you statutes and judgments, just as the LORD my God commanded me, that you should act according *to them* in the land which you go to possess. 6Therefore be careful to observe *them;* for this *is* your wisdom and your understanding in the sight of the peoples who will hear all these statutes, and say, 'Surely this great nation *is* a wise and understanding people.'

7"For what great nation *is there* that has God *so* near to it, as the LORD our God *is* to us, for whatever *reason* we may call upon Him? 8And what great nation *is there* that has *such* statutes and righteous judgments as are in all this law which I set before you this day? 9Only take heed to yourself, and diligently keep yourself, lest you forget the things your eyes have seen, and lest they depart from your heart all the days of your life. And teach them to your children and your grandchildren, 10*especially concerning* the day you stood before the LORD your God in Horeb, when the LORD said to me, 'Gather the people to Me, and I will let them hear My words, that they may learn to fear Me all the days they live on the earth, and *that* they may teach their children.'

11"Then you came near and stood at the foot of the mountain, and the mountain burned with fire to the midst of heaven, with darkness, cloud, and thick darkness. 12*And the LORD spoke to you out of the midst of the fire. You heard the sound

3:25–29 *A penalty to endure.* Because of his pride at Kadesh (Num. 20:1–13), Moses was not allowed to enter Canaan, even though he prayed earnestly for God to relent. He did see the land and give the people a leader to take them into the land. He also visited the land centuries later when Jesus was transfigured (Matt. 17:1–3). Some of the disappointments of life will have their compensations when the glory comes. Be patient!

CHAPTER 4

4:12, 13 Before he repeated the Law to Israel, Moses reminded them of their holy relationship with God and of their privileges as His chosen people. What other nation had heard the voice of God, had seen His power and glory, and had received His Word as their wisdom and their very life (vv. 1, 4, 25, 40)? When we take our blessings for granted, we are in danger of disobeying God.

of the words, but saw no form; *you* only *heard* a voice. 13So He declared to you His covenant which He commanded you to perform, the Ten Commandments; and He wrote them on two tablets of stone. 14And the LORD commanded me at that time to teach you statutes and judgments, that you might observe them in the land which you cross over to possess.

15*"Take careful heed to yourselves, for you saw no form when the LORD spoke to you at Horeb out of the midst of the fire, 16lest you act corruptly and make for yourselves a carved image in the form of any figure: the likeness of male or female, 17the likeness of any animal that *is* on the earth or the likeness of any winged bird that flies in the air, 18the likeness of anything that creeps on the ground or the likeness of any fish that *is* in the water beneath the earth. 19And *take heed,* lest you lift your eyes to heaven, and *when* you see the sun, the moon, and the stars, all the host of heaven, you feel driven to worship them and serve them, which the LORD your God has given to all the peoples under the whole heaven as a heritage. 20But the LORD has taken you and brought you out of the iron furnace, out of Egypt, to be His people, an inheritance, as you are this day. 21Furthermore the LORD was angry with me for your sakes, and swore that I would not cross over the Jordan, and that I would not enter the good land which the LORD your God is giving you as an inheritance. 22But I must die in this land, I must not cross over the Jordan; but you shall cross over and possess that good land. 23Take heed to yourselves, lest you forget the covenant of the LORD your God which He made with you, and make for yourselves a carved image in the form of anything which the LORD your God has forbidden you. 24*For the LORD your God *is* a consuming fire, a jealous God.

25"When you beget children and grandchildren and have grown old in the land, and act corruptly and make a carved image in the form of anything, and do evil in the sight of the LORD your God to provoke Him to anger, 26I call heaven and earth to witness against you this day, that you will soon utterly perish from the land which you cross over the Jordan to possess; you will not prolong *your* days in it, but will be utterly destroyed. 27And the LORD will scatter you among the peoples, and you will be left few in number among the nations where the LORD will drive you. 28And there you will serve gods, the work of men's hands, wood and stone, which neither see nor hear nor eat nor smell. 29But from there you will seek the LORD your God, and you will find *Him* if you seek Him with all your heart and with all your soul. 30When you are in distress, and all these things come upon you in the latter days, when you turn to the LORD your God and obey His voice 31(for the LORD your God *is* a merciful God), He will not forsake you nor destroy you, nor forget the covenant of your fathers which He swore to them.

32"For ask now concerning the days that are past, which were before you, since the day that God created man on the earth, and *ask* from one end of heaven to the other, whether *any* great *thing* like this has happened, or *anything* like it has been heard. 33Did *any* people *ever* hear the voice of God speaking out of the midst of the fire, as you have heard, and live? 34Or did God *ever* try to go *and* take for Himself a nation from the

4:15–23 On the basis of these privileges, Moses warned them to *take heed* lest they forget what God had done for them (v. 9), how God had come to them (v. 15), what God had said to them (v. 19), and what God expected of them because of His covenant (v. 23). To whom much is given, much shall be required.

4:24–31 He also warned them that disobedience would bring chastening. God forgives His people when they repent (vv. 29–31), but read Hebrews 12:25–29 before making plans to disobey God. He is a merciful God (v. 31), but He is also a jealous God (v. 24); He will not permit His children to sin successfully.

midst of *another* nation, by trials, by signs, by wonders, by war, by a mighty hand and an outstretched arm, and by great terrors, according to all that the LORD your God did for you in Egypt before your eyes? 35To you it was shown, that you might know that the LORD Himself *is* God; *there is* none other besides Him. 36Out of heaven He let you hear His voice, that He might instruct you; on earth He showed you His great fire, and you heard His words out of the midst of the fire. 37And because He loved your fathers, therefore He chose their descendants after them; and He brought you out of Egypt with His Presence, with His mighty power, 38driving out from before you nations greater and mightier than you, to bring you in, to give you their land *as* an inheritance, as *it is* this day. 39Therefore know this day, and consider *it* in your heart, that the LORD Himself *is* God in heaven above and on the earth beneath; *there is* no other. 40You shall therefore keep His statutes and His commandments which I command you today, that it may go well with you and with your children after you, and that you may prolong *your* days in the land which the LORD your God is giving you for all time."

41Then Moses set apart three cities on this side of the Jordan, toward the rising of the sun, 42that the manslayer might flee there, who kills his neighbor unintentionally, without having hated him in time past, and that by fleeing to one of these cities he might live: 43Bezer in the wilderness on the plateau for the Reubenites, Ramoth in Gilead for the Gadites, and Golan in Bashan for the Manassites.

44Now this *is* the law which Moses set before the children of Israel. 45These *are* the testimonies, the statutes, and the judgments which Moses spoke to the children of Israel after they came out of Egypt, 46on this side of the Jordan, in the valley opposite Beth Peor, in the land of Sihon king of the Amorites, who dwelt at Heshbon, whom Moses and the children of Israel defeated after they came out of Egypt. 47And they took possession of his land and the land of Og king of Bashan, two kings of the Amorites, who *were* on this side of the Jordan, toward the rising of the sun, 48from Aroer, which *is* on the bank of the River Arnon, even to Mount Sion*ⁱ* (that is, Hermon), 49and all the plain on the east side of the Jordan as far as the Sea of the Arabah, below the slopes of Pisgah.

5 And* Moses called all Israel, and said to them: "Hear, O Israel, the statutes and judgments which I speak in your hearing today, that you may learn them and be careful to observe them. 2The LORD our God made a covenant with us in Horeb. 3The LORD did not make this covenant with our fathers, but with us, those who *are* here today, all of us who *are* alive. 4The LORD talked with you face to face on the mountain from the midst of the fire. 5I stood between the LORD and you at that time, to declare to you the word of the LORD; for you were afraid because of the fire, and you did not go up the mountain. *He* said:

6 *"I *am* the LORD your God who brought you out of the land of Egypt, out of the house of bondage.

7 'You shall have no other gods before Me.

4:48 *ⁱ*Syriac reads *Sirion* (compare 3:9).

CHAPTER 5

5:1 God's people have three responsibilities when it comes to His commandments: hear them, learn them, and do them (v. 1). When we read the Word of God, we should hear the voice of God as the Spirit speaks to us personally. We must allow the Spirit to teach us God's truth and then empower us to obey it. The blessing comes in the *living* of the Word and not in the *learning* (James 1:21–25).

5:6–21 Most of Deuteronomy is an explanation and application of the commandments repeated here. God's laws are clear and simple; man's laws are complex. As we walk in love, we fulfill God's law in the power of the Holy Spirit (Rom. 8:1–4; 13:8–10).

8 'You shall not make for yourself a carved image—any likeness *of anything* that *is* in heaven above, or that *is* in the earth beneath, or that *is* in the water under the earth; 9you shall not bow down to them nor serve them. For I, the LORD your God, *am* a jealous God, visiting the iniquity of the fathers upon the children to the third and fourth *generations* of those who hate Me, 10but showing mercy to thousands, to those who love Me and keep My commandments.

11 'You shall not take the name of the LORD your God in vain, for the LORD will not hold *him* guiltless who takes His name in vain.

12 'Observe the Sabbath day, to keep it holy, as the LORD your God commanded you. 13Six days you shall labor and do all your work, 14but the seventh day *is* the Sabbath of the LORD your God. *In it* you shall do no work: you, nor your son, nor your daughter, nor your male servant, nor your female servant, nor your ox, nor your donkey, nor any of your cattle, nor your stranger who *is* within your gates, that your male servant and your female servant may rest as well as you. 15And remember that you were a slave in the land of Egypt, and the LORD your God brought you out from there by a mighty hand and by an outstretched arm; therefore the LORD your God commanded you to keep the Sabbath day.

16 'Honor your father and your mother, as the LORD your God has commanded you, that your days may be long, and that it may be well with you in the land which the LORD your God is giving you.

17 'You shall not murder.

18 'You shall not commit adultery.

19 'You shall not steal.

20 'You shall not bear false witness against your neighbor.

21 'You shall not covet your neighbor's wife; and you shall not desire your neighbor's house, his field, his male servant, his female servant, his ox, his donkey, or anything that *is* your neighbor's.'

22"These words the LORD spoke to all your assembly, in the mountain from the midst of the fire, the cloud, and the thick darkness, with a loud voice; and He added no more. And He wrote them on two tablets of stone and gave them to me.

23"So it was, when you heard the voice from the midst of the darkness, while the mountain was burning with fire, that you came near to me, all the heads of your tribes and your elders. 24And you said: 'Surely the LORD our God has shown us His glory and His greatness, and we have heard His voice from the midst of the fire. We have seen this day that God speaks with man; yet he *still* lives. 25Now therefore, why should we die? For this great fire will consume us; if we hear the voice of the LORD our God anymore, then we shall die. 26For who *is there* of all flesh who has heard the voice of the living God speaking from the midst of the fire, as we *have*, and lived? 27You go near and hear all that the LORD our God may say, and tell us all that the LORD our God says to you, and we will hear and do *it*.'

28"Then the LORD heard the voice of your words

when you spoke to me, and the LORD said to me:
'I have heard the voice of the words of this people
which they have spoken to you. They are right
in all that they have spoken. 29*Oh, that they had
such a heart in them that they would fear Me and
always keep all My commandments, that it might
be well with them and with their children forever!
30Go and say to them, "Return to your tents."
31But as for you, stand here by Me, and I will
speak to you all the commandments, the statutes,
and the judgments which you shall teach them,
that they may observe *them* in the land which I
am giving them to possess.'

32"Therefore you shall be careful to do as the
LORD your God has commanded you; you shall
not turn aside to the right hand or to the left.
33You shall walk in all the ways which the LORD
your God has commanded you, that you may live
and *that it may be* well with you, and *that* you
may prolong *your* days in the land which you shall
possess.

6 "Now this *is* the commandment, *and these are*
the statutes and judgments which the LORD
your God has commanded to teach you, that you
may observe *them* in the land which you are
crossing over to possess, 2that you may fear the
LORD your God, to keep all His statutes and His
commandments which I command you, you and
your son and your grandson, all the days of your
life, and that your days may be prolonged.
3Therefore hear, O Israel, and be careful to observe *it*, that it may be well with you, and that
you may multiply greatly as the LORD God of your
fathers has promised you—'a land flowing with
milk and honey.'*k*

4*"Hear, O Israel: The LORD our God, the LORD
is one!*l* 5*You shall love the LORD your God with
all your heart, with all your soul, and with all your
strength.

6"And these words which I command you today
shall be in your heart. 7You shall teach them diligently to your children, and shall talk of them
when you sit in your house, when you walk by
the way, when you lie down, and when you rise
up. 8You shall bind them as a sign on your hand,
and they shall be as frontlets between your eyes.
9You shall write them on the doorposts of your
house and on your gates.

10*"So it shall be, when the LORD your God
brings you into the land of which He swore to
your fathers, to Abraham, Isaac, and Jacob, to
give you large and beautiful cities which you did
not build, 11houses full of all good things, which
you did not fill, hewn-out wells which you did not
dig, vineyards and olive trees which you did not
plant—when you have eaten and are full—
12then beware, lest you forget the LORD who
brought you out of the land of Egypt, from the
house of bondage. 13You shall fear the LORD your
God and serve Him, and shall take oaths in His
name. 14You shall not go after other gods, the
gods of the peoples who *are* all around you
15(for the LORD your God *is* a jealous God among
you), lest the anger of the LORD your God be
aroused against you and destroy you from the
face of the earth.

16"You shall not tempt the LORD your God as

5:29 Beware a mere outward obedience to
the laws of God (Matt. 5:20ff.). We must
have a true fear of God in our hearts as
well as a love for Him (vv. 28–29). "Hear"
and "fear" are not contradictory commands;
in fact, they belong together (Deut. 4:10).

CHAPTER 6

6:4–9 Verse 4 is called "the Shema," from
the Hebrew word for "hear." The devout Jew
recites it several times a day to affirm his
faith in Jehovah. The worship of foreign gods
was always a threat to Israel, and this
statement of faith reminded the Jews that
Jehovah is the true and living God who alone
deserves worship and obedience. (See
1 John 5:21.)

6:5 We must love the Lord with *all* our
hearts by keeping *all* His Word *all* the days
of our lives (v. 2). He cannot accept
halfhearted worship or obedience (Eph. 6:6;
1 John 5:3).

6:10–19 How do we show our love to Him?
By hearing and obeying His Word and by
sharing it with others. If we love God, His
truth will be a part of our normal daily
conversation. We also show our love to Him
by appreciating His blessings. Times of
prosperity become times of temptation if we
receive the gifts but fail to thank the Giver
(vv. 10–15). (See Phil. 4:11–13; James
1:17.)

6:3 *k*Exodus 3:8   6:4 *l*Or *The LORD is our God, the LORD alone*
(that is, the only one)

you tempted *Him* in Massah. 17You shall diligently keep the commandments of the LORD your God, His testimonies, and His statutes which He has commanded you. 18And you shall do *what is* right and good in the sight of the LORD, that it may be well with you, and that you may go in and possess the good land of which the LORD swore to your fathers, 19to cast out all your enemies from before you, as the LORD has spoken.

20"When your son asks you in time to come, saying, 'What *is the meaning of* the testimonies, the statutes, and the judgments which the LORD our God has commanded you?' 21then you shall say to your son: 'We were slaves of Pharaoh in Egypt, and the LORD brought us out of Egypt with a mighty hand; 22and the LORD showed signs and wonders before our eyes, great and severe, against Egypt, Pharaoh, and all his household. 23Then He brought us out from there, that He might bring us in, to give us the land of which He swore to our fathers. 24And the LORD commanded us to observe all these statutes, to fear the LORD our God, for our good always, that He might preserve us alive, as *it is* this day. 25Then it will be righteousness for us, if we are careful to observe all these commandments before the LORD our God, as He has commanded us.'

CHAPTER 7

7:3–6 Israel had experienced the wrath of God when they allowed themselves to be seduced by the Moabites (Num. 25). Now they were entering a land where they would be surrounded by pagan worship. There could be no compromise. If the nation were defiled by the awful sins of the Canaanites, it would jeopardize the fulfilling of God's promise of the Savior. Israel had to be a separated people if they were to bless the whole world (Gen. 12:1–3).

7:7–26 Moses gives us some motives for personal obedience. To begin with, God has commanded us (vv. 1–5), and we belong to Him (vv. 6–8). He is faithful (vv. 9–11); what He promises, He will fulfill (vv. 12–26).
Believers today must maintain a separated position (2 Cor. 6:14–18; 1 John 2:15–17) while at the same time loving the lost and seeking to win them to Christ. How do we demolish the strongholds of the enemy? Read 2 Corinthians 10:1–6 and Ephesians 6:10–20.

7 "When the LORD your God brings you into the land which you go to possess, and has cast out many nations before you, the Hittites and the Girgashites and the Amorites and the Canaanites and the Perizzites and the Hivites and the Jebusites, seven nations greater and mightier than you, 2and when the LORD your God delivers them over to you, you shall conquer them *and* utterly destroy them. You shall make no covenant with them nor show mercy to them. 3*Nor shall you make marriages with them. You shall not give your daughter to their son, nor take their daughter for your son. 4For they will turn your sons away from following Me, to serve other gods; so the anger of the LORD will be aroused against you and destroy you suddenly. 5But thus you shall deal with them: you shall destroy their altars, and break down their *sacred* pillars, and cut down their wooden images,*m* and burn their carved images with fire.

6"For you *are* a holy people to the LORD your God; the LORD your God has chosen you to be a people for Himself, a special treasure above all the peoples on the face of the earth. 7*The LORD did not set His love on you nor choose you because you were more in number than any other people, for you were the least of all peoples; 8but because the LORD loves you, and because He would keep the oath which He swore to your fathers, the LORD has brought you out with a mighty hand, and redeemed you from the house of bondage, from the hand of Pharaoh king of Egypt.

9"Therefore know that the LORD your God, He *is* God, the faithful God who keeps covenant and mercy for a thousand generations with those who love Him and keep His commandments; 10and He repays those who hate Him to their face, to destroy them. He will not be slack with him who hates Him; He will repay him to his face. 11Therefore you shall keep the commandment, the

---

7:5 *m*Hebrew *Asherim,* Canaanite deities

statutes, and the judgments which I command you today, to observe them.

12"Then it shall come to pass, because you listen to these judgments, and keep and do them, that the LORD your God will keep with you the covenant and the mercy which He swore to your fathers. 13And He will love you and bless you and multiply you; He will also bless the fruit of your womb and the fruit of your land, your grain and your new wine and your oil, the increase of your cattle and the offspring of your flock, in the land of which He swore to your fathers to give you. 14You shall be blessed above all peoples; there shall not be a male or female barren among you or among your livestock. 15And the LORD will take away from you all sickness, and will afflict you with none of the terrible diseases of Egypt which you have known, but will lay *them* on all those who hate you. 16Also you shall destroy all the peoples whom the LORD your God delivers over to you; your eye shall have no pity on them; nor shall you serve their gods, for that *will be* a snare to you.

17"If you should say in your heart, 'These nations are greater than I; how can I dispossess them?'— 18you shall not be afraid of them, *but* you shall remember well what the LORD your God did to Pharaoh and to all Egypt: 19the great trials which your eyes saw, the signs and the wonders, the mighty hand and the outstretched arm, by which the LORD your God brought you out. So shall the LORD your God do to all the peoples of whom you are afraid. 20Moreover the LORD your God will send the hornet among them until those who are left, who hide themselves from you, are destroyed. 21You shall not be terrified of them; for the LORD your God, the great and awesome God, *is* among you. 22And the LORD your God will drive out those nations before you little by little; you will be unable to destroy them at once, lest the beasts of the field become *too* numerous for you. 23But the LORD your God will deliver them over to you, and will inflict defeat upon them until they are destroyed. 24And He will deliver their kings into your hand, and you will destroy their name from under heaven; no one shall be able to stand against you until you have destroyed them. 25You shall burn the carved images of their gods with fire; you shall not covet the silver or gold *that is* on them, nor take *it* for yourselves, lest you be snared by it; for it *is* an abomination to the LORD your God. 26Nor shall you bring an abomination into your house, lest you be doomed to destruction like it. You shall utterly detest it and utterly abhor it, for it *is* an accursed thing.

8 "Every* commandment which I command you today you must be careful to observe, that you may live and multiply, and go in and possess the land of which the LORD swore to your fathers. 2And you shall remember that the LORD your God led you all the way these forty years in the wilderness, to humble you *and* test you, to know what *was* in your heart, whether you would keep His commandments or not. 3So He humbled you, allowed you to hunger, and fed you with manna which you did not know nor did your fathers know, that He might make you know that man shall not live by bread alone; but man lives by every *word* that proceeds from the mouth of the LORD. 4Your garments did not wear out on you, nor did your foot swell these forty years. 5You

CHAPTER 8

8:1–5 If we will trust Him, God will bring us out (v. 14), lead us through (v. 15), and bring us in (v. 7). Whatever He starts, He finishes (Ps. 138:8; Phil. 1:6).

As He guides us, God tests us. He tests us by His Word (v. 1). Will we hear *every* word that He speaks, and will we obey? He also tests us by His ways (vv. 2–9), putting us into situations that help us to know our own hearts. When we become proud, God has to humble us. When we neglect His Word, He must remind us that His Word is our very life.

should know in your heart that as a man chastens his son, *so* the LORD your God chastens you.

6"Therefore you shall keep the commandments of the LORD your God, to walk in His ways and to fear Him. 7For the LORD your God is bringing you into a good land, a land of brooks of water, of fountains and springs, that flow out of valleys and hills; 8a land of wheat and barley, of vines and fig trees and pomegranates, a land of olive oil and honey; 9a land in which you will eat bread without scarcity, in which you will lack nothing; a land whose stones *are* iron and out of whose hills you can dig copper. 10*When you have eaten and are full, then you shall bless the LORD your God for the good land which He has given you.

11"Beware that you do not forget the LORD your God by not keeping His commandments, His judgments, and His statutes which I command you today, 12lest—*when* you have eaten and are full, and have built beautiful houses and dwell *in them;* 13and *when* your herds and your flocks multiply, and your silver and your gold are multiplied, and all that you have is multiplied; 14when your heart is lifted up, and you forget the LORD your God who brought you out of the land of Egypt, from the house of bondage; 15who led you through that great and terrible wilderness, *in which were* fiery serpents and scorpions and thirsty land where there was no water; who brought water for you out of the flinty rock; 16who fed you in the wilderness with manna, which your fathers did not know, that He might humble you and that He might test you, to do you good in the end— 17then you say in your heart, 'My power and the might of my hand have gained me this wealth.' 18"And you shall remember the LORD your God, for *it is* He who gives you power to get wealth, that He may establish His covenant which He swore to your fathers, as *it is* this day. 19Then it shall be, if you by any means forget the LORD your God, and follow other gods, and serve them and worship them, I testify against you this day that you shall surely perish. 20As the nations which the LORD destroys before you, so you shall perish, because you would not be obedient to the voice of the LORD your God.

9 "Hear, O Israel: You *are* to cross over the Jordan today, and go in to dispossess nations greater and mightier than yourself, cities great and fortified up to heaven, 2a people great and tall, the descendants of the Anakim, whom you know, and *of whom* you heard *it said,* 'Who can stand before the descendants of Anak?' 3Therefore understand today that the LORD your God *is* He who goes over before you *as* a consuming fire. He will destroy them and bring them down before you; so you shall drive them out and destroy them quickly, as the LORD has said to you.

4"Do not think in your heart, after the LORD your God has cast them out before you, saying, 'Because of my righteousness the LORD has brought me in to possess this land'; but *it is* because of the wickedness of these nations *that* the

---

8:10–20 God tests us by His wealth. If we love Him and feed on His Word, we will rejoice in Him and not just in His gifts. In times of prosperity, it is easy to forget the Lord who makes it possible for us to work and earn wealth.

Christians ask God's blessing on their food before they eat, but verse 10 tells us to bless God *after* we have eaten. This is one way to remember that God "gives us richly all things to enjoy" (1 Tim. 6:17).

Self-Confident People Who Failed—A wealthy farmer (Luke 12:13–21). A courageous apostle (Matt. 26:31–35). A mighty ruler (Dan. 4). A self-satisfied church (Rev. 3:14–22). Some successful businessmen (James 4:13–17). All those people failed. They apparently did not take these words to heart: "Do you see a man wise in his own eyes? There is more hope for a fool than for him" (Prov. 26:12).

LORD is driving them out from before you. 5*It is* not because of your righteousness or the uprightness of your heart *that* you go in to possess their land, but because of the wickedness of these nations *that* the LORD your God drives them out from before you, and that He may fulfill the word which the LORD swore to your fathers, to Abraham, Isaac, and Jacob. 6Therefore understand that the LORD your God is not giving you this good land to possess because of your righteousness, for you *are* a stiff-necked people.

7*"Remember! Do not forget how you provoked the LORD your God to wrath in the wilderness. From the day that you departed from the land of Egypt until you came to this place, you have been rebellious against the LORD. 8Also in Horeb you provoked the LORD to wrath, so that the LORD was angry *enough* with you to have destroyed you. 9When I went up into the mountain to receive the tablets of stone, the tablets of the covenant which the LORD made with you, then I stayed on the mountain forty days and forty nights. I neither ate bread nor drank water. 10Then the LORD delivered to me two tablets of stone written with the finger of God, and on them *were* all the words which the LORD had spoken to you on the mountain from the midst of the fire in the day of the assembly. 11And it came to pass, at the end of forty days and forty nights, *that* the LORD gave me the two tablets of stone, the tablets of the covenant.

12"Then the LORD said to me, 'Arise, go down quickly from here, for your people whom you brought out of Egypt have acted corruptly; they have quickly turned aside from the way which I commanded them; they have made themselves a molded image.'

13"Furthermore the LORD spoke to me, saying, 'I have seen this people, and indeed they are a stiff-necked people. 14Let Me alone, that I may destroy them and blot out their name from under heaven; and I will make of you a nation mightier and greater than they.'

15"So I turned and came down from the mountain, and the mountain burned with fire; and the two tablets of the covenant *were* in my two hands. 16And I looked, and behold, you had sinned against the LORD your God—had made for yourselves a molded calf! You had turned aside quickly from the way which the LORD had commanded you. 17Then I took the two tablets and threw them out of my two hands and broke them before your eyes. 18And I fell down before the LORD, as at the first, forty days and forty nights; I neither ate bread nor drank water, because of all your sin which you committed in doing wickedly in the sight of the LORD, to provoke Him to anger. 19For I was afraid of the anger and hot displeasure with which the LORD was angry with you, to destroy you. But the LORD listened to me at that time also. 20And the LORD was very angry with Aaron *and* would have destroyed him; so I prayed for Aaron also at the same time. 21Then I took your sin, the calf which you had made, and burned it with fire and crushed it *and* ground *it* very small, until it was as fine as dust; and I threw its dust into the brook that descended from the mountain.

22"Also at Taberah and Massah and Kibroth Hattaavah you provoked the LORD to wrath. 23Likewise, when the LORD sent you from Kadesh Barnea, saying, 'Go up and possess the land which

CHAPTER 9

9:7–29 Moses is pointing out dangers that God's people must avoid: forgetting God's goodness (chap. 6), compromising with the enemy (chap. 7), and becoming self-satisfied and complacent after great victory (chap. 8). In this chapter, he warns about a danger that all believers constantly face: the reappearance of an old sin. In Israel's case, that sin was rebellion against God.

"But we are a new generation!" the people might have argued. "The old generation that died in the wilderness was guilty of rebellion. We are different!"

But Moses warned *them*. He knew that human nature is the same from one generation to another and that people rarely learn from the mistakes of others. *The sin we think we have conquered is the one that will conquer us.* (See 1 Cor. 10:12.)

Your greatest fear may come before the battle (vv. 1–3), but your greatest danger may be after the battle (vv. 4–6). If the victory makes you proud, you will fall; but if God's blessing humbles you, you will succeed. God is able to make you stand (Rom. 14:4).

I have given you,' then you rebelled against the commandment of the LORD your God, and you did not believe Him nor obey His voice. 24You have been rebellious against the LORD from the day that I knew you.

25"Thus I prostrated myself before the LORD; forty days and forty nights I kept prostrating myself, because the LORD had said He would destroy you. 26Therefore I prayed to the LORD, and said: 'O Lord GOD, do not destroy Your people and Your inheritance whom You have redeemed through Your greatness, whom You have brought out of Egypt with a mighty hand. 27Remember Your servants, Abraham, Isaac, and Jacob; do not look on the stubbornness of this people, or on their wickedness or their sin, 28lest the land from which You brought us should say, "Because the LORD was not able to bring them to the land which He promised them, and because He hated them, He has brought them out to kill them in the wilderness." 29Yet they *are* Your people and Your inheritance, whom You brought out by Your mighty power and by Your outstretched arm.'

CHAPTER 10

10:1–11 Moses balances the two important themes of *law* (vv. 1–11) and *love* (vv. 12–22). Because God loves His people, He gives them His Word to nourish and guide them. *We cannot fully experience God's love for us unless we are obedient to His will.* The will of God is the expression of the love of God (Ps. 33:11).

There is no question that God loves His people (vv. 15–18). He has stated it clearly in His Word and has proved it in many ways, especially in giving His Son to die for the sins of the world (Rom. 5:8). We should love God (vv. 12–14) and prove it by our obedient service and our worship. If we love God, we will also love others (v. 19; 1 John 4:7–12).

10 "At* that time the LORD said to me, 'Hew for yourself two tablets of stone like the first, and come up to Me on the mountain and make yourself an ark of wood. 2And I will write on the tablets the words that were on the first tablets, which you broke; and you shall put them in the ark.'

3"So I made an ark of acacia wood, hewed two tablets of stone like the first, and went up the mountain, having the two tablets in my hand. 4And He wrote on the tablets according to the first writing, the Ten Commandments, which the LORD had spoken to you in the mountain from the midst of the fire in the day of the assembly; and the LORD gave them to me. 5Then I turned and came down from the mountain, and put the tablets in the ark which I had made; and there they are, just as the LORD commanded me."

6(Now the children of Israel journeyed from the wells of Bene Jaakan to Moserah, where Aaron died, and where he was buried; and Eleazar his son ministered as priest in his stead. 7From there they journeyed to Gudgodah, and from Gudgodah to Jotbathah, a land of rivers of water. 8At that time the LORD separated the tribe of Levi to bear the ark of the covenant of the LORD, to stand before the LORD to minister to Him and to bless in His name, to this day. 9Therefore Levi has no portion nor inheritance with his brethren; the LORD *is* his inheritance, just as the LORD your God promised him.)

10"As at the first time, I stayed in the mountain forty days and forty nights; the LORD also heard me at that time, *and* the LORD chose not to destroy you. 11Then the LORD said to me, 'Arise, begin *your* journey before the people, that they may go in and possess the land which I swore to their fathers to give them.'

12*"And now, Israel, what does the LORD your God require of you, but to fear the LORD your God, to walk in all His ways and to love Him, to serve the LORD your God with all your heart and with all your soul, 13*and* to keep the commandments of the LORD and His statutes which I command you today for your good? 14Indeed heaven and the highest heavens belong to the LORD your God, *also* the earth with all that *is* in it. 15The LORD delighted only in your fathers, to love them; and

10:12–16 God wants to write His Word on our hearts and make it a part of the inner person (2 Cor. 3:1–3). If you love the Word, meditate on it daily, and obey it, the Spirit will perform this wonderful work and transform your life.

He chose their descendants after them, you above all peoples, as *it is* this day. [16]Therefore circumcise the foreskin of your heart, and be stiff-necked no longer. [17]For the LORD your God *is* God of gods and Lord of lords, the great God, mighty and awesome, who shows no partiality nor takes a bribe. [18]He administers justice for the fatherless and the widow, and loves the stranger, giving him food and clothing. [19]Therefore love the stranger, for you were strangers in the land of Egypt. [20]You shall fear the LORD your God; you shall serve Him, and to Him you shall hold fast, and take oaths in His name. [21]He *is* your praise, and He *is* your God, who has done for you these great and awesome things which your eyes have seen. [22]Your fathers went down to Egypt with seventy persons, and now the LORD your God has made you as the stars of heaven in multitude.

11 "Therefore* you shall love the LORD your God, and keep His charge, His statutes, His judgments, and His commandments always. [2]Know today that *I do* not *speak* with your children, who have not known and who have not seen the chastening of the LORD your God, His greatness and His mighty hand and His outstretched arm— [3]His signs and His acts which He did in the midst of Egypt, to Pharaoh king of Egypt, and to all his land; [4]what He did to the army of Egypt, to their horses and their chariots: how He made the waters of the Red Sea overflow them as they pursued you, and *how* the LORD has destroyed them to this day; [5]what He did for you in the wilderness until you came to this place; [6]and what He did to Dathan and Abiram the sons of Eliab, the son of Reuben: how the earth opened its mouth and swallowed them up, their households, their tents, and all the substance that *was* in their possession, in the midst of all Israel— [7]but your eyes have seen every great act of the LORD which He did.

[8]*"Therefore you shall keep every commandment which I command you today, that you may be strong, and go in and possess the land which you cross over to possess, [9]and that you may prolong *your* days in the land which the LORD swore to give your fathers, to them and their descendants, 'a land flowing with milk and honey.'[n] [10]For the land which you go to possess *is* not like the land of Egypt from which you have come, where you sowed your seed and watered *it* by foot, as a vegetable garden; [11]but the land which you cross over to possess *is* a land of hills and valleys, which drinks water from the rain of heaven, [12]a land for which the LORD your God cares; the eyes of the LORD your God *are* always on it, from the beginning of the year to the very end of the year.

[13]'And it shall be that if you earnestly obey My commandments which I command you today, to love the LORD your God and serve Him with all your heart and with all your soul, [14]then I[o] will give *you* the rain for your land in its eason, the early rain and the latter rain, that you may gather in your grain, your new wine, and your oil. [15]And I will send grass in your fields for your

CHAPTER 11

11:1–7 What God did. Moses reminded the people of God's past mercies by using the phrase "what He did" five times. *They* did not win the battle in their own strength; God gave the victory. Note that Moses selected two examples of God's judgment, one from outside the nation (Egypt) and one from within the nation (the rebellion of Dathan and Abiram). The second is more dangerous than the first (Acts 20:28–30).

11:8–21 What God asks. He asks that His people obey Him because their obedience is their strength and life (vv. 8–9). They could not prosper in the land without God's constant care and blessing (Matt. 6:33). The Word in the heart will control the hand, the eyes and the tongue, and will protect and direct the household (vv. 18–19).

11:9 ⁿExodus 3:8   11:14 ᵒFollowing
Masoretic Text and Targum; Samaritan Pentateuch,
Septuagint, and Vulgate read *He*.

livestock, that you may eat and be filled.' [16]Take heed to yourselves, lest your heart be deceived, and you turn aside and serve other gods and worship them, [17]lest the LORD's anger be aroused against you, and He shut up the heavens so that there be no rain, and the land yield no produce, and you perish quickly from the good land which the LORD is giving you.

[18]"Therefore you shall lay up these words of mine in your heart and in your soul, and bind them as a sign on your hand, and they shall be as frontlets between your eyes. [19]You shall teach them to your children, speaking of them when you sit in your house, when you walk by the way, when you lie down, and when you rise up. [20]And you shall write them on the doorposts of your house and on your gates, [21]that your days and the days of your children may be multiplied in the land of which the LORD swore to your fathers to give them, like the days of the heavens above the earth.

[22]*"For if you carefully keep all these commandments which I command you to do—to love the LORD your God, to walk in all His ways, and to hold fast to Him— [23]then the LORD will drive out all these nations from before you, and you will dispossess greater and mightier nations than yourselves. [24]Every place on which the sole of your foot treads shall be yours: from the wilderness and Lebanon, from the river, the River Euphrates, even to the Western Sea,[p] shall be your territory. [25]No man shall be able to stand against you; the LORD your God will put the dread of you and the fear of you upon all the land where you tread, just as He has said to you.

[26]"Behold, I set before you today a blessing and a curse: [27]the blessing, if you obey the commandments of the LORD your God which I command you today; [28]and the curse, if you do not obey the commandments of the LORD your God, but turn aside from the way which I command you today, to go after other gods which you have not known. [29]Now it shall be, when the LORD your God has brought you into the land which you go to possess, that you shall put the blessing on Mount Gerizim and the curse on Mount Ebal. [30]*Are they not on the other side of the Jordan, toward the setting sun, in the land of the Canaanites who dwell in the plain opposite Gilgal, beside the terebinth trees of Moreh? [31]For you will cross over the Jordan and go in to possess the land which the LORD your God is giving you, and you will possess it and dwell in it. [32]And you shall be careful to observe all the statutes and judgments which I set before you today.

11:22–32 *What God promises.* God's "I will" is all the promise we need! If we choose to obey, God will bless, even though we may exerience trials and burdens. If we choose to disobey, God will still keep His promise and chasten us. If we love Him (vv. 1, 13, 22), we will obey Him, and in that obedience is life.

CHAPTER 12

Sometimes we think that a new location is the solution to all our problems, so we change jobs or addresses. It has well been said that a change in geography does not overcome a flaw in character. A change can bring out the best in us, but it might bring out the worst in us.

12:1–4 Moses warned that the new land could be a place of *entanglement* (vv. 1–4, 29–32) if the people disobeyed God. Today's pluralistic society tends to treat all religious faiths alike, but God demands that we worship and serve Him alone.

12 "These* *are* the statutes and judgments which you shall be careful to observe in the land which the LORD God of your fathers is giving you to possess, all the days that you live on the earth. [2]You shall utterly destroy all the places where the nations which you shall dispossess served their gods, on the high mountains and on the hills and under every green tree. [3]And you shall destroy their altars, break their *sacred* pillars, and burn their wooden images with fire; you shall cut down the carved images of their gods and destroy their names from that place. [4]You

---

11:24 [p]That is, the Mediterranean

shall not worship the LORD your God *with* such *things.*

5*"But you shall seek the place where the LORD your God chooses, out of all your tribes, to put His name for His dwelling place; and there you shall go. 6There you shall take your burnt offerings, your sacrifices, your tithes, the heave offerings of your hand, your vowed offerings, your freewill offerings, and the firstborn of your herds and flocks. 7And there you shall eat before the LORD your God, and you shall rejoice in all to which you have put your hand, you and your households, in which the LORD your God has blessed you.

8"You shall not at all do as we are doing here today—every man doing whatever *is* right in his own eyes— 9for as yet you have not come to the rest and the inheritance which the LORD your God is giving you. 10But *when* you cross over the Jordan and dwell in the land which the LORD your God is giving you to inherit, and He gives you rest from all your enemies round about, so that you dwell in safety, 11then there will be the place where the LORD your God chooses to make His name abide. There you shall bring all that I command you: your burnt offerings, your sacrifices, your tithes, the heave offerings of your hand, and all your choice offerings which you vow to the LORD. 12And you shall rejoice before the LORD your God, you and your sons and your daughters, your male and female servants, and the Levite who *is* within your gates, since he has no portion nor inheritance with you. 13Take heed to yourself that you do not offer your burnt offerings in every place that you see; 14but in the place which the LORD chooses, in one of your tribes, there you shall offer your burnt offerings, and there you shall do all that I command you.

15"However, you may slaughter and eat meat within all your gates, whatever your heart desires, according to the blessing of the LORD your God which He has given you; the unclean and the clean may eat of it, of the gazelle and the deer alike. 16Only you shall not eat the blood; you shall pour it on the earth like water. 17You may not eat within your gates the tithe of your grain or your new wine or your oil, of the firstborn of your herd or your flock, of any of your offerings which you vow, of your freewill offerings, or of the heave offering of your hand. 18But you must eat them before the LORD your God in the place which the LORD your God chooses, you and your son and your daughter, your male servant and your female servant, and the Levite who *is* within your gates; and you shall rejoice before the LORD your God in all to which you put your hands. 19Take heed to yourself that you do not forsake the Levite as long as you live in your land.

20"When the LORD your God enlarges your border as He has promised you, and you say, 'Let me eat meat,' because you long to eat meat, you may eat as much meat as your heart desires. 21If the place where the LORD your God chooses to put His name is too far from you, then you may slaughter from your herd and from your flock which the LORD has given you, just as I have commanded you, and you may eat within your gates as much as your heart desires. 22Just as the gazelle and the deer are eaten, so you may eat them; the unclean and the clean alike may eat them. 23Only be sure that you do not eat the blood, for the blood *is* the life; you may not eat the life with

12:5–19 The land would be a place of *enjoyment* (vv. 5–19) if they followed the Lord, for God would give them safety, rest, and blessing. We receive our spiritual inheritance by God's grace (Eph. 1:3), and we claim it by faith; but we enjoy it only if we are obedient to His will.

12:26–28 The land was to be a place of *enlargement* (vv. 26–28) as the people trusted God to give them victory. God wants to enlarge our lives; however, we must be careful that enlargement does not result in estrangement from God. It is folly to gain ground materially but lose it spiritually.

the meat. 24You shall not eat it; you shall pour it on the earth like water. 25You shall not eat it, that it may go well with you and your children after you, when you do *what is* right in the sight of the LORD. 26*Only the holy things which you have, and your vowed offerings, you shall take and go to the place which the LORD chooses. 27And you shall offer your burnt offerings, the meat and the blood, on the altar of the LORD your God; and the blood of your sacrifices shall be poured out on the altar of the LORD your God, and you shall eat the meat. 28Observe and obey all these words which I command you, that it may go well with you and your children after you forever, when you do *what is* good and right in the sight of the LORD your God.

29"When the LORD your God cuts off from before you the nations which you go to dispossess, and you displace them and dwell in their land, 30take heed to yourself that you are not ensnared to follow them, after they are destroyed from before you, and that you do not inquire after their gods, saying, 'How did these nations serve their gods? I also will do likewise.' 31You shall not worship the LORD your God in that way; for every abomination to the LORD which He hates they have done to their gods; for they burn even their sons and daughters in the fire to their gods.

32"Whatever I command you, be careful to observe it; you shall not add to it nor take away from it.

CHAPTER 13

13:1–5 In Moses' day, as in our day, some people who claimed to have miraculous gifts were not faithful to the Lord. The test is not the person's ability to perform miracles, for even Satan can do that (2 Cor. 11:13–15; 2 Thess. 2:9–12), but his or her fidelity to the truth of God. Any leader who tempts us away from the Lord and His Word is an enemy and must be rejected.

13 "If* there arises among you a prophet or a dreamer of dreams, and he gives you a sign or a wonder, 2and the sign or the wonder comes to pass, of which he spoke to you, saying, 'Let us go after other gods'—which you have not known—'and let us serve them,' 3you shall not listen to the words of that prophet or that dreamer of dreams, for the LORD your God is testing you to know whether you love the LORD your God with all your heart and with all your soul. 4You shall walk after the LORD your God and fear Him, and keep His commandments and obey His voice; you shall serve Him and hold fast to Him. 5But that prophet or that dreamer of dreams shall be put to death, because he has spoken in order to turn *you* away from the LORD your God, who brought you out of the land of Egypt and redeemed you from the house of bondage, to entice you from the way in which the LORD your God commanded you to walk. So you shall put away the evil from your midst.

13:6–11 Success does not determine truth, nor does personal affection. We must love truth more than we love people, no matter how painful our differences may be (Prov. 1:10ff.).

6*"If your brother, the son of your mother, your son or your daughter, the wife of your bosom, or your friend who is as your own soul, secretly entices you, saying, 'Let us go and serve other gods,' which you have not known, neither you nor your fathers, 7of the gods of the people which *are* all around you, near to you or far off from you, from *one* end of the earth to the *other* end of the earth, 8you shall not consent to him or listen to him, nor shall your eye pity him, nor shall you spare him or conceal him; 9but you shall surely kill him; your hand shall be first against him to put him to death, and afterward the hand of all the people. 10And you shall stone him with stones until he dies, because he sought to entice you away from the LORD your God, who brought you out of the land of Egypt, from the house of bondage. 11So all Israel shall hear and fear, and not again do such wickedness as this among you.

12*"If you hear someone in one of your cities, which the Lord your God gives you to dwell in, saying, 13'Corrupt men have gone out from among you and enticed the inhabitants of their city, saying, "Let us go and serve other gods" '—which you have not known— 14then you shall inquire, search out, and ask diligently. And *if it is* indeed true *and* certain *that* such an abomination was committed among you, 15you shall surely strike the inhabitants of that city with the edge of the sword, utterly destroying it, all that is in it and its livestock—with the edge of the sword. 16And you shall gather all its plunder into the middle of the street, and completely burn with fire the city and all its plunder, for the Lord your God. It shall be a heap forever; it shall not be built again. 17So none of the accursed things shall remain in your hand, that the Lord may turn from the fierceness of His anger and show you mercy, have compassion on you and multiply you, just as He swore to your fathers, 18because you have listened to the voice of the Lord your God, to keep all His commandments which I command you today, to do *what is* right in the eyes of the Lord your God.

14 "You *are* the children of the Lord your God; you shall not cut yourselves nor shave the front of your head for the dead. 2*For you *are* a holy people to the Lord your God, and the Lord has chosen you to be a people for Himself, a special treasure above all the peoples who *are* on the face of the earth.
3*"You shall not eat any detestable thing. 4These *are* the animals which you may eat: the ox, the sheep, the goat, 5the deer, the gazelle, the roe deer, the wild goat, the mountain goat,q the antelope, and the mountain sheep. 6And you may eat every animal with cloven hooves, having the hoof split into two parts, *and that* chews the cud, among the animals. 7Nevertheless, of those that chew the cud or have cloven hooves, you shall not eat, *such as* these: the camel, the hare, and the rock hyrax; for they chew the cud but do not have cloven hooves; they *are* unclean for you. 8Also the swine is unclean for you, because it has cloven hooves, yet *does* not *chew* the cud; you shall not eat their flesh or touch their dead carcasses.
9"These you may eat of all that *are* in the waters: you may eat all that have fins and scales. 10And whatever does not have fins and scales you shall not eat; it *is* unclean for you.
11"All clean birds you may eat. 12But these you shall not eat: the eagle, the vulture, the buzzard, 13the red kite, the falcon, and the kite after their kinds; 14every raven after its kind; 15the ostrich, the short-eared owl, the sea gull, and the hawk after their kinds; 16the little owl, the screech owl, the white owl, 17the jackdaw, the carrion vulture, the fisher owl, 18the stork, the heron after its kind, and the hoopoe and the bat.
19"Also every creeping thing that flies is unclean for you; they shall not be eaten. 20"You may eat all clean birds.
21"You shall not eat anything that dies *of itself;* you may give it to the alien who *is* within your gates, that he may eat it, or you may sell it to a

13:12–18 Numbers do not determine truth (vv. 12–18). If an entire city turned away from God, that is no reason for us to do so. God will stand with us (Matt. 10:28–42). Our allegiance must be "to the law and to the testimony" (Isa. 8:20).

CHAPTER 14

14:2 The children of the Lord must not be like the people of the world. The basic meaning of the Hebrew word translated "holy" is "to be different." God's people are different.

14:3–21 Although the Jewish dietary code does not apply to God's people today (1 Tim. 4:1–5), the spiritual principle remains: we must be a separated and obedient people. The lists of "clean" and "unclean" foods were reminders that the people must learn to distinguish between what God accepts and what He rejects. Review Leviticus 11:41–47.

14:5 qOr *addax*

14:22, 23 We should glorify God in what we receive and also in what we give (vv. 22–29). A tithe was 10 percent of the produce, which could be used as a sacrifice for joyful feasting before the Lord. A special tithe every third year supported the Levites and helped the poor.

In our receiving and in our giving, we should glorify God and joyfully serve Him. (See 1 Cor. 10:31.)

CHAPTER 15

15:4–6 The blessing of God ought to motivate us to be a blessing and a help to others. Note how often Moses mentions the blessing of God (vv. 4, 6, 10, 14, 18). God has opened His hand generously to us, and we should open our hands widely to others (v. 8). He blesses us so that we might be a blessing (Gen. 12:2).

15:10, 11 Not only must we have generous hands, but we should cultivate glad hearts as we share (v. 10). Giving is an occasion not for shrewd calculation (v. 9) but for jubilation! Paul may have had this verse in mind when he wrote "not grudgingly or of necessity; for God loves a cheerful giver" (2 Cor. 9:7).

foreigner; for you *are* a holy people to the LORD your God.

"You shall not boil a young goat in its mother's milk.

22*"You shall truly tithe all the increase of your grain that the field produces year by year. 23And you shall eat before the LORD your God, in the place where He chooses to make His name abide, the tithe of your grain and your new wine and your oil, of the firstborn of your herds and your flocks, that you may learn to fear the LORD your God always. 24But if the journey is too long for you, so that you are not able to carry *the tithe, or* if the place where the LORD your God chooses to put His name is too far from you, when the LORD your God has blessed you, 25then you shall exchange *it* for money, take the money in your hand, and go to the place which the LORD your God chooses. 26And you shall spend that money for whatever your heart desires: for oxen or sheep, for wine or similar drink, for whatever your heart desires; you shall eat there before the LORD your God, and you shall rejoice, you and your household. 27You shall not forsake the Levite who *is* within your gates, for he has no part nor inheritance with you.

28"At the end of *every* third year you shall bring out the tithe of your produce of that year and store *it* up within your gates. 29And the Levite, because he has no portion nor inheritance with you, and the stranger and the fatherless and the widow who *are* within your gates, may come and eat and be satisfied, that the LORD your God may bless you in all the work of your hand which you do.

15 "At the end of *every* seven years you shall grant a release *of debts.* 2And this *is* the form of the release: Every creditor who has lent *anything* to his neighbor shall release *it;* he shall not require *it* of his neighbor or his brother, because it is called the LORD's release. 3Of a foreigner you may require *it;* but you shall give up your claim to what is owed by your brother, 4*except when there may be no poor among you; for the LORD will greatly bless you in the land which the LORD your God is giving you to possess *as* an inheritance— 5only if you carefully obey the voice of the LORD your God, to observe with care all these commandments which I command you today. 6For the LORD your God will bless you just as He promised you; you shall lend to many nations, but you shall not borrow; you shall reign over many nations, but they shall not reign over you.

7"If there is among you a poor man of your brethren, within any of the gates in your land which the LORD your God is giving you, you shall not harden your heart nor shut your hand from your poor brother, 8but you shall open your hand wide to him and willingly lend him sufficient for his need, whatever he needs. 9Beware lest there be a wicked thought in your heart, saying, 'The seventh year, the year of release, is at hand,' and your eye be evil against your poor brother and you give him nothing, and he cry out to the LORD against you, and it become sin among you. 10*You shall surely give to him, and your heart should not be grieved when you give to him, because for this thing the LORD your God will bless you in all your works and in all to which you put your hand. 11For the poor will never cease from the land; therefore I command you, saying,

'You shall open your hand wide to your brother, to your poor and your needy, in your land.'

12"If your brother, a Hebrew man, or a Hebrew woman, is sold to you and serves you six years, then in the seventh year you shall let him go free from you. 13And when you send him away free from you, you shall not let him go away empty-handed; 14you shall supply him liberally from your flock, from your threshing floor, and from your winepress. *From what* the LORD has blessed you with, you shall give to him. 15You shall remember that you were a slave in the land of Egypt, and the LORD your God redeemed you; therefore I command you this thing today. 16*And if it happens that he says to you, 'I will not go away from you,' because he loves you and your house, since he prospers with you, 17then you shall take an awl and thrust *it* through his ear to the door, and he shall be your servant forever. Also to your female servant you shall do likewise. 18It shall not seem hard to you when you send him away free from you; for he has been worth a double hired servant in serving you six years. Then the LORD your God will bless you in all that you do.

19"All the firstborn males that come from your herd and your flock you shall sanctify to the LORD your God; you shall do no work with the firstborn of your herd, nor shear the firstborn of your flock. 20You and your household shall eat *it* before the LORD your God year by year in the place which the LORD chooses. 21But if there is a defect in it, *if it is* lame or blind *or has* any serious defect, you shall not sacrifice it to the LORD your God. 22You may eat it within your gates; the unclean and the clean *person* alike *may eat it, as if it were* a gazelle or a deer. 23Only you shall not eat its blood; you shall pour it on the ground like water.

16 "Observe* the month of Abib, and keep the Passover to the LORD your God, for in the month of Abib the LORD your God brought you out of Egypt by night. 2Therefore you shall sacrifice the Passover to the LORD your God, from the flock and the herd, in the place where the LORD chooses to put His name. 3You shall eat no leavened bread with it; seven days you shall eat unleavened bread with it, *that is,* the bread of affliction (for you came out of the land of Egypt in haste), that you may remember the day in which you came out of the land of Egypt all the days of your life. 4And no leaven shall be seen among you in all your territory for seven days, nor shall *any* of the meat which you sacrifice the first day at twilight remain overnight until morning.

5"You may not sacrifice the Passover within any of your gates which the LORD your God gives you; 6but at the place where the LORD your God chooses to make His name abide, there you shall sacrifice the Passover at twilight, at the going down of the sun, at the time you came out of Egypt. 7And you shall roast and eat *it* in the place which the LORD your God chooses, and in the morning you shall turn and go to your tents. 8Six days you shall eat unleavened bread, and on the seventh day there *shall be* a sacred assembly to the LORD your God. You shall do no work *on* it.

9*"You shall count seven weeks for yourself; begin to count the seven weeks from *the time* you begin *to put* the sickle to the grain. 10Then you shall keep the Feast of Weeks to the LORD your

15:16, 17 The greatest gift of all is the gift of ourselves because we love one another (vv. 16–17). First we give ourselves to the Lord (Rom. 12:1–2) and then to one another in loving service (2 Cor. 8:1–5). There is plenty of room in "The Fellowship of the Pierced Ear."

CHAPTER 16

From the seven feasts on the Jewish calendar (Lev. 23), Moses selected three to emphasize, and they bear a message to the believer today.

16:1–8 *Passover* looks to the past and reminds us that we have been redeemed by the blood of the Lamb of God (John 1:29; 1 Pet. 1:18–19). Redemption brings responsibility: feeding on the Lamb and removing from our lives all things that are wrong. (See 1 Cor. 5:1–8).

16:9–12 *Pentecost* speaks of renewal and the coming of the Spirit of God to His people (Acts 2). It is a harvest festival that calls us to enter into His service and help reap the harvest (Luke 10:2; John 4:33–38; Acts 1:8).

16:13–17 Tabernacles reminded the Jews that they had lived in booths as a pilgrim people in the wilderness. We are "sojourners and pilgrims" in this world (1 Pet. 2:11) and must not get too settled down. Tabernacles also looks to the future kingdom that God has promised His people when their pilgrim journey is ended. We need these three reminders today, lest we forget our redemption responsibilities.

CHAPTER 17

17:1–13 Presumption. God's Word reveals God's will and we must not go beyond what God permits. To transgress (v. 2) means to "cross the line," which is presumptuous sin. God says, "Thus far and no farther!" and we must obey. That obedience applied to sentences of judgment (vv. 8–13). The sinner who challenged the judgment of God's appointed leaders was destined to die. "Hear and fear!"

God with the tribute of a freewill offering from your hand, which you shall give as the LORD your God blesses you. 11You shall rejoice before the LORD your God, you and your son and your daughter, your male servant and your female servant, the Levite who is within your gates, the stranger and the fatherless and the widow who are among you, at the place where the LORD your God chooses to make His name abide. 12And you shall remember that you were a slave in Egypt, and you shall be careful to observe these statutes.

13*"You shall observe the Feast of Tabernacles seven days, when you have gathered from your threshing floor and from your winepress. 14And you shall rejoice in your feast, you and your son and your daughter, your male servant and your female servant and the Levite, the stranger and the fatherless and the widow, who are within your gates. 15Seven days you shall keep a sacred feast to the LORD your God in the place which the LORD chooses, because the LORD your God will bless you in all your produce and in all the work of your hands, so that you surely rejoice.

16"Three times a year all your males shall appear before the LORD your God in the place which He chooses: at the Feast of Unleavened Bread, at the Feast of Weeks, and at the Feast of Tabernacles; and they shall not appear before the LORD empty-handed. 17Every man shall give as he is able, according to the blessing of the LORD your God which He has given you.

18"You shall appoint judges and officers in all your gates, which the LORD your God gives you, according to your tribes, and they shall judge the people with just judgment. 19You shall not pervert justice; you shall not show partiality, nor take a bribe, for a bribe blinds the eyes of the wise and twists the words of the righteous. 20You shall follow what is altogether just, that you may live and inherit the land which the LORD your God is giving you.

21"You shall not plant for yourself any tree, as a wooden image, near the altar which you build for yourself to the LORD your God. 22You shall not set up a sacred pillar, which the LORD your God hates.

17 "You* shall not sacrifice to the LORD your God a bull or sheep which has any blemish or defect, for that is an abomination to the LORD your God.

2"If there is found among you, within any of your gates which the LORD your God gives you, a man or a woman who has been wicked in the sight of the LORD your God, in transgressing His covenant, 3who has gone and served other gods and worshiped them, either the sun or moon or any of the host of heaven, which I have not commanded, 4and it is told you, and you hear of it, then you shall inquire diligently. And if it is indeed true and certain that such an abomination has been committed in Israel, 5then you shall bring out to your gates that man or woman who has committed that wicked thing, and shall stone to death that man or woman with stones. 6Whoever is deserving of death shall be put to death on the testimony of two or three witnesses; he shall not be put to death on the testimony of one witness. 7The hands of the witnesses shall be the first against him to put him to death, and afterward the hands of all the people. So you shall put away the evil from among you.

⁸"If a matter arises which is too hard for you to judge, between degrees of guilt for bloodshed, between one judgment or another, or between one punishment or another, matters of controversy within your gates, then you shall arise and go up to the place which the LORD your God chooses. ⁹And you shall come to the priests, the Levites, and to the judge *there* in those days, and inquire *of them;* they shall pronounce upon you the sentence of judgment. ¹⁰You shall do according to the sentence which they pronounce upon you in that place which the LORD chooses. And you shall be careful to do according to all that they order you. ¹¹According to the sentence of the law in which they instruct you, according to the judgment which they tell you, you shall do; you shall not turn aside *to* the right hand or *to* the left from the sentence which they pronounce upon you. ¹²Now the man who acts presumptuously and will not heed the priest who stands to minister there before the LORD your God, or the judge, that man shall die. So you shall put away the evil from Israel. ¹³And all the people shall hear and fear, and no longer act presumptuously.

¹⁴*"When you come to the land which the LORD your God is giving you, and possess it and dwell in it, and say, 'I will set a king over me like all the nations that *are* around me,' ¹⁵you shall surely set a king over you whom the LORD your God chooses; *one* from among your brethren you shall set as king over you; you may not set a foreigner over you, who *is* not your brother. ¹⁶But he shall not multiply horses for himself, nor cause the people to return to Egypt to multiply horses, for the LORD has said to you, 'You shall not return that way again.' ¹⁷Neither shall he multiply wives for himself, lest his heart turn away; nor shall he greatly multiply silver and gold for himself.

¹⁸"Also it shall be, when he sits on the throne of his kingdom, that he shall write for himself a copy of this law in a book, from *the one* before the priests, the Levites. ¹⁹And it shall be with him, and he shall read it all the days of his life, that he may learn to fear the LORD his God and be careful to observe all the words of this law and these statutes, ²⁰that his heart may not be lifted above his brethren, that he may not turn aside from the commandment *to* the right hand or *to* the left, and that he may prolong *his* days in his kingdom, he and his children in the midst of Israel.

18 "The* priests, the Levites—all the tribe of Levi—shall have no part nor inheritance with Israel; they shall eat the offerings of the LORD made by fire, and His portion. ²Therefore they shall have no inheritance among their brethren; the LORD is their inheritance, as He said to them.

³"And this shall be the priest's due from the people, from those who offer a sacrifice, whether *it is* bull or sheep: they shall give to the priest the shoulder, the cheeks, and the stomach. ⁴The firstfruits of your grain and your new wine and your oil, and the first of the fleece of your sheep, you shall give him. ⁵For the LORD your God has chosen him out of all your tribes to stand to minister in the name of the LORD, him and his sons forever.

⁶"So if a Levite comes from any of your gates, from where he dwells among all Israel, and comes with all the desire of his mind to the place which the LORD chooses, ⁷then he may serve in the name

17:14–20 *Pride.* Israel did ask for a king, and God gave them Saul (1 Sam. 8—10). We do not know whether he obeyed verses 18–20, but we do know that he failed to obey God's will (1 Sam. 15). His successor David was a man of God's Word, but David's son Solomon committed all of the sins named in verses 16–17 (1 Kings 10—11). There was great prosperity for a time, but then the nation divided and turned from God.

Common citizens, priests, judges, and kings—all had an obligation to submit to God's Word and obey it. The higher the position, the greater the responsibility. "Hear and fear!"

CHAPTER 18

18:1–8 God's people should be a *generous* people, sharing what they have with those who serve (1 Cor. 9:1–14; 3 John 5–8). The priests and Levites depended on the sacrifices and the tithes for their sustenance, and an unfaithful people meant neglected servants. (See Neh. 13:10–14.)

18:9–14 They should also be a *separated* people. This is one of the strongest warnings in Scripture against occult practices, and it must be heeded today. Israel did not obey this command, and the land was defiled and the nation disciplined.

18:15–22 God's people must be a *discerning* people, listening to the Word, receiving it and obeying it. The Prophet mentioned here is Jesus Christ (Acts 3:18–23), but when He came, they did not recognize Him or receive Him (John 1:10–11; 5:43). The mark of a true prophet is that *everything* predicted comes to pass. The prophet is not 75 percent correct, but 100 percent correct!

CHAPTER 19

19:1–7 There was a court system in Israel but no police force. The innocent person had to be protected before the family of a victim attempted to take vengeance. The cities of refuge provided a place of escape where the manslayer could be tried to see whether the death was manslaughter or murder.

of the LORD his God as all his brethren the Levites *do*, who stand there before the LORD. 8They shall have equal portions to eat, besides what comes from the sale of his inheritance.

9*"When you come into the land which the LORD your God is giving you, you shall not learn to follow the abominations of those nations. 10There shall not be found among you *anyone* who makes his son or his daughter pass through the fire, *or one* who practices witchcraft, *or* a soothsayer, or one who interprets omens, or a sorcerer, 11or one who conjures spells, or a medium, or a spiritist, or one who calls up the dead. 12For all who do these things *are* an abomination to the LORD, and because of these abominations the LORD your God drives them out from before you. 13You shall be blameless before the LORD your God. 14For these nations which you will dispossess listened to soothsayers and diviners; but as for you, the LORD your God has not appointed such for you.

15*"The LORD your God will raise up for you a Prophet like me from your midst, from your brethren. Him you shall hear, 16according to all you desired of the LORD your God in Horeb in the day of the assembly, saying, 'Let me not hear again the voice of the LORD my God, nor let me see this great fire anymore, lest I die.'

17"And the LORD said to me: 'What they have spoken is good. 18I will raise up for them a Prophet like you from among their brethren, and will put My words in His mouth, and He shall speak to them all that I command Him. 19And it shall be *that* whoever will not hear My words, which He speaks in My name, I will require *it* of him. 20But the prophet who presumes to speak a word in My name, which I have not commanded him to speak, or who speaks in the name of other gods, that prophet shall die.' 21And if you say in your heart, 'How shall we know the word which the LORD has not spoken?'— 22when a prophet speaks in the name of the LORD, if the thing does not happen or come to pass, that *is* the thing which the LORD has not spoken; the prophet has spoken it presumptuously; you shall not be afraid of him.

19 "When* the LORD your God has cut off the nations whose land the LORD your God is giving you, and you dispossess them and dwell in their cities and in their houses, 2you shall separate three cities for yourself in the midst of your land which the LORD your God is giving you to possess. 3You shall prepare roads for yourself, and divide into three parts the territory of your land which the LORD your God is giving you to inherit, that any manslayer may flee there.

4"And this *is* the case of the manslayer who flees there, that he may live: Whoever kills his neighbor unintentionally, not having hated him in time past— 5as when *a man* goes to the woods with his neighbor to cut timber, and his hand swings a stroke with the ax to cut down the tree, and the head slips from the handle and strikes his neighbor so that he dies—he shall flee to one of these cities and live; 6lest the avenger of blood, while his anger is hot, pursue the manslayer and overtake him, because the way is long, and kill him, though he *was* not deserving of death, since he had not hated the victim in time past. 7Therefore I command you, saying, 'You shall separate three cities for yourself.'

8"Now if the LORD your God enlarges your territory, as He swore to your fathers, and gives you the land which He promised to give to your fathers, 9and if you keep all these commandments and do them, which I command you today, to love the LORD your God and to walk always in His ways, then you shall add three more cities for yourself besides these three, 10*lest innocent blood be shed in the midst of your land which the LORD your God is giving you *as* an inheritance, and *thus* guilt of bloodshed be upon you.

11"But if anyone hates his neighbor, lies in wait for him, rises against him and strikes him mortally, so that he dies, and he flees to one of these cities, 12then the elders of his city shall send and bring him from there, and deliver him over to the hand of the avenger of blood, that he may die. 13Your eye shall not pity him, but you shall put away *the guilt of* innocent blood from Israel, that it may go well with you.

14"You shall not remove your neighbor's landmark, which the men of old have set, in your inheritance which you will inherit in the land that the LORD your God is giving you to possess.

15"One witness shall not rise against a man concerning any iniquity or any sin that he commits; by the mouth of two or three witnesses the matter shall be established. 16If a false witness rises against any man to testify against him of wrongdoing, 17then both men in the controversy shall stand before the LORD, before the priests and the judges who serve in those days. 18And the judges shall make careful inquiry, and indeed, *if* the witness *is* a false witness, who has testified falsely against his brother, 19then you shall do to him as he thought to have done to his brother; so you shall put away the evil from among you. 20And those who remain shall hear and fear, and hereafter they shall not again commit such evil among you. 21Your eye shall not pity: life *shall be* for life, eye for eye, tooth for tooth, hand for hand, foot for foot.

20 "When* you go out to battle against your enemies, and see horses and chariots *and* people more numerous than you, do not be afraid of them; for the LORD your God *is* with you, who brought you up from the land of Egypt. 2So it shall be, when you are on the verge of battle, that the priest shall approach and speak to the people. 3And he shall say to them, 'Hear, O Israel: Today you are on the verge of battle with your enemies. Do not let your heart faint, do not be afraid, and do not tremble or be terrified because of them; 4for the LORD your God *is* He who goes with you, to fight for you against your enemies, to save you.'

5"Then the officers shall speak to the people, saying: 'What man *is there* who has built a new house and has not dedicated it? Let him go and return to his house, lest he die in the battle and another man dedicate it. 6Also what man *is there* who has planted a vineyard and has not eaten of it? Let him go and return to his house, lest he die in the battle and another man eat of it. 7And what man *is there* who is betrothed to a woman and has not married her? Let him go and return to his house, lest he die in the battle and another man marry her.'

8"The officers shall speak further to the people, and say, 'What man *is there who is* fearful and fainthearted? Let him go and return to his house,

19:10 The cities picture the salvation we have in Jesus Christ, the One to whom we have "fled for refuge" because death is pursuing us (Heb. 6:18; Rom. 6:23). The cities were appointed by God, and no other cities would do (Acts 4:12). They were accessible and available to all (Josh. 20:9; John 6:37), but the person had to believe God's Word and act on it. The roads to those cities were clearly marked and kept in good repair. The way was open and free.

However, in Christ we have something far better! The manslayer was tried to see if he were a murderer, but those who trust Christ shall never face judgment (John 5:24; Rom. 8:1). Our High Priest lives forever and intercedes for us; therefore, we can never be refused (Heb. 7:23–28). We are indeed guilty, but He forgives us by His grace—and He takes our punishment for us!

CHAPTER 20

Claiming our spiritual inheritance will involve battles as well as blessings, for the hosts of evil are against us (Eph. 6:10–13). God's words to Israel help us understand how to defeat the enemies we face.

20:1–4 *Before the battle: courage.* We walk by faith and not by sight (v. 1) and must never judge the victory by our own resources or the resources of the enemy. God gives us the power to overcome, so take courage from the fact that God is with us and fights for us. Read 2 Chronicles 20:1–23 for an exciting example of this truth.

20:10–20 *During the battle: obedience.* We must be totally devoted to the Lord if we are to win the battle (2 Tim. 2:4). The battlefield is no place for the fearful and fainthearted or the doubleminded. We must obey whatever battle plan God assigns to us, for the enemy often employs a different strategy.

20:15 *After the battle: complete conquest.* Even in defeat, the enemy is still the enemy and can entice us into sin. Remember what happened to Achan (Josh. 7) and King Saul (1 Sam. 15).

CHAPTER 21

Man is made in the image of God, and human life is precious in His sight. People are not to be treated like animals or things, and the laws in this chapter illustrate this truth.

21:1–9 *Murder.* The unlawful taking of a life is a tragedy that cannot be erased simply by burying a corpse. The heifer died instead of the culprit (Gen. 9:5–6), but the sacrifice did not atone for the murderer's sin. Rather, the sacrifice kept the land from being defiled by innocent blood (Deut. 19:10–13), and it reminded the people that life is precious.

lest the heart of his brethren faint[r] like his heart.' 9And so it shall be, when the officers have finished speaking to the people, that they shall make captains of the armies to lead the people.

10*"When you go near a city to fight against it, then proclaim an offer of peace to it. 11And it shall be that if they accept your offer of peace, and open to you, then all the people *who are* found in it shall be placed under tribute to you, and serve you. 12Now if *the city* will not make peace with you, but war against you, then you shall besiege it. 13And when the LORD your God delivers it into your hands, you shall strike every male in it with the edge of the sword. 14But the women, the little ones, the livestock, and all that is in the city, all its spoil, you shall plunder for yourself; and you shall eat the enemies' plunder which the LORD your God gives you. 15*Thus you shall do to all the cities *which are* very far from you, which *are* not of the cities of these nations.

16"But of the cities of these peoples which the LORD your God gives you *as* an inheritance, you shall let nothing that breathes remain alive, 17but you shall utterly destroy them: the Hittite and the Amorite and the Canaanite and the Perizzite and the Hivite and the Jebusite, just as the LORD your God has commanded you, 18lest they teach you to do according to all their abominations which they have done for their gods, and you sin against the LORD your God.

19"When you besiege a city for a long time, while making war against it to take it, you shall not destroy its trees by wielding an ax against them; if you can eat of them, do not cut them down to use in the siege, for the tree of the field *is* man's food. 20Only the trees which you know *are* not trees for food you may destroy and cut down, to build siegeworks against the city that makes war with you, until it is subdued.

21 "If* *anyone* is found slain, lying in the field in the land which the LORD your God is giving you to possess, *and* it is not known who killed him, 2then your elders and your judges shall go out and measure *the distance* from the slain man to the surrounding cities. 3And it shall be *that* the elders of the city nearest to the slain man will take a heifer which has not been worked *and* which has not pulled with a yoke. 4The elders of that city shall bring the heifer down to a valley with flowing water, which is neither plowed nor sown, and they shall break the heifer's neck there in the valley. 5Then the priests, the sons of Levi, shall come near, for the LORD your God has chosen them to minister to Him and to bless in the name of the LORD; by their word every controversy and every assault shall be *settled.* 6And all the elders of that city nearest to the slain *man* shall wash their hands over the heifer whose neck was broken in the valley. 7Then they shall answer and say, 'Our hands have not shed this blood, nor have our eyes seen *it.* 8Provide atonement, O LORD, for Your people Israel, whom You have redeemed, and do not lay innocent blood to the charge of Your people Israel.' And atonement shall be provided on their behalf for the blood.

20:8 rFollowing Masoretic Text and Targum; Samaritan Pentateuch, Septuagint, Syriac, and Vulgate read *lest he make his brother's heart faint.*

⁹So you shall put away the *guilt of* innocent blood from among you when you do *what is* right in the sight of the LORD.

¹⁰*"When you go out to war against your enemies, and the LORD your God delivers them into your hand, and you take them captive, ¹¹and you see among the captives a beautiful woman, and desire her and would take her for your wife, ¹²then you shall bring her home to your house, and she shall shave her head and trim her nails. ¹³She shall put off the clothes of her captivity, remain in your house, and mourn her father and her mother a full month; after that you may go in to her and be her husband, and she shall be your wife. ¹⁴And it shall be, if you have no delight in her, then you shall set her free, but you certainly shall not sell her for money; you shall not treat her brutally, because you have humbled her.

¹⁵"If a man has two wives, one loved and the other unloved, and they have borne him children, *both* the loved and the unloved, and *if* the firstborn son is of her who is unloved, ¹⁶then it shall be, on the day he bequeaths his possessions to his sons, *that* he must not bestow firstborn status on the son of the loved wife in preference to the son of the unloved, the *true* firstborn. ¹⁷But he shall acknowledge the son of the unloved wife *as* the firstborn by giving him a double portion of all that he has, for he *is* the beginning of his strength; the right of the firstborn *is* his.

¹⁸*"If a man has a stubborn and rebellious son who will not obey the voice of his father or the voice of his mother, and *who,* when they have chastened him, will not heed them, ¹⁹then his father and his mother shall take hold of him and bring him out to the elders of his city, to the gate of his city. ²⁰And they shall say to the elders of his city, 'This son of ours is stubborn and rebellious; he will not obey our voice; he is a glutton and a drunkard.' ²¹Then all the men of his city shall stone him to death with stones; so you shall put away the evil from among you, and all Israel shall hear and fear.

²²"If a man has committed a sin deserving of death, and he is put to death, and you hang him on a tree, ²³his body shall not remain overnight on the tree, but you shall surely bury him that day, so that you do not defile the land which the LORD your God is giving you *as* an inheritance; for he who is hanged *is* accursed of God.

22 "You* shall not see your brother's ox or his sheep going astray, and hide yourself from them; you shall certainly bring them back to your brother. ²And if your brother *is* not near you, or if you do not know him, then you shall bring it to your own house, and it shall remain with you until your brother seeks it; then you shall restore it to him. ³You shall do the same with his donkey, and so shall you do with his garment; with any lost thing of your brother's, which he has lost and you have found, you shall do likewise; you must not hide yourself.

⁴"You shall not see your brother's donkey or his ox fall down along the road, and hide yourself from them; you shall surely help him lift *them* up again.

⁵*"A woman shall not wear anything that pertains to a man, nor shall a man put on a woman's garment, for all who do so *are* an abomination to the LORD your God.

21:10–17 *Marriage.* Jews were forbidden to marry Canaanites (Deut. 7:1–4), so the captured wife mentioned in these verses had to come from another nation. Women in general, and captives in particular, had very little status in those days; but God protected her from abuse. No matter how much authority we have, we must not mistreat others or take advantage of them.

21:18–23 *Rebellion.* A rebellious son would grieve his parents, bring shame to his village, and be a bad example to other young men. The fear of death might deter some sons, or like the prodigal (Luke 15:11ff.), they might decide to leave home. To us, it seems like a drastic law, but God will not tolerate rebellion.

See our Lord in this chapter: He died for guilty sinners; He loved and married a foreign bride (Eph. 5:25ff.); He died for rebellious sinners; and He was hanged on a tree (Gal. 3:13).

CHAPTER 22

22:1–4 *Lost possessions.* God honors private ownership and demands honesty in the handling of other people's goods, even when it is not convenient. He also has compassion for animals (Exod. 23:5). We are stewards of all that God gives us, and we must be faithful.

22:5–12 *Lost distinctions.* The Bible makes it clear that "God is not the author of confusion" (1 Cor. 14:33), but confusion results when we ignore the distinctions God has made between men and women, animals, and even seeds and fabrics. Like the dietary laws, these rules reminded the Jews that they were a separated people, and the tassels on their clothing were an additional reminder.

22:13–30 *Lost reputations.* Here you see God's protection for the helpless in the land. It is a serious thing to bear false witness, particularly in the matter of sexual purity. A reputation can be ruined by people making false accusations. It is not enough simply to love virtue; sometimes we must also "put away the evil" (v. 21) and deal with sin.

6"If a bird's nest happens to be before you along the way, in any tree or on the ground, with young ones or eggs, with the mother sitting on the young or on the eggs, you shall not take the mother with the young; 7you shall surely let the mother go, and take the young for yourself, that it may be well with you and *that* you may prolong *your* days.

8"When you build a new house, then you shall make a parapet for your roof, that you may not bring guilt of bloodshed on your household if anyone falls from it.

9"You shall not sow your vineyard with different kinds of seed, lest the yield of the seed which you have sown and the fruit of your vineyard be defiled.

10"You shall not plow with an ox and a donkey together.

11"You shall not wear a garment of different sorts, *such as* wool and linen mixed together.

12"You shall make tassels on the four corners of the clothing with which you cover *yourself.*

13*"If any man takes a wife, and goes in to her, and detests her, 14and charges her with shameful conduct, and brings a bad name on her, and says, 'I took this woman, and when I came to her I found she *was* not a virgin,' 15then the father and mother of the young woman shall take and bring out *the evidence of* the young woman's virginity to the elders of the city at the gate. 16And the young woman's father shall say to the elders, 'I gave my daughter to this man as wife, and he detests her. 17Now he has charged her with shameful conduct, saying, "I found your daughter *was* not a virgin," and yet these *are the evidences of* my daughter's virginity.' And they shall spread the cloth before the elders of the city. 18Then the elders of that city shall take that man and punish him; 19and they shall fine him one hundred *shekels* of silver and give *them* to the father of the young woman, because he has brought a bad name on a virgin of Israel. And she shall be his wife; he cannot divorce her all his days.

20"But if the thing is true, *and evidences of* virginity are not found for the young woman, 21then they shall bring out the young woman to the door of her father's house, and the men of her city shall stone her to death with stones, because she has done a disgraceful thing in Israel, to play the harlot in her father's house. So you shall put away the evil from among you.

22"If a man is found lying with a woman married to a husband, then both of them shall die— the man that lay with the woman, and the woman; so you shall put away the evil from Israel.

23"If a young woman *who is* a virgin is betrothed to a husband, and a man finds her in the city and lies with her, 24then you shall bring them both out to the gate of that city, and you shall stone them to death with stones, the young woman because she did not cry out in the city, and the man because he humbled his neighbor's wife; so you shall put away the evil from among you.

25"But if a man finds a betrothed young woman in the countryside, and the man forces her and lies with her, then only the man who lay with her shall die. 26But you shall do nothing to the young woman; *there is* in the young woman no sin *deserving* of death, for just as when a man rises against his neighbor and kills him, even so *is* this matter. 27For he found her in the countryside, *and* the betrothed young woman cried out, but *there was* no one to save her.

28"If a man finds a young woman *who is* a virgin, who is not betrothed, and he seizes her and lies with her, and they are found out, 29then the man who lay with her shall give to the young woman's father fifty *shekels* of silver, and she shall be his wife because he has humbled her; he shall not be permitted to divorce her all his days.

30"A man shall not take his father's wife, nor uncover his father's bed.

23 "He* who is emasculated by crushing or mutilation shall not enter the assembly of the LORD.

2"One of illegitimate birth shall not enter the assembly of the LORD; even to the tenth generation none of his *descendants* shall enter the assembly of the LORD.

3"An Ammonite or Moabite shall not enter the assembly of the LORD; even to the tenth generation none of his *descendants* shall enter the assembly of the LORD forever, 4because they did not meet you with bread and water on the road when you came out of Egypt, and because they hired against you Balaam the son of Beor from Pethor of Mesopotamia,s to curse you. 5Nevertheless the LORD your God would not listen to Balaam, but the LORD your God turned the curse into a blessing for you, because the LORD your God loves you. 6You shall not seek their peace nor their prosperity all your days forever.

7"You shall not abhor an Edomite, for he *is* your brother. You shall not abhor an Egyptian, because you were an alien in his land. 8The children of the third generation born to them may enter the assembly of the LORD.

9"When the army goes out against your enemies, then keep yourself from every wicked thing. 10If there is any man among you who becomes unclean by some occurrence in the night, then he shall go outside the camp; he shall not come inside the camp. 11But it shall be, when evening comes, that he shall wash with water; and when the sun sets, he may come into the camp.

12"Also you shall have a place outside the camp, where you may go out; 13and you shall have an implement among your equipment, and when you sit down outside, you shall dig with it and turn and cover your refuse. 14*For the LORD your God walks in the midst of your camp, to deliver you and give your enemies over to you; therefore your camp shall be holy, that He may see no unclean thing among you, and turn away from you.

15"You shall not give back to his master the slave who has escaped from his master to you. 16He may dwell with you in your midst, in the place which he chooses within one of your gates, where it seems best to him; you shall not oppress him.

17*"There shall be no *ritual* harlott of the daughters of Israel, or a pervertedu one of the sons of Israel. 18You shall not bring the wages of a harlot or the price of a dog to the house of the LORD your God for any vowed offering, for both of these *are* an abomination to the LORD your God.

CHAPTER 23

23:1ff The phrase "enter the assembly," used six times in this chapter, refers to participation in religious activities rather than citizenship in the nation. God has the right to decide who shall approach Him in worship. (See Ps. 15; John 4:19–24.) Of course, in Jesus Christ, these distinctions have been removed (Gal. 3:26–29), and the gospel call is to "whoever" (Rev. 22:17).

23:14 These laws were required because God walked in the camp (v. 14); therefore, the camp had to be clean. Even matters of personal hygiene were important (vv. 9–14). Christ walks among His churches (Rev. 1:13; 2:1) and wants to see a holy people.

Verse 4 shows the sad consequences of sin, of both omission (the people did not help Israel) and commission (they hired Balaam). The kindness that we show to others, we also show to Christ (Matt. 25:31–46). One act of unkindness may bring years of sorrow.

23:17–20 Even the source of our money is God's concern (vv. 17–18). The pagan temples had religious prostitutes, male ("dogs") and female, and God would not accept their money earned by abominable means.

These miscellaneous regulations remind us that God is interested in the details of our lives. He wants us to be holy so that we may fellowship with Him (2 Cor. 6:14–18).

23:4 sHebrew *Aram Naharaim*   23:17 tHebrew *qedeshah*, feminine of *qadesh* (see following note) uHebrew *qadesh*, that is, one practicing sodomy and prostitution in religious rituals

19"You shall not charge interest to your brother—interest on money or food or anything that is lent out at interest. 20To a foreigner you may charge interest, but to your brother you shall not charge interest, that the LORD your God may bless you in all to which you set your hand in the land which you are entering to possess. 21"When you make a vow to the LORD your God, you shall not delay to pay it; for the LORD your God will surely require it of you, and it would be sin to you. 22But if you abstain from vowing, it shall not be sin to you. 23That which has gone from your lips you shall keep and perform, for you voluntarily vowed to the LORD your God what you have promised with your mouth.

24"When you come into your neighbor's vineyard, you may eat your fill of grapes at your pleasure, but you shall not put any in your container. 25When you come into your neighbor's standing grain, you may pluck the heads with your hand, but you shall not use a sickle on your neighbor's standing grain.

CHAPTER 24

24:1ff Knowing the sinfulness of the human heart, God gave these laws to promote happiness (v. 5) and to prevent oppression (v. 14) and the perversion of the law (v. 17).

24:1–5 Husbands and wives. God allowed divorced people to remarry; but this was a concession, not a commandment (Matt. 19:1–12). The divorced wife, protected by this law, could establish a new home, and she did not become a castaway. God wants happiness and holiness in our homes. We will enjoy those blessings if we obey Him and love one another.

24:6–18 Masters and servants. God sees how we treat those who depend on us for their living. We must never humiliate others because they have less money or authority than we do. When we start to get proud and insensitive, we should remember what we were before the Lord saved us (vv. 18, 22; Titus 3:3–8).

24 "When* a man takes a wife and marries her, and it happens that she finds no favor in his eyes because he has found some uncleanness in her, and he writes her a certificate of divorce, puts it in her hand, and sends her out of his house, 2when she has departed from his house, and goes and becomes another man's wife, 3if the latter husband detests her and writes her a certificate of divorce, puts it in her hand, and sends her out of his house, or if the latter husband dies who took her as his wife, 4then her former husband who divorced her must not take her back to be his wife after she has been defiled; for that is an abomination before the LORD, and you shall not bring sin on the land which the LORD your God is giving you as an inheritance.

5"When a man has taken a new wife, he shall not go out to war or be charged with any business; he shall be free at home one year, and bring happiness to his wife whom he has taken.

6*"No man shall take the lower or the upper millstone in pledge, for he takes one's living in pledge.

7"If a man is found kidnapping any of his brethren of the children of Israel, and mistreats him or sells him, then that kidnapper shall die; and you shall put away the evil from among you.

8"Take heed in an outbreak of leprosy, that you carefully observe and do according to all that the priests, the Levites, shall teach you; just as I commanded them, so you shall be careful to do. 9Remember what the LORD your God did to Miriam on the way when you came out of Egypt!

10"When you lend your brother anything, you shall not go into his house to get his pledge. 11You shall stand outside, and the man to whom you lend shall bring the pledge out to you. 12And if the man is poor, you shall not keep his pledge overnight. 13You shall in any case return the pledge to him again when the sun goes down, that he may sleep in his own garment and bless you; and it shall be righteousness to you before the LORD your God.

Helping Others—When others have needs, don't close your eyes (Prov. 28:27), your ears (Prov. 21:13), your hand, or your heart (Deut. 15:7; 1 John 3:17). Good words are not a substitute for good works (James 2:14–17; 1 John 3:18). When we share with the poor, we give to the Lord, and He sees to it that there are dividends for them and for us (Prov. 19:17).

¹⁴"You shall not oppress a hired servant *who is* poor and needy, *whether* one of your brethren or one of the aliens who *is* in your land within your gates. ¹⁵Each day you shall give *him* his wages, and not let the sun go down on it, for he *is* poor and has set his heart on it; lest he cry out against you to the LORD, and it be sin to you.

¹⁶"Fathers shall not be put to death for *their* children, nor shall children be put to death for *their* fathers; a person shall be put to death for his own sin.

¹⁷"You shall not pervert justice due the stranger or the fatherless, nor take a widow's garment as a pledge. ¹⁸But you shall remember that you were a slave in Egypt, and the LORD your God redeemed you from there; therefore I command you to do this thing.

¹⁹*"When you reap your harvest in your field, and forget a sheaf in the field, you shall not go back to get it; it shall be for the stranger, the fatherless, and the widow, that the LORD your God may bless you in all the work of your hands. ²⁰When you beat your olive trees, you shall not go over the boughs again; it shall be for the stranger, the fatherless, and the widow. ²¹When you gather the grapes of your vineyard, you shall not glean *it* afterward; it shall be for the stranger, the fatherless, and the widow. ²²And you shall remember that you were a slave in the land of Egypt; therefore I command you to do this thing.

25 "If* there is a dispute between men, and they come to court, that *the judges* may judge them, and they justify the righteous and condemn the wicked, ²then it shall be, if the wicked man deserves to be beaten, that the judge will cause him to lie down and be beaten in his presence, according to his guilt, with a certain number of blows. ³Forty blows he may give him *and* no more, lest he should exceed this and beat him with many blows above these, and your brother be humiliated in your sight.

⁴*"You shall not muzzle an ox while it treads out *the grain.*

⁵*"If brothers dwell together, and one of them dies and has no son, the widow of the dead man shall not be *married* to a stranger outside *the family;* her husband's brother shall go in to her, take her as his wife, and perform the duty of a husband's brother to her. ⁶And it shall be *that* the firstborn son which she bears will succeed to the name of his dead brother, that his name may not be blotted out of Israel. ⁷But if the man does not want to take his brother's wife, then let his brother's wife go up to the gate to the elders, and say, 'My husband's brother refuses to raise up a name to his brother in Israel; he will not perform the duty of my husband's brother.' ⁸Then the elders of his city shall call him and speak to him. But *if* he stands firm and says, 'I do not want to take her,' ⁹then his brother's wife shall come to him in the presence of the elders, remove his sandal from his foot, spit in his face, and answer and say, 'So shall it be done to the man who will not build up his brother's house.' ¹⁰And his name shall be called in Israel, 'The house of him who had his sandal removed.'

¹¹"If *two* men fight together, and the wife of one draws near to rescue her husband from the hand of the one attacking him, and puts out her hand and seizes him by the genitals, ¹²then you shall cut off her hand; your eye shall not pity *her.*

24:19–22 *Rich and poor.* God had special concern for the poor, and He depended on the generosity of His people to meet their needs. He promised to bless all who showed compassion to aliens, widows, and orphans. We should ask ourselves where we would be if others helped us to the same degree that we help others.

CHAPTER 25

25:1–3 The emphasis is on respecting people and treating them as fellow human beings, made in the image of God. It is wrong to humiliate others or take advantage of them (vv. 1–3, 11–12).

25:4 We also should have respect for animals (v. 4; see also Prov. 12:10). It would be frustrating for an ox to be in the midst of plenty and not be able to eat. The apostle Paul saw a much wider application of this verse (1 Cor. 9:1–14; 1 Tim. 5:17–18).

25:5–10 We should respect the family. This law was significant in Israel because of family and tribal inheritance. It does not apply today, but the principle is clear: the family carries on the life of the nation, and it must be protected.

25:13–16 We must have respect for truth and not be devious in our business dealings. Read Proverbs 11:1 and 20:10, and heed the warning of Proverbs 21:6.

CHAPTER 26

26:1–11 These two rituals were to be observed after the nation had entered Canaan and become an agricultural society. When they had reaped their first harvest, the people were to give the firstfruits to God to acknowledge Him as the Redeemer of the nation. God still wants us to put Him first and give Him glory for the blessings He freely bestows on us (Prov. 3:5–10).

26:12–15 They were also to present the "third-year tithe" to help support the Levites and the poor in the land. As with the ceremony of firstfruits, the people were to confess the Lord's goodness in blessing the land and giving the harvest.

13*"You shall not have in your bag differing weights, a heavy and a light. 14You shall not have in your house differing measures, a large and a small. 15You shall have a perfect and just weight, a perfect and just measure, that your days may be lengthened in the land which the LORD your God is giving you. 16For all who do such things, all who behave unrighteously, *are* an abomination to the LORD your God.

17"Remember what Amalek did to you on the way as you were coming out of Egypt, 18how he met you on the way and attacked your rear ranks, all the stragglers at your rear, when you *were* tired and weary; and he did not fear God. 19Therefore it shall be, when the LORD your God has given you rest from your enemies all around, in the land which the LORD your God is giving you to possess *as* an inheritance, *that* you will blot out the remembrance of Amalek from under heaven. You shall not forget.

26 "And* it shall be, when you come into the land which the LORD your God is giving you *as* an inheritance, and you possess it and dwell in it, 2that you shall take some of the first of all the produce of the ground, which you shall bring from your land that the LORD your God is giving you, and put *it* in a basket and go to the place where the LORD your God chooses to make His name abide. 3And you shall go to the one who is priest in those days, and say to him, 'I declare today to the LORD your God that I have come to the country which the LORD swore to our fathers to give us.'

4"Then the priest shall take the basket out of your hand and set it down before the altar of the LORD your God. 5And you shall answer and say before the LORD your God: 'My father *was* a Syrian,w about to perish, and he went down to Egypt and dwelt there, few in number; and there he became a nation, great, mighty, and populous. 6But the Egyptians mistreated us, afflicted us, and laid hard bondage on us. 7Then we cried out to the LORD God of our fathers, and the LORD heard our voice and looked on our affliction and our labor and our oppression. 8So the LORD brought us out of Egypt with a mighty hand and with an outstretched arm, with great terror and with signs and wonders. 9He has brought us to this place and has given us this land, "a land flowing with milk and honey";x 10and now, behold, I have brought the firstfruits of the land which you, O LORD, have given me.'

"Then you shall set it before the LORD your God, and worship before the LORD your God. 11So you shall rejoice in every good *thing* which the LORD your God has given to you and your house, you and the Levite and the stranger who *is* among you.

12*"When you have finished laying aside all the tithe of your increase in the third year—the year of tithing—and have given *it* to the Levite, the stranger, the fatherless, and the widow, so that they may eat within your gates and be filled, 13then you shall say before the LORD your God: 'I have removed the holy *tithe* from *my* house, and also have given them to the Levite, the stranger, the fatherless, and the widow, according

---

26:3 vSeptuagint reads *my.*   26:5 wOr *Aramean*
26:9 xExodus 3:8

to all Your commandments which You have commanded me; I have not transgressed Your commandments, nor have I forgotten *them*. 14I have not eaten any of it when in mourning, nor have I removed *any* of it for an unclean *use*, nor given *any* of it for the dead. I have obeyed the voice of the LORD my God, and have done according to all that You have commanded me. 15Look down from Your holy habitation, from heaven, and bless Your people Israel and the land which You have given us, just as You swore to our fathers, "a land flowing with milk and honey." 'y

16*"This day the LORD your God commands you to observe these statutes and judgments; therefore you shall be careful to observe them with all your heart and with all your soul. 17Today you have proclaimed the LORD to be your God, and that you will walk in His ways and keep His statutes, His commandments, and His judgments, and that you will obey His voice. 18Also today the LORD has proclaimed you to be His special people, just as He promised you, that *you* should keep all His commandments, 19and that He will set you high above all nations which He has made, in praise, in name, and in honor, and that you may be a holy people to the LORD your God, just as He has spoken."

27 Now* Moses, with the elders of Israel, commanded the people, saying: "Keep all the commandments which I command you today. 2*And it shall be, on the day when you cross over the Jordan to the land which the LORD your God is giving you, that you shall set up for yourselves large stones, and whitewash them with lime. 3You shall write on them all the words of this law, when you have crossed over, that you may enter the land which the LORD your God is giving you, 'a land flowing with milk and honey,'z just as the LORD God of your fathers promised you. 4Therefore it shall be, when you have crossed over the Jordan, *that* on Mount Ebal you shall set up these stones, which I command you today, and you shall whitewash them with lime. 5And there you shall build an altar to the LORD your God, an altar of stones; you shall not use an iron *tool* on them. 6You shall build with whole stones the altar of the LORD your God, and offer burnt offerings on it to the LORD your God. 7You shall offer peace offerings, and shall eat there, and rejoice before the LORD your God. 8And you shall write very plainly on the stones all the words of this law."

9Then Moses and the priests, the Levites, spoke to all Israel, saying, "Take heed and listen, O Israel: This day you have become the people of the LORD your God. 10Therefore you shall obey the voice of the LORD your God, and observe His commandments and His statutes which I command you today."

11And Moses commanded the people on the same day, saying, 12"These shall stand on Mount Gerizim to bless the people, when you have crossed over the Jordan: Simeon, Levi, Judah, Issachar, Joseph, and Benjamin; 13and these shall stand on Mount Ebal to curse: Reuben, Gad, Asher, Zebulun, Dan, and Naphtali.

14"And the Levites shall speak with a loud voice and say to all the men of Israel: 15*"Cursed *is* the

26:16–19 There is nothing wrong with special times of ceremony and celebration, especially when we make new beginnings. However, we must focus on worshiping God and not just observing a ceremony.

These two events remind us of the two great commandments, to love God first and then to love our neighbor. Grateful obedience is a hallmark of God's special people.

CHAPTER 27
27:1ff This ceremony was observed only once, after Israel entered the land and began to conquer it (Josh. 8:30–35). It was a solemn reminder to them that obedience to God was the secret of success (Josh. 1:8).

27:2–8 The Law was written on large stones so that everyone could read it. Today, as we read and meditate on God's Word, the Spirit writes it on our hearts and transforms us from within (2 Cor. 3:1–3, 18).

The ceremony was a renewal of the nation's covenant with God, for new beginnings deserve new acts of dedication. The burnt offering spoke of total dedication to God. The peace offerings, and the meal that followed, spoke of joyful fellowship with God.

27:15–26 The curses are related to the Law already given in the Ten Commandments and cover many aspects of personal life. Israel's obeying the Law did not deliver them from Egypt or take them into Canaan, but it did enable them to live together and enjoy the blessings of God.

None of us can wholly keep God's law or fully meet all His righteous demands. We give thanks for what Christ has done for us on the cross (Gal. 3:10–14) and what the Spirit does in our lives (Rom. 8:1–4).

26:15 yExodus 3:8   27:3 zExodus 3:8

one who makes a carved or molded image, an abomination to the LORD, the work of the hands of the craftsman, and sets *it* up in secret.'

"And all the people shall answer and say, 'Amen!'

16'Cursed *is* the one who treats his father or his mother with contempt.'

"And all the people shall say, 'Amen!'

17'Cursed *is* the one who moves his neighbor's landmark.'

"And all the people shall say, 'Amen!'

18'Cursed *is* the one who makes the blind to wander off the road.'

"And all the people shall say, 'Amen!'

19'Cursed *is* the one who perverts the justice due the stranger, the fatherless, and widow.'

"And all the people shall say, 'Amen!'

20'Cursed *is* the one who lies with his father's wife, because he has uncovered his father's bed.'

"And all the people shall say, 'Amen!'

21'Cursed *is* the one who lies with any kind of animal.'

"And all the people shall say, 'Amen!'

22'Cursed *is* the one who lies with his sister, the daughter of his father or the daughter of his mother.'

"And all the people shall say, 'Amen!'

23'Cursed *is* the one who lies with his mother-in-law.'

"And all the people shall say, 'Amen!'

24'Cursed *is* the one who attacks his neighbor secretly.'

"And all the people shall say, 'Amen!'

25'Cursed *is* the one who takes a bribe to slay an innocent person.'

"And all the people shall say, 'Amen!'

26'Cursed *is* the one who does not confirm *all* the words of this law.'

"And all the people shall say, 'Amen!' "

CHAPTER 28

28:1–14 God began with the blessings, but the major part of the address was given to the judgments. If this seems to be out of balance, just keep in mind that God knew their hearts (Deut. 5:29).

God promised to bless every area of their lives (vv. 2–6), including their political ventures (vv. 7, 13), their agriculture (vv. 8, 11–12), and their witness to the Gentiles (vv. 9–10). By being a separated and holy people, they would be a light to the Gentiles (Isa. 49:6), but they failed in their mission. Compare verse 10 with verse 25.

Obedience would lift them higher (vv. 1, 13), make them richer (vv. 3–6, 8), and keep them safer (v. 7). From a spiritual point of view, we can claim these promises today.

28 "Now* it shall come to pass, if you diligently obey the voice of the LORD your God, to observe carefully all His commandments which I command you today, that the LORD your God will set you high above all nations of the earth. 2And all these blessings shall come upon you and overtake you, because you obey the voice of the LORD your God:

3"Blessed *shall* you *be* in the city, and blessed *shall* you *be* in the country.

4"Blessed *shall be* the fruit of your body, the produce of your ground and the increase of your herds, the increase of your cattle and the offspring of your flocks.

5"Blessed *shall be* your basket and your kneading bowl.

6"Blessed *shall* you *be* when you come in, and blessed *shall* you *be* when you go out.

7"The LORD will cause your enemies who rise against you to be defeated before your face; they shall come out against you one way and flee before you seven ways.

8"The LORD will command the blessing on you in your storehouses and in all to which you set your hand, and He will bless you in the land which the LORD your God is giving you.

9"The LORD will establish you as a holy people to Himself, just as He has sworn to you, if you keep the commandments of the LORD your God and walk in His ways. 10Then all peoples of the earth shall see that you are called by the name of the LORD, and they shall be afraid of you.

11And the LORD will grant you plenty of goods, in the fruit of your body, in the increase of your livestock, and in the produce of your ground, in the land of which the LORD swore to your fathers to give you. 12The LORD will open to you His good treasure, the heavens, to give the rain to your land in its season, and to bless all the work of your hand. You shall lend to many nations, but you shall not borrow. 13And the LORD will make you the head and not the tail; you shall be above only, and not be beneath, if you heed the commandments of the LORD your God, which I command you today, and are careful to observe *them*. 14So you shall not turn aside from any of the words which I command you this day, *to* the right or the left, to go after other gods to serve them.

15*"But it shall come to pass, if you do not obey the voice of the LORD your God, to observe carefully all His commandments and His statutes which I command you today, that all these curses will come upon you and overtake you:

16"Cursed *shall* you *be* in the city, and cursed *shall* you *be* in the country.

17"Cursed *shall be* your basket and your kneading bowl.

18"Cursed *shall be* the fruit of your body and the produce of your land, the increase of your cattle and the offspring of your flocks.

19"Cursed *shall* you *be* when you come in, and cursed *shall* you *be* when you go out.

20"The LORD will send on you cursing, confusion, and rebuke in all that you set your hand to do, until you are destroyed and until you perish quickly, because of the wickedness of your doings in which you have forsaken Me. 21The LORD will make the plague cling to you until He has consumed you from the land which you are going to possess. 22The LORD will strike you with consumption, with fever, with inflammation, with severe burning fever, with the sword, with scorching, and with mildew; they shall pursue you until you perish. 23And your heavens which *are* over your head shall be bronze, and the earth which is under you *shall be* iron. 24The LORD will change the rain of your land to powder and dust; from the heaven it shall come down on you until you are destroyed.

25"The LORD will cause you to be defeated before your enemies; you shall go out one way against them and flee seven ways before them; and you shall become troublesome to all the kingdoms of the earth. 26Your carcasses shall be food for all the birds of the air and the beasts of the earth, and no one shall frighten *them* away. 27The LORD will strike you with the boils of Egypt, with tumors, with the scab, and with the itch, from which you cannot be healed. 28The LORD will strike you with madness and blindness and confusion of heart. 29And you shall grope at noonday, as a blind man gropes in darkness; you shall not prosper in your ways; you shall be only oppressed and plundered continually, and no one shall save you.

30"You shall betroth a wife, but another man shall lie with her; you shall build a house, but you shall not dwell in it; you shall plant a vineyard, but shall not gather its grapes. 31Your ox *shall be* slaughtered before your eyes, but you shall not eat of it; your donkey *shall be* violently taken away from before you, and shall not be restored to you; your sheep *shall be* given to your enemies, and you shall have no one to rescue them. 32Your sons and your daughters *shall be*

28:15–68 The curses are frightening, yet they eventually came upon the nation because the people turned from God to idols and disobeyed the Word of God. They did not *diligently* obey God, *carefully* observe His law, or *joyfully* do His will (vv. 1, 47). If we do not "serve the LORD with gladness" (Ps. 100:2), we will end up serving the enemy with sadness.

given to another people, and your eyes shall look and fail *with longing* for them all day long; and *there shall be* no strength in your hand. ³³A nation whom you have not known shall eat the fruit of your land and the produce of your labor, and you shall be only oppressed and crushed continually. ³⁴So you shall be driven mad because of the sight which your eyes see. ³⁵The LORD will strike you in the knees and on the legs with severe boils which cannot be healed, and from the sole of your foot to the top of your head.

³⁶"The LORD will bring you and the king whom you set over you to a nation which neither you nor your fathers have known, and there you shall serve other gods—wood and stone. ³⁷And you shall become an astonishment, a proverb, and a byword among all nations where the LORD will drive you.

³⁸"You shall carry much seed out to the field but gather little in, for the locust shall consume it. ³⁹You shall plant vineyards and tend *them,* but you shall neither drink *of* the wine nor gather the *grapes;* for the worms shall eat them. ⁴⁰You shall have olive trees throughout all your territory, but you shall not anoint *yourself* with the oil; for your olives shall drop off. ⁴¹You shall beget sons and daughters, but they shall not be yours; for they shall go into captivity. ⁴²Locusts shall consume all your trees and the produce of your land.

⁴³"The alien who *is* among you shall rise higher and higher above you, and you shall come down lower and lower. ⁴⁴He shall lend to you, but you shall not lend to him; he shall be the head, and you shall be the tail.

⁴⁵"Moreover all these curses shall come upon you and pursue and overtake you, until you are destroyed, because you did not obey the voice of the LORD your God, to keep His commandments and His statutes which He commanded you. ⁴⁶And they shall be upon you for a sign and a wonder, and on your descendants forever.

⁴⁷"Because you did not serve the LORD your God with joy and gladness of heart, for the abundance of everything, ⁴⁸therefore you shall serve your enemies, whom the LORD will send against you, in hunger, in thirst, in nakedness, and in need of everything; and He will put a yoke of iron on your neck until He has destroyed you. ⁴⁹The LORD will bring a nation against you from afar, from the end of the earth, *as swift* as the eagle flies, a nation whose language you will not understand, ⁵⁰a nation of fierce countenance, which does not respect the elderly nor show favor to the young. ⁵¹And they shall eat the increase of your livestock and the produce of your land, until you are destroyed; they shall not leave you grain or new wine or oil, *or* the increase of your cattle or the offspring of your flocks, until they have destroyed you.

⁵²"They shall besiege you at all your gates until your high and fortified walls, in which you trust, come down throughout all your land; and they shall besiege you at all your gates throughout all your land which the LORD your God has given you. ⁵³You shall eat the fruit of your own body, the flesh of your sons and your daughters whom the LORD your God has given you, in the siege and desperate straits in which your enemy shall distress you. ⁵⁴The sensitive and very refined man among you will be hostile toward his brother, toward the wife of his bosom, and toward the rest of his children whom he leaves behind, ⁵⁵so that

he will not give any of them the flesh of his children whom he will eat, because he has nothing left in the siege and desperate straits in which your enemy shall distress you at all your gates. 56The tender and delicate woman among you, who would not venture to set the sole of her foot on the ground because of her delicateness and sensitivity, will refuse*a* to the husband of her bosom, and to her son and her daughter, 57her placenta which comes out from between her feet and her children whom she bears; for she will eat them secretly for lack of everything in the siege and desperate straits in which your enemy shall distress you at all your gates.

58"If you do not carefully observe all the words of this law that are written in this book, that you may fear this glorious and awesome name, THE LORD YOUR GOD, 59then the LORD will bring upon you and your descendants extraordinary plagues—great and prolonged plagues—and serious and prolonged sicknesses. 60Moreover He will bring back on you all the diseases of Egypt, of which you were afraid, and they shall cling to you. 61Also every sickness and every plague, which *is* not written in this Book of the Law, will the LORD bring upon you until you are destroyed. 62You shall be left few in number, whereas you were as the stars of heaven in multitude, because you would not obey the voice of the LORD your God. 63And it shall be, *that* just as the LORD rejoiced over you to do you good and multiply you, so the LORD will rejoice over you to destroy you and bring you to nothing; and you shall be plucked from off the land which you go to possess.

64"Then the LORD will scatter you among all peoples, from one end of the earth to the other, and there you shall serve other gods, which neither you nor your fathers have known—wood and stone. 65And among those nations you shall find no rest, nor shall the sole of your foot have a resting place; but there the LORD will give you a trembling heart, failing eyes, and anguish of soul. 66Your life shall hang in doubt before you; you shall fear day and night, and have no assurance of life. 67In the morning you shall say, 'Oh, that it were evening!' And at evening you shall say, 'Oh, that it were morning!' because of the fear which terrifies your heart, and because of the sight which your eyes see. 68"And the LORD will take you back to Egypt in ships, by the way of which I said to you, 'You shall never see it again.' And there you shall be offered for sale to your enemies as male and female slaves, but no one will buy you."

29 These* *are* the words of the covenant which the LORD commanded Moses to make with the children of Israel in the land of Moab, besides the covenant which He made with them in Horeb.

2*Now Moses called all Israel and said to them: "You have seen all that the LORD did before your eyes in the land of Egypt, to Pharaoh and to all his servants and to all his land— 3the great trials which your eyes have seen, the signs, and those great wonders. 4Yet the LORD has not given you a heart to perceive and eyes to see and ears to hear, to this *very* day. 5And I have led you forty years in the wilderness. Your clothes have not worn out on you, and your sandals have not worn

---

28:56 *a*Literally *her eye shall be evil toward*

CHAPTER 29

29:1ff It is a serious thing to enter into a covenant with the Lord. He will keep His part of the agreement, but we are prone to disobey. If we are to be faithful, we need spiritual renewal for our eyes, ears, and hearts (v. 4). We need to see His hand at work, hear His Word, and love Him with all our hearts.

29:2–6 For forty years, the people saw miracles and heard words, yet they did not perceive what God was doing. They saw His acts but did not understand His ways (Ps. 103:7). They had seen God defeat the idols of Egypt, yet they still had idolatry in their hearts. What could have been spiritual experiences was only a series of historical events because they did not focus on the Lord.

out on your feet. 6You have not eaten bread, nor have you drunk wine or *similar* drink, that you may know that I *am* the LORD your God. 7And when you came to this place, Sihon king of Heshbon and Og king of Bashan came out against us to battle, and we conquered them. 8We took their land and gave it as an inheritance to the Reubenites, to the Gadites, and to half the tribe of Manasseh. 9Therefore keep the words of this covenant, and do them, that you may prosper in all that you do.

10"All of you stand today before the LORD your God: your leaders and your tribes and your elders and your officers, all the men of Israel, 11your little ones and your wives—also the stranger who *is* in your camp, from the one who cuts your wood to the one who draws your water— 12that you may enter into covenant with the LORD your God, and into His oath, which the LORD your God makes with you today, 13that He may establish you today as a people for Himself, and *that* He may be God to you, just as He has spoken to you, and just as He has sworn to your fathers, to Abraham, Isaac, and Jacob.

14"I make this covenant and this oath, not with you alone, 15but with *him* who stands here with us today before the LORD our God, as well as with *him* who *is* not here with us today 16(for you know that we dwelt in the land of Egypt and that we came through the nations which you passed by, 17and you saw their abominations and their idols which *were* among them—wood and stone and silver and gold); 18so that there may not be among you man or woman or family or tribe, whose heart turns away today from the LORD our God, to go *and* serve the gods of these nations, and that there may not be among you a root bearing bitterness or wormwood; 19and so it may not happen, when he hears the words of this curse, that he blesses himself in his heart, saying, 'I shall have peace, even though I follow the dictates[b] of my heart'—as though the drunkard could be included with the sober.

20"The LORD would not spare him; for then the anger of the LORD and His jealousy would burn against that man, and every curse that is written in this book would settle on him, and the LORD would blot out his name from under heaven. 21And the LORD would separate him from all the tribes of Israel for adversity, according to all the curses of the covenant that are written in this Book of the Law, 22so that the coming generation of your children who rise up after you, and the foreigner who comes from a far land, would say, when they see the plagues of that land and the sicknesses which the LORD has laid on it:

23'The whole land *is* brimstone, salt, and burning; it is not sown, nor does it bear, nor does any grass grow there, like the overthrow of Sodom and Gomorrah, Admah, and Zeboiim, which the LORD overthrew in His anger and His wrath.' 24All nations would say, 'Why has the LORD done so to this land? What does the heat of this great anger mean?' 25Then *people* would say: 'Because they have forsaken the covenant of the LORD God of their fathers, which He made with them when He brought them out of the land of Egypt; 26for they went and served other gods and worshiped them, gods that they did not know and that He

---

29:19 [b]Or *stubbornness*

had not given to them. 27Then the anger of the LORD was aroused against this land, to bring on it every curse that is written in this book. 28And the LORD uprooted them from their land in anger, in wrath, and in great indignation, and cast them into another land, as *it is* this day.'

29*"The secret *things belong* to the LORD our God, but those *things which are* revealed *belong* to us and to our children forever, that *we* may do all the words of this law.

30 "Now* it shall come to pass, when all these things come upon you, the blessing and the curse which I have set before you, and you call *them* to mind among all the nations where the LORD your God drives you, 2and you return to the LORD your God and obey His voice, according to all that I command you today, you and your children, with all your heart and with all your soul, 3that the LORD your God will bring you back from captivity, and have compassion on you, and gather you again from all the nations where the LORD your God has scattered you. 4If *any* of you are driven out to the farthest *parts* under heaven, from there the LORD your God will gather you, and from there He will bring you. 5Then the LORD your God will bring you to the land which your fathers possessed, and you shall possess it. He will prosper you and multiply you more than your fathers. 6And the LORD your God will circumcise your heart and the heart of your descendants, to love the LORD your God with all your heart and with all your soul, that you may live.

7"Also the LORD your God will put all these curses on your enemies and on those who hate you, who persecuted you. 8And you will again obey the voice of the LORD and do all His commandments which I command you today. 9The LORD your God will make you abound in all the work of your hand, in the fruit of your body, in the increase of your livestock, and in the produce of your land for good. For the LORD will again rejoice over you for good as He rejoiced over your fathers, 10if you obey the voice of the LORD your God, to keep His commandments and His statutes which are written in this Book of the Law, *and if* you turn to the LORD your God with all your heart and with all your soul.

11*"For this commandment which I command you today *is* not *too* mysterious for you, nor *is* it far off. 12It *is* not in heaven, that you should say, 'Who will ascend into heaven for us and bring it to us, that we may hear it and do it?' 13Nor *is* it beyond the sea, that you should say, 'Who will go over the sea for us and bring it to us, that we may hear it and do it?' 14But the word *is* very near you, in your mouth and in your heart, that you may do it.

15"See, I have set before you today life and good, death and evil, 16in that I command you today to love the LORD your God, to walk in His ways, and to keep His commandments, His statutes, and His judgments, that you may live and multiply; and the LORD your God will bless you in the land which you go to possess. 17But if your heart turns away so that you do not hear, and are drawn away, and worship other gods and serve them, 18I announce to you today that you shall surely perish; you shall not prolong *your* days in the land which you cross over the Jordan to go in and possess. 19I call heaven and earth as witnesses today against you, *that* I have set before

29:29 Our responsibility is to obey what we know and not pry into what we do not know (v. 29). Ponder Matthew 13:10–17, and then examine your spiritual perception.

CHAPTER 30

30:1–10 The purpose of chastening is restoration, not ruination. God knows what His people will do, so He makes provision for them to repent and return. He has done this for His people today (1 John 1:5—2:2).

Note the repetition of the little word *all*. God will send *all* His judgments among His people in *all* the nations (v. 1), so that with *all* their hearts and souls they will obey *all* He has commanded (v. 2). If we fail to deal with any sin, or if we ignore any word from God, our repentance will be incomplete.

30:11–20 The heart needs "spiritual surgery" if it is to love the Lord and obey Him (v. 6; Deut. 10:16; Jer. 4:4; Rom. 2:25–29). Every child of God has experienced this (Col. 2:11) and, by faith, can live victoriously. When we receive the Word in our hearts (vv. 11–14), we have both the desire and the dynamic to obey God and glorify Him. The heart of victory is the heart!

CHAPTER 31

31:1-3 Moses could have closed his life under a dark cloud of discouragement. Instead, he gave encouragement to his people as they faced the challenge of a new life in a new land under a new leader.

31:3-6 He encouraged *the people* (vv. 1-6) not to be afraid of the enemy because the Lord would go before them and give them victory. He gave a similar word of encouragement to *Joshua* (vv. 7-8). It would not be easy for Joshua to take the place of a great man like Moses, but he still had the God of Moses as his help.

31:9-13 Moses encouraged *the Levites* (vv. 9-13, 24-29) to protect and proclaim the Word of God and to teach it to the whole nation. If Israel did not enjoy the Word, they could not enjoy the blessings of God in their inheritance.

you life and death, blessing and cursing; therefore choose life, that both you and your descendants may live; 20that you may love the LORD your God, that you may obey His voice, and that you may cling to Him, for He *is* your life and the length of your days; and that you may dwell in the land which the LORD swore to your fathers, to Abraham, Isaac, and Jacob, to give them.''

31 Then* Moses went and spoke these words to all Israel. 2And he said to them: "I *am* one hundred and twenty years old today. I can no longer go out and come in. Also the LORD has said to me, 'You shall not cross over this Jordan.' 3*The LORD your God Himself crosses over before you; He will destroy these nations from before you, and you shall dispossess them. Joshua himself crosses over before you, just as the LORD has said. 4And the LORD will do to them as He did to Sihon and Og, the kings of the Amorites and their land, when He destroyed them. 5The LORD will give them over to you, that you may do to them according to every commandment which I have commanded you. 6Be strong and of good courage, do not fear nor be afraid of them; for the LORD your God, He *is* the One who goes with you. He will not leave you nor forsake you.''

7Then Moses called Joshua and said to him in the sight of all Israel, "Be strong and of good courage, for you must go with this people to the land which the LORD has sworn to their fathers to give them, and you shall cause them to inherit it. 8And the LORD, He *is* the One who goes before you. He will be with you, He will not leave you nor forsake you; do not fear nor be dismayed.''

9*So Moses wrote this law and delivered it to the priests, the sons of Levi, who bore the ark of the covenant of the LORD, and to all the elders of Israel. 10And Moses commanded them, saying: "At the end of *every* seven years, at the appointed time in the year of release, at the Feast of Tabernacles, 11when all Israel comes to appear before the LORD your God in the place which He chooses, you shall read this law before all Israel in their hearing. 12Gather the people together, men and women and little ones, and the stranger who *is* within your gates, that they may hear and that they may learn to fear the LORD your God and carefully observe all the words of this law, 13and *that* their children, who have not known it, may hear and learn to fear the LORD your God as long as you live in the land which you cross the Jordan to possess.''

14Then the LORD said to Moses, "Behold, the days approach when you must die; call Joshua, and present yourselves in the tabernacle of meeting, that I may inaugurate him.''

So Moses and Joshua went and presented themselves in the tabernacle of meeting. 15Now the LORD appeared at the tabernacle in a pillar of cloud, and the pillar of cloud stood above the door of the tabernacle.

16And the LORD said to Moses: "Behold, you will rest with your fathers; and this people will rise and play the harlot with the gods of the foreigners of the land, where they go *to be* among them, and they will forsake Me and break My covenant which I have made with them. 17Then My anger shall be aroused against them in that day, and I will forsake them, and I will hide My face from them, and they shall be devoured. And many evils and troubles shall befall them, so that they will say in that day, 'Have not these evils come upon us because our God *is* not among us?' 18And I will surely hide My face in that day because of all the evil which they have done, in that they have turned to other gods.

19"Now therefore, write down this song for yourselves, and teach it to the children of Israel; put it in their mouths, that this song may be a witness for Me against the children of Israel. 20When I have brought them to the land flowing with milk and honey, of which I swore to their fathers, and they have eaten and filled themselves and grown fat, then they will turn to other gods and serve them; and they will provoke Me and break My covenant. 21Then it shall be, when many evils and troubles have come upon them, that this song will testify against them as a witness; for it will not be forgotten in the mouths of their descendants, for I know the inclination of their behavior today, even before I have brought them to the land of which I swore *to give them.*"

22Therefore Moses wrote this song the same day, and taught it to the children of Israel. 23*Then He inaugurated Joshua the son of Nun, and said, "Be strong and of good courage; for you shall bring the children of Israel into the land of which I swore to them, and I will be with you."

24So it was, when Moses had completed writing the words of this law in a book, when they were finished, 25that Moses commanded the Levites, who bore the ark of the covenant of the LORD, saying: 26"Take this Book of the Law, and put it beside the ark of the covenant of the LORD your God, that it may be there as a witness against you; 27for I know your rebellion and your stiff neck. *If* today, while I am yet alive with you, you have been rebellious against the LORD, then how much more after my death? 28Gather to me all the elders of your tribes, and your officers, that I may speak these words in their hearing and call heaven and earth to witness against them. 29For I know that after my death you will become utterly corrupt, and turn aside from the way which I have commanded you. And evil will befall you in the latter days, because you will do evil in the sight of the LORD, to provoke Him to anger through the work of your hands."

30Then Moses spoke in the hearing of all the assembly of Israel the words of this song until they were ended:

32 "Give* ear, O heavens, and I will speak;
And hear, O earth, the words of my
mouth.
2   Let my teaching drop as the rain,
My speech distill as the dew,
As raindrops on the tender herb,
And as showers on the grass.
3   For I proclaim the name of the LORD:
Ascribe greatness to our God.
4   *He is* the Rock, His work *is* perfect;
For all His ways *are* justice,
A God of truth and without injustice;
Righteous and upright *is* He.

5   "They have corrupted themselves;
They are not His children,
Because of their blemish:
A perverse and crooked generation.
6   Do you thus deal with the LORD,
O foolish and unwise people?

31:23 God changes His workers, but His work goes on. No matter who our spiritual leaders are, we must love the Lord and live according to His Word. That is the secret of blessing and success. It is also the secret of being an encouragement to others.

CHAPTER 32

32:1–3 God gave Moses this song to teach the people so that they would learn to love and obey Him (Deut. 31:19–30). Our songs today should follow this pattern by revealing the greatness and goodness of the Lord and thus encouraging us to live for Him (v. 3).

32:4 The key image for God is "the Rock." It speaks of His stability in a changing world and His dependability in a demanding world (v. 4). The Rock is our Savior (v. 15), Father (v. 18), and Deliverer (vv. 30–31). He is all that we need.

Is He not your Father, *who* bought you?
Has He not made you and established you?

7　"Remember the days of old,
Consider the years of many generations.
Ask your father, and he will show you;
Your elders, and they will tell you:
8　When the Most High divided their
inheritance to the nations,
When He separated the sons of Adam,
He set the boundaries of the peoples
According to the number of the children of
Israel.
9　For the LORD's portion *is* His people;
Jacob *is* the place of His inheritance.

10　"He found him in a desert land
And in the wasteland, a howling wilderness;
He encircled him, He instructed him,
He kept him as the apple of His eye.
11　*As an eagle stirs up its nest,
Hovers over its young,
Spreading out its wings, taking them up,
Carrying them on its wings,
12　So the LORD alone led him,
And *there was* no foreign god with him.

13　"He made him ride in the heights of the earth,
That he might eat the produce of the fields;
He made him draw honey from the rock,
And oil from the flinty rock;
14　Curds from the cattle, and milk of the flock,
With fat of lambs;
And rams of the breed of Bashan, and goats,
With the choicest wheat;
And you drank wine, the blood of the
grapes.

15　"But Jeshurun grew fat and kicked;
You grew fat, you grew thick,
You are obese!
Then he forsook God *who* made him,
And scornfully esteemed the Rock of his
salvation.
16　They provoked Him to jealousy with foreign
gods;
With abominations they provoked Him to
anger.
17　They sacrificed to demons, not to God,
To gods they did not know,
To new *gods,* new arrivals
That your fathers did not fear.
18　Of the Rock *who* begot you, you are
unmindful,
And have forgotten the God who fathered
you.

19　"And when the LORD saw *it,* He spurned
them,
Because of the provocation of His sons and
His daughters.
20　And He said: 'I will hide My face from them,
I will see what their end *will be,*
For they *are* a perverse generation,
Children in whom *is* no faith.
21　They have provoked Me to jealousy by *what*
is not God;
They have moved Me to anger by their
foolish idols.
But I will provoke them to jealousy by *those*
who are not a nation;

32:11–14 Israel is compared to young eagles that must leave the nest and learn how to fly (vv. 11–12). But Israel is also God's treasure, and He will protect His people (vv. 34–35). Moses reminded them not to forget their beginning (v. 18) or ignore their "latter end" (v. 29). Moses compared God's Word to the rain and the dew (v. 2), which come down from heaven and bring life and refreshment to the earth. Much sharing of the Word may seem to be a waste, but the Word accomplishes God's purposes whether we see it or not (Isa. 55:10–11).

I will move them to anger by a foolish
 nation.
22 For a fire is kindled in My anger,
 And shall burn to the lowest hell;
 It shall consume the earth with her increase,
 And set on fire the foundations of the
  mountains.

23 'I will heap disasters on them;
 I will spend My arrows on them.
24 *They shall be* wasted with hunger,
 Devoured by pestilence and bitter
  destruction;
 I will also send against them the teeth of
  beasts,
 With the poison of serpents of the dust.
25 The sword shall destroy outside;
 There shall be terror within
 For the young man and virgin,
 The nursing child with the man of gray
  hairs.
26 I would have said, "I will dash them in
  pieces,
 I will make the memory of them to cease
  from among men,"
27 Had I not feared the wrath of the enemy,
 Lest their adversaries should
  misunderstand,
 Lest they should say, "Our hand *is* high;
 And it is not the LORD who has done all
  this." '

28 "For they *are* a nation void of counsel,
 Nor *is there any* understanding in them.
29 Oh, that they were wise, *that* they
  understood this,
 That they would consider their latter end!
30 How could one chase a thousand,
 And two put ten thousand to flight,
 Unless their Rock had sold them,
 And the LORD had surrendered them?
31 For their rock *is* not like our Rock,
 Even our enemies themselves *being* judges.
32 For their vine *is* of the vine of Sodom
 And of the fields of Gomorrah;
 Their grapes *are* grapes of gall,
 Their clusters *are* bitter.
33 Their wine *is* the poison of serpents,
 And the cruel venom of cobras.

34 'Is this not laid up in store with Me,
 Sealed up among My treasures?
35 Vengeance is Mine, and recompense;
 Their foot shall slip in *due* time;
 For the day of their calamity *is* at hand,
 And the things to come hasten upon them.'

36*"For the LORD will judge His people
 And have compassion on His servants,
 When He sees that *their* power is gone,
 And *there is* no one *remaining,* bond or free.
37 He will say: 'Where *are* their gods,
 The rock in which they sought refuge?
38 Who ate the fat of their sacrifices,
 And drank the wine of their drink offering?
 Let them rise and help you,
 And be your refuge.

39 'Now see that I, *even* I, *am* He,
 And *there is* no God besides Me;
 I kill and I make alive;
 I wound and I heal;

32:36–43 Much of this song is a warning
to the people that they were prone to forget
what God did for them and to turn from God
to idols. We do not know how often they
sang this song, but we do know that they
did not take it to heart. Do God's people
today pay attention to what they are singing?

Nor *is there any* who can deliver from My
 hand.
40 For I raise My hand to heaven,
 And say, *"As* I live forever,
41 If I whet My glittering sword,
 And My hand takes hold on judgment,
 I will render vengeance to My enemies,
 And repay those who hate Me.
42 I will make My arrows drunk with blood,
 And My sword shall devour flesh,
 With the blood of the slain and the captives,
 From the heads of the leaders of the
 enemy." '

43 "Rejoice, O Gentiles, *with* His people;[c]
 For He will avenge the blood of His
 servants,
 And render vengeance to His adversaries;
 He will provide atonement for His land *and*
 His people."

44So Moses came with Joshua[d] the son of Nun
and spoke all the words of this song in the hearing
of the people. 45Moses finished speaking all these
words to all Israel, 46and he said to them: "Set
your hearts on all the words which I testify among
you today, which you shall command your children to be careful to observe—all the words of
this law. 47For it *is* not a futile thing for you, because it *is* your life, and by this word you shall
prolong *your* days in the land which you cross
over the Jordan to possess."

48Then the LORD spoke to Moses that very same
day, saying: 49"Go up this mountain of the
Abarim, Mount Nebo, which *is* in the land of
Moab, across from Jericho; view the land of Canaan, which I give to the children of Israel as a
possession; 50and die on the mountain which you
ascend, and be gathered to your people, just as
Aaron your brother died on Mount Hor and was
gathered to his people; 51because you trespassed
against Me among the children of Israel at the
waters of Meribah Kadesh, in the Wilderness of
Zin, because you did not hallow Me in the midst
of the children of Israel. 52Yet you shall see the
land before you, though you shall not go there,
into the land which I am giving to the children
of Israel."

CHAPTER 33

33:1–29 Before viewing the land, Moses
viewed the future and told the tribes what
lay ahead. When Jacob gave his blessing
before he died, he revealed some of the sins
of his sons (Gen. 49), but Moses did not
do that. Instead, he focused primarily on the
relationship of the tribes with the Lord and
how each one would have a distinctive
character, blessing, and ministry.
 God's people are privileged to be in His
hand for safekeeping (John 10:28–29) and
at His feet for learning and obeying (v. 3).
 We are "between His shoulders," next to
His heart (v. 12), and He bears us with His
"everlasting arms" (v. 27). What more could
we want?

33 Now* this *is* the blessing with which Moses
the man of God blessed the children of Israel before his death. 2And he said:

"The LORD came from Sinai,
 And dawned on them from Seir;
 He shone forth from Mount Paran,
 And He came with ten thousands of saints;
 From His right hand
 Came a fiery law for them.
3 Yes, He loves the people;
 All His saints *are* in Your hand;
 They sit down at Your feet;
 Everyone receives Your words.
4 Moses commanded a law for us,
 A heritage of the congregation of Jacob.

32:43 [c]A Dead Sea Scroll fragment adds *And let all the gods
(angels) worship Him* (compare Septuagint and Hebrews 1:6).
32:44 [d]Hebrew *Hoshea* (compare Numbers 13:8, 16)

5   And He was King in Jeshurun,
     When the leaders of the people were
          gathered,
     All the tribes of Israel together.

6   "Let Reuben live, and not die,
     Nor let his men be few."

7And this he said of Judah:

     "Hear, LORD, the voice of Judah,
     And bring him to his people;
     Let his hands be sufficient for him,
     And may You be a help against his
          enemies."

8And of Levi he said:

     "*Let* Your Thummim and Your Urim *be* with
          Your holy one,
     Whom You tested at Massah,
     And with whom You contended at the
          waters of Meribah,
9   Who says of his father and mother,
     'I have not seen them';
     Nor did he acknowledge his brothers,
     Or know his own children;
     For they have observed Your word
     And kept Your covenant.
10   They shall teach Jacob Your judgments,
     And Israel Your law.
     They shall put incense before You,
     And a whole burnt sacrifice on Your altar.
11   Bless his substance, LORD,
     And accept the work of his hands;
     Strike the loins of those who rise against
          him,
     And of those who hate him, that they rise
          not again."

12Of Benjamin he said:

     "The beloved of the LORD shall dwell in safety
          by Him,
     Who shelters him all the day long;
     And he shall dwell between His shoulders."

13And of Joseph he said:

     "Blessed of the LORD *is* his land,
     With the precious things of heaven, with the
          dew,
     And the deep lying beneath,
14   With the precious fruits of the sun,
     With the precious produce of the months,
15   With the best things of the ancient
          mountains,
     With the precious things of the everlasting
          hills,
16   With the precious things of the earth and
          its fullness,
     And the favor of Him who dwelt in the bush.
     Let *the blessing* come 'on the head of
          Joseph,
     And on the crown of the head of him *who
          was* separate from his brothers.'*e*
17   His glory *is like* a firstborn bull,
     And his horns *like* the horns of the wild ox;

33:16 *e*Genesis 49:26

Together with them
He shall push the peoples
To the ends of the earth;
They *are* the ten thousands of Ephraim,
And they *are* the thousands of Manasseh."

18And of Zebulun he said:

"Rejoice, Zebulun, in your going out,
And Issachar in your tents!
19 They shall call the peoples *to* the mountain;
There they shall offer sacrifices of
    righteousness;
For they shall partake *of* the abundance of
    the seas
And *of* treasures hidden in the sand."

20And of Gad he said:

"Blessed *is* he who enlarges Gad;
He dwells as a lion,
And tears the arm and the crown of his
    head.
21 He provided the first *part* for himself,
Because a lawgiver's portion was reserved
    there.
He came *with* the heads of the people;
He administered the justice of the LORD,
And His judgments with Israel."

22And of Dan he said:

"Dan *is* a lion's whelp;
He shall leap from Bashan."

23And of Naphtali he said:

"O Naphtali, satisfied with favor,
And full of the blessing of the LORD,
Possess the west and the south."

24And of Asher he said:

"Asher *is* most blessed of sons;
Let him be favored by his brothers,
And let him dip his foot in oil.
25 *Your sandals *shall be* iron and bronze;
As your days, *so shall* your strength *be.*

26 "*There is* no one like the God of Jeshurun,
Who rides the heavens to help you,
And in His excellency on the clouds.
27 The eternal God *is your* refuge,
And underneath *are* the everlasting arms;
He will thrust out the enemy from before
    you,
And will say, 'Destroy!'
28 Then Israel shall dwell in safety,
The fountain of Jacob alone,
In a land of grain and new wine;
His heavens shall also drop dew.
29 Happy *are* you, O Israel!
Who *is* like you, a people saved by the LORD,
The shield of your help
And the sword of your majesty!
Your enemies shall submit to you,
And you shall tread down their high
    places."

33:25 Verse 25 is a good reminder to live a day at a time, as all creation lives (Matt. 6:25–34). The best way to destroy *today* is to regret *yesterday* and worry about *tomorrow*. Israel faced some difficult days, but God would be with them and help them *a day at a time.*

34 Then Moses went up from the plains of Moab to Mount Nebo, to the top of Pisgah, which is across from Jericho. And the LORD

showed him all the land of Gilead as far as Dan, [2]all Naphtali and the land of Ephraim and Manasseh, all the land of Judah as far as the Western Sea,[f] [3]the South, and the plain of the Valley of Jericho, the city of palm trees, as far as Zoar. [4]Then the LORD said to him, "This *is* the land of which I swore to give Abraham, Isaac, and Jacob, saying, 'I will give it to your descendants.' I have caused you to see *it* with your eyes, but you shall not cross over there."

[5]*So Moses the servant of the LORD died there in the land of Moab, according to the word of the LORD. [6]And He buried him in a valley in the land of Moab, opposite Beth Peor; but no one knows his grave to this day. [7]Moses *was* one hundred and twenty years old when he died. His eyes were not dim nor his natural vigor diminished. [8]And the children of Israel wept for Moses in the plains of Moab thirty days. So the days of weeping *and* mourning for Moses ended.

[9]Now Joshua the son of Nun was full of the spirit of wisdom, for Moses had laid his hands on him; so the children of Israel heeded him, and did as the LORD had commanded Moses.

[10]*But since then there has not arisen in Israel a prophet like Moses, whom the LORD knew face to face, [11]in all the signs and wonders which the LORD sent him to do in the land of Egypt, before Pharaoh, before all his servants, and in all his land, [12]and by all that mighty power and all the great terror which Moses performed in the sight of all Israel.

34:2 [f]That is, the Mediterranean

CHAPTER 34

34:5–8 When your time comes to die, the important thing is not the grandeur of your funeral but the greatness of your life. In fact, how you live now will determine how you will die then.

Moses lived in the heights, and he died in the heights. He often met God on the mountain, saw His glory, and experienced His grace. Keep your mind and heart "in the heavenlies" as you live on earth (Col. 3:1ff.).

34:10–12 Moses lived in God's will and died in God's will. You never have to fear life or death if you walk in obedience to the Lord. Moses died "the death of the righteous" (Num. 23:10) because he lived the life of the righteous.

Finally, Moses lived with a forward vision, and he died with a forward vision as he viewed the Promised Land. The nation so often wanted to go back to Egypt, but he challenged them to go forward to the inheritance God prepared for them.

It is good to plan your funeral, but it is also good to live your life in such a way that you will be missed when you are gone.

THE BOOKS OF HISTORY

The books of Joshua through Esther record key events in the history of Israel: their conquest of Canaan (Joshua); compromise with the enemy (Judges); the establishment of the kingdom, ending with a divided nation (1 and 2 Samuel—2 Chronicles); the captivity; and the return from exile (Ezra—Esther).

Israel's besetting sin was idolatry, and these books record the decay of the nation both politically and spiritually because the people turned away from God and His Word. Throughout the turbulent history, God was faithful to His people, sending them prophets to call them to repentance and helping them in their crises. But the people repeatedly turned away from God to serve heathen idols, and the Lord finally had to chasten them and send them into captivity. God preserved His people so that He might send the promised Redeemer and fulfill His covenant to Abraham that through Israel all nations would be blessed.

Political systems change, as do means of war and international diplomacy, but human nature is the same today as in the days of Joshua, David, Solomon, and Hezekiah. As you read the history of Israel, you will discover how contemporary it really is: "Righteousness exalts a nation, but sin is a reproach to any people" (Prov. 14:34).

JOSHUA

The book of Joshua records the dedication of the nation (chaps. 1—5), the defeat of the enemy (chaps. 6—12), and the division of the land (chaps. 13—24). Joshua leads Israel from victory to victory as they follow the Lord and claim their promised inheritance.

The man Joshua is a picture of our Lord Jesus Christ who won the victory over sin and Satan and who gives rest to those who trust Him (Heb. 4; Matt. 11:28–30). Joshua knew that he was second in command (Josh. 5:13–15), and his career illustrates the victory we have through faith (1 John 5:1–5). Each of us has a spiritual inheritance to claim, a "land" to conquer, and Joshua tells us how to do it. The word *inheritance* is used fifty-eight times in Joshua. (See Eph. 1:11; Col. 1:12.)

1 After* the death of Moses the servant of the LORD, it came to pass that the LORD spoke to Joshua the son of Nun, Moses' assistant, saying: 2"Moses My servant is dead. Now therefore, arise, go over this Jordan, you and all this people, to the land which I am giving to them—the children of Israel. 3Every place that the sole of your foot will tread upon I have given you, as I said to Moses. 4From the wilderness and this Lebanon as far as the great river, the River Euphrates, all the land of the Hittites, and to the Great Sea toward the going down of the sun, shall be your territory. 5*No man shall *be able to* stand before you all the days of your life; as I was with Moses, *so* I will be with you. I will not leave you nor forsake you. 6*Be strong and of good courage, for to this people you shall divide as an inheritance the land which I swore to their fathers to give them. 7Only be strong and very courageous, that you may observe to do according to all the law which Moses My servant commanded you; do not turn from it to the right hand or to the left, that you may prosper wherever you go. 8This Book of the Law shall not depart from your mouth, but you shall meditate in it day and night, that you may observe to do according to all that is written in it. For then you will make your way prosperous, and then you will have good success. 9Have I not commanded you? Be strong and of good courage; do not be afraid, nor be dismayed, for the LORD your God *is* with you wherever you go."

10Then Joshua commanded the officers of the people, saying, 11"Pass through the camp and command the people, saying, 'Prepare provisions for yourselves, for within three days you will cross over this Jordan, to go in to possess the land which the LORD your God is giving you to possess.' "

12And to the Reubenites, the Gadites, and half the tribe of Manasseh Joshua spoke, saying, 13"Remember the word which Moses the servant of the LORD commanded you, saying, 'The LORD your God is giving you rest and is giving you this

CHAPTER 1

1:1–4 God equips us. Joshua was not in an easy situation, facing a difficult assignment and replacing a great leader like Moses. But God had equipped him and prepared him for this very work. Joshua had faithfully served with Moses and was now qualified to lead. The task that you faithfully do today gets you ready for what God is preparing for you (Matt. 25:21).

1:5–18 God encourages us. The inheritance can be claimed only by the obedience of faith (v. 3), but faith and obedience demand courage. God encouraged Joshua by giving His promise (v. 6) and the assurance of His presence (v. 9) and by reminding him that his success came from the Word (vv. 7–8). God also encouraged Joshua through the people (vv. 16–18). Are you an encouragement to your leaders?

1:6–18 God enables us. "Be strong!" is much more than an admonition (vv. 6, 7, 18), for God's commandments are God's enablements. It was not Joshua's experience or skill that brought the victory; more than once, he was defeated. The victory came from the power of God that was released when they obeyed Him by faith. God still does the impossible (Luke 1:37)!

Joshua—Training for Leadership—Joshua did not seek a place of leadership, but he was called and trained by God to be successor to Moses. Joshua knew the rigors of slavery in Egypt. He also knew how to obey orders as he served with Moses (Exod. 24:13). He had courage to face the enemy (Exod. 17:8–16) and faith to believe God for victory (Num. 14:1–10). His given name was Hoshea ("salvation"), but Moses changed it to Joshua ("Jehovah is salvation"). Even Joshua's name reminded people that he had faith in God.

land.' ¹⁴Your wives, your little ones, and your livestock shall remain in the land which Moses gave you on this side of the Jordan. But you shall pass before your brethren armed, all your mighty men of valor, and help them, ¹⁵until the LORD has given your brethren rest, as He *gave* you, and they also have taken possession of the land which the LORD your God is giving them. Then you shall return to the land of your possession and enjoy it, which Moses the LORD's servant gave you on this side of the Jordan toward the sunrise."

¹⁶So they answered Joshua, saying, "All that you command us we will do, and wherever you send us we will go. ¹⁷Just as we heeded Moses in all things, so we will heed you. Only the LORD your God be with you, as He was with Moses. ¹⁸Whoever rebels against your command and does not heed your words, in all that you command him, shall be put to death. Only be strong and of good courage."

CHAPTER 2

2:1ff Joshua's sending the spies to Jericho was an act of wisdom, not unbelief (Prov. 20:18). The report of the two men encouraged Israel for the invasion (v. 24) and reminded them that God was fulfilling His promise to them (Deut. 2:25).

2:4–24 But the visit also meant the salvation of Rahab and her family. Although the Bible does not commend Rahab for her lies, it does commend her faith (Heb. 11:31) that revealed itself in works (James 2:25). Her faith saved her and her family from destruction (Josh. 6:17–19), and it resulted in her becoming an ancestress of the Messiah (Matt. 1:5). Once you begin to trust God and obey Him, you never know what He will do!

2 Now* Joshua the son of Nun sent out two men from Acacia Grove*ᵃ* to spy secretly, saying, "Go, view the land, especially Jericho."

So they went, and came to the house of a harlot named Rahab, and lodged there. ²And it was told the king of Jericho, saying, "Behold, men have come here tonight from the children of Israel to search out the country."

³So the king of Jericho sent to Rahab, saying, "Bring out the men who have come to you, who have entered your house, for they have come to search out all the country."

⁴*Then the woman took the two men and hid them. So she said, "Yes, the men came to me, but I did not know where they *were* from. ⁵And it happened as the gate was being shut, when it was dark, that the men went out. Where the men went I do not know; pursue them quickly, for you may overtake them." ⁶(But she had brought them up to the roof and hidden them with the stalks of flax, which she had laid in order on the roof.) ⁷Then the men pursued them by the road to the Jordan, to the fords. And as soon as those who pursued them had gone out, they shut the gate.

⁸Now before they lay down, she came up to them on the roof, ⁹and said to the men: "I know that the LORD has given you the land, that the terror of you has fallen on us, and that all the inhabitants of the land are fainthearted because of you. ¹⁰For we have heard how the LORD dried up the water of the Red Sea for you when you came out of Egypt, and what you did to the two kings of the Amorites who *were* on the other side of the Jordan, Sihon and Og, whom you utterly destroyed. ¹¹And as soon as we heard *these things*, our hearts melted; neither did there remain any more courage in anyone because of you, for the LORD your God, He *is* God in heaven above and on earth beneath. ¹²Now therefore, I beg you, swear to me by the LORD, since I have shown you kindness, that you also will show kindness to my father's house, and give me a true token, ¹³and spare my father, my mother, my brothers, my sisters, and all that they have, and deliver our lives from death."

¹⁴So the men answered her, "Our lives for yours, if none of you tell this business of ours.

2:1 ᵃHebrew *Shittim*

And it shall be, when the LORD has given us the land, that we will deal kindly and truly with you."

15Then she let them down by a rope through the window, for her house *was* on the city wall; she dwelt on the wall. 16And she said to them, "Get to the mountain, lest the pursuers meet you. Hide there three days, until the pursuers have returned. Afterward you may go your way."

17So the men said to her: "We *will be* blameless of this oath of yours which you have made us swear, 18unless, *when* we come into the land, you bind this line of scarlet cord in the window through which you let us down, and unless you bring your father, your mother, your brothers, and all your father's household to your own home. 19So it shall be *that* whoever goes outside the doors of your house into the street, his blood *shall be* on his own head, and we *will be* guiltless. And whoever is with you in the house, his blood *shall be* on our head if a hand is laid on him. 20And if you tell this business of ours, then we will be free from your oath which you made us swear."

21Then she said, "According to your words, so *be* it." And she sent them away, and they departed. And she bound the scarlet cord in the window.

22They departed and went to the mountain, and stayed there three days until the pursuers returned. The pursuers sought *them* all along the way, but did not find *them*. 23So the two men returned, descended from the mountain, and crossed over; and they came to Joshua the son of Nun, and told him all that had befallen them. 24And they said to Joshua, "Truly the LORD has delivered all the land into our hands, for indeed all the inhabitants of the country are fainthearted because of us."

3 Then* Joshua rose early in the morning; and they set out from Acacia Grove[b] and came to the Jordan, he and all the children of Israel, and lodged there before they crossed over. 2So it was, after three days, that the officers went through the camp; 3and they commanded the people, saying, "When you see the ark of the covenant of the LORD your God, and the priests, the Levites, bearing it, then you shall set out from your place and go after it. 4*Yet there shall be a space between you and it, about two thousand cubits by measure. Do not come near it, that you may know the way by which you must go, for you have not passed *this* way before."

5And Joshua said to the people, "Sanctify yourselves, for tomorrow the LORD will do wonders among you." 6Then Joshua spoke to the priests, saying, "Take up the ark of the covenant and cross over before the people."

So they took up the ark of the covenant and went before the people.

7And the LORD said to Joshua, "This day I will begin to exalt you in the sight of all Israel, that they may know that, as I was with Moses, *so* I will be with you. 8You shall command the priests who bear the ark of the covenant, saying, 'When you have come to the edge of the water of the Jordan, you shall stand in the Jordan.'"

9So Joshua said to the children of Israel, "Come here, and hear the words of the LORD your God." 10And Joshua said, "By this you shall know that

CHAPTER 3

3:1 Joshua was an early riser (v. 1; 6:12; 7:16; 8:10). He probably devoted that quiet time to praying and meditating on God's Word (Josh. 1:8; Ps. 63:1). This is a good example for us to follow today. (See Mark 1:35.)

3:4–11 We face an unknown future (v. 4) and need the Lord's presence as we step out each day. God goes before us and we must follow as He directs. God knows the way, leads the way and opens the way. He is "Lord of all the earth" (v. 11), and there is nothing for us to fear.

3:1 [b]Hebrew *Shittim*

3:13, 17 The priests had to get their feet wet before the nation could cross over, and that took faith. Your faith can encourage others in their walk with God. It takes great faith to walk through the water, but it takes even greater faith to walk *on the water* (Matt. 14:23–33). Are you still lingering on the banks or in the boat? The future is your friend when you follow the Lord and trust His promises.

CHAPTER 4

4:1–9 It is good to memorialize the great acts of the Lord, provided that the memorials do not become idols. Each new generation must learn what God has done for His people so that they will obey His Word and trust Him for the future (Ps. 78:1–8). When you have living faith in a living God, the past is not "dead history." It throbs with living reality.

"Crossing the Jordan" is not a picture of dying and going to heaven despite what some songs say. It illustrates the teaching of Romans 6: death to the old self-life and identification with Christ in resurrection power. Nobody but God can see the stones in the middle of the Jordan, but the record bears witness that they are there. So it is with the death and resurrection of Christ: we believe the record and thus experience the miracle.

the living God *is* among you, and *that* He will without fail drive out from before you the Canaanites and the Hittites and the Hivites and the Perizzites and the Girgashites and the Amorites and the Jebusites: 11Behold, the ark of the covenant of the Lord of all the earth is crossing over before you into the Jordan. 12Now therefore, take for yourselves twelve men from the tribes of Israel, one man from every tribe. 13*And it shall come to pass, as soon as the soles of the feet of the priests who bear the ark of the LORD, the Lord of all the earth, shall rest in the waters of the Jordan, *that* the waters of the Jordan shall be cut off, the waters that come down from upstream, and they shall stand as a heap."

14So it was, when the people set out from their camp to cross over the Jordan, with the priests bearing the ark of the covenant before the people, 15and as those who bore the ark came to the Jordan, and the feet of the priests who bore the ark dipped in the edge of the water (for the Jordan overflows all its banks during the whole time of harvest), 16that the waters which came down from upstream stood *still, and* rose in a heap very far away at Adam, the city that *is* beside Zaretan. So the waters that went down into the Sea of the Arabah, the Salt Sea, failed, *and* were cut off; and the people crossed over opposite Jericho. 17Then the priests who bore the ark of the covenant of the LORD stood firm on dry ground in the midst of the Jordan; and all Israel crossed over on dry ground, until all the people had crossed completely over the Jordan.

4 And* it came to pass, when all the people had completely crossed over the Jordan, that the LORD spoke to Joshua, saying: 2"Take for yourselves twelve men from the people, one man from every tribe, 3and command them, saying, 'Take for yourselves twelve stones from here, out of the midst of the Jordan, from the place where the priests' feet stood firm. You shall carry them over with you and leave them in the lodging place where you lodge tonight.' "

4Then Joshua called the twelve men whom he had appointed from the children of Israel, one man from every tribe; 5and Joshua said to them: "Cross over before the ark of the LORD your God into the midst of the Jordan, and each one of you take up a stone on his shoulder, according to the number of the tribes of the children of Israel, 6that this may be a sign among you when your children ask in time to come, saying, 'What do these stones *mean* to you?' 7Then you shall answer them that the waters of the Jordan were cut off before the ark of the covenant of the LORD; when it crossed over the Jordan, the waters of the Jordan were cut off. And these stones shall be for a memorial to the children of Israel forever."

8And the children of Israel did so, just as Joshua commanded, and took up twelve stones from the midst of the Jordan, as the LORD had spoken to Joshua, according to the number of the tribes of the children of Israel, and carried them over with them to the place where they lodged, and laid them down there. 9Then Joshua set up twelve stones in the midst of the Jordan, in the place where the feet of the priests who bore the ark of the covenant stood; and they are there to this day.

10So the priests who bore the ark stood in the midst of the Jordan until everything was finished that the LORD had commanded Joshua to speak to the people, according to all that Moses had commanded Joshua; and the people hurried and crossed over. 11Then it came to pass, when all the people had completely crossed over, that the ark of the LORD and the priests crossed over in the presence of the people. 12And the men of Reuben, the men of Gad, and half the tribe of Manasseh crossed over armed before the children of Israel, as Moses had spoken to them. 13About forty thousand prepared for war crossed over before the LORD for battle, to the plains of Jericho. 14On that day the LORD exalted Joshua in the sight of all Israel; and they feared him, as they had feared Moses, all the days of his life.

15Then the LORD spoke to Joshua, saying, 16"Command the priests who bear the ark of the Testimony to come up from the Jordan." 17Joshua therefore commanded the priests, saying, "Come up from the Jordan." 18And it came to pass, when the priests who bore the ark of the covenant of the LORD had come from the midst of the Jordan, and the soles of the priests' feet touched the dry land, that the waters of the Jordan returned to their place and overflowed all its banks as before.

19Now the people came up from the Jordan on the tenth *day* of the first month, and they camped in Gilgal on the east border of Jericho. 20And those twelve stones which they took out of the Jordan, Joshua set up in Gilgal. 21*Then he spoke to the children of Israel, saying: "When your children ask their fathers in time to come, saying, 'What *are* these stones?' 22then you shall let your children know, saying, 'Israel crossed over this Jordan on dry land'; 23for the LORD your God dried up the waters of the Jordan before you until you had crossed over, as the LORD your God did to the Red Sea, which He dried up before us until we had crossed over, 24that all the peoples of the earth may know the hand of the LORD, that it *is* mighty, that you may fear the LORD your God forever."

5 So* it was, when all the kings of the Amorites who *were* on the west side of the Jordan, and all the kings of the Canaanites who *were* by the sea, heard that the LORD had dried up the waters of the Jordan from before the children of Israel until wec had crossed over, that their heart melted; and there was no spirit in them any longer because of the children of Israel.

2*At that time the LORD said to Joshua, "Make flint knives for yourself, and circumcise the sons of Israel again the second time." 3So Joshua made flint knives for himself, and circumcised the sons of Israel at the hill of the foreskins.d 4And this *is* the reason why Joshua circumcised them: All the people who came out of Egypt who *were* males, all the men of war, had died in the wilderness on the way, after they had come out of Egypt. 5For all the people who came out had been circumcised, but all the people born in the wilderness, on the way as they came out of Egypt, had not been circumcised. 6For the children of Israel walked forty years in the wilderness, till all the people *who were* men of war, who came out of

4:21–24 The stones on the shore reminded the people that the old life was buried and they should "walk in newness of life" (Rom. 6:4; Col. 3:1ff.). Have you crossed the Jordan and set up your memorial of faith?

CHAPTER 5
5:1ff Israel had experienced a great miracle, the enemy was frightened, and God was at work. Now was the time for action! *But God told His people to wait.* Why? So that He might prepare them for the conquest of the land.

5:2–9 *We must deal with the past.* The new generation had not received the mark of the covenant (Gen. 17), so this ritual was a reaffirmation of their relationship with God. Circumcision symbolizes putting off what belongs to the sinful flesh (Rom. 8:13; Col. 2:11–12) and devoting the heart wholly to the Lord (Deut. 10:16; Jer. 4:4). The nation had experienced this *collectively* in crossing the Jordan, but it had to be made personal.

5:1 cFollowing Kethib; Qere, some Hebrew manuscripts and editions, Septuagint, Syriac, Targum, and Vulgate read *they*.
5:3 dHebrew *Gibeath Haaraloth*

5:10–12 *We must trust for the present.*
The nation stopped eating manna and started eating food that God naturally provided. There is a place for the miraculous, but God never wastes miracles. If we do the possible, He will do the impossible. The women baked unleavened bread for Passover, and the nation remembered how God had redeemed them from the land of Egypt.

5:13–15 *We must submit for the future.*
Joshua met Jesus Christ and learned that the Lord already had a plan for taking Jericho. All Joshua had to do was obey and remember that he was on "holy ground." From that time, whenever Joshua took off his shoes, it reminded him that he was second in command. That was the secret of his victory (2 Chron. 20:15).

CHAPTER 6
6:1–5 If God calls you to do His work, He will tell you how to do it. His plans may seem foolish to you, but they always work if you obey by faith (Isa. 55:8–11).
As we today seek to conquer territory for the Lord, we do not follow the same procedure Joshua used, but we must obey the same principles of faith and obedience. We use spiritual weapons to break down the barriers in men's minds and to claim them for Christ (2 Cor. 10:1–6).

Egypt, were consumed, because they did not obey the voice of the LORD—to whom the LORD swore that He would not show them the land which the LORD had sworn to their fathers that He would give us, "a land flowing with milk and honey."[e] 7Then Joshua circumcised their sons *whom* He raised up in their place; for they were uncircumcised, because they had not been circumcised on the way.

8So it was, when they had finished circumcising all the people, that they stayed in their places in the camp till they were healed. 9Then the LORD said to Joshua, "This day I have rolled away the reproach of Egypt from you." Therefore the name of the place is called Gilgal[f] to this day.

10*Now the children of Israel camped in Gilgal, and kept the Passover on the fourteenth day of the month at twilight on the plains of Jericho. 11And they ate of the produce of the land on the day after the Passover, unleavened bread and parched grain, on the very same day. 12Then the manna ceased on the day after they had eaten the produce of the land; and the children of Israel no longer had manna, but they ate the food of the land of Canaan that year.

13*And it came to pass, when Joshua was by Jericho, that he lifted his eyes and looked, and behold, a Man stood opposite him with His sword drawn in His hand. And Joshua went to Him and said to Him, "*Are* You for us or for our adversaries?"

14So He said, "No, but *as* Commander of the army of the LORD I have now come."

And Joshua fell on his face to the earth and worshiped, and said to Him, "What does my Lord say to His servant?"

15Then the Commander of the LORD's army said to Joshua, "Take your sandal off your foot, for the place where you stand *is* holy." And Joshua did so.

6 Now* Jericho was securely shut up because of the children of Israel; none went out, and none came in. 2And the LORD said to Joshua: "See! I have given Jericho into your hand, its king, *and* the mighty men of valor. 3You shall march around the city, all *you* men of war; you shall go all around the city once. This you shall do six days. 4And seven priests shall bear seven trumpets of rams' horns before the ark. But the seventh day you shall march around the city seven times, and the priests shall blow the trumpets. 5It shall come to pass, when they make a long *blast* with the ram's horn, *and* when you hear the sound of the trumpet, that all the people shall shout with a great shout; then the wall of the city will fall down flat. And the people shall go up every man straight before him."

6Then Joshua the son of Nun called the priests and said to them, "Take up the ark of the covenant, and let seven priests bear seven trumpets of rams' horns before the ark of the LORD." 7And he said to the people, "Proceed, and march around the city, and let him who is armed advance before the ark of the LORD."

8So it was, when Joshua had spoken to the people, that the seven priests bearing the seven trumpets of rams' horns before the LORD advanced and blew the trumpets, and the ark of the covenant

---

5:6 [e]Exodus 3:8   5:9 [f]Literally *Rolling*

of the LORD followed them. 9The armed men went before the priests who blew the trumpets, and the rear guard came after the ark, while *the priests* continued blowing the trumpets. 10Now Joshua had commanded the people, saying, "You shall not shout or make any noise with your voice, nor shall a word proceed out of your mouth, until the day I say to you, 'Shout!' Then you shall shout." 11So he had the ark of the LORD circle the city, going around *it* once. Then they came into the camp and lodged in the camp.

12And Joshua rose early in the morning, and the priests took up the ark of the LORD. 13Then seven priests bearing seven trumpets of rams' horns before the ark of the LORD went on continually and blew with the trumpets. And the armed men went before them. But the rear guard came after the ark of the LORD, while *the priests* continued blowing the trumpets. 14And the second day they marched around the city once and returned to the camp. So they did six days.

15But it came to pass on the seventh day that they rose early, about the dawning of the day, and marched around the city seven times in the same manner. On that day only they marched around the city seven times. 16And the seventh time it happened, when the priests blew the trumpets, that Joshua said to the people: "Shout, for the LORD has given you the city! 17*Now the city shall be doomed by the LORD to destruction, it and all who *are* in it. Only Rahab the harlot shall live, she and all who *are* with her in the house, because she hid the messengers that we sent. 18And you, by all means abstain from the accursed things, lest you become accursed when you take of the accursed things, and make the camp of Israel a curse, and trouble it. 19But all the silver and gold, and vessels of bronze and iron, *are* consecrated to the LORD; they shall come into the treasury of the LORD."

20So the people shouted when *the priests* blew the trumpets. And it happened when the people heard the sound of the trumpet, and the people shouted with a great shout, that the wall fell down flat. Then the people went up into the city, every man straight before him, and they took the city. 21And they utterly destroyed all that *was* in the city, both man and woman, young and old, ox and sheep and donkey, with the edge of the sword.

22But Joshua had said to the two men who had spied out the country, "Go into the harlot's house, and from there bring out the woman and all that she has, as you swore to her." 23And the young men who had been spies went in and brought out Rahab, her father, her mother, her brothers, and all that she had. So they brought out all her relatives and left them outside the camp of Israel. 24But they burned the city and all that *was* in it with fire. Only the silver and gold, and the vessels of bronze and iron, they put into the treasury of the house of the LORD. 25And Joshua spared Rahab the harlot, her father's household, and all that she had. So she dwells in Israel to this day, because she hid the messengers whom Joshua sent to spy out Jericho.

26*Then Joshua charged *them* at that time, saying, "Cursed *be* the man before the LORD who rises up and builds this city Jericho; he shall lay its foundation with his firstborn, and with his youngest he shall set up its gates."

27So the LORD was with Joshua, and his fame spread throughout all the country.

6:17–19 How could a holy, loving God command the killing of the entire population of a city? The people were wicked sinners with whom God had been patient for years (Gen. 15:16–21). They knew that judgment was coming (Josh. 2:9–11) and could have followed the example of Rahab and been delivered if they had exercised faith.

6:26 God was wiping the land clean so that His people would not be defiled and His great plan of salvation frustrated (Deut. 7:1–11). The Canaanites sinned against a flood of light, *just as people are doing today!* Christ died for the sins of the world. Individuals who do not trust Him will die in their own sins. Are you sharing the good news of the gospel?

7:1–5 *We can be tempted in the midst of victory.* The spies were tempted to be presumptuous and Achan to be covetous. Achan should have been attending to his military duties, but his eyes wandered and he walked into sin (v. 21; see also Gen. 3:6). He valued the spoils more than he valued obedience to God (Ps. 119:162). King Saul made the same mistake (1 Sam. 15).

7:10, 11 *We never sin alone.* God sees His people as one, so the sin of Achan was the sin of the whole nation. (See 1 Cor. 12:12–27.) One man's sin caused the death of thirty-six soldiers.

7:12 *Sin ultimately brings defeat.* The secret of success is knowing and obeying God's Word (Josh. 1:8), and Achan knew that. But he deliberately disobeyed God and brought defeat to the army, disgrace to the Lord, and dismay to his commander. Joshua started looking back instead of looking ahead (v. 7)!

7 But* the children of Israel committed a trespass regarding the accursed things, for Achan the son of Carmi, the son of Zabdi,ᵍ the son of Zerah, of the tribe of Judah, took of the accursed things; so the anger of the LORD burned against the children of Israel.

²Now Joshua sent men from Jericho to Ai, which *is* beside Beth Aven, on the east side of Bethel, and spoke to them, saying, "Go up and spy out the country." So the men went up and spied out Ai. ³And they returned to Joshua and said to him, "Do not let all the people go up, but let about two or three thousand men go up and attack Ai. Do not weary all the people there, for *the people of Ai are* few." ⁴So about three thousand men went up there from the people, but they fled before the men of Ai. ⁵And the men of Ai struck down about thirty-six men, for they chased them *from* before the gate as far as Shebarim, and struck them down on the descent; therefore the hearts of the people melted and became like water.

⁶Then Joshua tore his clothes, and fell to the earth on his face before the ark of the LORD until evening, he and the elders of Israel; and they put dust on their heads. ⁷And Joshua said, "Alas, Lord GOD, why have You brought this people over the Jordan at all—to deliver us into the hand of the Amorites, to destroy us? Oh, that we had been content, and dwelt on the other side of the Jordan! ⁸O Lord, what shall I say when Israel turns its back before its enemies? ⁹For the Canaanites and all the inhabitants of the land will hear *it,* and surround us, and cut off our name from the earth. Then what will You do for Your great name?"

¹⁰*So the LORD said to Joshua: "Get up! Why do you lie thus on your face? ¹¹Israel has sinned, and they have also transgressed My covenant which I commanded them. For they have even taken some of the accursed things, and have both stolen and deceived; and they have also put *it* among their own stuff. ¹²*Therefore the children of Israel could not stand before their enemies, *but* turned *their* backs before their enemies, because they have become doomed to destruction. Neither will I be with you anymore, unless you destroy the accursed from among you. ¹³Get up, sanctify the people, and say, 'Sanctify yourselves for tomorrow, because thus says the LORD God of Israel: "*There is* an accursed thing in your midst, O Israel; you cannot stand before your enemies until you take away the accursed thing from among you." ¹⁴In the morning therefore you shall be brought according to your tribes. And it shall be *that* the tribe which the LORD takes shall come according to families; and the family which the LORD takes shall come by households; and the household which the LORD takes shall come man by man. ¹⁵Then it shall be *that* he who is taken with the accursed thing shall be burned with fire, he and all that he has, because he has transgressed the covenant of the LORD, and because he has done a disgraceful thing in Israel.' "

¹⁶So Joshua rose early in the morning and brought Israel by their tribes, and the tribe of Judah was taken. ¹⁷He brought the clan of Judah, and he took the family of the Zarhites; and he brought the family of the Zarhites man by man,

---

7:1 ᵍCalled *Zimri* in 1 Chronicles 2:6

and Zabdi was taken. 18Then he brought his household man by man, and Achan the son of Carmi, the son of Zabdi, the son of Zerah, of the tribe of Judah, was taken.

19Now Joshua said to Achan, "My son, I beg you, give glory to the LORD God of Israel, and make confession to Him, and tell me now what you have done; do not hide *it* from me."

20*And Achan answered Joshua and said, "Indeed I have sinned against the LORD God of Israel, and this is what I have done: 21When I saw among the spoils a beautiful Babylonian garment, two hundred shekels of silver, and a wedge of gold weighing fifty shekels, I coveted them and took them. And there they are, hidden in the earth in the midst of my tent, with the silver under it."

22So Joshua sent messengers, and they ran to the tent; and there it was, hidden in his tent, with the silver under it. 23And they took them from the midst of the tent, brought them to Joshua and to all the children of Israel, and laid them out before the LORD. 24Then Joshua, and all Israel with him, took Achan the son of Zerah, the silver, the garment, the wedge of gold, his sons, his daughters, his oxen, his donkeys, his sheep, his tent, and all that he had, and they brought them to the Valley of Achor. 25*And Joshua said, "Why have you troubled us? The LORD will trouble you this day." So all Israel stoned him with stones; and they burned them with fire after they had stoned them with stones.

26Then they raised over him a great heap of stones, still there to this day. So the LORD turned from the fierceness of His anger. Therefore the name of that place has been called the Valley of Achor[h] to this day.

8 Now* the LORD said to Joshua: "Do not be afraid, nor be dismayed; take all the people of war with you, and arise, go up to Ai. See, I have given into your hand the king of Ai, his people, his city, and his land. 2*And you shall do to Ai and its king as you did to Jericho and its king. Only its spoil and its cattle you shall take as booty for yourselves. Lay an ambush for the city behind it."

3So Joshua arose, and all the people of war, to go up against Ai; and Joshua chose thirty thousand mighty men of valor and sent them away by night. 4And he commanded them, saying: "Behold, you shall lie in ambush against the city, behind the city. Do not go very far from the city, but all of you be ready. 5Then I and all the people who *are* with me will approach the city; and it will come about, when they come out against us as at the first, that we shall flee before them. 6For they will come out after us till we have drawn them from the city, for they will say, 'They *are* fleeing before us as at the first.' Therefore we will flee before them. 7Then you shall rise from the ambush and seize the city, for the LORD your God will deliver it into your hand. 8And it will be, when you have taken the city, *that* you shall set the city on fire. According to the commandment of the LORD you shall do. See, I have commanded you."

9Joshua therefore sent them out; and they went to lie in ambush, and stayed between Bethel and

7:20, 21 *Sin cannot be hidden forever.* There is a time to pray about a problem and a time to get up and deal with it. The punishment may seem severe to us, but Achan knew the rules. The main thing is the glory of God (v. 9).

7:25 The Jews raised another heap of stones, this time a witness to the trouble ("Achor") sin causes, but read Hosea 2:15 and rejoice.

CHAPTER 8

8:1 Never permit one failure to rob you of future victory. When God sees that we have obeyed His Word and sincerely dealt with sin, He comes with encouragement and guidance for the next step. It has well been said that the victorious Christian life is a series of new beginnings. (See Ps. 37:23–24.)

8:2 Had Achan only waited, he could have taken all the spoils he desired, but he ran ahead of God and lost everything. (See Matt. 6:33.)

7:26 [h]Literally *Trouble*

8:12–18 Joshua knew how to bring victory from defeat, for he used the original battle plan to deceive the inhabitants of Ai. Now *they* were the ones who were presumptuous, and it cost them their lives. The strategy in verse 26 was learned from Moses (Exod. 17:8–13).

Ai, on the west side of Ai; but Joshua lodged that night among the people. 10Then Joshua rose up early in the morning and mustered the people, and went up, he and the elders of Israel, before the people to Ai. 11And all the people of war who *were* with him went up and drew near; and they came before the city and camped on the north side of Ai. Now a valley *lay* between them and Ai. 12*So he took about five thousand men and set them in ambush between Bethel and Ai, on the west side of the city. 13And when they had set the people, all the army that *was* on the north of the city, and its rear guard on the west of the city, Joshua went that night into the midst of the valley.

14Now it happened, when the king of Ai saw *it,* that the men of the city hurried and rose early and went out against Israel to battle, he and all his people, at an appointed place before the plain. But he did not know that *there was* an ambush against him behind the city. 15And Joshua and all Israel made as if they were beaten before them, and fled by the way of the wilderness. 16So all the people who *were* in Ai were called together to pursue them. And they pursued Joshua and were drawn away from the city. 17There was not a man left in Ai or Bethel who did not go out after Israel. So they left the city open and pursued Israel.

18Then the LORD said to Joshua, "Stretch out the spear that *is* in your hand toward Ai, for I will give it into your hand." And Joshua stretched out the spear that *was* in his hand toward the city. 19So *those in* ambush arose quickly out of their place; they ran as soon as he had stretched out his hand, and they entered the city and took it, and hurried to set the city on fire. 20And when the men of Ai looked behind them, they saw, and behold, the smoke of the city ascended to heaven. So they had no power to flee this way or that way, and the people who had fled to the wilderness turned back on the pursuers.

21Now when Joshua and all Israel saw that the ambush had taken the city and that the smoke of the city ascended, they turned back and struck down the men of Ai. 22Then the others came out of the city against them; so they were *caught* in the midst of Israel, some on this side and some on that side. And they struck them down, so that they let none of them remain or escape. 23But the king of Ai they took alive, and brought him to Joshua.

24And it came to pass when Israel had made an end of slaying all the inhabitants of Ai in the field, in the wilderness where they pursued them, and when they all had fallen by the edge of the sword until they were consumed, that all the Israelites returned to Ai and struck it with the edge of the sword. 25So it was *that* all who fell that day, both men and women, *were* twelve thousand—all the people of Ai. 26For Joshua did not draw back his hand, with which he stretched out the spear, until he had utterly destroyed all the inhabitants of Ai. 27Only the livestock and the spoil of that city Israel took as booty for themselves, according to the word of the LORD which He had commanded Joshua. 28So Joshua burned Ai and made it a heap forever, a desolation to this day. 29And the king of Ai he hanged on a tree until evening. And as soon as the sun was down, Joshua commanded that they should take his corpse down from the tree, cast it at the entrance of the gate of the city, and raise over it a great heap of stones *that remains* to this day.

30*Now Joshua built an altar to the LORD God of Israel in Mount Ebal, 31as Moses the servant of the LORD had commanded the children of Israel, as it is written in the Book of the Law of Moses: "an altar of whole stones over which no man has wielded an iron *tool.*" And they offered on it burnt offerings to the LORD, and sacrificed peace offerings. 32And there, in the presence of the children of Israel, he wrote on the stones a copy of the law of Moses, which he had written. 33Then all Israel, with their elders and officers and judges, stood on either side of the ark before the priests, the Levites, who bore the ark of the covenant of the LORD, the stranger as well as he who was born among them. Half of them *were* in front of Mount Gerizim and half of them in front of Mount Ebal, as Moses the servant of the LORD had commanded before, that they should bless the people of Israel. 34And afterward he read all the words of the law, the blessings and the cursings, according to all that is written in the Book of the Law. 35There was not a word of all that Moses had commanded which Joshua did not read before all the assembly of Israel, with the women, the little ones, and the strangers who were living among them.

9 And it came to pass when all the kings who *were* on this side of the Jordan, in the hills and in the lowland and in all the coasts of the Great Sea toward Lebanon—the Hittite, the Amorite, the Canaanite, the Perizzite, the Hivite, and the Jebusite—heard *about it,* 2that they gathered together to fight with Joshua and Israel with one accord.

3*But when the inhabitants of Gibeon heard what Joshua had done to Jericho and Ai, 4they worked craftily, and went and pretended to be ambassadors. And they took old sacks on their donkeys, old wineskins torn and mended, 5old and patched sandals on their feet, and old garments on themselves; and all the bread of their provision was dry *and* moldy. 6And they went to Joshua, to the camp at Gilgal, and said to him and to the men of Israel, "We have come from a far country; now therefore, make a covenant with us."

7Then the men of Israel said to the Hivites, "Perhaps you dwell among us; so how can we make a covenant with you?"

8But they said to Joshua, "We *are* your servants."

And Joshua said to them, "Who *are* you, and where do you come from?"

9So they said to him: "From a very far country your servants have come, because of the name of the LORD your God; for we have heard of His fame, and all that He did in Egypt, 10and all that He did to the two kings of the Amorites who *were* beyond the Jordan—to Sihon king of Heshbon, and Og king of Bashan, who was at Ashtaroth. 11Therefore our elders and all the inhabitants of our country spoke to us, saying, 'Take provisions with you for the journey, and go to meet them, and say to them, "We *are* your servants; now therefore, make a covenant with us."' 12This bread of ours we took hot *for* our provision from our houses on the day we departed to come to

8:30–35 New victories ought to result in new steps of dedication (vv. 30–35). Joshua obeyed what Moses had commanded (Deut. 27), for obedience to the Word is the secret of success (Josh. 1:8).

CHAPTER 9

9:3–6 The Gibeonites knew that their neighbors were fighting a losing battle, for God was fighting for Israel, and no army could resist Him. So, they decided to use guile instead of muscle. If Satan does not defeat you by coming as the devouring lion (1 Pet. 5:8–9), he will try again as the deceiving serpent (2 Cor. 11:3). He never gives up.

8:31 'Deuteronomy 27:5, 6

9:14, 15 The humiliating defeat at Ai should have taught Joshua and the leaders to take time to pray and seek the mind of the Lord. After all, the Lord was the Commander of the army (Josh. 5:13–15). But they walked by sight and not by faith, and unbelief has a hard time waiting (Isa. 28:16; 30:1–2).

9:22, 23 Another defeat! The Lord lost glory, the leaders lost stature, and the nation lost a potential victory: "What agreement has the temple of God with idols?" (2 Cor. 6:16). But Joshua did not give up; rather, *he made his mistakes work for him* (vv. 21–27). That is the mark of a great leader.

CHAPTER 10

10:5, 6 When you make an agreement with the enemy, there is no end to the problems you create for yourself. Israel had to defend the very people they should have defeated. Imagine the servants commanding the masters (v. 6)!

you. But now look, it is dry and moldy. 13And these wineskins which we filled *were* new, and see, they are torn; and these our garments and our sandals have become old because of the very long journey."

14*Then the men of Israel took some of their provisions; but they did not ask counsel of the LORD. 15So Joshua made peace with them, and made a covenant with them to let them live; and the rulers of the congregation swore to them.

16And it happened at the end of three days, after they had made a covenant with them, that they heard that they *were* their neighbors who dwelt near them. 17Then the children of Israel journeyed and came to their cities on the third day. Now their cities *were* Gibeon, Chephirah, Beeroth, and Kirjath Jearim. 18But the children of Israel did not attack them, because the rulers of the congregation had sworn to them by the LORD God of Israel. And all the congregation complained against the rulers.

19Then all the rulers said to all the congregation, "We have sworn to them by the LORD God of Israel; now therefore, we may not touch them. 20This we will do to them: We will let them live, lest wrath be upon us because of the oath which we swore to them." 21And the rulers said to them, "Let them live, but let them be woodcutters and water carriers for all the congregation, as the rulers had promised them."

22*Then Joshua called for them, and he spoke to them, saying, "Why have you deceived us, saying, 'We *are* very far from you,' when you dwell near us? 23Now therefore, you *are* cursed, and none of you shall be freed from being slaves—woodcutters and water carriers for the house of my God."

24So they answered Joshua and said, "Because your servants were clearly told that the LORD your God commanded His servant Moses to give you all the land, and to destroy all the inhabitants of the land from before you; therefore we were very much afraid for our lives because of you, and have done this thing. 25And now, here we are, in your hands; do with us as it seems good and right to do to us." 26So he did to them, and delivered them out of the hand of the children of Israel, so that they did not kill them. 27And that day Joshua made them woodcutters and water carriers for the congregation and for the altar of the LORD, in the place which He would choose, even to this day.

10 Now it came to pass when Adoni-Zedek king of Jerusalem heard how Joshua had taken Ai and had utterly destroyed it—as he had done to Jericho and its king, so he had done to Ai and its king—and how the inhabitants of Gibeon had made peace with Israel and were among them, 2that they feared greatly, because Gibeon *was* a great city, like one of the royal cities, and because it *was* greater than Ai, and all its men *were* mighty. 3Therefore Adoni-Zedek king of Jerusalem sent to Hoham king of Hebron, Piram king of Jarmuth, Japhia king of Lachish, and Debir king of Eglon, saying, 4"Come up to me and help me, that we may attack Gibeon, for it has made peace with Joshua and with the children of Israel." 5*Therefore the five kings of the Amorites, the king of Jerusalem, the king of Hebron, the king of Jarmuth, the king of Lachish, *and* the king of Eglon, gathered together and went up, they and all their armies, and camped before Gibeon and made war against it.

6And the men of Gibeon sent to Joshua at the camp at Gilgal, saying, "Do not forsake your servants; come up to us quickly, save us and help us, for all the kings of the Amorites who dwell in the mountains have gathered together against us."

7*So Joshua ascended from Gilgal, he and all the people of war with him, and all the mighty men of valor. 8And the LORD said to Joshua, "Do not fear them, for I have delivered them into your hand; not a man of them shall stand before you." 9Joshua therefore came upon them suddenly, having marched all night from Gilgal. 10So the LORD routed them before Israel, killed them with a great slaughter at Gibeon, chased them along the road that goes to Beth Horon, and struck them down as far as Azekah and Makkedah. 11And it happened, as they fled before Israel and were on the descent of Beth Horon, that the LORD cast down large hailstones from heaven on them as far as Azekah, and they died. There were more who died from the hailstones than the children of Israel killed with the sword.

12Then Joshua spoke to the LORD in the day when the LORD delivered up the Amorites before the children of Israel, and he said in the sight of Israel:

> "Sun, stand still over Gibeon;
>   And Moon, in the Valley of Aijalon."
> 13 So the sun stood still,
>   And the moon stopped,
>   Till the people had revenge
>   Upon their enemies.

Is this not written in the Book of Jasher? So the sun stood still in the midst of heaven, and did not hasten to go down for about a whole day. 14And there has been no day like that, before it or after it, that the LORD heeded the voice of a man; for the LORD fought for Israel.

15*Then Joshua returned, and all Israel with him, to the camp at Gilgal.

16But these five kings had fled and hidden themselves in a cave at Makkedah. 17And it was told Joshua, saying, "The five kings have been found hidden in the cave at Makkedah." 18So Joshua said, "Roll large stones against the mouth of the cave, and set men by it to guard them. 19And do not stay there yourselves, but pursue your enemies, and attack their rear guard. Do not allow them to enter their cities, for the LORD your God has delivered them into your hand." 20Then it happened, while Joshua and the children of Israel made an end of slaying them with a very great slaughter, till they had finished, that those who escaped entered fortified cities. 21And all the people returned to the camp, to Joshua at Makkedah, in peace.

No one moved his tongue against any of the children of Israel.

22Then Joshua said, "Open the mouth of the cave, and bring out those five kings to me from the cave." 23And they did so, and brought out those five kings to him from the cave: the king of Jerusalem, the king of Hebron, the king of Jarmuth, the king of Lachish, and the king of Eglon.

24So it was, when they brought out those kings to Joshua, that Joshua called for all the men of Israel, and said to the captains of the men of war

10:7–14 God could have said, "You got yourself into this, so you can get yourself out!" But instead, He gave His people encouragement (v. 8) and fought for them from heaven (vv. 10–11). When Joshua needed more time to finish the battle, God stayed the sun and moon in answer to prayer. The Canaanites worshiped the heavenly bodies, so this miracle must have impressed them greatly. If we are doing the will of God, prayer has tremendous power.

10:15–43 Victory over the five kings opened the way for Joshua to attack southern Canaan until he had subdued the whole region. What began as a humiliating defense maneuver ended up a glorious series of victories: "If God is for us, who can be against us?" (Rom. 8:31).

who went with him, "Come near, put your feet on the necks of these kings." And they drew near and put their feet on their necks. 25Then Joshua said to them, "Do not be afraid, nor be dismayed; be strong and of good courage, for thus the LORD will do to all your enemies against whom you fight." 26And afterward Joshua struck them and killed them, and hanged them on five trees; and they were hanging on the trees until evening. 27So it was at the time of the going down of the sun *that* Joshua commanded, and they took them down from the trees, cast them into the cave where they had been hidden, and laid large stones against the cave's mouth, *which remain* until this very day.

28On that day Joshua took Makkedah, and struck it and its king with the edge of the sword. He utterly destroyed them*l*—all the people who *were* in it. He let none remain. He also did to the king of Makkedah as he had done to the king of Jericho.

29Then Joshua passed from Makkedah, and all Israel with him, to Libnah; and they fought against Libnah. 30And the LORD also delivered it and its king into the hand of Israel; he struck it and all the people who *were* in it with the edge of the sword. He let none remain in it, but did to its king as he had done to the king of Jericho.

31Then Joshua passed from Libnah, and all Israel with him, to Lachish; and they encamped against it and fought against it. 32And the LORD delivered Lachish into the hand of Israel, who took it on the second day, and struck it and all the people who *were* in it with the edge of the sword, according to all that he had done to Libnah. 33Then Horam king of Gezer came up to help Lachish; and Joshua struck him and his people, until he left him none remaining.

34From Lachish Joshua passed to Eglon, and all Israel with him; and they encamped against it and fought against it. 35They took it on that day and struck it with the edge of the sword; all the people who *were* in it he utterly destroyed that day, according to all that he had done to Lachish.

36So Joshua went up from Eglon, and all Israel with him, to Hebron; and they fought against it. 37And they took it and struck it with the edge of the sword—its king, all its cities, and all the people who *were* in it; he left none remaining, according to all that he had done to Eglon, but utterly destroyed it and all the people who *were* in it.

38Then Joshua returned, and all Israel with him, to Debir; and they fought against it. 39And he took it and its king and all its cities; they struck them with the edge of the sword and utterly destroyed all the people who *were* in it. He left none remaining; as he had done to Hebron, so he did to Debir and its king, as he had done also to Libnah and its king.

40So Joshua conquered all the land: the mountain country and the South*k* and the lowland and the wilderness slopes, and all their kings; he left none remaining, but utterly destroyed all that breathed, as the LORD God of Israel had commanded. 41And Joshua conquered them from Kadesh Barnea as far as Gaza, and all the country

10:28 *l*Following Masoretic Text and most authorities; many Hebrew manuscripts, some manuscripts of the Septuagint, and some manuscripts of the Targum read *it.*   10:40 *k*Hebrew *Negev,* and so throughout this book

of Goshen, even as far as Gibeon. 42All these kings and their land Joshua took at one time, because the LORD God of Israel fought for Israel. 43Then Joshua returned, and all Israel with him, to the camp at Gilgal.

11 And* it came to pass, when Jabin king of Hazor heard *these things*, that he sent to Jobab king of Madon, to the king of Shimron, to the king of Achshaph, 2and to the kings who *were* from the north, in the mountains, in the plain south of Chinneroth, in the lowland, and in the heights of Dor on the west, 3to the Canaanites in the east and in the west, the Amorite, the Hittite, the Perizzite, the Jebusite in the mountains, and the Hivite below Hermon in the land of Mizpah. 4So they went out, they and all their armies with them, *as* many people *as* the sand that *is* on the seashore in multitude, with very many horses and chariots. 5And when all these kings had met together, they came and camped together at the waters of Merom to fight against Israel.

6But the LORD said to Joshua, "Do not be afraid because of them, for tomorrow about this time I will deliver all of them slain before Israel. You shall hamstring their horses and burn their chariots with fire." 7So Joshua and all the people of war with him came against them suddenly by the waters of Merom, and they attacked them. 8And the LORD delivered them into the hand of Israel, who defeated them and chased them to Greater Sidon, to the Brook Misrephoth,*l* and to the Valley of Mizpah eastward; they attacked them until they left none of them remaining. 9So Joshua did to them as the LORD had told him: he hamstrung their horses and burned their chariots with fire.

10Joshua turned back at that time and took Hazor, and struck its king with the sword; for Hazor was formerly the head of all those kingdoms. 11And they struck all the people who *were* in it with the edge of the sword, utterly destroying *them*. There was none left breathing. Then he burned Hazor with fire.

12So all the cities of those kings, and all their kings, Joshua took and struck with the edge of the sword. He utterly destroyed them, as Moses the servant of the LORD had commanded. 13But *as for* the cities that stood on their mounds,*m* Israel burned none of them, except Hazor only, *which* Joshua burned. 14And all the spoil of these cities and the livestock, the children of Israel took as booty for themselves; but they struck every man with the edge of the sword until they had destroyed them, and they left none breathing. 15As the LORD had commanded Moses his servant, so Moses commanded Joshua, and so Joshua did. He left nothing undone of all that the LORD had commanded Moses.

16Thus Joshua took all this land: the mountain country, all the South, all the land of Goshen, the lowland, and the Jordan plain*n*—the mountains of Israel and its lowlands, 17from Mount Halak and the ascent to Seir, even as far as Baal Gad in the Valley of Lebanon below Mount Hermon. He captured all their kings, and struck them down and killed them. 18Joshua made war a long time

CHAPTERS 11—12

11:1–22 The enemy in the north of Canaan united to resist Israel's advance, and their forces were formidable. But God assured Joshua that he would win the battle, and he did. God assures us before the battle (11:6), fights for us during the battle (11:8), and commands us after the battle (11:9, 15). How we follow orders after the victory is as important as what we do before the battle begins.

11:8 *l*Hebrew *Misrephoth Maim* 11:13 *m*Hebrew *tel*, a heap of successive city ruins 11:16 *n*Hebrew *arabah*

with all those kings. ¹⁹There was not a city that made peace with the children of Israel, except the Hivites, the inhabitants of Gibeon. All *the others* they took in battle. ²⁰For it was of the LORD to harden their hearts, that they should come against Israel in battle, that He might utterly destroy them, *and* that they might receive no mercy, but that He might destroy them, as the LORD had commanded Moses.

²¹And at that time Joshua came and cut off the Anakim from the mountains: from Hebron, from Debir, from Anab, from all the mountains of Judah, and from all the mountains of Israel; Joshua utterly destroyed them with their cities. ²²None of the Anakim were left in the land of the children of Israel; they remained only in Gaza, in Gath, and in Ashdod.

²³*So Joshua took the whole land, according to all that the LORD had said to Moses; and Joshua gave it as an inheritance to Israel according to their divisions by their tribes. Then the land rested from war.

12 These *are* the kings of the land whom the children of Israel defeated, and whose land they possessed on the other side of the Jordan toward the rising of the sun, from the River Arnon to Mount Hermon, and all the eastern Jordan plain: ²*One king was* Sihon king of the Amorites, who dwelt in Heshbon *and* ruled half of Gilead, from Aroer, which is on the bank of the River Arnon, from the middle of that river, even as far as the River Jabbok, *which is* the border of the Ammonites, ³and the eastern Jordan plain from the Sea of Chinneroth as far as the Sea of the Arabah (the Salt Sea), the road to Beth Jeshimoth, and southward below the slopes of Pisgah. ⁴*The other king was* Og king of Bashan and his territory, *who was* of the remnant of the giants, who dwelt at Ashtaroth and at Edrei, ⁵and reigned over Mount Hermon, over Salcah, over all Bashan, as far as the border of the Geshurites and the Maachathites, and over half of Gilead *to* the border of Sihon king of Heshbon.

⁶These Moses the servant of the LORD and the children of Israel had conquered; and Moses the servant of the LORD had given it *as* a possession to the Reubenites, the Gadites, and half the tribe of Manasseh.

⁷And these *are* the kings of the country which Joshua and the children of Israel conquered on this side of the Jordan, on the west, from Baal Gad in the Valley of Lebanon as far as Mount Halak and the ascent to Seir, which Joshua gave to the tribes of Israel *as* a possession according to their divisions, ⁸in the mountain country, in the lowlands, in the *Jordan* plain, in the slopes, in the wilderness, and in the South—the Hittites, the Amorites, the Canaanites, the Perizzites, the Hivites, and the Jebusites: ⁹the king of Jericho, one; the king of Ai, which *is* beside Bethel, one; ¹⁰the king of Jerusalem, one; the king of Hebron, one; ¹¹the king of Jarmuth, one; the king of Lachish, one; ¹²the king of Eglon, one; the king of Gezer, one; ¹³the king of Debir, one; the king of Geder, one; ¹⁴the king of Hormah, one; the king of Arad, one; ¹⁵the king of Libnah, one; the king of Adullam, one; ¹⁶the king of Makkedah, one; the king of Bethel, one; ¹⁷the king of Tappuah, one; the king of Hepher, one; ¹⁸the king of Aphek, one; the king of Lasharon, one; ¹⁹the king of Madon, one; the king of Hazor, one; ²⁰the king of

11:23—12:24 Joshua conquered the whole land and did it to provide each Israelite with his inheritance from the Lord (11:23). God helped him defeat thirty-one kings and claim their land and their wealth for the Lord and His people. Our Joshua, the Son of God, has defeated every spiritual enemy and now reigns in heaven (Eph. 1:15–23; Col. 2:9–15). Through Him, we can "reign in life" (Rom. 5:17) and claim the victory.

Shimron Meron, one; the king of Achshaph, one; [21]the king of Taanach, one; the king of Megiddo, one; [22]the king of Kedesh, one; the king of Jokneam in Carmel, one; [23]the king of Dor in the heights of Dor, one; the king of the people of Gilgal, one; [24]the king of Tirzah, one—all the kings, thirty-one.

13 Now* Joshua was old, advanced in years. And the LORD said to him: "You are old, advanced in years, and there remains very much land yet to be possessed. [2]This is the land that yet remains: all the territory of the Philistines and all *that of* the Geshurites, [3]from Sihor, which *is* east of Egypt, as far as the border of Ekron northward (*which* is counted as Canaanite); the five lords of the Philistines—the Gazites, the Ashdodites, the Ashkelonites, the Gittites, and the Ekronites; also the Avites; [4]from the south, all the land of the Canaanites, and Mearah that belongs to the Sidonians as far as Aphek, to the border of the Amorites; [5]the land of the Gebalites,° and all Lebanon, toward the sunrise, from Baal Gad below Mount Hermon as far as the entrance to Hamath; [6]*all the inhabitants of the mountains from Lebanon as far as the Brook Misrephoth,ᵖ *and* all the Sidonians—them I will drive out from before the children of Israel; only divide it by lot to Israel as an inheritance, as I have commanded you. [7]Now therefore, divide this land as an inheritance to the nine tribes and half the tribe of Manasseh."

[8]With the other half-tribe the Reubenites and the Gadites received their inheritance, which Moses had given them, beyond the Jordan eastward, as Moses the servant of the LORD had given them: [9]from Aroer which *is* on the bank of the River Arnon, and the town that *is* in the midst of the ravine, and all the plain of Medeba as far as Dibon; [10]all the cities of Sihon king of the Amorites, who reigned in Heshbon, as far as the border of the children of Ammon; [11]Gilead, and the border of the Geshurites and Maachathites, all Mount Hermon, and all Bashan as far as Salcah; [12]all the kingdom of Og in Bashan, who reigned in Ashtaroth and Edrei, who remained of the remnant of the giants; for Moses had defeated and cast out these.

[13]Nevertheless the children of Israel did not drive out the Geshurites or the Maachathites, but the Geshurites and the Maachathites dwell among the Israelites until this day.

[14]Only to the tribe of Levi he had given no inheritance; the sacrifices of the LORD God of Israel made by fire *are* their inheritance, as He said to them.

[15]And Moses had given to the tribe of the children of Reuben *an inheritance* according to their families. [16]Their territory was from Aroer, which *is* on the bank of the River Arnon, and the city that *is* in the midst of the ravine, and all the plain by Medeba; [17]Heshbon and all its cities that *are* in the plain: Dibon, Bamoth Baal, Beth Baal Meon, [18]Jahaza, Kedemoth, Mephaath, [19]Kirjathaim, Sibmah, Zereth Shahar on the mountain of the valley, [20]Beth Peor, the slopes of Pisgah, and Beth Jeshimoth— [21]all the cities of the plain and all the kingdom of Sihon king of the Amorites, who

CHAPTER 13

13:1 Unlike some elderly people, Joshua lived in the future and not in the past. He had a job to do, and he wanted to complete it before he died. He was not satisfied to defeat thirty-one kings. He urged the tribes to possess the land they had conquered and claim it for the Lord.

13:6 No matter how much God has enabled you to accomplish in life, there is always much more land to possess. In the Christian life, we never stand still; we go either forward or backward. The challenge to the believer is Hebrews 6:1: "Let us go on!"

In all his ministry, Joshua was careful to follow the regulations laid down by Moses. Obedience to the Word guaranteed his success (Josh. 1:8).

13:5 °Or *Giblites*   13:6 ᵖHebrew *Misrephoth Maim*

reigned in Heshbon, whom Moses had struck with the princes of Midian: Evi, Rekem, Zur, Hur, and Reba, who *were* princes of Sihon dwelling in the country. ²²The children of Israel also killed with the sword Balaam the son of Beor, the soothsayer, among those who were killed by them. ²³And the border of the children of Reuben was the bank of the Jordan. This *was* the inheritance of the children of Reuben according to their families, the cities and their villages.

²⁴Moses also had given *an inheritance* to the tribe of Gad, to the children of Gad according to their families. ²⁵Their territory was Jazer, and all the cities of Gilead, and half the land of the Ammonites as far as Aroer, which *is* before Rabbah, ²⁶and from Heshbon to Ramath Mizpah and Betonim, and from Mahanaim to the border of Debir, ²⁷and in the valley Beth Haram, Beth Nimrah, Succoth, and Zaphon, the rest of the kingdom of Sihon king of Heshbon, with the Jordan as *its* border, as far as the edge of the Sea of Chinnereth, on the other side of the Jordan eastward. ²⁸This *is* the inheritance of the children of Gad according to their families, the cities and their villages.

²⁹Moses also had given *an inheritance* to the tribe of Manasseh; it was for half the tribe of the children of Manasseh according to their families: ³⁰Their territory was from Mahanaim, all Bashan, all the kingdom of Og king of Bashan, and all the towns of Jair which are in Bashan, sixty cities; ³¹half of Gilead, and Ashtaroth and Edrei, cities of the kingdom of Og in Bashan, *were* for the children of Machir the son of Manasseh, for half of the children of Machir according to their families.

³²These *are the areas* which Moses had distributed as an inheritance in the plains of Moab on the other side of the Jordan, by Jericho eastward. ³³*But to the tribe of Levi Moses had given no inheritance; the Lᴏʀᴅ God of Israel *was* their inheritance, as He had said to them.

14 These *are the areas* which the children of Israel inherited in the land of Canaan, which Eleazar the priest, Joshua the son of Nun, and the heads of the fathers of the tribes of the children of Israel distributed as an inheritance to them. ²Their inheritance *was* by lot, as the Lᴏʀᴅ had commanded by the hand of Moses, for the nine tribes and the half-tribe. ³For Moses had given the inheritance of the two tribes and the half-tribe on the other side of the Jordan; but to the Levites he had given no inheritance among them. ⁴For the children of Joseph were two tribes: Manasseh and Ephraim. And they gave no part to the Levites in the land, except cities to dwell *in*, with their common-lands for their livestock and their property. ⁵As the Lᴏʀᴅ had commanded Moses, so the children of Israel did; and they divided the land.

⁶*Then the children of Judah came to Joshua in Gilgal. And Caleb the son of Jephunneh the Kenizzite said to him: "You know the word which the Lᴏʀᴅ said to Moses the man of God concerning you and me in Kadesh Barnea. ⁷I *was* forty years old when Moses the servant of the Lᴏʀᴅ sent me from Kadesh Barnea to spy out the land, and I brought back word to him as *it was* in my heart. ⁸Nevertheless my brethren who went up with me made the heart of the people melt, but I wholly followed the Lᴏʀᴅ my God. ⁹So Moses swore on that day, saying, 'Surely the land where

13:33 Did the Levites feel left out? How could they, when God was their inheritance!

CHAPTER 14

14:6–11 Caleb illustrates the truth that "through faith and patience [we] inherit the promises" (Heb. 6:12). Along with Joshua, Caleb was eager to claim his inheritance over forty years before, but the nation had rebelled in unbelief. Patiently, Caleb endured the trials of the wilderness; he knew that his future was secure (Num. 14:24). That unbelieving generation had no hope, for they died in the wilderness, but Caleb had a "living hope" because of his faith (1 Pet. 1:3ff.).

your foot has trodden shall be your inheritance and your children's forever, because you have wholly followed the LORD my God.' 10And now, behold, the LORD has kept me alive, as He said, these forty-five years, ever since the LORD spoke this word to Moses while Israel wandered in the wilderness; and now, here I am this day, eighty-five years old. 11As yet I *am as* strong this day as on the day that Moses sent me; just as my strength *was* then, so now *is* my strength for war, both for going out and for coming in. 12*Now therefore, give me this mountain of which the LORD spoke in that day; for you heard in that day how the Anakim *were* there, and *that* the cities *were* great *and* fortified. It may be that the LORD *will be* with me, and I shall be able to drive them out as the LORD said."

13And Joshua blessed him, and gave Hebron to Caleb the son of Jephunneh as an inheritance. 14Hebron therefore became the inheritance of Caleb the son of Jephunneh the Kenizzite to this day, because he wholly followed the LORD God of Israel. 15And the name of Hebron formerly was Kirjath Arba (*Arba was* the greatest man among the Anakim).

Then the land had rest from war.

15 So* *this* was the lot of the tribe of the children of Judah according to their families: The border of Edom at the Wilderness of Zin southward *was* the extreme southern boundary. 2And their southern border began at the shore of the Salt Sea, from the bay that faces southward. 3Then it went out to the southern side of the Ascent of Akrabbim, passed along to Zin, ascended on the south side of Kadesh Barnea, passed along to Hezron, went up to Adar, and went around to Karkaa. 4*From there* it passed toward Azmon and went out to the Brook of Egypt; and the border ended at the sea. This shall be your southern border.

5The east border *was* the Salt Sea as far as the mouth of the Jordan.

And the border on the northern quarter *began* at the bay of the sea at the mouth of the Jordan. 6The border went up to Beth Hoglah and passed north of Beth Arabah; and the border went up to the stone of Bohan the son of Reuben. 7Then the border went up toward Debir from the Valley of Achor, and it turned northward toward Gilgal, which *is* before the Ascent of Adummim, which *is* on the south side of the valley. The border continued toward the waters of En Shemesh and ended at En Rogel. 8And the border went up by the Valley of the Son of Hinnom to the southern slope of the Jebusite *city* (which *is* Jerusalem). The border went up to the top of the mountain that *lies* before the Valley of Hinnom westward, which *is* at the end of the Valley of Rephaimq northward. 9Then the border went around from the top of the hill to the fountain of the water of Nephtoah, and extended to the cities of Mount Ephron. And the border went around to Baalah (which *is* Kirjath Jearim). 10Then the border turned westward from Baalah to Mount Seir, passed along to the side of Mount Jearim on the north (which *is* Chesalon), went down to Beth Shemesh, and passed on to Timnah. 11And the border went out to the side of Ekron northward.

14:12 What an example for us to follow! Age did not hinder him, the disappointments of the past did not embitter him, and giants did not frighten him! At a time in life when others were looking for security and ease, Caleb was saying, "Give me this mountain!" (v. 12). His secret? "He wholly followed the LORD God of Israel" (v. 14).

CHAPTER 15

15:1ff Had the people chosen their inheritance, there no doubt would have been competition and conflict; but the Lord assigned the territory, and the tribes submitted to His will.

"For who makes you differ from another?" asked Paul. "And what do you have that you did not receive?" (1 Cor. 4:7). John the Baptist said, "A man can receive nothing unless it has been given to him from heaven" (John 3:27).

Whenever you envy another's achievements or abilities, you are forgetting this basic spiritual principle. Whenever you complain to God because of what you are *not,* instead of praising Him for what you are, you need to listen again to Paul and John the Baptist.

15:8 qLiterally *Giants*

15:13–16 This is not to suggest that you become complacent. Caleb fought courageously to claim his God-given inheritance, and so did Othniel, his son-in-law. Caleb's daughter had faith to *ask* for additional blessings, and she received them. God gives—we possess by faith. We must accept whatever inheritance He grants us. The people could rest on Psalm 47:4 and the Levites on Psalm 16:5. Are you happy with the perfect choices that God makes?

Then the border went around to Shicron, passed along to Mount Baalah, and extended to Jabneel; and the border ended at the sea. ¹²The west border *was* the coastline of the Great Sea. This *is* the boundary of the children of Judah all around according to their families.

¹³*Now to Caleb the son of Jephunneh he gave a share among the children of Judah, according to the commandment of the LORD to Joshua, *namely*, Kirjath Arba, which *is* Hebron (*Arba was* the father of Anak). ¹⁴Caleb drove out the three sons of Anak from there: Sheshai, Ahiman, and Talmai, the children of Anak. ¹⁵Then he went up from there to the inhabitants of Debir (formerly the name of Debir *was* Kirjath Sepher).

¹⁶And Caleb said, "He who attacks Kirjath Sepher and takes it, to him I will give Achsah my daughter as wife." ¹⁷So Othniel the son of Kenaz, the brother of Caleb, took it; and he gave him Achsah his daughter as wife. ¹⁸Now it was so, when she came *to him*, that she persuaded him to ask her father for a field. So she dismounted from *her* donkey, and Caleb said to her, "What do you wish?" ¹⁹She answered, "Give me a blessing; since you have given me land in the South, give me also springs of water." So he gave her the upper springs and the lower springs.

²⁰This *was* the inheritance of the tribe of the children of Judah according to their families:

²¹The cities at the limits of the tribe of the children of Judah, toward the border of Edom in the South, were Kabzeel, Eder, Jagur, ²²Kinah, Dimonah, Adadah, ²³Kedesh, Hazor, Ithnan, ²⁴Ziph, Telem, Bealoth, ²⁵Hazor, Hadattah, Kerioth, Hezron (which *is* Hazor), ²⁶Amam, Shema, Moladah, ²⁷Hazar Gaddah, Heshmon, Beth Pelet, ²⁸Hazar Shual, Beersheba, Bizjothjah, ²⁹Baalah, Ijim, Ezem, ³⁰Eltolad, Chesil, Hormah, ³¹Ziklag, Madmannah, Sansannah, ³²Lebaoth, Shilhim, Ain, and Rimmon: all the cities *are* twenty-nine, with their villages.

³³In the lowland: Eshtaol, Zorah, Ashnah, ³⁴Zanoah, En Gannim, Tappuah, Enam, ³⁵Jarmuth, Adullam, Socoh, Azekah, ³⁶Sharaim, Adithaim, Gederah, and Gederothaim: fourteen cities with their villages; ³⁷Zenan, Hadashah, Migdal Gad, ³⁸Dilean, Mizpah, Joktheel, ³⁹Lachish, Bozkath, Eglon, ⁴⁰Cabbon, Lahmas,ʳ Kithlish, ⁴¹Gederoth, Beth Dagon, Naamah, and Makkedah: sixteen cities with their villages; ⁴²Libnah, Ether, Ashan, ⁴³Jiphtah, Ashnah, Nezib, ⁴⁴Keilah, Achzib, and Mareshah: nine cities with their villages; ⁴⁵Ekron, with its towns and villages; ⁴⁶from Ekron to the sea, all that *lay* near Ashdod, with their villages; ⁴⁷Ashdod with its towns and villages, Gaza with its towns and villages—as far as the Brook of Egypt and the Great Sea with *its* coastline.

⁴⁸And in the mountain country: Shamir, Jattir, Sochoh, ⁴⁹Dannah, Kirjath Sannah (which *is* Debir), ⁵⁰Anab, Eshtemoh, Anim, ⁵¹Goshen, Holon, and Giloh: eleven cities with their villages; ⁵²Arab, Dumah, Eshean, ⁵³Janum, Beth Tappuah, Aphekah, ⁵⁴Humtah, Kirjath Arba (which *is* Hebron), and Zior: nine cities with their villages; ⁵⁵Maon, Carmel, Ziph, Juttah, ⁵⁶Jezreel, Jokdeam, Zanoah, ⁵⁷Kain, Gibeah, and Timnah: ten cities with their villages; ⁵⁸Halhul, Beth Zur, Gedor,

15:40 ʳOr *Lahmam*

⁵⁹Maarath, Beth Anoth, and Eltekon: six cities with their villages; ⁶⁰Kirjath Baal (which *is* Kirjath Jearim) and Rabbah: two cities with their villages.

⁶¹In the wilderness: Beth Arabah, Middin, Secacah, ⁶²Nibshan, the City of Salt, and En Gedi: six cities with their villages.

⁶³As for the Jebusites, the inhabitants of Jerusalem, the children of Judah could not drive them out; but the Jebusites dwell with the children of Judah at Jerusalem to this day.

16 The* lot fell to the children of Joseph from the Jordan, by Jericho, to the waters of Jericho on the east, to the wilderness that goes up from Jericho through the mountains to Bethel, ²then went out from Bethel to Luz,ˢ passed along to the border of the Archites at Ataroth, ³and went down westward to the boundary of the Japhletites, as far as the boundary of Lower Beth Horon to Gezer; and it ended at the sea.

⁴So the children of Joseph, Manasseh and Ephraim, took their inheritance.

⁵The border of the children of Ephraim, according to their families, was *thus:* The border of their inheritance on the east side was Ataroth Addar as far as Upper Beth Horon.

⁶And the border went out toward the sea on the north side of Michmethath; then the border went around eastward to Taanath Shiloh, and passed by it on the east of Janohah. ⁷Then it went down from Janohah to Ataroth and Naarah,ᵗ reached to Jericho, and came out at the Jordan.

⁸The border went out from Tappuah westward to the Brook Kanah, and it ended at the sea. This *was* the inheritance of the tribe of the children of Ephraim according to their families. ⁹The separate cities for the children of Ephraim *were* among the inheritance of the children of Manasseh, all the cities with their villages.

¹⁰And they did not drive out the Canaanites who dwelt in Gezer; but the Canaanites dwell among the Ephraimites to this day and have become forced laborers.

17 There was also a lot for the tribe of Manasseh, for he *was* the firstborn of Joseph: *namely* for Machir the firstborn of Manasseh, the father of Gilead, because he was a man of war; therefore he was given Gilead and Bashan. ²And there was *a lot* for the rest of the children of Manasseh according to their families: for the children of Abiezer,ᵘ the children of Helek, the children of Asriel, the children of Shechem, the children of Hepher, and the children of Shemida; these *were* the male children of Manasseh the son of Joseph according to their families.

³But Zelophehad the son of Hepher, the son of Gilead, the son of Machir, the son of Manasseh, had no sons, but only daughters. And these *are* the names of his daughters: Mahlah, Noah, Hoglah, Milcah, and Tirzah. ⁴And they came near before Eleazar the priest, before Joshua the son of Nun, and before the rulers, saying, "The LORD commanded Moses to give us an inheritance among our brothers." Therefore, according to the commandment of the LORD, he gave them an inheritance among their father's brothers. ⁵Ten

CHAPTERS 16—17

16:1ff Ephraim and Manasseh were Joseph's two sons, born to him in Egypt. Jacob adopted them as his own and gave them a special blessing from the Lord (Gen. 48), which explains why these two tribes were given such valuable land in the heart of Canaan. Joseph had kept the family alive during seven years of famine, and his descendants reaped the benefits. They were wealthy because of Joseph's faith and love and Jacob's special blessing.

16:2 ˢSeptuagint reads *Bethel* (that is, Luz).   16:7 ᵗOr *Naaran* (compare 1 Chronicles 7:28)   17:2 ᵘCalled *Jeezer* in Numbers 26:30

shares fell to Manasseh, besides the land of Gilead and Bashan, which *were* on the other side of the Jordan, 6because the daughters of Manasseh received an inheritance among his sons; and the rest of Manasseh's sons had the land of Gilead.

7And the territory of Manasseh was from Asher to Michmethath, that *lies* east of Shechem; and the border went along south to the inhabitants of En Tappuah. 8Manasseh had the land of Tappuah, but Tappuah on the border of Manasseh *belonged* to the children of Ephraim. 9And the border descended to the Brook Kanah, southward to the brook. These cities of Ephraim *are* among the cities of Manasseh. The border of Manasseh *was* on the north side of the brook; and it ended at the sea.

10Southward *it was* Ephraim's, northward *it was* Manasseh's, and the sea was its border. Manasseh's territory was adjoining Asher on the north and Issachar on the east. 11And in Issachar and in Asher, Manasseh had Beth Shean and its towns, Ibleam and its towns, the inhabitants of Dor and its towns, the inhabitants of En Dor and its towns, the inhabitants of Taanach and its towns, and the inhabitants of Megiddo and its towns—three hilly regions. 12Yet the children of Manasseh could not drive out *the inhabitants of* those cities, but the Canaanites were determined to dwell in that land. 13And it happened, when the children of Israel grew strong, that they put the Canaanites to forced labor, but did not utterly drive them out.

14*Then the children of Joseph spoke to Joshua, saying, "Why have you given us *only* one lot and one share to inherit, since we *are* a great people, inasmuch as the LORD has blessed us until now?"

15So Joshua answered them, "If you *are* a great people, *then* go up to the forest *country* and clear a place for yourself there in the land of the Perizzites and the giants, since the mountains of Ephraim are too confined for you."

16But the children of Joseph said, "The mountain country is not enough for us; and all the Canaanites who dwell in the land of the valley have chariots of iron, *both those* who *are* of Beth Shean and its towns and *those* who *are* of the Valley of Jezreel."

17And Joshua spoke to the house of Joseph—to Ephraim and Manasseh—saying, "You *are* a great people and have great power; you shall not have *only* one lot, 18but the mountain country shall be yours. Although it *is* wooded, you shall cut it down, and its farthest extent shall be yours; for you shall drive out the Canaanites, though they have iron chariots *and* are strong."

17:14–18 However, we must not live only on what our ancestors have provided. We must also claim an inheritance for ourselves and our children (17:14–18). The two tribes did a lot of complaining but not much conquering! In the case of Zelophehad's daughters (17:3–6), they had not because they asked not (James 4:2). In the case of the two tribes, they had not because they claimed not. Are you guilty?

CHAPTERS 18—19

18:1 Since it was centrally located, Shiloh was the ideal place for the tabernacle. During the years of Israel's wanderings, the tabernacle was in the center of the camp. Now it was at the center of the land, accessible to all and a reminder that the fear of God must be at the heart of the nation. Beware the sin of neglect! It was not the enemy that prevented the tribes from claiming their inheritance; it was their own indifference and indolence. (See James 4:17.)

18 Now* the whole congregation of the children of Israel assembled together at Shiloh, and set up the tabernacle of meeting there. And the land was subdued before them. 2But there remained among the children of Israel seven tribes which had not yet received their inheritance.

3Then Joshua said to the children of Israel: "How long will you neglect to go and possess the land which the LORD God of your fathers has given you? 4Pick out from among you three men for *each* tribe, and I will send them; they shall rise and go through the land, survey it according to their inheritance, and come *back* to me. 5And they shall divide it into seven parts. Judah shall remain in their territory on the south, and the house of Joseph shall remain in their territory on the north.

6*You shall therefore survey the land in seven parts and bring *the survey* here to me, that I may cast lots for you here before the LORD our God. 7But the Levites have no part among you, for the priesthood of the LORD *is* their inheritance. And Gad, Reuben, and half the tribe of Manasseh have received their inheritance beyond the Jordan on the east, which Moses the servant of the LORD gave them."

8Then the men arose to go away; and Joshua charged those who went to survey the land, saying, "Go, walk through the land, survey it, and come back to me, that I may cast lots for you here before the LORD in Shiloh." 9So the men went, passed through the land, and wrote the survey in a book in seven parts by cities; and they came to Joshua at the camp in Shiloh. 10Then Joshua cast lots for them in Shiloh before the LORD, and there Joshua divided the land to the children of Israel according to their divisions.

11Now the lot of the tribe of the children of Benjamin came up according to their families, and the territory of their lot came out between the children of Judah and the children of Joseph. 12Their border on the north side began at the Jordan, and the border went up to the side of Jericho on the north, and went up through the mountains westward; it ended at the Wilderness of Beth Aven. 13The border went over from there toward Luz, to the side of Luz (which *is* Bethel) southward; and the border descended to Ataroth Addar, near the hill that *lies* on the south side of Lower Beth Horon.

14Then the border extended around the west side to the south, from the hill that *lies* before Beth Horon southward; and it ended at Kirjath Baal (which *is* Kirjath Jearim), a city of the children of Judah. This *was* the west side.

15The south side *began* at the end of Kirjath Jearim, and the border extended on the west and went out to the spring of the waters of Nephtoah. 16Then the border came down to the end of the mountain that *lies* before the Valley of the Son of Hinnom, which *is* in the Valley of the Rephaim[v] on the north, descended to the Valley of Hinnom, to the side of the Jebusite *city* on the south, and descended to En Rogel. 17And it went around from the north, went out to En Shemesh, and extended toward Geliloth, which is before the Ascent of Adummim, and descended to the stone of Bohan the son of Reuben. 18Then it passed along toward the north side of Arabah,[w] and went down to Arabah. 19And the border passed along to the north side of Beth Hoglah; then the border ended at the north bay at the Salt Sea, at the south end of the Jordan. This *was* the southern boundary.

20The Jordan was its border on the east side. This *was* the inheritance of the children of Benjamin, according to its boundaries all around, according to their families.

21Now the cities of the tribe of the children of Benjamin, according to their families, were Jericho, Beth Hoglah, Emek Keziz, 22Beth Arabah, Zemaraim, Bethel, 23Avim, Parah, Ophrah, 24Chephar Haammoni, Ophni, and Gaba: twelve cities with their villages; 25Gibeon, Ramah, Beeroth, 26Mizpah, Chephirah, Mozah, 27Rekem,

18:6–10 The surveyors gathered the facts, but God gave the guidance needed for the allocation of the land (18:8–10). We must cooperate with the Lord if we want to know His will. Although we must not *lean on* our own understanding (Prov. 3:6), we must have understanding in order for God to direct us.

18:16 vLiterally *Giants* 18:18 wOr *Beth Arabah* (compare 15:6 and 18:22)

Irpeel, Taralah, 28Zelah, Eleph, Jebus (which *is*
Jerusalem), Gibeath, *and* Kirjath: fourteen cities
with their villages. This was the inheritance of
the children of Benjamin according to their
families.

19 The second lot came out for Simeon, for
the tribe of the children of Simeon according to their families. And their inheritance was
within the inheritance of the children of Judah.
2They had in their inheritance Beersheba (Sheba),
Moladah, 3Hazar Shual, Balah, Ezem, 4Eltolad,
Bethul, Hormah, 5Ziklag, Beth Marcaboth, Hazar
Susah, 6Beth Lebaoth, and Sharuhen: thirteen cities and their villages; 7Ain, Rimmon, Ether, and
Ashan: four cities and their villages; 8and all the
villages that *were* all around these cities as far
as Baalath Beer, Ramah of the South. This *was*
the inheritance of the tribe of the children of
Simeon according to their families.
9The inheritance of the children of Simeon *was
included* in the share of the children of Judah,
for the share of the children of Judah was too
much for them. Therefore the children of Simeon
had *their* inheritance within the inheritance of
that people.
10The third lot came out for the children of
Zebulun according to their families, and the border of their inheritance was as far as Sarid.
11Their border went toward the west and to Mara-
lah, went to Dabbasheth, and extended along the
brook that is east of Jokneam. 12Then from Sarid
it went eastward toward the sunrise along the border of Chisloth Tabor, and went out toward Daberath, bypassing Japhia. 13And from there it
passed along on the east of Gath Hepher, toward
Eth Kazin, and extended to Rimmon, which borders on Neah. 14Then the border went around it
on the north side of Hannathon, and it ended in
the Valley of Jiphthah El. 15Included were Kat-
tath, Nahallal, Shimron, Idalah, and Bethlehem:
twelve cities with their villages. 16This *was* the
inheritance of the children of Zebulun according
to their families, these cities with their villages.
17The fourth lot came out to Issachar, for the
children of Issachar according to their families.
18And their territory went to Jezreel, and *included*
Chesulloth, Shunem, 19Haphraim, Shion, Anaha-
rath, 20Rabbith, Kishion, Abez, 21Remeth, En Gannim, En Haddah, and Beth Pazzez. 22And the border reached to Tabor, Shahazimah, and Beth
Shemesh; their border ended at the Jordan: sixteen cities with their villages. 23This *was* the inheritance of the tribe of the children of Issachar
according to their families, the cities and their
villages.
24The fifth lot came out for the tribe of the children of Asher according to their families. 25And
their territory included Helkath, Hali, Beten,
Achshaph, 26Alammelech, Amad, and Mishal; it
reached to Mount Carmel westward, along *the
Brook* Shihor Libnath. 27It turned toward the sunrise to Beth Dagon; and it reached to Zebulun and
to the Valley of Jiphthah El, then northward beyond Beth Emek and Neiel, bypassing Cabul
which was on the left, 28including Ebron,x Rehob,

19:28 xFollowing Masoretic Text, Targum, and Vulgate; a few
Hebrew manuscripts read *Abdon* (compare 21:30 and
1 Chronicles 6:74).

Hammon, and Kanah, as far as Greater Sidon.
29And the border turned to Ramah and to the fortified city of Tyre; then the border turned to Hosah,
and ended at the sea by the region of Achzib.
30Also Ummah, Aphek, and Rehob *were included:*
twenty-two cities with their villages. 31This *was*
the inheritance of the tribe of the children of
Asher according to their families, these cities with
their villages.

32The sixth lot came out to the children of Naphtali, for the children of Naphtali according to their
families. 33And their border began at Heleph, enclosing the territory from the terebinth tree in
Zaanannim, Adami Nekeb, and Jabneel, as far as
Lakkum; it ended at the Jordan. 34From Heleph
the border extended westward to Aznoth Tabor,
and went out from there toward Hukkok; it ad-
joined Zebulun on the south side and Asher on
the west side, and ended at Judah by the Jordan
toward the sunrise. 35And the fortified cities *are*
Ziddim, Zer, Hammath, Rakkath, Chinnereth,
36Adamah, Ramah, Hazor, 37Kedesh, Edrei, En
Hazor, 38Iron, Migdal El, Horem, Beth Anath, and
Beth Shemesh: nineteen cities with their villages.
39This *was* the inheritance of the tribe of the children of Naphtali according to their families, the
cities and their villages.

40The seventh lot came out for the tribe of the
children of Dan according to their families.
41And the territory of their inheritance was Zorah,
Eshtaol, Ir Shemesh, 42Shaalabbin, Aijalon, Jeth-
lah, 43Elon, Timnah, Ekron, 44Eltekeh, Gibbethon,
Baalath, 45Jehud, Bene Berak, Gath Rimmon,
46Me Jarkon, and Rakkon, with the region near
Joppa. 47And the border of the children of Dan
went beyond these, because the children of Dan
went up to fight against Leshem and took it; and
they struck it with the edge of the sword, took
possession of it, and dwelt in it. They called
Leshem, Dan, after the name of Dan their father.
48This *is* the inheritance of the tribe of the children
of Dan according to their families, these cities
with their villages.

49*When they had made an end of dividing the
land as an inheritance according to their borders,
the children of Israel gave an inheritance among
them to Joshua the son of Nun. 50According to
the word of the LORD they gave him the city which
he asked for, Timnath Serah in the mountains of
Ephraim; and he built the city and dwelt in it.
51These *were* the inheritances which Eleazar
the priest, Joshua the son of Nun, and the heads
of the fathers of the tribes of the children of Israel
divided as an inheritance by lot in Shiloh before
the LORD, at the door of the tabernacle of meeting.
So they made an end of dividing the country.

20 The* LORD also spoke to Joshua, saying,
2"Speak to the children of Israel, saying:
'Appoint for yourselves cities of refuge, of which
I spoke to you through Moses, 3that the slayer
who kills a person accidentally *or* unintentionally
may flee there; and they shall be your refuge from
the avenger of blood. 4And when he flees to one
of those cities, and stands at the entrance of the
gate of the city, and declares his case in the hearing of the elders of that city, they shall take him
into the city as one of them, and give him a place,
that he may dwell among them. 5Then if the
avenger of blood pursues him, they shall not deliver the slayer into his hand, because he struck
his neighbor unintentionally, but did not hate him

19:49–51 Joshua saw to it that the
distribution to the tribes was completed
before he received his own inheritance. The
city of Timnath was located in a
mountainous region where life would not be
easy. Joshua could have chosen the finest
place in the land, but he put others first and
let them take the best (1 Cor. 10:24; Phil.
2:1–4).

CHAPTER 20

20:1ff The cities of refuge are mentioned
in Exodus 21:12–13, Numbers 35, and
Deuteronomy 19, so you may want to review
those passages.

Jesus Christ is our "city of refuge" (Heb.
6:18–20), but the salvation He gives is in
contrast to the refuge given to the
manslayer. It is true that the sinner must
come to Christ (Matt. 11:28–30), but it is
also true that Christ first comes to us (Luke
19:10). The elders of the six cities did not
go seeking for people to help.

20:7 When we come to Christ, there is no trial to determine our guilt. We know we are guilty! That is why we fled to Him! We did not stand at the door and wait; we entered the open door (John 10:9) and were welcomed by the Savior, knowing that we would never face condemnation (John 5:24; Rom. 8:1). The manslayer had to remain in the city, but we "go in and out and find pasture" (John 10:9).

CHAPTER 21

21:1ff After the land was apportioned, the writer looked back and made one summary statement: *God keeps His promises* (v. 45).

beforehand. 6And he shall dwell in that city until he stands before the congregation for judgment, *and* until the death of the one who is high priest in those days. Then the slayer may return and come to his own city and his own house, to the city from which he fled.' "

7*So they appointed Kedesh in Galilee, in the mountains of Naphtali, Shechem in the mountains of Ephraim, and Kirjath Arba (which *is* Hebron) in the mountains of Judah. 8And on the other side of the Jordan, by Jericho eastward, they assigned Bezer in the wilderness on the plain, from the tribe of Reuben, Ramoth in Gilead, from the tribe of Gad, and Golan in Bashan, from the tribe of Manasseh. 9These were the cities appointed for all the children of Israel and for the stranger who dwelt among them, that whoever killed a person accidentally might flee there, and not die by the hand of the avenger of blood until he stood before the congregation.

21 Then* the heads of the fathers' *houses* of the Levites came near to Eleazar the priest, to Joshua the son of Nun, and to the heads of the fathers' *houses* of the tribes of the children of Israel. 2And they spoke to them at Shiloh in the land of Canaan, saying, "The LORD commanded through Moses to give us cities to dwell in, with their common-lands for our livestock." 3So the children of Israel gave to the Levites from their inheritance, at the commandment of the LORD, these cities and their common-lands:

4Now the lot came out for the families of the Kohathites. And the children of Aaron the priest, *who were* of the Levites, had thirteen cities by lot from the tribe of Judah, from the tribe of Simeon, and from the tribe of Benjamin. 5The rest of the children of Kohath had ten cities by lot from the families of the tribe of Ephraim, from the tribe of Dan, and from the half-tribe of Manasseh.

6And the children of Gershon had thirteen cities by lot from the families of the tribe of Issachar, from the tribe of Asher, from the tribe of Naphtali, and from the half-tribe of Manasseh in Bashan.

7The children of Merari according to their families had twelve cities from the tribe of Reuben, from the tribe of Gad, and from the tribe of Zebulun.

8And the children of Israel gave these cities with their common-lands by lot to the Levites, as the LORD had commanded by the hand of Moses.

9So they gave from the tribe of the children of Judah and from the tribe of the children of Simeon these cities which are designated by name, 10which were for the children of Aaron, one of the families of the Kohathites, *who were* of the children of Levi; for the lot was theirs first. 11And they gave them Kirjath Arba (*Arba was* the father of Anak), which *is* Hebron, in the mountains of Judah, with the common-land surrounding it. 12But the fields of the city and its villages they gave to Caleb the son of Jephunneh as his possession.

13Thus to the children of Aaron the priest they gave Hebron with its common-land (a city of refuge for the slayer), Libnah with its common-land, 14Jattir with its common-land, Eshtemoa with its common-land, 15Holon with its common-land, Debir with its common-land, 16Ain with its common-land, Juttah with its common-land, and Beth Shemesh with its common-land: nine cities from those two tribes; 17and from the tribe of Benjamin, Gibeon with its common-land, Geba with its common-land, 18Anathoth with its common-land, and Almon with its common-land: four cities. 19All the cities of the children of Aaron, the priests, *were* thirteen cities with their common-lands.

20And the families of the children of Kohath, the Levites, the rest of the children of Kohath, even they had the cities of their lot from the tribe of Ephraim. 21For they gave them Shechem with its common-land in the mountains of Ephraim (a city of refuge for the slayer), Gezer with its common-land, 22Kibzaim with its common-land, and Beth Horon with its common-land: four cities; 23and from the tribe of Dan, Eltekeh with its common-land, Gibbethon with its common-land, 24Aijalon with its common-land, *and* Gath Rimmon with its common-land: four cities; 25and from the half-tribe of Manasseh, Tanach with its common-land and Gath Rimmon with its common-land: two cities. 26All the ten cities with their common-lands *were* for the rest of the families of the children of Kohath.

27Also to the children of Gershon, of the families of the Levites, from the *other* half-tribe of Manasseh, *they gave* Golan in Bashan with its common-land (a city of refuge for the slayer), and Be Eshterah with its common-land: two cities; 28and from the tribe of Issachar, Kishion with its common-land, Daberath with its common-land, 29Jarmuth with its common-land, *and* En Gannim with its common-land: four cities; 30and from the tribe of Asher, Mishal with its common-land, Abdon with its common-land, 31Helkath with its common-land, and Rehob with its common-land: four cities; 32and from the tribe of Naphtali, Kedesh in Galilee with its common-land (a city of refuge for the slayer), Hammoth Dor with its common-land, and Kartan with its common-land: three cities. 33All the cities of the Gershonites according to their families *were* thirteen cities with their common-lands.

34And to the families of the children of Merari, the rest of the Levites, from the tribe of Zebulun, Jokneam with its common-land, Kartah with its common-land, 35Dimnah with its common-land, *and* Nahalal with its common-land: four cities; 36and from the tribe of Reuben, Bezer with its common-land, Jahaz with its common-land, 37Kedemoth with its common-land, and Mephaath with its common-land: four cities;y 38and from the tribe of Gad, Ramoth in Gilead with its common-land (a city of refuge for the slayer), Mahanaim with its common-land, 39Heshbon with its common-land, *and* Jazer with its common-land: four cities in all. 40So all the cities for the children of Merari according to their families, the rest of the families of the Levites, were *by* their lot twelve cities.

41All the cities of the Levites within the possession of the children of Israel *were* forty-eight cities with their common-lands. 42Every one of these cities had its common-land surrounding it; thus *were* all these cities.

43*So the LORD gave to Israel all the land of which He had sworn to give to their fathers, and they took possession of it and dwelt in it. 44*The LORD gave them rest all around, according to all

---

21:37 yFollowing Septuagint and Vulgate (compare 1 Chronicles 6:78, 79); Masoretic Text, Bomberg, and Targum omit verses 36 and 37.

21:43 God kept His promise and gave the land to Israel. He had promised it first to Abraham (Gen. 13:14–17), and then to his descendants (Gen. 17:8). On the basis of that promise, Joshua entered Canaan, defeated the enemy, and claimed the land for Israel.

21:44 God kept His promise and gave them rest from war, enabling them to conquer all their enemies and enjoy their inheritance (v. 44). (See Deut. 12:10; 25:19; Josh. 1:13.) We have spiritual rest today through Christ (Heb. 3—4) and will one day enter into eternal rest.

21:45 God kept His promise and scattered the Levites throughout Israel (Gen. 49:7). He gave them forty-eight towns, including the cities of refuge. It should have been a blessing to Israel to have these servants of God living in many different places and sharing the truth of the Word with the people (Deut. 33:10).

Not one word of His promises has failed (v. 45; Josh. 23:14; 1 Kings 8:56). You can trust the Word of God.

CHAPTER 22

22:1 Not only had the Lord kept His promises to Israel, but Reuben, Gad, and the half-tribe of Manasseh had kept their promise as well (Num. 32:25–32). It was time for them to cross the Jordan and join their families.

22:2, 3 Joshua *commended* them for their faithful service, something that all of us should do for those who have ministered well (1 Thess. 5:12–13). He also *commanded* them to obey the Lord and serve Him sincerely. Finally, he *cautioned* them not to become selfish but to share the spoils with their brethren. Perhaps Achan came to mind as Joshua spoke to them.

22:4 The land was at rest, but the eastern tribes were restless because the Jordan River separated them from their brethren. Would their children grow up and think they were not truly Israelites? They should have considered that when they chose the boundary!

that He had sworn to their fathers. And not a man of all their enemies stood against them; the LORD delivered all their enemies into their hand. 45*Not a word failed of any good thing which the LORD had spoken to the house of Israel. All came to pass.

22 Then* Joshua called the Reubenites, the Gadites, and half the tribe of Manasseh, 2*and said to them: "You have kept all that Moses the servant of the LORD commanded you, and have obeyed my voice in all that I commanded you. 3You have not left your brethren these many days, up to this day, but have kept the charge of the commandment of the LORD your God. 4*And now the LORD your God has given rest to your brethren, as He promised them; now therefore, return and go to your tents *and* to the land of your possession, which Moses the servant of the LORD gave you on the other side of the Jordan. 5But take careful heed to do the commandment and the law which Moses the servant of the LORD commanded you, to love the LORD your God, to walk in all His ways, to keep His commandments, to hold fast to Him, and to serve Him with all your heart and with all your soul." 6So Joshua blessed them and sent them away, and they went to their tents.

7Now to half the tribe of Manasseh Moses had given a possession in Bashan, but to the *other* half of it Joshua gave *a possession* among their brethren on this side of the Jordan, westward. And indeed, when Joshua sent them away to their tents, he blessed them, 8and spoke to them, saying, "Return with much riches to your tents, with very much livestock, with silver, with gold, with bronze, with iron, and with very much clothing. Divide the spoil of your enemies with your brethren."

9So the children of Reuben, the children of Gad, and half the tribe of Manasseh returned, and departed from the children of Israel at Shiloh, which *is* in the land of Canaan, to go to the country of Gilead. to the land of their possession, which they had obtained according to the word of the LORD by the hand of Moses.

10And when they came to the region of the Jordan which *is* in the land of Canaan, the children of Reuben, the children of Gad, and half the tribe of Manasseh built an altar there by the Jordan—a great, impressive altar. 11Now the children of Israel heard *someone* say, "Behold, the children of Reuben, the children of Gad, and half the tribe of Manasseh have built an altar on the frontier of the land of Canaan, in the region of the Jordan—on the children of Israel's side." 12And when the children of Israel heard *of it,* the whole congregation of the children of Israel gathered together at Shiloh to go to war against them.

13Then the children of Israel sent Phinehas the son of Eleazar the priest to the children of Reuben, to the children of Gad, and to half the tribe of Manasseh, into the land of Gilead, 14and with him ten rulers, one ruler each from the chief house of every tribe of Israel; and each one *was* the head of the house of his father among the divisions^z of Israel. 15Then they came to the children of Reuben, to the children of Gad, and to half the tribe of Manasseh, to the land of Gilead, and they spoke

---

22:14 ^z Literally *thousands*

with them, saying, [16]*"Thus says the whole congregation of the LORD: 'What treachery *is* this that you have committed against the God of Israel, to turn away this day from following the LORD, in that you have built for yourselves an altar, that you might rebel this day against the LORD? [17]*Is* the iniquity of Peor not enough for us, from which we are not cleansed till this day, although there was a plague in the congregation of the LORD, [18]but that you must turn away this day from following the LORD? And it shall be, if you rebel today against the LORD, that tomorrow He will be angry with the whole congregation of Israel. [19]Nevertheless, if the land of your possession *is* unclean, *then* cross over to the land of the possession of the LORD, where the LORD's tabernacle stands, and take possession among us; but do not rebel against the LORD, nor rebel against us, by building yourselves an altar besides the altar of the LORD our God. [20]Did not Achan the son of Zerah commit a trespass in the accursed thing, and wrath fell on all the congregation of Israel? And that man did not perish alone in his iniquity.'"

[21]Then the children of Reuben, the children of Gad, and half the tribe of Manasseh answered and said to the heads of the divisions[a] of Israel: [22]"The LORD God of gods, the LORD God of gods, He knows, and let Israel itself know—if *it is* in rebellion, or if in treachery against the LORD, do not save us this day. [23]If we have built ourselves an altar to turn from following the LORD, or if to offer on it burnt offerings or grain offerings, or if to offer peace offerings on it, let the LORD Himself require *an account.* [24]But in fact we have done it for fear, for a reason, saying, 'In time to come your descendants may speak to our descendants, saying, "What have you to do with the LORD God of Israel? [25]For the LORD has made the Jordan a border between you and us, *you* children of Reuben and children of Gad. You have no part in the LORD." So your descendants would make our descendants cease fearing the LORD.' [26]Therefore we said, 'Let us now prepare to build ourselves an altar, not for burnt offering nor for sacrifice, [27]but *that* it *may be* a witness between you and us and our generations after us, that we may perform the service of the LORD before Him with our burnt offerings, with our sacrifices, and with our peace offerings; that your descendants may not say to our descendants in time to come, "You have no part in the LORD."' [28]Therefore we said that it will be, when they say *this* to us or to our generations in time to come, that we may say, 'Here is the replica of the altar of the LORD which our fathers made, though not for burnt offerings nor for sacrifices; but it *is* a witness between you and us.' [29]Far be it from us that we should rebel against the LORD, and turn from following the LORD this day, to build an altar for burnt offerings, for grain offerings, or for sacrifices, besides the altar of the LORD our God which *is* before His tabernacle."

[30]Now when Phinehas the priest and the rulers of the congregation, the heads of the divisions[b] of Israel who *were* with him, heard the words that the children of Reuben, the children of Gad, and the children of Manasseh spoke, it pleased them.

22:16–34 The building of the altar was at first misunderstood as a declaration of war, but then it became a witness of peace and unity. It is too bad when God's people are forced to manufacture evidence to bear witness of their unity. Before you declare war on the brethren, stop to find out what is going on. Maybe you agree after all! Ponder Proverbs 18:13 and James 3:13–18.

22:21 [a]Literally *thousands*   22:30 [b]Literally *thousands*

31Then Phinehas the son of Eleazar the priest said to the children of Reuben, the children of Gad, and the children of Manasseh, "This day we perceive that the LORD *is* among us, because you have not committed this treachery against the LORD. Now you have delivered the children of Israel out of the hand of the LORD."

32And Phinehas the son of Eleazar the priest, and the rulers, returned from the children of Reuben and the children of Gad, from the land of Gilead to the land of Canaan, to the children of Israel, and brought back word to them. 33So the thing pleased the children of Israel, and the children of Israel blessed God; they spoke no more of going against them in battle, to destroy the land where the children of Reuben and Gad dwelt.

34The children of Reuben and the children of Gadᶜ called the altar, *Witness*, "For *it is* a witness between us that the LORD *is* God."

CHAPTER 23

23:1ff No matter how great leaders may be, they cannot last forever, although their work is never lost (1 John 2:17). Like his predecessor Moses, Joshua gave a farewell address, first to his leaders (chap. 23) and then to the people as a whole (chap. 24).

23:3–7 He magnified the Lord and not himself. No one would question that Joshua was a gifted leader and a great general, but he gave the glory to God.

23:8 He challenged the people to keep trusting God and claiming their inheritance. In the book of Judges, you will discover how their incomplete obedience led to compromise and severe discipline from the Lord. Joshua had warned them (v. 16), but they forgot his words. Triumph was turned into tragedy.

23 Now* it came to pass, a long time after the LORD had given rest to Israel from all their enemies round about, that Joshua was old, advanced in age. 2And Joshua called for all Israel, for their elders, for their heads, for their judges, and for their officers, and said to them:

"I am old, advanced in age. 3*You have seen all that the LORD your God has done to all these nations because of you, for the LORD your God *is* He who has fought for you. 4See, I have divided to you by lot these nations that remain, to be an inheritance for your tribes, from the Jordan, with all the nations that I have cut off, as far as the Great Sea westward. 5And the LORD your God will expel them from before you and drive them out of your sight. So you shall possess their land, as the LORD your God promised you. 6Therefore be very courageous to keep and to do all that is written in the Book of the Law of Moses, lest you turn aside from it to the right hand or to the left, 7*and* lest you go among these nations, these who remain among you. You shall not make mention of the name of their gods, nor cause *anyone* to swear *by them;* you shall not serve them nor bow down to them, 8*but you shall hold fast to the LORD your God, as you have done to this day. 9For the LORD has driven out from before you great and strong nations; but *as for* you, no one has been able to stand against you to this day. 10One man of you shall chase a thousand, for the LORD your God *is* He who fights for you, as He promised you. 11Therefore take careful heed to yourselves, that you love the LORD your God. 12Or else, if indeed you do go back, and cling to the remnant of these nations—these that remain among you— and make marriages with them, and go in to them and they to you, 13know for certain that the LORD your God will no longer drive out these nations from before you. But they shall be snares and traps to you, and scourges on your sides and thorns in your eyes, until you perish from this good land which the LORD your God has given you.

22:34 ᶜSeptuagint adds *and half the tribe of Manasseh*

Family Faith—Joshua was a great leader and a courageous general, and he was also a godly father who led his family in serving the Lord. He took seriously the example of Abraham (Gen. 18:19) and the exhortation of Moses (Deut. 6:4–9). Parents today need to take these Scriptures seriously, and also what Paul wrote in Ephesians 5:22—6:4.

14*"Behold, this day I *am* going the way of all the earth. And you know in all your hearts and in all your souls that not one thing has failed of all the good things which the LORD your God spoke concerning you. All have come to pass for you; not one word of them has failed. 15Therefore it shall come to pass, that as all the good things have come upon you which the LORD your God promised you, so the LORD will bring upon you all harmful things, until He has destroyed you from this good land which the LORD your God has given you. 16When you have transgressed the covenant of the LORD your God, which He commanded you, and have gone and served other gods, and bowed down to them, then the anger of the LORD will burn against you, and you shall perish quickly from the good land which He has given you."

24 Then* Joshua gathered all the tribes of Israel to Shechem and called for the elders of Israel, for their heads, for their judges, and for their officers; and they presented themselves before God. 2*And Joshua said to all the people, "Thus says the LORD God of Israel: 'Your fathers, *including* Terah, the father of Abraham and the father of Nahor, dwelt on the other side of the River^d in old times; and they served other gods. 3Then I took your father Abraham from the other side of the River, led him throughout all the land of Canaan, and multiplied his descendants and gave him Isaac. 4To Isaac I gave Jacob and Esau. To Esau I gave the mountains of Seir to possess, but Jacob and his children went down to Egypt. 5Also I sent Moses and Aaron, and I plagued Egypt, according to what I did among them. Afterward I brought you out. 6'Then I brought your fathers out of Egypt, and you came to the sea; and the Egyptians pursued your fathers with chariots and horsemen to the Red Sea. 7So they cried out to the LORD; and He put darkness between you and the Egyptians, brought the sea upon them, and covered them. And your eyes saw what I did in Egypt. Then you dwelt in the wilderness a long time. 8And I brought you into the land of the Amorites, who dwelt on the other side of the Jordan, and they fought with you. But I gave them into your hand, that you might possess their land, and I destroyed them from before you. 9Then Balak the son of Zippor, king of Moab, arose to make war against Israel, and sent and called Balaam the son of Beor to curse you. 10But I would not listen to Balaam; therefore he continued to bless you. So I delivered you out of his hand. 11Then you went over the Jordan and came to Jericho. And the men of

---

24:2 ^dHebrew *Nahar*, the Euphrates, and so in verses 3, 14, and 15

23:14, 15 He reminded them that God's Word never fails (v. 14) and must be obeyed completely if God is to continue His blessing on the land. Verse 7 explains how to wander from the Lord, and the nation did exactly that!

You are writing your own "farewell speech" right now. What will it sound like?

CHAPTER 24

24:1ff *Geography.* Joshua chose a meaningful place for his final message, for Shechem held many memories for Israel. There God appeared to Abraham (Gen. 12:6–7), and there Jacob had a "family revival" as he went to Bethel (Gen. 35:1–4). Shechem was near Mount Ebal where the people had rededicated themselves to the Lord after entering the land (Josh. 8:30–35). Being in a special place can sometimes make it easier for us to meet with God.

24:2–13 *History.* Joshua reviewed the history of Israel and reminded the people of God's grace and goodness in calling Abraham, delivering Israel from Egypt, and giving them their land. It is good to review the past and remember the mercies of the Lord.

Stones—Stones played an important role in the march of Israel through Canaan. The stones at the Jordan (4:1–9) reminded them of the miracle God performed as He opened the river; they also commemorated the people's death to the old life. The heap of stones in the Valley of Achor told of Achan's sin and the tragedy of covetousness and disobedience (7:25–26). The stones of the Law at Mount Ebal (8:31–32) spoke of Israel's dedication to God to obey His Word. The stone altar on the eastern bank of the Jordan was a witness to unity (22:10ff.), and the stone Joshua set up bore witness that the people promised to serve only the Lord (24:26–27). Over the years, those messengers became only monuments, and the people forgot what they meant. Today God's people still tend to forget what God would have us remember about our relationship with Him.

Jericho fought against you—*also* the Amorites, the Perizzites, the Canaanites, the Hittites, the Girgashites, the Hivites, and the Jebusites. But I delivered them into your hand. [12]I sent the hornet before you which drove them out from before you, *also* the two kings of the Amorites, *but* not with your sword or with your bow. [13]I have given you a land for which you did not labor, and cities which you did not build, and you dwell in them; you eat of the vineyards and olive groves which you did not plant.'

[14]*"Now therefore, fear the LORD, serve Him in sincerity and in truth, and put away the gods which your fathers served on the other side of the River and in Egypt. Serve the LORD! [15]*And if it seems evil to you to serve the LORD, choose for yourselves this day whom you will serve, whether the gods which your fathers served that *were* on the other side of the River, or the gods of the Amorites, in whose land you dwell. But as for me and my house, we will serve the LORD."

[16]So the people answered and said: "Far be it from us that we should forsake the LORD to serve other gods; [17]for the LORD our God *is* He who brought us and our fathers up out of the land of Egypt, from the house of bondage, who did those great signs in our sight, and preserved us in all the way that we went and among all the people through whom we passed. [18]And the LORD drove out from before us all the people, including the Amorites who dwelt in the land. We also will serve the LORD, for He *is* our God."

[19]But Joshua said to the people, "You cannot serve the LORD, for He *is* a holy God. He *is* a jealous God; He will not forgive your transgressions nor your sins. [20]If you forsake the LORD and serve foreign gods, then He will turn and do you harm and consume you, after He has done you good."

[21]And the people said to Joshua, "No, but we will serve the LORD!"

[22]So Joshua said to the people, "You *are* witnesses against yourselves that you have chosen the LORD for yourselves, to serve Him."

And they said, "*We are* witnesses!"

[23]*"Now therefore," *he said,* "put away the foreign gods which *are* among you, and incline your heart to the LORD God of Israel."

[24]And the people said to Joshua, "The LORD our God we will serve, and His voice we will obey!"

[25]So Joshua made a covenant with the people that day, and made for them a statute and an ordinance in Shechem.

[26]Then Joshua wrote these words in the Book of the Law of God. And he took a large stone, and set it up there under the oak that *was* by the sanctuary of the LORD. [27]And Joshua said to all the people, "Behold, this stone shall be a witness to us, for it has heard all the words of the LORD which He spoke to us. It shall therefore be a witness to you, lest you deny your God." [28]So Joshua let the people depart, each to his own inheritance.

[29]Now it came to pass after these things that Joshua the son of Nun, the servant of the LORD, died, *being* one hundred and ten years old. [30]And they buried him within the border of his inheritance at Timnath Serah, which *is* in the mountains of Ephraim, on the north side of Mount Gaash.

[31]Israel served the LORD all the days of Joshua, and all the days of the elders who outlived Joshua, who had known all the works of the LORD which He had done for Israel.

24:14 *Sincerity.* Our God is "a jealous God" in that He will not tolerate rivals. He will not be one of several gods in our lives; He must be Lord of all. Everybody serves some god, and if it is not the true God as revealed in Jesus Christ, it is a false god.

24:15 Joshua issued the challenge: "Choose for yourselves this day whom you will serve!" (v. 15). Have you chosen wisely?

32The bones of Joseph, which the children of Israel had brought up out of Egypt, they buried at Shechem, in the plot of ground which Jacob had bought from the sons of Hamor the father of Shechem for one hundred pieces of silver, and which had become an inheritance of the children of Joseph.

33And Eleazar the son of Aaron died. They buried him in a hill *belonging to* Phinehas his son, which was given to him in the mountains of Ephraim.

JUDGES

Judges is the book of "no king" (17:6; 18:1; 19:1; 21:25). God was their King, but the nation refused to obey Him. Their disobedience led to defeat (chaps. 1—2), discipline (chaps. 3—16) and decay (chaps. 17—21). Eight times we are told that the people "did evil" in God's sight and therefore had to be chastened. When God disciplined them, they cried out for mercy and were delivered, but then they lapsed back into their evil ways and had to be disciplined again.

In the book of Joshua, God was with *the whole nation* as they conquered the land. But in Judges, God turned from the nation and gave victory to *individuals* He called and empowered by His Spirit (3:10; 6:34; 11:29; etc.). Thirteen different judges are named in the book. Judges 2:16–19 is the best summary of Israel's history at this period—and a sad history it is.

We are living in a similar period today. God's people in general do not appear to be marching from victory to victory; but here and there, God enables selected servants, by the power of His Spirit, to accomplish great things for His glory. There will be no peace until there is a King in Israel.

CHAPTER 1

1:1 After the death of Joshua and the move of the two and a half tribes to the east of the Jordan, the nation did not function as one great army. Individual tribes fought to claim their inheritance, and often the tribes worked together; but something was definitely lost in the transition. God's people must endeavor "to keep the unity of the Spirit in the bond of peace" (Eph. 4:3).

1:8–26 What began with conquest (vv. 1–26) soon became compromise (vv. 27–36) as the defeated tribes gave in to the enemy. If we do not defeat the enemy completely, the enemy will eventually defeat us. Israel learned their ways and worshiped their gods, and the Lord had to chasten His people to bring them back. They forgot the warnings of Moses (Deut. 7) and Joshua (Josh. 23).

It has well been said, "The one thing we learn from history is that we do not learn from history." Read 2 Corinthians 6:14—7:1 and take it to heart.

1 Now* after the death of Joshua it came to pass that the children of Israel asked the LORD, saying, "Who shall be first to go up for us against the Canaanites to fight against them?"

2And the LORD said, "Judah shall go up. Indeed I have delivered the land into his hand."

3So Judah said to Simeon his brother, "Come up with me to my allotted territory, that we may fight against the Canaanites; and I will likewise go with you to your allotted territory." And Simeon went with him. 4Then Judah went up, and the LORD delivered the Canaanites and the Perizzites into their hand; and they killed ten thousand men at Bezek. 5And they found Adoni-Bezek in Bezek, and fought against him; and they defeated the Canaanites and the Perizzites. 6Then Adoni-Bezek fled, and they pursued him and caught him and cut off his thumbs and big toes. 7And Adoni-Bezek said, "Seventy kings with their thumbs and big toes cut off used to gather *scraps* under my table; as I have done, so God has repaid me." Then they brought him to Jerusalem, and there he died.

8*Now the children of Judah fought against Jerusalem and took it; they struck it with the edge of the sword and set the city on fire. 9And afterward the children of Judah went down to fight against the Canaanites who dwelt in the mountains, in the South,ª and in the lowland. 10Then Judah went against the Canaanites who dwelt in Hebron. (Now the name of Hebron *was* formerly Kirjath Arba.) And they killed Sheshai, Ahiman, and Talmai.

11From there they went against the inhabitants of Debir. (The name of Debir *was* formerly Kirjath Sepher.)

12Then Caleb said, "Whoever attacks Kirjath Sepher and takes it, to him I will give my daughter Achsah as wife." 13And Othniel the son of Kenaz, Caleb's younger brother, took it; so he gave him

---

1:9 ªHebrew *Negev,* and so throughout this book

his daughter Achsah as wife. [14]Now it happened, when she came *to him*, that she urged him[b] to ask her father for a field. And she dismounted from *her* donkey, and Caleb said to her, "What do you wish?" [15]So she said to him, "Give me a blessing; since you have given me land in the South, give me also springs of water."

And Caleb gave her the upper springs and the lower springs.

[16]Now the children of the Kenite, Moses' father-in-law, went up from the City of Palms with the children of Judah into the Wilderness of Judah, which *lies* in the South *near* Arad; and they went and dwelt among the people. [17]And Judah went with his brother Simeon, and they attacked the Canaanites who inhabited Zephath, and utterly destroyed it. So the name of the city was called Hormah. [18]Also Judah took Gaza with its territory, Ashkelon with its territory, and Ekron with its territory. [19]So the LORD was with Judah. And they drove out the mountaineers, but they could not drive out the inhabitants of the lowland, because they had chariots of iron. [20]And they gave Hebron to Caleb, as Moses had said. Then he expelled from there the three sons of Anak. [21]But the children of Benjamin did not drive out the Jebusites who inhabited Jerusalem; so the Jebusites dwell with the children of Benjamin in Jerusalem to this day.

[22]And the house of Joseph also went up against Bethel, and the LORD *was* with them. [23]So the house of Joseph sent men to spy out Bethel. (The name of the city *was* formerly Luz.) [24]And when the spies saw a man coming out of the city, they said to him, "Please show us the entrance to the city, and we will show you mercy." [25]So he showed them the entrance to the city, and they struck the city with the edge of the sword; but they let the man and all his family go. [26]And the man went to the land of the Hittites, built a city, and called its name Luz, which *is* its name to this day.

[27]However, Manasseh did not drive out *the inhabitants of* Beth Shean and its villages, or Taanach and its villages, or the inhabitants of Dor and its villages, or the inhabitants of Ibleam and its villages, or the inhabitants of Megiddo and its villages; for the Canaanites were determined to dwell in that land. [28]And it came to pass, when Israel was strong, that they put the Canaanites under tribute, but did not completely drive them out.

[29]Nor did Ephraim drive out the Canaanites who dwelt in Gezer; so the Canaanites dwelt in Gezer among them.

[30]Nor did Zebulun drive out the inhabitants of Kitron or the inhabitants of Nahalol; so the Canaanites dwelt among them, and were put under tribute.

[31]Nor did Asher drive out the inhabitants of Acco or the inhabitants of Sidon, or of Ahlab, Achzib, Helbah, Aphik, or Rehob. [32]So the Asherites dwelt among the Canaanites, the inhabitants of the land; for they did not drive them out.

[33]Nor did Naphtali drive out the inhabitants of Beth Shemesh or the inhabitants of Beth Anath; but they dwelt among the Canaanites, the inhabitants of the land. Nevertheless the inhabitants of

---

1:14 [b]Septuagint and Vulgate read *he urged her.*

Beth Shemesh and Beth Anath were put under tribute to them.

34And the Amorites forced the children of Dan into the mountains, for they would not allow them to come down to the valley; 35and the Amorites were determined to dwell in Mount Heres, in Aijalon, and in Shaalbim;*c* yet when the strength of the house of Joseph became greater, they were put under tribute.

36Now the boundary of the Amorites *was* from the Ascent of Akrabbim, from Sela, and upward.

CHAPTER 2

2:1 The tragedy of missed opportunities!

2 Then* the Angel of the LORD came up from Gilgal to Bochim, and said: "I led you up from Egypt and brought you to the land of which I swore to your fathers; and I said, 'I will never break My covenant with you. 2And you shall make no covenant with the inhabitants of this land; you shall tear down their altars.' But you have not obeyed My voice. Why have you done this? 3Therefore I also said, 'I will not drive them out before you; but they shall be *thorns* in your side,*d* and their gods shall be a snare to you.' "

4*So it was, when the Angel of the LORD spoke these words to all the children of Israel, that the people lifted up their voices and wept.

5Then they called the name of that place Bochim;*e* and they sacrificed there to the LORD. 6And when Joshua had dismissed the people, the children of Israel went each to his own inheritance to possess the land.

2:4, 5 *Opportunity for rededication.* It was at Gilgal that Israel first camped after crossing the Jordan (Josh. 4:19), and there they "rolled away" the old life (Josh. 5). But all they did this time was weep, and their weeping was not a sign of true repentance. It was a passing emotional experience that brought no change to their hearts.

7*So the people served the LORD all the days of Joshua, and all the days of the elders who outlived Joshua, who had seen all the great works of the LORD which He had done for Israel. 8Now Joshua the son of Nun, the servant of the LORD, died *when he was* one hundred and ten years old. 9And they buried him within the border of his inheritance at Timnath Heres, in the mountains of Ephraim, on the north side of Mount Gaash. 10When all that generation had been gathered to their fathers, another generation arose after them who did not know the LORD nor the work which He had done for Israel.

2:7 *Opportunity for training.* The older generation failed to teach the younger generation God's truth as Moses had commanded them (Deut. 6:1–9). It is bad enough that they forgot Joshua, their second greatest leader, but how could they forget the Lord? You will find the explanation in Deuteronomy 8.

11Then the children of Israel did evil in the sight of the LORD, and served the Baals; 12and they forsook the LORD God of their fathers, who had brought them out of the land of Egypt; and they followed other gods from *among* the gods of the people who *were* all around them, and they bowed down to them; and they provoked the LORD to anger. 13*They forsook the LORD and served Baal and the Ashtoreths.*f* 14And the anger of the LORD was hot against Israel. So He delivered them into the hands of plunderers who despoiled them; and He sold them into the hands of their enemies all around, so that they could no longer stand before their enemies. 15Wherever they went out, the hand of the LORD was against them for calamity, as the

2:13–15 *Opportunity for witness.* The nations in Canaan were in terrible bondage to ignorance, idolatry, and immorality, and they desperately needed to know the true God of Israel. But instead of giving illumination (Isa. 49:6), the Jews stooped to imitation and joined their neighbors in their sins. What an opportunity Israel missed, and what a price they paid!

1:35 *c*Spelled *Shaalabbin* in Joshua 19:42   2:3 *d*Septuagint, Targum, and Vulgate read *enemies to you.*   2:5 *e*Literally *Weeping*   2:13 *f*Canaanite goddesses

---

The Angel of the Lord—The Angel of the Lord in the Old Testament is generally agreed to be our Lord Jesus Christ who came to earth temporarily on occasion to deliver special messages or to accomplish special tasks. Among others, He ministered to Hagar (Gen. 16), Abraham (Gen. 22), Jacob (Gen. 31:11), and Moses (Exod. 3), and He appeared to Joshua (Josh. 5:13–15). Though we do not recognize them, the angels minister to God's people today (Heb. 1:14), and the Lord Jesus is with us as we walk with Him (Matt. 28:20; Heb. 13:5–6).

LORD had said, and as the LORD had sworn to them. And they were greatly distressed.

16Nevertheless, the LORD raised up judges who delivered them out of the hand of those who plundered them. 17Yet they would not listen to their judges, but they played the harlot with other gods, and bowed down to them. They turned quickly from the way in which their fathers walked, in obeying the commandments of the LORD; they did not do so. 18And when the LORD raised up judges for them, the LORD was with the judge and delivered them out of the hand of their enemies all the days of the judge; for the LORD was moved to pity by their groaning because of those who oppressed them and harassed them. 19*And it came to pass, when the judge was dead, that they reverted and behaved more corruptly than their fathers, by following other gods, to serve them and bow down to them. They did not cease from their own doings nor from their stubborn way.

20Then the anger of the LORD was hot against Israel; and He said, "Because this nation has transgressed My covenant which I commanded their fathers, and has not heeded My voice, 21I also will no longer drive out before them any of the nations which Joshua left when he died, 22so that through them I may test Israel, whether they will keep the ways of the LORD, to walk in them as their fathers kept *them,* or not." 23Therefore the LORD left those nations, without driving them out immediately; nor did He deliver them into the hand of Joshua.

3 Now* these *are* the nations which the LORD left, that He might test Israel by them, *that is,* all who had not known any of the wars in Canaan 2(this was only so that the generations of the children of Israel might be taught to know war, at least those who had not formerly known it), 3namely, five lords of the Philistines, all the Canaanites, the Sidonians, and the Hivites who dwelt in Mount Lebanon, from Mount Baal Hermon to the entrance of Hamath. 4And they were left, *that He might* test Israel by them, to know whether they would obey the commandments of the LORD, which He had commanded their fathers by the hand of Moses.

5*Thus the children of Israel dwelt among the Canaanites, the Hittites, the Amorites, the Perizzites, the Hivites, and the Jebusites. 6And they took their daughters to be their wives, and gave their daughters to their sons; and they served their gods.

7So the children of Israel did evil in the sight of the LORD. They forgot the LORD their God, and served the Baals and Asherahs.g 8*Therefore the anger of the LORD was hot against Israel, and He sold them into the hand of Cushan-Rishathaim king of Mesopotamia; and the children of Israel served Cushan-Rishathaim eight years. 9When the children of Israel cried out to the LORD, the LORD raised up a deliverer for the children of

---

3:7 9Name or symbol for Canaanite goddesses

2:19–23 In their relationship with God, the next generation, and their neighbors, Israel failed. Are we also failing in these ways today?

CHAPTER 3

3:1ff The presence of the enemy in the land was an opportunity for teaching, testing, and trusting. The younger generation could learn how to fight, and that would keep them from taking their inheritance for granted. God could test His people and encourage them to trust Him for victory. Even though the tribes had failed to drive out the enemy, God was still with His people and wanted to help them.

3:5–7 God's people must live *in* the world, but they must not live *like* the world. Israel forgot the Lord and adopted the ways of the enemy. It began with intermarriage, which led to the worship of idols. After all, when you visit your in-laws, you must be polite to their gods!

3:8–11 How humiliating that the pagan nations Israel imitated were used as the instruments of God's discipline! The conquerors were now the conquered. They regretted their sufferings, but they did not repent of their sins. They experienced a painful cycle of disobedience, discipline, despair, and deliverance, only to go back into disobedience again.

Chastening—The key passage is Hebrews 12:1–11. The word *chastening* means "child training" and refers to the process God uses to mature us and make us more like Jesus Christ. He tests us to bring out the best in us, but Satan tempts us to bring out the worst in us. If we persist in disobeying God, He will discipline us to bring us to submission. This is an act of love, a Father maturing a child and not a Judge punishing a criminal (Prov. 3:11–12).

Israel, who delivered them: Othniel the son of Kenaz, Caleb's younger brother. 10The Spirit of the LORD came upon him, and he judged Israel. He went out to war, and the LORD delivered Cushan-Rishathaim king of Mesopotamia into his hand; and his hand prevailed over Cushan-Rishathaim. 11So the land had rest for forty years. Then Othniel the son of Kenaz died.

12And the children of Israel again did evil in the sight of the LORD. So the LORD strengthened Eglon king of Moab against Israel, because they had done evil in the sight of the LORD. 13Then he gathered to himself the people of Ammon and Amalek, went and defeated Israel, and took possession of the City of Palms. 14So the children of Israel served Eglon king of Moab eighteen years.

15But when the children of Israel cried out to the LORD, the LORD raised up a deliverer for them: Ehud the son of Gera, the Benjamite, a left-handed man. By him the children of Israel sent tribute to Eglon king of Moab. 16Now Ehud made himself a dagger (it was double-edged and a cubit in length) and fastened it under his clothes on his right thigh. 17So he brought the tribute to Eglon king of Moab. (Now Eglon *was* a very fat man.) 18And when he had finished presenting the tribute, he sent away the people who had carried the tribute. 19But he himself turned back from the stone images that *were* at Gilgal, and said, "I have a secret message for you, O king."

He said, "Keep silence!" And all who attended him went out from him.

20So Ehud came to him (now he was sitting upstairs in his cool private chamber). Then Ehud said, "I have a message from God for you." So he arose from *his* seat. 21Then Ehud reached with his left hand, took the dagger from his right thigh, and thrust it into his belly. 22Even the hilt went in after the blade, and the fat closed over the blade, for he did not draw the dagger out of his belly; and his entrails came out. 23Then Ehud went out through the porch and shut the doors of the upper room behind him and locked them.

24When he had gone out, *Eglon's*[h] servants came to look, and *to their* surprise, the doors of the upper room were locked. So they said, "He is probably attending to his needs in the cool chamber." 25So they waited till they were embarrassed, and still he had not opened the doors of the upper room. Therefore they took the key and opened *them*. And there was their master, fallen dead on the floor.

26But Ehud had escaped while they delayed, and passed beyond the stone images and escaped to Seirah. 27And it happened, when he arrived, that he blew the trumpet in the mountains of Ephraim, and the children of Israel went down with him from the mountains; and he led them. 28Then he said to them, "Follow *me*, for the LORD has delivered your enemies the Moabites into your hand." So they went down after him, seized the fords of the Jordan leading to Moab, and did not allow anyone to cross over. 29And at that time they killed about ten thousand men of Moab, all stout men of valor; not a man escaped. 30So Moab was subdued that day under the hand of Israel. And the land had rest for eighty years.

31After him was Shamgar the son of Anath, who

3:24 [h]Literally *his*

killed six hundred men of the Philistines with an ox goad; and he also delivered Israel.

4 When Ehud was dead, the children of Israel again did evil in the sight of the LORD. ²So the LORD sold them into the hand of Jabin king of Canaan, who reigned in Hazor. The commander of his army *was* Sisera, who dwelt in Harosheth Hagoyim. ³And the children of Israel cried out to the LORD; for Jabin had nine hundred chariots of iron, and for twenty years he had harshly oppressed the children of Israel.

⁴*Now Deborah, a prophetess, the wife of Lapidoth, was judging Israel at that time. ⁵And she would sit under the palm tree of Deborah between Ramah and Bethel in the mountains of Ephraim. And the children of Israel came up to her for judgment. ⁶Then she sent and called for Barak the son of Abinoam from Kedesh in Naphtali, and said to him, "Has not the LORD God of Israel commanded, 'Go and deploy *troops* at Mount Tabor; take with you ten thousand men of the sons of Naphtali and of the sons of Zebulun; ⁷and against you I will deploy Sisera, the commander of Jabin's army, with his chariots and his multitude at the River Kishon; and I will deliver him into your hand'?"

⁸And Barak said to her, "If you will go with me, then I will go; but if you will not go with me, I will not go!"

⁹So she said, "I will surely go with you; nevertheless there will be no glory for you in the journey you are taking, for the LORD will sell Sisera into the hand of a woman." Then Deborah arose and went with Barak to Kedesh. ¹⁰And Barak called Zebulun and Naphtali to Kedesh; he went up with ten thousand men under his command,ⁱ and Deborah went up with him.

¹¹Now Heber the Kenite, of the children of Hobab the father-in-law of Moses, had separated himself from the Kenites and pitched his tent near the terebinth tree at Zaanaim, which *is* beside Kedesh.

¹²And they reported to Sisera that Barak the son of Abinoam had gone up to Mount Tabor. ¹³So Sisera gathered together all his chariots, nine hundred chariots of iron, and all the people who *were* with him, from Harosheth Hagoyim to the River Kishon.

¹⁴*Then Deborah said to Barak, "Up! For this *is* the day in which the LORD has delivered Sisera into your hand. Has not the LORD gone out before you?" So Barak went down from Mount Tabor with ten thousand men following him. ¹⁵And the LORD routed Sisera and all *his* chariots and all *his* army with the edge of the sword before Barak; and Sisera alighted from *his* chariot and fled away on foot. ¹⁶But Barak pursued the chariots and the army as far as Harosheth Hagoyim, and all the army of Sisera fell by the edge of the sword; not a man was left.

¹⁷However, Sisera had fled away on foot to the tent of Jael, the wife of Heber the Kenite; for *there was* peace between Jabin king of Hazor and the house of Heber the Kenite. ¹⁸And Jael went out to meet Sisera, and said to him, "Turn aside, my lord, turn aside to me; do not fear." And when he had turned aside with her into the tent, she covered him with a blanket.

4:10 ⁱLiterally *at his feet*

CHAPTER 4

4:4, 5 The society of that day was strongly masculine, so it was humiliating when women had leadership in the land (Isa. 3:12). The pages of church history record the names of godly women like Deborah who knew God's will, rallied God's people, and won God's victories; and we are grateful for them.

4:14–22 In Hebrews 11:32, Barak is named as a man of faith, but Deborah enlisted him and saved the day. What a strange victory! God used two women, a jug of milk, a hammer, a tent peg, and a storm (Judg. 5:4–5, 20–21) to defeat the enemy! (See 1 Cor. 1:26–29.)

19Then he said to her, "Please give me a little water to drink, for I am thirsty." So she opened a jug of milk, gave him a drink, and covered him. 20And he said to her, "Stand at the door of the tent, and if any man comes and inquires of you, and says, 'Is there any man here?' you shall say, 'No.' " 21Then Jael, Heber's wife, took a tent peg and took a hammer in her hand, and went softly to him and drove the peg into his temple, and it went down into the ground; for he was fast asleep and weary. So he died. 22And then, as Barak pursued Sisera, Jael came out to meet him, and said to him, "Come, I will show you the man whom you seek." And when he went into her *tent*, there lay Sisera, dead with the peg in his temple. 23*So on that day God subdued Jabin king of Canaan in the presence of the children of Israel. 24And the hand of the children of Israel grew stronger and stronger against Jabin king of Canaan, until they had destroyed Jabin king of Canaan.

4:23, 24 One person's faith and obedience can make a difference in history. Whether you are a leader like Deborah or a follower like Barak, be sure to be a *believer;* because faith makes the difference between defeat and victory.

CHAPTER 5

5:1ff Deborah and Barak cooperated in fighting the battle and also in praising the Lord (Ps. 149:6). Their song reveals some truths about our spiritual warfare in this world.

5:2 *Be willing to fight.* Leaders cannot lead unless soldiers are willing to obey. Are you a willing soldier?

5:4 *Know that the Lord goes before you.* The God of history can help you do exploits for Him today if you will trust Him and do His will. He is able!

5 Then* Deborah and Barak the son of Abinoam sang on that day, saying:

2 *"When leaders lead in Israel,
When the people willingly offer themselves,
Bless the LORD!

3 "Hear, O kings! Give ear, O princes!
I, *even* I, will sing to the LORD;
I will sing praise to the LORD God of Israel.

4 *"LORD, when You went out from Seir,
When You marched from the field of Edom,
The earth trembled and the heavens poured,
The clouds also poured water;
5 The mountains gushed before the LORD,
This Sinai, before the LORD God of Israel.

6 "In the days of Shamgar, son of Anath,
In the days of Jael,
The highways were deserted,
And the travelers walked along the byways.
7 Village life ceased, it ceased in Israel,
Until I, Deborah, arose,
Arose a mother in Israel.
8 They chose new gods;
Then *there was* war in the gates;
Not a shield or spear was seen among forty
thousand in Israel.
9 My heart *is* with the rulers of Israel
Who offered themselves willingly with the
people.
Bless the LORD!

10 "Speak, you who ride on white donkeys,
Who sit in judges' attire,
And who walk along the road.
11 Far from the noise of the archers, among
the watering places,
There they shall recount the righteous acts
of the LORD,
The righteous acts *for* His villagers in Israel;
Then the people of the LORD shall go down
to the gates.

12 "Awake, awake, Deborah!
Awake, awake, sing a song!
Arise, Barak, and lead your captives away,
O son of Abinoam!

13*"Then the survivors came down, the people
    against the nobles;
The LORD came down for me against the
    mighty.
14 From Ephraim *were* those whose roots were
    in Amalek.
After you, Benjamin, with your peoples,
From Machir rulers came down,
And from Zebulun those who bear the
    recruiter's staff.
15 And the princes of Issachar*ʲ were* with
    Deborah;
As Issachar, so *was* Barak
Sent into the valley under his command;*ᵏ*
Among the divisions of Reuben
There were great resolves of heart.
16 Why did you sit among the sheepfolds,
To hear the pipings for the flocks?
The divisions of Reuben have great
    searchings of heart.
17 Gilead stayed beyond the Jordan,
And why did Dan remain on ships?*ˡ*
Asher continued at the seashore,
And stayed by his inlets.
18 Zebulun *is* a people *who* jeopardized their
    lives to the point of death,
Naphtali also, on the heights of the
    battlefield.

19 "The kings came *and* fought,
Then the kings of Canaan fought
In Taanach, by the waters of Megiddo;
They took no spoils of silver.
20 They fought from the heavens;
The stars from their courses fought against
    Sisera.
21 The torrent of Kishon swept them away,
That ancient torrent, the torrent of Kishon.
O my soul, march on in strength!
22 Then the horses' hooves pounded,
The galloping, galloping of his steeds.
23 'Curse Meroz,' said the angel*ᵐ* of the LORD,
'Curse its inhabitants bitterly,
Because they did not come to the help of
    the LORD,
To the help of the LORD against the mighty.'

24 "Most blessed among women is Jael,
The wife of Heber the Kenite;
Blessed is she among women in tents.
25 He asked for water, she gave milk;
She brought out cream in a lordly bowl.
26 She stretched her hand to the tent peg,
Her right hand to the workmen's hammer;
She pounded Sisera, she pierced his head,
She split and struck through his temple.
27 At her feet he sank, he fell, he lay still;
At her feet he sank, he fell;
Where he sank, there he fell dead.

28 "The mother of Sisera looked through the
    window,
And cried out through the lattice,
'Why is his chariot *so* long in coming?
Why tarries the clatter of his chariots?'
29 Her wisest ladies answered her,
Yes, she answered herself,

5:13–18 *Do not let others discourage you.* Not all the tribes responded with faith and courage; in fact, some refused to get involved in the battle. Some sacrificed their lives while others stayed home.

5:15 *ʲ*Following Septuagint, Syriac, Targum, and Vulgate; Masoretic Text reads *And my princes in Issachar.* *ᵏ*Literally *at his feet* 5:17 *ˡ*Or *at ease* 5:23 *ᵐ*Or *Angel*

30 'Are they not finding and dividing the spoil:
To every man a girl *or* two;
For Sisera, plunder of dyed garments,
Plunder of garments embroidered and dyed,
Two pieces of dyed embroidery for the neck
of the looter?'

31*"Thus let all Your enemies perish, O LORD!
But *let* those who love Him *be* like the sun
When it comes out in full strength."

So the land had rest for forty years.

5:31 *Victors turn darkness into light.*
Israel was in despair and darkness before
Deborah took over (vv. 6–8), but she brought
the dawning of a new day. Are you the kind
of soldier who makes a difference in this
world?

6 Then the children of Israel did evil in the sight
of the LORD. So the LORD delivered them into
the hand of Midian for seven years, 2and the hand
of Midian prevailed against Israel. Because of the
Midianites, the children of Israel made for themselves the dens, the caves, and the strongholds
which *are* in the mountains. 3So it was, whenever
Israel had sown, Midianites would come up; also
Amalekites and the people of the East would come
up against them. 4Then they would encamp
against them and destroy the produce of the earth
as far as Gaza, and leave no sustenance for Israel,
neither sheep nor ox nor donkey. 5For they would
come up with their livestock and their tents, coming in as numerous as locusts; both they and their
camels were without number; and they would enter the land to destroy it. 6So Israel was greatly
impoverished because of the Midianites, and the
children of Israel cried out to the LORD.

7And it came to pass, when the children of Israel
cried out to the LORD because of the Midianites,
8that the LORD sent a prophet to the children of
Israel, who said to them, "Thus says the LORD God
of Israel: 'I brought you up from Egypt and
brought you out of the house of bondage; 9and I
delivered you out of the hand of the Egyptians
and out of the hand of all who oppressed you,
and drove them out before you and gave you their
land. 10Also I said to you, "I *am* the LORD your
God; do not fear the gods of the Amorites, in
whose land you dwell." But you have not obeyed
My voice.' "

11*Now the Angel of the LORD came and sat under the terebinth tree which *was* in Ophrah, which
belonged to Joash the Abiezrite, while his son
Gideon threshed wheat in the winepress, in order
to hide *it* from the Midianites. 12*And the Angel
of the LORD appeared to him, and said to him,
"The LORD *is* with you, you mighty man of valor!"

13Gideon said to Him, "O my lord,[n] if the LORD
is with us, why then has all this happened to us?
And where *are* all His miracles which our fathers
told us about, saying, 'Did not the LORD bring us
up from Egypt?' But now the LORD has forsaken
us and delivered us into the hands of the
Midianites."

14Then the LORD turned to him and said, "Go
in this might of yours, and you shall save Israel
from the hand of the Midianites. Have I not sent
you?"

CHAPTER 6

6:11 Gideon was an unlikely candidate for
God's "Hall of Fame" (Heb. 11:32). When
God called him, he was hiding. When God
spoke to him, he raised problems instead
of trusting promises. One of his favorite
words was *if* (vv. 13, 17, 36; Mark 9:22–23).
When Gideon did start to obey God, he
worked at night (v. 27) and had to have
repeated reassurance that the Lord was with
him.

6:12 But God saw the potential in Gideon
and even called him a "mighty man of valor"
(v. 12). God sees the potential in you and
says to you as He did to Simon, "You
are . . . You shall be" (John 1:42). He knows
your weaknesses and will accommodate
Himself to your needs so that He might
develop your faith.

6:13 [n]Hebrew *adoni,* used of man

"Putting Out the Fleece"—"Putting out the fleece" (asking God to do some special thing to
verify His will) is evidence of unbelief and not of faith. God stooped to Gideon's weakness and did
what he asked, and He may do that for you; but this is not the level on which God wants to meet
you. Immature faith needs signs for reassurance; mature faith takes God at His Word and obeys.

[15]So he said to Him, "O my Lord,[o] how can I
save Israel? Indeed my clan *is* the weakest in Manasseh, and I *am* the least in my father's house."
[16]And the LORD said to him, "Surely I will be
with you, and you shall defeat the Midianites as
one man."
[17]Then he said to Him, "If now I have found
favor in Your sight, then show me a sign that it
is You who talk with me. [18]Do not depart from
here, I pray, until I come to You and bring out
my offering and set *it* before You."

And He said, "I will wait until you come back."
[19]So Gideon went in and prepared a young goat,
and unleavened bread from an ephah of flour. The
meat he put in a basket, and he put the broth in
a pot; and he brought *them* out to Him under the
terebinth tree and presented *them*. [20]The Angel
of God said to him, "Take the meat and the unleavened bread and lay *them* on this rock, and
pour out the broth." And he did so.
[21]Then the Angel of the LORD put out the end
of the staff that *was* in His hand, and touched
the meat and the unleavened bread; and fire rose
out of the rock and consumed the meat and the
unleavened bread. And the Angel of the LORD departed out of his sight.
[22]*Now Gideon perceived that He *was* the Angel
of the LORD. So Gideon said, "Alas, O Lord GOD!
For I have seen the Angel of the LORD face to
face."
[23]Then the LORD said to him, "Peace *be* with
you; do not fear, you shall not die." [24]So Gideon
built an altar there to the LORD, and called it The-
LORD-*Is*-Peace.[p] To this day it *is* still in Ophrah
of the Abiezrites.
[25]Now it came to pass the same night that the
LORD said to him, "Take your father's young bull,
the second bull of seven years old, and tear down
the altar of Baal that your father has, and cut
down the wooden image[q] that *is* beside it; [26]and
build an altar to the LORD your God on top of
this rock in the proper arrangement, and take the
second bull and offer a burnt sacrifice with the
wood of the image which you shall cut down."
[27]So Gideon took ten men from among his servants and did as the LORD had said to him. But
because he feared his father's household and the
men of the city too much to do *it* by day, he did
it by night.
[28]And when the men of the city arose early in
the morning, there was the altar of Baal, torn
down; and the wooden image that *was* beside it
was cut down, and the second bull was being offered on the altar *which had been* built. [29]So they
said to one another, "Who has done this thing?"
And when they had inquired and asked, they said,
"Gideon the son of Joash has done this thing."
[30]Then the men of the city said to Joash, "Bring
out your son, that he may die, because he has
torn down the altar of Baal, and because he has
cut down the wooden image that *was* beside it."
[31]But Joash said to all who stood against him,
"Would you plead for Baal? Would you save him?
Let the one who would plead for him be put to
death by morning! If he *is* a god, let him plead
for himself, because his altar has been torn
down!" [32]Therefore on that day he called him

6:15 [o]Hebrew *Adonai*, used of God 6:24 [p]Hebrew *YHWH Shalom* 6:25 [q]Hebrew *Asherah*, a Canaanite goddess

6:22–24 For a man with a worried heart, "The-LORD-Is-Peace" was just what he needed (v. 24). You can enjoy God's peace today as you fight the battle (Phil. 4:4–9).

Jerubbaal,ʳ saying, "Let Baal plead against him, because he has torn down his altar."

33Then all the Midianites and Amalekites, the people of the East, gathered together; and they crossed over and encamped in the Valley of Jezreel. 34But the Spirit of the LORD came upon Gideon; then he blew the trumpet, and the Abiezrites gathered behind him. 35And he sent messengers throughout all Manasseh, who also gathered behind him. He also sent messengers to Asher, Zebulun, and Naphtali; and they came up to meet them.

36So Gideon said to God, "If You will save Israel by my hand as You have said— 37look, I shall put a fleece of wool on the threshing floor; if there is dew on the fleece only, and *it is* dry on all the ground, then I shall know that You will save Israel by my hand, as You have said." 38And it was so. When he rose early the next morning and squeezed the fleece together, he wrung the dew out of the fleece, a bowlful of water. 39Then Gideon said to God, "Do not be angry with me, but let me speak just once more: Let me test, I pray, just once more with the fleece; let it now be dry only on the fleece, but on all the ground let there be dew." 40And God did so that night. It was dry on the fleece only, but there was dew on all the ground.

CHAPTER 7

7:1 Imagine 32,000 Israelites facing 135,000 Midianites (Judg. 8:10), but it was the kind of situation that the Lord uses to glorify His name. When God is on your side, the size of the enemy is of no great concern, so keep your eyes on Him.

7:2–7 The really dangerous enemies were within the hearts of Gideon's soldiers. *Fear* was one of them (vv. 1–3), and it sent 22,000 men home (Deut. 20:1–9). *Overconfidence* was another enemy (vv. 4–8). God cut down the ranks from 10,000 to 300 so that the "army" had to trust completely in God. When God strips away your resources, it is not to impoverish your life but to enrich your faith.

7 Then* Jerubbaal (that *is,* Gideon) and all the people who *were* with him rose early and encamped beside the well of Harod, so that the camp of the Midianites was on the north side of them by the hill of Moreh in the valley.

2*And the LORD said to Gideon, "The people who *are* with you *are* too many for Me to give the Midianites into their hands, lest Israel claim glory for itself against Me, saying, 'My own hand has saved me.' 3Now therefore, proclaim in the hearing of the people, saying, 'Whoever *is* fearful and afraid, let him turn and depart at once from Mount Gilead.' " And twenty-two thousand of the people returned, and ten thousand remained.

4But the LORD said to Gideon, "The people *are* still *too* many; bring them down to the water, and I will test them for you there. Then it will be, *that* of whom I say to you, 'This one shall go with you,' the same shall go with you; and of whomever I say to you, 'This one shall not go with you,' the same shall not go." 5So he brought the people down to the water. And the LORD said to Gideon, "Everyone who laps from the water with his tongue, as a dog laps, you shall set apart by himself; likewise everyone who gets down on his knees to drink." 6And the number of those who lapped, *putting* their hand to their mouth, was three hundred men; but all the rest of the people got down on their knees to drink water. 7Then the LORD said to Gideon, "By the three hundred men who lapped I will save you, and deliver the Midianites into your hand. Let all the *other* people go, every man to his place." 8So the people took

---

6:32 ʳLiterally *Let Baal Plead*

Tests—We never know when God is using the everyday things of life to test our faith. The men in Gideon's army were tested by the way they drank water. Lot was tested by a disagreement over land (Gen. 13:6ff.). Israel was tested by thirst (Exod. 15:22–27), and Moses was tested by the complaining of the people (Num. 20:1–13). We must constantly be on guard because sometimes we do not know what the lesson was until we have failed the test!

provisions and their trumpets in their hands. And he sent away all *the rest of* Israel, every man to his tent, and retained those three hundred men. Now the camp of Midian was below him in the valley.

⁹It happened on the same night that the LORD said to him, "Arise, go down against the camp, for I have delivered it into your hand. ¹⁰But if you are afraid to go down, go down to the camp with Purah your servant, ¹¹and you shall hear what they say; and afterward your hands shall be strengthened to go down against the camp." Then he went down with Purah his servant to the outpost of the armed men who *were* in the camp. ¹²Now the Midianites and Amalekites, all the people of the East, were lying in the valley as numerous as locusts; and their camels *were* without number, as the sand by the seashore in multitude.

¹³And when Gideon had come, there was a man telling a dream to his companion. He said, "I have had a dream: *To my* surprise, a loaf of barley bread tumbled into the camp of Midian; it came to a tent and struck it so that it fell and overturned, and the tent collapsed."

¹⁴Then his companion answered and said, "This *is* nothing else but the sword of Gideon the son of Joash, a man of Israel! Into his hand God has delivered Midian and the whole camp."

¹⁵*And so it was, when Gideon heard the telling of the dream and its interpretation, that he worshiped. He returned to the camp of Israel, and said, "Arise, for the LORD has delivered the camp of Midian into your hand." ¹⁶Then he divided the three hundred men *into* three companies, and he put a trumpet into every man's hand, with empty pitchers, and torches inside the pitchers. ¹⁷And he said to them, "Look at me and do likewise; watch, and when I come to the edge of the camp you shall do as I do: ¹⁸When I blow the trumpet, I and all who *are* with me, then you also blow the trumpets on every side of the whole camp, and say, '*The sword of* the LORD and of Gideon!' "

¹⁹So Gideon and the hundred men who *were* with him came to the outpost of the camp at the beginning of the middle watch, just as they had posted the watch; and they blew the trumpets and broke the pitchers that *were* in their hands. ²⁰Then the three companies blew the trumpets and broke the pitchers—they held the torches in their left hands and the trumpets in their right hands for blowing—and they cried, "The sword of the LORD and of Gideon!" ²¹And every man stood in his place all around the camp; and the whole army ran and cried out and fled. ²²When the three hundred blew the trumpets, the LORD set every man's sword against his companion throughout the whole camp; and the army fled to Beth Acacia,ˢ toward Zererah, as far as the border of Abel Meholah, by Tabbath.

²³And the men of Israel gathered together from Naphtali, Asher, and all Manasseh, and pursued the Midianites.

²⁴Then Gideon sent messengers throughout all the mountains of Ephraim, saying, "Come down against the Midianites, and seize from them the watering places as far as Beth Barah and the Jordan." Then all the men of Ephraim gathered together and seized the watering places as far as

7:15–22 Like Joshua, Gideon worshiped God before going to battle (v. 15; Josh. 5:13–15), for he knew the source of his power. God used weak weapons to defeat a great host because Gideon and his men were living by faith: "For nothing restrains the LORD from saving by many or by few" (1 Sam. 14:6).

7:22 ˢHebrew *Beth Shittah*

CHAPTER 8

8:1ff It takes all kinds to make a nation (or a church), and a leader must know how to handle each one, especially after a great victory.

8:1–3 The critical. They were angry with Gideon because they were left out and did not share in the glory. Gideon tactfully gave them the "soft answer" that healed the wounds and prevented division (Prov. 15:1; Eph. 4:1–3). Better to do that than to start another war.

8:4–9 The cynical. They said, "You have not yet won the battle, so why should we help you?" The men of Succoth had no faith in God or appreciation for Gideon and his men, and their lack of love cost them dearly.

8:10–21 The cowardly. Executing two famous kings would be a great way to start a military career, but the lad was too immature to carry it out. We wonder if Gideon remembered his own fears and God's patience with him.

Beth Barah and the Jordan. 25And they captured two princes of the Midianites, Oreb and Zeeb. They killed Oreb at the rock of Oreb, and Zeeb they killed at the winepress of Zeeb. They pursued Midian and brought the heads of Oreb and Zeeb to Gideon on the other side of the Jordan.

8 Now* the men of Ephraim said to him, "Why have you done this to us by not calling us when you went to fight with the Midianites?" And they reprimanded him sharply.

2So he said to them, "What have I done now in comparison with you? Is not the gleaning of the grapes of Ephraim better than the vintage of Abiezer? 3God has delivered into your hands the princes of Midian, Oreb and Zeeb. And what was I able to do in comparison with you?" Then their anger toward him subsided when he said that.

4*When Gideon came to the Jordan, he and the three hundred men who were with him crossed over, exhausted but still in pursuit. 5Then he said to the men of Succoth, "Please give loaves of bread to the people who follow me, for they are exhausted, and I am pursuing Zebah and Zalmunna, kings of Midian."

6And the leaders of Succoth said, "Are the hands of Zebah and Zalmunna now in your hand, that we should give bread to your army?"

7So Gideon said, "For this cause, when the LORD has delivered Zebah and Zalmunna into my hand, then I will tear your flesh with the thorns of the wilderness and with briers!" 8Then he went up from there to Penuel and spoke to them in the same way. And the men of Penuel answered him as the men of Succoth had answered. 9So he also spoke to the men of Penuel, saying, "When I come back in peace, I will tear down this tower!"

10*Now Zebah and Zalmunna were at Karkor, and their armies with them, about fifteen thousand, all who were left of all the army of the people of the East; for one hundred and twenty thousand men who drew the sword had fallen. 11Then Gideon went up by the road of those who dwell in tents on the east of Nobah and Jogbehah; and he attacked the army while the camp felt secure. 12When Zebah and Zalmunna fled, he pursued them; and he took the two kings of Midian, Zebah and Zalmunna, and routed the whole army.

13Then Gideon the son of Joash returned from battle, from the Ascent of Heres. 14And he caught a young man of the men of Succoth and interrogated him; and he wrote down for him the leaders of Succoth and its elders, seventy-seven men. 15Then he came to the men of Succoth and said, "Here are Zebah and Zalmunna, about whom you ridiculed me, saying, 'Are the hands of Zebah and Zalmunna now in your hand, that we should give bread to your weary men?'" 16And he took the elders of the city, and thorns of the wilderness and briers, and with them he taught the men of Succoth. 17Then he tore down the tower of Penuel and killed the men of the city.

18And he said to Zebah and Zalmunna, "What kind of men were they whom you killed at Tabor?"

So they answered, "As you are, so were they; each one resembled the son of a king."

19Then he said, "They were my brothers, the sons of my mother. As the LORD lives, if you had let them live, I would not kill you." 20And he said to Jether his firstborn, "Rise, kill them!" But the youth would not draw his sword; for he was afraid, because he *was* still a youth.

21So Zebah and Zalmunna said, "Rise yourself, and kill us; for as a man *is, so is* his strength." So Gideon arose and killed Zebah and Zalmunna, and took the crescent ornaments that *were* on their camels' necks.

22*Then the men of Israel said to Gideon, "Rule over us, both you and your son, and your grandson also; for you have delivered us from the hand of Midian."

23But Gideon said to them, "I will not rule over you, nor shall my son rule over you; the LORD shall rule over you." 24Then Gideon said to them, "I would like to make a request of you, that each of you would give me the earrings from his plunder." For they had golden earrings, because they *were* Ishmaelites.

25So they answered, "We will gladly give *them*." And they spread out a garment, and each man threw into it the earrings from his plunder. 26Now the weight of the gold earrings that he requested was one thousand seven hundred *shekels* of gold, besides the crescent ornaments, pendants, and purple robes which *were* on the kings of Midian, and besides the chains that *were* around their camels' necks. 27Then Gideon made it into an ephod and set it up in his city, Ophrah. And all Israel played the harlot with it there. It became a snare to Gideon and to his house.

28Thus Midian was subdued before the children of Israel, so that they lifted their heads no more. And the country was quiet for forty years in the days of Gideon.

29Then Jerubbaal the son of Joash went and dwelt in his own house. 30Gideon had seventy sons who were his own offspring, for he had many wives. 31And his concubine who *was* in Shechem also bore him a son, whose name he called Abimelech. 32Now Gideon the son of Joash died at a good old age, and was buried in the tomb of Joash his father, in Ophrah of the Abiezrites.

33So it was, as soon as Gideon was dead, that the children of Israel again played the harlot with the Baals, and made Baal-Berith their god. 34Thus the children of Israel did not remember the LORD their God, who had delivered them from the hands of all their enemies on every side; 35nor did they show kindness to the house of Jerubbaal (Gideon) in accordance with the good he had done for Israel.

9 Then* Abimelech the son of Jerubbaal went to Shechem, to his mother's brothers, and spoke with them and with all the family of the house of his mother's father, saying, 2"Please speak in the hearing of all the men of Shechem: 'Which is better for you, that all seventy of the sons of Jerubbaal reign over you, or that one reign over you?' Remember that I *am* your own flesh and bone."

3And his mother's brothers spoke all these words concerning him in the hearing of all the men of Shechem; and their heart was inclined to follow Abimelech, for they said, "He is our brother." 4So they gave him seventy *shekels* of silver from the temple of Baal-Berith, with which Abimelech hired worthless and reckless men; and they followed him. 5Then he went to his father's house at Ophrah and killed his brothers, the seventy sons of Jerubbaal, on one stone. But Jotham the youngest son of Jerubbaal was left, because

8:22–35 *The compromising.* Unlike Abraham, Gideon became covetous and asked for a generous share of the loot (Gen. 14:18–24). This led to idolatry and apostasy because the heart of man is ever ready to indulge in sin.

CHAPTER 9

9:1–5 Gideon was a leader called of God, but Abimelech appointed himself and murdered his own brothers to become the leader. Absalom and Adonijah would make this mistake and pay for it dearly (2 Sam. 15; 1 Kings 1:5ff.).

9:7–15 Jotham's parable reveals that there is a price to pay for true leadership. *Others* had paid the price for Abimelech to rule, but he had sacrificed nothing himself. A true leader must often sacrifice richness (oil), sweetness, and joyfulness to serve the people. But if good men and women will not pay the price and lead, we have to settle for the bramble!

Abimelech's sin caught up with him, but he certainly did a lot of damage to his family and his people (Ps. 34:21; Prov. 11:3, 19).

he hid himself. 6And all the men of Shechem gathered together, all of Beth Millo, and they went and made Abimelech king beside the terebinth tree at the pillar that *was* in Shechem.

7*Now when they told Jotham, he went and stood on top of Mount Gerizim, and lifted his voice and cried out. And he said to them:

"Listen to me, you men of Shechem,
    That God may listen to you!

8 "The trees once went forth to anoint a king
        over them.
    And they said to the olive tree,
    'Reign over us!'
9 But the olive tree said to them,
    'Should I cease giving my oil,
    With which they honor God and men,
    And go to sway over trees?'

10 "Then the trees said to the fig tree,
    'You come *and* reign over us!'
11 But the fig tree said to them,
    'Should I cease my sweetness and my good
        fruit,
    And go to sway over trees?'

12 "Then the trees said to the vine,
    'You come *and* reign over us!'
13 But the vine said to them,
    'Should I cease my new wine,
    Which cheers *both* God and men,
    And go to sway over trees?'

14 "Then all the trees said to the bramble,
    'You come *and* reign over us!'
15 And the bramble said to the trees,
    'If in truth you anoint me as king over you,
    Then come *and* take shelter in my shade;
    But if not, let fire come out of the bramble
    And devour the cedars of Lebanon!'

16"Now therefore, if you have acted in truth and sincerity in making Abimelech king, and if you have dealt well with Jerubbaal and his house, and have done to him as he deserves— 17for my father fought for you, risked his life, and delivered you out of the hand of Midian; 18but you have risen up against my father's house this day, and killed his seventy sons on one stone, and made Abimelech, the son of his female servant, king over the men of Shechem, because he is your brother— 19if then you have acted in truth and sincerity with Jerubbaal and with his house this day, *then* rejoice in Abimelech, and let him also rejoice in you. 20But if not, let fire come from Abimelech and devour the men of Shechem and Beth Millo; and let fire come from the men of Shechem and from Beth Millo and devour Abimelech!" 21And Jotham ran away and fled; and he went to Beer and dwelt there, for fear of Abimelech his brother.

22After Abimelech had reigned over Israel three years, 23God sent a spirit of ill will between Abimelech and the men of Shechem; and the men of Shechem dealt treacherously with Abimelech, 24that the crime *done* to the seventy sons of Jerubbaal might be settled and their blood be laid on Abimelech their brother, who killed them, and on the men of Shechem, who aided him in the killing of his brothers. 25And the men of Shechem set men in ambush against him on the tops of the mountains, and they robbed all who passed by

them along that way; and it was told Abimelech.
26Now Gaal the son of Ebed came with his brothers and went over to Shechem; and the men of Shechem put their confidence in him. 27So they went out into the fields, and gathered *grapes* from their vineyards and trod *them,* and made merry. And they went into the house of their god, and ate and drank, and cursed Abimelech. 28Then Gaal the son of Ebed said, "Who *is* Abimelech, and who *is* Shechem, that we should serve him? *Is he* not the son of Jerubbaal, and *is not* Zebul his officer? Serve the men of Hamor the father of Shechem; but why should we serve him? 29If only this people were under my authority!*t* Then I would remove Abimelech." So he*u* said to Abimelech, "Increase your army and come out!"
30When Zebul, the ruler of the city, heard the words of Gaal the son of Ebed, his anger was aroused. 31And he sent messengers to Abimelech secretly, saying, "Take note! Gaal the son of Ebed and his brothers have come to Shechem; and here they are, fortifying the city against you. 32Now therefore, get up by night, you and the people who *are* with you, and lie in wait in the field. 33And it shall be, as soon as the sun is up in the morning, *that* you shall rise early and rush upon the city; and *when* he and the people who are with him come out against you, you may then do to them as you find opportunity."
34So Abimelech and all the people who *were* with him rose by night, and lay in wait against Shechem in four companies. 35When Gaal the son of Ebed went out and stood in the entrance to the city gate, Abimelech and the people who *were* with him rose from lying in wait. 36And when Gaal saw the people, he said to Zebul, "Look, people are coming down from the tops of the mountains!"
But Zebul said to him, "You see the shadows of the mountains as *if they were* men."
37So Gaal spoke again and said, "See, people are coming down from the center of the land, and another company is coming from the Diviners'*v* Terebinth Tree."
38Then Zebul said to him, "Where indeed *is* your mouth now, with which you said, 'Who is Abimelech, that we should serve him?' *Are* not these the people whom you despised? Go out, if you will, and fight with them now."
39So Gaal went out, leading the men of Shechem, and fought with Abimelech. 40And Abimelech chased him, and he fled from him; and many fell wounded, to the *very* entrance of the gate. 41Then Abimelech dwelt at Arumah, and Zebul drove out Gaal and his brothers, so that they would not dwell in Shechem.
42And it came about on the next day that the people went out into the field, and they told Abimelech. 43So he took his people, divided them into three companies, and lay in wait in the field. And he looked, and there were the people, coming out of the city; and he rose against them and attacked them. 44Then Abimelech and the company that *was* with him rushed forward and stood at the entrance of the gate of the city; and the *other* two companies rushed upon all who *were* in the fields and killed them. 45So Abimelech fought against the city all that day; he took the city and killed

9:29 *t*Literally *hand* *u*Following Masoretic Text and Targum; Dead Sea Scrolls read *they;* Septuagint reads *I.*
9:37 *v*Hebrew *Meonenim*

the people who *were* in it; and he demolished the city and sowed it with salt.

⁴⁶Now when all the men of the tower of Shechem had heard *that*, they entered the stronghold of the temple of the god Berith. ⁴⁷And it was told Abimelech that all the men of the tower of Shechem were gathered together. ⁴⁸Then Abimelech went up to Mount Zalmon, he and all the people who *were* with him. And Abimelech took an ax in his hand and cut down a bough from the trees, and took it and laid *it* on his shoulder; then he said to the people who were with him, "What you have seen me do, make haste *and* do as I *have* done." ⁴⁹So each of the people likewise cut down his own bough and followed Abimelech, put *them* against the stronghold, and set the stronghold on fire above them, so that all the people of the tower of Shechem died, about a thousand men and women.

⁵⁰Then Abimelech went to Thebez, and he encamped against Thebez and took it. ⁵¹But there was a strong tower in the city, and all the men and women—all the people of the city—fled there and shut themselves in; then they went up to the top of the tower. ⁵²So Abimelech came as far as the tower and fought against it; and he drew near the door of the tower to burn it with fire. ⁵³But a certain woman dropped an upper millstone on Abimelech's head and crushed his skull. ⁵⁴Then he called quickly to the young man, his armorbearer, and said to him, "Draw your sword and kill me, lest men say of me, 'A woman killed him.' " So his young man thrust him through, and he died. ⁵⁵And when the men of Israel saw that Abimelech was dead, they departed, every man to his place.

⁵⁶Thus God repaid the wickedness of Abimelech, which he had done to his father by killing his seventy brothers. ⁵⁷And all the evil of the men of Shechem God returned on their own heads, and on them came the curse of Jotham the son of Jerubbaal.

CHAPTER 10

10:1ff No great deeds of valor are recorded for either Tola or Jair, but they gave the nation forty-five years of peace. No foreign invaders are named, so these two judges served by solving the internal problems of the nation. They were administrators rather than generals; we need both.

10:6 When there are no battles to fight, we tend to take our blessings for granted, which can lead to sin (Deut. 8:7–20). The people forsook God and worshiped the gods of the enemy, and God had to chasten them by an invasion of the Ammonites.

10 After* Abimelech there arose to save Israel Tola the son of Puah, the son of Dodo, a man of Issachar; and he dwelt in Shamir in the mountains of Ephraim. ²He judged Israel twenty-three years; and he died and was buried in Shamir.

³After him arose Jair, a Gileadite; and he judged Israel twenty-two years. ⁴Now he had thirty sons who rode on thirty donkeys; they also had thirty towns, which are called "Havoth Jair"ʷ to this day, which *are* in the land of Gilead. ⁵And Jair died and was buried in Camon.

⁶*Then the children of Israel again did evil in the sight of the LORD, and served the Baals and the Ashtoreths, the gods of Syria, the gods of Sidon, the gods of Moab, the gods of the people of Ammon, and the gods of the Philistines; and they forsook the LORD and did not serve Him. ⁷So the anger of the LORD was hot against Israel; and He sold them into the hands of the Philistines and into the hands of the people of Ammon. ⁸From that year they harassed and oppressed the children of Israel for eighteen years—all the children of Israel who *were* on the other side of the Jordan

---

10:4 ʷLiterally *Towns of Jair* (compare Numbers 32:41 and Deuteronomy 3:14)

in the land of the Amorites, in Gilead. 9Moreover the people of Ammon crossed over the Jordan to fight against Judah also, against Benjamin, and against the house of Ephraim, so that Israel was severely distressed.

10*And the children of Israel cried out to the LORD, saying, "We have sinned against You, because we have both forsaken our God and served the Baals!"

11So the LORD said to the children of Israel, "*Did I not deliver you* from the Egyptians and from the Amorites and from the people of Ammon and from the Philistines? 12Also the Sidonians and Amalekites and Maonitesˣ oppressed you; and you cried out to Me, and I delivered you from their hand. 13Yet you have forsaken Me and served other gods. Therefore I will deliver you no more. 14Go and cry out to the gods which you have chosen; let them deliver you in your time of distress."

15And the children of Israel said to the LORD, "We have sinned! Do to us whatever seems best to You; only deliver us this day, we pray." 16So they put away the foreign gods from among them and served the LORD. And His soul could no longer endure the misery of Israel.

17Then the people of Ammon gathered together and encamped in Gilead. And the children of Israel assembled together and encamped in Mizpah. 18And the people, the leaders of Gilead, said to one another, "Who *is* the man who will begin the fight against the people of Ammon? He shall be head over all the inhabitants of Gilead."

11 Now* Jephthah the Gileadite was a mighty man of valor, but he *was* the son of a harlot; and Gilead begot Jephthah. 2Gilead's wife bore sons; and when his wife's sons grew up, they drove Jephthah out, and said to him, "You shall have no inheritance in our father's house, for you *are* the son of another woman." 3Then Jephthah fled from his brothers and dwelt in the land of Tob; and worthless men banded together with Jephthah and went out *raiding* with him.

4It came to pass after a time that the people of Ammon made war against Israel. 5And so it was, when the people of Ammon made war against Israel, that the elders of Gilead went to get Jephthah from the land of Tob. 6Then they said to Jephthah, "Come and be our commander, that we may fight against the people of Ammon."

7So Jephthah said to the elders of Gilead, "Did you not hate me, and expel me from my father's house? Why have you come to me now when you are in distress?"

8And the elders of Gilead said to Jephthah, "That is why we have turned again to you now, that you may go with us and fight against the people of Ammon, and be our head over all the inhabitants of Gilead."

9*So Jephthah said to the elders of Gilead, "If you take me back home to fight against the people of Ammon, and the LORD delivers them to me, shall I be your head?"

10And the elders of Gilead said to Jephthah, "The LORD will be a witness between us, if we do not do according to your words." 11Then Jephthah went with the elders of Gilead, and the

10:10 The confession in verse 10 was insincere, born out of suffering; but the confession in verse 15 was sincere because it was accompanied by repentance and a putting away of sin. (See 2 Cor. 7:8–11.) Remorse and regret are not the same as repentance. God is not impressed by hypocritical tears.

CHAPTER 11

11:1, 2 No person should be blamed for the circumstances surrounding his or her birth. Why permit the things you cannot control to burden your life? Learn to accept them, and the Lord will work out His purposes in His own time (Ps. 139:13–16). Opposition will one day give way to opportunity.

11:9, 10 There is every evidence that Jephthah was a sincere worshiper of the Lord. He negotiated with the elders in the hearing of the Lord and he knew the Scriptures. He was a man of faith and courage (Heb. 11:32) who depended on God's power for victory (v. 29).

10:12 ˣSome Septuagint manuscripts read *Midianites*.

people made him head and commander over them; and Jephthah spoke all his words before the LORD in Mizpah.

12Now Jephthah sent messengers to the king of the people of Ammon, saying, "What do you have against me, that you have come to fight against me in my land?"

13And the king of the people of Ammon answered the messengers of Jephthah, "Because Israel took away my land when they came up out of Egypt, from the Arnon as far as the Jabbok, and to the Jordan. Now therefore, restore those *lands* peaceably."

14So Jephthah again sent messengers to the king of the people of Ammon, 15and said to him, "Thus says Jephthah: 'Israel did not take away the land of Moab, nor the land of the people of Ammon; 16for when Israel came up from Egypt, they walked through the wilderness as far as the Red Sea and came to Kadesh. 17Then Israel sent messengers to the king of Edom, saying, "Please let me pass through your land." But the king of Edom would not heed. And in like manner they sent to the king of Moab, but he would not *consent.* So Israel remained in Kadesh. 18And they went along through the wilderness and bypassed the land of Edom and the land of Moab, came to the east side of the land of Moab, and encamped on the other side of the Arnon. But they did not enter the border of Moab, for the Arnon *was* the border of Moab. 19Then Israel sent messengers to Sihon king of the Amorites, king of Heshbon; and Israel said to him, "Please let us pass through your land into our place." 20But Sihon did not trust Israel to pass through his territory. So Sihon gathered all his people together, encamped in Jahaz, and fought against Israel. 21And the LORD God of Israel delivered Sihon and all his people into the hand of Israel, and they defeated them. Thus Israel gained possession of all the land of the Amorites, who inhabited that country. 22They took possession of all the territory of the Amorites, from the Arnon to the Jabbok and from the wilderness to the Jordan.

23'And now the LORD God of Israel has dispossessed the Amorites from before His people Israel; should you then possess it? 24Will you not possess whatever Chemosh your god gives you to possess? So whatever the LORD our God takes possession of before us, we will possess. 25And now, *are* you any better than Balak the son of Zippor, king of Moab? Did he ever strive against Israel? Did he ever fight against them? 26While Israel dwelt in Heshbon and its villages, in Aroer and its villages, and in all the cities along the banks of the Arnon, for three hundred years, why did you not recover *them* within that time? 27Therefore I have not sinned against you, but you wronged me by fighting against me. May the LORD, the Judge, render judgment this day between the children of Israel and the people of Ammon.' " 28However, the king of the people of Ammon did not heed the words which Jephthah sent him.

29Then the Spirit of the LORD came upon Jephthah, and he passed through Gilead and Manasseh, and passed through Mizpah of Gilead; and from Mizpah of Gilead he advanced *toward* the people of Ammon. 30And Jephthah made a vow to the LORD, and said, "If You will indeed deliver the people of Ammon into my hands, 31then it will be that whatever comes out of the doors of my house to meet me, when I return in peace from the people of Ammon, shall surely be the LORD's, and I will offer it up as a burnt offering."

³²So Jephthah advanced toward the people of Ammon to fight against them, and the LORD delivered them into his hands. ³³And he defeated them from Aroer as far as Minnith—twenty cities—and to Abel Keramim,ʸ with a very great slaughter. Thus the people of Ammon were subdued before the children of Israel.

³⁴When Jephthah came to his house at Mizpah, there was his daughter, coming out to meet him with timbrels and dancing; and she *was his* only child. Besides her he had neither son nor daughter. ³⁵*And it came to pass, when he saw her, that he tore his clothes, and said, "Alas, my daughter! You have brought me very low! You are among those who trouble me! For I have given my word to the LORD, and I cannot go back on it."

³⁶So she said to him, "My father, *if* you have given your word to the LORD, do to me according to what has gone out of your mouth, because the LORD has avenged you of your enemies, the people of Ammon." ³⁷Then she said to her father, "Let this thing be done for me: let me alone for two months, that I may go and wander on the mountains and bewail my virginity, my friends and I."

³⁸So he said, "Go." And he sent her away *for* two months; and she went with her friends, and bewailed her virginity on the mountains. ³⁹And it was so at the end of two months that she returned to her father, and he carried out his vow with her which he had vowed. She knew no man. And it became a custom in Israel ⁴⁰*that* the daughters of Israel went four days each year to lament the daughter of Jephthah the Gileadite.

12 Then* the men of Ephraim gathered together, crossed over toward Zaphon, and said to Jephthah, "Why did you cross over to fight against the people of Ammon, and did not call us to go with you? We will burn your house down on you with fire!"

²And Jephthah said to them, "My people and I were in a great struggle with the people of Ammon; and when I called you, you did not deliver me out of their hands. ³So when I saw that you would not deliver *me*, I took my life in my hands and crossed over against the people of Ammon; and the LORD delivered them into my hand. Why then have you come up to me this day to fight against me?" ⁴Now Jephthah gathered together all the men of Gilead and fought against Ephraim. And the men of Gilead defeated Ephraim, because they said, "You Gileadites *are* fugitives of Ephraim among the Ephraimites *and* among the Manassites." ⁵*The Gileadites seized the fords of the Jordan before the Ephraimites *arrived*. And when *any* Ephraimite who escaped said, "Let me cross over," the men of Gilead would say to him, "*Are* you an Ephraimite?" If he said, "No," ⁶then they would say to him, "Then say, 'Shibboleth'!" And he would say, "Sibboleth," for he could not pronounce *it* right. Then they would take him and kill him at the fords of the Jordan. There fell at that time forty-two thousand Ephraimites.

⁷*And Jephthah judged Israel six years. Then Jephthah the Gileadite died and was buried among the cities of Gilead.

11:35–40 Jephthah knew that God's law prohibited human sacrifices, and certainly the Lord would not have given victory on the basis of such an offer. Jephthah's daughter was dedicated to serve the Lord at the tabernacle and therefore remained unmarried. As a result, Jephthah had no descendants to carry on his great name. If she had been sacrificed, it is not likely that the maidens would have been allowed to commemorate the event annually, for that would have been imitating the heathen around them.

CHAPTER 12
12:1–6 The men of Ephraim could never rejoice in another's victory as long as they were left out (Judg. 8). Jephthah was not as patient and tactful as Gideon, and the result was a civil war that took 42,000 lives. "See how great a forest a little fire kindles!" (James 3:5). Proverbs 17:14 offers good counsel.

12:5, 6 The word *shibboleth* is in the English dictionary and means "a test for determining if you belong." If you do not conform *exactly* to what a group demands, you are rejected. Some Christians make these minor matters a test of spirituality and fellowship and bring division to the church.

12:7 We do not even know where Jephthah was buried! No matter; the Lord keeps the records, and this brave man will get His reward.

11:33 ʸLiterally *Plain of Vineyards*

8After him, Ibzan of Bethlehem judged Israel. 9He had thirty sons. And he gave away thirty daughters in marriage, and brought in thirty daughters from elsewhere for his sons. He judged Israel seven years. 10Then Ibzan died and was buried at Bethlehem.

11After him, Elon the Zebulunite judged Israel. He judged Israel ten years. 12And Elon the Zebulunite died and was buried at Aijalon in the country of Zebulun.

13*After him, Abdon the son of Hillel the Pirathonite judged Israel. 14He had forty sons and thirty grandsons, who rode on seventy young donkeys. He judged Israel eight years. 15Then Abdon the son of Hillel the Pirathonite died and was buried in Pirathon in the land of Ephraim, in the mountains of the Amalekites.

CHAPTER 13

13:1ff *Samson* means "sunny," and initially he did bring sunshine to his home and to Israel at a dark period in their history. But his life ended in the darkness because he did not fully obey the Lord. He *began* to deliver Israel from the Philistines (v. 5), but Samuel and David would finish the job.

13:5 How could a man fail when he had so much in his favor? He was born to godly parents who feared the Lord, prayed for wisdom, and obeyed His will. Samson was dedicated to the Lord as a lifelong Nazirite (Num. 6). A godly home is no guarantee of a godly life if the spiritual influence is rejected by the children. The parents were not at fault; Samson was.

13 Again* the children of Israel did evil in the sight of the LORD, and the LORD delivered them into the hand of the Philistines for forty years.

2Now there was a certain man from Zorah, of the family of the Danites, whose name *was* Manoah; and his wife *was* barren and had no children. 3And the Angel of the LORD appeared to the woman and said to her, "Indeed now, you are barren and have borne no children, but you shall conceive and bear a son. 4Now therefore, please be careful not to drink wine or *similar* drink, and not to eat anything unclean. 5*For behold, you shall conceive and bear a son. And no razor shall come upon his head, for the child shall be a Nazirite to God from the womb; and he shall begin to deliver Israel out of the hand of the Philistines."

6So the woman came and told her husband, saying, "A Man of God came to me, and His countenance *was* like the countenance of the Angel of God, very awesome; but I did not ask Him where He *was* from, and He did not tell me His name. 7And He said to me, 'Behold, you shall conceive and bear a son. Now drink no wine or *similar* drink, nor eat anything unclean, for the child shall be a Nazirite to God from the womb to the day of his death.'"

8Then Manoah prayed to the LORD, and said, "O my Lord, please let the Man of God whom You sent come to us again and teach us what we shall do for the child who will be born."

9And God listened to the voice of Manoah, and the Angel of God came to the woman again as she was sitting in the field; but Manoah her husband *was* not with her. 10Then the woman ran in haste and told her husband, and said to him, "Look, the Man who came to me the *other* day has just now appeared to me!"

11So Manoah arose and followed his wife. When he came to the Man, he said to Him, "Are You the Man who spoke to this woman?"

And He said, "I *am*."

12Manoah said, "Now let Your words come *to pass*! What will be the boy's rule of life, and his work?"

13So the Angel of the LORD said to Manoah, "Of all that I said to the woman let her be careful. 14She may not eat anything that comes from the vine, nor may she drink wine or *similar* drink, nor eat anything unclean. All that I commanded her let her observe."

15Then Manoah said to the Angel of the LORD, "Please let us detain You, and we will prepare a young goat for You."

16And the Angel of the LORD said to Manoah, "Though you detain Me, I will not eat your food. But if you offer a burnt offering, you must offer it to the LORD." (For Manoah did not know He *was* the Angel of the LORD.)

17Then Manoah said to the Angel of the LORD, "What *is* Your name, that when Your words come *to pass* we may honor You?"

18And the Angel of the LORD said to him, "Why do you ask My name, seeing it *is* wonderful?"

19So Manoah took the young goat with the grain offering, and offered it upon the rock to the LORD. And He did a wondrous thing while Manoah and his wife looked on— 20it happened as the flame went up toward heaven from the altar—the Angel of the LORD ascended in the flame of the altar! When Manoah and his wife saw *this*, they fell on their faces to the ground. 21When the Angel of the LORD appeared no more to Manoah and his wife, then Manoah knew that He *was* the Angel of the LORD.

22And Manoah said to his wife, "We shall surely die, because we have seen God!"

23But his wife said to him, "If the LORD had desired to kill us, He would not have accepted a burnt offering and a grain offering from our hands, nor would He have shown us all these *things*, nor would He have told us *such things* as these at this time."

24*So the woman bore a son and called his name Samson; and the child grew, and the LORD blessed him. 25And the Spirit of the LORD began to move upon him at Mahaneh Danᶻ between Zorah and Eshtaol.

14 Now* Samson went down to Timnah, and saw a woman in Timnah of the daughters of the Philistines. 2So he went up and told his father and mother, saying, "I have seen a woman in Timnah of the daughters of the Philistines; now therefore, get her for me as a wife."

3Then his father and mother said to him, "*Is there* no woman among the daughters of your brethren, or among all my people, that you must go and get a wife from the uncircumcised Philistines?"

And Samson said to his father, "Get her for me, for she pleases me well."

4But his father and mother did not know that it was of the LORD—that He was seeking an occasion to move against the Philistines. For at that time the Philistines had dominion over Israel.

5So Samson went down to Timnah with his father and mother, and came to the vineyards of Timnah.

Now *to his* surprise, a young lion *came* roaring against him. 6And the Spirit of the LORD came mightily upon him, and he tore the lion apart as one would have torn apart a young goat, though *he had* nothing in his hand. But he did not tell his father or his mother what he had done.

7Then he went down and talked with the woman; and she pleased Samson well. 8*After some time, when he returned to get her, he turned aside to see the carcass of the lion. And behold, a swarm of bees and honey *were* in the carcass of the lion. 9He took some of it in his hands and went along, eating. When he came to his father and mother, he gave *some* to them, and they also

13:24, 25 He began his ministry blessed by the Lord and closed his life mocked by a heathen crowd. Yes, in Samson's death, he killed many of the enemy, but how much better had he been a *living* sacrifice (Rom. 12:1–2) and not a dead one.

CHAPTER 14

14:1–5 Samson's decision, opposed by his parents (Deut. 7:1–4), was used by the Lord in His campaign against the Philistines. When God is not allowed to rule, He will overrule (Prov. 16:33), but that is not an excuse for sin (Rom. 3:8).

14:8, 9 Samson's next step of disobedience was in turning aside to contemplate a past victory (Prov. 4:27). The honey was defiled by the carcass, so Samson was defiled when he ate it (Num. 6:6). Beware defiled honey, no matter how sweet it is!

13:25 ᶻLiterally *Camp of Dan* (compare 18:12)

ate. But he did not tell them that he had taken the honey out of the carcass of the lion.

10So his father went down to the woman. And Samson gave a feast there, for young men used to do so. 11And it happened, when they saw him, that they brought thirty companions to be with him.

12Then Samson said to them, "Let me pose a riddle to you. If you can correctly solve and explain it to me within the seven days of the feast, then I will give you thirty linen garments and thirty changes of clothing. 13But if you cannot explain it to me, then you shall give me thirty linen garments and thirty changes of clothing."

And they said to him, "Pose your riddle, that we may hear it."

14*So he said to them:

> "Out of the eater came something to eat,
>   And out of the strong came something
>   sweet."

Now for three days they could not explain the riddle.

15But it came to pass on the seventh[a] day that they said to Samson's wife, "Entice your husband, that he may explain the riddle to us, or else we will burn you and your father's house with fire. Have you invited us in order to take what is ours? Is that not so?"

16Then Samson's wife wept on him, and said, "You only hate me! You do not love me! You have posed a riddle to the sons of my people, but you have not explained it to me."

And he said to her, "Look, I have not explained it to my father or my mother; so should I explain it to you?" 17Now she had wept on him the seven days while their feast lasted. And it happened on the seventh day that he told her, because she pressed him so much. Then she explained the riddle to the sons of her people. 18*So the men of the city said to him on the seventh day before the sun went down:

> "What is sweeter than honey?
>   And what is stronger than a lion?"

And he said to them:

> "If you had not plowed with my heifer,
>   You would not have solved my riddle!"

19Then the Spirit of the LORD came upon him mightily, and he went down to Ashkelon and killed thirty of their men, took their apparel, and gave the changes of clothing to those who had explained the riddle. So his anger was aroused, and he went back up to his father's house. 20And Samson's wife was given to his companion, who had been his best man.

15 After* a while, in the time of wheat harvest, it happened that Samson visited his wife with a young goat. And he said, "Let me go in to my wife, into her room." But her father would not permit him to go in.

2Her father said, "I really thought that you thoroughly hated her; therefore I gave her to your

14:14 Then Samson defiled his parents by sharing the honey with them, and at the wedding, he made a joke out of the whole experience. His lack of seriousness in obeying the Lord eventually led to his ruin. When all his plans fell apart, he should have turned to the Lord for guidance; instead, he continued on his own determined way.

14:18 We may ignore our sins, but our sins will not ignore us. We eventually reap what we sow.

CHAPTER 15

15:1–6 When life is motivated by retaliation, the consequences are usually painful. Responding to Samson's anger, his intended father-in-law retaliated by giving away Samson's bride. Then Samson retaliated by burning the Philistines' harvest, and the Philistines in turn burned the bride and her father. Who finally won?

14:15 aFollowing Masoretic Text, Targum, and Vulgate; Septuagint and Syriac read fourth.

companion. *Is* not her younger sister better than she? Please, take her instead."

3And Samson said to them, "This time I shall be blameless regarding the Philistines if I harm them!" 4Then Samson went and caught three hundred foxes; and he took torches, turned *the foxes* tail to tail, and put a torch between each pair of tails. 5When he had set the torches on fire, he let *the foxes* go into the standing grain of the Philistines, and burned up both the shocks and the standing grain, as well as the vineyards *and* olive groves.

6Then the Philistines said, "Who has done this?"

And they answered, "Samson, the son-in-law of the Timnite, because he has taken his wife and given her to his companion." So the Philistines came up and burned her and her father with fire.

7*Samson said to them, "Since you would do a thing like this, I will surely take revenge on you, and after that I will cease." 8So he attacked them hip and thigh with a great slaughter; then he went down and dwelt in the cleft of the rock of Etam.

9Now the Philistines went up, encamped in Judah, and deployed themselves against Lehi. 10And the men of Judah said, "Why have you come up against us?"

So they answered, "We have come up to arrest Samson, to do to him as he has done to us."

11Then three thousand men of Judah went down to the cleft of the rock of Etam, and said to Samson, "Do you not know that the Philistines rule over us? What *is* this you have done to us?"

And he said to them, "As they did to me, so I have done to them."

12But they said to him, "We have come down to arrest you, that we may deliver you into the hand of the Philistines."

Then Samson said to them, "Swear to me that you will not kill me yourselves."

13So they spoke to him, saying, "No, but we will tie you securely and deliver you into their hand; but we will surely not kill you." And they bound him with two new ropes and brought him up from the rock.

14When he came to Lehi, the Philistines came shouting against him. Then the Spirit of the LORD came mightily upon him; and the ropes that *were* on his arms became like flax that is burned with fire, and his bonds broke loose from his hands. 15He found a fresh jawbone of a donkey, reached out his hand and took it, and killed a thousand men with it. 16Then Samson said:

> "With the jawbone of a donkey,
> Heaps upon heaps,
> With the jawbone of a donkey
> I have slain a thousand men!"

17And so it was, when he had finished speaking, that he threw the jawbone from his hand, and called that place Ramath Lehi.*b*

18*Then he became very thirsty; so he cried out to the LORD and said, "You have given this great deliverance by the hand of Your servant; and now shall I die of thirst and fall into the hand of the uncircumcised?" 19So God split the hollow place that *is* in Lehi,*c* and water came out, and he drank;

15:7 Then the men of Judah became frightened and tried to get Samson out of the way. They would rather compromise with the enemy than declare war. Had Samson been a spiritual man, and not just a fighter, he could have led them forth to victory, but he preferred to work alone and not as the leader of a crusade.

15:18 All it took was *thirst* to remind Samson of his weakness and his total dependence on God. Had he prayed as earnestly for character as he did for physical help, he would have been a better man and a more successful judge. Like the prodigal son, he prayed, "Give me!" but he never did pray, "Make me!" (Luke 15:12, 19).

15:17 *b*Literally *Jawbone Height*   15:19 *c*Literally *Jawbone* (compare verse 14)

CHAPTER 16

16:1–3 Defilement. God had rescued Samson from so many tight places that he was sure he was invulnerable, so he continued to play with sin and defile himself. A Spirit-filled God-called leader has no right doing what Samson did. His body belonged to God (1 Cor. 6:12–20).

16:4–20 Deception. The harlot in Gaza deceived him and so did Delilah. You would think that by then Samson would have been alert to danger, but his conscience was defiled and his moral senses were destroyed. Samson even deceived *himself* by thinking he had everything under control (v. 20), but he was wrong.

and his spirit returned, and he revived. Therefore he called its name En Hakkore,*d* which is in Lehi to this day. 20And he judged Israel twenty years in the days of the Philistines.

16 Now* Samson went to Gaza and saw a harlot there, and went in to her. 2When the Gazites *were told,* "Samson has come here!" they surrounded *the place* and lay in wait for him all night at the gate of the city. They were quiet all night, saying, "In the morning, when it is daylight, we will kill him." 3And Samson lay *low* till midnight; then he arose at midnight, took hold of the doors of the gate of the city and the two gateposts, pulled them up, bar and all, put *them* on his shoulders, and carried them to the top of the hill that faces Hebron.

4*Afterward it happened that he loved a woman in the Valley of Sorek, whose name *was* Delilah. 5And the lords of the Philistines came up to her and said to her, "Entice him, and find out where his great strength *lies,* and by what *means* we may overpower him, that we may bind him to afflict him; and every one of us will give you eleven hundred *pieces* of silver."

6So Delilah said to Samson, "Please tell me where your great strength *lies,* and with what you may be bound to afflict you."

7And Samson said to her, "If they bind me with seven fresh bowstrings, not yet dried, then I shall become weak, and be like any *other* man."

8So the lords of the Philistines brought up to her seven fresh bowstrings, not yet dried, and she bound him with them. 9Now *men were* lying in wait, staying with her in the room. And she said to him, "The Philistines *are* upon you, Samson!" But he broke the bowstrings as a strand of yarn breaks when it touches fire. So the secret of his strength was not known.

10Then Delilah said to Samson, "Look, you have mocked me and told me lies. Now, please tell me what you may be bound with."

11So he said to her, "If they bind me securely with new ropes that have never been used, then I shall become weak, and be like any *other* man."

12Therefore Delilah took new ropes and bound him with them, and said to him, "The Philistines *are* upon you, Samson!" And *men were* lying in wait, staying in the room. But he broke them off his arms like a thread.

13Delilah said to Samson, "Until now you have mocked me and told me lies. Tell me what you may be bound with."

And he said to her, "If you weave the seven locks of my head into the web of the loom"—

14So she wove *it* tightly with the batten of the loom, and said to him, "The Philistines *are* upon you, Samson!" But he awoke from his sleep, and pulled out the batten and the web from the loom.

15Then she said to him, "How can you say, 'I love you,' when your heart *is* not with me? You have mocked me these three times, and have not told me where your great strength *lies.*" 16And it came to pass, when she pestered him daily with her words and pressed him, *so* that his soul was vexed to death, 17that he told her all his heart, and said to her, "No razor has ever come upon my head, for I *have been* a Nazirite to God from

15:19 *d*Literally *Spring of the Caller*

my mother's womb. If I am shaven, then my strength will leave me, and I shall become weak, and be like any *other* man."

18When Delilah saw that he had told her all his heart, she sent and called for the lords of the Philistines, saying, "Come up once more, for he has told me all his heart." So the lords of the Philistines came up to her and brought the money in their hand. 19Then she lulled him to sleep on her knees, and called for a man and had him shave off the seven locks of his head. Then she began to torment him,*e* and his strength left him. 20And she said, "The Philistines *are* upon you, Samson!" So he awoke from his sleep, and said, "I will go out as before, at other times, and shake myself free!" But he did not know that the LORD had departed from him.

21*Then the Philistines took him and put out his eyes, and brought him down to Gaza. They bound him with bronze fetters, and he became a grinder in the prison. 22However, the hair of his head began to grow again after it had been shaven.

23Now the lords of the Philistines gathered together to offer a great sacrifice to Dagon their god, and to rejoice. And they said:

"Our god has delivered into our hands
 Samson our enemy!"

24When the people saw him, they praised their god; for they said:

"Our god has delivered into our hands our
    enemy,
  The destroyer of our land,
  And the one who multiplied our dead."

25So it happened, when their hearts were merry, that they said, "Call for Samson, that he may perform for us." So they called for Samson from the prison, and he performed for them. And they stationed him between the pillars. 26Then Samson said to the lad who held him by the hand, "Let me feel the pillars which support the temple, so that I can lean on them." 27Now the temple was full of men and women. All the lords of the Philistines *were* there—about three thousand men and women on the roof watching while Samson performed.

28Then Samson called to the LORD, saying, "O Lord GOD, remember me, I pray! Strengthen me, I pray, just this once, O God, that I may with one *blow* take vengeance on the Philistines for my two eyes!" 29And Samson took hold of the two middle pillars which supported the temple, and he braced himself against them, one on his right and the other on his left. 30Then Samson said, "Let me die with the Philistines!" And he pushed with *all his* might, and the temple fell on the lords and all the people who *were* in it. So the dead that he killed at his death were more than he had killed in his life.

31And his brothers and all his father's household came down and took him, and brought *him* up and buried him between Zorah and Eshtaol in the tomb of his father Manoah. He had judged Israel twenty years.

16:21–30 *Destruction.* Someone has said that verse 21 describes the "blinding, binding, and grinding effects of sin." Samson walked in the darkness and died in the darkness. God forgave him and restored his strength, but He did not restore his sight or his ministry. Samson may have died in victory, but he lived in moral and spiritual defeat. He destroyed God's enemies, but he did not live like God's friend (John 15:14). What a tragedy!

16:19 *e*Following Masoretic Text, Targum, and Vulgate; Septuagint reads *he began to be weak.*

CHAPTER 17

17:1 There is an old saying: "As goes the home, so goes the nation." If that is true, Israel was in trouble; for everything about this home violated the law of God.

17:2–6 The family was devoted to idolatry. The son had established his own priesthood and was a thief, and the mother was guilty of speaking both curses and blessings (James 3:9–10). She was concerned more about her money than about her son's character.

17:7 The Levite was far more guilty than they were because he was especially called of God and was trained in the Law. He was not God's servant; he was a hireling. When offered a better situation by the Danites, he took it!

17:13 What a vivid example of Do-It-Yourself Religion! But is the situation any different today? People still ignore Isaiah 8:20 and do what is right in their own eyes.

CHAPTER 18

18:1ff Corruption in the home will eventually spread to society; in this case, it spread to a whole tribe. False doctrine is like yeast: it grows quietly in secret and affects everything it touches (Gal. 5:7–9). The Danites had claimed their inheritance (Josh. 19:40–48), but the enemy's invasion had forced them to relocate. Had the tribes stayed true to God, the enemy would not have dispossessed them, and they could have enjoyed their inheritance.

17 Now* there was a man from the mountains of Ephraim, whose name *was* Micah. 2*And he said to his mother, "The eleven hundred *shekels* of silver that were taken from you, and on which you put a curse, even saying it in my ears—here *is* the silver with me; I took it."

And his mother said, "*May you be* blessed by the LORD, my son!" 3So when he had returned the eleven hundred *shekels* of silver to his mother, his mother said, "I had wholly dedicated the silver from my hand to the LORD for my son, to make a carved image and a molded image; now therefore, I will return it to you." 4Thus he returned the silver to his mother. Then his mother took two hundred *shekels* of silver and gave them to the silversmith, and he made it into a carved image and a molded image; and they were in the house of Micah.

5The man Micah had a shrine, and made an ephod and household idols;*f* and he consecrated one of his sons, who became his priest. 6In those days *there was* no king in Israel; everyone did *what was* right in his own eyes.

7*Now there was a young man from Bethlehem in Judah, of the family of Judah; he *was* a Levite, and was staying there. 8The man departed from the city of Bethlehem in Judah to stay wherever he could find *a place*. Then he came to the mountains of Ephraim, to the house of Micah, as he journeyed. 9And Micah said to him, "Where do you come from?"

So he said to him, "I *am* a Levite from Bethlehem in Judah, and I am on my way to find *a place* to stay."

10Micah said to him, "Dwell with me, and be a father and a priest to me, and I will give you ten *shekels* of silver per year, a suit of clothes, and your sustenance." So the Levite went in. 11Then the Levite was content to dwell with the man; and the young man became like one of his sons to him. 12So Micah consecrated the Levite, and the young man became his priest, and lived in the house of Micah. 13*Then Micah said, "Now I know that the LORD will be good to me, since I have a Levite as priest!"

18 In* those days *there was* no king in Israel. And in those days the tribe of the Danites was seeking an inheritance for itself to dwell in; for until that day *their* inheritance among the tribes of Israel had not fallen to them. 2So the children of Dan sent five men of their family from their territory, men of valor from Zorah and Eshtaol, to spy out the land and search it. They said to them, "Go, search the land." So they went to the mountains of Ephraim, to the house of Micah, and lodged there. 3While they *were* at the house of Micah, they recognized the voice of the young Levite. They turned aside and said to him, "Who brought you here? What are you doing in this *place*? What do you have here?"

4He said to them, "Thus and so Micah did for me. He has hired me, and I have become his priest."

5So they said to him, "Please inquire of God, that we may know whether the journey on which we go will be prosperous."

6And the priest said to them, "Go in peace. The presence of the LORD *be* with you on your way."

7So the five men departed and went to Laish.

17:5 *f*Hebrew *teraphim*

They saw the people who *were* there, how they dwelt safely, in the manner of the Sidonians, quiet and secure. *There were* no rulers in the land who might put *them* to shame for anything. They *were* far from the Sidonians, and they had no ties with anyone.g

8Then *the spies* came back to their brethren at Zorah and Eshtaol, and their brethren said to them, "What *is* your *report?*"

9So they said, "Arise, let us go up against them. For we have seen the land, and indeed it *is* very good. *Would* you *do* nothing? Do not hesitate to go, *and* enter to possess the land. 10When you go, you will come to a secure people and a large land. For God has given it into your hands, a place where *there is* no lack of anything that *is* on the earth."

11And six hundred men of the family of the Danites went from there, from Zorah and Eshtaol, armed with weapons of war. 12Then they went up and encamped in Kirjath Jearim in Judah. (Therefore they call that place Mahaneh Danh to this day. There *it is,* west of Kirjath Jearim.) 13And they passed from there to the mountains of Ephraim, and came to the house of Micah.

14Then the five men who had gone to spy out the country of Laish answered and said to their brethren, "Do you know that there are in these houses an ephod, household idols, a carved image, and a molded image? Now therefore, consider what you should do." 15So they turned aside there, and came to the house of the young Levite man—to the house of Micah—and greeted him. 16*The six hundred men armed with their weapons of war, who *were* of the children of Dan, stood by the entrance of the gate. 17Then the five men who had gone to spy out the land went up. Entering there, they took the carved image, the ephod, the household idols, and the molded image. The priest stood at the entrance of the gate with the six hundred men *who were* armed with weapons of war.

18When these went into Micah's house and took the carved image, the ephod, the household idols, and the molded image, the priest said to them, "What are you doing?"

19And they said to him, "Be quiet, put your hand over your mouth, and come with us; be a father and a priest to us. *Is it* better for you to be a priest to the household of one man, or that you be a priest to a tribe and a family in Israel?" 20So the priest's heart was glad; and he took the ephod, the household idols, and the carved image, and took his place among the people.

21Then they turned and departed, and put the little ones, the livestock, and the goods in front of them. 22When they were a good way from the house of Micah, the men who *were* in the houses near Micah's house gathered together and overtook the children of Dan. 23And they called out to the children of Dan. So they turned around and said to Micah, "What ails you, that you have gathered such a company?"

24So he said, "You have taken away my gods which I made, and the priest, and you have gone away. Now what more do I have? How can you say to me, 'What ails you?' "

25And the children of Dan said to him, "Do not

18:16–20 What a way to find a new home! The Danites kidnapped the hireling priest of the false religion and stole the idols. Then they killed innocent people who were living in ignorant isolation, a dangerous thing in that day. The climax came when they set up their own center of idolatrous worship, in open disobedience to the Word of God.

18:7 gFollowing Masoretic Text, Targum, and Vulgate; Septuagint reads *with Syria.* 18:12 hLiterally *Camp of Dan*

let your voice be heard among us, lest angry men fall upon you, and you lose your life, with the lives of your household!'' 26Then the children of Dan went their way. And when Micah saw that they *were* too strong for him, he turned and went back to his house.

27So they took *the things* Micah had made, and the priest who had belonged to him, and went to Laish, to a people quiet and secure; and they struck them with the edge of the sword and burned the city with fire. 28*There was* no deliverer, because it *was* far from Sidon, and they had no ties with anyone. It was in the valley that belongs to Beth Rehob. So they rebuilt the city and dwelt there. 29And they called the name of the city Dan, after the name of Dan their father, who was born to Israel. However, the name of the city formerly *was* Laish.

30*Then the children of Dan set up for themselves the carved image; and Jonathan the son of Gershom, the son of Manasseh,ⁱ and his sons were priests to the tribe of Dan until the day of the captivity of the land. 31So they set up for themselves Micah's carved image which he made, all the time that the house of God was in Shiloh.

18:30, 31 They were living in a place where there was "no lack of anything that is on the earth" (v. 10); yet they lacked everything that God wanted to give them from heaven. Their false prosperity gave them false security that could not last.

CHAPTER 19

19:1ff The sad history of Israel moves now from idolatry to immorality and civil war. If sin is not dealt with, it spreads like a plague and destroys. The basic cause of Israel's plight was their independence from God and their indifference to His law. Nothing can be right when every man does what is right in his own eyes. It was a time of moral and spiritual darkness (Isa. 8:20).

19:6–25 The Levite was not a good example of a spiritual leader. He had a concubine, which was permitted and regulated by law but not really approved by God. His main interests were eating, drinking, and enjoying life. Had he been a man of discipline and spiritual wisdom, he would never have caused all the trouble. He had no godly influence on the people whose lives he touched, and his evil treatment of his concubine was inexcusable.

19 And* it came to pass in those days, when *there was* no king in Israel, that there was a certain Levite staying in the remote mountains of Ephraim. He took for himself a concubine from Bethlehem in Judah. 2But his concubine played the harlot against him, and went away from him to her father's house at Bethlehem in Judah, and was there four whole months. 3Then her husband arose and went after her, to speak kindly to her *and* bring her back, having his servant and a couple of donkeys with him. So she brought him into her father's house; and when the father of the young woman saw him, he was glad to meet him. 4Now his father-in-law, the young woman's father, detained him; and he stayed with him three days. So they ate and drank and lodged there.

5Then it came to pass on the fourth day that they arose early in the morning, and he stood to depart; but the young woman's father said to his son-in-law, "Refresh your heart with a morsel of bread, and afterward go your way."

6*So they sat down, and the two of them ate and drank together. Then the young woman's father said to the man, "Please be content to stay all night, and let your heart be merry." 7And when the man stood to depart, his father-in-law urged him; so he lodged there again. 8Then he arose early in the morning on the fifth day to depart, but the young woman's father said, "Please refresh your heart." So they delayed until afternoon; and both of them ate.

9And when the man stood to depart—he and his concubine and his servant—his father-in-law, the young woman's father, said to him, "Look, the day is now drawing toward evening; please spend the night. See, the day is coming to an end; lodge here, that your heart may be merry. Tomorrow go your way early, so that you may get home."

10However, the man was not willing to spend that night; so he rose and departed, and came opposite Jebus (that *is,* Jerusalem). With him were the two saddled donkeys; his concubine *was* also

---

18:30 ⁱSeptuagint and Vulgate read *Moses.*

with him. 11They *were* near Jebus, and the day
was far spent; and the servant said to his master,
"Come, please, and let us turn aside into this city
of the Jebusites and lodge in it."

12But his master said to him, "We will not turn
aside here into a city of foreigners, who *are* not
of the children of Israel; we will go on to Gibeah."
13So he said to his servant, "Come, let us draw
near to one of these places, and spend the night
in Gibeah or in Ramah." 14And they passed by
and went their way; and the sun went down on
them near Gibeah, which belongs to Benjamin.
15They turned aside there to go in to lodge in Gibeah. And when he went in, he sat down in the
open square of the city, for no one would take
them into *his* house to spend the night.

16Just then an old man came in from his work
in the field at evening, who also *was* from the
mountains of Ephraim; he was staying in Gibeah,
whereas the men of the place *were* Benjamites.
17And when he raised his eyes, he saw the traveler
in the open square of the city; and the old man
said, "Where are you going, and where do you
come from?"

18So he said to him, "We *are* passing from Bethlehem in Judah toward the remote mountains of
Ephraim; I *am* from there. I went to Bethlehem
in Judah; *now* I am going to the house of the LORD.
But there *is* no one who will take me into his
house, 19although we have both straw and fodder
for our donkeys, and bread and wine for myself,
for your female servant, and for the young man
who is with your servant; *there is* no lack of
anything."

20And the old man said, "Peace *be* with you!
However, *let* all your needs *be* my responsibility;
only do not spend the night in the open square."
21So he brought him into his house, and gave fodder to the donkeys. And they washed their feet,
and ate and drank.

22As they were enjoying themselves, suddenly
certain men of the city, perverted men,*ʲ* surrounded the house *and* beat on the door. They
spoke to the master of the house, the old man,
saying, "Bring out the man who came to your
house, that we may know him *carnally!*"

23But the man, the master of the house, went
out to them and said to them, "No, my brethren!
I beg you, do not act *so* wickedly! Seeing this man
has come into my house, do not commit this outrage. 24Look, *here is* my virgin daughter and *the
man's*ᵏ concubine; let me bring them out now.
Humble them, and do with them as you please;
but to this man do not do such a vile thing!"
25But the men would not heed him. So the man
took his concubine and brought *her* out to them.
And they knew her and abused her all night until
morning; and when the day began to break, they
let her go.

26Then the woman came as the day was dawning, and fell down at the door of the man's house
where her master *was*, till it was light.

27*When her master arose in the morning, and
opened the doors of the house and went out to
go his way, there was his concubine, fallen *at* the
door of the house with her hands on the threshold.
28And he said to her, "Get up and let us be going."
But there was no answer. So the man lifted her

19:27–30 When spiritual leaders fail to obey
God and set godly examples, the church and
the community suffer, and ultimately the
whole nation decays. One incident of
lawlessness can cause a national crisis. It
makes a difference when God's people are
truly salt and light in a decaying and dark
society (Matt. 5:13–16).

19:22 *ʲLiterally sons of Belial* 19:24 *ᵏLiterally his*

onto the donkey; and the man got up and went to his place.

²⁹When he entered his house he took a knife, laid hold of his concubine, and divided her into twelve pieces, limb by limb,ˡ and sent her throughout all the territory of Israel. ³⁰And so it was that all who saw it said, "No such deed has been done or seen from the day that the children of Israel came up from the land of Egypt until this day. Consider it, confer, and speak up!"

CHAPTER 20

20:1ff The chapter is a good illustration of James 3:13–18. When we operate on the basis of human wisdom, we create one problem after another, but when we pause to pray and seek the mind of the Lord, He shows us what to do.

20 So* all the children of Israel came out, from Dan to Beersheba, as well as from the land of Gilead, and the congregation gathered together as one man before the LORD at Mizpah. ²And the leaders of all the people, all the tribes of Israel, presented themselves in the assembly of the people of God, four hundred thousand foot soldiers who drew the sword. ³(Now the children of Benjamin heard that the children of Israel had gone up to Mizpah.)

Then the children of Israel said, "Tell *us*, how did this wicked deed happen?"

⁴So the Levite, the husband of the woman who was murdered, answered and said, "My concubine and I went into Gibeah, which belongs to Benjamin, to spend the night. ⁵And the men of Gibeah rose against me, and surrounded the house at night because of me. They intended to kill me, but instead they ravished my concubine so that she died. ⁶So I took hold of my concubine, cut her in pieces, and sent her throughout all the territory of the inheritance of Israel, because they committed lewdness and outrage in Israel. ⁷Look! All of you *are* children of Israel; give your advice and counsel here and now!"

⁸So all the people arose as one man, saying, "None *of us* will go to his tent, nor will any turn back to his house; ⁹but now this *is* the thing which we will do to Gibeah: *We will go up* against it by lot. ¹⁰We will take ten men out of *every* hundred throughout all the tribes of Israel, a hundred out of *every* thousand, and a thousand out of *every* ten thousand, to make provisions for the people, that when they come to Gibeah in Benjamin, they may repay all the vileness that they have done in Israel." ¹¹So all the men of Israel were gathered against the city, united together as one man.

20:13 The Benjamites did not seek the Lord, admit their guilt, or repent of their sins. There can be no peace unless sin is put away, but the people of Benjamin would not judge their own people in Gibeah. "So shall you put away the evil person from among you" is repeated nine times in Deuteronomy, and God expected His people to obey.

¹²Then the tribes of Israel sent men through all the tribe of Benjamin, saying, "What *is* this wickedness that has occurred among you? ¹³*Now therefore, deliver up the men, the perverted menᵐ who *are* in Gibeah, that we may put them to death and remove the evil from Israel!" But the children of Benjamin would not listen to the voice of their brethren, the children of Israel. ¹⁴Instead, the children of Benjamin gathered together from their cities to Gibeah, to go to battle against the children of Israel. ¹⁵And from their cities at that time the children of Benjamin numbered twenty-six thousand men who drew the sword, besides the inhabitants of Gibeah, who numbered seven hundred select men. ¹⁶Among all this people *were* seven hundred select men *who were* left-handed; every one could sling a stone at a hair's *breadth* and not miss. ¹⁷Now besides Benjamin, the men of Israel numbered four hundred thousand men who drew the sword; all of these *were* men of war.

19:29 ˡLiterally *with her bones*   20:13 ᵐLiterally *sons of Belial*

18Then the children of Israel arose and went up to the house of God[n] to inquire of God. They said, "Which of us shall go up first to battle against the children of Benjamin?"

The LORD said, "Judah first!"

19So the children of Israel rose in the morning and encamped against Gibeah. 20And the men of Israel went out to battle against Benjamin, and the men of Israel put themselves in battle array to fight against them at Gibeah. 21Then the children of Benjamin came out of Gibeah, and on that day cut down to the ground twenty-two thousand men of the Israelites. 22And the people, that is, the men of Israel, encouraged themselves and again formed the battle line at the place where they had put themselves in array on the first day. 23Then the children of Israel went up and wept before the LORD until evening, and asked counsel of the LORD, saying, "Shall I again draw near for battle against the children of my brother Benjamin?"

And the LORD said, "Go up against him."

24So the children of Israel approached the children of Benjamin on the second day. 25And Benjamin went out against them from Gibeah on the second day, and cut down to the ground eighteen thousand more of the children of Israel; all these drew the sword.

26*Then all the children of Israel, that is, all the people, went up and came to the house of God[o] and wept. They sat there before the LORD and fasted that day until evening; and they offered burnt offerings and peace offerings before the LORD. 27So the children of Israel inquired of the LORD (the ark of the covenant of God was there in those days, 28and Phinehas the son of Eleazar, the son of Aaron, stood before it in those days), saying, "Shall I yet again go out to battle against the children of my brother Benjamin, or shall I cease?"

And the LORD said, "Go up, for tomorrow I will deliver them into your hand."

29Then Israel set men in ambush all around Gibeah. 30And the children of Israel went up against the children of Benjamin on the third day, and put themselves in battle array against Gibeah as at the other times. 31So the children of Benjamin went out against the people, and were drawn away from the city. They began to strike down and kill some of the people, as at the other times, in the highways (one of which goes up to Bethel and the other to Gibeah) and in the field, about thirty men of Israel. 32And the children of Benjamin said, "They are defeated before us, as at first."

But the children of Israel said, "Let us flee and draw them away from the city to the highways." 33So all the men of Israel rose from their place and put themselves in battle array at Baal Tamar. Then Israel's men in ambush burst forth from their position in the plain of Geba. 34And ten thousand select men from all Israel came against Gibeah, and the battle was fierce. But the Benjamites[p] did not know that disaster was upon them. 35The LORD defeated Benjamin before Israel. And the children of Israel destroyed that day twenty-five thousand one hundred Benjamites; all these drew the sword.

20:26–28 God's people today need to deal with sin in their lives (2 Cor. 7:1) and in the church family (1 Cor. 5). Unconfessed sin is like uncontrolled disease: it spreads and it kills. Charles Spurgeon said, "Sin is the mother and nurse of all evil, the egg of all mischief, the fountain of all bitterness, the root of misery."

20:18 [n]Or Bethel   20:26 [o]Or Bethel   20:34 [p]Literally they

36So the children of Benjamin saw that they were defeated. The men of Israel had given ground to the Benjamites, because they relied on the men in ambush whom they had set against Gibeah. 37And the men in ambush quickly rushed upon Gibeah; the men in ambush spread out and struck the whole city with the edge of the sword. 38Now the appointed signal between the men of Israel and the men in ambush was that they would make a great cloud of smoke rise up from the city, 39whereupon the men of Israel would turn in battle. Now Benjamin had begun to strike *and* kill about thirty of the men of Israel. For they said, "Surely they are defeated before us, as *in* the first battle." 40But when the cloud began to rise from the city in a column of smoke, the Benjamites looked behind them, and there was the whole city going up *in smoke* to heaven. 41And when the men of Israel turned back, the men of Benjamin panicked, for they saw that disaster had come upon them. 42Therefore they turned *their backs* before the men of Israel in the direction of the wilderness; but the battle overtook them, and whoever *came* out of the cities they destroyed in their midst. 43They surrounded the Benjamites, chased them, *and* easily trampled them down as far as the front of Gibeah toward the east. 44And eighteen thousand men of Benjamin fell; all these *were* men of valor. 45Then theyq turned and fled toward the wilderness to the rock of Rimmon; and they cut down five thousand of them on the highways. Then they pursued them relentlessly up to Gidom, and killed two thousand of them. 46So all who fell of Benjamin that day were twenty-five thousand men who drew the sword; all these *were* men of valor.

47But six hundred men turned and fled toward the wilderness to the rock of Rimmon, and they stayed at the rock of Rimmon for four months. 48And the men of Israel turned back against the children of Benjamin, and struck them down with the edge of the sword—from *every* city, men and beasts, all who were found. They also set fire to all the cities they came to.

CHAPTER 21

21:1–3 After the tumult and the tempers calmed down, the nation discovered that their rash vow had created a new problem: a tribe in Israel was about to become extinct. If the people of Gibeah had dealt with sin as Moses had commanded, all of the trouble would have been avoided. The easy way always becomes the hard way.

21 Now* the men of Israel had sworn an oath at Mizpah, saying, "None of us shall give his daughter to Benjamin as a wife." 2Then the people came to the house of God,r and remained there before God till evening. They lifted up their voices and wept bitterly, 3and said, "O LORD God of Israel, why has this come to pass in Israel, that today there should be one tribe *missing* in Israel?"

4So it was, on the next morning, that the people rose early and built an altar there, and offered burnt offerings and peace offerings. 5The children of Israel said, "Who *is there* among all the tribes of Israel who did not come up with the assembly to the LORD?" For they had made a great oath concerning anyone who had not come up to the LORD at Mizpah, saying, "He shall surely be put to death." 6And the children of Israel grieved for Benjamin their brother, and said, "One tribe is cut off from Israel today. 7What shall we do for wives for those who remain, seeing we have sworn by the LORD that we will not give them our daughters as wives?"

8And they said, "What one *is there* from the tribes of Israel who did not come up to Mizpah

---

20:45 qSeptuagint reads *the rest.*   21:2 rOr *Bethel*

to the LORD?" And, in fact, no one had come to the camp from Jabesh Gilead to the assembly. ⁹For when the people were counted, indeed, not one of the inhabitants of Jabesh Gilead *was* there. ¹⁰So the congregation sent out there twelve thousand of their most valiant men, and commanded them, saying, "Go and strike the inhabitants of Jabesh Gilead with the edge of the sword, including the women and children. ¹¹And this *is* the thing that you shall do: You shall utterly destroy every male, and every woman who has known a man intimately." ¹²So they found among the inhabitants of Jabesh Gilead four hundred young virgins who had not known a man intimately; and they brought them to the camp at Shiloh, which is in the land of Canaan.

¹³*Then the whole congregation sent *word* to the children of Benjamin who *were* at the rock of Rimmon, and announced peace to them. ¹⁴So Benjamin came back at that time, and they gave them the women whom they had saved alive of the women of Jabesh Gilead; and yet they had not found enough for them.

¹⁵And the people grieved for Benjamin, because the LORD had made a void in the tribes of Israel.

¹⁶Then the elders of the congregation said, "What shall we do for wives for those who remain, since the women of Benjamin have been destroyed?" ¹⁷And they said, "*There must be* an inheritance for the survivors of Benjamin, that a tribe may not be destroyed from Israel. ¹⁸However, we cannot give them wives from our daughters, for the children of Israel have sworn an oath, saying, 'Cursed *be* the one who gives a wife to Benjamin.' " ¹⁹Then they said, "In fact, *there is* a yearly feast of the LORD in Shiloh, which *is* north of Bethel, on the east side of the highway that goes up from Bethel to Shechem, and south of Lebonah."

²⁰Therefore they instructed the children of Benjamin, saying, "Go, lie in wait in the vineyards, ²¹and watch; and just when the daughters of Shiloh come out to perform their dances, then come out from the vineyards, and every man catch a wife for himself from the daughters of Shiloh; then go to the land of Benjamin. ²²Then it shall be, when their fathers or their brothers come to us to complain, that we will say to them, 'Be kind to them for our sakes, because we did not take a wife for any of them in the war; for *it is* not *as though* you have given the *women* to them at this time, making yourselves guilty of your oath.' "

²³*And the children of Benjamin did so; they took enough wives for their number from those who danced, whom they caught. Then they went and returned to their inheritance, and they rebuilt the cities and dwelt in them. ²⁴So the children of Israel departed from there at that time, every man to his tribe and family; they went out from there, every man to his inheritance.

²⁵In those days *there was* no king in Israel; everyone did *what was* right in his own eyes.

21:13 The leaders of Israel became peacemakers (v. 13), and the tribes began working together to solve the problem. Their solution was a matter of semantics: Israel had vowed not to *give* them wives, but that did not prevent the men of Benjamin from going out and *taking* wives.

21:23–35 The apostle Paul came from the tribe of Benjamin. No doubt he was grateful for those four hundred women from Jabesh Gilead (v. 12) and the two hundred women who were kidnapped at Shiloh, for they kept the tribe alive.

RUTH

It seems incredible that this beautiful love story could occur during the dark days of the judges, but such is the grace of God. We are living in trying days today; yet God is at work in His world, getting a bride for His Son and accomplishing His eternal purposes. Never permit the bad news of man's sin to rob you of the good news of God's love and grace.

You see the providence of God at work in the lives of Naomi, Ruth, and Boaz, and you see another important link in the genealogy of the Savior. In Ruth 4:17, David is mentioned for the first time in the Bible.

The four chapters of Ruth are four acts in a drama: (1) tears, (2) toil, (3) trust, and (4) triumph. The book begins with funerals and ends with a wedding. Naomi moves from bitterness to blessedness, and Ruth moves from loneliness to love. What a picture of the grace of God!

CHAPTER 1

1:1–5 Naomi and her husband sinned when they left Judah for enemy country. Better to be hungry in the will of God than to have a full stomach and be out of His will. They planned to stay in Moab a short time, but their "sojourn" was long enough for their sons to marry. Then the sons and father died. You can run away from famine, but you cannot escape death.

1:6–18 Naomi sinned by urging her daughters-in-law to go home. She did not want to take two Moabite women back to Bethlehem with her and reveal the family's disobedience to God (Deut. 23:3). Imagine a Jewess sending them back to their false gods! But Ruth had come to trust in the God of Israel (vv. 16–17; 2:12), and she refused to go back.

1 Now* it came to pass, in the days when the judges ruled, that there was a famine in the land. And a certain man of Bethlehem, Judah, went to dwell in the country of Moab, he and his wife and his two sons. 2The name of the man *was* Elimelech, the name of his wife *was* Naomi, and the names of his two sons *were* Mahlon and Chilion—Ephrathites of Bethlehem, Judah. And they went to the country of Moab and remained there. 3Then Elimelech, Naomi's husband, died; and she was left, and her two sons. 4Now they took wives of the women of Moab: the name of the one *was* Orpah, and the name of the other Ruth. And they dwelt there about ten years. 5Then both Mahlon and Chilion also died; so the woman survived her two sons and her husband.

6*Then she arose with her daughters-in-law that she might return from the country of Moab, for she had heard in the country of Moab that the LORD had visited His people by giving them bread. 7Therefore she went out from the place where she was, and her two daughters-in-law with her; and they went on the way to return to the land of Judah. 8And Naomi said to her two daughters-in-law, "Go, return each to her mother's house. The LORD deal kindly with you, as you have dealt with the dead and with me. 9The LORD grant that you may find rest, each in the house of her husband."

So she kissed them, and they lifted up their voices and wept. 10And they said to her, "Surely we will return with you to your people."

11But Naomi said, "Turn back, my daughters; why will you go with me? *Are* there still sons in my womb, that they may be your husbands? 12Turn back, my daughters, go—for I am too old to have a husband. If I should say I have hope, *if* I should have a husband tonight and should also bear sons, 13would you wait for them till they were grown? Would you restrain yourselves from having husbands? No, my daughters; for it grieves me very much for your sakes that the hand of the LORD has gone out against me!"

14Then they lifted up their voices and wept again; and Orpah kissed her mother-in-law, but Ruth clung to her.

15And she said, "Look, your sister-in-law has gone back to her people and to her gods; return after your sister-in-law."

16But Ruth said:

"Entreat me not to leave you,
Or to turn back from following after you;
For wherever you go, I will go;
And wherever you lodge, I will lodge;
Your people *shall be* my people,
And your God, my God.
17 Where you die, I will die,
And there will I be buried.
The LORD do so to me, and more also,
If *anything but* death parts you and me."

18When she saw that she was determined to go with her, she stopped speaking to her.

19Now the two of them went until they came to Bethlehem. And it happened, when they had come to Bethlehem, that all the city was excited because of them; and the women said, "Is this Naomi?"

20*But she said to them, "Do not call me Naomi;a call me Mara,b for the Almighty has dealt very bitterly with me. 21*I went out full, and the LORD has brought me home again empty. Why do you call me Naomi, since the LORD has testified against me, and the Almighty has afflicted me?"

22So Naomi returned, and Ruth the Moabitess her daughter-in-law with her, who returned from the country of Moab. Now they came to Bethlehem at the beginning of barley harvest.

2 There was a relative of Naomi's husband, a man of great wealth, of the family of Elimelech. His name *was* Boaz. 2*So Ruth the Moabitess said to Naomi, "Please let me go to the field, and glean heads of grain after *him* in whose sight I may find favor."

And she said to her, "Go, my daughter."

3*Then she left, and went and gleaned in the field after the reapers. And she happened to come to the part of the field *belonging* to Boaz, who *was* of the family of Elimelech.

4Now behold, Boaz came from Bethlehem, and said to the reapers, "The LORD *be* with you!"

And they answered him, "The LORD bless you!"

5*Then Boaz said to his servant who was in charge of the reapers, "Whose young woman *is* this?"

6So the servant who was in charge of the reapers answered and said, "It *is* the young Moabite woman who came back with Naomi from the country of Moab. 7And she said, 'Please let me glean and gather after the reapers among the sheaves.' So she came and has continued from morning until now, though she rested a little in the house."

8Then Boaz said to Ruth, "You will listen, my daughter, will you not? Do not go to glean in another field, nor go from here, but stay close by my young women. 9Let your eyes *be* on the field which they reap, and go after them. Have I not commanded the young men not to touch you? And

---

1:20 aLiterally *Pleasant* bLiterally *Bitter*

1:20 Naomi sinned by getting bitter and blaming God for her plight. *Naomi* means "pleasant" and *Mara* means "bitter." But it was her decision to go to Moab, so why blame God? A "root of bitterness" can poison your life and the people around you (Deut. 29:18; Heb. 12:15), so avoid carrying grudges.

1:21 Although God does not prevent the painful consequences of our sins, He does overrule so that His purposes are fulfilled. By the grace of God, Naomi's emptiness will become fullness, and her sorrow will turn to joy.

CHAPTER 2

2:2 Ruth was a young believer, but she knew enough of the Word to understand that she was permitted to glean in the fields during the harvest (Lev. 19:9–10). She trusted the God who was concerned about widows and the poor (Exod. 22:22; Deut. 10:18), and He did not fail. When we trust God and obey Him, He begins to work on our behalf (Prov. 3:5–6).

2:3 There were at least two men in Bethlehem who could permanently deliver Ruth and Naomi from their poverty and loneliness, and God providentially led Ruth to the field of one of them, Boaz. (See Ps. 25:9; Isa. 42:16.) It was not the bitterness of Naomi but the faithfulness of Ruth that changed the picture.

2:5–9 Boaz protected Ruth and provided for her even before she discovered who he was. (On his part, it was probably love at first sight!) Instead of living on leftovers, Ruth became a friend of "the lord of the harvest" who gave her generous gifts. Can you see in all of this a picture of what Christ has done for His own?

Under His Wings (Ruth 2:12)—This image refers to the Holy of Holies in the tabernacle, where the wings of the cherubim overshadowed the mercy seat (Exod. 25:17–22). To be under His wings means to be in the place of security and fellowship with God (Pss. 36:7–8; 61:4; 91:1–4). Believers should abide in Him (John 15:1–10) and enter into the Holy of Holies (Heb. 10:19–25). God's people are "outside the camp" (Heb. 13:13) but living "inside the veil" in the Holy of Holies.

when you are thirsty, go to the vessels and drink from what the young men have drawn."

10So she fell on her face, bowed down to the ground, and said to him, "Why have I found favor in your eyes, that you should take notice of me, since I *am* a foreigner?"

11And Boaz answered and said to her, "It has been fully reported to me, all that you have done for your mother-in-law since the death of your husband, and *how* you have left your father and your mother and the land of your birth, and have come to a people whom you did not know before. 12The LORD repay your work, and a full reward be given you by the LORD God of Israel, under whose wings you have come for refuge."

13Then she said, "Let me find favor in your sight, my lord; for you have comforted me, and have spoken kindly to your maidservant, though I am not like one of your maidservants."

14Now Boaz said to her at mealtime, "Come here, and eat of the bread, and dip your piece of bread in the vinegar." So she sat beside the reapers, and he passed parched *grain* to her; and she ate and was satisfied, and kept some back. 15And when she rose up to glean, Boaz commanded his young men, saying, "Let her glean even among the sheaves, and do not reproach her. 16Also let *grain* from the bundles fall purposely for her; leave *it* that she may glean, and do not rebuke her."

17So she gleaned in the field until evening, and beat out what she had gleaned, and it was about an ephah of barley. 18Then she took *it* up and went into the city, and her mother-in-law saw what she had gleaned. So she brought out and gave to her what she had kept back after she had been satisfied.

19And her mother-in-law said to her, "Where have you gleaned today? And where did you work? Blessed be the one who took notice of you."

So she told her mother-in-law with whom she had worked, and said, "The man's name with whom I worked today *is* Boaz."

20Then Naomi said to her daughter-in-law, "Blessed *be* he of the LORD, who has not forsaken His kindness to the living and the dead!" And Naomi said to her, "This man *is* a relation of ours, one of our close relatives."

21Ruth the Moabitess said, "He also said to me, 'You shall stay close by my young men until they have finished all my harvest.'"

22And Naomi said to Ruth her daughter-in-law, "*It is* good, my daughter, that you go out with his young women, and that people do not meet you in any other field." 23So she stayed close by the young women of Boaz, to glean until the end of barley harvest and wheat harvest; and she dwelt with her mother-in-law.

CHAPTER 3

3:1–6 Naomi got rid of her bitterness and began to think of others. She told Ruth how to approach Boaz, her kinsman-redeemer (Lev. 25:23–55). He was a near relative who was able to redeem, but was he *willing* to redeem? Ruth would find out that night.

3 Then* Naomi her mother-in-law said to her, "My daughter, shall I not seek security for you, that it may be well with you? 2Now Boaz, whose young women you were with, *is he* not our relative? In fact, he is winnowing barley tonight

The Kinsman-Redeemer (Lev. 25:23–55)—This law helped to protect the poor from being exploited and the rich from taking property from one tribe to another. The redeemer had to be a near kinsman who was able to redeem and willing to redeem. He was not obligated to do so, but it was expected of him. To refuse was to hurt the family and tribe as well as his own reputation. By being born at Bethlehem, Jesus Christ became our near kinsman. He was able to save and willing to save; He saves all who will put their trust in Him.

at the threshing floor. 3Therefore wash yourself and anoint yourself, put on your *best* garment and go down to the threshing floor; *but* do not make yourself known to the man until he has finished eating and drinking. 4Then it shall be, when he lies down, that you shall notice the place where he lies; and you shall go in, uncover his feet, and lie down; and he will tell you what you should do."

5And she said to her, "All that you say to me I will do."

6So she went down to the threshing floor and did according to all that her mother-in-law instructed her. 7And after Boaz had eaten and drunk, and his heart was cheerful, he went to lie down at the end of the heap of grain; and she came softly, uncovered his feet, and lay down.

8Now it happened at midnight that the man was startled, and turned himself; and there, a woman was lying at his feet. 9*And he said, "Who *are* you?"

So she answered, "I *am* Ruth, your maidservant. Take your maidservant under your wing,c for you are a close relative."

10Then he said, "Blessed *are* you of the LORD, my daughter! For you have shown more kindness at the end than at the beginning, in that you did not go after young men, whether poor or rich. 11And now, my daughter, do not fear. I will do for you all that you request, for all the people of my town know that you *are* a virtuous woman. 12Now it is true that I *am* a close relative; however, there is a relative closer than I. 13Stay this night, and in the morning it shall be *that* if he will perform the duty of a close relative for you—good; let him do it. But if he does not want to perform the duty for you, then I will perform the duty for you, *as* the LORD lives! Lie down until morning."

14So she lay at his feet until morning, and she arose before one could recognize another. Then he said, "Do not let it be known that the woman came to the threshing floor." 15Also he said, "Bring the shawl that *is* on you and hold it." And when she held it, he measured six *ephahs* of barley, and laid *it* on her. Then shed went into the city.

16When she came to her mother-in-law, she said, "Is that you, my daughter?"

Then she told her all that the man had done for her. 17And she said, "These six *ephahs* of barley he gave me; for he said to me, 'Do not go empty-handed to your mother-in-law.'"

18Then she said, "Sit still, my daughter, until you know how the matter will turn out; for the man will not rest until he has concluded the matter this day."

4 Now* Boaz went up to the gate and sat down there; and behold, the close relative of whom Boaz had spoken came by. So Boaz said, "Come aside, friend,e sit down here." So he came aside and sat down. 2And he took ten men of the elders of the city, and said, "Sit down here." So they sat down. 3Then he said to the close relative, "Naomi, who has come back from the country of

3:9–18 She was already under the Lord's wings (2:12), but she requested to be under the wing of Boaz (v. 9). He was only too happy to comply! Up to that point, Ruth was doing all the work, but then Boaz went to work for Ruth (v. 18). It was time for Ruth to rest and wait, trusting her kinsman-redeemer.

Ruth is a good example for us to follow when we have needs to be met. She listened to instructions (vv. 1–4), obeyed (vv. 5–9), believed what her redeemer said (vv. 10–14), received his gifts (vv. 15–17), and waited in patience for him to do the rest (v. 18). When you are at the feet of your Redeemer, you have nothing to fear.

CHAPTER 4

4:1, 2 Five times in the first two verses we read about people *sitting down*. It was to be a deliberate and final transaction; Boaz was to pay the price to redeem Ruth. When our Savior finished the work of redemption, He sat down (Mark 16:19; Heb. 1:3; see also John 19:30).

3:9 cOr *Spread the corner of your garment over your maidservant*   3:15 dMany Hebrew manuscripts, Syriac, and Vulgate read *she;* Masoretic Text, Septuagint, and Targum read *he.*   4:1 eHebrew *peloni almoni;* literally *so and so*

4:5–12 Boaz planned the marriage privately but paid the price publicly. The other kinsman was able to redeem but not willing. He was afraid of harming his own inheritance. Jesus has made us a part of His inheritance (Eph. 1:11–14). What a contrast between chapters 1—2 and chapter 4: from tears to joy, from hard labor to rest, from emptiness to fullness, from fear to peace and assurance. And the thing that made the difference was *obeying the Word of God*. When Ruth put herself at the feet of her redeemer and entrusted herself to him, he took over and changed everything.

4:13–22 In chapter 1, Ruth had nothing but her faith. In chapter 2, she lived on leftovers, and in chapter 3, she received generous gifts. But once she belonged to Boaz, *everything he owned belonged to her.* Ponder Ephesians 1:3 and 2 Corinthians 8:9.

Moab, sold the piece of land which *belonged* to our brother Elimelech. 4And I thought to inform you, saying, 'Buy *it* back in the presence of the inhabitants and the elders of my people. If you will redeem *it*, redeem *it;* but if you*ƒ* will not redeem *it, then* tell me, that I may know; for *there is* no one but you to redeem *it*, and I *am* next after you.' "

And he said, "I will redeem *it*."

5*Then Boaz said, "On the day you buy the field from the hand of Naomi, you must also buy *it* from Ruth the Moabitess, the wife of the dead, to perpetuate*g* the name of the dead through his inheritance."

6And the close relative said, "I cannot redeem *it* for myself, lest I ruin my own inheritance. You redeem my right of redemption for yourself, for I cannot redeem *it*."

7Now this *was the custom* in former times in Israel concerning redeeming and exchanging, to confirm anything: one man took off his sandal and gave *it* to the other, and this *was* a confirmation in Israel.

8Therefore the close relative said to Boaz, "Buy *it* for yourself." So he took off his sandal. 9And Boaz said to the elders and all the people, "You *are* witnesses this day that I have bought all that was Elimelech's, and all that *was* Chilion's and Mahlon's, from the hand of Naomi. 10Moreover, Ruth the Moabitess, the widow of Mahlon, I have acquired as my wife, to perpetuate the name of the dead through his inheritance, that the name of the dead may not be cut off from among his brethren and from his position at the gate.*h* You *are* witnesses this day."

11And all the people who *were* at the gate, and the elders, said, "*We are* witnesses. The LORD make the woman who is coming to your house like Rachel and Leah, the two who built the house of Israel; and may you prosper in Ephrathah and be famous in Bethlehem. 12May your house be like the house of Perez, whom Tamar bore to Judah, because of the offspring which the LORD will give you from this young woman."

13*So Boaz took Ruth and she became his wife; and when he went in to her, the LORD gave her conception, and she bore a son. 14Then the women said to Naomi, "Blessed *be* the LORD, who has not left you this day without a close relative; and may his name be famous in Israel! 15And may he be to you a restorer of life and a nourisher of your old age; for your daughter-in-law, who loves you, who is better to you than seven sons, has borne him." 16Then Naomi took the child and laid him on her bosom, and became a nurse to him. 17Also the neighbor women gave him a name, saying, "There is a son born to Naomi." And they called his name Obed. He *is* the father of Jesse, the father of David.

18Now this *is* the genealogy of Perez: Perez begot Hezron; 19Hezron begot Ram, and Ram begot Amminadab; 20Amminadab begot Nahshon, and Nahshon begot Salmon;*i* 21Salmon begot Boaz, and Boaz begot Obed; 22Obed begot Jesse, and Jesse begot David.

4:4 *ƒ*Following many Hebrew manuscripts, Septuagint, Syriac, Targum, and Vulgate; Masoretic Text reads *he*.   4:5 *g*Literally *raise up*   4:10 *h*Probably his civic office   4:20 *i*Hebrew *Salmah*

1 SAMUEL

Three men are the center of attention in these books: Samuel (1 Sam. 1—7), Saul (1 Sam. 8—15) and David (1 Sam. 16—2 Sam. 24). Their careers overlap, of course, as the story of Israel's monarchy unfolds.

Samuel was the last of the judges, and Saul was the first of the kings. However, Saul was never meant to establish the dynasty because he was from the wrong tribe (Gen. 49:10). God chose David, from the tribe of Judah, to be His ruler. Saul was given to the people as a discipline because they rejected the Lord to have a king like other nations (Hos. 13:11).

These books show the hand of God at work in the affairs of men and nations. Men are free to make decisions, but God still guides and sees to it that His purposes are fulfilled.

1 Now there was a certain man of Ramathaim Zophim, of the mountains of Ephraim, and his name was Elkanah the son of Jeroham, the son of Elihu,ᵃ the son of Tohu,ᵇ the son of Zuph, an Ephraimite. 2*And he had two wives: the name of one was Hannah, and the name of the other Peninnah. Peninnah had children, but Hannah had no children. 3This man went up from his city yearly to worship and sacrifice to the LORD of hosts in Shiloh. Also the two sons of Eli, Hophni and Phinehas, the priests of the LORD, were there. 4And whenever the time came for Elkanah to make an offering, he would give portions to Peninnah his wife and to all her sons and daughters. 5But to Hannah he would give a double portion, for he loved Hannah, although the LORD had closed her womb. 6And her rival also provoked her severely, to make her miserable, because the LORD had closed her womb. 7So it was, year by year, when she went up to the house of the LORD, that she provoked her; therefore she wept and did not eat.

8Then Elkanah her husband said to her, "Hannah, why do you weep? Why do you not eat? And why is your heart grieved? Am I not better to you than ten sons?"

9So Hannah arose after they had finished eating and drinking in Shiloh. Now Eli the priest was sitting on the seat by the doorpost of the tabernacleᶜ of the LORD. 10*And she was in bitterness of soul, and prayed to the LORD and wept in anguish. 11Then she made a vow and said, "O LORD of hosts, if You will indeed look on the affliction of Your maidservant and remember me, and not forget Your maidservant, but will give Your maidservant a male child, then I will give him to the LORD all the days of his life, and no razor shall come upon his head."

12And it happened, as she continued praying before the LORD, that Eli watched her mouth. 13Now Hannah spoke in her heart; only her lips moved, but her voice was not heard. Therefore Eli thought she was drunk. 14So Eli said to her, "How long will you be drunk? Put your wine away from you!"

15But Hannah answered and said, "No, my lord, I am a woman of sorrowful spirit. I have drunk neither wine nor intoxicating drink, but have

CHAPTER 1

1:2 Grace. The name *Hannah* means "grace," and she needed God's grace to handle her burdens. Unfortunately, the home was divided, her rival provoked her, and she was childless. Out of this kind of sorrow and disappointment, God often builds great faith and sends special blessings. (See 1 Pet. 5:10.)

1:10—17 Faith. When you consider her situation at home and also the way Eli treated her, you find it remarkable that Hannah had any faith at all. But she did not become bitter against God, as Naomi had done (Ruth 1:19—22), nor did she create problems in the home. She asked God for a son, and God answered her prayer. No wonder Samuel ("heard by God") was a great man of prayer. Look at the mother God gave him!

1:1 ᵃSpelled *Eliel* in 1 Chronicles 6:34 ᵇSpelled *Toah* in 1 Chronicles 6:34   1:9 ᶜHebrew *heykal*, palace or temple

poured out my soul before the LORD. ¹⁶Do not consider your maidservant a wicked woman,ᵈ for out of the abundance of my complaint and grief I have spoken until now."

¹⁷Then Eli answered and said, "Go in peace, and the God of Israel grant your petition which you have asked of Him."

¹⁸And she said, "Let your maidservant find favor in your sight." So the woman went her way and ate, and her face was no longer *sad*.

¹⁹Then they rose early in the morning and worshiped before the LORD, and returned and came to their house at Ramah. And Elkanah knew Hannah his wife, and the LORD remembered her. ²⁰So it came to pass in the process of time that Hannah conceived and bore a son, and called his name Samuel,ᵉ *saying*, "Because I have asked for him from the LORD."

²¹Now the man Elkanah and all his house went up to offer to the LORD the yearly sacrifice and his vow. ²²*But Hannah did not go up, for she said to her husband, "*Not* until the child is weaned; then I will take him, that he may appear before the LORD and remain there forever."

²³So Elkanah her husband said to her, "Do what seems best to you; wait until you have weaned him. Only let the LORD establish Hisᶠ word." Then the woman stayed and nursed her son until she had weaned him.

²⁴Now when she had weaned him, she took him up with her, with three bulls,ᵍ one ephah of flour, and a skin of wine, and brought him to the house of the LORD in Shiloh. And the child *was* young. ²⁵Then they slaughtered a bull, and brought the child to Eli. ²⁶And she said, "O my lord! As your soul lives, my lord, I *am* the woman who stood by you here, praying to the LORD. ²⁷For this child I prayed, and the LORD has granted me my petition which I asked of Him. ²⁸Therefore I also have lent him to the LORD; as long as he lives he shall be lent to the LORD." So they worshiped the LORD there.

1:22–28 Obedience.

1:22–28 Obedience. Hannah's vow was not a "bargain" with the Lord but an expression of devotion: she would *give* her firstborn to God and not redeem him with a sacrifice (Exod. 13:11–16). A mother's prayers and a father's encouragement (vv. 21–23, 28) changed the destiny of an entire nation. Never underestimate the power of prayer or the value of one godly home.

CHAPTER 2

2:1–11 Singing. Most people would sing if they could *keep* their son, but Hannah sang because she could *give* her son to the service of the Lord. She glorified the Lord who does great things for His people. Mary's song is similar to Hannah's (Luke 1:46–55) because Mary had also made a sacrifice to the Lord (Luke 1:38). First the sacrifice, then the song (2 Chron. 29:27).

2 And* Hannah prayed and said:

"My heart rejoices in the LORD;
My hornʰ is exalted in the LORD.
I smile at my enemies,
Because I rejoice in Your salvation.

2 "No one is holy like the LORD,
For *there is* none besides You,
Nor *is there* any rock like our God.

3 "Talk no more so very proudly;
Let no arrogance come from your mouth,
For the LORD *is* the God of knowledge;
And by Him actions are weighed.

1:16 ᵈLiterally *daughter of Belial*   1:20 ᵉLiterally *Heard by God*   1:23 ᶠFollowing Masoretic Text, Targum, and Vulgate; Dead Sea Scrolls, Septuagint, and Syriac read *your*.
1:24 ᵍDead Sea Scrolls, Septuagint, and Syriac read a *three-year-old bull*.   2:1 ʰThat is, strength

---

Children—Children are a gift from God (Gen. 48:8–9), a heritage and a reward (Ps. 127:3), weapons to use in fighting the enemy (Ps. 127:4–5), a source of joy (Ps. 113:9), and a crown in their parents' old age (Prov. 17:6). It is a serious thing to abuse children (Matt. 18:1–6) or to neglect their spiritual training (Eph. 6:1–4). Christian witness is always one generation short of extinction. If we fail to train the children for Christ, we forfeit the future.

4 "The bows of the mighty men *are* broken,
   And those who stumbled are girded with
       strength.
5 *Those who were* full have hired themselves
       out for bread,
   And the hungry have ceased *to hunger*.
   Even the barren has borne seven,
   And she who has many children has become
       feeble.

6 "The LORD kills and makes alive;
   He brings down to the grave and brings up.
7 The LORD makes poor and makes rich;
   He brings low and lifts up.
8 He raises the poor from the dust
   And lifts the beggar from the ash heap,
   To set *them* among princes
   And make them inherit the throne of glory.

   "For the pillars of the earth *are* the LORD's,
   And He has set the world upon them.
9 He will guard the feet of His saints,
   But the wicked shall be silent in darkness.

   "For by strength no man shall prevail.
10 The adversaries of the LORD shall be broken
       in pieces;
   From heaven He will thunder against them.
   The LORD will judge the ends of the earth.

   "He will give strength to His king,
   And exalt the horn of His anointed."

11Then Elkanah went to his house at Ramah. But the child ministered to the LORD before Eli the priest.

12*Now the sons of Eli *were* corrupt;[i] they did not know the LORD. 13And the priests' custom with the people *was that* when any man offered a sacrifice, the priest's servant would come with a three-pronged fleshhook in his hand while the meat was boiling. 14Then he would thrust *it* into the pan, or kettle, or caldron, or pot; and the priest would take for himself all that the fleshhook brought up. So they did in Shiloh to all the Israelites who came there. 15Also, before they burned the fat, the priest's servant would come and say to the man who sacrificed, "Give meat for roasting to the priest, for he will not take boiled meat from you, but raw."

16And *if* the man said to him, "They should really burn the fat first; *then* you may take as *much* as your heart desires," he would then answer him, "No, but you must give *it* now; and if not, I will take *it* by force."

17Therefore the sin of the young men was very great before the LORD, for men abhorred the offering of the LORD.

18*But Samuel ministered before the LORD, *even* as a child, wearing a linen ephod. 19Moreover his mother used to make him a little robe, and bring *it* to him year by year when she came up with her husband to offer the yearly sacrifice. 20And Eli would bless Elkanah and his wife, and say, "The LORD give you descendants from this woman for the loan that was given to the LORD." Then they would go to their own home.

21And the LORD visited Hannah, so that she conceived and bore three sons and two daughters.

2:12–17 Sinning. Eli had lost his influence over his sons and as a result caused his family to lose the priesthood (1 Kings 2:26–27, 35). (See 1 Tim. 3:4–5.) It has well been said that the greatest evil comes from the corruption of the greatest good, and Eli's sons illustrate this truth.

2:18–26 Serving. Blessed are those parents who realize that their children are growing and facing new needs and struggles, and blessed are those children who grow "before the Lord" (Luke 2:52). God kept Samuel pure in the midst of a defiled environment because he had parents who loved him and prayed for him. Jesus has a special love for children, and we must love them, too.

2:12 [i]Literally *sons of Belial*

Meanwhile the child Samuel grew before the LORD.

22Now Eli was very old; and he heard everything his sons did to all Israel,*j* and how they lay with the women who assembled at the door of the tabernacle of meeting. 23So he said to them, "Why do you do such things? For I hear of your evil dealings from all the people. 24No, my sons! For *it is* not a good report that I hear. You make the LORD's people transgress. 25If one man sins against another, God will judge him. But if a man sins against the LORD, who will intercede for him?" Nevertheless they did not heed the voice of their father, because the LORD desired to kill them.

26And the child Samuel grew in stature, and in favor both with the LORD and men.

27Then a man of God came to Eli and said to him, "Thus says the LORD: 'Did I not clearly reveal Myself to the house of your father when they were in Egypt in Pharaoh's house? 28Did I not choose him out of all the tribes of Israel *to be* My priest, to offer upon My altar, to burn incense, and to wear an ephod before Me? And did I not give to the house of your father all the offerings of the children of Israel made by fire? 29Why do you kick at My sacrifice and My offering which I have commanded *in My* dwelling place, and honor your sons more than Me, to make yourselves fat with the best of all the offerings of Israel My people?' 30Therefore the LORD God of Israel says: 'I said indeed *that* your house and the house of your father would walk before Me forever.' But now the LORD says: 'Far be it from Me; for those who honor Me I will honor, and those who despise Me shall be lightly esteemed. 31Behold, the days are coming that I will cut off your arm and the arm of your father's house, so that there will not be an old man in your house. 32And you will see an enemy *in My* dwelling place, *despite* all the good which God does for Israel. And there shall not be an old man in your house forever. 33But any of your men *whom* I do not cut off from My altar shall consume your eyes and grieve your heart. And all the descendants of your house shall die in the flower of their age. 34Now this *shall be* a sign to you that will come upon your two sons, on Hophni and Phinehas: in one day they shall die, both of them. 35Then I will raise up for Myself a faithful priest *who* shall do according to what *is* in My heart and in My mind. I will build him a sure house, and he shall walk before My anointed forever. 36And it shall come to pass that everyone who is left in your house will come *and* bow down to him for a piece of silver and a morsel of bread, and say, "Please, put me in one of the priestly positions, that I may eat a piece of bread." ' "

CHAPTER 3

3:1ff *Sanctity.* A godly life can develop in spite of ungodly influences surrounding it. So it was with Moses in Egypt, Daniel in Babylon, and our Lord in Nazareth. Samuel was not isolated, but he was separated. He belonged to the Lord. Daily, he was in contact with sin, and yet he was not contaminated by it. He was a "living sacrifice" and experienced God's transforming power (Rom. 12:1–2).

3 Now* the boy Samuel ministered to the LORD before Eli. And the word of the LORD was rare in those days; *there was* no widespread revelation. 2And it came to pass at that time, while Eli *was* lying down in his place, and when his eyes had begun to grow so dim that he could not see, 3and before the lamp of God went out in the tabernacle*k* of the LORD where the ark of God *was,* and

---

2:22 *Following Masoretic Text, Targum, and Vulgate; Dead Sea Scrolls and Septuagint omit the rest of this verse.
3:3 *Hebrew *heykal,* palace or temple

while Samuel was lying down, [4]*that the LORD
called Samuel. And he answered, "Here I am!"
[5]So he ran to Eli and said, "Here I am, for you
called me."

And he said, "I did not call; lie down again."
And he went and lay down.

[6]Then the LORD called yet again, "Samuel!"

So Samuel arose and went to Eli, and said,
"Here I am, for you called me." He answered, "I
did not call, my son; lie down again." [7](Now Samuel did not yet know the LORD, nor was the word
of the LORD yet revealed to him.)

[8]And the LORD called Samuel again the third
time. So he arose and went to Eli, and said, "Here
I am, for you did call me."

Then Eli perceived that the LORD had called the
boy. [9]Therefore Eli said to Samuel, "Go, lie down;
and it shall be, if He calls you, that you must say,
'Speak, LORD, for Your servant hears.' " So Samuel went and lay down in his place.

[10]Now the LORD came and stood and called as
at other times, "Samuel! Samuel!"

And Samuel answered, "Speak, for Your servant hears."

[11]Then the LORD said to Samuel: "Behold, I will
do something in Israel at which both ears of
everyone who hears it will tingle. [12]In that day I
will perform against Eli all that I have spoken
concerning his house, from beginning to end.
[13]For I have told him that I will judge his house
forever for the iniquity which he knows, because
his sons made themselves vile, and he did not restrain them. [14]And therefore I have sworn to the
house of Eli that the iniquity of Eli's house shall
not be atoned for by sacrifice or offering forever."

[15]So Samuel lay down until morning,[l] and
opened the doors of the house of the LORD. And
Samuel was afraid to tell Eli the vision. [16]Then
Eli called Samuel and said, "Samuel, my son!"

He answered, "Here I am."

[17]And he said, "What is the word that the LORD
spoke to you? Please do not hide it from me. God
do so to you, and more also, if you hide anything
from me of all the things that He said to you."
[18]Then Samuel told him everything, and hid nothing from him. And he said, "It is the LORD. Let
Him do what seems good to Him."

[19]*So Samuel grew, and the LORD was with him
and let none of his words fall to the ground.
[20]And all Israel from Dan to Beersheba knew that
Samuel had been established as a prophet of the
LORD. [21]Then the LORD appeared again in Shiloh.
For the LORD revealed Himself to Samuel in Shiloh
by the word of the LORD.

4 And* the word of Samuel came to all Israel.[m]

Now Israel went out to battle against the

3:4–9 Authority. Even though Eli was not
the most godly example or mentor, young
Samuel submitted to his authority. We
submit to man's authority "for the Lord's
sake" (1 Pet. 2:13– 25), for we serve God,
not men. We trust Him to protect us and
work out His will even in the lives of ungodly
people.

3:19–21 Fidelity. God gave His message
to Samuel because He knew Samuel was
faithful. The lad was accustomed to being
alert to Eli's voice and to obeying
immediately, so when God spoke, Samuel
was ready. Being faithful in a few small
things prepares you for bigger things (Matt.
25:21). Hearing the voice of God did not
keep Samuel from doing the work of God
(v. 15); he went right back to the old tasks.
The nation would now listen to Samuel's
words, for they knew he was God's
spokesman.

CHAPTER 4

4:1ff Three tragedies are recorded here.

3:15 [l]Following Masoretic Text, Targum, and Vulgate;
Septuagint adds *and he arose in the morning.* 4:1 [m]Following
Masoretic Text and Targum; Septuagint and Vulgate add *And
it came to pass in those days that the Philistines gathered
themselves together to fight;* Septuagint adds further *against
Israel.*

Naming the Baby—Would you want your name to be Ichabod, "Where is the glory"? Or Ben-
Oni, "Son of my sorrow" (Gen. 35:16–20)? Or Jabez, "He will cause pain" (1 Chron. 4:9–10)? Or
Beriah, "Tragedy" (1 Chron. 7:23)? Our first birth identifies us with defeat, but the new birth identifies
us with victory (1 John 5:1–5). When you trust Jesus Christ, your life changes in many wonderful
ways.

4:3–5 Defeat. Eli's two sons wanted God's help but not God's holiness. They wanted God for the crisis experiences of life but not in their daily ministry (1 Sam. 2:12–17). They thought that the presence of the ark would assure victory, but their superstitious faith had no foundation. Beware "using" God to solve your problems if your life is not yielded to Him.

Philistines, and encamped beside Ebenezer; and the Philistines encamped in Aphek. 2Then the Philistines put themselves in battle array against Israel. And when they joined battle, Israel was defeated by the Philistines, who killed about four thousand men of the army in the field. 3*And when the people had come into the camp, the elders of Israel said, "Why has the LORD defeated us today before the Philistines? Let us bring the ark of the covenant of the LORD from Shiloh to us, that when it comes among us it may save us from the hand of our enemies." 4So the people sent to Shiloh, that they might bring from there the ark of the covenant of the LORD of hosts, who dwells *between* the cherubim. And the two sons of Eli, Hophni and Phinehas, *were* there with the ark of the covenant of God.

5And when the ark of the covenant of the LORD came into the camp, all Israel shouted so loudly that the earth shook. 6Now when the Philistines heard the noise of the shout, they said, "What *does* the sound of this great shout in the camp of the Hebrews *mean?*" Then they understood that the ark of the LORD had come into the camp. 7So the Philistines were afraid, for they said, "God has come into the camp!" And they said, "Woe to us! For such a thing has never happened before. 8Woe to us! Who will deliver us from the hand of these mighty gods? These *are* the gods who struck the Egyptians with all the plagues in the wilderness. 9Be strong and conduct yourselves like men, you Philistines, that you do not become servants of the Hebrews, as they have been to you. Conduct yourselves like men, and fight!"

10So the Philistines fought, and Israel was defeated, and every man fled to his tent. There was a very great slaughter, and there fell of Israel thirty thousand foot soldiers. 11Also the ark of God was captured; and the two sons of Eli, Hophni and Phinehas, died.

12Then a man of Benjamin ran from the battle line the same day, and came to Shiloh with his clothes torn and dirt on his head. 13Now when he came, there was Eli, sitting on a seat by the wayside watching,[n] for his heart trembled for the ark of God. And when the man came into the city and told *it*, all the city cried out. 14When Eli heard the noise of the outcry, he said, "What *does* the sound of this tumult *mean?*" And the man came quickly and told Eli. 15Eli was ninety-eight years old, and his eyes were so dim that he could not see.

16Then the man said to Eli, "I *am* he who came from the battle. And I fled today from the battle line."

And he said, "What happened, my son?"

17*So the messenger answered and said, "Israel has fled before the Philistines, and there has been a great slaughter among the people. Also your two sons, Hophni and Phinehas, are dead; and the ark of God has been captured."

18Then it happened, when he made mention of the ark of God, that Eli fell off the seat backward by the side of the gate; and his neck was broken and he died, for the man was old and heavy. And he had judged Israel forty years.

19Now his daughter-in-law, Phinehas' wife, was with child, *due* to be delivered; and when she

4:17–20 Death. The bad news from the battlefield brought death to Eli and his daughter-in-law. In Eli's case, it was a judgment from God; in the mother's case, it was the result of her burden for the glory of God. Phinehas was an ungodly man, but his wife must have been a godly woman to speak as she did.

4:13 [n]Following Masoretic Text and Vulgate; Septuagint reads *beside the gate watching the road.*

heard the news that the ark of God was captured, and that her father-in-law and her husband were dead, she bowed herself and gave birth, for her labor pains came upon her. 20And about the time of her death the women who stood by her said to her, "Do not fear, for you have borne a son." But she did not answer, nor did she regard *it*. 21*Then she named the child Ichabod,⁰ saying, "The glory has departed from Israel!" because the ark of God had been captured and because of her father-in-law and her husband. 22And she said, "The glory has departed from Israel, for the ark of God has been captured."

5 Then* the Philistines took the ark of God and brought it from Ebenezer to Ashdod. 2*When the Philistines took the ark of God, they brought it into the house of Dagonᵖ and set it by Dagon. 3And when the people of Ashdod arose early in the morning, there was Dagon, fallen on its face to the earth before the ark of the LORD. So they took Dagon and set it in its place again. 4And when they arose early the next morning, there was Dagon, fallen on its face to the ground before the ark of the LORD. The head of Dagon and both the palms of its hands *were* broken off on the threshold; only Dagon's torsoᵠ was left of it. 5Therefore neither the priests of Dagon nor any who come into Dagon's house tread on the threshold of Dagon in Ashdod to this day.

6But the hand of the LORD was heavy on the people of Ashdod, and He ravaged them and struck them with tumors,ʳ *both* Ashdod and its territory. 7And when the men of Ashdod saw how *it was,* they said, "The ark of the God of Israel must not remain with us, for His hand is harsh toward us and Dagon our god." 8*Therefore they sent and gathered to themselves all the lords of the Philistines, and said, "What shall we do with the ark of the God of Israel?"

And they answered, "Let the ark of the God of Israel be carried away to Gath." So they carried the ark of the God of Israel away. 9So it was, after they had carried it away, that the hand of the LORD was against the city with a very great destruction; and He struck the men of the city, both small and great, and tumors broke out on them.

10Therefore they sent the ark of God to Ekron. So it was, as the ark of God came to Ekron, that the Ekronites cried out, saying, "They have brought the ark of the God of Israel to us, to kill us and our people!" 11So they sent and gathered together all the lords of the Philistines, and said, "Send away the ark of the God of Israel, and let it go back to its own place, so that it does not kill us and our people." For there was a deadly destruction throughout all the city; the hand of God was very heavy there. 12And the men who did not die were stricken with the tumors, and the cry of the city went up to heaven.

6 Now* the ark of the LORD was in the country of the Philistines seven months. 2And the Philistines called for the priests and the diviners,

---

4:21 ⁰Literally *Inglorious*   5:2 ᵖA Philistine idol
5:4 ᵠFollowing Septuagint, Syriac, Targum, and Vulgate; Masoretic Text reads *Dagon.*   5:6 ʳProbably bubonic plague. Septuagint and Vulgate add here *And in the midst of their land rats sprang up, and there was a great death panic in the city.*

4:21, 22 *Departure.* The glory of God dwelt with Israel (Exod. 40:34–35; Rom. 9:4), but their sin forced God to depart at an hour when they most needed Him (Ps. 78:56–64). Israel had neither the ark nor the glory of God; they were naked before their enemies. Had they been concerned about God's glory, they would have repented of their sins and obeyed Him, but it was too late.

CHAPTER 5

5:1 The glory may have departed from Israel, but God was still in control and well able to defend His name. If you get depressed because the enemy seems to have "captured" the glory, rest assured that God is still on the throne.

5:2–7 God can reveal His glory even in a heathen temple, and all false gods must fall before Him. How much better it would have been for His glory to be revealed on the battlefield, but He could not give victory to a disobedient people. It would only have encouraged them more in their sin.

5:8–12 Instead of confessing their sin and trusting the true God of Israel, the people of Philistia tried to get rid of the ark. What a great opportunity they were passing by! But then, would you want to trust the god of the defeated enemy? Israel was a poor witness to the other nations, so they rejected Israel's God.

CHAPTER 6

6:1–12 God chastened the Philistines because they kept the ark, but He killed some of His own people because they looked into the ark (v. 19). The Israelites knew the Law (Num. 4:15, 20) and therefore were more responsible than the Philistines. Curiosity is important to learning and progress, but it is unwise to be unduly curious about holy things.

saying, "What shall we do with the ark of the LORD? Tell us how we should send it to its place."

3So they said, "If you send away the ark of the God of Israel, do not send it empty; but by all means return *it* to Him *with* a trespass offering. Then you will be healed, and it will be known to you why His hand is not removed from you."

4Then they said, "What *is* the trespass offering which we shall return to Him?"

They answered, "Five golden tumors and five golden rats, *according to* the number of the lords of the Philistines. For the same plague *was* on all of you and on your lords. 5Therefore you shall make images of your tumors and images of your rats that ravage the land, and you shall give glory to the God of Israel; perhaps He will lighten His hand from you, from your gods, and from your land. 6Why then do you harden your hearts as the Egyptians and Pharaoh hardened their hearts? When He did mighty things among them, did they not let the people go, that they might depart? 7Now therefore, make a new cart, take two milk cows which have never been yoked, and hitch the cows to the cart; and take their calves home, away from them. 8Then take the ark of the LORD and set it on the cart; and put the articles of gold which you are returning to Him *as* a trespass offering in a chest by its side. Then send it away, and let it go. 9And watch: if it goes up the road to its own territory, to Beth Shemesh, *then* He has done us this great evil. But if not, then we shall know that *it is* not His hand *that* struck us—it happened to us by chance."

10Then the men did so; they took two milk cows and hitched them to the cart, and shut up their calves at home. 11And they set the ark of the LORD on the cart, and the chest with the gold rats and the images of their tumors. 12Then the cows headed straight for the road to Beth Shemesh, *and* went along the highway, lowing as they went, and did not turn aside to the right hand or the left. And the lords of the Philistines went after them to the border of Beth Shemesh.

6:13–21 The men of Beth Shemesh were reaping the harvest when the cart with the ark came into view. The ark had been gone for six months, but the men did not allow that to keep them from working. Even in times of defeat, there are jobs to be done and people to feed.

Abinadab's house will become a tabernacle of the Lord, but should not every home be a holy dwelling place for Him? (See Isa. 4:4–5.)

13*Now *the people of* Beth Shemesh *were* reaping their wheat harvest in the valley; and they lifted their eyes and saw the ark, and rejoiced to see *it*. 14Then the cart came into the field of Joshua of Beth Shemesh, and stood there; a large stone *was* there. So they split the wood of the cart and offered the cows as a burnt offering to the LORD. 15The Levites took down the ark of the LORD and the chest that *was* with it, in which *were* the articles of gold, and put *them* on the large stone. Then the men of Beth Shemesh offered burnt offerings and made sacrifices the same day to the LORD. 16So when the five lords of the Philistines had seen *it*, they returned to Ekron the same day.

17These *are* the golden tumors which the Philistines returned *as* a trespass offering to the LORD: one for Ashdod, one for Gaza, one for Ashkelon, one for Gath, one for Ekron; 18and the golden rats, *according to* the number of all the cities of the Philistines *belonging* to the five lords, *both* fortified cities and country villages, even as far as the large *stone of* Abel on which they set the ark of the LORD, *which stone remains* to this day in the field of Joshua of Beth Shemesh.

19Then He struck the men of Beth Shemesh, because they had looked into the ark of the LORD.

He struck fifty thousand and seventy men[s] of the people, and the people lamented because the LORD had struck the people with a great slaughter.

20And the men of Beth Shemesh said, "Who is able to stand before this holy LORD God? And to whom shall it go up from us?" 21So they sent messengers to the inhabitants of Kirjath Jearim, saying, "The Philistines have brought back the ark of the LORD; come down *and* take it up with you."

7 Then* the men of Kirjath Jearim came and took the ark of the LORD, and brought it into the house of Abinadab on the hill, and consecrated Eleazar his son to keep the ark of the LORD.

2So it was that the ark remained in Kirjath Jearim a long time; it was there twenty years. And all the house of Israel lamented after the LORD.

3Then Samuel spoke to all the house of Israel, saying, "If you return to the LORD with all your hearts, *then* put away the foreign gods and the Ashtoreths[t] from among you, and prepare your hearts for the LORD, and serve Him only; and He will deliver you from the hand of the Philistines." 4So the children of Israel put away the Baals and the Ashtoreths,[u] and served the LORD only.

5And Samuel said, "Gather all Israel to Mizpah, and I will pray to the LORD for you." 6So they gathered together at Mizpah, drew water, and poured *it* out before the LORD. And they fasted that day, and said there, "We have sinned against the LORD." And Samuel judged the children of Israel at Mizpah.

7*Now when the Philistines heard that the children of Israel had gathered together at Mizpah, the lords of the Philistines went up against Israel. And when the children of Israel heard *of it,* they were afraid of the Philistines. 8So the children of Israel said to Samuel, "Do not cease to cry out to the LORD our God for us, that He may save us from the hand of the Philistines."

9And Samuel took a suckling lamb and offered *it as* a whole burnt offering to the LORD. Then Samuel cried out to the LORD for Israel, and the LORD answered him. 10Now as Samuel was offering up the burnt offering, the Philistines drew near to battle against Israel. But the LORD thundered with a loud thunder upon the Philistines that day, and so confused them that they were overcome before Israel. 11And the men of Israel went out of Mizpah and pursued the Philistines, and drove them back as far as below Beth Car. 12*Then Samuel took a stone and set *it* up between Mizpah and Shen, and called its name Ebenezer,[v] saying, "Thus far the LORD has helped us."

13So the Philistines were subdued, and they did not come anymore into the territory of Israel. And the hand of the LORD was against the Philistines all the days of Samuel. 14Then the cities which the Philistines had taken from Israel were restored to Israel, from Ekron to Gath; and Israel recovered its territory from the hands of the Philistines. Also there was peace between Israel and the Amorites.

15And Samuel judged Israel all the days of his life. 16He went from year to year on a circuit to Bethel, Gilgal, and Mizpah, and judged Israel in all those places. 17But he always returned to

CHAPTER 7

7:1–6 *Cleaning up.* The ark had been returned to Israel, but Israel had not returned to the Lord, so Samuel called them to repentance. They put away their foreign gods and then met at Mizpah to renew their covenant with the Lord. For years, God had been preparing Samuel for this strategic ministry, and he rescued the nation.

7:7, 8 *Looking up.* The Philistines thought that the assembly at Mizpah was preparation for war; however, Israel was not equipped for battle. But God's people use spiritual weapons to defeat the enemy: Samuel prayed, and God sent the enemy back in confusion. Samuel was born in answer to prayer, and he lived in dependence on prayer.

7:12 *Setting up.* *Ebenezer* means "stone of help." It was a memorial to God's helping His people from the beginning to that very day. Missionary J. Hudson Taylor had a plaque in his home that read, EBENEZER and JEHOVAH-JIREH. That means, "Thus far the Lord has helped us—The Lord will see to it." This takes care of the past and the future, so why worry about the present? God is in control!

6:19 [s]Or *He struck seventy men of the people and fifty oxen of a man*   7:3 [t]Canaanite goddesses   7:4 [u]Canaanite goddesses   7:12 [v]Literally *Stone of Help*

CHAPTER 8

8:1 It is possible to be faithful in ministry and yet close your life in disappointment. That is what happened to Samuel.

8:3 He was disappointed in his sons. They were not able to carry on their father's ministry because they did not follow their father's godly example. Eli's sons yielded to the lusts of the flesh (1 Sam. 2:12–17), while Samuel's sons were lovers of money.

8:4–10 He was disappointed in the nation, for they wanted a king. They used Samuel's sons as their excuse, but the real reason was their lack of faith in God. They wanted to be like the other nations and have a king lead them out to battle. Samuel's warnings about what the king would do made no impression on the people. Note the repetition of the phrase "he will take." He was disappointed in King Saul who rebelled against God and forfeited the crown. Much that Samuel worked for and prayed for seems to have turned out differently from what he expected, and yet he remained faithful to the Lord to the end. Leaders who are faithful to God may not always appear successful to men.

CHAPTER 9

9:1–3 The donkey was a prized animal (Job 1:3) and was used by royalty (1 Kings 1:33–34), but would you expect to find a nation's first king out looking for lost donkeys? Saul's obedience to his father, his concern for his father (v. 5), and his willingness to persevere in a hard task seemed to indicate character and future success.

Ramah, for his home *was* there. There he judged Israel, and there he built an altar to the LORD.

8 Now* it came to pass when Samuel was old that he made his sons judges over Israel. ²The name of his firstborn was Joel, and the name of his second, Abijah; *they were* judges in Beersheba. ³*But his sons did not walk in his ways; they turned aside after dishonest gain, took bribes, and perverted justice.

⁴*Then all the elders of Israel gathered together and came to Samuel at Ramah, ⁵and said to him, "Look, you are old, and your sons do not walk in your ways. Now make us a king to judge us like all the nations."

⁶But the thing displeased Samuel when they said, "Give us a king to judge us." So Samuel prayed to the LORD. ⁷And the LORD said to Samuel, "Heed the voice of the people in all that they say to you; for they have not rejected you, but they have rejected Me, that I should not reign over them. ⁸According to all the works which they have done since the day that I brought them up out of Egypt, even to this day—with which they have forsaken Me and served other gods—so they are doing to you also. ⁹Now therefore, heed their voice. However, you shall solemnly forewarn them, and show them the behavior of the king who will reign over them."

¹⁰So Samuel told all the words of the LORD to the people who asked him for a king. ¹¹And he said, "This will be the behavior of the king who will reign over you: He will take your sons and appoint *them* for his own chariots and *to be* his horsemen, and *some* will run before his chariots. ¹²He will appoint captains over his thousands and captains over his fifties, *will set some* to plow his ground and reap his harvest, and *some* to make his weapons of war and equipment for his chariots. ¹³He will take your daughters *to be* perfumers, cooks, and bakers. ¹⁴And he will take the best of your fields, your vineyards, and your olive groves, and give *them* to his servants. ¹⁵He will take a tenth of your grain and your vintage, and give it to his officers and servants. ¹⁶And he will take your male servants, your female servants, your finest young men,ʷ and your donkeys, and put *them* to his work. ¹⁷He will take a tenth of your sheep. And you will be his servants. ¹⁸And you will cry out in that day because of your king whom you have chosen for yourselves, and the LORD will not hear you in that day."

¹⁹Nevertheless the people refused to obey the voice of Samuel; and they said, "No, but we will have a king over us, ²⁰that we also may be like all the nations, and that our king may judge us and go out before us and fight our battles."

²¹And Samuel heard all the words of the people, and he repeated them in the hearing of the LORD. ²²So the LORD said to Samuel, "Heed their voice, and make them a king."

And Samuel said to the men of Israel, "Every man go to his city."

9 There* was a man of Benjamin whose name *was* Kish the son of Abiel, the son of Zeror, the son of Bechorath, the son of Aphiah, a Benjamite, a mighty man of power. ²And he had a

---

8:16 ʷSeptuagint reads *cattle.*

choice and handsome son whose name *was* Saul. *There was* not a more handsome person than he among the children of Israel. From his shoulders upward *he was* taller than any of the people.

3Now the donkeys of Kish, Saul's father, were lost. And Kish said to his son Saul, "Please take one of the servants with you, and arise, go and look for the donkeys." 4So he passed through the mountains of Ephraim and through the land of Shalisha, but they did not find *them.* Then they passed through the land of Shaalim, and *they were* not *there.* Then he passed through the land of the Benjamites, but they did not find *them.*

5When they had come to the land of Zuph, Saul said to his servant who *was* with him, "Come, let us return, lest my father cease *caring* about the donkeys and become worried about us."

6*And he said to him, "Look now, *there is* in this city a man of God, and *he is* an honorable man; all that he says surely comes to pass. So let us go there; perhaps he can show us the way that we should go."

7Then Saul said to his servant, "But look, *if we* go, what shall we bring the man? For the bread in our vessels is all gone, and *there is* no present to bring to the man of God. What do we have?"

8And the servant answered Saul again and said, "Look, I have here at hand one-fourth of a shekel of silver. I will give *that* to the man of God, to tell us our way." 9(Formerly in Israel, when a man went to inquire of God, he spoke thus: "Come, let us go to the seer"; for *he who is* now *called* a prophet was formerly called a seer.)

10Then Saul said to his servant, "Well said; come, let us go." So they went to the city where the man of God *was.*

11As they went up the hill to the city, they met some young women going out to draw water, and said to them, "Is the seer here?"

12And they answered them and said, "Yes, there he is, just ahead of you. Hurry now; for today he came to this city, because there is a sacrifice of the people today on the high place. 13As soon as you come into the city, you will surely find him before he goes up to the high place to eat. For the people will not eat until he comes, because he must bless the sacrifice; afterward those who are invited will eat. Now therefore, go up, for about this time you will find him." 14So they went up to the city. As they were coming into the city, there was Samuel, coming out toward them on his way up to the high place.

15Now the LORD had told Samuel in his ear the day before Saul came, saying, 16"Tomorrow about this time I will send you a man from the land of Benjamin, and you shall anoint him commander over My people Israel, that he may save My people from the hand of the Philistines; for I have looked upon My people, because their cry has come to Me."

17So when Samuel saw Saul, the LORD said to him, "There he is, the man of whom I spoke to you. This one shall reign over My people." 18Then Saul drew near to Samuel in the gate, and said, "Please tell me, where *is* the seer's house?"

19Samuel answered Saul and said, "I *am* the seer. Go up before me to the high place, for you shall eat with me today; and tomorrow I will let you go and will tell you all that *is* in your heart. 20But as for your donkeys that were lost three days ago, do not be anxious about them, for they have been found. And on whom *is* all the desire

9:6–8 How strange that Saul did not know about Samuel, and how disappointing that the only reason they visited Samuel was to find their lost animals! People often "use" religion to solve their problems and not to strengthen their character or overcome their sins.

9:21 Nevertheless, God used all of this to bring Saul to Samuel. Faithfulness in a small task led Saul to a new friend, a new calling and a new opportunity to serve God. Had he remained a humble servant, things would have been different in his life and in Israel (v. 21; 1 Sam. 15:17). But good beginnings are no guarantee of good endings.

of Israel? *Is it* not on you and on all your father's house?''

21*And Saul answered and said, *"Am* I not a Benjamite, of the smallest of the tribes of Israel, and my family the least of all the families of the tribeˣ of Benjamin? Why then do you speak like this to me?''

22Now Samuel took Saul and his servant and brought them into the hall, and had them sit in the place of honor among those who were invited; there *were* about thirty persons. 23And Samuel said to the cook, ''Bring the portion which I gave you, of which I said to you, 'Set it apart.' '' 24So the cook took up the thigh with its upper part and set *it* before Saul. And *Samuel* said, ''Here it is, what was kept back. *It* was set apart for you. Eat; for until this time it has been kept for you, since I said I invited the people.'' So Saul ate with Samuel that day.

25When they had come down from the high place into the city, *Samuel* spoke with Saul on the top of the house.ʸ 26They arose early; and it was about the dawning of the day that Samuel called to Saul on the top of the house, saying, ''Get up, that I may send you on your way.'' And Saul arose, and both of them went outside, he and Samuel.

27As they were going down to the outskirts of the city, Samuel said to Saul, ''Tell the servant to go on ahead of us.'' And he went on. ''But you stand here awhile, that I may announce to you the word of God.''

CHAPTER 10

10:1–7 Saul could not understand how a man like him could lead the nation of Israel, so God gave him a series of ''signs'' to assure him for his new responsibilities.

10 Then* Samuel took a flask of oil and poured it on his head, and kissed him and said: *"Is it* not because the LORD has anointed you commander over His inheritance?ᶻ 2When you have departed from me today, you will find two men by Rachel's tomb in the territory of Benjamin at Zelzah; and they will say to you, 'The donkeys which you went to look for have been found. And now your father has ceased caring about the donkeys and is worrying about you, saying, ''What shall I do about my son?'' ' 3Then you shall go on forward from there and come to the terebinth tree of Tabor. There three men going up to God at Bethel will meet you, one carrying three young goats, another carrying three loaves of bread, and another carrying a skin of wine. 4And they will greet you and give you two *loaves* of bread, which you shall receive from their hands. 5After that you shall come to the hill of God where the Philistine garrison *is*. And it will happen, when you have come there to the city, that you will meet a group of prophets coming down from the high place with a stringed instrument, a tambourine, a flute, and a harp before them; and they will be prophesying. 6Then the Spirit of the LORD will come upon you, and you will prophesy with them and be turned into another man. 7And let it be, when these signs

---

9:21 ˣLiterally *tribes*   9:25 ʸFollowing Masoretic Text and Targum; Septuagint omits *He spoke with Saul on the top of the house;* Septuagint and Vulgate add *And he prepared a bed for Saul on the top of the house, and he slept.*
10:1 ᶻFollowing Masoretic Text, Targum, and Vulgate; Septuagint reads *His people Israel; and you shall rule the people of the Lord;* Septuagint and Vulgate add *And you shall deliver His people from the hands of their enemies all around them. And this shall be a sign to you, that God has anointed you to be a prince.*

come to you, *that* you do as the occasion demands; for God *is* with you. 8You shall go down before me to Gilgal; and surely I will come down to you to offer burnt offerings *and* make sacrifices of peace offerings. Seven days you shall wait, till I come to you and show you what you should do."

9So it was, when he had turned his back to go from Samuel, that God gave him another heart; and all those signs came to pass that day. 10When they came there to the hill, there was a group of prophets to meet him; then the Spirit of God came upon him, and he prophesied among them. 11*And it happened, when all who knew him formerly saw that he indeed prophesied among the prophets, that the people said to one another, "What *is* this *that* has come upon the son of Kish? *Is* Saul also among the prophets?" 12Then a man from there answered and said, "But who *is* their father?" Therefore it became a proverb: "*Is* Saul also among the prophets?" 13And when he had finished prophesying, he went to the high place.

14Then Saul's uncle said to him and his servant, "Where did you go?"

So he said, "To look for the donkeys. When we saw that they were nowhere *to be found,* we went to Samuel."

15And Saul's uncle said, "Tell me, please, what Samuel said to you."

16*So Saul said to his uncle, "He told us plainly that the donkeys had been found." But about the matter of the kingdom, he did not tell him what Samuel had said.

17Then Samuel called the people together to the LORD at Mizpah, 18and said to the children of Israel, "Thus says the LORD God of Israel: 'I brought up Israel out of Egypt, and delivered you from the hand of the Egyptians *and* from the hand of all kingdoms and from those who oppressed you.' 19But you have today rejected your God, who Himself saved you from all your adversities and your tribulations; and you have said to Him, 'No, set a king over us!' Now therefore, present yourselves before the LORD by your tribes and by your clans."*a*

20And when Samuel had caused all the tribes of Israel to come near, the tribe of Benjamin was chosen. 21When he had caused the tribe of Benjamin to come near by their families, the family of Matri was chosen. And Saul the son of Kish was chosen. But when they sought him, he could not be found. 22Therefore they inquired of the LORD further, "Has the man come here yet?"

And the LORD answered, "There he is, hidden among the equipment."

23So they ran and brought him from there; and when he stood among the people, he was taller than any of the people from his shoulders upward. 24And Samuel said to all the people, "Do you see him whom the LORD has chosen, that *there is* no one like him among all the people?"

So all the people shouted and said, "Long live the king!"

25Then Samuel explained to the people the behavior of royalty, and wrote *it* in a book and laid *it* up before the LORD. And Samuel sent all the people away, every man to his house. 26And Saul also went home to Gibeah; and valiant *men* went with him, whose hearts God had touched. 27But some rebels said, "How can this man save us?"

10:11–13 A leader must trust God to solve problems (vv. 1–2), to provide needs (vv. 3–4), and to give the power needed for service (vv. 5–7). He must know how to hear God's Word and wait obediently on the Lord (v. 8). Saul began his ministry in the strength of these assurances, but as time went on, he trusted more and more in himself and rebelled against God's Word.

10:16–27 His modesty in saying nothing about the kingdom (v. 16) and his self-control in not answering his critics (v. 27) are commendable, but what about his hiding on coronation day? Was he genuinely humble, or was he unwilling to take responsibility? This much is sure: he did a great deal of "hiding" in the years of his leadership, but God found him out. As the book of Proverbs warns, "He who covers his sins will not prosper" (28:13).

10:19 *a*Literally *thousands*

CHAPTER 11

11:1–7 It is one thing to have authority and ability, but quite something else to prove yourself a leader. People respond to a crisis in different ways: some give in (vv. 1–3), but others give up (v. 4). Saul responded with anger and action and rallied the troops for battle.

11:6 God empowered Saul to fight the battle and win (v. 6). He had *stature* as well as authority; he had proved himself a leader. But it can be as dangerous after the victory as it is during the battle, for Saul was tempted to get rid of his critics (vv. 12–13; see also 1 Sam. 10:27). He gave God the glory and did not use his authority and success as weapons to attack his own people.

11:14, 15 Samuel had the right idea: it was time to renew their covenant with the Lord; and again, the nation met at historic Gilgal. Do the crises God permits in your life strengthen your faith? Do you use the victories He gives to glorify Him and help others?

CHAPTER 12

12:1 Samuel's message was the combination of a coronation address, a revival sermon, and a farewell speech. He pointed out the greatness of their sin in asking for a king and then called for new dedication. A key theme in the address is *witness* (vv. 3, 5).

12:2–5 *The witness of a godly leader.* The people had rejected a proven godly leader for a man who had won only one victory and whose devotion to the Lord was as yet unknown. Samuel was disappointed, but he left office knowing that his conscience was clear.

So they despised him, and brought him no presents. But he held his peace.

11 Then* Nahash the Ammonite came up and encamped against Jabesh Gilead; and all the men of Jabesh said to Nahash, "Make a covenant with us, and we will serve you."

²And Nahash the Ammonite answered them, "On this *condition* I will make *a covenant* with you, that I may put out all your right eyes, and bring reproach on all Israel."

³Then the elders of Jabesh said to him, "Hold off for seven days, that we may send messengers to all the territory of Israel. And then, if *there is* no one to save us, we will come out to you."

⁴So the messengers came to Gibeah of Saul and told the news in the hearing of the people. And all the people lifted up their voices and wept. ⁵Now there was Saul, coming behind the herd from the field; and Saul said, "What *troubles* the people, that they weep?" And they told him the words of the men of Jabesh. ⁶*Then the Spirit of God came upon Saul when he heard this news, and his anger was greatly aroused. ⁷So he took a yoke of oxen and cut them in pieces, and sent *them* throughout all the territory of Israel by the hands of messengers, saying, "Whoever does not go out with Saul and Samuel to battle, so it shall be done to his oxen."

And the fear of the LORD fell on the people, and they came out with one consent. ⁸When he numbered them in Bezek, the children of Israel were three hundred thousand, and the men of Judah thirty thousand. ⁹And they said to the messengers who came, "Thus you shall say to the men of Jabesh Gilead: 'Tomorrow, by *the time* the sun is hot, you shall have help.'" Then the messengers came and reported *it* to the men of Jabesh, and they were glad. ¹⁰Therefore the men of Jabesh said, "Tomorrow we will come out to you, and you may do with us whatever seems good to you."

¹¹So it was, on the next day, that Saul put the people in three companies; and they came into the midst of the camp in the morning watch, and killed Ammonites until the heat of the day. And it happened that those who survived were scattered, so that no two of them were left together.

¹²Then the people said to Samuel, "Who *is* he who said, 'Shall Saul reign over us?' Bring the men, that we may put them to death."

¹³But Saul said, "Not a man shall be put to death this day, for today the LORD has accomplished salvation in Israel."

¹⁴*Then Samuel said to the people, "Come, let us go to Gilgal and renew the kingdom there." ¹⁵So all the people went to Gilgal, and there they made Saul king before the LORD in Gilgal. There they made sacrifices of peace offerings before the LORD, and there Saul and all the men of Israel rejoiced greatly.

12 Now* Samuel said to all Israel: "Indeed I have heeded your voice in all that you said to me, and have made a king over you. ²*And now here is the king, walking before you; and I am old and gray headed, and look, my sons *are* with you. I have walked before you from my childhood to this day. ³Here I am. Witness against me before the LORD and before His anointed: Whose ox have I taken, or whose donkey have I taken, or whom have I cheated? Whom have I oppressed, or from whose hand have I received *any* bribe with which to blind my eyes? I will restore *it* to you."

⁴And they said, "You have not cheated us or oppressed us, nor have you taken anything from any man's hand."

⁵Then he said to them, "The LORD *is* witness against you, and His anointed *is* witness this day, that you have not found anything in my hand."

And they answered, *"He is* witness."

⁶*Then Samuel said to the people, "*It is* the LORD who raised up Moses and Aaron, and who brought your fathers up from the land of Egypt. ⁷Now therefore, stand still, that I may reason with you before the LORD concerning all the righteous acts of the LORD which He did to you and your fathers: ⁸When Jacob had gone into Egypt,ᵇ and your fathers cried out to the LORD, then the LORD sent Moses and Aaron, who brought your fathers out of Egypt and made them dwell in this place. ⁹And when they forgot the LORD their God, He sold them into the hand of Sisera, commander of the army of Hazor, into the hand of the Philistines, and into the hand of the king of Moab; and they fought against them. ¹⁰Then they cried out to the LORD, and said, 'We have sinned, because we have forsaken the LORD and served the Baals and Ashtoreths;ᶜ but now deliver us from the hand of our enemies, and we will serve You.' ¹¹And the LORD sent Jerubbaal,ᵈ Bedan,ᵉ Jephthah, and Samuel,ᶠ and delivered you out of the hand of your enemies on every side; and you dwelt in safety. ¹²And when you saw that Nahash king of the Ammonites came against you, you said to me, 'No, but a king shall reign over us,' when the LORD your God *was* your king.

¹³"Now therefore, here is the king whom you have chosen *and* whom you have desired. And take note, the LORD has set a king over you. ¹⁴If you fear the LORD and serve Him and obey His voice, and do not rebel against the commandment of the LORD, then both you and the king who reigns over you will continue following the LORD your God. ¹⁵However, if you do not obey the voice of the LORD, but rebel against the commandment of the LORD, then the hand of the LORD will be against you, as *it was* against your fathers.

¹⁶*"Now therefore, stand and see this great thing which the LORD will do before your eyes: ¹⁷Is today not the wheat harvest? I will call to the LORD, and He will send thunder and rain, that you may perceive and see that your wickedness is great, which you have done in the sight of the LORD, in asking a king for yourselves."

¹⁸So Samuel called to the LORD, and the LORD sent thunder and rain that day; and all the people greatly feared the LORD and Samuel.

¹⁹*And all the people said to Samuel, "Pray for your servants to the LORD your God, that we may not die; for we have added to all our sins the evil of asking a king for ourselves."

²⁰Then Samuel said to the people, "Do not fear. You have done all this wickedness; yet do not turn aside from following the LORD, but serve the LORD with all your heart. ²¹And do not turn aside; for *then you would go* after empty things which

12:6–15 *The witness of history.* The hand of the Lord was with them when they obeyed, but it was against them when they rebelled. Verse 14 emphasizes the same secret of success that God gave to Joshua (Josh. 1:8). Rebellion became King Saul's besetting sin, and it cost him the kingdom (1 Sam. 15:23).

12:16–18 *The witness of God's power.* What a man of prayer Samuel was, for it was most unusual to have thunder and rain at that time of year.

12:19–25 *The witness of the covenant.* The people had forsaken God, but He would not forsake them, for He is true to His Word. They had the assurance of God's faithfulness as well as the prayers and ministry of Samuel. Had the king maintained his friendship with Samuel and obeyed the Word, he would have led the nation to victory.

12:8 ᵇFollowing Masoretic Text, Targum, and Vulgate; Septuagint adds *and the Egyptians afflicted them.*
12:10 ᶜCanaanite goddesses   12:11 ᵈSyriac reads *Deborah*; Targum reads *Gideon.* ᵉSeptuagint and Syriac read *Barak;* Targum reads *Simson.* ᶠSyriac reads *Simson.*

CHAPTER 13

13:1ff Saul's second crisis came after he started to build a standing army, and he failed in four ways in this crisis.

13:2, 3 He failed to *act decisively.* It was Jonathan, not Saul, who declared war by attacking one of the Philistine garrisons. Saul took the credit and blew the trumpet to rally the people.

13:5–7 He failed to *inspire the people.* Some ran away, some hid, and some left the country! (People still dodge military service in the same ways.) Those who were faithful were fearful and the future looked bleak.

13:8, 9 He failed to *wait;* see also 1 Sam. 10:8). This was the first step in his rupture with Samuel and his rebellion against the Lord. Patience is a mark of character, and Saul's character was weak (James 1:1–8).

13:10–15 He failed to *tell the truth.* When David sinned, he came with confessions; when Saul sinned, he had only excuses. He lied to his best friend, and it cost him his crown. *And Saul would do it again* (1 Sam. 15:15). From that point, his course was downhill.

cannot profit or deliver, for they *are* nothing. 22For the LORD will not forsake His people, for His great name's sake, because it has pleased the LORD to make you His people. 23Moreover, as for me, far be it from me that I should sin against the LORD in ceasing to pray for you; but I will teach you the good and the right way. 24Only fear the LORD, and serve Him in truth with all your heart; for consider what great things He has done for you. 25But if you still do wickedly, you shall be swept away, both you and your king."

13 Saul* reigned one year; and when he had reigned two years over Israel,g 2*Saul chose for himself three thousand *men* of Israel. Two thousand were with Saul in Michmash and in the mountains of Bethel, and a thousand were with Jonathan in Gibeah of Benjamin. The rest of the people he sent away, every man to his tent.

3And Jonathan attacked the garrison of the Philistines that *was* in Geba, and the Philistines heard *of it.* Then Saul blew the trumpet throughout all the land, saying, "Let the Hebrews hear!" 4Now all Israel heard it said *that* Saul had attacked a garrison of the Philistines, and *that* Israel had also become an abomination to the Philistines. And the people were called together to Saul at Gilgal.

5*Then the Philistines gathered together to fight with Israel, thirtyh thousand chariots and six thousand horsemen, and people as the sand which *is* on the seashore in multitude. And they came up and encamped in Michmash, to the east of Beth Aven. 6When the men of Israel saw that they were in danger (for the people were distressed), then the people hid in caves, in thickets, in rocks, in holes, and in pits. 7And *some of* the Hebrews crossed over the Jordan to the land of Gad and Gilead.

As for Saul, he *was* still in Gilgal, and all the people followed him trembling. 8*Then he waited seven days, according to the time set by Samuel. But Samuel did not come to Gilgal; and the people were scattered from him. 9So Saul said, "Bring a burnt offering and peace offerings here to me." And he offered the burnt offering. 10*Now it happened, as soon as he had finished presenting the burnt offering, that Samuel came; and Saul went out to meet him, that he might greet him.

11And Samuel said, "What have you done?"

Saul said, "When I saw that the people were scattered from me, and *that* you did not come within the days appointed, and *that* the Philistines gathered together at Michmash, 12then I said, 'The Philistines will now come down on me at Gilgal, and I have not made supplication to the LORD.' Therefore I felt compelled, and offered a burnt offering."

13And Samuel said to Saul, "You have done foolishly. You have not kept the commandment

---

13:1 gThe Hebrew is difficult (compare 2 Samuel 5:4; 2 Kings 14:2; see also 2 Samuel 2:10; Acts 13:21).   13:5 hFollowing Masoretic Text, Septuagint, Targum, and Vulgate; Syriac and some manuscripts of the Septuagint read *three.*

Excuses—Evangelist Billy Sunday defined an *excuse* as "the skin of a reason stuffed with a lie." Benjamin Franklin said, "I never knew a man who was good at making excuses who was good at anything else." Adam made the first excuse for sin (Gen. 3:12), and many have followed his bad example. Excuses only make matters worse.

of the LORD your God, which He commanded you. For now the LORD would have established your kingdom over Israel forever. [14]But now your kingdom shall not continue. The LORD has sought for Himself a man after His own heart, and the LORD has commanded him *to be* commander over His people, because you have not kept what the LORD commanded you."

[15]Then Samuel arose and went up from Gilgal to Gibeah of Benjamin.[i] And Saul numbered the people present with him, about six hundred men.

[16]Saul, Jonathan his son, and the people present with them remained in Gibeah of Benjamin. But the Philistines encamped in Michmash. [17]Then raiders came out of the camp of the Philistines in three companies. One company turned onto the road to Ophrah, to the land of Shual, [18]another company turned to the road *to* Beth Horon, and another company turned *to* the road of the border that overlooks the Valley of Zeboim toward the wilderness.

[19]Now there was no blacksmith to be found throughout all the land of Israel, for the Philistines said, "Lest the Hebrews make swords or spears." [20]But all the Israelites would go down to the Philistines to sharpen each man's plowshare, his mattock, his ax, and his sickle; [21]and the charge for a sharpening was a pim[j] for the plowshares, the mattocks, the forks, and the axes, and to set the points of the goads. [22]So it came about, on the day of battle, that there was neither sword nor spear found in the hand of any of the people who *were* with Saul and Jonathan. But they were found with Saul and Jonathan his son.

[23]And the garrison of the Philistines went out to the pass of Michmash.

14 Now* it happened one day that Jonathan the son of Saul said to the young man who bore his armor, "Come, let us go over to the Philistines' garrison that *is* on the other side." But he did not tell his father. [2]And Saul was sitting in the outskirts of Gibeah under a pomegranate tree which *is* in Migron. The people who *were* with him *were* about six hundred men. [3]Ahijah the son of Ahitub, Ichabod's brother, the son of Phinehas, the son of Eli, the LORD's priest in Shiloh, was wearing an ephod. But the people did not know that Jonathan had gone.

[4]Between the passes, by which Jonathan sought to go over to the Philistines' garrison, *there was* a sharp rock on one side and a sharp rock on the other side. And the name of one *was* Bozez, and the name of the other Seneh. [5]The front of one faced northward opposite Michmash, and the other southward opposite Gibeah.

[6]Then Jonathan said to the young man who bore his armor, "Come, let us go over to the garrison of these uncircumcised; it may be that the LORD will work for us. For nothing restrains the LORD from saving by many or by few."

[7]So his armorbearer said to him, "Do all that is in your heart. Go then; here I am with you, according to your heart."

CHAPTER 14
14:1–14 Jonathan, not Saul, was the true leader in Israel. The contrast between the two is striking. Saul was sitting while Jonathan was attacking the enemy. Saul trusted his growing army, but Jonathan trusted God and did not depend on numbers (v. 6). Saul *watched* things happen, but Jonathan *made* things happen.

13:15 [i]Following Masoretic Text and Targum; Septuagint and Vulgate add *And the rest of the people went up after Saul to meet the people who fought against them, going from Gilgal to Gibeah in the hill of Benjamin.* 13:21 [j]About two-thirds shekel weight

8Then Jonathan said, "Very well, let us cross over to *these* men, and we will show ourselves to them. 9If they say thus to us, 'Wait until we come to you,' then we will stand still in our place and not go up to them. 10But if they say thus, 'Come up to us,' then we will go up. For the LORD has delivered them into our hand, and this *will be* a sign to us."

11So both of them showed themselves to the garrison of the Philistines. And the Philistines said, "Look, the Hebrews are coming out of the holes where they have hidden." 12Then the men of the garrison called to Jonathan and his armorbearer, and said, "Come up to us, and we will show you something."

Jonathan said to his armorbearer, "Come up after me, for the LORD has delivered them into the hand of Israel." 13And Jonathan climbed up on his hands and knees with his armorbearer after him; and they fell before Jonathan. And as he came after him, his armorbearer killed them. 14That first slaughter which Jonathan and his armorbearer made was about twenty men within about half an acre of land.[k]

15And there was trembling in the camp, in the field, and among all the people. The garrison and the raiders also trembled; and the earth quaked, so that it was a very great trembling. 16Now the watchmen of Saul in Gibeah of Benjamin looked, and *there* was the multitude, melting away; and they went here and there. 17Then Saul said to the people who *were* with him, "Now call the roll and see who has gone from us." And when they had called the roll, surprisingly, Jonathan and his armorbearer *were* not *there*. 18And Saul said to Ahijah, "Bring the ark[l] of God here" (for at that time the ark[m] of God was with the children of Israel). 19Now it happened, while Saul talked to the priest, that the noise which *was* in the camp of the Philistines continued to increase; so Saul said to the priest, "Withdraw your hand." 20Then Saul and all the people who *were* with him assembled, and they went to the battle; and indeed every man's sword was against his neighbor, *and there was* very great confusion. 21Moreover the Hebrews *who* were with the Philistines before that time, who went up with them into the camp *from the* surrounding *country*, they also joined the Israelites who *were* with Saul and Jonathan. 22Likewise all the men of Israel who had hidden in the mountains of Ephraim, *when* they heard that the Philistines fled, they also followed hard after them in the battle. 23So the LORD saved Israel that day, and the battle shifted to Beth Aven.

24*And the men of Israel were distressed that day, for Saul had placed the people under oath, saying, "Cursed *is* the man who eats *any* food until evening, before I have taken vengeance on my enemies." So none of the people tasted food. 25Now all *the people* of the land came to a forest; and there was honey on the ground. 26And when the people had come into the woods, there was the honey, dripping; but no one put his hand to his mouth, for the people feared the oath. 27But Jonathan had not heard his father charge the people with the oath; therefore he stretched out the

14:24 Saul tried to impress people with an oath, but Jonathan did what was necessary to fight the battle. Saul weakened the army; Jonathan strengthened the army and challenged it to new victories.

14:14 [k]Literally *half the area plowed by a yoke* (of oxen in a day)   14:18 [l]Following Masoretic Text, Targum, and Vulgate; Septuagint reads *ephod.* [m]Following Masoretic Text, Targum, and Vulgate; Septuagint reads *ephod.*

end of the rod that *was* in his hand and dipped it in a honeycomb, and put his hand to his mouth; and his countenance brightened. 28Then one of the people said, "Your father strictly charged the people with an oath, saying, 'Cursed *is* the man who eats food this day.' " And the people were faint.

29But Jonathan said, "My father has troubled the land. Look now, how my countenance has brightened because I tasted a little of this honey. 30How much better if the people had eaten freely today of the spoil of their enemies which they found! For now would there not have been a much greater slaughter among the Philistines?"

31Now they had driven back the Philistines that day from Michmash to Aijalon. So the people were very faint. 32And the people rushed on the spoil, and took sheep, oxen, and calves, and slaughtered *them* on the ground; and the people ate *them* with the blood. 33Then they told Saul, saying, "Look, the people are sinning against the Lord by eating with the blood!"

So he said, "You have dealt treacherously; roll a large stone to me this day." 34Then Saul said, "Disperse yourselves among the people, and say to them, 'Bring me here every man's ox and every man's sheep, slaughter *them* here, and eat; and do not sin against the Lord by eating with the blood.' " So every one of the people brought his ox with him that night, and slaughtered *it* there. 35Then Saul built an altar to the Lord. This was the first altar that he built to the Lord.

36Now Saul said, "Let us go down after the Philistines by night, and plunder them until the morning light; and let us not leave a man of them."

And they said, "Do whatever seems good to you."

Then the priest said, "Let us draw near to God here."

37So Saul asked counsel of God, "Shall I go down after the Philistines? Will You deliver them into the hand of Israel?" But He did not answer him that day. 38And Saul said, "Come over here, all you chiefs of the people, and know and see what this sin was today. 39For *as* the Lord lives, who saves Israel, though it be in Jonathan my son, he shall surely die." But not a man among all the people answered him. 40Then he said to all Israel, "You be on one side, and my son Jonathan and I will be on the other side."

And the people said to Saul, "Do what seems good to you."

41Therefore Saul said to the Lord God of Israel, "Give a perfect *lot*."n So Saul and Jonathan were taken, but the people escaped. 42And Saul said, "Cast *lots* between my son Jonathan and me." So Jonathan was taken. 43Then Saul said to Jonathan, "Tell me what you have done."

And Jonathan told him, and said, "I only tasted a little honey with the end of the rod that *was* in my hand. So now I must die!"

44*Saul answered, "God do so and more also; for you shall surely die, Jonathan."

45But the people said to Saul, "Shall Jonathan die, who has accomplished this great deliverance

14:44, 45 Saul was great on words but weak on deeds. (See Matt. 7:21–29.)

14:41 nFollowing Masoretic Text and Targum; Septuagint and Vulgate read *Why do You not answer Your servant today? If the injustice is with me or Jonathan my son, O Lord God of Israel, give proof; and if You say it is with Your people Israel, give holiness.*

in Israel? Certainly not! *As* the LORD lives, not one hair of his head shall fall to the ground, for he has worked with God this day." So the people rescued Jonathan, and he did not die.

⁴⁶Then Saul returned from pursuing the Philistines, and the Philistines went to their own place.

⁴⁷So Saul established his sovereignty over Israel, and fought against all his enemies on every side, against Moab, against the people of Ammon, against Edom, against the kings of Zobah, and against the Philistines. Wherever he turned, he harassed *them.*ᵒ ⁴⁸And he gathered an army and attacked the Amalekites, and delivered Israel from the hands of those who plundered them.

⁴⁹The sons of Saul were Jonathan, Jishui,ᵖ and Malchishua. And the names of his two daughters *were these:* the name of the firstborn Merab, and the name of the younger Michal. ⁵⁰The name of Saul's wife *was* Ahinoam the daughter of Ahimaaz. And the name of the commander of his army *was* Abner the son of Ner, Saul's uncle. ⁵¹Kish *was* the father of Saul, and Ner the father of Abner *was* the son of Abiel.

⁵²Now there was fierce war with the Philistines all the days of Saul. And when Saul saw any strong man or any valiant man, he took him for himself.

CHAPTER 15

15:1ff God's orders were clear, but Saul's motives were mixed (James 1:8). Look at the losses Saul incurred because he disobeyed God's word.

15 Samuel* also said to Saul, "The LORD sent me to anoint you king over His people, over Israel. Now therefore, heed the voice of the words of the LORD. ²Thus says the LORD of hosts: 'I will punish Amalek *for* what he did to Israel, how he ambushed him on the way when he came up from Egypt. ³Now go and attack Amalek, and utterly destroy all that they have, and do not spare them. But kill both man and woman, infant and nursing child, ox and sheep, camel and donkey.' "

⁴So Saul gathered the people together and numbered them in Telaim, two hundred thousand foot soldiers and ten thousand men of Judah. ⁵And Saul came to a city of Amalek, and lay in wait in the valley.

⁶Then Saul said to the Kenites, "Go, depart, get down from among the Amalekites, lest I destroy you with them. For you showed kindness to all the children of Israel when they came up out of Egypt." So the Kenites departed from among the Amalekites. ⁷And Saul attacked the Amalekites, from Havilah all the way to Shur, which is east of Egypt. ⁸He also took Agag king of the Amalekites alive, and utterly destroyed all the people with the edge of the sword. ⁹But Saul and the people spared Agag and the best of the sheep, the oxen, the fatlings, the lambs, and all *that was* good, and were unwilling to utterly destroy them. But everything despised and worthless, that they utterly destroyed.

¹⁰Now the word of the LORD came to Samuel, saying, ¹¹"I greatly regret that I have set up Saul

---

14:47 ᵒSeptuagint and Vulgate read *prospered.*
14:49 ᵖCalled *Abinadab* in 1 Chronicles 8:33 and 9:39

Obedience, Not Sacrifice—God's people face the constant temptation of substituting religious ritual for spiritual reality. Samuel's words (1 Sam. 15:22–23) do not belittle sacrifices. Rather, they point out that the condition of the heart determines the value of the sacrifice (Ps. 51:16–17). God is not enriched by our gifts (Ps. 50:12–14), but we are enriched if our gifts to Him are backed by obedient hearts (Hos. 6:6; Mic. 6:7–8). He accepts the worship only if He can accept the worshiper (Isa. 1:10ff.).

as king, for he has turned back from following Me, and has not performed My commandments." And it grieved Samuel, and he cried out to the LORD all night. 12So when Samuel rose early in the morning to meet Saul, it was told Samuel, saying, "Saul went to Carmel, and indeed, he set up a monument for himself; and he has gone on around, passed by, and gone down to Gilgal." 13Then Samuel went to Saul, and Saul said to him, "Blessed *are* you of the LORD! I have performed the commandment of the LORD."

14But Samuel said, "What then *is* this bleating of the sheep in my ears, and the lowing of the oxen which I hear?"

15*And Saul said, "They have brought them from the Amalekites; for the people spared the best of the sheep and the oxen, to sacrifice to the LORD your God; and the rest we have utterly destroyed."

16Then Samuel said to Saul, "Be quiet! And I will tell you what the LORD said to me last night."

And he said to him, "Speak on."

17So Samuel said, "When you *were* little in your own eyes, *were* you not head of the tribes of Israel? And did not the LORD anoint you king over Israel? 18Now the LORD sent you on a mission, and said, 'Go, and utterly destroy the sinners, the Amalekites, and fight against them until they are consumed.' 19Why then did you not obey the voice of the LORD? Why did you swoop down on the spoil, and do evil in the sight of the LORD?"

20And Saul said to Samuel, "But I have obeyed the voice of the LORD, and gone on the mission on which the LORD sent me, and brought back Agag king of Amalek; I have utterly destroyed the Amalekites. 21But the people took of the plunder, sheep and oxen, the best of the things which should have been utterly destroyed, to sacrifice to the LORD your God in Gilgal."

22So Samuel said:

"Has the LORD *as great* delight in burnt
    offerings and sacrifices,
As in obeying the voice of the LORD?
Behold, to obey is better than sacrifice,
And to heed than the fat of rams.
23 For rebellion *is as* the sin of witchcraft,
And stubbornness *is as* iniquity and
    idolatry.
Because you have rejected the word of the
    LORD,
He also has rejected you from *being* king."

24Then Saul said to Samuel, "I have sinned, for I have transgressed the commandment of the LORD and your words, because I feared the people and obeyed their voice. 25Now therefore, please pardon my sin, and return with me, that I may worship the LORD."

26*But Samuel said to Saul, "I will not return with you, for you have rejected the word of the LORD, and the LORD has rejected you from being king over Israel."

27*And as Samuel turned around to go away, *Saul* seized the edge of his robe, and it tore. 28So Samuel said to him, "The LORD has torn the kingdom of Israel from you today, and has given it to a neighbor of yours, *who is* better than you. 29And also the Strength of Israel will not lie nor relent. For He *is* not a man, that He should relent."

30Then he said, "I have sinned; *yet* honor me

15:15 He lost his *character,* for he lied to Samuel and tried to blame the people. Saul was very good at excuses.

15:26 He lost his *friend* Samuel (v. 35) who had anointed him, taught him, and prayed for him.

15:27, 28 He lost his *crown.* God took the kingdom from Saul and gave it to David.

Saul had many advantages as he began his reign, but he failed God and the people because he did not cultivate his spiritual life. He became proud (vv. 12, 17); he feared men rather than God (v. 24); he blamed others for his own sins (v. 21); and he was concerned more about his reputation than about his character (v. 30). He tried to substitute sacrifice for obedience, but God rejected him.

Is there a King Agag in your life?

now, please, before the elders of my people and
before Israel, and return with me, that I may worship the LORD your God." 31So Samuel turned
back after Saul, and Saul worshiped the LORD.
32Then Samuel said, "Bring Agag king of the
Amalekites here to me." So Agag came to him
cautiously.
And Agag said, "Surely the bitterness of death
is past."
33But Samuel said, "As your sword has made
women childless, so shall your mother be childless among women." And Samuel hacked Agag
in pieces before the LORD in Gilgal.
34Then Samuel went to Ramah, and Saul went
up to his house at Gibeah of Saul. 35And Samuel
went no more to see Saul until the day of his
death. Nevertheless Samuel mourned for Saul,
and the LORD regretted that He had made Saul
king over Israel.

16 Now* the LORD said to Samuel, "How long
will you mourn for Saul, seeing I have rejected him from reigning over Israel? Fill your
horn with oil, and go; I am sending you to Jesse
the Bethlehemite. For I have provided Myself a
king among his sons."
2And Samuel said, "How can I go? If Saul hears
it, he will kill me."
But the LORD said, "Take a heifer with you, and
say, 'I have come to sacrifice to the LORD.' 3Then
invite Jesse to the sacrifice, and I will show you
what you shall do; you shall anoint for Me the
one I name to you."
4So Samuel did what the LORD said, and went
to Bethlehem. And the elders of the town trembled
at his coming, and said, "Do you come peaceably?"
5And he said, "Peaceably; I have come to sacrifice to the LORD. Sanctify yourselves, and come
with me to the sacrifice." Then he consecrated
Jesse and his sons, and invited them to the
sacrifice.
6So it was, when they came, that he looked at
Eliab and said, "Surely the LORD's anointed *is* before Him!"
7*But the LORD said to Samuel, "Do not look at
his appearance or at his physical stature, because
I have refused him. For *the LORD does* not *see* as
man sees;[q] for man looks at the outward appearance, but the LORD looks at the heart."
8So Jesse called Abinadab, and made him pass
before Samuel. And he said, "Neither has the
LORD chosen this one." 9Then Jesse made Shammah pass by. And he said, "Neither has the LORD
chosen this one." 10Thus Jesse made seven of his
sons pass before Samuel. And Samuel said to
Jesse, "The LORD has not chosen these." 11And
Samuel said to Jesse, "Are all the young men
here?" Then he said, "There remains yet the
youngest, and there he is, keeping the sheep."
And Samuel said to Jesse, "Send and bring him.

CHAPTER 16

16:1 ***Reject what God rejects.*** You expect Samuel to mourn over Saul and his sin (1 Cor. 5:1–2), but mourning alone will not solve problems. There comes a time for action (Josh. 7:10ff.).

16:7 ***See as God sees.*** How strange that Samuel had not learned his lesson after the failure of Saul (1 Sam. 9:2; 10:23–24). God told Samuel that He would tell him the man of His choice (v. 3), but the old man was tempted to run ahead of the Lord. The heart determines the life (Prov. 4:23), and only God can see the heart (Acts 1:24–25).

16:7 [q]Septuagint reads *For God does not see as man sees;* Targum reads *It is not by the appearance of a man;* Vulgate reads *Nor do I judge according to the looks of a man.*

God Sees the Heart—God not only sees our hearts, but He searches them (1 Chron. 28:9) and knows our thoughts and motives (Heb. 4:12–13). We think we know our own hearts, but we do not (Jer. 17:9), so we had better accept God's verdict. We should be careful not to judge others since we cannot know their hearts (John 7:24; 1 Cor. 4:5).

For we will not sit down[r] till he comes here."
¹²So he sent and brought him in. Now he *was* ruddy, with bright eyes, and good-looking. And the LORD said, "Arise, anoint him; for this *is* the one!" ¹³Then Samuel took the horn of oil and anointed him in the midst of his brothers; and the Spirit of the LORD came upon David from that day forward. So Samuel arose and went to Ramah.

¹⁴*But the Spirit of the LORD departed from Saul, and a distressing spirit from the LORD troubled him. ¹⁵And Saul's servants said to him, "Surely, a distressing spirit from God is troubling you. ¹⁶Let our master now command your servants, *who are* before you, to seek out a man *who is* a skillful player on the harp. And it shall be that he will play it with his hand when the distressing spirit from God is upon you, and you shall be well."

¹⁷So Saul said to his servants, "Provide me now a man who can play well, and bring *him* to me." ¹⁸Then one of the servants answered and said, "Look, I have seen a son of Jesse the Bethlehemite, *who is* skillful in playing, a mighty man of valor, a man of war, prudent in speech, and a handsome person; and the LORD *is* with him."

¹⁹Therefore Saul sent messengers to Jesse, and said, "Send me your son David, who *is* with the sheep." ²⁰And Jesse took a donkey *loaded with* bread, a skin of wine, and a young goat, and sent *them* by his son David to Saul. ²¹So David came to Saul and stood before him. And he loved him greatly, and he became his armorbearer. ²²Then Saul sent to Jesse, saying, "Please let David stand before me, for he has found favor in my sight." ²³And so it was, whenever the spirit from God was upon Saul, that David would take a harp and play *it* with his hand. Then Saul would become refreshed and well, and the distressing spirit would depart from him.

17 Now* the Philistines gathered their armies together to battle, and were gathered at Sochoh, which *belongs* to Judah; they encamped between Sochoh and Azekah, in Ephes Dammim. ²And Saul and the men of Israel were gathered together, and they encamped in the Valley of Elah, and drew up in battle array against the Philistines. ³The Philistines stood on a mountain on one side, and Israel stood on a mountain on the other side, with a valley between them.

⁴And a champion went out from the camp of the Philistines, named Goliath, from Gath, whose height *was* six cubits and a span. ⁵*He had* a bronze helmet on his head, and he *was* armed with a coat of mail, and the weight of the coat *was* five thousand shekels of bronze. ⁶And *he had* bronze armor on his legs and a bronze javelin between his shoulders. ⁷Now the staff of his spear *was* like a

---

16:11 ʳFollowing Septuagint and Vulgate; Masoretic Text reads *turn around;* Targum and Syriac read *turn away.*

16:14–23 *Let God do the rest.* Samuel anointed David to be king and then departed from Bethlehem, for his work there was done. How would a shepherd boy get from the fields to the throne? That was not Samuel's responsibility; God would see to it. God used David's musical skill to bring him into the king's presence. Empowered by the Spirit (v. 13), David had nothing to fear.

(The ominous statement in v. 14 should be compared with David's prayer in Ps. 51:11.)

CHAPTER 17

17:1–11 *Opportunities.* God had prepared David for this occasion, for the private victories make possible the public victories (vv. 34–37). A seemingly trivial errand led to a challenging situation that brought glory to God and recognition to David. Be prepared; you never know when your opportunity will come.

David and the Lord Jesus—David is a picture of the Lord Jesus Christ, the Son of David. He was born in Bethlehem and misunderstood by his family; he was an obedient son and a conquering hero. The name *David* means "beloved," and Jesus is the Father's "beloved Son" (Matt. 3:17). David was anointed king long before he took the throne and ruled, and our Lord is King of kings even though He is not yet reigning on this earth. Like David, our Lord has had to experience rejection and exile before reigning.

weaver's beam, and his iron spearhead *weighed* six hundred shekels; and a shield-bearer went before him. 8Then he stood and cried out to the armies of Israel, and said to them, "Why have you come out to line up for battle? *Am* I not a Philistine, and you the servants of Saul? Choose a man for yourselves, and let him come down to me. 9If he is able to fight with me and kill me, then we will be your servants. But if I prevail against him and kill him, then you shall be our servants and serve us." 10And the Philistine said, "I defy the armies of Israel this day; give me a man, that we may fight together." 11When Saul and all Israel heard these words of the Philistine, they were dismayed and greatly afraid.

12Now David *was* the son of that Ephrathite of Bethlehem Judah, whose name *was* Jesse, and who had eight sons. And the man was old, advanced *in years*, in the days of Saul. 13The three oldest sons of Jesse had gone to follow Saul to the battle. The names of his three sons who went to the battle *were* Eliab the firstborn, next to him Abinadab, and the third Shammah. 14David *was* the youngest. And the three oldest followed Saul. 15But David occasionally went and returned from Saul to feed his father's sheep at Bethlehem.

16And the Philistine drew near and presented himself forty days, morning and evening.

17Then Jesse said to his son David, "Take now for your brothers an ephah of this dried *grain* and these ten loaves, and run to your brothers at the camp. 18And carry these ten cheeses to the captain of *their* thousand, and see how your brothers fare, and bring back news of them." 19Now Saul and they and all the men of Israel *were* in the Valley of Elah, fighting with the Philistines.

20So David rose early in the morning, left the sheep with a keeper, and took *the things* and went as Jesse had commanded him. And he came to the camp as the army was going out to the fight and shouting for the battle. 21For Israel and the Philistines had drawn up in battle array, army against army. 22And David left his supplies in the hand of the supply keeper, ran to the army, and came and greeted his brothers. 23Then as he talked with them, there was the champion, the Philistine of Gath, Goliath by name, coming up from the armies of the Philistines; and he spoke according to the same words. So David heard *them*. 24And all the men of Israel, when they saw the man, fled from him and were dreadfully afraid. 25So the men of Israel said, "Have you seen this man who has come up? Surely he has come up to defy Israel; and it shall be *that* the man who kills him the king will enrich with great riches, will give him his daughter, and give his father's house exemption *from taxes* in Israel."

26Then David spoke to the men who stood by him, saying, "What shall be done for the man who kills this Philistine and takes away the reproach from Israel? For who *is* this uncircumcised Philistine, that he should defy the armies of the living God?"

27And the people answered him in this manner, saying, "So shall it be done for the man who kills him."

28Now Eliab his oldest brother heard when he spoke to the men; and Eliab's anger was aroused against David, and he said, "Why did you come down here? And with whom have you left those few sheep in the wilderness? I know your pride and the insolence of your heart, for you have come down to see the battle."

29And David said, "What have I done now? *Is there* not a cause?" 30Then he turned from him toward another and said the same thing; and these people answered him as the first ones *did.*

31Now when the words which David spoke were heard, they reported *them* to Saul; and he sent for him. 32Then David said to Saul, "Let no man's heart fail because of him; your servant will go and fight with this Philistine."

33And Saul said to David, "You are not able to go against this Philistine to fight with him; for you *are* a youth, and he a man of war from his youth."

34But David said to Saul, "Your servant used to keep his father's sheep, and when a lion or a bear came and took a lamb out of the flock, 35I went out after it and struck it, and delivered *the lamb* from its mouth; and when it arose against me, I caught *it* by its beard, and struck and killed it. 36*Your servant has killed both lion and bear; and this uncircumcised Philistine will be like one of them, seeing he has defied the armies of the living God." 37Moreover David said, "The LORD, who delivered me from the paw of the lion and from the paw of the bear, He will deliver me from the hand of this Philistine."

And Saul said to David, "Go, and the LORD be with you!"

38So Saul clothed David with his armor, and he put a bronze helmet on his head; he also clothed him with a coat of mail. 39David fastened his sword to his armor and tried to walk, for he had not tested *them.* And David said to Saul, "I cannot walk with these, for I have not tested *them.*" So David took them off.

40Then he took his staff in his hand; and he chose for himself five smooth stones from the brook, and put them in a shepherd's bag, in a pouch which he had, and his sling was in his hand. And he drew near to the Philistine. 41So the Philistine came, and began drawing near to David, and the man who bore the shield *went* before him. 42And when the Philistine looked about and saw David, he disdained him; for he was *only* a youth, ruddy and good-looking. 43So the Philistine said to David, "*Am* I a dog, that you come to me with sticks?" And the Philistine cursed David by his gods. 44And the Philistine said to David, "Come to me, and I will give your flesh to the birds of the air and the beasts of the field!"

45Then David said to the Philistine, "You come to me with a sword, with a spear, and with a javelin. But I come to you in the name of the LORD of hosts, the God of the armies of Israel, whom you have defied. 46*This day the LORD will deliver you into my hand, and I will strike you and take your head from you. And this day I will give the carcasses of the camp of the Philistines to the birds of the air and the wild beasts of the earth, that all the earth may know that there is a God in Israel. 47Then all this assembly shall know that the LORD does not save with sword and spear; for the battle *is* the LORD's, and He will give you into our hands."

48So it was, when the Philistine arose and came and drew near to meet David, that David hurried and ran toward the army to meet the Philistine. 49Then David put his hand in his bag and took out a stone; and he slung *it* and struck the Philistine in his forehead, so that the stone sank into

17:36 Saul was losing strength, but David was growing in power; and Saul's diminishment would continue until Saul's tragic death. Saul stood head and shoulders above everybody else, but he was not big enough to meet Goliath. David was a man of faith, and God gave him spiritual stature. Great faith makes great men and women. David's only desire was to glorify the God of Israel (vv. 45–47).

17:46–58 Obstacles. Whenever you step out by faith, other people will often put obstacles in your way. David's brother ridiculed him (v. 28) and Saul bluntly told David, "You are not able!" (v. 33). Then Saul said, "If you must do it, do it my way," and he encumbered David with his heavy armor. David had to ignore the obstacles and keep his faith in the Lord. He had to do God's work in the way God wanted him to do it.

his forehead, and he fell on his face to the earth. 50So David prevailed over the Philistine with a sling and a stone, and struck the Philistine and killed him. But *there was* no sword in the hand of David. 51Therefore David ran and stood over the Philistine, took his sword and drew it out of its sheath and killed him, and cut off his head with it.

And when the Philistines saw that their champion was dead, they fled. 52Now the men of Israel and Judah arose and shouted, and pursued the Philistines as far as the entrance of the valleys and to the gates of Ekron. And the wounded of the Philistines fell along the road to Shaaraim, even as far as Gath and Ekron. 53Then the children of Israel returned from chasing the Philistines, and they plundered their tents. 54And David took the head of the Philistine and brought it to Jerusalem, but he put his armor in his tent.

55When Saul saw David going out against the Philistine, he said to Abner, the commander of the army, "Abner, whose son *is* this youth?"

And Abner said, "As your soul lives, O king, I do not know."

56So the king said, "Inquire whose son this young man *is*."

57Then, as David returned from the slaughter of the Philistine, Abner took him and brought him before Saul with the head of the Philistine in his hand. 58And Saul said to him, "Whose son *are* you, young man?"

So David answered, "*I am* the son of your servant Jesse the Bethlehemite."

CHAPTER 18

18:1ff As you read the history of Saul, you often find him with a spear in his hand. It was his symbol of authority and power, and he did not want anybody to forget that he was in charge. David had a harp in his hand—or a shepherd's crook or a sling or a sword. Whatever task God had for him to do, David was available to do it, and God received the glory.

18:8–11 When you are jealous over your authority and position, as Saul was, you become envious of others and sensitive to what people are saying about you. Saul became almost paranoid about David. First he was envious of David, then suspicious and afraid, then angry, and finally so hateful that he wanted to kill him.

18 Now* when he had finished speaking to Saul, the soul of Jonathan was knit to the soul of David, and Jonathan loved him as his own soul. 2Saul took him that day, and would not let him go home to his father's house anymore. 3Then Jonathan and David made a covenant, because he loved him as his own soul. 4And Jonathan took off the robe that *was* on him and gave it to David, with his armor, even to his sword and his bow and his belt.

5So David went out wherever Saul sent him, *and* behaved wisely. And Saul set him over the men of war, and he was accepted in the sight of all the people and also in the sight of Saul's servants. 6Now it had happened as they were coming *home*, when David was returning from the slaughter of the Philistine, that the women had come out of all the cities of Israel, singing and dancing, to meet King Saul, with tambourines, with joy, and with musical instruments. 7So the women sang as they danced, and said:

"Saul has slain his thousands,
And David his ten thousands."

8*Then Saul was very angry, and the saying displeased him; and he said, "They have ascribed to David ten thousands, and to me they have ascribed *only* thousands. Now *what* more can he have but the kingdom?" 9So Saul eyed David from that day forward.

10And it happened on the next day that the distressing spirit from God came upon Saul, and he prophesied inside the house. So David played *mu-*

17:52 sFollowing Masoretic Text, Syriac, Targum, and Vulgate; Septuagint reads *Gath*.

sic with his hand, as at other times; but *there was* a spear in Saul's hand. [11]And Saul cast the spear, for he said, "I will pin David to the wall!" But David escaped his presence twice.

[12]Now Saul was afraid of David, because the LORD was with him, but had departed from Saul. [13]Therefore Saul removed him from his presence, and made him his captain over a thousand; and he went out and came in before the people. [14]*And David behaved wisely in all his ways, and the LORD *was* with him. [15]Therefore, when Saul saw that he behaved very wisely, he was afraid of him. [16]But all Israel and Judah loved David, because he went out and came in before them.

[17]Then Saul said to David, "Here is my older daughter Merab; I will give her to you as a wife. Only be valiant for me, and fight the LORD's battles." For Saul thought, "Let my hand not be against him, but let the hand of the Philistines be against him."

[18]So David said to Saul, "Who *am* I, and what *is* my life *or* my father's family in Israel, that I should be son-in-law to the king?" [19]But it happened at the time when Merab, Saul's daughter, should have been given to David, that she was given to Adriel the Meholathite as a wife.

[20]Now Michal, Saul's daughter, loved David. And they told Saul, and the thing pleased him. [21]So Saul said, "I will give her to him, that she may be a snare to him, and that the hand of the Philistines may be against him." Therefore Saul said to David a second time, "You shall be my son-in-law today."

[22]And Saul commanded his servants, "Communicate with David secretly, and say, 'Look, the king has delight in you, and all his servants love you. Now therefore, become the king's son-in-law.'"

[23]So Saul's servants spoke those words in the hearing of David. And David said, "Does it seem to you *a* light *thing* to be a king's son-in-law, seeing I *am* a poor and lightly esteemed man?" [24]And the servants of Saul told him, saying, "In this manner David spoke."

[25]Then Saul said, "Thus you shall say to David: 'The king does not desire any dowry but one hundred foreskins of the Philistines, to take vengeance on the king's enemies.'" But Saul thought to make David fall by the hand of the Philistines. [26]So when his servants told David these words, it pleased David well to become the king's son-in-law. Now the days had not expired; [27]therefore David arose and went, he and his men, and killed two hundred men of the Philistines. And David brought their foreskins, and they gave them in full count to the king, that he might become the king's son-in-law. Then Saul gave him Michal his daughter as a wife. [28]Thus Saul saw and knew that the LORD *was* with David, and *that* Michal, Saul's daughter, loved him; [29]and Saul was still more afraid of David. So Saul became David's enemy continually. [30]Then the princes of the Philistines went out *to war*. And so it was, whenever they went out, *that* David behaved more wisely than all the servants of Saul, so that his name became highly esteemed.

19 Now* Saul spoke to Jonathan his son and to all his servants, that they should kill David; but Jonathan, Saul's son, delighted greatly in David. [2]So Jonathan told David, saying, "My father Saul seeks to kill you. Therefore please be

18:14–16 In that difficult situation, David acted with wisdom from God and trusted God to help him. David never considered Saul his enemy, which kept David in the place of God's blessing. David remained a humble servant in spite of his great victories, for he knew that God's anointing was upon him. God used those difficult experiences of conflict to help make David a great man of faith.

CHAPTER 19

19:1ff David was in constant danger, but God protected him, sometimes providentially (v. 10) and sometimes through the ministry of others. When the battles were all ended, David wrote, "He delivered me because He delighted in me" (Ps. 18:19). David's integrity before God was his strongest weapon during those years of persecution from Saul. You cannot control what people do to you, but you can control what you do with God.

19:3, 12–14 Jonathan was David's dearest friend, and he kept David informed of Saul's plans. Faith in God does not exclude a commonsense approach to life. Michal, Saul's daughter, risked her life to protect her husband, and until the day of his death, Samuel stood by David.

19:18–24 The "ultimate weapon" of the believer is spiritual, the power of God at work changing people (vv. 18–24; 2 Cor. 10:3–6). Had Saul repented and yielded himself to the Lord, he would have saved himself and his family a great deal of sorrow and trouble.

on your guard until morning, and stay in a secret *place* and hide. 3*And I will go out and stand beside my father in the field where you *are,* and I will speak with my father about you. Then what I observe, I will tell you."

4Thus Jonathan spoke well of David to Saul his father, and said to him, "Let not the king sin against his servant, against David, because he has not sinned against you, and because his works *have been* very good toward you. 5For he took his life in his hands and killed the Philistine, and the LORD brought about a great deliverance for all Israel. You saw *it* and rejoiced. Why then will you sin against innocent blood, to kill David without a cause?"

6So Saul heeded the voice of Jonathan, and Saul swore, "*As* the LORD lives, he shall not be killed." 7Then Jonathan called David, and Jonathan told him all these things. So Jonathan brought David to Saul, and he was in his presence as in times past.

8And there was war again; and David went out and fought with the Philistines, and struck them with a mighty blow, and they fled from him.

9Now the distressing spirit from the LORD came upon Saul as he sat in his house with his spear in his hand. And David was playing *music* with *his* hand. 10Then Saul sought to pin David to the wall with the spear, but he slipped away from Saul's presence; and he drove the spear into the wall. So David fled and escaped that night.

11Saul also sent messengers to David's house to watch him and to kill him in the morning. And Michal, David's wife, told him, saying, "If you do not save your life tonight, tomorrow you will be killed." 12So Michal let David down through a window. And he went and fled and escaped. 13And Michal took an image and laid *it* in the bed, put a cover of goats' *hair* for his head, and covered *it* with clothes. 14So when Saul sent messengers to take David, she said, "He *is* sick."

15Then Saul sent the messengers *back* to see David, saying, "Bring him up to me in the bed, that I may kill him." 16And when the messengers had come in, there was the image in the bed, with a cover of goats' *hair* for his head. 17Then Saul said to Michal, "Why have you deceived me like this, and sent my enemy away, so that he has escaped?"

And Michal answered Saul, "He said to me, 'Let me go! Why should I kill you?' "

18*So David fled and escaped, and went to Samuel at Ramah, and told him all that Saul had done to him. And he and Samuel went and stayed in Naioth. 19Now it was told Saul, saying, "Take note, David *is* at Naioth in Ramah!" 20Then Saul sent messengers to take David. And when they saw the group of prophets prophesying, and Samuel standing *as* leader over them, the Spirit of God came upon the messengers of Saul, and they also prophesied. 21And when Saul was told, he sent other messengers, and they prophesied likewise. Then Saul sent messengers again the third time, and they prophesied also. 22Then he also went to Ramah, and came to the great well that *is* at Sechu. So he asked, and said, "Where *are* Samuel and David?"

And *someone* said, "Indeed *they are* at Naioth in Ramah." 23So he went there to Naioth in Ramah. Then the Spirit of God was upon him also, and he went on and prophesied until he came to Naioth in Ramah. 24And he also stripped off his clothes and prophesied before Samuel in like manner, and lay down naked all that day and all that night. Therefore they say, *"Is Saul also among the prophets?"*[t]

20 Then* David fled from Naioth in Ramah, and went and said to Jonathan, "What have I done? What *is* my iniquity, and what *is* my sin before your father, that he seeks my life?"

2So Jonathan said to him, "By no means! You shall not die! Indeed, my father will do nothing either great or small without first telling me. And why should my father hide this thing from me? It *is* not *so!*"

3Then David took an oath again, and said, "Your father certainly knows that I have found favor in your eyes, and he has said, 'Do not let Jonathan know this, lest he be grieved.' But truly, *as* the LORD lives and *as* your soul lives, *there is* but a step between me and death."

4So Jonathan said to David, "Whatever you yourself desire, I will do *it* for you."

5And David said to Jonathan, "Indeed tomorrow *is* the New Moon, and I should not fail to sit with the king to eat. But let me go, that I may hide in the field until the third *day* at evening. 6If your father misses me at all, then say, 'David earnestly asked *permission* of me that he might run over to Bethlehem, his city, for *there is* a yearly sacrifice there for all the family.' 7If he says thus: '*It is* well,' your servant will be safe. But if he is very angry, be sure that evil is determined by him. 8Therefore you shall deal kindly with your servant, for you have brought your servant into a covenant of the LORD with you. Nevertheless, if there is iniquity in me, kill me yourself, for why should you bring me to your father?"

9But Jonathan said, "Far be it from you! For if I knew certainly that evil was determined by my father to come upon you, then would I not tell you?"

10Then David said to Jonathan, "Who will tell me, or what *if* your father answers you roughly?"

11And Jonathan said to David, "Come, let us go out into the field." So both of them went out into the field. 12Then Jonathan said to David: "The LORD God of Israel *is witness!* When I have sounded out my father sometime tomorrow, *or* the third *day*, and indeed *there is* good toward David, and I do not send to you and tell you, 13may the LORD do so and much more to Jonathan. But if it pleases my father *to do* you evil, then I will report it to you and send you away, that you may go in safety. And the LORD be with you as He has been with my father. 14And you shall not only show me the kindness of the LORD while I still live, that I may not die; 15but you shall not cut off your kindness from my house forever, no, not when the LORD has cut off every one of the enemies of David from the face of the earth." 16So Jonathan made *a covenant* with the house of David, *saying,* "Let the LORD require *it* at the hand of David's enemies."

17Now Jonathan again caused David to vow, because he loved him; for he loved him as he loved his own soul. 18Then Jonathan said to David, "Tomorrow *is* the New Moon; and you will be missed, because your seat will be empty. 19And *when* you have stayed three days, go down quickly and

CHAPTER 20

20:1ff It has well been said that faith is living without scheming. In the midst of the trials of life, we must beware lest we become weary, stop trusting God, and start scheming. We may be inclined to judge David, but perhaps we have done some scheming ourselves.

come to the place where you hid on the day of the deed; and remain by the stone Ezel. 20Then I will shoot three arrows to the side, as though I shot at a target; 21and there I will send a lad, *saying,* 'Go, find the arrows.' If I expressly say to the lad, 'Look, the arrows *are* on this side of you; get them and come'—then, as the LORD lives, *there is* safety for you and no harm. 22But if I say thus to the young man, 'Look, the arrows *are* beyond you'—go your way, for the LORD has sent you away. 23And as for the matter which you and I have spoken of, indeed the LORD *be* between you and me forever."

24Then David hid in the field. And when the New Moon had come, the king sat down to eat the feast. 25Now the king sat on his seat, as at other times, on a seat by the wall. And Jonathan arose,ᵘ and Abner sat by Saul's side, but David's place was empty. 26Nevertheless Saul did not say anything that day, for he thought, "Something has happened to him; he *is* unclean, surely he *is* unclean." 27And it happened the next day, the second *day* of the month, that David's place was empty. And Saul said to Jonathan his son, "Why has the son of Jesse not come to eat, either yesterday or today?"

28So Jonathan answered Saul, "David earnestly asked *permission* of me *to go* to Bethlehem. 29*And he said, 'Please let me go, for our family has a sacrifice in the city, and my brother has commanded me *to be there.* And now, if I have found favor in your eyes, please let me get away and see my brothers.' Therefore he has not come to the king's table."

30Then Saul's anger was aroused against Jonathan, and he said to him, "You son of a perverse, rebellious *woman!* Do I not know that you have chosen the son of Jesse to your own shame and to the shame of your mother's nakedness? 31For as long as the son of Jesse lives on the earth, you shall not be established, nor your kingdom. Now therefore, send and bring him to me, for he shall surely die."

32And Jonathan answered Saul his father, and said to him, "Why should he be killed? What has he done?" 33Then Saul cast a spear at him to kill him, by which Jonathan knew that it was determined by his father to kill David.

34So Jonathan arose from the table in fierce anger, and ate no food the second day of the month, for he was grieved for David, because his father had treated him shamefully.

35And so it was, in the morning, that Jonathan went out into the field at the time appointed with David, and a little lad *was* with him. 36Then he said to his lad, "Now run, find the arrows which I shoot." As the lad ran, he shot an arrow beyond him. 37When the lad had come to the place where the arrow was which Jonathan had shot, Jonathan cried out after the lad and said, "Is not the arrow beyond you?" 38And Jonathan cried out after the lad, "Make haste, hurry, do not delay!" So Jonathan's lad gathered up the arrows and came back to his master. 39But the lad did not know anything. Only Jonathan and David knew of the matter. 40Then Jonathan gave his weapons to his lad, and said to him, "Go, carry *them* to the city." 41As soon as the lad had gone, David arose from

---

20:29, 30 David and Jonathan lied to Saul, and it almost cost Jonathan his life. Jonathan had been altogether too optimistic about his father, and this experience helped to open his eyes. Jonathan tried to mediate between David and Saul instead of taking his stand with God's anointed. After all, as far as God was concerned, Saul was a "has been" (v. 13).

20:25 ᵘFollowing Masoretic Text, Syriac, Targum, and Vulgate; Septuagint reads *he sat across from Jonathan.*

a place toward the south, fell on his face to the ground, and bowed down three times. And they kissed one another; and they wept together, but David more so. ⁴²*Then Jonathan said to David, "Go in peace, since we have both sworn in the name of the LORD, saying, 'May the LORD be between you and me, and between your descendants and my descendants, forever.'" So he arose and departed, and Jonathan went into the city.

21 Now* David came to Nob, to Ahimelech the priest. And Ahimelech was afraid when he met David, and said to him, "Why *are* you alone, and no one is with you?"

²*So David said to Ahimelech the priest, "The king has ordered me on some business, and said to me, 'Do not let anyone know anything about the business on which I send you, or what I have commanded you.' And I have directed *my* young men to such and such a place. ³Now therefore, what have you on hand? Give *me* five *loaves of* bread in my hand, or whatever can be found."

⁴And the priest answered David and said, "There *is* no common bread on hand; but there is holy bread, if the young men have at least kept themselves from women."

⁵Then David answered the priest, and said to him, "Truly, women *have been* kept from us about three days since I came out. And the vessels of the young men are holy, and *the bread is* in effect common, even though it was consecrated in the vessel this day."

⁶So the priest gave him holy *bread;* for there was no bread there but the showbread which had been taken from before the LORD, in order to put hot bread *in its place* on the day when it was taken away.

⁷Now a certain man of the servants of Saul *was* there that day, detained before the LORD. And his name *was* Doeg, an Edomite, the chief of the herdsmen who *belonged* to Saul.

⁸And David said to Ahimelech, "Is there not here on hand a spear or a sword? For I have brought neither my sword nor my weapons with me, because the king's business required haste."

⁹So the priest said, "The sword of Goliath the Philistine, whom you killed in the Valley of Elah, there it is, wrapped in a cloth behind the ephod. If you will take that, take *it.* For *there is* no other except that one here."

And David said, "*There is* none like it; give it to me."

¹⁰Then David arose and fled that day from before Saul, and went to Achish the king of Gath. ¹¹And the servants of Achish said to him, "*Is* this not David the king of the land? Did they not sing of him to one another in dances, saying:

'Saul has slain his thousands,
And David his ten thousands'?"ᵛ

¹²Now David took these words to heart, and was very much afraid of Achish the king of Gath.

21:11 ᵛCompare 1 Samuel 18:7

20:42 Jonathan was also concerned about the future of his family (vv. 15, 42). David's promise to spare Jonathan's family made it possible for Mephibosheth to live (2 Sam. 9).

CHAPTER 21

21:1ff *Departure.* David lived as an exile for about ten years, during which time Saul tried to kill him and Saul's followers lied about him. Many people in Israel actually believed that David was a rebel against the king and that David was trying to destroy Saul. David had to leave his reputation with God and trust Him to silence the accusers.

21:2–15 *Deception.* It is disappointing to see David depending on lies for protection. He lied to the priest and to the king, but he could not lie to Doeg: "For the sons of this world are more shrewd in their generation than the sons of light" (Luke 16:8). Whenever you think you have "pulled off" a smart deal, you will find a Doeg ready to give you trouble (1 Sam. 22:9ff.; see also Ps. 52).

"Lying lips are an abomination to the LORD, but those who deal truthfully are His delight" (Prov. 12:22).

Is It Ever Right to Lie?—Scripture commands us to tell the truth and warns about the consequences of lying. Jesus is our example, for there was no deceit in His mouth (1 Pet. 2:22). We must always speak the truth in love (Eph. 4:15). If our telling the truth endangers others, silence is our best response. When David ran ahead of God, he found himself in trouble and lied. The safest thing is to stay away from those situations and to pray, "Lead us not into temptation."

13So he changed his behavior before them, pretended madness in their hands, scratched on the doors of the gate, and let his saliva fall down on his beard. 14Then Achish said to his servants, "Look, you see the man is insane. Why have you brought him to me? 15Have I need of madmen, that you have brought this *fellow* to play the madman in my presence? Shall this *fellow* come into my house?"

CHAPTER 22

22:1, 2 What a motley group gathered around the exiled king (1 Cor. 1:26–30)! A. W. Tozer used to say, "Don't follow any leader until you see the mark of the oil on his forehead." David had the anointing of God, and he represented the future in Israel. Yes, he made mistakes and was sometimes discouraged, but he was God's man and God used him.

22:7–19 Contrast Saul's approach to leadership. He could not challenge his men to a holy cause, so he tried to bribe them (v. 7) and play on their sympathy (v. 8). He depended on spies like Doeg, and he was not afraid to murder innocent priests just to let people know who was in charge. Saul was unwilling to kill the wicked Amalekites, but he murdered God's priests. Saul was fighting a losing battle, and he was desperate.

22 David* therefore departed from there and escaped to the cave of Adullam. So when his brothers and all his father's house heard *it,* they went down there to him. 2And everyone who *was* in distress, everyone who *was* in debt, and everyone *who was* discontented gathered to him. So he became captain over them. And there were about four hundred men with him.

3Then David went from there to Mizpah of Moab; and he said to the king of Moab, "Please let my father and mother come here with you, till I know what God will do for me." 4So he brought them before the king of Moab, and they dwelt with him all the time that David was in the stronghold.

5Now the prophet Gad said to David, "Do not stay in the stronghold; depart, and go to the land of Judah." So David departed and went into the forest of Hereth.

6When Saul heard that David and the men who *were* with him had been discovered—now Saul was staying in Gibeah under a tamarisk tree in Ramah, with his spear in his hand, and all his servants standing about him— 7*then Saul said to his servants who stood about him, "Hear now, you Benjamites! Will the son of Jesse give every one of you fields and vineyards, *and* make you all captains of thousands and captains of hundreds? 8All of you have conspired against me, and *there is* no one who reveals to me that my son has made a covenant with the son of Jesse; and *there is* not one of you who is sorry for me or reveals to me that my son has stirred up my servant against me, to lie in wait, as *it is* this day."

9Then answered Doeg the Edomite, who was set over the servants of Saul, and said, "I saw the son of Jesse going to Nob, to Ahimelech the son of Ahitub. 10And he inquired of the LORD for him, gave him provisions, and gave him the sword of Goliath the Philistine."

11So the king sent to call Ahimelech the priest, the son of Ahitub, and all his father's house, the priests who *were* in Nob. And they all came to the king. 12And Saul said, "Hear now, son of Ahitub!"

He answered, "Here I am, my lord."

13Then Saul said to him, "Why have you conspired against me, you and the son of Jesse, in that you have given him bread and a sword, and have inquired of God for him, that he should rise against me, to lie in wait, as it is this day?"

14So Ahimelech answered the king and said, "And who among all your servants *is as* faithful as David, who is the king's son-in-law, who goes at your bidding, and is honorable in your house? 15Did I then begin to inquire of God for him? Far be it from me! Let not the king impute anything to his servant, *or* to any in the house of my father. For your servant knew nothing of all this, little or much."

16And the king said, "You shall surely die, Ahimelech, you and all your father's house!"

17Then the king said to the guards who stood about him, "Turn and kill the priests of the LORD, because their hand also *is* with David, and because they knew when he fled and did not tell it to me." But the servants of the king would not lift their hands to strike the priests of the LORD. 18And the king said to Doeg, "You turn and kill the priests!" So Doeg the Edomite turned and struck the priests, and killed on that day eighty-five men who wore a linen ephod. 19Also Nob, the city of the priests, he struck with the edge of the sword, both men and women, children and nursing infants, oxen and donkeys and sheep— with the edge of the sword.

20*Now one of the sons of Ahimelech the son of Ahitub, named Abiathar, escaped and fled after David. 21And Abiathar told David that Saul had killed the LORD's priests. 22So David said to Abiathar, "I knew that day, when Doeg the Edomite *was* there, that he would surely tell Saul. I have caused *the death* of all the persons of your father's house. 23Stay with me; do not fear. For he who seeks my life seeks your life, but with me you *shall be* safe."

23 Then* they told David, saying, "Look, the Philistines are fighting against Keilah, and they are robbing the threshing floors."

2Therefore David inquired of the LORD, saying, "Shall I go and attack these Philistines?"

And the LORD said to David, "Go and attack the Philistines, and save Keilah."

3But David's men said to him, "Look, we are afraid here in Judah. How much more then if we go to Keilah against the armies of the Philistines?"

4Then David inquired of the LORD once again.

And the LORD answered him and said, "Arise, go down to Keilah. For I will deliver the Philistines into your hand." 5And David and his men went to Keilah and fought with the Philistines, struck them with a mighty blow, and took away their livestock. So David saved the inhabitants of Keilah.

6Now it happened, when Abiathar the son of Ahimelech fled to David at Keilah, *that* he went down *with* an ephod in his hand.

7And Saul was told that David had gone to Keilah. So Saul said, "God has delivered him into my hand, for he has shut himself in by entering a town that has gates and bars." 8Then Saul called all the people together for war, to go down to Keilah to besiege David and his men.

9When David knew that Saul plotted evil against him, he said to Abiathar the priest, "Bring the ephod here." 10Then David said, "O LORD God of Israel, Your servant has certainly heard that Saul seeks to come to Keilah to destroy the city for my sake. 11Will the men of Keilah deliver me into his hand? Will Saul come down, as Your servant has heard? O LORD God of Israel, I pray, tell Your servant."

And the LORD said, "He will come down."

12*Then David said, "Will the men of Keilah deliver me and my men into the hand of Saul?"

And the LORD said, "They will deliver *you.*"

13So David and his men, about six hundred, arose and departed from Keilah and went wherever they could go. Then it was told Saul that David had escaped from Keilah; so he halted the expedition.

14And David stayed in strongholds in the wilderness, and remained in the mountains in the

22:20–23 God in His providence gave David two great gifts: the ephod (1 Sam. 23:6) and a priest. He could always seek the will of the Lord as he planned his strategy. You have the Word of God and an interceding High Priest in heaven. Do you seek the mind of the Lord as you make decisions?

CHAPTER 23

23:1, 2 *Guidance.* A gifted leader like David might have been tempted to depend on his experience; instead, he turned to the Lord for the guidance he needed. Even the counsel of his men did not sway him once he knew the mind of the Lord.

23:12 *Treachery.* David rescued the citizens of Keilah, yet they planned to turn him and his men over to Saul! Do not expect everybody you help to appreciate what you have done. Do you appreciate what others have done for you?

23:16–18 *Love.* Although his father was out to kill David, Jonathan was brave enough to visit David and encourage him. That is what friendship is all about (Prov. 17:17). How tragic that Jonathan's hopes for the future were destroyed by his father's sins, but at least Jonathan was willing to be second man.

23:19–23 *Providence.* Ziph belonged to Judah (Josh. 15:24), so the citizens should have been loyal to David. They were obviously trying to curry favor with Saul, and they did not believe that David was their future king. God used an invasion of the Philistines to rescue David when it looked as if Saul's forces would win. No matter what men may do, God works out His purposes, and His providence does not fail.

Wilderness of Ziph. Saul sought him every day, but God did not deliver him into his hand. 15So David saw that Saul had come out to seek his life. And David *was* in the Wilderness of Ziph in a forest.w 16*Then Jonathan, Saul's son, arose and went to David in the woods and strengthened his hand in God. 17And he said to him, "Do not fear, for the hand of Saul my father shall not find you. You shall be king over Israel, and I shall be next to you. Even my father Saul knows that." 18So the two of them made a covenant before the LORD. And David stayed in the woods, and Jonathan went to his own house.

19*Then the Ziphites came up to Saul at Gibeah, saying, "Is David not hiding with us in strongholds in the woods, in the hill of Hachilah, which *is* on the south of Jeshimon? 20Now therefore, O king, come down according to all the desire of your soul to come down; and our part *shall be* to deliver him into the king's hand."

21And Saul said, "Blessed *are* you of the LORD, for you have compassion on me. 22Please go and find out for sure, and see the place where his hideout is, *and* who has seen him there. For I am told he is very crafty. 23See therefore, and take knowledge of all the lurking places where he hides; and come back to me with certainty, and I will go with you. And it shall be, if he is in the land, that I will search for him throughout all the clansx of Judah."

24So they arose and went to Ziph before Saul. But David and his men *were* in the Wilderness of Maon, in the plain on the south of Jeshimon. 25When Saul and his men went to seek *him,* they told David. Therefore he went down to the rock, and stayed in the Wilderness of Maon. And when Saul heard *that,* he pursued David in the Wilderness of Maon. 26Then Saul went on one side of the mountain, and David and his men on the other side of the mountain. So David made haste to get away from Saul, for Saul and his men were encircling David and his men to take them.

27But a messenger came to Saul, saying, "Hurry and come, for the Philistines have invaded the land!" 28Therefore Saul returned from pursuing David, and went against the Philistines; so they called that place the Rock of Escape.y 29Then David went up from there and dwelt in strongholds at En Gedi.

CHAPTER 24

24:1–4 *Circumstances.* People interpret events differently, depending on what they have in their hearts. Saul thought circumstances were safe, so he laid aside his spear and went into the cave. David's men saw a great opportunity for David to avenge himself, but David saw an opportunity to show mercy (Matt. 5:10–12; Rom. 12:17–21). David may have been Saul's enemy, but Saul was not David's enemy (v. 19). Compare verse 5 with 1 Samuel 15:27. Another tear in the robe.

24:5–7 *Conscience.* David's conscience was so tender that he was troubled after he cut off a corner of Saul's robe. He was humiliating the king, and David knew what it meant to respect authority. A sensitive conscience is a great treasure and a valuable guide. Don't lose it!

24 Now* it happened, when Saul had returned from following the Philistines, that it was told him, saying, "Take note! David *is* in the Wilderness of En Gedi." 2Then Saul took three thousand chosen men from all Israel, and went to seek David and his men on the Rocks of the Wild Goats. 3So he came to the sheepfolds by the road, where there *was* a cave; and Saul went in to attend to his needs. (David and his men were staying in the recesses of the cave.) 4Then the men of David said to him, "This is the day of which the LORD said to you, 'Behold, I will deliver your enemy into your hand, that you may do to him as it seems good to you.' " And David arose and secretly cut off a corner of Saul's robe. 5*Now it happened afterward that David's heart troubled him because he had cut Saul's *robe.* 6And he said

23:15 wOr *in Horesh*   23:23 xLiterally *thousands*
23:28 yHebrew *Sela Hammahlekoth*

to his men, "The Lord forbid that I should do this thing to my master, the Lord's anointed, to stretch out my hand against him, seeing he *is* the anointed of the Lord." 7So David restrained his servants with *these* words, and did not allow them to rise against Saul. And Saul got up from the cave and went on *his* way.

8David also arose afterward, went out of the cave, and called out to Saul, saying, "My lord the king!" And when Saul looked behind him, David stooped with his face to the earth, and bowed down. 9And David said to Saul: "Why do you listen to the words of men who say, 'Indeed David seeks your harm'? 10Look, this day your eyes have seen that the Lord delivered you today into my hand in the cave, and *someone* urged *me* to kill you. But *my eye* spared you, and I said, 'I will not stretch out my hand against my lord, for he *is* the Lord's anointed.' 11Moreover, my father, see! Yes, see the corner of your robe in my hand! For in that I cut off the corner of your robe, and did not kill you, know and see that *there is* neither evil nor rebellion in my hand, and I have not sinned against you. Yet you hunt my life to take it. 12Let the Lord judge between you and me, and let the Lord avenge me on you. But my hand shall not be against you. 13As the proverb of the ancients says, 'Wickedness proceeds from the wicked.' But my hand shall not be against you. 14After whom has the king of Israel come out? Whom do you pursue? A dead dog? A flea? 15Therefore let the Lord be judge, and judge between you and me, and see and plead my case, and deliver me out of your hand."

16*So it was, when David had finished speaking these words to Saul, that Saul said, "*Is* this your voice, my son David?" And Saul lifted up his voice and wept. 17Then he said to David: "You *are* more righteous than I; for you have rewarded me with good, whereas I have rewarded you with evil. 18And you have shown this day how you have dealt well with me; for when the Lord delivered me into your hand, you did not kill me. 19For if a man finds his enemy, will he let him get away safely? Therefore may the Lord reward you with good for what you have done to me this day. 20And now I know indeed that you shall surely be king, and that the kingdom of Israel shall be established in your hand. 21Therefore swear now to me by the Lord that you will not cut off my descendants after me, and that you will not destroy my name from my father's house."

22So David swore to Saul. And Saul went home, but David and his men went up to the stronghold.

25 Then* Samuel died; and the Israelites gathered together and lamented for him, and buried him at his home in Ramah. And David arose and went down to the Wilderness of Paran.z

2Now *there was* a man in Maon whose business *was* in Carmel, and the man *was* very rich. He had three thousand sheep and a thousand goats. And he was shearing his sheep in Carmel. 3The name of the man *was* Nabal, and the name of his wife Abigail. And *she was* a woman of good understanding and beautiful appearance; but the man *was* harsh and evil in *his* doings. He *was* of the house of Caleb.

24:16–22 Cowardice. Saul's tears were superficial and his conviction temporary; otherwise, he would have welcomed David and transferred the monarchy to him. He knew that David would be king, but he opposed it as long as he could. His greatest concern was that David spare his descendants, which David promised to do. However, it was Saul's sins, not David's revenge, that destroyed his family.

CHAPTER 25
25:1ff These events remind us we can live on several levels.

25:1 zFollowing Masoretic Text, Syriac, Targum, and Vulgate; Septuagint reads *Maon.*

4When David heard in the wilderness that Nabal was shearing his sheep, 5David sent ten young men; and David said to the young men, "Go up to Carmel, go to Nabal, and greet him in my name. 6And thus you shall say to him who lives in prosperity: 'Peace be to you, peace to your house, and peace to all that you have! 7Now I have heard that you have shearers. Your shepherds were with us, and we did not hurt them, nor was there anything missing from them all the while they were in Carmel. 8Ask your young men, and they will tell you. Therefore let my young men find favor in your eyes, for we come on a feast day. Please give whatever comes to your hand to your servants and to your son David.' "

9So when David's young men came, they spoke to Nabal according to all these words in the name of David, and waited.

10*Then Nabal answered David's servants, and said, "Who is David, and who is the son of Jesse? There are many servants nowadays who break away each one from his master. 11Shall I then take my bread and my water and my meat that I have killed for my shearers, and give it to men when I do not know where they are from?"

12So David's young men turned on their heels and went back; and they came and told him all these words. 13Then David said to his men, "Every man gird on his sword." So every man girded on his sword, and David also girded on his sword. And about four hundred men went with David, and two hundred stayed with the supplies.

14Now one of the young men told Abigail, Nabal's wife, saying, "Look, David sent messengers from the wilderness to greet our master; and he reviled them. 15But the men were very good to us, and we were not hurt, nor did we miss anything as long as we accompanied them, when we were in the fields. 16They were a wall to us both by night and day, all the time we were with them keeping the sheep. 17Now therefore, know and consider what you will do, for harm is determined against our master and against all his household. For he is such a scoundrel*a* that one cannot speak to him."

18Then Abigail made haste and took two hundred loaves of bread, two skins of wine, five sheep already dressed, five seahs of roasted grain, one hundred clusters of raisins, and two hundred cakes of figs, and loaded them on donkeys. 19And she said to her servants, "Go on before me; see, I am coming after you." But she did not tell her husband Nabal.

20So it was, as she rode on the donkey, that she went down under cover of the hill; and there were David and his men, coming down toward her, and she met them. 21*Now David had said, "Surely in vain I have protected all that this fellow has in the wilderness, so that nothing was missed of all that belongs to him. And he has repaid me evil for good. 22May God do so, and more also, to the enemies of David, if I leave one male of all who belong to him by morning light."

23Now when Abigail saw David, she dismounted quickly from the donkey, fell on her face before David, and bowed down to the ground. 24So she fell at his feet and said: "On me, my lord, on me let this iniquity be! And please let your maidservant speak in your ears, and hear the

---

25:10 We can return evil for good. Nabal did that when he refused to share his food with David's men. His name means "fool," and that is exactly what he was (Prov. 17:13).

25:21, 22 We can return evil for evil. David planned to do that before he was stopped. It is the natural thing to do because most of the world lives that way, and our hurt feelings cry out for revenge. And yet David had just shown mercy to Saul who had treated him far worse than had Nabal! How easy it is to lose perspective in the heat of anger.

25:17 aLiterally son of Belial

words of your maidservant. 25Please, let not my lord regard this scoundrel Nabal. For as his name is, so is he: Nabal^b is his name, and folly is with him! But I, your maidservant, did not see the young men of my lord whom you sent. 26Now therefore, my lord, as the LORD lives and as your soul lives, since the LORD has held you back from coming to bloodshed and from avenging yourself with your own hand, now then, let your enemies and those who seek harm for my lord be as Nabal. 27And now this present which your maidservant has brought to my lord, let it be given to the young men who follow my lord. 28*Please forgive the trespass of your maidservant. For the LORD will certainly make for my lord an enduring house, because my lord fights the battles of the LORD, and evil is not found in you throughout your days. 29Yet a man has risen to pursue you and seek your life, but the life of my lord shall be bound in the bundle of the living with the LORD your God; and the lives of your enemies He shall sling out, as from the pocket of a sling. 30And it shall come to pass, when the LORD has done for my lord according to all the good that He has spoken concerning you, and has appointed you ruler over Israel, 31that this will be no grief to you, nor offense of heart to my lord, either that you have shed blood without cause, or that my lord has avenged himself. But when the LORD has dealt well with my lord, then remember your maidservant."

32Then David said to Abigail: "Blessed is the LORD God of Israel, who sent you this day to meet me! 33And blessed is your advice and blessed are you, because you have kept me this day from coming to bloodshed and from avenging myself with my own hand. 34For indeed, as the LORD God of Israel lives, who has kept me back from hurting you, unless you had hurried and come to meet me, surely by morning light no males would have been left to Nabal!" 35So David received from her hand what she had brought him, and said to her, "Go up in peace to your house. See, I have heeded your voice and respected your person."

36Now Abigail went to Nabal, and there he was, holding a feast in his house, like the feast of a king. And Nabal's heart was merry within him, for he was very drunk; therefore she told him nothing, little or much, until morning light. 37So it was, in the morning, when the wine had gone from Nabal, and his wife had told him these things, that his heart died within him, and he became like a stone. 38Then it happened, after about ten days, that the LORD struck Nabal, and he died.

39So when David heard that Nabal was dead, he said, "Blessed be the LORD, who has pleaded the cause of my reproach from the hand of Nabal, and has kept His servant from evil! For the LORD has returned the wickedness of Nabal on his own head."

And David sent and proposed to Abigail, to take her as his wife. 40When the servants of David had come to Abigail at Carmel, they spoke to her saying, "David sent us to you, to ask you to become his wife."

41Then she arose, bowed her face to the earth, and said, "Here is your maidservant, a servant to wash the feet of the servants of my lord." 42So Abigail rose in haste and rode on a donkey,

25:28–31 We can overcome evil with good. God used Abigail to prevent David from becoming a murderer. She reminded David of Nabal's true character (vv. 23–25) and of David's efforts to do God's work (vv. 26–29). She also told him he would suffer when he remembered the incident in the future (vv. 30–31). This is good counsel to heed the next time you consider seeking revenge. Ponder Proverbs 20:22 and 24:29.

25:25 ^bLiterally *Fool*

attended by five of her maidens; and she followed the messengers of David, and became his wife. [43]David also took Ahinoam of Jezreel, and so both of them were his wives.

[44]But Saul had given Michal his daughter, David's wife, to Palti[c] the son of Laish, who *was* from Gallim.

26 Now* the Ziphites came to Saul at Gibeah, saying, "Is David not hiding in the hill of Hachilah, opposite Jeshimon?" [2]Then Saul arose and went down to the Wilderness of Ziph, having three thousand chosen men of Israel with him, to seek David in the Wilderness of Ziph. [3]And Saul encamped in the hill of Hachilah, which *is* opposite Jeshimon, by the road. But David stayed in the wilderness, and he saw that Saul came after him into the wilderness. [4]David therefore sent out spies, and understood that Saul had indeed come.

[5]So David arose and came to the place where Saul had encamped. And David saw the place where Saul lay, and Abner the son of Ner, the commander of his army. Now Saul lay within the camp, with the people encamped all around him. [6]Then David answered, and said to Ahimelech the Hittite and to Abishai the son of Zeruiah, brother of Joab, saying, "Who will go down with me to Saul in the camp?"

And Abishai said, "I will go down with you."

[7]*So David and Abishai came to the people by night; and there Saul lay sleeping within the camp, with his spear stuck in the ground by his head. And Abner and the people lay all around him. [8]Then Abishai said to David, "God has delivered your enemy into your hand this day. Now therefore, please, let me strike him at once with the spear, right to the earth; and I will not *have to strike* him a second time!"

[9]But David said to Abishai, "Do not destroy him; for who can stretch out his hand against the LORD's anointed, and be guiltless?" [10]David said furthermore, "As the LORD lives, the LORD shall strike him, or his day shall come to die, or he shall go out to battle and perish. [11]The LORD forbid that I should stretch out my hand against the LORD's anointed. But please, take now the spear and the jug of water that *are* by his head, and let us go." [12]So David took the spear and the jug of water *by* Saul's head, and they got away; and no man saw or knew *it* or awoke. For they *were* all asleep, because a deep sleep from the LORD had fallen on them.

[13]*Now David went over to the other side, and stood on the top of a hill afar off, a great distance *being* between them. [14]And David called out to the people and to Abner the son of Ner, saying, "Do you not answer, Abner?"

Then Abner answered and said, "Who *are* you, calling out to the king?"

[15]So David said to Abner, "*Are* you not a man? And who *is* like you in Israel? Why then have you not guarded your lord the king? For one of the people came in to destroy your lord the king.

26:1–4 Saul's tearful words did not mean much, for he continued to pursue David. In His mercy, God gave Saul another opportunity to repent, but the king's heart was too hard. Even while he slept, Saul kept his spear next to him to remind everybody that he was king. David took the spear from him, a significant action.

26:7–12 Abishai, David's nephew, was a brave man; but brave men are not always wise. He said, "You missed your first opportunity, so don't miss this one!" But David knew that God's hand, not his own, would have to strike Saul.

26:13–25 David's speech was designed to make Saul examine his heart. Was Saul chasing David because *God* told him to do so, or because he believed the lies his flattering officers told about David? Twice before, Saul had said "I have sinned" (1 Sam. 15:24, 30), but his words were not sincere then or on this occasion. He was correct when he called himself a fool. He was a fool in the way he treated Jonathan, David, Samuel, his army, his nation, and his God. He lived like a fool, and he died like a fool. (See Proverbs 26:11–12.)

CHAPTER 26

25:44 [c]Spelled *Paltiel* in 2 Samuel 3:15

"I Have Sinned!"—King Saul is not the only one who made this confession. Pharaoh said it (Exod. 9:27) and so did Balaam (Num. 22:34), Achan (Josh. 7:20), David (2 Sam. 12:13; 24:10, 17; Ps. 51:4), Judas (Matt. 27:4), and the prodigal son (Luke 15:18, 21). Which of these men do you think were really sincere?

16This thing that you have done *is* not good. *As* the LORD lives, you deserve to die, because you have not guarded your master, the LORD's anointed. And now see where the king's spear *is,* and the jug of water that *was* by his head."

17Then Saul knew David's voice, and said, "*Is* that your voice, my son David?"

David said, *"It is* my voice, my lord, O king." 18And he said, "Why does my lord thus pursue his servant? For what have I done, or what evil *is* in my hand? 19Now therefore, please, let my lord the king hear the words of his servant: If the LORD has stirred you up against me, let Him accept an offering. But if *it is* the children of men, *may* they *be* cursed before the LORD, for they have driven me out this day from sharing in the inheritance of the LORD, saying, 'Go, serve other gods.' 20So now, do not let my blood fall to the earth before the face of the LORD. For the king of Israel has come out to seek a flea, as when one hunts a partridge in the mountains."

21Then Saul said, "I have sinned. Return, my son David. For I will harm you no more, because my life was precious in your eyes this day. Indeed I have played the fool and erred exceedingly."

22And David answered and said, "Here is the king's spear. Let one of the young men come over and get it. 23May the LORD repay every man *for* his righteousness and his faithfulness; for the LORD delivered you into *my* hand today, but I would not stretch out my hand against the LORD's anointed. 24And indeed, as your life was valued much this day in my eyes, so let my life be valued much in the eyes of the LORD, and let Him deliver me out of all tribulation."

25Then Saul said to David, *"May* you *be* blessed, my son David! You shall both do great things and also still prevail."

So David went on his way, and Saul returned to his place.

27 And* David said in his heart, "Now I shall perish someday by the hand of Saul. *There is* nothing better for me than that I should speedily escape to the land of the Philistines; and Saul will despair of me, to seek me anymore in any part of Israel. So I shall escape out of his hand." 2*Then David arose and went over with the six hundred men who *were* with him to Achish the son of Maoch, king of Gath. 3So David dwelt with Achish at Gath, he and his men, each man with his household, *and* David with his two wives, Ahinoam the Jezreelitess, and Abigail the Carmelitess, Nabal's widow. 4And it was told Saul that David had fled to Gath; so he sought him no more.

5Then David said to Achish, "If I have now found favor in your eyes, let them give me a place in some town in the country, that I may dwell there. For why should your servant dwell in the royal city with you?" 6So Achish gave him Ziklag that day. Therefore Ziklag has belonged to the kings of Judah to this day. 7Now the time that David dwelt in the country of the Philistines was one full year and four months.

8And David and his men went up and raided the Geshurites, the Girzites,d and the Amalekites. For those nations *were* the inhabitants of the land from of old, as you go to Shur, even as far as the land of Egypt. 9Whenever David attacked the

---

❝*When the outlook is discouraging, try the uplook***❞**

CHAPTER 27

27:1 David won a great victory over Saul, only to be overwhelmed by despair. Such feelings are not unusual; you cannot have mountaintops without valleys. However, when you are feeling low, it is a dangerous thing to "talk to yourself" and make important decisions. David should have talked to the Lord. He and Abiathar could have sought the mind of God together.

27:2–12 David made some foolish decisions because he did not pause to inquire of the Lord. He stopped serving God and started thinking about survival: "For whoever desires to save his life will lose it" (Mark 8:35). He trusted the enemy for protection and did not trust the Lord. As a result, he had to scheme, kill, and lie to survive.

(continued)

27:8 *d*Or *Gezrites*

(continued from previous page)

When you are discouraged, ask a trusted Christian friend to pray with you, and seek the Lord's direction. Take time to talk about your feelings with your friend. You will gain a clearer perspective. *Make no impulsive decisions about significant matters.* Follow this advice: "Wait on the LORD; be of good courage, and He shall strengthen your heart" (Ps. 27:14).

CHAPTER 28

28:1–10 Saul had been fighting the wrong enemy for so long that when the real enemy appeared, the king was unprepared. God was not with him, and prayer was not answered (Prov. 1:20–33). When Saul began his reign, it was "the dawning of the day" (1 Sam. 9:26), but now he was walking in the darkness. Saul did not disguise himself (v. 8); *he revealed his true self.* Throughout his reign, he had been pretending, and the truth was coming out.

28:11–17 Depending on demonic forces, the medium planned to impersonate Samuel, but the Lord permitted Samuel to appear. The friend Saul grieved in life, he called for in death. Too late do we learn to appreciate those who tried to help us. Too late do we humble ourselves.

land, he left neither man nor woman alive, but took away the sheep, the oxen, the donkeys, the camels, and the apparel, and returned and came to Achish. ¹⁰Then Achish would say, "Where have you made a raid today?" And David would say, "Against the southern *area* of Judah, or against the southern *area* of the Jerahmeelites, or against the southern *area* of the Kenites." ¹¹David would save neither man nor woman alive, to bring *news* to Gath, saying, "Lest they should inform on us, saying, 'Thus David did.' " And thus *was* his behavior all the time he dwelt in the country of the Philistines. ¹²So Achish believed David, saying, "He has made his people Israel utterly abhor him; therefore he will be my servant forever."

28 Now* it happened in those days that the Philistines gathered their armies together for war, to fight with Israel. And Achish said to David, "You assuredly know that you will go out with me to battle, you and your men."

²So David said to Achish, "Surely you know what your servant can do."

And Achish said to David, "Therefore I will make you one of my chief guardians forever."

³Now Samuel had died, and all Israel had lamented for him and buried him in Ramah, in his own city. And Saul had put the mediums and the spiritists out of the land.

⁴Then the Philistines gathered together, and came and encamped at Shunem. So Saul gathered all Israel together, and they encamped at Gilboa. ⁵When Saul saw the army of the Philistines, he was afraid, and his heart trembled greatly. ⁶And when Saul inquired of the LORD, the LORD did not answer him, either by dreams or by Urim or by the prophets.

⁷Then Saul said to his servants, "Find me a woman who is a medium, that I may go to her and inquire of her."

And his servants said to him, "In fact, *there is* a woman who is a medium at En Dor."

⁸So Saul disguised himself and put on other clothes, and he went, and two men with him; and they came to the woman by night. And he said, "Please conduct a séance for me, and bring up for me the one I shall name to you."

⁹Then the woman said to him, "Look, you know what Saul has done, how he has cut off the mediums and the spiritists from the land. Why then do you lay a snare for my life, to cause me to die?"

¹⁰And Saul swore to her by the LORD, saying, "*As* the LORD lives, no punishment shall come upon you for this thing."

¹¹*Then the woman said, "Whom shall I bring up for you?"

And he said, "Bring up Samuel for me."

¹²When the woman saw Samuel, she cried out with a loud voice. And the woman spoke to Saul, saying, "Why have you deceived me? For you *are* Saul!"

¹³And the king said to her, "Do not be afraid. What did you see?"

Christians and the Occult—God forbade Israel to dabble in the occult (Exod. 22:18; Lev. 19:31; 20:6; Deut. 18:9–14), and these warnings should be heeded today, too. Sorcery is one of the works of the flesh that must be rejected (Gal. 5:20). Both Peter (Acts 8:9ff.) and Paul (Acts 13:6ff.) had harsh words for sorcerers. Seemingly innocent games that border on the occult can open the door to serious problems. As for seances, read what Isaiah 8:19 has to say.

And the woman said to Saul, "I saw a spirit[e] ascending out of the earth."

[14]So he said to her, "What *is* his form?"

And she said, "An old man is coming up, and he *is* covered with a mantle." And Saul perceived that it *was* Samuel, and he stooped with *his* face to the ground and bowed down.

[15]Now Samuel said to Saul, "Why have you disturbed me by bringing me up?"

And Saul answered, "I am deeply distressed; for the Philistines make war against me, and God has departed from me and does not answer me anymore, neither by prophets nor by dreams. Therefore I have called you, that you may reveal to me what I should do."

[16]Then Samuel said: "So why do you ask me, seeing the LORD has departed from you and has become your enemy? [17]And the LORD has done for Himself[f] as He spoke by me. For the LORD has torn the kingdom out of your hand and given it to your neighbor, David. [18]*Because you did not obey the voice of the LORD nor execute His fierce wrath upon Amalek, therefore the LORD has done this thing to you this day. [19]Moreover the LORD will also deliver Israel with you into the hand of the Philistines. And tomorrow you and your sons *will be* with me. The LORD will also deliver the army of Israel into the hand of the Philistines."

[20]Immediately Saul fell full length on the ground, and was dreadfully afraid because of the words of Samuel. And there was no strength in him, for he had eaten no food all day or all night.

[21]And the woman came to Saul and saw that he was severely troubled, and said to him, "Look, your maidservant has obeyed your voice, and I have put my life in my hands and heeded the words which you spoke to me. [22]Now therefore, please, heed also the voice of your maidservant, and let me set a piece of bread before you; and eat, that you may have strength when you go on *your* way."

[23]But he refused and said, "I will not eat."

So his servants, together with the woman, urged him; and he heeded their voice. Then he arose from the ground and sat on the bed. [24]Now the woman had a fatted calf in the house, and she hastened to kill it. And she took flour and kneaded *it*, and baked unleavened bread from it. [25]So she brought *it* before Saul and his servants, and they ate. Then they rose and went away that night.

29 Then* the Philistines gathered together all their armies at Aphek, and the Israelites encamped by a fountain which *is* in Jezreel. [2]And the lords of the Philistines passed in review by hundreds and by thousands, but David and his men passed in review at the rear with Achish. [3]Then the princes of the Philistines said, "What *are* these Hebrews *doing here?*"

And Achish said to the princes of the Philistines, "*Is* this not David, the servant of Saul king of Israel, who has been with me these days, or these years? And to this day I have found no fault in him since he defected *to me.*"

[4]But the princes of the Philistines were angry with him; so the princes of the Philistines said to him, "Make this fellow return, that he may go back to the place which you have appointed for him, and do not let him go down with us to battle,

28:18, 19 Saul's disobedience in the past led to darkness in the present and defeat and death in the future. When God gave him opportunities to repent, he ignored them. He did not "seek the LORD while He may be found" (Isa. 55:6).

CHAPTER 29

29:1–4 David was out of place, but God in His mercy cared for him. This is an encouragement to us when we sin, but it must not become an excuse for sin. That would be tempting God.

The king never once detected what was going on, so David must have been a gifted actor. However, what value is there in being successful at deception? Hypocrisy and lying destroyed King Saul.

28:13 [e]Hebrew *elohim*   28:17 [f]Or *him,* that is, David

29:5–7 The Lord used the song that got David into trouble with Saul (1 Sam. 18:7–9) to get him out of trouble with the Philistines. Saul was not David's enemy, and David did not want to meet him on the battlefield and fight against his own people. But when you fraternize with the enemy, you create difficult problems. Let us be grateful for Psalm 103:10–14.

lest in the battle he become our adversary. For with what could he reconcile himself to his master, if not with the heads of these men? 5*Is this not David, of whom they sang to one another in dances, saying:

'Saul has slain his thousands,
And David his ten thousands'?"g

6Then Achish called David and said to him, "Surely, as the LORD lives, you have been upright, and your going out and your coming in with me in the army is good in my sight. For to this day I have not found evil in you since the day of your coming to me. Nevertheless the lords do not favor you. 7Therefore return now, and go in peace, that you may not displease the lords of the Philistines."

8So David said to Achish, "But what have I done? And to this day what have you found in your servant as long as I have been with you, that I may not go and fight against the enemies of my lord the king?"

9Then Achish answered and said to David, "I know that you are as good in my sight as an angel of God; nevertheless the princes of the Philistines have said, 'He shall not go up with us to the battle.' 10Now therefore, rise early in the morning with your master's servants who have come with you.h And as soon as you are up early in the morning and have light, depart."

11So David and his men rose early to depart in the morning, to return to the land of the Philistines. And the Philistines went up to Jezreel.

CHAPTER 30

30:1–3 Relieved that he had been discharged from the war, David returned to Ziklag only to find tragedy. There are times when one problem follows hard on another. Had Saul slain the Amalekites as God commanded (1 Sam. 15), this raid would not have occurred. *Our* disobedience can cause problems for *others*.

30:6–8 A crisis does not make a person: it shows what a person is made of. Like his men, David wept and sorrowed, but unlike some of his men, he did not look for a scapegoat. In times of crisis, express your feelings honestly, but do not look for somebody to blame. Rather, get your strength from the Lord (v. 6) and seek His will (vv. 7–8). He is in complete control.

30 Now* it happened, when David and his men came to Ziklag, on the third day, that the Amalekites had invaded the South and Ziklag, attacked Ziklag and burned it with fire, 2and had taken captive the women and those who were there, from small to great; they did not kill anyone, but carried them away and went their way. 3So David and his men came to the city, and there it was, burned with fire; and their wives, their sons, and their daughters had been taken captive. 4Then David and the people who were with him lifted up their voices and wept, until they had no more power to weep. 5And David's two wives, Ahinoam the Jezreelitess, and Abigail the widow of Nabal the Carmelite, had been taken captive. 6*Now David was greatly distressed, for the people spoke of stoning him, because the soul of all the people was grieved, every man for his sons and his daughters. But David strengthened himself in the LORD his God.

7Then David said to Abiathar the priest, Ahimelech's son, "Please bring the ephod here to me." And Abiathar brought the ephod to David. 8So David inquired of the LORD, saying, "Shall I pursue this troop? Shall I overtake them?"

And He answered him, "Pursue, for you shall surely overtake them and without fail recover all."

9So David went, he and the six hundred men who were with him, and came to the Brook Besor,

---

29:5 gCompare 1 Samuel 18:7   29:10 hFollowing Masoretic Text, Targum, and Vulgate; Septuagint adds *and go to the place which I have selected for you there; and set no bothersome word in your heart, for you are good before me. And rise on your way.*

where those stayed who were left behind. ¹⁰But David pursued, he and four hundred men; for two hundred stayed *behind*, who were so weary that they could not cross the Brook Besor.

¹¹Then they found an Egyptian in the field, and brought him to David; and they gave him bread and he ate, and they let him drink water. ¹²And they gave him a piece of a cake of figs and two clusters of raisins. So when he had eaten, his strength came back to him; for he had eaten no bread nor drunk water for three days and three nights. ¹³*Then David said to him, "To whom do you *belong*, and where *are* you from?"

And he said, "I *am* a young man from Egypt, servant of an Amalekite; and my master left me behind, because three days ago I fell sick. ¹⁴We made an invasion of the southern *area* of the Cherethites, in the *territory* which *belongs* to Judah, and of the southern *area* of Caleb; and we burned Ziklag with fire."

¹⁵And David said to him, "Can you take me down to this troop?"

So he said, "Swear to me by God that you will neither kill me nor deliver me into the hands of my master, and I will take you down to this troop."

¹⁶And when he had brought him down, there they were, spread out over all the land, eating and drinking and dancing, because of all the great spoil which they had taken from the land of the Philistines and from the land of Judah. ¹⁷Then David attacked them from twilight until the evening of the next day. Not a man of them escaped, except four hundred young men who rode on camels and fled. ¹⁸So David recovered all that the Amalekites had carried away, and David rescued his two wives. ¹⁹And nothing of theirs was lacking, either small or great, sons or daughters, spoil or anything which they had taken from them; David recovered all. ²⁰Then David took all the flocks and herds they had driven before those *other* livestock, and said, "This *is* David's spoil."

²¹Now David came to the two hundred men who had been so weary that they could not follow David, whom they also had made to stay at the Brook Besor. So they went out to meet David and to meet the people who *were* with him. And when David came near the people, he greeted them. ²²Then all the wicked and worthless men[i] of those who went with David answered and said, "Because they did not go with us, we will not give them *any* of the spoil that we have recovered, except for every man's wife and children, that they may lead *them* away and depart."

²³But David said, "My brethren, you shall not do so with what the LORD has given us, who has preserved us and delivered into our hand the troop that came against us. ²⁴For who will heed you in this matter? But as his part *is* who goes down to the battle, so *shall* his part *be* who stays by the supplies; they shall share alike." ²⁵So it was, from that day forward; he made it a statute and an ordinance for Israel to this day.

²⁶Now when David came to Ziklag, he sent *some* of the spoil to the elders of Judah, to his friends, saying, "Here is a present for you from the spoil of the enemies of the LORD"— ²⁷to *those* who *were* in Bethel, *those* who *were* in Ramoth of the South, *those* who *were* in Jattir, ²⁸*those*

30:13–31 God uses the weak things of the world, even a sick boy who was left to die. When we do the possible, God does the impossible. The tragedy became victory, with profit for everybody.

30:22 [i]Literally *men of Belial*

who *were* in Aroer, *those* who *were* in Siphmoth, *those* who *were* in Eshtemoa, 29*those* who *were* in Rachal, *those* who *were* in the cities of the Je-rahmeelites, *those* who *were* in the cities of the Kenites, 30*those* who *were* in Hormah, *those* who *were* in Chorashan,ʲ *those* who *were* in Athach, 31*those* who *were* in Hebron, and to all the places where David himself and his men were accustomed to rove.

CHAPTER 31

31:1 Defeat. David won a battle and divided the spoils; Saul lost a battle and was stripped by the enemy. Gideon camped near Gilboa before his great victory over the Midianites (Judg. 7:1), but Gilboa would forever be associated with the defeat of Saul. Are you leaving behind monuments to victory or to defeat?

31:2–5 Death. Death reigned over Israel: their soldiers died, Saul and his armorbearer died, and Saul's sons died. Such is the high cost of one man's rebellion:."For to be carnally minded is death" (Rom. 8:6).

31:8–10 Disgrace. Had Israel won, God would have been glorified. Instead, the pagan idols were honored, and the dead were desecrated. It is bad enough to die in a losing battle, but not to be buried was an even greater disgrace.

31:11–13 Devotion. The brave men of Jabesh Gilead risked their lives to give Saul and his sons a decent burial. After all, Saul had rescued their city forty years before, and they were showing their gratitude (1 Sam. 11:1–11). David later honored them for their feat (2 Sam. 2:4–7).

31 Now* the Philistines fought against Israel; and the men of Israel fled from before the Philistines, and fell slain on Mount Gilboa. 2*Then the Philistines followed hard after Saul and his sons. And the Philistines killed Jonathan, Abinadab, and Malchishua, Saul's sons. 3The battle became fierce against Saul. The archers hit him, and he was severely wounded by the archers.

4Then Saul said to his armorbearer, "Draw your sword, and thrust me through with it, lest these uncircumcised men come and thrust me through and abuse me."

But his armorbearer would not, for he was greatly afraid. Therefore Saul took a sword and fell on it. 5And when his armorbearer saw that Saul was dead, he also fell on his sword, and died with him. 6So Saul, his three sons, his armorbearer, and all his men died together that same day.

7And when the men of Israel who *were* on the other side of the valley, and *those* who *were* on the other side of the Jordan, saw that the men of Israel had fled and that Saul and his sons were dead, they forsook the cities and fled; and the Philistines came and dwelt in them. 8*So it happened the next day, when the Philistines came to strip the slain, that they found Saul and his three sons fallen on Mount Gilboa. 9And they cut off his head and stripped off his armor, and sent *word* throughout the land of the Philistines, to proclaim *it in* the temple of their idols and among the people. 10Then they put his armor in the temple of the Ashtoreths, and they fastened his body to the wall of Beth Shan.ᵏ

11*Now when the inhabitants of Jabesh Gilead heard what the Philistines had done to Saul, 12all the valiant men arose and traveled all night, and took the body of Saul and the bodies of his sons from the wall of Beth Shan; and they came to Jabesh and burned them there. 13Then they took their bones and buried *them* under the tamarisk tree at Jabesh, and fasted seven days.

30:30 ʲOr *Borashan*   31:10 ᵏSpelled *Beth Shean* in Joshua 17:11 and elsewhere

2 SAMUEL

David the king is the central figure in this book that records his national victories (chaps. 1—10) and his personal defeats (chaps. 11—24). The turning point is his sin of adultery (chap. 11), the tragic consequences of which affected both his family and the nation. David confessed his sins, submitted to God's discipline, and spent the closing years of his reign preparing for the building of the temple. This book is an exposition of Proverbs 14:34 and 28:13.

1 Now it came to pass after the death of Saul, when David had returned from the slaughter of the Amalekites, and David had stayed two days in Ziklag, ²on the third day, behold, it happened that a man came from Saul's camp with his clothes torn and dust on his head. So it was, when he came to David, that he fell to the ground and prostrated himself.

³And David said to him, "Where have you come from?"

So he said to him, "I have escaped from the camp of Israel."

⁴*Then David said to him, "How did the matter go? Please tell me."

And he answered, "The people have fled from the battle, many of the people are fallen and dead, and Saul and Jonathan his son are dead also."

⁵So David said to the young man who told him, "How do you know that Saul and Jonathan his son are dead?"

⁶Then the young man who told him said, "As I happened by chance *to be* on Mount Gilboa, there was Saul, leaning on his spear; and indeed the chariots and horsemen followed hard after him. ⁷Now when he looked behind him, he saw me and called to me. And I answered, 'Here I am.' ⁸*And he said to me, 'Who *are* you?' So I answered him, 'I *am* an Amalekite.' ⁹He said to me again, 'Please stand over me and kill me, for anguish has come upon me, but my life still *remains* in me.' ¹⁰So I stood over him and killed him, because I was sure that he could not live after he had fallen. And I took the crown that *was* on his head and the bracelet that *was* on his arm, and have brought them here to my lord."

¹¹Therefore David took hold of his own clothes and tore them, and *so did* all the men who *were* with him. ¹²And they mourned and wept and fasted until evening for Saul and for Jonathan his son, for the people of the LORD and for the house of Israel, because they had fallen by the sword.

¹³Then David said to the young man who told him, "Where *are* you from?"

And he answered, "I *am* the son of an alien, an Amalekite."

¹⁴So David said to him, "How was it you were not afraid to put forth your hand to destroy the LORD's anointed?" ¹⁵Then David called one of the young men and said, "Go near, *and* execute him!" And he struck him so that he died. ¹⁶So David said to him, "Your blood *is* on your own head, for your own mouth has testified against you, saying, 'I have killed the LORD's anointed.'"

¹⁷Then David lamented with this lamentation over Saul and over Jonathan his son, ¹⁸and he told *them* to teach the children of Judah *the Song*

CHAPTER 1

1:4 Saul began his career *standing* (1 Sam. 10:23), but he closed his career *falling* (vv. 4, 10, 12, 19, 25, 27): "Therefore let him who thinks he stands take heed lest he fall" (1 Cor. 10:12). Natural abilities and great opportunities do not guarantee success. Saul was head and shoulders above everybody else, but he was not heart and soul yielded to God. Robert Murray M'Cheyne said, "It is not great talents God blesses so much as great likeness to Jesus."

1:8–18 The Amalekite tried to deceive David and win his favor, for his account contradicts the inspired record (1 Sam. 31). He did not know David! Saul was not David's enemy, so David could not rejoice over Israel's inglorious defeat. Do you have enemies whose sorrows make you happy? If you do, carefully consider Proverbs 24:17 and Romans 12:14–15.

1:19–21 David said only good things about Saul and praised him as a mighty warrior. Saul's treatment of David had been diabolical, but David's treatment of Saul was always kind and considerate (Lev. 19:18; Prov. 20:22; 24:29). Saul listened to men's lies and lost his crown; David obeyed God's Word and gained a kingdom.

of the Bow; indeed *it is* written in the Book of Jasher:

19*"The beauty of Israel is slain on your high
      places!
      How the mighty have fallen!
20   Tell *it* not in Gath,
      Proclaim *it* not in the streets of Ashkelon—
      Lest the daughters of the Philistines rejoice,
      Lest the daughters of the uncircumcised
         triumph.

21 "O mountains of Gilboa,
      Let there be no dew nor rain upon you,
      Nor fields of offerings.
      For the shield of the mighty is cast away
         there!
      The shield of Saul, not anointed with oil.
22   From the blood of the slain,
      From the fat of the mighty,
      The bow of Jonathan did not turn back,
      And the sword of Saul did not return empty.

23 "Saul and Jonathan *were* beloved and
         pleasant in their lives,
      And in their death they were not divided;
      They were swifter than eagles,
      They were stronger than lions.

24 "O daughters of Israel, weep over Saul,
      Who clothed you in scarlet, with luxury;
      Who put ornaments of gold on your apparel.

25 "How the mighty have fallen in the midst of
         the battle!
      Jonathan *was* slain in your high places.
26   I am distressed for you, my brother
         Jonathan;
      You have been very pleasant to me;
      Your love to me was wonderful,
      Surpassing the love of women.

27 "How the mighty have fallen,
      And the weapons of war perished!"

CHAPTER 2

2:1–7 David's tribe of Judah anointed him king and set up his headquarters in Hebron. But Abner, Saul's cousin (1 Sam. 14:50) and commander of his army, made Saul's son king in open defiance of God's will. Whenever we fail to submit to God's will, we cause division and bring destruction (James 3:13—4:1).

2 It* happened after this that David inquired of the LORD, saying, "Shall I go up to any of the cities of Judah?"
   And the LORD said to him, "Go up."
   David said, "Where shall I go up?"
   And He said, "To Hebron."
   2So David went up there, and his two wives also, Ahinoam the Jezreelitess, and Abigail the widow of Nabal the Carmelite. 3And David brought up the men who *were* with him, every man with his household. So they dwelt in the cities of Hebron.
   4Then the men of Judah came, and there they anointed David king over the house of Judah. And they told David, saying, "The men of Jabesh Gilead *were the ones* who buried Saul." 5So David sent messengers to the men of Jabesh Gilead, and said to them, "You *are* blessed of the LORD, for you have shown this kindness to your lord, to Saul, and have buried him. 6And now may the LORD show kindness and truth to you. I also will repay you this kindness, because you have done this thing. 7Now therefore, let your hands be strengthened, and be valiant; for your master Saul is dead, and also the house of Judah has anointed me king over them."
   8But* Abner the son of Ner, commander of

2:8–23 Three murders will occur before David becomes king of all the people: Asahel's (chap. 2), Abner's (chap. 3) and Ishbosheth's (chap. 4). All of that blood would not have been shed if the leaders had only submitted to God's chosen king instead of seeking their own advantage. Joab and Asahel were related to David (1 Chron. 2:16), so there were both family and national considerations. Had everybody put the glory of God and the good of the nation first, tragedies would have been avoided.

Saul's army, took Ishbosheth[a] the son of Saul and brought him over to Mahanaim; 9and he made him king over Gilead, over the Ashurites, over Jezreel, over Ephraim, over Benjamin, and over all Israel. 10Ishbosheth, Saul's son, *was* forty years old when he began to reign over Israel, and he reigned two years. Only the house of Judah followed David. 11And the time that David was king in Hebron over the house of Judah was seven years and six months.

12Now Abner the son of Ner, and the servants of Ishbosheth the son of Saul, went out from Mahanaim to Gibeon. 13And Joab the son of Zeruiah, and the servants of David, went out and met them by the pool of Gibeon. So they sat down, one on one side of the pool and the other on the other side of the pool. 14Then Abner said to Joab, "Let the young men now arise and compete before us."

And Joab said, "Let them arise."

15So they arose and went over by number, twelve from Benjamin, *followers* of Ishbosheth the son of Saul, and twelve from the servants of David. 16And each one grasped his opponent by the head and *thrust* his sword in his opponent's side; so they fell down together. Therefore that place was called the Field of Sharp Swords,[b] which *is* in Gibeon. 17So there was a very fierce battle that day, and Abner and the men of Israel were beaten before the servants of David.

18Now the three sons of Zeruiah were there: Joab and Abishai and Asahel. And Asahel *was as* fleet of foot as a wild gazelle. 19So Asahel pursued Abner, and in going he did not turn to the right hand or to the left from following Abner. 20Then Abner looked behind him and said, "*Are* you Asahel?"

He answered, "I *am.*"

21And Abner said to him, "Turn aside to your right hand or to your left, and lay hold on one of the young men and take his armor for yourself." But Asahel would not turn aside from following him. 22So Abner said again to Asahel, "Turn aside from following me. Why should I strike you to the ground? How then could I face your brother Joab?" 23However, he refused to turn aside. Therefore Abner struck him in the stomach with the blunt end of the spear, so that the spear came out of his back; and he fell down there and died on the spot. So it was *that* as many as came to the place where Asahel fell down and died, stood still.

24Joab and Abishai also pursued Abner. And the sun was going down when they came to the hill of Ammah, which *is* before Giah by the road to the Wilderness of Gibeon. 25Now the children of Benjamin gathered together behind Abner and became a unit, and took their stand on top of a hill. 26Then Abner called to Joab and said, "Shall the sword devour forever? Do you not know that it will be bitter in the latter end? How long will it be then until you tell the people to return from pursuing their brethren?"

27And Joab said, "*As* God lives, unless you had spoken, surely then by morning all the people would have given up pursuing their brethren." 28So Joab blew a trumpet; and all the people stood still and did not pursue Israel anymore, nor did they fight anymore. 29Then Abner and his men

---

2:8 [a]Called *Esh-Baal* in 1 Chronicles 8:33 and 9:39
2:16 [b]Hebrew *Helkath Hazzurim*

went on all that night through the plain, crossed over the Jordan, and went through all Bithron; and they came to Mahanaim.

30So Joab returned from pursuing Abner. And when he had gathered all the people together, there were missing of David's servants nineteen men and Asahel. 31But the servants of David had struck down, of Benjamin and Abner's men, three hundred and sixty men who died. 32Then they took up Asahel and buried him in his father's tomb, which *was in* Bethlehem. And Joab and his men went all night, and they came to Hebron at daybreak.

CHAPTER 3

3:1 Trusting in the Lord, David went "from strength to strength" (Ps. 84:7). He was God's anointed and knew that God would fulfill His promise and make him king over all Israel. When you walk by faith, you can wait on Him.

3:6–11 Abner also grew in strength (v. 6), not the strength of the Lord but political power. He had more authority than the king, for he had made Ishbosheth king. Abner's use of power to please himself was his downfall.

3 Now* there was a long war between the house of Saul and the house of David. But David grew stronger and stronger, and the house of Saul grew weaker and weaker.

2Sons were born to David in Hebron: His first-born was Amnon by Ahinoam the Jezreelitess; 3his second, Chileab, by Abigail the widow of Nabal the Carmelite; the third, Absalom the son of Maacah, the daughter of Talmai, king of Geshur; 4the fourth, Adonijah the son of Haggith; the fifth, Shephatiah the son of Abital; 5and the sixth, Ithream, by David's wife Eglah. These were born to David in Hebron.

6*Now it was so, while there was war between the house of Saul and the house of David, that Abner was strengthening *his hold* on the house of Saul. 7And Saul had a concubine, whose name *was* Rizpah, the daughter of Aiah. So *Ishbosheth* said to Abner, "Why have you gone in to my father's concubine?"

8Then Abner became very angry at the words of Ishbosheth, and said, "*Am* I a dog's head that belongs to Judah? Today I show loyalty to the house of Saul your father, to his brothers, and to his friends, and have not delivered you into the hand of David; and you charge me today with a fault concerning this woman? 9May God do so to Abner, and more also, if I do not do for David as the LORD has sworn to him— 10to transfer the kingdom from the house of Saul, and set up the throne of David over Israel and over Judah, from Dan to Beersheba." 11And he could not answer Abner another word, because he feared him.

12Then Abner sent messengers on his behalf to David, saying, "Whose *is* the land?" saying *also*, "Make your covenant with me, and indeed my hand *shall be* with you to bring all Israel to you."

13And *David* said, "Good, I will make a covenant with you. But one thing I require of you: you shall not see my face unless you first bring Michal, Saul's daughter, when you come to see my face." 14So David sent messengers to Ishbosheth, Saul's son, saying, "Give *me* my wife Michal, whom I betrothed to myself for a hundred foreskins of the Philistines." 15And Ishbosheth sent and took her from *her* husband, from Paltielᶜ the son of Laish. 16Then her husband went along with her to Bahurim, weeping behind her. So Abner said to him, "Go, return!" And he returned.

17Now Abner had communicated with the elders of Israel, saying, "In time past you were seeking for David *to be* king over you. 18Now then, do *it!* For the LORD has spoken of David, saying,

---

3:15 ᶜSpelled *Palti* in 1 Samuel 25:44

'By the hand of My servant David, I*d* will save My people Israel from the hand of the Philistines and the hand of all their enemies.' " 19And Abner also spoke in the hearing of Benjamin. Then Abner also went to speak in the hearing of David in Hebron all that seemed good to Israel and the whole house of Benjamin.

20So Abner and twenty men with him came to David at Hebron. And David made a feast for Abner and the men who *were* with him. 21Then Abner said to David, "I will arise and go, and gather all Israel to my lord the king, that they may make a covenant with you, and that you may reign over all that your heart desires." So David sent Abner away, and he went in peace.

22At that moment the servants of David and Joab came from a raid and brought much spoil with them. But Abner *was* not with David in Hebron, for he had sent him away, and he had gone in peace. 23When Joab and all the troops that *were* with him had come, they told Joab, saying, "Abner the son of Ner came to the king, and he sent him away, and he has gone in peace." 24Then Joab came to the king and said, "What have you done? Look, Abner came to you; why *is* it *that* you sent him away, and he has already gone? 25Surely you realize that Abner the son of Ner came to deceive you, to know your going out and your coming in, and to know all that you are doing."

26And when Joab had gone from David's presence, he sent messengers after Abner, who brought him back from the well of Sirah. But David did not know *it*. 27Now when Abner had returned to Hebron, Joab took him aside in the gate to speak with him privately, and there stabbed him in the stomach, so that he died for the blood of Asahel his brother.

28*Afterward, when David heard *it*, he said, "My kingdom and I *are* guiltless before the LORD forever of the blood of Abner the son of Ner. 29Let it rest on the head of Joab and on all his father's house; and let there never fail to be in the house of Joab one who has a discharge or is a leper, who leans on a staff or falls by the sword, or who lacks bread." 30So Joab and Abishai his brother killed Abner, because he had killed their brother Asahel at Gibeon in the battle.

31Then David said to Joab and to all the people who were with him, "Tear your clothes, gird yourselves with sackcloth, and mourn for Abner." And King David followed the coffin. 32So they buried Abner in Hebron; and the king lifted up his voice and wept at the grave of Abner, and all the people wept. 33And the king sang *a lament* over Abner and said:

"Should Abner die as a fool dies?
34 Your hands were not bound
    Nor your feet put into fetters;
    As a man falls before wicked men, *so* you
    fell."

Then all the people wept over him again.

35And when all the people came to persuade David to eat food while it was still day, David took an oath, saying, "God do so to me, and more also, if I taste bread or anything else till the sun goes down!" 36Now all the people took note *of*

3:28 David's way of life was reconciliation; he was a peacemaker. But Abner and Joab lived by retaliation: "All who take the sword will perish by the sword" (Matt. 26:52). Abner had murdered Asahel, and his sin had found him out. But Joab's deed was wicked, and David dissociated himself from it. Imagine Joab avenging his brother's blood at Hebron, a city of refuge!

3:18 *d*Following many Hebrew manuscripts, Septuagint, Syriac, and Targum; Masoretic Text reads *he*.

3:39 David was strong, yet he was weak (v. 39)! When we are weak in ourselves, the Lord can be strong through us (2 Cor. 12:7–10). We cannot control circumstances and people, but we can control what *we* say and do.

CHAPTER 4

4:5–7 Now for murder number three, committed by two men who did not know David's heart. When they heard that Abner was dead, they concluded that Ishbosheth would not remain king very long, so they murdered the king. They thought the act would please David and perhaps win them key positions in David's kingdom.

4:8 Verse 8 reveals the captains' stupidity. Saul was *not* David's enemy. *The Lord* did not avenge David. David was *not* pleased at what they did. What terrible things people do in the name of the Lord, thinking to please Him! How many "religious" wars and church conflicts have broken God's heart and disgraced His name!

4:11, 12 When you are tempted to retaliate, keep in mind that God's people do not "do evil that good may come" (Rom. 3:8). Rather, they "overcome evil with good" (Rom. 12:21).

CHAPTER 5

5:1, 2 When God's king ruled over His people, there was unity instead of division and civil war. All Israel submitted to God and to David, and there was peace among the brethren.

it, and it pleased them, since whatever the king did pleased all the people. 37For all the people and all Israel understood that day that it had not been the king's *intent* to kill Abner the son of Ner. 38Then the king said to his servants, "Do you not know that a prince and a great man has fallen this day in Israel? 39*And I *am* weak today, though anointed king; and these men, the sons of Zeruiah, *are* too harsh for me. The LORD shall repay the evildoer according to his wickedness."

4 When Saul's son*e* heard that Abner had died in Hebron, he lost heart, and all Israel was troubled. 2Now Saul's son *had* two men *who were* captains of troops. The name of one *was* Baanah and the name of the other Rechab, the sons of Rimmon the Beerothite, of the children of Benjamin. (For Beeroth also was *part* of Benjamin, 3because the Beerothites fled to Gittaim and have been sojourners there until this day.)

4Jonathan, Saul's son, had a son *who was* lame in *his* feet. He was five years old when the news about Saul and Jonathan came from Jezreel; and his nurse took him up and fled. And it happened, as she made haste to flee, that he fell and became lame. His name *was* Mephibosheth.*f*

5*Then the sons of Rimmon the Beerothite, Rechab and Baanah, set out and came at about the heat of the day to the house of Ishbosheth, who was lying on his bed at noon. 6And they came there, all the way into the house, *as though* to get wheat, and they stabbed him in the stomach. Then Rechab and Baanah his brother escaped. 7For when they came into the house, he was lying on his bed in his bedroom; then they struck him and killed him, beheaded him and took his head, and were all night escaping through the plain. 8*And they brought the head of Ishbosheth to David at Hebron, and said to the king, "Here is the head of Ishbosheth, the son of Saul your enemy, who sought your life; and the LORD has avenged my lord the king this day of Saul and his descendants."

9But David answered Rechab and Baanah his brother, the sons of Rimmon the Beerothite, and said to them, "*As* the LORD lives, who has redeemed my life from all adversity, 10when someone told me, saying, 'Look, Saul is dead,' thinking to have brought good news, I arrested him and had him executed in Ziklag—the one who *thought* I would give him a reward for *his* news. 11*How much more, when wicked men have killed a righteous person in his own house on his bed? Therefore, shall I not now require his blood at your hand and remove you from the earth?" 12So David commanded his young men, and they executed them, cut off their hands and feet, and hanged *them* by the pool in Hebron. But they took the head of Ishbosheth and buried *it* in the tomb of Abner in Hebron.

5 Then* all the tribes of Israel came to David at Hebron and spoke, saying, "Indeed we *are* your bone and your flesh. 2Also, in time past, when Saul was king over us, you were the one who led Israel out and brought them in; and the LORD said to you, 'You shall shepherd My people

---

4:1 *e*That is, Ishbosheth   4:4 *f*Called *Merib-Baal* in 1 Chronicles 8:34 and 9:40

Israel, and be ruler over Israel.' " ³*Therefore all the elders of Israel came to the king at Hebron, and King David made a covenant with them at Hebron before the LORD. And they anointed David king over Israel. ⁴David *was* thirty years old when he began to reign, *and* he reigned forty years. ⁵In Hebron he reigned over Judah seven years and six months, and in Jerusalem he reigned thirty-three years over all Israel and Judah.

⁶And the king and his men went to Jerusalem against the Jebusites, the inhabitants of the land, who spoke to David, saying, "You shall not come in here; but the blind and the lame will repel you," thinking, "David cannot come in here." ⁷Nevertheless David took the stronghold of Zion (that *is*, the City of David).

⁸Now David said on that day, "Whoever climbs up by way of the water shaft and defeats the Jebusites (the lame and the blind, *who are* hated by David's soul), *he shall be chief and captain.*"ᵍ Therefore they say, "The blind and the lame shall not come into the house."

⁹Then David dwelt in the stronghold, and called it the City of David. And David built all around from the Milloʰ and inward. ¹⁰So David went on and became great, and the LORD God of hosts *was* with him.

¹¹Then Hiram king of Tyre sent messengers to David, and cedar trees, and carpenters and masons. And they built David a house. ¹²So David knew that the LORD had established him as king over Israel, and that He had exalted His kingdom for the sake of His people Israel.

¹³And David took more concubines and wives from Jerusalem, after he had come from Hebron. Also more sons and daughters were born to David. ¹⁴Now these *are* the names of those who were born to him in Jerusalem: Shammua,ⁱ Shobab, Nathan, Solomon, ¹⁵Ibhar, Elishua,ʲ Nepheg, Japhia, ¹⁶Elishama, Eliada, and Eliphelet.

¹⁷Now when the Philistines heard that they had anointed David king over Israel, all the Philistines went up to search for David. And David heard *of it* and went down to the stronghold. ¹⁸The Philistines also went and deployed themselves in the Valley of Rephaim. ¹⁹So David inquired of the LORD, saying, "Shall I go up against the Philistines? Will You deliver them into my hand?"

And the LORD said to David, "Go up, for I will doubtless deliver the Philistines into your hand."

²⁰So David went to Baal Perazim, and David defeated them there; and he said, "The LORD has broken through my enemies before me, like a breakthrough of water." Therefore he called the name of that place Baal Perazim.ᵏ ²¹And they left their images there, and David and his men carried them away.

²²Then the Philistines went up once again and deployed themselves in the Valley of Rephaim. ²³Therefore David inquired of the LORD, and He said, "You shall not go up; circle around behind them, and come upon them in front of the mulberry trees. ²⁴And it shall be, when you hear the sound of marching in the tops of the mulberry trees, then you shall advance quickly. For then the LORD will go out before you to strike the camp

5:3 We should submit to Jesus Christ, the Son of David, for many reasons. He is God's Chosen One (v. 2), and we are "members of His body, of His flesh and of His bones" (Eph. 5:30). He is God's Anointed (the name *Christ* means "anointed one"), and He alone has the right to reign. He has proved Himself in battle and won the victory over our enemies.

As long as believers submit to someone other than the Lord Jesus Christ, division and dissension will exist among God's people. Unity comes not because we have a common enemy but because we obey a common King. (See 1 Cor. 1:10–31.)

5:8 ᵍCompare 1 Chronicles 11:6   5:9 ʰLiterally *The Landfill*
5:14 ⁱSpelled *Shimea* in 1 Chronicles 3:5   5:15 ʲSpelled *Elishama* in 1 Chronicles 3:6   5:20 ᵏLiterally *Master of Breakthroughs*

of the Philistines." 25And David did so, as the LORD commanded him; and he drove back the Philistines from Geba*l* as far as Gezer.

CHAPTER 6

6:1, 2 *Fervor.* David wanted to honor God by having the ark in the new capital of the land, Jerusalem (Matt. 6:33). The plan had all the marks of success: thirty thousand choice men assisted him, and the people were enthusiastic. David had lived among the Philistines so long that he unconsciously adopted their methods (1 Sam. 6) and ignored the law of God (Num. 4:15; 10:21). Why did he forget to consult God for the guidance he needed?

6:6–9 *Fear.* If the ark had been on the shoulders of the Levites, God would not have judged Uzzah, and David would not have been afraid. God's throne does not need man's hand to keep it steady and safe.

6:12–15 *Faith.* David was not one to quit because of a mistake, so he did it again— God's way. David expressed his worship and praise publicly, without shame, and God accepted them. Acts 3:1–10 is another example of fervent praise to God.

6 Again* David gathered all *the* choice *men* of Israel, thirty thousand. 2And David arose and went with all the people who *were* with him from Baale Judah to bring up from there the ark of God, whose name is called by the Name,*m* the LORD of Hosts, who dwells *between* the cherubim. 3So they set the ark of God on a new cart, and brought it out of the house of Abinadab, which *was* on the hill; and Uzzah and Ahio, the sons of Abinadab, drove the new cart.*n* 4And they brought it out of the house of Abinadab, which *was* on the hill, accompanying the ark of God; and Ahio went before the ark. 5Then David and all the house of Israel played *music* before the LORD on all kinds of *instruments of* fir wood, on harps, on stringed instruments, on tambourines, on sistrums, and on cymbals.

6*And when they came to Nachon's threshing floor, Uzzah put out *his* hand to the ark of God and took hold of it, for the oxen stumbled. 7Then the anger of the LORD was aroused against Uzzah, and God struck him there for *his* error; and he died there by the ark of God. 8And David became angry because of the LORD's outbreak against Uzzah; and he called the name of the place Perez Uzzah*o* to this day.

9David was afraid of the LORD that day; and he said, "How can the ark of the LORD come to me?" 10So David would not move the ark of the LORD with him into the City of David; but David took it aside into the house of Obed-Edom the Gittite. 11The ark of the LORD remained in the house of Obed-Edom the Gittite three months. And the LORD blessed Obed-Edom and all his household.

12*Now it was told King David, saying, "The LORD has blessed the house of Obed-Edom and all that *belongs* to him, because of the ark of God." So David went and brought up the ark of God from the house of Obed-Edom to the City of David with gladness. 13And so it was, when those bearing the ark of the LORD had gone six paces, that he sacrificed oxen and fatted sheep. 14Then David danced before the LORD with all *his* might; and David *was* wearing a linen ephod. 15So David and all the house of Israel brought up the ark of the LORD with shouting and with the sound of the trumpet.

16Now as the ark of the LORD came into the City of David, Michal, Saul's daughter, looked through a window and saw King David leaping and whirling before the LORD; and she despised him in her heart. 17So they brought the ark of the LORD, and set it in its place in the midst of the tabernacle that David had erected for it. Then David offered

---

5:25 *l*Following Masoretic Text, Targum, and Vulgate; Septuagint reads *Gibeon.* 6:2 *m*Septuagint, Targum, and Vulgate omit *by the Name;* many Hebrew manuscripts and Syriac read *there.* 6:3 *n*Septuagint adds *with the ark.* 6:8 *o*Literally *Outburst Against Uzzah*

Criticism—Never be afraid of honest criticism. If it is correct, the critic has helped you. If it is incorrect, you can help the critic. Either way, somebody is helped. When criticism is cruel, as was Michal's, look beyond the critic and leave the matter with God (Ps. 37). Elbert Hubbard observed, "To escape criticism—do nothing, say nothing, be nothing."

burnt offerings and peace offerings before the
LORD. [18]And when David had finished offering
burnt offerings and peace offerings, he blessed
the people in the name of the LORD of hosts.
[19]Then he distributed among all the people,
among the whole multitude of Israel, both the
women and the men, to everyone a loaf of bread,
a piece *of meat,* and a cake of raisins. So all the
people departed, everyone to his house.

[20]*Then David returned to bless his household.
And Michal the daughter of Saul came out to meet
David, and said, "How glorious was the king of
Israel today, uncovering himself today in the eyes
of the maids of his servants, as one of the base
fellows shamelessly uncovers himself!"

[21]So David said to Michal, "*It was* before the
LORD, who chose me instead of your father and
all his house, to appoint me ruler over the people
of the LORD, over Israel. Therefore I will play *music* before the LORD. [22]And I will be even more
undignified than this, and will be humble in my
own sight. But as for the maidservants of whom
you have spoken, by them I will be held in honor."

[23]Therefore Michal the daughter of Saul had no
children to the day of her death.

7 Now* it came to pass when the king was
dwelling in his house, and the LORD had given
him rest from all his enemies all around, [2]that
the king said to Nathan the prophet, "See now, I
dwell in a house of cedar, but the ark of God
dwells inside tent curtains."

[3]Then Nathan said to the king, "Go, do all that
is in your heart, for the LORD *is* with you."

[4]But it happened that night that the word of the
LORD came to Nathan, saying, [5]"Go and tell My
servant David, 'Thus says the LORD: "Would you
build a house for Me to dwell in? [6]For I have not
dwelt in a house since the time that I brought the
children of Israel up from Egypt, even to this day,
but have moved about in a tent and in a tabernacle. [7]Wherever I have moved about with all the
children of Israel, have I ever spoken a word to
anyone from the tribes of Israel, whom I commanded to shepherd My people Israel, saying,
'Why have you not built Me a house of cedar?' " '
[8]Now therefore, thus shall you say to My servant
David, 'Thus says the LORD of hosts: "I took you
from the sheepfold, from following the sheep, to
be ruler over My people, over Israel. [9]And I have
been with you wherever you have gone, and have
cut off all your enemies from before you, and
have made you a great name, like the name of
the great men who *are* on the earth. [10]Moreover
I will appoint a place for My people Israel, and
will plant them, that they may dwell in a place
of their own and move no more; nor shall the sons
of wickedness oppress them anymore, as previously, [11]since the time that I commanded judges
to be over My people Israel, and have caused you
to rest from all your enemies. Also the LORD tells
you that He will make you a house.*p*

[12]"When your days are fulfilled and you rest
with your fathers, I will set up your seed after
you, who will come from your body, and I will
establish his kingdom. [13]He shall build a house

6:20–23 *Folly.* Full of joy, David came home
to bless his family, only to have Michal
ridicule him. Not everybody gets the
blessing, and some people resent it when
others get blessed. She was unspiritual and
unsympathetic, and as a result, she became
unfruitful. Michal was David's first wife, and
she no doubt resented the other wives in
the home (Deut. 17:17).

When all else fails, take time to read God's
instructions.

CHAPTER 7

7:1, 2 How would you respond if God said
no to one of your greatest ambitions,
something that you were sure would please
Him? David wanted to build a house for the
Lord (Ps. 132), but God would not permit
him to do so. David was disappointed, and
his responses show us how to handle the
disappointments of life.

7:11 *p*That is, a royal dynasty

Forever!—Notice the "forevers" in 2 Samuel 7: a throne (v. 13), a kingdom (v. 16), a nation
(v. 24), a promise (v. 25), and a blessing (v. 29).

7:18 *He submitted to God's will.* David humbly accepted God's plan and did not try to change God's mind. He realized that God knows best.

7:21, 22 *He listened to God's word.* God would build a house (family) for David! The immediate reference is to Solomon, but ultimately the promise refers to Jesus Christ, the Son of David. If God says no to something, it is so that He may say yes to something better.

7:26–29 *He gave himself to worship.* David's words in verses 18–29 emphasize the greatness and the grace of God. Who was David that God should call him and bless him? Who was Israel that God should choose them? And who are we that God should save us and bless us? It has well been said, "Disappointments are His appointments." David believed that. Do you? Have you learned that there can be blessing in *un*answered prayer?

CHAPTER 8

8:1ff David's name is found twenty-one times in chapter 8. God magnified David's name because David did the will of God (v. 13). Exalt yourself and God will humble you, but humble yourself and God will exalt you (1 Pet. 5:5–6).

for My name, and I will establish the throne of his kingdom forever. [14]I will be his Father, and he shall be My son. If he commits iniquity, I will chasten him with the rod of men and with the blows of the sons of men. [15]But My mercy shall not depart from him, as I took *it* from Saul, whom I removed from before you. [16]And your house and your kingdom shall be established forever before you.*q* Your throne shall be established forever." '"

[17]According to all these words and according to all this vision, so Nathan spoke to David.

[18]*Then King David went in and sat before the LORD; and he said: "Who *am* I, O Lord GOD? And what is my house, that You have brought me this far? [19]And yet this was a small thing in Your sight, O Lord GOD; and You have also spoken of Your servant's house for a great while to come. *Is* this the manner of man, O Lord GOD? [20]Now what more can David say to You? For You, Lord GOD, know Your servant. [21]*For Your word's sake, and according to Your own heart, You have done all these great things, to make Your servant know *them*. [22]Therefore You are great, O Lord GOD.*r* For *there is* none like You, nor *is there any* God besides You, according to all that we have heard with our ears. [23]And who *is* like Your people, like Israel, the one nation on the earth whom God went to redeem for Himself as a people, to make for Himself a name—and to do for Yourself great and awesome deeds for Your land—before Your people whom You redeemed for Yourself from Egypt, the nations, and their gods? [24]For You have made Your people Israel Your very own people forever; and You, LORD, have become their God. [25]"Now, O LORD God, the word which You have spoken concerning Your servant and concerning his house, establish *it* forever and do as You have said. [26]*So let Your name be magnified forever, saying, 'The LORD of hosts *is* the God over Israel.' And let the house of Your servant David be established before You. [27]For You, O LORD of hosts, God of Israel, have revealed *this* to Your servant, saying, 'I will build you a house.' Therefore Your servant has found it in his heart to pray this prayer to You. [28]"And now, O Lord GOD, You are God, and Your words are true, and You have promised this goodness to Your servant. [29]Now therefore, let it please You to bless the house of Your servant, that it may continue before You forever; for You, O Lord GOD, have spoken *it*, and with Your blessing let the house of Your servant be blessed forever."

8 After* this it came to pass that David attacked the Philistines and subdued them. And David took Metheg Ammah from the hand of the Philistines. [2]Then he defeated Moab. Forcing them down to the ground, he measured them off with a line. With two lines he measured off those to be put to death, and with one full line those to be kept alive. So the Moabites became David's servants, *and* brought tribute. [3]David also defeated Hadadezer the son of Rehob, king of Zobah, as he went to recover his territory at the River Euphrates. [4]David took from him

7:16 *q*Septuagint reads *Me.*   7:22 *r*Targum and Syriac read O LORD God.

one thousand *chariots*, seven hundred[s] horsemen, and twenty thousand foot soldiers. Also David hamstrung all the chariot horses, except that he spared *enough* of them for one hundred chariots.

5When the Syrians of Damascus came to help Hadadezer king of Zobah, David killed twenty-two thousand of the Syrians. 6Then David put garrisons in Syria of Damascus; and the Syrians became David's servants, *and* brought tribute. So the LORD preserved David wherever he went. 7And David took the shields of gold that had belonged to the servants of Hadadezer, and brought them to Jerusalem. 8Also from Betah[t] and from Berothai, cities of Hadadezer, King David took a large amount of bronze.

9When Toi[u] king of Hamath heard that David had defeated all the army of Hadadezer, 10then Toi sent Joram[v] his son to King David, to greet him and bless him, because he had fought against Hadadezer and defeated him (for Hadadezer had been at war with Toi); and *Joram* brought with him articles of silver, articles of gold, and articles of bronze. 11*King David also dedicated these to the LORD, along with the silver and gold that he had dedicated from all the nations which he had subdued— 12from Syria,[w] from Moab, from the people of Ammon, from the Philistines, from Amalek, and from the spoil of Hadadezer the son of Rehob, king of Zobah.

13And David made *himself* a name when he returned from killing eighteen thousand Syrians[x] in the Valley of Salt. 14He also put garrisons in Edom; throughout all Edom he put garrisons, and all the Edomites became David's servants. And the LORD preserved David wherever he went.

15*So David reigned over all Israel; and David administered judgment and justice to all his people. 16Joab the son of Zeruiah *was* over the army; Jehoshaphat the son of Ahilud *was* recorder; 17Zadok the son of Ahitub and Ahimelech the son of Abiathar *were* the priests; Seraiah[y] *was* the scribe; 18Benaiah the son of Jehoiada *was over* both the Cherethites and the Pelethites; and David's sons were chief ministers.

9 Now* David said, "Is there still anyone who is left of the house of Saul, that I may show him kindness for Jonathan's sake?"

2And *there was* a servant of the house of Saul whose name *was* Ziba. So when they had called him to David, the king said to him, "Are you Ziba?"

He said, "At your service!"

3Then the king said, "Is there not still someone of the house of Saul, to whom I may show the kindness of God?"

And Ziba said to the king, "There is still a son of Jonathan *who is* lame in *his* feet."

4So the king said to him, "Where *is* he?"

And Ziba said to the king, "Indeed he *is* in the house of Machir the son of Ammiel, in Lo Debar."

5*Then King David sent and brought him out

8:11 God gave David victory, and David used each victory to serve the Lord (v. 11). David knew that he would not build the temple, but he risked his life to gather the wealth Solomon would need to do the job. If God gives your dream to somebody else, help him or her fulfill it.

8:15 David recovered lost territory and gained new territory, a good example for us to follow in our spiritual walk and warfare.

CHAPTER 9

9:1 Kindness is the key theme (vv. 1, 3, 7) of this chapter. Kindness is a fruit of the Spirit (Gal. 5:22) and an evidence of love (1 Cor. 13:4). David was practicing what is taught in Ephesians 4:32.

9:5–7 This event illustrates God's kindness to us in Christ (Eph. 2:7; Titus 3:4). As a part of the family of Saul, Mephibosheth had no claims on the kingdom; yet David treated him like one of his own sons. He did it for the sake of Jonathan (v. 7) in order to keep his covenant (1 Sam. 20:12–16). God has saved us for the sake of His Son, a part of the eternal covenant of redemption (Eph. 4:32; Heb. 13:20–21).

8:4 [s]Or *seven thousand* (compare 1 Chronicles 18:4)   8:8 [t]Spelled *Tibhath* in 1 Chronicles 18:8   8:9 [u]Spelled *Tou* in 1 Chronicles 18:9   8:10 [v]Spelled *Hadoram* in 1 Chronicles 18:10   8:12 [w]Septuagint, Syriac, and some Hebrew manuscripts read *Edom.*   8:13 [x]Septuagint, Syriac, and some Hebrew manuscripts read *Edomites* (compare 1 Chronicles 18:12).   8:17 [y]Spelled *Shavsha* in 1 Chronicles 18:16

of the house of Machir the son of Ammiel, from Lo Debar.

6Now when Mephibosheth the son of Jonathan, the son of Saul, had come to David, he fell on his face and prostrated himself. Then David said, "Mephibosheth?"

And he answered, "Here is your servant!"

7So David said to him, "Do not fear, for I will surely show you kindness for Jonathan your father's sake, and will restore to you all the land of Saul your grandfather; and you shall eat bread at my table continually."

8Then he bowed himself, and said, "What is your servant, that you should look upon such a dead dog as I?"

9And the king called to Ziba, Saul's servant, and said to him, "I have given to your master's son all that belonged to Saul and to all his house. 10You therefore, and your sons and your servants, shall work the land for him, and you shall bring in the harvest, that your master's son may have food to eat. But Mephibosheth your master's son shall eat bread at my table always." Now Ziba had fifteen sons and twenty servants.

11*Then Ziba said to the king, "According to all that my lord the king has commanded his servant, so will your servant do."

"As for Mephibosheth," said the king, "he shall eat at my tablez like one of the king's sons." 12Mephibosheth had a young son whose name was Micha. And all who dwelt in the house of Ziba were servants of Mephibosheth. 13So Mephibosheth dwelt in Jerusalem, for he ate continually at the king's table. And he was lame in both his feet.

CHAPTER 10

10 It* happened after this that the king of the people of Ammon died, and Hanun his son reigned in his place. 2Then David said, "I will show kindness to Hanun the son of Nahash, as his father showed kindness to me."

So David sent by the hand of his servants to comfort him concerning his father. And David's servants came into the land of the people of Ammon. 3And the princes of the people of Ammon said to Hanun their lord, "Do you think that David really honors your father because he has sent comforters to you? Has David not rather sent his servants to you to search the city, to spy it out, and to overthrow it?"

4Therefore Hanun took David's servants, shaved off half of their beards, cut off their garments in the middle, at their buttocks, and sent them away. 5*When they told David, he sent to meet them, because the men were greatly ashamed. And the king said, "Wait at Jericho until your beards have grown, and then return."

6When the people of Ammon saw that they had made themselves repulsive to David, the people of Ammon sent and hired the Syrians of Beth Rehob and the Syrians of Zoba, twenty thousand foot soldiers; and from the king of Maacah one thousand men, and from Ish-Tob twelve thousand men. 7Now when David heard of it, he sent Joab and all the army of the mighty men. 8Then the people of Ammon came out and put themselves in battle array at the entrance of the gate. And the Syrians of Zoba, Beth Rehob, Ish-Tob, and Maacah were by themselves in the field.

9:11–13 Mephibosheth did not need to fear (v. 7) because David would keep his word. The lame prince would have all his needs met and sit with the king every day. There was nothing to worry about! In the light of Ephesians 1:3 and 2:4–10, why should you worry? Henry Drummond wisely stated, "The greatest thing a man can do for his Heavenly Father is to be kind to some of His other children."

10:1–4 David's kindness to Mephibosheth was accepted, but his gesture of kindness to Hanun was rejected and led to the death of nearly fifty thousand men. Hanun's counselors were suspicious of David and questioned his motives because they judged David on the basis of what they would have done.

10:5 The King's servants are sometimes treated badly (Matt. 10:16ff.), but they need not fret: their King has everything in control, and some things heal with time. God cares for His own.

9:11 zSeptuagint reads David's table.

9When Joab saw that the battle line was against him before and behind, he chose some of Israel's best and put *them* in battle array against the Syrians. 10And the rest of the people he put under the command of Abishai his brother, that he might set *them* in battle array against the people of Ammon. 11Then he said, "If the Syrians are too strong for me, then you shall help me; but if the people of Ammon are too strong for you, then I will come and help you. 12*Be of good courage, and let us be strong for our people and for the cities of our God. And may the LORD do *what is* good in His sight."

13So Joab and the people who *were* with him drew near for the battle against the Syrians, and they fled before him. 14When the people of Ammon saw that the Syrians were fleeing, they also fled before Abishai, and entered the city. So Joab returned from the people of Ammon and went to Jerusalem.

15When the Syrians saw that they had been defeated by Israel, they gathered together. 16Then Hadadezer*a* sent and brought out the Syrians who *were* beyond the River,*b* and they came to Helam. And Shobach the commander of Hadadezer's army *went* before them. 17When it was told David, he gathered all Israel, crossed over the Jordan, and came to Helam. And the Syrians set themselves in battle array against David and fought with him. 18Then the Syrians fled before Israel; and David killed seven hundred charioteers and forty thousand horsemen of the Syrians, and struck Shobach the commander of their army, who died there. 19And when all the kings *who were* servants to Hadadezer*c* saw that they were defeated by Israel, they made peace with Israel and served them. So the Syrians were afraid to help the people of Ammon anymore.

11 It* happened in the spring of the year, at the time when kings go out *to battle,* that David sent Joab and his servants with him, and all Israel; and they destroyed the people of Ammon and besieged Rabbah. But David remained at Jerusalem.

2*Then it happened one evening that David arose from his bed and walked on the roof of the king's house. And from the roof he saw a woman bathing, and the woman *was* very beautiful to behold. 3So David sent and inquired about the woman. And someone said, "*Is* this not Bathsheba, the daughter of Eliam, the wife of Uriah the Hittite?" 4Then David sent messengers, and took her; and she came to him, and he lay with her, for she was cleansed from her impurity; and she returned to her house. 5And the woman conceived; so she sent and told David, and said, "I *am* with child."

6Then David sent to Joab, *saying,* "Send me Uriah the Hittite." And Joab sent Uriah to David. 7When Uriah had come to him, David asked how Joab was doing, and how the people were doing, and how the war prospered. 8*And David said to Uriah, "Go down to your house and wash your feet." So Uriah departed from the king's house, and a gift *of food* from the king followed him. 9But Uriah slept at the door of the king's house with all the servants of his lord, and did not go

10:12 Verse 12 is a good illustration of the biblical balance between divine sovereignty and human responsibility. The same God who ordains the end (victory in battle) also ordains the means to the end (courageous men who do their job well). Faith and works must always go together.

CHAPTER 11

11:1ff How we wish that "the matter of Uriah the Hittite" (1 Kings 15:5) were not in the Bible, but it is here for our warning and learning. Believers can thank God that *our* sins are not written down for everyone to read!

11:2–4 Disobedience. You start on the path to sin when you neglect duty. David was in more danger in Jerusalem than with his army on the battlefield. He laid aside his armor (Eph. 6:10ff.), allowed his eyes to wander, and lust took over (James 1:14–15).

11:8–13 Deception. Like our first parents, we try to cover our sins, but God will find us out (Gen. 3:7; Prov. 28:13). David the adulterer became a liar and a schemer, and then a murderer. Uriah was one of David's mighty men (2 Sam. 23:39). While David was sinning, Uriah and his fellow soldiers were risking their lives for him on the battlefield.

10:16 *a*Hebrew *Hadarezer* *b*That is, the Euphrates
10:19 *c*Hebrew *Hadarezer*

down to his house. ¹⁰So when they told David, saying, "Uriah did not go down to his house," David said to Uriah, "Did you not come from a journey? Why did you not go down to your house?"

¹¹And Uriah said to David, "The ark and Israel and Judah are dwelling in tents, and my lord Joab and the servants of my lord are encamped in the open fields. Shall I then go to my house to eat and drink, and to lie with my wife? As you live, and as your soul lives, I will not do this thing."

¹²Then David said to Uriah, "Wait here today also, and tomorrow I will let you depart." So Uriah remained in Jerusalem that day and the next. ¹³Now when David called him, he ate and drank before him; and he made him drunk. And at evening he went out to lie on his bed with the servants of his lord, but he did not go down to his house.

¹⁴In the morning it happened that David wrote a letter to Joab and sent it by the hand of Uriah. ¹⁵And he wrote in the letter, saying, "Set Uriah in the forefront of the hottest battle, and retreat from him, that he may be struck down and die." ¹⁶So it was, while Joab besieged the city, that he assigned Uriah to a place where he knew there were valiant men. ¹⁷Then the men of the city came out and fought with Joab. And some of the people of the servants of David fell; and Uriah the Hittite died also.

¹⁸*Then Joab sent and told David all the things concerning the war, ¹⁹and charged the messenger, saying, "When you have finished telling the matters of the war to the king, ²⁰if it happens that the king's wrath rises, and he says to you: 'Why did you approach so near to the city when you fought? Did you not know that they would shoot from the wall? ²¹Who struck Abimelech the son of Jerubbesheth?ᵈ Was it not a woman who cast a piece of a millstone on him from the wall, so that he died in Thebez? Why did you go near the wall?'—then you shall say, 'Your servant Uriah the Hittite is dead also.' "

²²So the messenger went, and came and told David all that Joab had sent by him. ²³And the messenger said to David, "Surely the men prevailed against us and came out to us in the field; then we drove them back as far as the entrance of the gate. ²⁴The archers shot from the wall at your servants; and some of the king's servants are dead, and your servant Uriah the Hittite is dead also."

²⁵Then David said to the messenger, "Thus you shall say to Joab: 'Do not let this thing displease you, for the sword devours one as well as another. Strengthen your attack against the city, and overthrow it.' So encourage him."

²⁶When the wife of Uriah heard that Uriah her husband was dead, she mourned for her husband. ²⁷And when her mourning was over, David sent and brought her to his house, and she became his wife and bore him a son. But the thing that David had done displeased the LORD.

11:18–21 Displeasure. From the human point of view, the scheme worked, but God was not pleased. See what David wrote in Psalms 5:4 and 11:5, and note Proverbs 6:16–19 and 1 Thessalonians 4:1–8. Before you yield to temptation . . . look back and recall God's goodness to you; look ahead and remember "the wages of sin"; look around and think of all the people who may be affected by what you do; look up and ask God for the strength to say no (1 Cor. 10:13).

CHAPTER 12

12:1–15 Chastening. For about a year, David hid his sins and suffered under the chastening hand of God (Ps. 32; Heb. 12:1–11). God gave David opportunity for repentance, but he refused to yield. Chastening proves God's love to us; our yielding proves our love to Him.

12 Then* the LORD sent Nathan to David. And he came to him, and said to him: "There were two men in one city, one rich and the other poor. ²The rich man had exceedingly many flocks and herds. ³But the poor man had nothing, except

---

11:21 ᵈSame as Jerubbaal (Gideon), Judges 6:32ff

one little ewe lamb which he had bought and nourished; and it grew up together with him and with his children. It ate of his own food and drank from his own cup and lay in his bosom; and it was like a daughter to him. 4And a traveler came to the rich man, who refused to take from his own flock and from his own herd to prepare one for the wayfaring man who had come to him; but he took the poor man's lamb and prepared it for the man who had come to him."

5So David's anger was greatly aroused against the man, and he said to Nathan, "As the LORD lives, the man who has done this shall surely die! 6*And he shall restore fourfold for the lamb, because he did this thing and because he had no pity."

7Then Nathan said to David, "You are the man! Thus says the LORD God of Israel: 'I anointed you king over Israel, and I delivered you from the hand of Saul. 8I gave you your master's house and your master's wives into your keeping, and gave you the house of Israel and Judah. And if that had been too little, I also would have given you much more! 9Why have you despised the commandment of the LORD, to do evil in His sight? You have killed Uriah the Hittite with the sword; you have taken his wife to be your wife, and have killed him with the sword of the people of Ammon. 10Now therefore, the sword shall never depart from your house, because you have despised Me, and have taken the wife of Uriah the Hittite to be your wife.' 11Thus says the LORD: 'Behold, I will raise up adversity against you from your own house; and I will take your wives before your eyes and give them to your neighbor, and he shall lie with your wives in the sight of this sun. 12For you did it secretly, but I will do this thing before all Israel, before the sun.' "

13*So David said to Nathan, "I have sinned against the LORD."

And Nathan said to David, "The LORD also has put away your sin; you shall not die. 14However, because by this deed you have given great occasion to the enemies of the LORD to blaspheme, the child also who is born to you shall surely die." 15Then Nathan departed to his house.

And the LORD struck the child that Uriah's wife bore to David, and it became ill. 16David therefore pleaded with God for the child, and David fasted and went in and lay all night on the ground. 17So the elders of his house arose and went to him, to raise him up from the ground. But he would not, nor did he eat food with them. 18Then on the seventh day it came to pass that the child died. And the servants of David were afraid to tell him that the child was dead. For they said, "Indeed, while the child was alive, we spoke to him, and he would not heed our voice. How can we tell him that the child is dead? He may do some harm!"

19When David saw that his servants were whispering, David perceived that the child was dead. Therefore David said to his servants, "Is the child dead?"

And they said, "He is dead."

20So David arose from the ground, washed and anointed himself, and changed his clothes; and he went into the house of the LORD and worshiped. Then he went to his own house; and when he requested, they set food before him, and he ate. 21Then his servants said to him, "What is this that you have done? You fasted and wept for the child

12:6 Conviction. How easy it is to condemn others! But beware: the sentence you pass on others will be passed on you (Matt. 7:1–5). David paid fourfold for his sins: the baby died, his daughter Tamar was raped, and his sons Absalom and Amnon were killed.

12:13 Confession. The Law said that both David and Bathsheba should die (Lev. 20:10). In His grace, God forgave their sins (Ps. 51); but in His government, He permitted them to reap what they had sown. First John 1:9 is a great promise, but it is not an excuse for sin. Remember, there are sad consequences of forgiven sin.

while he was alive, but when the child died, you arose and ate food."

22And he said, "While the child was alive, I fasted and wept; for I said, 'Who can tell *whether* the LORD[e] will be gracious to me, that the child may live?' 23But now he is dead; why should I fast? Can I bring him back again? I shall go to him, but he shall not return to me."

24*Then David comforted Bathsheba his wife, and went in to her and lay with her. So she bore a son, and he[f] called his name Solomon. Now the LORD loved him, 25and He sent *word* by the hand of Nathan the prophet: So he[g] called his name Jedidiah,[h] because of the LORD.

26Now Joab fought against Rabbah of the people of Ammon, and took the royal city. 27And Joab sent messengers to David, and said, "I have fought against Rabbah, and I have taken the city's water *supply.* 28Now therefore, gather the rest of the people together and encamp against the city and take it, lest I take the city and it be called after my name." 29So David gathered all the people together and went to Rabbah, fought against it, and took it. 30Then he took their king's crown from his head. Its weight *was* a talent of gold, with precious stones. And it was *set* on David's head. Also he brought out the spoil of the city in great abundance. 31And he brought out the people who *were* in it, and put *them to work* with saws and iron picks and iron axes, and made them cross over to the brick works. So he did to all the cities of the people of Ammon. Then David and all the people returned to Jerusalem.

12:24, 25 *Comfort.* God gave David another son and another crown. Saul lost his crown because he would not repent, but David always confessed his sin and rested on God's mercy (Rom. 5:20).

CHAPTER 13

13:1ff David now begins to reap the harvest of sowing to the flesh, the painful consequences of *forgiven* sin (2 Sam. 12:10; Gal. 6:7–8). Of all the trials of life, the most difficult to bear are those that come from our own family because of our failures.

13:2–20 So possessed was he by lust that Amnon made arrangements to sin. He knew that he was breaking God's law by violating a virgin whom he could not wed (Deut. 22:28–29; Lev. 20:17). Lust was replaced by hatred, for both are born of violence, and hatred resulted in Tamar's being ostracized in Israel.

13 After* this Absalom the son of David had a lovely sister, whose name *was* Tamar; and Amnon the son of David loved her. 2*Amnon was so distressed over his sister Tamar that he became sick; for she *was* a virgin. And it was improper for Amnon to do anything to her. 3But Amnon had a friend whose name *was* Jonadab the son of Shimeah, David's brother. Now Jonadab *was* a very crafty man. 4And he said to him, "Why *are* you, the king's son, becoming thinner day after day? Will you not tell me?"

Amnon said to him, "I love Tamar, my brother Absalom's sister."

5So Jonadab said to him, "Lie down on your bed and pretend to be ill. And when your father comes to see you, say to him, 'Please let my sister Tamar come and give me food, and prepare the food in my sight, that I may see *it* and eat it from her hand.' " 6Then Amnon lay down and pretended to be ill; and when the king came to see him, Amnon said to the king, "Please let Tamar my sister come and make a couple of cakes for me in my sight, that I may eat from her hand."

7And David sent home to Tamar, saying, "Now go to your brother Amnon's house, and prepare food for him." 8So Tamar went to her brother Amnon's house; and he was lying down. Then she took flour and kneaded *it,* made cakes in his sight, and baked the cakes. 9And she took the pan and placed *them* out before him, but he refused to eat. Then Amnon said, "Have everyone go out from

---

12:22 [e]A few Hebrew manuscripts and Syriac read *God.*
12:24 [f]Following Kethib, Septuagint, and Vulgate; Qere, a few Hebrew manuscripts, Syriac, and Targum read *she.*
12:25 [g]Qere, some Hebrew manuscripts, Syriac, and Targum read *she.* [h]Literally *Beloved of the LORD*

me." And they all went out from him. ¹⁰Then Amnon said to Tamar, "Bring the food into the bedroom, that I may eat from your hand." And Tamar took the cakes which she had made, and brought *them* to Amnon her brother in the bedroom. ¹¹Now when she had brought *them* to him to eat, he took hold of her and said to her, "Come, lie with me, my sister."

¹²But she answered him, "No, my brother, do not force me, for no such thing should be done in Israel. Do not do this disgraceful thing! ¹³And I, where could I take my shame? And as for you, you would be like one of the fools in Israel. Now therefore, please speak to the king; for he will not withhold me from you." ¹⁴However, he would not heed her voice; and being stronger than she, he forced her and lay with her.

¹⁵Then Amnon hated her exceedingly, so that the hatred with which he hated her *was* greater than the love with which he had loved her. And Amnon said to her, "Arise, be gone!"

¹⁶So she said to him, "No, indeed! This evil of sending me away *is* worse than the other that you did to me."

But he would not listen to her. ¹⁷Then he called his servant who attended him, and said, "Here! Put this *woman* out, away from me, and bolt the door behind her." ¹⁸Now she had on a robe of many colors, for the king's virgin daughters wore such apparel. And his servant put her out and bolted the door behind her.

¹⁹Then Tamar put ashes on her head, and tore her robe of many colors that *was* on her, and laid her hand on her head and went away crying bitterly. ²⁰And Absalom her brother said to her, "Has Amnon your brother been with you? But now hold your peace, my sister. He *is* your brother; do not take this thing to heart." So Tamar remained desolate in her brother Absalom's house.

²¹But when King David heard of all these things, he was very angry. ²²And Absalom spoke to his brother Amnon neither good nor bad. For Absalom hated Amnon, because he had forced his sister Tamar.

²³*And it came to pass, after two full years, that Absalom had sheepshearers in Baal Hazor, which *is* near Ephraim; so Absalom invited all the king's sons. ²⁴Then Absalom came to the king and said, "Kindly note, your servant has sheepshearers; please, let the king and his servants go with your servant."

²⁵But the king said to Absalom, "No, my son, let us not all go now, lest we be a burden to you." Then he urged him, but he would not go; and he blessed him.

²⁶Then Absalom said, "If not, please let my brother Amnon go with us."

And the king said to him, "Why should he go with you?" ²⁷But Absalom urged him; so he let Amnon and all the king's sons go with him.

²⁸Now Absalom had commanded his servants, saying, "Watch now, when Amnon's heart is merry with wine, and when I say to you, 'Strike Amnon!' then kill him. Do not be afraid. Have I not commanded you? Be courageous and valiant." ²⁹So the servants of Absalom did to Amnon as Absalom had commanded. Then all the king's sons arose, and each one got on his mule and fled.

³⁰And it came to pass, while they were on the way, that news came to David, saying, "Absalom has killed all the king's sons, and not one of them is left!" ³¹So the king arose and tore his garments

13:23–39 David's anger may have been restrained by his conscience, for he did nothing to punish Amnon. Absalom plotted, waited, and then avenged his sister by killing Amnon (James 1:15). David has now lost two sons to death and one to exile, and the situation will grow worse. The next time sin looks attractive to you, remember David's trials.

and lay on the ground, and all his servants stood by with their clothes torn. 32Then Jonadab the son of Shimeah, David's brother, answered and said, "Let not my lord suppose they have killed all the young men, the king's sons, for only Amnon is dead. For by the command of Absalom this has been determined from the day that he forced his sister Tamar. 33Now therefore, let not my lord the king take the thing to his heart, to think that all the king's sons are dead. For only Amnon is dead."

34Then Absalom fled. And the young man who was keeping watch lifted his eyes and looked, and there, many people were coming from the road on the hillside behind him.*i* 35And Jonadab said to the king, "Look, the king's sons are coming; as your servant said, so it is." 36So it was, as soon as he had finished speaking, that the king's sons indeed came, and they lifted up their voice and wept. Also the king and all his servants wept very bitterly.

37But Absalom fled and went to Talmai the son of Ammihud, king of Geshur. And *David* mourned for his son every day. 38So Absalom fled and went to Geshur, and was there three years. 39And King David*j* longed to go to*k* Absalom. For he had been comforted concerning Amnon, because he was dead.

CHAPTER 14

14:1–17 Nathan had told a story to help David do a right thing, repent of his sins (2 Sam. 12:1–6). This woman told a story to encourage David to do a wrong thing, restore Absalom without first insisting on repentance.

14 So* Joab the son of Zeruiah perceived that the king's heart *was* concerned about Absalom. 2And Joab sent to Tekoa and brought from there a wise woman, and said to her, "Please pretend to be a mourner, and put on mourning apparel; do not anoint yourself with oil, but act like a woman who has been mourning a long time for the dead. 3Go to the king and speak to him in this manner." So Joab put the words in her mouth.

4And when the woman of Tekoa spoke*l* to the king, she fell on her face to the ground and prostrated herself, and said, "Help, O king!"

5Then the king said to her, "What troubles you?"

And she answered, "Indeed I *am* a widow, my husband is dead. 6Now your maidservant had two sons; and the two fought with each other in the field, and *there was* no one to part them, but the one struck the other and killed him. 7And now the whole family has risen up against your maidservant, and they said, 'Deliver him who struck his brother, that we may execute him for the life of his brother whom he killed; and we will destroy the heir also.' So they would extinguish my ember that is left, and leave to my husband *neither* name nor remnant on the earth."

8Then the king said to the woman, "Go to your house, and I will give orders concerning you."

9And the woman of Tekoa said to the king, "My lord, O king, *let* the iniquity *be* on me and on my father's house, and the king and his throne *be* guiltless."

10So the king said, "Whoever says *anything* to

13:34 *i*Septuagint adds *And the watchman went and told the king, and said, "I see men from the way of Horonaim, from the regions of the mountains."* 13:39 *j*Following Masoretic Text, Syriac, and Vulgate; Septuagint reads *the spirit of the king;* Targum reads *the soul of King David.* *k*Following Masoretic Text and Targum; Septuagint and Vulgate read *ceased to pursue after.* 14:4 *l*Many Hebrew manuscripts, Septuagint, Syriac, and Vulgate read *came.*

you, bring him to me, and he shall not touch you anymore."

11Then she said, "Please let the king remember the LORD your God, and do not permit the avenger of blood to destroy anymore, lest they destroy my son."

And he said, "As the LORD lives, not one hair of your son shall fall to the ground."

12Therefore the woman said, "Please, let your maidservant speak *another* word to my lord the king."

And he said, "Say on."

13*So the woman said: "Why then have you schemed such a thing against the people of God? For the king speaks this thing as one who is guilty, *in that* the king does not bring his banished one home again. 14For we will surely die and *become* like water spilled on the ground, which cannot be gathered up again. Yet God does not take away a life; but He devises means, so that His banished ones are not expelled from Him. 15Now therefore, I have come to speak of this thing to my lord the king because the people have made me afraid. And your maidservant said, 'I will now speak to the king; it may be that the king will perform the request of his maidservant. 16For the king will hear and deliver his maidservant from the hand of the man *who would* destroy me and my son together from the inheritance of God.' 17Your maidservant said, 'The word of my lord the king will now be comforting; for as the angel of God, so *is* my lord the king in discerning good and evil. And may the LORD your God be with you.'"

18Then the king answered and said to the woman, "Please do not hide from me anything that I ask you."

And the woman said, "Please, let my lord the king speak."

19So the king said, "*Is* the hand of Joab with you in all this?" And the woman answered and said, "As you live, my lord the king, no one can turn to the right hand or to the left from anything that my lord the king has spoken. For your servant Joab commanded me, and he put all these words in the mouth of your maidservant. 20To bring about this change of affairs your servant Joab has done this thing; but my lord *is* wise, according to the wisdom of the angel of God, to know everything that *is* in the earth."

21And the king said to Joab, "All right, I have granted this thing. Go therefore, bring back the young man Absalom."

22Then Joab fell to the ground on his face and bowed himself, and thanked the king. And Joab said, "Today your servant knows that I have found favor in your sight, my lord, O king, in that the king has fulfilled the request of his servant."

23So Joab arose and went to Geshur, and brought Absalom to Jerusalem. 24And the king said, "Let him return to his own house, but do not let him see my face." So Absalom returned to his own house, but did not see the king's face.

25*Now in all Israel there was no one who was praised as much as Absalom for his good looks. From the sole of his foot to the crown of his head there was no blemish in him. 26And when he cut the hair of his head—at the end of every year he cut *it* because it was heavy on him—when he cut it, he weighed the hair of his head at two hundred shekels according to the king's standard. 27To Absalom were born three sons, and one daughter

14:13 Forgiveness that ignores justice is only a fiction. Even God does not restore a "banished one" (v. 13) without first paying the price to uphold His law. Forgiveness is not cheap; it is costly (Rom. 3:21–26). God demands that we repent and turn from sin. Jesus Christ had to die that we might be forgiven, for there is no other way.

14:25 God's forgiveness is complete; we can come into His presence and "see His face" (1 John 1:9—2:2). David restored Absalom's position, but he did not improve his character, so the young man returned to his sinful ways. The only thing weighty about Absalom was his hair; the rest of him was chaff. His good looks camouflaged a bad heart.

whose name *was* Tamar. She was a woman of beautiful appearance.

28And Absalom dwelt two full years in Jerusalem, but did not see the king's face. 29Therefore Absalom sent for Joab, to send him to the king, but he would not come to him. And when he sent again the second time, he would not come. 30So he said to his servants, "See, Joab's field is near mine, and he has barley there; go and set it on fire." And Absalom's servants set the field on fire.

31Then Joab arose and came to Absalom's house, and said to him, "Why have your servants set my field on fire?"

32And Absalom answered Joab, "Look, I sent to you, saying, 'Come here, so that I may send you to the king, to say, "Why have I come from Geshur? *It would be* better for me *to be* there still." ' Now therefore, let me see the king's face; but if there is iniquity in me, let him execute me."

33So Joab went to the king and told him. And when he had called for Absalom, he came to the king and bowed himself on his face to the ground before the king. Then the king kissed Absalom.

CHAPTER 15

15:1–6 *Enticement.* Absalom personified everything that God hates (Prov. 6:16–19). Unfortunately, many in Israel were deceived by him and believed his flattery and lies. They should have remained loyal to the Lord and to David, but recall what the crowd did to the Son of David (Matt. 27:15–26; Acts 3:14).

15 After* this it happened that Absalom provided himself with chariots and horses, and fifty men to run before him. 2Now Absalom would rise early and stand beside the way to the gate. So it was, whenever anyone who had a lawsuit came to the king for a decision, that Absalom would call to him and say, "What city *are* you from?" And he would say, "Your servant *is* from such and such a tribe of Israel." 3Then Absalom would say to him, "Look, your case *is* good and right; but *there is* no deputy of the king to hear you." 4Moreover Absalom would say, "Oh, that I were made judge in the land, and everyone who has any suit or cause would come to me; then I would give him justice." 5And *so* it was, whenever anyone came near to bow down to him, that he would put out his hand and take him and kiss him. 6In this manner Absalom acted toward all Israel who came to the king for judgment. So Absalom stole the hearts of the men of Israel.

7Now it came to pass after forty^m years that Absalom said to the king, "Please, let me go to Hebron and pay the vow which I made to the LORD. 8For your servant took a vow while I dwelt at Geshur in Syria, saying, 'If the LORD indeed brings me back to Jerusalem, then I will serve the LORD.' "

9And the king said to him, "Go in peace." So he arose and went to Hebron.

10Then Absalom sent spies throughout all the tribes of Israel, saying, "As soon as you hear the sound of the trumpet, then you shall say, 'Absalom reigns in Hebron!' " 11And with Absalom went two hundred men invited from Jerusalem, and they went along innocently and did not know anything. 12Then Absalom sent for Ahithophel the Gilonite, David's counselor, from his city—from Giloh—while he offered sacrifices. And the conspiracy grew strong, for the people with Absalom continually increased in number.

13Now a messenger came to David, saying, "The hearts of the men of Israel are with Absalom."

14So David said to all his servants who *were*

15:7 ^mSeptuagint manuscripts, Syriac, and Josephus read *four.*

with him at Jerusalem, "Arise, and let us flee, or we shall not escape from Absalom. Make haste to depart, lest he overtake us suddenly and bring disaster upon us, and strike the city with the edge of the sword."

15*And the king's servants said to the king, "We *are* your servants, *ready to do* whatever my lord the king commands." 16Then the king went out with all his household after him. But the king left ten women, concubines, to keep the house. 17And the king went out with all the people after him, and stopped at the outskirts. 18Then all his servants passed before him; and all the Chereth-ites, all the Pelethites, and all the Gittites, six hundred men who had followed him from Gath, passed before the king.

19Then the king said to Ittai the Gittite, "Why are you also going with us? Return and remain with the king. For you *are* a foreigner and also an exile from your own place. 20In fact, you came *only* yesterday. Should I make you wander up and down with us today, since I go I know not where? Return, and take your brethren back. Mercy and truth *be* with you."

21But Ittai answered the king and said, "*As* the LORD lives, and *as* my lord the king lives, surely in whatever place my lord the king shall be, whether in death or life, even there also your servant will be."

22So David said to Ittai, "Go, and cross over." Then Ittai the Gittite and all his men and all the little ones who *were* with him crossed over. 23And all the country wept with a loud voice, and all the people crossed over. The king himself also crossed over the Brook Kidron, and all the people crossed over toward the way of the wilderness.

24There was Zadok also, and all the Levites with him, bearing the ark of the covenant of God. And they set down the ark of God, and Abiathar went up until all the people had finished crossing over from the city. 25Then the king said to Zadok, "Carry the ark of God back into the city. If I find favor in the eyes of the LORD, He will bring me back and show me *both* it and His dwelling place. 26But if He says thus: 'I have no delight in you,' here I am, let Him do to me as seems good to Him." 27The king also said to Zadok the priest, "*Are* you *not* a seer? Return to the city in peace, and your two sons with you, Ahimaaz your son, and Jonathan the son of Abiathar. 28See, I will wait in the plains of the wilderness until word comes from you to inform me." 29Therefore Zadok and Abiathar carried the ark of God back to Jerusalem. And they remained there.

30So David went up by the Ascent of the *Mount of* Olives, and wept as he went up; and he had his head covered and went barefoot. And all the people who *were* with him covered their heads and went up, weeping as they went up. 31Then *someone* told David, saying, "Ahithophel *is* among the conspirators with Absalom." And David said, "O LORD, I pray, turn the counsel of Ahithophel into foolishness!"

32Now it happened when David had come to the top of *the mountain,* where he worshiped God—there was Hushai the Archite coming to meet him with his robe torn and dust on his head. 33David said to him, "If you go on with me, then you will become a burden to me. 34But if you return to the city, and say to Absalom, 'I will be your servant, O king; *as* I *was* your father's servant previously, so I *will* now also *be* your

15:15–37 Escape. A crisis helps to reveal who our loyal friends really are. David's servants were ready to obey (v. 15) and ready to die (v. 21). Ittai was a foreigner, yet he stayed with the king. The priests and David's counselor returned to the place of danger. David was a man of prayer, but he also used wise strategy. Ahithophel abandoned David and joined the rebellion. But he was Bathsheba's grandfather (2 Sam. 11:3; 23:34), so he took the opportunity for revenge.

Read the following psalms that many Bible students believe David wrote during the time of Absalom's rebellion: 3–4, 39, 41, 55, 61–63, and 143.

servant,' then you may defeat the counsel of Ahithophel for me. 35And *do* you not *have* Zadok and Abiathar the priests with you there? Therefore it will be *that* whatever you hear from the king's house, you shall tell to Zadok and Abiathar the priests. 36Indeed *they have* there with them their two sons, Ahimaaz, Zadok's *son*, and Jonathan, Abiathar's *son;* and by them you shall send me everything you hear."

37So Hushai, David's friend, went into the city. And Absalom came into Jerusalem.

CHAPTER 16

16:1ff In times of crisis, people respond in various ways. Expect to meet the following:

16:3 *The liar.* Ziba was an opportunist who took advantage of both David and Mephibosheth. In situations like this, heed Proverbs 18:13.

16:5–7 *The accuser.* Shimei was related to Saul and blamed David for the destruction of Saul's family and kingdom. David patiently "took it" and left the matter with the Lord. There are times when silence and submission are your best responses (1 Pet. 2:18–25).

16:9–12 *The avenger.* Abishai was usually quick to declare war (1 Sam. 26:1–11), but David took the better approach. (See Luke 22:47–53.)

16 When* David was a little past the top *of the mountain,* there was Ziba the servant of Mephibosheth, who met him with a couple of saddled donkeys, and on them two hundred *loaves* of bread, one hundred clusters of raisins, one hundred summer fruits, and a skin of wine. 2And the king said to Ziba, "What do you mean to do with these?"

So Ziba said, "The donkeys *are* for the king's household to ride on, the bread and summer fruit for the young men to eat, and the wine for those who are faint in the wilderness to drink."

3*Then the king said, "And where *is* your master's son?"

And Ziba said to the king, "Indeed he is staying in Jerusalem, for he said, 'Today the house of Israel will restore the kingdom of my father to me.'"

4So the king said to Ziba, "Here, all that *belongs* to Mephibosheth *is* yours."

And Ziba said, "I humbly bow before you, *that* I may find favor in your sight, my lord, O king!"

5*Now when King David came to Bahurim, there was a man from the family of the house of Saul, whose name *was* Shimei the son of Gera, coming from there. He came out, cursing continuously as he came. 6And he threw stones at David and at all the servants of King David. And all the people and all the mighty men *were* on his right hand and on his left. 7Also Shimei said thus when he cursed: "Come out! Come out! You bloodthirsty man, you rogue! 8The Lord has brought upon you all the blood of the house of Saul, in whose place you have reigned; and the Lord has delivered the kingdom into the hand of Absalom your son. So now you *are caught* in your own evil, because you are a bloodthirsty man!"

9*Then Abishai the son of Zeruiah said to the king, "Why should this dead dog curse my lord the king? Please, let me go over and take off his head!"

10But the king said, "What have I to do with you, you sons of Zeruiah? So let him curse, because the Lord has said to him, 'Curse David.' Who then shall say, 'Why have you done so?'"

11And David said to Abishai and all his servants, "See how my son who came from my own body seeks my life. How much more now *may this* Benjamite? Let him alone, and let him curse; for so the Lord has ordered him. 12It may be that the Lord will look on my affliction,n and that the Lord will repay me with good for his cursing this day." 13And as David and his men went along the road, Shimei went along the hillside opposite him and cursed as he went, threw stones at him and kicked up dust. 14Now the king and all the

---

16:12 nFollowing Kethib, Septuagint, Syriac, and Vulgate; Qere reads *my eyes;* Targum reads *tears of my eyes.*

people who *were* with him became weary; so they refreshed themselves there.

15*Meanwhile Absalom and all the people, the men of Israel, came to Jerusalem; and Ahithophel *was* with him. 16And so it was, when Hushai the Archite, David's friend, came to Absalom, that Hushai said to Absalom, "*Long* live the king! *Long* live the king!"

17So Absalom said to Hushai, "*Is* this your loyalty to your friend? Why did you not go with your friend?"

18And Hushai said to Absalom, "No, but whom the LORD and this people and all the men of Israel choose, his I will be, and with him I will remain. 19"Furthermore, whom should I serve? *Should I* not *serve* in the presence of his son? As I have served in your father's presence, so will I be in your presence."

20Then Absalom said to Ahithophel, "Give advice as to what we should do."

21And Ahithophel said to Absalom, "Go in to your father's concubines, whom he has left to keep the house; and all Israel will hear that you are abhorred by your father. Then the hands of all who are with you will be strong." 22So they pitched a tent for Absalom on the top of the house, and Absalom went in to his father's concubines in the sight of all Israel.

23Now the advice of Ahithophel, which he gave in those days, *was* as if one had inquired at the oracle of God. So *was* all the advice of Ahithophel both with David and with Absalom.

17 Moreover Ahithophel said to Absalom, "Now let me choose twelve thousand men, and I will arise and pursue David tonight. 2I will come upon him while he *is* weary and weak, and make him afraid. And all the people who *are* with him will flee, and I will strike only the king. 3Then I will bring back all the people to you. When all return except the man whom you seek, all the people will be at peace." 4And the saying pleased Absalom and all the elders of Israel.

5*Then Absalom said, "Now call Hushai the Archite also, and let us hear what he says too." 6And when Hushai came to Absalom, Absalom spoke to him, saying, "Ahithophel has spoken in this manner. Shall we do as he says? If not, speak up."

7So Hushai said to Absalom: "The advice that Ahithophel has given *is* not good at this time. 8For," said Hushai, "you know your father and his men, that they *are* mighty men, and they *are* enraged in their minds, like a bear robbed of her cubs in the field; and your father *is* a man of war, and will not camp with the people. 9Surely by now he is hidden in some pit, or in some *other* place. And it will be, when some of them are overthrown at the first, that whoever hears *it* will say, 'There is a slaughter among the people who follow Absalom.' 10And even he *who is* valiant, whose heart *is* like the heart of a lion, will melt completely. For all Israel knows that your father *is* a mighty man, and *those* who *are* with him *are* valiant men. 11Therefore I advise that all Israel be fully gathered to you, from Dan to Beersheba, like the sand that *is* by the sea for multitude, and that you go to battle in person. 12So we will come upon him in some place where he may be found, and we will fall on him as the dew falls on the ground. And of him and all the men who *are* with him there shall not be left so much as one. 13Moreover,

16:15–23 *The traitor.* Ahithophel had been David's esteemed counselor, but he turned traitor and sided with Absalom. He was the "Judas" in the camp (Ps. 55:12–14). David prayed about the problem (2 Sam. 15:31) and trusted God to work (Phil. 4:6–9), and He did.

CHAPTER 17

17:5–16 Hushai was a master of metaphors, and God used his skillful way with words to defeat Absalom. He compared David to an angry bear (v. 8) and a fierce lion (v. 10). Then he appealed to Absalom's pride by telling him to lead a large army ("like the sand" [v. 11]) and defeat David himself, coming upon David's men "as the dew falls" (v. 12). Absalom pictured himself as the conquering general, and pride did the rest (Prov. 16:18).

if he has withdrawn into a city, then all Israel shall bring ropes to that city; and we will pull it into the river, until there is not one small stone found there."

¹⁴So Absalom and all the men of Israel said, "The advice of Hushai the Archite *is* better than the advice of Ahithophel." For the LORD had purposed to defeat the good advice of Ahithophel, to the intent that the LORD might bring disaster on Absalom.

¹⁵Then Hushai said to Zadok and Abiathar the priests, "Thus and so Ahithophel advised Absalom and the elders of Israel, and thus and so I have advised. ¹⁶Now therefore, send quickly and tell David, saying, 'Do not spend this night in the plains of the wilderness, but speedily cross over, lest the king and all the people who *are* with him be swallowed up.'" ¹⁷*Now Jonathan and Ahimaaz stayed at En Rogel, for they dared not be seen coming into the city; so a female servant would come and tell them, and they would go and tell King David. ¹⁸Nevertheless a lad saw them, and told Absalom. But both of them went away quickly and came to a man's house in Bahurim, who had a well in his court; and they went down into it. ¹⁹Then the woman took and spread a covering over the well's mouth, and spread ground grain on it; and the thing was not known. ²⁰And when Absalom's servants came to the woman at the house, they said, "Where *are* Ahimaaz and Jonathan?"

So the woman said to them, "They have gone over the water brook."

And when they had searched and could not find *them,* they returned to Jerusalem. ²¹Now it came to pass, after they had departed, that they came up out of the well and went and told King David, and said to David, "Arise and cross over the water quickly. For thus has Ahithophel advised against you." ²²So David and all the people who *were* with him arose and crossed over the Jordan. By morning light not one of them was left who had not gone over the Jordan.

²³*Now when Ahithophel saw that his advice was not followed, he saddled a donkey, and arose and went home to his house, to his city. Then he put his household in order, and hanged himself, and died; and he was buried in his father's tomb.

²⁴Then David went to Mahanaim. And Absalom crossed over the Jordan, he and all the men of Israel with him. ²⁵And Absalom made Amasa captain of the army instead of Joab. This Amasa *was* the son of a man whose name *was* Jithra,ᵒ an Israelite,ᵖ who had gone in to Abigail the daughter of Nahash, sister of Zeruiah, Joab's mother. ²⁶So Israel and Absalom encamped in the land of Gilead.

²⁷Now it happened, when David had come to Mahanaim, that Shobi the son of Nahash from Rabbah of the people of Ammon, Machir the son of Ammiel from Lo Debar, and Barzillai the Gileadite from Rogelim, ²⁸brought beds and basins, earthen vessels and wheat, barley and flour, parched *grain* and beans, lentils and parched *seeds,* ²⁹honey and curds, sheep and cheese of the

17:17–22 David owed his life to the brave men who stayed in Jerusalem and kept the king informed of Absalom's plans, and also to an anonymous woman who protected the messengers. The people who helped him at Mahanaim were a gift of God. Jacob saw angels at Mahanaim (Gen. 32:1–2), but David's "angels" were loving people who cared for him. Behind all great leaders are devoted people whom God rewards but whose names we too soon forget.

17:23 Ahithophel saw that Absalom would lose the battle, and like Judas, he committed suicide (Matt. 27:1–5). He could counsel others, but he did not wisely counsel himself.

17:25 ᵒSpelled *Jether* in 1 Chronicles 2:17 and elsewhere
ᵖFollowing Masoretic Text, some manuscripts of the Septuagint, and Targum; some manuscripts of the Septuagint read *Ishmaelite* (compare 1 Chronicles 2:17); Vulgate reads *of Jezrael.*

herd, for David and the people who *were* with
him to eat. For they said, "The people are hungry
and weary and thirsty in the wilderness."

18 And* David numbered the people who *were*
with him, and set captains of thousands and
captains of hundreds over them. 2Then David sent
out one third of the people under the hand of Joab,
one third under the hand of Abishai the son of
Zeruiah, Joab's brother, and one third under the
hand of Ittai the Gittite. And the king said to the
people, "I also will surely go out with you myself."
3But the people answered, "You shall not go
out! For if we flee away, they will not care about
us; nor if half of us die, will they care about us.
But *you are* worth ten thousand of us now. For
you are now more help to us in the city."
4Then the king said to them, "Whatever seems
best to you I will do." So the king stood beside
the gate, and all the people went out by hundreds
and by thousands. 5Now the king had commanded
Joab, Abishai, and Ittai, saying, "*Deal* gently for
my sake with the young man Absalom." And all
the people heard when the king gave all the captains orders concerning Absalom.
6So the people went out into the field of battle
against Israel. And the battle was in the woods
of Ephraim. 7The people of Israel were overthrown there before the servants of David, and a
great slaughter of twenty thousand took place
there that day. 8For the battle there was scattered
over the face of the whole countryside, and the
woods devoured more people that day than the
sword devoured.
9Then Absalom met the servants of David. Absalom rode on a mule. The mule went under the
thick boughs of a great terebinth tree, and his
head caught in the terebinth; so he was left hanging between heaven and earth. And the mule
which *was* under him went on. 10Now a certain
man saw *it* and told Joab, and said, "I just saw
Absalom hanging in a terebinth tree!"
11So Joab said to the man who told him, "You
just saw *him!* And why did you not strike him
there to the ground? I would have given you ten
shekels of silver and a belt."
12But the man said to Joab, "Though I were to
receive a thousand *shekels* of silver in my hand,
I would not raise my hand against the king's son.
For in our hearing the king commanded you and
Abishai and Ittai, saying, 'Beware lest anyone
touch the young man Absalom!'[q] 13Otherwise I
would have dealt falsely against my own life. For
there is nothing hidden from the king, and you
yourself would have set yourself against *me*."
14Then Joab said, "I cannot linger with you."
And he took three spears in his hand and thrust
them through Absalom's heart, while he was *still*
alive in the midst of the terebinth tree. 15And ten
young men who bore Joab's armor surrounded
Absalom, and struck and killed him.
16So Joab blew the trumpet, and the people returned from pursuing Israel. For Joab held back
the people. 17And they took Absalom and cast him
into a large pit in the woods, and laid a very large
heap of stones over him. Then all Israel fled,
everyone to his tent.

18:12 [q]The ancient versions read *'Protect the young man Absalom for me!'*

CHAPTER 18

18:1–15 *Two armies.* There can be no neutrality when it comes to supporting and defending God's kingdom (Josh. 24:14–15; Matt. 12:30). We can understand a father's concern for his son, but there can be no gentleness when it comes to dealing with sin. David wanted love without justice, but with Joab it was justice without love. Only on the cross of Christ are love and justice both satisfied. God "did not spare His own Son" (Rom. 8:32).

18:18 Two monuments. Both Saul (1 Sam. 15:12) and Absalom set up monuments to their memory, but what do we remember about them? Joab and his men built the true monument: a heap of stones over the dead body of a proud rebel. The life you live is the monument you build, and ultimately the truth will come out.

18:19–33 Two messages. Ahimaaz had ambition and ability, but he lacked the maturity needed to minister to the king. Before you start to run, be sure you are the right person to deliver the message (Prov. 25:13).

18*Now Absalom in his lifetime had taken and set up a pillar for himself, which is in the King's Valley. For he said, "I have no son to keep my name in remembrance." He called the pillar after his own name. And to this day it is called Absalom's Monument.

19*Then Ahimaaz the son of Zadok said, "Let me run now and take the news to the king, how the LORD has avenged him of his enemies."

20And Joab said to him, "You shall not take the news this day, for you shall take the news another day. But today you shall take no news, because the king's son is dead." 21Then Joab said to the Cushite, "Go, tell the king what you have seen." So the Cushite bowed himself to Joab and ran.

22And Ahimaaz the son of Zadok said again to Joab, "But whatever happens, please let me also run after the Cushite."

So Joab said, "Why will you run, my son, since you have no news ready?"

23"But whatever happens," he said, "let me run."

So he said to him, "Run." Then Ahimaaz ran by way of the plain, and outran the Cushite.

24Now David was sitting between the two gates. And the watchman went up to the roof over the gate, to the wall, lifted his eyes and looked, and there was a man, running alone. 25Then the watchman cried out and told the king. And the king said, "If he is alone, there is news in his mouth." And he came rapidly and drew near.

26Then the watchman saw another man running, and the watchman called to the gatekeeper and said, "There is another man, running alone!"

And the king said, "He also brings news."

27So the watchman said, "I think the running of the first is like the running of Ahimaaz the son of Zadok."

And the king said, "He is a good man, and comes with good news."

28So Ahimaaz called out and said to the king, "All is well!" Then he bowed down with his face to the earth before the king, and said, "Blessed be the LORD your God, who has delivered up the men who raised their hand against my lord the king!"

29The king said, "Is the young man Absalom safe?"

Ahimaaz answered, "When Joab sent the king's servant and me your servant, I saw a great tumult, but I did not know what it was about."

30And the king said, "Turn aside and stand here." So he turned aside and stood still.

31Just then the Cushite came, and the Cushite said, "There is good news, my lord the king! For the LORD has avenged you this day of all those who rose against you."

32And the king said to the Cushite, "Is the young man Absalom safe?"

So the Cushite answered, "May the enemies of my lord the king, and all who rise against you to do harm, be like that young man!"

33Then the king was deeply moved, and went up to the chamber over the gate, and wept. And as he went, he said thus: "O my son Absalom—my son, my son Absalom—if only I had died in your place! O Absalom my son, my son!"

CHAPTER 19

19:1–8 Making wounds. Joab had to hurt David to help him: "Faithful are the wounds of a friend" (Prov. 27:6). David's sorrow over his dead son almost cost him the kingdom. It is right to mourn, but not to the point that we lose touch with reality.

19 And* Joab was told, "Behold, the king is weeping and mourning for Absalom." 2So the victory that day was turned into mourning for all the people. For the people heard it said

that day, "The king is grieved for his son."
3And the people stole back into the city that day,
as people who are ashamed steal away when they
flee in battle. 4But the king covered his face, and
the king cried out with a loud voice, "O my son
Absalom! O Absalom, my son, my son!"

5Then Joab came into the house to the king,
and said, "Today you have disgraced all your servants who today have saved your life, the lives
of your sons and daughters, the lives of your
wives and the lives of your concubines, 6in that
you love your enemies and hate your friends. For
you have declared today that you regard neither
princes nor servants; for today I perceive that if
Absalom had lived and all of us had died today,
then it would have pleased you well. 7Now therefore, arise, go out and speak comfort to your servants. For I swear by the LORD, if you do not go
out, not one will stay with you this night. And
that will be worse for you than all the evil that
has befallen you from your youth until now."
8Then the king arose and sat in the gate. And they
told all the people, saying, "There is the king, sitting in the gate." So all the people came before
the king.

For everyone of Israel had fled to his tent.

9*Now all the people were in a dispute throughout all the tribes of Israel, saying, "The king saved
us from the hand of our enemies, he delivered us
from the hand of the Philistines, and now he has
fled from the land because of Absalom. 10But Absalom, whom we anointed over us, has died in
battle. Now therefore, why do you say nothing
about bringing back the king?"

11So King David sent to Zadok and Abiathar
the priests, saying, "Speak to the elders of Judah,
saying, 'Why are you the last to bring the king
back to his house, since the words of all Israel
have come to the king, to his *very* house? 12You
are my brethren, you *are* my bone and my flesh.
Why then are you the last to bring back the king?'
13And say to Amasa, '*Are* you not my bone and
my flesh? God do so to me, and more also, if you
are not commander of the army before me continually in place of Joab.'" 14So he swayed the hearts
of all the men of Judah, just as *the heart of* one
man, so that they sent *this word* to the king: "Return, you and all your servants!"

15Then the king returned and came to the Jordan. And Judah came to Gilgal, to go to meet the
king, to escort the king across the Jordan. 16And
Shimei the son of Gera, a Benjamite, who *was*
from Bahurim, hurried and came down with the
men of Judah to meet King David. 17*There were*
a thousand men of Benjamin with him, and Ziba
the servant of the house of Saul, and his fifteen
sons and his twenty servants with him; and they
went over the Jordan before the king. 18Then
a ferryboat went across to carry over the
king's household, and to do what he thought
good.

Now Shimei the son of Gera fell down before
the king when he had crossed the Jordan. 19Then
he said to the king, "Do not let my lord impute
iniquity to me, or remember what wrong your servant did on the day that my lord the king left
Jerusalem, that the king should take *it* to heart.
20For I, your servant, know that I have sinned.
Therefore here I am, the first to come today of
all the house of Joseph to go down to meet my
lord the king."

21But Abishai the son of Zeruiah answered and

19:9–15 *Healing wounds.* It was time for
the whole nation to affirm loyalty to God's
chosen king, and David declared an
amnesty except in certain cases. The tribes
brought him back; he forgave Shimei and
Mephibosheth; he rewarded Barzillai.

said, "Shall not Shimei be put to death for this, because he cursed the LORD's anointed?"

22And David said, "What have I to do with you, you sons of Zeruiah, that you should be adversaries to me today? Shall any man be put to death today in Israel? For do I not know that today I *am* king over Israel?" 23Therefore the king said to Shimei, "You shall not die." And the king swore to him.

24Now Mephibosheth the son of Saul came down to meet the king. And he had not cared for his feet, nor trimmed his mustache, nor washed his clothes, from the day the king departed until the day he returned in peace. 25So it was, when he had come to Jerusalem to meet the king, that the king said to him, "Why did you not go with me, Mephibosheth?"

26And he answered, "My lord, O king, my servant deceived me. For your servant said, 'I will saddle a donkey for myself, that I may ride on it and go to the king,' because your servant *is* lame. 27And he has slandered your servant to my lord the king, but my lord the king *is* like the angel of God. Therefore do *what is* good in your eyes. 28For all my father's house were but dead men before my lord the king. Yet you set your servant among those who eat at your own table. Therefore what right have I still to cry out anymore to the king?"

29So the king said to him, "Why do you speak anymore of your matters? I have said, 'You and Ziba divide the land.'"

30Then Mephibosheth said to the king, "Rather, let him take it all, inasmuch as my lord the king has come back in peace to his own house."

31And Barzillai the Gileadite came down from Rogelim and went across the Jordan with the king, to escort him across the Jordan. 32Now Barzillai was a very aged man, eighty years old. And he had provided the king with supplies while he stayed at Mahanaim, for he *was* a very rich man. 33And the king said to Barzillai, "Come across with me, and I will provide for you while you are with me in Jerusalem."

34But Barzillai said to the king, "How long have I to live, that I should go up with the king to Jerusalem? 35I *am* today eighty years old. Can I discern between the good and bad? Can your servant taste what I eat or what I drink? Can I hear any longer the voice of singing men and singing women? Why then should your servant be a further burden to my lord the king? 36Your servant will go a little way across the Jordan with the king. And why should the king repay me *with* such a reward? 37Please let your servant turn back again, that I may die in my own city, near the grave of my father and mother. But here is your servant Chimham; let him cross over with my lord the king, and do for him what seems good to you."

38And the king answered, "Chimham shall cross over with me, and I will do for him what seems good to you. Now whatever you request of me, I will do for you." 39Then all the people went over the Jordan. And when the king had crossed over, the king kissed Barzillai and blessed him, and he returned to his own place.

40*Now the king went on to Gilgal, and Chimhamʳ went on with him. And all the people of Ju-

19:40–43 Opening wounds. Intertribal jealousy appeared again (Judg. 8:1; 12:1), and David faced a new rebellion (Prov. 13:10). Instead of using the soft answer (Prov. 15:1), the men of Judah held to their rights and made the situation worse. Romans 12:10 and Philippians 2:1–4 give the counsel we need.

19:40 ʳMasoretic Text reads *Chimhan.*

dah escorted the king, and also half the people of Israel. ⁴¹Just then all the men of Israel came to the king, and said to the king, "Why have our brethren, the men of Judah, stolen you away and brought the king, his household, and all David's men with him across the Jordan?"

⁴²So all the men of Judah answered the men of Israel, "Because the king *is* a close relative of ours. Why then are you angry over this matter? Have we ever eaten at the king's *expense?* Or has he given us any gift?"

⁴³And the men of Israel answered the men of Judah, and said, "We have ten shares in the king; therefore we also have more *right* to David than you. Why then do you despise us—were we not the first to advise bringing back our king?"

Yet the words of the men of Judah were fiercer than the words of the men of Israel.

20 And* there happened to be there a rebel,ˢ whose name *was* Sheba the son of Bichri, a Benjamite. And he blew a trumpet, and said:

"We have no share in David,
  Nor do we have inheritance in the son of
    Jesse;
  Every man to his tents, O Israel!"

²*So every man of Israel deserted David, *and* followed Sheba the son of Bichri. But the men of Judah, from the Jordan as far as Jerusalem, remained loyal to their king.

³Now David came to his house at Jerusalem. And the king took the ten women, his concubines whom he had left to keep the house, and put them in seclusion and supported them, but did not go in to them. So they were shut up to the day of their death, living in widowhood.

⁴*And the king said to Amasa, "Assemble the men of Judah for me within three days, and be present here yourself." ⁵So Amasa went to assemble *the men of* Judah. But he delayed longer than the set time which David had appointed him. ⁶And David said to Abishai, "Now Sheba the son of Bichri will do us more harm than Absalom. Take your lord's servants and pursue him, lest he find for himself fortified cities, and escape us." ⁷So Joab's men, with the Cherethites, the Pelethites, and all the mighty men, went out after him. And they went out of Jerusalem to pursue Sheba the son of Bichri. ⁸When they *were* at the large stone which *is* in Gibeon, Amasa came before them. Now Joab was dressed in battle armor; on it was a belt *with* a sword fastened in its sheath at his hips; and as he was going forward, it fell out. ⁹Then Joab said to Amasa, "*Are* you in health, my brother?" And Joab took Amasa by the beard with his right hand to kiss him. ¹⁰But Amasa did not notice the sword that *was* in Joab's hand. And he struck him with it in the stomach, and his entrails poured out on the ground; and he did not *strike* him again. Thus he died.

Then Joab and Abishai his brother pursued Sheba the son of Bichri. ¹¹Meanwhile one of Joab's men stood near Amasa, and said, "Whoever favors Joab and whoever *is* for David—follow Joab!" ¹²But Amasa wallowed in *his* blood in the middle of the highway. And when the man

CHAPTER 20

20:1ff Events create opportunities, and people use opportunities in different ways.

20:2, 3 Sheba saw the tribal conflict as an opportunity for promoting himself. Because he was a Benjamite, he hoped to get broad support from Saul's friends and David's enemies, and he almost succeeded. Once again, the people deserted God's chosen king for an opportunist.

20:4, 5 Amasa was chosen to lead David's army to victory (2 Sam. 19:13), but he delayed and lost his opportunity for greatness. However, Joab seized the opportunity, removed his replacement, won the battle and got his job back. Joab had murdered Abner, Absalom, and Amasa; yet David apparently did nothing to discipline him. Perhaps Joab knew too much about David (2 Sam. 11:6ff.).

20:1 ˢLiterally *man of Belial*

saw that all the people stood still, he moved Amasa from the highway to the field and threw a garment over him, when he saw that everyone who came upon him halted. 13When he was removed from the highway, all the people went on after Joab to pursue Sheba the son of Bichri.

14And he went through all the tribes of Israel to Abel and Beth Maachah and all the Berites. So they were gathered together and also went after *Sheba*.ᵗ 15Then they came and besieged him in Abel of Beth Maachah; and they cast up a siege mound against the city, and it stood by the rampart. And all the people who *were* with Joab battered the wall to throw it down.

16*Then a wise woman cried out from the city, "Hear, hear! Please say to Joab, 'Come nearby, that I may speak with you.'" 17When he had come near to her, the woman said, "*Are* you Joab?"

He answered, "I *am*."

Then she said to him, "Hear the words of your maidservant."

And he answered, "I am listening."

18So she spoke, saying, "They used to talk in former times, saying, 'They shall surely seek *guidance* at Abel,' and so they would end *disputes*. 19I *am among the* peaceable *and* faithful in Israel. You seek to destroy a city and a mother in Israel. Why would you swallow up the inheritance of the LORD?"

20And Joab answered and said, "Far be it, far be it from me, that I should swallow up or destroy! 21That *is* not so. But a man from the mountains of Ephraim, Sheba the son of Bichri by name, has raised his hand against the king, against David. Deliver him only, and I will depart from the city."

So the woman said to Joab, "Watch, his head will be thrown to you over the wall." 22Then the woman in her wisdom went to all the people. And they cut off the head of Sheba the son of Bichri, and threw *it* out to Joab. Then he blew a trumpet, and they withdrew from the city, every man to his tent. So Joab returned to the king at Jerusalem.

23And Joab *was* over all the army of Israel; Benaiah the son of Jehoiada *was* over the Cherethites and the Pelethites; 24Adoram *was* in charge of revenue; Jehoshaphat the son of Ahilud *was* recorder; 25Sheva *was* scribe; Zadok and Abiathar *were* the priests; 26and Ira the Jairite was a chief minister under David.

CHAPTER 21

21 Now* there was a famine in the days of David for three years, year after year; and David inquired of the LORD. And the LORD answered, "*It is* because of Saul and *his* bloodthirsty house, because he killed the Gibeonites." 2*So the king called the Gibeonites and spoke to them. Now the Gibeonites *were* not of the children of Israel, but of the remnant of the Amorites; the children of Israel had sworn protection to them, but Saul had sought to kill them in his zeal for the children of Israel and Judah.

3*Therefore David said to the Gibeonites, "What shall I do for you? And with what shall I make atonement, that you may bless the inheritance of the LORD?"

4And the Gibeonites said to him, "We will have no silver or gold from Saul or from his house, nor shall you kill any man in Israel for us."

20:16–22 The wise woman saw an opportunity to end the war and prevent many innocent people from being killed. Blessed are the peacemakers! Opportunities will come your way today. How will you use them?

21:1ff Promises are not to be made carelessly or broken with impunity. **God kept His promise.** If the nation obeyed God's law, He promised to bless them with rain and plenty, but if they disobeyed, He would discipline them. God often sent famines to discipline His people (Deut. 28:23–24).

21:2 Saul broke a promise. Israel's covenant with Gibeon (Josh. 9) had been honored for centuries, and then Saul violated it. Old sins can create new problems long after the sinners are dead.

21:3–13 David kept a promise. The law demanded fair and equal punishment for each crime (Exod. 21:23–25). Saul had killed innocent people, so his family had to pay the price to purge the innocent blood from the land (Deut. 19:11–13). David kept his promise to Mephibosheth (2 Sam. 9:7) and to Jonathan (1 Sam. 20:15–16) by sparing Mephibosheth's life. David also saw to it that the dead in Saul's family had decent burial.

20:14 ᵗLiterally *him*

So he said, "Whatever you say, I will do for you."

5Then they answered the king, "As for the man who consumed us and plotted against us, *that* we should be destroyed from remaining in any of the territories of Israel, 6let seven men of his descendants be delivered to us, and we will hang them before the LORD in Gibeah of Saul, *whom* the LORD chose."

And the king said, "I will give *them*."

7But the king spared Mephibosheth the son of Jonathan, the son of Saul, because of the LORD's oath that *was* between them, between David and Jonathan the son of Saul. 8So the king took Armoni and Mephibosheth, the two sons of Rizpah the daughter of Aiah, whom she bore to Saul, and the five sons of Michalu the daughter of Saul, whom she brought up for Adriel the son of Barzillai the Meholathite; 9and he delivered them into the hands of the Gibeonites, and they hanged them on the hill before the LORD. So they fell, *all* seven together, and were put to death in the days of harvest, in the first *days*, in the beginning of barley harvest.

10Now Rizpah the daughter of Aiah took sackcloth and spread it for herself on the rock, from the beginning of harvest until the late rains poured on them from heaven. And she did not allow the birds of the air to rest on them by day nor the beasts of the field by night.

11And David was told what Rizpah the daughter of Aiah, the concubine of Saul, had done. 12Then David went and took the bones of Saul, and the bones of Jonathan his son, from the men of Jabesh Gilead who had stolen them from the street of Beth Shan,v where the Philistines had hung them up, after the Philistines had struck down Saul in Gilboa. 13So he brought up the bones of Saul and the bones of Jonathan his son from there; and they gathered the bones of those who had been hanged. 14They buried the bones of Saul and Jonathan his son in the country of Benjamin in Zelah, in the tomb of Kish his father. So they performed all that the king commanded. And after that God heeded the prayer for the land.

15When the Philistines were at war again with Israel, David and his servants with him went down and fought against the Philistines; and David grew faint. 16*Then Ishbi-Benob, who *was* one of the sons of the giant, the weight of whose bronze spear *was* three hundred *shekels,* who was bearing a new *sword,* thought he could kill David. 17But Abishai the son of Zeruiah came to his aid, and struck the Philistine and killed him. Then the men of David swore to him, saying, "You shall go out no more with us to battle, lest you quench the lamp of Israel."

18Now it happened afterward that there was again a battle with the Philistines at Gob. Then Sibbechai the Hushathite killed Saph,w who *was* one of the sons of the giant. 19Again there was war at Gob with the Philistines, where Elhanan the son of Jaare-Oregimx the Bethlehemite killed *the brother of* Goliath the Gittite, the shaft of whose spear *was* like a weaver's beam.

20Yet again there was war at Gath, where there

21:16–22 *David made a promise.* Giants have a way of multiplying, and David discovered that he was not the giant killer he had been in his youth. There comes a time when we must give up some lesser things to protect the things that are more important. It was difficult for David to lay aside his armor and weapons, but it was a wise thing to do.

21:8 uOr *Merab* (compare 1 Samuel 18:19 and 25:44; 2 Samuel 3:14 and 6:23)   21:12 vSpelled *Beth Shean* in Joshua 17:11 and elsewhere   21:18 wSpelled *Sippai* in 1 Chronicles 20:4   21:19 xSpelled *Jair* in 1 Chronicles 20:5

was a man of *great* stature, who had six fingers on each hand and six toes on each foot, twenty-four in number; and he also was born to the giant. 21So when he defied Israel, Jonathan the son of Shimea,ʸ David's brother, killed him. 22These four were born to the giant in Gath, and fell by the hand of David and by the hand of his servants.

CHAPTER 22

22:1ff This psalm of victory is almost identical to Psalm 18. Note that David did not list Saul as one of his enemies (v. 1). What grace!

22:2–20 David did not take credit for any of his victories; he gave the glory to God. Nor was he ashamed to admit that he had cried out to God for deliverance and strength. His words should encourage us when we experience times of trial and testing.

22 Then* David spoke to the LORD the words of this song, on the day when the LORD had delivered him from the hand of all his enemies, and from the hand of Saul. 2*And he said:ᶻ

"The LORD *is* my rock and my fortress and
　　my deliverer;
3　The God of my strength, in whom I will
　　trust;
　My shield and the horn of my salvation,
　My stronghold and my refuge;
　My Savior, You save me from violence.
4　I will call upon the LORD, *who is worthy* to
　　be praised;
　So shall I be saved from my enemies.

5　"When the waves of death surrounded me,
　The floods of ungodliness made me afraid.
6　The sorrows of Sheol surrounded me;
　The snares of death confronted me.
7　In my distress I called upon the LORD,
　And cried out to my God;
　He heard my voice from His temple,
　And my cry *entered* His ears.

8　"Then the earth shook and trembled;
　The foundations of heavenᵃ quaked and
　　were shaken,
　Because He was angry.
9　Smoke went up from His nostrils,
　And devouring fire from His mouth;
　Coals were kindled by it.
10　He bowed the heavens also, and came down
　With darkness under His feet.
11　He rode upon a cherub, and flew;
　And He was seenᵇ upon the wings of the
　　wind.
12　He made darkness canopies around Him,
　Dark waters *and* thick clouds of the skies.
13　From the brightness before Him
　Coals of fire were kindled.

14　"The LORD thundered from heaven,
　And the Most High uttered His voice.
15　He sent out arrows and scattered them;
　Lightning bolts, and He vanquished them.
16　Then the channels of the sea were seen,
　The foundations of the world were
　　uncovered,
　At the rebuke of the LORD,
　At the blast of the breath of His nostrils.

17　"He sent from above, He took me,
　He drew me out of many waters.

21:21 ʸSpelled *Shammah* in 1 Samuel 16:9 and elsewhere
22:2 ᶻCompare Psalm 18   22:8 ᵃFollowing Masoretic Text, Septuagint, and Targum; Syriac and Vulgate read *hills* (compare Psalm 18:7).   22:11 ᵇFollowing Masoretic Text and Septuagint; many Hebrew manuscripts, Syriac, and Vulgate read *He flew* (compare Psalm 18:10); Targum reads *He spoke with power.*

18 He delivered me from my strong enemy,
    From those who hated me;
    For they were too strong for me.
19 They confronted me in the day of my
        calamity,
    But the LORD was my support.
20 He also brought me out into a broad place;
    He delivered me because He delighted in
        me.

21*"The LORD rewarded me according to my
        righteousness;
    According to the cleanness of my hands
    He has recompensed me.
22 For I have kept the ways of the LORD,
    And have not wickedly departed from my
        God.
23 For all His judgments *were* before me;
    And *as for* His statutes, I did not depart from
        them.
24 I was also blameless before Him,
    And I kept myself from my iniquity.
25 Therefore the LORD has recompensed me
        according to my righteousness,
    According to my cleanness in His eyes.*c*

26*"With the merciful You will show Yourself
        merciful;
    With a blameless man You will show
        Yourself blameless;
27 With the pure You will show Yourself pure;
    And with the devious You will show
        Yourself shrewd.
28 You will save the humble people;
    But Your eyes *are* on the haughty, *that* You
        may bring *them* down.

29 "For You *are* my lamp, O LORD;
    The LORD shall enlighten my darkness.
30 For by You I can run against a troop;
    By my God I can leap over a wall.
31 *As for* God, His way *is* perfect;
    The word of the LORD *is* proven;
    He *is* a shield to all who trust in Him.

32 "For who *is* God, except the LORD?
    And who *is* a rock, except our God?
33 God *is* my strength *and* power,*d*
    And He makes my*e* way perfect.
34 He makes my*f* feet like the *feet* of deer,
    And sets me on my high places.
35 He teaches my hands to make war,
    So that my arms can bend a bow of bronze.

36 "You have also given me the shield of Your
        salvation;
    Your gentleness has made me great.
37 You enlarged my path under me;
    So my feet did not slip.

22:21–24 Verses 21–24 are not a declaration of sinless perfection, for David was a sinner like any other man. They describe David's integrity of heart (Ps. 78:70–72). David obeyed the Word of God and trusted God to keep His promise and put him on the throne of Israel.

22:26–51 As he looked back on those years of danger and difficulty, David did not see the hardness of life; he saw the gentleness of God (v. 36). David affirmed that the yoke was easy and the burden was light (Matt. 11:28–30). Your life today may seem hard, but keep trusting and obeying. One of these days, God will give you your own victory song, and you will experience greatness from the gentle hand of God.

22:25 *c*Septuagint, Syriac, and Vulgate read *the cleanness of my hands in His sight* (compare Psalm 18:24); Targum reads *my cleanness before His word*.   22:33 *d*Dead Sea Scrolls, Septuagint, Syriac, and Vulgate read *It is God who arms me with strength* (compare Psalm 18:32); Targum reads *It is God who sustains me with strength*. *e*Following Qere, Septuagint, Syriac, Targum, and Vulgate (compare Psalm 18:32); Kethib reads *His*. 22:34 *f*Following Qere, Septuagint, Syriac, Targum, and Vulgate (compare Psalm 18:33); Kethib reads *His*.

38 "I have pursued my enemies and destroyed
  them;
  Neither did I turn back again till they were
  destroyed.
39 And I have destroyed them and wounded
  them,
  So that they could not rise;
  They have fallen under my feet.
40 For You have armed me with strength for
  the battle;
  You have subdued under me those who rose
  against me.
41 You have also given me the necks of my
  enemies,
  So that I destroyed those who hated me.
42 They looked, but *there was* none to save;
  Even to the LORD, but He did not answer
  them.
43 Then I beat them as fine as the dust of the
  earth;
  I trod them like dirt in the streets,
  And I spread them out.

44 "You have also delivered me from the
  strivings of my people;
  You have kept me as the head of the nations.
  A people I have not known shall serve me.
45 The foreigners submit to me;
  As soon as they hear, they obey me.
46 The foreigners fade away,
  And come frightenedᵍ from their hideouts.

47 "The LORD lives!
  Blessed *be* my Rock!
  Let God be exalted,
  The Rock of my salvation!
48 *It is* God who avenges me,
  And subdues the peoples under me;
49 He delivers me from my enemies.
  You also lift me up above those who rise
  against me;
  You have delivered me from the violent
  man.
50 Therefore I will give thanks to You, O LORD,
  among the Gentiles,
  And sing praises to Your name.

51 "*He is* the tower of salvation to His king,
  And shows mercy to His anointed,
  To David and his descendants
  forevermore."

23 Now* these *are* the last words of David.

  Thus says David the son of Jesse;
  Thus says the man raised up on high,
  The anointed of the God of Jacob,
  And the sweet psalmist of Israel:

2 "The Spirit of the LORD spoke by me,
  And His word *was* on my tongue.

CHAPTER 23

23:1–7 Leaders. Earlier in his reign, David wrote a long psalm about victory (2 Sam. 22), but when he closed his life, he wrote a beautiful brief song about leadership. Leaders must be called of God and empowered by Him (v. 1). They must be taught the Word of God by the Spirit of God (v. 2). They must be men and women of character who fear God (vv. 3–4). They are ruling for God, not for self.

22:46 ᵍFollowing Septuagint, Targum, and Vulgate (compare Psalm 18:45); Masoretic Text reads *gird themselves*.

A Cup of Water—David's hands accomplished many things as he held a sword, a spear and a harp. The finest thing he ever did was with a cup of water, for in making it a drink offering to the Lord, he revealed true character. "We can do no great things," said Mother Teresa, "only small things with great love."

3   The God of Israel said,
    The Rock of Israel spoke to me:
    'He who rules over men *must be* just,
    Ruling in the fear of God.
4   *And *he shall be* like the light of the morning
    when the sun rises,
    A morning without clouds,
    Like the tender grass *springing* out of the
    earth,
    By clear shining after rain.'

5   "Although my house *is* not so with God,
    Yet He has made with me an everlasting
    covenant,
    Ordered in all *things* and secure.
    For *this is* all my salvation and all *my* desire;
    Will He not make *it* increase?
6   But *the sons* of rebellion *shall* all *be* as
    thorns thrust away,
    Because they cannot be taken with hands.
7   But the man *who* touches them
    Must be armed with iron and the shaft of a
    spear,
    And they shall be utterly burned with fire
    in *their* place."

8*These *are* the names of the mighty men whom
David had: Josheb-Basshebeth[h] the Tachmonite,
chief among the captains.[i] He was called Adino
the Eznite, because he had killed eight hundred
men at one time. 9And after him *was* Eleazar the
son of Dodo,[j] the Ahohite, *one* of the three mighty
men with David when they defied the Philistines
who were gathered there for battle, and the men
of Israel had retreated. 10He arose and attacked
the Philistines until his hand was weary, and his
hand stuck to the sword. The LORD brought about
a great victory that day; and the people returned
after him only to plunder. 11And after him *was*
Shammah the son of Agee the Hararite. The Philistines had gathered together into a troop where
there was a piece of ground full of lentils. So the
people fled from the Philistines. 12But he stationed
himself in the middle of the field, defended it, and
killed the Philistines. So the LORD brought about
a great victory.
13Then three of the thirty chief men went down
at harvest time and came to David at the cave of
Adullam. And the troop of Philistines encamped
in the Valley of Rephaim. 14David *was* then in
the stronghold, and the garrison of the Philistines
was then *in* Bethlehem. 15And David said with
longing, "Oh, that someone would give me a drink
of the water from the well of Bethlehem, which
is by the gate!" 16So the three mighty men broke
through the camp of the Philistines, drew water
from the well of Bethlehem that *was* by the gate,
and took it and brought *it* to David. Nevertheless
he would not drink it, but poured it out to the
LORD. 17And he said, "Far be it from me, O LORD,
that I should do this! Is *this not* the blood of the
men who went in *jeopardy of* their lives?" Therefore he would not drink it.
These things were done by the three mighty
men.
18Now Abishai the brother of Joab, the son of

23:4 Two metaphors describe leadership
that is spiritual: the dawning of a new day,
and the springing up of grass after the rain
(v. 4). Saul brought darkness to the land,
but David brought light. Saul caused storms,
but David brought calm after the storm and
caused the storms to produce fruit. That is
leadership!

23:8–39 *Followers*. True leaders are not
afraid to surround themselves with people
of ability and then give them opportunities
for greatness. Those men were so close to
David that his whispered desires became
their marching orders (vv. 15–17). David
loved them so much that he would not
selfishly enjoy what had cost them dearly.
What an example those men are to us who
follow Jesus Christ!

23:8 [h]Literally *One Who Sits in the Seat* (compare 1 Chronicles
11:11) [i]Following Masoretic Text and Targum; Septuagint and
Vulgate read *the three*.   23:9 [j]Spelled *Dodai* in 1 Chronicles
27:4

Zeruiah, was chief of *another* three.[k] He lifted his spear against three hundred *men,* killed *them,* and won a name among *these* three. ¹⁹Was he not the most honored of three? Therefore he became their captain. However, he did not attain to the *first* three.

²⁰Benaiah *was* the son of Jehoiada, the son of a valiant man from Kabzeel, who had done many deeds. He had killed two lion-like heroes of Moab. He also had gone down and killed a lion in the midst of a pit on a snowy day. ²¹And he killed an Egyptian, a spectacular man. The Egyptian *had* a spear in his hand; so he went down to him with a staff, wrested the spear out of the Egyptian's hand, and killed him with his own spear. ²²These *things* Benaiah the son of Jehoiada did, and won a name among three mighty men. ²³He was more honored than the thirty, but he did not attain to the *first* three. And David appointed him over his guard.

²⁴Asahel the brother of Joab *was* one of the thirty; Elhanan the son of Dodo of Bethlehem, ²⁵Shammah the Harodite, Elika the Harodite, ²⁶Helez the Paltite, Ira the son of Ikkesh the Tekoite, ²⁷Abiezer the Anathothite, Mebunnai the Hushathite, ²⁸Zalmon the Ahohite, Maharai the Netophathite, ²⁹Heleb the son of Baanah (the Netophathite), Ittai the son of Ribai from Gibeah of the children of Benjamin, ³⁰Benaiah a Pirathonite, Hiddai from the brooks of Gaash, ³¹Abi-Albon the Arbathite, Azmaveth the Barhumite, ³²Eliahba the Shaalbonite (of the sons of Jashen), Jonathan, ³³Shammah the Hararite, Ahiam the son of Sharar the Hararite, ³⁴Eliphelet the son of Ahasbai, the son of the Maachathite, Eliam the son of Ahithophel the Gilonite, ³⁵Hezrai[l] the Carmelite, Paarai the Arbite, ³⁶Igal the son of Nathan of Zobah, Bani the Gadite, ³⁷Zelek the Ammonite, Naharai the Beerothite (armorbearer of Joab the son of Zeruiah), ³⁸Ira the Ithrite, Gareb the Ithrite, ³⁹*and* Uriah the Hittite: thirty-seven in all.

CHAPTER 24

24:1–9 *A stubborn heart.* There are sins of the spirit as well as sins of the flesh (2 Cor. 7:1). In his pride, David numbered the people, but he did not connect the census with the redemption money (Exod. 30:11–16) and seek to honor God. The Lord gave David nine months to change his mind, just long enough for the "pregnancy of sin" to give birth to death (James 1:13–15).

24 Again* the anger of the LORD was aroused against Israel, and He moved David against them to say, "Go, number Israel and Judah."

²So the king said to Joab the commander of the army who *was* with him, "Now go throughout all the tribes of Israel, from Dan to Beersheba, and count the people, that I may know the number of the people."

³And Joab said to the king, "Now may the LORD your God add to the people a hundred times more than there are, and may the eyes of my lord the king see *it.* But why does my lord the king desire this thing?" ⁴Nevertheless the king's word prevailed against Joab and against the captains of the army. Therefore Joab and the captains of the army went out from the presence of the king to count the people of Israel.

⁵And they crossed over the Jordan and camped in Aroer, on the right side of the town which *is* in the midst of the ravine of Gad, and toward Jazer. ⁶Then they came to Gilead and to the land of Tahtim Hodshi; they came to Dan Jaan and around to Sidon; ⁷and they came to the stronghold of Tyre and to all the cities of the Hivites and

---

23:18 ᵏFollowing Masoretic Text, Septuagint, and Vulgate; some Hebrew manuscripts and Syriac read *thirty;* Targum reads *the mighty men.*   23:35 ˡSpelled *Hezro* in 1 Chronicles 11:37

the Canaanites. Then they went out to South Judah *as far as* Beersheba. 8So when they had gone through all the land, they came to Jerusalem at the end of nine months and twenty days. 9Then Joab gave the sum of the number of the people to the king. And there were in Israel eight hundred thousand valiant men who drew the sword, and the men of Judah were five hundred thousand men.

10*And David's heart condemned him after he had numbered the people. So David said to the LORD, "I have sinned greatly in what I have done; but now, I pray, O LORD, take away the iniquity of Your servant, for I have done very foolishly."

11Now when David arose in the morning, the word of the LORD came to the prophet Gad, David's seer, saying, 12"Go and tell David, 'Thus says the LORD: "I offer you three *things;* choose one of them for yourself, that I may do *it* to you." ' " 13So Gad came to David and told him; and he said to him, "Shall sevenᵐ years of famine come to you in your land? Or shall you flee three months before your enemies, while they pursue you? Or shall there be three days' plague in your land? Now consider and see what answer I should take back to Him who sent me."

14And David said to Gad, "I am in great distress. Please let us fall into the hand of the LORD, for His mercies *are* great; but do not let me fall into the hand of man."

15*So the LORD sent a plague upon Israel from the morning till the appointed time. From Dan to Beersheba seventy thousand men of the people died. 16And when the angelⁿ stretched out His hand over Jerusalem to destroy it, the LORD relented from the destruction, and said to the angel who was destroying the people, "It is enough; now restrain your hand." And the angel of the LORD was by the threshing floor of Araunahᵒ the Jebusite.

17Then David spoke to the LORD when he saw the angel who was striking the people, and said, "Surely I have sinned, and I have done wickedly; but these sheep, what have they done? Let Your hand, I pray, be against me and against my father's house."

18*And Gad came that day to David and said to him, "Go up, erect an altar to the LORD on the threshing floor of Araunah the Jebusite." 19So David, according to the word of Gad, went up as the LORD commanded. 20Now Araunah looked, and saw the king and his servants coming toward him. So Araunah went out and bowed before the king with his face to the ground.

21Then Araunah said, "Why has my lord the king come to his servant?"

And David said, "To buy the threshing floor from you, to build an altar to the LORD, that the plague may be withdrawn from the people."

22Now Araunah said to David, "Let my lord the king take and offer up whatever *seems* good to him. Look, *here are* oxen for burnt sacrifice, and threshing implements and the yokes of the oxen for wood. 23All these, O king, Araunah has given to the king."

24:10–14 *A smitten heart.* David's sin was a sin of the will, so God asked him to make some decisions. He confessed his sin ("I have sinned *greatly*") and was forgiven, but he still had to suffer the consequences of sin.

24:15–17 *A suffering heart.* David had a shepherd's heart and longed to deliver his people. It is more difficult to watch those you love suffer than to endure it yourself.

24:18–25 *A sacrificing heart.* David did not take the easy way out. His repentance was sincere, and he paid the full price to prove it. Who pays for your sacrifices? Amazing grace! Solomon built the temple on the property that David purchased for his altar. Solomon was the son of Bathsheba. What amazing grace that God could take David's two great sins and build a temple out of them! (See Rom. 5:20.)

24:13 ᵐFollowing Masoretic Text, Syriac, Targum, and Vulgate; Septuagint reads *three* (compare 1 Chronicles 21:12). 24:16 ⁿOr *Angel* ᵒSpelled *Ornan* in 1 Chronicles 21:15

And Araunah said to the king, "May the LORD your God accept you."

24Then the king said to Araunah, "No, but I will surely buy *it* from you for a price; nor will I offer burnt offerings to the LORD my God with that which costs me nothing." So David bought the threshing floor and the oxen for fifty shekels of silver. 25And David built there an altar to the LORD, and offered burnt offerings and peace offerings. So the LORD heeded the prayers for the land, and the plague was withdrawn from Israel.

1 KINGS

As the names indicate, the books of 1 and 2 Kings record the history of the Jewish kings, from Solomon to Zedekiah. When the account begins, the nation is one (1 Kings 1—11). After Solomon's death, it divided (1 Kings 12—22); then both kingdoms went into captivity (2 Kings). The northern tribes were taken by Assyria (2 Kings 1—17), and the southern kingdom was taken by Babylon (2 Kings 18—25).

Israel was a nation greatly blessed by God, and yet it ended in disgrace and defeat. The cause was sin. Solomon worshiped the idols of the foreign nations, and the nation followed him. It took only one generation for the nation to decay and divide, as the false prophets and the worldly priests led the people astray. The leaders and the people would not listen to God's prophets and return to the true worship of Jehovah, so there was nothing left for God to do but discipline His people as He had warned (Deut. 28).

1 Now King David was old, advanced in years; and they put covers on him, but he could not get warm. 2Therefore his servants said to him, "Let a young woman, a virgin, be sought for our lord the king, and let her stand before the king, and let her care for him; and let her lie in your bosom, that our lord the king may be warm." 3So they sought for a lovely young woman throughout all the territory of Israel, and found Abishag the Shunammite, and brought her to the king. 4The young woman *was* very lovely; and she cared for the king, and served him; but the king did not know her.

5*Then Adonijah the son of Haggith exalted himself, saying, "I will be king"; and he prepared for himself chariots and horsemen, and fifty men to run before him. 6(And his father had not rebuked him at any time by saying, "Why have you done so?" He *was* also very good-looking. *His mother* had borne him after Absalom.) 7Then he conferred with Joab the son of Zeruiah and with Abiathar the priest, and they followed and helped Adonijah. 8But Zadok the priest, Benaiah the son of Jehoiada, Nathan the prophet, Shimei, Rei, and the mighty men who *belonged* to David were not with Adonijah.

9And Adonijah sacrificed sheep and oxen and fattened cattle by the stone of Zoheleth, which *is* by En Rogel; he also invited all his brothers, the king's sons, and all the men of Judah, the king's servants. 10But he did not invite Nathan the prophet, Benaiah, the mighty men, or Solomon his brother.

11*So Nathan spoke to Bathsheba the mother of Solomon, saying, "Have you not heard that Adonijah the son of Haggith has become king, and David our lord does not know *it?* 12Come, please, let me now give you advice, that you may save your own life and the life of your son Solomon. 13Go immediately to King David and say to him, 'Did you not, my lord, O king, swear to your maidservant, saying, "Assuredly your son Solomon shall reign after me, and he shall sit on my throne"? Why then has Adonijah become king?' 14Then, while you are still talking there with the king, I also will come in after you and confirm your words."

15So Bathsheba went into the chamber to the king. (Now the king was very old, and Abishag

CHAPTER 1

1:5–10 Some people are gullible and unwilling to learn from the past. Like Absalom, Adonijah was handsome, popular, and proud. His "I will be king!" sounds like another boast that ended in judgment (Isa. 14:12–15). Foolishly, Joab and Abiathar joined Adonijah and opposed God's man, Solomon, and they paid for it. They should have paid more attention to this pronouncement: "You shall not follow a crowd to do evil" (Exod. 23:2).

1:11–35 Sometimes leaders must be led, and Nathan and Bathsheba did it wisely. David had given up the sword (2 Sam. 21:15–17), and now he must give up the scepter. Wise is the leader who knows when to step aside. Solomon was God's choice for the throne (2 Sam. 12:24–25).

the Shunammite was serving the king.) 16And Bathsheba bowed and did homage to the king. Then the king said, "What is your wish?"

17Then she said to him, "My lord, you swore by the LORD your God to your maidservant, saying, 'Assuredly Solomon your son shall reign after me, and he shall sit on my throne.' 18So now, look! Adonijah has become king; and now, my lord the king, you do not know about it. 19He has sacrificed oxen and fattened cattle and sheep in abundance, and has invited all the sons of the king, Abiathar the priest, and Joab the commander of the army; but Solomon your servant he has not invited. 20And as for you, my lord, O king, the eyes of all Israel are on you, that you should tell them who will sit on the throne of my lord the king after him. 21Otherwise it will happen, when my lord the king rests with his fathers, that I and my son Solomon will be counted as offenders."

22And just then, while she was still talking with the king, Nathan the prophet also came in. 23So they told the king, saying, "Here is Nathan the prophet." And when he came in before the king, he bowed down before the king with his face to the ground. 24And Nathan said, "My lord, O king, have you said, 'Adonijah shall reign after me, and he shall sit on my throne'? 25For he has gone down today, and has sacrificed oxen and fattened cattle and sheep in abundance, and has invited all the king's sons, and the commanders of the army, and Abiathar the priest; and look! They are eating and drinking before him; and they say, 'Long live King Adonijah!' 26But he has not invited me—me your servant—nor Zadok the priest, nor Benaiah the son of Jehoiada, nor your servant Solomon. 27Has this thing been done by my lord the king, and you have not told your servant who should sit on the throne of my lord the king after him?"

28Then King David answered and said, "Call Bathsheba to me." So she came into the king's presence and stood before the king. 29And the king took an oath and said, "As the LORD lives, who has redeemed my life from every distress, 30just as I swore to you by the LORD God of Israel, saying, 'Assuredly Solomon your son shall be king after me, and he shall sit on my throne in my place,' so I certainly will do this day."

31Then Bathsheba bowed with her face to the earth, and paid homage to the king, and said, "Let my lord King David live forever!"

32And King David said, "Call to me Zadok the priest, Nathan the prophet, and Benaiah the son of Jehoiada." So they came before the king. 33The king also said to them, "Take with you the servants of your lord, and have Solomon my son ride on my own mule, and take him down to Gihon. 34There let Zadok the priest and Nathan the prophet anoint him king over Israel; and blow the horn, and say, 'Long live King Solomon!' 35Then you shall come up after him, and he shall come and sit on my throne, and he shall be king in my place. For I have appointed him to be ruler over Israel and Judah."

36Benaiah the son of Jehoiada answered the king and said, "Amen! May the LORD God of my lord the king say so too. 37As the LORD has been with my lord the king, even so may He be with Solomon, and make his throne greater than the throne of my lord King David."

38So Zadok the priest, Nathan the prophet, Benaiah the son of Jehoiada, the Cherethites, and the Pelethites went down and had Solomon ride on King David's mule, and took him to Gihon. ³⁹Then Zadok the priest took a horn of oil from the tabernacle and anointed Solomon. And they blew the horn, and all the people said, *"Long* live King Solomon!" ⁴⁰And all the people went up after him; and the people played the flutes and rejoiced with great joy, so that the earth *seemed to* split with their sound.

⁴¹Now Adonijah and all the guests who *were* with him heard *it* as they finished eating. And when Joab heard the sound of the horn, he said, "Why *is* the city in such a noisy uproar?" ⁴²While he was still speaking, there came Jonathan, the son of Abiathar the priest. And Adonijah said to him, "Come in, for you *are* a prominent man, and bring good news."

⁴³Then Jonathan answered and said to Adonijah, "No! Our lord King David has made Solomon king. ⁴⁴The king has sent with him Zadok the priest, Nathan the prophet, Benaiah the son of Jehoiada, the Cherethites, and the Pelethites; and they have made him ride on the king's mule. ⁴⁵So Zadok the priest and Nathan the prophet have anointed him king at Gihon; and they have gone up from there rejoicing, so that the city is in an uproar. This *is* the noise that you have heard. ⁴⁶Also Solomon sits on the throne of the kingdom. ⁴⁷And moreover the king's servants have gone to bless our lord King David, saying, 'May God make the name of Solomon better than your name, and may He make his throne greater than your throne.' Then the king bowed himself on the bed. ⁴⁸Also the king said thus, 'Blessed *be* the LORD God of Israel, who has given *one* to sit on my throne this day, while my eyes see *it!'* "

⁴⁹So all the guests who were with Adonijah were afraid, and arose, and each one went his way. ⁵⁰*Now Adonijah was afraid of Solomon; so he arose, and went and took hold of the horns of the altar. ⁵¹And it was told Solomon, saying, "Indeed Adonijah is afraid of King Solomon; for look, he has taken hold of the horns of the altar, saying, 'Let King Solomon swear to me today that he will not put his servant to death with the sword.' "

⁵²Then Solomon said, "If he proves himself a worthy man, not one hair of him shall fall to the earth; but if wickedness is found in him, he shall die." ⁵³So King Solomon sent them to bring him down from the altar. And he came and fell down before King Solomon; and Solomon said to him, "Go to your house."

2 Now* the days of David drew near that he should die, and he charged Solomon his son, saying: ²"I go the way of all the earth; be strong, therefore, and prove yourself a man. ³And keep the charge of the LORD your God: to walk in His ways, to keep His statutes, His commandments, His judgments, and His testimonies, as it is written in the Law of Moses, that you may prosper in all that you do and wherever you turn; ⁴that the LORD may fulfill His word which He spoke concerning me, saying, 'If your sons take heed to their way, to walk before Me in truth with all their heart and with all their soul,' He said, 'you shall not lack a man on the throne of Israel.'

⁵"Moreover you know also what Joab the son of Zeruiah did to me, *and* what he did to the two commanders of the armies of Israel, to Abner the son of Ner and Amasa the son of Jether, whom

1:50 Adonijah fled to the altar for safety, not for sanctity. Religion was something he used only for personal profit, but some insincere people today do the same thing.

CHAPTER 2

2:1–11 *The king died.* Death is an appointment we all must keep (Heb. 9:27), unless the Lord comes to take us home (1 Cor. 15:51ff.). Before he died, David gave Solomon wise counsel about the men who were a threat to the throne. It is good to know where the enemy is hiding. David had served his generation well (Acts 13:36).

he killed. And he shed the blood of war in peace-time, and put the blood of war on his belt that *was* around his waist, and on his sandals that *were* on his feet. 6Therefore do according to your wisdom, and do not let his gray hair go down to the grave in peace.

7"But show kindness to the sons of Barzillai the Gileadite, and let them be among those who eat at your table, for so they came to me when I fled from Absalom your brother.

8"And see, *you have* with you Shimei the son of Gera, a Benjamite from Bahurim, who cursed me with a malicious curse in the day when I went to Mahanaim. But he came down to meet me at the Jordan, and I swore to him by the LORD, say-ing, 'I will not put you to death with the sword.' 9Now therefore, do not hold him guiltless, for you *are* a wise man and know what you ought to do to him; but bring his gray hair down to the grave with blood."

10So David rested with his fathers, and was bur-ied in the City of David. 11The period that David reigned over Israel *was* forty years; seven years he reigned in Hebron, and in Jerusalem he reigned thirty-three years. 12*Then Solomon sat on the throne of his father David; and his kingdom was firmly established.

13Now Adonijah the son of Haggith came to Bathsheba the mother of Solomon. So she said, "Do you come peaceably?"

And he said, "Peaceably." 14Moreover he said, "I have something *to say* to you."

And she said, "Say it."

15Then he said, "You know that the kingdom was mine, and all Israel had set their expectations on me, that I should reign. However, the kingdom has been turned over, and has become my brother's; for it was his from the LORD. 16Now I ask one petition of you; do not deny me."

And she said to him, "Say it."

17Then he said, "Please speak to King Solomon, for he will not refuse you, that he may give me Abishag the Shunammite as wife."

18So Bathsheba said, "Very well, I will speak for you to the king."

19Bathsheba therefore went to King Solomon, to speak to him for Adonijah. And the king rose up to meet her and bowed down to her, and sat down on his throne and had a throne set for the king's mother; so she sat at his right hand. 20Then she said, "I desire one small petition of you; do not refuse me."

And the king said to her, "Ask it, my mother, for I will not refuse you."

21So she said, "Let Abishag the Shunammite be given to Adonijah your brother as wife."

22And King Solomon answered and said to his mother, "Now why do you ask Abishag the Shu-nammite for Adonijah? Ask for him the kingdom also—for he *is* my older brother—for him, and for Abiathar the priest, and for Joab the son of Zer-uiah." 23Then King Solomon swore by the LORD, saying, "May God do so to me, and more also, if Adonijah has not spoken this word against his own life! 24Now therefore, *as* the LORD lives, who has confirmed me and set me on the throne of David my father, and who has established a house*a* for me, as He promised, Adonijah shall be put to death today!"

2:12–25 *The usurper died.* Adonijah still wanted the throne and almost tricked Bathsheba into helping him. Since Abishag was one of David's concubines, claiming her would be the same as claiming the throne. Adonijah had planned a wedding, but he ended up at a funeral.

2:24 *a*That is, a royal dynasty

25So King Solomon sent by the hand of Benaiah the son of Jehoiada; and he struck him down, and he died.

26And to Abiathar the priest the king said, "Go to Anathoth, to your own fields, for you *are* deserving of death; but I will not put you to death at this time, because you carried the ark of the Lord GOD before my father David, and because you were afflicted every time my father was afflicted." 27So Solomon removed Abiathar from being priest to the LORD, that he might fulfill the word of the LORD which He spoke concerning the house of Eli at Shiloh.

28*Then news came to Joab, for Joab had defected to Adonijah, though he had not defected to Absalom. So Joab fled to the tabernacle of the LORD, and took hold of the horns of the altar. 29And King Solomon was told, "Joab has fled to the tabernacle of the LORD; there *he is,* by the altar." Then Solomon sent Benaiah the son of Jehoiada, saying, "Go, strike him down." 30So Benaiah went to the tabernacle of the LORD, and said to him, "Thus says the king, 'Come out!' "

And he said, "No, but I will die here." And Benaiah brought back word to the king, saying, "Thus said Joab, and thus he answered me."

31Then the king said to him, "Do as he has said, and strike him down and bury him, that you may take away from me and from the house of my father the innocent blood which Joab shed. 32So the LORD will return his blood on his head, because he struck down two men more righteous and better than he, and killed them with the sword—Abner the son of Ner, the commander of the army of Israel, and Amasa the son of Jether, the commander of the army of Judah—though my father David did not know *it.* 33Their blood shall therefore return upon the head of Joab and upon the head of his descendants forever. But upon David and his descendants, upon his house and his throne, there shall be peace forever from the LORD."

34So Benaiah the son of Jehoiada went up and struck and killed him; and he was buried in his own house in the wilderness. 35The king put Benaiah the son of Jehoiada in his place over the army, and the king put Zadok the priest in the place of Abiathar.

36*Then the king sent and called for Shimei, and said to him, "Build yourself a house in Jerusalem and dwell there, and do not go out from there anywhere. 37For it shall be, on the day you go out and cross the Brook Kidron, know for certain you shall surely die; your blood shall be on your own head."

38And Shimei said to the king, "The saying *is* good. As my lord the king has said, so your servant will do." So Shimei dwelt in Jerusalem many days.

39Now it happened at the end of three years, that two slaves of Shimei ran away to Achish the son of Maachah, king of Gath. And they told Shimei, saying, "Look, your slaves *are* in Gath!" 40So Shimei arose, saddled his donkey, and went to Achish at Gath to seek his slaves. And Shimei went and brought his slaves from Gath. 41And Solomon was told that Shimei had gone from Jerusalem to Gath and had come back. 42Then the king sent and called for Shimei, and said to him, "Did I not make you swear by the LORD, and warn you, saying, 'Know for certain that on the day you go out and travel anywhere, you shall surely die'?

2:28–34 The murderer died. Abiathar and Joab were both traitors, but Abiathar was spared because he was a priest. However, the exile removed the descendants of Eli from office as had been predicted years before (1 Sam. 2:30–35). Joab paid for murdering three men and also for his treachery to David. Benaiah was a priest (1 Chron. 27:5), but he was one of David's mighty men and Joab's successor as head of the army.

2:36–48 The accuser died. (See 2 Sam. 16:5–14; 19:18–23.) Had Shimei obeyed orders, he would have lived, but he defied the king and lost his life.

How true is the declaration: "Righteousness and justice are the foundation of His throne" (Ps. 97:2).

And you said to me, 'The word I have heard *is* good.' 43Why then have you not kept the oath of the Lord and the commandment that I gave you?" 44The king said moreover to Shimei, "You know, as your heart acknowledges, all the wickedness that you did to my father David; therefore the Lord will return your wickedness on your own head. 45But King Solomon *shall be* blessed, and the throne of David shall be established before the Lord forever."

46So the king commanded Benaiah the son of Jehoiada; and he went out and struck him down, and he died. Thus the kingdom was established in the hand of Solomon.

CHAPTER 3

3:1 *Politics.* The Jews were not forbidden to marry Egyptians, but Solomon's marriage to Pharaoh's daughter was the first step toward his breaking the law of God and bringing tragic consequences to himself and the people (1 Kings 11:1–8; see also Deut. 7:1–4). It was purely a political move designed to bring peace to the land, and it worked.

3:3–9 *Prayer.* How would you answer God's question: "What shall I give you?" Your answer reveals what you believe about yourself and the work God has called you to do. Solomon knew that he needed wisdom more than anything else, and God gave him that and much more (Matt. 6:33; Eph. 3:20–21). Prayer is not simply getting things from God. It is getting so that we might be able to give to others. Solomon's concern was ability to serve his people well.

3 Now* Solomon made a treaty with Pharaoh king of Egypt, and married Pharaoh's daughter; then he brought her to the City of David until he had finished building his own house, and the house of the Lord, and the wall all around Jerusalem. 2Meanwhile the people sacrificed at the high places, because there was no house built for the name of the Lord until those days. 3*And Solomon loved the Lord, walking in the statutes of his father David, except that he sacrificed and burned incense at the high places.

4Now the king went to Gibeon to sacrifice there, for that *was* the great high place: Solomon offered a thousand burnt offerings on that altar. 5At Gibeon the Lord appeared to Solomon in a dream by night; and God said, "Ask! What shall I give you?"

6And Solomon said: "You have shown great mercy to Your servant David my father, because he walked before You in truth, in righteousness, and in uprightness of heart with You; You have continued this great kindness for him, and You have given him a son to sit on his throne, as *it is* this day. 7Now, O Lord my God, You have made Your servant king instead of my father David, but I *am* a little child; I do not know *how* to go out or come in. 8And Your servant *is* in the midst of Your people whom You have chosen, a great people, too numerous to be numbered or counted. 9Therefore give to Your servant an understanding heart to judge Your people, that I may discern between good and evil. For who is able to judge this great people of Yours?"

10The speech pleased the Lord, that Solomon had asked this thing. 11Then God said to him: "Because you have asked this thing, and have not asked long life for yourself, nor have asked riches for yourself, nor have asked the life of your enemies, but have asked for yourself understanding to discern justice, 12behold, I have done according to your words; see, I have given you a wise and understanding heart, so that there has not been anyone like you before you, nor shall any like you arise after you. 13And I have also given you what you have not asked: both riches and honor, so that there shall not be anyone like you among the kings all your days. 14So if you walk in My ways, to keep My statutes and My commandments, as your father David walked, then I will lengthen your days."

15Then Solomon awoke; and indeed it had been a dream. And he came to Jerusalem and stood before the ark of the covenant of the Lord, offered up burnt offerings, offered peace offerings, and made a feast for all his servants.

3:16–28 *Perception.* Prostitutes had access to the king (Matt. 9:10–11)! The wisdom God gives is practical and helps us in the decisions of life (Prov. 1:1–7; James 1:5).

16*Now two women *who were* harlots came to the king, and stood before him. 17And one woman said, "O my lord, this woman and I dwell in the same house; and I gave birth while she *was* in the house. 18Then it happened, the third day after I had given birth, that this woman also gave birth. And we *were* together; no one *was* with us in the house, except the two of us in the house. 19And this woman's son died in the night, because she lay on him. 20So she arose in the middle of the night and took my son from my side, while your maidservant slept, and laid him in her bosom, and laid her dead child in my bosom. 21And when I rose in the morning to nurse my son, there he was, dead. But when I had examined him in the morning, indeed, he was not my son whom I had borne."

22Then the other woman said, "No! But the living one *is* my son, and the dead one *is* your son."

And the first woman said, "No! But the dead one *is* your son, and the living one *is* my son."

Thus they spoke before the king.

23And the king said, "The one says, 'This *is* my son, who lives, and your son *is* the dead one'; and the other says, 'No! But your son *is* the dead one, and my son *is* the living one.' " 24Then the king said, "Bring me a sword." So they brought a sword before the king. 25And the king said, "Divide the living child in two, and give half to one, and half to the other."

26Then the woman whose son *was* living spoke to the king, for she yearned with compassion for her son; and she said, "O my lord, give her the living child, and by no means kill him!"

But the other said, "Let him be neither mine nor yours, *but* divide *him*."

27So the king answered and said, "Give the first woman the living child, and by no means kill him; she *is* his mother."

28And all Israel heard of the judgment which the king had rendered; and they feared the king, for they saw that the wisdom of God *was* in him to administer justice.

4 So* King Solomon was king over all Israel. 2And these *were* his officials: Azariah the son of Zadok, the priest; 3Elihoreph and Ahijah, the sons of Shisha, scribes; Jehoshaphat the son of Ahilud, the recorder; 4Benaiah the son of Jehoiada, over the army; Zadok and Abiathar, the priests; 5Azariah the son of Nathan, over the officers; Zabud the son of Nathan, a priest *and* the king's friend; 6Ahishar, over the household; and Adoniram the son of Abda, over the labor force.

7And Solomon had twelve governors over all Israel, who provided food for the king and his household; each one made provision for one month of the year. 8These *are* their names: Ben-Hur,*b* in the mountains of Ephraim; 9Ben-Deker,*c* in Makaz, Shaalbim, Beth Shemesh, and Elon Beth Hanan; 10Ben-Hesed,*d* in Arubboth; to him *belonged* Sochoh and all the land of Hepher; 11Ben-Abinadab,*e in* all the regions of Dor; he had Taphath the daughter of Solomon as wife; 12Baana the son of Ahilud, *in* Taanach, Megiddo, and all Beth Shean, which *is* beside Zaretan below Jezreel, from Beth Shean to Abel Meholah, as far as the other side of Jokneam; 13Ben-Geber,*f* in Ramoth Gilead; to him *belonged* the towns of Jair

CHAPTER 4
4:1–19 Samuel's dire prediction came true (1 Sam. 8:10–18), for Solomon did a great deal of "taking." He divided the nation into twelve districts, each with a governor, and required each district to supply provisions for the royal household once a year. When you read the daily menu, you can see how difficult meeting those requirements must have been for the people (1 Kings 12:4).

4:8 *b*Literally *Son of Hur*   4:9 *c*Literally *Son of Deker*
4:10 *d*Literally *Son of Hesed*   4:11 *e*Literally *Son of Abinadab*
4:13 *f*Literally *Son of Geber*

the son of Manasseh, in Gilead; to him *also belonged* the region of Argob in Bashan—sixty large cities with walls and bronze gate-bars; [14]Ahinadab the son of Iddo, *in* Mahanaim; [15]Ahimaaz, in Naphtali; he also took Basemath the daughter of Solomon as wife; [16]Baanah the son of Hushai, in Asher and Aloth; [17]Jehoshaphat the son of Paruah, in Issachar; [18]Shimei the son of Elah, in Benjamin; [19]Geber the son of Uri, in the land of Gilead, *in* the country of Sihon king of the Amorites, and of Og king of Bashan. *He was* the only governor who *was* in the land.

[20]*Judah and Israel *were* as numerous as the sand by the sea in multitude, eating and drinking and rejoicing. [21]So Solomon reigned over all kingdoms from the River[g] *to* the land of the Philistines, as far as the border of Egypt. *They* brought tribute and served Solomon all the days of his life.

[22]Now Solomon's provision for one day was thirty kors of fine flour, sixty kors of meal, [23]ten fatted oxen, twenty oxen from the pastures, and one hundred sheep, besides deer, gazelles, roebucks, and fatted fowl.

[24]For he had dominion over all *the region* on this side of the River[h] from Tiphsah even to Gaza, namely over all the kings on this side of the River; and he had peace on every side all around him. [25]And Judah and Israel dwelt safely, each man under his vine and his fig tree, from Dan as far as Beersheba, all the days of Solomon.

[26]Solomon had forty[i] thousand stalls of horses for his chariots, and twelve thousand horsemen. [27]And these governors, each man in his month, provided food for King Solomon and for all who came to King Solomon's table. There was no lack in their supply. [28]They also brought barley and straw to the proper place, for the horses and steeds, each man according to his charge.

[29]*And God gave Solomon wisdom and exceedingly great understanding, and largeness of heart like the sand on the seashore. [30]Thus Solomon's wisdom excelled the wisdom of all the men of the East and all the wisdom of Egypt. [31]For he was wiser than all men—than Ethan the Ezrahite, and Heman, Chalcol, and Darda, the sons of Mahol; and his fame was in all the surrounding nations. [32]He spoke three thousand proverbs, and his songs were one thousand and five. [33]Also he spoke of trees, from the cedar tree of Lebanon even to the hyssop that springs out of the wall; he spoke also of animals, of birds, of creeping things, and of fish. [34]And men of all nations, from all the kings of the earth who had heard of his wisdom, came to hear the wisdom of Solomon.

5 Now Hiram king of Tyre sent his servants to Solomon, because he heard that they had anointed him king in place of his father, for Hiram

---

4:20 Verse 20 describes a prosperous people but not a spiritual people. Peace and prosperity do not always breed nobility of character, and rejoicing without responsibility is the way to ruin. As for Solomon's horses, read Deuteronomy 17:16.

4:29–34 Jesus Christ is "greater than Solomon" (Matt. 12:42) in wisdom (Col. 2:3), wealth (Col. 1:19; 2:9), and the bounty He shares with His people (Eph. 3:20–21). He does not promise you a life of "eat, drink, and be merry" (1 Kings 4:20), but He does promise to meet all your needs (Phil. 4:19) and never forsake you (Matt. 28:19–20; Heb. 13:5). One day you shall share His heavenly home and live with Him forever (John 14:1–6)!

4:21 [g]That is, the Euphrates   4:24 [h]That is, the Euphrates
4:26 [i]Following Masoretic Text and most other authorities; some manuscripts of the Septuagint read *four* (compare 2 Chronicles 9:25).

Pillars—The two pillars were called Jachin ("He will establish") and Boaz ("In Him is strength"). God provides stability and strength for His people because they worship Him. God's house was costly and beautiful, but it also needed stability and strength (Ps. 96:6).

had always loved David. ²Then Solomon sent to Hiram, saying:

3   You know how my father David could not
     build a house for the name of the LORD his
     God because of the wars which were fought
     against him on every side, until the LORD
     put *his foesʲ under the soles of his feet.
4   But now the LORD my God has given me
     rest on every side; *there is* neither adversary
     nor evil occurrence.
5   *And behold, I propose to build a house for
     the name of the LORD my God, as the LORD
     spoke to my father David, saying, "Your
     son, whom I will set on your throne in your
     place, he shall build the house for My
     name."
6   Now therefore, command that they cut
     down cedars for me from Lebanon; and my
     servants will be with your servants, and I
     will pay you wages for your servants
     according to whatever you say. For you
     know *there is* none among us who has skill
     to cut timber like the Sidonians.

⁷So it was, when Hiram heard the words of Solomon, that he rejoiced greatly and said,

     Blessed *be* the LORD this day, for He has
     given David a wise son over this great
     people!

⁸Then Hiram sent to Solomon, saying:

     I have considered *the message* which you
     sent me, *and* I will do all you desire
     concerning the cedar and cypress logs.
9   My servants shall bring *them* down from
     Lebanon to the sea; I will float them in rafts
     by sea to the place you indicate to me, and
     will have them broken apart there; then you
     can take *them* away. And you shall fulfill
     my desire by giving food for my household.

¹⁰Then Hiram gave Solomon cedar and cypress logs *according to* all his desire. ¹¹And Solomon gave Hiram twenty thousand kors of wheat *as* food for his household, and twentyᵏ kors of pressed oil. Thus Solomon gave to Hiram year by year.
¹²So the LORD gave Solomon wisdom, as He had promised him; and there was peace between Hiram and Solomon, and the two of them made a treaty together.
¹³Then King Solomon raised up a labor force out of all Israel; and the labor force was thirty thousand men. ¹⁴And he sent them to Lebanon, ten thousand a month in shifts: they were one month in Lebanon *and* two months at home; Adoniram *was* in charge of the labor force. ¹⁵Solomon had seventy thousand who carried burdens, and eighty thousand who quarried *stone* in the mountains, ¹⁶besides three thousand three hundredˡ from the chiefs of Solomon's deputies, who supervised the people who labored in the work. ¹⁷And the king commanded them to quarry large stones,

CHAPTERS 5—7

5:5–12 *Cooperation.* God gave David the design for the temple (1 Chron. 28:11–19), and David and the people provided most of the materials (1 Chron. 29). A gentile king, Hiram, supplied the timber, and a Canaanite work force (1 Kings 9:20–22) assisted the Jewish workers. It was a cooperative effort supervised by King Solomon. God is building His "holy temple" today (Eph. 2:19–22), and He uses the service of all kinds of people. Are you helping to build His church?

5:3 ʲLiterally *them*   5:11 ᵏFollowing Masoretic Text, Targum, and Vulgate; Septuagint and Syriac read *twenty thousand.*
5:16 ˡFollowing Masoretic Text, Targum, and Vulgate; Septuagint reads *three thousand six hundred.*

costly stones, *and* hewn stones, to lay the foundation of the temple.*m* [18]So Solomon's builders, Hiram's builders, and the Gebalites quarried *them;* and they prepared timber and stones to build the temple.

6 And it came to pass in the four hundred and eightieth[n] year after the children of Israel had come out of the land of Egypt, in the fourth year of Solomon's reign over Israel, in the month of Ziv, which *is* the second month, that he began to build the house of the LORD. [2]Now the house which King Solomon built for the LORD, its length *was* sixty cubits, its width twenty, and its height thirty cubits. [3]The vestibule in front of the sanctuary[o] of the house *was* twenty cubits long across the width of the house, *and* the width of *the vestibule*[p] extended ten cubits from the front of the house. [4]And he made for the house windows with beveled frames.

[5]Against the wall of the temple he built chambers all around, *against* the walls of the temple, all around the sanctuary and the inner sanctuary.[q] Thus he made side chambers all around it. [6]The lowest chamber *was* five cubits wide, the middle *was* six cubits wide, and the third *was* seven cubits wide; for he made narrow ledges around the outside of the temple, so that *the support beams* would not be fastened into the walls of the temple. [7]And the temple, when it was being built, was built with stone finished at the quarry, so that no hammer or chisel *or* any iron tool was heard in the temple while it was being built. [8]The doorway for the middle story[r] *was* on the right side of the temple. They went up by stairs to the middle *story,* and from the middle to the third.

[9]So he built the temple and finished it, and he paneled the temple with beams and boards of cedar. [10]And he built side chambers against the entire temple, each five cubits high; they were attached to the temple with cedar beams.

[11]Then the word of the LORD came to Solomon, saying: [12]"Concerning this temple which you are building, if you walk in My statutes, execute My judgments, keep all My commandments, and walk in them, then I will perform My word with you, which I spoke to your father David. [13]And I will dwell among the children of Israel, and will not forsake My people Israel."

[14]*So Solomon built the temple and finished it. [15]And he built the inside walls of the temple with cedar boards; from the floor of the temple to the ceiling he paneled the inside with wood; and he covered the floor of the temple with planks of cypress. [16]Then he built the twenty-cubit room at the rear of the temple, from floor to ceiling, with cedar boards; he built *it* inside as the inner sanctuary, as the Most Holy *Place.* [17]And in front of it the temple sanctuary was forty cubits *long.* [18]The inside of the temple was cedar, carved with

6:14–36 Construction. They built with gold, silver, and costly stones (1 Chron. 28:14—29:9), the same materials God wants in His church (1 Cor. 3:10–23; see also Prov. 2:1–9; 3:13–15; 8:10–11). Every detail was spelled out, and Solomon saw to it that the design was followed perfectly.

5:17 *m*Literally *house,* and so frequently throughout this book 6:1 *n*Following Masoretic Text, Targum, and Vulgate; Septuagint reads *fortieth.* 6:3 *o*Hebrew *heykal;* here the main room of the temple, elsewhere called the holy place (compare Exodus 26:33 and Ezekiel 41:1) *p*Literally *it* 6:5 *q*Hebrew *debir;* here the inner room of the temple, elsewhere called the Most Holy Place (compare verse 16) 6:8 *r*Following Masoretic Text and Vulgate; Septuagint reads *upper story;* Targum reads *ground story.*

ornamental buds and open flowers. All *was* cedar; there was no stone *to be* seen.

19And he prepared the inner sanctuary inside the temple, to set the ark of the covenant of the Lord there. 20The inner sanctuary *was* twenty cubits long, twenty cubits wide, and twenty cubits high. He overlaid it with pure gold, and overlaid the altar of cedar. 21So Solomon overlaid the inside of the temple with pure gold. He stretched gold chains across the front of the inner sanctuary, and overlaid it with gold. 22The whole temple he overlaid with gold, until he had finished all the temple; also he overlaid with gold the entire altar that *was* by the inner sanctuary.

23Inside the inner sanctuary he made two cherubim *of* olive wood, *each* ten cubits high. 24One wing of the cherub *was* five cubits, and the other wing of the cherub five cubits: ten cubits from the tip of one wing to the tip of the other. 25And the other cherub *was* ten cubits; both cherubim *were* of the same size and shape. 26The height of one cherub *was* ten cubits, and so *was* the other cherub. 27Then he set the cherubim inside the inner room;[s] and they stretched out the wings of the cherubim so that the wing of the one touched *one* wall, and the wing of the other cherub touched the other wall. And their wings touched each other in the middle of the room. 28Also he overlaid the cherubim with gold.

29Then he carved all the walls of the temple all around, both the inner and outer *sanctuaries,* with carved figures of cherubim, palm trees, and open flowers. 30And the floor of the temple he overlaid with gold, both the inner and outer *sanctuaries.*

31For the entrance of the inner sanctuary he made doors *of* olive wood; the lintel *and* doorposts *were* one-fifth *of the wall.* 32The two doors *were* of olive wood; and he carved on them figures of cherubim, palm trees, and open flowers, and overlaid *them* with gold; and he spread gold on the cherubim and on the palm trees. 33So for the door of the sanctuary he also made doorposts *of* olive wood, one-fourth *of the wall.* 34And the two doors *were of* cypress wood; two panels *comprised* one folding door, and two panels *comprised* the other folding door. 35Then he carved cherubim, palm trees, and open flowers *on them,* and overlaid *them* with gold applied evenly on the carved work.

36And he built the inner court with three rows of hewn stone and a row of cedar beams.

37In the fourth year the foundation of the house of the Lord was laid, in the month of Ziv. 38And in the eleventh year, in the month of Bul, which is the eighth month, the house was finished in all its details and according to all its plans. So he was seven years in building it.

7 But Solomon took thirteen years to build his own house; so he finished all his house.

2He also built the House of the Forest of Lebanon; its length *was* one hundred cubits, its width fifty cubits, and its height thirty cubits, with four rows of cedar pillars, and cedar beams on the pillars. 3And *it was* paneled with cedar above the beams that *were* on forty-five pillars, fifteen to a row. 4There were windows *with beveled frames* in three rows, and window *was* opposite window *in* three tiers. 5And all the doorways and door-

6:27 [s]Literally *house*

posts *had* rectangular frames; and window *was* opposite window *in* three tiers.

6He also made the Hall of Pillars: its length *was* fifty cubits, and its width thirty cubits; and in front of them *was* a portico with pillars, and a canopy *was* in front of them.

7Then he made a hall for the throne, the Hall of Judgment, where he might judge; and *it was* paneled with cedar from floor to ceiling.*t*

8And the house where he dwelt *had* another court inside the hall, of like workmanship. Solomon also made a house like this hall for Pharaoh's daughter, whom he had taken *as wife*.

9All these *were of* costly stones cut to size, trimmed with saws, inside and out, from the foundation to the eaves, and also on the outside to the great court. 10The foundation *was of* costly stones, large stones, some ten cubits and some eight cubits. 11And above *were* costly stones, hewn to size, and cedar wood. 12The great court *was* enclosed with three rows of hewn stones and a row of cedar beams. So were the inner court of the house of the LORD and the vestibule of the temple.

13Now King Solomon sent and brought Huram*u* from Tyre. 14He *was* the son of a widow from the tribe of Naphtali, and his father *was* a man of Tyre, a bronze worker; he was filled with wisdom and understanding and skill in working with all kinds of bronze work. So he came to King Solomon and did all his work.

15And he cast two pillars of bronze, each one eighteen cubits high, and a line of twelve cubits measured the circumference of each. 16Then he made two capitals *of* cast bronze, to set on the tops of the pillars. The height of one capital *was* five cubits, and the height of the other capital *was* five cubits. 17He made a lattice network, with wreaths of chainwork, for the capitals which *were* on top of the pillars: seven chains for one capital and seven for the other capital. 18So he made the pillars, and two rows of pomegranates above the network all around to cover the capitals that *were* on top; and thus he did for the other capital.

19The capitals which *were* on top of the pillars in the hall *were* in the shape of lilies, four cubits. 20The capitals on the two pillars also *had* pomegranates above, by the convex surface which *was* next to the network; and there *were* two hundred such pomegranates in rows on each of the capitals all around.

21Then he set up the pillars by the vestibule of the temple; he set up the pillar on the right and called its name Jachin, and he set up the pillar on the left and called its name Boaz. 22The tops of the pillars were in the shape of lilies. So the work of the pillars was finished.

23And he made the Sea of cast bronze, ten cubits from one brim to the other; *it was* completely round. Its height *was* five cubits, and a line of thirty cubits measured its circumference.

24Below its brim *were* ornamental buds encircling it all around, ten to a cubit, all the way around the Sea. The ornamental buds *were* cast in two rows when it was cast. 25It stood on twelve oxen: three looking toward the north, three looking toward the west, three looking toward the south, and three looking toward the east; the Sea

---

7:7 *t*Literally *floor,* that is, of the upper level   7:13 *u*Hebrew *Hiram* (compare 2 Chronicles 2:13, 14)

was set upon them, and all their back parts *pointed* inward. 26It *was* a handbreadth thick; and its brim was shaped like the brim of a cup, *like* a lily blossom. It contained two thousandᵛ baths.

27He also made ten carts of bronze; four cubits *was* the length of each cart, four cubits its width, and three cubits its height. 28And this *was* the design of the carts: They had panels, and the panels *were* between frames; 29on the panels that *were* between the frames *were* lions, oxen, and cherubim. And on the frames *was* a pedestal on top. Below the lions and oxen *were* wreaths of plaited work. 30Every cart had four bronze wheels and axles of bronze, and its four feet had supports. Under the laver *were* supports of cast *bronze* beside each wreath. 31Its opening inside the crown at the top *was* one cubit in diameter; and the opening *was* round, shaped *like* a pedestal, one and a half cubits in outside diameter; and also on the opening *were* engravings, but the panels were square, not round. 32Under the panels *were* the four wheels, and the axles of the wheels *were* *joined* to the cart. The height of a wheel *was* one and a half cubits. 33The workmanship of the wheels *was* like the workmanship of a chariot wheel; their axle pins, their rims, their spokes, and their hubs *were* all of cast *bronze*. 34And *there were* four supports at the four corners of each cart; its supports *were* part of the cart itself. 35On the top of the cart, at the height of half a cubit, *it was* perfectly round. And on the top of the cart, its flanges and its panels *were* of the same casting. 36On the plates of its flanges and on its panels he engraved cherubim, lions, and palm trees, wherever there was a clear space on each, with wreaths all around. 37Thus he made the ten carts. All of them were of the same mold, one measure, *and* one shape.

38Then he made ten lavers of bronze; each laver contained forty baths, *and* each laver *was* four cubits. On each of the ten carts *was* a laver. 39And he put five carts on the right side of the house, and five on the left side of the house. He set the Sea on the right side of the house, toward the southeast.

40Huramʷ made the lavers and the shovels and the bowls. So Huram finished doing all the work that he was to do for King Solomon *for* the house of the LORD: 41the two pillars, the *two* bowl-shaped capitals that *were* on top of the two pillars; the two networks covering the two bowl-shaped capitals which *were* on top of the pillars; 42four hundred pomegranates for the two networks (two rows of pomegranates for each network, to cover the two bowl-shaped capitals that *were* on top of the pillars); 43the ten carts, and ten lavers on the carts; 44one Sea, and twelve oxen under the Sea; 45the pots, the shovels, and the bowls.

All these articles which Huramˣ made for King Solomon *for* the house of the LORD *were of* burnished bronze. 46In the plain of Jordan the king had them cast in clay molds, between Succoth and Zaretan. 47And Solomon did not weigh all the articles, because *there were* so many; the weight of the bronze was not determined.

48*Thus Solomon had all the furnishings made for the house of the LORD: the altar of gold, and

---

7:26 ᵛOr *three thousand* (compare 2 Chronicles 4:5)
7:40 ʷHebrew *Hiram* (compare 2 Chronicles 2:13, 14)
7:45 ˣHebrew *Hiram* (compare 2 Chronicles 2:13, 14)

7:48–51 *Concern.* Wealth beyond measure went into the building of the temple, but the important thing was *obedience to the Lord* (1 Kings 6:11–13). God is not impressed with our buildings, for He provides everything we put into them (Isa. 66:1–2). He wants our loving obedience, and then He can make the buildings a blessing.

the table of gold on which *was* the showbread; [49]the lampstands of pure gold, five on the right *side* and five on the left in front of the inner sanctuary, with the flowers and the lamps and the wick-trimmers of gold; [50]the basins, the trimmers, the bowls, the ladles, and the censers of pure gold; and the hinges of gold, *both* for the doors of the inner room (the Most Holy *Place*) *and* for the doors of the main hall of the temple.

[51]So all the work that King Solomon had done for the house of the LORD was finished; and Solomon brought in the things which his father David had dedicated: the silver and the gold and the furnishings. He put them in the treasuries of the house of the LORD.

8:1–12 Solomon's temple was a place of glory. However, despite its extraordinary beauty, it was just another building until God moved in and consecrated it (Exod. 40:34–38). So it is with our lives (1 Cor. 6:19–20; Eph. 5:18) and our assemblies (1 Cor. 14:23–25). The presence of God is the important thing. A. W. Tozer aptly stated, "If God were to take the Holy Spirit out of this world, much of what the church is doing would go right on, *and nobody would know the difference.*"

8:14–21 The temple was a place of testimony (vv. 14–21, 56), bearing witness that God keeps His word. It was to be a place of prayer (vv. 22–53). Solomon was especially concerned that God hear the prayers of His own people as well as those of the stranger and foreigner. In later years, the religious leaders would turn the house of prayer into a den of thieves (Matt. 21:12–13).

8 Now* Solomon assembled the elders of Israel and all the heads of the tribes, the chief fathers of the children of Israel, to King Solomon in Jerusalem, that they might bring up the ark of the covenant of the LORD from the City of David, which *is* Zion. [2]Therefore all the men of Israel assembled with King Solomon at the feast in the month of Ethanim, which *is* the seventh month. [3]So all the elders of Israel came, and the priests took up the ark. [4]Then they brought up the ark of the LORD, the tabernacle of meeting, and all the holy furnishings that *were* in the tabernacle. The priests and the Levites brought them up. [5]Also King Solomon, and all the congregation of Israel who were assembled with him, *were* with him before the ark, sacrificing sheep and oxen that could not be counted or numbered for multitude. [6]Then the priests brought in the ark of the covenant of the LORD to its place, into the inner sanctuary of the temple, to the Most Holy *Place*, under the wings of the cherubim. [7]For the cherubim spread *their* two wings over the place of the ark, and the cherubim overshadowed the ark and its poles. [8]The poles extended so that the ends of the poles could be seen from the holy *place*, in front of the inner sanctuary; but they could not be seen from outside. And they are there to this day. [9]Nothing *was* in the ark except the two tablets of stone which Moses put there at Horeb, when the LORD made *a covenant* with the children of Israel, when they came out of the land of Egypt.

[10]And it came to pass, when the priests came out of the holy *place*, that the cloud filled the house of the LORD, [11]so that the priests could not continue ministering because of the cloud; for the glory of the LORD filled the house of the LORD.

[12]Then Solomon spoke:

"The LORD said He would dwell in the dark cloud.
[13] I have surely built You an exalted house,
And a place for You to dwell in forever."

[14]*Then the king turned around and blessed the whole assembly of Israel, while all the assembly

Who Is Justified?—Solomon prayed that God would condemn the wicked and justify the righteous (1 Kings 8:32). But through Jesus Christ, God justifies (declares righteous) *the wicked* (Rom. 4:5), and He does it on the basis of grace, not works. God cannot justify the righteous because *there are none* (Rom. 3:10).

The Heart of the Matter—Solomon's emphasis was on the heart: each one knows his own heart (1 Kings 8:38); God knows the heart (v. 39); we return to God with all our hearts (v. 48); God must incline our hearts to obedience (v. 58); God wants each of us to have a loyal heart (v. 61).

of Israel was standing. 15And he said: "Blessed
be the LORD God of Israel, who spoke with His
mouth to my father David, and with His hand has
fulfilled *it,* saying, 16'Since the day that I brought
My people Israel out of Egypt, I have chosen no
city from any tribe of Israel *in which* to build a
house, that My name might be there; but I chose
David to be over My people Israel.' 17Now it was
in the heart of my father David to build a temple^y
for the name of the LORD God of Israel. 18But the
LORD said to my father David, 'Whereas it was
in your heart to build a temple for My name, you
did well that it was in your heart. 19Nevertheless
you shall not build the temple, but your son who
will come from your body, he shall build the temple for My name.' 20So the LORD has fulfilled His
word which He spoke; and I have filled the position of my father David, and sit on the throne of
Israel, as the LORD promised; and I have built a
temple for the name of the LORD God of Israel.
21And there I have made a place for the ark, in
which *is* the covenant of the LORD which He made
with our fathers, when He brought them out of
the land of Egypt."

22Then Solomon stood before the altar of the
LORD in the presence of all the assembly of Israel,
and spread out his hands toward heaven; 23and
he said: "LORD God of Israel, *there is* no God in
heaven above or on earth below like You, who
keep *Your* covenant and mercy with Your servants who walk before You with all their hearts.
24You have kept what You promised Your servant
David my father; You have both spoken with Your
mouth and fulfilled *it* with Your hand, as *it is* this
day. 25Therefore, LORD God of Israel, now keep
what You promised Your servant David my father, saying, 'You shall not fail to have a man sit
before Me on the throne of Israel, only if your
sons take heed to their way, that they walk before
Me as you have walked before Me.' 26And now I
pray, O God of Israel, let Your word come true,
which You have spoken to Your servant David
my father.

27"But will God indeed dwell on the earth? Behold, heaven and the heaven of heavens cannot
contain You. How much less this temple which I
have built! 28Yet regard the prayer of Your servant and his supplication, O LORD my God, and
listen to the cry and the prayer which Your servant is praying before You today: 29that Your eyes
may be open toward this temple night and day,
toward the place of which You said, 'My name
shall be there,' that You may hear the prayer
which Your servant makes toward this place.
30And may You hear the supplication of Your servant and of Your people Israel, when they pray
toward this place. Hear in heaven Your dwelling
place; and when You hear, forgive.

31"When anyone sins against his neighbor, and
is forced to take an oath, and comes *and* takes
an oath before Your altar in this temple, 32then
hear in heaven, and act, and judge Your servants,
condemning the wicked, bringing his way on his
head, and justifying the righteous by giving him
according to his righteousness.

33"When Your people Israel are defeated before
an enemy because they have sinned against You,
and when they turn back to You and confess Your
name, and pray and make supplication to You in

8:17 ^yLiterally *house,* and so in verses 18–20

this temple, 34then hear in heaven, and forgive the sin of Your people Israel, and bring them back to the land which You gave to their fathers.

35"When the heavens are shut up and there is no rain because they have sinned against You, when they pray toward this place and confess Your name, and turn from their sin because You afflict them, 36then hear in heaven, and forgive the sin of Your servants, Your people Israel, that You may teach them the good way in which they should walk; and send rain on Your land which You have given to Your people as an inheritance.

37"When there is famine in the land, pestilence or blight or mildew, locusts or grasshoppers; when their enemy besieges them in the land of their cities; whatever plague or whatever sickness there is; 38whatever prayer, whatever supplication is made by anyone, or by all Your people Israel, when each one knows the plague of his own heart, and spreads out his hands toward this temple: 39then hear in heaven Your dwelling place, and forgive, and act, and give to everyone according to all his ways, whose heart You know (for You alone know the hearts of all the sons of men), 40that they may fear You all the days that they live in the land which You gave to our fathers.

41"Moreover, concerning a foreigner, who is not of Your people Israel, but has come from a far country for Your name's sake 42(for they will hear of Your great name and Your strong hand and Your outstretched arm), when he comes and prays toward this temple, 43hear in heaven Your dwelling place, and do according to all for which the foreigner calls to You, that all peoples of the earth may know Your name and fear You, as do Your people Israel, and that they may know that this temple which I have built is called by Your name.

44"When Your people go out to battle against their enemy, wherever You send them, and when they pray to the LORD toward the city which You have chosen and the temple which I have built for Your name, 45then hear in heaven their prayer and their supplication, and maintain their cause.

46"When they sin against You (for there is no one who does not sin), and You become angry with them and deliver them to the enemy, and they take them captive to the land of the enemy, far or near; 47yet when they come to themselves in the land where they were carried captive, and repent, and make supplication to You in the land of those who took them captive, saying, 'We have sinned and done wrong, we have committed wickedness'; 48and when they return to You with all their heart and with all their soul in the land of their enemies who led them away captive, and pray to You toward their land which You gave to their fathers, the city which You have chosen and the temple which I have built for Your name: 49then hear in heaven Your dwelling place their prayer and their supplication, and maintain their cause, 50and forgive Your people who have sinned against You, and all their transgressions which they have transgressed against You; and grant them compassion before those who took them captive, that they may have compassion on them 51(for they are Your people and Your inheritance, whom You brought out of Egypt, out of the iron furnace), 52that Your eyes may be open to the supplication of Your servant and the supplication of Your people Israel, to listen to them whenever they call to You. 53For You separated them from among all the peoples of the earth *to be* Your inheritance, as You spoke by Your servant Moses, when You brought our fathers out of Egypt, O Lord GOD."

54*And so it was, when Solomon had finished praying all this prayer and supplication to the LORD, that he arose from before the altar of the LORD, from kneeling on his knees with his hands spread up to heaven. 55Then he stood and blessed all the assembly of Israel with a loud voice, saying: 56"Blessed *be* the LORD, who has given rest to His people Israel, according to all that He promised. There has not failed one word of all His good promise, which He promised through His servant Moses. 57May the LORD our God be with us, as He was with our fathers. May He not leave us nor forsake us, 58that He may incline our hearts to Himself, to walk in all His ways, and to keep His commandments and His statutes and His judgments, which He commanded our fathers. 59And may these words of mine, with which I have made supplication before the LORD, be near the LORD our God day and night, that He may maintain the cause of His servant and the cause of His people Israel, as each day may require, 60*that all the peoples of the earth may know that the LORD *is* God; *there is* no other. 61Let your heart therefore be loyal to the LORD our God, to walk in His statutes and keep His commandments, as at this day."

62Then the king and all Israel with him offered sacrifices before the LORD. 63And Solomon offered a sacrifice of peace offerings, which he offered to the LORD, twenty-two thousand bulls and one hundred and twenty thousand sheep. So the king and all the children of Israel dedicated the house of the LORD. 64On the same day the king consecrated the middle of the court that *was* in front of the house of the LORD; for there he offered burnt offerings, grain offerings, and the fat of the peace offerings, because the bronze altar that *was* before the LORD *was* too small to receive the burnt offerings, the grain offerings, and the fat of the peace offerings.

65At that time Solomon held a feast, and all Israel with him, a great assembly from the entrance of Hamath to the Brook of Egypt, before the LORD our God, seven days and seven *more* days—fourteen days. 66On the eighth day he sent the people away; and they blessed the king, and went to their tents joyful and glad of heart for all the good that the LORD had done for His servant David, and for Israel His people.

9 And* it came to pass, when Solomon had finished building the house of the LORD and the king's house, and all Solomon's desire which he wanted to do, 2that the LORD appeared to Solomon the second time, as He had appeared to him at Gibeon. 3And the LORD said to him: "I have heard your prayer and your supplication that you have made before Me; I have consecrated this house which you have built to put My name there forever, and My eyes and My heart will be there perpetually. 4*Now if you walk before Me as your father David walked, in integrity of heart and in uprightness, to do according to all that I have commanded you, *and* if you keep My statutes and My judgments, 5then I will establish the throne of your kingdom over Israel forever, as I promised David your father, saying, 'You shall not fail to have a man on the throne of Israel.' 6*But* if you

8:54–61 It was a place of blessing and sacrifice (vv. 62–66). The two go together: we give our best to the Lord, and then we share our best with others. It is unfortunate that Solomon failed in the very thing he exhorted his people to remember—loyalty of heart (v. 61).

8:60 Finally, the temple was a place of witness to the world (vv. 41–43, 60), for Solomon had a "missionary vision" for the gentile nations. What an opportunity Israel had to win the lost people around them!

CHAPTER 9

9:1–3 *Assurance.* We dedicate, but only God can consecrate (sanctify) what we give Him. It is important to hear from God when a task has been completed, lest there be a letdown that can lead to discouragement (1 Kings 19). The phrases "My name . . . My eyes . . . My heart" (v. 3) indicate God's nearness to His people. He is identified with us; He watches over us; He loves us.

9:4–8 *Admonition.* Because He loves us, God warns us not to disobey Him. Solomon did not heed this warning, and God kept His promise and sent discipline. God would rather destroy His holy temple than permit His people to pollute it with their sin.

9:10–19 Agreement. Solomon was a successful maker of treaties with the Gentiles, and that ability helped to keep Israel out of war. However, there was a price to pay and a constant danger to avoid. Ultimately, Solomon was controlled by the gods of those nations (1 Kings 11).

or your sons at all turn from following Me, and do not keep My commandments *and* My statutes which I have set before you, but go and serve other gods and worship them, 7then I will cut off Israel from the land which I have given them; and this house which I have consecrated for My name I will cast out of My sight. Israel will be a proverb and a byword among all peoples. 8And *as for* this house, *which* is exalted, everyone who passes by it will be astonished and will hiss, and say, 'Why has the LORD done thus to this land and to this house?' 9Then they will answer, 'Because they forsook the LORD their God, who brought their fathers out of the land of Egypt, and have embraced other gods, and worshiped them and served them; therefore the LORD has brought all this calamity on them.' "

10*Now it happened at the end of twenty years, when Solomon had built the two houses, the house of the LORD and the king's house 11(Hiram the king of Tyre had supplied Solomon with cedar and cypress and gold, as much as he desired), *that* King Solomon then gave Hiram twenty cities in the land of Galilee. 12Then Hiram went from Tyre to see the cities which Solomon had given him, but they did not please him. 13So he said, "What *kind of* cities *are* these which you have given me, my brother?" And he called them the land of Cabul,z as they are to this day. 14Then Hiram sent the king one hundred and twenty talents of gold.

15And this *is* the reason for the labor force which King Solomon raised: to build the house of the LORD, his own house, the Millo,a the wall of Jerusalem, Hazor, Megiddo, and Gezer. 16(Pharaoh king of Egypt had gone up and taken Gezer and burned it with fire, had killed the Canaanites who dwelt in the city, and had given it *as* a dowry to his daughter, Solomon's wife.) 17And Solomon built Gezer, Lower Beth Horon, 18Baalath, and Tadmor in the wilderness, in the land *of Judah,* 19all the storage cities that Solomon had, cities for his chariots and cities for his cavalry, and whatever Solomon desired to build in Jerusalem, in Lebanon, and in all the land of his dominion.

20All the people *who were* left of the Amorites, Hittites, Perizzites, Hivites, and Jebusites, who *were* not of the children of Israel— 21that is, their descendants who were left in the land after them, whom the children of Israel had not been able to destroy completely—from these Solomon raised forced labor, as it is to this day. 22But of the children of Israel Solomon made no forced laborers, because they *were* men of war and his servants: his officers, his captains, commanders of his chariots, and his cavalry.

23Others *were* chiefs of the officials who *were* over Solomon's work: five hundred and fifty, who ruled over the people who did the work.

24But Pharaoh's daughter came up from the City of David to her house which Solomonb had built for her. Then he built the Millo.

25Now three times a year Solomon offered burnt offerings and peace offerings on the altar which he had built for the LORD, and he burned incense with them *on the altar* that *was* before the LORD. So he finished the temple.

26*King Solomon also built a fleet of ships at

9:26–28 Achievement. But everything looked grand as Solomon built buildings, walls, and ships and increased the wealth of the nation. They needed the warning of Revelation 3:17–18. The spiritual life of the nation was gradually decaying behind the veneer of prosperity.

9:13 zLiterally *Good for Nothing*   9:15 aLiterally *The Landfill*
9:24 bLiterally *he* (compare 2 Chronicles 8:11)

Ezion Geber, which *is* near Elath[c] on the shore of the Red Sea, in the land of Edom. 27Then Hiram sent his servants with the fleet, seamen who knew the sea, to work with the servants of Solomon. 28And they went to Ophir, and acquired four hundred and twenty talents of gold from there, and brought *it* to King Solomon.

10 Now* when the queen of Sheba heard of the fame of Solomon concerning the name of the LORD, she came to test him with hard questions. 2*She came to Jerusalem with a very great retinue, with camels that bore spices, very much gold, and precious stones; and when she came to Solomon, she spoke with him about all that was in her heart. 3So Solomon answered all her questions; there was nothing so difficult for the king that he could not explain *it* to her. 4And when the queen of Sheba had seen all the wisdom of Solomon, the house that he had built, 5the food on his table, the seating of his servants, the service of his waiters and their apparel, his cupbearers, and his entryway by which he went up to the house of the LORD, there was no more spirit in her. 6Then she said to the king: "It was a true report which I heard in my own land about your words and your wisdom. 7*However I did not believe the words until I came and saw with my own eyes; and indeed the half was not told me. Your wisdom and prosperity exceed the fame of which I heard. 8Happy *are* your men and happy *are* these your servants, who stand continually before you *and* hear your wisdom! 9Blessed be the LORD your God, who delighted in you, setting you on the throne of Israel! Because the LORD has loved Israel forever, therefore He made you king, to do justice and righteousness."

10Then she gave the king one hundred and twenty talents of gold, spices in great quantity, and precious stones. There never again came such abundance of spices as the queen of Sheba gave to King Solomon. 11Also, the ships of Hiram, which brought gold from Ophir, brought great *quantities* of almug[d] wood and precious stones from Ophir. 12And the king made steps of the almug wood for the house of the LORD and for the king's house, also harps and stringed instruments for singers. There never again came such almug wood, nor has the like been seen to this day.

13Now King Solomon gave the queen of Sheba all she desired, whatever she asked, besides what Solomon had given her according to the royal generosity. So she turned and went to her own country, she and her servants.

14The weight of gold that came to Solomon yearly was six hundred and sixty-six talents of gold, 15besides *that* from the traveling merchants, from the income of traders, from all the kings of Arabia, and from the governors of the country.

16And King Solomon made two hundred large shields *of* hammered gold; six hundred *shekels* of gold went into each shield. 17He also *made* three hundred shields *of* hammered gold; three minas of gold went into each shield. The king put them in the House of the Forest of Lebanon.

18Moreover the king made a great throne of ivory, and overlaid it with pure gold. 19The throne had six steps, and the top of the throne *was* round

CHAPTER 10

10:1 Our fame and God's name must go together (v. 1). If God magnifies your name (Josh. 3:7; 6:27), be sure He gets the glory (Ps. 135:13). Fame is a heavy burden to bear, and only God can help us do it wisely.

10:2–10 The queen traveled twelve hundred miles to see and hear Solomon. Her reasons were both personal and political, for she wanted to enter into trade agreements with the king. The people of Jesus' day rejected a "greater than Solomon" who was there among them (Matt. 12:42), and they were judged for it.

10:7 Do we take our blessings for granted? In spite of the queen's enthusiasm, perhaps even Solomon's servants got accustomed to hearing his wise words and beholding his great wealth (v. 8). Israel grew accustomed to the miracle of the manna (Num. 11), and the church at Ephesus grew accustomed to Christ's love (Rev. 2:1–7).

9:26 [c]Hebrew *Eloth* (compare 2 Kings 14:22)   10:11 [d]Or *algum* (compare 2 Chronicles 9:10, 11)

at the back; *there were* armrests on either side of the place of the seat, and two lions stood beside the armrests. 20Twelve lions stood there, one on each side of the six steps; nothing like *this* had been made for any *other* kingdom.

21All King Solomon's drinking vessels *were* gold, and all the vessels of the House of the Forest of Lebanon *were* pure gold. Not *one was* silver, for this was accounted as nothing in the days of Solomon. 22For the king had merchant ships*e* at sea with the fleet of Hiram. Once every three years the merchant ships came bringing gold, silver, ivory, apes, and monkeys.*f* 23So King Solomon surpassed all the kings of the earth in riches and wisdom.

24Now all the earth sought the presence of Solomon to hear his wisdom, which God had put in his heart. 25Each man brought his present: articles of silver and gold, garments, armor, spices, horses, and mules, at a set rate year by year.

26And Solomon gathered chariots and horsemen; he had one thousand four hundred chariots and twelve thousand horsemen, whom he stationed*g* in the chariot cities and with the king at Jerusalem. 27The king made silver *as common* in Jerusalem as stones, and he made cedar trees as abundant as the sycamores which *are* in the lowland.

28*Also Solomon had horses imported from Egypt and Keveh; the king's merchants bought them in Keveh at the *current* price. 29Now a chariot that was imported from Egypt cost six hundred *shekels* of silver, and a horse one hundred and fifty; and thus, through their agents,*h* they exported *them* to all the kings of the Hittites and the kings of Syria.

11 But* King Solomon loved many foreign women, as well as the daughter of Pharaoh: women of the Moabites, Ammonites, Edomites, Sidonians, *and* Hittites— 2from the nations of whom the LORD had said to the children of Israel, "You shall not intermarry with them, nor they with you. Surely they will turn away your hearts after their gods." Solomon clung to these in love. 3And he had seven hundred wives, princesses, and three hundred concubines; and his wives turned away his heart. 4For it was so, when Solomon was old, that his wives turned his heart after other gods; and his heart was not loyal to the LORD his God, as *was* the heart of his father David. 5For Solomon went after Ashtoreth the goddess of the Sidonians, and after Milcom the abomination of the Ammonites. 6Solomon did evil in the sight of the LORD, and did not fully follow the LORD, as *did* his father David. 7Then Solomon built a high place for Chemosh the abomination of Moab, on the hill that *is* east of Jerusalem, and for Molech the abomination of the people of Ammon. 8And he did likewise for all his foreign wives, who burned incense and sacrificed to their gods.

9*So the LORD became angry with Solomon, because his heart had turned from the LORD God of Israel, who had appeared to him twice, 10and had commanded him concerning this thing, that he

10:28, 29 Chariots and horses were another indication of decay (Deut. 17:17). And don't forget what Jesus said about all of Solomon's glory (Matt. 6:29).

CHAPTER 11

11:1–8 Apostasy. Solomon had wisdom for everybody else but would not apply it to himself (Rom. 2:21–24). The man who wrote Proverbs 4:23 did not obey it (v. 4; 1 Kings 8:61). The king was required to write a personal copy of Deuteronomy and study it (Deut. 17:18–20), so surely Solomon knew Deuteronomy 7:1–11; 17:17. It is one thing to know the Word but quite another thing to do it (James 1:22–25).

11:9 Anger. God's blessings are given by grace, but they are enjoyed by obedience. Solomon was disobedient, and yet surely he knew that the covenant included warnings about disobedience (2 Sam. 7:14; 1 Kings 3:14; 9:4–9).

10:22 *e*Literally *ships of Tarshish,* deep-sea vessels *f*Or *peacocks* 10:26 *g*Following Septuagint, Syriac, Targum, and Vulgate (compare 2 Chronicles 9:25); Masoretic Text reads *led.* 10:29 *h*Literally *by their hands*

should not go after other gods; but he did not keep what the LORD had commanded. 11Therefore the LORD said to Solomon, "Because you have done this, and have not kept My covenant and My statutes, which I have commanded you, I will surely tear the kingdom away from you and give it to your servant. 12Nevertheless I will not do it in your days, for the sake of your father David; I will tear it out of the hand of your son. 13However I will not tear away the whole kingdom; I will give one tribe to your son for the sake of my servant David, and for the sake of Jerusalem which I have chosen."

14*Now the LORD raised up an adversary against Solomon, Hadad the Edomite; he was a descendant of the king in Edom. 15For it happened, when David was in Edom, and Joab the commander of the army had gone up to bury the slain, after he had killed every male in Edom 16(because for six months Joab remained there with all Israel, until he had cut down every male in Edom), 17that Hadad fled to go to Egypt, he and certain Edomites of his father's servants with him. Hadad was still a little child. 18Then they arose from Midian and came to Paran; and they took men with them from Paran and came to Egypt, to Pharaoh king of Egypt, who gave him a house, apportioned food for him, and gave him land. 19And Hadad found great favor in the sight of Pharaoh, so that he gave him as wife the sister of his own wife, that is, the sister of Queen Tahpenes. 20Then the sister of Tahpenes bore him Genubath his son, whom Tahpenes weaned in Pharaoh's house. And Genubath was in Pharaoh's household among the sons of Pharaoh.

21So when Hadad heard in Egypt that David rested with his fathers, and that Joab the commander of the army was dead, Hadad said to Pharaoh, "Let me depart, that I may go to my own country."

22Then Pharaoh said to him, "But what have you lacked with me, that suddenly you seek to go to your own country?"

So he answered, "Nothing, but do let me go anyway."

23And God raised up another adversary against him, Rezon the son of Eliadah, who had fled from his lord, Hadadezer king of Zobah. 24So he gathered men to him and became captain over a band of raiders, when David killed those of Zobah. And they went to Damascus and dwelt there, and reigned in Damascus. 25He was an adversary of Israel all the days of Solomon (besides the trouble that Hadad caused); and he abhorred Israel, and reigned over Syria.

26Then Solomon's servant, Jeroboam the son of Nebat, an Ephraimite from Zereda, whose mother's name was Zeruah, a widow, also rebelled against the king.

27And this is what caused him to rebel against the king: Solomon had built the Millo and repaired the damages to the City of David his father. 28The man Jeroboam was a mighty man of valor; and Solomon, seeing that the young man was industrious, made him the officer over all the labor force of the house of Joseph.

29Now it happened at that time, when Jeroboam went out of Jerusalem, that the prophet Ahijah the Shilonite met him on the way; and he had clothed himself with a new garment, and the two were alone in the field. 30Then Ahijah took hold of the new garment that was on him, and tore it

11:14–43 Adversaries. God had a special love for Solomon (2 Sam. 12:24–25); therefore, He had to chasten him (Prov. 3:11–12). Hadad, Rezon, and Jeroboam all created problems for the king as the flimsy tissue of Israel's "peace" began to fall apart. Solomon even planned to murder his rival, Jeroboam! God was kind to Solomon only for the sake of David (v. 32), but how long can a nation (or a church or a family) live on the spiritual dividends of their ancestors' sacrifice and obedience?

into twelve pieces. ³¹And he said to Jeroboam, "Take for yourself ten pieces, for thus says the LORD, the God of Israel: 'Behold, I will tear the kingdom out of the hand of Solomon and will give ten tribes to you ³²(but he shall have one tribe for the sake of My servant David, and for the sake of Jerusalem, the city which I have chosen out of all the tribes of Israel), ³³because they haveⁱ forsaken Me, and worshiped Ashtoreth the goddess of the Sidonians, Chemosh the god of the Moabites, and Milcom the god of the people of Ammon, and have not walked in My ways to do *what is* right in My eyes and *keep* My statutes and My judgments, as *did* his father David. ³⁴However I will not take the whole kingdom out of his hand, because I have made him ruler all the days of his life for the sake of My servant David, whom I chose because he kept My commandments and My statutes. ³⁵But I will take the kingdom out of his son's hand and give it to you— ten tribes. ³⁶And to his son I will give one tribe, that My servant David may always have a lamp before Me in Jerusalem, the city which I have chosen for Myself, to put My name there. ³⁷So I will take you, and you shall reign over all your heart desires, and you shall be king over Israel. ³⁸Then it shall be, if you heed all that I command you, walk in My ways, and do *what is* right in My sight, to keep My statutes and My commandments, as My servant David did, then I will be with you and build for you an enduring house, as I built for David, and will give Israel to you. ³⁹And I will afflict the descendants of David because of this, but not forever.'"

⁴⁰Solomon therefore sought to kill Jeroboam. But Jeroboam arose and fled to Egypt, to Shishak king of Egypt, and was in Egypt until the death of Solomon.

⁴¹Now the rest of the acts of Solomon, all that he did, and his wisdom, *are* they not written in the book of the acts of Solomon? ⁴²And the period that Solomon reigned in Jerusalem over all Israel *was* forty years. ⁴³Then Solomon rested with his fathers, and was buried in the City of David his father. And Rehoboam his son reigned in his place.

CHAPTER 12

12:1–15 Rehoboam did not seek God's wisdom, as had his father before him (1 Kings 3). Instead, he turned to men for guidance and even then did not heed the right advice. Like some people who seek counsel today, he wanted somebody to tell him to do what he already decided to do. The new king grew up in luxury. What did he know about the burdens of the common people?

12 And* Rehoboam went to Shechem, for all Israel had gone to Shechem to make him king. ²So it happened, when Jeroboam the son of Nebat heard *it* (he was still in Egypt, for he had fled from the presence of King Solomon and had been dwelling in Egypt), ³that they sent and called him. Then Jeroboam and the whole assembly of Israel came and spoke to Rehoboam, saying, ⁴"Your father made our yoke heavy; now therefore, lighten the burdensome service of your father, and his heavy yoke which he put on us, and we will serve you."

⁵So he said to them, "Depart *for* three days, then come back to me." And the people departed.

⁶Then King Rehoboam consulted the elders who stood before his father Solomon while he still lived, and he said, "How do you advise *me* to answer these people?"

⁷And they spoke to him, saying, "If you will be a servant to these people today, and serve them, and answer them, and speak good words

---

11:33 ⁱFollowing Masoretic Text and Targum; Septuagint, Syriac, and Vulgate read *he has.*

to them, then they will be your servants forever."

8But he rejected the advice which the elders had given him, and consulted the young men who had grown up with him, who stood before him. 9And he said to them, "What advice do you give? How should we answer this people who have spoken to me, saying, 'Lighten the yoke which your father put on us'?"

10Then the young men who had grown up with him spoke to him, saying, "Thus you should speak to this people who have spoken to you, saying, 'Your father made our yoke heavy, but you make *it* lighter on us'—thus you shall say to them: 'My little *finger* shall be thicker than my father's waist! 11And now, whereas my father put a heavy yoke on you, I will add to your yoke; my father chastised you with whips, but I will chastise you with scourges!' "*j*

12So Jeroboam and all the people came to Rehoboam the third day, as the king had directed, saying, "Come back to me the third day." 13*Then the king answered the people roughly, and rejected the advice which the elders had given him; 14and he spoke to them according to the advice of the young men, saying, "My father made your yoke heavy, but I will add to your yoke; my father chastised you with whips, but I will chastise you with scourges!"*k* 15So the king did not listen to the people; for the turn *of events* was from the LORD, that He might fulfill His word, which the LORD had spoken by Ahijah the Shilonite to Jeroboam the son of Nebat.

16Now when all Israel saw that the king did not listen to them, the people answered the king, saying:

"What share have we in David?
    We have no inheritance in the son of Jesse.
    To your tents, O Israel!
    Now, see to your own house, O David!"

So Israel departed to their tents. 17But Rehoboam reigned over the children of Israel who dwelt in the cities of Judah.

18Then King Rehoboam sent Adoram, who *was* in charge of the revenue; but all Israel stoned him with stones, and he died. Therefore King Rehoboam mounted his chariot in haste to flee to Jerusalem. 19So Israel has been in rebellion against the house of David to this day.

20Now it came to pass when all Israel heard that Jeroboam had come back, they sent for him and called him to the congregation, and made him king over all Israel. There was none who followed the house of David, but the tribe of Judah only.

21And when Rehoboam came to Jerusalem, he assembled all the house of Judah with the tribe of Benjamin, one hundred and eighty thousand chosen *men* who were warriors, to fight against the house of Israel, that he might restore the kingdom to Rehoboam the son of Solomon. 22But the word of God came to Shemaiah the man of God, saying, 23"Speak to Rehoboam the son of Solomon, king of Judah, to all the house of Judah and Benjamin, and to the rest of the people, saying, 24'Thus says the LORD: "You shall not go up nor fight against your brethren the children of Israel. Let every man return to his house, for this thing is from Me." ' " Therefore they obeyed the

12:13 We lead by serving (Matt. 20:20–28), and a true leader seeks to lighten the loads people carry. (Compare Matt. 11:28–30 and 23:4.) The king used the people to build his authority instead of using his authority to build the people. The result was a divided nation as Ahijah predicted (1 Kings 11:29ff.). As much as we love unity, we must accept the fact that some divisions are of God.

12:11 *j*Literally *scorpions*   12:14 *k*Literally *scorpions*

12:28–33 Afraid that his people would return to Jerusalem to worship, Jeroboam established a "religion of convenience" (v. 28) and made it easy for the nation to sin. Abandoning the true worship of Jehovah, he repeated the sin of Aaron (Exod. 32). Patterned after the Mosaic system, his religion was popular, but it did not have God's approval (Hos. 13:2).

CHAPTER 13

13:1–10 *Courage.* The anonymous prophet received his message from God and delivered it to the king. It was fulfilled nearly three hundred years later by King Josiah (2 Kings 23:15–20). The prophet did not fear the king's threats or succumb to the king's bribes, both of which would have invalidated his ministry.

word of the LORD, and turned back, according to the word of the LORD.

25Then Jeroboam built Shechem in the mountains of Ephraim, and dwelt there. Also he went out from there and built Penuel. 26And Jeroboam said in his heart, "Now the kingdom may return to the house of David: 27If these people go up to offer sacrifices in the house of the LORD at Jerusalem, then the heart of this people will turn back to their lord, Rehoboam king of Judah, and they will kill me and go back to Rehoboam king of Judah."

28*Therefore the king asked advice, made two calves of gold, and said to the people, "It is too much for you to go up to Jerusalem. Here are your gods, O Israel, which brought you up from the land of Egypt!" 29And he set up one in Bethel, and the other he put in Dan. 30Now this thing became a sin, for the people went *to worship* before the one as far as Dan. 31He made shrines[l] on the high places, and made priests from every class of people, who were not of the sons of Levi.

32Jeroboam ordained a feast on the fifteenth day of the eighth month, like the feast that *was* in Judah, and offered sacrifices on the altar. So he did at Bethel, sacrificing to the calves that he had made. And at Bethel he installed the priests of the high places which he had made. 33So he made offerings on the altar which he had made at Bethel on the fifteenth day of the eighth month, in the month which he had devised in his own heart. And he ordained a feast for the children of Israel, and offered sacrifices on the altar and burned incense.

13 And* behold, a man of God went from Judah to Bethel by the word of the LORD, and Jeroboam stood by the altar to burn incense. 2Then he cried out against the altar by the word of the LORD, and said, "O altar, altar! Thus says the LORD: 'Behold, a child, Josiah by name, shall be born to the house of David; and on you he shall sacrifice the priests of the high places who burn incense on you, and men's bones shall be burned on you.' " 3And he gave a sign the same day, saying, "This *is* the sign which the LORD has spoken: Surely the altar shall split apart, and the ashes on it shall be poured out."

4So it came to pass when King Jeroboam heard the saying of the man of God, who cried out against the altar in Bethel, that he stretched out his hand from the altar, saying, "Arrest him!" Then his hand, which he stretched out toward him, withered, so that he could not pull it back to himself. 5The altar also was split apart, and the ashes poured out from the altar, according to the sign which the man of God had given by the word of the LORD. 6Then the king answered and said to the man of God, "Please entreat the favor of the LORD your God, and pray for me, that my hand may be restored to me."

So the man of God entreated the LORD, and the king's hand was restored to him, and became as before. 7Then the king said to the man of God, "Come home with me and refresh yourself, and I will give you a reward."

8But the man of God said to the king, "If you were to give me half your house, I would not go in with you; nor would I eat bread nor drink water

---

12:31 *l* Literally *a house*

in this place. 9For so it was commanded me by
the word of the LORD, saying, 'You shall not
eat bread, nor drink water, nor return by the
same way you came.'" 10So he went another
way and did not return by the way he came to
Bethel.

11*Now an old prophet dwelt in Bethel, and his
sons came and told him all the works that the
man of God had done that day in Bethel; they
also told their father the words which he had spoken to the king. 12And their father said to them,
"Which way did he go?" For his sons had seen^m
which way the man of God went who came from
Judah. 13Then he said to his sons, "Saddle the
donkey for me." So they saddled the donkey for
him; and he rode on it, 14and went after the man
of God, and found him sitting under an oak. Then
he said to him, "Are you the man of God who
came from Judah?"

And he said, "I am."

15Then he said to him, "Come home with me
and eat bread."

16And he said, "I cannot return with you nor
go in with you; neither can I eat bread nor drink
water with you in this place. 17For I have been
told by the word of the LORD, 'You shall not eat
bread nor drink water there, nor return by going
the way you came.'"

18He said to him, "I too am a prophet as you
are, and an angel spoke to me by the word of
the LORD, saying, 'Bring him back with you to
your house, that he may eat bread and drink water.'" (He was lying to him.)

19So he went back with him, and ate bread in
his house, and drank water.

20Now it happened, as they sat at the table, that
the word of the LORD came to the prophet who
had brought him back; 21*and he cried out to the
man of God who came from Judah, saying, "Thus
says the LORD: 'Because you have disobeyed the
word of the LORD, and have not kept the commandment which the LORD your God commanded
you, 22but you came back, ate bread, and drank
water in the place of which the LORD said to you,
"Eat no bread and drink no water," your corpse
shall not come to the tomb of your fathers.'"

23So it was, after he had eaten bread and after
he had drunk, that he saddled the donkey for him,
the prophet whom he had brought back. 24When
he was gone, a lion met him on the road and killed
him. And his corpse was thrown on the road,
and the donkey stood by it. The lion also stood
by the corpse. 25And there, men passed by and
saw the corpse thrown on the road, and the lion
standing by the corpse. Then they went and told
it in the city where the old prophet dwelt.

26Now when the prophet who had brought him
back from the way heard it, he said, "It is the
man of God who was disobedient to the word of
the LORD. Therefore the LORD has delivered him
to the lion, which has torn him and killed him,
according to the word of the LORD which He spoke
to him." 27And he spoke to his sons, saying, "Saddle the donkey for me." So they saddled it.
28Then he went and found his corpse thrown on
the road, and the donkey and the lion standing
by the corpse. The lion had not eaten the corpse
nor torn the donkey. 29And the prophet took up

13:11–19 *Compromise.* Had the prophet
continued to obey God's directions, he
would not have been killed, but gradually
he got out of the will of God. Instead of
hurrying home, he sat down (v. 14). Instead
of obeying his original commission from
God, he believed the lies of the old prophet.
The prophet ended up eating and drinking
with an enemy who pretended to be a friend.

13:21 Unless they can back it up from the
Word, beware when others know God's will
for your life. The sign found on some traffic
lights preaches a good sermon: OBEY YOUR
OWN SIGNAL.

13:12 ^mSeptuagint, Syriac, Targum, and Vulgate read *showed
him.*

the corpse of the man of God, laid it on the donkey, and brought it back. So the old prophet came to the city to mourn, and to bury him. 30Then he laid the corpse in his own tomb; and they mourned over him, *saying,* "Alas, my brother!" 31So it was, after he had buried him, that he spoke to his sons, saying, "When I am dead, then bury me in the tomb where the man of God *is* buried; lay my bones beside his bones. 32For the saying which he cried out by the word of the LORD against the altar in Bethel, and against all the shrines[n] on the high places which *are* in the cities of Samaria, will surely come to pass."

33After this event Jeroboam did not turn from his evil way, but again he made priests from every class of people for the high places; whoever wished, he consecrated him, and he became *one* of the priests of the high places. 34And this thing was the sin of the house of Jeroboam, so as to exterminate and destroy *it* from the face of the earth.

14 At* that time Abijah the son of Jeroboam became sick. 2And Jeroboam said to his wife, "Please arise, and disguise yourself, that they may not recognize you as the wife of Jeroboam, and go to Shiloh. Indeed, Ahijah the prophet *is* there, who told me that I *would be* king over this people. 3Also take with you ten loaves, *some* cakes, and a jar of honey, and go to him; he will tell you what will become of the child." 4And Jeroboam's wife did so; she arose and went to Shiloh, and came to the house of Ahijah. But Ahijah could not see, for his eyes were glazed by reason of his age.

5Now the LORD had said to Ahijah, "Here is the wife of Jeroboam, coming to ask you something about her son, for he *is* sick. Thus and thus you shall say to her; for it will be, when she comes in, that she will pretend *to be* another *woman.*"

6And so it was, when Ahijah heard the sound of her footsteps as she came through the door, he said, "Come in, wife of Jeroboam. Why do you pretend *to be* another *person?* For I *have been* sent to you *with* bad *news.* 7Go, tell Jeroboam, 'Thus says the LORD God of Israel: "Because I exalted you from among the people, and made you ruler over My people Israel, 8and tore the kingdom away from the house of David, and gave it to you; and *yet* you have not been as My servant David, who kept My commandments and who followed Me with all his heart, to do only *what was* right in My eyes; 9but you have done more evil than all who were before you, for you have gone and made for yourself other gods and molded images to provoke Me to anger, and have cast Me behind your back— 10therefore behold! I will bring disaster on the house of Jeroboam, and will cut off from Jeroboam every male in Israel, bond and free; I will take away the remnant of the house of Jeroboam, as one takes away refuse until it is all gone. 11The dogs shall eat whoever belongs to Jeroboam and dies in the city, and the birds of the air shall eat whoever dies in the field; for the LORD has spoken!"' 12*Arise therefore, go to your own house. When your feet enter the city, the child shall die. 13And all Israel shall mourn for him and bury him, for he is the only one of

CHAPTER 14

14:1–13 *Disguise.* Why did the king not consult one of the false gods he worshiped? And why not go to the Lord's prophet *personally* and *openly*? Because Jeroboam was a coward and did not want to weaken his "religious establishment." He did not dare identify himself publicly with the true worship of Jehovah, even though he knew that his own religious leaders could not help him.

14:12 *Death.* Abijah had good news about the son but bad news about everybody else in the royal family. God saw true devotion in the son and would not permit him to grow up in such an evil home. The boy was the only male to have a decent burial and be mourned. See verse 18 and 1 Kings 15:25–30 for the fulfillment.

13:32 [n]Literally *houses*

Jeroboam who shall come to the grave, because
in him there is found something good toward the
LORD God of Israel in the house of Jeroboam.
14"Moreover the LORD will raise up for Himself
a king over Israel who shall cut off the house of
Jeroboam; this is the day. What? Even now!
15For the LORD will strike Israel, as a reed is
shaken in the water. He will uproot Israel from
this good land which He gave to their fathers, and
will scatter them beyond the River,[o] because they
have made their wooden images,[p] provoking the
LORD to anger. 16And He will give Israel up because of the sins of Jeroboam, who sinned and
who made Israel sin."
17Then Jeroboam's wife arose and departed,
and came to Tirzah. When she came to the threshold of the house, the child died. 18And they buried
him; and all Israel mourned for him, according
to the word of the LORD which He spoke through
His servant Ahijah the prophet.
19Now the rest of the acts of Jeroboam, how
he made war and how he reigned, indeed they
are written in the book of the chronicles of the
kings of Israel. 20The period that Jeroboam
reigned *was* twenty-two years. So he rested with
his fathers. Then Nadab his son reigned in his
place.
21And Rehoboam the son of Solomon reigned
in Judah. Rehoboam *was* forty-one years old
when he became king. He reigned seventeen years
in Jerusalem, the city which the LORD had chosen
out of all the tribes of Israel, to put His name there.
His mother's name *was* Naamah, an Ammonitess.
22Now Judah did evil in the sight of the LORD,
and they provoked Him to jealousy with their sins
which they committed, more than all that their
fathers had done. 23For they also built for themselves high places, *sacred* pillars, and wooden images on every high hill and under every green
tree. 24And there were also perverted persons[q] in
the land. They did according to all the abominations of the nations which the LORD had cast out
before the children of Israel.
25It happened in the fifth year of King Rehoboam *that* Shishak king of Egypt came up against
Jerusalem. 26*And he took away the treasures of
the house of the LORD and the treasures of the
king's house; he took away everything. He also
took away all the gold shields which Solomon had
made. 27Then King Rehoboam made bronze
shields in their place, and committed *them* to the
hands of the captains of the guard, who guarded
the doorway of the king's house. 28And whenever
the king entered the house of the LORD, the guards
carried them, then brought them back into the
guardroom.
29Now the rest of the acts of Rehoboam, and
all that he did, *are* they not written in the book
of the chronicles of the kings of Judah? 30And
there was war between Rehoboam and Jeroboam
all *their* days. 31So Rehoboam rested with his fathers, and was buried with his fathers in the City
of David. His mother's name *was* Naamah, an
Ammonitess. Then Abijam[r] his son reigned in his
place.

14:26 *Decay.* Under King Rehoboam, Solomon's great kingdom lost both quantity (the tribes) and quality (the treasures). The costly golden shields (1 Kings 10:16–17) were replaced by bronze shields, but the guards and the king went through the same ceremony. What a picture of some lives and ministries today: everything looks the same, but the value has vanished. All we do is keep up appearances (Matt. 23).

14:15 [o]That is, the Euphrates [p]Hebrew *Asherim,* Canaanite deities 14:24 [q]Hebrew *qadesh,* that is, one practicing sodomy and prostitution in religious rituals 14:31 [r]Spelled *Abijah* in 2 Chronicles 12:16ff

15:4 A flickering lamp. God blessed Judah for David's sake, just as He blesses us for the sake of His beloved Son (Eph. 1:3) and because of the faithfulness of those who have gone before us. "Except in the matter of Uriah the Hittite"—and what a costly exception that was! Even a man who sinned greatly can be restored and become a blessing to others. But the lamp of truth was flickering, and Judah's sins would one day be judged.

15:9–19 An inconsistent ruler. Asa had a wonderful beginning to his reign but a disappointing ending. He was courageous enough to cleanse the temple of religious prostitutes and purge the land of idols, and he even dethroned his own grandmother. But instead of trusting the Lord for victory, he robbed the temple and bribed a pagan king to assist him in a war.

15 In the eighteenth year of King Jeroboam the son of Nebat, Abijam became king over Judah. 2He reigned three years in Jerusalem. His mother's name *was* Maachah the granddaughter of Abishalom. 3And he walked in all the sins of his father, which he had done before him; his heart was not loyal to the LORD his God, as was the heart of his father David. 4*Nevertheless for David's sake the LORD his God gave him a lamp in Jerusalem, by setting up his son after him and by establishing Jerusalem; 5because David did *what was* right in the eyes of the LORD, and had not turned aside from anything that He commanded him all the days of his life, except in the matter of Uriah the Hittite. 6And there was war between Rehoboam[s] and Jeroboam all the days of his life. 7Now the rest of the acts of Abijam, and all that he did, *are* they not written in the book of the chronicles of the kings of Judah? And there was war between Abijam and Jeroboam.

8So Abijam rested with his fathers, and they buried him in the City of David. Then Asa his son reigned in his place.

9*In the twentieth year of Jeroboam king of Israel, Asa became king over Judah. 10And he reigned forty-one years in Jerusalem. His grandmother's name *was* Maachah the granddaughter of Abishalom. 11Asa did *what was* right in the eyes of the LORD, as *did* his father David. 12And he banished the perverted persons[t] from the land, and removed all the idols that his fathers had made. 13Also he removed Maachah his grandmother from *being* queen mother, because she had made an obscene image of Asherah.[u] And Asa cut down her obscene image and burned *it* by the Brook Kidron. 14But the high places were not removed. Nevertheless Asa's heart was loyal to the LORD all his days. 15He also brought into the house of the LORD the things which his father had dedicated, and the things which he himself had dedicated: silver and gold and utensils.

16Now there was war between Asa and Baasha king of Israel all their days. 17And Baasha king of Israel came up against Judah, and built Ramah, that he might let none go out or come in to Asa king of Judah. 18Then Asa took all the silver and gold *that was* left in the treasuries of the house of the LORD and the treasuries of the king's house, and delivered them into the hand of his servants. And King Asa sent them to Ben-Hadad the son of Tabrimmon, the son of Hezion, king of Syria, who dwelt in Damascus, saying, 19"Let there be a treaty between you and me, as there was between my father and your father. See, I have sent you a present of silver and gold. Come and break your treaty with Baasha king of Israel, so that he will withdraw from me."

20So Ben-Hadad heeded King Asa, and sent the captains of his armies against the cities of Israel. He attacked Ijon, Dan, Abel Beth Maachah, and all Chinneroth, with all the land of Naphtali. 21Now it happened, when Baasha heard *it*, that he stopped building Ramah, and remained in Tirzah.

22Then King Asa made a proclamation throughout all Judah; none *was* exempted. And they took

---

15:6 [s]Following Masoretic Text, Septuagint, Targum, and Vulgate; some Hebrew manuscripts and Syriac read *Abijam*. 15:12 [t]Hebrew *qedeshim*, that is, those practicing sodomy and prostitution in religious rituals   15:13 [u]A Canaanite goddess

away the stones and timber of Ramah, which Baasha had used for building; and with them King Asa built Geba of Benjamin, and Mizpah.

23The rest of all the acts of Asa, all his might, all that he did, and the cities which he built, *are* they not written in the book of the chronicles of the kings of Judah? But in the time of his old age he was diseased in his feet. 24So Asa rested with his fathers, and was buried with his fathers in the City of David his father. Then Jehoshaphat his son reigned in his place.

25Now Nadab the son of Jeroboam became king over Israel in the second year of Asa king of Judah, and he reigned over Israel two years. 26And he did evil in the sight of the LORD, and walked in the way of his father, and in his sin by which he had made Israel sin.

27*Then Baasha the son of Ahijah, of the house of Issachar, conspired against him. And Baasha killed him at Gibbethon, which *belonged* to the Philistines, while Nadab and all Israel laid siege to Gibbethon. 28Baasha killed him in the third year of Asa king of Judah, and reigned in his place. 29And it was so, when he became king, *that* he killed all the house of Jeroboam. He did not leave to Jeroboam anyone that breathed, until he had destroyed him, according to the word of the LORD which He had spoken by His servant Ahijah the Shilonite, 30because of the sins of Jeroboam, which he had sinned and by which he had made Israel sin, because of his provocation with which he had provoked the LORD God of Israel to anger.

31Now the rest of the acts of Nadab, and all that he did, *are* they not written in the book of the chronicles of the kings of Israel? 32And there was war between Asa and Baasha king of Israel all their days.

33In the third year of Asa king of Judah, Baasha the son of Ahijah became king over all Israel in Tirzah, and *reigned* twenty-four years. 34He did evil in the sight of the LORD, and walked in the way of Jeroboam, and in his sin by which he had made Israel sin.

16 Then* the word of the LORD came to Jehu the son of Hanani, against Baasha, saying: 2"Inasmuch as I lifted you out of the dust and made you ruler over My people Israel, and you have walked in the way of Jeroboam, and have made My people Israel sin, to provoke Me to anger with their sins, 3*surely I will take away the posterity of Baasha and the posterity of his house, and I will make your house like the house of Jeroboam the son of Nebat. 4The dogs shall eat whoever belongs to Baasha and dies in the city, and the birds of the air shall eat whoever dies in the fields."

5Now the rest of the acts of Baasha, what he did, and his might, *are* they not written in the book of the chronicles of the kings of Israel? 6So Baasha rested with his fathers and was buried in Tirzah. Then Elah his son reigned in his place.

7And also the word of the LORD came by the prophet Jehu the son of Hanani against Baasha and his house, because of all the evil that he did in the sight of the LORD in provoking Him to anger with the work of his hands, in being like the house of Jeroboam, and because he killed them.

8In the twenty-sixth year of Asa king of Judah, Elah the son of Baasha became king over Israel, *and reigned* two years in Tirzah. 9Now his servant Zimri, commander of half *his* chariots, conspired

15:27–30 *A certain judgment.* God had promised that the house of Jeroboam would be destroyed, and Baasha was the instrument of that judgment. But Baasha repeated the sins of Jeroboam! Did he think that *he* would escape punishment?
F. von Logau commented, "Though the mills of God grind slowly, yet they grind exceeding small."

CHAPTER 16

16:1ff Whenever the kings or priests led the people into sin, God sent faithful prophets to warn them and to call them back to the true worship of Jehovah. Jehu was such a prophet; he was not afraid to give God's message of judgment to evil King Baasha. Are we today willing to take our stand against evil, or do we just drift with the crowd?

16:3 Baasha had imitated Jeroboam's sins, so he would suffer Jeroboam's judgment (1 Kings 14:7–11). God used Zimri to fulfill His word against Baasha. If we do not heed what God says, we must suffer His judgment.

16:12, 16 Zimri's reign was brief. Rather than fall into the hands of Omri and his faction, Zimri committed suicide. Omri, too, chose to disobey God and "did worse than all who were before him" (v. 25). And one of the worst things he did was to leave his son Ahab to reign over Israel.

against him as he was in Tirzah drinking himself drunk in the house of Arza, steward of *his* house in Tirzah. 10And Zimri went in and struck him and killed him in the twenty-seventh year of Asa king of Judah, and reigned in his place.

11Then it came to pass, when he began to reign, as soon as he was seated on his throne, *that* he killed all the household of Baasha; he did not leave him one male, neither of his relatives nor of his friends. 12*Thus Zimri destroyed all the household of Baasha, according to the word of the LORD, which He spoke against Baasha by Jehu the prophet, 13for all the sins of Baasha and the sins of Elah his son, by which they had sinned and by which they had made Israel sin, in provoking the LORD God of Israel to anger with their idols.

14Now the rest of the acts of Elah, and all that he did, *are* they not written in the book of the chronicles of the kings of Israel?

15In the twenty-seventh year of Asa king of Judah, Zimri had reigned in Tirzah seven days. And the people *were* encamped against Gibbethon, which *belonged* to the Philistines. 16Now the people *who were* encamped heard it said, "Zimri has conspired and also has killed the king." So all Israel made Omri, the commander of the army, king over Israel that day in the camp. 17Then Omri and all Israel with him went up from Gibbethon, and they besieged Tirzah. 18And it happened, when Zimri saw that the city was taken, that he went into the citadel of the king's house and burned the king's house down upon himself with fire, and died, 19because of the sins which he had committed in doing evil in the sight of the LORD, in walking in the way of Jeroboam, and in his sin which he had committed to make Israel sin.

20Now the rest of the acts of Zimri, and the treason he committed, *are* they not written in the book of the chronicles of the kings of Israel?

21Then the people of Israel were divided into two parts: half of the people followed Tibni the son of Ginath, to make him king, and half followed Omri. 22But the people who followed Omri prevailed over the people who followed Tibni the son of Ginath. So Tibni died and Omri reigned. 23In the thirty-first year of Asa king of Judah, Omri became king over Israel, *and reigned* twelve years. Six years he reigned in Tirzah. 24And he bought the hill of Samaria from Shemer for two talents of silver; then he built on the hill, and called the name of the city which he built, Samaria, after the name of Shemer, owner of the hill. 25Omri did evil in the eyes of the LORD, and did worse than all who *were* before him. 26For he walked in all the ways of Jeroboam the son of Nebat, and in his sin by which he had made Israel sin, provoking the LORD God of Israel to anger with their idols.

27Now the rest of the acts of Omri which he did, and the might that he showed, *are* they not written in the book of the chronicles of the kings of Israel?

28So Omri rested with his fathers and was buried in Samaria. Then Ahab his son reigned in his place.

29*In the thirty-eighth year of Asa king of Judah, Ahab the son of Omri became king over Israel; and Ahab the son of Omri reigned over Israel in Samaria twenty-two years. 30Now Ahab the son of Omri did evil in the sight of the LORD, more than all who *were* before him. 31And it came to

16:29–34 Ahab married a heathen princess, worshiped a heathen god, and provoked the Lord greatly. He made Baal worship a popular religion in Israel. Baal was the Canaanite storm god, and his worship was attractive to a nation that depended so much on rain. Besides, the rituals involved temple prostitutes, and that appealed to the baser appetites of the people.

pass, as though it had been a trivial thing for him to walk in the sins of Jeroboam the son of Nebat, that he took as wife Jezebel the daughter of Ethbaal, king of the Sidonians; and he went and served Baal and worshiped him. ³²Then he set up an altar for Baal in the temple of Baal, which he had built in Samaria. ³³And Ahab made a wooden image.ᵛ Ahab did more to provoke the LORD God of Israel to anger than all the kings of Israel who were before him. ³⁴In his days Hiel of Bethel built Jericho. He laid its foundation with Abiram his firstborn, and with his youngest *son* Segub he set up its gates, according to the word of the LORD, which He had spoken through Joshua the son of Nun.ʷ

17 And* Elijah the Tishbite, of the inhabitants of Gilead, said to Ahab, *"As* the LORD God of Israel lives, before whom I stand, there shall not be dew nor rain these years, except at my word."

²Then the word of the LORD came to him, saying, ³*"Get away from here and turn eastward, and hide by the Brook Cherith, which flows into the Jordan. ⁴And it will be *that* you shall drink from the brook, and I have commanded the ravens to feed you there."

⁵So he went and did according to the word of the LORD, for he went and stayed by the Brook Cherith, which flows into the Jordan. ⁶The ravens brought him bread and meat in the morning, and bread and meat in the evening; and he drank from the brook. ⁷*And it happened after a while that the brook dried up, because there had been no rain in the land.

⁸Then the word of the LORD came to him, saying, ⁹"Arise, go to Zarephath, which *belongs* to Sidon, and dwell there. See, I have commanded a widow there to provide for you." ¹⁰So he arose and went to Zarephath. And when he came to the gate of the city, indeed a widow *was* there gathering sticks. And he called to her and said, "Please bring me a little water in a cup, that I may drink." ¹¹And as she was going to get *it,* he called to her and said, "Please bring me a morsel of bread in your hand."

¹²So she said, "As the LORD your God lives, I do not have bread, only a handful of flour in a bin, and a little oil in a jar; and see, I *am* gathering a couple of sticks that I may go in and prepare it for myself and my son, that we may eat it, and die."

¹³And Elijah said to her, "Do not fear; go *and* do as you have said, but make me a small cake from it first, and bring *it* to me; and afterward make *some* for yourself and your son. ¹⁴For thus says the LORD God of Israel: 'The bin of flour shall not be used up, nor shall the jar of oil run dry, until the day the LORD sends rain on the earth.' "

¹⁵So she went away and did according to the word of Elijah; and she and he and her household ate for *many* days. ¹⁶The bin of flour was not used up, nor did the jar of oil run dry, according to the word of the LORD which He spoke by Elijah.

¹⁷Now it happened after these things *that* the son of the woman who owned the house became sick. And his sickness was so serious that there was no breath left in him. ¹⁸So she said to Elijah,

CHAPTER 17

17:1 Samuel grew up being recognized as God's prophet (1 Sam. 3:19–21), but Elijah *suddenly* appeared before Ahab declaring God's message. The drought, for which he had prayed (James 5:17), was Elijah's declaration of war against Ahab, Jezebel, and the storm god Baal. If the king and the people had humbled themselves before the Lord, He would have sent rain to the land (Deut. 11:13–17; 2 Chron. 7:12–15), but most of the nation trusted Baal, not Jehovah.

17:3 The drought had three more years to go (1 Kings 18:1; Luke 4:25), and God took care of His faithful servant (Ps. 37:3–6). During that time of "retirement," God led him, fed him, and enabled him to help others, including a *gentile* widow (Luke 4:25–26). When we walk by faith, God supplies our needs and opens doors of opportunity for us.

17:7 Be sure to trust the Provider and not the provision. Brooks dry up, but God never fails.

16:33 ᵛHebrew *Asherah,* a Canaanite goddess
16:34 ʷCompare Joshua 6:26

"What have I to do with you, O man of God? Have you come to me to bring my sin to remembrance, and to kill my son?" 19And he said to her, "Give me your son." So he took him out of her arms and carried him to the upper room where he was staying, and laid him on his own bed. 20Then he cried out to the LORD and said, "O LORD my God, have You also brought tragedy on the widow with whom I lodge, by killing her son?" 21And he stretched himself out on the child three times, and cried out to the LORD and said, "O LORD my God, I pray, let this child's soul come back to him." 22Then the LORD heard the voice of Elijah; and the soul of the child came back to him, and he revived.

23And Elijah took the child and brought him down from the upper room into the house, and gave him to his mother. And Elijah said, "See, your son lives!"

24Then the woman said to Elijah, "Now by this I know that you *are* a man of God, *and* that the word of the LORD in your mouth *is* the truth."

18 And it came to pass *after* many days that the word of the LORD came to Elijah, in the third year, saying, "Go, present yourself to Ahab, and I will send rain on the earth."

2So Elijah went to present himself to Ahab; and *there was* a severe famine in Samaria. 3And Ahab had called Obadiah, who *was* in charge of *his* house. (Now Obadiah feared the LORD greatly. 4For so it was, while Jezebel massacred the prophets of the LORD, that Obadiah had taken one hundred prophets and hidden them, fifty to a cave, and had fed them with bread and water.) 5*And Ahab had said to Obadiah, "Go into the land to all the springs of water and to all the brooks; perhaps we may find grass to keep the horses and mules alive, so that we will not have to kill any livestock." 6So they divided the land between them to explore it; Ahab went one way by himself, and Obadiah went another way by himself.

7*Now as Obadiah was on his way, suddenly Elijah met him; and he recognized him, and fell on his face, and said, "*Is* that you, my lord Elijah?"

8And he answered him, "*It is* I. Go, tell your master, 'Elijah *is* here.'"

9So he said, "How have I sinned, that you are delivering your servant into the hand of Ahab, to kill me? 10As the LORD your God lives, there is no nation or kingdom where my master has not sent someone to hunt for you; and when they said, '*He is* not *here,*' he took an oath from the kingdom or nation that they could not find you. 11And now you say, 'Go, tell your master, "Elijah *is* here"'! 12And it shall come to pass, *as soon as* I am gone from you, that the Spirit of the LORD will carry you to a place I do not know; so when I go and tell Ahab, and he cannot find you, he will kill me. But I your servant have feared the LORD from my youth. 13Was it not reported to my lord what I did when Jezebel killed the prophets of the LORD, how I hid one hundred men of the LORD's prophets, fifty to a cave, and fed them with bread and water? 14And now you say, 'Go, tell your master, "Elijah *is* here." ' He will kill me!"

15Then Elijah said, "*As* the LORD of hosts lives, before whom I stand, I will surely present myself to him today."

16So Obadiah went to meet Ahab, and told him; and Ahab went to meet Elijah.

17Then it happened, when Ahab saw Elijah, that

CHAPTER 18

18:5 *Searching for water.* Ahab's capital city suffered severely, but the godless rulers did not repent. It takes more than suffering to break a proud heart; it takes hearing and yielding to the word of God. But Ahab and Jezebel tried to silence God's word by killing God's prophets. They showed more concern for their animals than for their people. When a nation's leaders have their priorities confused, the nation will suffer greatly.

18:7–16 *Searching for Elijah.* Ahab wanted to kill Elijah (v. 10), but God protected His servant. To Ahab, Elijah was an enemy (1 Kings 21:20), but Ahab was his own worst enemy. We commend Obadiah for protecting the prophets, but that was not the final solution. Israel had to make a decision between Baal and Jehovah (Josh. 24:14–21).

Ahab said to him, "*Is that* you, O troubler of Israel?"

18And he answered, "I have not troubled Israel, but you and your father's house *have,* in that you have forsaken the commandments of the LORD and have followed the Baals. 19*Now therefore, send *and* gather all Israel to me on Mount Carmel, the four hundred and fifty prophets of Baal, and the four hundred prophets of Asherah,ˣ who eat at Jezebel's table."

20So Ahab sent for all the children of Israel, and gathered the prophets together on Mount Carmel. 21And Elijah came to all the people, and said, "How long will you falter between two opinions? If the LORD *is* God, follow Him; but if Baal, follow him." But the people answered him not a word. 22Then Elijah said to the people, "I alone am left a prophet of the LORD; but Baal's prophets *are* four hundred and fifty men. 23Therefore let them give us two bulls; and let them choose one bull for themselves, cut it in pieces, and lay *it* on the wood, but put no fire *under it;* and I will prepare the other bull, and lay *it* on the wood, but put no fire *under it.* 24Then you call on the name of your gods, and I will call on the name of the LORD; and the God who answers by fire, He is God."

So all the people answered and said, "It is well spoken."

25Now Elijah said to the prophets of Baal, "Choose one bull for yourselves and prepare *it* first, for you *are* many; and call on the name of your god, but put no fire *under it.*"

26So they took the bull which was given them, and they prepared *it,* and called on the name of Baal from morning even till noon, saying, "O Baal, hear us!" But *there was* no voice; no one answered. Then they leaped about the altar which they had made.

27And so it was, at noon, that Elijah mocked them and said, "Cry aloud, for he *is* a god; either he is meditating, or he is busy, or he is on a journey, *or* perhaps he is sleeping and must be awakened." 28So they cried aloud, and cut themselves, as was their custom, with knives and lances, until the blood gushed out on them. 29And when midday was past, they prophesied until the *time* of the offering of the *evening* sacrifice. But *there was* no voice; no one answered, no one paid attention.

30Then Elijah said to all the people, "Come near to me." So all the people came near to him. And he repaired the altar of the LORD *that was* broken down. 31And Elijah took twelve stones, according to the number of the tribes of the sons of Jacob, to whom the word of the LORD had come, saying, "Israel shall be your name."ʸ 32Then with the stones he built an altar in the name of the LORD; and he made a trench around the altar large enough to hold two seahs of seed. 33And he put the wood in order, cut the bull in pieces, and laid *it* on the wood, and said, "Fill four waterpots with water, and pour *it* on the burnt sacrifice and on the wood." 34Then he said, "Do *it* a second time," and they did *it* a second time; and he said, "Do *it* a third time," and they did *it* a third time. 35So the water ran all around the altar; and he also filled the trench with water.

36And it came to pass, at *the time of* the offering of the *evening* sacrifice, that Elijah the prophet came near and said, "LORD God of Abraham,

18:19–41 *Searching for God.* Baal was the storm god, so he should have been able to send rain, but he failed. Elijah rebuked the people (v. 21), repaired the altar (v. 30), and relied on the Lord (vv. 36–37), and God revealed Himself by sending fire (v. 38). In response to Elijah's prayer, God sent rain. Elijah was the man of the hour: he honored God, and God honored him.

Some may ask, "Where is the LORD God of Elijah?" (2 Kings 2:14). Perhaps the better question is, *Where are the Elijahs?*

18:19 ˣA Canaanite goddess   18:31 ʸGenesis 32:28

Isaac, and Israel, let it be known this day that You *are* God in Israel and I *am* Your servant, and *that* I have done all these things at Your word. [37]Hear me, O LORD, hear me, that this people may know that You *are* the LORD God, and *that* You have turned their hearts back *to You* again."

[38]Then the fire of the LORD fell and consumed the burnt sacrifice, and the wood and the stones and the dust, and it licked up the water that *was* in the trench. [39]Now when all the people saw *it*, they fell on their faces; and they said, "The LORD, He *is* God! The LORD, He *is* God!"

[40]And Elijah said to them, "Seize the prophets of Baal! Do not let one of them escape!" So they seized them; and Elijah brought them down to the Brook Kishon and executed them there.

[41]Then Elijah said to Ahab, "Go up, eat and drink; for *there is* the sound of abundance of rain." [42]So Ahab went up to eat and drink. And Elijah went up to the top of Carmel; then he bowed down on the ground, and put his face between his knees, [43]and said to his servant, "Go up now, look toward the sea."

So he went up and looked, and said, "*There is* nothing." And seven times he said, "Go again."

[44]Then it came to pass the seventh *time*, that he said, "There is a cloud, as small as a man's hand, rising out of the sea!" So he said, "Go up, say to Ahab, 'Prepare *your chariot,* and go down before the rain stops you.'"

[45]Now it happened in the meantime that the sky became black with clouds and wind, and there was a heavy rain. So Ahab rode away and went to Jezreel. [46]Then the hand of the LORD came upon Elijah; and he girded up his loins and ran ahead of Ahab to the entrance of Jezreel.

CHAPTER 19

19:1, 2 The "Elijah complex" can rob you of power and joy, so beware! Elijah went from victory to defeat because he started walking by sight and not by faith (v. 3). He believed the queen's words but not God's word, and he forgot how God had cared for him for three and a half years. Fear replaced faith, and he ran for his life.

19:4 He became concerned about saving himself rather than giving himself (Mark 8:34–38; John 12:23–28). Note the sequence: "your life" (v. 2), "his life" (v. 3), "my life" (v. 4). If he had said, "Take my life," as an act of surrender to God, the Lord would have worked in power; but his "Take my life" was a confession of pride and defeat. Beware when you think you are the only faithful one left!

19 And* Ahab told Jezebel all that Elijah had done, also how he had executed all the prophets with the sword. [2]Then Jezebel sent a messenger to Elijah, saying, "So let the gods do *to me,* and more also, if I do not make your life as the life of one of them by tomorrow about this time." [3]And when he saw *that,* he arose and ran for his life, and went to Beersheba, which *belongs* to Judah, and left his servant there.

[4]*But he himself went a day's journey into the wilderness, and came and sat down under a broom tree. And he prayed that he might die, and said, "It is enough! Now, LORD, take my life, for I *am* no better than my fathers!"

[5]Then as he lay and slept under a broom tree, suddenly an angel[z] touched him, and said to him, "Arise *and* eat." [6]Then he looked, and there by his head *was* a cake baked on coals, and a jar of water. So he ate and drank, and lay down again. [7]And the angel[a] of the LORD came back the second time, and touched him, and said, "Arise *and* eat, because the journey *is* too great for you." [8]So he arose, and ate and drank; and he went in the strength of that food forty days and forty nights as far as Horeb, the mountain of God.

19:5 [z]Or *Angel*   19:7 [a]Or *Angel*

They Wanted to Die! —Sometimes we feel so depressed about our work and ourselves that we wish God would call us home. Of course, had Elijah really *wanted* to die, Jezebel would have gladly accommodated him. But Elijah was not the only one to feel that way. Moses wanted to die (Num. 11:15), and so did Job (Job 3:20–21), Jeremiah (Jer. 8:3), and Jonah (Jon. 4:3). Of course, this is not the answer to despair because it is selfish and does not glorify God. The real answer is to *die to self* and trust God to work things out. "The future is your friend when Jesus is your Lord."

⁹And there he went into a cave, and spent the night in that place; and behold, the word of the LORD *came* to him, and He said to him, "What are you doing here, Elijah?"

¹⁰So he said, "I have been very zealous for the LORD God of hosts; for the children of Israel have forsaken Your covenant, torn down Your altars, and killed Your prophets with the sword. I alone am left; and they seek to take my life."

¹¹*Then He said, "Go out, and stand on the mountain before the LORD." And behold, the LORD passed by, and a great and strong wind tore into the mountains and broke the rocks in pieces before the LORD, *but* the LORD *was* not in the wind; and after the wind an earthquake, *but* the LORD *was* not in the earthquake; ¹²and after the earthquake a fire, *but* the LORD *was* not in the fire; and after the fire a still small voice.

¹³So it was, when Elijah heard *it*, that he wrapped his face in his mantle and went out and stood in the entrance of the cave. Suddenly a voice *came* to him, and said, "What are you doing here, Elijah?"

¹⁴And he said, "I have been very zealous for the LORD God of hosts; because the children of Israel have forsaken Your covenant, torn down Your altars, and killed Your prophets with the sword. I alone am left; and they seek to take my life."

¹⁵Then the LORD said to him: "Go, return on your way to the Wilderness of Damascus; and when you arrive, anoint Hazael *as* king over Syria. ¹⁶Also you shall anoint Jehu the son of Nimshi *as* king over Israel. And Elisha the son of Shaphat of Abel Meholah you shall anoint *as* prophet in your place. ¹⁷It shall be *that* whoever escapes the sword of Hazael, Jehu will kill; and whoever escapes the sword of Jehu, Elisha will kill. ¹⁸Yet I have reserved seven thousand in Israel, all whose knees have not bowed to Baal, and every mouth that has not kissed him."

¹⁹So he departed from there, and found Elisha the son of Shaphat, who *was* plowing *with* twelve yoke *of oxen* before him, and he was with the twelfth. Then Elijah passed by him and threw his mantle on him. ²⁰And he left the oxen and ran after Elijah, and said, "Please let me kiss my father and my mother, and *then* I will follow you."

And he said to him, "Go back again, for what have I done to you?"

²¹So *Elisha* turned back from him, and took a yoke of oxen and slaughtered them and boiled their flesh, using the oxen's equipment, and gave it to the people, and they ate. Then he arose and followed Elijah, and became his servant.

20 Now* Ben-Hadad the king of Syria gathered all his forces together; thirty-two kings *were* with him, with horses and chariots. And he went up and besieged Samaria, and made war against it. ²Then he sent messengers into the city to Ahab king of Israel, and said to him, "Thus says Ben-Hadad: ³'Your silver and your gold *are* mine; your loveliest wives and children are mine.' "

⁴And the king of Israel answered and said, "My lord, O king, just as you say, I and all that I have *are* yours."

⁵Then the messengers came back and said, "Thus speaks Ben-Hadad, saying, 'Indeed I have sent to you, saying, "You shall deliver to me your silver and your gold, your wives and your chil-

19:11, 12 God taught Elijah that He does not always work in the dramatic big events, such as the contest on Mount Carmel, but that He works by means of a "still small voice," ministries that are neither big nor loud. Elijah was not forsaken, for God was with him. He was not alone, for seven thousand people had not bowed to Baal. His work would go on, for God had a young man ready to take his place.

We need to obey these words: "Do not be afraid; only believe" (Mark 5:36).

CHAPTER 20

20:1–30 *Victory.* In His grace, God gave wicked King Ahab two victories over the enemy. The first victory was to teach Ahab that the Lord was the true God (v. 13), and the second was to show the enemy that Jehovah was not weak and limited like the heathen idols (v. 28). We must never think that we receive blessings because we deserve them.

dren''; 6but I will send my servants to you tomorrow about this time, and they shall search your house and the houses of your servants. And it shall be, *that* whatever is pleasant in your eyes, they will put *it* in their hands and take *it.*' "

7So the king of Israel called all the elders of the land, and said, "Notice, please, and see how this *man* seeks trouble, for he sent to me for my wives, my children, my silver, and my gold; and I did not deny him."

8And all the elders and all the people said to him, "Do not listen or consent."

9Therefore he said to the messengers of Ben-Hadad, "Tell my lord the king, 'All that you sent for to your servant the first time I will do, but this thing I cannot do.' "

And the messengers departed and brought back word to him.

10Then Ben-Hadad sent to him and said, "The gods do so to me, and more also, if enough dust is left of Samaria for a handful for each of the people who follow me."

11So the king of Israel answered and said, "Tell *him,* 'Let not the one who puts on *his armor* boast like the one who takes *it off.*' "

12And it happened when *Ben-Hadad* heard this message, as he and the kings *were* drinking at the command post, that he said to his servants, "Get ready." And they got ready to attack the city.

13Suddenly a prophet approached Ahab king of Israel, saying, "Thus says the LORD: 'Have you seen all this great multitude? Behold, I will deliver it into your hand today, and you shall know that I *am* the LORD.' "

14So Ahab said, "By whom?"

And he said, "Thus says the LORD: 'By the young leaders of the provinces.' "

Then he said, "Who will set the battle in order?"

And he answered, "You."

15Then he mustered the young leaders of the provinces, and there were two hundred and thirty-two; and after them he mustered all the people, all the children of Israel—seven thousand.

16So they went out at noon. Meanwhile Ben-Hadad and the thirty-two kings helping him were getting drunk at the command post. 17The young leaders of the provinces went out first. And Ben-Hadad sent out *a patrol,* and they told him, saying, "Men are coming out of Samaria!" 18So he said, "If they have come out for peace, take them alive; and if they have come out for war, take them alive."

19Then these young leaders of the provinces went out of the city with the army which followed them. 20And each one killed his man; so the Syrians fled, and Israel pursued them; and Ben-Hadad the king of Syria escaped on a horse with the cavalry. 21Then the king of Israel went out and attacked the horses and chariots, and killed the Syrians with a great slaughter.

22And the prophet came to the king of Israel and said to him, "Go, strengthen yourself; take note, and see what you should do, for in the spring of the year the king of Syria will come up against you."

23Then the servants of the king of Syria said to him, "Their gods *are* gods of the hills. Therefore they were stronger than we; but if we fight against them in the plain, surely we will be stronger than they. 24So do this thing: Dismiss the kings, each from his position, and put captains in their places; 25and you shall muster an army like the army that you have lost, horse for horse and chariot for chariot. Then we will fight against them in the plain; surely we will be stronger than they."

And he listened to their voice and did so.

26So it was, in the spring of the year, that Ben-Hadad mustered the Syrians and went up to Aphek to fight against Israel. 27And the children of Israel were mustered and given provisions, and they went against them. Now the children of Israel encamped before them like two little flocks of goats, while the Syrians filled the countryside.

28Then a man of God came and spoke to the king of Israel, and said, "Thus says the LORD: 'Because the Syrians have said, "The LORD is God of the hills, but He is not God of the valleys," therefore I will deliver all this great multitude into your hand, and you shall know that I am the LORD.' " 29And they encamped opposite each other for seven days. So it was that on the seventh day the battle was joined; and the children of Israel killed one hundred thousand foot soldiers of the Syrians in one day. 30But the rest fled to Aphek, into the city; then a wall fell on twenty-seven thousand of the men who were left.

And Ben-Hadad fled and went into the city, into an inner chamber.

31*Then his servants said to him, "Look now, we have heard that the kings of the house of Israel are merciful kings. Please, let us put sackcloth around our waists and ropes around our heads, and go out to the king of Israel; perhaps he will spare your life." 32So they wore sackcloth around their waists and put ropes around their heads, and came to the king of Israel and said, "Your servant Ben-Hadad says, 'Please let me live.' "

And he said, "Is he still alive? He is my brother."

33Now the men were watching closely to see whether any sign of mercy would come from him; and they quickly grasped at this word and said, "Your brother Ben-Hadad."

So he said, "Go, bring him." Then Ben-Hadad came out to him; and he had him come up into the chariot.

34So Ben-Hadad said to him, "The cities which my father took from your father I will restore; and you may set up marketplaces for yourself in Damascus, as my father did in Samaria."

Then Ahab said, "I will send you away with this treaty." So he made a treaty with him and sent him away.

35*Now a certain man of the sons of the prophets said to his neighbor by the word of the LORD, "Strike me, please." And the man refused to strike him. 36Then he said to him, "Because you have not obeyed the voice of the LORD, surely, as soon as you depart from me, a lion shall kill you." And as soon as he left him, a lion found him and killed him.

37And he found another man, and said, "Strike me, please." So the man struck him, inflicting a wound. 38Then the prophet departed and waited for the king by the road, and disguised himself with a bandage over his eyes. 39Now as the king passed by, he cried out to the king and said, "Your servant went out into the midst of the battle; and there, a man came over and brought a man to me, and said, 'Guard this man; if by any means he is missing, your life shall be for his life, or else you shall pay a talent of silver.' 40While your servant was busy here and there, he was gone."

Then the king of Israel said to him, "So shall your judgment be; you yourself have decided it."

20:31–34 Compromise. Instead of claiming complete victory and destroying Ben-Hadad (v. 42), Ahab entered into a treaty with him! King Saul made the same mistake with the king of the Amalekites (1 Sam. 15:8–9), and both kings lost their kingdoms because of their disobedience. When you think the battle is over, you may face your greatest danger and experience your greatest defeat.

20:35–43 Defeat. The Lord had given the king ample evidence that He was God, but Ahab persisted in hardening his heart. Too spiritually blind to know who the prophet was or what he was talking about, Ahab pronounced his own death sentence (v. 40). His pouting did not change anything (Prov. 19:3), but he refused to turn to the Lord.

CHAPTER 21

21:1–7 Covetousness. Ahab asked Naboth to break the law, but Naboth refused (Num. 36:7). The king thought that every man had his price, but Naboth was not for sale. "You shall not covet" is the last of the Ten Commandments (Exod. 20:17), but in breaking it, Ahab broke several of the other nine. Ahab and Jezebel put things ahead of God; they lied, murdered, and stole a man's property; and they tried to cover it up. How many commandments do we have to break to be guilty before God?

21:8–14 Conspiracy. Evil leaders could never succeed were it not for weak people who obey their orders. Jezebel did not fear God's name or believe in fasting, but she knew how to use both to get what she wanted. An innocent man died, but God saw it happen. Elijah found Ahab, Ahab's sin found Ahab (Num. 32:23), and the word of judgment was pronounced.

41And he hastened to take the bandage away from his eyes; and the king of Israel recognized him as one of the prophets. 42Then he said to him, "Thus says the LORD: 'Because you have let slip out of *your* hand a man whom I appointed to utter destruction, therefore your life shall go for his life, and your people for his people.'"

43So the king of Israel went to his house sullen and displeased, and came to Samaria.

21 And* it came to pass after these things *that* Naboth the Jezreelite had a vineyard which *was* in Jezreel, next to the palace of Ahab king of Samaria. 2So Ahab spoke to Naboth, saying, "Give me your vineyard, that I may have it for a vegetable garden, because it *is* near, next to my house; and for it I will give you a vineyard better than it. *Or,* if it seems good to you, I will give you its worth in money."

3But Naboth said to Ahab, "The LORD forbid that I should give the inheritance of my fathers to you!"

4So Ahab went into his house sullen and displeased because of the word which Naboth the Jezreelite had spoken to him; for he had said, "I will not give you the inheritance of my fathers." And he lay down on his bed, and turned away his face, and would eat no food. 5But Jezebel his wife came to him, and said to him, "Why is your spirit so sullen that you eat no food?"

6He said to her, "Because I spoke to Naboth the Jezreelite, and said to him, 'Give me your vineyard for money; or else, if it pleases you, I will give you *another* vineyard for it.' And he answered, 'I will not give you my vineyard.'"

7Then Jezebel his wife said to him, "You now exercise authority over Israel! Arise, eat food, and let your heart be cheerful; I will give you the vineyard of Naboth the Jezreelite."

8*And she wrote letters in Ahab's name, sealed *them* with his seal, and sent the letters to the elders and the nobles who *were* dwelling in the city with Naboth. 9She wrote in the letters, saying,

Proclaim a fast, and seat Naboth with high honor among the people; 10and seat two men, scoundrels, before him to bear witness against him, saying, You have blasphemed God and the king. *Then* take him out, and stone him, that he may die.

11So the men of his city, the elders and nobles who were inhabitants of his city, did as Jezebel had sent to them, as it *was* written in the letters which she had sent to them. 12They proclaimed a fast, and seated Naboth with high honor among the people. 13And two men, scoundrels, came in and sat before him; and the scoundrels witnessed against him, against Naboth, in the presence of the people, saying, "Naboth has blasphemed God and the king!" Then they took him outside the city and stoned him with stones, so that he died. 14Then they sent to Jezebel, saying, "Naboth has been stoned and is dead."

15And it came to pass, when Jezebel heard that Naboth had been stoned and was dead, that Jezebel said to Ahab, "Arise, take possession of the vineyard of Naboth the Jezreelite, which he refused to give you for money; for Naboth is not alive, but dead." 16So it was, when Ahab heard that Naboth was dead, that Ahab got up and went down to take possession of the vineyard of Naboth the Jezreelite.

17Then the word of the LORD came to Elijah the Tishbite, saying, 18"Arise, go down to meet Ahab king of Israel, who *lives* in Samaria. There *he is,* in the vineyard of Naboth, where he has gone down to take possession of it. 19You shall speak to him, saying, 'Thus says the LORD: "Have you murdered and also taken possession?"' And you shall speak to him, saying, 'Thus says the LORD: "In the place where dogs licked the blood of Naboth, dogs shall lick your blood, even yours."'"

20*So Ahab said to Elijah, "Have you found me, O my enemy?"

And he answered, "I have found *you,* because you have sold yourself to do evil in the sight of the LORD: 21'Behold, I will bring calamity on you. I will take away your posterity, and will cut off from Ahab every male in Israel, both bond and free. 22I will make your house like the house of Jeroboam the son of Nebat, and like the house of Baasha the son of Ahijah, because of the provocation with which you have provoked *Me* to anger, and made Israel sin.' 23And concerning Jezebel the LORD also spoke, saying, 'The dogs shall eat Jezebel by the wall*b* of Jezreel.' 24The dogs shall eat whoever belongs to Ahab and dies in the city, and the birds of the air shall eat whoever dies in the field."

25But there was no one like Ahab who sold himself to do wickedness in the sight of the LORD, because Jezebel his wife stirred him up. 26And he behaved very abominably in following idols, according to all *that* the Amorites had done, whom the LORD had cast out before the children of Israel.

27So it was, when Ahab heard those words, that he tore his clothes and put sackcloth on his body, and fasted and lay in sackcloth, and went about mourning.

28And the word of the LORD came to Elijah the Tishbite, saying, 29"See how Ahab has humbled himself before Me? Because he has humbled himself before Me, I will not bring the calamity in his days. In the days of his son I will bring the calamity on his house."

22 Now three years passed without war between Syria and Israel. 2Then it came to pass, in the third year, that Jehoshaphat the king of Judah went down to *visit* the king of Israel.

3And the king of Israel said to his servants, "Do you know that Ramoth in Gilead *is* ours, but we hesitate to take it out of the hand of the king of Syria?" 4*So he said to Jehoshaphat, "Will you go with me to fight at Ramoth Gilead?"

Jehoshaphat said to the king of Israel, "I *am* as you *are,* my people as your people, my horses as your horses." 5Also Jehoshaphat said to the king of Israel, "Please inquire for the word of the LORD today."

6Then the king of Israel gathered the prophets together, about four hundred men, and said to them, "Shall I go against Ramoth Gilead to fight, or shall I refrain?"

So they said, "Go up, for the Lord will deliver *it* into the hand of the king."

21:20, 21 *Clemency.* Ahab humbled himself before God, not because he felt the burden of his sins but because he faced the terror of death. God delayed the execution of the sentence, but it came just the same. Ahab had sold himself to do evil, and his master—sin—finally paid the wages (Rom. 6:23).

CHAPTER 22

22:4 *Fight your own battles.* Jehoshaphat had no reason to meddle in Ahab's wars. He made the mistake of marrying Ahab's daughter (2 Chron. 18:1; 2 Cor. 6:14–18), so there were family obligations to fulfill.

21:23 *b*Following Masoretic Text and Septuagint; some Hebrew manuscripts, Syriac, Targum, and Vulgate read *plot of ground* (compare 2 Kings 9:36).

7And Jehoshaphat said, "Is there not still a prophet of the LORD here, that we may inquire of Him?"c

8So the king of Israel said to Jehoshaphat, "There is still one man, Micaiah the son of Imlah, by whom we may inquire of the LORD; but I hate him, because he does not prophesy good concerning me, but evil."

And Jehoshaphat said, "Let not the king say such things!"

9Then the king of Israel called an officer and said, "Bring Micaiah the son of Imlah quickly!"

10The king of Israel and Jehoshaphat the king of Judah, having put on their robes, sat each on his throne, at a threshing floor at the entrance of the gate of Samaria; and all the prophets prophesied before them. 11Now Zedekiah the son of Chenaanah had made horns of iron for himself; and he said, "Thus says the LORD: 'With these you shall gore the Syrians until they are destroyed.' " 12And all the prophets prophesied so, saying, "Go up to Ramoth Gilead and prosper, for the LORD will deliver it into the king's hand."

13Then the messenger who had gone to call Micaiah spoke to him, saying, "Now listen, the words of the prophets with one accord encourage the king. Please, let your word be like the word of one of them, and speak encouragement."

14And Micaiah said, "As the LORD lives, whatever the LORD says to me, that I will speak."

15Then he came to the king; and the king said to him, "Micaiah, shall we go to war against Ramoth Gilead, or shall we refrain?"

And he answered him, "Go and prosper, for the LORD will deliver it into the hand of the king!"

16So the king said to him, "How many times shall I make you swear that you tell me nothing but the truth in the name of the LORD?"

17*Then he said, "I saw all Israel scattered on the mountains, as sheep that have no shepherd. And the LORD said, 'These have no master. Let each return to his house in peace.' "

18And the king of Israel said to Jehoshaphat, "Did I not tell you he would not prophesy good concerning me, but evil?"

19Then Micaiah said, "Therefore hear the word of the LORD: I saw the LORD sitting on His throne, and all the host of heaven standing by, on His right hand and on His left. 20And the LORD said, 'Who will persuade Ahab to go up, that he may fall at Ramoth Gilead?' So one spoke in this manner, and another spoke in that manner. 21Then a spirit came forward and stood before the LORD, and said, 'I will persuade him.' 22The LORD said to him, 'In what way?' So he said, 'I will go out and be a lying spirit in the mouth of all his prophets.' And the LORD said, 'You shall persuade him, and also prevail. Go out and do so.' 23Therefore look! The LORD has put a lying spirit in the mouth of all these prophets of yours, and the LORD has declared disaster against you."

24Now Zedekiah the son of Chenaanah went near and struck Micaiah on the cheek, and said, "Which way did the spirit from the LORD go from me to speak to you?"

25And Micaiah said, "Indeed, you shall see on that day when you go into an inner chamber to hide!"

26So the king of Israel said, "Take Micaiah, and

22:17–19 *Deliver your own message.* False prophets usually agree in their messages of success and glory. The messenger tried to get Micaiah to imitate them, but he gave the true message of the Lord. It was not easy to be a prophet in Israel in that day, but Micaiah was faithful.

22:7 cOr him

return him to Amon the governor of the city and to Joash the king's son; 27and say, 'Thus says the king: "Put this *fellow* in prison, and feed him with bread of affliction and water of affliction, until I come in peace." ' "

28But Micaiah said, "If you ever return in peace, the LORD has not spoken by me." And he said, "Take heed, all you people!"

29So the king of Israel and Jehoshaphat the king of Judah went up to Ramoth Gilead. 30And the king of Israel said to Jehoshaphat, "I will disguise myself and go into battle; but you put on your robes." So the king of Israel disguised himself and went into battle.

31Now the king of Syria had commanded the thirty-two captains of his chariots, saying, "Fight with no one small or great, but only with the king of Israel." 32*So it was, when the captains of the chariots saw Jehoshaphat, that they said, "Surely it *is* the king of Israel!" Therefore they turned aside to fight against him, and Jehoshaphat cried out. 33And it happened, when the captains of the chariots saw that it *was* not the king of Israel, that they turned back from pursuing him. 34Now a *certain* man drew a bow at random, and struck the king of Israel between the joints of his armor. So he said to the driver of his chariot, "Turn around and take me out of the battle, for I am wounded."

35The battle increased that day; and the king was propped up in his chariot, facing the Syrians, and died at evening. The blood ran out from the wound onto the floor of the chariot. 36Then, as the sun was going down, a shout went throughout the army, saying, "Every man to his city, and every man to his own country!"

37So the king died, and was brought to Samaria. And they buried the king in Samaria. 38Then *someone* washed the chariot at a pool in Samaria, and the dogs licked up his blood while the harlots bathed,*d* according to the word of the LORD which He had spoken.

39Now the rest of the acts of Ahab, and all that he did, the ivory house which he built and all the cities that he built, *are* they not written in the book of the chronicles of the kings of Israel? 40So Ahab rested with his fathers. Then Ahaziah his son reigned in his place.

41Jehoshaphat the son of Asa had become king over Judah in the fourth year of Ahab king of Israel. 42*Jehoshaphat *was* thirty-five years old when he became king, and he reigned twenty-five years in Jerusalem. His mother's name *was* Azubah the daughter of Shilhi. 43And he walked in all the ways of his father Asa. He did not turn aside from them, doing *what was* right in the eyes of the LORD. Nevertheless the high places were not taken away, *for* the people offered sacrifices and burned incense on the high places. 44Also Jehoshaphat made peace with the king of Israel.

45Now the rest of the acts of Jehoshaphat, the might that he showed, and how he made war, *are* they not written in the book of the chronicles of the kings of Judah? 46And the rest of the perverted persons,*e* who remained in the days of his father Asa, he banished from the land. 47*There was* then no king in Edom, only a deputy of the king.

22:32–34 *Know your own enemy.* Ahab cleverly tried to make Jehoshaphat a decoy and get him killed (Luke 16:8), but God overruled and Ahab was slain instead. The prophecy of 1 Kings 21:19 was fulfilled (v. 38). Paul may have had verse 31 in mind when he wrote Ephesians 6:12ff. Our real enemy is the god of this age and the prince of darkness, so let's not waste time and ammunition on lesser foes.

22:42–50 *Learn from your own mistakes.* When the new king of Israel, Jehoshaphat's brother-in-law, asked for a new alliance, Jehoshaphat refused. He had learned his lesson the hard way, but at least he had learned it and profited from his mistakes. He was a great and godly man, and we must not allow one event to discredit his service for the Lord.

22:38 *d*Syriac and Targum read *they washed his armor.*
22:46 *e*Hebrew *qadesh,* that is, one practicing sodomy and prostitution in religious rituals

⁴⁸Jehoshaphat made merchant ships*ᶠ* to go to Ophir for gold; but they never sailed, for the ships were wrecked at Ezion Geber. ⁴⁹Then Ahaziah the son of Ahab said to Jehoshaphat, "Let my servants go with your servants in the ships." But Jehoshaphat would not.

⁵⁰And Jehoshaphat rested with his fathers, and was buried with his fathers in the City of David his father. Then Jehoram his son reigned in his place.

⁵¹Ahaziah the son of Ahab became king over Israel in Samaria in the seventeenth year of Jehoshaphat king of Judah, and reigned two years over Israel. ⁵²He did evil in the sight of the LORD, and walked in the way of his father and in the way of his mother and in the way of Jeroboam the son of Nebat, who had made Israel sin; ⁵³for he served Baal and worshiped him, and provoked the LORD God of Israel to anger, according to all that his father had done.

22:48 *ᶠOr ships of Tarshish*

2 KINGS

This book records the collapse and captivity of the kingdom of Israel (chaps. 1—17) and the kingdom of Judah (chaps. 18—25). Spiritual decay led to political and social deterioration. In spite of the ministries of the prophets and the frequent chastenings God sent, Israel and Judah rebelled against the Lord and had to be judged. This is a warning to individuals (Prov. 29:1) and nations (Prov. 14:34) to listen to God's Word and obey it.

1 Moab* rebelled against Israel after the death of Ahab.

2Now Ahaziah fell through the lattice of his upper room in Samaria, and was injured; so he sent messengers and said to them, "Go, inquire of Baal-Zebub, the god of Ekron, whether I shall recover from this injury." 3*But the angel*a* of the LORD said to Elijah the Tishbite, "Arise, go up to meet the messengers of the king of Samaria, and say to them, 'Is it because there is no God in Israel that you are going to inquire of Baal-Zebub, the god of Ekron?' 4Now therefore, thus says the LORD: 'You shall not come down from the bed to which you have gone up, but you shall surely die.' " So Elijah departed.

5And when the messengers returned to him, he said to them, "Why have you come back?"

6*So they said to him, "A man came up to meet us, and said to us, 'Go, return to the king who sent you, and say to him, "Thus says the LORD: 'Is it because there is no God in Israel that you are sending to inquire of Baal-Zebub, the god of Ekron? Therefore you shall not come down from the bed to which you have gone up, but you shall surely die.' " ' "

7Then he said to them, "What kind of man was it who came up to meet you and told you these words?"

8So they answered him, "A hairy man wearing a leather belt around his waist."

And he said, "It is Elijah the Tishbite."

9Then the king sent to him a captain of fifty with his fifty men. So he went up to him; and there he was, sitting on the top of a hill. And he spoke to him: "Man of God, the king has said, 'Come down!' "

10*So Elijah answered and said to the captain of fifty, "If I am a man of God, then let fire come down from heaven and consume you and your fifty men." And fire came down from heaven and consumed him and his fifty. 11Then he sent to him another captain of fifty with his fifty men.

And he answered and said to him: "Man of God, thus has the king said, 'Come down quickly!' "

12So Elijah answered and said to them, "If I am a man of God, let fire come down from heaven and consume you and your fifty men." And the

CHAPTER 1

1:1ff "What kind of man was it?" is a key question. The messengers described Elijah's physical appearance, but they left out the most important thing. Elijah was "a man with a nature like ours" (James 5:17), but he was also a "man of God" (vv. 9–13). The physical description in verse 8 is incidental, yet that is what most people emphasize in their lives.

1:3–4 *He was guided by the Lord.* Elijah knew what was happening because he listened to God's voice (Ps. 25:4–5, 14). We today do not hear an audible voice, but we have His Spirit within us and His Word before us.

1:6 *He glorified the Lord.* The very idea of the king going to a false god for help! Elijah wanted Ahaziah to know that Jehovah alone was the true God and that the king had better bow humbly before the Lord.

1:10–12 *He trusted the Lord to care for him.* Elijah was one man against fifty-one soldiers, but the Lord protected him. Had the soldiers completely forgotten the fire that came down on Mount Carmel? The third captain humbled himself, and God spared him and his company.

1:3 *a*Or *Angel*

The Man of God—The title "man of God" was given first to Moses (Deut. 33:1), then to Samuel (1 Sam. 9:6–7), Elijah (1 Kings 1:9–13), Elisha (2 Kings 4:9), David (2 Chron. 8:14), and Timothy (1 Tim. 6:11). You need not be a prophet to be a godly person, nor do you display your godliness by calling down fire from heaven (Luke 9:51–56). God wants us to use "coals of fire" and turn enemies into friends (Rom. 12:14–21).

1:16 He did the Lord's will. He delivered the message to the king as he was commanded to do.

Can God's people today be men and women of God? Certainly! Ponder 1 Timothy 6:10–12 and 2 Timothy 3:14–17.

CHAPTER 2

2:2 Companions. Elisha's ministry began with Elijah saying, "Go back!" (1 Kings 19:20). Now Elijah is saying, "Stay here!" Elisha did not go back but faithfully served Elijah about ten years. And Elisha did not linger at Bethel or Jericho but walked with Elijah to the very end. Think of what Elisha would have missed had he tarried!

2:7 Spectators. The students had knowledge without experience. They were just spectators, yet they tried to tell the prophet what was going on! Elisha was not a spectator; he was right in the middle of what God was doing. What good is our knowledge of spiritual things if it does not make a difference in our lives?

fire of God came down from heaven and consumed him and his fifty.

13Again, he sent a third captain of fifty with his fifty men. And the third captain of fifty went up, and came and fell on his knees before Elijah, and pleaded with him, and said to him: "Man of God, please let my life and the life of these fifty servants of yours be precious in your sight. 14Look, fire has come down from heaven and burned up the first two captains of fifties with their fifties. But let my life now be precious in your sight."

15And the angel*b* of the LORD said to Elijah, "Go down with him; do not be afraid of him." So he arose and went down with him to the king. 16*Then he said to him, "Thus says the LORD: 'Because you have sent messengers to inquire of Baal-Zebub, the god of Ekron, *is it* because *there is* no God in Israel to inquire of His word? Therefore you shall not come down from the bed to which you have gone up, but you shall surely die.' "

17So *Ahaziah* died according to the word of the LORD which Elijah had spoken. Because he had no son, Jehoram*c* became king in his place, in the second year of Jehoram the son of Jehoshaphat, king of Judah.

18Now the rest of the acts of Ahaziah which he did, *are* they not written in the book of the chronicles of the kings of Israel?

2 And it came to pass, when the LORD was about to take up Elijah into heaven by a whirlwind, that Elijah went with Elisha from Gilgal. 2*Then Elijah said to Elisha, "Stay here, please, for the LORD has sent me on to Bethel."

But Elisha said, "*As* the LORD lives, and *as* your soul lives, I will not leave you!" So they went down to Bethel.

3Now the sons of the prophets who *were* at Bethel came out to Elisha, and said to him, "Do you know that the LORD will take away your master from over you today?"

And he said, "Yes, I know; keep silent!"

4Then Elijah said to him, "Elisha, stay here, please, for the LORD has sent me on to Jericho."

But he said, "*As* the LORD lives, and *as* your soul lives, I will not leave you!" So they came to Jericho.

5Now the sons of the prophets who *were* at Jericho came to Elisha and said to him, "Do you know that the LORD will take away your master from over you today?"

So he answered, "Yes, I know; keep silent!"

6Then Elijah said to him, "Stay here, please, for the LORD has sent me on to the Jordan."

But he said, "*As* the LORD lives, and *as* your soul lives, I will not leave you!" So the two of them went on. 7*And fifty men of the sons of the prophets went and stood facing *them* at a distance, while the two of them stood by the Jordan. 8Now Elijah took his mantle, rolled *it* up, and struck the water; and it was divided this way and that, so that the two of them crossed over on dry ground.

9And so it was, when they had crossed over, that Elijah said to Elisha, "Ask! What may I do for you, before I am taken away from you?"

1:15 *b*Or *Angel*   1:17 *c*The son of Ahab king of Israel (compare 3:1)

Elisha said, "Please let a double portion of your spirit be upon me."

¹⁰So he said, "You have asked a hard thing. *Nevertheless*, if you see me *when I am* taken from you, it shall be so for you; but if not, it shall not be *so*." ¹¹Then it happened, as they continued on and talked, that suddenly a chariot of fire *appeared* with horses of fire, and separated the two of them; and Elijah went up by a whirlwind into heaven.

¹²And Elisha saw *it*, and he cried out, "My father, my father, the chariot of Israel and its horsemen!" So he saw him no more. And he took hold of his own clothes and tore them into two pieces. ¹³He also took up the mantle of Elijah that had fallen from him, and went back and stood by the bank of the Jordan. ¹⁴*Then he took the mantle of Elijah that had fallen from him, and struck the water, and said, "Where *is* the Lᴏʀᴅ God of Elijah?" And when he also had struck the water, it was divided this way and that; and Elisha crossed over.

¹⁵Now when the sons of the prophets who *were* from Jericho saw him, they said, "The spirit of Elijah rests on Elisha." And they came to meet him, and bowed to the ground before him. ¹⁶Then they said to him, "Look now, there are fifty strong men with your servants. Please let them go and search for your master, lest perhaps the Spirit of the Lᴏʀᴅ has taken him up and cast him upon some mountain or into some valley."

And he said, "You shall not send anyone."

¹⁷But when they urged him till he was ashamed, he said, "Send *them!*" Therefore they sent fifty men, and they searched for three days but did not find him. ¹⁸And when they came back to him, for he had stayed in Jericho, he said to them, "Did I not say to you, 'Do not go'?"

¹⁹Then the men of the city said to Elisha, "Please notice, the situation of this city *is* pleasant, as my lord sees; but the water *is* bad, and the ground barren."

²⁰And he said, "Bring me a new bowl, and put salt in it." So they brought *it* to him. ²¹Then he went out to the source of the water, and cast in the salt there, and said, "Thus says the Lᴏʀᴅ: 'I have healed this water; from it there shall be no more death or barrenness.' " ²²So the water remains healed to this day, according to the word of Elisha which he spoke.

²³*Then he went up from there to Bethel; and as he was going up the road, some youths came from the city and mocked him, and said to him, "Go up, you baldhead! Go up, you baldhead!"

²⁴So he turned around and looked at them, and pronounced a curse on them in the name of the Lᴏʀᴅ. And two female bears came out of the woods and mauled forty-two of the youths.

²⁵Then he went from there to Mount Carmel, and from there he returned to Samaria.

3 Now Jehoram the son of Ahab became king over Israel at Samaria in the eighteenth year of Jehoshaphat king of Judah, and reigned twelve years. ²And he did evil in the sight of the Lᴏʀᴅ, but not like his father and mother; for he put away the *sacred* pillar of Baal that his father had made. ³Nevertheless he persisted in the sins of Jeroboam the son of Nebat, who had made Israel sin; he did not depart from them.

⁴Now Mesha king of Moab was a sheepbreeder, and he regularly paid the king of Israel one

2:14, 15 Doers. Elisha did not build a monument to Elijah. Instead, he trusted Elijah's God and did miracles. We cannot live *in* the past, *on* the past, or *for* the past. We must accept the heritage of the past and trust the living God for power today. There were problems to solve and needs to meet, and Elisha trusted God to help him. God's servants may leave us, but God's Spirit goes on working.

2:23–25 Mockers. They were not little children; the youths were old enough to know better. They mocked Elijah's going to heaven ("Go up!") and Elisha's personal appearance, and God rightly judged them for it. Today, God is patient with the mockers (2 Pet. 3), but one day, His judgment will fall on them.

hundred thousand lambs and the wool of one hundred thousand rams. 5But it happened, when Ahab died, that the king of Moab rebelled against the king of Israel.

6So King Jehoram went out of Samaria at that time and mustered all Israel. 7Then he went and sent to Jehoshaphat king of Judah, saying, "The king of Moab has rebelled against me. Will you go with me to fight against Moab?"

And he said, "I will go up; I *am* as you *are,* my people as your people, my horses as your horses." 8Then he said, "Which way shall we go up?"

And he answered, "By way of the Wilderness of Edom."

9So the king of Israel went with the king of Judah and the king of Edom, and they marched on that roundabout route seven days; and there was no water for the army, nor for the animals that followed them. 10And the king of Israel said, "Alas! For the LORD has called these three kings together to deliver them into the hand of Moab."

11But Jehoshaphat said, "*Is there* no prophet of the LORD here, that we may inquire of the LORD by him?"

So one of the servants of the king of Israel answered and said, "Elisha the son of Shaphat *is* here, who poured water on the hands of Elijah."

12And Jehoshaphat said, "The word of the LORD is with him." So the king of Israel and Jehoshaphat and the king of Edom went down to him.

13Then Elisha said to the king of Israel, "What have I to do with you? Go to the prophets of your father and the prophets of your mother."

But the king of Israel said to him, "No, for the LORD has called these three kings *together* to deliver them into the hand of Moab."

14*And Elisha said, "*As* the LORD of hosts lives, before whom I stand, surely were it not that I regard the presence of Jehoshaphat king of Judah, I would not look at you, nor see you. 15But now bring me a musician."

Then it happened, when the musician played, that the hand of the LORD came upon him. 16And he said, "Thus says the LORD: 'Make this valley full of ditches.' 17*For thus says the LORD: 'You shall not see wind, nor shall you see rain; yet that valley shall be filled with water, so that you, your cattle, and your animals may drink.' 18And this is a simple matter in the sight of the LORD; He will also deliver the Moabites into your hand. 19Also you shall attack every fortified city and every choice city, and shall cut down every good tree, and stop up every spring of water, and ruin every good piece of land with stones."

20Now it happened in the morning, when the grain offering was offered, that suddenly water came by way of Edom, and the land was filled with water.

21*And when all the Moabites heard that the kings had come up to fight against them, all who were able to bear arms and older were gathered; and they stood at the border. 22Then they rose up early in the morning, and the sun was shining on the water; and the Moabites saw the water on the other side *as* red as blood. 23And they said, "This is blood; the kings have surely struck swords and have killed one another; now therefore, Moab, to the spoil!"

24So when they came to the camp of Israel, Israel rose up and attacked the Moabites, so that they fled before them; and they entered *their* land,

---

CHAPTER 3

3:14 King Jehoshaphat was wrong to ally himself with the king of Israel (1 Kings 22), but Elisha did not withdraw from him because of that. The presence of the king of Judah was the only thing that motivated Elisha to help the kings in their plight. God still had a lamp in Judah for the sake of David.

3:17 The lack of water reminded all three kings that God was in control and their combined power meant nothing without Him. Samson had a similar experience (Judg. 15:18–20). The same water that meant salvation to the three armies brought defeat to overconfident Moab. (See Exod. 10:21–23; 2 Cor. 2:14–16.)

3:21–27 Hoping to get some good out of the war, the king of Moab attacked Edom alone, but he failed to conquer. In desperation, he even sacrificed the crown prince. The deed was so repulsive to Judah and Moab that they left the field in great anger against Israel for ever getting them involved. When you join forces with those who do not love God, you never know what will happen to embarrass or offend you or to disgrace the Lord's name.

killing the Moabites. 25Then they destroyed the cities, and each man threw a stone on every good piece of land and filled it; and they stopped up all the springs of water and cut down all the good trees. But they left the stones of Kir Haraseth *intact.* However the slingers surrounded and attacked it.

26And when the king of Moab saw that the battle was too fierce for him, he took with him seven hundred men who drew swords, to break through to the king of Edom, but they could not. 27Then he took his eldest son who would have reigned in his place, and offered him *as* a burnt offering upon the wall; and there was great indignation against Israel. So they departed from him and returned to *their own* land.

4 A* certain woman of the wives of the sons of the prophets cried out to Elisha, saying, "Your servant my husband is dead, and you know that your servant feared the LORD. And the creditor is coming to take my two sons to be his slaves."

2*So Elisha said to her, "What shall I do for you? Tell me, what do you have in the house?" And she said, "Your maidservant has nothing in the house but a jar of oil."

3Then he said, "Go, borrow vessels from everywhere, from all your neighbors—empty vessels; do not gather just a few. 4And when you have come in, you shall shut the door behind you and your sons; then pour it into all those vessels, and set aside the full ones."

5So she went from him and shut the door behind her and her sons, who brought *the vessels* to her; and she poured *it* out. 6Now it came to pass, when the vessels were full, that she said to her son, "Bring me another vessel."

And he said to her, "*There is* not another vessel." So the oil ceased. 7Then she came and told the man of God. And he said, "Go, sell the oil and pay your debt; and you *and* your sons live on the rest."

8Now it happened one day that Elisha went to Shunem, where there *was* a notable woman, and she persuaded him to eat some food. So it was, as often as he passed by, he would turn in there to eat some food. 9And she said to her husband, "Look now, I know that this *is* a holy man of God, who passes by us regularly. 10Please, let us make a small upper room on the wall; and let us put a bed for him there, and a table and a chair and a lampstand; so it will be, whenever he comes to us, he can turn in there."

11And it happened one day that he came there, and he turned in to the upper room and lay down there. 12Then he said to Gehazi his servant, "Call this Shunammite woman." When he had called her, she stood before him. 13And he said to him, "Say now to her, 'Look, you have been concerned for us with all this care. What *can* I do for you? Do you want me to speak on your behalf to the king or to the commander of the army?'"

She answered, "I dwell among my own people."

14So he said, "What then *is* to be done for her?"

And Gehazi answered, "Actually, she has no son, and her husband is old."

15So he said, "Call her." When he had called

CHAPTER 4

4:1ff Elisha ministered to individuals and accepted the hospitality of friends. He was like Jesus Christ in that respect, while Elijah was more like John the Baptist: alone, rugged, a preacher to the nation. Although God equips different people to work in different ways, He is Lord of all (1 Cor. 12:1–11). It is too bad people do not recognize this fact and receive the ministry no matter who the minister is (Luke 7:31–35; 1 Cor. 1:10–17).

4:2–44 A husband died, yet God met the needs of the family (vv. 1–7). A son died, yet God raised him and restored the family (vv. 8–37). A group of prophets almost died because of poisoned stew, yet God removed the danger (vv. 38–41). A group of believers would have died from starvation, but God multiplied the bread and sustained them (vv. 42–44). All of these miracles remind you to *give God what you have and let Him do what He wills.*

Three Important Questions—What are your answers to the three questions the prophet asked the Shunammite woman? "Is it well with you? Is it well with your husband [or wife]? Is it well with the child?" (2 Kings 4:26).

her, she stood in the doorway. 16Then he said, "About this time next year you shall embrace a son."

And she said, "No, my lord. Man of God, do not lie to your maidservant!"

17But the woman conceived, and bore a son when the appointed time had come, of which Elisha had told her.

18And the child grew. Now it happened one day that he went out to his father, to the reapers. 19And he said to his father, "My head, my head!"

So he said to a servant, "Carry him to his mother." 20When he had taken him and brought him to his mother, he sat on her knees till noon, and *then* died. 21And she went up and laid him on the bed of the man of God, shut *the door* upon him, and went out. 22Then she called to her husband, and said, "Please send me one of the young men and one of the donkeys, that I may run to the man of God and come back."

23So he said, "Why are you going to him today? *It is* neither the New Moon nor the Sabbath."

And she said, "*It is* well." 24Then she saddled a donkey, and said to her servant, "Drive, and go forward; do not slacken the pace for me unless I tell you." 25And so she departed, and went to the man of God at Mount Carmel.

So it was, when the man of God saw her afar off, that he said to his servant Gehazi, "Look, the Shunammite woman! 26Please run now to meet her, and say to her, '*Is it* well with you? *Is it* well with your husband? *Is it* well with the child?' "

And she answered, "*It is* well." 27Now when she came to the man of God at the hill, she caught him by the feet, but Gehazi came near to push her away. But the man of God said, "Let her alone; for her soul *is* in deep distress, and the LORD has hidden *it* from me, and has not told me."

28So she said, "Did I ask a son of my lord? Did I not say, 'Do not deceive me'?"

29Then he said to Gehazi, "Get yourself ready, and take my staff in your hand, and be on your way. If you meet anyone, do not greet him; and if anyone greets you, do not answer him; but lay my staff on the face of the child."

30And the mother of the child said, "As the LORD lives, and as your soul lives, I will not leave you." So he arose and followed her. 31*Now Gehazi went on ahead of them, and laid the staff on the face of the child; but *there was* neither voice nor hearing. Therefore he went back to meet him, and told him, saying, "The child has not awakened."

32When Elisha came into the house, there was the child, lying dead on his bed. 33He went in therefore, shut the door behind the two of them, and prayed to the LORD. 34And he went up and lay on the child, and put his mouth on his mouth, his eyes on his eyes, and his hands on his hands; and he stretched himself out on the child, and the flesh of the child became warm. 35He returned and walked back and forth in the house, and again went up and stretched himself out on him; then the child sneezed seven times, and the child opened his eyes. 36And he called Gehazi and said, "Call this Shunammite woman." So he called her. And when she came in to him, he said, "Pick up your son." 37So she went in, fell at his feet, and bowed to the ground; then she picked up her son and went out.

38And Elisha returned to Gilgal, and *there was* a famine in the land. Now the sons of the prophets *were* sitting before him; and he said to his servant,

4:31 Gehazi is declining spiritually, but the consequences will not appear until later. He was unkind to the Shunammite woman (v. 27; see also Matt. 15:23; Mark 10:13; Luke 9:49), and he had no power to help her. He went through the motions, but no life came. You can fellowship day after day with people of power, like the prophet Elisha, and still backslide. Beware!

"Put on the large pot, and boil stew for the sons of the prophets." [39]So one went out into the field to gather herbs, and found a wild vine, and gathered from it a lapful of wild gourds, and came and sliced *them* into the pot of stew, though they did not know *what they were.* [40]Then they served it to the men to eat. Now it happened, as they were eating the stew, that they cried out and said, "Man of God, *there is* death in the pot!" And they could not eat *it.*

[41]So he said, "Then bring some flour." And he put *it* into the pot, and said, "Serve *it* to the people, that they may eat." And there was nothing harmful in the pot.

[42]Then a man came from Baal Shalisha, and brought the man of God bread of the firstfruits, twenty loaves of barley bread, and newly ripened grain in his knapsack. And he said, "Give *it* to the people, that they may eat."

[43]But his servant said, "What? Shall I set this before one hundred men?"

He said again, "Give it to the people, that they may eat; for thus says the LORD: 'They shall eat and have *some* left over.' " [44]So he set *it* before them; and they ate and had *some* left over, according to the word of the LORD.

5 Now* Naaman, commander of the army of the king of Syria, was a great and honorable man in the eyes of his master, because by him the LORD had given victory to Syria. He was also a mighty man of valor, *but* a leper. [2]And the Syrians had gone out on raids, and had brought back captive a young girl from the land of Israel. She waited on Naaman's wife. [3]Then she said to her mistress, "If only my master *were* with the prophet who *is* in Samaria! For he would heal him of his leprosy." [4]And *Naaman* went in and told his master, saying, "Thus and thus said the girl who *is* from the land of Israel."

[5]*Then the king of Syria said, "Go now, and I will send a letter to the king of Israel."

So he departed and took with him ten talents of silver, six thousand *shekels* of gold, and ten changes of clothing. [6]Then he brought the letter to the king of Israel, which said,

Now be advised, when this letter comes to you, that I have sent Naaman my servant to you, that you may heal him of his leprosy.

[7]And it happened, when the king of Israel read the letter, that he tore his clothes and said, "*Am I God,* to kill and make alive, that this man sends a man to me to heal him of his leprosy? Therefore please consider, and see how he seeks a quarrel with me."

[8]So it was, when Elisha the man of God heard that the king of Israel had torn his clothes, that he sent to the king, saying, "Why have you torn your clothes? Please let him come to me, and he shall know that there is a prophet in Israel."

[9]Then Naaman went with his horses and chariot, and he stood at the door of Elisha's house. [10]And Elisha sent a messenger to him, saying, "Go and wash in the Jordan seven times, and your

CHAPTER 5

5:1–3 *Servants.* Servants played a major role in this miracle. The young Jewish girl gave a faithful witness for the Lord, and God used her testimony to get Naaman to visit Elisha. Naaman's servants encouraged him to obey the prophet, and his obedience led to his healing and his faith in Jehovah. No matter who or where you are, God can use your service. (See John 15:15.)

5:5, 6 *Suppositions.* The king of Syria thought the king of Israel could perform the miracle, and the false assumption almost led to a war. Naaman supposed that Elisha would use some religious ritual to remove the leprosy, and the supposition almost led to his going home still a leper. Gehazi supposed that he could get away with sin, but God judged him.

They Became Lepers—In the Bible, leprosy is used as a picture of sin (Lev. 13). Gehazi became a leper because of covetousness and deception. Miriam became a leper because of criticism and envy (Num. 12). King Uzziah became a leper because of pride (2 Chron. 26:16–23). If God did this to people today, would you be a leper? The hidden sins of the spirit are dangerous (2 Cor. 7:1)!

flesh shall be restored to you, and *you shall* be clean." ¹¹But Naaman became furious, and went away and said, "Indeed, I said to myself, 'He will surely come out *to me,* and stand and call on the name of the LORD his God, and wave his hand over the place, and heal the leprosy.' ¹²*Are* not the Abanah*ᵈ* and the Pharpar, the rivers of Damascus, better than all the waters of Israel? Could I not wash in them and be clean?" So he turned and went away in a rage. ¹³And his servants came near and spoke to him, and said, "My father, *if* the prophet had told you *to do* something great, would you not have done *it*? How much more then, when he says to you, 'Wash, and be clean'?" ¹⁴So he went down and dipped seven times in the Jordan, according to the saying of the man of God; and his flesh was restored like the flesh of a little child, and he was clean.

¹⁵And he returned to the man of God, he and all his aides, and came and stood before him; and he said, "Indeed, now I know that *there is* no God in all the earth, except in Israel; now therefore, please take a gift from your servant."

¹⁶But he said, "*As* the LORD lives, before whom I stand, I will receive nothing." And he urged him to take *it,* but he refused.

¹⁷So Naaman said, "Then, if not, please let your servant be given two mule-loads of earth; for your servant will no longer offer either burnt offering or sacrifice to other gods, but to the LORD. ¹⁸Yet in this thing may the LORD pardon your servant: when my master goes into the temple of Rimmon to worship there, and he leans on my hand, and I bow down in the temple of Rimmon—when I bow down in the temple of Rimmon, may the LORD please pardon your servant in this thing."

¹⁹Then he said to him, "Go in peace." So he departed from him a short distance.

²⁰*But Gehazi, the servant of Elisha the man of God, said, "Look, my master has spared Naaman this Syrian, while not receiving from his hands what he brought; but *as* the LORD lives, I will run after him and take something from him." ²¹So Gehazi pursued Naaman. When Naaman saw *him* running after him, he got down from the chariot to meet him, and said, "*Is* all well?"

²²And he said, "All *is* well. My master has sent me, saying, 'Indeed, just now two young men of the sons of the prophets have come to me from the mountains of Ephraim. Please give them a talent of silver and two changes of garments.' "

²³So Naaman said, "Please, take two talents." And he urged him, and bound two talents of silver in two bags, with two changes of garments, and handed *them* to two of his servants; and they carried *them* on ahead of him. ²⁴When he came to the citadel, he took *them* from their hand, and stored *them* away in the house; then he let the men go, and they departed. ²⁵Now he went in and stood before his master. Elisha said to him, "Where *did you* go, Gehazi?"

And he said, "Your servant did not go anywhere."

²⁶Then he said to him, "Did not my heart go *with you* when the man turned back from his chariot to meet you? *Is it* time to receive money and to receive clothing, olive groves and vineyards, sheep and oxen, male and female servants?

5:20–27 *Selfishness.* Naaman was healed completely by God's grace, but Gehazi robbed God of glory by asking Naaman for gifts. The Syrians would think that they had to pay God to get His help. Gehazi lied to Naaman, to Elisha, and to himself, but he could not lie to God. Gehazi became poor by getting rich.

5:12 *ᵈ*Following Kethib, Septuagint, and Vulgate; Qere, Syriac, and Targum read *Amanah*.

27Therefore the leprosy of Naaman shall cling to you and your descendants forever." And he went out from his presence leprous, *as white* as snow.

6 And* the sons of the prophets said to Elisha, "See now, the place where we dwell with you is too small for us. 2Please, let us go to the Jordan, and let every man take a beam from there, and let us make there a place where we may dwell."

So he answered, "Go."

3Then one said, "Please consent to go with your servants."

And he answered, "I will go." 4So he went with them. And when they came to the Jordan, they cut down trees. 5But as one was cutting down a tree, the iron *ax head* fell into the water; and he cried out and said, "Alas, master! For it was borrowed."

6So the man of God said, "Where did it fall?" And he showed him the place. So he cut off a stick, and threw *it* in there; and he made the iron float. 7Therefore he said, "Pick *it* up for yourself." So he reached out his hand and took it.

8*Now the king of Syria was making war against Israel; and he consulted with his servants, saying, "My camp *will be* in such and such a place." 9And the man of God sent to the king of Israel, saying, "Beware that you do not pass this place, for the Syrians are coming down there." 10Then the king of Israel sent *someone* to the place of which the man of God had told him. Thus he warned him, and he was watchful there, not just once or twice.

11Therefore the heart of the king of Syria was greatly troubled by this thing; and he called his servants and said to them, "Will you not show me which of us *is* for the king of Israel?"

12And one of his servants said, "None, my lord, O king; but Elisha, the prophet who *is* in Israel, tells the king of Israel the words that you speak in your bedroom."

13*So he said, "Go and see where he *is*, that I may send and get him."

And it was told him, saying, "Surely he *is* in Dothan."

14Therefore he sent horses and chariots and a great army there, and they came by night and surrounded the city. 15And when the servant of the man of God arose early and went out, there was an army, surrounding the city with horses and chariots. And his servant said to him, "Alas, my master! What shall we do?"

16So he answered, "Do not fear, for those who *are* with us *are* more than those who *are* with them." 17And Elisha prayed, and said, "LORD, I pray, open his eyes that he may see." Then the LORD opened the eyes of the young man, and he saw. And behold, the mountain *was* full of horses and chariots of fire all around Elisha. 18*So when *the Syrians* came down to him, Elisha prayed to the LORD, and said, "Strike this people, I pray, with blindness." And He struck them with blindness according to the word of Elisha.

19Now Elisha said to them, "This *is* not the way, nor *is* this the city. Follow me, and I will bring you to the man whom you seek." But he led them to Samaria.

20So it was, when they had come to Samaria, that Elisha said, "LORD, open the eyes of these *men*, that they may see." And the LORD opened their eyes, and they saw; and there *they were*, inside Samaria!

CHAPTER 6

6:1–7 *Doing the impossible.* All that we have is "borrowed," loaned to us by the Lord to get His work done (John 3:27). You can lose your cutting edge even while serving the Lord. But be honest about it, stop trying to chop without an ax head, and ask the Lord for help in recovering it. He alone can do the impossible if you trust Him.

6:8–12 *Knowing the unknowable.* Because Elisha knew what the enemy would do, Israel had the opportunity to escape surprise attacks. If you study God's Word, you can know the strategy of Satan and be able to defeat him.

6:13–17 *Seeing the invisible.* Many times we are afraid of the enemy because we walk by sight and not by faith. If God and His hosts are for us, who can be against us?

6:18–23 *Accomplishing the unthinkable.* Knowing that Elisha was his real enemy, the king of Syria tried to capture the prophet. *But Elisha captured them,* and he did it with prayer and kindness (Rom. 12:19–21; 2 Cor. 10:3–6). In the East, eating together is equivalent to making a covenant, so those soldiers could never attack Israel again.

21Now when the king of Israel saw them, he said to Elisha, "My father, shall I kill *them*? Shall I kill *them*?"

22But he answered, "You shall not kill *them*. Would you kill those whom you have taken captive with your sword and your bow? Set food and water before them, that they may eat and drink and go to their master." 23Then he prepared a great feast for them; and after they ate and drank, he sent them away and they went to their master. So the bands of Syrian *raiders* came no more into the land of Israel.

24And it happened after this that Ben-Hadad king of Syria gathered all his army, and went up and besieged Samaria. 25And there was a great famine in Samaria; and indeed they besieged it until a donkey's head was *sold* for eighty *shekels* of silver, and one-fourth of a kab of dove droppings for five *shekels* of silver.

26Then, as the king of Israel was passing by on the wall, a woman cried out to him, saying, "Help, my lord, O king!"

27And he said, "If the LORD does not help you, where can I find help for you? From the threshing floor or from the winepress?" 28Then the king said to her, "What is troubling you?"

And she answered, "This woman said to me, 'Give your son, that we may eat him today, and we will eat my son tomorrow.' 29So we boiled my son, and ate him. And I said to her on the next day, 'Give your son, that we may eat him'; but she has hidden her son."

30Now it happened, when the king heard the words of the woman, that he tore his clothes; and as he passed by on the wall, the people looked, and there underneath *he had* sackcloth on his body. 31Then he said, "God do so to me and more also, if the head of Elisha the son of Shaphat remains on him today!"

32But Elisha was sitting in his house, and the elders were sitting with him. And *the king* sent a man ahead of him, but before the messenger came to him, he said to the elders, "Do you see how this son of a murderer has sent someone to take away my head? Look, when the messenger comes, shut the door, and hold him fast at the door. *Is* not the sound of his master's feet behind him?" 33And while he was still talking with them, there was the messenger, coming down to him; and then *the king* said, "Surely this calamity *is* from the LORD; why should I wait for the LORD any longer?"

7 Then* Elisha said, "Hear the word of the LORD. Thus says the LORD: 'Tomorrow about this time a seah of fine flour *shall be sold* for a shekel, and two seahs of barley for a shekel, at the gate of Samaria.' "

2*So an officer on whose hand the king leaned answered the man of God and said, "Look, *if* the LORD would make windows in heaven, could this thing be?"

And he said, "In fact, you shall see *it* with your eyes, but you shall not eat of it."

3*Now there were four leprous men at the entrance of the gate; and they said to one another, "Why are we sitting here until we die? 4If we say, 'We will enter the city,' the famine *is* in the city, and we shall die there. And if we sit here, we die also. Now therefore, come, let us surrender to the army of the Syrians. If they keep us alive, we shall live; and if they kill us, we shall only die."

CHAPTER 7

7:1ff When times are tough, people may respond in the following ways: **Blaming.** Like his evil father Ahab who blamed Elijah for his woes, King Joram blamed Elisha for the plight of the city (1 Kings 18:17; 2 Kings 6:31), when in reality it was his own fault. He tore his clothes and wore sackcloth, but the king's actions did not impress God as long as his heart was hardened (2 Kings 6:30; Joel 2:12–14).

7:2 Doubting. The officer did not believe the word of God, and his unbelief caused his death (vv. 17–20). God will open the windows when we obey Him (Mal. 3:10).

7:3–8 Reasoning. The four lepers were logical in their reasoning: "If we give up, we will die. If we give in to the enemy, we may die, or we may live. Let's surrender to the enemy." But there was no enemy! God scattered them with a noise!

5And they rose at twilight to go to the camp of the Syrians; and when they had come to the outskirts of the Syrian camp, to their surprise no one *was* there. 6For the LORD had caused the army of the Syrians to hear the noise of chariots and the noise of horses—the noise of a great army; so they said to one another, "Look, the king of Israel has hired against us the kings of the Hittites and the kings of the Egyptians to attack us!" 7Therefore they arose and fled at twilight, and left the camp intact—their tents, their horses, and their donkeys—and they fled for their lives. 8And when these lepers came to the outskirts of the camp, they went into one tent and ate and drank, and carried from it silver and gold and clothing, and went and hid *them;* then they came back and entered another tent, and carried *some* from there *also,* and went and hid *it.*

9*Then they said to one another, "We are not doing right. This day *is* a day of good news, and we remain silent. If we wait until morning light, some punishment will come upon us. Now therefore, come, let us go and tell the king's household." 10So they went and called to the gatekeepers of the city, and told them, saying, "We went to the Syrian camp, and surprisingly no one *was* there, not a human sound—only horses and donkeys tied, and the tents intact." 11And the gatekeepers called out, and they told *it* to the king's household inside.

12So the king arose in the night and said to his servants, "Let me now tell you what the Syrians have done to us. They know that we *are* hungry; therefore they have gone out of the camp to hide themselves in the field, saying, 'When they come out of the city, we shall catch them alive, and get into the city.'"

13And one of his servants answered and said, "Please, let several *men* take five of the remaining horses which are left in the city. Look, they *may either become* like all the multitude of Israel that are left in it; or indeed, *I say,* they *may become* like all the multitude of Israel left from those who are consumed; so let us send them and see." 14Therefore they took two chariots with horses; and the king sent them in the direction of the Syrian army, saying, "Go and see." 15And they went after them to the Jordan; and indeed all the road *was* full of garments and weapons which the Syrians had thrown away in their haste. So the messengers returned and told the king. 16Then the people went out and plundered the tents of the Syrians. So a seah of fine flour was *sold* for a shekel, and two seahs of barley for a shekel, according to the word of the LORD.

17Now the king had appointed the officer on whose hand he leaned to have charge of the gate. But the people trampled him in the gate, and he died, just as the man of God had said, who spoke when the king came down to him. 18So it happened just as the man of God had spoken to the king, saying, "Two seahs of barley for a shekel, and a seah of fine flour for a shekel, shall be *sold* tomorrow about this time in the gate of Samaria."

19Then that officer had answered the man of God, and said, "Now look, *if* the LORD would make windows in heaven, could such a thing be?" And he had said, "In fact, you shall see *it* with your eyes, but you shall not eat of it." 20And so it happened to him, for the people trampled him in the gate, and he died.

7:9–16 *Sharing.* The lepers moved from giving up and giving in to giving out. Sharing the good news helped to save the city. We are living in a day of good news. Are you sharing it? We are here not to give in or give up but to give out.

CHAPTER 8

8:1 *God knows the future.* The Shunammite woman experienced three tragedies: the death of her son, the uprooting of her household, and the loss of her property. And yet she was faithful to the Lord and had been kind to God's servant (2 Kings 4:8ff.). God helped her escape the famine and then used the miracle of her son's resurrection to help her regain her property. Romans 8:28 certainly proved true in her life! You may wonder why God permits some of your trials, but wait and see how He will use them!

8:7–10 *God sees the heart.* When he was desperate, Ben-Hadad wanted Elisha's help, but he did not want Elisha's God. The prophet saw the murder in Hazael's heart, but Hazael denied it was there. We do not know how wicked our hearts really are (Jer. 17:9), and we must cry out to God for His help (Ps. 51:5–6, 10).

8:19 *God keeps His promises.* Jehoshaphat was a godly man, but he had married a daughter of Ahab (2 Chron. 18:1); and his son followed his bad example. Jehoram also followed the bad example of his father-in-law Ahab and allowed his evil wife to lead him into great sin. But God kept His promise to David (v. 19) and did not destroy Judah. He had purposes to fulfill through the godly remnant, for Judah would bring the Savior into the world.

8 Then* Elisha spoke to the woman whose son he had restored to life, saying, "Arise and go, you and your household, and stay wherever you can; for the LORD has called for a famine, and furthermore, it will come upon the land for seven years." ²So the woman arose and did according to the saying of the man of God, and she went with her household and dwelt in the land of the Philistines seven years.

³It came to pass, at the end of seven years, that the woman returned from the land of the Philistines; and she went to make an appeal to the king for her house and for her land. ⁴Then the king talked with Gehazi, the servant of the man of God, saying, "Tell me, please, all the great things Elisha has done." ⁵Now it happened, as he was telling the king how he had restored the dead to life, that there was the woman whose son he had restored to life, appealing to the king for her house and for her land. And Gehazi said, "My lord, O king, this *is* the woman, and this *is* her son whom Elisha restored to life." ⁶And when the king asked the woman, she told him.

So the king appointed a certain officer for her, saying, "Restore all that *was* hers, and all the proceeds of the field from the day that she left the land until now."

⁷*Then Elisha went to Damascus, and Ben-Hadad king of Syria was sick; and it was told him, saying, "The man of God has come here." ⁸And the king said to Hazael, "Take a present in your hand, and go to meet the man of God, and inquire of the LORD by him, saying, 'Shall I recover from this disease?'" ⁹So Hazael went to meet him and took a present with him, of every good thing of Damascus, forty camel-loads; and he came and stood before him, and said, "Your son Ben-Hadad king of Syria has sent me to you, saying, 'Shall I recover from this disease?'"

¹⁰And Elisha said to him, "Go, say to him, 'You shall certainly recover.' However the LORD has shown me that he will really die." ¹¹Then he set his countenance in a stare until he was ashamed; and the man of God wept. ¹²And Hazael said, "Why is my lord weeping?"

He answered, "Because I know the evil that you will do to the children of Israel: Their strongholds you will set on fire, and their young men you will kill with the sword; and you will dash their children, and rip open their women with child."

¹³So Hazael said, "But what *is* your servant—a dog, that he should do this gross thing?"

And Elisha answered, "The LORD has shown me that you *will become* king over Syria."

¹⁴Then he departed from Elisha, and came to his master, who said to him, "What did Elisha say to you?" And he answered, "He told me you would surely recover." ¹⁵But it happened on the next day that he took a thick cloth and dipped *it* in water, and spread *it* over his face so that he died; and Hazael reigned in his place.

¹⁶Now in the fifth year of Joram the son of Ahab, king of Israel, Jehoshaphat *having been* king of Judah, Jehoram the son of Jehoshaphat began to reign as king of Judah. ¹⁷He was thirty-two years old when he became king, and he reigned eight years in Jerusalem. ¹⁸And he walked in the way of the kings of Israel, just as the house of Ahab had done, for the daughter of Ahab was his wife; and he did evil in the sight of the LORD. ¹⁹*Yet the LORD would not destroy Judah, for the sake of his servant David, as He

promised him to give a lamp to him *and* his sons forever.

20In his days Edom revolted against Judah's authority, and made a king over themselves. 21So Joram*e* went to Zair, and all his chariots with him. Then he rose by night and attacked the Edomites who had surrounded him and the captains of the chariots; and the troops fled to their tents. 22Thus Edom has been in revolt against Judah's authority to this day. And Libnah revolted at that time.

23Now the rest of the acts of Joram, and all that he did, *are* they not written in the book of the chronicles of the kings of Judah? 24So Joram rested with his fathers, and was buried with his fathers in the City of David. Then Ahaziah his son reigned in his place.

25In the twelfth year of Joram the son of Ahab, king of Israel, Ahaziah the son of Jehoram, king of Judah, began to reign. 26Ahaziah *was* twenty-two years old when he became king, and he reigned one year in Jerusalem. His mother's name *was* Athaliah the granddaughter of Omri, king of Israel. 27And he walked in the way of the house of Ahab, and did evil in the sight of the LORD, like the house of Ahab, for he *was* the son-in-law of the house of Ahab.

28Now he went with Joram the son of Ahab to war against Hazael king of Syria at Ramoth Gilead; and the Syrians wounded Joram. 29Then King Joram went back to Jezreel to recover from the wounds which the Syrians had inflicted on him at Ramah, when he fought against Hazael king of Syria. And Ahaziah the son of Jehoram, king of Judah, went down to see Joram the son of Ahab in Jezreel, because he was sick.

9 And* Elisha the prophet called one of the sons of the prophets, and said to him, "Get yourself ready, take this flask of oil in your hand, and go to Ramoth Gilead. 2Now when you arrive at that place, look there for Jehu the son of Jehoshaphat, the son of Nimshi, and go in and make him rise up from among his associates, and take him to an inner room. 3Then take the flask of oil, and pour *it* on his head, and say, 'Thus says the LORD: "I have anointed you king over Israel." ' Then open the door and flee, and do not delay."

4So the young man, the servant of the prophet, went to Ramoth Gilead. 5And when he arrived, there *were* the captains of the army sitting; and he said, "I have a message for you, Commander."

Jehu said, "For which *one* of us?"

And he said, "For you, Commander." 6Then he arose and went into the house. And he poured the oil on his head, and said to him, "Thus says the LORD God of Israel: 'I have anointed you king over the people of the LORD, over Israel. 7You shall strike down the house of Ahab your master, that I may avenge the blood of My servants the prophets, and the blood of all the servants of the LORD, at the hand of Jezebel. 8For the whole house of Ahab shall perish; and I will cut off from Ahab all the males in Israel, both bond and free. 9So I will make the house of Ahab like the house of Jeroboam the son of Nebat, and like the house of Baasha the son of Ahijah. 10The dogs shall eat Jezebel on the plot *of ground* at Jezreel, and *there* shall *be* none to bury *her.*' " And he opened the door and fled.

CHAPTERS 9—10

9:1ff It is not pleasant to read the events recorded in these chapters, but we need to hear their message: *eventually sin is judged, and God's word is fulfilled.* God had ordained the anointing of Jehu (1 Kings 19:16) and the end of Ahab's family (1 Kings 21:21–26), and He kept His word.

❝*Sin is the only thing that God abhors. It brought Christ to the cross, it damns souls, it shuts heaven, it laid the foundations of hell.*❞

—Thomas Brooks

8:21 *e*Spelled *Jehoram* in verse 16

11Then Jehu came out to the servants of his master, and *one* said to him, "*Is* all well? Why did this madman come to you?"

And he said to them, "You know the man and his babble."

12And they said, "A lie! Tell us now."

So he said, "Thus and thus he spoke to me, saying, 'Thus says the LORD: "I have anointed you king over Israel." ' "

13Then each man hastened to take his garment and put *it* under him on the top of the steps; and they blew trumpets, saying, "Jehu is king!"

14So Jehu the son of Jehoshaphat, the son of Nimshi, conspired against Joram. (Now Joram had been defending Ramoth Gilead, he and all Israel, against Hazael king of Syria. 15But King Joram had returned to Jezreel to recover from the wounds which the Syrians had inflicted on him when he fought with Hazael king of Syria.) And Jehu said, "If you are so minded, let no one leave *or* escape from the city to go and tell *it* in Jezreel." 16So Jehu rode in a chariot and went to Jezreel, for Joram was laid up there; and Ahaziah king of Judah had come down to see Joram.

17Now a watchman stood on the tower in Jezreel, and he saw the company of Jehu as he came, and said, "I see a company of men."

And Joram said, "Get a horseman and send him to meet them, and let him say, '*Is it* peace?' "

18So the horseman went to meet him, and said, "Thus says the king: '*Is it* peace?' "

And Jehu said, "What have you to do with peace? Turn around and follow me."

So the watchman reported, saying, "The messenger went to them, but is not coming back."

19Then he sent out a second horseman who came to them, and said, "Thus says the king: '*Is it* peace?' "

And Jehu answered, "What have you to do with peace? Turn around and follow me."

20So the watchman reported, saying, "He went up to them and is not coming back; and the driving *is* like the driving of Jehu the son of Nimshi, for he drives furiously!"

21Then Joram said, "Make ready." And his chariot was made ready. Then Joram king of Israel and Ahaziah king of Judah went out, each in his chariot; and they went out to meet Jehu, and met him on the property of Naboth the Jezreelite. 22Now it happened, when Joram saw Jehu, that he said, "*Is it* peace, Jehu?"

So he answered, "What peace, as long as the harlotries of your mother Jezebel and her witchcraft *are so* many?"

23Then Joram turned around and fled, and said to Ahaziah, "Treachery, Ahaziah!" 24Now Jehu drew his bow with full strength and shot Jehoram between his arms; and the arrow came out at his heart, and he sank down in his chariot. 25Then *Jehu* said to Bidkar his captain, "Pick *him* up, *and* throw him into the tract of the field of Naboth the Jezreelite; for remember, when you and I were riding together behind Ahab his father, that the LORD laid this burden upon him: 26'Surely I saw yesterday the blood of Naboth and the blood of his sons,' says the LORD, 'and I will repay you in this plot,' says the LORD. Now therefore, take *and* throw him on the plot *of ground*, according to the word of the LORD."

27But when Ahaziah king of Judah saw *this*,

he fled by the road to Beth Haggan.*f* So Jehu pursued him, and said, "Shoot him also in the chariot." *And they shot him* at the Ascent of Gur, which is by Ibleam. Then he fled to Megiddo, and died there. 28And his servants carried him in the chariot to Jerusalem, and buried him in his tomb with his fathers in the City of David. 29In the eleventh year of Joram the son of Ahab, Ahaziah had become king over Judah.

30Now when Jehu had come to Jezreel, Jezebel heard *of it;* and she put paint on her eyes and adorned her head, and looked through a window. 31Then, as Jehu entered at the gate, she said, "*Is it* peace, Zimri, murderer of your master?"

32And he looked up at the window, and said, "Who *is* on my side? Who?" So two *or* three eunuchs looked out at him. 33Then he said, "Throw her down." So they threw her down, and *some* of her blood spattered on the wall and on the horses; and he trampled her underfoot. 34And when he had gone in, he ate and drank. Then he said, "Go now, see to this accursed *woman,* and bury her, for she was a king's daughter." 35*So they went to bury her, but they found no more of her than the skull and the feet and the palms of *her* hands. 36Therefore they came back and told him. And he said, "This *is* the word of the LORD, which He spoke by His servant Elijah the Tishbite, saying, 'On the plot *of ground* at Jezreel dogs shall eat the flesh of Jezebel;*g* 37and the corpse of Jezebel shall be as refuse on the surface of the field, in the plot at Jezreel, so that they shall not say, "Here *lies* Jezebel." ' "

10 Now* Ahab had seventy sons in Samaria. And Jehu wrote and sent letters to Samaria, to the rulers of Jezreel,*h* to the elders, and to those who reared Ahab's *sons,* saying:

2   Now as soon as this letter comes to you, since your master's sons *are* with you, and you have chariots and horses, a fortified city also, and weapons, 3choose the best qualified of your master's sons, set *him* on his father's throne, and fight for your master's house.

4But they were exceedingly afraid, and said, "Look, two kings could not stand up to him; how then can we stand?" 5And he who *was* in charge of the house, and he who *was* in charge of the city, the elders also, and those who reared *the sons,* sent to Jehu, saying, "We *are* your servants, we will do all you tell us; but we will not make anyone king. Do *what is* good in your sight." 6Then he wrote a second letter to them, saying:

If you *are* for me and will obey my voice, take the heads of the men, your master's sons, and come to me at Jezreel by this time tomorrow.

Now the king's sons, seventy persons, *were* with the great men of the city, *who* were rearing them. 7So it was, when the letter came to them, that they took the king's sons and slaughtered

9:35–37 King Joram of Israel was slain and so was King Ahaziah of Judah. Jezebel, the queen mother, was killed just as the prophet had predicted. Then Jehu wiped out all of Ahab's family and Ahaziah's relatives (who were also relatives of Ahab) and the followers of Baal.

10:1–9 Why was God so severe in His judgment? Because those leaders had turned the people away from the Lord and had polluted the nation. God had special work for His people to do (Gen. 12:1–3), and they could not do it if they were unfaithful to Him.

9:27 *f*Literally *The Garden House*   9:36 *g*1 Kings 21:23
10:1 *h*Following Masoretic Text, Syriac, and Targum; Septuagint reads *Samaria;* Vulgate reads *city.*

seventy persons, put their heads in baskets and sent *them* to him at Jezreel.

8Then a messenger came and told him, saying, "They have brought the heads of the king's sons." And he said, "Lay them in two heaps at the entrance of the gate until morning."

9So it was, in the morning, that he went out and stood, and said to all the people, "You *are* righteous. Indeed I conspired against my master and killed him; but who killed all these? 10Know now that nothing shall fall to the earth of the word of the LORD which the LORD spoke concerning the house of Ahab; for the LORD has done what He spoke by His servant Elijah." 11So Jehu killed all who remained of the house of Ahab in Jezreel, and all his great men and his close acquaintances and his priests, until he left him none remaining.

12And he arose and departed and went to Samaria. On the way, at Beth Eked[i] of the Shepherds, 13Jehu met with the brothers of Ahaziah king of Judah, and said, "Who *are* you?"

So they answered, "We *are* the brothers of Ahaziah; we have come down to greet the sons of the king and the sons of the queen mother."

14And he said, "Take them alive!" So they took them alive, and killed them at the well of Beth Eked, forty-two men; and he left none of them.

15Now when he departed from there, he met Jehonadab the son of Rechab, *coming* to meet him; and he greeted him and said to him, "Is your heart right, as my heart *is* toward your heart?"

And Jehonadab answered, "It is."

Jehu said, "If it is, give *me* your hand." So he gave *him* his hand, and he took him up to him into the chariot. 16Then he said, "Come with me, and see my zeal for the LORD." So they had him ride in his chariot. 17And when he came to Samaria, he killed all who remained to Ahab in Samaria, till he had destroyed them, according to the word of the LORD which He spoke to Elijah.

18Then Jehu gathered all the people together, and said to them, "Ahab served Baal a little, Jehu will serve him much. 19Now therefore, call to me all the prophets of Baal, all his servants, and all his priests. Let no one be missing, for I have a great sacrifice for Baal. Whoever is missing shall not live." But Jehu acted deceptively, with the intent of destroying the worshipers of Baal. 20And Jehu said, "Proclaim a solemn assembly for Baal." So they proclaimed *it.* 21Then Jehu sent throughout all Israel; and all the worshipers of Baal came, so that there was not a man left who did not come. So they came into the temple[j] of Baal, and the temple of Baal was full from one end to the other. 22And he said to the one in charge of the wardrobe, "Bring out vestments for all the worshipers of Baal." So he brought out vestments for them. 23Then Jehu and Jehonadab the son of Rechab went into the temple of Baal, and said to the worshipers of Baal, "Search and see that no servants of the LORD are here with you, but only the worshipers of Baal." 24So they went in to offer sacrifices and burnt offerings. Now Jehu had appointed for himself eighty men on the outside, and had said, "If any of the men whom I have brought into your hands escapes, *whoever lets him escape, it shall be* his life for the life of the other."

10:12 iOr *The Shearing House*   10:21 jLiterally *house,* and so elsewhere in this chapter

25Now it happened, as soon as he had made an end of offering the burnt offering, that Jehu said to the guard and to the captains, "Go in *and* kill them; let no one come out!" And they killed them with the edge of the sword; then the guards and the officers threw *them* out, and went into the inner room of the temple of Baal. 26And they brought the *sacred* pillars out of the temple of Baal and burned them. 27Then they broke down the *sacred* pillar of Baal, and tore down the temple of Baal and made it a refuse dump to this day. 28Thus Jehu destroyed Baal from Israel.

29*However Jehu did not turn away from the sins of Jeroboam the son of Nebat, who had made Israel sin, *that is,* from the golden calves that *were* at Bethel and Dan. 30And the LORD said to Jehu, "Because you have done well in doing *what is* right in My sight, *and* have done to the house of Ahab all that *was* in My heart, your sons shall sit on the throne of Israel to the fourth *generation.*" 31But Jehu took no heed to walk in the law of the LORD God of Israel with all his heart; for he did not depart from the sins of Jeroboam, who had made Israel sin.

32In those days the LORD began to cut off *parts* of Israel; and Hazael conquered them in all the territory of Israel 33from the Jordan eastward: all the land of Gilead—Gad, Reuben, and Manasseh—from Aroer, which *is* by the River Arnon, including Gilead and Bashan.

34Now the rest of the acts of Jehu, all that he did, and all his might, *are* they not written in the book of the chronicles of the kings of Israel? 35So Jehu rested with his fathers, and they buried him in Samaria. Then Jehoahaz his son reigned in his place. 36And the period that Jehu reigned over Israel in Samaria *was* twenty-eight years.

11 When* Athaliah the mother of Ahaziah saw that her son was dead, she arose and destroyed all the royal heirs. 2But Jehosheba, the daughter of King Joram, sister of Ahaziah, took Joash the son of Ahaziah, and stole him away from among the king's sons *who were* being murdered; and they hid him and his nurse in the bedroom, from Athaliah, so that he was not killed. 3So he was hidden with her in the house of the LORD for six years, while Athaliah reigned over the land.

4In the seventh year Jehoiada sent and brought the captains of hundreds—of the bodyguards and the escorts—and brought them into the house of the LORD to him. And he made a covenant with them and took an oath from them in the house of the LORD, and showed them the king's son. 5Then he commanded them, saying, "This *is* what you shall do: One-third of you who come on duty on the Sabbath shall be keeping watch over the king's house, 6one-third *shall be* at the gate of Sur, and one-third at the gate behind the escorts. You shall keep the watch of the house, lest it be broken down. 7The two contingents of you who go off duty on the Sabbath shall keep the watch of the house of the LORD for the king. 8But you shall surround the king on all sides, every man with his weapons in his hand; and whoever comes within range, let him be put to death. You are to be with the king as he goes out and as he comes in."

9So the captains of the hundreds did according to all that Jehoiada the priest commanded. Each of them took his men who were to be on duty on

10:29 After displaying all that zeal, Jehu should have set the example in his devotion to Jehovah, but he did not. A nation does not become righteous simply by removing evil; it must also establish godliness. An empty house is an invitation to even worse tenants (Matt. 12:43–45), and they eventually came—and the nation had to be judged.

CHAPTER 11

11:1–3 The future of David's royal line was at stake when the queen mother slaughtered all the heirs, and her wicked deed also threatened the fulfillment of the promise of the Messiah. Satan's seed was at war with God's seed (Gen. 3:15), but God won the battle. The future rested in one little boy whom God protected in the temple.

the Sabbath, with those who were going off duty on the Sabbath, and came to Jehoiada the priest. ¹⁰And the priest gave the captains of hundreds the spears and shields which *had belonged* to King David, that were in the temple of the LORD. ¹¹Then the escorts stood, every man with his weapons in his hand, all around the king, from the right side of the temple to the left side of the temple, by the altar and the house. ¹²And he brought out the king's son, put the crown on him, and *gave him* the Testimony;ᵏ they made him king and anointed him, and they clapped their hands and said, "Long live the king!"

¹³Now when Athaliah heard the noise of the escorts *and* the people, she came to the people *in* the temple of the LORD. ¹⁴When she looked, there was the king standing by a pillar according to custom; and the leaders and the trumpeters were by the king. All the people of the land were rejoicing and blowing trumpets. So Athaliah tore her clothes and cried out, "Treason! Treason!"

¹⁵And Jehoiada the priest commanded the captains of the hundreds, the officers of the army, and said to them, "Take her outside under guard, and slay with the sword whoever follows her." For the priest had said, "Do not let her be killed in the house of the LORD." ¹⁶So they seized her; and she went by way of the horses' entrance *into* the king's house, and there she was killed.

¹⁷*Then Jehoiada made a covenant between the LORD, the king, and the people, that they should be the LORD's people, and *also* between the king and the people. ¹⁸And all the people of the land went to the temple of Baal, and tore it down. They thoroughly broke in pieces its altars and images, and killed Mattan the priest of Baal before the altars. And the priest appointed officers over the house of the LORD. ¹⁹Then he took the captains of hundreds, the bodyguards, the escorts, and all the people of the land; and they brought the king down from the house of the LORD, and went by way of the gate of the escorts to the king's house. Then he sat on the throne of the kings. ²⁰So all the people of the land rejoiced; and the city was quiet, for they had slain Athaliah with the sword *in* the king's house. ²¹Jehoash *was* seven years old when he became king.

CHAPTER 12

11:17–21 Events around you may create doubts and fears in your heart, and you may wonder if God knows what is going on and if He cares. Rest assured that God not only knows and cares but that He is working out His purposes in spite of the evil deeds of wicked people. God does not need great armies to accomplish His plans. He can use a boy seven years old to change the course of a nation. Often when circumstances are the most difficult, God surprises you with a special victory. Trust Him!

12:1–5 Young Jehoash was fortunate to have as his counselor Jehoiada the priest, husband of the woman who had saved the king's life (2 Chron. 22:11). Jehoiada gave the king God's Word (2 Kings 11:12) and taught him how to obey it. The secret of success in any venture for God is to honor His Word (Josh. 1:8). Do you let others strengthen you in the faith, and do you appreciate their ministry to you?

12 In* the seventh year of Jehu, Jehoashˡ became king, and he reigned forty years in Jerusalem. His mother's name *was* Zibiah of Beersheba. ²Jehoash did *what was* right in the sight of the LORD all the days in which Jehoiada the priest instructed him. ³But the high places were not taken away; the people still sacrificed and burned incense on the high places.

⁴And Jehoash said to the priests, "All the money of the dedicated gifts that are brought into the house of the LORD—each man's census money, each man's assessment moneyᵐ—*and* all the money that a man purposes in his heart to bring into the house of the LORD, ⁵let the priests take *it* themselves, each from his constituency; and let them repair the damages of the temple, wherever any dilapidation is found."

⁶Now it was so, by the twenty-third year of King Jehoash, *that* the priests had not repaired the

---

11:12 ᵏThat is, the Law (compare Exodus 25:16, 21 and Deuteronomy 31:9)   12:1 ˡSpelled *Joash* in 11:2ff
12:4 ᵐCompare Leviticus 27:2ff

damages of the temple. [7]*So King Jehoash called Jehoiada the priest and the *other* priests, and said to them, "Why have you not repaired the damages of the temple? Now therefore, do not take *more* money from your constituency, but deliver it for repairing the damages of the temple." [8]And the priests agreed that they would neither receive *more* money from the people, nor repair the damages of the temple.

[9]Then Jehoiada the priest took a chest, bored a hole in its lid, and set it beside the altar, on the right side as one comes into the house of the LORD; and the priests who kept the door put there all the money brought into the house of the LORD. [10]So it was, whenever they saw that *there was* much money in the chest, that the king's scribe and the high priest came up and put it in bags, and counted the money that was found in the house of the LORD. [11]Then they gave the money, which had been apportioned, into the hands of those who did the work, who had the oversight of the house of the LORD; and they paid it out to the carpenters and builders who worked on the house of the LORD, [12]and to masons and stonecutters, and for buying timber and hewn stone, to repair the damage of the house of the LORD, and for all that was paid out to repair the temple. [13]However there were not made for the house of the LORD basins of silver, trimmers, sprinkling-bowls, trumpets, any articles of gold or articles of silver, from the money brought into the house of the LORD. [14]But they gave that to the workmen, and they repaired the house of the LORD with it. [15]Moreover they did not require an account from the men into whose hand they delivered the money to be paid to workmen, for they dealt faithfully. [16]The money from the trespass offerings and the money from the sin offerings was not brought into the house of the LORD. It belonged to the priests.

[17]Hazael king of Syria went up and fought against Gath, and took it; then Hazael set his face to go up to Jerusalem. [18]And Jehoash king of Judah took all the sacred things that his fathers, Jehoshaphat and Jehoram and Ahaziah, kings of Judah, had dedicated, and his own sacred things, and all the gold found in the treasuries of the house of the LORD and in the king's house, and sent *them* to Hazael king of Syria. Then he went away from Jerusalem.

[19]*Now the rest of the acts of Joash,[n] and all that he did, *are* they not written in the book of the chronicles of the kings of Judah?

[20]And his servants arose and formed a conspiracy, and killed Joash in the house of the Millo,[o] which goes down to Silla. [21]For Jozachar[p] the son of Shimeath and Jehozabad the son of Shomer,[q] his servants, struck him. So he died, and they buried him with his fathers in the City of David. Then Amaziah his son reigned in his place.

13 In* the twenty-third year of Joash[r] the son of Ahaziah, king of Judah, Jehoahaz the son of Jehu became king over Israel in Samaria, *and reigned* seventeen years. [2]And he did evil in the sight of the LORD, and followed the sins of

12:7–10 An idol-worshiping nation had allowed the temple to deteriorate. When we do not love God, we neglect the things important to God. A box by the altar was the ideal place for taking an offering. The sacrifices speak of our Lord's gracious work of redemption, and if that does not motivate us to give, nothing will (2 Cor. 8:9).

12:19 Jehoiada's death left Jehoash alone, and he led the nation back into sin (2 Chron. 24:15ff.). His religious zeal had not been very sincere. The king forgot the kindness of the high priest and even murdered his son. Jesus referred to this event in Matthew 23:34–35. It is not enough to promote religious works; we must have true devotion to God in our hearts. If your faith is "propped up" by others, what will you do when the "props" are gone?

CHAPTER 13

13:1–6 *Hands of oppression.* Jehoahaz followed the wrong example (v. 2) and brought Israel into bondage to foreign kings. Yet God was merciful to the disobedient king and His suffering people. As David wrote, "He has not dealt with us according to our sins, nor punished us according to our iniquities" (Ps. 103:10). Thank God for that!

12:19 [n]Spelled *Jehoash* in 12:1ff   12:20 [o]Literally *The Landfill*
12:21 [p]Called *Zabad* in 2 Chronicles 24:26   [q]Called *Shimrith* in 2 Chronicles 24:26   13:1 [r]Spelled *Jehoash* in 12:1ff

❝The opportunity that God sends does not wake up him who is asleep.**❞**

—Sengalese Proverb

13:16 *Hands of power.* Elisha was a dying man, yet he was able to communicate the power of God to the king. One man of God was equal in power to the whole army of Israel (v. 14)!

13:18 *Hands of opportunity.* Lacking spiritual discernment, the king did not understand the will of God as he followed the prophet's orders. Jehoash merely went through the motions, and as a result, he claimed only a limited victory over the enemy. He missed his opportunity and could never claim it again. What opportunity will God give you today that you may never have again?

Jeroboam the son of Nebat, who had made Israel sin. He did not depart from them.

³Then the anger of the LORD was aroused against Israel, and He delivered them into the hand of Hazael king of Syria, and into the hand of Ben-Hadad the son of Hazael, all *their* days. ⁴So Jehoahaz pleaded with the LORD, and the LORD listened to him; for He saw the oppression of Israel, because the king of Syria oppressed them. ⁵Then the LORD gave Israel a deliverer, so that they escaped from under the hand of the Syrians; and the children of Israel dwelt in their tents as before. ⁶Nevertheless they did not depart from the sins of the house of Jeroboam, who had made Israel sin, *but* walked in them; and the wooden imageˢ also remained in Samaria. ⁷For He left of the army of Jehoahaz only fifty horsemen, ten chariots, and ten thousand foot soldiers; for the king of Syria had destroyed them and made them like the dust at threshing.

⁸Now the rest of the acts of Jehoahaz, all that he did, and his might, *are* they not written in the book of the chronicles of the kings of Israel? ⁹So Jehoahaz rested with his fathers, and they buried him in Samaria. Then Joash his son reigned in his place.

¹⁰In the thirty-seventh year of Joash king of Judah, Jehoashᵗ the son of Jehoahaz became king over Israel in Samaria, *and reigned* sixteen years. ¹¹And he did evil in the sight of the LORD. He did not depart from all the sins of Jeroboam the son of Nebat, who made Israel sin, *but* walked in them.

¹²Now the rest of the acts of Joash, all that he did, and his might with which he fought against Amaziah king of Judah, *are* they not written in the book of the chronicles of the kings of Israel? ¹³So Joash rested with his fathers. Then Jeroboam sat on his throne. And Joash was buried in Samaria with the kings of Israel.

¹⁴Elisha had become sick with the illness of which he would die. Then Joash the king of Israel came down to him, and wept over his face, and said, "O my father, my father, the chariots of Israel and their horsemen!"

¹⁵And Elisha said to him, "Take a bow and some arrows." So he took himself a bow and some arrows. ¹⁶*Then he said to the king of Israel, "Put your hand on the bow." So he put his hand *on it,* and Elisha put his hands on the king's hands. ¹⁷And he said, "Open the east window"; and he opened *it.* Then Elisha said, "Shoot"; and he shot. And he said, "The arrow of the LORD's deliverance and the arrow of deliverance from Syria; for you must strike the Syrians at Aphek till you have destroyed *them.*" ¹⁸*Then he said, "Take the arrows"; so he took *them.* And he said to the king of Israel, "Strike the ground"; so he struck three times, and stopped. ¹⁹And the man of God was angry with him, and said, "You should have struck five or six times; then you would have struck Syria till you had destroyed *it!* But now you will strike Syria *only* three times."

²⁰Then Elisha died, and they buried him. And the *raiding* bands from Moab invaded the land in the spring of the year. ²¹So it was, as they were burying a man, that suddenly they spied a band *of raiders;* and they put the man in the tomb of

---

13:6 ˢHebrew *Asherah,* a Canaanite goddess   13:10 ᵗSpelled *Joash* in verse 9

Elisha; and when the man was let down and touched the bones of Elisha, he revived and stood on his feet.

22And Hazael king of Syria oppressed Israel all the days of Jehoahaz. 23But the LORD was gracious to them, had compassion on them, and regarded them, because of His covenant with Abraham, Isaac, and Jacob, and would not yet destroy them or cast them from His presence.

24Now Hazael king of Syria died. Then Ben-Hadad his son reigned in his place. 25And Jehoash*u* the son of Jehoahaz recaptured from the hand of Ben-Hadad, the son of Hazael, the cities which he had taken out of the hand of Jehoahaz his father by war. Three times Joash defeated him and recaptured the cities of Israel.

14 In* the second year of Joash the son of Jehoahaz, king of Israel, Amaziah the son of Joash, king of Judah, became king. 2He was twenty-five years old when he became king, and he reigned twenty-nine years in Jerusalem. His mother's name was Jehoaddan of Jerusalem. 3And he did *what was* right in the sight of the LORD, yet not like his father David; he did everything as his father Joash had done. 4However the high places were not taken away, and the people still sacrificed and burned incense on the high places.

5Now it happened, as soon as the kingdom was established in his hand, that he executed his servants who had murdered his father the king. 6But the children of the murderers he did not execute, according to what is written in the Book of the Law of Moses, in which the LORD commanded, saying, "Fathers shall not be put to death for their children, nor shall children be put to death for their fathers; but a person shall be put to death for his own sin."*v*

7He killed ten thousand Edomites in the Valley of Salt, and took Sela by war, and called its name Joktheel to this day.

8Then Amaziah sent messengers to Jehoash*w* the son of Jehoahaz, the son of Jehu, king of Israel, saying, "Come, let us face one another *in battle.*" 9And Jehoash king of Israel sent to Amaziah king of Judah, saying, "The thistle that *was* in Lebanon sent to the cedar that *was* in Lebanon, saying, 'Give your daughter to my son as wife'; and a wild beast that *was* in Lebanon passed by and trampled the thistle. 10*You have indeed defeated Edom, and your heart has lifted you up. Glory *in that,* and stay at home; for why should you meddle with trouble so that you fall— you and Judah with you?"

11But Amaziah would not heed. Therefore Jehoash king of Israel went out; so he and Amaziah king of Judah faced one another at Beth Shemesh, which *belongs* to Judah. 12And Judah was defeated by Israel, and every man fled to his tent. 13Then Jehoash king of Israel captured Amaziah king of Judah, the son of Jehoash, the son of Ahaziah, at Beth Shemesh; and he went to Jerusalem, and broke down the wall of Jerusalem from the Gate of Ephraim to the Corner Gate—four hundred cubits. 14And he took all the gold and silver, all the articles that were found in the house of

CHAPTER 14

14:1–5 King Amaziah made a fine beginning by following a good example, establishing justice in the land and obeying the Word of God (Deut. 24:16). But after he won a great victory over Edom, he became proud, and that led to his defeat.

14:10 Be content with your sphere of victory as the Lord gives you faith (Rom. 12:3). When you keep your eyes on the Lord, your victories will humble you, and God will get the glory. But when you forget the Lord, your victories will make you proud and lead you to defeat.

Beware the temptation to meddle. Learn to accept what God gives, stay at home, and do what He has called you to do. King Amaziah needed to heed Proverbs 16:18 and 26:17.

13:25 *u*Spelled *Joash* in verses 12–14, 25
14:6 *v*Deuteronomy 24:16　14:8 *w*Spelled *Joash* in 13:12ff and 2 Chronicles 25:17ff

the LORD and in the treasuries of the king's house, and hostages, and returned to Samaria.

15Now the rest of the acts of Jehoash which he did—his might, and how he fought with Amaziah king of Judah—*are* they not written in the book of the chronicles of the kings of Israel? 16So Jehoash rested with his fathers, and was buried in Samaria with the kings of Israel. Then Jeroboam his son reigned in his place.

17Amaziah the son of Joash, king of Judah, lived fifteen years after the death of Jehoash the son of Jehoahaz, king of Israel. 18Now the rest of the acts of Amaziah, *are* they not written in the book of the chronicles of the kings of Judah? 19And they formed a conspiracy against him in Jerusalem, and he fled to Lachish; but they sent after him to Lachish and killed him there. 20Then they brought him on horses, and he was buried at Jerusalem with his fathers in the City of David.

21And all the people of Judah took Azariah,ˣ who *was* sixteen years old, and made him king instead of his father Amaziah. 22He built Elath and restored it to Judah, after the king rested with his fathers.

23In the fifteenth year of Amaziah the son of Joash, king of Judah, Jeroboam the son of Joash, king of Israel, became king in Samaria, *and reigned* forty-one years. 24And he did evil in the sight of the LORD; he did not depart from all the sins of Jeroboam the son of Nebat, who had made Israel sin. 25He restored the territory of Israel from the entrance of Hamath to the Sea of the Arabah, according to the word of the LORD God of Israel, which He had spoken through His servant Jonah the son of Amittai, the prophet who *was* from Gath Hepher. 26For the LORD saw *that* the affliction of Israel *was* very bitter; and whether bond or free, there was no helper for Israel. 27And the LORD did not say that He would blot out the name of Israel from under heaven; but He saved them by the hand of Jeroboam the son of Joash.

28Now the rest of the acts of Jeroboam, and all that he did—his might, how he made war, and how he recaptured for Israel, from Damascus and Hamath, *what had belonged* to Judah—*are* they not written in the book of the chronicles of the kings of Israel? 29So Jeroboam rested with his fathers, the kings of Israel. Then Zechariah his son reigned in his place.

CHAPTER 15

15:1ff As the time of reckoning drew near, the kingdoms of Israel and Judah suffered under the rule of men whose godless lives brought more and more trouble. Conspiracies abounded as God's law was ignored.

15:5 But there were two exceptions: Azariah (Uzziah) and his son Jotham, who followed his father's example. Unfortunately, Uzziah became proud and wanted to serve as a priest. The Lord punished him by making him a leper (2 Chron. 26:16ff.). It is the lesson of 2 Kings 14:10 all over again: accept the sphere of blessing God gives you and do not meddle with matters that are beyond you. (See Ps. 131.)

15 In* the twenty-seventh year of Jeroboam king of Israel, Azariah the son of Amaziah, king of Judah, became king. 2He was sixteen years old when he became king, and he reigned fifty-two years in Jerusalem. His mother's name *was* Jecholiah of Jerusalem. 3And he did *what was* right in the sight of the LORD, according to all that his father Amaziah had done, 4except that the high places were not removed; the people still sacrificed and burned incense on the high places. 5*Then the LORD struck the king, so that he was a leper until the day of his death; so he dwelt in an isolated house. And Jotham the king's son *was* over the *royal* house, judging the people of the land.

6Now the rest of the acts of Azariah, and all

14:21 ˣCalled *Uzziah* in 2 Chronicles 26:1ff, Isaiah 6:1, and elsewhere

that he did, *are* they not written in the book of the chronicles of the kings of Judah? 7So Azariah rested with his fathers, and they buried him with his fathers in the City of David. Then Jotham his son reigned in his place.

8In the thirty-eighth year of Azariah king of Judah, Zechariah the son of Jeroboam reigned over Israel in Samaria six months. 9And he did evil in the sight of the LORD, as his fathers had done; he did not depart from the sins of Jeroboam the son of Nebat, who had made Israel sin. 10Then Shallum the son of Jabesh conspired against him, and struck and killed him in front of the people; and he reigned in his place.

11Now the rest of the acts of Zechariah, indeed they *are* written in the book of the chronicles of the kings of Israel.

12This *was* the word of the LORD which He spoke to Jehu, saying, "Your sons shall sit on the throne of Israel to the fourth *generation*."ʸ And so it was.

13Shallum the son of Jabesh became king in the thirty-ninth year of Uzziahᶻ king of Judah; and he reigned a full month in Samaria. 14For Menahem the son of Gadi went up from Tirzah, came to Samaria, and struck Shallum the son of Jabesh in Samaria and killed him; and he reigned in his place.

15Now the rest of the acts of Shallum, and the conspiracy which he led, indeed they *are* written in the book of the chronicles of the kings of Israel. 16Then from Tirzah, Menahem attacked Tiphsah, all who *were* there, and its territory. Because they did not surrender, therefore he attacked *it*. All the women there who were with child he ripped open.

17In the thirty-ninth year of Azariah king of Judah, Menahem the son of Gadi became king over Israel, *and reigned* ten years in Samaria. 18And he did evil in the sight of the LORD; he did not depart all his days from the sins of Jeroboam the son of Nebat, who had made Israel sin. 19Pulᵃ king of Assyria came against the land; and Menahem gave Pul a thousand talents of silver, that his hand might be with him to strengthen the kingdom under his control. 20And Menahem exacted the money from Israel, from all the very wealthy, from each man fifty shekels of silver, to give to the king of Assyria. So the king of Assyria turned back, and did not stay there in the land.

21Now the rest of the acts of Menahem, and all that he did, *are* they not written in the book of the chronicles of the kings of Israel? 22So Menahem rested with his fathers. Then Pekahiah his son reigned in his place.

23In the fiftieth year of Azariah king of Judah, Pekahiah the son of Menahem became king over Israel in Samaria, *and reigned* two years. 24And he did evil in the sight of the LORD; he did not depart from the sins of Jeroboam the son of Nebat, who had made Israel sin. 25Then Pekah the son of Remaliah, an officer of his, conspired against him and killed him in Samaria, in the citadel of the king's house, along with Argob and Arieh; and with him were fifty men of Gilead. He killed him and reigned in his place.

26Now the rest of the acts of Pekahiah, and all

15:12 ʸ2 Kings 10:30   15:13 ᶻCalled *Azariah* in 14:21ff and 15:1ff   15:19 ᵃThat is, Tiglath-Pileser III (compare verse 29)

that he did, indeed they *are* written in the book of the chronicles of the kings of Israel.

27In the fifty-second year of Azariah king of Judah, Pekah the son of Remaliah became king over Israel in Samaria, *and reigned* twenty years. 28And he did evil in the sight of the LORD; he did not depart from the sins of Jeroboam the son of Nebat, who had made Israel sin. 29In the days of Pekah king of Israel, Tiglath-Pileser king of Assyria came and took Ijon, Abel Beth Maachah, Janoah, Kedesh, Hazor, Gilead, and Galilee, all the land of Naphtali; and he carried them captive to Assyria. 30Then Hoshea the son of Elah led a conspiracy against Pekah the son of Remaliah, and struck and killed him; so he reigned in his place in the twentieth year of Jotham the son of Uzziah.

31Now the rest of the acts of Pekah, and all that he did, indeed they *are* written in the book of the chronicles of the kings of Israel.

32In the second year of Pekah the son of Remaliah, king of Israel, Jotham the son of Uzziah, king of Judah, began to reign. 33He was twenty-five years old when he became king, and he reigned sixteen years in Jerusalem. His mother's name *was* Jerusha[b] the daughter of Zadok. 34And he did *what was* right in the sight of the LORD; he did according to all that his father Uzziah had done. 35However the high places were not removed; the people still sacrificed and burned incense on the high places. He built the Upper Gate of the house of the LORD.

36Now the rest of the acts of Jotham, and all that he did, *are* they not written in the book of the chronicles of the kings of Judah? 37In those days the LORD began to send Rezin king of Syria and Pekah the son of Remaliah against Judah. 38So Jotham rested with his fathers, and was buried with his fathers in the City of David his father. Then Ahaz his son reigned in his place.

16 In the seventeenth year of Pekah the son of Remaliah, Ahaz the son of Jotham, king of Judah, began to reign. 2*Ahaz *was* twenty years old when he became king, and he reigned sixteen years in Jerusalem; and he did not do *what was* right in the sight of the LORD his God, as his father David *had done.* 3But he walked in the way of the kings of Israel; indeed he made his son pass through the fire, according to the abominations of the nations whom the LORD had cast out from before the children of Israel. 4And he sacrificed and burned incense on the high places, on the hills, and under every green tree.

5Then Rezin king of Syria and Pekah the son of Remaliah, king of Israel, came up to Jerusalem to *make* war; and they besieged Ahaz but could not overcome *him.* 6At that time Rezin king of Syria captured Elath for Syria, and drove the men of Judah from Elath. Then the Edomites[c] went to Elath, and dwell there to this day.

7So Ahaz sent messengers to Tiglath-Pileser king of Assyria, saying, "I *am* your servant and your son. Come up and save me from the hand of the king of Syria and from the hand of the king of Israel, who rise up against me." 8*And Ahaz took the silver and gold that was found in the house of the LORD, and in the treasuries of the

16:2, 3 *Ahaz was a failure in his walk.* He followed the wicked example of the kings of Israel. He was a descendant of David and should have obeyed the Word of God and trusted the God of the Word. Consciously or unconsciously, each of us follows various examples, and we must be sure they are the examples God wants us to follow.

16:8 *Ahaz was a failure in his warfare.* Because he had no faith in God, he was defeated by the enemy (1 John 5:4–5). He robbed God's temple to buy protection and he offered his son to a heathen god to secure help.

15:33 [b]Spelled *Jerushah* in 2 Chronicles 27:1   16:6 [c]Some ancient authorities read *Syrians.*

king's house, and sent *it as* a present to the king of Assyria. ⁹So the king of Assyria heeded him; for the king of Assyria went up against Damascus and took it, carried *its people* captive to Kir, and killed Rezin.

¹⁰Now King Ahaz went to Damascus to meet Tiglath-Pileser king of Assyria, and saw an altar that *was* at Damascus; and King Ahaz sent to Urijah the priest the design of the altar and its pattern, according to all its workmanship. ¹¹Then Urijah the priest built an altar according to all that King Ahaz had sent from Damascus. So Urijah the priest made *it* before King Ahaz came back from Damascus. ¹²And when the king came back from Damascus, the king saw the altar; and the king approached the altar and made offerings on it. ¹³So he burned his burnt offering and his grain offering; and he poured his drink offering and sprinkled the blood of his peace offerings on the altar. ¹⁴He also brought the bronze altar which *was* before the LORD, from the front of the temple—from between the *new* altar and the house of the LORD—and put it on the north side of the *new* altar. ¹⁵*Then King Ahaz commanded Urijah the priest, saying, "On the great *new* altar burn the morning burnt offering, the evening grain offering, the king's burnt sacrifice, and his grain offering, with the burnt offering of all the people of the land, their grain offering, and their drink offerings; and sprinkle on it all the blood of the burnt offering and all the blood of the sacrifice. And the bronze altar shall be for me to inquire by." ¹⁶Thus did Urijah the priest, according to all that King Ahaz commanded.

¹⁷And King Ahaz cut off the panels of the carts, and removed the lavers from them; and he took down the Sea from the bronze oxen that *were* under it, and put it on a pavement of stones. ¹⁸Also he removed the Sabbath pavilion which they had built in the temple, and he removed the king's outer entrance from the house of the LORD, on account of the king of Assyria.

¹⁹Now the rest of the acts of Ahaz which he did, *are* they not written in the book of the chronicles of the kings of Judah? ²⁰So Ahaz rested with his fathers, and was buried with his fathers in the City of David. Then Hezekiah his son reigned in his place.

17 In the twelfth year of Ahaz king of Judah, Hoshea the son of Elah became king of Israel in Samaria, *and he reigned* nine years. ²And he did evil in the sight of the LORD, but not as the kings of Israel who were before him. ³*Shalmaneser king of Assyria came up against him; and Hoshea became his vassal, and paid him tribute money. ⁴And the king of Assyria uncovered a conspiracy by Hoshea; for he had sent messengers to So, king of Egypt, and brought no tribute to the king of Assyria, as *he had done* year by year. Therefore the king of Assyria shut him up, and bound him in prison.

⁵Now the king of Assyria went throughout all the land, and went up to Samaria and besieged it for three years. ⁶In the ninth year of Hoshea, the king of Assyria took Samaria and carried Israel away to Assyria, and placed them in Halah and by the Habor, the River of Gozan, and in the cities of the Medes.

⁷*For so it was that the children of Israel had sinned against the LORD their God, who had brought them up out of the land of Egypt, from

16:15 *Ahaz also failed in his worship.* Instead of following the divine pattern for the altar, he borrowed a pattern from a heathen temple (Exod. 25:40; 26:30). God's people do not need the novelties of the world (Rom. 12:2), no matter how attractive they may be. It is tragic when we try to worship God after the pattern of the world and not after the heavenly pattern. Building a different altar did not make Ahaz a better person. Are you looking for "religious novelties," or do you follow the pattern given by God in His Word?

CHAPTER 17

17:3 God's long-suffering ran out, and He called for Assyria to carry Israel away. What God did to Israel He can do to groups and individuals today. Consider some of their sins.

17:7 *They forgot God's mercy* in saving them from Egyptian bondage. One of the best ways to remain true to the Lord is to remind yourself of all He has done for you (Ps. 103).

17:8 *They imitated the ungodly* so that the true worship of Jehovah was corrupted by worldly practices. At first, they did those things secretly, but then the pagan practices were openly added to their worship of God.

17:13–18 *They turned a deaf ear to the preaching of the prophets* and rejected the law of the Lord. When God disciplined them, they only hardened themselves more.

17:25–41 *"They feared the Lord"* but manufactured their own religion! Jehovah was "the God of the land" (v. 27) but not the only god. God rejected the religion of the Samaritans (John 4:19–24) as He rejects today all worship that is not "in spirit and truth."

under the hand of Pharaoh king of Egypt; and they had feared other gods, 8*and had walked in the statutes of the nations whom the LORD had cast out from before the children of Israel, and of the kings of Israel, which they had made. 9Also the children of Israel secretly did against the LORD their God things that *were* not right, and they built for themselves high places in all their cities, from watchtower to fortified city. 10They set up for themselves *sacred* pillars and wooden images*d* on every high hill and under every green tree. 11There they burned incense on all the high places, like the nations whom the LORD had carried away before them; and they did wicked things to provoke the LORD to anger, 12for they served idols, of which the LORD had said to them, "You shall not do this thing."

13*Yet the LORD testified against Israel and against Judah, by all of His prophets, every seer, saying, "Turn from your evil ways, and keep My commandments *and* My statutes, according to all the law which I commanded your fathers, and which I sent to you by My servants the prophets." 14Nevertheless they would not hear, but stiffened their necks, like the necks of their fathers, who did not believe in the LORD their God. 15And they rejected His statutes and His covenant that He had made with their fathers, and His testimonies which He had testified against them; they followed idols, became idolaters, and *went* after the nations who *were* all around them, *concerning* whom the LORD had charged them that they should not do like them. 16So they left all the commandments of the LORD their God, made for themselves a molded image *and* two calves, made a wooden image and worshiped all the host of heaven, and served Baal. 17And they caused their sons and daughters to pass through the fire, practiced witchcraft and soothsaying, and sold themselves to do evil in the sight of the LORD, to provoke Him to anger. 18Therefore the LORD was very angry with Israel, and removed them from His sight; there was none left but the tribe of Judah alone.

19Also Judah did not keep the commandments of the LORD their God, but walked in the statutes of Israel which they made. 20And the LORD rejected all the descendants of Israel, afflicted them, and delivered them into the hand of plunderers, until He had cast them from His sight. 21For He tore Israel from the house of David, and they made Jeroboam the son of Nebat king. Then Jeroboam drove Israel from following the LORD, and made them commit a great sin. 22For the children of Israel walked in all the sins of Jeroboam which he did; they did not depart from them, 23until the LORD removed Israel out of His sight, as He had said by all His servants the prophets. So Israel was carried away from their own land to Assyria, *as it is* to this day.

24Then the king of Assyria brought *people* from Babylon, Cuthah, Ava, Hamath, and from Sepharvaim, and placed *them* in the cities of Samaria instead of the children of Israel; and they took possession of Samaria and dwelt in its cities. 25*And it was so, at the beginning of their dwelling there, *that* they did not fear the LORD; therefore the LORD sent lions among them, which killed *some* of them. 26So they spoke to the king of As-

---

17:10 *d*Hebrew *Asherim*, Canaanite deities

syria, saying, "The nations whom you have removed and placed in the cities of Samaria do not know the rituals of the God of the land; therefore He has sent lions among them, and indeed, they are killing them because they do not know the rituals of the God of the land." 27Then the king of Assyria commanded, saying, "Send there one of the priests whom you brought from there; let him go and dwell there, and let him teach them the rituals of the God of the land." 28Then one of the priests whom they had carried away from Samaria came and dwelt in Bethel, and taught them how they should fear the LORD.

29However every nation continued to make gods of its own, and put *them* in the shrines on the high places which the Samaritans had made, *every* nation in the cities where they dwelt. 30The men of Babylon made Succoth Benoth, the men of Cuth made Nergal, the men of Hamath made Ashima, 31and the Avites made Nibhaz and Tartak; and the Sepharvites burned their children in fire to Adrammelech and Anammelech, the gods of Sepharvaim. 32So they feared the LORD, and from every class they appointed for themselves priests of the high places, who sacrificed for them in the shrines of the high places. 33They feared the LORD, yet served their own gods—according to the rituals of the nations from among whom they were carried away.

34To this day they continue practicing the former rituals; they do not fear the LORD, nor do they follow their statutes or their ordinances, or the law and commandment which the LORD had commanded the children of Jacob, whom He named Israel, 35with whom the LORD had made a covenant and charged them, saying: "You shall not fear other gods, nor bow down to them nor serve them nor sacrifice to them; 36but the LORD, who brought you up from the land of Egypt with great power and an outstretched arm, Him you shall fear, Him you shall worship, and to Him you shall offer sacrifice. 37And the statutes, the ordinances, the law, and the commandment which He wrote for you, you shall be careful to observe forever; you shall not fear other gods. 38And the covenant that I have made with you, you shall not forget, nor shall you fear other gods. 39But the LORD your God you shall fear; and He will deliver you from the hand of all your enemies." 40However they did not obey, but they followed their former rituals. 41So these nations feared the LORD, yet served their carved images; also their children and their children's children have continued doing as their fathers did, even to this day.

18 Now* it came to pass in the third year of Hoshea the son of Elah, king of Israel, *that* Hezekiah the son of Ahaz, king of Judah, began to reign. 2He was twenty-five years old when he became king, and he reigned twenty-nine years in Jerusalem. His mother's name *was* Abi[e] the daughter of Zechariah. 3And he did *what was* right in the sight of the LORD, according to all that his father David had done.

4He removed the high places and broke the *sacred* pillars, cut down the wooden image[f] and broke in pieces the bronze serpent that Moses had made; for until those days the children of Israel

CHAPTERS 18—19

18:1–6 *An idol within.* Hezekiah removed all the idols from the land, including the brazen serpent that Moses had made (Num. 21:5–9). It is easy for God's people to make idols out of good things that outlive their usefulness.

❝*Prayer is not conquering God's reluctance, but taking hold of God's willingness.*❞

—Phillips Brooks

18:2 eCalled *Abijah* in 2 Chronicles 29:1ff   18:4 fHebrew *Asherah*, a Canaanite goddess

burned incense to it, and called it Nehushtan.ᵍ
5He trusted in the LORD God of Israel, so that after
him was none like him among all the kings of
Judah, nor who were before him. 6For he held
fast to the LORD; he did not depart from following
Him, but kept His commandments, which the
LORD had commanded Moses. 7The LORD was with
him; he prospered wherever he went. And he rebelled against the king of Assyria and did not
serve him. 8He subdued the Philistines, as far as
Gaza and its territory, from watchtower to fortified city.

9Now it came to pass in the fourth year of King
Hezekiah, which was the seventh year of Hoshea
the son of Elah, king of Israel, that Shalmaneser
king of Assyria came up against Samaria and besieged it. 10And at the end of three years they
took it. In the sixth year of Hezekiah, that is, the
ninth year of Hoshea king of Israel, Samaria was
taken. 11Then the king of Assyria carried Israel
away captive to Assyria, and put them in Halah
and by the Habor, the River of Gozan, and in the
cities of the Medes, 12because they did not obey
the voice of the LORD their God, but transgressed
His covenant and all that Moses the servant of
the LORD had commanded; and they would neither
hear nor do them.

13And in the fourteenth year of King Hezekiah,
Sennacherib king of Assyria came up against all
the fortified cities of Judah and took them.
14Then Hezekiah king of Judah sent to the king
of Assyria at Lachish, saying, "I have done wrong;
turn away from me; whatever you impose on me
I will pay." And the king of Assyria assessed
Hezekiah king of Judah three hundred talents of
silver and thirty talents of gold. 15So Hezekiah
gave him all the silver that was found in the house
of the LORD and in the treasuries of the king's
house. 16At that time Hezekiah stripped the gold
from the doors of the temple of the LORD, and from
the pillars which Hezekiah king of Judah had
overlaid, and gave it to the king of Assyria.

17*Then the king of Assyria sent the Tartan,ʰ
the Rabsaris,ⁱ and the Rabshakehʲ from Lachish,
with a great army against Jerusalem, to King
Hezekiah. And they went up and came to Jerusalem. When they had come up, they went and stood
by the aqueduct from the upper pool, which was
on the highway to the Fuller's Field. 18And when
they had called to the king, Eliakim the son of
Hilkiah, who was over the household, Shebna the
scribe, and Joah the son of Asaph, the recorder,
came out to them. 19Then the Rabshakeh said to
them, "Say now to Hezekiah, 'Thus says the great
king, the king of Assyria: "What confidence is
this in which you trust? 20You speak of having
plans and power for war; but they are mere
words. And in whom do you trust, that you rebel
against me? 21Now look! You are trusting in the
staff of this broken reed, Egypt, on which if a man
leans, it will go into his hand and pierce it. So is
Pharaoh king of Egypt to all who trust in him.
22But if you say to me, 'We trust in the LORD our
God,' is it not He whose high places and whose
altars Hezekiah has taken away, and said to Judah and Jerusalem, 'You shall worship before this
altar in Jerusalem'?"' 23Now therefore, I urge

18:17–37 An enemy without. Having
conquered Israel, Assyria wanted to capture
Judah. The nation was divided three ways:
some wanted to give up to Assyria, others
wanted to go to Egypt for help, and a
minority wanted to trust the Lord for
deliverance. Note the emphasis on the word
trust in 18:19–25, and note that the enemy
always has a bargain to offer (18:23).
However, each bargain has a fatal "until"
attached to it (18:31–32).

18:4 ᵍLiterally Bronze Thing　18:17 ʰA title, probably
Commander in Chief ⁱA title, probably Chief Officer ʲA title,
probably Chief of Staff or Governor

you, give a pledge to my master the king of Assyria, and I will give you two thousand horses—if you are able on your part to put riders on them! 24How then will you repel one captain of the least of my master's servants, and put your trust in Egypt for chariots and horsemen? 25Have I now come up without the LORD against this place to destroy it? The LORD said to me, 'Go up against this land, and destroy it.' "

26Then Eliakim the son of Hilkiah, Shebna, and Joah said to the Rabshakeh, "Please speak to your servants in Aramaic, for we understand it; and do not speak to us in Hebrew*k* in the hearing of the people who are on the wall."

27But the Rabshakeh said to them, "Has my master sent me to your master and to you to speak these words, and not to the men who sit on the wall, who will eat and drink their own waste with you?"

28Then the Rabshakeh stood and called out with a loud voice in Hebrew, and spoke, saying, "Hear the word of the great king, the king of Assyria! 29Thus says the king: 'Do not let Hezekiah deceive you, for he shall not be able to deliver you from his hand; 30nor let Hezekiah make you trust in the LORD, saying, "The LORD will surely deliver us; this city shall not be given into the hand of the king of Assyria." ' 31Do not listen to Hezekiah; for thus says the king of Assyria: 'Make peace with me by a present and come out to me; and every one of you eat from his own vine and every one from his own fig tree, and every one of you drink the waters of his own cistern; 32until I come and take you away to a land like your own land, a land of grain and new wine, a land of bread and vineyards, a land of olive groves and honey, that you may live and not die. But do not listen to Hezekiah, lest he persuade you, saying, "The LORD will deliver us." 33Has any of the gods of the nations at all delivered its land from the hand of the king of Assyria? 34Where are the gods of Hamath and Arpad? Where are the gods of Sepharvaim and Hena and Ivah? Indeed, have they delivered Samaria from my hand? 35Who among all the gods of the lands have delivered their countries from my hand, that the LORD should deliver Jerusalem from my hand?' "

36But the people held their peace and answered him not a word; for the king's commandment was, "Do not answer him." 37Then Eliakim the son of Hilkiah, who was over the household, Shebna the scribe, and Joah the son of Asaph, the recorder, came to Hezekiah with their clothes torn, and told him the words of the Rabshakeh.

19 And* so it was, when King Hezekiah heard it, that he tore his clothes, covered himself with sackcloth, and went into the house of the LORD. 2Then he sent Eliakim, who was over the household, Shebna the scribe, and the elders of the priests, covered with sackcloth, to Isaiah the prophet, the son of Amoz. 3And they said to him, "Thus says Hezekiah: 'This day is a day of trouble, and rebuke, and blasphemy; for the children have come to birth, but there is no strength to bring them forth. 4It may be that the LORD your God will hear all the words of the Rabshakeh, whom his master the king of Assyria has sent to reproach the living God, and will rebuke the words

19:1–37 *An encouragement above.*
Hezekiah depended on the Word of God and prayer; he spread the matter before the Lord. His only desire was to glorify the Lord before that heathen army (19:19). God gave him a message of peace and victory (19:6–7), and the enemy was defeated. God knows the battles you fight, and He will give you the help you need. Spread the matter before Him in faith, and seek to glorify His name.

18:26 *k*Literally *Judean*

which the LORD your God has heard. Therefore lift up *your* prayer for the remnant that is left.' "

⁵So the servants of King Hezekiah came to Isaiah. ⁶And Isaiah said to them, "Thus you shall say to your master, 'Thus says the LORD: "Do not be afraid of the words which you have heard, with which the servants of the king of Assyria have blasphemed Me. ⁷Surely I will send a spirit upon him, and he shall hear a rumor and return to his own land; and I will cause him to fall by the sword in his own land."' "

⁸Then *the* Rabshakeh returned and found the king of Assyria warring against Libnah, for he heard that he had departed from Lachish. ⁹And the king heard concerning Tirhakah king of Ethiopia, "Look, he has come out to make war with you." So he again sent messengers to Hezekiah, saying, ¹⁰"Thus you shall speak to Hezekiah king of Judah, saying: 'Do not let your God in whom you trust deceive you, saying, "Jerusalem shall not be given into the hand of the king of Assyria." ¹¹Look! You have heard what the kings of Assyria have done to all lands by utterly destroying them; and shall you be delivered? ¹²Have the gods of the nations delivered those whom my fathers have destroyed, Gozan and Haran and Rezeph, and the people of Eden who *were* in Telassar? ¹³Where *is* the king of Hamath, the king of Arpad, and the king of the city of Sepharvaim, Hena, and Ivah?' "

¹⁴And Hezekiah received the letter from the hand of the messengers, and read it; and Hezekiah went up to the house of the LORD, and spread it before the LORD. ¹⁵Then Hezekiah prayed before the LORD, and said: "O LORD God of Israel, *the One* who dwells *between* the cherubim, You are God, You alone, of all the kingdoms of the earth. You have made heaven and earth. ¹⁶Incline Your ear, O LORD, and hear; open Your eyes, O LORD, and see; and hear the words of Sennacherib, which he has sent to reproach the living God. ¹⁷Truly, LORD, the kings of Assyria have laid waste the nations and their lands, ¹⁸and have cast their gods into the fire; for they *were* not gods, but the work of men's hands—wood and stone. Therefore they destroyed them. ¹⁹Now therefore, O LORD our God, I pray, save us from his hand, that all the kingdoms of the earth may know that You *are* the LORD God, You alone."

²⁰Then Isaiah the son of Amoz sent to Hezekiah, saying, "Thus says the LORD God of Israel: 'Because you have prayed to Me against Sennacherib king of Assyria, I have heard.' ²¹This *is* the word which the LORD has spoken concerning him:

'The virgin, the daughter of Zion,
    Has despised you, laughed you to scorn;
The daughter of Jerusalem
    Has shaken *her* head behind your back!

22 'Whom have you reproached and
        blasphemed?
    Against whom have you raised *your* voice,
    And lifted up your eyes on high?
    Against the Holy *One* of Israel.
23 By your messengers you have reproached
        the Lord,
    And said: "By the multitude of my chariots
    I have come up to the height of the
        mountains,
    To the limits of Lebanon;
    I will cut down its tall cedars

And its choice cypress trees;
I will enter the extremity of its borders,
To its fruitful forest.
24 I have dug and drunk strange water,
And with the soles of my feet I have
dried up
All the brooks of defense."

25 'Did you not hear long ago
How I made it,
From ancient times that I formed it?
Now I have brought it to pass,
That you should be
For crushing fortified cities *into* heaps of
ruins.
26 Therefore their inhabitants had little power;
They were dismayed and confounded;
They were *as* the grass of the field
And the green herb,
As the grass on the housetops
And *grain* blighted before it is grown.

27 'But I know your dwelling place,
Your going out and your coming in,
And your rage against Me.
28 Because your rage against Me and your
tumult
Have come up to My ears,
Therefore I will put My hook in your nose
And My bridle in your lips,
And I will turn you back
By the way which you came.

29'This *shall be* a sign to you:

You shall eat this year such as grows of
itself,
And in the second year what springs from
the same;
Also in the third year sow and reap,
Plant vineyards and eat the fruit of them.
30 And the remnant who have escaped of the
house of Judah
Shall again take root downward,
And bear fruit upward.
31 For out of Jerusalem shall go a remnant,
And those who escape from Mount Zion.
The zeal of the LORD of hosts*ˡ* will do this.'

32"Therefore thus says the LORD concerning the
king of Assyria:

'He shall not come into this city,
Nor shoot an arrow there,
Nor come before it with shield,
Nor build a siege mound against it.
33 By the way that he came,
By the same shall he return;
And he shall not come into this city,'
Says the LORD.
34 'For I will defend this city, to save it
For My own sake and for My servant
David's sake.' "

35And it came to pass on a certain night that
the angel*ᵐ* of the LORD went out, and killed in
the camp of the Assyrians one hundred and

19:31 *ˡ*Following many Hebrew manuscripts and ancient
versions (compare Isaiah 37:32); Masoretic Text omits *of
hosts*. 19:35 *ᵐ*Or *Angel*

eighty-five thousand; and when *people* arose early in the morning, there were the corpses—all dead. [36]So Sennacherib king of Assyria departed and went away, returned *home,* and remained at Nineveh. [37]Now it came to pass, as he was worshiping in the temple of Nisroch his god, that his sons Adrammelech and Sharezer struck him down with the sword; and they escaped into the land of Ararat. Then Esarhaddon his son reigned in his place.

CHAPTER 20

20:1–11 Verse 6 suggests that this event took place while Jerusalem was under siege by Assyria. It was bad enough that Judah was in danger, but the king was about to die. Sometimes it seems that troubles come in packs! Death is the last enemy we face (1 Cor. 15:26), and only God can give us victory over death.
Hezekiah was delivered because he prayed and used the means God provided for healing. Believing prayer can move God even to alter things in His universe just to meet our needs.

20 In* those days Hezekiah was sick and near death. And Isaiah the prophet, the son of Amoz, went to him and said to him, "Thus says the LORD: 'Set your house in order, for you shall die, and not live.' "

[2]Then he turned his face toward the wall, and prayed to the LORD, saying, [3]"Remember now, O LORD, I pray, how I have walked before You in truth and with a loyal heart, and have done *what was* good in Your sight." And Hezekiah wept bitterly.

[4]And it happened, before Isaiah had gone out into the middle court, that the word of the LORD came to him, saying, [5]"Return and tell Hezekiah the leader of My people, 'Thus says the LORD, the God of David your father: "I have heard your prayer, I have seen your tears; surely I will heal you. On the third day you shall go up to the house of the LORD. [6]And I will add to your days fifteen years. I will deliver you and this city from the hand of the king of Assyria; and I will defend this city for My own sake, and for the sake of My servant David." ' "

[7]Then Isaiah said, "Take a lump of figs." So they took and laid *it* on the boil, and he recovered.

[8]And Hezekiah said to Isaiah, "What *is* the sign that the LORD will heal me, and that I shall go up to the house of the LORD the third day?"

[9]Then Isaiah said, "This is the sign to you from the LORD, that the LORD will do the thing which He has spoken: *shall* the shadow go forward ten degrees or go backward ten degrees?"

[10]And Hezekiah answered, "It is an easy thing for the shadow to go down ten degrees; no, but let the shadow go backward ten degrees."

[11]So Isaiah the prophet cried out to the LORD, and He brought the shadow ten degrees backward, by which it had gone down on the sundial of Ahaz.

20:13–19 Hezekiah escaped the lion (1 Pet. 5:8) but succumbed to the serpent (vv. 12–19). He let the enemy know his secrets! Again, it was *pride: "my* house, *my* treasures, *my* days." His great victory over Assyria gave him false confidence as he entertained the Babylonians. He mortgaged his people's future by what he did and was thankful the defeat would not come in his own day.
Your decisions today will affect others tomorrow. Make the right decisions!

[12]At that time Berodach-Baladan[n] the son of Baladan, king of Babylon, sent letters and a present to Hezekiah, for he heard that Hezekiah had been sick. [13]*And Hezekiah was attentive to them, and showed them all the house of his treasures—the silver and gold, the spices and precious ointment, and all[o] his armory—all that was found among his treasures. There was nothing in his house or in all his dominion that Hezekiah did not show them.

[14]Then Isaiah the prophet went to King Hezekiah, and said to him, "What did these men say, and from where did they come to you?"

So Hezekiah said, "They came from a far country, from Babylon."

[15]And he said, "What have they seen in your house?"

20:12 [n]Spelled *Merodach-Baladan* in Isaiah 39:1
20:13 [o]Following many Hebrew manuscripts, Syriac, and Targum; Masoretic Text omits *all.*

So Hezekiah answered, "They have seen all that *is* in my house; there is nothing among my treasures that I have not shown them."

16Then Isaiah said to Hezekiah, "Hear the word of the LORD: 17'Behold, the days are coming when all that *is* in your house, and what your fathers have accumulated until this day, shall be carried to Babylon; nothing shall be left,' says the LORD. 18'And they shall take away some of your sons who will descend from you, whom you will beget; and they shall be eunuchs in the palace of the king of Babylon.'"

19So Hezekiah said to Isaiah, "The word of the LORD which you have spoken *is* good!" For he said, "Will there not be peace and truth at least in my days?"

20Now the rest of the acts of Hezekiah—all his might, and how he made a pool and a tunnel and brought water into the city—*are* they not written in the book of the chronicles of the kings of Judah? 21So Hezekiah rested with his fathers. Then Manasseh his son reigned in his place.

21 Manasseh* *was* twelve years old when he became king, and he reigned fifty-five years in Jerusalem. His mother's name *was* Hephzibah. 2And he did evil in the sight of the LORD, according to the abominations of the nations whom the LORD had cast out before the children of Israel. 3For he rebuilt tne high places which Hezekiah his father had destroyed; he raised up altars for Baal, and made a wooden image,p as Ahab king of Israel had done; and he worshiped all the host of heavenq and served them. 4He also built altars in the house of the LORD, of which the LORD had said, "In Jerusalem I will put My name." 5And he built altars for all the host of heaven in the two courts of the house of the LORD. 6Also he made his son pass through the fire, practiced soothsaying, used witchcraft, and consulted spiritists and mediums. He did much evil in the sight of the LORD, to provoke *Him* to anger. 7He even set a carved image of Asherahr that he had made, in the house of which the LORD had said to David and to Solomon his son, "In this house and in Jerusalem, which I have chosen out of all the tribes of Israel, I will put My name forever; 8and I will not make the feet of Israel wander anymore from the land which I gave their fathers—only if they are careful to do according to all that I have commanded them, and according to all the law that My servant Moses commanded them." 9But they paid no attention, and Manasseh seduced them to do more evil than the nations whom the LORD had destroyed before the children of Israel.

10And the LORD spoke by His servants the prophets, saying, 11"Because Manasseh king of Judah has done these abominations (he has acted more wickedly than all the Amorites who *were* before him, and has also made Judah sin with his idols), 12therefore thus says the LORD God of Israel: 'Behold, *I* am bringing *such* calamity upon Jerusalem and Judah, that whoever hears of it, both his ears will tingle. 13And I will stretch over Jerusalem the measuring line of Samaria and the plummet of the house of Ahab; I will wipe Jerusalem as *one* wipes a dish, wiping *it* and turning *it* upside down. 14*So I will forsake the remnant of

21:3 pHebrew *Asherah,* a Canaanite goddess qThe gods of the Assyrians   21:7 rA Canaanite goddess

CHAPTER 21

21:1 Wicked King Ahaz fathered godly Hezekiah, and Hezekiah fathered evil King Manasseh whom the Lord allowed to reign for fifty-five years. King Manasseh was the father of godly King Josiah. Manasseh began his reign doing evil, but at the end of his life, he repented (2 Chron. 33:12). Josiah sought the Lord early in his life but closed his life disobeying God (2 Chron. 35:20ff.).

21:14–17 God's ways are not our ways; He is free to work as He chooses. People who claim to see clear patterns in history or who lock divine providence into a fixed formula must keep this in mind. God punishes the disobedient and vindicates His people but not always in the way or at the time that we expect. Ponder Psalm 73.

Sometimes God permits evil men to rule so that He may test His people or chasten them. We sometimes can do very little about world affairs, but we can pray for persons in authority (1 Tim. 2:1–8) and be faithful to obey God (Rom. 13).

My inheritance and deliver them into the hand of their enemies; and they shall become victims of plunder to all their enemies, 15because they have done evil in My sight, and have provoked Me to anger since the day their fathers came out of Egypt, even to this day.' "

16Moreover Manasseh shed very much innocent blood, till he had filled Jerusalem from one end to another, besides his sin by which he made Judah sin, in doing evil in the sight of the LORD.

17Now the rest of the acts of Manasseh—all that he did, and the sin that he committed—*are* they not written in the book of the chronicles of the kings of Judah? 18So Manasseh rested with his fathers, and was buried in the garden of his own house, in the garden of Uzza. Then his son Amon reigned in his place.

19Amon *was* twenty-two years old when he became king, and he reigned two years in Jerusalem. His mother's name *was* Meshullemeth the daughter of Haruz of Jotbah. 20And he did evil in the sight of the LORD, as his father Manasseh had done. 21So he walked in all the ways that his father had walked; and he served the idols that his father had served, and worshiped them. 22He forsook the LORD God of his fathers, and did not walk in the way of the LORD.

23Then the servants of Amon conspired against him, and killed the king in his own house. 24But the people of the land executed all those who had conspired against King Amon. Then the people of the land made his son Josiah king in his place.

25Now the rest of the acts of Amon which he did, *are* they not written in the book of the chronicles of the kings of Judah? 26And he was buried in his tomb in the garden of Uzza. Then Josiah his son reigned in his place.

CHAPTER 22

22:1ff At the age of sixteen, Josiah began to seek the Lord and live for Him. Was his mother a special godly influence in his life? Her name means "beloved" and is very much like the Lord's "pet name" for Solomon (2 Sam. 12:25). Certainly Hilkiah the high priest saw to it that the young king honored the Lord. Never underestimate the power of godly influence.

Manasseh rebuilt everything that his father tore down (2 Kings 21:3), but Josiah tore down what Manasseh built up (2 Chron. 34:3–7). But reformation alone will not change people; there must be repentance and renewal within the heart. That came with the finding of the Law in the temple. (Imagine losing the Word of God in the house of God!)

22:8–12 It is good to *have* God's Word; it is even better to *hear* God's Word; but the greatest blessing of all is to *heed* God's Word (James 1:19–25). The king humbled himself before the Lord, and God spared the land.

22 Josiah* *was* eight years old when he became king, and he reigned thirty-one years in Jerusalem. His mother's name *was* Jedidah the daughter of Adaiah of Bozkath. 2And he did *what was* right in the sight of the LORD, and walked in all the ways of his father David; he did not turn aside to the right hand or to the left.

3Now it came to pass, in the eighteenth year of King Josiah, *that* the king sent Shaphan the scribe, the son of Azaliah, the son of Meshullam, to the house of the LORD, saying: 4"Go up to Hilkiah the high priest, that he may count the money which has been brought into the house of the LORD, which the doorkeepers have gathered from the people. 5And let them deliver it into the hand of those doing the work, who are the overseers in the house of the LORD; let them give it to those who *are* in the house of the LORD doing the work, to repair the damages of the house— 6to carpenters and builders and masons—and to buy timber and hewn stone to repair the house. 7However there need be no accounting made with them of the money delivered into their hand, because they deal faithfully."

8*Then Hilkiah the high priest said to Shaphan the scribe, "I have found the Book of the Law in the house of the LORD." And Hilkiah gave the book to Shaphan, and he read it. 9So Shaphan the scribe went to the king, bringing the king word, saying, "Your servants have gathered the money that was found in the house, and have delivered it into the hand of those who do the work, who oversee the house of the LORD." 10Then Shaphan the scribe showed the king, saying, "Hilkiah the priest has given me a book." And Shaphan read it before the king.

11Now it happened, when the king heard the words of the Book of the Law, that he tore his clothes. 12Then the king commanded Hilkiah the priest, Ahikam the son of Shaphan, Achbors the son of Michaiah, Shaphan the scribe, and Asaiah a servant of the king, saying, 13"Go, inquire of the LORD for me, for the people and for all Judah, concerning the words of this book that has been found; for great is the wrath of the LORD that is aroused against us, because our fathers have not obeyed the words of this book, to do according to all that is written concerning us."

14So Hilkiah the priest, Ahikam, Achbor, Shaphan, and Asaiah went to Huldah the prophetess, the wife of Shallum the son of Tikvah, the son of Harhas, keeper of the wardrobe. (She dwelt in Jerusalem in the Second Quarter.) And they spoke with her. 15Then she said to them, "Thus says the LORD God of Israel, 'Tell the man who sent you to Me, 16"Thus says the LORD: 'Behold, I will bring calamity on this place and on its inhabitants—all the words of the book which the king of Judah has read— 17because they have forsaken Me and burned incense to other gods, that they might provoke Me to anger with all the works of their hands. Therefore My wrath shall be aroused against this place and shall not be quenched.' " ' 18But as for the king of Judah, who sent you to inquire of the LORD, in this manner you shall speak to him, 'Thus says the LORD God of Israel: "Concerning the words which you have heard— 19*because your heart was tender, and you humbled yourself before the LORD when you heard what I spoke against this place and against its inhabitants, that they would become a desolation and a curse, and you tore your clothes and wept before Me, I also have heard you," says the LORD. 20Surely, therefore, I will gather you to your fathers, and you shall be gathered to your grave in peace; and your eyes shall not see all the calamity which I will bring on this place." ' " So they brought back word to the king.

23 Now the king sent them to gather all the elders of Judah and Jerusalem to him. 2The king went up to the house of the LORD with all the men of Judah, and with him all the inhabitants of Jerusalem—the priests and the prophets and all the people, both small and great. And he read in their hearing all the words of the Book of the Covenant which had been found in the house of the LORD.

3Then the king stood by a pillar and made a covenant before the LORD, to follow the LORD and to keep His commandments and His testimonies and His statutes, with all his heart and all his soul, to perform the words of this covenant that were written in this book. And all the people took a stand for the covenant. 4*And the king commanded Hilkiah the high priest, the priests of the second order, and the doorkeepers, to bring out of the temple of the LORD all the articles that were made for Baal, for Asherah,t and for all the host of heaven;u and he burned them outside Jerusalem in the fields of Kidron, and carried their ashes to Bethel. 5Then he removed the idolatrous priests

22:19 Have you "lost" the Word of God somewhere, even in the midst of a religious life? Does God still speak to you, and do you obey?

CHAPTER 23

23:4–8 The temple was really in bad shape when Josiah began his reformation. The priests had lost the Word of God in the temple (22:8) and had permitted idolatrous things to accumulate there. When God's truth is neglected, it is easy for the false to move in and take over. Perhaps our lives and our churches could use a good "housecleaning" occasionally!

22:12 sAbdon the son of Micah in 2 Chronicles 34:20
23:4 tA Canaanite goddess uThe gods of the Assyrians

whom the kings of Judah had ordained to burn incense on the high places in the cities of Judah and in the places all around Jerusalem, and those who burned incense to Baal, to the sun, to the moon, to the constellations, and to all the host of heaven. 6And he brought out the wooden image[v] from the house of the LORD, to the Brook Kidron outside Jerusalem, burned it at the Brook Kidron and ground it to ashes, and threw its ashes on the graves of the common people. 7Then he tore down the ritual booths of the perverted persons[w] that were in the house of the LORD, where the women wove hangings for the wooden image. 8And he brought all the priests from the cities of Judah, and defiled the high places where the priests had burned incense, from Geba to Beersheba; also he broke down the high places at the gates which were at the entrance of the Gate of Joshua the governor of the city, which were to the left of the city gate. 9Nevertheless the priests of the high places did not come up to the altar of the LORD in Jerusalem, but they ate unleavened bread among their brethren.

10And he defiled Topheth, which is in the Valley of the Son[x] of Hinnom, that no man might make his son or his daughter pass through the fire to Molech. 11Then he removed the horses that the kings of Judah had dedicated to the sun, at the entrance to the house of the LORD, by the chamber of Nathan-Melech, the officer who was in the court; and he burned the chariots of the sun with fire. 12The altars that were on the roof, the upper chamber of Ahaz, which the kings of Judah had made, and the altars which Manasseh had made in the two courts of the house of the LORD, the king broke down and pulverized there, and threw their dust into the Brook Kidron. 13*Then the king defiled the high places that were east of Jerusalem, which were on the south of the Mount of Corruption, which Solomon king of Israel had built for Ashtoreth the abomination of the Sidonians, for Chemosh the abomination of the Moabites, and for Milcom the abomination of the people of Ammon. 14And he broke in pieces the sacred pillars and cut down the wooden images, and filled their places with the bones of men.

15Moreover the altar that was at Bethel, and the high place which Jeroboam the son of Nebat, who made Israel sin, had made, both that altar and the high place he broke down; and he burned the high place and crushed it to powder, and burned the wooden image. 16As Josiah turned, he saw the tombs that were there on the mountain. And he sent and took the bones out of the tombs and burned them on the altar, and defiled it according to the word of the LORD which the man of God proclaimed, who proclaimed these words. 17Then he said, "What gravestone is this that I see?"

So the men of the city told him, "It is the tomb of the man of God who came from Judah and proclaimed these things which you have done against the altar of Bethel."

18And he said, "Let him alone; let no one move his bones." So they let his bones alone, with the bones of the prophet who came from Samaria.

19Now Josiah also took away all the shrines of the high places that were in the cities of Samaria,

23:13 Josiah's work was the fulfillment of the prophecy that had been made years before (1 Kings 13:1–5). As he obeyed the Word of God, he removed what was evil and practiced what was good. The observance of Passover reminded the people that they belonged to the Lord and must put evil out of their lives.

23:6 vHebrew Asherah, a Canaanite goddess 23:7 wHebrew qedeshim, that is, those practicing sodomy and prostitution in religious rituals 23:10 xKethib reads Sons.

which the kings of Israel had made to provoke the LORD[y] to anger; and he did to them according to all the deeds he had done in Bethel. 20He executed all the priests of the high places who *were* there, on the altars, and burned men's bones on them; and he returned to Jerusalem.

21Then the king commanded all the people, saying, "Keep the Passover to the LORD your God, as *it is* written in this Book of the Covenant." 22Such a Passover surely had never been held since the days of the judges who judged Israel, nor in all the days of the kings of Israel and the kings of Judah. 23But in the eighteenth year of King Josiah this Passover was held before the LORD in Jerusalem. 24Moreover Josiah put away those who consulted mediums and spiritists, the household gods and idols, all the abominations that were seen in the land of Judah and in Jerusalem, that he might perform the words of the law which were written in the book that Hilkiah the priest found in the house of the LORD. 25Now before him there was no king like him, who turned to the LORD with all his heart, with all his soul, and with all his might, according to all the Law of Moses; nor after him did *any* arise like him.

26Nevertheless the LORD did not turn from the fierceness of His great wrath, with which His anger was aroused against Judah, because of all the provocations with which Manasseh had provoked Him. 27And the LORD said, "I will also remove Judah from My sight, as I have removed Israel, and will cast off this city Jerusalem which I have chosen, and the house of which I said, 'My name shall be there.'"[z]

28Now the rest of the acts of Josiah, and all that he did, *are* they not written in the book of the chronicles of the kings of Judah? 29*In his days Pharaoh Necho king of Egypt went to the aid of the king of Assyria, to the River Euphrates; and King Josiah went against him. And *Pharaoh Necho* killed him at Megiddo when he confronted him. 30Then his servants moved his body in a chariot from Megiddo, brought him to Jerusalem, and buried him in his own tomb. And the people of the land took Jehoahaz the son of Josiah, anointed him, and made him king in his father's place.

31Jehoahaz *was* twenty-three years old when he became king, and he reigned three months in Jerusalem. His mother's name *was* Hamutal the daughter of Jeremiah of Libnah. 32And he did evil in the sight of the LORD, according to all that his fathers had done. 33Now Pharaoh Necho put him in prison at Riblah in the land of Hamath, that he might not reign in Jerusalem; and he imposed on the land a tribute of one hundred talents of silver and a talent of gold. 34Then Pharaoh Necho made Eliakim the son of Josiah king in place of his father Josiah, and changed his name to Jehoiakim. And *Pharaoh* took Jehoahaz and went to Egypt, and he[a] died there.

35So Jehoiakim gave the silver and gold to Pharaoh; but he taxed the land to give money according to the command of Pharaoh; he exacted the silver and gold from the people of the land, from

23:29 It is sad that Josiah became proud and dared Pharaoh to fight him (2 Chron. 35:20–25). That led to his death and the ultimate downfall of the kingdom of Judah. Amaziah had made the same mistake (2 Kings 14:9–20).

23:19 [y]Following Septuagint, Syriac, and Vulgate; Masoretic Text and Targum omit *the LORD*.   23:27 [z]1 Kings 8:29
23:34 [a]That is, Jehoahaz

every one according to his assessment, to give *it* to Pharaoh Necho. ³⁶Jehoiakim *was* twenty-five years old when he became king, and he reigned eleven years in Jerusalem. His mother's name *was* Zebudah the daughter of Pedaiah of Rumah. ³⁷And he did evil in the sight of the LORD, according to all that his fathers had done.

24 In* his days Nebuchadnezzar king of Babylon came up, and Jehoiakim became his vassal *for* three years. Then he turned and rebelled against him. ²And the LORD sent against him *raiding* bands of Chaldeans, bands of Syrians, bands of Moabites, and bands of the people of Ammon; He sent them against Judah to destroy it, according to the word of the LORD which He had spoken by His servants the prophets. ³Surely at the commandment of the LORD *this* came upon Judah, to remove *them* from His sight because of the sins of Manasseh, according to all that he had done, ⁴and also because of the innocent blood that he had shed; for he had filled Jerusalem with innocent blood, which the LORD would not pardon.

⁵Now the rest of the acts of Jehoiakim, and all that he did, *are* they not written in the book of the chronicles of the kings of Judah? ⁶So Jehoiakim rested with his fathers. Then Jehoiachin his son reigned in his place.

⁷And the king of Egypt did not come out of his land anymore, for the king of Babylon had taken all that belonged to the king of Egypt from the Brook of Egypt to the River Euphrates.

⁸Jehoiachin *was* eighteen years old when he became king, and he reigned in Jerusalem three months. His mother's name *was* Nehushta the daughter of Elnathan of Jerusalem. ⁹And he did evil in the sight of the LORD, according to all that his father had done.

¹⁰At that time the servants of Nebuchadnezzar king of Babylon came up against Jerusalem, and the city was besieged. ¹¹And Nebuchadnezzar king of Babylon came against the city, as his servants were besieging it. ¹²Then Jehoiachin king of Judah, his mother, his servants, his princes, and his officers went out to the king of Babylon; and the king of Babylon, in the eighth year of his reign, took him prisoner.

¹³And he carried out from there all the treasures of the house of the LORD and the treasures of the king's house, and he cut in pieces all the articles of gold which Solomon king of Israel had made in the temple of the LORD, as the LORD had said. ¹⁴Also he carried into captivity all Jerusalem: all the captains and all the mighty men of valor, ten thousand captives, and all the craftsmen and smiths. None remained except the poorest people of the land. ¹⁵And he carried Jehoiachin captive to Babylon. The king's mother, the king's wives, his officers, and the mighty of the land he carried into captivity from Jerusalem to Babylon. ¹⁶All the valiant men, seven thousand, and craftsmen and smiths, one thousand, all *who were* strong *and* fit for war, these the king of Babylon brought captive to Babylon.

¹⁷Then the king of Babylon made Mattaniah,

CHAPTERS 24—25

24:1–4 A series of weak and ungodly rulers led Judah into ruin as the sins of Manasseh came up for judgment. The consequences of decisions may not appear immediately, but they eventually come. Leaders may forget their decisions, but their decisions will not forget them. "Be sure your sin will find you out" is the sure word of God (Num. 32:23).

Submit to God—The governor urged the Jews to submit to God's chastening in Babylon and be good citizens (2 Kings 25:24). The prophet Jeremiah wrote them a letter saying the same thing (Jer. 29). When God chastens us, we only make matters worse when we resent it and resist it. We should yield to our Father's loving will and let Him work out His purposes (Heb. 12:1–11).

Jehoiachin's[b] uncle, king in his place, and changed his name to Zedekiah.

[18]Zedekiah *was* twenty-one years old when he became king, and he reigned eleven years in Jerusalem. His mother's name *was* Hamutal the daughter of Jeremiah of Libnah. [19]He also did evil in the sight of the LORD, according to all that Jehoiakim had done. [20]For because of the anger of the LORD *this* happened in Jerusalem and Judah, that He finally cast them out from His presence. Then Zedekiah rebelled against the king of Babylon.

25 Now* it came to pass in the ninth year of his reign, in the tenth month, on the tenth *day* of the month, *that* Nebuchadnezzar king of Babylon and all his army came against Jerusalem and encamped against it; and they built a siege wall against it all around. [2]So the city was besieged until the eleventh year of King Zedekiah. [3]By the ninth *day* of the *fourth* month the famine had become so severe in the city that there was no food for the people of the land.

[4]Then the city wall was broken through, and all the men of war *fled* at night by way of the gate between two walls, which was by the king's garden, even though the Chaldeans *were* still encamped all around against the city. And *the king*[c] went by way of the plain.[d] [5]But the army of the Chaldeans pursued the king, and they overtook him in the plains of Jericho. All his army was scattered from him. [6]So they took the king and brought him up to the king of Babylon at Riblah, and they pronounced judgment on him. [7]Then they killed the sons of Zedekiah before his eyes, put out the eyes of Zedekiah, bound him with bronze fetters, and took him to Babylon.

[8]And in the fifth month, on the seventh *day* of the month (which *was* the nineteenth year of King Nebuchadnezzar king of Babylon), Nebuzaradan the captain of the guard, a servant of the king of Babylon, came to Jerusalem. [9]He burned the house of the LORD and the king's house; all the houses of Jerusalem, that is, all the houses of the great, he burned with fire. [10]And all the army of the Chaldeans who *were with* the captain of the guard broke down the walls of Jerusalem all around.

[11]Then Nebuzaradan the captain of the guard carried away captive the rest of the people *who* remained in the city and the defectors who had deserted to the king of Babylon, with the rest of the multitude. [12]But the captain of the guard left *some* of the poor of the land as vinedressers and farmers. [13]The bronze pillars that *were* in the house of the LORD, and the carts and the bronze Sea that *were* in the house of the LORD, the Chaldeans broke in pieces, and carried their bronze to Babylon. [14]They also took away the pots, the shovels, the trimmers, the spoons, and all the bronze utensils with which the priests ministered. [15]The firepans and the basins, the things of solid gold and solid silver, the captain of the guard took away. [16]The two pillars, one Sea, and the carts, which Solomon had made for the house of the LORD, the bronze of all these articles was beyond measure. [17]The height of one pillar *was* eighteen cubits, and the capital on it *was* of bronze. The

25:1–17 The nation had been rotting away at the center for years and was no match for the mighty Babylonian army. The king was captured, the city and temple were destroyed, and the people were taken into captivity. During the period of the judges, God had chastened them *in* the land; now He would chasten them *outside* their land. If they wanted to live like the idolaters, let them live *with* the idolaters.

As they were led off into captivity, do you think any of the people remembered Solomon's prayer to God (1 Kings 8:46–53) or God's message to Solomon (1 Kings 9:1–9)?

24:17 [b]Literally *his*   25:4 [c]Literally *he* [d]Or *Arabah*, that is, the Jordan Valley

height of the capital was three cubits, and the network and pomegranates all around the capital
were all of bronze. The second pillar was the
same, with a network.

18And the captain of the guard took Seraiah the
chief priest, Zephaniah the second priest, and the
three doorkeepers. 19He also took out of the city
an officer who had charge of the men of war, five
men of the king's close associates who were found
in the city, the chief recruiting officer of the army,
who mustered the people of the land, and sixty
men of the people of the land *who were* found in
the city. 20So Nebuzaradan, captain of the guard,
took these and brought them to the king of Babylon at Riblah. 21Then the king of Babylon struck
them and put them to death at Riblah in the land
of Hamath. Thus Judah was carried away captive
from its own land.

22Then he made Gedaliah the son of Ahikam,
the son of Shaphan, governor over the people who
remained in the land of Judah, whom Nebuchadnezzar king of Babylon had left. 23Now when all
the captains of the armies, they and *their* men,
heard that the king of Babylon had made Gedaliah
governor, they came to Gedaliah at Mizpah—Ishmael the son of Nethaniah, Johanan the son of
Careah, Seraiah the son of Tanhumeth the Netophathite, and Jaazaniahe the son of a Maachathite, they and their men. 24And Gedaliah took
an oath before them and their men, and said to
them, "Do not be afraid of the servants of the
Chaldeans. Dwell in the land and serve the king
of Babylon, and it shall be well with you."

25But it happened in the seventh month that Ishmael the son of Nethaniah, the son of Elishama,
of the royal family, came with ten men and struck
and killed Gedaliah, the Jews, as well as the Chaldeans who were with him at Mizpah. 26And all
the people, small and great, and the captains of
the armies, arose and went to Egypt; for they were
afraid of the Chaldeans.

27Now it came to pass in the thirty-seventh year
of the captivity of Jehoiachin king of Judah, in
the twelfth month, on the twenty-seventh *day* of
the month, *that* Evil-Merodachf king of Babylon,
in the year that he began to reign, released Jehoiachin king of Judah from prison. 28He spoke kindly
to him, and gave him a more prominent seat than
those of the kings who *were* with him in Babylon.
29So Jehoiachin changed from his prison garments, and he ate bread regularly before the king
all the days of his life. 30And as for his provisions,
there was a regular ration given him by the king,
a portion for each day, all the days of his life.

25:23 eSpelled *Jezaniah* in Jeremiah 40:8   25:27 fLiterally
Man of Marduk

1 and 2 CHRONICLES

The record in these books parallels that in Samuel and Kings. The focus is on David and the kingdom of Judah and the viewpoint is that of the priests. The opening genealogy takes you from Adam to Saul (1 Chron. 1—10), and that is followed by an account of David's reign (chaps. 11—29). Second Chronicles opens with the reign of Solomon (chaps. 1—9) and then describes the kings of Judah from the division of the kingdom to the captivity (chaps. 10—36).

These books were important to the Jews who returned to the land after the captivity. The genealogy established their tribal connections, something especially significant to the priests (Ezra 2:59—62). The people needed David's example of godliness, and the emphasis on the temple was needed at a time when it had to be rebuilt. The books of 1 and 2 Chronicles encourage people seeking to rebuild in a time of change and difficulty.

As you read 1 and 2 Chronicles, you will want to note the cross-references to Samuel and Kings and compare complementary passages.

1 CHRONICLES

CHAPTERS 1—9

1:ff You see nine chapters of unfamiliar names, many of them hard to pronounce, and you are tempted to skip them and get to the story. But stop to consider the importance of these chapters.

These names belonged to real people who once lived on this earth. Now most of them are forgotten, their names buried in an ancient list. One day *you* will be a name in a record file somewhere. History may forget you, but heaven never will. Are you living in the light of eternity (1 John 2:15–17)? Make your life count today.

These names were written on earth because these people were born on earth. The most vital listing is in heaven, the names of those who have been born again through faith in Jesus Christ (Luke 10:20; Phil. 4:3).

Is your name written there?

These names belonged to what we would call "ordinary people." They were not all great men of faith like Abraham and David, but they all played a part in the working out of God's plan in this world. You may not consider yourself of consequence, but you are; every child of God has a place in God's heart and in His plan. Make yourself available to Him for the task He wants you to do, no matter how humble or unrecognized it may seem to you or to others.

These names belonged to Jews, one nation, called of God to witness for Him in a dark and wicked world. They were not always faithful, but through them, the world received witness of the one true and living God. They gave us the written Word of God, and in due time, they gave us the Savior. If nothing else, pause to give thanks for Israel, and "pray for the peace of Jerusalem" (Ps. 122:6).

(continued)

1 Adam,* Seth, Enosh, ²Cainan,ᵃ Mahalalel, Jared, ³Enoch, Methuselah, Lamech, ⁴Noah,ᵇ Shem, Ham, and Japheth.

⁵The sons of Japheth *were* Gomer, Magog, Madai, Javan, Tubal, Meshech, and Tiras. ⁶The sons of Gomer *were* Ashkenaz, Diphath,ᶜ and Togarmah. ⁷The sons of Javan *were* Elishah, Tarshishah,ᵈ Kittim, and Rodanim.ᵉ

⁸The sons of Ham *were* Cush, Mizraim, Put, and Canaan. ⁹The sons of Cush *were* Seba, Havilah, Sabta,ᶠ Raama,ᵍ and Sabtecha. The sons of Raama *were* Sheba and Dedan. ¹⁰Cush begot Nimrod; he began to be a mighty one on the earth. ¹¹Mizraim begot Ludim, Anamim, Lehabim, Naphtuhim, ¹²Pathrusim, Casluhim (from whom came the Philistines and the Caphtorim). ¹³Canaan begot Sidon, his firstborn, and Heth; ¹⁴the Jebusite, the Amorite, and the Girgashite; ¹⁵the Hivite, the Arkite, and the Sinite; ¹⁶the Arvadite, the Zemarite, and the Hamathite.

¹⁷The sons of Shem *were* Elam, Asshur, Arphaxad, Lud, Aram, Uz, Hul, Gether, and Meshech.ʰ ¹⁸Arphaxad begot Shelah, and Shelah begot Eber. ¹⁹To Eber were born two sons: the name of one *was* Peleg,ⁱ for in his days the earth was divided; and his brother's name *was* Joktan. ²⁰Joktan begot Almodad, Sheleph, Hazarmaveth, Jerah, ²¹Hadoram, Uzal, Diklah, ²²Ebal,ʲ Abimael, Sheba, ²³Ophir, Havilah, and Jobab. All these *were* the sons of Joktan.

²⁴Shem, Arphaxad, Shelah, ²⁵Eber, Peleg, Reu, ²⁶Serug, Nahor, Terah, ²⁷and Abram, who *is* Abraham. ²⁸The sons of Abraham *were* Isaac and Ishmael.

²⁹These *are* their genealogies: The firstborn of Ishmael *was* Nebajoth; then Kedar, Adbeel, Mibsam, ³⁰Mishma, Dumah, Massa, Hadad,ᵏ Tema, ³¹Jetur, Naphish, and Kedemah. These *were* the sons of Ishmael.

³²Now the sons born to Keturah, Abraham's concubine, *were* Zimran, Jokshan, Medan, Midian, Ishbak, and Shuah. The sons of Jokshan *were* Sheba and Dedan. ³³The sons of Midian *were* Ephah, Epher, Hanoch, Abida, and Eldaah. All these *were* the children of Keturah.

³⁴And Abraham begot Isaac. The sons of Isaac *were* Esau and Israel. ³⁵The sons of Esau *were* Eliphaz, Reuel, Jeush, Jaalam, and Korah. ³⁶And the sons of Eliphaz *were* Teman, Omar, Zephi,ˡ Gatam, *and* Kenaz; and *by* Timna,ᵐ Amalek. ³⁷The sons of Reuel *were* Nahath, Zerah, Shammah, and Mizzah.

³⁸The sons of Seir *were* Lotan, Shobal, Zibeon, Anah, Dishon, Ezer, and Dishan. ³⁹And the sons

---

1:2 ᵃHebrew *Qenan*   1:4 ᵇFollowing Masoretic Text and Vulgate; Septuagint adds *the sons of Noah.*   1:6 ᶜSpelled *Riphath* in Genesis 10:3   1:7 ᵈSpelled *Tarshish* in Genesis 10:4   ᵉSpelled *Dodanim* in Genesis 10:4   1:9 ᶠSpelled *Sabtah* in Genesis 10:7   ᵍSpelled *Raamah* in Genesis 10:7   1:17 ʰSpelled *Mash* in Genesis 10:23   1:19 ⁱLiterally *Division*   1:22 ʲSpelled *Obal* in Genesis 10:28   1:30 ᵏSpelled *Hadar* in Genesis 25:15   1:36 ˡSpelled *Zepho* in Genesis 36:11   ᵐCompare Genesis 36:12

of Lotan *were* Hori and Homam; Lotan's sister *was* Timna. 40The sons of Shobal *were* Alian,*n* Manahath, Ebal, Shephi,*o* and Onam. The sons of Zibeon *were* Ajah and Anah. 41The son of Anah *was* Dishon. The sons of Dishon *were* Hamran,*p* Eshban, Ithran, and Cheran. 42The sons of Ezer *were* Bilhan, Zaavan, *and* Jaakan.*q* The sons of Dishan *were* Uz and Aran.

43Now these *were* the kings who reigned in the land of Edom before a king reigned over the children of Israel: Bela the son of Beor, and the name of his city was Dinhabah. 44And when Bela died, Jobab the son of Zerah of Bozrah reigned in his place. 45When Jobab died, Husham of the land of the Temanites reigned in his place. 46And when Husham died, Hadad the son of Bedad, who attacked Midian in the field of Moab, reigned in his place. The name of his city *was* Avith. 47When Hadad died, Samlah of Masrekah reigned in his place. 48And when Samlah died, Saul of Rehoboth-by-the-River reigned in his place. 49When Saul died, Baal-Hanan the son of Achbor reigned in his place. 50And when Baal-Hanan died, Hadad*r* reigned in his place; and the name of his city was Pai.*s* His wife's name was Mehetabel the daughter of Matred, the daughter of Mezahab. 51Hadad died also. And the chiefs of Edom were Chief Timnah, Chief Aliah,*t* Chief Jetheth, 52Chief Aholibamah, Chief Elah, Chief Pinon, 53Chief Kenaz, Chief Teman, Chief Mibzar, 54Chief Magdiel, and Chief Iram. These *were* the chiefs of Edom.

2 These *were* the sons of Israel: Reuben, Simeon, Levi, Judah, Issachar, Zebulun, 2Dan, Joseph, Benjamin, Naphtali, Gad, and Asher.

3The sons of Judah *were* Er, Onan, and Shelah. *These* three were born to him by the daughter of Shua, the Canaanitess. Er, the firstborn of Judah, was wicked in the sight of the LORD; so He killed him. 4And Tamar, his daughter-in-law, bore him Perez and Zerah. All the sons of Judah *were* five.

5The sons of Perez *were* Hezron and Hamul. 6The sons of Zerah *were* Zimri, Ethan, Heman, Calcol, and Dara—five of them in all.

7The son of Carmi *was* Achar,*u* the troubler of Israel, who transgressed in the accursed thing.

8The son of Ethan *was* Azariah.

9Also the sons of Hezron who were born to him *were* Jerahmeel, Ram, and Chelubai.*v* 10Ram begot Amminadab, and Amminadab begot Nahshon, leader of the children of Judah; 11Nahshon begot Salma,*w* and Salma begot Boaz; 12Boaz begot Obed, and Obed begot Jesse; 13Jesse begot Eliab his firstborn, Abinadab the second, Shimea*x* the third, 14Nethanel the fourth, Raddai the fifth, 15Ozem the sixth, *and* David the seventh.

16Now their sisters *were* Zeruiah and Abigail. And the sons of Zeruiah *were* Abishai, Joab, and Asahel—three. 17Abigail bore Amasa; and the father of Amasa *was* Jether the Ishmaelite.*y*

(continued from previous page)
For different reasons, some names stand out in this list. Abram had his name changed (1:27). Achan is identified as a troublemaker (2:7). Jabez had a sad name ("He will cause pain" [4:9–10]), but he overcame the stigma because he trusted the Lord. Reuben sinned away his birthright, which was given to the sons of Joseph (5:1). Joseph had refused to sin, so God honored him (Gen. 39). A father's sin can make a difference to the future of his family.

Read these chapters carefully. Here and there, you may meet some people who will warn you, challenge you, and even encourage you.

1:40 *n*Spelled *Alvan* in Genesis 36:23 *o*Spelled *Shepho* in Genesis 36:23   1:41 *p*Spelled *Hemdan* in Genesis 36:26 1:42 *q*Spelled *Akan* in Genesis 36:27   1:50 *r*Spelled *Hadar* in Genesis 36:39 *s*Spelled *Pau* in Genesis 36:39   1:51 *t*Spelled *Alvah* in Genesis 36:40   2:7 *u*Spelled *Achan* in Joshua 7:1 and elsewhere   2:9 *v*Spelled *Caleb* in 2:18, 42 2:11 *w*Spelled *Salmon* in Ruth 4:21 and Luke 3:32 2:13 *x*Spelled *Shammah* in 1 Samuel 16:9 and elsewhere 2:17 *y*Compare 2 Samuel 17:25

18Caleb the son of Hezron had children by Azubah, *his* wife, and by Jerioth. Now these were her sons: Jesher, Shobab, and Ardon. 19When Azubah died, Caleb took Ephrath[z] as his wife, who bore him Hur. 20And Hur begot Uri, and Uri begot Bezalel.

21Now afterward Hezron went in to the daughter of Machir the father of Gilead, whom he married when he *was* sixty years old; and she bore him Segub. 22Segub begot Jair, who had twenty-three cities in the land of Gilead. 23(Geshur and Syria took from them the towns of Jair, with Kenath and its towns—sixty towns.) All these *belonged to* the sons of Machir the father of Gilead. 24After Hezron died in Caleb Ephrathah, Hezron's wife Abijah bore him Ashhur the father of Tekoa.

25The sons of Jerahmeel, the firstborn of Hezron, *were* Ram, the firstborn, and Bunah, Oren, Ozem, *and* Ahijah. 26Jerahmeel had another wife, whose name was Atarah; she was the mother of Onam. 27The sons of Ram, the firstborn of Jerahmeel, were Maaz, Jamin, and Eker. 28The sons of Onam were Shammai and Jada. The sons of Shammai *were* Nadab and Abishur.

29And the name of the wife of Abishur *was* Abihail, and she bore him Ahban and Molid. 30The sons of Nadab *were* Seled and Appaim; Seled died without children. 31The son of Appaim *was* Ishi, the son of Ishi *was* Sheshan, and Sheshan's son *was* Ahlai. 32The sons of Jada, the brother of Shammai, *were* Jether and Jonathan; Jether died without children. 33The sons of Jonathan *were* Peleth and Zaza. These were the sons of Jerahmeel.

34Now Sheshan had no sons, only daughters. And Sheshan had an Egyptian servant whose name *was* Jarha. 35Sheshan gave his daughter to Jarha his servant as wife, and she bore him Attai. 36Attai begot Nathan, and Nathan begot Zabad; 37Zabad begot Ephlal, and Ephlal begot Obed; 38Obed begot Jehu, and Jehu begot Azariah; 39Azariah begot Helez, and Helez begot Eleasah; 40Eleasah begot Sismai, and Sismai begot Shallum; 41Shallum begot Jekamiah, and Jekamiah begot Elishama.

42The descendants of Caleb the brother of Jerahmeel *were* Mesha, his firstborn, who was the father of Ziph, and the sons of Mareshah the father of Hebron. 43The sons of Hebron *were* Korah, Tappuah, Rekem, and Shema. 44Shema begot Raham the father of Jorkoam, and Rekem begot Shammai. 45And the son of Shammai *was* Maon, and Maon *was* the father of Beth Zur.

46Ephah, Caleb's concubine, bore Haran, Moza, and Gazez; and Haran begot Gazez. 47And the sons of Jahdai *were* Regem, Jotham, Geshan, Pelet, Ephah, and Shaaph.

48Maachah, Caleb's concubine, bore Sheber and Tirhanah. 49She also bore Shaaph the father of Madmannah, Sheva the father of Machbenah and the father of Gibea. And the daughter of Caleb *was* Achsah.

50These were the descendants of Caleb: The sons of Hur, the firstborn of Ephrathah, *were* Shobal the father of Kirjath Jearim, 51Salma the father of Bethlehem, *and* Hareph the father of Beth Gader.

52And Shobal the father of Kirjath Jearim had descendants: Haroeh, *and* half of the *families of*

2:19 [z]Spelled *Ephrathah* elsewhere

Manuhoth.ᵃ ⁵³The families of Kirjath Jearim *were* the Ithrites, the Puthites, the Shumathites, and the Mishraites. From these came the Zorathites and the Eshtaolites.

⁵⁴The sons of Salma *were* Bethlehem, the Netophathites, Atroth Beth Joab, half of the Manahethites, and the Zorites.

⁵⁵And the families of the scribes who dwelt at Jabez *were* the Tirathites, the Shimeathites, *and* the Suchathites. These *were* the Kenites who came from Hammath, the father of the house of Rechab.

3 Now these were the sons of David who were born to him in Hebron: The firstborn *was* Amnon, by Ahinoam the Jezreelitess; the second, Daniel,ᵇ by Abigail the Carmelitess; ²the third, Absalom the son of Maacah, the daughter of Talmai, king of Geshur; the fourth, Adonijah the son of Haggith; ³the fifth, Shephatiah, by Abital; the sixth, Ithream, by his wife Eglah.

⁴*These* six were born to him in Hebron. There he reigned seven years and six months, and in Jerusalem he reigned thirty-three years. ⁵And these were born to him in Jerusalem: Shimea,ᶜ Shobab, Nathan, and Solomon—four by Bathshuaᵈ the daughter of Ammiel.ᵉ ⁶Also *there* were Ibhar, Elishama,ᶠ Eliphelet,ᵍ ⁷Nogah, Nepheg, Japhia, ⁸Elishama, Eliada,ʰ and Eliphelet—nine *in all.* ⁹*These were* all the sons of David, besides the sons of the concubines, and Tamar their sister.

¹⁰Solomon's son *was* Rehoboam; Abijahⁱ *was* his son, Asa his son, Jehoshaphat his son, ¹¹Joramʲ his son, Ahaziah his son, Joashᵏ his son, ¹²Amaziah his son, Azariahˡ his son, Jotham his son, ¹³Ahaz his son, Hezekiah his son, Manasseh his son, ¹⁴Amon his son, *and* Josiah his son. ¹⁵The sons of Josiah *were* Johanan the firstborn, the second Jehoiakim, the third Zedekiah, and the fourth Shallum.ᵐ ¹⁶The sons of Jehoiakim *were* Jeconiah his son *and* Zedekiahⁿ his son.

¹⁷And the sons of Jeconiahᵒ *were* Assir,ᵖ Shealtiel his son, ¹⁸*and* Malchiram, Pedaiah, Shenazzar, Jecamiah, Hoshama, and Nedabiah. ¹⁹The sons of Pedaiah *were* Zerubbabel and Shimei. The sons of Zerubbabel *were* Meshullam, Hananiah, Shelomith their sister, ²⁰and Hashubah, Ohel, Berechiah, Hasadiah, and Jushab-Hesed—five *in all.*

²¹The sons of Hananiah *were* Pelatiah and Jeshaiah, the sons of Rephaiah, the sons of Arnan, the sons of Obadiah, and the sons of Shechaniah. ²²The son of Shechaniah was Shemaiah. The sons of Shemaiah *were* Hattush, Igal, Bariah, Neariah, and Shaphat—six *in all.* ²³The sons of Neariah *were* Elioenai, Hezekiah, and Azrikam—three *in all.* ²⁴The sons of Elioenai *were* Hodaviah, Eliashib, Pelaiah, Akkub, Johanan, Delaiah, and Anani—seven *in all.*

2:52 ᵃSame as *the Manahethites,* verse 54   3:1 ᵇCalled *Chileab* in 2 Samuel 3:3   3:5 ᶜSpelled *Shammua* in 14:4 and 2 Samuel 5:14 ᵈSpelled *Bathsheba* in 2 Samuel 11:3 ᵉCalled *Eliam* in 2 Samuel 11:3   3:6 ᶠSpelled *Elishua* in 14:5 and 2 Samuel 5:15 ᵍSpelled *Elpelet* in 14:5   3:8 ʰSpelled *Beeliada* in 14:7   3:10 ⁱSpelled *Abijam* in 1 Kings 15:1   3:11 ʲSpelled *Jehoram* in 2 Kings 1:17 and 8:16 ᵏSpelled *Jehoash* in 2 Kings 12:1   3:12 ˡCalled *Uzziah* in Isaiah 6:1   3:15 ᵐCalled *Jehoahaz* in 2 Kings 23:31   3:16 ⁿCompare 2 Kings 24:17 3:17 ᵒAlso called *Coniah* in Jeremiah 22:24 and *Jehoiachin* in 2 Kings 24:8 ᵖOr *Jeconiah the captive were*

4 The sons of Judah *were* Perez, Hezron, Carmi,
Hur, and Shobal. 2And Reaiah the son of Sho-
bal begot Jahath, and Jahath begot Ahumai and
Lahad. These *were* the families of the Zorathites.
3These *were* the sons *of the father* of Etam:
Jezreel, Ishma, and Idbash; and the name of their
sister *was* Hazelelponi; 4and Penuel *was* the father of Gedor, and Ezer *was the* father of Hushah.
These *were* the sons of Hur, the firstborn of
Ephrathah the father of Bethlehem.
5And Ashhur the father of Tekoa had two wives,
Helah and Naarah. 6Naarah bore him Ahuzzam,
Hepher, Temeni, and Haahashtari. These *were* the
sons of Naarah. 7The sons of Helah *were* Zereth,
Zohar, and Ethnan; 8and Koz begot Anub, Zobe-
bah, and the families of Aharhel the son of
Harum.
9Now Jabez was more honorable than his
brothers, and his mother called his name Jabez,[q]
saying, "Because I bore *him* in pain." 10And Jabez
called on the God of Israel saying, "Oh, that You
would bless me indeed, and enlarge my territory,
that Your hand would be with me, and that You
would keep *me* from evil, that I may not cause
pain!" So God granted him what he requested.
11Chelub the brother of Shuhah begot Mehir,
who *was* the father of Eshton. 12And Eshton begot
Beth-Rapha, Paseah, and Tehinnah the father of
Ir-Nahash. These *were* the men of Rechah.
13The sons of Kenaz *were* Othniel and Seraiah.
The sons of Othniel *were* Hathath,[r] 14and Meonothai *who* begot Ophrah. Seraiah begot Joab the
father of Ge Harashim,[s] for they were craftsmen.
15The sons of Caleb the son of Jephunneh *were*
Iru, Elah, and Naam. The son of Elah *was* Kenaz.
16The sons of Jehallelel *were* Ziph, Ziphah, Tiria,
and Asarel. 17The sons of Ezrah *were* Jether,
Mered, Epher, and Jalon. And *Mered's wife*[t] *bore*
Miriam, Shammai, and Ishbah the father of Eshtemoa. 18(His wife Jehudijah[u] bore Jered the father of Gedor, Heber the father of Sochoh, and
Jekuthiel the father of Zanoah.) And these were
the sons of Bithiah the daughter of Pharaoh,
whom Mered took.
19The sons of Hodiah's wife, the sister of Na-
ham, *were* the fathers of Keilah the Garmite and
of Eshtemoa the Maachathite. 20And the sons of
Shimon *were* Amnon, Rinnah, Ben-Hanan, and
Tilon. And the sons of Ishi *were* Zoheth and Ben-
Zoheth.
21The sons of Shelah the son of Judah *were* Er
the father of Lecah, Laadah the father of Mareshah, and the families of the house of the linen
workers of the house of Ashbea; 22also Jokim, the
men of Chozeba, and Joash; Saraph, who ruled
in Moab, and Jashubi-Lehem. Now the records
are ancient. 23These *were* the potters and those
who dwell at Netaim[v] and Gederah;[w] there they
dwelt with the king for his work.
24The sons of Simeon *were* Nemuel, Jamin,
Jarib,[x] Zerah,[y] *and* Shaul, 25Shallum his son, Mibsam his son, and Mishma his son. 26And the sons
of Mishma *were* Hamuel his son, Zacchur his son,
and Shimei his son. 27Shimei had sixteen sons and
six daughters; but his brothers did not have many

4:9 [q]Literally *He Will Cause Pain* 4:13 [r]Septuagint and Vulgate add *and Meonothai*. 4:14 [s]Literally *Valley of Craftsmen* 4:17 [t]Literally *she* 4:18 [u]Or *His Judean wife* 4:23 [v]Literally *Plants* [w]Literally *Hedges* 4:24 [x]Called *Jachin* in Genesis 46:10 [y]Called *Zohar* in Genesis 46:10

children, nor did any of their families multiply as much as the children of Judah.
28They dwelt at Beersheba, Moladah, Hazar Shual, 29Bilhah, Ezem, Tolad, 30Bethuel, Hormah, Ziklag, 31Beth Marcaboth, Hazar Susim, Beth Biri, and at Shaaraim. These *were* their cities until the reign of David. 32And their villages *were* Etam, Ain, Rimmon, Tochen, and Ashan—five cities— 33and all the villages that *were* around these cities as far as Baal.z These *were* their dwelling places, and they maintained their genealogy: 34Meshobab, Jamlech, and Joshah the son of Amaziah; 35Joel, and Jehu the son of Joshibiah, the son of Seraiah, the son of Asiel; 36Elioenai, Jaakobah, Jeshohaiah, Asaiah, Adiel, Jesimiel, and Benaiah; 37Ziza the son of Shiphi, the son of Allon, the son of Jedaiah, the son of Shimri, the son of Shemaiah— 38these mentioned by name *were* leaders in their families, and their father's house increased greatly.

39So they went to the entrance of Gedor, as far as the east side of the valley, to seek pasture for their flocks. 40And they found rich, good pasture, and the land *was* broad, quiet, and peaceful; for some Hamites formerly lived there.

41These recorded by name came in the days of Hezekiah king of Judah; and they attacked their tents and the Meunites who were found there, and utterly destroyed them, as it is to this day. So they dwelt in their place, because *there was* pasture for their flocks there. 42Now *some* of them, five hundred men of the sons of Simeon, went to Mount Seir, having as their captains Pelatiah, Neariah, Rephaiah, and Uzziel, the sons of Ishi. 43And they defeated the rest of the Amalekites who had escaped. They have dwelt there to this day.

5 Now the sons of Reuben the firstborn of Israel—he *was* indeed the firstborn, but because he defiled his father's bed, his birthright was given to the sons of Joseph, the son of Israel, so that the genealogy is not listed according to the birthright; 2yet Judah prevailed over his brothers, and from him *came* a ruler, although the birthright was Joseph's— 3the sons of Reuben the firstborn of Israel were Hanoch, Pallu, Hezron, and Carmi.

4The sons of Joel *were* Shemaiah his son, Gog his son, Shimei his son, 5Micah his son, Reaiah his son, Baal his son, 6and Beerah his son, whom Tiglath-Pilesera king of Assyria carried into captivity. He *was* leader of the Reubenites. 7And his brethren by their families, when the genealogy of their generations was registered: the chief, Jeiel, and Zechariah, 8and Bela the son of Azaz, the son of Shema, the son of Joel, who dwelt in Aroer, as far as Nebo and Baal Meon. 9Eastward they settled as far as the entrance of the wilderness this side of the River Euphrates, because their cattle had multiplied in the land of Gilead.
10Now in the days of Saul they made war with the Hagrites, who fell by their hand; and they dwelt in their tents throughout the entire *area* east of Gilead.

11And the children of Gad dwelt next to them in the land of Bashan as far as Salcah: 12Joel *was* the chief, Shapham the next, then Jaanai and

---

4:33 zOr *Baalath Beer* (compare Joshua 19:8)   5:6 aHebrew *Tilgath-Pilneser*

Shaphat in Bashan, 13and their brethren of their father's house: Michael, Meshullam, Sheba, Jorai, Jachan, Zia, and Eber—seven *in all.* 14These *were* the children of Abihail the son of Huri, the son of Jaroah, the son of Gilead, the son of Michael, the son of Jeshishai, the son of Jahdo, the son of Buz; 15Ahi the son of Abdiel, the son of Guni, *was* chief of their father's house. 16And *the Gadites* dwelt in Gilead, in Bashan and in its villages, and in all the common-lands of Sharon within their borders. 17All these were registered by genealogies in the days of Jotham king of Judah, and in the days of Jeroboam king of Israel.

18The sons of Reuben, the Gadites, and half the tribe of Manasseh *had* forty-four thousand seven hundred and sixty valiant men, men able to bear shield and sword, to shoot with the bow, and skillful in war, who went to war. 19They made war with the Hagrites, Jetur, Naphish, and Nodab. 20And they were helped against them, and the Hagrites were delivered into their hand, and all who *were* with them, for they cried out to God in the battle. He heeded their prayer, because they put their trust in Him. 21Then they took away their livestock—fifty thousand of their camels, two hundred and fifty thousand of their sheep, and two thousand of their donkeys—also one hundred thousand of their men; 22for many fell dead, because the war *was* God's. And they dwelt in their place until the captivity.

23So the children of the half-tribe of Manasseh dwelt in the land. Their *numbers* increased from Bashan to Baal Hermon, that is, to Senir, or Mount Hermon. 24These *were* the heads of their fathers' houses: Epher, Ishi, Eliel, Azriel, Jeremiah, Hodaviah, and Jahdiel. They were mighty men of valor, famous men, *and* heads of their fathers' houses.

25And they were unfaithful to the God of their fathers, and played the harlot after the gods of the peoples of the land, whom God had destroyed before them. 26So the God of Israel stirred up the spirit of Pul king of Assyria, that is, Tiglath-Pileser[b] king of Assyria. He carried the Reubenites, the Gadites, and the half-tribe of Manasseh into captivity. He took them to Halah, Habor, Hara, and the river of Gozan to this day.

6 The sons of Levi *were* Gershon, Kohath, and Merari. 2The sons of Kohath *were* Amram, Izhar, Hebron, and Uzziel. 3The children of Amram *were* Aaron, Moses, and Miriam. And the sons of Aaron *were* Nadab, Abihu, Eleazar, and Ithamar. 4Eleazar begot Phinehas, *and* Phinehas begot Abishua; 5Abishua begot Bukki, and Bukki begot Uzzi; 6Uzzi begot Zerahiah, and Zerahiah begot Meraioth; 7Meraioth begot Amariah, and Amariah begot Ahitub; 8Ahitub begot Zadok, and Zadok begot Ahimaaz; 9Ahimaaz begot Azariah, and Azariah begot Johanan; 10Johanan begot Azariah (it was he who ministered as priest in the temple that Solomon built in Jerusalem); 11Azariah begot Amariah, and Amariah begot Ahitub; 12Ahitub begot Zadok, and Zadok begot Shallum; 13Shallum begot Hilkiah, and Hilkiah begot Azariah; 14Azariah begot Seraiah, and Seraiah begot Jehozadak. 15Jehozadak went *into captivity* when the LORD carried Judah and Jerusalem into captivity by the hand of Nebuchadnezzar.

5:26 *b*Hebrew *Tilgath-Pilneser*

16The sons of Levi *were* Gershon,[c] Kohath, and Merari. 17These are the names of the sons of Gershon: Libni and Shimei. 18The sons of Kohath *were* Amram, Izhar, Hebron, and Uzziel. 19The sons of Merari *were* Mahli and Mushi. Now these *are* the families of the Levites according to their fathers: 20Of Gershon *were* Libni his son, Jahath his son, Zimmah his son, 21Joah his son, Iddo his son, Zerah his son, *and* Jeatherai his son. 22The sons of Kohath *were* Amminadab his son, Korah his son, Assir his son, 23Elkanah his son, Ebiasaph his son, Assir his son, 24Tahath his son, Uriel his son, Uzziah his son, and Shaul his son. 25The sons of Elkanah *were* Amasai and Ahimoth. 26As for Elkanah,[d] the sons of Elkanah *were* Zophai[e] his son, Nahath[f] his son, 27Eliab[g] his son, Jeroham his son, *and* Elkanah his son. 28The sons of Samuel *were* Joel[h] the firstborn, and Abijah the second.[i] 29The sons of Merari *were* Mahli, Libni his son, Shimei his son, Uzzah his son, 30Shimea his son, Haggiah his son, *and* Asaiah his son.

31Now these are the men whom David appointed over the service of song in the house of the LORD, after the ark came to rest. 32They were ministering with music before the dwelling place of the tabernacle of meeting, until Solomon had built the house of the LORD in Jerusalem, and they served in their office according to their order.

33And these *are* the ones who ministered with their sons: Of the sons of the Kohathites *were* Heman the singer, the son of Joel, the son of Samuel, 34the son of Elkanah, the son of Jeroham, the son of Eliel,[j] the son of Toah,[k] 35the son of Zuph, the son of Elkanah, the son of Mahath, the son of Amasai, 36the son of Elkanah, the son of Joel, the son of Azariah, the son of Zephaniah, 37the son of Tahath, the son of Assir, the son of Ebiasaph, the son of Korah, 38the son of Izhar, the son of Kohath, the son of Levi, the son of Israel. 39And his brother Asaph, who stood at his right hand, *was* Asaph the son of Berachiah, the son of Shimea, 40the son of Michael, the son of Baaseiah, the son of Malchijah, 41the son of Ethni, the son of Zerah, the son of Adaiah, 42the son of Ethan, the son of Zimmah, the son of Shimei, 43the son of Jahath, the son of Gershon, the son of Levi.

44Their brethren, the sons of Merari, on the left hand, *were* Ethan the son of Kishi, the son of Abdi, the son of Malluch, 45the son of Hashabiah, the son of Amaziah, the son of Hilkiah, 46the son of Amzi, the son of Bani, the son of Shamer, 47the son of Mahli, the son of Mushi, the son of Merari, the son of Levi.

48And their brethren, the Levites, *were* appointed to every kind of service of the tabernacle of the house of God.

49But Aaron and his sons offered sacrifices on the altar of burnt offering and on the altar of incense, for all the work of the Most Holy *Place,* and to make atonement for Israel, according to all that Moses the servant of God had commanded. 50Now these *are* the sons of Aaron: Eleazar his son, Phinehas his son, Abishua his son,

---

6:16 [c]Hebrew *Gershom* (alternate spelling of *Gershon,* as in verses 1, 17, 20, 43, 62, and 71)   6:26 [d]Compare verse 35   [e]Spelled *Zuph* in verse 35 and 1 Samuel 1:1 [f]Compare verse 34   6:27 [g]Compare verse 34   6:28 [h]Following Septuagint, Syriac, and Arabic (compare verse 33 and 1 Samuel 8:2) [i]Hebrew *Vasheni*   6:34 [j]Spelled *Elihu* in 1 Samuel 1:1 [k]Spelled *Tohu* in 1 Samuel 1:1

51Bukki his son, Uzzi his son, Zerahiah his son, 52Meraioth his son, Amariah his son, Ahitub his son, 53Zadok his son, *and* Ahimaaz his son.

54Now these *are* their dwelling places throughout their settlements in their territory, for they were *given* by lot to the sons of Aaron, of the family of the Kohathites: 55They gave them Hebron in the land of Judah, with its surrounding common-lands. 56But the fields of the city and its villages they gave to Caleb the son of Jephunneh. 57And to the sons of Aaron they gave *one of* the cities of refuge, Hebron; also Libnah with its common-lands, Jattir, Eshtemoa with its common-lands, 58Hilen*ˡ* with its common-lands, Debir with its common-lands, 59Ashan*ᵐ* with its common-lands, and Beth Shemesh with its common-lands. 60And from the tribe of Benjamin: Geba with its common-lands, Alemeth*ⁿ* with its common-lands, and Anathoth with its common-lands. All their cities among their families *were* thirteen.

61To the rest of the family of the tribe of the Kohathites *they gave* by lot ten cities from half the tribe of Manasseh. 62And to the sons of Gershon, throughout their families, *they gave* thirteen cities from the tribe of Issachar, from the tribe of Asher, from the tribe of Naphtali, and from the tribe of Manasseh in Bashan. 63To the sons of Merari, throughout their families, *they gave* twelve cities from the tribe of Reuben, from the tribe of Gad, and from the tribe of Zebulun. 64So the children of Israel gave *these* cities with their common-lands to the Levites. 65And they gave by lot from the tribe of the children of Judah, from the tribe of the children of Simeon, and from the tribe of the children of Benjamin these cities which are called by *their* names.

66Now some of the families of the sons of Kohath *were given* cities as their territory from the tribe of Ephraim. 67And they gave them *one of* the cities of refuge, Shechem with its common-lands, in the mountains of Ephraim, also Gezer with its common-lands, 68Jokmeam with its common-lands, Beth Horon with its common-lands, 69Aijalon with its common-lands, and Gath Rimmon with its common-lands. 70And from the half-tribe of Manasseh: Aner with its common-lands and Bileam with its common-lands, for the rest of the family of the sons of Kohath.

71From the family of the half-tribe of Manasseh the sons of Gershon *were given* Golan in Bashan with its common-lands and Ashtaroth with its common-lands. 72And from the tribe of Issachar: Kedesh with its common-lands, Daberath with its common-lands, 73Ramoth with its common-lands, and Anem with its common-lands. 74And from the tribe of Asher: Mashal with its common-lands, Abdon with its common-lands, 75Hukok with its common-lands, and Rehob with its common-lands. 76And from the tribe of Naphtali: Kedesh in Galilee with its common-lands, Hammon with its common-lands, and Kirjathaim with its common-lands.

77From the tribe of Zebulun the rest of the children of Merari *were given* Rimmon*ᵒ* with its common-lands and Tabor with its common-lands. 78And on the other side of the Jordan, across from

---

6:58 ˡSpelled *Holon* in Joshua 21:15   6:59 ᵐSpelled *Ain* in Joshua 21:16   6:60 ⁿSpelled *Almon* in Joshua 21:18
6:77 ᵒHebrew *Rimmono*, alternate spelling of *Rimmon;* see 4:32

Jericho, on the east side of the Jordan, *they were given* from the tribe of Reuben: Bezer in the wilderness with its common-lands, Jahzah with its common-lands, [79]Kedemoth with its common-lands, and Mephaath with its common-lands. [80]And from the tribe of Gad: Ramoth in Gilead with its common-lands, Mahanaim with its common-lands, [81]Heshbon with its common-lands, and Jazer with its common-lands.

7 The sons of Issachar *were* Tola, Puah,[p] Jashub, and Shimron—four *in all.* [2]The sons of Tola *were* Uzzi, Rephaiah, Jeriel, Jahmai, Jibsam, and Shemuel, heads of their father's house. *The sons* of Tola *were* mighty men of valor in their generations; their number in the days of David *was* twenty-two thousand six hundred. [3]The son of Uzzi *was* Izrahiah, and the sons of Izrahiah *were* Michael, Obadiah, Joel, and Ishiah. All five of them *were* chief men. [4]And with them, by their generations, according to their fathers' houses, *were* thirty-six thousand troops ready for war; for they had many wives and sons.

[5]Now their brethren among all the families of Issachar *were* mighty men of valor, listed by their genealogies, eighty-seven thousand in all.

[6]*The sons* of Benjamin *were* Bela, Becher, and Jediael—three *in all.* [7]The sons of Bela were Ezbon, Uzzi, Uzziel, Jerimoth, and Iri—five *in all.* They *were* heads of *their* fathers' houses, and they were listed by their genealogies, twenty-two thousand and thirty-four mighty men of valor.

[8]The sons of Becher *were* Zemirah, Joash, Eliezer, Elioenai, Omri, Jerimoth, Abijah, Anathoth, and Alemeth. All these *are* the sons of Becher. [9]And they were recorded by genealogy according to their generations, heads of their fathers' houses, twenty thousand two hundred mighty men of valor. [10]The son of Jediael *was* Bilhan, and the sons of Bilhan *were* Jeush, Benjamin, Ehud, Chenaanah, Zethan, Tharshish, and Ahishahar.

[11]All these sons of Jediael *were* heads of their fathers' houses; *there were* seventeen thousand two hundred mighty men of valor fit to go out for war *and* battle. [12]Shuppim and Huppim[q] *were* the sons of Ir, *and* Hushim *was* the son of Aher.

[13]The sons of Naphtali *were* Jahziel,[r] Guni, Jezer, and Shallum,[s] the sons of Bilhah.

[14]The descendants of Manasseh: his Syrian concubine bore him Machir the father of Gilead, the father of Asriel.[t] [15]Machir took as his wife *the sister* of Huppim and Shuppim,[u] whose name *was* Maachah. The name of *Gilead's* grandson[v] *was* Zelophehad,[w] but Zelophehad begot only daughters. [16](Maachah the wife of Machir bore a son, and she called his name Peresh. The name of his brother *was* Sheresh, and his sons *were* Ulam and Rakem. [17]The son of Ulam *was* Bedan.) These *were* the descendants of Gilead the son of Machir, the son of Manasseh.

[18]His sister Hammoleketh bore Ishhod, Abiezer, and Mahlah.

[19]And the sons of Shemida were Ahian, Shechem, Likhi, and Aniam.

7:1 [p]Spelled *Puvah* in Genesis 46:13 7:12 [q]Called *Hupham* in Numbers 26:39 7:13 [r]Spelled *Jahzeel* in Genesis 46:24 [s]Spelled *Shillem* in Genesis 46:24 7:14 [t]The son of Gilead (compare Numbers 26:30, 31) 7:15 [u]Compare verse 12 [v]Literally *the second* [w]Compare Numbers 26:30–33

20The sons of Ephraim *were* Shuthelah, Bered his son, Tahath his son, Eladah his son, Tahath his son, 21Zabad his son, Shuthelah his son, and Ezer and Elead. The men of Gath who were born in *that* land killed *them* because they came down to take away their cattle. 22Then Ephraim their father mourned many days, and his brethren came to comfort him.

23And when he went in to his wife, she conceived and bore a son; and he called his name Beriah,x because tragedy had come upon his house. 24Now his daughter *was* Sheerah, who built Lower and Upper Beth Horon and Uzzen Sheerah; 25and Rephah *was* his son, *as well* as Resheph, and Telah his son, Tahan his son, 26Laadan his son, Ammihud his son, Elishama his son, 27Nuny his son, and Joshua his son.

28Now their possessions and dwelling places *were* Bethel and its towns: to the east Naaran, to the west Gezer and its towns, and Shechem and its towns, as far as Ayyahz and its towns; 29and by the borders of the children of Manasseh *were* Beth Shean and its towns, Taanach and its towns, Megiddo and its towns, Dor and its towns. In these dwelt the children of Joseph, the son of Israel.

30The sons of Asher *were* Imnah, Ishvah, Ishvi, Beriah, and their sister Serah. 31The sons of Beriah *were* Heber and Malchiel, who was the father of Birzaith.a 32And Heber begot Japhlet, Shomer,b Hotham,c and their sister Shua. 33The sons of Japhlet *were* Pasach, Bimhal, and Ashvath. These *were* the children of Japhlet. 34The sons of Shemer *were* Ahi, Rohgah, Jehubbah, and Aram. 35And the sons of his brother Helem *were* Zophah, Imna, Shelesh, and Amal. 36The sons of Zophah *were* Suah, Harnepher, Shual, Beri, Imrah, 37Bezer, Hod, Shamma, Shilshah, Jithran,d and Beera. 38The sons of Jether *were* Jephunneh, Pispah, and Ara. 39The sons of Ulla *were* Arah, Haniel, and Rizia.

40All these *were* the children of Asher, heads of *their* fathers' houses, choice men, mighty men of valor, chief leaders. And they were recorded by genealogies among the army fit for battle; their number *was* twenty-six thousand.

8 Now Benjamin begot Bela his firstborn, Ashbel the second, Aharahe the third, 2Nohah the fourth, and Rapha the fifth. 3The sons of Bela *were* Addar,f Gera, Abihud, 4Abishua, Naaman, Ahoah, 5Gera, Shephuphan, and Huram.

6These *are* the sons of Ehud, who were the heads of the fathers' *houses* of the inhabitants of Geba, and who forced them to move to Manahath: 7Naaman, Ahijah, and Gera who forced them to move. He begot Uzza and Ahihud.

8Also Shaharaim had children in the country of Moab, after he had sent away Hushim and Baara his wives. 9By Hodesh his wife he begot Jobab, Zibia, Mesha, Malcam, 10Jeuz, Sachiah, and Mirmah. These *were* his sons, heads of their fathers' *houses*.

11And by Hushim he begot Abitub and Elpaal. 12The sons of Elpaal *were* Eber, Misham, and

---

7:23 xLiterally *In Tragedy*   7:27 yHebrew *Non*   7:28 zMany Hebrew manuscripts, Bomberg, Septuagint, Targum, and Vulgate read *Gazza*.   7:31 aOr *Birzavith* or *Birzoth* 7:32 bSpelled *Shemer* in verse 34 cSpelled *Helem* in verse 35   7:37 dSpelled *Jether* in verse 38   8:1 eSpelled *Ahiram* in Numbers 26:38   8:3 fCalled *Ard* in Numbers 26:40

Shemed, who built Ono and Lod with its towns;
[13]and Beriah and Shema, who *were* heads of
their fathers' *houses* of the inhabitants of Aijalon,
who drove out the inhabitants of Gath. [14]Ahio,
Shashak, Jeremoth, [15]Zebadiah, Arad, Eder,
[16]Michael, Ispah, and Joha *were* the sons of
Beriah. [17]Zebadiah, Meshullam, Hizki, Heber,
[18]Ishmerai, Jizliah, and Jobab *were* the sons of
Elpaal. [19]Jakim, Zichri, Zabdi, [20]Elienai, Zillethai,
Eliel, [21]Adaiah, Beraiah, and Shimrath *were* the
sons of Shimei. [22]Ishpan, Eber, Eliel, [23]Abdon,
Zichri, Hanan, [24]Hananiah, Elam, Antothijah,
[25]Iphdeiah, and Penuel *were* the sons of Shashak.
[26]Shamsherai, Shehariah, Athaliah, [27]Jaareshiah,
Elijah, and Zichri *were* the sons of Jeroham.

[28]These *were* heads of the fathers' *houses* by
their generations, chief men. These dwelt in
Jerusalem.

[29]Now the father of Gibeon, whose wife's name
was Maacah, dwelt at Gibeon. [30]And his firstborn
son *was* Abdon, then Zur, Kish, Baal, Nadab,
[31]Gedor, Ahio, Zecher, [32]and Mikloth, *who* begot
Shimeah.[g] They also dwelt alongside their relatives in Jerusalem, with their brethren. [33]Ner[h] begot Kish, Kish begot Saul, and Saul begot Jonathan, Malchishua, Abinadab,[i] and Esh-Baal.[j]
[34]The son of Jonathan *was* Merib-Baal,[k] and
Merib-Baal begot Micah. [35]The sons of Micah
were Pithon, Melech, Tarea, and Ahaz. [36]And
Ahaz begot Jehoaddah;[l] Jehoaddah begot Alemeth, Azmaveth, and Zimri; and Zimri begot
Moza. [37]Moza begot Binea, Raphah[m] his son,
Eleasah his son, *and* Azel his son.

[38]Azel had six sons whose names *were* these:
Azrikam, Bocheru, Ishmael, Sheariah, Obadiah,
and Hanan. All these *were* the sons of Azel.
[39]And the sons of Eshek his brother *were* Ulam
his firstborn, Jeush the second, and Eliphelet the
third.

[40]The sons of Ulam were mighty men of valor—
archers. *They* had many sons and grandsons, one
hundred and fifty *in all*. These *were* all sons of
Benjamin.

9 So all Israel was recorded by genealogies, and
indeed, they *were* inscribed in the book of the
kings of Israel. But Judah was carried away captive to Babylon because of their unfaithfulness.
[2]And the first inhabitants who *dwelt* in their possessions in their cities *were* Israelites, priests, Levites, and the Nethinim.

[3]Now in Jerusalem the children of Judah dwelt,
and some of the children of Benjamin, and of the
children of Ephraim and Manasseh: [4]Uthai the
son of Ammihud, the son of Omri, the son of Imri,
the son of Bani, of the descendants of Perez, the
son of Judah. [5]Of the Shilonites: Asaiah the firstborn and his sons. [6]Of the sons of Zerah: Jeuel,
and their brethren—six hundred and ninety.
[7]Of the sons of Benjamin: Sallu the son of Meshullam, the son of Hodaviah, the son of Hassenuah;
[8]Ibneiah the son of Jeroham; Elah the son of Uzzi,
the son of Michri; Meshullam the son of Shephatiah, the son of Reuel, the son of Ibnijah; [9]and
their brethren, according to their generations—

8:32 [g]Spelled *Shimeam* in 9:38   8:33 [h]Also the son of Gibeon
(compare 9:36, 39) [i]Called *Jishui* in 1 Samuel 14:49 [j]Called
Ishbosheth in 2 Samuel 2:8 and elsewhere   8:34 [k]Called
Mephibosheth in 2 Samuel 4:4   8:36 [l]Spelled *Jarah* in 9:42
8:37 [m]Spelled *Rephaiah* in 9:43

nine hundred and fifty-six. All these men *were* heads of a father's *house* in their fathers' houses.

10Of the priests: Jedaiah, Jehoiarib, and Jachin; 11Azariah the son of Hilkiah, the son of Meshullam, the son of Zadok, the son of Meraioth, the son of Ahitub, the officer over the house of God; 12Adaiah the son of Jeroham, the son of Pashur, the son of Malchijah; Maasai the son of Adiel, the son of Jahzerah, the son of Meshullam, the son of Meshillemith, the son of Immer; 13and their brethren, heads of their fathers' *houses*—one thousand seven hundred and sixty. *They were* very able men for the work of the service of the house of God.

14Of the Levites: Shemaiah the son of Hasshub, the son of Azrikam, the son of Hashabiah, of the sons of Merari; 15Bakbakkar, Heresh, Galal, and Mattaniah the son of Micah, the son of Zichri, the son of Asaph; 16Obadiah the son of Shemaiah, the son of Galal, the son of Jeduthun; and Berechiah the son of Asa, the son of Elkanah, who lived in the villages of the Netophathites.

17And the gatekeepers *were* Shallum, Akkub, Talmon, Ahiman, and their brethren. Shallum *was* the chief. 18Until then *they had been* gatekeepers for the camps of the children of Levi at the King's Gate on the east.

19Shallum the son of Kore, the son of Ebiasaph, the son of Korah, and his brethren, from his father's house, the Korahites, *were* in charge of the work of the service, gatekeepers of the tabernacle. Their fathers had been keepers of the entrance to the camp of the LORD. 20And Phinehas the son of Eleazar had been the officer over them in time past; the LORD *was* with him. 21Zechariah the son of Meshelemiah *was* keeper of the door of the tabernacle of meeting.

22All those chosen as gatekeepers *were* two hundred and twelve. They were recorded by their genealogy, in their villages. David and Samuel the seer had appointed them to their trusted office. 23So they and their children *were* in charge of the gates of the house of the LORD, the house of the tabernacle, by assignment. 24The gatekeepers were assigned to the four directions: the east, west, north, and south. 25And their brethren in their villages *had* to come with them from time to time for seven days. 26For in this trusted office *were* four chief gatekeepers; they were Levites. And they had charge over the chambers and treasuries of the house of God. 27And they lodged *all* around the house of God because they *had* the responsibility, and they *were* in charge of opening *it* every morning.

28Now *some* of them were in charge of the serving vessels, for they brought them in and took them out by count. 29*Some* of them *were* appointed over the furnishings and over all the implements of the sanctuary, and over the fine flour and the wine and the oil and the incense and the spices. 30And *some* of the sons of the priests made the ointment of the spices.

31Mattithiah of the Levites, the firstborn of Shallum the Korahite, had the trusted office over the things that were baked in the pans. 32And some of their brethren of the sons of the Kohathites *were* in charge of preparing the showbread for every Sabbath.

33These are the singers, heads of the fathers' *houses* of the Levites, *who lodged* in the chambers, *and were* free *from other duties;* for they were employed in *that* work day and night.

34These heads of the fathers' *houses* of the Levites *were* heads throughout their generations. They dwelt at Jerusalem.

35Jeiel the father of Gibeon, whose wife's name *was* Maacah, dwelt at Gibeon. 36His firstborn son *was* Abdon, then Zur, Kish, Baal, Ner, Nadab, 37Gedor, Ahio, Zechariah,[n] and Mikloth. 38And Mikloth begot Shimeam.[o] They also dwelt alongside their relatives in Jerusalem, with their brethren. 39Ner begot Kish, Kish begot Saul, and Saul begot Jonathan, Malchishua, Abinadab, and Esh-Baal. 40The son of Jonathan *was* Merib-Baal, and Merib-Baal begot Micah. 41The sons of Micah *were* Pithon, Melech, Tahrea,[p] *and Ahaz.*[q] 42And Ahaz begot Jarah;[r] Jarah begot Alemeth, Azmaveth, and Zimri; and Zimri begot Moza; 43Moza begot Binea, Rephaiah[s] his son, Eleasah his son, and Azel his son.

44And Azel had six sons whose names *were* these: Azrikam, Bocheru, Ishmael, Sheariah, Obadiah, and Hanan; these *were* the sons of Azel.

10 Now* the Philistines fought against Israel; and the men of Israel fled from before the Philistines, and fell slain on Mount Gilboa. 2Then the Philistines followed hard after Saul and his sons. And the Philistines killed Jonathan, Abinadab, and Malchishua, Saul's sons. 3The battle became fierce against Saul. The archers hit him, and he was wounded by the archers. 4Then Saul said to his armorbearer, "Draw your sword, and thrust me through with it, lest these uncircumcised men come and abuse me." But his armorbearer would not, for he was greatly afraid. Therefore Saul took a sword and fell on it. 5And when his armorbearer saw that Saul was dead, he also fell on his sword and died. 6So Saul and his three sons died, and all his house died together. 7And when all the men of Israel who *were* in the valley saw that they had fled and that Saul and his sons were dead, they forsook their cities and fled; then the Philistines came and dwelt in them.

8So it happened the next day, when the Philistines came to strip the slain, that they found Saul and his sons fallen on Mount Gilboa. 9And they stripped him and took his head and his armor, and sent word *throughout* the land of the Philistines to proclaim the news *in the temple* of their idols and among the people. 10Then they put his armor in the temple of their gods, and fastened his head in the temple of Dagon.

11And when all Jabesh Gilead heard all that the Philistines had done to Saul, 12all the valiant men arose and took the body of Saul and the bodies of his sons; and they brought them to Jabesh, and buried their bones under the tamarisk tree at Jabesh, and fasted seven days.

13*So Saul died for his unfaithfulness which he had committed against the LORD, because he did not keep the word of the LORD, and also because he consulted a medium for guidance. 14But *he* did not inquire of the LORD; therefore He killed him, and turned the kingdom over to David the son of Jesse.

CHAPTER 10

10:1–5 King Saul's life is ignored as the writer focuses on his death. He was a man with a good beginning and a tragic ending, and the reason is given in verses 13–14: he was unfaithful to the Lord and disobeyed His Word.

First Samuel 13—31 records Saul's gradual decline. He ran ahead of the Lord and offered a sacrifice. He spared King Agag and then lied to the Lord about it. He wanted recognition from Samuel and the people even though God had deserted him. He envied David and tried to destroy him. He wasted God-given opportunities for repentance. Finally, he turned to Satan for help and ended up committing suicide.

10:13, 14 Not belonging to the tribe of Judah, Saul was never meant to establish the dynasty (Gen. 49:10), but that was not the cause of his sin. He could have been a godly leader and prepared the way for David, but Saul would not obey. Alexander Whyte quoted a relevant comment by Thomas Shepard: "Oh, the grievous shipwrecks of some great ships! We see some boards and planks lying in the mud at low water, but that is all!"

9:37 [n]Called *Zecher* in 8:31   9:38 [o]Spelled *Shimeah* in 8:32
9:41 [p]Spelled *Tarea* in 8:35 [q]Following Arabic, Syriac, Targum, and Vulgate (compare 8:35); Masoretic Text and Septuagint omit *and Ahaz.*   9:42 [r]Spelled *Jehoaddah* in 8:36
9:43 [s]Spelled *Raphah* in 8:37

CHAPTER 11

11:1–3 Some people become leaders because God chooses them in a special way and anoints them for a special work. That is how David came to the throne. In contrast to Saul, David was faithful to the Lord.

11:8 Others become leaders because people like David challenge them to do their best. Joab became head of the army because he conquered a stronghold, and all of David's "mighty men" won their way into the inner circle of heroes. David was a mighty leader, but he could not accomplish anything alone. We all need one another.

11:18, 19 Greatness is often shown more in little things than in big things. Real leaders see greatness in places where others may see little or nothing. David did not see water in the vessel; he saw the blood of the men who risked their lives to satisfy his desire.

It is not what a thing *is* or *does* that impresses a leader, but what a thing *costs his people.* D. L. Moody observed, "There are many of us that are willing to do great things for the Lord; but few of us are willing to do little things." And only God can make the "little things" great!

11 Then* all Israel came together to David at Hebron, saying, "Indeed we *are* your bone and your flesh. 2Also, in time past, even when Saul was king, you *were* the one who led Israel out and brought them in; and the LORD your God said to you, 'You shall shepherd My people Israel, and be ruler over My people Israel.' " 3Therefore all the elders of Israel came to the king at Hebron, and David made a covenant with them at Hebron before the LORD. And they anointed David king over Israel, according to the word of the LORD by Samuel.

4And David and all Israel went to Jerusalem, which is Jebus, where the Jebusites *were,* the inhabitants of the land. 5But the inhabitants of Jebus said to David, "You shall not come in here!" Nevertheless David took the stronghold of Zion (that is, the City of David). 6Now David said, "Whoever attacks the Jebusites first shall be chief and captain." And Joab the son of Zeruiah went up first, and became chief. 7Then David dwelt in the stronghold; therefore they called it the City of David. 8*And he built the city around it, from the Millo*t* to the surrounding area. Joab repaired the rest of the city. 9So David went on and became great, and the LORD of hosts *was* with him.

10Now these *were* the heads of the mighty men whom David had, who strengthened themselves with him in his kingdom, with all Israel, to make him king, according to the word of the LORD concerning Israel.

11And this *is* the number of the mighty men whom David had: Jashobeam the son of a Hachmonite, chief of the captains;*u* he had lifted up his spear against three hundred, killed *by him* at one time.

12After him *was* Eleazar the son of Dodo, the Ahohite, who *was one* of the three mighty men. 13He was with David at Pasdammim. Now there the Philistines were gathered for battle, and there was a piece of ground full of barley. So the people fled from the Philistines. 14But they stationed themselves in the middle of *that* field, defended it, and killed the Philistines. So the LORD brought about a great victory.

15Now three of the thirty chief men went down to the rock to David, into the cave of Adullam; and the army of the Philistines encamped in the Valley of Rephaim. 16David *was* then in the stronghold, and the garrison of the Philistines *was* then in Bethlehem. 17And David said with longing, "Oh, that someone would give me a drink of water from the well of Bethlehem, which is by the gate!" 18*So the three broke through the camp of the Philistines, drew water from the well of Bethlehem that *was* by the gate, and took *it* and brought *it* to David. Nevertheless David would not drink it, but poured it out to the LORD. 19And he said, "Far be it from me, O my God, that I should do this! Shall I drink the blood of these men *who have put* their lives *in* jeopardy? For at the risk of their lives they brought it." Therefore he would not drink it. These things were done by the three mighty men.

20Abishai the brother of Joab was chief of *another* three.*v* He had lifted up his spear against

---

11:8 *t*Literally *The Landfill*   11:11 *u*Following Qere; Kethib, Septuagint, and Vulgate read *the thirty* (compare 2 Samuel 23:8).   11:20 *v*Following Masoretic Text, Septuagint, and Vulgate; Syriac reads *thirty.*

three hundred *men*, killed *them*, and won a name among *these* three. [21]Of the three he was more honored than the other two men. Therefore he became their captain. However he did not attain to the *first* three.

[22]Benaiah was the son of Jehoiada, the son of a valiant man from Kabzeel, who had done many deeds. He had killed two lion-like heroes of Moab. He also had gone down and killed a lion in the midst of a pit on a snowy day. [23]And he killed an Egyptian, a man of *great* height, five cubits tall. In the Egyptian's hand *there was* a spear like a weaver's beam; and he went down to him with a staff, wrested the spear out of the Egyptian's hand, and killed him with his own spear. [24]These *things* Benaiah the son of Jehoiada did, and won a name among three mighty men. [25]Indeed he was more honored than the thirty, but he did not attain to the *first* three. And David appointed him over his guard.

[26]Also the mighty warriors *were* Asahel the brother of Joab, Elhanan the son of Dodo of Bethlehem, [27]Shammoth the Harorite,[w] Helez the Pelonite,[x] [28]Ira the son of Ikkesh the Tekoite, Abiezer the Anathothite, [29]Sibbechai the Hushathite, Ilai the Ahohite, [30]Maharai the Netophathite, Heled[y] the son of Baanah the Netophathite, [31]Ithai[z] the son of Ribai of Gibeah, of the sons of Benjamin, Benaiah the Pirathonite, [32]Hurai[a] of the brooks of Gaash, Abiel[b] the Arbathite, [33]Azmaveth the Baharumite,[c] Eliahba the Shaalbonite, [34]the sons of Hashem the Gizonite, Jonathan the son of Shageh the Hararite, [35]Ahiam the son of Sacar the Hararite, Eliphal the son of Ur, [36]Hepher the Mecherathite, Ahijah the Pelonite, [37]Hezro the Carmelite, Naarai the son of Ezbai, [38]Joel the brother of Nathan, Mibhar the son of Hagri, [39]Zelek the Ammonite, Naharai the Berothite[d] (the armorbearer of Joab the son of Zeruiah), [40]Ira the Ithrite, Gareb the Ithrite, [41]Uriah the Hittite, Zabad the son of Ahlai, [42]Adina the son of Shiza the Reubenite (a chief of the Reubenites) and thirty with him, [43]Hanan the son of Maachah, Joshaphat the Mithnite, [44]Uzzia the Ashterathite, Shama and Jeiel the sons of Hotham the Aroerite, [45]Jediael the son of Shimri, and Joha his brother, the Tizite, [46]Eliel the Mahavite, Jeribai and Joshaviah the sons of Elnaam, Ithmah the Moabite, [47]Eliel, Obed, and Jaasiel the Mezobaite.

12 Now* these *were* the men who came to David at Ziklag while he was still a fugitive from Saul the son of Kish; and they *were* among the mighty men, helpers in the war, [2]armed with bows, using both the right hand and the left in *hurling* stones and *shooting* arrows with the bow. *They were* of Benjamin, Saul's brethren.

[3]The chief *was* Ahiezer, then Joash, the sons of Shemaah the Gibeathite; Jeziel and Pelet the sons of Azmaveth; Berachah, and Jehu the Anathothite; [4]Ishmaiah the Gibeonite, a mighty man among the thirty, and over the thirty; Jeremiah, Jahaziel, Johanan, and Jozabad the Gederathite;

CHAPTER 12

12:1, 2 Saul *drafted* men into his army (1 Sam. 14:52) while David *attracted* them because of his character and leadership. In fact, some of his best men came from Saul's tribe! Saul seemed to bring out the worst in people while David brought out the best.

11:27 [w]Spelled *Harodite* in 2 Samuel 23:25 [x]Called *Paltite* in 2 Samuel 23:26   11:30 [y]Spelled *Heleb* in 2 Samuel 23:29 and *Heldai* in 1 Chronicles 27:15   11:31 [z]Spelled *Ittai* in 2 Samuel 23:29   11:32 [a]Spelled *Hiddai* in 2 Samuel 23:30 [b]Spelled *Abi-Albon* in 2 Samuel 23:31   11:33 [c]Spelled *Barhumite* in 2 Samuel 23:31   11:39 [d]Spelled *Beerothite* in 2 Samuel 23:37

5Eluzai, Jerimoth, Bealiah, Shemariah, and Shephatiah the Haruphite; 6Elkanah, Jisshiah, Azarel, Joezer, and Jashobeam, the Korahites; 7and Joelah and Zebadiah the sons of Jeroham of Gedor.

8*Some* Gadites joined David at the stronghold in the wilderness, mighty men of valor, men trained for battle, who could handle shield and spear, whose faces *were like* the faces of lions, and *were* as swift as gazelles on the mountains: 9Ezer the first, Obadiah the second, Eliab the third, 10Mishmannah the fourth, Jeremiah the fifth, 11Attai the sixth, Eliel the seventh, 12Johanan the eighth, Elzabad the ninth, 13Jeremiah the tenth, and Machbanai the eleventh. 14These *were* from the sons of Gad, captains of the army; the least was over a hundred, and the greatest was over a thousand. 15These *are* the ones who crossed the Jordan in the first month, when it had overflowed all its banks; and they put to flight all *those* in the valleys, to the east and to the west.

16Then some of the sons of Benjamin and Judah came to David at the stronghold. 17*And David went out to meet them, and answered and said to them, "If you have come peaceably to me to help me, my heart will be united with you; but if to betray me to my enemies, since *there is* no wrong in my hands, may the God of our fathers look and bring judgment." 18Then the Spirit came upon Amasai, chief of the captains, *and he said:*

> "*We are* yours, O David;
> We *are* on your side, O son of Jesse!
> Peace, peace to you,
> And peace to your helpers!
> For your God helps you."

So David received them, and made them captains of the troop.

19And *some* from Manasseh defected to David when he was going with the Philistines to battle against Saul; but they did not help them, for the lords of the Philistines sent him away by agreement, saying, "He may defect to his master Saul *and endanger* our heads." 20When he went to Ziklag, those of Manasseh who defected to him were Adnah, Jozabad, Jediael, Michael, Jozabad, Elihu, and Zillethai, captains of the thousands who *were* from Manasseh. 21And they helped David against the bands *of raiders,* for they *were* all mighty men of valor, and they were captains in the army. 22For at *that* time they came to David day by day to help him, until *it was* a great army, like the army of God.

23Now these *were* the numbers of the divisions *that were* equipped for war, *and* came to David at Hebron to turn *over* the kingdom of Saul to him, according to the word of the LORD: 24of the sons of Judah bearing shield and spear, six thousand eight hundred armed for war; 25of the sons of Simeon, mighty men of valor fit for war, seven thousand one hundred; 26of the sons of Levi four thousand six hundred; 27Jehoiada, the leader of the Aaronites, and with him three thousand seven hundred; 28Zadok, a young man, a valiant warrior, and from his father's house twenty-two captains; 29of the sons of Benjamin, relatives of Saul, three thousand (until then the greatest part of them had remained loyal to the house of Saul); 30of the sons of Ephraim twenty thousand eight hundred, mighty men of valor, famous men throughout their father's house; 31of the half-tribe

12:17 If Jesus Christ were recruiting an army on earth today, how many of us would qualify? He seeks skilled people (v. 2), trained people (v. 8), people not afraid to get their feet wet (v. 15). He wants soldiers with loyal hearts (vv. 16–18) who know how to keep rank and face the enemy together (vv. 33, 38). He needs people who understand the times (v. 32).

Are you a volunteer? Are you willing for the Lord to make you qualified? The only winning army is the Lord's army. "The real great man is the man who makes every man feel great," according to Gilbert K. Chesterton.

of Manasseh eighteen thousand, who were designated by name to come and make David king; 32of the sons of Issachar who had understanding of the times, to know what Israel ought to do, their chiefs were two hundred; and all their brethren were at their command; 33of Zebulun there were fifty thousand who went out to battle, expert in war with all weapons of war, stouthearted men who could keep ranks; 34of Naphtali one thousand captains, and with them thirty-seven thousand with shield and spear; 35of the Danites who could keep battle formation, twenty-eight thousand six hundred; 36of Asher, those who could go out to war, able to keep battle formation, forty thousand; 37of the Reubenites and the Gadites and the half-tribe of Manasseh, from the other side of the Jordan, one hundred and twenty thousand armed for battle with every *kind* of weapon of war.

38All these men of war, who could keep ranks, came to Hebron with a loyal heart, to make David king over all Israel; and all the rest of Israel *were* of one mind to make David king. 39And they were there with David three days, eating and drinking, for their brethren had prepared for them. 40Moreover those who were near to them, from as far away as Issachar and Zebulun and Naphtali, were bringing food on donkeys and camels, on mules and oxen—provisions of flour and cakes of figs and cakes of raisins, wine and oil and oxen and sheep abundantly, for *there was* joy in Israel.

13 Then* David consulted with the captains of thousands and hundreds, *and* with every leader. 2And David said to all the assembly of Israel, "If *it seems* good to you, and if it is of the LORD our God, let us send out to our brethren everywhere *who are* left in all the land of Israel, and with them to the priests and Levites *who are* in their cities *and* their common-lands, that they may gather together to us; 3and let us bring the ark of our God back to us, for we have not inquired at it since the days of Saul." 4Then all the assembly said that they would do so, for the thing was right in the eyes of all the people.

5So David gathered all Israel together, from Shihor in Egypt to as far as the entrance of Hamath, to bring the ark of God from Kirjath Jearim. 6And David and all Israel went up to Baalah,e to Kirjath Jearim, which belonged to Judah, to bring up from there the ark of God the LORD, who dwells *between* the cherubim, where *His* name is proclaimed. 7So they carried the ark of God on a new cart from the house of Abinadab, and Uzza and Ahio drove the cart. 8*Then David and all Israel played *music* before God with all *their* might, with singing, on harps, on stringed instruments, on tambourines, on cymbals, and with trumpets.

9And when they came to Chidon'sf threshing floor, Uzza put out his hand to hold the ark, for the oxen stumbled. 10Then the anger of the LORD was aroused against Uzza, and He struck him because he put his hand to the ark; and he died there before God. 11And David became angry because of the LORD's outbreak against Uzza; therefore that place is called Perez Uzzag to this day. 12David was afraid of God that day, saying, "How can I bring the ark of God to me?"

13:6 eCalled *Baale Judah* in 2 Samuel 6:2   13:9 fCalled *Nachon* in 2 Samuel 6:6   13:11 gLiterally *Outburst Against Uzza*

CHAPTER 13

13:1–4 A unanimous decision is not always a right decision, and enthusiasm is not the best test of truth. Were David's motives mixed as he sought to bring the ark home? Was the king subtly promoting himself as well as glorifying the Lord (v. 3)? Perhaps.

13:8–12 One thing is sure: David did not pause to seek the Lord's direction in the venture. It was his habit to seek the will of God before he acted, but that time, he failed. Any Levite could have told him how to do the job!

The ark was God's throne (Ps. 99:1), and the throne of God does not depend on the hand of man for support or protection. Had the ark been where it belonged, on the shoulders of the Levites, Uzza would have lived. No matter how successful at the beginning, man's methods *without God* will ultimately fail. The time to find out how to do His work is before the job begins, not after the funeral.

¹³So David would not move the ark with him into the City of David, but took it aside into the house of Obed-Edom the Gittite. ¹⁴The ark of God remained with the family of Obed-Edom in his house three months. And the LORD blessed the house of Obed-Edom and all that he had.

14 Now Hiram king of Tyre sent messengers to David, and cedar trees, with masons and carpenters, to build him a house. ²*So David knew that the LORD had established him as king over Israel, for his kingdom was highly exalted for the sake of His people Israel.

³*Then David took more wives in Jerusalem, and David begot more sons and daughters. ⁴And these are the names of his children whom he had in Jerusalem: Shammua,^h Shobab, Nathan, Solomon, ⁵Ibhar, Elishua,ⁱ Elpelet,^j ⁶Nogah, Nepheg, Japhia, ⁷Elishama, Beeliada,^k and Eliphelet.

⁸Now when the Philistines heard that David had been anointed king over all Israel, all the Philistines went up to search for David. And David heard *of it* and went out against them. ⁹Then the Philistines went and made a raid on the Valley of Rephaim. ¹⁰*And David inquired of God, saying, "Shall I go up against the Philistines? Will You deliver them into my hand?"

The LORD said to him, "Go up, for I will deliver them into your hand."

¹¹So they went up to Baal Perazim, and David defeated them there. Then David said, "God has broken through my enemies by my hand like a breakthrough of water." Therefore they called the name of that place Baal Perazim.^l ¹²And when they left their gods there, David gave a commandment, and they were burned with fire.

¹³Then the Philistines once again made a raid on the valley. ¹⁴Therefore David inquired again of God, and God said to him, "You shall not go up after them; circle around them, and come upon them in front of the mulberry trees. ¹⁵And it shall be, when you hear a sound of marching in the tops of the mulberry trees, then you shall go out to battle, for God has gone out before you to strike the camp of the Philistines." ¹⁶So David did as God commanded him, and they drove back the army of the Philistines from Gibeon as far as Gezer. ¹⁷Then the fame of David went out into all lands, and the LORD brought the fear of him upon all nations.

15 David* built houses for himself in the City of David; and he prepared a place for the ark of God, and pitched a tent for it. ²Then David said, "No one may carry the ark of God but the Levites, for the LORD has chosen them to carry the ark of God and to minister before Him forever." ³And David gathered all Israel together at Jerusalem, to bring up the ark of the LORD to its place, which he had prepared for it. ⁴Then David assembled the children of Aaron and the Levites: ⁵of the sons of Kohath, Uriel the chief, and one hundred and twenty of his brethren; ⁶of the sons of Merari, Asaiah the chief, and two hundred and twenty of his brethren; ⁷of the sons of Gershom, Joel the chief, and one hundred and thirty of his brethren; ⁸of the sons of Elizaphan, Shemaiah the

---

CHAPTER 14

14:2 David had his disappointments, but he did not allow them to keep him from getting things done. It has been said that the only people who never make mistakes are the people who never make anything. To permit past blunders to keep us from fulfilling present duties is to make those blunders even worse.

14:3 As you seek to serve the Lord, you will discover that friends will help you (v. 1), the Lord will establish you (v. 2), and the enemy will fight you (vv. 8–17). Building and battling are normal experiences in the life of faith (Luke 14:25–33). Be like Nehemiah's workers on the wall, and have a tool in one hand and a ready weapon in the other (Neh. 4:17).

14:10–17 Twice David sought the mind of the Lord as he confronted his old enemies. Unlike Joshua at Ai, he did not assume that what worked once would work again (Josh. 7). Depending on past victories is a good way to guarantee future defeats. Ponder Judges 16:20–22.

CHAPTER 15

15:1–15 Do God's work biblically. David turned the work over to the Levites, and 870 of them united to bring the ark to Jerusalem. They had no problems because they did it God's way.

14:4 ^hSpelled *Shimea* in 3:5   14:5 ⁱSpelled *Elishama* in 3:6
^jSpelled *Eliphelet* in 3:6   14:7 ^kSpelled *Eliada* in 3:8
14:11 ^lLiterally *Master of Breakthroughs*

chief, and two hundred of his brethren; 9of the sons of Hebron, Eliel the chief, and eighty of his brethren; 10of the sons of Uzziel, Amminadab the chief, and one hundred and twelve of his brethren.

11And David called for Zadok and Abiathar the priests, and for the Levites: for Uriel, Asaiah, Joel, Shemaiah, Eliel, and Amminadab. 12He said to them, "You *are* the heads of the fathers' *houses* of the Levites; sanctify yourselves, you and your brethren, that you may bring up the ark of the LORD God of Israel to *the place* I have prepared for it. 13For because you *did* not *do it* the first *time,* the LORD our God broke out against us, because we did not consult Him about the proper order."

14So the priests and the Levites sanctified themselves to bring up the ark of the LORD God of Israel. 15And the children of the Levites bore the ark of God on their shoulders, by its poles, as Moses had commanded according to the word of the LORD.

16*Then David spoke to the leaders of the Levites to appoint their brethren *to be* the singers accompanied by instruments of music, stringed instruments, harps, and cymbals, by raising the voice with resounding joy. 17So the Levites appointed Heman the son of Joel; and of his brethren, Asaph the son of Berechiah; and of their brethren, the sons of Merari, Ethan the son of Kushaiah; 18and with them their brethren of the second *rank:* Zechariah, Ben,m Jaaziel, Shemiramoth, Jehiel, Unni, Eliab, Benaiah, Maaseiah, Mattithiah, Elipheleh, Mikneiah, Obed-Edom, and Jeiel, the gatekeepers; 19the singers, Heman, Asaph, and Ethan, *were* to sound the cymbals of bronze; 20Zechariah, Aziel, Shemiramoth, Jehiel, Unni, Eliab, Maaseiah, and Benaiah, with strings according to Alamoth; 21Mattithiah, Elipheleh, Mikneiah, Obed-Edom, Jeiel, and Azaziah, to direct with harps on the Sheminith; 22Chenaniah, leader of the Levites, was instructor *in charge of* the music, because he *was* skillful; 23Berechiah and Elkanah *were* doorkeepers for the ark; 24Shebaniah, Joshaphat, Nethanel, Amasai, Zechariah, Benaiah, and Eliezer, the priests, were to blow the trumpets before the ark of God; and Obed-Edom and Jehiah, doorkeepers for the ark.

25*So David, the elders of Israel, and the captains over thousands went to bring up the ark of the covenant of the LORD from the house of Obed-Edom with joy. 26And so it was, when God helped the Levites who bore the ark of the covenant of the LORD, that they offered seven bulls and seven rams. 27*David was clothed with a robe of fine linen, as were all the Levites who bore the ark, the singers, and Chenaniah the music master *with* the singers. David also wore a linen ephod. 28Thus all Israel brought up the ark of the covenant of the LORD with shouting and with the sound of the horn, with trumpets and with cymbals, making music with stringed instruments and harps.

29And it happened, *as* the ark of the covenant of the LORD came to the City of David, that Michal, Saul's daughter, looked through a window and saw King David whirling and playing music; and she despised him in her heart.

15:16–25 Do God's work joyfully. They served "the LORD with gladness" (Ps. 100:2). Singers and musicians joined their talents in praising the Lord joyfully (vv. 16, 24). Harps, horns, trumpets, and even cymbals accompanied the singers' hymns of thanksgiving and praise.

15:25, 26 Do God's work sacrificially. If they are to be acceptable to the Lord, our worship and service must come from the altar where a price has been paid. Cheap ministry is powerless ministry that cannot bless people or glorify the Lord.

15:27–29 Do God's work fervently. It was an enthusiastic procession with the Levites singing and playing instruments, the people shouting, and David leading them in praising the Lord. There are times when you should be silent before the Lord, but there are times when He wants to hear your praise. Vance Havner noted, "Too many church services start at eleven o'clock sharp and end at twelve o'clock dull."

15:18 mFollowing Masoretic Text and Vulgate; Septuagint omits *Ben.*

CHAPTER 16

16:1–3 Special times of praise and celebration are good to have, but you cannot live on these experiences. A satisfying walk with the Lord depends on daily worship of the Lord. That is why David assigned Asaph and the Levites their work in the ministry of worship "as every day's work required" (v. 37). Sacrifice and praise were parts of their daily service, as they should be in your life.

16:8–36 The main thing is to focus on the Lord, and David did just that in the special psalm he wrote. (For parallels, see Pss. 96; 105.) "The LORD" is named fourteen times as David reminds the people of God's works (vv. 8–13), God's words (vv. 14–22) and God's wonder (vv. 23–36)—His glory, greatness, and goodness. The excitement of the day would disappear, but the inspired song of praise would remain for all generations to use in worshiping God.

16 So* they brought the ark of God, and set it in the midst of the tabernacle that David had erected for it. Then they offered burnt offerings and peace offerings before God. ²And when David had finished offering the burnt offerings and the peace offerings, he blessed the people in the name of the LORD. ³Then he distributed to everyone of Israel, both man and woman, to everyone a loaf of bread, a piece *of meat,* and a cake of raisins.

⁴And he appointed some of the Levites to minister before the ark of the LORD, to commemorate, to thank, and to praise the LORD God of Israel: ⁵Asaph the chief, and next to him Zechariah, *then* Jeiel, Shemiramoth, Jehiel, Mattithiah, Eliab, Benaiah, and Obed-Edom: Jeiel with stringed instruments and harps, but Asaph made music with cymbals; ⁶Benaiah and Jahaziel the priests regularly *blew* the trumpets before the ark of the covenant of God.

⁷On that day David first delivered *this psalm* into the hand of Asaph and his brethren, to thank the LORD:

8 *Oh, give thanks to the LORD!
   Call upon His name;
   Make known His deeds among the peoples!
9 Sing to Him, sing psalms to Him;
   Talk of all His wondrous works!
10 Glory in His holy name;
   Let the hearts of those rejoice who seek the
       LORD!
11 Seek the LORD and His strength;
   Seek His face evermore!
12 Remember His marvelous works which He
       has done,
   His wonders, and the judgments of His
       mouth,
13 O seed of Israel His servant,
   You children of Jacob, His chosen ones!

14 He *is* the LORD our God;
   His judgments *are* in all the earth.
15 Remember His covenant forever,
   The word which He commanded, for a
       thousand generations,
16 *The covenant which* He made with
       Abraham,
   And His oath to Isaac,
17 And confirmed it to Jacob for a statute,
   To Israel *for* an everlasting covenant,
18 Saying, "To you I will give the land of
       Canaan
   As the allotment of your inheritance,"
19 When you were few in number,
   Indeed very few, and strangers in it.

20 When they went from one nation to another,
   And from *one* kingdom to another people,
21 He permitted no man to do them wrong;
   Yes, He rebuked kings for their sakes,
22 *Saying,* "Do not touch My anointed ones,
   And do My prophets no harm."ⁿ

23 Sing to the LORD, all the earth;
   Proclaim the good news of His salvation
       from day to day.
24 Declare His glory among the nations,
   His wonders among all peoples.

16:22 ⁿCompare verses 8–22 with Psalm 105:1–15

25 For the LORD *is* great and greatly to be praised;
He *is* also to be feared above all gods.
26 For all the gods of the peoples *are* idols,
But the LORD made the heavens.
27 Honor and majesty *are* before Him;
Strength and gladness are in His place.

28 Give to the LORD, O families of the peoples,
Give to the LORD glory and strength.
29 Give to the LORD the glory *due* His name;
Bring an offering, and come before Him.
Oh, worship the LORD in the beauty of holiness!
30 Tremble before Him, all the earth.
The world also is firmly established,
It shall not be moved.

31 Let the heavens rejoice, and let the earth be glad;
And let them say among the nations, "The LORD reigns."
32 Let the sea roar, and all its fullness;
Let the field rejoice, and all that *is* in it.
33 Then the trees of the woods shall rejoice before the LORD,
For He is coming to judge the earth.[o]

34 Oh, give thanks to the LORD, for *He is* good!
For His mercy *endures* forever.[p]
35 And say, "Save us, O God of our salvation;
Gather us together, and deliver us from the Gentiles,
To give thanks to Your holy name,
To triumph in Your praise."

36 Blessed *be* the LORD God of Israel
From everlasting to everlasting![q]

And all the people said, "Amen!" and praised the LORD.
37So he left Asaph and his brothers there before
the ark of the covenant of the LORD to minister
before the ark regularly, as every day's work required; 38and Obed-Edom with his sixty-eight
brethren, including Obed-Edom the son of Jeduthun, and Hosah, *to be* gatekeepers; 39and Zadok
the priest and his brethren the priests, before the
tabernacle of the LORD at the high place that *was*
at Gibeon, 40*to offer burnt offerings to the LORD
on the altar of burnt offering regularly morning
and evening, and *to do* according to all that is
written in the Law of the LORD which He commanded Israel; 41and with them Heman and Jeduthun and the rest who were chosen, who were
designated by name, to give thanks to the LORD,
because His mercy *endures* forever; 42and with
them Heman and Jeduthun, to sound aloud with
trumpets and cymbals and the musical instruments of God. Now the sons of Jeduthun *were*
gatekeepers.
43Then all the people departed, every man to
his house; and David returned to bless his house.

17 Now it came to pass, when David was dwelling in his house, that David said to Nathan the prophet, "See now, I dwell in a house

16:33 [o]Compare verses 23–33 with Psalm 96:1–13
16:34 [p]Compare verse 34 with Psalm 106:1 16:36 [q]Compare verses 35, 36 with Psalm 106:47, 48

16:40 But after you have worshiped, remember to witness to the lost (v. 23) and to do your part in getting the Gospel out to the nations of the world (vv. 24, 31). Archbishop William Temple pointed out the essential nature of worship: "For to worship is to quicken the conscience by the holiness of God, to feed the mind with the truth of God, to purge the imagination by the beauty of God, to open the heart to the love of God, to devote the will to the purpose of God."

CHAPTER 17

17:1–4 Nathan was too quick to encourage David in the noble enterprise of building a house for the Lord (Josh. 9:14). How did Nathan know that was God's will for David? But the prophet's ear was ever open to God's voice (Amos 3:7), and he received from God the words that he delivered to David the next day.

of cedar, but the ark of the covenant of the LORD *is* under tent curtains."

²Then Nathan said to David, "Do all that *is* in your heart, for God *is* with you."

³But it happened that night that the word of God came to Nathan, saying, ⁴"Go and tell My servant David, 'Thus says the LORD: "You shall not build Me a house to dwell in. ⁵For I have not dwelt in a house since the time that I brought up Israel, even to this day, but have gone from tent to tent, and from *one* tabernacle *to another.* ⁶Wherever I have moved about with all Israel, have I ever spoken a word to any of the judges of Israel, whom I commanded to shepherd My people, saying, 'Why have you not built Me a house of cedar?' " ' ⁷*Now therefore, thus shall you say to My servant David, 'Thus says the LORD of hosts: "I took you from the sheepfold, from following the sheep, to be ruler over My people Israel. ⁸And I have been with you wherever you have gone, and have cut off all your enemies from before you, and have made you a name like the name of the great men who *are* on the earth. ⁹Moreover I will appoint a place for My people Israel, and will plant them, that they may dwell in a place of their own and move no more; nor shall the sons of wickedness oppress them anymore, as previously, ¹⁰since the time that I commanded judges *to be* over My people Israel. Also I will subdue all your enemies. Furthermore I tell you that the LORD will build you a house.ʳ ¹¹And it shall be, when your days are fulfilled, when you must go *to be* with your fathers, that I will set up your seed after you, who will be of your sons; and I will establish his kingdom. ¹²He shall build Me a house, and I will establish his throne forever. ¹³I will be his Father, and he shall be My son; and I will not take My mercy away from him, as I took *it* from *him* who was before you. ¹⁴And I will establish him in My house and in My kingdom forever; and his throne shall be established forever." ' "

¹⁵According to all these words and according to all this vision, so Nathan spoke to David.

¹⁶Then King David went in and sat before the LORD; and he said: "Who *am* I, O LORD God? And what *is* my house, that You have brought me this far? ¹⁷And *yet* this was a small thing in Your sight, O God; and You have *also* spoken of Your servant's house for a great while to come, and have regarded me according to the rank of a man of high degree, O LORD God. ¹⁸What more can David *say* to You for the honor of Your servant? For You know Your servant. ¹⁹O LORD, for Your servant's sake, and according to Your own heart, You have done all this greatness, in making known all these great things. ²⁰O LORD, *there is* none like You, nor *is there any* God besides You, according to all that we have heard with our ears. ²¹And who *is* like Your people Israel, the one nation on the earth whom God went to redeem for Himself *as* a people—to make for Yourself a name by great and awesome deeds, by driving out nations from before Your people whom You redeemed from Egypt? ²²For You have made Your people Israel Your very own people forever; and You, LORD, have become their God.

²³"And now, O LORD, the word which You have spoken concerning Your servant and concerning his house, *let it* be established forever, and do

17:7 Ten times in this chapter David is called "servant." The servant does not command the master; the master commands the servant. And what a wonderful Master the Lord is! Whether we look at the past ("I took you" [v. 7]; "I have been with you" [v. 8]), or the future (God says "I will" ten times), we see the grace and goodness of the Lord. How David was humbled by the goodness of the Lord!

17:23 It is one thing to *know* God's promises and quite something else to *claim them by faith.* Like a little child, David went in and "sat before the LORD." He thanked God for the mercies He had promised, and then he said, "Lord, do it!" Faith turns God's promises into reality, but before praying, take time to praise Him.

17:10 ʳThat is, a royal dynasty

as You have said. 24So let it be established, that
Your name may be magnified forever, saying,
'The LORD of hosts, the God of Israel, is Israel's
God.' And let the house of Your servant David
be established before You. 25For You, O my God,
have revealed to Your servant that You will build
him a house. Therefore Your servant has found
it in his heart to pray before You. 26And now,
LORD, You are God, and have promised this goodness to Your servant. 27Now You have been
pleased to bless the house of Your servant, that
it may continue before You forever; for You have
blessed it, O LORD, and it shall be blessed forever."

18 After* this it came to pass that David attacked the Philistines, subdued them, and
took Gath and its towns from the hand of the Philistines. 2Then he defeated Moab, and the Moabites
became David's servants, and brought tribute.
3And David defeated Hadadezerˢ king of Zobah
as far as Hamath, as he went to establish his
power by the River Euphrates. 4David took from
him one thousand chariots, seven thousandᵗ
horsemen, and twenty thousand foot soldiers.
Also David hamstrung all the chariot horses, except that he spared enough of them for one hundred chariots.
5When the Syrians of Damascus came to help
Hadadezer king of Zobah, David killed twenty-
two thousand of the Syrians. 6Then David put garrisons in Syria of Damascus; and the Syrians became David's servants, and brought tribute. So
the LORD preserved David wherever he went.
7*And David took the shields of gold that were on
the servants of Hadadezer, and brought them to
Jerusalem. 8Also from Tibhathᵘ and from Chun,
cities of Hadadezer, David brought a large
amount of bronze, with which Solomon made the
bronze Sea, the pillars, and the articles of bronze.
9Now when Touᵛ king of Hamath heard that
David had defeated all the army of Hadadezer
king of Zobah, 10he sent Hadoramʷ his son to
King David, to greet him and bless him, because
he had fought against Hadadezer and defeated
him (for Hadadezer had been at war with Tou);
and Hadoram brought with him all kinds of articles of gold, silver, and bronze. 11*King David also
dedicated these to the LORD, along with the silver
and gold that he had brought from all these nations—from Edom, from Moab, from the people
of Ammon, from the Philistines, and from
Amalek.
12Moreover Abishai the son of Zeruiah killed
eighteen thousand Edomitesˣ in the Valley of Salt.
13He also put garrisons in Edom, and all the

18:3 ˢHebrew Hadarezer, and so throughout chapters 18 and
19   18:4 ᵗOr seven hundred (compare 2 Samuel 8:4)
18:8 ᵘSpelled Betah in 2 Samuel 8:8   18:9 ᵛSpelled Toi in
2 Samuel 8:9, 10   18:10 ʷSpelled Joram in 2 Samuel 8:10
18:12 ˣOr Syrians (compare 2 Samuel 8:13)

CHAPTER 18

18:1ff David defeated four great enemies
because the Lord was with him. But David
saw them as more than wars: they were
opportunities to claim more territory for the
Lord and gather more wealth for His
treasury. He looked beyond the battle to the
temple.

18:7 David reasoned, "If I cannot build the
Lord's temple, at least I can help my son
do it." One generation's victories can help
build the next generation's temples. David
dedicated to the Lord the spoils he won and
the gifts and tribute he received. (See
1 Chron. 28.)

18:11 Each enemy can give you something
to help build God's work on earth.
Temptation is the opportunity to get the
treasure without first winning the battle. Faith
overcomes the enemy and claims the spoils
for the Lord.

Benaiah—In the Old Testament record, the name Benaiah belongs to at least a dozen men, but
the most fascinating of all is the man mentioned in 1 Chronicles 18:17. He was born a priest
(1 Chron. 27:5) but became a soldier. He began his military career as one of David's mighty men
(2 Sam. 23:20–23) and was put over David's personal bodyguard. Eventually, Benaiah became head
of Solomon's army (1 Kings 2:35). He could have enjoyed a relatively safe and easy life as a priest,
but he chose the dangerous life of a soldier to serve his king. He "killed a lion in the midst of a pit
on a snowy day" (2 Sam. 23:20). Frank Boreham wrote, "He met the worst of enemies, in the worst
of places, under the worst of conditions; and he won." What a man!

CHAPTER 19

19:1–4 If you fear a person and consider him or her your enemy, nothing that person does will please you. Instead of taking his or her words and actions at face value, you get suspicious. Malice poisons us to the point that our ears hear nothing good and our eyes see nothing good, no matter what that person may say or do. (See 1 Pet. 2:1–3.)

19:6 Hanun's actions were a public offense against David, so he had to act, especially when he saw the Ammonites getting ready for war. But what should Christians do when they are handed evil in return for good?

19:8 Consider these verses when deciding what action to take: "Love . . . does not seek its own, is not provoked, thinks no evil" (1 Cor. 13:5); "In return for my love they are my accusers, but I give myself to prayer" (Ps. 109:4); "Father, forgive them, for they do not know what they do" (Luke 23:34). Ponder Matthew 5:10–12, 43–48, and then ask God to help you practice it. Francis Bacon commented on the situation: "In taking revenge, a man is but even with his enemy; but in passing it over, he is superior."

Edomites became David's servants. And the LORD preserved David wherever he went. ¹⁴So David reigned over all Israel, and administered judgment and justice to all his people. ¹⁵Joab the son of Zeruiah *was* over the army; Jehoshaphat the son of Ahilud *was* recorder; ¹⁶Zadok the son of Ahitub and Abimelech the son of Abiathar *were* the priests; Shavshaʸ *was* the scribe; ¹⁷Benaiah the son of Jehoiada *was* over the Cherethites and the Pelethites; and David's sons *were* chief ministers at the king's side.

19 It* happened after this that Nahash the king of the people of Ammon died, and his son reigned in his place. ²Then David said, "I will show kindness to Hanun the son of Nahash, because his father showed kindness to me." So David sent messengers to comfort him concerning his father. And David's servants came to Hanun in the land of the people of Ammon to comfort him.

³And the princes of the people of Ammon said to Hanun, "Do you think that David really honors your father because he has sent comforters to you? Did his servants not come to you to search and to overthrow and to spy out the land?"

⁴Therefore Hanun took David's servants, shaved them, and cut off their garments in the middle, at their buttocks, and sent them away. ⁵Then *some* went and told David about the men; and he sent to meet them, because the men were greatly ashamed. And the king said, "Wait at Jericho until your beards have grown, and *then* return."

⁶*When the people of Ammon saw that they had made themselves repulsive to David, Hanun and the people of Ammon sent a thousand talents of silver to hire for themselves chariots and horsemen from Mesopotamia,ᶻ from Syrian Maacah, and from Zobah.ᵃ ⁷So they hired for themselves thirty-two thousand chariots, with the king of Maacah and his people, who came and encamped before Medeba. Also the people of Ammon gathered together from their cities, and came to battle.

⁸*Now when David heard *of it,* he sent Joab and all the army of the mighty men. ⁹Then the people of Ammon came out and put themselves in battle array before the gate of the city, and the kings who had come *were* by themselves in the field.

¹⁰When Joab saw that the battle line was against him before and behind, he chose some of Israel's best, and put *them* in battle array against the Syrians. ¹¹And the rest of the people he put under the command of Abishai his brother, and they set *themselves* in battle array against the people of Ammon. ¹²Then he said, "If the Syrians are too strong for me, then you shall help me; but if the people of Ammon are too strong for you, then I will help you. ¹³Be of good courage, and let us be strong for our people and for the cities of our God. And may the LORD do *what is* good in His sight."

¹⁴So Joab and the people who *were* with him drew near for the battle against the Syrians, and they fled before him. ¹⁵When the people of Ammon saw that the Syrians were fleeing, they also

18:16 ʸSpelled *Seraiah* in 2 Samuel 8:17   19:6 ᶻHebrew *Aram Naharaim* ᵃSpelled *Zoba* in 2 Samuel 10:6

fled before Abishai his brother, and entered the city. So Joab went to Jerusalem.

16Now when the Syrians saw that they had been defeated by Israel, they sent messengers and brought the Syrians who were beyond the River,b and Shophachc the commander of Hadadezer's army *went* before them. 17When it was told David, he gathered all Israel, crossed over the Jordan and came upon them, and set up in battle array against them. So when David had set up in *battle* array against the Syrians, they fought with him. 18Then the Syrians fled before Israel; and David killed seven thousandd charioteers and forty thousand foot soldierse of the Syrians, and killed Shophach the commander of the army. 19And when the servants of Hadadezer saw that they were defeated by Israel, they made peace with David and became his servants. So the Syrians were not willing to help the people of Ammon anymore.

20 It* happened in the spring of the year, at the time kings go out *to battle*, that Joab led out the armed forces and ravaged the country of the people of Ammon, and came and besieged Rabbah. But David stayed at Jerusalem. And Joab defeated Rabbah and overthrew it. 2*Then David took their king's crown from his head, and found it to weigh a talent of gold, and *there were* precious stones in it. And it was set on David's head. Also he brought out the spoil of the city in great abundance. 3And he brought out the people who *were* in it, and put *them* to workf with saws, with iron picks, and with axes. So David did to all the cities of the people of Ammon. Then David and all the people returned *to* Jerusalem.

4*Now it happened afterward that war broke out at Gezer with the Philistines, at which time Sibbechai the Hushathite killed Sippai,g *who was one* of the sons of the giant. And they were subdued.

5Again there was war with the Philistines, and Elhanan the son of Jairh killed Lahmi the brother of Goliath the Gittite, the shaft of whose spear *was* like a weaver's beam.

6Yet again there was war at Gath, where there was a man of *great* stature, with twenty-four fingers and toes, six *on each hand* and six *on each foot*; and he also was born to the giant. 7So when he defied Israel, Jonathan the son of Shimea,i David's brother, killed him.

8These were born to the giant in Gath, and they fell by the hand of David and by the hand of his servants.

21 Now* Satan stood up against Israel, and moved David to number Israel. 2So David said to Joab and to the leaders of the people, "Go, number Israel from Beersheba to Dan, and bring the number of them to me that I may know *it*." 3And Joab answered, "May the LORD make His people a hundred times more than they are. But, my lord the king, *are* they not all my lord's servants? Why then does my lord require this thing? Why should he be a cause of guilt in Israel?"

CHAPTER 20

20:1ff Not a word is offered here about David's tarrying in Jerusalem and committing adultery with the wife of Uriah, one of his mighty men. But the story had already been written in 2 Samuel, and there was no need to repeat it. However, the writer gave an account of David's sin of numbering the people (chap. 21). Sins of the spirit can be more insidious than sins of the flesh (2 Cor. 7:1). You may be tempted more often by pride than by the lusts of the flesh.

20:2 Joab and the army won the war, but David came to the battlefield in time to direct the final victory and then claim the crown. It was a heavy one: seventy-five pounds of gold! But all crowns are heavy, for it is not an easy thing to be a leader.

20:4 Giants have a way of multiplying! David had killed Goliath, but other giants remained; and God had His servants ready to defeat them. We remember David and Goliath and tend to forget these other heroes, but God remembers them.

CHAPTER 21

21:1-6 Pride: David and Joab. Satan attacks leaders and it behooves us to pray for them. He appealed to David's pride by encouraging him to find out the size of his kingdom. David was stubborn as well as proud, and his attitude got Israel into real trouble.

19:16 bThat is, the Euphrates cSpelled *Shobach* in 2 Samuel 10:16   19:18 dOr *seven hundred* (compare 2 Samuel 10:18) eOr *horsemen* (compare 2 Samuel 10:18)   20:3 fSeptuagint reads *cut them.*   20:4 gSpelled *Saph* in 2 Samuel 21:18 20:5 hSpelled *Jaare-Oregim* in 2 Samuel 21:19   20:7 iSpelled *Shimeah* in 2 Samuel 21:21 and *Shammah* in 1 Samuel 16:9

4Nevertheless the king's word prevailed against Joab. Therefore Joab departed and went throughout all Israel and came to Jerusalem. 5Then Joab gave the sum of the number of the people to David. All Israel *had* one million one hundred thousand men who drew the sword, and Judah *had* four hundred and seventy thousand men who drew the sword. 6But he did not count Levi and Benjamin among them, for the king's word was abominable to Joab.

7*And God was displeased with this thing; therefore He struck Israel. 8So David said to God, "I have sinned greatly, because I have done this thing; but now, I pray, take away the iniquity of Your servant, for I have done very foolishly."

9Then the LORD spoke to Gad, David's seer, saying, 10"Go and tell David, saying, 'Thus says the LORD: "I offer you three *things;* choose one of them for yourself, that I may do *it* to you." ' "

11So Gad came to David and said to him, "Thus says the LORD: 'Choose for yourself, 12either three*j* years of famine, or three months to be defeated by your foes with the sword of your enemies overtaking *you,* or else for three days the sword of the LORD—the plague in the land, with the angel*k* of the LORD destroying throughout all the territory of Israel.' Now consider what answer I should take back to Him who sent me."

13And David said to Gad, "I am in great distress. Please let me fall into the hand of the LORD, for His mercies *are* very great; but do not let me fall into the hand of man."

14So the LORD sent a plague upon Israel, and seventy thousand men of Israel fell. 15And God sent an angel to Jerusalem to destroy it. As he*l* was destroying, the LORD looked and relented of the disaster, and said to the angel who was destroying, "It is enough; now restrain your*m* hand." And the angel of the LORD stood by the threshing floor of Ornan*n* the Jebusite.

16Then David lifted his eyes and saw the angel of the LORD standing between earth and heaven, having in his hand a drawn sword stretched out over Jerusalem. So David and the elders, clothed in sackcloth, fell on their faces. 17And David said to God, "Was it not I who commanded the people to be numbered? I am the one who has sinned and done evil indeed; but these sheep, what have they done? Let Your hand, I pray, O LORD my God, be against me and my father's house, but not against Your people that they should be plagued."

18*Therefore, the angel of the LORD commanded Gad to say to David that David should go and erect an altar to the LORD on the threshing floor of Ornan the Jebusite. 19So David went up at the word of Gad, which he had spoken in the name of the LORD. 20Now Ornan turned and saw the angel; and his four sons *who were* with him hid themselves, but Ornan continued threshing wheat. 21So David came to Ornan, and Ornan looked and saw David. And he went out from the threshing floor, and bowed before David with *his* face to the ground. 22Then David said to Ornan, "Grant me the place of *this* threshing floor, that I may build an altar on it to the LORD. You shall

21:7–17 *Humility: David and the Lord.* When David realized his sins, he confessed to the Lord and was forgiven, but he still had to bear the consequences (Gal. 6:7–8). Dressed in sackcloth, David publicly begged God to stop the plague. What a picture of humility!

21:18–20 *Obedience: David and Ornan.* In the hour of penitence and prayer, we will hear a word from God. Gad brought that word to David. David could have claimed the property and sacrifices, but the Lord would not have been pleased. David said "I will not take what is yours for the LORD, nor offer burnt offerings with that which costs me nothing" (v. 24). Do you look for the easy way out when sin catches up with you? Our Savior did not have it easy when He paid for our sins on the cross.

21:12 *j*Or *seven* (compare 2 Samuel 24:13) *k*Or *Angel,* and so elsewhere in this chapter   21:15 *l*Or *He* *m*Or *Your* *n*Spelled *Araunah* in 2 Samuel 24:16

grant it to me at the full price, that the plague may be withdrawn from the people."

23But Ornan said to David, "Take *it* to yourself, and let my lord the king do *what is* good in his eyes. Look, I *also* give *you* the oxen for burnt offerings, the threshing implements for wood, and the wheat for the grain offering; I give *it* all."

24Then King David said to Ornan, "No, but I will surely buy *it* for the full price, for I will not take what is yours for the LORD, nor offer burnt offerings with *that which* costs *me* nothing." 25So David gave Ornan six hundred shekels of gold by weight for the place. 26And David built there an altar to the LORD, and offered burnt offerings and peace offerings, and called on the LORD; and He answered him from heaven by fire on the altar of burnt offering.

27So the LORD commanded the angel, and he returned his sword to its sheath.

28At that time, when David saw that the LORD had answered him on the threshing floor of Ornan the Jebusite, he sacrificed there. 29For the tabernacle of the LORD and the altar of the burnt offering, which Moses had made in the wilderness, *were* at that time at the high place in Gibeon. 30But David could not go before it to inquire of God, for he was afraid of the sword of the angel of the LORD.

22 Then David said, "This *is* the house of the LORD God, and this *is* the altar of burnt offering for Israel." 2So David commanded to gather the aliens who *were* in the land of Israel; and he appointed masons to cut hewn stones to build the house of God. 3And David prepared iron in abundance for the nails of the doors of the gates and for the joints, and bronze in abundance beyond measure, 4and cedar trees in abundance; for the Sidonians and those from Tyre brought much cedar wood to David.

5*Now David said, "Solomon my son *is* young and inexperienced, and the house to be built for the LORD *must be* exceedingly magnificent, famous and glorious throughout all countries. I will now make preparation for it." So David made abundant preparations before his death.

6Then he called for his son Solomon, and charged him to build a house for the LORD God of Israel. 7And David said to Solomon: "My son, as for me, it was in my mind to build a house to the name of the LORD my God; 8but the word of the LORD came to me, saying, 'You have shed much blood and have made great wars; you shall not build a house for My name, because you have shed much blood on the earth in My sight. 9Behold, a son shall be born to you, who shall be a man of rest; and I will give him rest from all his enemies all around. His name shall be Solomon,o for I will give peace and quietness to Israel in his days. 10*He shall build a house for My name, and he shall be My son, and I *will be* his Father; and I will establish the throne of his kingdom over Israel forever.' 11*Now, my son, may the LORD be with you; and may you prosper, and build the house of the LORD your God, as He has said to you. 12Only may the LORD give you wisdom and understanding, and give you charge concerning Israel, that you may keep the law of the LORD your God. 13Then you will prosper, if you take care to

22:9 oLiterally *Peaceful*

CHAPTER 22

22:5 Preparation. So David made "abundant preparations before his death." He was making preparations not for dying but for building the temple. (The idea of *preparation* is found five times in this chapter.) For years, David had been preparing for this great project and gathering materials (vv. 3–4). He had risked his life in battle and claimed the spoils for the Lord. His reputation was that of a soldier, but his heart was that of a builder.

22:10 Promise. David claimed God's promise and used it to encourage his son, a young man with little practical experience. The work we do is for God, and it must be our best.

22:11–13 Prosperity. You cannot escape the basic principle stated in Joshua 1:8: if we obey God's Word, He will prosper our work. David had collected over forty million tons of gold and silver, but all that wealth was of no value apart from the blessing of God.

fulfill the statutes and judgments with which the LORD charged Moses concerning Israel. Be strong and of good courage; do not fear nor be dismayed. [14]Indeed I have taken much trouble to prepare for the house of the LORD one hundred thousand talents of gold and one million talents of silver, and bronze and iron beyond measure, for it is so abundant. I have prepared timber and stone also, and you may add to them. [15]Moreover *there are* workmen with you in abundance: woodsmen and stonecutters, and all types of skillful men for every kind of work. [16]Of gold and silver and bronze and iron *there is* no limit. Arise and begin working, and the LORD be with you."

[17]*David also commanded all the leaders of Israel to help Solomon his son, *saying,* [18]"*Is not the LORD your God with you? And has He *not* given you rest on every side? For He has given the inhabitants of the land into my hand, and the land is subdued before the LORD and before His people. [19]Now set your heart and your soul to seek the LORD your God. Therefore arise and build the sanctuary of the LORD God, to bring the ark of the covenant of the LORD and the holy articles of God into the house that is to be built for the name of the LORD."

22:17–19 Partners. We cannot do God's work alone; we need helpers. Leaders, stonemasons, timber cutters—all were a part of the work, and each worker was important.

CHAPTERS 23—27

23:1–32 A beautiful and costly temple is a waste of money unless ministry is going on for the good of God's people and the glory of God. So, before he died, David organized the temple workers and put them under proper leadership: "Let all things be done decently and in order" (1 Cor. 14:40).

23 So* when David was old and full of days, he made his son Solomon king over Israel. [2]And he gathered together all the leaders of Israel, with the priests and the Levites. [3]Now the Levites were numbered from the age of thirty years and above; and the number of individual males was thirty-eight thousand. [4]Of these, twenty-four thousand *were* to look after the work of the house of the LORD, six thousand *were* officers and judges, [5]four thousand *were* gatekeepers, and four thousand praised the LORD with *musical* instruments, "which I made," *said David,* "for giving praise."

[6]Also David separated them into divisions among the sons of Levi: Gershon, Kohath, and Merari.

[7]Of the Gershonites: Laadan[p] and Shimei. [8]The sons of Laadan: the first Jehiel, then Zetham and Joel—three *in all.* [9]The sons of Shimei: Shelomith, Haziel, and Haran—three *in all.* These were the heads of the fathers' *houses* of Laadan. [10]And the sons of Shimei: Jahath, Zina,[q] Jeush, and Beriah. These *were* the four sons of Shimei. [11]Jahath was the first and Zizah the second. But Jeush and Beriah did not have many sons; therefore they were assigned as one father's house.

[12]The sons of Kohath: Amram, Izhar, Hebron, and Uzziel—four *in all.* [13]The sons of Amram: Aaron and Moses; and Aaron was set apart, he and his sons forever, that he should sanctify the most holy things, to burn incense before the LORD, to minister to Him, and to give the blessing in His name forever. [14]Now the sons of Moses the man of God were reckoned to the tribe of Levi. [15]The sons of Moses *were* Gershon[r] and Eliezer. [16]Of the sons of Gershon, Shebuel[s] *was* the first. [17]Of the descendants of Eliezer, Rehabiah was the first. And Eliezer had no other sons, but the sons of Rehabiah were very many. [18]Of the sons of Izhar, Shelomith *was* the first. [19]Of the sons of

---

23:7 [p]Spelled *Libni* in Exodus 6:17   23:10 [q]Septuagint and Vulgate read *Zizah* (compare verse 11).   23:15 [r]Hebrew *Gershom* (compare 6:16)   23:16 [s]Spelled *Shubael* in 24:20

Hebron, Jeriah *was* the first, Amariah the second, Jahaziel the third, and Jekameam the fourth. 20Of the sons of Uzziel, Michah *was* the first and Jesshiah the second.

21The sons of Merari *were* Mahli and Mushi. The sons of Mahli *were* Eleazar and Kish. 22And Eleazar died, and had no sons, but only daughters; and their brethren, the sons of Kish, took them *as wives.* 23The sons of Mushi *were* Mahli, Eder, and Jeremoth—three *in all.*

24These *were* the sons of Levi by their fathers' houses—the heads of the fathers' *houses* as they were counted individually by the number of their names, who did the work for the service of the house of the LORD, from the age of twenty years and above.

25For David said, "The LORD God of Israel has given rest to His people, that they may dwell in Jerusalem forever"; 26and also to the Levites, "They shall no longer carry the tabernacle, or any of the articles for its service." 27For by the last words of David the Levites *were* numbered from twenty years old and above; 28because their duty *was* to help the sons of Aaron in the service of the house of the LORD, in the courts and in the chambers, in the purifying of all holy things and the work of the service of the house of God, 29both with the showbread and the fine flour for the grain offering, with the unleavened cakes and *what is baked in* the pan, with what is mixed and with all kinds of measures and sizes; 30to stand every morning to thank and praise the LORD, and likewise at evening; 31and at every presentation of a burnt offering to the LORD on the Sabbaths and on the New Moons and on the set feasts, by number according to the ordinance governing them, regularly before the LORD; 32and that they should attend to the needs of the tabernacle of meeting, the needs of the holy *place,* and the needs of the sons of Aaron their brethren in the work of the house of the LORD.

24 Now* *these are* the divisions of the sons of Aaron. The sons of Aaron *were* Nadab, Abihu, Eleazar, and Ithamar. 2And Nadab and Abihu died before their father, and had no children; therefore Eleazar and Ithamar ministered as priests. 3Then David with Zadok of the sons of Eleazar, and Ahimelech of the sons of Ithamar, divided them according to the schedule of their service.

4There were more leaders found of the sons of Eleazar than of the sons of Ithamar, and *thus* they were divided. Among the sons of Eleazar *were* sixteen heads of *their* fathers' houses, and eight heads of their fathers' houses among the sons of Ithamar. 5Thus they were divided by lot, one group as another, for there were officials of the sanctuary and officials *of the house* of God, from the sons of Eleazar and from the sons of Ithamar. 6And the scribe, Shemaiah the son of Nethanel, *one of* the Levites, wrote them down before the king, the leaders, Zadok the priest, Ahimelech the son of Abiathar, and the heads of the fathers' *houses* of the priests and Levites, one father's house taken for Eleazar and *one* for Ithamar.

7Now the first lot fell to Jehoiarib, the second to Jedaiah, 8the third to Harim, the fourth to Seorim, 9the fifth to Malchijah, the sixth to Mijamin, 10the seventh to Hakkoz, the eighth to Abijah, 11the ninth to Jeshua, the tenth to Shecaniah, 12the eleventh to Eliashib, the twelfth to Jakim,

24:1–31 The work of the Lord called for dedicated service from many kinds of people: priests, Levites, musicians, treasurers, gatekeepers, soldiers, and state officers. Each of us has a calling from the Lord and we must be faithful to take our place and do our job. We are helping to build the church, and we must give God our best (Matt. 16:18; Eph. 2:19–22).

13the thirteenth to Huppah, the fourteenth to Jeshebeab, 14the fifteenth to Bilgah, the sixteenth to Immer, 15the seventeenth to Hezir, the eighteenth to Happizzez,*t* 16the nineteenth to Pethahiah, the twentieth to Jehezekel,*u* 17the twenty-first to Jachin, the twenty-second to Gamul, 18the twenty-third to Delaiah, the twenty-fourth to Maaziah.

19This *was* the schedule of their service for coming into the house of the LORD according to their ordinance by the hand of Aaron their father, as the LORD God of Israel had commanded him.

20And the rest of the sons of Levi: of the sons of Amram, Shubael;*v* of the sons of Shubael, Jehdeiah. 21Concerning Rehabiah, of the sons of Rehabiah, the first *was* Isshiah. 22Of the Izharites, Shelomoth;*w* of the sons of Shelomoth, Jahath. 23Of the sons *of Hebron,x* Jeriah *was the first,y* Amariah the second, Jahaziel the third, *and* Jekameam the fourth. 24Of the sons of Uzziel, Michah; of the sons of Michah, Shamir. 25The brother of Michah, Isshiah; of the sons of Isshiah, Zechariah. 26The sons of Merari *were* Mahli and Mushi; the son of Jaaziah, Beno. 27The sons of Merari by Jaaziah *were* Beno, Shoham, Zaccur, and Ibri. 28Of Mahli: Eleazar, who had no sons. 29Of Kish: the son of Kish, Jerahmeel.

30Also the sons of Mushi *were* Mahli, Eder, and Jerimoth. These *were* the sons of the Levites according to their fathers' houses.

31These also cast lots just as their brothers the sons of Aaron did, in the presence of King David, Zadok, Ahimelech, and the heads of the fathers' *houses* of the priests and Levites. The chief fathers *did* just as their younger brethren.

25:1–7 Being a musician himself, David was no doubt especially concerned that the music in the temple be the finest available. God gave him people who were skillful and trained (25:7), but their task was not to magnify their talents: they were to glorify their Lord (25:3). Do you open and close each day with praise to the Lord (23:30)?

25 Moreover* David and the captains of the army separated for the service *some* of the sons of Asaph, of Heman, and of Jeduthun, who *should* prophesy with harps, stringed instruments, and cymbals. And the number of the skilled men performing their service was: 2Of the sons of Asaph: Zaccur, Joseph, Nethaniah, and Asharelah;*z* the sons of Asaph *were* under the direction of Asaph, who prophesied according to the order of the king. 3Of Jeduthun, the sons of Jeduthun: Gedaliah, Zeri,*a* Jeshaiah, Shimei, Hashabiah, and Mattithiah, six,*b* under the direction of their father Jeduthun, who prophesied with a harp to give thanks and to praise the LORD. 4Of Heman, the sons of Heman: Bukkiah, Mattaniah, Uzziel,*c* Shebuel,*d* Jerimoth,*e* Hananiah, Hanani, Eliathah, Giddalti, Romamti-Ezer, Joshbekashah, Mallothi, Hothir, *and* Mahazioth. 5All these *were* the sons of Heman the king's seer in the words of God, to exalt his horn.*f* For God gave Heman fourteen sons and three daughters.

24:15 *Septuagint and Vulgate read *Aphses*.
24:16 *Masoretic Text reads *Jehezkel*.   24:20 *Spelled *Shebuel* in 23:16   24:22 *Spelled *Shelomith* in 23:18
24:23 *Supplied from 23:19 (following some Hebrew manuscripts and Septuagint manuscripts) *Supplied from 23:19 (following some Hebrew manuscripts and Septuagint manuscripts)   25:2 *Spelled *Jesharelah* in verse 14
25:3 *Spelled *Jizri* in verse 11 *Shimei*, appearing in one Hebrew and several Septuagint manuscripts, completes the total of six sons (compare verse 17).   25:4 *Spelled *Azarel* in verse 18 *Spelled *Shubael* in verse 20 *Spelled *Jeremoth* in verse 22   25:5 *That is, to increase his power or influence

6All these *were* under the direction of their father for the music *in* the house of the LORD, with cymbals, stringed instruments, and harps, for the service of the house of God. Asaph, Jeduthun, and Heman *were* under the authority of the king. 7So the number of them, with their brethren who were instructed in the songs of the LORD, all who were skillful, *was* two hundred and eighty-eight.

8And they cast lots for their duty, the small as well as the great, the teacher with the student.

9Now the first lot for Asaph came out for Joseph; the second for Gedaliah, him with his brethren and sons, twelve; 10the third for Zaccur, his sons and his brethren, twelve; 11the fourth for Jizri,*g* his sons and his brethren, twelve; 12the fifth for Nethaniah, his sons and his brethren, twelve; 13the sixth for Bukkiah, his sons and his brethren, twelve; 14the seventh for Jesharelah,*h* his sons and his brethren, twelve; 15the eighth for Jeshaiah, his sons and his brethren, twelve; 16the ninth for Mattaniah, his sons and his brethren, twelve; 17the tenth for Shimei, his sons and his brethren, twelve; 18the eleventh for Azarel,*i* his sons and his brethren, twelve; 19the twelfth for Hashabiah, his sons and his brethren, twelve; 20the thirteenth for Shubael,*j* his sons and his brethren, twelve; 21the fourteenth for Mattithiah, his sons and his brethren, twelve; 22the fifteenth for Jeremoth,*k* his sons and his brethren, twelve; 23the sixteenth for Hananiah, his sons and his brethren, twelve; 24the seventeenth for Joshbekashah, his sons and his brethren, twelve; 25the eighteenth for Hanani, his sons and his brethren, twelve; 26the nineteenth for Mallothi, his sons and his brethren, twelve; 27the twentieth for Eliathah, his sons and his brethren, twelve; 28the twenty-first for Hothir, his sons and his brethren, twelve; 29the twenty-second for Giddalti, his sons and his brethren, twelve; 30the twenty-third for Mahazioth, his sons and his brethren, twelve; 31the twenty-fourth for Romamti-Ezer, his sons and his brethren, twelve.

26 Concerning the divisions of the gatekeepers: of the Korahites, Meshelemiah the son of Kore, of the sons of Asaph. 2And the sons of Meshelemiah *were* Zechariah the firstborn, Jediael the second, Zebadiah the third, Jathniel the fourth, 3Elam the fifth, Jehohanan the sixth, Eliehoenai the seventh.

4Moreover the sons of Obed-Edom *were* Shemaiah the firstborn, Jehozabad the second, Joah the third, Sacar the fourth, Nethanel the fifth, 5Ammiel the sixth, Issachar the seventh, Peulthai the eighth; for God blessed him.

6Also to Shemaiah his son were sons born who governed their fathers' houses, because they *were* men of great ability. 7The sons of Shemaiah *were* Othni, Rephael, Obed, and Elzabad, whose brothers Elihu and Semachiah *were* able men.

8All these *were* of the sons of Obed-Edom, they and their sons and their brethren, able men with strength for the work: sixty-two of Obed-Edom.

9And Meshelemiah had sons and brethren, eighteen able men.

10Also Hosah, of the children of Merari, had

25:11 *g*Spelled *Zeri* in verse 3   25:14 *h*Spelled *Asharelah* in verse 2   25:18 *i*Spelled *Uzziel* in verse 4   25:20 *j*Spelled *Shebuel* in verse 4   25:22 *k*Spelled *Jerimoth* in verse 4

sons: Shimri the first (for *though* he was not the firstborn, his father made him the first), [11]Hilkiah the second, Tebaliah the third, Zechariah the fourth; all the sons and brethren of Hosah *were* thirteen.

[12]Among these *were* the divisions of the gatekeepers, among the chief men, *having* duties just like their brethren, to serve in the house of the LORD. [13]And they cast lots for each gate, the small as well as the great, according to their father's house. [14]The lot for the East *Gate* fell to Shelemiah. Then they cast lots *for* his son Zechariah, a wise counselor, and his lot came out for the North Gate; [15]to Obed-Edom the South Gate, and to his sons the storehouse.[l] [16]To Shuppim and Hosah *the lot came out* for the West Gate, with the Shallecheth Gate on the ascending highway— watchman opposite watchman. [17]On the east were *six* Levites, on the north four each day, on the south four each day, and for the storehouse[m] two by two. [18]As for the Parbar[n] on the west, *there were* four on the highway *and* two at the Parbar. [19]These were the divisions of the gatekeepers among the sons of Korah and among the sons of Merari.

[20]Of the Levites, Ahijah *was* over the treasuries of the house of God and over the treasuries of the dedicated things. [21]The sons of Laadan, the descendants of the Gershonites of Laadan, heads of their fathers' *houses,* of Laadan the Gershonite: Jehieli. [22]The sons of Jehieli, Zetham and Joel his brother, *were* over the treasuries of the house of the LORD. [23]Of the Amramites, the Izharites, the Hebronites, and the Uzzielites: [24]Shebuel the son of Gershom, the son of Moses, *was* overseer of the treasuries. [25]And his brethren by Eliezer *were* Rehabiah his son, Jeshaiah his son, Joram his son, Zichri his son, and Shelomith his son.

[26]This Shelomith and his brethren *were* over all the treasuries of the dedicated things which King David and the heads of fathers' *houses,* the captains over thousands and hundreds, and the captains of the army, had dedicated. [27]Some of the spoils won in battles they dedicated to maintain the house of the LORD. [28]And all that Samuel the seer, Saul the son of Kish, Abner the son of Ner, and Joab the son of Zeruiah had dedicated, every dedicated *thing,* was under the hand of Shelomith and his brethren.

[29]Of the Izharites, Chenaniah and his sons *performed* duties as officials and judges over Israel outside Jerusalem.

[30]Of the Hebronites, Hashabiah and his brethren, one thousand seven hundred able men, had the oversight of Israel on the west side of the Jordan for all the business of the LORD, and in the service of the king. [31]Among the Hebronites, Jerijah *was* head of the Hebronites according to his genealogy of the fathers. In the fortieth year of the reign of David they were sought, and there were found among them capable men at Jazer of Gilead. [32]And his brethren *were* two thousand seven hundred able men, heads of fathers' *houses,* whom King David made officials over the Reubenites, the Gadites, and the half-tribe of Manasseh, for every matter pertaining to God and the affairs of the king.

26:15 [l]Hebrew *asuppim*   26:17 [m]Hebrew *asuppim*
26:18 [n]Probably a court or colonnade extending west of the temple

27 And the children of Israel, according to their number, the heads of fathers' *houses,* the captains of thousands and hundreds and their officers, served the king in every matter of the *military* divisions. *These divisions* came in and went out month by month throughout all the months of the year, each division *having* twenty-four thousand.

2Over the first division for the first month *was* Jashobeam the son of Zabdiel, and in his division *were* twenty-four thousand; 3*he was* of the children of Perez, and the chief of all the captains of the army for the first month. 4Over the division of the second month *was* Dodai⁰ an Ahohite, and of his division Mikloth also *was* the leader; in his division *were* twenty-four thousand. 5The third captain of the army for the third month *was* Benaiah, the son of Jehoiada the priest, who was chief; in his division *were* twenty-four thousand. 6This was the Benaiah *who was* mighty *among* the thirty, and was over the thirty; in his division *was* Ammizabad his son. 7The fourth *captain* for the fourth month *was* Asahel the brother of Joab, and Zebadiah his son after him; in his division *were* twenty-four thousand. 8The fifth *captain* for the fifth month *was* Shamhuth𝑝 the Izrahite; in his division were twenty-four thousand. 9The sixth *captain* for the sixth month *was* Ira the son of Ikkesh the Tekoite; in his division *were* twenty-four thousand. 10The seventh *captain* for the seventh month *was* Helez the Pelonite, of the children of Ephraim; in his division *were* twenty-four thousand. 11The eighth *captain* for the eighth month *was* Sibbechai the Hushathite, of the Zarhites; in his division *were* twenty-four thousand. 12The ninth *captain* for the ninth month *was* Abiezer the Anathothite, of the Benjamites; in his division *were* twenty-four thousand. 13The tenth *captain* for the tenth month *was* Maharai the Netophathite, of the Zarhites; in his division *were* twenty-four thousand. 14The eleventh *captain* for the eleventh month *was* Benaiah the Pirathonite, of the children of Ephraim; in his division *were* twenty-four thousand. 15The twelfth *captain* for the twelfth month *was* Heldai𝑞 the Netophathite, of Othniel; in his division *were* twenty-four thousand.

16Furthermore, over the tribes of Israel: the officer over the Reubenites *was* Eliezer the son of Zichri; over the Simeonites, Shephatiah the son of Maachah; 17*over* the Levites, Hashabiah the son of Kemuel; over the Aaronites, Zadok; 18*over* Judah, Elihu, *one* of David's brothers; *over* Issachar, Omri the son of Michael; 19*over* Zebulun, Ishmaiah the son of Obadiah; *over* Naphtali, Jerimoth the son of Azriel; 20*over* the children of Ephraim, Hoshea the son of Azaziah; *over* the half-tribe of Manasseh, Joel the son of Pedaiah; 21*over* the half-*tribe* of Manasseh in Gilead, Iddo the son of Zechariah; *over* Benjamin, Jaasiel the son of Abner; 22*over* Dan, Azarel the son of Jeroham. These *were* the leaders of the tribes of Israel.

23But David did not take the number of those twenty years old and under, because the LORD had said He would multiply Israel like the stars of the heavens. 24Joab the son of Zeruiah began a

---

27:4 ⁰Hebrew *Dodai,* usually spelled *Dodo* (compare 2 Samuel 23:9)   27:8 𝑝Spelled *Shammoth* in 11:27 and *Shammah* in 2 Samuel 23:11   27:15 𝑞Spelled *Heled* in 11:30 and *Heleb* in 2 Samuel 23:29

census, but he did not finish, for wrath came upon Israel because of this census; nor was the number recorded in the account of the chronicles of King David.

25And Azmaveth the son of Adiel *was* over the king's treasuries; and Jehonathan the son of Uzziah was over the storehouses in the field, in the cities, in the villages, and in the fortresses. 26Ezri the son of Chelub was over those who did the work of the field for tilling the ground. 27And Shimei the Ramathite *was* over the vineyards, and Zabdi the Shiphmite was over the produce of the vineyards for the supply of wine. 28Baal-Hanan the Gederite was over the olive trees and the sycamore trees that *were* in the lowlands, and Joash *was* over the store of oil. 29And Shitrai the Sharonite *was* over the herds that fed in Sharon, and Shaphat the son of Adlai was over the herds *that were* in the valleys. 30Obil the Ishmaelite *was* over the camels, Jehdeiah the Meronothite *was* over the donkeys, 31and Jaziz the Hagrite *was* over the flocks. All these *were* the officials over King David's property.

32Also Jehonathan, David's uncle, *was* a counselor, a wise man, and a scribe; and Jehiel the son of Hachmoni *was* with the king's sons. 33Ahithophel *was* the king's counselor, and Hushai the Archite *was* the king's companion. 34After Ahithophel *was* Jehoiada the son of Benaiah, then Abiathar. And the general of the king's army *was* Joab.

28 Now David assembled at Jerusalem all the leaders of Israel: the officers of the tribes and the captains of the divisions who served the king, the captains over thousands and captains over hundreds, and the stewards over all the substance and possessions of the king and of his sons, with the officials, the valiant men, and all the mighty men of valor. 2*Then King David rose to his feet and said, "Hear me, my brethren and my people: I *had* it in my heart to build a house of rest for the ark of the covenant of the LORD, and for the footstool of our God, and had made preparations to build it. 3But God said to me, 'You shall not build a house for My name, because you *have been* a man of war and have shed blood.' 4However the LORD God of Israel chose me above all the house of my father to be king over Israel forever, for He has chosen Judah *to be* the ruler. And of the house of Judah, the house of my father, and among the sons of my father, He was pleased with me to make *me* king over all Israel. 5And of all my sons (for the LORD has given me many sons) He has chosen my son Solomon to sit on the throne of the kingdom of the LORD over Israel. 6Now He said to me, 'It is your son Solomon *who* shall build My house and My courts; for I have chosen him *to be* My son, and I will be his Father. 7Moreover I will establish his kingdom forever, if he is steadfast to observe My commandments and My judgments, as it is this day.' 8Now therefore, in the sight of all Israel, the assembly of the LORD, and in the hearing of our God, be careful to seek out all the commandments of the LORD your God, that you may possess this good land, and leave *it* as an inheritance for your children after you forever.

9*"As for you, my son Solomon, know the God of your father, and serve Him with a loyal heart and with a willing mind; for the LORD searches all hearts and understands all the intent of the

CHAPTERS 28—29

28:2 *A disappointed heart.* Instead of complaining because he could not build God's house, David began preparing to help Solomon do the job. David served his own generation and generations to come because he unselfishly served the Lord. When disappointments come into your life, how do you handle them?

28:9 *A loyal heart.* Solomon had all that he needed for building the temple, but the most important thing only he could supply: a heart loyal to God. His motives had to be right, or his work would not be blessed.

thoughts. If you seek Him, He will be found by you; but if you forsake Him, He will cast you off forever. [10]Consider now, for the LORD has chosen you to build a house for the sanctuary; be strong, and do it."

[11]Then David gave his son Solomon the plans for the vestibule, its houses, its treasuries, its upper chambers, its inner chambers, and the place of the mercy seat; [12]and the plans for all that he had by the Spirit, of the courts of the house of the LORD, of all the chambers all around, of the treasuries of the house of God, and of the treasuries for the dedicated things; [13]also for the division of the priests and the Levites, for all the work of the service of the house of the LORD, and for all the articles of service in the house of the LORD. [14]*He gave* gold by weight for *things* of gold, for all articles used in every kind of service; also *silver* for all articles of silver by weight, for all articles used in every kind of service; [15]the weight for the lampstands of gold, and their lamps of gold, by weight for each lampstand and its lamps; for the lampstands of silver by weight, for the lampstand and its lamps, according to the use of each lampstand. [16]And by weight *he gave* gold for the tables of the showbread, for each table, and silver for the tables of silver; [17]also pure gold for the forks, the basins, the pitchers of pure gold, and the golden bowls—*he gave gold* by weight for every bowl; and for the silver bowls, *silver* by weight for every bowl; [18]and refined gold by weight for the altar of incense, and for the construction of the chariot, that is, the gold cherubim that spread *their wings* and overshadowed the ark of the covenant of the LORD. [19]"All *this*," *said David,* "the LORD made me understand in writing, by *His* hand upon me, all the works of these plans."

[20]And David said to his son Solomon, "Be strong and of good courage, and do *it*; do not fear nor be dismayed, for the LORD God—my God—*will be* with you. He will not leave you nor forsake you, until you have finished all the work for the service of the house of the LORD. [21]*Here are* the divisions of the priests and the Levites for all the service of the house of God; and every willing craftsman *will be* with you for all manner of workmanship, for every kind of service; also the leaders and all the people *will be* completely at your command."

29 Furthermore King David said to all the assembly: "My son Solomon, whom alone God has chosen, *is* young and inexperienced; and the work *is* great, because the temple[r] *is* not for man but for the LORD God. [2]Now for the house of my God I have prepared with all my might: gold for *things to be made of* gold, silver for *things of* silver, bronze for *things of* bronze, iron for *things of* iron, wood for *things of* wood, onyx stones, *stones* to be set, glistening stones of various colors, all kinds of precious stones, and marble slabs in abundance. [3]Moreover, because I have set my affection on the house of my God, I have given to the house of my God, over and above all that I have prepared for the holy house, my own special treasure of gold and silver: [4]three thousand talents of gold, of the gold of Ophir, and

29:1 [r]Literally *palace*

seven thousand talents of refined silver, to overlay the walls of the houses; [5]the gold for *things* of gold and the silver for *things of* silver, and for all kinds of work *to be done* by the hands of craftsmen. Who *then* is willing to consecrate himself this day to the LORD?"

[6]Then the leaders of the fathers' *houses,* leaders of the tribes of Israel, the captains of thousands and of hundreds, with the officers over the king's work, offered willingly. [7]They gave for the work of the house of God five thousand talents and ten thousand darics of gold, ten thousand talents of silver, eighteen thousand talents of bronze, and one hundred thousand talents of iron. [8]And whoever had *precious* stones gave *them* to the treasury of the house of the LORD, into the hand of Jehiel[s] the Gershonite. [9]*Then the people rejoiced, for they had offered willingly, because with a loyal heart they had offered willingly to the LORD; and King David also rejoiced greatly.

[10]Therefore David blessed the LORD before all the assembly; and David said:

> "Blessed are You, LORD God of Israel, our
>   Father, forever and ever.
> [11] Yours, O LORD, *is* the greatness,
>   The power and the glory,
>   The victory and the majesty;
>   For all *that is* in heaven and in earth *is*
>   *Yours;*
>   Yours *is* the kingdom, O LORD,
>   And You are exalted as head over all.
> [12] Both riches and honor *come* from You,
>   And You reign over all.
>   In Your hand *is* power and might;
>   In Your hand *it is* to make great
>   And to give strength to all.
>
> [13] "Now therefore, our God,
>   We thank You
>   And praise Your glorious name.
> [14] But who *am* I, and who *are* my people,
>   That we should be able to offer so willingly
>   as this?
>   For all things *come* from You,
>   And of Your own we have given You.
> [15] For we *are* aliens and pilgrims before You,
>   As *were* all our fathers;
>   Our days on earth *are* as a shadow,
>   And without hope.

[16]"O LORD our God, all this abundance that we have prepared to build You a house for Your holy name is from Your hand, and *is* all Your own. [17]*I know also, my God, that You test the heart and have pleasure in uprightness. As for me, in the uprightness of my heart I have willingly offered all these *things;* and now with joy I have seen Your people, who are present here to offer willingly to You. [18]O LORD God of Abraham, Isaac, and Israel, our fathers, keep this forever in the intent of the thoughts of the heart of Your people, and fix their heart toward You. [19]And give my son Solomon a loyal heart to keep Your commandments and Your testimonies and Your statutes, to do all *these things,* and to build the temple[t] for which I have made provision."

29:9, 17 *A generous heart.* The people joined their king in generously giving to the Lord. Of course, whatever we give Him, He has first given us (29:11–15). There were even gifts from the past, from Samuel, Saul, and Abner (26:28).

29:17, 18 *A devoted heart.* "Fix their heart toward You" means "Keep them loyal and devoted to You." In his latter years, Solomon's heart turned away from the Lord (1 Kings 11:3). That can happen to any of us, so we must heed Proverbs 4:23. Why should we generously give to the Lord? David's song of praise in 29:10–15 presents some reasons: God is great (vv. 10–12); God deserves glory (v. 13); God has given so much to us (v. 14); life is short and we must make it count (v. 15). Take comfort in this truth: "He who does the will of God abides forever" (1 John 2:17).

29:8 [s]Possibly the same as *Jehieli* (compare 26:21, 22)
29:19 [t]Literally *palace*

20Then David said to all the assembly, "Now bless the LORD your God." So all the assembly blessed the LORD God of their fathers, and bowed their heads and prostrated themselves before the LORD and the king.

21And they made sacrifices to the LORD and offered burnt offerings to the LORD on the next day: a thousand bulls, a thousand rams, a thousand lambs, with their drink offerings, and sacrifices in abundance for all Israel. 22So they ate and drank before the LORD with great gladness on that day. And they made Solomon the son of David king the second time, and anointed *him* before the LORD *to be* the leader, and Zadok *to be* priest. 23Then Solomon sat on the throne of the LORD as king instead of David his father, and prospered; and all Israel obeyed him. 24All the leaders and the mighty men, and also all the sons of King David, submitted themselves to King Solomon. 25So the LORD exalted Solomon exceedingly in the sight of all Israel, and bestowed on him *such* royal majesty as had not been on any king before him in Israel.

26Thus David the son of Jesse reigned over all Israel. 27And the period that he reigned over Israel *was* forty years; seven years he reigned in Hebron, and thirty-three *years* he reigned in Jerusalem. 28So he died in a good old age, full of days and riches and honor; and Solomon his son reigned in his place. 29Now the acts of King David, first and last, indeed they *are* written in the book of Samuel the seer, in the book of Nathan the prophet, and in the book of Gad the seer, 30with all his reign and his might, and the events that happened to him, to Israel, and to all the kingdoms of the lands.

2 CHRONICLES

CHAPTER 1

1:1 *The ruler.* God "exalted him exceedingly." Solomon could strengthen his kingdom, but only God could exalt his name. If Solomon had tried to exalt himself, God would have disciplined him (1 Pet.5:5).

1:6 *The worshiper.* Solomon's hands were filled with sacrifices for the Lord; his ears were open to the word of the Lord; his heart was devoted to the service of the Lord. His great desire was to be capable of serving his people with wisdom, and God granted that desire. Have you asked God for wisdom (James 1:5)?

1:14–17 *The trader.* King Solomon had a flair for foreign trade. In spite of the admonition in Deuteronomy 17:16–17, he amassed silver and gold and multiplied horses. David had only 100 chariots (1 Chron. 18:4), but his son added 1,300 more. Trade brought wealth to the nation, but it may have been the beginning of Solomon's downfall (1 Kings 11). Oliver Goldsmith wrote, "Ill fares the land, to hastening ills a prey, / Where wealth accumulates and men decay."

1 Now* Solomon the son of David was strengthened in his kingdom, and the LORD his God *was* with him and exalted him exceedingly.

2And Solomon spoke to all Israel, to the captains of thousands and of hundreds, to the judges, and to every leader in all Israel, the heads of the fathers' *houses.* 3Then Solomon, and all the assembly with him, went to the high place that *was* at Gibeon; for the tabernacle of meeting with God was there, which Moses the servant of the LORD had made in the wilderness. 4But David had brought up the ark of God from Kirjath Jearim to *the place* David had prepared for it, for he had pitched a tent for it at Jerusalem. 5Now the bronze altar that Bezalel the son of Uri, the son of Hur, had made, he put*a* before the tabernacle of the LORD; Solomon and the assembly sought Him *there.* 6*And Solomon went up there to the bronze altar before the LORD, which *was* at the tabernacle of meeting, and offered a thousand burnt offerings on it.

7On that night God appeared to Solomon, and said to him, "Ask! What shall I give you?"

8And Solomon said to God: "You have shown great mercy to David my father, and have made me king in his place. 9Now, O LORD God, let Your promise to David my father be established, for You have made me king over a people like the dust of the earth in multitude. 10Now give me wisdom and knowledge, that I may go out and come in before this people; for who can judge this great people of Yours?"

11Then God said to Solomon: "Because this was in your heart, and you have not asked riches or wealth or honor or the life of your enemies, nor have you asked long life—but have asked wisdom and knowledge for yourself, that you may judge My people over whom I have made you king— 12wisdom and knowledge *are* granted to you; and I will give you riches and wealth and honor, such as none of the kings have had who *were* before you, nor shall any after you have the like."

13So Solomon came to Jerusalem from the high place that *was* at Gibeon, from before the tabernacle of meeting, and reigned over Israel. 14*And Solomon gathered chariots and horsemen; he had one thousand four hundred chariots and twelve thousand horsemen, whom he stationed in the chariot cities and with the king in Jerusalem. 15Also the king made silver and gold as common in Jerusalem as stones, and he made cedars as abundant as the sycamores which *are* in the lowland. 16And Solomon had horses imported from Egypt and Keveh; the king's merchants bought them in Keveh at the *current* price. 17They also acquired and imported from Egypt a chariot for six hundred *shekels* of silver, and a horse for one hundred and fifty; thus, through their agents,*b* they exported them to all the kings of the Hittites and the kings of Syria.

1:5 *a*Some authorities read *it was there.* 1:17 *b*Literally *by their hands*

2 Then* Solomon determined to build a temple for the name of the LORD, and a royal house for himself. ²Solomon selected seventy thousand men to bear burdens, eighty thousand to quarry *stone* in the mountains, and three thousand six hundred to oversee them.

³Then Solomon sent to Hiram^c king of Tyre, saying:

As you have dealt with David my father, and sent him cedars to build himself a house to dwell in, *so deal with me.* ⁴Behold, I am building a temple for the name of the LORD my God, to dedicate *it* to Him, to burn before Him sweet incense, for the continual showbread, for the burnt offerings morning and evening, on the Sabbaths, on the New Moons, and on the set feasts of the LORD our God. This *is an ordinance* forever to Israel.

5   And the temple which I build *will be* great, for our God is greater than all gods. ⁶But who is able to build Him a temple, since heaven and the heaven of heavens cannot contain Him? Who *am* I then, that I should build Him a temple, except to burn sacrifice before Him?

7   Therefore send me at once a man skillful to work in gold and silver, in bronze and iron, in purple and crimson and blue, who has skill to engrave with the skillful men who are with me in Judah and Jerusalem, whom David my father provided. ⁸Also send me cedar and cypress and algum logs from Lebanon, for I know that your servants have skill to cut timber in Lebanon; and indeed my servants *will be* with your servants, ⁹to prepare timber for me in abundance, for the temple which I am about to build *shall be* great and wonderful.

10   And indeed I will give to your servants, the woodsmen who cut timber, twenty thousand kors of ground wheat, twenty thousand kors of barley, twenty thousand baths of wine, and twenty thousand baths of oil.

¹¹Then Hiram king of Tyre answered in writing, which he sent to Solomon:

Because the LORD loves His people, He has made you king over them.

¹²Hiram^d also said:

Blessed *be* the LORD God of Israel, who made heaven and earth, for He has given King David a wise son, endowed with prudence and understanding, who will build a temple for the LORD and a royal house for himself!

13   And now I have sent a skillful man, endowed with understanding, Huram^e my

CHAPTERS 2—4

2:1ff The plans for both the temple and the tabernacle were given by God; in both projects, the people were permitted to share their gifts. There was one difference: God's Spirit equipped two Jewish men to make the tabernacle and its furnishings (Exod. 31), but an artisan from outside Israel supervised the construction of the temple. Had God's Spirit failed to equip anybody for the task? Or was that another one of Solomon's ways to build strong bonds with his neighbors?

2:3 ^cHebrew *Huram* (compare 1 Kings 5:1)   2:12 ^dHebrew *Huram* (compare 1 Kings 5:1)   2:13 ^eSpelled *Hiram* in 1 Kings 7:13

master[f] *craftsman* 14(the son of a woman of the daughters of Dan, and his father was a man of Tyre), skilled to work in gold and silver, bronze and iron, stone and wood, purple and blue, fine linen and crimson, and to make any engraving and to accomplish any plan which may be given to him, with your skillful men and with the skillful men of my lord David your father.

15 Now therefore, the wheat, the barley, the oil, and the wine which my lord has spoken of, let him send to his servants. 16And we will cut wood from Lebanon, as much as you need; we will bring it to you in rafts by sea to Joppa, and you will carry it up to Jerusalem.

17Then Solomon numbered all the aliens who *were* in the land of Israel, after the census in which David his father had numbered them; and there were found to be one hundred and fifty-three thousand six hundred. 18And he made seventy thousand of them bearers of burdens, eighty thousand stonecutters in the mountain, and three thousand six hundred overseers to make the people work.

3 Now Solomon began to build the house of the LORD at Jerusalem on Mount Moriah, where *the* LORD[g] had appeared to his father David, at the place that David had prepared on the threshing floor of Ornan[h] the Jebusite. 2And he began to build on the second *day* of the second month in the fourth year of his reign.

3This is the foundation which Solomon laid for building the house of God: The length *was* sixty cubits (by cubits according to the former measure) and the width twenty cubits. 4And the vestibule that *was* in front *of the sanctuary*[i] was twenty cubits long across the width of the house, and the height *was* one hundred and[j] twenty. He overlaid the inside with pure gold. 5The larger room[k] he paneled with cypress which he overlaid with fine gold, and he carved palm trees and chainwork on it. 6*And he decorated the house with precious stones for beauty, and the gold *was* gold from Parvaim. 7He also overlaid the house—the beams and doorposts, its walls and doors—with gold; and he carved cherubim on the walls.

8And he made the Most Holy Place. Its length was according to the width of the house, twenty cubits, and its width twenty cubits. He overlaid it with six hundred talents of fine gold. 9The weight of the nails *was* fifty shekels of gold; and he overlaid the upper area with gold. 10In the Most Holy Place he made two cherubim, fashioned by carving, and overlaid them with gold. 11The wings of the cherubim *were* twenty cubits in *overall* length: one wing *of the one cherub was* five cubits, touching the wall of the room, and the other wing *was* five cubits, touching the wing of the other

3:6 At least his motives were pure: he built the house "for the name of the LORD" (2:1). He used the best materials ("pure gold," "fine gold"), and he laid a good foundation (3:3). The apostle Paul surely had Solomon's temple in mind when he wrote 1 Corinthians 3:10–17.

---

[f]Literally *father* (compare 1 Kings 7:13, 14)   3:1 [g]Literally *He,* following Masoretic Text and Vulgate; Septuagint reads *the* LORD; Targum reads *the Angel of the LORD.* [h]Spelled *Araunah* in 2 Samuel 24:16ff   3:4 [i]The main room of the temple; elsewhere called the holy place (compare 1 Kings 6:3) [j]Following Masoretic Text, Septuagint, and Vulgate; Arabic, some manuscripts of the Septuagint, and Syriac omit *one hundred and.*   3:5 [k]Literally *house*

cherub; 12one wing of the other cherub was five cubits, touching the wall of the room, and the other wing also was five cubits, touching the wing of the other cherub. 13The wings of these cherubim spanned twenty cubits overall. They stood on their feet, and they faced inward. 14And he made the veil of blue, purple, crimson, and fine linen, and wove cherubim into it.

15Also he made in front of the temple*l* two pillars thirty-five*m* cubits high, and the capital that was on the top of each of them was five cubits. 16He made wreaths of chainwork, as in the inner sanctuary, and put them on top of the pillars; and he made one hundred pomegranates, and put them on the wreaths of chainwork. 17*Then he set up the pillars before the temple, one on the right hand and the other on the left; he called the name of the one on the right hand Jachin, and the name of the one on the left Boaz.

4 Moreover he made a bronze altar: twenty cubits was its length, twenty cubits its width, and ten cubits its height.
2Then he made the Sea of cast bronze, ten cubits from one brim to the other; it was completely round. Its height was five cubits, and a line of thirty cubits measured its circumference. 3And under it was the likeness of oxen encircling it all around, ten to a cubit, all the way around the Sea. The oxen were cast in two rows, when it was cast. 4It stood on twelve oxen: three looking toward the north, three looking toward the west, three looking toward the south, and three looking toward the east; the Sea was set upon them, and all their back parts pointed inward. 5It was a handbreadth thick; and its brim was shaped like the brim of a cup, like a lily blossom. It contained three thousand*n* baths.
6He also made ten lavers, and put five on the right side and five on the left, to wash in them; such things as they offered for the burnt offering they would wash in them, but the Sea was for the priests to wash in. 7And he made ten lampstands of gold according to their design, and set them in the temple, five on the right side and five on the left. 8He also made ten tables, and placed them in the temple, five on the right side and five on the left. And he made one hundred bowls of gold.
9Furthermore he made the court of the priests, and the great court and doors for the court; and he overlaid these doors with bronze. 10He set the Sea on the right side, toward the southeast.
11Then Huram made the pots and the shovels and the bowls. So Huram finished doing the work that he was to do for King Solomon for the house of God: 12the two pillars and the bowl-shaped capitals that were on top of the two pillars; the two networks covering the two bowl-shaped capitals which were on top of the pillars; 13four hundred pomegranates for the two networks (two rows of pomegranates for each network, to cover the two bowl-shaped capitals that were on the pillars); 14he also made carts and the lavers on the carts; 15one Sea and twelve oxen under it; 16also the pots, the shovels, the forks—and all their articles Huram his master*o* craftsman made of burnished

3:17 The pillars (3:17) in God's spiritual temple, the church, are dedicated people who serve Him devotedly (Gal. 2:9). Are you a pillar, or must you lean on others?

3:15 *l*Literally house *m*Or eighteen (compare 1 Kings 7:15; 2 Kings 25:17; and Jeremiah 52:21) 4:5 *n*Or two thousand (compare 1 Kings 7:26) 4:16 *o*Literally father

bronze for King Solomon for the house of the LORD.

[17]In the plain of Jordan the king had them cast in clay molds, between Succoth and Zeredah.[p] [18]And Solomon had all these articles made in such great abundance that the weight of the bronze was not determined.

[19]Thus Solomon had all the furnishings made for the house of God: the altar of gold and the tables on which *was* the showbread; [20]the lampstands with their lamps of pure gold, to burn in the prescribed manner in front of the inner sanctuary, [21]with the flowers and the lamps and the wick-trimmers of gold, of purest gold; [22]the trimmers, the bowls, the ladles, and the censers of pure gold. As for the entry of the sanctuary, its inner doors to the Most Holy *Place*, and the doors of the main hall of the temple, *were* gold.

CHAPTER 5

5:1ff The beautiful temple was empty until God's throne was put in place (vv. 2–10) and God's glory filled the house (vv. 13–14). When Moses dedicated the tabernacle, the glory came in when the work was finished (Exod. 40:33–38). It was the song of praise that brought the glory into the temple. When you worship with God's people, does your praise increase His glory in the assembly?

5:10 The tables of the Law were still in the ark (v. 10), but the pot of manna and Aaron's rod were no longer there (Heb. 9:4). Some things God does are temporary, and we must not make permanent institutions out of them.

5:11–14 David had carefully organized the priests and Levites, but that order was forgotten as they led the worship on that holy day (v. 11). There are times when the Spirit of God ignores our plans and procedures and reveals God's glory in a new way. Let Him do it! We are not to worship organization; we are to worship God.

5 So* all the work that Solomon had done for the house of the LORD was finished; and Solomon brought in the things which his father David had dedicated: the silver and the gold and all the furnishings. And he put *them* in the treasuries of the house of God.

[2]Now Solomon assembled the elders of Israel and all the heads of the tribes, the chief fathers of the children of Israel, in Jerusalem, that they might bring the ark of the covenant of the LORD up from the City of David, which *is* Zion. [3]Therefore all the men of Israel assembled with the king at the feast, which *was* in the seventh month. [4]So all the elders of Israel came, and the Levites took up the ark. [5]Then they brought up the ark, the tabernacle of meeting, and all the holy furnishings that *were* in the tabernacle. The priests and the Levites brought them up. [6]Also King Solomon, and all the congregation of Israel who were assembled with him before the ark, were sacrificing sheep and oxen that could not be counted or numbered for multitude. [7]Then the priests brought in the ark of the covenant of the LORD to its place, into the inner sanctuary of the temple,[q] to the Most Holy *Place*, under the wings of the cherubim. [8]For the cherubim spread *their* wings over the place of the ark, and the cherubim overshadowed the ark and its poles. [9]The poles extended so that the ends of the poles of the ark could be seen from *the holy place*, in front of the inner sanctuary; but they could not be seen from outside. And they are there to this day. [10]*Nothing was in the ark except the two tablets which Moses put *there* at Horeb, when the LORD made *a covenant* with the children of Israel, when they had come out of Egypt.

[11]*And it came to pass when the priests came out of the Most Holy *Place* (for all the priests who *were* present had sanctified themselves, without keeping to their divisions), [12]and the Levites *who were* the singers, all those of Asaph and Heman and Jeduthun, with their sons and their brethren, stood at the east end of the altar, clothed in white linen, having cymbals, stringed instruments and harps, and with them one hundred and twenty priests sounding with trumpets— [13]indeed it came to pass, when the trumpeters and singers *were* as one, to make one sound to be heard in praising and thanking the LORD, and when they lifted up their voice with the trumpets and cymbals and

---

4:17 [p]Spelled *Zaretan* in 1 Kings 7:46   5:7 [q]Literally *house*

instruments of music, and praised the LORD, *saying:*

"*For He is* good,
For His mercy *endures* forever,"[r]

that the house, the house of the LORD, was filled with a cloud, [14]so that the priests could not continue ministering because of the cloud; for the glory of the LORD filled the house of God.

6 Then* Solomon spoke:

"The LORD said
He would dwell in the dark cloud.
2   *I have surely built You an exalted house,
And a place for You to dwell in forever."

[3]Then the king turned around and blessed the whole assembly of Israel, while all the assembly of Israel was standing. [4]And he said: "Blessed *be* the LORD God of Israel, who has fulfilled with His hands *what* He spoke with His mouth to my father David, saying, [5]'Since the day that I brought My people out of the land of Egypt, I have chosen no city from any tribe of Israel *in which* to build a house, that My name might be there, nor did I choose any man to be a ruler over My people Israel. [6]Yet I have chosen Jerusalem, that My name may be there, and I have chosen David to be over My people Israel.' [7]Now it was in the heart of my father David to build a temple[s] for the name of the LORD God of Israel. [8]But the LORD said to my father David, 'Whereas it was in your heart to build a temple for My name, you did well in that it was in your heart. [9]Nevertheless you shall not build the temple, but your son who will come from your body, he shall build the temple for My name.' [10]So the LORD has fulfilled His word which He spoke, and I have filled the position of my father David, and sit on the throne of Israel, as the LORD promised; and I have built the temple for the name of the LORD God of Israel. [11]And there I have put the ark, in which *is* the covenant of the LORD which He made with the children of Israel."

[12]*Then *Solomon*[t] stood before the altar of the LORD in the presence of all the assembly of Israel, and spread out his hands [13](for Solomon had made a bronze platform five cubits long, five cubits wide, and three cubits high, and had set it in the midst of the court; and he stood on it, knelt down on his knees before all the assembly of Israel, and spread out his hands toward heaven); [14]and he said: "LORD God of Israel, *there is* no God in heaven or on earth like You, who keep *Your* covenant and mercy with Your servants who walk before You with all their hearts. [15]You have kept what You promised Your servant David my father; You have both spoken with Your mouth and fulfilled *it* with Your hand, as *it is* this day. [16]Therefore, LORD God of Israel, now keep what You promised Your servant David my father, saying, 'You shall not fail to have a man sit before Me on the throne of Israel, only if your sons take heed to their way, that they walk in My law as you have walked before Me.' [17]And now, O LORD God of Israel, let Your word come true, which You have spoken to Your servant David.

CHAPTER 6

6:1ff In his dedication address and prayer, King Solomon looked in five different directions.

6:2–11 *He looked back.* He recalled how God chose him to build the temple.

6:12–21 *He looked up.* He asked God to fulfill the covenant promises He had made with David. The covenant included the coming into this world of the Son of David, Jesus Christ, who was born of the house of David.

5:13 [r]Compare Psalm 106:1   6:7 [s]Literally *house,* and so in verses 8–10   6:12 [t]Literally *he* (compare 1 Kings 8:22)

18"But will God indeed dwell with men on the earth? Behold, heaven and the heaven of heavens cannot contain You. How much less this temple[u] which I have built! 19Yet regard the prayer of Your servant and his supplication, O LORD my God, and listen to the cry and the prayer which Your servant is praying before You: 20that Your eyes may be open toward this temple day and night, toward the place where *You* said *You would* put Your name, that You may hear the prayer which Your servant makes toward this place. 21And may You hear the supplications of Your servant and of Your people Israel, when they pray toward this place. Hear from heaven Your dwelling place, and when You hear, forgive.

22*"If anyone sins against his neighbor, and is forced to take an oath, and comes *and* takes an oath before Your altar in this temple, 23then hear from heaven, and act, and judge Your servants, bringing retribution on the wicked by bringing his way on his own head, and justifying the righteous by giving him according to his righteousness.

24"Or if Your people Israel are defeated before an enemy because they have sinned against You, and return and confess Your name, and pray and make supplication before You in this temple, 25then hear from heaven and forgive the sin of Your people Israel, and bring them back to the land which You gave to them and their fathers.

26"When the heavens are shut up and there is no rain because they have sinned against You, when they pray toward this place and confess Your name, and turn from their sin because You afflict them, 27then hear *in* heaven, and forgive the sin of Your servants, Your people Israel, that You may teach them the good way in which they should walk; and send rain on Your land which You have given to Your people as an inheritance.

28"When there is famine in the land, pestilence or blight or mildew, locusts or grasshoppers; when their enemies besiege them in the land of their cities; whatever plague or whatever sickness *there is;* 29whatever prayer, whatever supplication is *made* by anyone, or by all Your people Israel, when each one knows his own burden and his own grief, and spreads out his hands to this temple: 30then hear from heaven Your dwelling place, and forgive, and give to everyone according to all his ways, whose heart You know (for You alone know the hearts of the sons of men), 31that they may fear You, to walk in Your ways as long as they live in the land which You gave to our fathers.

32*"Moreover, concerning a foreigner, who is not of Your people Israel, but has come from a far country for the sake of Your great name and Your mighty hand and Your outstretched arm, when they come and pray in this temple; 33then hear from heaven Your dwelling place, and do according to all for which the foreigner calls to You, that all peoples of the earth may know Your name and fear You, as *do* Your people Israel, and that they may know that this temple which I have built is called by Your name.

34"When Your people go out to battle against their enemies, wherever You send them, and when they pray to You toward this city which You have chosen and the temple which I have

6:22–31 *He looked ahead.* Solomon asked God to help His people in various trials of life, particularly to forgive them when they sinned. Coming to the temple, or looking toward the temple, and praying to God would bring them forgiveness. In this chapter, there are numerous references to prayer.

6:32–35 *He looked around.* The king called on God to help the Gentiles. The temple was to be "a house of prayer for all nations" (Isa. 56:7); God's desire was that Israel bring blessing to all the world (Gen. 12:1–3).

6:18 [u]Literally *house*

built for Your name, 35then hear from heaven their prayer and their supplication, and maintain their cause.

36*"When they sin against You (for *there is* no one who does not sin), and You become angry with them and deliver them to the enemy, and they take them captive to a land far or near; 37yet when they come to themselves in the land where they were carried captive, and repent, and make supplication to You in the land of their captivity, saying, 'We have sinned, we have done wrong, and have committed wickedness'; 38and *when* they return to You with all their heart and with all their soul in the land of their captivity, where they have been carried captive, and pray toward their land which You gave to their fathers, the city which You have chosen, and toward the temple which I have built for Your name: 39then hear from heaven Your dwelling place their prayer and their supplications, and maintain their cause, and forgive Your people who have sinned against You. 40Now, my God, I pray, let Your eyes be open and *let* Your ears *be* attentive to the prayer *made* in this place.

41*"Now therefore,
  Arise, O LORD God, to Your resting place,
  You and the ark of Your strength.
  Let Your priests, O LORD God, be clothed
    with salvation,
  And let Your saints rejoice in goodness.

42 "O LORD God, do not turn away the face of
    Your Anointed;
  Remember the mercies of Your servant
    David."*v*

7 When* Solomon had finished praying, fire came down from heaven and consumed the burnt offering and the sacrifices; and the glory of the LORD filled the temple.*w* 2And the priests could not enter the house of the LORD, because the glory of the LORD had filled the LORD's house. 3*When all the children of Israel saw how the fire came down, and the glory of the LORD on the temple, they bowed their faces to the ground on the pavement, and worshiped and praised the LORD, *saying:*

  "For *He is* good,
  For His mercy *endures* forever."*x*

4Then the king and all the people offered sacrifices before the LORD. 5King Solomon offered a sacrifice of twenty-two thousand bulls and one hundred and twenty thousand sheep. So the king and all the people dedicated the house of God. 6And the priests attended to their services; the Levites also with instruments of the music of the LORD, which King David had made to praise the LORD, saying, "For His mercy *endures* forever,"*y* whenever David offered praise by their ministry. The priests sounded trumpets opposite them, while all Israel stood.

7Furthermore Solomon consecrated the middle of the court that *was* in front of the house of the LORD; for there he offered burnt offerings and the fat of the peace offerings, because the bronze altar

6:36–40 *He looked within.* He ended his prayer by pleading for forgiveness for sinning Israel. His words must have been very meaningful to the Jews taken captive to Babylon four centuries later.

6:41, 42 The temple is gone, but the record of that great day of dedication remains to encourage and bless God's people. Read the chapter again, and note the promises you can claim today. In his closing prayer, Solomon asked God to bless everybody present: the priests, the people, and himself as God's anointed king. But any blessing that came would result from God's mercy and His promises to David. David could not build the temple or attend the dedication service, but he was there just the same!

CHAPTER 7

7:1, 2 *Fire and glory.* The fire came to devour, and the glory came to dwell. There was glory at the start of the service (2 Chron. 5:14) and glory at the close! But there could be no glory apart from the sacrifices that took care of the sins of the people. Isaiah saw God's glory, but before he was ready for service, he had to feel the fire (Isa. 6:1–8). Most of us want the glory, but we resist the fire.

7:3–10 *Falling and feasting.* This demonstration of God's power and glory brought the people to their knees, but when the service ended, they rejoiced with feasting. Contradictory? Not in the least. We are to "serve the LORD with fear, and rejoice with trembling" (Ps. 2:11). It was said of Moses and some others: "So they saw God, and they ate and drank" (Exod. 24:11).

6:42 *v*Compare Psalm 132:8–10 7:1 *w*Literally *house*
7:3 *x*Compare Psalm 106:1 7:6 *y*Compare Psalm 106:1

which Solomon had made was not able to receive the burnt offerings, the grain offerings, and the fat.

8At that time Solomon kept the feast seven days, and all Israel with him, a very great assembly from the entrance of Hamath to the Brook of Egypt.z 9And on the eighth day they held a sacred assembly, for they observed the dedication of the altar seven days, and the feast seven days. 10On the twenty-third day of the seventh month he sent the people away to their tents, joyful and glad of heart for the good that the LORD had done for David, for Solomon, and for His people Israel. 11Thus Solomon finished the house of the LORD and the king's house; and Solomon successfully accomplished all that came into his heart to make in the house of the LORD and in his own house.

12*Then the LORD appeared to Solomon by night, and said to him: "I have heard your prayer, and have chosen this place for Myself as a house of sacrifice. 13When I shut up heaven and there is no rain, or command the locusts to devour the land, or send pestilence among My people, 14if My people who are called by My name will humble themselves, and pray and seek My face, and turn from their wicked ways, then I will hear from heaven, and will forgive their sin and heal their land. 15Now My eyes will be open and My ears attentive to prayer *made* in this place. 16For now I have chosen and sanctified this house, that My name may be there forever; and My eyes and My heart will be there perpetually. 17As for you, if you walk before Me as your father David walked, and do according to all that I have commanded you, and if you keep My statutes and My judgments, 18then I will establish the throne of your kingdom, as I covenanted with David your father, saying, 'You shall not fail to have a man as ruler in Israel.'

19"But if you turn away and forsake My statutes and My commandments which I have set before you, and go and serve other gods, and worship them, 20then I will uproot them from My land which I have given them; and this house which I have sanctified for My name I will cast out of My sight, and will make it a proverb and a byword among all peoples.

21"And *as for* this house, which is exalted, everyone who passes by it will be astonished and say, 'Why has the LORD done thus to this land and this house?' 22Then they will answer, 'Because they forsook the LORD God of their fathers, who brought them out of the land of Egypt, and embraced other gods, and worshiped them and served them; therefore He has brought all this calamity on them.'"

CHAPTER 8

8 It* came to pass at the end of twenty years, when Solomon had built the house of the LORD and his own house, 2that the cities which Hirama had given to Solomon, Solomon built them; and he settled the children of Israel there. 3And Solomon went to Hamath Zobah and seized it. 4He also built Tadmor in the wilderness, and all the storage cities which he built in Hamath. 5He built Upper Beth Horon and Lower Beth Horon, fortified cities *with* walls, gates, and bars, 6also Baal-

---

7:12 Promise and warning. What an encouragement to know that God hears our prayers! God graciously granted what the king asked for, but He added a word of caution: "These blessings are given when My children obey." Disobedience brings discipline, not because God hates us but because He loves us and wants to bless us even more. Prayer went up, fire came down, and glory moved in. Could you ask for more?

8:1ff David was known for his battles, Solomon for his buildings. It was a time of peace, so the opportunities and resources for building were available.

7:8 ᶻThat is, the Shihor (compare 1 Chronicles 13:5)
8:2 ªHebrew *Huram* (compare 2 Chronicles 2:3)

ath and all the storage cities that Solomon had, and all the chariot cities and the cities of the cavalry, and all that Solomon desired to build in Jerusalem, in Lebanon, and in all the land of his dominion.

7All the people *who were* left of the Hittites, Amorites, Perizzites, Hivites, and Jebusites, who *were* not of Israel— 8that is, their descendants who were left in the land after them, whom the children of Israel did not destroy—from these Solomon raised forced labor, as it is to this day. 9But Solomon did not make the children of Israel servants for his work. Some *were* men of war, captains of his officers, captains of his chariots, and his cavalry. 10And others *were* chiefs of the officials of King Solomon: two hundred and fifty, who ruled over the people.

11*Now Solomon brought the daughter of Pharaoh up from the City of David to the house he had built for her, for he said, "My wife shall not dwell in the house of David king of Israel, because *the places* to which the ark of the LORD has come are holy."

12*Then Solomon offered burnt offerings to the LORD on the altar of the LORD which he had built before the vestibule, 13according to the daily rate, offering according to the commandment of Moses, for the Sabbaths, the New Moons, and the three appointed yearly feasts—the Feast of Unleavened Bread, the Feast of Weeks, and the Feast of Tabernacles. 14And, according to the order of David his father, he appointed the divisions of the priests for their service, the Levites for their duties (to praise and serve before the priests) as the duty of each day required, and the gatekeepers by their divisions at each gate; for so David the man of God had commanded. 15They did not depart from the command of the king to the priests and Levites concerning any matter or concerning the treasuries.

16Now all the work of Solomon was well-ordered from*b* the day of the foundation of the house of the LORD until it was finished. So the house of the LORD was completed.

17Then Solomon went to Ezion Geber and Elath*c* on the seacoast, in the land of Edom. 18And Hiram sent him ships by the hand of his servants, and servants who knew the sea. They went with the servants of Solomon to Ophir, and acquired four hundred and fifty talents of gold from there, and brought it to King Solomon.

9 Now* when the queen of Sheba heard of the fame of Solomon, she came to Jerusalem to test Solomon with hard questions, *having* a very great retinue, camels that bore spices, gold in abundance, and precious stones; and when she came to Solomon, she spoke with him about all that was in her heart. 2So Solomon answered all her questions; there was nothing so difficult for Solomon that he could not explain it to her. 3And when the queen of Sheba had seen the wisdom of Solomon, the house that he had built, 4the food on his table, the seating of his servants, the service of his waiters and their apparel, his cupbearers and their apparel, and his entryway

8:11 It is disappointing that Solomon married a foreign woman who could not be identified with the Lord's throne. God wants each home to be a tabernacle (Isa. 4:5–6); He wants His children to enjoy His presence (2 Cor. 6:14—7:1). Apparently in this decision, Solomon was concerned more about politics than about piety.

8:12–16 Solomon was faithful in his public worship despite these inconsistencies in his life, and he continued to increase the wealth of the nation. But the people were not growing in the things of the Lord. Alexander Whyte wrote that "the secret worm . . . was gnawing all the time in the royal staff upon which Solomon leaned."

The most important part of your life is the part that only God sees. Are you concerned about character—or reputation?

CHAPTER 9

9:1ff Wealth and wisdom are the central themes of this chapter; gold is mentioned sixteen times and wisdom six times. According to King Solomon, wisdom is better than wealth (Prov. 3:13–15; 8:10–11), although most people today would probably rather have money. They measure life by prices, not values.

8:16 *b*Following Septuagint, Syriac, and Vulgate; Masoretic Text reads *as far as*.   8:17 *c*Hebrew *Eloth* (compare 2 Kings 14:22)

by which he went up to the house of the LORD, there was no more spirit in her.

5Then she said to the king: "*It was* a true report which I heard in my own land about your words and your wisdom. 6However I did not believe their words until I came and saw with my own eyes; and indeed the half of the greatness of your wisdom was not told me. You exceed the fame of which I heard. 7Happy *are* your men and happy *are* these your servants, who stand continually before you and hear your wisdom! 8Blessed be the LORD your God, who delighted in you, setting you on His throne *to be* king for the LORD your God! Because your God has loved Israel, to establish them forever, therefore He made you king over them, to do justice and righteousness."

9And she gave the king one hundred and twenty talents of gold, spices in great abundance, and precious stones; there never were any spices such as those the queen of Sheba gave to King Solomon.

10Also, the servants of Hiram and the servants of Solomon, who brought gold from Ophir, brought algum*d* wood and precious stones. 11And the king made walkways *of* the algum*e* wood for the house of the LORD and for the king's house, also harps and stringed instruments for singers; and there were none such *as these* seen before in the land of Judah.

12Now King Solomon gave to the queen of Sheba all she desired, whatever she asked, *much more* than she had brought to the king. So she turned and went to her own country, she and her servants.

13The weight of gold that came to Solomon yearly was six hundred and sixty-six talents of gold, 14besides *what* the traveling merchants and traders brought. And all the kings of Arabia and governors of the country brought gold and silver to Solomon. 15And King Solomon made two hundred large shields of hammered gold; six hundred *shekels* of hammered gold went into each shield. 16*He* also *made* three hundred shields of hammered gold; three hundred *shekels*f of gold went into each shield. The king put them in the House of the Forest of Lebanon.

17Moreover the king made a great throne of ivory, and overlaid it with pure gold. 18The throne *had* six steps, with a footstool of gold, *which were* fastened to the throne; there were armrests on either side of the place of the seat, and two lions stood beside the armrests. 19Twelve lions stood there, one on each side of the six steps; nothing like *this* had been made for any *other* kingdom.

20All King Solomon's drinking vessels *were* gold, and all the vessels of the House of the Forest of Lebanon *were* pure gold. Not *one was* silver, for this was accounted as nothing in the days of Solomon. 21For the king's ships went to Tarshish with the servants of Hiram.g Once every three years the merchant shipsh came, bringing gold, silver, ivory, apes, and monkeys.i

22*So King Solomon surpassed all the kings of the earth in riches and wisdom. 23And all the

9:22, 23 If you want gold, silver, and jewels, you must dig for them. Very little treasure lies on the ground, convenient to pick up. If you want wisdom, you must "seek her as silver, and search for her as for hidden treasures" (Prov. 2:4). That means work! It means taking time to read, meditate, pray, and put truth into practice.

9:10 dOr *almug* (compare 1 Kings 10:11, 12)   9:11 eOr *almug* (compare 1 Kings 10:11, 12)   9:16 fOr *three minas* (compare 1 Kings 10:17)   9:21 gHebrew *Huram* (compare 1 Kings 10:22) hLiterally *ships of Tarshish*, deep-sea vessels iOr *peacocks*

kings of the earth sought the presence of Solomon to hear his wisdom, which God had put in his heart. 24Each man brought his present: articles of silver and gold, garments, armor, spices, horses, and mules, at a set rate year by year.

25Solomon had four thousand stalls for horses and chariots, and twelve thousand horsemen whom he stationed in the chariot cities and with the king at Jerusalem.

26So he reigned over all the kings from the River*j* to the land of the Philistines, as far as the border of Egypt. 27*The king made silver *as common* in Jerusalem as stones, and he made cedar trees as abundant as the sycamores which *are* in the lowland. 28And they brought horses to Solomon from Egypt and from all lands.

29Now the rest of the acts of Solomon, first and last, *are* they not written in the book of Nathan the prophet, in the prophecy of Ahijah the Shilonite, and in the visions of Iddo the seer concerning Jeroboam the son of Nebat? 30Solomon reigned in Jerusalem over all Israel forty years. 31Then Solomon rested with his fathers, and was buried in the City of David his father. And Rehoboam his son reigned in his place.

10 And* Rehoboam went to Shechem, for all Israel had gone to Shechem to make him king. 2So it happened, when Jeroboam the son of Nebat heard *it* (he was in Egypt, where he had fled from the presence of King Solomon), that Jeroboam returned from Egypt. 3Then they sent for him and called him. And Jeroboam and all Israel came and spoke to Rehoboam, saying, 4"Your father made our yoke heavy; now therefore, lighten the burdensome service of your father and his heavy yoke which he put on us, and we will serve you."

5So he said to them, "Come back to me after three days." And the people departed.

6Then King Rehoboam consulted the elders who stood before his father Solomon while he still lived, saying, "How do you advise *me* to answer these people?"

7And they spoke to him, saying, "If you are kind to these people, and please them, and speak good words to them, they will be your servants forever."

8But he rejected the advice which the elders had given him, and consulted the young men who had grown up with him, who stood before him. 9And he said to them, "What advice do you give? How should we answer this people who have spoken to me, saying, 'Lighten the yoke which your father put on us'?"

10Then the young men who had grown up with him spoke to him, saying, "Thus you should speak to the people who have spoken to you, saying, 'Your father made our yoke heavy, but you make *it* lighter on us'—thus you shall say to them: 'My little *finger* shall be thicker than my father's waist! 11And now, whereas my father put a heavy yoke on you, I will add to your yoke; my father chastised you with whips, but I *will chastise you* with scourges!'"*k*

12So Jeroboam and all the people came to Rehoboam on the third day, as the king had directed, saying, "Come back to me the third day." 13Then

9:27 The only convenient materials you will find are wood, hay, and straw, but they will not last (1 Cor. 3:10–15). To sacrifice the permanent for the immediate is folly, not wisdom.

CHAPTERS 10—11
10:1–11 The chronicler does not mention Solomon's apostasy or God's warning (1 Kings 11—13), but he does record Rehoboam's folly. You would think *younger* men would recommend easier lives for the people, for youth is generally a carefree time. But the king's friends did not have to bear any of the burdens, and their decision made them appear strong. They used the people to advance their authority instead of using their authority to help the people. (See Matt. 23:4; Gal. 6:2.)

9:26 *j*That is, the Euphrates   10:11 *k*Literally *scorpions*

the king answered them roughly. King Rehoboam rejected the advice of the elders, [14]and he spoke to them according to the advice of the young men, saying, "My father[l] made your yoke heavy, but I will add to it; my father chastised you with whips, but I *will chastise you* with scourges!"[m] [15]So the king did not listen to the people; for the turn *of events* was from God, that the Lord might fulfill His word, which He had spoken by the hand of Ahijah the Shilonite to Jeroboam the son of Nebat.

[16]Now when all Israel *saw* that the king did not listen to them, the people answered the king, saying:

> "What share have we in David?
> *We have* no inheritance in the son of Jesse.
> Every man to your tents, O Israel!
> Now see to your own house, O David!"

So all Israel departed to their tents. [17]But Rehoboam reigned over the children of Israel who dwelt in the cities of Judah.

[18]Then King Rehoboam sent Hadoram, who *was* in charge of revenue; but the children of Israel stoned him with stones, and he died. Therefore King Rehoboam mounted *his* chariot in haste to flee to Jerusalem. [19]So Israel has been in rebellion against the house of David to this day.

11 Now when Rehoboam came to Jerusalem, he assembled from the house of Judah and Benjamin one hundred and eighty thousand chosen *men* who were warriors, to fight against Israel, that he might restore the kingdom to Rehoboam. [2]But the word of the Lord came to Shemaiah the man of God, saying, [3]"Speak to Rehoboam the son of Solomon, king of Judah, and to all Israel in Judah and Benjamin, saying, [4]*Thus says the Lord: "You shall not go up or fight against your brethren! Let every man return to his house, for this thing is from Me." ' " Therefore they obeyed the words of the Lord, and turned back from attacking Jeroboam.

[5]So Rehoboam dwelt in Jerusalem, and built cities for defense in Judah. [6]And he built Bethlehem, Etam, Tekoa, [7]Beth Zur, Sochoh, Adullam, [8]Gath, Mareshah, Ziph, [9]Adoraim, Lachish, Azekah, [10]Zorah, Aijalon, and Hebron, which are in Judah and Benjamin, fortified cities. [11]And he fortified the strongholds, and put captains in them, and stores of food, oil, and wine. [12]Also in every city *he put* shields and spears, and made them very strong, having Judah and Benjamin on his side.

[13]And from all their territories the priests and the Levites who *were* in all Israel took their stand with him. [14]For the Levites left their commonlands and their possessions and came to Judah and Jerusalem, for Jeroboam and his sons had rejected them from serving as priests to the Lord. [15]Then he appointed for himself priests for the high places, for the demons, and the calf idols which he had made. [16]And after *the Levites left,*[n] those from all the tribes of Israel, such as set their

11:4–14 Some divisions are of God (11:4), even though they create problems and cause hurts. For one thing, divisions force people to make decisions, and the decisions they make reveal the kind of people they are. The priests and Levites left Israel and came to Judah because they wanted to serve in the true temple and be ruled by a king from David's line.

God's program for this world is to bring things together in Christ (Eph. 1:10), and He will succeed despite man's rebellion. The devil's program is to tear things apart. Which side are you helping?

10:14 [l]Following many Hebrew manuscripts, Septuagint, Syriac, and Vulgate (compare verse 10 and 1 Kings 12:14); Masoretic Text reads *I.* [m]Literally *scorpions*   11:16 [n]Literally *after them*

heart to seek the LORD God of Israel, came to Jerusalem to sacrifice to the LORD God of their fathers. 17So they strengthened the kingdom of Judah, and made Rehoboam the son of Solomon strong for three years, because they walked in the way of David and Solomon for three years.

18Then Rehoboam took for himself as wife Mahalath the daughter of Jerimoth the son of David, *and of* Abihail the daughter of Eliah the son of Jesse. 19And she bore him children: Jeush, Shamariah, and Zaham. 20After her he took Maachah the granddaughter° of Absalom; and she bore him Abijah, Attai, Ziza, and Shelomith. 21Now Rehoboam loved Maachah the granddaughter of Absalom more than all his wives and his concubines; for he took eighteen wives and sixty concubines, and begot twenty-eight sons and sixty daughters. 22And Rehoboam appointed Abijah the son of Maachah as chief, *to be* leader among his brothers; for he *intended* to make him king. 23He dealt wisely, and dispersed some of his sons throughout all the territories of Judah and Benjamin, to every fortified city; and he gave them provisions in abundance. He also sought many wives *for them.*

12 Now* it came to pass, when Rehoboam had established the kingdom and had strengthened himself, that he forsook the law of the LORD, and all Israel along with him. 2*And it happened in the fifth year of King Rehoboam *that* Shishak king of Egypt came up against Jerusalem, because they had transgressed against the LORD, 3with twelve hundred chariots, sixty thousand horsemen, and people without number who came with him out of Egypt—the Lubim and the Sukkiim and the Ethiopians. 4And he took the fortified cities of Judah and came to Jerusalem.

5Then Shemaiah the prophet came to Rehoboam and the leaders of Judah, who were gathered together in Jerusalem because of Shishak, and said to them, "Thus says the LORD: 'You have forsaken Me, and therefore I also have left you in the hand of Shishak.'"

6So the leaders of Israel and the king humbled themselves; and they said, "The LORD *is* righteous."

7Now when the LORD saw that they humbled themselves, the word of the LORD came to Shemaiah, saying, "They have humbled themselves; *therefore* I will not destroy them, but I will grant them some deliverance. My wrath shall not be poured out on Jerusalem by the hand of Shishak. 8Nevertheless they will be his servants, that they may distinguish My service from the service of the kingdoms of the nations."

9*So Shishak king of Egypt came up against Jerusalem, and took away the treasures of the house of the LORD and the treasures of the king's house; he took everything. He also carried away the gold shields which Solomon had made. 10Then King Rehoboam made bronze shields in their place, and committed *them* to the hands of the captains of the guard, who guarded the doorway of the king's house. 11And whenever the king entered the house of the LORD, the guard would go and bring them out; then they would take them back

CHAPTER 12

12:1ff Rehoboam refused to serve the Lord or the people, so he ended up serving Egypt. God wanted him to learn the difference between His easy yoke and the heavy yoke of sin (v. 8; Deut. 28:47–48). Some people must learn the hard way. Are you one of them?

12:2–4 No matter how strong you think you are, your strength becomes weakness if you forsake the Lord. Rehoboam relied on his fortified cities for protection, and the Egyptians took every one of them. His son Abijah would rely on the Lord and win a great victory (2 Chron. 13:18). Where is your faith today?

12:9, 12 Solomon's treasures became Egypt's spoils because the king turned away from God. The king and the elders humbled themselves before God, but they could not escape the consequences of their sin. God spared them from wrath, but He permitted them to suffer. Alexander Maclaren stated, "Every sin is a mistake, as well as a wrong; and the epitaph for the sinner is, 'Thou fool!' "

11:20 °Literally *daughter,* but in the broader sense of granddaughter (compare 2 Chronicles 13:2)

into the guardroom. 12When he humbled himself, the wrath of the LORD turned from him, so as not to destroy *him* completely; and things also went well in Judah.

13Thus King Rehoboam strengthened himself in Jerusalem and reigned. Now Rehoboam *was* forty-one years old when he became king; and he reigned seventeen years in Jerusalem, the city which the LORD had chosen out of all the tribes of Israel, to put His name there. His mother's name *was* Naamah, an Ammonitess. 14And he did evil, because he did not prepare his heart to seek the LORD.

15The acts of Rehoboam, first and last, *are* they not written in the book of Shemaiah the prophet, and of Iddo the seer concerning genealogies? And *there were* wars between Rehoboam and Jeroboam all their days. 16So Rehoboam rested with his fathers, and was buried in the City of David. Then Abijah^p his son reigned in his place.

13 In* the eighteenth year of King Jeroboam, Abijah became king over Judah. 2He reigned three years in Jerusalem. His mother's name *was* Michaiah^q the daughter of Uriel of Gibeah.

And there was war between Abijah and Jeroboam. 3Abijah set the battle in order with an army of valiant warriors, four hundred thousand choice men. Jeroboam also drew up in battle formation against him with eight hundred thousand choice men, mighty men of valor.

4Then Abijah stood on Mount Zemaraim, which *is* in the mountains of Ephraim, and said, "Hear me, Jeroboam and all Israel: 5Should you not know that the LORD God of Israel gave the dominion over Israel to David forever, to him and his sons, by a covenant of salt? 6Yet Jeroboam the son of Nebat, the servant of Solomon the son of David, rose up and rebelled against his lord. 7Then worthless rogues gathered to him, and strengthened themselves against Rehoboam the son of Solomon, when Rehoboam was young and inexperienced and could not withstand them. 8And now you think to withstand the kingdom of the LORD, which is in the hand of the sons of David; and you *are* a great multitude, and with you are the gold calves which Jeroboam made for you as gods. 9Have you not cast out the priests of the LORD, the sons of Aaron, and the Levites, and made for yourselves priests, like the peoples of *other* lands, so that whoever comes to consecrate himself with a young bull and seven rams may be a priest of *things that are* not gods? 10But as for us, the LORD *is* our God, and we have not forsaken Him; and the priests who minister to the LORD *are* the sons of Aaron, and the Levites *attend* to *their* duties. 11And they burn to the LORD every morning and every evening burnt sacrifices and sweet incense; *they* also *set* the showbread *in order on* the pure *gold* table, and the lampstand of gold with its lamps to burn every evening; for we keep the command of the LORD our God, but you have forsaken Him. 12*Now look, God Himself *is* with us as *our* head, and His priests with sounding trumpets to sound the alarm against you. O children of Israel, do not fight against the

---

CHAPTER 13

13:1ff The army of Israel had strategy and great numbers, but it did not have God. It was twice as big as Judah's army (Luke 14:31–32), but by the time the battle was over, Israel had lost 500,000 soldiers.

13:12 "God Himself is with us as our head," King Abijah announced (v. 12). He obviously believed that "If God is for us, who can be against us?" (Rom. 8:31). Abijah had his faith in the God of the covenant who always keeps His promises (v. 5). He was living by faith and not by sight.

12:16 ^pSpelled *Abijam* in 1 Kings 14:31   13:2 ^qSpelled *Maachah* in 11:20, 21 and 1 Kings 15:2

LORD God of your fathers, for you shall not prosper!"

13But Jeroboam caused an ambush to go around behind them; so they were in front of Judah, and the ambush *was* behind them. 14And when Judah looked around, to their surprise the battle line *was* at both front and rear; and they cried out to the LORD, and the priests sounded the trumpets. 15Then the men of Judah gave a shout; and as the men of Judah shouted, it happened that God struck Jeroboam and all Israel before Abijah and Judah. 16And the children of Israel fled before Judah, and God delivered them into their hand. 17Then Abijah and his people struck them with a great slaughter; so five hundred thousand choice men of Israel fell slain. 18*Thus the children of Israel were subdued at that time; and the children of Judah prevailed, because they relied on the LORD God of their fathers.

19And Abijah pursued Jeroboam and took cities from him: Bethel with its villages, Jeshanah with its villages, and Ephrainʳ with its villages. 20So Jeroboam did not recover strength again in the days of Abijah; and the LORD struck him, and he died.

21But Abijah grew mighty, married fourteen wives, and begot twenty-two sons and sixteen daughters. 22Now the rest of the acts of Abijah, his ways, and his sayings *are* written in the annals of the prophet Iddo.

14 So* Abijah rested with his fathers, and they buried him in the City of David. Then Asa his son reigned in his place. In his days the land was quiet for ten years.

2Asa did *what was* good and right in the eyes of the LORD his God, 3for he removed the altars of the foreign *gods* and the high places, and broke down the *sacred* pillars and cut down the wooden images. 4He commanded Judah to seek the LORD God of their fathers, and to observe the law and the commandment. 5He also removed the high places and the incense altars from all the cities of Judah, and the kingdom was quiet under him. 6And he built fortified cities in Judah, for the land had rest; he had no war in those years, because the LORD had given him rest. 7Therefore he said to Judah, "Let us build these cities and make walls around *them*, and towers, gates, and bars, *while* the land *is* yet before us, because we have sought the LORD our God; we have sought *Him*, and He has given us rest on every side." So they built and prospered. 8And Asa had an army of three hundred thousand from Judah who carried shields and spears, and from Benjamin two hundred and eighty thousand men who carried shields and drew bows; all these *were* mighty men of valor.

9Then Zerah the Ethiopian came out against them with an army of a million men and three hundred chariots, and he came to Mareshah. 10So Asa went out against him, and they set the troops in battle array in the Valley of Zephathah at Mareshah. 11And Asa cried out to the LORD his God, and said, "LORD, *it is* nothing for You to help, whether with many or with those who have no power; help us, O LORD our God, for we rest on You, and in Your name we go against this

13:18 For a brief moment, it looked like Israel would win, but God gave Judah the victory. Their "secret weapon" was back in Jerusalem: their faithful worship of the Lord (vv. 8–11). They kept the commandments of the Lord, and He kept His promises to them. Public victories are the result of private ministries to the Lord. Those who rejoice before the Lord can rely on the Lord.

CHAPTERS 14—16

14:1ff Asa is another sad example of a man who made a splendid beginning but had a tragic ending. Early in his reign, he relied on the Lord, and God gave him a great victory. Then he believed the prophet's message and removed the idols from the land and called the people to reaffirm their allegiance to the Lord. He even deposed the queen mother for her idolatry!

13:19 ʳOr *Ephron*

multitude. O LORD, You *are* our God; do not let man prevail against You!"

12So the LORD struck the Ethiopians before Asa and Judah, and the Ethiopians fled. 13And Asa and the people who *were* with him pursued them to Gerar. So the Ethiopians were overthrown, and they could not recover, for they were broken before the LORD and His army. And they carried away very much spoil. 14Then they defeated all the cities around Gerar, for the fear of the LORD came upon them; and they plundered all the cities, for there was exceedingly much spoil in them. 15They also attacked the livestock enclosures, and carried off sheep and camels in abundance, and returned to Jerusalem.

15 Now the Spirit of God came upon Azariah the son of Oded. 2And he went out to meet Asa, and said to him: "Hear me, Asa, and all Judah and Benjamin. The LORD *is* with you while you are with Him. If you seek Him, He will be found by you; but if you forsake Him, He will forsake you. 3For a long time Israel *has been* without the true God, without a teaching priest, and without law; 4but when in their trouble they turned to the LORD God of Israel, and sought Him, He was found by them. 5And in those times *there was* no peace to the one who went out, nor to the one who came in, but great turmoil *was* on all the inhabitants of the lands. 6So nation was destroyed by nation, and city by city, for God troubled them with every adversity. 7But you, be strong and do not let your hands be weak, for your work shall be rewarded!"

8And when Asa heard these words and the prophecy of Odeds the prophet, he took courage, and removed the abominable idols from all the land of Judah and Benjamin and from the cities which he had taken in the mountains of Ephraim; and he restored the altar of the LORD that *was* before the vestibule of the LORD. 9Then he gathered all Judah and Benjamin, and those who dwelt with them from Ephraim, Manasseh, and Simeon, for they came over to him in great numbers from Israel when they saw that the LORD his God was with him.

10So they gathered together at Jerusalem in the third month, in the fifteenth year of the reign of Asa. 11And they offered to the LORD at that time seven hundred bulls and seven thousand sheep from the spoil they had brought. 12Then they entered into a covenant to seek the LORD God of their fathers with all their heart and with all their soul; 13and whoever would not seek the LORD God of Israel was to be put to death, whether small or great, whether man or woman. 14Then they took an oath before the LORD with a loud voice, with shouting and trumpets and rams' horns. 15And all Judah rejoiced at the oath, for they had sworn with all their heart and sought Him with all their soul; and He was found by them, and the LORD gave them rest all around.

16Also he removed Maachah, the mother of Asa the king, from *being* queen mother, because she had made an obscene image of Asherah;*t* and Asa cut down her obscene image, then crushed and

---

15:8 *sFollowing Masoretic Text and Septuagint; Syriac and Vulgate read *Azariah the son of Oded* (compare verse 1).
15:16 *fA Canaanite deity

burned *it* by the Brook Kidron. 17But the high places were not removed from Israel. Nevertheless the heart of Asa was loyal all his days.

18He also brought into the house of God the things that his father had dedicated and that he himself had dedicated: silver and gold and utensils. 19And there was no war until the thirty-fifth year of the reign of Asa.

16 In* the thirty-sixth year of the reign of Asa, Baasha king of Israel came up against Judah and built Ramah, that he might let none go out or come in to Asa king of Judah. 2Then Asa brought silver and gold from the treasuries of the house of the LORD and of the king's house, and sent to Ben-Hadad king of Syria, who dwelt in Damascus, saying, 3*"Let there be* a treaty between you and me, as there was between my father and your father. See, I have sent you silver and gold; come, break your treaty with Baasha king of Israel, so that he will withdraw from me."

4So Ben-Hadad heeded King Asa, and sent the captains of his armies against the cities of Israel. They attacked Ijon, Dan, Abel Maim, and all the storage cities of Naphtali. 5Now it happened, when Baasha heard *it,* that he stopped building Ramah and ceased his work. 6Then King Asa took all Judah, and they carried away the stones and timber of Ramah, which Baasha had used for building; and with them he built Geba and Mizpah.

7And at that time Hanani the seer came to Asa king of Judah, and said to him: "Because you have relied on the king of Syria, and have not relied on the LORD your God, therefore the army of the king of Syria has escaped from your hand. 8Were the Ethiopians and the Lubim not a huge army with very many chariots and horsemen? Yet, because you relied on the LORD, He delivered them into your hand. 9For the eyes of the LORD run to and fro throughout the whole earth, to show Himself strong on behalf of *those* whose heart *is* loyal to Him. In this you have done foolishly; therefore from now on you shall have wars." 10Then Asa was angry with the seer, and put him in prison, for *he was* enraged at him because of this. And Asa oppressed *some* of the people at that time.

11Note that the acts of Asa, first and last, are indeed written in the book of the kings of Judah and Israel. 12And in the thirty-ninth year of his reign, Asa became diseased in his feet, and his malady was severe; yet in his disease he did not seek the LORD, but the physicians.

13So Asa rested with his fathers; he died in the forty-first year of his reign. 14*They buried him in his own tomb, which he had made for himself in the City of David; and they laid him in the bed which was filled with spices and various ingredients prepared in a mixture of ointments. They made a very great burning for him.

17 Then Jehoshaphat his son reigned in his place, and strengthened himself against Israel. 2And he placed troops in all the fortified cities of Judah, and set garrisons in the land of Judah and in the cities of Ephraim which Asa his father had taken. 3*Now the LORD was with Jehoshaphat, because he walked in the former ways of his

16:1–10 But when he had been king thirty-six years, he stopped relying on the Lord. He took the Lord's treasures and bought protection from a heathen king! The prophet Hanani told the king what was wrong: his heart was not loyal to the Lord (16:9). Instead of humbling himself and obeying, as he had done before, in anger Asa resisted the Word and God's servant (James 1:19). When we are wrong, we should admit it instead of trying to resist God. God is much stronger than our stubbornness.

16:14 God is with us—seek Him (15:2). God answers prayer—trust Him (15:4). God rewards faithfulness—obey Him (15:7). You never outgrow the ability to sin. Noah was a mature man when he got drunk (Gen. 9:20–23), and so was Abraham when he lied about his wife (Gen. 12:10ff.). Moses was a seasoned leader when he lost his temper (Num. 20), and so was David when he committed adultery and murder. Asa's corpse lay on a bed of fragrant spices, but his name was not as fragrant as it had been. Ponder Proverbs 10:7, Ecclesiastes 7:1 and 1 Corinthians 10:12.

CHAPTERS 17—18

17:3–5 Jehoshaphat's life is described in Psalm 1:1–3. He walked in the right counsel (17:3), he delighted in God's ways (17:6), and he was fruitful in his service, sharing the Word with the people (17:7–9). He practiced the fear of the Lord, so he was protected by the fear of the Lord. When you fear God, you need fear nothing else (Ps. 112).

father David; he did not seek the Baals, [4]but sought the God[u] of his father, and walked in His commandments and not according to the acts of Israel. [5]Therefore the LORD established the kingdom in his hand; and all Judah gave presents to Jehoshaphat, and he had riches and honor in abundance. [6]And his heart took delight in the ways of the LORD; moreover he removed the high places and wooden images from Judah.

[7]Also in the third year of his reign he sent his leaders, Ben-Hail, Obadiah, Zechariah, Nethanel, and Michaiah, to teach in the cities of Judah. [8]And with them *he sent* Levites: Shemaiah, Nethaniah, Zebadiah, Asahel, Shemiramoth, Jehonathan, Adonijah, Tobijah, and Tobadonijah—the Levites; and with them Elishama and Jehoram, the priests. [9]So they taught in Judah, and *had* the Book of the Law of the LORD with them; they went throughout all the cities of Judah and taught the people.

[10]And the fear of the LORD fell on all the kingdoms of the lands that *were* around Judah, so that they did not make war against Jehoshaphat. [11]Also *some* of the Philistines brought Jehoshaphat presents and silver as tribute; and the Arabians brought him flocks, seven thousand seven hundred rams and seven thousand seven hundred male goats.

[12]So Jehoshaphat became increasingly powerful, and he built fortresses and storage cities in Judah. [13]He had much property in the cities of Judah; and the men of war, mighty men of valor, *were* in Jerusalem.

[14]These *are* their numbers, according to their fathers' houses. Of Judah, the captains of thousands: Adnah the captain, and with him three hundred thousand mighty men of valor; [15]and next to him *was* Jehohanan the captain, and with him two hundred and eighty thousand; [16]and next to him *was* Amasiah the son of Zichri, who willingly offered himself to the LORD, and with him two hundred thousand mighty men of valor. [17]Of Benjamin: Eliada a mighty man of valor, and with him two hundred thousand men armed with bow and shield; [18]and next to him *was* Jehozabad, and with him one hundred and eighty thousand prepared for war. [19]These served the king, besides those the king put in the fortified cities throughout all Judah.

18:1 But Jehoshaphat married the wrong wife, joined the wrong allies, fought the wrong war, and almost came to the wrong end. By walking "in the counsel of the ungodly" and sitting with the scornful (18:9; Ps. 1:1), the king found himself in serious trouble. He had to listen to false prophets and go to battle with a king depending on false confidence.

18

Jehoshaphat* had riches and honor in abundance; and by marriage he allied himself with Ahab. [2]After some years he went down to *visit* Ahab in Samaria; and Ahab killed sheep and oxen in abundance for him and the people who were with him, and persuaded him to go up *with him* to Ramoth Gilead. [3]So Ahab king of Israel said to Jehoshaphat king of Judah, "Will you go with me *against* Ramoth Gilead?"

And he answered him, "I *am* as you *are,* and my people as your people; *we will be* with you in the war."

[4]Also Jehoshaphat said to the king of Israel, "Please inquire for the word of the LORD today." [5]Then the king of Israel gathered the prophets together, four hundred men, and said to them, "Shall we go to war against Ramoth Gilead, or shall I refrain?"

17:4 [u]Septuagint reads LORD God.

So they said, "Go up, for God will deliver it into the king's hand."

6But Jehoshaphat said, "*Is there* not still a prophet of the LORD here, that we may inquire of Him?"ᵛ

7So the king of Israel said to Jehoshaphat, "*There is* still one man by whom we may inquire of the LORD; but I hate him, because he never prophesies good concerning me, but always evil. He *is* Micaiah the son of Imla."

And Jehoshaphat said, "Let not the king say such things!"

8Then the king of Israel called one *of his* officers and said, "Bring Micaiah the son of Imla quickly!"

9The king of Israel and Jehoshaphat king of Judah, clothed in *their* robes, sat each on his throne; and they sat at a threshing floor at the entrance of the gate of Samaria; and all the prophets prophesied before them. 10*Now Zedekiah the son of Chenaanah had made horns of iron for himself; and he said, "Thus says the LORD: 'With these you shall gore the Syrians until they are destroyed.'"

11And all the prophets prophesied so, saying, "Go up to Ramoth Gilead and prosper, for the LORD will deliver *it* into the king's hand."

12Then the messenger who had gone to call Micaiah spoke to him, saying, "Now listen, the words of the prophets with one accord encourage the king. Therefore please let your word be like *the word of* one of them, and speak encouragement."

13And Micaiah said, "As the LORD lives, whatever my God says, that I will speak."

14Then he came to the king; and the king said to him, "Micaiah, shall we go to war against Ramoth Gilead, or shall I refrain?"

And he said, "Go and prosper, and they shall be delivered into your hand!"

15So the king said to him, "How many times shall I make you swear that you tell me nothing but the truth in the name of the LORD?"

16Then he said, "I saw all Israel scattered on the mountains, as sheep that have no shepherd. And the LORD said, 'These have no master. Let each return to his house in peace.'"

17And the king of Israel said to Jehoshaphat, "Did I not tell you he would not prophesy good concerning me, but evil?"

18Then *Micaiah* said, "Therefore hear the word of the LORD: I saw the LORD sitting on His throne, and all the host of heaven standing on His right hand and His left. 19And the LORD said, 'Who will persuade Ahab king of Israel to go up, that he may fall at Ramoth Gilead?' So one spoke in this manner, and another spoke in that manner. 20Then a spirit came forward and stood before the LORD, and said, 'I will persuade him.' The LORD said to him, 'In what way?' 21So he said, 'I will go out and be a lying spirit in the mouth of all his prophets.' And the LORD said, 'You shall persuade *him* and also prevail; go out and do so.' 22Therefore look! The LORD has put a lying spirit in the mouth of these prophets of yours, and the LORD has declared disaster against you."

23Then Zedekiah the son of Chenaanah went near and struck Micaiah on the cheek, and said, "Which way did the spirit from the LORD go from me to speak to you?"

18:10 The pressure to conform is greater today than in that day. Are you resisting it? Can you detect the false prophet and his message, or are you impressed with his "visual aids" and pleasing message (18:10)? Read the last three verses of Psalm 1 and beware!

18:6 ᵛOr *him*

24And Micaiah said, "Indeed you shall see on that day when you go into an inner chamber to hide!"

25Then the king of Israel said, "Take Micaiah, and return him to Amon the governor of the city and to Joash the king's son; 26and say, 'Thus says the king: "Put this *fellow* in prison, and feed him with bread of affliction and water of affliction, until I return in peace."' "

27But Micaiah said, "If you ever return in peace, the LORD has not spoken by me." And he said, "Take heed, all you people!"

28So the king of Israel and Jehoshaphat the king of Judah went up to Ramoth Gilead. 29And the king of Israel said to Jehoshaphat, "I will disguise myself and go into battle; but you put on your robes." So the king of Israel disguised himself, and they went into battle.

30Now the king of Syria had commanded the captains of the chariots who *were* with him, saying, "Fight with no one small or great, but only with the king of Israel."

31So it was, when the captains of the chariots saw Jehoshaphat, that they said, "It *is* the king of Israel!" Therefore they surrounded him to attack; but Jehoshaphat cried out, and the LORD helped him, and God diverted them from him. 32For so it was, when the captains of the chariots saw that it was not the king of Israel, that they turned back from pursuing him. 33Now a certain man drew a bow at random, and struck the king of Israel between the joints of his armor. So he said to the driver of his chariot, "Turn around and take me out of the battle, for I am wounded." 34The battle increased that day, and the king of Israel propped *himself* up in *his* chariot facing the Syrians until evening; and about the time of sunset he died.

CHAPTER 19

19:1 Jehoshaphat returned home safely only because God was gracious to him and protected him in the battle. When we are out of the will of God and get into places of danger, we tempt God, and it is a sin to tempt God and force Him to work miracles on our behalf. That is the way Satan tempted the Lord Jesus (Matt. 4:5–7).

19:4–11 He submitted to God's Word and went back to ministering to his people. While he was away fighting somebody else's battle, his own people were being neglected (Song of Sol. 1:6). Like a good shepherd, he sought the lost and brought them back to the Lord (Ezek. 34:1–10), and he saw to it that the people were protected by honest judges and served by godly priests.

19:9 Note the emphasis on the fear of the Lord (vv. 7, 9). Jehoshaphat had sinned, but God forgave him. The result of forgiveness should be the fear of the Lord (Ps. 130:4). John Calvin wrote, "True piety consists . . . in a pure and true zeal which loves God altogether, and reveres Him truly as Lord, embraces his justice and dreads to offend Him more than to die."

19 Then* Jehoshaphat the king of Judah returned safely to his house in Jerusalem. 2And Jehu the son of Hanani the seer went out to meet him, and said to King Jehoshaphat, "Should you help the wicked and love those who hate the LORD? Therefore the wrath of the LORD *is* upon you. 3Nevertheless good things are found in you, in that you have removed the wooden images from the land, and have prepared your heart to seek God."

4*So Jehoshaphat dwelt at Jerusalem; and he went out again among the people from Beersheba to the mountains of Ephraim, and brought them back to the LORD God of their fathers. 5Then he set judges in the land throughout all the fortified cities of Judah, city by city, 6and said to the judges, "Take heed to what you are doing, for you do not judge for man but for the LORD, who *is* with you in the judgment. 7Now therefore, let the fear of the LORD be upon you; take care and do *it,* for *there is* no iniquity with the LORD our God, no partiality, nor taking of bribes."

8Moreover in Jerusalem, for the judgment of the LORD and for controversies, Jehoshaphat appointed some of the Levites and priests, and some of the chief fathers of Israel, when they returned to Jerusalem.w 9*And he commanded them, saying, "Thus you shall act in the fear of the LORD,

---

19:8 wSeptuagint and Vulgate read *for the inhabitants of Jerusalem.*

faithfully and with a loyal heart: ¹⁰Whatever case comes to you from your brethren who dwell in their cities, whether of bloodshed or offenses against law or commandment, against statutes or ordinances, you shall warn them, lest they trespass against the LORD and wrath come upon you and your brethren. Do this, and you will not be guilty. ¹¹And take notice: Amariah the chief priest *is* over you in all matters of the LORD; and Zebadiah the son of Ishmael, the ruler of the house of Judah, for all the king's matters; also the Levites *will be* officials before you. Behave courageously, and the LORD will be with the good."

20 It happened after this *that* the people of Moab with the people of Ammon, and *others* with them besides the Ammonites,ˣ came to battle against Jehoshaphat. ²Then some came and told Jehoshaphat, saying, "A great multitude is coming against you from beyond the sea, from Syria;ʸ and they are in Hazazon Tamar" (which *is* En Gedi). ³*And Jehoshaphat feared, and set himself to seek the LORD, and proclaimed a fast throughout all Judah. ⁴So Judah gathered together to ask *help* from the LORD; and from all the cities of Judah they came to seek the LORD.

⁵Then Jehoshaphat stood in the assembly of Judah and Jerusalem, in the house of the LORD, before the new court, ⁶and said: "O LORD God of our fathers, *are* You not God in heaven, and do You *not* rule over all the kingdoms of the nations, and in Your hand *is there not* power and might, so that no one is able to withstand You? ⁷*Are* You not our God, *who* drove out the inhabitants of this land before Your people Israel, and gave it to the descendants of Abraham Your friend forever? ⁸And they dwell in it, and have built You a sanctuary in it for Your name, saying, ⁹'If disaster comes upon us—sword, judgment, pestilence, or famine—we will stand before this temple and in Your presence (for Your name *is* in this temple), and cry out to You in our affliction, and You will hear and save.' ¹⁰And now, here are the people of Ammon, Moab, and Mount Seir—whom You would not let Israel invade when they came out of the land of Egypt, but they turned from them and did not destroy them— ¹¹here they are, rewarding us by coming to throw us out of Your possession which You have given us to inherit. ¹²O our God, will You not judge them? For we have no power against this great multitude that is coming against us; nor do we know what to do, but our eyes *are* upon You."

¹³Now all Judah, with their little ones, their wives, and their children, stood before the LORD. ¹⁴*Then the Spirit of the LORD came upon Jahaziel the son of Zechariah, the son of Benaiah, the son of Jeiel, the son of Mattaniah, a Levite of the sons of Asaph, in the midst of the assembly. ¹⁵And he said, "Listen, all you of Judah and you inhabitants of Jerusalem, and you, King Jehoshaphat! Thus says the LORD to you: 'Do not be afraid nor dismayed because of this great multitude, for the battle *is* not yours, but God's. ¹⁶Tomorrow go down against them. They will surely come up by the Ascent of Ziz, and you will

CHAPTER 20

20:3, 4 Seek the Lord. When you see big problems on the horizon, seek the Lord before you do anything else. What does that mean? It means to do what Jehoshaphat and Judah did. They remembered who God is (v. 6), what He did in the past (v. 7) and what He said He would do in the future (vv. 8–9). It means to trust Him and keep your eyes on Him by faith (v. 12).

20:14–20 Hear the Lord. God always has a special word for those who turn to Him for help. When you face a battle, spend much time in His Word and in prayer, for then He will give you that needed word of encouragement.

20:1 ˣFollowing Masoretic Text and Vulgate; Septuagint reads *Meunites* (compare 26:7).   20:2 ʸFollowing Masoretic Text, Septuagint, and Vulgate; some Hebrew manuscripts and Old Latin read *Edom.*

find them at the end of the brook before the Wilderness of Jeruel. [17]You will not *need* to fight in this *battle*. Position yourselves, stand still and see the salvation of the LORD, who is with you, O Judah and Jerusalem!' Do not fear or be dismayed; tomorrow go out against them, for the LORD *is* with you."

[18]And Jehoshaphat bowed his head with *his* face to the ground, and all Judah and the inhabitants of Jerusalem bowed before the LORD, worshiping the LORD. [19]Then the Levites of the children of the Kohathites and of the children of the Korahites stood up to praise the LORD God of Israel with voices loud and high.

[20]So they rose early in the morning and went out into the Wilderness of Tekoa; and as they went out, Jehoshaphat stood and said, "Hear me, O Judah and you inhabitants of Jerusalem: Believe in the LORD your God, and you shall be established; believe His prophets, and you shall prosper." [21]*And when he had consulted with the people, he appointed those who should sing to the LORD, and who should praise the beauty of holiness, as they went out before the army and were saying:

> "Praise the LORD,
> For His mercy *endures* forever."[z]

[22]Now when they began to sing and to praise, the LORD set ambushes against the people of Ammon, Moab, and Mount Seir, who had come against Judah; and they were defeated. [23]For the people of Ammon and Moab stood up against the inhabitants of Mount Seir to utterly kill and destroy *them*. And when they had made an end of the inhabitants of Seir, they helped to destroy one another.

[24]So when Judah came to a place overlooking the wilderness, they looked toward the multitude; and there *were* their dead bodies, fallen on the earth. No one had escaped.

[25]When Jehoshaphat and his people came to take away their spoil, they found among them an abundance of valuables on the dead bodies,[a] and precious jewelry, which they stripped off for themselves, more than they could carry away; and they were three days gathering the spoil because there was so much. [26]*And on the fourth day they assembled in the Valley of Berachah, for there they blessed the LORD; therefore the name of that place was called The Valley of Berachah[b] until this day. [27]Then they returned, every man of Judah and Jerusalem, with Jehoshaphat in front of them, to go back to Jerusalem with joy, for the LORD had made them rejoice over their enemies. [28]So they came to Jerusalem, with stringed instruments and harps and trumpets, to the house of the LORD. [29]And the fear of God was on all the kingdoms of *those* countries when they heard that the LORD had fought against the enemies of Israel. [30]Then the realm of Jehoshaphat was quiet, for his God gave him rest all around.

[31]So Jehoshaphat was king over Judah. *He was* thirty-five years old when he became king, and he reigned twenty-five years in Jerusalem. His mother's name *was* Azubah the daughter of

---

20:21–23 *Praise the Lord.* The battle was won by the singers, standing in the most dangerous place of all—between two armies. But they sang the Lord's praises and routed the enemy. The choir praised God after God gave the word (v. 19), before the battle (v. 21), and after the victory (vv. 26–28), a good pattern for us to follow in our praise.

20:26 In Hebrew, *Berachah* means "blessing" (v. 26). Even a valley can become a place of blessing if we learn how to praise the Lord. "Prayer changes things" is a familiar saying that is certainly true. But it is also true that "praise changes things." Why? Because true praise changes people, and God can work in and through people who praise Him. True praise involves faith, hope, and love, the strongest weapons in the Christian armory.

20:21 [z]Compare Psalm 106:1   20:25 [a]A few Hebrew manuscripts, Old Latin, and Vulgate read *garments;* Septuagint reads *armor.*   20:26 [b]Literally *Blessing*

Shilhi. 32And he walked in the way of his father Asa, and did not turn aside from it, doing *what was* right in the sight of the LORD. 33Nevertheless the high places were not taken away, for as yet the people had not directed their hearts to the God of their fathers.

34Now the rest of the acts of Jehoshaphat, first and last, indeed they *are* written in the book of Jehu the son of Hanani, which *is* mentioned in the book of the kings of Israel.

35After this Jehoshaphat king of Judah allied himself with Ahaziah king of Israel, who acted very wickedly. 36And he allied himself with him to make ships to go to Tarshish, and they made the ships in Ezion Geber. 37But Eliezer the son of Dodavah of Mareshah prophesied against Jehoshaphat, saying, "Because you have allied yourself with Ahaziah, the LORD has destroyed your works." Then the ships were wrecked, so that they were not able to go to Tarshish.

21 And Jehoshaphat rested with his fathers, and was buried with his fathers in the City of David. Then Jehoram his son reigned in his place. 2He had brothers, the sons of Jehoshaphat: Azariah, Jehiel, Zechariah, Azaryahu, Michael, and Shephatiah; all these *were* the sons of Jehoshaphat king of Israel. 3*Their father gave them great gifts of silver and gold and precious things, with fortified cities in Judah; but he gave the kingdom to Jehoram, because he *was* the firstborn.

4Now when Jehoram was established over the kingdom of his father, he strengthened himself and killed all his brothers with the sword, and also *others* of the princes of Israel.

5Jehoram *was* thirty-two years old when he became king, and he reigned eight years in Jerusalem. 6And he walked in the way of the kings of Israel, just as the house of Ahab had done, for he had the daughter of Ahab as a wife; and he did evil in the sight of the LORD. 7Yet the LORD would not destroy the house of David, because of the covenant that He had made with David, and since He had promised to give a lamp to him and to his sons forever.

8*In his days Edom revolted against Judah's authority, and made a king over themselves. 9So Jehoram went out with his officers, and all his chariots with him. And he rose by night and attacked the Edomites who had surrounded him and the captains of the chariots. 10Thus Edom has been in revolt against Judah's authority to this day. At that time Libnah revolted against his rule, because he had forsaken the LORD God of his fathers. 11Moreover he made high places in the mountains of Judah, and caused the inhabitants of Jerusalem to commit harlotry, and led Judah astray.

12*And a letter came to him from Elijah the prophet, saying,

Thus says the LORD God of your father David:
Because you have not walked in the ways of Jehoshaphat your father, or in the ways of Asa king of Judah, 13but have walked in the way of the kings of Israel, and have made Judah and the inhabitants of Jerusalem to play the harlot like the harlotry of the house of Ahab, and also have killed your brothers, those of your father's household, *who were* better than yourself,

CHAPTER 21

21:3 God kept His promise to maintain David's descendants on the throne of Judah, but He also kept His promise to chasten them if they disobeyed Him (2 Sam. 7:12–17). He disciplined Jehoram in several ways.

21:8–11 To begin with, Jehoram's rule began to disintegrate as the Edomites revolted and the Philistines invaded. Even the Levitical city of Libnah revolted (v. 10; Josh. 21:13). Life starts to fall apart when you stop obeying the Lord.

21:12–15 Elijah's letter warned the king and gave him opportunity to repent, but Jehoram went his own way. What a privilege to get a letter from a famous prophet! And what a tragedy to treat it with disdain. The king died in severe pain, and nobody regretted it. Yet he was the son of the great Jehoshaphat.

If you received a loving letter of warning today, how would you respond to it?

¹⁴behold, the LORD will strike your people with a serious affliction—your children, your wives, and all your possessions; ¹⁵and you *will become* very sick with a disease of your intestines, until your intestines come out by reason of the sickness, day by day.

¹⁶Moreover the LORD stirred up against Jehoram the spirit of the Philistines and the Arabians who *were* near the Ethiopians. ¹⁷And they came up into Judah and invaded it, and carried away all the possessions that were found in the king's house, and also his sons and his wives, so that there was not a son left to him except Jehoahaz,ᶜ the youngest of his sons. ¹⁸After all this the LORD struck him in his intestines with an incurable disease. ¹⁹Then it happened in the course of time, after the end of two years, that his intestines came out because of his sickness; so he died in severe pain. And his people made no burning for him, like the burning for his fathers.

²⁰He was thirty-two years old when he became king. He reigned in Jerusalem eight years and, to no one's sorrow, departed. However they buried him in the City of David, but not in the tombs of the kings.

22 Then the inhabitants of Jerusalem made Ahaziah his youngest son king in his place, for the raiders who came with the Arabians into the camp had killed all the older *sons.* So Ahaziah the son of Jehoram, king of Judah, reigned. ²Ahaziah *was* forty-twoᵈ years old when he became king, and he reigned one year in Jerusalem. His mother's name *was* Athaliah the granddaughter of Omri. ³*He also walked in the ways of the house of Ahab, for his mother advised him to do wickedly. ⁴Therefore he did evil in the sight of the LORD, like the house of Ahab; for they were his counselors after the death of his father, to his destruction. ⁵He also followed their advice, and went with Jehoramᵉ the son of Ahab king of Israel to war against Hazael king of Syria at Ramoth Gilead; and the Syrians wounded Joram. ⁶Then he returned to Jezreel to recover from the wounds which he had received at Ramah, when he fought against Hazael king of Syria. And Azariahᶠ the son of Jehoram, king of Judah, went down to see Jehoram the son of Ahab in Jezreel, because he was sick.

⁷His going to Joram was God's occasion for Ahaziah's downfall; for when he arrived, he went out with Jehoram against Jehu the son of Nimshi, whom the LORD had anointed to cut off the house of Ahab. ⁸And it happened, when Jehu was executing judgment on the house of Ahab, and found the princes of Judah and the sons of Ahaziah's brothers who served Ahaziah, that he killed them. ⁹Then he searched for Ahaziah; and they caught him (he was hiding in Samaria), and brought him to Jehu. When they had killed him, they buried him, "because," they said, "he is the son of Je-

CHAPTERS 22—23

22:3–12 Corruption. The British poet Samuel Taylor Coleridge called mothers "the holiest thing alive," but you could not apply those words to Athaliah. Imagine a mother teaching her son how to sin! She was the Old Testament version of Herodias (Matt. 14:1–12), just the opposite of godly Hannah (1 Sam. 1—2). But what else would you expect from the daughter of Jezebel and Ahab? Athaliah was the only woman to rule over the kingdom of Judah, and it was a rule of evil.

21:17 ᶜElsewhere called *Ahaziah* (compare 2 Chronicles 22:1) 22:2 ᵈOr *twenty-two* (compare 2 Kings 8:26) 22:5 ᵉAlso spelled *Joram* (compare verses 5 and 7; 2 Kings 8:28; and elsewhere) 22:6 ᶠSome Hebrew manuscripts, Septuagint, Syriac, Vulgate, and 2 Kings 8:29 read *Ahaziah.*

hoshaphat, who sought the LORD with all his heart."

So the house of Ahaziah had no one to assume power over the kingdom.

10Now when Athaliah the mother of Ahaziah saw that her son was dead, she arose and destroyed all the royal heirs of the house of Judah. 11But Jehoshabeath,g the daughter of the king, took Joash the son of Ahaziah, and stole him away from among the king's sons who were being murdered, and put him and his nurse in a bedroom. So Jehoshabeath, the daughter of King Jehoram, the wife of Jehoiada the priest (for she was the sister of Ahaziah), hid him from Athaliah so that she did not kill him. 12And he was hidden with them in the house of God for six years, while Athaliah reigned over the land.

23 In the seventh year Jehoiada strengthened himself, *and made a* covenant with the captains of hundreds: Azariah the son of Jeroham, Ishmael the son of Jehohanan, Azariah the son of Obed, Maaseiah the son of Adaiah, and Elishaphat the son of Zichri. 2And they went throughout Judah and gathered the Levites from all the cities of Judah, and the chief fathers of Israel, and they came to Jerusalem.

3Then all the assembly made a covenant with the king in the house of God. And he said to them, "Behold, the king's son shall reign, as the LORD has said of the sons of David. 4This *is* what you shall do: One-third of you entering on the Sabbath, of the priests and the Levites, *shall be* keeping watch over the doors; 5one-third *shall be* at the king's house; and one-third at the Gate of the Foundation. All the people *shall be* in the courts of the house of the LORD. 6But let no one come into the house of the LORD except the priests and those of the Levites who serve. They may go in, for they *are* holy; but all the people shall keep the watch of the LORD. 7And the Levites shall surround the king on all sides, every man with his weapons in his hand; and whoever comes into the house, let him be put to death. You are to be with the king when he comes in and when he goes out."

8So the Levites and all Judah did according to all that Jehoiada the priest commanded. And each man took his men who were to be on duty on the Sabbath, with those who were going *off duty* on the Sabbath; for Jehoiada the priest had not dismissed the divisions. 9And Jehoiada the priest gave to the captains of hundreds the spears and the large and small shields which *had belonged* to King David, that *were* in the temple of God. 10Then he set all the people, every man with his weapon in his hand, from the right side of the temple to the left side of the temple, along by the altar and by the temple, all around the king. 11*And they brought out the king's son, put the crown on him, gave *him* the Testimony,h and made him king. Then Jehoiada and his sons anointed him, and said, "*Long* live the king!"

12Now when Athaliah heard the noise of the people running and praising the king, she came to the people *in* the temple of the LORD. 13When she looked, there was the king standing by his

23:11–15 Coronation. But God had another woman on the scene, the godly wife of the high priest, and she did the will of God in saving the infant Joash. At the right time, her husband orchestrated the coronation of Joash and the condemnation of Athaliah. Note the three covenants involved: with the army (23:1), with the king (23:3), and with the Lord (23:16).

22:11 gSpelled *Jehosheba* in 2 Kings 11:2　23:11 hThat is, the Law (compare Exodus 25:16, 21; 31:18)

pillar at the entrance; and the leaders and the trumpeters *were* by the king. All the people of the land were rejoicing and blowing trumpets, also the singers with musical instruments, and those who led in praise. So Athaliah tore her clothes and said, "Treason! Treason!"

14And Jehoiada the priest brought out the captains of hundreds who were set over the army, and said to them, "Take her outside under guard, and slay with the sword whoever follows her." For the priest had said, "Do not kill her in the house of the LORD."

15So they seized her; and she went by way of the entrance of the Horse Gate *into* the king's house, and they killed her there.

16Then Jehoiada made a covenant between himself, the people, and the king, that they should be the LORD's people. 17And all the people went to the temple*ᶦ* of Baal, and tore it down. They broke in pieces its altars and images, and killed Mattan the priest of Baal before the altars. 18*Also Jehoiada appointed the oversight of the house of the LORD to the hand of the priests, the Levites, whom David had assigned in the house of the LORD, to offer the burnt offerings of the LORD, as *it is* written in the Law of Moses, with rejoicing and with singing, *as it was established* by David. 19And he set the gatekeepers at the gates of the house of the LORD, so that no one *who was* in any way unclean should enter.

20Then he took the captains of hundreds, the nobles, the governors of the people, and all the people of the land, and brought the king down from the house of the LORD; and they went through the Upper Gate to the king's house, and set the king on the throne of the kingdom. 21So all the people of the land rejoiced; and the city was quiet, for they had slain Athaliah with the sword.

23:18 Contribution. We cannot escape David! He provided the king (23:3), the weapons (23:9), and the temple organization and music (23:18). But how long can Judah live on the dividends of the spiritual investments made by godly men and women of previous generations? *How long can God's church live today?*

CHAPTER 24

24:1, 2 Joash did many fine things, but he was a "leaner." As long as godly Jehoiada was on the scene, the king obeyed the Lord, and the temple prospered. But after the high priest died, the king began listening to other counselors; soon he led the nation into sin.

24 Joash* *was* seven years old when he became king, and he reigned forty years in Jerusalem. His mother's name *was* Zibiah of Beersheba. 2Joash did *what was* right in the sight of the LORD all the days of Jehoiada the priest. 3And Jehoiada took two wives for him, and he had sons and daughters.

4Now it happened after this *that* Joash set his heart on repairing the house of the LORD. 5Then he gathered the priests and the Levites, and said to them, "Go out to the cities of Judah, and gather from all Israel money to repair the house of your God from year to year, and see that you do it quickly."

However the Levites did not do it quickly. 6So the king called Jehoiada the chief *priest,* and said to him, "Why have you not required the Levites to bring in from Judah and from Jerusalem the collection, *according to the commandment* of Moses the servant of the LORD and of the assembly of Israel, for the tabernacle of witness?" 7For the sons of Athaliah, that wicked woman, had broken into the house of God, and had also presented all the dedicated things of the house of the LORD to the Baals.

8Then at the king's command they made a chest, and set it outside at the gate of the house of the LORD. 9And they made a proclamation throughout Judah and Jerusalem to bring to the LORD the col-

---

23:17 ᶦLiterally *house*

lection *that* Moses the servant of God *had imposed* on Israel in the wilderness. ¹⁰Then all the leaders and all the people rejoiced, brought their contributions, and put *them* into the chest until all had given. ¹¹So it was, at that time, when the chest was brought to the king's official by the hand of the Levites, and when they saw that *there was* much money, that the king's scribe and the high priest's officer came and emptied the chest, and took it and returned it to its place. Thus they did day by day, and gathered money in abundance.

¹²The king and Jehoiada gave it to those who did the work of the service of the house of the Lord; and they hired masons and carpenters to repair the house of the Lord, and also those who worked in iron and bronze to restore the house of the Lord. ¹³So the workmen labored, and the work was completed by them; they restored the house of God to its original condition and reinforced it. ¹⁴When they had finished, they brought the rest of the money before the king and Jehoiada; they made from it articles for the house of the Lord, articles for serving and offering, spoons and vessels of gold and silver. And they offered burnt offerings in the house of the Lord continually all the days of Jehoiada.

¹⁵But Jehoiada grew old and was full of days, and he died; *he was* one hundred and thirty years old when he died. ¹⁶And they buried him in the City of David among the kings, because he had done good in Israel, both toward God and His house.

¹⁷*Now after the death of Jehoiada the leaders of Judah came and bowed down to the king. And the king listened to them. ¹⁸Therefore they left the house of the Lord God of their fathers, and served wooden images and idols; and wrath came upon Judah and Jerusalem because of their trespass. ¹⁹Yet He sent prophets to them, to bring them back to the Lord; and they testified against them, but they would not listen.

²⁰Then the Spirit of God came upon Zechariah the son of Jehoiada the priest, who stood above the people, and said to them, "Thus says God: 'Why do you transgress the commandments of the Lord, so that you cannot prosper? Because you have forsaken the Lord, He also has forsaken you.' " ²¹So they conspired against him, and at the command of the king they stoned him with stones in the court of the house of the Lord. ²²Thus Joash the king did not remember the kindness which Jehoiada his father had done to him, but killed his son; and as he died, he said, "The Lord look on *it*, and repay!"

²³So it happened in the spring of the year *that* the army of Syria came up against him; and they came to Judah and Jerusalem, and destroyed all the leaders of the people from among the people, and sent all their spoil to the king of Damascus. ²⁴For the army of the Syrians came with a small company of men; but the Lord delivered a very great army into their hand, because they had forsaken the Lord God of their fathers. So they executed judgment against Joash. ²⁵*And when they had withdrawn from him (for they left him severely wounded), his own servants conspired against him because of the blood of the sonsʲ of

24:25 ʲSeptuagint and Vulgate read *son* (compare verses 20–22).

24:17 When you truly obey God's Word, you do it regardless of the messenger. If you lean on others and fail to develop spiritual depth, your spiritual life will be gone when those people are gone. Joash would not listen to the prophets and he even killed one of them (vv. 19–21). God abandoned the people, the army was defeated (v. 24; see also Deut. 32:30), and the king was assassinated.

24:25 The godly priest was buried with the kings (v. 16), but the ungodly king was not (v. 25). Joash was untrue to his friends and treated them like enemies (Prov. 27:6, 10, 17). He refused to listen to God and became another example of a man who made a good beginning but came to a tragic ending. Henry Ford commented, "My best friend is the one who brings out the best in me."

Jehoiada the priest, and killed him on his bed. So he died. And they buried him in the City of David, but they did not bury him in the tombs of the kings.

26These are the ones who conspired against him: Zabad[k] the son of Shimeath the Ammonitess, and Jehozabad the son of Shimrith[l] the Moabitess. 27Now *concerning* his sons, and the many oracles about him, and the repairing of the house of God, indeed they *are* written in the annals of the book of the kings. Then Amaziah his son reigned in his place.

25 Amaziah *was* twenty-five years old *when* he became king, and he reigned twenty-nine years in Jerusalem. His mother's name *was* Jehoaddan of Jerusalem. 2*And he did *what was* right in the sight of the LORD, but not with a loyal heart.

3Now it happened, as soon as the kingdom was established for him, that he executed his servants who had murdered his father the king. 4However he did not execute their children, but *did* as *it is* written in the Law in the Book of Moses, where the LORD commanded, saying, "The fathers shall not be put to death for their children, nor shall the children be put to death for their fathers; but a person shall die for his own sin."[m]

5Moreover Amaziah gathered Judah together and set over them captains of thousands and captains of hundreds, according to *their* fathers' houses, throughout all Judah and Benjamin; and he numbered them from twenty years old and above, and found them to be three hundred thousand choice *men, able* to go to war, who could handle spear and shield. 6*He also hired one hundred thousand mighty men of valor from Israel for one hundred talents of silver. 7But a man of God came to him, saying, "O king, do not let the army of Israel go with you, for the LORD is not with Israel—*not with* any of the children of Ephraim. 8But if you go, be gone! Be strong in battle! *Even so,* God shall make you fall before the enemy; for God has power to help and to overthrow."

9Then Amaziah said to the man of God, "But what *shall we* do about the hundred talents which I have given to the troops of Israel?"

And the man of God answered, "The LORD is able to give you much more than this." 10So Amaziah discharged the troops that had come to him from Ephraim, to go back home. Therefore their anger was greatly aroused against Judah, and they returned home in great anger.

11Then Amaziah strengthened himself, and leading his people, he went to the Valley of Salt and killed ten thousand of the people of Seir. 12Also the children of Judah took captive ten thousand alive, brought them to the top of the rock, and cast them down from the top of the rock, so that they all were dashed in pieces.

13But as for the soldiers of the army which Amaziah had discharged, so that they would not go with him to battle, they raided the cities of Judah from Samaria to Beth Horon, killed three thousand in them, and took much spoil.

14Now it was so, after Amaziah came from the

CHAPTER 25

25:2 Amaziah was halfhearted in his religious life and was not loyal to the Lord. Instead of trusting God for victory, he hired men from Israel; then he worried about the money he would lose if he obeyed the Lord! Once you start measuring obedience by profit and loss, you are not living by faith (Matt. 6:33). When you start asking yourself, "Is it profitable?" instead of "Is it right?" you had better read Philippians 2:1–11 and Hebrews 11:24–26.

25:6–10 Amaziah argued with God's will but finally obeyed it; then the army became angry with him and declared war! They had been paid, so they should have gone home rejoicing, but they wanted a chance to fight and get spoils of war. Such is the wickedness of the human heart. Amaziah lost money and was upset; the soldiers made money and were angry. Money does not satisfy the heart.

24:26 [k]Or *Jozachar* (compare 2 Kings 12:21) [l]Or *Shomer* (compare 2 Kings 12:21)   25:4 [m]Deuteronomy 24:16

slaughter of the Edomites, that he brought the gods of the people of Seir, set them up *to be* his gods, and bowed down before them and burned incense to them. 15*Therefore the anger of the LORD was aroused against Amaziah, and He sent him a prophet who said to him, "Why have you sought the gods of the people, which could not rescue their own people from your hand?"

16So it was, as he talked with him, that *the king* said to him, "Have we made you the king's counselor? Cease! Why should you be killed?"

Then the prophet ceased, and said, "I know that God has determined to destroy you, because you have done this and have not heeded my advice."

17Now Amaziah king of Judah asked advice and sent to Joash[n] the son of Jehoahaz, the son of Jehu, king of Israel, saying, "Come, let us face one another *in battle.*"

18And Joash king of Israel sent to Amaziah king of Judah, saying, "The thistle that *was* in Lebanon sent to the cedar that was in Lebanon, saying, 'Give your daughter to my son as wife'; and a wild beast that *was* in Lebanon passed by and trampled the thistle. 19Indeed you say that you have defeated the Edomites, and your heart is lifted up to boast. Stay at home now; why should you meddle with trouble, that you should fall— you and Judah with you?"

20But Amaziah would not heed, for it *came* from God, that He might give them into the hand *of their enemies,* because they sought the gods of Edom. 21So Joash king of Israel went out; and he and Amaziah king of Judah faced one another at Beth Shemesh, which *belongs* to Judah. 22And Judah was defeated by Israel, and every man fled to his tent. 23Then Joash the king of Israel captured Amaziah king of Judah, the son of Joash, the son of Jehoahaz, at Beth Shemesh; and he brought him to Jerusalem, and broke down the wall of Jerusalem from the Gate of Ephraim to the Corner Gate—four hundred cubits. 24And *he took* all the gold and silver, all the articles that were found in the house of God with Obed-Edom, the treasures of the king's house, and hostages, and returned to Samaria.

25Amaziah the son of Joash, king of Judah, lived fifteen years after the death of Joash the son of Jehoahaz, king of Israel. 26Now the rest of the acts of Amaziah, from first to last, indeed *are* they not written in the book of the kings of Judah and Israel? 27After the time that Amaziah turned away from following the LORD, they made a conspiracy against him in Jerusalem, and he fled to Lachish; but they sent after him to Lachish and killed him there. 28Then they brought him on horses and buried him with his fathers in the City of Judah.

26 Now* all the people of Judah took Uzziah,[o] who *was* sixteen years old, and made him king instead of his father Amaziah. 2He built

---

25:17 [n]Spelled *Jehoash* in 2 Kings 14:8ff   26:1 [o]Called *Azariah* in 2 Kings 14:21ff

25:15, 16 The king refused to hear God's servant and threatened to kill him, but in the end, Amaziah died. He lived for the wrong values and by the wrong counsel, and he died a failure. God is seeking disciples who are wholehearted (Matt. 6:19–24).

CHAPTER 26

26:1–5 The *starting point* in Uzziah's success was his seeking God and wanting to do His will (v. 5). Unlike his father, Uzziah was a man wholly given to the Lord. He believed and practiced Joshua 1:8 and Psalm 1:1–3.

The Peril of Pride—In his pride, Moses lost his temper and was kept out of the Promised Land (Num. 20:1–13). Pride kept Joshua from seeking God's will at Ai, and he lost the battle (Josh. 7). King Nebuchadnezzar's pride turned him into an animal (Dan. 4), and Peter's pride led to his denial of Christ (Luke 22:31–34). "No matter how dear you are to God," said Charles Haddon Spurgeon, "if pride is harbored in your spirit, He will whip it out of you. They that go up in their own estimation must come down again by His discipline."

Elath[p] and restored it to Judah, after the king rested with his fathers.

3Uzziah *was* sixteen years old when he became king, and he reigned fifty-two years in Jerusalem. His mother's name was Jecholiah of Jerusalem. 4And he did *what was* right in the sight of the LORD, according to all that his father Amaziah had done. 5He sought God in the days of Zechariah, who had understanding in the visions[q] of God; and as long as he sought the LORD, God made him prosper.

6Now he went out and made war against the Philistines, and broke down the wall of Gath, the wall of Jabneh, and the wall of Ashdod; and he built cities *around* Ashdod and among the Philistines. 7God helped him against the Philistines, against the Arabians who lived in Gur Baal, and against the Meunites. 8Also the Ammonites brought tribute to Uzziah. His fame spread as far as the entrance of Egypt, for he became exceedingly strong.

9And Uzziah built towers in Jerusalem at the Corner Gate, at the Valley Gate, and at the corner buttress of the wall; then he fortified them. 10Also he built towers in the desert. He dug many wells, for he had much livestock, both in the lowlands and in the plains; *he also had* farmers and vinedressers in the mountains and in Carmel, for he loved the soil.

11Moreover Uzziah had an army of fighting men who went out to war by companies, according to the number on their roll as prepared by Jeiel the scribe and Maaseiah the officer, under the hand of Hananiah, *one* of the king's captains. 12The total number of chief officers[r] of the mighty men of valor *was* two thousand six hundred. 13And under their authority *was* an army of three hundred and seven thousand five hundred, that made war with mighty power, to help the king against the enemy. 14Then Uzziah prepared for them, for the entire army, shields, spears, helmets, body armor, bows, and slings *to cast* stones. 15And he made devices in Jerusalem, invented by skillful men, to be on the towers and the corners, to shoot arrows and large stones. So his fame spread far and wide, for he was marvelously helped till he became strong.

16*But when he was strong his heart was lifted up, to *his* destruction, for he transgressed against the LORD his God by entering the temple of the LORD to burn incense on the altar of incense. 17So Azariah the priest went in after him, and with him were eighty priests of the LORD—valiant men. 18And they withstood King Uzziah, and said to him, "*It is* not for you, Uzziah, to burn incense to the LORD, but for the priests, the sons of Aaron, who are consecrated to burn incense. Get out of the sanctuary, for you have trespassed! You *shall have* no honor from the LORD God."

19*Then Uzziah became furious; and he *had* a censer in his hand to burn incense. And while he was angry with the priests, leprosy broke out on his forehead, before the priests in the house of the LORD, beside the incense altar. 20And Azariah the chief priest and all the priests looked at him, and there, on his forehead, he *was* leprous;

26:16–18 The *turning point* was his pride (v. 16). He became famous (vv. 8, 15) and strong, and God helped him wonderfully (vv. 7, 15); but he could not handle success. If God's blessings do not humble us, they will eventually destroy us. It is true that "a man's pride will bring him low" (Prov. 29:23; see also Prov. 11:2; 16:18).

26:19–21 The *finishing point* was his isolation as a leper (vv. 19–21). Not content to be a king, he also wanted to be a priest. He did not respect the boundaries God had established, so God shut him in a narrow place as a leper. God gives the wide places to those He can trust with freedom (Ps. 18:16–19).

Uzziah did not commit a gross sin of the flesh. *He sinned in the realm of spiritual things.* It is possible to disobey God in the temple with a censer in your hand, but if you do, expect God to deal with you drastically.

26:2 [p]Hebrew *Eloth*   26:5 [q]Several Hebrew manuscripts, Septuagint, Syriac, Targum, and Arabic read *fear*.
26:12 [r]Literally *chief fathers*

so they thrust him out of that place. Indeed he also hurried to get out, because the LORD had struck him.

²¹King Uzziah was a leper until the day of his death. He dwelt in an isolated house, because he was a leper; for he was cut off from the house of the LORD. Then Jotham his son *was* over the king's house, judging the people of the land.

²²Now the rest of the acts of Uzziah, from first to last, the prophet Isaiah the son of Amoz wrote. ²³So Uzziah rested with his fathers, and they buried him with his fathers in the field of burial which *belonged* to the kings, for they said, "He is a leper." Then Jotham his son reigned in his place.

27 Jotham* *was* twenty-five years old when he became king, and he reigned sixteen years in Jerusalem. His mother's name *was* Jerushahˢ the daughter of Zadok. ²And he did *what was* right in the sight of the LORD, according to all that his father Uzziah had done (although he did not enter the temple of the LORD). But still the people acted corruptly.

³He built the Upper Gate of the house of the LORD, and he built extensively on the wall of Ophel. ⁴Moreover he built cities in the mountains of Judah, and in the forests he built fortresses and towers. ⁵He also fought with the king of the Ammonites and defeated them. And the people of Ammon gave him in that year one hundred talents of silver, ten thousand kors of wheat, and ten thousand of barley. The people of Ammon paid this to him in the second and third years also. ⁶So Jotham became mighty, because he prepared his ways before the LORD his God.

⁷Now the rest of the acts of Jotham, and all his wars and his ways, indeed they *are* written in the book of the kings of Israel and Judah. ⁸*He was twenty-five years old when he became king, and he reigned sixteen years in Jerusalem. ⁹So Jotham rested with his fathers, and they buried him in the City of David. Then Ahaz his son reigned in his place.

28 Ahaz* *was* twenty years old when he became king, and he reigned sixteen years in Jerusalem; and he did not do *what was* right in the sight of the LORD, as his father David *had* done. ²For he walked in the ways of the kings of Israel, and made molded images for the Baals. ³*He burned incense in the Valley of the Son of Hinnom, and burned his children in the fire, according to the abominations of the nations whom the LORD had cast out before the children of Israel. ⁴And he sacrificed and burned incense on the high places, on the hills, and under every green tree.

⁵Therefore the LORD his God delivered him into the hand of the king of Syria. They defeated him, and carried away a great multitude of them as captives, and brought *them* to Damascus. Then he was also delivered into the hand of the king of Israel, who defeated him with a great slaughter. ⁶For Pekah the son of Remaliah killed one hundred and twenty thousand in Judah in one day, all valiant men, because they had forsaken the LORD God of their fathers. ⁷Zichri, a mighty man of Ephraim, killed Maaseiah the king's son, Azrikam the officer over the house, and Elkanah *who*

CHAPTER 27

27:1, 2 Uzziah sinned and was disciplined by the Lord, but that one event did not destroy his godly influence. His son Jotham followed his father's example but avoided his father's sin, and the Lord honored him.

27:8, 9 Jotham lived a brief life and had a short reign, but he was faithful to the Lord. It is not how long we live that counts but *how* we live. Although Jotham's chapter in Chronicles is short, 1 John 2:17 is still true.

CHAPTER 28

28:1, 2 The spiritual leadership that began with Uzziah and continued with Jotham disappeared with Ahaz. We wonder why the godly examples of his father and grandfather did Ahaz no good. Historians tell us that Ahaz was co-regent with his father for four years, which means he started when he was sixteen. Did Ahaz become proud? Did he listen to wrong counsel?

28:3 The Ammonite god Molech was worshiped in the Valley of the Son of Hinnom. The king even put his children on the heathen altar. When a father is disobedient to God, often the children suffer most. King Josiah defiled the place (2 Kings 23:10) and made it a garbage dump. The word *gehenna* came to refer to the place of eternal judgment, hell.

27:1 ˢSpelled *Jerusha* in 2 Kings 15:33

28:9–11 Judah experienced a humiliating defeat from Israel, but God mercifully overruled and rescued the people. It was a prophet, not a king or general, who saved the day.

was second to the king. [8]And the children of Israel carried away captive of their brethren two hundred thousand women, sons, and daughters; and they also took away much spoil from them, and brought the spoil to Samaria.

[9]*But a prophet of the LORD was there, whose name *was* Oded; and he went out before the army that came to Samaria, and said to them: "Look, because the LORD God of your fathers was angry with Judah, He has delivered them into your hand; but you have killed them in a rage *that* reaches up to heaven. [10]And now you propose to force the children of Judah and Jerusalem to be your male and female slaves; *but are* you not also guilty before the LORD your God? [11]Now hear me, therefore, and return the captives, whom you have taken captive from your brethren, for the fierce wrath of the LORD *is* upon you."

[12]Then some of the heads of the children of Ephraim, Azariah the son of Johanan, Berechiah the son of Meshillemoth, Jehizkiah the son of Shallum, and Amasa the son of Hadlai, stood up against those who came from the war, [13]and said to them, "You shall not bring the captives here, for we *already* have offended the LORD. You intend to add to our sins and to our guilt; for our guilt is great, and *there is* fierce wrath against Israel." [14]So the armed men left the captives and the spoil before the leaders and all the assembly. [15]Then the men who were designated by name rose up and took the captives, and from the spoil they clothed all who were naked among them, dressed them and gave them sandals, gave them food and drink, and anointed them; and they let all the feeble ones ride on donkeys. So they brought them to their brethren at Jericho, the city of palm trees. Then they returned to Samaria.

[16]At the same time King Ahaz sent to the kings[f] of Assyria to help him. [17]For again the Edomites had come, attacked Judah, and carried away captives. [18]The Philistines also had invaded the cities of the lowland and of the South of Judah, and had taken Beth Shemesh, Aijalon, Gederoth, Sochoh with its villages, Timnah with its villages, and Gimzo with its villages; and they dwelt there. [19]For the LORD brought Judah low because of Ahaz king of Israel, for he had encouraged moral decline in Judah and had been continually unfaithful to the LORD. [20]Also Tiglath-Pileser[u] king of Assyria came to him and distressed him, and did not assist him. [21]For Ahaz took part *of the treasures* from the house of the LORD, from the house of the king, and from the leaders, and he gave *it* to the king of Assyria; but he did not help him.

28:22–27 Instead of repenting and returning to the God of his father and grandfather, Ahaz adopted the gods of the victorious enemy. It seemed logical to him because the enemy was winning! Instead of going by the Word of God, he took the pragmatic approach (Prov. 3:5–6). Have you ever done that? It is dangerous!

[22]*Now in the time of his distress King Ahaz became increasingly unfaithful to the LORD. This *is that* King Ahaz. [23]For he sacrificed to the gods of Damascus which had defeated him, saying, "Because the gods of the kings of Syria help them, I will sacrifice to them that they may help me." But they were the ruin of him and of all Israel. [24]So Ahaz gathered the articles of the house of God, cut in pieces the articles of the house of God, shut up the doors of the house of the LORD, and made for himself altars in every corner of Jerusalem. [25]And in every single city of Judah he made high places to burn incense to other gods, and

28:16 'Septuagint, Syriac, and Vulgate read *king* (compare verse 20).   28:20 ᵘHebrew *Tilgath-Pilneser*

provoked to anger the LORD God of his fathers. 26Now the rest of his acts and all his ways, from first to last, indeed they *are* written in the book of the kings of Judah and Israel. 27So Ahaz rested with his fathers, and they buried him in the city, in Jerusalem; but they did not bring him into the tombs of the kings of Israel. Then Hezekiah his son reigned in his place.

29 Hezekiah* became king *when he was* twenty-five years old, and he reigned twenty-nine years in Jerusalem. His mother's name *was* Abijahᵛ the daughter of Zechariah. 2And he did *what was* right in the sight of the LORD, according to all that his father David had done.

3In the first year of his reign, in the first month, he opened the doors of the house of the LORD and repaired them. 4Then he brought in the priests and the Levites, and gathered them in the East Square, 5and said to them: "Hear me, Levites! Now sanctify yourselves, sanctify the house of the LORD God of your fathers, and carry out the rubbish from the holy *place*. 6*For our fathers have trespassed and done evil in the eyes of the LORD our God; they have forsaken Him, have turned their faces away from the dwelling place of the LORD, and turned *their* backs *on Him*. 7They have also shut up the doors of the vestibule, put out the lamps, and have not burned incense or offered burnt offerings in the holy *place* to the God of Israel. 8Therefore the wrath of the LORD fell upon Judah and Jerusalem, and He has given them up to trouble, to desolation, and to jeering, as you see with your eyes. 9For indeed, because of this our fathers have fallen by the sword; and our sons, our daughters, and our wives *are* in captivity.

10"Now *it is* in my heart to make a covenant with the LORD God of Israel, that His fierce wrath may turn away from us. 11My sons, do not be negligent now, for the LORD has chosen you to stand before Him, to serve Him, and that you should minister to Him and burn incense."

12Then these Levites arose: Mahath the son of Amasai and Joel the son of Azariah, of the sons of the Kohathites; of the sons of Merari, Kish the son of Abdi and Azariah the son of Jehallelel; of the Gershonites, Joah the son of Zimmah and Eden the son of Joah; 13of the sons of Elizaphan, Shimri and Jeiel; of the sons of Asaph, Zechariah and Mattaniah; 14of the sons of Heman, Jehiel and Shimei; and of the sons of Jeduthun, Shemaiah and Uzziel.

15*And they gathered their brethren, sanctified themselves, and went according to the commandment of the king, at the words of the LORD, to cleanse the house of the LORD. 16Then the priests went into the inner part of the house of the LORD to cleanse *it*, and brought out all the debris that they found in the temple of the LORD to the court of the house of the LORD. And the Levites took *it* out and carried *it* to the Brook Kidron.

17Now they began to sanctify on the first *day* of the first month, and on the eighth day of the month they came to the vestibule of the LORD. So they sanctified the house of the LORD in eight days, and on the sixteenth day of the first month they finished.

CHAPTER 29

29:1–3 When Hezekiah became king, the situation at the temple was not unlike the condition of some churches today (v. 7). Closed doors speak of no access to God and no service for God. He has set before us an open door (Rev. 3:8), and we close it.

29:6 The lamps were out, which indicates no witness (Matt. 5:16), and the incense altar was cold, which signifies that no prayer was going up to God (Ps. 141:2). There were no sacrifices on the altar (Rom. 12:1–2), but there was plenty of rubbish in the temple. No wonder the nation was experiencing the wrath of God instead of the blessing of God.

29:15–31 Hezekiah's formula for revival was simple: sanctification, sacrifice, and song. He started with the priests and Levites, for if God's servants are not clean, God cannot bless their work. Then the priests sanctified the temple, offered the sacrifices, and sang the song of the Lord.

29:1 ᵛSpelled *Abi* in 2 Kings 18:2

18Then they went in to King Hezekiah and said, "We have cleansed all the house of the LORD, the altar of burnt offerings with all its articles, and the table of the showbread with all its articles. 19Moreover all the articles which King Ahaz in his reign had cast aside in his transgression we have prepared and sanctified; and there they *are*, before the altar of the LORD."

20Then King Hezekiah rose early, gathered the rulers of the city, and went up to the house of the LORD. 21And they brought seven bulls, seven rams, seven lambs, and seven male goats for a sin offering for the kingdom, for the sanctuary, and for Judah. Then he commanded the priests, the sons of Aaron, to offer *them* on the altar of the LORD. 22So they killed the bulls, and the priests received the blood and sprinkled *it* on the altar. Likewise they killed the rams and sprinkled the blood on the altar. They also killed the lambs and sprinkled the blood on the altar. 23Then they brought out the male goats *for* the sin offering before the king and the assembly, and they laid their hands on them. 24And the priests killed them; and they presented their blood on the altar as a sin offering to make an atonement for all Israel, for the king commanded *that* the burnt offering and the sin offering *be made* for all Israel.

25And he stationed the Levites in the house of the LORD with cymbals, with stringed instruments, and with harps, according to the commandment of David, of Gad the king's seer, and of Nathan the prophet; for thus *was* the commandment of the LORD by his prophets. 26The Levites stood with the instruments of David, and the priests with the trumpets. 27Then Hezekiah commanded *them* to offer the burnt offering on the altar. And when the burnt offering began, the song of the LORD *also* began, with the trumpets and with the instruments of David king of Israel. 28So all the assembly worshiped, the singers sang, and the trumpeters sounded; all *this continued* until the burnt offering was finished. 29And when they had finished offering, the king and all who were present with him bowed and worshiped. 30Moreover King Hezekiah and the leaders commanded the Levites to sing praise to the LORD with the words of David and of Asaph the seer. So they sang praises with gladness, and they bowed their heads and worshiped.

31Then Hezekiah answered and said, "Now *that* you have consecrated yourselves to the LORD, come near, and bring sacrifices and thank offerings into the house of the LORD." So the assembly brought in sacrifices and thank offerings, and as many as were of a willing heart *brought* burnt offerings. 32And the number of the burnt offerings which the assembly brought was seventy bulls, one hundred rams, *and* two hundred lambs; all these *were* for a burnt offering to the LORD. 33The consecrated things *were* six hundred bulls and three thousand sheep. 34But the priests were too few, so that they could not skin all the burnt offerings; therefore their brethren the Levites helped them until the work was ended and until the *other* priests had sanctified themselves, for the Levites were more diligent in sanctifying themselves than the priests. 35Also the burnt offerings *were* in abundance, with the fat of the peace offerings and *with* the drink offerings for *every* burnt offering.

So the service of the house of the LORD was set in order. 36*Then Hezekiah and all the people

29:36 It all happened suddenly, but what happened was not new or novel. It was simply a return to the ways of the Lord (Jer. 6:16).

rejoiced that God had prepared the people, since the events took place so suddenly.

30 And* Hezekiah sent to all Israel and Judah, and also wrote letters to Ephraim and Manasseh, that they should come to the house of the LORD at Jerusalem, to keep the Passover to the LORD God of Israel. ²For the king and his leaders and all the assembly in Jerusalem had agreed to keep the Passover in the second month. ³*For they could not keep it at the regular time,ʷ because a sufficient number of priests had not consecrated themselves, nor had the people gathered together at Jerusalem. ⁴And the matter pleased the king and all the assembly. ⁵So they resolved to make a proclamation throughout all Israel, from Beersheba to Dan, that they should come to keep the Passover to the LORD God of Israel at Jerusalem, since they had not done it for a long time in the prescribed manner.

⁶Then the runners went throughout all Israel and Judah with the letters from the king and his leaders, and spoke according to the command of the king: "Children of Israel, return to the LORD God of Abraham, Isaac, and Israel; then He will return to the remnant of you who have escaped from the hand of the kings of Assyria. ⁷And do not be like your fathers and your brethren, who trespassed against the LORD God of their fathers, so that He gave them up to desolation, as you see. ⁸Now do not be stiff-necked, as your fathers were, but yield yourselves to the LORD; and enter His sanctuary, which He has sanctified forever, and serve the LORD your God, that the fierceness of His wrath may turn away from you. ⁹For if you return to the LORD, your brethren and your children will be treated with compassion by those who lead them captive, so that they may come back to this land; for the LORD your God is gracious and merciful, and will not turn His face from you if you return to Him."

¹⁰So the runners passed from city to city through the country of Ephraim and Manasseh, as far as Zebulun; but they laughed at them and mocked them. ¹¹Nevertheless some from Asher, Manasseh, and Zebulun humbled themselves and came to Jerusalem. ¹²Also the hand of God was on Judah to give them singleness of heart to obey the command of the king and the leaders, at the word of the LORD.

¹³Now many people, a very great assembly, gathered at Jerusalem to keep the Feast of Unleavened Bread in the second month. ¹⁴They arose and took away the altars that were in Jerusalem, and they took away all the incense altars and cast them into the Brook Kidron. ¹⁵Then they slaughtered the Passover lambs on the fourteenth day of the second month. The priests and the Levites were ashamed, and sanctified themselves, and brought the burnt offerings to the house of the LORD. ¹⁶They stood in their place according to their custom, according to the Law of Moses the man of God; the priests sprinkled the blood received from the hand of the Levites. ¹⁷*For there were many in the assembly who had not sanctified themselves; therefore the Levites had charge of the slaughter of the Passover lambs for everyone who was not clean, to sanctify them to the LORD.

30:3 ʷThat is, the first month (compare Leviticus 23:5); literally at that time

CHAPTER 30

30:1 When God's Spirit is at work, Jesus Christ will be glorified, and God's people will be unified. Hezekiah called the whole nation back to the celebration of the Passover, the feast that depicts Jesus Christ, the Lamb of God, and many participated with oneness of heart (v. 12). What an occasion of blessing it was!

30:3–10 How tragic that the spiritual leaders were to blame for delaying the event (v. 3). How tragic that some of the people laughed at the invitation (v. 10; Matt. 22:1–14). But how wonderful that God blessed abundantly, healed the people and sent them home rejoicing (vv. 21, 23, 25, 26). The people who turned down the invitation missed a special opportunity.

30:17–27 God looks at the heart and does not permit ceremonial matters to get in the way of His grace (1 Sam. 15:22; Ps. 50:7–15; 51:16–17; Hos. 6:6). Hezekiah saw to it that the people were taught the Word (v. 22) because the Word nourishes the heart and cleanses the life, long after the memories of great events have faded away. The people experienced great joy as a result of sharing in the Passover feast (v. 26). The Jews would have great joy at the dedication of the walls of Jerusalem (Neh. 12:43). Other people who experienced great joy from the Lord are the wise men (Matt. 2:10), the apostles (Luke 24:52), and the new believers in Samaria (Acts 8:8). The message of the gospel is good news of great joy (Luke 2:10). Are you sharing it with others?

578

18For a multitude of the people, many from Ephraim, Manasseh, Issachar, and Zebulun, had not cleansed themselves, yet they ate the Passover contrary to what was written. But Hezekiah prayed for them, saying, "May the good LORD provide atonement for everyone 19who prepares his heart to seek God, the LORD God of his fathers, though *he is* not *cleansed* according to the purification of the sanctuary." 20And the LORD listened to Hezekiah and healed the people.

21So the children of Israel who were present at Jerusalem kept the Feast of Unleavened Bread seven days with great gladness; and the Levites and the priests praised the LORD day by day, *singing* to the LORD, accompanied by loud instruments. 22And Hezekiah gave encouragement to all the Levites who taught the good knowledge of the LORD; and they ate throughout the feast seven days, offering peace offerings and making confession to the LORD God of their fathers.

23Then the whole assembly agreed to keep *the feast* another seven days, and they kept it *another* seven days with gladness. 24For Hezekiah king of Judah gave to the assembly a thousand bulls and seven thousand sheep, and the leaders gave to the assembly a thousand bulls and ten thousand sheep; and a great number of priests sanctified themselves. 25The whole assembly of Judah rejoiced, also the priests and Levites, all the assembly that came from Israel, the sojourners who came from the land of Israel, and those who dwelt in Judah. 26So there was great joy in Jerusalem, for since the time of Solomon the son of David, king of Israel, *there had* been nothing like this in Jerusalem. 27Then the priests, the Levites, arose and blessed the people, and their voice was heard; and their prayer came *up* to His holy dwelling place, to heaven.

31 Now* when all this was finished, all Israel who were present went out to the cities of Judah and broke the sacred pillars in pieces, cut down the wooden images, and threw down the high places and the altars—from all Judah, Benjamin, Ephraim, and Manasseh—until they had utterly destroyed them all. Then all the children of Israel returned to their own cities, every man to his possession.

2*And Hezekiah appointed the divisions of the priests and the Levites according to their divisions, each man according to his service, the priests and Levites for burnt offerings and peace offerings, to serve, to give thanks, and to praise in the gates of the campx of the LORD. 3*The king also *appointed* a portion of his possessions for the burnt offerings: for the morning and evening burnt offerings, the burnt offerings for the Sabbaths and the New Moons and the set feasts, as *it is* written in the Law of the LORD.

4Moreover he commanded the people who dwelt in Jerusalem to contribute support for the priests and the Levites, that they might devote themselves to the Law of the LORD.

5As soon as the commandment was circulated, the children of Israel brought in abundance the firstfruits of grain and wine, oil and honey, and of all the produce of the field; and they brought in abundantly the tithe of everything. 6And the children of Israel and Judah, who dwelt in the

---

CHAPTER 31

31:1ff When you come back to walk with the Lord, the evidences of the new life are there to see.

Cleansing. For too long, the worship of Jehovah had taken place alongside the worship of the heathen gods; that would now end. The people assisted the king in destroying the obscene images and pagan altars. After all, the nation had just celebrated Passover, and the week following Passover was to be a time of "housecleaning" (Exod. 12:15–20).

31:2 Serving. It is not enough to get rid of the bad; we must also establish and strengthen the good. The king made certain the priests obeyed God's law and ministered at the temple. Had the priests been ministering faithfully to begin with, the nation would not have gone into apostasy.

31:3, 4 Giving. If the priests are to serve, the people must support them. One of the first signs of spiritual awakening is the generosity of those whose hearts God has touched. Nobody had to plead or urge; the giving came from the hearts of people who were right with God.

31:2 xThat is, the temple

cities of Judah, brought the tithe of oxen and sheep; also the tithe of holy things which were consecrated to the LORD their God they laid in heaps.

7In the third month they began laying them in heaps, and they finished in the seventh month. 8And when Hezekiah and the leaders came and saw the heaps, they blessed the LORD and His people Israel. 9Then Hezekiah questioned the priests and the Levites concerning the heaps. 10And Azariah the chief priest, from the house of Zadok, answered him and said, "Since *the people* began to bring the offerings into the house of the LORD, we have had enough to eat and have plenty left, for the LORD has blessed His people; and what is left *is* this great abundance."

11Now Hezekiah commanded *them* to prepare rooms in the house of the LORD, and they prepared them. 12Then they faithfully brought in the offerings, the tithes, and the dedicated things; Cononiah the Levite had charge of them, and Shimei his brother *was* the next. 13Jehiel, Azaziah, Nahath, Asahel, Jerimoth, Jozabad, Eliel, Ismachiah, Mahath, and Benaiah *were* overseers under the hand of Cononiah and Shimei his brother, at the commandment of Hezekiah the king and Azariah the ruler of the house of God. 14Kore the son of Imnah the Levite, the keeper of the East Gate, *was* over the freewill offerings to God, to distribute the offerings of the LORD and the most holy things. 15And under him *were* Eden, Miniamin, Jeshua, Shemaiah, Amariah, and Shecaniah, *his* faithful assistants in the cities of the priests, to distribute allotments to their brethren by divisions, to the great as well as the small.

16Besides those males from three years old and up who were written in the genealogy, they distributed to everyone who entered the house of the LORD his daily portion for the work of his service, by his division, 17and to the priests who were written in the genealogy according to their father's house, and to the Levites from twenty years old and up according to their work, by their divisions, 18and to all who were written in the genealogy— their little ones and their wives, their sons and daughters, the whole company of them—for in their faithfulness they sanctified themselves in holiness.

19Also for the sons of Aaron the priests, *who were* in the fields of the common-lands of their cities, in every single city, *there were* men who were designated by name to distribute portions to all the males among the priests and to all who were listed by genealogies among the Levites.

20Thus Hezekiah did throughout all Judah, and he did what *was* good and right and true before the LORD his God. 21And in every work that he began in the service of the house of God, in the law and in the commandment, to seek his God, he did *it* with all his heart. So he prospered.

32 After* these deeds of faithfulness, Sennacherib king of Assyria came and entered Judah; he encamped against the fortified cities, thinking to win them over to himself. 2*And when Hezekiah saw that Sennacherib had come, and that his purpose was to make war against Jerusalem, 3he consulted with his leaders and commandersʸ to stop the water from the springs which

---

32:3 ʸLiterally *mighty men*

CHAPTER 32

32:1ff Testings usually come after times of great blessing, and Hezekiah faced three of them.

32:2–22 *War.* After other times of awakening, the nation was given protection and rest from enemies (2 Chron. 15:15; 20:29–30), but this time, God allowed the enemy to come in. God was testing the faith of the king and the people to see how deep it really was. It is one thing to participate in a huge religious meeting, but quite something else to have your land invaded and your capital city threatened.

were outside the city; and they helped him. 4Thus many people gathered together who stopped all the springs and the brook that ran through the land, saying, "Why should the kingsz of Assyria come and find much water?" 5And he strengthened himself, built up all the wall that was broken, raised *it* up to the towers, and *built* another wall outside; also he repaired the Milloa *in* the City of David, and made weapons and shields in abundance. 6Then he set military captains over the people, gathered them together to him in the open square of the city gate, and gave them encouragement, saying, 7"Be strong and courageous; do not be afraid nor dismayed before the king of Assyria, nor before all the multitude that *is* with him; for *there are* more with us than with him. 8With him *is* an arm of flesh; but with us *is* the LORD our God, to help us and to fight our battles." And the people were strengthened by the words of Hezekiah king of Judah.

9After this Sennacherib king of Assyria sent his servants to Jerusalem (but he and all the forces with him *laid siege* against Lachish), to Hezekiah king of Judah, and to all Judah who *were* in Jerusalem, saying, 10"Thus says Sennacherib king of Assyria: 'In what do you trust, that you remain under siege in Jerusalem? 11Does not Hezekiah persuade you to give yourselves over to die by famine and by thirst, saying, "The LORD our God will deliver us from the hand of the king of Assyria"? 12Has not the same Hezekiah taken away His high places and His altars, and commanded Judah and Jerusalem, saying, "You shall worship before one altar and burn incense on it"? 13Do you not know what I and my fathers have done to all the peoples of *other* lands? Were the gods of the nations of those lands in any way able to deliver their lands out of my hand? 14Who *was there* among all the gods of those nations that my fathers utterly destroyed that could deliver his people from my hand, that your God should be able to deliver you from my hand? 15Now therefore, do not let Hezekiah deceive you or persuade you like this, and do not believe him; for no god of any nation or kingdom was able to deliver his people from my hand or the hand of my fathers. How much less will your God deliver you from my hand?'"

16Furthermore, his servants spoke against the LORD God and against His servant Hezekiah.

17He also wrote letters to revile the LORD God of Israel, and to speak against Him, saying, "As the gods of the nations of *other* lands have not delivered their people from my hand, so the God of Hezekiah will not deliver His people from my hand." 18Then they called out with a loud voice in Hebrewb to the people of Jerusalem who *were* on the wall, to frighten them and trouble them, that they might take the city. 19And they spoke against the God of Jerusalem, as against the gods of the people of the earth—the work of men's hands.

20Now because of this King Hezekiah and the prophet Isaiah, the son of Amoz, prayed and cried out to heaven. 21Then the LORD sent an angel who cut down every mighty man of valor, leader, and captain in the camp of the king of Assyria. So

---

32:4 zFollowing Masoretic Text and Vulgate; Arabic, Septuagint, and Syriac read *king.* 32:5 aLiterally *The Landfill* 32:18 bLiterally *Judean*

he returned shamefaced to his own land. And when he had gone into the temple of his god, some of his own offspring struck him down with the sword there. 22Thus the LORD saved Hezekiah and the inhabitants of Jerusalem from the hand of Sennacherib the king of Assyria, and from the hand of all *others,* and guided them[c] on every side. 23And many brought gifts to the LORD at Jerusalem, and presents to Hezekiah king of Judah, so that he was exalted in the sight of all nations thereafter.

24*In those days Hezekiah was sick and near death, and he prayed to the LORD; and He spoke to him and gave him a sign. 25But Hezekiah did not repay according to the favor *shown* him, for his heart was lifted up; therefore wrath was looming over him and over Judah and Jerusalem. 26Then Hezekiah humbled himself for the pride of his heart, he and the inhabitants of Jerusalem, so that the wrath of the LORD did not come upon them in the days of Hezekiah.

27Hezekiah had very great riches and honor. And he made himself treasuries for silver, for gold, for precious stones, for spices, for shields, and for all kinds of desirable items; 28storehouses for the harvest of grain, wine, and oil; and stalls for all kinds of livestock, and folds for flocks.[d] 29Moreover he provided cities for himself, and possessions of flocks and herds in abundance; for God had given him very much property. 30This same Hezekiah also stopped the water outlet of Upper Gihon, and brought the water by tunnel[e] to the west side of the City of David. Hezekiah prospered in all his works.

31*However, *regarding* the ambassadors of the princes of Babylon, whom they sent to him to inquire about the wonder that was *done* in the land, God withdrew from him, in order to test him, that He might know all *that was* in his heart.

32Now the rest of the acts of Hezekiah, and his goodness, indeed they *are* written in the vision of Isaiah the prophet, the son of Amoz, *and* in the book of the kings of Judah and Israel. 33So Hezekiah rested with his fathers, and they buried him in the upper tombs of the sons of David; and all Judah and the inhabitants of Jerusalem honored him at his death. Then Manasseh his son reigned in his place.

33 Manasseh* *was* twelve years old when he became king, and he reigned fifty-five years in Jerusalem. 2But he did evil in the sight of the LORD, according to the abominations of the nations whom the LORD had cast out before the children of Israel. 3For he rebuilt the high places which Hezekiah his father had broken down; he raised up altars for the Baals, and made wooden images; and he worshiped all the host of heaven[f] and served them. 4He also built altars in the house of the LORD, of which the LORD had said, "In Jerusalem shall My name be forever." 5And he built altars for all the host of heaven in the two courts of the house of the LORD. 6Also he caused his sons

32:24 Sickness. Hezekiah's illness was both a national and a personal crisis, for he did not have any sons to take the throne. God had promised that David's family would never lack for a man on the throne, so Hezekiah prayed that he might be able to live and have a son.

32:31 Honor. Hezekiah weathered the invasion and the illness, but he capitulated to pride. It began when he failed to thank God for sparing his life, and apparently even God's chastening did not cure him. The extent of his wealth and the praises of the visiting dignitaries made Hezekiah proud, and God had to deal with him.

We have learned that if Satan cannot conquer us when he comes as the lion (1 Pet. 5:8), he will come again as the serpent (2 Cor. 11:1–3). You may be in greater danger when things are going well than when you are fighting a battle, so keep alert.

CHAPTER 33

33:1–9 Manasseh rebuilt what his father had torn down and then tore it down again so he could rebuild. (Compare Gen. 26:18.) He did not learn from the past or listen to the prophets, so he had to live with the punishment God sent him. Some people only learn the hard way.

32:22 [c]Septuagint reads *gave them rest;* Vulgate reads *gave them treasures.* 32:28 [d]Following Septuagint and Vulgate; Arabic and Syriac omit *folds for flocks;* Masoretic Text reads *flocks for sheepfolds.* 32:30 [e]Literally *brought it straight* (compare 2 Kings 20:20) 33:3 [f]The gods of the Assyrians

33:12, 13 How gracious of God to see Manasseh's repentance, hear his prayer, and restore him to Jerusalem. But even God's forgiveness could not automatically nullify the king's bad example or undo the terrible damage he had done in the land. Sin has consequences long after sinners are forgiven (2 Kings 23:26; 24:3).

God is ready and willing to forgive, and we should seek that forgiveness early. The longer we wait, the more damage we do; the more damage we do, the more we and others will suffer because of our sins.

to pass through the fire in the Valley of the Son of Hinnom; he practiced soothsaying, used witchcraft and sorcery, and consulted mediums and spiritists. He did much evil in the sight of the LORD, to provoke Him to anger. [7]He even set a carved image, the idol which he had made, in the house of God, of which God had said to David and to Solomon his son, "In this house and in Jerusalem, which I have chosen out of all the tribes of Israel, I will put My name forever; [8]and I will not again remove the foot of Israel from the land which I have appointed for your fathers—only if they are careful to do all that I have commanded them, according to the whole law and the statutes and the ordinances by the hand of Moses." [9]So Manasseh seduced Judah and the inhabitants of Jerusalem to do more evil than the nations whom the LORD had destroyed before the children of Israel.

[10]And the LORD spoke to Manasseh and his people, but they would not listen. [11]Therefore the LORD brought upon them the captains of the army of the king of Assyria, who took Manasseh with hooks,[g] bound him with bronze *fetters,* and carried him off to Babylon. [12]*Now when he was in affliction, he implored the LORD his God, and humbled himself greatly before the God of his fathers, [13]and prayed to Him; and He received his entreaty, heard his supplication, and brought him back to Jerusalem into his kingdom. Then Manasseh knew that the LORD *was* God.

[14]After this he built a wall outside the City of David on the west side of Gihon, in the valley, as far as the entrance of the Fish Gate; and *it* enclosed Ophel, and he raised it to a very great height. Then he put military captains in all the fortified cities of Judah. [15]He took away the foreign gods and the idol from the house of the LORD, and all the altars that he had built in the mount of the house of the LORD and in Jerusalem; and he cast *them* out of the city. [16]He also repaired the altar of the LORD, sacrificed peace offerings and thank offerings on it, and commanded Judah to serve the LORD God of Israel. [17]Nevertheless the people still sacrificed on the high places, *but* only to the LORD their God.

[18]*Now the rest of the acts of Manasseh, his prayer to his God, and the words of the seers who spoke to him in the name of the LORD God of Israel, indeed they *are written* in the book[h] of the kings of Israel. [19]Also his prayer and *how* God received his entreaty, and all his sin and trespass, and the sites where he built high places and set up wooden images and carved images, before he was humbled, indeed they *are* written among the sayings of Hozai.[i] [20]So Manasseh rested with his fathers, and they buried him in his own house. Then his son Amon reigned in his place.

[21]Amon *was* twenty-two years old when he became king, and he reigned two years in Jerusalem. [22]But he did evil in the sight of the LORD, as his father Manasseh had done; for Amon sacrificed to all the carved images which his father Manasseh had made, and served them. [23]And he did not humble himself before the LORD, as his

---

33:11 [g]That is, nose hooks (compare 2 Kings 19:28)
33:18 [h]Literally *words*   33:19 [i]Septuagint reads *the seers.*

father Manasseh had humbled himself; but Amon trespassed more and more.

24Then his servants conspired against him, and killed him in his own house. 25But the people of the land executed all those who had conspired against King Amon. Then the people of the land made his son Josiah king in his place.

34 Josiah *was* eight years old when he became king, and he reigned thirty-one years in Jerusalem. 2And he did *what was* right in the sight of the LORD, and walked in the ways of his father David; *he* did *not* turn aside to the right hand or to the left.

3For in the eighth year of his reign, while he was still young, he began to seek the God of his father David; and in the twelfth year he began to purge Judah and Jerusalem of the high places, the wooden images, the carved images, and the molded images. 4They broke down the altars of the Baals in his presence, and the incense altars which *were* above them he cut down; and the wooden images, the carved images, and the molded images he broke in pieces, and made dust of them and scattered *it* on the graves of those who had sacrificed to them. 5He also burned the bones of the priests on their altars, and cleansed Judah and Jerusalem. 6And *so he did* in the cities of Manasseh, Ephraim, and Simeon, as far as Naphtali and all around, with axes.*j* 7When he had broken down the altars and the wooden images, had beaten the carved images into powder, and cut down all the incense altars throughout all the land of Israel, he returned to Jerusalem.

8In the eighteenth year of his reign, when he had purged the land and the temple,*k* he sent Shaphan the son of Azaliah, Maaseiah the governor of the city, and Joah the son of Joahaz the recorder, to repair the house of the LORD his God. 9When they came to Hilkiah the high priest, they delivered the money that was brought into the house of God, which the Levites who kept the doors had gathered from the hand of Manasseh and Ephraim, from all the remnant of Israel, from all Judah and Benjamin, and *which* they had brought back to Jerusalem. 10Then they put *it* in the hand of the foremen who had the oversight of the house of the LORD; and they gave it to the workmen who worked in the house of the LORD, to repair and restore the house. 11They gave *it* to the craftsmen and builders to buy hewn stone and timber for beams, and to floor the houses which the kings of Judah had destroyed. 12And the men did the work faithfully. Their overseers *were* Jahath and Obadiah the Levites, of the sons of Merari, and Zechariah and Meshullam, of the sons of the Kohathites, to supervise. *Others of* the Levites, all of whom were skillful with instruments of music, 13*were* over the burden bearers and *were* overseers of all who did work in any kind of service. And *some* of the Levites *were* scribes, officers, and gatekeepers.

14*Now when they brought out the money that was brought into the house of the LORD, Hilkiah the priest found the Book of the Law of the LORD *given* by Moses. 15Then Hilkiah answered and said to Shaphan the scribe, "I have found the Book of the Law in the house of the LORD." And Hilkiah gave the book to Shaphan. 16So Shaphan

CHAPTER 34

34:14, 15 *Find the Book.* The greatest treasure you have is not money but the Word of God, which too often is "lost" amid the "rubbish" you can easily accumulate. Do you treasure God's Word? (See Ps. 119:14, 72, 127, 162.) Is it "buried" somewhere?

34:6 *l*Literally *swords*   34:8 *k*Literally *house*

34:18, 19 Read the Book. God's Word is not a relic to admire in a religious museum. They did not put the Book back in its niche in the temple. Rather, they read it publicly and honored it as the living Word of God.

34:27 Obey the Book. The king trembled at God's Word (Isa. 66:2) and immediately sent for God's message. There is always a fresh word from the Lord as you read the Bible and seek His will.

34:29, 30 Share the Book. The king gathered the people to the temple to hear God's Word. It is good to be a receiver of the Word, but it is also good to be a transmitter and share it with others (1 Thess. 1:6–10).

34:31 Stand for the Word. The king and the people made a covenant with the Lord and took their stand publicly. After all, the result of Bible knowledge ought to be obedience and service, a living commitment to the God of the Word.

carried the book to the king, bringing the king word, saying, "All that was committed to your servants they are doing. [17]And they have gathered the money that was found in the house of the LORD, and have delivered it into the hand of the overseers and the workmen." [18]*Then Shaphan the scribe told the king, saying, "Hilkiah the priest has given me a book." And Shaphan read it before the king.

[19]Thus it happened, when the king heard the words of the Law, that he tore his clothes. [20]Then the king commanded Hilkiah, Ahikam the son of Shaphan, Abdon[l] the son of Micah, Shaphan the scribe, and Asaiah a servant of the king, saying, [21]"Go, inquire of the LORD for me, and for those who are left in Israel and Judah, concerning the words of the book that is found; for great is the wrath of the LORD that is poured out on us, because our fathers have not kept the word of the LORD, to do according to all that is written in this book."

[22]So Hilkiah and those the king had appointed went to Huldah the prophetess, the wife of Shallum the son of Tokhath,[m] the son of Hasrah,[n] keeper of the wardrobe. (She dwelt in Jerusalem in the Second Quarter.) And they spoke to her to that effect.

[23]Then she answered them, "Thus says the LORD God of Israel, 'Tell the man who sent you to Me, [24]"Thus says the LORD: 'Behold, I will bring calamity on this place and on its inhabitants, all the curses that are written in the book which they have read before the king of Judah, [25]because they have forsaken Me and burned incense to other gods, that they might provoke Me to anger with all the works of their hands. Therefore My wrath will be poured out on this place, and not be quenched.' " ' [26]But as for the king of Judah, who sent you to inquire of the LORD, in this manner you shall speak to him, 'Thus says the LORD God of Israel: "Concerning the words which you have heard— [27]*because your heart was tender, and you humbled yourself before God when you heard His words against this place and against its inhabitants, and you humbled yourself before Me, and you tore your clothes and wept before Me, I also have heard you," says the LORD. [28]"Surely I will gather you to your fathers, and you shall be gathered to your grave in peace; and your eyes shall not see all the calamity which I will bring on this place and its inhabitants." ' " So they brought back word to the king.

[29]*Then the king sent and gathered all the elders of Judah and Jerusalem. [30]The king went up to the house of the LORD, with all the men of Judah and the inhabitants of Jerusalem—the priests and the Levites, and all the people, great and small. And he read in their hearing all the words of the Book of the Covenant which had been found in the house of the LORD. [31]*Then the king stood in his place and made a covenant before the LORD, to follow the LORD, and to keep His commandments and His testimonies and His statutes with all his heart and all his soul, to perform the words of the covenant that were written in this book. [32]And he made all who were present in Jerusalem and Benjamin take a stand. So the inhabitants of

34:20 [l]Achbor the son of Michaiah in 2 Kings 22:12
34:22 [m]Spelled Tikvah in 2 Kings 22:14 [n]Spelled Harhas in 2 Kings 22:14

Jerusalem did according to the covenant of God, the God of their fathers. 33Thus Josiah removed all the abominations from all the country that *belonged* to the children of Israel, and made all who were present in Israel diligently serve the LORD their God. All his days they did not depart from following the LORD God of their fathers.

35 Now* Josiah kept a Passover to the LORD in Jerusalem, and they slaughtered the Passover *lambs* on the fourteenth *day* of the first month. 2And he set the priests in their duties and encouraged them for the service of the house of the LORD. 3Then he said to the Levites who taught all Israel, who were holy to the LORD: "Put the holy ark in the house which Solomon the son of David, king of Israel, built. *It shall* no longer *be* a burden on *your* shoulders. Now serve the LORD your God and His people Israel. 4Prepare *yourselves* according to your fathers' houses, according to your divisions, following the written instruction of David king of Israel and the written instruction of Solomon his son. 5And stand in the holy *place* according to the divisions of the fathers' houses of your brethren the *lay* people, and *according to* the division of the father's house of the Levites. 6So slaughter the Passover *offerings,* consecrate yourselves, and prepare *them* for your brethren, that *they* may do according to the word of the LORD by the hand of Moses."

7Then Josiah gave the *lay* people lambs and young goats from the flock, all for Passover *offerings* for all who were present, to the number of thirty thousand, as well as three thousand cattle; these *were* from the king's possessions. 8And his leaders gave willingly to the people, to the priests, and to the Levites. Hilkiah, Zechariah, and Jehiel, rulers of the house of God, gave to the priests for the Passover *offerings* two thousand six hundred *from the flock,* and three hundred cattle. 9Also Conaniah, his brothers Shemaiah and Nethanel, and Hashabiah and Jeiel and Jozabad, chief of the Levites, gave to the Levites for Passover *offerings* five thousand *from the flock* and five hundred cattle.

10So the service was prepared, and the priests stood in their places, and the Levites in their divisions, according to the king's command. 11And they slaughtered the Passover *offerings;* and the priests sprinkled *the blood* with their hands, while the Levites skinned *the animals.* 12Then they removed the burnt offerings that *they* might give them to the divisions of the fathers' houses of the *lay* people, to offer to the LORD, as *it is* written in the Book of Moses. And so *they did* with the cattle. 13Also they roasted the Passover *offerings* with fire according to the ordinance; but the *other* holy *offerings* they boiled in pots, in caldrons, and in pans, and divided *them* quickly among all the *lay* people. 14Then afterward they prepared portions for themselves and for the priests, because the priests, the sons of Aaron, *were busy* in offering burnt offerings and fat until night; therefore the Levites prepared portions for themselves and for the priests, the sons of Aaron. 15And the singers, the sons of Asaph, *were* in their places, according to the command of David, Asaph, Heman, and Jeduthun the king's seer. Also the gatekeepers were at each gate; they did not have to leave their position, because their brethren the Levites prepared portions for them.

16So all the service of the LORD was prepared

CHAPTER 35

35:1–19 *Remembering the past.* Passover is the great feast of Jewish liberation, when the nation recalls its deliverance from Egypt (Exod. 13:1–10). Following the example of godly Hezekiah (2 Chron. 30), Josiah held a feast and called the people to praise God. As in the days of Hezekiah, the spiritual leaders had to be encouraged to do their jobs. Too often those who should be leading are standing in the way.

35:20–27 ***Mortgaging the future.*** If God defeated Egypt in the days of Moses, surely He could do it again for Josiah! Without seeking the mind of the Lord, Josiah meddled in a war that had nothing to do with Judah, and it led to his death. A disguise is no protection if we have disobeyed God (v. 22; 2 Chron. 18:29). Judah was back in bondage to Egypt!

35:21 We wonder what the future of Judah might have been had Josiah heeded the warning God gave him. Strange as it seems, God can speak through messengers who may not even know Him (John 11:49–52).

CHAPTER 36

36:1ff Second Chronicles opens telling how the temple was built. It closes telling how and why the temple of God was destroyed.

36:7, 14 First the enemy *robbed the temple,* taking the treasures of the Lord to their pagan temple in Babylon. You expect an enemy to do this, but you do not expect the priests and people to *defile* their own temple! While Nebuchadnezzar was taking Jerusalem to Babylon, the Jewish leaders were bringing Babylon to Jerusalem! Do we ever learn?

the same day, to keep the Passover and to offer
burnt offerings on the altar of the LORD, according
to the command of King Josiah. 17And the children of Israel who were present kept the Passover
at that time, and the Feast of Unleavened Bread
for seven days. 18There had been no Passover kept
in Israel like that since the days of Samuel the
prophet; and none of the kings of Israel had kept
such a Passover as Josiah kept, with the priests
and the Levites, all Judah and Israel who were
present, and the inhabitants of Jerusalem. 19In the
eighteenth year of the reign of Josiah this Passover was kept.

20*After all this, when Josiah had prepared the
temple, Necho king of Egypt came up to fight
against Carchemish by the Euphrates; and Josiah
went out against him. 21*But he sent messengers
to him, saying, "What have I to do with you, king
of Judah? *I have* not *come* against you this day,
but against the house with which I have war; for
God commanded me to make haste. Refrain *from
meddling with* God, who *is* with me, lest He destroy you." 22Nevertheless Josiah would not turn
his face from him, but disguised himself so that
he might fight with him, and did not heed the
words of Necho from the mouth of God. So he
came to fight in the Valley of Megiddo.

23And the archers shot King Josiah; and the
king said to his servants, "Take me away, for I
am severely wounded." 24His servants therefore
took him out of that chariot and put him in the
second chariot that he had, and they brought him
to Jerusalem. So he died, and was buried in *one
of* the tombs of his fathers. And all Judah and
Jerusalem mourned for Josiah.

25Jeremiah also lamented for Josiah. And to this
day all the singing men and the singing women
speak of Josiah in their lamentations. They made
it a custom in Israel; and indeed they *are* written
in the Laments.

26Now the rest of the acts of Josiah and his
goodness, according to *what was* written in the
Law of the LORD, 27and his deeds from first to
last, indeed they *are* written in the book of the
kings of Israel and Judah.

36 Then* the people of the land took Jehoahaz
the son of Josiah, and made him king in
his father's place in Jerusalem. 2Jehoahaz[o] *was*
twenty-three years old when he became king, and
he reigned three months in Jerusalem. 3Now the
king of Egypt deposed him at Jerusalem; and he
imposed on the land a tribute of one hundred talents of silver and a talent of gold. 4Then the king
of Egypt made *Jehoahaz's*[p] brother Eliakim king
over Judah and Jerusalem, and changed his name
to Jehoiakim. And Necho took Jehoahaz[q] his
brother and carried him off to Egypt.

5Jehoiakim *was* twenty-five years old when he
became king, and he reigned eleven years in Jerusalem. And he did evil in the sight of the LORD
his God. 6Nebuchadnezzar king of Babylon came
up against him, and bound him in bronze *fetters*
to carry him off to Babylon. 7*Nebuchadnezzar
also carried off *some* of the articles from the house
of the LORD to Babylon, and put them in his temple
at Babylon. 8Now the rest of the acts of Jehoiakim,
the abominations which he did, and what was

36:2 [o]Masoretic Text reads *Joahaz.* 36:4 [p]Literally *his*
[q]Masoretic Text reads *Joahaz.*

found against him, indeed they *are* written in the book of the kings of Israel and Judah. Then Jehoiachin his son reigned in his place.

⁹Jehoiachin *was* eightʳ years old when he became king, and he reigned in Jerusalem three months and ten days. And he did evil in the sight of the Lord. ¹⁰At the turn of the year King Nebuchadnezzar summoned *him* and took him to Babylon, with the costly articles from the house of the Lord, and made Zedekiah, *Jehoiakim'sˢ* brother, king over Judah and Jerusalem.

¹¹Zedekiah *was* twenty-one years old when he became king, and he reigned eleven years in Jerusalem. ¹²He did evil in the sight of the Lord his God, *and* did not humble himself before Jeremiah the prophet, *who spoke* from the mouth of the Lord. ¹³And he also rebelled against King Nebuchadnezzar, who had made him swear *an oath* by God; but he stiffened his neck and hardened his heart against turning to the Lord God of Israel. ¹⁴Moreover all the leaders of the priests and the people transgressed more and more, *according* to all the abominations of the nations, and defiled the house of the Lord which He had consecrated in Jerusalem.

¹⁵And the Lord God of their fathers sent *warnings* to them by His messengers, rising up early and sending *them,* because He had compassion on His people and on His dwelling place. ¹⁶But they mocked the messengers of God, despised His words, and scoffed at His prophets, until the wrath of the Lord arose against His people, till *there was* no remedy.

¹⁷*Therefore He brought against them the king of the Chaldeans, who killed their young men with the sword in the house of their sanctuary, and had no compassion on young man or virgin, on the aged or the weak; He gave *them* all into his hand. ¹⁸*And all the articles from the house of God, great and small, the treasures of the house of the Lord, and the treasures of the king and of his leaders, all *these* he took to Babylon. ¹⁹Then they burned the house of God, broke down the wall of Jerusalem, burned all its palaces with fire, and destroyed all its precious possessions. ²⁰And those who escaped from the sword he carried away to Babylon, where they became servants to him and his sons until the rule of the kingdom of Persia, ²¹to fulfill the word of the Lord by the mouth of Jeremiah, until the land had enjoyed her Sabbaths. As long as she lay desolate she kept Sabbath, to fulfill seventy years.

²²Now in the first year of Cyrus king of Persia, that the word of the Lord by the mouth of Jeremiah might be fulfilled, the Lord stirred up the spirit of Cyrus king of Persia, so that he made a proclamation throughout all his kingdom, and also *put it* in writing, saying,

23   *Thus says Cyrus king of Persia:
        All the kingdoms of the earth the Lord God
        of heaven has given me. And He has
        commanded me to build Him a house at
        Jerusalem which is in Judah. Who *is* among
        you of all His people? May the Lord his God
        be with him, and let him go up!

36:17 The next step was *death in the temple.* God had shown compassion to His people (v. 15), but the enemy showed no compassion at all. The people fled to the temple, hoping for God's protection, but it was too late. The house of prayer had become a den of thieves.

36:18, 19 Finally, the temple was *destroyed,* just as Jeremiah had warned (Jer. 25—26). The nation had disobeyed the Word of God in many ways, including ignoring the Sabbatical Years (Lev. 25:1–7; 26:27–35). The only thing left was judgment.

36:23 But the book closes with an announcement of the *rebuilding* of the temple, something that Jeremiah also prophesied (29:10). Even in wrath, God remembers mercy (Hab. 3:2).

36:9 ʳSome Hebrew manuscripts, Septuagint, Syriac, and 2 Kings 24:8 read *eighteen.*   36:10 ˢLiterally *his* (compare 2 Kings 24:17)

EZRA and NEHEMIAH

In 606–605 B.C., the Babylonians began their conquest of Jerusalem, deporting many of the people and finally destroying the city and the temple in 587–586 B.C. In 538, Cyrus issued a proclamation allowing the Jews to return to their land and rebuild their temple, and nearly fifty thousand returned under the leadership of Zerubbabel (Ezra 1—6). The seventy years of captivity were ended. In spite of difficulty and delay, the temple was completed in 515.

Ezra the scribe went to Jerusalem in 458 with about two thousand Jews, including some Levites to help in the temple ministry (Ezra 7—10). In 444 B.C., Nehemiah, a layman, went to rebuild the walls (Neh. 1—6) and rededicate the people (Neh. 7—13).

Following their restoration to the land, the Jewish nation experienced times of trial and reproach, but the Lord saw them through. The emphasis in Ezra and Nehemiah is on trusting God for a new beginning and doing His work—no matter what obstacles and opposition are encountered. Although the days may be dark, God is there to guide us, protect us, and help us.

EZRA

1 Now* in the first year of Cyrus king of Persia, that the word of the LORD by the mouth of Jeremiah might be fulfilled, the LORD stirred up the spirit of Cyrus king of Persia, so that he made a proclamation throughout all his kingdom, and also *put it* in writing, saying,

2 *Thus says Cyrus king of Persia:
All the kingdoms of the earth the LORD God of heaven has given me. And He has commanded me to build Him a house at Jerusalem which *is* in Judah. ³Who *is* among you of all His people? May his God be with him, and let him go up to Jerusalem which *is* in Judah, and build the house of the LORD God of Israel (He *is* God), which *is* in Jerusalem. ⁴And whoever is left in any place where he dwells, let the men of his place help him with silver and gold, with goods and livestock, besides the freewill offerings for the house of God which *is* in Jerusalem.

⁵*Then the heads of the fathers' *houses* of Judah and Benjamin, and the priests and the Levites, with all whose spirits God had moved, arose to go up and build the house of the LORD which *is* in Jerusalem. ⁶And all those who *were* around them encouraged them with articles of silver and gold, with goods and livestock, and with precious things, besides all *that* was willingly offered.

⁷King Cyrus also brought out the articles of the house of the LORD, which Nebuchadnezzar had taken from Jerusalem and put in the temple of his gods; ⁸and Cyrus king of Persia brought them out by the hand of Mithredath the treasurer, and counted them out to Sheshbazzar the prince of Judah. ⁹This *is* the number of them: thirty gold platters, one thousand silver platters, twenty-nine knives, ¹⁰thirty gold basins, four hundred and ten silver basins of a similar *kind, and* one thousand other articles. ¹¹All the articles of gold and silver *were* five thousand four hundred. All *these* Sheshbazzar took with the captives who were brought from Babylon to Jerusalem.

2 Nowᵃ these *are* the people of the province who came back from the captivity, of those who had been carried away, whom Nebuchadnezzar the king of Babylon had carried away to Babylon, and who returned to Jerusalem and Judah, everyone to his *own* city. ²*Those* who came with Zerubbabel *were* Jeshua, Nehemiah, Seraiah, Reelaiah, Mordecai, Bilshan, Mispar,ᵇ Bigvai, Rehum,ᶜ *and* Baanah. The number of the men of the people of Israel: ³the people of Parosh, two thousand one hundred and seventy-two; ⁴the people of Shephatiah, three hundred and seventy-two; ⁵the people of Arah, seven hundred and seventy-five; ⁶the people of Pahath-Moab, of the people of Jeshua *and* Joab, two thousand eight hundred and twelve; ⁷the

2:1 ᵃCompare this chapter with Nehemiah 7:6–73.
2:2 ᵇSpelled *Mispereth* in Nehemiah 7:7 ᶜSpelled *Nehum* in Nehemiah 7:7

CHAPTERS 1—2

1:1 The book opens with the closing words of 2 Chronicles, for God's plan was not finished. Judah had rejected Jeremiah's warning, but the prophet's words came true. God is at work in human history. His purposes will be accomplished, regardless of the nations' activities. Jeremiah warned of coming judgment, but he also promised restoration; and the promise was fulfilled (Jer. 29:10).

1:2–4 From God's Word to the king's word! Cyrus fulfilled a prophecy given a century and a half before (Isa. 44:28). God can use even a pagan ruler to accomplish His divine purposes. When the words and actions of world leaders disturb you, just remember that God is still on the throne and has things in control.

1:5, 6 Not all the Jews of the captivity wanted to return to a desolate land. Some of those who did not go at least encouraged the others and helped with the expenses, as did some of their Babylonian neighbors (1:4, 6).

The trip was difficult, and life in the land was demanding; however, the courageous Jews paid the price to do God's will. No matter how you may have failed in the past, God gives you an opportunity for a new beginning.

people of Elam, one thousand two hundred and fifty-four; ⁸the people of Zattu, nine hundred and forty-five; ⁹the people of Zaccai, seven hundred and sixty; ¹⁰the people of Bani,ᵈ six hundred and forty-two; ¹¹the people of Bebai, six hundred and twenty-three; ¹²the people of Azgad, one thousand two hundred and twenty-two; ¹³the people of Adonikam, six hundred and sixty-six; ¹⁴the people of Bigvai, two thousand and fifty-six; ¹⁵the people of Adin, four hundred and fifty-four; ¹⁶the people of Ater of Hezekiah, ninety-eight; ¹⁷the people of Bezai, three hundred and twenty-three; ¹⁸the people of Jorah,ᵉ one hundred and twelve; ¹⁹the people of Hashum, two hundred and twenty-three; ²⁰the people of Gibbar,ᶠ ninety-five; ²¹the people of Bethlehem, one hundred and twenty-three; ²²the men of Netophah, fifty-six; ²³the men of Anathoth, one hundred and twenty-eight; ²⁴the people of Azmaveth,ᵍ forty-two; ²⁵the people of Kirjath Arim,ʰ Chephirah, and Beeroth, seven hundred and forty-three; ²⁶the people of Ramah and Geba, six hundred and twenty-one; ²⁷the men of Michmas, one hundred and twenty-two; ²⁸the men of Bethel and Ai, two hundred and twenty-three; ²⁹the people of Nebo, fifty-two; ³⁰the people of Magbish, one hundred and fifty-six; ³¹the people of the other Elam, one thousand two hundred and fifty-four; ³²the people of Harim, three hundred and twenty; ³³the people of Lod, Hadid, and Ono, seven hundred and twenty-five; ³⁴the people of Jericho, three hundred and forty-five; ³⁵the people of Senaah, three thousand six hundred and thirty.

³⁶The priests: the sons of Jedaiah, of the house of Jeshua, nine hundred and seventy-three; ³⁷the sons of Immer, one thousand and fifty-two; ³⁸the sons of Pashhur, one thousand two hundred and forty-seven; ³⁹the sons of Harim, one thousand and seventeen.

⁴⁰The Levites: the sons of Jeshua and Kadmiel, of the sons of Hodaviah,ⁱ seventy-four.

⁴¹The singers: the sons of Asaph, one hundred and twenty-eight.

⁴²The sons of the gatekeepers: the sons of Shallum, the sons of Ater, the sons of Talmon, the sons of Akkub, the sons of Hatita, and the sons of Shobai, one hundred and thirty-nine *in* all.

⁴³The Nethinim: the sons of Ziha, the sons of Hasupha, the sons of Tabbaoth, ⁴⁴the sons of Keros, the sons of Siaha,ʲ the sons of Padon, ⁴⁵the sons of Lebanah, the sons of Hagabah, the sons of Akkub, ⁴⁶the sons of Hagab, the sons of Shalmai, the sons of Hanan, ⁴⁷the sons of Giddel, the sons of Gahar, the sons of Reaiah, ⁴⁸the sons of Rezin, the sons of Nekoda, the sons of Gazzam, ⁴⁹the sons of Uzza, the sons of Paseah, the sons of Besai, ⁵⁰the sons of Asnah, the sons of Meunim, the sons of Nephusim,ᵏ ⁵¹the sons of Bakbuk, the sons of Hakupha, the sons of Harhur, ⁵²the sons of Bazluth,ˡ the sons of Mehida, the sons of Harsha, ⁵³the sons of Barkos, the sons of Sisera, the sons of Tamah, ⁵⁴the sons of Neziah, and the sons of Hatipha.

55The sons of Solomon's servants: the sons of
Sotai, the sons of Sophereth, the sons of Peruda,[m]
56the sons of Jaala, the sons of Darkon, the sons
of Giddel, 57the sons of Shephatiah, the sons of
Hattil, the sons of Pochereth of Zebaim, and the
sons of Ami.[n] 58All the Nethinim and the children
of Solomon's servants were three hundred and
ninety-two.
59And these *were* the ones who came up from
Tel Melah, Tel Harsha, Cherub, Addan,[o] and Immer; but they could not identify their father's
house or their genealogy,[p] whether they *were* of
Israel: 60the sons of Delaiah, the sons of Tobiah,
and the sons of Nekoda, six hundred and fifty-
two; 61and of the sons of the priests: the sons of
Habaiah, the sons of Koz,[q] and the sons of Barzillai, who took a wife of the daughters of Barzillai
the Gileadite, and was called by their name.
62These sought their listing *among* those who
were registered by genealogy, but they were not
found; therefore they *were excluded* from the
priesthood as defiled. 63And the governor[r] said
to them that they should not eat of the most holy
things till a priest could consult with the Urim
and Thummim.
64The whole assembly together *was* forty-two
thousand three hundred *and* sixty, 65besides their
male and female servants, of whom *there were*
seven thousand three hundred and thirty-seven;
and they had two hundred men and women singers. 66Their horses *were* seven hundred and thirty-
six, their mules two hundred and forty-five,
67their camels four hundred and thirty-five, and
their donkeys six thousand seven hundred and
twenty.
68*Some* of the heads of the fathers' *houses,*
when they came to the house of the LORD which *is*
in Jerusalem, offered freely for the house of God,
to erect it in its place: 69According to their ability, they gave to the treasury for the work sixty-
one thousand gold drachmas, five thousand minas
of silver, and one hundred priestly garments.
70So the priests and the Levites, *some* of the
people, the singers, the gatekeepers, and the Nethinim, dwelt in their cities, and all Israel in their
cities.

3 And* when the seventh month had come, and
the children of Israel *were* in the cities, the
people gathered together as one man to Jerusalem. 2*Then Jeshua the son of Jozadak[s] and his
brethren the priests, and Zerubbabel the son of
Shealtiel and his brethren, arose and built the altar of the God of Israel, to offer burnt offerings
on it, as *it is* written in the Law of Moses the
man of God. 3Though fear *had come* upon them
because of the people of those countries, they set
the altar on its bases; and they offered burnt offerings on it to the LORD, *both* the morning and evening burnt offerings. 4*They also kept the Feast
of Tabernacles, as *it is* written, and *offered* the

2:55 [m]Spelled *Perida* in Nehemiah 7:57 2:57 [n]Spelled *Amon* in Nehemiah 7:59 2:59 [o]Spelled *Addon* in Nehemiah 7:61 [p]Literally *seed* 2:61 [q]Or *Hakkoz* 2:63 [r]Hebrew *Tirshatha* 3:2 [s]Spelled *Jehozadak* in 1 Chronicles 6:14

CHAPTER 3

3:1ff How do you go about restoring things after God's chastening hand has been removed?

3:2–6 *Put worship first.* There was no temple as yet, but that did not hinder them from setting up an altar and sacrificing to God. This is an illustration of Matthew 6:33. They needed to worship God for their own sake as well for a witness to the people around them.

3:4 *Celebrate God's goodness.* It was time for the Feast of Tabernacles, a joyful feast of thanksgiving. Times were tough, but the people obeyed the Word and praised the Lord. This in itself would be a testimony to the Gentiles, and it would do their own hearts good. It is always the right time to praise the Lord.

The Future—You cannot change the past, but the past can change you, either for better or for worse. It all depends on how you look at it. The past can be a rudder that guides you or an anchor that hinders you. Leave your past mistakes with God, and look to the future by faith.

daily burnt offerings in the number required by ordinance for each day. [5]Afterwards *they offered* the regular burnt offering, and *those* for New Moons and for all the appointed feasts of the LORD that were consecrated, and *those* of everyone who willingly offered a freewill offering to the LORD. [6]From the first day of the seventh month they began to offer burnt offerings to the LORD, although the foundation of the temple of the LORD had not been laid. [7]They also gave money to the masons and the carpenters, and food, drink, and oil to the people of Sidon and Tyre to bring cedar logs from Lebanon to the sea, to Joppa, according to the permission which they had from Cyrus king of Persia.

[8]Now in the second month of the second year of their coming to the house of God at Jerusalem, Zerubbabel the son of Shealtiel, Jeshua the son of Jozadak,[t] and the rest of their brethren the priests and the Levites, and all those who had come out of the captivity to Jerusalem, began *work* and appointed the Levites from twenty years old and above to oversee the work of the house of the LORD. [9]Then Jeshua *with* his sons and brothers, Kadmiel *with* his sons, and the sons of Judah,[u] arose as one to oversee those working on the house of God: the sons of Henadad *with* their sons and their brethren the Levites.

[10]*When the builders laid the foundation of the temple of the LORD, the priests stood[v] in their apparel with trumpets, and the Levites, the sons of Asaph, with cymbals, to praise the LORD, according to the ordinance of David king of Israel. [11]And they sang responsively, praising and giving thanks to the LORD:

> "For *He is* good,
> For His mercy *endures* forever toward
> Israel."[w]

Then all the people shouted with a great shout, when they praised the LORD, because the foundation of the house of the LORD was laid.
[12]*But many of the priests and Levites and heads of the fathers' *houses,* old men who had seen the first temple, wept with a loud voice when the foundation of this temple was laid before their eyes. Yet many shouted aloud for joy, [13]so that the people could not discern the noise of the shout of joy from the noise of the weeping of the people, for the people shouted with a loud shout, and the sound was heard afar off.

4 Now* when the adversaries of Judah and Benjamin heard that the descendants of the captivity were building the temple of the LORD God of Israel, [2]*they came to Zerubbabel and the heads of the fathers' *houses,* and said to them, "Let us build with you, for we seek your God as you *do; and* we have sacrificed to Him since the days of Esarhaddon king of Assyria, who brought us here." [3]But Zerubbabel and Jeshua and the rest of the heads of the fathers' *houses* of Israel said to them, "You may do nothing with us to build a house for our God; but we alone will build to the LORD God of Israel, as King Cyrus the king of

3:10, 11 *Establish the foundations.* The Scriptures told them all they needed to know to rebuild the temple, and they followed God's plan. The foundation is the most important part of the building, for it determines the size, shape, and strength of the structure. Do you have the right foundations for your life?

3:12, 13 *Look to the future.* The old people looked back and wept while the young people looked ahead and rejoiced. Tears and cheers, not too different from what is happening in families and churches today. The men were able to work together but not praise God together. If you concentrate on your past, you are sure to rob yourself of a glorious future (Phil. 3:12–14).

CHAPTER 4

4:1 As soon as God starts to bless, the enemy starts to battle. Satan is a destroyer, and he gets angry when God's people unite to build. He has three favorite weapons.

4:2, 3 *Cooperation.* The people were descendants of the Jews who intermarried with the Gentiles the Assyrians brought to the land (2 Kings 17:24ff.). The "mixed multitude" would have corrupted the Jews and interfered with the work (Exod. 12:38; Num. 11:4). Beware volunteers; they may be working for the enemy!

⁶⁶*There is no need to fear; if we keep within the moral frontiers of God, we can say boldly, 'The Lord is my helper.'* ⁹⁹
—Oswald Chambers

3:8 [t]Spelled *Jehozadak* in 1 Chronicles 6:14　3:9 [u]Or *Hodaviah* (compare 2:40)　3:10 [v]Following Septuagint, Syriac, and Vulgate; Masoretic Text reads *they stationed the priests.*　3:11 [w]Compare Psalm 136:1

Persia has commanded us." 4*Then the people of the land tried to discourage the people of Judah. They troubled them in building, 5and hired counselors against them to frustrate their purpose all the days of Cyrus king of Persia, even until the reign of Darius king of Persia.

6*In the reign of Ahasuerus, in the beginning of his reign, they wrote an accusation against the inhabitants of Judah and Jerusalem.

7In the days of Artaxerxes also, Bishlam, Mithredath, Tabel, and the rest of their companions wrote to Artaxerxes king of Persia; and the letter *was* written in Aramaic script, and translated into the Aramaic language. 8Rehumˣ the commander and Shimshai the scribe wrote a letter against Jerusalem to King Artaxerxes in this fashion:

9   Fromʸ Rehum the commander, Shimshai the scribe, and the rest of their companions—
     representatives of the Dinaites, the Apharsathchites, the Tarpelites, the people of Persia and Erech and Babylon and Shushan,ᶻ the Dehavites, the Elamites, 10and the rest of the nations whom the great and noble Osnapper took captive and settled in the cities of Samaria and the remainder beyond the Riverᵃ—and so forth.ᵇ

11(This *is* a copy of the letter that they sent him)

To King Artaxerxes from your servants, the men *of the region* beyond the River, and so forth:ᶜ

12   Let it be known to the king that the Jews who came up from you have come to us at Jerusalem, and are building the rebellious and evil city, and are finishing *its* walls and repairing the foundations. 13Let it now be known to the king that, if this city is built and the walls completed, they will not pay tax, tribute, or custom, and the king's treasury will be diminished. 14Now because we receive support from the palace, it was not proper for us to see the king's dishonor; therefore we have sent and informed the king, 15that search may be made in the book of the records of your fathers. And you will find in the book of the records and know that this city *is* a rebellious city, harmful to kings and provinces, and that they have incited sedition within the city in former times, for which cause this city was destroyed.

16   We inform the king that if this city is rebuilt and its walls are completed, the result will be that you will have no dominion beyond the River.

17The king sent an answer:

To Rehum the commander, *to* Shimshai the scribe, *to* the rest of their companions who dwell in Samaria, and *to* the remainder beyond the River:

4:4, 5 *Intimidation.* Discouragement and fear are effective weapons, especially when the work is already difficult. When you start to experience fear, lean on Isaiah 12:2.

4:6–24 *Legislation.* The people of the world will use "official influence" to hinder God's work. From their viewpoint, Jerusalem had been a rebellious city, and the king would certainly be concerned about taxes. The tactic worked, and the construction had to stop.

But God was still at work!

4:8 ˣThe original language of Ezra 4:8 through 6:18 is Aramaic.
4:9 ʸLiterally *Then* ᶻOr *Susa*   4:10 ᵃThat is, the Euphrates
ᵇLiterally *and now*   4:11 ᶜLiterally *and now*

Peace, and so forth.[d]

18 The letter which you sent to us has been clearly read before me. [19]And I gave the command, and a search has been made, and it was found that this city in former times has revolted against kings, and rebellion and sedition have been fostered in it. [20]There have also been mighty kings over Jerusalem, who have ruled over all *the region* beyond the River; and tax, tribute, and custom were paid to them. [21]Now give the command to make these men cease, that this city may not be built until the command is given by me.

22 Take heed now that you do not fail to do this. Why should damage increase to the hurt of the kings?

[23]Now when the copy of King Artaxerxes' letter *was* read before Rehum, Shimshai the scribe, and their companions, they went up in haste to Jerusalem against the Jews, and by force of arms made them cease. [24]Thus the work of the house of God which *is* at Jerusalem ceased, and it was discontinued until the second year of the reign of Darius king of Persia.

CHAPTERS 5—6

5:1ff About fifteen years elapse between 4:24 and 5:1. During that time, God prepared two prophets to renew and strengthen the work. After all, God's Word commenced the project (Ezra 1:1), so only God's Word could continue it and complete it (Gal. 3:3). When God wants to get something done, He sends His servants with His Word, for nothing but our unbelief can hinder the power of the Word. Even the pagan king had to bow before the Word of God!

5:5 When God's Word is with you and God's eye is upon you (5:5), your work will prosper (6:14; see also Josh. 1:8; Ps. 1:1–3). Revival comes when God's people heed God's Word and do what God tells them to do. Read Haggai's four sermons of encouragement and rebuke and see what true "revival preaching" is like. Do those messages speak to you now?

5 Then* the prophet Haggai and Zechariah the son of Iddo, prophets, prophesied to the Jews who *were* in Judah and Jerusalem, in the name of the God of Israel, *who was* over them. [2]So Zerubbabel the son of Shealtiel and Jeshua the son of Jozadak[e] rose up and began to build the house of God which *is* in Jerusalem; and the prophets of God *were* with them, helping them.

[3]At the same time Tattenai the governor of *the region* beyond the River[f] and Shethar-Boznai and their companions came to them and spoke thus to them: "Who has commanded you to build this temple and finish this wall?" [4]Then, accordingly, we told them the names of the men who were constructing this building. [5]*But the eye of their God was upon the elders of the Jews, so that they could not make them cease till a report could go to Darius. Then a written answer was returned concerning this *matter*. [6]This is a copy of the letter that Tattenai sent:

The governor of *the region* beyond the River, and Shethar-Boznai, and his companions, the Persians who *were* in the *region* beyond the River, to Darius the king.

[7](They sent a letter to him, in which was written thus)

To Darius the king:

All peace.

8 Let it be known to the king that we went into the province of Judea, to the temple of the great God, which is being built with heavy stones, and timber is being laid in the walls; and this work goes on diligently and prospers in their hands.

4:17 [d]Literally *and now*   5:2 [e]Spelled *Jehozadak* in 1 Chronicles 6:14   5:3 [f]That is, the Euphrates

9 Then we asked those elders, *and* spoke thus
to them: "Who commanded you to build this
temple and to finish these walls?" 10We also
asked them their names to inform you, that
we might write the names of the men who
were chief among them.

11 And thus they returned us an answer,
saying: "We are the servants of the God of
heaven and earth, and we are rebuilding the
temple that was built many years ago, which
a great king of Israel built and completed.
12But because our fathers provoked the God
of heaven to wrath, He gave them into the
hand of Nebuchadnezzar king of Babylon,
the Chaldean, *who* destroyed this temple
and carried the people away to Babylon.
13However, in the first year of Cyrus king
of Babylon, King Cyrus issued a decree to
build this house of God. 14Also, the gold and
silver articles of the house of God, which
Nebuchadnezzar had taken from the temple
that *was* in Jerusalem and carried into the
temple of Babylon—those King Cyrus took
from the temple of Babylon, and they were
given to one named Sheshbazzar, whom he
had made governor. 15And he said to him,
'Take these articles; go, carry them to the
temple *site* that *is* in Jerusalem, and let the
house of God be rebuilt on its former site.'
16Then the same Sheshbazzar came *and* laid
the foundation of the house of God which
is in Jerusalem; but from that time even
until now it has been under construction,
and it is not finished."

17 Now therefore, if *it seems* good to the king,
let a search be made in the king's treasure
house, which *is* there in Babylon, whether
it is *so* that a decree was issued by King
Cyrus to build this house of God at
Jerusalem, and let the king send us his
pleasure concerning this *matter.*

6 Then King Darius issued a decree, and a
search was made in the archives,g where the
treasures were stored in Babylon. 2And at Achme-
tha,h in the palace that *is* in the province of Media,
a scroll was found, and in it a record *was* written
thus:

3 In the first year of King Cyrus, King Cyrus
issued a decree *concerning* the house of God
at Jerusalem: "Let the house be rebuilt, the
place where they offered sacrifices; and let
the foundations of it be firmly laid, its height
sixty cubits *and* its width sixty cubits,
4*with* three rows of heavy stones and one
row of new timber. Let the expenses be paid
from the king's treasury. 5Also let the gold
and silver articles of the house of God,
which Nebuchadnezzar took from the
temple which *is* in Jerusalem and brought
to Babylon, be restored and taken back to
the temple which *is* in Jerusalem, *each* to
its place; and deposit *them* in the house of
God"—

6:1 gLiterally *house of the scrolls*   6:2 hProbably *Ecbatana,*
the ancient capital of Media

6 Now *therefore,* Tattenai, governor of *the region* beyond the River, and Shethar-Boznai, and your companions the Persians who *are* beyond the River, keep yourselves far from there. 7Let the work of this house of God alone; let the governor of the Jews and the elders of the Jews build this house of God on its site.

8 Moreover I issue a decree *as to* what you shall do for the elders of these Jews, for the building of this house of God: Let the cost be paid at the king's expense from taxes *on the region* beyond the River; this is to be given immediately to these men, so that they are not hindered. 9And whatever they need—young bulls, rams, and lambs for the burnt offerings of the God of heaven, wheat, salt, wine, and oil, according to the request of the priests who *are* in Jerusalem—let it be given them day by day without fail, 10that they may offer sacrifices of sweet aroma to the God of heaven, and pray for the life of the king and his sons.

11 Also I issue a decree that whoever alters this edict, let a timber be pulled from his house and erected, and let him be hanged on it; and let his house be made a refuse heap because of this. 12And may the God who causes His name to dwell there destroy any king or people who put their hand to alter it, or to destroy this house of God which is in Jerusalem. I Darius issue a decree; let it be done diligently.

13Then Tattenai, governor of *the region* beyond the River, Shethar-Boznai, and their companions diligently did according to what King Darius had sent. 14So the elders of the Jews built, and they prospered through the prophesying of Haggai the prophet and Zechariah the son of Iddo. And they built and finished *it,* according to the commandment of the God of Israel, and according to the command of Cyrus, Darius, and Artaxerxes king of Persia. 15*Now the temple was finished on the third day of the month of Adar, which was in the sixth year of the reign of King Darius. 16Then the children of Israel, the priests and the Levites and the rest of the descendants of the captivity, celebrated the dedication of this house of God with joy. 17And they offered sacrifices at the dedication of this house of God, one hundred bulls, two hundred rams, four hundred lambs, and as a sin offering for all Israel twelve male goats, according to the number of the tribes of Israel. 18They assigned the priests to their divisions and the Levites to their divisions, over the service of God in Jerusalem, as it is written in the Book of Moses.

19And the descendants of the captivity kept the Passover on the fourteenth *day* of the first month. 20For the priests and the Levites had purified themselves; all of them *were ritually* clean. And they slaughtered the Passover *lambs* for all the descendants of the captivity, for their brethren the priests, and for themselves. 21Then the children of Israel who had returned from the captivity ate together with all who had separated themselves from the filth of the nations of the land in order to seek the LORD God of Israel. 22And they kept the Feast of Unleavened Bread seven days with joy; for the LORD made them joyful, and turned

6:15–22 The project began with mingled joy and tears (3:8–13), but it ended with all the people rejoicing (6:16–22). The traditional feast took on new joy because of what God had done for His people.

the heart of the king of Assyria toward them, to strengthen their hands in the work of the house of God, the God of Israel.

7 Now* after these things, in the reign of Artaxerxes king of Persia, Ezra the son of Seraiah, the son of Azariah, the son of Hilkiah, ²the son of Shallum, the son of Zadok, the son of Ahitub, ³the son of Amariah, the son of Azariah, the son of Meraioth, ⁴the son of Zerahiah, the son of Uzzi, the son of Bukki, ⁵the son of Abishua, the son of Phinehas, the son of Eleazar, the son of Aaron the chief priest— ⁶this Ezra came up from Babylon; and he *was* a skilled scribe in the Law of Moses, which the LORD God of Israel had given. The king granted him all his request, according to the hand of the LORD his God upon him. ⁷Some of the children of Israel, the priests, the Levites, the singers, the gatekeepers, and the Nethinim came up to Jerusalem in the seventh year of King Artaxerxes. ⁸And Ezra came to Jerusalem in the fifth month, which *was* in the seventh year of the king. ⁹On the first *day* of the first month he began *his* journey from Babylon, and on the first *day* of the fifth month he came to Jerusalem, according to the good hand of his God upon him. ¹⁰*For Ezra had prepared his heart to seek the Law of the LORD, and to do *it*, and to teach statutes and ordinances in Israel.

¹¹This *is* a copy of the letter that King Artaxerxes gave Ezra the priest, the scribe, expert in the words of the commandments of the LORD, and of His statutes to Israel:

12   Artaxerxes,ⁱ king of kings,

To Ezra the priest, a scribe of the Law of the God of heaven:

Perfect *peace,* and so forth.ʲ

13   I issue a decree that all those of the people of Israel and the priests and Levites in my realm, who volunteer to go up to Jerusalem, may go with you. ¹⁴*And whereas you are being sent by the king and his seven counselors to inquire concerning Judah and Jerusalem, with regard to the Law of your God which *is* in your hand; ¹⁵and *whereas you are* to carry the silver and gold which the king and his counselors have freely offered to the God of Israel, whose dwelling *is* in Jerusalem; ¹⁶and *whereas* all the silver and gold that you may find in all the province of Babylon, along with the freewill offering of the people and the priests, *are to be* freely offered for the house of their God in Jerusalem— ¹⁷now therefore, be careful to buy with this money bulls, rams, and lambs, with their grain offerings and their drink offerings, and offer them on the altar of the house of your God in Jerusalem.

CHAPTERS 7—8

7:1ff There is a gap of fifty-seven years between the completion of the temple and the arrival of Ezra. Unfortunately, the people had lapsed into sin; and it was Ezra's task to bring them back to the Lord. One of the emphases in these chapters is *hands.*

7:10 *God's hand.* Ezra was a gifted man, but he could do nothing unless God's hand was upon him and the people traveling with him. God's hand is a *providing* hand (7:6; 8:18), a *protecting* hand (8:22, 31), an *encouraging* hand (7:28), and a *guiding* hand (7:9).

7:14 *Ezra's hand.* God's Word was in Ezra's heart as well as his hand (7:10), and it was the Word that the people needed. There can be no cleansing or reviving apart from the Word of God.

7:12 ⁱThe original language of Ezra 7:12–26 is Aramaic.
ʲLiterally *and now*

A Balanced Life—According to Ezra 7:10, Ezra studied God's Word, obeyed God's Word, and taught God's Word. He was like the person Jesus spoke about in Matthew 13:52: a student (learning) who was a disciple (living) and a householder (sharing). Having a balanced life is most important.

18 And whatever seems good to you and your brethren to do with the rest of the silver and the gold, do it according to the will of your God. 19Also the articles that are given to you for the service of the house of your God, deliver in full before the God of Jerusalem. 20And whatever more may be needed for the house of your God, which you may have occasion to provide, pay *for it* from the king's treasury.

21 And I, *even* I, Artaxerxes the king, issue a decree to all the treasurers who *are in the region* beyond the River, that whatever Ezra the priest, the scribe of the Law of the God of heaven, may require of you, let it be done diligently, 22up to one hundred talents of silver, one hundred kors of wheat, one hundred baths of wine, one hundred baths of oil, and salt without prescribed limit. 23Whatever is commanded by the God of heaven, let it diligently be done for the house of the God of heaven. For why should there be wrath against the realm of the king and his sons?

24 Also we inform you that it shall not be lawful to impose tax, tribute, or custom *on* any of the priests, Levites, singers, gatekeepers, Nethinim, or servants of this house of God. 25And you, Ezra, according to your God-given wisdom, set magistrates and judges who may judge all the people who *are in the region* beyond the River, all such as know the laws of your God; and teach those who do not know *them*. 26Whoever will not observe the law of your God and the law of the king, let judgment be executed speedily on him, whether *it be* death, or banishment, or confiscation of goods, or imprisonment.

27Blessed *be* the LORD God of our fathers, who has put *such a thing* as this in the king's heart, to beautify the house of the LORD which *is* in Jerusalem, 28and has extended mercy to me before the king and his counselors, and before all the king's mighty princes.

So I was encouraged, as the hand of the LORD my God *was* upon me; and I gathered leading men of Israel to go up with me.

8 These *are* the heads of their fathers' *houses*, and *this is* the genealogy of those who went up with me from Babylon, in the reign of King Artaxerxes: 2of the sons of Phinehas, Gershom; of the sons of Ithamar, Daniel; of the sons of David, Hattush; 3of the sons of Shecaniah, of the sons of Parosh, Zechariah; and registered with him *were* one hundred and fifty males; 4of the sons of Pahath-Moab, Eliehoenai the son of Zerahiah, and with him two hundred males; 5of the sons of Shechaniah,ᵏ Ben-Jahaziel, and with him three hundred males; 6of the sons of Adin, Ebed the son of Jonathan, and with him fifty males; 7of the sons of Elam, Jeshaiah the son of Athaliah, and with him seventy males; 8of the sons of Shephatiah, Zebadiah the son of Michael, and with him eighty males; 9of the sons of Joab, Obadiah the son of Jehiel, and with him two hundred

---

8:5 ᵏFollowing Masoretic Text and Vulgate; Septuagint reads *the sons of Zatho, Shechaniah*.

and eighteen males; [10]of the sons of Shelomith,[l] Ben-Josiphiah, and with him one hundred and sixty males; [11]of the sons of Bebai, Zechariah the son of Bebai, and with him twenty-eight males; [12]of the sons of Azgad, Johanan the son of Hakkatan, and with him one hundred and ten males; [13]of the last sons of Adonikam, whose names *are* these—Eliphelet, Jeiel, and Shemaiah—and with them sixty males; [14]also of the sons of Bigvai, Uthai and Zabbud, and with them seventy males.

[15]Now I gathered them by the river that flows to Ahava, and we camped there three days. And I looked among the people and the priests, and found none of the sons of Levi there. [16]Then I sent for Eliezer, Ariel, Shemaiah, Elnathan, Jarib, Elnathan, Nathan, Zechariah, and Meshullam, leaders; also for Joiarib and Elnathan, men of understanding. [17]And I gave them a command for Iddo the chief man at the place Casiphia, and I told them what they should say to Iddo *and* his brethren[m] the Nethinim at the place Casiphia— that they should bring us servants for the house of our God. [18]Then, by the good hand of our God upon us, they brought us a man of understanding, of the sons of Mahli the son of Levi, the son of Israel, namely Sherebiah, with his sons and brothers, eighteen men; [19]and Hashabiah, and with him Jeshaiah of the sons of Merari, his brothers and their sons, twenty men; [20]also of the Nethinim, whom David and the leaders had appointed for the service of the Levites, two hundred and twenty Nethinim. All of them were designated by name.

[21]Then I proclaimed a fast there at the river of Ahava, that we might humble ourselves before our God, to seek from Him the right way for us and our little ones and all our possessions. [22]For I was ashamed to request of the king an escort of soldiers and horsemen to help us against the enemy on the road, because we had spoken to the king, saying, "The hand of our God *is* upon all those for good who seek Him, but His power and His wrath *are* against all those who forsake Him." [23]So we fasted and entreated our God for this, and He answered our prayer.

[24]And I separated twelve of the leaders of the priests—Sherebiah, Hashabiah, and ten of their brethren with them— [25]and weighed out to them the silver, the gold, and the articles, the offering for the house of our God which the king and his counselors and his princes, and all Israel *who were* present, had offered. [26]*I weighed into their hand six hundred and fifty talents of silver, silver articles *weighing* one hundred talents, one hundred talents of gold, [27]twenty gold basins *worth* a thousand drachmas, and two vessels of fine polished bronze, precious as gold. [28]And I said to them, "You *are* holy to the Lord; the articles *are* holy also; and the silver and the gold *are* a freewill offering to the Lord God of your fathers. [29]Watch and keep *them* until you weigh *them* before the leaders of the priests and the Levites and heads of the fathers' *houses* of Israel in Jerusalem, *in* the chambers of the house of the Lord." [30]So the priests and the Levites received the silver and the gold and the articles by weight, to bring *them* to Jerusalem to the house of our God.

8:26–33 The Jews' hands. The hands of the people carried the treasures of the Lord, faithfully delivered to the temple at the end of the journey. When you meet the Lord, you will "weigh in" and find out how faithful you have been with what He has given you. Heed the words of 8:29: "Watch and keep!"

8:10 [l]Following Masoretic Text and Vulgate; Septuagint reads *the sons of Banni, Shelomith*.   8:17 [m]Following Vulgate; Masoretic Text reads *to Iddo his brother;* Septuagint reads *to their brethren.*

CHAPTER 9

9:1–4 *Astonished*. For at least three reasons, the Jewish remnant should have obeyed God's Word about marriage. To begin with, God had been good to bring them back to the land. He had also chastened them in Babylon, and they knew from their own past the consequences of compromise. No wonder Ezra was astonished.

9:5–9 *Ashamed*. Ezra used several images to show their plight. They were like drowning men because of their sins (v. 6), and yet they sinned more. They were a little peg on which so much future was hanging (v. 8), a remnant that had to serve as a wall against the awful encroachments of sin (v. 9). If the nation was polluted, how could Messiah be born (v. 2)?

9:10–15 *Alarmed*. God had revealed His Word, and they did not obey it. God had shown them grace (v. 8), and they did not appreciate it. God had held back punishment (v. 13; Ps. 103:10), and they took advantage of it. All God could do now was punish them even more.

As he prayed, Ezra trembled (v. 4), knelt (v. 5), and bowed down (v. 6) because nobody could stand before God (v. 15; Ps. 130:3).

31Then we departed from the river of Ahava on the twelfth *day* of the first month, to go to Jerusalem. And the hand of our God was upon us, and He delivered us from the hand of the enemy and from ambush along the road. 32So we came to Jerusalem, and stayed there three days.

33Now on the fourth day the silver and the gold and the articles were weighed in the house of our God by the hand of Meremoth the son of Uriah the priest, and with him *was* Eleazar the son of Phinehas; with them *were* the Levites, Jozabad the son of Jeshua and Noadiah the son of Binnui, 34with the number *and* weight of everything. All the weight was written down at that time.

35The children of those who had been carried away captive, who had come from the captivity, offered burnt offerings to the God of Israel: twelve bulls for all Israel, ninety-six rams, seventy-seven lambs, and twelve male goats *as* a sin offering. All *this was* a burnt offering to the LORD.

36And they delivered the king's orders to the king's satraps and the governors *in the region* beyond the River. So they gave support to the people and the house of God.

9 When* these things were done, the leaders came to me, saying, "The people of Israel and the priests and the Levites have not separated themselves from the peoples of the lands, with respect to the abominations of the Canaanites, the Hittites, the Perizzites, the Jebusites, the Ammonites, the Moabites, the Egyptians, and the Amorites. 2For they have taken some of their daughters *as wives* for themselves and their sons, so that the holy seed is mixed with the peoples of *those* lands. Indeed, the hand of the leaders and rulers has been foremost in this trespass." 3So when I heard this thing, I tore my garment and my robe, and plucked out some of the hair of my head and beard, and sat down astonished. 4Then everyone who trembled at the words of the God of Israel assembled to me, because of the transgression of those who had been carried away captive, and I sat astonished until the evening sacrifice.

5*At the evening sacrifice I arose from my fasting; and having torn my garment and my robe, I fell on my knees and spread out my hands to the LORD my God. 6And I said: "O my God, I am too ashamed and humiliated to lift up my face to You, my God; for our iniquities have risen higher than *our* heads, and our guilt has grown up to the heavens. 7Since the days of our fathers to this day we *have been* very guilty, and for our iniquities we, our kings, *and* our priests have been delivered into the hand of the kings of the lands, to the sword, to captivity, to plunder, and to humiliation, as *it is* this day. 8And now for a little while grace has been *shown* from the LORD our God, to leave us a remnant to escape, and to give us a peg in His holy place, that our God may enlighten our eyes and give us a measure of revival in our bondage. 9For we *were* slaves. Yet our God did not forsake us in our bondage; but He extended mercy to us in the sight of the kings of Persia, to revive us, to repair the house of our God, to rebuild its ruins, and to give us a wall in Judah and Jerusalem. 10*And now, O our God, what shall we say after this? For we have forsaken Your commandments, 11which You commanded by Your servants the prophets, saying, 'The land which you are entering to possess is an unclean land, with the uncleanness of the peoples of the lands, with their abominations which have filled it from one end to another with their impurity. 12Now therefore, do not give your daughters as wives for their sons, nor take their daughters to your sons; and never seek their peace or prosperity, that you may be strong and eat the good of the land, and leave *it* as an inheritance to your children forever.' 13And after all that has come upon us for our evil deeds and for our great guilt, since You our God have punished us less than our iniquities *deserve,* and have given us *such* deliverance as this, 14should we again break Your commandments, and join in marriage with the people *committing* these abominations? Would You not be angry with us until You had consumed *us,* so that *there would be* no remnant or survivor? 15O LORD God of Israel, You *are* righteous, for we are left as a remnant, as *it is* this day. Here we *are* before You, in our guilt, though no one can stand before You because of this!"

10 Now while Ezra was praying, and while he was confessing, weeping, and bowing down before the house of God, a very large assembly of men, women, and children gathered to him from Israel; for the people wept very bitterly. 2*And Shechaniah the son of Jehiel, *one* of the sons of Elam, spoke up and said to Ezra, "We have trespassed against our God, and have taken pagan wives from the peoples of the land; yet now there is hope in Israel in spite of this. 3*Now therefore, let us make a covenant with our God to put away all these wives and those who have been born to them, according to the advice of my master and of those who tremble at the commandment of our God; and let it be done according to the law. 4Arise, for *this* matter *is* your *responsibility.* We also *are* with you. Be of good courage, and do *it.*"

5Then Ezra arose, and made the leaders of the priests, the Levites, and all Israel swear an oath that they would do according to this word. So they swore an oath. 6Then Ezra rose up from before the house of God, and went into the chamber of Jehohanan the son of Eliashib; and *when* he came there, he ate no bread and drank no water, for he mourned because of the guilt of those from the captivity.

7And they issued a proclamation throughout Judah and Jerusalem to all the descendants of the captivity, that they must gather at Jerusalem, 8and that whoever would not come within three days, according to the instructions of the leaders and elders, all his property would be confiscated, and he himself would be separated from the assembly of those from the captivity.

9So all the men of Judah and Benjamin gathered at Jerusalem within three days. It *was* the ninth month, on the twentieth of the month; and all the people sat in the open square of the house of God, trembling because of *this* matter and because of heavy rain. 10Then Ezra the priest stood up and said to them, "You have transgressed and have taken pagan wives, adding to the guilt of Israel. 11Now therefore, make confession to the LORD God of your fathers, and do His will; separate yourselves from the peoples of the land, and from the pagan wives."

CHAPTER 10

10:2 When things look dark, there is always a ray of hope. Shechaniah encouraged the people to confess their sins and obey the Word. He may have been thinking of God's promises in Exodus 34:6–7, Isaiah 55:6–7, and Jeremiah 3:11–13. Believers today turn to 1 John 1:9.

10:3 But confession must not be a routine thing that comes only from the lips. We must tremble at God's Word (Ezra 9:4; 10:3; Isa. 66:2) and truly bring Him a broken heart (Ps. 51:16–17). That explains why Ezra fasted and prayed, for he identified himself with the people in their sins. Note the pronouns in Ezra 9:6–15.

Our Hope—God's people have hope because of salvation (Rom. 5:1–2), suffering (Rom. 5:3), the Word of God (Rom. 15:4), and the Spirit of God (Rom. 15:13). Of course, there could be no hope were it not for the resurrection of Jesus Christ (1 Pet. 1:3). He is our Hope (1 Tim. 1:1).

12Then all the assembly answered and said with a loud voice, "Yes! As you have said, so we must do. 13But *there are* many people; *it is* the season for heavy rain, and we are not able to stand outside. Nor *is this* the work of one or two days, for *there are* many of us who have transgressed in this matter. 14Please, let the leaders of our entire assembly stand; and let all those in our cities who have taken pagan wives come at appointed times, together with the elders and judges of their cities, until the fierce wrath of our God is turned away from us in this matter." 15*Only Jonathan the son of Asahel and Jahaziah the son of Tikvah opposed this, and Meshullam and Shabbethai the Levite gave them support.

16Then the descendants of the captivity did so. And Ezra the priest, *with* certain heads of the fathers' *households,* were set apart by the fathers' *households,* each of them by name; and they sat down on the first day of the tenth month to examine the matter. 17By the first day of the first month they finished *questioning* all the men who had taken pagan wives.

18And among the sons of the priests who had taken pagan wives *the following* were found of the sons of Jeshua the son of Jozadak,[n] and his brothers: Maaseiah, Eliezer, Jarib, and Gedaliah. 19And they gave their promise that they would put away their wives; and *being* guilty, *they* presented a ram of the flock as their trespass offering.

20Also of the sons of Immer: Hanani and Zebadiah; 21of the sons of Harim: Maaseiah, Elijah, Shemaiah, Jehiel, and Uzziah; 22of the sons of Pashhur: Elioenai, Maaseiah, Ishmael, Nethanel, Jozabad, and Elasah.

23Also of the Levites: Jozabad, Shimei, Kelaiah (the same *is* Kelita), Pethahiah, Judah, and Eliezer.

24Also of the singers: Eliashib; and of the gatekeepers: Shallum, Telem, and Uri.

25And others of Israel: of the sons of Parosh: Ramiah, Jeziah, Malchiah, Mijamin, Eleazar, Malchijah, and Benaiah; 26of the sons of Elam: Mattaniah, Zechariah, Jehiel, Abdi, Jeremoth, and Eliah; 27of the sons of Zattu: Elioenai, Eliashib, Mattaniah, Jeremoth, Zabad, and Aziza; 28of the sons of Bebai: Jehohanan, Hananiah, Zabbai, *and* Athlai; 29of the sons of Bani: Meshullam, Malluch, Adaiah, Jashub, Sheal, *and* Ramoth;[o] 30of the sons of Pahath-Moab: Adna, Chelal, Benaiah, Maaseiah, Mattaniah, Bezalel, Binnui, and Manasseh; 31of the sons of Harim: Eliezer, Ishijah, Malchijah, Shemaiah, Shimeon, 32Benjamin, Malluch, *and* Shemariah; 33of the sons of Hashum: Mattenai, Mattattah, Zabad, Eliphelet, Jeremai, Manasseh, *and* Shimei; 34of the sons of Bani: Maadai, Amram, Uel, 35Benaiah, Bedeiah, Cheluh,[p] 36Vaniah, Meremoth, Eliashib, 37Mattaniah, Mattenai, Jaasai,[q] 38Bani, Binnui, Shimei, 39Shelemiah, Nathan, Adaiah, 40Machnadebai, Shashai, Sharai, 41Azarel, Shelemiah, Shemariah, 42Shallum, Amariah, *and* Joseph; 43of the sons of Nebo: Jeiel, Mattithiah, Zabad, Zebina, Jaddai,[r] Joel, *and* Benaiah.

44All these had taken pagan wives, and *some* of them had wives *by whom* they had children.

10:15 Not everybody agreed to obey, but those who did submit to Ezra confessed their sins publicly, offered a sacrifice, and put away their pagan wives and children. The experience was painful for them, but it was the only way to keep the nation pure (Matt. 18:7–9). There is no easy way to deal with sin.

10:18 [n]Spelled *Jehozadak* in 1 Chronicles 6:14   10:29 [o]Or *Jeremoth*   10:35 [p]Or *Cheluhi,* or *Cheluhu*   10:37 [q]Or *Jaasu*   10:43 [r]Or *Jaddu*

NEHEMIAH

1 The* words of Nehemiah the son of Hachaliah. It came to pass in the month of Chislev, *in* the twentieth year, as I was in Shushan*ª* the citadel, ²that Hanani one of my brethren came with men from Judah; and I asked them concerning the Jews who had escaped, who had survived the captivity, and concerning Jerusalem. ³And they said to me, "The survivors who are left from the captivity in the province *are* there in great distress and reproach. The wall of Jerusalem *is* also broken down, and its gates *are* burned with fire."

⁴*So it was, when I heard these words, that I sat down and wept, and mourned *for many* days; I was fasting and praying before the God of heaven.

⁵And I said: "I pray, LORD God of heaven, O great and awesome God, *You* who keep *Your* covenant and mercy with those who love You*ᵇ* and observe Your*ᶜ* commandments, ⁶please let Your ear be attentive and Your eyes open, that You may hear the prayer of Your servant which I pray before You now, day and night, for the children of Israel Your servants, and confess the sins of the children of Israel which we have sinned against You. Both my father's house and I have sinned. ⁷We have acted very corruptly against You, and have not kept the commandments, the statutes, nor the ordinances which You commanded Your servant Moses. ⁸Remember, I pray, the word that You commanded Your servant Moses, saying, '*If you are unfaithful, I will scatter you among the nations;*ᵈ ⁹but *if you return to Me, and keep My commandments and do them, though some of you were cast out to the farthest part of the heavens, yet I will gather them from there, and bring them to the place which I have chosen as a dwelling for My name.'*ᵉ ¹⁰*Now these *are* Your servants and Your people, whom You have redeemed by Your great power, and by Your strong hand. ¹¹O Lord, I pray, please let Your ear be attentive to the prayer of Your servant, and to the prayer of Your servants who desire to fear Your name; and let Your servant prosper this day, I pray, and grant him mercy in the sight of this man."

For I was the king's cupbearer.

2 And* it came to pass in the month of Nisan, in the twentieth year of King Artaxerxes, *when* wine *was* before him, that I took the wine and gave it to the king. Now I had never been sad in his presence before. ²Therefore the king said to me, "Why *is* your face sad, since you *are* not sick? This *is* nothing but sorrow of heart."

So I became dreadfully afraid, ³and said to the

CHAPTER 1

1:1–3 *Great distress.* Nehemiah enjoyed security and prestige as the king's cupbearer, so there was no reason for him to ask about the needs of people hundreds of miles away. But he loved Jerusalem and was concerned about the welfare of his people (Jer. 15:5). How do you respond when you learn that others are hurting?

1:4–9 *A great God.* Nehemiah was a man of prayer; you will find ten of his prayers in this book (1:4ff.; 2:4; 4:4; 5:19; 6:9, 14; 13:14, 22, 29, 31). He believed in a great God (1:5; 4:14; 8:6; 9:32) who kept His promises, forgave sin, and helped His people when they called on Him. Like Ezra before him, Nehemiah identified himself with the sins and sorrows of the nation (Ezra 9:5ff.).

1:10, 11 *Great power.* Nehemiah did more than weep and pray; he made himself available to the Lord to get the job done. He depended on God's great power to work in and through him (Eph. 3:20–21). He was not content merely to *get* answers to prayer: he wanted to *be* an answer to prayer. Has God used you lately to be an answer to somebody's prayers?

CHAPTER 2

2:1–3 *Waiting.* Nehemiah did not suddenly quit his job and hurry to Jerusalem. He prayed and faithfully worked for four months, waiting to approach the king in the Lord's time. Waiting may be much harder than working, but it is dangerous to rush ahead of the Lord.

1:1 *ª*Or *Susa*   1:5 *ᵇ*Literally *Him* *ᶜ*Literally *His*   1:8 *ᵈ*Leviticus 26:33   1:9 *ᵉ*Deuteronomy 30:2–5

You Can Make the Difference—It was a day of reproach for the people of God (Neh. 1:3; 2:17; 5:9; 6:13). The great city of Jerusalem was no longer beautiful (Ps. 50:2), and the Jews were no longer powerful. But one man made the difference! Nehemiah led the Jews from great reproach (1:3) to great rejoicing (12:43). God is still seeking men and women willing to sacrifice to do His work. Are you available?

2:4 *Praying.* Nehemiah's "telegraph prayers" were effective because he spent much time alone with God. The throne of grace in heaven has greater authority than any throne on earth (Eph. 1:15–23). Are you in the habit of talking to God during your daily activities?

2:5–8 *Explaining.* Nehemiah had been planning his work carefully, so he was able to give the king satisfactory answers. Prayer and concern are not substitutes for clear thinking and adequate organization.

2:12–16 *Preparing.* Nehemiah paid attention to this advice: "Whoever believes will not act hastily" (Isa. 28:16). Before enlisting the leaders, Nehemiah became personally acquainted with the needs (v. 11; Ezra 8:32). Dedicated leaders are awake when others are asleep, but they see more in the darkness than others do in the light (Prov. 20:18).

king, "May the king live forever! Why should my face not be sad, when the city, the place of my fathers' tombs, *lies* waste, and its gates are burned with fire?"

4*Then the king said to me, "What do you request?"

So I prayed to the God of heaven. 5*And I said to the king, "If it pleases the king, and if your servant has found favor in your sight, I ask that you send me to Judah, to the city of my fathers' tombs, that I may rebuild it."

6Then the king said to me (the queen also sitting beside him), "How long will your journey be? And when will you return?" So it pleased the king to send me; and I set him a time.

7Furthermore I said to the king, "If it pleases the king, let letters be given to me for the governors *of the region* beyond the River,*f* that they must permit me to pass through till I come to Judah, 8and a letter to Asaph the keeper of the king's forest, that he must give me timber to make beams for the gates of the citadel which *pertains* to the temple,*g* for the city wall, and for the house that I will occupy." And the king granted *them* to me according to the good hand of my God upon me.

9Then I went to the governors *in the region* beyond the River, and gave them the king's letters. Now the king had sent captains of the army and horsemen with me. 10When Sanballat the Horonite and Tobiah the Ammonite official*h* heard *of it,* they were deeply disturbed that a man had come to seek the well-being of the children of Israel.

11So I came to Jerusalem and was there three days. 12*Then I arose in the night, I and a few men with me; I told no one what my God had put in my heart to do at Jerusalem; nor was there any animal with me, except the one on which I rode. 13And I went out by night through the Valley Gate to the Serpent Well and the Refuse Gate, and viewed the walls of Jerusalem which were broken down and its gates which were burned with fire. 14Then I went on to the Fountain Gate and to the King's Pool, but *there was* no room for the animal under me to pass. 15So I went up in the night by the valley, and viewed the wall; then I turned back and entered by the Valley Gate, and so returned. 16And the officials did not know where I had gone or what I had done; I had not yet told the Jews, the priests, the nobles, the officials, or the others who did the work.

17Then I said to them, "You see the distress that we *are* in, how Jerusalem *lies* waste, and its gates are burned with fire. Come and let us build the wall of Jerusalem, that we may no longer be a reproach." 18And I told them of the hand of my God which had been good upon me, and also of the king's words that he had spoken to me.

So they said, "Let us rise up and build." Then they set their hands to *this* good *work.*

19But when Sanballat the Horonite, Tobiah the Ammonite official, and Geshem the Arab heard *of it,* they laughed at us and despised us, and said, "What *is* this thing that you are doing? Will you rebel against the king?"

20So I answered them, and said to them, "The God of heaven Himself will prosper us; therefore

---

2:7 *f*That is, the Euphrates, and so elsewhere in this book
2:8 *g*Literally *house*   2:10 *h*Literally *servant,* and so elsewhere in this book

we His servants will arise and build, but you have no heritage or right or memorial in Jerusalem."

3 Then* Eliashib the high priest rose up with his brethren the priests and built the Sheep Gate; they consecrated it and hung its doors. They built as far as the Tower of the Hundred,ᶦ *and* consecrated it, then as far as the Tower of Hananel. 2Next to *Eliashibʲ* the men of Jericho built. And next to them Zaccur the son of Imri built.

3Also the sons of Hassenaah built the Fish Gate; they laid its beams and hung its doors with its bolts and bars. 4And next to them Meremoth the son of Urijah, the son of Koz,ᵏ made repairs. Next to them Meshullam the son of Berechiah, the son of Meshezabel, made repairs. Next to them Zadok the son of Baana made repairs. 5Next to them the Tekoites made repairs; but their nobles did not put their shouldersᶦ to the work of their Lord.

6Moreover Jehoiada the son of Paseah and Meshullam the son of Besodeiah repaired the Old Gate; they laid its beams and hung its doors, with its bolts and bars. 7And next to them Melatiah the Gibeonite, Jadon the Meronothite, the men of Gibeon and Mizpah, repaired the residenceᵐ of the governor *of the region* beyond the River. 8Next to him Uzziel the son of Harhaiah, one of the goldsmiths, made repairs. Also next to him Hananiah, oneⁿ of the perfumers, made repairs; and they fortified Jerusalem as far as the Broad Wall. 9And next to them Rephaiah the son of Hur, leader of half the district of Jerusalem, made repairs. 10*Next to them Jedaiah the son of Harumaph made repairs in front of his house. And next to him Hattush the son of Hashabniah made repairs.

11Malchijah the son of Harim and Hashub the son of Pahath-Moab repaired another section, as well as the Tower of the Ovens. 12And next to him was Shallum the son of Hallohesh, leader of half the district of Jerusalem; he and his daughters made repairs.

13Hanun and the inhabitants of Zanoah repaired the Valley Gate. They built it, hung its doors with its bolts and bars, and *repaired* a thousand cubits of the wall as far as the Refuse Gate.

14Malchijah the son of Rechab, leader of the district of Beth Haccerem, repaired the Refuse Gate; he built it and hung its doors with its bolts and bars.

15Shallun the son of Col-Hozeh, leader of the district of Mizpah, repaired the Fountain Gate; he built it, covered it, hung its doors with its bolts and bars, and repaired the wall of the Pool of Shelah by the King's Garden, as far as the stairs that go down from the City of David. 16After him Nehemiah the son of Azbuk, leader of half the district of Beth Zur, made repairs as far as *the place* in front of the tombsᵒ of David, to the man-made pool, and as far as the House of the Mighty.

17After him the Levites, *under* Rehum the son

CHAPTER 3

3:1ff The workers were involved in building, repairing (the word is used forty times) and fortifying (v. 8), ministries needed in the church today. The walls and gates were important for the protection of the people and the beauty of the city.

3:1–32 There is a place of ministry for everybody who has a mind to work: priests (v. 1), rulers (vv. 12–19), craftsmen (v. 8), and dedicated women (v. 12). God sometimes brings outsiders to help us (vv. 2, 5, 7), and some people are willing to do extra work (vv. 11, 19, 21). The significant thing is that they cooperated as they served the Lord. But don't be surprised if some people do nothing (v. 5), including some leaders. Just keep on working!

3:10 The best place to start working is at your own house. If each of us served the Lord first at home, what a difference it would make in the work of the Lord!

3:1 ᶦHebrew *Hammeah*, also at 12:39   3:2 ʲLiterally *On his hand*   3:4 ᵏOr *Hakkoz*   3:5 ᶦLiterally *necks*   3:7 ᵐLiterally *throne*   3:8 ⁿLiterally *the son*   3:16 ᵒSeptuagint, Syriac, and Vulgate read *tomb*.

Who Does the Work?—Some people are *constructionists,* helping to get the job done. Others are *destructionists,* busy tearing things down. A third group is made up of *obstructionists* who create problems for the people doing the work. In which group are you?

of Bani, made repairs. Next to him Hashabiah, leader of half the district of Keilah, made repairs for his district. [18]After him their brethren, *under* Bavai[p] the son of Henadad, leader of the *other* half of the district of Keilah, made repairs. [19]And next to him Ezer the son of Jeshua, the leader of Mizpah, repaired another section in front of the Ascent to the Armory at the buttress. [20]After him Baruch the son of Zabbai[q] carefully repaired the other section, from the buttress to the door of the house of Eliashib the high priest. [21]After him Meremoth the son of Urijah, the son of Koz,[r] repaired another section, from the door of the house of Eliashib to the end of the house of Eliashib.

[22]And after him the priests, the men of the plain, made repairs. [23]After him Benjamin and Hasshub made repairs opposite their house. After them Azariah the son of Maaseiah, the son of Ananiah, made repairs by his house. [24]After him Binnui the son of Henadad repaired another section, from the house of Azariah to the buttress, even as far as the corner. [25]Palal the son of Uzai *made repairs* opposite the buttress, and on the tower which projects from the king's upper house that *was* by the court of the prison. After him Pedaiah the son of Parosh *made repairs*.

[26]Moreover the Nethinim who dwelt in Ophel *made repairs* as far as *the place* in front of the Water Gate toward the east, and on the projecting tower. [27]After them the Tekoites repaired another section, next to the great projecting tower, and as far as the wall of Ophel.

[28]Beyond the Horse Gate the priests made repairs, each in front of his *own* house. [29]After them Zadok the son of Immer made repairs in front of his *own* house. After him Shemaiah the son of Shechaniah, the keeper of the East Gate, made repairs. [30]After him Hananiah the son of Shelemiah, and Hanun, the sixth son of Zalaph, repaired another section. After him Meshullam the son of Berechiah made repairs in front of his dwelling. [31]After him Malchijah, one of the goldsmiths, made repairs as far as the house of the Nethinim and of the merchants, in front of the Miphkad[s] Gate, and as far as the upper room at the corner. [32]And between the upper room at the corner, as far as the Sheep Gate, the goldsmiths and the merchants made repairs.

CHAPTER 4

4:1ff The enemy knows what we are doing and will be quick to fight us. Expect opposition, and be ready for it. Note the different weapons that the enemy used then and still uses today.

4:2–8 *Mockery*. The enemy wants you to think that your work is not important, that you are too weak to do it, and that if you finish it, it will not last. In other words, he wants you to believe that it is not worth it all, so you might as well quit. Just keep in mind that it is God's work and therefore a great work (v. 19; 6:3). Keep the greatness of God before your eyes (v. 14; 1:5, 10).

4 But* it so happened, when Sanballat heard that we were rebuilding the wall, that he was furious and very indignant, and mocked the Jews. [2]*And he spoke before his brethren and the army of Samaria, and said, "What are these feeble Jews doing? Will they fortify themselves? Will they offer sacrifices? Will they complete it in a day? Will they revive the stones from the heaps of rubbish— *stones* that are burned?"

3:18 [p]Following Masoretic Text and Vulgate; some Hebrew manuscripts, Septuagint, and Syriac read *Binnui* (compare verse 24).   3:20 [q]A few Hebrew manuscripts, Syriac, and Vulgate read *Zaccai*.   3:21 [r]Or *Hakkoz*   3:31 [s]Literally *Inspection* or *Recruiting*

"Watch and Pray!"—This means trusting God while at the same time being alert to what the enemy is doing. It is the way to be ready for Christ's return (Mark 13:33) and to be victorious over temptation (Mark 14:38) and Satan (Eph. 6:18). It is also the way to have open doors for ministry and make the most of them (Col. 4:2–6).

³Now Tobiah the Ammonite *was* beside him, and he said, "Whatever they build, if even a fox goes up *on it,* he will break down their stone wall."

⁴Hear, O our God, for we are despised; turn their reproach on their own heads, and give them as plunder to a land of captivity! ⁵Do not cover their iniquity, and do not let their sin be blotted out from before You; for they have provoked *You* to anger before the builders.

⁶So we built the wall, and the entire wall was joined together up to half its *height,* for the people had a mind to work.

⁷*Now it happened, when Sanballat, Tobiah, the Arabs, the Ammonites, and the Ashdodites heard that the walls of Jerusalem were being restored and the gaps were beginning to be closed, that they became very angry, ⁸and all of them conspired together to come *and* attack Jerusalem and create confusion. ⁹Nevertheless we made our prayer to our God, and because of them we set a watch against them day and night.

¹⁰*Then Judah said, "The strength of the laborers is failing, and *there is* so much rubbish that we are not able to build the wall."

¹¹And our adversaries said, "They will neither know nor see anything, till we come into their midst and kill them and cause the work to cease."

¹²So it was, when the Jews who dwelt near them came, that they told us ten times, "From whatever place you turn, *they will be* upon us."

¹³Therefore I positioned *men* behind the lower parts of the wall, at the openings; and I set the people according to their families, with their swords, their spears, and their bows. ¹⁴And I looked, and arose and said to the nobles, to the leaders, and to the rest of the people, "Do not be afraid of them. Remember the Lord, great and awesome, and fight for your brethren, your sons, your daughters, your wives, and your houses."

¹⁵And it happened, when our enemies heard that it was known to us, and *that* God had brought their plot to nothing, that all of us returned to the wall, everyone to his work. ¹⁶So it was, from that time on, *that* half of my servants worked at construction, while the other half held the spears, the shields, the bows, and *wore* armor; and the leaders *were* behind all the house of Judah. ¹⁷Those who built on the wall, and those who carried burdens, loaded themselves so that with one hand they worked at construction, and with the other held a weapon. ¹⁸Every one of the builders had his sword girded at his side as he built. And the one who sounded the trumpet *was* beside me.

¹⁹Then I said to the nobles, the rulers, and the rest of the people, "The work *is* great and extensive, and we are separated far from one another on the wall. ²⁰Wherever you hear the sound of the trumpet, rally to us there. Our God will fight for us."

²¹So we labored in the work, and half of *the men*ᵗ held the spears from daybreak until the stars appeared. ²²At the same time I also said to the people, "Let each man and his servant stay at night in Jerusalem, that they may be our guard by night and a working party by day." ²³So neither I, my brethren, my servants, nor the men of the guard who followed me took off our clothes, *except* that everyone took them off for washing.

4:7–9 *Threats.* If your enemy cannot fool you, he will try to frighten you. The people practiced Ephesians 6:10–18; they armed themselves, prayed, and kept working.

4:10–23 *Fear.* The Jews living outside the city came to work with frightening tales about the enemy's plans. Again, the greatness of God helps us overcome the fear of man (v. 14), plus our willingness to stay on the job despite the sacrifices that may be required.

4:21 ᵗLiterally *them*

CHAPTER 5

5:1 Now the enemy attacks from inside the nation, and Nehemiah must deal with selfishness and greed among his people. The wealthier Jews took advantage of the famine and economic crisis to exploit their own people (Hag. 1:7–11). How did Nehemiah respond?

5:6 *Anger.* There is a righteous anger against sin that itself is not sinful (Eph. 4:26). Although it is difficult not to get angry with people, we must try to focus on what they do rather than who they are. (See Exod. 32:19; Mark 3:5.) A person who lacks anger may also lack conviction and courage.

5:7 *Deliberation.* It was not Nehemiah's practice to exercise leadership without first thinking things through (Prov. 18:13; 29:22). No doubt he also prayed for God's wisdom.

5:7–13 *Resolution.* Once he decided what to do, he did it! He appealed to their love ("brother" in v. 7) and their devotion to the Word of God (Exod. 22:25). He reminded them of the fear of God and their witness to the enemy (v. 9).

5:14–19 *Example.* Had Nehemiah not been an unselfish and sacrificing man, he could not have appealed as he did (Matt. 7:1–5). He had helped the people generously and did not take advantage of his position as governor. A clear conscience is a mighty weapon in God's hands.

❝*It is easy to fly into a passion—anybody can do that—but to be angry with the right person to the right extent and at the right time and with the right object and in the right way—that is not easy, and it is not everyone who can do it.*❞

Aristotle

5 And* there was a great outcry of the people and their wives against their Jewish brethren. ²For there were those who said, "We, our sons, and our daughters *are* many; therefore let us get grain, that we may eat and live."

³There were also *some* who said, "We have mortgaged our lands and vineyards and houses, that we might buy grain because of the famine."

⁴There were also those who said, "We have borrowed money for the king's tax *on* our lands and vineyards. ⁵Yet now our flesh *is* as the flesh of our brethren, our children as their children; and indeed we are forcing our sons and our daughters to be slaves, and *some* of our daughters have been brought into slavery. *It is* not in our power *to* redeem *them,* for other men have our lands and vineyards."

⁶*And I became very angry when I heard their outcry and these words. ⁷*After serious thought, I rebuked the nobles and rulers, and said to them, "Each of you is exacting usury from his brother." So I called a great assembly against them. ⁸And I said to them, "According to our ability we have redeemed our Jewish brethren who were sold to the nations. Now indeed, will you even sell your brethren? Or should they be sold to us?" Then they were silenced and found nothing to say. ⁹Then I said, "What you are doing *is* not good. Should you not walk in the fear of our God because of the reproach of the nations, our enemies? ¹⁰I also, *with* my brethren and my servants, am lending them money and grain. Please, let us stop this usury! ¹¹Restore now to them, even this day, their lands, their vineyards, their olive groves, and their houses, also a hundredth of the money and the grain, the new wine and the oil, that you have charged them."

¹²So they said, "We will restore *it,* and will require nothing from them; we will do as you say." Then I called the priests, and required an oath from them that they would do according to this promise. ¹³Then I shook out the fold of my garmentᵘ and said, "So may God shake out each man from his house, and from his property, who does not perform this promise. Even thus may he be shaken out and emptied." And all the assembly said, "Amen!" and praised the LORD. Then the people did according to this promise.

¹⁴*Moreover, from the time that I was appointed to be their governor in the land of Judah, from the twentieth year until the thirty-second year of King Artaxerxes, twelve years, neither I nor my brothers ate the governor's provisions. ¹⁵But the former governors who *were* before me laid burdens on the people, and took from them bread and wine, besides forty shekels of silver. Yes, even their servants bore rule over the people, but I did not do so, because of the fear of God. ¹⁶Indeed, I also continued the work on this wall, and weᵛ did not buy any land. All my servants *were* gathered there for the work.

¹⁷And at my table *were* one hundred and fifty Jews and rulers, besides those who came to us from the nations around us. ¹⁸Now *that* which was prepared daily *was* one ox *and* six choice sheep. Also fowl were prepared for me, and once

5:13 ᵘLiterally *my lap*   5:16 ᵛFollowing Masoretic Text; Septuagint, Syriac, and Vulgate read *I.*

every ten days an abundance of all kinds of wine. Yet in spite of this I did not demand the governor's provisions, because the bondage was heavy on this people.

¹⁹Remember me, my God, for good, *according to* all that I have done for this people.

6 Now* it happened when Sanballat, Tobiah, Geshem the Arab, and the rest of our enemies heard that I had rebuilt the wall, and *that* there were no breaks left in it (though at that time I had not hung the doors in the gates), ²*that Sanballat and Geshem sent to me, saying, "Come, let us meet together among the villages in the plain of Ono." But they thought to do me harm.

³So I sent messengers to them, saying, "I *am* doing a great work, so that I cannot come down. Why should the work cease while I leave it and go down to you?"

⁴But they sent me this message four times, and I answered them in the same manner.

⁵*Then Sanballat sent his servant to me as before, the fifth time, with an open letter in his hand. ⁶In it *was* written:

It is reported among the nations, and Geshem^w says, *that* you and the Jews plan to rebel; therefore, according to these rumors, you are rebuilding the wall, that you may be their king. ⁷And you have also appointed prophets to proclaim concerning you at Jerusalem, saying, "*There is* a king in Judah!" Now these matters will be reported to the king. So come, therefore, and let us consult together.

⁸Then I sent to him, saying, "No such things as you say are being done, but you invent them in your own heart."

⁹For they all *were trying to* make us afraid, saying, "Their hands will be weakened in the work, and it will not be done."

Now therefore, O God, strengthen my hands.

¹⁰*Afterward I came to the house of Shemaiah the son of Delaiah, the son of Mehetabel, who *was* a secret informer; and he said, "Let us meet together in the house of God, within the temple, and let us close the doors of the temple, for they are coming to kill you; indeed, at night they will come to kill you."

¹¹And I said, "Should such a man as I flee? And who *is there* such as I who would go into the temple to save his life? I will not go in!" ¹²Then I perceived that God had not sent him at all, but that he pronounced *this* prophecy against me because Tobiah and Sanballat had hired him. ¹³For this reason he *was* hired, so that I should be afraid and act that way and sin, so *that* they might have *cause* for an evil report, that they might reproach me.

¹⁴My God, remember Tobiah and Sanballat, according to these their works, and the prophetess

---

CHAPTER 6

6:1 As long as God's people sin against one another, the enemy can rest, but as soon as sin has been dealt with, the enemy must attack once more. Here are some more weapons he uses.

6:2–4 *Guile.* Beware when the enemy is smiling and holding out his arms to hug you! We must say no to invitations that compromise our witness (2 Cor. 6:14—7:1) and take us away from the great work God has called us to do.

6:5–9 *Accusation.* Satan is both a liar and an accuser (Rev. 12:10); he seeks to slander God's servants (Job 1:6ff.). When you have a clear conscience (Acts 24:16) and you know how to pray, this weapon will fail to frighten you or stop your work.

6:10–19 *Fear.* Jesus had His Judas and Nehemiah had his Shemaiah, an informer who tried to frighten Nehemiah. There were also "family informers" opposing the work (vv. 17–19). But Nehemiah was a true shepherd and not a hireling (v. 13; John 10:11–15). He was not going to flee. The work was completed in a record fifty-two days, and God was glorified.

6:6 ^wHebrew *Gashmu*

Keep on Course—A true leader will not desert his or her post, but a hireling flees when the going is tough (Prov. 28:1). The enemy tried to get Jesus to flee, but He refused to alter His course (Luke 13:31–33). Paul continued on his course even though he knew that suffering lay before him (Acts 20:22–24; 21:13). We must always flee sin and temptation (Gen. 39:12; 1 Cor. 6:18; 1 Tim. 6:11; 2 Tim. 2:22), but we must not flee the place of duty.

Noadiah and the rest of the prophets who would have made me afraid.

15So the wall was finished on the twenty-fifth *day* of Elul, in fifty-two days. 16And it happened, when all our enemies heard *of it,* and all the nations around us saw *these things,* that they were very disheartened in their own eyes; for they perceived that this work was done by our God.

17Also in those days the nobles of Judah sent many letters to Tobiah, and *the letters of* Tobiah came to them. 18For many in Judah were pledged to him, because he was the son-in-law of Shechaniah the son of Arah, and his son Jehohanan had married the daughter of Meshullam the son of Berechiah. 19Also they reported his good deeds before me, and reported my words to him. Tobiah sent letters to frighten me.

7 Then it was, when the wall was built and I had hung the doors, when the gatekeepers, the singers, and the Levites had been appointed, 2that I gave the charge of Jerusalem to my brother Hanani, and Hananiah the leader of the citadel, for he *was* a faithful man and feared God more than many.

3*And I said to them, "Do not let the gates of Jerusalem be opened until the sun is hot; and while they stand *guard,* let them shut and bar the doors; and appoint guards from among the inhabitants of Jerusalem, one at his watch station and another in front of his own house."

4Now the city *was* large and spacious, but the people in it *were* few, and the houses *were* not rebuilt. 5Then my God put it into my heart to gather the nobles, the rulers, and the people, that they might be registered by genealogy. And I found a register of the genealogy of those who had come up in the first *return,* and found written in it:

6   *These^x *are* the people of the province who came back from the captivity, of those who had been carried away, whom Nebuchadnezzar the king of Babylon had carried away, and who returned to Jerusalem and Judah, everyone to his city.

7   Those who came with Zerubbabel *were* Jeshua, Nehemiah, Azariah, Raamiah, Nahamani, Mordecai, Bilshan, Mispereth,^y Bigvai, Nehum, and Baanah.

The number of the men of the people of Israel: 8the sons of Parosh, two thousand one hundred and seventy-two;
9the sons of Shephatiah, three hundred and seventy-two;
10the sons of Arah, six hundred and fifty-two;
11the sons of Pahath-Moab, of the sons of Jeshua and Joab, two thousand eight hundred and eighteen;
12the sons of Elam, one thousand two hundred and fifty-four;
13the sons of Zattu, eight hundred and forty-five;
14the sons of Zaccai, seven hundred and sixty;

CHAPTERS 7—8

7:3 *The city of God.* Every ministry and home needs gatekeepers and guards, for after a work is finished, it must be protected from the enemy (2 John 8). We also need leaders with courage and integrity. After all, there is a battle going on!

7:6–73 *The people of God.* The record of the original returnees helped Nehemiah determine who should become a citizen of Jerusalem, for he did not want any of the "mixed multitude" to come in and cause more trouble. One of the most difficult things in the Christian life is maintaining the purity of the faith and of the fellowship.

7:6 ^xCompare verses 6–72 with Ezra 2:1–70 7:7 ^ySpelled *Mispar* in Ezra 2:2

15the sons of Binnui,z six hundred and forty-eight;

16the sons of Bebai, six hundred and twenty-eight;

17the sons of Azgad, two thousand three hundred and twenty-two;

18the sons of Adonikam, six hundred and sixty-seven;

19the sons of Bigvai, two thousand and sixty-seven;

20the sons of Adin, six hundred and fifty-five;

21the sons of Ater of Hezekiah, ninety-eight;

22the sons of Hashum, three hundred and twenty-eight;

23the sons of Bezai, three hundred and twenty-four;

24the sons of Hariph,a one hundred and twelve;

25the sons of Gibeon,b ninety-five;

26the men of Bethlehem and Netophah, one hundred and eighty-eight;

27the men of Anathoth, one hundred and twenty-eight;

28the men of Beth Azmaveth,c forty-two;

29the men of Kirjath Jearim, Chephirah, and Beeroth, seven hundred and forty-three;

30the men of Ramah and Geba, six hundred and twenty-one;

31the men of Michmas, one hundred and twenty-two;

32the men of Bethel and Ai, one hundred and twenty-three;

33the men of the other Nebo, fifty-two;

34the sons of the other Elam, one thousand two hundred and fifty-four;

35the sons of Harim, three hundred and twenty;

36the sons of Jericho, three hundred and forty-five;

37the sons of Lod, Hadid, and Ono, seven hundred and twenty-one;

38the sons of Senaah, three thousand nine hundred and thirty.

39   The priests: the sons of Jedaiah, of the house of Jeshua, nine hundred and seventy-three;

40the sons of Immer, one thousand and fifty-two;

41the sons of Pashhur, one thousand two hundred and forty-seven;

42the sons of Harim, one thousand and seventeen.

43   The Levites: the sons of Jeshua, of Kadmiel, and of the sons of Hodevah,d seventy-four.

44   The singers: the sons of Asaph, one hundred and forty-eight.

45   The gatekeepers: the sons of Shallum,
     the sons of Ater,
     the sons of Talmon,
     the sons of Akkub,
     the sons of Hatita,

7:15 zSpelled *Bani* in Ezra 2:10   7:24 aCalled *Jorah* in Ezra
2:18   7:25 bCalled *Gibbar* in Ezra 2:20   7:28 cCalled
Azmaveth in Ezra 2:24   7:43 dSpelled *Hodaviah* in Ezra 2:40

the sons of Shobai, one hundred and thirty-
eight.

46 The Nethinim: the sons of Ziha,
    the sons of Hasupha,
    the sons of Tabbaoth,
    47the sons of Keros,
    the sons of Sia,*e*
    the sons of Padon,
    48the sons of Lebana,*f*
    the sons of Hagaba,*g*
    the sons of Salmai,*h*
    49the sons of Hanan,
    the sons of Giddel,
    the sons of Gahar,
    50the sons of Reaiah,
    the sons of Rezin,
    the sons of Nekoda,
    51the sons of Gazzam,
    the sons of Uzza,
    the sons of Paseah,
    52the sons of Besai,
    the sons of Meunim,
    the sons of Nephishesim,*i*
    53the sons of Bakbuk,
    the sons of Hakupha,
    the sons of Harhur,
    54the sons of Bazlith,*j*
    the sons of Mehida,
    the sons of Harsha,
    55the sons of Barkos,
    the sons of Sisera,
    the sons of Tamah,
    56the sons of Neziah,
    and the sons of Hatipha.

57 The sons of Solomon's servants:
    the sons of Sotai,
    the sons of Sophereth,
    the sons of Perida,*k*
    58the sons of Jaala,
    the sons of Darkon,
    the sons of Giddel,
    59the sons of Shephatiah,
    the sons of Hattil,
    the sons of Pochereth of Zebaim,
    and the children of Amon.*l*
    60All the Nethinim, and the sons of
    Solomon's servants, *were* three hundred
    and ninety-two.

61 And these *were* the ones who came up from
    Tel Melah, Tel Harsha, Cherub, Addon,*m*
    and Immer, but they could not identify their
    father's house nor their lineage, whether
    they *were* of Israel: 62the sons of Delaiah,
    the sons of Tobiah,
    the sons of Nekoda, six hundred and forty-
    two;
    63and of the priests: the sons of Habaiah,
    the sons of Koz,*n*
    the sons of Barzillai, who took a wife of the
    daughters of Barzillai the Gileadite, and was
    called by their name.

7:47 *e*Spelled *Siaha* in Ezra 2:44   7:48 *f*Masoretic Text reads
*Lebanah. g*Masoretic Text reads *Hogabah. h*Or *Shalmai,* or
Shamlai   7:52 *i*Spelled *Nephusim* in Ezra 2:50   7:54 *j*Spelled
Bazluth in Ezra 2:52   7:57 *k*Spelled *Peruda* in Ezra 2:55
7:59 *l*Spelled *Ami* in Ezra 2:57   7:61 *m*Spelled *Addan* in Ezra
2:59   7:63 *n*Or *Hakkoz*

64These sought their listing *among* those who were registered by genealogy, but it was not found; therefore they were excluded from the priesthood as defiled. 65And the governor° said to them that they should not eat of the most holy things till a priest could consult with the Urim and Thummim.

66 Altogether the whole assembly *was* forty-two thousand three hundred and sixty, 67besides their male and female servants, of whom *there were* seven thousand three hundred and thirty-seven; and they had two hundred and forty-five men and women singers. 68Their horses were seven hundred and thirty-six, their mules two hundred and forty-five, 69*their* camels four hundred and thirty-five, *and* donkeys six thousand seven hundred and twenty.

70 And some of the heads of the fathers' houses gave to the work. The governor° gave to the treasury one thousand gold drachmas, fifty basins, and five hundred and thirty priestly garments. 71Some of the heads of the fathers' *houses* gave to the treasury of the work twenty thousand gold drachmas, and two thousand two hundred silver minas. 72And that which the rest of the people gave *was* twenty thousand gold drachmas, two thousand silver minas, and sixty-seven priestly garments.

73So the priests, the Levites, the gatekeepers, the singers, *some* of the people, the Nethinim, and all Israel dwelt in their cities.

When the seventh month came, the children of Israel *were* in their cities.

8 Now* all the people gathered together as one man in the open square that *was* in front of the Water Gate; and they told Ezra the scribe to bring the Book of the Law of Moses, which the LORD had commanded Israel. 2So Ezra the priest brought the Law before the assembly of men and women and all who *could* hear with understanding on the first day of the seventh month. 3Then he read from it in the open square that *was* in front of the Water Gate from morning until midday, before the men and women and those who could understand; and the ears of all the people *were attentive* to the Book of the Law.

4So Ezra the scribe stood on a platform of wood which they had made for the purpose; and beside him, at his right hand, stood Mattithiah, Shema, Anaiah, Urijah, Hilkiah, and Maaseiah; and at his left hand Pedaiah, Mishael, Malchijah, Hashum, Hashbadana, Zechariah, *and* Meshullam. 5And Ezra opened the book in the sight of all the people, for he was *standing* above all the people; and when he opened it, all the people stood up. 6And Ezra blessed the LORD, the great God.

Then all the people answered, "Amen, Amen!" while lifting up their hands. And they bowed their heads and worshiped the LORD with *their* faces to the ground.

7Also Jeshua, Bani, Sherebiah, Jamin, Akkub, Shabbethai, Hodijah, Maaseiah, Kelita, Azariah,

8:1–8 *The Word of God.* When Nehemiah arrived in Jerusalem in 444 B.C., Ezra was already there, instructing the people in God's law. When the work of rebuilding was completed, Ezra held a great "Bible conference" during the Feast of Tabernacles. The emphasis in chapter 8 is on "the Book" (vv. 1, 3, 5, 8, 18). They honored God's Word by standing when it was opened (v. 5), listening when it was read, and seeking to understand it when it was explained (vv. 2–3, 7–8, 12–13). They rejoiced at understanding the Word (v. 12) and at obeying the Word (v. 17; James 1:25).

7:65 °Hebrew *Tirshatha*   7:70 °Hebrew *Tirshatha*

Jozabad, Hanan, Pelaiah, and the Levites, helped the people to understand the Law; and the people *stood* in their place. 8So they read distinctly from the book, in the Law of God; and they gave the sense, and helped *them* to understand the reading.

9And Nehemiah, who *was* the governor,*q* Ezra the priest *and* scribe, and the Levites who taught the people said to all the people, "This day *is* holy to the LORD your God; do not mourn nor weep." For all the people wept, when they heard the words of the Law.

10Then he said to them, "Go your way, eat the fat, drink the sweet, and send portions to those for whom nothing is prepared; for *this* day *is* holy to our Lord. Do not sorrow, for the joy of the LORD is your strength."

11So the Levites quieted all the people, saying, "Be still, for the day *is* holy; do not be grieved." 12And all the people went their way to eat and drink, to send portions and rejoice greatly, because they understood the words that were declared to them.

13Now on the second day the heads of the fathers' *houses* of all the people, with the priests and Levites, were gathered to Ezra the scribe, in order to understand the words of the Law. 14And they found written in the Law, which the LORD had commanded by Moses, that the children of Israel should dwell in booths during the feast of the seventh month, 15and that they should announce and proclaim in all their cities and in Jerusalem, saying, "Go out to the mountain, and bring olive branches, branches of oil trees, myrtle branches, palm branches, and branches of leafy trees, to make booths, as *it is* written."

16Then the people went out and brought *them* and made themselves booths, each one on the roof of his house, or in their courtyards or the courts of the house of God, and in the open square of the Water Gate and in the open square of the Gate of Ephraim. 17So the whole assembly of those who had returned from the captivity made booths and sat under the booths; for since the days of Joshua the son of Nun until that day the children of Israel had not done so. And there was very great gladness. 18Also day by day, from the first day until the last day, he read from the Book of the Law of God. And they kept the feast seven days; and on the eighth day *there was* a sacred assembly, according to the *prescribed* manner.

9 Now* on the twenty-fourth day of this month the children of Israel were assembled with fasting, in sackcloth, and with dust on their heads.*r* 2Then those of Israelite lineage separated themselves from all foreigners; and they stood and confessed their sins and the iniquities of their fathers. 3And they stood up in their place and read from the Book of the Law of the LORD their God *for one*-fourth of the day; and *for another* fourth they confessed and worshiped the LORD their God.

4Then Jeshua, Bani, Kadmiel, Shebaniah, Bunni, Sherebiah, Bani, *and* Chenani stood on the stairs of the Levites and cried out with a loud voice to the LORD their God. 5*And the Levites, Jeshua, Kadmiel, Bani, Hashabniah, Sherebiah, Hodijah, Shebaniah, *and* Pethahiah, said:

9:1–4 The Feast of Tabernacles was a time of joy, but when it ended, the people took an extra day for hearing the Word, confessing sin, and worshiping the Lord. This is a balanced ministry: the Word reveals our sin and God's forgiveness; confession brings forgiveness; and forgiveness should lead to praise.

9:5 The people stood up to hear the Word (8:5), and the choir encouraged them to stand up and praise the Lord (v. 5)! He is the God of creation (v. 6), the God of the covenant (vv. 7–8), and the God of redemption (vv. 9–15). He is long-suffering with His people and meets their needs even when they do not obey His commands (vv. 16–31). The song ended with the people entering into a covenant with the Lord (vv. 32–38).

8:9 *q*Hebrew *Tirshatha*   9:1 *r*Literally *earth on them*

"Stand up *and* bless the LORD your God
Forever and ever!

"Blessed be Your glorious name,
Which is exalted above all blessing and
    praise!
6 *You alone *are* the LORD;
You have made heaven,
The heaven of heavens, with all their host,
The earth and everything on it,
The seas and all that is in them,
And You preserve them all.
The host of heaven worships You.

7 "You *are* the LORD God,
Who chose Abram,
And brought him out of Ur of the Chaldeans,
And gave him the name Abraham;
8 You found his heart faithful before You,
And made a covenant with him
To give the land of the Canaanites,
The Hittites, the Amorites,
The Perizzites, the Jebusites,
And the Girgashites—
To give *it* to his descendants.
You have performed Your words,
For You *are* righteous.

9 "You saw the affliction of our fathers in
    Egypt,
And heard their cry by the Red Sea.
10 You showed signs and wonders against
    Pharaoh,
Against all his servants,
And against all the people of his land.
For You knew that they acted proudly
    against them.
So You made a name for Yourself, as *it is*
    this day.
11 And You divided the sea before them,
So that they went through the midst of the
    sea on the dry land;
And their persecutors You threw into the
    deep,
As a stone into the mighty waters.
12 Moreover You led them by day with a
    cloudy pillar,
And by night with a pillar of fire,
To give them light on the road
Which they should travel.

13 "You came down also on Mount Sinai,
And spoke with them from heaven,
And gave them just ordinances and true
    laws,
Good statutes and commandments.
14 You made known to them Your holy
    Sabbath,
And commanded them precepts, statutes
    and laws,
By the hand of Moses Your servant.
15 You gave them bread from heaven for their
    hunger,
And brought them water out of the rock for
    their thirst,
And told them to go in to possess the land
Which You had sworn to give them.

16 "But they and our fathers acted proudly,
Hardened their necks,
And did not heed Your commandments.

9:6–38 It is a beautiful summary of God's ministry to Israel. He brought them out (v. 7), brought them through (v. 11), brought them in (v. 23), and saved them from their enemies (v. 27). But what a record of Israel's sins! However, God invites His people to make new beginnings and to let Him bury the past.

17 They refused to obey,
   And they were not mindful of Your wonders
   That You did among them.
   But they hardened their necks,
   And in their rebellion[s]
   They appointed a leader
   To return to their bondage.
   But You *are* God,
   Ready to pardon,
   Gracious and merciful,
   Slow to anger,
   Abundant in kindness,
   And did not forsake them.

18 "Even when they made a molded calf for
     themselves,
   And said, 'This *is* your god
   That brought you up out of Egypt,'
   And worked great provocations,
19 Yet in Your manifold mercies
   You did not forsake them in the wilderness.
   The pillar of the cloud did not depart from
     them by day,
   To lead them on the road;
   Nor the pillar of fire by night,
   To show them light,
   And the way they should go.
20 You also gave Your good Spirit to instruct
     them,
   And did not withhold Your manna from
     their mouth,
   And gave them water for their thirst.
21 Forty years You sustained them in the
     wilderness;
   They lacked nothing;
   Their clothes did not wear out[t]
   And their feet did not swell.

22 "Moreover You gave them kingdoms and
     nations,
   And divided them into districts.[u]
   So they took possession of the land of
     Sihon,
   The land of[v] the king of Heshbon,
   And the land of Og king of Bashan.
23 You also multiplied their children as the
     stars of heaven,
   And brought them into the land
   Which You had told their fathers
   To go in and possess.
24 So the people went in
   And possessed the land;
   You subdued before them the inhabitants
     of the land,
   The Canaanites,
   And gave them into their hands,
   With their kings
   And the people of the land,
   That they might do with them as they
     wished.
25 And they took strong cities and a rich land,
   And possessed houses full of all goods,
   Cisterns *already* dug, vineyards, olive
     groves,
   And fruit trees in abundance.
   So they ate and were filled and grew fat,

9:17 [s]Following Masoretic Text and Vulgate; Septuagint reads
in Egypt.   9:21 [t]Compare Deuteronomy 29:5   9:22 [u]Literally
corners [v]Following Masoretic Text and Vulgate; Septuagint
omits *The land of.*

And delighted themselves in Your great
  goodness.

26 "Nevertheless they were disobedient
  And rebelled against You,
  Cast Your law behind their backs
  And killed Your prophets, who testified
    against them
  To turn them to Yourself;
  And they worked great provocations.
27 Therefore You delivered them into the hand
    of their enemies,
  Who oppressed them;
  And in the time of their trouble,
  When they cried to You,
  You heard from heaven;
  And according to Your abundant mercies
  You gave them deliverers who saved them
  From the hand of their enemies.

28 "But after they had rest,
  They again did evil before You.
  Therefore You left them in the hand of their
    enemies,
  So that they had dominion over them;
  Yet when they returned and cried out to
    You,
  You heard from heaven;
  And many times You delivered them
    according to Your mercies,
29 And testified against them,
  That You might bring them back to Your
    law.
  Yet they acted proudly,
  And did not heed Your commandments,
  But sinned against Your judgments,
  'Which if a man does, he shall live by them.'*w*
  And they shrugged their shoulders,
  Stiffened their necks,
  And would not hear.
30 Yet for many years You had patience with
    them,
  And testified against them by Your Spirit
    in Your prophets.
  Yet they would not listen;
  Therefore You gave them into the hand of
    the peoples of the lands.
31 Nevertheless in Your great mercy
  You did not utterly consume them nor
    forsake them;
  For You *are* God, gracious and merciful.

32 "Now therefore, our God,
  The great, the mighty, and awesome God,
  Who keeps covenant and mercy:
  Do not let all the trouble seem small before
    You
  That has come upon us,
  Our kings and our princes,
  Our priests and our prophets,
  Our fathers and on all Your people,
  From the days of the kings of Assyria until
    this day.
33 However You *are* just in all that has befallen
    us;
  For You have dealt faithfully,
  But we have done wickedly.
34 Neither our kings nor our princes,
  Our priests nor our fathers,

9:29 *w* Leviticus 18:5

Have kept Your law,
Nor heeded Your commandments and Your
testimonies,
With which You testified against them.
35 For they have not served You in their
kingdom,
Or in the many good *things* that You gave
them,
Or in the large and rich land which You set
before them;
Nor did they turn from their wicked
works.

36 "Here we *are,* servants today!
And the land that You gave to our fathers,
To eat its fruit and its bounty,
Here we *are,* servants in it!
37 And it yields much increase to the kings
You have set over us,
Because of our sins;
Also they have dominion over our bodies
and our cattle
At their pleasure;
And we *are* in great distress.

38 "And because of all this,
We make a sure *covenant* and write *it;*
Our leaders, our Levites, *and* our priests seal
it."

CHAPTERS 10—11

10:1–27 It is one thing to attend a feast, sing praises to God, and hear the Bible read and explained, and quite something else to commit yourself to obey the will of God. The eighty-four men who put their seal to the covenant wanted God and the people to know that they were serious about obedience. These names represented whole families (v. 28), so that more people were involved in this solemn commitment than are named in chapter 10.

10:28–39 Their dedication was public, and it was also specific and included obedience with regard to marriage (v. 30), the Sabbath and the Sabbatical year (v. 31), their support of the temple (v. 32) and their gifts and sacrifices for the temple ministry (vv. 33–39). Their dedication was costly, but it was worthy of all that God had done for them. When we are right with God, we will support His work and His house: "We will not neglect the house of our God" (v. 39).

❝*Most church members live so far below the standard, you'd have to backslide to be in fellowship. We are so subnormal that if we were to become normal, people would think we were abnormal.*❞

—Vance Havner

10 Now* those who placed *their* seal on *the document were:*
Nehemiah the governor, the son of Hacaliah, and Zedekiah, 2Seraiah, Azariah, Jeremiah, 3Pashhur, Amariah, Malchijah, 4Hattush, Shebaniah, Malluch, 5Harim, Meremoth, Obadiah, 6Daniel, Ginnethon, Baruch, 7Meshullam, Abijah, Mijamin, 8Maaziah, Bilgai, *and* Shemaiah. These *were* the priests.
9The Levites: Jeshua the son of Azaniah, Binnui of the sons of Henadad, *and* Kadmiel.
10Their brethren: Shebaniah, Hodijah, Kelita, Pelaiah, Hanan, 11Micha, Rehob, Hashabiah, 12Zaccur, Sherebiah, Shebaniah, 13Hodijah, Bani, *and* Beninu.
14The leaders of the people: Parosh, Pahath-Moab, Elam, Zattu, Bani, 15Bunni, Azgad, Bebai, 16Adonijah, Bigvai, Adin, 17Ater, Hezekiah, Azzur, 18Hodijah, Hashum, Bezai, 19Hariph, Anathoth, Nebai, 20Magpiash, Meshullam, Hezir, 21Meshezabel, Zadok, Jaddua, 22Pelatiah, Hanan, Anaiah, 23Hoshea, Hananiah, Hasshub, 24Hallohesh, Pilha, Shobek, 25Rehum, Hashabnah, Maaseiah, 26Ahijah, Hanan, Anan, 27Malluch, Harim, *and* Baanah.
28*Now the rest of the people—the priests, the Levites, the gatekeepers, the singers, the Nethinim, and all those who had separated themselves from the peoples of the lands to the Law of God, their wives, their sons, and their daughters, everyone who had knowledge and understanding—29these joined with their brethren, their nobles, and entered into a curse and an oath to walk in God's Law, which was given by Moses the servant of God, and to observe and do all the commandments of the LORD our Lord, and His ordinances and His statutes: 30We would not give our daughters as wives to the peoples of the land, nor take their daughters for our sons; 31if the peoples of the land brought wares or any grain to sell on the Sabbath day, we would not buy it from them

on the Sabbath, or on a holy day; and we would forego the seventh year's *produce* and the exacting of every debt.

32Also we made ordinances for ourselves, to exact from ourselves yearly one-third of a shekel for the service of the house of our God: 33for the showbread, for the regular grain offering, for the regular burnt offering of the Sabbaths, the New Moons, and the set feasts; for the holy things, for the sin offerings to make atonement for Israel, and all the work of the house of our God. 34We cast lots among the priests, the Levites, and the people, for *bringing* the wood offering into the house of our God, according to our fathers' houses, at the appointed times year by year, to burn on the altar of the LORD our God as *it is* written in the Law.

35And *we made ordinances* to bring the firstfruits of our ground and the firstfruits of all fruit of all trees, year by year, to the house of the LORD; 36to bring the firstborn of our sons and our cattle, as *it is* written in the Law, and the firstborn of our herds and our flocks, to the house of our God, to the priests who minister in the house of our God; 37to bring the firstfruits of our dough, our offerings, the fruit from all kinds of trees, *the* new wine and oil, to the priests, to the storerooms of the house of our God; and to bring the tithes of our land to the Levites, for the Levites should receive the tithes in all our farming communities. 38And the priest, the descendant of Aaron, shall be with the Levites when the Levites receive tithes; and the Levites shall bring up a tenth of the tithes to the house of our God, to the rooms of the storehouse.

39For the children of Israel and the children of Levi shall bring the offering of the grain, of the new wine and the oil, to the storerooms where the articles of the sanctuary *are, where* the priests who minister and the gatekeepers and the singers *are;* and we will not neglect the house of our God.

11 Now the leaders of the people dwelt at Jerusalem; the rest of the people cast lots to bring one out of ten to dwell in Jerusalem, the holy city, and nine-tenths *were to dwell* in *other* cities. 2And the people blessed all the men who willingly offered themselves to dwell at Jerusalem.

3These *are* the heads of the province who dwelt in Jerusalem. (But in the cities of Judah everyone dwelt in his own possession in their cities—Israelites, priests, Levites, Nethinim, and descendants of Solomon's servants.) 4Also in Jerusalem dwelt *some* of the children of Judah and of the children of Benjamin.

The children of Judah: Athaiah the son of Uzziah, the son of Zechariah, the son of Amariah, the son of Shephatiah, the son of Mahalalel, of the children of Perez; 5and Maaseiah the son of Baruch, the son of Col-Hozeh, the son of Hazaiah, the son of Adaiah, the son of Joiarib, the son of Zechariah, the son of Shiloni. 6All the sons of Perez who dwelt at Jerusalem *were* four hundred and sixty-eight valiant men.

7And these are the sons of Benjamin: Sallu the son of Meshullam, the son of Joed, the son of Pedaiah, the son of Kolaiah, the son of Maaseiah, the son of Ithiel, the son of Jeshaiah; 8and after him Gabbai *and* Sallai, nine hundred and twenty-eight. 9Joel the son of Zichri *was* their overseer, and Judah the son of Senuah[x] *was* second over the city.

10Of the priests: Jedaiah the son of Joiarib, and Jachin; 11Seraiah the son of Hilkiah, the son of Meshullam, the son of Zadok, the son of Meraioth, the son of Ahitub, *was* the leader of the house of God. 12Their brethren who did the work of the house *were* eight hundred and twenty-two; and Adaiah the son of Jeroham, the son of Pelaliah, the son of Amzi, the son of Zechariah, the son of Pashhur, the son of Malchijah, 13and his brethren, heads of the fathers' *houses, were* two hundred and forty-two; and Amashai the son of Azarel, the son of Ahzai, the son of Meshillemoth, the son of Immer, 14and their brethren, mighty men of valor, *were* one hundred and twenty-eight. Their overseer *was* Zabdiel the son of *one of* the great men.[y]

15Also of the Levites: Shemaiah the son of Hasshub, the son of Azrikam, the son of Hashabiah, the son of Bunni; 16Shabbethai and Jozabad, of the heads of the Levites, *had* the oversight of the business outside of the house of God; 17Mattaniah the son of Micha,[z] the son of Zabdi, the son of Asaph, the leader *who* began the thanksgiving with prayer; Bakbukiah, the second among his brethren; and Abda the son of Shammua, the son of Galal, the son of Jeduthun. 18All the Levites in the holy city *were* two hundred and eighty-four.

19Moreover the gatekeepers, Akkub, Talmon, and their brethren who kept the gates, *were* one hundred and seventy-two.

20And the rest of Israel, of the priests *and* Levites, *were* in all the cities of Judah, everyone in his inheritance. 21But the Nethinim dwelt in Ophel. And Ziha and Gishpa *were* over the Nethinim.

22Also the overseer of the Levites at Jerusalem *was* Uzzi the son of Bani, the son of Hashabiah, the son of Mattaniah, the son of Micha, of the sons of Asaph, the singers in charge of the service of the house of God. 23For *it was* the king's command concerning them that a certain portion should be for the singers, a quota day by day. 24Pethahiah the son of Meshezabel, of the children of Zerah the son of Judah, *was* the king's deputy[a] in all matters concerning the people.

25And as for the villages with their fields, *some* of the children of Judah dwelt in Kirjath Arba and its villages, Dibon and its villages, Jekabzeel and its villages; 26in Jeshua, Moladah, Beth Pelet, 27Hazar Shual, and Beersheba and its villages; 28in Ziklag and Meconah and its villages; 29in En Rimmon, Zorah, Jarmuth, 30Zanoah, Adullam, and their villages; in Lachish and its fields; in Azekah and its villages. They dwelt from Beersheba to the Valley of Hinnom.

31Also the children of Benjamin from Geba *dwelt* in Michmash, Aija, and Bethel, and their villages; 32in Anathoth, Nob, Ananiah; 33in Hazor, Ramah, Gittaim; 34in Hadid, Zeboim, Neballat; 35in Lod, Ono, *and* the Valley of Craftsmen. 36Some of the Judean divisions of Levites *were* in Benjamin.

11:9 [x]Or *Hassenuah*   11:14 [y]Or *the son of Haggedolim*
11:17 [z]Or *Michah*   11:24 [a]Literally *at the king's hand*

12 Now these *are* the priests and the Levites who came up with Zerubbabel the son of Shealtiel, and Jeshua: Seraiah, Jeremiah, Ezra, [2]Amariah, Malluch, Hattush, [3]Shechaniah, Rehum, Meremoth, [4]Iddo, Ginnethoi,[b] Abijah, [5]Mijamin, Maadiah, Bilgah, [6]Shemaiah, Joiarib, Jedaiah, [7]Sallu, Amok, Hilkiah, *and* Jedaiah.

These *were* the heads of the priests and their brethren in the days of Jeshua.

[8]Moreover the Levites *were* Jeshua, Binnui, Kadmiel, Sherebiah, Judah, *and* Mattaniah *who led* the thanksgiving *psalms,* he and his brethren. [9]Also Bakbukiah and Unni, their brethren, *stood* across from them in *their* duties.

[10]Jeshua begot Joiakim, Joiakim begot Eliashib, Eliashib begot Joiada, [11]Joiada begot Jonathan, and Jonathan begot Jaddua.

[12]Now in the days of Joiakim, the priests, the heads of the fathers' *houses were:* of Seraiah, Meraiah; of Jeremiah, Hananiah; [13]of Ezra, Meshullam; of Amariah, Jehohanan; [14]of Melichu,[c] Jonathan; of Shebaniah,[d] Joseph; [15]of Harim,[e] Adna; of Meraioth,[f] Helkai; [16]of Iddo, Zechariah; of Ginnethon, Meshullam; [17]of Abijah, Zichri; *the son of* Minjamin;[g] of Moadiah,[h] Piltai; [18]of Bilgah, Shammua; of Shemaiah, Jehonathan; [19]of Joiarib, Mattenai; of Jedaiah, Uzzi; [20]of Sallai,[i] Kallai; of Amok, Eber; [21]of Hilkiah, Hashabiah; *and* of Jedaiah, Nethanel.

[22]During the reign of Darius the Persian, a record *was also kept* of the Levites and priests *who had been* heads of their fathers' *houses* in the days of Eliashib, Joiada, Johanan, and Jaddua. [23]The sons of Levi, the heads of the fathers' *houses* until the days of Johanan the son of Eliashib, *were* written in the book of the chronicles.

[24]And the heads of the Levites *were* Hashabiah, Sherebiah, and Jeshua the son of Kadmiel, with their brothers across from them, to praise *and* give thanks, group alternating with group, according to the command of David the man of God. [25]Mattaniah, Bakbukiah, Obadiah, Meshullam, Talmon, and Akkub *were* gatekeepers keeping the watch at the storerooms of the gates. [26]These *lived* in the days of Joiakim the son of Jeshua, the son of Jozadak,[j] and in the days of Nehemiah the governor, and of Ezra the priest, the scribe.

[27]*Now at the dedication of the wall of Jerusalem they sought out the Levites in all their places, to bring them to Jerusalem to celebrate the dedication with gladness, both with thanksgivings and singing, *with* cymbals and stringed instruments and harps. [28]And the sons of the singers gathered together from the countryside around Jerusalem, from the villages of the Netophathites, [29]from the house of Gilgal, and from the fields of Geba and Azmaveth; for the singers had built themselves villages all around Jerusalem. [30]Then the priests and Levites purified themselves, and purified the people, the gates, and the wall.

[31]*So I brought the leaders of Judah up on the wall, and appointed two large thanksgiving choirs. *One* went to the right hand on the wall

---

CHAPTER 12

12:27 Completion. Any work that we do for God succeeds only because of His working in us (Phil. 2:12–13). Therefore, that work must be dedicated to Him for His glory. Otherwise, we may become proud, and the work then becomes an idol that takes God's rightful place in our lives (Deut. 8:11–20).

12:31 Celebration. The emphasis is on joy and thanksgiving to God. The work was finished, the enemy was humiliated, and the Lord was glorified; so why not rejoice? Nehemiah and Ezra each led one of the two choirs as they sang their way around the city walls and met at the temple area. The sound of the joy "was heard afar off" (v. 43; Ezra 3:12–13).

12:4 [b]Or *Ginnethon* (compare verse 16)   12:14 [c]Or *Malluch* (compare verse 2)   [d]Or *Shechaniah* (compare verse 3)
12:15 [e]Or *Rehum* (compare verse 3)   [f]Or *Meremoth* (compare verse 3)   12:17 [g]Or *Mijamin* (compare verse 5)   [h]Or *Maadiah* (compare verse 5)   12:20 [i]Or *Sallu* (compare verse 7)
12:26 [j]Spelled *Jehozadak* in 1 Chronicles 6:14

toward the Refuse Gate. [32]After them went Hoshaiah and half of the leaders of Judah, [33]and Azariah, Ezra, Meshullam, [34]Judah, Benjamin, Shemaiah, Jeremiah, [35]and some of the priests' sons with trumpets—Zechariah the son of Jonathan, the son of Shemaiah, the son of Mattaniah, the son of Michaiah, the son of Zaccur, the son of Asaph, [36]and his brethren, Shemaiah, Azarel, Milalai, Gilalai, Maai, Nethanel, Judah, *and* Hanani, with the musical instruments of David the man of God. And Ezra the scribe *went* before them. [37]By the Fountain Gate, in front of them, they went up the stairs of the City of David, on the stairway of the wall, beyond the house of David, as far as the Water Gate eastward.

[38]The other thanksgiving choir went the opposite *way,* and I *was* behind them with half of the people on the wall, going past the Tower of the Ovens as far as the Broad Wall, [39]and above the Gate of Ephraim, above the Old Gate, above the Fish Gate, the Tower of Hananel, the Tower of the Hundred, as far as the Sheep Gate; and they stopped by the Gate of the Prison.

[40]So the two thanksgiving choirs stood in the house of God, likewise I and the half of the rulers with me; [41]and the priests, Eliakim, Maaseiah, Minjamin,[k] Michaiah, Elioenai, Zechariah, *and* Hananiah, with trumpets; [42]also Maaseiah, Shemaiah, Eleazar, Uzzi, Jehohanan, Malchijah, Elam, and Ezer. The singers sang loudly with Jezrahiah the director.

[43]Also that day they offered great sacrifices, and rejoiced, for God had made them rejoice with great joy; the women and the children also rejoiced, so that the joy of Jerusalem was heard afar off.

[44]And at the same time some were appointed over the rooms of the storehouse for the offerings, the firstfruits, and the tithes, to gather into them from the fields of the cities the portions specified by the Law for the priests and Levites; for Judah rejoiced over the priests and Levites who ministered. [45]*Both the singers and the gatekeepers kept the charge of their God and the charge of the purification, according to the command of David *and* Solomon his son. [46]For in the days of David and Asaph of old *there were* chiefs of the singers, and songs of praise and thanksgiving to God. [47]In the days of Zerubbabel and in the days of Nehemiah all Israel gave the portions for the singers and the gatekeepers, a portion for each day. They also consecrated *holy things* for the Levites, and the Levites consecrated *them* for the children of Aaron.

12:45 *Cleansing.* Of what value is a dedicated wall without dedicated people? Verse 30 parallels Isaiah 1:16 and 2 Corinthians 7:1. A singing people should be a sanctified people.

CHAPTER 13

After the big celebration, then what? The work of a spiritual leader is never finished, for the enemy never quits. How sad it is to read that during Nehemiah's absence from the city, the Jews gradually stopped keeping the covenant they had made with God (10:28–39). By the time Nehemiah returned, the people were terribly backslidden.

13 On that day they read from the Book of Moses in the hearing of the people, and in it was found written that no Ammonite or Moabite should ever come into the assembly of God, [2]because they had not met the children of Israel with bread and water, but hired Balaam against

12:41 [k]Or *Mijamin* (compare verse 5)

A Worthy Role Model—Nehemiah was a layman who loved Jerusalem and the temple and wanted the city to glorify God. He is a good example for all of us to follow in his devotion to duty, his discipline in planning and doing his work, his dedication to the Word of God, and his dependence on prayer. He did not use his authority selfishly but humbly and sacrificially served God and the people. He did not run from difficulties or dangers but trusted God to help him face them honestly and solve them successfully.

them to curse them. However, our God turned the curse into a blessing. 3*So it was, when they had heard the Law, that they separated all the mixed multitude from Israel.

4Now before this, Eliashib the priest, having authority over the storerooms of the house of our God, *was* allied with Tobiah. 5And he had prepared for him a large room, where previously they had stored the grain offerings, the frankincense, the articles, the tithes of grain, the new wine and oil, which were commanded *to be given* to the Levites and singers and gatekeepers, and the offerings for the priests. 6But during all this I was not in Jerusalem, for in the thirty-second year of Artaxerxes king of Babylon I had returned to the king. Then after certain days I obtained leave from the king, 7and I came to Jerusalem and discovered the evil that Eliashib had done for Tobiah, in preparing a room for him in the courts of the house of God. 8And it grieved me bitterly; therefore I threw all the household goods of Tobiah out of the room. 9Then I commanded them to cleanse the rooms; and I brought back into them the articles of the house of God, with the grain offering and the frankincense.

10I also realized that the portions for the Levites had not been given *them;* for each of the Levites and the singers who did the work had gone back to his field. 11So I contended with the rulers, and said, "Why is the house of God forsaken?" And I gathered them together and set them in their place. 12*Then all Judah brought the tithe of the grain and the new wine and the oil to the storehouse. 13And I appointed as treasurers over the storehouse Shelemiah the priest and Zadok the scribe, and of the Levites, Pedaiah; and next to them *was* Hanan the son of Zaccur, the son of Mattaniah; for they were considered faithful, and their task *was* to distribute to their brethren.

14Remember me, O my God, concerning this, and do not wipe out my good deeds that I have done for the house of my God, and for its services!

15*In those days I saw *people* in Judah treading wine presses on the Sabbath, and bringing in sheaves, and loading donkeys with wine, grapes, figs, and all *kinds of* burdens, which they brought into Jerusalem on the Sabbath day. And I warned *them* about the day on which they were selling provisions. 16Men of Tyre dwelt there also, who brought in fish and all kinds of goods, and sold *them* on the Sabbath to the children of Judah, and in Jerusalem.

17Then I contended with the nobles of Judah, and said to them, "What evil thing *is* this that you do, by which you profane the Sabbath day? 18Did not your fathers do thus, and did not our God bring all this disaster on us and on this city? Yet you bring added wrath on Israel by profaning the Sabbath."

19So it was, at the gates of Jerusalem, as it began to be dark before the Sabbath, that I commanded the gates to be shut, and charged that they must not be opened till after the Sabbath. Then I posted *some* of my servants at the gates, *so that* no burdens would be brought in on the Sabbath day. 20Now the merchants and sellers of all kinds of wares lodged outside Jerusalem once or twice.

21Then I warned them, and said to them, "Why do you spend the night around the wall? If you do *so* again, I will lay hands on you!" From that time on they came no *more* on the Sabbath.

13:3 Separation. The people had mixed with the pagans, the priest had let the enemy into the temple, and Jewish parents were allowing their children to marry pagan mates (vv. 23–27). The walls of the city were still strong, but the spiritual walls of separation were crumbling.

13:12 Stewardship. The people had promised to support the temple ministry but had not been faithful to bring the required tithes and offerings. Decreased giving is often a sign of diminished spiritual vitality.

13:15–22 Sacrifice. God gave them six days for work and business and asked for only one day for Himself, but some people robbed Him of that. They were actually robbing themselves of blessing and of the opportunity to witness to the pagans around them.

Nehemiah was resolute, and the secret of his courage was prayer (vv. 14, 22, 29, 31). Are you willing to be different from others to the glory of God?

22And I commanded the Levites that they should cleanse themselves, and that they should go and guard the gates, to sanctify the Sabbath day.

Remember me, O my God, *concerning* this also, and spare me according to the greatness of Your mercy!

23In those days I also saw Jews *who* had married women of Ashdod, Ammon, *and* Moab. 24And half of their children spoke the language of Ashdod, and could not speak the language of Judah, but spoke according to the language of one or the other people.

25So I contended with them and cursed them, struck some of them and pulled out their hair, and made them swear by God, *saying*, "You shall not give your daughters as wives to their sons, nor take their daughters for your sons or yourselves. 26Did not Solomon king of Israel sin by these things? Yet among many nations there was no king like him, who was beloved of his God; and God made him king over all Israel. Nevertheless pagan women caused even him to sin. 27Should we then hear of your doing all this great evil, transgressing against our God by marrying pagan women?"

28And *one* of the sons of Joiada, the son of Eliashib the high priest, *was* a son-in-law of Sanballat the Horonite; therefore I drove him from me.

29Remember them, O my God, because they have defiled the priesthood and the covenant of the priesthood and the Levites.

30Thus I cleansed them of everything pagan. I also assigned duties to the priests and the Levites, each to his service, 31and *to bringing* the wood offering and the firstfruits at appointed times.

Remember me, O my God, for good!

ESTHER

Esther and Ruth are the only books in the Bible named after women. Ruth was a Gentile who married a Jew, while Esther was a Jewess who married a Gentile. Both were women of faith and courage; both helped to save the nation of Israel, Ruth by the birth of a son and Esther by the death of an enemy.

The Persians conquered Babylon in 539 B.C. The events in the book of Esther occurred at Susa (Shushan; Esth. 1:2; see also Neh. 1:1), where the king's winter palace was located, and they belong between chapters 6 and 7 of Ezra. The king who married Esther was Xerxes I (the name Ahasuerus was a title, like Pharaoh); the events in the book cover about ten years, from his third year (1:3) to his twelfth year (3:7).

The name of God is not mentioned in this book, but the hand of God is seen throughout the account. A primary lesson is that God is sovereign in the nations of the world, and His people must surrender and do His will. The Jews who were struggling in Jerusalem and Judah needed the encouragement of this book and the reminder that God keeps His covenant promises (Gen. 12:1–3).

1 Now it came to pass in the days of Ahasuerus*a* (this *was* the Ahasuerus who reigned over one hundred and twenty-seven provinces, from India to Ethiopia), ²in those days when King Ahasuerus sat on the throne of his kingdom, which *was* in Shushan*b* the citadel, ³*that* in the third year of his reign he made a feast for all his officials and servants—the powers of Persia and Media, the nobles, and the princes of the provinces *being* before him— ⁴*when he showed the riches of his glorious kingdom and the splendor of his excellent majesty for many days, one hundred and eighty days *in all*.

⁵And when these days were completed, the king made a feast lasting seven days for all the people who were present in Shushan the citadel, from great to small, in the court of the garden of the king's palace. ⁶*There were* white and blue linen *curtains* fastened with cords of fine linen and purple on silver rods and marble pillars; *and the* couches *were* of gold and silver on a *mosaic* pavement of alabaster, turquoise, and white and black marble. ⁷*And they served drinks in golden vessels, each vessel being different from the other, with royal wine in abundance, according to the generosity of the king. ⁸In accordance with the law, the drinking was not compulsory; for so the king had ordered all the officers of his household, that they should do according to each man's pleasure.

⁹Queen Vashti also made a feast for the women *in* the royal palace which *belonged* to King Ahasuerus.

¹⁰On the seventh day, when the heart of the king was merry with wine, he commanded Mehuman, Biztha, Harbona, Bigtha, Abagtha, Zethar, and Carcas, seven eunuchs who served in the presence of King Ahasuerus, ¹¹to bring Queen Vashti before the king, *wearing* her royal crown, in order to show her beauty to the people and the officials,

CHAPTER 1

1:4 A man is very poor if he can show *all* his glory and wealth in six months! It will take eternal ages for us to begin to fathom the riches of God's grace and glory (Eph. 1:18). Where is the glory of Xerxes today?

1:7 A man is poor if he must entertain his guests with "wine in abundance." What began as a royal banquet degenerated into a drunken party (Prov. 20:1; 23:29–31). Queen Vashti was wise to refuse to attend such a feast (Prov. 23:20). She lost her crown, but she kept her integrity.

1:1 *a*Generally identified with Xerxes I (485–464 B.C.)
1:2 *b*Or *Susa,* and so throughout this book

1:12 A man is poor if he lets his temper get the best of him (Prov. 14:17; 16:32). Xerxes made some foolish decisions, which is what usually happens when anger takes over. But God was in control, working out His plan even through a proud pagan monarch (Prov. 21:1).

for she *was* beautiful to behold. 12*But Queen Vashti refused to come at the king's command *brought* by *his* eunuchs; therefore the king was furious, and his anger burned within him.

13Then the king said to the wise men who understood the times (for this *was* the king's manner toward all who knew law and justice, 14those closest to him *being* Carshena, Shethar, Admatha, Tarshish, Meres, Marsena, and Memucan, the seven princes of Persia and Media, who had access to the king's presence, *and* who ranked highest in the kingdom): 15"What *shall we* do to Queen Vashti, according to law, because she did not obey the command of King Ahasuerus *brought to her* by the eunuchs?"

16And Memucan answered before the king and the princes: "Queen Vashti has not only wronged the king, but also all the princes, and all the people who *are* in all the provinces of King Ahasuerus. 17For the queen's behavior will become known to all women, so that they will despise their husbands in their eyes, when they report, 'King Ahasuerus commanded Queen Vashti to be brought in before him, but she did not come.' 18This very day the *noble* ladies of Persia and Media will say to all the king's officials that they have heard of the behavior of the queen. Thus *there will be* excessive contempt and wrath. 19If it pleases the king, let a royal decree go out from him, and let it be recorded in the laws of the Persians and the Medes, so that it will not be altered, that Vashti shall come no more before King Ahasuerus; and let the king give her royal position to another who is better than she. 20When the king's decree which he will make is proclaimed throughout all his empire (for it is great), all wives will honor their husbands, both great and small."

21And the reply pleased the king and the princes, and the king did according to the word of Memucan. 22Then he sent letters to all the king's provinces, to each province in its own script, and to every people in their own language, that each man should be master in his own house, and speak in the language of his own people.

CHAPTER 2

2:1–18 The selection of Esther and the detection of the plotters may seem to be events that do not belong together, but they were both part of God's plan to save His people. Esther's coronation was a grand public affair, while Mordecai's service to the king was rather private. But God would use Esther's position and Mordecai's service to fulfill His purposes.

2 After* these things, when the wrath of King Ahasuerus subsided, he remembered Vashti, what she had done, and what had been decreed against her. 2Then the king's servants who attended him said: "Let beautiful young virgins be sought for the king; 3and let the king appoint officers in all the provinces of his kingdom, that they may gather all the beautiful young virgins to Shushan the citadel, into the women's quarters, under the custody of Hegaic the king's eunuch, custodian of the women. And let beauty preparations be given *them*. 4Then let the young woman who pleases the king be queen instead of Vashti."

This thing pleased the king, and he did so.

5In Shushan the citadel there was a certain Jew whose name *was* Mordecai the son of Jair, the son of Shimei, the son of Kish, a Benjamite. 6Kishd had been carried away from Jerusalem with the captives who had been captured with Jeconiahe king of Judah, whom Nebuchadnezzar the king of Babylon had carried away. 7And *Mordecai* had brought up Hadassah, that *is,* Esther,

2:3 cHebrew *Hege*   2:6 dLiterally *Who* eSame as *Jehoiachin,* 2 Kings 24:6 and elsewhere

his uncle's daughter, for she had neither father nor mother. The young woman *was* lovely and beautiful. When her father and mother died, Mordecai took her as his own daughter.

8So it was, when the king's command and decree were heard, and when many young women were gathered at Shushan the citadel, *under* the custody of Hegai, that Esther also was taken to the king's palace, into the care of Hegai the custodian of the women. 9Now the young woman pleased him, and she obtained his favor; so he readily gave beauty preparations to her, besides her allowance. Then seven choice maidservants were provided for her from the king's palace, and he moved her and her maidservants to the best *place* in the house of the women.

10Esther had not revealed her people or family, for Mordecai had charged her not to reveal *it*. 11And every day Mordecai paced in front of the court of the women's quarters, to learn of Esther's welfare and what was happening to her.

12Each young woman's turn came to go in to King Ahasuerus after she had completed twelve months' preparation, according to the regulations for the women, for thus were the days of their preparation apportioned: six months with oil of myrrh, and six months with perfumes and preparations for beautifying women. 13Thus *prepared*, *each* young woman went to the king, and she was given whatever she desired to take with her from the women's quarters to the king's palace. 14In the evening she went, and in the morning she returned to the second house of the women, to the custody of Shaashgaz, the king's eunuch who kept the concubines. She would not go in to the king again unless the king delighted in her and called for her by name.

15Now when the turn came for Esther the daughter of Abihail the uncle of Mordecai, who had taken her as his daughter, to go in to the king, she requested nothing but what Hegai the king's eunuch, the custodian of the women, advised. And Esther obtained favor in the sight of all who saw her. 16So Esther was taken to King Ahasuerus, into his royal palace, in the tenth month, which *is* the month of Tebeth, in the seventh year of his reign. 17The king loved Esther more than all the *other* women, and she obtained grace and favor in his sight more than all the virgins; so he set the royal crown upon her head and made her queen instead of Vashti. 18Then the king made a great feast, the Feast of Esther, for all his officials and servants; and he proclaimed a holiday in the provinces and gave gifts according to the generosity of a king.

19*When virgins were gathered together a second time, Mordecai sat within the king's gate. 20Now Esther had not revealed her family and her people, just as Mordecai had charged her, for Esther obeyed the command of Mordecai as when she was brought up by him.

21In those days, while Mordecai sat within the king's gate, two of the king's eunuchs, Bigthan and Teresh, doorkeepers, became furious and sought to lay hands on King Ahasuerus. 22So the matter became known to Mordecai, who told Queen Esther, and Esther informed the king in Mordecai's name. 23And when an inquiry was made into the matter, it was confirmed, and both were hanged on a gallows; and it was written in the book of the chronicles in the presence of the king.

2:19–23 You may be prone to believe that God works only in the "important events" of life. All events are important if you are living in the will of God. Mordecai was not immediately rewarded for saving the king's life, but God would take care of it at the right time (chap. 6). Do your duty today, and let God take care of the consequences.

CHAPTER 3

3:1–11 The king promoted an evil man and approved a wicked project. No doubt many of the Jews were asking, "Why has God permitted such a thing?" The fact that God permits evil in this world does not mean that evil is good or that God is unconcerned or unable to help. When men do not allow Him to rule, He overrules, and He always accomplishes His purposes.

3:5 No matter how you examine Haman, he is a wicked man. Promote him and he gets proud. Ignore him and he becomes angry and takes out his anger on a whole race. (Prejudice usually works that way.) Make him rich and he uses his money to destroy and not to build.

Everything about Haman was hateful to the Lord (Prov. 6:16–19), but He did not interfere with Haman's evil deeds. Haman's sins would ultimately destroy him and be used by God for the good of Israel.

3 After* these things King Ahasuerus promoted Haman, the son of Hammedatha the Agagite, and advanced him and set his seat above all the princes who *were* with him. ²And all the king's servants who *were* within the king's gate bowed and paid homage to Haman, for so the king had commanded concerning him. But Mordecai would not bow or pay homage. ³Then the king's servants who *were* within the king's gate said to Mordecai, "Why do you transgress the king's command?" ⁴Now it happened, when they spoke to him daily and he would not listen to them, that they told *it* to Haman, to see whether Mordecai's words would stand; for *Mordecai* had told them that he *was* a Jew. ⁵*When Haman saw that Mordecai did not bow or pay him homage, Haman was filled with wrath. ⁶But he disdained to lay hands on Mordecai alone, for they had told him of the people of Mordecai. Instead, Haman sought to destroy all the Jews who *were* throughout the whole kingdom of Ahasuerus—the people of Mordecai.

⁷In the first month, which is the month of Nisan, in the twelfth year of King Ahasuerus, they cast Pur (that *is*, the lot), before Haman to determine the day and the month,ᶠ until *it fell on the* twelfth *month,*ᵍ which *is* the month of Adar.

⁸Then Haman said to King Ahasuerus, "There is a certain people scattered and dispersed among the people in all the provinces of your kingdom; their laws *are* different from all *other* people's, and they do not keep the king's laws. Therefore it *is* not fitting for the king to let them remain. ⁹If it pleases the king, let *a decree* be written that they be destroyed, and I will pay ten thousand talents of silver into the hands of those who do the work, to bring *it* into the king's treasuries."

¹⁰So the king took his signet ring from his hand and gave it to Haman, the son of Hammedatha the Agagite, the enemy of the Jews. ¹¹And the king said to Haman, "The money and the people *are* given to you, to do with them as seems good to you."

¹²Then the king's scribes were called on the thirteenth day of the first month, and *a decree* was written according to all that Haman commanded—to the king's satraps, to the governors who *were* over each province, to the officials of all people, to every province according to its script, and to every people in their language. In the name of King Ahasuerus it was written, and sealed with the king's signet ring. ¹³And the letters were sent by couriers into all the king's provinces, to destroy, to kill, and to annihilate all the Jews, both young and old, little children and women, in one day, on the thirteenth *day* of the twelfth *month,* which *is* the month of Adar, and to plunder their possessions.ʰ ¹⁴A copy of the doc-

---

3:7 ᶠSeptuagint adds *to destroy the people of Mordecai in one day;* Vulgate adds *the nation of the Jews should be destroyed.* ᵍFollowing Masoretic Text and Vulgate; Septuagint reads *and the lot fell on the fourteenth of the month.* 3:13 ʰSeptuagint adds the text of the letter here.

Prejudice—"Prejudice is the dislike for all that is unlike," said Israel Zangwill, author and Zionist leader. When Haman said that the Jews were a different people (3:8), he was right, and that difference meant salvation for the world. Mark Twain called anti-Semitism "the swollen envy of pigmy minds." From Pharaoh to Hitler, every leader who has tried to destroy the Jews has tasted the wrath of God. No race is perfect, including the Jews, but no race should be singled out for oppression as they have been. God's covenant with Abraham still stands (Gen. 12:1–3).

ument was to be issued as law in every province, being published for all people, that they should be ready for that day. ¹⁵The couriers went out, hastened by the king's command; and the decree was proclaimed in Shushan the citadel. So the king and Haman sat down to drink, but the city of Shushan was perplexed.

4 When* Mordecai learned all that had happened, he tore his clothes and put on sackcloth and ashes, and went out into the midst of the city. He cried out with a loud and bitter cry. ²He went as far as the front of the king's gate, for no one *might* enter the king's gate clothed with sackcloth. ³And in every province where the king's command and decree arrived, *there was* great mourning among the Jews, with fasting, weeping, and wailing; and many lay in sackcloth and ashes.

⁴So Esther's maids and eunuchs came and told her, and the queen was deeply distressed. Then she sent garments to clothe Mordecai and take his sackcloth away from him, but he would not accept *them.* ⁵Then Esther called Hathach, *one* of the king's eunuchs whom he had appointed to attend her, and she gave him a command concerning Mordecai, to learn what and why this *was.* ⁶So Hathach went out to Mordecai in the city square that *was* in front of the king's gate. ⁷And Mordecai told him all that had happened to him, and the sum of money that Haman had promised to pay into the king's treasuries to destroy the Jews. ⁸He also gave him a copy of the written decree for their destruction, which was given at Shushan, that he might show it to Esther and explain it to her, and that he might command her to go in to the king to make supplication to him and plead before him for her people. ⁹So Hathach returned and told Esther the words of Mordecai.

¹⁰Then Esther spoke to Hathach, and gave him a command for Mordecai: ¹¹*"All the king's servants and the people of the king's provinces know that any man or woman who goes into the inner court to the king, who has not been called, *he has* but one law: put *all* to death, except the one to whom the king holds out the golden scepter, that he may live. Yet I myself have not been called to go in to the king these thirty days." ¹²So they told Mordecai Esther's words.

¹³And Mordecai told *them* to answer Esther: "Do not think in your heart that you will escape in the king's palace any more than all the other Jews. ¹⁴*For if you remain completely silent at this time, relief and deliverance will arise for the Jews from another place, but you and your father's house will perish. Yet who knows whether you have come to the kingdom for *such* a time as this?"

¹⁵Then Esther told *them* to reply to Mordecai: ¹⁶"Go, gather all the Jews who are present in Shushan, and fast for me; neither eat nor drink for three days, night or day. My maids and I will fast likewise. And so I will go to the king, which *is* against the law; and if I perish, I perish!"

¹⁷So Mordecai went his way and did according to all that Esther commanded him.ᶠ

CHAPTER 4

4:1–3 *An irrepressible grief.* A crisis does not make a person; it shows what a person is made of. In spite of the danger involved, Mordecai publicly displayed his grief and let people know his position. He would not stand by and do nothing when the authorities were about to slaughter innocent people, including children.

4:11 *An inaccessible king.* Oriental monarchs were supposed to hear only good news; they reigned in a world of illusion, sheltered from reality. Even the queen had to have permission to talk to him! How different it is with the King of kings. He has worn the sackcloth of sorrow, He knows how we feel, and He gives us free access to His throne (Heb. 10:19–22).

4:14, 16 *An incomparable opportunity.* God uses people to accomplish His purposes, and Esther was God's prepared servant for that hour (v. 14; Eph. 2:10). God accomplishes His purposes even if we disobey His call, *but we are the losers.* Mordecai did not want Esther's gifts; he wanted her life surrendered to the Lord. She became a living sacrifice to accomplish the work of God (Rom. 12:1).

4:17 ᶠSeptuagint adds a prayer of Mordecai here.

CHAPTER 5

5:1ff Sometimes it takes a crisis to remind us that we never serve the Lord alone. Esther enjoyed comfort and ease in the palace, but now she had a difficult task to perform. Her people were fasting and seeking God's help for her; she could not have succeeded alone.

5:9–12 Poor Haman was basking in false glory, boasting about false wealth, enjoying false happiness, and resting on false confidence. He did not realize that the shadow of death was over him. But is he much different from the proud unbelievers of this day who build their lives on illusions?

5:14 Esther sensed that this was not the right time to reveal her nationality. The delay of one day gave Haman opportunity to have the gallows built on which he would be hanged. Promoted by the king, honored by the queen, and advised by his wife, Haman appears to have all his problems solved! But read Psalm 37.

CHAPTER 6

6:1–3 *Providence.* If any chapter in the book of Esther reveals the providence of God, it is this one. (*Providence* [*pro,* "before"; *video,* "to see"] means "to see beforehand.") God kept the king awake, led the reader to the record about Mordecai, and had Haman arrive at just the right time. All of that happened behind the scenes, so Esther, Mordecai, and the Jews did not know about it. God is working on your behalf today, so trust Him (Rom. 8:28).

6:4–9 *Conceit.* Haman hated Mordecai so much that he got up very early to ask for his enemy's death. And Haman loved Haman so much that he could not imagine the king honoring anyone but himself! The proud man has a mirror in which he sees himself; the humble man has a window through which he sees others (Rom. 12:10; Phil. 2:3–4). Haman's pride destroyed him (Prov. 16:18; 18:12).

❝❝*Humility is the source of all true greatness: pride is ever impatient, ready to be offended. He who thinks nothing is due to him, never thinks himself ill-treated.*❞❞

Fenelon

5 Now* it happened on the third day that Esther put on *her* royal *robes* and stood in the inner court of the king's palace, across from the king's house, while the king sat on his royal throne in the royal house, facing the entrance of the house.ʲ ²So it was, when the king saw Queen Esther standing in the court, *that* she found favor in his sight, and the king held out to Esther the golden scepter that *was* in his hand. Then Esther went near and touched the top of the scepter. ³And the king said to her, "What do you wish, Queen Esther? What *is* your request? It shall be given to you—up to half the kingdom!" ⁴So Esther answered, "If it pleases the king, let the king and Haman come today to the banquet that I have prepared for him." ⁵Then the king said, "Bring Haman quickly, that he may do as Esther has said." So the king and Haman went to the banquet that Esther had prepared. ⁶At the banquet of wine the king said to Esther, "What *is* your petition? It shall be granted you. What *is* your request, up to half the kingdom? It shall be done!" ⁷Then Esther answered and said, "My petition and request *is this:* ⁸If I have found favor in the sight of the king, and if it pleases the king to grant my petition and fulfill my request, then let the king and Haman come to the banquet which I will prepare for them, and tomorrow I will do as the king has said."

⁹*So Haman went out that day joyful and with a glad heart; but when Haman saw Mordecai in the king's gate, and that he did not stand or tremble before him, he was filled with indignation against Mordecai. ¹⁰Nevertheless Haman restrained himself and went home, and he sent and called for his friends and his wife Zeresh. ¹¹Then Haman told them of his great riches, the multitude of his children, everything in which the king had promoted him, and how he had advanced him above the officials and servants of the king.

¹²Moreover Haman said, "Besides, Queen Esther invited no one but me to come in with the king to the banquet that she prepared; and tomorrow I am again invited by her, along with the king. ¹³Yet all this avails me nothing, so long as I see Mordecai the Jew sitting at the king's gate." ¹⁴*Then his wife Zeresh and all his friends said to him, "Let a gallows be made, fifty cubits high, and in the morning suggest to the king that Mordecai be hanged on it; then go merrily with the king to the banquet."

And the thing pleased Haman; so he had the gallows made.

6 That* night the king could not sleep. So one was commanded to bring the book of the records of the chronicles; and they were read before the king. ²And it was found written that Mordecai had told of Bigthana and Teresh, two of the king's eunuchs, the doorkeepers who had sought to lay hands on King Ahasuerus. ³Then the king said, "What honor or dignity has been bestowed on Mordecai for this?"

And the king's servants who attended him said, "Nothing has been done for him."

⁴*So the king said, "Who *is* in the court?" Now Haman had *just* entered the outer court of the

---

5:1 ʲSeptuagint adds many extra details in verses 1 and 2.

king's palace to suggest that the king hang Morde-cai on the gallows that he had prepared for him.

5The king's servants said to him, "Haman is there, standing in the court."

And the king said, "Let him come in."

6So Haman came in, and the king asked him, "What shall be done for the man whom the king delights to honor?"

Now Haman thought in his heart, "Whom would the king delight to honor more than me?"

7And Haman answered the king, "*For* the man whom the king delights to honor, 8let a royal robe be brought which the king has worn, and a horse on which the king has ridden, which has a royal crest placed on its head. 9Then let this robe and horse be delivered to the hand of one of the king's most noble princes, that he may array the man whom the king delights to honor. Then parade him on horseback through the city square, and proclaim before him: 'Thus shall it be done to the man whom the king delights to honor!' "

10*Then the king said to Haman, "Hurry, take the robe and the horse, as you have suggested, and do so for Mordecai the Jew who sits within the king's gate! Leave nothing undone of all that you have spoken."

11So Haman took the robe and the horse, ar-rayed Mordecai and led him on horseback through the city square, and proclaimed before him, "Thus shall it be done to the man whom the king delights to honor!"

12Afterward Mordecai went back to the king's gate. But Haman hurried to his house, mourning and with his head covered. 13When Haman told his wife Zeresh and all his friends everything that had happened to him, his wise men and his wife Zeresh said to him, "If Mordecai, before whom you have begun to fall, is of Jewish descent, you will not prevail against him but will surely fall before him."

14While they *were* still talking with him, the king's eunuchs came, and hastened to bring Haman to the banquet which Esther had pre-pared.

7 So the king and Haman went to dine with Queen Esther. 2And on the second day, at the banquet of wine, the king again said to Esther, "What *is* your petition, Queen Esther? It shall be granted you. And what *is* your request, up to half the kingdom? It shall be done!"

3*Then Queen Esther answered and said, "If I have found favor in your sight, O king, and if it pleases the king, let my life be given me at my petition, and my people at my request. 4For we have been sold, my people and I, to be destroyed, to be killed, and to be annihilated. Had we been sold as male and female slaves, I would have held my tongue, although the enemy could never com-pensate for the king's loss."

5*So King Ahasuerus answered and said to Queen Esther, "Who is he, and where is he, who

6:10–14 *Disgrace.* What a humiliating experience! Haman had to dress Mordecai in the robes he wanted to wear, put him on the horse he wanted to ride, and then lead him—a Jew—through the busiest part of the city! That should have been a warning to Haman that his plot would fail, and his wife's words only confirmed it. Had he heeded the warning and humbled himself, his life would have been spared, but pride does not easily give in to truth.

CHAPTER 7

7:3, 4 The wise person knows *what* to say and *how* and *when* to say it (Prov. 15:28; 16:23). In her brief reply to the king's question, Esther revealed her nationality (2:10, 20), her danger, and the presence of an enemy in the palace. She gave no names but waited to see the reaction of the king. God gives us the wisdom we need when we need it (James 1:5).

7:5–8 What a blow to the king's pride to learn that the man he had promoted and honored was only a self-seeking traitor: "As messengers of death is the king's wrath" (Prov. 16:14). Haman took Mordecai's place on the gallows, and the king's anger was appeased: "The righteous is delivered from trouble, and it comes to the wicked instead" (Prov. 11:8).

The Prosperity of the Wicked—Today it seems that the wicked are prospering and the righteous are suffering, but one day that will change (Prov. 11:8). Pharaoh had the Jewish boy babies drowned and God drowned his army in the Red Sea (Exod. 14:19ff.). Daniel was delivered from the lions' den, and the people who falsely accused him took his place and were slain (Dan. 6). Peter was delivered from prison, and his guards were executed (Acts 12). King Herod killed James and was slain by God (Acts 12). Read and ponder Psalm 73.

would dare presume in his heart to do such a thing?"

6And Esther said, "The adversary and enemy *is* this wicked Haman!"

So Haman was terrified before the king and queen.

7Then the king arose in his wrath from the banquet of wine *and went* into the palace garden; but Haman stood before Queen Esther, pleading for his life, for he saw that evil was determined against him by the king. 8When the king returned from the palace garden to the place of the banquet of wine, Haman had fallen across the couch where Esther *was*. Then the king said, "Will he also assault the queen while I *am* in the house?"

As the word left the king's mouth, they covered Haman's face. 9*Now Harbonah, one of the eunuchs, said to the king, "Look! The gallows, fifty cubits high, which Haman made for Mordecai, who spoke good on the king's behalf, is standing at the house of Haman."

Then the king said, "Hang him on it!"

10So they hanged Haman on the gallows that he had prepared for Mordecai. Then the king's wrath subsided.

8 On that day King Ahasuerus gave Queen Esther the house of Haman, the enemy of the Jews. And Mordecai came before the king, for Esther had told how he *was related* to her. 2So the king took off his signet ring, which he had taken from Haman, and gave it to Mordecai; and Esther appointed Mordecai over the house of Haman.

3Now Esther spoke again to the king, fell down at his feet, and implored him with tears to counteract the evil of Haman the Agagite, and the scheme which he had devised against the Jews. 4And the king held out the golden scepter toward Esther. So Esther arose and stood before the king, 5and said, "If it pleases the king, and if I have found favor in his sight and the thing *seems* right to the king and I am pleasing in his eyes, let it be written to revoke the letters devised by Haman, the son of Hammedatha the Agagite, which he wrote to annihilate the Jews who *are* in all the king's provinces. 6For how can I endure to see the evil that will come to my people? Or how can I endure to see the destruction of my countrymen?"

7*Then King Ahasuerus said to Queen Esther and Mordecai the Jew, "Indeed, I have given Esther the house of Haman, and they have hanged him on the gallows because he *tried to* lay his hand on the Jews. 8You yourselves write *a decree* concerning the Jews, as you please, in the king's name, and seal *it* with the king's signet ring; for whatever is written in the king's name and sealed with the king's signet ring no one can revoke."

9So the king's scribes were called at that time, in the third month, which *is* the month of Sivan, on the twenty-third *day;* and it was written, according to all that Mordecai commanded, to the Jews, the satraps, the governors, and the princes of the provinces from India to Ethiopia, one hundred and twenty-seven provinces *in all,* to every province in its own script, to every people in their own language, and to the Jews in their own script and language. 10And he wrote in the name of King Ahasuerus, sealed *it* with the king's signet ring,

7:9, 10 Beware if you are digging a pit for an enemy; you may fall in it yourself (Ps. 7:14–16). An enemy is a costly thing, a luxury that is too expensive to maintain.

CHAPTER 8

8:7, 8 Esther had exposed the enemy and saved her own life, but what about her people? The king himself could not revoke his edict, but he could issue another edict.

He gave the Jews the right to arm and protect themselves and gave them nine months to get ready. The people of the land got the message: the king did not want the Jews to be harmed.

Can you see here an illustration of how God solved the sinner's plight? You were under condemnation because of the law of sin and death (Rom. 3:23; 6:23). God did not revoke that law—He *obeyed* it! He sent His Son to die for our sins and to bring in "the law of the Spirit of life" (Rom. 8:2). Any sinner who believes the message and trusts the Savior will receive everlasting life (John 3:15–16).

and sent letters by couriers on horseback, riding on royal horses bred from swift steeds.*k*

11By these letters the king permitted the Jews who *were* in every city to gather together and protect their lives—to destroy, kill, and annihilate all the forces of any people or province that would assault them, *both* little children and women, and to plunder their possessions, 12on one day in all the provinces of King Ahasuerus, on the thirteenth *day* of the twelfth month, which *is* the month of Adar.*l* 13A copy of the document was to be issued as a decree in every province and published for all people, so that the Jews would be ready on that day to avenge themselves on their enemies. 14*The couriers who rode on royal horses went out, hastened and pressed on by the king's command. And the decree was issued in Shushan the citadel.

15So Mordecai went out from the presence of the king in royal apparel of blue and white, with a great crown of gold and a garment of fine linen and purple; and the city of Shushan rejoiced and was glad. 16The Jews had light and gladness, joy and honor. 17And in every province and city, wherever the king's command and decree came, the Jews had joy and gladness, a feast and a holiday. Then many of the people of the land became Jews, because fear of the Jews fell upon them.

9 Now* in the twelfth month, that *is,* the month of Adar, on the thirteenth day, *the time* came for the king's command and his decree to be executed. On the day that the enemies of the Jews had hoped to overpower them, the opposite occurred, in that the Jews themselves overpowered those who hated them. 2The Jews gathered together in their cities throughout all the provinces of King Ahasuerus to lay hands on those who sought their harm. And no one could withstand them, because fear of them fell upon all people. 3And all the officials of the provinces, the satraps, the governors, and all those doing the king's work, helped the Jews, because the fear of Mordecai fell upon them. 4For Mordecai *was* great in the king's palace, and his fame spread throughout all the provinces; for this man Mordecai became increasingly prominent. 5Thus the Jews defeated all their enemies with the stroke of the sword, with slaughter and destruction, and did what they pleased with those who hated them.

6And in Shushan the citadel the Jews killed and destroyed five hundred men. 7Also Parshandatha, Dalphon, Aspatha, 8Poratha, Adalia, Aridatha, 9Parmashta, Arisai, Aridai, and Vajezatha—10the ten sons of Haman the son of Hammedatha, the enemy of the Jews—they killed; but they did not lay a hand on the plunder.

11On that day the number of those who were killed in Shushan the citadel was brought to the king. 12And the king said to Queen Esther, "The Jews have killed and destroyed five hundred men in Shushan the citadel, and the ten sons of Haman. What have they done in the rest of the king's provinces? Now what *is* your petition? It shall be

8:14 But that is not the end. We are the King's couriers, sent into the world by His authority to share the good news that *condemned sinners need not die!* Just as those couriers "hastened and pressed on by the king's command," so we must get the gospel to the ends of the earth as quickly as possible. After all, people will perish unless we tell them the good news!

CHAPTERS 9—10

9:1 We discover that the Jews had many enemies throughout the king's provinces. Had Haman's plan succeeded, the nation would have been annihilated. We are not told how these enemies had been persecuting God's people, but their day of reckoning finally came. God kept His covenant promise to Abraham (Gen. 12:1–3).

8:10 *k*Literally *sons of the swift horses*   8:12 *l*Septuagint adds the text of the letter here.

Trust in Him—"Never be afraid to trust an unknown future to a known God," said Corrie ten Boom. And Dr. Bob Jones, Sr., advised, "Never doubt in the darkness what God has told you in the light."

granted to you. Or what *is* your further request? It shall be done."

13Then Esther said, "If it pleases the king, let it be granted to the Jews who *are* in Shushan to do again tomorrow according to today's decree, and let Haman's ten sons be hanged on the gallows."

14So the king commanded this to be done; the decree was issued in Shushan, and they hanged Haman's ten sons.

15And the Jews who *were* in Shushan gathered together again on the fourteenth day of the month of Adar and killed three hundred men at Shushan; but they did not lay a hand on the plunder.

16The remainder of the Jews in the king's provinces gathered together and protected their lives, had rest from their enemies, and killed seventy-five thousand of their enemies; but they did not lay a hand on the plunder. 17*This was* on the thirteenth day of the month of Adar. And on the fourteenth of *the month*m they rested and made it a day of feasting and gladness.

18But the Jews who *were* at Shushan assembled together on the thirteenth *day*, as well as on the fourteenth; and on the fifteenth of *the month*n they rested, and made it a day of feasting and gladness. 19Therefore the Jews of the villages who dwelt in the unwalled towns celebrated the fourteenth day of the month of Adar *with* gladness and feasting, as a holiday, and for sending presents to one another.

20And Mordecai wrote these things and sent letters to all the Jews, near and far, who *were* in all the provinces of King Ahasuerus, 21to establish among them that they should celebrate yearly the fourteenth and fifteenth days of the month of Adar, 22as the days on which the Jews had rest from their enemies, as the month which was turned from sorrow to joy for them, and from mourning to a holiday; that they should make them days of feasting and joy, of sending presents to one another and gifts to the poor. 23So the Jews accepted the custom which they had begun, as Mordecai had written to them, 24because Haman, the son of Hammedatha the Agagite, the enemy of all the Jews, had plotted against the Jews to annihilate them, and had cast Pur (that *is*, the lot), to consume them and destroy them; 25but when *Esther*o came before the king, he commanded by letter that this*p* wicked plot which *Haman* had devised against the Jews should return on his own head, and that he and his sons should be hanged on the gallows.

26So they called these days Purim, after the name Pur. Therefore, because of all the words of this letter, what they had seen concerning this matter, and what had happened to them, 27the Jews established and imposed it upon themselves and their descendants and all who would join them, that without fail they should celebrate these two days every year, according to the written *instructions* and according to the *prescribed* time, 28that these days *should be* remembered and kept throughout every generation, every family, every province, and every city, that these days of Purim should not fail *to be observed* among the Jews, and *that* the memory of them should not perish among their descendants.

9:17 It is a good thing to set aside days for special remembrance and celebration. We need to remind ourselves of what the Lord has done and show our gratitude to Him. The Feast of Purim (*pur* means "lots" [3:7; 9:26]) is a time of great gladness and feasting. (See Ps. 30.)

9:17 mLiterally *it*   9:18 nLiterally *it*   9:25 oLiterally *she* or *it*   PLiterally *his*

29Then Queen Esther, the daughter of Abihail, with Mordecai the Jew, wrote with full authority to confirm this second letter about Purim. 30And *Mordecai* sent letters to all the Jews, to the one hundred and twenty-seven provinces of the kingdom of Ahasuerus, *with* words of peace and truth, 31to confirm these days of Purim at their *appointed* time, as Mordecai the Jew and Queen Esther had prescribed for them, and as they had decreed for themselves and their descendants concerning matters of their fasting and lamenting. 32So the decree of Esther confirmed these matters of Purim, and it was written in the book.

10 And* King Ahasuerus imposed tribute on the land and *on* the islands of the sea. 2Now all the acts of his power and his might, and the account of the greatness of Mordecai, to which the king advanced him, *are* they not written in the book of the chronicles of the kings of Media and Persia? 3For Mordecai the Jew *was* second to King Ahasuerus, and was great among the Jews and well received by the multitude of his brethren, seeking the good of his people and speaking peace to all his countrymen.*q*

10:3 *q*Literally *seed*. Septuagint and Vulgate add a dream of Mordecai here; Vulgate adds six more chapters.

10:1, 2 God turned defeat into victory (9:1–3) and sorrow into joy (9:22). Of course, God does not write a "happy ending" *on earth* for every life story. Some of God's choicest saints have had to suffer and even die for the faith (Heb. 11:36–40). But God still writes that last chapter, even if it looks to us like failure. Ponder Paul's words in 2 Corinthians 4:7–18, and look forward with joy to the future God has planned for you (1 Cor. 2:9–10).

JOB

Most of this book is poetry, but it is not fiction. Job was a real person in a real place who suffered real trials (Ezek. 14:14–20). James points to Job as an example of endurance, which means faithfulness under trial (James 5:11). Job did get impatient with himself, his circumstances, and his friends, but he did not turn away from his faith in God.

The book describes three encounters: Job and Satan (chaps. 1—2), Job and his friends (chaps. 3—37), and Job and the Lord (chaps. 38—42). His friends did their best to convince Job he was suffering because he was a sinner, but Job refused to compromise his integrity. In spite of some rash statements, Job spoke the truth, but his friends did not (Job 42:7).

It is usually said that the book of Job deals with this question: "Why do the godly suffer?" Actually, the theme goes deeper than that. Satan accused Job of serving God *only because God blessed him.* Unfortunately, there are still people like that, people with "commercial faith" who say to God, "If you bless me, I will serve You!" (See Satan's temptation of Christ in Matt. 4:8–10.)

The basic question is not "Why do the righteous suffer?" (there are many answers to that question) but "Is our God worthy of our worship and service, or must He 'buy' us with His blessings?" Satan was not only slandering Job; he was also slandering the Lord! He was saying, "God would not have any followers if He did not reward them!"

As you read, note the many images used by the speakers. These similes and metaphors help us see ourselves, the world of nature, life and death and, most of all, almighty God. (God is called "Almighty" thirty-one times in Job.) Job suffered so that you and I might learn some valuable lessons about what it really means to trust the Lord.

1 There was a man in the land of Uz, whose name *was* Job; and that man was blameless and upright, and one who feared God and shunned evil. 2And seven sons and three daughters were born to him. 3Also, his possessions were seven thousand sheep, three thousand camels, five hundred yoke of oxen, five hundred female donkeys, and a very large household, so that this man was the greatest of all the people of the East.

4And his sons would go and feast *in their* houses, each on his *appointed* day, and would send and invite their three sisters to eat and drink with them. 5So it was, when the days of feasting had run their course, that Job would send and sanctify them, and he would rise early in the morning and offer burnt offerings *according to* the number of them all. For Job said, "It may be that my sons have sinned and cursed^a God in their hearts." Thus Job did regularly.

6*Now there was a day when the sons of God came to present themselves before the Lord, and Satan^b also came among them. 7And the Lord said to Satan, "From where do you come?"

So Satan answered the Lord and said, "From going to and fro on the earth, and from walking back and forth on it."

8*Then the Lord said to Satan, "Have you considered My servant Job, that *there is* none like him on the earth, a blameless and upright man, one who fears God and shuns evil?"

CHAPTER 1

1:6–12 Job knew nothing about Satan's challenge to God and had no idea that the enemy was using him as a reason for slandering the Lord. Neither did Job know that God would use his sufferings to defeat Satan. God's people are soldiers on the battlefield, but there are times when they *are* the battlefield!

1:8 If you obey God only because He blesses you, the shallowness of your faith will show up in the testing time (Matt. 7:24–27; 13:20–21). Faith that cannot be tested cannot be trusted (James 1:1–8; 1 Pet. 1:3–9).

1:5 ^{a}Literally *blessed*, but used here in the evil sense, and so in verse 11 and 2:5, 9   1:6 ^{b}Literally *the Adversary*, and so throughout this book

⁹So Satan answered the LORD and said, "Does Job fear God for nothing? ¹⁰Have You not made a hedge around him, around his household, and around all that he has on every side? You have blessed the work of his hands, and his possessions have increased in the land. ¹¹*But now, stretch out Your hand and touch all that he has, and he will surely curse You to Your face!"

¹²And the LORD said to Satan, "Behold, all that he has *is* in your power; only do not lay a hand on his *person*."

So Satan went out from the presence of the LORD.

¹³Now there was a day when his sons and daughters *were* eating and drinking wine in their oldest brother's house; ¹⁴and a messenger came to Job and said, "The oxen were plowing and the donkeys feeding beside them, ¹⁵when the Sabeansᶜ raided *them* and took them away—indeed they have killed the servants with the edge of the sword; and I alone have escaped to tell you!"

¹⁶While he *was* still speaking, another also came and said, "The fire of God fell from heaven and burned up the sheep and the servants, and consumed them; and I alone have escaped to tell you!"

¹⁷While he *was* still speaking, another also came and said, "The Chaldeans formed three bands, raided the camels and took them away, yes, and killed the servants with the edge of the sword; and I alone have escaped to tell you!"

¹⁸While he *was* still speaking, another also came and said, "Your sons and daughters *were* eating and drinking wine in their oldest brother's house, ¹⁹and suddenly a great wind came from

1:11 When Satan accuses you before God (or to yourself), remember that Jesus Christ is your defending Advocate in heaven; turn your case over to Him (Zech. 3; Rom. 8:31–39; 1 John 2:1–2; Rev. 12:10).

1:15 ᶜLiterally *Sheba* (compare 6:19)

Satan—Origin. Satan is a rebellious angel who was judged by God and fell from holiness to wickedness (Isa. 14:12–15). The angels who fell with him make up his army of spirits opposed to God and God's people (Eph. 6:10–13; Luke 11:18). Because Satan is a created being, he is not equal to God; though he possesses tremendous wisdom and power, Satan is always subject to God's will.

Nature. He is a liar and murderer (John 8:44); an adversary (1 Pet. 5:8–9); the god of this age (2 Cor. 4:4); the ruler of this world (John 12:31; 14:30; 16:11; 1 John 5:19); a deceiver (2 Cor. 11:3); a destroyer (Rev. 9:11; *Abaddon* means "destruction"); and a counterfeiter of God (Matt. 13:24–30, 36–43; 2 Cor. 11:13–15). The word *Satan* means "adversary," and *devil* means "slanderer, accuser" (Zech. 3:1–5).

Works. Satan can seek to deceive your mind (Gen. 3:1ff.; Matt. 16:21–23; 2 Cor. 11:3); snatch away God's Word (Matt. 13:19); attack your body (Job 2:4–7; 2 Cor. 12:7); control your will (1 Chron. 21:1ff.; 2 Tim. 2:26); destroy your possessions (Job 1:13ff.); hinder your work for the Lord (1 Thess. 2:18); make you proud (1 Tim. 3:6–7); cause persecution (Rev. 2:10); and tempt you to sin (Matt. 4:1ff.). When you have sinned, he can accuse you and discourage you (2 Cor. 2:6–11). You must claim God's forgiveness by faith (1 John 1:9).

Defeat. In His life, death, resurrection, and ascension, Christ defeated Satan and his evil hosts (John 12:31–33; Eph. 1:15—2:10; Col. 2:13–15). God's people must *recognize* the devil and know when he is at work (2 Cor. 2:11); *respect* him, because he is powerful and subtle (1 Pet. 5:8); and *resist* him with the Word of God and prayer (Matt. 4:1–11; James 4:7; Eph. 6:17–18). The believer must wear the whole armor of God (Eph. 6:10ff.) and use the spiritual equipment. There is overcoming power in the blood of Christ (Rev. 12:11) and the power of the Spirit (1 John 4:4).

"Nor give place to the devil" (Eph. 4:27). In Ephesians 4:17–32, Paul names some sins that can give Satan a foothold in your life: lust, lying, anger, stealing, corrupt speech, evil speaking, an unforgiving spirit, bitterness, malice, and so forth. Any sinful thing that belonged to your old life can be used by the devil to ruin your new life, so be sure to keep your heart clean before the Lord.

Future. Satan still has access to heaven (Job 1—2; Zech. 3) but one day will be thrown out (Rev. 12:7–12). When the Lord Jesus comes to establish His kingdom, He will cast Satan into hell, the lake of fire, where he will be tormented forever (Rev. 19:11—20:3). Hell was prepared for Satan and his angels, but people who reject Christ and believe Satan's lies will suffer in hell with him (Matt. 25:41; Rev. 20:11–15).

across[d] the wilderness and struck the four corners of the house, and it fell on the young people, and they are dead; and I alone have escaped to tell you!"

20Then Job arose, tore his robe, and shaved his head; and he fell to the ground and worshiped. 21And he said:

> "Naked I came from my mother's womb,
> And naked shall I return there.
> The LORD gave, and the LORD has taken away;
> Blessed be the name of the LORD."

22In all this Job did not sin nor charge God with wrong.

2 Again there was a day when the sons of God came to present themselves before the LORD, and Satan came also among them to present himself before the LORD. 2And the LORD said to Satan, "From where do you come?"

Satan answered the LORD and said, "From going to and fro on the earth, and from walking back and forth on it."

3Then the LORD said to Satan, "Have you considered My servant Job, that *there is* none like him on the earth, a blameless and upright man, one who fears God and shuns evil? And still he holds fast to his integrity, although you incited Me against him, to destroy him without cause."

4*So Satan answered the LORD and said, "Skin for skin! Yes, all that a man has he will give for his life. 5*But stretch out Your hand now, and touch his bone and his flesh, and he will surely curse You to Your face!"

6And the LORD said to Satan, "Behold, he *is* in your hand, but spare his life."

7So Satan went out from the presence of the LORD, and struck Job with painful boils from the sole of his foot to the crown of his head. 8And he took for himself a potsherd with which to scrape himself while he sat in the midst of the ashes.

9Then his wife said to him, "Do you still hold fast to your integrity? Curse God and die!"

10*But he said to her, "You speak as one of the foolish women speaks. Shall we indeed accept good from God, and shall we not accept adversity?" In all this Job did not sin with his lips.

11Now when Job's three friends heard of all this adversity that had come upon him, each one came from his own place—Eliphaz the Temanite, Bildad the Shuhite, and Zophar the Naamathite. For they had made an appointment together to come and

---

CHAPTER 2

2:4, 5 Satan's prediction about Job was wrong, which shows that he cannot foresee the future as God can. Instead of hearing Job say, "Cursed be the name of the Lord!" Satan heard, "Blessed be the name of the Lord!" Job had lost his wealth and his children, yet he did not blame God. (See James 1:2–12; 1 Pet. 1:3–9.)

2:5 Satan never gives up (Luke 4:13). He suggested to God a new test for Job: personal physical suffering (2 Cor. 12:1–10). Pain can weaken our resistance and make everything feel and look worse than it really is. More than one person who has victoriously survived tragedy has fallen apart under the onslaughts of pain.

2:10 What kept Job going? His faith in God and his personal integrity. God had no cause to inflict pain on Job (v. 3), and Job knew that he was right in his relationship with God (Job 23:10–12; 27:1–6). God would use Job to refute the explanation of his friends, to silence the accusation of the devil, and to strengthen the determination of all who will suffer in the will of God. If today you are perplexed about something in your life, wait on the Lord and let Him work out His hidden purposes.

1:19 [d]Septuagint omits *across*.

God Will Provide—Are health and wealth necessarily marks of God's blessing? Are sickness and poverty proof that we are out of God's will? To the Old Testament Jew, the answer would be yes to both questions. God promised to bless Israel physically and materially if they obeyed His law (Deut. 28). The nation of Israel was like a little child that had to be taught by means of rewards and punishments. But these old covenant blessings are not guaranteed to God's people under the new covenant today. With the coming of Jesus Christ to earth, the "childhood" period of Israel's history ended (Gal. 4:1–7). Our Lord was poor, and so were the apostles and many of the great men and women of faith (2 Cor. 8:9; 6:4–10; Heb. 11:36–40). Paul lived with a physical affliction (2 Cor. 12:7–10), and one of his most beloved workers almost died from illness (Phil. 2:25–30; see also 2 Tim. 4:20). It is the wicked who seem to be prospering today, not the righteous, but one day, God will turn things around (Ps. 73). God has promised to meet your needs (Matt. 6:25–34; Phil. 4:19), so stop fretting and trust Him to provide.

mourn with him, and to comfort him. 12And when they raised their eyes from afar, and did not recognize him, they lifted their voices and wept; and each one tore his robe and sprinkled dust on his head toward heaven. 13So they sat down with him on the ground seven days and seven nights, and no one spoke a word to him, for they saw that *his* grief was very great.

3 After this Job opened his mouth and cursed the day of his *birth.* 2And Job spoke, and said:

3 *"May the day perish on which I was born,
   And the night *in which* it was said,
   'A male child is conceived.'
4 May that day be darkness;
   May God above not seek it,
   Nor the light shine upon it.
5 May darkness and the shadow of death
      claim it;
   May a cloud settle on it;
   May the blackness of the day terrify it.
6 *As for* that night, may darkness seize it;
   May it not rejoice[e] among the days of the
      year,
   May it not come into the number of the
      months.
7 Oh, may that night be barren!
   May no joyful shout come into it!
8 May those curse it who curse the day,
   Those who are ready to arouse Leviathan.
9 May the stars of its morning be dark;
   May it look for light, but *have* none,
   And not see the dawning of the day;
10 Because it did not shut up the doors of my
      mother's womb,
   Nor hide sorrow from my eyes.

11*"Why did I not die at birth?
   Why did I *not* perish when I came from the
      womb?
12 Why did the knees receive me?
   Or why the breasts, that I should nurse?
13 For now I would have lain still and been
      quiet,
   I would have been asleep;
   Then I would have been at rest
14 With kings and counselors of the earth,
   Who built ruins for themselves,
15 Or with princes who had gold,
   Who filled their houses *with* silver;
16 Or *why* was I not hidden like a stillborn
      child,
   Like infants who never saw light?
17 There the wicked cease *from* troubling,
   And there the weary are at rest.
18 *There* the prisoners rest together;
   They do not hear the voice of the oppressor.
19 The small and great are there,
   And the servant *is* free from his master.

20 "Why is light given to him who is in misery,
   And life to the bitter of soul,

3:6 eSeptuagint, Syriac, Targum, and Vulgate read *be joined.*

CHAPTER 3
3:3–10 Job did not curse God, but he did curse the night of his conception and the day of his birth. The prophet Jeremiah did the same thing one dismal day (Jer. 20:14–18). When you hurt, physically and emotionally, you are prone to lose perspective and forget the joys of the past. Times of suffering can be times of remembering God's goodness and thanking Him for all you have received from His hand. Ponder Psalm 77.

3:11–26 Job asks the question "Why?" seven times in this monologue (vv. 11, 12, 16, 20, 23). "Why?" is an easy question to ask but a very difficult one to answer. Suppose God had told Job the reasons behind his troubles. Would that have solved his problems? After all, God's people live on promises, not on explanations.

A Spiritual Diet—According to Job 3:24, Job was "feeding" on his grief and could not eat. Some people feed on their tears (Ps. 42:3), and others feed on their sins (Job 20:12–19). How much better to feed on God's Word (Jer. 15:16; Matt. 4:4), His will (John 4:34), and His faithfulness (Ps. 37:3).

21 Who long for death, but it does not *come,*
   And search for it more than hidden
       treasures;
22 Who rejoice exceedingly,
   And are glad when they can find the grave?
23 *Why is light given* to a man whose way is
       hidden,
   And whom God has hedged in?
24 *For my sighing comes before I eat,^f
   And my groanings pour out like water.
25 For the thing I greatly feared has come upon
       me,
   And what I dreaded has happened to me.
26 I am not at ease, nor am I quiet;
   I have no rest, for trouble comes."

4 Then* Eliphaz the Temanite answered and
   said:

2 "If one attempts a word with you, will you
       become weary?
   But who can withhold himself from
       speaking?
3 *Surely you have instructed many,
   And you have strengthened weak hands.
4 Your words have upheld him who was
       stumbling,
   And you have strengthened the feeble
       knees;
5 But now it comes upon you, and you are
       weary;
   It touches you, and you are troubled.
6 *Is* not your reverence your confidence?
   And the integrity of your ways your hope?

7 "Remember now, who *ever* perished being
       innocent?
   Or where were the upright *ever* cut off?
8 Even as I have seen,
   Those who plow iniquity
   And sow trouble reap the same.
9 By the blast of God they perish,
   And by the breath of His anger they are
       consumed.
10 The roaring of the lion,
   The voice of the fierce lion,
   And the teeth of the young lions are broken.
11 The old lion perishes for lack of prey,
   And the cubs of the lioness are scattered.

12 *"Now a word was secretly brought to me,
   And my ear received a whisper of it.
13 In disquieting thoughts from the visions of
       the night,
   When deep sleep falls on men,
14 Fear came upon me, and trembling,
   Which made all my bones shake.
15 Then a spirit passed before my face;
   The hair on my body stood up.
16 It stood still,
   But I could not discern its appearance.
   A form *was* before my eyes;
   There was silence;
   Then I heard a voice *saying:*
17 'Can a mortal be more righteous than God?
   Can a man be more pure than his Maker?
18 If He puts no trust in His servants,
   If He charges His angels with error,

3:24–26 It is too bad that Job's three friends listened to Job's *words* instead of to his *feelings.* They decided to tell Job why he was suffering, but they only made his situation worse. Suffering people need love, acceptance, and patient encouragement, not arguments and accusations.

CHAPTERS 4—5

4:1ff The three friends sincerely meant to console Job, but they ended up condemning him and taking Satan's place! Why? Because each of them saw Job's plight from his own narrow perspective and failed to identify with Job's perplexity and pain. We all need to obey Romans 12:9–16.

4:3–6 Eliphaz asked Job why he did not practice what he preached (4:1–6), a fine way to start encouraging a hurting friend! He told Job that sinners always reap what they sow (4:7–11), suggesting that it was Job's fault that he was now poor and sick instead of being rich and healthy. What encouragement!

4:12–21 Then Eliphaz shared his "experience with God" (4:12–21) on which he based his whole interpretation of life. Avoid those who make *their* experience the only test of truth. The Word of God does not change, but experiences do. We are all different, and God deals with each of us in ways suitable to our needs, our natures and our level of maturity.

3:24 ^f Literally *my bread*

19 How much more those who dwell in houses
        of clay,
      Whose foundation is in the dust,
      Who are crushed before a moth?
20 They are broken in pieces from morning till
        evening;
      They perish forever, with no one regarding.
21 Does not their own excellence go away?
      They die, even without wisdom.'

5 "Call out now;
      Is there anyone who will answer you?
      And to which of the holy ones will you turn?
2   For wrath kills a foolish man,
      And envy slays a simple one.
3   I have seen the foolish taking root,
      But suddenly I cursed his dwelling place.
4   His sons are far from safety,
      They are crushed in the gate,
      And *there is* no deliverer.
5   Because the hungry eat up his harvest,
      Taking it even from the thorns,ᵍ
      And a snare snatches their substance.ʰ
6   For affliction does not come from the dust,
      Nor does trouble spring from the ground;
7   Yet man is born to trouble,
      As the sparks fly upward.

8 *"But as for me, I would seek God,
      And to God I would commit my cause—
9   Who does great things, and unsearchable,
      Marvelous things without number.
10 He gives rain on the earth,
      And sends waters on the fields.
11 He sets on high those who are lowly,
      And those who mourn are lifted to safety.
12 He frustrates the devices of the crafty,
      So that their hands cannot carry out their
        plans.
13 He catches the wise in their own craftiness,
      And the counsel of the cunning comes
        quickly upon them.
14 They meet with darkness in the daytime,
      And grope at noontime as in the night.
15 But He saves the needy from the sword,
      From the mouth of the mighty,
      And from their hand.
16 So the poor have hope,
      And injustice shuts her mouth.

17 "Behold, happy *is* the man whom God
        corrects;
      Therefore do not despise the chastening of
        the Almighty.
18 For He bruises, but He binds up;
      He wounds, but His hands make whole.
19 He shall deliver you in six troubles,
      Yes, in seven no evil shall touch you.
20 In famine He shall redeem you from death,
      And in war from the power of the sword.
21 You shall be hidden from the scourge of the
        tongue,
      And you shall not be afraid of destruction
        when it comes.
22 You shall laugh at destruction and famine,
      And you shall not be afraid of the beasts
        of the earth.

5:8 Eliphaz closed his speech by telling Job
to seek God and submit (5:8), and to accept
His correction (5:17); then God would bless
him again. But his suggestion played right
into Satan's hands: "Does Job fear God for
nothing?" (1:9). Eliphaz had the same
theology as the devil and did not know it!

5:5 ᵍSeptuagint reads *They shall not be taken from evil men;*
Vulgate reads *And the armed man shall take him by violence.*
ʰSeptuagint reads *The might shall draw them off;* Vulgate
reads *And the thirsty shall drink up their riches.*

23　For you shall have a covenant with the
stones of the field,
And the beasts of the field shall be at peace
with you.
24　You shall know that your tent *is* in peace;
You shall visit your dwelling and find
nothing amiss.
25　You shall also know that your descendants
shall be many,
And your offspring like the grass of the
earth.
26　You shall come to the grave at a full age,
As a sheaf of grain ripens in its season.
27　*Behold, this we have searched out;
It *is* true.
Hear it, and know for yourself."

5:27 If you want to help others, listen with your heart as well as your ears; try not to make your experience the only test of truth. We all "know in part" (1 Cor. 13:9).

CHAPTERS 6—7

6:1–7 Job admits that his words were rash (6:3), and he explains why: his grief was a burden that his friends did not feel or try to help him carry. God was shooting poisoned arrows at Job, and his friends were not applying medicine to his painful wounds. One day God will change our burdens into glory (2 Cor. 4:16–18), but until then, we must bear one another's burdens (Gal. 6:2) and relieve one another's wounds (Luke 10:25–37; Acts 16:33).

6 Then* Job answered and said:

2　"Oh, that my grief were fully weighed,
And my calamity laid with it on the scales!
3　For then it would be heavier than the sand
of the sea—
Therefore my words have been rash.
4　For the arrows of the Almighty *are* within
me;
My spirit drinks in their poison;
The terrors of God are arrayed against me.
5　Does the wild donkey bray when it has
grass,
Or does the ox low over its fodder?
6　Can flavorless food be eaten without salt?
Or is there *any* taste in the white of an egg?
7　My soul refuses to touch them;
They *are* as loathsome food to me.

8　"Oh, that I might have my request,
That God would grant *me* the thing that I
long for!
9　That it would please God to crush me,
That He would loose His hand and cut me
off!
10　Then I would still have comfort;
Though in anguish I would exult,
He will not spare;
For I have not concealed the words of the
Holy One.

11　"What strength do I have, that I should hope?
And what *is* my end, that I should prolong
my life?
12　*Is* my strength the strength of stones?
Or *is* my flesh bronze?
13　*Is* my help not within me?
And is success driven from me?

14　"To him who is afflicted, kindness *should be
shown* by his friend,
Even though he forsakes the fear of the
Almighty.
15　*My brothers have dealt deceitfully like a
brook,
Like the streams of the brooks that pass
away,
16　Which are dark because of the ice,
And into which the snow vanishes.
17　When it is warm, they cease to flow;
When it is hot, they vanish from their place.
18　The paths of their way turn aside,
They go nowhere and perish.
19　The caravans of Tema look,
The travelers of Sheba hope for them.

6:15–18 The friends were like desert brooks that dry up when they are most needed. The thirsty travelers hope for refreshment, but they are disappointed (6:14–23). Do you disappoint hurting people by being critical and failing to care?

20 They are disappointed because they were
      confident;
   They come there and are confused.
21 For now you are nothing,
   You see terror and are afraid.
22 Did I ever say, 'Bring *something* to me'?
   Or, 'Offer a bribe for me from your wealth'?
23 Or, 'Deliver me from the enemy's hand'?
   Or, 'Redeem me from the hand of
      oppressors'?

24 "Teach me, and I will hold my tongue;
   Cause me to understand wherein I have
      erred.
25 How forceful are right words!
   But what does your arguing prove?
26 Do you intend to rebuke *my* words,
   And the speeches of a desperate one, *which
      are* as wind?
27 Yes, you overwhelm the fatherless,
   And you undermine your friend.
28 Now therefore, be pleased to look at me;
   For I would never lie to your face.
29 Yield now, let there be no injustice!
   Yes, concede, my righteousness still stands!
30 Is there injustice on my tongue?
   Cannot my taste discern the unsavory?

7 "Is* *there* not a time of hard service for man
      on earth?
   Are not his days also like the days of a hired
      man?
2   Like a servant who earnestly desires the
      shade,
   And like a hired man who eagerly looks for
      his wages,
3   So I have been allotted months of futility,
   And wearisome nights have been appointed
      to me.
4   When I lie down, I say, 'When shall I arise,
   And the night be ended?'
   For I have had my fill of tossing till dawn.
5   My flesh is caked with worms and dust,
   My skin is cracked and breaks out afresh.

6   "My days are swifter than a weaver's shuttle,
   And are spent without hope.
7   Oh, remember that my life *is* a breath!
   My eye will never again see good.
8   The eye of him who sees me will see me
      no *more*;
   While your *eyes* are upon me, I shall no
      longer *be*.
9   *As* the cloud disappears and vanishes away,
   So he who goes down to the grave does not
      come up.
10   He shall never return to his house,
   Nor shall his place know him anymore.

11   "Therefore I will not restrain my mouth;
   I will speak in the anguish of my spirit;
   I will complain in the bitterness of my soul.
12   *Am* I a sea, or a sea serpent,
   That You set a guard over me?
13   When I say, 'My bed will comfort me,
   My couch will ease my complaint,'
14   Then You scare me with dreams
   And terrify me with visions,
15   So that my soul chooses strangling
   And death rather than my body.*i*

7:1–10 In chapter 7, Job talks to God about the seeming futility of his life. Why should God keep him alive? What is all this suffering accomplishing? Job is like a weary hired man who gets no wages (7:1–5). His life rushes by like the shuttle on a loom; it is like a breath and a cloud (7:6–10; James 4:13–17). Job is a target (6:4; 7:20), but what is God aiming at?

7:15 *i* Literally *my bones*

7:20, 21 "If I am a great sinner," says Job, "then either pardon my sins or take my life. Either way, I will find some peace." (See 6:9–10; 7:15, 20–21.) It seems a logical argument, but God's thoughts are not our thoughts; what seems meaningless to us is reasonable to God (Isa. 55:8–9). We must walk by faith.

Hurting people need encouragement, not argument. Ask God to make your words like healing medicine (Prov. 12:18) and refreshing water (Prov. 18:4). Start the day praying for wisdom to say the right things at the right times (Isa. 50:4).

CHAPTER 8

8:1–7 **Theology.** Eliphaz emphasized the sinfulness of man, and Bildad majored on the justice of God. Both men were right in their doctrine but wrong in their conclusion. They locked God into a formula and refused to let Him exercise His freedom to do what He wants to do. Before the book ends, Job and his friends will discover that God is much greater than the words they used in speaking about Him. Have you limited God? Do you know the living God or only theological words?

8:8–10 **History.** Bildad was a devoted traditionalist who called his witnesses from the past. There is nothing wrong with our learning from the past, provided it does not turn the present into a museum and the future into a cemetery. Someone has said, "Tradition is the living face of dead people, while traditionalism is the dead face of living people." Is the past encouraging you or embalming you?

8:11–22 **Science.** Bildad argues from nature: for every effect, there is a cause. If Job is suffering, there must be a cause, and since God is just, that cause has to be Job's sin. But God's dealings with His people cannot be studied in a laboratory. Science has its place, but it cannot explain God. He is too great for man's feeble instruments.

16 I loathe *my life;*
   I would not live forever.
   Let me alone,
   For my days *are but* a breath.

17 "What *is* man, that You should exalt him,
    That You should set Your heart on him,
18 That You should visit him every morning,
    And test him every moment?
19 How long?
    Will You not look away from me,
    And let me alone till I swallow my saliva?
20 *Have I sinned?
    What have I done to You, O watcher of men?
    Why have You set me as Your target,
    So that I am a burden to myself?*ʲ*
21 Why then do You not pardon my transgression,
    And take away my iniquity?
    For now I will lie down in the dust,
    And You will seek me diligently,
    But I *will* no longer *be.*"

8 Then* Bildad the Shuhite answered and said:

2 "How long will you speak these *things,*
   And the words of your mouth *be like* a strong wind?
3 Does God subvert judgment?
   Or does the Almighty pervert justice?
4 If your sons have sinned against Him,
   He has cast them away for their transgression.
5 If you would earnestly seek God
   And make your supplication to the Almighty,
6 If you *were* pure and upright,
   Surely now He would awake for you,
   And prosper your rightful dwelling place.
7 Though your beginning was small,
   Yet your latter end would increase abundantly.

8 *"For inquire, please, of the former age,
   And consider the things discovered by their fathers;
9 For we *were born* yesterday, and know nothing,
   Because our days on earth *are* a shadow.
10 Will they not teach you and tell you,
    And utter words from their heart?

11*"Can the papyrus grow up without a marsh?
    Can the reeds flourish without water?
12 While it *is* yet green *and* not cut down,
    It withers before any *other* plant.
13 So *are* the paths of all who forget God;
    And the hope of the hypocrite shall perish,
14 Whose confidence shall be cut off,
    And whose trust *is* a spider's web.
15 He leans on his house, but it does not stand.
    He holds it fast, but it does not endure.
16 He grows green in the sun,
    And his branches spread out in his garden.
17 His roots wrap around the rock heap,
    And look for a place in the stones.

7:20 ʲFollowing Masoretic Text, Targum, and Vulgate; Septuagint and Jewish tradition read *to You.*

18 If he is destroyed from his place,
Then *it* will deny him, *saying,* 'I have not
seen you.'

19 "Behold, this is the joy of His way,
And out of the earth others will grow.
20 Behold, God will not cast away the
blameless,
Nor will He uphold the evildoers.
21 He will yet fill your mouth with laughing,
And your lips with rejoicing.
22 Those who hate you will be clothed with
shame,
And the dwelling place of the wicked will
come to nothing."[k]

9 Then* Job answered and said:

2 "Truly I know *it is* so,
But how can a man be righteous before
God?
3 *If one wished to contend with Him,
He could not answer Him one time out of a
thousand.
4 *God is* wise in heart and mighty in strength.
Who has hardened *himself* against Him and
prospered?
5 He removes the mountains, and they do not
know
When He overturns them in His anger;
6 He shakes the earth out of its place,
And its pillars tremble;
7 He commands the sun, and it does not rise;
He seals off the stars;
8 He alone spreads out the heavens,
And treads on the waves of the sea;
9 He made the Bear, Orion, and the Pleiades,
And the chambers of the south;
10 He does great things past finding out,
Yes, wonders without number.
11 If He goes by me, I do not see *Him;*
If He moves past, I do not perceive Him;
12 If He takes away, who can hinder Him?
Who can say to Him, 'What are You doing?'
13 God will not withdraw His anger,
The allies of the proud[l] lie prostrate beneath
Him.

14*"How then can I answer Him,
And choose my words *to reason* with Him?
15 For though I were righteous, I could not
answer Him;
I would beg mercy of my Judge.
16 If I called and He answered me,
I would not believe that He was listening
to my voice.
17 For He crushes me with a tempest,
And multiplies my wounds without cause.
18 He will not allow me to catch my breath,
But fills me with bitterness.
19 If *it is a matter* of strength, indeed *He is*
strong;
And if of justice, who will appoint my day
in court?
20 Though I were righteous, my own mouth
would condemn me;
Though I *were* blameless, it would prove me
perverse.

CHAPTERS 9—10

9:1, 2 Job accepted Bildad's affirmation that
God is just, but doing that did not solve his
problem. "I am blameless," he said (9:21);
"therefore, why should God condemn me?"
Job then shared three complaints.

9:3–13 *"I cannot contend with Him."* God
is so much greater and stronger than we
are, who would dare to declare war on Him?
God is wise and powerful; we are ignorant
and weak.

9:14–35 *"I cannot answer Him."* If God
and Job went to court, Job would not have
an argument to present. God is the Judge,
He has all power, and nobody can contend
with Him. Meanwhile, life goes by swiftly,
like a fast runner, a ship and an eagle. For
Job to put on a smiling face (v. 27) will not
change his circumstances. It would be
hypocrisy.

8:22 [k]Literally *will not be*   9:13 [l]Hebrew *rahab*

21 "I am blameless, yet I do not know myself;
   I despise my life.
22 It *is* all one *thing*;
   Therefore I say, 'He destroys the blameless
     and the wicked.'
23 If the scourge slays suddenly,
   He laughs at the plight of the innocent.
24 The earth is given into the hand of the
    wicked.
   He covers the faces of its judges.
   If it is not *He*, who else could it be?

25 "Now my days are swifter than a runner;
   They flee away, they see no good.
26 They pass by like swift ships,
   Like an eagle swooping on its prey.
27 If I say, 'I will forget my complaint,
   I will put off my sad face and wear a smile,'
28 I am afraid of all my sufferings;
   I know that You will not hold me innocent.
29 *If* I am condemned,
   Why then do I labor in vain?
30 If I wash myself with snow water,
   And cleanse my hands with soap,
31 Yet You will plunge me into the pit,
   And my own clothes will abhor me.

32 "For *He is* not a man, as I *am,*
   That I may answer Him,
   And that we should go to court together.
33 Nor is there any mediator between us,
   Who may lay his hand on us both.
34 Let Him take His rod away from me,
   And do not let dread of Him terrify me.
35 *Then* I would speak and not fear Him,
   But it is not so with me.

10 "My* soul loathes my life;
   I will give free course to my complaint,
   I will speak in the bitterness of my soul.
2 I will say to God, 'Do not condemn me;
   Show me why You contend with me.
3 *Does it* seem good to You that You should
    oppress,
   That You should despise the work of Your
    hands,
   And smile on the counsel of the wicked?
4 Do You have eyes of flesh?
   Or do You see as man sees?
5 *Are* Your days like the days of a mortal
    man?
   Are Your years like the days of a mighty
    man,
6 That You should seek for my iniquity
   And search out my sin,
7 Although You know that I am not wicked,
   And *there is* no one who can deliver from
    Your hand?

8 'Your hands have made me and fashioned
    me,
   An intricate unity;
   Yet You would destroy me,
9 Remember, I pray, that You have made me
    like clay.
   And will You turn me into dust again?
10 Did You not pour me out like milk,
   And curdle me like cheese,
11 Clothe me with skin and flesh,
   And knit me together with bones and
    sinews?

10:1–22 *"I cannot understand Him."* God made Job, and He seems to be destroying His own work. Why was Job born to begin with? God could have saved Himself a lot of trouble!

The answer to these complaints is in 9:33—a mediator, someone who could bring Job and God together. You have that Mediator in Jesus Christ, God's Son (1 Tim. 2:5; Heb. 12:24). As both God and man, Jesus understands your needs and can do something about them. Are you complaining—or trusting Him?

12 You have granted me life and favor,
    And Your care has preserved my spirit.

13 'And these *things* You have hidden in Your
        heart;
    I know that this *was* with You:
14 If I sin, then You mark me,
    And will not acquit me of my iniquity.
15 If I am wicked, woe to me;
    Even *if* I am righteous, I cannot lift up my
        head.
    I am full of disgrace;
    See my misery!
16 If *my head* is exalted,
    You hunt me like a fierce lion,
    And again You show Yourself awesome
        against me.
17 You renew Your witnesses against me,
    And increase Your indignation toward me;
    Changes and war are *ever* with me.

18 'Why then have You brought me out of the
        womb?
    Oh, that I had perished and no eye had seen
        me!
19 I would have been as though I had not been.
    I would have been carried from the womb
        to the grave.
20 Are not my days few?
    Cease! Leave me alone, that I may take a
        little comfort,
21 Before I go *to the place from which* I shall
        not return,
    To the land of darkness and the shadow of
        death,
22 A land as dark as darkness *itself,*
    As the shadow of death, without any order,
    Where even the light *is* like darkness.' "

11 Then* Zophar the Naamathite answered
        and said:

2 "Should not the multitude of words be
        answered?
    And should a man full of talk be vindicated?
3 Should your empty talk make men hold
        their peace?
    And when you mock, should no one rebuke
        you?
4 For you have said,
    'My doctrine *is* pure,
    And I am clean in your eyes.'
5 But oh, that God would speak,
    And open His lips against you,
6 That He would show you the secrets of
        wisdom!
    For *they would* double *your* prudence.
    Know therefore that God exacts from you
    Less than your iniquity *deserves.*

7 "Can you search out the deep things of God?
    Can you find out the limits of the Almighty?
8 *They are* higher than heaven— what can
        you do?
    Deeper than Sheol— what can you know?
9 Their measure *is* longer than the earth
    And broader than the sea.

10 "If He passes by, imprisons, and gathers *to*
        judgment,
    Then who can hinder Him?

CHAPTER 11
11:1–8 Job has heard two points of the
sermon from his friends: man is sinful
(Eliphaz), and God is just (Bildad). Zophar
now finishes the sermon with the third point:
God punishes sin and gives less than we
really deserve (v. 6). "Things could be
worse!" is a cruel statement to make to
somebody who has lost everything.

11 For He knows deceitful men;
    He sees wickedness also.
    Will He not then consider *it?*
12 For an empty-headed man will be wise,
    When a wild donkey's colt is born a man.

13*"If you would prepare your heart,
    And stretch out your hands toward Him;
14 If iniquity *were* in your hand, *and you* put
    it far away,
    And would not let wickedness dwell in your
    tents;
15 Then surely you could lift up your face
    without spot;
    Yes, you could be steadfast, and not fear;
16 Because you would forget *your* misery,
    And remember *it* as waters *that have*
    passed away,
17 And *your* life would be brighter than
    noonday.
    Though you were dark, you would be like
    the morning.
18 And you would be secure, because there is
    hope;
    Yes, you would dig *around you, and* take
    your rest in safety.
19 You would also lie down, and no one would
    make *you* afraid;
    Yes, many would court your favor.
20 But the eyes of the wicked will fail,
    And they shall not escape,
    And their hope—loss of life!"

11:13 People in pain think that their suffering is worse than anybody else's, so do not argue with them. Zophar responded to Job's words, not his feelings, and that was a mistake. He told Job to repent and seek God, promising that God would hear him. He warned Job that if he did not repent, he would die (v. 20).

You cannot measure pain or the greatness of God (vv. 7–9). These are dead-end streets. Instead, *lose yourself in the measureless love and power of God* (Eph. 3:14–21). God is not found at the end of an argument, but He is near to those who call on Him.

CHAPTERS 12—14

12:1–25 *"My life."* Job replied to all three friends and reminded them that *he* had wisdom as well as they. In fact, all creation knew the things that they said to him. God is great: His hand made everything (v. 6), and His hand keeps everything alive (v. 10). Job wanted to die and escape his suffering, but God held his life in His hand (Acts 17:24–28; Col. 1:16–17). If your life is in God's hand, have you anything to fear?

12 Then* Job answered and said:

2 "No doubt you *are* the people,
    And wisdom will die with you!
3 But I have understanding as well as you;
    I *am* not inferior to you.
    Indeed, who does not *know* such things as
    these?

4 "I am one mocked by his friends,
    Who called on God, and He answered him,
    The just and blameless *who is* ridiculed.
5 A lamp^m is despised in the thought of one
    who is at ease;
    It is made ready for those whose feet slip.
6 The tents of robbers prosper,
    And those who provoke God are secure—
    In what God provides by His hand.

12:5 ^m Or *disaster*

What About Suicide?—The life of every living thing is in God's hand (Job 12:10). He has numbered our days (Job 14:5) and set a limit beyond which we cannot go (Ps. 139:16). But can we determine a limit *sooner than He planned?* Is suicide permissible? Job's wife counseled her husband to curse God and thereby invite His judgment, but Job rejected that suggestion as foolish (Job 2:9–10). Job wanted to die (Job 6:8–10; 7:15–16) but did not assume that he had the right to take his own life. Our lives are in God's hand, and our times are in His hand (Ps. 31:15). There is no incident in the Bible of a godly person committing suicide. Saul had rebelled against God (1 Sam. 31:3–5); Ahithophel had turned against the king (2 Sam. 17:23); Zimri was a rebel and a conspirator (1 Kings 16:8–20); and Judas betrayed the Lord (Matt. 27:4–5). Samson's death (Judg. 16:23ff.) appears to be more martyrdom than suicide. The sixth commandment forbids murder (Exod. 20:13). Man is made in the image of God, and we have no right to attack that image, even if we are suffering greatly. In the Bible, men like Moses, Elijah, and Jonah became discouraged and wanted to die, but they did not attempt to take their own lives. "To run away from trouble is a form of cowardice," wrote Aristotle, "and while it is true that the suicide braves death, he does it not for some noble object but to escape some ill." Ponder 2 Timothy 4:6–8.

7 "But now ask the beasts, and they will teach
     you;
   And the birds of the air, and they will tell
     you;
8 Or speak to the earth, and it will teach you;
   And the fish of the sea will explain to you.
9 Who among all these does not know
   That the hand of the LORD has done this,
10 In whose hand *is* the life of every living
     thing,
   And the breath of all mankind?
11 Does not the ear test words
   And the mouth taste its food?
12 Wisdom *is* with aged men,
   And with length of days, understanding.

13 "With Him *are* wisdom and strength,
   He has counsel and understanding.
14 If He breaks *a thing* down, it cannot be
     rebuilt;
   If He imprisons a man, there can be no
     release.
15 If He withholds the waters, they dry up;
   If He sends them out, they overwhelm the
     earth.
16 With Him *are* strength and prudence.
   The deceived and the deceiver *are* His.
17 He leads counselors away plundered,
   And makes fools of the judges.
18 He loosens the bonds of kings,
   And binds their waist with a belt.
19 He leads princes*ⁿ* away plundered,
   And overthrows the mighty.
20 He deprives the trusted ones of speech,
   And takes away the discernment of the
     elders.
21 He pours contempt on princes,
   And disarms the mighty.
22 He uncovers deep things out of darkness,
   And brings the shadow of death to light.
23 He makes nations great, and destroys them;
   He enlarges nations, and guides them.
24 He takes away the understanding*º* of the
     chiefs of the people of the earth,
   And makes them wander in a pathless
     wilderness.
25 They grope in the dark without light,
   And He makes them stagger like a drunken
     man.

13 "Behold,* my eye has seen all *this,*
   My ear has heard and understood it.
2 What you know, I also know;
   I *am* not inferior to you.
3 But I would speak to the Almighty,
   And I desire to reason with God.
4 But you forgers of lies,
   You *are* all worthless physicians.
5 Oh, that you would be silent,
   And it would be your wisdom!
6 Now hear my reasoning,
   And heed the pleadings of my lips.
7 Will you speak wickedly for God,
   And talk deceitfully for Him?
8 Will you show partiality for Him?
   Will you contend for God?
9 Will it be well when He searches you out?
   Or can you mock Him as one mocks a man?

13:1–28 *"My faith."* In the previous chapter,
Job saw God as Creator, but now he sees
Him as Judge. "I desire to reason with God"
(v. 3) means "I want to meet Him in court."
Job would rather meet a just God than
"worthless physicians" like his friends.
When you seek to help others, keep in mind
that you are a witness and not a prosecuting
attorney. Even if God did condemn him, Job
would still trust Him (v. 15). What faith!

12:19 *ⁿ*Literally *priests,* but not in a technical sense
12:24 *º*Literally *heart*

¹⁰ He will surely rebuke you
If you secretly show partiality.
¹¹ Will not His excellence make you afraid,
And the dread of Him fall upon you?
¹² Your platitudes *are* proverbs of ashes,
Your defenses are defenses of clay.

¹³ "Hold your peace with me, and let me speak,
Then let come on me what *may!*
¹⁴ Why do I take my flesh in my teeth,
And put my life in my hands?
¹⁵ Though He slay me, yet will I trust Him.
Even so, I will defend my own ways before
Him.
¹⁶ He also *shall* be my salvation,
For a hypocrite could not come before Him.
¹⁷ Listen carefully to my speech,
And to my declaration with your ears.
¹⁸ See now, I have prepared *my* case,
I know that I shall be vindicated.
¹⁹ Who *is* he *who* will contend with me?
If now I hold my tongue, I perish.
²⁰ "Only two *things* do not do to me,
Then I will not hide myself from You:
²¹ Withdraw Your hand far from me,
And let not the dread of You make me
afraid.
²² Then call, and I will answer;
Or let me speak, then You respond to me.
²³ How many *are* my iniquities and sins?
Make me know my transgression and my
sin.
²⁴ Why do You hide Your face,
And regard me as Your enemy?
²⁵ Will You frighten a leaf driven to and fro?
And will You pursue dry stubble?
²⁶ For You write bitter things against me,
And make me inherit the iniquities of my
youth.
²⁷ You put my feet in the stocks,
And watch closely all my paths.
You set a limit^p for the soles of my feet.

²⁸ "Man^q decays like a rotten thing,
Like a garment that is moth-eaten.

14:1–32 *"My hope."* Like a flower, man is
born to die. He disappears like a shadow
(v. 2) or like evaporating water (v. 11). Man's
days are numbered (vv. 5–6), but does he
have a future? Even a tree will grow again
after it is cut down (v. 7), but what about
man? The truth about resurrection was not
fully revealed in Old Testament days, but
Job still rested his hope on God. God has
revealed the blessed hope that His people
have because of faith in Jesus Christ (John
11:25–26; 1 Cor. 15; 2 Tim. 1:9–10).
"In spite of my sufferings," said Job, "my
life, my faith, and my hope are in God." Is
that your testimony?

14 "Man* *who is* born of woman
Is of few days and full of trouble.
² He comes forth like a flower and fades
away;
He flees like a shadow and does not
continue.
³ And do You open Your eyes on such a one,
And bring me^r to judgment with Yourself?
⁴ Who can bring a clean *thing* out of an
unclean?
No one!
⁵ Since his days *are* determined,
The number of his months *is* with You;
You have appointed his limits, so that he
cannot pass.
⁶ Look away from him that he may rest,
Till like a hired man he finishes his day.

⁷ "For there is hope for a tree,
If it is cut down, that it will sprout again,
And that its tender shoots will not cease.

13:27 ^pLiterally *inscribe a print*   13:28 ^qLiterally *He*
14:3 ^rSeptuagint, Syriac, and Vulgate read *him.*

8 Though its root may grow old in the earth,
   And its stump may die in the ground,
9 Yet at the scent of water it will bud
   And bring forth branches like a plant.
10 But man dies and is laid away;
   Indeed he breathes his last
   And where is he?
11 As water disappears from the sea,
   And a river becomes parched and dries up,
12 So man lies down and does not rise.
   Till the heavens are no more,
   They will not awake
   Nor be roused from their sleep.

13 "Oh, that You would hide me in the grave,
   That You would conceal me until Your
       wrath is past,
   That You would appoint me a set time, and
       remember me!
14 If a man dies, shall he live again?
   All the days of my hard service I will wait,
   Till my change comes.
15 You shall call, and I will answer You;
   You shall desire the work of Your hands.
16 For now You number my steps,
   But do not watch over my sin.
17 My transgression is sealed up in a bag,
   And You covers my iniquity.

18 "But as a mountain falls and crumbles away,
   And as a rock is moved from its place;
19 As water wears away stones,
   And as torrents wash away the soil of the
       earth;
   So You destroy the hope of man.
20 You prevail forever against him, and he
       passes on;
   You change his countenance and send him
       away.
21 His sons come to honor, and he does not
       know it;
   They are brought low, and he does not
       perceive it.
22 But his flesh will be in pain over it,
   And his soul will mourn over it."

15 Then* Eliphaz the Temanite answered and
   said:

2 "Should a wise man answer with empty
       knowledge,
   And fill himself with the east wind?
3 Should he reason with unprofitable talk,
   Or by speeches with which he can do no
       good?
4 Yes, you cast off fear,
   And restrain prayer before God.
5 For your iniquity teaches your mouth,
   And you choose the tongue of the crafty.
6 Your own mouth condemns you, and not I;
   Yes, your own lips testify against you.

7 "Are you the first man who was born?
   Or were you made before the hills?
8 Have you heard the counsel of God?
   Do you limit wisdom to yourself?
9 What do you know that we do not know?
   What do you understand that is not in us?

CHAPTER 15

15:1–13 The wise man. Eliphaz thought himself a wise man, so he rebuked Job for his sins. For one thing, Job's words were so much "hot air" and revealed that he had no fear of God. Job claimed to be wise but was really surpassed in that virtue by his three friends, all of whom were older than he. (Is age a guarantee of wisdom?) Most of all, Job had refused the "consolations" God had sent him through his friends (v. 11). If the words of the three men were "gentle," what would their harsh words be like! How difficult it is for us accurately to hear ourselves or see ourselves.

14:17 sLiterally plaster over

15:14–35 The wicked man. Eliphaz painted this picture of Job. All of us are born in sin (vv. 14–16; Rom. 3:9–23), but some sinners are worse than others. Eliphaz described the fate of the wicked: pain, fear, dreadful noises, hunger, poverty, darkness, and then death. Eliphaz did not explain why the ungodly seem to prosper in this world while the godly often suffer. His theology was "cut and dried." He had an answer for everything, but he had no help for Job.

10 Both the gray-haired and the aged *are* among us,
   Much older than your father.
11 *Are* the consolations of God too small for you,
   And the word *spoken gently*[t] with you?
12 Why does your heart carry you away,
   And what do your eyes wink at,
13 That you turn your spirit against God,
   And let *such* words go out of your mouth?

14*"What *is* man, that he could be pure?
   And *he who is* born of a woman, that he could be righteous?
15 If *God* puts no trust in His saints,
   And the heavens are not pure in His sight,
16 How much less man, *who is* abominable and filthy,
   Who drinks iniquity like water!

17 "I will tell you, hear me;
   What I have seen I will declare,
18 What wise men have told,
   Not hiding *anything received* from their fathers,
19 To whom alone the land was given,
   And no alien passed among them:
20 The wicked man writhes with pain all *his* days,
   And the number of years is hidden from the oppressor.
21 Dreadful sounds *are* in his ears;
   In prosperity the destroyer comes upon him.
22 He does not believe that he will return from darkness,
   For a sword is waiting for him.
23 He wanders about for bread, *saying,* 'Where is it?'
   He knows that a day of darkness is ready at his hand.
24 Trouble and anguish make him afraid;
   They overpower him, like a king ready for battle.
25 For he stretches out his hand against God,
   And acts defiantly against the Almighty,
26 Running stubbornly against Him
   With his strong, embossed shield.

27 "Though he has covered his face with his fatness,
   And made *his* waist heavy with fat,
28 He dwells in desolate cities,
   In houses which no one inhabits,
   Which are destined to become ruins.
29 He will not be rich,
   Nor will his wealth continue,
   Nor will his possessions overspread the earth.
30 He will not depart from darkness;
   The flame will dry out his branches,
   And by the breath of His mouth he will go away.
31 Let him not trust in futile *things,* deceiving himself,
   For futility will be his reward.
32 It will be accomplished before his time,
   And his branch will not be green.

15:11 [t]Septuagint reads *a secret thing.*

33 He will shake off his unripe grape like a
     vine,
   And cast off his blossom like an olive tree.
34 For the company of hypocrites *will be*
     barren,
   And fire will consume the tents of bribery.
35 They conceive trouble and bring forth
     futility;
   Their womb prepares deceit."

16

Then* Job answered and said:

2 "I have heard many such things;
   Miserable comforters *are* you all!
3 Shall words of wind have an end?
   Or what provokes you that you answer?
4 I also could speak as you *do,*
   If your soul were in my soul's place.
   I could heap up words against you,
   And shake my head at you;
5 *But* I would strengthen you with my mouth,
   And the comfort of my lips would relieve
     your grief.

6 "Though I speak, my grief is not relieved;
   And *if* I remain silent, how am I eased?
7 But now He has worn me out;
   You have made desolate all my company.
8 You have shriveled me up,
   And it is a witness *against me;*
   My leanness rises up against me
   And bears witness to my face.
9 *He tears *me* in His wrath, and hates me;
   He gnashes at me with His teeth;
   My adversary sharpens His gaze on me.
10 They gape at me with their mouth,
   They strike me reproachfully on the cheek,
   They gather together against me.
11 God has delivered me to the ungodly,
   And turned me over to the hands of the
     wicked.
12 I was at ease, but He has shattered me;
   He also has taken *me* by my neck, and
     shaken me to pieces;
   He has set me up for His target,
13 His archers surround me.
   He pierces my heart*u* and does not pity;
   He pours out my gall on the ground.
14 He breaks me with wound upon wound;
   He runs at me like a warrior.*v*

15 "I have sewn sackcloth over my skin,
   And laid my head*w* in the dust.
16 My face is flushed from weeping,
   And on my eyelids *is* the shadow of death;
17 Although no violence *is* in my hands,
   And my prayer *is* pure.

18 "O earth, do not cover my blood,
   And let my cry have no *resting* place!
19 Surely even now my witness *is* in heaven,
   And my evidence *is* on high.
20 My friends scorn me;
   My eyes pour out *tears* to God.
21 Oh, that one might plead for a man with
     God,
   As a man *pleads* for his neighbor!

CHAPTERS 16—17

16:1–8 *No comfort.* Job's three friends
were indeed "miserable comforters." They
only added to his pain. If the situation were
reversed, Job would have spoken words of
strength and help to them in their suffering.
Their words wore him out and made him
shrivel up, as when a desert wind blows.
Does God use your words to bring new life
to others (Prov. 15:4)?

16:9–22 *No defense.* Job told what God did
to him. God was an adversary against whom
Job had no defense. God permitted the
people in Job's life to gape at him, shoot at
him, and scorn him. Job was in a battle! If
only he had a mediator who could represent
him in heaven and bring justice (vv. 18–22)!
(See Job 9:33.)

16:13 *u*Literally *kidneys*   16:14 *v*Vulgate reads *giant.*
16:15 *w*Literally *horn*

17:1–16 *No hope.* Job had expressed hope that God would vindicate him even after death (14:14), but his hope was almost gone (v. 15; 6:11; 7:6; 14:19). All he saw in his future was a decaying body, death, and the grave (vv. 1, 13). Once again, Job cried out for a representative before God (v. 3), somebody who would put up security for him ("shake hands") and get his case settled. Jesus Christ is Advocate and Mediator for His people and their hope (1 Tim. 1:1). He gave His own blood as security (Heb. 9:12ff.), and those who trust Him always have living hope (1 Pet. 1:3ff.).

22 For when a few years are finished,
     I shall go the way of no return.

17 "My* spirit is broken,
       My days are extinguished,
       The grave *is ready* for me.
2   *Are* not mockers with me?
       And does not my eye dwell on their
          provocation?

3   "Now put down a pledge for me with
        Yourself.
     Who *is he who* will shake hands with me?
4   For You have hidden their heart from
        understanding;
     Therefore You will not exalt *them.*
5   He who speaks flattery to *his* friends,
     Even the eyes of his children will fail.

6   "But He has made me a byword of the people,
     And I have become one in whose face men
        spit.
7   My eye has also grown dim because of
        sorrow,
     And all my members *are* like shadows.
8   Upright *men* are astonished at this,
     And the innocent stirs himself up against
        the hypocrite.
9   Yet the righteous will hold to his way,
     And he who has clean hands will be
        stronger and stronger.

10 "But please, come back again, all of you,ˣ
     For I shall not find *one* wise *man* among
        you.
11   My days are past,
     My purposes are broken off,
     Even the thoughts of my heart.
12   They change the night into day;
     'The light *is* near,' *they say,* in the face of
        darkness.
13   If I wait *for* the grave *as* my house,
     If I make my bed in the darkness,
14   If I say to corruption, 'You *are* my father,'
     And to the worm, 'You *are* my mother and
        my sister,'
15   Where then *is* my hope?
     As for my hope, who can see it?
16   *Will* they go down to the gates of Sheol?
     Shall *we have* rest together in the dust?"

CHAPTER 18

18:1 Since Job brought up the matter of death and the grave, Bildad decided to elaborate on the subject. He painted some vivid pictures of the death of the wicked.

18 Then* Bildad the Shuhite answered and
       said:

2   "How long *till* you put an end to words?
     Gain understanding, and afterward we will
        speak.
3   Why are we counted as beasts,
     And regarded as stupid in your sight?
4   You who tear yourself in anger,
     Shall the earth be forsaken for you?
     Or shall the rock be removed from its place?

18:5, 6 *It is like a light put out.* For the lost sinner, death does indeed mean darkness, but not for those who have faith in Christ (Prov. 4:18). Believers go to heaven where there is no darkness (Rev. 21:25); unbelievers go to hell where there is no light (Matt. 22:13).

5   *"The light of the wicked indeed goes out,
     And the flame of his fire does not shine.
6   The light is dark in his tent,
     And his lamp beside him is put out.

17:10 ˣFollowing some Hebrew manuscripts, Septuagint, Syriac, and Vulgate; Masoretic Text and Targum read *all of them.*

7 *The steps of his strength are shortened,
   And his own counsel casts him down.
8 For he is cast into a net by his own feet,
   And he walks into a snare.
9 The net takes *him* by the heel,
   And a snare lays hold of him.
10 A noose *is* hidden for him on the ground,
   And a trap for him in the road.
11 *Terrors frighten him on every side,
   And drive him to his feet.
12 His strength is starved,
   And destruction *is* ready at his side.
13 It devours patches of his skin;
   The firstborn of death devours his limbs.
14 He is uprooted from the shelter of his tent,
   And they parade him before the king of
   terrors.
15 *They dwell in his tent *who are* none of his;
   Brimstone is scattered on his dwelling.
16 His roots are dried out below,
   And his branch withers above.
17 The memory of him perishes from the earth,
   And he has no name among the renowned.y
18 He is driven from light into darkness,
   And chased out of the world.
19 He has neither son nor posterity among his
   people,
   Nor any remaining in his dwellings.
20 Those in the west are astonished at his day,
   As those in the east are frightened.
21 Surely such *are* the dwellings of the wicked,
   And this *is* the place *of him who* does not
   know God."

19 Then* Job answered and said:

2 "How long will you torment my soul,
   And break me in pieces with words?
3 These ten times you have reproached me;
   You are not ashamed *that* you have
   wronged me.z
4 And if indeed I have erred,
   My error remains with me.
5 *If indeed you exalt *yourselves* against me,
   And plead my disgrace against me,
6 Know then that God has wronged me,
   And has surrounded me with His net.

7 "If I cry out concerning wrong, I am not
   heard.
   If I cry aloud, *there is* no justice.
8 He has fenced up my way, so that I cannot
   pass;
   And He has set darkness in my paths.
9 He has stripped me of my glory,
   And taken the crown *from* my head.
10 He breaks me down on every side,
   And I am gone;
   My hope He has uprooted like a tree.
11 He has also kindled His wrath against me,
   And He counts me as *one of* His enemies.

18:7–10 *It is like an animal trapped.* The
wicked man tries to run away, but the path
is filled with devices to catch him. Bildad
named six different kinds of traps—but it
takes only one. There is no escape when
your time comes.

18:11–14 *It is like a criminal pursued.* As
he tries to escape "the king of terrors," the
criminal runs, falls down, gets weary, and
finally is caught. (See Heb. 9:27.)

18:15–20 *It is like a tree rooted up.* The
tree seemed strong and solid, but the roots
were already dry and death could easily pull
the tree up. People even forget that the tree
was once there!
  This is the death of the wicked, not the
death of the righteous. For those who trust
Jesus Christ, death means "to be absent
from the body and to be present with the
Lord" (2 Cor. 5:1–8). Is that your
confidence?

CHAPTER 19
19:1–4 *Wronged by his comforters.* Their
harsh words tormented him, broke him, and
reproached him. Why should they go on?
After all, it was not *their* sin that God was
punishing, but *his* sin, and they were only
making matters worse.

19:5–12 *Wronged by God.* Why should
one sinner receive so much punishment?
Bildad's description of death (chap. 18) was
Job's description of his life (vv. 7–12)! He
was a "living dead man," and his hope was
gone.

18:17 yLiterally *before the outside,* meaning distinguished,
famous   19:3 zA Jewish tradition reads *make yourselves
strange to me.*

They Had Faith—Job 19:25–27 is one of the great declarations of faith found in the Bible. Other
important statements of faith were made by Ruth (Ruth 1:16–17), Jeremiah (Lam. 3:22–24), the
three Hebrew men (Dan. 3:16–18), Habakkuk (Hab. 3:17–19), a Roman centurion (Matt. 8:5–13), a
Canaanite mother (Matt. 15:21–28), Peter (Matt. 16:13–20), and Paul (Acts 20:24).

19:13–22 *Wronged by his family and friends.* Those closest to him stayed farthest from him, and those who should have shown him respect only mocked him. Job was a lonely man crying out for pity, but nobody answered. Ask God to help you be sensitive to the cries of those who hurt, no matter what others may do.

19:22–27 Job still had faith in God! If he died, he would see God, and one day, he would have a new body from God. This promise gives great confidence to God's people (John 11:25–26; 1 Cor. 15:50–58).

CHAPTER 20

20:1–3 Zophar's speech is an echo of Bildad's (chap. 18) as he describes the fate of the wicked man. The speech did not apply to Job, but it should be taken to heart by self-confident, successful people who leave God out of their lives.

20:4–11 *Success is temporary.* No matter how rich, famous, or secure he may be, the wicked person will eventually perish. Zophar used graphic images: he will go away like refuse (v. 7, human excrement) or like a dream or night vision (v. 8). Here today, gone tomorrow! Ponder James 4:13–17 and 1 John 2:17.

12 His troops come together
    And build up their road against me;
    They encamp all around my tent.

13*"He has removed my brothers far from me,
    And my acquaintances are completely
        estranged from me.
14 My relatives have failed,
    And my close friends have forgotten me.
15 Those who dwell in my house, and my
        maidservants,
    Count me as a stranger;
    I am an alien in their sight.
16 I call my servant, but he gives no answer;
    I beg him with my mouth.
17 My breath is offensive to my wife,
    And I am repulsive to the children of my
        own body.
18 Even young children despise me;
    I arise, and they speak against me.
19 All my close friends abhor me,
    And those whom I love have turned against
        me.
20 My bone clings to my skin and to my flesh,
    And I have escaped by the skin of my teeth.

21 "Have pity on me, have pity on me, O you
        my friends,
    For the hand of God has struck me!
22 *Why do you persecute me as God *does*,
    And are not satisfied with my flesh?

23 "Oh, that my words were written!
    Oh, that they were inscribed in a book!
24 That they were engraved on a rock
    With an iron pen and lead, forever!
25 For I know *that* my Redeemer lives,
    And He shall stand at last on the earth;
26 And after my skin is destroyed, this *I know*,
    That in my flesh I shall see God,
27 Whom I shall see for myself,
    And my eyes shall behold, and not another.
    How my heart yearns within me!
28 If you should say, 'How shall we persecute
        him?'—
    Since the root of the matter is found in me,
29 Be afraid of the sword for yourselves;
    For wrath *brings* the punishment of the
        sword,
    That you may know *there is* a judgment."

20 Then* Zophar the Naamathite answered
    and said:

2 "Therefore my anxious thoughts make me
        answer,
    Because of the turmoil within me.
3 I have heard the rebuke that reproaches me,
    And the spirit of my understanding causes
        me to answer.

4 *"Do you *not* know this of old,
    Since man was placed on earth,
5 That the triumphing of the wicked is short,
    And the joy of the hypocrite is *but* for a
        moment?
6 Though his haughtiness mounts up to the
        heavens,
    And his head reaches to the clouds,
7 *Yet* he will perish forever like his own
        refuse;

Those who have seen him will say, 'Where
is he?'
8 He will fly away like a dream, and not be
found;
Yes, he will be chased away like a vision
of the night.
9 The eye *that* saw him will *see him* no more,
Nor will his place behold him anymore.
10 His children will seek the favor of the poor,
And his hands will restore his wealth.
11 His bones are full of his youthful vigor,
But it will lie down with him in the dust.

12*"Though evil is sweet in his mouth,
And he hides it under his tongue,
13 *Though* he spares it and does not forsake
it,
But still keeps it in his mouth,
14 *Yet* his food in his stomach turns sour;
It becomes cobra venom within him.
15 He swallows down riches
And vomits them up again;
God casts them out of his belly.
16 He will suck the poison of cobras;
The viper's tongue will slay him.
17 He will not see the streams,
The rivers flowing with honey and cream.
18 He will restore that for which he labored,
And will not swallow *it* down;
From the proceeds of business
He will get no enjoyment.
19 For he has oppressed *and* forsaken the poor,
He has violently seized a house which he
did not build.

20*"Because he knows no quietness in his
heart,[a]
He will not save anything he desires.
21 Nothing is left for him to eat;
Therefore his well-being will not last.
22 In his self-sufficiency he will be in distress;
Every hand of misery will come against him.
23 *When* he is about to fill his stomach,
God will cast on him the fury of His wrath,
And will rain *it* on him while he is eating.
24 He will flee from the iron weapon;
A bronze bow will pierce him through.
25 It is drawn, and comes out of the body;
Yes, the glittering *point comes* out of his
gall.
Terrors *come* upon him;
26 Total darkness *is* reserved for his treasures.
An unfanned fire will consume him;
It shall go ill with him who is left in his tent.
27 *The heavens will reveal his iniquity,
And the earth will rise up against him.
28 The increase of his house will depart,
And his goods will flow away in the day of
His wrath.
29 This *is* the portion from God for a wicked
man,
The heritage appointed to him by God."

21 Then* Job answered and said:

2 "Listen carefully to my speech,
And let this be your consolation.
3 Bear with me that I may speak,
And after I have spoken, keep mocking.

20:12–19 *Life is bitter.* Dainty food
becomes poison and wealth makes him sick.
The things he thought he would enjoy only
bring pain to him. Riches without God can
never give anyone true enjoyment (1 Tim.
6:1–10).

20:20–29 *Life is painful.* He has no peace
because everybody has declared war on
him, including God, who rains judgment on
him. Arrows (note 6:4), terrors, darkness,
and fire are his lot, and then—the end.

20:27 Zophar tried to frighten Job into
confessing his sins and "getting right with
God," but his approach did not work. The
fear of God is a legitimate motive for
obedience (Matt. 10:28), but it is not the only
motive and it must be tempered by love
(2 Cor. 5:10–11, 14).

CHAPTER 21

21:1–3 Bildad and Zophar tried to use logic
to silence Job, and their reasoning went like
this: (a) God blesses the righteous but
makes the wicked suffer; (b) Job is suffering;
(c) therefore, Job is wicked. How
reasonable!

20:20 [a]Literally *belly*

21:4–16 But Job questioned their basic premise. He had often seen the wicked enjoying great blessing: long life, many descendants, peace and safety, riches, success, and days filled with joy. Yes, the wicked die, but even their death is often quick and easy (Ps. 73:1–14).

4 *"As for me, *is* my complaint against man?
  And if *it were,* why should I not be
    impatient?
5 Look at me and be astonished;
  Put *your* hand over *your* mouth.
6 Even when I remember I am terrified,
  And trembling takes hold of my flesh.
7 Why do the wicked live *and* become old,
  Yes, become mighty in power?
8 Their descendants are established with
    them in their sight,
  And their offspring before their eyes.
9 Their houses *are* safe from fear,
  Neither *is* the rod of God upon them.
10 Their bull breeds without failure;
   Their cow calves without miscarriage.
11 They send forth their little ones like a flock,
   And their children dance.
12 They sing to the tambourine and harp,
   And rejoice to the sound of the flute.
13 They spend their days in wealth,
   And in a moment go down to the grave.*b*
14 Yet they say to God, 'Depart from us,
   For we do not desire the knowledge of Your
     ways.
15 Who *is* the Almighty, that we should serve
     Him?
   And what profit do we have if we pray to
     Him?'
16 Indeed their prosperity *is* not in their hand;
   The counsel of the wicked is far from me.

17 "How often is the lamp of the wicked put out?
   How often does their destruction come upon
     them,
   The sorrows *God* distributes in His anger?
18 They are like straw before the wind,
   And like chaff that a storm carries away.
19 *They say,* 'God lays up one's*c* iniquity for
     his children';
   Let Him recompense him, that he may know
     it.
20 Let his eyes see his destruction,
   And let him drink of the wrath of the
     Almighty.
21 For what does he care about his household
     after him,
   When the number of his months is cut in
     half?

22 "Can *anyone* teach God knowledge,
   Since He judges those on high?
23 One dies in his full strength,
   Being wholly at ease and secure;
24 His pails*d* are full of milk,
   And the marrow of his bones is moist.
25 Another man dies in the bitterness of his
     soul,
   Never having eaten with pleasure.

21:13 *b*Or *Sheol*   21:19 *c*Literally *his*   21:24 *d*Septuagint and Vulgate read *bowels;* Syriac reads *sides;* Targum reads *breasts.*

It's an Illusion—Now we can better understand why the three friends were so hard on Job: *they were afraid that trials might come to them as they did to Job.* They protected themselves with a false theology that was born in the pit of hell: "If we obey God, He will bless us and protect us from suffering." Job detected their fear (6:21) and refuted their reasoning, which made them angry. The three friends had a very shallow view of God and of faith and life, while Job penetrated the deep things of God. People who trust a false theology are living a life of illusion that one day will vanish.

26 They lie down alike in the dust,
   And worms cover them.

27 *"Look, I know your thoughts,
   And the schemes *with which* you would
      wrong me.
28 For you say,
   'Where *is* the house of the prince?
   And where *is* the tent,^{e}
   The dwelling place of the wicked?'
29 Have you not asked those who travel the
      road?
   And do you not know their signs?
30 For the wicked are reserved for the day of
      doom;
   They shall be brought out on the day of
      wrath.
31 Who condemns his way to his face?
   And who repays him *for what* he has done?
32 Yet he shall be brought to the grave,
   And a vigil kept over the tomb.
33 The clods of the valley shall be sweet to him;
   Everyone shall follow him,
   As countless *have gone* before him.
34 *How then can you comfort me with empty
      words,
   Since falsehood remains in your answers?"

22 Then* Eliphaz the Temanite answered and
   said:

2 *"Can a man be profitable to God,
   Though he who is wise may be profitable
      to himself?
3 *Is it* any pleasure to the Almighty that you
      are righteous?
   Or *is it* gain *to Him* that you make your
      ways blameless?

4 "Is it because of your fear of Him that He
      corrects you,
   And enters into judgment with you?
5 *Is* not your wickedness great,
   And your iniquity without end?
6 For you have taken pledges from your
      brother for no reason,
   And stripped the naked of their clothing.
7 You have not given the weary water to
      drink,
   And you have withheld bread from the
      hungry.
8 But the mighty man possessed the land,
   And the honorable man dwelt in it.
9 You have sent widows away empty,
   And the strength of the fatherless was
      crushed.
10 Therefore snares *are* all around you,
   And sudden fear troubles you,
11 Or darkness *so that* you cannot see;
   And an abundance of water covers you.

21:28 ^{e}Vulgate omits *the tent*.

21:27–33 Job's friends were looking at the *outside* of things and ignoring the heart (John 7:24). The test of godly character is not success but *what people think about God* (vv. 14–15). The ungodly ask, "What will we get out of it if we obey God?" But that is Satan's approach (Job 1:6–11) *and the three friends agreed with him!*

21:34 If comfort and wealth are evidences of holiness, our Lord was not holy, for He had little earthly comfort and wealth, and He died a terrible death on the cross. Perhaps you need to examine your own "logic" and see if you are thinking like God or like the devil (Ps. 1:1; Matt. 16:21–28).

CHAPTER 22

22:1 Satan and Job's friends all agreed that Job was a sinner at heart and that he obeyed God only because God blessed him. The fact that Job still trusted God after losing his children and his wealth should have proved to them that his faith was not "commercial."

22:2–11 Eliphaz then took a new approach, asking whether Job's righteousness *did God any good*. (Compare v. 2 with Job 21:15.) God is just and does what is right; therefore, He is not influenced by man's good deeds. Eliphaz then named sins that Job must have committed (vv. 4–11), sins Job thought God could not see (vv. 12–20), sins God would forgive if Job would only repent (vv. 21–30). It was the same argument in a new dress, and Satan could not have done better.
   Like any loving parent, our heavenly Father delights in the obedience of His children and finds pleasure in their worship, service, and growth. Whether you are rich or poor, healthy or sick, your highest joy ought to be to please Him (Ps. 40:8; John 8:29).

Pleasing God—We please the Lord by living holy lives (Col. 1:10; 1 Thess. 4:1ff.), being devoted fully to Him as soldiers (2 Tim. 2:4), living by faith (Heb. 11:5–6), giving generously (Phil. 4:18), obeying parents (Col. 3:20), and accepting and using our spiritual gifts (1 Cor. 12:18). The Father is well pleased with His Son (Matt. 3:17; 17:5), and when we seek to honor Him, we please the Father. God takes delight in the way of the believer who obeys His will (Ps. 37:23).

12 "Is not God in the height of heaven?
And see the highest stars, how lofty they
are!
13 And you say, 'What does God know?
Can He judge through the deep darkness?
14 Thick clouds cover Him, so that He cannot
see,
And He walks above the circle of heaven.'
15 Will you keep to the old way
Which wicked men have trod,
16 Who were cut down before their time,
Whose foundations were swept away by a
flood?
17 They said to God, 'Depart from us!
What can the Almighty do to them?'ᶠ
18 Yet He filled their houses with good *things;*
But the counsel of the wicked is far from
me.

19 "The righteous see *it* and are glad,
And the innocent laugh at them:
20 'Surely our adversariesᵍ are cut down,
And the fire consumes their remnant.'

21 "Now acquaint yourself with Him, and be at
peace;
Thereby good will come to you.
22 Receive, please, instruction from His mouth,
And lay up His words in your heart.
23 If you return to the Almighty, you will be
built up;
You will remove iniquity far from your
tents.
24 Then you will lay your gold in the dust,
And the *gold* of Ophir among the stones of
the brooks.
25 Yes, the Almighty will be your goldʰ
And your precious silver;
26 For then you will have your delight in the
Almighty,
And lift up your face to God.
27 You will make your prayer to Him,
He will hear you,
And you will pay your vows.
28 You will also declare a thing,
And it will be established for you;
So light will shine on your ways.
29 When they cast *you* down, and you say,
'Exaltation *will come!'*
Then He will save the humble *person.*
30 He will *even* deliver one who is not
innocent;
Yes, he will be delivered by the purity of
your hands."

CHAPTERS 23—24

23:1–9 In the courtroom. Job still wanted
to meet God and get a fair trial, but he did
not know where to find Him. In the end, when
God showed up and asked Job to present
his case, Job was speechless. Why?
Because beholding the majesty of God
made all his arguments useless. He had
seen God, and that was all that mattered!

23

Then* Job answered and said:

2 "Even today my complaint is bitter;
Myⁱ hand is listless because of my groaning.
3 Oh, that I knew where I might find Him,
That I might come to His seat!
4 I would present *my* case before Him,
And fill my mouth with arguments.
5 I would know the words *which* He would
answer me,

22:17 ᶠSeptuagint and Syriac read *us.*   22:20 ᵍSeptuagint
reads *substance.*   22:25 ʰThe ancient versions suggest
defense; Hebrew reads *gold* as in verse 24.   23:2 ⁱFollowing
Masoretic Text, Targum, and Vulgate; Septuagint and Syriac
read *His.*

And understand what He would say to me.
6   Would He contend with me in His great
        power?
     No! But He would take *note* of me.
7   There the upright could reason with Him,
     And I would be delivered forever from my
        Judge.

8   "Look, I go forward, but He is not *there*,
     And backward, but I cannot perceive Him;
9   When He works on the left hand, I cannot
        behold *Him*;
     When He turns to the right hand, I cannot
        see *Him*.
10   *But He knows the way that I take;
     When He has tested me, I shall come forth
        as gold.
11   My foot has held fast to His steps;
     I have kept His way and not turned aside.
12   I have not departed from the commandment
        of His lips;
     I have treasured the words of His mouth
     More than my necessary *food*.

13   "But He *is* unique, and who can make Him
        change?
     And *whatever* His soul desires, *that* He
        does.
14   For He performs *what is* appointed for me,
     And many such *things are* with Him.
15   Therefore I am terrified at His presence;
     When I consider *this*, I am afraid of Him.
16   For God made my heart weak,
     And the Almighty terrifies me;
17   Because I was not cut off from the presence
        of darkness,
     And He did *not* hide deep darkness from
        my face.

24 "*Since** times are not hidden from the
        Almighty,
     Why do those who know Him see not His
        days?

2   "*Some* remove landmarks;
     They seize flocks violently and feed *on*
        them;
3   They drive away the donkey of the
        fatherless;
     They take the widow's ox as a pledge.
4   They push the needy off the road;
     All the poor of the land are forced to hide.
5   Indeed, *like* wild donkeys in the desert,
     They go out to their work, searching for
        food.
     The wilderness *yields* food for them *and* for
        their children.
6   They gather their fodder in the field
     And glean in the vineyard of the wicked.
7   They spend the night naked, without
        clothing,
     And have no covering in the cold.
8   They are wet with the showers of the
        mountains,
     And huddle around the rock for want of
        shelter.

9   "*Some* snatch the fatherless from the breast,
     And take a pledge from the poor.
10   They cause *the poor* to go naked, without
        clothing;

23:10–17 *In the furnace.* The important
thing is not to win an argument with God
but to become more like God. For that to
happen, you often need the furnace of
affliction (1 Pet. 1:6–9), which separates the
dross from the pure gold and leaves you a
better person. You cannot control the
temperature of the furnace or the duration
of the testing time, but you can obey Him
(23:11) and feed on His Word (23:12).

24:1–25 *On the watchtower.* Job again
presented proof that all sinners are not
immediately judged by God. As it were, he
took his friends into the watchtower and
pointed out various kinds of sinners who
seemed to be getting away with their evil
deeds. Job did not deny the fact of God's
judgment (vv. 22–24), but he did affirm that
man could not fully explain how He worked.
    When there are more questions in your
life than answers, and when the furnace is
hot, remember Abraham's great statement
of faith: "Shall not the Judge of all the earth
do right?" (Gen. 18:25; see also 2 Tim. 4:8).

And they take away the sheaves from the
  hungry.
11 They press out oil within their walls,
  And tread winepresses, yet suffer thirst.
12 The dying groan in the city,
  And the souls of the wounded cry out;
  Yet God does not charge *them* with wrong.

13 "There are those who rebel against the light;
  They do not know its ways
  Nor abide in its paths.
14 The murderer rises with the light;
  He kills the poor and needy;
  And in the night he is like a thief.
15 The eye of the adulterer waits for the
  twilight,
  Saying, 'No eye will see me';
  And he disguises *his* face.
16 In the dark they break into houses
  Which they marked for themselves in the
  daytime;
  They do not know the light.
17 For the morning is the same to them as the
  shadow of death;
  If *someone* recognizes *them,*
  They are in the terrors of the shadow of
  death.

18 "They *should be* swift on the face of the
  waters,
  Their portion *should be* cursed in the earth,
  So that no *one would* turn into the way of
  their vineyards.
19 As drought and heat consume the snow
  waters,
  So the grave[j] *consumes those who* have
  sinned.
20 The womb *should* forget him,
  The worm *should* feed sweetly on him;
  He *should* be remembered no more,
  And wickedness *should* be broken like a
  tree.
21 For he preys on the barren *who* do not bear,
  And does no good for the widow.

22 "But *God* draws the mighty away with His
  power;
  He rises up, but no *man* is sure of life.
23 He gives them security, and they rely *on it;*
  Yet His eyes *are* on their ways.
24 They are exalted for a little while,
  Then they are gone.
  They are brought low;
  They are taken out of the way like all *others;*
  They dry out like the heads of grain.

25 "Now if *it is* not *so,* who will prove me a
  liar,
  And make my speech worth nothing?"

CHAPTERS 25—26

25:1–6 Bildad's brief speech (the shortest
in the book) emphasized the greatness of
God (25:1–3) and the nothingness of man
(25:4–6). God finds no righteousness in any
part of His creation, including the angels,
so how could He find it in Job? Again, Bildad
was trying to get Job to confess, but he
failed. It is too bad Bildad did not encourage
Job with the other attributes of God, such
as His love, mercy, and grace.

25
Then* Bildad the Shuhite answered and
said:

2 "Dominion and fear *belong* to Him;
  He makes peace in His high places.
3 Is there any number to His armies?
  Upon whom does His light not rise?

24:19 *j* Or *Sheol*

4   How then can man be righteous before God?
     Or how can he be pure *who is* born of a
         woman?
5   If even the moon does not shine,
     And the stars are not pure in His sight,
6   How much less man, *who is* a maggot,
     And a son of man, *who is* a worm?"

26 But* Job answered and said:

2   "How have you helped *him who is* without
         power?
     How have you saved the arm *that has* no
         strength?
3   How have you counseled *one who has* no
         wisdom?
     And *how* have you declared sound advice
         to many?
4   To whom have you uttered words?
     And whose spirit came from you?

5   *"The dead tremble,
     Those under the waters and those
         inhabiting them.
6   Sheol *is* naked before Him,
     And Destruction has no covering.
7   He stretches out the north over empty space;
     He hangs the earth on nothing.
8   He binds up the water in His thick clouds,
     Yet the clouds are not broken under it.
9   He covers the face of *His* throne,
     And spreads His cloud over it.
10   He drew a circular horizon on the face of
         the waters,
     At the boundary of light and darkness.
11   The pillars of heaven tremble,
     And are astonished at His rebuke.
12   He stirs up the sea with His power,
     And by His understanding He breaks up the
         storm.
13   By His Spirit He adorned the heavens;
     His hand pierced the fleeing serpent.
14   Indeed these *are* the mere edges of His
         ways,
     And how small a whisper we hear of Him!
     But the thunder of His power who can
         understand?"

27 Moreover* Job continued his discourse, and
     said:

2   "As God lives, *who* has taken away my
         justice,
     And the Almighty, *who* has made my soul
         bitter,
3   As long as my breath *is* in me,
     And the breath of God in my nostrils,
4   My lips will not speak wickedness,
     Nor my tongue utter deceit.
5   Far be it from me
     That I should say you are right;
     Till I die I will not put away my integrity
         from me.
6   My righteousness I hold fast, and will not
         let it go;
     My heart shall not reproach *me* as long as
         I live.
7   "May my enemy be like the wicked,
     And he who rises up against me like the
         unrighteous.

26:1ff Job's reply (chaps. 26—31) is almost like the "summing up" argument of an attorney. In 26:1–4, he rebuked Bildad for giving him no help at all. These verses suggest ways by which we can help others today, so let us not fail as Bildad did. Your words can bring help and hope to people who desperately need them.

26:5–14 Nobody can escape the eye of God, not even the dead (26:5–6). No matter where you are in creation, He sees you: in the heavens (26:7–9, 13), on the earth (26:10–11), and on the seas (26:12). But the voice of God in creation is only a whisper and we see only the "fringes" of His ways (26:14). Creation clearly reveals the power and wisdom of God, but the grace and mercy of God are seen but dimly.

As you try to help others, keep in mind that "we know in part" (1 Cor. 13:9). It will keep you humble and make you more useful.

CHAPTERS 27—28

27:1–23 Justice. Job still wanted to take God to court and get his case settled. He was bitter (v. 2; 3:20) because God would not solve his problems *on his terms*. Trials can make you bitter or better, depending on how you relate to God. If you see Him as an unkind Judge, you will be bitter; if you see Him as a loving Father, you will be better.

Job was right in holding to his integrity (2:9–10). His friends urged him to admit his sins, even if he had not committed them, because that would gain him the favor of God. (Satan's philosophy again!) Job described the judgment of the wicked man, but he did not say that he qualified.

❝*Knowledge is proud that he has learned so much; wisdom is humble that he knows no more.*❞

—William Cowper

8   For what is the hope of the hypocrite,
    Though he may gain *much*,
    If God takes away his life?
9   Will God hear his cry
    When trouble comes upon him?
10 Will he delight himself in the Almighty?
    Will he always call on God?

11 "I will teach you about the hand of God;
    What *is* with the Almighty I will not conceal.
12 Surely all of you have seen *it*;
    Why then do you behave with complete
    nonsense?

13 "This is the portion of a wicked man with
        God,
    And the heritage of oppressors, received
        from the Almighty:
14 If his children are multiplied, *it is* for the
        sword;
    And his offspring shall not be satisfied with
        bread.
15 Those who survive him shall be buried in
        death,
    And their[k] widows shall not weep,
16 Though he heaps up silver like dust,
    And piles up clothing like clay—
17 He may pile *it* up, but the just will wear *it*,
    And the innocent will divide the silver.
18 He builds his house like a moth,[l]
    Like a booth *which* a watchman makes.
19 The rich man will lie down,
    But not be gathered *up*;[m]
    He opens his eyes,
    And he *is* no more.
20 Terrors overtake him like a flood;
    A tempest steals him away in the night.
21 The east wind carries him away, and he is
        gone;
    It sweeps him out of his place.
22 It hurls against him and does not spare;
    He flees desperately from its power.
23 *Men* shall clap their hands at him,
    And shall hiss him out of his place.

28:1–26 Wisdom. "Where is wisdom found?" is Job's key question (vv. 12, 20). Does it have to be mined like silver and gold (Prov. 2:1–9)? In one sense, yes, for wisdom is not found on the surface of things. You must dig into the Word of God and into life if you would have the wisdom of God (Prov. 8:10–11). True wisdom begins with the fear of the Lord (v. 28; Prov. 1:7; 9:10; 15:33; 19:23). When we reverence Him and seek to please Him, He teaches us His wisdom and His way (Isa. 33:6; James 1:5).

28

1   "Surely* there is a mine for silver,
    And a place *where* gold is refined.
2   Iron is taken from the earth,
    And copper *is* smelted *from* ore.
3   *Man* puts an end to darkness,
    And searches every recess
    For ore in the darkness and the shadow of
        death.
4   He breaks open a shaft away from people;
    In places forgotten by feet
    They hang far away from men;
    They swing to and fro.
5   *As for* the earth, from it comes bread,
    But underneath it is turned up as by fire;
6   Its stones *are* the source of sapphires,
    And it contains gold dust.
7   *That* path no bird knows,
    Nor has the falcon's eye seen it.

27:15 [k]Literally *his*   27:18 [l]Following Masoretic Text and Vulgate; Septuagint and Syriac read *spider* (compare 8:14); Targum reads *decay*.   27:19 [m]Following Masoretic Text and Targum; Septuagint and Syriac read *But shall not add* (that is, do it again); Vulgate reads *But take away nothing*.

8   The proud lions[n] have not trodden it,
     Nor has the fierce lion passed over it.
9   He puts his hand on the flint;
     He overturns the mountains at the roots.
10 He cuts out channels in the rocks,
     And his eye sees every precious thing.
11 He dams up the streams from trickling;
     What is hidden he brings forth to light.

12 "But where can wisdom be found?
     And where *is* the place of understanding?
13 Man does not know its value,
     Nor is it found in the land of the living.
14 The deep says, '*It is* not in me';
     And the sea says, '*It is* not with me.'
15 It cannot be purchased for gold,
     Nor can silver be weighed *for* its price.
16 It cannot be valued in the gold of Ophir,
     In precious onyx or sapphire.
17 Neither gold nor crystal can equal it,
     Nor can it be exchanged for jewelry of fine
       gold.
18 No mention shall be made of coral or quartz,
     For the price of wisdom *is* above rubies.
19 The topaz of Ethiopia cannot equal it,
     Nor can it be valued in pure gold.

20 "From where then does wisdom come?
     And where *is* the place of understanding?
21 It is hidden from the eyes of all living,
     And concealed from the birds of the air.
22 Destruction and Death say,
     'We have heard a report about it with our
       ears.'
23 God understands its way,
     And He knows its place.
24 For He looks to the ends of the earth,
     And sees under the whole heavens,
25 To establish a weight for the wind,
     And apportion the waters by measure.
26 When He made a law for the rain,
     And a path for the thunderbolt,
27 Then He saw *wisdom*[o] and declared it;
     He prepared it, indeed, He searched it out.
28 And to man He said,
     'Behold, the fear of the Lord, that *is* wisdom,
     And to depart from evil *is* understanding.'"

29 Job* further continued his discourse, and
       said:

2   "Oh, that I were as *in* months past,
     As *in* the days *when* God watched over me;
3   When His lamp shone upon my head,
     And when by His light I walked *through*
       darkness;
4   Just as I was in the days of my prime,
     When the friendly counsel of God *was* over
       my tent;
5   When the Almighty *was* yet with me,
     When my children *were* around me;
6   When my steps were bathed with cream,[p]
     And the rock poured out rivers of oil for
       me!

28:8 [n]Literally *sons of pride*, figurative of the great lions
28:27 [o]Literally *it*   29:6 [p]Masoretic Text reads *wrath;* ancient
versions and some Hebrew manuscripts read *cream* (compare
20:17).

CHAPTERS 29—30

29:1ff *Longing for the past.* When life is
difficult, it is normal to look back to "the good
old days" and want to turn back the clock.
But that approach is selfish (note how many
times Job says "I" and "my") and only adds
to your pain. It makes enjoying happiness
more important than experiencing holiness.
Job listed some of the blessings he had
enjoyed and some of the services he had
performed for others, and all of that should
have prepared him to face his trials with
confidence.

The past must be more than a memory;
it must be a ministry. Today will soon be a
yesterday. Are you using today to grow in
the Lord so you are prepared for tomorrow?
Is life an investment or just an enjoyment?

7   "When I went out to the gate by the city,
    When I took my seat in the open square,
8   The young men saw me and hid,
    And the aged arose *and* stood;
9   The princes refrained from talking,
    And put *their* hand on their mouth;
10 The voice of nobles was hushed,
    And their tongue stuck to the roof of their
        mouth.
11 When the ear heard, then it blessed me,
    And when the eye saw, then it approved
        me;
12 Because I delivered the poor who cried out,
    The fatherless and *the one who* had no
        helper.
13 The blessing of a perishing *man* came upon
        me,
    And I caused the widow's heart to sing for
        joy.
14 I put on righteousness, and it clothed me;
    My justice *was* like a robe and a turban.
15 I *was* eyes to the blind,
    And I *was* feet to the lame.
16 I *was* a father to the poor,
    And I searched out the case *that* I did not
        know.
17 I broke the fangs of the wicked,
    And plucked the victim from his teeth.

18 "Then I said, 'I shall die in my nest,
    And multiply *my* days as the sand.
19 My root *is* spread out to the waters,
    And the dew lies all night on my branch.
20 My glory *is* fresh within me,
    And my bow is renewed in my hand.'

21 "*Men* listened to me and waited,
    And kept silence for my counsel.
22 After my words they did not speak again,
    And my speech settled on them *as dew*.
23 They waited for me *as* for the rain,
    And they opened their mouth wide *as* for
        the spring rain.
24 *If* I mocked at them, they did not believe
        it,
    And the light of my countenance they did
        not cast down.
25 I chose the way for them, and sat as chief;
    So I dwelt as a king in the army,
    As one *who* comforts mourners.

30 "But* now they mock at me, *men* younger
        than I,
    Whose fathers I disdained to put with the
        dogs of my flock.
2   Indeed, of what *profit* is the strength of their
        hands to me?
    Their vigor has perished.
3   *They are* gaunt from want and famine,
    Fleeing late to the wilderness, desolate and
        waste,
4   Who pluck mallow by the bushes,
    And broom tree roots *for* their food.
5   They were driven out from among *men*,
    They shouted at them as *at* a thief.
6   *They had* to live in the clefts of the valleys,
    In caves of the earth and the rocks.
7   Among the bushes they brayed,
    Under the nettles they nestled.
8   *They were* sons of fools,
    Yes, sons of vile men;
    They were scourged from the land.

30:1ff *Lamenting the present*. "But now,"
says Job (vv. 1, 16), and he launches into
his complaint about his sufferings. His
friends mock him (vv. 1–15), his body hurts
him (vv. 16–19), his God has deserted him
(vv. 20–23), and his hope has fled from him
(vv. 24–31). He cannot return to the past,
endure the present, or face the future!
Whenever your circumstances lead you
to join Job in the "dust and ashes" (v. 19),
remember that the Lord Jesus once was
there (Ps. 22:15) and knows how you feel.
He is adequate for your yesterdays and
tomorrows as well as your todays (Heb.
13:8). Do not just remember your past
enjoyments; also remember God's past
mercies (Ps. 77:1–12), and trust Him for the
future.

❝*The good old days are often a
combination of a bad memory and
a good imagination.*❞

9 "And now I am their taunting song;
   Yes, I am their byword.
10 They abhor me, they keep far from me;
   They do not hesitate to spit in my face.
11 Because He has loosed my[q] bowstring and
      afflicted me,
   They have cast off restraint before me.
12 At *my* right *hand* the rabble arises;
   They push away my feet,
   And they raise against me their ways of
      destruction.
13 They break up my path,
   They promote my calamity;
   They have no helper.
14 They come as broad breakers;
   Under the ruinous storm they roll along.
15 Terrors are turned upon me;
   They pursue my honor as the wind,
   And my prosperity has passed like a cloud.

16 "And now my soul is poured out because of
      my *plight;*
   The days of affliction take hold of me.
17 My bones are pierced in me at night,
   And my gnawing pains take no rest.
18 By great force my garment is disfigured;
   It binds me about as the collar of my coat.
19 He has cast me into the mire,
   And I have become like dust and ashes.

20 "I cry out to You, but You do not answer
      me;
   I stand up, and You regard me.
21 *But* You have become cruel to me;
   With the strength of Your hand You oppose
      me.
22 You lift me up to the wind and cause me to
      ride *on it;*
   You spoil my success.
23 For I know *that* You will bring me *to* death,
   And *to* the house appointed for all living.

24 "Surely He would not stretch out *His* hand
      against a heap of ruins,
   If they cry out when He destroys *it.*
25 Have I not wept for him who was in trouble?
   Has *not* my soul grieved for the poor?
26 But when I looked for good, evil came *to*
      me;
   And when I waited for light, then came
      darkness.
27 My heart is in turmoil and cannot rest;
   Days of affliction confront me.
28 I go about mourning, but not in the sun;
   I stand up in the assembly *and* cry out for
      help.
29 I am a brother of jackals,
   And a companion of ostriches.
30 My skin grows black and falls from me;
   My bones burn with fever.
31 My harp is *turned* to mourning,
   And my flute to the voice of those who weep.

31 "I* have made a covenant with my eyes;
   Why then should I look upon a young
      woman?
2 For what *is* the allotment of God from
      above,

30:11 [q]Following Masoretic Text, Syriac, and Targum;
Septuagint and Vulgate read *His.*

CHAPTER 31

31:1ff As he concluded his final defense,
Job named specific sins and denied that he
had committed them. He knew that God
watched him (v. 4) and weighed him (v. 6),
and he was not afraid to speak. He wanted
more than anything else for God to speak
and either accuse him or defend him (v. 35).

This chapter helps you take inventory of
your spiritual life. Do you have eyes that
wander lustfully (vv. 1–4) or feet that move
deceitfully (vv. 5–8)? Has lust been fulfilled
in overt sin (vv. 9–12)? Have you treated
others as God wants them treated (vv. 13–
23)? Have you coveted wealth or been
proud of what you possess (vv. 24–28)?
How do you respond to the suffering of an
enemy (vv. 29–30) or the needs of a
stranger (vv. 31–34)? Are you a faithful
steward of the natural resources God gives
(vv. 38–40)?

Job has seen himself and is satisfied, but
he has not yet seen God. When he does,
he will change his opinion of himself and
get started on the road to victory.

And the inheritance of the Almighty from
   on high?
3 *Is* it not destruction for the wicked,
   And disaster for the workers of iniquity?
4 Does He not see my ways,
   And count all my steps?

5 "If I have walked with falsehood,
   Or if my foot has hastened to deceit,
6 Let me be weighed on honest scales,
   That God may know my integrity.
7 If my step has turned from the way,
   Or my heart walked after my eyes,
   Or if any spot adheres to my hands,
8 *Then* let me sow, and another eat;
   Yes, let my harvest be rooted out.

9 "If my heart has been enticed by a woman,
   Or *if* I have lurked at my neighbor's door,
10 *Then* let my wife grind for another,
   And let others bow down over her.
11 For that *would be* wickedness;
   Yes, it *would be* iniquity *deserving of*
    judgment.
12 For that *would be* a fire *that* consumes to
    destruction,
   And would root out all my increase.

13 "If I have despised the cause of my male or
    female servant
   When they complained against me,
14 What then shall I do when God rises up?
   When He punishes, how shall I answer
    Him?
15 Did not He who made me in the womb make
    them?
   Did not the same One fashion us in the
    womb?

16 "If I have kept the poor from *their* desire,
   Or caused the eyes of the widow to fail,
17 Or eaten my morsel by myself,
   So that the fatherless could not eat of it
18 (But from my youth I reared him as a father,
   And from my mother's womb I guided *the*
    widow*ʳ*);
19 If I have seen anyone perish for lack of
    clothing,
   Or any poor *man* without covering;
20 If his heart*ˢ* has not blessed me,
   And *if* he was *not* warmed with the fleece
    of my sheep;
21 If I have raised my hand against the
    fatherless,
   When I saw I had help in the gate;
22 *Then* let my arm fall from my shoulder,
   Let my arm be torn from the socket.
23 For destruction *from* God *is* a terror to me,
   And because of His magnificence I cannot
    endure.

24 "If I have made gold my hope,
   Or said to fine gold, '*You are* my
    confidence';
25 If I have rejoiced because my wealth *was*
    great,
   And because my hand had gained much;
26 If I have observed the sun*ᵗ* when it shines,
   Or the moon moving *in* brightness,

31:18 ʳLiterally *her* (compare verse 16) 31:20 ˢLiterally *loins*
31:26 ᵗLiterally *light*

27 So that my heart has been secretly enticed,
   And my mouth has kissed my hand;
28 This also *would be* an iniquity *deserving of*
      judgment,
   For I would have denied God *who is* above.

29 "If I have rejoiced at the destruction of him
      who hated me,
   Or lifted myself up when evil found him
30 (Indeed I have not allowed my mouth to sin
   By asking for a curse on his soul);
31 If the men of my tent have not said,
   'Who is there that has not been satisfied with
      his meat?'
32 (*But* no sojourner had to lodge in the street,
   For I have opened my doors to the
      traveler*u*);
33 If I have covered my transgressions as
      Adam,
   By hiding my iniquity in my bosom,
34 Because I feared the great multitude,
   And dreaded the contempt of families,
   So that I kept silence
   And did not go out of the door—
35 Oh, that I had one to hear me!
   Here is my mark.
   Oh, that the Almighty would answer me,
   That my Prosecutor had written a book!
36 Surely I would carry it on my shoulder,
   And bind it on me *like* a crown;
37 I would declare to Him the number of my
      steps;
   Like a prince I would approach Him.

38 "If my land cries out against me,
   And its furrows weep together;
39 If I have eaten its fruit*v* without money,
   Or caused its owners to lose their lives;
40 *Then* let thistles grow instead of wheat,
   And weeds instead of barley."

The words of Job are ended.

32 So* these three men ceased answering Job,
because he *was* righteous in his own eyes.
²Then the wrath of Elihu, the son of Barachel the
Buzite, of the family of Ram, was aroused against
Job; his wrath was aroused because he justified
himself rather than God. ³Also against his three
friends his wrath was aroused, because they had
found no answer, and yet had condemned Job.
    ⁴Now because they *were* years older than he,
Elihu had waited to speak to Job.*w* ⁵When Elihu
saw that *there was* no answer in the mouth of
these three men, his wrath was aroused.
    ⁶*So Elihu, the son of Barachel the Buzite, an-
swered and said:

    "I *am* young in years, and you *are* very old;
    Therefore I was afraid,
    And dared not declare my opinion to you.
7 I said, 'Age*x* should speak,
    And multitude of years should teach
       wisdom.'

CHAPTERS 32—33

32:1–5 Anger. Elihu was polite in his
waiting and kind in his speaking, but he was
an angry young man (32:1–5). He was angry
with Job for accusing God and with the three
friends for failing to convince Job of his sins.
Elihu agreed with their view that Job was a
sinner, but he disagreed with their
arguments. We must beware when our
speech is motivated by self-righteous anger.

32:6–17 Pride. As the youngest man in the
group, Elihu knew his place, but he was still
quite sure of himself. The discussion needed
his opinion (32:6, 10, 17) because
everybody else was wrong. He was bursting
with words (32:18–20) and could not hold
them in. That is the time to ask God for self-
control and wisdom, lest your words do more
harm than good.

31:32 *u*Following Septuagint, Syriac, Targum, and Vulgate;
Masoretic Text reads *road*.   31:39 *v*Literally *its strength*
32:4 *w*Vulgate reads *till Job had spoken.*   32:7 *x*Literally *Days,*
that is, years

8 But *there is* a spirit in man,
And the breath of the Almighty gives him
understanding.
9 Great men[y] are not *always* wise,
Nor do the aged *always* understand justice.

10 "Therefore I say, 'Listen to me,
I also will declare my opinion.'
11 Indeed I waited for your words,
I listened to your reasonings, while you
searched out what to say.
12 I paid close attention to you;
And surely not one of you convinced Job,
Or answered his words—
13 Lest you say,
'We have found wisdom';
God will vanquish him, not man.
14 Now he has not directed *his* words against
me;
So I will not answer him with your words.

15 "They are dismayed and answer no more;
Words escape them.
16 And I have waited, because they did not
speak,
Because they stood still *and* answered no
more.
17 I also will answer my part,
I too will declare my opinion.
18 For I am full of words;
The spirit within me compels me.
19 Indeed my belly *is* like wine *that* has no
vent;
It is ready to burst like new wineskins.
20 I will speak, that I may find relief;
I must open my lips and answer.
21 Let me not, I pray, show partiality to
anyone;
Nor let me flatter any man.
22 For I do not know how to flatter,
Else my Maker would soon take me away.

33:1–8 *Knowledge.* Elihu was sure he was right and challenged Job to refute him (33:1–8). He had not yet learned that Job needed understanding and love and not accusations and arguments. Like the three friends, Elihu had a great many facts in his mind but very little truth in his heart.

33:9–33 He quoted Job's own words (33:9–11) and explained that God owed him no explanation of what He was doing (33:13). God may speak in dreams (33:14–18), in trials (33:19–30), and through people (33:31–33). God had used all three in Job's life, and Job had rejected them! No wonder Job was miserable!
God may indeed teach us valuable lessons at night, in times of pain. Are we listening?

33

"But* please, Job, hear my speech,
And listen to all my words.
2 Now, I open my mouth;
My tongue speaks in my mouth.
3 My words *come* from my upright heart;
My lips utter pure knowledge.
4 The Spirit of God has made me,
And the breath of the Almighty gives me
life.
5 If you can answer me,
Set *your words* in order before me;
Take your stand.
6 Truly I *am* as your spokesman[z] before God;
I also have been formed out of clay.
7 Surely no fear of me will terrify you,
Nor will my hand be heavy on you.

8 "Surely you have spoken in my hearing,
And I have heard the sound of *your* words,
saying,
9 *'I *am* pure, without transgression;
I *am* innocent, and *there is* no iniquity in
me.
10 Yet He finds occasions against me,
He counts me as His enemy;
11 He puts my feet in the stocks,
He watches all my paths.'

32:9 [y]Or *Men of many years*   33:6 [z]Literally *as your mouth*

12 "Look, *in* this you are not righteous.
   I will answer you,
      For God is greater than man.
13 Why do you contend with Him?
   For He does not give an accounting of any
      of His words.
14 For God may speak in one way, or in
      another,
   Yet man does not perceive it.
15 In a dream, in a vision of the night,
   When deep sleep falls upon men,
   While slumbering on their beds,
16 Then He opens the ears of men,
   And seals their instruction.
17 In order to turn man *from his* deed,
   And conceal pride from man,
18 He keeps back his soul from the Pit,
   And his life from perishing by the sword.

19 "*Man* is also chastened with pain on his bed,
   And with strong *pain* in many of his bones,
20 So that his life abhors bread,
   And his soul succulent food.
21 His flesh wastes away from sight,
   And his bones stick out *which once* were
      not seen.
22 Yes, his soul draws near the Pit,
   And his life to the executioners.

23 "If there is a messenger for him,
   A mediator, one among a thousand,
   To show man His uprightness,
24 Then He is gracious to him, and says,
   'Deliver him from going down to the Pit;
   I have found a ransom';
25 His flesh shall be young like a child's,
   He shall return to the days of his youth.
26 He shall pray to God, and He will delight
      in him,
   He shall see His face with joy,
   For He restores to man His righteousness.
27 Then he looks at men and says,
   'I have sinned, and perverted *what was*
      right,
   And it did not profit me.'
28 He will redeem his[a] soul from going down
      to the Pit,
   And his[b] life shall see the light.

29 "Behold, God works all these *things,*
   Twice, *in fact,* three *times* with a man,
30 To bring back his soul from the Pit,
   That he may be enlightened with the light
      of life.

31 "Give ear, Job, listen to me;
   Hold your peace, and I will speak.
32 If you have anything to say, answer me;
   Speak, for I desire to justify you.
33 If not, listen to me;
   Hold your peace, and I will teach you
      wisdom."

34

Elihu* further answered and said:

2 "Hear my words, you wise *men;*
   Give ear to me, you who have knowledge.
3 For the ear tests words
   As the palate tastes food.

33:28 [a]Or *my* (Kethib) [b]Or *my* (Kethib)

CHAPTERS 34—35

34:1–30 God is just. Elihu must have been a good listener because he was able to quote Job's words. However, Elihu listened with his ears and not with his heart, which made his speeches harsh and unkind. He was too sure of himself and kept reminding Job and his friends to listen to him (vv. 2, 10, 16, 34). Were their minds wandering?

4   Let us choose justice for ourselves;
     Let us know among ourselves what *is* good.

5   "For Job has said, 'I am righteous,
     But God has taken away my justice;
6   Should I lie concerning my right?
     My wound *is* incurable, *though I am* without
       transgression.'
7   What man *is* like Job,
     Who drinks scorn like water,
8   Who goes in company with the workers of
       iniquity,
     And walks with wicked men?
9   For he has said, 'It profits a man nothing
     That he should delight in God.'

10   "Therefore listen to me, you men of
      understanding:
     Far be it from God *to do* wickedness,
     And *from* the Almighty to *commit* iniquity.
11   For He repays man *according to* his work,
     And makes man to find a reward according
      to *his* way.
12   Surely God will never do wickedly,
     Nor will the Almighty pervert justice.
13   Who gave Him charge over the earth?
     Or who appointed *Him over* the whole
      world?
14   If He should set His heart on it,
     If He should gather to Himself His Spirit and
      His breath,
15   All flesh would perish together,
     And man would return to dust.

16   "If *you have* understanding, hear this;
     Listen to the sound of my words:
17   Should one who hates justice govern?
     Will you condemn *Him who is* most just?
18   *Is it fitting* to say to a king, '*You are*
      worthless,'
     And to nobles, '*You are* wicked'?
19   Yet He is not partial to princes,
     Nor does He regard the rich more than the
      poor;
     For they *are* all the work of His hands.
20   In a moment they die, in the middle of the
      night;
     The people are shaken and pass away;
     The mighty are taken away without a hand.

21   "For His eyes *are* on the ways of man,
     And He sees all his steps.
22   There is no darkness nor shadow of death
     Where the workers of iniquity may hide
      themselves.
23   For He need not further consider a man,
     That he should go before God in judgment.
24   He breaks in pieces mighty men without
      inquiry,
     And sets others in their place.
25   Therefore He knows their works;
     He overthrows *them* in the night,
     And they are crushed.
26   He strikes them as wicked *men*
     In the open sight of others,
27   Because they turned back from Him,
     And would not consider any of His ways,
28   So that they caused the cry of the poor to
      come to Him;
     For He hears the cry of the afflicted.
29   When He gives quietness, who then can
     make trouble?

And when He hides *His* face, who then can
    see Him,
Whether *it is* against a nation or a man
    alone?—
30 That the hypocrite should not reign,
    Lest the people be ensnared.

31*"For has *anyone* said to God,
    'I have borne *chastening;*
    I will offend no more;
32 Teach me *what* I do not see;
    If I have done iniquity, I will do no more'?
33 Should He repay *it* according to your *terms,*
    Just because you disavow it?
    You must choose, and not I;
    Therefore speak what you know.

34 "Men of understanding say to me,
    Wise men who listen to me:
35 'Job speaks without knowledge,
    His words *are* without wisdom.'
36 Oh, that Job were tried to the utmost,
    Because *his* answers *are like* those of
        wicked men!
37 For he adds rebellion to his sin;
    He claps *his hands* among us,
    And multiplies his words against God."

35 Moreover* Elihu answered and said:

2 "Do you think this is right?
    Do you say,
    'My righteousness is more than God's'?
3 For you say,
    'What advantage will it be to You?
    What profit shall I have, more than *if* I had
        sinned?'

4 "I will answer you,
    And your companions with you.
5 Look to the heavens and see;
    And behold the clouds—
    They are higher than you.
6 If you sin, what do you accomplish against
        Him?
    Or, *if* your transgressions are multiplied,
        what do you do to Him?
7 If you are righteous, what do you give Him?
    Or what does He receive from your hand?
8 Your wickedness affects a man such as you,
    And your righteousness a son of man.

9 "Because of the multitude of oppressions
        they cry out;
    They cry out for help because of the arm
        of the mighty.
10 *But no one says, 'Where *is* God my Maker,
    Who gives songs in the night,
11 Who teaches us more than the beasts of the
        earth,
    And makes us wiser than the birds of
        heaven?'
12 There they cry out, but He does not answer,
    Because of the pride of evil men.
13 Surely God will not listen to empty *talk,*
    Nor will the Almighty regard it.
14 Although you say you do not see Him,
    Yet justice *is* before Him, and you must wait
        for Him.
15 And now, because He has not punished in
        His anger,
    Nor taken much notice of folly,

34:31–37 It was the same old argument:
God is just and therefore cannot be accused
of sin or partiality. God sees all we do and
judges sin righteously. Job has rebelled
against God and ought to confess and get
right with God!

35:1ff *God is great.* How important did Job
think he was in God's sight? Can his sin or
his righteousness affect God? That was only
pride on Job's part (vv. 12–13). But Job *was*
important to God, so much so that God and
Satan had a discussion in heaven about him!

35:10 The greatness of God does not mean
that He is far from us and unconcerned
about us. He is great in His love (Eph. 2:4),
mercy (Ps. 86:13), and kindness (Ps. 117:2).
He may not immediately take away your
trials, but He can give you a song in the
night (v. 10; Ps. 42:8; 77:6; 119:62).

❝*Any man can sing in the
day. . . . It is easy to sing when
we can read the notes by daylight;
but he is the skillful singer who can
sing when there is not a ray of light
by which to read. . . . Songs in the
night come only from God; they are
not in the power of man.*❞

—Charles Haddon Spurgeon

16 Therefore Job opens his mouth in vain;
   He multiplies words without knowledge."

CHAPTERS 36—37

36:1ff Elihu criticized Job for questioning
God, but he did not judge himself for
speaking "on God's behalf." What pride that
any man should claim to have "perfect
knowledge" and be able to serve as God's
spokesman and defender! The apostle Paul
had been to heaven and back, and had
learned great mysteries, yet he never made
claims like that (Rom. 11:33–36). No matter
how smart you think you are, you never
know enough to "play God" in somebody's
life.

36:5–21 *"Behold, God is mighty"* in power
and understanding. He blesses the obedient
but judges the ungodly and the hypocrite.
(We have heard that someplace before.)

36 Elihu* also proceeded and said:

2 "Bear with me a little, and I will show you
   That *there are* yet words to speak on God's
   behalf.
3 I will fetch my knowledge from afar;
   I will ascribe righteousness to my Maker.
4 For truly my words *are* not false;
   One who is perfect in knowledge *is* with
   you.

5 *"Behold, God *is* mighty, but despises *no one;*
   He *is* mighty in strength of understanding.
6 He does not preserve the life of the wicked,
   But gives justice to the oppressed.
7 He does not withdraw His eyes from the
   righteous;
   But *they are* on the throne with kings,
   For He has seated them forever,
   And they are exalted.
8 And if *they are* bound in fetters,
   Held in the cords of affliction,
9 Then He tells them their work and their
   transgressions—
   That they have acted defiantly.
10 He also opens their ear to instruction,
   And commands that they turn from iniquity.
11 If they obey and serve *Him,*
   They shall spend their days in prosperity,
   And their years in pleasures.
12 But if they do not obey,
   They shall perish by the sword,
   And they shall die without knowledge.*c*

13 "But the hypocrites in heart store up wrath;
   They do not cry for help when He binds
   them.
14 They die in youth,
   And their life *ends* among the perverted
   persons.*d*
15 He delivers the poor in their affliction,
   And opens their ears in oppression.

16 "Indeed He would have brought you out of
   dire distress,
   Into a broad place where *there is* no
   restraint;
   And what is set on your table *would be* full
   of richness.
17 But you are filled with the judgment due the
   wicked;
   Judgment and justice take hold *of you.*
18 Because *there is* wrath, *beware* lest He take
   you away with *one* blow;
   For a large ransom would not help you
   avoid *it.*
19 Will your riches,
   Or all the mighty forces,
   Keep you from distress?
20 Do not desire the night,
   When people are cut off in their place.
21 Take heed, do not turn to iniquity,
   For you have chosen this rather than
   affliction.

36:12 *c*Masoretic Text reads *as one without knowledge.*
36:14 *d*Hebrew *qedeshim,* that is, those practicing sodomy
and prostitution in religious rituals

22*"Behold, God is exalted by His power;
  Who teaches like Him?
23 Who has assigned Him His way,
  Or who has said, 'You have done wrong'?

24 "Remember to magnify His work,
  Of which men have sung.
25 Everyone has seen it;
  Man looks on *it* from afar.

26*"Behold, God *is* great, and we do not know
    Him;
  Nor can the number of His years *be*
    discovered.
27 For He draws up drops of water,
  Which distill as rain from the mist,
28 Which the clouds drop down
  And pour abundantly on man.
29 Indeed, can *anyone* understand the
    spreading of clouds,
  The thunder from His canopy?
30 Look, He scatters His light upon it,
  And covers the depths of the sea.
31 For by these He judges the peoples;
  He gives food in abundance.
32 He covers *His* hands with lightning,
  And commands it to strike.
33 His thunder declares it,
  The cattle also, concerning the rising *storm.*

37 "At this also my heart trembles,
  And leaps from its place.
2 Hear attentively the thunder of His voice,
  And the rumbling *that* comes from His
    mouth.
3 He sends it forth under the whole heaven,
  His lightning to the ends of the earth.
4 After it a voice roars;
  He thunders with His majestic voice,
  And He does not restrain them when His
    voice is heard.
5 God thunders marvelously with His voice;
  He does great things which we cannot
    comprehend.
6 For He says to the snow, 'Fall *on* the earth';
  Likewise to the gentle rain and the heavy
    rain of His strength.
7 He seals the hand of every man,
  That all men may know His work.
8 The beasts go into dens,
  And remain in their lairs.
9 From the chamber *of the south* comes the
    whirlwind,
  And cold from the scattering winds *of the
    north.*
10 By the breath of God ice is given,
  And the broad waters are frozen.
11 Also with moisture He saturates the thick
    clouds;
  He scatters His bright clouds.
12 And they swirl about, being turned by His
    guidance,

36:22–25 *"Behold, God is exalted,"* and no one can teach Him what is right or accuse Him of doing what is wrong. He is sovereign in all that He does.

36:26—37:24 *"Behold, God is great,"* and we cannot know Him. (But Elihu claimed to be the spokesman for God!) A storm may have been brewing about that time, and Elihu used it as an example of God's greatness: the water cycle (36:27–28), the clouds, the thunder and lightning. The thunder is God's voice (37:2–5), and the weather is His servant.

How should we respond to the evidences of God's greatness in nature? We should see the majesty of God, thank Him for His provision, and obey and fear Him. But Job knew all this before Elihu was born! Nature does reveal the greatness of God; but it is in Jesus Christ that we see the grace of God, and grace meets our needs.

The Creator and His Creation—When Jesus spoke about nature, He usually emphasized the nearness of God and His care for His people. The Father knows the price of the sparrows, and He observes when they fall to the earth (Matt. 10:29–30). He feeds the birds, even though they never sow or reap (Matt. 6:25–27), and He makes the flowers beautiful, even though they last such a short time (Matt. 6:28–34). We are more valuable to God than the sparrows are, and we live much longer than the flowers, so surely the Father will care for us. Today, God's creation is in travail because of sin (Rom. 8:22); but the Creator is our Father, and we can trust Him to care for us.

That they may do whatever He commands them
On the face of the whole earth.*e*
13 He causes it to come,
Whether for correction,
Or for His land,
Or for mercy.

14 "Listen to this, O Job;
Stand still and consider the wondrous works of God.
15 Do you know when God dispatches them,
And causes the light of His cloud to shine?
16 Do you know how the clouds are balanced,
Those wondrous works of Him who is perfect in knowledge?
17 Why *are* your garments hot,
When He quiets the earth by the south *wind*?
18 With Him, have you spread out the skies,
Strong as a cast metal mirror?

19 "Teach us what we should say to Him,
For we can prepare nothing because of the darkness.
20 Should He be told that I *wish to* speak?
If a man were to speak, surely he would be swallowed up.
21 Even now *men* cannot look at the light *when it is* bright in the skies,
When the wind has passed and cleared them.
22 He comes from the north *as* golden *splendor*;
With God *is* awesome majesty.
23 *As for* the Almighty, we cannot find Him;
He is excellent in power,
In judgment and abundant justice;
He does not oppress.
24 Therefore men fear Him;
He shows no partiality to any *who are* wise of heart."

CHAPTERS 38—39

38:1ff The storm finally broke on the five men seated on the ash heap, and God spoke to Job out of the storm. We do not enjoy it when the storm comes, but if we listen for His voice, the storm will accomplish good things in our lives. When the storm was over, Job was ready to meet God and help his friends.

38:2 God's Word is light (Ps. 119:105, 130), but too often our words bring darkness. Words without knowledge are like lamps that shed darkness instead of light and only make the situation worse. Elihu recognized this in Job's speeches (34:35; 35:16), but Job did not recognize it. Be sure your words are true; otherwise, you will find yourself in the darkness. (See 1 John 1:5–10 and note the repeated phrase "if we say.")

38:4 Job claimed to know a great deal about God (27:11), so God examined him on several subjects: creation (38:4–11), the regulating of nature (38:12–30), the stars and clouds in the heavens (38:31–38), and the ways of the animals and birds (38:39—39:30). Needless to say, Job failed the examination—and so would you and I.
   The problems of life are solved not by *reasons* but by *relationships*. Job wanted to reason with God, but what he really needed was to rest in God. Job saw God's greatness and his own littleness, and that was the turning point. However, the smaller we are in our own eyes, the greater God makes us in His sight.

38 Then* the LORD answered Job out of the whirlwind, and said:

2 *"Who *is* this who darkens counsel
By words without knowledge?
3 Now prepare yourself like a man;
I will question you, and you shall answer Me.

4 *"Where were you when I laid the foundations of the earth?
Tell *Me*, if you have understanding.
5 Who determined its measurements?
Surely you know!
Or who stretched the line upon it?
6 To what were its foundations fastened?
Or who laid its cornerstone,
7 When the morning stars sang together,
And all the sons of God shouted for joy?

8 "Or *who* shut in the sea with doors,
When it burst forth *and* issued from the womb;
9 When I made the clouds its garment,
And thick darkness its swaddling band;

37:12 *e*Literally *the world of the earth*

10 When I fixed My limit for it,
    And set bars and doors;
11 When I said,
    'This far you may come, but no farther,
    And here your proud waves must stop!'

12 "Have you commanded the morning since
        your days *began,*
    And caused the dawn to know its place,
13 That it might take hold of the ends of the
        earth,
    And the wicked be shaken out of it?
14 It takes on form like clay *under* a seal,
    And stands out like a garment.
15 From the wicked their light is withheld,
    And the upraised arm is broken.

16 "Have you entered the springs of the sea?
    Or have you walked in search of the depths?
17 Have the gates of death been revealed to
        you?
    Or have you seen the doors of the shadow
        of death?
18 Have you comprehended the breadth of the
        earth?
    Tell *Me,* if you know all this.

19 "Where *is* the way *to* the dwelling of light?
    And darkness, where *is* its place,
20 That you may take it to its territory,
    That you may know the paths *to* its home?
21 Do you know *it,* because you were born
        then,
    Or *because* the number of your days *is*
        great?

22 "Have you entered the treasury of snow,
    Or have you seen the treasury of hail,
23 Which I have reserved for the time of
        trouble,
    For the day of battle and war?
24 By what way is light diffused,
    Or the east wind scattered over the earth?

25 "Who has divided a channel for the
        overflowing *water,*
    Or a path for the thunderbolt,
26 To cause it to rain on a land *where there is*
        no one,
    A wilderness in which *there is* no man;
27 To satisfy the desolate waste,
    And cause to spring forth the growth of
        tender grass?
28 Has the rain a father?
    Or who has begotten the drops of dew?
29 From whose womb comes the ice?
    And the frost of heaven, who gives it birth?
30 The waters harden like stone,
    And the surface of the deep is frozen.

31 "Can you bind the cluster of the Pleiades,
    Or loose the belt of Orion?
32 Can you bring out Mazzaroth*f* in its season?
    Or can you guide the Great Bear with its
        cubs?
33 Do you know the ordinances of the
        heavens?
    Can you set their dominion over the earth?

38:32 *f* Literally *Constellations*

34 "Can you lift up your voice to the clouds,
That an abundance of water may cover you?
35 Can you send out lightnings, that they may go,
And say to you, 'Here we *are!*'?
36 Who has put wisdom in the mind?*g*
Or who has given understanding to the heart?
37 Who can number the clouds by wisdom?
Or who can pour out the bottles of heaven,
38 When the dust hardens in clumps,
And the clods cling together?

39 "Can you hunt the prey for the lion,
Or satisfy the appetite of the young lions,
40 When they crouch in *their* dens,
Or lurk in their lairs to lie in wait?
41 Who provides food for the raven,
When its young ones cry to God,
And wander about for lack of food?

39 "Do you know the time when the wild mountain goats bear young?
Or can you mark when the deer gives birth?
2 Can you number the months *that* they fulfill?
Or do you know the time when they bear young?
3 They bow down,
They bring forth their young,
They deliver their offspring.*h*
4 Their young ones are healthy,
They grow strong with grain;
They depart and do not return to them.

5 "Who set the wild donkey free?
Who loosed the bonds of the onager,
6 Whose home I have made the wilderness,
And the barren land his dwelling?
7 He scorns the tumult of the city;
He does not heed the shouts of the driver.
8 The range of the mountains *is* his pasture,
And he searches after every green thing.

9 "Will the wild ox be willing to serve you?
Will he bed by your manger?
10 Can you bind the wild ox in the furrow with ropes?
Or will he plow the valleys behind you?
11 Will you trust him because his strength *is* great?
Or will you leave your labor to him?
12 Will you trust him to bring home your grain,
And gather *it* to your threshing floor?

13 "The wings of the ostrich wave proudly,
But are her wings and pinions *like the* kindly stork's?
14 For she leaves her eggs on the ground,
And warms them in the dust;
15 She forgets that a foot may crush them,
Or that a wild beast may break them.
16 She treats her young harshly, as though *they were* not hers;
Her labor is in vain, without concern,
17 Because God deprived her of wisdom,
And did not endow her with understanding.

❝I had a million questions to ask God: but when I met Him, they all fled my mind; and it didn't seem to matter.**❞**
—Christopher Morley

38:36 *g*Literally *inward parts*　39:3 *h*Literally *pangs,* figurative of offspring

18 When she lifts herself on high,
    She scorns the horse and its rider.

19 "Have you given the horse strength?
    Have you clothed his neck with thunder?[i]
20 Can you frighten him like a locust?
    His majestic snorting strikes terror.
21 He paws in the valley, and rejoices in *his*
        strength;
    He gallops into the clash of arms.
22 He mocks at fear, and is not frightened;
    Nor does he turn back from the sword.
23 The quiver rattles against him,
    The glittering spear and javelin.
24 He devours the distance with fierceness and
        rage;
    Nor does he come to a halt because the
        trumpet *has* sounded.
25 At *the blast of* the trumpet he says, 'Aha!'
    He smells the battle from afar,
    The thunder of captains and shouting.

26 "Does the hawk fly by your wisdom,
    And spread its wings toward the south?
27 Does the eagle mount up at your command,
    And make its nest on high?
28 On the rock it dwells and resides,
    On the crag of the rock and the stronghold.
29 From there it spies out the prey;
    Its eyes observe from afar.
30 Its young ones suck up blood;
    And where the slain *are*, there it *is*."

40 Moreover the LORD answered Job, and said:

2 *"Shall the one who contends with the
        Almighty correct *Him*?
    He who rebukes God, let him answer it."

3*Then Job answered the LORD and said:

4 "Behold, I am vile;
    What shall I answer You?
    I lay my hand over my mouth.
5 Once I have spoken, but I will not answer;
    Yes, twice, but I will proceed no further."

6*Then the LORD answered Job out of the whirlwind, and said:

7 "Now prepare yourself like a man;
    I will question you, and you shall answer
        Me:

8 "Would you indeed annul My judgment?
    Would you condemn Me that you may be
        justified?
9 Have you an arm like God?
    Or can you thunder with a voice like His?
10 Then adorn yourself *with* majesty and
        splendor,
    And array yourself with glory and beauty.
11 Disperse the rage of your wrath;
    Look on everyone *who is* proud, and humble
        him.
12 Look on everyone *who is* proud, *and* bring
        him low;
    Tread down the wicked in their place.

CHAPTERS 40—41

40:2 God finally gave Job the one thing he
wanted most, the opportunity to meet Him
in court and defend his case. Suppose God
gave you the same opportunity. What would
you say to Him? Would you rather meet God
in court or at the throne of grace? The more
you meet Him at the throne of grace, the
less interested you will be to meet Him in
court.

40:3–5 But Job had nothing much to say!
He saw himself as insignificant and ignorant
and totally unable to face God. The
revelation of God completely stopped his
mouth. But when we are silent, we can hear
God's voice better, even if we are in a storm.

40:6–14 God asked Job many humbling
questions, but they can be summarized in
these three: (1) "Are you My equal?" (40:6–
14); (2) "Can you explain the behemoth?"
(40:15–24); (3) "Can you control
Leviathan?" (chap. 41). The behemoth was
probably the hippopotamus and the
Leviathan the crocodile. Job certainly would
be afraid to fight these two creatures, *but
he was not afraid to challenge God, their
Creator!* Job could not control them, but he
wanted to tell God what to do!

39:19 [i]Or *a mane*

40:15—41:34 God made each living thing, including man, suited to its environment and task. But man is not content to be the creature: he wants to be the Creator (Rom. 1:25); and that is Satan's promise to him if he will disobey God (Gen. 3:5). The next time you hear that invitation from Satan, look at God's creation and remember that you are not God.

13 Hide them in the dust together,
Bind their faces in hidden *darkness*.
14 Then I will also confess to you
That your own right hand can save you.

15*"Look now at the behemoth,ʲ which I made
along with you;
He eats grass like an ox.
16 See now, his strength *is* in his hips,
And his power *is* in his stomach muscles.
17 He moves his tail like a cedar;
The sinews of his thighs are tightly knit.
18 His bones *are like* beams of bronze,
His ribs like bars of iron.
19 He *is* the first of the ways of God;
Only He who made him can bring near His sword.
20 Surely the mountains yield food for him,
And all the beasts of the field play there.
21 He lies under the lotus trees,
In a covert of reeds and marsh.
22 The lotus trees cover him *with* their shade;
The willows by the brook surround him.
23 Indeed the river may rage,
Yet he is not disturbed;
He is confident, though the Jordan gushes into his mouth,
24 *Though* he takes it in his eyes,
Or one pierces *his* nose with a snare.

41 "Can you draw out Leviathanᵏ with a hook,
Or *snare* his tongue with a line *which* you lower?
2 Can you put a reed through his nose,
Or pierce his jaw with a hook?
3 Will he make many supplications to you?
Will he speak softly to you?
4 Will he make a covenant with you?
Will you take him as a servant forever?
5 Will you play with him as *with* a bird,
Or will you leash him for your maidens?
6 Will *your* companions make a banquetˡ of him?
Will they apportion him among the merchants?
7 Can you fill his skin with harpoons,
Or his head with fishing spears?
8 Lay your hand on him;
Remember the battle—
Never do it again!
9 Indeed, *any* hope of *overcoming* him is false;
Shall *one not* be overwhelmed at the sight of him?
10 No one *is so* fierce that he would dare stir him up.
Who then is able to stand against Me?
11 Who has preceded Me, that I should pay *him*?
Everything under heaven is Mine.

40:15 ʲA large animal, exact identity unknown   41:1 ᵏA large sea creature, exact identity unknown   41:6 ˡOr *bargain over him*

The Value of Silence—God cannot do much for us as long as we are busy telling Him what to do. He must shut our mouths, as He did with Job (40:4), Moses (Deut. 3:26), and David (Ps. 39:9). The lost sinner's mouth must be stopped (Matt. 22:12; Rom. 3:19). One day, the whole earth will be silent before the glory of the Lord (Hab. 2:20).

12 "I will not conceal[m] his limbs,
   His mighty power, or his graceful
      proportions.
13 Who can remove his outer coat?
   Who can approach *him* with a double
      bridle?
14 Who can open the doors of his face,
   With his terrible teeth all around?
15 *His* rows of scales are *his* pride,
   Shut up tightly *as with* a seal;
16 One is so near another
   That no air can come between them;
17 They are joined one to another,
   They stick together and cannot be parted.
18 His sneezings flash forth light,
   And his eyes *are* like the eyelids of the
      morning.
19 Out of his mouth go burning lights;
   Sparks of fire shoot out.
20 Smoke goes out of his nostrils,
   As *from* a boiling pot and burning rushes.
21 His breath kindles coals,
   And a flame goes out of his mouth.
22 Strength dwells in his neck,
   And sorrow dances before him.
23 The folds of his flesh are joined together;
   They are firm on him and cannot be moved.
24 His heart is as hard as stone,
   Even as hard as the lower *millstone.*
25 When he raises himself up, the mighty are
      afraid;
   Because of his crashings they are beside[n]
      themselves.
26 *Though* the sword reaches him, it cannot
      avail;
   Nor does spear, dart, or javelin.
27 He regards iron as straw,
   And bronze as rotten wood.
28 The arrow cannot make him flee;
   Slingstones become like stubble to him.
29 Darts are regarded as straw;
   He laughs at the threat of javelins.
30 His undersides *are* like sharp potsherds;
   He spreads pointed *marks* in the mire.
31 He makes the deep boil like a pot;
   He makes the sea like a pot of ointment.
32 He leaves a shining wake behind him;
   One would think the deep had white hair.
33 On earth there is nothing like him,
   Which is made without fear.
34 *He beholds every high *thing;*
   He *is* king over all the children of pride."

42
Then* Job answered the Lord and said:

2 "I know that You can do everything,
   And that no purpose *of Yours* can be
      withheld from You.
3 *You asked,* 'Who *is* this who hides counsel
      without knowledge?'
   Therefore I have uttered what I did not
      understand,
   Things too wonderful for me, which I did
      not know.
4 Listen, please, and let me speak;
   You said, 'I will question you, and you shall
      answer Me.'

CHAPTER 42

42:1–6 *Job the sinner.* Job had said some rash things during this discussion, but unlike his friends, he had spoken the truth about God (v. 7). Job had a new understanding of God's power and purpose (v. 2), and he realized that he had to repent. Job's sufferings gave him a new vision of himself and of the glory and greatness of God (Heb. 12:11).

41:12 *m*Literally *keep silent about*   41:25 *n*Or *purify themselves*

5 "I have heard of You by the hearing of the
    ear,
    But now my eye sees You.
6   Therefore I abhor *myself*,
    And repent in dust and ashes."

42:7 *Job the servant.* Four times in verses 7–8, God called Job "My servant." Although he had weaknesses and failures, *Job served God during his time of suffering.* By maintaining his faith in God in spite of trials, Job unknowingly silenced the devil and revealed to the world that God is worthy of our trust and worship, no matter how much He allows us to suffer. In the will of God, trials work *for* us, not *against* us (Rom. 8:28; 2 Cor. 4:16–18); therefore, we can work for God as we suffer. Suffering can be a ministry.

42:8 *Job the intercessor.* The friends had said some unkind things *to* Job and some terrible things *about* Job, *yet he forgave them and prayed for them.* The friends had to do what they admonished Job to do: confess their sins and repent. Do you pray for people who have wronged you (Matt. 5:43–48)? Do you pray for condemnation or restoration?

42:12–17 *Job the receiver.* Job had wanted to go to court and argue law, but instead he went to the altar and experienced grace. He received forgiveness, friends, family, wealth and honor, twice as much as he had before. God does not guarantee this kind of happy ending *in this life* to everybody who goes through trials (Heb. 11:36–40), but He does promise to reward all who are true to Him (Rev. 2:10). Job came out of the furnace a better person (Job 23:10), and so can you if you will trust God and let Him have His way.

7*And so it was, after the Lord had spoken these words to Job, that the Lord said to Eliphaz the Temanite, "My wrath is aroused against you and your two friends, for you have not spoken of Me *what is* right, as My servant Job *has*. 8*Now therefore, take for yourselves seven bulls and seven rams, go to My servant Job, and offer up for yourselves a burnt offering; and My servant Job shall pray for you. For I will accept him, lest I deal with you *according to your* folly; because you have not spoken of Me *what is* right, as My servant Job *has*."

9So Eliphaz the Temanite and Bildad the Shuhite *and* Zophar the Naamathite went and did as the Lord commanded them; for the Lord had accepted Job. 10And the Lord restored Job's losses° when he prayed for his friends. Indeed the Lord gave Job twice as much as he had before. 11Then all his brothers, all his sisters, and all those who had been his acquaintances before, came to him and ate food with him in his house; and they consoled him and comforted him for all the adversity that the Lord had brought upon him. Each one gave him a piece of silver and each a ring of gold. 12*Now the Lord blessed the latter *days* of Job more than his beginning; for he had fourteen thousand sheep, six thousand camels, one thousand yoke of oxen, and one thousand female donkeys. 13He also had seven sons and three daughters. 14And he called the name of the first Jemimah, the name of the second Keziah, and the name of the third Keren-Happuch. 15In all the land were found no women *so* beautiful as the daughters of Job; and their father gave them an inheritance among their brothers. 16After this Job lived one hundred and forty years, and saw his children and grandchildren *for* four generations. 17So Job died, old and full of days.

42:10 °Literally *Job's captivity,* that is, what was captured from Job

The Trials of Job—If you feel your sufferings are beyond what anybody else has experienced, consider Job's trials. He was shot at like an enemy (6:4; 16:12–13), hunted like a wild animal (10:16), covered by darkness (19:8), uprooted like a tree (19:10), and put into a furnace (23:10). His wife discouraged him, his three friends attacked him and the Lord seemed to abandon him. However, the greatest example of endurance in suffering is the Lord Jesus (Heb. 12:1–3). He was forsaken *even by the Father* and suffered the shameful death of the cross. He was made sin for us, yet He was sinless. There was no cause of suffering or death in Him, yet He willingly yielded to the Father's will. He endured, He conquered, and we can conquer in and through Him. Job's suffering makes it clear that God is worthy of our obedience—no matter what "profit" or "loss" may come from obeying Him. God is not obligated to make the righteous healthy and rich or the wicked sick and poor. Our Lord's death and resurrection make it possible for God to *transform* our suffering into glory, not simply *replace* it with glory. Job's suffering was replaced with earthly glory, but the believer's suffering will be transformed into heavenly glory. Therefore, our sufferings are not in vain, for the Lord is working out His glorious purposes.

PSALMS

This book is the hymnal of the Bible. The word *psalm* comes from a Greek word that means "a poem sung to musical accompaniment." Many psalms were sung in the Jewish temple, and the New Testament church also used psalms in worship (1 Cor. 14:26; Eph. 5:19; Col. 3:16). Some of the church's hymns and praise songs today are based on these inspired poems.

The psalms express man's praise to God for who He is and what He does. They also express man's need of God in times of trial and his confidence that God will help. You will find in the psalms a full range of human emotions, from ecstatic joy to despair and contrition. You will also find a revelation of God that brings comfort and encouragement when you trust Him.

That explains why the book of Psalms is so greatly beloved by God's people, for each of us can identify with the writers as they found God's grace sufficient in the experiences of life. No matter what your circumstances or feelings may be, there is a psalm that perfectly fits your situation.

The book is divided into five sections, each one ending with a doxology: (1) Pss. 1—41; (2) Pss. 42—72; (3) Pss. 73—89; (4) Pss. 90—106; and (5) Pss. 107—150.

Book One: Psalms 1—41

PSALM 1

B lessed* *is* the man
   Who walks not in the counsel of the
      ungodly,
   Nor stands in the path of sinners,
   Nor sits in the seat of the scornful;
2   But his delight *is* in the law of the LORD,
   And in His law he meditates day and
      night.
3   He shall be like a tree
   Planted by the rivers of water,
   That brings forth its fruit in its season,
   Whose leaf also shall not wither;
   And whatever he does shall prosper.

PSALM 1

1:1–3 *Blessing.* God enjoys blessing your life, but you must be "blessable." That means having *discernment* (v. 1), avoiding the steps that lead to sin: considering sin (walking), contemplating sin (standing), being comfortable in sin (sitting). Watch that first step!

Blessing involves *delight* (v. 2). The Word guides your walk and rejoices your heart (Jer. 15:16). Meditation is to your inner

(continued)

Where to Look in the Psalms

When you cannot sleep	Psalms 3—4
When you have sinned	Psalms 32; 51
When you are ill	Psalm 31
When you need God's guidance	Psalm 25
When you are traveling	Psalm 121
When people create problems	Psalm 37
When you are downcast	Psalms 42—43
When sinners seem to succeed	Psalm 73
When you are afraid	Psalms 27; 91
When you "feel old"	Psalm 102
When you worry about the future	Psalm 34
When you think about death	Psalm 116
When you are in deep waters	Psalms 124; 130
When problems seem bigger than God	Psalm 139
When you just want to praise Him	Psalm 103

(continued from previous page)
person what digestion is to your body: you make the Word a part of your life and you grow.

Blessing involves *dependence* (v. 3). Your spiritual roots go deep into the resources of God's grace, and you bear fruit because His life is at work in you.

1:4–6 Perishing. How tragic that anyone is perishing when Jesus offers abundant life! Contrast *tree* and *chaff* if you want to see the difference between the godly and the ungodly. The godly receive blessing but the ungodly receive judgment. The psalm starts with "blessed" and ends with "perish." The choice is yours.

PSALM 2

2:1–3 God hears. He hears the raging of the nations and the plots of the rulers. What do they want? *Freedom from God!* But the way to real freedom is by submission and not by rebellion. To throw off God's will is to invite bondage and destruction.

2:4 God laughs. Puny man does not worry God with all his noise and threats. God is on His throne and has everything in control. When the world's noise frightens you, turn to the Lord and let Him take over (Acts 4:23–31).

2:5–12 God speaks. God the Father announces that His King is enthroned in the heavenly Zion where the nations cannot touch Him. God the Son announces that the nations are His, so their rebellion is futile (vv. 7–9). Finally, God the Spirit invites the rebels to submit and be blessed instead of destroyed (vv. 10–12).

Over the noise of the nations, listen for the assuring voice of God.

4 *The ungodly *are* not so,
But *are* like the chaff which the wind drives away.
5 Therefore the ungodly shall not stand in the judgment,
Nor sinners in the congregation of the righteous.

6 For the LORD knows the way of the righteous,
But the way of the ungodly shall perish.

PSALM 2

Why* do the nations rage,
And the people plot a vain thing?
2 The kings of the earth set themselves,
And the rulers take counsel together,
Against the LORD and against His Anointed,
saying,
3 "Let us break Their bonds in pieces
And cast away Their cords from us."

4 *He who sits in the heavens shall laugh;
The LORD shall hold them in derision.
5 *Then He shall speak to them in His wrath,
And distress them in His deep displeasure:
6 "Yet I have set My King
On My holy hill of Zion."

7 "I will declare the decree:
The LORD has said to Me,
'You *are* My Son,
Today I have begotten You.
8 Ask of Me, and I will give You
The nations *for* Your inheritance,
And the ends of the earth *for* Your possession.
9 You shall break[a] them with a rod of iron;
You shall dash them to pieces like a potter's vessel.' "

2:9 [a]Following Masoretic Text and Targum; Septuagint, Syriac, and Vulgate read *rule* (compare Revelation 2:27).

Jesus Christ in the Psalms (Luke 24:44)

The King	Ps. 2 with Acts 4:25–26; 13:33; Ps. 118:26 with Matt. 21:9
The Son of man	Ps. 8; Heb. 2:6–11
The Resurrection	Ps. 16 with Acts 2:25–31; Ps. 22:21–31 with Heb. 2:12
The Crucifixion	Ps. 22:1–21; Matt. 27:35–46
The Shepherd	Ps. 23; John 10
The sacrifice for our sins	Ps. 40:6–8; Heb. 10:1–10
Judas's betrayal	Ps. 41:9; John 13:18–19
The royal Bridegroom	Ps. 45; Heb. 1:8–9
The Ascension	Ps. 68:18; Eph. 4:7–16
The rejection	Ps. 69:4 with John 15:25; Ps. 69:8 with John 7:3–5; Ps. 69:9 with John 2:17 and Rom. 15:3
The eternal Son	Ps. 102:25–27; Heb. 1:10–12
The divine King-Priest	Ps. 110; Matt. 22:41–45; Acts 2:34–35; Heb. 1:13; 7:17–21; 10:12–13
The Stone	Ps. 118:22–23 with Matt. 21:42

10 Now therefore, be wise, O kings;
    Be instructed, you judges of the earth.
11 Serve the LORD with fear,
    And rejoice with trembling.
12 Kiss the Son,[b] lest He[c] be angry,
    And you perish in the way,
    When His wrath is kindled but a little.
    Blessed are all those who put their trust in
    Him.

PSALM 3

A Psalm of David when he fled from Absalom his son.

LORD, how they have increased who trouble me!
    Many are they who rise up against me.
2   Many are they who say of me,
    "There is no help for him in God."   Selah

3   But You, O LORD, are a shield for me,
    My glory and the One who lifts up my head.
4   I cried to the LORD with my voice,
    And He heard me from His holy hill.
                                                Selah

5   *I lay down and slept;
    I awoke, for the LORD sustained me.
6   *I will not be afraid of ten thousands of
    people
    Who have set themselves against me all
    around.

7   Arise, O LORD;
    Save me, O my God!
    For You have struck all my enemies on the
    cheekbone;
    You have broken the teeth of the ungodly.
8   Salvation belongs to the LORD.
    Your blessing is upon Your people.   Selah

PSALM 4

To the Chief Musician. With stringed instruments. A Psalm
of David.

Hear* me when I call, O God of my
    righteousness!
    You have relieved me in my distress;
    Have mercy on me, and hear my prayer.

2   *How long, O you sons of men,
    Will you turn my glory to shame?
    How long will you love worthlessness
    And seek falsehood?   Selah
3   But know that the LORD has set apart[d] for
    Himself him who is godly;
    The LORD will hear when I call to Him.

4   *Be angry, and do not sin.
    Meditate within your heart on your bed, and
    be still.   Selah
5   Offer the sacrifices of righteousness,
    And put your trust in the LORD.

6   *There are many who say,
    "Who will show us any good?"
    LORD, lift up the light of Your countenance
    upon us.

2:12 [b]Septuagint and Vulgate read Embrace discipline;
Targum reads Receive instruction. [c]Septuagint reads the
LORD.   4:3 [d]Many Hebrew manuscripts, Septuagint, Targum,
and Vulgate read made wonderful.

PSALM 3

3:5 If worry keeps you from getting a good
night's sleep, Psalms 3 and 4 are what you
need. Both psalms were probably written
when David was exiled from Jerusalem
because his son Absalom had stolen the
kingdom (2 Sam. 15—18). Psalm 3 is a
morning psalm (v. 5), and Psalm 4 is an
evening psalm (v. 8).

3:6 How was David able to sleep when he
was in such danger? The enemy was
against him (vv. 1, 6) but David knew that
God was for him. God surrounds you (v. 3),
sustains you (v. 5), and saves you (v. 7).
When people discourage you (v. 2), God lifts
up your head and keeps you going (v. 3).
    God never sleeps (Ps. 121:3–4), so why
should you stay awake and worry?

❝*If you can't sleep, don't count
sheep—talk to the Shepherd!***❞**

PSALM 4

4:1 David wrote this psalm as he was about
to retire for the night (v. 8). He could not
do much about the war around him, but he
could do something about the war within
him. He did not want to lie in bed and worry,
so he committed himself and his situation
to the Lord.

4:2, 3 He asked. Asking the Lord for help
is still a good way to deal with inner turmoil
(Phil. 4:6–7).

4:4, 5 He believed. He faced his anger
honestly and gave it to the Lord (Eph. 4:26).
Instead of lying in bed and thinking about
your problems, meditate on the Lord and
offer Him sacrifices of praise.

4:6–8 He received. In the darkness, he saw
the face of God and received light. In his
sorrow, he discovered the gift of gladness.
In the time of battle, he received peace. God
did not immediately change the situation, but
He did change David; He can do the same
for you.

7   You have put gladness in my heart,
    More than in the season that their grain and
    wine increased.
8   I will both lie down in peace, and sleep;
    For You alone, O LORD, make me dwell in
    safety.

PSALM 5

To the Chief Musician. With flutes.*e* A Psalm of David.

G ive* ear to my words, O LORD,
    Consider my meditation.
2   Give heed to the voice of my cry,
    My King and my God,
    For to You I will pray.
3   My voice You shall hear in the morning,
    O LORD;
    In the morning I will direct *it* to You,
    And I will look up.

4   For You *are* not a God who takes pleasure
    in wickedness,
    Nor shall evil dwell with You.
5   The boastful shall not stand in Your sight;
    You hate all workers of iniquity.
6   *You shall destroy those who speak
    falsehood;
    The LORD abhors the bloodthirsty and
    deceitful man.

7   *But as for me, I will come into Your house
    in the multitude of Your mercy;
    In fear of You I will worship toward Your
    holy temple.
8   Lead me, O LORD, in Your righteousness
    because of my enemies;
    Make Your way straight before my face.

9   *For *there is* no faithfulness in their mouth;
    Their inward part *is* destruction;
    Their throat *is* an open tomb;
    They flatter with their tongue.
10 Pronounce them guilty, O God!
    Let them fall by their own counsels;
    Cast them out in the multitude of their
    transgressions,
    For they have rebelled against You.

11 *But let all those rejoice who put their trust
    in You;
    Let them ever shout for joy, because You
    defend them;
    Let those also who love Your name
    Be joyful in You.
12 For You, O LORD, will bless the righteous;
    With favor You will surround him as *with*
    a shield.

PSALM 6

To the Chief Musician. With stringed instruments. On an
eight-stringed harp.*f* A Psalm of David.

O * LORD, do not rebuke me in Your anger,
    Nor chasten me in Your hot displeasure.

5:title *e*Hebrew *nehiloth*   6:title *f*Hebrew *sheminith*

PSALM 5

5:1 When he served in King Saul's court, David was often attacked by some of Saul's officers who flattered the king and lied about David (vv. 4–6, 9). King Saul actually believed that David was trying to steal the throne. When people lie about you, follow David's example and pray about the matter. Note his requests.

5:6 *Hear me.* David began the day with his heart lifted up to God. God knew the sinful words of the liars, but He also heard the believing prayers of His servant.

5:7, 8 *Lead me.* David had to be careful because Saul and his leaders were watching him and his life was in danger. He worshiped God and asked for God's daily direction.

5:9, 10 *Protect me.* David did not fight Saul or Saul's men; he left those battles to the Lord. He trusted God to care for him, and God did not fail.

5:11, 12 *Bless me.* Protection is the last thing named (v. 12). Beyond that, David was blessed with joy, confidence, and a deeper love for the Lord. Times of suffering can be times of growing if we let the Lord have His way.

PSALM 6

6:1 This psalm grew out of an experience of sickness and pain, when David thought he was going to die. Besides that, he had to put up with the attacks of his enemies who wanted him to die. It was a time of deep discouragement for David, but he did not waver in his faith.

The Penitential Psalms—Psalms 6, 32, 38, 51, 102, 130, and 143 are known as "The Penitential Psalms." You may use these psalms as your own prayers when you want to confess sin and ask for God's forgiveness (1 John 1:9).

2 *Have mercy on me, O LORD, for I *am* weak;
   O LORD, heal me, for my bones are troubled.
3 My soul also is greatly troubled;
   But You, O LORD—how long?

4 Return, O LORD, deliver me!
   Oh, save me for Your mercies' sake!
5 For in death *there is* no remembrance of
     You;
   In the grave who will give You thanks?

6 *I am weary with my groaning;
   All night I make my bed swim;
   I drench my couch with my tears.
7 My eye wastes away because of grief;
   It grows old because of all my enemies.

8 *Depart from me, all you workers of iniquity;
   For the LORD has heard the voice of my
     weeping.
9 The LORD has heard my supplication;
   The LORD will receive my prayer.
10 Let all my enemies be ashamed and greatly
     troubled;
   Let them turn back *and* be ashamed
     suddenly.

PSALM 7

A Meditation*g* of David, which he sang to the LORD
concerning the words of Cush, a Benjamite.

O* LORD my God, in You I put my trust;
   Save me from all those who persecute me;
   And deliver me,
2 *Lest they tear me like a lion,
   Rending *me* in pieces, while *there is* none
     to deliver.

3 O LORD my God, if I have done this:
   If there is iniquity in my hands,
4 If I have repaid evil to him who was at peace
     with me,
   Or have plundered my enemy without
     cause,
5 Let the enemy pursue me and overtake *me;*
   Yes, let him trample my life to the earth,
   And lay my honor in the dust.   Selah

6 *Arise, O LORD, in Your anger;
   Lift Yourself up because of the rage of my
     enemies;
   Rise up for me*h* *to* the judgment You have
     commanded!
7 So the congregation of the peoples shall
     surround You;
   For their sakes, therefore, return on high.
8 The LORD shall judge the peoples;
   Judge me, O LORD, according to my
     righteousness,
   And according to my integrity within me.

9 Oh, let the wickedness of the wicked come
     to an end,
   But establish the just;
   For the righteous God tests the hearts and
     minds.

6:2–5 As he prayed, he asked for mercy for his body (vv. 1–2) and his soul (vv. 3–5). Mercy means that God does not give us what we deserve, and grace means that He gives us what we do not deserve. What a loving God He is!

6:6, 7 David reminded God of his tears of repentance and confession (vv. 6–7). His bed should have been a place of rest, but it had become a place of trial as God chastened him.

6:8–10 But there is a happy ending: David was assured and his enemies were ashamed (vv. 8–10)! God heard and answered his prayers! When the night is dark and long, keep on trusting, and the dawn will come in God's good time.

PSALM 7

7:1 We do not know what Cush said about David, but apparently he was one of the "court liars" who flattered Saul and made life difficult for David (1 Sam. 24:9). When you have a "Cush" in your life, do what David did.

7:2–5 *Be honest with God.* David did not say that the enemy was telling the truth, but he was willing for God to examine him and punish him. He had nothing to hide.

7:6–13 *Let God be the judge.* It is wise to let God be the judge because His judgment is always right (1 Cor. 4:3–5). We do not see ourselves and others as He sees, so it is best to turn the matter over to Him. David was careful to maintain his integrity (v. 8) and let God be his defense (v. 10).

7:title *g*Hebrew *Shiggaion*   7:6 *h*Following Masoretic Text,
Targum, and Vulgate; Septuagint reads *O LORD my God.*

10 My defense *is* of God,
    Who saves the upright in heart.

11 God *is* a just judge,
    And God is angry *with the wicked* every
      day.
12 If he does not turn back,
    He will sharpen His sword;
    He bends His bow and makes it ready.
13 He also prepares for Himself instruments of
      death;
    He makes His arrows into fiery shafts.

14 *Behold, *the wicked* brings forth iniquity;
    Yes, he conceives trouble and brings forth
      falsehood.
15 He made a pit and dug it out,
    And has fallen into the ditch *which* he made.
16 His trouble shall return upon his own
      head,
    And his violent dealing shall come down on
      his own crown.

17 *I will praise the LORD according to His
      righteousness,
    And will sing praise to the name of the LORD
      Most High.

PSALM 8

To the Chief Musician. On the instrument of Gath.*ⁱ* A Psalm
of David.

O* LORD, our Lord,
    How excellent *is* Your name in all the earth,
    Who have set Your glory above the
      heavens!

2   Out of the mouth of babes and nursing
      infants
    You have ordained strength,
    Because of Your enemies,
    That You may silence the enemy and the
      avenger.

3   When I consider Your heavens, the work
      of Your fingers,
    The moon and the stars, which You have
      ordained,
4   What is man that You are mindful of him,
    And the son of man that You visit him?
5   *For You have made him a little lower than
      the angels,ʲ
    And You have crowned him with glory and
      honor.

6   *You have made him to have dominion over
      the works of Your hands;
    You have put all *things* under his feet,
7   All sheep and oxen—
    Even the beasts of the field,
8   The birds of the air,
    And the fish of the sea
    That pass through the paths of the seas.

9   O LORD, our Lord,
    How excellent *is* Your name in all the
      earth!

7:14–16 *Wait on the Lord.* Sin has a way
of bringing its own punishment if we wait
long enough. It is like giving birth to pain
and trouble (v. 14; James 1:14–15), falling
into a pit (v. 15), or getting back the trouble
that they tried to impose on others (v. 16).

7:17 *Give God thanks.* What does it matter
that men slander us, so long as the
righteousness of God prevails and the name
of the Lord is glorified!

PSALM 8

8:1 The universe is vast and full of
grandeur, so why should God pay any
attention to weak and insignificant men and
women? *But He does!* He can use the
weakness of babes to reveal His great
strength (Matt. 21:16) and to defeat the
enemy (the way David defeated Goliath
[1 Sam. 17]). If He can use infants, surely
He can use anybody.

8:5 You are important because God made
you in His image (v. 5; Gen. 1:26–28). Sin
has marred that image, but in Jesus Christ,
that image can be restored (2 Cor. 3:18; Col.
3:10).

8:6–8 You are important because God has
shared His dominion with you (vv. 6–8). Man
lost that dominion when he sinned, but
Jesus Christ has regained it (Heb. 2:6–8).
Can you think of occasions when Jesus
Christ proved that He had dominion over
beasts, birds, and fish?

8:9 Yes, you are important to God, and He
has a purpose for you to fulfill. He wants
you to "reign in life" through His Son (Rom.
5:17), for you are enthroned in the
heavenlies with Him (Eph. 2:6). Why live like
a slave when you can live like a sovereign?

8:title *ⁱHebrew *Al Gittith*   8:5 *ʲHebrew *Elohim, God;*
Septuagint, Syriac, Targum, and Jewish tradition translate as
angels.

PSALM 9

To the Chief Musician. To *the tune of* "Death of the Son."[k]
A Psalm of David.

I* will praise *You,* O Lord, with my whole heart;
    I will tell of all Your marvelous works.
2 I will be glad and rejoice in You;
    I will sing praise to Your name, O Most
    High.

3 When my enemies turn back,
    They shall fall and perish at Your presence.
4 For You have maintained my right and my
    cause;
    You sat on the throne judging in
    righteousness.
5 You have rebuked the nations,
    You have destroyed the wicked;
    You have blotted out their name forever and
    ever.

6 O enemy, destructions are finished forever!
    And you have destroyed cities;
    Even their memory has perished.
7 *But the Lord shall endure forever;
    He has prepared His throne for judgment.
8 He shall judge the world in righteousness,
    And He shall administer judgment for the
    peoples in uprightness.

9 The Lord also will be a refuge for the
    oppressed,
    A refuge in times of trouble.
10 And those who know Your name will put
    their trust in You;
    For You, Lord, have not forsaken those who
    seek You.

11 Sing praises to the Lord, who dwells in
    Zion!
    Declare His deeds among the people.
12 When He avenges blood, He remembers
    them;
    He does not forget the cry of the humble.

13 *Have mercy on me, O Lord!
    Consider my trouble from those who hate
    me,
    You who lift me up from the gates of
    death,
14 That I may tell of all Your praise
    In the gates of the daughter of Zion.
    I will rejoice in Your salvation.

15 The nations have sunk down in the pit
    which they made;
    In the net which they hid, their own foot is
    caught.
16 The Lord is known *by* the judgment He
    executes;
    The wicked is snared in the work of his own
    hands.
             Meditation.[l]   Selah

17 The wicked shall be turned into hell,
    And all the nations that forget God.
18 For the needy shall not always be forgotten;
    The expectation of the poor shall *not* perish
    forever.

PSALM 9

9:1–6 Praise. God had won a victory for David, so he sang a song of praise to the Lord. It was not a personal battle. Because David was doing *God's* will, the Lord maintained his cause. Take time to praise the Lord for the victories He graciously gives you.

9:7–12 Promise. David looked ahead to the time when God would finally judge sin and establish His righteous kingdom. His people do not need to worry: He is their Refuge and will never forsake them (Heb. 13:5). The Father forsook His Son on the cross, but He will not forsake you.

9:13–20 Prayer. From considering the past and the future, David turned to his present need as he prayed for God's help. His need was for mercy; his motive was that he might praise the Lord and tell others of His salvation. Why? Because there is a place called hell (v. 17) and God's salvation is the only escape from that terrible place.

Paul advised, "Knowing, therefore, the terror of the Lord, we persuade men" (2 Cor. 5:11).

> ❝The safest road to hell is the gradual one—the gentle slope, soft underfoot, without sudden turnings, without milestones, without signposts.❞
>
> —C. S. Lewis

9:title [k]Hebrew *Muth Labben*   9:16 [l]Hebrew *Higgaion*

19 Arise, O LORD,
    Do not let man prevail;
    Let the nations be judged in Your sight.
20 Put them in fear, O LORD,
    That the nations may know themselves *to*
        be but men.   Selah

PSALM 10

PSALM 10

10:1–4 *Does God hide?* "Why do the wicked prosper?" is a perennial question God's people ask. As they consider the suffering of the godly and the security of the ungodly, they feel that God has forgotten and forsaken His people. He is hiding.

10:5–13 *Does God hear?* Note the repetition of "He has said in his heart" (vv. 6, 11, 13). God hears what the ungodly say and does not approve of their pride and rebellion. The ungodly announces, "I shall not be moved! God does not see what I do! Even if He does, He will never judge me!" What arrogance!

10:14–18 *Does God help?* Of course He does! He sees the trouble of His people, feels their grief, and helps them in the right way at the right time. After all, the Lord is King! It may look as though the ungodly are winning the day, but the Lord will triumph in the end.

Why* do You stand afar off, O LORD?
    Why do You hide in times of trouble?
2   The wicked in *his* pride persecutes the poor;
    Let them be caught in the plots which they
        have devised.

3   For the wicked boasts of his heart's desire;
    He blesses the greedy *and* renounces the
        LORD.
4   The wicked in his proud countenance does
        not seek *God;*
    God *is* in none of his thoughts.

5   *His ways are always prospering;
    Your judgments *are* far above, out of his
        sight;
    As for all his enemies, he sneers at them.
6   He has said in his heart, "I shall not be
        moved;
    I shall never be in adversity."
7   His mouth is full of cursing and deceit and
        oppression;
    Under his tongue *is* trouble and iniquity.

8   He sits in the lurking places of the villages;
    In the secret places he murders the
        innocent;
    His eyes are secretly fixed on the helpless.
9   He lies in wait secretly, as a lion in his
        den;
    He lies in wait to catch the poor;
    He catches the poor when he draws him into
        his net.
10 So he crouches, he lies low,
    That the helpless may fall by his strength.
11 He has said in his heart,
    "God has forgotten;
    He hides His face;
    He will never see."

12 Arise, O LORD!
    O God, lift up Your hand!
    Do not forget the humble.
13 Why do the wicked renounce God?
    He has said in his heart,
    "You will not require *an account.*"

14 *But You have seen, for You observe trouble
        and grief,
    To repay *it* by Your hand.
    The helpless commits himself to You;
    You are the helper of the fatherless.
15 Break the arm of the wicked and the evil
        man;
    Seek out his wickedness *until* You find
        none.

16 The LORD *is* King forever and ever;
    The nations have perished out of His land.
17 LORD, You have heard the desire of the
        humble;
    You will prepare their heart;
    You will cause Your ear to hear,

18 To do justice to the fatherless and the
       oppressed,
    That the man of the earth may oppress no
       more.

PSALM 11

To the Chief Musician. A Psalm of David.

In* the LORD I put my trust;
       How can you say to my soul,
    "Flee *as* a bird to your mountain"?
2   *For look! The wicked bend *their* bow,
       They make ready their arrow on the string,
    That they may shoot secretly at the upright
       in heart.
3   *If the foundations are destroyed,
       What can the righteous do?

4   The LORD *is* in His holy temple,
    The LORD's throne *is* in heaven;
    His eyes behold,
    His eyelids test the sons of men.
5   The LORD tests the righteous,
    But the wicked and the one who loves
       violence His soul hates.
6   Upon the wicked He will rain coals;
    Fire and brimstone and a burning wind
    Shall be the portion of their cup.

7   For the LORD *is* righteous,
    He loves righteousness;
    His countenance beholds the upright.[m]

PSALM 12

To the Chief Musician. On an eight-stringed harp.[n] A Psalm
of David.

Help,* LORD, for the godly man ceases!
       For the faithful disappear from among the
       sons of men.
2   They speak idly everyone with his neighbor;
    With flattering lips *and* a double heart they
       speak.

3   *May the LORD cut off all flattering lips,
    And the tongue that speaks proud things,
4   Who have said,
    "With our tongue we will prevail;
    Our lips *are* our own;
    Who *is* lord over us?"

5   "For the oppression of the poor, for the
       sighing of the needy,
    Now I will arise," says the LORD;
    "I will set *him* in the safety for which he
       yearns."

6   *The words of the LORD *are* pure words,
    Like silver tried in a furnace of earth,
    Purified seven times.
7   You shall keep them, O LORD,
    You shall preserve them from this
       generation forever.

8   The wicked prowl on every side,
    When vileness is exalted among the sons
       of men.

"*It is always too soon to quit.*"
—V. Raymond Edman

PSALM 11

11:1 David was in great difficulty. Around him, the archers were getting ready to shoot. Under him, the foundations of society were shaking. What should he do? What would you do?

11:2 When you are in that kind of situation, your first thought may be to get away as fast as you can. Even David's friends advised him to act like the bird and fly away. It is right to flee from temptation (Gen. 39:11–13) but not from duty (Neh. 6:10–11; Luke 13:31; John 10:12–13). Instead of flying away like a frightened bird, you should trust God and "mount up with wings like eagles" (Isa. 40:31).

11:3 If the foundations are destroyed, *lay the foundations again.* That is what Ezra did (Ezra 3:8ff.) and what each new generation may have to do. David became king of Israel and laid the foundations for a godly society. After all, God is still on His throne (v. 4) and will one day judge the wicked (vv. 5–6). If you love righteousness, God is on your side (v. 7).

PSALM 12

12:1, 2 *David's words.* In the previous psalm, David saw the *foundations* failing; in this one, the *faithful* were vanishing from the earth (v. 1). The godly remnant was getting smaller and smaller, and David was feeling very much alone. No wonder he cried out, "Help, Lord!"

12:3–5 *Man's words.* What made David conclude that godliness was on the decline? *The way people spoke.* David heard flattering words, proud words, and oppressive words, and he knew that God was displeased. In our "age of communication," are you able to discern what is true and right? When you speak, is it communication or manipulation?

12:6–8 *God's words.* God's Word is pure, proved, and preserved, and you can depend on it. So much of what man says is cheap and temporary, but God's Word is like pure silver that is valuable and lasting. Let your words be controlled by His Word and God will make your words valuable (Prov. 10:20; 25:11).

11:7 [m]Or *The upright beholds His countenance*
12:title [n]Hebrew *sheminith*

13:1–2 *Asking.* Four times David asked, "How long?" He had prayed, but God had hidden Himself and not answered. David had examined his heart and knew of no reason why God should abandon him. The longer God waited, the more the enemy would succeed. When you have this same feeling, do what David did and talk to God with an honest and humble heart.

13:3, 4 *Arguing.* Would God be glorified by David's defeat? Would God's cause be helped by David's death? Should the enemy rejoice while God's people suffer? David reasoned with God but did not try to tell God what to do. Sometimes prayer means wrestling.

13:5, 6 *Affirming.* Faith does not always give answers, but it does give encouragement. No matter how successful the enemy appears to be, you can trust the Lord, rejoice in the Lord, sing to the Lord and know that He will always deal bountifully with you.

❝*It is faith's work to claim and challenge lovingkindness out of all the roughest strokes of God.*❞
—Samuel Rutherford

14:2 The contrast is between the generation of the wicked and the generation of the righteous (v. 5). The latter group is made up of those who have trusted the Lord and seek Him and His will (Ps. 24:6).

14:3 The generation of the wicked is composed of people who are "practical atheists": God is not in their hearts, no matter what they may say and do outwardly. They can live without God! They disobey God and exploit people made in the image of God. They are corrupt (v. 1), and so they do corrupt things.

14:4 The generation of the righteous calls on the Lord and He answers (v. 4). God dwells with these people (v. 5), protects them (v. 6), and gives them joyful hope
(continued)

PSALM 13

To the Chief Musician. A Psalm of David.

H̲ow* long, O LORD? Will You forget me forever?
How long will You hide Your face from me?
2   How long shall I take counsel in my soul,
Having sorrow in my heart daily?
How long will my enemy be exalted over me?

3   *Consider *and* hear me, O LORD my God;
Enlighten my eyes,
Lest I sleep the *sleep of* death;
4   Lest my enemy say,
"I have prevailed against him";
Lest those who trouble me rejoice when I am moved.

5   *But I have trusted in Your mercy;
My heart shall rejoice in Your salvation.
6   I will sing to the LORD,
Because He has dealt bountifully with me.

PSALM 14

To the Chief Musician. A Psalm of David.

T̲he fool has said in his heart,
"*There is* no God."
They are corrupt,
They have done abominable works,
There is none who does good.

2   *The LORD looks down from heaven upon the children of men,
To see if there are any who understand, who seek God.
3   *They have all turned aside,
They have together become corrupt;
There is none who does good,
No, not one.

4   *Have all the workers of iniquity no knowledge,
Who eat up my people *as* they eat bread,
And do not call on the LORD?
5   There they are in great fear,
For God *is* with the generation of the righteous.
6   You shame the counsel of the poor,
But the LORD *is* his refuge.

7   Oh, that the salvation of Israel *would come* out of Zion!
When the LORD brings back the captivity of His people,
Let Jacob rejoice *and* Israel be glad.

Don't Despair—"How long?" is a question frequently asked in the Psalms: 6:3; 35:17; 74:10; 79:5; 80:4; 82:2; 89:46; 90:13; and 94:3. Time seems to rush by when we are enjoying life but to linger when we are suffering. God knows how long our trials should last because He knows exactly what we need (1 Pet. 1:6–8).

PSALM 15

A Psalm of David.

Lord,* who may abide in Your tabernacle?
Who may dwell in Your holy hill?

2 *He who walks uprightly,
And works righteousness,
And speaks the truth in his heart;
3 He *who* does not backbite with his tongue,
Nor does evil to his neighbor,
Nor does he take up a reproach against
his friend;
4 *In whose eyes a vile person is despised,
But he honors those who fear the Lord;
He *who* swears to his own hurt and does
not change;
5 He *who* does not put out his money at usury,
Nor does he take a bribe against the
innocent.

He who does these *things* shall never be
moved.

PSALM 16

A Michtam of David.

Preserve* me, O God, for in You I put my trust.

2 O my soul, you have said to the Lord,
"You *are* my Lord,
My goodness is nothing apart from You."
3 *As for the saints who *are* on the earth,
"They are the excellent ones, in whom is all
my delight."

4 Their sorrows shall be multiplied who
hasten *after* another god;
Their drink offerings of blood I will not
offer,
Nor take up their names on my lips.

(continued from previous page)
(v. 7). The group may not be large, but it is
precious to God; and the future of God's
program rests with it.
    Of which group are you a member? Have
you made your allegiance known?

PSALM 15

15:1 David loved God's house and longed
to dwell there and fellowship with God (Ps.
27:4–5). He yearned to be like the priests
who lived in the tabernacle and had constant
access to holy things. David wished he could
even be a guest and pay God a visit, but
did he qualify? Does anybody qualify?

15:2 God's children have open access into
His presence through the work of Jesus
Christ (Heb. 10:19–25). He is our High Priest
and Advocate in heaven, and He welcomes
us. We come on the basis of His
righteousness, not our own. But we had
better be sure we have experienced the
cleansing of Hebrews 10:22 before we rush
into His presence.

15:4 This psalm helps us examine our walk,
our works, and our words (v. 2). The
inventory includes our relationship with
others (vv. 3–4), how we keep our promises,
and how we use our money (v. 5). Meditating
on this psalm and pondering these
"qualifications" could help us deepen our
relationship with God.

PSALM 16

16:1 You have taken a giant step toward
true Christian maturity when you can say
(continued)

Psalms and Hymns

Some of our best-loved songs are based on psalms.

Title	Composer	Psalm
"A Mighty Fortress"	Luther	Ps. 46
"O God, Our Help in Ages Past"	Watts	Ps. 90
"The King of Love My Shepherd Is"	Baker	Ps. 23
"Joy to the World"	Watts	Ps. 98
"Ivory Palaces"	Barraclough	Ps. 45
"O Worship the King"	Grant	Ps. 104
"All People That on Earth Do Dwell"	Kethe	Ps. 100
"Praise, My Soul, the King of Heaven"	Lyte	Ps. 103
"Glorious Things of Thee Are Spoken"	Newton	Ps. 87
"Under His Wings"	Cushing	Ps. 91

(continued from previous page)
to the Lord *and mean it,* "My goodness is nothing apart from You" (v. 2).

16:3 *Good fellowship.* God's people are not perfect, but we should delight in their fellowship and not in the fellowship of the world's crowd (2 Cor. 6:14–18). The world needs our witness, but we must take care not to start loving the world (1 John 2:15–17).

16:5 *Good heritage.* Not just God's gifts, but God Himself! What a joy it is to let God choose your inheritance for you instead of acting like the world and fighting for your "place in the sun."

16:7 *Good counsel.* God gives wisdom if you will ask Him (James 1:5). God teaches you in the darkness as well as in the light. These verses are summarized in Matthew 6:33.

16:8 *Good hope.* This passage is one of the few in the Old Testament dealing with resurrection. It refers to the resurrection of Christ (Acts 2:22–32), and that is what gives us our hope (1 Pet. 1:3).

PSALM 17

17:1 "God is Spirit" (John 4:24) and therefore does not have a body. Sometimes Scripture uses the parts of the human body to describe God's activities with respect to His people. He does not have eyes, but He sees us; He does not have ears, but He hears our cries. David referred to four of these in this psalm.

17:2 *God's ears.* The enemy opposed David's just cause, so he cried out to God for vindication. David's prayer was sincere, and he wanted God to judge righteously.

17:3 *God's eyes.* David had nothing to hide. His heart was right and his walk was righteous. You must be able to say the same of your heart and walk if you expect God to answer your prayers (Ps. 66:18).

17:6 *God's hand.* David trusted not his own hand but the hand of God to protect him and to defeat the enemy. The pride of the enemy grieved David because he wanted God alone to be glorified.

5 *O LORD, *You are* the portion of my inheritance and my cup;
You maintain my lot.
6 The lines have fallen to me in pleasant *places;*
Yes, I have a good inheritance.

7 *I will bless the LORD who has given me counsel;
My heart also instructs me in the night seasons.
8 *I have set the LORD always before me;
Because *He is* at my right hand I shall not be moved.

9 Therefore my heart is glad, and my glory rejoices;
My flesh also will rest in hope.
10 For You will not leave my soul in Sheol,
Nor will You allow Your Holy One to see corruption.
11 You will show me the path of life;
In Your presence *is* fullness of joy;
At Your right hand *are* pleasures forevermore.

PSALM 17

A Prayer of David.

Hear* a just cause, O LORD,
Attend to my cry;
Give ear to my prayer *which is* not from deceitful lips.
2 *Let my vindication come from Your presence;
Let Your eyes look on the things that are upright.

3 *You have tested my heart;
You have visited *me* in the night;
You have tried me and have found nothing;
I have purposed that my mouth shall not transgress.
4 Concerning the works of men,
By the word of Your lips,
I have kept away from the paths of the destroyer.
5 Uphold my steps in Your paths,
That my footsteps may not slip.

6 *I have called upon You, for You will hear me, O God;
Incline Your ear to me, *and* hear my speech.
7 Show Your marvelous lovingkindness by Your right hand,
O You who save those who trust *in You*
From those who rise up *against them.*
8 Keep me as the apple of Your eye;
Hide me under the shadow of Your wings,
9 From the wicked who oppress me,
From my deadly enemies who surround me.

10 They have closed up their fat *hearts;*
With their mouths they speak proudly.
11 They have now surrounded us in our steps;
They have set their eyes, crouching down to the earth,
12 As a lion is eager to tear his prey,
And like a young lion lurking in secret places.

13 Arise, O Lord,
  Confront him, cast him down;
  Deliver my life from the wicked with Your
      sword,
14 With Your hand from men, O Lord,
  From men of the world *who have* their
      portion in *this* life,
  And whose belly You fill with Your hidden
      treasure.
  They are satisfied with children,
  And leave the rest of their *possession* for
      their babes.

15 *As for me, I will see Your face in
      righteousness;
  I shall be satisfied when I awake in Your
      likeness.

PSALM 18

To the Chief Musician. A Psalm of David the servant of the
Lord, who spoke to the Lord the words of this song on the
day that the Lord delivered him from the hand of all his
enemies and from the hand of Saul. And he said:

I* will love You, O Lord, my strength.
2   The Lord is my rock and my fortress and
      my deliverer;
  My God, my strength, in whom I will trust;
  My shield and the horn of my salvation, my
      stronghold.
3 *I will call upon the Lord, *who is worthy* to
      be praised;
  So shall I be saved from my enemies.

4 *The pangs of death surrounded me,
  And the floods of ungodliness made me
      afraid.
5 The sorrows of Sheol surrounded me;
  The snares of death confronted me.
6 In my distress I called upon the Lord,
  And cried out to my God;
  He heard my voice from His temple,
  And my cry came before Him, *even* to His
      ears.

7 Then the earth shook and trembled;
  The foundations of the hills also quaked and
      were shaken,
  Because He was angry.
8 Smoke went up from His nostrils,
  And devouring fire from His mouth;
  Coals were kindled by it.
9 He bowed the heavens also, and came down
  With darkness under His feet.
10 And He rode upon a cherub, and flew;
  He flew upon the wings of the wind.
11 He made darkness His secret place;
  His canopy around Him *was* dark waters
  And thick clouds of the skies.
12 From the brightness before Him,
  His thick clouds passed with hailstones and
      coals of fire.

13 The Lord thundered from heaven,
  And the Most High uttered His voice,
  Hailstones and coals of fire.°

17:15 *God's likeness.* God has in mind this
goal when He permits you to go through
trials: He wants to make you more like His
Son (Rom. 8:29; 2 Cor. 3:18). Although this
verse may refer to future resurrection
(1 John 3:1–3; see also 1 Cor. 15:49), it
can be applied to life today. Our Lord goes
with us into the furnace so that we may be
more like Him when we come out of it (Dan.
3:19–25).

PSALM 18

18:1 David sang this song after God
delivered him from his enemies and
established him as the king of Israel. (See
our comments on 2 Sam. 22.) But keep in
mind that he often sang to God in the midst
of his trials. It is easier to sing after the
victory; it takes faith to sing *during* the battle.
As David looked back on those difficult
years, what did he see?

18:3 *God's faithfulness.* God saved David,
protected him, and strengthened him when
Saul and his men were out to kill him. Is
God your refuge and your strength (Ps.
46:1)?

18:4 *God's righteousness.* Those had
been stormy years for David, yet God
rescued him and upheld His dedicated
servant. David had obeyed God's Word and
accomplished God's will, so God rewarded
him. When the storms come, remember that
God is greater than the storms and will help
you see the rainbow.

18:13 °Following Masoretic Text, Targum, and Vulgate; a few
Hebrew manuscripts and Septuagint omit *Hailstones and
coals of fire.*

14 He sent out His arrows and scattered the
foe,
Lightnings in abundance, and He
vanquished them.
15 Then the channels of the sea were seen,
The foundations of the world were
uncovered
At Your rebuke, O LORD,
At the blast of the breath of Your nostrils.

16 He sent from above, He took me;
He drew me out of many waters.
17 He delivered me from my strong enemy,
From those who hated me,
For they were too strong for me.
18 They confronted me in the day of my
calamity,
But the LORD was my support.
19 He also brought me out into a broad place;
He delivered me because He delighted in
me.

20 The LORD rewarded me according to my
righteousness;
According to the cleanness of my hands
He has recompensed me.
21 For I have kept the ways of the LORD,
And have not wickedly departed from my
God.
22 For all His judgments *were* before me,
And I did not put away His statutes from
me.
23 I was also blameless before Him,
And I kept myself from my iniquity.
24 Therefore the LORD has recompensed me
according to my righteousness,
According to the cleanness of my hands in
His sight.

25 With the merciful You will show Yourself
merciful;
With a blameless man You will show
Yourself blameless;
26 With the pure You will show Yourself
pure;
And with the devious You will show
Yourself shrewd.
27 For You will save the humble people,
But will bring down haughty looks.

28 *For You will light my lamp;
The LORD my God will enlighten my
darkness.
29 For by You I can run against a troop,
By my God I can leap over a wall.
30 *As for* God, His way *is* perfect;
The word of the LORD is proven;
He *is* a shield to all who trust in Him.

31 For who *is* God, except the LORD?
And who *is* a rock, except our God?
32 *It is* God who arms me with strength,
And makes my way perfect.
33 He makes my feet like the *feet of* deer,
And sets me on my high places.
34 He teaches my hands to make war,
So that my arms can bend a bow of bronze.

35 You have also given me the shield of Your
salvation;
Your right hand has held me up,
Your gentleness has made me great.

18:28 God's gentleness. God did many
things to make David a great soldier, but
His gentleness made David what he was
(v. 35). God was doing more than winning
wars; He was building character. It humbled
David to think that God would condescend
to call him, equip him, and help him (Ps.
8:3–5). (See Ps. 113:6; Isa. 57:15–16.)

36 You enlarged my path under me,
   So my feet did not slip.

37 *I have pursued my enemies and overtaken
      them;
   Neither did I turn back again till they were
      destroyed.
38 I have wounded them,
   So that they could not rise;
   They have fallen under my feet.
39 For You have armed me with strength for
      the battle;
   You have subdued under me those who rose
      up against me.
40 You have also given me the necks of my
      enemies,
   So that I destroyed those who hated me.
41 They cried out, but *there was* none to save;
   Even to the LORD, but He did not answer
      them.
42 Then I beat them as fine as the dust before
      the wind;
   I cast them out like dirt in the streets.

43 You have delivered me from the strivings
      of the people;
   You have made me the head of the nations;
   A people I have not known shall serve me.
44 As soon as they hear of me they obey me;
   The foreigners submit to me.
45 The foreigners fade away,
   And come frightened from their hideouts.

46 The LORD lives!
   Blessed *be* my Rock!
   Let the God of my salvation be exalted.
47 *It is* God who avenges me,
   And subdues the peoples under me;
48 He delivers me from my enemies.
   You also lift me up above those who rise
      against me;
   You have delivered me from the violent
      man.
49 Therefore I will give thanks to You, O LORD,
      among the Gentiles,
   And sing praises to Your name.

50 Great deliverance He gives to His king,
   And shows mercy to His anointed,
   To David and his descendants forevermore.

PSALM 19

To the Chief Musician. A Psalm of David.

The* heavens declare the glory of God;
And the firmament shows His handiwork.
2 Day unto day utters speech,
   And night unto night reveals knowledge.
3 *There is* no speech nor language
   Where their voice is not heard.
4 Their line[p] has gone out through all the
      earth,
   And their words to the end of the world.

   In them He has set a tabernacle for the sun,
5 Which *is* like a bridegroom coming out of
      his chamber,

18:37 *God's exaltedness.* David did not take credit for his victories; he gave all the glory to the Lord. Whatever David had, God gave it to him; whatever he was, God made him; whatever he did, God enabled him. Blessed be the name of the Lord!

PSALM 19

19:1 God reveals Himself in creation (vv. 1–6), in the Scriptures (vv. 7–11), and in your heart as you worship Him (vv. 12–14). To be properly "educated" in spiritual things, you must seek to master three books: the book of nature, the Bible, and the book of humanity. A scientist studies the book of nature and a psychologist the book of human nature, but if they ignore God's Book, their conclusions may be wrong. Keep balanced. All truth is God's truth.

19:4 [p]Septuagint, Syriac, and Vulgate read *sound;* Targum reads *business.*

And rejoices like a strong man to run its
race.
6   Its rising *is* from one end of heaven,
And its circuit to the other end;
And there is nothing hidden from its heat.

7   *The law of the LORD *is* perfect, converting
the soul;
The testimony of the LORD *is* sure, making
wise the simple;
8   The statutes of the LORD *are* right, rejoicing
the heart;
The commandment of the LORD *is* pure,
enlightening the eyes;
9   The fear of the LORD *is* clean, enduring
forever;
The judgments of the LORD *are* true *and*
righteous altogether.
10 More to be desired *are they* than gold,
Yea, than much fine gold;
Sweeter also than honey and the
honeycomb.
11 Moreover by them Your servant is warned,
And in keeping them *there is* great reward.

12 Who can understand *his* errors?
Cleanse me from secret *faults.*
13 Keep back Your servant also from
presumptuous *sins;*
Let them not have dominion over me.
Then I shall be blameless,
And I shall be innocent of great
transgression.

14 *Let the words of my mouth and the
meditation of my heart
Be acceptable in Your sight,
O LORD, my strength and my Redeemer.

PSALM 20

To the Chief Musician. A Psalm of David.

May* the LORD answer you in the day of
trouble;
May the name of the God of Jacob defend
you;
2   May He send you help from the sanctuary,
And strengthen you out of Zion;
3   May He remember all your offerings,
And accept your burnt sacrifice.   Selah

4   *May He grant you according to your heart's
desire,
And fulfill all your purpose.
5   We will rejoice in your salvation,
And in the name of our God we will set up
our banners!
May the LORD fulfill all your petitions.

6   Now I know that the LORD saves His
anointed;
He will answer him from His holy heaven
With the saving strength of His right hand.

19:7 The goal of all study is a knowledge of Jesus Christ and of yourself. Verses 7–11 tell you what the Bible can do for you if only you will read it, meditate on it, and obey it. The better you understand your Bible and obey it, the more you will appreciate God's creation and the better you will understand yourself and others. God's Word is the basic book.

19:14 Open each day beholding God's glory in Jesus Christ (v. 1). Enter each day with the devotion of a bridegroom and the determination of an athlete (vv. 4–5). At the end of the day, what you have done will please Him (v. 14).

PSALM 20

20:1–3 *A day of trouble.* David was going out to battle, and he and his people gathered to pray. His secret of victory was the name of the Lord (v. 1), the Lord he worshiped sincerely and sacrificially.

20:4 *A day of triumph.* Again, it is in the name of the Lord that you fight the forces of evil (v. 5). God hears and answers prayer and sends you the help you need.

What's in a Name?—In the Bible, names are important because the name represents the person. When somebody had a life-changing experience, the name was often changed. For example, Abram became Abraham and Sarai became Sarah (Gen. 17), and Simon was given the name Peter (John 1:42). The Bible records many names of God, and all of them can be trusted. (See Pss. 9:10; 33:21; 44:5.)

7 *Some *trust* in chariots, and some in horses;
But we will remember the name of the LORD our God.
8 They have bowed down and fallen;
But we have risen and stand upright.

9 Save, LORD!
May the King answer us when we call.

PSALM 21

To the Chief Musician. A Psalm of David.

The* king shall have joy in Your strength, O LORD;
And in Your salvation how greatly shall he rejoice!
2 *You have given him his heart's desire,
And have not withheld the request of his lips. Selah

3 For You meet him with the blessings of goodness;
You set a crown of pure gold upon his head.
4 He asked life from You, *and* You gave *it* to him—
Length of days forever and ever.
5 His glory *is* great in Your salvation;
Honor and majesty You have placed upon him.
6 For You have made him most blessed forever;
You have made him exceedingly glad with Your presence.
7 For the king trusts in the LORD,
And through the mercy of the Most High he shall not be moved.

8 *Your hand will find all Your enemies;
Your right hand will find those who hate You.
9 You shall make them as a fiery oven in the time of Your anger;
The LORD shall swallow them up in His wrath,
And the fire shall devour them.
10 Their offspring You shall destroy from the earth,
And their descendants from among the sons of men.
11 For they intended evil against You;
They devised a plot *which* they are not able *to perform.*
12 Therefore You will make them turn their back;
You will make ready *Your arrows* on Your string toward their faces.

13 *Be exalted, O LORD, in Your own strength!
We will sing and praise Your power.

PSALM 22

To the Chief Musician. Set to "The Deer of the Dawn."[q] A Psalm of David.

My* God, My God, why have You forsaken Me?
Why are You so far from helping Me,
And from the words of My groaning?

22:title [q]Hebrew *Aijeleth Hashahar*

20:7 ***A day of trust.*** David had a great name, but the name of the Lord is much greater. Some people have names that cannot be trusted, but God's name has never failed. Your days of trouble can become days of triumph if you trust in the name of the Lord.

PSALM 21

21:1 If Psalm 20 is a prayer before the battle, Psalm 21 is the praise after the victory. Too often we forget to praise God when He answers prayer and gives us what we requested. (See Luke 17:11–19.)

21:2–7 ***God and the king.*** God gave David strength to win the battle and then gave him honor and majesty from the victory. Before the battle, David asked God to spare his life, and God gave him his request. God responded to David's faith by protecting him, and David responded to God's blessings by praising Him. David rejoiced in God's strength and salvation (v. 1) and in His presence with him (v. 6).

21:8–12 ***God and the enemy.*** These were the enemies of God because they wanted to destroy His people Israel. David fought the Lord's battles, and the Lord gave victory. God kept His promise to Abraham (Gen. 12:1–3).

21:13 ***God and the nation.*** Now the whole congregation praises the Lord. Individual praise in private is important, but we should share the joy with others and let them praise God with us. Praise Ye the Lord!

PSALM 22

22:1–21 ***Crucifixion.*** Because he was a prophet (Acts 2:30), David was able to write about the Messiah centuries before He came. Crucifixion was not a Jewish form of capital punishment, yet David described it accurately. As you read, you see Jesus at Calvary: His cry to the Father (v. 1; Matt. 27:46); the period of darkness (v. 2; Matt. 27:45); the ridicule of the people (vv. 6–8; Matt. 27:39–44); His thirst and pain (vv. 14–15; John 19:28); His pierced hands and feet (v. 16; Luke 24:39); and the gambling for His clothes (v. 18; John 19:23–24). Remember, He endured all of these things for you.

2 O My God, I cry in the daytime, but You
do not hear;
And in the night season, and am not silent.

3 But You *are* holy,
Enthroned in the praises of Israel.
4 Our fathers trusted in You;
They trusted, and You delivered them.
5 They cried to You, and were delivered;
They trusted in You, and were not ashamed.

6 But I *am* a worm, and no man;
A reproach of men, and despised by the
people.
7 All those who see Me ridicule Me;
They shoot out the lip, they shake the head,
saying,
8 "He trusted[r] in the LORD, let Him rescue Him;
Let Him deliver Him, since He delights in
Him!"

9 But You *are* He who took Me out of the
womb;
You made Me trust *while* on My mother's
breasts.
10 I was cast upon You from birth.
From My mother's womb
You *have been* My God.
11 Be not far from Me,
For trouble *is* near;
For *there is* none to help.

12 Many bulls have surrounded Me;
Strong *bulls* of Bashan have encircled Me.
13 They gape at Me *with* their mouths,
Like a raging and roaring lion.

14 I am poured out like water,
And all My bones are out of joint;
My heart is like wax;
It has melted within Me.
15 My strength is dried up like a potsherd,
And My tongue clings to My jaws;
You have brought Me to the dust of death.

16 For dogs have surrounded Me;
The congregation of the wicked has
enclosed Me.
They pierced[s] My hands and My feet;
17 I can count all My bones.
They look *and* stare at Me.
18 They divide My garments among them,
And for My clothing they cast lots.

19 But You, O LORD, do not be far from Me;
O My Strength, hasten to help Me!
20 Deliver Me from the sword,
My precious *life* from the power of the dog.
21 Save Me from the lion's mouth
And from the horns of the wild oxen!

You have answered Me.

22:8 [r]Septuagint, Syriac, and Vulgate read *hoped;* Targum
reads *praised.* 22:16 [s]Following some Hebrew manuscripts,
Septuagint, Syriac, Vulgate; Masoretic Text reads *Like a lion.*

The Shepherd Psalms—Psalms 22, 23, and 24 are sometimes called the "Shepherd Psalms"
because they speak of Jesus Christ in His shepherding ministry. In Psalm 22, the Good Shepherd
dies for the sheep (John 10:11). In Psalm 23, the Great Shepherd lives and cares for the sheep
(Heb. 13:20–21). In Psalm 24, the Chief Shepherd returns in glory for the sheep (1 Pet. 5:4). If you
are one of His sheep, your every need is met as you trust Him and follow His leading.

22 *I will declare Your name to My brethren;
   In the midst of the assembly I will praise
      You.
23 You who fear the Lord, praise Him!
   All you descendants of Jacob, glorify Him,
   And fear Him, all you offspring of Israel!
24 For He has not despised nor abhorred the
      affliction of the afflicted;
   Nor has He hidden His face from Him;
   But when He cried to Him, He heard.

25 My praise *shall be* of You in the great
      assembly;
   I will pay My vows before those who fear
      Him.
26 The poor shall eat and be satisfied;
   Those who seek Him will praise the Lord.
   Let your heart live forever!

27 *All the ends of the world
   Shall remember and turn to the Lord,
   And all the families of the nations
   Shall worship before You.[t]
28 For the kingdom *is* the Lord's,
   And He rules over the nations.

29 All the prosperous of the earth
   Shall eat and worship;
   All those who go down to the dust
   Shall bow before Him,
   Even he who cannot keep himself alive.

30 A posterity shall serve Him.
   It will be recounted of the Lord to the *next*
      generation.
31 They will come and declare His
      righteousness to a people who will be
      born,
   That He has done *this.*

PSALM 23

A Psalm of David.

The* Lord *is* my shepherd;
      I shall not want.
2   *He makes me to lie down in green pastures;
      He leads me beside the still waters.
3   *He restores my soul;
      He leads me in the paths of righteousness
      For His name's sake.

4   *Yea, though I walk through the valley of
         the shadow of death,
      I will fear no evil;
      For You *are* with me;
      Your rod and Your staff, they comfort me.

5   You prepare a table before me in the
         presence of my enemies;
      You anoint my head with oil;
      My cup runs over.
6   *Surely goodness and mercy shall follow me
      All the days of my life;
      And I will dwell[u] in the house of the Lord
      Forever.

22:27 [t]Following Masoretic Text, Septuagint, and Targum;
Arabic, Syriac, and Vulgate read *Him.*   23:6 [u]Following
Septuagint, Syriac, Targum, and Vulgate; Masoretic Text
reads *return.*

22:22–26 Resurrection. The Savior is no
longer on the cross but is alive and in the
midst of His people, leading them in praise
for the mighty victory God has won (Heb.
2:11–12). The first day of the week is the
memorial to His resurrection, and we follow
His example by meeting with God's people
and praising the Lord. Resurrection day is
victory day!

22:27 Coronation. Christ shares the
blessings of Calvary with His church (v. 22),
with Israel (v. 23), and with the whole world
(vv. 27–31). We must get the message out
to every nation that Jesus Christ is Savior
and King (v. 27): "The Father has sent the
Son as Savior of the world" (1 John 4:14).

PSALM 23

23:1 Though Psalm 23 is often read at
funerals, its message applies to the days
of your life right now (v. 6). The Savior who
died for you also lives for you and cares
for you, the way a shepherd cares for the
sheep (John 10:1–18). If you can say, "The
Lord is *my* Shepherd," you can also say,
"I shall not want."

23:2 The Shepherd feeds us and leads us.
Sheep must have grass and water to live,
and the shepherd finds those essential
elements for them. God meets the everyday
needs of your life as you follow Him (Ps.
37:25; Phil. 4:18). Never worry!

23:3 If we wander, He seeks us and
restores us, as He did with David, Jonah,
and Peter. When we need to know which
way to go, He shows us the right path and
then goes before us to prepare the way.
Even in the places of danger, we need not
be afraid. (Note the change from "He" in
vv. 1–3 to "You" in vv. 4–5.) He is with you!

23:4 At the end of the dark valley, He has
a special blessing for you: you drink of the
refreshing water of life, and you receive the
Spirit's anointing. The Shepherd is there to
care for every hurt and heal every bruise.

23:6 One day, you will look back at your
life and see that it was only "goodness and
mercy," and that includes the valley
experiences. If life is difficult today, just keep
following the Shepherd; He will never lead
you where He cannot care for you.

24:1 Psalm 22 points to our Lord's grace in dying for us, and Psalm 23 explains His goodness in caring for us. This psalm reveals His glory in coming for us.

Glory in creation (1–2). These verses remind you of Psalms 8 and 19. The world today is in travail because of sin, but the Creator will one day set His creation free (Rom. 8:18–23).

Glory in salvation (3–6). Psalm 15 is a parallel, and both passages emphasize the fact that nobody but the Lord Jesus Christ can meet God's qualifications to live in His holy palace. We are all like Jacob, but He is "the God of Jacob" (Ps. 46:7) and will forgive us and let us live with Him forever!

Glory in the kingdom (7–10). These verses may originally have celebrated David's return to Jerusalem from a great victory, but they speak to us of our King of glory. When He rode into Jerusalem, Jesus came in humility and tears (Luke 19:29–44); but when He comes again, it will be in power and great glory (Matt. 24:29ff.). Your Shepherd is the King of glory!

25:1 This psalm is helpful when you are making decisions and seeking God's will. What kind of people does God guide?

25:2 *Those who glorify Him.* If you want His will for His glory, He will show you the right path. If you have selfish motives, He may let you have your way, and then you will regret it.

25:3 *Those who wait.* You are not wasting time when you wait on the Lord in prayer.

25:4 *Those who ask.* God wants to show you His ways, teach you His paths, and lead you in His truths. The Word of God and prayer always go together, so spend time in His Word. If you ask Him sincerely, He will answer you clearly.

25:6 *Those who are clean.* Psalm 66:18 applies here, as does 1 John 1:9.

25:8 *Those who submit.* God does not guide rebels, but He joyfully leads those who fear Him and submit to His will (Ps. 32:8–9). Keep your eyes on the Lord and let Him have His way. He knows where He is going and what He is doing, so follow Him by faith.

PSALM 24

A Psalm of David.

The* earth is the LORD's, and all its fullness,
The world and those who dwell therein.
2 For He has founded it upon the seas,
And established it upon the waters.

3 Who may ascend into the hill of the LORD?
Or who may stand in His holy place?
4 He who has clean hands and a pure heart,
Who has not lifted up his soul to an idol,
Nor sworn deceitfully.
5 He shall receive blessing from the LORD,
And righteousness from the God of his salvation.
6 This is Jacob, the generation of those who seek Him,
Who seek Your face.   Selah

7 Lift up your heads, O you gates!
And be lifted up, you everlasting doors!
And the King of glory shall come in.
8 Who is this King of glory?
The LORD strong and mighty,
The LORD mighty in battle.
9 Lift up your heads, O you gates!
Lift up, you everlasting doors!
And the King of glory shall come in.
10 Who is this King of glory?
The LORD of hosts,
He is the King of glory.   Selah

PSALM 25

A Psalm of David.

To* You, O LORD, I lift up my soul.
2 *O my God, I trust in You;
Let me not be ashamed;
Let not my enemies triumph over me.
3 *Indeed, let no one who waits on You be ashamed;
Let those be ashamed who deal treacherously without cause.

4 *Show me Your ways, O LORD;
Teach me Your paths.
5 Lead me in Your truth and teach me,
For You are the God of my salvation;
On You I wait all the day.

6 *Remember, O LORD, Your tender mercies and Your lovingkindnesses,
For they are from of old.
7 Do not remember the sins of my youth, nor my transgressions;
According to Your mercy remember me,
For Your goodness' sake, O LORD.

8 *Good and upright is the LORD;
Therefore He teaches sinners in the way.
9 The humble He guides in justice,
And the humble He teaches His way.
10 All the paths of the LORD are mercy and truth,
To such as keep His covenant and His testimonies.
11 For Your name's sake, O LORD,
Pardon my iniquity, for it is great.

12 Who is the man that fears the LORD?
   Him shall He[v] teach in the way He[w] chooses.
13 He himself shall dwell in prosperity,
   And his descendants shall inherit the
      earth.
14 The secret of the LORD is with those who
      fear Him,
   And He will show them His covenant.
15 My eyes are ever toward the LORD,
   For He shall pluck my feet out of the
      net.

16 Turn Yourself to me, and have mercy on
      me,
   For I am desolate and afflicted.
17 The troubles of my heart have enlarged;
   Bring me out of my distresses!
18 Look on my affliction and my pain,
   And forgive all my sins.
19 Consider my enemies, for they are many;
   And they hate me with cruel hatred.
20 Keep my soul, and deliver me;
   Let me not be ashamed, for I put my trust
      in You.
21 *Let integrity and uprightness preserve
      me,
   For I wait for You.

22 Redeem Israel, O God,
   Out of all their troubles!

PSALM 26

A Psalm of David.

Vindicate* me, O LORD,
   For I have walked in my integrity.
   I have also trusted in the LORD;
   I shall not slip.
2 Examine me, O LORD, and prove me;
   Try my mind and my heart.
3 For Your lovingkindness is before my
      eyes,
   And I have walked in Your truth.
4 I have not sat with idolatrous mortals,
   Nor will I go in with hypocrites.
5 I have hated the assembly of evildoers,
   And will not sit with the wicked.

6 *I will wash my hands in innocence;
   So I will go about Your altar, O LORD,
7 That I may proclaim with the voice of
      thanksgiving,
   And tell of all Your wondrous works.
8 LORD, I have loved the habitation of Your
      house,
   And the place where Your glory dwells.

9 Do not gather my soul with sinners,
   Nor my life with bloodthirsty men,
10 In whose hands is a sinister scheme,
   And whose right hand is full of bribes.

11 *But as for me, I will walk in my integrity;
   Redeem me and be merciful to me.
12 My foot stands in an even place;
   In the congregations I will bless the
      LORD.

❝On every level of life from housework to heights of prayer, in all judgment and all efforts to get things done, hurry and impatience are sure marks of the amateur.❞
—Evelyn Underhill

25:21 The enemy was slandering David again, and he had no way to vindicate himself. Samuel Johnson called slander "the revenge of a coward," and it is. What should you do when people spread lies about you?

PSALM 26

26:1–5 Examine yourself. Is your life what it ought to be? Let God test your mind and heart (Ps. 139:23–24). In your walking, standing (v. 12), and sitting, are you keeping yourself clean (Ps. 1:1)? Sometimes God allows the enemy to attack us just to make us take time for a personal inventory.

26:6 Focus on the Lord. If you look at others, you will be upset, and if you look at yourself too long, you may get discouraged, *so focus your attention on the Lord.* Match your defects with His perfections and claim what you need from Him.

26:11 Keep serving the Lord. The enemy wants nothing better than to upset you and get you on a detour (Neh. 6:1–14). Continue to walk with the Lord and serve Him, come what may. Bless the Lord and don't complain. God will vindicate you in His time and in His own way.

❝Look at others and be distressed; look at self and be depressed; look at Jesus and you will be blessed.❞
—Anonymous

PSALM 27

A Psalm of David.

T**he*** LORD *is* my light and my salvation;
  Whom shall I fear?
  The LORD *is* the strength of my life;
  Of whom shall I be afraid?
2 When the wicked came against me
  To eat up my flesh,
  My enemies and foes,
  They stumbled and fell.
3 Though an army may encamp against me,
  My heart shall not fear;
  Though war may rise against me,
  In this I *will be* confident.

4 *One *thing* I have desired of the LORD,
  That will I seek:
  That I may dwell in the house of the LORD
  All the days of my life,
  To behold the beauty of the LORD,
  And to inquire in His temple.
5 For in the time of trouble
  He shall hide me in His pavilion;
  In the secret place of His tabernacle
  He shall hide me;
  He shall set me high upon a rock.

6 And now my head shall be lifted up above
    my enemies all around me;
  Therefore I will offer sacrifices of joy in His
    tabernacle;
  I will sing, yes, I will sing praises to the
    LORD.

7 *Hear, O LORD, *when* I cry with my voice!
  Have mercy also upon me, and answer
    me.
8 *When You said,* "Seek My face,"
  My heart said to You, "Your face, LORD, I
    will seek."
9 Do not hide Your face from me;
  Do not turn Your servant away in anger;
  You have been my help;
  Do not leave me nor forsake me,
  O God of my salvation.
10 When my father and my mother forsake me,
  Then the LORD will take care of me.

11 *Teach me Your way, O LORD,
  And lead me in a smooth path, because of
    my enemies.
12 Do not deliver me to the will of my
    adversaries;
  For false witnesses have risen against me,
  And such as breathe out violence.
13 *I would have lost heart,* unless I had
    believed
  That I would see the goodness of the LORD
  In the land of the living.

14 *Wait on the LORD;
  Be of good courage,
  And He shall strengthen your heart;
  Wait, I say, on the LORD!

PSALM 28

A Psalm of David.

T**o*** You I will cry, O LORD my Rock:
  Do not be silent to me,

PSALM 27

27:1 What makes you afraid? Darkness? But the Lord is your light. Danger? He is also your salvation. Deficiency? He is your strength. Then why be afraid? See what He does for you.

27:4 *God saves you.* Because he was not a priest, David could not actually go into the tabernacle, but he could still rest in the Lord and trust Him as his refuge. The New Testament equivalent for this is "Abide in Me" (John 15:1–11). In Him is perfect safety.

27:7 *God smiles on you.* You must go beyond merely seeking God's help. *Seek His face* (Num. 6:22–27). The smile of God is all you need to overcome the scowls of men.

27:11 *God shows you the way.* Satan wants to trap you, but the Lord will show you the safe way. Believe His promise and walk by faith. His goodness will be with you.

27:14 *God strengthens you.* We need strength for the battle and strength for the journey, and God abundantly provides. Be sure to take time to wait on the Lord (Isa. 40:31). If you run ahead of Him or lag behind, you will be a perfect target for the enemy.

PSALM 28

28:1–5 *Requesting.* David's enemies were undermining his reputation and his work, so he turned to the Lord with two special requests: that God would speak to him (vv. 1–2) and that God would save him (vv. 3–5). God speaks to us in answered prayer. "If You are silent," said David, "I might just as well be dead! And if You don't deliver me, You are treating me like the enemy!" Pretty powerful arguments!

Lest, if You *are* silent to me,
I become like those who go down to the pit.
2 Hear the voice of my supplications
When I cry to You,
When I lift up my hands toward Your holy
    sanctuary.

3 Do not take me away with the wicked
And with the workers of iniquity,
Who speak peace to their neighbors,
But evil *is* in their hearts.
4 Give them according to their deeds,
And according to the wickedness of their
    endeavors;
Give them according to the work of their
    hands;
Render to them what they deserve.
5 Because they do not regard the works of
    the LORD,
Nor the operation of His hands,
He shall destroy them
And not build them up.

6 *Blessed *be* the LORD,
Because He has heard the voice of my
    supplications!
7 The LORD *is* my strength and my shield;
My heart trusted in Him, and I am helped;
Therefore my heart greatly rejoices,
And with my song I will praise Him.

8 The LORD *is* their strength,ˣ
And He *is* the saving refuge of His anointed.
9 Save Your people,
And bless Your inheritance;
Shepherd them also,
And bear them up forever.

PSALM 29

A Psalm of David.

Give* unto the LORD, O you mighty ones,
    Give unto the LORD glory and strength.
2 Give unto the LORD the glory due to His
    name;
Worship the LORD in the beauty of holiness.

3 *The voice of the LORD *is* over the waters;
The God of glory thunders;
The LORD *is* over many waters.
4 The voice of the LORD *is* powerful;
The voice of the LORD *is* full of majesty.

5 The voice of the LORD breaks the cedars,
Yes, the LORD splinters the cedars of
    Lebanon.
6 He makes them also skip like a calf,
Lebanon and Sirion like a young wild ox.
7 The voice of the LORD divides the flames of
    fire.

8 The voice of the LORD shakes the
    wilderness;
The LORD shakes the Wilderness of Kadesh.
9 The voice of the LORD makes the deer give
    birth,
And strips the forests bare;
And in His temple everyone says, "Glory!"

God moves in a mysterious way,
    His wonders to perform;
He plants His footsteps in the sea,
    and rides upon the storm,
Ye fearful saints, fresh courage
    take; the clouds ye so much
    dread;
Are big with mercy, and shall
    break;
With blessing on your head.

—William Cowper

28:6–9 *Rejoicing.* God heard him and
helped him, and He does the same for you
today as you trust Him. You can rejoice in
the Lord even when you cannot rejoice in
yourselves or your circumstances. Trust
God to be your strength, your song, and your
salvation (Isa. 12:2). He is the faithful
Shepherd who can carry both you and your
burdens.

PSALM 29

29:1–2 *Praise before the storm.* David
called on the angels in heaven to ascribe
praise to God. You never know when a
storm is coming, so be sure you are
worshiping Him and giving Him all the glory.
The greatest beauty of all is the beauty of
holiness, and it comes from worshiping the
Lord.

29:3–9 *Power in the storm.* First the
thunder rolled over the Mediterranean Sea.
Then the storm broke and moved across the
land. Seven times the storm is called "the
voice of the LORD." (See Rev. 10:3–4.) What
power there is in a storm! Even the angels
shout, "Glory!" as they watch it!

28:8 ˣFollowing Masoretic Text and Targum; Septuagint,
Syriac, and Vulgate read *the strength of His people*.

29:10, 11 Peace after the storm. David may have seen a rainbow and remembered God's promise given after the Flood (Gen. 9:8–17). God sat as King at the Flood, and He is still King! No storm is greater than God. If you trust Him, the storm will bring glory to God. If life is stormy just now, worship Him and wait on Him. The storm will pass, and He will give you peace.

PSALM 30

30:1 In this song of praise (vv. 1, 4, 11–12) David expressed his thanks to God for the changes God sent to his life.

30:2 From sickness to health. God had healed David and lifted him up from the grave. His sickness had been a discipline from God because of David's pride and self-sufficiency (vv. 6–7). Perhaps it was in connection with the sin of numbering the people (1 Chron. 21).

30:4 From weeping to joy. There is a contrast between God's momentary anger and His gift of lasting joy, between weeping and joy, and between the night and the morning. Things may seem dark to you now, but wait for His morning to dawn. He can change everything in a hurry!

30:8 From mourning to singing. David humbled himself before God and begged for help and mercy. When God saw that the discipline had done its work, He healed David and forgave his sins. David changed clothes, picked up his harp, and began to sing praises to the Lord.

30:12 No matter how dark the night, dawn will come. No matter how heavy your heart, one day there will be a song. Wait patiently and trust the Lord. "His favor is for life" (v. 5).

❝*Joys are always on the way to us. They are always traveling to us through the darkness of the night. There is never a night when they are not coming.*❞
—Amy Carmichael

31:1 Foes. David's enemies persecuted him, lied about him, and spread a net to catch him. Where could he turn for help? Only to the Lord! If the hand of the enemy is against you (vv. 8, 15), find safety in the hand of the Lord (vv. 5, 15; John 10:27–29). Jesus quoted verse 5 when He was on the cross (Luke 23:46).

---

10 *The LORD sat *enthroned* at the Flood,
   And the LORD sits as King forever.
11 The LORD will give strength to His people;
   The LORD will bless His people with peace.

PSALM 30

A Psalm. A Song at the dedication of the house of David.

I* will extol You, O LORD, for You have lifted me up,
   And have not let my foes rejoice over me.
2 *O LORD my God, I cried out to You,
   And You healed me.
3 O LORD, You brought my soul up from the grave;
   You have kept me alive, that I should not go down to the pit.ʸ

4 *Sing praise to the LORD, you saints of His,
   And give thanks at the remembrance of His holy name.ᶻ
5 For His anger *is but for* a moment,
   His favor *is for* life;
   Weeping may endure for a night,
   But joy *comes* in the morning.

6 Now in my prosperity I said,
   "I shall never be moved."
7 LORD, by Your favor You have made my mountain stand strong;
   You hid Your face, *and* I was troubled.

8 *I cried out to You, O LORD;
   And to the LORD I made supplication:
9 "What profit *is there* in my blood,
   When I go down to the pit?
   Will the dust praise You?
   Will it declare Your truth?
10 Hear, O LORD, and have mercy on me;
   LORD, be my helper!"

11 You have turned for me my mourning into dancing;
   You have put off my sackcloth and clothed me with gladness,
12 *To the end that *my* glory may sing praise to You and not be silent.
   O LORD my God, I will give thanks to You forever.

PSALM 31

To the Chief Musician. A Psalm of David.

In* You, O LORD, I put my trust;
   Let me never be ashamed;
   Deliver me in Your righteousness.
2 Bow down Your ear to me,
   Deliver me speedily;
   Be my rock of refuge,
   A fortress of defense to save me.

3 For You *are* my rock and my fortress;
   Therefore, for Your name's sake,
   Lead me and guide me.

30:3 ʸFollowing Qere and Targum; Kethib, Septuagint, Syriac, and Vulgate read *from those who descend to the pit.*
30:4 ᶻOr *His holiness*

4   Pull me out of the net which they have
        secretly laid for me,
    For You *are* my strength.
5   Into Your hand I commit my spirit;
    You have redeemed me, O LORD God of
        truth.

6   I have hated those who regard useless idols;
    But I trust in the LORD.
7   *I will be glad and rejoice in Your mercy,
    For You have considered my trouble;
    You have known my soul in adversities,
8   And have not shut me up into the hand of
        the enemy;
    You have set my feet in a wide place.

9   Have mercy on me, O LORD, for I am in
        trouble;
    My eye wastes away with grief,
    Yes, my soul and my body!
10 For my life is spent with grief,
    And my years with sighing;
    My strength fails because of my iniquity,
    And my bones waste away.
11 I am a reproach among all my enemies,
    But especially among my neighbors,
    And *am* repulsive to my acquaintances;
    Those who see me outside flee from me.
12 I am forgotten like a dead man, out of
        mind;
    I am like a broken vessel.
13 For I hear the slander of many;
    Fear *is* on every side;
    While they take counsel together against
        me,
    They scheme to take away my life.

14 *But as for me, I trust in You, O LORD;
    I say, "You *are* my God."
15 My times *are* in Your hand;
    Deliver me from the hand of my enemies,
    And from those who persecute me.
16 Make Your face shine upon Your servant;
    Save me for Your mercies' sake.
17 Do not let me be ashamed, O LORD, for I
        have called upon You;
    Let the wicked be ashamed;
    Let them be silent in the grave.
18 Let the lying lips be put to silence,
    Which speak insolent things proudly and
        contemptuously against the righteous.

19 Oh, how great *is* Your goodness,
    Which You have laid up for those who fear
        You,
    Which You have prepared for those who
        trust in You
    In the presence of the sons of men!
20 You shall hide them in the secret place of
        Your presence
    From the plots of man;
    You shall keep them secretly in a pavilion
    From the strife of tongues.

21 Blessed *be* the LORD,
    For He has shown me His marvelous
        kindness in a strong city!
22 For I said in my haste,
    "I am cut off from before Your eyes";
    Nevertheless You heard the voice of my
        supplications
    When I cried out to You.

31:7 Feelings. David was ill, possibly as the result of his own disobedience (vv. 9–13). God can use enemies and sickness to chasten us and bring us to a place of submission. David's enemies laughed at him and his friends ignored him. All David could do was turn to the Lord for help, and the Lord did not fail him.

31:14 Faith. The emphasis is on David's faith in the Lord. Because of his faith, David was not ashamed (v. 1) but rejoiced in God (vv. 6–7) and enjoyed the smile of God upon his life (vv. 14–16; Num. 6:22–27). He knew that God's goodness would carry him through (v. 19).

True faith is never alone, for it leads to love and hope (vv. 23–24), which give you the courage you need to win the battle, whether the foe is within or without.

23 Oh, love the LORD, all you His saints!
For the LORD preserves the faithful,
And fully repays the proud person.
24 Be of good courage,
And He shall strengthen your heart,
All you who hope in the LORD.

PSALM 32

PSALM 32

32:1 This penitential psalm grew out of David's experiences with the Lord after he had committed adultery and had tried to hide his sins (2 Sam. 11—12). When you refuse to confess your sins, the Lord must deal with you to bring you to repentance (Prov. 28:13). The longer you wait, the more miserable you will be, as you can see in David's experience. You must face the following:

32:2 The debt against you. God sees what you do and keeps a record of it. David had covered his sins on earth, but you could not cover the record in heaven. When we confess, God wipes the record clean (1 John 1:9).

32:3 The pain within you. Sin affects the body, and God's disciplines are painful but needful (Heb. 12:1–11). David became like an old man carrying a heavy burden.

32:6 The flood around you. God uses difficult circumstances to bring you back to Himself. In fact, because of his sins, David went through many deep waters with his family.

32:8 The road before you. David was like a stubborn animal that needed to be broken. When you are out of the will of God, your decisions will often create problems instead of solve them. The way gets harder.

32:10 David went from silence (v. 3) to singing (v. 7) because he finally was honest with God and confessed his sins (vv. 5–6).

PSALM 33

33:1–5 God's Word in worship. We dare not separate worship from the Word of God, for we must worship "in truth" (John 4:24). The better we know the Scriptures, the better we will be able to praise Him (Col. 3:16ff.).

A Psalm of David. A Contemplation.*a*

Blessed* *is he whose* transgression *is* forgiven,
Whose sin *is* covered.
2 *Blessed *is* the man to whom the LORD does not impute iniquity,
And in whose spirit *there is* no deceit.

3 *When I kept silent, my bones grew old
Through my groaning all the day long.
4 For day and night Your hand was heavy upon me;
My vitality was turned into the drought of summer.   Selah
5 I acknowledged my sin to You,
And my iniquity I have not hidden.
I said, "I will confess my transgressions to the LORD,"
And You forgave the iniquity of my sin.   Selah

6 *For this cause everyone who is godly shall pray to You
In a time when You may be found;
Surely in a flood of great waters
They shall not come near him.
7 You *are* my hiding place;
You shall preserve me from trouble;
You shall surround me with songs of deliverance.   Selah

8 *I will instruct you and teach you in the way you should go;
I will guide you with My eye.
9 Do not be like the horse *or* like the mule,
Which have no understanding,
Which must be harnessed with bit and bridle,
Else they will not come near you.

10 *Many sorrows *shall be* to the wicked;
But he who trusts in the LORD, mercy shall surround him.
11 Be glad in the LORD and rejoice, you righteous;
And shout for joy, all *you* upright in heart!

PSALM 33

Rejoice* in the LORD, O you righteous!
For praise from the upright is beautiful.
2 Praise the LORD with the harp;
Make melody to Him with an instrument of ten strings.
3 Sing to Him a new song;
Play skillfully with a shout of joy.

4 For the word of the LORD *is* right,
And all His work *is* done in truth.

❝*Blessed are the single-hearted, for they shall enjoy much peace . . . If you refuse to be hurried and pressed, if you stay your soul on God, nothing can keep you from that clearness of spirit which is life and peace. In that stillness you will know what His will is.***❞**
—Amy Carmichael

32:title *a*Hebrew *Maschil*

5   He loves righteousness and justice;
     The earth is full of the goodness of the LORD.

6   *By the word of the LORD the heavens were
        made,
     And all the host of them by the breath of
        His mouth.
7   He gathers the waters of the sea together
        as a heap;[b]
     He lays up the deep in storehouses.

8   Let all the earth fear the LORD;
     Let all the inhabitants of the world stand
        in awe of Him.
9   For He spoke, and it was *done;*
     He commanded, and it stood fast.

10   *The LORD brings the counsel of the nations
        to nothing;
     He makes the plans of the peoples of no
        effect.
11   The counsel of the LORD stands forever,
     The plans of His heart to all generations.
12   Blessed *is* the nation whose God *is* the LORD,
     The people He has chosen as His own
        inheritance.

13   The LORD looks from heaven;
     He sees all the sons of men.
14   From the place of His dwelling He looks
        On all the inhabitants of the earth;
15   He fashions their hearts individually;
     He considers all their works.

16   No king *is* saved by the multitude of an
        army;
     A mighty man is not delivered by great
        strength.
17   A horse *is* a vain hope for safety;
     Neither shall it deliver *any* by its great
        strength.

18   *Behold, the eye of the LORD *is* on those who
        fear Him,
     On those who hope in His mercy,
19   To deliver their soul from death,
     And to keep them alive in famine.

20   Our soul waits for the LORD;
     He *is* our help and our shield.
21   For our heart shall rejoice in Him,
     Because we have trusted in His holy name.
22   *Let Your mercy, O LORD, be upon us,
     Just as we hope in You.

PSALM 34

A Psalm of David when he pretended madness before
Abimelech, who drove him away, and he departed.

I* will bless the LORD at all times;
     His praise *shall* continually *be* in my mouth.
2   *My soul shall make its boast in the LORD;
     The humble shall hear *of it* and be glad.
3   Oh, magnify the LORD with me,
     And let us exalt His name together.

4   I sought the LORD, and He heard me,
     And delivered me from all my fears.

33:6–9 *God's Word in creation.* God
spoke the universe into existence (Gen. 1;
John 1:1–3), and His Word controls it (Ps.
147:15–18). What a powerful Word it is!

33:10–17 *God's Word in history.* The
nations may confederate and rebel against
God, but His Word will prevail (Ps. 2).
Military strength is no guarantee of success.
God has a plan for the nations, and He will
fulfill it (Acts 17:24–28).

33:18–22 *God's Word in your life.* The
Word that created and controls the universe
can also control your life. When you trust
His Word and obey it, all the universe works
for you. When you abandon that Word, all
the universe works against you (Jon. 1).

33:22 Never fear the will of God because
it comes from the heart of God (v. 11).

PSALM 34

34:1 Fearful that Saul would kill him, David
fled to Gath and sought the protection of
the enemy (1 Sam. 21:10—22:2). But you
are never safe out of the will of God, and
David had to lie to escape. This psalm is
David's personal testimony of what God did
for him.

34:2–10 *"I will bless."* David had every
reason to praise the Lord, for the Lord had
rescued him from certain death. When you
call on the Lord in faith, He saves
(vv. 4–6), He keeps (v. 7), and He
satisfies (vv. 8–10). Why run to the enemy
when you can run to the Lord and be safe?

33:7 [b]Septuagint, Targum, and Vulgate read *in a vessel.*

5 They looked to Him and were radiant,
  And their faces were not ashamed.
6 This poor man cried out, and the LORD heard
  him,
  And saved him out of all his troubles.
7 The angel[c] of the LORD encamps all around
    those who fear Him,
  And delivers them.

8 Oh, taste and see that the LORD *is* good;
  Blessed *is* the man *who* trusts in Him!
9 Oh, fear the LORD, you His saints!
  There is no want to those who fear Him.
10 The young lions lack and suffer hunger;
  But those who seek the LORD shall not lack
    any good *thing.*

11 *Come, you children, listen to me;
  I will teach you the fear of the LORD.
12 Who *is* the man *who* desires life,
  And loves *many* days, that he may see good?
13 Keep your tongue from evil,
  And your lips from speaking deceit.
14 Depart from evil and do good;
  Seek peace and pursue it.

15 The eyes of the LORD *are* on the righteous,
  And His ears *are open* to their cry.
16 The face of the LORD *is* against those who
    do evil,
  To cut off the remembrance of them from
    the earth.

17 *The righteous* cry out, and the LORD hears,
  And delivers them out of all their troubles.
18 The LORD *is* near to those who have a
    broken heart,
  And saves such as have a contrite spirit.

19 Many *are* the afflictions of the righteous,
  But the LORD delivers him out of them all.
20 He guards all his bones;
  Not one of them is broken.
21 Evil shall slay the wicked,
  And those who hate the righteous shall be
    condemned.
22 The LORD redeems the soul of His servants,
  And none of those who trust in Him shall
    be condemned.

PSALM 35

A Psalm of David.

Plead* my cause, O LORD, with those who strive
    with me;
  Fight against those who fight against me.
2 *Take hold of shield and buckler,
  And stand up for my help.
3 Also draw out the spear,
  And stop those who pursue me.
  Say to my soul,
  "I *am* your salvation."

4 Let those be put to shame and brought to
    dishonor
  Who seek after my life;
  Let those be turned back and brought to
    confusion
  Who plot my hurt.

34:11–22 "I will teach." David wanted the next generation to know the Lord and trust Him. He gave some wise counsel about how to have "good days" (vv. 12–14; 1 Pet. 3:8–12), and he urged them to call on the Lord in the time of trouble. God's eyes see your needs, God's ears hear your prayers, and God is near you when your heart is broken.

When God does something special for you, tell somebody else. The next generation needs to know that God is alive.

PSALM 35

35:1 Like David, you need God's deliverance from two different enemies.

35:2, 3 *Those who attack you.* There are places in this world where it is a dangerous thing to be a Christian, and their number may increase. After all, Satan is a murderer (John 8:44) and would destroy all of God's people if he could. But the Lord fights for us. He has effective weapons (vv. 2–3) and knows the enemy's plots (v. 4). If you belong to the Lord, He is responsible to care for you.

34:7 [c]Or *Angel*

5 Let them be like chaff before the wind,
   And let the angel[d] of the LORD chase *them*.
6 Let their way be dark and slippery,
   And let the angel of the LORD pursue them.
7 For without cause they have hidden their
      net for me *in* a pit,
   Which they have dug without cause for my
      life.
8 Let destruction come upon him
      unexpectedly,
   And let his net that he has hidden catch
      himself;
   Into that very destruction let him fall.

9 And my soul shall be joyful in the LORD;
   It shall rejoice in His salvation.
10 All my bones shall say,
   "LORD, who *is* like You,
   Delivering the poor from him who is too
      strong for him,
   Yes, the poor and the needy from him who
      plunders him?"

11 *Fierce witnesses rise up;
   They ask me *things* that I do not know.
12 They reward me evil for good,
   To the sorrow of my soul.
13 But as for me, when they were sick,
   My clothing *was* sackcloth;
   I humbled myself with fasting;
   And my prayer would return to my own
      heart.
14 I paced about as though *he were* my friend
      or brother;
   I bowed down heavily, as one who mourns
      for his mother.

15 But in my adversity they rejoiced
   And gathered together;
   Attackers gathered against me,
   And I did not know *it;*
   They tore *at me* and did not cease;
16 With ungodly mockers at feasts
   They gnashed at me with their teeth.

17 Lord, how long will You look on?
   Rescue me from their destructions,
   My precious *life* from the lions.
18 I will give You thanks in the great assembly;
   I will praise You among many people.

19 Let them not rejoice over me who are
      wrongfully my enemies;
   Nor let them wink with the eye who hate
      me without a cause.
20 For they do not speak peace,
   But they devise deceitful matters
   Against *the* quiet ones in the land.
21 They also opened their mouth wide against
      me,
   And said, "Aha, aha!
   Our eyes have seen *it*."

22 *This* You have seen, O LORD;
   Do not keep silence.
   O Lord, do not be far from me.
23 Stir up Yourself, and awake to my
      vindication,
   To my cause, my God and my Lord.

35:11, 12 *Those who accuse you.* Satan
is an accuser as well as a murderer (Rev.
12:10), so David had to move from the
battlefield to the courtroom where his
enemies were lying about him. His prayer
changed from "Fight for me!" to "Vindicate
me!" (vv. 23–24). But his concern was that
God's name, not his own, be magnified
(v. 27). When the enemy slanders your
name, he attacks the name of the Lord as
well.

35:5 [d]Or *Angel*

24 Vindicate me, O Lord my God, according
   to Your righteousness;
   And let them not rejoice over me.
25 Let them not say in their hearts, "Ah, so
   we would have it!"
   Let them not say, "We have swallowed him
   up."

26 Let them be ashamed and brought to mutual
   confusion
   Who rejoice at my hurt;
   Let them be clothed with shame and
   dishonor
   Who exalt themselves against me.

27 Let them shout for joy and be glad,
   Who favor my righteous cause;
   And let them say continually,
   "Let the Lord be magnified,
   Who has pleasure in the prosperity of His
   servant."
28 *And my tongue shall speak of Your
   righteousness
   And of Your praise all the day long.

35:28 Note the results: "And my soul shall be joyful" (v. 9); "And my tongue shall speak of Your righteousness" (v. 28). Joy on the inside and witness on the outside!

PSALM 36

To the Chief Musician. A Psalm of David the servant of the Lord.

PSALM 36

36:1–4 Man's wickedness. David had seen a good deal of life and knew what human nature was like. He knew his own heart as well! But in this psalm, he shared a special oracle that God gave him. The sinner flatters himself that he "gets away" with sin. He lives on lies as he plots against the godly. His words and his works are evil, but that does not bother him.

An* oracle within my heart concerning the
   transgression of the wicked:
   There is no fear of God before his eyes.
2 For he flatters himself in his own eyes,
   When he finds out his iniquity *and* when
   he hates.
3 The words of his mouth *are* wickedness and
   deceit;
   He has ceased to be wise *and* to do good.
4 He devises wickedness on his bed;
   He sets himself in a way *that is* not good;
   He does not abhor evil.

36:5–7 God's faithfulness. What a vivid contrast to the unfaithfulness of the sinner! God can be trusted always to do what is right, and the safest place in the world is under His shadow in the Holy of Holies (v. 7).

5 *Your mercy, O Lord, *is* in the heavens;
   Your faithfulness *reaches* to the clouds.
6 Your righteousness *is* like the great
   mountains;
   Your judgments *are* a great deep;
   O Lord, You preserve man and beast.

7 How precious *is* Your lovingkindness,
   O God!
   Therefore the children of men put their trust
   under the shadow of Your wings.
8 *They are abundantly satisfied with the
   fullness of Your house,
   And You give them drink from the river of
   Your pleasures.
9 For with You *is* the fountain of life;
   In Your light we see light.

36:8–12 The believer's blessedness. God satisfies His people with the water of life and the light of life. He protects from the enemy and provides for every need. The word "pleasures" in verse 8 is *Eden* in the Hebrew. When you dwell in God, you are in Paradise!

10 Oh, continue Your lovingkindness to those
   who know You,
   And Your righteousness to the upright in
   heart.
11 Let not the foot of pride come against me,
   And let not the hand of the wicked drive
   me away.
12 There the workers of iniquity have fallen;
   They have been cast down and are not able
   to rise.

PSALM 37

A Psalm of David.

Do* not fret because of evildoers,
Nor be envious of the workers of iniquity.
2 For they shall soon be cut down like the grass,
And wither as the green herb.

3 *Trust in the LORD, and do good;
Dwell in the land, and feed on His faithfulness.
4 *Delight yourself also in the LORD,
And He shall give you the desires of your heart.

5 *Commit your way to the LORD,
Trust also in Him,
And He shall bring it to pass.
6 He shall bring forth your righteousness as the light,
And your justice as the noonday.

7 *Rest in the LORD, and wait patiently for Him;
Do not fret because of him who prospers in his way,
Because of the man who brings wicked schemes to pass.
8 Cease from anger, and forsake wrath;
Do not fret—it only causes harm.

9 For evildoers shall be cut off;
But those who wait on the LORD,
They shall inherit the earth.
10 For yet a little while and the wicked shall be no more;
Indeed, you will look carefully for his place,
But it shall be no more.
11 But the meek shall inherit the earth,
And shall delight themselves in the abundance of peace.

12 The wicked plots against the just,
And gnashes at him with his teeth.
13 The Lord laughs at him,
For He sees that his day is coming.
14 The wicked have drawn the sword
And have bent their bow,
To cast down the poor and needy,
To slay those who are of upright conduct.
15 Their sword shall enter their own heart,
And their bows shall be broken.

16 A little that a righteous man has
Is better than the riches of many wicked.
17 For the arms of the wicked shall be broken,
But the LORD upholds the righteous.

18 The LORD knows the days of the upright,
And their inheritance shall be forever.
19 They shall not be ashamed in the evil time,
And in the days of famine they shall be satisfied.
20 But the wicked shall perish;
And the enemies of the LORD,
Like the splendor of the meadows, shall vanish.
Into smoke they shall vanish away.

21 The wicked borrows and does not repay,
But the righteous shows mercy and gives.

PSALM 37

37:1 This psalm shares the wisdom of an old man who had walked with the Lord (v. 25). He had battled with evil men and knew the frustration of seeing the wicked prosper and the righteous suffer. As he reviewed the past, he gave some wise counsel to keep us from fretting against the Lord when things are not going the way we want them to go.

37:3 "Trust in the LORD." If you walk by sight and not by faith, you will find it easy to fret. (See Ps. 73.) The wicked seem to be prospering, but they will not last (vv. 35–36). Believe what God says in His Word because that is where you find reality.

37:4 "Delight in the LORD." Find all your joy and pleasure in His will. Make Him your delight, and your desires will be in His will. Living to please the Lord sets you free from fretting about what men are doing.

37:5 "Commit your way to the LORD." When you trust Him and delight in Him, how could you do anything other than commit your way to Him? Let God guide your steps, choose your joys, protect your name, and bless your work.

37:7 "Rest in the LORD." Restlessness is an evidence of unbelief. Faith rests in the Lord and enjoys "the peace of God, which surpasses all understanding" (Phil. 4:7). God sometimes waits in answering prayer so that He might strengthen our patience (James 1:2–8).

❝ 'Rest in the Lord; wait patiently for Him.' In Hebrew, 'Be silent to God and let Him mold thee.' Keep still and He will mold thee to the right shape. ❞

—Martin Luther

22 For *those* blessed by Him shall inherit the
earth,
But *those* cursed by Him shall be cut off.

23 The steps of a *good* man are ordered by the
LORD,
And He delights in his way.
24 Though he fall, he shall not be utterly cast
down;
For the LORD upholds *him with* His hand.

25 I have been young, and *now* am old;
Yet I have not seen the righteous forsaken,
Nor his descendants begging bread.
26 *He is* ever merciful, and lends;
And his descendants *are* blessed.

27 Depart from evil, and do good;
And dwell forevermore.
28 For the LORD loves justice,
And does not forsake His saints;
They are preserved forever,
But the descendants of the wicked shall be
cut off.
29 The righteous shall inherit the land,
And dwell in it forever.

30 The mouth of the righteous speaks wisdom,
And his tongue talks of justice.
31 The law of his God *is* in his heart;
None of his steps shall slide.

32 The wicked watches the righteous,
And seeks to slay him.
33 The LORD will not leave him in his hand,
Nor condemn him when he is judged.

37:34 *"Wait on the LORD."* For what are you
waiting? *The inheritance God has for you*
(vv. 11, 18, 22, 29, 34). The wicked have
only temporary pleasure on earth, but God's
people have eternal treasure in heaven. You
will one day receive your inheritance, so be
patient.

34 *Wait on the LORD,
And keep His way,
And He shall exalt you to inherit the
land;
When the wicked are cut off, you shall see
it.
35 I have seen the wicked in great power,
And spreading himself like a native green
tree.
36 Yet he passed away,[e] and behold, he *was*
no *more;*
Indeed I sought him, but he could not be
found.

37 Mark the blameless *man,* and observe the
upright;
For the future of *that* man *is* peace.
38 But the transgressors shall be destroyed
together;
The future of the wicked shall be cut off.

39 But the salvation of the righteous *is* from
the LORD;
He is their strength in the time of trouble.
40 And the LORD shall help them and deliver
them;
He shall deliver them from the wicked,
And save them,
Because they trust in Him.

37:36 [e]Following Masoretic Text, Septuagint, and Targum;
Syriac and Vulgate read *I passed by.*

PSALM 38

A Psalm of David. To bring to remembrance.

O* LORD, do not rebuke me in Your wrath,
   Nor chasten me in Your hot displeasure!
2 *For Your arrows pierce me deeply,
   And Your hand presses me down.

3 *There is no soundness in my flesh
   Because of Your anger,
   Nor any health in my bones
   Because of my sin.
4 For my iniquities have gone over my head;
   Like a heavy burden they are too heavy for
      me.
5 My wounds are foul and festering
   Because of my foolishness.

6 I am troubled, I am bowed down greatly;
   I go mourning all the day long.
7 For my loins are full of inflammation,
   And there is no soundness in my flesh.
8 I am feeble and severely broken;
   I groan because of the turmoil of my heart.

9 Lord, all my desire is before You;
   And my sighing is not hidden from You.
10 My heart pants, my strength fails me;
   As for the light of my eyes, it also has gone
      from me.

11 *My loved ones and my friends stand aloof
      from my plague,
   And my relatives stand afar off.
12 Those also who seek my life lay snares for
      me;
   Those who seek my hurt speak of
      destruction,
   And plan deception all the day long.

13 But I, like a deaf man, do not hear;
   And I am like a mute who does not open
      his mouth.
14 Thus I am like a man who does not hear,
   And in whose mouth is no response.

15 *For in You, O LORD, I hope;
   You will hear, O Lord my God.
16 For I said, "Hear me, lest they rejoice over
      me,
   Lest, when my foot slips, they exalt
      themselves against me."

17 For I am ready to fall,
   And my sorrow is continually before me.
18 For I will declare my iniquity;
   I will be in anguish over my sin.
19 But my enemies are vigorous, and they are
      strong;
   And those who hate me wrongfully have
      multiplied.
20 Those also who render evil for good,
   They are my adversaries, because I follow
      what is good.

PSALM 38

38:1 This is the third of the Penitential
Psalms (cf. Ps. 6), and it reveals what
happens to you when you sin.

38:2 What God does. God loves you too
much to allow you to sin and get away with
it. If you disobey, He will first rebuke you
and then chasten you. He will shoot His
arrows from a distance or come closer and
put His hand on you, but He will let you know
that He is displeased.

38:3–10 What sin does. David suffered
from sickness because of his sin (Ps.
32:3–5). He carried a heavy burden and was
crushed under it. He sighed and panted and
was ready to quit. Sin comes as a friend to
entice you and then becomes a master to
enslave you.

38:11 What people do. Sin puts a wall
between you and those who can help you,
but it builds a bridge between you and those
who want to exploit you and hurt you.

38:15–20 What the sinner must do. The
only hope is to confess sin and cry out to
God for mercy. He promises to forgive, so
claim His promise.

What Happens to Sins—When you trust Christ, what does God do with your sins? He takes
them away (John 1:29); forgets them (Heb. 10:17); washes them away (Isa. 1:18); blots them out
(Isa. 43:25); wipes them out like a cloud (Isa. 44:22); pardons them (Isa. 55:7); and buries them in
the depths of the sea (Mic. 7:19).

21 Do not forsake me, O LORD;
   O my God, be not far from me!
22 Make haste to help me,
   O Lord, my salvation!

PSALM 39

To the Chief Musician. To Jeduthun. A Psalm of David.

I* said, "I will guard my ways,
    Lest I sin with my tongue;
    I will restrain my mouth with a muzzle,
    While the wicked are before me."
2 I was mute with silence,
    I held my peace *even* from good;
    And my sorrow was stirred up.
3 My heart was hot within me;
    While I was musing, the fire burned.
    Then I spoke with my tongue:

4 "LORD, make me to know my end,
    And what *is* the measure of my days,
    That I may know how frail I *am.*
5 Indeed, You have made my days *as*
      handbreadths,
    And my age *is* as nothing before You;
    Certainly every man at his best state *is* but
      vapor.   Selah
6 Surely every man walks about like a
      shadow;
    Surely they busy themselves in vain;
    He heaps up *riches,*
    And does not know who will gather them.

7 "And now, Lord, what do I wait for?
    My hope *is* in You.
8 Deliver me from all my transgressions;
    Do not make me the reproach of the foolish.
9 *I was mute, I did not open my mouth,
    Because it was You who did *it.*
10 Remove Your plague from me;
    I am consumed by the blow of Your hand.
11 When with rebukes You correct man for
      iniquity,
    You make his beauty melt away like a moth;
    Surely every man *is* vapor.   Selah

12 *"Hear my prayer, O LORD,
    And give ear to my cry;
    Do not be silent at my tears;
    For I *am* a stranger with You,
    A sojourner, as all my fathers *were.*
13 Remove Your gaze from me, that I may
      regain strength,
    Before I go away and am no more."

PSALM 40

To the Chief Musician. A Psalm of David.

I* waited patiently for the LORD;
    And He inclined to me,
    And heard my cry.

PSALM 39

39:1 *God's silence to David.* David had sinned, and God was correcting him. Chastening is a sign of God's love (Heb. 12:5–11), so submit to His will and let Him have His way. God had been silent to David (v. 12), and that worried him. Was he going to die (Ps. 28:1)?

39:9 *David's silence to God.* David was silent before the Lord and did not argue with Him (v. 9; see also Lev. 10:3; 1 Sam. 3:18). David accepted God's will and submitted meekly. He prayed that God would forgive him and help him, and God answered in His mercy.

39:12 *David's silence before the wicked.* When wicked men came to visit him in his sickness, David tried to be silent before them (Matt. 7:6). But he finally had to speak and remind himself and them that man was frail and life was short. Life is only a handbreadth long, a vapor that comes and goes (James 4:14) and a mere shadow. We are strangers and sojourners (v. 12), and the journey is not a long one. Why gather riches when you cannot take them with you when you go? Silence sometimes is louder than speech. Know when to speak and when to be silent.

PSALM 40

40:1–3 *Waiting.* While experiencing trials at the hands of his enemies, David asked God for help, but the answer did not come immediately. He waited—and then God worked! What a change took place: David went from a pit to a highway, from miry clay to a rock, and from crying to singing!

The Ultimate Sacrifice—Psalm 40:6–8 is quoted in Hebrews 10:1–14 as referring to Jesus Christ. He came to hear God's will (the open ear [Isa. 50:4–6]) and to do God's work (the prepared body). His body was prepared in Mary's womb by the Holy Spirit (Luke 1:26–38; see also Isa. 7:14). Jesus delighted to do the Father's will because the Word was in His heart (John 4:34; 8:29). If you delight in God's Word, you will delight in God's will (Ps. 1:1–3). Jesus Christ is the sacrifice for sins that God has appointed, and in His death, He fulfilled the Old Testament sacrifices. His one sacrifice has settled the sin question once and for all—forever.

2   He also brought me up out of a horrible pit,
    Out of the miry clay,
    And set my feet upon a rock,
    And established my steps.
3   He has put a new song in my mouth—
    Praise to our God;
    Many will see *it* and fear,
    And will trust in the LORD.

4   *Blessed *is* that man who makes the LORD
    his trust,
    And does not respect the proud, nor such
    as turn aside to lies.
5   Many, O LORD my God, *are* Your wonderful
    works
    Which You have done;
    And Your thoughts toward us
    Cannot be recounted to You in order;
    If I would declare and speak *of them,*
    They are more than can be numbered.

6   Sacrifice and offering You did not desire;
    My ears You have opened.
    Burnt offering and sin offering You did not
    require.
7   Then I said, "Behold, I come;
    In the scroll of the book *it is* written of me.
8   I delight to do Your will, O my God,
    And Your law *is* within my heart."

9   I have proclaimed the good news of
    righteousness
    In the great assembly;
    Indeed, I do not restrain my lips,
    O LORD, You Yourself know.
10 I have not hidden Your righteousness within
    my heart;
    I have declared Your faithfulness and Your
    salvation;
    I have not concealed Your lovingkindness
    and Your truth
    From the great assembly.

11 *Do not withhold Your tender mercies from
    me, O LORD;
    Let Your lovingkindness and Your truth
    continually preserve me.
12 For innumerable evils have surrounded me;
    My iniquities have overtaken me, so that I
    am not able to look up;
    They are more than the hairs of my head;
    Therefore my heart fails me.

13 Be pleased, O LORD, to deliver me;
    O LORD, make haste to help me!
14 Let them be ashamed and brought to mutual
    confusion
    Who seek to destroy my life;
    Let them be driven backward and brought
    to dishonor
    Who wish me evil.
15 Let them be confounded because of their
    shame,
    Who say to me, "Aha, aha!"

16 *Let all those who seek You rejoice and be
    glad in You;
    Let such as love Your salvation say
    continually,
    "The LORD be magnified!"
17 But I *am* poor and needy;
    Yet the LORD thinks upon me.

40:4–10 *Witnessing.* When God does a great thing for you, share it with others. God's works and thoughts ought to be a part of your daily conversation. Share the good news by what you say and do. God can use your witness to bring others to Himself (v. 3).

40:11–15 *Warring.* So often David found himself surrounded by danger, and all he could do was turn to the Lord for help. You may not be battling against armies, but you are part of a spiritual warfare that demands diligence and devotion (Eph. 6:10ff.).

40:16, 17 *Worshiping.* No matter what the problem, David took time to worship the Lord. When you do this, it helps to put things into perspective, and you see what God is doing for you. The important thing is that God is magnified. You may get impatient with Him, but He thinks about you and is working everything together for your good (Jer. 29:11).

You *are* my help and my deliverer;
Do not delay, O my God.

PSALM 41

To the Chief Musician. A Psalm of David.

B lessed* *is* he who considers the poor;
    The LORD will deliver him in time of trouble.
2   The LORD will preserve him and keep him
     alive,
    And he will be blessed on the earth;
    You will not deliver him to the will of his
     enemies.
3   The LORD will strengthen him on his bed
     of illness;
    You will sustain him on his sickbed.

4   I said, "LORD, be merciful to me;
    Heal my soul, for I have sinned against
     You."
5   My enemies speak evil of me:
    "When will he die, and his name perish?"
6   And if he comes to see *me,* he speaks lies;
    His heart gathers iniquity to itself;
    When he goes out, he tells *it.*

7   *All who hate me whisper together against
     me;
    Against me they devise my hurt.
8   "An evil disease," *they say,* "clings to him.
    And *now* that he lies down, he will rise up
     no more."
9   Even my own familiar friend in whom I
     trusted,
    Who ate my bread,
    Has lifted up *his* heel against me.

10   *But You, O LORD, be merciful to me, and
     raise me up,
    That I may repay them.
11   By this I know that You are well pleased
     with me,
    Because my enemy does not triumph over
     me.
12   As for me, You uphold me in my integrity,
    And set me before Your face forever.

13   Blessed *be* the LORD God of Israel
    From everlasting to everlasting!
    Amen and Amen.

Book Two: Psalms 42—72

PSALM 42

To the Chief Musician. A Contemplation^f of the sons of Korah.

A s the deer pants for the water brooks,
    So pants my soul for You, O God.
2   *My soul thirsts for God, for the living God.
    When shall I come and appear before God?^{g}
3   My tears have been my food day and night,
    While they continually say to me,
    "Where *is* your God?"

4   When I remember these *things,*
    I pour out my soul within me.

PSALM 41

41:1–3 As David lay sick, he *looked back* and recalled that he had been merciful to others and had helped the poor. This encouraged him, for he knew that God would help him (Deut. 15:1–11). God is merciful to those who show mercy to others (Matt. 5:7). When you are in pain, it is good to have a clear conscience to encourage you.

41:7–9 Then David *looked around* and saw that his enemies were gossiping about him and wishing he were dead. Even his close friend turned against him. If this happens to you, keep in mind that it also happened to Jesus (John 13:18). Greater than the pain of sickness is the pain of having a treacherous "friend."

41:10–13 Finally, David *looked up,* and that solved his problems. No matter what others might say, God was well pleased with David, and that was all that mattered. Let David's enemies spread their gossip. God would raise him up, hold him up, and give him the light of His countenance. Sometimes, how you feel depends on where you look.

❝*When a man gets to despair he knows that all his thinking will never get him out. He will only get out by the sheer creative effort of God. Consequently he is in the right attitude to receive from God that which he cannot gain for himself.*❞

—Oswald Chambers

42:title ^{f}Hebrew *Maschil*   42:2 ^{g}Following Masoretic Text and Vulgate; some Hebrew manuscripts, Septuagint, Syriac, and Targum read *I see the face of God.*

For I used to go with the multitude;
I went with them to the house of God,
With the voice of joy and praise,
With a multitude that kept a pilgrim feast.

5 *Why are you cast down, O my soul?
And *why* are you disquieted within me?
Hope in God, for I shall yet praise Him
For the help of His countenance.[h]

6 O my God,[i] my soul is cast down within me;
Therefore I will remember You from the
land of the Jordan,
And from the heights of Hermon,
From the Hill Mizar.
7 Deep calls unto deep at the noise of Your
waterfalls;
All Your waves and billows have gone over
me.
8 *The LORD will command His lovingkindness
in the daytime,
And in the night His song *shall be* with me—
A prayer to the God of my life.

9 I will say to God my Rock,
"Why have You forgotten me?
Why do I go mourning because of the
oppression of the enemy?"
10 *As* with a breaking of my bones,
My enemies reproach me,
While they say to me all day long,
"Where *is* your God?"

11 Why are you cast down, O my soul?
And why are you disquieted within me?
Hope in God;
For I shall yet praise Him,
The help of my countenance and my God.

PSALM 43

Vindicate me, O God,
And plead my cause against an ungodly
nation;
Oh, deliver me from the deceitful and unjust
man!
2 For You *are* the God of my strength;
Why do You cast me off?
Why do I go mourning because of the
oppression of the enemy?

3 *Oh, send out Your light and Your truth!
Let them lead me;
Let them bring me to Your holy hill
And to Your tabernacle.
4 Then I will go to the altar of God,
To God my exceeding joy;
And on the harp I will praise You,
O God, my God.

5 *Why are you cast down, O my soul?
And why are you disquieted within me?
Hope in God;
For I shall yet praise Him,
The help of my countenance and my God.

42:5 [h]Following Masoretic Text and Targum; a few Hebrew manuscripts, Septuagint, Syriac, and Vulgate read *The help of my countenance, my God.* 42:6 [i]Following Masoretic Text and Targum; a few Hebrew manuscripts, Septuagint, Syriac, and Vulgate put *my God* at the end of verse 5.

PSALMS 42—43

42:5 The refrain "Why are you cast down, O my soul?" ties these two psalms together (42:5, 11; 43:5). Why was the writer so depressed?

42:8 For one thing, God seemed far from him in his hour of need (42:1–3). He felt like a thirsty deer in the desert, searching for water. But the Lord is never far away; He is near even when you do not recognize Him (Isa. 41:10; Heb. 13:5; Ps. 46:7).

43:3 The writer's depression was aggravated because he looked back at "the good old days" (42:4–6). He longed to return to Jerusalem and minister in the temple. Sometimes retirement or a change of residence will make people depressed. The older we get, the less we enjoy change.

The discouraging talk of others was a third contributing factor (42:3, 9–10): "Has God forgotten you? Where is your God?" The answer is in Psalm 115. Listen to God and not to the foolish talk of men.

43:5 What should you do when depression starts to control you? "Hope in God" (42:5, 11; 43:5). Look at the future and not at the past. If you feel drowned by circumstances, keep in mind that they are *His* waves and billows (42:7), and He knows what is best for you. Stop feeding on your feelings (42:3) and start feeding on His Word (43:3). God will guard you and guide you, no matter how miserable you may feel. God is greater than your feelings. Walk by faith and He will see you through.

PSALM 44

PSALM 44

44:1 The nation was facing a crisis, and it seemed that God had forsaken His people and was helping the enemy (vv. 9–16). Israel was a scattered people, shamed and scorned. What do you do when it looks like God is on the side of the enemy?

44:2, 3 *You remember what God did.* This does not mean living in the past but learning from the past. Your situation may be painful, but God has not changed. He can still work wonders and glorify His name.

44:4–8 *You trust in Him.* If you trust your own resources, you will fail. Sometimes God allows defeat just to remind you that you must trust Him and Him alone.

44:17–26 *You remain faithful to Him, come what may.* Remember Satan's lie about Job (Job 1:6–12)? Is yours a "commercial" faith? Are you faithful to God only because He does good things for you? God tests your faith to see if it is sincere (1 Pet. 1:6–9). Trust Him even though you may not fully understand what He is doing (Job 13:15).

PSALM 44

To the Chief Musician. A Contemplation/ of the sons of Korah.

We* have heard with our ears, O God,
Our fathers have told us,
The deeds You did in their days,
In days of old:
2 *You drove out the nations with Your hand,
But them You planted;
You afflicted the peoples, and cast them out.
3 For they did not gain possession of the land
by their own sword,
Nor did their own arm save them;
But it was Your right hand, Your arm, and
the light of Your countenance,
Because You favored them.

4 *You are my King, O God;*ᵏ
Command*ˡ* victories for Jacob.
5 Through You we will push down our
enemies;
Through Your name we will trample those
who rise up against us.
6 For I will not trust in my bow,
Nor shall my sword save me.
7 But You have saved us from our enemies,
And have put to shame those who hated us.
8 In God we boast all day long,
And praise Your name forever.   Selah

9 But You have cast *us* off and put us to
shame,
And You do not go out with our armies.
10 You make us turn back from the enemy,
And those who hate us have taken spoil for
themselves.
11 You have given us up like sheep *intended*
for food,
And have scattered us among the nations.
12 You sell Your people for *next to* nothing,
And are not enriched by selling them.

13 You make us a reproach to our neighbors,
A scorn and a derision to those all around
us.
14 You make us a byword among the nations,
A shaking of the head among the peoples.
15 My dishonor *is* continually before me,
And the shame of my face has covered me,
16 Because of the voice of him who reproaches
and reviles,
Because of the enemy and the avenger.

17 *All this has come upon us;
But we have not forgotten You,
Nor have we dealt falsely with Your
covenant.
18 Our heart has not turned back,
Nor have our steps departed from Your
way;
19 But You have severely broken us in the
place of jackals,
And covered us with the shadow of death.

20 If we had forgotten the name of our God,
Or stretched out our hands to a foreign god,

44:title *ˡHebrew Maschil*   44:4 *ᵏFollowing Masoretic Text and Targum; Septuagint and Vulgate read and my God. ˡFollowing Masoretic Text and Targum; Septuagint, Syriac, and Vulgate read Who commands.*

21 Would not God search this out?
For He knows the secrets of the heart.
22 Yet for Your sake we are killed all day
long;
We are accounted as sheep for the
slaughter.

23 Awake! Why do You sleep, O Lord?
Arise! Do not cast *us* off forever.
24 Why do You hide Your face,
And forget our affliction and our
oppression?
25 For our soul is bowed down to the dust;
Our body clings to the ground.
26 Arise for our help,
And redeem us for Your mercies' sake.

PSALM 45

To the Chief Musician. Set to "The Lilies."*m* A
Contemplation*n* of the sons of Korah. A Song of Love.

My* heart is overflowing with a good theme;
I recite my composition concerning the
King;
My tongue *is* the pen of a ready writer.

2 *You are fairer than the sons of men;
Grace is poured upon Your lips;
Therefore God has blessed You forever.
3 *Gird Your sword upon *Your* thigh, O Mighty
One,
With Your glory and Your majesty.
4 And in Your majesty ride prosperously
because of truth, humility, *and*
righteousness;
And Your right hand shall teach You
awesome things.
5 Your arrows *are* sharp in the heart of the
King's enemies;
The peoples fall under You.

6 *Your throne, O God, *is* forever and ever;
A scepter of righteousness *is* the scepter of
Your kingdom.
7 You love righteousness and hate
wickedness;
Therefore God, Your God, has anointed
You
With the oil of gladness more than Your
companions.
8 All Your garments are scented with myrrh
and aloes *and* cassia,
Out of the ivory palaces, by which they have
made You glad.
9 Kings' daughters *are* among Your
honorable women;
At Your right hand stands the queen in gold
from Ophir.

10 Listen, O daughter,
Consider and incline your ear;
Forget your own people also, and your
father's house;
11 So the King will greatly desire your beauty;
Because He *is* your Lord, worship Him.
12 And the daughter of Tyre *will come* with a
gift;

PSALM 45

45:1 Written for a royal wedding, this psalm
is messianic (vv. 6–7; Heb. 1:8–9) and
shows us Christ the Royal Bridegroom.

45:2 His beauty. When He was here on
earth, Jesus had no special beauty that
would attract people (Isa. 53:2). It is the
beauty of His character, His words, and His
works that makes us love Him (1 Pet. 1:8).

45:3 His battles. He came a Savior, but He
was also a warrior and defeated Satan (Matt.
12:25–29; Col. 2:15). He conquers today
through His people as we yield to Him and
practice truth, humility, and righteousness.
One day He will come to conquer all the
kingdoms of the world (Rev. 11:15; 19:11–
21).

45:6 His bounties. Who else has an eternal
throne, a righteous scepter, gladness, and
the fragrance of grace and glory? If you
know the King, you share all His bounties.

45:title *m*Hebrew *Shoshannim* *n*Hebrew *Maschil*

The rich among the people will seek your favor.

13 *The royal daughter *is* all glorious within *the palace;*
Her clothing *is* woven with gold.

14 She shall be brought to the King in robes of many colors;
The virgins, her companions who follow her, shall be brought to You.

15 With gladness and rejoicing they shall be brought;
They shall enter the King's palace.

16 Instead of Your fathers shall be Your sons,
Whom You shall make princes in all the earth.

17 I will make Your name to be remembered in all generations;
Therefore the people shall praise You forever and ever.

PSALM 46

To the Chief Musician. A Psalm of the sons of Korah. A Song for Alamoth.

God* *is* our refuge and strength,
A very present help in trouble.

2 *Therefore we will not fear,
Even though the earth be removed,
And though the mountains be carried into the midst of the sea;

3 *Though* its waters roar *and* be troubled,
Though the mountains shake with its swelling.　　　　　　Selah

4 *There is* a river whose streams shall make glad the city of God,
The holy *place* of the tabernacle of the Most High.

5 God *is* in the midst of her, she shall not be moved;
God shall help her, just at the break of dawn.

6 The nations raged, the kingdoms were moved;
He uttered His voice, the earth melted.

7 The LORD of hosts *is* with us;
The God of Jacob *is* our refuge.　　　Selah

8 Come, behold the works of the LORD,
Who has made desolations in the earth.

9 He makes wars cease to the end of the earth;
He breaks the bow and cuts the spear in two;
He burns the chariot in the fire.

10 *Be still, and know that I *am* God;
I will be exalted among the nations,
I will be exalted in the earth!

11 The LORD of hosts *is* with us;
The God of Jacob *is* our refuge.　　　Selah

45:13 His bride. This is a picture of the church (Eph. 5:25ff.), all those who have been saved through faith in Christ. The Bridegroom is ready (v. 8), the attendants are ready (v. 9), and the bride is brought to the King with rejoicing. What a wedding that will be (Rev. 19:1–10)! Are you eagerly looking forward to being there?

PSALM 46

46:1 Some Bible students believe that this psalm was written in connection with the dramatic deliverance of Jerusalem from the Assyrians (2 Kings 18—20). This song was the inspiration for Martin Luther's "A Mighty Fortress Is Our God," and it can be an inspiration to you today.

46:2, 3 When things are changing and threatening around you, focus your attention on God. He is with you (His presence); He is a refuge (His protection); He helps you (His power). Your world may be shaken with convulsions (vv. 2–3), but He has a river to give you peace (v. 4). You may be in the midst of battles, but He will end the war victoriously (vv. 8–9).

46:10 "Be still" (v. 10) means "take your hands off, relax." God knows what He is doing, and His timing is perfect (v. 5). When it is all over, He will be exalted (v. 10), and you will be blessed.

Wise Counsel—When you are nervous and fidgety, wanting to interfere with God's plans for your life, remember these three admonitions: "Be still!" (Ps. 46:10); "Stand still!" (Exod. 14:13); and "Sit still!" (Ruth 3:18).

PSALM 47

To the Chief Musician. A Psalm of the sons of Korah.

O h,* clap your hands, all you peoples!
　　Shout to God with the voice of triumph!
2　*For the Lord Most High *is* awesome;
　　He is a great King over all the earth.
3　He will subdue the peoples under us,
　　And the nations under our feet.
4　He will choose our inheritance for us,
　　The excellence of Jacob whom He loves.
　　　　　　　　　　　　　　　　　　Selah

5　God has gone up with a shout,
　　The Lord with the sound of a trumpet.
6　*Sing praises to God, sing praises!
　　Sing praises to our King, sing praises!
7　For God *is* the King of all the earth;
　　Sing praises with understanding.

8　*God reigns over the nations;
　　God sits on His holy throne.
9　The princes of the people have gathered together,
　　The people of the God of Abraham.
　　For the shields of the earth *belong* to God;
　　He is greatly exalted.

PSALM 48

A Song. A Psalm of the sons of Korah.

G reat* *is* the Lord, and greatly to be praised
　　In the city of our God,
　　In His holy mountain.
2　*Beautiful in elevation,
　　The joy of the whole earth,
　　Is Mount Zion *on* the sides of the north,
　　The city of the great King.
3　God *is* in her palaces;
　　He is known as her refuge.

4　For behold, the kings assembled,
　　They passed by together.
5　They saw *it, and* so they marveled;
　　They were troubled, they hastened away.
6　Fear took hold of them there,
　　And pain, as of a woman in birth pangs,
7　*As when* You break the ships of Tarshish
　　With an east wind.

8　As we have heard,
　　So we have seen
　　In the city of the Lord of hosts,
　　In the city of our God:
　　God will establish it forever.　　　　Selah

9　*We have thought, O God, on Your lovingkindness,
　　In the midst of Your temple.
10　According to Your name, O God,
　　So *is* Your praise to the ends of the earth;
　　Your right hand is full of righteousness.
11　Let Mount Zion rejoice,
　　Let the daughters of Judah be glad,
　　Because of Your judgments.

12　*Walk about Zion,
　　And go all around her.
　　Count her towers;
13　Mark well her bulwarks;
　　Consider her palaces;

PSALM 47

47:1 If you prefer quiet meditative worship, this psalm will challenge you, for it describes a praise celebration that involves hand-clapping, shouting, and loud singing. The cause of this excitement is the greatness of Christ our King. (If that does not excite you, what will? Get excited about these things:

47:2–4 *His great victory.* We do not know what military victory the psalmist was celebrating, but as believers today, we walk in Christ's spiritual victory (2 Cor. 2:14). Like Joshua, we submit to our Captain and trust Him to win the battle (Josh. 5:13–15). That is something to shout about!

47:6 *His great throne.* What a picture of the ascension of our Lord, returning to heaven and sitting at the right hand of God! Satan may be the god of this age, but Jesus is King of all the earth. That is something to shout about!

47:8 *His great reign.* His kingdom is a spiritual kingdom today, but He still rules in the affairs of men. One day, Christ will reign on earth, and His people shall reign with Him (Rev. 1:5–6; 5:9–10; 11:15–18). That is something to shout about!

PSALM 48

48:1 Like Psalm 46, this psalm celebrates God's deliverance of Jerusalem from an invading army (vv. 4–7). To Christian believers, Jerusalem and Mount Zion speak of "the Jerusalem above" (Gal. 4:26) and the heavenly Zion (Heb. 12:18–24) where their citizenship is recorded (Phil. 3:20).

48:2–8 *Look at the city.* It is the city of God, the Holy City, beautiful and joyful. But to the enemy who do not know the Lord, it is an awesome place that speaks of judgment. Ponder your heavenly destiny so that you may live a happier and holier life.

48:9–11 *Enjoy the city.* It is a place of God's loving-kindness and righteousness, where His name is praised and His people rejoice. You are not in the heavenly city yet, but you can still enjoy "the powers of the age to come" (Heb. 6:5). "Little faith will take your soul to heaven," said Charles Spurgeon, "but great faith will bring heaven to your soul."

48:12, 13 *Celebrate the city.* Tell others what God has prepared for His people and invite them to become citizens of Zion by faith ⌐ Christ (Luke 10:20). To know the God of glory is to know a faithful Guide who will care for you in life and take you to Mount Zion when you die. What more could you want?

"If you read history you will find that the Christians who did most for the present world were precisely those who thought most of the next. It is since Christians have largely ceased to think of the other world that they have become so ineffective in this."

—C. S. Lewis

PSALM 49

49:1, 2 Whether you are rich or poor, this psalm is for you (v. 2) because it deals with two important subjects: death and money. "Do not boast in your wealth or trust in your wealth," wrote the psalmist, and he explained why.

49:5–9 *Your wealth cannot prevent death.* When Queen Elizabeth I was dying, she said, "All my possessions for one moment of time." Although money can buy medicine and professional help, it cannot buy God off when the death angel comes to claim you.

49:10 *Your wealth cannot go with you.* The dead bodies of both men and beasts turn to dust in the grave, and the rich are not exempt from this end. When a believer dies, the spirit goes to be with the Lord (2 Cor. 5:1–8), but you cannot take your wealth with you (v. 17). However, you can send it ahead as you share it with others in the name of the Lord (Matt. 6:19–34).

49:16 *Your wealth cannot buy permanent fame.* Men praise the rich while they live, honor them when they die (and perhaps hope to inherit something), and then forget them. The rich man can build himself a monument, but he cannot make people remember him.

Verse 15 reveals the believer's assurance of future resurrection (1 Thess. 4:13–18). That is what conquers death and makes life worth living (1 Cor. 15:58; 1 Pet. 1:3).

"There are no pockets in shrouds."

—Jewish Proverb

That you may tell *it* to the generation following.
14 For this *is* God,
Our God forever and ever;
He will be our guide
Even to death.[o]

PSALM 49

To the Chief Musician. A Psalm of the sons of Korah.

Hear* this, all peoples;
Give ear, all inhabitants of the world,
2 Both low and high,
Rich and poor together.
3 My mouth shall speak wisdom,
And the meditation of my heart *shall give* understanding.
4 I will incline my ear to a proverb;
I will disclose my dark saying on the harp.

5 *Why should I fear in the days of evil,
When the iniquity at my heels surrounds me?
6 Those who trust in their wealth
And boast in the multitude of their riches,
7 None *of them* can by any means redeem *his* brother,
Nor give to God a ransom for him—
8 For the redemption of their souls *is* costly,
And it shall cease forever—
9 That he should continue to live eternally,
And not see the Pit.

10 *For he sees wise men die;
Likewise the fool and the senseless person perish,
And leave their wealth to others.
11 Their inner thought *is that* their houses *will last* forever,[p]
Their dwelling places to all generations;
They call *their* lands after their own names.
12 Nevertheless man, *though* in honor, does not remain;[q]
He is like the beasts *that* perish.

13 This is the way of those who *are* foolish,
And of their posterity who approve their sayings. Selah
14 Like sheep they are laid in the grave;
Death shall feed on them;
The upright shall have dominion over them in the morning;
And their beauty shall be consumed in the grave, far from their dwelling.
15 But God will redeem my soul from the power of the grave,
For He shall receive me. Selah

16 *Do not be afraid when one becomes rich,
When the glory of his house is increased;
17 For when he dies he shall carry nothing away;
His glory shall not descend after him.

48:14 [o]Following Masoretic Text and Syriac; Septuagint and Vulgate read *Forever.* 49:11 [p]Septuagint, Syriac, Targum, and Vulgate read *Their graves shall be their houses forever.* 49:12 [q]Following Masoretic Text and Targum; Septuagint, Syriac, and Vulgate read *understand* (compare verse 20).

18 Though while he lives he blesses himself
    (For *men* will praise you when you do well
        for yourself),
19 He shall go to the generation of his fathers;
    They shall never see light.
20 A man *who is* in honor, yet does not
        understand,
    Is like the beasts *that* perish.

PSALM 50

A Psalm of Asaph.

T he* Mighty One, God the LORD,
    Has spoken and called the earth
    From the rising of the sun to its going down.
2 *Out of Zion, the perfection of beauty,
    God will shine forth.
3 Our God shall come, and shall not keep
        silent;
    A fire shall devour before Him,
    And it shall be very tempestuous all around
        Him.

4 He shall call to the heavens from above,
    And to the earth, that He may judge His
        people:
5 "Gather My saints together to Me,
    Those who have made a covenant with Me
        by sacrifice."
6 Let the heavens declare His righteousness,
    For God Himself *is* Judge.   Selah

7 "Hear, O My people, and I will speak,
    O Israel, and I will testify against you;
    I *am* God, your God!
8 I will not rebuke you for your sacrifices
    Or your burnt offerings,
    Which are continually before Me.
9 I will not take a bull from your house,
    Nor goats out of your folds.
10 For every beast of the forest *is* Mine,
    And the cattle on a thousand hills.
11 I know all the birds of the mountains,
    And the wild beasts of the field *are* Mine.

12 "If I were hungry, I would not tell you;
    For the world *is* Mine, and all its fullness.
13 Will I eat the flesh of bulls,
    Or drink the blood of goats?
14 Offer to God thanksgiving,
    And pay your vows to the Most High.
15 Call upon Me in the day of trouble;
    I will deliver you, and you shall glorify Me."

16 *But to the wicked God says:
    "What *right* have you to declare My statutes,
    Or take My covenant in your mouth,
17 Seeing you hate instruction
    And cast My words behind you?
18 When you saw a thief, you consented[r] with
        him,
    And have been a partaker with adulterers.
19 You give your mouth to evil,
    And your tongue frames deceit.
20 You sit *and* speak against your brother;
    You slander your own mother's son.
21 These *things* you have done, and I kept
        silent;

PSALM 50

50:1 This psalm describes a courtroom scene. God is judge, witness and jury, and He brings an indictment against two kinds of "religious sinners."

50:2, 3 *Insincere worshipers.* He calls the court to order, not with the rap of a gavel but with the revelation of His glory (vv. 1–3). He indicts His people who offer sacrifices insincerely—their worship is just empty routine—and hope to "earn" God's blessing. God does not need the things we give Him (Acts 17:24–25), but we need to give Him spiritual sacrifices of thanksgiving, praise, and obedience (vv. 14–15, 23).

❝For to worship is to quicken the conscience by the holiness of God, to feed the mind with the truth of God, to purge the imagination by the beauty of God, to open the heart to the love of God, to devote the will to the purpose of God.**❞**
    —William Temple

50:16–20 *Hypocritical worshipers.* Here the issue is not sacrifices but the covenant they made with God. They profess one thing and practice another (Titus 1:16); they are guilty of theft, adultery, deceit, and slander. They thought that God's silence meant escape from punishment, but they were wrong (Eccles. 8:11).

50:18 ʳSeptuagint, Syriac, Targum, and Vulgate read *ran*.

You thought that I was altogether like you;
But I will rebuke you,
And set *them* in order before your eyes.

50:22 Judgment begins with God's people, not with the lost world (1 Pet. 4:17). Heed the warning of verse 22 and accept the admonition of verse 23.

22*"Now consider this, you who forget God,
Lest I tear *you* in pieces,
And *there be* none to deliver:
23 Whoever offers praise glorifies Me;
And to him who orders *his* conduct *aright*
I will show the salvation of God."

PSALM 51

To the Chief Musician. A Psalm of David when Nathan the prophet went to him, after he had gone in to Bathsheba.

Have* mercy upon me, O God,
According to Your lovingkindness;
According to the multitude of Your tender mercies,
Blot out my transgressions.
2   *Wash me thoroughly from my iniquity,
And cleanse me from my sin.

PSALM 51

51:1 This is the fourth of the Penitential Psalms. Like Psalm 32, it came out of David's sin with Bathsheba (2 Sam. 11—12) and his futile attempt to cover it up. If any chapter in the Bible reveals the high cost of sinning, it is this one.

3   *For I acknowledge my transgressions,
And my sin *is* always before me.
4   *Against You, You only, have I sinned,
And done *this* evil in Your sight—
That You may be found just when You speak,s
And blameless when You judge.

51:2 *Sin hurts the sinner.* David's whole being was affected by his sin: his eyes (v. 3), mind (v. 6), ears (v. 8), heart (v. 10), spirit (v. 10), and mouth (vv. 13–15). He lost fellowship with God (v. 11) and the joy of the Lord (v. 12). Are the pleasures of sin worth paying this great price?

5   Behold, I was brought forth in iniquity,
And in sin my mother conceived me.
6   Behold, You desire truth in the inward parts,
And in the hidden *part* You will make me to know wisdom.

51:3 *Sin hurts others.* Sin can bring tragic consequences to the lives of others (James 1:13–16), especially one's family. David's sin led to Uriah's death. Bathsheba's baby died. David's lovely daughter Tamar was violated by her brother Amnon, who was then killed by Absalom, who in turn was slain by Joab. Is a fleeting moment of sinful pleasure worth a lifetime of sorrow?

7   Purge me with hyssop, and I shall be clean;
Wash me, and I shall be whiter than snow.
8   Make me hear joy and gladness,
That the bones You have broken may rejoice.
9   Hide Your face from my sins,
And blot out all my iniquities.

51:4 *Sin hurts God.* We hurt ourselves and others when we sin, but primarily, our sins are against God (v. 4). Sin makes us dirty (vv. 2, 7). Sin is rebellion against God's holy law. If you want to know how much sin hurts God, go to Calvary and see His Son dying for the sins of the world. God is love, and our selfish sins break His heart.

10 *Create in me a clean heart, O God,
And renew a steadfast spirit within me.
11 Do not cast me away from Your presence,
And do not take Your Holy Spirit from me.

12 Restore to me the joy of Your salvation,
And uphold me *by Your* generous Spirit.
13 *Then* I will teach transgressors Your ways,
And sinners shall be converted to You.

51:10 God is merciful and gracious and forgives when we come in repentance and faith (1 John 1:9). David did not want "cheap" forgiveness; he came with a broken heart.

14 Deliver me from the guilt of bloodshed,
O God,
The God of my salvation,
And my tongue shall sing aloud of Your righteousness.
15 O Lord, open my lips,
And my mouth shall show forth Your praise.
16 For You do not desire sacrifice, or else I would give *it;*
You do not delight in burnt offering.

●●*How sad it is to have to live with the consequences of* forgiven *sin.*●●

—William Culbertson

51:4 sSeptuagint, Targum, and Vulgate read *in Your words.*

David's Prayer—"Blot out my transgressions" was David's prayer (Ps. 51:1). To see how God answers, read Isaiah 43:25; 44:22; Micah 7:18–19; Acts 3:19; and Hebrews 10:14–18.

17   The sacrifices of God *are* a broken spirit,
      A broken and a contrite heart—
      These, O God, You will not despise.

18   Do good in Your good pleasure to Zion;
      Build the walls of Jerusalem.
19   Then You shall be pleased with the
          sacrifices of righteousness,
      With burnt offering and whole burnt
          offering;
      Then they shall offer bulls on Your altar.

PSALM 52

To the Chief Musician. A Contemplation[t] of David when Doeg
the Edomite went and told Saul, and said to him, "David
has gone to the house of Ahimelech."

Why* do you boast in evil, O mighty man?
      The goodness of God *endures* continually.
2   *Your tongue devises destruction,
      Like a sharp razor, working deceitfully.
3   You love evil more than good,
      Lying rather than speaking righteousness.
                                            Selah
4   You love all devouring words,
      You deceitful tongue.

5   God shall likewise destroy you forever;
      He shall take you away, and pluck you out
          of *your* dwelling place,
      And uproot you from the land of the living.
                                            Selah
6   The righteous also shall see and fear,
      And shall laugh at him, *saying,*
7 *"Here is the man *who* did not make God his
          strength,
      But trusted in the abundance of his riches,
      And strengthened himself in his
          wickedness."

8   But I *am* like a green olive tree in the house
          of God;
      I trust in the mercy of God forever and
          ever.
9   I will praise You forever,
      Because You have done *it;*
      And in the presence of Your saints
      I will wait on Your name, for *it is* good.

PSALM 53

To the Chief Musician. Set to "Mahalath." A Contemplation[u]
of David.

The* fool has said in his heart,
      "*There is* no God."
      They are corrupt, and have done
          abominable iniquity;
      There is none who does good.

2   God looks down from heaven upon the
          children of men,
      To see if there are *any* who understand, who
          seek God.
3   *Every one of them has turned aside;
      They have together become corrupt;
      There is none who does good,
      No, not one.

52:title [t]Hebrew *Maschil*   53:title [u]Hebrew *Maschil*

PSALM 52

52:1 Doeg was an evil man who curried
favor with King Saul by spying on David
(1 Sam. 21—22). When David learned what
Doeg had done, he turned to God for help,
for God is the only One who can justly deal
with our enemies.

52:2 The tongue can be a force for good
or for evil. Doeg's tongue was boastful,
deceitful, and destructive, like a sharp razor
(vv. 1–4). David focused on the goodness
of God, not the badness of men, because
he knew that God's justice would ultimately
prevail.

52:7 Doeg looked like a strong luxuriant
tree, but he would be rooted up (vv. 5–7)
while David would be fresh and fruitful
(v. 8; Ps. 37:34–38). God protected David's
name because David trusted God's name
(v. 9). More people call their sons "David"
than "Doeg."

PSALM 53

53:1 In this adaptation of Psalm 14, "God"
(Elohim) is used instead of "Lord"
(Jehovah); verse 5 has more words; and
verse 6 has fewer words. Some psalms were
adapted by the musicians for various uses
in the temple worship. One of the wonders
of Scripture is that it can be applied to every
situation.

53:3 What you think concerning God helps
to determine your character and conduct.
The fool ignores God and exploits people
made in the image of God. Many people
are "practical atheists"; they may claim to
believe there is a God, but they live as
though He did not exist. Are you guilty of
this?
      God will have the last word!

4 Have the workers of iniquity no knowledge,
   Who eat up my people *as* they eat bread,
   And do not call upon God?
5 There they are in great fear
   Where no fear was,
   For God has scattered the bones of him who
       encamps against you;
   You have put *them* to shame,
   Because God has despised them.

6 Oh, that the salvation of Israel would come
       out of Zion!
   When God brings back the captivity of His
       people,
   Let Jacob rejoice *and* Israel be glad.

PSALM 54

To the Chief Musician. With stringed instruments.ᵛ A
Contemplationʷ of David when the Ziphites went and said
to Saul, "Is David not hiding with us?"

S ave* me, O God, by Your name,
     And vindicate me by Your strength.
2   Hear my prayer, O God;
     Give ear to the words of my mouth.
3   For strangers have risen up against me,
     And oppressors have sought after my life;
     They have not set God before them.   Selah

4   *Behold, God *is* my helper;
     The Lord *is* with those who uphold my life.
5   He will repay my enemies for their evil.
     Cut them off in Your truth.

6   I will freely sacrifice to You;
     I will praise Your name, O LORD, for *it is*
         good.
7   For He has delivered me out of all trouble;
     And my eye has seen *its desire* upon my
         enemies.

PSALM 55

To the Chief Musician. With stringed instruments.ˣ A
Contemplationʸ of David.

G ive* ear to my prayer, O God,
     And do not hide Yourself from my
         supplication.
2   Attend to me, and hear me;
     I am restless in my complaint, and moan
         noisily,
3   Because of the voice of the enemy,
     Because of the oppression of the wicked;
     For they bring down trouble upon me,
     And in wrath they hate me.

4   My heart is severely pained within me,
     And the terrors of death have fallen upon
         me.
5   Fearfulness and trembling have come upon
         me,
     And horror has overwhelmed me.
6   *So I said, "Oh, that I had wings like a dove!
     I would fly away and be at rest.
7   Indeed, I would wander far off,
     And remain in the wilderness.   Selah

PSALM 54

54:1 David had not bothered the Ziphites,
yet they turned against him to win favor with
King Saul (1 Sam. 23:15–23). The world
does not love God's people and even
strangers will create problems for you while
you seek to serve the Lord.

54:4, 5 Do what David did: pray for God to
take charge, protect you and vindicate you
against your enemies. God hears (v. 2) and
God helps (v. 4). When the answer comes,
be sure you take time to praise the Lord
(v. 6).

PSALM 55

55:1 Troubles around him (vv. 1–3), terrors
within him (vv. 4–5), and treachery next to
him (vv. 12–15, 21) combined to make David
wish he could get away from it all (v. 6). It
was not easy being God's anointed king, for
with the privileges came great burdens and
responsibilities, and God's enemies became
David's enemies. Leadership is not easy.

55:6 David wanted wings like a dove so he
could fly *away from* the storm. What he
really needed were wings like an eagle so
he could fly *above* the storm. How do you
get them? By going into the Holy of Holies,
under the shadow of His wings (Pss. 57:1;
91:1–4). When you call on the Lord (v. 16)
and cast your burdens on Him (v. 22), He
enables you to overcome.

54:title ᵛHebrew *neginoth* ʷHebrew *Maschil*   55:title ˣHebrew
neginoth ʸHebrew *Maschil*

8   *I would hasten my escape
    From the windy storm *and* tempest.".

9   Destroy, O Lord, *and* divide their tongues,
    For I have seen violence and strife in the
        city.
10 Day and night they go around it on its walls;
    Iniquity and trouble *are* also in the midst
        of it.
11 Destruction *is* in its midst;
    Oppression and deceit do not depart from
        its streets.

12 For *it is* not an enemy *who* reproaches me;
    Then I could bear *it.*
    Nor *is it* one *who* hates me who has exalted
        himself against me;
    Then I could hide from him.
13 But *it was* you, a man my equal,
    My companion and my acquaintance.
14 We took sweet counsel together,
    And walked to the house of God in the
        throng.

15 Let death seize them;
    Let them go down alive into hell,
    For wickedness *is* in their dwellings *and*
        among them.

16 As for me, I will call upon God,
    And the LORD shall save me.
17 Evening and morning and at noon
    I will pray, and cry aloud,
    And He shall hear my voice.
18 He has redeemed my soul in peace from the
        battle *that was* against me,
    For there were many against me.
19 God will hear, and afflict them,
    Even He who abides from of old.   Selah
    Because they do not change,
    Therefore they do not fear God.

20 He has put forth his hands against those
        who were at peace with him;
    He has broken his covenant.
21 *The words* of his mouth were smoother than
        butter,
    But war *was* in his heart;
    His words were softer than oil,
    Yet they *were* drawn swords.

22 Cast your burden on the LORD,
    And He shall sustain you;
    He shall never permit the righteous to be
        moved.

23 But You, O God, shall bring them down to
        the pit of destruction;
    Bloodthirsty and deceitful men shall not live
        out half their days;
    But I will trust in You.

PSALM 56

To the Chief Musician. Set to "The Silent Dove in Distant
Lands."² A Michtam of David when the Philistines captured
him in Gath.

B e* merciful to me, O God, for man would
        swallow me up;
    Fighting all day he oppresses me.

56:title ²Hebrew *Jonath Elem Rechokim*

55:8 You cannot fly beyond the storm
because you will find problems everywhere,
but you can fly above the storm. God permits
the burdens you face today to help you "win
your wings." Claim verse 22 and 1 Peter
5:7.

PSALM 56

56:1 David prayed this prayer while he was
in danger in enemy country (1 Sam. 21:10–
15). After God delivered him, he wrote
Psalm 34 as an expression of praise. When
you are in the midst of trouble, remember
these truths about God.

2 My enemies would hound *me* all day,
   For *there are* many who fight against me,
   O Most High.

3 Whenever I am afraid,
   I will trust in You.
4 In God (I will praise His word),
   In God I have put my trust;
   I will not fear.
   What can flesh do to me?

5 All day they twist my words;
   All their thoughts *are* against me for evil.
6 They gather together,
   They hide, they mark my steps,
   When they lie in wait for my life.
7 Shall they escape by iniquity?
   In anger cast down the peoples, O God!

8 *You number my wanderings;
   Put my tears into Your bottle;
   Are they not in Your book?
9 *When I cry out *to You,*
   Then my enemies will turn back;
   This I know, because God *is* for me.
10 In God (I will praise *His* word),
   In the LORD (I will praise *His* word),
11 In God I have put my trust;
   I will not be afraid.
   What can man do to me?

12 Vows *made* to You *are binding* upon me,
   O God;
   I will render praises to You,
13 For You have delivered my soul from death.
   Have You not *kept* my feet from falling,
   That I may walk before God
   In the light of the living?

PSALM 57

To the Chief Musician. Set to "Do Not Destroy."[a] A Michtam of David when he fled from Saul into the cave.

B e* merciful to me, O God, be merciful to me!
   For my soul trusts in You;
   And in the shadow of Your wings I will
       make my refuge,
   Until *these* calamities have passed by.

2 I will cry out to God Most High,
   To God who performs *all things* for me.
3 He shall send from heaven and save me;
   He reproaches the one who would swallow
       me up.   Selah
   God shall send forth His mercy and His
       truth.

4 My soul *is* among lions;
   I lie *among* the sons of men
   Who are set on fire,
   Whose teeth *are* spears and arrows,
   And their tongue a sharp sword.
5 Be exalted, O God, above the heavens;
   Let Your glory *be* above all the earth.

6 *They have prepared a net for my steps;
   My soul is bowed down;

56:8 *God sees where you are.* David should not have been in Gath to begin with, but the Lord was gracious to go with him and help him. God understands your situation far better than you do! ***God knows how you feel.*** He not only knows your tears, but He records them and retains them! Why? So that one day He may transform them into gems of joy and glory. No tears are ever wasted when you follow Him.

56:9 *God hears when you call.* Terrors and tears must be handled with trust (vv. 3–4, 10–11). But be sure your motive is not just deliverance. He delivers us that we might delight in Him and serve Him (vv. 12–13). The highest purpose of prayer is the glory of God.

PSALM 57

57:1 This psalm and Psalm 142 are "cave" psalms that can give you great encouragement. Your own "cave" may be a sickroom, a difficult place of ministry, or even a home where there is tension or trouble. If you do what David did, you will experience peace and victory even in the cave.

57:6 David's faith transformed his cave into a Holy of Holies (v. 1)! His confidence was not in the rocks but "under His wings." (See Ruth 2:12.) In spite of sharp teeth (v. 4), nets and pits (v. 6), David was sure of God's help.

57:title [a]Hebrew *Al Tashcheth*

They have dug a pit before me;
Into the midst of it they *themselves* have
   fallen.   Selah

7 *My heart is steadfast, O God, my heart is
   steadfast;
   I will sing and give praise.
8 Awake, my glory!
   Awake, lute and harp!
   I will awaken the dawn.

9 I will praise You, O Lord, among the
   peoples;
   I will sing to You among the nations.
10 For Your mercy reaches unto the heavens,
   And Your truth unto the clouds.

11 Be exalted, O God, above the heavens;
   Let Your glory *be* above all the earth.

PSALM 58

To the Chief Musician. Set to "Do Not Destroy."[b] A Michtam
of David.

D o* you indeed speak righteousness, you silent
   ones?
   Do you judge uprightly, you sons of men?
2 No, in heart you work wickedness;
   You weigh out the violence of your hands
   in the earth.

3 The wicked are estranged from the womb;
   They go astray as soon as they are born,
   speaking lies.
4 Their poison *is* like the poison of a serpent;
   They are like the deaf cobra *that* stops its
   ear,
5 Which will not heed the voice of charmers,
   Charming ever so skillfully.

6 *Break their teeth in their mouth, O God!
   Break out the fangs of the young lions,
   O Lord!
7 Let them flow away as waters *which* run
   continually;
   When he bends *his bow,*
   Let his arrows be as if cut in pieces.
8 *Let them be* like a snail which melts away
   as it goes,
   Like a stillborn child of a woman, that they
   may not see the sun.

9 *Before your pots can feel *the burning*
   thorns,
   He shall take them away as with a
   whirlwind,
   As in His living and burning wrath.
10 *The righteous shall rejoice when he sees the
   vengeance;
   He shall wash his feet in the blood of the
   wicked,
11 *So that men will say,
   "Surely *there is* a reward for the righteous;
   Surely He is God who judges in the earth."

58:title [b]Hebrew *Al Tashcheth*

57:7 His desire was not just to escape but
to exalt the Lord (vv. 5, 11). In fact, when
he awakened the next morning, he picked
up his harp and sang praises to God!

Trust Him; exalt Him; sing praises to Him.
This approach worked for David in his cave,
and it will work for you in your cave.

PSALM 58

58:1 In words that may seem unchristian
to us, David denounced the unjust rulers of
his day, people who promoted evil by
condemning the righteous and defending the
wicked. In a prayer that would probably not
be "Amened" in churches today, he asked
God to judge sinners and establish
righteousness on the earth.

58:6 David used many images as he prayed
for their judgment: "Make them toothless
lions! Let them disappear like water on the
sand or like the slime of a snail! Make them
broken arrows! Let them be like stillborn
children! Let them burn up like fuel under a
pot! Let them be taken away in a whirlwind!"

58:9 You will find similar passages in other
Psalms, such as 35:1–8, 26; 59:11–15;
69:22–28; 109:6–20; and 139:19–22. These
verses seem to contradict the admonition
of Matthew 5:43–48 and the examples of
Luke 23:34 and Acts 7:60. How should
today's Christian respond?

58:10 Because he was God's chosen king,
David's enemies were God's enemies (Ps.
139:21–22). No doubt his personal feelings
were involved in these prayers, but his great
concern was the righteousness of God and
the good of God's people. David had the
authority to denounce *national* enemies; we
have the privilege of forgiving *personal*
enemies.

58:11 But you cannot forgive enemies until
you realize how wicked their words and
deeds are. A holy anger against sin, and a
forgiving spirit toward sinners, is the mark
of a true child of God. The person who has
no concern to oppose wickedness in this
world does not know the sinfulness of sin
or the holiness of God. That believer needs
some backbone!

One day, God will judge the wicked. When
you pray the first three petitions of the Lord's
Prayer, you are expressing briefly what
David wrote in vivid detail. David left all
judgment to the Lord but did his part to
further God's holy will on the earth. If more
saints today felt a holy anger against sin
(Ps. 4:4; Eph. 4:26), the church might have
a more effective ministry as the salt of the
earth and the light of the world.

59:1–7 *I will pray.* David compared his enemies to dogs prowling the city streets and growling over the garbage. Saul was after him again (1 Sam. 19:1–11), and only the Lord could deliver David.

59:8–15 *I will wait.* David's wife helped him escape that time, but David faced several years of danger and exile before he received his rightful throne. Twice he could have killed Saul, but he refused to do so. He knew that God would deal with his enemies in His way and in His time (1 Sam. 26:8–11).

❝*If the Jews cursed more bitterly than the pagans this was, I think, at least in part because they took right and wrong more seriously. For if we look at their railings we find that they are usually angry not simply because these things have been done to them but because these things are manifestly wrong, are hateful to God as well as to the victim.*❞

—C. S. Lewis

PSALM 59

To the Chief Musician. Set to "Do Not Destroy."*c* A Michtam of David when Saul sent men, and they watched the house in order to kill him.

Deliver* me from my enemies, O my God;
  Defend me from those who rise up against me.
2 Deliver me from the workers of iniquity,
  And save me from bloodthirsty men.

3 For look, they lie in wait for my life;
  The mighty gather against me,
  Not *for* my transgression nor *for* my sin,
  O LORD.
4 They run and prepare themselves through no fault *of mine.*

  Awake to help me, and behold!
5 You therefore, O LORD God of hosts, the God of Israel,
  Awake to punish all the nations;
  Do not be merciful to any wicked transgressors.   Selah

6 At evening they return,
  They growl like a dog,
  And go all around the city.
7 Indeed, they belch with their mouth;
  Swords *are* in their lips;
  For *they* say, "Who hears?"

8 *But You, O LORD, shall laugh at them;
  You shall have all the nations in derision.
9 I will wait for You, O You his Strength;*d*
  For God *is* my defense.
10 My God of mercy*e* shall come to meet me;
  God shall let me see *my desire* on my enemies.

11 Do not slay them, lest my people forget;
  Scatter them by Your power,
  And bring them down,
  O Lord our shield.
12 *For* the sin of their mouth *and* the words of their lips,
  Let them even be taken in their pride,
  And for the cursing and lying *which* they speak.
13 Consume *them* in wrath, consume *them,*
  That they *may* not *be;*
  And let them know that God rules in Jacob
  To the ends of the earth.   Selah

14 And at evening they return,
  They growl like a dog,
  And go all around the city.
15 They wander up and down for food,
  And howl*f* if they are not satisfied.

59:title *c*Hebrew *Al Tashcheth*   59:9 *d*Following Masoretic Text and Syriac; some Hebrew manuscripts, Septuagint, Targum, and Vulgate read *my Strength.*   59:10 *e*Following Qere; some Hebrew manuscripts, Septuagint, and Vulgate read *My God, His mercy;* Kethib, some Hebrew manuscripts and Targum read *O God, my mercy;* Syriac reads *O God, Your mercy.*   59:15 *f*Following Septuagint and Vulgate; Masoretic Text, Syriac, and Targum read *spend the night.*

16 *But I will sing of Your power;
Yes, I will sing aloud of Your mercy in the
morning;
For You have been my defense
And refuge in the day of my trouble.
17 To You, O my Strength, I will sing praises;
For God *is* my defense,
My God of mercy.

PSALM 60

To the Chief Musician. Set to "Lily of the Testimony."ᵍ A
Michtam of David. For teaching. When he fought against
Mesopotamia and Syria of Zobah, and Joab returned and
killed twelve thousand Edomites in the Valley of Salt.

O* God, You have cast us off;
You have broken us down;
You have been displeased;
Oh, restore us again!
2 You have made the earth tremble;
You have broken it;
Heal its breaches, for it is shaking.
3 You have shown Your people hard things;
You have made us drink the wine of
confusion.

4 *You have given a banner to those who fear
You,
That it may be displayed because of the
truth.   Selah
5 *That Your beloved may be delivered,
Save *with* Your right hand, and hear me.

6 *God has spoken in His holiness:
"I will rejoice;
I will divide Shechem
And measure out the Valley of Succoth.
7 Gilead *is* Mine, and Manasseh *is* Mine;
Ephraim also *is* the helmet for My head;
Judah *is* My lawgiver.
8 Moab *is* My washpot;
Over Edom I will cast My shoe;
Philistia, shout in triumph because of Me."

9 Who will bring me *to* the strong city?
Who will lead me to Edom?
10 *Is it* not You, O God, *who* cast us off?
And You, O God, *who* did not go out with
our armies?
11 Give us help from trouble,
For the help of man *is* useless.
12 Through God we will do valiantly,
For *it is* He *who* shall tread down our
enemies.ʰ

PSALM 61

To the Chief Musician. On a stringed instrument.ⁱ A Psalm
of David.

Hear* my cry, O God;
Attend to my prayer.
2 *From the end of the earth I will cry to You,
When my heart is overwhelmed;
Lead me to the rock that is higher than I.

60:title ᵍHebrew *Shushan Eduth*   60:12 ʰCompare verses 5–
12 with 108:6–13   61:title ⁱHebrew *neginah*

59:16, 17 *I will sing.* David had a song in the morning because God gave him joy in the morning (Ps. 30:5). Things often look worse at night, so wait for the morning; God will give you your song of praise.

PSALM 60

60:1–3 *Broken.* David and Joab were leading the armies of Israel against two enemies in the north when a third enemy invaded in the south. When you get one problem solved, another one comes along! It seemed that God had abandoned His people and that the end was near.

60:4 *Bold.* But David did not run away. Instead, he boldly lifted God's banner of truth and listened for God's word of assurance (vv. 4–8). The Lord is our banner (Exod. 17:8–16), and we can trust Him to give the victory.

60:5 *Beloved.* His banner over us is love (Song of Sol. 2:4; Rom. 8:37). The name *David* means "beloved." God's people are beloved not in themselves but in Jesus Christ, the Beloved One (Matt. 3:17; Eph. 1:6). In the midst of life's battles, remember that God loves you.

60:6 *Believing.* God assured David that He was in control of the nations, so David and Joab stepped out by faith and won both battles. When you feel broken, you are still His beloved. If you believe, you can boldly win the battle. March under God's banner of truth!

PSALM 61

61:1 *Distance.* No matter how far away you go, God hears your prayers, for His ears are open to the cries of His children (Ps. 34:15). David was far from the house of God, yet the Lord heard his prayer and answered.

61:2 *Depth.* No matter how far down you sink, God can lift you up. When life overwhelms you, take time to pray. Let God lift you up and put you on the Rock that will never sink.

Daily Benefits—When daily we obey God (Ps. 61:8), praise His name (Ps. 72:15), and pray (Ps. 88:9), then daily He shares His benefits (Ps. 88:9).

61:3 Danger. Prayer brings you into the Holy of Holies, under the shadow of His wings (Exod. 25:20), where God's glory dwells. God preserves and protects His own until that hour when He calls them to Himself.

61:8 Delight. Do you find delight in prayer, or is prayer only an "emergency exercise" to get you out of trouble? David ended the psalm with an expression of praise and an affirmation of obedience. Prayer changes things, but prayer also changes people, starting with the one who does the praying!

PSALM 62

62:1 Waiting on the Lord (vv. 1, 5) does not mean being idle or indifferent because sometimes waiting is harder than working. For your waiting to be meaningful and spiritually productive, do what David did. **Wait silently.** This means not telling your trials to everybody who will listen or even telling them repeatedly to the Lord. When a child rests in the arms of the mother or father, there is no need to make noise. Much talk is sometimes evidence of little faith.

62:5 Wait expectantly. God will work as you trust Him and let Him have His way. Your hope is not in human or material resources (vv. 9–10) but in the power of God (v. 11).

62:8 Wait continually. It is not easy to wait "at all times," especially when you feel that God is not following your schedule. If your times are in His hands (Ps. 31:15), you will have perfect peace as you wait for Him to work (Isa. 26:3).

PSALM 63

63:1 This psalm probably grew out of David's painful experience during the rebellion led by his son Absalom (2 Sam. 15:13–23). Imagine the king having to leave his comfortable palace and flee to the wilderness to hide! When you find yourself in a "wilderness" situation, take inventory of the things that really are important. Just as David did in vv. 2, 4, and 6.

3   *For You have been a shelter for me,
A strong tower from the enemy.
4   I will abide in Your tabernacle forever;
I will trust in the shelter of Your wings.
                          Selah

5   For You, O God, have heard my vows;
You have given *me* the heritage of those
who fear Your name.
6   You will prolong the king's life,
His years as many generations.
7   He shall abide before God forever.
Oh, prepare mercy and truth, *which* may
preserve him!

8   *So I will sing praise to Your name forever,
That I may daily perform my vows.

PSALM 62

To the Chief Musician. To Jeduthun. A Psalm of David.

Truly* my soul silently *waits* for God;
    From Him *comes* my salvation.
2   He only *is* my rock and my salvation;
He is my defense;
I shall not be greatly moved.

3   How long will you attack a man?
You shall be slain, all of you,
Like a leaning wall and a tottering fence.
4   They only consult to cast *him* down from
his high position;
They delight in lies;
They bless with their mouth,
But they curse inwardly.   Selah

5   *My soul, wait silently for God alone,
For my expectation *is* from Him.
6   He only *is* my rock and my salvation;
He is my defense;
I shall not be moved.
7   In God *is* my salvation and my glory;
The rock of my strength,
And my refuge, *is* in God.

8   *Trust in Him at all times, you people;
Pour out your heart before Him;
God *is* a refuge for us.   Selah

9   Surely men of low degree *are* a vapor,
Men of high degree *are* a lie;
If they are weighed on the scales,
They *are* altogether *lighter* than vapor.
10 Do not trust in oppression,
Nor vainly hope in robbery;
If riches increase,
Do not set *your* heart *on them.*

11 God has spoken once,
Twice I have heard this:
That power *belongs* to God.
12 Also to You, O Lord, *belongs* mercy;
For You render to each one according to
his work.

PSALM 63

A Psalm of David when he was in the wilderness of Judah.

O* God, You *are* my God;
    Early will I seek You;
    My soul thirsts for You;
    My flesh longs for You

In a dry and thirsty land
Where there is no water.
2 *So I have looked for You in the sanctuary,
   To see Your power and Your glory.

3 Because Your lovingkindness *is* better than
      life,
   My lips shall praise You.
4 *Thus I will bless You while I live;
   I will lift up my hands in Your name.
5 My soul shall be satisfied as with marrow
      and fatness,
   And my mouth shall praise You with joyful
      lips.

6 *When I remember You on my bed,
   I meditate on You in the *night* watches.
7 Because You have been my help,
   Therefore in the shadow of Your wings I
      will rejoice.
8 My soul follows close behind You;
   Your right hand upholds me.

9 But those *who* seek my life, to destroy *it*,
   Shall go into the lower parts of the earth.
10 They shall fall by the sword;
   They shall be a portion for jackals.

11 But the king shall rejoice in God;
   Everyone who swears by Him shall glory;
   But the mouth of those who speak lies shall
      be stopped.

PSALM 64

To the Chief Musician. A Psalm of David.

Hear* my voice, O God, in my meditation;
   Preserve my life from fear of the enemy.
2 Hide me from the secret plots of the wicked,
   From the rebellion of the workers of
      iniquity,
3 Who sharpen their tongue like a sword,
   And bend *their bows to shoot* their
      arrows—bitter words,
4 That they may shoot in secret at the
      blameless;
   Suddenly they shoot at him and do not fear.

5 *They encourage themselves *in* an evil
      matter;
   They talk of laying snares secretly;
   They say, "Who will see them?"
6 They devise iniquities:
   "We have perfected a shrewd scheme."
   Both the inward thought and the heart of
      man are deep.

7 *But God shall shoot at them *with* an arrow;
   Suddenly they shall be wounded.
8 So He will make them stumble over their
      own tongue;
   All who see them shall flee away.

63:2 *"I still have God."* The God you
worship in the sanctuary is with you in your
difficulty. If you hunger and thirst after Him,
He will satisfy you (Matt. 5:6).

63:4 *"I still have a song."* David could not
go to the altar and offer sacrifices to God,
but he could lift his hands and his voice as
"spiritual sacrifices" (Heb. 13:15). When you
praise God, your inner person is nourished
(v. 5), and you are satisfied.

63:6 *"I still have joy in the Lord."* If you
cannot rejoice in your situation, you can
always rejoice in your Savior: His past help
(v. 6), His present protection (v. 7), and His
future guidance (v. 8). He hides you and
holds you, so you have nothing to fear.

PSALM 64

64:1 *David's fear of the enemy.* The king
asked to be preserved not from the enemy
but from the *fear* of the enemy. Fear and
faith cannot live in the same heart (Mark
4:40). If the enemy can make you afraid,
he has almost won the battle. A calm heart
makes a confident soldier.

64:5 *The enemy's fear of nothing.* They
"do not fear" (v. 4) to form secret plans or
lead open insurrections. (Absalom's
rebellion, perhaps?) Their words are like
swords and arrows, and they set hidden
traps. It looks like David is defeated!

64:7 *The fear of the Lord.* "But God" is
the turning point in the story. When the
enemy least expect it, God shoots at them,
and they fall into their own traps. "All men
shall fear" (v. 9), and the righteous shall be
glad.

Conquering Fear—On March 4, 1933, during the dark days of the depression, President Franklin
D. Roosevelt said in a radio speech, "The only thing we have to fear is fear itself." On September
7, 1851, the naturalist Henry David Thoreau wrote in his journal, "Nothing is so much to be feared
as fear." Three centuries before that, the French essayist Montaigne wrote, "The thing of which I
have most fear is fear." People in all ages of history have fought their fears in one way or another,
but the only thing that really conquers fear is faith in the Lord: "I will trust and not be afraid" (Isa.
12:2).

9   All men shall fear,
And shall declare the work of God;
For they shall wisely consider His doing.

10   The righteous shall be glad in the LORD, and
trust in Him.
And all the upright in heart shall glory.

PSALM 65

To the Chief Musician. A Psalm of David. A Song.

Praise* is awaiting You, O God, in Zion;
And to You the vow shall be performed.
2   O You who hear prayer,
To You all flesh will come.
3   Iniquities prevail against me;
As for our transgressions,
You will provide atonement for them.

4   Blessed *is the man* You choose,
And cause to approach *You,*
That he may dwell in Your courts.
We shall be satisfied with the goodness of
Your house,
Of Your holy temple.

5   *By awesome deeds in righteousness You
will answer us,
O God of our salvation,
You who are the confidence of all the ends
of the earth,
And of the far-off seas;
6   Who established the mountains by His
strength,
Being clothed with power;
7   You who still the noise of the seas,
The noise of their waves,
And the tumult of the peoples.
8   They also who dwell in the farthest parts
are afraid of Your signs;
You make the outgoings of the morning and
evening rejoice.

9   *You visit the earth and water it,
You greatly enrich it;
The river of God is full of water;
You provide their grain,
For so You have prepared it.
10   You water its ridges abundantly,
You settle its furrows;
You make it soft with showers,
You bless its growth.

11   You crown the year with Your goodness,
And Your paths drip *with* abundance.
12   They drop *on* the pastures of the wilderness,
And the little hills rejoice on every side.
13   The pastures are clothed with flocks;
The valleys also are covered with grain;
They shout for joy, they also sing.

PSALM 66

To the Chief Musician. A Song. A Psalm.

Make* a joyful shout to God, all the earth!
2 Sing out the honor of His name;
Make His praise glorious.
3   Say to God,
"How awesome are Your works!
Through the greatness of Your power

PSALM 65

65:1–4 *The worship goes up.* This is a
harvest psalm for believers who want to
thank God for His goodness and care during
another year. Praise and prayer go up to
the Lord from the hearts of grateful people.
We are told that "in everything [we are to]
give thanks" (1 Thess. 5:18).

65:5 *The witness reaches out.* The ends
of the earth need to hear about the God of
grace and glory. He reveals Himself to them
in creation, but they must be told the good
news of salvation: God has provided
atonement (v. 3). God blesses you that you
in turn might be a blessing to others.

65:9–13 *The wealth comes down.* How
good He is to send the rain, fill the rivers,
and water the fields! The fields provide food
for the flocks, and they rejoice at His
kindness. We take the rain for granted until
it does not fall, and then we learn how much
we need it.
You can find joy in God's goodness at
the beginning and ending of each day
(v. 8), so do not wait until the "crowning"
of the year to praise Him (v. 11).

PSALM 66

66:1–4 *Come and praise.* He invites the
whole world to praise the Lord because God
loves the world and sent His Son to be the
Savior of the world. When you know Jesus
as your Savior, you have something to sing
about, but do not do it alone. Share the
praise!

Your enemies shall submit themselves to
   You.
4 All the earth shall worship You
   And sing praises to You;
   They shall sing praises *to* Your name."
                                                    Selah

5 *Come and see the works of God;
   He is awesome *in His* doing toward the sons
      of men.
6 He turned the sea into dry *land;*
   They went through the river on foot.
   There we will rejoice in Him.
7 He rules by His power forever;
   His eyes observe the nations;
   Do not let the rebellious exalt themselves.
                                                    Selah

8 Oh, bless our God, you peoples!
   And make the voice of His praise to be
      heard,
9 Who keeps our soul among the living,
   And does not allow our feet to be moved.
10 For You, O God, have tested us;
   You have refined us as silver is refined.
11 You brought us into the net;
   You laid affliction on our backs.
12 You have caused men to ride over our
      heads;
   We went through fire and through water;
   But You brought us out to rich *fulfillment.*

13 *I will go into Your house with burnt
      offerings;
   I will pay You my vows,
14 Which my lips have uttered
   And my mouth has spoken when I was in
      trouble.
15 I will offer You burnt sacrifices of fat
      animals,
   With the sweet aroma of rams;
   I will offer bulls with goats.   Selah

16 *Come *and* hear, all you who fear God,
   And I will declare what He has done for my
      soul.
17 I cried to Him with my mouth,
   And He was extolled with my tongue.
18 If I regard iniquity in my heart,
   The Lord will not hear.
19 *But* certainly God has heard *me;*
   He has attended to the voice of my prayer.

20 Blessed *be* God,
   Who has not turned away my prayer,
   Nor His mercy from me!

PSALM 67

To the Chief Musician. On stringed instruments./ A Psalm.
A Song.

God* be merciful to us and bless us,
   And cause His face to shine upon us,
                                                    Selah
2 *That Your way may be known on earth,
   Your salvation among all nations.
3 *Let the peoples praise You, O God;
   Let all the peoples praise You.

66:5–12 *Come and see.* This brief review
of Israel's history mentions the Exodus
(v. 6), the conquest of Canaan (v. 7), and
the nation's times of trial (vv. 10–12). When
you go through testing in the will of God,
keep in mind that the same God who brings
you in will see you through and make you
better for having been in the furnace.

66:13 *Come and sacrifice.* Have you ever
made promises to God when you have been
in the furnace of suffering? Did you keep
those promises? When the test was over,
did you praise God for what you learned?

66:16 *Come and hear.* David wanted to tell
others that God answers prayer. Worship
should lead to witness to the glory of God.
   The Lord and David say, "Come!"

PSALM 67

67:1 This missionary psalm exhorts us to
get the message out to all the nations of
the world. Why?

67:2 Because they need *light* (vv. 1–2). The
lost walk in darkness and need the light of
God's face to shine upon them (2 Cor.
4:3–6). They have lost their way and are
headed for eternal darkness. Does that
burden you?

67:3 Because they need *joy* (vv. 3–4a). Sin
gives pleasure for only a short time, but in
Christ there are "pleasures forevermore"
(Ps. 16:11). How can we keep to ourselves
the joy that Jesus gives?

67:title /Hebrew *neginoth*

67:4 Because they need *righteousness* (v. 4b), which can come only through faith in Jesus Christ (Rom. 3:21–31). Man's righteousness can never satisfy the demands of God's holy law.

67:5 Because they need *life* (vv. 5–7). "The field is the world" (Matt. 13:38), but that field is not producing fruit to the glory of God. Only with God's life and blessing can the harvest of righteousness come.
If every believer did what you do about missions, would *all* the people of the earth be praising the Lord?

PSALM 68

68:1 This victory psalm celebrated how God blew the enemy away like smoke and melted them like wax (v. 2). It pictures three triumphal processions.

68:2–5 The victorious nation. Great victories were nothing new to Israel, for God had been with them from the beginning. He had delivered them from Egypt and led them through the wilderness into the Promised Land. He gave them Mount Zion and dwelt with them there. What a history of victory! Have you reviewed lately all that God has done for you?

4 *Oh, let the nations be glad and sing for joy!
For You shall judge the people righteously,
And govern the nations on earth.   Selah

5 *Let the peoples praise You, O God;
Let all the peoples praise You.
6 *Then* the earth shall yield her increase;
God, our own God, shall bless us.
7 God shall bless us,
And all the ends of the earth shall fear Him.

PSALM 68

To the Chief Musician. A Psalm of David. A Song.

Let* God arise,
    Let His enemies be scattered;
Let those also who hate Him flee before
    Him.
2 *As smoke is driven away,
So drive *them* away;
As wax melts before the fire,
So let the wicked perish at the presence of
    God.
3 But let the righteous be glad;
Let them rejoice before God;
Yes, let them rejoice exceedingly.

4 Sing to God, sing praises to His name;
Extol Him who rides on the clouds,[k]
By His name YAH,
And rejoice before Him.

5 A father of the fatherless, a defender of
    widows,
Is God in His holy habitation.
6 God sets the solitary in families;
He brings out those who are bound into
    prosperity;
But the rebellious dwell in a dry *land.*

7 O God, when You went out before Your
    people,
When You marched through the wilderness,
                    Selah
8 The earth shook;
The heavens also dropped *rain* at the
    presence of God;
Sinai itself *was moved* at the presence of
    God, the God of Israel.
9 You, O God, sent a plentiful rain,
Whereby You confirmed Your inheritance,
When it was weary.
10 Your congregation dwelt in it;
You, O God, provided from Your goodness
    for the poor.

11 The Lord gave the word;
Great *was* the company of those who
    proclaimed *it:*
12 "Kings of armies flee, they flee,
And she who remains at home divides the
    spoil.
13 Though you lie down among the sheepfolds,
You will be like the wings of a dove covered
    with silver,
And her feathers with yellow gold."
14 When the Almighty scattered kings in it,
It was *white* as snow in Zalmon.

68:4 [k]Masoretic Text reads *deserts;* Targum reads *heavens* (compare verse 34 and Isaiah 19:1).

15 A mountain of God *is* the mountain of
      Bashan;
    A mountain *of many* peaks *is* the mountain
      of Bashan.
16 Why do you fume with envy, you mountains
      of *many* peaks?
    This is the mountain *which* God desires to
      dwell in;
    Yes, the LORD will dwell *in it* forever.

17 *The chariots of God *are* twenty thousand,
    Even thousands of thousands;
    The Lord is among them *as in* Sinai, in the
      Holy *Place.*
18 You have ascended on high,
    You have led captivity captive;
    You have received gifts among men,
    Even *from* the rebellious,
    That the LORD God might dwell *there.*

19 *Blessed *be* the Lord,
    Who daily loads us *with benefits,*
    The God of our salvation!   Selah
20 Our God *is* the God of salvation;
    And to GOD the Lord *belong* escapes from
      death.

21 But God will wound the head of His
      enemies,
    The hairy scalp of the one who still goes
      on in his trespasses.
22 The Lord said, "I will bring back from
      Bashan,
    I will bring *them* back from the depths of
      the sea,
23 That your foot may crush *them*[l] in blood,
    And the tongues of your dogs *may have*
      their portion from *your* enemies."

24 They have seen Your procession, O God,
    The procession of my God, my King, into
      the sanctuary.
25 The singers went before, the players on
      instruments *followed* after;
    Among *them were* the maidens playing
      timbrels.
26 Bless God in the congregations,
    The Lord, from the fountain of Israel.
27 There *is* little Benjamin, their leader,
    The princes of Judah *and* their company,
    The princes of Zebulun *and* the princes of
      Naphtali.

28 Your God has commanded[m] your strength;
    Strengthen, O God, what You have done for
      us.
29 Because of Your temple at Jerusalem,
    Kings will bring presents to You.
30 Rebuke the beasts of the reeds,
    The herd of bulls with the calves of the
      peoples,
    Till everyone submits himself with pieces of
      silver.
    Scatter the peoples *who* delight in war.
31 Envoys will come out of Egypt;
    Ethiopia will quickly stretch out her hands
      to God.

68:17, 18 *The victorious Savior.* Paul
quoted verse 18 in Ephesians 4:8 and
applied it to the ascension of Jesus Christ.
Believers today are part of a spiritual army,
marching in a triumphal procession (2 Cor.
2:14; Col. 2:15) and claiming their
inheritance. They are seated with Christ in
the heavenlies (Eph. 2:4–6) using their
spiritual gifts to serve Him on earth. What
a victory!

68:19–35 *The victorious singers.* The
happy procession reached the sanctuary
where they lifted their praises to God and
asked for His continued strength as new
enemies attacked (vv. 28, 34–35). The God
of past victories would not forsake them as
they trusted Him and obeyed His will (2 Cor.
1:8–11).
    Are you marching like a conqueror in a
victory celebration or like a mourner in a
funeral procession?

68:23 [l]Septuagint, Syriac, Targum, and Vulgate read *you may
dip your foot.*   68:28 [m]Septuagint, Syriac, Targum, and
Vulgate read *Command, O God.*

32 Sing to God, you kingdoms of the earth;
   Oh, sing praises to the Lord,   Selah
33 To Him who rides on the heaven of heavens,
   which were of old!
   Indeed, He sends out His voice, a mighty
   voice.
34 Ascribe strength to God;
   His excellence *is* over Israel,
   And His strength *is* in the clouds.
35 O God, *You are* more awesome than Your
   holy places.
   The God of Israel *is* He who gives strength
   and power to *His* people.

Blessed *be* God!

PSALM 69

To the Chief Musician. Set to "The Lilies."[n] A Psalm of David.

S ave* me, O God!
   For the waters have come up to *my* neck.
2 I sink in deep mire,
   Where *there is* no standing;
   I have come into deep waters,
   Where the floods overflow me.
3 I am weary with my crying;
   My throat is dry;
   My eyes fail while I wait for my God.

4 *Those who hate me without a cause
   Are more than the hairs of my head;
   They are mighty who would destroy me,
   Being my enemies wrongfully;
   Though I have stolen nothing,
   I *still* must restore *it.*

5 O God, You know my foolishness;
   And my sins are not hidden from You.
6 Let not those who wait for You, O Lord GOD
   of hosts, be ashamed because of me;
   Let not those who seek You be confounded
   because of me, O God of Israel.
7 Because for Your sake I have borne
   reproach;
   Shame has covered my face.
8 I have become a stranger to my brothers,
   And an alien to my mother's children;
9 Because zeal for Your house has eaten me
   up,
   And the reproaches of those who reproach
   You have fallen on me.
10 When I wept *and chastened* my soul with
   fasting,
   That became my reproach.
11 I also made sackcloth my garment;
   I became a byword to them.
12 Those who sit in the gate speak against me,
   And I *am* the song of the drunkards.

13 But as for me, my prayer *is* to You,
   O LORD, *in* the acceptable time;
   O God, in the multitude of Your mercy,
   Hear me in the truth of Your salvation.
14 Deliver me out of the mire,
   And let me not sink;
   Let me be delivered from those who hate
   me,
   And out of the deep waters.

PSALM 69

69:1 Psalm 69 begins with sinking (vv. 1–3, 14–15) but ends with singing (vv. 30–36). It goes from prayer to praise, from reproach (vv. 7, 9, 10, 19, 20) to rejoicing, because David poured out his heart to the Lord. No matter how painful your situation may be, tell God exactly how you feel.

69:4 This is a messianic psalm. Out of David's sufferings, the Lord revealed His Son. (Compare v. 4 with John 15:25, v. 8 with John 7:3–5, v. 9 with John 2:17, v. 21 with Matt. 27:48, and v. 25 with Acts 1:20.) One purpose God has in allowing His people to suffer is that they might become more like Jesus Christ. That makes it worth it all!

❛❛*I would rather play with forked lightning, or take in my hand living wires with their fiery current, than speak a reckless word against any servant of Christ, or idly repeat the slanderous darts which thousands of Christians are hurling on others, to the hurt of their own souls and bodies.*❜❜
—A. B. Simpson

69:title [n]Hebrew *Shoshannim*

15 Let not the floodwater overflow me,
   Nor let the deep swallow me up;
   And let not the pit shut its mouth on me.

16 Hear me, O Lord, for Your lovingkindness
     is good;
   Turn to me according to the multitude of
     Your tender mercies.
17 And do not hide Your face from Your
     servant,
   For I am in trouble;
   Hear me speedily.
18 Draw near to my soul, *and* redeem it;
   Deliver me because of my enemies.

19 You know my reproach, my shame, and my
     dishonor;
   My adversaries *are* all before You.
20 Reproach has broken my heart,
   And I am full of heaviness;
   I looked *for someone* to take pity, but *there
     was* none;
   And for comforters, but I found none.
21 They also gave me gall for my food,
   And for my thirst they gave me vinegar to
     drink.

22 *Let their table become a snare before
     them,
   And their well-being a trap.
23 Let their eyes be darkened, so that they do
     not see;
   And make their loins shake continually.
24 Pour out Your indignation upon them,
   And let Your wrathful anger take hold of
     them.
25 Let their dwelling place be desolate;
   Let no one live in their tents.
26 For they persecute the *ones* You have
     struck,
   And talk of the grief of those You have
     wounded.
27 Add iniquity to their iniquity,
   And let them not come into Your
     righteousness.
28 Let them be blotted out of the book of the
     living,
   And not be written with the righteous.

29 *But I *am* poor and sorrowful;
   Let Your salvation, O God, set me up on
     high.
30 I will praise the name of God with a song,
   And will magnify Him with thanksgiving.
31 *This* also shall please the Lord better than
     an ox *or* bull,
   Which has horns and hooves.
32 The humble shall see *this and* be glad;
   And you who seek God, your hearts shall
     live.
33 For the Lord hears the poor,
   And does not despise His prisoners.

34 Let heaven and earth praise Him,
   The seas and everything that moves in them.
35 For God will save Zion
   And build the cities of Judah,
   That they may dwell there and possess it.
36 Also, the descendants of His servants shall
     inherit it,
   And those who love His name shall dwell
     in it.

69:22 This is also an imprecatory psalm (vv. 22–28; review the comments on Ps. 58). Paul quoted these words in Romans 11:9–10, applying them to unbelieving Israel. In attacking King David, the enemy were also rebelling against God and inviting their own judgment.

69:29 It is not easy to bear reproach because we want to be accepted and approved by others. But in the battle against sin, God's soldiers are often falsely accused and lied about. When this happens to you, remember that it also happened to David and to Jesus. You are in good company! Meditate on Isaiah 54:17.

PSALM 70

To the Chief Musician. *A Psalm* of David. To bring to remembrance.

M*ake* haste,* O God, to deliver me!
Make haste to help me, O Lord!

2 Let them be ashamed and confounded
Who seek my life;
Let them be turned back° and confused
Who desire my hurt.
3 Let them be turned back because of their shame,
Who say, "Aha, aha!"

4 *Let all those who seek You rejoice and be glad in You;
And let those who love Your salvation say continually,
"Let God be magnified!"

5 *But I *am* poor and needy;
Make haste to me, O God!
You *are* my help and my deliverer;
O Lord, do not delay.

PSALM 71

I*n* You, O Lord, I put my trust;
Let me never be put to shame.
2 Deliver me in Your righteousness, and cause me to escape;
Incline Your ear to me, and save me.
3 Be my strong refuge,
To which I may resort continually;
You have given the commandment to save me,
For You *are* my rock and my fortress.

4 Deliver me, O my God, out of the hand of the wicked,
Out of the hand of the unrighteous and cruel man.
5 For You are my hope, O Lord God;
You are my trust from my youth.
6 By You I have been upheld from birth;
You are He who took me out of my mother's womb.
My praise *shall be* continually of You.

7 I have become as a wonder to many,
But You *are* my strong refuge.
8 Let my mouth be filled *with* Your praise
And with Your glory all the day.

9 Do not cast me off in the time of old age;
Do not forsake me when my strength fails.

PSALM 70

70:1 David was in a hurry when he wrote this brief psalm because God was *not* in a hurry! Three times he cried, "Make haste!" and he ended with, "Do not delay!" Like Peter sinking into the water, he did not have time for a long prayer. All he could cry was, "Lord, save me!" (See Matt. 14:30.)

70:4 Why does God delay answering your prayers? Surely He can see your desperate situation. He promises to give "grace to help in time of need" (Heb. 4:16), which can be translated "grace for well-timed help." *Your Father's timing is never wrong.*

70:5 When God waits, He may have a better gift for you than what you are asking Him for (Isa. 30:18). His delays are neither denials nor defeats, so put your times in His hands and wait on the Lord (Ps. 31:15).

PSALM 71

71:1 The psalmist reviews a life of dependence on God. The Lord cared for him at birth, and he trusted the Lord as a youth (vv. 5–6). God taught him when he was young (v. 17) and was with him during his mature years. Now he is old, and he prays that God will not abandon him (vv. 9, 18).

70:2 °Following Masoretic Text, Septuagint, Targum, and Vulgate; some Hebrew manuscripts and Syriac read *be appalled* (compare 40:15).

God's Perfect Timing—Joseph in prison had to wait for God to free him and then to reconcile him to his brothers. Israel had to wait for deliverance from Egypt, and Moses had to wait through ten difficult plagues before Pharaoh would let the people go. Joshua and Caleb had to wait forty years before claiming their inheritance, and the delay was not their fault. David had to wait to receive his throne. Mary and Martha had to wait for Jesus to come to Bethany, and while they waited, their brother died (John 11). God is not in a hurry even when we are, and His schedule is better than ours.

10 For my enemies speak against me;
   And those who lie in wait for my life take
      counsel together,
11 Saying, "God has forsaken him;
   Pursue and take him, for *there is* none to
      deliver *him.*"

12 O God, do not be far from me;
   O my God, make haste to help me!
13 Let them be confounded *and* consumed
   Who are adversaries of my life;
   Let them be covered *with* reproach and
      dishonor
   Who seek my hurt.

14 But I will hope continually,
   And will praise You yet more and more.
15 My mouth shall tell of Your righteousness
   And Your salvation all the day,
   For I do not know *their* limits.
16 I will go in the strength of the Lord GOD;
   I will make mention of Your righteousness,
      of Yours only.

17 *O God, You have taught me from my youth;
   And to this *day* I declare Your wondrous
      works.
18 *Now also when *I am* old and grayheaded,
   O God, do not forsake me,
   Until I declare Your strength to *this*
      generation,
   Your power to everyone *who* is to come.

19 Also Your righteousness, O God, *is* very
      high,
   You who have done great things;
   O God, who *is* like You?
20 *You,* who have shown me great and severe
      troubles,
   Shall revive me again,
   And bring me up again from the depths of
      the earth.
21 You shall increase my greatness,
   And comfort me on every side.

22 Also with the lute I will praise You—
   And Your faithfulness, O my God!
   To You I will sing with the harp,
   O Holy One of Israel.
23 My lips shall greatly rejoice when I sing to
      You,
   And my soul, which You have redeemed.
24 My tongue also shall talk of Your
      righteousness all the day long;
   For they are confounded,
   For they are brought to shame
   Who seek my hurt.

PSALM 72

A Psalm of Solomon.

Give* the king Your judgments, O God,
   And Your righteousness to the king's Son.
2 *He will judge Your people with
      righteousness,
   And Your poor with justice.

71:17 As you read this psalm, you discover the ideal way to spend old age as a Christian. Devote time to prayer and trust the Lord to help you. Instead of complaining about what is wrong, praise God for His righteousness and goodness. Practice continual prayer (v. 3), continual praise (vv. 6, 8), and continual hope (v. 14).

71:18 Depend on His strength and use every opportunity to witness for Him (vv. 15–16). Ask God to make you a walking wonder (v. 7) who will point people to Christ. Keep a song on your lips and in your heart. After all, the best is yet to come!

PSALM 72
72:1 Solomon prayed for blessing on his reign when he followed David. A young man, Solomon knew he could not succeed without the help of the Lord. The psalm also pictures our Lord Jesus when He reigns as King of kings and Lord of lords.

72:2–4 Solomon asked for wisdom to administer justice to his people (vv. 1–7), and God granted his request (1 Kings 3). His reign was like a refreshing shower that made the earth fruitful and beautiful (2 Sam. 23:1–7). God can give you wisdom for your tasks (James 1:5) and make you a blessing to others. Do you bring refreshing showers or storms?

Glory Overcomes Gloom—When things around you look dark, just remind yourself that God will one day fill the earth with His glory (Num. 14:21; Pss. 22:27–28; 86:9; Isa. 6:3; Hab. 2:14). Trust Him to see you through (Jude 24–25).

3   The mountains will bring peace to the
     people,
     And the little hills, by righteousness.
4   He will bring justice to the poor of the
     people;
     He will save the children of the needy,
     And will break in pieces the oppressor.

5   They shall fear You[p]
     As long as the sun and moon endure,
     Throughout all generations.
6   He shall come down like rain upon the grass
     before mowing,
     Like showers *that* water the earth.
7   In His days the righteous shall flourish,
     And abundance of peace,
     Until the moon is no more.

8   He shall have dominion also from sea to sea,
     And from the River to the ends of the earth.
9   Those who dwell in the wilderness will bow
     before Him,
     And His enemies will lick the dust.
10 The kings of Tarshish and of the isles
     Will bring presents;
     The kings of Sheba and Seba
     Will offer gifts.
11 Yes, all kings shall fall down before Him;
     All nations shall serve Him.

12 For He will deliver the needy when he cries,
     The poor also, and *him* who has no helper.
13 He will spare the poor and needy,
     And will save the souls of the needy.
14 He will redeem their life from oppression
     and violence;
     And precious shall be their blood in His
     sight.

15 And He shall live;
     And the gold of Sheba will be given to Him;
     Prayer also will be made for Him
     continually,
     And daily He shall be praised.

16 *There will be an abundance of grain in the
     earth,
     On the top of the mountains;
     Its fruit shall wave like Lebanon;
     And *those* of the city shall flourish like grass
     of the earth.

17 His name shall endure forever;
     His name shall continue as long as the sun.
     And *men* shall be blessed in Him;
     All nations shall call Him blessed.

18 Blessed *be* the LORD God, the God of Israel,
     Who only does wondrous things!
19 *And blessed *be* His glorious name forever!
     And let the whole earth be filled *with* His
     glory.
     Amen and Amen.

20 The prayers of David the son of Jesse are
     ended.

72:16 Peace and security prospered while Solomon was on the throne, and Israel's domain was extended. Of course, verses 8–11 especially apply to the Lord Jesus and His glorious reign yet to come, but He can give you peace and safety today as you yield to Him. He wants you to "reign in life" right now (Rom. 5:17).

72:19 God's purpose is to fill the whole earth with His glory (v. 19) as He unites all things in Christ (Eph. 1:10). Are you helping to extend His glory on the earth?

72:5 [p]Following Masoretic Text and Targum; Septuagint and Vulgate read *They shall continue.*

Book Three: Psalms 73—89

PSALM 73

A Psalm of Asaph.

Truly* God *is* good to Israel,
   To such as are pure in heart.
2 *But as for me, my feet had almost stumbled;
   My steps had nearly slipped.
3 For I *was* envious of the boastful,
   When I saw the prosperity of the wicked.

4 *For *there are* no pangs in their death,
   But their strength *is* firm.
5 They *are* not in trouble *as other* men,
   Nor are they plagued like *other* men.
6 Therefore pride serves as their necklace;
   Violence covers them *like* a garment.
7 Their eyes bulge*q* with abundance;
   They have more than heart could wish.
8 They scoff and speak wickedly *concerning*
      oppression;
   They speak loftily.
9 They set their mouth against the heavens,
   And their tongue walks through the earth.

10 Therefore his people return here,
   And waters of a full *cup* are drained by
      them.
11 And they say, "How does God know?
   And is there knowledge in the Most High?"
12 Behold, these *are* the ungodly,
   Who are always at ease;
   They increase *in* riches.
13 Surely I have cleansed my heart *in* vain,
   And washed my hands in innocence.
14 For all day long I have been plagued,
   And chastened every morning.

15 If I had said, "I will speak thus,"
   Behold, I would have been untrue to the
      generation of Your children.
16 When I thought *how* to understand this,
   It *was* too painful for me—
17 Until I went into the sanctuary of God;
   Then I understood their end.

18 Surely You set them in slippery places;
   You cast them down to destruction.
19 Oh, how they are *brought* to desolation, as
      in a moment!
   They are utterly consumed with terrors.
20 As a dream when *one* awakes,
   So, Lord, when You awake,
   You shall despise their image.

21 Thus my heart was grieved,
   And I was vexed in my mind.
22 I *was* so foolish and ignorant;
   I was *like* a beast before You.
23 Nevertheless I *am* continually with You;
   You hold *me* by my right hand.
24 You will guide me with Your counsel,
   And afterward receive me *to* glory.

25 *Whom have I in heaven *but* You?
   And *there is* none upon earth *that* I desire
      besides You.

73:7 *q*Targum reads *face bulges;* Septuagint, Syriac, and
Vulgate read *iniquity bulges.*

PSALM 73

73:1 The psalm begins with "God is good"
and ends with "It is good" (v. 28), but
between those statements, things are not
so good!

73:2 The philosopher. Asaph's basic
premise was correct: God is good. But when
he pondered the success of the wicked and
the sorrows of the righteous, he began to
falter in his faith. It seemed that he was
wasting his time and energy being faithful
to God because the unfaithful received all
the blessings. *He did not realize that what
he called "good" was not what God would
call "good."* He was walking by sight and
not by faith.

73:4 The worshiper. The turning point
came when he went into the sanctuary and
started looking at things from God's
viewpoint. *The important thing is not so
much what you own or enjoy but where you
are going.* What good is an easy death
(v. 4) if it ushers you into pain? When life
seems unfair, take time to worship and get
your spiritual vision properly focused.

73:25 The friend. Asaph realized that
because he had God as his Friend, he
needed nothing else. He had more than the
wicked, and what he had would last forever.
God would hold him, guide him, strengthen
him, satisfy his spiritual desires—and one
day, take him to heaven!
   We are not philosophers, living on man's
explanations. We are pilgrims, living on
God's promises, *and His promises never
fail.*

PSALM 74

74:1–8 What we see. Written probably after the destruction of the temple, this psalm reveals the anguish of one who deeply loved God and could not understand why He permitted such desecration. Israel was His flock and His inheritance, and Mount Zion was His dwelling-place; yet He allowed evil men to destroy His people and His house. Why, O Lord?

74:9–17 What we do not see. God is King, but we do not see His hand working as in past centuries. We see no signs, and we have no prophet to interpret the times and give us God's message. One of God's judgments is to leave His people without a word of guidance because they have refused to obey His will.

---

26 My flesh and my heart fail;
But God *is* the strength of my heart and my portion forever.

27 For indeed, those who are far from You shall perish;
You have destroyed all those who desert You for harlotry.

28 But *it is* good for me to draw near to God;
I have put my trust in the Lord GOD,
That I may declare all Your works.

PSALM 74

A Contemplation[r] of Asaph.

O* God, why have You cast *us* off forever?
Why does Your anger smoke against the sheep of Your pasture?

2 Remember Your congregation, *which* You have purchased of old,
The tribe of Your inheritance, *which* You have redeemed—
This Mount Zion where You have dwelt.

3 Lift up Your feet to the perpetual desolations.
The enemy has damaged everything in the sanctuary.

4 Your enemies roar in the midst of Your meeting place;
They set up their banners *for* signs.

5 They seem like men who lift up
Axes among the thick trees.

6 And now they break down its carved work, all at once,
With axes and hammers.

7 They have set fire to Your sanctuary;
They have defiled the dwelling place of Your name to the ground.

8 They said in their hearts,
"Let us destroy them altogether."
They have burned up all the meeting places of God in the land.

9 *We do not see our signs;
There is no longer any prophet;
Nor *is there* any among us who knows how long.

10 O God, how long will the adversary reproach?
Will the enemy blaspheme Your name forever?

11 Why do You withdraw Your hand, even Your right hand?
Take it out of Your bosom and destroy *them.*

12 For God *is* my King from of old,
Working salvation in the midst of the earth.

13 You divided the sea by Your strength;
You broke the heads of the sea serpents in the waters.

14 You broke the heads of Leviathan in pieces,
And gave him *as* food to the people inhabiting the wilderness.

15 You broke open the fountain and the flood;
You dried up mighty rivers.

16 The day *is* Yours, the night also *is* Yours;
You have prepared the light and the sun.

74:title [r]Hebrew *Maschil*

17   You have set all the borders of the earth;
     You have made summer and winter.

18   Remember this, *that* the enemy has
         reproached, O Lord,
     And *that* a foolish people has blasphemed
         Your name.
19   *Oh, do not deliver the life of Your turtledove
         to the wild beast!
     Do not forget the life of Your poor forever.
20   Have respect to the covenant;
     For the dark places of the earth are full of
         the haunts of cruelty.
21   Oh, do not let the oppressed return
         ashamed!
     Let the poor and needy praise Your
         name.

22   Arise, O God, plead Your own cause;
     Remember how the foolish man reproaches
         You daily.
23   Do not forget the voice of Your enemies;
     The tumult of those who rise up against You
         increases continually.

PSALM 75

To the Chief Musician. Set to "Do Not Destroy."s A Psalm
of Asaph. A Song.

W e* give thanks to You, O God, we give
         thanks!
     For Your wondrous works declare *that*
         Your name is near.

2   "When I choose the proper time,
         I will judge uprightly.
3   The earth and all its inhabitants are
         dissolved;
     I set up its pillars firmly.   Selah

4   *"I said to the boastful, 'Do not deal
         boastfully,'
     And to the wicked, 'Do not lift up the
         horn.
5   Do not lift up your horn on high;
     Do *not* speak with a stiff neck.' "

6   For exaltation *comes* neither from the
         east
     Nor from the west nor from the south.
7   But God *is* the Judge:
     He puts down one,
     And exalts another.
8   For in the hand of the Lord *there is* a
         cup,
     And the wine is red;
     It is fully mixed, and He pours it out;
     Surely its dregs shall all the wicked of the
         earth
     Drain *and* drink down.

9   But I will declare forever,
     I will sing praises to the God of Jacob.

10   *"All the horns of the wicked I will also cut
         off,
     But the horns of the righteous shall be
         exalted."

75:title $Hebrew *Al Tashcheth*

74:19 *What we want to see.* Surely Asaph
knew that the sins of the nation caused the
invasion of the enemy and the destruction
of the temple. As a faithful Jew, he wanted
to see the city and the people delivered and
the enemy defeated. That would happen in
due time, when God's discipline of His
people was ended and their rebellion
conquered (Heb. 12:9–11). Meanwhile, all
he could do was weep, pray, trust God, and
wait.

PSALM 75

75:1, 2 God is the Judge; His people are
only His witnesses. We can tell others about
His great works (v. 1) and His gracious
warnings (vv. 4–5), but we cannot tell them
when His judgment will fall. God will choose
the proper time, and His judgment will be
just.

75:4 The proud rulers of the nations think
they are secure, but the God who set them
up can also pull them down (1 Sam. 2:7–8;
Dan. 4:25). The wicked think they are getting
away with their evil deeds, but one day they
must drink the wine of God's wrath.

75:10 Meanwhile, God's children continue
to sing His praises because they are sure
God knows what He is doing. The world
needs our witness, and worship is the
greatest witness of all. The next time you
are disturbed by the evil in the world, pause
and praise the Lord.

❝_Judgment for an evil thing is many times delayed some day or two, some century or two, but it is sure as life, it is sure as death._**❞**

—Thomas Carlyle

PSALM 76

76:1 God is to be praised. We do not know what military victory is celebrated here, but it brought great glory to the Lord. The enemy's fortresses (v. 4), soldiers (v. 5),and equipment (v. 6) were unable to stand before the Lord of hosts. It is encouraging to know that God is for us in the battles of life.

76:7 God is to be feared. Man's fury does not frighten God (Ps. 2:1–4). In fact, He uses it to bring Himself glory, like a woman wearing a special garment (v. 10). God is long-suffering, but one day He will arise to judge the wicked. Meanwhile, His people must also fear Him and be faithful to keep their vows to Him (v. 11). Never trifle with God.

PSALM 77

77:1 Joyless days of trouble and sleepless nights of despair plagued the psalmist. Why? Not because of unbelief but because of faith. Because he believed in the Lord, he wrestled with himself and with God. He could not understand why the Lord did not keep His promises and deliver His people from bondage. What do you do in a situation like that?

77:2 Of course, you pray (v. 1) and tell God just how you feel. Reach out to Him in the night seasons (v. 2), _but do not refuse the comfort that He sends._ He will remind you of His past works and wonders, and the more you meditate on them, the better you will feel.

PSALM 76

To the Chief Musician. On stringed instruments.[t] A Psalm of Asaph. A Song.

In* Judah God is known;
    His name is great in Israel.
2 In Salem[u] also is His tabernacle,
    And His dwelling place in Zion.
3 There He broke the arrows of the bow,
    The shield and sword of battle.   Selah

4 You are more glorious and excellent
    Than the mountains of prey.
5 The stouthearted were plundered;
    They have sunk into their sleep;
    And none of the mighty men have found
      the use of their hands.
6 At Your rebuke, O God of Jacob,
    Both the chariot and horse were cast into a
      dead sleep.

7 *You, Yourself, are to be feared;
    And who may stand in Your presence
    When once You are angry?
8 You caused judgment to be heard from
      heaven;
    The earth feared and was still,
9 When God arose to judgment,
    To deliver all the oppressed of the earth.
                  Selah

10 Surely the wrath of man shall praise You;
    With the remainder of wrath You shall gird
    Yourself.

11 Make vows to the LORD your God, and pay
    them;
    Let all who are around Him bring presents
    to Him who ought to be feared.
12 He shall cut off the spirit of princes;
    He is awesome to the kings of the earth.

PSALM 77

To the Chief Musician. To Jeduthun. A Psalm of Asaph.

I* cried out to God with my voice—
    To God with my voice;
    And He gave ear to me.
2 *In the day of my trouble I sought the Lord;
    My hand was stretched out in the night
      without ceasing;
    My soul refused to be comforted.
3 I remembered God, and was troubled;
    I complained, and my spirit was
      overwhelmed.   Selah

4 You hold my eyelids open;
    I am so troubled that I cannot speak.
5 I have considered the days of old,
    The years of ancient times.
6 I call to remembrance my song in the night;
    I meditate within my heart,
    And my spirit makes diligent search.

7 Will the Lord cast off forever?
    And will He be favorable no more?
8 Has His mercy ceased forever?
    Has His promise failed forevermore?

76:title [t]Hebrew neginoth   76:2 [u]That is, Jerusalem

9   Has God forgotten to be gracious?
Has He in anger shut up His tender mercies?
           Selah

10   And I said, "This *is* my anguish;
But I will remember the years of the right
   hand of the Most High."
11   I will remember the works of the LORD;
Surely I will remember Your wonders of
   old.
12   I will also meditate on all Your work,
And talk of Your deeds.
13   Your way, O God, *is* in the sanctuary;
Who *is* so great a God as *our* God?
14   *You *are* the God who does wonders;
You have declared Your strength among the
   peoples.
15   You have with *Your* arm redeemed Your
   people,
The sons of Jacob and Joseph.   Selah

16   The waters saw You, O God;
The waters saw You, they were afraid;
The depths also trembled.
17   The clouds poured out water;
The skies sent out a sound;
Your arrows also flashed about.
18   The voice of Your thunder *was* in the
   whirlwind;
The lightnings lit up the world;
The earth trembled and shook.
19   Your way *was* in the sea,
Your path in the great waters,
And Your footsteps were not known.
20   You led Your people like a flock
By the hand of Moses and Aaron.

PSALM 78

A Contemplation^v of Asaph.

G ive* ear, O my people, *to* my law;
   Incline your ears to the words of my
     mouth.
2   I will open my mouth in a parable;
I will utter dark sayings of old,
3   Which we have heard and known,
And our fathers have told us.
4   We will not hide *them* from their children,
Telling to the generation to come the praises
   of the LORD,
And His strength and His wonderful works
   that He has done.

5   *For He established a testimony in Jacob,
And appointed a law in Israel,
Which He commanded our fathers,
That they should make them known to their
   children;
6   That the generation to come might know
   them,
The children *who* would be born,
That they may arise and declare *them* to
   their children,
7   That they may set their hope in God,
And not forget the works of God,
But keep His commandments;
8   And may not be like their fathers,
A stubborn and rebellious generation,

77:14 Asaph meditated on Israel's exodus from Egypt and recalled that God kept the people waiting by the Red Sea, that it was night, and that deliverance came just in the nick of time. The people were afraid and certain that God had forgotten them, but He showed His power and humiliated the enemy.

His way is a holy way (v. 13) and a hidden way (v. 19). You need not understand it; just follow as He leads you.

     ❝*What are all histories but God manifesting Himself?*❞
     —Oliver Cromwell

PSALM 78

78:1 This long psalm reviews the history of Israel: the Exodus (vv. 12–16, 42–53); their wilderness journey (vv. 17–41); the conquest of Canaan (vv. 54–55); and disciplines God sent them there (vv. 56–64). A nation's true history is a record not of how the people treated one another but of how they treated God.

78:5–8 But why the long history lesson? For the sake of the generations to follow (vv. 1–8). The Jews were commanded to teach their children the works and ways of the Lord so that each generation would know the Lord and trust Him (Deut. 6:1–9). We have the same obligation today. When Israel stopped doing this, the nation forsook the Lord and God had to chasten them (Judg. 2:7–10).

78:title ^vHebrew *Maschil*

A generation *that* did not set its heart
   aright,
And whose spirit was not faithful to God.

9   The children of Ephraim, *being* armed *and*
       carrying bows,
     Turned back in the day of battle.
10   They did not keep the covenant of God;
     They refused to walk in His law,
11   And forgot His works
     And His wonders that He had shown them.

12   Marvelous things He did in the sight of their
       fathers,
     In the land of Egypt, *in* the field of Zoan.
13   He divided the sea and caused them to pass
       through;
     And He made the waters stand up like a
       heap.
14   In the daytime also He led them with the
       cloud,
     And all the night with a light of fire.
15   He split the rocks in the wilderness,
     And gave *them* drink in abundance like the
       depths.
16   He also brought streams out of the rock,
     And caused waters to run down like rivers.

17   But they sinned even more against Him
     By rebelling against the Most High in the
       wilderness.
18   And they tested God in their heart
     By asking for the food of their fancy.
19   Yes, they spoke against God:
     They said, "Can God prepare a table in the
       wilderness?
20   Behold, He struck the rock,
     So that the waters gushed out,
     And the streams overflowed.
     Can He give bread also?
     Can He provide meat for His people?"

21   Therefore the LORD heard *this* and was
       furious;
     So a fire was kindled against Jacob,
     And anger also came up against Israel,
22   Because they did not believe in God,
     And did not trust in His salvation.
23   Yet He had commanded the clouds above,
     And opened the doors of heaven,
24   Had rained down manna on them to eat,
     And given them of the bread of heaven.
25   Men ate angels' food;
     He sent them food to the full.

26   He caused an east wind to blow in the
       heavens;
     And by His power He brought in the south
       wind.
27   He also rained meat on them like the dust,
     Feathered fowl like the sand of the seas;
28   And He let *them* fall in the midst of their
       camp,
     All around their dwellings.
29   So they ate and were well filled,
     For He gave them their own desire.
30   They were not deprived of their craving;
     But while their food *was* still in their
       mouths,
31   The wrath of God came against them,
     And slew the stoutest of them,
     And struck down the choice *men* of Israel.

32 In spite of this they still sinned,
    And did not believe in His wondrous works.
33 Therefore their days He consumed in
        futility,
    And their years in fear.

34 When He slew them, then they sought Him;
    And they returned and sought earnestly for
        God.
35 Then they remembered that God *was* their
        rock,
    And the Most High God their Redeemer.
36 Nevertheless they flattered Him with their
        mouth,
    And they lied to Him with their tongue;
37 For their heart was not steadfast with Him,
    Nor were they faithful in His covenant.
38 But He, *being* full of compassion, forgave
        their iniquity,
    And did not destroy *them.*
    Yes, many a time He turned His anger away,
    And did not stir up all His wrath;
39 For He remembered that they *were but*
        flesh,
    A breath that passes away and does not
        come again.

40 *How often they provoked Him in the
        wilderness,
    And grieved Him in the desert!
41 Yes, again and again they tempted God,
    And limited the Holy One of Israel.
42 They did not remember His power:
    The day when He redeemed them from the
        enemy,
43 When He worked His signs in Egypt,
    And His wonders in the field of Zoan;
44 Turned their rivers into blood,
    And their streams, that they could not drink.
45 He sent swarms of flies among them, which
        devoured them,
    And frogs, which destroyed them.
46 He also gave their crops to the caterpillar,
    And their labor to the locust.
47 He destroyed their vines with hail,
    And their sycamore trees with frost.
48 He also gave up their cattle to the hail,
    And their flocks to fiery lightning.
49 He cast on them the fierceness of His anger,
    Wrath, indignation, and trouble,
    By sending angels of destruction *among
        them.*
50 He made a path for His anger;
    He did not spare their soul from death,
    But gave their life over to the plague,
51 And destroyed all the firstborn in Egypt,
    The first of *their* strength in the tents of
        Ham.
52 But He made His own people go forth like
        sheep,
    And guided them in the wilderness like a
        flock;
53 And He led them on safely, so that they did
        not fear;
    But the sea overwhelmed their enemies.
54 And He brought them to His holy border,
    This mountain *which* His right hand had
        acquired.
55 He also drove out the nations before them,
    Allotted them an inheritance by survey,
    And made the tribes of Israel dwell in their
        tents.

78:40 Israel was a rebellious nation, but
God was gracious and gave the people
opportunities to start again. This is not an
excuse for us to sin and tempt God, but it
is an encouragement to repent when we do
sin.

56 Yet they tested and provoked the Most High
    God,
    And did not keep His testimonies,
57 But turned back and acted unfaithfully like
    their fathers;
    They were turned aside like a deceitful
    bow.
58 For they provoked Him to anger with their
    high places,
    And moved Him to jealousy with their
    carved images.
59 When God heard *this,* He was furious,
    And greatly abhorred Israel,
60 So that He forsook the tabernacle of Shiloh,
    The tent He had placed among men,
61 And delivered His strength into captivity,
    And His glory into the enemy's hand.
62 He also gave His people over to the sword,
    And was furious with His inheritance.
63 The fire consumed their young men,
    And their maidens were not given in
    marriage.
64 Their priests fell by the sword,
    And their widows made no lamentation.

65 Then the Lord awoke as *from* sleep,
    Like a mighty man who shouts because of
    wine.
66 And He beat back His enemies;
    He put them to a perpetual reproach.

67 Moreover He rejected the tent of Joseph,
    And did not choose the tribe of Ephraim,
68 But chose the tribe of Judah,
    Mount Zion which He loved.
69 And He built His sanctuary like the heights,
    Like the earth which He has established
    forever.
70 *He also chose David His servant,
    And took him from the sheepfolds;
71 From following the ewes that had young He
    brought him,
    To shepherd Jacob His people,
    And Israel His inheritance.
72 So he shepherded them according to the
    integrity of his heart,
    And guided them by the skillfulness of his
    hands.

78:70 God's answer to Israel's needs was to give them a spiritual leader, David, the shepherd. He had both integrity (the heart) and ability (the hands), and he sought to serve the Lord and love the flock of Israel. People have not changed; they still rebel against God. There is still a need for faithful instructors in the home (vv. 1–8) and leaders in the nation (vv. 70–72). Do all you can to help the next generation serve the Lord acceptably.

PSALM 79

79:1–3 Once again Asaph is lamenting the invasion of the enemy (cf. Ps. 74). He had several concerns.
God's inheritance. The temple was defiled, the city destroyed, and the people slain. God permitted these things to happen to His inheritance! But God would rather destroy His inheritance than allow His people to sin and rebel.

PSALM 79

A Psalm of Asaph.

O* God, the nations have come into Your
    inheritance;
    Your holy temple they have defiled;
    They have laid Jerusalem in heaps.
2   The dead bodies of Your servants
    They have given *as* food for the birds of the
    heavens,
    The flesh of Your saints to the beasts of the
    earth.
3   Their blood they have shed like water all
    around Jerusalem,
    And *there was* no one to bury *them.*
4   We have become a reproach to our
    neighbors,
    A scorn and derision to those who are
    around us.

5   How long, LORD?
    Will You be angry forever?
    Will Your jealousy burn like fire?

6 *Pour out Your wrath on the nations that do
   not know You,
   And on the kingdoms that do not call on
      Your name.
7 For they have devoured Jacob,
   And laid waste his dwelling place.

8 Oh, do not remember former iniquities
      against us!
   Let Your tender mercies come speedily to
      meet us,
   For we have been brought very low.
9 Help us, O God of our salvation,
   For the glory of Your name;
   And deliver us, and provide atonement for
      our sins,
   For Your name's sake!
10 *Why should the nations say,
   "Where is their God?"
   Let there be known among the nations in
      our sight
   The avenging of the blood of Your servants
   which has been shed.

11 Let the groaning of the prisoner come
      before You;
   According to the greatness of Your power
   Preserve those who are appointed to die;
12 And return to our neighbors sevenfold into
      their bosom
   Their reproach with which they have
      reproached You, O Lord.

13 *So we, Your people and sheep of Your
      pasture,
   Will give You thanks forever;
   We will show forth Your praise to all
      generations.

PSALM 80

To the Chief Musician. Set to "The Lilies."ʷ A Testimonyˣ
of Asaph. A Psalm.

Give* ear, O Shepherd of Israel,
   You who lead Joseph like a flock;
   You who dwell between the cherubim, shine
      forth!
2 *Before Ephraim, Benjamin, and Manasseh,
   Stir up Your strength,
   And come and save us!

3 Restore us, O God;
   Cause Your face to shine,
   And we shall be saved!

4 O LORD God of hosts,
   How long will You be angry
   Against the prayer of Your people?
5 You have fed them with the bread of tears,
   And given them tears to drink in great
      measure.
6 You have made us a strife to our neighbors,
   And our enemies laugh among themselves.

7 Restore us, O God of hosts;
   Cause Your face to shine,
   And we shall be saved!

79:6 God's name. What will the heathen nations say about Israel and Israel's God? The corpses and ruins bore witness to something that the world needed to know: *God is holy and does not tolerate disobedience.* Asaph confessed the sins of the nation and asked God to honor His name before the nations (vv. 8–10, 13).

79:10 God's wrath. Asaph asserted, "Pour out Your wrath" (v. 6)! "Avenge our blood" (v. 10)! Years later, that prayer was answered, and God punished Babylon for the way she treated Israel.

79:13 God's people. They are "Your servants" and "Your saints" (v. 2), "the sheep of Your pasture" (v. 13). Care for them, Lord! Deliver them! God did care for them, but He also chastened them so that they might learn to obey His will.
   When you want God to be harder on others than He is on you, it is time to start seeing your sins the way God sees them.

PSALM 80

80:1 Asaph prayed for the restoration and illumination of God's people by the shining of God's face (vv. 3, 7, 19; Num. 6:22–27). He gave two pictures of the nation.

80:2–7 A flock. Israel was like a flock of sheep led by God (Pss. 77:20; 78:52): "We are His people and the sheep of His pasture" (Ps. 100:3). But they were *wayward* sheep who would not follow the Shepherd. So, instead of enjoying green pastures and still waters (Ps. 23:2), they were enduring tears and the reproach of the enemy (v. 5).

80:title ʷHebrew *Shoshannim* ˣHebrew *Eduth*

80:8 *A vine.* This picture parallels Isaiah 5 and our Lord's parables in Matthew 21:28–46. Israel was a fruitful vineyard until she turned from the Lord and began to worship the gods of the nations. God used those very nations to discipline His people and destroy the vineyard. The prayer in verses 17–18 was partially answered when some of the people returned to the land after the captivity, but it is fully realized in Jesus Christ.

80:16 God's people today are sheep in the flock (John 10) and branches in the Vine (John 15). Do not take your blessings for granted. He is seeking faithfulness and fruitfulness.

PSALM 81

81:1–10 *The things that were.* This section is an invitation for the people to participate in a joyful celebration, probably Passover. Asaph gave them two reasons for sharing: obedience (it was God's ordinance) and gratitude (all God had done for them). It is good to set aside special times to meditate on the work of the Lord in your life.

8 *You have brought a vine out of Egypt;
You have cast out the nations, and planted it.
9 You prepared *room* for it,
And caused it to take deep root,
And it filled the land.
10 The hills were covered with its shadow,
And the mighty cedars with its boughs.
11 She sent out her boughs to the Sea,ʸ
And her branches to the River.ᶻ

12 Why have You broken down her hedges,
So that all who pass by the way pluck her *fruit*?
13 The boar out of the woods uproots it,
And the wild beast of the field devours it.

14 Return, we beseech You, O God of hosts;
Look down from heaven and see,
And visit this vine
15 And the vineyard which Your right hand has planted,
And the branch *that* You made strong for Yourself.
16 *It is* burned with fire, *it is* cut down;
They perish at the rebuke of Your countenance.
17 Let Your hand be upon the man of Your right hand,
Upon the son of man *whom* You made strong for Yourself.
18 Then we will not turn back from You;
Revive us, and we will call upon Your name.

19 Restore us, O LORD God of hosts;
Cause Your face to shine,
And we shall be saved!

PSALM 81

To the Chief Musician. On an instrument of Gath.ᵃ A Psalm of Asaph.

Sing* aloud to God our strength;
Make a joyful shout to the God of Jacob.
2 Raise a song and strike the timbrel,
The pleasant harp with the lute.

3 Blow the trumpet at the time of the New Moon,
At the full moon, on our solemn feast day.
4 For this *is* a statute for Israel,
A law of the God of Jacob.
5 This He established in Joseph *as* a testimony,
When He went throughout the land of Egypt,
Where I heard a language I did not understand.

6 "I removed his shoulder from the burden;
His hands were freed from the baskets.
7 You called in trouble, and I delivered you;
I answered you in the secret place of thunder;
I tested you at the waters of Meribah.
Selah

80:11 ʸThat is, the Mediterranean ᶻThat is, the Euphrates
81:title ᵃHebrew *Al Gittith*

8 "Hear, O My people, and I will admonish you!
  O Israel, if you will listen to Me!
9 There shall be no foreign god among you;
  Nor shall you worship any foreign god.
10 I *am* the LORD your God,
  Who brought you out of the land of Egypt;
  Open your mouth wide, and I will fill it.

11*"But My people would not heed My voice,
  And Israel would *have* none of Me.
12 So I gave them over to their own stubborn
  heart,
  To walk in their own counsels.

13*"Oh, that My people would listen to Me,
  That Israel would walk in My ways!
14 I would soon subdue their enemies,
  And turn My hand against their adversaries.
15 The haters of the LORD would pretend
  submission to Him,
  But their fate would endure forever.
16 He would have fed them also with the finest
  of wheat;
  And with honey from the rock I would have
  satisfied you."

PSALM 82

A Psalm of Asaph.

God* stands in the congregation of the mighty;
  He judges among the gods.*b*
2 How long will you judge unjustly,
  And show partiality to the wicked?   Selah
3 Defend the poor and fatherless;
  Do justice to the afflicted and needy.
4 Deliver the poor and needy;
  Free *them* from the hand of the wicked.

5 *They do not know, nor do they understand;
  They walk about in darkness;
  All the foundations of the earth are
  unstable.

6 *I said, "You *are* gods,*c*
  And all of you *are* children of the Most High.
7 But you shall die like men,
  And fall like one of the princes."

8 Arise, O God, judge the earth;
  For You shall inherit all nations.

PSALM 83

A Song. A Psalm of Asaph.

Do* not keep silent, O God!
  Do not hold Your peace,
  And do not be still, O God!
2 For behold, Your enemies make a tumult;
  And those who hate You have lifted up their
  head.
3 They have taken crafty counsel against
  Your people,
  And consulted together against Your
  sheltered ones.
4 They have said, "Come, and let us cut them
  off from *being* a nation,

82:1 *b*Hebrew *elohim, mighty ones;* that is, the judges
82:6 *c*Hebrew *elohim, mighty ones;* that is, the judges

81:11, 12 *The things that are.* In spite of
all that God did for His people, they would
not listen to His Word or do His will. One
of God's most painful judgments is to permit
you to have your own way. For a time, you
enjoy it; then you learn how much you have
missed.

**81:13–16 *The things that might have
been.*** Had they obeyed, they would have
experienced victory instead of defeat,
fullness instead of emptiness, and the best
instead of the worst. They could have looked
back with rejoicing, but instead they had to
remember with regret.
  The things that might have been *will be*
if *today* you let the Master have His way.

PSALM 82

82:1–4 *The throne in heaven.* The Lord
stands as Judge and indicts the human
judges for their failure to defend the poor
and needy and condemn the wicked. Their
partiality made a farce out of the legal
system God ordained for Israel (Lev. 19:15;
Prov. 24:23–25). What does He think of our
judicial system today?

82:5 *The foundations on earth.* The
foundations for peace and order in society
are righteousness and justice (Pss. 89:14;
97:2). Whether in the home, church, or
government, abandoning righteousness and
justice makes the very foundations tremble
(Ps. 11:3) and brings darkness where there
should be light.

82:6–8 *The graves under the earth.* The
human judges are called "gods" because
the Hebrew word *elohim* means "mighty
ones." (It is also one of the names for God.)
Leadership is a serious thing, for leaders
stand in the place of God and will one day
answer to Him. The selfish judges may have
their days of pleasure, but one day they will
die, and then what? The judges will be
judged righteously by the Judge of all the
earth, and there will be no escape.

PSALM 83

83:1–8 Asaph was perplexed (vv. 1–8).
Israel was in danger, but God was silent and
inactive. The nations were noisily forming a
military confederacy against the Jews, but
God was speechless and seemingly doing
nothing. The enemy wanted to destroy the
nation (v. 4) and take the land (v. 12), and
apparently God was going to let them do it.

That the name of Israel may be remembered
no more.''

5   For they have consulted together with one
consent;
They form a confederacy against You:
6   The tents of Edom and the Ishmaelites;
Moab and the Hagrites;
7   Gebal, Ammon, and Amalek;
Philistia with the inhabitants of Tyre;
8   Assyria also has joined with them;
They have helped the children of Lot.
Selah

9   *Deal with them as *with* Midian,
As *with* Sisera,
As *with* Jabin at the Brook Kishon,
10   Who perished at En Dor,
Who became *as* refuse on the earth.
11   Make their nobles like Oreb and like Zeeb,
Yes, all their princes like Zebah and
Zalmunna,
12   Who said, "Let us take for ourselves
The pastures of God for a possession."

13   O my God, make them like the whirling
dust,
Like the chaff before the wind!
14   As the fire burns the woods,
And as the flame sets the mountains on fire,
15   So pursue them with Your tempest,
And frighten them with Your storm.
16   *Fill their faces with shame,
That they may seek Your name, O LORD.
17   Let them be confounded and dismayed
forever;
Yes, let them be put to shame and perish,
18   *That they may know that You, whose name
alone *is* the LORD,
Are the Most High over all the earth.

PSALM 84

To the Chief Musician. On an instrument of Gath.[d] A Psalm
of the sons of Korah.

How* lovely *is* Your tabernacle,
O LORD of hosts!
2   My soul longs, yes, even faints
For the courts of the LORD;
My heart and my flesh cry out for the living
God.

3   Even the sparrow has found a home,
And the swallow a nest for herself,
Where she may lay her young—
Even Your altars, O LORD of hosts,
My King and my God.
4   *Blessed *are* those who dwell in Your house;
They will still be praising You.   Selah

5   *Blessed *is* the man whose strength *is* in You,
Whose heart *is* set on pilgrimage.
6   *As they* pass through the Valley of Baca,
They make it a spring;
The rain also covers it with pools.
7   They go from strength to strength;
Each one appears before God in Zion.[e]

83:9–13 So, Asaph prayed (vv. 9–18) and
reminded God of what He did to Israel's
enemies during the days of the judges (vv.
9–12). Then he shifted from history to nature
and asked God to send a storm to wipe them
out (vv. 13–15).

83:16 Asaph had a purpose in mind—not
just the safety of Israel but the glory of the
Lord (vv. 16–18). Some of the enemy
soldiers might even trust in the God of Israel!
It was not important that Israel's name be
preserved (v. 4), but it was important that
God's name be glorified.

83:18 When it seems that God is saying and
doing nothing, rest assured that He is
working on your behalf. He is not as noisy
as the enemy, but He is more powerful; *and
He will win.*

PSALM 84

84:1 The Jews were required to go to
Jerusalem three times each year, to
celebrate Passover, Pentecost, and the
Feast of Tabernacles. The author of this
psalm was unable to join the pilgrimage,
even though his soul yearned to be there.
Life has its disappointments, but the three
beatitudes in this psalm tell you how to
handle them.

84:4 *The blessing of dwelling.* Perhaps
the priests and Levites took for granted their
privilege of dwelling in the courts of the Lord,
but the psalmist did not. God's altars were
to him what a nest was to a bird, a place
of safety and satisfaction. Abiding in the Lord
is not a matter of geography, for you can
worship Him and love Him wherever you are.
When life disappoints you, abide in Him.

84:5 *The blessing of desiring.* What is in
your heart is what counts. He would rather
serve in the temple than be served
anywhere else. When your desires are
godly, the Lord will give you all you need.
When life disappoints you, be sure your
heart's desires are pleasing to God.

84:title [d]Hebrew *Al Gittith*   84:7 [e]Septuagint, Syriac, and
Vulgate read *The God of gods shall be seen.*

8 O Lord God of hosts, hear my prayer;
   Give ear, O God of Jacob!   Selah
9 O God, behold our shield,
   And look upon the face of Your anointed.

10 For a day in Your courts *is* better than a
   thousand.
   I would rather be a doorkeeper in the house
   of my God
   Than dwell in the tents of wickedness.
11 For the Lord God *is* a sun and shield;
   The Lord will give grace and glory;
   No good *thing* will He withhold
   From those who walk uprightly.

12 *O Lord of hosts,
   Blessed *is* the man who trusts in You!

PSALM 85

To the Chief Musician. A Psalm of the sons of Korah.

L ord,* You have been favorable to Your land;
   You have brought back the captivity of
   Jacob.
2 You have forgiven the iniquity of Your
   people;
   You have covered all their sin.   Selah
3 You have taken away all Your wrath;
   You have turned from the fierceness of Your
   anger.

4 *Restore us, O God of our salvation,
   And cause Your anger toward us to cease.
5 Will You be angry with us forever?
   Will You prolong Your anger to all
   generations?
6 Will You not revive us again,
   That Your people may rejoice in You?
7 Show us Your mercy, Lord,
   And grant us Your salvation.

8 *I will hear what God the Lord will speak,
   For He will speak peace
   To His people and to His saints;
   But let them not turn back to folly.
9 Surely His salvation *is* near to those who
   fear Him,
   That glory may dwell in our land.

10 Mercy and truth have met together;
   Righteousness and peace have kissed.
11 Truth shall spring out of the earth,
   And righteousness shall look down from
   heaven.
12 Yes, the Lord will give *what is* good;
   And our land will yield its increase.
13 Righteousness will go before Him,
   And shall make His footsteps *our* pathway.

PSALM 86

A Prayer of David.

B ow* down Your ear, O Lord, hear me;
   For I *am* poor and needy.
2 Preserve my life, for I *am* holy;
   You *are* my God;
   Save Your servant who trusts in You!
3 Be merciful to me, O Lord,
   For I cry to You all day long.
4 Rejoice the soul of Your servant,
   For to You, O Lord, I lift up my soul.

84:12 *The blessing of depending.* God's pilgrims go "from strength to strength" and "from faith to faith" (Rom. 1:17). As you trust the Lord, He gives "grace and glory," for He is your sun (provision) and shield (protection). He gives you all you need on the pilgrimage of life. When life disappoints you, depend on the Lord for what you really need.

PSALM 85

85:1–3 *Restoration.* We do not know from what crisis the Lord had delivered His people; perhaps it was the captivity in Babylon. His wrath had ended, their sins were forgiven, and they had come home again. In times of divine chastening, rest on Psalm 30:5.

85:4–7 *Revival.* When the refugees got back to the land, life was difficult, and they were ready to give up. God had forgiven their sins, but that did not make life a paradise. They wanted new life from God so they could rejoice in Him. New beginnings should lead to experiences of new life.

85:8 *Responsibility.* God forgives us that we might fear and serve Him (Ps. 130:4). You must hear and obey His Word and trust Him to send the needed increase. Mercy and truth met in His passion when Jesus died for the sin of the world. Righteousness and peace meet in His person: King of righteousness and King of peace (Heb. 7:1–3).
God's chastening is for your good, and He is with you when it is ended. He will help you make a fresh new start for His glory.

> ❝*It is no use to pray for the old days; stand square where you are and make the present better than any past has been. Base all on your relationship to God and go forward, and presently you will find that what is emerging is infinitely better than the past ever was.*❞
>
> —Oswald Chambers

PSALM 86

86:1 *"Preserve my life."* David was in trouble again. As he always did, he turned to the Lord for help, and he presented some reasons why God should answer him. God was *his* God, and he was God's servant. God was merciful, and he needed mercy. He wanted God alone to be glorified in the victory. God is good and great and ready to help.

86:11 *"Unite my heart."* A divided heart leads only to instability (James 1:5–8), because you cannot serve two masters (Matt. 6:22–24). With a single heart, fear the Lord, learn from the Lord, obey the Lord, and praise His name.

86:14 *"Strengthen my hand."* David's strength and experience were inadequate to face the foe; he needed the strength of the Lord. David knew his theology (v. 15; Exod. 34:6; Neh. 9:17), and that helped him in his praying. The better you know God, the better you can approach Him with your needs.

❝*What man needs is not a boost from below but a birth from above.*❞

—Vance Havner

PSALM 87

87:1 The earthly Mount Zion is a figure of the heavenly Zion, the city of God and God's redeemed people (Gal. 4:21–31; Heb. 12:18–24). As you ponder this psalm, take inventory of your spiritual life.

87:2 *On what are you building?* Are you building your life on God's foundation (1 Cor. 3:11)? "Salvation is of the Jews" (John 4:22), for God's gracious work in this world came through Israel (Gen. 12:1–3). Your Bible is a Jewish book, and the Savior came from the tribe of Judah. When the church was born, the Holy Spirit came on Jewish believers in the temple in Jerusalem. To obey Him is to build on an unfailing foundation (Matt. 7:21–29).

87:4 *Where is your citizenship?* Some people like to boast about the place of their birth, but the "once-born" do not have the blessings of the "twice-born." Through faith in Christ, God's children are enrolled in the heavenly Zion (Luke 10:20; Phil. 3:20; 4:3)— and will live with the Father forever.

87:7 *What are your joys?* Jerusalem is one of the few ancient cities that is not built by a river. The psalmist found all his joys in Jerusalem, and he wanted nothing more. By faith, you can drink of the river of His pleasures (Pss. 36:8; 46:4) and be satisfied.

5 For You, Lord, *are* good, and ready to forgive,
And abundant in mercy to all those who call upon You.

6 Give ear, O Lᴏʀᴅ, to my prayer;
And attend to the voice of my supplications.
7 In the day of my trouble I will call upon You,
For You will answer me.

8 Among the gods *there is* none like You, O Lord;
Nor *are there any works* like Your works.
9 All nations whom You have made
Shall come and worship before You, O Lord,
And shall glorify Your name.
10 For You *are* great, and do wondrous things;
You alone *are* God.

11 *Teach me Your way, O Lᴏʀᴅ;
I will walk in Your truth;
Unite my heart to fear Your name.
12 I will praise You, O Lord my God, with all my heart,
And I will glorify Your name forevermore.
13 For great *is* Your mercy toward me,
And You have delivered my soul from the depths of Sheol.

14 *O God, the proud have risen against me,
And a mob of violent *men* have sought my life,
And have not set You before them.
15 But You, O Lord, *are* a God full of compassion, and gracious,
Longsuffering and abundant in mercy and truth.

16 Oh, turn to me, and have mercy on me!
Give Your strength to Your servant,
And save the son of Your maidservant.
17 Show me a sign for good,
That those who hate me may see *it* and be ashamed,
Because You, Lᴏʀᴅ, have helped me and comforted me.

PSALM 87

A Psalm of the sons of Korah. A Song.

His* foundation *is* in the holy mountains.
2*The Lᴏʀᴅ loves the gates of Zion
More than all the dwellings of Jacob.
3 Glorious things are spoken of you,
O city of God!   Selah

4 *"I will make mention of Rahab and Babylon
to those who know Me;
Behold, O Philistia and Tyre, with Ethiopia:
'This *one* was born there.' "

5 And of Zion it will be said,
"This *one* and that *one* were born in her;
And the Most High Himself shall establish her."
6 The Lᴏʀᴅ will record,
When He registers the peoples:
"This *one* was born there."   Selah

7 *Both the singers and the players on instruments *say*,
"All my springs *are* in you."

PSALM 88

A Song. A Psalm of the sons of Korah. To the Chief Musician. Set to "Mahalath Leannoth." A Contemplation[f] of Heman the Ezrahite.

O* LORD, God of my salvation,
 I have cried out day and night before You.
2 Let my prayer come before You;
 Incline Your ear to my cry.

3 *For my soul is full of troubles,
 And my life draws near to the grave.
4 I am counted with those who go down to the pit;
 I am like a man *who has* no strength,
5 Adrift among the dead,
 Like the slain who lie in the grave,
 Whom You remember no more,
 And who are cut off from Your hand.

6 You have laid me in the lowest pit,
 In darkness, in the depths.
7 Your wrath lies heavy upon me,
 And You have afflicted *me* with all Your waves.   Selah
8 You have put away my acquaintances far from me;
 You have made me an abomination to them;
 I am shut up, and I cannot get out;
9 *My eye wastes away because of affliction.

 LORD, I have called daily upon You;
 I have stretched out my hands to You.
10 Will You work wonders for the dead?
 Shall the dead arise *and* praise You?
                                    Selah
11 Shall Your lovingkindness be declared in the grave?
 Or Your faithfulness in the place of destruction?
12 Shall Your wonders be known in the dark?
 And Your righteousness in the land of forgetfulness?

13 *But to You I have cried out, O LORD,
 And in the morning my prayer comes before You.
14 LORD, why do You cast off my soul?
 Why do You hide Your face from me?
15 I *have been* afflicted and ready to die from *my* youth;
 I suffer Your terrors;
 I am distraught.
16 Your fierce wrath has gone over me;
 Your terrors have cut me off.
17 They came around me all day long like water;
 They engulfed me altogether.
18 Loved one and friend You have put far from me,
 And my acquaintances into darkness.

PSALM 89

A Contemplation[g] of Ethan the Ezrahite.

I* will sing of the mercies of the LORD forever;
 With my mouth will I make known Your faithfulness to all generations.

88:title [f]Hebrew *Maschil*   89:title [g]Hebrew *Maschil*

PSALM 88

88:1 This is one of the few psalms that does not end on a note of glorious victory. When Heman wrote it, he was suffering greatly, and God had not given him relief. *But he kept on praying and trusting God* (vv. 1–2, 9, 13).

88:3 The next time you want to say, "Nobody knows how I feel!" take time to read this psalm. How did Heman feel? Like a dead man buried in a dark pit. Like a drowning man sinking under cold waves and billows. Like a defiled man watching everybody run away and leave him alone. Most of all, he felt like a doomed man whom God had forsaken.

88:9 But Heman did not give up. Instead, he looked by faith to God, the God of wonders, loving-kindness, and faithfulness (vv. 10–12). He cried out to God and told Him just how he felt. Your feelings may change, but God never changes. You can trust Him even in the dark, even when you seem to be drowning.

88:13 God knows how you feel (Heb. 4:14–16) and is working out His purposes for you. The final verses of your "psalm" have not been written yet, but God knows what they are, so wait for Him. They are worth waiting for!

PSALM 89

89:1 God made a covenant with David that he would always have a descendant on his throne and that the Davidic line would rule forever (2 Sam. 7). But Ethan the Ezrahite had a problem. One of the Davidic kings had been defeated in war and had lost his throne (vv. 38–45). It seemed to Ethan that God had broken His covenant (vv. 3, 28, 34, 39) and that God was not faithful to His people.

89:2 *Faithfulness* is a key word in this psalm (vv. 1, 2, 5, 8, 24, 33). God's faithfulness is seen from generation to generation (vv. 1–4), among His people (vv. 5–10), in creation (vv. 11–13), among the nations (vv. 14–18), and toward David and his family (vv. 19–37). Ethan knew all of this because he knew the Scriptures, but recent events seemed to deny the truthfulness of the covenant and the faithfulness of the Lord.

89:6 Ethan's problem was caused by spiritual shortsightedness. The ultimate fulfillment of the Davidic covenant is in Jesus Christ, the Son of David (Matt. 1:1), and He will reign forever (Luke 1:26–33). God's faithfulness does not fail!

89:19 When Jeremiah viewed the destruction of Jerusalem, he may have felt as Ethan did when the king was defeated and dethroned. Instead of questioning God's faithfulness, Jeremiah reaffirmed it: "Great is Your faithfulness" (Lam. 3:23). Never judge God's faithfulness on the basis of what you see or how you feel. His promises do not fail (2 Cor. 1:18–20).

2 *For I have said, "Mercy shall be built up forever;
  Your faithfulness You shall establish in the very heavens."

3 "I have made a covenant with My chosen,
  I have sworn to My servant David:
4 'Your seed I will establish forever,
  And build up your throne to all generations.' "   Selah

5 And the heavens will praise Your wonders, O LORD;
  Your faithfulness also in the assembly of the saints.
6 *For who in the heavens can be compared to the LORD?
  Who among the sons of the mighty can be likened to the LORD?
7 God is greatly to be feared in the assembly of the saints,
  And to be held in reverence by all *those* around Him.
8 O LORD God of hosts,
  Who *is* mighty like You, O LORD?
  Your faithfulness also surrounds You.
9 You rule the raging of the sea;
  When its waves rise, You still them.
10 You have broken Rahab in pieces, as one who is slain;
  You have scattered Your enemies with Your mighty arm.

11 The heavens *are* Yours, the earth also *is* Yours;
  The world and all its fullness, You have founded them.
12 The north and the south, You have created them;
  Tabor and Hermon rejoice in Your name.
13 You have a mighty arm;
  Strong is Your hand, *and* high is Your right hand.
14 Righteousness and justice *are* the foundation of Your throne;
  Mercy and truth go before Your face.
15 Blessed *are* the people who know the joyful sound!
  They walk, O LORD, in the light of Your countenance.
16 In Your name they rejoice all day long,
  And in Your righteousness they are exalted.
17 For You *are* the glory of their strength,
  And in Your favor our horn is exalted.
18 For our shield *belongs* to the LORD,
  And our king to the Holy One of Israel.

19 *Then You spoke in a vision to Your holy one,[h]
  And said: "I have given help to *one who is* mighty;
  I have exalted one chosen from the people.
20 I have found My servant David;
  With My holy oil I have anointed him,
21 With whom My hand shall be established;
  Also My arm shall strengthen him.
22 The enemy shall not outwit him,
  Nor the son of wickedness afflict him.

89:19 [h]Following many Hebrew manuscripts; Masoretic Text, Septuagint, Targum, and Vulgate read *holy ones.*

23 I will beat down his foes before his face,
    And plague those who hate him.

24 "But My faithfulness and My mercy *shall be*
        with him,
    And in My name his horn shall be exalted.
25 Also I will set his hand over the sea,
    And his right hand over the rivers.
26 He shall cry to Me, 'You *are* my Father,
    My God, and the rock of my salvation.'
27 Also I will make him *My* firstborn,
    The highest of the kings of the earth.
28 My mercy I will keep for him forever,
    And My covenant shall stand firm with him.
29 His seed also I will make *to endure* forever,
    And his throne as the days of heaven.

30 "If his sons forsake My law
    And do not walk in My judgments,
31 If they break My statutes
    And do not keep My commandments,
32 Then I will punish their transgression with
        the rod,
    And their iniquity with stripes.
33 Nevertheless My lovingkindness I will not
        utterly take from him,
    Nor allow My faithfulness to fail.
34 My covenant I will not break,
    Nor alter the word that has gone out of My
        lips.
35 Once I have sworn by My holiness;
    I will not lie to David:
36 His seed shall endure forever,
    And his throne as the sun before Me;
37 It shall be established forever like the moon,
    Even *like* the faithful witness in the sky."
                                                        Selah

38 But You have cast off and abhorred,
    You have been furious with Your anointed.
39 You have renounced the covenant of Your
        servant;
    You have profaned his crown *by casting it*
        to the ground.
40 You have broken down all his hedges;
    You have brought his strongholds to ruin.
41 All who pass by the way plunder him;
    He is a reproach to his neighbors.
42 You have exalted the right hand of his
        adversaries;
    You have made all his enemies rejoice.
43 You have also turned back the edge of his
        sword,
    And have not sustained him in the battle.
44 You have made his glory cease,
    And cast his throne down to the ground.
45 The days of his youth You have shortened;
    You have covered him with shame.   Selah

46 How long, LORD?
    Will You hide Yourself forever?
    Will Your wrath burn like fire?
47 Remember how short my time is;
    For what futility have You created all the
        children of men?
48 What man can live and not see death?
    Can he deliver his life from the power of
        the grave?   Selah

49 Lord, where *are* Your former
        lovingkindnesses,
    Which You swore to David in Your truth?

50 Remember, Lord, the reproach of Your
   servants—
   How I bear in my bosom *the reproach of*
   all the many peoples,
51 With which Your enemies have reproached,
   O LORD,
   With which they have reproached the
   footsteps of Your anointed.

52 Blessed *be* the LORD forevermore!
   Amen and Amen.

Book Four: Psalms 90—106

PSALM 90

A Prayer of Moses the man of God.

LORD,* You have been our dwelling place[*i*] in all
   generations.
2 *Before the mountains were brought forth,
   Or ever You had formed the earth and the
   world,
   Even from everlasting to everlasting, You
   are God.

3 You turn man to destruction,
   And say, "Return, O children of men."
4 *For a thousand years in Your sight
   Are like yesterday when it is past,
   And *like* a watch in the night.
5 You carry them away *like* a flood;
   They are like a sleep.
   In the morning they are like grass *which*
   grows up:
6 In the morning it flourishes and grows up;
   In the evening it is cut down and withers.

7 For we have been consumed by Your anger,
   And by Your wrath we are terrified.
8 You have set our iniquities before You,
   Our secret *sins* in the light of Your
   countenance.
9 For all our days have passed away in Your
   wrath;
   We finish our years like a sigh.
10 The days of our lives *are* seventy years;
   And if by reason of strength *they are* eighty
   years,
   Yet their boast *is* only labor and sorrow;
   For it is soon cut off, and we fly away.
11 Who knows the power of Your anger?
   For as the fear of You, *so is* Your wrath.
12 So teach *us* to number our days,
   That we may gain a heart of wisdom.

13 Return, O LORD!
   How long?
   And have compassion on Your servants.
14 Oh, satisfy us early with Your mercy,
   That we may rejoice and be glad all our
   days!
15 Make us glad according to the days *in which*
   You have afflicted us,
   The years *in which* we have seen evil.

90:1 *Septuagint, Targum, and Vulgate read *refuge*.

PSALM 90

90:1 The somber tone of this psalm
suggests that Moses may have written it
when the nation rebelled in unbelief at
Kadesh Barnea (Num. 13—14). God
announced that everybody twenty years old
and older would die within the next forty
years. No wonder Moses prayed, "So teach
us to number our days" (v. 12).

90:2 We number our years, but it is wiser
to number our days, for we live a day at a
time. Life is brief, like the changing of the
guard, or taking a nap, or mowing the lawn
(vv. 3–6). In the camp of Israel, a twenty-
year-old would not live beyond sixty, and
the older people would never make it to
eighty (v. 10). It was a funeral march for
forty long years!

90:4 In the light of eternity (vv. 1–4), life is
brief—no matter how long you live. You
need God's help to use your days wisely
(v. 12) and joyfully (vv. 14–15). There is real
satisfaction in doing God's will (v. 14; 1 John
2:17), revealing God's glory (v. 16) and
growing in God's beauty (v. 17). In spite of
the burdens of life and the brevity of life,
life is worth living when you trust the Lord.

The Land of the Living—Charles Spurgeon told about a man who said to a dying believer,
"Farewell, friend! I shall never see you again in the land of the living!" The dying Christian replied,
"I *shall* see you again in the land of the living where I am going. *This* is the land of the dying!"

16 Let Your work appear to Your servants,
    And Your glory to their children.
17 And let the beauty of the LORD our God be
        upon us,
    And establish the work of our hands for us;
    Yes, establish the work of our hands.

PSALM 91

He* who dwells in the secret place of the Most
    High
        Shall abide under the shadow of the
            Almighty.
2   *I will say of the LORD, "*He is* my refuge and
        my fortress;
    My God, in Him I will trust."

3   *Surely He shall deliver you from the snare
        of the fowler[j]
    And from the perilous pestilence.
4   He shall cover you with His feathers,
    And under His wings you shall take refuge;
    His truth *shall be your* shield and buckler.
5   You shall not be afraid of the terror by
        night,
    Nor of the arrow *that* flies by day,
6   *Nor* of the pestilence *that* walks in
        darkness,
    Nor of the destruction *that* lays waste at
        noonday.

7   A thousand may fall at your side,
    And ten thousand at your right hand;
    But it shall not come near you.
8   Only with your eyes shall you look,
    And see the reward of the wicked.

9   Because you have made the LORD, *who is*
        my refuge,
    Even the Most High, your dwelling place,
10 No evil shall befall you,
    Nor shall any plague come near your
        dwelling;
11 For He shall give His angels charge over
        you,
    To keep you in all your ways.
12 In *their* hands they shall bear you up,
    Lest you dash your foot against a stone.
13 You shall tread upon the lion and the cobra,
    The young lion and the serpent you shall
        trample underfoot.

14*"Because he has set his love upon Me,
        therefore I will deliver him;
    I will set him on high, because he has known
        My name.
15 He shall call upon Me, and I will answer
        him;
    I *will be* with him in trouble;
    I will deliver him and honor him.
16 With long life I will satisfy him,
    And show him My salvation."

PSALM 92

A Psalm. A Song for the Sabbath day.

It* is good to give thanks to the LORD,
    And to sing praises to Your name, O Most
        High;

91:3 [j]That is, one who catches birds in a trap or snare

PSALM 91

91:1 What a relief to turn to this psalm and
move out of the shadows into the sunshine!
In light of the sobering admonitions of Psalm
90, we appreciate even more the sublime
assurances of Psalm 91.

91:2 The theme is *security:* God preserves
those who abide in Him and love Him. These
promises are not for people who run to the
Lord only in times of danger but for those
who *dwell* in His presence (v. 1) and make
the Holy of Holies their *habitation* (v. 9).

91:3–6 What are the dangers we face?
Snares and pestilences (v. 3), arrows (v. 5),
plagues (v. 10), stones (vv. 11–12), and
lions and snakes (v. 13; perhaps referring
to Satan). You can easily give the modern
equivalents for these ancient perils that
Jewish travelers faced.

91:14–16 The abiding life (vv. 1–4)
produces the assuring life (vv. 5–13), the
life without fear, which leads to the
abounding life (vv. 14–16), the life of victory
and peace. The safest place in the world is
under the shadow of the Almighty.

PSALM 92

92:1 It is good to thank the Lord *for every
day He gives you* (vv. 1–4). As the day
begins, you can look ahead by faith and
praise Him for His loving-kindness. As the
day ends, you can look back and praise Him
for His faithfulness.

> **"**It does not pay to get sour as you get old. I pity a man who lives in the past. He lives on stale manna. He gets stunted.**"**
>
> —D. L. Moody

92:5 It is good to thank the Lord *that you are part of what is eternal* (vv. 5–9). You cannot understand eternity, but you can have eternal life through faith in Christ; and you can live for what is eternal (1 John 2:17). Ponder 1 Corinthians 15:58.

92:10 It is even good to thank the Lord *for old age* (vv. 10–15). In old age, those who live for Christ become fresh (v. 10), flourishing (vv. 12–13), fruitful (v. 14), and faithful (v. 15). Instead of complaining, they are praising the Lord and witnessing for Him.

PSALM 93

93:1 When the floods are rising (v. 3), lay hold of three anchors that will steady you.

93:2–4 *God's throne.* No matter what may come to you today, "the LORD reigns!" God is sovereign and everything is under control. His majestic throne is strong, established, and everlasting. His throne is above the floods, but He is with you in your trials and will see you through (Isa. 43:1–2).

93:5 *God's testimonies.* You can trust the Word of God because it never fails (Josh. 21:45; 23:14). Cling to His testimonies (Ps. 119:31) and withstand the floods by faith.
God's temple. God's throne was the mercy seat in the Holy of Holies (Ps. 99:1), and there His glory rested. Satan himself cannot dethrone our Lord, and the men who attempt it are attempting vanity (Ps. 2:1–3). When the storms come and the floods rise, you can experience peace, for "the LORD is in His holy temple. Let all the earth keep silence before Him" (Hab. 2:20).

PSALM 94

94:1 God alone can judge and punish the wicked (vv. 1–3), but God's people must stand up and be counted in the battle for truth (v. 16). It is easier to be a spectator or an advisor than to be a soldier. When you enter the battle against evil, rely on God.

2 To declare Your lovingkindness in the morning,
And Your faithfulness every night,
3 On an instrument of ten strings,
On the lute,
And on the harp,
With harmonious sound.
4 For You, LORD, have made me glad through Your work;
I will triumph in the works of Your hands.

5 *O LORD, how great are Your works!
Your thoughts are very deep.
6 A senseless man does not know,
Nor does a fool understand this.
7 When the wicked spring up like grass,
And when all the workers of iniquity flourish,
It is that they may be destroyed forever.

8 But You, LORD, *are* on high forevermore.
9 For behold, Your enemies, O LORD,
For behold, Your enemies shall perish;
All the workers of iniquity shall be scattered.

10 *But my horn You have exalted like a wild ox;
I have been anointed with fresh oil.
11 My eye also has seen *my desire* on my enemies;
My ears hear *my desire* on the wicked
Who rise up against me.

12 The righteous shall flourish like a palm tree,
He shall grow like a cedar in Lebanon.
13 Those who are planted in the house of the LORD
Shall flourish in the courts of our God.
14 They shall still bear fruit in old age;
They shall be fresh and flourishing,
15 To declare that the LORD is upright;
He is my rock, and *there is* no unrighteousness in Him.

PSALM 93

The* LORD reigns, He is clothed with majesty;
The LORD is clothed,
He has girded Himself with strength.
Surely the world is established, so that it cannot be moved.
2 *Your throne *is* established from of old;
You *are* from everlasting.

3 The floods have lifted up, O LORD,
The floods have lifted up their voice;
The floods lift up their waves.
4 The LORD on high *is* mightier
Than the noise of many waters,
Than the mighty waves of the sea.

5 *Your testimonies are very sure;
Holiness adorns Your house,
O LORD, forever.

PSALM 94

O* LORD God, to whom vengeance belongs—
O God, to whom vengeance belongs, shine forth!

2 *Rise up, O Judge of the earth;
   Render punishment to the proud.
3 LORD, how long will the wicked,
   How long will the wicked triumph?

4 They utter speech, *and* speak insolent
      things;
   All the workers of iniquity boast in
      themselves.
5 They break in pieces Your people, O LORD,
   And afflict Your heritage.
6 They slay the widow and the stranger,
   And murder the fatherless.
7 Yet they say, "The LORD does not see,
   Nor does the God of Jacob understand."

8 Understand, you senseless among the
      people;
   And *you* fools, when will you be wise?
9 He who planted the ear, shall He not hear?
   He who formed the eye, shall He not see?
10 He who instructs the nations, shall He not
      correct,
   He who teaches man knowledge?
11 The LORD knows the thoughts of man,
   That they *are* futile.

12 *Blessed *is* the man whom You instruct,
      O LORD,
   And teach out of Your law,
13 That You may give him rest from the days
      of adversity,
   Until the pit is dug for the wicked.
14 For the LORD will not cast off His people,
   Nor will He forsake His inheritance.
15 But judgment will return to righteousness,
   And all the upright in heart will follow it.

16 *Who will rise up for me against the
      evildoers?
   Who will stand up for me against the
      workers of iniquity?
17 Unless the LORD *had been* my help,
   My soul would soon have settled in silence.
18 If I say, "My foot slips,"
   Your mercy, O LORD, will hold me up.
19 In the multitude of my anxieties within me,
   Your comforts delight my soul.

20 Shall the throne of iniquity, which devises
      evil by law,
   Have fellowship with You?
21 They gather together against the life of the
      righteous,
   And condemn innocent blood.
22 But the LORD has been my defense,
   And my God the rock of my refuge.
23 He has brought on them their own iniquity,
   And shall cut them off in their own
      wickedness;
   The LORD our God shall cut them off.

PSALM 95

O h* come, let us sing to the LORD!
   Let us shout joyfully to the Rock of our
      salvation.
2   Let us come before His presence with
      thanksgiving;
   Let us shout joyfully to Him with psalms.
3   For the LORD *is* the great God,
   And the great King above all gods.

94:2 *God knows all about the enemy.* He hears their insolent speech, He sees their wicked deeds, and He will eventually bring them to judgment. The Captain of your salvation will not be caught off guard!

94:12 *God will teach you what to do.* The basic "Handbook for Battle" is the Word of God, and God will teach you what you need to know. Gideon was an ordinary farmer when God called him, and yet he became a mighty warrior because he let God teach him (Judg. 6—7). Even though he was hiding from the enemy, God called him a "mighty man of valor" (Judg. 6:11–12).

94:16 *God will help you fight.* God is for you if you are against what He is against. When you fight, He will help you. If you slip, He will hold you. If you worry, He will comfort you, and if you are attacked, He will defend you.
   Who is on the Lord's side? Are you?

PSALM 95
95:1–7 *God is great!* This is a call to jubilant worship, not just participation in services as usual. He invites us to "shout joyfully" and to "kneel before the LORD." Why? Because God is great! He is a great Creator and a great King, and we are privileged to be His people.

95:8–11 *God is grieved.* The opposite of a worshiping heart that pleases the Lord is a hard heart that grieves the Lord. Imagine seeing God's wonders and not submitting gladly to Him! The unbelieving Jews paid a high price for their sin: they died in the wilderness and never entered the Promised Land (Heb. 3—4).

Do you want to enjoy your life of faith? Then take time to see the greatness of God and to praise Him. Do you want to inherit all that God has planned for you in this life? Then give yourself to worship and praise. A hard heart leads to a hard life, so keep your heart tender before God.

PSALM 96

96:1 In this invitation to worship the Lord, you are given three admonitions.

96:2 *Sing to the Lord.* Sing a *new song* because you have had a new experience with Him. Sing a *worship hymn* because God is glorious (v. 3) and great (vv. 4–5). Sing a *gospel song* because the nations need to hear the good news of salvation. Sing a *song of victory* and reveal the strength of the Lord. Sing a *song of devotion* and reveal the beauty of the Lord.

96:7 *Give to the Lord.* Give Him glory with your lips and heart, and give Him offerings with your hands. God does not need your gifts (Acts 17:24–25), but you need to bring your gifts to God. He deserves the best (Mal. 1:6–14).

96:11 *Look for the Lord.* All nature is eagerly anticipating the Lord's return, for then creation will be set free (Rom. 8:18–25). The oppressed people will be vindicated, and sinners will be judged when Jesus Christ comes to reign. God's people shall reign with Christ and then worship Him perfectly. Hallelujah!

4 In His hand *are* the deep places of the earth;
The heights of the hills *are* His also.
5 The sea *is* His, for He made it;
And His hands formed the dry *land.*

6 Oh come, let us worship and bow down;
Let us kneel before the Lord our Maker.
7 For He *is* our God,
And we *are* the people of His pasture,
And the sheep of His hand.

*Today, if you will hear His voice:
8 *"Do not harden your hearts, as in the rebellion,[k]
As *in* the day of trial[l] in the wilderness,
9 When your fathers tested Me;
They tried Me, though they saw My work.
10 For forty years I was grieved with *that* generation,
And said, 'It *is* a people who go astray in their hearts,
And they do not know My ways.'
11 So I swore in My wrath,
'They shall not enter My rest.'"

PSALM 96

Oh,* sing to the Lord a new song!
Sing to the Lord, all the earth.
2 *Sing to the Lord, bless His name;
Proclaim the good news of His salvation from day to day.
3 Declare His glory among the nations,
His wonders among all peoples.

4 For the Lord *is* great and greatly to be praised;
He *is* to be feared above all gods.
5 For all the gods of the peoples *are* idols,
But the Lord made the heavens.
6 Honor and majesty *are* before Him;
Strength and beauty *are* in His sanctuary.

7 *Give to the Lord, O families of the peoples,
Give to the Lord glory and strength.
8 Give to the Lord the glory *due* His name;
Bring an offering, and come into His courts.
9 Oh, worship the Lord in the beauty of holiness!
Tremble before Him, all the earth.

10 Say among the nations, "The Lord reigns;
The world also is firmly established,
It shall not be moved;
He shall judge the peoples righteously."

11 *Let the heavens rejoice, and let the earth be glad;
Let the sea roar, and all its fullness;
12 Let the field be joyful, and all that *is* in it.
Then all the trees of the woods will rejoice before the Lord.
13 For He is coming, for He is coming to judge the earth.
He shall judge the world with righteousness,
And the peoples with His truth.

95:8 [k]Or *Meribah* [l]Or *Massah*   97:12 [m]Or *His holiness*

PSALM 97

T he* LORD reigns;
Let the earth rejoice;
Let the multitude of isles be glad!

2 *Clouds and darkness surround Him;
Righteousness and justice *are* the
foundation of His throne.
3 A fire goes before Him,
And burns up His enemies round about.
4 His lightnings light the world;
The earth sees and trembles.
5 The mountains melt like wax at the
presence of the LORD,
At the presence of the Lord of the whole
earth.
6 The heavens declare His righteousness,
And all the peoples see His glory.

7 *Let all be put to shame who serve carved
images,
Who boast of idols.
Worship Him, all *you* gods.
8 Zion hears and is glad,
And the daughters of Judah rejoice
Because of Your judgments, O LORD.
9 For You, LORD, *are* most high above all the
earth;
You are exalted far above all gods.

10 *You who love the LORD, hate evil!
He preserves the souls of His saints;
He delivers them out of the hand of the
wicked.
11 Light is sown for the righteous,
And gladness for the upright in heart.
12 Rejoice in the LORD, you righteous,
And give thanks at the remembrance of His
holy name.*m*

PSALM 98

A Psalm.

O h,* sing to the LORD a new song!
For He has done marvelous things;
His right hand and His holy arm have
gained Him the victory.
2 The LORD has made known His salvation;
His righteousness He has revealed in the
sight of the nations.
3 He has remembered His mercy and His
faithfulness to the house of Israel;
All the ends of the earth have seen the
salvation of our God.

4 *Shout joyfully to the LORD, all the earth;
Break forth in song, rejoice, and sing
praises.
5 Sing to the LORD with the harp,
With the harp and the sound of a psalm,
6 With trumpets and the sound of a horn;
Shout joyfully before the LORD, the King.

PSALM 97

97:1 "The LORD reigns!" Not "the LORD *will*
reign," but "the LORD reigns!" Right now! In
another psalm the Lord declared, "I have
set My King on My holy hill of Zion" (Ps.
2:6). We are children of the King.

97:2–6 *Let the earth be glad.* You may not
see much righteousness and justice in the
world today, but that does not mean God
has been dethroned. For reasons we do not
fully understand, God permits evil men to
exploit the earth and its people, but one day
He will come in power and glory and set
things right.

97:7–9 *Let Israel be glad.* Israel has played
the key part in God's gracious plan of
salvation, witnessing the true God, passing
the Bible on to us, and giving us the Savior.
The nation has suffered much, but one day
her Messiah King will come in glory and fulfill
the promises made to the patriarchs.

97:10 *Let the righteous be glad.* This
group includes all of God's people, sinners
declared righteous through faith in Jesus
Christ (Rom. 3:21—4:8). They love the Lord
and rejoice in the Lord. If you are yielded
to the King, you have good reason to be
glad, so joyfully tell the world, "The Lord
reigns!"

PSALM 98

98:1 *Why should we praise the Lord?*
Because of His redemption (v. 1), the
revelation of His righteousness (v. 2), and
the remembrance of His mercy (v. 3). That
should keep you busy singing His praises
for a long time!

98:4 *How should we praise the Lord?*
With a joyful shout and song (v. 4), and with
musical instruments skillfully played to
please Him (vv. 5–6). Let voices and
instruments join in praising the Lord! Not
religious entertainment but the joyful
expression of praise to God.

A New Song—The psalmist often exhorts us to "sing a new song" (Pss. 33:3; 40:3; 96:1; 98:1;
144:9; 149:1). The word translated "new" means "fresh, new in quality." The song may be an old
one, but our growth in the Lord and our new experiences of His grace enable us to sing an old
song with fresh new meaning and blessing. This explains why the Lord allows us to go through
trials. He is tuning us up to praise Him in a new way!

98:7 *Who should praise the Lord?* Everybody in the world—and all the world of nature (vv. 7–9). The anticipation of His coming excites creation, and you should be a part of their excitement. Joy to the world—the Lord has come!

PSALM 99

99:1 "He is holy" (vv. 3, 5, 9), and He is high (v. 2); therefore, give God the honor due Him.

99:2, 3 *Fear Him.* The greatness of God makes the earth shake, and it should make the people tremble (Isa. 64:1–5). Even the demons tremble when they think of God (James 2:19). It is frightening to hear how carelessly many people speak *about* God or *to* God. It is even more frightening to see how carelessly people live, as though God will never require an accounting from them.

99:4 *Exalt Him.* The Lord is exalted in strength, righteousness, and holiness. One way to exalt Him is by your worship, but you must back that up by a consistent walk. Christ should be magnified in your body so that the lost around you may realize how great He is (1 Cor. 6:19–20; Phil. 1:19–26).

99:6 *Call on Him.* Three great men of prayer are mentioned to encourage you in your praying. They were not perfect, but they heard God's word, obeyed it, and God answered when they called. The Word of God and prayer must always go together (John 15:7; Acts 6:4), and so must prayer and obedience (Ps. 66:18).

PSALM 100

100:1 The hymn "Old Hundredth" ("All People That on Earth Do Dwell") is based on this psalm, as is the familiar "Doxology." Thanking the Lord is something we must do with our lives as well as with our lips. How shall we do it?

100:2 *By serving.* "Enter to worship— depart to serve" should be written clearly above the door to the church sanctuary. Too many people serve themselves and not the Lord, and too often we do not serve the Lord "with gladness." The Lord loves a cheerful servant.

100:3 *By submitting.* As creatures, we submit to the Creator who made us. As sheep, we submit to the Shepherd who died for us and now leads us in His paths. He not only made us, but *He is making us* as we yield to Him (Eph. 2:10). Submission means fulfillment.

100:4 *By sacrificing.* As priests, we are privileged to offer spiritual sacrifices to the Lord (1 Pet. 2:5). They include our songs
(continued)

7 *Let the sea roar, and all its fullness,
 The world and those who dwell in it;
8 Let the rivers clap *their* hands;
 Let the hills be joyful together before the
 Lord,
9 For He is coming to judge the earth.
 With righteousness He shall judge the
 world,
 And the peoples with equity.

PSALM 99

The* Lord reigns;
 Let the peoples tremble!
 He dwells *between* the cherubim;
 Let the earth be moved!
2 *The Lord *is* great in Zion,
 And He *is* high above all the peoples.
3 Let them praise Your great and awesome
 name—
 He *is* holy.

4 *The King's strength also loves justice;
 You have established equity;
 You have executed justice and
 righteousness in Jacob.
5 Exalt the Lord our God,
 And worship at His footstool—
 He *is* holy.

6 *Moses and Aaron were among His priests,
 And Samuel was among those who called
 upon His name;
 They called upon the Lord, and He
 answered them.
7 He spoke to them in the cloudy pillar;
 They kept His testimonies and the
 ordinance He gave them.

8 You answered them, O Lord our God;
 You were to them God-Who-Forgives,
 Though You took vengeance on their
 deeds.
9 Exalt the Lord our God,
 And worship at His holy hill;
 For the Lord our God *is* holy.

PSALM 100

A Psalm of Thanksgiving.

Make* a joyful shout to the Lord, all you lands!
 2*Serve the Lord with gladness;
 Come before His presence with singing.
3 *Know that the Lord, He *is* God;
 It is He *who* has made us, and not we
 ourselves;[n]
 We are His people and the sheep of His
 pasture.

4 *Enter into His gates with thanksgiving,
 And into His courts with praise.
 Be thankful to Him, *and* bless His name.
5 For the Lord *is* good;
 His mercy *is* everlasting,
 And His truth *endures* to all generations.

100:3 [n]Following Kethib, Septuagint, and Vulgate; Qere, many Hebrew manuscripts, and Targum read *we are His*.

PSALM 101

A Psalm of David.

I* will sing of mercy and justice;
    To You, O LORD, I will sing praises.

2   I will behave wisely in a perfect way.
    Oh, when will You come to me?
    I will walk within my house with a perfect
      heart.

3   I will set nothing wicked before my eyes;
    I hate the work of those who fall away;
    It shall not cling to me.
4   A perverse heart shall depart from me;
    I will not know wickedness.

5   Whoever secretly slanders his neighbor,
    Him I will destroy;
    The one who has a haughty look and a
      proud heart,
    Him I will not endure.

6   My eyes *shall be* on the faithful of the land,
    That they may dwell with me;
    He who walks in a perfect way,
    He shall serve me.
7   He who works deceit shall not dwell within
      my house;
    He who tells lies shall not continue in my
      presence.
8   *Early I will destroy all the wicked of the
      land,
    That I may cut off all the evildoers from the
      city of the LORD.

PSALM 102

A Prayer of the afflicted, when he is overwhelmed and pours
out his complaint before the LORD.

Hear my prayer, O LORD,
    And let my cry come to You.
2   *Do not hide Your face from me in the day
      of my trouble;
    Incline Your ear to me;
    In the day that I call, answer me speedily.

3   *For my days are consumed like smoke,
    And my bones are burned like a hearth.
4   My heart is stricken and withered like
      grass,
    So that I forget to eat my bread.
5   Because of the sound of my groaning
    My bones cling to my skin.
6   I am like a pelican of the wilderness;
    I am like an owl of the desert.
7   I lie awake,
    And am like a sparrow alone on the
      housetop.

8   My enemies reproach me all day long;
    Those who deride me swear an oath against
      me.
9   For I have eaten ashes like bread,
    And mingled my drink with weeping,
10   Because of Your indignation and Your
      wrath;
    For You have lifted me up and cast me
      away.
11   My days *are* like a shadow that lengthens,
    And I wither away like grass.

(continued from previous page)
of praise (Heb. 13:15), good works (Heb. 13:16), and material gifts (Phil. 4:15–18). Because of who He is (v. 5) and what He does for us, He is certainly worthy of our joyful thanks.

PSALM 101

101:1 Determination and dedication characterize this psalm as David says "I will" nine times and "shall" six times. He wanted a perfect (blameless) heart (v. 2), not a perverse (twisted) heart (v. 4) or a proud heart (v. 5). To be "perfect" before the Lord does not mean to be sinless; it means to be sincere and without pretense. John called it "walking in the light" (1 John 1:5–10).

101:8 David wanted justice in the land and the city (v. 8), just as we do today. But civic righteousness must begin in the heart and in the home (vv. 2, 7). Yes, we need honest people enforcing just laws, but we also need godly people living holy lives, starting at home.
    We must be careful what we look at (v. 3) and listen to (v. 5), and with whom we fellowship (vv. 6–7). In a world full of illusion, we must avoid lies and must walk in God's wisdom (vv. 7, 2). Unlike David, we do not have authority to execute judgment on the wicked. But if our hearts and homes are what God wants them to be, our influence will be felt in the city and the nation.

PSALM 102

102:1 God enjoys endless years, but we endure shortened days (vv. 23–24), troubled days (v. 2), days that disappear like smoke, grass, and a shadow (vv. 3, 4, 11). We sit alone like birds in a desert and dying patients in a hospital (vv. 5–9). How depressing!

---

⁹⁹*Strength of character may be acquired at work, but beauty of character is learned at home. There the affections are trained. There the gentle life reaches us, the true heaven life. In one word, the family circle is the supreme conductor of Christianity.***⁹⁹**

—Phillips Brooks

102:3 Do you ever have days like that? If you do, beware. Looking at yourself and your feelings will only make things worse. Do what the writer of this penitential psalm did: look by faith to the Lord. Things will be different when you look from yourself to God and say, "But You."

102:12 *"But You shall endure."* If you know Jesus Christ by faith, you possess eternal life (1 John 5:11–13). So, living in a world of death and decay need not be a threat to you because you will live forever with the Lord (1 Thess. 4:13–18).

102:25 *"But You are the same."* As you grow older, you may find yourself resisting change. Loved ones move away or die, your body weakens, the world changes, and it is easy to become bitter and afraid. But God does not change (Heb. 13:5–8), and He is your Friend and Guide to the very end (Ps. 73:24).

The temporary things will change, but the things eternal will last (2 Cor. 4:11–18).

12 *But You, O LORD, shall endure forever,
And the remembrance of Your name to all generations.
13 You will arise *and* have mercy on Zion;
For the time to favor her,
Yes, the set time, has come.
14 For Your servants take pleasure in her stones,
And show favor to her dust.
15 So the nations shall fear the name of the LORD,
And all the kings of the earth Your glory.
16 For the LORD shall build up Zion;
He shall appear in His glory.
17 He shall regard the prayer of the destitute,
And shall not despise their prayer.

18 This will be written for the generation to come,
That a people yet to be created may praise the LORD.
19 For He looked down from the height of His sanctuary;
From heaven the LORD viewed the earth,
20 To hear the groaning of the prisoner,
To release those appointed to death,
21 To declare the name of the LORD in Zion,
And His praise in Jerusalem,
22 When the peoples are gathered together,
And the kingdoms, to serve the LORD.

23 He weakened my strength in the way;
He shortened my days.
24 I said, "O my God,
Do not take me away in the midst of my days;
Your years *are* throughout all generations.
25 *Of old You laid the foundation of the earth,
And the heavens *are* the work of Your hands.
26 They will perish, but You will endure;
Yes, they will all grow old like a garment;
Like a cloak You will change them,
And they will be changed.
27 But You *are* the same,
And Your years will have no end.
28 The children of Your servants will continue,
And their descendants will be established before You."

"Abide with Me"

Swift to its close ebbs out life's little day;
Earth's joys grow dim, its glories pass away;
Change and decay in all around I see;
O Thou who changest not, abide with me.

I fear no foe, with Thee at hand to bless;
Ills have no weight, and tears no bitterness.
Where is death's sting? where, grave, thy victory?
I triumph still, if Thou abide with me.

—Henry Francis Lyte

PSALM 103

A Psalm of David.

Bless* the LORD, O my soul;
  And all that is within me, *bless* His holy
    name!
2 Bless the LORD, O my soul,
  And forget not all His benefits:
3 *Who forgives all your iniquities,
  Who heals all your diseases,
4 *Who redeems your life from destruction,
  Who crowns you with lovingkindness and
    tender mercies,
5 *Who satisfies your mouth with good *things,*
  So that your youth is renewed like the
    eagle's.

6 The LORD executes righteousness
  And justice for all who are oppressed.
7 He made known His ways to Moses,
  His acts to the children of Israel.
8 The LORD *is* merciful and gracious,
  Slow to anger, and abounding in mercy.
9 He will not always strive *with us,*
  Nor will He keep *His anger* forever.
10 He has not dealt with us according to our
    sins,
  Nor punished us according to our iniquities.

11 For as the heavens are high above the earth,
  So great is His mercy toward those who fear
    Him;
12 As far as the east is from the west,
  So far has He removed our transgressions
    from us.
13 As a father pities *his* children,
  So the LORD pities those who fear Him.
14 For He knows our frame;
  He remembers that we *are* dust.

15 *As for* man, his days *are* like grass;
  As a flower of the field, so he flourishes.
16 For the wind passes over it, and it is gone,
  And its place remembers it no more.º
17 But the mercy of the LORD *is* from
      everlasting to everlasting
  On those who fear Him,
  And His righteousness to children's
    children,
18 To such as keep His covenant,
  And to those who remember His
    commandments to do them.

19 The LORD has established His throne in
    heaven,
  And His kingdom rules over all.

20 Bless the LORD, you His angels,
  Who excel in strength, who do His word,
  Heeding the voice of His word.

103:16 ºCompare Job 7:10

PSALM 103

103:1 David makes no requests in this psalm. All he does is praise the Lord for three wonderful blessings, which he names in verses 3–5 and then explains in the rest of the psalm.

103:3 *Forgiveness.* Forgiveness is like healing when you are sick (1 Pet. 2:24), relief when you are burdened (vv. 11–12; Lev. 16:20–22; John 1:29), and reconciliation when you have hurt someone (vv. 13–14). All of this comes because Jesus died for your sins on the cross and you have trusted Him.

103:4 *Redemption.* God redeemed the nation from bondage and from difficulties they faced on their journey to Canaan. He frees us that He might be our Master and care for us forever. When He crowns us, He transforms slaves into kings (Rom. 5:17). What grace!

103:5 *Satisfaction.* Man is frail and temporary, but believers enjoy "eternal youth" and spiritual renewal. David compares it to the eagle that looks old but still soars upward with new strength (Isa. 40:31).
  You belong to the King who rules over everything (v. 19)! The angels praise Him (vv. 20–22), so why not join in their worship?

Renewal—Just as God renews the face of the earth and brings it new life and beauty (Ps. 104:30), so He can renew your life if you will let Him. It begins with a renewed mind (Rom. 12:1–2) as you permit the Spirit to teach you God's Word (Eph. 4:23; Col. 3:10). Wait before the Lord in worship, and He will renew strength (Isa. 40:31). When you walk by faith, you have a constant experience of renewal in spite of the changes of life (2 Cor. 4:16–18). There is always something new to enjoy when you "walk in newness of life" (Rom. 6:4).

21 Bless the LORD, all *you* His hosts,
    You ministers of His, who do His pleasure.
22 Bless the LORD, all His works,
    In all places of His dominion.

   *Bless the LORD, O my soul!

PSALM 104

Bless* the LORD, O my soul!

    O LORD my God, You are very great:
    You are clothed with honor and majesty,
2 Who cover *Yourself* with light as *with* a
    garment,
    Who stretch out the heavens like a curtain.

3 *He lays the beams of His upper chambers
    in the waters,
    Who makes the clouds His chariot,
    Who walks on the wings of the wind,
4 Who makes His angels spirits,
    His ministers a flame of fire.

5 *You who* laid the foundations of the
    earth,
    So *that* it should not be moved forever,
6 You covered it with the deep as *with* a
    garment;
    The waters stood above the mountains.
7 At Your rebuke they fled;
    At the voice of Your thunder they hastened
    away.
8 They went up over the mountains;
    They went down into the valleys,
    To the place which You founded for them.
9 You have set a boundary that they may not
    pass over,
    That they may not return to cover the
    earth.

10 *He sends the springs into the valleys;
    They flow among the hills.
11 They give drink to every beast of the field;
    The wild donkeys quench their thirst.
12 By them the birds of the heavens have their
    home;
    They sing among the branches.
13 He waters the hills from His upper
    chambers;
    The earth is satisfied with the fruit of Your
    works.

PSALM 104

104:1 Psalm 104 praises God for His fullness as Creator, Psalm 105 for His faithfulness as Redeemer, and Psalm 106 for His forgiveness as Savior of His people. How easy it is to take for granted the world that God created! We see the blemishes but not the blessings, and we forget what kind of world God gave us.

104:3 It is a place of *greatness,* not the greatness of man but the greatness of God. The psalmist compared creation to the building of a house: laying the foundations, putting up the beams, hanging the curtains, and taking care of the water system. Only a great and wise God could make this kind of world.

104:10 It is a place of *goodness.* He provides life, water, food and homes for man and beast and also the birds, and He sees to it they are cared for. Everything in creation is God's gift to us to enjoy (1 Tim. 6:17).

"This Is My Father's World"

This is my Father's world,
Oh, let me ne'er forget
That though the wrong seems oft so strong,
God is the ruler yet.
This is my Father's world;
Why should my heart be sad?
The Lord is king; let the heavens ring.
God reigns; let the earth be glad.
        —Maltbie D. Babcock

14 He causes the grass to grow for the cattle,
    And vegetation for the service of man,
    That he may bring forth food from the earth,
15 And wine *that* makes glad the heart of man,
    Oil to make *his* face shine,
    And bread *which* strengthens man's heart.
16 The trees of the LORD are full *of sap*,
    The cedars of Lebanon which He planted,
17 Where the birds make their nests;
    The stork has her home in the fir trees.
18 The high hills *are* for the wild goats;
    The cliffs are a refuge for the rock badgers.P

19 He appointed the moon for seasons;
    The sun knows its going down.
20 You make darkness, and it is night,
    In which all the beasts of the forest creep
        about.
21 The young lions roar after their prey,
    And seek their food from God.
22 *When* the sun rises, they gather together
    And lie down in their dens.
23 Man goes out to his work
    And to his labor until the evening.

24 O LORD, how manifold are Your works!
    In wisdom You have made them all.
    The earth is full of Your possessions—
25 This great and wide sea,
    In which *are* innumerable teeming things,
    Living things both small and great.
26 There the ships sail about;
    There is that Leviathan
    Which You have made to play there.

27 These all wait for You,
    That You may give *them* their food in due
        season.
28 *What* You give them they gather in;
    You open Your hand, they are filled with
        good.
29 You hide Your face, they are troubled;
    You take away their breath, they die and
        return to their dust.
30 You send forth Your Spirit, they are created;
    And You renew the face of the earth.

31 *May the glory of the LORD endure forever;
    May the LORD rejoice in His works.
32 He looks on the earth, and it trembles;
    He touches the hills, and they smoke.

33 I will sing to the LORD as long as I live;
    I will sing praise to my God while I have
        my being.
34 May my meditation be sweet to Him;
    I will be glad in the LORD.
35 May sinners be consumed from the earth,
    And the wicked be no more.

    Bless the LORD, O my soul!
    Praise the LORD!

PSALM 105

Oh,* give thanks to the LORD!
    Call upon His name;
    Make known His deeds among the peoples!

104:31 It is a place of *gladness*. God rejoices over creation (v. 31), and we should be "glad in the LORD" (v. 34). Creation is a window through which we see God, not a mirror in which we see ourselves; and the more we see Him, the happier we should be. Only this will make us good stewards of God's creation.

PSALM 105
105:1 The previous psalm extols the Creator, while this one exalts the Redeemer and His providential care for His people, Israel.

104:18 POr *rock hyrax* (compare Leviticus 11:5)

105:2 *His deeds.* When you read the history of Israel, you are encouraged by God's mighty and marvelous deeds wrought for His needy people (Rom. 15:4). You want to praise Him, rejoice in Him, seek Him, and tell others about Him.

105:7 *His covenant.* God bound Himself by an oath to only one nation, Israel. He gave His promise to Abraham (Gen. 12:1–3) and then reaffirmed it to his descendants. The covenant was their assurance that they would inherit the land. God's new covenant people have the assurance that their future inheritance is secure (Matt. 26:26–29; Heb. 8:6–13).

105:16 *His servants.* God sent Joseph to Egypt to preserve Jacob's family so they could become a nation. He sent Moses to Egypt to deliver His people. He sent Aaron to assist Moses and serve as high priest for a sinful people. God always has a man or woman ready to send when a job must be done. He waits to hear you say, "Here am I! Send me!" (Isa. 6:8).

2 *Sing to Him, sing psalms to Him;
  Talk of all His wondrous works!
3 Glory in His holy name;
  Let the hearts of those rejoice who seek the
    LORD!
4 Seek the LORD and His strength;
  Seek His face evermore!
5 Remember His marvelous works which He
    has done,
  His wonders, and the judgments of His
    mouth,
6 O seed of Abraham His servant,
  You children of Jacob, His chosen ones!

7 *He *is* the LORD our God;
  His judgments *are* in all the earth.
8 He remembers His covenant forever,
  The word *which* He commanded, for a
    thousand generations,
9 *The covenant* which He made with
    Abraham,
  And His oath to Isaac,
10 And confirmed it to Jacob for a statute,
  To Israel *as* an everlasting covenant,
11 Saying, "To you I will give the land of
    Canaan
  As the allotment of your inheritance,"
12 When they were few in number,
  Indeed very few, and strangers in it.

13 When they went from one nation to another,
  From *one* kingdom to another people,
14 He permitted no one to do them wrong;
  Yes, He rebuked kings for their sakes,
15 *Saying,* "Do not touch My anointed ones,
  And do My prophets no harm."

16 *Moreover He called for a famine in the land;
  He destroyed all the provision of bread.
17 He sent a man before them—
  Joseph—*who* was sold as a slave.
18 They hurt his feet with fetters,
  He was laid in irons.
19 Until the time that his word came to pass,
  The word of the LORD tested him.
20 The king sent and released him,
  The ruler of the people let him go free.
21 He made him lord of his house,
  And ruler of all his possessions,
22 To bind his princes at his pleasure,
  And teach his elders wisdom.

23 Israel also came into Egypt,
  And Jacob dwelt in the land of Ham.
24 He increased His people greatly,
  And made them stronger than their
    enemies.
25 He turned their heart to hate His people,
  To deal craftily with His servants.

26 He sent Moses His servant,
  And Aaron whom He had chosen.
27 They performed His signs among them,
  And wonders in the land of Ham.
28 He sent darkness, and made *it* dark;
  And they did not rebel against His word.
29 He turned their waters into blood,
  And killed their fish.
30 Their land abounded with frogs,
  Even in the chambers of their kings.
31 He spoke, and there came swarms of flies,
  And lice in all their territory.

32 He gave them hail for rain,
  And flaming fire in their land.
33 He struck their vines also, and their fig
    trees,
  And splintered the trees of their territory.
34 He spoke, and locusts came,
  Young locusts without number,
35 And ate up all the vegetation in their land,
  And devoured the fruit of their ground.
36 He also destroyed all the firstborn in their
    land,
  The first of all their strength.

37 He also brought them out with silver and
    gold,
  And *there was* none feeble among His
    tribes.
38 Egypt was glad when they departed,
  For the fear of them had fallen upon them.
39 He spread a cloud for a covering,
  And fire to give light in the night.
40 *The people* asked, and He brought quail,
  And satisfied them with the bread of
    heaven.
41 He opened the rock, and water gushed out;
  It ran in the dry places *like* a river.

42 For He remembered His holy promise,
  And Abraham His servant.
43 He brought out His people with joy,
  His chosen ones with gladness.
44 He gave them the lands of the Gentiles,
  And they inherited the labor of the nations,
45 That they might observe His statutes
  And keep His laws.

  Praise the LORD!

PSALM 106

Praise* the LORD!

  Oh, give thanks to the LORD, for *He is* good!
  For His mercy *endures* forever.

2 Who can utter the mighty acts of the LORD?
  Who can declare all His praise?
3 Blessed *are* those who keep justice,
  And he who does*q* righteousness at all
    times!

4 Remember me, O LORD, with the favor *You
    have toward* Your people.
  Oh, visit me with Your salvation,
5 That I may see the benefit of Your chosen
    ones,
  That I may rejoice in the gladness of Your
    nation,
  That I may glory with Your inheritance.

6 *We have sinned with our fathers,
  We have committed iniquity,
  We have done wickedly.
7 Our fathers in Egypt did not understand
    Your wonders;
  They did not remember the multitude of
    Your mercies,
  But rebelled by the sea—the Red Sea.

PSALM 106
106:1 In light of God's goodness to Israel,
you would have expected the nation to
submit to Him and serve Him gratefully.
Instead, they sinned and had to be
disciplined many times. Before you judge
them, however, consider whether you may
be guilty of some of the same sins they
committed.

106:6 God delivered Israel from Egypt, but
they soon forgot His mercy and ignored His
counsel (vv. 6–23). He gave them manna,
and they lusted for meat. They criticized their
leaders. They worshiped a golden idol and
would have been destroyed had Moses not
interceded for them.

106:3 *q*Septuagint, Syriac, Targum, and Vulgate read *those
who do.*

8 Nevertheless He saved them for His name's
sake,
That He might make His mighty power
known.
9 He rebuked the Red Sea also, and it dried
up;
So He led them through the depths,
As through the wilderness.
10 He saved them from the hand of him who
hated *them,*
And redeemed them from the hand of the
enemy.
11 The waters covered their enemies;
There was not one of them left.
12 Then they believed His words;
They sang His praise.

13 They soon forgot His works;
They did not wait for His counsel,
14 But lusted exceedingly in the
wilderness,
And tested God in the desert.
15 And He gave them their request,
But sent leanness into their soul.

16 When they envied Moses in the camp,
And Aaron the saint of the LORD,
17 The earth opened up and swallowed
Dathan,
And covered the faction of Abiram.
18 A fire was kindled in their company;
The flame burned up the wicked.

19 They made a calf in Horeb,
And worshiped the molded image.
20 Thus they changed their glory
Into the image of an ox that eats grass.
21 They forgot God their Savior,
Who had done great things in Egypt,
22 Wondrous works in the land of Ham,
Awesome things by the Red Sea.
23 Therefore He said that He would destroy
them,
Had not Moses His chosen one stood before
Him in the breach,
To turn away His wrath, lest He destroy
them.

106:24 They came to the border of the
Promised Land and refused to go in (vv. 24–
27). While wandering in the wilderness, they
compromised with the heathen nations (vv.
28–31). Their stubborn attitude even made
Moses sin (vv. 32–33). Once in the land,
they compromised with the wicked nations,
and God had to chasten them repeatedly
(vv. 34–43).

24 *Then they despised the pleasant land;
They did not believe His word,
25 But complained in their tents,
And did not heed the voice of the LORD.
26 Therefore He raised His hand *in an oath*
against them,
To overthrow them in the wilderness,
27 To overthrow their descendants among the
nations,
And to scatter them in the lands.

28 They joined themselves also to Baal of
Peor,
And ate sacrifices made to the dead.
29 Thus they provoked *Him* to anger with their
deeds,
And the plague broke out among them.
30 Then Phinehas stood up and intervened,
And the plague was stopped.
31 And that was accounted to him for
righteousness
To all generations forevermore.

32 They angered *Him* also at the waters of
strife,[r]
So that it went ill with Moses on account
of them;
33 Because they rebelled against His Spirit,
So that he spoke rashly with his lips.

34 *They did not destroy the peoples,
Concerning whom the LORD had
commanded them,
35 But they mingled with the Gentiles
And learned their works;
36 They served their idols,
Which became a snare to them.
37 They even sacrificed their sons
And their daughters to demons,
38 And shed innocent blood,
The blood of their sons and daughters,
Whom they sacrificed to the idols of
Canaan;
And the land was polluted with blood.
39 Thus they were defiled by their own works,
And played the harlot by their own deeds.

40 Therefore the wrath of the LORD was
kindled against His people,
So that He abhorred His own inheritance.
41 And He gave them into the hand of the
Gentiles,
And those who hated them ruled over them.
42 Their enemies also oppressed them,
And they were brought into subjection
under their hand.
43 Many times He delivered them;
But they rebelled in their counsel,
And were brought low for their iniquity.

44 Nevertheless He regarded their affliction,
When He heard their cry;
45 And for their sake He remembered His
covenant,
And relented according to the multitude of
His mercies.
46 He also made them to be pitied
By all those who carried them away captive.

47 Save us, O LORD our God,
And gather us from among the Gentiles,
To give thanks to Your holy name,
To triumph in Your praise.

48 Blessed *be* the LORD God of Israel
From everlasting to everlasting!
And let all the people say, "Amen!"

Praise the LORD!

Book Five: Psalms 107—150

PSALM 107

O h,* give thanks to the LORD, for *He is* good!
For His mercy *endures* forever.
2 Let the redeemed of the LORD say *so*,
Whom He has redeemed from the hand of
the enemy,
3 And gathered out of the lands,
From the east and from the west,
From the north and from the south.

106:34 Were it not for His covenant, God
would have destroyed them. But He forgave
them and allowed them to have many new
beginnings. Finally He had to disperse them
among the Gentiles (v. 47).
Paul gives you most of the story in
1 Corinthians 10:1–13. Take it to heart!

PSALM 107
107:1 How easy it is to take God's mercy
for granted! Ingratitude seems to be natural
to the sinful human heart (vv. 8, 15, 21, 31;
Rom. 1:21ff.). Here are four pictures of
God's mercy toward sinners and how they
responded.

106:32 [r]Or *Meribah*

107:4–9 *Travelers.* Being lost in the wilderness without food or drink would be a frightful experience. God not only saved them but led them to the safety of the city. Did they take time to thank Him?

107:10 *Prisoners.* They were in prison because they had rebelled against God's will, so they deserved to suffer. But when they cried out to God, He heard them and set them free. Did they take time to thank Him?

107:17 *Sufferers.* We move from the prison to the hospital where people were dying because of their foolish way of life. They had "made their own bed" and should lie in it, but God mercifully healed them. Did they take time to show their appreciation?

107:23 *Sailors.* Dangers on the water usually exceed dangers on the land, for where can you go for help in the midst of a violent storm? You can only look up, which is what they did, and the Lord rescued them. He calmed the storm, and He brought them to their desired destination (John 6:15–21).

4   *They wandered in the wilderness in a
     desolate way;
     They found no city to dwell in.
5   Hungry and thirsty,
     Their soul fainted in them.
6   Then they cried out to the LORD in their
     trouble,
     And He delivered them out of their
     distresses.
7   And He led them forth by the right way,
     That they might go to a city for a dwelling
     place.
8   Oh, that *men* would give thanks to the LORD
     for His goodness,
     And *for* His wonderful works to the children
     of men!
9   For He satisfies the longing soul,
     And fills the hungry soul with goodness.

10   *Those who sat in darkness and in the
     shadow of death,
     Bound in affliction and irons—
11   Because they rebelled against the words of
     God,
     And despised the counsel of the Most High,
12   Therefore He brought down their heart with
     labor;
     They fell down, and *there was* none to help.
13   Then they cried out to the LORD in their
     trouble,
     And He saved them out of their distresses.
14   He brought them out of darkness and the
     shadow of death,
     And broke their chains in pieces.
15   Oh, that *men* would give thanks to the LORD
     for His goodness,
     And *for* His wonderful works to the children
     of men!
16   For He has broken the gates of bronze,
     And cut the bars of iron in two.

17   *Fools, because of their transgression,
     And because of their iniquities, were
     afflicted.
18   Their soul abhorred all manner of food,
     And they drew near to the gates of death.
19   Then they cried out to the LORD in their
     trouble,
     And He saved them out of their distresses.
20   He sent His word and healed them,
     And delivered *them* from their destructions.
21   Oh, that *men* would give thanks to the LORD
     for His goodness,
     And *for* His wonderful works to the children
     of men!
22   Let them sacrifice the sacrifices of
     thanksgiving,
     And declare His works with rejoicing.

23   *Those who go down to the sea in ships,
     Who do business on great waters,
24   They see the works of the LORD,
     And His wonders in the deep.
25   For He commands and raises the stormy
     wind,
     Which lifts up the waves of the sea.
26   They mount up to the heavens,
     They go down again to the depths;
     Their soul melts because of trouble.
27   They reel to and fro, and stagger like a
     drunken man,
     And are at their wits' end.

28 Then they cry out to the LORD in their
        trouble,
    And He brings them out of their distresses.
29 He calms the storm,
        So that its waves are still.
30 Then they are glad because they are quiet;
        So He guides them to their desired haven.
31 Oh, that *men* would give thanks to the LORD
        for His goodness,
    And *for* His wonderful works to the children
        of men!
32 Let them exalt Him also in the assembly of
        the people,
    And praise Him in the company of the
        elders.

33 *He turns rivers into a wilderness,
        And the watersprings into dry ground;
34 A fruitful land into barrenness,
        For the wickedness of those who dwell in
        it.
35 He turns a wilderness into pools of water,
        And dry land into watersprings.
36 There He makes the hungry dwell,
        That they may establish a city for a dwelling
        place,
37 And sow fields and plant vineyards,
        That they may yield a fruitful harvest.
38 He also blesses them, and they multiply
        greatly;
    And He does not let their cattle decrease.

39 When they are diminished and brought low
        Through oppression, affliction and sorrow,
40 He pours contempt on princes,
        And causes them to wander in the
        wilderness *where there is* no way;
41 Yet He sets the poor on high, far from
        affliction,
    And makes *their* families like a flock.
42 The righteous see *it* and rejoice,
        And all iniquity stops its mouth.

43 Whoever *is* wise will observe these *things,*
        And they will understand the
        lovingkindness of the LORD.

PSALM 108

A Song. A Psalm of David.

O* God, my heart is steadfast;
        I will sing and give praise, even with my
        glory.
2 *Awake, lute and harp!
        I will awaken the dawn.
3 I will praise You, O LORD, among the
        peoples,
    And I will sing praises to You among the
        nations.
4 For Your mercy *is* great above the heavens,
        And Your truth *reaches* to the clouds.

5 Be exalted, O God, above the heavens,
        And Your glory above all the earth;
6 That Your beloved may be delivered,
        Save *with* Your right hand, and hear me.

7 *God has spoken in His holiness:
        "I will rejoice;
    I will divide Shechem
        And measure out the Valley of Succoth.
8 Gilead *is* Mine; Manasseh *is* Mine;

107:33 *Farmers.* Only God can send the
rain that turns the wilderness into a garden,
and only God can make the cattle multiply.
We eat and are full, but do we take time to
thank the Lord for giving us food (Deut.
6:10–13)? Be wise and understand the
loving-kindness of the Lord.

PSALM 108
108:1 This psalm is adapted from Psalm
57:7–11 (vv. 1–5) and Psalm 60:5–12 (vv.
6–13). It is the song of a warrior, and in it,
David makes three affirmations.

108:2–5 *"I will praise."* A steadfast heart
is a singing heart because confidence in
God gives you something to sing about.
David arose early in the morning to sing to
the Lord. Worship is good preparation for
warfare.

108:7 *"I will listen."* God heard the voice
of David, and then David listened to the
voice of God. It was a word of assurance
as the king went out to battle: "All nations
are mine, and I can do with them as I
please."

Ephraim also *is* the helmet for My head;
Judah *is* My lawgiver.
9 Moab *is* My washpot;
Over Edom I will cast My shoe;
Over Philistia I will triumph."

10 *Who will bring me *into* the strong city?
Who will lead me to Edom?
11 *Is it* not *You*, O God, *who* cast us off?
And *You*, O God, *who* did not go out with
our armies?
12 Give us help from trouble,
For the help of man is useless.
13 Through God we will do valiantly,
For *it is* He *who* shall tread down our
enemies.[s]

108:10 *"I will conquer."* God leads us into the battle, helps us capture the enemy's strongholds, and gives us the victory. Verse 13 is David's version of Philippians 4:13. It was true for him, and it is true for you today.

PSALM 109

To the Chief Musician. A Psalm of David.

Do* not keep silent,
O God of my praise!
2 For the mouth of the wicked and the mouth
of the deceitful
Have opened against me;
They have spoken against me with a lying
tongue.
3 They have also surrounded me with words
of hatred,
And fought against me without a cause.
4 In return for my love they are my accusers,
But I *give myself to* prayer.
5 *Thus they have rewarded me evil for good,
And hatred for my love.

6 Set a wicked man over him,
And let an accuser[t] stand at his right hand.
7 When he is judged, let him be found guilty,
And let his prayer become sin.
8 Let his days be few,
And let another take his office.
9 Let his children be fatherless,
And his wife a widow.
10 Let his children continually be vagabonds,
and beg;
Let them seek *their bread*[u] also from their
desolate places.
11 Let the creditor seize all that he has,
And let strangers plunder his labor.
12 Let there be none to extend mercy to him,
Nor let there be any to favor his fatherless
children.
13 Let his posterity be cut off,
And in the generation following let their
name be blotted out.

PSALM 109

109:1 When people have lied about you, spoken hatefully to you, and rewarded you evil for good, you would benefit from reading this psalm. When your heart is wounded within (v. 22) and there is no way to set the record straight, take it to the Lord and tell Him how you feel.

109:5 Verses 5–20 record another of King David's "imprecatory prayers." (See the comments on Ps. 58.) He asks God to judge the man who lied about him (vv. 6–8) and also to judge the man's children (vv. 9–13). He even asks that the man's ancestors' sins come up before God for judgment (vv. 14–16), and that the liar reap just what he has sown (vv. 18–20).

14 Let the iniquity of his fathers be
remembered before the LORD,
And let not the sin of his mother be blotted
out.
15 Let them be continually before the LORD,
That He may cut off the memory of them
from the earth;
16 Because he did not remember to show
mercy,
But persecuted the poor and needy man,

108:13 [s]Compare verses 6–13 with 60:5–12   109:6 [t]Hebrew *satan*   109:10 [u]Following Masoretic Text and Targum; Septuagint and Vulgate read *be cast out.*

That he might even slay the broken in heart.
17 As he loved cursing, so let it come to him;
As he did not delight in blessing, so let it
be far from him.
18 As he clothed himself with cursing as with
his garment,
So let it enter his body like water,
And like oil into his bones.
19 Let it be to him like the garment which
covers him,
And for a belt with which he girds himself
continually.
20 *Let* this *be* the LORD's reward to my
accusers,
And to those who speak evil against my
person.

21 *But You, O GOD the Lord,
Deal with me for Your name's sake;
Because Your mercy *is* good, deliver me.
22 For I *am* poor and needy,
And my heart is wounded within me.
23 I am gone like a shadow when it lengthens;
I am shaken off like a locust.
24 My knees are weak through fasting,
And my flesh is feeble from lack of fatness.
25 I also have become a reproach to them;
When they look at me, they shake their
heads.

26 Help me, O LORD my God!
Oh, save me according to Your mercy,
27 That they may know that this *is* Your
hand—
That You, LORD, have done it!
28 Let them curse, but You bless;
When they arise, let them be ashamed,
But let Your servant rejoice.
29 Let my accusers be clothed with shame,
And let them cover themselves with their
own disgrace as with a mantle.

30 I will greatly praise the LORD with my
mouth;
Yes, I will praise Him among the multitude.
31 For He shall stand at the right hand of the
poor,
To save *him* from those who condemn him.

PSALM 110

A Psalm of David.

The* LORD said to my Lord,
"Sit at My right hand,
Till I make Your enemies Your footstool."
2 *The LORD shall send the rod of Your
strength out of Zion.
Rule in the midst of Your enemies!
3 Your people *shall be* volunteers
In the day of Your power;
In the beauties of holiness, from the womb
of the morning,
You have the dew of Your youth.
4 *The LORD has sworn
And will not relent,
"You *are* a priest forever
According to the order of Melchizedek."

5 *The Lord *is* at Your right hand;
He shall execute kings in the day of His
wrath.

109:21 When you feel that way, give the Lord the opportunity to heal your wounded heart (Ps. 147:3). No matter how God deals with your enemies, be sure you praise Him. And remember, He is long-suffering with sinners—including you! The best way to get rid of an enemy is to leave him or her with the Lord.

PSALM 110

110:1 This psalm is quoted in the New Testament more than any other one. It was quoted by Jesus (Matt. 22:41–46) and Peter (Acts 2:32–36), and the writer of Hebrews quoted it (or alluded to it) many times.
   The Lord. Jesus focused on the real issue when He asked, "If Messiah is David's Son, how can Messiah be David's Lord?" There is only one answer: Messiah must come as a man *through the family of David.* Messiah is both eternal God and man, divine and human. He is seated in the place of glory and authority.

110:2 *The King.* This is a picture of victory over Messiah's enemies. The final victory has not yet been won, but He still rules in the midst of His enemies. Are you one of His volunteers in the battle against sin?

110:4 *The Priest.* Hebrews 7—10 expounds this verse, and the background for it is in Genesis 14. Melchizedek and Jesus Christ are the only king-priests God has accepted. As King, Jesus can deal with the circumstances around you; as Priest, He can help with the feelings and weaknesses within you.

110:5 *The Judge.* A day of wrath is coming when the Lord Jesus will deal with His enemies once and for all (Rev. 19:11—20:15). He will be victorious and His head lifted up in exaltation.
   If you know Him as God's Son and your High Priest, obey Him as your King, and seek to win others before He comes as Judge.

> **"***All men naturally desire to know, but what does knowledge avail without the fear of God?***"**
> —Thomas à Kempis

111:1 Psalm 111 is for people who study. It explains how to be a student who pleases the Lord and grows in understanding of truth. *Start with worship.* The lower you bow before the Lord, the more He will instruct you. Go right to the Source!

111:2 *See God in His works.* Whether it is science or history, you are examining God's works in this world. His works are great and glorious, revealing His power and wisdom. To see the creation but ignore the Creator is to move into idolatry and sin (Rom. 1:18ff.).

111:7 *See God in His Word.* The Word of God and the book of nature do not contradict each other, for the same Author wrote them. The theories of scholars come and go, but God's Word stands forever.

111:10 *Obey what God teaches you.* The search into truth is not simply an academic endeavor of the mind; it must involve your whole person. If you are willing to *do* God's truth, He will teach you (John 7:17). F. W. Robertson said, "Obedience is the organ of spiritual knowledge." All truth is God's truth. If you love truth, learn truth, and live truth, the truth will set you free (John 8:31–32).

112:1 "Blessed is the man who fears the LORD," says verse 1; and verses 7–8 declare, "He will not be afraid." When you fear the Lord, you need not fear anything else. The fear of God is the fear that conquers fear.

112:2 This applies to fears about your family (v. 2) and your finances (v. 3), and even fear of the dark (v. 4). If you dread making decisions, the Lord will help you (vv. 5–6). When you fear the Lord, you need not fear bad news (vv. 7–8) because you know He is in control of all things (Rom. 8:28).

6   He shall judge among the nations,
     He shall fill *the places* with dead bodies,
     He shall execute the heads of many
       countries.
7   He shall drink of the brook by the wayside;
     Therefore He shall lift up the head.

PSALM 111

Praise* the LORD!

    I will praise the LORD with *my* whole
      heart,
    In the assembly of the upright and *in* the
      congregation.

2   *The works of the LORD *are* great,
     Studied by all who have pleasure in
      them.
3   His work *is* honorable and glorious,
     And His righteousness endures forever.
4   He has made His wonderful works to be
      remembered;
     The LORD *is* gracious and full of compassion.
5   He has given food to those who fear
      Him;
     He will ever be mindful of His covenant.
6   He has declared to His people the power of
      His works,
     In giving them the heritage of the nations.

7   *The works of His hands *are* verity and
      justice;
     All His precepts *are* sure.
8   They stand fast forever and ever,
     And are done in truth and uprightness.
9   He has sent redemption to His people;
     He has commanded His covenant forever:
     Holy and awesome *is* His name.

10 *The fear of the LORD *is* the beginning of
      wisdom;
     A good understanding have all those who
      do *His commandments.*
     His praise endures forever.

PSALM 112

Praise* the LORD!

    Blessed *is* the man *who* fears the LORD,
    Who delights greatly in His
      commandments.

2   *His descendants will be mighty on earth;
     The generation of the upright will be
      blessed.
3   Wealth and riches *will be* in his house,
     And his righteousness endures forever.
4   Unto the upright there arises light in the
      darkness;
     He is gracious, and full of compassion, and
      righteous.
5   A good man deals graciously and lends;
     He will guide his affairs with discretion.
6   Surely he will never be shaken;
     The righteous will be in everlasting
      remembrance.
7   He will not be afraid of evil tidings;

His heart is steadfast, trusting in the LORD.
8 His heart *is* established;
He will not be afraid,
Until he sees *his desire* upon his enemies.

9 *He has dispersed abroad,
He has given to the poor;
His righteousness endures forever;
His horn will be exalted with honor.
10 The wicked will see *it* and be grieved;
He will gnash his teeth and melt away;
The desire of the wicked shall perish.

PSALM 113

Praise* the LORD!

Praise, O servants of the LORD,
Praise the name of the LORD!
2 *Blessed be the name of the LORD
From this time forth and forevermore!
3 *From the rising of the sun to its going
down
The LORD's name *is* to be praised.

4 *The LORD *is* high above all nations,
His glory above the heavens.
5 Who *is* like the LORD our God,
Who dwells on high,
6 Who humbles Himself to behold
The things that are in the heavens and in
the earth?

7 He raises the poor out of the dust,
And lifts the needy out of the ash heap,
8 That He may seat *him* with princes—
With the princes of His people.
9 He grants the barren woman a home,
Like a joyful mother of children.

Praise the LORD!

PSALM 114

When* Israel went out of Egypt,
The house of Jacob from a people of strange
language,
2 Judah became His sanctuary,
And Israel His dominion.

3 *The sea saw *it* and fled;
Jordan turned back.
4 The mountains skipped like rams,
The little hills like lambs.
5 What ails you, O sea, that you fled?
O Jordan, *that* you turned back?
6 O mountains, *that* you skipped like
rams?
O little hills, like lambs?

7 *Tremble, O earth, at the presence of the
Lord,
At the presence of the God of Jacob,
8 Who turned the rock *into* a pool of
water,
The flint into a fountain of waters.

112:9 You need not be afraid to give
because God will use your gifts and reward
you (v. 9). And do not be alarmed at your
enemies; God will take care of them as well
(v. 10).
    Isaiah proclaimed, "The LORD of hosts. . . .
Let Him be your fear, and let Him be your
dread" (Isa. 8:13).

PSALM 113
113:1 A concise manual of worship is
presented here.
    Who should worship. "Servants of the
LORD" includes all of God's people, for those
who have trusted Him surely would want to
live for Him.

113:2 **When we worship.** Start right now
and keep on going! It is always time to praise
the Lord. Make every breath a hymn of
worship.

113:3 **Where we worship.** His name should
be praised from east to west, all day long,
no matter where we are. If you find yourself
in a place where you cannot praise the Lord,
maybe you do not belong there.

113:4 **Why we worship.** Because of who
God is (vv. 4–6) and what God does (vv.
7–9). The better you know God, the more
you will worship Him. The more you
experience His grace in daily life, the more
praise you will bring to Him.
    If you have a problem praising the Lord
from sunup to sundown, what will you do
for all eternity?

PSALM 114
114:1 This beautiful poem celebrates the
exodus of Israel from Egypt. The sea, the
river, the mountains, and the hills all made
way for the people of God as they marched
in triumph. Even the rocks became Israel's
servants and gave them water to drink.

114:3 God brings us out (v. 1), takes us
through (v. 3), and leads us over (v. 4).
When you are following Him, no obstacle
can keep you from the goal He has set for
you, except your sin and unbelief.

114:7 When you are in the will of God, all
of creation works for you to accomplish
God's purposes. You are God's sanctuary
(1 Cor. 6:19–20); let Him have dominion in
your life (v. 2).

Praise the Lord!—Mary's joyful song of praise (Luke 1:46–55) echoes Psalm 113:7–9. God's
grace makes kings out of beggars and joyful mothers out of the barren. Praise the Lord!

PSALM 115

PSALM 115

115:1 The message of this psalm raises some important questions for you to answer.

115:2 *"Where is your God?"* Gentiles visiting Jerusalem would notice the absence of idols. Back home, they could point to their gods and introduce you to the craftsman who made them. Is your God in heaven, ruling over all? Are you trusting something less than God?

115:4, 9 *"What is your God like?"* Be careful! You become like the god you worship (v. 8). The living God can see you, hear your prayers, walk with you and help you. He can speak to you from His Word.

115:18 *"Do you praise your God?"* He has blessed you; have you blessed Him? He has given you promises; do you trust Him? He is the *living* God; does your life glorify Him?

PSALM 116

116:1 *From danger to deliverance.* The psalmist almost died (v. 3), possibly because people lied to him (v. 11). But when he cried out to the Lord, the Lord saved him (v. 8). The death of a believer is precious to the Lord; He will not permit it to be merely an accident (v. 15). This does not mean that God *enjoys* the death of one of His own. Rather, it means that He values His own so much that He makes death an appointment. It is a part of a loving plan (Pss. 31:15; 139:16).

PSALM 115

Not* unto us, O Lord, not unto us,
　But to Your name give glory,
　Because of Your mercy,
　Because of Your truth.
2　*Why should the Gentiles say,
　"So where *is* their God?"

3　But our God *is* in heaven;
　He does whatever He pleases.
4　*Their idols *are* silver and gold,
　The work of men's hands.
5　They have mouths, but they do not speak;
　Eyes they have, but they do not see;
6　They have ears, but they do not hear;
　Noses they have, but they do not smell;
7　They have hands, but they do not handle;
　Feet they have, but they do not walk;
　Nor do they mutter through their throat.
8　Those who make them are like them;
　So is everyone who trusts in them.

9　O Israel, trust in the Lord;
　He *is* their help and their shield.
10　O house of Aaron, trust in the Lord;
　He *is* their help and their shield.
11　You who fear the Lord, trust in the Lord;
　He *is* their help and their shield.

12　The Lord has been mindful of *us;*
　He will bless *us;*
　He will bless the house of Israel;
　He will bless the house of Aaron.
13　He will bless those who fear the Lord,
　Both small and great.

14　May the Lord give you increase more and
　　more,
　You and your children.
15　*May* you *be* blessed by the Lord,
　Who made heaven and earth.

16　The heaven, *even* the heavens, *are* the
　　Lord's;
　But the earth He has given to the children
　　of men.
17　The dead do not praise the Lord,
　Nor any who go down into silence.
18　*But we will bless the Lord
　From this time forth and forevermore.

Praise the Lord!

PSALM 116

I* love the Lord, because He has heard
　My voice *and* my supplications.
2　Because He has inclined His ear to me,
　Therefore I will call *upon Him* as long as I
　　live.

The Living God—The Bible uses human illustrations to explain divine attributes. God is spirit and does not have a body, but He can see you, hear you, and walk with you. After all, *we* can do those things, and we are made in the image of God. If we fail to trust the Lord and worship Him, we might just as well worship a dead idol! Do you have living faith in the living God?

The Good Hand of Our God—When God wanted to create a world, He merely had to use His fingers (Ps. 8:3). To save lost sinners, He had to bare His arm (Isa. 53:1). When He wants to accomplish a task, He uses His mighty hand (Ezra 7:6, 9, 28; Neh. 2:8).

3   The pains of death surrounded me,
     And the pangs of Sheol laid hold of me;
     I found trouble and sorrow.
4   Then I called upon the name of the LORD:
     "O LORD, I implore You, deliver my soul!"

5   Gracious *is* the LORD, and righteous;
     Yes, our God *is* merciful.
6   *The LORD preserves the simple;
     I was brought low, and He saved me.
7   Return to your rest, O my soul,
     For the LORD has dealt bountifully with you.

8   For You have delivered my soul from death,
     My eyes from tears,
     And my feet from falling.
9   I will walk before the LORD
     In the land of the living.
10 I believed, therefore I spoke,
     "I am greatly afflicted."
11 I said in my haste,
     "All men *are* liars."

12 What shall I render to the LORD
     For all His benefits toward me?
13 I will take up the cup of salvation,
     And call upon the name of the LORD.
14 I will pay my vows to the LORD
     Now in the presence of all His people.

15 Precious in the sight of the LORD
     Is the death of His saints.

16 *O LORD, truly I *am* Your servant;
     I *am* Your servant, the son of Your
       maidservant;
     You have loosed my bonds.
17 I will offer to You the sacrifice of
     thanksgiving,
     And will call upon the name of the LORD.
18 I will pay my vows to the LORD
     Now in the presence of all His people,
19 In the courts of the LORD's house,
     In the midst of you, O Jerusalem.

     Praise the LORD!

PSALM 117

Praise* the LORD, all you Gentiles!
    Laud Him, all you peoples!
2   *For His merciful kindness is great toward
     us,
     And the truth of the LORD *endures* forever.

     Praise the LORD!

PSALM 118

Oh,* give thanks to the LORD, for *He is* good!
    For His mercy *endures* forever.

2   Let Israel now say,
     "His mercy *endures* forever."

116:6, 7 *From agitation to rest.* He was surrounded by the pains of death and was worried about his future, but the Lord gave him rest (v. 7).

116:16, 17 *From prayer to praise.* Praise is the logical response when God has answered prayer and seen you through your difficulties. Note these assertions: "I will walk" (v. 9); "I will offer . . . the sacrifice of thanksgiving" (v. 17); "I will pay my vows" (v. 18); and "I will call upon Him as long as I live" (v. 2).

PSALM 117

117:1 This short psalm is about a big subject: helping all the nations to praise the Lord. God called Israel to be a blessing to all the nations of the world (Gen. 12:1–3), just as He has called His church to take the gospel to the whole world (Matt. 28:18–20).

117:2 The nations are worshiping false gods, so what do we tell them about the true God? That His mercy is great and His truth is enduring. What He does is merciful and what He says is dependable.

   God blesses you so that you might be a blessing to others, not only the people you see every day but people you will never see until you get to heaven. Are you helping the peoples of the world learn about Jesus?

❝*The Spirit of Christ is the spirit of missions, and the nearer we get to Him the more intensely missionary we must become.***❞**

—Henry Martyn

PSALM 118

118:1 The Jewish people sing Psalms 113 to 118 at Passover, so this is one of the songs that Jesus sang before He went to the Garden to pray (Matt. 26:30). If you knew you were going to be executed unjustly, would you be able to sing praises to the Lord?

A Song of Faith—"The LORD is my strength and song, and He has become my salvation" (Ps. 118:14)—Israel sang those words when they were delivered from the Egyptian army at the Red Sea (Exod. 15:2). They will sing those words again when God gathers them from the nations and restores them to their land (Isa. 11:10—12:2). It is a song you may sing today by faith.

3   Let the house of Aaron now say,
    "His mercy *endures* forever."
4   Let those who fear the LORD now say,
    "His mercy *endures* forever."

5   I called on the LORD in distress;
    The LORD answered me *and set me* in a
       broad place.
6   The LORD *is* on my side;
    I will not fear.
    What can man do to me?
7   The LORD is for me among those who help
       me;
    Therefore I shall see *my desire* on those who
       hate me.
8   *It is* better to trust in the LORD
    Than to put confidence in man.
9   *It is* better to trust in the LORD
    Than to put confidence in princes.

10 All nations surrounded me,
    But in the name of the LORD I will destroy
       them.
11 They surrounded me,
    Yes, they surrounded me;
    But in the name of the LORD I will destroy
       them.
12 They surrounded me like bees;
    They were quenched like a fire of thorns;
    For in the name of the LORD I will destroy
       them.
13 You pushed me violently, that I might fall,
    But the LORD helped me.
14 The LORD *is* my strength and song,
    And He has become my salvation.[v]

15 The voice of rejoicing and salvation
    Is in the tents of the righteous;
    The right hand of the LORD does valiantly.
16 The right hand of the LORD is exalted;
    The right hand of the LORD does valiantly.
17 I shall not die, but live,
    And declare the works of the LORD.
18 The LORD has chastened me severely,
    But He has not given me over to death.

19 Open to me the gates of righteousness;
    I will go through them,
    And I will praise the LORD.
20 This is the gate of the LORD,
    Through which the righteous shall enter.

21 I will praise You,
    For You have answered me,
    And have become my salvation.

22 The stone *which* the builders rejected
    Has become the chief cornerstone.
23 This was the LORD's doing;
    It *is* marvelous in our eyes.
24 This *is* the day the LORD has made;
    We will rejoice and be glad in it.

25 *Save now, I pray, O LORD;
    O LORD, I pray, send now prosperity.
26 Blessed *is* he who comes in the name of the
       LORD!
    We have blessed you from the house of the
       LORD.

118:25 This is also a messianic psalm. The
crowds shouted verses 25–26 as Jesus rode
into Jerusalem on Palm Sunday (Matt. 21:9),
and Jesus quoted verses 22–23 in His
debate with the religious leaders (Matt.
21:33–46).

118:14 ᵛCompare Exodus 15:2

27 God *is* the LORD,
    And He has given us light;
    Bind the sacrifice with cords to the horns
        of the altar.
28 *You *are* my God, and I will praise You;
    You are my God, I will exalt You.

29 Oh, give thanks to the LORD, for *He is* good!
    For His mercy *endures* forever.

PSALM 119

א ALEPH

B lessed* *are* the undefiled in the way,
        Who walk in the law of the LORD!
2   Blessed *are* those who keep His
        testimonies,
    Who seek Him with the whole heart!
3   They also do no iniquity;
    They walk in His ways.
4   You have commanded *us*
    To keep Your precepts diligently.
5   Oh, that my ways were directed
    To keep Your statutes!
6   Then I would not be ashamed,
    When I look into all Your commandments.
7   I will praise You with uprightness of heart,
    When I learn Your righteous judgments.
8   I will keep Your statutes;
    Oh, do not forsake me utterly!

ב BETH

9   *How can a young man cleanse his way?
    By taking heed according to Your word.
10 With my whole heart I have sought You;
    Oh, let me not wander from Your
        commandments!
11 Your word I have hidden in my heart,
    That I might not sin against You.
12 Blessed *are* You, O LORD!
    Teach me Your statutes.
13 With my lips I have declared
    All the judgments of Your mouth.
14 I have rejoiced in the way of Your
        testimonies,
    As *much as* in all riches.
15 I will meditate on Your precepts,
    And contemplate Your ways.
16 I will delight myself in Your statutes;
    I will not forget Your word.

ג GIMEL

17 *Deal bountifully with Your servant,
    That I may live and keep Your word.
18 Open my eyes, that I may see
    Wondrous things from Your law.
19 I *am* a stranger in the earth;
    Do not hide Your commandments from
        me.
20 My soul breaks with longing
    For Your judgments at all times.
21 You rebuke the proud—the cursed,
    Who stray from Your commandments.
22 Remove from me reproach and contempt,
    For I have kept Your testimonies.
23 Princes also sit *and* speak against me,
    But Your servant meditates on Your
        statutes.
24 Your testimonies also *are* my delight
    And my counselors.

118:28 But it is also a song of praise, thanking God for deliverance from a difficult situation (vv. 10–14). The name of the Lord (vv. 10–12) and the hand of the Lord (vv. 15–16) can give you the victory you need. When you are hemmed in by the enemy (vv. 10–12), cry out to God and He will put you into "a broad place" (v. 5). He will open the gates for you and give you new freedom (vv. 19–20).

Claim verse 24 for every day that you live.

PSALM 119

119:1ff The theme of this unique psalm is the Word of God. Every verse except five (84, 90, 121, 122, 132) refers to God's Word, what it is and what it can do in your life if you let it. The arrangement is also unique. There are twenty-two sections of eight lines each, and the lines in each individual section begin with the same letter of the Hebrew alphabet. The first eight lines begin with *Aleph,* the next eight with *Beth,* and so on through all twenty-two letters. This may have been a device to help people memorize the psalm.

The writer had a great love for the Word of God and was persecuted because he obeyed God and opposed sin. Most of the verses are either prayers for God's help or affirmations of the writer's faith in God's truth despite his difficulties. Meditating on this psalm ought to make you love and treasure the Word of God more and obey it more willingly.

Our approach will be to emphasize in each section one special ministry of the Word to your life.

119:1–8 Knowing and obeying God's Word will bring blessings to your life, some of which are given in the following sections. But if God is to bless you, you must sincerely seek the Lord and not just study the Bible. It is not facts in the head but truth in the heart that makes you grow in the Lord. Review Psalm 1.

119:9–16 Here is the first blessing: God's Word can keep you clean. You must heed God's Word (v. 9) and hide God's Word in your heart (v. 11). Campbell Morgan said of the Bible: "The best book, in the best place, for the best purpose." You must also rejoice in God's Word, delight in it and meditate on it. Meditation is to your inner person what digestion is to your body.

119:17–24 God's Word will guide you on the pilgrim path of life. You are a stranger on the earth (v. 19; 1 Pet. 2:11), and you need a "road map" to help you know the way. That road map is the Bible. Ask God to open your eyes to the Word (v. 18) and keep your eyes on the way (v. 21; Prov. 3:1–6; 4:25–27). Let your Bible be your trusted counselor (v. 24).

❝*Everywhere among Conservatives we find persons who are Bible-taught but not Spirit-taught. They conceive truth to be something which they can grasp with the mind. If a man holds to the fundamentals of the Christian faith he is thought to possess divine truth. But it does not follow. There is no truth apart from the Spirit.*❞

—A. W. Tozer

119:25–32 The Word of God brings you the blessing of life (v. 25) because it *has* life (Heb. 4:12), *imparts* life (1 Pet. 1:23–25), and *nourishes* life (1 Pet. 2:1–3). God's Word can revive and strengthen you (v. 28), even when you are in the dust. Nine times in this psalm the writer prayed for new life from the Lord (vv. 25, 37, 40, 88, 107, 149, 154, 156, 159). No need to stay in the dust when there is life for you in the Word of God!

119:33–40 If you want real values, get them from the Word of God (v. 37). How tragic that so many people waste time, energy, and money on things that amount to little or nothing (Isa. 55:2). The Hebrew word translated "worthless things" means "that which is nothing (vanity) because it is false." The word was used of idols. What your heart covets (v. 36), your eyes will see, and then you will make wrong decisions. This is what happened to Lot (Gen. 13).

ד DALETH

25 *My soul clings to the dust;
   Revive me according to Your word.
26 I have declared my ways, and You answered me;
   Teach me Your statutes.
27 Make me understand the way of Your precepts;
   So shall I meditate on Your wonderful works.
28 My soul melts from heaviness;
   Strengthen me according to Your word.
29 Remove from me the way of lying,
   And grant me Your law graciously.
30 I have chosen the way of truth;
   Your judgments I have laid *before me.*
31 I cling to Your testimonies;
   O LORD, do not put me to shame!
32 I will run the course of Your commandments,
   For You shall enlarge my heart.

ה HE

33 *Teach me, O LORD, the way of Your statutes,
   And I shall keep it *to* the end.
34 Give me understanding, and I shall keep Your law;
   Indeed, I shall observe it with *my* whole heart.
35 Make me walk in the path of Your commandments,
   For I delight in it.
36 Incline my heart to Your testimonies,
   And not to covetousness.
37 Turn away my eyes from looking at worthless things,
   And revive me in Your way.ʷ
38 Establish Your word to Your servant,
   Who *is devoted* to fearing You.
39 Turn away my reproach which I dread,
   For Your judgments *are* good.
40 Behold, I long for Your precepts;
   Revive me in Your righteousness.

119:37 ʷFollowing Masoretic Text, Septuagint, and Vulgate; Targum reads *Your words.*

   The Word of God—Psalm 119 contains ten different names for the Word of God: *word, law, saying, statutes, way, commandments, path, testimonies, precepts,* and *judgments.* Each name indicates what the Word is and how we should respond to it. The writer pictured the Word of God as water (v. 9), treasure (vv. 14, 72, 127, 162), a companion and counselor (v. 24), a song (v. 54), honey (v. 103), light (vv. 105, 130), and a heritage (v. 111). Meditate on these pictures and see what they mean to your personal life of faith.
   Heavenly Meditaton—When you truly delight in the Word, you will have a desire to meditate on it and make it a part of your life. In Psalm 119, the writer connects "delight" and "meditation" (vv. 15–16, 23–24, 47–48, 77–78). Cultivate an appetite for the Word of God.
   Proper Values—The psalmist had the right values. He would rather have God's Word than food (v. 103), sleep (vv. 55, 62, 147–48), or money (vv. 14, 72, 127, 162).
   Honor His Word—You have been thinking about what the Word of God will do for you if you allow it to work in your life. Now it is time to discover what you must do with God's Word. You must do more than simply read it, although that is necessary. You should also love it (v. 97), treasure it (v. 72), learn it (vv. 26–27), memorize it (v. 11), meditate on it (v. 15), believe it (v. 42), and practice it (vv. 1–4). The way you treat your Bible is the way you treat your Lord, for it is His Word to your heart.

ו WAW

41 *Let Your mercies come also to me,
   O LORD—
   Your salvation according to Your word.
42 So shall I have an answer for him who
   reproaches me,
   For I trust in Your word.
43 And take not the word of truth utterly out
   of my mouth,
   For I have hoped in Your ordinances.
44 So shall I keep Your law continually,
   Forever and ever.
45 And I will walk at liberty,
   For I seek Your precepts.
46 I will speak of Your testimonies also before
   kings,
   And will not be ashamed.
47 And I will delight myself in Your
   commandments,
   Which I love.
48 My hands also I will lift up to Your
   commandments,
   Which I love,
   And I will meditate on Your statutes.

ז ZAYIN

49 *Remember the word to Your servant,
   Upon which You have caused me to hope.
50 This *is* my comfort in my affliction,
   For Your word has given me life.
51 The proud have me in great derision,
   Yet I do not turn aside from Your law.
52 I remembered Your judgments of old,
   O LORD,
   And have comforted myself.
53 Indignation has taken hold of me
   Because of the wicked, who forsake Your
   law.
54 Your statutes have been my songs
   In the house of my pilgrimage.
55 I remember Your name in the night,
   O LORD,
   And I keep Your law.
56 This has become mine,
   Because I kept Your precepts.

ח HETH

57 *You are* my portion, O LORD;
   I have said that I would keep Your words.
58 I entreated Your favor with *my* whole
   heart;
   Be merciful to me according to Your word.
59 I thought about my ways,
   And turned my feet to Your testimonies.
60 I made haste, and did not delay
   To keep Your commandments.
61 The cords of the wicked have bound me,
   But I have not forgotten Your law.
62 At midnight I will rise to give thanks to
   You,
   Because of Your righteous judgments.
63 I *am* a companion of all who fear You,
   And of those who keep Your precepts.
64 The earth, O LORD, is full of Your mercy;
   Teach me Your statutes.

ט TETH

65 *You have dealt well with Your servant,
   O LORD, according to Your word.
66 Teach me good judgment and knowledge,
   For I believe Your commandments.

119:41–48 *Freedom* is another blessing God will give you if you love and obey His Word (v. 45). His Word is truth (v. 43), and the truth sets you free (John 8:32). Disobedience may seem like freedom, but it is really bondage (2 Pet. 2:19). When you obey God's Word, you enjoy true freedom because His Word is "the law of liberty" (James 2:12). Law and liberty are not enemies; they are coworkers in your life in building character and bringing joy.

119:49–56 The Word of God will bring *comfort* to your life if you will let it. The writer suffered affliction and persecution because of his faith, but the Word gave him comfort and hope. When the days are difficult and the nights are long, remember God's promises and God's name, and He will comfort you. (See vv. 76, 82, 92.)

119:57–64 If you are true to God's Word, you will have friends who are worth having (v. 63). Solomon taught this same lesson in Proverbs 2 (see also Prov. 13:20). If you walk with the wicked, they will bind you (v. 61), but if you walk with God's people, they will help you to enjoy life and liberty. People who love the Word will be glad to see you (v. 74) and will turn to you and help you (v. 79).

119:65–72 The Word of God can encourage you in times of affliction (vv. 67, 71; see also vv. 50, 92). What life does to you depends upon what life finds in you. If the Word is in your mind and heart, affliction can bring out the best in you. If not, it may bring out the worst in you. The school of suffering never graduates any students, so ask God to teach you the lessons He wants you to learn.

67　Before I was afflicted I went astray,
　　But now I keep Your word.
68　You *are* good, and do good;
　　Teach me Your statutes.
69　The proud have forged a lie against me,
　　But I will keep Your precepts with *my*
　　　whole heart.
70　Their heart is as fat as grease,
　　But I delight in Your law.
71　*It is* good for me that I have been afflicted,
　　That I may learn Your statutes.
72　The law of Your mouth *is* better to me
　　Than thousands of *coins of* gold and silver.

׳ YOD

73　*Your hands have made me and fashioned
　　　me;
　　Give me understanding, that I may learn
　　　Your commandments.
74　Those who fear You will be glad when they
　　　see me,
　　Because I have hoped in Your word.
75　I know, O LORD, that Your judgments *are*
　　　right,
　　And *that* in faithfulness You have afflicted
　　　me.
76　Let, I pray, Your merciful kindness be for
　　　my comfort,
　　According to Your word to Your servant.
77　Let Your tender mercies come to me, that
　　　I may live;
　　For Your law *is* my delight.
78　Let the proud be ashamed,
　　For they treated me wrongfully with
　　　falsehood;
　　But I will meditate on Your precepts.
79　Let those who fear You turn to me,
　　Those who know Your testimonies.
80　Let my heart be blameless regarding Your
　　　statutes,
　　That I may not be ashamed.

כ KAPH

81　*My soul faints for Your salvation,
　　But I hope in Your word.
82　My eyes fail *from searching* Your word,
　　Saying, "When will You comfort me?"
83　For I have become like a wineskin in
　　　smoke,
　　Yet I do not forget Your statutes.
84　How many *are* the days of Your servant?
　　When will You execute judgment on those
　　　who persecute me?
85　The proud have dug pits for me,
　　Which *is* not according to Your law.
86　All Your commandments *are* faithful;
　　They persecute me wrongfully;
　　Help me!
87　They almost made an end of me on
　　　earth,
　　But I did not forsake Your precepts.
88　Revive me according to Your
　　　lovingkindness,
　　So that I may keep the testimony of Your
　　　mouth.

ל LAMED

89　*Forever, O LORD,
　　Your word is settled in heaven.
90　Your faithfulness *endures* to all
　　　generations;
　　You established the earth, and it abides.

119:73–80 God made you and knows best how you should manage your life. The Bible is His how-to-do-it manual for making life work successfully (v. 73). It tells you how to use your body and mind, how to handle your time and money, and how to make right decisions. Obeying it can keep you from getting into trouble and hurting yourself and others. Do not wait until "all else fails" before you read the instructions! It may be too late!

119:81–88 The Word of God will help you get victory over your enemies (vv. 84–87). When your eyes are failing and your soul is fainting, the Word will give you strength and comfort. When it looks like the end has come, God's Word helps you make a new beginning. Your worst enemy is on the inside, so let the Word work in your heart.

119:89–96 If you trust God's Word, you will have a solid foundation in a world that offers you no stability. The Word of God is settled; nothing can change it or destroy it (v. 152; Matt. 24:35). God is faithful and His Word can be trusted. The same Word that created the world (v. 90) and runs the world (v. 91) will also govern your life and make it secure.

91   They continue this day according to Your
         ordinances,
      For all *are* Your servants.
92   Unless Your law *had been* my delight,
      I would then have perished in my affliction.
93   I will never forget Your precepts,
      For by them You have given me life.
94   I *am* Yours, save me;
      For I have sought Your precepts.
95   The wicked wait for me to destroy me,
      But I will consider Your testimonies.
96   I have seen the consummation of all
         perfection,
      But Your commandment *is* exceedingly
         broad.

ב MEM
97   *Oh, how I love Your law!
      It *is* my meditation all the day.
98   You, through Your commandments, make
         me wiser than my enemies;
      For they *are* ever with me.
99   I have more understanding than all my
         teachers,
      For Your testimonies *are* my meditation.
100   I understand more than the ancients,
      Because I keep Your precepts.
101   I have restrained my feet from every evil
         way,
      That I may keep Your word.
102   I have not departed from Your judgments,
      For You Yourself have taught me.
103   How sweet are Your words to my taste,
      Sweeter than honey to my mouth!
104   Through Your precepts I get
         understanding;
      Therefore I hate every false way.

ן NUN
105   *Your word *is* a lamp to my feet
      And a light to my path.
106   I have sworn and confirmed
      That I will keep Your righteous judgments.
107   I am afflicted very much;
      Revive me, O LORD, according to Your
         word.
108   Accept, I pray, the freewill offerings of my
         mouth, O LORD,
      And teach me Your judgments.
109   My life *is* continually in my hand,
      Yet I do not forget Your law.
110   The wicked have laid a snare for me,
      Yet I have not strayed from Your precepts.
111   Your testimonies I have taken as a heritage
         forever,
      For they *are* the rejoicing of my heart.
112   I have inclined my heart to perform Your
         statutes
      Forever, to the very end.

ס SAMEK
113   *I hate the double-minded,
      But I love Your law.
114   You *are* my hiding place and my shield;
      I hope in Your word.
115   Depart from me, you evildoers,
      For I will keep the commandments of my
         God!
116   Uphold me according to Your word, that I
         may live;
      And do not let me be ashamed of my hope.
117   Hold me up, and I shall be safe,

119:97–104 Those who love God's Word and obey it develop a practical wisdom for guiding their lives. It is dangerous to learn from your enemies (v. 98), and both your teachers and your elderly friends may not know what you need to know (vv. 99–100). Learn all you can from every good source, but let God, not man, be your teacher (John 14:26; 16:13–15).

119:105–112 In a dark world, God's Word can be your light (v. 105) to keep you from the traps and detours of the enemy (v. 110). God gives you the light you need a step at a time. If you want more light, you must obey what He says; then more light will come (John 7:17). God sends the light into your heart (v. 130) and gives you the wisdom you need.

119:113–120 Doubleminded people are unstable people (James 1:8), and unstable people eventually fall. If you put God's Word first in your life, it will hold you up and you will not fall (vv. 116–17; 2 Pet. 3:17–18; Jude 20–25). Cultivate a holy fear of the Lord and His Word (v. 120) and you will not be ashamed of your hope (v. 116).

And I shall observe Your statutes
continually.
118 You reject all those who stray from Your
statutes,
For their deceit *is* falsehood.
119 You put away all the wicked of the earth
like dross;
Therefore I love Your testimonies.
120 My flesh trembles for fear of You,
And I am afraid of Your judgments.

ע AYIN

121 *I have done justice and righteousness;
Do not leave me to my oppressors.
122 Be surety for Your servant for good;
Do not let the proud oppress me.
123 My eyes fail *from seeking* Your salvation
And Your righteous word.
124 Deal with Your servant according to Your
mercy,
And teach me Your statutes.
125 I *am* Your servant;
Give me understanding,
That I may know Your testimonies.
126 *It is* time for *You* to act, O LORD,
For they have regarded Your law as
void.
127 Therefore I love Your commandments
More than gold, yes, than fine gold!
128 Therefore all *Your* precepts *concerning* all
things
I consider *to be* right;
I hate every false way.

פ PE

129 *Your testimonies are wonderful;
Therefore my soul keeps them.
130 The entrance of Your words gives light;
It gives understanding to the simple.
131 I opened my mouth and panted,
For I longed for Your commandments.
132 Look upon me and be merciful to me,
As Your custom *is* toward those who love
Your name.
133 Direct my steps by Your word,
And let no iniquity have dominion over
me.
134 Redeem me from the oppression of man,
That I may keep Your precepts.
135 Make Your face shine upon Your servant,
And teach me Your statutes.
136 Rivers of water run down from my eyes,
Because *men* do not keep Your law.

צ TSADDE

137 *Righteous *are* You, O LORD,
And upright *are* Your judgments.
138 Your testimonies, *which* You have
commanded,
Are righteous and very faithful.
139 My zeal has consumed me,
Because my enemies have forgotten Your
words.
140 Your word *is* very pure;
Therefore Your servant loves it.
141 I *am* small and despised,
Yet I do not forget Your precepts.
142 Your righteousness *is* an everlasting
righteousness,
And Your law *is* truth.
143 Trouble and anguish have overtaken me,
Yet Your commandments *are* my delights.

119:121–128 God's Word will assure you and enable you when you feel the oppression of the enemy (vv. 121–22). God's people are aliens in enemy territory, and only the Word can protect them from the lies of the oppressor. But you must accept *all* that God's Word says about *all things;* if you love the truth, you must also hate the false (v. 128).

119:129–136 When you live by the Word of God, your life becomes wonderful because the Word of God is wonderful (v. 129). The Spirit shows you wonderful things in the Word (v. 18) and enables you to meditate on His wonderful works (v. 27). God transforms your mind and enables you to escape the dull conformity of the world (Rom. 12:1–2). His light shines within you (v. 130) and His face shines upon you (v. 135), so that you become a light in a dark world (Phil. 2:14–16).

119:137–144 A key word of this section is *righteousness*. No matter how zealous we may be for God's truth (v. 139), we must also have His righteousness if we are going to succeed. The Word helps us practice righteousness in a sinful world. There is no substitute for integrity, which comes from loving the Word and obeying it.

144   The righteousness of Your testimonies *is*
      everlasting;
      Give me understanding, and I shall live.

פ QOPH

145 *I cry out with *my* whole heart;
      Hear me, O LORD!
      I will keep Your statutes.
146 I cry out to You;
      Save me, and I will keep Your testimonies.
147 I rise before the dawning of the morning,
      And cry for help;
      I hope in Your word.
148 My eyes are awake through the *night*
      watches,
      That I may meditate on Your word.
149 Hear my voice according to Your
      lovingkindness;
      O LORD, revive me according to Your
      justice.
150 They draw near who follow after
      wickedness;
      They are far from Your law.
151 You *are* near, O LORD,
      And all Your commandments *are* truth.
152 Concerning Your testimonies,
      I have known of old that You have founded
      them forever.

ר RESH

153 *Consider my affliction and deliver me,
      For I do not forget Your law.
154 Plead my cause and redeem me;
      Revive me according to Your word.
155 Salvation *is* far from the wicked,
      For they do not seek Your statutes.
156 Great *are* Your tender mercies, O LORD;
      Revive me according to Your judgments.
157 Many *are* my persecutors and my enemies,
      Yet I do not turn from Your testimonies.
158 I see the treacherous, and am disgusted,
      Because they do not keep Your word.
159 Consider how I love Your precepts;
      Revive me, O LORD, according to Your
      lovingkindness.
160 The entirety of Your word *is* truth,
      And every one of Your righteous
      judgments *endures* forever.

ש SHIN

161 *Princes persecute me without a cause,
      But my heart stands in awe of Your word.
162 I rejoice at Your word
      As one who finds great treasure.
163 I hate and abhor lying,
      But I love Your law.
164 Seven times a day I praise You,
      Because of Your righteous judgments.
165 Great peace have those who love Your law,
      And nothing causes them to stumble.
166 LORD, I hope for Your salvation,
      And I do Your commandments.
167 My soul keeps Your testimonies,
      And I love them exceedingly.
168 I keep Your precepts and Your testimonies,
      For all my ways *are* before You.

ת TAU

169 *Let my cry come before You, O LORD;
      Give me understanding according to Your
      word.

119:145–152 In this section, the psalmist is crying out to God in prayer and reminding us that the Word of God helps us to pray in the will of God. The Word of God and prayer must never be separated (Acts 6:4); if they are, we will get out of balance. The better we know the Word, the more effectively we will pray (John 15:7), and the more effectively we pray, the better we will learn the Word.

119:153–160 One of the most difficult things in the life of faith is to be accused by Satan and ungodly people. "Plead my cause," prayed the psalmist (v. 154), and God defended him. When the enemy accuses you, let the Word of God assure you (Zech. 3), for the Word is truth (v. 160; John 17:17). If Satan tries to drag you into court, read Romans 8:31–39.

119:161–168 Knowing the Word of God and obeying it will bring joy to your heart, the kind of joy you would have if you found a buried treasure (v. 162) or inherited a fortune (v. 111). If material wealth is your goal, God's Word will not be a joy to you; but if you love the Word more than money (v. 127), you will have eternal spiritual treasures. Along with joy, you will experience love (vv. 163, 167), peace (v. 165), and hope (v. 166)—treasures money cannot buy.

119:169–176 If you put the Word of God first in your life, you will have something to sing about (vv. 171, 172, 175). Spontaneously, you will find yourself *singing God's Word* and turning statutes into songs (v. 54)! When your heart delights in God's law (v. 174), your lips must declare God's praise (Matt. 12:34). After all, you talk about the things that you love. When God's Word fills your heart, the right words will come out of your mouth (Col. 3:16; 4:6).

120ff "THE SONGS OF ASCENTS"
The next fifteen psalms are known as "the
Songs of Ascents." They are thought to be
the songs the Jewish pilgrims sang when
they went up to Jerusalem for the feasts
three times each year. Whoever made this
selection chose four psalms by David and
one by Solomon; the other ten are
anonymous.

The Hebrew word translated "ascents"
also means "degrees," and for this reason
some scholars relate this special collection
to King Hezekiah and his experience related
in Isaiah 38. The fifteen psalms mark the
fifteen years added to his life, and the ten
anonymous psalms are a reminder of the
shadow going back ten degrees.

The emphasis in this "hymnal within the
hymnal" is on trusting the God of Mount
Zion, even in the midst of suffering and trial.
The writers describe both the trials and the
triumphs of the people of God and reveal
that God is with His people—no matter what
the difficulty.

PSALM 120

120:1 Deliverance. The familiar rhyme
"Sticks and stones will break my bones, but
names will never hurt me" is not always true.
Words *can* hurt us, and the psalmist felt
them keenly. Only God can deliver you from
lies and their destructive power, and only
God can judge the liars. Just be sure you
are "valiant for the truth" in your own life
(Jer. 9:3).

120:5 Endurance. God did not change the
psalmist's circumstances; he had to remain
among people who hated him and lied about
him. But God gave him the endurance he
needed to be faithful under pressure. God
can easily change your circumstances, but
He needs your help if He is to change you.
Before God gives deliverance, He first must
give endurance.

PSALM 121

121:1 God is your Helper. The God who
made the hills is the God who gives you
help. He is a God of the hills and the valleys
(1 Kings 20:23–30), and His help is available
to all who will call upon Him.

121:3 God is your Keeper. The pilgrims
traveled together for fellowship and safety
because the roads were dangerous. The
dangers in modern society are just as great,
if not greater. But God goes *before you* (vv.
3–4) and stays awake to guide you and
guard your path. He is *next to you* (v. 5)
and *over you* (v. 6), and He will take you
safely to Zion (vv. 7–8).

170 Let my supplication come before You;
     Deliver me according to Your word.
171 My lips shall utter praise,
     For You teach me Your statutes.
172 My tongue shall speak of Your word,
     For all Your commandments *are*
     righteousness.
173 Let Your hand become my help,
     For I have chosen Your precepts.
174 I long for Your salvation, O LORD,
     And Your law *is* my delight.
175 Let my soul live, and it shall praise
     You;
     And let Your judgments help me.
176 I have gone astray like a lost sheep;
     Seek Your servant,
     For I do not forget Your commandments.

PSALM 120

A Song of Ascents.

In* my distress I cried to the LORD,
     And He heard me.
2   Deliver my soul, O LORD, from lying
     lips
     And from a deceitful tongue.

3   What shall be given to you,
     Or what shall be done to you,
     You false tongue?
4   Sharp arrows of the warrior,
     With coals of the broom tree!

5   *Woe is me, that I dwell in Meshech,
     That I dwell among the tents of Kedar!
6   My soul has dwelt too long
     With one who hates peace.
7   I *am for* peace;
     But when I speak, they *are* for war.

PSALM 121

A Song of Ascents.

I* will lift up my eyes to the hills—
     From whence comes my help?
2   My help *comes* from the LORD,
     Who made heaven and earth.

3   *He will not allow your foot to be moved;
     He who keeps you will not slumber.
4   Behold, He who keeps Israel
     Shall neither slumber nor sleep.

5   The LORD *is* your keeper;
     The LORD *is* your shade at your right
     hand.
6   The sun shall not strike you by day,
     Nor the moon by night.

7   The LORD shall preserve you from all evil;
     He shall preserve your soul.
8   The LORD shall preserve your going out and
     your coming in
     From this time forth, and even forevermore.

See His Greatness—Be sure you lift your eyes high enough so that you see by faith the great
God who cares for you. The ten spies in Canaan did not look high enough: they saw the giants and
the walls but not the Lord far above all (Num. 13:28–33). When things on earth seem too big for
you to handle, lift your eyes to God by meditating on Isaiah 40 (note v. 26). He is able!

PSALM 122

A Song of Ascents. Of David.

I* was glad when they said to me,
  "Let us go into the house of the LORD."
2   *Our feet have been standing
    Within your gates, O Jerusalem!

3   Jerusalem is built
    As a city that is compact together,
4   Where the tribes go up,
    The tribes of the LORD,
    To the Testimony of Israel,
    To give thanks to the name of the LORD.
5   For thrones are set there for judgment,
    The thrones of the house of David.

6   *Pray for the peace of Jerusalem:
    "May they prosper who love you.
7   Peace be within your walls,
    Prosperity within your palaces."
8   For the sake of my brethren and
      companions,
    I will now say, "Peace be within you."
9   Because of the house of the LORD our God
    I will seek your good.

PSALM 123

A Song of Ascents.

Unto* You I lift up my eyes,
  O You who dwell in the heavens.
2   *Behold, as the eyes of servants look to the
      hand of their masters,
    As the eyes of a maid to the hand of her
      mistress,
    So our eyes look to the LORD our God,
    Until He has mercy on us.

3   *Have mercy on us, O LORD, have mercy on
      us!
    For we are exceedingly filled with contempt.
4   Our soul is exceedingly filled
    With the scorn of those who are at ease,
    With the contempt of the proud.

PSALM 124

A Song of Ascents. Of David.

"If* it had not been the LORD who was on our
    side,"
    Let Israel now say—
2   "If it had not been the LORD who was on our
      side,
    When men rose up against us,
3   *Then they would have swallowed us alive,
    When their wrath was kindled against us;
4   Then the waters would have overwhelmed
      us,
    The stream would have gone over our soul;
5   Then the swollen waters
    Would have gone over our soul."

6   Blessed be the LORD,
    Who has not given us as prey to their teeth.
7   Our soul has escaped as a bird from the
      snare of the fowlers;ˣ
    The snare is broken, and we have escaped.

124:7 ˣThat is, persons who catch birds in a trap or snare

PSALM 122

122:1 "Let us go." Do you really rejoice when you have opportunity to go to God's house and worship Him? We today can travel easily to a place of worship, but the ancient Jews had to walk a long distance. Yet the pilgrim was happy to go to God's house.

122:2–5 "Let us praise." How the people loved Jerusalem! It was a holy place because the temple was there, an honored place because David's throne was there, and a happy place because the tribes were there to celebrate the greatness and goodness of God.

122:6 "Let us pray." Do you pray for the peace and prosperity of the people in your local "house of God"? Do you pray for God's people Israel? There can be no peace in our world until the Prince of Peace rules His people and there is peace in Jerusalem.

PSALM 123

123:1 Throughout their history, the Jews have often had to endure the scorn and contempt of their enemies. The world does not love God's people. As we make our way on the narrow road that leads to Zion, we run up against the crowd going in the other direction.
  Look to God's heaven. If you look at the enemy, you will get discouraged, so look by faith to the God of the universe who reigns in heaven. Psalm 121 shows you how.

123:2 Look to God's hand. He is the Master, we are the servants, and He tenderly cares for His own. Just be sure your ears are open to whatever orders your Master wants to give you.

123:3 Look for His help. Adequate mercy is available for you when your heart is filled with pain. Let God's words of strength drown out the enemy's words of scorn.

PSALM 124

124:1 The Lord is on your side when people want to devour you (vv. 1–3), when circumstances seem to drown you (vv. 4–5), and when Satan tries to deceive you (vv. 6–8).

124:3 You can usually detect man's anger, and you can feel it when circumstances overwhelm you. But Satan's traps might catch you if you are not careful. In His death, resurrection, and ascension, Jesus Christ has not only set you free from the snares, but He has broken the snares and they can never trap you again unless you let them.
  You are free as a bird, so use your wings of faith and live in the heavenlies!

125:1 Trusting the Lord means *security and stability* (vv. 1–2). Built on Mount Zion and surrounded by the mountains, Jerusalem was an impregnable fortress. The pilgrims felt safe when they arrived there after their dangerous journey. As a citizen of the heavenly Zion, you are safe in the Lord's care.

125:3 Trusting the Lord also means *sovereignty* (v. 3), bowing down to the God who holds the righteous scepter. Wickedness in our world is a temptation even to the righteous, so keep submitted to Him.

125:4 *Sanctity* (vv. 4–5) is a third result of trusting the Lord. When you walk by faith, you avoid the dangerous detours that lead you away from the path of righteousness. God has made you safe that you might be submitted, and your submission should lead to separated living: "Faith without works is dead" (James 2:20).

PSALM 126

126:1 This song probably celebrates Jerusalem's deliverance from the Assyrian army in the days of Hezekiah (2 Kings 18—19). It all happened so quickly that the people thought they were dreaming, and even the other nations had to admit the greatness of God.

126:4 But deliverance is just the beginning; God always wants to do something more. He wants to make us rivers of blessing (v. 4), like the dry wadis in the desert that become rushing torrents in the rainy season. If God sends you "showers of blessing," share the blessing with others.

126:5, 6 He also wants you to get to work in the harvest (vv. 5–6). Whether it is plowing the field (Luke 9:62), sowing the seed, or reaping the sheaves, God has a place for you. If you water the seed with your tears, you will one day rejoice as you bring in the sheaves. This is the formula for a harvest: going, weeping, sowing, reaping.

PSALM 127

127:1, 2 Do not forget the Lord. Jesus warned, "Without Me you can do nothing" (John 15:5), and that truth is illustrated in this psalm. What good is all your working, watching, and waking if the Lord is not with you? Long hours and sleepless nights are a waste apart from the blessing of the Lord. This psalm is not a plea for idleness, for God expects you to work and watch. But *(continued)*

8 Our help *is* in the name of the LORD,
Who made heaven and earth.

PSALM 125

A Song of Ascents.

Those* who trust in the LORD
Are like Mount Zion,
Which cannot be moved, *but* abides forever.
2 As the mountains surround Jerusalem,
So the LORD surrounds His people
From this time forth and forever.

3 *For the scepter of wickedness shall not rest
On the land allotted to the righteous,
Lest the righteous reach out their hands to
iniquity.

4 *Do good, O LORD, to *those who are* good,
And to *those who are* upright in their hearts.

5 As for such as turn aside to their crooked
ways,
The LORD shall lead them away
With the workers of iniquity.

Peace *be* upon Israel!

PSALM 126

A Song of Ascents.

When* the LORD brought back the captivity of
Zion,
We were like those who dream.
2 Then our mouth was filled with laughter,
And our tongue with singing.
Then they said among the nations,
"The LORD has done great things for them."
3 The LORD has done great things for us,
And we are glad.

4 *Bring back our captivity, O LORD,
As the streams in the South.

5 *Those who sow in tears
Shall reap in joy.
6 He who continually goes forth weeping,
Bearing seed for sowing,
Shall doubtless come again with rejoicing,
Bringing his sheaves *with him.*

PSALM 127

A Song of Ascents. Of Solomon.

Unless* the LORD builds the house,
They labor in vain who build it;
Unless the LORD guards the city,
The watchman stays awake in vain.
2 *It is* vain for you to rise up early,
To sit up late,
To eat the bread of sorrows;
For so He gives His beloved sleep.

3 *Behold, children *are* a heritage from the
LORD,
The fruit of the womb *is* a reward.

His Grace—"Great things He has done!" is the theme of many people who have experienced God's grace. Samuel preached about it (1 Sam. 12:24); David thanked the Lord for it (2 Sam. 7:21, 23); Mary sang about it (Luke 1:49); and the healed demoniac told everybody about it (Luke 8:39).

4   Like arrows in the hand of a warrior,
     So *are* the children of one's youth.
5   Happy *is* the man who has his quiver full
        of them;
     They shall not be ashamed,
     But shall speak with their enemies in the
        gate.

PSALM 128

A Song of Ascents.

Blessed *is* every one who fears the LORD,
     Who walks in His ways.

2   When you eat the labor of your hands,
     You *shall be* happy, and *it shall be* well with
        you.
3   Your wife *shall be* like a fruitful vine
     In the very heart of your house,
     Your children like olive plants
     All around your table.
4   Behold, thus shall the man be blessed
     Who fears the LORD.

5   The LORD bless you out of Zion,
     And may you see the good of Jerusalem
     All the days of your life.
6   Yes, may you see your children's children.

     Peace *be* upon Israel!

PSALM 129

A Song of Ascents.

"Many* a time they have afflicted me from
     my youth,"
     Let Israel now say—
2   "Many a time they have afflicted me from
        my youth;
     Yet they have not prevailed against me.
3   *The plowers plowed on my back;
     They made their furrows long."
4   *The LORD *is* righteous;
     He has cut in pieces the cords of the wicked.

5   Let all those who hate Zion
     Be put to shame and turned back.
6   Let them be as the grass *on* the housetops,
     Which withers before it grows up,
7   With which the reaper does not fill his hand,
     Nor he who binds sheaves, his arms.
8   *Neither let those who pass by them say,
     "The blessing of the LORD *be* upon you;
     We bless you in the name of the LORD!"

PSALM 130

A Song of Ascents.

Out* of the depths I have cried to You, O LORD;
2   *Lord, hear my voice!
     Let Your ears be attentive
     To the voice of my supplications.

3   *If You, LORD, should mark iniquities,
     O Lord, who could stand?
4   But *there is* forgiveness with You,
     That You may be feared.

5   *I wait for the LORD, my soul waits,
     And in His word I do hope.

(continued from previous page)
He wants to work in you and to accomplish
His will (Phil. 2:12–13).

127:3–5 *Do not neglect your family.* What
good are a lovely house and a big income
if the people in your life are robbed of the
joys of a happy home? Children are a gift
and a heritage, so appreciate them and
guard them. They are like fruit, so lovingly
cultivate them. They can be arrows for
fighting the Lord's battles, so keep them
polished and sharp and aimed in the right
direction. Give yourself to building a *home*,
not just a house, and building for the *future*,
not just the present.

❝*The beauty of the house is order;
The blessing of the house is
contentment; The glory of the house
is hospitality; The crown of the
house is godliness.*❞
—An old motto often placed
above fireplaces

PSALM 129

129:1 Israel's afflictions are compared to
the plowing of a field. Think of what it would
feel like to be face down in the dirt while a
plow goes down your back! How do you
handle a situation like that?

129:3 First, you accept it from the Lord. *If
the Lord is allowing people to plow your
back, that is happening because He has
planned a harvest.* Just be sure you plant
the right kind of seed. If you plant anger
and malice, you will not reap the blessings
of the Lord.

129:4 Second, you trust the Lord to help
you. In His own time, He will stop the plows
*and cut the cords so they cannot plow
anymore.* All their efforts will be useless.

129:8 Third, you wait for the Lord to judge
your enemies. He will put them to shame
and make them wither like grass on a sod
roof. On the other hand, God's people will
hear God's blessing in their ears and have
God's blessing in their hands.
     Plowing times can be productive times.

PSALM 130

130:1 As you ponder this psalm, see
yourself in four different situations, and learn
what it means to trust the mercy of the Lord.

130:2 In the depths. The depths of despair overwhelm you. You are drowning, and all you can do is cry out to God. He hears—
and He rescues you!

130:3 In the court. You are on trial, facing your sins, and you have no defense. The Judge pays the penalty, and *you are forgiven!*

130:5 In the dark. You are waiting patiently, yet it seems morning will never come. But the sun rises, and God gives you the dawning of a new day!

130:7 On the block. You are a slave, bound by your own sins, and you are about to sell yourself to a terrible master. But the Savior comes and purchases you and sets you free!
What a wonderful salvation you have!

PSALM 131

131:1 Most children naturally resist weaning because they want to continue enjoying the special attention of mother and the security it brings. Children do not realize that the traumatic experience of weaning is the first step toward maturity and freedom.
From birth to death, life is a series of weanings, and God never takes anything from you without giving you something better. You may weep and try to hold on to the past, but God tenderly leads you toward the future.

131:2 Weaned children discover who they are and what they can do. They have quiet hearts and no desire to go back to babyhood. They live for the future and watch for the special things that come to children growing up. They learn to obey, for only then can they fully experience all that the Father has for them.
As you mature in the Lord, you must "put away childish things" (1 Cor. 13:11). When God weans you away from something, do not fret; He has something better to take its place.

PSALM 132

132:1 Some students believe that this psalm was written when the Jewish exiles returned to their land from Babylon. This theory explains why David is mentioned. It was a difficult time as the Jews tried to rebuild their temple, their city, and their nation, and their beloved King David had been involved in these endeavors. The returned exiles wanted God to remember His covenant with David and restore their land.

132:2, 3 The temple. David yearned to build the temple, but the Lord chose his son Solomon instead. However, David provided the plans for the temple (1 Chron. 28:11–19) and much of the wealth needed. Would
(continued)

6 My soul *waits* for the Lord
More than those who watch for the morning—
Yes, more than those who watch for the morning.

7 *O Israel, hope in the LORD;
For with the LORD *there is* mercy,
And with Him *is* abundant redemption.
8 And He shall redeem Israel
From all his iniquities.

PSALM 131

A Song of Ascents. Of David.

LORD,* my heart is not haughty,
Nor my eyes lofty.
Neither do I concern myself with great matters,
Nor with things too profound for me.

2 *Surely I have calmed and quieted my soul,
Like a weaned child with his mother;
Like a weaned child *is* my soul within me.

3 O Israel, hope in the LORD
From this time forth and forever.

PSALM 132

A Song of Ascents.

LORD,* remember David
And all his afflictions;
2 *How he swore to the LORD,
And vowed to the Mighty One of Jacob:
3 "Surely I will not go into the chamber of my house,
Or go up to the comfort of my bed;
4 I will not give sleep to my eyes
Or slumber to my eyelids,
5 Until I find a place for the LORD,
A dwelling place for the Mighty One of Jacob."

6 Behold, we heard of it in Ephrathah;
We found it in the fields of the woods.ʸ
7 Let us go into His tabernacle;
Let us worship at His footstool.
8 Arise, O LORD, to Your resting place,
You and the ark of Your strength.
9 Let Your priests be clothed with righteousness,
And let Your saints shout for joy.

10 *For Your servant David's sake,
Do not turn away the face of Your Anointed.

11 The LORD has sworn *in* truth to David;
He will not turn from it:
"I will set upon your throne the fruit of your body.
12 If your sons will keep My covenant
And My testimony which I shall teach them,
Their sons also shall sit upon your throne forevermore."

13 *For the LORD has chosen Zion;
He has desired *it* for His dwelling place:

132:6 ʸHebrew *Jaar*

14 "This *is* My resting place forever;
   Here I will dwell, for I have desired it.
15 I will abundantly bless her provision;
   I will satisfy her poor with bread.
16 I will also clothe her priests with salvation,
   And her saints shall shout aloud for joy.
17 There I will make the horn of David
      grow;
   I will prepare a lamp for My Anointed.
18 His enemies I will clothe with shame,
   But upon Himself His crown shall flourish."

PSALM 133

A Song of Ascents. Of David.

B ehold,* how good and how pleasant *it is*
   For brethren to dwell together in unity!

2 *It is* like the precious oil upon the head,
   Running down on the beard,
   The beard of Aaron,
   Running down on the edge of his garments.
3 *It is* like the dew of Hermon,
   Descending upon the mountains of Zion;
   For there the LORD commanded the
      blessing—
   Life forevermore.

PSALM 134

A Song of Ascents.

B ehold,* bless the LORD,
   All *you* servants of the LORD,
   Who by night stand in the house of the
      LORD!
2 *Lift up your hands *in* the sanctuary,
   And bless the LORD.

3 *The LORD who made heaven and earth
   Bless you from Zion!

PSALM 135

P raise* the LORD!

   Praise the name of the LORD;
   Praise *Him,* O you servants of the LORD!
2 You who stand in the house of the LORD,
   In the courts of the house of our God,
3 Praise the LORD, for the LORD *is* good;
   Sing praises to His name, for *it is* pleasant.
4 *For the LORD has chosen Jacob for Himself,
   Israel for His special treasure.

5 *For I know that the LORD *is* great,
   And our Lord *is* above all gods.
6 Whatever the LORD pleases He does,
   In heaven and in earth,
   In the seas and in all deep places.
7 He causes the vapors to ascend from the
      ends of the earth;
   He makes lightning for the rain;
   He brings the wind out of His treasuries.

8 *He destroyed the firstborn of Egypt,
   Both of man and beast.
9 He sent signs and wonders into the midst
      of you, O Egypt,
   Upon Pharaoh and all his servants.
10 He defeated many nations
   And slew mighty kings—

(continued from previous page)
God desert His people as they tried to
rebuild the temple that meant so much to
David?

132:10 *The throne.* God promised that
David's line would continue on the throne
(2 Sam. 7), but now Israel was without a
king. In fact, there would be no king until
Jesus came, and they would reject Him. One
day, He will return and restore David's
throne (Luke 1:30–33; Acts 15:14–18).

132:13 *The city.* Jerusalem was in ruins,
but it was the City of David and would not
be forgotten by the Lord. He would dwell
there, bless the people, and give them joy.
He would restore power (the horn) and light
(the lamp) and make the city a testimony
to the nations.
   When the going is tough, remember those
feeble Jews who sacrificed to restore what
sin had destroyed. They prepared the way
for the Son of God who came to their city
and temple and gave His life for the sins of
the world.

PSALM 133

133:1 It is one thing for a group of people
to *journey together* to Jerusalem for a feast
and quite something else for them to *live
together* day after day. Abraham and Lot,
Isaac and his family, Jacob and Laban, and
Joseph's brothers remind us that brethren
do not always dwell together in unity.

133:2 Unity must come down from above,
like the oil running down Aaron's beard and
bathing the twelve jewels on the breastplate
(Exod. 29:5–7), or like the dew descending
on the mountains. You can manufacture
uniformity by manipulating people and
exerting pressure, but true unity can come
only from God by His Spirit.

133:3 Unity is good like the dew and
produces fruitfulness. It is pleasant like the
oil and produces a lovely fragrance.
Divisions among God's people produce
opposite results. Have you heeded the
admonition of Ephesians 4:1–6?

PSALM 134

134:1 Have you ever given thanks for the
people who work the night shift? Were it not
for them, you would have no electricity or
water at night, no fire or police protection,
or no emergency service at the hospital.
While you are asleep, others are serving.
Be grateful!

134:2 But do the people on the night shift
give thanks? Perhaps not. The psalmist
admonished the priests in the temple to give
thanks as they served God and the people
at night. It may have been a lonely ministry,
but it was an important ministry.

134:3 Your High Priest in heaven intercedes for you day and night. He never grows weary or impatient. Have you told Him you are thankful for His faithful ministry? Are you willing to be like Him and serve others, even on the night shift?

PSALM 135

135:1 The psalmist opened his song praising the Lord four times (vv. 1–3), and he ended it blessing the Lord four times (vv. 19–21). In between, he gave four excellent reasons why the Lord deserves your heartfelt praise.

135:4 To begin with, He is the God of *salvation* (v. 4). In His grace, He chose you; in His mercy, He made you His special treasure. You belong to Him. He values you and He loves you.

135:5 He is the God of *creation* (vv. 5–7), which means He provides for you day after day and gives you the things you need. He is in charge of the storms and uses them to accomplish His perfect will.

135:8 He is the God of *history* (vv. 8–14). The Jews prided themselves in the fact that God worked especially on behalf of their nation. He worked for Israel and through Israel to bring about His great plan of salvation.

135:15 He is the God of *celebration* (vv. 15–18). These verses parallel Psalm 115 and show the greatness of the living God in contrast to the dead idols of the nations. Celebrate the Lord today! Bless His holy name!

PSALM 136

136:1 Two choirs sang this psalm. One choir sang the first line of each verse, and the other choir answered, "For His mercy endures forever." This was not vain repetition (Matt. 6:7), for the second choir was offering inspired praise to the Lord. You can never say too much about the mercy of God!

136:4 God reveals His mercy by giving you a wonderful creation to use and to enjoy (vv. 4–9). Just think, He had everything ready for our first parents when He made them! It is too bad that many people are such poor stewards of God's creation gifts. Never take for granted the wonderful world you live in.

136:10 He reveals His mercy in His care for you, helping you fight your battles and defeat your enemies (vv. 10–25). Israel was not always faithful to God, but that is where His mercy comes in! He was faithful to them. The God of heaven is caring for you on earth! His mercy endures forever!

11 Sihon king of the Amorites,
Og king of Bashan,
And all the kingdoms of Canaan—
12 And gave their land *as* a heritage,
A heritage to Israel His people.

13 Your name, O LORD, *endures* forever,
Your fame, O LORD, throughout all generations.
14 For the LORD will judge His people,
And He will have compassion on His servants.

15 *The idols of the nations *are* silver and gold,
The work of men's hands.
16 They have mouths, but they do not speak;
Eyes they have, but they do not see;
17 They have ears, but they do not hear;
Nor is there *any* breath in their mouths.
18 Those who make them are like them;
So is everyone who trusts in them.

19 Bless the LORD, O house of Israel!
Bless the LORD, O house of Aaron!
20 Bless the LORD, O house of Levi!
You who fear the LORD, bless the LORD!
21 Blessed be the LORD out of Zion,
Who dwells in Jerusalem!

Praise the LORD!

PSALM 136

Oh,* give thanks to the LORD, for *He is* good!
For His mercy *endures* forever.
2 Oh, give thanks to the God of gods!
For His mercy *endures* forever.
3 Oh, give thanks to the Lord of lords!
For His mercy *endures* forever:

4 *To Him who alone does great wonders,
For His mercy *endures* forever;
5 To Him who by wisdom made the heavens,
For His mercy *endures* forever;
6 To Him who laid out the earth above the waters,
For His mercy *endures* forever;
7 To Him who made great lights,
For His mercy *endures* forever—
8 The sun to rule by day,
For His mercy *endures* forever;
9 The moon and stars to rule by night,
For His mercy *endures* forever.

10 *To Him who struck Egypt in their firstborn,
For His mercy *endures* forever;
11 And brought out Israel from among them,
For His mercy *endures* forever;
12 With a strong hand, and with an outstretched arm,
For His mercy *endures* forever;
13 To Him who divided the Red Sea in two,
For His mercy *endures* forever;
14 And made Israel pass through the midst of it,
For His mercy *endures* forever;
15 But overthrew Pharaoh and his army in the Red Sea,
For His mercy *endures* forever;
16 To Him who led His people through the wilderness,
For His mercy *endures* forever;

17 To Him who struck down great kings,
        For His mercy *endures* forever;
18 And slew famous kings,
        For His mercy *endures* forever—
19 Sihon king of the Amorites,
        For His mercy *endures* forever;
20 And Og king of Bashan,
        For His mercy *endures* forever—
21 And gave their land as a heritage,
        For His mercy *endures* forever;
22 A heritage to Israel His servant,
        For His mercy *endures* forever.

23 Who remembered us in our lowly state,
        For His mercy *endures* forever;
24 And rescued us from our enemies,
        For His mercy *endures* forever;
25 Who gives food to all flesh,
        For His mercy *endures* forever.

26 Oh, give thanks to the God of heaven!
        For His mercy *endures* forever.

PSALM 137

B y* the rivers of Babylon,
        There we sat down, yea, we wept
        When we remembered Zion.
2   *We hung our harps
        Upon the willows in the midst of it.
3   For there those who carried us away captive
            asked of us a song,
        And those who plundered us *requested*
            mirth,
        Saying, "Sing us *one* of the songs of Zion!"

4   How shall we sing the LORD's song
        In a foreign land?
5   *If I forget you, O Jerusalem,
        Let my right hand forget *its skill!*
6   If I do not remember you,
        Let my tongue cling to the roof of my
            mouth—
        If I do not exalt Jerusalem
        Above my chief joy.

7   *Remember, O LORD, against the sons of
            Edom
        The day of Jerusalem,
        Who said, "Raze *it,* raze *it,*
        To its very foundation!"

8   O daughter of Babylon, who are to be
            destroyed,
        Happy the one who repays you as you have
            served us!
9   Happy the one who takes and dashes
        Your little ones against the rock!

PSALM 138

A Psalm of David.

I * will praise You with my whole heart;
        Before the gods I will sing praises to You.
2   I will worship toward Your holy temple,
        And praise Your name
        For Your lovingkindness and Your truth;
        For You have magnified Your word above
            all Your name.
3   In the day when I cried out, You answered
            me,
        And made me bold *with* strength in my soul.

PSALM 137

137:1 This psalm came out of Israel's exile in Babylon, and it can serve as an inventory of your spiritual life today.

What makes you weep? The Jews wept as they remembered the past, but they did not weep over their sins. They wept because their sins caught up with them, not because they had sinned.

137:2 *What makes you sing?* They lost their song, so they hung up their harps. David had a similar experience (Ps. 32:1–7). Can you sing praises to God in a difficult place (Acts 16:25)? Can you praise the Lord at all times?

137:5 *What makes you yearn?* What is the ache in your heart? What do you long for more than anything else? Is it in God's will?

137:7 *What makes you angry?* God had promised to judge Babylon (Isa. 13; note v. 16), so they were praying in His will; but the note of anguish is missing. (See the entry on Ps. 58 for comments on the "imprecatory psalms.") If you love the Lord, you must hate evil (Ps. 97:10; Rom. 12:9) but leave the judgment to the Lord (Rom. 12:17–21).

PSALM 138

138:1 Walking "in the midst of trouble" did not hinder the psalmist's *worship* (vv. 1–3). If anything, it helped him to pray and to praise the Lord even more. David could not go to the temple, so he worshiped "toward the temple"; and God helped him.

138:4 His troubles did not hinder his *witness* (vv. 4–6). David may have been among the Gentiles when he wrote this psalm, but he was careful to share the Word and instruct them on singing God's praises. Trouble can be God's way to open doors for you to share the gospel.

138:7 His troubles did not hinder his *walk* (vv. 7–8). God revived David and enabled him to defeat his foes. Best of all, God perfected His plan for David and made him a better man (Eph. 2:10; Phil. 2:12–13). You may think that your troubles give you an excuse to stop living for the Lord. This psalm says that just the opposite is true! Read it again and follow David's example.

PSALM 139

139:1 If you are faithful to the Lord, this psalm will encourage you. If you are trying to hide from the Lord, this psalm will make you realize you are fighting a losing battle.

139:2 He knows what you do. He knows you personally and intimately, so do not try to fool Him. Be open and honest with God, and rest in His love (1 John 4:18). His eye is upon you, and you have nothing to fear.

139:7 He knows where you go. What a comfort to know that God is with you and cares for you! Whether you go up or down, east or west, He is there (Heb. 13:5). Sinners try to hide *from* God, but believers hide *in* God.

139:13 He knows what you are. After all, He made you, planned your potential, and ordered your days. This is not some kind of fatalism that paralyzes you. It is the wise plan of a loving Father who knows what is best for you. Accept what you are as His gift to you, and then use it wisely as your gift to Him. You are *unique;* God made you that way.

4 *All the kings of the earth shall praise You,
   O Lord,
   When they hear the words of Your mouth.
5 Yes, they shall sing of the ways of the Lord,
   For great *is* the glory of the Lord.
6 Though the Lord *is* on high,
   Yet He regards the lowly;
   But the proud He knows from afar.

7 *Though I walk in the midst of trouble, You
   will revive me;
   You will stretch out Your hand
   Against the wrath of my enemies,
   And Your right hand will save me.
8 The Lord will perfect *that which* concerns
   me;
   Your mercy, O Lord, *endures* forever;
   Do not forsake the works of Your hands.

PSALM 139

For the Chief Musician. A Psalm of David.

O * Lord, You have searched me and known *me.*
2 *You know my sitting down and my rising
   up;
   You understand my thought afar off.
3 You comprehend my path and my lying
   down,
   And are acquainted with all my ways.
4 For *there is* not a word on my tongue,
   But behold, O Lord, You know it altogether.
5 You have hedged me behind and before,
   And laid Your hand upon me.
6 *Such* knowledge *is* too wonderful for me;
   It is high, I cannot *attain* it.

7 *Where can I go from Your Spirit?
   Or where can I flee from Your presence?
8 If I ascend into heaven, You *are* there;
   If I make my bed in hell, behold, You *are*
   there.
9 *If* I take the wings of the morning,
   And dwell in the uttermost parts of the sea,
10 Even there Your hand shall lead me,
   And Your right hand shall hold me.
11 If I say, "Surely the darkness shall fall[z] on
   me,"
   Even the night shall be light about me;
12 Indeed, the darkness shall not hide from
   You,
   But the night shines as the day;
   The darkness and the light *are* both alike
   to You.

13 *For You formed my inward parts;
   You covered me in my mother's womb.
14 I will praise You, for I am fearfully *and*
   wonderfully made;[a]
   Marvelous are Your works,
   And *that* my soul knows very well.
15 My frame was not hidden from You,
   When I was made in secret,
   And skillfully wrought in the lowest parts
   of the earth.
16 Your eyes saw my substance, being yet
   unformed.

139:11 [z]Vulgate and Symmachus read *cover.*
139:14 [a]Following Masoretic Text and Targum; Septuagint, Syriac, and Vulgate read *You are fearfully wonderful.*

And in Your book they all were written,
The days fashioned for me,
When *as yet there were* none of them.

17 *How precious also are Your thoughts to me,
   O God!
   How great is the sum of them!
18 *If I should count them, they would be more
   in number than the sand;
   When I awake, I am still with You.

19 Oh, that You would slay the wicked, O God!
   Depart from me, therefore, you bloodthirsty
   men.
20 For they speak against You wickedly;
   Your enemies take *Your name* in vain.[b]
21 Do I not hate them, O LORD, who hate You?
   And do I not loathe those who rise up
   against You?
22 I hate them with perfect hatred;
   I count them my enemies.

23 *Search me, O God, and know my heart;
   Try me, and know my anxieties;
24 And see if *there is any* wicked way in me,
   And lead me in the way everlasting.

PSALM 140

To the Chief Musician. A Psalm of David.

Deliver* me, O LORD, from evil men;
   Preserve me from violent men,
2 Who plan evil things in *their* hearts;
   They continually gather together *for* war.
3 They sharpen their tongues like a serpent;
   The poison of asps *is* under their lips.
                                      Selah

4 Keep me, O LORD, from the hands of the
   wicked;
   Preserve me from violent men,
   Who have purposed to make my steps
   stumble.
5 The proud have hidden a snare for me, and
   cords;
   They have spread a net by the wayside;
   They have set traps for me.   Selah

6 *I said to the LORD: "You *are* my God;
   Hear the voice of my supplications, O LORD.
7 O GOD the Lord, the strength of my
   salvation,
   You have covered my head in the day of
   battle.
8 Do not grant, O LORD, the desires of the
   wicked;
   Do not further his *wicked* scheme,
   Lest they be exalted.   Selah

9 "As *for* the head of those who surround me,
   Let the evil of their lips cover them;
10 Let burning coals fall upon them;
   Let them be cast into the fire,
   Into deep pits, that they rise not up again.
11 Let not a slanderer be established in the
   earth;
   Let evil hunt the violent man to overthrow
   him."

139:17 *He knows what you think.* The psalmist pondered the thoughts of God and in this way cultivated the presence of God in his life. "You are to meditate on these things" (Phil. 4:8).

139:18 *He knows what you love.* Take these words to heart: "You who love the LORD, hate evil" (Ps. 97:10); "Love not the world" (1 John 2:15–17).

139:23 *He knows what you desire.* You do not know your own heart as well as you may think you do (Jer. 17:9–10). Let God search you and deal with the things that make you anxious. Let Him lead you. He knows where you ought to go.

PSALM 140

140:1 Satan fights anyone who is doing the will of God, and David was no exception. You must pray for Christian leaders especially, for they are prime targets for the evil one. The enemy has two favorite weapons: poisonous tongues (vv. 1–3) and hidden traps (vv. 4–5). He slanders God's leaders (sometimes using the lips of professed Christians), and he sets traps for them, hoping to trip them up.

140:6 David depended on prayer (vv. 6–11), God's promise (v. 12), and praise (v. 13). God hates a lying tongue (Prov. 6:17) and will one day judge slanderers. Meanwhile, maintain your character before God and let Him take care of your reputation. So live that when people hear lies about you, they will not believe them.

139:20 [b]Septuagint and Vulgate read *They take your cities in vain*.

12 I know that the LORD will maintain
    The cause of the afflicted,
    And justice for the poor.
13 Surely the righteous shall give thanks to
    Your name;
    The upright shall dwell in Your presence.

PSALM 141

A Psalm of David.

L ORD,* I cry out to You;
    Make haste to me!
    Give ear to my voice when I cry out to You.
2   Let my prayer be set before You *as* incense,
    The lifting up of my hands *as* the evening
        sacrifice.

3   *Set a guard, O LORD, over my mouth;
    Keep watch over the door of my lips.
4   Do not incline my heart to any evil thing,
    To practice wicked works
    With men who work iniquity;
    And do not let me eat of their delicacies.

5   *Let the righteous strike me;
    It shall be a kindness.
    And let him rebuke me;
    It shall be as excellent oil;
    Let my head not refuse it.

    For still my prayer *is* against the deeds of
        the wicked.
6   Their judges are overthrown by the sides
        of the cliff,
    And they hear my words, for they are sweet.
7   Our bones are scattered at the mouth of the
        grave,
    As when one plows and breaks up the earth.

8   *But my eyes *are* upon You, O GOD the Lord;
    In You I take refuge;
    Do not leave my soul destitute.
9   Keep me from the snares they have laid for
        me,
    And from the traps of the workers of
        iniquity.
10 Let the wicked fall into their own nets,
    While I escape safely.

PSALM 142

A Contemplation of David. A Prayer when he was in the
cave.

I * cry out to the LORD with my voice;
    With my voice to the LORD I make my
        supplication.
2   *I pour out my complaint before Him;
    I declare before Him my trouble.

3   *When my spirit was overwhelmed within
        me,
    Then You knew my path.
    In the way in which I walk
    They have secretly set a snare for me.
4   *Look on *my* right hand and see,
    For *there is* no one who acknowledges me;
    Refuge has failed me;
    No one cares for my soul.

PSALM 141

141:1, 2 "My voice . . . my hands." David
was away from God's house, but he knew
he could worship the Lord even without a
priest or an altar. His prayer would be like
the incense on the golden altar (Exod.
30:1–10), and the lifting of his hands in
praise like the burnt offering on the brazen
altar (Exod. 29:38–41; Heb. 13:15). No
matter where you are, worship the Lord!

141:3, 4 "My mouth . . . my lips." When
evil is near you, and evil people tempt you,
it is easy to say the wrong thing. It is the
heart that needs protection (Matt. 12:34–37).

141:5–7 "My head." "Faithful are the
wounds of a friend" (Prov. 27:6): they may
hurt, but like oil, they heal. Watch out for
the kisses—and delicacies (v. 4)—of the
enemy.

141:8 "My eyes." Keep your eyes of faith
on the Lord, and He will direct and protect
your steps.
    David gave *himself* to the Lord as the
evening sacrifice, every part of his being
(Rom. 12:1–2). This is the highest kind of
worship and the greatest privilege.

PSALM 142

142:1 Another of David's "cave" psalms
(Ps. 57; see also 1 Sam. 22:1–2, 24:1ff.),
Psalm 142 is filled with assurances you can
claim when you find yourself in a difficult
place.

142:2 God hears your prayers. There are
times when prayer is worship (Ps. 141:1),
and there are times when prayer is warfare.
In the heat of the battle, pour out your heart
to the Lord and tell Him how you feel and
what you need. Turn the cave into a Holy
of Holies.

142:3 God knows your path. David walked
in God's will, but the enemy lied about him
and set traps to catch him. Walk with the
Lord a step at a time and He will see you
through (Ps. 16:11; Prov. 3:5–6).

142:4 God knows your pain. David felt
completely abandoned, but he knew the
Lord was with him (2 Tim. 4:16–18). When
you feel like nobody cares, remember that
He cares for you (1 Pet. 5:7).

142:title °Hebrew *Maschil*

5 *I cried out to You, O LORD:
   I said, "You *are* my refuge,
   My portion in the land of the living.
6 *Attend to my cry,
   For I am brought very low;
   Deliver me from my persecutors,
   For they are stronger than I.
7 Bring my soul out of prison,
   That I may praise Your name;
   The righteous shall surround me,
   For You shall deal bountifully with me."

PSALM 143

A Psalm of David.

Hear* my prayer, O LORD,
   Give ear to my supplications!
   In Your faithfulness answer me,
   And in Your righteousness.
2 *Do not enter into judgment with Your
      servant,
   For in Your sight no one living is righteous.

3 For the enemy has persecuted my soul;
   He has crushed my life to the ground;
   He has made me dwell in darkness,
   Like those who have long been dead.
4 Therefore my spirit is overwhelmed within
      me;
   My heart within me is distressed.

5 I remember the days of old;
   I meditate on all Your works;
   I muse on the work of Your hands.
6 I spread out my hands to You;
   My soul *longs* for You like a thirsty land.
                                          Selah

7 *Answer me speedily, O LORD;
   My spirit fails!
   Do not hide Your face from me,
   Lest I be like those who go down into the
      pit.
8 Cause me to hear Your lovingkindness in
      the morning,
   For in You do I trust;
   Cause me to know the way in which I should
      walk,
   For I lift up my soul to You.
9 Deliver me, O LORD, from my enemies;
   In You I take shelter.*d*
10 *Teach me to do Your will,
   For You *are* my God;
   Your Spirit *is* good.
   Lead me in the land of uprightness.

11 *Revive me, O LORD, for Your name's sake!
   For Your righteousness' sake bring my soul
      out of trouble.
12 In Your mercy cut off my enemies,
   And destroy all those who afflict my soul;
   For I *am* Your servant.

PSALM 144

A Psalm of David.

Blessed* *be* the LORD my Rock,
   Who trains my hands for war,
   And my fingers for battle—

143:9 *d*Septuagint and Vulgate read *To You I flee.*

142:5 *God is your portion.* If you have
God, what more do you need? One with God
is a majority, so be wholly satisfied with Him.

142:6, 7 *God will be praised.* It may not
look like it now, but one day your trials will
turn out for your good and God's glory. Start
praising Him now—by faith—and you will be
"tuned up" when the answer comes.

PSALM 143

143:1 Unless you have been engaged in the
Lord's battles, you may not understand this
prayer, for it is the cry of a soldier in combat.
It is also a penitential prayer.

143:2–6 *"Hear me."* Depend on God's
grace and faithfulness, not on your
righteousness. Tell God what is happening
in your life. David was in the dust and in
the darkness. He felt like a thirsty man dying
in a desert.

143:7–9 *"Answer me."* When God does not
answer prayer, it is as though His face turns
away from us and we sink into the grave.
Do you find strength and joy in answered
prayer?

143:10 *"Teach me."* David met with the
Lord each morning and got his orders for
the day. Without those orders, he did not
know how to walk. Trust God's Spirit to lead
you as you yield yourself to Him.

143:11 *"Revive me."* David was in the dust
(v. 3), and only God could raise him up.
David wanted to fight the Lord's battles and
establish righteousness in the land. True
prayer means that we serve God, not that
God serves us (v. 12).

PSALM 144

144:1 This is another battle song to help
you in your spiritual warfare.
   Let God train you *before the battle* (vv.
1–4). In yourself, you are nothing, but God
loves you and equips you for what lies
ahead. God does not always explain how
He prepares you, so accept His disciplines
by faith. David fought a lion and a bear
before God let him fight a giant. Each
morning, put on the whole armor of God and
be ready for the trumpet call (Eph. 6:10–18).

2 My lovingkindness and my fortress,
   My high tower and my deliverer,
   My shield and *the One* in whom I take
      refuge,
   Who subdues my people[e] under me.

3 LORD, what *is* man, that You take knowledge
      of him?
   Or the son of man, that You are mindful of
      him?
4 Man is like a breath;
   His days *are* like a passing shadow.

5 *Bow down Your heavens, O LORD, and come
      down;
   Touch the mountains, and they shall smoke.
6 Flash forth lightning and scatter them;
   Shoot out Your arrows and destroy them.
7 Stretch out Your hand from above;
   Rescue me and deliver me out of great
      waters,
   From the hand of foreigners,
8 Whose mouth speaks lying words,
   And whose right hand *is* a right hand of
      falsehood.

9 *I will sing a new song to You, O God;
   On a harp of ten strings I will sing praises
      to You,
10 *The One* who gives salvation to kings,
   Who delivers David His servant
   From the deadly sword.

11 Rescue me and deliver me from the hand
      of foreigners,
   Whose mouth speaks lying words,
   And whose right hand *is* a right hand of
      falsehood—
12 That our sons *may be* as plants grown up
      in their youth;
   That our daughters *may be* as pillars,
   Sculptured in palace style;
13 *That* our barns *may be* full,
   Supplying all kinds of produce;
   That our sheep may bring forth thousands
   And ten thousands in our fields;
14 *That* our oxen *may be* well laden;
   That there be no breaking in or going out;
   That there be no outcry in our streets.
15 Happy *are* the people who are in such a
      state;
   Happy *are* the people whose God *is* the
      LORD!

144:5–8 Let God help you *in the battle* (vv. 5–8). God's hand is there to strengthen and deliver you, so do not be afraid to engage the enemy. You are fighting the Lord's battles; He will not abandon you (2 Chron. 20:14–19).

144:9–15 Sing God's praises *after the battle* (vv. 9–15). Thank Him for all He has done for you personally (vv. 9–11), for your family (v. 12), and for your nation (vv. 13–15).

PSALM 145

A Praise of David.

I *will extol You, my God, O King;
   And I will bless Your name forever and
      ever.
2 Every day I will bless You,
   And I will praise Your name forever and
      ever.
3 Great *is* the LORD, and greatly to be praised;
   And His greatness *is* unsearchable.

4 *One generation shall praise Your works to
      another,

PSALM 145

145:1 David extols the Lord for His greatness (v. 3), grace (vv. 8, 17), goodness (v. 9), glory (vv. 11–12), and generosity (vv. 15–16). If you are having a hard time praising the Lord today, that should help get you started! God's people will praise Him forever, so we had better learn to do it day by day (v. 2).

145:4 David extols the Lord as an encouragement to others. Members of each generation need to learn to praise the Lord (vv. 4–7), so your praise is an example and witness to them. Are others growing in their worship because of you?

144:2 [e]Following Masoretic Text, Septuagint, and Vulgate; Syriac and Targum read *the peoples* (compare 18:47).

And shall declare Your mighty acts.
5   If will meditate on the glorious splendor of
       Your majesty,
     And on Your wondrous works.^g
6   *Men* shall speak of the might of Your
       awesome acts,
     And I will declare Your greatness.
7   They shall utter the memory of Your great
       goodness,
     And shall sing of Your righteousness.

8   The LORD *is* gracious and full of compassion,
     Slow to anger and great in mercy.
9   The LORD *is* good to all,
     And His tender mercies *are* over all His
       works.

10 *All Your works shall praise You, O LORD,
     And Your saints shall bless You.
11 They shall speak of the glory of Your
       kingdom,
     And talk of Your power,
12 To make known to the sons of men His
       mighty acts,
     And the glorious majesty of His kingdom.
13 Your kingdom *is* an everlasting kingdom,
     And Your dominion *endures* throughout all
       generations.^h

14 *The LORD upholds all who fall,
     And raises up all *who are* bowed down.
15 The eyes of all look expectantly to You,
     And You give them their food in due season.
16 You open Your hand
     And satisfy the desire of every living thing.

17 The LORD *is* righteous in all His ways,
     Gracious in all His works.
18 The LORD *is* near to all who call upon Him,
     To all who call upon Him in truth.
19 He will fulfill the desire of those who fear
       Him;
     He also will hear their cry and save them.
20 The LORD preserves all who love Him,
     But all the wicked He will destroy.
21 My mouth shall speak the praise of the
       LORD,
     And all flesh shall bless His holy name
     Forever and ever.

PSALM 146

Praise* the LORD!

   Praise the LORD, O my soul!
2 While I live I will praise the LORD;
     I will sing praises to my God while I have
       my being.

3 *Do not put your trust in princes,
     Nor in a son of man, in whom *there is* no
       help.
4 His spirit departs, he returns to his earth;
     In that very day his plans perish.

145:10 David hears all God's works praising Him (v. 10). Nature takes on new meaning and new beauty when you realize this (Ps. 19:1–6).

145:14 When you live a life of praise, you have the Lord's help in every situation. If you stumble, He helps you up (v. 14). If you are hungry, He feeds you (vv. 15–16). If you call, He draws near (v. 18). No wonder David blessed the Lord so much!

PSALM 146

146:1 Praise is an evidence of *life* (vv. 1–2), not just physical life, but the life of God in the heart. In heaven, it is all praise; in hell, there is no praise; here on earth, you must make a choice.

146:3, 4 Praise is an encouragement to *faith* (vv. 3–4). When you have faith in somebody—your doctor, for instance—you praise that person to others. When your faith is low, your praise will gradually subside, but when you major on praise, your faith will grow.

145:5 ^fFollowing Masoretic Text and Targum; Dead Sea Scrolls, Septuagint, Syriac, and Vulgate read *They*. ^gLiterally *on the words of Your wondrous works*   145:13 ^hFollowing Masoretic Text and Targum; Dead Sea Scrolls, Septuagint, Syriac, and Vulgate add *The LORD is faithful in all His words, And holy in all His works*.

146:5 Praise is an encouragement to *hope* (vv. 5–7). When your hope is in the Lord, you can praise Him no matter what the circumstances may be. Faith is the upward look, and hope is the forward look.

146:8 Praise is an encouragement to *love* (vv. 8–10), your love for God and others, and God's love for you. When you love someone, you trust that person, and greater trust brings greater love.
Life, faith, hope, and love—all are bound up in the experience of praise.

PSALM 147

147:1 Praising the Lord is the highest exercise of your faculties. He is worthy of praise, and you should praise Him whether or not you think your praise is accomplishing anything in your life. However, there are some blessings that come to those who worship Him in truth.

147:2 Praise brings spiritual beauty to God's people (v. 1; Pss. 27:4, 29:2; 149:4). It builds His work and unifies His people (v. 2). It heals the inner person (v. 3) and lifts the fallen (v. 6). Praise is good medicine!

147:7 Praise makes God's world real and personal to you (vv. 7–9, 15–18), even the storms; and it is great protection against the enemy (vv. 12–14). Praise pleases the Lord and enables Him to work in your life (vv. 10–11).
Praise must never become a pragmatic device for getting blessing from God. When you sincerely praise Him, the blessing will come. Praise changes things—and people.

5 *Happy *is he* who *has* the God of Jacob for his help,
  Whose hope *is* in the LORD his God,
6 Who made heaven and earth,
  The sea, and all that *is* in them;
  Who keeps truth forever,
7 Who executes justice for the oppressed,
  Who gives food to the hungry.
  The LORD gives freedom to the prisoners.

8 *The LORD opens *the eyes of* the blind;
  The LORD raises those who are bowed down;
  The LORD loves the righteous.
9 The LORD watches over the strangers;
  He relieves the fatherless and widow;
  But the way of the wicked He turns upside down.

10 The LORD shall reign forever—
  Your God, O Zion, to all generations.

  Praise the LORD!

PSALM 147

Praise* the LORD!
  For *it is* good to sing praises to our God;
  For *it is* pleasant, *and* praise is beautiful.

2 *The LORD builds up Jerusalem;
  He gathers together the outcasts of Israel.
3 He heals the brokenhearted
  And binds up their wounds.
4 He counts the number of the stars;
  He calls them all by name.
5 Great *is* our Lord, and mighty in power;
  His understanding *is* infinite.
6 The LORD lifts up the humble;
  He casts the wicked down to the ground.

7 *Sing to the LORD with thanksgiving;
  Sing praises on the harp to our God,
8 Who covers the heavens with clouds,
  Who prepares rain for the earth,
  Who makes grass to grow on the mountains.
9 He gives to the beast its food,
  And to the young ravens that cry.

10 He does not delight in the strength of the horse;
  He takes no pleasure in the legs of a man.
11 The LORD takes pleasure in those who fear Him,
  In those who hope in His mercy.

12 Praise the LORD, O Jerusalem!
  Praise your God, O Zion!
13 For He has strengthened the bars of your gates;
  He has blessed your children within you.
14 He makes peace *in* your borders,
  And fills you with the finest wheat.

15 He sends out His command *to the* earth;
  His word runs very swiftly.
16 He gives snow like wool;
  He scatters the frost like ashes;
17 He casts out His hail like morsels;
  Who can stand before His cold?
18 He sends out His word and melts them;
  He causes His wind to blow, *and* the waters flow.

19 He declares His word to Jacob,
His statutes and His judgments to Israel.
20 He has not dealt thus with any nation;
And *as for His* judgments, they have not
known them.

*Praise the LORD!

PSALM 148

Praise* the LORD!

Praise the LORD from the heavens;
Praise Him in the heights!
2 *Praise Him, all His angels;
Praise Him, all His hosts!
3 Praise Him, sun and moon;
Praise Him, all you stars of light!
4 Praise Him, you heavens of heavens,
And you waters above the heavens!

5 Let them praise the name of the LORD,
For He commanded and they were created.
6 He also established them forever and ever;
He made a decree which shall not pass
away.

7 *Praise the LORD from the earth,
You great sea creatures and all the depths;
8 Fire and hail, snow and clouds;
Stormy wind, fulfilling His word;
9 Mountains and all hills;
Fruitful trees and all cedars;
10 Beasts and all cattle;
Creeping things and flying fowl;
11 *Kings of the earth and all peoples;
Princes and all judges of the earth;
12 Both young men and maidens;
Old men and children.

13 Let them praise the name of the LORD,
For His name alone is exalted;
His glory *is* above the earth and heaven.
14 And He has exalted the horn of His people,
The praise of all His saints—
Of the children of Israel,
A people near to Him.

Praise the LORD!

PSALM 149

Praise* the LORD!

Sing to the LORD a new song,
And His praise in the assembly of saints.

2 Let Israel rejoice in their Maker;
Let the children of Zion be joyful in their
King.
3 Let them praise His name with the dance;
Let them sing praises to Him with the
timbrel and harp.
4 For the LORD takes pleasure in His people;
He will beautify the humble with salvation.

PSALM 148

148:1 When it comes to praising the Lord, the psalmist will not permit anyone or anything in all creation to escape.

148:2 *The heavens.* He starts with the angels, then summons the heavenly bodies, and even includes the clouds! God created them, established them, and controls them. They should praise Him—and they do!

148:7 *The earth.* Whether the depths of the sea or the heights of the mountains, the winds or the fruitful trees, all should praise the Lord—and they do! When the weather is bad, it is good to know that even the storms fulfill God's Word (v. 8).

148:11 *Mankind.* Made in God's image, men and women have more reason to praise God than does any other thing in creation. And when you have been saved by God's grace, your motive is even greater. Praise the Lord!

PSALM 149

149:1 God's people should be a singing people. They should sing *in the sanctuary* (vv. 1–4) because God is their Savior (v. 1), their Maker, and their King (v. 2). You are reminded again that praise pleases God and beautifies God's people (v. 4; Ps. 147:1, 11).

How Do You Mend a Broken Heart?—The God who numbers and names the stars knows about your broken heart and can heal it—*if* you give all the pieces to Him (Ps. 147:3–4).

149:5 You should sing *at home* (v. 5), even when in bed! Sing when you wake up in the morning, when you take a nap, when you go to bed at night. If it is a bed of illness, sing to the Lord even more.

149:6 Sing to the Lord *on the battlefield* (vv. 6–9). God's Word is your sword (Eph. 6:17; Heb. 4:12), and it should be on your lips as well as in your hand. Praise is a wonderful weapon for defeating the enemy.

PSALM 150

150:1 It is only right that the closing song in the Hebrew hymnal be an invitation to praise the Lord. The word *praise* is used thirteen times here. **Where should we praise Him?** Locally and universally, in the temple and in the vast heavens (v. 1). In other words, wherever you are, praise the Lord!

150:2 Why should we praise Him? Because of what He does and who He is (v. 2). The better you know God's character and works, the more you will praise Him and the more you will enjoy praising Him.

150:3 How should we praise Him? With voices and instruments, including the cymbals, and with our bodies expressing the joy we feel within (vv. 3–5). The whole person should be one living sacrifice that praises the Lord.

150:6 Who should praise Him? "Everything that has breath" (v. 6). But things that do not have breath praise Him (Ps. 148:7–9), so we have even more reason to do so! Our breath comes from Him (Acts 17:25), so we ought to use it to praise His name. Breath is the weakest thing we have, but we can devote it to the highest service, praising the Lord.

5 *Let the saints be joyful in glory;
Let them sing aloud on their beds.
6 *Let the high praises of God *be* in their mouth,
And a two-edged sword in their hand,
7 To execute vengeance on the nations,
And punishments on the peoples;
8 To bind their kings with chains,
And their nobles with fetters of iron;
9 To execute on them the written judgment—
This honor have all His saints.

Praise the LORD!

PSALM 150

Praise* the LORD!

Praise God in His sanctuary;
Praise Him in His mighty firmament!
2 *Praise Him for His mighty acts;
Praise Him according to His excellent greatness!

3 *Praise Him with the sound of the trumpet;
Praise Him with the lute and harp!
4 Praise Him with the timbrel and dance;
Praise Him with stringed instruments and flutes!
5 Praise Him with loud cymbals;
Praise Him with clashing cymbals!

6 *Let everything that has breath praise the LORD.

Praise the LORD!

PROVERBS

A *proverb* has been defined as a "short statement based on long experience." The Hebrew word translated "proverb" means "to be like," and many of the proverbs are contrasts or comparisons. The proverbs deal with the ethical and moral aspects of life. They are practical, not theoretical, and point the way to godly character and a fulfilled life.

The theme of Proverbs is wisdom, the right use of knowledge. This wisdom is more than an intellectual pursuit; it also involves devotion to the Lord. The wise person fears the Lord, trusts Him, and seeks to obey His will. The wisdom described in Proverbs is like a spiritual "sixth sense." It enables you to evaluate circumstances and people and make the right decisions in life.

Since a proverb is only the statement of a general truth, it must not be taken for a divine promise. David and Jesus both pleased the Lord, but they still had enemies (Prov. 16:7); and more than one obedient child of God has died young (Prov. 10:27). Not all godly people have houses full of money (Prov. 15:6), and many godless people eat well (Prov. 13:25). In the light of eternity, the wicked are the losers—no matter how successful they may be—but Proverbs focuses primarily on this life, not the next.

These wise sayings are "distilled truth" made practical for daily living. You find in them principles, warnings, and counsels that really work *when you fear the Lord and want to please Him.* The book of Proverbs is not a do-it-yourself success kit for the greedy but a guidebook for the godly.

Most of the book was written by Solomon (1:1; see also 1 Kings 4:32), with contributions from other writers (22:17; 24:23; 30:1; 31:1). "The men of Hezekiah" (25:1) probably edited the book to its present form.

Proverbs covers a wide range of subjects, and the verses are not arranged in topical order. In our meditations, we will concentrate on a major emphasis in each chapter, and from time to time, we will bring together verses that relate to a common theme.

1 The proverbs of Solomon the son of David, king of Israel:

2 *To know wisdom and instruction,
To perceive the words of understanding,
3 To receive the instruction of wisdom,
Justice, judgment, and equity;
4 To give prudence to the simple,
To the young man knowledge and discretion—
5 A wise *man* will hear and increase learning,
And a man of understanding will attain wise counsel,
6 To understand a proverb and an enigma,
The words of the wise and their riddles.

7 *The fear of the LORD *is* the beginning of knowledge,
But fools despise wisdom and instruction.

8 My son, hear the instruction of your father,
And do not forsake the law of your mother;

CHAPTER 1

1:2–6 The importance of wisdom. All you need for success is yours when you receive God's wisdom. "Success" means much more than making a living. It means making a life that honors God and serves others. Wisdom is more important than riches and power (Prov. 8:12–21) because wisdom helps you build for all eternity.

1:7–19 The instruction of wisdom. "The fear of the LORD" means reverence for God and respect for His Word, a willingness to listen and a promptness to obey. God uses different people to teach you wisdom, and you must be alert to each lesson. Note the warnings: "Do not forsake! Do not consent! Do not walk!" God says no that He might say yes.

Who Is Wise?—The truly wise person will hear the Word of God (Prov. 1:5) and obey it (Prov. 12:15); store up what is learned (Prov. 9:9; 10:14); win the lost (Prov. 11:30); turn from sin (Prov. 14:16); control the tongue (Prov. 10:19; 16:23); and be diligent (Prov. 10:5). The wise person will inherit glory (Prov. 3:35); bring joy to others (Prov. 10:1; 15:20); have his or her needs met (Prov. 21:20); and have strength for war (Prov. 24:5–6).

9   For they *will be* a graceful ornament on your
     head,
     And chains about your neck.

10   My son, if sinners entice you,
     Do not consent.
11   If they say, "Come with us,
     Let us lie in wait to *shed* blood;
     Let us lurk secretly for the innocent without
     cause;
12   Let us swallow them alive like Sheol,*a*
     And whole, like those who go down to the
     Pit;
13   We shall find all *kinds* of precious
     possessions,
     We shall fill our houses with spoil;
14   Cast in your lot among us,
     Let us all have one purse"—
15   My son, do not walk in the way with them,
     Keep your foot from their path;
16   For their feet run to evil,
     And they make haste to shed blood.
17   Surely, in vain the net is spread
     In the sight of any bird;
18   But they lie in wait for their *own* blood,
     They lurk secretly for their *own* lives.
19   So *are* the ways of everyone who is greedy
     for gain;
     It takes away the life of its owners.

1:20–33 *The invitation of wisdom.*
Wisdom is like a lovely woman inviting
hungry people to a great feast (Prov. 1:20–
33; 8:1ff.; 9:1ff.). Folly is like an evil woman
seducing the ignorant into sin (5:1ff.; 6:20ff.;
7:1ff.). Accept wisdom's call and you will be
blessed; accept folly's call and you will be
destroyed.

20   *Wisdom calls aloud outside;
     She raises her voice in the open squares.
21   She cries out in the chief concourses,*b*
     At the openings of the gates in the city
     She speaks her words:
22   "How long, you simple ones, will you love
     simplicity?
     For scorners delight in their scorning,
     And fools hate knowledge.
23   Turn at my rebuke;
     Surely I will pour out my spirit on you;
     I will make my words known to you.
24   Because I have called and you refused,
     I have stretched out my hand and no one
     regarded,
25   Because you disdained all my counsel,
     And would have none of my rebuke,
26   I also will laugh at your calamity;
     I will mock when your terror comes,
27   When your terror comes like a storm,
     And your destruction comes like a
     whirlwind,
     When distress and anguish come upon you.

28   "Then they will call on me, but I will not
     answer;
     They will seek me diligently, but they will
     not find me.
29   Because they hated knowledge
     And did not choose the fear of the LORD,
30   They would have none of my counsel
     And despised my every rebuke.
31   Therefore they shall eat the fruit of their
     own way,
     And be filled to the full with their own
     fancies.
32   For the turning away of the simple will slay
     them,

1:12 *a*Or *the grave*   1:21 *b*Septuagint, Syriac, and Targum
read *top of the walls;* Vulgate reads *the head of multitudes.*

And the complacency of fools will destroy
  them;
33 But whoever listens to me will dwell safely,
  And will be secure, without fear of evil."

2 My* son, if you receive my words,
  And treasure my commands within you,
2 So that you incline your ear to wisdom,
  And apply your heart to understanding;
3 Yes, if you cry out for discernment,
  And lift up your voice for understanding,
4 If you seek her as silver,
  And search for her as *for* hidden treasures;
5 Then you will understand the fear of the
    LORD,
  And find the knowledge of God.
6 For the LORD gives wisdom;
  From His mouth *come* knowledge and
    understanding;
7 He stores up sound wisdom for the upright;
  He is a shield to those who walk uprightly;
8 He guards the paths of justice,
  And preserves the way of His saints.
9 Then you will understand righteousness and
    justice,
  Equity *and* every good path.

10 When wisdom enters your heart,
  And knowledge is pleasant to your soul,
11 Discretion will preserve you;
  Understanding will keep you,
12 To deliver you from the way of evil,
  From the man who speaks perverse things,
13 From those who leave the paths of
    uprightness
  To walk in the ways of darkness;
14 Who rejoice in doing evil,
  And delight in the perversity of the wicked;
15 Whose ways *are* crooked,
  And *who are* devious in their paths;
16 To deliver you from the immoral woman,
  From the seductress *who* flatters with her
    words,
17 Who forsakes the companion of her youth,
  And forgets the covenant of her God.
18 For her house leads down to death,
  And her paths to the dead;
19 None who go to her return,
  Nor do they regain the paths of life—
20 So you may walk in the way of goodness,
  And keep *to* the paths of righteousness.
21 For the upright will dwell in the land,
  And the blameless will remain in it;
22 But the wicked will be cut off from the earth,
  And the unfaithful will be uprooted from it.

3 My* son, do not forget my law,
  But let your heart keep my commands;
2 For length of days and long life
  And peace they will add to you.

CHAPTER 2

2:1ff Wisdom is not only a person to know
(chap. 1) but also a path to walk. The word
path is used seven times in this chapter. It
suggests to us that life involves direction,
decision, and determination, just like walking
a path. God will do His part (vv. 6–9) if you
do your part (vv. 1–5).
  The path of wisdom is a guarded path
(v. 8) and a good path (v. 9) that leads to
life (v. 19) and righteousness (v. 20). The
path of folly is a dark (v. 13) and devious
(v. 15) path that leads to death (v. 18).
  If you want to walk on the path of God's
wisdom, heed the admonitions in verses
1–5.

CHAPTER 3

3:1–8 *Your heart.* What you do with your
heart determines what you do with your
life (Prov. 4:23). Cultivate an obedient
heart (v. 1) that receives God's Word (v. 3;
2 Cor. 3:1–3) and a trusting heart that obeys
(vv. 5–6). Verse 5 does not suggest that you
ignore your mind or common sense, but that
you not lean only on them and reject God's
way.

The Path of the Unwise—Wisdom addresses three kinds of people: the simple, the scorner, and
the fool. The *simple* are people who believe everything (Prov. 14:15). They have no understanding
(Prov. 7:7; 9:4) and cannot see the road ahead (Prov. 22:3; 27:12). *Scorners* think they know
everything (Prov. 21:24), so they never attain wisdom (Prov. 14:6) or even profit from rebuke (Prov.
9:7–8; 13:1; 15:12). They are great troublemakers (Prov. 22:10) who ought to be punished (Prov.
19:29; 21:11). *Fools* are self-confident (Prov. 12:15; 28:26) and hate instruction (Prov. 1:7, 22; 23:9).
They speak proudly (Prov. 10:18; 14:3), love to fight (Prov. 18:6–7; 27:3), meddle (Prov. 20:3), speak
without thinking (Prov. 18:13; 19:11), and mock at sin (Prov. 14:9). They are not helped by discipline
(Prov. 17:10; 27:22) and will finally fall (Prov. 10:8, 10, 14).

3 Let not mercy and truth forsake you;
   Bind them around your neck,
   Write them on the tablet of your heart,
4 *And* so find favor and high esteem
   In the sight of God and man.

5 Trust in the LORD with all your heart,
   And lean not on your own understanding;
6 In all your ways acknowledge Him,
   And He shall direct*c* your paths.

7 Do not be wise in your own eyes;
   Fear the LORD and depart from evil.
8 It will be health to your flesh,*d*
   And strength*e* to your bones.

3:9–18 *Your possessions.* Put God first in the way you use His wealth (Matt. 6:33) and major on the things that money cannot buy (vv. 13–18). When God corrects you, accept it as an evidence of His love (Heb. 12:5–6).

9 *Honor the LORD with your possessions,
   And with the firstfruits of all your increase;
10 So your barns will be filled with plenty,
   And your vats will overflow with new wine.

11 My son, do not despise the chastening of
      the LORD,
   Nor detest His correction;
12 For whom the LORD loves He corrects,
   Just as a father the son *in whom* he delights.

13 Happy *is* the man *who* finds wisdom,
   And the man *who* gains understanding;
14 For her proceeds *are* better than the profits
      of silver,
   And her gain than fine gold.
15 She *is* more precious than rubies,
   And all the things you may desire cannot
      compare with her.
16 Length of days *is* in her right hand,
   In her left hand riches and honor.
17 Her ways *are* ways of pleasantness,
   And all her paths *are* peace.
18 She *is* a tree of life to those who take hold
      of her,
   And happy *are all* who retain her.

19 The LORD by wisdom founded the earth;
   By understanding He established the
      heavens;
20 By His knowledge the depths were broken
      up,
   And clouds drop down the dew.

3:21–26 *Your conduct.* Let every part of your body be controlled by God's wisdom (Rom. 12:1–2). Sleep is one of the tests of faith and true surrender to God (Ps. 4).

21 *My son, let them not depart from your
      eyes—
   Keep sound wisdom and discretion;
22 So they will be life to your soul
   And grace to your neck.
23 Then you will walk safely in your way,
   And your foot will not stumble.
24 When you lie down, you will not be afraid;
   Yes, you will lie down and your sleep will
      be sweet.
25 Do not be afraid of sudden terror,
   Nor of trouble from the wicked when it
      comes;
26 For the LORD will be your confidence,
   And will keep your foot from being caught.

3:27–35 *Your neighbors.* If you want God's blessing on your home, be a blessing to those around you. Share what you have and never plan evil against others (Rom. 12:9–21).

27 *Do not withhold good from those to whom
      it is due,

3:6 *c*Or *make smooth* or *straight*   3:8 *d*Literally *navel,* figurative of the body *e*Literally *drink* or *refreshment*

When it is in the power of your hand to do
    so.
28 Do not say to your neighbor,
"Go, and come back,
And tomorrow I will give *it,*"
When *you have* it with you.
29 Do not devise evil against your neighbor,
For he dwells by you for safety's sake.
30 Do not strive with a man without cause,
If he has done you no harm.

31 Do not envy the oppressor,
And choose none of his ways;
32 For the perverse *person is* an abomination
    to the LORD,
But His secret counsel *is* with the upright.
33 The curse of the LORD *is* on the house of
    the wicked,
But He blesses the home of the just.
34 Surely He scorns the scornful,
But gives grace to the humble.
35 The wise shall inherit glory,
But shame shall be the legacy of fools.

4 Hear,* *my* children, the instruction of a
    father,
And give attention to know understanding;
2 For I give you good doctrine:
Do not forsake my law.
3 When I was my father's son,
Tender and the only one in the sight of my
    mother,
4 He also taught me, and said to me:
"Let your heart retain my words;
Keep my commands, and live.
5 Get wisdom! Get understanding!
Do not forget, nor turn away from the words
    of my mouth.
6 Do not forsake her, and she will preserve
    you;
Love her, and she will keep you.
7 Wisdom *is* the principal thing;
Therefore get wisdom.
And in all your getting, get understanding.
8 Exalt her, and she will promote you;
She will bring you honor, when you
    embrace her.
9 She will place on your head an ornament
    of grace;
A crown of glory she will deliver to you."

10 Hear, my son, and receive my sayings,
And the years of your life will be many.
11 I have taught you in the way of wisdom;
I have led you in right paths.
12 When you walk, your steps will not be
    hindered,
And when you run, you will not stumble.
13 Take firm hold of instruction, do not let go;
Keep her, for she *is* your life.

14 Do not enter the path of the wicked,
And do not walk in the way of evil.
15 Avoid it, do not travel on it;
Turn away from it and pass on.

CHAPTER 4

4:1ff The wise person encourages others
to hear the Word and find wisdom. The
father received wisdom when he was a boy,
and he admonished his children to do the
same. Live today so that your counsel and
example will influence others and help them
live wisely.

When you have wisdom, you have
protection (v. 6) and promotion (vv. 8–9) and
you will have the freedom to make progress
(v. 12). As you obey His Word, the light will
get brighter on the path of life (v. 18). But
this is not true if you are on the path of the
wicked.

Again, Solomon emphasized having your
whole person controlled by God's Word
(vv. 20–27; Col. 3:16). This will guide you
on the right path and keep you from detours.

Samson on the Wrong Path—Samson was a gifted man who ignored many of the instructions
given in Proverbs 1—4. Read Judges 13—16 and note that he did not seek God's wisdom but went
his own rebellious way. He took his eyes off the right path and ended up on the path of darkness
and death. He chose the wrong friends and followed folly instead of wisdom. Had he allowed the
Word to control his whole person, Samson would have brought blessing to himself and glory to
God.

16 For they do not sleep unless they have done evil;
And their sleep is taken away unless they make *someone* fall.

17 For they eat the bread of wickedness,
And drink the wine of violence.

18 But the path of the just *is* like the shining sun,*ƒ*
That shines ever brighter unto the perfect day.

19 The way of the wicked *is* like darkness;
They do not know what makes them stumble.

20 My son, give attention to my words;
Incline your ear to my sayings.

21 Do not let them depart from your eyes;
Keep them in the midst of your heart;

22 For they *are* life to those who find them,
And health to all their flesh.

23 Keep your heart with all diligence,
For out of it *spring* the issues of life.

24 Put away from you a deceitful mouth,
And put perverse lips far from you.

25 Let your eyes look straight ahead,
And your eyelids look right before you.

26 Ponder the path of your feet,
And let all your ways be established.

27 Do not turn to the right or the left;
Remove your foot from evil.

CHAPTER 5

5:1ff In a world that has commercialized sex and turned adultery into entertainment, this warning is desperately needed. Few people believe that there are tragic consequences to sexual sin, but Solomon names some of them.

What begins as something "sweet" gradually turns into something bitter; what is "life" becomes death; and the end is hell (vv. 4–5). You lose honor, years of life, wealth, and joy (vv. 7–14), and what you think is freedom is really the worst kind of bondage (vv. 21–23). The physical consequences alone ought to make a person want to obey God (v. 11).

Sex in marriage should be like drinking refreshing water from a clean fountain, while illicit sex is like drinking at a sewer (vv. 15–20). The Hebrew word translated "enraptured" in verse 19 means "intoxicated." When husband and wife love each other as God wants them to, the water turns into wine! (See John 2:1–11.)

5

1 My* son, pay attention to my wisdom;
Lend your ear to my understanding,

2 That you may preserve discretion,
And your lips may keep knowledge.

3 For the lips of an immoral woman drip honey,
And her mouth *is* smoother than oil;

4 But in the end she is bitter as wormwood,
Sharp as a two-edged sword.

5 Her feet go down to death,
Her steps lay hold of hell.*g*

6 Lest you ponder *her* path of life—
Her ways are unstable;
You do not know *them*.

7 Therefore hear me now, *my* children,
And do not depart from the words of my mouth.

8 Remove your way far from her,
And do not go near the door of her house,

9 Lest you give your honor to others,
And your years to the cruel *one;*

10 Lest aliens be filled with your wealth,
And your labors *go* to the house of a foreigner;

11 And you mourn at last,
When your flesh and your body are consumed,

12 And say:
"How I have hated instruction,
And my heart despised correction!

4:18 *ƒ*Literally *light*   5:5 *g*Or *Sheol*

Sexual Sin—Sexual immorality is like walking a path that leads to death (Prov. 2:16–22) and hell (Prov. 5:5); like deliberately burning and wounding yourself (Prov. 6:20–35); like being slaughtered as an animal (Prov. 7:6–27); like closing your eyes and falling into a pit (Prov. 22:14; 23:26–28). Ponder Hebrews 13:4.

13 I have not obeyed the voice of my teachers,
    Nor inclined my ear to those who instructed
        me!
14 I was on the verge of total ruin,
    In the midst of the assembly and
        congregation.''

15 Drink water from your own cistern,
    And running water from your own well.
16 Should your fountains be dispersed abroad,
    Streams of water in the streets?
17 Let them be only your own,
    And not for strangers with you.
18 Let your fountain be blessed,
    And rejoice with the wife of your youth.
19 As a loving deer and a graceful doe,
    Let her breasts satisfy you at all times;
    And always be enraptured with her love.
20 For why should you, my son, be enraptured
        by an immoral woman,
    And be embraced in the arms of a
        seductress?

21 For the ways of man are before the eyes of
        the LORD,
    And He ponders all his paths.
22 His own iniquities entrap the wicked man,
    And he is caught in the cords of his sin.
23 He shall die for lack of instruction,
    And in the greatness of his folly he shall
        go astray.

6 My* son, if you become surety for your
        friend,
    If you have shaken hands in pledge for a
        stranger,
2   You are snared by the words of your mouth;
    You are taken by the words of your mouth.
3   So do this, my son, and deliver yourself;
    For you have come into the hand of your
        friend:
    Go and humble yourself;
    Plead with your friend.
4   Give no sleep to your eyes,
    Nor slumber to your eyelids.
5   Deliver yourself like a gazelle from the hand
        of the hunter,
    And like a bird from the hand of the fowler.ʰ

6   *Go to the ant, you sluggard!
    Consider her ways and be wise,
7   Which, having no captain,
    Overseer or ruler,
8   Provides her supplies in the summer,
    And gathers her food in the harvest.
9   How long will you slumber, O sluggard?
    When will you rise from your sleep?
10 A little sleep, a little slumber,
    A little folding of the hands to sleep—
11 So shall your poverty come on you like a
        prowler,
    And your need like an armed man.

CHAPTER 6

6:1–5 Deliver yourself. Wicked works will
ensnare you (Prov. 5:22), but so will reckless
words. You must be careful when you make
promises. If you do not learn to say no, you
will end up in bondage, and the price will
be very high. Better to humble yourself and
get free than to let your pride ruin you.

6:6–11 Teach yourself. Learn from the
world of nature (Prov. 30:15–31). The ant
makes good use of opportunities to prepare
for the future, but the sluggard is aimless
and lazy and ends up in poverty. The
preacher who used this text was correct
when he titled his sermon "Rock-A-Bye,
Lullaby, Bye-Bye."

6:5 ʰThat is, one who catches birds in a trap or snare

The Sluggard—The sluggard likes to sleep (Prov. 6:6–11; 24:30–34) and expects everybody else
to serve him (Prov. 12:27; 19:24). He dreams of wealth but ends up poor (Prov. 13:4; 21:25–26).
He is good at excuses (Prov. 20:4; 22:13; 26:13–16) but poor at performance (Prov. 10:26). He is
not a builder but a destroyer (Prov. 18:9).

6:12–35 *Guard yourself.* Watch out for the wicked man (vv. 12–19) and the evil woman (vv. 20–35). Hate what God hates and love what God loves and you will enjoy what God enjoys.

12 *A worthless person, a wicked man,
   Walks with a perverse mouth;
13 He winks with his eyes,
   He shuffles his feet,
   He points with his fingers;
14 Perversity *is* in his heart,
   He devises evil continually,
   He sows discord.
15 Therefore his calamity shall come suddenly;
   Suddenly he shall be broken without
      remedy.

16 These six *things* the LORD hates,
   Yes, seven *are* an abomination to Him:
17 A proud look,
   A lying tongue,
   Hands that shed innocent blood,
18 A heart that devises wicked plans,
   Feet that are swift in running to evil,
19 A false witness *who* speaks lies,
   And one who sows discord among brethren.

20 My son, keep your father's command,
   And do not forsake the law of your mother.
21 Bind them continually upon your heart;
   Tie them around your neck.
22 When you roam, they† will lead you;
   When you sleep, they will keep you;
   And *when* you awake, they will speak with
      you.
23 For the commandment *is* a lamp,
   And the law a light;
   Reproofs of instruction *are* the way of life,
24 To keep you from the evil woman,
   From the flattering tongue of a seductress.
25 Do not lust after her beauty in your heart,
   Nor let her allure you with her eyelids.
26 For by means of a harlot
   A man is reduced to a crust of bread;
   And an adulteress† will prey upon his
      precious life.
27 Can a man take fire to his bosom,
   And his clothes not be burned?
28 Can one walk on hot coals,
   And his feet not be seared?
29 So *is* he who goes in to his neighbor's wife;
   Whoever touches her shall not be innocent.

30 *People* do not despise a thief
   If he steals to satisfy himself when he is
      starving.
31 Yet *when* he is found, he must restore
      sevenfold;
   He may have to give up all the substance
      of his house.
32 Whoever commits adultery with a woman
      lacks understanding;
   He *who* does so destroys his own soul.
33 Wounds and dishonor he will get,
   And his reproach will not be wiped away.
34 For jealousy *is* a husband's fury;
   Therefore he will not spare in the day of
      vengeance.
35 He will accept no recompense,
   Nor will he be appeased though you give
      many gifts.

6:22 †Literally *it*   6:26 †Literally *a man's wife,* that is, of another

7 My* son, keep my words,
And treasure my commands within you.
2 Keep my commands and live,
And my law as the apple of your eye.
3 Bind them on your fingers;
Write them on the tablet of your heart.
4 Say to wisdom, "You *are* my sister,"
And call understanding *your* nearest kin,
5 That they may keep you from the immoral
woman,
From the seductress *who* flatters with her
words.

6 For at the window of my house
I looked through my lattice,
7 And saw among the simple,
I perceived among the youths,
A young man devoid of understanding,
8 Passing along the street near her corner;
And he took the path to her house
9 In the twilight, in the evening,
In the black and dark night.

10 And there a woman met him,
With the attire of a harlot, and a crafty
heart.
11 She *was* loud and rebellious,
Her feet would not stay at home.
12 At times *she was* outside, at times in the
open square,
Lurking at every corner.
13 So she caught him and kissed him;
With an impudent face she said to him:
14 "*I have* peace offerings with me;
Today I have paid my vows.
15 So I came out to meet you,
Diligently to seek your face,
And I have found you.
16 I have spread my bed with tapestry,
Colored coverings of Egyptian linen.
17 I have perfumed my bed
With myrrh, aloes, and cinnamon.
18 Come, let us take our fill of love until
morning;
Let us delight ourselves with love.
19 For my husband *is* not at home;
He has gone on a long journey;
20 He has taken a bag of money with him,
And will come home on the appointed day."

21 With her enticing speech she caused him
to yield,
With her flattering lips she seduced him.
22 Immediately he went after her, as an ox
goes to the slaughter,
Or as a fool to the correction of the stocks,^{k}
23 Till an arrow struck his liver.
As a bird hastens to the snare,
He did not know it *would cost* his life.

24 Now therefore, listen to me, *my* children;
Pay attention to the words of my mouth:
25 Do not let your heart turn aside to her ways,
Do not stray into her paths;
26 For she has cast down many wounded,
And all who were slain by her were strong
men.
27 Her house *is* the way to hell,^{l}
Descending to the chambers of death.

CHAPTER 7

7:1ff When wisdom is your sister, you will
not be seduced by the temptress (vv. 1–5;
Ps. 119:11). Your feet will not go near her
house. And if she should come after you,
your heart will see through all her
enticements and have no desire for her.

Expensive tapestries cannot cover the
ugliness of sin, and the most aromatic spices
cannot turn the stench of sin into fragrant
perfume (vv. 16–17). No matter what
temptation is offered you, look beyond the
externals and see it as it really is.

You are made in the image of God, but
sin drags you down to the level of a beast
(vv. 22–23) and eventually to the level of
Satan himself (v. 27)! Is it worth it?

7:22 ^{k}Septuagint, Syriac, and Targum read *as a dog to bonds;*
Vulgate reads *as a lamb . . . to bonds.*   7:27 ^{l}Or *Sheol*

CHAPTER 8

8:6 *Listen!* Wisdom's first call was from the crowded city square (1:20ff.), but now she is "where the paths meet" (v. 2). When you are confronted with truth, you are at a place of decision, and the decision you make will have inevitable consequences. Keep your ears open and listen to God's wisdom (vv. 6, 32, 34).

8:17 *Love!* Wisdom says, "I love those who love me." Love wisdom rather than wealth (vv. 10–11, 18–21), for wisdom enriches you for eternity. Verses 22–31 make you think of Jesus Christ, who is the Wisdom of God (1 Cor. 1:30; Col. 2:3). To love wisdom is to love Christ, and when you love Christ, you live for Him.

8 Does not wisdom cry out,
And understanding lift up her voice?
2 She takes her stand on the top of the high hill,
Beside the way, where the paths meet.
3 She cries out by the gates, at the entry of the city,
At the entrance of the doors:
4 "To you, O men, I call,
And my voice *is* to the sons of men.
5 O you simple ones, understand prudence,
And you fools, be of an understanding heart.
6 *Listen, for I will speak of excellent things,
And from the opening of my lips *will come* right things;
7 For my mouth will speak truth;
Wickedness *is* an abomination to my lips.
8 All the words of my mouth *are* with righteousness;
Nothing crooked or perverse *is* in them.
9 They *are* all plain to him who understands,
And right to those who find knowledge.
10 Receive my instruction, and not silver,
And knowledge rather than choice gold;
11 For wisdom *is* better than rubies,
And all the things one may desire cannot be compared with her.

12 "I, wisdom, dwell with prudence,
And find out knowledge *and* discretion.
13 The fear of the LORD *is* to hate evil;
Pride and arrogance and the evil way
And the perverse mouth I hate.
14 Counsel *is* mine, and sound wisdom;
I *am* understanding, I have strength.
15 By me kings reign,
And rulers decree justice.
16 By me princes rule, and nobles,
All the judges of the earth.*m*
17 *I love those who love me,
And those who seek me diligently will find me.
18 Riches and honor *are* with me,
Enduring riches and righteousness.
19 My fruit *is* better than gold, yes, than fine gold,
And my revenue than choice silver.
20 I traverse the way of righteousness,
In the midst of the paths of justice,
21 That I may cause those who love me to inherit wealth,
That I may fill their treasuries.

22 "The LORD possessed me at the beginning of His way,
Before His works of old.
23 I have been established from everlasting,
From the beginning, before there was ever an earth.
24 When *there were* no depths I was brought forth,
When *there were* no fountains abounding with water.
25 Before the mountains were settled,
Before the hills, I was brought forth;
26 While as yet He had not made the earth or the fields,

8:16 *m*Masoretic Text, Syriac, Targum, and Vulgate read *righteousness;* Septuagint, Bomberg, and some manuscripts and editions read *earth.*

Or the primal dust of the world.
27 When He prepared the heavens, I *was* there,
    When He drew a circle on the face of the
        deep,
28 When He established the clouds above,
    When He strengthened the fountains of the
        deep,
29 When He assigned to the sea its limit,
    So that the waters would not transgress His
        command,
    When He marked out the foundations of the
        earth,
30 Then I was beside Him *as* a master
        craftsman;[n]
    And I was daily *His* delight,
    Rejoicing always before Him,
31 Rejoicing in His inhabited world,
    And my delight *was* with the sons of men.

32 "Now therefore, listen to me, *my* children,
    For blessed *are those who* keep my ways.
33 Hear instruction and be wise,
    And do not disdain *it.*
34 *Blessed is the man who listens to me,
    Watching daily at my gates,
    Waiting at the posts of my doors.
35 For whoever finds me finds life,
    And obtains favor from the LORD;
36 But he who sins against me wrongs his own
        soul;
    All those who hate me love death."

9   Wisdom* has built her house,
    She has hewn out her seven pillars;
2   She has slaughtered her meat,
    She has mixed her wine,
    She has also furnished her table.
3   She has sent out her maidens,
    She cries out from the highest places of the
        city,
4   "Whoever *is* simple, let him turn in here!"
    As for him who lacks understanding, she
        says to him,
5   "Come, eat of my bread
    And drink of the wine I have mixed.
6   Forsake foolishness and live,
    And go in the way of understanding.

7   *"He who corrects a scoffer gets shame for
        himself,
    And he who rebukes a wicked *man only*
        harms himself.
8   Do not correct a scoffer, lest he hate you;
    Rebuke a wise *man,* and he will love you.
9   Give *instruction* to a wise *man,* and he will
        be still wiser;
    Teach a just *man,* and he will increase in
        learning.

10 *"The fear of the LORD *is* the beginning of
        wisdom,
    And the knowledge of the Holy One *is*
        understanding.

8:30 [n]A Jewish tradition reads *one brought up.*

8:34 *Linger!* Spend time daily at wisdom's door as you read God's Word and meditate on His truth. According to verse 14, God will give you counsel (what to do), wisdom (how to do it), understanding (why you do it), and strength (the ability to do it). Instead of serving as a slave, you will reign as a king (vv. 15–16).

CHAPTER 9

9:1–6, 13–18 *Come and dine!* You see two houses and hear two invitations. Wisdom offers you a banquet of bread, meat, and wine; folly offers you stolen bread and water. Wisdom promises you life, but if you eat at folly's table, you will die. Which house will you enter?

9:7–9 *Come and learn!* Scoffers know so much that nobody can teach them anything, but the wise learn from rebuke. You may not enjoy it when somebody reproves you, but it will do you good. (See Ps. 141:5.)

9:10–12 *Come and live!* Wisdom multiplies days (v. 11). Those who abuse their bodies with sin usually cut their lives short, but when you follow wisdom, you can add years to your life—and life to your years! God gives a fullness of experience to those who obey Him.

Rebuke—The way you respond to criticism and rebuke reveals the kind of person you are (Prov. 9:7–9). Scoffers will not listen to rebuke (Prov. 13:1) or love those who rebuke them (Prov. 15:12). The wise person knows that rebuke is evidence of love (Prov. 27:5) and will value it (Prov. 25:12) and gain understanding from it (Prov. 19:25). Ponder Proverbs 27:6.

11 For by me your days will be multiplied,
   And years of life will be added to you.
12 If you are wise, you are wise for yourself,
   And *if* you scoff, you will bear *it* alone."

13 A foolish woman is clamorous;
   She is simple, and knows nothing.
14 For she sits at the door of her house,
   On a seat *by* the highest places of the city,
15 To call to those who pass by,
   Who go straight on their way:
16 "Whoever *is* simple, let him turn in here";
   And *as for* him who lacks understanding,
      she says to him,
17 "Stolen water is sweet,
   And bread *eaten* in secret is pleasant."
18 But he does not know that the dead *are*
      there,
   That her guests *are* in the depths of hell.°

CHAPTER 10

10:1ff *Wise* and *righteous* are key words in this chapter, and they go together, for the wise practice righteousness and the righteous grow in wisdom.
The wise bring joy and not grief to their parents (v. 1). They will take advantage of God-given opportunities (v. 5) and will obey orders (v. 8). Wise people gather knowledge (v. 14) and share it with others (vv. 13, 21, 31). They also know when to be quiet (v. 19). They do not jest about sin (v. 23) but are serious about obeying the Lord.
The righteous have God's protection and provision (vv. 2–3, 24–25), and He blesses them in life (v. 6) and after death (v. 7). Their words give life (vv. 11, 20–21, 31–32), and their works prosper (v. 16). Their future is secure (v. 30) and joyful (v. 28).
If you are wise and righteous, those traits will be revealed by your words (vv. 6, 11, 14, 20–21, 31–32) as well as by your works.

10 The* proverbs of Solomon:

A wise son makes a glad father,
But a foolish son *is* the grief of his mother.

2 Treasures of wickedness profit nothing,
  But righteousness delivers from death.
3 The LORD will not allow the righteous soul
     to famish,
  But He casts away the desire of the wicked.

4 He who has a slack hand becomes poor,
  But the hand of the diligent makes rich.
5 He who gathers in summer *is* a wise son;
  He who sleeps in harvest *is* a son who
     causes shame.

6 Blessings *are* on the head of the righteous,
  But violence covers the mouth of the
     wicked.
7 The memory of the righteous *is* blessed,
  But the name of the wicked will rot.

8 The wise in heart will receive commands,
  But a prating fool will fall.

9 He who walks with integrity walks securely,
  But he who perverts his ways will become
     known.

10 He who winks with the eye causes trouble,
   But a prating fool will fall.

11 The mouth of the righteous *is* a well of life,
   But violence covers the mouth of the
      wicked.

12 Hatred stirs up strife,
   But love covers all sins.

13 Wisdom is found on the lips of him who has
      understanding,
   But a rod *is* for the back of him who is
      devoid of understanding.

9:18 °Or *Sheol*

The Tongue of the Righteous—The wise person's words are like silver (Prov. 10:20), a tree of life (Prov. 15:4), food (Prov. 10:21), refreshing water (Prov. 10:11; 18:4), and medicine (Prov. 12:18). They should be seasoned with salt (Col. 4:6) and must not become destructive (James 3:1–12).

14 Wise *people* store up knowledge,
    But the mouth of the foolish *is* near
        destruction.

15 The rich man's wealth *is* his strong city;
    The destruction of the poor *is* their poverty.

16 The labor of the righteous *leads* to life,
    The wages of the wicked to sin.

17 He who keeps instruction *is in* the way of
        life,
    But he who refuses correction goes astray.

18 Whoever hides hatred *has* lying lips,
    And whoever spreads slander *is* a fool.

19 In the multitude of words sin is not lacking,
    But he who restrains his lips *is* wise.
20 The tongue of the righteous *is* choice silver;
    The heart of the wicked *is worth* little.
21 The lips of the righteous feed many,
    But fools die for lack of wisdom.ᴾ

22 The blessing of the Lᴏʀᴅ makes *one* rich,
    And He adds no sorrow with it.

23 To do evil *is* like sport to a fool,
    But a man of understanding has wisdom.
24 The fear of the wicked will come upon
        him,
    And the desire of the righteous will be
        granted.
25 When the whirlwind passes by, the wicked
        is no *more*,
    But the righteous *has* an everlasting
        foundation.

26 As vinegar to the teeth and smoke to the
        eyes,
    So *is* the lazy *man* to those who send
        him.

27 The fear of the Lᴏʀᴅ prolongs days,
    But the years of the wicked will be
        shortened.
28 The hope of the righteous *will be* gladness,
    But the expectation of the wicked will
        perish.
29 The way of the Lᴏʀᴅ *is* strength for the
        upright,
    But destruction *will come* to the workers of
        iniquity.

30 The righteous will never be removed,
    But the wicked will not inhabit the earth.
31 The mouth of the righteous brings forth
        wisdom,
    But the perverse tongue will be cut out.
32 The lips of the righteous know what is
        acceptable,
    But the mouth of the wicked *what is*
        perverse.

11 Dishonest* scales *are* an abomination to the
        Lᴏʀᴅ,
    But a just weight *is* His delight.

2   When pride comes, then comes shame;
    But with the humble *is* wisdom.

CHAPTER 11
11:1ff The contrast is between the
righteous and the wicked. God delights in
the righteous (v. 20) and delivers them from
lust (v. 6), death (v. 4), trouble (v. 8), and
gossip (v. 9). God also delivers their families
(v. 21).
    God guides the upright in their integrity
(v. 3) because they desire what God desires
(v. 23). They sow righteousness (v. 18) and
flourish like a healthy tree (vv. 28, 30). The
upright are a blessing to others (vv. 10–11),
and they gain a sure reward (v. 18).
    Reread the chapter and discover what
happens to the wicked.

3 The integrity of the upright will guide them,
But the perversity of the unfaithful will
destroy them.
4 Riches do not profit in the day of wrath,
But righteousness delivers from death.
5 The righteousness of the blameless will
direct^q his way aright,
But the wicked will fall by his own
wickedness.
6 The righteousness of the upright will deliver
them,
But the unfaithful will be caught by *their*
lust.

7 When a wicked man dies, *his* expectation
will perish,
And the hope of the unjust perishes.
8 The righteous is delivered from trouble,
And it comes to the wicked instead.
9 The hypocrite with *his* mouth destroys his
neighbor,
But through knowledge the righteous will
be delivered.
10 When it goes well with the righteous, the
city rejoices;
And when the wicked perish, *there is*
jubilation.
11 By the blessing of the upright the city is
exalted,
But it is overthrown by the mouth of the
wicked.

12 He who is devoid of wisdom despises his
neighbor,
But a man of understanding holds his peace.

13 A talebearer reveals secrets,
But he who is of a faithful spirit conceals a
matter.

14 Where *there is* no counsel, the people fall;
But in the multitude of counselors *there is*
safety.

15 He who is surety for a stranger will suffer,
But one who hates being surety is secure.

16 A gracious woman retains honor,
But ruthless *men* retain riches.
17 The merciful man does good for his own
soul,
But *he who is* cruel troubles his own flesh.
18 The wicked *man* does deceptive work,
But he who sows righteousness *will have* a
sure reward.
19 As righteousness *leads* to life,
So he who pursues evil *pursues it* to his own
death.
20 Those who are of a perverse heart *are* an
abomination to the LORD,
But *the* blameless in their ways *are* His
delight.
21 *Though they join* forces,^r the wicked will not
go unpunished;
But the posterity of the righteous will be
delivered.

22 *As* a ring of gold in a swine's snout,
So is a lovely woman who lacks discretion.

11:5 ^qOr *make smooth* or *straight*   11:21 ^rLiterally *hand to
hand*

23 The desire of the righteous *is* only good,
    But the expectation of the wicked *is* wrath.

24 There is *one* who scatters, yet increases
        more;
    And there is *one* who withholds more than
        is right,
    But it *leads* to poverty.
25 The generous soul will be made rich,
    And he who waters will also be watered
        himself.
26 The people will curse him who withholds
        grain,
    But blessing *will be* on the head of him who
        sells *it.*

27 He who earnestly seeks good finds favor,
    But trouble will come to him who seeks *evil.*

28 He who trusts in his riches will fall,
    But the righteous will flourish like foliage.

29 He who troubles his own house will inherit
        the wind,
    And the fool *will be* servant to the wise of
        heart.

30 The fruit of the righteous *is a* tree of life,
    And he who wins souls *is* wise.

31 If the righteous will be recompensed on the
        earth,
    How much more the ungodly and the sinner.

12 Whoever* loves instruction loves
        knowledge,
    But he who hates correction *is* stupid.

2   A good *man* obtains favor from the LORD,
    But a man of wicked intentions He will
        condemn.

3   A man is not established by wickedness,
    But the root of the righteous cannot be
        moved.

4   An excellent⁵ wife *is* the crown of her
        husband,
    But she who causes shame *is* like rottenness
        in his bones.

5   The thoughts of the righteous *are* right,
    But the counsels of the wicked *are* deceitful.
6   The words of the wicked *are,* "Lie in wait
        for blood,"
    But the mouth of the upright will deliver
        them.

7   The wicked are overthrown and *are* no
        more,
    But the house of the righteous will stand.

CHAPTER 12

12:1ff God uses the mouth of the righteous
to bring deliverance (v. 6), but the mouth
of the wicked brings bondage (v. 13). Right
words must begin with right thoughts (v. 5)
and a love for learning (v. 1), and this is
where the ungodly person fails.

Right words bring good to others (Prov.
10:21) and also to those who speak them
(v. 14; Prov. 13:2). With your words, you
can help to heal those who have been hurt
(v. 18) and who have suffered because of
lies (vv. 19–22). You can bring joy to those
who are depressed and worried (v. 25).

Be alert today for God-given opportunities
to speak healing words to hurting people.

12:4 ⁵Literally *A wife of valor*

Liars—Because He is a God of truth, the Lord hates a lying tongue (Prov. 6:17; 12:22). With lies,
people cover their true feelings (Prov. 10:18) and promote hypocrisy (Prov. 26:23–26). Liars do not
last (Prov. 12:19), but lies can go on for years and do great damage. Wealth gained by lies is
fleeting (Prov. 21:6), and all liars will one day be punished (Prov. 19:5, 9). If God hates lies, we
must hate them, too (Prov. 13:5). Ponder Ephesians 4:17–32.

8 A man will be commended according to his
    wisdom,
But he who is of a perverse heart will be
    despised.

9 Better *is the one* who is slighted but has a
    servant,
Than he who honors himself but lacks
    bread.

10 A righteous *man* regards the life of his
    animal,
But the tender mercies of the wicked *are*
    cruel.

11 He who tills his land will be satisfied with
    bread,
But he who follows frivolity *is* devoid of
    understanding.[t]

12 The wicked covet the catch of evil *men,*
But the root of the righteous yields *fruit.*
13 The wicked is ensnared by the transgression
    of *his* lips,
But the righteous will come through trouble.
14 A man will be satisfied with good by the
    fruit of *his* mouth,
And the recompense of a man's hands will
    be rendered to him.

15 The way of a fool *is* right in his own eyes,
But he who heeds counsel *is* wise.
16 A fool's wrath is known at once,
But a prudent *man* covers shame.

17 He *who* speaks truth declares
    righteousness,
But a false witness, deceit.
18 There is one who speaks like the piercings
    of a sword,
But the tongue of the wise *promotes* health.
19 The truthful lip shall be established forever,
But a lying tongue *is* but for a moment.
20 Deceit is in the heart of those who devise
    evil,
But counselors of peace have joy.
21 No grave trouble will overtake the
    righteous,
But the wicked shall be filled with evil.
22 Lying lips *are* an abomination to the
    LORD,
But those who deal truthfully *are* His
    delight.

23 A prudent man conceals knowledge,
But the heart of fools proclaims foolishness.

24 The hand of the diligent will rule,
But the lazy *man* will be put to forced
    labor.

25 Anxiety in the heart of man causes
    depression,
But a good word makes it glad.

26 The righteous should choose his friends
    carefully,
For the way of the wicked leads them astray.

12:11 [t]Literally *heart*

27 The lazy *man* does not roast what he took
   in hunting,
   But diligence *is* man's precious possession.

28 In the way of righteousness *is* life,
   And in *its* pathway *there is* no death.

13 A* wise son *heeds* his father's instruction,
   But a scoffer does not listen to rebuke.

2 A man shall eat well by the fruit of *his*
   mouth,
   But the soul of the unfaithful feeds on
   violence.

3 He who guards his mouth preserves his life,
   But he who opens wide his lips shall have
   destruction.

4 The soul of a lazy *man* desires, and *has*
   nothing;
   But the soul of the diligent shall be made
   rich.

5 A righteous *man* hates lying,
   But a wicked *man* is loathsome and comes
   to shame.

6 Righteousness guards *him whose* way is
   blameless,
   But wickedness overthrows the sinner.

7 There is one who makes himself rich, yet
   has nothing;
   And one who makes himself poor, yet *has*
   great riches.

8 The ransom of a man's life *is* his riches,
   But the poor does not hear rebuke.

9 The light of the righteous rejoices,
   But the lamp of the wicked will be put
   out.

10 By pride comes nothing but strife,
   But with the well-advised *is* wisdom.

11 Wealth *gained by* dishonesty will be
   diminished,
   But he who gathers by labor will increase.

12 Hope deferred makes the heart sick,
   But *when* the desire comes, *it is* a tree of
   life.

13 He who despises the word will be destroyed,
   But he who fears the commandment will be
   rewarded.

14 The law of the wise *is* a fountain of life,
   To turn *one* away from the snares of
   death.

15 Good understanding gains favor,
   But the way of the unfaithful *is* hard.

16 Every prudent *man* acts with knowledge,
   But a fool lays open *his* folly.

CHAPTER 13

13:1ff This chapter gives some practical
counsel on how to be wise. First, listen to
rebuke and instruction (v. 1) and learn to
take advice (v. 10) and discipline (v. 24).
Walk with the wise (v. 20) and listen to their
conversation (v. 14), and you will become
more like them. As you meditate on the
Word of God, you walk with the wisest of
the wise, so do not neglect the Scriptures
(v. 13).

   The chapter also offers counsel
concerning wealth. Diligent people will work
and gain wealth (v. 4) and not get it
dishonestly (v. 11). Verse 7 cautions you
not to be rich in the things money can buy
while you ignore the things money cannot
buy. The rich are often poorer than the poor
when it comes to what really counts!

Discipline—"Spare the rod and spoil the child" is an old English proverb that was probably based
on a similar Latin proverb. The Bible's version is Proverbs 13:24. When parents discipline their children
in love, they follow the example of the Lord Himself (Prov. 3:11–12; Heb. 12:5–6; Rev. 3:19). The
purpose is improvement (Prov. 22:15), not the venting of anger, and their only desire must be the
welfare of the child (Prov. 19:18; 23:13–14; 29:15, 17).

17 A wicked messenger falls into trouble,
    But a faithful ambassador *brings* health.

18 Poverty and shame *will come* to him who
        disdains correction,
    But he who regards a rebuke will be
        honored.

19 A desire accomplished is sweet to the soul,
    But *it is* an abomination to fools to depart
        from evil.

20 He who walks with wise *men* will be wise,
    But the companion of fools will be
        destroyed.

21 Evil pursues sinners,
    But to the righteous, good shall be repaid.

22 A good *man* leaves an inheritance to his
        children's children,
    But the wealth of the sinner is stored up for
        the righteous.

23 Much food *is in* the fallow *ground* of the
        poor,
    And for lack of justice there is waste.ᵘ

24 He who spares his rod hates his son,
    But he who loves him disciplines him
        promptly.

25 The righteous eats to the satisfying of his
        soul,
    But the stomach of the wicked shall be in
        want.

CHAPTER 14

14:1ff Watch out for fools (v. 7)! Wisdom builds but folly destroys (v. 1), and the tent of the godly is stronger than the house of the wicked (v. 11). When you obey the Word of God, you build on a solid foundation (Matt. 7:21–27).

Watch out for fools! Their speech can tear you down (v. 7), for their words are like a rod that hurts (v. 3). You cannot trust what they say (v. 8); they mock at sin (v. 9); and they rage in their self-confidence (v. 16). Be sure to watch out for their temper (vv. 17, 29); it can get you and them into trouble.

When you fear the Lord, your walk will be marked by uprightness (vv. 2, 16), confidence (v. 26), and protection (v. 27). The fear of the Lord is better than the folly of fools.

14 The* wise woman builds her house,
    But the foolish pulls it down with her hands.

2   He who walks in his uprightness fears the
        LORD,
    But *he who is* perverse in his ways despises
        Him.

3   In the mouth of a fool *is* a rod of pride,
    But the lips of the wise will preserve them.

4   Where no oxen *are*, the trough *is* clean;
    But much increase *comes* by the strength
        of an ox.

5   A faithful witness does not lie,
    But a false witness will utter lies.

6   A scoffer seeks wisdom and does not *find
        it*,
    But knowledge *is* easy to him who
        understands.

7   Go from the presence of a foolish man,
    When you do not perceive *in him* the lips
        of knowledge.

8   The wisdom of the prudent *is* to understand
        his way,
    But the folly of fools *is* deceit.

9   Fools mock at sin,
    But among the upright *there is* favor.

13:23 ᵘLiterally *what is swept away*

10   The heart knows its own bitterness,
      And a stranger does not share its joy.

11   The house of the wicked will be overthrown,
      But the tent of the upright will flourish.

12   There is a way *that seems* right to a man,
      But its end *is* the way of death.

13   Even in laughter the heart may sorrow,
      And the end of mirth *may be* grief.

14   The backslider in heart will be filled with
         his own ways,
      But a good man *will be satisfied* from
         above.ᵛ

15   The simple believes every word,
      But the prudent considers well his steps.
16   A wise *man* fears and departs from evil,
      But a fool rages and is self-confident.
17   A quick-tempered *man* acts foolishly,
      And a man of wicked intentions is hated.
18   The simple inherit folly,
      But the prudent are crowned with
         knowledge.
19   The evil will bow before the good,
      And the wicked at the gates of the righteous.

20   The poor *man* is hated even by his own
         neighbor,
      But the rich *has* many friends.
21   He who despises his neighbor sins;
      But he who has mercy on the poor, happy
         is he.

22   Do they not go astray who devise evil?
      But mercy and truth *belong* to those who
         devise good.

23   In all labor there is profit,
      But idle chatterʷ *leads* only to poverty.

24   The crown of the wise is their riches,
      But the foolishness of fools *is* folly.

25   A true witness delivers souls,
      But a deceitful *witness* speaks lies.

26   In the fear of the LORD *there is* strong
         confidence,
      And His children will have a place of refuge.
27   The fear of the LORD *is* a fountain of life,
      To turn *one* away from the snares of death.

28   In a multitude of people *is* a king's honor,
      But in the lack of people *is* the downfall of
         a prince.

29   *He who is* slow to wrath has great
         understanding,
      But *he who is* impulsiveˣ exalts folly.

30   A sound heart *is* life to the body,
      But envy *is* rottenness to the bones.

31   He who oppresses the poor reproaches his
         Maker,

14:14 ᵛLiterally *from above himself*   14:23 ʷLiterally *talk of the
lips*   14:29 ˣLiterally *short of spirit*

But he who honors Him has mercy on the
needy.

32 The wicked is banished in his wickedness,
But the righteous has a refuge in his death.

33 Wisdom rests in the heart of him who has
understanding,
But *what is* in the heart of fools is made
known.

34 Righteousness exalts a nation,
But sin *is* a reproach to *any* people.

35 The king's favor *is* toward a wise servant,
But his wrath *is against* him who causes
shame.

CHAPTER 15

15:1ff When you open your mouth, you let
people know whether you are foolish or
wise. The wise share knowledge and are
like fruitful trees that feed many (v. 4). Fools
pour out words that accomplish nothing
(v. 2).

The wise know how to control anger
(v. 18) and respond to anger (v. 1). The "soft
answer" is neither deception nor flattery, but
saying the right thing (v. 28) at the right time
(v. 23) in the right spirit (v. 1).

What comes out of the mouth begins in
the heart (Matt. 12:35), so maintain a joyful
heart before the Lord (vv. 13, 15) and fill
your heart with His truth (v. 14). God sees
your heart; do not try to hide anything from
Him (v. 11).

Most of all, ask God for help in saying
the right thing (vv. 8, 29). David's prayer in
Psalm 141:3–4 is a good place to start.

15 A* soft answer turns away wrath,
But a harsh word stirs up anger.

2 The tongue of the wise uses knowledge
rightly,
But the mouth of fools pours forth
foolishness.

3 The eyes of the LORD *are* in every place,
Keeping watch on the evil and the good.

4 A wholesome tongue *is* a tree of life,
But perverseness in it breaks the spirit.

5 A fool despises his father's instruction,
But he who receives correction is prudent.

6 *In* the house of the righteous *there is* much
treasure,
But in the revenue of the wicked is trouble.

7 The lips of the wise disperse knowledge,
But the heart of the fool *does* not *do* so.

8 The sacrifice of the wicked *is* an
abomination to the LORD,
But the prayer of the upright *is* His delight.

9 The way of the wicked *is* an abomination
to the LORD,
But He loves him who follows
righteousness.

10 Harsh discipline *is* for him who forsakes the
way,
And he who hates correction will die.

11 Hell[y] and Destruction[z] *are* before the LORD;
So how much more the hearts of the sons
of men.

12 A scoffer does not love one who corrects
him,
Nor will he go to the wise.

13 A merry heart makes a cheerful
countenance,
But by sorrow of the heart the spirit is
broken.

14 The heart of him who has understanding
seeks knowledge,
But the mouth of fools feeds on foolishness.

15:11 [y]Or *Sheol* [z]Hebrew *Abaddon*

15 All the days of the afflicted *are* evil,
But he who is of a merry heart *has* a
continual feast.

16 Better *is* a little with the fear of the LORD,
Than great treasure with trouble.

17 Better *is* a dinner of herbs^a where love is,
Than a fatted calf with hatred.

18 A wrathful man stirs up strife,
But *he who is* slow to anger allays
contention.

19 The way of the lazy *man is* like a hedge of
thorns,
But the way of the upright *is* a highway.

20 A wise son makes a father glad,
But a foolish man despises his mother.

21 Folly *is* joy *to him who is* destitute of
discernment,
But a man of understanding walks
uprightly.

22 Without counsel, plans go awry,
But in the multitude of counselors they are
established.

23 A man has joy by the answer of his mouth,
And a word *spoken* in due season, how good
it is!

24 The way of life *winds* upward for the
wise,
That he may turn away from hell^b below.

25 The LORD will destroy the house of the
proud,
But He will establish the boundary of the
widow.

26 The thoughts of the wicked *are* an
abomination to the LORD,
But *the words* of the pure *are* pleasant.

27 He who is greedy for gain troubles his own
house,
But he who hates bribes will live.

28 The heart of the righteous studies how to
answer,
But the mouth of the wicked pours forth
evil.

29 The LORD *is* far from the wicked,
But He hears the prayer of the righteous.

30 The light of the eyes rejoices the heart,
And a good report makes the bones
healthy.^c

31 The ear that hears the rebukes of life
Will abide among the wise.

32 He who disdains instruction despises his
own soul,
But he who heeds rebuke gets
understanding.

15:17 ^a Or *vegetables*   15:24 ^b Or *Sheol*   15:30 ^c Literally *fat*

33 The fear of the Lord *is* the instruction of
wisdom,
And before honor *is* humility.

16 The* preparations of the heart *belong* to
man,
But the answer of the tongue *is* from the
Lord.

2 All the ways of a man *are* pure in his own
eyes,
But the Lord weighs the spirits.

3 Commit your works to the Lord,
And your thoughts will be established.

4 The Lord has made all for Himself,
Yes, even the wicked for the day of doom.

5 *Everyone proud in heart *is* an abomination
to the Lord;
Though they join forces,[d] none will go
unpunished.

6 In mercy and truth
Atonement is provided for iniquity;
And by the fear of the Lord *one* departs
from evil.

7 *When a man's ways please the Lord,
He makes even his enemies to be at peace
with him.

8 Better *is* a little with righteousness,
Than vast revenues without justice.

9 A man's heart plans his way,
But the Lord directs his steps.

10 Divination *is* on the lips of the king;
His mouth must not transgress in judgment.
11 Honest weights and scales *are* the Lord's;
All the weights in the bag *are* His work.
12 *It is* an abomination for kings to commit
wickedness,
For a throne is established by righteousness.
13 Righteous lips *are* the delight of kings,
And they love him who speaks *what is*
right.
14 As messengers of death *is* the king's
wrath,
But a wise man will appease it.
15 In the light of the king's face *is* life,
And his favor *is* like a cloud of the latter
rain.

16 How much better to get wisdom than gold!
And to get understanding is to be chosen
rather than silver.

17 The highway of the upright *is* to depart from
evil;
He who keeps his way preserves his soul.

18 Pride *goes* before destruction,
And a haughty spirit before a fall.
19 Better *to be* of a humble spirit with the
lowly,
Than to divide the spoil with the proud.

16:1–3, 23 *A prepared heart* is a heart that receives God's truth and submits to God's will. Since the mouth speaks what the heart has treasured up, the Lord can guide your words when your heart is prepared (Matt. 10:19–20).

16:5, 18, 19 *A proud heart*. Pride is one sin that God especially hates. It leads to all kinds of trouble and robs you of the blessing of the Lord.

16:7, 9, 25 *A purposeful heart*. If your heart is not devoted to God's purposes, then it will lead you astray. Take time to think and pray, meditate on the Word, and make your plans; and then trust the Lord to guide you.

16:5 [d]Literally *hand to hand*

20 *He who heeds the word wisely will find
     good,
     And whoever trusts in the LORD, happy *is*
     he.

21 The wise in heart will be called prudent,
     And sweetness of the lips increases
     learning.

22 Understanding *is* a wellspring of life to him
     who has it.
     But the correction of fools *is* folly.

23 The heart of the wise teaches his mouth,
     And adds learning to his lips.

24 Pleasant words *are like* a honeycomb,
     Sweetness to the soul and health to the
     bones.

25 There is a way *that seems* right to a
     man,
     But its end *is* the way of death.

26 The person who labors, labors for himself,
     For his *hungry* mouth drives him *on.*

27 *An ungodly man digs up evil,
     And *it is* on his lips like a burning fire.

28 A perverse man sows strife,
     And a whisperer separates the best of
     friends.

29 A violent man entices his neighbor,
     And leads him in a way *that is* not good.

30 He winks his eye to devise perverse
     things;
     He purses his lips *and* brings about evil.

31 The silver-haired head *is* a crown of glory,
     If it is found in the way of righteousness.

32 *He who is* slow to anger *is* better than the
     mighty,
     And he who rules his spirit than he who
     takes a city.

33 The lot is cast into the lap,
     But its every decision *is* from the LORD.

17 Better *is* a dry morsel with quietness,
     Than a house full of feasting*e* *with* strife.

2   A wise servant will rule over a son who
     causes shame,
     And will share an inheritance among the
     brothers.

3   The refining pot *is* for silver and the furnace
     for gold,
     But the LORD tests the hearts.

4 *An evildoer gives heed to false lips;
     A liar listens eagerly to a spiteful tongue.

5 *He who mocks the poor reproaches his
     Maker;
     He who is glad at calamity will not go
     unpunished.

16:20–24 *A prudent heart.* When wisdom
is your food and drink, then you will be able
to make prudent decisions. A prudent heart
is revealed by lips that speak sweet words
of wisdom.

16:27–30 *A perverse heart.* What is in the
heart eventually comes out in the life, and
the life described here is anything but
beautiful or useful. No wonder Proverbs 4:23
is in God's Word! Are you heeding it?

CHAPTER 17

17:4 Use this chapter as the basis for a
spiritual inventory. God has many ways of
testing your heart (v. 3).
   What do you listen to? Your ears will
hear what your heart loves, so guard your
inner affections.

17:5 *What do you rejoice in?* Are you glad
when others suffer? Do you use the plight
of others to promote yourself?

17:1 *e*Or *sacrificial meals*

17:9 *What do you talk about?* Do morsels of gossip bring delight to your heart, and do you enjoy sharing them with others? The best thing is to cover sin and let God deal with it.

17:10, 13, 14 *What do you get angry at?* Do you accept criticism or respond with anger? Do you think of ways to retaliate, or do you try to stop disagreements at the beginning?

17:23 *What do you give in to?* "Every man has his price," claims the world, but it must not be true of believers. Is your conscience for sale?

6 Children's children *are* the crown of old men,
And the glory of children *is* their father.

7 Excellent speech is not becoming to a fool,
Much less lying lips to a prince.

8 A present *is* a precious stone in the eyes of its possessor;
Wherever he turns, he prospers.

9 *He who covers a transgression seeks love,
But he who repeats a matter separates friends.

10 *Rebuke is more effective for a wise *man*
Than a hundred blows on a fool.

11 An evil *man* seeks only rebellion;
Therefore a cruel messenger will be sent against him.

12 Let a man meet a bear robbed of her cubs,
Rather than a fool in his folly.

13 Whoever rewards evil for good,
Evil will not depart from his house.

14 The beginning of strife *is like* releasing water;
Therefore stop contention before a quarrel starts.

15 He who justifies the wicked, and he who condemns the just,
Both of them alike *are* an abomination to the LORD.

16 Why *is there* in the hand of a fool the purchase price of wisdom,
Since *he has* no heart *for it?*

17 A friend loves at all times,
And a brother is born for adversity.

18 A man devoid of understanding shakes hands in a pledge,
And becomes surety for his friend.

19 He who loves transgression loves strife,
And he who exalts his gate seeks destruction.

20 He who has a deceitful heart finds no good,
And he who has a perverse tongue falls into evil.

21 He who begets a scoffer *does so* to his sorrow,
And the father of a fool has no joy.

22 A merry heart does good, *like* medicine,[f]
But a broken spirit dries the bones.

23 *A wicked *man* accepts a bribe behind the back[g]
To pervert the ways of justice.

17:22 [f]Or *makes medicine even better*   17:23 [g]Literally *from the bosom*

24 Wisdom *is* in the sight of him who has
      understanding,
    But the eyes of a fool *are* on the ends of
      the earth.

25 A foolish son *is* a grief to his father,
    And bitterness to her who bore him.

26 Also, to punish the righteous *is* not good,
    Nor to strike princes for *their* uprightness.

27 He who has knowledge spares his words,
    And a man of understanding is of a calm
      spirit.
28 Even a fool is counted wise when he holds
      his peace;
    When he shuts his lips, *he is considered*
      perceptive.

18 A* man who isolates himself seeks his own
      desire;
    He rages against all wise judgment.

2   A fool has no delight in understanding,
    But in expressing his own heart.

3   When the wicked comes, contempt comes
      also;
    And with dishonor *comes* reproach.

4   The words of a man's mouth *are* deep
      waters;
    The wellspring of wisdom *is* a flowing
      brook.

5   *It is* not good to show partiality to the
      wicked,
    Or to overthrow the righteous in judgment.

6   A fool's lips enter into contention,
    And his mouth calls for blows.
7   A fool's mouth *is* his destruction,
    And his lips *are* the snare of his soul.
8   The words of a talebearer *are* like tasty
      trifles,*h*
    And they go down into the inmost body.

9   He who is slothful in his work
    Is a brother to him who is a great destroyer.

10 The name of the LORD *is* a strong tower;
    The righteous run to it and are safe.
11 The rich man's wealth *is* his strong city,
    And like a high wall in his own esteem.

12 Before destruction the heart of a man is
      haughty,
    And before honor *is* humility.

18:8 *h*A Jewish tradition reads *wounds.*

CHAPTER 18

18:1ff *Friends.* Friendship has its risks
(v. 19), but the isolated person is not wise
(v. 1). We belong to each other, and we need
each other (v. 14). We may have many
acquaintances, but we have few real friends.
The person with too many friends may end
up in trouble (v. 24 margin). Be a true friend
and God will give you true friends who will
stick close to you throughout life.

Fools. Fools do not make good friends
for many reasons. For one thing, they like
to talk so much that they do not hear what
others say (v. 2). Their foolish words cause
fights (vv. 6–7) and inward pain (v. 8). Their
impatience to speak makes them jump to
conclusions (vv. 13, 17), and that creates
problems (v. 5). The only hope for fools is
that they will stop talking and start to listen
to wisdom (v. 15).

❝*No one can develop freely in this
world and find a full life without
feeling understood by at least one
person.*❞

—Paul Tournier

True Friends—A real friend can be trusted (Prov. 11:13; 17:9) and will stay with you when you
are in trouble (Prov. 17:17; 25:19). Friends love you too much to pamper you (Prov. 27:6, 17), and
their counsel helps you (Prov. 27:9). A real friend is good for generations (Prov. 27:10)! Some people
do not make good friends: those who tempt you to sin (Prov. 1:10ff.); gluttons (Prov. 28:7); drunkards
(Prov. 23:20–21); gossips (Prov. 20:19); the violent and angry (Prov. 16:29; 22:24–25); and flatterers
(Prov. 27:14). Your best friends are those who have Jesus Christ as their Friend and seek to be like
Him (John 15:12–15).

13 He who answers a matter before he hears
it,
It *is* folly and shame to him.

14 The spirit of a man will sustain him in
sickness,
But who can bear a broken spirit?

15 The heart of the prudent acquires
knowledge,
And the ear of the wise seeks knowledge.

16 A man's gift makes room for him,
And brings him before great men.

17 The first *one* to plead his cause *seems* right,
Until his neighbor comes and examines him.

18 Casting lots causes contentions to cease,
And keeps the mighty apart.

19 A brother offended *is harder to win* than a
strong city,
And contentions *are* like the bars of a castle.

20 A man's stomach shall be satisfied from the
fruit of his mouth;
From the produce of his lips he shall be
filled.

21 Death and life *are* in the power of the
tongue,
And those who love it will eat its fruit.

22 *He who* finds a wife finds a good *thing,*
And obtains favor from the LORD.

23 The poor *man* uses entreaties,
But the rich answers roughly.

24 A man *who has* friends must himself be
friendly,[i]
But there is a friend *who* sticks closer than
a brother.

CHAPTER 19

19:1 Rich and poor. It is better to be rich
in character and poor in wealth, especially
when that wealth is acquired by deception
(vv. 1, 22). If friendship is based on wealth,
it is not friendship at all (vv. 4, 6–7). True
friendship goes much deeper. Be careful
how you treat the poor because God is
concerned about them (v. 17).

19:3 Wise and foolish. Wise people submit
to the Lord and walk a straight way, but fools
argue with the Lord and twist their way
(v. 3). Wealth is no evidence of wisdom
(v. 10); in fact, a fool only wastes wealth.

19 Better* *is* the poor who walks in his integrity
Than *one who is* perverse in his lips, and
is a fool.

2 Also it is not good *for* a soul *to be* without
knowledge,
And he sins who hastens with *his* feet.

3 *The foolishness of a man twists his way,
And his heart frets against the LORD.

4 Wealth makes many friends,
But the poor is separated from his friend.

18:24 [i]Following Greek manuscripts, Syriac, Targum, and
Vulgate; Masoretic Text reads *may come to ruin.*

The Poor—Some people become poor because of having wrong values (Prov. 16:16), being lazy
(Prov. 10:4; 14:23), following sinful pleasures (Prov. 21:17; 23:21), refusing good counsel (Prov.
13:18), and not planning carefully (Prov. 21:5). But some are poor because they cannot help it.
They may be the victims of injustice (Prov. 22:22–23) or have such heavy debts they cannot succeed
(Prov. 22:7). You should show mercy to the poor (Prov. 14:21, 31; 19:17; 21:13), for the same Lord
made us all (Prov. 22:2).

5   A false witness will not go unpunished,
    And *he who* speaks lies will not escape.

6   Many entreat the favor of the nobility,
    And every man *is* a friend to one who gives
        gifts.
7   All the brothers of the poor hate him;
    How much more do his friends go far from
        him!
    He may pursue *them with* words, *yet* they
        abandon *him.*

8   He who gets wisdom loves his own soul;
    He who keeps understanding will find good.

9   A false witness will not go unpunished,
    And *he who* speaks lies shall perish.

10 Luxury is not fitting for a fool,
    Much less for a servant to rule over princes.

11 The discretion of a man makes him slow to
        anger,
    And his glory *is* to overlook a transgression.

12 The king's wrath *is* like the roaring of a lion,
    But his favor *is* like dew on the grass.

13 *A foolish son *is* the ruin of his father,
    And the contentions of a wife *are* a
        continual dripping.

14 Houses and riches *are* an inheritance from
        fathers,
    But a prudent wife *is* from the LORD.

15 Laziness casts *one* into a deep sleep,
    And an idle person will suffer hunger.

16 He who keeps the commandment keeps his
        soul,
    But he who is careless^j of his ways will die.

17 He who has pity on the poor lends to the
        LORD,
    And He will pay back what he has given.

18 Chasten your son while there is hope,
    And do not set your heart on his
        destruction.^k

19 *A man of* great wrath will suffer
        punishment;
    For if you rescue *him,* you will have to do
        it again.

20 Listen to counsel and receive instruction,
    That you may be wise in your latter days.

21 There are many plans in a man's heart,
    Nevertheless the LORD's counsel—that will
        stand.

22 What is desired in a man is kindness,
    And a poor man is better than a liar.

19:13 *Fathers and sons.* Every father wants wise sons who will use their inheritance wisely (vv. 13–14). Lazy sons only bring poverty (v. 15). The father who chastens his son will help him build character (v. 18), but the son who chases his father away will bring shame and reproach (v. 26). Sons who listen to their fathers (and their Father in heaven) will stay on the right path (v. 27). (This paragraph can also be applied to mothers and daughters.)

19:16 ^jLiterally *despises,* figurative of recklessness or carelessness   19:18 ^kLiterally *to put him to death;* a Jewish tradition reads *on his crying.*

23 The fear of the LORD *leads* to life,
   And *he who has it* will abide in satisfaction;
   He will not be visited with evil.

24 A lazy *man* buries his hand in the bowl,[l]
   And will not so much as bring it to his
      mouth again.

25 Strike a scoffer, and the simple will become
      wary;
   Rebuke one who has understanding, *and* he
      will discern knowledge.

26 He who mistreats *his* father *and* chases
      away *his* mother
   Is a son who causes shame and brings
      reproach.

27 Cease listening to instruction, my son,
   And you will stray from the words of
      knowledge.

28 A disreputable witness scorns justice,
   And the mouth of the wicked devours
      iniquity.

29 Judgments are prepared for scoffers,
   And beatings for the backs of fools.

CHAPTER 20

20:1ff If you are wise, you will consider the
consequences of your decisions and
actions. You will ask, "What about
afterward?"
The afterward of strong drink (v. 1) is not
pleasant, and the afterward of starting
trouble (v. 2) could be dangerous. Better to
stop the trouble at the beginning (v. 3).
Sleep is essential to good health, but the
afterward of too much sleep is poverty (vv.
4, 13). A crooked business deal may be
profitable financially, but you will not enjoy
the aftertaste (v. 17). You may enjoy getting
your inheritance now, but afterward it may
do you more harm than good (v. 21).
Remember what happened to the prodigal
son (Luke 15:11ff.).
Rash promises have an afterward of
regret (v. 25; Eccles. 5:1–7), but loving
discipline has an afterward of reform.
Ponder Hebrews 12:3–11, and especially
note v. 11.

20 Wine* *is* a mocker,
   Strong drink *is* a brawler,
   And whoever is led astray by it is not wise.

2 The wrath[m] of a king *is* like the roaring of
      a lion;
   Whoever provokes him to anger sins
      against his own life.

3 *It is* honorable for a man to stop striving,
   Since any fool can start a quarrel.

4 The lazy *man* will not plow because of
      winter;
   He will beg during harvest and *have*
      nothing.

5 Counsel in the heart of man *is like* deep
      water,
   But a man of understanding will draw it out.

6 Most men will proclaim each his own
      goodness,
   But who can find a faithful man?

7 The righteous *man* walks in his integrity;
   His children *are* blessed after him.

8 A king who sits on the throne of judgment
   Scatters all evil with his eyes.

19:24 *l*Septuagint and Syriac read *bosom;* Targum and
Vulgate read *armpit.*   20:2 *m*Literally *fear* or *terror* which is
produced by the king's wrath

Lazy People—The book of Proverbs has nothing good to say about laziness. Even the feeble
ants are more diligent than the sluggard (6:6–11)! It is shameful to sleep when there is work to do
(10:4–5; 24:30–34). One of these days, the lazy person will be forced to work (10:24) to get something
to eat (19:15). Lazy people can think up many excuses not to work (20:4; 22:13; 26:13–16), and
nothing anybody says will do them any good.

9 Who can say, "I have made my heart clean,
   I am pure from my sin"?

10 Diverse weights *and* diverse measures,
   They *are* both alike, an abomination to the
   LORD.

11 Even a child is known by his deeds,
   Whether what he does *is* pure and right.

12 The hearing ear and the seeing eye,
   The LORD has made them both.

13 Do not love sleep, lest you come to poverty;
   Open your eyes, *and* you will be satisfied
     with bread.

14 "*It is* good for nothing,"[n] cries the buyer;
   But when he has gone his way, then he
     boasts.

15 There is gold and a multitude of rubies,
   But the lips of knowledge *are* a precious
     jewel.

16 Take the garment of one who is surety *for*
     a stranger,
   And hold it as a pledge *when it* is for a
     seductress.

17 Bread gained by deceit *is* sweet to a man,
   But afterward his mouth will be filled with
     gravel.

18 Plans are established by counsel;
   By wise counsel wage war.

19 He who goes about *as* a talebearer reveals
     secrets;
   Therefore do not associate with one who
     flatters with his lips.

20 Whoever curses his father or his mother,
   His lamp will be put out in deep darkness.

21 An inheritance gained hastily at the
     beginning
   Will not be blessed at the end.

22 Do not say, "I will recompense evil";
   Wait for the LORD, and He will save you.

23 Diverse weights *are* an abomination to the
     LORD,
   And dishonest scales *are* not good.

24 A man's steps *are* of the LORD;
   How then can a man understand his own
     way?

25 *It is* a snare for a man to devote rashly
     something as holy,
   And afterward to reconsider *his* vows.

26 A wise king sifts out the wicked,
   And brings the threshing wheel over them.

27 The spirit of a man *is* the lamp of the LORD,
   Searching all the inner depths of his heart.[o]

20:14 [n]Literally *evil, evil*   20:27 [o]Literally *the rooms of the
belly*

28 Mercy and truth preserve the king,
And by lovingkindness he upholds his throne.

29 The glory of young men *is* their strength,
And the splendor of old men *is* their gray head.

30 Blows that hurt cleanse away evil,
As *do* stripes the inner depths of the heart.[p]

CHAPTER 21

21:1ff God can turn hearts (v. 1) and accomplish His purposes. He can also test hearts to see what we are really like (v. 2). He wants both righteousness and justice in our lives, not simply empty religious ceremonies (v. 3; 1 Sam. 15:22; Mark 12:38–44). Note the emphasis on justice (vv. 3, 7, and 15).

God sees the wicked—their pride (v. 4), violence (v. 7), evil desires (v. 10), false confidence (v. 12), sinful sacrifices (v. 27), and hardness of heart (v. 29)—and He will judge them in due time.

The wicked may try to outmaneuver God, but God will have His way (v. 30; Prov. 19:21). No matter what resources men may lean on, only God can give success (v. 31). Use whatever means God provides, but put your faith in God alone.

21

The* king's heart *is* in the hand of the LORD,
Like the rivers of water; He turns it wherever He wishes.

2 Every way of a man *is* right in his own eyes,
But the LORD weighs the hearts.

3 To do righteousness and justice
Is more acceptable to the LORD than sacrifice.

4 A haughty look, a proud heart,
And the plowing[q] of the wicked *are* sin.

5 The plans of the diligent *lead* surely to plenty,
But *those of* everyone *who is* hasty, surely to poverty.

6 Getting treasures by a lying tongue
Is the fleeting fantasy of those who seek death.[r]

7 The violence of the wicked will destroy them,[s]
Because they refuse to do justice.

8 The way of a guilty man *is* perverse;[t]
But *as for* the pure, his work *is* right.

9 Better to dwell in a corner of a housetop,
Than in a house shared with a contentious woman.

10 The soul of the wicked desires evil;
His neighbor finds no favor in his eyes.

11 When the scoffer is punished, the simple is made wise;
But when the wise is instructed, he receives knowledge.

12 The righteous *God* wisely considers the house of the wicked,
Overthrowing the wicked for *their* wickedness.

13 Whoever shuts his ears to the cry of the poor
Will also cry himself and not be heard.

14 A gift in secret pacifies anger,
And a bribe behind the back,[u] strong wrath.

20:30 [p]Literally *the rooms of the belly* 21:4 [q]Or *lamp* 21:6 [r]Septuagint reads *Pursue vanity on the snares of death;* Vulgate reads *Is vain and foolish, and shall stumble on the snares of death;* Targum reads *They shall be destroyed, and they shall fall who seek death.* 21:7 [s]Literally *drag them away* 21:8 [t]Or *The way of a man is perverse and strange* 21:14 [u]Literally *in the bosom*

15 *It is* a joy for the just to do justice,
But destruction *will come* to the workers of
iniquity.

16 A man who wanders from the way of
understanding
Will rest in the assembly of the dead.

17 He who loves pleasure *will be* a poor man;
He who loves wine and oil will not be rich.

18 The wicked *shall be* a ransom for the
righteous,
And the unfaithful for the upright.

19 Better to dwell in the wilderness,
Than with a contentious and angry woman.

20 *There is* desirable treasure,
And oil in the dwelling of the wise,
But a foolish man squanders it.

21 He who follows righteousness and mercy
Finds life, righteousness and honor.

22 A wise *man* scales the city of the mighty,
And brings down the trusted stronghold.

23 Whoever guards his mouth and tongue
Keeps his soul from troubles.

24 A proud *and* haughty *man*—"Scoffer" *is* his
name;
He acts with arrogant pride.

25 The desire of the lazy *man* kills him,
For his hands refuse to labor.

26 He covets greedily all day long,
But the righteous gives and does not spare.

27 The sacrifice of the wicked *is* an
abomination;
How much more *when* he brings it with
wicked intent!

28 A false witness shall perish,
But the man who hears *him* will speak
endlessly.

29 A wicked man hardens his face,
But *as for* the upright, he establishes^v his
way.

30 *There is* no wisdom or understanding
Or counsel against the LORD.

31 The horse *is* prepared for the day of battle,
But deliverance *is* of the LORD.

22 A* good name is to be chosen rather than
great riches,
Loving favor rather than silver and gold.

21:29 ^vQere and Septuagint read *understands.*

CHAPTER 22

22:1ff If you measure life by riches, you will
be disappointed. God made both the rich
and the poor (v. 2), and both are important
to Him. (See Luke 6:20–26; James 2:1–13.)

Major on character—a good name—and
not on great wealth (v. 1). Money can buy
fame but not a good name. If you are proud,
all you may get is money, but if you are
humble, God will give honor and life along
with the wealth He wants you to have
(v. 4).

Do not allow debt to put you into bondage
(v. 7) or the love of money to cause you to
oppress others (vv. 16, 22–23). If you give
gifts to the rich just to get their favor, you
will end up poor.

No matter how rich or poor you may be,
it is integrity that really counts. Even the
king, probably the richest person in the land,
pays attention to people of character
(vv. 11, 29). And do not forget the King of
kings before whom you will one day stand.

Properly View Wealth—The book of Proverbs issues a number of stern warnings about wealth.
Wealth cannot give you peace (15:16) or wisdom (16:16), but it can create pride (18:11, 23) and
trouble (15:6, 27) and friends who will not last (14:20). You should fear God (22:4) and share with
others what God gives to you (11:24–25; 19:17). Watch out when somebody promises to make you
rich in a hurry because those schemes backfire and leave you poor (20:21; 28:20, 22). The way to
gain wealth is through hard work (10:4, 22) and faithfulness to the Lord.

2 The rich and the poor have this in common,
   The LORD *is* the maker of them all.

3 A prudent *man* foresees evil and hides
      himself,
   But the simple pass on and are punished.

4 By humility *and* the fear of the LORD
   Are riches and honor and life.

5 Thorns *and* snares *are* in the way of the
      perverse;
   He who guards his soul will be far from
      them.

6 Train up a child in the way he should go,
   And when he is old he will not depart from
      it.

7 The rich rules over the poor,
   And the borrower *is* servant to the lender.

8 He who sows iniquity will reap sorrow,
   And the rod of his anger will fail.

9 He who has a generous eye will be blessed,
   For he gives of his bread to the poor.

10 Cast out the scoffer, and contention will
      leave;
   Yes, strife and reproach will cease.

11 He who loves purity of heart
   And has grace on his lips,
   The king *will be* his friend.

12 The eyes of the LORD preserve knowledge,
   But He overthrows the words of the
      faithless.

13 The lazy *man* says, "*There is* a lion outside!
   I shall be slain in the streets!"

14 The mouth of an immoral woman *is* a deep
      pit;
   He who is abhorred by the LORD will fall
      there.

15 Foolishness *is* bound up in the heart of a
      child;
   The rod of correction will drive it far from
      him.

16 He who oppresses the poor to increase his
      riches,
   And he who gives to the rich, *will* surely
      come to poverty.

17 Incline your ear and hear the words of the
      wise,
   And apply your heart to my knowledge;
18 For *it is* a pleasant thing if you keep them
      within you;
   Let them all be fixed upon your lips,
19 So that your trust may be in the LORD;
   I have instructed you today, even you.
20 Have I not written to you excellent things
   Of counsels and knowledge,
21 That I may make you know the certainty
      of the words of truth,
   That you may answer words of truth
   To those who send to you?

22 Do not rob the poor because he *is* poor,
   Nor oppress the afflicted at the gate;
23 For the LORD will plead their cause,
   And plunder the soul of those who plunder
      them.

24 Make no friendship with an angry man,
   And with a furious man do not go,
25 Lest you learn his ways
   And set a snare for your soul.

26 Do not be one of those who shakes hands
      in a pledge,
   One of those who is surety for debts;
27 If you have nothing *with which* to pay,
   Why should he take away your bed from
      under you?

28 Do not remove the ancient landmark
   Which your fathers have set.

29 Do you see a man *who* excels in his work?
   He will stand before kings;
   He will not stand before unknown *men*.

23 When* you sit down to eat with a ruler,
   Consider carefully what *is* before you;
2 And put a knife to your throat
   If you *are* a man given to appetite.
3 Do not desire his delicacies,
   For they *are* deceptive food.

4 Do not overwork to be rich;
   Because of your own understanding, cease!
5 Will you set your eyes on that which is not?
   For *riches* certainly make themselves wings;
   They fly away like an eagle *toward* heaven.

6 Do not eat the bread of a miser,ᵂ
   Nor desire his delicacies;
7 For as he thinks in his heart, so *is* he.
   "Eat and drink!" he says to you,
   But his heart is not with you.
8 The morsel you have eaten, you will vomit
      up,
   And waste your pleasant words.

9 *Do not speak in the hearing of a fool,
   For he will despise the wisdom of your
      words.

10 Do not remove the ancient landmark,
   Nor enter the fields of the fatherless;
11 For their Redeemer *is* mighty;
   He will plead their cause against you.

23:6 ᵂLiterally *one who has an evil eye*

CHAPTER 23

23:1–8 The repeated "do not" reminds you that there are some things God does not want His children to do.

Do not desire luxuries (vv. 1–3), even when the rich offer them to you. You may get an appetite for such things and start living to get rich (vv. 4–5). But riches fly away, while character remains for eternity. At the same time, do not get friendly with miserly people (vv. 6–8). No matter how much they offer you, their hearts are not with you. It is not the food on the table but the love in the heart that makes fellowship real and lasting.

23:9–11 Do not speak carelessly around fools (v. 9), for they will misunderstand and misquote you and get you into trouble. Do not change the boundaries that men and God have made (vv. 10–11; 22:28; Deut. 19:14). This is robbery and oppression, and God will judge it.

Respect the Truth—"Buy the truth, and do not sell it" is the advice of Proverbs 23:23. Lot sold the truth for a home in the city (Gen. 13:1–13), and Esau sold the truth for a mess of pottage (Gen. 25:29–34). King Saul sold the truth for the support of the people (1 Sam. 15:24–35). Judas sold the truth for thirty pieces of silver (Matt. 26:14–16), and Pilate sold the truth for the approval of the crowd (Mark 15:15). It is not worth it!

Beware Strong Drink!—The Bible does not demand total abstinence, but it does magnify it and warn against the sin of drunkenness. Strong drink is a mocker (Prov. 20:1): it promises one thing but gives another. Instead of wealth, it gives poverty (Prov. 21:17; 23:20–21); instead of pleasure, it gives misery (Prov. 23:29–35). For a short time, the drinker feels good, but then things start to change. Alcoholics can be saved and changed by the grace of God (1 Cor. 6:9–11). You must be careful not to cause others to stumble because of the things you do (Rom. 14:14–23).

23:13–18, 22 Do not fail to discipline your child (vv. 13–14), so that he or she might have wisdom and bring you joy (vv. 15–16). No matter what other families may do, do not envy sinners (vv. 17–18), but trust the Lord and obey Him. Set a good example by respecting your parents (v. 22).

23:19–21, 29–35 Do not mix with drunkards and gluttons lest you become like them (vv. 19–21). Do not even look at the wine (vv. 29–35) lest you end up embarrassed and bruised.

23:23 Do not sell the truth at any price! It costs something to live by the truth, but it costs even more to abandon the truth.

12 Apply your heart to instruction,
    And your ears to words of knowledge.

13 *Do not withhold correction from a child,
    For *if* you beat him with a rod, he will not
       die.
14 You shall beat him with a rod,
    And deliver his soul from hell.ˣ

15 My son, if your heart is wise,
    My heart will rejoice—indeed, I myself;
16 Yes, my inmost being will rejoice
    When your lips speak right things.

17 Do not let your heart envy sinners,
    But *be zealous* for the fear of the LORD all
       the day;
18 For surely there is a hereafter,
    And your hope will not be cut off.

19 *Hear, my son, and be wise;
    And guide your heart in the way.
20 Do not mix with winebibbers,
    Or with gluttonous eaters of meat;
21 For the drunkard and the glutton will come
       to poverty,
    And drowsiness will clothe *a man* with rags.

22 Listen to your father who begot you,
    And do not despise your mother when she
       is old.

23 *Buy the truth, and do not sell *it,*
    Also wisdom and instruction and
       understanding.

24 The father of the righteous will greatly
       rejoice,
    And he who begets a wise *child* will delight
       in him.
25 Let your father and your mother be glad,
    And let her who bore you rejoice.

26 My son, give me your heart,
    And let your eyes observe my ways.
27 For a harlot *is* a deep pit,
    And a seductress *is* a narrow well.
28 She also lies in wait as *for* a victim,
    And increases the unfaithful among men.

29 Who has woe?
    Who has sorrow?
    Who has contentions?
    Who has complaints?
    Who has wounds without cause?
    Who has redness of eyes?
30 Those who linger long at the wine,
    Those who go in search of mixed wine.
31 Do not look on the wine when it is red,
    When it sparkles in the cup,
    When it swirls around smoothly;
32 At the last it bites like a serpent,
    And stings like a viper.
33 Your eyes will see strange things,
    And your heart will utter perverse things.
34 Yes, you will be like one who lies down in
       the midst of the sea,
    Or like one who lies at the top of the mast,
       saying:

23:14 ˣOr *Sheol*

35 "They have struck me, *but* I was not hurt;
They have beaten me, but I did not feel *it*.
When shall I awake, that I may seek another
    drink?"

24 Do* not be envious of evil men,
Nor desire to be with them;
2 For their heart devises violence,
And their lips talk of troublemaking.

3 Through wisdom a house is built,
And by understanding it is established;
4 By knowledge the rooms are filled
With all precious and pleasant riches.

5 A wise man *is* strong,
Yes, a man of knowledge increases
    strength;
6 For by wise counsel you will wage your own
    war,
And in a multitude of counselors *there is*
    safety.

7 Wisdom *is* too lofty for a fool;
He does not open his mouth in the gate.

8 He who plots to do evil
Will be called a schemer.
9 The devising of foolishness *is* sin,
And the scoffer *is* an abomination to men.

10 *If* you faint in the day of adversity,
Your strength *is* small.

11 *Deliver *those who* are drawn toward death,
And hold back *those* stumbling to the
    slaughter.
12 If you say, "Surely we did not know this,"
Does not He who weighs the hearts consider
    it?
He who keeps your soul, does He *not* know
    it?
And will He *not* render to *each* man
    according to his deeds?

13 My son, eat honey because *it is* good,
And the honeycomb *which is* sweet to your
    taste;
14 So *shall* the knowledge of wisdom *be* to
    your soul;
If you have found *it*, there is a prospect,
And your hope will not be cut off.

15 Do not lie in wait, O wicked *man*, against
    the dwelling of the righteous;
Do not plunder his resting place;
16 For a righteous *man* may fall seven times
    And rise again,
But the wicked shall fall by calamity.

17 Do not rejoice when your enemy falls,
And do not let your heart be glad when he
    stumbles;

CHAPTER 24
24:1ff The wise person builds while others
tear down (vv. 1–4) and is strong for the
battles of life (vv. 5–6). There is no need to
faint (v. 10); and if you fall, you need not
stay down (vv. 15–16). (See Ps. 37:23–24.)

24:11ff The wise person seeks to deliver
people who have been unjustly condemned
(vv. 11–12). If you hide your head and fail
to help when you can, God will judge you
(James 4:17). At the same time, be careful
not to rejoice when an enemy falls (vv. 17–
18), fret when the wicked prosper (vv. 19–
20), or pay back those who may have hurt
you (vv. 28–29).

Honey—Honey was one of the sweetest things in the Jewish diet, and Solomon used it to teach
some important lessons. He warned about the sweet words of the harlot (Prov. 5:3) that would lead
only to bitterness. Studying may not be easy for you, but knowledge is like honey, so learn to enjoy
it (Prov. 24:13–14). When people praise you, they are feeding you honey (Prov. 25:27), so do not
eat too much of it! If you take too much, it will make you sick (Prov. 25:16), so learn to be satisfied
without it (Prov. 27:7). You cannot live on honey, and you cannot live on praise.

18 Lest the LORD see *it*, and it displease Him,
And He turn away His wrath from him.

19 Do not fret because of evildoers,
Nor be envious of the wicked;
20 For there will be no prospect for the evil
    man;
The lamp of the wicked will be put out.

21 My son, fear the LORD and the king;
Do not associate with those given to change;
22 For their calamity will rise suddenly,
And who knows the ruin those two can
    bring?

23 These *things* also *belong* to the wise:

It *is* not good to show partiality in judgment.
24 *He who says to the wicked, "You *are*
    righteous,"
Him the people will curse;
Nations will abhor him.
25 But those who rebuke *the wicked* will have
    delight,
And a good blessing will come upon them.

26 He who gives a right answer kisses the lips.

27 Prepare your outside work,
Make it fit for yourself in the field;
And afterward build your house.

28 Do not be a witness against your neighbor
    without cause,
For would you deceive^y with your lips?
29 Do not say, "I will do to him just as he has
    done to me;
I will render to the man according to his
    work."

30 I went by the field of the lazy *man,*
And by the vineyard of the man devoid of
    understanding;
31 And there it was, all overgrown with thorns;
Its surface was covered with nettles;
Its stone wall was broken down.
32 When I saw *it,* I considered *it* well;
I looked on *it and* received instruction:
33 A little sleep, a little slumber,
A little folding of the hands to rest;
34 So shall your poverty come *like* a prowler,
And your need like an armed man.

25 These also *are* proverbs of Solomon which
the men of Hezekiah king of Judah copied:

2 *It is* the glory of God to conceal a matter,
But the glory of kings *is* to search out a
    matter.

3 *As* the heavens for height and the earth for
    depth,
So the heart of kings *is* unsearchable.

24:28 ^ySeptuagint and Vulgate read *Do not deceive.*

24:27, 30–34 The wise person labors while there is opportunity (v. 27) and does not live for ease and pleasure (vv. 30–34; 6:6–11). Follow the example of your Master (John 9:4).

CHAPTER 25

25:2–7 *Leaders.* People in authority must know what is going on. God has the right to conceal things, but nobody should hide things from the leader. However, a wise leader knows how to keep his counsel (v. 3) and share his plans at the right time. The wise leader gets rid of evil associates and does what is right. Verses 6–7 remind us of our Lord's parable in Luke 14:7–8. Humility leads to honor, but self-promotion leads to shame.

Handling Disputes—The time to stop a dispute is when it begins (Prov. 17:14; 30:32–33). As much as possible, do not let arguments get started (Prov. 20:3). Some people contribute to peace (Prov. 12:20); others contribute to war (Prov. 22:10; 26:21); and there are some people that nobody can get along with (Prov. 29:9). God blesses the peacemakers (Matt. 5:9), so let God's wisdom direct you and use you to make peace (James 3:13–18).

4   Take away the dross from silver,
    And it will go to the silversmith *for* jewelry.
5   Take away the wicked from before the
        king,
    And his throne will be established in
        righteousness.

6   Do not exalt yourself in the presence of the
        king,
    And do not stand in the place of the great;
7   For *it is* better that he say to you,
    "Come up here,"
    Than that you should be put lower in the
        presence of the prince,
    Whom your eyes have seen.

8   *Do not go hastily to court;
    For what will you do in the end,
    When your neighbor has put you to shame?
9   Debate your case with your neighbor,
    And do not disclose the secret to another;
10 Lest he who hears *it* expose your shame,
    And your reputation be ruined.

11 A word fitly spoken *is like* apples of gold
    In settings of silver.
12 *Like* an earring of gold and an ornament
        of fine gold
    Is a wise rebuker to an obedient ear.

13 Like the cold of snow in time of harvest
    Is a faithful messenger to those who send
        him,
    For he refreshes the soul of his masters.

14 Whoever falsely boasts of giving
    Is like clouds and wind without rain.

15 By long forbearance a ruler is persuaded,
    And a gentle tongue breaks a bone.

16 Have you found honey?
    Eat only as much as you need,
    Lest you be filled with it and vomit.

17 Seldom set foot in your neighbor's house,
    Lest he become weary of you and hate
        you.

18 A man who bears false witness against his
        neighbor
    Is like a club, a sword, and a sharp arrow.

19 Confidence in an unfaithful *man* in time of
        trouble
    Is like a bad tooth and a foot out of joint.

20 *Like* one who takes away a garment in cold
        weather,
    And like vinegar on soda,
    Is one who sings songs to a heavy heart.

21 *If your enemy is hungry, give him bread to
        eat;
    And if he is thirsty, give him water to drink;
22 For *so* you will heap coals of fire on his
        head,
    And the Lord will reward you.

23 The north wind brings forth rain,
    And a backbiting tongue an angry
        countenance.

25:8–19 Neighbors. Keep problems between you and your neighbor and try to settle them out of court (Matt. 5:21–26). Let your words be appropriate (vv. 11–12) and helpful (v. 13), and keep your promises (v. 14). Do not be a neighborhood pest (v. 17) or troublemaker (v. 18). Be dependable (v. 19)!

25:21, 22 Enemies. Paul quoted these words in Romans 12:20, and Elisha practiced them (2 Kings 6:8–23) and so did Jesus and the early believers (Luke 22:49–51; Acts 7:59–60).

24 *It is* better to dwell in a corner of a housetop,
Than in a house shared with a contentious
woman.

25 *As* cold water to a weary soul,
So *is* good news from a far country.

26 A righteous *man* who falters before the
wicked
Is like a murky spring and a polluted well.

27 *It is* not good to eat much honey;
So to seek one's own glory *is not* glory.

28 Whoever *has* no rule over his own spirit
Is like a city broken down, without walls.

CHAPTER 26

26:1–12 Solomon names some people you should avoid, and the first is the *fool*. You cannot change him by promotion (vv. 1, 8), correction (v. 3), or admonition (vv. 4–5). If you answer a fool, do not stoop to his level of folly or you will make him think you have elevated him to wisdom. No matter how much you correct him, he goes right back into folly (v. 11; 2 Pet. 2:22).

26 As* snow in summer and rain in harvest,
So honor is not fitting for a fool.

2 Like a flitting sparrow, like a flying
swallow,
So a curse without cause shall not alight.

3 A whip for the horse,
A bridle for the donkey,
And a rod for the fool's back.

4 Do not answer a fool according to his folly,
Lest you also be like him.

5 Answer a fool according to his folly,
Lest he be wise in his own eyes.

6 He who sends a message by the hand of a
fool
Cuts off *his own* feet *and* drinks violence.

7 *Like* the legs of the lame that hang limp
Is a proverb in the mouth of fools.

8 Like one who binds a stone in a sling
Is he who gives honor to a fool.

9 *Like* a thorn *that* goes into the hand of a
drunkard
Is a proverb in the mouth of fools.

10 The great *God* who formed everything
Gives the fool *his* hire and the transgressor
his wages.ᶻ

11 As a dog returns to his own vomit,
So a fool repeats his folly.

12 Do you see a man wise in his own eyes?
There is more hope for a fool than for him.

26:13–16 The second is the *sluggard,* who has excuses for everything. He has motion but no progress (v. 14) and is even too lazy to feed himself (v. 15)! You are wasting your time trying to help him (v. 16; 27:22).

13 *The lazy *man* says, "*There is* a lion in the
road!
A fierce lion *is* in the streets!"

14 *As* a door turns on its hinges,
So *does* the lazy *man* on his bed.

15 The lazy *man* buries his hand in the bowl;ᵃ
It wearies him to bring it back to his mouth.

16 The lazy *man is* wiser in his own eyes
Than seven men who can answer sensibly.

26:17–28 The *troublemaker* is the third problem person. This category includes meddlers (v. 17), pranksters (vv. 18–19), talebearers (vv. 20–22), and deceivers (vv. 23–28).
Are you anywhere in this chapter?

17 *He who passes by *and* meddles in a quarrel
not his own
Is like one who takes a dog by the ears.

18 Like a madman who throws firebrands,
arrows, and death,

19 *Is* the man *who* deceives his neighbor,
And says, "I was only joking!"

26:10 ᶻThe Hebrew is difficult; ancient and modern translators differ greatly.   26:15 ᵃCompare 19:24

20 Where *there is* no wood, the fire goes
        out;
     And where *there is* no talebearer, strife
        ceases.
21 *As* charcoal *is* to burning coals, and wood
        to fire,
     So *is* a contentious man to kindle strife.
22 The words of a talebearer *are* like tasty
        trifles,
     And they go down into the inmost body.

23 Fervent lips with a wicked heart
     Are like earthenware covered with silver
        dross.

24 He who hates, disguises *it* with his lips,
     And lays up deceit within himself;
25 When he speaks kindly, do not believe him,
     For *there are* seven abominations in his
        heart;
26 *Though his* hatred is covered by deceit,
     His wickedness will be revealed before the
        assembly.

27 Whoever digs a pit will fall into it,
     And he who rolls a stone will have it roll
        back on him.

28 A lying tongue hates *those who are* crushed
        by it,
     And a flattering mouth works ruin.

27 Do not boast about tomorrow,
     For you do not know what a day may bring
        forth.

2 Let another man praise you, and not your
        own mouth;
     A stranger, and not your own lips.

3 A stone *is* heavy and sand *is* weighty,
     But a fool's wrath *is* heavier than both of
        them.

4 Wrath *is* cruel and anger a torrent,
     But who *is* able to stand before jealousy?

5 Open rebuke *is* better
     Than love carefully concealed.

6 *Faithful *are* the wounds of a friend,
     But the kisses of an enemy *are* deceitful.

7 A satisfied soul loathes the honeycomb,
     But to a hungry soul every bitter thing *is*
        sweet.

8 Like a bird that wanders from its nest
     Is a man who wanders from his place.

9 Ointment and perfume delight the heart,
     And the sweetness of a man's friend *gives
        delight* by hearty counsel.

10 Do not forsake your own friend or your
        father's friend,

CHAPTER 27

27:6 True friendship will occasionally
involve wounds (vv. 5–6) as you speak the
truth in love (Eph. 4:15) because friendship
cannot be built on deception or envy (v. 4).
    Friends should encourage each other with
loving counsel (v. 9) and honest praise
(v. 2). But beware flattery (v. 14)! The way
you respond to praise reveals your
character, just as a jeweler's furnace reveals
the nature of the precious metal (v. 21).
Praise brought out the best in David but the
worst in Saul (1 Sam. 18:1–16). What does
it do to you?
    Friends should be faithful to each other
(v. 10; 17:17), but you also need to be loyal
to family and neighbors (v. 10). You never
can tell when you may need them or they
may need you! Not everybody will become
a close friend, so do not get so exclusive
that you neglect other people.

❝*Flattery is not communication;*
     it is manipulation.❞

Don't Fall for Flattery—Sincere praise can be an encouragement, but flattery only does harm
(Prov. 26:28). Beware the kisses of an enemy (Prov. 27:6; 2 Sam. 20:9–10; Matt. 26:48–50)! There
are times when flattery may seem the only way to save a friendship, but afterward, you will regret it
(Prov. 28:23). The flatterer is like a hunter who spreads his net (Prov. 29:5), so be on your guard.

Nor go to your brother's house in the day
    of your calamity;
Better *is* a neighbor nearby than a brother
    far away.

11 My son, be wise, and make my heart glad,
    That I may answer him who reproaches me.

12 A prudent *man* foresees evil *and* hides
    himself;
    The simple pass on *and* are punished.

13 Take the garment of him who is surety for
    a stranger,
    And hold it in pledge *when* he is surety for
    a seductress.

14 He who blesses his friend with a loud voice,
    rising early in the morning,
    It will be counted a curse to him.

15 A continual dripping on a very rainy day
    And a contentious woman are alike;
16 Whoever restrains her restrains the wind,
    And grasps oil with his right hand.

17 As iron sharpens iron,
    So a man sharpens the countenance of his
    friend.

18 Whoever keeps the fig tree will eat its fruit;
    So he who waits on his master will be
    honored.

19 As in water face *reflects* face,
    So a man's heart *reveals* the man.

20 Hell[b] and Destruction[c] are never full;
    So the eyes of man are never satisfied.

21 The refining pot *is* for silver and the furnace
    for gold,
    And a man *is valued* by what others say of
    him.

22 Though you grind a fool in a mortar with a
    pestle along with crushed grain,
    Yet his foolishness will not depart from him.

23 Be diligent to know the state of your flocks,
    And attend to your herds;
24 For riches *are* not forever,
    Nor does a crown *endure* to all generations.
25 *When* the hay is removed, and the tender
    grass shows itself,
    And the herbs of the mountains are
    gathered in,
26 The lambs *will provide* your clothing,
    And the goats the price of a field;
27 *You shall have* enough goats' milk for your
    food,
    For the food of your household,
    And the nourishment of your maidservants.

CHAPTER 28

28:2ff As crime increases, the government must pass more laws and hire more people to enforce them (v. 2). When you break God's law, you promote the wicked; when you obey His law, you promote righteousness (v. 4) and enable God to answer your prayers (v. 9). Read Romans 13 and see what God says about Christian citizens.

Wicked rulers are like fierce animals (v. 15) who drive the righteous into hiding (vv. 12, 28). This includes ignorant leaders and those grasping after money (v. 16). The people in that day could not vote to replace leaders or correct laws, so all they could do was protect themselves.

When laws and leaders are unjust, usually the poor suffer and the rich profit. But even a poor person can have integrity (v. 6) and understanding (v. 11) and faith that God will meet his needs (v. 27). Is there someone you should help today?

28 The wicked flee when no one pursues,
    But the righteous are bold as a lion.

2 *Because of the transgression of a land,
    many *are* its princes;

27:20 [b]Or *Sheol* [c]Hebrew *Abaddon*

But by a man of understanding *and* knowledge
Right will be prolonged.

3 A poor man who oppresses the poor
Is like a driving rain which leaves no food.

4 Those who forsake the law praise the wicked,
But such as keep the law contend with them.

5 Evil men do not understand justice,
But those who seek the LORD understand all.

6 Better *is* the poor who walks in his integrity
Than one perverse *in his* ways, though he *be* rich.

7 Whoever keeps the law *is* a discerning son,
But a companion of gluttons shames his father.

8 One who increases his possessions by usury and extortion
Gathers it for him who will pity the poor.

9 One who turns away his ear from hearing the law,
Even his prayer *is* an abomination.

10 Whoever causes the upright to go astray in an evil way,
He himself will fall into his own pit;
But the blameless will inherit good.

11 The rich man *is* wise in his own eyes,
But the poor who has understanding searches him out.

12 When the righteous rejoice, *there is* great glory;
But when the wicked arise, men hide themselves.

13 He who covers his sins will not prosper,
But whoever confesses and forsakes *them* will have mercy.

14 Happy *is* the man who is always reverent,
But he who hardens his heart will fall into calamity.

15 *Like* a roaring lion and a charging bear
Is a wicked ruler over poor people.

16 A ruler who lacks understanding *is* a great oppressor,
But he who hates covetousness will prolong *his* days.

17 A man burdened with bloodshed will flee into a pit;
Let no one help him.

18 Whoever walks blamelessly will be saved,
But *he who is* perverse *in his* ways will suddenly fall.

19 He who tills his land will have plenty of bread,
But he who follows frivolity will have poverty enough!

20 A faithful man will abound with blessings,
But he who hastens to be rich will not go
unpunished.

21 To show partiality *is* not good,
Because for a piece of bread a man will
transgress.

22 A man with an evil eye hastens after riches,
And does not consider that poverty will
come upon him.

23 He who rebukes a man will find more favor
afterward
Than he who flatters with the tongue.

24 Whoever robs his father or his mother,
And says, "*It is* no transgression,"
The same *is* companion to a destroyer.

25 He who is of a proud heart stirs up strife,
But he who trusts in the LORD will be
prospered.

26 He who trusts in his own heart is a fool,
But whoever walks wisely will be delivered.

27 He who gives to the poor will not lack,
But he who hides his eyes will have many
curses.

28 When the wicked arise, men hide
themselves;
But when they perish, the righteous
increase.

29 He who is often rebuked, *and* hardens *his*
neck,
Will suddenly be destroyed, and that
without remedy.

2 *When the righteous are in authority, the
people rejoice;
But when a wicked *man* rules, the people
groan.

3 Whoever loves wisdom makes his father
rejoice,
But a companion of harlots wastes *his*
wealth.

4 The king establishes the land by justice,
But he who receives bribes overthrows it.

5 A man who flatters his neighbor
Spreads a net for his feet.

6 By transgression an evil man is snared,
But the righteous sings and rejoices.

7 The righteous considers the cause of the
poor,
But the wicked does not understand *such*
knowledge.

8 Scoffers set a city aflame,
But wise *men* turn away wrath.

CHAPTER 29

29:2ff When honest people enforce the law,
there is joy (v. 2), and society is established
with security and order (v. 4). A few leaders
who scoff at the law can endanger things,
so the wise must be ready to act (v. 8). Of
course, even a wise leader cannot change
some people (v. 9).

Leaders must act on the basis of truth and
not lies (vv. 12, 14). The foundation for law
is God's truth, and where that is preached
and obeyed, there will be happiness (v. 18).
If leaders try to please people, or if they fear
people, they will get into trouble; but if they
obey the Lord, He will bless them (vv. 25–
27).

Everybody must practice self-control in
feelings (vv. 11, 22) and words (v. 20). We
may not be able to run the government, but
we can manage the kingdom within our own
hearts (Prov. 16:32; 25:28).

Bribery—Bribery erodes the very foundation of the law and of the land (Prov. 29:4) and must be
hated as an enemy (Prov. 15:27). It perverts justice (Prov. 17:23), provides offices for dishonest
people (Prov. 18:16), purchases favors (Prov. 19:6), and pacifies people without solving problems
(Prov. 21:14). The person whose integrity is for sale is not fit to govern.

9 *If* a wise man contends with a foolish man,
   Whether *the fool* rages or laughs, *there is*
      no peace.

10 The bloodthirsty hate the blameless,
    But the upright seek his well-being.*d*

11 A fool vents all his feelings,*e*
    But a wise *man* holds them back.

12 If a ruler pays attention to lies,
    All his servants *become* wicked.

13 The poor *man* and the oppressor have this
       in common:
    The LORD gives light to the eyes of both.

14 The king who judges the poor with truth,
    His throne will be established forever.

15 The rod and rebuke give wisdom,
    But a child left *to himself* brings shame to
       his mother.

16 When the wicked are multiplied,
       transgression increases;
    But the righteous will see their fall.

17 Correct your son, and he will give you rest;
    Yes, he will give delight to your soul.

18 Where *there is* no revelation,*f* the people
       cast off restraint;
    But happy *is* he who keeps the law.

19 A servant will not be corrected by mere
       words;
    For though he understands, he will not
       respond.

20 Do you see a man hasty in his words?
    There is more hope for a fool than for him.

21 He who pampers his servant from childhood
    Will have him as a son in the end.

22 An angry man stirs up strife,
    And a furious man abounds in
       transgression.

23 A man's pride will bring him low,
    But the humble in spirit will retain honor.

24 Whoever is a partner with a thief hates his
       own life;
    He swears to tell the truth,*g* but reveals
       nothing.

25 The fear of man brings a snare,
    But whoever trusts in the LORD shall be safe.

26 Many seek the ruler's favor,
    But justice for man *comes* from the LORD.

27 An unjust man *is* an abomination to the
       righteous,

29:10 *d*Literally *soul*   29:11 *e*Literally *spirit*   29:18 *f*Or
prophetic vision   29:24 *g*Literally *hears the adjuration*

And *he who is* upright in the way *is* an
abomination to the wicked.

30 The words of Agur the son of Jakeh, *his*
utterance. This man declared to Ithiel—to
Ithiel and Ucal:

2   Surely I *am* more stupid than *any* man,
And do not have the understanding of a
man.
3   I neither learned wisdom
Nor have knowledge of the Holy One.

4   Who has ascended into heaven, or
descended?
Who has gathered the wind in His fists?
Who has bound the waters in a garment?
Who has established all the ends of the
earth?
What *is* His name, and what *is* His Son's
name,
If you know?

5   Every word of God *is* pure;
He *is* a shield to those who put their trust
in Him.
6   Do not add to His words,
Lest He rebuke you, and you be found a liar.

7   Two *things* I request of You
(Deprive me not before I die):
8   Remove falsehood and lies far from me;
Give me neither poverty nor riches—
Feed me with the food allotted to me;
9   Lest I be full and deny *You,*
And say, "Who *is* the LORD?"
Or lest I be poor and steal,
And profane the name of my God.

10 Do not malign a servant to his master,
Lest he curse you, and you be found guilty.

11 *There is* a generation *that* curses its father,
And does not bless its mother.
12 *There is* a generation *that is* pure in its own
eyes,
Yet is not washed from its filthiness.
13 *There is* a generation— oh, how lofty are
their eyes!
And their eyelids are lifted up.
14 *There is* a generation whose teeth *are like*
swords,
And whose fangs *are like* knives,
To devour the poor from off the earth,
And the needy from *among* men.

15 *The leech has two daughters—
Give *and* Give!

There are three *things that* are never
satisfied,
Four never say, "Enough!":
16 The grave,[h]

30:16 [h]Or *Sheol*

CHAPTER 30

30:15, 16 Agur's reverence for God
(vv. 2–4) and His Word (vv. 5–6) proves that
he was a wise man worth listening to. He
had the right attitude toward wealth (vv.
7–9; Phil. 4:10) and the family (v. 17), and
he was concerned about a generation that
had turned away from God (vv. 11–14). He
shares some lessons with you.
Some things are never satisfied. The
leech wants more blood, the grave wants
more dead, the barren mother yearns for
children, the earth thirsts for more water, and
the fire wants more fuel (Prov. 26:20–21).
Dissatisfaction creates many problems in
our world.

Respect in the Home—Proverbs has much to say about the home. When children walk in wisdom,
they bring joy to their parents (10:1; 15:20; 17:21, 25; 19:26; 23:24–25). It is tragic when children do
not respect their parents (23:22; 30:17), when they speak evil of them (20:20), waste their money
with the wrong friends (28:7; 29:3), and rob their parents (28:24). Early discipline helps a child learn
to respect parental authority and appreciate parental love (13:24; 19:18; 22:15).

The barren womb,
The earth *that* is not satisfied with water—
And the fire never says, "Enough!"

17 The eye *that* mocks *his* father,
And scorns obedience to *his* mother,
The ravens of the valley will pick it out,
And the young eagles will eat it.

18 *There are three *things which* are too
wonderful for me,
Yes, four *which* I do not understand:
19 The way of an eagle in the air,
The way of a serpent on a rock,
The way of a ship in the midst of the sea,
And the way of a man with a virgin.

20 This *is* the way of an adulterous woman:
She eats and wipes her mouth,
And says, "I have done no wickedness."

21 *For three *things* the earth is perturbed,
Yes, for four it cannot bear up:
22 For a servant when he reigns,
A fool when he is filled with food,
23 A hateful *woman* when she is married,
And a maidservant who succeeds her
mistress.

24 *There are four *things which* are little on the
earth,
But they *are* exceedingly wise:
25 The ants *are* a people not strong,
Yet they prepare their food in the summer;
26 The rock badgers^i are a feeble folk,
Yet they make their homes in the crags;
27 The locusts have no king,
Yet they all advance in ranks;
28 The spider^j skillfully grasps with its hands,
And it is in kings' palaces.

29 *There are three *things which* are majestic
in pace,
Yes, four *which* are stately in walk:
30 A lion, *which is* mighty among beasts
And does not turn away from any;
31 A greyhound,^k
A male goat also,
And a king *whose* troops *are* with him.^l

32 If you have been foolish in exalting yourself,
Or if you have devised evil, *put your* hand
on *your* mouth.
33 For *as* the churning of milk produces butter,
And wringing the nose produces blood,
So the forcing of wrath produces strife.

31 The words of King Lemuel, the utterance
which his mother taught him:

2 What, my son?
And what, son of my womb?
And what, son of my vows?
3 Do not give your strength to women,
Nor your ways to that which destroys
kings.

**30:18, 19 *Some things must never lose
their wonder.*** Science may explain the flight
of birds, the movements of snakes, the
currents of the ocean, and human sexuality,
but that does not take away their wonder.
Life and love are not explained by laboratory
experiments or the convenient formulas of
the experts. As you go through life, do not
lose your sense of wonder.

**30:21–23 *Some things always seem to
cause trouble.*** Servants do not always
know how to handle the luxury and authority
of the throne (Prov. 19:10), so they create
problems instead of solving them. Folly and
hatred are not changed by food and
marriage; if anything, they become worse.
Genesis 16 illustrates what happens when
a maidservant gets promoted.

**30:24–28 *Some small things are very big
in wisdom.*** The ants are wise to prepare,
the badgers to protect, the locusts to
cooperate, and the spiders to get into the
best places and hold on. Good examples
for you to follow!

**30:29–33 *Some things are made for
honor.*** The lion, greyhound, and male goat
are regal because God made them that way.
The dog is not a lion and the goat is not a
beautiful dog, but each has its own kind of
honor. The king is regal because of his office
and his official trappings (such as an army).
If you exalt yourself (v. 32), you will have
only artificial honor. If you let God fulfill in
you the purpose for which He made you,
you will have true honor.

30:26 ^iOr *hyraxes*   30:28 ^jOr *lizard*   30:31 ^kExact identity
unknown ^lA Jewish tradition reads *a king against whom there
is no uprising.*

4   *It is* not for kings, O Lemuel,
    It is not for kings to drink wine,
    Nor for princes intoxicating drink;
5   Lest they drink and forget the law,
    And pervert the justice of all the afflicted.
6   Give strong drink to him who is perishing,
    And wine to those who are bitter of heart.
7   Let him drink and forget his poverty,
    And remember his misery no more.

8   Open your mouth for the speechless,
    In the cause of all *who are* appointed to
        die.^m
9   Open your mouth, judge righteously,
    And plead the cause of the poor and needy.
10 *Who^n can find a virtuous^o wife?
    For her worth *is* far above rubies.
11 The heart of her husband safely trusts
        her;
    So he will have no lack of gain.
12 She does him good and not evil
    All the days of her life.
13 She seeks wool and flax,
    And willingly works with her hands.
14 She is like the merchant ships,
    She brings her food from afar.
15 She also rises while it is yet night,
    And provides food for her household,
    And a portion for her maidservants.
16 She considers a field and buys it;
    From her profits she plants a vineyard.
17 She girds herself with strength,
    And strengthens her arms.
18 She perceives that her merchandise *is*
        good,
    And her lamp does not go out by night.
19 She stretches out her hands to the distaff,
    And her hand holds the spindle.
20 She extends her hand to the poor,
    Yes, she reaches out her hands to the needy.
21 She is not afraid of snow for her household,
    For all her household *is* clothed with scarlet.
22 She makes tapestry for herself;
    Her clothing *is* fine linen and purple.
23 Her husband is known in the gates,
    When he sits among the elders of the
        land.
24 She makes linen garments and sells *them*,
    And supplies sashes for the merchants.
25 Strength and honor *are* her clothing;
    She shall rejoice in time to come.
26 She opens her mouth with wisdom,
    And on her tongue *is* the law of kindness.
27 She watches over the ways of her
        household,
    And does not eat the bread of idleness.
28 Her children rise up and call her blessed;
    Her husband *also,* and he praises her:
29 "Many daughters have done well,
    But you excel them all."
30 Charm *is* deceitful and beauty *is* passing,
    But a woman *who* fears the LORD, she shall
        be praised.
31 Give her of the fruit of her hands,
    And let her own works praise her in the
        gates.

CHAPTER 31

31:10–31 The book of Proverbs opens with warnings about evil women but closes with a description of a godly woman. Everything about this woman is praiseworthy.

Look at *her hands.* She is a willing worker (vv. 13, 19), and her work is fruitful (v. 31). She cooks, sews, manages real estate, and even plants a garden. Her family needs nothing, and she is generous to the poor (v. 20).

Her mouth speaks wisdom (v. 26), and she gives wise counsel to her family and friends. *Her eyes* are alert to opportunities (vv. 13, 16) and to the needs of the home (v. 27).

Most important, *her heart* is faithful to the Lord and to her husband (vv. 11–12, 30). It is no surprise that she is praised, by her children and husband (vv. 28–29) and by her works (v. 31).

Compare verse 30 with 1 Peter 3:1–6 and find out what kind of beauty really lasts.

31:8 ^m Literally *sons of passing away*   31:10 ^n Verses 10 through 31 are an alphabetic acrostic in Hebrew (compare Psalm 119). ^o Literally *a wife of valor,* in the sense of all forms of excellence

ECCLESIASTES

His name is not mentioned in the book, but King Solomon probably wrote it. He calls himself "the Preacher," which means "one who calls an assembly and discusses a topic." The Greek word for "assembly" is *ekklesia* (the New Testament word for "church"), and the book's title comes from this word. As the wisest, wealthiest, and most powerful man of his day, Solomon certainly had the opportunity and resources to do the things mentioned in Ecclesiastes.

In this book, Solomon seeks to answer the question, "Is life worth living?" First, he states the problem and argues for the negative (chaps. 1—2). Then he examines the problem from many different angles (chaps. 3—10) and argues for the positive. He concludes that life is worth living if you put God first and obey His Word (chaps. 11—12).

Called a pessimistic book, Ecclesiastes is actually realistic. Solomon looked at life and death, success and failure, time and events, and wrote some wise counsel about how to live a meaningful life in a world of contradictions and seeming futility. When viewed apart from God ("under the sun"), life is indeed "vanity" (futility); but when you live for Christ, life is never "in vain" (1 Cor. 15:58).

Six times Solomon advises you to enjoy life *now* and be grateful for God's gifts (2:24; 3:12-15, 22; 5:18-20; 8:15; 9:7-10; 11:9-10). This is not the pleasure-seeking philosophy of the epicurean ("eat, drink, and be merry, for tomorrow we die") but the joyful outlook of the believer who accepts life as God's gift to enjoy and employ for His glory (1 Tim. 6:17-19).

1 The words of the Preacher, the son of David, king in Jerusalem.

2 *"Vanity[a] of vanities," says the Preacher;
"Vanity of vanities, all *is* vanity."

3 What profit has a man from all his labor
In which he toils under the sun?
4 *One* generation passes away, and *another* generation comes;
But the earth abides forever.
5 The sun also rises, and the sun goes down,
And hastens to the place where it arose.
6 The wind goes toward the south,
And turns around to the north;
The wind whirls about continually,
And comes again on its circuit.
7 All the rivers run into the sea,
Yet the sea *is* not full;
To the place from which the rivers come,
There they return again.
8 All things *are* full of labor;
Man cannot express *it*.
The eye is not satisfied with seeing,
Nor the ear filled with hearing.

9 That which has been *is* what will be,
That which *is* done is what will be done,
And *there is* nothing new under the sun.
10 Is there anything of which it may be said,
"See, this *is* new"?
It has already been in ancient times before us.

1:2 [a]Or *Absurdity, Frustration, Futility, Nonsense;* and so throughout this book

CHAPTER 1

1:2ff When Solomon began his discussion, he was convinced that life was meaningless. Perhaps you feel the same way at times and for the same reasons. When you look around, you see nature functioning as it has since creation (vv. 2–8). When you look back, you see history only repeating itself (vv. 9–11). When you look within, you find (as Solomon did) that your wisdom and experience cannot explain the mysteries of life or solve life's problems (vv. 12–18). Vanity of vanities!

Solomon's big mistake was to leave God out of the picture and forget that God has broken into creation and done new things. He stopped the sun for Joshua (Josh. 10:12) and moved it back for Hezekiah (Isa. 38:8). He opened both the sea (Exod. 14) and the river (Josh. 3) for His people. God is in charge of the world and human history, and what He does is not "vain."

Knowledge can increase sorrow *if you*
(continued)

❝*Nine-tenths of our unhappiness is selfishness and is an insult cast in the face of God.*❞
—G. H. Morrison

(continued from previous page)
leave out the God of wisdom and the wisdom of God. Satan promises knowledge apart from God (Gen. 2:17; 3:1–5), but it leads only to sin and death. Be sure to grow in grace as you grow in knowledge (2 Pet. 3:17–18), or knowledge will make you critical and cynical.

CHAPTER 2

2:1ff God made life for enjoyment and investment (1 Tim. 6:17–19), but Solomon decided to turn it into experiment. He tested his heart with pleasure (vv. 1–3), works (vv. 4–6), and the acquisition of wealth (vv. 7–9), and he discovered that they did not satisfy. These things can bring a certain amount of enjoyment while you are doing them, but when it is all over, you feel empty (vv. 10–11). *Enjoyment without God is only entertainment, not enrichment;* you cannot live on entertainment.
At that point Solomon became cynical and hated life (vv. 12–23; see also Ps. 34:11–14; 1 Pet. 3:10–12). "Why bother to do all these things," he asked, "when I am going to die anyway? Who will remember me?"
Paul's answer is found in 1 Corinthians 15:58 and John's in 1 John 2:17. Instead of complaining about what you do not have, thank God for what you do have *and enjoy it* (vv. 24–26).

11 *There is* no remembrance of former *things,*
Nor will there be any remembrance of *things* that are to come
By *those* who will come after.

12I, the Preacher, was king over Israel in Jerusalem. 13And I set my heart to seek and search out by wisdom concerning all that is done under heaven; this burdensome task God has given to the sons of man, by which they may be exercised. 14I have seen all the works that are done under the sun; and indeed, all *is* vanity and grasping for the wind.

15 *What is* crooked cannot be made straight,
And what is lacking cannot be numbered.

16I communed with my heart, saying, "Look, I have attained greatness, and have gained more wisdom than all who were before me in Jerusalem. My heart has understood great wisdom and knowledge." 17And I set my heart to know wisdom and to know madness and folly. I perceived that this also is grasping for the wind.

18 For in much wisdom *is* much grief,
And he who increases knowledge increases sorrow.

2 I* said in my heart, "Come now, I will test you with mirth; therefore enjoy pleasure"; but surely, this also *was* vanity. 2I said of laughter— "Madness!"; and of mirth, "What does it accomplish?" 3I searched in my heart *how* to gratify my flesh with wine, while guiding my heart with wisdom, and how to lay hold on folly, till I might see what *was* good for the sons of men to do under heaven all the days of their lives.

4I made my works great, I built myself houses, and planted myself vineyards. 5I made myself gardens and orchards, and I planted all *kinds* of fruit trees in them. 6I made myself water pools from which to water the growing trees of the grove. 7I acquired male and female servants, and had servants born in my house. Yes, I had greater possessions of herds and flocks than all who were in Jerusalem before me. 8I also gathered for myself silver and gold and the special treasures of kings and of the provinces. I acquired male and female singers, the delights of the sons of men, *and* musical instruments[b] of all kinds.

9So I became great and excelled more than all who were before me in Jerusalem. Also my wisdom remained with me.

10 Whatever my eyes desired I did not keep from them.
I did not withhold my heart from any pleasure,
For my heart rejoiced in all my labor;
And this was my reward from all my labor.
11 Then I looked on all the works that my hands had done
And on the labor in which I had toiled;

2:8 *b*Exact meaning unknown

The Cynic—Henry Ward Beecher described a cynic as a person who "never sees a good quality in a man, and never fails to see a bad one. He is the human owl, vigilant in darkness, and blind to light, mousing for vermin, and never seeing noble game."

And indeed all *was* vanity and grasping for
   the wind.
There was no profit under the sun.
12 Then I turned myself to consider wisdom
   and madness and folly;
For what *can* the man *do* who succeeds the
   king?—
Only what he has already done.
13 Then I saw that wisdom excels folly
As light excels darkness.
14 The wise man's eyes *are* in his head,
But the fool walks in darkness.
Yet I myself perceived
That the same event happens to them all.

15 So I said in my heart,
"As it happens to the fool,
It also happens to me,
And why was I then more wise?"
Then I said in my heart,
"This also *is* vanity."
16 For *there is* no more remembrance of the
   wise than of the fool forever,
Since all that now *is* will be forgotten in the
   days to come.
And how does a wise *man* die?
As the fool!

17Therefore I hated life because the work that was
done under the sun *was* distressing to me, for all
is vanity and grasping for the wind.
18Then I hated all my labor in which I had toiled
under the sun, because I must leave it to the man
who will come after me. 19And who knows
whether he will be wise or a fool? Yet he will
rule over all my labor in which I toiled and in
which I have shown myself wise under the sun.
This also *is* vanity. 20Therefore I turned my heart
and despaired of all the labor in which I had toiled
under the sun. 21For there is a man whose labor
is with wisdom, knowledge, and skill; yet he must
leave his heritage to a man who has not labored
for it. This also *is* vanity and a great evil. 22For
what has man for all his labor, and for the striving
of his heart with which he has toiled under the
sun? 23For all his days *are* sorrowful, and his work
burdensome; even in the night his heart takes no
rest. This also is vanity.
24Nothing *is* better for a man *than* that he
should eat and drink, and *that* his soul should
enjoy good in his labor. This also, I saw, was from
the hand of God. 25For who can eat, or who can
have enjoyment, more than I?c 26For *God* gives
wisdom and knowledge and joy to a man who *is*
good in His sight; but to the sinner He gives the
work of gathering and collecting, that he may give
to *him who is* good before God. This also *is* vanity
and grasping for the wind.

3   To* everything *there is* a season,
     A time for every purpose under heaven:

2   A time to be born,
       And a time to die;
     A time to plant,
       And a time to pluck *what is* planted;

2:25 cFollowing Masoretic Text, Targum, and Vulgate; some
Hebrew manuscripts, Septuagint, and Syriac read *without
Him.*

CHAPTER 3

3:1–8 *Balance.* When life is especially
difficult, we are prone to see only one side
of the situation. In these statements,
Solomon reminds you that God is in control
of life and keeps everything balanced. You
feel pain when there is bereavement, but
you feel joy when there is birth. You are
not always weeping, but neither are you
always laughing. Job knew this principle,
and it gave him strength in his trials (Job
1:21).

3   A time to kill,
    And a time to heal;
  A time to break down,
    And a time to build up;
4   A time to weep,
    And a time to laugh;
  A time to mourn,
    And a time to dance;
5   A time to cast away stones,
    And a time to gather stones;
  A time to embrace,
    And a time to refrain from embracing;
6   A time to gain,
    And a time to lose;
  A time to keep,
    And a time to throw away;
7   A time to tear,
    And a time to sew;
  A time to keep silence,
    And a time to speak;
8   A time to love,
    And a time to hate;
  A time of war,
    And a time of peace.

9What profit has the worker from that in which he labors? 10*I have seen the God-given task with which the sons of men are to be occupied. 11He has made everything beautiful in its time. Also He has put eternity in their hearts, except that no one can find out the work that God does from beginning to end.

12I know that nothing *is* better for them than to rejoice, and to do good in their lives, 13and also that every man should eat and drink and enjoy the good of all his labor—it *is* the gift of God.

14   I know that whatever God does,
    It shall be forever.
    Nothing can be added to it,
    And nothing taken from it.
    God does *it*, that men should fear before
      Him.
15   That which is has already been,
    And what is to be has already been;
    And God requires an account of what is
      past.

16Moreover I saw under the sun:

  In the place of judgment,
  Wickedness *was* there;
  And *in* the place of righteousness,
  Iniquity *was* there.

17I said in my heart,

  "God shall judge the righteous and the
    wicked,
  For *there is* a time there for every purpose
    and for every work."

18*I said in my heart, "Concerning the condition of the sons of men, God tests them, that they may see that they themselves are *like* animals." 19For what happens to the sons of men also happens to animals; one thing befalls them: as one dies, so dies the other. Surely, they all have one breath; man has no advantage over animals, for all *is* vanity. 20All go to one place: all are from the dust, and all return to dust. 21Who knows the spirit of the sons of men, which goes upward, and

3:10–14 *Beauty.* It may not look like it now, but God will bring beauty out of all that happens (Rom. 8:28; Isa. 61:1–7). No matter what the seed looks like, the flower will be beautiful, so give God time to work. You were made for the eternal; in Christ, you now share eternal life, the life of God (1 John 5:9–13).

3:18–22 *Burial.* Again, Solomon faces the fact of death, as he will several times in this book. Both people and animals die and are buried, and their bodies go to the same place: the dust. The spirit of man goes to meet God (v. 21). One day, God will bring beauty even out of the dust (1 Cor. 15:35–58)! Enjoy today and thank God for all He gives you.

the spirit of the animal, which goes down to the earth?*d* *22*So I perceived that nothing *is* better than that a man should rejoice in his own works, for that *is* his heritage. For who can bring him to see what will happen after him?

4 Then* I returned and considered all the oppression that is done under the sun:

> And look! The tears of the oppressed,
> But they have no comforter—
> On the side of their oppressors *there is* power,
> But they have no comforter.
> 2 Therefore I praised the dead who were already dead,
> More than the living who are still alive.
> 3 Yet, better than both *is* he who has never existed,
> Who has not seen the evil work that is done under the sun.

*4*Again, I saw that for all toil and every skillful work a man is envied by his neighbor. This also *is* vanity and grasping for the wind.

> 5 The fool folds his hands
> And consumes his own flesh.
> 6 Better a handful *with* quietness
> Than both hands full, *together with* toil and grasping for the wind.

*7*Then I returned, and I saw vanity under the sun:

> 8 There is one alone, without companion:
> He has neither son nor brother.
> Yet *there is* no end to all his labors,
> Nor is his eye satisfied with riches.
> *But he never asks,*
> "For whom do I toil and deprive myself of good?"
> This also *is* vanity and a grave misfortune.
>
> 9 Two *are* better than one,
> Because they have a good reward for their labor.
> 10 For if they fall, one will lift up his companion.
> But woe to him *who is* alone when he falls,
> For *he has* no one to help him up.
> 11 Again, if two lie down together, they will keep warm;
> But how can one be warm *alone?*
> 12 Though one may be overpowered by another, two can withstand him.
> And a threefold cord is not quickly broken.
>
> 13 Better a poor and wise youth
> Than an old and foolish king who will be admonished no more.
> 14 For he comes out of prison to be king,
> Although he was born poor in his kingdom.
> 15 I saw all the living who walk under the sun;
> They were with the second youth who stands in his place.

CHAPTER 4

4:1–12 Have you ever wished you could just get away from it all? People get on your nerves, circumstances ruin your plans, and the best solution to the problem seems to be to "go it alone." But is it the best solution?

As Solomon looked at the problems of life, he saw adversity and inequality (vv. 1–6), but he realized that *nobody can make it alone.* The solitary worker may get all the profits, but he is so busy making money that he has no time to enjoy it (vv. 7–8). And how rich will he be in the grave?

There are risks in society as well as rewards, but the rewards are greater. If you fall and break a leg, or if you are in danger, you are thankful to have a friend at your side to help you (vv. 9–12). We all need times of solitude, but nobody can be independent. Life is tough enough even when we have friends to encourage us. What would it be like if we had to do it alone?

Loneliness is the first thing which God's eye named not good. *(See Gen. 2:18.)*
—John Milton

16 *There was* no end of all the people over
whom he was made king;
Yet those who come afterward will not
rejoice in him.
Surely this also *is* vanity and grasping for
the wind.

CHAPTER 5

5:1–7 Do not speak rashly. Your mouth
can cause you to sin, especially when you
pray hypocritically or make rash promises
to God. Hasty words and lying words do not
please God, nor will He accept excuses
when you fail to keep your vow. Do not live
in a dream world of religious fantasy,
expressed by words alone. Be honest with
God (1 John 1:5–10).

5 Walk* prudently when you go to the house
of God; and draw near to hear rather than to
give the sacrifice of fools, for they do not know
that they do evil.

2 Do not be rash with your mouth,
And let not your heart utter anything hastily
before God.
For God *is* in heaven, and you on earth;
Therefore let your words be few.
3 For a dream comes through much activity,
And a fool's voice *is known* by *his* many
words.

4 When you make a vow to God, do not delay
to pay it;
For *He has* no pleasure in fools.
Pay what you have vowed—
5 Better not to vow than to vow and not pay.

5:8, 9 Do not marvel at wrongs. This does
not mean that you should *approve* them,
but do not be surprised when they happen.
The poor Jews in Solomon's day had to put
up with selfish bureaucrats who had to be
paid off before they would help. (Have times
changed?) Certainly you should work to see
that justice is done, but do not be
disappointed if many of your efforts fail.

5:10–20 Do not covet wealth. The poor
think all their problems will be solved with
more money, and the rich have problems
because of their money! Money does not
satisfy (v. 10) or guarantee peace (v. 12).
You can buy sleep, but you cannot buy
peace. Be thankful that God not only shares
His gifts with you but also enables you to
enjoy them. Not everybody can do that.

6Do not let your mouth cause your flesh to sin,
nor say before the messenger *of God* that it *was*
an error. Why should God be angry at your excuse*e* and destroy the work of your hands?
7For in the multitude of dreams and many words
there is also vanity. But fear God.
8*If you see the oppression of the poor, and the
violent perversion of justice and righteousness in
a province, do not marvel at the matter; for high
official watches over high official, and higher officials are over them.
9Moreover the profit of the land is for all; *even*
the king is served from the field.

10 *He who loves silver will not be satisfied with
silver;
Nor he who loves abundance, with increase.
This also *is* vanity.

11 When goods increase,
They increase who eat them;
So what profit have the owners
Except to see *them* with their eyes?

12 The sleep of a laboring man *is* sweet,
Whether he eats little or much;
But the abundance of the rich will not
permit him to sleep.

13 There is a severe evil *which* I have seen
under the sun:
Riches kept for their owner to his hurt.
14 But those riches perish through misfortune;
When he begets a son, *there is* nothing in
his hand.
15 As he came from his mother's womb, naked
shall he return,
To go as he came;
And he shall take nothing from his labor
Which he may carry away in his hand.

16 And this also *is* a severe evil—
Just exactly as he came, so shall he go.

••*O God, give us serenity to accept
what cannot be changed, courage
to change what should be changed,
and wisdom to distinguish the one
from the other.***••*
—Reinhold Niebuhr

5:6 *e*Literally *voice*

And what profit has he who has labored for the wind?

17 All his days he also eats in darkness,
And *he has* much sorrow and sickness and anger.

18Here is what I have seen: *It is* good and fitting *for one* to eat and drink, and to enjoy the good of all his labor in which he toils under the sun all the days of his life which God gives him; for it *is* his heritage. 19As for every man to whom God has given riches and wealth, and given him power to eat of it, to receive his heritage and rejoice in his labor—this *is* the gift of God. 20For he will not dwell unduly on the days of his life, because God keeps *him* busy with the joy of his heart.

6 There* is an evil which I have seen under the sun, and it *is* common among men: 2A man to whom God has given riches and wealth and honor, so that he lacks nothing for himself of all he desires; yet God does not give him power to eat of it, but a foreigner consumes it. This *is* vanity, and it *is* an evil affliction.

3If a man begets a hundred *children* and lives many years, so that the days of his years are many, but his soul is not satisfied with goodness, or indeed he has no burial, I say *that* a stillborn child *is* better than he— 4for it comes in vanity and departs in darkness, and its name is covered with darkness. 5Though it has not seen the sun or known *anything,* this has more rest than that man, 6even if he lives a thousand years twice— but has not seen goodness. Do not all go to one place?

7 All the labor of man *is* for his mouth,
And yet the soul is not satisfied.
8 For what more has the wise *man* than the fool?
What does the poor man have,
Who knows *how* to walk before the living?
9 Better *is* the sight of the eyes than the wandering of desire.
This also *is* vanity and grasping for the wind.

10 Whatever one is, he has been named already,
For it is known that he *is* man;
And he cannot contend with Him who is mightier than he.
11 Since there are many things that increase vanity,
How *is* man the better?

12For who knows what *is* good for man in life, all the days of his vain life which he passes like a shadow? Who can tell a man what will happen after him under the sun?

7 A* good name *is* better than precious ointment,
And the day of death than the day of one's birth;
2 Better to go to the house of mourning
Than to go to the house of feasting,
For that *is* the end of all men;
And the living will take *it* to heart.
3 Sorrow *is* better than laughter,

CHAPTER 6

6:1ff *Accept what you have.* Instead of looking around for something different (v. 9), accept what you now have as God's gift. This does not suggest laziness or resignation because God expects you to make good use of what He gives you (Matt. 25:14–30).

Enjoy what you have. How tragic to have riches and a long life but not be able to enjoy them! The poor man wishes for more while the rich man wishes he could enjoy even a part of what he has (Prov. 15:16–17).

Enjoy what you have TODAY. Life passes by like a shadow, and you do not know the future (v. 12). In the will of God, make the most of today's opportunities and blessings, and you will be ready for what lies ahead.

CHAPTER 7

7:1–12 *The better life.* The better life involves some "bitter things," such as sorrow and rebuke, but the bitter things can make life better. On the day of your birth, you were given a name. On the day of your death, that name will be either putrid or fragrant, depending on how you lived. If you have a good name, your death will be better than your birth *because nothing will be able to hurt your name.* In that sense, the end is better than the beginning (v. 8). Sorrow and rebuke can teach you lessons that will not be learned any other way (Prov. 27:5–6, 12).

❝*A man is rich in proportion to the number of things he can afford to let alone.*❞
—Henry David Thoreau

For by a sad countenance the heart is made
  better.
4   The heart of the wise *is* in the house of
       mourning,
    But the heart of fools *is* in the house of
       mirth.

5   *It is* better to hear the rebuke of the wise
    Than for a man to hear the song of fools.
6   For like the crackling of thorns under a pot,
    So *is* the laughter of the fool.
    This also is vanity.
7   Surely oppression destroys a wise *man's*
       reason,
    And a bribe debases the heart.

8   The end of a thing *is* better than its
       beginning;
    The patient in spirit *is* better than the proud
       in spirit.
9   Do not hasten in your spirit to be angry,
    For anger rests in the bosom of fools.
10   Do not say,
    "Why were the former days better than
       these?"
    For you do not inquire wisely concerning
       this.

11   Wisdom *is* good with an inheritance,
    And profitable to those who see the
       sun.
12   For wisdom *is* a defense *as* money *is* a
       defense,
    But the excellence of knowledge *is that*
       wisdom gives life to those who have
       it.

13   *Consider the work of God;
    For who can make straight what He has
       made crooked?
14   In the day of prosperity be joyful,
    But in the day of adversity consider:
    Surely God has appointed the one as well
       as the other,
    So that man can find out nothing *that will*
       come after him.

15   I have seen everything in my days of vanity:

    There is a just *man* who perishes in his
       righteousness,
    And there is a wicked *man* who prolongs
       life in his wickedness.

16   Do not be overly righteous,
    Nor be overly wise:
    Why should you destroy yourself?
17   Do not be overly wicked,
    Nor be foolish:
    Why should you die before your time?
18   *It is* good that you grasp this,
    And also not remove your hand from the
       other;
    For he who fears God will escape them all.

19   Wisdom strengthens the wise
    More than ten rulers of the city.
20   For *there is* not a just man on earth who
       does good
    And does not sin.

21   Also do not take to heart everything people
       say,

7:13–18 *The balanced life.* God gives both prosperity and adversity, and He knows how much and how long. Instead of peering into the future (v. 14b), live in the present and learn to profit from both pain and pleasure (Phil. 4:10–13). In verses 16–17, Solomon did not suggest that you play it safe and get the best of both worlds. The tenses of the verbs in Hebrew give the meaning, "Do not claim to be righteous and wise." You are still on the way and have not arrived yet (Phil. 3:12–16). That is why God balances your life with trials and triumphs: to keep you from getting proud and set in your ways.

Lest you hear your servant cursing you.
22 For many times, also, your own heart has known
   That even you have cursed others.

23 All this I have proved by wisdom.
   I said, "I will be wise";
   But it *was* far from me.
24 As for that which is far off and exceedingly deep,
   Who can find it out?
25 I applied my heart to know,
   To search and seek out wisdom and the reason *of things*,
   To know the wickedness of folly,
   Even of foolishness *and* madness.
26 And I find more bitter than death
   The woman whose heart *is* snares and nets,
   Whose hands *are* fetters.
   He who pleases God shall escape from her,
   But the sinner shall be trapped by her.

27 "Here is what I have found," says the Preacher,
   "*Adding* one thing to the other to find out the reason,
28 Which my soul still seeks but I cannot find:
   One man among a thousand I have found,
   But a woman among all these I have not found.
29 Truly, this only I have found:
   That God made man upright,
   But they have sought out many schemes."

8 Who* *is* like a wise *man*?
   And who knows the interpretation of a thing?
   A man's wisdom makes his face shine,
   And the sternness of his face is changed.

2I say, "Keep the king's commandment for the sake of your oath to God. 3Do not be hasty to go from his presence. Do not take your stand for an evil thing, for he does whatever pleases him."

4 Where the word of a king *is, there is* power;
   And who may say to him, "What are you doing?"
5 He who keeps his command will experience nothing harmful;
   And a wise man's heart discerns both time and judgment,
6 Because for every matter there is a time and judgment,
   Though the misery of man increases greatly.
7 For he does not know what will happen;
   So who can tell him when it will occur?
8 No one has power over the spirit to retain the spirit,
   And no one has power in the day of death.
   There is no release from that war,
   And wickedness will not deliver those who are given to it.

9All this I have seen, and applied my heart to every work that is done under the sun: *There is*

CHAPTER 8

8:1ff You will not always get things your way, so learn to deal wisely with disagreements. A shining face is better than a stern (impudent) face, and it is wisdom that makes the face shine. Learn to smile—and to laugh!

As much as possible, submit to authority, do what you are told, and keep your promises. Do not get angry and resign, but do not be a partner in anything wrong: "We ought to obey God rather than men" (Acts 5:29). Wise people have discernment and know the right time to speak and to act (v. 6; James 1:5).

There are many injustices (vv. 10–13) and mysteries (vv. 14–17) in this life. Leave them with God and do what He calls you to do. There are still many enjoyable things in life *if* you do not make yourself the most important person to be pleased. Put God first and serve others, and life will become meaningful and joyful.

❝*To consider persons and events and situations only in the light of their effect upon myself is to live on the doorstep of hell.*❞

—Thomas Merton

How Do You React?—Solomon recommends that you "do not take to heart everything people say." Proud people are alert to what others say about them and quick to react and retaliate. This keeps the fires burning and robs everybody of peace and joy. Charles Spurgeon advises, "You cannot stop people's tongues, and therefore the best thing to do is to stop your own ears and never mind what is spoken.

a time in which one man rules over another to his own hurt.

10Then I saw the wicked buried, who had come and gone from the place of holiness, and they were forgotten*f* in the city where they had so done. This also *is* vanity. 11Because the sentence against an evil work is not executed speedily, therefore the heart of the sons of men is fully set in them to do evil. 12Though a sinner does evil a hundred *times,* and his *days* are prolonged, yet I surely know that it will be well with those who fear God, who fear before Him. 13But it will not be well with the wicked; nor will he prolong *his* days, *which are* as a shadow, because he does not fear before God.

14There is a vanity which occurs on earth, that there are just *men* to whom it happens according to the work of the wicked; again, there are wicked *men* to whom it happens according to the work of the righteous. I said that this also *is* vanity.

15So I commended enjoyment, because a man has nothing better under the sun than to eat, drink, and be merry; for this will remain with him in his labor *all* the days of his life which God gives him under the sun.

16When I applied my heart to know wisdom and to see the business that is done on earth, even though one sees no sleep day or night, 17then I saw all the work of God, that a man cannot find out the work that is done under the sun. For though a man labors to discover *it,* yet he will not find *it;* moreover, though a wise *man* attempts to know *it,* he will not be able to find *it.*

9 For* I considered all this in my heart, so that I could declare it all: that the righteous and the wise and their works *are* in the hand of God. People know neither love nor hatred *by* anything *they see* before them. 2All things *come* alike to all:

> One event *happens* to the righteous and the
>   wicked;
> To the good,*g* the clean, and the unclean;
> To him who sacrifices and him who does
>   not sacrifice.
> As *is* the good, so *is* the sinner;
> He who takes an oath as *he* who fears an
>   oath.

3This *is* an evil in all that is done under the sun: that one thing *happens* to all. Truly the hearts of the sons of men are full of evil; madness *is* in their hearts while they live, and after that *they* go to the dead. 4But for him who is joined to all the living there is hope, for a living dog is better than a dead lion.

> 5   For the living know that they will die;
>   But the dead know nothing,
>   And they have no more reward,
>   For the memory of them is forgotten.
> 6   Also their love, their hatred, and their envy
>   have now perished;
>   Nevermore will they have a share
>   In anything done under the sun.

CHAPTER 9

9:1ff Death is a fact of life. You can avoid thinking about it, but you cannot avoid the appointment (Heb. 9:27). The only way to be prepared for death is to receive God's gift of eternal life through faith in Jesus Christ (John 3:16; Rom. 6:23; 1 John 5:9–13), and then obey God's will until He calls you.

The reality of death need not rob you of the enjoyments of life. God wants you to enjoy feasts (vv. 7–8) and family (v. 9) and the work He has called you to do (v. 10). Life is unpredictable (v. 11), but it need not be irrational. Let God give you wisdom to use each day profitably for His glory (vv. 16–18). The thought of death should energize you, not paralyze you (Phil. 1:19–26; 2 Tim. 4:6–8).

8:10 *f*Some Hebrew manuscripts, Septuagint, and Vulgate read *praised.*   9:2 *g*Septuagint, Syriac, and Vulgate read *good and bad.*

7 Go, eat your bread with joy,
   And drink your wine with a merry heart;
   For God has already accepted your works.
8 Let your garments always be white,
   And let your head lack no oil.

9Live joyfully with the wife whom you love all the days of your vain life which He has given you under the sun, all your days of vanity; for that *is* your portion in life, and in the labor which you perform under the sun. 10Whatever your hand finds to do, do *it* with your might; for *there is* no work or device or knowledge or wisdom in the grave where you are going.
   11I returned and saw under the sun that—

   The race *is* not to the swift,
   Nor the battle to the strong,
   Nor bread to the wise,
   Nor riches to men of understanding,
   Nor favor to men of skill;
   But time and chance happen to them all.
12 For man also does not know his time:
   Like fish taken in a cruel net,
   Like birds caught in a snare,
   So the sons of men *are* snared in an evil time,
   When it falls suddenly upon them.

13This wisdom I have also seen under the sun, and it *seemed* great to me: 14*There was* a little city with few men in it; and a great king came against it, besieged it, and built great snares[h] around it. 15Now there was found in it a poor wise man, and he by his wisdom delivered the city. Yet no one remembered that same poor man.
   16Then I said:

   "Wisdom *is* better than strength.
   Nevertheless the poor man's wisdom *is* despised,
   And his words are not heard.
17 Words of the wise, *spoken* quietly, *should be* heard
   Rather than the shout of a ruler of fools.
18 Wisdom *is* better than weapons of war;
   But one sinner destroys much good."

10 Dead* flies putrefy[i] the perfumer's ointment,
   And cause it to give off a foul odor;
   So does a little folly to one respected for wisdom *and* honor.
2 A wise man's heart *is* at his right hand,
   But a fool's heart at his left.
3 Even when a fool walks along the way,
   He lacks wisdom,
   And he shows everyone that he *is* a fool.
4 If the spirit of the ruler rises against you,
   Do not leave your post;
   For conciliation pacifies great offenses.

5 There is an evil I have seen under the sun,
   As an error proceeding from the ruler:
6 Folly is set in great dignity,
   While the rich sit in a lowly place.

9:14 [h]Septuagint, Syriac, and Vulgate read *bulwarks*.
10:1 [i]Targum and Vulgate omit *putrefy*.

CHAPTER 10
10:1ff The wiser you are, the more damage even a little folly can do to both your character and your reputation. The world seems to honor the fool and humiliate the honorable (vv. 5–7), but that is no reason for you to permit even a little folly in your life.

In Bible times, the right hand stood for honor and the left hand for dishonor (Matt. 25:33, 41). Verse 2 is another way of saying what Solomon wrote in Proverbs 4:23. If you guard your heart, you will avoid folly in your work (vv. 8–10) and your words (vv. 11–14). Verse 10 is Solomon's version of, "Don't work harder, work smarter!" Don't lose your cutting edge!

Leaders who live for themselves are only wasting time, resources, and opportunities for service, and that is folly (vv. 16–19). Yes, they have a good time at the expense of the citizens, but eventually, their folly will catch up with them.

Are there any "dead flies" that need to be taken out of the perfume of your life?

7 I have seen servants on horses,
While princes walk on the ground like
servants.

8 He who digs a pit will fall into it,
And whoever breaks through a wall will be
bitten by a serpent.
9 He who quarries stones may be hurt by
them,
And he who splits wood may be endangered
by it.
10 If the ax is dull,
And one does not sharpen the edge,
Then he must use more strength;
But wisdom brings success.

11 A serpent may bite when *it is* not charmed;
The babbler is no different.
12 The words of a wise man's mouth *are*
gracious,
But the lips of a fool shall swallow him up;
13 The words of his mouth begin with
foolishness,
And the end of his talk *is* raving madness.
14 A fool also multiplies words.
No man knows what is to be;
Who can tell him what will be after him?
15 The labor of fools wearies them,
For they do not even know how to go to
the city!

16 Woe to you, O land, when your king *is* a
child,
And your princes feast in the morning!
17 Blessed *are* you, O land, when your king *is*
the son of nobles,
And your princes feast at the proper time—
For strength and not for drunkenness!
18 Because of laziness the building decays,
And through idleness of hands the house
leaks.
19 A feast is made for laughter,
And wine makes merry;
But money answers everything.

20 Do not curse the king, even in your thought;
Do not curse the rich, even in your bedroom;
For a bird of the air may carry your voice,
And a bird in flight may tell the matter.

CHAPTER 11

11:1, 2 *Live by faith*. Solomon owned a
fleet of merchant ships (1 Kings 9:26–28)
that helped add to his great wealth. Life is
like that: you have to launch out by faith if
you hope to get anywhere. Limiting yourself
to one ship may lead to disaster, so trust
God to guide you in several endeavors.

11:3–5 *Avoid excuses*. The weather is
rarely right for what the farmer wants to do,
but he does it anyway. You cannot explain
the growth of the unborn child, but that does
not stop people from having families!

❝*One must wait until the evening
to see how splendid the day has
been.*❞
—Sophocles

11 Cast* your bread upon the waters,
For you will find it after many days.
2 Give a serving to seven, and also to eight,
For you do not know what evil will be on
the earth.

3 *If the clouds are full of rain,
They empty *themselves* upon the earth;
And if a tree falls to the south or the north,
In the place where the tree falls, there it
shall lie.
4 He who observes the wind will not sow,
And he who regards the clouds will not
reap.

5 As you do not know what *is* the way of the
wind,*
Or how the bones *grow* in the womb of her
who is with child,

11:5 *Or spirit*

So you do not know the works of God who makes everything.

6 *In the morning sow your seed,
And in the evening do not withhold your hand;
For you do not know which will prosper,
Either this or that,
Or whether both alike *will be* good.

7 Truly the light is sweet,
And *it is* pleasant for the eyes to behold the sun;

8 But if a man lives many years
And rejoices in them all,
Yet let him remember the days of darkness,
For they will be many.
All that is coming *is* vanity.

9 *Rejoice, O young man, in your youth,
And let your heart cheer you in the days of your youth;
Walk in the ways of your heart,
And in the sight of your eyes;
But know that for all these
God will bring you into judgment.

10 Therefore remove sorrow from your heart,
And put away evil from your flesh,
For childhood and youth *are* vanity.

12 Remember* now your Creator in the days of your youth,
Before the difficult days come,
And the years draw near when you say,
"I have no pleasure in them":

2 While the sun and the light,
The moon and the stars,
Are not darkened,
And the clouds do not return after the rain;

3 In the day when the keepers of the house tremble,
And the strong men bow down;
When the grinders cease because they are few,
And those that look through the windows grow dim;

4 When the doors are shut in the streets,
And the sound of grinding is low;
When one rises up at the sound of a bird,
And all the daughters of music are brought low.

5 Also they are afraid of height,
And of terrors in the way;
When the almond tree blossoms,
The grasshopper is a burden,
And desire fails.
For man goes to his eternal home,
And the mourners go about the streets.

6 *Remember your Creator* before the silver cord is loosed,[k]
Or the golden bowl is broken,
Or the pitcher shattered at the fountain,
Or the wheel broken at the well.

7 Then the dust will return to the earth as it was,
And the spirit will return to God who gave it.

8 "Vanity of vanities," says the Preacher,
"All *is* vanity."

11:6–8 *Work hard.* Get started early in the morning, and keep in mind that night is coming "when no one can work" (John 9:4). You will get older and one day not be able to work as much, so use your opportunities while you can. If dawn is sweet to you, your sleep at night will be sweet (Eccles. 5:12).

11:9, 10 *Please God.* The best way to remove sorrow is to avoid evil and walk in the fear of the Lord. The sooner you start, the happier your life will be. Childhood and youth are transient; you have but a short time to lay those important foundations. But it is never too late to make a new beginning and do it right.

CHAPTER 12

12:1–7 What are your days like at this stage in life?
  Days of decline. Solomon makes one last plea: make use of your opportunities while you can, before you get old and the storms come (v. 2). This poetic description of old age is quite graphic: trembling limbs and poor vision (v. 3); deafness and nervousness (v. 4); fear, gray hair, loss of appetite and then—death (vv. 5–7; 2 Cor. 4:16–18).

12:6 [k]Following Qere and Targum; Kethib reads *removed;* Septuagint and Vulgate read *broken.*

12:9–12 *Days of learning.* Listen to what God says and be admonished, no matter how old you are. You are never too old to get wiser—or to act like a fool! You can read many books about many subjects, but major on understanding God's Word and living a life of wisdom. His words are like nails: you can depend on them. They are goads: they prod you to do His will.

12:13, 14 *Days of obedience.* If you fear God, you need fear nothing else; you are safe in the Father's will. So live that God could publish a book about you and you would not be ashamed for the whole world to read it. Live with eternity in view, and the ravages of time will not distress you.

⁹*And moreover, because the Preacher was wise, he still taught the people knowledge; yes, he pondered and sought out *and* set in order many proverbs. ¹⁰The Preacher sought to find acceptable words; and *what was* written *was* upright—words of truth. ¹¹The words of the wise are like goads, and the words of scholars*ˡ* are like well-driven nails, given by one Shepherd. ¹²And further, my son, be admonished by these. Of making many books *there is* no end, and much study *is* wearisome to the flesh.

¹³*Let us hear the conclusion of the whole matter:

Fear God and keep His commandments,
For this is man's all.
¹⁴   For God will bring every work into
        judgment,
    Including every secret thing,
    Whether good or evil.

12:11 *ˡLiterally masters of the assemblies*

THE SONG OF SOLOMON

Jewish tradition sees this book picturing Jehovah's love for Israel, and Christians see it illustrating Christ's love for the church (Eph. 5:23–33) as well as the individual believer (John 14:21–24).

The "plot" centers on King Solomon's love for a humble maiden. Courtship (1:1—3:5) leads to marriage (3:6—5:1) and then to the joys and trials of married love (5:2—8:14). The book is indeed a beautiful presentation of the love of husband and wife, for the Jews accepted sexuality as a precious gift from God, a holy expression of true commitment in marriage.

The Song of Solomon is also an expression of the love relationship of the believer and the Savior. Christ calls us away from the trivial things of life that we might enjoy a deeper communion with Him. This communion is not without difficulties and disciplines, but it leads to a happier and holier life.

As you read the Song of Solomon, be sure to distinguish the various people speaking. Many recent translations of the Bible, such as the New King James Version, will identify them for you. Also keep in mind that this is a poem for mature people, rich in Oriental imagery, and must be "felt" as well as read. Solomon wrote Ecclesiastes for the inquiring mind, Proverbs for the obedient will, and the Song of Solomon for the loving heart. It takes all three for a balanced life.

1 The song of songs, which *is* Solomon's.

THE SHULAMITE*a*
2 *Let him kiss me with the kisses of his
    mouth—
    For your*b* love *is* better than wine.
3 Because of the fragrance of your good
    ointments,
    Your name *is* ointment poured forth;
    Therefore the virgins love you.
4 Draw me away!

THE DAUGHTERS OF JERUSALEM
    We will run after you.*c*

THE SHULAMITE
    The king has brought me into his chambers.

THE DAUGHTERS OF JERUSALEM
    We will be glad and rejoice in you.*d*

    We will remember your*e* love more than
    wine.

THE SHULAMITE
    Rightly do they love you.*f*

5 I *am* dark, but lovely,
    O daughters of Jerusalem,
    Like the tents of Kedar,
    Like the curtains of Solomon.

CHAPTER 1
1:2ff Christ loves you, no matter what you may see in yourself (vv. 5–6, 8, 15). Be sure that your love for Him is expressed in both words (vv. 2–3, 16) and deeds (John 14:21–24). Spend time with Him and enjoy His love as you would food and drink (vv. 2, 12) and the fragrance of sweet perfume (vv. 3, 12–13; John 12:1–8).

Your love relationship must never become stagnant because He wants to lead you into deeper experiences in His chambers (v. 4) and His banquet hall (2:4). Never be afraid to follow Him, for His love will never lead you astray. Enjoyment and enrichment will be yours as you commune with Him.

At the same time, never neglect your work (v. 6); faithful service is one way you show Him your love. You do not choose between Mary and Martha (Luke 10:38–42), for both service and devotion belong to the balanced Christian life. Also, do not allow yourself to become isolated from others. Follow His flock and His footsteps and you will walk in paths of loving fellowship (John 21:15–25).

1:2 *a*A Palestinian young woman (compare 6:13). The speaker and audience are identified according to the number, gender, and person of the Hebrew words. Occasionally the identity is not certain. *b*Masculine singular, that is, the Beloved
1:4 *c*Masculine singular, that is, the Beloved *d*Feminine singular, that is, the Shulamite *e*Masculine singular, that is, the Beloved *f*Masculine singular, that is, the Beloved

> **❝**The historical books I may compare to the outer courts of the temple; the gospels, the epistles and the psalms bring us into the holy place, or the court of the priests; but the Song of Solomon is the most holy place—the holy of holies, before which the veil still hangs to many an untaught believer.**❞**
> —Charles Haddon Spurgeon

> **❝**Love is the greatest thing that God can give us; for Himself is love: and it is the greatest thing we can give to God.**❞**
> —Jeremy Taylor

CHAPTER 2

2:1ff As you grow in your love for Christ, you must expect a variety of experiences, both pleasant and painful. You will enjoy His shade (v. 3), His banquets (vv. 4–5), and His tender expressions of love (v. 6). But you must also expect mountains (v. 8), walls (v. 9), winter seasons (v. 11), and enemies that creep in and try to destroy your work (v. 15).

You never know when your Lord will come to you for a time of communion, so be ever alert. When you least expect it, He will come (v. 8), stand (v. 9), look (v. 9), and speak (v. 10). No obstacle stands between Him and you *except the ones you put up yourself*. He leaps over the mountains because He yearns to be with you and lift you higher (v. 14).

When you spend time in loving communion with Christ, it is like springtime after the winter (vv. 10–13) and the dawning of a new day (v. 17).

6 Do not look upon me, because I *am* dark,
Because the sun has tanned me.
My mother's sons were angry with me;
They made me the keeper of the vineyards,
But my own vineyard I have not kept.

(To Her Beloved)

7 Tell me, O you whom I love,
Where you feed *your* flock,
Where you make *it* rest at noon.
For why should I be as one who veils herself[g]
By the flocks of your companions?

The Beloved

8 If you do not know, O fairest among women,
Follow in the footsteps of the flock,
And feed your little goats
Beside the shepherds' tents.
9 I have compared you, my love,
To my filly among Pharaoh's chariots.
10 Your cheeks are lovely with ornaments,
Your neck with chains *of gold*.

The Daughters of Jerusalem

11 We will make you[h] ornaments of gold
With studs of silver.

The Shulamite

12 While the king *is* at his table,
My spikenard sends forth its fragrance.
13 A bundle of myrrh *is* my beloved to me,
That lies all night between my breasts.
14 My beloved *is* to me a cluster of henna blooms
In the vineyards of En Gedi.

The Beloved .

15 Behold, you *are* fair, my love!
Behold, you *are* fair!
You *have* dove's eyes.

The Shulamite

16 Behold, you *are* handsome, my beloved!
Yes, pleasant!
Also our bed *is* green.
17 The beams of our houses *are* cedar,
And our rafters of fir.

2 I* *am* the rose of Sharon,
And the lily of the valleys.

The Beloved

2 Like a lily among thorns,
So is my love among the daughters.

The Shulamite

3 Like an apple tree among the trees of the woods,
So *is* my beloved among the sons.
I sat down in his shade with great delight,
And his fruit *was* sweet to my taste.

The Shulamite to the Daughters of Jerusalem

4 He brought me to the banqueting house,
And his banner over me *was* love.
5 Sustain me with cakes of raisins,
Refresh me with apples,
For I *am* lovesick.

1:7 [g]Septuagint, Syriac, and Vulgate read *wanders*.
1:11 [h]Feminine singular, that is, the Shulamite

6 His left hand *is* under my head,
And his right hand embraces me.
7 I charge you, O daughters of Jerusalem,
By the gazelles or by the does of the field,
Do not stir up nor awaken love
Until it pleases.

THE SHULAMITE
8 The voice of my beloved!
Behold, he comes
Leaping upon the mountains,
Skipping upon the hills.
9 My beloved is like a gazelle or a young stag.
Behold, he stands behind our wall;
He is looking through the windows,
Gazing through the lattice.

10 My beloved spoke, and said to me:
"Rise up, my love, my fair one,
And come away.
11 For lo, the winter is past,
The rain is over *and* gone.
12 The flowers appear on the earth;
The time of singing has come,
And the voice of the turtledove
Is heard in our land.
13 The fig tree puts forth her green figs,
And the vines *with* the tender grapes
Give a good smell.
Rise up, my love, my fair one,
And come away!

14 "O my dove, in the clefts of the rock,
In the secret *places* of the cliff,
Let me see your face,
Let me hear your voice;
For your voice *is* sweet,
And your face *is* lovely."

HER BROTHERS
15 Catch us the foxes,
The little foxes that spoil the vines,
For our vines *have* tender grapes.

THE SHULAMITE
16 My beloved *is* mine, and I *am* his.
He feeds *his flock* among the lilies.

"Jesus, the Very Thought of Thee"

When once Thou visitest the heart
Jesus, the very thought of Thee
With sweetness fills my breast;
But sweeter far Thy face to see,
And in Thy bosom rest.

When once Thou visitest the heart
Then truth begins to shine,
Then earthly vanities depart,
Then kindles love divine.

Twelfth-century Latin hymn,
attributed to Bernard of Clairvaux;
translated by Edward Caswall

(TO HER BELOVED)

(TO HER BELOVED)

17 Until the day breaks
And the shadows flee away,
Turn, my beloved,
And be like a gazelle
Or a young stag
Upon the mountains of Bether.*i*

THE SHULAMITE

3 By* night on my bed I sought the one I love;
I sought him, but I did not find him.
2 "I will rise now," *I said,*
"And go about the city;
In the streets and in the squares
I will seek the one I love."
I sought him, but I did not find him.
3 The watchmen who go about the city found me;
I said,
"Have you seen the one I love?"

4 *Scarcely had I passed by them,
When I found the one I love.
I held him and would not let him go,
Until I had brought him to the house of my mother,
And into the chamber of her who conceived me.

5 I charge you, O daughters of Jerusalem,
By the gazelles or by the does of the field,
Do not stir up nor awaken love
Until it pleases.

THE SHULAMITE

6 *Who *is* this coming out of the wilderness
Like pillars of smoke,
Perfumed with myrrh and frankincense,
With all the merchant's fragrant powders?
7 Behold, it *is* Solomon's couch,
With sixty valiant men around it,
Of the valiant of Israel.
8 They all hold swords,
Being expert in war.
Every man *has* his sword on his thigh
Because of fear in the night.

9 Of the wood of Lebanon
Solomon the King
Made himself a palanquin:*j*
10 He made its pillars *of* silver,
Its support *of* gold,
Its seat *of* purple,
Its interior paved *with* love
By the daughters of Jerusalem.
11 Go forth, O daughters of Zion,
And see King Solomon with the crown
With which his mother crowned him
On the day of his wedding,
The day of the gladness of his heart.

THE BELOVED

4 Behold,* you *are* fair, my love!
Behold, you *are* fair!
You *have* dove's eyes behind your veil.
Your hair *is* like a flock of goats,
Going down from Mount Gilead.
2 Your teeth *are* like a flock of shorn *sheep*
Which have come up from the washing,

CHAPTER 3

3:1–3 *Seeking.* There are times when the Lord comes to you (2:8), but there are also times when you should seek Him. It was not easy for her to leave the comfort and security of the bed for the danger of the street, but love cannot rest until it finds its beloved. Do you have that kind of love?

3:4, 5 *Finding.* She was not satisfied with information from the watchmen; she wanted personal communion with her beloved. It is not enough merely to listen to what others say about Jesus, as helpful as that may be. Press on until you enjoy Him personally.

3:6–11 *Enjoying.* In a triumphant and beautiful wedding procession, Solomon claims his bride and takes her home. The church is awaiting the Lord's glorious coming, but as we wait, we experience His love and joy (vv. 10–11; John 15:9–11). Find your delight in Him today and the joys of heaven will be greater.

CHAPTER 4

4:1–8 Do you want to experience His love? ***Listen to His words.*** He wants to tell you how fair you are in His sight because of His grace (Eph. 1:6). If you listen to what others say about you, you may be led astray, and if you listen to yourself, you may become discouraged. Believe His Word and rest in His love. Let your heart listen for His voice.

2:17 *i*Literally *Separation*   3:9 *j*A portable enclosed chair

Every one of which bears twins,
And none *is* barren among them.
3 Your lips *are* like a strand of scarlet,
And your mouth is lovely.
Your temples behind your veil
Are like a piece of pomegranate.
4 Your neck *is* like the tower of David,
Built for an armory,
On which hang a thousand bucklers,
All shields of mighty men.
5 Your two breasts *are* like two fawns,
Twins of a gazelle,
Which feed among the lilies.

6 Until the day breaks
And the shadows flee away,
I will go my way to the mountain of
myrrh
And to the hill of frankincense.

7 You *are* all fair, my love,
And *there is* no spot in you.
8 Come with me from Lebanon, *my* spouse,
With me from Lebanon.
Look from the top of Amana,
From the top of Senir and Hermon,
From the lions' dens,
From the mountains of the leopards.

9 *You have ravished my heart,
My sister, *my* spouse;
You have ravished my heart
With one *look* of your eyes,
With one link of your necklace.
10 How fair is your love,
My sister, *my* spouse!
How much better than wine is your love,
And the scent of your perfumes
Than all spices!
11 Your lips, O *my* spouse,
Drip as the honeycomb;
Honey and milk *are* under your tongue;
And the fragrance of your garments
Is like the fragrance of Lebanon.

12 *A garden enclosed
Is my sister, *my* spouse,
A spring shut up,
A fountain sealed.
13 Your plants *are* an orchard of pomegranates
With pleasant fruits,
Fragrant henna with spikenard,
14 Spikenard and saffron,
Calamus and cinnamon,
With all trees of frankincense,
Myrrh and aloes,
With all the chief spices—
15 A fountain of gardens,
A well of living waters,
And streams from Lebanon.

THE SHULAMITE
16 Awake, O north *wind*,
And come, O south!
Blow upon my garden,
That its spices may flow out.
Let my beloved come to his garden
And eat its pleasant fruits.

THE BELOVED
5 I* have come to my garden, my sister, *my*
spouse;

4:9–11 *Look to Him in love.* You cannot see Him physically, but you can still love Him (1 Pet. 1:8). See Him in His Word, in the world He has made, and in His providential care for you each day. Tell Him that you love Him!

4:12–16 *Live to please Him.* A garden, spring, and fountain are not useful if they are shut up, so open your life to Him and let Him bring out of you all that will delight Him and help others. Sometimes He must send trials to bring out the best blessings (v. 16). You are His unique garden and He is the loving Gardener (John 20:15), and He will cultivate your life and make it fruitful as you commune with Him (John 15:1–8).

When the Lord comes to your garden, let Him enjoy your love (5:1; John 20:11–18).

CHAPTER 5

5:1ff No matter where you are or what you are doing, fix your heart on the Lord and keep alert to His voice. You never know when He may come to have fellowship with you.

When He comes, He will speak and knock, *and you must respond to Him immediately.* No excuses! She heard his knock and his voice, and she saw his hand, but she did not yield to his call. When finally she opened the door, he was gone, even though he left a token blessing behind (v. 5). Better to have your beloved than any blessing he might give.

A loving heart will seek the Lord, no matter what the cost (vv. 6–8). How much better it would have been for her to respond to Him when she first heard His call. But she does not blame her Beloved; she gladly tells others how wonderful He is (vv. 10–16).

An affectionate heart is an alert heart, quick to respond to the Beloved's calls.

I have gathered my myrrh with my spice;
I have eaten my honeycomb with my honey;
I have drunk my wine with my milk.

(To His Friends)

Eat, O friends!
Drink, yes, drink deeply,
O beloved ones!

The Shulamite

2   I sleep, but my heart is awake;
It is the voice of my beloved!
He knocks, *saying,*
"Open for me, my sister, my love,
My dove, my perfect one;
For my head is covered with dew,
My locks with the drops of the night."

3   I have taken off my robe;
How can I put it on *again?*
I have washed my feet;
How can I defile them?
4   My beloved put his hand
By the latch *of the door,*
And my heart yearned for him.
5   I arose to open for my beloved,
And my hands dripped *with* myrrh,
My fingers with liquid myrrh,
On the handles of the lock.

6   I opened for my beloved,
But my beloved had turned away *and* was
gone.
My heart leaped up when he spoke.
I sought him, but I could not find him;
I called him, but he gave me no answer.
7   The watchmen who went about the city
found me.
They struck me, they wounded me;
The keepers of the walls
Took my veil away from me.
8   I charge you, O daughters of Jerusalem,
If you find my beloved,
That you tell him I *am* lovesick!

The Daughters of Jerusalem

9   What *is* your beloved
More than *another* beloved,
O fairest among women?
What *is* your beloved
More than *another* beloved,
That you so charge us?

The Shulamite

10   My beloved *is* white and ruddy,
Chief among ten thousand.
11   His head *is like* the finest gold;
His locks *are* wavy,
And black as a raven.
12   His eyes *are* like doves
By the rivers of waters,
Washed with milk,
And fitly set.
13   His cheeks *are* like a bed of spices,
Banks of scented herbs.
His lips *are* lilies,
Dripping liquid myrrh.

14   His hands *are* rods of gold
Set with beryl.
His body *is* carved ivory
Inlaid *with* sapphires.

15 His legs *are* pillars of marble
   Set on bases of fine gold.
   His countenance *is* like Lebanon,
   Excellent as the cedars.
16 His mouth *is* most sweet,
   Yes, he *is* altogether lovely.
   This *is* my beloved,
   And this *is* my friend,
   O daughters of Jerusalem!

THE DAUGHTERS OF JERUSALEM

6 Where* has your beloved gone,
   O fairest among women?
   Where has your beloved turned aside,
   That we may seek him with you?

THE SHULAMITE

2 My beloved has gone to his garden,
   To the beds of spices,
   To feed *his flock* in the gardens,
   And to gather lilies.
3 I *am* my beloved's,
   And my beloved *is* mine.
   He feeds *his flock* among the lilies.

THE BELOVED

4 O my love, you *are as* beautiful as Tirzah,
   Lovely as Jerusalem,
   Awesome as *an army* with banners!
5 Turn your eyes away from me,
   For they have overcome me.
   Your hair *is* like a flock of goats
   Going down from Gilead.
6 Your teeth *are* like a flock of sheep
   Which have come up from the washing;
   Every one bears twins,
   And none *is* barren among them.
7 Like a piece of pomegranate
   Are your temples behind your veil.

8 There are sixty queens
   And eighty concubines,
   And virgins without number.
9 My dove, my perfect one,
   Is the only one,
   The only one of her mother,
   The favorite of the one who bore her.
   The daughters saw her
   And called her blessed,
   The queens and the concubines,
   And they praised her.

10 Who is she who looks forth as the morning,
   Fair as the moon,
   Clear as the sun,
   Awesome as *an army* with banners?

THE SHULAMITE

11 I went down to the garden of nuts
   To see the verdure of the valley,
   To see whether the vine had budded
   And the pomegranates had bloomed.
12 Before I was even aware,
   My soul had made me
   As the chariots of my noble people.ᵏ

THE BELOVED AND HIS FRIENDS

13 Return, return, O Shulamite;
   Return, return, that we may look upon you!

CHAPTER 6

6:1ff The friends of the bride noticed that her Beloved was missing, and they asked about Him (v. 1). Often others can tell when we are out of fellowship with the Lord. Of course, we know where He is (v. 2) and what we must do to be reconciled to Him (1 John 1:9). We know that we belong to Him (v. 3) and that He still loves us and sees beauty in us (vv. 4–10) in spite of our lack of loving response. Contrast verse 3 with 2:16 and 7:10.

The bride went where her beloved was (v. 11) that she might be forgiven and restored. If we are to be reconciled to him and enjoy his communion once more, we must go back to the place where we left him (Gen. 13:3). Instead of being beaten (5:7), she is now in his glorious triumphal procession (vv. 10–12; 2 Cor. 2:14), sitting regally in the lead chariot!

Her friends begged her to remain that they might enjoy her beauty (v. 13). Do God's people today impress the world with their beauty and Christlikeness? Perhaps we need to meet the Beloved in His garden.

6:12 ᵏHebrew *Ammi Nadib*

CHAPTER 7

7:1–5 *He admires you.* Once more, the Beloved tells His wife how attractive she is to Him. This reminds us that husbands and wives need to express their love to each other often and find their joy freely in each other. Perhaps we would use different similes today, but each of these descriptions was meaningful in that day.

7:6–13 *He desires you.* What incredible love that He should want to share His life with sinners such as we are (1 John 3:1)! Verse 10 is an improvement over 2:16 and 6:3, for it focuses on His desire for us and not just on our relationship with Him. Ask Him to go with you to some special place where you can give Him your love (vv. 11–13). There are times when He invites you (2:10ff.), but He enjoys it when you invite Him.

THE SHULAMITE

What would you see in the Shulamite—
As it were, the dance of the two
    camps?^{l}

THE BELOVED

7 How* beautiful are your feet in sandals,
    O prince's daughter!
    The curves of your thighs *are* like
        jewels,
    The work of the hands of a skillful
        workman.
2 Your navel *is* a rounded goblet;
    It lacks no blended beverage.
    Your waist *is* a heap of wheat
    Set about with lilies.
3 Your two breasts *are* like two fawns,
    Twins of a gazelle.
4 Your neck *is* like an ivory tower,
    Your eyes *like* the pools in Heshbon
    By the gate of Bath Rabbim.
    Your nose *is* like the tower of Lebanon
    Which looks toward Damascus.
5 Your head *crowns* you like *Mount* Carmel,
    And the hair of your head *is* like purple;
    A king *is* held captive by *your* tresses.

6 *How fair and how pleasant you are,
    O love, with your delights!
7 This stature of yours is like a palm tree,
    And your breasts *like* its clusters.
8 I said, "I will go up to the palm tree,
    I will take hold of its branches."
    Let now your breasts be like clusters of the
        vine,
    The fragrance of your breath like
        apples,
9 And the roof of your mouth like the best
        wine.

THE SHULAMITE

The wine goes *down* smoothly for my
    beloved,
    Moving gently the lips of sleepers.^{m}
10 I *am* my beloved's,
    And his desire *is* toward me.

11 Come, my beloved,
    Let us go forth to the field;
    Let us lodge in the villages.
12 Let us get up early to the vineyards;
    Let us see if the vine has budded,
    Whether the grape blossoms are open,
    And the pomegranates are in bloom.
    There I will give you my love.
13 The mandrakes give off a fragrance,
    And at our gates *are* pleasant *fruits,*
    All manner, new and old,
    Which I have laid up for you, my
        beloved.

6:13 ^{l}Hebrew *Mahanaim* 7:9 ^{m}Septuagint, Syriac, and Vulgate read *lips and teeth.*

Lovely Feet—We do not usually think of feet as attractive parts of the body (7:1), but our Lord wants us to have beautiful feet, spiritually speaking. Our feet should be clean (John 13:1–11) and shod (Luke 15:22; Eph. 6:15) and busy carrying the good news of salvation (Isa. 52:7; Rom. 10:15). Defiled feet and disobedient feet will grieve His heart and make it difficult for Him to fellowship with us as He desires.

8

Oh,* that you were like my brother,
Who nursed at my mother's breasts!
If I should find you outside,
I would kiss you;
I would not be despised.

2 I would lead you *and* bring you
Into the house of my mother,
She *who* used to instruct me.
I would cause you to drink of spiced wine,
Of the juice of my pomegranate.

(To the Daughters of Jerusalem)

3 *His left hand *is* under my head,
And his right hand embraces me.

4 I charge you, O daughters of Jerusalem,
Do not stir up nor awaken love
Until it pleases.

A Relative

5 Who *is* this coming up from the wilderness,
Leaning upon her beloved?

I awakened you under the apple tree.
There your mother brought you forth;
There she *who* bore you brought *you*
forth.

The Shulamite to Her Beloved

6 *Set me as a seal upon your heart,
As a seal upon your arm;
For love *is as* strong as death,
Jealousy *as* cruel as the grave;[n]
Its flames *are* flames of fire,
A most vehement[o] flame.

7 Many waters cannot quench love,
Nor can the floods drown it.
If a man would give for love
All the wealth of his house,
It would be utterly despised.

The Shulamite's Brothers

8 *We have a little sister,
And she has no breasts.
What shall we do for our sister
In the day when she is spoken for?

9 If she *is* a wall,
We will build upon her
A battlement of silver;
And if she *is* a door,
We will enclose her
With boards of cedar.

The Shulamite

10 I *am* a wall,
And my breasts like towers;
Then I became in his eyes
As one who found peace.

11 Solomon had a vineyard at Baal Hamon;
He leased the vineyard to keepers;
Everyone was to bring for its fruit
A thousand silver coins.

(To Solomon)

12 My own vineyard *is* before me.
You, O Solomon, *may have* a thousand,
And those who tend its fruit two hundred.

8:6 [n]Or *Sheol* [o]Literally *A flame of Yah* (a poetic form of *YHWH,*
the Lord)

CHAPTER 8

8:1, 2 *Imagining love*. When you love
someone, you think about that person and
imagine all kinds of wonderful experiences
together. But true love cannot remain only
in the mind; it has to be fulfilled in life. An
imaginary love for Christ is fatal to a vital
Christian life.

8:3–5 *Experiencing love*. Your love for Him
must be a living and growing experience,
not something you manufacture yourself.
You can commune with Him in private
worship, lean on Him in the wilderness, and
enjoy Him in the field. Everywhere, He
awaits your affection.

8:6, 7 *Cherishing love*. Solomon used
three images to illustrate true love. The
seal speaks of ownership, two lovers belonging
only to each other until separated by death.
This is the permanence of love. The fire
reminds us of the power of love—nothing
can quench it. And the wealth illustrates the
preciousness of love.

8:8, 9 *Protecting love*. The picture is that
of a family, protecting a young daughter until
she is old enough to marry. If she is a "door"
(open to everybody), she must be protected,
but if she is a "wall," she has the integrity
to protect herself.

❝*I ask you, Lord Jesus, to develop
in me, your lover, an immeasurable
urge towards you, an affection that
is unbounded, a longing that is
unrestrained, a fervor that throws
discretion to the winds! There is no
one more blessed than he who dies
because he loves so much. No
creature can love God too much.*❞

—Richard Rolle

8:13 *Listening for love.* The Savior listens for your voice (v. 13; 2:14), and you must listen for His voice (2:8; 5:2). He will speak to you through His Word and by His Holy Spirit, so be attentive.

THE BELOVED
13 *You who dwell in the gardens,
    The companions listen for your voice—
    Let me hear it!

THE SHULAMITE
14 Make haste, my beloved,
    And be like a gazelle
    Or a young stag
    On the mountains of spices.

ISAIAH

The book of Isaiah may be compared to the whole Bible because it has two parts, like the two testaments. In the Old Testament section (chaps. 1—39), the prophet condemns the sins of Judah and warns of coming judgment. In the New Testament section (chaps. 40—66), he prophesies Judah's deliverance from Babylonian captivity. Throughout both sections, he announces the establishment of God's glorious kingdom. The first section primarily highlights law and condemnation, while the second emphasizes grace and glorious redemption. "The Holy One of Israel" is one of Isaiah's favorite names for the Lord.

The name *Isaiah* means "the salvation of Jehovah," and the prophet deals with four different kinds of salvation: (1) Judah's national salvation from the attacks of other nations; (2) Judah's salvation from the Babylonian captivity; (3) the future salvation of the Jews when their kingdom is established; and (4) the personal salvation of the sinner who puts his faith in the Redeemer.

Isaiah prophesied seven hundred years before Christ, in a period of international tension. Egypt, Syria, Israel (the northern kingdom), Babylon, and Assyria had their eyes on Judah, and the leaders of Judah tried to play one nation against another in their attempt to avoid war. Isaiah warned them not to trust in politics but to trust the Lord and obey His Word. The leaders did not listen, and Judah was eventually taken captive by Babylon. Isaiah's book guided and comforted the exiles both during and after their captivity.

As you read this book, you will see how believers should respond to international conflicts, political decay in the nation, and religious decay among the people, including the religious leaders. Isaiah ministered at a time when "religion" was popular but not spiritual, and the ministry at the temple was only a formality. The nation as a whole was corrupt, but God had His faithful remnant just as He does today.

Tradition says that the prophet Isaiah was sawed in half by King Manasseh. Hebrews 11:37 is said to refer to his death.

1 The* vision of Isaiah the son of Amoz, which he saw concerning Judah and Jerusalem in the days of Uzziah, Jotham, Ahaz, *and* Hezekiah, kings of Judah.

2 Hear, O heavens, and give ear, O earth!
For the LORD has spoken:
"I have nourished and brought up children,
And they have rebelled against Me;
3 The ox knows its owner
And the donkey its master's crib;
But Israel does not know,
My people do not consider."

4 Alas, sinful nation,
A people laden with iniquity,
A brood of evildoers,
Children who are corrupters!
They have forsaken the LORD,
They have provoked to anger
The Holy One of Israel,
They have turned away backward.

5 Why should you be stricken again?
You will revolt more and more.

CHAPTER 1

1:1ff Isaiah had access to four different kings, but his great concern was the spiritual state of the nation and not the political success of the leaders. There is a place for diplomacy and political action, for God established human government; but the leaders' faith must be in God's truth and not in man's schemes.

Outwardly, the nation seemed prosperous and even religious, but God saw a different picture. His people were rebellious children, lower than animals (vv. 2–3). They were sick with sin, like lepers (vv. 4–6), and their "garden city" had become another Sodom and Gomorrah (vv. 7–9).

Their popular religious meetings were futile and a grief to the Lord (vv. 10–15). In fact, their religious activities defiled the people instead of making them clean (vv. 16–20; Matt. 23:25–28). The wife of Jehovah was now a harlot (v. 21); their
(continued)

The Virtue of Cleanliness—It is good to pray, "Wash me" (Ps. 51:7), but keep in mind that God says, "Wash yourselves" (Isa. 1:16). Paul wrote, "Let us cleanse ourselves" (2 Cor. 7:1). Follow that advice and keep yourself clean!

(continued from previous page)
treasures were now cheap (vv. 22–26); and their garden was destined to be destroyed by fire (vv. 27–31).

Sin breaks God's heart, cheapens a nation or an individual, and invites the judgment of God. God graciously offers His forgiveness if we will repent (vv. 18–20).

The whole head is sick,
And the whole heart faints.
6 From the sole of the foot even to the head,
There is no soundness in it,
But wounds and bruises and putrefying sores;
They have not been closed or bound up,
Or soothed with ointment.

7 Your country *is* desolate,
Your cities *are* burned with fire;
Strangers devour your land in your presence;
And *it is* desolate, as overthrown by strangers.
8 So the daughter of Zion is left as a booth in a vineyard,
As a hut in a garden of cucumbers,
As a besieged city.
9 Unless the LORD of hosts
Had left to us a very small remnant,
We would have become like Sodom,
We would have been made like Gomorrah.

10 Hear the word of the LORD,
You rulers of Sodom;
Give ear to the law of our God,
You people of Gomorrah:
11 "To what purpose *is* the multitude of your sacrifices to Me?"
Says the LORD.
"I have had enough of burnt offerings of rams
And the fat of fed cattle.
I do not delight in the blood of bulls,
Or of lambs or goats.

12 "When you come to appear before Me,
Who has required this from your hand,
To trample My courts?
13 Bring no more futile sacrifices;
Incense is an abomination to Me.
The New Moons, the Sabbaths, and the calling of assemblies—
I cannot endure iniquity and the sacred meeting.
14 Your New Moons and your appointed feasts
My soul hates;
They are a trouble to Me,
I am weary of bearing *them*.
15 When you spread out your hands,
I will hide My eyes from you;
Even though you make many prayers,
I will not hear.
Your hands are full of blood.

16 "Wash yourselves, make yourselves clean;
Put away the evil of your doings from before My eyes.
Cease to do evil,
17 Learn to do good;
Seek justice,
Rebuke the oppressor;[a]
Defend the fatherless,
Plead for the widow.

18 "Come now, and let us reason together,"
Says the LORD,
"Though your sins are like scarlet,
They shall be as white as snow;

1:17 [a]Some ancient versions read *the oppressed.*

Though they are red like crimson,
They shall be as wool.
19 If you are willing and obedient,
   You shall eat the good of the land;
20 But if you refuse and rebel,
   You shall be devoured by the sword";
   For the mouth of the LORD has spoken.

21 How the faithful city has become a harlot!
   It was full of justice;
   Righteousness lodged in it,
   But now murderers.
22 Your silver has become dross,
   Your wine mixed with water.
23 Your princes *are* rebellious,
   And companions of thieves;
   Everyone loves bribes,
   And follows after rewards.
   They do not defend the fatherless,
   Nor does the cause of the widow come
      before them.

24 Therefore the Lord says,
   The LORD of hosts, the Mighty One of Israel,
   "Ah, I will rid Myself of My adversaries,
   And take vengeance on My enemies.
25 I will turn My hand against you,
   And thoroughly purge away your dross,
   And take away all your alloy.
26 I will restore your judges as at the first,
   And your counselors as at the beginning.
   Afterward you shall be called the city of
      righteousness, the faithful city."

27 Zion shall be redeemed with justice,
   And her penitents with righteousness.
28 The destruction of transgressors and of
      sinners *shall be* together,
   And those who forsake the LORD shall be
      consumed.
29 For they[b] shall be ashamed of the terebinth
      trees
   Which you have desired;
   And you shall be embarrassed because of
      the gardens
   Which you have chosen.
30 For you shall be as a terebinth whose leaf
      fades,
   And as a garden that has no water.
31 The strong shall be as tinder,
   And the work of it as a spark;
   Both will burn together,
   And no one shall quench *them.*

2 The word that Isaiah the son of Amoz saw
   concerning Judah and Jerusalem.

2 *Now it shall come to pass in the latter days
   That the mountain of the LORD's house
   Shall be established on the top of the
      mountains,
   And shall be exalted above the hills;
   And all nations shall flow to it.
3 Many people shall come and say,
   "Come, and let us go up to the mountain of
      the LORD,
   To the house of the God of Jacob;
   He will teach us His ways,

CHAPTER 2

2:2–4 The house of the Lord. In the
previous chapter, Isaiah looked *within* the
heart of the nation; now he looks *ahead* to
the future glorious kingdom God promised
His people. Instead of being a place for
corrupt worship, the temple will be a center
of truth and blessing for Jews and Gentiles.
Instead of international conflict, there will be
peace. When world conditions distress you,
remember that things will not always be like
this.

1:29 *b*Following Masoretic Text, Septuagint, and Vulgate;
some Hebrew manuscripts and Targum read *you.*

And we shall walk in His paths."
For out of Zion shall go forth the law,
And the word of the LORD from Jerusalem.

4   He shall judge between the nations,
And rebuke many people;
They shall beat their swords into
    plowshares,
And their spears into pruning hooks;
Nation shall not lift up sword against nation,
Neither shall they learn war anymore.

2:5–9 *The light of the Lord.* Judah was borrowing new religious ideas from the gentile nations and not walking in God's truth. Their faith was in material progress and not in the Lord. How they needed to get back to the light of God's Word! In our own day, astrology and Eastern religions have replaced the Bible, and making money is more important than serving the Lord.

5   *O house of Jacob, come and let us walk
In the light of the LORD.

6   For You have forsaken Your people, the
    house of Jacob,
Because they are filled with eastern ways;
They *are* soothsayers like the Philistines,
And they are pleased with the children of
    foreigners.

7   Their land is also full of silver and gold,
And there is no end to their treasures;
Their land is also full of horses,
And there is no end to their chariots.

8   Their land is also full of idols;
They worship the work of their own hands,
That which their own fingers have made.

9   People bow down,
And each man humbles himself;
Therefore do not forgive them.

2:10–22 *The day of the Lord.* This is a time of judgment from the Lord that can apply locally, as with Judah, or worldwide, as in the end times. Man's pride will be brought low, and all that man lives for will be destroyed. God patiently waits as people rebel against the truth, but in the end, sin will be judged and the Lord will be exalted (vv. 11, 17). God will protect His believing remnant when that day of judgment comes (1 Thess. 1:10; 5:9–10).

10 *Enter into the rock, and hide in the dust,
From the terror of the LORD
And the glory of His majesty.

11 The lofty looks of man shall be humbled,
The haughtiness of men shall be bowed
    down,
And the LORD alone shall be exalted in that
    day.

12 For the day of the LORD of hosts
Shall come upon everything proud and
    lofty,
Upon everything lifted up—
And it shall be brought low—

13 Upon all the cedars of Lebanon *that are*
    high and lifted up,
And upon all the oaks of Bashan;

14 Upon all the high mountains,
And upon all the hills *that are* lifted up;

15 Upon every high tower,
And upon every fortified wall;

16 Upon all the ships of Tarshish,
And upon all the beautiful sloops.

17 The loftiness of man shall be bowed down,
And the haughtiness of men shall be
    brought low;
The LORD alone will be exalted in that day,

18 But the idols He shall utterly abolish.

19 They shall go into the holes of the rocks,
And into the caves of the earth,
From the terror of the LORD
And the glory of His majesty,
When He arises to shake the earth mightily.

20 In that day a man will cast away his idols
    of silver
And his idols of gold,
Which they made, *each* for himself to
    worship,
To the moles and bats,

21 To go into the clefts of the rocks,
    And into the crags of the rugged rocks,
    From the terror of the LORD
    And the glory of His majesty,
    When He arises to shake the earth mightily.

22 Sever yourselves from such a man,
    Whose breath *is* in his nostrils;
    For of what account is he?

3 For* behold, the Lord, the LORD of hosts,
    Takes away from Jerusalem and from
        Judah
    The stock and the store,
    The whole supply of bread and the whole
        supply of water;
2   The mighty man and the man of war,
    The judge and the prophet,
    And the diviner and the elder;
3   The captain of fifty and the honorable man,
    The counselor and the skillful artisan,
    And the expert enchanter.

4   "I will give children *to be* their princes,
    And babes shall rule over them.
5   The people will be oppressed,
    Every one by another and every one by his
        neighbor;
    The child will be insolent toward the elder,
    And the base toward the honorable."

6   When a man takes hold of his brother
    In the house of his father, *saying,*
    "You have clothing;
    You be our ruler,
    And *let* these ruins *be* under your power,"c
7   In that day he will protest, saying,
    "I cannot cure *your* ills,
    For in my house *is* neither food nor clothing;
    Do not make me a ruler of the people."

8   For Jerusalem stumbled,
    And Judah is fallen,
    Because their tongue and their doings
    Are against the LORD,
    To provoke the eyes of His glory.
9   The look on their countenance witnesses
        against them,
    And they declare their sin as Sodom;
    They do not hide *it.*
    Woe to their soul!
    For they have brought evil upon themselves.

10 "Say to the righteous that *it shall be* well *with*
        them,
    For they shall eat the fruit of their doings.
11 Woe to the wicked! *It shall be* ill *with him,*
    For the reward of his hands shall be given
        him.
12 *As for* My people, children *are* their
        oppressors,
    And women rule over them.
    O My people! Those who lead you cause you
        to err,
    And destroy the way of your paths."

13 The LORD stands up to plead,
    And stands to judge the people.

CHAPTER 3

3:1ff The leaders of Judah trusted substitutes that would not help them in the coming day of judgment: natural resources, material wealth, military might, political experience, and even "religion" (vv. 1–3). God would take away in His wrath everything that dethroned Him in the hearts of the people.

But that was not all. God would replace their proud leaders with weaklings, nobodies without ability, who would oppress the people (vv. 4–8). Why? Because the nation not only sinned but boasted about it openly!

Isaiah was especially grieved because the women of the land had become addicted to wealth and fashion and were more interested in social status than spiritual character. The day would come when their artificial glamour would be gone and they would be sitting in the dust. (See 1 Pet. 3:1–6.) So many men would die in the coming war that the women would do anything to get a husband (Isa. 4:1).

Beware living on substitutes!

3:6 cLiterally *hand*

14 The LORD will enter into judgment
With the elders of His people
And His princes:
"For you have eaten up the vineyard;
The plunder of the poor *is* in your houses.
15 What do you mean by crushing My people
And grinding the faces of the poor?"
Says the Lord GOD of hosts.

16Moreover the LORD says:

"Because the daughters of Zion are haughty,
And walk with outstretched necks
And wanton eyes,
Walking and mincing *as* they go,
Making a jingling with their feet,
17 Therefore the Lord will strike with a scab
The crown of the head of the daughters of
Zion,
And the LORD will uncover their secret
parts."

18 In that day the Lord will take away the
finery:
The jingling anklets, the scarves, and the
crescents;
19 The pendants, the bracelets, and the veils;
20 The headdresses, the leg ornaments, and the
headbands;
The perfume boxes, the charms,
21   and the rings;
The nose jewels,
22   the festal apparel, and the mantles;
The outer garments, the purses,
23   and the mirrors;
The fine linen, the turbans, and the robes.

24And so it shall be:

Instead of a sweet smell there will be a
stench;
Instead of a sash, a rope;
Instead of well-set hair, baldness;
Instead of a rich robe, a girding of
sackcloth;
And branding instead of beauty.
25 Your men shall fall by the sword,
And your mighty in the war.

26 Her gates shall lament and mourn,
And she *being* desolate shall sit on the
ground.

4 And* in that day seven women shall take
hold of one man, saying,
"We will eat our own food and wear our own
apparel;
Only let us be called by your name,
To take away our reproach."
2 In that day the Branch of the LORD shall be
beautiful and glorious;
And the fruit of the earth *shall be* excellent
and appealing
For those of Israel who have escaped.

3And it shall come to pass that *he who is* left
in Zion and remains in Jerusalem will be called
holy—everyone who is recorded among the living
in Jerusalem. 4When the Lord has washed away
the filth of the daughters of Zion, and purged the
blood of Jerusalem from her midst, by the spirit
of judgment and by the spirit of burning, 5then

CHAPTER 4

4:1ff "In that day" refers to the coming
kingdom when the Lord will be exalted (Isa.
2:11, 17). Isaiah looked beyond the
impending crisis to the glory that one day
would come to Israel.
It will be a day of glory and not shame
as Jesus Christ (the "Branch of the LORD"
[Isa. 11:1; Jer. 33:15]) reigns on earth
(v. 2). It will be a time when the nation will
be washed and sanctified (vv. 5–6) and
every home on Mount Zion will become a
"tabernacle of God" with the distinctive pillar
of glory above it (Exod. 40:34ff.).
But why should we wait for these
blessings when God can give them to us
now? He will wash us clean (Isa. 1:18), set
us apart for Himself, and bless us in our
homes with His presence. Perhaps it is time
we followed Vance Havner's advice and
started living "in kingdom come."

the LORD will create above every dwelling place of Mount Zion, and above her assemblies, a cloud and smoke by day and the shining of a flaming fire by night. For over all the glory there *will be* a covering. 6And there will be a tabernacle for shade in the daytime from the heat, for a place of refuge, and for a shelter from storm and rain.

5 Now* let me sing to my Well-beloved
A song of my Beloved regarding His
   vineyard:

My Well-beloved has a vineyard
On a very fruitful hill.
2 He dug it up and cleared out its stones,
And planted it with the choicest vine.
He built a tower in its midst,
And also made a winepress in it;
So He expected *it* to bring forth *good*
   grapes,
But it brought forth wild grapes.

3 "And now, O inhabitants of Jerusalem and
   men of Judah,
Judge, please, between Me and My
   vineyard.
4 What more could have been done to My
   vineyard
That I have not done in it?
Why then, when I expected *it* to bring forth
   good grapes,
Did it bring forth wild grapes?
5 And now, please let Me tell you what I will
   do to My vineyard:
I will take away its hedge, and it shall be
   burned;
And break down its wall, and it shall be
   trampled down.
6 I will lay it waste;
It shall not be pruned or dug,
But there shall come up briers and thorns.
I will also command the clouds
That they rain no rain on it."

7 For the vineyard of the LORD of hosts *is* the
   house of Israel,
And the men of Judah are His pleasant
   plant.
He looked for justice, but behold,
   oppression;
For righteousness, but behold, a cry *for help.*

8 *Woe to those who join house to house;
They add field to field,
Till *there is* no place
Where they may dwell alone in the midst
   of the land!
9 In my hearing the LORD of hosts *said,*
"Truly, many houses shall be desolate,
Great and beautiful ones, without
   inhabitant.
10 For ten acres of vineyard shall yield one
   bath,
And a homer of seed shall yield one ephah."

CHAPTER 5

5:1–7 This chapter contains a song (vv. 1–7), a lament (vv. 8–23), and a judgment (vv. 24–30).

The nation of Israel is the Vineyard for which God did so much (Matt. 21:33–46). The people's sin was ingratitude, taking their blessings for granted and using them selfishly. Instead of serving the Lord, they served themselves, and the result was a corrupted nation.

5:8–23 The lament names some specific sins of the nation ("wild grapes" [v. 2]), sins that people still commit today. The rich stole from the poor (vv. 8–10), and people lived for sensual pleasure rather than godly enrichment (vv. 11–17). Confident of their own wisdom (v. 21), they questioned God's counsel (vv. 18–19) and for a price changed His words (vv. 20–23). There was no justice in the land because evil leaders turned from the truth of God's Word.

Significant Vines—There are three symbolic vines in Scripture. The past vine is Israel (Ps. 80; Isa. 3:14; 5:1–7; Jer. 2:21; 12:10; Ezek. 15; Hos. 10:1). The present vine is Christ and His church (John 15). The future vine is "the vine of the earth," the corrupt world system of the last days that is destined for judgment (Rev. 14:14–20).

11 Woe to those who rise early in the morning,
   That they may follow intoxicating drink;
   Who continue until night, *till* wine inflames
      them!
12 The harp and the strings,
   The tambourine and flute,
   And wine are in their feasts;
   But they do not regard the work of the LORD,
   Nor consider the operation of His hands.

13 Therefore my people have gone into
      captivity,
   Because *they have* no knowledge;
   Their honorable men *are* famished,
   And their multitude dried up with thirst.
14 Therefore Sheol has enlarged itself
   And opened its mouth beyond measure;
   Their glory and their multitude and their
      pomp,
   And he who is jubilant, shall descend into
      it.
15 People shall be brought down,
   Each man shall be humbled,
   And the eyes of the lofty shall be humbled.
16 But the LORD of hosts shall be exalted in
      judgment,
   And God who is holy shall be hallowed in
      righteousness.
17 Then the lambs shall feed in their pasture,
   And in the waste places of the fat ones
      strangers shall eat.

18 Woe to those who draw iniquity with cords
      of vanity,
   And sin as if with a cart rope;
19 That say, "Let Him make speed *and* hasten
      His work,
   That we may see *it;*
   And let the counsel of the Holy One of Israel
      draw near and come,
   That we may know *it.*"

20 Woe to those who call evil good, and good
      evil;
   Who put darkness for light, and light for
      darkness;
   Who put bitter for sweet, and sweet for
      bitter!

21 Woe to *those who are* wise in their own
      eyes,
   And prudent in their own sight!

22 Woe to men mighty at drinking wine,
   Woe to men valiant for mixing intoxicating
      drink,
23 Who justify the wicked for a bribe,
   And take away justice from the righteous
      man!

24 *Therefore, as the fire devours the stubble,
   And the flame consumes the chaff,
   So their root will be as rottenness,
   And their blossom will ascend like dust;
   Because they have rejected the law of the
      LORD of hosts,
   And despised the word of the Holy One of
      Israel.
25 Therefore the anger of the LORD is aroused
      against His people;
   He has stretched out His hand against them
   And stricken them,

5:24–30 God was angry; His hand of judgment was stretched out against His people (v. 25; 9:12, 17, 21; 10:4; 14:27). Judgment comes like a prairie fire (v. 24) when the invading army conquers the land (vv. 26–30).

Today, He stretches out His hands in love, inviting sinners to repent (Isa. 65:2; Rom. 10:21); but tomorrow, He will stretch them out in wrath.

And the hills trembled.
Their carcasses *were* as refuse in the midst
  of the streets.

For all this His anger is not turned away,
But His hand *is* stretched out still.

26 He will lift up a banner to the nations from
  afar,
And will whistle to them from the end of
  the earth;
Surely they shall come with speed, swiftly.
27 No one will be weary or stumble among
  them,
No one will slumber or sleep;
Nor will the belt on their loins be loosed,
Nor the strap of their sandals be broken;
28 Whose arrows *are* sharp,
And all their bows bent;
Their horses' hooves will seem like flint,
And their wheels like a whirlwind.
29 Their roaring *will be* like a lion,
They will roar like young lions;
Yes, they will roar
And lay hold of the prey;
They will carry *it* away safely,
And no one will deliver.
30 In that day they will roar against them
Like the roaring of the sea.
And if *one* looks to the land,
Behold, darkness *and* sorrow;
And the light is darkened by the clouds.

6 In* the year that King Uzziah died, I saw the
Lord sitting on a throne, high and lifted up,
and the train of His *robe* filled the temple. ²Above
it stood seraphim; each one had six wings: with
two he covered his face, with two he covered his
feet, and with two he flew. ³And one cried to another and said:

"Holy, holy, holy *is* the LORD of hosts;
  The whole earth *is* full of His glory!"

⁴And the posts of the door were shaken by the
voice of him who cried out, and the house was
filled with smoke.
⁵*So I said:

"Woe *is* me, for I am undone!
Because I *am* a man of unclean lips,
And I dwell in the midst of a people of
  unclean lips;
For my eyes have seen the King,
The LORD of hosts."

⁶Then one of the seraphim flew to me, having
in his hand a live coal *which* he had taken with
the tongs from the altar. ⁷And he touched my
mouth *with it,* and said:

"Behold, this has touched your lips;
Your iniquity is taken away,
And your sin purged."

⁸*Also I heard the voice of the Lord, saying:

CHAPTER 6

6:1–4 *Sight: he saw the Lord.* Isaiah had
a life-changing vision of Jesus Christ (John
12:38–41). The throne of Judah had
changed occupants, but God was still on His
throne and in perfect control of everything.
When you worship, focus on God's holiness,
sovereignty, and glory. When things on earth
are discouraging, start looking at things from
heaven's point of view.

6:5–7 *Insight: he saw himself.* Isaiah had
pronounced woes on other people, but now
he cried, "Woe is me!" He admitted that he
was a sinner, he confessed his sin, and the
Lord cleansed him. Were it not for the
sacrifice on the altar, we could never
approach the throne.

6:8–13 *Vision: he saw the need.* True
worship leads to service. You hear God's
call, and you respond with obedience. God
did not send Isaiah to a receptive people
or give him an easy message to preach. But
when you have seen the Lord and felt His
touch, you can obey His will without fear.

His Majesty—"Men are never duly touched and impressed with a conviction of their insignificance,
until they have contrasted themselves with the majesty of God," wrote John Calvin. This was true
not only of Isaiah but also of Job (Job 42:5–6), Daniel (Dan. 10:16–17), Peter (Luke 5:8), and John
(Rev. 1:17).

"Whom shall I send,
And who will go for Us?"

Then I said, "Here *am* I! Send me."
9And He said, "Go, and tell this people:

'Keep on hearing, but do not understand;
Keep on seeing, but do not perceive.'

10 "Make the heart of this people dull,
And their ears heavy,
And shut their eyes;
Lest they see with their eyes,
And hear with their ears,
And understand with their heart,
And return and be healed."

11Then I said, "Lord, how long?"
And He answered:

"Until the cities are laid waste and without
inhabitant,
The houses are without a man,
The land is utterly desolate,
12   The LORD has removed men far away,
And the forsaken places *are* many in the
midst of the land.
13   But yet a tenth *will be* in it,
And will return and be for consuming,
As a terebinth tree or as an oak,
Whose stump *remains* when it is cut down.
So the holy seed *shall be* its stump."

CHAPTER 7

7:1, 2 Fear. King Ahaz was frightened
(vv. 2, 4, 16) because Syria and Israel united
to depose him and crown a new king in
Judah. Assyria and Egypt were also on the
move, so it was not an encouraging time.
When circumstances threaten you, what do
you do? Alas, Ahaz trusted in his own
wisdom and made a treaty with the king of
Assyria, only to see him break it.

7 Now* it came to pass in the days of Ahaz the
son of Jotham, the son of Uzziah, king of Judah, *that* Rezin king of Syria and Pekah the son
of Remaliah, king of Israel, went up to Jerusalem
to *make* war against it, but could not prevail
against it. 2And it was told to the house of David,
saying, "Syria's forces are deployed in Ephraim."
So his heart and the heart of his people were
moved as the trees of the woods are moved with
the wind.
3Then the LORD said to Isaiah, "Go out now to
meet Ahaz, you and Shear-Jashubᵈ your son, at
the end of the aqueduct from the upper pool, on
the highway to the Fuller's Field, 4and say to him:
'Take heed, and be quiet; do not fear or be faint-

7:3 ᵈLiterally *A Remnant Shall Return*

He Shall Be Immanuel—Isaiah 7—12 is sometimes called the "Book of Immanuel" (Isa. 7:14;
8:8, 10). *Immanuel* means "God with us." God gave this prophecy to the whole "house of David"
(Isa. 7:13) and not just to King Ahaz; it refers ultimately to the Lord Jesus Christ (Matt. 1:18–25).
He is God, and He is "God with us."
     Isaiah the Evangelical—Isaiah is called "the evangelical prophet" because he says so much
about Jesus Christ. Isaiah writes about His birth (7:14; Matt. 1:23); the ministry of John the Baptist
(40:1–6; Matt. 3); His own ministry in the Spirit (61:1–2; Luke 4:17–19); His rejection by the nation
(6:9–13; Matt. 13:10–15; John 12:38); the Stone of stumbling (8:14; 28:16; Matt. 21:42; Rom.
9:32–33; 1 Pet. 2:6); His ministry to the Gentiles (49:6; Luke 2:32; Acts 13:47); His future kingdom
(11:1–9; Rev. 12:10); and His atoning death on the cross (53:1ff.; Mark 10:25).
     Jesus' Birth—The virgin birth of Jesus Christ is a basic doctrine of the Christian faith, for the
Son of God could never be born as you were born. Every baby is a new creation, but Jesus Christ
existed from eternity. He was not only born, but He "came into the world" (John 3:17; 10:36; 16:28).
According to Isaiah 9:6, the Child was born (His human nature) and the Son was given (His divine
nature). The holy Son of God could not partake of sinful human nature. His body was miraculously
conceived by the Holy Spirit in Mary's womb (Luke 1:26–38; Heb. 10:5). He did no sin (1 Pet. 2:22);
"in Him there is no sin" (1 John 3:5); He knew no sin (2 Cor. 5:21). Hallelujah, what a Savior!

hearted for these two stubs of smoking firebrands, for the fierce anger of Rezin and Syria, and the son of Remaliah. 5Because Syria, Ephraim, and the son of Remaliah have plotted evil against you, saying, 6"Let us go up against Judah and trouble it, and let us make a gap in its wall for ourselves, and set a king over them, the son of Tabel"— 7thus says the Lord GOD:

"It shall not stand,
Nor shall it come to pass.
8 For the head of Syria *is* Damascus,
    And the head of Damascus *is* Rezin.
    Within sixty-five years Ephraim will be
       broken,
    So that it will not *be* a people.
9 The head of Ephraim *is* Samaria,
    And the head of Samaria *is* Remaliah's
       son.
    If you will not believe,
    Surely you shall not be established." ' "

10*Moreover the LORD spoke again to Ahaz, saying, 11"Ask a sign for yourself from the LORD your God; ask it either in the depth or in the height above."

12But Ahaz said, "I will not ask, nor will I test the LORD!"

13Then he said, "Hear now, O house of David! *Is it* a small thing for you to weary men, but will you weary my God also? 14*Therefore the Lord Himself will give you a sign: Behold, the virgin shall conceive and bear a Son, and shall call His name Immanuel.*e* 15Curds and honey He shall eat, that He may know to refuse the evil and choose the good. 16For before the Child shall know to refuse the evil and choose the good, the land that you dread will be forsaken by both her kings. 17The LORD will bring the king of Assyria upon you and your people and your father's house— days that have not come since the day that Ephraim departed from Judah."

18 And it shall come to pass in that day
    That the LORD will whistle for the fly
    That *is* in the farthest part of the rivers of
       Egypt,
    And for the bee that *is* in the land of Assyria.
19 They will come, and all of them will rest
    In the desolate valleys and in the clefts of
       the rocks,
    And on all thorns and in all pastures.

20 In the same day the Lord will shave with a
       hired razor,
    With those from beyond the River,*f* with the
       king of Assyria,
    The head and the hair of the legs,
    And will also remove the beard.

21 It shall be in that day
    That a man will keep alive a young cow
       and two sheep;
22 So it shall be, from the abundance of milk
       they give,
    That he will eat curds;
    For curds and honey everyone will eat who
       is left in the land.

7:10–13 Faith. Isaiah's word to the king was from God and could be trusted. Ahaz pretended to be very spiritual when he refused to ask for a sign, but his rejection of the sign was actually a rejection of the Lord and His messenger. God's Word goes to work when we believe it and act on it. Ahaz only talked about it!

7:14–25 Fulfillment. Both Syria and Israel were eventually out of the picture as Isaiah had promised, but Assyria became the new threat. Israel was invaded by Assyria in 722 B.C., and the nation came to an end. The Assyrians invaded Judah in the days of King Hezekiah, but God defeated them. However, Assyria humbled Judah because God's people would not trust God's Word. It is *faith* in God, not faith in man's treaties, that brings the victory.

7:14 *e*Literally *God-With-Us*   7:20 *f*That is, the Euphrates

23 It shall happen in that day,
　　That wherever there could be a thousand
　　　vines
　　Worth a thousand *shekels* of silver,
　　It will be for briers and thorns.
24 With arrows and bows men will come there,
　　Because all the land will become briers and
　　　thorns.

25 And to any hill which could be dug with
　　　the hoe,
　　You will not go there for fear of briers and
　　　thorns;
　　But it will become a range for oxen
　　And a place for sheep to roam.

8 Moreover* the LORD said to me, "Take a large
scroll, and write on it with a man's pen concerning Maher-Shalal-Hash-Baz.ᵍ ²And I will take
for Myself faithful witnesses to record, Uriah the
priest and Zechariah the son of Jeberechiah."
³Then I went to the prophetess, and she conceived and bore a son. Then the LORD said to me,
"Call his name Maher-Shalal-Hash-Baz; ⁴for before the child shall have knowledge to cry 'My
father' and 'My mother,' the riches of Damascus
and the spoil of Samaria will be taken away before the king of Assyria."
⁵The LORD also spoke to me again, saying:

6 "Inasmuch as these people refused
　　The waters of Shiloah that flow softly,
　　And rejoice in Rezin and in Remaliah's son;
7 Now therefore, behold, the Lord brings up
　　　over them
　　The waters of the River,ʰ strong and
　　　mighty—
　　The king of Assyria and all his glory;
　　He will go up over all his channels
　　And go over all his banks.
8 He will pass through Judah,
　　He will overflow and pass over,
　　He will reach up to the neck;
　　And the stretching out of his wings
　　Will fill the breadth of Your land,
　　　O Immanuel.ⁱ

9 "Be shattered, O you peoples, and be broken
　　　in pieces!
　　Give ear, all you from far countries.
　　Gird yourselves, but be broken in pieces;
　　Gird yourselves, but be broken in pieces.
10 Take counsel together, but it will come to
　　　nothing;
　　Speak the word, but it will not stand,
　　For God *is* with us."ʲ

¹¹*For the LORD spoke thus to me with a strong
hand, and instructed me that I should not walk
in the way of this people, saying:

12 "Do not say, 'A conspiracy,'
　　Concerning all that this people call a
　　　conspiracy,
　　Nor be afraid of their threats, nor be
　　　troubled.

CHAPTER 8

8:1–10 Two rivers. The lengthy name in
verse 1 means "Speed to the spoil! Hasten
to the booty!" It refers to the victory Assyria
would win over Syria (Damascus) and Israel
(Samaria). This would give Assyria a clear
path to Judah, so Ahaz's treaty did not work.
He rejected the quiet waters of Shiloah (a
reference to a spring in Jerusalem) for the
flood waters of the Euphrates (a reference
to Assyria). God's wisdom brings peace, but
man's wisdom brings confusion (James
3:13–18).

8:11–15 Two fears. If you fear God, you
need not fear the threats of men. Make
Jesus Lord in your life, and He will take care
of your fears (1 Pet. 3:13–17). Christ is the
Stone of refuge for His people but a snare
to those who reject Him.

8:1 ᵍLiterally *Speed the Spoil, Hasten the Booty*　8:7 ʰThat
is, the Euphrates　8:8 ⁱLiterally *God-With-Us*　8:10 ʲHebrew
Immanuel

13 The LORD of hosts, Him you shall hallow;
   Let Him be your fear,
   And let Him be your dread.
14 He will be as a sanctuary,
   But a stone of stumbling and a rock of
      offense
   To both the houses of Israel,
   As a trap and a snare to the inhabitants of
      Jerusalem.
15 And many among them shall stumble;
   They shall fall and be broken,
   Be snared and taken."

16 *Bind up the testimony,
   Seal the law among my disciples.
17 And I will wait on the LORD,
   Who hides His face from the house of Jacob;
   And I will hope in Him.
18 Here am I and the children whom the LORD
      has given me!
   We are for signs and wonders in Israel
   From the LORD of hosts,
   Who dwells in Mount Zion.

19And when they say to you, "Seek those who
are mediums and wizards, who whisper and mutter," should not a people seek their God? Should
they seek the dead on behalf of the living?
20To the law and to the testimony! If they do not
speak according to this word, it is because there
is no light in them. 21They will pass through it hard-pressed and
hungry; and it shall happen, when they are hun-
gry, that they will be enraged and curse their king
and their God, and look upward. 22Then they will
look to the earth, and see trouble and darkness,
gloom of anguish; and they will be driven into
darkness.

9 Nevertheless* the gloom will not be upon
     her who is distressed,
   As when at first He lightly esteemed
   The land of Zebulun and the land of
      Naphtali,
   And afterward more heavily oppressed her,
   By the way of the sea, beyond the Jordan,
   In Galilee of the Gentiles.
2 The people who walked in darkness
   Have seen a great light;
   Those who dwelt in the land of the shadow
      of death,
   Upon them a light has shined.

3 You have multiplied the nation
   And increased its joy;ᵏ
   They rejoice before You
   According to the joy of harvest,
   As men rejoice when they divide the spoil.
4 For You have broken the yoke of his burden
   And the staff of his shoulder,
   The rod of his oppressor,
   As in the day of Midian.
5 For every warrior's sandal from the noisy
      battle,
   And garments rolled in blood,
   Will be used for burning and fuel of fire.

9:3 ᵏFollowing Qere and Targum; Kethib and Vulgate read not
increased joy; Septuagint reads Most of the people You
brought down in Your joy.

8:16–22 Two authorities. The Word of God
is the only authority for the believer, even if
circumstances seem to challenge it. In
Isaiah's day, the leaders were even
consulting mediums (Deut. 18:10–12)! Let
the Word be your light in this dark world
(Ps. 119:105).

CHAPTER 9

9:1ff What a difference it makes in our lives
that Jesus Christ came and died for our sins!
And what a difference it will make in this
world when He comes to sit on David's
throne and rule righteously!
   Jesus is the difference between light and
darkness, life and death (v. 2). He is also
the difference between joy and sorrow,
freedom and bondage (vv. 3–4). As you wait
for His return, be sure the government of
your life is on His shoulders. Let Him be to
you all that His names proclaim, for every
name that He bears is a blessing that He
shares.
   The proud will be judged (vv. 8–21), as
was Israel (the northern kingdom) when
Assyria took the nation captive. First, God
chastened them in love; and when they
would not submit, He judged them
(vv. 13–14). They were led astray by the
very people who should have led them in
the right way (v. 16; Lam. 4:13).
   Our God is a God of grace and truth (John
1:17). If you acknowledge His truth, you can
receive His grace (Ps. 51:3–4); but if you
reject His truth, His hand of judgment must
be stretched out to you. Which will it be?

6 For unto us a Child is born,
Unto us a Son is given;
And the government will be upon His
shoulder.
And His name will be called
Wonderful, Counselor, Mighty God,
Everlasting Father, Prince of Peace.

7 Of the increase of *His* government and
peace
There will be no end,
Upon the throne of David and over His
kingdom,
To order it and establish it with judgment
and justice
From that time forward, even forever.
The zeal of the LORD of hosts will perform
this.

8 The Lord sent a word against Jacob,
And it has fallen on Israel.

9 All the people will know—
Ephraim and the inhabitant of Samaria—
Who say in pride and arrogance of heart:

10 "The bricks have fallen down,
But we will rebuild with hewn stones;
The sycamores are cut down,
But we will replace *them* with cedars."

11 Therefore the LORD shall set up
The adversaries of Rezin against him,
And spur his enemies on,

12 The Syrians before and the Philistines
behind;
And they shall devour Israel with an open
mouth.

For all this His anger is not turned away,
But His hand *is* stretched out still.

13 For the people do not turn to Him who
strikes them,
Nor do they seek the LORD of hosts.

14 Therefore the LORD will cut off head and tail
from Israel,
Palm branch and bulrush in one day.

15 The elder and honorable, he *is* the head;
The prophet who teaches lies, he *is* the tail.

16 For the leaders of this people cause *them*
to err,
And *those who are* led by them are
destroyed.

17 Therefore the Lord will have no joy in their
young men,
Nor have mercy on their fatherless and
widows;
For everyone *is* a hypocrite and an evildoer,
And every mouth speaks folly.

For all this His anger is not turned away,
But His hand *is* stretched out still.

18 For wickedness burns as the fire;
It shall devour the briers and thorns,
And kindle in the thickets of the forest;
They shall mount up *like* rising smoke.

19 Through the wrath of the LORD of hosts
The land is burned up,
And the people shall be as fuel for the fire;
No man shall spare his brother.

20 And he shall snatch on the right hand
And be hungry;
He shall devour on the left hand
And not be satisfied;

Every man shall eat the flesh of his own
   arm.
21 Manasseh *shall devour* Ephraim, and
   Ephraim Manasseh;
Together they *shall be* against Judah.

For all this His anger is not turned away,
But His hand *is* stretched out still.

10

"Woe* to those who decree unrighteous
   decrees,
Who write misfortune,
Which they have prescribed
2 To rob the needy of justice,
And to take what is right from the poor of
   My people,
That widows may be their prey,
And *that* they may rob the fatherless.
3 What will you do in the day of punishment,
And in the desolation *which* will come from
   afar?
To whom will you flee for help?
And where will you leave your glory?
4 Without Me they shall bow down among the
   prisoners,
And they shall fall among the slain."

For all this His anger is not turned away,
But His hand *is* stretched out still.

5 *"Woe to Assyria, the rod of My anger
And the staff in whose hand is My
   indignation.
6 I will send him against an ungodly nation,
And against the people of My wrath
I will give him charge,
To seize the spoil, to take the prey,
And to tread them down like the mire of
   the streets.
7 Yet he does not mean so,
Nor does his heart think so;
But *it is* in his heart to destroy,
And cut off not a few nations.
8 For he says,
'*Are* not my princes altogether kings?
9 *Is* not Calno like Carchemish?
Is not Hamath like Arpad?
Is not Samaria like Damascus?
10 As my hand has found the kingdoms of the
   idols,
Whose carved images excelled those of
   Jerusalem and Samaria,
11 As I have done to Samaria and her idols,
Shall I not do also to Jerusalem and her
   idols?' "

12Therefore it shall come to pass, when the Lord
has performed all His work on Mount Zion and
on Jerusalem, *that He will say,* "I will punish the
fruit of the arrogant heart of the king of Assyria,
and the glory of his haughty looks."
13For he says:

"By the strength of my hand I have done *it,*
And by my wisdom, for I am prudent;
Also I have removed the boundaries of the
   people,
And have robbed their treasuries;
So I have put down the inhabitants like a
   valiant *man.*
14 My hand has found like a nest the riches
   of the people,

CHAPTER 10

10:1–4 *Greed.* The leaders in Israel were
greedy for gain. They used unjust laws to
support their selfish practices as they robbed
the poor and needy. Just before God's
judgment fell on the nation, the rich were
prospering and the poor languishing. "What
will you do in the day of punishment?"
(v. 3) is a question we all must answer. What
good is all your wealth if you are not
prepared to meet God?

10:5–19 *Pride.* Assyria was God's tool for
punishing Israel (vv. 5, 15), but the tool
cannot boast about what it does. Assyria
was proud of its conquests, so God had to
humble its people and judge them for their
evil deeds. The army would vanish like trees
in a forest fire. Nineveh, the capital of
Assyria, was conquered by Babylon in 612
B.C. Nations may boast, but God has the
last word.

And as one gathers eggs *that are* left,
I have gathered all the earth;
And there was no one who moved *his* wing,
Nor opened *his* mouth with even a peep."

15 Shall the ax boast itself against him who
chops with it?
Or shall the saw exalt itself against him who
saws with it?
As if a rod could wield *itself* against those
who lift it up,
Or as if a staff could lift up, *as if it were*
not wood!
16 Therefore the Lord, the Lord[l] of hosts,
Will send leanness among his fat ones;
And under his glory
He will kindle a burning
Like the burning of a fire.
17 So the Light of Israel will be for a fire,
And his Holy One for a flame;
It will burn and devour
His thorns and his briers in one day.
18 And it will consume the glory of his forest
and of his fruitful field,
Both soul and body;
And they will be as when a sick man wastes
away.
19 Then the rest of the trees of his forest
Will be so few in number
That a child may write them.

20 *And it shall come to pass in that day
That the remnant of Israel,
And such as have escaped of the house of
Jacob,
Will never again depend on him who
defeated them,
But will depend on the LORD, the Holy One
of Israel, in truth.
21 The remnant will return, the remnant of
Jacob,
To the Mighty God.
22 For though your people, O Israel, be as the
sand of the sea,
A remnant of them will return;
The destruction decreed shall overflow with
righteousness.
23 For the Lord GOD of hosts
Will make a determined end
In the midst of all the land.

24Therefore thus says the Lord GOD of hosts:
"O My people, who dwell in Zion, do not be afraid
of the Assyrian. He shall strike you with a rod
and lift up his staff against you, in the manner
of Egypt. 25For yet a very little while and the indignation will cease, as will My anger in their destruction." 26And the LORD of hosts will stir up a
scourge for him like the slaughter of Midian at
the rock of Oreb; *as* His rod was on the sea, so
will He lift it up in the manner of Egypt.

27 It shall come to pass in that day
That his burden will be taken away from
your shoulder,
And his yoke from your neck,
And the yoke will be destroyed because of
the anointing oil.

10:20–34 *Hope.* In His grace, God saved
a remnant and permitted them to return to
the land. God also promised Judah that
Assyria would not capture Jerusalem
(vv. 24–27; Isa. 37). The tall proud tree
(Assyria) would be cut down to size (vv. 33–
34)! Even in the midst of wrath, God gives
His people hope.

10:16 [l]Following Bomberg; Masoretic Text and Dead Sea
Scrolls read YHWH (*the* LORD).

28   He has come to Aiath,
      He has passed Migron;
      At Michmash he has attended to his
          equipment.
29   They have gone along the ridge,
      They have taken up lodging at Geba.
      Ramah is afraid,
      Gibeah of Saul has fled.
30   Lift up your voice,
      O daughter of Gallim!
      Cause it to be heard as far as Laish—
      O poor Anathoth!^m
31   Madmenah has fled,
      The inhabitants of Gebim seek refuge.
32   As yet he will remain at Nob that day;
      He will shake his fist at the mount of the
          daughter of Zion,
      The hill of Jerusalem.

33   Behold, the Lord,
      The Lᴏʀᴅ of hosts,
      Will lop off the bough with terror;
      Those of high stature *will be* hewn down,
      And the haughty will be humbled.
34   He will cut down the thickets of the forest
          with iron,
      And Lebanon will fall by the Mighty One.

11 There* shall come forth a Rod from the stem
          of Jesse,
      And a Branch shall grow out of his roots.
2   The Spirit of the Lᴏʀᴅ shall rest upon Him,
      The Spirit of wisdom and understanding,
      The Spirit of counsel and might,
      The Spirit of knowledge and of the fear of
          the Lᴏʀᴅ.

3   His delight *is* in the fear of the Lᴏʀᴅ,
      And He shall not judge by the sight of His
          eyes,
      Nor decide by the hearing of His ears;
4   But with righteousness He shall judge the
          poor,
      And decide with equity for the meek of the
          earth;
      He shall strike the earth with the rod of His
          mouth,
      And with the breath of His lips He shall slay
          the wicked.
5   Righteousness shall be the belt of His loins,
      And faithfulness the belt of His waist.

6   "The wolf also shall dwell with the lamb,
      The leopard shall lie down with the young
          goat,
      The calf and the young lion and the fatling
          together;
      And a little child shall lead them.
7   The cow and the bear shall graze;
      Their young ones shall lie down together;
      And the lion shall eat straw like the ox.
8   The nursing child shall play by the cobra's
          hole,
      And the weaned child shall put his hand in
          the viper's den.
9   They shall not hurt nor destroy in all My
          holy mountain,

CHAPTERS 11—12

11:1–10 *Reign.* God cuts down the tall trees (Isa. 10:33–34), but He builds a great kingdom from a tiny shoot (v. 1). Our Savior had a humble beginning at a time when David's family was in dishonor; but in the end, His kingdom will prevail over all earthly powers. He will bring peace on earth and the glory of God will cover the earth. Are you praying, "Thy kingdom come"?

10:30 *ᵐFollowing Masoretic Text, Targum, and Vulgate; Septuagint and Syriac read Listen to her, O Anathoth.*

For the earth shall be full of the knowledge
  of the LORD
As the waters cover the sea.

10 "And in that day there shall be a Root of
  Jesse,
Who shall stand as a banner to the people;
For the Gentiles shall seek Him,
And His resting place shall be glorious."

11:11–16 Return. The humble Root is now the leader of an army! He defeats the enemy and gathers His people to their land, and He also rallies the Gentiles who seek Him. It is the picture of another "exodus" as God dries up the waters and makes a highway for His people. But this time there will be no wilderness wandering!

11 *It shall come to pass in that day
  That the Lord shall set His hand again the
  second time
To recover the remnant of His people who
  are left,
From Assyria and Egypt,
From Pathros and Cush,
From Elam and Shinar,
From Hamath and the islands of the sea.

12 He will set up a banner for the nations,
And will assemble the outcasts of Israel,
And gather together the dispersed of Judah
From the four corners of the earth.
13 Also the envy of Ephraim shall depart,
And the adversaries of Judah shall be cut
  off;
Ephraim shall not envy Judah,
And Judah shall not harass Ephraim.
14 But they shall fly down upon the shoulder
  of the Philistines toward the west;
Together they shall plunder the people of
  the East;
They shall lay their hand on Edom and
  Moab;
And the people of Ammon shall obey them.
15 The LORD will utterly destroy[n] the tongue
  of the Sea of Egypt;
With His mighty wind He will shake His fist
  over the River,[o]
And strike it in the seven streams,
And make *men* cross over dryshod.
16 There will be a highway for the remnant of
  His people
Who will be left from Assyria,
As it was for Israel
In the day that he came up from the land
  of Egypt.

12:1–6 Rejoicing. Worshiping people give thanks to the Lord for saving them and bringing them home again. Witnessing people tell all the nations of the greatness of God. Compare verse 2 with Exodus 15:2 and Psalm 118:14, and be sure to believe this "song" for yourself.

12 And* in that day you will say:

"O LORD, I will praise You;
Though You were angry with me,
Your anger is turned away, and You
  comfort me.
2 Behold, God *is* my salvation,
I will trust and not be afraid;
'For YAH, the LORD, *is* my strength and song;
He also has become my salvation.' "[p]

3 Therefore with joy you will draw water
From the wells of salvation.

4 And in that day you will say:

"Praise the LORD, call upon His name;
Declare His deeds among the peoples,

11:15 [n]Following Masoretic Text and Vulgate; Septuagint,
Syriac, and Targum read *dry up*. [o]That is, the Euphrates
12:2 [p]Exodus 15:2

Make mention that His name is exalted.
5 Sing to the LORD,
For He has done excellent things;
This *is* known in all the earth.
6 Cry out and shout, O inhabitant of Zion,
For great *is* the Holy One of Israel in your
  midst!"

13

The* burden against Babylon which Isaiah
the son of Amoz saw.

2 "Lift up a banner on the high mountain,
Raise your voice to them;
Wave your hand, that they may enter the
  gates of the nobles.
3 I have commanded My sanctified ones;
I have also called My mighty ones for My
  anger—
Those who rejoice in My exaltation."

4 The noise of a multitude in the mountains,
Like that of many people!
A tumultuous noise of the kingdoms of
  nations gathered together!
The LORD of hosts musters
The army for battle.
5 They come from a far country,
From the end of heaven—
The LORD and His weapons of indignation,
To destroy the whole land.

6 Wail, for the day of the LORD *is* at hand!
It will come as destruction from the
  Almighty.
7 Therefore all hands will be limp,
Every man's heart will melt,
8 And they will be afraid.
Pangs and sorrows will take hold of *them;*
They will be in pain as a woman in
  childbirth;
They will be amazed at one another;
Their faces *will be like* flames.

9 Behold, the day of the LORD comes,
Cruel, with both wrath and fierce anger,
To lay the land desolate;
And He will destroy its sinners from it.
10 For the stars of heaven and their
  constellations
Will not give their light;
The sun will be darkened in its going
  forth,
And the moon will not cause its light to
  shine.

11 "I will punish the world for *its* evil,
And the wicked for their iniquity;
I will halt the arrogance of the proud,
And will lay low the haughtiness of the
  terrible.
12 I will make a mortal more rare than fine
  gold,
A man more than the golden wedge of
  Ophir.
13 Therefore I will shake the heavens,
And the earth will move out of her place,
In the wrath of the LORD of hosts
And in the day of His fierce anger.
14 It shall be as the hunted gazelle,
And as a sheep that no man takes up;
Every man will turn to his own people,
And everyone will flee to his own land.

CHAPTER 13

13:1ff In chapters 13—23, Isaiah
announces God's judgment on ten gentile
peoples as well as on His own people in
Judah and Israel. He begins with Babylon,
which would one day swallow up the
Assyrians, take Judah captive and then itself
be defeated by the Medes and Persians
(vv. 17–22). The rise and the fall of nations
are in the hands of God (Dan. 4:25, 32; Acts
17:26). God can even use heathen soldiers
to do His work and can call them "My
sanctified ones" (v. 3). He is sovereign.

In the defeat of Babylon, Isaiah saw a
picture of the final "day of the Lord" when
the world will taste the judgment of God.
God is long-suffering with sinners, but there
comes a time when His judgment must fall.
Isaiah's message against Babylon was
fulfilled, and the city and empire are no
more.

In Scripture, Babylon symbolizes the
world system confederated against God
(Gen. 11). Like Babylon in Isaiah's day, the
world today seems so successful and
invincible; but one day, the whole system
will fall (Rev. 17—18). That is why God calls
His people to separate themselves from it
(2 Cor. 6:14–18).

15   Everyone who is found will be thrust
        through,
     And everyone who is captured will fall by
        the sword.
16   Their children also will be dashed to pieces
        before their eyes;
     Their houses will be plundered
     And their wives ravished.

17   "Behold, I will stir up the Medes against
        them,
     Who will not regard silver;
     And *as for* gold, they will not delight in it.
18   Also *their* bows will dash the young men
        to pieces,
     And they will have no pity on the fruit of
        the womb;
     Their eye will not spare children.
19   And Babylon, the glory of kingdoms,
     The beauty of the Chaldeans' pride,
     Will be as when God overthrew Sodom and
        Gomorrah.
20   It will never be inhabited,
     Nor will it be settled from generation to
        generation;
     Nor will the Arabian pitch tents there,
     Nor will the shepherds make their
        sheepfolds there.
21   But wild beasts of the desert will lie there,
     And their houses will be full of owls;
     Ostriches will dwell there,
     And wild goats will caper there.
22   The hyenas will howl in their citadels,
     And jackals in their pleasant palaces.
     Her time *is* near to come,
     And her days will not be prolonged."

14 For the LORD will have mercy on Jacob, and
     will still choose Israel, and settle them in
their own land. The strangers will be joined with
them, and they will cling to the house of Jacob.
2Then people will take them and bring them to
their place, and the house of Israel will possess
them for servants and maids in the land of the
LORD; they will take them captive whose captives
they were, and rule over their oppressors.
3It shall come to pass in the day the LORD gives
you rest from your sorrow, and from your fear
and the hard bondage in which you were made
to serve, 4that you will take up this proverb
against the king of Babylon, and say:

     "How the oppressor has ceased,
        The golden*q* city ceased!
5   The LORD has broken the staff of the wicked,
        The scepter of the rulers;
6   He who struck the people in wrath with a
        continual stroke,
     He who ruled the nations in anger,
        Is persecuted *and* no one hinders.
7   The whole earth is at rest *and* quiet;
        They break forth into singing.
8   Indeed the cypress trees rejoice over you,
        And the cedars of Lebanon,
     Saying, 'Since you were cut down,
        No woodsman has come up against us.'

9   "Hell from beneath is excited about you,
        To meet *you* at your coming;

14:4 *q*Or *insolent*

It stirs up the dead for you,
All the chief ones of the earth;
It has raised up from their thrones
All the kings of the nations.
10 They all shall speak and say to you:
'Have you also become as weak as we?
Have you become like us?
11 Your pomp is brought down to Sheol,
And the sound of your stringed instruments;
The maggot is spread under you,
And worms cover you.'

12*'How you are fallen from heaven,
O Lucifer,[r] son of the morning!
How you are cut down to the ground,
You who weakened the nations!
13 For you have said in your heart:
'I will ascend into heaven,
I will exalt my throne above the stars of
God;
I will also sit on the mount of the
congregation
On the farthest sides of the north;
14 I will ascend above the heights of the clouds,
I will be like the Most High.'
15 Yet you shall be brought down to Sheol,
To the lowest depths of the Pit.

16 "Those who see you will gaze at you,
And consider you, *saying:*
'*Is* this the man who made the earth tremble,
Who shook kingdoms,
17 Who made the world as a wilderness
And destroyed its cities,
Who did not open the house of his
prisoners?'

18 "All the kings of the nations,
All of them, sleep in glory,
Everyone in his own house;
19 But you are cast out of your grave
Like an abominable branch,
Like the garment of those who are slain,
Thrust through with a sword,
Who go down to the stones of the pit,
Like a corpse trodden underfoot.
20 You will not be joined with them in burial,
Because you have destroyed your land
And slain your people.
The brood of evildoers shall never be
named.
21 Prepare slaughter for his children
Because of the iniquity of their fathers,
Lest they rise up and possess the land,
And fill the face of the world with cities."

22 "For I will rise up against them," says the
LORD of hosts,
"And cut off from Babylon the name and
remnant,
And offspring and posterity," says the LORD.
23 "I will also make it a possession for the
porcupine,
And marshes of muddy water;
I will sweep it with the broom of
destruction," says the LORD of hosts.

24 The LORD of hosts has sworn, saying,
"Surely, as I have thought, so it shall come
to pass,

CHAPTER 14

14:12–15 There is more to the fall of
Babylon than the deposing of a proud king
(vv. 3–11, 16–21) or the destroying of a
great city (vv. 22–23). Behind the evil
Babylonian system was Lucifer ("Day Star"),
the enemy of God (vv. 12–15). As God
taunts the king of Babylon, He also speaks
to Satan who motivated and energized him.
    It appears that Lucifer was an angel who
rebelled against God and wanted to take to
himself the worship that belonged only to
God. "I will be like the Most High" (v. 14)
is the ambition of the evil one and the
temptation he puts before man (Gen. 3:5).
The world today worships and serves "the
creature rather than the Creator" (Rom.
1:25). Man is his own god; in worshiping
and serving only himself, he plays right into
the hands of the evil one.
    The Christian's ambition is to be like Jesus
Christ in all things, "conformed to the image
of His Son" (Rom. 8:29). Contrast Isaiah
14:12–15 with Philippians 2:1–11 if you want
to see the difference between Satan's
approach and our Lord's approach.

14:12 'Literally *Day Star*

And as I have purposed, *so* it shall stand:

25 That I will break the Assyrian in My land,
And on My mountains tread him underfoot.
Then his yoke shall be removed from them,
And his burden removed from their
shoulders.

26 This *is* the purpose that is purposed against
the whole earth,
And this *is* the hand that is stretched out
over all the nations.

27 For the LORD of hosts has purposed,
And who will annul *it*?
His hand *is* stretched out,
And who will turn it back?"

28This is the burden which came in the year that
King Ahaz died.

29 "Do not rejoice, all you of Philistia,
Because the rod that struck you is broken;
For out of the serpent's roots will come forth
a viper,
And its offspring *will be* a fiery flying
serpent.

30 The firstborn of the poor will feed,
And the needy will lie down in safety;
I will kill your roots with famine,
And it will slay your remnant.

31 Wail, O gate! Cry, O city!
All you of Philistia *are* dissolved;
For smoke will come from the north,
And no one *will be* alone in his appointed
times."

32 What will they answer the messengers of
the nation?
That the LORD has founded Zion,
And the poor of His people shall take refuge
in it.

CHAPTERS 15—16

15:1ff The nation of Moab (chapters 15—16) was born out of Lot's incestuous union with one of his daughters (Gen. 19:30–38). It was a proud nation that would not honor the God of Israel but trusted in its fortifications. Pride is a sin that God hates (Prov. 6:16–17), whether in nations or in individuals, and it leads to judgment.

When the Assyrians invaded, the Moabites turned from boasting to weeping (vv. 1–4) and fleeing (vv. 5–9). They had faith in their fortifications, but everything failed them. Contrast this with Isaiah 2:10–11. They should have made peace with Judah (16:1–2) and gone to Jerusalem for asylum. God had promised to protect Judah from the Assyrian army (10:24ff.) because that was where David's throne was (16:5).

The prophet looked beyond this event to the time when the Son of God would sit on David's throne and bring in righteousness and justice (16:5). God could do without Moab; but He had a covenant with David (2 Sam. 7), and He would be faithful to His promises. Judah was safe because the people trusted the Lord.

15 The* burden against Moab.

Because in the night Ar of Moab is laid
waste
And destroyed,
Because in the night Kir of Moab is laid
waste
And destroyed,

2 He has gone up to the templeˢ and Dibon,
To the high places to weep.
Moab will wail over Nebo and over Medeba;
On all their heads *will be* baldness,
And every beard cut off.

3 In their streets they will clothe themselves
with sackcloth;
On the tops of their houses
And in their streets
Everyone will wail, weeping bitterly.

4 Heshbon and Elealeh will cry out,
Their voice shall be heard as far as Jahaz;
Therefore the armed soldiersᵗ of Moab will
cry out;
His life will be burdensome to him.

5 "My heart will cry out for Moab;
His fugitives *shall flee* to Zoar,
Like a three-year-old heifer.ᵘ

15:2 ˢHebrew *bayith,* literally *house*   15:4 ᵗFollowing Masoretic Text, Targum, and Vulgate; Septuagint and Syriac read *loins.*   15:5 ᵘOr *The Third Eglath,* an unknown city (compare Jeremiah 48:34)

For by the Ascent of Luhith
They will go up with weeping;
For in the way of Horonaim
They will raise up a cry of destruction,
6 For the waters of Nimrim will be desolate,
For the green grass has withered away;
The grass fails, there is nothing green.
7 Therefore the abundance they have gained,
And what they have laid up,
They will carry away to the Brook of the
   Willows.
8 For the cry has gone all around the borders
   of Moab,
Its wailing to Eglaim
And its wailing to Beer Elim.
9 For the waters of Dimon[v] will be full of
   blood;
Because I will bring more upon Dimon,[w]
Lions upon him who escapes from Moab,
And on the remnant of the land."

16 Send the lamb to the ruler of the land,
From Sela to the wilderness,
To the mount of the daughter of Zion.
2 For it shall be as a wandering bird thrown
   out of the nest;
So shall be the daughters of Moab at the
   fords of the Arnon.

3 "Take counsel, execute judgment;
Make your shadow like the night in the
   middle of the day;
Hide the outcasts,
Do not betray him who escapes.
4 Let My outcasts dwell with you, O Moab;
Be a shelter to them from the face of the
   spoiler.
For the extortioner is at an end,
Devastation ceases,
The oppressors are consumed out of the
   land.
5 In mercy the throne will be established;
And One will sit on it in truth, in the
   tabernacle of David,
Judging and seeking justice and hastening
   righteousness."

6 We have heard of the pride of Moab—
He is very proud—
Of his haughtiness and his pride and his
   wrath;
But his lies *shall* not *be* so.
7 Therefore Moab shall wail for Moab;
Everyone shall wail.
For the foundations of Kir Hareseth you
   shall mourn;
Surely *they are* stricken.

8 For the fields of Heshbon languish,
And the vine of Sibmah;
The lords of the nations have broken down
   its choice plants,
Which have reached to Jazer
And wandered through the wilderness.
Her branches are stretched out,
They are gone over the sea.

15:9 [v]Following Masoretic Text and Targum; Dead Sea Scrolls
and Vulgate read *Dibon;* Septuagint reads *Rimon.* [w]Following
Masoretic Text and Targum; Dead Sea Scrolls and Vulgate
read *Dibon;* Septuagint reads *Rimon.*

9   Therefore I will bewail the vine of Sibmah,
    With the weeping of Jazer;
    I will drench you with my tears,
    O Heshbon and Elealeh;
    For battle cries have fallen
    Over your summer fruits and your harvest.

10   Gladness is taken away,
    And joy from the plentiful field;
    In the vineyards there will be no singing,
    Nor will there be shouting;
    No treaders will tread out wine in the
      presses;
    I have made their shouting cease.
11   Therefore my heart shall resound like a
      harp for Moab,
    And my inner being for Kir Heres.

12   And it shall come to pass,
    When it is seen that Moab is weary on the
      high place,
    That he will come to his sanctuary to pray;
    But he will not prevail.

13This *is* the word which the LORD has spoken concerning Moab since that time. 14But now the LORD has spoken, saying, "Within three years, as the years of a hired man, the glory of Moab will be despised with all that great multitude, and the remnant *will be* very small *and* feeble."

CHAPTER 17

17:1ff The northern kingdom of Israel had allied with Syria (Damascus), and both would fall to the Assyrians. If the people you trust do not trust the Lord, their judgment may become your judgment.
God's judgment on Israel is pictured by a sunset and a heavy person losing weight (v. 4), as well as a field that has no fruit for the gleaners (vv. 5–6). Israel had decayed beyond hope, and all her efforts at recovery were wasted (vv. 10–11).
If only they had turned to God before the sun set or the disease wasted away the body or the blight destroyed the harvest! But they trusted their own idols and not the true God (vv. 7–8). How easy it is to put confidence in the work of your own hands and not in the God who made those hands!
The judgment carried them off, like houses before a flood (vv. 12–13a) or chaff and tumbleweeds before the wind (v. 13b). Israel could have had the quiet waters of Shiloah (8:6), but they chose the turbulent waters of Assyria.
The will of God is your greatest security.

17 The* burden against Damascus.

  "Behold, Damascus will cease from *being* a
    city,
    And it will be a ruinous heap.
2   The cities of Aroer *are* forsaken;ˣ
    They will be for flocks
    Which lie down, and no one will make *them*
      afraid.
3   The fortress also will cease from Ephraim,
    The kingdom from Damascus,
    And the remnant of Syria;
    They will be as the glory of the children of
      Israel,"
    Says the LORD of hosts.

4   "In that day it shall come to pass
    That the glory of Jacob will wane,
    And the fatness of his flesh grow lean.
5   It shall be as when the harvester gathers
      the grain,
    And reaps the heads with his arm;
    It shall be as he who gathers heads of grain
    In the Valley of Rephaim.
6   Yet gleaning grapes will be left in it,
    Like the shaking of an olive tree,
    Two *or* three olives at the top of the
      uppermost bough,
    Four *or* five in its most fruitful branches,"
    Says the LORD God of Israel.

7   In that day a man will look to his Maker,
    And his eyes will have respect for the Holy
      One of Israel.
8   He will not look to the altars,
    The work of his hands;

17:2 ˣFollowing Masoretic Text and Vulgate; Septuagint reads *It shall be forsaken forever;* Targum reads *Its cities shall be forsaken and desolate.*

He will not respect what his fingers have
　　made,
Nor the wooden images^y nor the incense
　　altars.

9　In that day his strong cities will be as a
　　　forsaken bough^z
　　And an uppermost branch,^a
　　Which they left because of the children of
　　　Israel;
　　And there will be desolation.

10　Because you have forgotten the God of your
　　　salvation,
　　And have not been mindful of the Rock of
　　　your stronghold,
　　Therefore you will plant pleasant plants
　　And set out foreign seedlings;
11　In the day you will make your plant to grow,
　　And in the morning you will make your seed
　　　to flourish;
　　But the harvest *will be* a heap of ruins
　　In the day of grief and desperate sorrow.

12　Woe to the multitude of many people
　　Who make a noise like the roar of the seas,
　　And to the rushing of nations
　　That make a rushing like the rushing of
　　　mighty waters!
13　The nations will rush like the rushing of
　　　many waters;
　　But *God* will rebuke them and they will flee
　　　far away,
　　And be chased like the chaff of the
　　　mountains before the wind,
　　Like a rolling thing before the whirlwind.
14　Then behold, at eventide, trouble!
　　And before the morning, he *is* no more.
　　This *is* the portion of those who plunder us,
　　And the lot of those who rob us.

18

Woe* to the land shadowed with buzzing
　　wings,
　　Which *is* beyond the rivers of Ethiopia,
2　Which sends ambassadors by sea,
　　Even in vessels of reed on the waters,
　　　saying,
　　"Go, swift messengers, to a nation tall and
　　　smooth *of skin,*
　　To a people terrible from their beginning
　　　onward,
　　A nation powerful and treading down,
　　Whose land the rivers divide."

3　All inhabitants of the world and dwellers
　　　on the earth:
　　When he lifts up a banner on the mountains,
　　　you see *it;*
　　And when he blows a trumpet, you hear *it.*
4　For so the LORD said to me,
　　"I will take My rest,
　　And I will look from My dwelling place
　　Like clear heat in sunshine,
　　Like a cloud of dew in the heat of harvest."
5　For before the harvest, when the bud is
　　　perfect
　　And the sour grape is ripening in the flower,

CHAPTER 18

18:1ff The people of Ethiopia (ancient
Cush) sent ambassadors to Israel, hoping
to form a strong alliance against Assyria,
but the venture was doomed to fail. God was
not in it, because all of man's clever ideas
are worthless if they run contrary to the will
of God (1 Cor. 3:18–20). First find His will,
then do it!

The Assyrian invasion was God's plan,
and He would not intervene until He
accomplished His divine purposes. He
would hover over the scene like summer
heat or the morning dew (vv. 3–4). When
the time was right, He would reap the
harvest (v. 5) and leave the corpses to the
scavengers (v. 6). It is not a very pretty
scene, but that is the way civilization is
moving today (Matt. 24:28; Rev. 19:17–21).

Those clean-shaven ambassadors should
have gone to Jerusalem with a gift for the
Lord. They should have been humble
worshipers, not haughty negotiators (v. 7),
and trusted the God of Israel, not their
armies or treaties (Ps. 20:7).

17:8 ^yHebrew *Asherim,* Canaanite deities   17:9 ^zSeptuagint
reads *Hivites;* Targum reads *laid waste;* Vulgate reads *as the
plows.* ^aSeptuagint reads *Amorites;* Targum reads *in ruins;*
Vulgate reads *corn.*

He will both cut off the sprigs with pruning
  hooks
And take away *and* cut down the branches.
6 They will be left together for the mountain
  birds of prey
And for the beasts of the earth;
The birds of prey will summer on them,
And all the beasts of the earth will winter
  on them.

7 In that time a present will be brought to the
  LORD of hosts
From[b] a people tall and smooth *of skin,*
And from a people terrible from their
  beginning onward,
A nation powerful and treading down,
Whose land the rivers divide—
To the place of the name of the LORD of
  hosts,
To Mount Zion.

19 The* burden against Egypt.

Behold, the LORD rides on a swift cloud,
And will come into Egypt;
The idols of Egypt will totter at His
  presence,
And the heart of Egypt will melt in its midst.

2 "I will set Egyptians against Egyptians;
Everyone will fight against his brother,
And everyone against his neighbor,
City against city, kingdom against kingdom.
3 The spirit of Egypt will fail in its midst;
I will destroy their counsel,
And they will consult the idols and the
  charmers,
The mediums and the sorcerers.
4 And the Egyptians I will give
Into the hand of a cruel master,
And a fierce king will rule over them,"
Says the Lord, the LORD of hosts.

5 The waters will fail from the sea,
And the river will be wasted and dried up.
6 The rivers will turn foul;
The brooks of defense will be emptied and
  dried up;
The reeds and rushes will wither.
7 The papyrus reeds by the River,[c] by the
  mouth of the River,
And everything sown by the River,
Will wither, be driven away, and be no
  more.
8 The fishermen also will mourn;
All those will lament who cast hooks into
  the River,
And they will languish who spread nets on
  the waters.

CHAPTER 19

19:1ff A strong faction in Judah advised the
king to get help from Egypt (Isa. 31), but
Isaiah warned that Egypt could not help
them. Why? Because the Lord had
discouraged and divided the Egyptians
(vv. 1–2), their counsel was from the devil
(v. 3), and they were heading for bondage
themselves (v. 4). Furthermore, their
economy was about to fail (vv. 5–10). How
could they help?
The counselors in Egypt were supposed
to be very wise, but God said they were
deluded fools (vv. 11–13). God's people get
their wisdom from God, not from the world
(James 1:5). The wisdom of Egypt would
lead them into staggering and humiliating
defeat (vv. 14–15).
In verses 16–25, the prophet sees the
future of both the Jews and the Egyptians,
when the Lord will establish His kingdom.
The situation will be reversed, with Egypt
turning to Israel for help (vv. 16–17)! In fact,
the Egyptians will worship the God of Israel
(vv. 18–21)! The nations will no longer battle
but will visit one another on God's highway.

18:7 [b]Following Dead Sea Scrolls, Septuagint, and Vulgate;
Masoretic Text omits *From;* Targum reads *To.* 19:7 [c]That is,
the Nile

Going Down to Egypt—When Abraham faced a famine in Canaan, he went down to Egypt for
help, and he almost lost his wife (Gen. 12:10—13:4). After the Exodus, God led His people so they
would not want to go back to Egypt (Exod. 13:17–22). During their wilderness wanderings, the people
wanted to go back (Num. 11; 14), but God would not permit it. Isaiah warned against it (32:1ff.), and
so did Jeremiah (42—43). The book of Hebrews uses this image to warn believers not to go back in
unbelief but to go forward in faith (3:7–19; 6:1).

9 Moreover those who work in fine flax
  And those who weave fine fabric will be
   ashamed;
10 And its foundations will be broken.
  All who make wages *will be* troubled of
   soul.

11 Surely the princes of Zoan *are* fools;
  Pharaoh's wise counselors give foolish
   counsel.
  How do you say to Pharaoh, "I *am* the son
   of the wise,
  The son of ancient kings?"
12 Where *are* they?
  Where are your wise men?
  Let them tell you now,
  And let them know what the L ORD of hosts
   has purposed against Egypt.
13 The princes of Zoan have become fools;
  The princes of Noph[d] are deceived;
  They have also deluded Egypt,
  Those who are the mainstay of its tribes.
14 The L ORD has mingled a perverse spirit in
   her midst;
  And they have caused Egypt to err in all
   her work,
  As a drunken man staggers in his vomit.
15 Neither will there be *any* work for Egypt,
  Which the head or tail,
  Palm branch or bulrush, may do.[e]

16In that day Egypt will be like women, and will
be afraid and fear because of the waving of the
hand of the L ORD of hosts, which He waves over
it. 17And the land of Judah will be a terror to
Egypt; everyone who makes mention of it will be
afraid in himself, because of the counsel of the
L ORD of hosts which He has determined against
it.

18In that day five cities in the land of Egypt will
speak the language of Canaan and swear by the
L ORD of hosts; one will be called the City of
Destruction.[f]

19In that day there will be an altar to the L ORD
in the midst of the land of Egypt, and a pillar to
the L ORD at its border. 20And it will be for a sign
and for a witness to the L ORD of hosts in the land
of Egypt; for they will cry to the L ORD because
of the oppressors, and He will send them a Savior
and a Mighty One, and He will deliver them.
21Then the L ORD will be known to Egypt, and the
Egyptians will know the L ORD in that day, and
will make sacrifice and offering; yes, they will
make a vow to the L ORD and perform *it.* 22And
the L ORD will strike Egypt, He will strike and heal
it; they will return to the L ORD, and He will be
entreated by them and heal them.

23In that day there will be a highway from Egypt
to Assyria, and the Assyrian will come into Egypt
and the Egyptian into Assyria, and the Egyptians
will serve with the Assyrians.

24In that day Israel will be one of three with
Egypt and Assyria—a blessing in the midst of the
land, 25whom the L ORD of hosts shall bless, saying,
"Blessed *is* Egypt My people, and Assyria the
work of My hands, and Israel My inheritance."

19:13 *d*That is, ancient Memphis 19:15 *e*Compare Isaiah
9:14–16 19:18 *f*Some Hebrew manuscripts, Arabic, Dead
Sea Scrolls, Targum, and Vulgate read *Sun;* Septuagint reads
Asedek (literally *Righteousness*).

CHAPTER 20

20:1ff This brief chapter records two object lessons that the Lord used to try to convince the people not to form unholy alliances. The first was the defeat of Ashdod by the Assyrians. The people of this Philistine city had depended on Egypt and Ethiopia to help them, but their help failed. Why then should God's people trust Egypt and Ethiopia? Remember, the one thing we learn from history is that we do not learn from history. "It can't happen here!"

The second object lesson was personified by Isaiah the prophet who for three years did not wear his prophetic garb or his sandals. He looked like a prisoner of war, which is what the Egyptians and Ethiopians eventually became (vv. 3–4). God's people did not take it to heart, and eventually they were led off to Babylon.

God uses things we see and hear to help us make the right decisions. Do we really pay attention?

CHAPTER 21

21:3, 4 Three pictures help us better understand what is involved in faithful ministry.

The woman in travail. If you are faithful to your calling, your ministry will not be easy. Isaiah was distressed as he saw what God was doing in the world. He felt like a woman in travail; it was very painful for him to "give birth" to his message.

21:5–9, 11, 12 *The watchman.* While the prophet was anxiously watching so he could warn the people, the nation's leaders were carelessly feasting and thinking only of themselves (v. 5). The watchman sees both night (trouble) and morning (blessing), and that is how it will be until Jesus comes. The most important thing is that the watchman be faithful to warn when danger is coming (Ezek. 25:12–14).

❝*Preaching that costs nothing accomplishes nothing.***❞**

—John Henry Jowett

---

20 In* the year that Tartan^g came to Ashdod, when Sargon the king of Assyria sent him, and he fought against Ashdod and took it, 2at the same time the Lord spoke by Isaiah the son of Amoz, saying, "Go, and remove the sackcloth from your body, and take your sandals off your feet." And he did so, walking naked and barefoot.

3Then the Lord said, "Just as My servant Isaiah has walked naked and barefoot three years *for* a sign and a wonder against Egypt and Ethiopia, 4so shall the king of Assyria lead away the Egyptians as prisoners and the Ethiopians as captives, young and old, naked and barefoot, with their buttocks uncovered, to the shame of Egypt. 5Then they shall be afraid and ashamed of Ethiopia their expectation and Egypt their glory. 6And the inhabitant of this territory will say in that day, 'Surely such *is* our expectation, wherever we flee for help to be delivered from the king of Assyria; and how shall we escape?'"

21 The burden against the Wilderness of the Sea.

> As whirlwinds in the South pass through,
> *So* it comes from the desert, from a terrible land.

2   A distressing vision is declared to me;
> The treacherous dealer deals treacherously,
> And the plunderer plunders.
> Go up, O Elam!
> Besiege, O Media!
> All its sighing I have made to cease.

3   *Therefore my loins are filled with pain;
> Pangs have taken hold of me, like the pangs of a woman in labor.
> I was distressed when *I* heard *it;*
> I was dismayed when *I* saw *it.*

4   My heart wavered, fearfulness frightened me;
> The night for which I longed He turned into fear for me.

5   *Prepare the table,
> Set a watchman in the tower,
> Eat and drink.
> Arise, you princes,
> Anoint the shield!

6   For thus has the Lord said to me:
> "Go, set a watchman,
> Let him declare what he sees."

7   And he saw a chariot *with* a pair of horsemen,
> A chariot of donkeys, *and* a chariot of camels,
> And he listened earnestly with great care.

8   Then he cried, "A lion,^h my Lord!
> I stand continually on the watchtower in the daytime;
> I have sat at my post every night.

9   And look, here comes a chariot of men *with* a pair of horsemen!"
> Then he answered and said,
> "Babylon is fallen, is fallen!
> And all the carved images of her gods
> He has broken to the ground."

20:1 ^gOr *the Commander in Chief*   21:8 ^hDead Sea Scrolls read *Then the observer cried.*

10 *Oh, my threshing and the grain of my floor!
That which I have heard from the LORD of
hosts,
The God of Israel,
I have declared to you.

11The burden against Dumah.

He calls to me out of Seir,
"Watchman, what of the night?
Watchman, what of the night?"
12 The watchman said,
"The morning comes, and also the night.
If you will inquire, inquire;
Return! Come back!"

13The burden against Arabia.

In the forest in Arabia you will lodge,
O you traveling companies of Dedanites.
14 O inhabitants of the land of Tema,
Bring water to him who is thirsty;
With their bread they met him who fled.
15 For they fled from the swords, from the
drawn sword,
From the bent bow, and from the distress
of war.

16For thus the LORD has said to me: "Within a
year, according to the year of a hired man, all
the glory of Kedar will fail; 17and the remainder
of the number of archers, the mighty men of the
people of Kedar, will be diminished; for the LORD
God of Israel has spoken it."

22 The* burden against the Valley of Vision.

What ails you now, that you have all gone
up to the housetops,
2 You who are full of noise,
A tumultuous city, a joyous city?
Your slain men are not slain with the sword,
Nor dead in battle.
3 All your rulers have fled together;
They are captured by the archers.
All who are found in you are bound
together;
They have fled from afar.
4 *Therefore I said, "Look away from me,
I will weep bitterly;
Do not labor to comfort me
Because of the plundering of the daughter
of my people."

5 For it is a day of trouble and treading down
and perplexity
By the Lord GOD of hosts
In the Valley of Vision—
Breaking down the walls
And of crying to the mountain.
6 Elam bore the quiver
With chariots of men and horsemen,
And Kir uncovered the shield.
7 It shall come to pass that your choicest
valleys
Shall be full of chariots,
And the horsemen shall set themselves in
array at the gate.

8 *He removed the protection of Judah.
You looked in that day to the armor of the
House of the Forest;

21:10 The threshing floor. Why would Isaiah be distressed at the fall of the city of Babylon? (This was not the destruction of the city but a temporary takeover by a rival power.) Isaiah had hoped Babylon would stop the advances of Assyria and thus save the Jews from suffering. He saw them being winnowed and crushed by the enemy. He longed for a calm evening of his life (v. 4); instead, he had to carry distressing burdens to the end.

CHAPTER 22
22:1 Isaiah's vision was probably of the Assyrian attack on Jerusalem (chaps. 36—37), and one of the messages of the chapter is this: when a crisis occurs, different people respond in different ways.

22:4 The prophet saw events from a spiritual viewpoint and was burdened.

22:8–11 The city leaders depended on their defenses and did not call for fasting and prayer.

9   You also saw the damage to the city of
     David,
     That it was great;
     And you gathered together the waters of the
     lower pool.
10   You numbered the houses of Jerusalem,
     And the houses you broke down
     To fortify the wall.
11   You also made a reservoir between the two
     walls
     For the water of the old pool.
     But you did not look to its Maker,
     Nor did you have respect for Him who
     fashioned it long ago.

22:12–14 The people feasted and expected the worst. They had no faith in God (1 Cor. 15:32).

12 *And in that day the Lord GOD of hosts
     Called for weeping and for mourning,
     For baldness and for girding with sackcloth.
13   But instead, joy and gladness,
     Slaying oxen and killing sheep,
     Eating meat and drinking wine:
     "Let us eat and drink, for tomorrow we die!"

14   Then it was revealed in my hearing by the
     LORD of hosts,
     "Surely for this iniquity there will be no
     atonement for you,
     Even to your death," says the Lord GOD of
     hosts.

22:15–19 Shebna used his office for personal gain, and the crisis brought him only shame. In taking inventory of the city's resources, somebody uncovered his deceit and exposed him. Instead of enjoying retirement, security, and a fine burial, he experienced captivity, exile, and a lonely death.

15 *Thus says the Lord GOD of hosts:

     "Go, proceed to this steward,
     To Shebna, who is over the house, and say:
16   'What have you here, and whom have you
     here,
     That you have hewn a sepulcher here,
     As he who hews himself a sepulcher on
     high,
     Who carves a tomb for himself in a rock?
17   Indeed, the LORD will throw you away
     violently,
     O mighty man,
     And will surely seize you.
18   He will surely turn violently and toss you
     like a ball
     Into a large country;
     There you shall die, and there your glorious
     chariots
     Shall be the shame of your master's house.
19   So I will drive you out of your office,
     And from your position he will pull you
     down.*

22:20–25 The crisis brought out the best in Eliakim. He was a servant who was a father to the people, a person who could be trusted with authority (the keys), and a strong peg on which the nation could put their burdens. He is the kind of leader needed today.

20 *Then it shall be in that day,
     That I will call My servant Eliakim the son
     of Hilkiah;
21   I will clothe him with your robe
     And strengthen him with your belt;
     I will commit your responsibility into his
     hand.
     He shall be a father to the inhabitants of
     Jerusalem
     And to the house of Judah.
22   The key of the house of David
     I will lay on his shoulder;
     So he shall open, and no one shall shut;

22:19 *Septuagint omits he will pull you down; Syriac, Targum, and Vulgate read I will pull you down.*

And he shall shut, and no one shall open.
23 I will fasten him *as* a peg in a secure place,
And he will become a glorious throne to his
father's house.

24'They will hang on him all the glory of his
father's house, the offspring and the posterity, all
vessels of small quantity, from the cups to all the
pitchers. 25In that day,' says the LORD of hosts,
'the peg that is fastened in the secure place will
be removed and be cut down and fall, and the
burden that *was* on it will be cut off; for the LORD
has spoken.' "

23 The* burden against Tyre.

Wail, you ships of Tarshish!
For it is laid waste,
So that there is no house, no harbor;
From the land of Cyprus*j* it is revealed to
them.

2 Be still, you inhabitants of the coastland,
You merchants of Sidon,
Whom those who cross the sea have filled.*k*
3 And on great waters the grain of Shihor,
The harvest of the River,*l* *is* her revenue;
And she is a marketplace for the nations.

4 Be ashamed, O Sidon;
For the sea has spoken,
The strength of the sea, saying,
"I do not labor, nor bring forth children;
Neither do I rear young men,
Nor bring up virgins."
5 When the report *reaches* Egypt,
They also will be in agony at the report of
Tyre.

6 Cross over to Tarshish;
Wail, you inhabitants of the coastland!
7 *Is* this your joyous *city,*
Whose antiquity *is* from ancient days,
Whose feet carried her far off to dwell?
8 Who has taken this counsel against Tyre,
the crowning *city,*
Whose merchants *are* princes,
Whose traders *are* the honorable of the
earth?
9 The LORD of hosts has purposed it,
To bring to dishonor the pride of all glory,
To bring into contempt all the honorable of
the earth.

10 Overflow through your land like the River,*m*
O daughter of Tarshish;
There is no more strength.
11 He stretched out His hand over the sea,
He shook the kingdoms;
The LORD has given a commandment
against Canaan
To destroy its strongholds.
12 And He said, "You will rejoice no more,
O you oppressed virgin daughter of Sidon.

CHAPTER 23

23:1ff Tyre and Sidon were Phoenician
cities that brought great wealth to the nation
by shipping and trading. It seemed incredible
that such a successful economy would be
wiped out, but it happened just as the
prophet warned. Some of the people were
stunned into silence (v. 2), while others
openly expressed their grief by wailing
(vv. 1, 6, 14). It seems that people who rarely
weep over anything else will weep when
they have money problems. The joy left the
city (v. 7).

Assyria put Tyre and Sidon out of
business for seventy years, and then they
were restored.

God considered the business of Tyre and
Sidon as nothing but fornication (v. 17; Rev.
17:1–2). They were harlots promoting
themselves and ready to sell themselves at
the highest price (v. 16). But some of their
goods would be used to help rebuild the
temple of the Lord (v. 18; Ezra 3:7).

Men may think they control the economy
and what they do with their profits, but God
makes the final decision.

23:1 *j*Hebrew *Kittim,* western lands, especially Cyprus
23:2 *k*Following Masoretic Text and Vulgate; Septuagint and
Targum read *passing over the water;* Dead Sea Scrolls read
your messengers passing over the sea.   23:3 *l*That is, the
Nile   23:10 *m*That is, the Nile

Arise, cross over to Cyprus;
There also you will have no rest."

13 Behold, the land of the Chaldeans,
This people *which* was not;
Assyria founded it for wild beasts of the
   desert.
They set up its towers,
They raised up its palaces,
And brought it to ruin.

14 Wail, you ships of Tarshish!
For your strength is laid waste.

15Now it shall come to pass in that day that Tyre
will be forgotten seventy years, according to the
days of one king. At the end of seventy years it
will happen to Tyre as *in* the song of the harlot:

16 "Take a harp, go about the city,
You forgotten harlot;
Make sweet melody, sing many songs,
That you may be remembered."

17And it shall be, at the end of seventy years,
that the LORD will deal with Tyre. She will return
to her hire, and commit fornication with all the
kingdoms of the world on the face of the earth.
18Her gain and her pay will be set apart for the
LORD; it will not be treasured nor laid up, for her
gain will be for those who dwell before the LORD,
to eat sufficiently, and for fine clothing.

CHAPTER 24

24:1ff The whole earth is now the focus of
attention and not just individual nations and
cities. The Lord made the earth and is King
over all the earth (Ps. 47:2), so He has a
right to do what He pleases. He will punish
sinners because they have not respected
His covenant (v. 5; Gen. 9:8–17) or cared
for the earth as faithful stewards of His gifts.
They have disobeyed His will, claimed the
earth for themselves, and abused it selfishly.
   When that time of judgment comes, God
will pay no attention to anyone's economic
or social status (vv. 2–3). The joyful feast
will become a funeral (vv. 7–13); those who
try to escape will be trapped (vv. 17–18);
and proud leaders will become prisoners (vv.
21–23). The Lord will humble the "haughty
people" (v. 4) and the "exalted ones"
(v. 21).
   But Isaiah ends on a note of triumph: the
Lord will reign gloriously (v. 23)! Will you
be reigning with Him?

24 Behold,* the LORD makes the earth empty
and makes it waste,
Distorts its surface
And scatters abroad its inhabitants.
2 And it shall be:
As with the people, so with the priest;
As with the servant, so with his master;
As with the maid, so with her mistress;
As with the buyer, so with the seller;
As with the lender, so with the borrower;
As with the creditor, so with the debtor.
3 The land shall be entirely emptied and
   utterly plundered,
For the LORD has spoken this word.

4 The earth mourns *and* fades away,
The world languishes *and* fades away;
The haughty people of the earth languish.
5 The earth is also defiled under its
   inhabitants,
Because they have transgressed the laws,
Changed the ordinance,
Broken the everlasting covenant.
6 Therefore the curse has devoured the earth,
And those who dwell in it are desolate.
Therefore the inhabitants of the earth are
   burned,
And few men *are* left.

7 The new wine fails, the vine languishes,
All the merry-hearted sigh.
8 The mirth of the tambourine ceases,
The noise of the jubilant ends,
The joy of the harp ceases.
9 They shall not drink wine with a song;
Strong drink is bitter to those who drink it.
10 The city of confusion is broken down;
Every house is shut up, so that none may
go in.

11 *There is* a cry for wine in the streets,
    All joy is darkened,
    The mirth of the land is gone.
12 In the city desolation is left,
    And the gate is stricken with destruction.
13 When it shall be thus in the midst of the
        land among the people,
    It shall be like the shaking of an olive tree,
    Like the gleaning of grapes when the
        vintage is done.

14 They shall lift up their voice, they shall sing;
    For the majesty of the LORD
    They shall cry aloud from the sea.
15 Therefore glorify the LORD in the dawning
        light,
    The name of the LORD God of Israel in the
        coastlands of the sea.
16 From the ends of the earth we have heard
        songs:
    "Glory to the righteous!"
    But I said, "I am ruined, ruined!
    Woe to me!
    The treacherous dealers have dealt
        treacherously,
    Indeed, the treacherous dealers have dealt
        very treacherously."

17 Fear and the pit and the snare
    Are upon you, O inhabitant of the earth.
18 And it shall be
    That he who flees from the noise of the fear
    Shall fall into the pit,
    And he who comes up from the midst of
        the pit
    Shall be caught in the snare;
    For the windows from on high are open,
    And the foundations of the earth are
        shaken.

19 The earth is violently broken,
    The earth is split open,
    The earth is shaken exceedingly.
20 The earth shall reel to and fro like a
        drunkard,
    And shall totter like a hut;
    Its transgression shall be heavy upon it,
    And it will fall, and not rise again.

21 It shall come to pass in that day
    That the LORD will punish on high the host
        of exalted ones,
    And on the earth the kings of the earth.
22 They will be gathered together,
    As prisoners are gathered in the pit,
    And will be shut up in the prison;
    After many days they will be punished.
23 Then the moon will be disgraced
    And the sun ashamed;
    For the LORD of hosts will reign
    On Mount Zion and in Jerusalem
    And before His elders, gloriously.

25 O* LORD, You *are* my God.
    I will exalt You,
    I will praise Your name,
    For You have done wonderful *things;*
    Your counsels of old *are* faithfulness *and*
        truth.
2   For You have made a city a ruin,
    A fortified city a ruin,
    A palace of foreigners to be a city no more;

CHAPTER 25

25:1–3, 10–12 The prophet now addresses
God instead of the people and praises Him
for who He is and what He has done.
Isaiah's knowledge of God's truth did not
make him proud; it humbled him and moved
him to worship the Lord.

God is Judge. "The city" ultimately refers
to Babylon (Rev. 18:1—19:5), but it applies
to anything man makes and uses to defy
God. It does not take God long to wipe out
a nation or destroy a city.

25:4, 5 God is Refuge. Tribulation is like a storm, but He is the Refuge; it is like desert heat, but He is the Cloud that blots out the hot rays. God silences the noise of the enemy and brings peace.

25:6–9 God is Host. The Jews pictured the future kingdom as a great feast with God as the Host (Matt. 8:10–12; Rev. 19:6–9). But the feast will do more than sustain life; it will give life, for death will be destroyed forever (Rev. 20:11–15; 21:4). Can you join the praise expressed in verse 9?

CHAPTERS 26—27

26:1ff The phrase "in that day" links chapters 26 and 27 (26:1; 27:1, 2, 12, 13) and focuses attention on the glory of God in the promised kingdom (26:15). Knowing that the future is secure in the Lord is an encouragement when you suffer (Rom. 8:18–25; 2 Cor. 5:1–8).

Israel sings to the Lord. The proud enemy has been brought down (vv. 5–6), and God has given peace to His people (vv. 3, 12). The city of Jerusalem, where the Redeemer will reign, is strong and righteous after having been weak and defiled; and the nation's time of tribulation will be ended. This is not something the Jews will do for themselves, for they will be like women in travail who give birth only to wind (vv. 16–18). God will do it, and His people will praise Him for His mercy.

It will never be rebuilt.
3 Therefore the strong people will glorify You;
  The city of the terrible nations will fear You.
4 *For You have been a strength to the poor,
  A strength to the needy in his distress,
  A refuge from the storm,
  A shade from the heat;
  For the blast of the terrible ones *is* as a storm *against* the wall.
5 You will reduce the noise of aliens,
  As heat in a dry place;
  As heat in the shadow of a cloud,
  The song of the terrible ones will be diminished.

6 *And in this mountain
  The LORD of hosts will make for all people
  A feast of choice pieces,
  A feast of wines on the lees,
  Of fat things full of marrow,
  Of well-refined wines on the lees.
7 And He will destroy on this mountain
  The surface of the covering cast over all people,
  And the veil that is spread over all nations.
8 He will swallow up death forever,
  And the Lord GOD will wipe away tears from all faces;
  The rebuke of His people
  He will take away from all the earth;
  For the LORD has spoken.

9 And it will be said in that day:
  "Behold, this *is* our God;
  We have waited for Him, and He will save us.
  This *is* the LORD;
  We have waited for Him;
  We will be glad and rejoice in His salvation."

10 For on this mountain the hand of the LORD will rest,
  And Moab shall be trampled down under Him,
  As straw is trampled down for the refuse heap.
11 And He will spread out His hands in their midst
  As a swimmer reaches out to swim,
  And He will bring down their pride
  Together with the trickery of their hands.
12 The fortress of the high fort of your walls
  He will bring down, lay low,
  And bring to the ground, down to the dust.

26 In* that day this song will be sung in the land of Judah:

"We have a strong city;
  God will appoint salvation *for* walls and bulwarks.

The Peace of God—When you trust Jesus Christ to save you, your sins are forgiven (Col. 2:13), and you have peace with God (Rom. 5:1). He will never call you into judgment for them (John 5:24; Rom. 8:1). You may also enjoy "the peace of God" in your heart and mind as you pray (Phil. 4:6–7) and fix your mind on Him (Isa. 26:3; Phil. 4:8–9; Col. 3:1ff.). "The peace of God" is not the absence of problems; it is the presence of divine sufficiency in the midst of problems (Isa. 26:4; Phil. 4:13, 19). George Morrison said, "Peace is the possession of adequate resources"; and those resources come from the Lord when you yield heart and mind to Him.

2 Open the gates,
   That the righteous nation which keeps the
      truth may enter in.
3 You will keep *him* in perfect peace,
   Whose mind *is* stayed *on You,*
   Because he trusts in You.
4 Trust in the LORD forever,
   For in YAH, the LORD, *is* everlasting
      strength.[n]
5 For He brings down those who dwell on
      high,
   The lofty city;
   He lays it low,
   He lays it low to the ground,
   He brings it down to the dust.
6 The foot shall tread it down—
   The feet of the poor
   And the steps of the needy."

7 The way of the just *is* uprightness;
   O Most Upright,
   You weigh the path of the just.
8 Yes, in the way of Your judgments,
   O LORD, we have waited for You;
   The desire of *our* soul *is* for Your name
   And for the remembrance of You.
9 With my soul I have desired You in the
      night,
   Yes, by my spirit within me I will seek You
      early;
   For when Your judgments *are* in the earth,
   The inhabitants of the world will learn
      righteousness.

10 Let grace be shown to the wicked,
   Yet he will not learn righteousness;
   In the land of uprightness he will deal
      unjustly,
   And will not behold the majesty of the LORD.
11 LORD, *when* Your hand is lifted up, they will
      not see.
   But they will see and be ashamed
   For *their* envy of people;
   Yes, the fire of Your enemies shall devour
      them.

12 LORD, You will establish peace for us,
   For You have also done all our works in
      us.
13 O LORD our God, masters besides You
   Have had dominion over us;
   But by You only we make mention of Your
      name.
14 *They are* dead, they will not live;
   They are deceased, they will not rise.
   Therefore You have punished and
      destroyed them,
   And made all their memory to perish.
15 You have increased the nation, O LORD,
   You have increased the nation;
   You are glorified;
   You have expanded all the borders of the
      land.

16 LORD, in trouble they have visited You,
   They poured out a prayer *when* Your
      chastening *was* upon them.
17 As a woman with child
   Is in pain and cries out in her pangs,

26:4 [n]Or *Rock of Ages*

When she draws near the time of her
   delivery,
So have we been in Your sight, O LORD.
18 We have been with child, we have been in
       pain;
   We have, as it were, brought forth wind;
   We have not accomplished any deliverance
       in the earth,
   Nor have the inhabitants of the world fallen.

19 Your dead shall live;
   Together with my dead body° they shall
       arise.
   Awake and sing, you who dwell in dust;
   For your dew *is like* the dew of herbs,
   And the earth shall cast out the dead.

20 Come, my people, enter your chambers,
   And shut your doors behind you;
   Hide yourself, as it were, for a little moment,
   Until the indignation is past.
21 For behold, the LORD comes out of His place
   To punish the inhabitants of the earth for
       their iniquity;
   The earth will also disclose her blood,
   And will no more cover her slain.

27 In* that day the LORD with His severe sword,
   great and strong,
   Will punish Leviathan the fleeing serpent,
   Leviathan that twisted serpent;
   And He will slay the reptile that *is* in the
       sea.

27:2–5 *The Lord sings about Israel.* In
chapter 5, God sang about the failure of the
vineyard, Israel. But here the theme is the
fruitfulness of the nation and God's care over
it. In that day, the enemy will be defeated
(v. 1), and God will gather His people back
to their land (vv. 12–13). From Israel,
blessings shall flow to the whole world
(v. 6).

2   *In that day sing to her,
   "A vineyard of red wine!ᴾ
3   I, the LORD, keep it,
   I water it every moment;
   Lest any hurt it,
   I keep it night and day.
4   Fury *is* not in Me.
   Who would set briers *and* thorns
   Against Me in battle?
   I would go through them,
   I would burn them together.
5   Or let him take hold of My strength,
   That he may make peace with Me;
   And he shall make peace with Me."

6   Those who come He shall cause to take root
       in Jacob;
   Israel shall blossom and bud,
   And fill the face of the world with fruit.

7   Has He struck Israel as He struck those who
       struck him?
   Or has He been slain according to the
       slaughter of those who were slain by Him?
8   In measure, by sending it away,
   You contended with it.
   He removes *it* by His rough wind
   In the day of the east wind.
9   Therefore by this the iniquity of Jacob will
       be covered;

26:19 °Following Masoretic Text and Vulgate; Syriac and
Targum read *their dead bodies;* Septuagint reads *those in
the tombs.*   27:2 ᴾFollowing Masoretic Text (Kittel's *Biblia
Hebraica*), Bomberg, and Vulgate; Masoretic Text (*Biblia
Hebraica Stuttgartensia*), some Hebrew manuscripts, and
Septuagint read *delight;* Targum reads *choice vineyard.*

And this *is* all the fruit of taking away his
  sin:
When he makes all the stones of the altar
Like chalkstones that are beaten to dust,
Wooden images[q] and incense altars shall
  not stand.

10 Yet the fortified city *will be* desolate,
The habitation forsaken and left like a
  wilderness;
There the calf will feed, and there it will
  lie down
And consume its branches.
11 When its boughs are withered, they will be
  broken off;
The women come *and* set them on fire.
For it *is* a people of no understanding;
Therefore He who made them will not have
  mercy on them,
And He who formed them will show them
  no favor.

12 And it shall come to pass in that day
That the LORD will thresh,
From the channel of the River[r] to the Brook
  of Egypt;
And you will be gathered one by one,
O you children of Israel.

13 So it shall be in that day:
The great trumpet will be blown;
They will come, who are about to perish in
  the land of Assyria,
And they who are outcasts in the land of
  Egypt,
And shall worship the LORD in the holy
  mount at Jerusalem.

28 Woe* to the crown of pride, to the
  drunkards of Ephraim,
Whose glorious beauty *is* a fading flower
Which *is* at the head of the verdant valleys,
To those who are overcome with wine!
2 Behold, the Lord has a mighty and strong
  one,
Like a tempest of hail and a destroying
  storm,
Like a flood of mighty waters overflowing,
Who will bring *them* down to the earth with
  His hand.
3 The crown of pride, the drunkards of
  Ephraim,
Will be trampled underfoot;
4 And the glorious beauty is a fading flower
Which *is* at the head of the verdant valley,
Like the first fruit before the summer,
Which an observer sees;
He eats it up while it is still in his hand.

5 In that day the LORD of hosts will be
For a crown of glory and a diadem of beauty
To the remnant of His people,
6 For a spirit of justice to him who sits in
  judgment,
And for strength to those who turn back the
  battle at the gate.

27:9 [q]Hebrew *Asherim,* Canaanite deities 27:12 [r]That is, the Euphrates

CHAPTER 28

28:1–13 The prophet addressed the northern tribes (Ephraim) and indicted them for drunkenness (vv. 1–8) and an unteachable spirit (vv. 9–13). The religious leaders told Isaiah not to talk to them like children (vv. 9–10); after all, they knew the Law! But God would talk to them through the Assyrians whose tongue Israel would not understand. If God's people will not listen to His voice from the Word, they may have to listen to foreign voices that speak no peace and show no love.

It was a confident time in Israel, but their prosperity would fade like a trampled flower (vv. 1, 3–4), be carried away in a storm and flood (v. 2), and be swallowed like fruit (v. 4). Judgment was at the gate (v. 6).

7   But they also have erred through wine,
    And through intoxicating drink are out of
        the way;
    The priest and the prophet have erred
        through intoxicating drink,
    They are swallowed up by wine,
    They are out of the way through
        intoxicating drink;
    They err in vision, they stumble *in*
        judgment.
8   For all tables are full of vomit *and* filth;
    No place *is clean.*

9   "Whom will he teach knowledge?
    And whom will he make to understand the
        message?
    Those *just* weaned from milk?
    Those *just* drawn from the breasts?
10 For precept *must be* upon precept, precept
        upon precept,
    Line upon line, line upon line,
    Here a little, there a little."

11 For with stammering lips and another
        tongue
    He will speak to this people,
12 To whom He said, "This *is* the rest *with
        which*
    You may cause the weary to rest,"
    And, "This *is* the refreshing";
    Yet they would not hear.
13 But the word of the LORD was to them,
    "Precept upon precept, precept upon precept,
    Line upon line, line upon line,
    Here a little, there a little,"
    That they might go and fall backward, and
        be broken
    And snared and caught.

28:14–29 Then Isaiah denounced the sin of Judah, which was trusting false gods (vv. 14–15). Jesus Christ is God's Stone and He alone is a sure Refuge from the storm (Isa. 8:14; Matt. 21:42–44; Eph. 2:20). You have as much protection from lies as you do from a blanket that is too short! God is seeking a harvest and knows exactly how to handle the soil and the seeds (vv. 23–29). God's people may not enjoy the plowing and threshing, but the results are worth it.

14 *Therefore hear the word of the LORD, you
        scornful men,
    Who rule this people who *are* in Jerusalem,
15 Because you have said, "We have made a
        covenant with death,
    And with Sheol we are in agreement.
    When the overflowing scourge passes
        through,
    It will not come to us,
    For we have made lies our refuge,
    And under falsehood we have hidden
        ourselves."

16 Therefore thus says the Lord GOD:

    "Behold, I lay in Zion a stone for a
        foundation,
    A tried stone, a precious cornerstone, a sure
        foundation;
    Whoever believes will not act hastily.
17 Also I will make justice the measuring line,
    And righteousness the plummet;
    The hail will sweep away the refuge of
        lies,
    And the waters will overflow the hiding
        place.
18 Your covenant with death will be annulled,
    And your agreement with Sheol will not
        stand;
    When the overflowing scourge passes
        through,
    Then you will be trampled down by it.
19 As often as it goes out it will take you;

For morning by morning it will pass over,
And by day and by night;
It will be a terror just to understand the
   report."

20 For the bed is too short to stretch out *on,*
And the covering so narrow that one cannot
   wrap himself *in it.*
21 For the LORD will rise up as *at* Mount
   Perazim,
He will be angry as in the Valley of
   Gibeon--
That He may do His work, His awesome
   work,
And bring to pass His act, His unusual act.
22 Now therefore, do not be mockers,
Lest your bonds be made strong;
For I have heard from the Lord GOD of
   hosts,
A destruction determined even upon the
   whole earth.

23 Give ear and hear my voice,
Listen and hear my speech.
24 Does the plowman keep plowing all day to
   sow?
Does he keep turning his soil and breaking
   the clods?
25 When he has leveled its surface,
Does he not sow the black cummin
And scatter the cummin,
Plant the wheat in rows,
The barley in the appointed place,
And the spelt in its place?
26 For He instructs him in right judgment,
His God teaches him.

27 For the black cummin is not threshed with
   a threshing sledge,
Nor is a cartwheel rolled over the cummin;
But the black cummin is beaten out with a
   stick,
And the cummin with a rod.
28 Bread *flour* must be ground;
Therefore he does not thresh it forever,
Break *it with* his cartwheel,
Or crush it *with* his horsemen.
29 This also comes from the LORD of hosts,
Who is wonderful in counsel *and* excellent
   in guidance.

29 "Woe* to Ariel,ˢ to Ariel, the city *where*
   David dwelt!
Add year to year;
Let feasts come around.
2 Yet I will distress Ariel;
There shall be heaviness and sorrow,
And it shall be to Me as Ariel.
3 I will encamp against you all around,
I will lay siege against you with a mound,
And I will raise siegeworks against you.
4 You shall be brought down,
You shall speak out of the ground;
Your speech shall be low, out of the dust;
Your voice shall be like a medium's, out of
   the ground;
And your speech shall whisper out of the
   dust.

CHAPTER 29
29:1–8 The prophet presented three
descriptions of Ariel ("lion of God"), the city
of Jerusalem.
   A besieged city. The immediate
reference is to God's victory over Assyria
(Isa. 36—37), but the final application is to
His defeat of the armies that will surround
Jerusalem in the last days (Zech. 14:1–3).
The enemy will be like dust and chaff. They
will wake up and discover their dreams of
success have become nightmares of defeat.
God knows how and when to deliver His
people.

29:1 ˢThat is, Jerusalem

5 "Moreover the multitude of your foes
   Shall be like fine dust,
   And the multitude of the terrible ones
   Like chaff that passes away;
   Yes, it shall be in an instant, suddenly.
6 You will be punished by the LORD of hosts
   With thunder and earthquake and great
      noise,
   With storm and tempest
   And the flame of devouring fire.
7 The multitude of all the nations who fight
      against Ariel,
   Even all who fight against her and her
      fortress,
   And distress her,
   Shall be as a dream of a night vision.
8 It shall even be as when a hungry man
      dreams,
   And look—he eats;
   But he awakes, and his soul is still empty;
   Or as when a thirsty man dreams,
   And look—he drinks;
   But he awakes, and indeed *he is* faint,
   And his soul still craves:
   So the multitude of all the nations shall be,
   Who fight against Mount Zion."

29:9–16 *A blind city.* God's people were like drunken sleeping blind men trying to read a sealed book! They had no understanding of spiritual things nor did they worship God in the Spirit (Matt. 15:8–9). Even more, they made their own plans (political alliances) and thought God did not know (vv. 15–16)! Does the clay know more than the Potter (Rom. 9:20)? Can the thing made fool the Maker?

9 *Pause and wonder!
   Blind yourselves and be blind!
   They are drunk, but not with wine;
   They stagger, but not with intoxicating
      drink.
10 For the LORD has poured out on you
   The spirit of deep sleep,
   And has closed your eyes, namely, the
      prophets;
   And He has covered your heads, *namely,*
      the seers.

11The whole vision has become to you like the words of a book that is sealed, which *men* deliver to one who is literate, saying, "Read this, please." And he says, "I cannot, for it *is* sealed." 12Then the book is delivered to one who is illiterate, saying, "Read this, please." And he says, "I am not literate." 13Therefore the Lord said:

   "Inasmuch as these people draw near with
      their mouths
   And honor Me with their lips,
   But have removed their hearts far from Me,
   And their fear toward Me is taught by the
      commandment of men,
14 Therefore, behold, I will again do a
      marvelous work
   Among this people,
   A marvelous work and a wonder;
   For the wisdom of their wise *men* shall
      perish,
   And the understanding of their prudent *men*
      shall be hidden."

15 Woe to those who seek deep to hide their
      counsel far from the LORD,
   And their works are in the dark;
   They say, "Who sees us?" and, "Who knows
      us?"
16 Surely you have things turned around!
   Shall the potter be esteemed as the clay;
   For shall the thing made say of him who
      made it,

"He did not make me"?
Or shall the thing formed say of him who
    formed it,
"He has no understanding"?

17 *Is it not yet a very little while
    Till Lebanon shall be turned into a fruitful
        field,
    And the fruitful field be esteemed as a
        forest?
18 In that day the deaf shall hear the words
        of the book,
    And the eyes of the blind shall see out of
        obscurity and out of darkness.
19 The humble also shall increase *their* joy in
        the LORD,
    And the poor among men shall rejoice
    In the Holy One of Israel.
20 For the terrible one is brought to nothing,
    The scornful one is consumed,
    And all who watch for iniquity are cut off—
21 Who make a man an offender by a word,
    And lay a snare for him who reproves in
        the gate,
    And turn aside the just by empty words.

22Therefore thus says the LORD, who redeemed
Abraham, concerning the house of Jacob:

    "Jacob shall not now be ashamed,
    Nor shall his face now grow pale;
23 But when he sees his children,
    The work of My hands, in his midst,
    They will hallow My name,
    And hallow the Holy One of Jacob,
    And fear the God of Israel.
24 These also who erred in spirit will come to
        understanding,
    And those who complained will learn
        doctrine."

30 "Woe* to the rebellious children," says the
    LORD,
    "Who take counsel, but not of Me,
    And who devise plans, but not of My Spirit,
    That they may add sin to sin;
2 Who walk to go down to Egypt,
    And have not asked My advice,
    To strengthen themselves in the strength of
        Pharaoh,
    And to trust in the shadow of Egypt!
3 Therefore the strength of Pharaoh
    Shall be your shame,
    And trust in the shadow of Egypt
    Shall be *your* humiliation.
4 For his princes were at Zoan,
    And his ambassadors came to Hanes.
5 They were all ashamed of a people *who*
        could not benefit them,
    Or be help or benefit,
    But a shame and also a reproach."

6The burden against the beasts of the South.

    Through a land of trouble and anguish,
    From which *came* the lioness and lion,
    The viper and fiery flying serpent,
    They will carry their riches on the backs
        of young donkeys,
    And their treasures on the humps of
        camels,
    To a people *who* shall not profit;

29:17–24 *A blessed city.* When the Lord
returns and establishes His kingdom, things
will change! God's people will hear and see
His truth, rejoice in it, and honor the Holy
One of Israel. But you need not wait to have
Him change your life. Give Him an honest
heart, and let the Potter have His way in
your life.

CHAPTERS 30—31

30:1ff When Assyria threatened Judah, the
leaders did not immediately turn to God for
help but trusted in diplomacy (chaps. 30–
31). Their ambassadors went through
dangerous territory (vv. 6–7) to go to Egypt,
but Egypt could not help Judah. Egypt was
as helpful as a shadow (vv. 1–5), a wall
about to fall down (vv. 12–13), or a broken
clay vessel (v. 14). The Egyptians were only
men, not God (31:1–3). Are you trusting
things that cannot help you while the Lord
waits for you to come to Him for help
(vv. 15, 18)?

Those who wait on the Lord for help will
experience blessings, such as answered
prayer (vv. 18–19), God's guidance (vv. 20–
21), cleansing (v. 22), fruitfulness (vv. 23–
26), victory (vv. 27–33; 31:4–9), and a song
(v. 29).

The horses of Egypt can never take the
place of the chariots of God (Ps. 20:7–8).

7 For the Egyptians shall help in vain and to
   no purpose.
Therefore I have called her
   Rahab-Hem-Shebeth.[t]

8 Now go, write it before them on a tablet,
And note it on a scroll,
That it may be for time to come,
Forever and ever:
9 That this *is* a rebellious people,
Lying children,
Children *who* will not hear the law of the
   L ORD;
10 Who say to the seers, "Do not see,"
And to the prophets, "Do not prophesy to
   us right things;
Speak to us smooth things, prophesy
   deceits.
11 Get out of the way,
Turn aside from the path,
Cause the Holy One of Israel
To cease from before us."

12 Therefore thus says the Holy One of Israel:

   "Because you despise this word,
And trust in oppression and perversity,
And rely on them,
13 Therefore this iniquity shall be to you
Like a breach ready to fall,
A bulge in a high wall,
Whose breaking comes suddenly, in an
   instant.
14 And He shall break it like the breaking of
   the potter's vessel,
Which is broken in pieces;
He shall not spare.
So there shall not be found among its
   fragments
A shard to take fire from the hearth,
Or to take water from the cistern."

15 For thus says the Lord G OD, the Holy One of
Israel:

   "In returning and rest you shall be saved;
In quietness and confidence shall be your
   strength."
But you would not,
16 And you said, "No, for we will flee on
   horses"—
Therefore you shall flee!
And, "We will ride on swift *horses*"—
Therefore those who pursue you shall be
   swift!

17 One thousand *shall flee* at the threat of one,
At the threat of five you shall flee,
Till you are left as a pole on top of a
   mountain
And as a banner on a hill.

18 Therefore the L ORD will wait, that He may
   be gracious to you;
And therefore He will be exalted, that He
   may have mercy on you.
For the L ORD *is* a God of justice;
Blessed *are* all those who wait for Him.

30:7 [t]Literally *Rahab Sits Idle*

19 For the people shall dwell in Zion at
    Jerusalem;
  You shall weep no more.
  He will be very gracious to you at the sound
    of your cry;
  When He hears it, He will answer you.
20 And *though* the Lord gives you
  The bread of adversity and the water of
    affliction,
  Yet your teachers will not be moved into a
    corner anymore,
  But your eyes shall see your teachers.
21 Your ears shall hear a word behind you,
    saying,
  "This *is* the way, walk in it,"
  Whenever you turn to the right hand
  Or whenever you turn to the left.
22 You will also defile the covering of your
    images of silver,
  And the ornament of your molded images
    of gold.
  You will throw them away as an unclean
    thing;
  You will say to them, "Get away!"

23 Then He will give the rain for your seed
  With which you sow the ground,
  And bread of the increase of the earth;
  It will be fat and plentiful.
  In that day your cattle will feed
  In large pastures.
24 Likewise the oxen and the young donkeys
    that work the ground
  Will eat cured fodder,
  Which has been winnowed with the shovel
    and fan.
25 There will be on every high mountain
  And on every high hill
  Rivers *and* streams of waters,
  In the day of the great slaughter,
  When the towers fall.
26 Moreover the light of the moon will be as
    the light of the sun,
  And the light of the sun will be sevenfold,
  As the light of seven days,
  In the day that the LORD binds up the bruise
    of His people
  And heals the stroke of their wound.

27 Behold, the name of the LORD comes from
    afar,
  Burning *with* His anger,
  And *His* burden *is* heavy;
  His lips are full of indignation,
  And His tongue like a devouring fire.
28 His breath is like an overflowing stream,
  Which reaches up to the neck,
  To sift the nations with the sieve of futility;
  And *there shall be* a bridle in the jaws of
    the people,
  Causing *them* to err.

29 You shall have a song
  As in the night *when* a holy festival is kept,
  And gladness of heart as when one goes
    with a flute,
  To come into the mountain of the LORD,
  To the Mighty One of Israel.
30 The LORD will cause His glorious voice to
    be heard,
  And show the descent of His arm,
  With the indignation of *His* anger

And the flame of a devouring fire,
With scattering, tempest, and hailstones.
31 For through the voice of the LORD
Assyria will be beaten down,
As He strikes with the rod.
32 And *in* every place where the staff of
   punishment passes,
Which the LORD lays on him,
It will be with tambourines and harps;
And in battles of brandishing He will fight
   with it.
33 For Tophet *was* established of old,
Yes, for the king it is prepared.
He has made *it* deep and large;
Its pyre *is* fire with much wood;
The breath of the LORD, like a stream of
   brimstone,
Kindles it.

31 Woe to those who go down to Egypt for
   help,
And rely on horses,
Who trust in chariots because *they are*
   many,
And in horsemen because they are very
   strong,
But who do not look to the Holy One of
   Israel,
Nor seek the LORD!
2 Yet He also *is* wise and will bring disaster,
And will not call back His words,
But will arise against the house of evildoers,
And against the help of those who work
   iniquity.
3 Now the Egyptians *are* men, and not
      God;
And their horses are flesh, and not spirit.
When the LORD stretches out His hand,
Both he who helps will fall,
And he who is helped will fall down;
They all will perish together.

4For thus the LORD has spoken to me:

"As a lion roars,
And a young lion over his prey
(When a multitude of shepherds is
   summoned against him,
He will not be afraid of their voice
Nor be disturbed by their noise),
So the LORD of hosts will come down
To fight for Mount Zion and for its hill.
5 Like birds flying about,
So will the LORD of hosts defend Jerusalem.
Defending, He will also deliver *it*;
Passing over, He will preserve *it*."

6Return *to Him* against whom the children of
Israel have deeply revolted. 7For in that day every
man shall throw away his idols of silver and his
idols of gold—sin, which your own hands have
made for yourselves.

8 "Then Assyria shall fall by a sword not of
      man,
And a sword not of mankind shall devour
   him.
But he shall flee from the sword,
And his young men shall become forced
   labor.
9 He shall cross over to his stronghold for
   fear,

And his princes shall be afraid of the
    banner,"
Says the LORD,
Whose fire *is* in Zion
And whose furnace *is* in Jerusalem.

32 Behold,* a king will reign in righteousness,
    And princes will rule with justice.
2   A man will be as a hiding place from the
        wind,
    And a cover from the tempest,
    As rivers of water in a dry place,
    As the shadow of a great rock in a weary
        land.
3   *The eyes of those who see will not be dim,
    And the ears of those who hear will listen.
4   Also the heart of the rash will understand
        knowledge,
    And the tongue of the stammerers will be
        ready to speak plainly.

5   The foolish person will no longer be called
        generous,
    Nor the miser said *to be* bountiful;
6   For the foolish person will speak
        foolishness,
    And his heart will work iniquity:
    To practice ungodliness,
    To utter error against the LORD,
    To keep the hungry unsatisfied,
    And he will cause the drink of the thirsty
        to fail.
7   Also the schemes of the schemer *are* evil;
    He devises wicked plans
    To destroy the poor with lying words,
    Even when the needy speaks justice.
8   But a generous man devises generous
        things,
    And by generosity he shall stand.

9   *Rise up, you women who are at ease,
    Hear my voice;
    You complacent daughters,
    Give ear to my speech.
10 In a year and *some* days
    You will be troubled, you complacent
        women;
    For the vintage will fail,
    The gathering will not come.
11 Tremble, you *women* who are at ease;
    Be troubled, you complacent ones;
    Strip yourselves, make yourselves bare,
    And gird *sackcloth* on *your* waists.

12 People shall mourn upon their breasts
    For the pleasant fields, for the fruitful vine.
13 On the land of my people will come up
        thorns *and* briers,
    Yes, on all the happy homes *in* the joyous
        city;
14 Because the palaces will be forsaken,
    The bustling city will be deserted.
    The forts and towers will become lairs
        forever,
    A joy of wild donkeys, a pasture of flocks—
15 Until the Spirit is poured upon us from on
        high,
    And the wilderness becomes a fruitful field,
    And the fruitful field is counted as a forest.

16 *Then justice will dwell in the wilderness,
    And righteousness remain in the fruitful
        field.

CHAPTER 32

32:1, 2 *Dependable people.* Although our
Lord fits this description (Isa. 25:4), the
prophet is speaking primarily about leaders
in the kingdom. They should be both *rocks*
and *rivers,* providing *security* and
sufficiency. Rocks do not move or change,
while rivers are ever moving and changing.
Leaders must be both consistent and
adaptable, combining the faithfulness of the
rock with the fruitfulness of the river.

32:3–8 *Wise people.* Fools, scoundrels,
and schemers abounded in Isaiah's day and
made the nation weak. But God wants
people whose eyes, ears, and hearts are
open to spiritual truth, people who are able
to share that truth clearly with others.

32:9–15 *Concerned people.* Isaiah had a
special burden for the careless women of
the land (Isa. 3:16ff.; see also Amos 6:1ff.),
for wives and mothers can have great
influence for good or for evil. They were
living at ease as God's judgment was about
to fall. Their happy homes were about to
be destroyed, but they did not seem to care.

32:16–20 *Peaceful people.* The prophet
ends on a happy note, describing the peace
and prosperity of the future kingdom. There
can be no lasting peace without
righteousness, and Jesus Christ is our "King
of righteousness" and "King of peace" (Heb.
7:1–3).

17 The work of righteousness will be peace,
And the effect of righteousness, quietness
and assurance forever.
18 My people will dwell in a peaceful
habitation,
In secure dwellings, and in quiet resting
places,
19 Though hail comes down on the forest,
And the city is brought low in humiliation.

20 Blessed *are* you who sow beside all waters,
Who send out freely the feet of the ox and
the donkey.

CHAPTER 33

33:1ff The prophet looked out at the horizon and saw the plunderer coming to conquer the land. Then he looked around at some of the people in the nation who helped cause this judgment: the traitors who sold out to the enemy (v. 1); the ambassadors who sought help from Egypt (v. 7); and the religious hypocrites who pretended to serve God (v. 14; 1:10–20; 29:13). All of this was discouraging, but one thing encouraged Isaiah: a godly remnant that trusted the Lord and interceded for the land (vv. 2–4, 14–15). When you pray, you see the Lord exalted (vv. 5–6), you hear His words of encouragement (vv. 10–13), and you view your King in glory and power (vv. 17–24). Are you looking in the right direction? Are you a part of the godly remnant of intercessors?

33 Woe* to you who plunder, though you *have*
not been plundered;
And you who deal treacherously, though
they have not dealt treacherously with
you!
When you cease plundering,
You will be plundered;
When you make an end of dealing
treacherously,
They will deal treacherously with you.

2 O LORD, be gracious to us;
We have waited for You.
Be their^u arm every morning,
Our salvation also in the time of trouble.
3 At the noise of the tumult the people shall
flee;
When You lift Yourself up, the nations shall
be scattered;
4 And Your plunder shall be gathered
Like the gathering of the caterpillar;
As the running to and fro of locusts,
He shall run upon them.

5 The LORD is exalted, for He dwells on high;
He has filled Zion with justice and
righteousness.
6 Wisdom and knowledge will be the stability
of your times,
And the strength of salvation;
The fear of the LORD *is* His treasure.

7 Surely their valiant ones shall cry outside,
The ambassadors of peace shall weep
bitterly.
8 The highways lie waste,
The traveling man ceases.
He has broken the covenant,
He has despised the cities,^v
He regards no man.
9 The earth mourns *and* languishes,
Lebanon is shamed *and* shriveled;
Sharon is like a wilderness,
And Bashan and Carmel shake off *their*
fruits.

10 "Now I will rise," says the LORD;
"Now I will be exalted,

33:2 ^uSeptuagint omits *their;* Syriac, Targum, and Vulgate read *our.* 33:8 ^vFollowing Masoretic Text and Vulgate; Dead Sea Scrolls read *witnesses;* Septuagint omits *cities;* Targum reads *They have been removed from their cities.*

It's a Promise—All the plunderers will be plundered, and all the traitors will themselves be betrayed (Isa. 33:1). We reap what we sow (Gal. 6:7–8).

Now I will lift Myself up.
11 You shall conceive chaff,
You shall bring forth stubble;
Your breath, *as* fire, shall devour you.
12 And the people shall be *like* the burnings
of lime;
Like thorns cut up they shall be burned in
the fire.
13 Hear, you *who are* afar off, what I have
done;
And you *who are* near, acknowledge My
might."

14 The sinners in Zion are afraid;
Fearfulness has seized the hypocrites:
"Who among us shall dwell with the
devouring fire?
Who among us shall dwell with everlasting
burnings?"
15 He who walks righteously and speaks
uprightly,
He who despises the gain of oppressions,
Who gestures with his hands, refusing
bribes,
Who stops his ears from hearing of
bloodshed,
And shuts his eyes from seeing evil:
16 He will dwell on high;
His place of defense *will be* the fortress of
rocks;
Bread will be given him,
His water *will be* sure.

17 Your eyes will see the King in His beauty;
They will see the land that is very far off.
18 Your heart will meditate on terror:
"Where *is* the scribe?
Where *is* he who weighs?
Where *is* he who counts the towers?"
19 You will not see a fierce people,
A people of obscure speech, beyond
perception,
Of a stammering tongue *that you* cannot
understand.

20 Look upon Zion, the city of our appointed
feasts;
Your eyes will see Jerusalem, a quiet home,
A tabernacle *that* will not be taken down;
Not one of its stakes will ever be removed,
Nor will any of its cords be broken.
21 But there the majestic LORD *will be* for us
A place of broad rivers *and* streams,
In which no galley with oars will sail,
Nor majestic ships pass by
22 (For the LORD *is* our Judge,
The LORD *is* our Lawgiver,
The LORD *is* our King;
He will save us);
23 Your tackle is loosed,
They could not strengthen their mast,
They could not spread the sail.

Then the prey of great plunder is divided;
The lame take the prey.
24 And the inhabitant will not say, "I am sick";
The people who dwell in it *will be* forgiven
their iniquity.

34 Come* near, you nations, to hear;
And heed, you people!
Let the earth hear, and all that is in it,

CHAPTER 34

34:1ff From judgment upon His people,
God turns to warn about judgment upon the
whole world. It will be like slaughtering whole
armies (v. 3), shaking heaven (v. 4), and
sacrificing people like animals (vv. 5–7).
God will also judge the land (vv. 8–17)
and make it a wilderness. When you read
the judgments described in Revelation
6—19, you see what ruin will come to the
earth. Isaiah specifically names Edom, one
of Israel's longtime enemies; but no nation
will escape.
Why this indignation? "For the cause of
Zion" (v. 8). God fights *against* His people
if they disobey Him, but He fights *for* them
when His chastening has accomplished its
purposes. He will keep His covenant with
Abraham and Abraham's descendants
(Gen. 12:1–3).

The world and all things that come forth
   from it.
2 For the indignation of the LORD *is* against
   all nations,
And *His* fury against all their armies;
He has utterly destroyed them,
He has given them over to the slaughter.
3 Also their slain shall be thrown out;
Their stench shall rise from their corpses,
And the mountains shall be melted with
   their blood.
4 All the host of heaven shall be dissolved,
And the heavens shall be rolled up like a
   scroll;
All their host shall fall down
As the leaf falls from the vine,
And as *fruit* falling from a fig tree.

5 "For My sword shall be bathed in heaven;
Indeed it shall come down on Edom,
And on the people of My curse, for
   judgment.
6 The sword of the LORD is filled with blood,
It is made overflowing with fatness,
With the blood of lambs and goats,
With the fat of the kidneys of rams.
For the LORD has a sacrifice in Bozrah,
And a great slaughter in the land of Edom.
7 The wild oxen shall come down with them,
And the young bulls with the mighty bulls;
Their land shall be soaked with blood,
And their dust saturated with fatness."

8 For *it is* the day of the LORD's vengeance,
The year of recompense for the cause of
   Zion.
9 Its streams shall be turned into pitch,
And its dust into brimstone;
Its land shall become burning pitch.
10 It shall not be quenched night or day;
Its smoke shall ascend forever.
From generation to generation it shall lie
   waste;
No one shall pass through it forever and
   ever.
11 But the pelican and the porcupine shall
   possess it,
Also the owl and the raven shall dwell in
   it.
And He shall stretch out over it
The line of confusion and the stones of
   emptiness.
12 They shall call its nobles to the kingdom,
But none *shall be* there, and all its princes
   shall be nothing.

13 And thorns shall come up in its palaces,
Nettles and brambles in its fortresses;
It shall be a habitation of jackals,
A courtyard for ostriches.
14 The wild beasts of the desert shall also meet
   with the jackals,
And the wild goat shall bleat to its
   companion;
Also the night creature shall rest there,
And find for herself a place of rest.
15 There the arrow snake shall make her nest
   and lay *eggs*
And hatch, and gather *them* under her
   shadow;
There also shall the hawks be gathered,
Every one with her mate.

16 "Search from the book of the LORD, and read:
   Not one of these shall fail;
   Not one shall lack her mate.
   For My mouth has commanded it, and His
      Spirit has gathered them.
17 He has cast the lot for them,
   And His hand has divided it among them
      with a measuring line.
   They shall possess it forever;
   From generation to generation they shall
      dwell in it.".

35 The* wilderness and the wasteland shall be
         glad for them,
   And the desert shall rejoice and blossom as
      the rose;
2 It shall blossom abundantly and rejoice,
   Even with joy and singing.
   The glory of Lebanon shall be given to it,
   The excellence of Carmel and Sharon.
   They shall see the glory of the LORD,
   The excellency of our God.

3 Strengthen the weak hands,
   And make firm the feeble knees.
4 Say to those *who are* fearful-hearted,
   "Be strong, do not fear!
   Behold, your God will come *with*
      vengeance,
   With the recompense of God;
   He will come and save you."

5 Then the eyes of the blind shall be opened,
   And the ears of the deaf shall be unstopped.
6 Then the lame shall leap like a deer,
   And the tongue of the dumb sing.
   For waters shall burst forth in the
      wilderness,
   And streams in the desert.
7 The parched ground shall become a pool,
   And the thirsty land springs of water;
   In the habitation of jackals, where each lay,
   There shall be grass with reeds and rushes.

8 A highway shall be there, and a road,
   And it shall be called the Highway of
      Holiness.
   The unclean shall not pass over it,
   But it *shall be* for others.
   Whoever walks the road, although a fool,
   Shall not go astray.

CHAPTER 35

35:1ff Once again, God balances the announcement of judgment with the assurance of glory. He wants sinners to repent and believers to be encouraged. When Jesus Christ comes to reign, marvelous changes will take place.

The desolate wilderness will become a beautiful garden (vv. 1–2, 7). Human history began in a garden, but man's sin turned the garden into a desert. God's creation will rejoice when it is set free from the bondage of sin (Isa. 55:12–13; Rom. 8:18–25).

The weak will be strong, and the disabled will be handicapped no longer (vv. 3–6). The wanderers will never lose their way as they walk safely on God's Highway of Holiness (vv. 8–9), and the weepers will have their sorrows turned into joy (v. 10).

As you wait for these physical blessings, you can enjoy them in a spiritual way. God can give you deliverance, fruitfulness, strength, holiness, and joy as you yield to Him.

The Desert Will Bloom—Eighty-nine workers were accidentally killed during the building of Boulder (Hoover) Dam. The memorial plaque reads: "For those who died that the desert might bloom." One day, the desert will bloom to the glory of God because Jesus Christ died on the cross for the sins of the world.

"O For a Thousand Tongues to Sing"

Hear Him, ye deaf;
His praise, ye dumb, Your loosened tongues employ;
Ye blind, behold your Saviour come;
And leap, ye lame, for joy!

Charles Wesley

9 No lion shall be there,
Nor shall *any* ravenous beast go up on it;
It shall not be found there.
But the redeemed shall walk *there*,

10 And the ransomed of the LORD shall return,
And come to Zion with singing,
With everlasting joy on their heads.
They shall obtain joy and gladness,
And sorrow and sighing shall flee away.

CHAPTER 36

36:1ff Chapters 36—39 are historical and describe three special tests that King Hezekiah faced: enemy invasion (chaps. 36—37), sickness (chap. 38), and flattery (chap. 39). See 2 Kings 18—19 and 2 Chronicles 32 for additional data.

The prophet warned that the Assyrian army was coming, and now it surrounded Jerusalem.

Assyria conquered Israel and then moved into Judah where it captured every fortified city. From the words of the Rabshakeh (army field commander), you can learn much about warfare against your own spiritual enemy, the devil.

Satan is proud and confident of victory. He tries to frighten you into surrendering. He knows that the most important thing is *where you put your faith* (v. 4). Are you trusting the world, yourself or the Lord (vv. 6–7)?

The enemy offers to give you something in return for your obedience (vv. 8, 16), *but there is always an "until" involved* (v. 17)! He wants you to think that his gifts are as good as the Lord's gifts and that the Lord cannot be trusted to help you (vv. 14–15, 18).

Use the shield of faith to quench those fiery darts (Eph. 6:16) *and never negotiate with Satan* (v. 21). Do what Hezekiah did: ask the Lord for help and believe His Word.

36 Now* it came to pass in the fourteenth year of King Hezekiah *that* Sennacherib king of Assyria came up against all the fortified cities of Judah and took them. ²Then the king of Assyria sent *the* Rabshakeh[w] with a great army from Lachish to King Hezekiah at Jerusalem. And he stood by the aqueduct from the upper pool, on the highway to the Fuller's Field. ³And Eliakim the son of Hilkiah, who was over the household, Shebna the scribe, and Joah the son of Asaph, the recorder, came out to him.

⁴Then *the* Rabshakeh said to them, "Say now to Hezekiah, 'Thus says the great king, the king of Assyria: "What confidence is this in which you trust? ⁵I say you speak of having plans and power for war; but *they are* mere words. Now in whom do you trust, that you rebel against me? ⁶Look! You are trusting in the staff of this broken reed, Egypt, on which if a man leans, it will go into his hand and pierce it. So *is* Pharaoh king of Egypt to all who trust in him.

⁷"But if you say to me, 'We trust in the LORD our God,' *is it* not He whose high places and whose altars Hezekiah has taken away, and said to Judah and Jerusalem, 'You shall worship before this altar'?" ' ⁸Now therefore, I urge you, give a pledge to my master the king of Assyria, and I will give you two thousand horses—if you are able on your part to put riders on them! ⁹How then will you repel one captain of the least of my master's servants, and put your trust in Egypt for chariots and horsemen? ¹⁰Have I now come up without the LORD against this land to destroy it? The LORD said to me, 'Go up against this land, and destroy it.' "

¹¹Then Eliakim, Shebna, and Joah said to *the* Rabshakeh, "Please speak to your servants in Aramaic, for we understand *it;* and do not speak to us in Hebrew[x] in the hearing of the people who *are* on the wall."

¹²But *the* Rabshakeh said, "Has my master sent me to your master and to you to speak these words, and not to the men who sit on the wall, who will eat and drink their own waste with you?"

¹³Then *the* Rabshakeh stood and called out with a loud voice in Hebrew, and said, "Hear the words of the great king, the king of Assyria! ¹⁴Thus says the king: 'Do not let Hezekiah deceive you, for he will not be able to deliver you; ¹⁵nor let Hezekiah make you trust in the LORD, saying, "The LORD will surely deliver us; this city will not be given into the hand of the king of Assyria." ' ¹⁶Do not listen to Hezekiah; for thus says the king of Assyria: 'Make *peace* with me *by a* present and come out to me; and every one of you eat from his own vine and every one from his own fig tree, and every one of you drink the waters of his own

36:2 ʷA title, probably *Chief of Staff* or *Governor*
36:11 ˣLiterally *Judean*

cistern; 17until I come and take you away to a land like your own land, a land of grain and new wine, a land of bread and vineyards. 18*Beware* lest Hezekiah persuade you, saying, "The LORD will deliver us." Has any one of the gods of the nations delivered its land from the hand of the king of Assyria? 19Where *are* the gods of Hamath and Arpad? Where *are* the gods of Sepharvaim? Indeed, have they delivered Samaria from my hand? 20Who among all the gods of these lands have delivered their countries from my hand, that the LORD should deliver Jerusalem from my hand?' "

21But they held their peace and answered him not a word; for the king's commandment was, "Do not answer him." 22Then Eliakim the son of Hilkiah, who *was* over the household, Shebna the scribe, and Joah the son of Asaph, the recorder, came to Hezekiah with *their* clothes torn, and told him the words of *the* Rabshakeh.

37 And* so it was, when King Hezekiah heard it, that he tore his clothes, covered himself with sackcloth, and went into the house of the LORD. 2Then he sent Eliakim, who *was* over the household, Shebna the scribe, and the elders of the priests, covered with sackcloth, to Isaiah the prophet, the son of Amoz. 3And they said to him, "Thus says Hezekiah: 'This day *is* a day of trouble and rebuke and blasphemy; for the children have come to birth, but *there is* no strength to bring them forth. 4It may be that the LORD your God will hear the words of *the* Rabshakeh, whom his master the king of Assyria has sent to reproach the living God, and will rebuke the words which the LORD your God has heard. Therefore lift up *your* prayer for the remnant that is left.' "

5So the servants of King Hezekiah came to Isaiah. 6And Isaiah said to them, "Thus you shall say to your master, 'Thus says the LORD: "Do not be afraid of the words which you have heard, with which the servants of the king of Assyria have blasphemed Me. 7Surely I will send a spirit upon him, and he shall hear a rumor and return to his own land; and I will cause him to fall by the sword in his own land." ' "

8Then *the* Rabshakeh returned, and found the king of Assyria warring against Libnah, for he heard that he had departed from Lachish. 9And the king heard concerning Tirhakah king of Ethiopia, "He has come out to make war with you." So when he heard *it*, he sent messengers to Hezekiah, saying, 10"Thus you shall speak to Hezekiah king of Judah, saying: 'Do not let your God in whom you trust deceive you, saying, "Jerusalem shall not be given into the hand of the king of Assyria." 11Look! You have heard what the kings of Assyria have done to all lands by utterly destroying them; and shall you be delivered? 12Have the gods of the nations delivered those whom my fathers have destroyed, Gozan and Haran and Rezeph, and the people of Eden who *were* in Telassar? 13Where *is* the king of Hamath, the king of Arpad, and the king of the city of Sepharvaim, Hena, and Ivah?' "

14And Hezekiah received the letter from the hand of the messengers, and read it; and Hezekiah went up to the house of the LORD, and spread it before the LORD. 15Then Hezekiah prayed to the LORD, saying: 16"O LORD of hosts, God of Israel, *the* One who dwells *between* the cherubim, You *are* God, You alone, of all the kingdoms of the

CHAPTER 37

37:1ff Not all victories are as dramatic as this one, but Hezekiah's experience shows you what to do when you are attacked by the enemy.

Take your burdens to the Lord. It is good to talk things over with others, but only the Lord can work in your heart and turn fear into faith. God knows everything the enemy says and writes, and He has a perfect plan. By faith, take everything to Him in prayer.

Listen for God's message. The words of the enemy will discourage you, but God's Word will encourage you. In every battle, His word to you is, "Do not be afraid" (v. 6). After all, He has everything under control.

Seek to glorify God alone. More than anything else, Hezekiah was concerned for the glory of God (vv. 4, 16–20). "Hallowed be Thy name" must be your primary prayer.

Trust God to work. Sennacherib defied the God of Israel, and yet he died in the house of his god *who could not protect him.* God can handle the enemy far better than you can.

Trust God after the victory. The Assyrians had devastated the land, but God promised to feed His people and give them a harvest. Your future is in God's hands.

❝*The future is as bright as the promises of God.*❞

—William Carey

earth. You have made heaven and earth. [17]Incline Your ear, O LORD, and hear; open Your eyes, O LORD, and see; and hear all the words of Sennacherib, which he has sent to reproach the living God. [18]Truly, LORD, the kings of Assyria have laid waste all the nations and their lands, [19]and have cast their gods into the fire; for they *were* not gods, but the work of men's hands—wood and stone. Therefore they destroyed them. [20]Now therefore, O LORD our God, save us from his hand, that all the kingdoms of the earth may know that You *are* the LORD, You alone."

[21]Then Isaiah the son of Amoz sent to Hezekiah, saying, "Thus says the LORD God of Israel, 'Because you have prayed to Me against Sennacherib king of Assyria, [22]this *is* the word which the LORD has spoken concerning him:

> "The virgin, the daughter of Zion,
> Has despised you, laughed you to scorn;
> The daughter of Jerusalem
> Has shaken *her* head behind your back!

23 "Whom have you reproached and
>   blasphemed?
> Against whom have you raised *your* voice,
> And lifted up your eyes on high?
> Against the Holy One of Israel.
24 By your servants you have reproached the
>   Lord,
> And said, 'By the multitude of my chariots
> I have come up to the height of the
>   mountains,
> To the limits of Lebanon;
> I will cut down its tall cedars
> *And* its choice cypress trees;
> I will enter its farthest height,
> To its fruitful forest.
25 I have dug and drunk water,
> And with the soles of my feet I have dried
>   up
> All the brooks of defense.'

26 "Did you not hear long ago
> *How* I made it,
> From ancient times that I formed it?
> Now I have brought it to pass,
> That you should be
> For crushing fortified cities *into* heaps of
>   ruins.
27 Therefore their inhabitants *had* little power;
> They were dismayed and confounded;
> They were *as* the grass of the field
> And the green herb,
> *As* the grass on the housetops
> And grain blighted before it is grown.

28 "But I know your dwelling place,
> Your going out and your coming in,
> And your rage against Me.
29 Because your rage against Me and your
>   tumult
> Have come up to My ears,
> Therefore I will put My hook in your nose
> And My bridle in your lips,
> And I will turn you back
> By the way which you came." '

30"This *shall be* a sign to you:

> You shall eat this year such as grows of
>   itself,

And the second year what springs from the
   same;
Also in the third year sow and reap,
Plant vineyards and eat the fruit of them.
31   And the remnant who have escaped of the
   house of Judah
Shall again take root downward,
And bear fruit upward.
32   For out of Jerusalem shall go a remnant,
And those who escape from Mount Zion.
The zeal of the LORD of hosts will do this.

33"Therefore thus says the LORD concerning the
king of Assyria:

'He shall not come into this city,
Nor shoot an arrow there,
Nor come before it with shield,
Nor build a siege mound against it.
34   By the way that he came,
By the same shall he return;
And he shall not come into this city,'
Says the LORD.
35   'For I will defend this city, to save it
For My own sake and for My servant
   David's sake.'"

36Then the angel*y* of the LORD went out, and
killed in the camp of the Assyrians one hundred
and eighty-five thousand; and when *people* arose
early in the morning, there were the corpses—all
dead. 37So Sennacherib king of Assyria departed
and went away, returned *home*, and remained at
Nineveh. 38Now it came to pass, as he was worshiping in the house of Nisroch his god, that his
sons Adrammelech and Sharezer struck him
down with the sword; and they escaped into the
land of Ararat. Then Esarhaddon his son reigned
in his place.

38 In* those days Hezekiah was sick and near
death. And Isaiah the prophet, the son of
Amoz, went to him and said to him, "Thus says
the LORD: 'Set your house in order, for you shall
die and not live.'"
2Then Hezekiah turned his face toward the wall,
and prayed to the LORD, 3and said, "Remember
now, O LORD, I pray, how I have walked before
You in truth and with a loyal heart, and have done
what is good in Your sight." And Hezekiah wept
bitterly.
4And the word of the LORD came to Isaiah, saying, 5"Go and tell Hezekiah, 'Thus says the LORD,
the God of David your father: "I have heard your
prayer, I have seen your tears; surely I will add
to your days fifteen years. 6I will deliver you and
this city from the hand of the king of Assyria,
and I will defend this city." ' 7And this *is* the sign
to you from the LORD, that the LORD will do this
thing which He has spoken: 8Behold, I will bring
the shadow on the sundial, which has gone down
with the sun on the sundial of Ahaz, ten degrees
backward." So the sun returned ten degrees on
the dial by which it had gone down.

9This is the writing of Hezekiah king of Judah,
when he had been sick and had recovered from
his sickness:

❝*If you are swept off your feet, it
is time to get on your knees.***❞**
                                    —Frederick Beck

CHAPTER 38
38:1ff In the prime of life (v. 10), Hezekiah
contracted a boil (v. 21) that so infected his
body that he was told he would die (v. 1).
All this happened before the events of
chapters 36 and 37 (v. 6), but Hezekiah
knew Assyria was coming. What a
predicament to be in!
   The king's prayer was certainly a normal
response. After all, most believers want to
go on living and serving God. He was
concerned, too, about the future of the
nation in view of the Assyrian advance. At
any rate, God not only answered his prayer
but even gave him a special sign to
encourage his faith.
   Hezekiah pictured death as going through
a gate (v. 10), taking down a tent (v. 12),
being cut from a loom and rolled up (v. 12),
and being attacked by a beast (v. 13). But
he clung to the Word of God (v. 17) and
gave praise to God for all He did (vv. 16–
20).
   Difficult experiences should give us a new
appreciation for life and a new desire to live
for the Lord.

10 I said,
  "In the prime of my life
    I shall go to the gates of Sheol;
    I am deprived of the remainder of my
      years."
11 I said,
  "I shall not see YAH,
    The LORD[z] in the land of the living;
    I shall observe man no more among the
      inhabitants of the world.[a]
12 My life span is gone,
    Taken from me like a shepherd's tent;
    I have cut off my life like a weaver.
    He cuts me off from the loom;
    From day until night You make an end of
      me.
13 I have considered until morning—
    Like a lion,
    So He breaks all my bones;
    From day until night You make an end of
      me.
14 Like a crane *or* a swallow, so I chattered;
    I mourned like a dove;
    My eyes fail *from looking* upward.
    O LORD,[b] I am oppressed;
    Undertake for me!

15 "What shall I say?
    He has both spoken to me,[c]
    And He Himself has done *it*.
    I shall walk carefully all my years
    In the bitterness of my soul.
16 O Lord, by these *things men* live;
    And in all these *things is* the life of my spirit;
    So You will restore me and make me live.
17 Indeed *it was* for *my own* peace
    That I had great bitterness;
    But You have lovingly *delivered* my soul
      from the pit of corruption,
    For You have cast all my sins behind Your
      back.
18 For Sheol cannot thank You,
    Death cannot praise You;
    Those who go down to the pit cannot hope
      for Your truth.
19 The living, the living man, he shall praise
      You,
    As I *do* this day;
    The father shall make known Your truth to
      the children.

20 "The LORD *was ready* to save me;
    Therefore we will sing my songs with
      stringed instruments
    All the days of our life, in the house of the
      LORD."

21Now Isaiah had said, "Let them take a lump
of figs, and apply *it* as a poultice on the boil, and
he shall recover."
22And Hezekiah had said, "What *is* the sign that
I shall go up to the house of the LORD?"

38:11 [z]Hebrew *YAH, YAH* [a]Following some Hebrew
manuscripts; Masoretic Text and Vulgate read *rest;* Septuagint
omits *among the inhabitants of the world;* Targum reads *land.*
38:14 [b]Following Bomberg; Masoretic Text and Dead Sea
Scrolls read *Lord.* 38:15 [c]Following Masoretic Text and
Vulgate; Dead Sea Scrolls and Targum read *And shall I say
to Him;* Septuagint omits first half of this verse.

39 At* that time Merodach-Baladan[d] the son of Baladan, king of Babylon, sent letters and a present to Hezekiah, for he heard that he had been sick and had recovered. 2And Hezekiah was pleased with them, and showed them the house of his treasures—the silver and gold, the spices and precious ointment, and all his armory—all that was found among his treasures. There was nothing in his house or in all his dominion that Hezekiah did not show them.

3Then Isaiah the prophet went to King Hezekiah, and said to him, "What did these men say, and from where did they come to you?"

So Hezekiah said, "They came to me from a far country, from Babylon."

4And he said, "What have they seen in your house?"

So Hezekiah answered, "They have seen all that *is* in my house; there is nothing among my treasures that I have not shown them."

5Then Isaiah said to Hezekiah, "Hear the word of the LORD of hosts: 6'Behold, the days are coming when all that *is* in your house, and what your fathers have accumulated until this day, shall be carried to Babylon; nothing shall be left,' says the LORD. 7'And they shall take away *some* of your sons who will descend from you, whom you will beget; and they shall be eunuchs in the palace of the king of Babylon.' "

8So Hezekiah said to Isaiah, "The word of the LORD which you have spoken *is* good!" For he said, "At least there will be peace and truth in my days."

40 "Comfort,* yes, comfort My people!" Says your God.

2 "Speak comfort to Jerusalem, and cry out to her,
   That her warfare is ended,
   That her iniquity is pardoned;
   For she has received from the LORD's hand
   Double for all her sins."

3 The voice of one crying in the wilderness:
   "Prepare the way of the LORD;
   Make straight in the desert[e]
   A highway for our God.
4 Every valley shall be exalted
   And every mountain and hill brought low;
   The crooked places shall be made straight
   And the rough places smooth;
5 The glory of the LORD shall be revealed,
   And all flesh shall see *it* together;
   For the mouth of the LORD has spoken."

6 The voice said, "Cry out!"
   And he[f] said, "What shall I cry?"

39:1 [d]Spelled *Berodach-Baladan* in 2 Kings 20:12
40:3 [e]Following Masoretic Text, Targum, and Vulgate; Septuagint omits *in the desert*.   40:6 [f]Following Masoretic Text and Targum; Dead Sea Scrolls, Septuagint, and Vulgate read *I*.

CHAPTER 39

39:1ff This was the third test (2 Chron. 32:31), and the king failed miserably. What could not be accomplished through an army or an illness was accomplished through flattery. If Satan cannot succeed as a lion, then he comes as a serpent: "Faithful are the wounds of a friend, but the kisses of an enemy are deceitful" (Prov. 27:6).

The kisses. The king of Babylon wanted one thing: Judah's cooperation in opposing the Assyrians. The enemy is a liar and uses every excuse to get entry into your life. It was foolish for Hezekiah to welcome them and show them the royal treasures, but pride took over and discernment disappeared. Ephesians 4:17–32 lists some "footholds" you can give Satan in your life.

The wounds. Isaiah did not fear the king but told him truthfully that Babylon was the real enemy *and one day would conquer Judah.* However, instead of repenting, Hezekiah felt relieved that the judgment would not come in his day. How shortsighted can a man of faith become! Had he no concern for the future of his people?

CHAPTER 40

40:1–11 Voices. Though Isaiah wrote a century before the fall of Judah, his words greatly encouraged the exiles when they read them in Babylon. The voice of *comfort* (vv. 1–5) tells you that God knows how to measure your chastening and that He forgives and gives you a new beginning. The voice of *confidence* (vv. 6–8) assures you that His Word stands in spite of the frailty of man. The voice of *conquest* (vv. 9–11) is *your* voice as you share the good news with others. Shout it aloud!

Wound with Truth—It is not always easy to deliver God's message to those who need it. It takes courage to wound a friend. Nathan faced King David with the truth (2 Sam. 12), and Isaiah confronted both Ahaz (Isa. 7) and Hezekiah (Isa. 39). The apostle Paul fearlessly confronted Peter (Gal. 2:11ff.). One writer observed, "A lying tongue hates those who are crushed by it, and a flattering mouth works ruin" (Prov. 26:28). Speak the truth in love (Eph. 4:15) and give wounds that heal.

"All flesh *is* grass,
And all its loveliness *is* like the flower of
  the field.
7 The grass withers, the flower fades,
Because the breath of the LORD blows upon
  it;
Surely the people *are* grass.
8 The grass withers, the flower fades,
But the word of our God stands forever."

9 O Zion,
You who bring good tidings,
Get up into the high mountain;
O Jerusalem,
You who bring good tidings,
Lift up your voice with strength,
Lift *it* up, be not afraid;
Say to the cities of Judah, "Behold your
  God!"

10 Behold, the Lord GOD shall come with a
  strong *hand*,
And His arm shall rule for Him;
Behold, His reward *is* with Him,
And His work before Him.
11 He will feed His flock like a shepherd;
He will gather the lambs with His arm,
And carry *them* in His bosom,
And gently lead those who are with young.

40:12–24 Vision. Returning to the land and rebuilding the nation seemed impossible tasks to the exiles, so Isaiah invited them to behold the greatness of God. God is greater than every burden you bear and every challenge you face. Babylon was but a drop in the bucket to God! The world's false gods can do nothing to hinder the working of your great God, so trust Him to see you through.

12 *Who has measured the waters[g] in the
  hollow of His hand,
Measured heaven with a span
And calculated the dust of the earth in a
  measure?
Weighed the mountains in scales
And the hills in a balance?
13 Who has directed the Spirit of the LORD,
Or *as* His counselor has taught Him?
14 With whom did He take counsel, and *who*
  instructed Him,
And taught Him in the path of justice?
Who taught Him knowledge,
And showed Him the way of understanding?

15 Behold, the nations *are* as a drop in a
  bucket,
And are counted as the small dust on the
  scales;
Look, He lifts up the isles as a very little
  thing.
16 And Lebanon *is* not sufficient to burn,
Nor its beasts sufficient for a burnt offering.
17 All nations before Him *are* as nothing,
And they are counted by Him less than
  nothing and worthless.

18 To whom then will you liken God?
Or what likeness will you compare to Him?
19 The workman molds an image,
The goldsmith overspreads it with gold,
And the silversmith casts silver chains.
20 Whoever *is* too impoverished for *such* a
  contribution
Chooses a tree *that* will not rot;
He seeks for himself a skillful workman
To prepare a carved image *that* will not
  totter.

40:12 [g]Following Masoretic Text, Septuagint, and Vulgate;
Dead Sea Scrolls read *waters of the sea;* Targum reads
waters of the world.

21 Have you not known?
    Have you not heard?
    Has it not been told you from the beginning?
    Have you not understood from the
        foundations of the earth?
22 *It is* He who sits above the circle of the
        earth,
    And its inhabitants *are* like grasshoppers,
    Who stretches out the heavens like a
        curtain,
    And spreads them out like a tent to dwell
        in.
23 He brings the princes to nothing;
    He makes the judges of the earth useless.

24 Scarcely shall they be planted,
    Scarcely shall they be sown,
    Scarcely shall their stock take root in the
        earth,
    When He will also blow on them,
    And they will wither,
    And the whirlwind will take them away like
        stubble.

25*"To whom then will you liken Me,
    Or *to whom* shall I be equal?" says the Holy
        One.
26 Lift up your eyes on high,
    And see who has created these *things,*
    Who brings out their host by number;
    He calls them all by name,
    By the greatness of His might
    And the strength of *His* power;
    Not one is missing.

27 Why do you say, O Jacob,
    And speak, O Israel:
    "My way is hidden from the LORD,
    And my just claim is passed over by my
        God"?
28 Have you not known?
    Have you not heard?
    The everlasting God, the LORD,
    The Creator of the ends of the earth,
    Neither faints nor is weary.
    His understanding is unsearchable.
29 He gives power to the weak,
    And to *those who have* no might He
        increases strength.
30 Even the youths shall faint and be weary,
    And the young men shall utterly fall,
31 But those who wait on the LORD
    Shall renew *their* strength;
    They shall mount up with wings like eagles,
    They shall run and not be weary,
    They shall walk and not faint.

41 "Keep* silence before Me, O coastlands,
    And let the people renew *their* strength!
    Let them come near, then let them speak;
    Let us come near together for judgment.

2   "Who raised up one from the east?
    Who in righteousness called him to His feet?
    Who gave the nations before him,
    And made *him* rule over kings?
    Who gave *them* as the dust *to* his sword,
    As driven stubble to his bow?
3   Who pursued them, *and* passed safely
    By the way *that* he had not gone with his
        feet?
4   Who has performed and done *it,*

40:25–31 *Victory.* You may be weak like grass (vv. 6–8), sheep (v. 11), dust (v. 15), grasshoppers (v. 22), and even worms (41:14); but if you trust the power of God, you can be like an eagle, a runner, and a patient pilgrim (vv. 28–31). In the emergencies of life, God helps you soar; in the daily routine of life, He helps you patiently walk. Both are the working of His mighty power (Eph. 3:20–21).

CHAPTER 41

41:1–7 As the exiles prepared to return to their land, they looked around, saw other nations, and were afraid (vv. 1–7). But God was (and is) in control of the nations, and He raised up Cyrus to do His bidding (vv. 2, 25). The false gods of the nations are no match for the true God of Israel.

Calling the generations from the beginning?
'I, the LORD, am the first;
And with the last I *am* He.'"

5   The coastlands saw *it* and feared,
The ends of the earth were afraid;
They drew near and came.
6   Everyone helped his neighbor,
And said to his brother,
"Be of good courage!"
7   So the craftsman encouraged the goldsmith;
He who smooths *with* the hammer *inspired*
him who strikes the anvil,
Saying, "It *is* ready for the soldering";
Then he fastened it with pegs,
That it might not totter.

41:8–20 Then the exiles looked at one another and asked, "Are we able to travel to our land and rebuild our nation?" But God gave them assurance: "You are My servant! Fear not, for I am with you! I will help you!" He can make a toothless worm into a sharp threshing instrument (v. 15)! He can transform the arid desert into a garden (vv. 17–20).

8 *"But you, Israel, *are* My servant,
Jacob whom I have chosen,
The descendants of Abraham My friend.
9   *You* whom I have taken from the ends of
the earth,
And called from its farthest regions,
And said to you,
'You *are* My servant,
I have chosen you and have not cast you
away:
10   Fear not, for I *am* with you;
Be not dismayed, for I *am* your God.
I will strengthen you,
Yes, I will help you,
I will uphold you with My righteous right
hand.'

11 "Behold, all those who were incensed against
you
Shall be ashamed and disgraced;
They shall be as nothing,
And those who strive with you shall perish.
12   You shall seek them and not find them—
Those who contended with you.
Those who war against you
Shall be as nothing,
As a nonexistent thing.
13   For I, the LORD your God, will hold your
right hand,
Saying to you, 'Fear not, I will help you.'

14 "Fear not, you worm Jacob,
You men of Israel!
I will help you," says the LORD
And your Redeemer, the Holy One of Israel.
15 "Behold, I will make you into a new threshing
sledge with sharp teeth;
You shall thresh the mountains and beat
them small,
And make the hills like chaff.
16   You shall winnow them, the wind shall
carry them away,

Servanthood—"Servant" is a key concept in the second half of Isaiah's prophecy. It refers to the nation of Israel (41:8–9); to Cyrus, king of Persia, who defeated Babylon (41:2; 44:28—45:1); and to the Lord Jesus Christ, God's "Suffering Servant," who died for the sins of the world (52:13—53:12).

Fear Not—The admonition "fear not" is often repeated in Isaiah, backed up by various reasons why God's people need not be afraid. God is with us no matter what the circumstances, and He strengthens us and helps us no matter what the task (41:10). He holds us as He helps us (41:13–14). He will not forsake us because He made us and redeemed us, and we belong to Him (43:1, 5) He was with us before we were born, and He has a purpose for us to fulfill in this world today (44:2). How can we be afraid when God's words are sure and He is the Rock of our salvation (44:8)?

And the whirlwind shall scatter them;
You shall rejoice in the LORD,
And glory in the Holy One of Israel.

17 "The poor and needy seek water, but *there
    is* none,
Their tongues fail for thirst.
I, the LORD, will hear them;
I, the God of Israel, will not forsake them.
18 I will open rivers in desolate heights,
And fountains in the midst of the valleys;
I will make the wilderness a pool of water,
And the dry land springs of water.
19 I will plant in the wilderness the cedar and
    the acacia tree,
The myrtle and the oil tree;
I will set in the desert the cypress tree *and*
    the pine
And the box tree together,
20 That they may see and know,
And consider and understand together,
That the hand of the LORD has done this,
And the Holy One of Israel has created it.

21*"Present your case," says the LORD.
"Bring forth your strong *reasons,*" says the
    King of Jacob.
22 "Let them bring forth and show us what will
    happen;
Let them show the former things, what they
    were,
That we may consider them,
And know the latter end of them;
Or declare to us things to come.
23 Show the things that are to come hereafter,
That we may know that you *are* gods;
Yes, do good or do evil,
That we may be dismayed and see *it*
    together.
24 Indeed you *are* nothing,
And your work *is* nothing;
He who chooses you *is* an abomination.

25 "I have raised up one from the north,
And he shall come;
From the rising of the sun he shall call on
    My name;
And he shall come against princes as
    though mortar,
As the potter treads clay.
26 Who has declared from the beginning, that
    we may know?
And former times, that we may say, 'He *is*
    righteous'?
Surely *there is* no one who shows,
Surely *there is* no one who declares,
Surely *there is* no one who hears your
    words.
27 The first time *I said* to Zion,
'Look, there they are!'
And I will give to Jerusalem one who brings
    good tidings.
28 For I looked, and *there was* no man;
I looked among them, but *there was* no
    counselor,
Who, when I asked of them, could answer
    a word.
29 Indeed they *are* all worthless;[h]

41:21–29 Finally, they looked ahead and
wondered about the future. God knows the
future (the idols do not!) and has everything
under control, so there is no need to worry.
    As you contemplate your situation and
face an unknown future, are you trusting
Him? God's promise is still "I will help you"
(vv. 10, 13, 14), and He will keep it!

41:29 [h]Following Masoretic Text and Vulgate; Dead Sea
Scrolls, Syriac, and Targum read *nothing;* Septuagint omits
the first line.

Their works *are* nothing;
Their molded images *are* wind and
   confusion.

CHAPTER 42

42:1–13 God helped His Servant, Jesus Christ. Matthew 12:18–21 applies this to our Lord in His earthly ministry to the needy. He was chosen by God and empowered by God, so He did not get discouraged and quit. Jesus Christ lived and served by faith, trusting His Father to meet His needs, and that is the way you must live today. His power is available to you.

42 "Behold!* My Servant whom I uphold,
My Elect One *in whom* My soul delights!
I have put My Spirit upon Him;
He will bring forth justice to the Gentiles.
2 He will not cry out, nor raise *His voice*,
Nor cause His voice to be heard in the street.
3 A bruised reed He will not break,
And smoking flax He will not quench;
He will bring forth justice for truth.
4 He will not fail nor be discouraged,
Till He has established justice in the earth;
And the coastlands shall wait for His law."

5 Thus says God the LORD,
Who created the heavens and stretched
   them out,
Who spread forth the earth and that which
   comes from it,
Who gives breath to the people on it,
And spirit to those who walk on it:
6 "I, the LORD, have called You in
   righteousness,
And will hold Your hand;
I will keep You and give You as a covenant
   to the people,
As a light to the Gentiles,
7 To open blind eyes,
To bring out prisoners from the prison,
Those who sit in darkness from the prison
   house.
8 I *am* the LORD, that *is* My name;
And My glory I will not give to another,
Nor My praise to carved images.
9 Behold, the former things have come to
   pass,
And new things I declare;
Before they spring forth I tell you of them."

10 Sing to the LORD a new song,
And His praise from the ends of the earth,
You who go down to the sea, and all that
   is in it,
You coastlands and you inhabitants of
   them!
11 Let the wilderness and its cities lift up *their
   voice*,
The villages *that* Kedar inhabits.
Let the inhabitants of Sela sing,
Let them shout from the top of the
   mountains.
12 Let them give glory to the LORD,
And declare His praise in the coastlands.
13 The LORD shall go forth like a mighty man;
He shall stir up *His* zeal like a man of war.
He shall cry out, yes, shout aloud;
He shall prevail against His enemies.

14*"I have held My peace a long time,
I have been still and restrained Myself.
Now I will cry like a woman in labor,
I will pant and gasp at once.
15 I will lay waste the mountains and hills,
And dry up all their vegetation;
I will make the rivers coastlands,
And I will dry up the pools.
16 I will bring the blind by a way they did not
   know;
I will lead them in paths they have not
   known.

42:14–25 God helped His servant, Israel. Weak as they were, the nation returned to the land after their years of captivity. They were spiritually blind and obstinate, but God led them and worked on their behalf. **God helps His servants today.** When you belong to God's family, your Father is ready to forgive and restore you. Putting life back together again may appear impossible, but the Lord will work for you if you let Him. He can do new things (v. 9), guide you on new paths (v. 16), and give you a new song (v. 10).

I will make darkness light before them,
And crooked places straight.
These things I will do for them,
And not forsake them.
17 They shall be turned back,
They shall be greatly ashamed,
Who trust in carved images,
Who say to the molded images,
'You *are* our gods.'

18 "Hear, you deaf;
And look, you blind, that you may see.
19 Who *is* blind but My servant,
Or deaf as My messenger *whom* I send?
Who *is* blind as *he who is* perfect,
And blind as the LORD's servant?
20 Seeing many things, but you do not observe;
Opening the ears, but he does not hear."

21 The LORD is well pleased for His
    righteousness' sake;
He will exalt the law and make *it* honorable.
22 But this *is* a people robbed and plundered;
All of them are snared in holes,
And they are hidden in prison houses;
They are for prey, and no one delivers;
For plunder, and no one says, "Restore!"

23 Who among you will give ear to this?
Who will listen and hear for the time to
    come?
24 Who gave Jacob for plunder, and Israel to
    the robbers?
Was it not the LORD,
He against whom we have sinned?
For they would not walk in His ways,
Nor were they obedient to His law.
25 Therefore He has poured on him the fury
    of His anger
And the strength of battle;
It has set him on fire all around,
Yet he did not know;
And it burned him,
Yet he did not take *it* to heart.

43

But* now, thus says the LORD, who created
    you, O Jacob,
And He who formed you, O Israel:
"Fear not, for I have redeemed you;
I have called *you* by your name;
You *are* Mine.
2 When you pass through the waters, I *will
    be* with you;
And through the rivers, they shall not
    overflow you.
When you walk through the fire, you shall
    not be burned,
Nor shall the flame scorch you.
3 For I *am* the LORD your God,
The Holy One of Israel, your Savior;
I gave Egypt for your ransom,
Ethiopia and Seba in your place.
4 Since you were precious in My sight,
You have been honored,
And I have loved you;
Therefore I will give men for you,
And people for your life.
5 Fear not, for I *am* with you;
I will bring your descendants from the east,
And gather you from the west;
6 I will say to the north, 'Give them up!'
And to the south, 'Do not keep them back!'

CHAPTER 43

43:1ff There is no reason to be afraid when
you realize what God has done for you. He
formed you (v. 1) and made you for Himself
(v. 21) and for His glory (v. 7). When you
trusted Jesus Christ, God redeemed you
(v. 1) and blotted out all your sins (v. 25).
He is "the LORD, your Holy One, the Creator
of Israel, your King" (v. 15). He loves you
(v. 4) and knows your name (v. 1). What a
privilege to belong to such a great and
gracious God!

Even more, God promises to be with you
(v. 5) and take you through the water and
the fire (v. 2). At the Exodus, He took Israel
through the Red Sea and defeated the
Egyptian army (vv. 16–17). Perhaps the
three Hebrew heroes claimed this promise
when they faced the fiery furnace (Dan. 3).

In spite of all the ministry He shares with
us, God does not get weary as we do
(40:28); but we can weary Him with our
empty religious ritual and our sins (vv. 22–
24). You are precious in His sight (v. 4), so
do not cheapen yourself by disobeying Him.

Bring My sons from afar,
And My daughters from the ends of the
earth—
7 Everyone who is called by My name,
Whom I have created for My glory;
I have formed him, yes, I have made him."

8 Bring out the blind people who have eyes,
And the deaf who have ears.
9 Let all the nations be gathered together,
And let the people be assembled.
Who among them can declare this,
And show us former things?
Let them bring out their witnesses, that they
may be justified;
Or let them hear and say, "It is truth."
10 "You are My witnesses," says the LORD,
"And My servant whom I have chosen,
That you may know and believe Me,
And understand that I am He.
Before Me there was no God formed,
Nor shall there be after Me.
11 I, even I, am the LORD,
And besides Me there is no savior.
12 I have declared and saved,
I have proclaimed,
And there was no foreign god among you;
Therefore you are My witnesses,"
Says the LORD, "that I am God.
13 Indeed before the day was, I am He;
And there is no one who can deliver out of
My hand;
I work, and who will reverse it?"

14 Thus says the LORD, your Redeemer,
The Holy One of Israel:
"For your sake I will send to Babylon,
And bring them all down as fugitives—
The Chaldeans, who rejoice in their ships.
15 I am the LORD, your Holy One,
The Creator of Israel, your King."

16 Thus says the LORD, who makes a way in
the sea
And a path through the mighty waters,
17 Who brings forth the chariot and horse,
The army and the power
(They shall lie down together, they shall not
rise;
They are extinguished, they are quenched
like a wick):
18 "Do not remember the former things,
Nor consider the things of old.
19 Behold, I will do a new thing,
Now it shall spring forth;
Shall you not know it?
I will even make a road in the wilderness
And rivers in the desert.
20 The beast of the field will honor Me,
The jackals and the ostriches,
Because I give waters in the wilderness
And rivers in the desert,
To give drink to My people, My chosen.
21 This people I have formed for Myself;
They shall declare My praise.

22 "But you have not called upon Me, O Jacob;
And you have been weary of Me, O Israel.
23 You have not brought Me the sheep for your
burnt offerings,
Nor have you honored Me with your
sacrifices.

I have not caused you to serve with grain
    offerings,
Nor wearied you with incense.
24 You have bought Me no sweet cane with
    money,
Nor have you satisfied Me with the fat of
    your sacrifices;
But you have burdened Me with your sins,
You have wearied Me with your iniquities.

25 "I, *even* I, *am* He who blots out your
    transgressions for My own sake;
And I will not remember your sins.
26 Put Me in remembrance;
Let us contend together;
State your *case*, that you may be acquitted.
27 Your first father sinned,
And your mediators have transgressed
    against Me.
28 Therefore I will profane the princes of the
    sanctuary;
I will give Jacob to the curse,
And Israel to reproaches.

44

"Yet* hear me now, O Jacob My servant,
And Israel whom I have chosen.
2 Thus says the LORD who made you
And formed you from the womb, *who* will
    help you:
'Fear not, O Jacob My servant;
And you, Jeshurun, whom I have chosen.
3 For I will pour water on him who is thirsty,
And floods on the dry ground;
I will pour My Spirit on your descendants,
And My blessing on your offspring;
4 They will spring up among the grass
Like willows by the watercourses.'
5 One will say, 'I *am* the LORD's';
Another will call *himself* by the name of
    Jacob;
Another will write *with* his hand, 'The
    LORD's,'
And name *himself* by the name of Israel.

6 "Thus says the LORD, the King of Israel,
And his Redeemer, the LORD of hosts:
'I *am* the First and I *am* the Last;
Besides Me *there is* no God.
7 And who can proclaim as I do?
Then let him declare it and set it in order
    for Me,
Since I appointed the ancient people.
And the things that are coming and shall
    come,
Let them show these to them.
8 Do not fear, nor be afraid;
Have I not told you from that time, and
    declared *it*?
You *are* My witnesses.
Is there a God besides Me?
Indeed *there is* no other Rock;
I know not *one*.' "

CHAPTER 44

44:1–8 *The faithfulness of God.* Once
again, God reminds His people that He
formed them, chose them, and would help
them. There is no need to be afraid, for God
meets every need (vv. 2–5) and keeps every
promise (vv. 6–8). He knows what lies ahead
and helps you prepare yourself to meet it.

Even a Pagan Ruler—The gods of the nations could not predict the future, but the Lord told
Isaiah what would happen. A ruler named Cyrus would conquer Babylon and allow the Jews to
return to their land (44:28; 45:1). Cyrus founded the Persian Empire, which defeated Babylon in 539
B.C. (Dan. 5:30). The next year, he issued the famous decree that permitted the Jews to go back to
their land and rebuild their temple (Ezra 1:1–6). If God can use a pagan ruler to serve His people
and fulfill His Word, you have no reason to be afraid of what people may say or do. The predictions
of astrologers and other "prophets" are ashes. God's Word is the true light in the darkness (2 Pet.
1:19–21).

44:9–20 *The folly of idolatry.* Israel learned in Babylon the futility and folly of idolatry. How easy it is to trust something other than the Lord, including the things we manufacture. Those who trust false gods will be afraid (v. 11) and become like the gods they worship (v. 18; Ps. 115:1–8). Their bodies may feast on excellent food (v. 19), but their souls feed on ashes (v. 20). They live on substitutes.

9 *Those who make an image, all of them *are* useless,
And their precious things shall not profit;
They *are* their own witnesses;
They neither see nor know, that they may be ashamed.

10 Who would form a god or mold an image
That profits him nothing?

11 Surely all his companions would be ashamed;
And the workmen, they *are* mere men.
Let them all be gathered together,
Let them stand up;
Yet they shall fear,
They shall be ashamed together.

12 The blacksmith with the tongs works one in the coals,
Fashions it with hammers,
And works it with the strength of his arms.
Even so, he is hungry, and his strength fails;
He drinks no water and is faint.

13 The craftsman stretches out *his* rule,
He marks one out with chalk;
He fashions it with a plane,
He marks it out with the compass,
And makes it like the figure of a man,
According to the beauty of a man, that it may remain in the house.

14 He cuts down cedars for himself,
And takes the cypress and the oak;
He secures *it* for himself among the trees of the forest.
He plants a pine, and the rain nourishes *it.*

15 Then it shall be for a man to burn,
For he will take some of it and warm himself;
Yes, he kindles *it* and bakes bread;
Indeed he makes a god and worships *it;*
He makes it a carved image, and falls down to it.

16 He burns half of it in the fire;
With this half he eats meat;
He roasts a roast, and is satisfied.
He even warms *himself* and says,
"Ah! I am warm,
I have seen the fire."

17 And the rest of it he makes into a god,
His carved image.
He falls down before it and worships *it,*
Prays to it and says,
"Deliver me, for you *are* my god!"

18 They do not know nor understand;
For He has shut their eyes, so that they cannot see,
And their hearts, so that they cannot understand.

19 And no one considers in his heart,
Nor *is there* knowledge nor understanding to say,
"I have burned half of it in the fire,
Yes, I have also baked bread on its coals;
I have roasted meat and eaten *it;*
And shall I make the rest of it an abomination?
Shall I fall down before a block of wood?"

20 He feeds on ashes;
A deceived heart has turned him aside;

And he cannot deliver his soul,
Nor say, "*Is there* not a lie in my right
    hand?"

21*"Remember these, O Jacob,
And Israel, for you *are* My servant;
I have formed you, you *are* My servant;
O Israel, you will not be forgotten by Me!
22 I have blotted out, like a thick cloud, your
        transgressions,
And like a cloud, your sins.
Return to Me, for I have redeemed you."

23 Sing, O heavens, for the LORD has done *it!*
Shout, you lower parts of the earth;
Break forth into singing, you mountains,
O forest, and every tree in it!
For the LORD has redeemed Jacob,
And glorified Himself in Israel.

24 Thus says the LORD, your Redeemer,
And He who formed you from the womb:
"I *am* the LORD, who makes all *things,*
Who stretches out the heavens all alone,
Who spreads abroad the earth by Myself;
25 Who frustrates the signs of the babblers,
And drives diviners mad;
Who turns wise men backward,
And makes their knowledge foolishness;
26 Who confirms the word of His servant,
And performs the counsel of His
        messengers;
Who says to Jerusalem, 'You shall be
        inhabited,'
To the cities of Judah, 'You shall be built,'
And I will raise up her waste places;
27 Who says to the deep, 'Be dry!
And I will dry up your rivers';
28 Who says of Cyrus, '*He is* My shepherd,
And he shall perform all My pleasure,
Saying to Jerusalem, "You shall be built,"
And to the temple, "Your foundation shall
        be laid."'

45 "Thus* says the LORD to His anointed,
To Cyrus, whose right hand I have held—
To subdue nations before him
And loose the armor of kings,
To open before him the double doors,
So that the gates will not be shut:
2 'I will go before you
And make the crooked places† straight;
I will break in pieces the gates of bronze
And cut the bars of iron.
3 I will give you the treasures of darkness
And hidden riches of secret places,
That you may know that I, the LORD,
Who call *you* by your name,
Am the God of Israel.

45:2 †Dead Sea Scrolls and Septuagint read *mountains;*
Targum reads *I will trample down the walls;* Vulgate reads *I
will humble the great ones of the earth.*

44:21–28 *The future of Israel.* Just like the
exodus from Egypt (Exod. 14—15), the
nation's exodus from Babylon would be a
time of redemption and rejoicing, and God
would confirm His Word to His people.
Jerusalem would be restored and the temple
rebuilt, and God would even use a pagan
ruler to accomplish His purposes! He is the
God of the impossible, so do what He
commands.

CHAPTER 45

45:1–7 God makes declarations to Cyrus,
to the Jews, and to the gentile nations; and
in these messages, He speaks to His people
today.
  His message to Cyrus was one of
sovereignty, focusing on His uniqueness:
Jehovah is the Creator and the Lord of
history. Cyrus did not even know the Lord;
yet the Lord called him by name and used
him to accomplish His purposes. When life
seems to be tumbling in, remember that God
is on the throne and is sovereign.

Look Now!—The famous British preacher Charles Haddon Spurgeon (1834–92) was converted
to Christ when he heard a layman preach a sermon based on Isaiah 45:22. "He was an ignorant
man," said Spurgeon in later years. "He could not say much; he was obliged to keep to his text.
Thank God for that." The preacher looked at young Spurgeon and said, "Young man, you are very
miserable. Young man, look! In God's name, look, and look now!" Spurgeon said, "I did look, blessed
be God! I know I looked then and there, and he who but that minute before had been near despair
had the fullness of joy and hope." Have you looked to Christ by faith and received His gift of salvation?

4 For Jacob My servant's sake,
And Israel My elect,
I have even called you by your name;
I have named you, though you have not
known Me.
5 I *am* the LORD, and *there is* no other;
There is no God besides Me.
I will gird you, though you have not known
Me,
6 That they may know from the rising of the
sun to its setting
That *there is* none besides Me.
I *am* the LORD, and *there is* no other;
7 I form the light and create darkness,
I make peace and create calamity;
I, the LORD, do all these *things.*'

45:8–19 His message to Israel emphasized *submission.* God can tell the rain clouds what to do, but His own people resist Him. This is like the clay telling the potter what to do (Jer. 18) or the child scolding the parents. If Israel would trust Him, they could share in the great things He was doing. Cyrus would cooperate with the Lord, and he did not even know Him!

8 *"Rain down, you heavens, from above,
And let the skies pour down righteousness;
Let the earth open, let them bring forth
salvation,
And let righteousness spring up together.
I, the LORD, have created it.

9 "Woe to him who strives with his Maker!
Let the potsherd *strive* with the potsherds
of the earth!
Shall the clay say to him who forms it,
'What are you making?'
Or shall your handiwork *say,* 'He has no
hands'?
10 Woe to him who says to *his* father, 'What
are you begetting?'
Or to the woman, 'What have you brought
forth?' "

11 Thus says the LORD,
The Holy One of Israel, and his Maker:
"Ask Me of things to come concerning My
sons;
And concerning the work of My hands, you
command Me.
12 I have made the earth,
And created man on it.
I—My hands—stretched out the heavens,
And all their host I have commanded.
13 I have raised him up in righteousness,
And I will direct all his ways;
He shall build My city
And let My exiles go free,
Not for price nor reward,"
Says the LORD of hosts.

14Thus says the LORD:

"The labor of Egypt and merchandise of
Cush
And of the Sabeans, men of stature,
Shall come over to you, and they shall be
yours;
They shall walk behind you,
They shall come over in chains;
And they shall bow down to you.
They will make supplication to you, *saying,*
'Surely God *is* in you,
And *there is* no other;
There is no other God.' "

15 Truly You *are* God, who hide Yourself,
O God of Israel, the Savior!
16 They shall be ashamed
And also disgraced, all of them;

They shall go in confusion together,
Who are makers of idols.
17 *But* Israel shall be saved by the LORD
With an everlasting salvation;
You shall not be ashamed or disgraced
Forever and ever.

18 For thus says the LORD,
Who created the heavens,
Who is God,
Who formed the earth and made it,
Who has established it,
Who did not create it in vain,
Who formed it to be inhabited:
"I *am* the LORD, and *there is* no other.
19 I have not spoken in secret,
In a dark place of the earth;
I did not say to the seed of Jacob,
'Seek Me in vain';
I, the LORD, speak righteousness,
I declare things that are right.

20*"Assemble yourselves and come;
Draw near together,
You *who have* escaped from the nations.
They have no knowledge,
Who carry the wood of their carved image,
And pray to a god *that* cannot save.
21 Tell and bring forth *your case;*
Yes, let them take counsel together.
Who has declared this from ancient time?
Who has told it from that time?
Have not I, the LORD?
And *there is* no other God besides Me,
A just God and a Savior;
There is none besides Me.

22 "Look to Me, and be saved,
All you ends of the earth!
For I *am* God, and *there is* no other.
23 I have sworn by Myself;
The word has gone out of My mouth *in*
righteousness,
And shall not return,
That to Me every knee shall bow,
Every tongue shall take an oath.
24 He shall say,
'Surely in the LORD I have righteousness and
strength.
To Him *men* shall come,
And all shall be ashamed
Who are incensed against Him.
25 In the LORD all the descendants of Israel
Shall be justified, and shall glory.' "

46 Bel* bows down, Nebo stoops;
Their idols were on the beasts and on the
cattle.
Your carriages *were* heavily loaded,
A burden to the weary *beast.*
2 They stoop, they bow down together;
They could not deliver the burden,
But have themselves gone into captivity.

45:20–25 The message to the Gentiles was one of *salvation.* God's purpose through Israel was that all nations be blessed (Gen. 12:1–3). One day God will gather His people and establish His kingdom, and then the nations will know the true God and trust the Savior. Meanwhile, we must get the message of salvation to every tribe and nation.

CHAPTERS 46—47

46:1ff In chapters 46 and 47 the prophet speaks to the Babylonians and warns them that judgment is coming because of their many sins.
He begins with their idolatry (chap. 46) and contrasts Jehovah and the gods of Babylon. The idols must be carried, but Jehovah is a God who carries His people. The false gods cannot predict the future or control history, but Jehovah does both. The idols are all alike, but Jehovah is the only true God and there is none like Him. Rejoice that you can worship the true and living God (Ps. 115)!

There Is No Substitute—An idol is a substitute for God, something that we value and serve other than God. We trust it and sacrifice for it; but in the end, it can do us no good. Isaiah mocked the idols of the nations and affirmed repeatedly that Jehovah was the only true and living God (40:18–20; 41:5–7; 44:9–20; 45:15–21; 46:1–7). Martin Luther said that "all such as rely and depend upon their art, wisdom, strength, sanctity, riches, honor, power, or anything else" are guilty of worshiping idols.

3 "Listen to Me, O house of Jacob,
  And all the remnant of the house of Israel,
  Who have been upheld *by Me* from birth,
  Who have been carried from the womb:
4 Even to *your* old age, I *am* He,
  And *even* to gray hairs I will carry *you!*
  I have made, and I will bear;
  Even I will carry, and will deliver *you.*

5 "To whom will you liken Me, and make *Me*
    equal
  And compare Me, that we should be alike?
6 They lavish gold out of the bag,
  And weigh silver on the scales;
  They hire a goldsmith, and he makes it a
    god;
  They prostrate themselves, yes, they
    worship.
7 They bear it on the shoulder, they carry it
  And set it in its place, and it stands;
  From its place it shall not move.
  Though *one* cries out to it, yet it cannot
    answer
  Nor save him out of his trouble.

8 "Remember this, and show yourselves men;
  Recall to mind, O you transgressors.
9 Remember the former things of old,
  For I *am* God, and *there is* no other;
  I am God, and *there is* none like Me,
10 Declaring the end from the beginning,
  And from ancient times *things* that are not
    yet done,
  Saying, 'My counsel shall stand,
  And I will do all My pleasure,'
11 Calling a bird of prey from the east,
  The man who executes My counsel, from a
    far country.
  Indeed I have spoken *it;*
  I will also bring it to pass.
  I have purposed *it;*
  I will also do it.

12 "Listen to Me, you stubborn-hearted,
  Who *are* far from righteousness:
13 I bring My righteousness near, it shall not
    be far off;
  My salvation shall not linger.
  And I will place salvation in Zion,
  For Israel My glory.

47 "Come* down and sit in the dust,
  O virgin daughter of Babylon;
  Sit on the ground without a throne,
  O daughter of the Chaldeans!
  For you shall no more be called
  Tender and delicate.
2 Take the millstones and grind meal.
  Remove your veil,
  Take off the skirt,
  Uncover the thigh,
  Pass through the rivers.
3 Your nakedness shall be uncovered,
  Yes, your shame will be seen;
  I will take vengeance,
  And I will not arbitrate with a man."

4 *As for* our Redeemer, the LORD of hosts *is*
    His name,
  The Holy One of Israel.

5 "Sit in silence, and go into darkness,
  O daughter of the Chaldeans;

47:1ff God then accused the Babylonians of being proud (vv. 1–3), having no humanity (vv. 4–7), living for pleasure (vv. 8–9), and depending on occult practices (vv. 10–15), sins that are prevalent today. The "Lady of Kingdoms" would sit in the dust like a barren widow, and the astrologers and stargazers would be burned to stubble. Why did they not see the fire coming?
Nations and kingdoms have their day, but God reigns as King. Just be sure you are not learning the practices of Babylon.

For you shall no longer be called
The Lady of Kingdoms.
6 I was angry with My people;
I have profaned My inheritance,
And given them into your hand.
You showed them no mercy;
On the elderly you laid your yoke very
heavily.
7 And you said, 'I shall be a lady forever,'
So that you did not take these *things* to
heart,
Nor remember the latter end of them.

8 "Therefore hear this now, *you who are* given
to pleasures,
Who dwell securely,
Who say in your heart, 'I *am,* and *there is*
no one else besides me;
I shall not sit *as* a widow,
Nor shall I know the loss of children';
9 But these two *things* shall come to you
In a moment, in one day:
The loss of children, and widowhood.
They shall come upon you in their fullness
Because of the multitude of your sorceries,
For the great abundance of your
enchantments.

10 "For you have trusted in your wickedness;
You have said, 'No one sees me';
Your wisdom and your knowledge have
warped you;
And you have said in your heart,
'I *am,* and *there is* no one else besides me.'
11 Therefore evil shall come upon you;
You shall not know from where it arises.
And trouble shall fall upon you;
You will not be able to put it off.
And desolation shall come upon you
suddenly,
Which you shall not know.

12 "Stand now with your enchantments
And the multitude of your sorceries,
In which you have labored from your
youth—
Perhaps you will be able to profit,
Perhaps you will prevail.
13 You are wearied in the multitude of your
counsels;
Let now the astrologers, the stargazers,
And the monthly prognosticators
Stand up and save you
From what shall come upon you.
14 Behold, they shall be as stubble,
The fire shall burn them;
They shall not deliver themselves
From the power of the flame;
It shall not *be* a coal to be warmed by,
Nor a fire to sit before!
15 Thus shall they be to you
With whom you have labored,
Your merchants from your youth;
They shall wander each one to his quarter.
No one shall save you.

48 "Hear* this, O house of Jacob,
Who are called by the name of Israel,
And have come forth from the wellsprings
of Judah;
Who swear by the name of the LORD,
And make mention of the God of Israel,

CHAPTER 48

48:1ff *Rebuke.* When you end up in trouble
because you did not listen to sound advice,
the last thing you want to hear is somebody
saying, "I told you so!" But that is just what
God says to Israel in this chapter. He had
warned them that their sins would bring
judgment, but they hardened their necks and
closed their ears. It was time to repent and
seek forgiveness.

Refining. The captivity was about to end.
It had been a time of refining for the nation
(v. 10; Job 23:10; 1 Pet. 1:7), but they had
learned to turn from idols and trust Jehovah
alone. If you resist, the fire will burn you
and make you hard; if you submit, the fire
will purify you and make you tender.

Renewing. God declares new things (Isa.
42:9) and does new things (Isa. 43:19), and
His people can hear new things (v. 6). Verse
20 has its parallel in 2 Corinthians 6:14–18.
As you obey God, He leads you (v. 17),
gives you peace (v. 18), and meets your
needs (v. 21). No matter how weak you are,
you can lean on Him (v. 2).

But not in truth or in righteousness;
2 For they call themselves after the holy city,
And lean on the God of Israel;
The Lord of hosts *is* His name:

3 "I have declared the former things from the
      beginning;
They went forth from My mouth, and I
      caused them to hear it.
Suddenly I did *them*, and they came to pass.
4 Because I knew that you *were* obstinate,
And your neck *was* an iron sinew,
And your brow bronze,
5 Even from the beginning I have declared *it*
      to you;
Before it came to pass I proclaimed *it* to you,
Lest you should say, 'My idol has done
      them,
And my carved image and my molded
      image
Have commanded them.'

6 "You have heard;
See all this.
And will you not declare *it*?
I have made you hear new things from this
      time,
Even hidden things, and you did not know
      them.
7 They are created now and not from the
      beginning;
And before this day you have not heard
      them,
Lest you should say, 'Of course I knew
      them.'
8 Surely you did not hear,
Surely you did not know;
Surely from long ago your ear was not
      opened.
For I knew that you would deal very
      treacherously,
And were called a transgressor from the
      womb.

9 "For My name's sake I will defer My anger,
And *for* My praise I will restrain it from you,
So that I do not cut you off.
10 Behold, I have refined you, but not as silver;
I have tested you in the furnace of affliction.
11 For My own sake, for My own sake, I will
      do *it*;
For how should *My name* be profaned?
And I will not give My glory to another.

12 "Listen to Me, O Jacob,
And Israel, My called:
I *am* He, I *am* the First,
I *am* also the Last.
13 Indeed My hand has laid the foundation of
      the earth,
And My right hand has stretched out the
      heavens;
When I call to them,
They stand up together.

14 "All of you, assemble yourselves, and hear!
Who among them has declared these
      things?
The Lord loves him;
He shall do His pleasure on Babylon,
And His arm *shall be against* the Chaldeans.
15 I, *even* I, have spoken;

Yes, I have called him,
I have brought him, and his way will
    prosper.

16 "Come near to Me, hear this:
I have not spoken in secret from the
    beginning;
From the time that it was, I *was* there.
And now the Lord GOD and His Spirit
Have^j sent Me."

17 Thus says the LORD, your Redeemer,
The Holy One of Israel:
"I *am* the LORD your God,
Who teaches you to profit,
Who leads you by the way you should go.
18 Oh, that you had heeded My
    commandments!
Then your peace would have been like a
    river,
And your righteousness like the waves of
    the sea.
19 Your descendants also would have been like
    the sand,
And the offspring of your body like the
    grains of sand;
His name would not have been cut off
Nor destroyed from before Me."

20 Go forth from Babylon!
Flee from the Chaldeans!
With a voice of singing,
Declare, proclaim this,
Utter it to the end of the earth;
Say, "The LORD has redeemed
His servant Jacob!"
21 And they did not thirst
When He led them through the deserts;
He caused the waters to flow from the rock
    for them;
He also split the rock, and the waters
    gushed out.

22 "*There is* no peace," says the LORD, "for the
    wicked."

49 "Listen,* O coastlands, to Me,
And take heed, you peoples from afar!
The LORD has called Me from the womb;
From the matrix of My mother He has made
    mention of My name.
2 And He has made My mouth like a sharp
    sword;
In the shadow of His hand He has hidden
    Me,
And made Me a polished shaft;
In His quiver He has hidden Me."

3 "And He said to me,
'You *are* My servant, O Israel,
In whom I will be glorified.'
4 Then I said, 'I have labored in vain,
I have spent my strength for nothing and
    in vain;
Yet surely my just reward *is* with the LORD,
And my work with my God.' "

5 "And now the LORD says,
Who formed Me from the womb *to be* His
    Servant,

48:16 ^j The Hebrew verb is singular.

CHAPTER 49

49:1ff The Servant is the Lord Jesus Christ,
to whom several meaningful names are
given.

He is God's *weapon* to conquer the
enemy (vv. 1–2; Heb. 4:12; Rev. 1:16;
19:15) and to bring salvation to the nations.
He is God's *Israel* (v. 3), accomplishing what
the nation failed to accomplish, namely,
bringing God's salvation to the Gentiles.

He is a *light* (v. 6) to guide the Gentiles
to God (Luke 1:79; Acts 13:47); and He is
the *covenant of God* (v. 8), fulfilling all the
promises God made to the fathers (Isa. 42:6;
Rom. 15:8–13; 2 Cor. 1:20). The nation's
return to the land was a picture of their final
return when Messiah comes (vv. 8–13).

There are times when you wonder if God
really cares about you (v. 14), but He
assures you that you are not forgotten. You
are His beloved child (v. 15; Ps. 27:10), and
He will never forget your name (v. 16). He
will gather His family and bring them home
(vv. 19–23).

To bring Jacob back to Him,
So that Israel is gathered to Him[k]
(For I shall be glorious in the eyes of the
    LORD,
And My God shall be My strength),
6   Indeed He says,
    'It is too small a thing that You should be
        My Servant
    To raise up the tribes of Jacob,
    And to restore the preserved ones of Israel;
    I will also give You as a light to the Gentiles,
    That You should be My salvation to the ends
        of the earth.' "

7   Thus says the LORD,
    The Redeemer of Israel, their Holy One,
    To Him whom man despises,
    To Him whom the nation abhors,
    To the Servant of rulers:
    "Kings shall see and arise,
    Princes also shall worship,
    Because of the LORD who is faithful,
    The Holy One of Israel;
    And He has chosen You."

8 Thus says the LORD:

    "In an acceptable time I have heard You,
    And in the day of salvation I have helped
        You;
    I will preserve You and give You
    As a covenant to the people,
    To restore the earth,
    To cause them to inherit the desolate
        heritages;
9   That You may say to the prisoners, 'Go
        forth,'
    To those who *are* in darkness, 'Show
        yourselves.'

    "They shall feed along the roads,
    And their pastures *shall be* on all desolate
        heights.
10   They shall neither hunger nor thirst,
    Neither heat nor sun shall strike them;
    For He who has mercy on them will lead
        them,
    Even by the springs of water He will guide
        them.
11   I will make each of My mountains a road,
    And My highways shall be elevated.
12   Surely these shall come from afar;
    Look! Those from the north and the west,
    And these from the land of Sinim."

13   Sing, O heavens!
    Be joyful, O earth!
    And break out in singing, O mountains!
    For the LORD has comforted His people,
    And will have mercy on His afflicted.

14   But Zion said, "The LORD has forsaken me,
    And my Lord has forgotten me."

15   "Can a woman forget her nursing child,
    And not have compassion on the son of her
        womb?
    Surely they may forget,

49:5 [k]Qere, Dead Sea Scrolls, and Septuagint read *is
gathered to Him;* Kethib reads *is not gathered.*

Yet I will not forget you.
16 See, I have inscribed you on the palms *of
      My hands;*
   Your walls *are* continually before Me.
17 Your sons[l] shall make haste;
   Your destroyers and those who laid you
      waste
   Shall go away from you.
18 Lift up your eyes, look around and see;
   All these gather together *and* come to you.
   As I live," says the LORD,
   "You shall surely clothe yourselves with
      them all as an ornament,
   And bind them *on you* as a bride *does.*

19 "For your waste and desolate places,
   And the land of your destruction,
   Will even now be too small for the
      inhabitants;
   And those who swallowed you up will be
      far away.
20 The children you will have,
   After you have lost the others,
   Will say again in your ears,
   'The place *is* too small for me;
   Give me a place where I may dwell.'
21 Then you will say in your heart,
   'Who has begotten these for me,
   Since I have lost my children and am
      desolate,
   A captive, and wandering to and fro?
   And who has brought these up?
   There I was, left alone;
   But these, where *were* they?'"

22 Thus says the Lord GOD:

   "Behold, I will lift My hand in an oath to the
      nations,
   And set up My standard for the peoples;
   They shall bring your sons in *their* arms,
   And your daughters shall be carried on *their*
      shoulders;
23 Kings shall be your foster fathers,
   And their queens your nursing mothers;
   They shall bow down to you with *their* faces
      to the earth,
   And lick up the dust of your feet.
   Then you will know that I *am* the LORD,
   For they shall not be ashamed who wait for
      Me."

24 Shall the prey be taken from the mighty,
   Or the captives of the righteous[m] be
      delivered?

25 But thus says the LORD:

   "Even the captives of the mighty shall be
      taken away,
   And the prey of the terrible be delivered;
   For I will contend with him who contends
      with you,
   And I will save your children.
26 I will feed those who oppress you with their
      own flesh,

49:17 [l]Dead Sea Scrolls, Septuagint, Targum, and Vulgate
read *builders.*   49:24 [m]Following Masoretic Text and Targum;
Dead Sea Scrolls, Syriac, and Vulgate read *the mighty;*
Septuagint reads *unjustly.*

And they shall be drunk with their own
  blood as with sweet wine.
All flesh shall know
That I, the LORD, *am* your Savior,
And your Redeemer, the Mighty One of
  Jacob."

CHAPTER 50

50:1 *The unfaithful wife.* Israel was "married to Jehovah" when she accepted His covenant at Sinai. But the nation eventually turned to idols, committed spiritual adultery, and sold herself into slavery; and God had to put her away (Hos. 1—4). God will restore His chosen people one day just as He forgives and restores believers today who turn from sin and obey Him (James 4:1–10).

50:4–9 *The faithful Servant.* This is our Lord Jesus Christ with a ready tongue and an open ear (vv. 4–5), a set face (v. 7; Luke 9:51), and a body surrendered to suffering (v. 6). What an example for us to follow as we seek to serve the Lord (Rom. 12:1–12).

50:10, 11 *The perplexed disciple.* People who fear God and obey Him can still end up in the darkness of perplexity. Then they are tempted to light their own fires and try to find their way out by themselves. Instead, trust the Lord, wait on Him, and He will give you the light you need when you need it.

50 Thus* says the LORD:

"Where *is* the certificate of your mother's
  divorce,
Whom I have put away?
Or which of My creditors *is it* to whom I
  have sold you?
For your iniquities you have sold
  yourselves,
And for your transgressions your mother
  has been put away.

2 Why, when I came, *was there* no man?
Why, when I called, *was there* none to
  answer?
Is My hand shortened at all that it cannot
  redeem?
Or have I no power to deliver?
Indeed with My rebuke I dry up the sea,
I make the rivers a wilderness;
Their fish stink because *there is* no water,
And die of thirst.

3 I clothe the heavens with blackness,
And I make sackcloth their covering."

4 *"The Lord GOD has given Me
The tongue of the learned,
That I should know how to speak
A word in season to *him who is* weary.
He awakens Me morning by morning,
He awakens My ear
To hear as the learned.

5 The Lord GOD has opened My ear;
And I was not rebellious,
Nor did I turn away.

6 I gave My back to those who struck
    Me,
And My cheeks to those who plucked out
  the beard;
I did not hide My face from shame and
  spitting.

7 "For the Lord GOD will help Me;
Therefore I will not be disgraced;
Therefore I have set My face like a flint,
And I know that I will not be ashamed.

8 *He is* near who justifies Me;
Who will contend with Me?
Let us stand together.
Who *is* My adversary?
Let him come near Me.

9 Surely the Lord GOD will help Me;
Who *is* he *who* will condemn Me?
Indeed they will all grow old like a garment;
The moth will eat them up.

10*"Who among you fears the LORD?
Who obeys the voice of His Servant?
Who walks in darkness
And has no light?
Let him trust in the name of the LORD
And rely upon his God.

11 Look, all you who kindle a fire,
Who encircle *yourselves* with sparks:
Walk in the light of your fire and in the
  sparks you have kindled—

This you shall have from My hand:
You shall lie down in torment.

51 "Listen* to Me, you who follow after
righteousness,
You who seek the LORD:
Look to the rock *from which* you were
hewn,
And to the hole of the pit *from which* you
were dug.
2 Look to Abraham your father,
And to Sarah *who* bore you;
For I called him alone,
And blessed him and increased him."

3 For the LORD will comfort Zion,
He will comfort all her waste places;
He will make her wilderness like Eden,
And her desert like the garden of the LORD;
Joy and gladness will be found in it,
Thanksgiving and the voice of melody.

4 "Listen to Me, My people;
And give ear to Me, O My nation:
For law will proceed from Me,
And I will make My justice rest
As a light of the peoples.
5 My righteousness *is* near,
My salvation has gone forth,
And My arms will judge the peoples;
The coastlands will wait upon Me,
And on My arm they will trust.
6 *Lift up your eyes to the heavens,
And look on the earth beneath.
For the heavens will vanish away like
smoke,
The earth will grow old like a garment,
And those who dwell in it will die in like
manner;
But My salvation will be forever,
And My righteousness will not be abolished.

7 "Listen to Me, you who know righteousness,
You people in whose heart *is* My law:
Do not fear the reproach of men,
Nor be afraid of their insults.
8 For the moth will eat them up like a
garment,
And the worm will eat them like wool;
But My righteousness will be forever,
And My salvation from generation to
generation."

9 Awake, awake, put on strength,
O arm of the LORD!
Awake as in the ancient days,
In the generations of old.
Are You not *the arm* that cut Rahab apart,
And wounded the serpent?

10 *Are* You not *the One* who dried up the sea,
The waters of the great deep;
That made the depths of the sea a road
For the redeemed to cross over?
11 *So the ransomed of the LORD shall return,
And come to Zion with singing,
With everlasting joy on their heads.
They shall obtain joy and gladness;
Sorrow and sighing shall flee away.

12 "I, *even* I, *am* He who comforts you.
Who *are* you that you should be afraid

CHAPTER 51

51:1, 2 As the nation prepared to leave
Babylon and return home, they needed to
strengthen their faith in Jehovah God. God
told them to do the following:
   Look back! God urged His people to
recall their spiritual roots: the call of
Abraham (vv. 1–2) and the exodus from
Egypt (vv. 9–10, 15). They are a covenant
people, and God will not break His promises.
They are a redeemed people, and God will
care for them. Take time to remember your
spiritual roots; you will be encouraged in
your faith.

51:6 *Look up!* He said, "Lift up your eyes"
(v. 6; Gen. 15:1–6). Again, Isaiah tells the
people to consider God's creation and
remember what a great God He is and how
lasting is His Word (40:6–8, 12–14). When
you are prone to fret, remember that the
Creator is your Father, and you have nothing
to fear.

51:11 *Look ahead!* The wilderness will
become a Garden of Eden (v. 3), and the
people will "exodus" from Babylon and
return joyfully to Zion (v. 11). The ultimate
fulfillment will be when the kingdom is
established and all of Israel's enemies will
be defeated.

Of a man *who* will die,
And of the son of a man *who* will be made
   like grass?
13 And you forget the L ORD your Maker,
Who stretched out the heavens
And laid the foundations of the earth;
You have feared continually every day
Because of the fury of the oppressor,
When *he has* prepared to destroy.
And where *is* the fury of the oppressor?
14 The captive exile hastens, that he may be
   loosed,
That he should not die in the pit,
And that his bread should not fail.
15 But I *am* the L ORD your God,
Who divided the sea whose waves roared—
The L ORD of hosts *is* His name.
16 And I have put My words in your mouth;
I have covered you with the shadow of My
   hand,
That I may plant the heavens,
Lay the foundations of the earth,
And say to Zion, 'You *are* My people.' "

17 Awake, awake!
Stand up, O Jerusalem,
You who have drunk at the hand of the L ORD
The cup of His fury;
You have drunk the dregs of the cup of
   trembling,
And drained *it* out.
18 *There is* no one to guide her
Among all the sons she has brought forth;
Nor *is there any* who takes her by the hand
Among all the sons she has brought up.
19 These two *things* have come to you;
Who will be sorry for you?—
Desolation and destruction, famine and
   sword—
By whom will I comfort you?
20 Your sons have fainted,
They lie at the head of all the streets,
Like an antelope in a net;
They are full of the fury of the L ORD,
The rebuke of your God.

21 Therefore please hear this, you afflicted,
And drunk but not with wine.
22 Thus says your Lord,
The L ORD and your God,
Who pleads the cause of His people:
"See, I have taken out of your hand
The cup of trembling,
The dregs of the cup of My fury;
You shall no longer drink it.
23 But I will put it into the hand of those who
   afflict you,
Who have said to you,[n]
'Lie down, that we may walk over you.'
And you have laid your body like the
   ground,
And as the street, for those who walk over."

CHAPTER 52

52:1 It is a new day and time for God's people to *wake up* (51:9, 17; Rom. 13:11–14). The night of trial is over, and God will do a new thing for them. This is a new day for you, so wake up to God's blessing (Lam. 3:22–23).

It is also time to *dress up,* for the feast is about to begin. God has forgiven His people and brought them home, and it is time to rejoice (v. 9; Luke 15:22–24).

52 Awake,* awake!
Put on your strength, O Zion;
Put on your beautiful garments,
O Jerusalem, the holy city!
For the uncircumcised and the unclean
Shall no longer come to you.

51:23 [n]Literally *your soul*

2   Shake yourself from the dust, arise;
     Sit down, O Jerusalem!
     Loose yourself from the bonds of your neck,
     O captive daughter of Zion!

3For thus says the LORD:

   "You have sold yourselves for nothing,
   And you shall be redeemed without
      money."

4For thus says the Lord GOD:

   "My people went down at first
   Into Egypt to dwell there;
   Then the Assyrian oppressed them without
      cause.
5   Now therefore, what have I here," says the
        LORD,
   "That My people are taken away for nothing?
   Those who rule over them
   Make them wail,"o says the LORD,
   "And My name *is* blasphemed continually
      every day.
6   Therefore My people shall know My name;
     Therefore *they shall know* in that day
     That I *am* He who speaks:
     'Behold, *it is* I.' "

7   *How beautiful upon the mountains
     Are the feet of him who brings good news,
     Who proclaims peace,
     Who brings glad tidings of good *things,*
     Who proclaims salvation,
     Who says to Zion,
   "Your God reigns!"
8   Your watchmen shall lift up *their* voices,
     With their voices they shall sing together;
     For they shall see eye to eye
     When the LORD brings back Zion.
9   Break forth into joy, sing together,
     You waste places of Jerusalem!
     For the LORD has comforted His people,
     He has redeemed Jerusalem.
10   The LORD has made bare His holy arm
     In the eyes of all the nations;
     And all the ends of the earth shall see
     The salvation of our God.

11   *Depart! Depart! Go out from there,
     Touch no unclean *thing;*
     Go out from the midst of her,
     Be clean,
     You who bear the vessels of the LORD.
12   For you shall not go out with haste,
     Nor go by flight;
     For the LORD will go before you,
     And the God of Israel *will be* your rear
        guard.

13   Behold, My Servant shall deal prudently;
     He shall be exalted and extolled and be very
        high.
14   Just as many were astonished at you,
     So His visage was marred more than any
        man,
     And His form more than the sons of men;

52:7–10 It is time to *speak up* and tell the world what God has done for His people. Paul applies this to the sharing of the gospel with the lost (Rom. 10:15).

52:11, 12 It is time to *clean up.* As the exiles left Babylon, they were not to defile themselves but be clean and carry the holy vessels back to Zion. There is always a new "Babylon" for God's people to flee if they would keep themselves clean (Rev. 18:1–8). As you obey, God goes before you and behind you, so you need not be afraid of the enemy.

52:5 °Dead Sea Scrolls read *Mock;* Septuagint reads *Marvel and wail;* Targum reads *Boast themselves;* Vulgate reads *Treat them unjustly.*

¹⁵ So shall He sprinkle^p many nations.
Kings shall shut their mouths at Him;
For what had not been told them they shall
see,
And what they had not heard they shall
consider.

CHAPTER 53

53:1ff This chapter is about Jesus Christ,
God's perfect sacrifice for the sins of the
world (Acts 8:26–40). It actually begins in
52:13 where the prophet tells us that the
Servant suffered for doing God's will and yet
was highly exalted by the Lord. Humiliation
and exaltation, suffering and glory, are key
themes in this prophecy.

Consider the humiliation of His birth and
life (vv. 1–3) as well as the humiliation of
His trial and His sufferings and death
(vv. 4–9). Consider the glory of the salvation
He purchased for you on the cross (vv. 10–
12). The Father was pleased, not that His
Son suffered, but that His sacrifice
accomplished eternal salvation. God's
justice was satisfied, and believing sinners
can be justified (v. 11; Rom. 3:21–31).

Consider the pictures of the Savior: a
beaten servant (52:13–14), a root (v. 2), an
innocent lamb (v. 7), an offering for sin
(v. 10), a woman in travail giving birth to
spiritual "seed" (vv. 10–11), and a victorious
general (v. 12). Hallelujah, what a Savior!
Yet people still do not believe in Him
(v. 1). Instead, they despise and reject Him
(v. 2) and laugh at the message of the Cross
(1 Cor. 1:18–25). But heaven praises the
Lamb of God (Rev. 5), and His people on
earth glory in His cross (Gal. 6:14). Are you
among them?

53 ¹ Who* has believed our report?
And to whom has the arm of the LORD been
revealed?
² For He shall grow up before Him as a tender
plant,
And as a root out of dry ground.
He has no form or comeliness;
And when we see Him,
There is no beauty that we should desire
Him.
³ He is despised and rejected by men,
A Man of sorrows and acquainted with
grief.
And we hid, as it were, *our* faces from Him;
He was despised, and we did not esteem
Him.

⁴ Surely He has borne our griefs
And carried our sorrows;
Yet we esteemed Him stricken,
Smitten by God, and afflicted.
⁵ But He *was* wounded for our transgressions,
He was bruised for our iniquities;
The chastisement for our peace *was* upon
Him,
And by His stripes we are healed.
⁶ All we like sheep have gone astray;
We have turned, every one, to his own way;
And the LORD has laid on Him the iniquity
of us all.

⁷ He was oppressed and He was afflicted,
Yet He opened not His mouth;
He was led as a lamb to the slaughter,
And as a sheep before its shearers is silent,
So He opened not His mouth.
⁸ He was taken from prison and from
judgment,
And who will declare His generation?
For He was cut off from the land of the
living;
For the transgressions of My people He was
stricken.
⁹ And they^q made His grave with the
wicked—
But with the rich at His death,
Because He had done no violence,
Nor *was any* deceit in His mouth.

¹⁰ Yet it pleased the LORD to bruise Him;
He has put *Him* to grief.
When You make His soul an offering for
sin,

52:15 ^pOr *startle*   53:9 ^qLiterally *he* or *He*

He Paid the Price—Isaiah 53 is cited or alluded to frequently in the New Testament. (Along with
the passages in the Gospels that describe Christ's sufferings, death, and burial, see John 1:29;
12:38; Acts 8:26–40; Rom. 10:16; Heb. 9:28; 1 Pet. 2:21–25; Rev. 5.) The chapter teaches
substitutionary atonement, that the innocent Son of God died in the place of guilty sinners and paid
the price for sin. We do not understand all that was involved in that "holy transaction" on the cross,
but we do know that it accomplished salvation for a lost world.

He shall see *His* seed, He shall prolong *His* days,
And the pleasure of the LORD shall prosper in His hand.

11 He shall see the labor of His soul,*r and be satisfied.
By His knowledge My righteous Servant shall justify many,
For He shall bear their iniquities.

12 Therefore I will divide Him a portion with the great,
And He shall divide the spoil with the strong,
Because He poured out His soul unto death,
And He was numbered with the transgressors,
And He bore the sin of many,
And made intercession for the transgressors.

54 "Sing,* O barren,
You *who* have not borne!
Break forth into singing, and cry aloud,
You *who* have not labored with child!
For more *are* the children of the desolate
Than the children of the married woman,"
says the LORD.

2 "Enlarge the place of your tent,
And let them stretch out the curtains of your dwellings;
Do not spare;
Lengthen your cords,
And strengthen your stakes.

3 For you shall expand to the right and to the left,
And your descendants will inherit the nations,
And make the desolate cities inhabited.

4 "Do not fear, for you will not be ashamed;
Neither be disgraced, for you will not be put to shame;
For you will forget the shame of your youth,
And will not remember the reproach of your widowhood anymore.

5 For your Maker *is* your husband,
The LORD of hosts *is* His name;
And your Redeemer *is* the Holy One of Israel;
He is called the God of the whole earth.

6 For the LORD has called you
Like a woman forsaken and grieved in spirit,
Like a youthful wife when you were refused,"
Says your God.

7 "For a mere moment I have forsaken you,
But with great mercies I will gather you.

8 With a little wrath I hid My face from you for a moment;
But with everlasting kindness I will have mercy on you,"
Says the LORD, your Redeemer.

9 "For this *is* like the waters of Noah to Me;
For as I have sworn

CHAPTER 54

54:1ff The future regathering and restoring of Israel is a picture of the wonderful changes God makes when trials and sufferings end.

The barren woman gives birth to so many children that the family tent must be enlarged (vv. 1–3). The widow loses her shame and is wed once again, this time to Jehovah (vv. 4–6). The storm is over and God gives peace (vv. 7–15), and the covenant sign of the rainbow is in the sky (v. 10).

Times of chastening or suffering may seem spiritually barren to you, but God uses them to give birth to blessings. Times of sorrow and reproach are painful, but they can lead to greater joys. Storms are frightening, but they polish God's jewels (vv. 11–12) and bring Him glory. It is painful to go through the furnace (vv. 16–17), but God uses the experience to make you a stronger and better tool.

The best is yet to come!

❝❝*We say, 'sorrow, disaster, calamity'; God says, 'chastening,' and it sounds sweet to Him though it is a discord to our ears. Don't faint when you are rebuked, and don't despise the chastenings of the Lord. 'In your patience possess ye your souls.'* **❞❞**

—Oswald Chambers

53:11 *r*Following Masoretic Text, Targum, and Vulgate; Dead Sea Scrolls and Septuagint read *From the labor of His soul He shall see light.*

That the waters of Noah would no longer
cover the earth,
So have I sworn
That I would not be angry with you, nor
rebuke you.
10 For the mountains shall depart
And the hills be removed,
But My kindness shall not depart from
you,
Nor shall My covenant of peace be
removed,"
Says the LORD, who has mercy on you.

11 "O you afflicted one,
Tossed with tempest, *and* not comforted,
Behold, I will lay your stones with colorful
gems,
And lay your foundations with sapphires.
12 I will make your pinnacles of rubies,
Your gates of crystal,
And all your walls of precious stones.
13 All your children *shall be* taught by the
LORD,
And great *shall be* the peace of your
children.
14 In righteousness you shall be established;
You shall be far from oppression, for you
shall not fear;
And from terror, for it shall not come near
you.
15 Indeed they shall surely assemble, *but* not
because of Me.
Whoever assembles against you shall fall
for your sake.

16 "Behold, I have created the blacksmith
Who blows the coals in the fire,
Who brings forth an instrument for his
work;
And I have created the spoiler to destroy.
17 No weapon formed against you shall
prosper,
And every tongue *which* rises against you
in judgment
You shall condemn.
This *is* the heritage of the servants of the
LORD,
And their righteousness *is* from Me,"
Says the LORD.

CHAPTER 55

55:1, 2 Again, the prophet depicts the changes God makes in the lives of those who turn from their sins and trust the Savior. ***From substitutes to reality.*** The lost sinner is bankrupt because he spends all he has for what cannot satisfy. When you hear God's Word and obey, you start to enjoy the water of life and the bread of life, found in Jesus Christ (John 4; 6).

55:3–5 ***From death to life.*** Compare verse 3 with John 5:24. Jesus is the fulfillment of the covenant God made with David (2 Sam. 7; Acts 13:34). When you trust Him, you share in His life and His victories.

55 "Ho!* Everyone who thirsts,
Come to the waters;
And you who have no money,
Come, buy and eat.
Yes, come, buy wine and milk
Without money and without price.
2 Why do you spend money for *what is* not
bread,
And your wages for *what* does not satisfy?
Listen carefully to Me, and eat *what is* good,
And let your soul delight itself in
abundance.
3 *Incline your ear, and come to Me.
Hear, and your soul shall live;
And I will make an everlasting covenant
with you—
The sure mercies of David.
4 Indeed I have given him *as* a witness to the
people,
A leader and commander for the people.
5 Surely you shall call a nation you do not
know,

And nations *who* do not know you shall run
to you,
Because of the LORD your God,
And the Holy One of Israel;
For He has glorified you."

6 *Seek the LORD while He may be found,
Call upon Him while He is near.
7 Let the wicked forsake his way,
And the unrighteous man his thoughts;
Let him return to the LORD,
And He will have mercy on him;
And to our God,
For He will abundantly pardon.

55:6, 7 *From guilt to pardon.* When the sinner repents and turns to Christ by faith, God shows mercy and grants pardon. But do not delay (Prov. 1:20–33)!

8 *"For My thoughts *are* not your thoughts,
Nor *are* your ways My ways," says the
LORD.
9 "For *as* the heavens are higher than the
earth,
So are My ways higher than your ways,
And My thoughts than your thoughts.

55:8–11 *From fear to certainty.* God's ways are beyond man's comprehension, but you can be sure He is accomplishing His purposes in His times. Like the rain and snow that seem to be wasted, God's Word accomplishes His will on the earth.

10 "For as the rain comes down, and the snow
from heaven,
And do not return there,
But water the earth,
And make it bring forth and bud,
That it may give seed to the sower
And bread to the eater,
11 So shall My word be that goes forth from
My mouth;
It shall not return to Me void,
But it shall accomplish what I please,
And it shall prosper *in the thing* for which
I sent it.

12 *"For you shall go out with joy,
And be led out with peace;
The mountains and the hills
Shall break forth into singing before you,
And all the trees of the field shall clap *their*
hands.
13 Instead of the thorn shall come up the
cypress tree,
And instead of the brier shall come up the
myrtle tree;
And it shall be to the LORD for a name,
For an everlasting sign *that* shall not be cut
off."

55:12, 13 *From wilderness to paradise.* Sin turns the garden into a desert (Isa. 5:3–6; 32:12–15), but grace transforms the desert into a joyful and fruitful garden. Abundant satisfaction, pardon, and joy are available to all who accept God's gracious invitation.

CHAPTER 56

56:1ff It was God's purpose that through Israel the Gentiles might come to know the true God and His salvation (Gen. 12:1–3). But instead, Israel adopted the false gods of the Gentiles! Their leaders were like blind watchmen, greedy watchdogs that could not bark, and shepherds concerned only for themselves (vv. 9–12)! No wonder the nation went into captivity! And what a warning to spiritual leaders today!

56

Thus* says the LORD:

"Keep justice, and do righteousness,
For My salvation *is* about to come,
And My righteousness to be revealed.
2 Blessed *is* the man *who* does this,
And the son of man *who* lays hold on it;
Who keeps from defiling the Sabbath,
And keeps his hand from doing any evil."

3 Do not let the son of the foreigner
Who has joined himself to the LORD
Speak, saying,
"The LORD has utterly separated me from His
people";
Nor let the eunuch say,
"Here I am, a dry tree."
4 For thus says the LORD:
"To the eunuchs who keep My Sabbaths,
And choose what pleases Me,
And hold fast My covenant,

But God did not abandon the Gentiles. The "outcast" foreigner is accepted (vv. 6–8), and the eunuch is welcomed (vv. 3–5; Deut. 23:1). In Jesus Christ, the wall between Jews and Gentiles is broken down; and any sinner can come to the Savior and find forgiveness and acceptance (Eph. 2).

Jesus quoted from verse 7 when He cleansed the temple in Jerusalem (Matt. 21:13). How tragic that the religious leaders had turned a place of worship and witness into a den of thieves. Would any Gentile want to know the God of Israel after seeing the Court of the Gentiles made into a marketplace? But what do outsiders see when they attend our church services today (1 Cor. 14:23–25)?

5 Even to them I will give in My house
And within My walls a place and a name
Better than that of sons and daughters;
I will give them[s] an everlasting name
That shall not be cut off.

6 "Also the sons of the foreigner
Who join themselves to the LORD, to serve
  Him,
And to love the name of the LORD, to be His
  servants—
Everyone who keeps from defiling the
  Sabbath,
And holds fast My covenant—
7 Even them I will bring to My holy mountain,
And make them joyful in My house of
  prayer.
Their burnt offerings and their sacrifices
Will be accepted on My altar;
For My house shall be called a house of
  prayer for all nations."
8 The Lord GOD, who gathers the outcasts of
  Israel, says,
"Yet I will gather to him
Others besides those who are gathered to
  him."

9 All you beasts of the field, come to devour,
All you beasts in the forest.
10 His watchmen *are* blind,
They are all ignorant;
They *are* all dumb dogs,
They cannot bark;
Sleeping, lying down, loving to slumber.
11 Yes, *they are* greedy dogs
Which never have enough.
And they *are* shepherds
Who cannot understand;
They all look to their own way,
Every one for his own gain,
From his *own* territory.
12 "Come," *one says,* "I will bring wine,
And we will fill ourselves with intoxicating
  drink;
Tomorrow will be as today,
And much more abundant."

CHAPTER 57

57:1, 2 Deterioration. When God wants to judge His people, He sometimes takes the godly leaders away; and they are spared the pain of seeing their nation deteriorate and then go into judgment (vv. 1–2; 3:1–5). Do you appreciate the men and women God has given to provide spiritual leadership, and do you encourage them?

57:3–13 Denunciation. This description of the godless society in Judah seems quite contemporary. God denounced them for lying, worshiping idols, indulging in sexual sins, sacrificing their children, and mocking the godly. These people had no fear of God because He did not immediately send judgment, but their day was coming.

57 The* righteous perishes,
And no man takes *it* to heart;
Merciful men *are* taken away,
While no one considers
That the righteous is taken away from evil.
2 He shall enter into peace;
They shall rest in their beds,
Each one walking *in* his uprightness.

3 *"But come here,
You sons of the sorceress,
You offspring of the adulterer and the
  harlot!
4 Whom do you ridicule?
Against whom do you make a wide mouth
And stick out the tongue?
Are you not children of transgression,
Offspring of falsehood,
5 Inflaming yourselves with gods under every
  green tree,
Slaying the children in the valleys,
Under the clefts of the rocks?

56:5 [s]Literally *him*

6   Among the smooth *stones* of the stream
     Is your portion;
     They, they, *are* your lot!
     Even to them you have poured a drink
       offering,
     You have offered a grain offering.
     Should I receive comfort in these?

7   "On a lofty and high mountain
     You have set your bed;
     Even there you went up
     To offer sacrifice.
8   Also behind the doors and their posts
     You have set up your remembrance;
     For you have uncovered yourself *to those
       other* than Me,
     And have gone up to them;
     You have enlarged your bed
     And made *a covenant* with them;
     You have loved their bed,
     Where you saw *their* nudity.*t*
9   You went to the king with ointment,
     And increased your perfumes;
     You sent your messengers far off,
     And *even* descended to Sheol.
10   You are wearied in the length of your way;
     Yet you did not say, 'There is no hope.'
     You have found the life of your hand;
     Therefore you were not grieved.

11   "And of whom have you been afraid, or
      feared,
     That you have lied
     And not remembered Me,
     Nor taken *it* to your heart?
     Is it not because I have held My peace from
      of old
     That you do not fear Me?
12   I will declare your righteousness
     And your works,
     For they will not profit you.
13   When you cry out,
     Let your collection *of idols* deliver you.
     But the wind will carry them all away,
     A breath will take *them*.
     But he who puts his trust in Me shall possess
      the land,
     And shall inherit My holy mountain."

14   *And one shall say,
     "Heap it up! Heap it up!
     Prepare the way,
     Take the stumbling block out of the way of
      My people."

15   For thus says the High and Lofty One
     Who inhabits eternity, whose name *is* Holy:
     "I dwell in the high and holy *place,*
     With him *who* has a contrite and humble
      spirit,
     To revive the spirit of the humble,
     And to revive the heart of the contrite ones.
16   For I will not contend forever,
     Nor will I always be angry;
     For the spirit would fail before Me,
     And the souls *which* I have made.
17   For the iniquity of his covetousness
     I was angry and struck him;

57:14–21 Dedication. Even in a godless society, here and there are dedicated people who have fellowship with God. God longs to dwell with His people (John 14:21–24), and He will if they are humble and contrite (Ps. 51:17; Isa. 66:2). Does God "feel at home" in your heart (Eph. 3:14–21)?

57:8 *t* Literally *hand,* a euphemism

I hid and was angry,
And he went on backsliding in the way of
his heart.
18 I have seen his ways, and will heal him;
I will also lead him,
And restore comforts to him
And to his mourners.

19 "I create the fruit of the lips:
Peace, peace to *him who is* far off and to
him who is near,"
Says the LORD,
"And I will heal him."
20 But the wicked *are* like the troubled sea,
When it cannot rest,
Whose waters cast up mire and dirt.

21 "*There is* no peace,"
Says my God, "for the wicked."

CHAPTER 58

58:1--3 When you strive to be a spiritual person, you fight the constant battle of "ritual versus reality." It is much easier to go through the external activities of religion than it is to love God from your heart and let that love touch the lives of others. It is a matter not of either/or but of both/and: worshiping God from the heart and serving others in love. James stated, "Faith without works is dead" (2:20).

The orthodox faith was popular in Judah at that time, and people enjoyed learning the Word and even participating in fasts (vv. 2–3). But when the services were over, the worshipers went back to exploiting people and pleasing themselves.

What a difference it makes when we repent and return to the Lord (vv. 8–12)! We have light instead of darkness, healing instead of disease, righteousness instead of defilement, glory instead of disgrace; and life becomes a watered garden, not a dismal swamp.

58 "Cry* aloud, spare not;
Lift up your voice like a trumpet;
Tell My people their transgression,
And the house of Jacob their sins.
2 Yet they seek Me daily,
And delight to know My ways,
As a nation that did righteousness,
And did not forsake the ordinance of their
God.
They ask of Me the ordinances of justice;
They take delight in approaching God.
3 'Why have we fasted,' *they say,* 'and You
have not seen?
Why have we afflicted our souls, and You
take no notice?'

"In fact, in the day of your fast you find
pleasure,
And exploit all your laborers.
4 Indeed you fast for strife and debate,
And to strike with the fist of wickedness.
You will not fast as *you do* this day,
To make your voice heard on high.
5 Is it a fast that I have chosen,
A day for a man to afflict his soul?
Is it to bow down his head like a bulrush,
And to spread out sackcloth and ashes?
Would you call this a fast,
And an acceptable day to the LORD?

6 "*Is* this not the fast that I have chosen:
To loose the bonds of wickedness,
To undo the heavy burdens,
To let the oppressed go free,
And that you break every yoke?
7 *Is it* not to share your bread with the
hungry,
And that you bring to your house the poor
who are cast out;
When you see the naked, that you cover
him,
And not hide yourself from your own flesh?
8 Then your light shall break forth like the
morning,
Your healing shall spring forth speedily,
And your righteousness shall go before
you;
The glory of the LORD shall be your rear
guard.
9 Then you shall call, and the LORD will
answer;
You shall cry, and He will say, 'Here I *am.*'

"If you take away the yoke from your midst,
The pointing of the finger, and speaking
wickedness,
10 *If* you extend your soul to the hungry
And satisfy the afflicted soul,
Then your light shall dawn in the darkness,
And your darkness shall *be* as the noonday.
11 The LORD will guide you continually,
And satisfy your soul in drought,
And strengthen your bones;
You shall be like a watered garden,
And like a spring of water, whose waters
do not fail.
12 Those from among you
Shall build the old waste places;
You shall raise up the foundations of many
generations;
And you shall be called the Repairer of the
Breach,
The Restorer of Streets to Dwell In.

13 "If you turn away your foot from the
Sabbath,
From doing your pleasure on My holy day,
And call the Sabbath a delight,
The holy *day* of the LORD honorable,
And shall honor Him, not doing your own
ways,
Nor finding your own pleasure,
Nor speaking *your own* words,
14 Then you shall delight yourself in the LORD;
And I will cause you to ride on the high hills
of the earth,
And feed you with the heritage of Jacob
your father.
The mouth of the LORD has spoken."

59 Behold,* the LORD's hand is not shortened,
That it cannot save;
Nor His ear heavy,
That it cannot hear.
2 But your iniquities have separated you from
your God;
And your sins have hidden *His* face from
you,
So that He will not hear.
3 For your hands are defiled with blood,
And your fingers with iniquity;
Your lips have spoken lies,
Your tongue has muttered perversity.

4 *No one calls for justice,
Nor does *any* plead for truth.
They trust in empty words and speak lies;
They conceive evil and bring forth iniquity.
5 They hatch vipers' eggs and weave the
spider's web;
He who eats of their eggs dies,
And *from* that which is crushed a viper
breaks out.

6 *Their webs will not become garments,
Nor will they cover themselves with their
works;
Their works *are* works of iniquity,
And the act of violence *is* in their hands.
7 Their feet run to evil,
And they make haste to shed innocent
blood;
Their thoughts *are* thoughts of iniquity;
Wasting and destruction *are* in their paths.
8 The way of peace they have not known,

❝God will bless Elijah and send rain on Israel, but Elijah must pray for it. If the chosen nation is to prosper, Samuel must plead for it. If the Jews are to be delivered, Daniel must intercede. God will bless Paul, and the nations shall be converted, but Paul must pray. . . . Let me have your prayers, and I can do anything! Let me be without my people's prayers, and I can do nothing!**❞**
—Charles Haddon Spurgeon

CHAPTER 59
59:1–3 The images in this chapter teach important spiritual truths.
Hands. God's hand is unable to work when our hands are defiled with sin. Our prayers accomplish nothing (Ps. 66:18), and His power is absent from our lives and ministries.

59:4, 5 *Poison.* A lie is not just a sound in the air or a sentence on paper. It has a life of its own and gives birth to all kinds of trouble. Try to live on lies, and they will poison you. When lies finally "hatch," they will bite you and may kill you (James 1:13–16).

59:6–8 *Spiders' webs.* Trying to hide behind lies and hypocritical religious works is like clothing yourself with a spider's web. The sins described here were committed by *religious* people. No wonder God withheld His blessings! Is He doing that today?

59:9–15 Traffic jam. It is dark. The pedestrians on the streets are blind and are acting like beasts. Truth has fallen in the street and progress has ceased. The "traffic officers" (justice and righteousness) are standing far off because the people will not let them exercise authority.

59:16–21 Manhunt. God searched for one person to intercede for His people, but He found none, so He did the work Himself. Are you an intercessor? Are you concerned about the "traffic jam" that hinders God's work and robs God of glory?

And *there is* no justice in their ways;
They have made themselves crooked paths;
Whoever takes that way shall not know
    peace.
9 *Therefore justice is far from us,
    Nor does righteousness overtake us;
    We look for light, but there is darkness!
    For brightness, *but* we walk in blackness!
10 We grope for the wall like the blind,
    And we grope as if *we had* no eyes;
    We stumble at noonday as at twilight;
    We are as dead *men* in desolate places.
11 We all growl like bears,
    And moan sadly like doves;
    We look for justice, but *there is* none;
    For salvation, *but* it is far from us.
12 For our transgressions are multiplied before
        You,
    And our sins testify against us;
    For our transgressions *are* with us,
    And *as for* our iniquities, we know them:
13 In transgressing and lying against the LORD,
    And departing from our God,
    Speaking oppression and revolt,
    Conceiving and uttering from the heart
        words of falsehood.
14 Justice is turned back,
    And righteousness stands afar off;
    For truth is fallen in the street,
    And equity cannot enter.
15 So truth fails,
    And he *who* departs from evil makes
        himself a prey.

Then the LORD saw *it*, and it displeased Him
    That *there was* no justice.
16 *He saw that *there was* no man,
    And wondered that *there was* no
        intercessor;
    Therefore His own arm brought salvation
        for Him;
    And His own righteousness, it sustained
        Him.
17 For He put on righteousness as a
        breastplate,
    And a helmet of salvation on His head;
    He put on the garments of vengeance for
        clothing,
    And was clad with zeal as a cloak.
18 According to *their* deeds, accordingly He
        will repay,
    Fury to His adversaries,
    Recompense to His enemies;
    The coastlands He will fully repay.
19 So shall they fear
    The name of the LORD from the west,
    And His glory from the rising of the sun;
    When the enemy comes in like a flood,
    The Spirit of the LORD will lift up a standard
        against him.

20 "The Redeemer will come to Zion,
    And to those who turn from transgression
        in Jacob,"
    Says the LORD.

21"As for Me," says the LORD, "this *is* My covenant with them: My Spirit who *is* upon you, and My words which I have put in your mouth, shall not depart from your mouth, nor from the mouth of your descendants, nor from the mouth of your descendants' descendants," says the LORD, "from this time and forevermore."

60

Arise,* shine;
For your light has come!
And the glory of the LORD is risen upon you.
2   For behold, the darkness shall cover the
        earth,
    And deep darkness the people;
    But the LORD will arise over you,
    And His glory will be seen upon you.
3   The Gentiles shall come to your light,
    And kings to the brightness of your rising.

4 *"Lift up your eyes all around, and see:
    They all gather together, they come to you;
    Your sons shall come from afar,
    And your daughters shall be nursed at your
        side.
5   Then you shall see and become radiant,
    And your heart shall swell with joy;
    Because the abundance of the sea shall be
        turned to you,
    The wealth of the Gentiles shall come to
        you.
6   The multitude of camels shall cover your
        land,
    The dromedaries of Midian and Ephah;
    All those from Sheba shall come;
    They shall bring gold and incense,
    And they shall proclaim the praises of the
        LORD.
7   All the flocks of Kedar shall be gathered
        together to you,
    The rams of Nebaioth shall minister to you;
    They shall ascend with acceptance on My
        altar,
    And I will glorify the house of My glory.

8   "Who are these who fly like a cloud,
    And like doves to their roosts?
9   Surely the coastlands shall wait for Me;
    And the ships of Tarshish will come first,
    To bring your sons from afar,
    Their silver and their gold with them,
    To the name of the LORD your God,
    And to the Holy One of Israel,
    Because He has glorified you.

10 *"The sons of foreigners shall build up your
        walls,
    And their kings shall minister to you;
    For in My wrath I struck you,
    But in My favor I have had mercy on you.
11 Therefore your gates shall be open
        continually;
    They shall not be shut day or night,
    That men may bring to you the wealth of
        the Gentiles,
    And their kings in procession.
12 For the nation and kingdom which will not
        serve you shall perish,
    And those nations shall be utterly ruined.

13 "The glory of Lebanon shall come to you,
    The cypress, the pine, and the box tree
        together,
    To beautify the place of My sanctuary;
    And I will make the place of My feet
        glorious.
14 Also the sons of those who afflicted you
    Shall come bowing to you,

CHAPTER 60

60:1–3, 19–22 Light (Rev. 21—22). As Isaiah looked ahead to the redeemed people and the restored city of Zion, the thing that impressed him most was *glory* (vv. 1, 2, 7, 9, 13, 19, 21). It would be the dawning of a new day for the nation. Ponder John 17:22–24; Romans 8:18; and 1 Peter 5:10.

60:4–9 Unity. The nations will stream to the light of Israel, and Jews and Gentiles will unite in worshiping and serving God. Our world is plagued by division and conflict, but one day God will give peace.

60:10–18 Joy. God's favor and mercy will enrich His people as He surrounds them with beauty and joy. Zion's citizens will know the Lord and give Him praise.

And all those who despised you shall fall
    prostrate at the soles of your feet;
And they shall call you The City of the LORD,
Zion of the Holy One of Israel.

15 "Whereas you have been forsaken and hated,
So that no one went through *you,*
I will make you an eternal excellence,
A joy of many generations.
16 You shall drink the milk of the Gentiles,
And milk the breast of kings;
You shall know that I, the LORD, *am* your
    Savior
And your Redeemer, the Mighty One of
    Jacob.

17 "Instead of bronze I will bring gold,
Instead of iron I will bring silver,
Instead of wood, bronze,
And instead of stones, iron.
I will also make your officers peace,
And your magistrates righteousness.
18 Violence shall no longer be heard in your
    land,
Neither wasting nor destruction within your
    borders;
But you shall call your walls Salvation,
And your gates Praise.

19 "The sun shall no longer be your light by day,
Nor for brightness shall the moon give light
    to you;
But the LORD will be to you an everlasting
    light,
And your God your glory.
20 Your sun shall no longer go down,
Nor shall your moon withdraw itself;
For the LORD will be your everlasting light,
And the days of your mourning shall be
    ended.
21 Also your people *shall* all *be* righteous;
They shall inherit the land forever,
The branch of My planting,
The work of My hands,
That I may be glorified.
22 A little one shall become a thousand,
And a small one a strong nation.
I, the LORD, will hasten it in its time."

CHAPTER 61

61:1–3 *Release.* Jesus took these verses as His text when He preached in Nazareth (Luke 4:16ff.) and announced that He was ushering in the Year of Jubilee (Lev. 25). It is a time of releasing the slaves, canceling all debts, and making a new beginning. Today, those who trust Christ begin to enjoy their Jubilee; those who reject Him face judgment.

61:4–6 *Renewal.* The land of Judah was in ruins after the Babylonian captivity, but God would help the people repair and rebuild. The whole nation would become priests of the Lord (1 Pet. 2:5, 9) and servants of God.

61 "The* Spirit of the Lord God *is* upon Me,
Because the LORD has anointed Me
To preach good tidings to the poor;
He has sent Me to heal the brokenhearted,
To proclaim liberty to the captives,
And the opening of the prison to *those who
    are* bound;
2 To proclaim the acceptable year of the LORD,
And the day of vengeance of our God;
To comfort all who mourn,
3 To console those who mourn in Zion,
To give them beauty for ashes,
The oil of joy for mourning,
The garment of praise for the spirit of
    heaviness;
That they may be called trees of
    righteousness,
The planting of the LORD, that He may be
    glorified."

4 *And they shall rebuild the old ruins,
They shall raise up the former desolations,
And they shall repair the ruined cities,
The desolations of many generations.

5 Strangers shall stand and feed your flocks,
  And the sons of the foreigner
  Shall be your plowmen and your
      vinedressers.
6 But you shall be named the priests of the
      Lord,
  They shall call you the servants of our God.
  You shall eat the riches of the Gentiles,
  And in their glory you shall boast.
7 *Instead of your shame *you shall have* double
      honor,
  And *instead of* confusion they shall rejoice
      in their portion.
  Therefore in their land they shall possess
      double;
  Everlasting joy shall be theirs.

8 "For I, the Lord, love justice;
  I hate robbery for burnt offering;
  I will direct their work in truth,
  And will make with them an everlasting
      covenant.
9 Their descendants shall be known among
      the Gentiles,
  And their offspring among the people.
  All who see them shall acknowledge them,
  That they *are* the posterity *whom* the Lord
      has blessed."

10 I will greatly rejoice in the Lord,
   My soul shall be joyful in my God;
   For He has clothed me with the garments
       of salvation,
   He has covered me with the robe of
       righteousness,
   As a bridegroom decks *himself* with
       ornaments,
   And as a bride adorns *herself* with her
       jewels.
11 For as the earth brings forth its bud,
   As the garden causes the things that are
       sown in it to spring forth,
   So the Lord God will cause righteousness
       and praise to spring forth before all the
       nations.

62 For* Zion's sake I will not hold My peace,
   And for Jerusalem's sake I will not rest,
   Until her righteousness goes forth as
       brightness,
   And her salvation as a lamp *that* burns.
2 The Gentiles shall see your righteousness,
  And all kings your glory.
  You shall be called by a new name,
  Which the mouth of the Lord will name.
3 You shall also be a crown of glory
  In the hand of the Lord,
  And a royal diadem
  In the hand of your God.
4 You shall no longer be termed Forsaken,
  Nor shall your land any more be termed
      Desolate;
  But you shall be called Hephzibah,u and
      your land Beulah;v
  For the Lord delights in you,
  And your land shall be married.
5 For *as* a young man marries a virgin,
  So shall your sons marry you;

61:7–11 *Rejoicing.* Instead of shame, there would be rejoicing and everlasting joy. It would be like going from a funeral to a wedding (Luke 5:27–39) and from a desert to a beautiful garden!
Have you entered your Jubilee?

CHAPTER 62

62:1ff God's promises should become our prayers. Isaiah prayed that Jerusalem might be restored (v. 1), and he urged the watchmen and all of God's people to pray as well (vv. 6–7). The psalmist also prayed "for the peace of Jerusalem" (Ps. 122:6). When there is peace in Jerusalem, there will be peace in the world.
   The nation's restoration will be as joyful as a wedding (vv. 4–5; 61:10). *Beulah* means "married," and *Hephzibah* means "My delight is in her." The people were "divorced" from God because of their unfaithfulness, and He was not delighted in them; but that will change when God cleanses their sins.
   Now is the time to make ready, for the King is coming to Zion (vv. 10–12; Matt. 21:5; Rev. 22:12)!

62:4 uLiterally *My Delight Is in Her* vLiterally *Married*

And *as* the bridegroom rejoices over the
   bride,
So shall your God rejoice over you.

6   I have set watchmen on your walls,
       O Jerusalem;
   They shall never hold their peace day or
       night.
   You who make mention of the LORD, do not
       keep silent,
7   And give Him no rest till He establishes
   And till He makes Jerusalem a praise in the
       earth.

8   The LORD has sworn by His right hand
   And by the arm of His strength:
   "Surely I will no longer give your grain
       As food for your enemies;
   And the sons of the foreigner shall not drink
       your new wine,
   For which you have labored.
9   But those who have gathered it shall eat it,
   And praise the LORD;
   Those who have brought it together shall
       drink it in My holy courts."

10 Go through,
   Go through the gates!
   Prepare the way for the people;
   Build up,
   Build up the highway!
   Take out the stones,
   Lift up a banner for the peoples!

11 Indeed the LORD has proclaimed
   To the end of the world:
   "Say to the daughter of Zion,
   'Surely your salvation is coming;
   Behold, His reward *is* with Him,
   And His work before Him.' "
12 And they shall call them The Holy People,
   The Redeemed of the LORD;
   And you shall be called Sought Out,
   A City Not Forsaken.

CHAPTER 63

63:1–6 *Indignation.* When Jesus Christ
returns to establish His kingdom, He will
come as a conquering warrior (Rev. 19:11–
21). When He came the first time, He was
a servant who shed His blood for sinners;
but the next time, the sinners will shed their
blood in a futile defense against the Lord.
The Year of Jubilee will become the "day
of vengeance" (Isa. 61:1–2).

63 Who* *is* this who comes from Edom,
   With dyed garments from Bozrah,
   This *One who is* glorious in His apparel,
   Traveling in the greatness of His strength?—

   "I who speak in righteousness, mighty to
       save."

2   Why *is* Your apparel red,
   And Your garments like one who treads in
       the winepress?

3   "I have trodden the winepress alone,
   And from the peoples no one *was* with Me.
   For I have trodden them in My anger,
   And trampled them in My fury;
   Their blood is sprinkled upon My garments,
   And I have stained all My robes.
4   For the day of vengeance *is* in My heart,
   And the year of My redeemed has come.

Are Your Trials Overwhelming?—Isaiah said, "In all their affliction He was afflicted" (63:9). God
not only goes with you in the difficulties of life (Isa. 43:2), but He knows how you feel. Your High
Priest in heaven is able to sympathize with you because He has experienced the trials and temptations
of life (Heb. 2:17–18; 4:14–16). You should cast "all your care upon Him, for He cares for you"
(1 Pet. 5:7).

5   I looked, but *there was* no one to help,
     And I wondered
     That *there was* no one to uphold;
     Therefore My own arm brought salvation
        for Me;
     And My own fury, it sustained Me.
6   I have trodden down the peoples in My
        anger,
     Made them drunk in My fury,
     And brought down their strength to the
        earth."

7   *I will mention the lovingkindnesses of the
        LORD
     And the praises of the LORD,
     According to all that the LORD has bestowed
        on us,
     And the great goodness toward the house
        of Israel,
     Which He has bestowed on them according
        to His mercies,
     According to the multitude of His
        lovingkindnesses.
8   For He said, "Surely they *are* My people,
     Children *who* will not lie."
     So He became their Savior.
9   In all their affliction He was afflicted,
     And the Angel of His Presence saved them;
     In His love and in His pity He redeemed
        them;
     And He bore them and carried them
     All the days of old.
10   But they rebelled and grieved His Holy
        Spirit;
     So He turned Himself against them as an
        enemy,
     And He fought against them.

11   Then he remembered the days of old,
     Moses *and* his people, *saying:*
     "Where *is* He who brought them up out of
        the sea
     With the shepherd of His flock?
     Where *is* He who put His Holy Spirit within
        them,
12   Who led *them* by the right hand of Moses,
     With His glorious arm,
     Dividing the water before them
     To make for Himself an everlasting name,
13   Who led them through the deep,
     As a horse in the wilderness,
     That they might not stumble?"

14   As a beast goes down into the valley,
     And the Spirit of the LORD causes him to
        rest,
     So You lead Your people,
     To make Yourself a glorious name.

15   *Look down from heaven,
     And see from Your habitation, holy and
        glorious.
     Where *are* Your zeal and Your strength,
     The yearning of Your heart and Your
        mercies toward me?
     Are they restrained?
16   Doubtless You *are* our Father,
     Though Abraham was ignorant of us,
     And Israel does not acknowledge us.
     You, O LORD, *are* our Father;
     Our Redeemer from Everlasting *is* Your
        name.

63:7–14 Compassion. Jesus will defeat His enemies, but He will save His own people (v. 8). The emphasis is on lovingkindness, goodness, mercy, and love. God cares for His children and promises them glory (1 Thess. 5:9–10). Just as He saved them in the days of Moses, so He will save them in the latter days.

63:15–19 Intercession. Isaiah continues to pray for his people (62:1). As a child pleading with a father, he begs God to return and overcome the enemy. He longs to see the temple restored and the people obeying their Lord. Have you joined in that prayer?

CHAPTER 64

64:1–4 The missing demonstration. When the enemy attacked Jerusalem, the Lord held His peace and did not intervene. The Jews were both defeated and disgraced before their foes. Is this somewhat parallel to the situation of God's people today? Demonstrations of divine power are easily found in history books but not readily found among God's people today. Why?

64:5–7 The missing intercession. Isaiah once again emphasizes the importance of prayer (62:1, 6–7; 63:15–19). God wonders that there is no intercessor (Isa. 59:16), nobody who will get stirred up about the need for confessing sin and seeking God's face. Until we pray and get right with God, He will not reveal His power (2 Chron. 7:14).

64:8–12 The missing submission. The clay should yield to the Potter, and the children should obey the Father (Isa. 29:16; 45:9–10; Jer. 18; Rom. 9:20–21). No wonder the temple, the city, and the land were desolate, for God cannot bless those who rebel against Him. If God is going to "come down" with His power, we must fall down in surrender to Him.

17 O LORD, why have You made us stray from
     Your ways,
     And hardened our heart from Your fear?
     Return for Your servants' sake,
     The tribes of Your inheritance.
18 Your holy people have possessed *it* but a
     little while;
     Our adversaries have trodden down Your
     sanctuary.
19 We have become *like* those of old, over
     whom You never ruled,
     Those who were never called by Your name.

64 Oh,* that You would rend the heavens!
     That You would come down!
     That the mountains might shake at Your
     presence—
2 As fire burns brushwood,
     As fire causes water to boil—
     To make Your name known to Your
     adversaries,
     That the nations may tremble at Your
     presence!
3 When You did awesome things *for which*
     we did not look,
     You came down,
     The mountains shook at Your presence.
4 For since the beginning of the world
     Men have not heard nor perceived by the
     ear,
     Nor has the eye seen any God besides You,
     Who acts for the one who waits for Him.
5 *You meet him who rejoices and does
     righteousness,
     Who remembers You in Your ways.
     You are indeed angry, for we have sinned—
     In these ways we continue;
     And we need to be saved.

6 But we are all like an unclean *thing,*
     And all our righteousnesses *are* like filthy
     rags;
     We all fade as a leaf,
     And our iniquities, like the wind,
     Have taken us away.
7 And *there is* no one who calls on Your
     name,
     Who stirs himself up to take hold of You;
     For You have hidden Your face from us,
     And have consumed us because of our
     iniquities.

8 *But now, O LORD,
     You *are* our Father;
     We *are* the clay, and You our potter;
     And all we *are* the work of Your hand.
9 Do not be furious, O LORD,
     Nor remember iniquity forever;
     Indeed, please look—we all *are* Your
     people!
10 Your holy cities are a wilderness,
     Zion is a wilderness,
     Jerusalem a desolation.
11 Our holy and beautiful temple,
     Where our fathers praised You,

Riches Beyond Compare—Paul quoted Isaiah 64:4 in 1 Corinthians 2:9. Some people think this refers to heaven, but Paul applied it to the Christian life *here and now* (1 Cor. 2:10). When you read the Word of God and let the Spirit teach you, you can find out the wonderful things God has done for you and will do for you as you trust and obey. Your Bible is your "passbook" to the Bank of Heaven; it tells you how rich you are in Jesus Christ (Eph. 1:3, 7, 18; 2:7; 3:8, 16).

Is burned up with fire;
And all our pleasant things are laid waste.
12 Will You restrain Yourself because of these
   things, O LORD?
   Will You hold Your peace, and afflict us
   very severely?

65 "I* was sought by *those who* did not ask *for*
     Me;
   I was found by *those who* did not seek Me.
   I said, 'Here I am, here I am,'
   To a nation *that* was not called by My name.
2 I have stretched out My hands all day long
      to a rebellious people,
   Who walk in a way *that is* not good,
   According to their own thoughts;
3 A people who provoke Me to anger
      continually to My face;
   Who sacrifice in gardens,
   And burn incense on altars of brick;
4 Who sit among the graves,
   And spend the night in the tombs;
   Who eat swine's flesh,
   And the broth of abominable things is *in*
      their vessels;
5 Who say, 'Keep to yourself,
   Do not come near me,
   For I am holier than you!'
   These *are* smoke in My nostrils,
   A fire that burns all the day.

6 "Behold, *it is* written before Me:
   I will not keep silence, but will repay—
   Even repay into their bosom—
7 Your iniquities and the iniquities of your
      fathers together,"
   Says the LORD,
   "Who have burned incense on the mountains
   And blasphemed Me on the hills;
   Therefore I will measure their former work
   into their bosom."

8*Thus says the LORD:

   "As the new wine is found in the cluster,
   And *one* says, 'Do not destroy it,
   For a blessing *is* in it,'
   So will I do for My servants' sake,
   That I may not destroy them all.
9 I will bring forth descendants from Jacob,
   And from Judah an heir of My mountains;
   My elect shall inherit it,
   And My servants shall dwell there.
10 Sharon shall be a fold of flocks,
   And the Valley of Achor a place for herds
      to lie down,
   For My people who have sought Me.

11 "But you *are* those who forsake the LORD,
   Who forget My holy mountain,
   Who prepare a table for Gad,ʷ
   And who furnish a drink offering for Meni.ˣ
12 Therefore I will number you for the sword,
   And you shall all bow down to the
      slaughter;
   Because, when I called, you did not answer;
   When I spoke, you did not hear,

CHAPTER 65

65:1–7 The rebels. God pleaded with His
people to turn from their sins and come back
to Him, but they refused. They acted so
pious and yet were guilty of many sins:
worshiping idols, following occult practices,
violating dietary laws, and blaspheming
God. But if the Jews rejected God's call, the
Gentiles responded in their stead (Rom.
10:20–21; Matt. 21:43).

65:8–16 The remnant. God always has His
faithful remnant, like a few grapes after the
harvest (Deut. 24:21); and He uses them
as the nucleus of a new beginning. The
rebels will be judged, but the remnant ("My
servants") will be blessed.

❝We should all be concerned
about the future because we will
have to spend the rest of our lives
there.❞
— Charles F. Kettering

65:11 ʷLiterally *Troop* or *Fortune,* a pagan deity ˣLiterally
Number or *Destiny,* a pagan deity

But did evil before My eyes,
And chose *that* in which I do not delight.''

13Therefore thus says the Lord GOD:

"Behold, My servants shall eat,
But you shall be hungry;
Behold, My servants shall drink,
But you shall be thirsty;
Behold, My servants shall rejoice,
But you shall be ashamed;
14 Behold, My servants shall sing for joy of
heart,
But you shall cry for sorrow of heart,
And wail for grief of spirit.
15 You shall leave your name as a curse to My
chosen;
For the Lord GOD will slay you,
And call His servants by another name;
16 So that he who blesses himself in the earth
Shall bless himself in the God of truth;
And he who swears in the earth
Shall swear by the God of truth;
Because the former troubles are forgotten,
And because they are hidden from My
eyes.

65:17–25 *The regeneration.* That is what Jesus called the kingdom God has prepared for His people (Matt. 19:28). The blessings named are in contrast to the judgments listed in Deuteronomy 28:15ff. It will be a time of joy and fulfillment when the blessing of the Lord flows without interference from man.

17*"For behold, I create new heavens and a new
earth;
And the former shall not be remembered
or come to mind.
18 But be glad and rejoice forever in what I
create;
For behold, I create Jerusalem *as a*
rejoicing,
And her people a joy.
19 I will rejoice in Jerusalem,
And joy in My people;
The voice of weeping shall no longer be
heard in her,
Nor the voice of crying.

20 "No more shall an infant from there *live but
a few* days,
Nor an old man who has not fulfilled his
days;
For the child shall die one hundred years
old,
But the sinner *being* one hundred years old
shall be accursed.
21 They shall build houses and inhabit *them;*
They shall plant vineyards and eat their
fruit.
22 They shall not build and another inhabit;
They shall not plant and another eat;
For as the days of a tree, *so shall be* the
days of My people,
And My elect shall long enjoy the work of
their hands.
23 They shall not labor in vain,
Nor bring forth children for trouble;
For they *shall be* the descendants of the
blessed of the LORD,
And their offspring with them.

24 "It shall come to pass
That before they call, I will answer;
And while they are still speaking, I will
hear.
25 The wolf and the lamb shall feed together,
The lion shall eat straw like the ox,
And dust *shall be* the serpent's food.

They shall not hurt nor destroy in all My
holy mountain,"
Says the LORD.

66 Thus* says the LORD:

"Heaven *is* My throne,
And earth *is* My footstool.
Where *is* the house that you will build
Me?
And where *is* the place of My rest?
2 For all those *things* My hand has made,
And all those *things* exist,"
Says the LORD.
"But on this *one* will I look:
On *him who is* poor and of a contrite spirit,
And who trembles at My word.

3 "He who kills a bull *is as if* he slays a man;
He who sacrifices a lamb, *as if* he breaks a
dog's neck;
He who offers a grain offering, *as if he offers*
swine's blood;
He who burns incense, *as if* he blesses an
idol.
Just as they have chosen their own ways,
And their soul delights in their
abominations,
4 So will I choose their delusions,
And bring their fears on them;
Because, when I called, no one answered,
When I spoke they did not hear;
But they did evil before My eyes,
And chose *that* in which I do not delight."

5 Hear the word of the LORD,
You who tremble at His word:
"Your brethren who hated you,
Who cast you out for My name's sake,
said,
'Let the LORD be glorified,
That we may see your joy.'
But they shall be ashamed."

6 The sound of noise from the city!
A voice from the temple!
The voice of the LORD,
Who fully repays His enemies!

7 *"Before she was in labor, she gave birth;
Before her pain came,
She delivered a male child.
8 Who has heard such a thing?
Who has seen such things?
Shall the earth be made to give birth in one
day?
Or shall a nation be born at once?
For as soon as Zion was in labor,
She gave birth to her children.
9 Shall I bring to the time of birth, and not
cause delivery?" says the LORD.
"Shall I who cause delivery shut up *the
womb*?" says your God.

CHAPTER 66

66:1–6 *Trembling.* How can anyone build
a house for the Lord when He made
everything (Isa. 40:25–26)? He is so great
that He uses the earth for His footstool
(v. 1)! But with all of His greatness, God
deigns to dwell with the humble (v. 2; 57:15),
those who tremble at His word and seek to
glorify Him (v. 5).

66:7–13 *Travailing.* The restoration of
Israel's kingdom will be as sudden and joyful
as the birth of a baby. The travail of their
tribulation will give birth to glory, and God
will love them just like a mother (v. 13). It
will be a time of peace and joy.

Tremble at His Word—To "tremble at God's word" (Isa. 66:2, 5) means to respect what God
says and fear to disobey it (Ps. 119:120). The Jews experienced this when Ezra exposed their sins
(Ezra 9:4; 10:3), and the prophet Habakkuk experienced it when he saw the vision of God's judgment
(Hab. 3:16). Saul of Tarsus trembled when he met the Lord (Acts 9:6). However, King Jehoiakim
did not tremble at the Word; he tried to destroy it (Jer. 36), and that led to his destruction (Prov.
13:13). Paul urged, "Work out your own salvation [Christian life] with fear and trembling" (Phil. 2:12).

10 "Rejoice with Jerusalem,
   And be glad with her, all you who love
     her;
   Rejoice for joy with her, all you who mourn
     for her;
11 That you may feed and be satisfied
   With the consolation of her bosom,
   That you may drink deeply and be delighted
   With the abundance of her glory."

12For thus says the LORD:

"Behold, I will extend peace to her like a
   river,
And the glory of the Gentiles like a flowing
   stream.
Then you shall feed;
On *her* sides shall you be carried,
And be dandled on *her* knees.
13 As one whom his mother comforts,
   So I will comfort you;
   And you shall be comforted in Jerusalem."

14 *When you see *this*, your heart shall rejoice,
   And your bones shall flourish like grass;
   The hand of the LORD shall be known to His
     servants,
   And *His* indignation to His enemies.
15 For behold, the LORD will come with fire
   And with His chariots, like a whirlwind,
   To render His anger with fury,
   And His rebuke with flames of fire.
16 For by fire and by His sword
   The LORD will judge all flesh;
   And the slain of the LORD shall be many.

17 "Those who sanctify themselves and purify
     themselves,
   To go to the gardens
   After an *idol* in the midst,
   Eating swine's flesh and the abomination
     and the mouse,
   Shall be consumed together," says the LORD.

18"For I *know* their works and their thoughts. It shall be that I will gather all nations and tongues; and they shall come and see My glory. 19I will set a sign among them; and those among them who escape I will send to the nations: *to* Tarshish and Pul[y] and Lud, who draw the bow, and Tubal and Javan, *to* the coastlands afar off who have not heard My fame nor seen My glory. And they shall declare My glory among the Gentiles. 20Then they shall bring all your brethren for an offering to the LORD out of all nations, on horses and in chariots and in litters, on mules and on camels, to My holy mountain Jerusalem," says the LORD, "as the children of Israel bring an offering in a clean vessel into the house of the LORD. 21And I will also take some of them for priests *and* Levites," says the LORD.

22 "For as the new heavens and the new earth
   Which I will make shall remain before Me,"
     says the LORD,
   "So shall your descendants and your name
     remain.

66:14–24 *Triumphing.* God will defeat His enemies (vv. 14–17), summon the gentile nations to share the glory (vv. 18–19), and make Israel a holy offering to the Lord (vv. 20–24). Isaiah opened his prophecy indicting Israel for her religious hypocrisy (chap. 1), but he ended it promising that her worship will be acceptable to the Lord.

66:19 [y]Following Masoretic Text and Targum; Septuagint reads *Put* (compare Jeremiah 46:9).

23 And it shall come to pass
  That from one New Moon to another,
  And from one Sabbath to another,
  All flesh shall come to worship before Me,"
    says the LORD.

24 "And they shall go forth and look
  Upon the corpses of the men
  Who have transgressed against Me.
  For their worm does not die,
  And their fire is not quenched.
  They shall be an abhorrence to all flesh."

JEREMIAH

The prophet Jeremiah ministered in Judah during the last forty years of the nation's history, from 627 to perhaps 582 B.C. In spite of his faithful preaching of the Word, Jeremiah watched the nation decline until Judah was taken captive by the Babylonians and Jerusalem and the temple were destroyed. He expressed his grief vividly in the book of Lamentations.

He was a priest called to be a prophet, a sensitive man called to confront kings, false prophets, and hypocritical priests. He was bold before men but broken before God, and we call him "the weeping prophet." When Jesus was here on earth, the people identified Him with the prophet Jeremiah (Matt. 16:14). Jeremiah's life was not easy, and his ministry did not appear successful. But he was faithful to the Lord and accomplished God's will.

After describing his call to ministry (chap. 1), Jeremiah records his messages to Judah, pleading with the people to repent (chaps. 2—33). He shares some of his personal sufferings (chaps. 34—45) and sermons to the gentile nations (chaps. 46—51). The last chapter reviews the fall of the city and the nation (chap. 52).

Jeremiah is a master of imagery who creates many word pictures to give his message. As you read his prophecy, use your imagination and "see" what Jeremiah is saying. Also, note the occasional personal disclosures in the book, particularly the honest expressions of the prophet's feelings. Jeremiah reveals his own heart as he preaches about the broken heart of God.

CHAPTER 1

1:4–10 Kings and rulers come and go, but the Word of God remains and accomplishes God's work in the world. Yet God needs a voice to herald the Word, and nobody feels adequate for the task.

Hearing. God's word to Jeremiah was, "You will be what I want you to be, go where I want you to go, and say what I want you to say. I supervised your conception, I consecrated you, and now I am ordaining you." If God calls you, believe what He says and obey Him. You may not feel up to it, but your adequacy comes from God, not from yourself.

1 The words of Jeremiah the son of Hilkiah, of the priests who *were* in Anathoth in the land of Benjamin, ²to whom the word of the LORD came in the days of Josiah the son of Amon, king of Judah, in the thirteenth year of his reign. ³It came also in the days of Jehoiakim the son of Josiah, king of Judah, until the end of the eleventh year of Zedekiah the son of Josiah, king of Judah, until the carrying away of Jerusalem captive in the fifth month.

⁴*Then the word of the LORD came to me, saying:

5 "Before I formed you in the womb I knew you;
Before you were born I sanctified you;
I ordained you a prophet to the nations."

⁶Then said I:

"Ah, Lord GOD!
Behold, I cannot speak, for I *am* a youth."

⁷But the LORD said to me:

Are You Available?—Moses did not feel adequate for the task when God called him, but the Lord reassured him (Exod. 3—4). "And who is sufficient for these things?" asked Paul (2 Cor. 2:16); and his answer was, "Our sufficiency is from God" (2 Cor. 4:5–6). When God calls you to do a task for Him, He does not ask you to be adequate; He only asks you to be available.

God's Touch—The touch of God makes the difference between success and failure. God touched Isaiah's lips to give him purity (Isa. 6:1–7) and Jeremiah's lips to give him power (Jer. 1:9–10; Luke 21:15). He touched Jacob's hip and gave him a limp (Gen. 32:25), thus helping him to become a "prince with God." God touched Daniel and set him on his feet (Dan. 8:18), gave him strength (Dan. 10:18), and opened his mouth for ministry (Dan. 10:15–16). The call of God and the touch of God must go together or we fail.

"Do not say, 'I *am* a youth,'
For you shall go to all to whom I send
    you,
And whatever I command you, you shall
    speak.
8 Do not be afraid of their faces,
For I *am* with you to deliver you," says the
    LORD.

9Then the LORD put forth His hand and touched
my mouth, and the LORD said to me:

"Behold, I have put My words in your mouth.
10   See, I have this day set you over the nations
        and over the kingdoms,
     To root out and to pull down,
     To destroy and to throw down,
     To build and to plant."

11*Moreover the word of the LORD came to me,
saying, "Jeremiah, what do you see?"
    And I said, "I see a branch of an almond tree."
12Then the LORD said to me, "You have seen
well, for I am ready to perform My word."
13And the word of the LORD came to me the
second time, saying, "What do you see?"
    And I said, "I see a boiling pot, and it is facing
away from the north."
14Then the LORD said to me:

"Out of the north calamity shall break forth
On all the inhabitants of the land.
15 For behold, I am calling
All the families of the kingdoms of the
    north," says the LORD;
"They shall come and each one set his throne
At the entrance of the gates of Jerusalem,
Against all its walls all around,
And against all the cities of Judah.
16 I will utter My judgments
Against them concerning all their
    wickedness,
Because they have forsaken Me,
Burned incense to other gods,
And worshiped the works of their own
    hands.

17*"Therefore prepare yourself and arise,
And speak to them all that I command you.
Do not be dismayed before their faces,
Lest I dismay you before them.
18 For behold, I have made you this day
A fortified city and an iron pillar,
And bronze walls against the whole land—
Against the kings of Judah,
Against its princes,
Against its priests,
And against the people of the land.
19 They will fight against you,
But they shall not prevail against you.
For I *am* with you," says the LORD, "to
    deliver you."

2 Moreover* the word of the LORD came to me,
saying, 2"Go and cry in the hearing of Jerusalem, saying, 'Thus says the LORD:

"I remember you,
The kindness of your youth,
The love of your betrothal,
When you went after Me in the wilderness,
In a land not sown.

❛❛*Jeremiah lived about sixty years.
Across that life span there is no sign
of decay or shriveling. Always he
was pushing out the borders of
reality, exploring new territory.
And always he was vigorous in
battle, challenging and contesting
the shoddy, the false, the vile.*❜❜
—Eugene H. Peterson

1:11–16 Seeing. God's servants must have
open eyes as well as open ears, for God
can "speak" through what they see. In
Hebrew, the words almond and watch are
similar. God watches over His Word to
perform what He says. Our job is
proclamation; His job is performance.
Babylon came from the north and destroyed
Judah and Jerusalem.

1:17–19 Doing. It was difficult for youthful
Jeremiah to confront his elders with a
message of denunciation, but God made
him and God was with him. God's
messengers must be walls and not shifting
sand.

CHAPTER 2

2:1ff Why was judgment coming to the
nation of Judah? Because the people were
unfaithful to God and had mixed the worship
of Jehovah with the worship of heathen
idols. Religion was very popular in Judah,
but it was not very spiritual.
    Judah was an unfaithful wife who had not
maintained her "honeymoon love" (vv. 2, 32;
Rev. 2:4). The people were a wasted
harvest devoured by the enemy (v. 3). They
forgot what God did for them and turned to
false gods (vv. 4–8). It was like exchanging
a pure artesian well for a dirty, leaky cistern
(vv. 9–13).
    They were stubborn animals that hated
the yoke (v. 20) and a degenerate vine that
bore no fruit (v. 21; Isa. 5). Their sins were
so deep that they could not be washed away
(v. 22). Like wild animals in heat (vv. 23–
25), they lusted after sin; yet they denied
that they had sinned (vv. 33–36)!
    The last picture is that of prisoners of war,
marching away with their hands on their
heads (v. 37). What the people thought was
freedom turned out to be slavery.

3   Israel *was* holiness to the LORD,
    The firstfruits of His increase.
    All that devour him will offend;
    Disaster will come upon them," says the
        LORD.' "

⁴Hear the word of the LORD, O house of Jacob
and all the families of the house of Israel. ⁵Thus
says the LORD:

    "What injustice have your fathers found in
        Me,
    That they have gone far from Me,
    Have followed idols,
    And have become idolaters?
6   Neither did they say, 'Where *is* the LORD,
    Who brought us up out of the land of Egypt,
    Who led us through the wilderness,
    Through a land of deserts and pits,
    Through a land of drought and the shadow
        of death,
    Through a land that no one crossed
    And where no one dwelt?'
7   I brought you into a bountiful country,
    To eat its fruit and its goodness.
    But when you entered, you defiled My land
    And made My heritage an abomination.
8   The priests did not say, 'Where *is* the LORD?'
    And those who handle the law did not know
        Me;
    The rulers also transgressed against Me;
    The prophets prophesied by Baal,
    And walked after *things that* do not profit.

9   "Therefore I will yet bring charges against
        you," says the LORD,
    "And against your children's children I will
        bring charges.
10 For pass beyond the coasts of Cyprus*ᵃ* and
        see,
    Send to Kedar*ᵇ* and consider diligently,
    And see if there has been such *a thing.*
11 Has a nation changed *its* gods,
    Which *are* not gods?
    But My people have changed their Glory
    For *what* does not profit.
12 Be astonished, O heavens, at this,
    And be horribly afraid;
    Be very desolate," says the LORD.
13 "For My people have committed two evils:
    They have forsaken Me, the fountain of
        living waters,
    And hewn themselves cisterns—broken
        cisterns that can hold no water.

14 "*Is* Israel a servant?
    Is he a homeborn *slave?*
    Why is he plundered?
15 The young lions roared at him, *and* growled;
    They made his land waste;
    His cities are burned, without inhabitant.
16 Also the people of Noph*ᶜ* and Tahpanhes
    Have broken the crown of your head.
17 Have you not brought this on yourself,
    In that you have forsaken the LORD your
        God
    When He led you in the way?

2:10 *ᵃ*Hebrew *Kittim,* western lands, especially Cyprus *ᵇ*In the
northern Arabian desert, representative of the eastern cultures
2:16 *ᶜ*That is, Memphis in ancient Egypt

18 And now why take the road to Egypt,
To drink the waters of Sihor?
Or why take the road to Assyria,
To drink the waters of the River?*d*

19 Your own wickedness will correct you,
And your backslidings will rebuke you.
Know therefore and see that *it is* an evil
and bitter *thing*
That you have forsaken the LORD your God,
And the fear of Me *is* not in you,"
Says the Lord GOD of hosts.

20 "For of old I have broken your yoke *and* burst
your bonds;
And you said, 'I will not transgress,'
When on every high hill and under every
green tree
You lay down, playing the harlot.

21 Yet I had planted you a noble vine, a seed
of highest quality.
How then have you turned before Me
Into the degenerate plant of an alien vine?

22 For though you wash yourself with lye, and
use much soap,
Yet your iniquity is marked before Me,"
says the Lord GOD.

23 "How can you say, 'I am not polluted,
I have not gone after the Baals'?
See your way in the valley;
Know what you have done:
You are a swift dromedary breaking loose
in her ways,

24 A wild donkey used to the wilderness,
That sniffs at the wind in her desire;
In her time of mating, who can turn her
away?
All those who seek her will not weary
themselves;
In her month they will find her.

25 Withhold your foot from being unshod, and
your throat from thirst.
But you said, 'There is no hope.
No! For I have loved aliens, and after them
I will go.'

26 "As the thief is ashamed when he is found
out,
So is the house of Israel ashamed;
They and their kings and their princes, and
their priests and their prophets,

27 Saying to a tree, 'You *are* my father,'
And to a stone, 'You gave birth to me.'
For they have turned *their* back to Me, and
not *their* face.
But in the time of their trouble
They will say, 'Arise and save us.'

28 But where *are* your gods that you have
made for yourselves?
Let them arise,
If they can save you in the time of your
trouble;
For *according to* the number of your cities
Are your gods, O Judah.

29 "Why will you plead with Me?
You all have transgressed against Me," says
the LORD.

2:18 *d*That is, the Euphrates

30 "In vain I have chastened your children;
They received no correction.
Your sword has devoured your prophets
Like a destroying lion.

31 "O generation, see the word of the LORD!
Have I been a wilderness to Israel,
Or a land of darkness?
Why do My people say, 'We are lords;
We will come no more to You'?
32 Can a virgin forget her ornaments,
Or a bride her attire?
Yet My people have forgotten Me days
without number.

33 "Why do you beautify your way to seek love?
Therefore you have also taught
The wicked women your ways.
34 Also on your skirts is found
The blood of the lives of the poor innocents.
I have not found it by secret search,
But plainly on all these things.
35 Yet you say, 'Because I am innocent,
Surely His anger shall turn from me.'
Behold, I will plead My case against you,
Because you say, 'I have not sinned.'
36 Why do you gad about so much to change
your way?
Also you shall be ashamed of Egypt as you
were ashamed of Assyria.
37 Indeed you will go forth from him
With your hands on your head;
For the LORD has rejected your trusted allies,
And you will not prosper by them.

3 "They say, 'If a man divorces his wife,
And she goes from him
And becomes another man's,
May he return to her again?'
Would not that land be greatly polluted?
But you have played the harlot with many
lovers;
Yet return to Me," says the LORD.

2 "Lift up your eyes to the desolate heights and
see:
Where have you not lain *with men?*
By the road you have sat for them
Like an Arabian in the wilderness;
And you have polluted the land
With your harlotries and your wickedness.
3 Therefore the showers have been withheld,
And there has been no latter rain.
You have had a harlot's forehead;
You refuse to be ashamed.
4 Will you not from this time cry to Me,
'My Father, You *are* the guide of my youth?
5 Will He remain angry forever?
Will He keep it to the end?'
Behold, you have spoken and done evil
things,
As you were able."

6*The LORD said also to me in the days of Josiah
the king: "Have you seen what backsliding Israel

CHAPTER 3

3:6 The word *backsliding* is used seven
times in this chapter. Judah was gradually
sliding away from the Lord and ignoring His
loving pleas. What is *backsliding* like?
Backsliding is like harlotry. The nation
was "married" to Jehovah at Sinai when
God gave her His covenant. But Judah
became an unfaithful wife whose love was
growing cold (Jer. 2:2) and whose "lovers"
were many. God could "divorce" His defiled
wife; but if He did, *she could not return to
Him* (Deut. 24:1–4). So, instead of divorcing
her, God warned her (vv. 3, 6–10). However,
she would not listen. He begged her to
return, for returning is the only remedy for
backsliding; but she refused.
Backsliding is like sickness (v. 22). It
begins with a secret "infection" of sin, which
leads to loss of spiritual appetite, gradual
decline and, if not attended to, death. God
heals our backsliding if we honestly accept
His diagnosis and humbly return to Him.

Backsliding—*Backsliding* is an Old Testament word used only by Isaiah (57:17), Jeremiah, and
Hosea (11:7; 14:4). It means "disloyalty," "faithlessness." Most Christians do not *jump* into sin and
get away from God's will. They gradually decline spiritually, then find themselves in trouble
and wonder how it happened. They leave their first love (Rev. 2:4) and start living for the flesh and
not the Spirit (Gal. 3:1–3). That is why our Lord admonished us to watch and pray (Matt. 26:41).
When we least expect it, the germ of sin can enter the system.

has done? She has gone up on every high mountain and under every green tree, and there played the harlot. 7And I said, after she had done all these *things*, 'Return to Me.' But she did not return. And her treacherous sister Judah saw it. 8Then I saw that for all the causes for which backsliding Israel had committed adultery, I had put her away and given her a certificate of divorce; yet her treacherous sister Judah did not fear, but went and played the harlot also. 9So it came to pass, through her casual harlotry, that she defiled the land and committed adultery with stones and trees. 10And yet for all this her treacherous sister Judah has not turned to Me with her whole heart, but in pretense," says the LORD.

11Then the LORD said to me, "Backsliding Israel has shown herself more righteous than treacherous Judah. 12Go and proclaim these words toward the north, and say:

'Return, backsliding Israel,' says the
    LORD;
'I will not cause My anger to fall on you.
For I *am* merciful,' says the LORD;
'I will not remain angry forever.
13   Only acknowledge your iniquity,
    That you have transgressed against the
        LORD your God,
    And have scattered your charms
    To alien deities under every green tree,
    And you have not obeyed My voice,' says
        the LORD.

14"Return, O backsliding children," says the LORD; "for I am married to you. I will take you, one from a city and two from a family, and I will bring you to Zion. 15And I will give you shepherds according to My heart, who will feed you with knowledge and understanding.

16"Then it shall come to pass, when you are multiplied and increased in the land in those days," says the LORD, "that they will say no more, 'The ark of the covenant of the LORD.' It shall not come to mind, nor shall they remember it, nor shall they visit *it,* nor shall it be made anymore.

17"At that time Jerusalem shall be called The Throne of the LORD, and all the nations shall be gathered to it, to the name of the LORD, to Jerusalem. No more shall they follow the dictates of their evil hearts.

18"In those days the house of Judah shall walk with the house of Israel, and they shall come together out of the land of the north to the land that I have given as an inheritance to your fathers.

19"But I said:

'How can I put you among the children
And give you a pleasant land,
A beautiful heritage of the hosts of nations?'

"And I said:

'You shall call Me, "My Father,"
And not turn away from Me.'
20   Surely, *as* a wife treacherously departs from
        her husband,
    So have you dealt treacherously with Me,
    O house of Israel," says the LORD.

21   A voice was heard on the desolate heights,
    Weeping *and* supplications of the children
        of Israel.

For they have perverted their way;
They have forgotten the LORD their
       God.

22 "Return, you backsliding children,
       And I will heal your backslidings."

"Indeed we do come to You,
For You are the LORD our God.
23   Truly, in vain *is salvation hoped for* from
       the hills,
       And from the multitude of mountains;
Truly, in the LORD our God
       Is the salvation of Israel.
24   For shame has devoured
The labor of our fathers from our youth—
Their flocks and their herds,
Their sons and their daughters.
25   We lie down in our shame,
And our reproach covers us.
For we have sinned against the LORD our
       God,
We and our fathers,
From our youth even to this day,
And have not obeyed the voice of the LORD
       our God."

4   "If you will return, O Israel," says the LORD,
       "Return to Me;
       And if you will put away your abominations
       out of My sight,
       Then you shall not be moved.
2   And you shall swear, 'The LORD lives,'
       In truth, in judgment, and in righteousness;
       The nations shall bless themselves in Him,
       And in Him they shall glory."

3*For thus says the LORD to the men of Judah
and Jerusalem:

"Break up your fallow ground,
And do not sow among thorns.
4   *Circumcise yourselves to the LORD,
       And take away the foreskins of your hearts,
       You men of Judah and inhabitants of
       Jerusalem,
       Lest My fury come forth like fire,
       And burn so that no one can quench *it,*
       Because of the evil of your doings."

5*Declare in Judah and proclaim in Jerusalem,
and say:

"Blow the trumpet in the land;
Cry, 'Gather together,'
And say, 'Assemble yourselves,
And let us go into the fortified cities.'
6   Set up the standard toward Zion.
Take refuge! Do not delay!
For I will bring disaster from the north,
And great destruction."

7   The lion has come up from his thicket,
And the destroyer of nations is on his way.
He has gone forth from his place
To make your land desolate.
Your cities will be laid waste,
Without inhabitant.
8   For this, clothe yourself with sackcloth,
Lament and wail.
For the fierce anger of the LORD
Has not turned back from us.

CHAPTER 4

4:3 Over forty times in his book, Jeremiah calls for God's people to return to the Lord. To describe what that is like, he uses several images.

It is like *plowing*. Hard hearts need plowing up so they can receive the seed of the Word and bear fruit.

4:4 It is like *performing surgery*. The Jews put their confidence in external religious ritual and did not let God operate on their hearts (Deut. 10:12–16; 30:6; Rom. 2:28–29). He wants truth deep within the heart (Ps. 51:6).

4:5, 6, 19–21 It is like *joining the army*. The backslider is serving the enemy; but then he hears the trumpet call, realizes he is a traitor, and returns to obey his commander.

9 "And it shall come to pass in that day," says
    the LORD,
"*That* the heart of the king shall perish,
    And the heart of the princes;
    The priests shall be astonished,
    And the prophets shall wonder."

10 Then I said, "Ah, Lord GOD!
    Surely You have greatly deceived this
        people and Jerusalem,
    Saying, 'You shall have peace,'
    Whereas the sword reaches to the heart."

11 At that time it will be said
    To this people and to Jerusalem,
"A dry wind of the desolate heights *blows*
    in the wilderness
    Toward the daughter of My people—
    Not to fan or to cleanse—
12 A wind too strong for these will come for
    Me;
    Now I will also speak judgment against
        them."

13 "Behold, he shall come up like clouds,
    And his chariots like a whirlwind.
    His horses are swifter than eagles.
    Woe to us, for we are plundered!"

14 *O Jerusalem, wash your heart from
        wickedness,
    That you may be saved.
    How long shall your evil thoughts lodge
        within you?
15 For a voice declares from Dan
    And proclaims affliction from Mount
        Ephraim:
16 "Make mention to the nations,
    Yes, proclaim against Jerusalem,
    That watchers come from a far country
    And raise their voice against the cities of
        Judah.
17 Like keepers of a field they are against her
        all around,
    Because she has been rebellious against
        Me," says the LORD.
18 "Your ways and your doings
    Have procured these *things* for you.
    This *is* your wickedness,
    Because it is bitter,
    Because it reaches to your heart."

19 O my soul, my soul!
    I am pained in my very heart!
    My heart makes a noise in me;
    I cannot hold my peace,
    Because you have heard, O my soul,
    The sound of the trumpet,
    The alarm of war.
20 Destruction upon destruction is cried,
    For the whole land is plundered.
    Suddenly my tents are plundered,
    And my curtains in a moment.
21 How long will I see the standard,
    And hear the sound of the trumpet?

22 "For My people *are* foolish,
    They have not known Me.
    They *are* silly children,
    And they have no understanding.
    They *are* wise to do evil,
    But to do good they have no knowledge."

4:14 It is like *taking a bath*. When we confess our sins, God cleanses us (1 John 1:9) and gives us a new beginning (Ps. 51:1–2, 10–11).

4:22 It is like *growing up*. Believers should be childlike but not childish (Matt. 11:16–17). Backsliders are foolish, like disobedient children who are only hurting themselves.
    No wonder God repeatedly calls to His backslidden people, "Return! Return!"

23 I beheld the earth, and indeed *it was* without
form, and void;
And the heavens, they *had* no light.
24 I beheld the mountains, and indeed they
trembled,
And all the hills moved back and forth.
25 I beheld, and indeed *there was* no man,
And all the birds of the heavens had fled.
26 I beheld, and indeed the fruitful land *was* a
wilderness,
And all its cities were broken down
At the presence of the LORD,
By His fierce anger.

27For thus says the LORD:

"The whole land shall be desolate;
Yet I will not make a full end.
28 For this shall the earth mourn,
And the heavens above be black,
Because I have spoken.
I have purposed and will not relent,
Nor will I turn back from it.
29 The whole city shall flee from the noise of
the horsemen and bowmen.
They shall go into thickets and climb up on
the rocks.
Every city *shall be* forsaken,
And not a man shall dwell in it.

30 "And *when* you *are* plundered,
What will you do?
Though you clothe yourself with crimson,
Though you adorn *yourself* with ornaments
of gold,
Though you enlarge your eyes with paint,
In vain you will make yourself fair;
Your lovers will despise you;
They will seek your life.

31 "For I have heard a voice as of a woman in
labor,
The anguish as of her who brings forth her
first child,
The voice of the daughter of Zion bewailing
herself;
She spreads her hands, *saying,*
'Woe *is* me now, for my soul is weary
Because of murderers!'

CHAPTER 5

5:1–9 *Looking for a man.* God would have
spared Sodom had He found ten righteous
men (Gen. 18:26–32); but to spare
Jerusalem, He would have settled for *one!*
Yet Jeremiah could not find one, not even
among the "great men" who were spiritual
leaders in the city. Never underestimate the
importance of one person living wholly for
the Lord. Perhaps you can be that "righteous
one" in your home or place of employment.

5:3 *Looking for truth.* The eyes of the Lord
search for people who are faithful to Him
and His Word. They may be in the minority
and they may be persecuted, but they are
God's own people and He will bless them.

5 "Run* to and fro through the streets of
Jerusalem;
See now and know;
And seek in her open places
If you can find a man,
If there is *anyone* who executes judgment,
Who seeks the truth,
And I will pardon her.
2 Though they say, 'As the LORD lives,'
Surely they swear falsely."

3 *O LORD, *are* not Your eyes on the truth?
You have stricken them,
But they have not grieved;
You have consumed them,
But they have refused to receive correction.

A Righteous Man—Henry Varley said to evangelist D. L. Moody, "The world has yet to see what
God can do with and for and through and in a man who is fully and wholly consecrated to Him."
Moody asked God to make him that man, and the Lord gave him his request. God used Moody in a
marvelous way, and his work is still being blessed around the world.

They have made their faces harder than
    rock;
They have refused to return.

4   Therefore I said, "Surely these *are* poor.
    They are foolish;
    For they do not know the way of the LORD,
    The judgment of their God.
5   I will go to the great men and speak to them,
    For they have known the way of the LORD,
    The judgment of their God."

    But these have altogether broken the yoke
    And burst the bonds.
6   Therefore a lion from the forest shall slay
    them,
    A wolf of the deserts shall destroy them;
    A leopard will watch over their cities.
    Everyone who goes out from there shall be
    torn in pieces,
    Because their transgressions are many;
    Their backslidings have increased.

7   "How shall I pardon you for this?
    Your children have forsaken Me
    And sworn by *those that are* not gods.
    When I had fed them to the full,
    Then they committed adultery
    And assembled themselves by troops in the
    harlots' houses.
8   They were *like* well-fed lusty stallions;
    Every one neighed after his neighbor's wife.
9   Shall I not punish *them* for these *things*?"
    says the LORD.
    "And shall I not avenge Myself on such a
    nation as this?

10 "Go up on her walls and destroy,
    But do not make a complete end.
    Take away her branches,
    For they *are* not the LORD's.
11 For the house of Israel and the house of
    Judah
    Have dealt very treacherously with Me,"
    says the LORD.

12 They have lied about the LORD,
    And said, "*It is* not He.
    Neither will evil come upon us,
    Nor shall we see sword or famine.
13 And the prophets become wind,
    For the word *is* not in them.
    Thus shall it be done to them."

14Therefore thus says the LORD God of hosts:

    "Because you speak this word,
    Behold, I will make My words in your mouth
    fire,
    And this people wood,
    And it shall devour them.
15 Behold, I will bring a nation against you
    from afar,
    O house of Israel," says the LORD.
    "It *is* a mighty nation,
    It *is* an ancient nation,
    A nation whose language you do not know,
    Nor can you understand what they say.
16 Their quiver *is* like an open tomb;
    They *are* all mighty men.
17 And they shall eat up your harvest and your
    bread,

Which your sons and daughters should eat.
They shall eat up your flocks and your
herds;
They shall eat up your vines and your fig
trees;
They shall destroy your fortified cities,
In which you trust, with the sword.

18"Nevertheless in those days," says the LORD,
"I will not make a complete end of you. 19And it
will be when you say, 'Why does the LORD our
God do all these *things* to us?' then you shall answer them, 'Just as you have forsaken Me and
served foreign gods in your land, so you shall
serve aliens in a land *that is* not yours.'

5:20–25 *Looking but not seeing.* The eyes
of the spiritual leaders were blind to God
and what God was doing (Isa. 6:10; Matt.
13:15). They were also blind to the judgment
about to fall on the nation. The waves of
the sea know where to stop, but Judah's
leaders went beyond the limits God had set.
They might be popular and prosperous, but
their prosperity would destroy them.

20*"'Declare this in the house of Jacob
And proclaim it in Judah, saying,
21 'Hear this now, O foolish people,
Without understanding,
Who have eyes and see not,
And who have ears and hear not:
22 Do you not fear Me?' says the LORD.
'Will you not tremble at My presence,
Who have placed the sand as the bound of
the sea,
By a perpetual decree, that it cannot pass
beyond it?
And though its waves toss to and fro,
Yet they cannot prevail;
Though they roar, yet they cannot pass over
it.
23 But this people has a defiant and rebellious
heart;
They have revolted and departed.
24 They do not say in their heart,
"Let us now fear the LORD our God,
Who gives rain, both the former and the
latter, in its season.
He reserves for us the appointed weeks of
the harvest."
25 Your iniquities have turned these *things*
away,
And your sins have withheld good from you.

26 'For among My people are found wicked
men;
They lie in wait as one who sets snares;
They set a trap;
They catch men.
27 As a cage is full of birds,
So their houses *are* full of deceit.
Therefore they have become great and
grown rich.
28 They have grown fat, they are sleek;
Yes, they surpass the deeds of the wicked;
They do not plead the cause,
The cause of the fatherless;
Yet they prosper,
And the right of the needy they do not
defend.
29 Shall I not punish *them* for these *things?'*
says the LORD.
'Shall I not avenge Myself on such a nation
as this?'

30 "An astonishing and horrible thing
Has been committed in the land:
31 The prophets prophesy falsely,
And the priests rule by their *own* power;
And My people love *to have it* so.
But what will you do in the end?

6 "O you children of Benjamin,
Gather yourselves to flee from the midst of
Jerusalem!
Blow the trumpet in Tekoa,
And set up a signal-fire in Beth Haccerem;
For disaster appears out of the north,
And great destruction.
2 I have likened the daughter of Zion
To a lovely and delicate woman.
3 The shepherds with their flocks shall come
to her.
They shall pitch *their* tents against her all
around.
Each one shall pasture in his own place."

4 "Prepare war against her;
Arise, and let us go up at noon.
Woe to us, for the day goes away,
For the shadows of the evening are
lengthening.
5 Arise, and let us go by night,
And let us destroy her palaces."

6For thus has the LORD of hosts said:

"Cut down trees,
And build a mound against Jerusalem.
This *is* the city to be punished.
She *is* full of oppression in her midst.
7 As a fountain wells up with water,
So she wells up with her wickedness.
Violence and plundering are heard in her.
Before Me continually *are* grief and wounds.
8 Be instructed, O Jerusalem,
Lest My soul depart from you;
Lest I make you desolate,
A land not inhabited."

9Thus says the LORD of hosts:

"They shall thoroughly glean as a vine the
remnant of Israel;
As a grape-gatherer, put your hand back
into the branches."

10 *To whom shall I speak and give warning,
That they may hear?
Indeed their ear *is* uncircumcised,
And they cannot give heed.
Behold, the word of the LORD is a reproach
to them;
They have no delight in it.
11 Therefore I am full of the fury of the LORD.
I am weary of holding *it* in.
"I will pour it out on the children outside,
And on the assembly of young men
together;
For even the husband shall be taken with
the wife,
The aged with *him who is* full of days.
12 And their houses shall be turned over to
others,

CHAPTER 6

6:10, 17 The watchman. The prophet saw
the invasion coming and warned the people,
but they would not listen to him (v. 10). The
delicate woman (Jerusalem) would be
ruined (v. 2); the sun was going down
(vv. 4–5); and the harvest of sin would be
reaped (v. 9).

Heart Trouble—The false prophets in Judah, like the false teachers today, dealt superficially with
the problems in society, but Jeremiah dealt with *the heart*. The word *heart* appears more than sixty
times in his prophecy, and one of his favorite phrases is "the imagination of his heart." The heart is
deceitful and wicked (Jer. 17:9), and only God can change it (Jer. 31:31–34). Honest diagnosis by a
faithful physician is the first step toward recovery, but too many people prefer the superficial
encouragement that says "Peace, peace!"

6:14 *The physician.* Jeremiah saw the sickness and wounds of the nation and pointed to God as the only source of healing (3:22). The false prophets gave a superficial diagnosis and a false remedy, which led the nation into judgment (Lam. 2:14). Beware of religious teachers who look only at the surface and never get to the heart of the problem.

6:16 *The guide.* Jeremiah saw the people wondering which way to go. The "new religions" confused them, so he called them back to God's Word. Seek "the old paths" of the Word, not to try to repeat "the good old days," but to go forward to do God's will in your day.

Fields and wives together;
For I will stretch out My hand
Against the inhabitants of the land," says
   the LORD.
13 "Because from the least of them even to the
      greatest of them,
Everyone *is* given to covetousness;
And from the prophet even to the priest,
Everyone deals falsely.
14 *They have also healed the hurt of My people
      slightly,
Saying, 'Peace, peace!'
When *there is* no peace.
15 Were they ashamed when they had
      committed abomination?
No! They were not at all ashamed;
Nor did they know how to blush.
Therefore they shall fall among those who
      fall;
At the time I punish them,
They shall be cast down," says the LORD.

16*Thus says the LORD:

"Stand in the ways and see,
And ask for the old paths, where the good
      way *is*,
And walk in it;
Then you will find rest for your souls.
But they said, 'We will not walk *in it.*'
17 Also, I set watchmen over you, *saying,*
'Listen to the sound of the trumpet!'
But they said, 'We will not listen.'
18 Therefore hear, you nations,
And know, O congregation, what *is* among
      them.
19 Hear, O earth!
Behold, I will certainly bring calamity on
      this people—
The fruit of their thoughts,
Because they have not heeded My words
Nor My law, but rejected it.
20 For what purpose to Me
Comes frankincense from Sheba,
And sweet cane from a far country?
Your burnt offerings *are* not acceptable,
Nor your sacrifices sweet to Me."

21Therefore thus says the LORD:

"Behold, I will lay stumbling blocks before
      this people,
And the fathers and the sons together shall
      fall on them.
The neighbor and his friend shall perish."

22Thus says the LORD:

"Behold, a people comes from the north
      country,
And a great nation will be raised from the
      farthest parts of the earth.
23 They will lay hold on bow and spear;
They *are* cruel and have no mercy;
Their voice roars like the sea;
And they ride on horses,
As men of war set in array against you,
   O daughter of Zion."

24 We have heard the report of it;
Our hands grow feeble.
Anguish has taken hold of us,
Pain as of a woman in labor.

25 Do not go out into the field,
   Nor walk by the way.
   Because of the sword of the enemy,
   Fear *is* on every side.
26 O daughter of my people,
   Dress in sackcloth
   And roll about in ashes!
   Make mourning *as for* an only son, most
      bitter lamentation;
   For the plunderer will suddenly come upon
      us.

27*"I have set you *as* an assayer *and* a fortress
      among My people,
   That you may know and test their way.
28 They *are* all stubborn rebels, walking as
      slanderers.
   They are bronze and iron,
   They *are* all corrupters;
29 The bellows blow fiercely,
   The lead is consumed by the fire;
   The smelter refines in vain,
   For the wicked are not drawn off.
30 *People* will call them rejected silver,
   Because the LORD has rejected them."

6:27–30 *The assayer.* Jeremiah's words were like a fire (23:29) that separated the precious metal from the dross. But the people chose to be cheap alloy instead of precious gold and silver: all God's judgments were in vain.

7 The* word that came to Jeremiah from the LORD, saying, 2"Stand in the gate of the LORD's house, and proclaim there this word, and say, 'Hear the word of the LORD, all *you of* Judah who enter in at these gates to worship the LORD!'" 3Thus says the LORD of hosts, the God of Israel: "Amend your ways and your doings, and I will cause you to dwell in this place. 4Do not trust in these lying words, saying, 'The temple of the LORD, the temple of the LORD, the temple of the LORD *are* these.'

5"For if you thoroughly amend your ways and your doings, if you thoroughly execute judgment between a man and his neighbor, 6if you do not oppress the stranger, the fatherless, and the widow, and do not shed innocent blood in this place, or walk after other gods to your hurt, 7then I will cause you to dwell in this place, in the land that I gave to your fathers forever and ever.

8"Behold, you trust in lying words that cannot profit. 9Will you steal, murder, commit adultery, swear falsely, burn incense to Baal, and walk after other gods whom you do not know, 10and *then* come and stand before Me in this house which is called by My name, and say, 'We are delivered to do all these abominations'? 11Has this house, which is called by My name, become a den of thieves in your eyes? Behold, I, even I, have seen *it*," says the LORD.

12"But go now to My place which *was* in Shiloh, where I set My name at the first, and see what I did to it because of the wickedness of My people Israel. 13And now, because you have done all these works," says the LORD, "and I spoke to you, rising up early and speaking, but you did not hear, and I called you, but you did not answer, 14therefore I will do to the house which is called by My name, in which you trust, and to this place which I gave to you and your fathers, as I have

CHAPTER 7

7:1ff God told Jeremiah to preach a sermon at the gate of the temple and tell the people that their confidence was unfounded because they were trusting the wrong things. The false prophets were saying, "Nothing can happen to Jerusalem because the temple is here" (v. 4); "We are safe because we offer sacrifices to the Lord" (v. 21); "We have the ark of God's covenant, the throne of the Lord" (3:16); and "We have the law of God" (8:8).

The temple, the sacrifices, the ark, and the Law were indeed precious things, but they could not be used to please God apart from the sincere devotion of the people to the Lord. The people were hiding their sins behind religion (vv. 8–15, 21–27). The so-called revival under King Josiah (2 Kings 22—23) was merely a surface reformation; it did not change the hearts of the people.

Never be satisfied with surface religion; be sure that God ministers to your heart and that you obey Him from the heart (Eph. 6:6). The only way to have confidence is to build on the Rock (Matt. 7:21–29), and the only way to build on the Rock is to obey what He says.

The True Source of Confidence—In what do you put your confidence? In lying words from optimistic false teachers (Jer. 7:4, 8)? In riches (Ps. 52:7)? In important people (Ps. 146:3–4; Amos 6:1)? In the intuitions of your own heart (Prov. 28:26)? In excellent equipment (Isa. 31:1)? In your own experience and expertise (Ps. 44:6)? Or in the living God (Ps. 118:8–9; Prov. 3:21–26)?

done to Shiloh. 15And I will cast you out of My sight, as I have cast out all your brethren—the whole posterity of Ephraim.

16"Therefore do not pray for this people, nor lift up a cry or prayer for them, nor make intercession to Me; for I will not hear you. 17Do you not see what they do in the cities of Judah and in the streets of Jerusalem? 18The children gather wood, the fathers kindle the fire, and the women knead dough, to make cakes for the queen of heaven; and *they* pour out drink offerings to other gods, that they may provoke Me to anger. 19Do they provoke Me to anger?" says the LORD. "*Do they* not *provoke* themselves, to the shame of their own faces?"

20Therefore thus says the Lord GOD: "Behold, My anger and My fury will be poured out on this place—on man and on beast, on the trees of the field and on the fruit of the ground. And it will burn and not be quenched."

21Thus says the LORD of hosts, the God of Israel: "Add your burnt offerings to your sacrifices and eat meat. 22For I did not speak to your fathers, or command them in the day that I brought them out of the land of Egypt, concerning burnt offerings or sacrifices. 23But this is what I commanded them, saying, 'Obey My voice, and I will be your God, and you shall be My people. And walk in all the ways that I have commanded you, that it may be well with you.' 24Yet they did not obey or incline their ear, but followed the counsels *and* the dictates of their evil hearts, and went backward and not forward. 25Since the day that your fathers came out of the land of Egypt until this day, I have even sent to you all My servants the prophets, daily rising up early and sending *them*. 26Yet they did not obey Me or incline their ear, but stiffened their neck. They did worse than their fathers.

27"Therefore you shall speak all these words to them, but they will not obey you. You shall also call to them, but they will not answer you.

28"So you shall say to them, 'This *is* a nation that does not obey the voice of the LORD their God nor receive correction. Truth has perished and has been cut off from their mouth. 29Cut off your hair and cast *it* away, and take up a lamentation on the desolate heights; for the LORD has rejected and forsaken the generation of His wrath.' 30For the children of Judah have done evil in My sight," says the LORD. "They have set their abominations in the house which is called by My name, to pollute it. 31And they have built the high places of Tophet, which *is* in the Valley of the Son of Hinnom, to burn their sons and their daughters in the fire, which I did not command, nor did it come into My heart.

32"Therefore behold, the days are coming," says the LORD, "when it will no more be called Tophet, or the Valley of the Son of Hinnom, but the Valley of Slaughter; for they will bury in Tophet until there is no room. 33The corpses of this people will be food for the birds of the heaven and for the beasts of the earth. And no one will frighten *them* away. 34Then I will cause to cease from the cities of Judah and from the streets of Jerusalem the voice of mirth and the voice of gladness, the voice of the bridegroom and the voice of the bride. For the land shall be desolate.

8 "At that time," says the LORD, "they shall bring out the bones of the kings of Judah, and

the bones of its princes, and the bones of the priests, and the bones of the prophets, and the bones of the inhabitants of Jerusalem, out of their graves. ²They shall spread them before the sun and the moon and all the host of heaven, which they have loved and which they have served and after which they have walked, which they have sought and which they have worshiped. They shall not be gathered nor buried; they shall be like refuse on the face of the earth. ³Then death shall be chosen rather than life by all the residue of those who remain of this evil family, who remain in all the places where I have driven them," says the LORD of hosts.

⁴"Moreover you shall say to them, 'Thus says the LORD:

"Will they fall and not rise?
Will one turn away and not return?
5 *Why has this people slidden back,
Jerusalem, in a perpetual backsliding?
They hold fast to deceit,
They refuse to return.
6 I listened and heard,
But they do not speak aright.
No man repented of his wickedness,
Saying, 'What have I done?'
Everyone turned to his own course,
As the horse rushes into tne battle.

7 "Even the stork in the heavens
Knows her appointed times;
And the turtledove, the swift, and the
swallow
Observe the time of their coming.
But My people do not know the judgment
of the LORD.

8 "How can you say, 'We *are* wise,
And the law of the LORD *is* with us'?
Look, the false pen of the scribe certainly
works falsehood.
9 The wise men are ashamed,
They are dismayed and taken.
Behold, they have rejected the word of the
LORD;
So what wisdom do they have?
10 Therefore I will give their wives to others,
And their fields to those who will inherit
them;
Because from the least even to the greatest
Everyone is given to covetousness;
From the prophet even to the priest
Everyone deals falsely.
11 For they have healed the hurt of the
daughter of My people slightly,
Saying, 'Peace, peace!'
When *there is* no peace.
12 Were they ashamed when they had
committed abomination?
No! They were not at all ashamed,
Nor did they know how to blush.
Therefore they shall fall among those who
fall;
In the time of their punishment
They shall be cast down," says the LORD.

13 "I will surely consume them," says the
LORD.
"No grapes *shall be* on the vine,
Nor figs on the fig tree,
And the leaf shall fade;

CHAPTER 8

8:5–12 Four times in this chapter, Jeremiah asks and answers the question, "Why?" ***Why are they backsliding?*** The answer is plain: they believe lies and will not heed the truth of God's Word. They will not admit their sins or repent of their sins. They are happy with the superficial ministry of the false prophets (v. 11) and the right it gives them to be religious and still live in sin.

8:14–17 Why are they sitting still?
Because they do not really believe the enemy is coming! They have false confidence based on lying words, so they are at peace.

8:19 Why did they provoke God? Because they believed they could serve both the Lord and their idols. They did not abandon the Lord; they just made Him one of their many gods. But the Lord will not accept equality with any other god, for He is God alone.
Just as an unfaithful husband or wife provokes a spouse, so the unfaithful child of God grieves the heart of the Lord.

8:22 Why is there no recovery? Because the people did not heed God's warning and His long-suffering reached its limit. Had they plowed their hearts (4:3), there could have been a harvest of repentance; but it was too late. The sickness was too far gone, and no medicine was available.
When God calls you to return, do not wait too long. Seek the Lord while He may be found (Isa. 55:6–7).

CHAPTER 9

9:1ff Most people want to stop their weeping, but Jeremiah wanted to weep more, so burdened was he for his people. The easiest thing for him would have been escape (Ps. 55:6–7). However, like a true shepherd, he stayed with the people and sought to minister to them.
He would not be the only one weeping, for he saw the day coming when the wailing women would lament the death of the nation (vv. 17–21). They used their tongues like bows (v. 3) to shoot the arrows of deceit (v. 8), and they went from evil to evil. Are you among those who are valiant for the truth (v. 3)? If you are, you know that the only thing to glory in is the Lord of glory (v. 24). It is not our minds, our might, or our money that wins the day (v. 23) but our faith in God and our desire to glorify Him.

And *the things* I have given them shall pass away from them." ' "

14*"Why do we sit still?
Assemble yourselves,
And let us enter the fortified cities,
And let us be silent there.
For the LORD our God has put us to silence
And given us water of gall to drink,
Because we have sinned against the LORD.

15 "*We* looked for peace, but no good *came;*
And for a time of health, and there was trouble!

16 The snorting of His horses was heard from Dan.
The whole land trembled at the sound of the neighing of His strong ones;
For they have come and devoured the land and all that is in it,
The city and those who dwell in it."

17 "For behold, I will send serpents among you,
Vipers which cannot be charmed,
And they shall bite you," says the LORD.

18 I would comfort myself in sorrow;
My heart *is* faint in me.

19 *Listen! The voice,
The cry of the daughter of my people
From a far country:
"Is not the LORD in Zion?
Is not her King in her?"

"Why have they provoked Me to anger
With their carved images—
With foreign idols?"

20 "The harvest is past,
The summer is ended,
And we are not saved!"

21 For the hurt of the daughter of my people I am hurt.
I am mourning;
Astonishment has taken hold of me.

22 *Is there* no balm in Gilead,
Is there no physician there?
Why then is there no recovery
For the health of the daughter of my people?

9 Oh,* that my head were waters,
And my eyes a fountain of tears,
That I might weep day and night
For the slain of the daughter of my people!

2 Oh, that I had in the wilderness
A lodging place for travelers;
That I might leave my people,
And go from them!
For they *are* all adulterers,
An assembly of treacherous men.

3 "And *like* their bow they have bent their tongues *for* lies.
They are not valiant for the truth on the earth.

Pilgrim's Progress—Life never stands still and Judah was going "from evil to evil" (Jer. 9:3). Those who know Jesus Christ can go "from faith to faith" (Rom. 1:17), "from strength to strength" (Ps. 84:7), and "from glory to glory" (2 Cor. 3:18). That is the kind of progress God's pilgrims should make!

For they proceed from evil to evil,
And they do not know Me," says the LORD.
4 "Everyone take heed to his neighbor,
And do not trust any brother;
For every brother will utterly supplant,
And every neighbor will walk with
    slanderers.
5 Everyone will deceive his neighbor,
And will not speak the truth;
They have taught their tongue to speak lies;
They weary themselves to commit iniquity.
6 Your dwelling place *is* in the midst of deceit;
Through deceit they refuse to know Me,"
    says the LORD.

7Therefore thus says the LORD of hosts:

"Behold, I will refine them and try them;
For how shall I deal with the daughter of
    My people?
8 Their tongue *is* an arrow shot out;
It speaks deceit;
One speaks peaceably to his neighbor with
    his mouth,
But in his heart he lies in wait.
9 Shall I not punish them for these *things*?"
    says the LORD.
"Shall I not avenge Myself on such a nation
    as this?"

10 I will take up a weeping and wailing for the
    mountains,
And for the dwelling places of the
    wilderness a lamentation,
Because they are burned up,
So that no one can pass through;
Nor can *men* hear the voice of the cattle.
Both the birds of the heavens and the beasts
    have fled;
They are gone.

11 "I will make Jerusalem a heap of ruins, a den
    of jackals.
I will make the cities of Judah desolate,
    without an inhabitant."

12Who *is* the wise man who may understand
this? And *who is he* to whom the mouth of the
LORD has spoken, that he may declare it? Why
does the land perish *and* burn up like a wilderness, so that no one can pass through?
13And the LORD said, "Because they have forsaken My law which I set before them, and have
not obeyed My voice, nor walked according to it,
14but they have walked according to the dictates
of their own hearts and after the Baals, which
their fathers taught them," 15therefore thus says
the LORD of hosts, the God of Israel: "Behold, I
will feed them, this people, with wormwood, and
give them water of gall to drink. 16I will scatter
them also among the Gentiles, whom neither they
nor their fathers have known. And I will send a
sword after them until I have consumed them."
17Thus says the LORD of hosts:

"Consider and call for the mourning women,
That they may come;
And send for skillful wailing women,
That they may come.
18 Let them make haste
And take up a wailing for us,
That our eyes may run with tears,

And our eyelids gush with water.
19 For a voice of wailing is heard from Zion:
    'How we are plundered!
    We are greatly ashamed,
    Because we have forsaken the land,
    Because we have been cast out of our
        dwellings.' "

20 Yet hear the word of the LORD, O women,
    And let your ear receive the word of His
        mouth;
    Teach your daughters wailing,
    And everyone her neighbor a lamentation.
21 For death has come through our windows,
    Has entered our palaces,
    To kill off the children—*no longer to be*
        outside!
    And the young men—*no longer* on the
        streets!

22 Speak, "Thus says the LORD:

    'Even the carcasses of men shall fall as
        refuse on the open field,
    Like cuttings after the harvester,
    And no one shall gather *them*.' "

23Thus says the LORD:

    "Let not the wise *man* glory in his wisdom,
    Let not the mighty *man* glory in his might,
    Nor let the rich *man* glory in his riches;
24 But let him who glories glory in this,
    That he understands and knows Me,
    That I *am* the LORD, exercising
        lovingkindness, judgment, and
        righteousness in the earth.
    For in these I delight," says the LORD.

25"Behold, the days are coming," says the LORD,
"that I will punish all *who are* circumcised with
the uncircumcised— 26Egypt, Judah, Edom, the
people of Ammon, Moab, and all *who are* in the
farthest corners, who dwell in the wilderness. For
all *these* nations *are* uncircumcised, and all the
house of Israel *are* uncircumcised in the heart."

CHAPTER 10

10:1ff Jeremiah spoke to both Israel
(already in exile) and Judah and reminded
them that they belonged to the true God,
the living God, the everlasting King (v. 10)
about whom they could say, "There is none
like You" (vv. 6–7). He is the Creator of
everything (vv. 11–13).
Then why should they fear the idols of
the nations or seek their help? The idols
have no breath, so they are dead. They
cannot speak. They must be propped up or
carried because they have no strength. (See
Ps. 115; Isa. 40:18–20.) They are indeed
futile!
Today's idols are much more subtle, but
they are just as worthless when it comes
to a life that is real: money and the things
money can buy, position, authority, fame,
and so forth. When we trust and serve
anything other than God, we practice
idolatry.
We have been told, "Little children, keep
yourselves from idols" (1 John 5:21).

10 Hear* the word which the LORD speaks to
    you, O house of Israel.
2Thus says the LORD:

    "Do not learn the way of the Gentiles;
    Do not be dismayed at the signs of heaven,
    For the Gentiles are dismayed at them.
3   For the customs of the peoples *are* futile;
    For *one* cuts a tree from the forest,
    The work of the hands of the workman, with
        the ax.
4   They decorate it with silver and gold;
    They fasten it with nails and hammers
    So that it will not topple.
5   They *are* upright, like a palm tree,
    And they cannot speak;
    They must be carried,
    Because they cannot go *by themselves*.
    Do not be afraid of them,
    For they cannot do evil,
    Nor can they do any good."

6   Inasmuch as *there is* none like You, O LORD
    (You *are* great, and Your name *is* great in
        might),

7 Who would not fear You, O King of the
       nations?
    For this is Your rightful due.
    For among all the wise *men* of the nations,
    And in all their kingdoms,
    There is none like You.
8 But they are altogether dull-hearted and
       foolish;
    A wooden idol *is* a worthless doctrine.
9 Silver is beaten into plates;
    It is brought from Tarshish,
    And gold from Uphaz,
    The work of the craftsman
    And of the hands of the metalsmith;
    Blue and purple *are* their clothing;
    They *are* all the work of skillful *men*.
10 But the LORD *is* the true God;
    He *is* the living God and the everlasting
       King.
    At His wrath the earth will tremble,
    And the nations will not be able to endure
       His indignation.

11Thus you shall say to them: "The gods that
have not made the heavens and the earth shall
perish from the earth and from under these heavens."

12 He has made the earth by His power,
    He has established the world by His
       wisdom,
    And has stretched out the heavens at His
       discretion.
13 When He utters His voice,
    There is a multitude of waters in the
       heavens:
    "And He causes the vapors to ascend from
       the ends of the earth.
    He makes lightning for the rain,
    He brings the wind out of His treasuries."e
14 Everyone is dull-hearted, without
       knowledge;
    Every metalsmith is put to shame by an
       image;
    For his molded image *is* falsehood,
    And *there is* no breath in them.
15 They *are* futile, a work of errors;
    In the time of their punishment they shall
       perish.
16 The Portion of Jacob *is* not like them,
    For He *is* the Maker of all *things,*
    And Israel *is* the tribe of His inheritance;
    The LORD of hosts *is* His name.
17 Gather up your wares from the land,
    O inhabitant of the fortress!

18For thus says the LORD:

    "Behold, I will throw out at this time
    The inhabitants of the land,
    And will distress them,
    That they may find *it so.*"

19 Woe is me for my hurt!
    My wound is severe.
    But I say, "Truly this *is* an infirmity,
    And I must bear it."
20 My tent is plundered,

10:13 ePsalm 135:7

And all my cords are broken;
My children have gone from me,
And they *are* no more.
There is no one to pitch my tent anymore,
Or set up my curtains.

21 For the shepherds have become
    dull-hearted,
And have not sought the LORD;
Therefore they shall not prosper,
And all their flocks shall be scattered.
22 Behold, the noise of the report has come,
And a great commotion out of the north
    country,
To make the cities of Judah desolate, a den
    of jackals.

23 O LORD, I know the way of man *is* not in
    himself;
It is not in man who walks to direct his own
    steps.
24 O LORD, correct me, but with justice;
Not in Your anger, lest You bring me to
    nothing.
25 Pour out Your fury on the Gentiles, who do
    not know You,
And on the families who do not call on Your
    name;
For they have eaten up Jacob,
Devoured him and consumed him,
And made his dwelling place desolate.

CHAPTER 11

11:1–5 Deliverance. Jehovah repeatedly reminded His people of their deliverance from Egypt and the covenant He made with them at Sinai. He reminded them of His grace in giving them the Promised Land. Why turn to idols when all their blessings came from the Lord?

11:6–8 Disobedience. Israel accepted the covenant (Exod. 19:8) but then disobeyed the law of God. The new generation accepted the covenant as found in Deuteronomy, entered the land, and eventually turned to idols.

11:9–17 Disaster. The Babylonians would come, capture the nation, and destroy Jerusalem and the temple. God *would not* defend His people and their false gods *could not,* and He would not even answer the prayers of His servant.

11 The* word that came to Jeremiah from the LORD, saying, 2"Hear the words of this covenant, and speak to the men of Judah and to the inhabitants of Jerusalem; 3and say to them, 'Thus says the LORD God of Israel: "Cursed *is* the man who does not obey the words of this covenant 4which I commanded your fathers in the day I brought them out of the land of Egypt, from the iron furnace, saying, 'Obey My voice, and do according to all that I command you; so shall you be My people, and I will be your God,' 5that I may establish the oath which I have sworn to your fathers, to give them 'a land flowing with milk and honey,'*f* as *it is* this day." ' "
And I answered and said, "So be it, LORD."
6*Then the LORD said to me, "Proclaim all these words in the cities of Judah and in the streets of Jerusalem, saying: 'Hear the words of this covenant and do them. 7For I earnestly exhorted your fathers in the day I brought them up out of the land of Egypt, until this day, rising early and exhorting, saying, "Obey My voice." 8Yet they did not obey or incline their ear, but everyone followed the dictates of his evil heart; therefore I will bring upon them all the words of this covenant, which I commanded *them* to do, but *which* they have not done.' "
9*And the LORD said to me, "A conspiracy has been found among the men of Judah and among the inhabitants of Jerusalem. 10They have turned back to the iniquities of their forefathers who refused to hear My words, and they have gone after

---

11:5 *f*Exodus 3:8

Docile Lambs—Both Jeremiah and Jesus were like sheep led to the slaughter (Jer. 11:19; Isa. 53:7). They did not fight back but committed themselves to God and trusted Him to work (1 Pet. 2:18–24).

other gods to serve them; the house of Israel and the house of Judah have broken My covenant which I made with their fathers."

11Therefore thus says the LORD: "Behold, I will surely bring calamity on them which they will not be able to escape; and though they cry out to Me, I will not listen to them. 12Then the cities of Judah and the inhabitants of Jerusalem will go and cry out to the gods to whom they offer incense, but they will not save them at all in the time of their trouble. 13For *according to* the number of your cities were your gods, O Judah; and *according to* the number of the streets of Jerusalem you have set up altars to *that* shameful thing, altars to burn incense to Baal.

14"So do not pray for this people, or lift up a cry or prayer for them; for I will not hear *them* in the time that they cry out to Me because of their trouble.

15 "What has My beloved to do in My house,
Having done lewd deeds with many?
And the holy flesh has passed from you.
When you do evil, then you rejoice.
16 The LORD called your name,
Green Olive Tree, Lovely *and* of Good Fruit.
With the noise of a great tumult
He has kindled fire on it,
And its branches are broken.

17"For the LORD of hosts, who planted you, has pronounced doom against you for the evil of the house of Israel and of the house of Judah, which they have done against themselves to provoke Me to anger in offering incense to Baal."

18*Now the LORD gave me knowledge *of it*, and I know *it;* for You showed me their doings. 19But I *was* like a docile lamb brought to the slaughter; and I did not know that they had devised schemes against me, *saying*, "Let us destroy the tree with its fruit, and let us cut him off from the land of the living, that his name may be remembered no more."

20 But, O LORD of hosts,
You who judge righteously,
Testing the mind and the heart,
Let me see Your vengeance on them,
For to You I have revealed my cause.

21"Therefore thus says the LORD concerning the men of Anathoth who seek your life, saying, 'Do not prophesy in the name of the LORD, lest you die by our hand'— 22therefore thus says the LORD of hosts: 'Behold, I will punish them. The young men shall die by the sword, their sons and their daughters shall die by famine; 23and there shall be no remnant of them, for I will bring catastrophe on the men of Anathoth, *even* the year of their punishment.'"

12 Righteous* *are* You, O LORD, when I plead with You;
Yet let me talk with You about *Your* judgments.
Why does the way of the wicked prosper?
Why are those happy who deal so treacherously?
2 You have planted them, yes, they have taken root;
They grow, yes, they bear fruit.

11:18–23 *Defense.* The prophet's own friends and relatives tried to silence him and then slay him, but God defended His servant. Jeremiah took his life in his hands when he preached, but nothing stopped him. He was bold before men because he was broken before God.

CHAPTER 12

12:1–4 *Perplexity.* "Why do the wicked prosper?" is asked not only by Jeremiah, Job (21:7), and Asaph (Ps. 73), but also by many believers who suffer because of their faithfulness to God. The wicked treated Jeremiah like a sacrificial lamb (11:19), but he wanted God to slaughter them (v. 3)! Would that have solved the problem?

❝His *promises are checks to be cashed, not mere mottoes to hang on the wall.*❞

—Vance Havner

You *are* near in their mouth
But far from their mind.

3   But You, O LORD, know me;
You have seen me,
And You have tested my heart toward You.
Pull them out like sheep for the slaughter,
And prepare them for the day of slaughter.
4   How long will the land mourn,
And the herbs of every field wither?
The beasts and birds are consumed,
For the wickedness of those who dwell
there,
Because they said, "He will not see our final
end."

5   *"If you have run with the footmen, and they
have wearied you,
Then how can you contend with horses?
And *if* in the land of peace,
In which you trusted, *they wearied you,*
Then how will you do in the floodplain^g of
the Jordan?
6   For even your brothers, the house of your
father,
Even they have dealt treacherously with
you;
Yes, they have called a multitude after you.
Do not believe them,
Even though they speak smooth words to
you.

7   *"I have forsaken My house, I have left My
heritage;
I have given the dearly beloved of My soul
into the hand of her enemies.
8   My heritage is to Me like a lion in the forest;
It cries out against Me;
Therefore I have hated it.
9   My heritage *is* to Me *like* a speckled vulture;
The vultures all around *are* against her.
Come, assemble all the beasts of the field,
Bring them to devour!

10 "Many rulers^h have destroyed My vineyard,
They have trodden My portion underfoot,
They have made My pleasant portion a
desolate wilderness.
11 They have made it desolate;
Desolate, it mourns to Me;
The whole land is made desolate,
Because no one takes *it* to heart.
12 The plunderers have come
On all the desolate heights in the
wilderness,
For the sword of the LORD shall devour
From *one* end of the land to the *other* end
of the land;
No flesh shall have peace.
13 They have sown wheat but reaped thorns;
They have put themselves to pain *but* do
not profit.
But be ashamed of your harvest
Because of the fierce anger of the LORD."

14 *Thus says the LORD: "Against all My evil
neighbors who touch the inheritance which I have
caused My people Israel to inherit—behold, I will
pluck them out of their land and pluck out the

12:5, 6 *Perspective.* God's answer helped to prepare His servant for the trials ahead. Serving God is a blessed privilege, but it is also a difficult task; *and it gets more and more difficult.* Jeremiah would go from racing with men to racing with horses, from a land of peace to the thickets of the Jordan. This is the only way we can mature in life and service.

12:7–13 *Plunder.* The people depended on the temple (7:4), but God had forsaken it. The enemy was about to come like vultures eating a corpse (v. 9) or strangers tramping down a vineyard or a garden (vv. 10–13).

12:14–17 *Promise.* God chastens, but His compassions do not fail (Lam. 3:22–24). He promised to judge the invading nations and one day free Judah from her exile and bring her back to her land, and He kept His promise.
The prophet asked for *explanations,* but God met his need by giving him *promises.* When you cannot explain God's ways, you can still trust His promises.

12:5 ^{g}Or *thicket*   12:10 ^{h}Literally *shepherds* or *pastors*

house of Judah from among them. 15Then it shall be, after I have plucked them out, that I will return and have compassion on them and bring them back, everyone to his heritage and everyone to his land. 16And it shall be, if they will learn carefully the ways of My people, to swear by My name, 'As the LORD lives,' as they taught My people to swear by Baal, then they shall be established in the midst of My people. 17But if they do not obey, I will utterly pluck up and destroy that nation," says the LORD.

13 Thus* the LORD said to me: "Go and get yourself a linen sash, and put it around your waist, but do not put it in water." 2So I got a sash according to the word of the LORD, and put *it* around my waist.

3And the word of the LORD came to me the second time, saying, 4"Take the sash that you acquired, which *is* around your waist, and arise, go to the Euphrates,ⁱ and hide it there in a hole in the rock." 5So I went and hid it by the Euphrates, as the LORD commanded me.

6Now it came to pass after many days that the LORD said to me, "Arise, go to the Euphrates, and take from there the sash which I commanded you to hide there." 7Then I went to the Euphrates and dug, and I took the sash from the place where I had hidden it; and there was the sash, ruined. It was profitable for nothing.

8Then the word of the LORD came to me, saying, 9"Thus says the LORD: 'In this manner I will ruin the pride of Judah and the great pride of Jerusalem. 10This evil people, who refuse to hear My words, who follow the dictates of their hearts, and walk after other gods to serve them and worship them, shall be just like this sash which is profitable for nothing. 11For as the sash clings to the waist of a man, so I have caused the whole house of Israel and the whole house of Judah to cling to Me,' says the LORD, 'that they may become My people, for renown, for praise, and for glory; but they would not hear.'

12*"Therefore you shall speak to them this word: 'Thus says the LORD God of Israel: "Every bottle shall be filled with wine." '

"And they will say to you, 'Do we not certainly know that every bottle will be filled with wine?' 13"Then you shall say to them, 'Thus says the LORD: "Behold, I will fill all the inhabitants of this land—even the kings who sit on David's throne, the priests, the prophets, and all the inhabitants of Jerusalem—with drunkenness! 14And I will dash them one against another, even the fathers and the sons together," says the LORD. "I will not pity nor spare nor have mercy, but will destroy them." ' "

15 *Hear and give ear:
      Do not be proud,
      For the LORD has spoken.
16   Give glory to the LORD your God
      Before He causes darkness,
      And before your feet stumble
      On the dark mountains,
      And while you are looking for light,
      He turns it into the shadow of death
      And makes *it* dense darkness.
17   But if you will not hear it,

CHAPTER 13

13:1–11 Jeremiah sometimes preached object lesson sermons, parables in action using familiar things. Like our Lord's parables, they got the attention of the people and awakened the interest of the indifferent.

The sash was probably part of the priestly garments, which would make it especially holy. As long as the people clung to God in humble obedience, He was glorified. When they defiled themselves in pride, they became ruined and useless like the sash under the rock. Too proud to repent, Judah ended up in the darkness (vv. 15–17).

13:12–14 The bottles represented the leaders and the people who were all empty of spiritual life. God would fill them with drunkenness, which symbolizes judgment (25:15–25). Then He would smash the bottles and show no pity.

13:15–22 The flock is a familiar picture of God's people (Ps. 100:3). Their leaders were to be like loving shepherds; instead, they were selfish hirelings. The sheep would be taken to slaughter by the invaders.

My soul will weep in secret for *your* pride;
My eyes will weep bitterly
And run down with tears,
Because the LORD's flock has been taken
   captive.

18 Say to the king and to the queen mother,
"Humble yourselves;
Sit down,
For your rule shall collapse, the crown of
   your glory."
19 The cities of the South shall be shut up,
And no one shall open *them;*
Judah shall be carried away captive, all of
   it;
It shall be wholly carried away captive.

20 Lift up your eyes and see
Those who come from the north.
Where *is* the flock *that* was given to you,
Your beautiful sheep?
21 What will you say when He punishes you?
For you have taught them
To be chieftains, to be head over you.
Will not pangs seize you,
Like a woman in labor?
22 And if you say in your heart,
"Why have these things come upon me?"
For the greatness of your iniquity
Your skirts have been uncovered,
Your heels made bare.
23 *Can the Ethiopian change his skin or the
   leopard its spots?
Then may you also do good who are
   accustomed to do evil.

24 "Therefore I will scatter them like stubble
That passes away by the wind of the
   wilderness.
25 This is your lot,
The portion of your measures from Me,"
   says the LORD,
"Because you have forgotten Me
And trusted in falsehood.
26 Therefore I will uncover your skirts over
   your face,
That your shame may appear.
27 I have seen your adulteries
And your *lustful* neighings,
The lewdness of your harlotry,
Your abominations on the hills in the fields.
Woe to you, O Jerusalem!
Will you still not be made clean?"

13:23 *The Ethiopian and the leopard* were
reminders that Judah's sin was deeper than
the skin and could not easily be removed
by some superficial means. Disobedience
was such a habit with the people that it was
part of their very nature.
Useless, broken, and slaughtered
because of sin too deep to be removed:
those are the sad consequences of pride
and disobedience.

CHAPTER 14

14:1–6 *No hope.* God sent a drought to
Judah to bring His people to repentance,
but the chastening did no good. The people
mourned for the land but not for their sins.
They were sorry for their plight but not for
their evil ways.

> **❝**Now may the God of hope fill
> you with all joy and peace in
> believing, that you may abound in
> hope by the power of the Holy
> Spirit.**❞**
> —Paul (Rom. 15:13)

14 The* word of the LORD that came to Jeremiah concerning the droughts.

2 "Judah mourns,
And her gates languish;
They mourn for the land,
And the cry of Jerusalem has gone up.
3 Their nobles have sent their lads for water;
They went to the cisterns *and* found no
   water.
They returned with their vessels empty;
They were ashamed and confounded
And covered their heads.
4 Because the ground is parched,
For there was no rain in the land,
The plowmen were ashamed;
They covered their heads.
5 Yes, the deer also gave birth in the field,

But left because there was no grass.
6   And the wild donkeys stood in the desolate
        heights;
    They sniffed at the wind like jackals;
    Their eyes failed because *there was* no
        grass."

7   *O Lord, though our iniquities testify against
        us,
    Do it for Your name's sake;
    For our backslidings are many,
    We have sinned against You.
8   O the Hope of Israel, his Savior in time of
        trouble,
    Why should You be like a stranger in the
        land,
    And like a traveler *who* turns aside to tarry
        for a night?
9   Why should You be like a man astonished,
    Like a mighty one *who* cannot save?
    Yet You, O Lord, *are* in our midst,
    And we are called by Your name;
    Do not leave us!

10*Thus says the Lord to this people:

    "Thus they have loved to wander;
    They have not restrained their feet.
    Therefore the Lord does not accept them;
    He will remember their iniquity now,
    And punish their sins."

11Then the Lord said to me, "Do not pray for
this people, for *their* good. 12When they fast, I
will not hear their cry; and when they offer burnt
offering and grain offering, I will not accept them.
But I will consume them by the sword, by the famine, and by the pestilence."
13Then I said, "Ah, Lord God! Behold, the
prophets say to them, 'You shall not see the
sword, nor shall you have famine, but I will give
you assured peace in this place.'"
14And the Lord said to me, "The prophets
prophesy lies in My name. I have not sent them,
commanded them, nor spoken to them; they
prophesy to you a false vision, divination, a
worthless thing, and the deceit of their heart.
15Therefore thus says the Lord concerning the
prophets who prophesy in My name, whom I did
not send, and who say, 'Sword and famine shall
not be in this land'—'By sword and famine those
prophets shall be consumed! 16And the people to
whom they prophesy shall be cast out in the
streets of Jerusalem because of the famine and
the sword; they will have no one to bury them—
them nor their wives, their sons nor their daughters—for I will pour their wickedness on them.'
17"Therefore you shall say this word to them:

    'Let my eyes flow with tears night and
        day,
    And let them not cease;
    For the virgin daughter of my people
    Has been broken with a mighty stroke, with
        a very severe blow.
18   If I go out to the field,
    Then behold, those slain with the sword!
    And if I enter the city,
    Then behold, those sick from famine!
    Yes, both prophet and priest go about in a
        land they do not know.'"

14:7–9 Hope. Their only hope was in the
Lord, but He would not do anything for them
as long as they refused to return to Him.
Instead of being King in residence, God was
a tourist passing through the land and a
warrior unable to help. If God is not with
us, everything will be against us.

14:10–22 False hope. Their religious
activities could not save them because their
hearts were far from God. The messages
of the false prophets gave the people only
a false hope for peace and healing that
never came (v. 19). They prayed to the idols,
but the idols could not send rain.
    Sometimes all you can do when God is
a stranger in the land is to imitate Jeremiah
and get alone and weep. Wait on the Lord
with a broken heart (vv. 17, 22).

19 Have You utterly rejected Judah?
    Has Your soul loathed Zion?
    Why have You stricken us so that *there is*
       no healing for us?
    We looked for peace, but *there was* no good;
    And for the time of healing, and there was
       trouble.
20 We acknowledge, O LORD, our wickedness
    And the iniquity of our fathers,
    For we have sinned against You.
21 Do not abhor *us,* for Your name's sake;
    Do not disgrace the throne of Your glory.
    Remember, do not break Your covenant
       with us.
22 Are there any among the idols of the nations
       that can cause rain?
    Or can the heavens give showers?
    Are You not He, O LORD our God?
    Therefore we will wait for You,
    Since You have made all these.

15 Then* the LORD said to me, "*Even* if Moses and Samuel stood before Me, My mind *would* not *be* favorable toward this people. Cast *them* out of My sight, and let them go forth. 2And it shall be, if they say to you, 'Where should we go?' then you shall tell them, 'Thus says the LORD:

"Such as *are* for death, to death;
And such as *are* for the sword, to the sword;
And such as *are* for the famine, to the
   famine;
And such as *are* for the captivity, to the
   captivity." '

3"And I will appoint over them four forms *of destruction,*" says the LORD: "the sword to slay, the dogs to drag, the birds of the heavens and the beasts of the earth to devour and destroy. 4I will hand them over to trouble, to all kingdoms of the earth, because of Manasseh the son of Hezekiah, king of Judah, for what he did in Jerusalem.

5 "For who will have pity on you, O Jerusalem?
    Or who will bemoan you?
    Or who will turn aside to ask how you are
       doing?
6 You have forsaken Me," says the LORD,
    "You have gone backward.
    Therefore I will stretch out My hand against
       you and destroy you;
    I am weary of relenting!
7 And I will winnow them with a winnowing
       fan in the gates of the land;
    I will bereave *them* of children;
    I will destroy My people,
    Since they do not return from their ways.
8 Their widows will be increased to Me more
       than the sand of the seas;
    I will bring against them,
    Against the mother of the young men,
    A plunderer at noonday;
    I will cause anguish and terror to fall on
       them suddenly.

9 "She languishes who has borne seven;
    She has breathed her last;
    Her sun has gone down
    While *it was* yet day;
    She has been ashamed and confounded.

CHAPTER 15

15:1–9 The chapter presents Jeremiah in several different roles in his spiritual ministry.

The mourner. Jeremiah did not rejoice that the people were facing either captivity or death. He was a man with a broken heart. He knew that the nation deserved their fate, but it pained him just the same. Jesus felt that pain when He wept over Jerusalem in His day (Luke 19:41–44). Does the wickedness of today's world break your heart?

●●*To be a true minister to men is always to accept new happiness and new distress, both of them forever deepening and entering into closer and more inseparable union with each other the more profound and spiritual the ministry becomes. The man who gives himself to other men can never be a wholly sad man; but no more can he be a man of unclouded gladness.*●●

—Phillips Brooks

And the remnant of them I will deliver to
    the sword
Before their enemies," says the LORD.

10 *Woe is me, my mother,
    That you have borne me,
    A man of strife and a man of contention to
      the whole earth!
    I have neither lent for interest,
    Nor have men lent to me for interest.
    Every one of them curses me.

11The LORD said:

"Surely it will be well with your remnant;
    Surely I will cause the enemy to intercede
      with you
    In the time of adversity and in the time of
      affliction.
12 Can anyone break iron,
    The northern iron and the bronze?
13 Your wealth and your treasures
    I will give as plunder without price,
    Because of all your sins,
    Throughout your territories.
14 And I will make *you* cross over with/ your
      enemies
    Into a land *which* you do not know;
    For a fire is kindled in My anger,
    Which shall burn upon you."

15 *O LORD, You know;
    Remember me and visit me,
    And take vengeance for me on my
      persecutors.
    In Your enduring patience, do not take me
      away.
    Know that for Your sake I have suffered
      rebuke.
16 Your words were found, and I ate them,
    And Your word was to me the joy and
      rejoicing of my heart;
    For I am called by Your name,
    O LORD God of hosts.
17 I did not sit in the assembly of the mockers,
    Nor did I rejoice;
    I sat alone because of Your hand,
    For You have filled me with indignation.
18 Why is my pain perpetual
    And my wound incurable,
    Which refuses to be healed?
    Will You surely be to me like an unreliable
      stream,
    As waters *that* fail?

19*Therefore thus says the LORD:

"If you return,
    Then I will bring you back;
    You shall stand before Me;
    If you take out the precious from the vile,
    You shall be as My mouth.
    Let them return to you,
    But you must not return to them.
20 And I will make you to this people a fortified
      bronze wall;
    And they will fight against you,
    But they shall not prevail against you;

15:10 *The troublemaker.* Jeremiah did not preach "smooth words" as the false prophets did (12:6), and his messages made people curse him. Sometimes you must cause problems before you can solve problems.

15:15–18 *The sufferer.* The prophet experienced the loneliness of leadership and the anguish of ministry, but God encouraged him as he fed on the Word. God may not take away the pain in your heart, but He can balance it with His joy.

15:19–21 *The separator.* The prophet had to be careful to preach only the true Word of God and not mix it with lies as the false prophets did. As a wall, he brought division; but God would defend him from the attacks of the people. God did not keep him out of the battle, but He did bring Jeremiah through.

15:14 /Following Masoretic Text and Vulgate; Septuagint,
Syriac, and Targum read *cause you to serve* (compare 17:4).

For I *am* with you to save you
And deliver you," says the LORD.
21 "I will deliver you from the hand of the
  wicked,
And I will redeem you from the grip of the
  terrible."

CHAPTER 16

16:2 God gave His servant four prohibitions. ***Do not take a wife.*** A godly wife can be a great encouragement to a minister, but Jeremiah had to serve alone. His singleness was a witness to the nation that homes would be destroyed. (See 1 Cor. 7:25–33.)

16:5 *Do not mourn.* People were dying because of the drought, but Jeremiah was not to join in mourning. Why? Because the dead were better off than those who would perish in the siege. The prophet was a living witness that God's comfort was taken from His people.

16:8 *Do not celebrate.* There were weddings as well as funerals, but what joy could they bring knowing that death was imminent? When people asked Jeremiah about his strange behavior, he would have opportunity to declare the Word of God.

16:14, 15 *Do not look back.* He ended with a message of hope: the future restoration of the nation will be greater than the exodus from Egypt. In the discouraging hours of life, God is working out His purposes, so take refuge in Him.

16 The word of the LORD also came to me, saying, 2*"You shall not take a wife, nor shall you have sons or daughters in this place." 3For thus says the LORD concerning the sons and daughters who are born in this place, and concerning their mothers who bore them and their fathers who begot them in this land: 4"They shall die gruesome deaths; they shall not be lamented nor shall they be buried, *but* they shall be like refuse on the face of the earth. They shall be consumed by the sword and by famine, and their corpses shall be meat for the birds of heaven and for the beasts of the earth."

5*For thus says the LORD: "Do not enter the house of mourning, nor go to lament or bemoan them; for I have taken away My peace from this people," says the LORD, "lovingkindness and mercies. 6Both the great and the small shall die in this land. They shall not be buried; neither shall men lament for them, cut themselves, nor make themselves bald for them. 7Nor shall *men* break *bread* in mourning for them, to comfort them for the dead; nor shall *men* give them the cup of consolation to drink for their father or their mother. 8*Also you shall not go into the house of feasting to sit with them, to eat and drink."

9For thus says the LORD of hosts, the God of Israel: "Behold, I will cause to cease from this place, before your eyes and in your days, the voice of mirth and the voice of gladness, the voice of the bridegroom and the voice of the bride.

10"And it shall be, when you show this people all these words, and they say to you, 'Why has the LORD pronounced all this great disaster against us? Or what *is* our iniquity? Or what *is* our sin that we have committed against the LORD our God?' 11then you shall say to them, 'Because your fathers have forsaken Me,' says the LORD; 'they have walked after other gods and have served them and worshiped them, and have forsaken Me and not kept My law. 12And you have done worse than your fathers, for behold, each one follows the dictates of his own evil heart, so that no one listens to Me. 13Therefore I will cast you out of this land into a land that you do not know, neither you nor your fathers; and there you shall serve other gods day and night, where I will not show you favor.'

14*"Therefore behold, the days are coming," says the LORD, "that it shall no more be said, 'The LORD lives who brought up the children of Israel from the land of Egypt,' 15but, 'The LORD lives who brought up the children of Israel from the land of the north and from all the lands where He had driven them.' For I will bring them back into their land which I gave to their fathers.

16"Behold, I will send for many fishermen," says the LORD, "and they shall fish them; and afterward I will send for many hunters, and they shall hunt them from every mountain and every hill, and out of the holes of the rocks. 17For My eyes *are* on all their ways; they are not hidden from My face, nor is their iniquity hidden from My eyes. 18And first I will repay double for their iniquity and their sin, because they have defiled

My land; they have filled My inheritance with the carcasses of their detestable and abominable idols."

19   O Lord, my strength and my fortress,
      My refuge in the day of affliction,
      The Gentiles shall come to You
      From the ends of the earth and say,
      "Surely our fathers have inherited lies,
      Worthlessness and unprofitable *things*."
20   Will a man make gods for himself,
      Which *are* not gods?

21   "Therefore behold, I will this once cause
              them to know,
      I will cause them to know
      My hand and My might;
      And they shall know that My name *is* the
              Lord.

17 "The* sin of Judah *is* written with a pen of
              iron;
      With the point of a diamond *it is* engraved
      On the tablet of their heart,
      And on the horns of your altars,
2   While their children remember
      Their altars and their wooden images^k
      By the green trees on the high hills.
3   O My mountain in the field,
      I will give as plunder your wealth, all your
              treasures,
      And your high places of sin within all your
              borders.
4   And you, even yourself,
      Shall let go of your heritage which I gave
              you;
      And I will cause you to serve your enemies
      In the land which you do not know;
      For you have kindled a fire in My anger
      which shall burn forever."

5*Thus says the Lord:

      "Cursed *is* the man who trusts in man
      And makes flesh his strength,
      Whose heart departs from the Lord.
6   For he shall be like a shrub in the desert,
      And shall not see when good comes,
      But shall inhabit the parched places in the
              wilderness,
      In a salt land *which is* not inhabited.

7   "Blessed *is* the man who trusts in the Lord,
      And whose hope is the Lord.
8   For he shall be like a tree planted by the
              waters,
      Which spreads out its roots by the river,
      And will not fear^l when heat comes;
      But its leaf will be green,
      And will not be anxious in the year of
              drought,
      Nor will cease from yielding fruit.

17:2 ^kHebrew *Asherim,* Canaanite deities   17:8 ^lQere and Targum read *see.*

CHAPTER 17

17:1 *The engraver.* When we sin, we write it on our hearts, and only God can erase it when we repent and trust Him. He writes His Word on our hearts so we will get victory over sin (Ps. 119:11; 2 Cor. 3:1–3). The altar was to be a place of remitting sin, not recording sin; but their sins were engraved even there.

17:5–8 *The farmer.* Faith in the Lord makes you a deeply rooted tree that survives the drought. Faith in man makes you a shrub in the desert.

Where Are You Written?—Those who will not trust the Lord have neither salvation nor security and are "written in the earth" (Jer. 17:13). Those who trust the Lord are written in heaven (Luke 10:20) in the Lamb's Book of Life (Rev. 21:27). When our Lord wrote on the ground (John 8:6, 8), was He perhaps referring to Jeremiah 17:13?

17:9, 10 *The doctor.* The heart is "sick," and only the Great Physician can diagnose its problems and bring the necessary healing. Think of Jeremiah 17:9 the next time you say, "If I know my own heart!" You may be surprised what God sees there!

17:12–18 *The worshiper.* The throne of Judah had decayed, but because the prophet saw God's glorious throne on high, he had hope. God's throne room is our sanctuary, and He welcomes us to come to get the help we need.

9 *"The heart *is* deceitful above all *things,*
  And desperately wicked;
  Who can know it?
10 I, the LORD, search the heart,
  I test the mind,
  Even to give every man according to his
      ways,
  According to the fruit of his doings.

11 "As a partridge that broods but does not
      hatch,
  So is he who gets riches, but not by right;
  It will leave him in the midst of his days,
  And at his end he will be a fool."

12 *A glorious high throne from the beginning
  Is the place of our sanctuary.
13 O LORD, the hope of Israel,
  All who forsake You shall be ashamed.

  "Those who depart from Me
  Shall be written in the earth,
  Because they have forsaken the LORD,
  The fountain of living waters."

14 Heal me, O LORD, and I shall be healed;
  Save me, and I shall be saved,
  For You *are* my praise.
15 Indeed they say to me,
  "Where *is* the word of the LORD?
  Let it come now!"
16 As for me, I have not hurried away from
      being a shepherd *who* follows You,
  Nor have I desired the woeful day;
  You know what came out of my lips;
  It was right there before You.
17 Do not be a terror to me;
  You *are* my hope in the day of doom.
18 Let them be ashamed who persecute me,
  But do not let me be put to shame;
  Let them be dismayed,
  But do not let me be dismayed.
  Bring on them the day of doom,
  And destroy them with double destruction!

19Thus the LORD said to me: "Go and stand in the gate of the children of the people, by which the kings of Judah come in and by which they go out, and in all the gates of Jerusalem; 20and say to them, 'Hear the word of the LORD, you kings of Judah, and all Judah, and all the inhabitants of Jerusalem, who enter by these gates. 21Thus says the LORD: "Take heed to yourselves, and bear no burden on the Sabbath day, nor bring *it* in by the gates of Jerusalem; 22nor carry a burden out of your houses on the Sabbath day, nor do any work, but hallow the Sabbath day, as I commanded your fathers. 23But they did not obey nor incline their ear, but made their neck stiff, that they might not hear nor receive instruction.

24"And it shall be, if you heed Me carefully," says the LORD, "to bring no burden through the gates of this city on the Sabbath day, but hallow the Sabbath day, to do no work in it, 25then shall enter the gates of this city kings and princes sitting on the throne of David, riding in chariots and on horses, they and their princes, accompanied by the men of Judah and the inhabitants of Jerusalem; and this city shall remain forever. 26And they shall come from the cities of Judah and from the places around Jerusalem, from the land of Benjamin and from the lowland, from the mountains and from the South, bringing burnt offerings and sacrifices, grain offerings and incense, bringing sacrifices of praise to the house of the LORD.

27"But if you will not heed Me to hallow the Sabbath day, such as not carrying a burden when entering the gates of Jerusalem on the Sabbath day, then I will kindle a fire in its gates, and it shall devour the palaces of Jerusalem, and it shall not be quenched." ' "

18 The* word which came to Jeremiah from the LORD, saying: 2"Arise and go down to the potter's house, and there I will cause you to hear My words." 3Then I went down to the potter's house, and there he was, making something at the wheel. 4And the vessel that he made of clay was marred in the hand of the potter; so he made it again into another vessel, as it seemed good to the potter to make.

5Then the word of the LORD came to me, saying: 6"O house of Israel, can I not do with you as this potter?" says the LORD. "Look, as the clay *is* in the potter's hand, so *are* you in My hand, O house of Israel! 7The instant I speak concerning a nation and concerning a kingdom, to pluck up, to pull down, and to destroy *it,* 8if that nation against whom I have spoken turns from its evil, I will relent of the disaster that I thought to bring upon it. 9And the instant I speak concerning a nation and concerning a kingdom, to build and to plant *it,* 10if it does evil in My sight so that it does not obey My voice, then I will relent concerning the good with which I said I would benefit it.

11"Now therefore, speak to the men of Judah and to the inhabitants of Jerusalem, saying, 'Thus says the LORD: "Behold, I am fashioning a disaster and devising a plan against you. Return now every one from his evil way, and make your ways and your doings good." ' "

12And they said, "That is hopeless! So we will walk according to our own plans, and we will every one obey the dictates of his evil heart."

13Therefore thus says the LORD:

"Ask now among the Gentiles,
    Who has heard such things?
    The virgin of Israel has done a very horrible
        thing.
14 Will *a man* leave the snow water of
        Lebanon,
    Which comes from the rock of the field?
    Will the cold flowing waters be forsaken for
        strange waters?

15 "Because My people have forgotten Me,
    They have burned incense to worthless
        idols.
    And they have caused themselves to
        stumble in their ways,
    From the ancient paths,
    To walk in pathways and not on a highway,
16 To make their land desolate *and* a perpetual
        hissing;
    Everyone who passes by it will be
        astonished
    And shake his head.

CHAPTER 18—19

18:1–11 *Mending the vessel.* Individual believers are God's vessels (Acts 9:15; 2 Cor. 4:7), but the reference here is to the nation of Israel, a chosen vessel to bring God's blessing to the world. Romans 9:1–5 tells you what God put into the vessel. Many times in her history, when the nation would not yield to God, He made her again. She was marred but still in His hands. She was marred but had potential. She was marred and He made her again; and He will do the same for anyone who yields to His will (Rom. 9:19–21).

Earthen Vessels—We have the spiritual treasure in earthen vessels (2 Cor. 4:7) so that we might share it with others. A vessel does not manufacture; it only contains and shares. All God asks is that we are clean, empty, and available. He will do the rest.

17 I will scatter them as with an east wind
    before the enemy;
I will show them[m] the back and not the face
In the day of their calamity."

18Then they said, "Come and let us devise plans against Jeremiah; for the law shall not perish from the priest, nor counsel from the wise, nor the word from the prophet. Come and let us attack him with the tongue, and let us not give heed to any of his words."

19 Give heed to me, O LORD,
    And listen to the voice of those who contend
      with me!
20 Shall evil be repaid for good?
    For they have dug a pit for my life.
Remember that I stood before You
To speak good for them,
To turn away Your wrath from them.
21 Therefore deliver up their children to the
    famine,
And pour out their *blood*
By the force of the sword;
Let their wives *become* widows
And bereaved of their children.
Let their men be put to death,
Their young men *be* slain
By the sword in battle.
22 Let a cry be heard from their houses,
When You bring a troop suddenly upon
    them;
For they have dug a pit to take me,
And hidden snares for my feet.
23 Yet, LORD, You know all their counsel
Which is against me, to slay *me.*
Provide no atonement for their iniquity,
Nor blot out their sin from Your sight;
But let them be overthrown before You.
Deal *thus* with them
In the time of Your anger.

19:1–13 *Breaking the vessel.* However, if the vessel becomes hardened, it cannot be made again. All God can do is break it, and that is what He did when Babylon captured Judah. The nation was beyond repair. The Valley of the Son of Hinnom was a site for pagan worship, but Josiah turned it into a garbage dump (2 Kings 23:10). In the Greek it is *Gehenna,* the New Testament word for "hell." *Tophet* (vv. 12–13) means "burning." Jeremiah gave a new name to the place: "the Valley of Slaughter" (v. 6). People with hard hearts and stiff necks (v. 15) may be easily broken.

19 Thus* says the LORD: "Go and get a potter's earthen flask, and *take* some of the elders of the people and some of the elders of the priests. 2And go out to the Valley of the Son of Hinnom, which *is* by the entry of the Potsherd Gate; and proclaim there the words that I will tell you, 3and say, 'Hear the word of the LORD, O kings of Judah and inhabitants of Jerusalem. Thus says the LORD of hosts, the God of Israel: "Behold, I will bring such a catastrophe on this place, that whoever hears of it, his ears will tingle. 4"Because they have forsaken Me and made this an alien place, because they have burned incense in it to other gods whom neither they, their fathers, nor the kings of Judah have known, and have filled this place with the blood of the innocents 5(they have also built the high places of Baal, to burn their sons with fire *for* burnt offerings to Baal, which I did not command or speak, nor did it come into My mind), 6therefore behold, the days are coming," says the LORD, "that this place shall no more be called Tophet or the Valley of the Son of Hinnom, but the Valley of Slaughter. 7And I will make void the counsel of Judah and Jerusalem in this place, and I will cause them to fall by the sword before their enemies and by the

---

18:17 [m]Following Septuagint, Syriac, Targum, and Vulgate; Masoretic Text reads *look them in.*

hands of those who seek their lives; their corpses I will give as meat for the birds of the heaven and for the beasts of the earth. 8I will make this city desolate and a hissing; everyone who passes by it will be astonished and hiss because of all its plagues. 9And I will cause them to eat the flesh of their sons and the flesh of their daughters, and everyone shall eat the flesh of his friend in the siege and in the desperation with which their enemies and those who seek their lives shall drive them to despair." '

10"Then you shall break the flask in the sight of the men who go with you, 11and say to them, 'Thus says the LORD of hosts: "Even so I will break this people and this city, as one breaks a potter's vessel, which cannot be made whole again; and they shall bury them in Tophet till there is no place to bury. 12Thus I will do to this place," says the LORD, "and to its inhabitants, and make this city like Tophet. 13And the houses of Jerusalem and the houses of the kings of Judah shall be defiled like the place of Tophet, because of all the houses on whose roofs they have burned incense to all the host of heaven, and poured out drink offerings to other gods." ' "

14Then Jeremiah came from Tophet, where the LORD had sent him to prophesy; and he stood in the court of the Lord's house and said to all the people, 15"Thus says the LORD of hosts, the God of Israel: 'Behold, I will bring on this city and on all her towns all the doom that I have pronounced against it, because they have stiffened their necks that they might not hear My words.' "

20 Now* Pashhur the son of Immer, the priest who was also chief governor in the house of the LORD, heard that Jeremiah prophesied these things. 2Then Pashhur struck Jeremiah the prophet, and put him in the stocks that were in the high gate of Benjamin, which was by the house of the LORD.

3And it happened on the next day that Pashhur brought Jeremiah out of the stocks. Then Jeremiah said to him, "The LORD has not called your name Pashhur, but Magor-Missabib.[n] 4For thus says the LORD: 'Behold, I will make you a terror to yourself and to all your friends; and they shall fall by the sword of their enemies, and your eyes shall see it. I will give all Judah into the hand of

---

20:3 [n]Literally Fear on Every Side

CHAPTER 20

20:1ff Jeremiah went from joy (v. 13) to despair (vv. 14–18), from bold proclamation (vv. 1–6) to burdened prayer (vv. 7–12). God's servants are human and have changes in their feelings. If we were in danger as he was, we might feel and act as he did.

As officer second to the high priest, Pashhur had a job of punishing persons who committed offenses against the temple, and his main target was Jeremiah. Religious people who have no saving faith in the Lord oppose those who have a true experience and message. Jesus was crucified by the Pharisees, who were certainly religious, and the disciples were scourged in the synagogues (Matt. 10:17).

Jeremiah gave Pashhur a new name: "Fear on every side." He was successful in the temple, but his success would vanish when the enemy appeared. Let God take care of the people who create problems for you.

Once again, the prophet was bold before men but broken before God. Always tell the Lord just how you feel and let Him apply the medicine to your heart. When He answers your prayers, sing His praises! The enemy waits for you to stumble (vv. 10–11), but the Lord can hold you up (Jude 24–25).

A Personal Lament—"I wish I had never been born!" Job felt that way when he was suffering (Job 3), and now Jeremiah takes up the lament (Jer. 20:14–18; see also 15:10). But when we speak that way, we seem to forget all the wonderful blessings we have enjoyed throughout life. Suffering has a way of erasing the happy memories and putting sad memories in their place. Remembering His mercies helps encourage us in times of trial.

When Upon Life's Billows

When upon life's billows you are tempest-tossed,
When you are discouraged, thinking all is lost,
Count your many blessings, name them one by one,
And it will surprise you what the Lord has done.

Johnson Oatman, Jr.

the king of Babylon, and he shall carry them captive to Babylon and slay them with the sword. ⁵Moreover I will deliver all the wealth of this city, all its produce, and all its precious things; all the treasures of the kings of Judah I will give into the hand of their enemies, who will plunder them, seize them, and carry them to Babylon. ⁶And you, Pashhur, and all who dwell in your house, shall go into captivity. You shall go to Babylon, and there you shall die, and be buried there, you and all your friends, to whom you have prophesied lies.' "

7   O LORD, You induced me, and I was
        persuaded;
     You are stronger than I, and have prevailed.
     I am in derision daily;
     Everyone mocks me.
8   For when I spoke, I cried out;
     I shouted, "Violence and plunder!"
     Because the word of the LORD was made to
        me
     A reproach and a derision daily.
9   Then I said, "I will not make mention of
        Him,
     Nor speak anymore in His name."
     But *His word* was in my heart like a burning
        fire
     Shut up in my bones;
     I was weary of holding *it* back,
     And I could not.
10   For I heard many mocking:
     "Fear on every side!"
     "Report," *they say,* "and we will report it!"
     All my acquaintances watched for my
        stumbling, *saying,*
     "Perhaps he can be induced;
     Then we will prevail against him,
     And we will take our revenge on him."

11   But the LORD *is* with me as a mighty,
        awesome One.
     Therefore my persecutors will stumble, and
        will not prevail.
     They will be greatly ashamed, for they will
        not prosper.
     Their everlasting confusion will never be
        forgotten.
12   But, O LORD of hosts,
     You who test the righteous,
     And see the mind and heart,
     Let me see Your vengeance on them;
     For I have pleaded my cause before You.

13   Sing to the LORD! Praise the LORD!
     For He has delivered the life of the poor
     From the hand of evildoers.

14   Cursed *be* the day in which I was born!
     Let the day not be blessed in which my
        mother bore me!
15   Let the man *be* cursed
     Who brought news to my father, saying,
     "A male child has been born to you!"
     Making him very glad.
16   And let that man be like the cities
     Which the LORD overthrew, and did not
        relent;
     Let him hear the cry in the morning
     And the shouting at noon,
17   Because he did not kill me from the womb,
     That my mother might have been my grave,

And her womb always enlarged *with me.*
18 Why did I come forth from the womb to see
      labor and sorrow,
    That my days should be consumed with
      shame?

21 The* word which came to Jeremiah from the LORD when King Zedekiah sent to him Pashhur the son of Melchiah, and Zephaniah the son of Maaseiah, the priest, saying, 2"Please inquire of the LORD for us, for Nebuchadnezzar° king of Babylon makes war against us. Perhaps the LORD will deal with us according to all His wonderful works, that *the king* may go away from us."

3Then Jeremiah said to them, "Thus you shall say to Zedekiah, 4'Thus says the LORD God of Israel: "Behold, I will turn back the weapons of war that *are* in your hands, with which you fight against the king of Babylon and the Chaldeans^p who besiege you outside the walls; and I will assemble them in the midst of this city. 5I Myself will fight against you with an outstretched hand and with a strong arm, even in anger and fury and great wrath. 6I will strike the inhabitants of this city, both man and beast; they shall die of a great pestilence. 7And afterward," says the LORD, "I will deliver Zedekiah king of Judah, his servants and the people, and such as are left in this city from the pestilence and the sword and the famine, into the hand of Nebuchadnezzar king of Babylon, into the hand of their enemies, and into the hand of those who seek their life; and he shall strike them with the edge of the sword. He shall not spare them, or have pity or mercy." '

8*"Now you shall say to this people, 'Thus says the LORD: "Behold, I set before you the way of life and the way of death. 9He who remains in this city shall die by the sword, by famine, and by pestilence; but he who goes out and defects to the Chaldeans who besiege you, he shall live, and his life shall be as a prize to him. 10For I have set My face against this city for adversity and not for good," says the LORD. "It shall be given into the hand of the king of Babylon, and he shall burn it with fire." '

11*"And concerning the house of the king of Judah, *say,* 'Hear the word of the LORD, 12O house of David! Thus says the LORD:

"Execute judgment in the morning;
  And deliver *him who is* plundered
  Out of the hand of the oppressor,
  Lest My fury go forth like fire
  And burn so that no one can quench *it,*
  Because of the evil of your doings.

13 "Behold, I *am* against you, O inhabitant of
    the valley,
  And rock of the plain," says the LORD,
  "Who say, 'Who shall come down against
    us?
  Or who shall enter our dwellings?'
14 But I will punish you according to the fruit
    of your doings," says the LORD;
  "I will kindle a fire in its forest,
  And it shall devour all things around it." ' "

21:1–7 The prophet delivered three messages, and the first was *to the king.* Zedekiah, the last king of Judah, rebelled against Babylon and ended up being captured and seeing his sons slain (2 Kings 24—25). Although he was not a man of faith, he wanted God's help. Jeremiah told him, "Babylon is not fighting against you, *God is!*" People ignore the Lord until they desperately need His help, and then they discover He is their enemy.

21:8–10 The second message was *to the people,* giving them the choice between life or death. Because of this counsel, Jeremiah was considered a traitor; but it was God's word to the people, and those who obeyed it lived.

21:11–14 The recipients of the third message were *members of the house of David,* Judah's kings (vv. 11–14). Josiah was Judah's last good king; the four kings who followed him were evil men whose doom Jeremiah announced. Had the kings led the nation in repentance, God would have shown mercy, but they persisted in their sins.

Jeremiah was not a popular preacher, but his message was faithful. Those who heeded him lived; those who resisted the Word died.

21:2 °Hebrew *Nebuchadrezzar,* and so elsewhere
21:4 ^pOr *Babylonians*

CHAPTER 22

22:1–9 The prophet addressed four kings of Judah, beginning with Zedekiah, the last king, and then taking the preceding kings in the order of their reign.

He reminded *Zedekiah* that he sat on the throne of *David* but was not ruling as David ruled. Not only would Zedekiah's palace be ruined, but the house (dynasty) of David would have no king until the Messiah would come.

22:10–17 He reminded *Shallum* (Jehoahaz that his father Josiah had been a godly man but Shallum was not following his example. His besetting sin was covetousness (v. 17). He reigned only three months before being taken to Egypt where he died.

22 Thus* says the LORD: "Go down to the
house of the king of Judah, and there speak
this word, 2and say, 'Hear the word of the LORD,
O king of Judah, you who sit on the throne of
David, you and your servants and your people
who enter these gates! 3Thus says the LORD: "Execute judgment and righteousness, and deliver the
plundered out of the hand of the oppressor. Do
no wrong and do no violence to the stranger, the
fatherless, or the widow, nor shed innocent blood
in this place. 4For if you indeed do this thing, then
shall enter the gates of this house, riding on
horses and in chariots, accompanied by servants
and people, kings who sit on the throne of David.
5But if you will not hear these words, I swear by
Myself," says the LORD, "that this house shall become a desolation." ' "

6For thus says the LORD to the house of the king
of Judah:

"You *are* Gilead to Me,
The head of Lebanon;
Yet I surely will make you a wilderness,
Cities *which* are not inhabited.
7 I will prepare destroyers against you,
Everyone with his weapons;
They shall cut down your choice cedars
And cast *them* into the fire.

8And many nations will pass by this city; and
everyone will say to his neighbor, 'Why has the
LORD done so to this great city?' 9Then they will
answer, 'Because they have forsaken the covenant
of the LORD their God, and worshiped other gods
and served them.' "

10 *Weep not for the dead, nor bemoan him;
Weep bitterly for him who goes away,
For he shall return no more,
Nor see his native country.

11For thus says the LORD concerning Shallum[q]
the son of Josiah, king of Judah, who reigned instead of Josiah his father, who went from this
place: "He shall not return here anymore, 12but
he shall die in the place where they have led him
captive, and shall see this land no more.

13 "Woe to him who builds his house by
unrighteousness
And his chambers by injustice,
Who uses his neighbor's service without
wages
And gives him nothing for his work,
14 Who says, 'I will build myself a wide house
with spacious chambers,
And cut out windows for it,
Paneling *it* with cedar
And painting *it* with vermilion.'

15 "Shall you reign because you enclose
yourself in cedar?
Did not your father eat and drink,
And do justice and righteousness?
Then *it was* well with him.
16 He judged the cause of the poor and needy;
Then *it was* well.
Was not this knowing Me?" says the
LORD.

22:11 [q]Also called *Jehoahaz*

17 "Yet your eyes and your heart *are* for nothing
    but your covetousness,
For shedding innocent blood,
And practicing oppression and violence."

18*Therefore thus says the LORD concerning Jehoiakim the son of Josiah, king of Judah:

"They shall not lament for him,
    Saying, 'Alas, my brother!' or 'Alas, my
    sister!'
They shall not lament for him,
    Saying, 'Alas, master!' or 'Alas, his glory!'
19 He shall be buried with the burial of a
    donkey,
    Dragged and cast out beyond the gates of
    Jerusalem.

20 "Go up to Lebanon, and cry out,
    And lift up your voice in Bashan;
    Cry from Abarim,
    For all your lovers are destroyed.
21 I spoke to you in your prosperity,
    But you said, 'I will not hear.'
    This *has been* your manner from your
    youth,
    That you did not obey My voice.
22 The wind shall eat up all your rulers,
    And your lovers shall go into captivity;
    Surely then you will be ashamed and
    humiliated
    For all your wickedness.
23 O inhabitant of Lebanon,
    Making your nest in the cedars,
    How gracious will you be when pangs come
    upon you,
    Like the pain of a woman in labor?

24*"As I live," says the LORD, "though Coniah[r]
the son of Jehoiakim, king of Judah, were the signet on My right hand, yet I would pluck you off;
25and I will give you into the hand of those who
seek your life, and into the hand *of those* whose
face you fear—the hand of Nebuchadnezzar king
of Babylon and the hand of the Chaldeans.
26So I will cast you out, and your mother who
bore you, into another country where you were
not born; and there you shall die. 27But to the land
to which they desire to return, there they shall
not return.

28 "Is this man Coniah a despised, broken idol—
    A vessel in which *is* no pleasure?
    Why are they cast out, he and his
    descendants,
    And cast into a land which they do not
    know?
29 O earth, earth, earth,
    Hear the word of the LORD!
30 Thus says the LORD:
    'Write this man down as childless,
    A man *who* shall not prosper in his days;
    For none of his descendants shall prosper,
    Sitting on the throne of David,
    And ruling anymore in Judah.'"

23 "Woe* to the shepherds who destroy and
    scatter the sheep of My pasture!" says the
LORD. 2Therefore thus says the LORD God of Israel

22:24 [r]Also called *Jeconiah* and *Jehoiachin*

22:18–23 *Jehoiakim* would not listen to the
voice of God. Even the animals know and
obey their Creator (Isa. 1:2–3), but the heir
to David's throne would not hear David's
God. Instead of having the usual state
funeral, the king was buried in disgrace.

22:24–30 *Coniah* (Jeconiah; Jehoiachin)
was apparently very popular, but the idol
would fall and be smashed. He had several
children, but none of them would inherit the
throne of David. Coniah was a castaway
(vv. 26, 28) who by his sins jeopardized his
future and the future of his family and the
nation.
    When we do not learn from the past or
hear God and obey Him in the present, we
destroy our future.

CHAPTER 23

23:1–8 God expects the leaders of His
people to be shepherds who love, guide, and
care for them. But the shepherds in Judah
at that time were selfish and disloyal to
God's covenant.
    The kings scattered the people and did
not protect them or provide for them. But
one day God's King will gather them and
establish His kingdom in righteousness. The
more we are like Jesus Christ today, the
better we will serve others in love.

against the shepherds who feed My people: "You have scattered My flock, driven them away, and not attended to them. Behold, I will attend to you for the evil of your doings," says the LORD. ³"But I will gather the remnant of My flock out of all countries where I have driven them, and bring them back to their folds; and they shall be fruitful and increase. ⁴I will set up shepherds over them who will feed them; and they shall fear no more, nor be dismayed, nor shall they be lacking," says the LORD.

⁵ "Behold, *the* days are coming," says the
    LORD,
    "That I will raise to David a Branch of
        righteousness;
    A King shall reign and prosper,
    And execute judgment and righteousness in
        the earth.
⁶ In His days Judah will be saved,
    And Israel will dwell safely;
    Now this *is* His name by which He will be
        called:

THE LORD OUR RIGHTEOUSNESS.ˢ

⁷"Therefore, behold, *the* days are coming," says the LORD, "that they shall no longer say, 'As the LORD lives who brought up the children of Israel from the land of Egypt,' ⁸but, 'As the LORD lives who brought up and led the descendants of the house of Israel from the north country and from all the countries where I had driven them.' And they shall dwell in their own land."

23:9–40 *The prophets and priests* did not give the people spiritual direction, nor were they examples of godliness. People who lack spiritual direction will lack spiritual discernment and believe anything. The false prophets invented their visions and passed them off as oracles from God. They did not get their messages from God. What they said was chaff compared to the wheat (v. 28).

No wonder false teachers are so popular! The sinful human heart does not want to be burned and broken by the fire and hammer of the Word of God. It prefers the chaff, even though chaff gives no nourishment.

Be sure that the people who give you spiritual counsel are called by God, walk with God, and obey God's Word. The false prophets' dreams eventually become nightmares.

⁹ *My heart within me is broken
    Because of the prophets;
    All my bones shake.
    I am like a drunken man,
    And like a man whom wine has overcome,
    Because of the LORD,
    And because of His holy words.
¹⁰ For the land is full of adulterers;
    For because of a curse the land mourns.
    The pleasant places of the wilderness are
        dried up.
    Their course of life is evil,
    And their might *is* not right.

¹¹ "For both prophet and priest are profane;
    Yes, in My house I have found their
        wickedness," says the LORD.
¹² "Therefore their way shall be to them
    Like slippery *ways;*
    In the darkness they shall be driven on
    And fall in them;
    For I will bring disaster on them,
    The year of their punishment," says the
        LORD.
¹³ "And I have seen folly in the prophets of
        Samaria:
    They prophesied by Baal
    And caused My people Israel to err.
¹⁴ Also I have seen a horrible thing in the
        prophets of Jerusalem:
    They commit adultery and walk in lies;
    They also strengthen the hands of evildoers,
    So that no one turns back from his
        wickedness.
    All of them are like Sodom to Me,
    And her inhabitants like Gomorrah.

23:6 ˢHebrew *YHWH Tsidkenu*

15"Therefore thus says the LORD of hosts concerning the prophets:

'Behold, I will feed them with wormwood,
And make them drink the water of gall;
For from the prophets of Jerusalem
Profaneness has gone out into all the land.' "

16Thus says the LORD of hosts:

"Do not listen to the words of the prophets
    who prophesy to you.
They make you worthless;
They speak a vision of their own heart,
Not from the mouth of the LORD.
17 They continually say to those who despise
    Me,
'The LORD has said, "You shall have peace" ';
And to everyone who walks according to
    the dictates of his own heart, they say,
'No evil shall come upon you.' "

18 For who has stood in the counsel of the
    LORD,
And has perceived and heard His word?
Who has marked His word and heard it?
19 Behold, a whirlwind of the LORD has gone
    forth in fury—
A violent whirlwind!
It will fall violently on the head of the
    wicked.
20 The anger of the LORD will not turn back
Until He has executed and performed the
    thoughts of His heart.
In the latter days you will understand it
    perfectly.

21 "I have not sent these prophets, yet they
    ran.
I have not spoken to them, yet they
    prophesied.
22 But if they had stood in My counsel,
And had caused My people to hear My
    words,
Then they would have turned them from
    their evil way
And from the evil of their doings.

23 "Am I a God near at hand," says the LORD,
    "And not a God afar off?
24 Can anyone hide himself in secret places,
So I shall not see him?" says the LORD;
"Do I not fill heaven and earth?" says the
    LORD.

25"I have heard what the prophets have said
who prophesy lies in My name, saying, 'I have
dreamed, I have dreamed!' 26How long will this
be in the heart of the prophets who prophesy lies?
Indeed they are prophets of the deceit of their
own heart, 27who try to make My people forget
My name by their dreams which everyone tells
his neighbor, as their fathers forgot My name for
Baal.

28 "The prophet who has a dream, let him tell
    a dream;
And he who has My word, let him speak
    My word faithfully.
What is the chaff to the wheat?" says the
    LORD.
29 "Is not My word like a fire?" says the LORD,

"And like a hammer *that* breaks the rock in pieces?

30"Therefore behold, I *am* against the prophets," says the LORD, "who steal My words every one from his neighbor. 31Behold, I *am* against the prophets," says the LORD, "who use their tongues and say, 'He says.' 32Behold, I *am* against those who prophesy false dreams," says the LORD, "and tell them, and cause My people to err by their lies and by their recklessness. Yet I did not send them or command them; therefore they shall not profit this people at all," says the LORD.

33"So when these people or the prophet or the priest ask you, saying, 'What is the oracle of the LORD?' you shall then say to them, 'What oracle?'*t* I will even forsake you," says the LORD. 34"And *as for* the prophet and the priest and the people who say, 'The oracle of the LORD!' I will even punish that man and his house. 35Thus every one of you shall say to his neighbor, and every one to his brother, 'What has the LORD answered?' and, 'What has the LORD spoken?' 36And the oracle of the LORD you shall mention no more. For every man's word will be his oracle, for you have perverted the words of the living God, the LORD of hosts, our God. 37Thus you shall say to the prophet, 'What has the LORD answered you?' and, 'What has the LORD spoken?' 38But since you say, 'The oracle of the LORD!' therefore thus says the LORD: 'Because you say this word, "The oracle of the LORD!" and I have sent to you, saying, "Do not say, 'The oracle of the LORD!' " 39therefore behold, I, even I, will utterly forget you and forsake you, and the city that I gave you and your fathers, and *will cast you* out of My presence. 40And I will bring an everlasting reproach upon you, and a perpetual shame, which shall not be forgotten.' "

CHAPTER 24

24:1ff The firstfruits were to be offered to the Lord as a sacrifice of thanksgiving for His goodness. Israel was to be like firstfruits to the Lord (Jer. 2:3), but the nation was not wholly devoted to God. Like the two baskets of figs, most of the people were bad, and only a remnant were good because they obeyed God.

What life does to us depends on what life finds in us. The godly remnant experienced good things from God during the exile, but the ungodly citizens were consumed by trouble. The godly remnant made the best of a bad situation because they trusted the Lord (Rom. 8:28).

The important thing is a heart that knows the Lord and is wholly devoted to Him (v. 7). You may not be able to control the situation, but you can control how you respond to it and to God. You are to "keep your heart with all diligence, for out of it spring the issues of life" (Prov. 4:23). Believers today are to be "a kind of firstfruits of His creatures" (James 1:18), and we want to give Him the best.

24 The* LORD showed me, and there were two baskets of figs set before the temple of the LORD, after Nebuchadnezzar king of Babylon had carried away captive Jeconiah the son of Jehoiakim, king of Judah, and the princes of Judah with the craftsmen and smiths, from Jerusalem, and had brought them to Babylon. 2One basket *had* very good figs, like the figs *that are* first ripe; and the other basket *had* very bad figs which could not be eaten, they were so bad. 3Then the LORD said to me, "What do you see, Jeremiah?"

And I said, "Figs, the good figs, very good; and the bad, very bad, which cannot be eaten, they are so bad."

4Again the word of the LORD came to me, saying, 5"Thus says the LORD, the God of Israel: 'Like these good figs, so will I acknowledge those who are carried away captive from Judah, whom I have sent out of this place for *their own* good, into the land of the Chaldeans. 6For I will set My eyes on them for good, and I will bring them back to this land; I will build them and not pull *them* down, and I will plant them and not pluck *them* up. 7Then I will give them a heart to know Me, that I *am* the LORD; and they shall be My people, and I will be their God, for they shall return to Me with their whole heart.

8'And as the bad figs which cannot be eaten, they are so bad'—surely thus says the LORD—'so

---

23:33 *f*Septuagint, Targum, and Vulgate read '*You are the burden.*'

will I give up Zedekiah the king of Judah, his princes, the residue of Jerusalem who remain in this land, and those who dwell in the land of Egypt. 9I will deliver them to trouble into all the kingdoms of the earth, for *their* harm, *to be* a reproach and a byword, a taunt and a curse, in all places where I shall drive them. 10And I will send the sword, the famine, and the pestilence among them, till they are consumed from the land that I gave to them and their fathers.' "

25 The word that came to Jeremiah concerning all the people of Judah, in the fourth year of Jehoiakim the son of Josiah, king of Judah (which *was* the first year of Nebuchadnezzar king of Babylon), 2which Jeremiah the prophet spoke to all the people of Judah and to all the inhabitants of Jerusalem, saying: 3*"From the thirteenth year of Josiah the son of Amon, king of Judah, even to this day, this *is* the twenty-third year in which the word of the LORD has come to me; and I have spoken to you, rising early and speaking, but you have not listened. 4And the LORD has sent to you all His servants the prophets, rising early and sending *them*, but you have not listened nor inclined your ear to hear. 5They said, 'Repent now everyone of his evil way and his evil doings, and dwell in the land that the LORD has given to you and your fathers forever and ever. 6Do not go after other gods to serve them and worship them, and do not provoke Me to anger with the works of your hands; and I will not harm you.' 7Yet you have not listened to Me," says the LORD, "that you might provoke Me to anger with the works of your hands to your own hurt.

8*"Therefore thus says the LORD of hosts: 'Because you have not heard My words, 9behold, I will send and take all the families of the north,' says the LORD, 'and Nebuchadnezzar the king of Babylon, My servant, and will bring them against this land, against its inhabitants, and against these nations all around, and will utterly destroy them, and make them an astonishment, a hissing, and perpetual desolations. 10Moreover I will take from them the voice of mirth and the voice of gladness, the voice of the bridegroom and the voice of the bride, the sound of the millstones and the light of the lamp. 11And this whole land shall be a desolation *and* an astonishment, and these nations shall serve the king of Babylon seventy years.

12'Then it will come to pass, when seventy years are completed, *that* I will punish the king of Babylon and that nation, the land of the Chaldeans, for their iniquity,' says the LORD; 'and I will make it a perpetual desolation. 13So I will bring on that land all My words which I have pronounced against it, all that is written in this book, which Jeremiah has prophesied concerning all the nations. 14(For many nations and great kings shall be served by them also; and I will repay them according to their deeds and according to the works of their own hands.)' "

15For thus says the LORD God of Israel to me: "Take this wine cup of fury from My hand, and

CHAPTER 25

25:3 Imagine preaching for twenty-three years and seeing no visible results! Jeremiah was faithful to his calling even though the people opposed him and would not hear God's Word. We are judged by God according to our faithfulness, not our outward success. By men's standards, Jeremiah would be considered a failure (1 Cor. 4:1–5).

25:8–38 The Babylonian captivity was God's way of punishing the rebels and purifying the godly remnant of the nation. The nation was deaf to God's Word (vv. 4, 7, 8), but that Word would be fulfilled, not only to Israel, but to all the nations to which God sent it by His prophet.

God is long-suffering toward disobedient people and gives them many opportunities for repentance, but eventually He must act. He will be like a host who makes his guests drunk (vv. 15–29), a lion that attacks the flock (vv. 30–31, 34–38), a whirlwind that sweeps across the nation and destroys it (vv. 32–33).

Judah's Punishment—According to 2 Chronicles 36:20–21, the Lord punished Judah for seventy years because that was the number of Sabbatical Years they had not observed (Lev. 25:1–7). The people did not rest on the weekly Sabbath (Jer. 17:19–27), and they did not give the land its rest every seven years (Lev. 26:27–35). When we keep to ourselves what belongs to God, we eventually lose it and suffer in the process.

cause all the nations, to whom I send you, to drink it. ¹⁶And they will drink and stagger and go mad because of the sword that I will send among them."

¹⁷Then I took the cup from the LORD's hand, and made all the nations drink, to whom the LORD had sent me: ¹⁸Jerusalem and the cities of Judah, its kings and its princes, to make them a desolation, an astonishment, a hissing, and a curse, as *it is* this day; ¹⁹Pharaoh king of Egypt, his servants, his princes, and all his people; ²⁰all the mixed multitude, all the kings of the land of Uz, all the kings of the land of the Philistines (namely, Ashkelon, Gaza, Ekron, and the remnant of Ashdod); ²¹Edom, Moab, and the people of Ammon; ²²all the kings of Tyre, all the kings of Sidon, and the kings of the coastlands which *are* across the sea; ²³Dedan, Tema, Buz, and all *who are* in the farthest corners; ²⁴all the kings of Arabia and all the kings of the mixed multitude who dwell in the desert; ²⁵all the kings of Zimri, all the kings of Elam, and all the kings of the Medes; ²⁶all the kings of the north, far and near, one with another; and all the kingdoms of the world which *are* on the face of the earth. Also the king of Sheshachᵘ shall drink after them.

²⁷"Therefore you shall say to them, 'Thus says the LORD of hosts, the God of Israel: "Drink, be drunk, and vomit! Fall and rise no more, because of the sword which I will send among you."' ²⁸And it shall be, if they refuse to take the cup from your hand to drink, then you shall say to them, 'Thus says the LORD of hosts: "You shall certainly drink! ²⁹For behold, I begin to bring calamity on the city which is called by My name, and should you be utterly unpunished? You shall not be unpunished, for I will call for a sword on all the inhabitants of the earth," says the LORD of hosts.'

³⁰"Therefore prophesy against them all these words, and say to them:

'The LORD will roar from on high,
And utter His voice from His holy
    habitation;
He will roar mightily against His fold.
He will give a shout, as those who tread *the
    grapes*,
Against all the inhabitants of the earth.
31   A noise will come to the ends of the earth—
For the LORD has a controversy with the
    nations;
He will plead His case with all flesh.
He will give those *who are* wicked to the
    sword,' says the LORD."

³²Thus says the LORD of hosts:

"Behold, disaster shall go forth
From nation to nation,
And a great whirlwind shall be raised up
From the farthest parts of the earth.

³³"And at that day the slain of the LORD shall be from *one* end of the earth even to the *other* end of the earth. They shall not be lamented, or gathered, or buried; they shall become refuse on the ground.

25:26 ᵘA code word for Babylon (compare 51:41)

34 "Wail, shepherds, and cry!
   Roll about *in the ashes,*
   You leaders of the flock!
   For the days of your slaughter and your
       dispersions are fulfilled;
   You shall fall like a precious vessel.
35 And the shepherds will have no way to flee,
   Nor the leaders of the flock to escape.
36 A voice of the cry of the shepherds,
   And a wailing of the leaders to the flock
       will be heard.
   For the LORD has plundered their pasture,
37 And the peaceful dwellings are cut down
   Because of the fierce anger of the LORD.
38 He has left His lair like the lion;
   For their land is desolate
   Because of the fierceness of the Oppressor,
   And because of His fierce anger."

26 In* the beginning of the reign of Jehoiakim the son of Josiah, king of Judah, this word came from the LORD, saying, 2"Thus says the LORD: 'Stand in the court of the LORD's house, and speak to all the cities of Judah, which come to worship *in* the LORD's house, all the words that I command you to speak to them. Do not diminish a word. 3Perhaps everyone will listen and turn from his evil way, that I may relent concerning the calamity which I purpose to bring on them because of the evil of their doings.' 4And you shall say to them, 'Thus says the LORD: "If you will not listen to Me, to walk in My law which I have set before you, 5to heed the words of My servants the prophets whom I sent to you, both rising up early and sending *them* (but you have not heeded), 6then I will make this house like Shiloh, and will make this city a curse to all the nations of the earth."' "

7*So the priests and the prophets and all the people heard Jeremiah speaking these words in the house of the LORD. 8Now it happened, when Jeremiah had made an end of speaking all that the LORD had commanded *him* to speak to all the people, that the priests and the prophets and all the people seized him, saying, "You will surely die! 9Why have you prophesied in the name of the LORD, saying, 'This house shall be like Shiloh, and this city shall be desolate, without an inhabitant'?" And all the people were gathered against Jeremiah in the house of the LORD.

10When the princes of Judah heard these things, they came up from the king's house to the house of the LORD and sat down in the entry of the New Gate of the LORD's *house.* 11And the priests and the prophets spoke to the princes and all the people, saying, "This man deserves to die! For he has prophesied against this city, as you have heard with your ears."

12Then Jeremiah spoke to all the princes and all the people, saying: "The LORD sent me to prophesy against this house and against this city with all the words that you have heard. 13Now therefore, amend your ways and your doings, and obey the voice of the LORD your God; then the LORD will relent concerning the doom that He has pronounced against you. 14As for me, here I am, in

CHAPTER 26

26:1–6, 12–15 How patient the Lord is with us! He keeps speaking to us and pleading with us to listen. "Listen and turn—hear and heed!" is His loving message to us. Will we obey?

26:7–11 How prone human nature is to resist the Word! The leaders should have called for a time of fasting and prayer, but instead they called for the execution of God's prophet! Are we "swift to hear, slow to speak, slow to wrath" (James 1:19)? Do we want what is right for us and the nation, or what is popular?

A Special Family—God used Ahikam, the son of Shaphan, to rescue Jeremiah. Shaphan was the man who found the Book of the Law when Josiah was restoring the temple (2 Kings 22:3–13). His son Gemariah begged King Jehoiakim not to destroy the book Jeremiah had written (Jer. 36:25). The whole family was devoted to God's Word, and God used it to help His servants.

26:17–19 How wise are those who learn from the past! The elders knew the Word of God and the history of the nation, and they were able to guide the mob toward sanity and justice.

26:20–24 How safe are those who are faithful to God when everything seems against them! Jeremiah stood his ground, and God protected him. Urijah ran away and was captured and killed. The safest place in the world is in the will of God, for there you are ready to live or die.

CHAPTER 27—28

27:1ff Jeremiah wore a yoke (28:10) to convey his message that Judah must surrender to Babylon. He delivered his "yoke sermon" three times: first to some ambassadors who had come to form an alliance (vv. 1–11); next to King Zedekiah (vv. 12–15); and then publicly to the priests and people (vv. 16–22). The false prophets were giving the nation false hopes, but Jeremiah told them the truth. Nebuchadnezzar was God's servant, doing God's will; and all nations should submit to him. If they accepted his yoke, they would live; if they rejected it, they would die.

God is in charge of yokes. The yoke He gives you is the right one for you, no matter who may put it on your shoulders. God can even use unsaved people to help you do His will. Accept every yoke as the yoke of God and He will transform it from bondage to blessing. Break the light yoke and the next yoke will be heavier. Everyone must wear a yoke.

your hand; do with me as seems good and proper to you. 15But know for certain that if you put me to death, you will surely bring innocent blood on yourselves, on this city, and on its inhabitants; for truly the LORD has sent me to you to speak all these words in your hearing."

16So the princes and all the people said to the priests and the prophets, "This man does not deserve to die. For he has spoken to us in the name of the LORD our God."

17*Then certain of the elders of the land rose up and spoke to all the assembly of the people, saying: 18"Micah of Moresheth prophesied in the days of Hezekiah king of Judah, and spoke to all the people of Judah, saying, 'Thus says the LORD of hosts:

"Zion shall be plowed *like* a field,
Jerusalem shall become heaps of ruins,
And the mountain of the temple[v]
Like the bare hills of the forest." '[w]

19Did Hezekiah king of Judah and all Judah ever put him to death? Did he not fear the LORD and seek the LORD's favor? And the LORD relented concerning the doom which He had pronounced against them. But we are doing great evil against ourselves."

20*Now there was also a man who prophesied in the name of the LORD, Urijah the son of Shemaiah of Kirjath Jearim, who prophesied against this city and against this land according to all the words of Jeremiah. 21And when Jehoiakim the king, with all his mighty men and all the princes, heard his words, the king sought to put him to death; but when Urijah heard *it,* he was afraid and fled, and went to Egypt. 22Then Jehoiakim the king sent men to Egypt: Elnathan the son of Achbor, and *other* men *who went* with him to Egypt. 23And they brought Urijah from Egypt and brought him to Jehoiakim the king, who killed him with the sword and cast his dead body into the graves of the common people.

24Nevertheless the hand of Ahikam the son of Shaphan was with Jeremiah, so that they should not give him into the hand of the people to put him to death.

27 In* the beginning of the reign of Jehoiakim[x] the son of Josiah, king of Judah, this word came to Jeremiah from the LORD, saying,[y] 2"Thus says the LORD to me: 'Make for yourselves bonds and yokes, and put them on your neck, 3and send them to the king of Edom, the king of Moab, the king of the Ammonites, the king of Tyre, and the king of Sidon, by the hand of the messengers who come to Jerusalem to Zedekiah king of Judah. 4And command them to say to their masters, "Thus says the LORD of hosts, the God of Israel— thus you shall say to your masters: 5'I have made the earth, the man and the beast that *are* on the ground, by My great power and by My outstretched arm, and have given it to whom it seemed proper to Me. 6And now I have given all these lands into the hand of Nebuchadnezzar the king of Babylon, My servant; and the beasts of the field I have also given him to serve him.

26:18 [v]Literally *house* [w]Compare Micah 3:12 27:1 [x]Following Masoretic Text, Targum, and Vulgate; some Hebrew manuscripts, Arabic, and Syriac read *Zedekiah* (compare 27:3, 12; 28:1). [y]Septuagint omits verse 1.

7So all nations shall serve him and his son and his son's son, until the time of his land comes; and then many nations and great kings shall make him serve them. 8And it shall be, *that* the nation and kingdom which will not serve Nebuchadnezzar the king of Babylon, and which will not put its neck under the yoke of the king of Babylon, that nation I will punish,' says the LORD, 'with the sword, the famine, and the pestilence, until I have consumed them by his hand. 9Therefore do not listen to your prophets, your diviners, your dreamers, your soothsayers, or your sorcerers, who speak to you, saying, "You shall not serve the king of Babylon." 10For they prophesy a lie to you, to remove you far from your land; and I will drive you out, and you will perish. 11But the nations that bring their necks under the yoke of the king of Babylon and serve him, I will let them remain in their own land,' says the LORD, 'and they shall till it and dwell in it.' " ' "

12I also spoke to Zedekiah king of Judah according to all these words, saying, "Bring your necks under the yoke of the king of Babylon, and serve him and his people, and live! 13Why will you die, you and your people, by the sword, by the famine, and by the pestilence, as the LORD has spoken against the nation that will not serve the king of Babylon? 14Therefore do not listen to the words of the prophets who speak to you, saying, 'You shall not serve the king of Babylon,' for they prophesy a lie to you; 15for I have not sent them," says the LORD, "yet they prophesy a lie in My name, that I may drive you out, and that you may perish, you and the prophets who prophesy to you."

16Also I spoke to the priests and to all this people, saying, "Thus says the LORD: 'Do not listen to the words of your prophets who prophesy to you, saying, "Behold, the vessels of the LORD's house will now shortly be brought back from Babylon"; for they prophesy a lie to you. 17Do not listen to them; serve the king of Babylon, and live! Why should this city be laid waste? 18But if they *are* prophets, and if the word of the LORD is with them, let them now make intercession to the LORD of hosts, that the vessels which are left in the house of the LORD, *in* the house of the king of Judah, and at Jerusalem, do not go to Babylon.'

19"For thus says the LORD of hosts concerning the pillars, concerning the Sea, concerning the carts, and concerning the remainder of the vessels that remain in this city, 20which Nebuchadnezzar king of Babylon did not take, when he carried away captive Jeconiah the son of Jehoiakim, king of Judah, from Jerusalem to Babylon, and all the nobles of Judah and Jerusalem— 21yes, thus says the LORD of hosts, the God of Israel, concerning the vessels that remain in the house of the LORD, and in the house of the king of Judah and of Jerusalem: 22'They shall be carried to Babylon, and there they shall be until the day that I visit them,' says the LORD. 'Then I will bring them up and restore them to this place.' "

28 And it happened in the same year, at the beginning of the reign of Zedekiah king of

Yokes—The nation broke God's yoke by her sins (Jer. 2:20; 5:5), and those sins became a heavy yoke (Lam. 1:14). This led to the even heavier yoke of Babylonian captivity. But God promised to remove the heavy yoke and give His people a new beginning (Jer. 30:8–11). Your youth is the best time to learn to wear the yoke (Lam. 3:27). Let God "break you" and control you now, and the future will be bright. Jesus said, "My yoke is easy and My burden is light" (Matt. 11:28–30).

Judah, in the fourth year *and* in the fifth month, *that* Hananiah the son of Azur the prophet, who *was* from Gibeon, spoke to me in the house of the LORD in the presence of the priests and of all the people, saying, ²"Thus speaks the LORD of hosts, the God of Israel, saying: 'I have broken the yoke of the king of Babylon. ³Within two full years I will bring back to this place all the vessels of the LORD's house, that Nebuchadnezzar king of Babylon took away from this place and carried to Babylon. ⁴And I will bring back to this place Jeconiah the son of Jehoiakim, king of Judah, with all the captives of Judah who went to Babylon,' says the LORD, 'for I will break the yoke of the king of Babylon.' "

⁵Then the prophet Jeremiah spoke to the prophet Hananiah in the presence of the priests and in the presence of all the people who stood in the house of the LORD, ⁶and the prophet Jeremiah said, "Amen! The LORD do so; the LORD perform your words which you have prophesied, to bring back the vessels of the LORD's house and all who were carried away captive, from Babylon to this place. ⁷Nevertheless hear now this word that I speak in your hearing and in the hearing of all the people: ⁸The prophets who have been before me and before you of old prophesied against many countries and great kingdoms—of war and disaster and pestilence. ⁹As for the prophet who prophesies of peace, when the word of the prophet comes to pass, the prophet will be known *as* one whom the LORD has truly sent."

¹⁰Then Hananiah the prophet took the yoke off the prophet Jeremiah's neck and broke it. ¹¹And Hananiah spoke in the presence of all the people, saying, "Thus says the LORD: 'Even so I will break the yoke of Nebuchadnezzar king of Babylon from the neck of all nations within the space of two full years.' " And the prophet Jeremiah went his way.

¹²Now the word of the LORD came to Jeremiah, after Hananiah the prophet had broken the yoke from the neck of the prophet Jeremiah, saying, ¹³"Go and tell Hananiah, saying, 'Thus says the LORD: "You have broken the yokes of wood, but you have made in their place yokes of iron." ¹⁴For thus says the LORD of hosts, the God of Israel: "I have put a yoke of iron on the neck of all these nations, that they may serve Nebuchadnezzar king of Babylon; and they shall serve him. I have given him the beasts of the field also." ' "

¹⁵Then the prophet Jeremiah said to Hananiah the prophet, "Hear now, Hananiah, the LORD has not sent you, but you make this people trust in a lie. ¹⁶Therefore thus says the LORD: 'Behold, I will cast you from the face of the earth. This year you shall die, because you have taught rebellion against the LORD.' "

¹⁷So Hananiah the prophet died the same year in the seventh month.

29 Now these *are* the words of the letter that Jeremiah the prophet sent from Jerusalem to the remainder of the elders who were carried away captive—to the priests, the prophets, and all the people whom Nebuchadnezzar had carried

Far From Home—God's people in the world today are somewhat like the Jewish exiles in Babylon, for we are away from our heavenly home and living among those who do not accept our way of life. "Seek the peace of the city" (Jer. 29:7) is good counsel for us to follow as strangers on this earth. Peter explains how we should do this in 1 Peter 2:11—3:19.

away captive from Jerusalem to Babylon. 2(This happened after Jeconiah the king, the queen mother, the eunuchs, the princes of Judah and Jerusalem, the craftsmen, and the smiths had departed from Jerusalem.) 3*The letter was sent by* the hand of Elasah the son of Shaphan, and Gemariah the son of Hilkiah, whom Zedekiah king of Judah sent to Babylon, to Nebuchadnezzar king of Babylon, saying,

4   Thus says the LORD of hosts, the God of Israel, to all who were carried away captive, whom I have caused to be carried away from Jerusalem to Babylon:

5   *Build houses and dwell *in them;* plant gardens and eat their fruit. 6Take wives and beget sons and daughters; and take wives for your sons and give your daughters to husbands, so that they may bear sons and daughters—that you may be increased there, and not diminished. 7And seek the peace of the city where I have caused you to be carried away captive, and pray to the LORD for it; for in its peace you will have peace. 8For thus says the LORD of hosts, the God of Israel: Do not let your prophets and your diviners who are in your midst deceive you, nor listen to your dreams which you cause to be dreamed. 9For they prophesy falsely to you in My name; I have not sent them, says the LORD.

10   *For thus says the LORD: After seventy years are completed at Babylon, I will visit you and perform My good word toward you, and cause you to return to this place. 11*For I know the thoughts that I think toward you, says the LORD, thoughts of peace and not of evil, to give you a future and a hope. 12Then you will call upon Me and go and pray to Me, and I will listen to you. 13And you will seek Me and find *Me,* when you search for Me with all your heart. 14I will be found by you, says the LORD, and I will bring you back from your captivity; I will gather you from all the nations and from all the places where I have driven you, says the LORD, and I will bring you to the place from which I cause you to be carried away captive.

15   Because you have said, "The LORD has raised up prophets for us in Babylon"— 16therefore thus says the LORD concerning the king who sits on the throne of David, concerning all the people who dwell in this city, and concerning your brethren who have not gone out with you into captivity— 17thus says the LORD of hosts: Behold, I will send on them the sword, the famine, and the pestilence, and will make them like rotten figs that cannot be eaten, they are so bad. 18And I will pursue them with the sword, with famine, and with pestilence; and I will deliver them to trouble among all the kingdoms of the earth—to be a curse, an astonishment, a hissing, and a reproach among all the nations where I have driven them, 19because they have not heeded My words, says the LORD, which I sent to them by My servants the prophets, rising up early

CHAPTER 29

29:5–7 In 597 B.C., the Babylonians began to deport the Jews to Babylon. Jeremiah's letter to the exiles helps us understand how we can make the best of a difficult situation.

Accept it. Live as normal a life as you can and put up with inconveniences without complaining. Try to be a blessing to others. Be a peacemaker, not a troublemaker.

29:10–14 *Be patient.* God has the timing all worked out, and His plans never fail. He knows how long and how much.

29:11 *Trust God.* Verse 11 is a powerful promise to claim when you are "in exile." God thinks about you personally and is planning for you. His plans are for peace, not war, so you need not fear the future. His plans are purposeful, so let Him work out His will. No matter how difficult your situation may be, do not waste your suffering by resisting God.

29:21–32 *Avoid false hopes.* It is human to indulge in false hopes and grasp at every straw, but this approach leads to despair. Avoid the subtle voices of the false teachers with their false hopes (v. 8). The Word of God will tell you what to do.

CHAPTER 30

30:1ff Jeremiah saw in Judah's exile a picture of the future day of national suffering ("the time of Jacob's trouble" [v. 7]), when the Jews will go through tribulation. He also saw in their restoration from exile a promise of the regathering of Israel in the latter days.

Judah had sinned, so God had to correct them in love; but He would not permit their enemies to take advantage of them. God is faithful to His people even when they are not faithful to Him (2 Tim. 2:12–13). He chastens us so that He might heal us (vv. 12–17). The trials that He sends may be like bitter medicine, but they have a way of healing the sinful heart: "Now no chastening seems to be joyful for the present, but grievous; nevertheless, afterward it yields the peaceable fruit of righteousness to those who have been trained by it" (Heb. 12:11). In times of suffering, live for the joys of "afterward."

and sending *them;* neither would you heed, says the LORD. 20Therefore hear the word of the LORD, all you of the captivity, whom I have sent from Jerusalem to Babylon.

21 *Thus says the LORD of hosts, the God of Israel, concerning Ahab the son of Kolaiah, and Zedekiah the son of Maaseiah, who prophesy a lie to you in My name: Behold, I will deliver them into the hand of Nebuchadnezzar king of Babylon, and he shall slay them before your eyes. 22And because of them a curse shall be taken up by all the captivity of Judah who *are* in Babylon, saying, "The LORD make you like Zedekiah and Ahab, whom the king of Babylon roasted in the fire"; 23because they have done disgraceful things in Israel, have committed adultery with their neighbors' wives, and have spoken lying words in My name, which I have not commanded them. Indeed I know, and *am* a witness, says the LORD.

24 You shall also speak to Shemaiah the Nehelamite, saying, 25Thus speaks the LORD of hosts, the God of Israel, saying: You have sent letters in your name to all the people who *are* at Jerusalem, to Zephaniah the son of Maaseiah the priest, and to all the priests, saying, 26"The LORD has made you priest instead of Jehoiada the priest, so that there should be officers *in* the house of the LORD over every man *who* is demented and considers himself a prophet, that you should put him in prison and in the stocks. 27Now therefore, why have you not rebuked Jeremiah of Anathoth who makes himself a prophet to you? 28For he has sent to us *in* Babylon, saying, 'This *captivity is* long; build houses and dwell *in them*, and plant gardens and eat their fruit.' "

29 Now Zephaniah the priest read this letter in the hearing of Jeremiah the prophet. 30Then the word of the LORD came to Jeremiah, saying: 31Send to all those in captivity, saying, Thus says the LORD concerning Shemaiah the Nehelamite: Because Shemaiah has prophesied to you, and I have not sent him, and he has caused you to trust in a lie— 32therefore thus says the LORD: Behold, I will punish Shemaiah the Nehelamite and his family: he shall not have anyone to dwell among this people, nor shall he see the good that I will do for My people, says the LORD, because he has taught rebellion against the LORD.

30 The* word that came to Jeremiah from the LORD, saying, 2"Thus speaks the LORD God of Israel, saying: 'Write in a book for yourself all the words that I have spoken to you. 3For behold, the days are coming,' says the LORD, 'that I will bring back from captivity My people Israel and Judah,' says the LORD. 'And I will cause them to return to the land that I gave to their fathers, and they shall possess it.' "

4Now these *are* the words that the LORD spoke concerning Israel and Judah.

5"For thus says the LORD:

'We have heard a voice of trembling,
Of fear, and not of peace.
6 Ask now, and see,
Whether a man is ever in labor with child?
So why do I see every man *with* his hands
   on his loins
Like a woman in labor,
And all faces turned pale?
7 Alas! For that day *is* great,
So that none *is* like it;
And it *is* the time of Jacob's trouble,
But he shall be saved out of it.

8 'For it shall come to pass in that day,'
Says the LORD of hosts,
'*That* I will break his yoke from your
   neck,
And will burst your bonds;
Foreigners shall no more enslave them.
9 But they shall serve the LORD their God,
And David their king,
Whom I will raise up for them.

10 'Therefore do not fear, O My servant Jacob,'
   says the LORD,
'Nor be dismayed, O Israel;
For behold, I will save you from afar,
And your seed from the land of their
   captivity.
Jacob shall return, have rest and be quiet,
And no one shall make *him* afraid.
11 For I *am* with you,' says the LORD, 'to save
   you;
Though I make a full end of all nations
   where I have scattered you,
Yet I will not make a complete end of you.
But I will correct you in justice,
And will not let you go altogether
   unpunished.'

12 "For thus says the LORD:

'Your affliction *is* incurable,
Your wound *is* severe.
13 *There is* no one to plead your cause,
That you may be bound up;
You have no healing medicines.
14 All your lovers have forgotten you;
They do not seek you;
For I have wounded you with the wound of
   an enemy,
With the chastisement of a cruel one,
For the multitude of your iniquities,
Because your sins have increased.
15 Why do you cry about your affliction?
Your sorrow *is* incurable.
Because of the multitude of your iniquities,
Because your sins have increased,
I have done these things to you.

16 'Therefore all those who devour you shall
   be devoured;
And all your adversaries, every one of them,
   shall go into captivity;
Those who plunder you shall become
   plunder,
And all who prey upon you I will make a
   prey.
17 For I will restore health to you
And heal you of your wounds,' says the
   LORD,
'Because they called you an outcast *saying:*

"This *is* Zion;
No one seeks her." '

18"Thus says the LORD:

'Behold, I will bring back the captivity of
    Jacob's tents,
And have mercy on his dwelling places;
The city shall be built upon its own mound,
And the palace shall remain according to
    its own plan.
19   Then out of them shall proceed
        thanksgiving
And the voice of those who make merry;
I will multiply them, and they shall not
    diminish;
I will also glorify them, and they shall not
    be small.
20   Their children also shall be as before,
And their congregation shall be established
    before Me;
And I will punish all who oppress them.
21   Their nobles shall be from among them,
And their governor shall come from their
    midst;
Then I will cause him to draw near,
And he shall approach Me;
For who *is* this who pledged his heart to
    approach Me?' says the LORD.
22   'You shall be My people,
And I will be your God.' "

23   Behold, the whirlwind of the LORD
Goes forth with fury,
A continuing whirlwind;
It will fall violently on the head of the
    wicked.
24   The fierce anger of the LORD will not return
    until He has done it,
And until He has performed the intents of
    His heart.

In the latter days you will consider it.

31 "At the same time," says the LORD, "I will
be the God of all the families of Israel, and
they shall be My people."
2Thus says the LORD:

"The people who survived the sword
Found grace in the wilderness—
Israel, when I went to give him rest."

3   *The LORD has appeared of old to me, *saying*:
"Yes, I have loved you with an everlasting
    love;
Therefore with lovingkindness I have drawn
    you.
4   Again I will build you, and you shall be
    rebuilt,
O virgin of Israel!
You shall again be adorned with your
    tambourines,
And shall go forth in the dances of those
    who rejoice.
5   You shall yet plant vines on the mountains
    of Samaria;
The planters shall plant and eat *them* as
    ordinary food.
6   For there shall be a day
When the watchmen will cry on Mount
    Ephraim,

CHAPTER 31

31:3–6 The tragedy of sin is that it keeps
God from being to us all that He wants to
be.

He is our Lover. The image of marriage
is frequently found in both Jeremiah and
Hosea. When we disobey God, we sin not
only against His law but also against His
love. We break the heart of God when we
give our love to what He hates.

'Arise, and let us go up *to* Zion,
To the LORD our God.' "

7*For thus says the LORD:

"Sing with gladness for Jacob,
And shout among the chief of the nations;
Proclaim, give praise, and say,
'O LORD, save Your people,
The remnant of Israel!'
8   Behold, I will bring them from the north
        country,
And gather them from the ends of the earth,
Among them the blind and the lame,
The woman with child
And the one who labors with child, together;
A great throng shall return there.
9   They shall come with weeping,
And with supplications I will lead them.
I will cause them to walk by the rivers of
        waters,
In a straight way in which they shall not
        stumble;
For I am a Father to Israel,
And Ephraim *is* My firstborn.

10*"Hear the word of the LORD, O nations,
And declare *it* in the isles afar off, and
        say,
'He who scattered Israel will gather him,
And keep him as a shepherd *does* his flock.'
11   For the LORD has redeemed Jacob,
And ransomed him from the hand of one
        stronger than he.
12   Therefore they shall come and sing in the
        height of Zion,
Streaming to the goodness of the LORD—
For wheat and new wine and oil,
For the young of the flock and the herd;
Their souls shall be like a well-watered
        garden,
And they shall sorrow no more at all.

13 "Then shall the virgin rejoice in the dance,
And the young men and the old, together;
For I will turn their mourning to joy,
Will comfort them,
And make them rejoice rather than sorrow.
14   I will satiate the soul of the priests with
        abundance,
And My people shall be satisfied with My
        goodness, says the LORD."

15*Thus says the LORD:

"A voice was heard in Ramah,
Lamentation *and* bitter weeping,
Rachel weeping for her children,
Refusing to be comforted for her children,
Because they *are* no more."

16Thus says the LORD:

"Refrain your voice from weeping,
And your eyes from tears;
For your work shall be rewarded, says the
        LORD,
And they shall come back from the land of
        the enemy.
17   There is hope in your future, says the LORD,
That *your* children shall come back to their
        own border.

31:7–9 *He is our Father.* Israel is His firstborn; He redeemed the people in Egypt (Exod. 4:22). God wants to be a Father to us (2 Cor. 6:14–16), but our sins stand in the way.

31:10–12 *He is our Shepherd.* The flock of Israel was smitten and scattered, but the Lord was caring for it just the same. No matter how dark the day, the Shepherd will find you, lead you, and give you a song.

31:15–40 *He is our Comforter.* What lamentation there was when homes were broken up and people were carried off to a foreign land! But God gave the word of comfort: they will come home again. He promised them a new covenant that would change their hearts, and we have that covenant in Jesus Christ (Heb. 8; 10:1–25).

18 "I have surely heard Ephraim bemoaning
      himself:
   'You have chastised me, and I was chastised,
   Like an untrained bull;
   Restore me, and I will return,
   For You *are* the LORD my God.
19   Surely, after my turning, I repented;
   And after I was instructed, I struck myself
      on the thigh;
   I was ashamed, yes, even humiliated,
   Because I bore the reproach of my youth.'
20   *Is* Ephraim My dear son?
   Is he a pleasant child?
   For though I spoke against him,
   I earnestly remember him still;
   Therefore My heart yearns for him;
   I will surely have mercy on him, says the
      LORD.

21 "Set up signposts,
   Make landmarks;
   Set your heart toward the highway,
   The way in *which* you went.
   Turn back, O virgin of Israel,
   Turn back to these your cities.
22   How long will you gad about,
   O you backsliding daughter?
   For the LORD has created a new thing in the
      earth—
   A woman shall encompass a man."

23Thus says the LORD of hosts, the God of Israel:
"They shall again use this speech in the land of
Judah and in its cities, when I bring back their
captivity: 'The LORD bless you, O home of justice,
and mountain of holiness!' 24And there shall dwell
in Judah itself, and in all its cities together, farmers and those going out with flocks. 25For I have
satiated the weary soul, and I have replenished
every sorrowful soul."

26After this I awoke and looked around, and
my sleep was sweet to me.

27"Behold, the days are coming, says the LORD,
that I will sow the house of Israel and the house
of Judah with the seed of man and the seed of
beast. 28And it shall come to pass, *that* as I have
watched over them to pluck up, to break down,
to throw down, to destroy, and to afflict, so I will
watch over them to build and to plant, says the
LORD. 29In those days they shall say no more:

   'The fathers have eaten sour grapes,
   And the children's teeth are set on edge.'

30But every one shall die for his own iniquity;
every man who eats the sour grapes, his teeth shall
be set on edge.

31"Behold, the days are coming, says the LORD,
when I will make a new covenant with the house
of Israel and with the house of Judah— 32not according to the covenant that I made with their
fathers in the day *that* I took them by the hand
to lead them out of the land of Egypt, My covenant
which they broke, though I was a husband to
them,ᶻ says the LORD. 33But this *is* the covenant
that I will make with the house of Israel after
those days, says the LORD: I will put My law in
their minds, and write it on their hearts; and I

31:32 ᶻFollowing Masoretic Text, Targum, and Vulgate;
Septuagint and Syriac read *and I turned away from them.*

will be their God, and they shall be My people. [34]No more shall every man teach his neighbor, and every man his brother, saying, 'Know the LORD,' for they all shall know Me, from the least of them to the greatest of them, says the LORD. For I will forgive their iniquity, and their sin I will remember no more."

35 Thus says the LORD,
Who gives the sun for a light by day,
The ordinances of the moon and the stars
   for a light by night,
Who disturbs the sea,
And its waves roar
(The LORD of hosts *is* His name):

36 "If those ordinances depart
From before Me, says the LORD,
Then the seed of Israel shall also cease
From being a nation before Me forever."

[37]Thus says the LORD:

"If heaven above can be measured,
And the foundations of the earth searched
   out beneath,
I will also cast off all the seed of Israel
For all that they have done, says the LORD.

[38]"Behold, the days are coming, says the LORD, that the city shall be built for the LORD from the Tower of Hananel to the Corner Gate. [39]The surveyor's line shall again extend straight forward over the hill Gareb; then it shall turn toward Goath. [40]And the whole valley of the dead bodies and of the ashes, and all the fields as far as the Brook Kidron, to the corner of the Horse Gate toward the east, *shall be* holy to the LORD. It shall not be plucked up or thrown down anymore forever."

32 The* word that came to Jeremiah from the LORD in the tenth year of Zedekiah king of Judah, which was the eighteenth year of Nebuchadnezzar. [2]For then the king of Babylon's army besieged Jerusalem, and Jeremiah the prophet was shut up in the court of the prison, which *was in* the king of Judah's house. [3]For Zedekiah king of Judah had shut him up, saying, "Why do you prophesy and say, 'Thus says the LORD: "Behold, I will give this city into the hand of the king of Babylon, and he shall take it; [4]and Zedekiah king of Judah shall not escape from the hand of the Chaldeans, but shall surely be delivered into the hand of the king of Babylon, and shall speak with him face to face,[a] and see him eye to eye; [5]then he shall lead Zedekiah to Babylon, and there he shall be until I visit him," says the LORD; "though you fight with the Chaldeans, you shall not succeed" '?"

[6]And Jeremiah said, "The word of the LORD came to me, saying, [7]'Behold, Hanamel the son of Shallum your uncle will come to you, saying, "Buy my field which *is* in Anathoth, for the right of redemption *is* yours to buy *it*." ' [8]Then Hanamel my uncle's son came to me in the court of the prison according to the word of the LORD, and said to me, 'Please buy my field that *is* in Anathoth, which *is* in the country of Benjamin; for

CHAPTER 32

32:1ff "Put your money where your mouth is!" is an American saying that means "Practice what you preach!" Jeremiah had been preaching that the Jews would one day return from exile, so God made him prove that he really believed God's promise. Whenever you share the Word with people, expect to be tested. This is the only way they can tell the reality of your faith.

How foolish to purchase property in a town occupied by the enemy! But if you believe that there is a future for that land, you will not hesitate to buy it. God's people live in the future tense and measure today's decisions in the light of tomorrow's certainties.

You may feel let down after you have made a great step of faith, and that is the time to pray and let the Lord speak to you and assure you. People may laugh at you, but rest in the Lord and allow Him to encourage you.

32:4 [a]Literally *mouth to mouth*

the right of inheritance *is* yours, and the redemption yours; buy *it* for yourself.' Then I knew that this was the word of the LORD. 9So I bought the field from Hanamel, the son of my uncle who *was* in Anathoth, and weighed *out to* him the money—seventeen shekels of silver. 10And I signed the deed and sealed *it*, took witnesses, and weighed the money on the scales. 11So I took the purchase deed, *both* that which was sealed *according to* the law and custom, and that which was open; 12and I gave the purchase deed to Baruch the son of Neriah, son of Mahseiah, in the presence of Hanamel my uncle's *son*, and in the presence of the witnesses who signed the purchase deed, before all the Jews who sat in the court of the prison.

13"Then I charged Baruch before them, saying, 14'Thus says the LORD of hosts, the God of Israel: "Take these deeds, both this purchase deed which is sealed and this deed which is open, and put them in an earthen vessel, that they may last many days." 15For thus says the LORD of hosts, the God of Israel: "Houses and fields and vineyards shall be possessed again in this land." '

16"Now when I had delivered the purchase deed to Baruch the son of Neriah, I prayed to the LORD, saying: 17'Ah, Lord GOD! Behold, You have made the heavens and the earth by Your great power and outstretched arm. There is nothing too hard for You. 18*You* show lovingkindness to thousands, and repay the iniquity of the fathers into the bosom of their children after them—the Great, the Mighty God, whose name *is* the LORD of hosts. 19*You are* great in counsel and mighty in work, for your eyes *are* open to all the ways of the sons of men, to give everyone according to his ways and according to the fruit of his doings. 20You have set signs and wonders in the land of Egypt, to this day, and in Israel and among *other* men; and You have made Yourself a name, as it is this day. 21You have brought Your people Israel out of the land of Egypt with signs and wonders, with a strong hand and an outstretched arm, and with great terror; 22You have given them this land, of which You swore to their fathers to give them—"a land flowing with milk and honey."*b* 23And they came in and took possession of it, but they have not obeyed Your voice or walked in Your law. They have done nothing of all that You commanded them to do; therefore You have caused all this calamity to come upon them.

24'Look, the siege mounds! They have come to the city to take it; and the city has been given into the hand of the Chaldeans who fight against it, because of the sword and famine and pestilence. What You have spoken has happened; there You see *it*! 25And You have said to me, O Lord GOD, "Buy the field for money, and take witnesses"!—yet the city has been given into the hand of the Chaldeans.' "

26Then the word of the LORD came to Jeremiah, saying, 27"Behold, I *am* the LORD, the God of all flesh. Is there anything too hard for Me? 28Therefore thus says the LORD: 'Behold, I will give this city into the hand of the Chaldeans, into the hand of Nebuchadnezzar king of Babylon, and he shall take it. 29And the Chaldeans who fight against this city shall come and set fire to this city and burn it, with the houses on whose roofs they have offered incense to Baal and poured out

---

32:22 *b*Exodus 3:8

drink offerings to other gods, to provoke Me to anger; 30because the children of Israel and the children of Judah have done only evil before Me from their youth. For the children of Israel have provoked Me only to anger with the work of their hands,' says the LORD. 31'For this city has been to Me *a provocation of* My anger and My fury from the day that they built it, even to this day; so I will remove it from before My face 32because of all the evil of the children of Israel and the children of Judah, which they have done to provoke Me to anger—they, their kings, their princes, their priests, their prophets, the men of Judah, and the inhabitants of Jerusalem. 33And they have turned to Me the back, and not the face; though I taught them, rising up early and teaching *them,* yet they have not listened to receive instruction. 34But they set their abominations in the house which is called by My name, to defile it. 35And they built the high places of Baal which *are* in the Valley of the Son of Hinnom, to cause their sons and their daughters to pass through *the fire* to Molech, which I did not command them, nor did it come into My mind that they should do this abomination, to cause Judah to sin.'

36"Now therefore, thus says the LORD, the God of Israel, concerning this city of which you say, 'It shall be delivered into the hand of the king of Babylon by the sword, by the famine, and by the pestilence: 37Behold, I will gather them out of all countries where I have driven them in My anger, in My fury, and in great wrath; I will bring them back to this place, and I will cause them to dwell safely. 38They shall be My people, and I will be their God; 39then I will give them one heart and one way, that they may fear Me forever, for the good of them and their children after them. 40And I will make an everlasting covenant with them, that I will not turn away from doing them good; but I will put My fear in their hearts so that they will not depart from Me. 41Yes, I will rejoice over them to do them good, and I will assuredly plant them in this land, with all My heart and with all My soul.'

42"For thus says the LORD: 'Just as I have brought all this great calamity on this people, so I will bring on them all the good that I have promised them. 43And fields will be bought in this land of which you say, "It is desolate, without man or beast; it has been given into the hand of the Chaldeans." 44Men will buy fields for money, sign deeds and seal *them,* and take witnesses, in the land of Benjamin, in the places around Jerusalem, in the cities of Judah, in the cities of the mountains, in the cities of the lowland, and in the cities of the South; for I will cause their captives to return,' says the LORD."

33 Moreover* the word of the LORD came to Jeremiah a second time, while he was still shut up in the court of the prison, saying, 2"Thus says the LORD who made it, the LORD who formed it to establish it (the LORD *is* His name): 3'Call to Me, and I will answer you, and show you great and mighty things, which you do not know.'

4"For thus says the LORD, the God of Israel, concerning the houses of this city and the houses of the kings of Judah, which have been pulled down *to fortify*c against the siege mounds and the

33:4 cCompare Isaiah 22:10

CHAPTER 33

33:1ff Men may shut up God's servant, but they cannot shut out God's Word (2 Tim. 2:9). The Word comes to you—no matter where you are—if your heart is open to the Lord. God sometimes has a "second" message for you, so be alert.

God sent his imprisoned prophet a message of encouragement. The "sick" nation would one day have health; the defiled nation would be cleansed; war would give way to peace; and the truth of God would conquer the lies of the false prophets. There would be wedding songs, not funeral dirges; and righteousness would reign from the throne of David.

When will this occur? When Jesus Christ, the Son of David, reigns on earth (23:5–6) and makes Jerusalem a city of righteousness. Meanwhile, as He reigns in our lives, we can be His servants and minister to those who need these same blessings. Through us, the Lord can bring to others the life-changing message of spiritual health, cleansing, and peace, and they can start rebuilding what sin has torn down.

sword: 5'They come to fight with the Chaldeans, but *only* to fill their places[d] with the dead bodies of men whom I will slay in My anger and My fury, all for whose wickedness I have hidden My face from this city. 6Behold, I will bring it health and healing; I will heal them and reveal to them the abundance of peace and truth. 7And I will cause the captives of Judah and the captives of Israel to return, and will rebuild those places as at the first. 8I will cleanse them from all their iniquity by which they have sinned against Me, and I will pardon all their iniquities by which they have sinned and by which they have transgressed against Me. 9Then it shall be to Me a name of joy, a praise, and an honor before all nations of the earth, who shall hear all the good that I do to them; they shall fear and tremble for all the goodness and all the prosperity that I provide for it.'

10"Thus says the LORD: 'Again there shall be heard in this place—of which you say, "It *is* desolate, without man and without beast"—in the cities of Judah, in the streets of Jerusalem that are desolate, without man and without inhabitant and without beast, 11the voice of joy and the voice of gladness, the voice of the bridegroom and the voice of the bride, the voice of those who will say:

> "Praise the LORD of hosts,
> For the LORD *is* good,
> For His mercy *endures* forever"—

and of those *who will* bring the sacrifice of praise into the house of the LORD. For I will cause the captives of the land to return as at the first,' says the LORD.

12"Thus says the LORD of hosts: 'In this place which is desolate, without man and without beast, and in all its cities, there shall again be a dwelling place of shepherds causing *their* flocks to lie down. 13In the cities of the mountains, in the cities of the lowland, in the cities of the South, in the land of Benjamin, in the places around Jerusalem, and in the cities of Judah, the flocks shall again pass under the hands of him who counts *them*,' says the LORD.

14'Behold, the days are coming,' says the LORD, 'that I will perform that good thing which I have promised to the house of Israel and to the house of Judah:

15 'In those days and at that time
    I will cause to grow up to David
    A Branch of righteousness;
    He shall execute judgment and
        righteousness in the earth.
16 In those days Judah will be saved,
    And Jerusalem will dwell safely.
    And this *is the name* by which she will be
        called:

THE LORD OUR RIGHTEOUSNESS.'[e]

17"For thus says the LORD: 'David shall never lack a man to sit on the throne of the house of Israel; 18nor shall the priests, the Levites, lack a man to offer burnt offerings before Me, to kindle grain offerings, and to sacrifice continually.' "

19And the word of the LORD came to Jeremiah, saying, 20"Thus says the LORD: 'If you can break

---

33:5 [d]Compare 2 Kings 23:14   33:16 [e]Compare 23:5, 6

My covenant with the day and My covenant with the night, so that there will not be day and night in their season, 21then My covenant may also be broken with David My servant, so that he shall not have a son to reign on his throne, and with the Levites, the priests, My ministers. 22As the host of heaven cannot be numbered, nor the sand of the sea measured, so will I multiply the descendants of David My servant and the Levites who minister to Me.' "

23Moreover the word of the LORD came to Jeremiah, saying, 24"Have you not considered what these people have spoken, saying, 'The two families which the LORD has chosen, He has also cast them off'? Thus they have despised My people, as if they should no more be a nation before them.

25"Thus says the LORD: 'If My covenant is not with day and night, and if I have not appointed the ordinances of heaven and earth, 26then I will cast away the descendants of Jacob and David My servant, so that I will not take any of his descendants to be rulers over the descendants of Abraham, Isaac, and Jacob. For I will cause their captives to return, and will have mercy on them.' "

34 The* word which came to Jeremiah from the LORD, when Nebuchadnezzar king of Babylon and all his army, all the kingdoms of the earth under his dominion, and all the people, fought against Jerusalem and all its cities, saying, 2"Thus says the LORD, the God of Israel: 'Go and speak to Zedekiah king of Judah and tell him, "Thus says the LORD: 'Behold, I will give this city into the hand of the king of Babylon, and he shall burn it with fire. 3And you shall not escape from his hand, but shall surely be taken and delivered into his hand; your eyes shall see the eyes of the king of Babylon, he shall speak with you face to face,f and you shall go to Babylon.' " ' 4Yet hear the word of the LORD, O Zedekiah king of Judah! Thus says the LORD concerning you: 'You shall not die by the sword. 5You shall die in peace; as in the ceremonies of your fathers, the former kings who were before you, so they shall burn incense for you and lament for you, saying, "Alas, lord!" For I have pronounced the word, says the LORD.' "

6Then Jeremiah the prophet spoke all these words to Zedekiah king of Judah in Jerusalem, 7when the king of Babylon's army fought against Jerusalem and all the cities of Judah that were left, against Lachish and Azekah; for only these fortified cities remained of the cities of Judah.

8*This is the word that came to Jeremiah from the LORD, after King Zedekiah had made a covenant with all the people who were at Jerusalem to proclaim liberty to them: 9that every man should set free his male and female slave—a Hebrew man or woman—that no one should keep a Jewish brother in bondage. 10Now when all the princes and all the people, who had entered into the covenant, heard that everyone should set free his male and female slaves, that no one should keep them in bondage anymore, they obeyed and let them go. 11But afterward they changed their minds and made the male and female slaves return, whom they had set free, and brought them into subjection as male and female slaves.

12Therefore the word of the LORD came to

CHAPTER 34

34:1–7 Bondage to the enemy. When the enemy finally broke through the city wall, King Zedekiah would try to escape but would fail (2 Kings 25:1–7). Jeremiah told the king to submit to Babylon, but he would not obey. Therefore, the king would be captured, bound and blinded, and taken to Babylon where he would die. His bondage to sin led to bondage to the enemy. He destroyed himself.

34:8–22 Bondage to the brethren. The Jews were not to enslave their brethren; and every seven years, their servants were to be set free (Exod. 21:1–11; Deut. 15:12–18). The people in Jerusalem obeyed this law during the siege; but when the Babylonian army retreated because of the Egyptian army (v. 21; 37:5–10), the people took their slaves back again! The owners had obeyed when things were difficult, hoping to appease the Lord; but when things got better, they changed their minds (Ps. 66:13–14).

Obedience must come from devotion within us (Eph. 6:6) and not depend on circumstances around us. These masters were in greater slavery than their servants because they did not seek to please the Lord.

34:3 fLiterally mouth to mouth

Jeremiah from the LORD, saying, 13"Thus says the LORD, the God of Israel: 'I made a covenant with your fathers in the day that I brought them out of the land of Egypt, out of the house of bondage, saying, 14"At the end of seven years let every man set free his Hebrew brother, who has been sold to him; and when he has served you six years, you shall let him go free from you." But your fathers did not obey Me nor incline their ear. 15Then you recently turned and did what was right in My sight—every man proclaiming liberty to his neighbor; and you made a covenant before Me in the house which is called by My name. 16Then you turned around and profaned My name, and every one of you brought back his male and female slaves, whom he had set at liberty, at their pleasure, and brought them back into subjection, to be your male and female slaves.'

17"Therefore thus says the LORD: 'You have not obeyed Me in proclaiming liberty, every one to his brother and every one to his neighbor. Behold, I proclaim liberty to you,' says the LORD—'to the sword, to pestilence, and to famine! And I will deliver you to trouble among all the kingdoms of the earth. 18And I will give the men who have transgressed My covenant, who have not performed the words of the covenant which they made before Me, when they cut the calf in two and passed between the parts of it— 19the princes of Judah, the princes of Jerusalem, the eunuchs, the priests, and all the people of the land who passed between the parts of the calf— 20I will give them into the hand of their enemies and into the hand of those who seek their life. Their dead bodies shall be for meat for the birds of the heaven and the beasts of the earth. 21And I will give Zedekiah king of Judah and his princes into the hand of their enemies, into the hand of those who seek their life, and into the hand of the king of Babylon's army which has gone back from you. 22Behold, I will command,' says the LORD, 'and cause them to return to this city. They will fight against it and take it and burn it with fire; and I will make the cities of Judah a desolation without inhabitant.' "

CHAPTER 35

35:1ff The founder of the Rechabite family had assisted Jehu in removing Baal worship from the land (2 Kings 10:15–17), so they had a godly heritage. When the Babylonian army moved in, the Rechabites had to abandon their nomadic way of life and enter Jerusalem for safety.

They abandoned their tents, but they did not abandon their standards. Even though they were in the house of the Lord with a prophet of the Lord, they refused to drink wine. The Rechabites did not ask others to agree with their tradition, but they would not violate it themselves. They were a loyal clan.

Man's tradition is not necessarily bad, unless it is contradicted by or substituted for God's truth (Matt. 15:1–20). You may not agree with the traditions of others, but are you as devoted to God's Word as they are to their traditions? The Jews refused to obey *the very law of God,* but the Rechabites obeyed *human traditions.* What an indictment against the Jews who claimed to know the true God! Is it an indictment against us today?

35 The* word which came to Jeremiah from the LORD in the days of Jehoiakim the son of Josiah, king of Judah, saying, 2"Go to the house of the Rechabites, speak to them, and bring them into the house of the LORD, into one of the chambers, and give them wine to drink."

3Then I took Jaazaniah the son of Jeremiah, the son of Habazziniah, his brothers and all his sons, and the whole house of the Rechabites, 4and I brought them into the house of the LORD, into the chamber of the sons of Hanan the son of Igdaliah, a man of God, which *was* by the chamber of the princes, above the chamber of Maaseiah the son of Shallum, the keeper of the door. 5Then I set before the sons of the house of the Rechabites bowls full of wine, and cups; and I said to them, "Drink wine."

6But they said, "We will drink no wine, for Jonadab the son of Rechab, our father, commanded us, saying, 'You shall drink no wine, you nor your sons, forever. 7You shall not build a house, sow seed, plant a vineyard, nor have *any of these;* but all your days you shall dwell in tents, that you may live many days in the land where you are sojourners.' 8Thus we have obeyed the voice of Jonadab the son of Rechab, our father, in all that he charged us, to drink no wine all our days, we, our wives, our sons, or our daughters, 9nor to build ourselves houses to dwell in; nor do we have vineyard, field, or seed. 10But we have dwelt in tents, and have obeyed and done according to all that Jonadab our father commanded us. 11But it came to pass, when Nebuchadnezzar king of Babylon came up into the land, that we said, 'Come, let us go to Jerusalem for fear of the army of the Chaldeans and for fear of the army of the Syrians.' So we dwell at Jerusalem."

12Then came the word of the LORD to Jeremiah, saying, 13"Thus says the LORD of hosts, the God of Israel: 'Go and tell the men of Judah and the inhabitants of Jerusalem, "Will you not receive instruction to obey My words?" says the LORD. 14"The words of Jonadab the son of Rechab, which he commanded his sons, not to drink wine, are performed; for to this day they drink none, and obey their father's commandment. But although I have spoken to you, rising early and speaking, you did not obey Me. 15I have also sent to you all My servants the prophets, rising up early and sending *them*, saying, 'Turn now everyone from his evil way, amend your doings, and do not go after other gods to serve them; then you will dwell in the land which I have given you and your fathers.' But you have not inclined your ear, nor obeyed Me. 16Surely the sons of Jonadab the son of Rechab have performed the commandment of their father, which he commanded them, but this people has not obeyed Me."'

17"Therefore thus says the LORD God of hosts, the God of Israel: 'Behold, I will bring on Judah and on all the inhabitants of Jerusalem all the doom that I have pronounced against them; because I have spoken to them but they have not heard, and I have called to them but they have not answered.'"

18And Jeremiah said to the house of the Rechabites, "Thus says the LORD of hosts, the God of Israel: 'Because you have obeyed the commandment of Jonadab your father, and kept all his precepts and done according to all that he commanded you, 19therefore thus says the LORD of hosts, the God of Israel: "Jonadab the son of Rechab shall not lack a man to stand before Me forever."'"

36 Now* it came to pass in the fourth year of Jehoiakim the son of Josiah, king of Judah, *that* this word came to Jeremiah from the LORD, saying: 2"Take a scroll of a book and write on it all the words that I have spoken to you against Israel, against Judah, and against all the nations, from the day I spoke to you, from the days of Josiah even to this day. 3It may be that the house of Judah will hear all the adversities which I purpose to bring upon them, that everyone may turn from his evil way, that I may forgive their iniquity and their sin."

4Then Jeremiah called Baruch the son of Neriah; and Baruch wrote on a scroll of a book, at the instruction of Jeremiah,g all the words of the LORD which He had spoken to him. 5*And Jeremiah commanded Baruch, saying, "I *am* confined, I cannot go into the house of the LORD. 6You go, therefore, and read from the scroll which you

CHAPTER 36

36:1–4 *God's Word written.* Unlike any other book, the Bible is God's Word, inspired by the Spirit of God (2 Tim. 3:13–17; 2 Pet. 1:19–21). Therefore, it can be trusted, and it must be obeyed.

36:5–16 *God's Word announced.* God uses human instruments to declare His divine Word to men: "And how shall they hear without a preacher?" (Rom. 10:14).

❝*The deathless Book has survived three great dangers: the negligence of its friends; the false systems built upon it; the warfare of those who have hated it.*❞

—Isaac Taylor

have written at my instruction,[h] the words of the LORD, in the hearing of the people in the LORD's house on the day of fasting. And you shall also read them in the hearing of all Judah who come from their cities. [7]It may be that they will present their supplication before the LORD, and everyone will turn from his evil way. For great is the anger and the fury that the LORD has pronounced against this people." [8]And Baruch the son of Neriah did according to all that Jeremiah the prophet commanded him, reading from the book the words of the LORD in the LORD's house.

[9]Now it came to pass in the fifth year of Jehoiakim the son of Josiah, king of Judah, in the ninth month, that they proclaimed a fast before the LORD to all the people in Jerusalem, and to all the people who came from the cities of Judah to Jerusalem. [10]Then Baruch read from the book the words of Jeremiah in the house of the LORD, in the chamber of Gemariah the son of Shaphan the scribe, in the upper court at the entry of the New Gate of the LORD's house, in the hearing of all the people.

[11]When Michaiah the son of Gemariah, the son of Shaphan, heard all the words of the LORD from the book, [12]he then went down to the king's house, into the scribe's chamber; and there all the princes were sitting—Elishama the scribe, Delaiah the son of Shemaiah, Elnathan the son of Achbor, Gemariah the son of Shaphan, Zedekiah the son of Hananiah, and all the princes. [13]Then Michaiah declared to them all the words that he had heard when Baruch read the book in the hearing of the people. [14]Therefore all the princes sent Jehudi the son of Nethaniah, the son of Shelemiah, the son of Cushi, to Baruch, saying, "Take in your hand the scroll from which you have read in the hearing of the people, and come." So Baruch the son of Neriah took the scroll in his hand and came to them. [15]And they said to him, "Sit down now, and read it in our hearing." So Baruch read it in their hearing.

[16]Now it happened, when they had heard all the words, that they looked in fear from one to another, and said to Baruch, "We will surely tell the king of all these words." [17]And they asked Baruch, saying, "Tell us now, how did you write all these words—at his instruction?"[i]

[18]So Baruch answered them, "He proclaimed with his mouth all these words to me, and I wrote them with ink in the book."

[19]Then the princes said to Baruch, "Go and hide, you and Jeremiah; and let no one know where you are."

36:20–26 God's Word destroyed. The king should have been copying the Law for himself (Deut. 17:18–20) and heeding its message. Instead, he destroyed what Jeremiah had spoken and Baruch had written. You can try to destroy the Bible, but you will fail.

[20]*And they went to the king, into the court; but they stored the scroll in the chamber of Elishama the scribe, and told all the words in the hearing of the king. [21]So the king sent Jehudi to bring the scroll, and he took it from Elishama the scribe's chamber. And Jehudi read it in the hearing of the king and in the hearing of all the princes who stood beside the king. [22]Now the king was sitting in the winter house in the ninth month, with a fire burning on the hearth before him. [23]And it happened, when Jehudi had read three or four columns, that the king cut it with the scribe's knife and cast it into the fire that was

---

36:6 [h]Literally from my mouth   36:17 [i]Literally with his mouth

on the hearth, until all the scroll was consumed in the fire that *was* on the hearth. 24Yet they were not afraid, nor did they tear their garments, the king nor any of his servants who heard all these words. 25Nevertheless Elnathan, Delaiah, and Gemariah implored the king not to burn the scroll; but he would not listen to them. 26And the king commanded Jerahmeel the king's*j* son, Seraiah the son of Azriel, and Shelemiah the son of Abdeel, to seize Baruch the scribe and Jeremiah the prophet, but the LORD hid them.

27*Now after the king had burned the scroll with the words which Baruch had written at the instruction of Jeremiah,*k* the word of the LORD came to Jeremiah, saying: 28"Take yet another scroll, and write on it all the former words that were in the first scroll which Jehoiakim the king of Judah has burned. 29And you shall say to Jehoiakim king of Judah, 'Thus says the LORD: "You have burned this scroll, saying, 'Why have you written in it that the king of Babylon will certainly come and destroy this land, and cause man and beast to cease from here?' " 30Therefore thus says the LORD concerning Jehoiakim king of Judah: "He shall have no one to sit on the throne of David, and his dead body shall be cast out to the heat of the day and the frost of the night. 31I will punish him, his family, and his servants for their iniquity; and I will bring on them, on the inhabitants of Jerusalem, and on the men of Judah all the doom that I have pronounced against them; but they did not heed." ' "

32Then Jeremiah took another scroll and gave it to Baruch the scribe, the son of Neriah, who wrote on it at the instruction of Jeremiah*l* all the words of the book which Jehoiakim king of Judah had burned in the fire. And besides, there were added to them many similar words.

37 Now* King Zedekiah the son of Josiah reigned instead of Coniah the son of Jehoiakim, whom Nebuchadnezzar king of Babylon made king in the land of Judah. 2But neither he nor his servants nor the people of the land gave heed to the words of the LORD which He spoke by the prophet Jeremiah.

3And Zedekiah the king sent Jehucal the son of Shelemiah, and Zephaniah the son of Maaseiah, the priest, to the prophet Jeremiah, saying, "Pray now to the LORD our God for us." 4Now Jeremiah was coming and going among the people, for they had not *yet* put him in prison. 5Then Pharaoh's army came up from Egypt; and when the Chaldeans who were besieging Jerusalem heard news of them, they departed from Jerusalem.

6Then the word of the LORD came to the prophet Jeremiah, saying, 7"Thus says the LORD, the God of Israel, 'Thus you shall say to the king of Judah, who sent you to Me to inquire of Me: "Behold, Pharaoh's army which has come up to help you will return to Egypt, to their own land. 8And the Chaldeans shall come back and fight against this city, and take it and burn it with fire." ' 9Thus says the LORD: 'Do not deceive yourselves, saying, "The Chaldeans will surely depart from us," for they will not depart. 10For though you had

36:27–32 *God's Word preserved.* The king and his family are gone and would be forgotten were it not for the Book he tried to destroy! God's Word will endure: "Forever, O LORD, Your word is settled in heaven" (Ps. 119:89); "Heaven and earth will pass away, but My words will by no means pass away" (Matt. 24:35).

CHAPTER 37

37:1–10 *Expect to be "used."* Zedekiah wanted the intercession of the man of God but not the instruction of the Word of God. He never should have separated the two (John 15:7; Acts 6:4). He wanted God to be his servant and deliver the city, but he was not willing to be God's servant and obey the Word. Do you ask God for help only in emergencies, or do you seek His direction each day?

36:26 *j*Hebrew *Hammelech*   36:27 *k*Literally *from Jeremiah's mouth*   36:32 *l*Literally *from Jeremiah's mouth*

37:11–15 Expect to be misunderstood. While going on an innocent trip, Jeremiah was arrested, beaten, and put into prison! (See Acts 16:16–24.) The ungodly look for every opportunity to persecute the godly.

37:16, 17 Expect to be ignored. It did not worry the king that God's servant was in prison illegally and suffering miserably. The king would not be seen with Jeremiah, but he still wanted Jeremiah's help.

37:18–21 Expect to be cared for by God. The Lord had promised Jeremiah years before that He would care for him (1:8, 19), and He kept His promise. Jeremiah did not have an easy life, but he had a good conscience, for he knew he had been faithful to God.

CHAPTER 38

38:1ff Zedekiah was a weak king who was more interested in being popular with his friends than in being right with God. Since he was a doubleminded man, he was "unstable in all his ways" (James 1:8).

First, he allowed some of his friends to arrest Jeremiah and put him in a dungeon. Next, he let Ebed-Melech and thirty guards rescue Jeremiah and take him to a safe place. Then, Zedekiah had a private meeting with Jeremiah to ask for help! If the king had accepted God's message and obeyed it, he would have had the courage to stand up to his unbelieving friends and do what was right.

Jeremiah sank in the mire (v. 6), but the king was sinking even deeper (v. 22). His fear (v. 19) and unbelief ruined him. He could have saved himself and his people had he submitted to the Lord. Instead, he trusted his friends, and they dragged him down into the mire of disgrace and defeat.

defeated the whole army of the Chaldeans who fight against you, and there remained only wounded men among them, they would rise up, every man in his tent, and burn the city with fire.' "

11*And it happened, when the army of the Chaldeans left the siege of Jerusalem for fear of Pharaoh's army, 12that Jeremiah went out of Jerusalem to go into the land of Benjamin to claim his property there among the people. 13And when he was in the Gate of Benjamin, a captain of the guard was there whose name was Irijah the son of Shelemiah, the son of Hananiah; and he seized Jeremiah the prophet, saying, "You are defecting to the Chaldeans!"

14Then Jeremiah said, "False! I am not defecting to the Chaldeans." But he did not listen to him. So Irijah seized Jeremiah and brought him to the princes. 15Therefore the princes were angry with Jeremiah, and they struck him and put him in prison in the house of Jonathan the scribe. For they had made that the prison.

16*When Jeremiah entered the dungeon and the cells, and Jeremiah had remained there many days, 17then Zedekiah the king sent and took him out. The king asked him secretly in his house, and said, "Is there any word from the LORD?"

And Jeremiah said, "There is." Then he said, "You shall be delivered into the hand of the king of Babylon!"

18*Moreover Jeremiah said to King Zedekiah, "What offense have I committed against you, against your servants, or against this people, that you have put me in prison? 19Where now are your prophets who prophesied to you, saying, 'The king of Babylon will not come against you or against this land?' 20Therefore please hear now, O my lord the king. Please, let my petition be accepted before you, and do not make me return to the house of Jonathan the scribe, lest I die there."

21Then Zedekiah the king commanded that they should commit Jeremiah to the court of the prison, and that they should give him daily a piece of bread from the bakers' street, until all the bread in the city was gone. Thus Jeremiah remained in the court of the prison.

38 Now* Shephatiah the son of Mattan, Gedaliah the son of Pashhur, Jucalm the son of Shelemiah, and Pashhur the son of Malchiah heard the words that Jeremiah had spoken to all the people, saying, 2"Thus says the LORD: 'He who remains in this city shall die by the sword, by famine, and by pestilence; but he who goes over to the Chaldeans shall live; his life shall be as a prize to him, and he shall live.'n 3Thus says the LORD: 'This city shall surely be given into the hand of the king of Babylon's army, which shall take it.' "

4Therefore the princes said to the king, "Please, let this man be put to death, for thus he weakens the hands of the men of war who remain in this city, and the hands of all the people, by speaking such words to them. For this man does not seek the welfare of this people, but their harm."

5Then Zedekiah the king said, "Look, he is in your hand. For the king can do nothing against

---

38:1 mSame as Jehucal (compare 37:3)   38:2 nCompare 21:9

you." 6So they took Jeremiah and cast him into the dungeon of Malchiah the king's° son, which *was* in the court of the prison, and they let Jeremiah down with ropes. And in the dungeon *there was* no water, but mire. So Jeremiah sank in the mire.

7Now Ebed-Melech the Ethiopian, one of the eunuchs, who was in the king's house, heard that they had put Jeremiah in the dungeon. When the king was sitting at the Gate of Benjamin, 8Ebed-Melech went out of the king's house and spoke to the king, saying: 9"My lord the king, these men have done evil in all that they have done to Jeremiah the prophet, whom they have cast into the dungeon, and he is likely to die from hunger in the place where he is. For *there is* no more bread in the city." 10Then the king commanded Ebed-Melech the Ethiopian, saying, "Take from here thirty men with you, and lift Jeremiah the prophet out of the dungeon before he dies." 11So Ebed-Melech took the men with him and went into the house of the king under the treasury, and took from there old clothes and old rags, and let them down by ropes into the dungeon to Jeremiah. 12Then Ebed-Melech the Ethiopian said to Jeremiah, "Please put these old clothes and rags under your armpits, under the ropes." And Jeremiah did so. 13So they pulled Jeremiah up with ropes and lifted him out of the dungeon. And Jeremiah remained in the court of the prison.

14Then Zedekiah the king sent and had Jeremiah the prophet brought to him at the third entrance of the house of the LORD. And the king said to Jeremiah, "I will ask you something. Hide nothing from me."

15Jeremiah said to Zedekiah, "If I declare *it* to you, will you not surely put me to death? And if I give you advice, you will not listen to me."

16So Zedekiah the king swore secretly to Jeremiah, saying, "As the LORD lives, who made our very souls, I will not put you to death, nor will I give you into the hand of these men who seek your life."

17Then Jeremiah said to Zedekiah, "Thus says the LORD, the God of hosts, the God of Israel: 'If you surely surrender to the king of Babylon's princes, then your soul shall live; this city shall not be burned with fire, and you and your house shall live. 18But if you do not surrender to the king of Babylon's princes, then this city shall be given into the hand of the Chaldeans; they shall burn it with fire, and you shall not escape from their hand.' "

19And Zedekiah the king said to Jeremiah, "I am afraid of the Jews who have defected to the Chaldeans, lest they deliver me into their hand, and they abuse me."

20But Jeremiah said, "They shall not deliver *you*. Please, obey the voice of the LORD which I speak to you. So it shall be well with you, and your soul shall live. 21But if you refuse to surrender, this *is* the word that the LORD has shown me: 22'Now behold, all the women who are left in the king of Judah's house *shall be* surrendered to the king of Babylon's princes, and those *women* shall say:

"Your close friends have set upon you
And prevailed against you;

38:6 °Hebrew *Hammelech*

Your feet have sunk in the mire,
And they have turned away again.' "

23'So they shall surrender all your wives and children to the Chaldeans. You shall not escape from their hand, but shall be taken by the hand of the king of Babylon. And you shall cause this city to be burned with fire.' "

24Then Zedekiah said to Jeremiah, "Let no one know of these words, and you shall not die. 25But if the princes hear that I have talked with you, and they come to you and say to you, 'Declare to us now what you have said to the king, and also what the king said to you; do not hide *it* from us, and we will not put you to death,' 26then you shall say to them, 'I presented my request before the king, that he would not make me return to Jonathan's house to die there.' "

27Then all the princes came to Jeremiah and asked him. And he told them according to all these words that the king had commanded. So they stopped speaking with him, for the conversation had not been heard. 28Now Jeremiah remained in the court of the prison until the day that Jerusalem was taken. And he was *there* when Jerusalem was taken.

CHAPTER 39

39:4–7 God rewarded Zedekiah for his wickedness (vv. 1–10). The king thought he could escape, but the enemy caught up with him. The last thing Zedekiah saw was the execution of his own sons; then he was blinded. He walked by sight and ended up in darkness. He lived to serve himself and lost everything. He learned the truth of these words: "Be sure your sin will find you out" (Num. 32:23).

39 In the ninth year of Zedekiah king of Judah, in the tenth month, Nebuchadnezzar king of Babylon and all his army came against Jerusalem, and besieged it. 2In the eleventh year of Zedekiah, in the fourth month, on the ninth *day* of the month, the city was penetrated.

3Then all the princes of the king of Babylon came in and sat in the Middle Gate: Nergal-Sharezer, Samgar-Nebo, Sarsechim, Rabsaris,p Nergal-Sarezer, Rabmag,q with the rest of the princes of the king of Babylon.

4*So it was, when Zedekiah the king of Judah and all the men of war saw them, that they fled and went out of the city by night, by way of the king's garden, by the gate between the two walls. And he went out by way of the plain.r 5But the Chaldean army pursued them and overtook Zedekiah in the plains of Jericho. And when they had captured him, they brought him up to Nebuchadnezzar king of Babylon, to Riblah in the land of Hamath, where he pronounced judgment on him. 6Then the king of Babylon killed the sons of Zedekiah before his eyes in Riblah; the king of Babylon also killed all the nobles of Judah. 7Moreover he put out Zedekiah's eyes, and bound him with bronze fetters to carry him off to Babylon. 8And the Chaldeans burned the king's house and the houses of the people with fire, and broke down the walls of Jerusalem. 9Then Nebuzaradan the captain of the guard carried away captive to Babylon the remnant of the people who remained in the city and those who defected to him, with the rest of the people who remained. 10But Nebuzaradan the captain of the guard left in the land of Judah the poor people, who had nothing, and gave them vineyards and fields at the same time.

11*Now Nebuchadnezzar king of Babylon gave charge concerning Jeremiah to Nebuzaradan the captain of the guard, saying, 12"Take him and look after him, and do him no harm; but do to

39:11–14 God rewarded Jeremiah for his faithfulness (vv. 11–14). For forty difficult years, he courageously proclaimed God's Word, even though the people refused to obey it. If you measure ministry by "results," Jeremiah was a failure. Given his freedom, he chose to remain with his people and minister to them. He had a shepherd's heart.

39:3 pA title, probably *Chief Officer;* also verse 13 qA title, probably *Troop Commander;* also verse 13   39:4 rOr *the arabah,* that is, the Jordan Valley

him just as he says to you." [13]So Nebuzaradan the captain of the guard sent Nebushasban, Rab-saris, Nergal-Sharezer, Rabmag, and all the king of Babylon's chief officers; [14]then they sent *some-one* to take Jeremiah from the court of the prison, and committed him to Gedaliah the son of Ahi-kam, the son of Shaphan, that he should take him home. So he dwelt among the people.

[15]*Meanwhile the word of the LORD had come to Jeremiah while he was shut up in the court of the prison, saying, [16]"Go and speak to Ebed-Melech the Ethiopian, saying, 'Thus says the LORD of hosts, the God of Israel: "Behold, I will bring My words upon this city for adversity and not for good, and they shall be *performed* in that day before you. [17]But I will deliver you in that day," says the LORD, "and you shall not be given into the hand of the men of whom you *are* afraid. [18]For I will surely deliver you, and you shall not fall by the sword; but your life shall be as a prize to you, because you have put your trust in Me," says the LORD.' "

40

The* word that came to Jeremiah from the LORD after Nebuzaradan the captain of the guard had let him go from Ramah, when he had taken him bound in chains among all who were carried away captive from Jerusalem and Judah, who were carried away captive to Babylon.

[2]And the captain of the guard took Jeremiah and said to him: "The LORD your God has pro-nounced this doom on this place. [3]Now the LORD has brought *it*, and has done just as He said. Be-cause you *people* have sinned against the LORD, and not obeyed His voice, therefore this thing has come upon you. [4]And now look, I free you this day from the chains that *were* on your hand. If it seems good to you to come with me to Babylon, come, and I will look after you. But if it seems wrong for you to come with me to Babylon, re-main here. See, all the land *is* before you; wher-ever it seems good and convenient for you to go, go there."

[5]Now while Jeremiah had not yet gone back, *Nebuzaradan said,* "Go back to Gedaliah the son of Ahikam, the son of Shaphan, whom the king of Babylon has made governor over the cities of Judah, and dwell with him among the people. Or go wherever it seems convenient for you to go." So the captain of the guard gave him rations and a gift and let him go. [6]Then Jeremiah went to Gedaliah the son of Ahikam, to Mizpah, and dwelt with him among the people who were left in the land.

[7]*And when all the captains of the armies who *were* in the fields, they and their men, heard that the king of Babylon had made Gedaliah the son of Ahikam governor in the land, and had commit-ted to him men, women, children, and the poorest of the land who had not been carried away captive to Babylon, [8]then they came to Gedaliah at Mizpah—Ishmael the son of Nethaniah, Johanan and Jonathan the sons of Kareah, Seraiah the son of Tanhumeth, the sons of Ephai the Netophathite, and Jezaniah[s] the son of a Maachathite, they and their men. [9]And Gedaliah the son of Ahikam, the son of Shaphan, took an oath before them and their men, saying, "Do not be afraid to serve the

39:15–18 God rewarded Ebed-Melech for his kindness (38:7–13). Now we know why this foreigner rescued Jeremiah: he had put his faith in the God of Israel (v. 18). It must have been Jeremiah's witness that won him. An outsider trusted the God of Israel, but the Jews would not trust Him!

CHAPTER 40—41

40:1–6 Liberty. God has a word for you in the crisis hours of life, so take time to listen. In this case, it came from the mouth of a Babylonian officer who knew Jeremiah's prophecies. If you could go where you wanted, where would it be? Jeremiah chose to remain with the hurting people of the land. What an encouragement he must have been to them!

40:7–12 Authority. God has ordained that men live under authority (Rom. 13); otherwise, there is chaos. Gedaliah told the people exactly what Jeremiah had counseled: submit to the enemy and seek to live normal lives. Are you praying for those in authority (1 Tim. 2:1–3)? Their job is not easy, and they need God's help.

40:8 [s]Spelled *Jaazaniah* in 2 Kings 25:23

Chaldeans. Dwell in the land and serve the king of Babylon, and it shall be well with you. ¹⁰As for me, I will indeed dwell at Mizpah and serve the Chaldeans who come to us. But you, gather wine and summer fruit and oil, put *them* in your vessels, and dwell in your cities that you have taken." ¹¹Likewise, when all the Jews who *were* in Moab, among the Ammonites, in Edom, and who *were* in all the countries, heard that the king of Babylon had left a remnant of Judah, and that he had set over them Gedaliah the son of Ahikam, the son of Shaphan, ¹²then all the Jews returned out of all places where they had been driven, and came to the land of Judah, to Gedaliah at Mizpah, and gathered wine and summer fruit in abundance.

¹³*Moreover Johanan the son of Kareah and all the captains of the forces that *were* in the fields came to Gedaliah at Mizpah, ¹⁴and said to him, "Do you certainly know that Baalis the king of the Ammonites has sent Ishmael the son of Nethaniah to murder you?" But Gedaliah the son of Ahikam did not believe them.

¹⁵Then Johanan the son of Kareah spoke secretly to Gedaliah in Mizpah, saying, "Let me go, please, and I will kill Ishmael the son of Nethaniah, and no one will know *it*. Why should he murder you, so that all the Jews who are gathered to you would be scattered, and the remnant in Judah perish?"

¹⁶But Gedaliah the son of Ahikam said to Johanan the son of Kareah, "You shall not do this thing, for you speak falsely concerning Ishmael."

40:13—41:3 Treachery. Was Gedaliah a bit naive? Did he have too much faith in human nature? Perhaps, but he should at least have taken precautions to protect his life. Ishmael was loyal to Zedekiah (41:1) and rejected the rule of the governor. His love for the fallen king was greater than his love for God, others, and the nation. He was more concerned about revenge than righteousness. What could have been a peaceful transition became a civil war—all because of one man's wickedness.

41 Now it came to pass in the seventh month *that* Ishmael the son of Nethaniah, the son of Elishama, of the royal family and of the officers of the king, came with ten men to Gedaliah the son of Ahikam, at Mizpah. And there they ate bread together in Mizpah. ²Then Ishmael the son of Nethaniah, and the ten men who were with him, arose and struck Gedaliah the son of Ahikam, the son of Shaphan, with the sword, and killed him whom the king of Babylon had made governor over the land. ³Ishmael also struck down all the Jews who were with him, *that is,* with Gedaliah at Mizpah, and the Chaldeans who were found there, the men of war.

⁴And it happened, on the second day after he had killed Gedaliah, when as yet no one knew *it,* ⁵that certain men came from Shechem, from Shiloh, and from Samaria, eighty men with their beards shaved and their clothes torn, having cut themselves, with offerings and incense in their hand, to bring *them* to the house of the LORD. ⁶Now Ishmael the son of Nethaniah went out from Mizpah to meet them, weeping as he went along; and it happened as he met them that he said to them, "Come to Gedaliah the son of Ahikam!" ⁷So it was, when they came into the midst of the city, that Ishmael the son of Nethaniah killed them *and cast them* into the midst of a pit, he and the men who were with him. ⁸But ten men were found among them who said to Ishmael, "Do not kill us, for we have treasures of wheat, barley, oil, and honey in the field." So he desisted and did not kill them among their brethren. ⁹Now the pit into which Ishmael had cast all the dead bodies of the men whom he had slain, because of Gedaliah, *was* the same one Asa the king had made for fear of Baasha king of Israel. Ishmael the son of Nethaniah filled it with *the* slain. ¹⁰Then Ish-

mael carried away captive all the rest of the people who *were* in Mizpah, the king's daughters and
all the people who remained in Mizpah, whom
Nebuzaradan the captain of the guard had committed to Gedaliah the son of Ahikam. And Ishmael the son of Nethaniah carried them away captive and departed to go over to the Ammonites.

11But when Johanan the son of Kareah and all
the captains of the forces that *were* with him
heard of all the evil that Ishmael the son of Nethaniah had done, 12they took all the men and went
to fight with Ishmael the son of Nethaniah; and
they found him by the great pool that *is* in Gibeon.
13So it was, when all the people who *were* with
Ishmael saw Johanan the son of Kareah, and all
the captains of the forces who *were* with him, that
they were glad. 14Then all the people whom Ishmael had carried away captive from Mizpah
turned around and came back, and went to Johanan the son of Kareah. 15But Ishmael the son
of Nethaniah escaped from Johanan with eight
men and went to the Ammonites.

16Then Johanan the son of Kareah, and all the
captains of the forces that were with him, took
from Mizpah all the rest of the people whom he
had recovered from Ishmael the son of Nethaniah
after he had murdered Gedaliah the son of Ahikam—the mighty men of war and the women and
the children and the eunuchs, whom he had
brought back from Gibeon. 17And they departed
and dwelt in the habitation of Chimham, which
is near Bethlehem, as they went on their way to
Egypt, 18because of the Chaldeans; for they were
afraid of them, because Ishmael the son of Nethaniah had murdered Gedaliah the son of Ahikam,
whom the king of Babylon had made governor
in the land.

42 Now* all the captains of the forces, Johanan
the son of Kareah, Jezaniah the son of
Hoshaiah, and all the people, from the least to
the greatest, came near 2and said to Jeremiah the
prophet, "Please, let our petition be acceptable
to you, and pray for us to the LORD your God,
for all this remnant (since we are left *but* a few
of many, as you can see), 3that the LORD your God
may show us the way in which we should walk
and the thing we should do."

4Then Jeremiah the prophet said to them, "I
have heard. Indeed, I will pray to the LORD your
God according to your words, and it shall be, *that*
whatever the LORD answers you, I will declare *it*
to you. I will keep nothing back from you."

5So they said to Jeremiah, "Let the LORD be a
true and faithful witness between us, if we do not
do according to everything which the LORD your
God sends us by you. 6Whether *it is* pleasing or
displeasing, we will obey the voice of the LORD
our God to whom we send you, that it may be
well with us when we obey the voice of the LORD
our God."

7And it happened after ten days that the word
of the LORD came to Jeremiah. 8Then he called
Johanan the son of Kareah, all the captains of
the forces which *were* with him, and all the people
from the least even to the greatest, 9and said to
them, "Thus says the LORD, the God of Israel, to
whom you sent me to present your petition before
Him: 10'If you will still remain in this land, then
I will build you and not pull *you* down, and I will
plant you and not pluck *you* up. For I relent concerning the disaster that I have brought upon you.

CHAPTER 42

42:1ff "Back to Egypt!" was Israel's cry
whenever they found themselves in trouble.
It was true in the days of Moses (Exod. 16:3;
17:3; Num. 11:4–6; 14:1–5) and Isaiah (Isa.
30:1–5; 31:1–3), and now in the trying days
after the Babylonian conquest (41:17). God
had told them to stay in the land, but they
were afraid to obey.

They had already made up their minds
to go, but they thought it would be good to
ask the prophet to pray for them: "Pray for
us! We will obey!" How pious their words
sounded! (See Matt. 15:7–9.) Have you ever
tried to fool God with pious prayers and
promises?

Jeremiah prayed and waited for God's
word for that hour. Perhaps God did have
another plan for the people. No, God's plan
had not been changed. God told them not
to be afraid; He told them to stay in the land
and trust His care. But God also told His
servant that the leaders were hypocrites and
not to be trusted.

Faith and patience go together (Heb. 6:12;
10:36): "Whosoever believes will not act
hastily" (Isa. 28:16).

66*Solemn prayers, rapturous
devotions, are but repeated
hypocrisies unless the heart and
mind be conformable to them.***99**

—William Law

11Do not be afraid of the king of Babylon, of whom you are afraid; do not be afraid of him,' says the LORD, 'for I *am* with you, to save you and deliver you from his hand. 12And I will show you mercy, that he may have mercy on you and cause you to return to your own land.'

13"But if you say, 'We will not dwell in this land,' disobeying the voice of the LORD your God, 14saying, 'No, but we will go to the land of Egypt where we shall see no war, nor hear the sound of the trumpet, nor be hungry for bread, and there we will dwell'— 15Then hear now the word of the LORD, O remnant of Judah! Thus says the LORD of hosts, the God of Israel: 'If you wholly set your faces to enter Egypt, and go to dwell there, 16then it shall be *that* the sword which you feared shall overtake you there in the land of Egypt; the famine of which you were afraid shall follow close after you there *in* Egypt; and there you shall die. 17So shall it be with all the men who set their faces to go to Egypt to dwell there. They shall die by the sword, by famine, and by pestilence. And none of them shall remain or escape from the disaster that I will bring upon them.'

18"For thus says the LORD of hosts, the God of Israel: 'As My anger and My fury have been poured out on the inhabitants of Jerusalem, so will My fury be poured out on you when you enter Egypt. And you shall be an oath, an astonishment, a curse, and a reproach; and you shall see this place no more.'

19"The LORD has said concerning you, O remnant of Judah, 'Do not go to Egypt!' Know certainly that I have admonished you this day. 20For you were hypocrites in your hearts when you sent me to the LORD your God, saying, 'Pray for us to the LORD our God, and according to all that the LORD your God says, so declare to us and we will do *it*.' 21And I have this day declared *it* to you, but you have not obeyed the voice of the LORD your God, or anything which He has sent you by me. 22Now therefore, know certainly that you shall die by the sword, by famine, and by pestilence in the place where you desire to go to dwell."

CHAPTER 43

43:1ff Everything Jeremiah had predicted had come true, but they called him a false prophet! Once you have decided to disobey the Lord, you can always find excuses for rejecting God's truth. It must have been painful for Baruch and Jeremiah to endure the slander of those arrogant men, people they had helped for many years. But Jesus was treated the same way, so Jeremiah was experiencing "the fellowship of His sufferings" (Phil. 3:10).

God had the last word: their trip to Egypt would be a death march. *The only safe place is in the will of God.* The army from which the Jews fled in Judah would come to Egypt and judge them because no one can run away from problems.

43 Now* it happened, when Jeremiah had stopped speaking to all the people all the words of the LORD their God, for which the LORD their God had sent him to them, all these words, 2that Azariah the son of Hoshaiah, Johanan the son of Kareah, and all the proud men spoke, saying to Jeremiah, "You speak falsely! The LORD our God has not sent you to say, 'Do not go to Egypt to dwell there.' 3But Baruch the son of Neriah has set you against us, to deliver us into the hand of the Chaldeans, that they may put us to death or carry us away captive to Babylon." 4So Johanan the son of Kareah, all the captains of the forces, and all the people would not obey the voice of the LORD, to remain in the land of Judah. 5But Johanan the son of Kareah and all the captains of the forces took all the remnant of Judah who had returned to dwell in the land of Judah, from all nations where they had been driven— 6men, women, children, the king's daughters, and every person whom Nebuzaradan the captain of the guard had left with Gedaliah the son of Ahikam, the son of Shaphan, and Jeremiah the prophet and Baruch the son of Neriah. 7So they went to the land of Egypt, for they did

not obey the voice of the LORD. And they went as far as Tahpanhes.

8Then the word of the LORD came to Jeremiah in Tahpanhes, saying, 9"Take large stones in your hand, and hide them in the sight of the men of Judah, in the clay in the brick courtyard which *is* at the entrance to Pharaoh's house in Tahpanhes; 10and say to them, 'Thus says the LORD of hosts, the God of Israel: "Behold, I will send and bring Nebuchadnezzar the king of Babylon, My servant, and will set his throne above these stones that I have hidden. And he will spread his royal pavilion over them. 11When he comes, he shall strike the land of Egypt *and deliver* to death *those appointed* for death, and to captivity *those appointed* for captivity, and to the sword *those appointed* for the sword. 12I*t* will kindle a fire in the houses of the gods of Egypt, and he shall burn them and carry them away captive. And he shall array himself with the land of Egypt, as a shepherd puts on his garment, and he shall go out from there in peace. 13He shall also break the sacred pillars of Beth Shemesh*u* that *are* in the land of Egypt; and the houses of the gods of the Egyptians he shall burn with fire." ' "

44 The* word that came to Jeremiah concerning all the Jews who dwell in the land of Egypt, who dwell at Migdol, at Tahpanhes, at Noph,*v* and in the country of Pathros, saying, 2"Thus says the LORD of hosts, the God of Israel: 'You have seen all the calamity that I have brought on Jerusalem and on all the cities of Judah; and behold, this day they *are* a desolation, and no one dwells in them, 3because of their wickedness which they have committed to provoke Me to anger, in that they went to burn incense *and* to serve other gods whom they did not know, they nor you nor your fathers. 4However I have sent to you all My servants the prophets, rising early and sending *them,* saying, "Oh, do not do this abominable thing that I hate!" 5But they did not listen or incline their ear to turn from their wickedness, to burn no incense to other gods. 6So My fury and My anger were poured out and kindled in the cities of Judah and in the streets of Jerusalem; and they are wasted *and* desolate, as it is this day.'

7"Now therefore, thus says the LORD, the God of hosts, the God of Israel: 'Why do you commit *this* great evil against yourselves, to cut off from you man and woman, child and infant, out of Judah, leaving none to remain, 8in that you provoke Me to wrath with the works of your hands, burning incense to other gods in the land of Egypt where you have gone to dwell, that you may cut yourselves off and be a curse and a reproach among all the nations of the earth? 9Have you forgotten the wickedness of your fathers, the wickedness of the kings of Judah, the wickedness of their wives, your own wickedness, and the wickedness of your wives, which they committed in the land of Judah and in the streets of Jerusalem? 10They have not been humbled, to this day, nor have they feared; they have not walked in

CHAPTER 44

44:1ff How shall God bring His people to the place where He can bless and enjoy them? He sent His servants with the Word, but people would not listen. He chastened them with drought, but they did not repent. Then He allowed the enemy to humiliate them, but the people still would not obey the will of God.

Perhaps it would be different in Egypt. No, the change in geography did not change their hearts. They practiced their idolatry in Egypt, they even defended it! Before King Josiah's reform, when they bowed down to idols, "they had plenty of food, were well-off, and saw no trouble" (v. 17)—as if those things are tests of truth! The wicked may prosper, but that is no excuse to sin.

In His mercy, God would rescue a small remnant of His people. The rest would be slain in the land they thought was so safe. Was God watching over them? Yes, but not for blessing (v. 27).

43:12 'Following Masoretic Text and Targum; Septuagint, Syriac, and Vulgate read *He.* 43:13 *u*Literally *House of the Sun,* ancient On; later called Heliopolis 44:1 *v*That is, ancient Memphis

My law or in My statutes that I set before you and your fathers.'

11"Therefore thus says the LORD of hosts, the God of Israel: 'Behold, I will set My face against you for catastrophe and for cutting off all Judah. 12And I will take the remnant of Judah who have set their faces to go into the land of Egypt to dwell there, and they shall all be consumed *and* fall in the land of Egypt. They shall be consumed by the sword *and* by famine. They shall die, from the least to the greatest, by the sword and by famine; and they shall be an oath, an astonishment, a curse and a reproach! 13For I will punish those who dwell in the land of Egypt, as I have punished Jerusalem, by the sword, by famine, and by pestilence, 14so that none of the remnant of Judah who have gone into the land of Egypt to dwell there shall escape or survive, lest they return to the land of Judah, to which they desire to return and dwell. For none shall return except those who escape.' "

15Then all the men who knew that their wives had burned incense to other gods, with all the women who stood by, a great multitude, and all the people who dwelt in the land of Egypt, in Pathros, answered Jeremiah, saying: 16"*As for the word that you have spoken to us in the name of the LORD, we will not listen to you!* 17But we will certainly do whatever has gone out of our own mouth, to burn incense to the queen of heaven and pour out drink offerings to her, as we have done, we and our fathers, our kings and our princes, in the cities of Judah and in the streets of Jerusalem. For *then* we had plenty of food, were well-off, and saw no trouble. 18But since we stopped burning incense to the queen of heaven and pouring out drink offerings to her, we have lacked everything and have been consumed by the sword and by famine."

19*The women also said,* "And when we burned incense to the queen of heaven and poured out drink offerings to her, did we make cakes for her, to worship her, and pour out drink offerings to her without our husbands' *permission?*"

20Then Jeremiah spoke to all the people—the men, the women, and all the people who had given him *that* answer—saying: 21"The incense that you burned in the cities of Judah and in the streets of Jerusalem, you and your fathers, your kings and your princes, and the people of the land, did not the LORD remember them, and did it *not* come into His mind? 22So the LORD could no longer bear *it,* because of the evil of your doings *and* because of the abominations which you committed. Therefore your land is a desolation, an astonishment, a curse, and without an inhabitant, as *it is* this day. 23Because you have burned incense and because you have sinned against the LORD, and have not obeyed the voice of the LORD or walked in His law, in His statutes or in His testimonies, therefore this calamity has happened to you, as *at* this day."

24Moreover Jeremiah said to all the people and to all the women, "Hear the word of the LORD, all Judah who *are* in the land of Egypt! 25Thus says the LORD of hosts, the God of Israel, saying: 'You and your wives have spoken with your mouths and fulfilled with your hands, saying, "We will surely keep our vows that we have made, to burn incense to the queen of heaven and pour out drink offerings to her." You will surely keep your vows and perform your vows!' 26Therefore hear the word of the LORD, all Judah who dwell in the land of Egypt: 'Behold, I have sworn by My great name,' says the LORD, 'that My name shall no more be named in the mouth of any man of Judah in all the land of Egypt, saying, "The Lord GOD lives." 27Behold, I will watch over them for adversity and not for good. And all the men of Judah who *are* in the land of Egypt shall be consumed by the sword and by famine, until there is an end to them. 28Yet a small number who escape the sword shall return from the land of Egypt to the land of Judah; and all the remnant of Judah, who have gone to the land of Egypt to dwell there, shall know whose words will stand, Mine or theirs. 29And this *shall be* a sign to you,' says the LORD, 'that I will punish you in this place, that you may know that My words will surely stand against you for adversity.'

30"Thus says the LORD: 'Behold, I will give Pharaoh Hophra king of Egypt into the hand of his enemies and into the hand of those who seek his life, as I gave Zedekiah king of Judah into the hand of Nebuchadnezzar king of Babylon, his enemy who sought his life.' "

45 The* word that Jeremiah the prophet spoke to Baruch the son of Neriah, when he had written these words in a book at the instruction of Jeremiah,ʷ in the fourth year of Jehoiakim the son of Josiah, king of Judah, saying, 2"Thus says the LORD, the God of Israel, to you, O Baruch: 3'You said, "Woe is me now! For the LORD has added grief to my sorrow. I fainted in my sighing, and I find no rest." '

4"Thus you shall say to him, 'Thus says the LORD: "Behold, what I have built I will break down, and what I have planted I will pluck up, that is, this whole land. 5And do you seek great things for yourself? Do not seek *them;* for behold, I will bring adversity on all flesh," says the LORD. "But I will give your life to you as a prize in all places, wherever you go." ' "

46 The* word of the LORD which came to Jeremiah the prophet against the nations. 2Against Egypt.

Concerning the army of Pharaoh Necho, king of Egypt, which was by the River Euphrates in Carchemish, and which Nebuchadnezzar king of Babylon defeated in the fourth year of Jehoiakim the son of Josiah, king of Judah:

3   "Order the buckler and shield,
      And draw near to battle!
4   Harness the horses,
      And mount up, you horsemen!
      Stand forth with *your* helmets,
      Polish the spears,
      Put on the armor!
5   Why have I seen them dismayed *and* turned
         back?
      Their mighty ones are beaten down;
      They have speedily fled,
      And did not look back,

45:1 ʷLiterally *from Jeremiah's mouth*

CHAPTER 45

45:1ff This brief chapter focuses on Jeremiah's faithful secretary, Baruch, who shared the prophet's trials and sorrows. It records an event that occurred after Baruch wrote a second copy of the prophecy because Jehoiakim had burned the original (chap. 36).

God sees your work. What a disappointment it was when Baruch heard that everything he had written had gone up in smoke. When it seems like your work and witness are useless, remember for whom you are doing them.

God knows your trials. Baruch could have had an easier life, but he chose to identify himself with the most unpopular man in the land. Why? Because he believed in the Lord and relied on His Word.

God hears your words. Like any servant of God, Baruch had his difficult days when he felt everything was falling apart. God heard in Baruch's cry a dangerous desire for "great things." If he had not identified with the prophet, how great Baruch might have been!

God meets your needs. Suppose Baruch had become a great man in the kingdom? Where was the kingdom then? Baruch was alive and cared for because he was associated with Jeremiah. If you are going to seek great things, seek them for God, not for yourself.

CHAPTER 46

46:1–26 Jeremiah was a prophet to the nations as well as to Judah (1:5), and his book closes with prophecies concerning the nations, beginning with Egypt.

Josiah, Judah's last good king, was slain at Carchemish when he fought Egypt (2 Chron. 35:20–27); but now Egypt would be defeated at Carchemish by the Babylonians. The Egyptians thought they were like the Nile, rising up to flood the enemy, but they would fail (vv. 7–10).

When God looked at the Egyptians, He did not see a mighty river. He saw a heifer that would be bitten by the Babylonian fly (v. 20), and her allies were fat bulls heading for the slaughter (v. 21; see also v. 10). The army of Babylon was like grasshoppers in number (vv. 23–24), and Egypt would flee like a frightened serpent (v. 22). God had spoken!

Baruch, An Honorable Servant—Baruch's brother Seraiah was an officer in the king's court (Jer. 32:12; 51:59), so he might have gotten an appointment for Baruch; but God chose Baruch to be His servant and His servant's servant. Beware selfish ambitions that run contrary to the will of God; *God may let you succeed!* (See Matt. 20:20–28.)

For fear *was* all around," says the LORD.
6 "Do not let the swift flee away,
    Nor the mighty man escape;
    They will stumble and fall
    Toward the north, by the River Euphrates.

7 "Who *is* this coming up like a flood,
    Whose waters move like the rivers?
8 Egypt rises up like a flood,
    And *its* waters move like the rivers;
    And he says, 'I will go up *and* cover the
      earth,
    I will destroy the city and its inhabitants.'
9 Come up, O horses, and rage, O chariots!
    And let the mighty men come forth:
    The Ethiopians and the Libyans who handle
      the shield,
    And the Lydians who handle *and* bend the
      bow.
10 For this *is* the day of the Lord GOD of hosts,
    A day of vengeance,
    That He may avenge Himself on His
      adversaries.
    The sword shall devour;
    It shall be satiated and made drunk with
      their blood;
    For the Lord GOD of hosts has a sacrifice
    In the north country by the River Euphrates.

11 "Go up to Gilead and take balm,
    O virgin, the daughter of Egypt;
    In vain you will use many medicines;
    You shall not be cured.
12 The nations have heard of your shame,
    And your cry has filled the land;
    For the mighty man has stumbled against
      the mighty;
    They both have fallen together."

13 The word that the LORD spoke to Jeremiah the prophet, how Nebuchadnezzar king of Babylon would come *and* strike the land of Egypt.

14 "Declare in Egypt, and proclaim in Migdol;
    Proclaim in Noph˟ and in Tahpanhes;
    Say, 'Stand fast and prepare yourselves,
    For the sword devours all around you.'
15 Why are your valiant *men* swept away?
    They did not stand
    Because the LORD drove them away.
16 He made many fall;
    Yes, one fell upon another.
    And they said, 'Arise!
    Let us go back to our own people
    And to the land of our nativity
    From the oppressing sword.'
17 They cried there,
    'Pharaoh, king of Egypt, *is but* a noise.
    He has passed by the appointed time!'

18 "As I live," says the King,
    Whose name *is* the LORD of hosts,
    "Surely as Tabor *is* among the mountains
    And as Carmel by the sea, *so* he shall come.
19 O you daughter dwelling in Egypt,
    Prepare yourself to go into captivity!
    For Nophʸ shall be waste and desolate,
      without inhabitant.

46:14 ˟That is, ancient Memphis   46:19 ʸThat is, ancient Memphis

20 "Egypt *is* a very pretty heifer,
   But destruction comes, it comes from the
      north.
21 Also her mercenaries are in her midst like
      fat bulls,
   For they also are turned back,
   They have fled away together.
   They did not stand,
   For the day of their calamity had come upon
      them,
   The time of their punishment.
22 Her noise shall go like a serpent,
   For they shall march with an army
   And come against her with axes,
   Like those who chop wood.

23 "They shall cut down her forest," says the
      LORD,
   "Though it cannot be searched,
   Because they *are* innumerable,
   And more numerous than grasshoppers.
24 The daughter of Egypt shall be ashamed;
   She shall be delivered into the hand
   Of the people of the north."

25The LORD of hosts, the God of Israel, says:
"Behold, I will bring punishment on Amon[z] of
No,[a] and Pharaoh and Egypt, with their gods and
their kings—Pharaoh and those who trust in him.
26And I will deliver them into the hand of those
who seek their lives, into the hand of Nebuchadnezzar king of Babylon and the hand of his servants. Afterward it shall be inhabited as in the
days of old," says the LORD.

27*"But do not fear, O My servant Jacob,
   And do not be dismayed, O Israel!
   For behold, I will save you from afar,
   And your offspring from the land of their
      captivity;
   Jacob shall return, have rest and be at ease;
   No one shall make *him* afraid.
28 Do not fear, O Jacob My servant," says the
      LORD,
   "For I *am* with you;
   For I will make a complete end of all the
      nations
   To which I have driven you,
   But I will not make a complete end of you.
   I will rightly correct you,
   For I will not leave you wholly unpunished."

47 The* word of the LORD that came to Jeremiah the prophet against the Philistines, before Pharaoh attacked Gaza.
2Thus says the LORD:

   "Behold, waters rise out of the north,
   And shall be an overflowing flood;
   They shall overflow the land and all that is
      in it,
   The city and those who dwell within;
   Then the men shall cry,
   And all the inhabitants of the land shall
      wail.
3 At the noise of the stamping hooves of his
      strong horses,
   At the rushing of his chariots,
   At the rumbling of his wheels,

46:27, 28 God gave a message of peace
to His people in captivity: they would return
to their land and be established again. They
had to be corrected in love, but they would
not be destroyed: "I will save you . . . I am
with you." What words of encouragement!
Claim them today!

CHAPTER 47—48
47:1ff The Egyptians had defeated Philistia,
but the Babylonians would destroy both
Philistia (chap. 47) and Moab (chap. 48).
The Babylonian army would be like a rising
river (v. 2) and a sword in the hands of the
Lord (v. 6).

46:25 [z]A sun god [a]That is, ancient Thebes

The fathers will not look back for *their*
children,
Lacking courage,
4   Because of the day that comes to plunder
all the Philistines,
To cut off from Tyre and Sidon every helper
who remains;
For the LORD shall plunder the Philistines,
The remnant of the country of Caphtor.
5   Baldness has come upon Gaza,
Ashkelon is cut off
With the remnant of their valley.
How long will you cut yourself?

6   "O you sword of the LORD,
How long until you are quiet?
Put yourself up into your scabbard,
Rest and be still!
7   How can it be quiet,
Seeing the LORD has given it a charge
Against Ashkelon and against the seashore?
There He has appointed it."

48 Against* Moab.
Thus says the LORD of hosts, the God of
Israel:

"Woe to Nebo!
For it is plundered,
Kirjathaim is shamed *and* taken;
The high stronghold[b] is shamed and
dismayed—
2   No more praise of Moab.
In Heshbon they have devised evil against
her:
'Come, and let us cut her off as a nation.'
You also shall be cut down, O Madmen![c]
The sword shall pursue you;
3   A voice of crying *shall be* from Horonaim:
'Plundering and great destruction!'

4   "Moab is destroyed;
Her little ones have caused a cry to be
heard;[d]
5   For in the Ascent of Luhith they ascend with
continual weeping;
For in the descent of Horonaim the enemies
have heard a cry of destruction.

6   "Flee, save your lives!
And be like the juniper[e] in the wilderness.
7   For because you have trusted in your works
and your treasures,
You also shall be taken.
And Chemosh shall go forth into captivity,
His priests and his princes together.
8   And the plunderer shall come against every
city;
No one shall escape.
The valley also shall perish,
And the plain shall be destroyed,
As the LORD has spoken.

9   "Give wings to Moab,
That she may flee and get away;
For her cities shall be desolate,
Without any to dwell in them.

48:1ff Moab was known for its pride (vv. 29, 42), so the Lord brought those people low. They relied on a false god and trusted material wealth (v. 7), so their god was captured and their wealth was plundered. They lost all their defenses! Moab was also known for its wine. But the vessels would be emptied and broken, and the people would become drunk with God's wrath (vv. 12, 26, 38). The Babylonians were God's "wine-workers" to give Moab a "new taste" they had never had before (v. 11). Sometimes God has to pour us "from vessel to vessel" to make us what He wants us to be. The bottles were broken (v. 12), the staff was broken (v. 17), and their arm was broken (v. 25): "How she is broken down!" (v. 39). Had Moab been broken *before* the Lord, she would not have been broken *by* the Lord.

48:1 [b]Hebrew *Misgab*   48:2 [c]A city of Moab   48:4 [d]Following
Masoretic Text, Targum, and Vulgate; Septuagint reads
Proclaim it in Zoar.   48:6 [e]Or *Aroer,* a city of Moab

10   Cursed *is* he who does the work of the Lord
        deceitfully,
     And cursed *is* he who keeps back his sword
        from blood.

11   "Moab has been at ease from his[f] youth;
     He has settled on his dregs,
     And has not been emptied from vessel to
        vessel,
     Nor has he gone into captivity.
     Therefore his taste remained in him,
     And his scent has not changed.

12   "Therefore behold, the days are coming,"
        says the Lord,
     "That I shall send him wine-workers
     Who will tip him over
     And empty his vessels
     And break the bottles.
13   Moab shall be ashamed of Chemosh,
     As the house of Israel was ashamed of
        Bethel, their confidence.

14   "How can you say, 'We *are* mighty
     And strong men for the war'?
15   Moab is plundered and gone up *from* her
        cities;
     Her chosen young men have gone down to
        the slaughter," says the King,
     Whose name *is* the Lord of hosts.

16   "The calamity of Moab *is* near at hand,
     And his affliction comes quickly.
17   Bemoan him, all you who are around him;
     And all you who know his name,
     Say, 'How the strong staff is broken,
     The beautiful rod!'

18   "O daughter inhabiting Dibon,
     Come down from *your* glory,
     And sit in thirst;
     For the plunderer of Moab has come against
        you,
     He has destroyed your strongholds.
19   O inhabitant of Aroer,
     Stand by the way and watch;
     Ask him who flees
     And her who escapes;
     Say, 'What has happened?'
20   Moab is shamed, for he is broken down.
     Wail and cry!
     Tell it in Arnon, that Moab is plundered.

21   "And judgment has come on the plain
        country:
     On Holon and Jahzah and Mephaath,
22   On Dibon and Nebo and Beth Diblathaim,
23   On Kirjathaim and Beth Gamul and Beth
        Meon,
24   On Kerioth and Bozrah,
     On all the cities of the land of Moab,
     Far or near.
25   The horn of Moab is cut off,
     And his arm is broken," says the Lord.

26   "Make him drunk,
     Because he exalted *himself* against the
        Lord.

48:11 [f]The Hebrew uses masculine and feminine pronouns
interchangeably in this chapter.

Moab shall wallow in his vomit,
And he shall also be in derision.
27 For was not Israel a derision to you?
Was he found among thieves?
For whenever you speak of him,
You shake *your head in scorn.*
28 You who dwell in Moab,
Leave the cities and dwell in the rock,
And be like the dove *which* makes her nest
In the sides of the cave's mouth.

29 "We have heard the pride of Moab
(He *is* exceedingly proud),
Of his loftiness and arrogance and pride,
And of the haughtiness of his heart."

30 "I know his wrath," says the LORD,
"But it *is* not right;
His lies have made nothing right.
31 Therefore I will wail for Moab,
And I will cry out for all Moab;
I*g* will mourn for the men of Kir Heres.
32 O vine of Sibmah! I will weep for you with
the weeping of Jazer.
Your plants have gone over the sea,
They reach to the sea of Jazer.
The plunderer has fallen on your summer
fruit and your vintage.
33 Joy and gladness are taken
From the plentiful field
And from the land of Moab;
I have caused wine to fail from the
winepresses;
No one will tread with joyous shouting—
Not joyous shouting!

34 "From the cry of Heshbon to Elealeh and to
Jahaz
They have uttered their voice,
From Zoar to Horonaim,
Like a three-year-old heifer;*h*
For the waters of Nimrim also shall be
desolate.

35 "Moreover," says the LORD,
"I will cause to cease in Moab
The one who offers *sacrifices* in the high
places
And burns incense to his gods.
36 Therefore My heart shall wail like flutes for
Moab,
And like flutes My heart shall wail
For the men of Kir Heres.
Therefore the riches they have acquired
have perished.

37 "For every head *shall be* bald, and every
beard clipped;
On all the hands *shall be* cuts, and on the
loins sackcloth—
38 A general lamentation
On all the housetops of Moab,
And in its streets;
For I have broken Moab like a vessel in
which *is* no pleasure," says the LORD.
39 "They shall wail:
'How she is broken down!

48:31 *g*Following Dead Sea Scrolls, Septuagint, and Vulgate;
Masoretic Text reads *He*.   48:34 *h*Or *The Third Eglath,* an
unknown city (compare Isaiah 15:5)

How Moab has turned her back with
   shame!'
So Moab shall be a derision
And a dismay to all those about her."

40For thus says the LORD:

"Behold, one shall fly like an eagle,
   And spread his wings over Moab.
41 Kerioth is taken,
   And the strongholds are surprised;
   The mighty men's hearts in Moab on that
      day shall be
   Like the heart of a woman in birth pangs.
42 And Moab shall be destroyed as a people,
   Because he exalted *himself* against the
      LORD.
43 Fear and the pit and the snare *shall be* upon
      you,
   O inhabitant of Moab," says the LORD.
44 "He who flees from the fear shall fall into
      the pit,
   And he who gets out of the pit shall be
      caught in the snare.
   For upon Moab, upon it I will bring
   The year of their punishment," says the
      LORD.

45 "Those who fled stood under the shadow of
      Heshbon
   Because of exhaustion.
   But a fire shall come out of Heshbon,
   A flame from the midst of Sihon,
   And shall devour the brow of Moab,
   The crown of the head of the sons of tumult.
46 Woe to you, O Moab!
   The people of Chemosh perish;
   For your sons have been taken captive,
   And your daughters captive.

47 "Yet I will bring back the captives of Moab
   In the latter days," says the LORD.

Thus far *is* the judgment of Moab.

49

Against* the Ammonites.
Thus says the LORD:

"Has Israel no sons?
   Has he no heir?
   Why *then* does Milcom¹ inherit Gad,
   And his people dwell in its cities?
2 Therefore behold, the days are coming,"
      says the LORD,
   "That I will cause to be heard an alarm of
      war
   In Rabbah of the Ammonites;
   It shall be a desolate mound,
   And her villages shall be burned with fire.
   Then Israel shall take possession of his
      inheritance," says the LORD.

49:1 ¹Hebrew *Malcam,* literally *their king,* a god of the
Ammonites; also called *Molech* (compare verse 3)

CHAPTER 49

49:1–6 The Ammonites and Moabites were
descended from Lot (Gen. 19:30–38) and
were enemies of the Jews. Milcom (Molech)
was the god of the Ammonites, worshiped
in terrible orgies that involved the sacrificing
of children. His name means "the reigning
one," but he would reign no more. He would
go into captivity and not be able to rescue
himself, which is what happens to all false
gods.

Our Merciful God—In His wrath, God remembers mercy (Hab. 3:2). He gave promises to the
Jews (46:27–28), the Moabites (48:47), the Ammonites (49:6), and the people of Elam (49:39). These
nations did not reappear on the scene when the Jews went back to their land, but they will be
included when the Lord restores His people at the return of Christ and the establishment of His
kingdom.

3 "Wail, O Heshbon, for Ai is plundered!
   Cry, you daughters of Rabbah,
   Gird yourselves with sackcloth!
   Lament and run to and fro by the walls;
   For Milcom shall go into captivity
   With his priests and his princes together.
4 Why do you boast in the valleys,
   Your flowing valley, O backsliding
      daughter?
   Who trusted in her treasures, *saying,*
   'Who will come against me?'
5 Behold, I will bring fear upon you,"
   Says the Lord GOD of hosts,
   "From all those who are around you;
   You shall be driven out, everyone headlong,
   And no one will gather those who wander
      off.
6 But afterward I will bring back
   The captives of the people of Ammon," says
      the LORD.

7*Against Edom.
Thus says the LORD of hosts:

   "*Is* wisdom no more in Teman?
   Has counsel perished from the prudent?
   Has their wisdom vanished?
8 Flee, turn back, dwell in the depths,
      O inhabitants of Dedan!
   For I will bring the calamity of Esau upon
      him,
   The time *that* I will punish him.
9 If grape-gatherers came to you,
   Would they not leave *some* gleaning
      grapes?
   If thieves by night,
   Would they not destroy until they have
      enough?
10 But I have made Esau bare;
   I have uncovered his secret places,*j*
   And he shall not be able to hide himself.
   His descendants are plundered,
   His brethren and his neighbors,
   And he *is* no more.
11 Leave your fatherless children,
   I will preserve *them* alive;
   And let your widows trust in Me."

12For thus says the LORD: "Behold, those whose
judgment *was* not to drink of the cup have assuredly drunk. And *are* you the one who will altogether go unpunished? You shall not go unpunished, but you shall surely drink *of it.* 13For I have
sworn by Myself," says the LORD, "that Bozrah
shall become a desolation, a reproach, a waste,
and a curse. And all its cities shall be perpetual
wastes."

14 I have heard a message from the LORD,
   And an ambassador has been sent to the
      nations:
   "Gather together, come against her,
   And rise up to battle!

15 "For indeed, I will make you small among
      nations,
   Despised among men.
16 Your fierceness has deceived you,
   The pride of your heart,

49:7–22 The Edomites were the descendants of Esau, brother of Jacob (Gen. 36), and they, too, hated the Jews. They were recognized for their great wisdom (Obad. 8), but they would not be wise enough to stop the Babylonian invasion. Their judgment would be like the stripping of a vineyard (v. 9), getting drunk (v. 12), the destroying of Sodom and Gomorrah (v. 18), the attacking of a lion from the Jordan thicket (v. 19), and the sudden swooping down of an eagle (v. 22). There was no escape!

49:10 *j* Compare Obadiah 5, 6

O you who dwell in the clefts of the rock,
Who hold the height of the hill!
Though you make your nest as high as the
  eagle,
I will bring you down from there," says the
  LORD.[k]

17 "Edom also shall be an astonishment;
Everyone who goes by it will be astonished
And will hiss at all its plagues.
18 As in the overthrow of Sodom and
    Gomorrah
And their neighbors," says the LORD,
"No one shall remain there,
Nor shall a son of man dwell in it.

19 "Behold, he shall come up like a lion from
    the floodplain[l] of the Jordan
Against the dwelling place of the strong;
But I will suddenly make him run away from
  her.
And who is a chosen man that I may
  appoint over her?
For who is like Me?
Who will arraign Me?
And who is that shepherd
Who will withstand Me?"

20 Therefore hear the counsel of the LORD that
    He has taken against Edom,
And His purposes that He has proposed
  against the inhabitants of Teman:
Surely the least of the flock shall draw them
  out;
Surely He shall make their dwelling places
  desolate with them.
21 The earth shakes at the noise of their fall;
At the cry its noise is heard at the Red Sea.
22 Behold, He shall come up and fly like the
    eagle,
And spread His wings over Bozrah;
The heart of the mighty men of Edom in
  that day shall be
Like the heart of a woman in birth pangs.

23*Against Damascus.

"Hamath and Arpad are shamed,
For they have heard bad news.
They are fainthearted;
There is trouble on the sea;
It cannot be quiet.
24 Damascus has grown feeble;
She turns to flee,
And fear has seized her.
Anguish and sorrows have taken her like a
  woman in labor.
25 Why is the city of praise not deserted, the
    city of My joy?
26 Therefore her young men shall fall in her
    streets,
And all the men of war shall be cut off in
  that day," says the LORD of hosts.
27 "I will kindle a fire in the wall of Damascus,
And it shall consume the palaces of Ben-
  Hadad."[m]

49:23–39 Damascus would be feeble and
fearful, like a woman in labor (v. 24); and
Kedar, Hazor, and Elam would be scattered
to the wind like chaff (vv. 32, 36). All these
proud kingdoms felt secure in resisting the
Lord, and He bore with them in His long-
suffering. But their day of opportunity ran
out, and all God could do was judge them.

49:16 [k]Compare Obadiah 3, 4   49:19 [l]Or thicket
49:27 [m]Compare Amos 1:4

²⁸Against Kedar and against the kingdoms of Hazor, which Nebuchadnezzar king of Babylon shall strike.
Thus says the LORD:

"Arise, go up to Kedar,
And devastate the men of the East!
²⁹ Their tents and their flocks they shall take away.
They shall take for themselves their curtains,
All their vessels and their camels;
And they shall cry out to them,
'Fear *is* on every side!'

³⁰ "Flee, get far away! Dwell in the depths,
O inhabitants of Hazor!" says the LORD.
"For Nebuchadnezzar king of Babylon has taken counsel against you,
And has conceived a plan against you.

³¹ "Arise, go up to the wealthy nation that dwells securely," says the LORD,
"Which has neither gates nor bars,
Dwelling alone.
³² Their camels shall be for booty,
And the multitude of their cattle for plunder.
I will scatter to all winds those in the farthest corners,
And I will bring their calamity from all its sides," says the LORD.
³³ "Hazor shall be a dwelling for jackals, a desolation forever;
No one shall reside there,
Nor son of man dwell in it."

³⁴The word of the LORD that came to Jeremiah the prophet against Elam, in the beginning of the reign of Zedekiah king of Judah, saying, ³⁵"Thus says the LORD of hosts:

'Behold, I will break the bow of Elam,
The foremost of their might.
³⁶ Against Elam I will bring the four winds
From the four quarters of heaven,
And scatter them toward all those winds;
There shall be no nations where the outcasts of Elam will not go.
³⁷ For I will cause Elam to be dismayed before their enemies
And before those who seek their life.
I will bring disaster upon them,
My fierce anger,' says the LORD;
'And I will send the sword after them
Until I have consumed them.
³⁸ I will set My throne in Elam,
And will destroy from there the king and the princes,' says the LORD.

³⁹ 'But it shall come to pass in the latter days:
I will bring back the captives of Elam,' says the LORD."

CHAPTER 50—51

50:1ff This prophecy (chaps. 50—51) was given in the fourth year of Zedekiah's reign, and Jeremiah sent it with Baruch's brother, Seraiah, to be read publicly in Babylon (51:59—64). In Scripture, Babylon symbolizes man's worldly system organized in opposition to God (Gen. 11:1—9; Rev. 17—18).

The Persians would come out of the north, defeat Babylon, and leave it desolate (50:3). Babylon had been God's hammer (50:23), cup (51:7), and "battle-ax" (51:20—23) to bring His judgment to the sinful nations; but now her sins would be judged, particularly her brutal treatment of Israel (51:34—35).

Throughout this prophecy, God gives words of hope to His people still in captivity. Both Israel and Judah will be reunited and restored to their land (50:4—5). The scattered flock will be gathered (50:6—7, 17) and the sinful nation forgiven (50:19—20). They are guilty of sin, but God the Judge will plead their case (50:33—34). The forsaken wife will be reunited to her Husband (51:5), and the nation will be vindicated (51:10).

How will all of this happen? By the power of the God of Israel who is not like the dead idols of the heathen (51:15—19). His people must flee this evil system (51:6, 45—48) and separate themselves wholly to the Lord (2 Cor. 6:14—7:1; Rev. 18:4). Babylon is still a desolation, and that ruin is a reminder that God is Governor of the nations and Judge of all the earth. Israel is still among the nations because her God is the Maker of all things (51:19).

50 The* word that the LORD spoke against Babylon *and* against the land of the Chaldeans by Jeremiah the prophet.

² "Declare among the nations,
Proclaim, and set up a standard;
Proclaim—do not conceal *it*—
Say, 'Babylon is taken, Bel is shamed.

Merodach[n] is broken in pieces;
Her idols are humiliated,
Her images are broken in pieces.'
3 For out of the north a nation comes up
against her,
Which shall make her land desolate,
And no one shall dwell therein.
They shall move, they shall depart,
Both man and beast.

4 "In those days and in that time," says the
LORD,
"The children of Israel shall come,
They and the children of Judah together;
With continual weeping they shall come,
And seek the LORD their God.
5 They shall ask the way to Zion,
With their faces toward it, *saying,*
'Come and let us join ourselves to the LORD
In a perpetual covenant
That will not be forgotten.'

6 "My people have been lost sheep.
Their shepherds have led them astray;
They have turned them away *on the*
mountains.
They have gone from mountain to hill;
They have forgotten their resting place.
7 All who found them have devoured them;
And their adversaries said, 'We have not
offended,
Because they have sinned against the LORD,
the habitation of justice,
The LORD, the hope of their fathers.'

8 "Move from the midst of Babylon,
Go out of the land of the Chaldeans;
And be like the rams before the flocks.
9 For behold, I will raise and cause to come
up against Babylon
An assembly of great nations from the north
country,
And they shall array themselves against
her;
From there she shall be captured.
Their arrows *shall be* like *those* of an expert
warrior;[o]
None shall return in vain.
10 And Chaldea shall become plunder;
All who plunder her shall be satisfied," says
the LORD.

11 "Because you were glad, because you
rejoiced,
You destroyers of My heritage,
Because you have grown fat like a heifer
threshing grain,
And you bellow like bulls,
12 Your mother shall be deeply ashamed;
She who bore you shall be ashamed.
Behold, the least of the nations *shall be* a
wilderness,
A dry land and a desert.
13 Because of the wrath of the LORD
She shall not be inhabited,

50:2 [n]A Babylonian god; sometimes spelled *Marduk*
50:9 [o]Following some Hebrew manuscripts, Septuagint, and
Syriac; Masoretic Text, Targum, and Vulgate read *a warrior
who makes childless.*

But she shall be wholly desolate.
Everyone who goes by Babylon shall be
    horrified
And hiss at all her plagues.

14 "Put yourselves in array against Babylon all
    around,
All you who bend the bow;
Shoot at her, spare no arrows,
For she has sinned against the LORD.
15 Shout against her all around;
She has given her hand,
Her foundations have fallen,
Her walls are thrown down;
For it is the vengeance of the LORD.
Take vengeance on her.
As she has done, so do to her.
16 Cut off the sower from Babylon,
And him who handles the sickle at harvest
    time.
For fear of the oppressing sword
Everyone shall turn to his own people,
And everyone shall flee to his own land.

17 "Israel is like scattered sheep;
The lions have driven him away.
First the king of Assyria devoured him;
Now at last this Nebuchadnezzar king of
    Babylon has broken his bones."

18Therefore thus says the LORD of hosts, the God
of Israel:

"Behold, I will punish the king of Babylon
    and his land,
As I have punished the king of Assyria.
19 But I will bring back Israel to his home,
And he shall feed on Carmel and Bashan;
His soul shall be satisfied on Mount
    Ephraim and Gilead.
20 In those days and in that time," says the
    LORD,
"The iniquity of Israel shall be sought, but
    there shall be none;
And the sins of Judah, but they shall not
    be found;
For I will pardon those whom I preserve.

21 "Go up against the land of Merathaim,
    against it,
And against the inhabitants of Pekod.
Waste and utterly destroy them," says the
    LORD,
"And do according to all that I have
    commanded you.
22 A sound of battle is in the land,
And of great destruction.
23 How the hammer of the whole earth has
    been cut apart and broken!
How Babylon has become a desolation
    among the nations!
I have laid a snare for you;
24 You have indeed been trapped, O Babylon,
And you were not aware;
You have been found and also caught,
Because you have contended against the
    LORD.
25 The LORD has opened His armory,
And has brought out the weapons of His
    indignation;
For this is the work of the Lord GOD of hosts
In the land of the Chaldeans.

26 Come against her from the farthest border;
Open her storehouses;
Cast her up as heaps of ruins,
And destroy her utterly;
Let nothing of her be left.
27 Slay all her bulls,
Let them go down to the slaughter.
Woe to them!
For their day has come, the time of their
punishment.
28 The voice of those who flee and escape from
the land of Babylon
Declares in Zion the vengeance of the LORD
our God,
The vengeance of His temple.

29 "Call together the archers against Babylon.
All you who bend the bow, encamp against
it all around;
Let none of them escape.[p]
Repay her according to her work;
According to all she has done, do to her;
For she has been proud against the LORD,
Against the Holy One of Israel.
30 Therefore her young men shall fall in the
streets,
And all her men of war shall be cut off in
that day," says the LORD.
31 "Behold, I *am* against you,
O most haughty one!" says the Lord GOD
of hosts;
"For your day has come,
The time *that* I will punish you.[q]
32 The most proud shall stumble and fall,
And no one will raise him up;
I will kindle a fire in his cities,
And it will devour all around him."

33 Thus says the LORD of hosts:

"The children of Israel *were* oppressed,
Along with the children of Judah;
All who took them captive have held them
fast;
They have refused to let them go.
34 Their Redeemer *is* strong;
The LORD of hosts *is* His name.
He will thoroughly plead their case,
That He may give rest to the land,
And disquiet the inhabitants of Babylon.

35 "A sword *is* against the Chaldeans," says the
LORD,
"Against the inhabitants of Babylon,
And against her princes and her wise men.
36 A sword *is* against the soothsayers, and they
will be fools.
A sword *is* against her mighty men, and they
will be dismayed.
37 A sword *is* against their horses,
Against their chariots,
And against all the mixed peoples who *are*
in her midst;
And they will become like women.
A sword *is* against her treasures, and they
will be robbed.

50:29 [p]Qere, some Hebrew manuscripts, Septuagint, and Targum add *to her*. 50:31 [q]Following Masoretic Text and Targum; Septuagint and Vulgate read *The time of your punishment*.

38　A drought[r] *is* against her waters, and they
　　　will be dried up.
　　For it *is* the land of carved images,
　　And they are insane with *their* idols.

39　"Therefore the wild desert beasts shall dwell
　　　there with the jackals,
　　And the ostriches shall dwell in it.
　　It shall be inhabited no more forever,
　　Nor shall it be dwelt in from generation to
　　　generation.
40　As God overthrew Sodom and Gomorrah
　　And their neighbors," says the Lord,
　　"*So* no one shall reside there,
　　Nor son of man dwell in it.

41　"Behold, a people shall come from the north,
　　And a great nation and many kings
　　Shall be raised up from the ends of the
　　　earth.
42　They shall hold the bow and the lance;
　　They *are* cruel and shall not show mercy.
　　Their voice shall roar like the sea;
　　They shall ride on horses,
　　Set in array, like a man for the battle,
　　Against you, O daughter of Babylon.

43　"The king of Babylon has heard the report
　　　about them,
　　And his hands grow feeble;
　　Anguish has taken hold of him,
　　Pangs as of a woman in childbirth.

44　"Behold, he shall come up like a lion from
　　　the floodplains[s] of the Jordan
　　Against the dwelling place of the strong;
　　But I will make them suddenly run away
　　　from her.
　　And who *is* a chosen *man that* I may
　　　appoint over her?
　　For who *is* like Me?
　　Who will arraign Me?
　　And who *is* that shepherd
　　Who will withstand Me?"

45　Therefore hear the counsel of the Lord that
　　　He has taken against Babylon,
　　And His purposes that He has proposed
　　　against the land of the Chaldeans:
　　Surely the least of the flock shall draw them
　　　out;
　　Surely He will make their dwelling place
　　　desolate with them.
46　At the noise of the taking of Babylon
　　The earth trembles,
　　And the cry is heard among the nations.

51

Thus says the Lord:

　"Behold, I will raise up against Babylon,
　Against those who dwell in Leb Kamai,[t]
　A destroying wind.
2　And I will send winnowers to Babylon,
　Who shall winnow her and empty her land.
　For in the day of doom

50:38 [r]Following Masoretic Text, Targum, and Vulgate; Syriac
reads *sword;* Septuagint omits *A drought is.*　50:44 [s]Or
thicket　51:1 [t]A code word for Chaldea (Babylonia); may be
translated *The Midst of Those Who Rise Up Against Me*

They shall be against her all around.
3 Against *her* let the archer bend his bow,
And lift himself up against *her* in his armor.
Do not spare her young men;
Utterly destroy all her army.
4 Thus the slain shall fall in the land of the
Chaldeans,
And *those* thrust through in her streets.
5 For Israel is not forsaken, nor Judah,
By his God, the LORD of hosts,
Though their land was filled with sin against
the Holy One of Israel."

6 Flee from the midst of Babylon,
And every one save his life!
Do not be cut off in her iniquity,
For this *is* the time of the LORD's vengeance;
He shall recompense her.
7 Babylon *was* a golden cup in the LORD's
hand,
That made all the earth drunk.
The nations drank her wine;
Therefore the nations are deranged.
8 Babylon has suddenly fallen and been
destroyed.
Wail for her!
Take balm for her pain;
Perhaps she may be healed.

9 We would have healed Babylon,
But she is not healed.
Forsake her, and let us go everyone to his
own country;
For her judgment reaches to heaven and is
lifted up to the skies.
10 The LORD has revealed our righteousness.
Come and let us declare in Zion the work
of the LORD our God.

11 Make the arrows bright!
Gather the shields!
The LORD has raised up the spirit of the
kings of the Medes.
For His plan *is* against Babylon to destroy
it,
Because it *is* the vengeance of the LORD,
The vengeance for His temple.
12 Set up the standard on the walls of Babylon;
Make the guard strong,
Set up the watchmen,
Prepare the ambushes.
For the LORD has both devised and done
What He spoke against the inhabitants of
Babylon.
13 O you who dwell by many waters,
Abundant in treasures,
Your end has come,
The measure of your covetousness.
14 The LORD of hosts has sworn by Himself:
"Surely I will fill you with men, as with
locusts,
And they shall lift up a shout against
you."

15 He has made the earth by His power;
He has established the world by His
wisdom,
And stretched out the heaven by His
understanding.
16 When He utters *His* voice—
There is a multitude of waters in the
heavens:

"He causes the vapors to ascend from the
ends of the earth;
He makes lightnings for the rain;
He brings the wind out of His treasuries."u

17 Everyone is dull-hearted, without
knowledge;
Every metalsmith is put to shame by the
carved image;
For his molded image *is* falsehood,
And *there is* no breath in them.
18 They *are* futile, a work of errors;
In the time of their punishment they shall
perish.
19 The Portion of Jacob *is* not like them,
For He *is* the Maker of all things;
And *Israel is* the tribe of His inheritance.
The LORD of hosts *is* His name.

20 "You *are* My battle-ax *and* weapons of war:
For with you I will break the nation in
pieces;
With you I will destroy kingdoms;
21 With you I will break in pieces the horse
and its rider;
With you I will break in pieces the chariot
and its rider;
22 With you also I will break in pieces man
and woman;
With you I will break in pieces old and
young;
With you I will break in pieces the young
man and the maiden;
23 With you also I will break in pieces the
shepherd and his flock;
With you I will break in pieces the farmer
and his yoke of oxen;
And with you I will break in pieces
governors and rulers.

24 "And I will repay Babylon
And all the inhabitants of Chaldea
For all the evil they have done
In Zion in your sight," says the LORD.

25 "Behold, I *am* against you, O destroying
mountain,
Who destroys all the earth," says the LORD.
"And I will stretch out My hand against you,
Roll you down from the rocks,
And make you a burnt mountain.
26 They shall not take from you a stone for a
corner
Nor a stone for a foundation,
But you shall be desolate forever," says the
LORD.

27 Set up a banner in the land,
Blow the trumpet among the nations!
Prepare the nations against her,
Call the kingdoms together against her:
Ararat, Minni, and Ashkenaz.
Appoint a general against her;
Cause the horses to come up like the
bristling locusts.
28 Prepare against her the nations,
With the kings of the Medes,
Its governors and all its rulers,
All the land of his dominion.

51:16 uPsalm 135:7

29 And the land will tremble and sorrow;
For every purpose of the LORD shall be
performed against Babylon,
To make the land of Babylon a desolation
without inhabitant.
30 The mighty men of Babylon have ceased
fighting,
They have remained in their strongholds;
Their might has failed,
They became *like* women;
They have burned her dwelling places,
The bars of her *gate* are broken.
31 One runner will run to meet another,
And one messenger to meet another,
To show the king of Babylon that his city
is taken on *all* sides;
32 The passages are blocked,
The reeds they have burned with fire,
And the men of war are terrified.

33For thus says the LORD of hosts, the God of
Israel:

"The daughter of Babylon *is* like a threshing
floor
When it is time to thresh her;
Yet a little while
And the time of her harvest will come."

34 "Nebuchadnezzar the king of Babylon
Has devoured me, he has crushed me;
He has made me an empty vessel,
He has swallowed me up like a monster;
He has filled his stomach with my
delicacies,
He has spit me out.
35 Let the violence *done* to me and my flesh
be upon Babylon,"
The inhabitant of Zion will say;
"And my blood be upon the inhabitants of
Chaldea!"
Jerusalem will say.

36Therefore thus says the LORD:

"Behold, I will plead your case and take
vengeance for you.
I will dry up her sea and make her springs
dry.
37 Babylon shall become a heap,
A dwelling place for jackals,
An astonishment and a hissing,
Without an inhabitant.
38 They shall roar together like lions,
They shall growl like lions' whelps.
39 In their excitement I will prepare their
feasts;
I will make them drunk,
That they may rejoice,
And sleep a perpetual sleep
And not awake," says the LORD.
40 "I will bring them down
Like lambs to the slaughter,
Like rams with male goats.

41 "Oh, how Sheshach[v] is taken!
Oh, how the praise of the whole earth is
seized!
How Babylon has become desolate among
the nations!

51:41 [v]A code word for Babylon (compare 25:26)

42 The sea has come up over Babylon;
   She is covered with the multitude of its
      waves.
43 Her cities are a desolation,
   A dry land and a wilderness,
   A land where no one dwells,
   Through which no son of man passes.
44 I will punish Bel in Babylon,
   And I will bring out of his mouth what he
      has swallowed;
   And the nations shall not stream to him
      anymore.
   Yes, the wall of Babylon shall fall.

45 "My people, go out of the midst of her!
   And let everyone deliver himself from the
      fierce anger of the LORD.
46 And lest your heart faint,
   And you fear for the rumor that *will be*
      heard in the land
   (A rumor will come *one* year,
   And after that, in *another* year
   A rumor *will come,*
   And violence in the land,
   Ruler against ruler),
47 Therefore behold, the days are coming
   That I will bring judgment on the carved
      images of Babylon;
   Her whole land shall be ashamed,
   And all her slain shall fall in her midst.
48 Then the heavens and the earth and all that
      is in them
   Shall sing joyously over Babylon;
   For the plunderers shall come to her from
      the north," says the LORD.

49 As Babylon *has caused* the slain of Israel
      to fall,
   So at Babylon the slain of all the earth shall
      fall.
50 You who have escaped the sword,
   Get away! Do not stand still!
   Remember the LORD afar off,
   And let Jerusalem come to your mind.

51 We are ashamed because we have heard
      reproach.
   Shame has covered our faces,
   For strangers have come into the
      sanctuaries of the LORD's house.

52 "Therefore behold, the days are coming,"
      says the LORD,
   "That I will bring judgment on her carved
      images,
   And throughout all her land the wounded
      shall groan.
53 Though Babylon were to mount up to
      heaven,
   And though she were to fortify the height
      of her strength,
   Yet from Me plunderers would come to
      her," says the LORD.

54 The sound of a cry *comes* from Babylon,
   And great destruction from the land of the
      Chaldeans,
55 Because the LORD is plundering Babylon
   And silencing her loud voice,
   Though her waves roar like great waters,
   And the noise of their voice is uttered,
56 Because the plunderer comes against her,
      against Babylon,

And her mighty men are taken.
Every one of their bows is broken;
For the LORD *is* the God of recompense,
He will surely repay.

57 "And I will make drunk
Her princes and wise men,
Her governors, her deputies, and her mighty
men.
And they shall sleep a perpetual sleep
And not awake," says the King,
Whose name *is* the LORD of hosts.

58Thus says the LORD of hosts:

"The broad walls of Babylon shall be utterly
broken,
And her high gates shall be burned with fire;
The people will labor in vain,
And the nations, because of the fire;
And they shall be weary."

59The word which Jeremiah the prophet commanded Seraiah the son of Neriah, the son of Mahseiah, when he went with Zedekiah the king of Judah to Babylon in the fourth year of his reign. And Seraiah *was* the quartermaster. 60So Jeremiah wrote in a book all the evil that would come upon Babylon, all these words that are written against Babylon. 61And Jeremiah said to Seraiah, "When you arrive in Babylon and see it, and read all these words, 62then you shall say, 'O LORD, You have spoken against this place to cut it off, so that none shall remain in it, neither man nor beast, but it shall be desolate forever.' 63Now it shall be, when you have finished reading this book, *that* you shall tie a stone to it and throw it out into the Euphrates. 64Then you shall say, 'Thus Babylon shall sink and not rise from the catastrophe that I will bring upon her. And they shall be weary.'"
Thus far *are* the words of Jeremiah.

52 Zedekiah* *was* twenty-one years old when he became king, and he reigned eleven years in Jerusalem. His mother's name *was* Hamutal the daughter of Jeremiah of Libnah. 2He also did evil in the sight of the LORD, according to all that Jehoiakim had done. 3For because of the anger of the LORD *this* happened in Jerusalem and Judah, till He finally cast them out from His presence. Then Zedekiah rebelled against the king of Babylon.
4Now it came to pass in the ninth year of his reign, in the tenth month, on the tenth *day* of the month, *that* Nebuchadnezzar king of Babylon and all his army came against Jerusalem and encamped against it; and *they* built a siege wall against it all around. 5So the city was besieged until the eleventh year of King Zedekiah. 6By the fourth month, on the ninth day of the month, the famine had become so severe in the city that there was no food for the people of the land. 7Then the city wall was broken through, and all the men of war fled and went out of the city at night by way of the gate between the two walls, which *was* by the king's garden, even though the Chaldeans *were* near the city all around. And they went by way of the plain.w

CHAPTER 52
52:1–11, 24–27 Jeremiah's prophecy opens with God saying, "I am ready to perform My word" (1:12); and it closes with evidence that God did what He said He would do. This chapter parallels 2 Kings 24—25 and also Jeremiah 39; and it sets the stage for your reading of Lamentations.
Zedekiah was a rebel, not only against the king of Babylon but also against the Lord; and he lost both battles. He led his sons and his leaders into death and himself into darkness and bondage (Judg. 16:20–21). The religious leaders who had persecuted Jeremiah were slain by the enemy (vv. 24—27).

52:7 wOr *the arabah*, that is, the Jordan Valley

52:12–23 The *temple* was plundered despite the promises given by the false prophets (27:19—28:4). The walls were broken down, and the city and the temple were burned. God would rather destroy His city and His house than permit His people to sin successfully. If they will not glorify Him in obedience, they must honor Him in judgment.

52:28–30 The *people* were deported to remain in captivity for seventy years (25:1–14). The words of Jeremiah were precious to them during those difficult years, just as God's Word should be precious to His people "in exile" in this world today. Follow Jeremiah's good example and joyfully feed on His Word (15:16).

8But the army of the Chaldeans pursued the king, and they overtook Zedekiah in the plains of Jericho. All his army was scattered from him. 9So they took the king and brought him up to the king of Babylon at Riblah in the land of Hamath, and he pronounced judgment on him. 10Then the king of Babylon killed the sons of Zedekiah before his eyes. And he killed all the princes of Judah in Riblah. 11He also put out the eyes of Zedekiah; and the king of Babylon bound him in bronze fetters, took him to Babylon, and put him in prison till the day of his death.

12*Now in the fifth month, on the tenth *day* of the month (which *was* the nineteenth year of King Nebuchadnezzar king of Babylon), Nebuzaradan, the captain of the guard, *who* served the king of Babylon, came to Jerusalem. 13He burned the house of the LORD and the king's house; all the houses of Jerusalem, that is, all the houses of the great, he burned with fire. 14And all the army of the Chaldeans who *were* with the captain of the guard broke down all the walls of Jerusalem all around. 15Then Nebuzaradan the captain of the guard carried away captive *some* of the poor people, the rest of the people who remained in the city, the defectors who had deserted to the king of Babylon, and the rest of the craftsmen. 16But Nebuzaradan the captain of the guard left *some* of the poor of the land as vinedressers and farmers.

17The bronze pillars that *were* in the house of the LORD, and the carts and the bronze Sea that *were* in the house of the LORD, the Chaldeans broke in pieces, and carried all their bronze to Babylon. 18They also took away the pots, the shovels, the trimmers, the bowls, the spoons, and all the bronze utensils with which the priests ministered. 19The basins, the firepans, the bowls, the pots, the lampstands, the spoons, and the cups, whatever *was* solid gold and whatever *was* solid silver, the captain of the guard took away. 20The two pillars, one Sea, the twelve bronze bulls which *were* under *it, and* the carts, which King Solomon had made for the house of the LORD— the bronze of all these articles was beyond measure. 21Now *concerning* the pillars: the height of one pillar *was* eighteen cubits, a measuring line of twelve cubits could measure its circumference, and its thickness *was* four fingers; *it was* hollow. 22A capital of bronze *was* on it; and the height of one capital *was* five cubits, with a network and pomegranates all around the capital, all of bronze. The second pillar, with pomegranates was the same. 23There were ninety-six pomegranates on the sides; all the pomegranates, all around on the network, *were* one hundred.

24The captain of the guard took Seraiah the chief priest, Zephaniah the second priest, and the three doorkeepers. 25He also took out of the city an officer who had charge of the men of war, seven men of the king's close associates who were found in the city, the principal scribe of the army who mustered the people of the land, and sixty men of the people of the land who were found in the midst of the city. 26And Nebuzaradan the captain of the guard took these and brought them to the king of Babylon at Riblah. 27Then the king of Babylon struck them and put them to death at Riblah in the land of Hamath. Thus Judah was carried away captive from its own land.

28*These *are* the people whom Nebuchadnezzar carried away captive: in the seventh year, three thousand and twenty-three Jews; [29]in the eighteenth year of Nebuchadnezzar he carried away captive from Jerusalem eight hundred and thirty-two persons; [30]in the twenty-third year of Nebuchadnezzar, Nebuzaradan the captain of the guard carried away captive of the Jews seven hundred and forty-five persons. All the persons *were* four thousand six hundred.

[31]Now it came to pass in the thirty-seventh year of the captivity of Jehoiachin king of Judah, in the twelfth month, on the twenty-fifth *day* of the month, *that* Evil-Merodach[x] king of Babylon, in the first *year* of his reign, lifted up the head of Jehoiachin king of Judah and brought him out of prison. [32]And he spoke kindly to him and gave him a more prominent seat than those of the kings who *were* with him in Babylon. [33]So Jehoiachin changed from his prison garments, and he ate bread regularly before the king all the days of his life. [34]And as for his provisions, there was a regular ration given him by the king of Babylon, a portion for each day until the day of his death, all the days of his life.

52:31 [x]Or *Awil-Marduk*

LAMENTATIONS

As the name indicates, this is a book of "funeral dirges," written by Jeremiah after the destruction of Jerusalem in 586 B.C. His heart was broken, and his grief reveals the broken heart of God. God had to chasten His people, and it grieved Him to do it.

The verses in chapters 1—2 and 4—5 follow the successive letters of the Hebrew alphabet. Chapter 3 has sixty-six verses, and each triad of verses begins with a successive letter. The turning point in Jeremiah's grief is found in chapter 3, although he gives expressions of faith and hope here and there in his lament.

Sin is costly, God must punish sin, but God's mercy never fails: these are the key lessons of Lamentations.

CHAPTER 1

1:1ff Is sin worth it? Sin promises to enrich you, but in the end it robs you of the good things God has given you. Jerusalem had been a popular princess; now she had become a lonely widow who was a slave (vv. 1–2). Once she had enjoyed splendor, but now her glory was gone (v. 6). All she had left were memories (v. 7), and remembering only made the pain greater. She had refused the yoke of submission to the Lord (Jer. 27—28), but now she had to wear the yoke of the enemy (v. 14; Jer. 5:5).

Does anybody care? There was no one to comfort the people (vv. 2, 9, 16–17, 21). Even those who beheld the ruins showed no concern (v. 12). Former friends who praised her were now enemies who despised her (vv. 2, 8). Even the Lord was like an enemy to His people. The people who encourage you in your sin will discourage you in your suffering.

Can anybody question God? "The LORD is righteous," but His people had been rebellious (vv. 18, 20). Read the chapter again and note the words used to describe their sin. Jeremiah had warned them, but they listened instead to the false prophets (2:14; 4:13). God is holy, and sin must be judged.

1 How* lonely sits the city
That *was* full of people!
How like a widow is she,
Who *was* great among the nations!
The princess among the provinces
Has become a slave!

2 She weeps bitterly in the night,
Her tears *are* on her cheeks;
Among all her lovers
She has none to comfort *her*.
All her friends have dealt treacherously
  with her;
They have become her enemies.

3 Judah has gone into captivity,
Under affliction and hard servitude;
She dwells among the nations,
She finds no rest;
All her persecutors overtake her in dire
  straits.

4 The roads to Zion mourn
Because no one comes to the set feasts.
All her gates are desolate;
Her priests sigh,
Her virgins are afflicted,
And she *is* in bitterness.

5 Her adversaries have become the master,
Her enemies prosper;
For the LORD has afflicted her
Because of the multitude of her
  transgressions.
Her children have gone into captivity before
  the enemy.

6 And from the daughter of Zion
All her splendor has departed.
Her princes have become like deer
That find no pasture,
That flee without strength
Before the pursuer.

Those Who Pass By—Lamentations 1:12 is sometimes applied to our Lord Jesus Christ when He hung on the cross. Except for a small group of followers who stayed at the cross, nobody else offered Him any sympathy. They mocked Him and added to His pain. Yet, *He did it for you and me!* He felt the anger of God against *our* sins. Do we have compassion on those who suffer, or do we pass by "on the other side" (Luke 10:25–37)?

7   In the days of her affliction and roaming,
      Jerusalem remembers all her pleasant
         things
      That she had in the days of old.
      When her people fell into the hand of the
         enemy,
      With no one to help her,
      The adversaries saw her
      And mocked at her downfall.[a]

8   Jerusalem has sinned gravely,
      Therefore she has become vile.[b]
      All who honored her despise her
      Because they have seen her nakedness;
      Yes, she sighs and turns away.

9   Her uncleanness *is* in her skirts;
      She did not consider her destiny;
      Therefore her collapse was awesome;
      She had no comforter.
    "O Lord, behold my affliction,
      For *the* enemy is exalted!"

10   The adversary has spread his hand
      Over all her pleasant things;
      For she has seen the nations enter her
         sanctuary,
      Those whom You commanded
      Not to enter Your assembly.

11   All her people sigh,
      They seek bread;
      They have given their valuables for food to
         restore life.
    "See, O Lord, and consider,
      For I am scorned."

12   "*Is it* nothing to you, all you who pass by?
      Behold and see
      If there is any sorrow like my sorrow,
      Which has been brought on me,
      Which the Lord has inflicted
      In the day of His fierce anger.

13   "From above He has sent fire into my bones,
      And it overpowered them;
      He has spread a net for my feet
      And turned me back;
      He has made me desolate
      And faint all the day.

14   "The yoke of my transgressions was bound;[c]
      They were woven together by His hands,
      And thrust upon my neck.
      He made my strength fail;
      The Lord delivered me into the hands of
         those whom I am not able to withstand.

15   "The Lord has trampled underfoot all my
         mighty *men* in my midst;
      He has called an assembly against me
      To crush my young men;
      The Lord trampled *as* in a winepress
      The virgin daughter of Judah.

1:7 [a]Vulgate reads *her Sabbaths.* 1:8 [b]Septuagint and
Vulgate read *moved* or *removed.* 1:14 [c]Following Masoretic
Text and Targum; Septuagint, Syriac, and Vulgate read
watched over.

16 "For these *things* I weep;
My eye, my eye overflows with water;
Because the comforter, who should restore
my life,
Is far from me.
My children are desolate
Because the enemy prevailed."

17 Zion spreads out her hands,
But no one comforts her;
The LORD has commanded concerning
Jacob
That those around him *become* his
adversaries;
Jerusalem has become an unclean thing
among them.

18 "The LORD is righteous,
For I rebelled against His commandment.
Hear now, all peoples,
And behold my sorrow;
My virgins and my young men
Have gone into captivity.

19 "I called for my lovers,
But they deceived me;
My priests and my elders
Breathed their last in the city,
While they sought food
To restore their life.

20 "See, O LORD, that I *am* in distress;
My soul is troubled;
My heart is overturned within me,
For I have been very rebellious.
Outside the sword bereaves,
At home *it is* like death.

21 "They have heard that I sigh,
But no one comforts me.
All my enemies have heard of my trouble;
They are glad that You have done *it*.
Bring on the day You have announced,
That they may become like me.

22 "Let all their wickedness come before You,
And do to them as You have done to me
For all my transgressions;
For my sighs *are* many,
And my heart *is* faint."

2 How the Lord has covered the daughter
of Zion
With a cloud in His anger!
He cast down from heaven to the earth
The beauty of Israel,
And did not remember His footstool
In the day of His anger.

2 The Lord has swallowed up and has not
pitied
All the dwelling places of Jacob.
He has thrown down in His wrath
The strongholds of the daughter of Judah;
He has brought *them* down to the ground;
He has profaned the kingdom and its
princes.

3 He has cut off in fierce anger
Every horn of Israel;
He has drawn back His right hand
From before the enemy.

He has blazed against Jacob like a flaming
   fire
Devouring all around.

4   Standing like an enemy, He has bent His
     bow;
With His right hand, like an adversary,
He has slain all *who were* pleasing to His
   eye;
On the tent of the daughter of Zion,
He has poured out His fury like fire.

5   *The Lord was like an enemy.
He has swallowed up Israel,
He has swallowed up all her palaces;
He has destroyed her strongholds,
And has increased mourning and
   lamentation
In the daughter of Judah.

6   He has done violence to His tabernacle,
As if it were a garden;
He has destroyed His place of assembly;
The LORD has caused
The appointed feasts and Sabbaths to be
   forgotten in Zion.
In His burning indignation He has spurned
   the king and the priest.

7   The Lord has spurned His altar,
He has abandoned His sanctuary;
He has given up the walls of her palaces
Into the hand of the enemy.
They have made a noise in the house of the
   LORD
As on the day of a set feast.

8   The LORD has purposed to destroy
The wall of the daughter of Zion.
He has stretched out a line;
He has not withdrawn His hand from
   destroying;
Therefore He has caused the rampart and
   wall to lament;
They languished together.

9   Her gates have sunk into the ground;
He has destroyed and broken her bars.
Her king and her princes *are* among the
   nations;
The Law *is* no *more*,
And her prophets find no vision from the
   LORD.

10   The elders of the daughter of Zion
Sit on the ground *and* keep silence;
They throw dust on their heads
And gird themselves with sackcloth.
The virgins of Jerusalem
Bow their heads to the ground.

11   My eyes fail with tears,
My heart is troubled;
My bile is poured on the ground
Because of the destruction of the daughter
   of my people,
Because the children and the infants
Faint in the streets of the city.

12   They say to their mothers,
"Where *is* grain and wine?"
As they swoon like the wounded

CHAPTER 2

2:5, 6, 8, 9, 11, 22 *Sin brings destruction*
(Jer. 5:6, 10, 17). History records that
Babylon was the enemy, but Jeremiah said
that God was the enemy (vv. 4–5). He
supervised the destruction of the walls and
defenses (vv. 5, 8–9), the temple (vv. 6–7),
and the people (vv. 10–12); Babylon was
just His battle-ax (Jer. 51:20–23).

In the streets of the city,
As their life is poured out
In their mothers' bosom.

13   How shall I console you?
To what shall I liken you,
O daughter of Jerusalem?
What shall I compare with you, that I may
    comfort you,
O virgin daughter of Zion?
For your ruin *is* spread wide as the sea;
Who can heal you?

14   Your prophets have seen for you
False and deceptive visions;
They have not uncovered your iniquity,
To bring back your captives,
But have envisioned for you false
    prophecies and delusions.

15   *All who pass by clap *their* hands at you;
They hiss and shake their heads
At the daughter of Jerusalem:
"*Is* this the city that is called
'The perfection of beauty,
The joy of the whole earth'?"

16   All your enemies have opened their mouth
    against you;
They hiss and gnash *their* teeth.
They say, "We have swallowed *her* up!
Surely this *is* the day we have waited for;
We have found *it,* we have seen *it!* "

17   The LORD has done what He purposed;
He has fulfilled His word
Which He commanded in days of old.
He has thrown down and has not pitied,
And He has caused an enemy to rejoice over
    you;
He has exalted the horn of your adversaries.

18   Their heart cried out to the Lord,
"O wall of the daughter of Zion,
Let tears run down like a river day and
    night;
Give yourself no relief;
Give your eyes no rest.

19   "Arise, cry out in the night,
At the beginning of the watches;
Pour out your heart like water before the
    face of the Lord.
Lift your hands toward Him
For the life of your young children,
Who faint from hunger at the head of every
    street."

20   "See, O LORD, and consider!
To whom have You done this?
Should the women eat their offspring,
The children they have cuddled?*d*
Should the priest and prophet be slain
In the sanctuary of the Lord?

21   "Young and old lie
On the ground in the streets;
My virgins and my young men
Have fallen by the sword;

2:15, 16 *Sin brings disgrace.* The passersby not only offer no comfort (1:12) but contribute to Jerusalem's shame (v. 15). The enemy boasts of a great victory but does not give glory to God. All the faithful remnant could do was trust the purposes of God (v. 17) and cry out to Him for mercy (vv. 18–20).

2:20 *d*Vulgate reads *a span long.*

You have slain *them* in the day of Your
  anger,
You have slaughtered *and* not pitied.

22 "You have invited as to a feast day
The terrors that surround me.
In the day of the LORD's anger
There was no refugee or survivor.
Those whom I have borne and brought up
My enemies have destroyed."

3 I* *am* the man *who* has seen affliction by
  the rod of His wrath.
2 He has led me and made *me* walk
In darkness and not *in* light.
3 Surely He has turned His hand against me
Time and time again throughout the day.

4 He has aged my flesh and my skin,
And broken my bones.
5 He has besieged me
And surrounded *me* with bitterness and
  woe.
6 He has set me in dark places
Like the dead of long ago.

7 He has hedged me in so that I cannot get
  out;
He has made my chain heavy.
8 Even when I cry and shout,
He shuts out my prayer.
9 He has blocked my ways with hewn stone;
He has made my paths crooked.

10 He *has been* to me a bear lying in wait,
Like a lion in ambush.
11 He has turned aside my ways and torn me
  in pieces;
He has made me desolate.
12 He has bent His bow
And set me up as a target for the arrow.

13 He has caused the arrows of His quiver
To pierce my loins.*e*
14 I have become the ridicule of all my
  people—
Their taunting song all the day.
15 He has filled me with bitterness,
He has made me drink wormwood.

16 He has also broken my teeth with gravel,
And covered me with ashes.
17 You have moved my soul far from peace;
I have forgotten prosperity.
18 And I said, "My strength and my hope
Have perished from the LORD."

19 *Remember my affliction and roaming,
The wormwood and the gall.
20 My soul still remembers
And sinks within me.
21 This I recall to my mind,
Therefore I have hope.

3:13 *e*Literally *kidneys*

CHAPTER 3

3:1–18 This central chapter marks the
turning point in Jeremiah's experience of
grief and prayer. As he *looked at himself,*
he saw an aged man on a winding path in
the dark, being pursued by lions. The more
he considered his feelings, the more
hopeless he felt.

3:19–39 Then he looked away from himself
and by faith *looked to the Lord.* Now he can
say, "I have hope" (v. 21). Why? Because
of God's mercies, compassions, and
faithfulness: "For He does not afflict
willingly" (v. 33; Hos. 11:8–9), and He "will
not cast off forever" (v. 31). God does not
enjoy having to chasten His people; but as
a loving Father, He must do it (Prov. 3:11–
12).

A New Day—If God's compassions are "new every morning" (Lam. 3:23), you have the right to
claim them daily. Let each morning be for you the dawn of a new day. Start over again, no matter
how many times you failed the day before. If God's mercies never fail, depend on them during the
day. He is faithful, and His faithfulness will not fail.

22 *Through* the LORD's mercies we are not
consumed,
Because His compassions fail not.
23 *They are* new every morning;
Great *is* Your faithfulness.
24 "The LORD *is* my portion," says my soul,
"Therefore I hope in Him!"

25 The LORD *is* good to those who wait for Him,
To the soul *who* seeks Him.
26 *It is* good that *one* should hope and wait
quietly
For the salvation of the LORD.
27 *It is* good for a man to bear
The yoke in his youth.

28 Let him sit alone and keep silent,
Because *God* has laid *it* on him;
29 Let him put his mouth in the dust—
There may yet be hope.
30 Let him give *his* cheek to the one who
strikes him,
And be full of reproach.

31 For the Lord will not cast off forever.
32 Though He causes grief,
Yet He will show compassion
According to the multitude of His mercies.
33 For He does not afflict willingly,
Nor grieve the children of men.

34 To crush under one's feet
All the prisoners of the earth,
35 To turn aside the justice *due* a man
Before the face of the Most High,
36 Or subvert a man in his cause—
The Lord does not approve.

37 Who *is* he *who* speaks and it comes to pass,
When the Lord has not commanded *it*?
38 *Is it* not from the mouth of the Most High
That woe and well-being proceed?
39 Why should a living man complain,
A man for the punishment of his sins?

3:40–66 Finally, Jeremiah *looked to the people* (vv. 40–66) and called for a time of prayer and confession of sin. The "weeping prophet" (vv. 48–49) pleaded with the people to lift their hearts and hands to the Lord and ask Him for forgiveness and mercy. What did God do for His suffering servant? "You drew near on the day I called on You, and said, 'Do not fear!'" (v. 57). Wait before the Lord (vv. 25–26), and He will speak to you from His Word.

40 *Let us search out and examine our ways,
And turn back to the LORD;
41 Let us lift our hearts and hands
To God in heaven.
42 We have transgressed and rebelled;
You have not pardoned.

43 You have covered *Yourself* with anger
And pursued us;
You have slain *and* not pitied.
44 You have covered Yourself with a cloud,
That prayer should not pass through.
45 You have made us an offscouring and refuse
In the midst of the peoples.

46 All our enemies
Have opened their mouths against us.
47 Fear and a snare have come upon us,
Desolation and destruction.
48 My eyes overflow with rivers of water
For the destruction of the daughter of my
people.

49 My eyes flow and do not cease,
Without interruption,
50 Till the LORD from heaven
Looks down and sees.

51 My eyes bring suffering to my soul
    Because of all the daughters of my city.

52 My enemies without cause
    Hunted me down like a bird.
53 They silenced[f] my life in the pit
    And threw stones at me.
54 The waters flowed over my head;
    I said, "I am cut off!"

55 I called on Your name, O LORD,
    From the lowest pit.
56 You have heard my voice:
    "Do not hide Your ear
    From my sighing, from my cry for help."
57 You drew near on the day I called on You,
    And said, "Do not fear!"

58 O Lord, You have pleaded the case for my
        soul;
    You have redeemed my life.
59 O LORD, You have seen *how* I am wronged;
    Judge my case.
60 You have seen all their vengeance,
    All their schemes against me.

61 You have heard their reproach, O LORD,
    All their schemes against me,
62 The lips of my enemies
    And their whispering against me all the day.
63 Look at their sitting down and their rising
        up;
    I *am* their taunting song.

64 Repay them, O LORD,
    According to the work of their hands.
65 Give them a veiled[g] heart;
    Your curse *be* upon them!
66 In Your anger,
    Pursue and destroy them
    From under the heavens of the LORD.

4   How* the gold has become dim!
    How changed the fine gold!
    The stones of the sanctuary are scattered
    At the head of every street.

2   The precious sons of Zion,
    Valuable as fine gold,
    How they are regarded as clay pots,
    The work of the hands of the potter!

3   Even the jackals present their breasts
    To nurse their young;
    But the daughter of my people *is* cruel,
    Like ostriches in the wilderness.

4   The tongue of the infant clings
    To the roof of its mouth for thirst;
    The young children ask for bread,
    But no one breaks *it* for them.

5   Those who ate delicacies
    Are desolate in the streets;
    Those who were brought up in scarlet
    Embrace ash heaps.

6   The punishment of the iniquity of the
        daughter of my people

CHAPTER 4

4:1ff The greatest destruction from sin is not to buildings but to people. In God's sight, His people had been like gold and precious gems (Exod. 19:5), but now they were only cheap clay pots. People accustomed to luxuries could not find the necessities of life (v. 5). The healthy young men were but walking corpses and would be better off dead (vv. 7–9). If you want to cheapen yourself and others, sin will help you do it.

The children suffered the most (vv. 4, 10; 2:20) as children often do when parents sin. And it all came about because the leaders of the land would not obey the Word of God but listened to false teachers (v. 13; 2:14). God's Word to Joshua is still true (Josh. 1:8), and the Lord still keeps His promises.

❝*I'm against sin. I'll kick it as long as I've got a foot, and I'll fight it as long as I've got a fist. I'll butt it as long as I've got a head. I'll bite it as long as I've got a tooth. When I'm old and fistless and footless and toothless, I'll gum it till I go home to Glory and it goes home to perdition.*❞

—Billy Sunday

3:53 [f]Septuagint reads *put to death.*   3:65 [g]A Jewish tradition reads *sorrow of.*

Is greater than the punishment of the sin
   of Sodom,
Which was overthrown in a moment,
With no hand to help her!

7   Her Nazirites[h] were brighter than snow
And whiter than milk;
They were more ruddy in body than rubies,
Like sapphire in their appearance.

8   *Now* their appearance is blacker than soot;
They go unrecognized in the streets;
Their skin clings to their bones,
It has become as dry as wood.

9   *Those* slain by the sword are better off
Than *those* who die of hunger;
For these pine away,
Stricken *for lack* of the fruits of the field.

10   The hands of the compassionate women
Have cooked their own children;
They became food for them
In the destruction of the daughter of my
   people.

11   The LORD has fulfilled His fury,
He has poured out His fierce anger.
He kindled a fire in Zion,
And it has devoured its foundations.

12   The kings of the earth,
And all inhabitants of the world,
Would not have believed
That the adversary and the enemy
Could enter the gates of Jerusalem—

13   Because of the sins of her prophets
And the iniquities of her priests,
Who shed in her midst
The blood of the just.

14   They wandered blind in the streets;
They have defiled themselves with blood,
So that no one would touch their garments.

15   They cried out to them,
"Go away, unclean!
Go away, go away,
Do not touch us!"
When they fled and wandered,
Those among the nations said,
"They shall no longer dwell *here.*"

16   The face[i] of the LORD scattered them;
He no longer regards them.
The people do not respect the priests
Nor show favor to the elders.

17   Still our eyes failed us,
Watching vainly for our help;
In our watching we watched
For a nation *that* could not save *us.*

18   They tracked our steps
So that we could not walk in our streets.
Our end was near;
Our days were over,
For our end had come.

4:7 [h]Or *nobles*   4:16 [i]Targum reads *anger.*

19 Our pursuers were swifter
   Than the eagles of the heavens.
   They pursued us on the mountains
   And lay in wait for us in the wilderness.

20 The breath of our nostrils, the anointed of
      the LORD,
   Was caught in their pits,
   Of whom we said, "Under his shadow
   We shall live among the nations."

21 Rejoice and be glad, O daughter of Edom,
   You who dwell in the land of Uz!
   The cup shall also pass over to you
   And you shall become drunk and make
      yourself naked.

22 *The punishment of* your iniquity is
      accomplished,
   O daughter of Zion;
   He will no longer send you into captivity.
   He will punish your iniquity,
   O daughter of Edom;
   He will uncover your sins!

5

Remember,* O LORD, what has come
   upon us;
Look, and behold our reproach!
2 Our inheritance has been turned over to
      aliens,
   And our houses to foreigners.
3 We have become orphans and waifs,
   Our mothers *are* like widows.
4 We pay for the water we drink,
   And our wood comes at a price.
5 *They* pursue at our heels;*j*
   We labor *and* have no rest.
6 We have given our hand *to* the Egyptians
   And the Assyrians, to be satisfied with
      bread.
7 Our fathers sinned *and are* no more,
   But we bear their iniquities.
8 Servants rule over us;
   There is none to deliver *us* from their hand.
9 We get our bread *at the risk* of our lives,
   Because of the sword in the wilderness.
10 Our skin is hot as an oven,
   Because of the fever of famine.
11 They ravished the women in Zion,
   The maidens in the cities of Judah.
12 Princes were hung up by their hands,
   And elders were not respected.
13 Young men ground at the millstones;
   Boys staggered under *loads of* wood.
14 The elders have ceased *gathering at* the
      gate,
   And the young men from their music.

15 The joy of our heart has ceased;
   Our dance has turned into mourning.
16 The crown has fallen *from* our head.
   Woe to us, for we have sinned!
17 Because of this our heart is faint;
   Because of these *things* our eyes grow dim;
18 Because of Mount Zion which is desolate,
   With foxes walking about on it.

CHAPTER 5

5:1–18 *Remember.* There is no prayer in
chapter 4, but now the people pray to God
and describe their reproach. They have lost
their freedom, their joy, and their inheritance,
and they are paying dearly just to stay
alive—all because of the sins of their fathers.
God knows your needs and will not forget
you (Isa. 49:14–18).

5:5 *j* Literally *necks*

5:19 *Rule.* They had lost their crown (v. 16), but God was still on His throne (v. 19). The defeat of Judah was not the victory of the false gods of Babylon! No matter how hopeless you feel, no matter how difficult the present situation may be, God is still ruling in this universe, and He will not forsake you.

5:20–22 *Renew and restore.* God's chastening is proof that He loves you and has not forsaken you (Heb. 12:5–11). One day, He will take you out of the furnace and give you a new start. You will be a new and better person if you let Him have His way.

19 *You, O LORD, remain forever;
   Your throne from generation to generation.
20 *Why do You forget us forever,
   *And forsake us for so long a time?
21 Turn us back to You, O LORD, and we will
      be restored;
   Renew our days as of old,
22 Unless You have utterly rejected us,
   *And are very angry with us!

EZEKIEL

While Jeremiah was ministering to the people in Judah, Ezekiel was ministering to the exiles in Babylon. He was taken to Babylon in 597 B.C. with the second deportation; and five years later, he received his call to ministry (592 B.C.). Like Jeremiah, he was a priest who was called to be a prophet; and also like Jeremiah, he preached action sermons that caught the attention of the people.

There are four sections to the book: (1) God's call of Ezekiel (chaps. 1—3); (2) God's judgment on Jerusalem (chaps. 4—24); (3) God's judgment on the nations (chaps. 25—32); and (4) God's restoration of His people (chaps. 33—48).

Ezekiel's prophecy emphasizes the glory of God and the honor of God's name. Sixty-seven times the statement "I am the LORD" is found in this book, and several times God is said to act "for [His] name's sake" so that His holy name would "not be profaned." Had the people of Judah been concerned for the honor of the Lord, He would not have dishonored them before their enemies.

1 Now it came to pass in the thirtieth year, in the fourth *month,* on the fifth *day* of the month, as I *was* among the captives by the River Chebar, *that* the heavens were opened and I saw visions^a of God. 2On the fifth *day* of the month, which *was* in the fifth year of King Jehoiachin's captivity, 3the word of the LORD came expressly to Ezekiel the priest, the son of Buzi, in the land of the Chaldeans^b by the River Chebar; and the hand of the LORD was upon him there.

4*Then I looked, and behold, a whirlwind was coming out of the north, a great cloud with raging fire engulfing itself; and brightness *was* all around it and radiating out of its midst like the color of amber, out of the midst of the fire. 5Also from within it *came* the likeness of four living creatures. And this *was* their appearance: they had the likeness of a man. 6Each one had four faces, and each one had four wings. 7Their legs *were* straight, and the soles of their feet *were* like the soles of calves' feet. They sparkled like the color of burnished bronze. 8The hands of a man *were* under their wings on their four sides; and each of the four had faces and wings. 9Their wings touched one another. *The creatures* did not turn when they went, but each one went straight forward.

10As for the likeness of their faces, *each* had the face of a man; each of the four had the face of a lion on the right side, each of the four had the face of an ox on the left side, and each of the four had the face of an eagle. 11Thus *were* their faces. Their wings stretched upward; two *wings* of each one touched one another, and two covered their bodies. 12And each one went straight forward; they went wherever the spirit wanted to go, and they did not turn when they went.

13As for the likeness of the living creatures, their appearance *was* like burning coals of fire, like the appearance of torches going back and forth among the living creatures. The fire was bright, and out of the fire went lightning. 14And

CHAPTER 1

1:4–21 At the age of thirty, when he could have started serving in the temple (Num. 4:3), Ezekiel was called to serve as God's prophet in Babylon. He was in captivity, but that did not keep the heavens from opening so that he could see the glory of God (Rev. 1:9ff.).

He saw God's providence. The vision shows how God is working in His world. What looks like a storm to us is the tool of His providence, the wheels spinning within the wheels and the living creatures going back and forth like lightning. It is all too much for us to understand but not for God to control. Romans 8:28 still stands!

1:1 ^{a}Following Masoretic Text, Septuagint, and Vulgate; Syriac and Targum read *a vision.* 1:3 ^{b}Or *Babylonians,* and so elsewhere in this book

1:22–27 He saw God's throne. Far above the storm, the wheels, the living creatures, and the firmament is God's throne ruling over all. It looked as though Nebuchadnezzar was ruling everything, but God was still on His throne: "The LORD sits as King forever" (Ps. 29:10). The next time you face a storm, look high enough to see God's exalted throne.

1:28 He saw the rainbow. Usually you see the rainbow when the storm is over (Gen. 9:8–17), and only an arc at that. Ezekiel saw the rainbow during the storm, and it completely encircled the throne! A symbol of God's grace, the rainbow assures us that the Lord is with us and will not forsake us, especially when we are going through a storm.

CHAPTERS 2—3

2:1ff After the vision came the voice, which is as it ought to be. God's Word endures after the memory of visions fades (2 Pet. 1:16–21). Ezekiel had all the qualities that make for success in serving the Lord. He saw God's glory and fell on his face in humble worship (1:28). Only a vision of the glorious throne of God can sustain you when the way grows difficult.

He stood on his feet, was filled with the Spirit, and listened to the Word of God (2:1–5). He fed on the Word, which gave him what he needed to speak God's Word (2:6—3:3). In this, he was like Jeremiah (Jer. 15:16), John (Rev. 10:9), and Jesus (Matt. 4:4).

He set his face to do God's will (3:4–11; Isa. 50:7; Luke 9:51). Several times in the book God tells him to "set his face" against something. Ezekiel depended on the hand of God to strengthen him (3:12–14). He sat with the people and identified with their pain (3:15), and he waited patiently for God's word to come to him (3:16–23). When God spoke, He made Ezekiel a watchman and told him to stay home and be quiet until he received the message to speak. His solitude and silence were signs to the people that God was angry with them for rejecting His Word. Ezekiel knew that he had been called at a difficult time to do a difficult work with a difficult people, and yet he obeyed the Lord. Little did he know the price he would have to pay to be a watchman, but he was faithful.

the living creatures ran back and forth, in appearance like a flash of lightning.

15Now as I looked at the living creatures, behold, a wheel *was* on the earth beside each living creature with its four faces. 16The appearance of the wheels and their workings *was* like the color of beryl, and all four had the same likeness. The appearance of their workings *was*, as it were, a wheel in the middle of a wheel. 17When they moved, they went toward any one of four directions; they did not turn aside when they went. 18As for their rims, they were so high they were awesome; and their rims *were* full of eyes, all around the four of them. 19When the living creatures went, the wheels went beside them; and when the living creatures were lifted up from the earth, the wheels were lifted up. 20Wherever the spirit wanted to go, they went, *because* there the spirit went; and the wheels were lifted together with them, for the spirit of the living creatures^c *was* in the wheels. 21When those went, *these* went; when those stood, *these* stood; and when those were lifted up from the earth, the wheels were lifted up together with them, for the spirit of the living creatures^d *was* in the wheels.

22*The likeness of the firmament above the heads of the living creatures^e *was* like the color of an awesome crystal, stretched out over their heads. 23And under the firmament their wings *spread out* straight, one toward another. Each one had two which covered one side, and each one had two which covered the other side of the body. 24When they went, I heard the noise of their wings, like the noise of many waters, like the voice of the Almighty, a tumult like the noise of an army; and when they stood still, they let down their wings. 25A voice came from above the firmament that *was* over their heads; whenever they stood, they let down their wings.

26And above the firmament over their heads *was* the likeness of a throne, in appearance like a sapphire stone; on the likeness of the throne *was* a likeness with the appearance of a man high above it. 27Also from the appearance of His waist and upward I saw, as it were, the color of amber with the appearance of fire all around within it; and from the appearance of His waist and downward I saw, as it were, the appearance of fire with brightness all around. 28*Like the appearance of a rainbow in a cloud on a rainy day, so *was* the appearance of the brightness all around it. This *was* the appearance of the likeness of the glory of the LORD.

So when I saw *it*, I fell on my face, and I heard a voice of One speaking.

2 And* He said to me, "Son of man, stand on your feet, and I will speak to you." 2Then the

---

1:20 ^cLiterally *living creature;* Septuagint and Vulgate read *spirit of life;* Targum reads *creatures.* 1:21 ^dLiterally *living creature;* Septuagint and Vulgate read *spirit of life;* Targum reads *creatures.* 1:22 ^eFollowing Septuagint, Targum, and Vulgate; Masoretic Text reads *living creature.*

Faithful Watchmen—It is a serious thing to be a watchman, for the destiny of precious souls is at stake (Ezek. 3:16–21; 33:1–9). The watchman must be alert to every opportunity and must not be afraid to sound the alarm. False watchmen are not faithful (Isa. 56:10–12) and will have much to answer for at the Judgment. Paul was a faithful watchman who was able to say, "I am innocent of the blood of all men. For I have not shunned to declare to you the whole counsel of God" (Acts 20:26–27).

Spirit entered me when He spoke to me, and set me on my feet; and I heard Him who spoke to me. ³And He said to me: "Son of man, I am sending you to the children of Israel, to a rebellious nation that has rebelled against Me; they and their fathers have transgressed against Me to this very day. ⁴For *they are* impudent and stubborn children. I am sending you to them, and you shall say to them, 'Thus says the Lord GOD.' ⁵As for them, whether they hear or whether they refuse— for they *are* a rebellious house—yet they will know that a prophet has been among them.

⁶"And you, son of man, do not be afraid of them nor be afraid of their words, though briers and thorns *are* with you and you dwell among scorpions; do not be afraid of their words or dismayed by their looks, though they *are* a rebellious house. ⁷You shall speak My words to them, whether they hear or whether they refuse, for they *are* rebellious. ⁸But you, son of man, hear what I say to you. Do not be rebellious like that rebellious house; open your mouth and eat what I give you."

⁹Now when I looked, there was a hand stretched out to me; and behold, a scroll of a book *was* in it. ¹⁰Then He spread it before me; and *there was* writing on the inside and on the outside, and written on it *were* lamentations and mourning and woe.

3 Moreover He said to me, "Son of man, eat what you find; eat this scroll, and go, speak to the house of Israel." ²So I opened my mouth, and He caused me to eat that scroll.

³And He said to me, "Son of man, feed your belly, and fill your stomach with this scroll that I give you." So I ate, and it was in my mouth like honey in sweetness.

⁴Then He said to me: "Son of man, go to the house of Israel and speak with My words to them. ⁵For you *are* not sent to a people of unfamiliar speech and of hard language, *but* to the house of Israel, ⁶not to many people of unfamiliar speech and of hard language, whose words you cannot understand. Surely, had I sent you to them, they would have listened to you. ⁷But the house of Israel will not listen to you, because they will not listen to Me; for all the house of Israel *are* impudent and hard-hearted. ⁸Behold, I have made your face strong against their faces, and your forehead strong against their foreheads. ⁹Like adamant stone, harder than flint, I have made your forehead; do not be afraid of them, nor be dismayed at their looks, though they *are* a rebellious house."

¹⁰Moreover He said to me: "Son of man, receive into your heart all My words that I speak to you, and hear with your ears. ¹¹And go, get to the captives, to the children of your people, and speak to them and tell them, 'Thus says the Lord GOD,' whether they hear, or whether they refuse."

¹²Then the Spirit lifted me up, and I heard behind me a great thunderous voice: "Blessed *is* the glory of the LORD from His place!" ¹³*I* also *heard* the noise of the wings of the living creatures that touched one another, and the noise of the wheels beside them, and a great thunderous noise. ¹⁴So the Spirit lifted me up and took me away, and I went in bitterness, in the heat of my spirit; but the hand of the LORD was strong upon me. ¹⁵Then I came to the captives at Tel Abib, who dwelt by the River Chebar; and I sat where they sat, and remained there astonished among them seven days.

16Now it came to pass at the end of seven days that the word of the LORD came to me, saying, 17"Son of man, I have made you a watchman for the house of Israel; therefore hear a word from My mouth, and give them warning from Me: 18When I say to the wicked, 'You shall surely die,' and you give him no warning, nor speak to warn the wicked from his wicked way, to save his life, that same wicked *man* shall die in his iniquity; but his blood I will require at your hand. 19Yet, if you warn the wicked, and he does not turn from his wickedness, nor from his wicked way, he shall die in his iniquity; but you have delivered your soul.

20"Again, when a righteous *man* turns from his righteousness and commits iniquity, and I lay a stumbling block before him, he shall die; because you did not give him warning, he shall die in his sin, and his righteousness which he has done shall not be remembered; but his blood I will require at your hand. 21Nevertheless if you warn the righteous *man* that the righteous should not sin, and he does not sin, he shall surely live because he took warning; also you will have delivered your soul."

22Then the hand of the LORD was upon me there, and He said to me, "Arise, go out into the plain, and there I shall talk with you."

23So I arose and went out into the plain, and behold, the glory of the LORD stood there, like the glory which I saw by the River Chebar; and I fell on my face. 24Then the Spirit entered me and set me on my feet, and spoke with me and said to me: "Go, shut yourself inside your house. 25And you, O son of man, surely they will put ropes on you and bind you with them, so that you cannot go out among them. 26I will make your tongue cling to the roof of your mouth, so that you shall be mute and not be one to rebuke them, for they *are* a rebellious house. 27But when I speak with you, I will open your mouth, and you shall say to them, 'Thus says the Lord GOD.' He who hears, let him hear; and he who refuses, let him refuse; for they *are* a rebellious house.

CHAPTERS 4—5

4:1–3 Ezekiel began his public ministry with four action sermons that declared God's judgment against Jerusalem. First, he "played war" to demonstrate the siege of the city (chaps. 4—5). The iron plate represented the barrier between God and His people (Lam. 3:43–44). Nothing could stop Babylon from capturing the city.

4:4–8 Then, he lay bound for part of each day, 390 days on left side and then 40 days on the right, to show how many years both Israel and Judah had sinned. How long-suffering God was during those years and how they broke His heart (6:9)!

4 "You* also, son of man, take a clay tablet and lay it before you, and portray on it a city, Jerusalem. 2Lay siege against it, build a siege wall against it, and heap up a mound against it; set camps against it also, and place battering rams against it all around. 3Moreover take for yourself an iron plate, and set it *as* an iron wall between you and the city. Set your face against it, and it shall be besieged, and you shall lay siege against it. This *will be* a sign to the house of Israel.

4*"Lie also on your left side, and lay the iniquity of the house of Israel upon it. *According* to the number of the days that you lie on it, you shall bear their iniquity. 5For I have laid on you the years of their iniquity, according to the number of the days, three hundred and ninety days; so you shall bear the iniquity of the house of Israel. 6And when you have completed them, lie again on your right side; then you shall bear the iniquity of the house of Judah forty days. I have laid on you a day for each year.

7"Therefore you shall set your face toward the siege of Jerusalem; your arm *shall be* uncovered, and you shall prophesy against it. 8And surely I will restrain you so that you cannot turn from one side to another till you have ended the days of your siege.

9*"'Also take for yourself wheat, barley, beans, lentils, millet, and spelt; put them into one vessel, and make bread of them for yourself. *During* the number of days that you lie on your side, three hundred and ninety days, you shall eat it. 10And your food which you eat *shall be* by weight, twenty shekels a day; from time to time you shall eat it. 11You shall also drink water by measure, one-sixth of a hin; from time to time you shall drink. 12And you shall eat it *as* barley cakes; and bake it using fuel of human waste in their sight."

13Then the LORD said, "So shall the children of Israel eat their defiled bread among the Gentiles, where I will drive them."

14So I said, "Ah, Lord GOD! Indeed I have never defiled myself from my youth till now; I have never eaten what died of itself or was torn by beasts, nor has abominable flesh ever come into my mouth."

15Then He said to me, "See, I am giving you cow dung instead of human waste, and you shall prepare your bread over it."

16Moreover He said to me, "Son of man, surely I will cut off the supply of bread in Jerusalem; they shall eat bread by weight and with anxiety, and shall drink water by measure and with dread, 17that they may lack bread and water, and be dismayed with one another, and waste away because of their iniquity.

5 "And* you, son of man, take a sharp sword, take it as a barber's razor, and pass *it* over your head and your beard; then take scales to weigh and divide the hair. 2You shall burn with fire one-third in the midst of the city, when the days of the siege are finished; then you shall take one-third and strike around *it* with the sword, and one-third you shall scatter in the wind: I will draw out a sword after them. 3You shall also take a small number of them and bind them in the edge of your *garment.* 4Then take some of them again and throw them into the midst of the fire, and burn them in the fire. From there a fire will go out into all the house of Israel.

5"Thus says the Lord GOD: 'This *is* Jerusalem; I have set her in the midst of the nations and the countries all around her. 6She has rebelled against My judgments by doing wickedness more than the nations, and against My statutes more than the countries that *are* all around her; for they have refused My judgments, and they have not walked in My statutes.' 7Therefore thus says the Lord GOD: 'Because you have multiplied *disobedience* more than the nations that *are* all around you, have not walked in My statutes nor kept My judgments, nor even done*f* according to the judgments of the nations that *are* all around you'— 8therefore thus says the Lord GOD: 'Indeed I, even I, *am* against you and will execute judgments in your midst in the sight of the nations. 9And I will do among you what I have never done, and the like of which I will never do again, because of all your abominations. 10Therefore fathers shall eat *their* sons in your midst, and sons shall eat their fathers; and I will execute judgments among you, and all of you who remain I will scatter to all the winds.

4:9–17 During those fourteen months and ten days, Ezekiel had to ration his food and water as the people in Jerusalem would do. Compare verse 14 with Acts 10:14. Though he was not serving as a priest, Ezekiel still obeyed the priestly code. No doubt the people watched him day after day and told others about his bizarre behavior, and that helped to spread the message.

5:1ff His fourth sign involved shaving his head and face, a real sacrifice for a Jew. The hair represented the people in Jerusalem who faced three destinies: death by famine, death by the sword, and dispersion among the nations (Deut. 28:47–57). But a believing remnant would be protected and saved by the Lord.

Why was God angry with His people? Because they rebelled against His law (v. 6), defiled His temple (v. 11), and did more abominations than the heathen nations around them (vv. 6–7). They did not glorify the Lord but used all His blessings to promote their sin.

Three hundred and ninety years is a long time to continue in sin! We can only marvel at the long-suffering of the Lord (2 Pet. 3:1–9).

5:7 *f*Following Masoretic Text, Septuagint, Targum, and Vulgate; many Hebrew manuscripts and Syriac read *but have done* (compare 11:12).

11'Therefore, *as* I live,' says the Lord GOD, 'surely, because you have defiled My sanctuary with all your detestable things and with all your abominations, therefore I will also diminish *you*; My eye will not spare, nor will I have any pity. 12One-third of you shall die of the pestilence, and be consumed with famine in your midst; and one-third shall fall by the sword all around you; and I will scatter another third to all the winds, and I will draw out a sword after them.

13'Thus shall My anger be spent, and I will cause My fury to rest upon them, and I will be avenged; and they shall know that I, the LORD, have spoken *it* in My zeal, when I have spent My fury upon them. 14Moreover I will make you a waste and a reproach among the nations that *are* all around you, in the sight of all who pass by.

15'So it^g shall be a reproach, a taunt, a lesson, and an astonishment to the nations that *are* all around you, when I execute judgments among you in anger and in fury and in furious rebukes. I, the LORD, have spoken. 16When I send against them the terrible arrows of famine which shall be for destruction, which I will send to destroy you, I will increase the famine upon you and cut off your supply of bread. 17So I will send against you famine and wild beasts, and they will bereave you. Pestilence and blood shall pass through you, and I will bring the sword against you. I, the LORD, have spoken.' "

CHAPTERS 6—7

6:1–7, 11–14 Ruin. The signs were over; now the prophet gave two sermons. Judgment was coming to the mountains and valleys where the people carried on their idolatrous worship. The whole system would be destroyed and the people with it. It was the end!

6:8–10 Repentance. In grace, God would spare a remnant that would remember Him and repent of their sins. The sin that breaks the heart of God should break our hearts as well.

6 Now* the word of the LORD came to me, saying: 2"Son of man, set your face toward the mountains of Israel, and prophesy against them, 3and say, 'O mountains of Israel, hear the word of the Lord GOD! Thus says the Lord GOD to the mountains, to the hills, to the ravines, and to the valleys: "Indeed I, *even* I, will bring a sword against you, and I will destroy your high places. 4Then your altars shall be desolate, your incense altars shall be broken, and I will cast down your slain *men* before your idols. 5And I will lay the corpses of the children of Israel before their idols, and I will scatter your bones all around your altars. 6In all your dwelling places the cities shall be laid waste, and the high places shall be desolate, so that your altars may be laid waste and made desolate, your idols may be broken and made to cease, your incense altars may be cut down, and your works may be abolished. 7The slain shall fall in your midst, and you shall know that I *am* the LORD.

8*"Yet I will leave a remnant, so that you may have *some* who escape the sword among the nations, when you are scattered through the countries. 9Then those of you who escape will remember Me among the nations where they are carried captive, because I was crushed by their adulterous heart which has departed from Me, and by their eyes which play the harlot after their idols; they will loathe themselves for the evils which they committed in all their abominations. 10And they shall know that I *am* the LORD; I have not said in vain that I would bring this calamity upon them."

11'Thus says the Lord GOD: "Pound your fists and stamp your feet, and say, 'Alas, for all the evil abominations of the house of Israel! For they shall fall by the sword, by famine, and by pestilence. 12He who is far off shall die by the pesti-

---

5:15 ^{g}Septuagint, Syriac, Targum, and Vulgate read *you*.

lence, he who is near shall fall by the sword, and he who remains and is besieged shall die by the famine. Thus will I spend My fury upon them. [13]Then you shall know that I *am* the LORD, when their slain are among their idols all around their altars, on every high hill, on all the mountaintops, under every green tree, and under every thick oak, wherever they offered sweet incense to all their idols. [14]So I will stretch out My hand against them and make the land desolate, yes, more desolate than the wilderness toward Diblah, in all their dwelling places. Then they shall know that I *am* the LORD.' " ' "

7 Moreover* the word of the LORD came to me, saying, [2]"And you, son of man, thus says the Lord GOD to the land of Israel:

'An end! The end has come upon the four
   corners of the land.
3 Now the end *has come* upon you,
   And I will send My anger against you;
   I will judge you according to your ways,
   And I will repay you for all your
      abominations.
4 My eye will not spare you,
   Nor will I have pity;
   But I will repay your ways,
   And your abominations will be in your
      midst;
   Then you shall know that I *am* the LORD!'

[5]"Thus says the Lord GOD:

'A disaster, a singular disaster;
   Behold, it has come!
6 An end has come,
   The end has come;
   It has dawned for you;
   Behold, it has come!
7 Doom has come to you, you who dwell in
      the land;
   The time has come,
   A day of trouble *is* near,
   And not of rejoicing in the mountains.
8 Now upon you I will soon pour out My fury,
   And spend My anger upon you;
   I will judge you according to your ways,
   And I will repay you for all your
      abominations.

9 'My eye will not spare,
   Nor will I have pity;
   I will repay you according to your ways,
   And your abominations will be in your
      midst.
   Then you shall know that I *am* the LORD
      who strikes.

10 'Behold, the day!
   Behold, it has come!
   Doom has gone out;
   The rod has blossomed,
   Pride has budded.
11 Violence has risen up into a rod of
      wickedness;
   None of them *shall remain,*
   None of their multitude,
   None of them;
   Nor *shall there be* wailing for them.
12 The time has come,
   The day draws near.

7:1ff *Repayment.* Four times God says, "I will repay" (vv. 3–4, 8–9; See also Gal. 6:6–8). All the things Judah trusted will not help them, not money (v. 19), idols (vv. 20–22), or their leaders (7:23–27).

   It was the end: "The end has come!" (vv. 2, 3, 6); "Then they shall know that I am the LORD" (v. 27).

'Let not the buyer rejoice,
Nor the seller mourn,
For wrath *is* on their whole multitude.
13 For the seller shall not return to what has
been sold,
Though he may still be alive;
For the vision concerns the whole multitude,
And it shall not turn back;
No one will strengthen himself
Who lives in iniquity.

14 'They have blown the trumpet and made
everyone ready,
But no one goes to battle;
For My wrath *is* on all their multitude.
15 The sword *is* outside,
And the pestilence and famine within.
Whoever *is* in the field
Will die by the sword;
And whoever *is* in the city,
Famine and pestilence will devour him.

16 'Those who survive will escape and be on
the mountains
Like doves of the valleys,
All of them mourning,
Each for his iniquity.
17 Every hand will be feeble,
And every knee will be *as* weak *as* water.
18 They will also be girded with sackcloth;
Horror will cover them;
Shame *will be* on every face,
Baldness on all their heads.

19 'They will throw their silver into the streets,
And their gold will be like refuse;
Their silver and their gold will not be able
to deliver them
In the day of the wrath of the LORD;
They will not satisfy their souls,
Nor fill their stomachs,
Because it became their stumbling block of
iniquity.

20 'As for the beauty of his ornaments,
He set it in majesty;
But they made from it
The images of their abominations—
Their detestable things;
Therefore I have made it
Like refuse to them.
21 I will give it as plunder
Into the hands of strangers,
And to the wicked of the earth as spoil;
And they shall defile it.
22 I will turn My face from them,
And they will defile My secret place;
For robbers shall enter it and defile it.

23 'Make a chain,
For the land is filled with crimes of blood,
And the city is full of violence.
24 Therefore I will bring the worst of the
Gentiles,
And they will possess their houses;
I will cause the pomp of the strong to cease,
And their holy places shall be defiled.
25 Destruction comes;
They will seek peace, but *there shall be*
none.
26 Disaster will come upon disaster,
And rumor will be upon rumor.

Then they will seek a vision from a prophet;
But the law will perish from the priest,
And counsel from the elders.

27 'The king will mourn,
The prince will be clothed with desolation,
And the hands of the common people will
    tremble.
I will do to them according to their way,
And according to what they deserve I will
    judge them;
Then they shall know that I *am* the LORD!' "

8 And* it came to pass in the sixth year, in the sixth *month,* on the fifth *day* of the month, as I sat in my house with the elders of Judah sitting before me, that the hand of the Lord GOD fell upon me there. ²Then I looked, and there was a likeness, like the appearance of fire—from the appearance of His waist and downward, fire; and from His waist and upward, like the appearance of brightness, like the color of amber. ³He stretched out the form of a hand, and took me by a lock of my hair; and the Spirit lifted me up between earth and heaven, and brought me in visions of God to Jerusalem, to the door of the north gate of the inner *court,* where the seat of the image of jealousy *was,* which provokes to jealousy. ⁴And behold, the glory of the God of Israel *was* there, like the vision that I saw in the plain.

⁵Then He said to me, "Son of man, lift your eyes now toward the north." So I lifted my eyes toward the north, and there, north of the altar gate, was this image of jealousy in the entrance.

⁶Furthermore He said to me, "Son of man, do you see what they are doing, the great abominations that the house of Israel commits here, to make Me go far away from My sanctuary? Now turn again, you will see greater abominations." ⁷So He brought me to the door of the court; and when I looked, there was a hole in the wall. ⁸Then He said to me, "Son of man, dig into the wall"; and when I dug into the wall, there was a door.

⁹And He said to me, "Go in, and see the wicked abominations which they are doing there." ¹⁰So I went in and saw, and there—every sort of creeping thing, abominable beasts, and all the idols of the house of Israel, portrayed all around on the walls. ¹¹And there stood before them seventy men of the elders of the house of Israel, and in their midst stood Jaazaniah the son of Shaphan. Each man had a censer in his hand, and a thick cloud of incense went up. ¹²Then He said to me, "Son of man, have you seen what the elders of the house of Israel do in the dark, every man in the room of his idols? For they say, 'The LORD does not see us, the LORD has forsaken the land.' "

¹³And He said to me, "Turn again, *and* you will see greater abominations that they are doing." ¹⁴So He brought me to the door of the north gate of the LORD's house; and to my dismay, women were sitting there weeping for Tammuz.

¹⁵Then He said to me, "Have you seen *this,* O son of man? Turn again, you will see greater abominations than these." ¹⁶So He brought me into the inner court of the LORD's house; and there, at the door of the temple of the LORD, between the porch and the altar, *were* about twenty-five men with their backs toward the temple of the LORD and their faces toward the east, and they were worshiping the sun toward the east.

CHAPTER 8

8:1ff Chapters 8—11 constitute a vision God gave to Ezekiel of the defilement of the temple (chap. 8), the destruction of the people (chap. 9), and the departure of God's glory from His house (chaps. 10—11). The vision burdened Ezekiel to pray (9:8) and prepared him to preach the Word (11:25). God will one day judge our evil world. Knowing this, what does it motivate you to do?

What happened in the temple was indicative of what was happening in the nation: it was given over to the worship of idols. There was an image at the door, and there were idolatrous pictures in the inner chamber. Men and women worshiped idols openly, and others did it "in the dark" (v. 12); but all were guilty. When sin comes in at the door of a person's life, it eventually moves to the inner chambers and takes over. Ponder Proverbs 4:23.

This sin brought violence to the land (v. 17) and removed God's glory from His house (v. 6). What a price to pay for sin!

17And He said to me, "Have you seen *this*, O son of man? Is it a trivial thing to the house of Judah to commit the abominations which they commit here? For they have filled the land with violence; then they have returned to provoke Me to anger. Indeed they put the branch to their nose. 18Therefore I also will act in fury. My eye will not spare nor will I have pity; and though they cry in My ears with a loud voice, I will not hear them."

9 Then He called out in my hearing with a loud voice, saying, "Let those who have charge over the city draw near, each *with* a deadly weapon in his hand." 2And suddenly six men came from the direction of the upper gate, which faces north, each with his battle-ax in his hand. One man among them *was* clothed with linen and had a writer's inkhorn at his side. They went in and stood beside the bronze altar.

3*Now the glory of the God of Israel had gone up from the cherub, where it had been, to the threshold of the temple.*h* And He called to the man clothed with linen, who *had* the writer's inkhorn at his side; 4*and the LORD said to him, "Go through the midst of the city, through the midst of Jerusalem, and put a mark on the foreheads of the men who sigh and cry over all the abominations that are done within it."

5To the others He said in my hearing, "Go after him through the city and kill; do not let your eye spare, nor have any pity. 6Utterly slay old *and* young men, maidens and little children and women; but do not come near anyone on whom *is* the mark; and begin at My sanctuary." So they began with the elders who *were* before the temple. 7Then He said to them, "Defile the temple, and fill the courts with the slain. Go out!" And they went out and killed in the city.

8So it was, that while they were killing them, I was left *alone*; and I fell on my face and cried out, and said, "Ah, Lord GOD! Will You destroy all the remnant of Israel in pouring out Your fury on Jerusalem?"

9Then He said to me, "The iniquity of the house of Israel and Judah *is* exceedingly great, and the land is full of bloodshed, and the city full of perversity; for they say, 'The LORD has forsaken the land, and the LORD does not see!' 10And as for Me also, My eye will neither spare, nor will I have pity, *but* I will recompense their deeds on their own head."

11Just then, the man clothed with linen, who *had* the inkhorn at his side, reported back and said, "I have done as You commanded me."

10 And* I looked, and there in the firmament that was above the head of the cherubim, there appeared something like a sapphire stone, having the appearance of the likeness of a throne. 2*Then He spoke to the man clothed with linen,

---

CHAPTER 9

9:3 The glory of God moved from the Holy of Holies and began to depart from the temple: "Ichabod—the glory has departed" (1 Sam. 4:19–22; Jer. 7:1–15). Without the glory of God, the temple was just another building; and without the presence of God, we are just like other people (Exod. 33:12–16).

9:4–7 God's judgment begins with His people (v. 6; 1 Pet. 4:17), for greater privileges bring greater responsibilities. Either we judge our sins, or God will judge them (1 Cor. 11:31).

Even in His wrath, God is merciful and saves a believing remnant, those who "sigh and cry" over the sins of God's people (v.4). Are you among "the sighers and criers"? Like Ezekiel, are you interceding and asking for mercy?

CHAPTER 10

10:1 The throne. If all you do is look at the sins of the land, you will end up very discouraged. Do as the prophet did: lift your eyes higher and get a new vision of the throne of God (Jer. 17:12).

10:2–17 The fire. Coals from the altar brought cleansing to Isaiah (Isa. 6:6–7), but they brought judgment to Jerusalem. The altar is the place where sin is atoned for because sin is judged. Had the nation sought God's mercy and obeyed His Word, the coals would have brought cleansing. Yet even in the midst of terrible judgment, God's "wheels" were still turning and His purposes being worked out in the world.

9:3 *h*Literally *house*

The Fullness of the Spirit—In Old Testament times, the Spirit came upon people temporarily for special reasons, but Jesus promised that the Holy Spirit would stay with His church forever (John 14:16). God took His Spirit from King Saul (1 Sam. 16:14), and David prayed that the Spirit would not depart from him (Ps. 51:11). Our prayer must be that we not grieve the Spirit (Eph. 4:30), lie to the Spirit (Acts 5), or quench the Spirit (1 Thess. 5:19) but have the Spirit's fullness for life and service each day (Eph. 5:18ff.).

and said, "Go in among the wheels, under the cherub, fill your hands with coals of fire from among the cherubim, and scatter *them* over the city." And he went in as I watched.

3Now the cherubim were standing on the south side of the temple*ⁱ* when the man went in, and the cloud filled the inner court. 4Then the glory of the LORD went up from the cherub, *and paused* over the threshold of the temple; and the house was filled with the cloud, and the court was full of the brightness of the LORD's glory. 5And the sound of the wings of the cherubim was heard *even* in the outer court, like the voice of Almighty God when He speaks.

6Then it happened, when He commanded the man clothed in linen, saying, "Take fire from among the wheels, from among the cherubim," that he went in and stood beside the wheels. 7And the cherub stretched out his hand from among the cherubim to the fire that *was* among the cherubim, and took *some of it* and put *it* into the hands of the *man* clothed with linen, who took *it* and went out. 8The cherubim appeared to have the form of a man's hand under their wings.

9And when I looked, there were four wheels by the cherubim, one wheel by one cherub and another wheel by each other cherub; the wheels appeared *to have* the color of a beryl stone. 10*As for* their appearance, all four looked alike—as it were, a wheel in the middle of a wheel. 11When they went, they went toward *any of* their four directions; they did not turn aside when they went, but followed in the direction the head was facing. They did not turn aside when they went. 12And their whole body, with their back, their hands, their wings, and the wheels that the four had, *were* full of eyes all around. 13As for the wheels, they were called in my hearing, "Wheel."

14Each one had four faces: the first face *was* the face of a cherub, the second face the face of a man, the third the face of a lion, and the fourth the face of an eagle. 15And the cherubim were lifted up. This *was* the living creature I saw by the River Chebar. 16When the cherubim went, the wheels went beside them; and when the cherubim lifted their wings to mount up from the earth, the same wheels also did not turn from beside them. 17When *the cherubimʲ* stood still, *the wheels* stood still, and when *oneᵏ* was lifted up, *the otherˡ* lifted itself up, for the spirit of the living creature *was* in them.

18*Then the glory of the LORD departed from the threshold of the temple and stood over the cherub. 19And the cherubim lifted their wings and mounted up from the earth in my sight. When they went out, the wheels *were* beside them; and they stood at the door of the east gate of the LORD's house, and the glory of the God of Israel *was* above them.

20This *is* the living creature I saw under the God of Israel by the River Chebar, and I knew they *were* cherubim. 21Each one had four faces and each one four wings, and the likeness of the hands of a man *was* under their wings. 22And the likeness of their faces *was* the same *as* the faces which I had seen by the River Chebar, their appearance and their persons. They each went straight forward.

10:18, 19 *The glory.* God will not share His glory with idols (Isa. 42:8); therefore, He had to abandon His house. His glory moved to the door of the east gate, poised to move again (11:22–23). If the nation would not glorify God in their obedience, they would glorify Him in judgment.

10:3 *ⁱ*Literally *house,* also in verses 4 and 18   10:17 *ʲ*Literally *they ᵏ*Literally *they ˡ*Literally *they*

CHAPTER 11

11:1–12 *The caldron*. The leaders in Jerusalem committed two errors. First, they rested on a false confidence that since the deportation was ended, nothing terrible could happen to them. Jerusalem was safe. The second error was that they were the "choice meat" and the people they had slain (the "sighers and criers" of 9:4) were only "scraps." Pride and false confidence made them arrogant.

But God saw things differently. The slain people were the "choice meat," and the leaders of the city were the "scraps." The evil men would try to flee the sword, but God would meet them "at the border." They would *almost* make it! Then the city would indeed be a caldron where God would pour out His anger (chap. 24).

11:14–20 *The sanctuary*. The remnant might be taken from their city and temple, but they could not lose the presence of their God. They would one day be regathered, renewed, and restored to their land. There is always hope.

11:22, 23 *The glory*. Judgment cannot fall as long as God's glory dwells in the city, so the glory moved out to the Mount of Olives. This parallels Matthew 23:38—24:3. If in your character and conduct you major on the glory of God, you need not fear the judgment of God.

11 Then* the Spirit lifted me up and brought me to the East Gate of the LORD's house, which faces eastward; and there at the door of the gate were twenty-five men, among whom I saw Jaazaniah the son of Azzur, and Pelatiah the son of Benaiah, princes of the people. 2And He said to me: "Son of man, these *are* the men who devise iniquity and give wicked counsel in this city, 3who say, '*The time is* not near to build houses; this *city is* the caldron, and we *are* the meat.' 4Therefore prophesy against them, prophesy, O son of man!"

5Then the Spirit of the LORD fell upon me, and said to me, "Speak! 'Thus says the LORD: "Thus you have said, O house of Israel; for I know the things that come into your mind. 6You have multiplied your slain in this city, and you have filled its streets with the slain." 7Therefore thus says the Lord GOD: "Your slain whom you have laid in its midst, they *are* the meat, and this *city is* the caldron; but I shall bring you out of the midst of it. 8You have feared the sword; and I will bring a sword upon you," says the Lord GOD. 9"And I will bring you out of its midst, and deliver you into the hands of strangers, and execute judgments on you. 10You shall fall by the sword. I will judge you at the border of Israel. Then you shall know that I *am* the LORD. 11This *city* shall not be your caldron, nor shall you be the meat in its midst. I will judge you at the border of Israel. 12And you shall know that I *am* the LORD; for you have not walked in My statutes nor executed My judgments, but have done according to the customs of the Gentiles which *are* all around you." ' "

13Now it happened, while I was prophesying, that Pelatiah the son of Benaiah died. Then I fell on my face and cried with a loud voice, and said, "Ah, Lord GOD! Will You make a complete end of the remnant of Israel?"

14*Again the word of the LORD came to me, saying, 15"Son of man, your brethren, your relatives, your countrymen, and all the house of Israel in its entirety, *are* those about whom the inhabitants of Jerusalem have said, 'Get far away from the LORD; this land has been given to us as a possession.' 16Therefore say, 'Thus says the Lord GOD: "Although I have cast them far off among the Gentiles, and although I have scattered them among the countries, yet I shall be a little sanctuary for them in the countries where they have gone." ' 17Therefore say, 'Thus says the Lord GOD: "I will gather you from the peoples, assemble you from the countries where you have been scattered, and I will give you the land of Israel." ' 18And they will go there, and they will take away all its detestable things and all its abominations from there. 19Then I will give them one heart, and I will put a new spirit within them,*m* and take the stony heart out of their flesh, and give them a heart of flesh, 20that they may walk in My statutes and keep My judgments and do them; and they shall be My people, and I will be their God. 21But *as for those* whose hearts follow the desire for their detestable things and their abominations, I will recompense their deeds on their own heads," says the Lord GOD.

22*So the cherubim lifted up their wings, with the wheels beside them, and the glory of the God

---

11:19 *m*Literally *you*

of Israel *was* high above them. ²³And the glory of the LORD went up from the midst of the city and stood on the mountain, which *is* on the east side of the city.

²⁴Then the Spirit took me up and brought me in a vision by the Spirit of God into Chaldea,ⁿ to those in captivity. And the vision that I had seen went up from me. ²⁵So I spoke to those in captivity of all the things the LORD had shown me.

12 Now the word of the LORD came to me, saying: ²"Son of man, you dwell in the midst of a rebellious house, which has eyes to see but does not see, and ears to hear but does not hear; for they *are* a rebellious house.

³*"Therefore, son of man, prepare your belongings for captivity, and go into captivity by day in their sight. You shall go from your place into captivity to another place in their sight. It may be that they will consider, though they *are* a rebellious house. ⁴By day you shall bring out your belongings in their sight, as though going into captivity; and at evening you shall go in their sight, like those who go into captivity. ⁵Dig through the wall in their sight, and carry your belongings out through it. ⁶In their sight you shall bear *them* on *your* shoulders *and* carry *them* out at twilight; you shall cover your face, so that you cannot see the ground, for I have made you a sign to the house of Israel."

⁷So I did as I was commanded. I brought out my belongings by day, as though going into captivity, and at evening I dug through the wall with my hand. I brought *them* out at twilight, *and* I bore *them* on *my* shoulder in their sight.

⁸And in the morning the word of the LORD came to me, saying, ⁹"Son of man, has not the house of Israel, the rebellious house, said to you, 'What are you doing?' ¹⁰Say to them, 'Thus says the Lord GOD: "This burden *concerns* the prince in Jerusalem and all the house of Israel who are among them." ' ¹¹Say, 'I *am* a sign to you. As I have done, so shall it be done to them; they shall be carried away into captivity.' ¹²And the prince who *is* among them shall bear *his* belongings on *his* shoulder at twilight and go out. They shall dig through the wall to carry *them* out through it. He shall cover his face, so that he cannot see the ground with *his* eyes. ¹³I will also spread My net over him, and he shall be caught in My snare. I will bring him to Babylon, *to* the land of the Chaldeans; yet he shall not see it, though he shall die there. ¹⁴I will scatter to every wind all who *are* around him to help him, and all his troops; and I will draw out the sword after them.

¹⁵"Then they shall know that I *am* the LORD, when I scatter them among the nations and disperse them throughout the countries. ¹⁶But I will spare a few of their men from the sword, from famine, and from pestilence, that they may declare all their abominations among the Gentiles wherever they go. Then they shall know that I *am* the LORD."

¹⁷*Moreover the word of the LORD came to me, saying, ¹⁸"Son of man, eat your bread with quaking, and drink your water with trembling and anxiety. ¹⁹And say to the people of the land, 'Thus says the Lord GOD to the inhabitants of Jerusalem

---

CHAPTER 12

12:3–16 When people become spiritually blind and deaf, God uses unusual means to get His Word across to them. Ezekiel preached two more action sermons to warn them that judgment was at hand. The prophet lived the message he was declaring.

First, his actions in the morning portrayed the people who were packing to go into captivity, while his actions in the evening portrayed the futile attempt of King Zedekiah to escape. God knew what would occur, and nobody could alter His plans.

12:17–20 Second, Ezekiel's actions at his meals portrayed the terror the people would experience in spite of their believing that the worst was past. The false prophets said that people like Ezekiel and Jeremiah were "doomsayers" and their dire predictions would not occur. But God's Word never fails, and it is always fulfilled on time.

God does not ask you to do bizarre things as He did Ezekiel, but can others tell by your life-style that you believe Jesus is coming and that He will one day judge the world (2 Pet. 3:10–18)? Is your life an action sermon that catches the attention of people who are blind and deaf to God's truth?

and to the land of Israel: "They shall eat their bread with anxiety, and drink their water with dread, so that her land may be emptied of all who are in it, because of the violence of all those who dwell in it. ²⁰Then the cities that are inhabited shall be laid waste, and the land shall become desolate; and you shall know that I *am* the LORD." ' "

²¹And the word of the LORD came to me, saying, ²²"Son of man, what *is* this proverb *that* you people have about the land of Israel, which says, 'The days are prolonged, and every vision fails'? ²³Tell them therefore, 'Thus says the Lord GOD: "I will lay this proverb to rest, and they shall no more use it as a proverb in Israel." But say to them, "The days are at hand, and the fulfillment of every vision. ²⁴For no more shall there be any false vision or flattering divination within the house of Israel. ²⁵For I *am* the LORD. I speak, and the word which I speak will come to pass; it will no more be postponed; for in your days, O rebellious house, I will say the word and perform it," says the Lord GOD.' "

²⁶Again the word of the LORD came to me, saying, ²⁷"Son of man, look, the house of Israel is saying, 'The vision that he sees *is* for many days from now, and he prophesies of times far off.' ²⁸Therefore say to them, 'Thus says the Lord GOD: "None of My words will be postponed any more, but the word which I speak will be done," says the Lord GOD.' "

CHAPTER 13

13:1ff *False prophets.* Imagine being called to preach against the preachers! Why were those prophets so dangerous? Because they invented their messages and did not get them from the mouth of God. Instead of being shepherds who faithfully led the flock, they were foxes living on refuse. Spiritually speaking, the false prophets were religious scavengers, living among ruins they had made themselves.

13:10, 16 *False peace.* This was also Jeremiah's word of warning (Jer. 6:14; 8:11), and yet the people rejected it. Even though he was running away from God, Jonah was able to sleep in a storm (Jon. 1:5). Having confidence in our feelings is not the same as having confidence from God.

13:11–16 *False protection.* No matter how strong the wall looked, it would not survive the storm. God wanted to wash things white (Isa. 1:18), but the false prophets whitewashed things. The common people rejoiced at the comforting words of the false prophets, but the "sighers and criers" were saddened by them (v. 22). John asserted, "I have no greater joy than to hear that my children walk in truth" (3 John 4).

13 And* the word of the LORD came to me, saying, ²"Son of man, prophesy against the prophets of Israel who prophesy, and say to those who prophesy out of their own heart, 'Hear the word of the LORD!' "

³Thus says the Lord GOD: "Woe to the foolish prophets, who follow their own spirit and have seen nothing! ⁴O Israel, your prophets are like foxes in the deserts. ⁵You have not gone up into the gaps to build a wall for the house of Israel to stand in battle on the day of the LORD. ⁶They have envisioned futility and false divination, saying, 'Thus says the LORD!' But the LORD has not sent them; yet they hope that the word may be confirmed. ⁷Have you not seen a futile vision, and have you not spoken false divination? You say, 'The LORD says,' but I have not spoken."

⁸Therefore thus says the Lord GOD: "Because you have spoken nonsense and envisioned lies, therefore I *am* indeed against you," says the Lord GOD. ⁹"My hand will be against the prophets who envision futility and who divine lies; they shall not be in the assembly of My people, nor be written in the record of the house of Israel, nor shall they enter into the land of Israel. Then you shall know that I *am* the Lord GOD.

¹⁰*"Because, indeed, because they have seduced My people, saying, 'Peace!' when *there is* no peace—and one builds a wall, and they plaster it with untempered *mortar*— ¹¹*say to those who plaster *it* with untempered *mortar*, that it will fall. There will be flooding rain, and you, O great hailstones, shall fall; and a stormy wind shall tear *it* down. ¹²Surely, when the wall has fallen, will it not be said to you, 'Where *is* the mortar with which you plastered *it*?' "

¹³Therefore thus says the Lord GOD: "I will cause a stormy wind to break forth in My fury; and there shall be a flooding rain in My anger, and great hailstones in fury to consume *it*.

¹⁴So I will break down the wall you have plastered with untempered *mortar*, and bring it down to the ground, so that its foundation will be uncovered; it will fall, and you shall be consumed in the midst of it. Then you shall know that I *am* the LORD.

¹⁵"Thus will I accomplish My wrath on the wall and on those who have plastered it with untempered *mortar;* and I will say to you, 'The wall *is* no *more,* nor those who plastered it, ¹⁶*that is,* the prophets of Israel who prophesy concerning Jerusalem, and who see visions of peace for her when *there is* no peace,' " says the Lord GOD.

¹⁷"Likewise, son of man, set your face against the daughters of your people, who prophesy out of their own heart; prophesy against them, ¹⁸and say, 'Thus says the Lord GOD: "Woe to the *women* who sew *magic* charms on their sleevesº and make veils for the heads of people of every height to hunt souls! Will you hunt the souls of My people, and keep yourselves alive? ¹⁹And will you profane Me among My people for handfuls of barley and for pieces of bread, killing people who should not die, and keeping people alive who should not live, by your lying to My people who listen to lies?"

²⁰"Therefore thus says the Lord GOD: "Behold, I *am* against your *magic* charms by which you hunt souls there like birds. I will tear them from your arms, and let the souls go, the souls you hunt like birds. ²¹I will also tear off your veils and deliver My people out of your hand, and they shall no longer be as prey in your hand. Then you shall know that I *am* the LORD.

²²"Because with lies you have made the heart of the righteous sad, whom I have not made sad; and you have strengthened the hands of the wicked, so that he does not turn from his wicked way to save his life. ²³Therefore you shall no longer envision futility nor practice divination; for I will deliver My people out of your hand, and you shall know that I *am* the LORD." ' "

14 Now* some of the elders of Israel came to me and sat before me. ²And the word of the LORD came to me, saying, ³"Son of man, these men have set up their idols in their hearts, and put before them that which causes them to

---

13:18 ºLiterally *over all the joints of My hands;* Vulgate reads *under every elbow;* Septuagint and Targum read *on all elbows of the hands.*

CHAPTER 14

14:1ff The prophet had seen idols in the temple in Jerusalem (chap. 8), but now he saw idols in the hearts of the elders in Babylon (vv. 3, 4, 7). God had disciplined those men by taking them from Judah to Babylon, and He had been merciful to them in sparing their lives; yet nothing brought them to repentance. They pretended to be spiritual by inquiring of Ezekiel, but God saw their hearts and told His servant the truth (Heb. 4:13).

Judgment was inevitable: famine, hungry beasts, war, and pestilence (Rev. 6:1–8). Noah saved his family (Heb. 11:7), Daniel rescued his friends (Dan. 2), and Job prayed for his three friends and delivered them (Job 42:7–10); but *nobody's intercession would save Jerusalem or anybody in it.* A person's righteousness could save only himself or herself; it could not save another.

Cherishing sin in the heart will lead to practicing sin in the life: "For as he thinks in his heart, so is he" (Prov. 23:7). A good prayer for all of us is Psalm 139:23–24.

Jesus' Righteousness—Sinners are saved from God's eternal wrath not by their righteousness (Titus 3:4–7) but the righteousness of Jesus Christ, the Son of God and the Savior of the world (Isa. 53:6; 2 Cor. 5:21). Not only that, but He is in heaven today, interceding for His people at the right hand of God (Heb. 4:14–16; 1 John 2:1–2). *This is not an excuse for us to sin,* but it is an encouragement to know that our future is secure because of what He did for us on the cross and what He is now doing for us in heaven.

Depth of mercy,
Can there be Mercy still reserved for me?
Can my God His wrath forbear,
Me, the chief of sinners, spare?

There for me the Saviour stands,
Holding forth His wounded hands;
God is love! I know, I feel,
Jesus weeps and loves me still.
—Charles Wesley

stumble into iniquity. Should I let Myself be inquired of at all by them?

4"Therefore speak to them, and say to them, 'Thus says the Lord GOD: "Everyone of the house of Israel who sets up his idols in his heart, and puts before him what causes him to stumble into iniquity, and then comes to the prophet, I the LORD will answer him who comes, according to the multitude of his idols, 5that I may seize the house of Israel by their heart, because they are all estranged from Me by their idols." '

6"Therefore say to the house of Israel, 'Thus says the Lord GOD: "Repent, turn away from your idols, and turn your faces away from all your abominations. 7For anyone of the house of Israel, or of the strangers who dwell in Israel, who separates himself from Me and sets up his idols in his heart and puts before him what causes him to stumble into iniquity, then comes to a prophet to inquire of him concerning Me, I the LORD will answer him by Myself. 8I will set My face against that man and make him a sign and a proverb, and I will cut him off from the midst of My people. Then you shall know that I am the LORD.

9"And if the prophet is induced to speak anything, I the LORD have induced that prophet, and I will stretch out My hand against him and destroy him from among My people Israel. 10And they shall bear their iniquity; the punishment of the prophet shall be the same as the punishment of the one who inquired, 11that the house of Israel may no longer stray from Me, nor be profaned anymore with all their transgressions, but that they may be My people and I may be their God," says the Lord GOD.' "

12The word of the LORD came again to me, saying: 13"Son of man, when a land sins against Me by persistent unfaithfulness, I will stretch out My hand against it; I will cut off its supply of bread, send famine on it, and cut off man and beast from it. 14Even if these three men, Noah, Daniel, and Job, were in it, they would deliver only themselves by their righteousness," says the Lord GOD.

15"If I cause wild beasts to pass through the land, and they empty it, and make it so desolate that no man may pass through because of the beasts, 16even though these three men were in it, as I live," says the Lord GOD, "they would deliver neither sons nor daughters; only they would be delivered, and the land would be desolate.

17"Or if I bring a sword on that land, and say, 'Sword, go through the land,' and I cut off man and beast from it, 18even though these three men were in it, as I live," says the Lord GOD, "they would deliver neither sons nor daughters, but only they themselves would be delivered.

19"Or if I send a pestilence into that land and pour out My fury on it in blood, and cut off from it man and beast, 20even though Noah, Daniel, and Job were in it, as I live," says the Lord GOD, "they would deliver neither son nor daughter; they would deliver only themselves by their righteousness."

21For thus says the Lord GOD: "How much more it shall be when I send My four severe judgments on Jerusalem—the sword and famine and wild beasts and pestilence—to cut off man and beast from it? 22Yet behold, there shall be left in it a remnant who will be brought out, both sons and daughters; surely they will come out to you, and you will see their ways and their doings. Then you will be comforted concerning the disaster that

I have brought upon Jerusalem, all that I have brought upon it. 23And they will comfort you, when you see their ways and their doings; and you shall know that I have done nothing without cause that I have done in it," says the Lord GOD.

15 Then* the word of the LORD came to me, saying: 2"Son of man, how is the wood of the vine *better* than any other wood, the vine branch which is among the trees of the forest? 3Is wood taken from it to make any object? Or can *men* make a peg from it to hang any vessel on? 4Instead, it is thrown into the fire for fuel; the fire devours both ends of it, and its middle is burned. Is it useful for *any* work? 5Indeed, when it was whole, no object could be made from it. How much less will it be useful for *any* work when the fire has devoured it, and it is burned?

6"Therefore thus says the Lord GOD: 'Like the wood of the vine among the trees of the forest, which I have given to the fire for fuel, so I will give up the inhabitants of Jerusalem; 7and I will set My face against them. They will go out from *one* fire, but *another* fire shall devour them. Then you shall know that I *am* the LORD, when I set My face against them. 8Thus I will make the land desolate, because they have persisted in unfaithfulness,' says the Lord GOD."

16 Again* the word of the LORD came to me, saying, 2"Son of man, cause Jerusalem to know her abominations, 3and say, 'Thus says the Lord GOD to Jerusalem: "Your birth and your nativity *are* from the land of Canaan; your father *was* an Amorite and your mother a Hittite. 4As for your nativity, on the day you were born your navel cord was not cut, nor were you washed in water to cleanse *you;* you were not rubbed with salt nor wrapped in swaddling cloths. 5No eye pitied you, to do any of these things for you, to have compassion on you; but you were thrown out into the open field, when you yourself were loathed on the day you were born.

6"And when I passed by you and saw you struggling in your own blood, I said to you in your blood, 'Live!' Yes, I said to you in your blood, 'Live!' 7I made you thrive like a plant in the field; and you grew, matured, and became very beautiful. *Your* breasts were formed, your hair grew, but you *were* naked and bare.

8"When I passed by you again and looked upon you, indeed your time *was* the time of love; so I spread My wing over you and covered your nakedness. Yes, I swore an oath to you and entered into a covenant with you, and you became Mine," says the Lord GOD.

9"Then I washed you in water; yes, I thoroughly washed off your blood, and I anointed you with oil. 10I clothed you in embroidered cloth and gave you sandals of badger skin; I clothed you with fine linen and covered you with silk. 11I adorned you with ornaments, put bracelets on your wrists, and a chain on your neck. 12And I put a jewel in your nose, earrings in your ears, and a beautiful crown on your head. 13Thus you were adorned with gold and silver, and your clothing *was of* fine linen, silk, and embroidered cloth. You ate *pastry of* fine flour, honey, and oil. You were exceedingly beautiful, and succeeded to royalty. 14Your fame went out among the nations because of your beauty, for it *was* perfect through My

CHAPTERS 15—16

15:1ff *Unfruitfulness.* The vine was a familiar emblem of Israel (Ps. 80:8–13; Isa. 5:1–7). Vines are good for only two things: bearing or burning. You do not build with wood from the vine because it does not lend itself to being cut and shaped. If the vine does not bear fruit, it is useless, and that was the condition of God's people in Ezekiel's day. If you share the life of God through faith in Jesus Christ, let that life reveal itself in the fruit you bear for His glory.

16:1ff *Unfaithfulness.* Israel was the wife of Jehovah only because of His grace and love. She was in wretched shape when He called her and saved her. He showered her with gifts, which she used to commit spiritual adultery as she worshiped the idols of the other nations. She was both an adulterous wife who broke the marriage covenant and a harlot who paid others to sin with her. God judged Sodom and Israel (Samaria, the northern kingdom), but that did not deter Judah; she went right on sinning. No wonder God became angry and judged the people.

In Romans 7:4, Paul applies these two images in chapters 15 and 16 to believers: we are "married to another—to Him who was raised from the dead, that we should bear fruit to God." Jesus Christ wants our single-hearted devotion as we share our love with Him (2 Cor. 11:2–3).

> ❝*Lord, let me not live to be useless.* ❞
>
> —John Wesley

splendor which I had bestowed on you," says the Lord GOD.

15"But you trusted in your own beauty, played the harlot because of your fame, and poured out your harlotry on everyone passing by who *would have* it. 16You took some of your garments and adorned multicolored high places for yourself, and played the harlot on them. *Such* things should not happen, nor be. 17You have also taken your beautiful jewelry from My gold and My silver, which I had given you, and made for yourself male images and played the harlot with them. 18You took your embroidered garments and covered them, and you set My oil and My incense before them. 19Also My food which I gave you— the pastry of fine flour, oil, and honey *which* I fed you—you set it before them as sweet incense; and *so* it was," says the Lord GOD.

20"Moreover you took your sons and your daughters, whom you bore to Me, and these you sacrificed to them to be devoured. *Were* your *acts* of harlotry a small matter, 21that you have slain My children and offered them up to them by causing them to pass through *the fire?* 22And in all your abominations and acts of harlotry you did not remember the days of your youth, when you were naked and bare, struggling in your blood.

23"Then it was so, after all your wickedness— 'Woe, woe to you!' says the Lord GOD— 24*that* you also built for yourself a shrine, and made a high place for yourself in every street. 25You built your high places at the head of every road, and made your beauty to be abhorred. You offered yourself to everyone who passed by, and multiplied your acts of harlotry. 26You also committed harlotry with the Egyptians, your very fleshly neighbors, and increased your acts of harlotry to provoke Me to anger.

27"Behold, therefore, I stretched out My hand against you, diminished your allotment, and gave you up to the will of those who hate you, the daughters of the Philistines, who were ashamed of your lewd behavior. 28You also played the harlot with the Assyrians, because you were insatiable; indeed you played the harlot with them and still were not satisfied. 29Moreover you multiplied your acts of harlotry as far as the land of the trader, Chaldea; and even then you were not satisfied.

30"How degenerate is your heart!" says the Lord GOD, "seeing you do all these *things,* the deeds of a brazen harlot.

31"You erected your shrine at the head of every road, and built your high place in every street. Yet you were not like a harlot, because you scorned payment. 32*You are* an adulterous wife, *who* takes strangers instead of her husband. 33Men make payment to all harlots, but you made your payments to all your lovers, and hired them to come to you from all around for your harlotry. 34You are the opposite of *other* women in your harlotry, because no one solicited you to be a harlot. In that you gave payment but no payment was given you, therefore you are the opposite."

35'Now then, O harlot, hear the word of the LORD! 36Thus says the Lord GOD: "Because your filthiness was poured out and your nakedness uncovered in your harlotry with your lovers, and with all your abominable idols, and because of the blood of your children which you gave to them, 37surely, therefore, I will gather all your lovers with whom you took pleasure, all those you loved, *and* all those you hated; I will gather them from all around against you and will uncover your nakedness to them, that they may see all your nakedness. [38]And I will judge you as women who break wedlock or shed blood are judged; I will bring blood upon you in fury and jealousy. [39]I will also give you into their hand, and they shall throw down your shrines and break down your high places. They shall also strip you of your clothes, take your beautiful jewelry, and leave you naked and bare.

[40]"They shall also bring up an assembly against you, and they shall stone you with stones and thrust you through with their swords. [41]They shall burn your houses with fire, and execute judgments on you in the sight of many women; and I will make you cease playing the harlot, and you shall no longer hire lovers. [42]So I will lay to rest My fury toward you, and My jealousy shall depart from you. I will be quiet, and be angry no more. [43]Because you did not remember the days of your youth, but agitated Me[p] with all these *things,* surely I will also recompense your deeds on *your own* head," says the Lord GOD. "And you shall not commit lewdness in addition to all your abominations.

[44]"Indeed everyone who quotes proverbs will use *this* proverb against you: 'Like mother, like daughter!' [45]You *are* your mother's daughter, loathing husband and children; and you *are* the sister of your sisters, who loathed their husbands and children; your mother *was* a Hittite and your father an Amorite.

[46]"Your elder sister *is* Samaria, who dwells with her daughters to the north of you; and your younger sister, who dwells to the south of you, *is* Sodom and her daughters. [47]You did not walk in their ways nor act according to their abominations; but, as *if that were* too little, you became more corrupt than they in all your ways.

[48]"*As* I live," says the Lord GOD, "neither your sister Sodom nor her daughters have done as you and your daughters have done. [49]Look, this was the iniquity of your sister Sodom: She and her daughter had pride, fullness of food, and abundance of idleness; neither did she strengthen the hand of the poor and needy. [50]And they were haughty and committed abomination before Me; therefore I took them away as I saw *fit.*[q]

[51]"Samaria did not commit half of your sins; but you have multiplied your abominations more than they, and have justified your sisters by all the abominations which you have done. [52]You who judged your sisters, bear your own shame also, because the sins which you committed were more abominable than theirs; they are more righteous than you. Yes, be disgraced also, and bear your own shame, because you justified your sisters.

[53]"When I bring back their captives, the captives of Sodom and her daughters, and the captives of Samaria and her daughters, then *I will also bring back* the captives of your captivity among them, [54]that you may bear your own shame and be disgraced by all that you did when you comforted them. [55]When your sisters, Sodom

---

16:43 [p]Following Septuagint, Syriac, Targum, and Vulgate; Masoretic Text reads *were agitated with Me.*   16:50 [q]Vulgate reads *you saw;* Septuagint reads *he saw;* Targum reads *as was revealed to Me.*

and her daughters, return to their former state, and Samaria and her daughters return to their former state, then you and your daughters will return to your former state. [56]For your sister Sodom was not a byword in your mouth in the days of your pride, [57]before your wickedness was uncovered. It was like the time of the reproach of the daughters of Syria[r] and all *those* around her, and of the daughters of the Philistines, who despise you everywhere. [58]You have paid for your lewdness and your abominations," says the LORD. [59]For thus says the Lord GOD: "I will deal with you as you have done, who despised the oath by breaking the covenant.

[60]"Nevertheless I will remember My covenant with you in the days of your youth, and I will establish an everlasting covenant with you. [61]Then you will remember your ways and be ashamed, when you receive your older and your younger sisters; for I will give them to you for daughters, but not because of My covenant with you. [62]And I will establish My covenant with you. Then you shall know that I *am* the LORD, [63]that you may remember and be ashamed, and never open your mouth anymore because of your shame, when I provide you an atonement for all you have done," says the Lord GOD.' "

CHAPTER 17

17:1ff God used allegories to arouse interest and capture attention. Jesus used parables for the same purpose (Matt. 13:10–17).

The great eagle (Nebuchadnezzar) came to Jerusalem (Lebanon) and took to Babylon the top branch of the cedar (King Jehoiachin). He left some of the seed (King Zedekiah), which grew into a low vine. Zedekiah made a covenant to be loyal to Babylon, but then he broke it (vv. 15, 16, 18) and turned to Egypt for help (vv. 7–8; Jer. 37). The result? The king of Babylon will come back and destroy the lowly vine of Judah (vv. 9–10).

The cedar represents the Davidic dynasty. One day God will take a lowly young twig from David's line (Jesus Christ) and will establish His glorious kingdom (Isa. 11:1–9). But before He can enter into that glory, He must suffer for the sins of the world. "O come, let us adore Him, Christ, the Lord!"

17 And[*] the word of the LORD came to me, saying, [2]"Son of man, pose a riddle, and speak a parable to the house of Israel, [3]and say, 'Thus says the Lord GOD:

> "A great eagle with large wings and long pinions,
> Full of feathers of various colors,
> Came to Lebanon
> And took from the cedar the highest branch.
> 4 He cropped off its topmost young twig
> And carried it to a land of trade;
> He set it in a city of merchants.
> 5 Then he took some of the seed of the land
> And planted it in a fertile field;
> He placed *it* by abundant waters
> *And* set it like a willow tree.
> 6 And it grew and became a spreading vine of low stature;
> Its branches turned toward him,
> But its roots were under it.
> So it became a vine,
> Brought forth branches,
> And put forth shoots.
>
> 7 "But there was another[s] great eagle with large wings and many feathers;
> And behold, this vine bent its roots toward him,
> And stretched its branches toward him,
> From the garden terrace where it had been planted,
> That he might water it.
> 8 It was planted in good soil by many waters,
> To bring forth branches, bear fruit,
> *And* become a majestic vine." '

[9]"Say, 'Thus says the Lord GOD:

16:57 [r]Following Masoretic Text, Septuagint, Targum, and Vulgate; many Hebrew manuscripts and Syriac read *Edom*.
17:7 [s]Following Septuagint, Syriac, and Vulgate; Masoretic Text and Targum read *one*.

"Will it thrive?
Will he not pull up its roots,
Cut off its fruit,
And leave it to wither?
All of its spring leaves will wither,
And no great power or many people
Will be needed to pluck it up by its roots.
10   Behold, *it is* planted,
Will it thrive?
Will it not utterly wither when the east wind
   touches it?
It will wither in the garden terrace where
   it grew." ' "

11Moreover the word of the LORD came to me, saying, 12"Say now to the rebellious house: 'Do you not know what these *things mean?*' Tell *them,* 'Indeed the king of Babylon went to Jerusalem and took its king and princes, and led them with him to Babylon. 13And he took the king's offspring, made a covenant with him, and put him under oath. He also took away the mighty of the land, 14that the kingdom might be brought low and not lift itself up, *but* that by keeping his covenant it might stand. 15But he rebelled against him by sending his ambassadors to Egypt, that they might give him horses and many people. Will he prosper? Will he who does such *things* escape? Can he break a covenant and still be delivered?

16'As I live,' says the Lord GOD, 'surely in the place *where* the king *dwells* who made him king, whose oath he despised and whose covenant he broke—with him in the midst of Babylon he shall die. 17Nor will Pharaoh with *his* mighty army and great company do anything in the war, when they heap up a siege mound and build a wall to cut off many persons. 18Since he despised the oath by breaking the covenant, and in fact gave his hand and still did all these *things,* he shall not escape.' "

19Therefore thus says the Lord GOD: "*As* I live, surely My oath which he despised, and My covenant which he broke, I will recompense on his own head. 20I will spread My net over him, and he shall be taken in My snare. I will bring him to Babylon and try him there for the treason which he committed against Me. 21All his fugitives[t] with all his troops shall fall by the sword, and those who remain shall be scattered to every wind; and you shall know that I, the LORD, have spoken."

22Thus says the Lord GOD: "I will take also *one* of the highest branches of the high cedar and set *it* out. I will crop off from the topmost of its young twigs a tender one, and will plant *it* on a high and prominent mountain. 23On the mountain height of Israel I will plant it; and it will bring forth boughs, and bear fruit, and be a majestic cedar. Under it will dwell birds of every sort; in the shadow of its branches they will dwell. 24And all the trees of the field shall know that I, the LORD, have brought down the high tree and exalted the low tree, dried up the green tree and made the dry tree flourish; I, the LORD, have spoken and have done *it.*"

17:21 *t*Following Masoretic Text and Vulgate; many Hebrew manuscripts and Syriac read *choice men;* Targum reads *mighty men;* Septuagint omits *All his fugitives.*

CHAPTER 18

18:1ff Have you ever accused God of not being fair? The Jews were doing that (vv. 25, 29–30) and quoting a familiar proverb to argue their case (v. 2; Jer. 31:29–30). If the fathers did the sinning, why should their children do the suffering? Is not God unjust when He punishes the children for the fathers' sins?

But God does not do that, nor does He take pleasure in sending judgment (vv. 23, 32). He would gladly forgive sinners if they would only repent. God judges *individuals*—regardless of what their fathers have done (vv. 4, 20). You cannot claim your father's righteousness, nor can you be punished for your father's sin. You might be punished *by* your father's sin, but that is another matter (Deut. 5:9).

The supreme need is for a "new heart and a new spirit" (v. 31), which can come only through faith in Christ. "Turn and live!" is God's loving call to sinners today. It is a matter not of fairness but of grace.

18 The* word of the LORD came to me again, saying, 2"What do you mean when you use this proverb concerning the land of Israel, saying:

'The fathers have eaten sour grapes,
And the children's teeth are set on edge'?

3"*As* I live," says the Lord GOD, "you shall no longer use this proverb in Israel.

4 "Behold, all souls are Mine;
The soul of the father
As well as the soul of the son is Mine;
The soul who sins shall die.
5 But if a man is just
And does what is lawful and right;
6 If he has not eaten on the mountains,
Nor lifted up his eyes to the idols of the
house of Israel,
Nor defiled his neighbor's wife,
Nor approached a woman during her
impurity;
7 If he has not oppressed anyone,
But has restored to the debtor his pledge;
Has robbed no one by violence,
But has given his bread to the hungry
And covered the naked with clothing;
8 If he has not exacted usury
Nor taken any increase,
But has withdrawn his hand from iniquity
And executed true judgment between man
and man;
9 *If* he has walked in My statutes
And kept My judgments faithfully—
He *is* just;
He shall surely live!"
Says the Lord GOD.

10 "If he begets a son *who is* a robber
Or a shedder of blood,
Who does any of these *things*
11 And does none of those *duties*,
But has eaten on the mountains
Or defiled his neighbor's wife;
12 If he has oppressed the poor and needy,
Robbed by violence,
Not restored the pledge,
Lifted his eyes to the idols,
Or committed abomination;
13 If he has exacted usury
Or taken increase—
Shall he then live?
He shall not live!
If he has done any of these abominations,
He shall surely die;
His blood shall be upon him.

14 "*If*, however, he begets a son
Who sees all the sins which his father has
done,
And considers but does not do likewise;
15 *Who* has not eaten on the mountains,
Nor lifted his eyes to the idols of the house
of Israel,
Nor defiled his neighbor's wife;

Punishment for Sins—God does not punish the innocent for the guilty *except in the case of His Son.* On the cross, Jesus took the punishment for your sins. God has no pleasure in the death of the wicked, "yet it pleased the LORD to bruise Him" (Isa. 53:10), "for Christ also suffered once for sins, the just for the unjust, that He might bring us to God" (1 Pet. 3:18).

16 Has not oppressed anyone,
    Nor withheld a pledge,
    Nor robbed by violence,
    But has given his bread to the hungry
    And covered the naked with clothing;
17 *Who* has withdrawn his hand from the
        poor[u]
    And not received usury or increase,
    But has executed My judgments
    And walked in My statutes—
    He shall not die for the iniquity of his father;
    He shall surely live!

18 "*As for* his father,
    Because he cruelly oppressed,
    Robbed his brother by violence,
    And did what *is* not good among his people,
    Behold, he shall die for his iniquity.

19"Yet you say, 'Why should the son not bear the guilt of the father?' Because the son has done what is lawful and right, and has kept all My statutes and observed them, he shall surely live. 20The soul who sins shall die. The son shall not bear the guilt of the father, nor the father bear the guilt of the son. The righteousness of the righteous shall be upon himself, and the wickedness of the wicked shall be upon himself.

21"But if a wicked man turns from all his sins which he has committed, keeps all My statutes, and does what is lawful and right, he shall surely live; he shall not die. 22None of the transgressions which he has committed shall be remembered against him; because of the righteousness which he has done, he shall live. 23Do I have any pleasure at all that the wicked should die?" says the Lord GOD, "*and* not that he should turn from his ways and live?

24"But when a righteous man turns away from his righteousness and commits iniquity, and does according to all the abominations that the wicked *man* does, shall he live? All the righteousness which he has done shall not be remembered; because of the unfaithfulness of which he is guilty and the sin which he has committed, because of them he shall die.

25"Yet you say, 'The way of the Lord is not fair.' Hear now, O house of Israel, is it not My way which is fair, and your ways which are not fair? 26When a righteous *man* turns away from his righteousness, commits iniquity, and dies in it, it is because of the iniquity which he has done that he dies. 27Again, when a wicked *man* turns away from the wickedness which he committed, and does what is lawful and right, he preserves himself alive. 28Because he considers and turns away from all the transgressions which he committed, he shall surely live; he shall not die. 29Yet the house of Israel says, 'The way of the Lord is not fair.' O house of Israel, is it not My ways which are fair, and your ways which are not fair?

30"Therefore I will judge you, O house of Israel, every one according to his ways," says the Lord GOD. "Repent, and turn from all your transgressions, so that iniquity will not be your ruin. 31Cast away from you all the transgressions which you have committed, and get yourselves a new

18:17 uFollowing Masoretic Text, Targum, and Vulgate; Septuagint reads *iniquity* (compare verse 8).

heart and a new spirit. For why should you die, O house of Israel? ³²For I have no pleasure in the death of one who dies," says the Lord GOD. "Therefore turn and live!"

CHAPTER 19

19:1–9 Jeremiah was not the only prophet to write funeral dirges. Ezekiel wrote this one five years before Jerusalem fell. He used two familiar images of the nation in speaking about the fate of their kings.
The lioness. The lion is the royal animal, and Ezekiel was speaking about the rulers of the land: Jehoahaz (vv. 2–4; Jer. 22:11–12), who died in Egypt; and the present king, Zedekiah (vv. 5–9), who was blinded and taken to Babylon (Jer. 39). None of Judah's "cubs" succeeded in saving the land because they resisted the Word of God.

19 "Moreover* take up a lamentation for the princes of Israel, ²and say:

'What *is* your mother? A lioness:
She lay down among the lions;
Among the young lions she nourished her
　　cubs.
3　She brought up one of her cubs,
And he became a young lion;
He learned to catch prey,
And he devoured men.
4　The nations also heard of him;
He was trapped in their pit,
And they brought him with chains to the
　　land of Egypt.

5　'When she saw that she waited, *that* her
　　hope was lost,
She took another of her cubs *and* made him
　　a young lion.
6　He roved among the lions,
And became a young lion;
He learned to catch prey;
He devoured men.
7　He knew their desolate places,ᵛ
And laid waste their cities;
The land with its fullness was desolated
By the noise of his roaring.
8　Then the nations set against him from the
　　provinces on every side,
And spread their net over him;
He was trapped in their pit.
9　They put him in a cage with chains,
And brought him to the king of Babylon;
They brought him in nets,
That his voice should no longer be heard
　　on the mountains of Israel.

19:10–14 The vine. We have met this image of Israel several times already. The prophet had spoken *about* Zedekiah, but now he speaks *to* Zedekiah and tells him that the beautiful, luxuriant vine would be withered by the east wind (v. 12; 17:10), plucked up, and planted in Babylon. That would be the end of David's line; there would be no strong branch out of which to make a scepter—until the birth of Jesus Christ, the Son of David (Matt. 1:1; Luke 1:30–33)! Judah will supply the scepter (Gen. 49:8–10).
When it looks like man has done his worst and everything is at an end, remember that God always has the last word—and His "Last Word" is His Son, Jesus Christ (Heb. 1:1–2).

10　*'Your mother *was* like a vine in your
　　bloodline,ʷ
Planted by the waters,
Fruitful and full of branches
Because of many waters.
11　She had strong branches for scepters of
　　rulers.
She towered in stature above the thick
　　branches,
And was seen in her height amid the dense
　　foliage.
12　But she was plucked up in fury,
She was cast down to the ground,
And the east wind dried her fruit.
Her strong branches were broken and
　　withered;
The fire consumed them.
13　And now she *is* planted in the wilderness,
In a dry and thirsty land.
14　Fire has come out from a rod of her
　　branches

19:7 ᵛSeptuagint reads *He stood in insolence;* Targum reads *He destroyed its palaces;* Vulgate reads *He learned to make widows.*　19:10 ʷLiterally *blood,* following Masoretic Text, Syriac, and Vulgate; Septuagint reads *like a flower on a pomegranate tree;* Targum reads *in your likeness.*

And devoured her fruit,
So that she has no strong branch— a scepter
    for ruling.' "

This *is* a lamentation, and has become a lamentation.

20 It* came to pass in the seventh year, in the fifth *month*, on the tenth *day* of the month, *that* certain of the elders of Israel came to inquire of the LORD, and sat before me. ²Then the word of the LORD came to me, saying, ³"Son of man, speak to the elders of Israel, and say to them, 'Thus says the Lord GOD: "Have you come to inquire of Me? *As* I live," says the Lord GOD, "I will not be inquired of by you." ' ⁴Will you judge them, son of man, will you judge *them*? Then make known to them the abominations of their fathers.

⁵"Say to them, 'Thus says the Lord GOD: "On the day when I chose Israel and raised My hand in an oath to the descendants of the house of Jacob, and made Myself known to them in the land of Egypt, I raised My hand in an oath to them, saying, 'I *am* the LORD your God.' ⁶On that day I raised My hand in an oath to them, to bring them out of the land of Egypt into a land that I had searched out for them, 'flowing with milk and honey,'ˣ the glory of all lands. ⁷Then I said to them, 'Each of you, throw away the abominations which are before his eyes, and do not defile yourselves with the idols of Egypt. I *am* the LORD your God.' ⁸But they rebelled against Me and would not obey Me. They did not all cast away the abominations which were before their eyes, nor did they forsake the idols of Egypt. Then I said, 'I will pour out My fury on them and fulfill My anger against them in the midst of the land of Egypt.' ⁹But I acted for My name's sake, that it should not be profaned before the Gentiles among whom they *were,* in whose sight I had made Myself known to them, to bring them out of the land of Egypt.

¹⁰"Therefore I made them go out of the land of Egypt and brought them into the wilderness. ¹¹And I gave them My statutes and showed them My judgments, 'which, *if* a man does, he shall live by them.'ʸ ¹²Moreover I also gave them My Sabbaths, to be a sign between them and Me, that they might know that I *am* the LORD who sanctifies them. ¹³Yet the house of Israel rebelled against Me in the wilderness; they did not walk in My statutes; they despised My judgments, 'which, *if* a man does, he shall live by them';ᶻ and they greatly defiled My Sabbaths. Then I said I would pour out My fury on them in the wilderness, to consume them. ¹⁴But I acted for My name's sake, that it should not be profaned before the Gentiles, in whose sight I had brought them out. ¹⁵So I also raised My hand in an oath to them in the wilderness, that I would not bring them into

---

CHAPTER 20

20:1–32 *History.* In his message to the Jewish elders, Ezekiel reviewed the nation's history: the Exodus (vv. 1–9), the wilderness journey (vv. 10–17), and the conquest of their land (vv. 18–32). He pointed out two facts: (1) the nation was guilty of repeated rebellion against the Lord (vv. 8, 13, 21), and (2) the Lord acted as He did for His name's sake (vv. 9, 14, 22). He could easily have destroyed the nation, but what would the Gentiles have said about Israel's God?

Repeated rebellion against God's will is serious. The Lord is long-suffering, but we must never take this for granted. Eventually He must chasten His rebellious children for His name's sake. If we do not glorify Him by obeying His commandments, we must glorify Him by submitting to His chastening (Heb. 12).

20:6 ˣExodus 3:8   20:11 ʸLeviticus 18:5
20:13 ᶻLeviticus 18:5

Honor God's Name—For His name's sake, the Lord forgives our sins (1 John 2:12), guides us (Pss. 23:3; 31:3), deals with us (Ps. 109:21), and revives us (Ps. 143:11). For His name's sake, we ought to serve Him (3 John 7; Rev. 2:3), sacrifice for Him (Matt. 19:29), and be willing to suffer reproach (Matt. 10:22; 24:9). All that we do should be for the honor and glory of God's name (1 Cor. 10:31).

the land which I had given *them,* 'flowing with milk and honey,'*ᵃ* the glory of all lands, ¹⁶because they despised My judgments and did not walk in My statutes, but profaned My Sabbaths; for their heart went after their idols. ¹⁷Nevertheless My eye spared them from destruction. I did not make an end of them in the wilderness.

¹⁸"But I said to their children in the wilderness, 'Do not walk in the statutes of your fathers, nor observe their judgments, nor defile yourselves with their idols. ¹⁹I *am* the LORD your God: Walk in My statutes, keep My judgments, and do them; ²⁰hallow My Sabbaths, and they will be a sign between Me and you, that you may know that I *am* the LORD your God.'

²¹"Notwithstanding, the children rebelled against Me; they did not walk in My statutes, and were not careful to observe My judgments, 'which, *if* a man does, he shall live by them';*ᵇ* but they profaned My Sabbaths. Then I said I would pour out My fury on them and fulfill My anger against them in the wilderness. ²²Nevertheless I withdrew My hand and acted for My name's sake, that it should not be profaned in the sight of the Gentiles, in whose sight I had brought them out. ²³Also I raised My hand in an oath to those in the wilderness, that I would scatter them among the Gentiles and disperse them throughout the countries, ²⁴because they had not executed My judgments, but had despised My statutes, profaned My Sabbaths, and their eyes were fixed on their fathers' idols.

²⁵"Therefore I also gave them up to statutes *that were* not good, and judgments by which they could not live; ²⁶and I pronounced them unclean because of their ritual gifts, in that they caused all their firstborn to pass through *the fire,* that I might make them desolate and that they might know that I am the LORD."'

²⁷"Therefore, son of man, speak to the house of Israel, and say to them, 'Thus says the Lord GOD: "In this too your fathers have blasphemed Me, by being unfaithful to Me. ²⁸When I brought them into the land *concerning* which I had raised My hand in an oath to give them, and they saw all the high hills and all the thick trees, there they offered their sacrifices and provoked Me with their offerings. There they also sent up their sweet aroma and poured out their drink offerings. ²⁹Then I said to them, 'What *is* this high place to which you go?' So its name is called Bamah*ᶜ* to this day." ' ³⁰Therefore say to the house of Israel, 'Thus says the Lord GOD: "Are you defiling yourselves in the manner of your fathers, and committing harlotry according to their abominations? ³¹For when you offer your gifts and make your sons pass through the fire, you defile yourselves with all your idols, even to this day. So shall I be inquired of by you, O house of Israel? *As* I live," says the Lord GOD, "I will not be inquired of by you. ³²What you have in your mind shall never be, when you say, 'We will be like the Gentiles, like the families in other countries, serving wood and stone.'

³³*"As* I live," says the Lord GOD, "surely with a mighty hand, with an outstretched arm, and with fury poured out, I will rule over you. ³⁴I will bring you out from the peoples and gather you

---

20:33–44 Hope. God chastens us that He might restore us, and there is always hope. The repeated "I will" statements assure us that God is working for us and not against us: "I will bring you out! I will plead! I will bring you in! I will accept you!" Why does He do it? "For [His] name's sake" (v. 44).

20:15 *ᵃ*Exodus 3:8   20:21 *ᵇ*Leviticus 18:5   20:29 *ᶜ*Literally *High Place*

out of the countries where you are scattered, with a mighty hand, with an outstretched arm, and with fury poured out. 35And I will bring you into the wilderness of the peoples, and there I will plead My case with you face to face. 36Just as I pleaded My case with your fathers in the wilderness of the land of Egypt, so I will plead My case with you," says the Lord God.

37"I will make you pass under the rod, and I will bring you into the bond of the covenant; 38I will purge the rebels from among you, and those who transgress against Me; I will bring them out of the country where they dwell, but they shall not enter the land of Israel. Then you will know that I *am* the Lord.

39"As for you, O house of Israel," thus says the Lord God: "Go, serve every one of you his idols—and hereafter—if you will not obey Me; but profane My holy name no more with your gifts and your idols. 40For on My holy mountain, on the mountain height of Israel," says the Lord God, "there all the house of Israel, all of them in the land, shall serve Me; there I will accept them, and there I will require your offerings and the firstfruits of your sacrifices, together with all your holy things. 41I will accept you as a sweet aroma when I bring you out from the peoples and gather you out of the countries where you have been scattered; and I will be hallowed in you before the Gentiles. 42Then you shall know that I *am* the Lord, when I bring you into the land of Israel, into the country *for* which I raised My hand in an oath to give to your fathers. 43And there you shall remember your ways and all your doings with which you were defiled; and you shall loathe yourselves in your own sight because of all the evils that you have committed. 44Then you shall know that I *am* the Lord, when I have dealt with you for My name's sake, not according to your wicked ways nor according to your corrupt doings, O house of Israel," says the Lord God.' "

45Furthermore the word of the Lord came to me, saying, 46"Son of man, set your face toward the south; preach against the south and prophesy against the forest land, the South,*d* 47and say to the forest of the South, 'Hear the word of the Lord! Thus says the Lord God: "Behold, I will kindle a fire in you, and it shall devour every green tree and every dry tree in you; the blazing flame shall not be quenched, and all faces from the south to the north shall be scorched by it. 48All flesh shall see that I, the Lord, have kindled it; it shall not be quenched." ' "

49Then I said, "Ah, Lord God! They say of me, 'Does he not speak parables?' "

21 And* the word of the Lord came to me, saying, 2"Son of man, set your face toward Jerusalem, preach against the holy places, and prophesy against the land of Israel; 3and say to the land of Israel, 'Thus says the Lord: "Behold, I *am* against you, and I will draw My sword out of its sheath and cut off both righteous and wicked from you. 4Because I will cut off both righteous and wicked from you, therefore My sword shall go out of its sheath against all flesh from south *to* north, 5that all flesh may know that I, the Lord, have drawn My sword out of its sheath; it shall

20:46 *d*Hebrew *Negev*

CHAPTER 21

21:1ff Jeremiah called Babylon God's battle-ax (Jer. 51:20–23), and Ezekiel called Babylon God's sword. (The word *sword* is used more than a dozen times in this chapter.) God pulled His sword out of the scabbard (vv. 1–7), prepared it for use (vv. 8–17), and then pointed it toward Jerusalem (vv. 18–27) and Ammon (vv. 28–32). The Ammonites had united with Judah against Babylon but had escaped invasion. However, their judgment eventually came.

God uses unbelievers to accomplish His purposes and can even overrule their pagan methods of making decisions (vv. 18–23; Prov. 16:33). God's people did not obey the declared will of God, but the pagan nations obeyed God and did not know it. What a paradox!

The prophet's responses to this message attracted the attention of the people, for he sighed (vv. 6–7) and wailed (v. 12). What is your response to the message of the coming judgment of God (2 Pet. 3:10–18)?

not return anymore." ' [6]Sigh therefore, son of man, with a breaking heart, and sigh with bitterness before their eyes. [7]And it shall be when they say to you, 'Why are you sighing?' that you shall answer, 'Because of the news; when it comes, every heart will melt, all hands will be feeble, every spirit will faint, and all knees will be weak *as* water. Behold, it is coming and shall be brought to pass,' says the Lord GOD."

[8]Again the word of the LORD came to me, saying, [9]"Son of man, prophesy and say, 'Thus says the LORD!' Say:

'A sword, a sword is sharpened
And also polished!
10 Sharpened to make a dreadful slaughter,
Polished to flash like lightning!
Should we then make mirth?
It despises the scepter of My son,
As it does all wood.
11 And He has given it to be polished,
That it may be handled;
This sword is sharpened, and it is polished
To be given into the hand of the slayer.'

12 "Cry and wail, son of man;
For it will be against My people,
Against all the princes of Israel.
Terrors including the sword will be against
My people;
Therefore strike *your* thigh.

13 "Because *it is* a testing,
And what if *the sword* despises even the
scepter?
The scepter shall be no *more*,"

says the Lord GOD.

14 "You therefore, son of man, prophesy,
And strike *your* hands together.
The third time let the sword do double
damage.
It *is* the sword *that* slays,
The sword that slays the great *men*,
That enters their private chambers.
15 I have set the point of the sword against
all their gates,
That the heart may melt and many may
stumble.
Ah! *It is* made bright;
It is grasped for slaughter:

16 "Swords at the ready!
Thrust right!
Set your blade!
Thrust left—
Wherever your edge is ordered!

17 "I also will beat My fists together,
And I will cause My fury to rest;
I, the LORD, have spoken."

[18]The word of the LORD came to me again, saying: [19]"And son of man, appoint for yourself two ways for the sword of the king of Babylon to go; both of them shall go from the same land. Make a sign; put *it* at the head of the road to the city. [20]Appoint a road for the sword to go to Rabbah of the Ammonites, and to Judah, into fortified Jerusalem. [21]For the king of Babylon stands at the parting of the road, at the fork of the two roads,

to use divination: he shakes the arrows, he consults the images, he looks at the liver. 22In his right hand is the divination for Jerusalem: to set up battering rams, to call for a slaughter, to lift the voice with shouting, to set battering rams against the gates, to heap up a *siege* mound, and to build a wall. 23And it will be to them like a false divination in the eyes of those who have sworn oaths with them; but he will bring their iniquity to remembrance, that they may be taken.

24"Therefore thus says the Lord GOD: 'Because you have made your iniquity to be remembered, in that your transgressions are uncovered, so that in all your doings your sins appear—because you have come to remembrance, you shall be taken in hand.

25'Now to you, O profane, wicked prince of Israel, whose day has come, whose iniquity *shall* end, 26thus says the Lord GOD:

"Remove the turban, and take off the crown;
    Nothing *shall remain* the same.
    Exalt the humble, and humble the exalted.
27 Overthrown, overthrown,
    I will make it overthrown!
    It shall be no *longer*,
    Until He comes whose right it is,
    And I will give it *to Him."* '

28"And you, son of man, prophesy and say, 'Thus says the Lord GOD concerning the Ammonites and concerning their reproach,' and say:

'A sword, a sword *is* drawn,
    Polished for slaughter,
    For consuming, for flashing—
29 While they see false visions for you,
    While they divine a lie to you,
    To bring you on the necks of the wicked,
        the slain
    Whose day has come,
    Whose iniquity *shall* end.

30 'Return *it* to its sheath.
    I will judge you
    In the place where you were created,
    In the land of your nativity.
31 I will pour out My indignation on you;
    I will blow against you with the fire of My
        wrath,
    And deliver you into the hands of brutal
        men *who are* skillful to destroy.
32 You shall be fuel for the fire;
    Your blood shall be in the midst of the land.
    You shall not be remembered,
    For I the LORD have spoken.' "

22 Moreover* the word of the LORD came to me, saying, 2"Now, son of man, will you judge, will you judge the bloody city? Yes, show her all her abominations! 3Then say, 'Thus says the Lord GOD: "The city sheds blood in her own midst, that her time may come; and she makes idols within herself to defile herself. 4You have

CHAPTER 22

22:1–16 Four images stand out in this chapter.

The court. The prophet became a prosecuting attorney as he indicted Judah for her sins, proving that the leaders and the common people alike were guilty of breaking the law of God.

People in the Breach—In the history of Israel, God raised up "gap people" to stand in the breach and stay off the judgment. Moses and Phinehas were such men (Ps. 106:23, 30), as were Joseph (Ps. 105:17) and Samuel (1 Sam. 3). Had the people heeded the messages of Jeremiah, God would have spared them, but they refused to obey. Today, God needs "gap people" with the courage to stand for what is right, even if they must stand alone.

become guilty by the blood which you have shed, and have defiled yourself with the idols which you have made. You have caused your days to draw near, and have come to *the end of* your years; therefore I have made you a reproach to the nations, and a mockery to all countries. 5*Those* near and *those* far from you will mock you as infamous *and* full of tumult.

6"Look, the princes of Israel: each one has used his power to shed blood in you. 7In you they have made light of father and mother; in your midst they have oppressed the stranger; in you they have mistreated the fatherless and the widow. 8You have despised My holy things and profaned My Sabbaths. 9In you are men who slander to cause bloodshed; in you are those who eat on the mountains; in your midst they commit lewdness. 10In you men uncover their fathers' nakedness; in you they violate women who are set apart during their impurity. 11One commits abomination with his neighbor's wife; another lewdly defiles his daughter-in-law; and another in you violates his sister, his father's daughter. 12In you they take bribes to shed blood; you take usury and increase; you have made profit from your neighbors by extortion, and have forgotten Me," says the Lord God.

13"Behold, therefore, I beat My fists at the dishonest profit which you have made, and at the bloodshed which has been in your midst. 14Can your heart endure, or can your hands remain strong, in the days when I shall deal with you? I, the LORD, have spoken, and will do *it*. 15I will scatter you among the nations, disperse you throughout the countries, and remove your filthiness completely from you. 16You shall defile yourself in the sight of the nations; then you shall know that I *am* the LORD." ' "

17*The word of the LORD came to me, saying, 18"Son of man, the house of Israel has become dross to Me; they *are* all bronze, tin, iron, and lead, in the midst of a furnace; they have become dross from silver. 19Therefore thus says the Lord God: 'Because you have all become dross, therefore behold, I will gather you into the midst of Jerusalem. 20As *men* gather silver, bronze, iron, lead, and tin into the midst of a furnace, to blow fire on it, to melt *it;* so I will gather *you* in My anger and in My fury, and I will leave *you there* and melt you. 21Yes, I will gather you and blow on you with the fire of My wrath, and you shall be melted in its midst. 22As silver is melted in the midst of a furnace, so shall you be melted in its midst; then you shall know that I, the LORD, have poured out My fury on you.' "

23*And the word of the LORD came to me, saying, 24"Son of man, say to her: 'You *are* a land that is not cleansed[e] or rained on in the day of indignation.' 25The conspiracy of her prophets[f] in her midst is like a roaring lion tearing the prey; they have devoured people; they have taken treasure and precious things; they have made many widows in her midst. 26Her priests have violated My law and profaned My holy things; they have not distinguished between the holy and unholy, nor have they made known *the difference* between

22:17–22 The furnace. Jerusalem would indeed become like a furnace when the army of Babylon encamped around it. But there was no good metal left in the city; all was dross. The nation had been cheapened by sin.

22:23–27 The jungle. The prophets were like lions and the princes like wolves, all fighting to get what they could from the people. Like animals, the priests did not make a difference between what was holy and what was unclean (Matt. 7:6).

22:24 eFollowing Masoretic Text, Syriac, and Vulgate; Septuagint reads *showered upon.*   22:25 fFollowing Masoretic Text and Vulgate; Septuagint reads *princes;* Targum reads *scribes.*

the unclean and the clean; and they have hidden their eyes from My Sabbaths, so that I am profaned among them. 27Her princes in her midst *are* like wolves tearing the prey, to shed blood, to destroy people, and to get dishonest gain. 28*Her prophets plastered them with untempered *mortar,* seeing false visions, and divining lies for them, saying, 'Thus says the Lord GOD,' when the LORD had not spoken. 29The people of the land have used oppressions, committed robbery, and mistreated the poor and needy; and they wrongfully oppress the stranger. 30So I sought for a man among them who would make a wall, and stand in the gap before Me on behalf of the land, that I should not destroy it; but I found no one. 31Therefore I have poured out My indignation on them; I have consumed them with the fire of My wrath; and I have recompensed their deeds on their own heads," says the Lord GOD.

23 The* word of the LORD came again to me, saying:

2 "Son of man, there were two women,
    The daughters of one mother.
3 They committed harlotry in Egypt,
    They committed harlotry in their youth;
    Their breasts were there embraced,
    Their virgin bosom was there pressed.
4 Their names: Oholah^g the elder and
        Oholibah^h her sister;
    They were Mine,
    And they bore sons and daughters.
    As for their names,
    Samaria *is* Oholah, and Jerusalem *is*
        Oholibah.

5 "Oholah played the harlot even though she
        was Mine;
    And she lusted for her lovers, the
        neighboring Assyrians,
6 *Who were* clothed in purple,
    Captains and rulers,
    All of them desirable young men,
    Horsemen riding on horses.
7 Thus she committed her harlotry with them,
    All of them choice men of Assyria;
    And with all for whom she lusted,
    With all their idols, she defiled herself.
8 She has never given up her harlotry *brought*
        from Egypt,
    For in her youth they had lain with her,
    Pressed her virgin bosom,
    And poured out their immorality upon her.

9 "Therefore I have delivered her
    Into the hand of her lovers,
    Into the hand of the Assyrians,
    For whom she lusted.
10 They uncovered her nakedness,
    Took away her sons and daughters,
    And slew her with the sword;
    She became a byword among women,
    For they had executed judgment on her.

11"Now although her sister Oholibah saw *this,* she became more corrupt in her lust than she,

22:28–31 *The wall.* With their false visions and messages, the prophets whitewashed the nation's sins and covered its weaknesses. (See chap. 13.) God is still looking for people who will not only build strong walls but *become walls* by standing in the gap in the hour of danger.

CHAPTER 23

23:1ff Because the Jewish nation was wedded to Jehovah, idolatry was the same as infidelity. They were giving themselves to foreign gods and committing harlotry and adultery. That is why God brought judgment on His people.

Oholah ("her tent") represents Samaria, the northern kingdom; and Oholibah ("My tent is in her") represents the southern kingdom of Judah. The Samaritans had devised their own religion, but God dwelt in Judah because of His covenant with David. What they did in His temple grieved Him greatly (vv. 36–39; 1 Cor. 6:19–20). God judged Samaria in 722 B.C. when He permitted Assyria to take them captive, but Judah did not profit from that lesson. Judah persisted in sin, so God had to judge them.

When God judges sin in others, never say, "That will never happen to me! I can get away with my sin!" God waits for us to repent, and we must not try His patience (Eccles. 8:11). In the end, our sins punish us, and we learn afresh that He is the Lord (v. 49). God wants single-hearted devotion from His bride (2 Cor. 11:1–4; James 4:1–10).

23:4 ^gLiterally *Her Own Tabernacle* ^hLiterally *My Tabernacle Is in Her*

and in her harlotry more corrupt than her sister's harlotry.

12 "She lusted for the neighboring Assyrians,
Captains and rulers,
Clothed most gorgeously,
Horsemen riding on horses,
All of them desirable young men.
13 Then I saw that she was defiled;
Both *took* the same way.
14 But she increased her harlotry;
She looked at men portrayed on the wall,
Images of Chaldeans portrayed in
vermilion,
15 Girded with belts around their waists,
Flowing turbans on their heads,
All of them looking like captains,
In the manner of the Babylonians of
Chaldea,
The land of their nativity.
16 As soon as her eyes saw them,
She lusted for them
And sent messengers to them in Chaldea.

17 "Then the Babylonians came to her, into the
bed of love,
And they defiled her with their immorality;
So she was defiled by them, and alienated
herself from them.
18 She revealed her harlotry and uncovered
her nakedness.
Then I alienated Myself from her,
As I had alienated Myself from her sister.

19 "Yet she multiplied her harlotry
In calling to remembrance the days of her
youth,
When she had played the harlot in the land
of Egypt.
20 For she lusted for her paramours,
Whose flesh *is like* the flesh of donkeys,
And whose issue *is like* the issue of horses.
21 Thus you called to remembrance the
lewdness of your youth,
When the Egyptians pressed your bosom
Because of your youthful breasts.

22 "Therefore, Oholibah, thus says the Lord GOD:

'Behold, I will stir up your lovers against
you,
From whom you have alienated yourself,
And I will bring them against you from
every side:
23 The Babylonians,
All the Chaldeans,
Pekod, Shoa, Koa,
All the Assyrians with them,
All of them desirable young men,
Governors and rulers,
Captains and men of renown,
All of them riding on horses.
24 And they shall come against you
With chariots, wagons, and war-horses,
With a horde of people.
They shall array against you
Buckler, shield, and helmet all around.

'I will delegate judgment to them,
And they shall judge you according to their
judgments.
25 I will set My jealousy against you,

And they shall deal furiously with you;
They shall remove your nose and your ears,
And your remnant shall fall by the sword;
They shall take your sons and your
    daughters,
And your remnant shall be devoured by fire.
26   They shall also strip you of your clothes
And take away your beautiful jewelry.

27   'Thus I will make you cease your lewdness
        and your harlotry
    Brought from the land of Egypt,
    So that you will not lift your eyes to them,
    Nor remember Egypt anymore.'

28"For thus says the Lord GOD: 'Surely I will deliver you into the hand of those you hate, into the hand *of those* from whom you alienated yourself. 29They will deal hatefully with you, take away all you have worked for, and leave you naked and bare. The nakedness of your harlotry shall be uncovered, both your lewdness and your harlotry. 30I will do these *things* to you because you have gone as a harlot after the Gentiles, because you have become defiled by their idols. 31You have walked in the way of your sister; therefore I will put her cup in your hand.'
32"Thus says the Lord GOD:

    'You shall drink of your sister's cup,
    The deep and wide one;
    You shall be laughed to scorn
    And held in derision;
    It contains much.
33   You will be filled with drunkenness and
        sorrow,
    The cup of horror and desolation,
    The cup of your sister Samaria.
34   You shall drink and drain it,
    You shall break its shards,
    And tear at your own breasts;
    For I have spoken,'
    Says the Lord GOD.

35"Therefore thus says the Lord GOD:

    'Because you have forgotten Me and cast Me
        behind your back,
    Therefore you shall bear the *penalty*
    Of your lewdness and your harlotry.' "

36The LORD also said to me: "Son of man, will you judge Oholah and Oholibah? Then declare to them their abominations. 37For they have committed adultery, and blood *is* on their hands. They have committed adultery with their idols, and even sacrificed their sons whom they bore to Me, passing them through *the fire,* to devour *them.* 38Moreover they have done this to Me: They have defiled My sanctuary on the same day and profaned My Sabbaths. 39For after they had slain their children for their idols, on the same day they came into My sanctuary to profane it; and indeed thus they have done in the midst of My house.
40"Furthermore you sent for men to come from afar, to whom a messenger *was* sent; and there they came. And you washed yourself for them, painted your eyes, and adorned yourself with ornaments. 41You sat on a stately couch, with a table prepared before it, on which you had set My incense and My oil. 42The sound of a carefree multitude *was* with her, and Sabeans *were* brought

from the wilderness with men of the common sort, who put bracelets on their wrists and beautiful crowns on their heads. 43Then I said concerning *her who had grown* old in adulteries, 'Will they commit harlotry with her now, and she *with them?*' 44Yet they went in to her, as men go in to a woman who plays the harlot; thus they went in to Oholah and Oholibah, the lewd women. 45But righteous men will judge them after the manner of adulteresses, and after the manner of women who shed blood, because they *are* adulteresses, and blood *is* on their hands.

46"For thus says the Lord GOD: 'Bring up an assembly against them, give them up to trouble and plunder. 47The assembly shall stone them with stones and execute them with their swords; they shall slay their sons and their daughters, and burn their houses with fire. 48Thus I will cause lewdness to cease from the land, that all women may be taught not to practice your lewdness. 49They shall repay you for your lewdness, and you shall pay for your idolatrous sins. Then you shall know that I *am* the Lord GOD.' "

CHAPTER 24

24:1–14 *The death of a city.* Ezekiel was far away in Babylon, yet he knew what was happening in Jerusalem (Amos 3:7; John 15:15). The parable of the pot (11:3) revealed the city's wickedness. As the fire of judgment grew hotter, only the scum appeared, and then the pot and everything in it were destroyed. The date was January 15, 588 B.C., when Nebuchadnezzar began the siege of Jerusalem.

24 Again,* in the ninth year, in the tenth month, on the tenth *day* of the month, the word of the LORD came to me, saying, 2"Son of man, write down the name of the day, this very day—the king of Babylon started his siege against Jerusalem this very day. 3And utter a parable to the rebellious house, and say to them, 'Thus says the Lord GOD:

"Put on a pot, set *it* on,
    And also pour water into it.
4 Gather pieces *of meat* in it,
    Every good piece,
    The thigh and the shoulder.
    Fill *it* with choice cuts;
5 Take the choice of the flock.
    Also pile *fuel* bones under it,
    Make it boil well,
    And let the cuts simmer in it."

6'Therefore thus says the Lord GOD:

"Woe to the bloody city,
    To the pot whose scum *is* in it,
    And whose scum is not gone from it!
    Bring it out piece by piece,
    On which no lot has fallen.
7 For her blood is in her midst;
    She set it on top of a rock;
    She did not pour it on the ground,
    To cover it with dust.
8 That it may raise up fury and take
        vengeance,
    I have set her blood on top of a rock,
    That it may not be covered."

9'Therefore thus says the Lord GOD:

"Woe to the bloody city!
    I too will make the pyre great.
10 Heap on the wood,
    Kindle the fire;
    Cook the meat well,
    Mix in the spices,
    And let the cuts be burned up.

11 "Then set the pot empty on the coals,
    That it may become hot and its bronze may
        burn,

That its filthiness may be melted in it,
That its scum may be consumed.
12 She has grown weary with lies,
And her great scum has not gone from her.
Let her scum *be* in the fire!
13 In your filthiness *is* lewdness.
Because I have cleansed you, and you were
not cleansed,
You will not be cleansed of your filthiness
anymore,
Till I have caused My fury to rest upon you.
14 I, the LORD, have spoken *it;*
It shall come to pass, and I will do *it;*
I will not hold back,
Nor will I spare,
Nor will I relent;
According to your ways
And according to your deeds
They[*] will judge you,"
Says the Lord GOD.' "

15*Also the word of the LORD came to me, saying, 16"Son of man, behold, I take away from you
the desire of your eyes with one stroke; yet you
shall neither mourn nor weep, nor shall your tears
run down. 17Sigh in silence, make no mourning
for the dead; bind your turban on your head, and
put your sandals on your feet; do not cover *your*
lips, and do not eat man's bread *of sorrow.*"

18So I spoke to the people in the morning, and
at evening my wife died; and the next morning I
did as I was commanded.

19And the people said to me, "Will you not tell
us what these *things signify* to us, that you behave
so?"

20Then I answered them, "The word of the LORD
came to me, saying, 21'Speak to the house of Israel, "Thus says the Lord GOD: 'Behold, I will profane My sanctuary, your arrogant boast, the desire of your eyes, the delight of your soul; and
your sons and daughters whom you left behind
shall fall by the sword. 22And you shall do as I
have done; you shall not cover *your* lips nor eat
man's bread *of sorrow.* 23Your turbans shall be
on your heads and your sandals on your feet; you
shall neither mourn nor weep, but you shall pine
away in your iniquities and mourn with one another. 24Thus Ezekiel is a sign to you; according
to all that he has done you shall do; and when
this comes, you shall know that I *am* the Lord
GOD.' "

25'And you, son of man—*will it* not *be* in the
day when I take from them their stronghold, their
joy and their glory, the desire of their eyes, and
that on which they set their minds, their sons and
their daughters: 26on that day one who escapes
will come to you to let *you* hear *it* with *your* ears;
27on that day your mouth will be opened to him
who has escaped; you shall speak and no longer
be mute. Thus you will be a sign to them, and
they shall know that I *am* the LORD.' "

25 The* word of the LORD came to me, saying,
2"Son of man, set your face against the

24:14 'Septuagint, Syriac, Targum, and Vulgate read *I*.

24:15–27 The death of a wife. During his
years of ministry, Ezekiel had paid a price
to "act out" some of his sermons (chap. 12),
but none was as costly as this one. The life
you live is the greatest sermon you can ever
preach. The city of Jerusalem was the
delight of the Jews, but she would be
buried—*and that was what the nation
deserved.* Ezekiel told the people in the
morning that his wife would die, just as he
had told them for years that their beloved
city would be destroyed; in the evening, his
words came true.

If the people wanted to mourn at all, they
should have mourned over their sins and
not over the loss of their city and temple.
But it was too late. They should have heeded
this advice: "Seek the Lord while He may
be found" (Isa. 55:6).

CHAPTER 25

25:1ff God's judgment begins with God's
people (Ezek. 9:6). If *they* are judged for
their sins, what will happen to those who
do not know the Lord (1 Pet. 4:17–18)?

In chapters 25—32, Ezekiel described
God's judgment of the gentile nations
surrounding Judah. The Jews had sinned
against God's love and law, but the gentile
nations had sinned against God's people.
Note the repetition of "because"; God's
judgments are reasonable.

The Ammonites rejoiced at the fall of
Judah and the captivity of the people (vv.
1–7), so God promised to destroy them.
Moab (vv. 8–11) said that the Jews were
like any other nation (20:32), which meant
that Ammon had no reverence for Jehovah.
He was just like the idols of the other
nations! (See Ps. 115.)

The Edomites (vv. 12–14) actually helped
the Babylonians instead of assisting the
Jews, who were their relatives (Ps. 137:7;
Obad. 11–14). The Philistines saw an
opportunity to pay back an old debt and vent
their hatred of God's people.

Although Judah sinned, they were still the
people of God. God will not defend our sins,
*but He will defend His people and allow
no outsiders to touch us without His
permission.* God's chastening is born out of
His love, while man's revenge is born out
of hatred. That is why David prayed as he
did in 2 Samuel 24:14.

"Restore Such a One"—When other believers are experiencing God's chastening or are suffering
the consequences of their sins, what is your attitude toward them? Do you pray for them and encourage
them to seek the Lord and yield to His will, or do you add to their trials? Ponder Galatians 6:1–5,
Hebrews 12:12–17, and Matthew 7:12.

Ammonites, and prophesy against them. 3Say to the Ammonites, 'Hear the word of the Lord GOD! Thus says the Lord GOD: "Because you said, 'Aha!' against My sanctuary when it was profaned, and against the land of Israel when it was desolate, and against the house of Judah when they went into captivity, 4indeed, therefore, I will deliver you as a possession to the men of the East, and they shall set their encampments among you and make their dwellings among you; they shall eat your fruit, and they shall drink your milk. 5And I will make Rabbah a stable for camels and Ammon a resting place for flocks. Then you shall know that I *am* the LORD.''

6'For thus says the Lord GOD: "Because you clapped *your* hands, stamped your feet, and rejoiced in heart with all your disdain for the land of Israel, 7indeed, therefore, I will stretch out My hand against you, and give you as plunder to the nations; I will cut you off from the peoples, and I will cause you to perish from the countries; I will destroy you, and you shall know that I *am* the LORD.''

8'Thus says the Lord GOD: "Because Moab and Seir say, 'Look! The house of Judah *is* like all the nations,' 9therefore, behold, I will clear the territory of Moab of cities, of the cities on its frontier, the glory of the country, Beth Jeshimoth, Baal Meon, and Kirjathaim. 10To the men of the East I will give it as a possession, together with the Ammonites, that the Ammonites may not be remembered among the nations. 11And I will execute judgments upon Moab, and they shall know that I *am* the LORD.''

12'Thus says the Lord GOD: "Because of what Edom did against the house of Judah by taking vengeance, and has greatly offended by avenging itself on them,'' 13therefore thus says the Lord GOD: "I will also stretch out My hand against Edom, cut off man and beast from it, and make it desolate from Teman; Dedan shall fall by the sword. 14I will lay My vengeance on Edom by the hand of My people Israel, that they may do in Edom according to My anger and according to My fury; and they shall know My vengeance,'' says the Lord GOD.

15'Thus says the Lord GOD: "Because the Philistines dealt vengefully and took vengeance with a spiteful heart, to destroy because of the old hatred,'' 16therefore thus says the Lord GOD: "I will stretch out My hand against the Philistines, and I will cut off the Cherethites and destroy the remnant of the seacoast. 17I will execute great vengeance on them with furious rebukes; and they shall know that I *am* the LORD, when I lay My vengeance upon them.'' ''

CHAPTERS 26—28

26:1ff The judgment of the proud and wealthy cities of Tyre and Sidon is the theme of chapter 26 through 28, described in three vivid pictures.

The scraping of a rock. The city of Tyre seemed impregnable, but Nebuchadnezzar would besiege it and Alexander the Great would wipe it off the face of the earth in 332 B.C. Tyre would become a bare rock, a place only for drying fishing nets (vv. 4, 14). What a rebuke to civic pride!

26 And* it came to pass in the eleventh year, on the first *day* of the month, *that* the word of the LORD came to me, saying, 2"Son of man, because Tyre has said against Jerusalem, 'Aha! She is broken who *was* the gateway of the peoples; now she is turned over to me; I shall be filled; she is laid waste.'

3"Therefore thus says the Lord GOD: 'Behold, I *am* against you, O Tyre, and will cause many nations to come up against you, as the sea causes its waves to come up. 4And they shall destroy the walls of Tyre and break down her towers; I will also scrape her dust from her, and make her like the top of a rock. 5It shall be *a place for* spreading nets in the midst of the sea, for I have spoken,' says the Lord GOD; 'it shall become plunder for the nations. 6Also her daughter *villages* which *are* in the fields shall be slain by the sword. Then they shall know that I am the LORD.'

7"For thus says the Lord GOD: 'Behold, I will bring against Tyre from the north Nebuchadnezzar[j] king of Babylon, king of kings, with horses, with chariots, and with horsemen, and an army with many people. 8He will slay with the sword your daughter *villages* in the fields; he will heap up a siege mound against you, build a wall against you, and raise a defense against you. 9He will direct his battering rams against your walls, and with his axes he will break down your towers. 10Because of the abundance of his horses, their dust will cover you; your walls will shake at the noise of the horsemen, the wagons, and the chariots, when he enters your gates, as men enter a city that has been breached. 11With the hooves of his horses he will trample all your streets; he will slay your people by the sword, and your strong pillars will fall to the ground. 12They will plunder your riches and pillage your merchandise; they will break down your walls and destroy your pleasant houses; they will lay your stones, your timber, and your soil in the midst of the water. 13I will put an end to the sound of your songs, and the sound of your harps shall be heard no more. 14I will make you like the top of a rock; you shall be *a place for* spreading nets, and you shall never be rebuilt, for I the LORD have spoken,' says the Lord GOD.

15"Thus says the Lord GOD to Tyre: 'Will the coastlands not shake at the sound of your fall, when the wounded cry, when slaughter is made in the midst of you? 16Then all the princes of the sea will come down from their thrones, lay aside their robes, and take off their embroidered garments; they will clothe themselves with trembling; they will sit on the ground, tremble *every* moment, and be astonished at you. 17And they will take up a lamentation for you, and say to you:

"How you have perished,
    O one inhabited by seafaring men,
    O renowned city,
    Who was strong at sea,
    She and her inhabitants,
    Who caused their terror *to be* on all her
        inhabitants!
18 Now the coastlands tremble on the day of
        your fall;
    Yes, the coastlands by the sea are troubled
        at your departure." '

19"For thus says the Lord GOD: 'When I make you a desolate city, like cities that are not inhabited, when I bring the deep upon you, and great waters cover you, 20then I will bring you down with those who descend into the Pit, to the people of old, and I will make you dwell in the lowest part of the earth, in places desolate from antiquity, with those who go down to the Pit, so that you may never be inhabited; and I shall establish glory in the land of the living. 21I will make you a terror, and you *shall be* no *more;* though you are sought for, you will never be found again,' says the Lord GOD."

26:7 [j]Hebrew *Nebuchadrezzar*, and so elsewhere in this book

27:1ff *The sinking of a ship.* Ezekiel described Tyre as a beautiful and costly ship, loaded with riches and growing wealthy as it did business with all the nations. But the ship would be broken and would sink, and all the merchants would lament the loss of their great wealth. What a rebuke to covetousness!

27 The* word of the LORD came again to me, saying, 2"Now, son of man, take up a lamentation for Tyre, 3and say to Tyre, 'You who are situated at the entrance of the sea, merchant of the peoples on many coastlands, thus says the Lord GOD:

"O Tyre, you have said,
'I *am* perfect in beauty.'
4   Your borders *are* in the midst of the seas.
Your builders have perfected your beauty.
5   They made all *your* planks of fir trees from
Senir;
They took a cedar from Lebanon to make
you a mast.
6   *Of* oaks from Bashan they made your oars;
The company of Ashurites have inlaid your
planks
With ivory from the coasts of Cyprus.*k*
7   Fine embroidered linen from Egypt was
what you spread for your sail;
Blue and purple from the coasts of Elishah
was what covered you.

8   "Inhabitants of Sidon and Arvad were your
oarsmen;
Your wise men, O Tyre, were in you;
They became your pilots.
9   Elders of Gebal and its wise men
Were in you to caulk your seams;
All the ships of the sea
And their oarsmen were in you
To market your merchandise.

10   "Those from Persia, Lydia,*l* and Libya*m*
Were in your army as men of war;
They hung shield and helmet in you;
They gave splendor to you.
11   Men of Arvad with your army *were* on your
walls *all* around,
And the men of Gammad were in your
towers;
They hung their shields on your walls *all*
around;
They made your beauty perfect.

12"Tarshish *was* your merchant because of your many luxury goods. They gave you silver, iron, tin, and lead for your goods. 13Javan, Tubal, and Meshech *were* your traders. They bartered human lives and vessels of bronze for your merchandise. 14Those from the house of Togarmah traded for your wares with horses, steeds, and mules. 15The men of Dedan *were* your traders; many isles *were* the market of your hand. They brought you ivory tusks and ebony as payment. 16Syria *was* your merchant because of the abundance of goods you made. They gave you for your wares emeralds, purple, embroidery, fine linen, corals, and rubies. 17Judah and the land of Israel *were* your traders. They traded for your merchandise wheat of Minnith, millet, honey, oil, and balm. 18Damascus *was* your merchant because of the abundance of goods you made, because of your many luxury items, with the wine of Helbon and with white wool. 19Dan and Javan paid for your wares, traversing back and forth. Wrought iron,

27:6 *k*Hebrew *Kittim*, western lands, especially Cyprus
27:10 *l*Hebrew *Lud* *m*Hebrew *Put*

cassia, and cane were among your merchandise.
²⁰Dedan *was* your merchant in saddlecloths for
riding. ²¹Arabia and all the princes of Kedar *were*
your regular merchants. They traded with you in
lambs, rams, and goats. ²²The merchants of Sheba
and Raamah *were* your merchants. They traded
for your wares the choicest spices, all kinds of
precious stones, and gold. ²³Haran, Canneh, Eden,
the merchants of Sheba, Assyria, *and* Chilmad
were your merchants. ²⁴These *were* your merchants in choice items—in purple clothes, in embroidered garments, in chests of multicolored apparel, in sturdy woven cords, which were in your
marketplace.

²⁵ "The ships of Tarshish were carriers of your
        merchandise.
    You were filled and very glorious in the
        midst of the seas.
²⁶ Your oarsmen brought you into many
        waters,
    But the east wind broke you in the midst
        of the seas.

²⁷ "Your riches, wares, and merchandise,
    Your mariners and pilots,
    Your caulkers and merchandisers,
    All your men of war who *are* in you,
    And the entire company which *is* in your
        midst,
    Will fall into the midst of the seas on the
        day of your ruin.
²⁸ The common-land will shake at the sound
        of the cry of your pilots.

²⁹ "All who handle the oar,
    The mariners,
    All the pilots of the sea
    Will come down from their ships *and* stand
        on the shore.
³⁰ They will make their voice heard because
        of you;
    They will cry bitterly and cast dust on their
        heads;
    They will roll about in ashes;
³¹ They will shave themselves completely bald
        because of you,
    Gird themselves with sackcloth,
    And weep for you
    With bitterness of heart *and* bitter wailing.
³² In their wailing for you
    They will take up a lamentation,
    And lament for you:
    'What *city is* like Tyre,
    Destroyed in the midst of the sea?

³³ 'When your wares went out by sea,
    You satisfied many people;
    You enriched the kings of the earth
    With your many luxury goods and your
        merchandise.
³⁴ But you are broken by the seas in the depths
        of the waters;
    Your merchandise and the entire company
        will fall in your midst.
³⁵ All the inhabitants of the isles will be
        astonished at you;
    Their kings will be greatly afraid,
    And *their* countenance will be troubled.
³⁶ The merchants among the peoples will hiss
        at you;

You will become a horror, and *be* no more
  forever.' " ' "

28 The* word of the LORD came to me again,
saying, 2"Son of man, say to the prince of
Tyre, 'Thus says the Lord GOD:

"Because your heart *is* lifted up,
And you say, '*I am* a god,
I sit *in* the seat of gods,
In the midst of the seas,'
Yet you *are* a man, and not a god,
Though you set your heart as the heart of
  a god
3   (Behold, you *are* wiser than Daniel!
There is no secret that can be hidden from
  you!
4   With your wisdom and your understanding
You have gained riches for yourself,
And gathered gold and silver into your
  treasuries;
5   By your great wisdom in trade you have
  increased your riches,
And your heart is lifted up because of your
  riches),"

6"Therefore thus says the Lord GOD:

"Because you have set your heart as the heart
  of a god,
7   Behold, therefore, I will bring strangers
  against you,
The most terrible of the nations;
And they shall draw their swords against
  the beauty of your wisdom,
And defile your splendor.
8   They shall throw you down into the Pit,
And you shall die the death of the slain
In the midst of the seas.

9   "Will you still say before him who slays you,
'*I am* a god'?
But you *shall be* a man, and not a god,
In the hand of him who slays you.
10   You shall die the death of the uncircumcised
By the hand of aliens;
For I have spoken," says the Lord GOD.' "

11Moreover the word of the LORD came to me,
saying, 12"Son of man, take up a lamentation for
the king of Tyre, and say to him, 'Thus says the
Lord GOD:

"You *were* the seal of perfection,
Full of wisdom and perfect in beauty.
13   You were in Eden, the garden of God;
Every precious stone *was* your covering:
The sardius, topaz, and diamond,
Beryl, onyx, and jasper,
Sapphire, turquoise, and emerald with gold.
The workmanship of your timbrels and
  pipes
Was prepared for you on the day you were
  created.

14   "You *were* the anointed cherub who covers;
I established you;
You were on the holy mountain of God;
You walked back and forth in the midst of
  fiery stones.
15   You *were* perfect in your ways from the day
  you were created,
Till iniquity was found in you.

28:1ff *The dethroning of a king.* The king
of Tyre thought he was God, and his heart
was lifted up with pride. Surely Satan was
the cause of this (Gen. 3:5). In fact, God
may have been addressing Satan in verses
11–19, for the description surely fits. Pride
lifted him up, but God cast him down. What
a rebuke to his feeble attempt to take the
place of God!

16 "By the abundance of your trading
  You became filled with violence within,
  And you sinned;
  Therefore I cast you as a profane thing
  Out of the mountain of God;
  And I destroyed you, O covering cherub,
  From the midst of the fiery stones.

17 "Your heart was lifted up because of your
       beauty;
  You corrupted your wisdom for the sake of
       your splendor;
  I cast you to the ground,
  I laid you before kings,
  That they might gaze at you.

18 "You defiled your sanctuaries
  By the multitude of your iniquities,
  By the iniquity of your trading;
  Therefore I brought fire from your midst;
  It devoured you,
  And I turned you to ashes upon the earth
  In the sight of all who saw you.
19   All who knew you among the peoples are
       astonished at you;
  You have become a horror,
  And *shall be* no more forever." ' "

20Then the word of the LORD came to me, saying,
21"Son of man, set your face toward Sidon, and
prophesy against her, 22and say, 'Thus says the
Lord GOD:

  "Behold, I *am* against you, O Sidon;
  I will be glorified in your midst;
  And they shall know that I *am* the LORD,
  When I execute judgments in her and am
       hallowed in her.
23   For I will send pestilence upon her,
  And blood in her streets;
  The wounded shall be judged in her
       midst
  By the sword against her on every side;
  Then they shall know that I *am* the LORD.

24"And there shall no longer be a pricking brier
or a painful thorn for the house of Israel from
among all *who are* around them, who despise
them. Then they shall know that I *am* the Lord
GOD."
25'Thus says the Lord GOD: "When I have gathered the house of Israel from the peoples among
whom they are scattered, and am hallowed in
them in the sight of the Gentiles, then they will
dwell in their own land which I gave to My servant
Jacob. 26And they will dwell safely there, build
houses, and plant vineyards; yes, they will dwell
securely, when I execute judgments on all those
around them who despise them. Then they shall
know that I *am* the LORD their God." ' "

29 In* the tenth year, in the tenth *month,* on
   the twelfth *day* of the month, the word of
the LORD came to me, saying, 2"Son of man, set
your face against Pharaoh king of Egypt, and
prophesy against him, and against all Egypt.
3Speak, and say, 'Thus says the Lord GOD:

  "Behold, I *am* against you,
  O Pharaoh king of Egypt,
  O great monster who lies in the midst of
       his rivers,

CHAPTERS 29—32

29:1ff Chapters 29 through 32 focus on
Egypt, the nation that the Jews trusted
instead of trusting the Lord (Isa. 30:1–7;
31:1–3). Ezekiel detailed four illustrations of
the coming judgment of Egypt.

   The capturing of a monster. The king
of Egypt thought he was a great monster,
guarding his royal river; but God said he was
only a weak reed in the river (vv. 6–7). God
would capture the monster and show
Pharaoh that He owned the Nile River and
could do with it what He pleased. The
Babylonians would come and plunder Egypt,
and Pharaoh would not be able to stop them.

Who has said, 'My River[n] is my own;
I have made it for myself.'
4   But I will put hooks in your jaws,
And cause the fish of your rivers to stick
to your scales;
I will bring you up out of the midst of your
rivers,
And all the fish in your rivers will stick to
your scales.
5   I will leave you in the wilderness,
You and all the fish of your rivers;
You shall fall on the open field;
You shall not be picked up or gathered.[o]
I have given you as food
To the beasts of the field
And to the birds of the heavens.

6   "Then all the inhabitants of Egypt
Shall know that I am the LORD,
Because they have been a staff of reed to
the house of Israel.
7   When they took hold of you with the hand,
You broke and tore all their shoulders;[p]
When they leaned on you,
You broke and made all their backs quiver."

8'Therefore thus says the Lord GOD: "Surely I will bring a sword upon you and cut off from you man and beast. 9And the land of Egypt shall become desolate and waste; then they will know that I am the LORD, because he said, 'The River is mine, and I have made it.' 10Indeed, therefore, I am against you and against your rivers, and I will make the land of Egypt utterly waste and desolate, from Migdol[q] to Syene, as far as the border of Ethiopia. 11Neither foot of man shall pass through it nor foot of beast pass through it, and it shall be uninhabited forty years. 12I will make the land of Egypt desolate in the midst of the countries that are desolate; and among the cities that are laid waste, her cities shall be desolate forty years; and I will scatter the Egyptians among the nations and disperse them throughout the countries."

13'Yet, thus says the Lord GOD: "At the end of forty years I will gather the Egyptians from the peoples among whom they were scattered. 14I will bring back the captives of Egypt and cause them to return to the land of Pathros, to the land of their origin, and there they shall be a lowly kingdom. 15It shall be the lowliest of kingdoms; it shall never again exalt itself above the nations, for I will diminish them so that they will not rule over the nations anymore. 16No longer shall it be the confidence of the house of Israel, but will remind them of their iniquity when they turned to follow them. Then they shall know that I am the Lord GOD." ' "

17And it came to pass in the twenty-seventh year, in the first month, on the first day of the month, that the word of the LORD came to me, saying, 18"Son of man, Nebuchadnezzar king of Babylon caused his army to labor strenuously against Tyre; every head was made bald, and every shoulder rubbed raw; yet neither he nor his army received wages from Tyre, for the labor

29:3 [n]That is, the Nile   29:5 [o]Following Masoretic Text, Septuagint, and Vulgate; some Hebrew manuscripts and Targum read buried.   29:7 [p]Following Masoretic Text and Vulgate; Septuagint and Syriac read hand.   29:10 [q]Or tower

which they expended on it. ¹⁹Therefore thus says the Lord GOD: 'Surely I will give the land of Egypt to Nebuchadnezzar king of Babylon; he shall take away her wealth, carry off her spoil, and remove her pillage; and that will be the wages for his army. ²⁰I have given him the land of Egypt *for* his labor, because they worked for Me,' says the Lord GOD.

²¹*In that day I will cause the horn of the house of Israel to spring forth, and I will open your mouth to speak in their midst. Then they shall know that I *am* the LORD.' "

30 The word of the LORD came to me again, saying, ²"Son of man, prophesy and say, 'Thus says the Lord GOD:

> "Wail, 'Woe to the day!'
> 3 For the day *is* near,
>   Even the day of the LORD *is* near;
>   It will be a day of clouds, the time of the
>   Gentiles.
> 4 The sword shall come upon Egypt,
>   And great anguish shall be in Ethiopia,
>   When the slain fall in Egypt,
>   And they take away her wealth,
>   And her foundations are broken down.

⁵"Ethiopia, Libya,^r Lydia,^s all the mingled people, Chub, and the men of the lands who are allied, shall fall with them by the sword."

⁶'Thus says the LORD:

> "Those who uphold Egypt shall fall,
>   And the pride of her power shall come
>   down.
>   From Migdol *to* Syene
>   Those within her shall fall by the sword,"
>   Says the Lord GOD.
> 7 "They shall be desolate in the midst of the
>   desolate countries,
>   And her cities shall be in the midst of the
>   cities *that are* laid waste.
> 8 Then they will know that I *am* the LORD,
>   When I have set a fire in Egypt
>   And all her helpers are destroyed.
> 9 On that day messengers shall go forth from
>   Me in ships
>   To make the careless Ethiopians afraid,
>   And great anguish shall come upon them,
>   As on the day of Egypt;
>   For indeed it is coming!"

¹⁰'Thus says the Lord GOD:

> "I will also make a multitude of Egypt to
>   cease
>   By the hand of Nebuchadnezzar king of
>   Babylon.
> 11 He and his people with him, the most
>   terrible of the nations,
>   Shall be brought to destroy the land;
>   They shall draw their swords against
>   Egypt,
>   And fill the land with the slain.
> 12 I will make the rivers dry,
>   And sell the land into the hand of the
>   wicked;

30:5 ^rHebrew *Put* ^sHebrew *Lud*

I will make the land waste, and all that is
    in it,
By the hand of aliens.
I, the LORD, have spoken."

13'Thus says the Lord GOD:

"I will also destroy the idols,
    And cause the images to cease from
       Noph;[t]
    There shall no longer be princes from the
       land of Egypt;
    I will put fear in the land of Egypt.
14 I will make Pathros desolate,
    Set fire to Zoan,
    And execute judgments in No.[u]
15 I will pour My fury on Sin,[y] the strength of
       Egypt;
    I will cut off the multitude of No,
16 And set a fire in Egypt;
    Sin shall have great pain,
    No shall be split open,
    And Noph *shall be in* distress daily.
17 The young men of Aven[w] and Pi Beseth
       shall fall by the sword,
    And these *cities* shall go into captivity.
18 At Tehaphnehes[x] the day shall also be
       darkened,[y]
    When I break the yokes of Egypt there.
    And her arrogant strength shall cease in
       her;
    As for her, a cloud shall cover her,
    And her daughters shall go into captivity.
19 Thus I will execute judgments on Egypt,
    Then they shall know that I *am* the
       LORD." ' "

20And it came to pass in the eleventh year, in the first *month,* on the seventh *day* of the month, *that* the word of the LORD came to me, saying, 21*"Son of man, I have broken the arm of Pharaoh king of Egypt; and see, it has not been bandaged for healing, nor a splint put on to bind it, to make it strong enough to hold a sword. 22Therefore thus says the Lord GOD: 'Surely I *am* against Pharaoh king of Egypt, and will break his arms, both the strong one and the one that was broken; and I will make the sword fall out of his hand. 23I will scatter the Egyptians among the nations, and disperse them throughout the countries. 24I will strengthen the arms of the king of Babylon and put My sword in his hand; but I will break Pharaoh's arms, and he will groan before him with the groanings of a mortally wounded *man.* 25Thus I will strengthen the arms of the king of Babylon, but the arms of Pharaoh shall fall down; they shall know that I *am* the LORD, when I put My sword into the hand of the king of Babylon and he stretches it out against the land of Egypt. 26I will scatter the Egyptians among the nations and disperse them throughout the countries. Then they shall know that I *am* the LORD.' "

30:21–26 *The breaking of arms.* God would break Pharaoh's arm and not allow it to heal, but He would strengthen Nebuchadnezzar's arms and give him victory over Egypt and her many allies. No more would God's people turn to Egypt for help.

30:13 [t]That is, ancient Memphis 30:14 [u]That is, ancient Thebes 30:15 [y]That is, ancient Pelusium 30:17 [w]That is, ancient On (Heliopolis) 30:18 [x]Spelled *Tahpanhes* in Jeremiah 43:7 and elsewhere [y]Following many Hebrew manuscripts, Bomberg, Septuagint, Syriac, Targum, and Vulgate; Masoretic Text reads *refrained.*

31 Now* it came to pass in the eleventh year, in the third *month*, on the first *day* of the month, *that* the word of the LORD came to me, saying, 2"Son of man, say to Pharaoh king of Egypt and to his multitude:

'Whom are you like in your greatness?
3   Indeed Assyria *was* a cedar in Lebanon,
     With fine branches that shaded the forest,
     And of high stature;
     And its top was among the thick boughs.
4   The waters made it grow;
     Underground waters gave it height,
     With their rivers running around the place
          where it was planted,
     And sent out rivulets to all the trees of the
          field.

5   'Therefore its height was exalted above all
          the trees of the field;
     Its boughs were multiplied,
     And its branches became long because of
          the abundance of water,
     As it sent them out.
6   All the birds of the heavens made their nests
          in its boughs;
     Under its branches all the beasts of the field
          brought forth their young;
     And in its shadow all great nations made
          their home.

7   'Thus it was beautiful in greatness and in
          the length of its branches,
     Because its roots reached to abundant
          waters.
8   The cedars in the garden of God could not
          hide it;
     The fir trees were not like its boughs,
     And the chestnutᶻ trees were not like its
          branches;
     No tree in the garden of God was like it in
          beauty.
9   I made it beautiful with a multitude of
          branches,
     So that all the trees of Eden envied it,
     That *were* in the garden of God.'

10"Therefore thus says the Lord GOD: 'Because you have increased in height, and it set its top among the thick boughs, and its heart was lifted up in its height, 11therefore I will deliver it into the hand of the mighty one of the nations, and he shall surely deal with it; I have driven it out for its wickedness. 12And aliens, the most terrible of the nations, have cut it down and left it; its branches have fallen on the mountains and in all the valleys; its boughs lie broken by all the rivers of the land; and all the peoples of the earth have gone from under its shadow and left it.

13   'On its ruin will remain all the birds of the
          heavens,
     And all the beasts of the field will come to
          its branches—

14'So that no trees by the waters may ever again exalt themselves for their height, nor set their tops among the thick boughs, that no tree which drinks

31:1ff *The cutting down of a great tree.*
This message was for Pharaoh, who thought his nation was indestructible. Assyria once had the same idea, but look what God did to her. God would rebuke Pharaoh's pride, cut down his nation, and cast it into hell (vv. 15, 17).

31:8 ᶻHebrew *armon*

water may ever be high enough to reach up to them.

> 'For they have all been delivered to death,
> To the depths of the earth,
> Among the children of men who go down
>   to the Pit.'

15"Thus says the Lord GOD: 'In the day when it went down to hell, I caused mourning. I covered the deep because of it. I restrained its rivers, and the great waters were held back. I caused Lebanon to mourn for it, and all the trees of the field wilted because of it. 16I made the nations shake at the sound of its fall, when I cast it down to hell together with those who descend into the Pit; and all the trees of Eden, the choice and best of Lebanon, all that drink water, were comforted in the depths of the earth. 17They also went down to hell with it, with those *slain* by the sword; and *those who were* its *strong* arm dwelt in its shadows among the nations.

18'To which of the trees in Eden will you then be likened in glory and greatness? Yet you shall be brought down with the trees of Eden to the depths of the earth; you shall lie in the midst of the uncircumcised, with *those* slain by the sword. This *is* Pharaoh and all his multitude,' says the Lord GOD."

32:1ff *The trapping of animals.* Egypt was strong and active like a young lion, but the nation would be caught in God's net and go down into the Pit with all the other great nations of that era.

Remember that God is the King and rules among the nations as He pleases. What He does has one grand purpose: that the nations may know He is the Lord (29:6, 9; 30:8, 19, 26). When nations and rulers start to think they are gods, God has to remind them that He alone is the God of all the earth. Nebuchadnezzar himself had to learn that lesson (Dan. 4).

32 And* it came to pass in the twelfth year, in the twelfth *month*, on the first *day* of the month, *that* the word of the LORD came to me, saying, 2"Son of man, take up a lamentation for Pharaoh king of Egypt, and say to him:

> 'You are like a young lion among the
>   nations,
> And you *are* like a monster in the seas,
> Bursting forth in your rivers,
> Troubling the waters with your feet,
> And fouling their rivers.'

3"Thus says the Lord GOD:

> 'I will therefore spread My net over you with
>   a company of many people,
> And they will draw you up in My net.
> 4   Then I will leave you on the land;
> I will cast you out on the open fields,
> And cause to settle on you all the birds of
>   the heavens.
> And with you I will fill the beasts of the
>   whole earth.
> 5   I will lay your flesh on the mountains,
> And fill the valleys with your carcass.
> 6   'I will also water the land with the flow of
>   your blood,
> *Even* to the mountains;
> And the riverbeds will be full of you.
> 7   When *I* put out your light,
> I will cover the heavens, and make its stars
>   dark;
> I will cover the sun with a cloud,
> And the moon shall not give her light.
> 8   All the bright lights of the heavens I will
>   make dark over you,
> And bring darkness upon your land,'
> Says the Lord GOD.

9'I will also trouble the hearts of many peoples, when I bring your destruction among the nations,

into the countries which you have not known.
10Yes, I will make many peoples astonished at
you, and their kings shall be horribly afraid of
you when I brandish My sword before them; and
they shall tremble *every* moment, every man for
his own life, in the day of your fall.'

11"For thus says the Lord GOD: 'The sword of
the king of Babylon shall come upon you. 12By
the swords of the mighty warriors, all of them
the most terrible of the nations, I will cause your
multitude to fall.

> 'They shall plunder the pomp of Egypt,
> And all its multitude shall be destroyed.
> 13 Also I will destroy all its animals
> From beside its great waters;
> The foot of man shall muddy them no more,
> Nor shall the hooves of animals muddy
> them.
> 14 Then I will make their waters clear,
> And make their rivers run like oil,'
> Says the Lord GOD.

> 15 'When I make the land of Egypt desolate,
> And the country is destitute of all that once
> filled it,
> When I strike all who dwell in it,
> Then they shall know that I *am* the LORD.

> 16 'This *is* the lamentation
> With which they shall lament her;
> The daughters of the nations shall lament
> her;
> They shall lament for her, for Egypt,
> And for all her multitude,'
> Says the Lord GOD."

17It came to pass also in the twelfth year, on
the fifteenth *day* of the month, *that* the word of
the LORD came to me, saying:

> 18 "Son of man, wail over the multitude of
> Egypt,
> And cast them down to the depths of the
> earth,
> Her and the daughters of the famous
> nations,
> With those who go down to the Pit:
> 19 'Whom do you surpass in beauty?
> Go down, be placed with the
> uncircumcised.'

> 20 "They shall fall in the midst of *those* slain
> by the sword;
> She is delivered to the sword,
> Drawing her and all her multitudes.
> 21 The strong among the mighty
> Shall speak to him out of the midst of hell
> With those who help him:
> 'They have gone down,
> They lie with the uncircumcised, slain by
> the sword.'

> 22 "Assyria *is* there, and all her company,
> With their graves all around her,
> All of them slain, fallen by the sword.
> 23 Her graves are set in the recesses of the Pit,
> And her company is all around her grave,
> All of them slain, fallen by the sword,
> Who caused terror in the land of the living.

> 24 "There *is* Elam and all her multitude,
> All around her grave,

All of them slain, fallen by the sword,
Who have gone down uncircumcised to the
    lower parts of the earth,
Who caused their terror in the land of the
    living;
Now they bear their shame with those who
    go down to the Pit.
25 They have set her bed in the midst of the
    slain,
With all her multitude,
With her graves all around it,
All of them uncircumcised, slain by the
    sword;
Though their terror was caused
In the land of the living,
Yet they bear their shame
With those who go down to the Pit;
It was put in the midst of the slain.

26 "There *are* Meshech and Tubal and all their
    multitudes,
With all their graves around it,
All of them uncircumcised, slain by the
    sword,
Though they caused their terror in the land
    of the living.
27 They do not lie with the mighty
Who are fallen of the uncircumcised,
Who have gone down to hell with their
    weapons of war;
They have laid their swords under their
    heads,
But their iniquities will be on their bones,
Because of the terror of the mighty in the
    land of the living.
28 Yes, you shall be broken in the midst of the
    uncircumcised,
And lie with *those* slain by the sword.

29 "There *is* Edom,
Her kings and all her princes,
Who despite their might
Are laid beside *those* slain by the sword;
They shall lie with the uncircumcised,
And with those who go down to the Pit.
30 There *are* the princes of the north,
All of them, and all the Sidonians,
Who have gone down with the slain
In shame at the terror which they caused
    by their might;
They lie uncircumcised with *those* slain by
    the sword,
And bear their shame with those who go
    down to the Pit.

31 "Pharaoh will see them
And be comforted over all his multitude,
Pharaoh and all his army,
Slain by the sword,"
Says the Lord GOD.

32 "For I have caused My terror in the land of
    the living;
And he shall be placed in the midst of the
    uncircumcised
With *those* slain by the sword,
Pharaoh and all his multitude,"
Says the Lord GOD.

CHAPTER 33

33:1–11 *God warns.* God had ordained
Ezekiel to be a watchman (3:16ff.), but now
the people were to ordain their own
watchmen in each territory. The three key
words are *sword, trumpet,* and *blood.* When
you see the sword coming, blow the trumpet
and warn the people; otherwise, their blood
will be on your hands (Acts 20:26–27). (See
Prov. 24:10–12.)

33 Again* the word of the LORD came to me,
saying, 2"Son of man, speak to the children
of your people, and say to them: 'When I bring

the sword upon a land, and the people of the land take a man from their territory and make him their watchman, 3when he sees the sword coming upon the land, if he blows the trumpet and warns the people, 4then whoever hears the sound of the trumpet and does not take warning, if the sword comes and takes him away, his blood shall be on his *own* head. 5He heard the sound of the trumpet, but did not take warning; his blood shall be upon himself. But he who takes warning will save his life. 6But if the watchman sees the sword coming and does not blow the trumpet, and the people are not warned, and the sword comes and takes *any* person from among them, he is taken away in his iniquity; but his blood I will require at the watchman's hand.'

7"So you, son of man: I have made you a watchman for the house of Israel; therefore you shall hear a word from My mouth and warn them for Me. 8When I say to the wicked, 'O wicked *man,* you shall surely die!' and you do not speak to warn the wicked from his way, that wicked *man* shall die in his iniquity; but his blood I will require at your hand. 9Nevertheless if you warn the wicked to turn from his way, and he does not turn from his way, he shall die in his iniquity; but you have delivered your soul.

10"Therefore you, O son of man, say to the house of Israel: 'Thus you say, "If our transgressions and our sins *lie* upon us, and we pine away in them, how can we then live?" ' 11Say to them: '*As* I live,' says the Lord GOD, 'I have no pleasure in the death of the wicked, but that the wicked turn from his way and live. Turn, turn from your evil ways! For why should you die, O house of Israel?'

12*"Therefore you, O son of man, say to the children of your people: 'The righteousness of the righteous man shall not deliver him in the day of his transgression; as for the wickedness of the wicked, he shall not fall because of it in the day that he turns from his wickedness; nor shall the righteous be able to live because of *his righteousness* in the day that he sins.' 13When I say to the righteous *that* he shall surely live, but he trusts in his own righteousness and commits iniquity, none of his righteous works shall be remembered; but because of the iniquity that he has committed, he shall die. 14Again, when I say to the wicked, 'You shall surely die,' if he turns from his sin and does what is lawful and right, 15if the wicked restores the pledge, gives back what he has stolen, and walks in the statutes of life without committing iniquity, he shall surely live; he shall not die. 16None of his sins which he has committed shall be remembered against him; he has done what is lawful and right; he shall surely live.

17"Yet the children of your people say, 'The way of the LORD is not fair.' But it is their way which is not fair! 18When the righteous turns from his righteousness and commits iniquity, he shall die because of it. 19But when the wicked turns from his wickedness and does what is lawful and right, he shall live because of it. 20Yet you say, 'The way of the LORD is not fair.' O house of Israel, I will judge every one of you according to his own ways."

21*"And it came to pass in the twelfth year of our captivity, in the tenth *month,* on the fifth *day* of the month, *that* one who had escaped from Jerusalem came to me and said, "The city has been captured!"

33:12–20 *God is fair.* Review chapter 18 where Ezekiel defended God's fairness in sending judgment to His people. This is a plea for repentance, for God wants each of us to have a broken and a contrite heart (Ps. 51:17). We should not judge God but allow Him to judge us. (See Mic. 7:18–19; Heb. 10:11–18.)

33:21–29 *God judges.* For seven years, the prophet had been silent except when delivering a message (3:26). His words about Jerusalem had been fulfilled, and he could engage in normal conversation again. But his first words had to do with the nation's sins! How could the people call God unfair when they were so guilty before the law of God?

22Now the hand of the LORD had been upon me the evening before the man came who had escaped. And He had opened my mouth; so when he came to me in the morning, my mouth was opened, and I was no longer mute.

23Then the word of the LORD came to me, saying: 24"Son of man, they who inhabit those ruins in the land of Israel are saying, 'Abraham was only one, and he inherited the land. But we are many; the land has been given to us as a possession.'

25"Therefore say to them, 'Thus says the Lord GOD: "You eat meat with blood, you lift up your eyes toward your idols, and shed blood. Should you then possess the land? 26You rely on your sword, you commit abominations, and you defile one another's wives. Should you then possess the land?"'

27"Say thus to them, 'Thus says the Lord GOD: "As I live, surely those who are in the ruins shall fall by the sword, and the one who is in the open field I will give to the beasts to be devoured, and those who are in the strongholds and caves shall die of the pestilence. 28For I will make the land most desolate, her arrogant strength shall cease, and the mountains of Israel shall be so desolate that no one will pass through. 29Then they shall know that I am the LORD, when I have made the land most desolate because of all their abominations which they have committed."'

30*"As for you, son of man, the children of your people are talking about you beside the walls and in the doors of the houses; and they speak to one another, everyone saying to his brother, 'Please come and hear what the word is that comes from the LORD.' 31So they come to you as people do, they sit before you as My people, and they hear your words, but they do not do them; for with their mouth they show much love, but their hearts pursue their own gain. 32Indeed you are to them as a very lovely song of one who has a pleasant voice and can play well on an instrument; for they hear your words, but they do not do them. 33And when this comes to pass—surely it will come—then they will know that a prophet has been among them."

33:30–33 God sees the heart. Imagine calling a watchman's warnings "a very lovely song"! They did not take God's Word seriously; if they had, they would have obeyed it (James 1:21–27). Complimenting the preacher is not the same as obeying the Master. (See Isa. 29:13; Matt. 15:8–9.)

CHAPTER 34

34:1ff The watchman serves the people in times of danger, but the shepherd cares for them day after day; and we need both. The civil and religious leaders were expected to shepherd the nation by feeding them, uniting them, and protecting them from enemies. But Israel's leaders exploited the flock in order to feed themselves, scattered the flock, and failed to protect the flock from danger. See Acts 20 for Paul's example of faithful shepherding.

One day God will seek His people and bring them back to their land, and He will be their shepherd. Note the "I will" statements in this message, and see what assurance they bring to hearts even today.

Today, Jesus Christ is the Great Shepherd of the sheep (Heb. 13:20–21), and He cares for His own. He sends "showers of blessing" on the dry land and makes it into a garden (vv. 26, 29). What a difference it makes when the Lord is in control!

34 And* the word of the LORD came to me, saying, 2"Son of man, prophesy against the shepherds of Israel, prophesy and say to them, 'Thus says the Lord GOD to the shepherds: "Woe to the shepherds of Israel who feed themselves! Should not the shepherds feed the flocks? 3You eat the fat and clothe yourselves with the wool; you slaughter the fatlings, but you do not feed the flock. 4The weak you have not strengthened, nor have you healed those who were sick, nor bound up the broken, nor brought back what was driven away, nor sought what was lost; but with force and cruelty you have ruled them. 5So they were scattered because there was no shepherd; and they became food for all the beasts of the field when they were scattered. 6My sheep wandered through all the mountains, and on every high hill; yes, My flock was scattered over the whole face of the earth, and no one was seeking or searching for them."

7'Therefore, you shepherds, hear the word of the LORD: 8"As I live," says the Lord GOD, "surely because My flock became a prey, and My flock became food for every beast of the field, because there was no shepherd, nor did My shepherds search for My flock, but the shepherds fed themselves and did not feed My flock"— [9]therefore, O shepherds, hear the word of the LORD! [10]Thus says the Lord GOD: "Behold, I *am* against the shepherds, and I will require My flock at their hand; I will cause them to cease feeding the sheep, and the shepherds shall feed themselves no more; for I will deliver My flock from their mouths, that they may no longer be food for them."

[11]'For thus says the Lord GOD: "Indeed I Myself will search for My sheep and seek them out. [12]As a shepherd seeks out his flock on the day he is among his scattered sheep, so will I seek out My sheep and deliver them from all the places where they were scattered on a cloudy and dark day. [13]And I will bring them out from the peoples and gather them from the countries, and will bring them to their own land; I will feed them on the mountains of Israel, in the valleys and in all the inhabited places of the country. [14]I will feed them in good pasture, and their fold shall be on the high mountains of Israel. There they shall lie down in a good fold and feed in rich pasture on the mountains of Israel. [15]I will feed My flock, and I will make them lie down," says the Lord GOD. [16]"I will seek what was lost and bring back what was driven away, bind up the broken and strengthen what was sick; but I will destroy the fat and the strong, and feed them in judgment."

[17]'And *as for* you, O My flock, thus says the Lord GOD: "Behold, I shall judge between sheep and sheep, between rams and goats. [18]*Is it* too little for you to have eaten up the good pasture, that you must tread down with your feet the residue of your pasture—and to have drunk of the clear waters, that you must foul the residue with your feet? [19]And *as for* My flock, they eat what you have trampled with your feet, and they drink what you have fouled with your feet."

[20]'Therefore thus says the Lord GOD to them: "Behold, I Myself will judge between the fat and the lean sheep. [21]Because you have pushed with side and shoulder, butted all the weak ones with your horns, and scattered them abroad, [22]therefore I will save My flock, and they shall no longer be a prey; and I will judge between sheep and sheep. [23]I will establish one shepherd over them, and he shall feed them—My servant David. He shall feed them and be their shepherd. [24]And I, the LORD, will be their God, and My servant David a prince among them; I, the LORD, have spoken.

[25]"I will make a covenant of peace with them, and cause wild beasts to cease from the land; and they will dwell safely in the wilderness and sleep in the woods. [26]I will make them and the places all around My hill a blessing; and I will cause showers to come down in their season; there shall be showers of blessing. [27]Then the trees of the field shall yield their fruit, and the earth shall yield her increase. They shall be safe in their land; and they shall know that I *am* the LORD, when I have broken the bands of their yoke and delivered them from the hand of those who enslaved them. [28]And they shall no longer be a prey for the nations, nor shall beasts of the land devour them; but they shall dwell safely, and no one shall make *them* afraid. [29]I will raise up for them a garden of renown, and they shall no longer be consumed with hunger in the land, nor bear the shame of the Gentiles anymore. [30]Thus they shall know that I, the LORD their God, *am* with them, and they,

the house of Israel, *are* My people," says the Lord GOD.'"

31"You are My flock, the flock of My pasture; you *are* men, *and* I *am* your God," says the Lord GOD.

CHAPTER 35

35:5 God announced blessing for Jacob, but He pronounced judgment on Edom, the descendants of Jacob's brother Esau (25:12–14). The Edomites were guilty of sins that are still practiced today.

Hatred. Their grudge went all the way back to Genesis 27, and they would not forgive and forget. How tragic that brothers could not dwell together in unity (Ps. 133)!

35:11 *Anger and envy.* When you hate others, you are envious of their blessings and angry when they succeed. The Edomites revealed their anger when they helped the Babylonians ravage Jerusalem (Obad. 10–14). Are you envious when others succeed and glad when they fail? Then you may be carrying a grudge. Beware! The judgment you want to fall on your enemy may fall on you (v. 15)!

35:12 *Pride.* The Edomites boasted of their great security in the rocks (Obad. 1–4), but God would bring them down in humiliation (Jer. 49). God still resists the proud— whether in nations or individuals—but gives grace to the humble (1 Pet. 5:5).

CHAPTER 36

36:1 From this chapter on, the prophet focuses on reinhabiting the land, rebuilding the temple, and restoring the kingdom to the glory of God.

In His grace, God will bring the land from desolation to delight (vv. 33–36), and His people from dispersion to regathering (v. 24) and from defilement to cleansing (vv. 25–29). God will remove the disgrace of the people and bring great glory to His name (vv. 20–23). "I am for you!" says the Lord (v. 9); and "if God is for us, who can be against us?" (Rom. 8:31).

There is no future for those who persist in their sins, but those who confess and forsake their sins shall always find mercy with God (Prov. 28:13).

35 Moreover the word of the LORD came to me, saying, 2"Son of man, set your face against Mount Seir and prophesy against it, 3and say to it, 'Thus says the Lord GOD:

"Behold, O Mount Seir, I *am* against you;
I will stretch out My hand against you,
And make you most desolate;
4   I shall lay your cities waste,
And you shall be desolate.
Then you shall know that I *am* the LORD.

5*"Because you have had an ancient hatred, and have shed *the blood of* the children of Israel by the power of the sword at the time of their calamity, *when* their iniquity *came to an* end, 6therefore, *as* I live," says the Lord GOD, "I will prepare you for blood, and blood shall pursue you; since you have not hated blood, therefore blood shall pursue you. 7Thus I will make Mount Seir most desolate, and cut off from it the one who leaves and the one who returns. 8And I will fill its mountains with the slain; on your hills and in your valleys and in all your ravines those who are slain by the sword shall fall. 9I will make you perpetually desolate, and your cities shall be uninhabited; then you shall know that I *am* the LORD.

10"Because you have said, 'These two nations and these two countries shall be mine, and we will possess them,' although the LORD was there, 11*therefore, *as* I live," says the Lord GOD, "I will do according to your anger and according to the envy which you showed in your hatred against them; and I will make Myself known among them when I judge you. 12*Then you shall know that I *am* the LORD. I have heard all your blasphemies which you have spoken against the mountains of Israel, saying, 'They are desolate; they are given to us to consume.' 13Thus with your mouth you have boasted against Me and multiplied your words against Me; I have heard *them.*"

14Thus says the Lord GOD: "The whole earth will rejoice when I make you desolate. 15As you rejoiced because the inheritance of the house of Israel was desolate, so I will do to you; you shall be desolate, O Mount Seir, as well as all of Edom— all of it! Then they shall know that I *am* the LORD.'"

36 "And* you, son of man, prophesy to the mountains of Israel, and say, 'O mountains of Israel, hear the word of the LORD! 2Thus says the Lord GOD: "Because the enemy has said of you, 'Aha! The ancient heights have become our possession,'"' 3therefore prophesy, and say, 'Thus says the Lord GOD: "Because they made *you* desolate and swallowed you up on every side, so that you became the possession of the rest of the nations, and you are taken up by the lips of talkers and slandered by the people"— 4therefore, O mountains of Israel, hear the word of the Lord GOD! Thus says the Lord GOD to the mountains, the hills, the rivers, the valleys, the desolate wastes, and the cities that have been forsaken, which became plunder and mockery to the rest of the nations all around— [5]therefore thus says the Lord GOD: "Surely I have spoken in My burning jealousy against the rest of the nations and against all Edom, who gave My land to themselves as a possession, with wholehearted joy *and* spiteful minds, in order to plunder its open country." '

[6]"Therefore prophesy concerning the land of Israel, and say to the mountains, the hills, the rivers, and the valleys, 'Thus says the Lord GOD: "Behold, I have spoken in My jealousy and My fury, because you have borne the shame of the nations." [7]Therefore thus says the Lord GOD: "I have raised My hand in an oath that surely the nations that *are* around you shall bear their own shame. [8]But you, O mountains of Israel, you shall shoot forth your branches and yield your fruit to My people Israel, for they are about to come. [9]For indeed I *am* for you, and I will turn to you, and you shall be tilled and sown. [10]I will multiply men upon you, all the house of Israel, all of it; and the cities shall be inhabited and the ruins rebuilt. [11]I will multiply upon you man and beast; and they shall increase and bear young; I will make you inhabited as in former times, and do better *for you* than at your beginnings. Then you shall know that I *am* the LORD. [12]Yes, I will cause men to walk on you, My people Israel; they shall take possession of you, and you shall be their inheritance; no more shall you bereave them *of children.*"

[13]'Thus says the Lord GOD: "Because they say to you, 'You devour men and bereave your nation *of children,*' [14]therefore you shall devour men no more, nor bereave your nation anymore," says the Lord GOD. [15]Nor will I let you hear the taunts of the nations anymore, nor bear the reproach of the peoples anymore, nor shall you cause your nation to stumble anymore," says the Lord GOD.' "

[16]Moreover the word of the LORD came to me, saying: [17]"Son of man, when the house of Israel dwelt in their own land, they defiled it by their own ways and deeds; to Me their way was like the uncleanness of a woman in her customary impurity. [18]Therefore I poured out My fury on them for the blood they had shed on the land, and for their idols *with which* they had defiled it. [19]So I scattered them among the nations, and they were dispersed throughout the countries; I judged them according to their ways and their deeds. [20]When they came to the nations, wherever they went, they profaned My holy name—when they said of them, 'These *are* the people of the LORD, *and* yet they have gone out of His land.' [21]But I had concern for My holy name, which the house of Israel had profaned among the nations wherever they went.

[22]"Therefore say to the house of Israel, 'Thus says the Lord GOD: "I do not do *this* for your sake, O house of Israel, but for My holy name's sake, which you have profaned among the nations

Grudges—Some people nurse a grudge the way a mother nurses a child: they love it, cherish it, and cannot live without it. But they forget that the child is growing and may one day turn on them and destroy them. A grudge against an enemy is a very expensive thing, no matter how much enjoyment you may get nursing it. Ponder Matthew 5:21–26, 43–48.

Confessing Sin—There is a difference between merely *admitting* sin and *confessing* sin. When we have confessed our sins sincerely to the Lord, we despise them and forsake them; even their very memory upsets us (Ezek. 36:31; see also 6:9). If the memory of your sin is pleasant to you and you enjoy "tasting it" from time to time (Ps. 10:7), you have not really confessed it to the Lord. A false confession is worse than no confession at all.

wherever you went. 23And I will sanctify My great name, which has been profaned among the nations, which you have profaned in their midst; and the nations shall know that I *am* the LORD," says the Lord GOD, "when I am hallowed in you before their eyes. 24For I will take you from among the nations, gather you out of all countries, and bring you into your own land. 25Then I will sprinkle clean water on you, and you shall be clean; I will cleanse you from all your filthiness and from all your idols. 26I will give you a new heart and put a new spirit within you; I will take the heart of stone out of your flesh and give you a heart of flesh. 27I will put My Spirit within you and cause you to walk in My statutes, and you will keep My judgments and do *them.* 28Then you shall dwell in the land that I gave to your fathers; you shall be My people, and I will be your God. 29I will deliver you from all your uncleannesses. I will call for the grain and multiply it, and bring no famine upon you. 30And I will multiply the fruit of your trees and the increase of your fields, so that you need never again bear the reproach of famine among the nations. 31Then you will remember your evil ways and your deeds that *were* not good; and you will loathe yourselves in your own sight, for your iniquities and your abominations. 32Not for your sake do I do *this,*" says the Lord GOD, "let it be known to you. Be ashamed and confounded for your own ways, O house of Israel!"

33'Thus says the Lord GOD: "On the day that I cleanse you from all your iniquities, I will also enable *you* to dwell in the cities, and the ruins shall be rebuilt. 34The desolate land shall be tilled instead of lying desolate in the sight of all who pass by. 35So they will say, 'This land that was desolate has become like the garden of Eden; and the wasted, desolate, and ruined cities *are now* fortified *and* inhabited.' 36Then the nations which are left all around you shall know that I, the LORD, have rebuilt the ruined places *and* planted what was desolate. I, the LORD, have spoken *it*, and I will do *it*."

37'Thus says the Lord GOD: "I will also let the house of Israel inquire of Me to do this for them: I will increase their men like a flock. 38Like a flock *offered as* holy *sacrifices,* like the flock at Jerusalem on its feast days, so shall the ruined cities be filled with flocks of men. Then they shall know that I *am* the LORD." ' "

CHAPTER 37

37:1–14 *Resurrection.* The nation seemed to be hopeless, like an army of skeletons in a desert. But God can give life through His Word (vv. 4, 7) and His Spirit (v. 14; the Hebrew word for "breath" also means "Spirit"). One day, the nation of Israel will be resurrected spiritually and will know their God.

37 The* hand of the LORD came upon me and brought me out in the Spirit of the LORD, and set me down in the midst of the valley; and it *was* full of bones. 2Then He caused me to pass by them all around, and behold, *there were* very many in the open valley; and indeed *they were* very dry. 3And He said to me, "Son of man, can these bones live?"

So I answered, "O Lord GOD, You know."

4Again He said to me, "Prophesy to these bones, and say to them, 'O dry bones, hear the word of the LORD! 5Thus says the Lord GOD to these bones: "Surely I will cause breath to enter into you, and

The Breath of Life—The breath of God was breathed into man at creation (Gen. 2:7), into the Word when it was written (2 Tim. 3:16), and upon the disciples to empower them for ministry (John 20:22). It will one day sweep over God's chosen people and make them a new nation. Meanwhile, God longs to send the "wind of revival" to His church; and He will, if we honor His Word, pray, and depend on the Spirit of God.

you shall live. [6]I will put sinews on you and bring flesh upon you, cover you with skin and put breath in you; and you shall live. Then you shall know that I *am* the LORD." ' "

[7]So I prophesied as I was commanded; and as I prophesied, there was a noise, and suddenly a rattling; and the bones came together, bone to bone. [8]Indeed, as I looked, the sinews and the flesh came upon them, and the skin covered them over; but *there was* no breath in them.

[9]Also He said to me, "Prophesy to the breath, prophesy, son of man, and say to the breath, 'Thus says the Lord GOD: "Come from the four winds, O breath, and breathe on these slain, that they may live." ' " [10]So I prophesied as He commanded me, and breath came into them, and they lived, and stood upon their feet, an exceedingly great army.

[11]Then He said to me, "Son of man, these bones are the whole house of Israel. They indeed say, 'Our bones are dry, our hope is lost, and we ourselves are cut off!' [12]Therefore prophesy and say to them, 'Thus says the Lord GOD: "Behold, O My people, I will open your graves and cause you to come up from your graves, and bring you into the land of Israel. [13]Then you shall know that I *am* the LORD, when I have opened your graves, O My people, and brought you up from your graves. [14]I will put My Spirit in you, and you shall live, and I will place you in your own land. Then you shall know that I, the LORD, have spoken *it* and performed *it*," says the LORD.' "

[15]*Again the word of the LORD came to me, saying, [16]"As for you, son of man, take a stick for yourself and write on it: 'For Judah and for the children of Israel, his companions.' Then take another stick and write on it, 'For Joseph, the stick of Ephraim, and *for* all the house of Israel, his companions.' [17]Then join them one to another for yourself into one stick, and they will become one in your hand.

[18]"And when the children of your people speak to you, saying, 'Will you not show us what you *mean* by these?'— [19]say to them, 'Thus says the Lord GOD: "Surely I will take the stick of Joseph, which *is* in the hand of Ephraim, and the tribes of Israel, his companions; and I will join them with it, with the stick of Judah, and make them one stick, and they will be one in My hand." ' [20]And the sticks on which you write will be in your hand before their eyes.

[21]"Then say to them, 'Thus says the Lord GOD: "Surely I will take the children of Israel from among the nations, wherever they have gone, and will gather them from every side and bring them into their own land; [22]and I will make them one nation in the land, on the mountains of Israel; and one king shall be king over them all; they shall no longer be two nations, nor shall they ever be divided into two kingdoms again. [23]They shall not defile themselves anymore with their idols, nor with their detestable things, nor with any of their transgressions; but I will deliver them from all their dwelling places in which they have sinned, and will cleanse them. Then they shall be My people, and I will be their God.

[24]"David My servant *shall be* king over them, and they shall all have one shepherd; they shall also walk in My judgments and observe My statutes, and do them. [25]Then they shall dwell in the land that I have given to Jacob My servant, where your fathers dwelt; and they shall dwell there,

37:15–28 *Reconciliation.* Not only will the dead nation receive life, but the divided nation will be united in a covenant of peace. There will be no more "Ephraim" and "Judah," but one nation with one king and one temple.

According to Ephesians 2, God is doing this today. He is raising lost sinners from the dead (Eph. 2:1–10) and reconciling Jews and Gentiles into one temple (Eph. 2:11–22). These spiritual miracles take place when you and I share the life-giving Word in the power of the Spirit of God.

they, their children, and their children's children, forever; and My servant David *shall be* their prince forever. 26Moreover I will make a covenant of peace with them, and it shall be an everlasting covenant with them; I will establish them and multiply them, and I will set My sanctuary in their midst forevermore. 27My tabernacle also shall be with them; indeed I will be their God, and they shall be My people. 28The nations also will know that I, the LORD, sanctify Israel, when My sanctuary is in their midst forevermore." ' "

CHAPTERS 38—39

38:1ff God's people will have enemies until the very establishing of the kingdom. Chapters 38 and 39 describe a coalition of gentile nations in the latter days (v. 16) as they attack Israel when she is at peace in her land (v. 14). God will defeat the invaders with an earthquake (vv. 19–20), a storm (v. 22), and the confusion of the enemy so they start to kill each other (v. 21). Why does God do this? So that the nations will know that He is the Lord (39:6) and that His name is holy (39:7), and so that Israel will know that He is their God (39:21ff.). In punishing them, God hid His face (39:23–24); but now He will reveal Himself to them and they will receive His Spirit (39:29).
The day will come for God's people when every enemy will be defeated, every sin washed away, and every believer sharing in the glorious reign of the Son of God. What a day that will be!

38 Now* the word of the LORD came to me, saying, 2"Son of man, set your face against Gog, of the land of Magog, the prince of Rosh,*a* Meshech, and Tubal, and prophesy against him, 3and say, 'Thus says the Lord GOD: "Behold, I *am* against you, O Gog, the prince of Rosh, Meshech, and Tubal. 4I will turn you around, put hooks into your jaws, and lead you out, with all your army, horses, and horsemen, all splendidly clothed, a great company *with* bucklers and shields, all of them handling swords. 5Persia, Ethiopia,*b* and Libya*c* are with them, all of them *with* shield and helmet; 6Gomer and all its troops; the house of Togarmah *from* the far north and all its troops— many people *are* with you.

7"Prepare yourself and be ready, you and all your companies that are gathered about you; and be a guard for them. 8After many days you will be visited. In the latter years you will come into the land of those brought back from the sword *and* gathered from many people on the mountains of Israel, which had long been desolate; they were brought out of the nations, and now all of them dwell safely. 9You will ascend, coming like a storm, covering the land like a cloud, you and all your troops and many peoples with you."

10'Thus says the Lord GOD: "On that day it shall come to pass *that* thoughts will arise in your mind, and you will make an evil plan: 11You will say, 'I will go up against a land of unwalled villages; I will go to a peaceful people, who dwell safely, all of them dwelling without walls, and having neither bars nor gates'— 12to take plunder and to take booty, to stretch out your hand against the waste places *that are again* inhabited, and against a people gathered from the nations, who have acquired livestock and goods, who dwell in the midst of the land. 13Sheba, Dedan, the merchants of Tarshish, and all their young lions will say to you, 'Have you come to take plunder? Have you gathered your army to take booty, to carry away silver and gold, to take away livestock and goods, to take great plunder?' " '

14"Therefore, son of man, prophesy and say to Gog, 'Thus says the Lord GOD: "On that day when My people Israel dwell safely, will you not know *it*? 15Then you will come from your place out of the far north, you and many peoples with you, all of them riding on horses, a great company and a mighty army. 16You will come up against My people Israel like a cloud, to cover the land. It will be in the latter days that I will bring you against My land, so that the nations may know Me, when I am hallowed in you, O Gog, before their eyes." 17Thus says the Lord GOD: "Are *you*

38:2 *a*Targum, Vulgate, and Aquila read *chief prince of* (also verse 3). 38:5 *b*Hebrew *Cush* *c*Hebrew *Put*

he of whom I have spoken in former days by My servants the prophets of Israel, who prophesied for years in those days that I would bring you against them?

18"And it will come to pass at the same time, when Gog comes against the land of Israel," says the Lord GOD, "*that* My fury will show in My face. 19For in My jealousy *and* in the fire of My wrath I have spoken: 'Surely in that day there shall be a great earthquake in the land of Israel, 20so that the fish of the sea, the birds of the heavens, the beasts of the field, all creeping things that creep on the earth, and all men who *are* on the face of the earth shall shake at My presence. The mountains shall be thrown down, the steep places shall fall, and every wall shall fall to the ground.' 21I will call for a sword against Gog throughout all My mountains," says the Lord GOD. "Every man's sword will be against his brother. 22And I will bring him to judgment with pestilence and bloodshed; I will rain down on him, on his troops, and on the many peoples who *are* with him, flooding rain, great hailstones, fire, and brimstone. 23Thus I will magnify Myself and sanctify Myself, and I will be known in the eyes of many nations. Then they shall know that I *am* the LORD." '

39 "And you, son of man, prophesy against Gog, and say, 'Thus says the Lord GOD: "Behold, I *am* against you, O Gog, the prince of Rosh,*d* Meshech, and Tubal; 2and I will turn you around and lead you on, bringing you up from the far north, and bring you against the mountains of Israel. 3Then I will knock the bow out of your left hand, and cause the arrows to fall out of your right hand. 4You shall fall upon the mountains of Israel, you and all your troops and the peoples who *are* with you; I will give you to birds of prey of every sort and *to* the beasts of the field to be devoured. 5You shall fall on the open field; for I have spoken," says the Lord GOD. 6"And I will send fire on Magog and on those who live in security in the coastlands. Then they shall know that I *am* the LORD. 7So I will make My holy name known in the midst of My people Israel, and I will not *let them* profane My holy name anymore. Then the nations shall know that I *am* the LORD, the Holy One in Israel. 8Surely it is coming, and it shall be done," says the Lord GOD. "This *is* the day of which I have spoken.

9"Then those who dwell in the cities of Israel will go out and set on fire and burn the weapons, both the shields and bucklers, the bows and arrows, the javelins and spears; and they will make fires with them for seven years. 10They will not take wood from the field nor cut down *any* from the forests, because they will make fires with the weapons; and they will plunder those who plundered them, and pillage those who pillaged them," says the Lord GOD.

11"It will come to pass in that day *that* I will give Gog a burial place there in Israel, the valley of those who pass by east of the sea; and it will obstruct travelers, because there they will bury Gog and all his multitude. Therefore they will call *it* the Valley of Hamon Gog.*e* 12For seven months the house of Israel will be burying them, in order

---

39:1 *d*Targum, Vulgate and Aquila read *chief prince of.*
39:11 *e*Literally *The Multitude of Gog*

to cleanse the land. 13Indeed all the people of the land will be burying, and they will gain renown for it on the day that I am glorified," says the Lord GOD. 14"They will set apart men regularly employed, with the help of a search party,ᶠ to pass through the land and bury those bodies remaining on the ground, in order to cleanse it. At the end of seven months they will make a search. 15The search party will pass through the land; and *when anyone* sees a man's bone, he shall set up a marker by it, till the buriers have buried it in the Valley of Hamon Gog. 16*The* name of *the* city *will* also *be* Hamonah. Thus they shall cleanse the land." '

17"And as for you, son of man, thus says the Lord GOD, 'Speak to every sort of bird and to every beast of the field:

"Assemble yourselves and come;
    Gather together from all sides to My
        sacrificial meal
    Which I am sacrificing for you,
    A great sacrificial meal on the mountains
        of Israel,
    That you may eat flesh and drink blood.
18   You shall eat the flesh of the mighty,
    Drink the blood of the princes of the earth,
    Of rams and lambs,
    Of goats and bulls,
    All of them fatlings of Bashan.
19   You shall eat fat till you are full,
    And drink blood till you are drunk,
    At My sacrificial meal
    Which I am sacrificing for you.
20   You shall be filled at My table
    With horses and riders,
    With mighty men
    And with all the men of war," says the Lord
        GOD.

21"I will set My glory among the nations; all the nations shall see My judgment which I have executed, and My hand which I have laid on them. 22So the house of Israel shall know that I *am* the LORD their God from that day forward. 23The Gentiles shall know that the house of Israel went into captivity for their iniquity; because they were unfaithful to Me, therefore I hid My face from them. I gave them into the hand of their enemies, and they all fell by the sword. 24According to their uncleanness and according to their transgressions I have dealt with them, and hidden My face from them." '

25"Therefore thus says the Lord GOD: 'Now I will bring back the captives of Jacob, and have mercy on the whole house of Israel; and I will be jealous for My holy name— 26after they have borne their shame, and all their unfaithfulness in which they were unfaithful to Me, when they dwelt safely in their *own* land and no one made *them* afraid. 27When I have brought them back from the peoples and gathered them out of their enemies' lands, and I am hallowed in them in the sight of many nations, 28then they shall know that I *am* the LORD their God, who sent them into captivity among the nations, but also brought them back to their land, and left none of them captive any longer. 29And I will not hide My face from

---

39:14 ᶠLiterally *those who pass through*

them anymore; for I shall have poured out My Spirit on the house of Israel,' says the Lord GOD."

40 In* the twenty-fifth year of our captivity, at the beginning of the year, on the tenth *day* of the month, in the fourteenth year after the city was captured, on the very same day the hand of the LORD was upon me; and He took me there. ²In the visions of God He took me into the land of Israel and set me on a very high mountain; on it toward the south *was* something like the structure of a city. ³He took me there, and behold, *there was* a man whose appearance *was* like the appearance of bronze. He had a line of flax and a measuring rod in his hand, and he stood in the gateway.

⁴And the man said to me, "Son of man, look with your eyes and hear with your ears, and fix your mind on everything I show you; for you *were* brought here so that I might show *them* to you. Declare to the house of Israel everything you see." ⁵Now there was a wall all around the outside of the temple.ᵍ In the man's hand was a measuring rod six cubits *long, each being a* cubit and a handbreadth; and he measured the width of the wall structure, one rod; and the height, one rod.

⁶Then he went to the gateway which faced east; and he went up its stairs and measured the threshold of the gateway, *which was* one rod wide, and the other threshold *was* one rod wide. ⁷Each gate chamber *was* one rod long and one rod wide; between the gate chambers *was a space of* five cubits; and the threshold of the gateway by the vestibule of the inside gate *was* one rod. ⁸He also measured the vestibule of the inside gate, one rod. ⁹Then he measured the vestibule of the gateway, eight cubits; and the gateposts, two cubits. The vestibule of the gate *was* on the inside. ¹⁰In the eastern gateway *were* three gate chambers on one side and three on the other; the three *were* all the same size; also the gateposts were of the same size on this side and that side.

¹¹He measured the width of the entrance to the gateway, ten cubits; *and* the length of the gate, thirteen cubits. ¹²*There was* a space in front of the gate chambers, one cubit *on this side* and one cubit on that side; the gate chambers *were* six cubits on this side and six cubits on that side. ¹³Then he measured the gateway from the roof of *one* gate chamber to the roof of the other; the width *was* twenty-five cubits, as door faces door. ¹⁴He measured the gateposts, sixty cubits high, and the court all around the gateway *extended* to the gatepost. ¹⁵*From* the front of the entrance gate to the front of the vestibule of the inner gate *was* fifty cubits. ¹⁶*There were* beveled window *frames* in the gate chambers and in their intervening archways on the inside of the gateway all around, and likewise in the vestibules. *There were* windows all around on the inside. And on each gatepost *were* palm trees.

¹⁷Then he brought me into the outer court; and *there were* chambers and a pavement made all around the court; thirty chambers faced the pavement. ¹⁸The pavement was by the side of the gateways, corresponding to the length of the gateways; *this was* the lower pavement. ¹⁹Then he measured the width from the front of the lower

---

CHAPTERS 40—43

40:1ff The city of Jerusalem and the temple had been destroyed, the land had been taken over by the Babylonians, and the people had been scattered or exiled. It was not a time of good news. But Ezekiel did what God's people always must do in times of trial: he looked ahead to the glorious future God had planned. One day the scattered people would be regathered and the defiled people cleansed. The land would be restored to beauty and fruitfulness, and there would be a new city, a new temple, and a new priesthood serving the Lord in holiness.

This vision of a glorious land and temple was to be declared to the people (40:4) so that they would repent of their sins (43:10). We today do not understand the significance of all these details; however, Israel will understand them in that day, and their understanding will bring about a change in their lives.

The assurance of a glorious future helps to sustain God's people during the trials of life (John 17:22–24; 1 Pet. 1:1–9). It should also be a stimulus to holy living. (The word *holy* is used thirty-five times in chaps. 41—48.) For Christians, heaven is not simply a *destination;* it is a *motivation.* It should make a difference in your life today because you know you are going to heaven. Does it?

The temple will be a place of sacrifice and singing and a place where *God's glory will dwell* (43:1–5). Ezekiel had described how the glory left the old temple (11:22–23), and now he describes how the glory returns and fills the house (43:1–5; 44:4). The beauty and grandeur of the temple mean nothing if God is not present.

Today, the bodies of God's people are His temple (1 Cor. 6:19–20), and so is His church (Eph. 2:19–22). Just as God has a beautiful plan for His future temple in Jerusalem, so He has a plan for His people individually (Eph. 2:10) and His church collectively. We are to be a holy temple, dedicated to Him alone; we are to radiate the glory of God.

40:5 ᵍLiterally *house,* and so elsewhere in this book

gateway to the front of the inner court exterior, one hundred cubits toward the east and the north.

20On the outer court was also a gateway facing north, and he measured its length and its width. 21Its gate chambers, three on this side and three on that side, its gateposts and its archways, had the same measurements as the first gate; its length *was* fifty cubits and its width twenty-five cubits. 22Its windows and those of its archways, and also its palm trees, *had* the same measurements as the gateway facing east; it was ascended by seven steps, and its archway *was* in front of it. 23A gate of the inner court was opposite the northern gateway, just as the eastern *gateway;* and he measured from gateway to gateway, one hundred cubits.

24After that he brought me toward the south, and there a gateway was facing south; and he measured its gateposts and archways according to these same measurements. 25There were windows in it and in its archways all around like those windows; its length *was* fifty cubits and its width twenty-five cubits. 26Seven steps led up to it, and its archway *was* in front of them; and it had palm trees on its gateposts, one on this side and one on that side. 27There was also a gateway on the inner court, facing south; and he measured from gateway to gateway toward the south, one hundred cubits.

28Then he brought me to the inner court through the southern gateway; he measured the southern gateway according to these same measurements. 29Also its gate chambers, its gateposts, and its archways *were* according to these same measurements; *there were* windows in it and in its archways all around; *it was* fifty cubits long and twenty-five cubits wide. 30There were archways all around, twenty-five cubits long and five cubits wide. 31Its archways faced the outer court, palm trees *were* on its gateposts, and going up to it *were* eight steps.

32And he brought me into the inner court facing east; he measured the gateway according to these same measurements. 33Also its gate chambers, its gateposts, and its archways *were* according to these same measurements; and *there were* windows in it and in its archways all around; *it was* fifty cubits long and twenty-five cubits wide. 34Its archways faced the outer court, and palm trees *were* on its gateposts on this side and on that side; and going up to it *were* eight steps.

35Then he brought me to the north gateway and measured *it* according to these same measurements— 36also its gate chambers, its gateposts, and its archways. It had windows all around; its length *was* fifty cubits and its width twenty-five cubits. 37Its gateposts faced the outer court, palm trees *were* on its gateposts on this side and on that side, and going up to it *were* eight steps.

38There was a chamber and its entrance by the gateposts of the gateway, where they washed the burnt offering. 39In the vestibule of the gateway *were* two tables on this side and two tables on that side, on which to slay the burnt offering, the sin offering, and the trespass offering. 40At the outer side of the vestibule, as one goes up to the entrance of the northern gateway, *were* two tables; and on the other side of the vestibule of the gateway *were* two tables. 41Four tables *were* on this side and four tables on that side, by the side of the gateway, eight tables on which they slaughtered *the sacrifices.* 42There were also four tables of hewn stone for the burnt offering, one cubit and a half long, one cubit and a half wide, and one cubit high; on these they laid the instruments with which they slaughtered the burnt offering and the sacrifice. 43Inside *were* hooks, a handbreadth wide, fastened all around; and the flesh of the sacrifices *was* on the tables.

44Outside the inner gate *were* the chambers for the singers in the inner court, one facing south at the side of the northern gateway, and the other facing north at the side of the southern gateway. 45Then he said to me, "This chamber which faces south *is* for the priests who have charge of the temple. 46The chamber which faces north *is* for the priests who have charge of the altar; these *are* the sons of Zadok, from the sons of Levi, who come near the LORD to minister to Him."

47And he measured the court, one hundred cubits long and one hundred cubits wide, foursquare. The altar *was* in front of the temple. 48Then he brought me to the vestibule of the temple and measured the doorposts of the vestibule, five cubits on this side and five cubits on that side; and the width of the gateway was three cubits on this side and three cubits on that side. 49The length of the vestibule *was* twenty cubits, and the width eleven cubits; and by the steps which led up to it *there were* pillars by the doorposts, one on this side and another on that side.

41 Then he brought me into the sanctuary[h] and measured the doorposts, six cubits wide on one side and six cubits wide on the other side—the width of the tabernacle. 2The width of the entryway *was* ten cubits, and the side walls of the entrance *were* five cubits on this side and five cubits on the other side; and he measured its length, forty cubits, and its width, twenty cubits.

3Also he went inside and measured the doorposts, two cubits; and the entrance, six cubits *high;* and the width of the entrance, seven cubits. 4He measured the length, twenty cubits; and the width, twenty cubits, beyond the sanctuary; and he said to me, "This *is* the Most Holy *Place.*"

5Next, he measured the wall of the temple, six cubits. The width of each side chamber all around the temple *was* four cubits on every side. 6The side chambers *were* in three stories, one above the other, thirty chambers in each story; they rested on ledges which *were* for the side chambers all around, that they might be supported, but not fastened to the wall of the temple. 7As one went up from story to story, the side chambers became wider all around, because their supporting ledges in the wall of the temple ascended like steps; therefore the width of the structure increased as one went up *from* the lowest *story* to the highest by way of the middle one. 8I also saw an elevation all around the temple; it was the foundation of the side chambers, a full rod, *that is,* six cubits high. 9The thickness of the outer wall of the side chambers *was* five cubits, and so also the remaining terrace by the place of the side chambers of the temple. 10And between *it and* the *wall* chambers was a width of twenty cubits all around the temple on every side. 11The doors of the side chambers opened on the terrace, one door toward

41:1 [h]Hebrew *heykal,* here the main room of the temple, sometimes called the *holy place* (compare Exodus 26:33)

the north and another toward the south; and the width of the terrace *was* five cubits all around.

12The building that faced the separating courtyard at its western end *was* seventy cubits wide; the wall of the building *was* five cubits thick all around, and its length ninety cubits.

13So he measured the temple, one hundred cubits long; and the separating courtyard with the building and its walls *was* one hundred cubits long; 14also the width of the eastern face of the temple, including the separating courtyard, *was* one hundred cubits. 15He measured the length of the building behind it, facing the separating courtyard, with its galleries on the one side and on the other side, one hundred cubits, as well as the inner temple and the porches of the court, 16their doorposts and the beveled window frames. And the galleries all around their three stories opposite the threshold were paneled with wood from the ground to the windows—the windows were covered— 17from the space above the door, even to the inner room,¹ as well as outside, and on every wall all around, inside and outside, by measure.

18And *it was* made with cherubim and palm trees, a palm tree between cherub and cherub. *Each* cherub had two faces, 19so that the face of a man *was* toward a palm tree on one side, and the face of a young lion toward a palm tree on the other side; thus *it was* made throughout the temple all around. 20From the floor to the space above the door, and on the wall of the sanctuary, cherubim and palm trees *were* carved.

21The doorposts of the temple *were* square, *as was* the front of the sanctuary; their appearance was similar. 22The altar *was* of wood, three cubits high, and its length two cubits. Its corners, its length, and its sides *were* of wood; and he said to me, "This *is* the table that *is* before the LORD."

23The temple and the sanctuary had two doors. 24The doors had two panels *apiece,* two folding panels: two *panels* for one door and two panels for the other *door.* 25Cherubim and palm trees *were* carved on the doors of the temple just as they *were* carved on the walls. A wooden canopy *was* on the front of the vestibule outside. 26*There were* beveled window *frames* and palm trees on one side and on the other, on the sides of the vestibule—also on the side chambers of the temple and on the canopies.

42 Then he brought me out into the outer court, by the way toward the north; and he brought me into the chamber which *was* opposite the separating courtyard, and which *was* opposite the building toward the north. 2Facing the length, *which was* one hundred cubits (the width was fifty cubits), was the north door. 3Opposite the inner court of twenty *cubits,* and opposite the pavement of the outer court, *was* gallery against gallery in three *stories.* 4In front of the chambers, toward the inside, *was* a walk ten cubits wide, at a distance of one cubit; and their doors faced north. 5Now the upper chambers *were* shorter, because the galleries took away *space* from them more than from the lower and middle stories of the building. 6For they *were* in three *stories* and did not have pillars like the pillars of the courts; therefore *the upper level* was shortened more than the

---

41:17 ¹Literally *house,* here *the Most Holy Place*

lower and middle levels from the ground up. [7]And a wall which *was* outside ran parallel to the chambers, at the front of the chambers, toward the outer court; its length *was* fifty cubits. [8]The length of the chambers toward the outer court *was* fifty cubits, whereas that facing the temple *was* one hundred cubits. [9]At the lower chambers *was* the entrance on the east side, as one goes into them from the outer court.

[10]Also *there were* chambers in the thickness of the wall of the court toward the east, opposite the separating courtyard and opposite the building. [11]*There was* a walk in front of them also, and their appearance *was* like the chambers which *were* toward the north; they *were* as long and as wide as the others, and all their exits and entrances *were* according to plan. [12]And corresponding to the doors of the chambers that *were* facing south, as one enters them, *there was* a door in front of the walk, the way directly in front of the wall toward the east.

[13]Then he said to me, "The north chambers *and* the south chambers, which *are* opposite the separating courtyard, *are* the holy chambers where the priests who approach the LORD shall eat the most holy offerings. There they shall lay the most holy offerings—the grain offering, the sin offering, and the trespass offering—for the place *is* holy. [14]When the priests enter them, they shall not go out of the holy *chamber* into the outer court; but there they shall leave their garments in which they minister, for they *are* holy. They shall put on other garments; then they may approach *that* which *is* for the people."

[15]Now when he had finished measuring the inner temple, he brought me out through the gateway that faces toward the east, and measured it all around. [16]He measured the east side with the measuring rod,[j] five hundred rods by the measuring rod all around. [17]He measured the north side, five hundred rods by the measuring rod all around. [18]He measured the south side, five hundred rods by the measuring rod. [19]He came around to the west side *and* measured five hundred rods by the measuring rod. [20]He measured it on the four sides; it had a wall all around, five hundred *cubits* long and five hundred wide, to separate the holy areas from the common.

43 Afterward he brought me to the gate, the gate that faces toward the east. [2]And behold, the glory of the God of Israel came from the way of the east. His voice *was* like the sound of many waters; and the earth shone with His glory. [3]*It was* like the appearance of the vision which I saw—like the vision which I saw when I[k] came to destroy the city. The visions *were* like the vision which I saw by the River Chebar; and I fell on my face. [4]And the glory of the LORD came into the temple by way of the gate which faces

42:16 [j]Compare 40:5   43:3 [k]Some Hebrew manuscripts and Vulgate read *He*.

Future Sacrifices—Since Jesus Christ has fulfilled all the Old Testament sacrifices in Himself (Heb. 10:1–18), why will God reinstate them in the future temple worship? Certainly not for the purpose of dealing with sin, for Christ's sacrifice did that once and for all, and the blood of bulls and goats never did take away sin (Heb. 10:1–4). It seems that these future sacrifices, like the Lord's Supper today, will be memorials of what Jesus did. They will teach the Jews the meaning of their ancient religion in the light of the Cross.

toward the east. ⁵The Spirit lifted me up and brought me into the inner court; and behold, the glory of the LORD filled the temple.

⁶Then I heard *Him* speaking to me from the temple, while a man stood beside me. ⁷And He said to me, "Son of man, *this is* the place of My throne and the place of the soles of My feet, where I will dwell in the midst of the children of Israel forever. No more shall the house of Israel defile My holy name, they nor their kings, by their harlotry or with the carcasses of their kings on their high places. ⁸When they set their threshold by My threshold, and their doorpost by My doorpost, with a wall between them and Me, they defiled My holy name by the abominations which they committed; therefore I have consumed them in My anger. ⁹Now let them put their harlotry and the carcasses of their kings far away from Me, and I will dwell in their midst forever.

¹⁰"Son of man, describe the temple to the house of Israel, that they may be ashamed of their iniquities; and let them measure the pattern. ¹¹And if they are ashamed of all that they have done, make known to them the design of the temple and its arrangement, its exits and its entrances, its entire design and all its ordinances, all its forms and all its laws. Write *it* down in their sight, so that they may keep its whole design and all its ordinances, and perform them. ¹²This *is* the law of the temple: The whole area surrounding the mountaintop *is* most holy. Behold, this *is* the law of the temple.

¹³"These are the measurements of the altar in cubits (the *cubit is* one cubit and a handbreadth): the base one cubit high and one cubit wide, with a rim all around its edge of one span. This *is* the height of the altar: ¹⁴from the base on the ground to the lower ledge, two cubits; the width of the ledge, one cubit; from the smaller ledge to the larger ledge, four cubits; and the width of the ledge, *one* cubit. ¹⁵The altar hearth *is* four cubits high, with four horns extending upward from the hearth. ¹⁶The altar hearth *is* twelve cubits long, twelve wide, square at its four corners; ¹⁷the ledge, fourteen *cubits* long and fourteen wide on its four sides, with a rim of half a cubit around it; its base, one cubit all around; and its steps face toward the east."

¹⁸And He said to me, "Son of man, thus says the Lord GOD: 'These *are* the ordinances for the altar on the day when it is made, for sacrificing burnt offerings on it, and for sprinkling blood on it. ¹⁹You shall give a young bull for a sin offering to the priests, the Levites, who are of the seed of Zadok, who approach Me to minister to Me,' says the Lord GOD. ²⁰You shall take some of its blood and put *it* on the four horns of the altar, on the four corners of the ledge, and on the rim around it; thus you shall cleanse it and make atonement for it. ²¹Then you shall also take the bull of the sin offering, and burn it in the appointed place of the temple, outside the sanctuary. ²²On the second day you shall offer a kid of the goats without blemish for a sin offering; and they shall cleanse the altar, as they cleansed *it* with the bull. ²³When you have finished cleansing *it,* you shall offer a young bull without blemish, and a ram from the flock without blemish. ²⁴When you offer them before the LORD, the priests shall throw salt on them, and they will offer them up *as* a burnt offering to the LORD. ²⁵Every day for seven days you shall prepare a goat *for* a sin offering; they shall also

prepare a young bull and a ram from the flock, both without blemish. 26Seven days they shall make atonement for the altar and purify it, and so consecrate *it*. 27When these days are over it shall be, on the eighth day and thereafter, that the priests shall offer your burnt offerings and your peace offerings on the altar; and I will accept you,' says the Lord GOD."

44 Then* He brought me back to the outer gate of the sanctuary which faces toward the east, but it *was* shut. 2And the LORD said to me, "This gate shall be shut; it shall not be opened, and no man shall enter by it, because the LORD God of Israel has entered by it; therefore it shall be shut. 3As *for* the prince, *because* he *is* the prince, he may sit in it to eat bread before the LORD; he shall enter by way of the vestibule of the gateway, and go out the same way."

4Also He brought me by way of the north gate to the front of the temple; so I looked, and behold, the glory of the LORD filled the house of the LORD; and I fell on my face. 5And the LORD said to me, "Son of man, mark well, see with your eyes and hear with your ears, all that I say to you concerning all the ordinances of the house of the LORD and all its laws. Mark well who may enter the house and all who go out from the sanctuary.

6"Now say to the rebellious, to the house of Israel, 'Thus says the Lord GOD: "O house of Israel, let Us have no more of all your abominations. 7When you brought in foreigners, uncircumcised in heart and uncircumcised in flesh, to be in My sanctuary to defile it—My house—and when you offered My food, the fat and the blood, then they broke My covenant because of all your abominations. 8And you have not kept charge of My holy things, but you have set *others* to keep charge of My sanctuary for you." 9Thus says the Lord GOD: "No foreigner, uncircumcised in heart or uncircumcised in flesh, shall enter My sanctuary, including any foreigner who *is* among the children of Israel.

10"And the Levites who went far from Me, when Israel went astray, who strayed away from Me after their idols, they shall bear their iniquity. 11Yet they shall be ministers in My sanctuary, *as* gatekeepers of the house and ministers of the house; they shall slay the burnt offering and the sacrifice for the people, and they shall stand before them to minister to them. 12Because they ministered to them before their idols and caused the house of Israel to fall into iniquity, therefore I have raised My hand in an oath against them," says the Lord GOD, "that they shall bear their iniquity. 13And they shall not come near Me to minister to Me as priest, nor come near any of My holy things, nor into the Most Holy *Place;* but they shall bear their shame and their abominations which they have committed. 14Nevertheless I will make them keep charge of the temple, for all its work, and for all that has to be done in it.

15"But the priests, the Levites, the sons of Zadok, who kept charge of My sanctuary when the children of Israel went astray from Me, they shall come near Me to minister to Me; and they shall stand before Me to offer to Me the fat and the blood," says the Lord GOD. 16"They shall enter My sanctuary, and they shall come near My table to minister to Me, and they shall keep My charge. 17And it shall be, whenever they shall enter the gates of the inner court, that they shall put on linen

CHAPTERS 44—46

44:1ff Somebody must serve in the new temple, so God gave Ezekiel instructions concerning the Levites and priests and the manner of worship He wanted. Note the emphasis on the word *My:* My sanctuary, My food, My covenant, My holy things, My table, and so on. One reason the temple was destroyed is that the priests and Levites forgot it was the house of God, and they did in it whatever they pleased.

What a privilege it is to minister for the Lord! You wonder why people would want to give their privileges to others, especially men who were not qualified (vv. 4–9). Never lose the wonder of belonging to God and being asked to serve Him (Mal. 1:6—2:9). Such an attitude always leads to sin.

Unfaithfulness in service can lead to loss of privileges (vv. 10–14), but faithfulness can mean being able to draw near to serve the Lord (vv. 15ff.). The priests had to be careful what they wore, what they ate and drank and how they looked. How could they teach the people to have discernment (v. 23) if they did not practice discernment?

The prince will worship only at the threshold of the gate and the people only at the entrance (46:2–3), but we have the great privilege today of entering into the presence of God (Heb. 10:19–25). However, like the prince, we should not return from worship as we came; things should be different because we have met with the Lord (46:9). And we must not forget the daily burnt offering (46:13; Rom. 12:1–2).

garments; no wool shall come upon them while they minister within the gates of the inner court or within the house. ¹⁸They shall have linen turbans on their heads and linen trousers on their bodies; they shall not clothe themselves with *anything that causes* sweat. ¹⁹When they go out to the outer court, to the *outer* court to the people, they shall take off their garments in which they have ministered, leave them in the holy chambers, and put on other garments; and in their holy garments they shall not sanctify the people.

²⁰"They shall neither shave their heads, nor let their hair grow long, but they shall keep their hair well trimmed. ²¹No priest shall drink wine when he enters the inner court. ²²They shall not take as wife a widow or a divorced woman, but take virgins of the descendants of the house of Israel, or widows of priests.

²³"And they shall teach My people *the difference* between the holy and the unholy, and cause them to discern between the unclean and the clean. ²⁴In controversy they shall stand as judges, *and* judge it according to My judgments. They shall keep My laws and My statutes in all My appointed meetings, and they shall hallow My Sabbaths.

²⁵"They shall not defile *themselves* by coming near a dead person. Only for father or mother, for son or daughter, for brother or unmarried sister may they defile themselves. ²⁶After he is cleansed, they shall count seven days for him. ²⁷And on the day that he goes to the sanctuary to minister in the sanctuary, he must offer his sin offering in the inner court," says the Lord GOD.

²⁸"It shall be, in regard to their inheritance, *that* I *am* their inheritance. You shall give them no possession in Israel, for I *am* their possession. ²⁹They shall eat the grain offering, the sin offering, and the trespass offering; every dedicated thing in Israel shall be theirs. ³⁰The best of all firstfruits of any kind, and every sacrifice of any kind from all your sacrifices, shall be the priest's; also you shall give to the priest the first of your ground meal, to cause a blessing to rest on your house. ³¹The priests shall not eat anything, bird or beast, that died naturally or was torn *by wild beasts.*

45 "Moreover, when you divide the land by lot into inheritance, you shall set apart a district for the LORD, a holy section of the land; its length *shall be* twenty-five thousand *cubits,* and the width ten thousand. It *shall be* holy throughout its territory all around. ²Of this there shall be a square plot for the sanctuary, five hundred by five hundred *rods,* with fifty cubits around it for an open space. ³So this is the district you shall measure: twenty-five thousand *cubits* long and ten thousand wide; in it shall be the sanctuary, the Most Holy *Place.* ⁴It shall be a holy *section* of the land, belonging to the priests, the ministers of the sanctuary, who come near to minister to the LORD; it shall be a place for their houses and a holy place for the sanctuary. ⁵*An area* twenty-five thousand *cubits* long and ten thousand wide shall belong to the Levites, the ministers of the temple; they shall have twenty chambers as a possession.ⁱ

45:5 ⁱFollowing Masoretic Text, Targum, and Vulgate; Septuagint reads *a possession, cities of dwelling.*

6"You shall appoint as the property of the city *an area* five thousand *cubits* wide and twenty-five thousand long, adjacent to the district of the holy *section;* it shall belong to the whole house of Israel.

7"The prince shall have *a section* on one side and the other of the holy district and the city's property; and bordering on the holy district and the city's property, extending westward on the west side and eastward on the east side, the length *shall be* side by side with one of the *tribal* portions, from the west border to the east border. 8The land shall be his possession in Israel; and My princes shall no more oppress My people, but they shall give *the rest of* the land to the house of Israel, according to their tribes."

9"Thus says the Lord GOD: "Enough, O princes of Israel! Remove violence and plundering, execute justice and righteousness, and stop dispossessing My people," says the Lord GOD. 10"You shall have honest scales, an honest ephah, and an honest bath. 11The ephah and the bath shall be of the same measure, so that the bath contains one-tenth of a homer, and the ephah one-tenth of a homer; their measure shall be according to the homer. 12The shekel *shall be* twenty gerahs; twenty shekels, twenty-five shekels, *and* fifteen shekels shall be your mina.

13"This *is* the offering which you shall offer: you shall give one-sixth of an ephah from a homer of wheat, and one-sixth of an ephah from a homer of barley. 14The ordinance concerning oil, the bath of oil, *is* one-tenth of a bath from a kor. A kor *is* a homer or ten baths, for ten baths *are* a homer. 15And one lamb shall be given from a flock of two hundred, from the rich pastures of Israel. These shall be for grain offerings, burnt offerings, and peace offerings, to make atonement for them," says the Lord GOD. 16"All the people of the land shall give this offering for the prince in Israel. 17Then it shall be the prince's part *to give* burnt offerings, grain offerings, and drink offerings, at the feasts, the New Moons, the Sabbaths, and at all the appointed seasons of the house of Israel. He shall prepare the sin offering, the grain offering, the burnt offering, and the peace offerings to make atonement for the house of Israel."

18"Thus says the Lord GOD: "In the first *month,* on the first *day* of the month, you shall take a young bull without blemish and cleanse the sanctuary. 19The priest shall take some of the blood of the sin offering and put *it* on the doorposts of the temple, on the four corners of the ledge of the altar, and on the gateposts of the gate of the inner court. 20And so you shall do on the seventh *day* of the month for everyone who has sinned unintentionally or in ignorance. Thus you shall make atonement for the temple.

21"In the first *month,* on the fourteenth day of the month, you shall observe the Passover, a feast of seven days; unleavened bread shall be eaten. 22And on that day the prince shall prepare for himself and for all the people of the land a bull *for* a sin offering. 23On the seven days of the feast he shall prepare a burnt offering to the LORD, seven bulls and seven rams without blemish, daily for seven days, and a kid of the goats daily *for* a sin offering. 24And he shall prepare a grain offering of one ephah for each bull and one ephah for each ram, together with a hin of oil for each ephah.

25"In the seventh *month,* on the fifteenth day

of the month, at the feast, he shall do likewise for seven days, according to the sin offering, the burnt offering, the grain offering, and the oil."

46 ¹Thus says the Lord GOD: "The gateway of the inner court that faces toward the east shall be shut the six working days; but on the Sabbath it shall be opened, and on the day of the New Moon it shall be opened. ²The prince shall enter by way of the vestibule of the gateway from the outside, and stand by the gatepost. The priests shall prepare his burnt offering and his peace offerings. He shall worship at the threshold of the gate. Then he shall go out, but the gate shall not be shut until evening. ³Likewise the people of the land shall worship at the entrance to this gateway before the LORD on the Sabbaths and the New Moons. ⁴The burnt offering that the prince offers to the LORD on the Sabbath day *shall be* six lambs without blemish, and a ram without blemish; ⁵and the grain offering *shall be one* ephah for a ram, and the grain offering for the lambs, as much as he wants to give, as well as a hin of oil with every ephah. ⁶On the day of the New Moon *it shall be* a young bull without blemish, six lambs, and a ram; they shall be without blemish. ⁷He shall prepare a grain offering of an ephah for a bull, an ephah for a ram, as much as he wants to give for the lambs, and a hin of oil with every ephah. ⁸When the prince enters, he shall go in by way of the vestibule of the gateway, and go out the same way.

⁹"But when the people of the land come before the LORD on the appointed feast days, whoever enters by way of the north gate to worship shall go out by way of the south gate; and whoever enters by way of the south gate shall go out by way of the north gate. He shall not return by way of the gate through which he came, but shall go out through the opposite gate. ¹⁰The prince shall then be in their midst. When they go in, he shall go in; and when they go out, he shall go out. ¹¹At the festivals and the appointed feast days the grain offering shall be an ephah for a bull, an ephah for a ram, as much as he wants to give for the lambs, and a hin of oil with every ephah.

¹²"Now when the prince makes a voluntary burnt offering or voluntary peace offering to the LORD, the gate that faces toward the east shall then be opened for him; and he shall prepare his burnt offering and his peace offerings as he did on the Sabbath day. Then he shall go out, and after he goes out the gate shall be shut.

¹³"You shall daily make a burnt offering to the LORD *of* a lamb of the first year without blemish; you shall prepare it every morning. ¹⁴And you shall prepare a grain offering with it every morning, a sixth of an ephah, and a third of a hin of oil to moisten the fine flour. This grain offering is a perpetual ordinance, to be made regularly to the LORD. ¹⁵Thus they shall prepare the lamb, the grain offering, and the oil, *as* a regular burnt offering every morning."

¹⁶Thus says the Lord GOD: "If the prince gives a gift *of some* of his inheritance to any of his sons, it shall belong to his sons; it is their possession by inheritance. ¹⁷But if he gives a gift of some of his inheritance to one of his servants, it shall be his until the year of liberty, after which it shall return to the prince. But his inheritance shall belong to his sons; it shall become theirs. ¹⁸Moreover the prince shall not take any of the

people's inheritance by evicting them from their property; he shall provide an inheritance for his sons from his own property, so that none of My people may be scattered from his property." ' "

19Now he brought me through the entrance, which *was* at the side of the gate, into the holy chambers of the priests which face toward the north; and there a place *was* situated at their extreme western end. 20And he said to me, "This *is* the place where the priests shall boil the trespass offering and the sin offering, *and* where they shall bake the grain offering, so that they do not bring *them* out into the outer court to sanctify the people."

21Then he brought me out into the outer court and caused me to pass by the four corners of the court; and in fact, in every corner of the court *there was another* court. 22In the four corners of the court *were* enclosed courts, forty *cubits* long and thirty wide; all four corners *were* the same size. 23*There was* a row *of building stones* all around in them, all around the four of them; and cooking hearths were made under the rows of stones all around. 24And he said to me, "These *are* the kitchens where the ministers of the temple shall boil the sacrifices of the people."

47 Then* he brought me back to the door of the temple; and there was water, flowing from under the threshold of the temple toward the east, for the front of the temple faced east; the water was flowing from under the right side of the temple, south of the altar. 2He brought me out by way of the north gate, and led me around on the outside to the outer gateway that faces east; and there was water, running out on the right side.

3And when the man went out to the east with the line in his hand, he measured one thousand cubits, and he brought me through the waters; the water *came up to my* ankles. 4Again he measured one thousand and brought me through the waters; the water *came up to my* knees. Again he measured one thousand and brought me through; the water *came up to my* waist. 5Again he measured one thousand, *and it was* a river that I could not cross; for the water was too deep, water in which one must swim, a river that could not be crossed. 6He said to me, "Son of man, have you seen *this?*" Then he brought me and returned me to the bank of the river.

7When I returned, there, along the bank of the river, *were* very many trees on one side and the other. 8Then he said to me: "This water flows toward the eastern region, goes down into the valley, and enters the sea. *When it* reaches the sea, *its* waters are healed. 9And it shall be *that* every living thing that moves, wherever the rivers go, will live. There will be a very great multitude of fish, because these waters go there; for they will be healed, and everything will live wherever the river goes. 10It shall be *that* fishermen will stand by it from En Gedi to En Eglaim; they will be *places* for spreading their nets. Their fish will be of the same kinds as the fish of the Great Sea, exceedingly many. 11But its swamps and marshes will not be healed; they will be given over to salt. 12Along the bank of the river, on this side and that, will grow all *kinds of* trees used for food; their leaves will not wither, and their fruit will not fail. They will bear fruit every month, because their water flows from the sanctuary. Their fruit will be for food, and their leaves for medicine."

CHAPTERS 47—48

47:1–12 *Depths.* This river speaks of the healing and life-giving power of the Holy Spirit of God (cf. John 7:37–39; Zech. 14:8). No matter how deep you want to go into the things of God, the opportunity is there. It's tragic that too many linger in the shallows when they could be enjoying the depths.

47:13—48:34 *Dimensions.* God assigns our inheritance (Ps. 47:4), and He will keep His promise to Abraham (Gen. 13:14–17; 15:17–21) and give Israel their land.

13*Thus says the Lord GOD: "These *are* the borders by which you shall divide the land as an inheritance among the twelve tribes of Israel. Joseph *shall have two* portions. 14You shall inherit it equally with one another; for I raised My hand in an oath to give it to your fathers, and this land shall fall to you as your inheritance.

15"This *shall be* the border of the land on the north: from the Great Sea, *by* the road to Hethlon, as one goes to Zedad, 16Hamath, Berothah, Sibraim (which *is* between the border of Damascus and the border of Hamath), to Hazar Hatticon (which *is* on the border of Hauran). 17Thus the boundary shall be from the Sea to Hazar Enan, the border of Damascus; and as for the north, northward, it is the border of Hamath. *This is* the north side.

18"On the east side you shall mark out the border from between Hauran and Damascus, and between Gilead and the land of Israel, along the Jordan, and along the eastern side of the sea. *This is* the east side.

19"The south side, toward the South,*m* *shall be* from Tamar to the waters of Meribah by Kadesh, along the brook to the Great Sea. *This is* the south side, toward the South.

20"The west side *shall be* the Great Sea, from the *southern* boundary until one comes to a point opposite Hamath. This *is* the west side.

21"Thus you shall divide this land among yourselves according to the tribes of Israel. 22It shall be that you will divide it by lot as an inheritance for yourselves, and for the strangers who dwell among you and who bear children among you. They shall be to you as native-born among the children of Israel; they shall have an inheritance with you among the tribes of Israel. 23And it shall be *that* in whatever tribe the stranger dwells, there you shall give *him* his inheritance," says the Lord GOD.

48 "Now these *are* the names of the tribes: From the northern border along the road to Hethlon at the entrance of Hamath, to Hazar Enan, the border of Damascus northward, in the direction of Hamath, *there shall be* one *section for* Dan from its east to its west side; 2by the border of Dan, from the east side to the west, one *section for* Asher; 3by the border of Asher, from the east side to the west, one *section for* Naphtali; 4by the border of Naphtali, from the east side to the west, one *section for* Manasseh; 5by the border of Manasseh, from the east side to the west, one *section for* Ephraim; 6by the border of Ephraim, from the east side to the west, one *section for* Reuben; 7by the border of Reuben, from the east side to the west, one *section for* Judah; 8by the border of Judah, from the east side to the west, shall be the district which you shall set apart, twenty-five

47:19 *m*Hebrew *Negev*

Jehovah—*Jehovah-Shammah* is one of nine special names of God found in the Old Testament. The others are: *Jehovah-Jireh*—"the Lord will see to it" (Gen. 22:14); *Jehovah-Rophe*—"the Lord who heals" (Exod. 15:26); *Jehovah-Nissi*—"the Lord our Banner" (Exod. 17:15); *Jehovah-M'Kaddesh*—"the Lord who sanctifies" (Lev. 20:8); *Jehovah-Shalom*—"the Lord our peace" (Judg. 6:24); *Jehovah-Tsidkenu*—"the Lord our righteousness" (Jer. 23:6); *Jehovah-Rohi*—"the Lord my shepherd" (Ps. 23:1); and *Jehovah-Sebaoth*—"the Lord of hosts [armies]" (Ps. 46:7). The Lord is to us all that we need, no matter what that need may be.

thousand *cubits* in width, and *in* length the same as one of the *other* portions, from the east side to the west, with the sanctuary in the center.

9"The district that you shall set apart for the LORD *shall be* twenty-five thousand *cubits* in length and ten thousand in width. 10To these—to the priests—the holy district shall belong: on the north twenty-five thousand *cubits in length,* on the west ten thousand in width, on the east ten thousand in width, and on the south twenty-five thousand in length. The sanctuary of the LORD shall be in the center. 11*It shall be* for the priests of the sons of Zadok, who are sanctified, who have kept My charge, who did not go astray when the children of Israel went astray, as the Levites went astray. 12And *this* district of land that is set apart shall be to them a thing most holy by the border of the Levites.

13"Opposite the border of the priests, the Levites *shall have an area* twenty-five thousand *cubits* in length and ten thousand in width; its entire length *shall be* twenty-five thousand and its width ten thousand. 14And they shall not sell or exchange any of it; they may not alienate this best *part* of the land, for *it is* holy to the LORD.

15"The five thousand *cubits* in width that remain, along the edge of the twenty-five thousand, shall be for general use by the city, for dwellings and common-land; and the city shall be in the center. 16These *shall be* its measurements: the north side four thousand five hundred *cubits,* the south side four thousand five hundred, the east side four thousand five hundred, and the west side four thousand five hundred. 17The common-land of the city shall be: to the north two hundred and fifty *cubits,* to the south two hundred and fifty, to the east two hundred and fifty, and to the west two hundred and fifty. 18The rest of the length, alongside the district of the holy *section, shall be* ten thousand *cubits* to the east and ten thousand to the west. It shall be adjacent to the district of the holy *section,* and its produce shall be food for the workers of the city. 19The workers of the city, from all the tribes of Israel, shall cultivate it. 20The entire district *shall be* twenty-five thousand *cubits* by twenty-five thousand *cubits,* foursquare. You shall set apart the holy district with the property of the city.

21"The rest *shall belong* to the prince, on one side and on the other of the holy district and of the city's property, next to the twenty-five thousand *cubits* of the *holy* district as far as the eastern border, and westward next to the twenty-five thousand as far as the western border, adjacent to the *tribal* portions; *it shall belong* to the prince. It shall be the holy district, and the sanctuary of the temple *shall be* in the center. 22Moreover, apart from the possession of the Levites and the possession of the city *which are* in the midst of what *belongs* to the prince, *the area* between the border of Judah and the border of Benjamin shall belong to the prince.

23"As for the rest of the tribes, from the east side to the west, Benjamin *shall have* one *section;* 24by the border of Benjamin, from the east side to the west, Simeon *shall have* one *section;* 25by the border of Simeon, from the east side to the west, Issachar *shall have* one *section;* 26by the border of Issachar, from the east side to the west, Zebulun *shall have* one *section;* 27by the border of Zebulun, from the east side to the west, Gad *shall have* one *section;* 28by the border of Gad, on the south side, toward the South,[n] the border shall be from Tamar *to* the waters of Meribah *by* Kadesh, along the brook to the Great Sea. [29]This *is* the land which you shall divide by lot as an inheritance among the tribes of Israel, and these *are* their portions," says the Lord GOD.

[30]"These *are* the exits of the city. On the north side, measuring four thousand five hundred *cubits* [31](the gates of the city *shall be* named after the tribes of Israel), the three gates northward: one gate for Reuben, one gate for Judah, and one gate for Levi; [32]on the east side, four thousand five hundred *cubits*, three gates: one gate for Joseph, one gate for Benjamin, and one gate for Dan; [33]on the south side, measuring four thousand five hundred *cubits*, three gates: one gate for Simeon, one gate for Issachar, and one gate for Zebulun; [34]on the west side, four thousand five hundred *cubits* with their three gates: one gate for Gad, one gate for Asher, and one gate for Naphtali. [35]*All the way around *shall be* eighteen thousand *cubits*; and the name of the city from *that* day *shall be*: THE LORD *IS* THERE."[o]

48:28 [n]Hebrew *Negev*   48:35 [o]Hebrew *YHWH Shammah*

48:35 *Distinction.* The important thing about the land is not the river or the borders but the glorious presence of God. The new name for the city of Jerusalem will be *Jehovah-Shammah*—"the Lord is there!" The Lord had departed from Jerusalem because of the sins of the people, but He will return to dwell with them and bless them. When you are discouraged about the way things are going on earth, lift your eyes to heaven by pondering Revelation 21:1–8. Just think of it: we shall live forever *where the Lord is*! Are you looking by faith for that future city (Heb. 11:13–16)?

DANIEL

When Nebuchadnezzar began his conquest of Judah in 605 B.C., he deported a number of Jews to Babylon, including Daniel and his friends, who were probably teenagers at the time. God blessed Daniel and gave him important places of service under four different rulers who represented three different kingdoms. When you read about Daniel, you meet a man of God who was faithful to the Lord and glorified Him in the enemy's land.

The emphasis in Daniel is on the sovereign will of God in the affairs of nations (4:25). In a series of dreams and visions, God showed Daniel the course of gentile history until the establishing of the promised kingdom on earth.

Chapters 1 and 6 are historical and reveal Daniel's godly integrity. Chapters 2—5 record his interpretations of the dreams and visions of *others*; in chapters 7—12, he receives his own visions from God and shares with us their meanings.

With Babylon's taking of Jerusalem, the "times of the Gentiles" began (Luke 21:24) and will continue until Christ returns to set up His glorious kingdom. God is in control of history and will work out His perfect plan. God also wants to have control in your life, as He did in Daniel's life; and He will—if, like Daniel, you determine in your heart to serve Him faithfully. Daniel was a man of personal integrity who had nothing to fear because he feared the Lord and served Him.

1 In the third year of the reign of Jehoiakim king of Judah, Nebuchadnezzar king of Babylon came to Jerusalem and besieged it. 2And the Lord gave Jehoiakim king of Judah into his hand, with some of the articles of the house of God, which he carried into the land of Shinar to the house of his god; and he brought the articles into the treasure house of his god.

3Then the king instructed Ashpenaz, the master of his eunuchs, to bring some of the children of Israel and some of the king's descendants and some of the nobles, 4young men in whom *there was* no blemish, but good-looking, gifted in all wisdom, possessing knowledge and quick to understand, who *had* ability to serve in the king's palace, and whom they might teach the language and literature of the Chaldeans. 5And the king appointed for them a daily provision of the king's delicacies and of the wine which he drank, and three years of training for them, so that at the end of *that time* they might serve before the king. 6Now from among those of the sons of Judah were Daniel, Hananiah, Mishael, and Azariah. 7To them the chief of the eunuchs gave names: he gave Daniel *the name* Belteshazzar; to Hananiah, Shadrach; to Mishael, Meshach; and to Azariah, Abed-Nego.

8*But Daniel purposed in his heart that he would not defile himself with the portion of the king's delicacies, nor with the wine which he drank;

CHAPTER 1

1:8 The world always wants the best (vv. 3–4), but these young men determined to give their best to the Lord. It is possible to serve the Lord even in Babylon. Think of Joseph in Egypt and Esther in Persia. Don't complain about the place where God puts you. Ask Him to use you while you are there.

The world wants to change you and make you a "conformer," but God can help you become a "transformer" (Rom. 12:1–2). Daniel and his friends had a new home, strange new names, new teachings, and were even offered a new diet; but they kept the same heart's dedication to the Lord (Prov. 4:23).

God can give us favor in difficult places (v. 9). Daniel was courteous to his guards and did not create problems for them. He was following the counsel of Jeremiah (Jer. 29) and the example of Joseph (Gen. 39:4).

When everything in your life is upset and you find yourself in new circumstances that you cannot control, let the Lord take over and work out the plan He has in mind. If your heart is right with Him, His hand will work for you.

Dare to Be a Daniel

Dare to be a Daniel, / Dare to stand alone!
Dare to have a purpose firm! / Dare to make it known!

Philip P. Bliss

therefore he requested of the chief of the eunuchs that he might not defile himself. [9]Now God had brought Daniel into the favor and goodwill of the chief of the eunuchs. [10]And the chief of the eunuchs said to Daniel, "I fear my lord the king, who has appointed your food and drink. For why should he see your faces looking worse than the young men who *are* your age? Then you would endanger my head before the king."

[11]So Daniel said to the steward[a] whom the chief of the eunuchs had set over Daniel, Hananiah, Mishael, and Azariah, [12]"Please test your servants for ten days, and let them give us vegetables to eat and water to drink. [13]Then let our appearance be examined before you, and the appearance of the young men who eat the portion of the king's delicacies; and as you see fit, *so* deal with your servants." [14]So he consented with them in this matter, and tested them ten days.

[15]And at the end of ten days their features appeared better and fatter in flesh than all the young men who ate the portion of the king's delicacies. [16]Thus the steward took away their portion of delicacies and the wine that they were to drink, and gave them vegetables.

[17]As for these four young men, God gave them knowledge and skill in all literature and wisdom; and Daniel had understanding in all visions and dreams.

[18]Now at the end of the days, when the king had said that they should be brought in, the chief of the eunuchs brought them in before Nebuchadnezzar. [19]Then the king interviewed them,[b] and among them all none was found like Daniel, Hananiah, Mishael, and Azariah; therefore they served before the king. [20]And in all matters of wisdom *and* understanding about which the king examined them, he found them ten times better than all the magicians *and* astrologers who *were* in all his realm. [21]Thus Daniel continued until the first year of King Cyrus.

2 Now* in the second year of Nebuchadnezzar's reign, Nebuchadnezzar had dreams; and his spirit was *so* troubled that his sleep left him. [2]Then the king gave the command to call the magicians, the astrologers, the sorcerers, and the Chaldeans to tell the king his dreams. So they came and stood before the king. [3]And the king said to them, "I have had a dream, and my spirit is anxious to know the dream."

[4]Then the Chaldeans spoke to the king in Aramaic,[c] "O king, live forever! Tell your servants the dream, and we will give the interpretation."

[5]The king answered and said to the Chaldeans, "My decision is firm: if you do not make known the dream to me, and its interpretation, you shall be cut in pieces, and your houses shall be made an ash heap. [6]However, if you tell the dream and its interpretation, you shall receive from me gifts, rewards, and great honor. Therefore tell me the dream and its interpretation."

CHAPTER 2

2:1ff Nebuchadnezzar could conquer empires, but he could not conquer his own anger (v. 12; 3:13, 19; Prov. 16:32). He understood how to defeat the enemy, but he could not understand the message of God. Daniel had patience and self-control and could explain the mysteries of God. A pure heart is better than a powerful throne. Daniel and his friends knew the "God of heaven" who is merciful (v. 18), answers prayer (vv. 19–23; James 1:5), reveals secrets (v. 28), establishes rulers (v. 37), and will one day set up His kingdom (v. 44).

Because the four men could not come to God's throne, they had no fear of Nebuchadnezzar's throne.

When he explained the dream, Daniel gave the glory to God and shared the credit with his three friends. He also saved the lives of the king's wise men (the Chaldeans) when he could have exposed them as frauds. The presence of a believer can mean deliverance for unbelievers (Job 42:7–10; Acts 27:21–25), and we must be forgiving to our enemies. After all, we want to win them to the Savior.

1:11 [a]Hebrew *Melzar,* also in verse 16   1:19 [b]Literally *talked with them*   2:4 [c]The original language of Daniel 2:4b through 7:28 is Aramaic.

Progress?—From the human point of view, the kingdoms of the world look like metal; but from the divine point of view, they are like beasts (Dan. 7). Note that the value of the metal decreases as history unfolds, until the nations end up a weak mixture of iron and clay (Dan. 2:41–43). God does not see "progress" in what man does; He sees only increasing weakness.

7They answered again and said, "Let the king tell his servants the dream, and we will give its interpretation."

8The king answered and said, "I know for certain that you would gain time, because you see that my decision is firm: 9if you do not make known the dream to me, *there is only* one decree for you! For you have agreed to speak lying and corrupt words before me till the time has changed. Therefore tell me the dream, and I shall know that you can give me its interpretation."

10The Chaldeans answered the king, and said, "There is not a man on earth who can tell the king's matter; therefore no king, lord, or ruler has *ever* asked such things of any magician, astrologer, or Chaldean. 11*It is* a difficult thing that the king requests, and there is no other who can tell it to the king except the gods, whose dwelling is not with flesh."

12For this reason the king was angry and very furious, and gave the command to destroy all the wise *men* of Babylon. 13So the decree went out, and they began killing the wise *men;* and they sought Daniel and his companions, to kill *them.*

14Then with counsel and wisdom Daniel answered Arioch, the captain of the king's guard, who had gone out to kill the wise *men* of Babylon; 15he answered and said to Arioch the king's captain, "Why is the decree from the king so urgent?" Then Arioch made the decision known to Daniel.

16So Daniel went in and asked the king to give him time, that he might tell the king the interpretation. 17Then Daniel went to his house, and made the decision known to Hananiah, Mishael, and Azariah, his companions, 18that they might seek mercies from the God of heaven concerning this secret, so that Daniel and his companions might not perish with the rest of the wise *men* of Babylon. 19Then the secret was revealed to Daniel in a night vision. So Daniel blessed the God of heaven.

20Daniel answered and said:

> "Blessed be the name of God forever and
>   ever,
>   For wisdom and might are His.
> 21 And He changes the times and the seasons;
>   He removes kings and raises up kings;
>   He gives wisdom to the wise
>   And knowledge to those who have
>   understanding.
> 22 He reveals deep and secret things;
>   He knows what *is* in the darkness,
>   And light dwells with Him.
>
> 23 "I thank You and praise You,
>   O God of my fathers;
>   You have given me wisdom and might,
>   And have now made known to me what we
>   asked of You,
>   For You have made known to us the king's
>   demand."

24Therefore Daniel went to Arioch, whom the king had appointed to destroy the wise *men* of Babylon. He went and said thus to him: "Do not destroy the wise *men* of Babylon; take me before the king, and I will tell the king the interpretation."

25Then Arioch quickly brought Daniel before the king, and said thus to him, "I have found a man of the captives[d] of Judah, who will make known to the king the interpretation."

26The king answered and said to Daniel, whose name *was* Belteshazzar, "Are you able to make known to me the dream which I have seen, and its interpretation?"

27Daniel answered in the presence of the king, and said, "The secret which the king has demanded, the wise *men*, the astrologers, the magicians, and the soothsayers cannot declare to the king. 28But there is a God in heaven who reveals secrets, and He has made known to King Nebuchadnezzar what will be in the latter days. Your dream, and the visions of your head upon your bed, were these: 29As for you, O king, thoughts came *to* your *mind while* on your bed, *about* what would come to pass after this; and He who reveals secrets has made known to you what will be. 30But as for me, this secret has not been revealed to me because I have more wisdom than anyone living, but for *our* sakes who make known the interpretation to the king, and that you may know the thoughts of your heart.

31"You, O king, were watching; and behold, a great image! This great image, whose splendor *was* excellent, stood before you; and its form *was* awesome. 32This image's head *was* of fine gold, its chest and arms of silver, its belly and thighs[e] of bronze, 33its legs of iron, its feet partly of iron and partly of clay.[f] 34You watched while a stone was cut out without hands, which struck the image on its feet of iron and clay, and broke them in pieces. 35Then the iron, the clay, the bronze, the silver, and the gold were crushed together, and became like chaff from the summer threshing floors; the wind carried them away so that no trace of them was found. And the stone that struck the image became a great mountain and filled the whole earth.

36"This *is* the dream. Now we will tell the interpretation of it before the king. 37You, O king, *are* a king of kings. For the God of heaven has given you a kingdom, power, strength, and glory; 38and wherever the children of men dwell, or the beasts of the field and the birds of the heaven, He has given *them* into your hand, and has made you ruler over them all—you *are* this head of gold. 39But after you shall arise another kingdom inferior to yours; then another, a third kingdom of bronze, which shall rule over all the earth. 40And the fourth kingdom shall be as strong as iron, inasmuch as iron breaks in pieces and shatters everything; and like iron that crushes, *that kingdom* will break in pieces and crush all the others. 41Whereas you saw the feet and toes, partly of potter's clay and partly of iron, the kingdom shall be divided; yet the strength of the iron shall be in it, just as you saw the iron mixed with ceramic clay. 42And *as* the toes of the feet *were* partly of iron and partly of clay, *so* the kingdom shall be partly strong and partly fragile. 43As you saw iron mixed with ceramic clay, they will mingle with the seed of men; but they will not adhere to one another, just as iron does not mix with clay. 44And in the days of these kings the God of heaven will set up a kingdom which shall never be destroyed; and the kingdom shall not be left

---

2:25 [d]Literally *of the sons of the captivity*   2:32 [e]Or *sides*
2:33 [f]Or *baked clay,* and so in verses 34, 35, and 42

to other people; it shall break in pieces and consume all these kingdoms, and it shall stand forever. 45Inasmuch as you saw that the stone was cut out of the mountain without hands, and that it broke in pieces the iron, the bronze, the clay, the silver, and the gold—the great God has made known to the king what will come to pass after this. The dream is certain, and its interpretation is sure."

46Then King Nebuchadnezzar fell on his face, prostrate before Daniel, and commanded that they should present an offering and incense to him. 47The king answered Daniel, and said, "Truly your God is the God of gods, the Lord of kings, and a revealer of secrets, since you could reveal this secret." 48Then the king promoted Daniel and gave him many great gifts; and he made him ruler over the whole province of Babylon, and chief administrator over all the wise men of Babylon. 49Also Daniel petitioned the king, and he set Shadrach, Meshach, and Abed-Nego over the affairs of the province of Babylon; but Daniel sat in the gateg of the king.

3 Nebuchadnezzar* the king made an image of gold, whose height was sixty cubits and its width six cubits. He set it up in the plain of Dura, in the province of Babylon. 2And King Nebuchadnezzar sent word to gather together the satraps, the administrators, the governors, the counselors, the treasurers, the judges, the magistrates, and all the officials of the provinces, to come to the dedication of the image which King Nebuchadnezzar had set up. 3So the satraps, the administrators, the governors, the counselors, the treasurers, the judges, the magistrates, and all the officials of the provinces gathered together for the dedication of the image that King Nebuchadnezzar had set up; and they stood before the image that Nebuchadnezzar had set up. 4Then a herald cried aloud: "To you it is commanded, O peoples, nations, and languages, 5that at the time you hear the sound of the horn, flute, harp, lyre, and psaltery, in symphony with all kinds of music, you shall fall down and worship the gold image that King Nebuchadnezzar has set up; 6and whoever does not fall down and worship shall be cast immediately into the midst of a burning fiery furnace."

7So at that time, when all the people heard the sound of the horn, flute, harp, and lyre, in symphony with all kinds of music, all the people, nations, and languages fell down and worshiped the gold image which King Nebuchadnezzar had set up.

8*Therefore at that time certain Chaldeans came forward and accused the Jews. 9They spoke and said to King Nebuchadnezzar, "O king, live forever! 10You, O king, have made a decree that everyone who hears the sound of the horn, flute, harp, lyre, and psaltery, in symphony with all kinds of music, shall fall down and worship the gold image; 11and whoever does not fall down and worship shall be cast into the midst of a burning fiery furnace. 12There are certain Jews whom you have set over the affairs of the province of Babylon: Shadrach, Meshach, and Abed-Nego; these men, O king, have not paid due regard to you.

CHAPTER 3
3:1–7 This event involves three kinds of people, all of whom are still in our world.
   Conformers. Nebuchadnezzar was not content to be the "head of gold" (2:38); he wanted to be represented by a whole image of gold! The people were happy to conform to his desires as long as he spared their lives and gave them what they needed.

3:8–12 Informers. These were some of the Chaldeans whose lives Daniel and his friends had saved. Unsaved people do not always appreciate what believers do for them. These men wanted only to win the king's favor and get the high offices he had given to the three Jews (2:49).

2:49 gThat is, the king's court

3:13–30 *Transformers* (Rom. 12:1–2). The three men did not know for sure that God would deliver them; but even if He did not, they would still obey the Lord and not worship the king and his idol. Were they trusting Isaiah 41:10 and 43:2? The fire brought them two blessings: the Lord came and walked with them, and they were set free from their bonds. Fellowship and freedom are often found in the midst of the furnace if you are committed to the Lord.

They do not serve your gods or worship the gold image which you have set up."

13*Then Nebuchadnezzar, in rage and fury, gave the command to bring Shadrach, Meshach, and Abed-Nego. So they brought these men before the king. 14Nebuchadnezzar spoke, saying to them, "*Is it* true, Shadrach, Meshach, and Abed-Nego, *that* you do not serve my gods or worship the gold image which I have set up? 15Now if you are ready at the time you hear the sound of the horn, flute, harp, lyre, *and* psaltery, in symphony with all kinds of music, and you fall down and worship the image which I have made, *good!* But if you do not worship, you shall be cast immediately into the midst of a burning fiery furnace. And who *is* the god who will deliver you from my hands?"

16Shadrach, Meshach, and Abed-Nego answered and said to the king, "O Nebuchadnezzar, we have no need to answer you in this matter. 17If that *is the case,* our God whom we serve is able to deliver us from the burning fiery furnace, and He will deliver *us* from your hand, O king. 18But if not, let it be known to you, O king, that we do not serve your gods, nor will we worship the gold image which you have set up."

19Then Nebuchadnezzar was full of fury, and the expression on his face changed toward Shadrach, Meshach, and Abed-Nego. He spoke and commanded that they heat the furnace seven times more than it was usually heated. 20And he commanded certain mighty men of valor who *were* in his army to bind Shadrach, Meshach, and Abed-Nego, *and* cast *them* into the burning fiery furnace. 21Then these men were bound in their coats, their trousers, their turbans, and their *other* garments, and were cast into the midst of the burning fiery furnace. 22Therefore, because the king's command was urgent, and the furnace exceedingly hot, the flame of the fire killed those men who took up Shadrach, Meshach, and Abed-Nego. 23And these three men, Shadrach, Meshach, and Abed-Nego, fell down bound into the midst of the burning fiery furnace.

24Then King Nebuchadnezzar was astonished; and he rose in haste *and* spoke, saying to his counselors, "Did we not cast three men bound into the midst of the fire?"

They answered and said to the king, "True, O king."

25"Look!" he answered, "I see four men loose, walking in the midst of the fire; and they are not hurt, and the form of the fourth is like the Son of God."*h*

26Then Nebuchadnezzar went near the mouth of the burning fiery furnace *and* spoke, saying, "Shadrach, Meshach, and Abed-Nego, servants of the Most High God, come out, and come *here.*" Then Shadrach, Meshach, and Abed-Nego came from the midst of the fire. 27And the satraps, administrators, governors, and the king's counselors gathered together, and they saw these men on whose bodies the fire had no power; the hair of their head was not singed nor were their garments affected, and the smell of fire was not on them.

28Nebuchadnezzar spoke, saying, "Blessed be the God of Shadrach, Meshach, and Abed-Nego, who sent His Angel*i* and delivered His servants who trusted in Him, and they have frustrated the

---

3:25 *h*Or *a son of the gods*   3:28 *i*Or *angel*

king's word, and yielded their bodies, that they should not serve nor worship any god except their own God! 29Therefore I make a decree that any people, nation, or language which speaks anything amiss against the God of Shadrach, Meshach, and Abed-Nego shall be cut in pieces, and their houses shall be made an ash heap; because there is no other God who can deliver like this."

30Then the king promoted Shadrach, Meshach, and Abed-Nego in the province of Babylon.

4 Nebuchadnezzar the king,

> To all peoples, nations, and languages that
> dwell in all the earth:
>
> Peace be multiplied to you.

2 I thought it good to declare the signs and
wonders that the Most High God has
worked for me.

3 How great *are* His signs,
And how mighty His wonders!
His kingdom *is* an everlasting kingdom,
And His dominion *is* from generation to
generation.

4 *I, Nebuchadnezzar, was at rest in my
house, and flourishing in my palace. 5I saw
a dream which made me afraid, and the
thoughts on my bed and the visions of my
head troubled me. 6Therefore I issued a
decree to bring in all the wise *men* of
Babylon before me, that they might make
known to me the interpretation of the
dream. 7Then the magicians, the
astrologers, the Chaldeans, and the
soothsayers came in, and I told them the
dream; but they did not make known to me
its interpretation. 8But at last Daniel came
before me (his name *is* Belteshazzar,
according to the name of my god; in him *is*
the Spirit of the Holy God), and I told the
dream before him, *saying:* 9"Belteshazzar,
chief of the magicians, because I know that
the Spirit of the Holy God *is* in you, and
no secret troubles you, explain to me the
visions of my dream that I have seen, and
its interpretation.

10 "These *were* the visions of my head *while*
on my bed:

> I was looking, and behold,
> A tree in the midst of the earth,
> And its height was great.
11 The tree grew and became strong;
> Its height reached to the heavens,
> And it could be seen to the ends of all the
> earth.
12 Its leaves *were* lovely,
> Its fruit abundant,
> And in it *was* food for all.
> The beasts of the field found shade under
> it,
> The birds of the heavens dwelt in its
> branches,
> And all flesh was fed from it.

13 "I saw in the visions of my head *while* on
my bed, and there was a watcher, a holy

CHAPTER 4

4:4–9 Nebuchadnezzar's second dream accomplished three things: it warned the king that his pride would lead to judgment (v. 37; Prov. 16:18); it exposed the incompetence of his magicians (vv. 6–7); and it gave Daniel another opportunity to glorify the God of heaven.

It was not easy for Daniel to give the king the message of the dream. Nebuchadnezzar had a short temper, and he might have ordered Daniel to be killed. Nathan had a similar situation when he had to confront David with his sins (2 Sam. 12). But when your ways please the Lord, you do not worry about your enemies (Prov. 16:7).

one, coming down from heaven. [14]He cried aloud and said thus:

'Chop down the tree and cut off its branches,
Strip off its leaves and scatter its fruit.
Let the beasts get out from under it,
And the birds from its branches.
[15] Nevertheless leave the stump and roots in
    the earth,
Bound with a band of iron and bronze,
In the tender grass of the field.
Let it be wet with the dew of heaven,
And *let* him graze with the beasts
On the grass of the earth.
[16] Let his heart be changed from *that of* a man,
Let him be given the heart of a beast,
And let seven times[j] pass over him.

[17] 'This decision *is* by the decree of the
    watchers,
And the sentence by the word of the holy
    ones,
In order that the living may know
That the Most High rules in the kingdom
    of men,
Gives it to whomever He will,
And sets over it the lowest of men.'

[18] "This dream I, King Nebuchadnezzar, have seen. Now you, Belteshazzar, declare its interpretation, since all the wise *men* of my kingdom are not able to make known to me the interpretation; but you *are* able, for the Spirit of the Holy God *is* in you."

[19] Then Daniel, whose name was Belteshazzar, was astonished for a time, and his thoughts troubled him. *So* the king spoke, and said, "Belteshazzar, do not let the dream or its interpretation trouble you." Belteshazzar answered and said, "My lord, *may* the dream concern those who hate you, and its interpretation concern your enemies!

[20] "The tree that you saw, which grew and became strong, whose height reached to the heavens and which *could be seen* by all the earth, [21]whose leaves *were* lovely and its fruit abundant, in which *was* food for all, under which the beasts of the field dwelt, and in whose branches the birds of the heaven had their home— [22]it *is* you, O king, who have grown and become strong; for your greatness has grown and reaches to the heavens, and your dominion to the end of the earth.

[23] "And inasmuch as the king saw a watcher, a holy one, coming down from heaven and saying, 'Chop down the tree and destroy it, but leave its stump and roots in the earth, *bound* with a band of iron and bronze in the tender grass of the field; let it be wet with the dew of heaven, and let him graze with the beasts of the field, till seven times pass over him'; [24]this is the interpretation, O king, and this is the decree of the Most High, which has come upon my lord the king: [25]They shall drive you from men, your

4:16 [j]Possibly *seven years,* and so in verses 23, 25, and 32

dwelling shall be with the beasts of the field, and they shall make you eat grass like oxen. They shall wet you with the dew of heaven, and seven times shall pass over you, till you know that the Most High rules in the kingdom of men, and gives it to whomever He chooses.

26 "And inasmuch as they gave the command to leave the stump *and* roots of the tree, your kingdom shall be assured to you, after you come to know that Heaven rules. 27Therefore, O king, let my advice be acceptable to you; break off your sins by *being* righteous, and your iniquities by showing mercy to *the* poor. Perhaps there may be a lengthening of your prosperity."

28 *All *this* came upon King Nebuchadnezzar. 29At the end of the twelve months he was walking about the royal palace of Babylon. 30The king spoke, saying, "Is not this great Babylon, that I have built for a royal dwelling by my mighty power and for the honor of my majesty?"

31 While the word *was still* in the king's mouth, a voice fell from heaven: "King Nebuchadnezzar, to you it is spoken: the kingdom has departed from you! 32And they shall drive you from men, and your dwelling *shall be* with the beasts of the field. They shall make you eat grass like oxen; and seven times shall pass over you, until you know that the Most High rules in the kingdom of men, and gives it to whomever He chooses."

33 That very hour the word was fulfilled concerning Nebuchadnezzar; he was driven from men and ate grass like oxen; his body was wet with the dew of heaven till his hair had grown like eagles' *feathers* and his nails like birds' *claws*.

34 And at the end of the time*k* I, Nebuchadnezzar, lifted my eyes to heaven, and my understanding returned to me; and I blessed the Most High and praised and honored Him who lives forever:

For His dominion *is* an everlasting
    dominion,
And His kingdom *is* from generation to
    generation.
35 All the inhabitants of the earth *are* reputed
    as nothing;
He does according to His will in the army
    of heaven
And *among* the inhabitants of the earth.
No one can restrain His hand
Or say to Him, "What have You done?"

36 At the same time my reason returned to me, and for the glory of my kingdom, my honor and splendor returned to me. My counselors and nobles resorted to me, I was restored to my kingdom, and excellent majesty was added to me. 37Now I, Nebuchadnezzar, praise and extol and honor the King of heaven, all of whose

4:28–36 God gave the king a year's opportunity for repentance (v. 29), but he continued in his sins. Then God humbled him. The king learned his lesson, and when he was restored, he gave glory to God.

No matter what position we have in life, God gave it to us, and He is sovereign. When man tries to take the place of God, he becomes like a beast. God still resists the proud but gives grace to the humble (Prov. 3:34).

4:34 *k*Literally *days*

works *are* truth, and His ways justice. And those who walk in pride He is able to put down.

CHAPTER 5

5:1–4 The events in this chapter occurred several years after those recorded in chapter 4. Belshazzar was coregent with his father Nabonidus, which explains why Daniel was named *third* ruler in the kingdom (v. 29). The king may have been new, but the sin was old: pride and self-confidence. At that very hour, Darius was besieging the city; but so certain was Belshazzar of his defenses that he ridiculed Jehovah and praised the false gods of Babylon. It was Proverbs 16:7 over again.

5 Belshazzar* the king made a great feast for a thousand of his lords, and drank wine in the presence of the thousand. 2While he tasted the wine, Belshazzar gave the command to bring the gold and silver vessels which his father Nebuchadnezzar had taken from the temple which *had been* in Jerusalem, that the king and his lords, his wives, and his concubines might drink from them. 3Then they brought the gold vessels that had been taken from the temple of the house of God which *had been* in Jerusalem; and the king and his lords, his wives, and his concubines drank from them. 4They drank wine, and praised the gods of gold and silver, bronze and iron, wood and stone.

5In the same hour the fingers of a man's hand appeared and wrote opposite the lampstand on the plaster of the wall of the king's palace; and the king saw the part of the hand that wrote. 6Then the king's countenance changed, and his thoughts troubled him, so that the joints of his hips were loosened and his knees knocked against each other. 7The king cried aloud to bring in the astrologers, the Chaldeans, and the soothsayers. The king spoke, saying to the wise *men* of Babylon, "Whoever reads this writing, and tells me its interpretation, shall be clothed with purple and *have* a chain of gold around his neck; and he shall be the third ruler in the kingdom." 8Now all the king's wise *men* came, but they could not read the writing, or make known to the king its interpretation. 9Then King Belshazzar was greatly troubled, his countenance was changed, and his lords were astonished.

10The queen, because of the words of the king and his lords, came to the banquet hall. The queen spoke, saying, "O king, live forever! Do not let your thoughts trouble you, nor let your countenance change. 11There is a man in your kingdom in whom *is* the Spirit of the Holy God. And in the days of your father, light and understanding and wisdom, like the wisdom of the gods, were found in him; and King Nebuchadnezzar your father—your father the king—made him chief of the magicians, astrologers, Chaldeans, *and* soothsayers. 12Inasmuch as an excellent spirit, knowledge, understanding, interpreting dreams, solving riddles, and explaining enigmas*l* were found in this Daniel, whom the king named Belteshazzar, now let Daniel be called, and he will give the interpretation."

13Then Daniel was brought in before the king. The king spoke, and said to Daniel, "*Are* you that Daniel who is one of the captives*m* from Judah, whom my father the king brought from Judah? 14I have heard of you, that the Spirit of God *is* in you, and *that* light and understanding and excellent wisdom are found in you. 15Now the wise *men*, the astrologers, have been brought in before me, that they should read this writing and make known to me its interpretation, but they could not give the interpretation of the thing. 16And I have heard of you, that you can give interpretations and explain enigmas. Now if you can read the

---

5:12 *l*Literally *untying knots,* and so in verse 16
5:13 *m*Literally *of the sons of the captivity*

writing and make known to me its interpretation, you shall be clothed with purple and *have* a chain of gold around your neck, and shall be the third ruler in the kingdom."

17Then Daniel answered, and said before the king, "Let your gifts be for yourself, and give your rewards to another; yet I will read the writing to the king, and make known to him the interpretation. 18O king, the Most High God gave Nebuchadnezzar your father a kingdom and majesty, glory and honor. 19And because of the majesty that He gave him, all peoples, nations, and languages trembled and feared before him. Whomever he wished, he executed; whomever he wished, he kept alive; whomever he wished, he set up; and whomever he wished, he put down. 20But when his heart was lifted up, and his spirit was hardened in pride, he was deposed from his kingly throne, and they took his glory from him. 21Then he was driven from the sons of men, his heart was made like the beasts, and his dwelling *was* with the wild donkeys. They fed him with grass like oxen, and his body was wet with the dew of heaven, till he knew that the Most High God rules in the kingdom of men, and appoints over it whomever He chooses.

22"But you his son, Belshazzar, have not humbled your heart, although you knew all this. 23And you have lifted yourself up against the Lord of heaven. They have brought the vessels of His house before you, and you and your lords, your wives and your concubines, have drunk wine from them. And you have praised the gods of silver and gold, bronze and iron, wood and stone, which do not see or hear or know; and the God who *holds* your breath in His hand and owns all your ways, you have not glorified. 24Then the fingers[n] of the hand were sent from Him, and this writing was written.

25"And this is the inscription that was written:

MENE,[o] MENE, TEKEL,[p] UPHARSIN.[q]

26This *is* the interpretation of *each* word. MENE: God has numbered your kingdom, and finished it; 27TEKEL: You have been weighed in the balances, and found wanting; 28PERES: Your kingdom has been divided, and given to the Medes and Persians."[r] 29Then Belshazzar gave the command, and they clothed Daniel with purple and *put* a chain of gold around his neck, and made a proclamation concerning him that he should be the third ruler in the kingdom.

30*That very night Belshazzar, king of the Chaldeans, was slain. 31And Darius the Mede received the kingdom, *being* about sixty-two years old.

6 It* pleased Darius to set over the kingdom one hundred and twenty satraps, to be over the whole kingdom; 2and over these, three governors, of whom Daniel *was* one, that the satraps might give account to them, so that the king would suffer no loss. 3Then this Daniel distinguished himself above the governors and satraps, because an excellent spirit *was* in him; and the king gave thought to setting him over the whole realm.

5:30 God gave Nebuchadnezzar a year to repent, but He judged Belshazzar *that very night.* The king had not learned from those who had gone before, and Daniel told him so (vv. 17–23). But it was too late!

The self-confident sinner had better beware (Luke 11:16–21), and so should a proud world that says, "peace and safety!" (1 Thess. 5:1–11). In Noah's day and in Abraham's day, judgment came when people least expected it (Luke 17:26–32). It will happen again.

CHAPTER 6

6:1–5 Daniel faced three crises, and the Lord gave him victory in each one.

The work crisis. When the other officers heard that Daniel might be promoted, they were envious and wanted to get rid of him. The unbelieving world does not want a believer in charge, even if he or she is gifted and efficient. The light always reveals what happens in the darkness (Eph. 5:8–13).

5:24 [n]Literally *palm*   5:25 [o]Literally *a mina (50 shekels)* from the verb "to number"   [p]Literally *a shekel* from the verb "to weigh"   [q]Literally *and half-shekels* from the verb "to divide"   5:28 [r]Aramaic *Paras,* consonant with *Peres*

6:6–17 The prayer crisis. The officers lied when they used the word *all,* for that gave the king the idea that Daniel agreed with them. But no laws or threats could keep Daniel from his times of prayer. Is prayer to you a matter of life and death? It was to Daniel!

6:18–28 The faith crisis. God did not keep Daniel *out of* the den; He protected him *in* the den. Why? Because Daniel had faith in the Lord (v. 23; Heb. 11:33) and was faithful to the Lord (Ps. 18:17–24). Perhaps Daniel meditated on Psalm 37:1–15 and Proverbs 11:8.
When the lions are about to attack, trust the Lord and claim His promises.

⁴So the governors and satraps sought to find *some* charge against Daniel concerning the kingdom; but they could find no charge or fault, because he *was* faithful; nor was there any error or fault found in him. ⁵Then these men said, "We shall not find any charge against this Daniel unless we find *it* against him concerning the law of his God."

⁶*So these governors and satraps thronged before the king, and said thus to him: "King Darius, live forever! ⁷All the governors of the kingdom, the administrators and satraps, the counselors and advisors, have consulted together to establish a royal statute and to make a firm decree, that whoever petitions any god or man for thirty days, except you, O king, shall be cast into the den of lions. ⁸Now, O king, establish the decree and sign the writing, so that it cannot be changed, according to the law of the Medes and Persians, which does not alter." ⁹Therefore King Darius signed the written decree.

¹⁰Now when Daniel knew that the writing was signed, he went home. And in his upper room, with his windows open toward Jerusalem, he knelt down on his knees three times that day, and prayed and gave thanks before his God, as was his custom since early days.

¹¹Then these men assembled and found Daniel praying and making supplication before his God. ¹²And they went before the king, and spoke concerning the king's decree: "Have you not signed a decree that every man who petitions any god or man within thirty days, except you, O king, shall be cast into the den of lions?"
The king answered and said, "The thing *is* true, according to the law of the Medes and Persians, which does not alter."

¹³So they answered and said before the king, "That Daniel, who is one of the captivesˢ from Judah, does not show due regard for you, O king, or for the decree that you have signed, but makes his petition three times a day."

¹⁴And the king, when he heard *these* words, was greatly displeased with himself, and set *his* heart on Daniel to deliver him; and he labored till the going down of the sun to deliver him. ¹⁵Then these men approached the king, and said to the king, "Know, O king, that *it is* the law of the Medes and Persians that no decree or statute which the king establishes may be changed."

¹⁶So the king gave the command, and they brought Daniel and cast *him* into the den of lions. *But* the king spoke, saying to Daniel, "Your God, whom you serve continually, He will deliver you." ¹⁷Then a stone was brought and laid on the mouth of the den, and the king sealed it with his own signet ring and with the signets of his lords, that the purpose concerning Daniel might not be changed.

¹⁸*Now the king went to his palace and spent the night fasting; and no musiciansᵗ were brought before him. Also his sleep went from him. ¹⁹Then the king arose very early in the morning and went in haste to the den of lions. ²⁰And when he came to the den, he cried out with a lamenting voice to Daniel. The king spoke, saying to Daniel, "Daniel, servant of the living God, has your God, whom you serve continually, been able to deliver you from the lions?"

6:13 ˢLiterally *of the sons of the captivity* 6:18 ᵗExact meaning unknown

²¹Then Daniel said to the king, "O king, live forever! ²²My God sent His angel and shut the lions' mouths, so that they have not hurt me, because I was found innocent before Him; and also, O king, I have done no wrong before you."

²³Now the king was exceedingly glad for him, and commanded that they should take Daniel up out of the den. So Daniel was taken up out of the den, and no injury whatever was found on him, because he believed in his God.

²⁴And the king gave the command, and they brought those men who had accused Daniel, and they cast *them* into the den of lions—them, their children, and their wives; and the lions overpowered them, and broke all their bones in pieces before they ever came to the bottom of the den.

²⁵Then King Darius wrote:

To all peoples, nations, and languages that dwell in all the earth:

Peace be multiplied to you.

26   I make a decree that in every dominion of my kingdom *men must* tremble and fear before the God of Daniel.

For He *is* the living God,
And steadfast forever;
His kingdom *is the one* which shall not be destroyed,
And His dominion *shall endure* to the end.
27   He delivers and rescues,
And He works signs and wonders
In heaven and on earth,
Who has delivered Daniel from the power of the lions.

²⁸So this Daniel prospered in the reign of Darius and in the reign of Cyrus the Persian.

7 In* the first year of Belshazzar king of Babylon, Daniel had a dream and visions of his head *while* on his bed. Then he wrote down the dream, telling the main facts.ᵘ

²Daniel spoke, saying, "I saw in my vision by night, and behold, the four winds of heaven were stirring up the Great Sea. ³And four great beasts came up from the sea, each different from the other. ⁴The first *was* like a lion, and had eagle's wings. I watched till its wings were plucked off; and it was lifted up from the earth and made to stand on two feet like a man, and a man's heart was given to it.

⁵"And suddenly another beast, a second, like a

7:1 ᵘLiterally *the head* (or *chief*) *of the words*

CHAPTER 7

7:1–8 *A vision of world history.* Man views human kingdoms as valuable metals (chap. 2), but God sees them as vicious animals that fight and devour each other. Human history will culminate in a worldwide kingdom under a satanic world ruler (Antichrist) who will defy God and eventually be defeated by God's Son.

Daniel's Vision—Daniel's vision in chapter 7 parallels what Nebuchadnezzar saw in his dream (chap. 2). The lion (v. 4) is Babylon, the head of gold. The bear (v. 5) is Media-Persia, the arms and chest of silver. The leopard (v. 6) is Greece, the thigh of brass. The dreadful beast (v. 7) is Rome, the legs of iron. The little horn (v. 8) represents Antichrist and his kingdom, the toes of iron and clay. The Ancient of Days on the throne (vv. 9–14) parallels the smiting stone.

Bible Prophecy—How should believers respond when they get an understanding of God's prophetic Word? Daniel was affected physically by his visions and was left weak and prostrate (7:15, 28; 8:17–18, 27; 10:8). Those who are proud of a knowledge of Bible prophecy may have learned only what it *says* and not what it *means*. Revelation always brings responsibility with it. If we really believe these things, we will obey what God tells us to do.

bear. It was raised up on one side, and *had* three ribs in its mouth between its teeth. And they said thus to it: 'Arise, devour much flesh!'

⁶"After this I looked, and there was another, like a leopard, which had on its back four wings of a bird. The beast also had four heads, and dominion was given to it.

⁷"After this I saw in the night visions, and behold, a fourth beast, dreadful and terrible, exceedingly strong. It had huge iron teeth; it was devouring, breaking in pieces, and trampling the residue with its feet. It *was* different from all the beasts that *were* before it, and it had ten horns. ⁸I was considering the horns, and there was another horn, a little one, coming up among them, before whom three of the first horns were plucked out by the roots. And there, in this horn, *were* eyes like the eyes of a man, and a mouth speaking pompous words.

7:9–14 *A vision of heaven.* While the beasts are fighting on earth, God is holding court in heaven, and everything is under His control. Jesus Christ will one day establish a righteous kingdom that nobody will overthrow.

9 *"I watched till thrones were put in place,
  And the Ancient of Days was seated;
  His garment *was* white as snow,
  And the hair of His head *was* like pure wool.
  His throne *was* a fiery flame,
  Its wheels a burning fire;
10 A fiery stream issued
  And came forth from before Him.
  A thousand thousands ministered to Him;
  Ten thousand times ten thousand stood
   before Him.
  The court° was seated,
  And the books were opened.

11"I watched then because of the sound of the pompous words which the horn was speaking; I watched till the beast was slain, and its body destroyed and given to the burning flame. ¹²As for the rest of the beasts, they had their dominion taken away, yet their lives were prolonged for a season and a time.

13 "I was watching in the night visions,
  And behold, *One* like the Son of Man,
  Coming with the clouds of heaven!
  He came to the Ancient of Days,
  And they brought Him near before Him.
14 Then to Him was given dominion and glory
   and a kingdom,
  That all peoples, nations, and languages
   should serve Him.
  His dominion *is* an everlasting dominion,
  Which shall not pass away,
  And His kingdom *the one*
  Which shall not be destroyed.

15*"I, Daniel, was grieved in my spirit within *my* body, and the visions of my head troubled me. ¹⁶I came near to one of those who stood by, and asked him the truth of all this. So he told me and made known to me the interpretation of these things: ¹⁷'Those great beasts, which are four, *are* four kings° *which* arise out of the earth. ¹⁸But the saints of the Most High shall receive the kingdom, and possess the kingdom forever, even forever and ever.'

19"Then I wished to know the truth about the fourth beast, which was different from all the oth-

7:15–28 *A vision of saints on earth.* These "saints" are believers during the end times, just before the Lord returns to set up His kingdom. But what Daniel says about them has spiritual application to believers today. They are involved in a war (v. 21) and suffer persecution (v. 25), but they will receive the kingdom (v. 18) and reign with Christ (v. 27). When the course of world history depresses you, look at events from heaven's point of view.

7:10 °Or *judgment*   7:17 °Representing their kingdoms (compare verse 23)

ers, exceedingly dreadful, *with* its teeth of iron and its nails of bronze, *which* devoured, broke in pieces, and trampled the residue with its feet; 20and the ten horns that *were* on its head, and the other *horn* which came up, before which three fell, namely, that horn which had eyes and a mouth which spoke pompous words, whose appearance *was* greater than his fellows.

21"I was watching; and the same horn was making war against the saints, and prevailing against them, 22until the Ancient of Days came, and a judgment was made *in favor* of the saints of the Most High, and the time came for the saints to possess the kingdom.

23"Thus he said:

'The fourth beast shall be
A fourth kingdom on earth,
Which shall be different from all *other* kingdoms,
And shall devour the whole earth,
Trample it and break it in pieces.
24 The ten horns *are* ten kings
Who shall arise from this kingdom.
And another shall rise after them;
He shall be different from the first *ones,*
And shall subdue three kings.
25 He shall speak *pompous* words against the Most High,
Shall persecutex the saints of the Most High,
And shall intend to change times and law.
Then *the saints* shall be given into his hand
For a time and times and half a time.

26 'But the court shall be seated,
And they shall take away his dominion,
To consume and destroy *it* forever.
27 Then the kingdom and dominion,
And the greatness of the kingdoms under the whole heaven,
Shall be given to the people, the saints of the Most High.
His kingdom *is* an everlasting kingdom,
And all dominions shall serve and obey Him.'

28"This *is* the end of the account.y As for me, Daniel, my thoughts greatly troubled me, and my countenance changed; but I kept the matter in my heart."

8 In the third year of the reign of King Belshazzar a vision appeared *to* me—to me, Daniel—after the one that appeared to me the first time. 2*I saw in the vision, and it so happened while I was looking, that I *was* in Shushan, the citadel, which *is* in the province of Elam; and I saw in the vision that I was by the River Ulai. 3Then I lifted my eyes and saw, and there, standing beside the river, was a ram which had two horns, and the two horns *were* high; but one *was* higher than the other, and the higher *one* came up last. 4I saw the ram pushing westward, northward, and southward, so that no animal could withstand him; nor *was there any* that could deliver from his hand, but he did according to his will and became great.

5*And as I was considering, suddenly a male

CHAPTER 8

8:2–4 Daniel saw himself in the Persian capital, for Persia would be the next world power after Babylon. In this vision, God pictured Persia as a ram and Greece (the next power) as a male goat (vv. 19–22). We have moved from wild beasts to beasts that have been domesticated.

8:5–26 The "notable horn" (v. 5) is Alexander the Great, who conquered many nations, including Persia, and built a great kingdom. After his death, his kingdom was divided into four parts by four of his generals (v. 8). The "little horn" (vv. 9–14) represents the evil general, Antiochus Epiphanes, who invaded Palestine, defiled the Jewish temple, and put the Jews under bondage. He is a picture of the world ruler to come, the Antichrist (vv. 15–26).

goat came from the west, across the surface of the whole earth, without touching the ground; and the goat *had* a notable horn between his eyes. 6Then he came to the ram that had two horns, which I had seen standing beside the river, and ran at him with furious power. 7And I saw him confronting the ram; he was moved with rage against him, attacked the ram, and broke his two horns. There was no power in the ram to withstand him, but he cast him down to the ground and trampled him; and there was no one that could deliver the ram from his hand.

8Therefore the male goat grew very great; but when he became strong, the large horn was broken, and in place of it four notable ones came up toward the four winds of heaven. 9And out of one of them came a little horn which grew exceedingly great toward the south, toward the east, and toward the Glorious *Land.* 10And it grew up to the host of heaven; and it cast down *some* of the host and *some* of the stars to the ground, and trampled them. 11He even exalted *himself* as high as the Prince of the host; and by him the daily *sacrifices* were taken away, and the place of His sanctuary was cast down. 12Because of transgression, an army was given over *to the horn* to oppose the daily *sacrifices;* and he cast truth down to the ground. He did *all this* and prospered.

13Then I heard a holy one speaking; and *another* holy one said to that certain *one* who was speaking, "How long *will* the vision *be, concerning* the daily *sacrifices* and the transgression of desolation, the giving of both the sanctuary and the host to be trampled underfoot?"

14And he said to me, "For two thousand three hundred days;z then the sanctuary shall be cleansed."

15Then it happened, when I, Daniel, had seen the vision and was seeking the meaning, that suddenly there stood before me one having the appearance of a man. 16And I heard a man's voice between *the banks of* the Ulai, who called, and said, "Gabriel, make this *man* understand the vision." 17So he came near where I stood, and when he came I was afraid and fell on my face; but he said to me, "Understand, son of man, that the vision *refers* to the time of the end."

18Now, as he was speaking with me, I was in a deep sleep with my face to the ground; but he touched me, and stood me upright. 19And he said, "Look, I am making known to you what shall happen in the latter time of the indignation; for at the appointed time the end *shall be.* 20The ram which you saw, having the two horns—*they are* the kings of Media and Persia. 21And the male goat *is* the kingdoma of Greece. The large horn that *is* between its eyes *is* the first king. 22As for the broken *horn* and the four that stood up in its place, four kingdoms shall arise out of that nation, but not with its power.

23 "And in the latter time of their kingdom,
    When the transgressors have reached their
        fullness,
    A king shall arise,
    Having fierce features,
    Who understands sinister schemes.

8:14 zLiterally *evening-mornings*   8:21 aLiterally *king,* representing his kingdom (compare 7:17, 23)

24 His power shall be mighty, but not by his
    own power;
He shall destroy fearfully,
And shall prosper and thrive;
He shall destroy the mighty, and *also* the
    holy people.

25 "Through his cunning
He shall cause deceit to prosper under his
    rule;[b]
And he shall exalt *himself* in his heart.
He shall destroy many in *their* prosperity.
He shall even rise against the Prince of
    princes;
But he shall be broken without *human*
    means.[c]

26 "And the vision of the evenings and
    mornings
Which was told is true;
Therefore seal up the vision,
For *it refers* to many days *in the future."*

27*And I, Daniel, fainted and was sick for days;
afterward I arose and went about the king's business. I was astonished by the vision, but no one
understood it.

9 In* the first year of Darius the son of Ahasuerus, of the lineage of the Medes, who was
made king over the realm of the Chaldeans—
2in the first year of his reign I, Daniel, understood
by the books the number of the years *specified*
by the word of the LORD through Jeremiah the
prophet, that He would accomplish seventy years
in the desolations of Jerusalem.

3*Then I set my face toward the Lord God to
make request by prayer and supplications, with
fasting, sackcloth, and ashes. 4And I prayed to
the LORD my God, and made confession, and said,
"O Lord, great and awesome God, who keeps His
covenant and mercy with those who love Him,
and with those who keep His commandments,
5we have sinned and committed iniquity, we have
done wickedly and rebelled, even by departing
from Your precepts and Your judgments. 6Neither
have we heeded Your servants the prophets, who
spoke in Your name to our kings and our princes,
to our fathers and all the people of the land.
7O Lord, righteousness *belongs* to You, but to us
shame of face, as *it is* this day—to the men of
Judah, to the inhabitants of Jerusalem and all Israel, those near and those far off in all the countries to which You have driven them, because of
the unfaithfulness which they have committed
against You.

8:25 [b]Literally *hand* [c]Literally *hand*

8:27 Daniel was so overwhelmed by the
vision that he became ill and could not do
his work! He could never be the same again,
knowing what God had planned for his
people in the latter days. How does Bible
prophecy affect you?

CHAPTER 9

9:1, 2 Insight. Even though he received
visions from God and could interpret
dreams, Daniel still read the Scriptures and
sought to understand them. While pondering
Jeremiah 25, he understood that the seventy
years of Jewish captivity would soon end.
Not all world events have prophetic
significance, but God's people should keep
their eyes open.

9:3–19 *Intercession.* The Word of God and
prayer go together (Acts 6:4), as do prayer
and fasting (Acts 13:3). Compare this prayer
with the prayers in Nehemiah 9 and Ezra
9. Daniel emphasized the sinfulness of
himself and his people and the
righteousness of God, and he asked for
God's forgiveness. Note that he especially
prayed for Jerusalem. Had he read Jeremiah
29:10–14 and 30:10–24?

The Seventy Weeks—The seventy weeks are in three periods: seven weeks (49 years), sixty-
two weeks (434 years), and one week (7 years). The first period starts in 444 B.C. with the decree
allowing the Jews to return to their land and rebuild the city. The next sixty-two weeks (434 years)
take us up to the time of Christ (vv. 24, 26). The "missing" seventieth week is fulfilled in the end
times and parallels Revelation 6—19. The "prince who is to come" (v. 26) is the Antichrist, who will
make a covenant with the Jews to protect them for seven years. After three and one-half years, he
will break the covenant and usher in a terrible time of trouble for the world. That final seven-year
period climaxes with the return of Christ, the defeat of His enemies, and the establishment of His
kingdom on earth (Matt. 24:29–31; Rev. 19). The New Testament declares, "Known to God from
eternity are all His works" (Acts 15:18).

8"O Lord, to us *belongs* shame of face, to our kings, our princes, and our fathers, because we have sinned against You. 9To the Lord our God *belong* mercy and forgiveness, though we have rebelled against Him. 10We have not obeyed the voice of the LORD our God, to walk in His laws, which He set before us by His servants the prophets. 11Yes, all Israel has transgressed Your law, and has departed so as not to obey Your voice; therefore the curse and the oath written in the Law of Moses the servant of God have been poured out on us, because we have sinned against Him. 12And He has confirmed His words, which He spoke against us and against our judges who judged us, by bringing upon us a great disaster; for under the whole heaven such has never been done as what has been done to Jerusalem.

13"As *it is* written in the Law of Moses, all this disaster has come upon us; yet we have not made our prayer before the LORD our God, that we might turn from our iniquities and understand Your truth. 14Therefore the LORD has kept the disaster in mind, and brought it upon us; for the LORD our God *is* righteous in all the works which He does, though we have not obeyed His voice. 15And now, O Lord our God, who brought Your people out of the land of Egypt with a mighty hand, and made Yourself a name, as *it is* this day—we have sinned, we have done wickedly!

16"O Lord, according to all Your righteousness, I pray, let Your anger and Your fury be turned away from Your city Jerusalem, Your holy mountain; because for our sins, and for the iniquities of our fathers, Jerusalem and Your people *are* a reproach to all *those* around us. 17Now therefore, our God, hear the prayer of Your servant, and his supplications, and for the Lord's sake cause Your face to shine on Your sanctuary, which is desolate. 18O my God, incline Your ear and hear; open Your eyes and see our desolations, and the city which is called by Your name; for we do not present our supplications before You because of our righteous deeds, but because of Your great mercies. 19O Lord, hear! O Lord, forgive! O Lord, listen and act! Do not delay for Your own sake, my God, for Your city and Your people are called by Your name."

20*Now while I *was* speaking, praying, and confessing my sin and the sin of my people Israel, and presenting my supplication before the LORD my God for the holy mountain of my God, 21yes, while I *was* speaking in prayer, the man Gabriel, whom I had seen in the vision at the beginning, being caused to fly swiftly, reached me about the time of the evening offering. 22And he informed *me*, and talked with me, and said, "O Daniel, I have now come forth to give you skill to understand. 23At the beginning of your supplications the command went out, and I have come to tell *you*, for you *are* greatly beloved; therefore consider the matter, and understand the vision:

24 "Seventy weeks[d] are determined
    For your people and for your holy city,
    To finish the transgression,
    To make an end of[e] sins,

9:20–27 Instruction. God gave Daniel a preview of Jewish history. Jerusalem would be rebuilt and the temple restored. Messiah would come and die. An evil prince would break his covenant with the Jews and trigger desolation. But God would triumph, and Jerusalem would become truly a holy city. Men are free to make decisions and even rebel against God if they want to, but He will accomplish His purposes in the world. With confidence, you can pray, "Thy kingdom come!"

9:24 [d]Literally *sevens,* and so throughout the chapter
[e]Following Qere, Septuagint, Syriac, and Vulgate; Kethib and Theodotion read *To seal up.*

To make reconciliation for iniquity,
To bring in everlasting righteousness,
To seal up vision and prophecy,
And to anoint the Most Holy.

25 "Know therefore and understand,
   That from the going forth of the command
   To restore and build Jerusalem
   Until Messiah the Prince,
   There shall be seven weeks and sixty-two
      weeks;
   The street*ᶠ* shall be built again, and the
      wall,*ᵍ*
   Even in troublesome times.

26 "And after the sixty-two weeks
   Messiah shall be cut off, but not for Himself;
   And the people of the prince who is to come
   Shall destroy the city and the sanctuary.
   The end of it *shall be* with a flood,
   And till the end of the war desolations are
      determined.
27 Then he shall confirm a covenant with many
      for one week;
   But in the middle of the week
   He shall bring an end to sacrifice and
      offering.
   And on the wing of abominations shall be
      one who makes desolate,
   Even until the consummation, which is
      determined,
   Is poured out on the desolate."

10 In the third year of Cyrus king of Persia a
message was revealed to Daniel, whose
name was called Belteshazzar. The message *was*
true, but the appointed time *was* long;*ʰ* and he
understood the message, and had understanding
of the vision. 2*In those days I, Daniel, was mourning three full weeks. 3I ate no pleasant food, no
meat or wine came into my mouth, nor did I anoint
myself at all, till three whole weeks were fulfilled.
4Now on the twenty-fourth day of the first
month, as I was by the side of the great river,
that *is*, the Tigris,*ⁱ* 5I lifted my eyes and looked,
and behold, a certain man clothed in linen, whose
waist *was* girded with gold of Uphaz! 6His body
was like beryl, his face like the appearance of
lightning, his eyes like torches of fire, his arms
and feet like burnished bronze in color, and the
sound of his words like the voice of a multitude.
7And I, Daniel, alone saw the vision, for the men
who were with me did not see the vision; but a
great terror fell upon them, so that they fled to
hide themselves. 8Therefore I was left alone when
I saw this great vision, and no strength remained
in me; for my vigor was turned to frailty in me,
and I retained no strength. 9Yet I heard the sound
of his words; and while I heard the sound of his
words I was in a deep sleep on my face, with my
face to the ground.
10*Suddenly, a hand touched me, which made
me tremble on my knees and *on* the palms of my
hands. 11*And he said to me, "O Daniel, man
greatly beloved, understand the words that I
speak to you, and stand upright, for I have now
been sent to you." While he was speaking this
word to me, I stood trembling.

9:25 *ᶠOr open square ᵍOr moat* 10:1 *ʰOr and of great conflict*
10:4 *ⁱHebrew Hiddekel*

CHAPTER 10

10:2, 3, 8, 9 The Jewish exiles had returned
to the land and were rebuilding the temple
when Daniel had this experience. He had
been fasting for three weeks, and the vision
of the angel left him even more weakened.
When you pray for deeper experiences with
the Lord, expect to pay a price.

10:10, 16, 18, 19 *God touches us.* God's
touch awakened and aroused Daniel (v. 10),
enabled him to speak (v. 16), and gave him
strength (vv. 18–19). By His Word, God
gives us the peace and power that we need
(v. 19).

10:11, 12, 19 *God assures us.* Daniel was
a man "greatly beloved" by the Lord (vv.
11, 19). The Father loves us as He loves
His Son (John 17:23) and wants to share
His love with us (John 14:21–23). God also
said, "Fear not" (vv. 12, 19). You can rest
today in the love of God and His promise
that you need not be afraid.

10:12–14, 20 God instructs us. Why did it take so long for the angel to come to Daniel? Because of a spiritual battle in the heavenlies (vv. 12–13, 20; Eph. 6:10ff.).

When you pray, you become a part of spiritual warfare, so do not take lightly your times of prayer. The angel also instructed Daniel about the future of his people (v. 14), explained in chapters 11—12.

Daniel's companions did not see the vision or hear the voice, but in terror fled away. God still needs people like Daniel who see the glory of God, hear the Word of God, feel God's touch, and enter into the spiritual battle.

CHAPTER 11

11:2ff God revealed to Daniel a summary of what would happen to his people now that they were restored as a nation. They would not have an easy time of it! The chapter describes wars involving armies from the north (Syria) and south (Egypt) as well as from Greece (vv. 3–4). The words *forces [arms], army, anger,* and *intrigue* describe the course of history. Have things changed much in the world?

At verse 36, the angel shifts to the latter days and describes the program of Antichrist. Read 2 Thessalonians 2 and Revelation 13.

What should God's people do in such times of conflict and destruction? They should be strong in the Lord, carry out daring deeds of faith, and share the truth with others, despite persecution and possible death (vv. 32–33). Bad times challenge good people.

12*Then he said to me, "Do not fear, Daniel, for from the first day that you set your heart to understand, and to humble yourself before your God, your words were heard; and I have come because of your words. 13But the prince of the kingdom of Persia withstood me twenty-one days; and behold, Michael, one of the chief princes, came to help me, for I had been left alone there with the kings of Persia. 14Now I have come to make you understand what will happen to your people in the latter days, for the vision *refers* to *many* days yet *to come*."

15When he had spoken such words to me, I turned my face toward the ground and became speechless. 16And suddenly, *one* having the likeness of the sonsʲ of men touched my lips; then I opened my mouth and spoke, saying to him who stood before me, "My lord, because of the vision my sorrows have overwhelmed me, and I have retained no strength. 17For how can this servant of my lord talk with you, my lord? As for me, no strength remains in me now, nor is any breath left in me."

18Then again, *the one* having the likeness of a man touched me and strengthened me. 19And he said, "O man greatly beloved, fear not! Peace *be* to you; be strong, yes, be strong!"

So when he spoke to me I was strengthened, and said, "Let my lord speak, for you have strengthened me."

20Then he said, "Do you know why I have come to you? And now I must return to fight with the prince of Persia; and when I have gone forth, indeed the prince of Greece will come. 21But I will tell you what is noted in the Scripture of Truth. (No one upholds me against these, except Michael your prince.

11 "Also in the first year of Darius the Mede, I, *even* I, stood up to confirm and strengthen him.) 2*And now I will tell you the truth: Behold, three more kings will arise in Persia, and the fourth shall be far richer than *them* all; by his strength, through his riches, he shall stir up all against the realm of Greece. 3Then a mighty king shall arise, who shall rule with great dominion, and do according to his will. 4And when he has arisen, his kingdom shall be broken up and divided toward the four winds of heaven, but not among his posterity nor according to his dominion with which he ruled; for his kingdom shall be uprooted, even for others besides these.

5"Also the king of the South shall become strong, as well as *one* of his princes; and he shall gain power over him and have dominion. His dominion *shall be* a great dominion. 6And at the end of *some* years they shall join forces, for the daughter of the king of the South shall go to the king of the North to make an agreement; but she shall not retain the power of her authority,ᵏ and neither he nor his authorityˡ shall stand; but she shall be given up, with those who brought her, and with him who begot her, and with him who strengthened her in *those* times. 7But from a branch of her roots *one* shall arise in his place, who shall come with an army, enter the fortress of the king of the North, and deal with them and prevail.

10:16 ʲTheodotion and Vulgate read *the son;* Septuagint reads *a hand.*   11:6 ᵏLiterally *arm* ˡLiterally *arm*

8And he shall also carry their gods captive to Egypt, with their princes[m] *and* their precious articles of silver and gold; and he shall continue *more* years than the king of the North.

9"Also *the king of the North* shall come to the kingdom of the king of the South, but shall return to his own land. 10However his sons shall stir up strife, and assemble a multitude of great forces; and *one* shall certainly come and overwhelm and pass through; then he shall return to his fortress and stir up strife.

11"And the king of the South shall be moved with rage, and go out and fight with him, with the king of the North, who shall muster a great multitude; but the multitude shall be given into the hand of his *enemy.* 12When he has taken away the multitude, his heart will be lifted up; and he will cast down tens of thousands, but he will not prevail. 13For the king of the North will return and muster a multitude greater than the former, and shall certainly come at the end of some years with a great army and much equipment.

14"Now in those times many shall rise up against the king of the South. Also, violent men[n] of your people shall exalt themselves in fulfillment of the vision, but they shall fall. 15So the king of the North shall come and build a siege mound, and take a fortified city; and the forces[o] of the South shall not withstand *him.* Even his choice troops *shall have* no strength to resist. 16But he who comes against him shall do according to his own will, and no one shall stand against him. He shall stand in the Glorious Land with destruction in his power.[p]

17"He shall also set his face to enter with the strength of his whole kingdom, and upright ones[q] with him; thus shall he do. And he shall give him the daughter of women to destroy it; but she shall not stand *with him,* or be for him. 18After this he shall turn his face to the coastlands, and shall take many. But a ruler shall bring the reproach against them to an end; and with the reproach removed, he shall turn back on him. 19Then he shall turn his face toward the fortress of his own land; but he shall stumble and fall, and not be found.

20"There shall arise in his place one who imposes taxes *on* the glorious kingdom; but within a few days he shall be destroyed, but not in anger or in battle. 21And in his place shall arise a vile person, to whom they will not give the honor of royalty; but he shall come in peaceably, and seize the kingdom by intrigue. 22With the force[r] of a flood they shall be swept away from before him and be broken, and also the prince of the covenant. 23And after the league *is made* with him he shall act deceitfully, for he shall come up and become strong with a small *number of* people. 24He shall enter peaceably, even into the richest places of the province; and he shall do *what* his fathers have not done, nor his forefathers: he shall disperse among them the plunder, spoil, and riches; and he shall devise his plans against the strongholds, but *only* for a time.

25"He shall stir up his power and his courage against the king of the South with a great army. And the king of the South shall be stirred up to

---

11:8 [m]Or *molded images*   11:14 [n]Or *robbers,* literally *sons of breakage*   11:15 [o]Literally *arms*   11:16 [p]Literally *hand*   11:17 [q]Or *bring equitable terms*   11:22 [r]Literally *arms*

battle with a very great and mighty army; but he shall not stand, for they shall devise plans against him. 26Yes, those who eat of the portion of his delicacies shall destroy him; his army shall be swept away, and many shall fall down slain. 27Both these kings' hearts *shall be* bent on evil, and they shall speak lies at the same table; but it shall not prosper, for the end *will* still be at the appointed time. 28While returning to his land with great riches, his heart shall be *moved* against the holy covenant; so he shall do *damage* and return to his own land.

29"At the appointed time he shall return and go toward the south; but it shall not be like the former or the latter. 30For ships from Cyprus[s] shall come against him; therefore he shall be grieved, and return in rage against the holy covenant, and do *damage*.

"So he shall return and show regard for those who forsake the holy covenant. 31And forces[t] shall be mustered by him, and they shall defile the sanctuary fortress; then they shall take away the daily *sacrifices,* and place *there* the abomination of desolation. 32Those who do wickedly against the covenant he shall corrupt with flattery; but the people who know their God shall be strong, and carry out *great exploits.* 33And those of the people who understand shall instruct many; yet *for many* days they shall fall by sword and flame, by captivity and plundering. 34Now when they fall, they shall be aided with a little help; but many shall join with them by intrigue. 35And *some* of those of understanding shall fall, to refine them, purify *them,* and make *them* white, *until* the time of the end; because *it is* still for the appointed time.

36"Then the king shall do according to his own will: he shall exalt and magnify himself above every god, shall speak blasphemies against the God of gods, and shall prosper till the wrath has been accomplished; for what has been determined shall be done. 37He shall regard neither the God[u] of his fathers nor the desire of women, nor regard any god; for he shall exalt himself above *them* all. 38But in their place he shall honor a god of fortresses; and a god which his fathers did not know he shall honor with gold and silver, with precious stones and pleasant things. 39Thus he shall act against the strongest fortresses with a foreign god, which he shall acknowledge, *and* advance *its* glory; and he shall cause them to rule over many, and divide the land for gain.

40"At the time of the end the king of the South shall attack him; and the king of the North shall come against him like a whirlwind, with chariots, horsemen, and with many ships; and he shall enter the countries, overwhelm *them,* and pass through. 41He shall also enter the Glorious Land, and many *countries* shall be overthrown; but these shall escape from his hand: Edom, Moab, and the prominent people of Ammon. 42He shall stretch out his hand against the countries, and the land of Egypt shall not escape. 43He shall have power over the treasures of gold and silver, and over all the precious things of Egypt; also the Libyans and Ethiopians *shall follow* at his heels. 44But news from the east and the north shall trou-

---

11:30 [s]Hebrew *Kittim,* western lands, especially Cyprus
11:31 [t]Literally *arms* 11:37 [u]Or *gods*

ble him; therefore he shall go out with great fury to destroy and annihilate many. 45And he shall plant the tents of his palace between the seas and the glorious holy mountain; yet he shall come to his end, and no one will help him.

12 "At* that time Michael shall stand up,
        The great prince who stands *watch* over
             the sons of your people;
        And there shall be a time of trouble,
        Such as never was since there was a nation,
        Even to that time.
        And at that time your people shall be
             delivered,
        Every one who is found written in the book.
2   And many of those who sleep in the dust
             of the earth shall awake,
        Some to everlasting life,
        Some to shame *and* everlasting contempt.
3   Those who are wise shall shine
        Like the brightness of the firmament,
        And those who turn many to righteousness
        Like the stars forever and ever.

4"But you, Daniel, shut up the words, and seal the book until the time of the end; many shall run to and fro, and knowledge shall increase."

5Then I, Daniel, looked; and there stood two others, one on this riverbank and the other on that riverbank. 6And *one* said to the man clothed in linen, who *was* above the waters of the river, "How long shall the fulfillment of these wonders *be?*"

7Then I heard the man clothed in linen, who *was* above the waters of the river, when he held up his right hand and his left hand to heaven, and swore by Him who lives forever, that *it shall be* for a time, times, and half *a time;* and when the power of the holy people has been completely shattered, all these *things* shall be finished.

8Although I heard, I did not understand. Then I said, "My lord, what *shall be* the end of these *things?*"

9And he said, "Go *your way,* Daniel, for the words *are* closed up and sealed till the time of the end. 10Many shall be purified, made white, and refined, but the wicked shall do wickedly; and none of the wicked shall understand, but the wise shall understand.

11"And from the time *that* the daily *sacrifice* is taken away, and the abomination of desolation is set up, *there shall be* one thousand two hundred and ninety days. 12Blessed *is* he who waits, and comes to the one thousand three hundred and thirty-five days.

13"But you, go *your way* till the end; for you shall rest, and will arise to your inheritance at the end of the days."

CHAPTER 12

12:1ff Keep in mind that this prophecy has to do with the Jewish people in the end times. But it gives encouragement to all of God's people in every generation to know that God is in control and will accomplish His purposes in spite of the forces of evil.

God assures His servant that the living believers will be delivered (v. 1) and the ones who die will be resurrected to shine in glory (v. 2; Matt. 13:43). No matter what kind of affliction or tribulation God permits you to experience, He is still in control.

What, then, are your responsibilities? To seek to win others to the Savior (v. 3), to leave the hidden things with the Lord (vv. 8–9), to grow in holiness (v. 10), and to wait on the Lord and rest in Him (vv. 12–13). This is the way Bible prophecy should affect us personally.

THE MINOR PROPHETS

The prophets Jonah, Amos, and Hosea ministered in the northern kingdom (Israel, Ephraim) before it was taken by Assyria in 722 B.C. In the southern kingdom (Judah), Joel, Micah, Zephaniah, Nahum, Habakkuk, and Obadiah served prior to the Babylonian captivity. Ezekiel and Daniel, who are considered major prophets, ministered during the captivity; and Haggai, Zechariah, and Malachi ministered to the Jewish remnant after their return to the land from exile. Their messages are not "minor" as far as content is concerned; "minor" refers only to their size. Most of the minor prophets have a threefold message: the sin of the people; the coming judgment of God; and the future restoration of Israel. The promise of hope is present even in the message of judgment.

HOSEA

Hosea preached in the northern kingdom when the nation was prospering outwardly but decaying inwardly and facing certain judgment. He is a master of imagery; as you read, notice the many comparisons he makes ("like a dry land," "like a morning cloud," etc.).

The overriding image in his book is that of *marriage*. Hosea married a woman who bore him three children and then deserted him and became a prostitute. He finally had to buy her back out of the slave market (3:1–2)! Hosea's painful experience was a sermon to the nation. Israel was married to Jehovah but committed "spiritual adultery" and turned to idols. That in turn led to moral decay in the nation. The nation would suffer for her sins, but the Lord would one day redeem her and restore her.

The development of the book is as follows: Hosea's marriage, (chaps. 1—3); Israel's sins, (chaps. 4—7); Israel's judgment (chaps. 8—10); and Israel's future restoration (chaps. 11—14).

It is easy for the church today to prostitute itself to the world and still claim to be faithful to the Lord (James 4:4–10). The warning of Revelation 2:4–5 must be heeded!

1 The word of the LORD that came to Hosea the son of Beeri, in the days of Uzziah, Jotham, Ahaz, *and* Hezekiah, kings of Judah, and in the days of Jeroboam the son of Joash, king of Israel. ²*When the LORD began to speak by Hosea, the LORD said to Hosea:

"Go, take yourself a wife of harlotry
And children of harlotry,
For the land has committed great harlotry
By *departing* from the LORD."

³So he went and took Gomer the daughter of Diblaim, and she conceived and bore him a son. ⁴*Then the LORD said to him:

"Call his name Jezreel,
For in a little *while*
I will avenge the bloodshed of Jezreel on the house of Jehu,
And bring an end to the kingdom of the house of Israel.
5 It shall come to pass in that day
That I will break the bow of Israel in the Valley of Jezreel."

⁶*And she conceived again and bore a daughter. Then *God* said to him:

"Call her name Lo-Ruhamah,ᵃ
For I will no longer have mercy on the house of Israel,

1:6 ᵃLiterally *No-Mercy*

CHAPTER 1

1:2 Gomer was not a harlot when Hosea married her, but God warned him that she would be unfaithful. Like Ezekiel, Hosea had to "live" his message before the people, and that was not an easy thing to do. Expect to pay a price if you want to have a ministry to others (2 Cor. 1:3–11).

1:4 The names of the three children summarize the spiritual history of Israel. *Jezreel* means "God will sow" (2:22–23) and refers to Jehu's slaughter of his enemies at Jezreel (2 Kings 9—10). He went too far in his zeal, and his descendants would suffer for it when Assyria would take the land. God's judgments come—no matter how long He seems to wait.

1:6 *Lo-Ruhamah* means "no mercy," which is the situation of Israel today (3:4). Although God is providentially guiding the Jewish nation, they are not enjoying God's mercies as before.

Jezreel—The Valley of Jezreel has been a battlefield for many different armies. Saul launched his last battle there (1 Sam. 29:1), and there Jehu destroyed the house of Ahab as well as some innocent people (2 Kings 9—10). When Assyria took Israel, they fought on the plain of Jezreel; and there God avenged the innocent blood shed by Jehu. But Hosea saw a new future for Jezreel (1:11—2:1). Israel and Judah would be united and restored to the land, and they would experience the blessing of God. God would "sow" them in the land (2:21–23) to bear fruit for the glory of God. Only God can give new meanings to old names and wipe out painful associations with old places. Even the Valley of Achor, where Achan died (Josh. 7:16–26), will become a door of hope (2:15).

But I will utterly take them away.[b]
7   Yet I will have mercy on the house of Judah,
Will save them by the LORD their God,
And will not save them by bow,
Nor by sword or battle,
By horses or horsemen.''

8Now when she had weaned Lo-Ruhamah, she conceived and bore a son. 9*Then *God* said:

"Call his name Lo-Ammi,[c]
For you *are* not My people,
And I will not be your *God*.

10*"Yet the number of the children of Israel
Shall be as the sand of the sea,
Which cannot be measured or numbered.
And it shall come to pass
In the place where it was said to them,
'You *are* not My people,'[d]
There it shall be said to them,
'*You are* sons of the living God.'
11   Then the children of Judah and the children
of Israel
Shall be gathered together,
And appoint for themselves one head;
And they shall come up out of the land,
For great *will be* the day of Jezreel!

2 Say to your brethren, 'My people,'[e]
And to your sisters, 'Mercy[f] *is shown.'*

2 *"Bring charges against your mother, bring
charges;
For she *is* not My wife, nor *am* I her
Husband!
Let her put away her harlotries from her
sight,
And her adulteries from between her
breasts;
3   Lest I strip her naked
And expose her, as in the day she was born,
And make her like a wilderness,
And set her like a dry land,
And slay her with thirst.

4   "I will not have mercy on her children,
For they *are* the children of harlotry.
5   For their mother has played the harlot;
She who conceived them has behaved
shamefully.
For she said, 'I will go after my lovers,
Who give *me* my bread and my water,
My wool and my linen,
My oil and my drink.'

6   "Therefore, behold,
I will hedge up your way with thorns,
And wall her in,
So that she cannot find her paths.
7   She will chase her lovers,
But not overtake them;
Yes, she will seek them, but not find *them*.
Then she will say,
'I will go and return to my first husband,

1:9 *Lo-Ammi* means "not my people" and speaks of God's temporary rejection of the nation because of their sins.

1:10—2:1 Hosea closes with a great affirmation of hope! God will gather His people, claim them once again, and show them mercy. The names of the children will be changed to "My People" and "Mercy." No matter how dark the day, God promises us hope if we will return to Him in sincere repentance.

CHAPTERS 2—3
2:2–8 God makes four declarations in chapters 2 and 3.
I will not have mercy. Israel accepted God's gifts but used them to worship idols. Do we ever use our God-given resources for things that grieve Him? God withheld His mercy and allowed the nation to sink deeper into sin. What a tragedy!

---

[b]Or *That I may forgive them at all*   1:9 [c]Literally *Not-My-People*   1:10 [d]Hebrew *lo-ammi* (compare verse 9)
2:1 [e]Hebrew *Ammi* (compare 1:9, 10)   [f]Hebrew *Ruhamah* (compare 1:6)

For then *it was* better for me than now.'
8　For she did not know
That I gave her grain, new wine, and oil,
And multiplied her silver and gold—
Which they prepared for Baal.

9 *"Therefore I will return and take away
My grain in its time
And My new wine in its season,
And will take back My wool and My linen,
Given to cover her nakedness.
10　Now I will uncover her lewdness in the sight
of her lovers,
And no one shall deliver her from My hand.
11　I will also cause all her mirth to cease,
Her feast days,
Her New Moons,
Her Sabbaths—
All her appointed feasts.

12　"And I will destroy her vines and her fig
trees,
Of which she has said,
'These *are* my wages that my lovers have
given me.'
So I will make them a forest,
And the beasts of the field shall eat them.
13　I will punish her
For the days of the Baals to which she
burned incense.
She decked herself with her earrings and
jewelry,
And went after her lovers;
But Me she forgot," says the LORD.

14 *"Therefore, behold, I will allure her,
Will bring her into the wilderness,
And speak comfort to her.
15　I will give her her vineyards from there,
And the Valley of Achor as a door of
hope;
She shall sing there,
As in the days of her youth,
As in the day when she came up from the
land of Egypt.

16　"And it shall be, in that day,"
Says the LORD,
"*That* you will call Me 'My Husband,'g
And no longer call Me 'My Master,'h
17　For I will take from her mouth the names
of the Baals,
And they shall be remembered by their
name no more.
18　In that day I will make a covenant for them
With the beasts of the field,
With the birds of the air,
And *with* the creeping things of the ground.
Bow and sword of battle I will shatter from
the earth,
To make them lie down safely.

19　"I will betroth you to Me forever;
Yes, I will betroth you to Me
In righteousness and justice,
In lovingkindness and mercy;
20　I will betroth you to Me in faithfulness,
And you shall know the LORD.

2:9–13 *I will punish her.* He did this by taking away His blessings, especially the land's fruitfulness. The people were still outwardly worshiping God (v. 11), but their hearts were with the idols.

2:14–20; 3:1–5 *I will allure her.* Just as Hosea reclaimed his wife, so God will one day reclaim His people, renew His "marriage vows," and restore His people to blessing (Jer. 3:1–20). This will occur in the latter days after Israel has suffered greatly at the hands of the Gentiles. There is hope!

2:16 gHebrew *Ishi* hHebrew *Baali*

2:21—3:5 *I will sow her.* *Jezreel* means "God will sow" (1:4–5) and refers to God's planting His people again in their land where He will love them and bless them. The names will be changed (2:23)! Note the declaration from the unfaithful wife: "I will go and return to my first husband" (v. 7; Luke 15:18). When we return to our first love (Rev. 2:4–5), we can enjoy the first blessings.

21*"It shall come to pass in that day
　　That I will answer," says the LORD;
"I will answer the heavens,
　　And they shall answer the earth.
22　The earth shall answer
　　With grain,
　　With new wine,
　　And with oil;
　　They shall answer Jezreel.*ᶦ*
23　Then I will sow her for Myself in the earth,
　　And I will have mercy on *her who had* not
　　　obtained mercy;*ʲ*
　　Then I will say to *those who were* not My
　　　people,*ᵏ*
　　'You *are* My people!'
　　And they shall say, '*You are* my God!' "

3 Then the LORD said to me, "Go again, love a woman *who is* loved by a lover*ᶦ* and is committing adultery, just like the love of the LORD for the children of Israel, who look to other gods and love *the* raisin cakes *of the pagans.*" ²So I bought her for myself for fifteen *shekels* of silver, and one and one-half homers of barley. ³And I said to her, "You shall stay with me many days; you shall not play the harlot, nor shall you have a man—so, too, *will I be* toward you." ⁴For the children of Israel shall abide many days without king or prince, without sacrifice or sacred pillar, without ephod or teraphim. ⁵Afterward the children of Israel shall return and seek the LORD their God and David their king. They shall fear the LORD and His goodness in the latter days.

CHAPTERS 4—5

4:1–10 *Ignorance.* What you don't know *can* hurt you! The priests and prophets did not teach the Word or help the people know God. The religious services were popular, but the people were being destroyed for lack of true spiritual knowledge. It was only a religious routine (Matt. 15:1–9).

4 Hear* the word of the LORD,
　　You children of Israel,
　　For the LORD *brings* a charge against the
　　　inhabitants of the land:

　　"There is no truth or mercy
　　Or knowledge of God in the land.
2　*By* swearing and lying,
　　Killing and stealing and committing
　　　adultery,
　　They break all restraint,
　　With bloodshed upon bloodshed.
3　Therefore the land will mourn;
　　And everyone who dwells there will waste
　　　away
　　With the beasts of the field
　　And the birds of the air;
　　Even the fish of the sea will be taken away.

4　"Now let no man contend, or rebuke another;
　　For your people *are* like those who contend
　　　with the priest.
5　Therefore you shall stumble in the day;
　　The prophet also shall stumble with you in
　　　the night;
　　And I will destroy your mother.
6　My people are destroyed for lack of
　　　knowledge.
　　Because you have rejected knowledge,
　　I also will reject you from being priest for
　　　Me;
　　Because you have forgotten the law of your
　　　God,
　　I also will forget your children.

2:22 *ᶦLiterally God Will Sow*　2:23 *ʲHebrew lo-ruhamah*
ᵏHebrew lo-ammi　3:1 *ᶦLiterally friend or husband*

7   "The more they increased,
    The more they sinned against Me;
    I will change[m] their glory[n] into shame.
8   They eat up the sin of My people;
    They set their heart on their iniquity.
9   And it shall be: like people, like priest.
    So I will punish them for their ways,
    And reward them for their deeds.
10 For they shall eat, but not have enough;
    They shall commit harlotry, but not
        increase;
    Because they have ceased obeying the LORD.

11* "Harlotry, wine, and new wine enslave the
        heart.
12 My people ask counsel from their wooden
        idols,
    And their staff informs them.
    For the spirit of harlotry has caused *them*
        to stray,
    And they have played the harlot against
        their God.
13 They offer sacrifices on the mountaintops,
    And burn incense on the hills,
    Under oaks, poplars, and terebinths,
    Because their shade *is* good.
    Therefore your daughters commit harlotry,
    And your brides commit adultery.

14 "I will not punish your daughters when they
        commit harlotry,
    Nor your brides when they commit adultery;
    For *the men* themselves go apart with
        harlots,
    And offer sacrifices with a ritual harlot.[o]
    Therefore people *who* do not understand
        will be trampled.

15 "Though you, Israel, play the harlot,
    Let not Judah offend.
    Do not come up to Gilgal,
    Nor go up to Beth Aven,
    Nor swear an oath, *saying,* 'As the LORD
        lives'—

16 "For Israel is stubborn
    Like a stubborn calf;
    Now the LORD will let them forage
    Like a lamb in open country.

17 "Ephraim *is* joined to idols,
    Let him alone.
18 Their drink is rebellion,
    They commit harlotry continually.
    Her rulers dearly love dishonor.[p]
19 The wind has wrapped her up in its wings,
    And they shall be ashamed because of their
        sacrifices.

5   "Hear* this, O priests!
    Take heed, O house of Israel!
    Give ear, O house of the king!
    For yours *is* the judgment,

4:11–19 *Idolatry.* The key word here is
harlotry, which is what idolatry really is. Like
Hosea's wife Gomer, Israel had forsaken the
true God and gone after idols. What is God's
response? "Let him alone!" (v. 17).

5:1ff *Indignation.* Any faithful husband
would be indignant if his wife defiled herself
by unfaithfulness (v. 3). Instead of pursuing
Israel, God withdrew Himself and His
blessings (v. 6; 4:17) and let them reap what
they had sown. But His judgment was at
work: the water was gathering behind the
dam (5:10); the moth was silently destroying
the fabric of society (v. 12); the rottenness
in the bones would lead to death (vv. 12–
13). Then the Assyrian lion would spring
(v. 14) and the nation would be conquered.
    God withdraws so that we may realize
what we are missing and want Him to come
back to us again (v. 15). There is no reason
to stumble (5:5; 4:5) or to be stubborn (4:16)
when God will welcome us if we will
sincerely seek Him.

4:7 *m*Following Masoretic Text, Septuagint, and Vulgate;
scribal tradition, Syriac, and Targum read *They will
change.* *n*Following Masoretic Text, Septuagint, Syriac,
Targum, and Vulgate; scribal tradition reads *My glory.*
4:14 *o*Compare Deuteronomy 23:18   4:18 *p*Hebrew is difficult;
a Jewish tradition reads *Her rulers shamefully love, 'Give!'*

Because you have been a snare to Mizpah
And a net spread on Tabor.
2 The revolters are deeply involved in
slaughter,
Though I rebuke them all.
3 I know Ephraim,
And Israel is not hidden from Me;
For now, O Ephraim, you commit harlotry;
Israel is defiled.

4 "They do not direct their deeds
Toward turning to their God,
For the spirit of harlotry is in their midst,
And they do not know the LORD.
5 The pride of Israel testifies to his face;
Therefore Israel and Ephraim stumble in
their iniquity;
Judah also stumbles with them.

6 "With their flocks and herds
They shall go to seek the LORD,
But they will not find *Him;*
He has withdrawn Himself from them.
7 They have dealt treacherously with the
LORD,
For they have begotten pagan children.
Now a New Moon shall devour them and
their heritage.

8 "Blow the ram's horn in Gibeah,
The trumpet in Ramah!
Cry aloud *at* Beth Aven,
'*Look* behind you, O Benjamin!'
9 Ephraim shall be desolate in the day of
rebuke;
Among the tribes of Israel I make known
what is sure.

10 "The princes of Judah are like those who
remove a landmark;
I will pour out my wrath on them like water.
11 Ephraim is oppressed *and* broken in
judgment,
Because he willingly walked by *human*
precept.
12 Therefore I *will be* to Ephraim like a moth,
And to the house of Judah like rottenness.

13 "When Ephraim saw his sickness,
And Judah *saw* his wound,
Then Ephraim went to Assyria
And sent to King Jareb;
Yet he cannot cure you,
Nor heal you of your wound.
14 For I *will be* like a lion to Ephraim,
And like a young lion to the house of Judah.
I, *even* I, will tear *them* and go away;
I will take *them* away, and no one shall
rescue.
15 I will return again to My place
Till they acknowledge their offense.
Then they will seek My face;
In their affliction they will earnestly seek
Me."

CHAPTERS 6—7

6:1–3 *Like the rain.* When we come back
to God, He brings the dawning of a new
day with the refreshing showers. The God
who chastens us also heals and revives us.
Why do we delay? Because of what *we* are
like!

6 Come,* and let us return to the LORD;
For He has torn, but He will heal us;
He has stricken, but He will bind us up.
2 After two days He will revive us;
On the third day He will raise us up,
That we may live in His sight.
3 Let us know,

Let us pursue the knowledge of the LORD.
His going forth is established as the
   morning;
He will come to us like the rain,
Like the latter *and* former rain to the earth.

4 *"O Ephraim, what shall I do to you?
  O Judah, what shall I do to you?
  For your faithfulness is like a morning
   cloud,
  And like the early dew it goes away.
5 Therefore I have hewn *them* by the
   prophets,
  I have slain them by the words of My mouth;
  And your judgments *are like* light *that* goes
   forth.
6 For I desire mercy and not sacrifice,
  And the knowledge of God more than burnt
   offerings.

7 "But like men*q* they transgressed the
   covenant;
  There they dealt treacherously with Me.
8 Gilead *is* a city of evildoers
  And defiled with blood.
9 As bands of robbers lie in wait for a man,
  So the company of priests murder on the
   way to Shechem;
  Surely they commit lewdness.
10 I have seen a horrible thing in the house of
   Israel:
  There *is* the harlotry of Ephraim;
  Israel is defiled.
11 Also, O Judah, a harvest is appointed for
   you,
  When I return the captives of My people.

7 "When I would have healed Israel,
  Then the iniquity of Ephraim was
   uncovered,
  And the wickedness of Samaria.
  For they have committed fraud;
  A thief comes in;
  A band of robbers takes spoil outside.
2 They do not consider in their hearts
  That I remember all their wickedness;
  Now their own deeds have surrounded
   them;
  They are before My face.
3 They make a king glad with their
   wickedness,
  And princes with their lies.

4 *"They *are* all adulterers.
  Like an oven heated by a baker—
  He ceases stirring *the fire* after kneading
   the dough,
  Until it is leavened.
5 In the day of our king
  Princes have made *him* sick, inflamed with
   wine;
  He stretched out his hand with scoffers.
6 They prepare their heart like an oven,
  While they lie in wait;
  Their baker*r* sleeps all night;
  In the morning it burns like a flaming fire.

6:4–6 *Like a morning cloud and the dew.*
Israel's loyalty did not last but vanished like
a cloud and evaporated like the dew. They
brought sacrifices and engaged in religious
services, but those activities made no
difference in the way they lived. Their
sacrifices were substitutes for obedience
(1 Sam. 15:21–23; Amos 5:21–24).

7:4–7 *Like an oven.* The desire for sin can
smolder like a fire in an oven and then blaze
forth when the opportunity comes. If you
have "burning desires," be sure that they
are under God's control or they may destroy
you.

6:7 *q*Or *like Adam*   7:6 *r*Following Masoretic Text and Vulgate;
Syriac and Targum read *Their anger;* Septuagint reads
Ephraim.

7:8–10 *Like a cake not turned.* If the fire is not watched, it can burn the cake, and then the cake must be thrown away. The people were "half-baked": there was no depth to their religious experience. The nation was aging and did not realize it, and national death would come much sooner than the people realized.

7:11, 12 *Like a silly dove.* In their foreign policy, the officials flitted between Egypt and Assyria, playing one against the other; eventually the nation was trapped. Instead of trusting the Lord and obeying His Word, they depended on politics and failed.

7:15, 16 *Like a deceitful bow.* God could not depend on His people. They sinned against Him, lied to Him, and did not profit from His discipline. He tried to straighten them out, but they preferred to be substandard. In the battle against evil, are you a weapon that God can depend on?

CHAPTER 8

8:1ff The trumpet was blown in Israel to warn of impending battle (Num. 10:9). In this case, Assyria was coming, and there would be no escape. Israel claimed to know God (v. 2) and yet disobeyed Him (Titus 1:16). They made kings and rulers without seeking God's will, and they made idols in defiance of the Lord. The famous calf of Samaria would be destroyed (1 Kings 12:28–30) when the eagle swooped down (v. 1) and the whirlwind came (v. 7). What seems a lovely soft wind today can become a storm tomorrow (Acts 27:13–15).

Israel had become like a piece of junk pottery on the trash heap (v. 8). They trusted the gentile nations to protect them but left God out of their plans (vv. 9–10). Israel multiplied altars (v. 11; 10:1) and Judah multiplied fortifications (v. 14), but neither could deliver from judgment. Israel would be taken by Assyria and Judah by Babylon, and God's judgment would fall on a sinful people. When God blows the trumpet, we had better wake up and listen!

7 They are all hot, like an oven,
And have devoured their judges;
All their kings have fallen.
None among them calls upon Me.

8 *"Ephraim has mixed himself among the peoples;
Ephraim is a cake unturned.

9 Aliens have devoured his strength,
But he does not know *it;*
Yes, gray hairs are here and there on him,
Yet he does not know *it.*

10 And the pride of Israel testifies to his face,
But they do not return to the LORD their God,
Nor seek Him for all this.

11 *"Ephraim also is like a silly dove, without sense—
They call to Egypt,
They go to Assyria.

12 Wherever they go, I will spread My net on them;
I will bring them down like birds of the air;
I will chastise them
According to what their congregation has heard.

13 "Woe to them, for they have fled from Me!
Destruction to them,
Because they have transgressed against Me!
Though I redeemed them,
Yet they have spoken lies against Me.

14 They did not cry out to Me with their heart
When they wailed upon their beds.

"They assemble together for^s grain and new wine,
They rebel against Me;^{t}

15 *Though I disciplined *and* strengthened their arms,
Yet they devise evil against Me;

16 They return, *but* not to the Most High;^{u}
They are like a treacherous bow.
Their princes shall fall by the sword
For the cursings of their tongue.
This *shall be* their derision in the land of Egypt.

8 "*Set* the trumpet^v to your mouth!
He shall come like an eagle against the house of the LORD,
Because they have transgressed My covenant
And rebelled against My law.

2 Israel will cry to Me,
'My God, we know You!'

3 Israel has rejected the good;
The enemy will pursue him.

4 "They set up kings, but not by Me;
They made princes, but I did not acknowledge *them.*
From their silver and gold
They made idols for themselves—

7:14 ^{s}Following Masoretic Text and Targum; Vulgate reads *thought upon;* Septuagint reads *slashed themselves for* (compare 1 Kings 18:28). ^{t}Following Masoretic Text, Syriac, and Targum; Septuagint omits *They rebel against Me;* Vulgate reads *They departed from Me.*   7:16 ^{u}Or *upward*
8:1 ^{v}Hebrew *shophar,* ram's horn

That they might be cut off.
5 Your calf is rejected, O Samaria!
My anger is aroused against them—
How long until they attain to innocence?
6 For from Israel is even this:
A workman made it, and it is not God;
But the calf of Samaria shall be broken to
pieces.

7 "They sow the wind,
And reap the whirlwind.
The stalk has no bud;
It shall never produce meal.
If it should produce,
Aliens would swallow it up.
8 Israel is swallowed up;
Now they are among the Gentiles
Like a vessel in which is no pleasure.
9 For they have gone up to Assyria,
Like a wild donkey alone by itself;
Ephraim has hired lovers.
10 Yes, though they have hired among the
nations,
Now I will gather them;
And they shall sorrow a little,w
Because of the burdenx of the king of
princes.

11 "Because Ephraim has made many altars for
sin,
They have become for him altars for
sinning.
12 I have written for him the great things of
My law,
But they were considered a strange thing.
13 For the sacrifices of My offerings they
sacrifice flesh and eat it,
But the LORD does not accept them.
Now He will remember their iniquity and
punish their sins.
They shall return to Egypt.

14 "For Israel has forgotten his Maker,
And has built temples;y
Judah also has multiplied fortified cities;
But I will send fire upon his cities,
And it shall devour his palaces."

9 Do* not rejoice, O Israel, with joy like other
peoples,
For you have played the harlot against your
God.
You have made love for hire on every
threshing floor.
2 The threshing floor and the winepress
Shall not feed them,
And the new wine shall fail in her.

3 They shall not dwell in the LORD's land,
But Ephraim shall return to Egypt,
And shall eat unclean things in Assyria.
4 They shall not offer wine offerings to the
LORD,
Nor shall their sacrifices be pleasing to Him.
It shall be like bread of mourners to them;
All who eat it shall be defiled.
For their bread shall be for their own life;
It shall not come into the house of the LORD.

CHAPTERS 9—10

9:1ff The name *Ephraim* means "twice fruitful," and Hosea used that fact as the basis for his message in chapters 9 and 10. There would be no fruitfulness *in the harvest* (vv. 1–9) because poverty was coming and God would judge the land (Deut. 28:38–42). That would be the end of harvest joy (9:1). Ephraim would no longer be known as the fruitful land.

There would also be no more fruitfulness *in the home* (vv. 10–17). Why allow them to bear children who would only worship idols and then be murdered by the Assyrian invaders? The fruitful womb was always a blessing to the Jewish people (Pss. 127:3–5; 128:3–4), but now the miscarrying womb would be a blessing.

What was wrong with Israel? They tried to serve two masters (10:1–2), they lied to God (10:4), they worshiped idols (10:5–6), and their hearts were hard and needed plowing up (10:12). They sowed the wrong seed in the wrong kind of soil and yet expected to reap the right harvest!

Have you pondered Galatians 6:7–8 lately?

8:10 wOr *begin to diminish* xOr *oracle* 8:14 yOr *palaces*

5   What will you do in the appointed day,
    And in the day of the feast of the LORD?
6   For indeed they are gone because of
      destruction.
    Egypt shall gather them up;
    Memphis shall bury them.
    Nettles shall possess their valuables of
      silver;
    Thorns *shall be* in their tents.

7   The days of punishment have come;
    The days of recompense have come.
    Israel knows!
    The prophet *is* a fool,
    The spiritual man *is* insane,
    Because of the greatness of your iniquity
      and great enmity.
8   The watchman of Ephraim *is* with my
      God;
    But the prophet *is* a fowler'sᶻ snare in all
      his ways—
    Enmity in the house of his God.
9   They are deeply corrupted,
    As in the days of Gibeah.
    He will remember their iniquity;
    He will punish their sins.

10 "I found Israel
    Like grapes in the wilderness;
    I saw your fathers
    As the firstfruits on the fig tree in its first
      season.
    But they went to Baal Peor,
    And separated themselves *to that* shame;
    They became an abomination like the thing
      they loved.
11 *As for* Ephraim, their glory shall fly away
      like a bird—
    No birth, no pregnancy, and no conception!
12 Though they bring up their children,
    Yet I will bereave them to the last man.
    Yes, woe to them when I depart from them!
13 Just as I saw Ephraim like Tyre, planted in
      a pleasant place,
    So Ephraim will bring out his children to
      the murderer."

14 Give them, O LORD—
    What will You give?
    Give them a miscarrying womb
    And dry breasts!

15 "All their wickedness *is* in Gilgal,
    For there I hated them.
    Because of the evil of their deeds
    I will drive them from My house;
    I will love them no more.
    All their princes *are* rebellious.
16 Ephraim is stricken,
    Their root is dried up;
    They shall bear no fruit.
    Yes, were they to bear children,
    I would kill the darlings of their womb."

17 My God will cast them away,
    Because they did not obey Him;
    And they shall be wanderers among the
      nations.

9:8 ᶻThat is, one who catches birds in a trap or snare

10 Israel empties *his* vine;
He brings forth fruit for himself.
According to the multitude of his fruit
He has increased the altars;
According to the bounty of his land
They have embellished *his* sacred pillars.
2   Their heart is divided;
Now they are held guilty.
He will break down their altars;
He will ruin their sacred pillars.

3   For now they say,
"We have no king,
Because we did not fear the Lord.
And as for a king, what would he do for
us?"
4   They have spoken words,
Swearing falsely in making a covenant.
Thus judgment springs up like hemlock in
the furrows of the field.

5   The inhabitants of Samaria fear
Because of the calf*a* of Beth Aven.
For its people mourn for it,
And its priests shriek for it—
Because its glory has departed from it.
6   *The idol* also shall be carried to Assyria
As a present for King Jareb.
Ephraim shall receive shame,
And Israel shall be ashamed of his own
counsel.

7   *As for* Samaria, her king is cut off
Like a twig on the water.
8   Also the high places of Aven, the sin of
Israel,
Shall be destroyed.
The thorn and thistle shall grow on their
altars;
They shall say to the mountains, "Cover
us!"
And to the hills, "Fall on us!"

9   "O Israel, you have sinned from the days of
Gibeah;
There they stood.
The battle in Gibeah against the children
of iniquity*b*
Did not overtake them.
10   When *it is* My desire, I will chasten them.
Peoples shall be gathered against them
When I bind them for their two
transgressions.*c*
11   Ephraim *is* a trained heifer
That loves to thresh *grain*;
But I harnessed her fair neck,
I will make Ephraim pull *a plow*.
Judah shall plow;
Jacob shall break his clods."

12   Sow for yourselves righteousness;
Reap in mercy;
Break up your fallow ground,
For *it is* time to seek the Lord,
Till He comes and rains righteousness on
you.

10:5 *a*Literally *calves*   10:9 *b*So read many Hebrew
manuscripts, Septuagint, and Vulgate; Masoretic Text reads
unruliness.   10:10 *c*Or *in their two habitations*

13 You have plowed wickedness;
    You have reaped iniquity.
    You have eaten the fruit of lies,
    Because you trusted in your own way,
    In the multitude of your mighty men.
14 Therefore tumult shall arise among your
        people,
    And all your fortresses shall be plundered
    As Shalman plundered Beth Arbel in the
        day of battle—
    A mother dashed in pieces upon *her*
        children.
15 Thus it shall be done to you, O Bethel,
    Because of your great wickedness.
    At dawn the king of Israel
    Shall be cut off utterly.

CHAPTERS 11—12

11:1–4 Chapters 11 and 12 form a history lesson that reveals the sins of the people as Hosea reviews the history of Israel and of Jacob.

Ingratitude. Israel took for granted their covenant relationship with the Lord, forgetting that He chose them (Deut. 7:6–11). In love He delivered a child from Egypt, carried him, fed him, and taught him to walk and work; and that child abandoned Him for idols. What ingratitude!

11:5–11 Hardness of heart. They followed their own plans and gave no thought to the will of God. When God rebuked them, they did not repent. The soil of their hearts was hard (10:12), but God's heart was tender toward them. He could not destroy them as He did the cities of the plain (Gen. 14:2, 8). No, one day He will call for them with a lion's roar, and they will come with trembling hearts.

11 "When* Israel *was* a child, I loved him,
     And out of Egypt I called My son.
2   *As* they called them,*d*
     So they went from them;*e*
     They sacrificed to the Baals,
     And burned incense to carved images.

3   "I taught Ephraim to walk,
     Taking them by their arms;*f*
     But they did not know that I healed them.
4   I drew them with gentle cords,*g*
     With bands of love,
     And I was to them as those who take the
         yoke from their neck.*h*
     I stooped *and* fed them.

5   *"He shall not return to the land of Egypt;
     But the Assyrian shall be his king,
     Because they refused to repent.
6   And the sword shall slash in his cities,
     Devour his districts,
     And consume *them,*
     Because of their own counsels.
7   My people are bent on backsliding from
         Me.
     Though they call to the Most High,*i*
     None at all exalt *Him.*

8   "How can I give you up, Ephraim?
     How can I hand you over, Israel?
     How can I make you like Admah?
     How can I set you like Zeboiim?
     My heart churns within Me;
     My sympathy is stirred.
9   I will not execute the fierceness of My
         anger;
     I will not again destroy Ephraim.
     For I *am* God, and not man,
     The Holy One in your midst;
     And I will not come with terror.*j*

10   "They shall walk after the LORD.
     He will roar like a lion.
     When He roars,
     Then *His* sons shall come trembling from
         the west;

11:2 *d*Following Masoretic Text and Vulgate; Septuagint reads *Just as I called them;* Targum interprets as *I sent prophets to a thousand of them.* *e*Following Masoretic Text, Targum, and Vulgate; Septuagint reads *from My face.*   11:3 *f*Some Hebrew manuscripts, Septuagint, Syriac, and Vulgate read *My arms.*   11:4 *g*Literally *cords of a man* *h*Literally *jaws*
11:7 *i*Or *upward*   11:9 *j*Or *I will not enter a city*

11 They shall come trembling like a bird from
      Egypt,
   Like a dove from the land of Assyria.
   And I will let them dwell in their houses,"
   Says the LORD.

12 *"Ephraim has encircled Me with lies,
   And the house of Israel with deceit;
   But Judah still walks with God,
   Even with the Holy One[k] *who is* faithful.

12 "Ephraim feeds on the wind,
      And pursues the east wind;
   He daily increases lies and desolation.
   Also they make a covenant with the
      Assyrians,
   And oil is carried to Egypt.

2 "The LORD also *brings* a charge against
      Judah,
   And will punish Jacob according to his
      ways;
   According to his deeds He will recompense
      him.
3 He took his brother by the heel in the womb,
   And in his strength he struggled with God.[l]
4 Yes, he struggled with the Angel and
      prevailed;
   He wept, and sought favor from Him.
   He found Him *in* Bethel,
   And there He spoke to us—
5 That is, the LORD God of hosts.
   The LORD *is* His memorable name.
6 So you, by *the help of* your God, return;
   Observe mercy and justice,
   And wait on your God continually.

7 *"A cunning Canaanite!
   Deceitful scales *are* in his hand;
   He loves to oppress.
8 And Ephraim said,
   'Surely I have become rich,
   I have found wealth for myself;
   In all my labors
   They shall find in me no iniquity that *is* sin.'

9 "But I *am* the LORD your God,
   Ever since the land of Egypt;
   I will again make you dwell in tents,
   As in the days of the appointed feast.
10 I have also spoken by the prophets,
   And have multiplied visions;
   I have given symbols through the witness
      of the prophets."

11 Though Gilead *has* idols—
   Surely they are vanity—
   Though they sacrifice bulls in Gilgal,
   Indeed their altars *shall be* heaps in the
      furrows of the field.

12 Jacob fled to the country of Syria;
   Israel served for a spouse,
   And for a wife he tended *sheep*.
13 By a prophet the LORD brought Israel out
      of Egypt,
   And by a prophet he was preserved.
14 Ephraim provoked *Him* to anger most
      bitterly;

11:12—12:6 *Deceitfulness.* Both Israel and Judah (the southern kingdom) are included in this message. The prophet reviews the history of Jacob their founder and sees his deceit in his descendants. Jacob tried to trip up Esau at birth (Gen. 25:26); he fought with God (Gen. 32:22–32); but he returned to Bethel and found God's blessing again (Gen. 35). The time had come for Israel and Judah to return to God and repent of their sins (Hos. 12:6).

12:7, 8 *Boasting.* "I have become rich!" was their boast, but it was an empty boast and just a lot of wind (v. 1). Why? Because they made their money deceitfully by cheating the poor, and such wealth can never last. Read and ponder Revelation 3:14–22.

11:12 [k]Or *holy ones*   12:3 [l]Compare Genesis 32:28

CHAPTERS 13—14

13:1ff Ephraim had been a great tribe in Israel (Gen. 48:10–20). Now it would become like the clouds, the dew, the chaff, and the smoke—*nothing* (13:3). But God would be to the people like a lion, a leopard, and a bear (vv. 7–8)!

God had saved them from Egypt and in the wilderness, and He could have saved them from Assyria; but they trusted their wealth, their kings, and their foreign policy.

Now the east wind would dry them up (v. 15), and the "twice fruitful" Ephraim would be fruitful no more.

But we can always heed God's loving call to repentance. If we return to Him, He will receive us (14:2–3), restore us (14:4), and revive us (14:5–9). The desert will become a fruitful garden where the roots go deep. Instead of ugliness, there will be beauty; instead of a stench, there will be fragrance. What a difference it makes when we obey Him!

God does not want our material sacrifices so much as the "sacrifices of our lips" (14:2; Heb. 13:15). He wants to hear words from our hearts that are honest and sincere, and He wants to see faith that depends on His mercy alone. Will you be a stumbling sinner (14:1, 9) or a forgiven sinner?

Therefore his Lord will leave the guilt of
  his bloodshed upon him,
And return his reproach upon him.

13 When* Ephraim spoke, trembling,
  He exalted *himself* in Israel;
  But when he offended through Baal
  worship, he died.
2 Now they sin more and more,
  And have made for themselves molded
    images,
  Idols of their silver, according to their skill;
  All of it *is* the work of craftsmen.
  They say of them,
  "Let the men who sacrifice*m* kiss the calves!"
3 Therefore they shall be like the morning
    cloud
  And like the early dew that passes away,
  Like chaff blown off from a threshing floor
  And like smoke from a chimney.

4 "Yet I *am* the LORD your God
  Ever since the land of Egypt,
  And you shall know no God but Me;
  For *there is* no savior besides Me.
5 I knew you in the wilderness,
  In the land of great drought.
6 When they had pasture, they were filled;
  They were filled and their heart was
    exalted;
  Therefore they forgot Me.

7 "So I will be to them like a lion;
  Like a leopard by the road I will lurk;
8 I will meet them like a bear deprived *of her
    cubs;*
  I will tear open their rib cage,
  And there I will devour them like a lion.
  The wild beast shall tear them.

9 "O Israel, you are destroyed,*n*
  But your help*o is* from Me.
10 I will be your King;*p*
  Where *is any other,*
  That he may save you in all your cities?
  And your judges to whom you said,
  'Give me a king and princes'?
11 I gave you a king in My anger,
  And took *him* away in My wrath.

12 "The iniquity of Ephraim *is* bound up;
  His sin *is* stored up.
13 The sorrows of a woman in childbirth shall
    come upon him.
  He *is* an unwise son,
  For he should not stay long where children
    are born.

14 "I will ransom them from the power of the
    grave;*q*
  I will redeem them from death.
  O Death, I will be your plagues!*r*
  O Grave,*s* I will be your destruction!*t*
  Pity is hidden from My eyes."

13:2 *m*Or *those who offer human sacrifice* 13:9 *n*Literally *it or he destroyed you* *o*Literally *in your help* 13:10 *p*Septuagint, Syriac, Targum, and Vulgate read *Where is your king?* 13:14 *q*Or *Sheol* *r*Septuagint reads *where is your punishment?* *s*Or *Sheol* *t*Septuagint reads *where is your sting?*

15 Though he is fruitful among *his* brethren,
   An east wind shall come;
   The wind of the LORD shall come up from
      the wilderness.
   Then his spring shall become dry,
   And his fountain shall be dried up.
   He shall plunder the treasury of every
      desirable prize.
16 Samaria is held guilty,u
   For she has rebelled against her God.
   They shall fall by the sword,
   Their infants shall be dashed in pieces,
   And their women with child ripped open.

14 O Israel, return to the LORD your God,
   For you have stumbled because of your
      iniquity;
 2 Take words with you,
   And return to the LORD.
   Say to Him,
   "Take away all iniquity;
   Receive *us* graciously,
   For we will offer the sacrificesᵛ of our lips.
 3 Assyria shall not save us,
   We will not ride on horses,
   Nor will we say anymore to the work of our
      hands, '*You are* our gods.'
   For in You the fatherless finds mercy."

 4 "I will heal their backsliding,
   I will love them freely,
   For My anger has turned away from him.
 5 I will be like the dew to Israel;
   He shall grow like the lily,
   And lengthen his roots like Lebanon.
 6 His branches shall spread;
   His beauty shall be like an olive tree,
   And his fragrance like Lebanon.
 7 Those who dwell under his shadow shall
      return;
   They shall be revived *like* grain,
   And grow like a vine.
   Their scentw *shall be* like the wine of
      Lebanon.

 8 "Ephraim *shall say*, 'What have I to do
      anymore with idols?'
   I have heard and observed him.
   I *am* like a green cypress tree;
   Your fruit is found in Me."

 9 Who *is* wise?
   Let him understand these things.
   Who is prudent?
   Let him know them.
   For the ways of the LORD *are* right;
   The righteous walk in them,
   But transgressors stumble in them.

13:16 ᵘSeptuagint reads *shall be disfigured.*   14:2 ᵛLiterally
bull calves; Septuagint reads *fruit.*   14:7 ʷLiterally
remembrance

JOEL

The prophet Joel ministered in Judah at a time when drought and a plague of locusts had devastated the economy. He used the phrase "the day of the LORD" (1:15; 2:1, 11, 31; 3:14) to describe both their present calamity (1:1—2:27) and the future judgment that would come upon the whole world (2:28—3:21). God's "army" of locusts (2:11, 20, 25) was but a picture of a future army that would invade the land in the last days. Joel called the nation to repent (2:12–17) and promised that the Lord would forgive and bless them (2:18–27). He also promised blessings in the last days when Israel's tribulation would be ended (2:28–32; 3:18–21). God's message of judgment is not left without a promise of hope.

Campbell Morgan wrote, "It is always the day of the Lord." No matter what calamities may come to men and nations, He is always in control, and these calamities remind us of the greater judgment yet to come.

1 The word of the LORD that came to Joel the son of Pethuel.

CHAPTER 1

1:2–4 The prophet gives us four instructions to follow when we find ourselves in difficult circumstances, instructions that should be heeded by individuals and nations. **Hear.** Listen to God's Word and let Him interpret events for you. God raises up people to encourage us to turn to Him for help.

2 *Hear this, you elders,
    And give ear, all you inhabitants of the land!
    Has *anything like* this happened in your days,
    Or even in the days of your fathers?
3   Tell your children about it,
    Let your children *tell* their children,
    And their children another generation.

4   What the chewing locust[a] left, the swarming locust has eaten;
    What the swarming locust left, the crawling locust has eaten;
    And what the crawling locust left, the consuming locust has eaten.

1:5–7 *Awake.* When Joel looked at the dying vines and trees, he addressed the drinkers and told them to wake up and weep. But they should shed tears not because the wine is gone but because their sins have brought judgment on the land.

5   *Awake, you drunkards, and weep;
    And wail, all you drinkers of wine,
    Because of the new wine,
    For it has been cut off from your mouth.
6   For a nation has come up against My land,
    Strong, and without number;
    His teeth *are* the teeth of a lion,
    And he has the fangs of a fierce lion.
7   He has laid waste My vine,
    And ruined My fig tree;
    He has stripped it bare and thrown *it* away;
    Its branches are made white.

1:8–18 *Lament.* The fields, orchards, vineyards, flocks, and herds were all ruined; and Joel called for the farmers to lament (v. 11) and for the priests to repent (vv. 13–14). It is time to seek the Lord!

8   *Lament like a virgin girded with sackcloth
    For the husband of her youth.
9   The grain offering and the drink offering
    Have been cut off from the house of the LORD;
    The priests mourn, who minister to the LORD.
10 The field is wasted,
    The land mourns;
    For the grain is ruined,
    The new wine is dried up,
    The oil fails.

1:4 [a]Exact identity of these locusts is unknown.

11 Be ashamed, you farmers,
    Wail, you vinedressers,
    For the wheat and the barley;
    Because the harvest of the field has
        perished.
12 The vine has dried up,
    And the fig tree has withered;
    The pomegranate tree,
    The palm tree also,
    And the apple tree—
    All the trees of the field are withered;
    Surely joy has withered away from the sons
        of men.

13 Gird yourselves and lament, you priests;
    Wail, you who minister before the altar;
    Come, lie all night in sackcloth,
    You who minister to my God;
    For the grain offering and the drink offering
    Are withheld from the house of your God.
14 Consecrate a fast,
    Call a sacred assembly;
    Gather the elders
    And all the inhabitants of the land
    Into the house of the LORD your God,
    And cry out to the LORD.

15 Alas for the day!
    For the day of the LORD *is* at hand;
    It shall come as destruction from the
        Almighty.
16 Is not the food cut off before our eyes,
    Joy and gladness from the house of our
        God?
17 The seed shrivels under the clods,
    Storehouses are in shambles;
    Barns are broken down,
    For the grain has withered.
18 How the animals groan!
    The herds of cattle are restless,
    Because they have no pasture;
    Even the flocks of sheep suffer punishment.*b*

19 *O LORD, to You I cry out;
    For fire has devoured the open pastures,
    And a flame has burned all the trees of the
        field.
20 The beasts of the field also cry out to You,
    For the water brooks are dried up,
    And fire has devoured the open pastures.

2 Blow* the trumpet in Zion,
    And sound an alarm in My holy mountain!
    Let all the inhabitants of the land tremble;
    For the day of the LORD is coming,
    For it is at hand:
2   A day of darkness and gloominess,
    A day of clouds and thick darkness,
    Like the morning *clouds* spread over the
        mountains.
    A people *come,* great and strong,

1:19, 20 Cry out. The prophet set the
example by crying out to God for His mercy
and help. Perhaps he claimed God's
promise in 2 Chronicles 7:14. It is not
enough for us to weep over the sad
consequences of our sins; we must also
weep over our sins.

CHAPTER 2
2:1–11 The trumpet of warning. The
calamities that come to our lives should
awaken us and remind us that the Lord is
in control. The locusts were God's army
(vv. 11, 20, 25), and the day was "the day
of the LORD." This is a sobering truth, but it
is also a comforting truth (2 Sam. 24:14).
The Lord who wounds will also heal (Hos.
6:1).

1:18 *b*Septuagint and Vulgate read *are made desolate.*

Restoration—The Lord said, "So I will restore to you the years that the . . . locust has eaten"
(Joel 2:25). God promised them bumper crops that would make up for all they had lost because of
the drought and the locust plague. "Lost years can never be restored literally," said Charles Spurgeon.
"Time once past is gone forever. . . . You cannot have back your time; but there is a strange and
wonderful way in which God can give back to you the wasted blessings, the unripened fruits of
years over which you mourned. The fruits of wasted years may yet be yours."

The like of whom has never been;
Nor will there ever be any *such* after them,
Even for many successive generations.

3   A fire devours before them,
And behind them a flame burns;
The land *is* like the Garden of Eden before
    them,
And behind them a desolate wilderness;
Surely nothing shall escape them.
4   Their appearance is like the appearance of
    horses;
And like swift steeds, so they run.
5   With a noise like chariots
Over mountaintops they leap,
Like the noise of a flaming fire that devours
    the stubble,
Like a strong people set in battle array.

6   Before them the people writhe in pain;
All faces are drained of color.[c]
7   They run like mighty men,
They climb the wall like men of war;
Every one marches in formation,
And they do not break ranks.
8   They do not push one another;
Every one marches in his own column.[d]
Though they lunge between the weapons,
They are not cut down.[e]
9   They run to and fro in the city,
They run on the wall;
They climb into the houses,
They enter at the windows like a thief.

10   The earth quakes before them,
The heavens tremble;
The sun and moon grow dark,
And the stars diminish their brightness.
11   The LORD gives voice before His army,
For His camp is very great;
For strong *is the One* who executes His
    word.
For the day of the LORD *is* great and very
    terrible;
Who can endure it?

12*"Now, therefore," says the LORD,
"Turn to Me with all your heart,
With fasting, with weeping, and with
    mourning."
13   So rend your heart, and not your garments;
Return to the LORD your God,
For He *is* gracious and merciful,
Slow to anger, and of great kindness;
And He relents from doing harm.
14   Who knows *if* He will turn and relent,
And leave a blessing behind Him—
A grain offering and a drink offering
For the LORD your God?

15   Blow the trumpet in Zion,
Consecrate a fast,
Call a sacred assembly;
16   Gather the people,
Sanctify the congregation,
Assemble the elders,
Gather the children and nursing babes;

2:12–17 *The trumpet of weeping.* The prophet summoned the people to return to God with fasting and confession. Never be afraid to come to the Lord in honesty and humility because He is "gracious and merciful, slow to anger, and of great kindness" (v. 13). As you pray, think about magnifying the glory of God (v. 17) as well as escaping the suffering that sin causes.

2:6 [c]Septuagint, Targum, and Vulgate read *gather blackness.*
2:8 [d]Literally *his own highway* [e]That is, they are not halted by losses

Let the bridegroom go out from his
chamber,
And the bride from her dressing room.
17 Let the priests, who minister to the LORD,
Weep between the porch and the altar;
Let them say, "Spare Your people, O LORD,
And do not give Your heritage to reproach,
That the nations should rule over them.
Why should they say among the peoples,
'Where *is* their God?'"

18 *Then the LORD will be zealous for His land,
And pity His people.
19 The LORD will answer and say to His people,
"Behold, I will send you grain and new wine
and oil,
And you will be satisfied by them;
I will no longer make you a reproach among
the nations.

20 "But I will remove far from you the northern
army,
And will drive him away into a barren and
desolate land,
With his face toward the eastern sea
And his back toward the western sea;
His stench will come up,
And his foul odor will rise,
Because he has done monstrous things."

21 Fear not, O land;
Be glad and rejoice,
For the LORD has done marvelous things!
22 Do not be afraid, you beasts of the field;
For the open pastures are springing up,
And the tree bears its fruit;
The fig tree and the vine yield their strength.
23 Be glad then, you children of Zion,
And rejoice in the LORD your God;
For He has given you the former rain
faithfully,*f*
And He will cause the rain to come down
for you—
The former rain,
And the latter rain in the first *month*.
24 The threshing floors shall be full of wheat,
And the vats shall overflow with new wine
and oil.

25 "So I will restore to you the years that the
swarming locust has eaten,
The crawling locust,
The consuming locust,
And the chewing locust,*g*
My great army which I sent among you.
26 You shall eat in plenty and be satisfied,
And praise the name of the LORD your
God,
Who has dealt wondrously with you;
And My people shall never be put to shame.
27 Then you shall know that I *am* in the midst
of Israel:
I *am* the LORD your God
And there is no other.
My people shall never be put to shame.

28 "And it shall come to pass afterward
That I will pour out My Spirit on all flesh;

2:18–32 *The promise of blessing.* God
promised to remove their reproach and
restore His blessings to the land.
"Monstrous things" (v. 20) will be replaced
by "marvelous things" from the Lord (v. 21),
and joy will take the place of fear. Verses
28–32 refer especially to the future day of
the Lord, but Peter's use of them at
Pentecost (Acts 2:16–21) suggests that they
have a spiritual application today.

2:23 *f*Or *the teacher of righteousness* 2:25 *g*Compare 1:4

Your sons and your daughters shall
  prophesy,
Your old men shall dream dreams,
Your young men shall see visions.
29 And also on *My* menservants and on *My*
  maidservants
  I will pour out My Spirit in those days.

30 "And I will show wonders in the heavens and
  in the earth:
  Blood and fire and pillars of smoke.
31 The sun shall be turned into darkness,
  And the moon into blood,
  Before the coming of the great and awesome
  day of the LORD.
32 And it shall come to pass
  That whoever calls on the name of the LORD
  Shall be saved.
  For in Mount Zion and in Jerusalem there
  shall be deliverance,
  As the LORD has said,
  Among the remnant whom the LORD calls.

CHAPTER 3

3:1–8 Four vivid pictures describe God's
future dealings with His people and the
nations.

The court. In the last days, God will
summon the gentile nations to court and
judge them for the sins they have committed
against Israel: scattering them, dividing up
their land, treating them like slaves, and
robbing them of wealth. This judgment has
been long in coming, but it will come.

3 "For* behold, in those days and at that
  time,
  When I bring back the captives of Judah
  and Jerusalem,
2 I will also gather all nations,
  And bring them down to the Valley of
  Jehoshaphat;
  And I will enter into judgment with them
  there
  On account of My people, My heritage
  Israel,
  Whom they have scattered among the
  nations;
  They have also divided up My land.
3 They have cast lots for My people,
  Have given a boy *as payment* for a harlot,
  And sold a girl for wine, that they may
  drink.

4 "Indeed, what have you to do with Me,
  O Tyre and Sidon, and all the coasts of
  Philistia?
  Will you retaliate against Me?
  But if you retaliate against Me,
  Swiftly and speedily I will return your
  retaliation upon your own head;
5 Because you have taken My silver and My
  gold,
  And have carried into your temples My
  prized possessions,
6 Also the people of Judah and the people of
  Jerusalem
  You have sold to the Greeks,
  That you may remove them far from their
  borders.

7 "Behold, I will raise them
  Out of the place to which you have sold
  them,
  And will return your retaliation upon your
  own head.
8 I will sell your sons and your daughters
  Into the hand of the people of Judah,

War, Not Peace—Joel 3:10 expresses the opposite thought from Isaiah 2:4 and Micah 4:3. Isaiah
and Micah describe the future glorious kingdom when the world will have peace instead of war.
Joel's call was, "Prepare for war!" (3:9).

And they will sell them to the Sabeans,[h]
To a people far off;
For the LORD has spoken.''

9 *Proclaim this among the nations:
"Prepare for war!
Wake up the mighty men,
Let all the men of war draw near,
Let them come up.
10 Beat your plowshares into swords
And your pruning hooks into spears;
Let the weak say, 'I *am* strong.' ''
11 Assemble and come, all you nations,
And gather together all around.
Cause Your mighty ones to go down there,
O LORD.

12 "Let the nations be wakened, and come up
to the Valley of Jehoshaphat;
For there I will sit to judge all the
surrounding nations.
13 Put in the sickle, for the harvest is ripe.
Come, go down;
For the winepress is full,
The vats overflow—
For their wickedness *is* great.''

14 *Multitudes, multitudes in the valley of
decision!
For the day of the LORD *is* near in the valley
of decision.
15 The sun and moon will grow dark,
And the stars will diminish their brightness.
16 The LORD also will roar from Zion,
And utter His voice from Jerusalem;
The heavens and earth will shake;
But the LORD will be a shelter for His people,
And the strength of the children of Israel.

17 "So you shall know that I *am* the LORD your
God,
Dwelling in Zion My holy mountain.
Then Jerusalem shall be holy,
And no aliens shall ever pass through her
again.''

18 *And it will come to pass in that day
That the mountains shall drip with new
wine,
The hills shall flow with milk,
And all the brooks of Judah shall be flooded
with water;
A fountain shall flow from the house of the
LORD
And water the Valley of Acacias.

19 "Egypt shall be a desolation,
And Edom a desolate wilderness,
Because of violence *against* the people of
Judah,
For they have shed innocent blood in their
land.
20 But Judah shall abide forever,
And Jerusalem from generation to
generation.
21 For I will acquit them of the guilt of
bloodshed, whom I had not acquitted;
For the LORD dwells in Zion.''

3:9–13 The harvest. God will call the nations to conflict and reap a final harvest (Isa. 63:1–6; Rev. 14:14–20). But His people will be strong, and God will uphold their cause.

3:14–17 The storm. The nations will feel the wrath of God, but He will care for His people with shelter and with strength. (See Pss. 46; 91.)

3:18–21 The garden. The book opens with drought and famine but closes with a description of a land of milk and honey. God will forgive His people and graciously dwell with them. He will give them a new beginning.

What the future holds for you depends on your relationship with the Lord. If you trust Jesus Christ as Savior, you will never be called into court (John 5:24; Rom. 8:1–4), and you never need fear the storm.

3:8 [h]Literally *Shebaites* (compare Isaiah 60:6 and Ezekiel 27:22)

AMOS

The prophet Amos came from Judah, but his ministry was primarily to Israel, the northern kingdom. He was a herdsman/farmer (7:14–15), and his book contains many rural allusions. He did not have the formal training of a prophet but was called of God and effectively preached God's Word.

Under Jeroboam II, the northern kingdom was enjoying a time of peace and prosperity; interest in "religion" was high. But the "revival" was shallow and had little effect on the everyday life of the people. The rich were getting richer, and the poor had no one to defend them. Amos warned that God was sending judgment to Israel and the nations around her, and in 722 B.C., Assyria brought that judgment.

The book contains eight *accusations* against the nations (chaps. 1—2), three *messages* about the sins of Israel (chaps. 3—6), and five *visions* of future judgment (chaps. 7—9). The book ends with the promise of restoration for God's people (9:11–15; see also Acts 15:14–17).

The name *Amos* means "to be burdened" (2:13), and he certainly was burdened because of the sins of his people.

CHAPTERS 1—2

1:3ff In chapters 1 and 2 Amos denounces the sins of six gentile nations before he pronounces judgment on Judah (2:4–5) and Israel (2:6–16). God did not give His law to the gentile nations, but He still held them accountable for their sins against humanity. Israel and Judah sinned against God's law (2:4) and God's love (2:9–12); but the Gentiles sinned against their "inner law," their conscience (Rom. 2:12–16).
The Gentiles sinned against their fellowman. Amos condemned their brutality, slavery, revenge, murder, and thievery. The nations seemed to get away with their sins but God eventually caught up with them. He is long-suffering, but He is also holy.

1 The words of Amos, who was among the sheepbreeders[a] of Tekoa, which he saw concerning Israel in the days of Uzziah king of Judah, and in the days of Jeroboam the son of Joash, king of Israel, two years before the earthquake.
2And he said:

"The LORD roars from Zion,
And utters His voice from Jerusalem;
The pastures of the shepherds mourn,
And the top of Carmel withers."

3*Thus says the LORD:

"For three transgressions of Damascus, and
for four,
I will not turn away its *punishment*,
Because they have threshed Gilead with
implements of iron.
4 But I will send a fire into the house of
Hazael,
Which shall devour the palaces of
Ben-Hadad.
5 I will also break the *gate* bar of Damascus,
And cut off the inhabitant from the Valley
of Aven,
And the one who holds the scepter from
Beth Eden.
The people of Syria shall go captive to Kir,"
Says the LORD.

6Thus says the LORD:

"For three transgressions of Gaza, and for
four,
I will not turn away its *punishment*,
Because they took captive the whole
captivity
To deliver *them* up to Edom.

1:1 aCompare 2 Kings 3:4

7   But I will send a fire upon the wall of Gaza,
Which shall devour its palaces.

8   I will cut off the inhabitant from Ashdod,
And the one who holds the scepter from
   Ashkelon;
I will turn My hand against Ekron,
And the remnant of the Philistines shall
   perish,"
Says the Lord God.

9Thus says the Lord:

"For three transgressions of Tyre, and for
   four,
I will not turn away its *punishment,*
Because they delivered up the whole
   captivity to Edom,
And did not remember the covenant of
   brotherhood.

10   But I will send a fire upon the wall of
   Tyre,
Which shall devour its palaces."

11Thus says the Lord:

"For three transgressions of Edom, and for
   four,
I will not turn away its *punishment,*
Because he pursued his brother with the
   sword,
And cast off all pity;
His anger tore perpetually,
And he kept his wrath forever.

12   But I will send a fire upon Teman,
Which shall devour the palaces of Bozrah."

13Thus says the Lord:

"For three transgressions of the people of
   Ammon, and for four,
I will not turn away its *punishment,*
Because they ripped open the women with
   child in Gilead,
That they might enlarge their territory.

14   But I will kindle a fire in the wall of Rabbah,
And it shall devour its palaces,
Amid shouting in the day of battle,
And a tempest in the day of the whirlwind.

15   Their king shall go into captivity,
He and his princes together,"
Says the Lord.

2

Thus says the Lord:

"For three transgressions of Moab, and for
   four,
I will not turn away its *punishment,*
Because he burned the bones of the king
   of Edom to lime.

2   But I will send a fire upon Moab,
And it shall devour the palaces of Kerioth;
Moab shall die with tumult,
With shouting *and* trumpet sound.

3   And I will cut off the judge from its midst,
And slay all its princes with him,"
Says the Lord.

4*Thus says the Lord:

"For three transgressions of Judah, and for
   four,
I will not turn away its *punishment,*

2:4ff Being the chosen people of God,
Israel and Judah had a greater responsibility
before the Lord. In one way or another, they
violated all the Ten Commandments; and
that meant God would have to judge them
(2:13–16).

If God judges *lost* people for their sins,
what will He do to those who claim to know
Him? Privilege brings responsibility (Luke
12:48), and where there is responsibility,
there will be accountability. The people of
Israel and Judah rejoiced when they heard
Amos condemn their neighbors; but then he
condemned *God's people* for their sins, and
that was not acceptable to them.

Is God being long-suffering toward you?
Is His judgment of others a warning to you?
Are you heeding it?

Because they have despised the law of the
  LORD,
And have not kept His commandments.
Their lies lead them astray,
Lies which their fathers followed.
5   But I will send a fire upon Judah,
And it shall devour the palaces of
  Jerusalem."

6Thus says the LORD:

"For three transgressions of Israel, and for
  four,
I will not turn away its *punishment*,
Because they sell the righteous for silver,
And the poor for a pair of sandals.
7   They pant after[b] the dust of the earth *which
  is* on the head of the poor,
And pervert the way of the humble.
A man and his father go in to the *same* girl,
To defile My holy name.
8   They lie down by every altar on clothes
  taken in pledge,
And drink the wine of the condemned *in* the
  house of their god.

9   "Yet *it was* I *who* destroyed the Amorite
  before them,
Whose height *was* like the height of the
  cedars,
And he *was as* strong as the oaks;
Yet I destroyed his fruit above
And his roots beneath.
10   Also *it was* I *who* brought you up from the
  land of Egypt,
And led you forty years through the
  wilderness,
To possess the land of the Amorite.
11   I raised up some of your sons as prophets,
And some of your young men as Nazirites.
Is it not so, O you children of Israel?"
  Says the LORD.
12 "But you gave the Nazirites wine to drink,
And commanded the prophets saying,
'Do not prophesy!'

13 "Behold, I am weighed down by you,
As a cart full of sheaves is weighed down.
14   Therefore flight shall perish from the swift,
The strong shall not strengthen his power,
Nor shall the mighty deliver himself;
15   He shall not stand who handles the bow,
The swift of foot shall not escape,
Nor shall he who rides a horse deliver
  himself.
16   The most courageous men of might
Shall flee naked in that day,"
  Says the LORD.

CHAPTER 3

3:1, 2 Past. This is another reminder that
privilege brings responsibility. The Lord
delivered the Jews from Egypt and called
them to be His special people. *That was why
He was punishing them.* God's gracious
election of Israel did not give them the right
to disobey Him, and the same truth applies
to the church today. Election involves
responsibility (John 15:16; Eph. 1:4; 1 Pet.
2:4–5, 9).

3 Hear* this word that the LORD has spoken
against you, O children of Israel, against the
whole family which I brought up from the land
of Egypt, saying:

2   "You only have I known of all the families
  of the earth;
Therefore I will punish you for all your
  iniquities."

2:7 [b]Or *trample on*

3 *Can two walk together, unless they are
  agreed?
4 Will a lion roar in the forest, when he has
  no prey?
  Will a young lion cry out of his den, if he
  has caught nothing?
5 Will a bird fall into a snare on the earth,
  where there is no trap for it?
  Will a snare spring up from the earth, if it
  has caught nothing at all?
6 If a trumpet is blown in a city, will not the
  people be afraid?
  If there is calamity in a city, will not the
  LORD have done *it?*

7 Surely the Lord GOD does nothing,
  Unless He reveals His secret to His servants
  the prophets.
8 A lion has roared!
  Who will not fear?
  The Lord GOD has spoken!
  Who can but prophesy?

9 "Proclaim in the palaces at Ashdod,c
  And in the palaces in the land of Egypt, and
  say:
  'Assemble on the mountains of Samaria;
  See great tumults in her midst,
  And the oppressed within her.
10 For they do not know to do right,'
  Says the LORD,
  'Who store up violence and robbery in their
  palaces.' "

11*Therefore thus says the Lord GOD:

  "An adversary *shall be* all around the land;
  He shall sap your strength from you,
  And your palaces shall be plundered."

12Thus says the LORD:

  "As a shepherd takes from the mouth of a
  lion
  Two legs or a piece of an ear,
  So shall the children of Israel be taken out
  Who dwell in Samaria—
  In the corner of a bed and on the edged of
  a couch!
13 Hear and testify against the house of
  Jacob,"
  Says the Lord GOD, the God of hosts,
14 "That in the day I punish Israel for their
  transgressions,
  I will also visit *destruction* on the altars of
  Bethel;
  And the horns of the altar shall be cut off
  And fall to the ground.
15 I will destroy the winter house along with
  the summer house;
  The houses of ivory shall perish,
  And the great houses shall have an end,"
  Says the LORD.

4 Hear* this word, you cows of Bashan, who
  are on the mountain of Samaria,
  Who oppress the poor,

3:9 cFollowing Masoretic Text; Septuagint reads *Assyria.*
3:12 dThe Hebrew is uncertain.

3:3–10 *Present.* What right did a common
herdsman like Amos have to denounce his
own people and warn of judgment? He and
God were walking together because they
agreed (v. 3). God was roaring like a lion
(1:2; vv. 4, 8) and setting the trap for sinners
(v. 5). Amos was blowing the trumpet to
warn people (v. 6) because God had shared
His secrets with him (v. 7; Ps. 25:14). In
spite of his humble origins, Amos was God's
servant.

3:11–15 *Future.* If a shepherd lost an
animal, he had to pay for it, unless he could
prove that a beast killed it. He did that by
bringing home some of the parts that were
not devoured. Israel could hear the lion roar,
but the nation would not repent. Soon, only
a remnant would be left.

CHAPTER 4

4:1ff "Yet you have not returned to Me!" is
the sad refrain of this chapter (vv. 6, 8, 9,
10, 11). God's disciplines are for the purpose
of restoration, to bring people to true
repentance.

God used several means of discipline—
drought, famine, crop diseases, locusts,
plagues, war, and local catastrophes
(v. 11)—and yet the people did not get the
message. They had met with God's
disciplines, but the next step was to *meet
God Himself* (v. 12). He was personally
coming to judge them.

What a tragedy that the people kept living
in luxury (vv. 1–3) and carrying out their
religious duties (vv. 4–5) while ignoring the
call of God. It took courage for Amos to call
the wealthy women "cows" and to picture
them being led away to slaughter. In their
comfort and prosperity, the people thought
they were immune from judgment, but it
came just the same.

Are you prepared to meet your God?

Who crush the needy,
Who say to your husbands,*e* "Bring *wine*,
  let us drink!"
2 The Lord GOD has sworn by His holiness:
"Behold, the days shall come upon you
When He will take you away with
  fishhooks,
And your posterity with fishhooks.
3 You will go out *through* broken *walls,*
Each one straight ahead of her,
And you will be cast into Harmon,"
Says the LORD.

4 "Come to Bethel and transgress,
At Gilgal multiply transgression;
Bring your sacrifices every morning,
Your tithes every three days.*f*
5 Offer a sacrifice of thanksgiving with
  leaven,
Proclaim *and* announce the freewill
  offerings;
For this you love,
You children of Israel!"
Says the Lord GOD.
6 "Also I gave you cleanness of teeth in all your
  cities.
And lack of bread in all your places;
Yet you have not returned to Me,"
Says the LORD.

7 "I also withheld rain from you,
When *there were* still three months to the
  harvest.
I made it rain on one city,
I withheld rain from another city.
One part was rained upon,
And where it did not rain the part withered.
8 So two *or* three cities wandered to another
  city to drink water,
But they were not satisfied;
Yet you have not returned to Me,"
Says the LORD.

9 "I blasted you with blight and mildew.
When your gardens increased,
Your vineyards,
Your fig trees,
And your olive trees,
The locust devoured *them;*
Yet you have not returned to Me,"
Says the LORD.

10 "I sent among you a plague after the manner
  of Egypt;
Your young men I killed with a sword,
Along with your captive horses;
I made the stench of your camps come up
  into your nostrils;
Yet you have not returned to Me,"
Says the LORD.

4:1 *e*Literally *their lords* or *their masters*   4:4 *f*Or *years*
(compare Deuteronomy 14:28)

"Religion"—The prophet Amos denounced luxury and urged the people to care for the poor of the land. He particularly condemned their expensive houses (3:15; 5:11), their drinking (4:1), their complacency (6:1), and their costly parties (6:3–6; 8:10). The rich got their money by exploiting the poor (5:11–15). Yet those wealthy people were "religious" and faithfully participated in the temple services (4:4–5; 5:21–27). Their "religion" was only a masquerade to cover their sins. Are professed believers guilty of any of these sins today?

11 "I overthrew *some* of you,
As God overthrew Sodom and Gomorrah,
And you were like a firebrand plucked from
   the burning;
Yet you have not returned to Me,"
Says the LORD.

12 "Therefore thus will I do to you, O Israel;
Because I will do this to you,
Prepare to meet your God, O Israel!"

13 For behold,
He who forms mountains,
And creates the wind,
Who declares to man what his[g] thought *is*,
And makes the morning darkness,
Who treads the high places of the earth—
The LORD God of hosts *is* His name.

5 Hear* this word which I take up against you,
a lamentation, O house of Israel:

2   The virgin of Israel has fallen;
She will rise no more.
She lies forsaken on her land;
There is no one to raise her up.

3For thus says the Lord GOD:

"The city that goes out by a thousand
Shall have a hundred left,
And that which goes out by a hundred
Shall have ten left to the house of Israel."

4*For thus says the LORD to the house of Israel:

"Seek Me and live;
5   But do not seek Bethel,
Nor enter Gilgal,
Nor pass over to Beersheba;
For Gilgal shall surely go into captivity,
And Bethel shall come to nothing.
6   Seek the LORD and live,
Lest He break out like fire *in* the house of
   Joseph,
And devour *it*,
With no one to quench *it* in Bethel—
7   You who turn justice to wormwood,
And lay righteousness to rest in the earth!"

8   He made the Pleiades and Orion;
He turns the shadow of death into morning
And makes the day dark as night;
He calls for the waters of the sea
And pours them out on the face of the earth;
The LORD *is* His name.
9   He rains ruin upon the strong,
So that fury comes upon the fortress.

CHAPTER 5

5:1–3 *Lamentation.* This is a funeral dirge for a nation that was dead and left unburied. The Assyrians would come, and Israel would be taken captive. Israel thought she was a lovely virgin, but she was only a fallen corpse, left to rot. No wonder Amos wept!

5:4–15 *Invitation.* But God still gives His gracious invitation: "Seek Me and live" (vv. 4, 6, 14). The people flocked to their holy places with their sacrifices, but that would not save them. The nation would not listen to the Lord's servants (v. 10), so the Lord told them to be quiet (v. 13). God knows our sins, and yet in mercy He calls us to come to Him for cleansing. What a gracious God!

4:13 ⁹Or *His*

Jesus' Coming—When you pray, "Thy kingdom come," be sure that you mean it. Do you really want the Lord Jesus to return today, or will His coming upset your plans? Some of God's people will be ashamed when they meet Him (1 John 2:28), while others will welcome Him with joy (1 Thess. 2:19–20).

The joyful anticipation of His coming is a great motivation for holy living (1 John 3:1–3) and faithful service (Luke 12:35–48).

Justice—Amos 5:24 is a key verse in the book. There was gross injustice in the land as the rich exploited the poor and the religious leaders did nothing about it. God wants justice to be like a mighty river that cleanses society of evil and refreshes everything it touches.

10 They hate the one who rebukes in the gate,
And they abhor the one who speaks
uprightly.
11 Therefore, because you tread down the poor
And take grain taxes from him,
Though you have built houses of hewn
stone,
Yet you shall not dwell in them;
You have planted pleasant vineyards,
But you shall not drink wine from them.
12 For I know your manifold transgressions
And your mighty sins:
Afflicting the just *and* taking bribes;
Diverting the poor *from justice* at the gate.
13 Therefore the prudent keep silent at that
time,
For it *is* an evil time.

14 Seek good and not evil,
That you may live;
So the LORD God of hosts will be with you,
As you have spoken.
15 Hate evil, love good;
Establish justice in the gate.
It may be that the LORD God of hosts
Will be gracious to the remnant of Joseph.

5:16–27 Condemnation. Amos saw the day of the Lord approaching, a day of judgment, darkness, and despair. The people had a false confidence that "the day of the LORD" would bring blessing to the nation (vv. 18–20), not unlike some believers today who think of the return of Christ only as an escape to heaven. God would send judgment in spite of their religious activities and generous gifts of sacrifices (Isa. 1:12–23). God still wants obedience and not sacrifice.

16*Therefore the LORD God of hosts, the Lord,
says this:

"*There shall be* wailing in all streets,
And they shall say in all the highways,
'Alas! Alas!'
They shall call the farmer to mourning,
And skillful lamenters to wailing.
17 In all vineyards *there shall be* wailing,
For I will pass through you,"
Says the LORD.

18 Woe to you who desire the day of the LORD!
For what good *is* the day of the LORD to you?
It *will be* darkness, and not light.
19 It *will be* as though a man fled from a lion,
And a bear met him!
Or *as though* he went into the house,
Leaned his hand on the wall,
And a serpent bit him!
20 *Is* not the day of the LORD darkness, and
not light?
Is it not very dark, with no brightness in
it?

21 "I hate, I despise your feast days,
And I do not savor your sacred assemblies.
22 Though you offer Me burnt offerings and
your grain offerings,
I will not accept *them,*
Nor will I regard your fattened peace
offerings.
23 Take away from Me the noise of your songs,
For I will not hear the melody of your
stringed instruments.
24 But let justice run down like water,
And righteousness like a mighty stream.

25 "Did you offer Me sacrifices and offerings
In the wilderness forty years, O house of
Israel?
26 You also carried Sikkuth[h] your king[i]

5:26 [h]A pagan deity [i]Septuagint and Vulgate read *tabernacle of Moloch.*

And Chiun,[j] your idols,
The star of your gods,
Which you made for yourselves.
27 Therefore I will send you into captivity
beyond Damascus,"
Says the LORD, whose name *is* the God of
hosts.

6 Woe[*] to you *who are* at ease in Zion,
And trust in Mount Samaria,
Notable persons in the chief nation,
To whom the house of Israel comes!
2 Go over to Calneh and see;
And from there go to Hamath the great;
Then go down to Gath of the Philistines.
Are you better than these kingdoms?
Or is their territory greater than your
territory?

3 *Woe to* you who put far off the day of
doom,
Who cause the seat of violence to come
near;
4 Who lie on beds of ivory,
Stretch out on your couches,
Eat lambs from the flock
And calves from the midst of the stall;
5 Who sing idly to the sound of stringed
instruments,
And invent for yourselves musical
instruments like David;
6 Who drink wine from bowls,
And anoint yourselves with the best
ointments,
But are not grieved for the affliction of
Joseph.
7 Therefore they shall now go captive as the
first of the captives,
And those who recline at banquets shall be
removed.

8 The Lord GOD has sworn by Himself,
The LORD God of hosts says:
"I abhor the pride of Jacob,
And hate his palaces;
Therefore I will deliver up *the* city
And all that is in it."

9*Then it shall come to pass, that if ten men
remain in one house, they shall die. 10And when
a relative *of the dead,* with one who will burn
the bodies, picks up the bodies[k] to take them out
of the house, he will say to one inside the house,
"*Are there* any more with you?"
Then someone will say, "None."
And he will say, "Hold your tongue! For we dare
not mention the name of the LORD."

11 For behold, the LORD gives a command:
He will break the great house into bits,
And the little house into pieces.

12 *Do horses run on rocks?
Does *one* plow *there* with oxen?
Yet you have turned justice into gall,
And the fruit of righteousness into
wormwood,
13 You who rejoice over Lo Debar,[l]

CHAPTER 6

6:1–8 The nation was guilty of complacency
born of false confidence (vv. 1–2), trusting
the military leaders and not the Lord. The
people were also guilty of self-indulgence
and unconcern for hurting persons of the
land (vv. 3–8). After all, the day of judgment
was far away! Or was it?

6:9–14 God appointed three judgments for
them: death (vv. 9–10), destruction (vv. 11–
13), and defeat (v. 14). The banqueters
would become corpses, and the great
houses would be left in ruins. The leaders
boasted of their recent victories (v. 13), but
Assyria would bring defeat.

6:12 Horses cannot safely run on the rocky
cliffs, and oxen cannot plow there. But Israel
was not as smart as the animals, for she
was attempting the impossible: trying to
escape judgment by disobeying the Lord.
"We are an exception to the rule!" was the
confident boast, but the people did not
escape. Their sins found them out.

---

[j]A pagan deity   6:10 [k]Literally *bones*   6:13 [l]Literally *Nothing*

Who say, "Have we not taken Karnaim[m] for ourselves
By our own strength?"

14 "But, behold, I will raise up a nation against you,
O house of Israel,"
Says the LORD God of hosts;
"And they will afflict you from the entrance of Hamath
To the Valley of the Arabah."

CHAPTER 7

7:1–9 Defending his people. The closing three chapters record five visions that describe the future of Israel. Eleven times the prophet refers to God as "the LORD God," the Sovereign Ruler over all things. After the first two visions, Amos interceded for the people, and the Lord relented. But Amos did not intercede after the third vision, for the nation had been measured and was found wanting. God weighs us (Prov. 21:2; Dan. 5:27) and measures us by His standards, and His examination is always accurate.

7 Thus* the Lord GOD showed me: Behold, He formed locust swarms at the beginning of the late crop; indeed *it was* the late crop after the king's mowings. 2And so it was, when they had finished eating the grass of the land, that I said:

"O Lord GOD, forgive, I pray!
Oh, that Jacob may stand,
For he *is* small!"
3   *So* the LORD relented concerning this.
"It shall not be," said the LORD.

4Thus the Lord GOD showed me: Behold, the Lord GOD called for conflict by fire, and it consumed the great deep and devoured the territory. 5Then I said:

"O Lord GOD, cease, I pray!
Oh, that Jacob may stand,
For he *is* small!"
6   *So* the LORD relented concerning this.
"This also shall not be," said the Lord GOD.

7Thus He showed me: Behold, the Lord stood on a wall *made* with a plumb line, with a plumb line in His hand. 8And the LORD said to me, "Amos, what do you see?"
And I said, "A plumb line."
Then the Lord said:

"Behold, I am setting a plumb line
In the midst of My people Israel;
I will not pass by them anymore.
9   The high places of Isaac shall be desolate,
And the sanctuaries of Israel shall be laid waste.
I will rise with the sword against the house of Jeroboam."

7:10–17 Defending his ministry. Here is a conflict between two ministries—priest and prophet, the institutional and the radical. The priest seeks to conserve the past while the prophet threatens the present because he wants to preserve the future. There is also a conflict between structure and ministry. Amaziah was a man of position while Amos was a humble farmer with a commission from the Lord. But Amos did not back down; he remained true to his calling and let God deal with Amaziah.
If you were to choose either Amaziah or Amos to be your spiritual leader, which would you select—and why?

10*Then Amaziah the priest of Bethel sent to Jeroboam king of Israel, saying, "Amos has conspired against you in the midst of the house of Israel. The land is not able to bear all his words. 11For thus Amos has said:

'Jeroboam shall die by the sword,
And Israel shall surely be led away captive
From their own land.' "

---

[m]Literally *Horns,* symbol of strength

Called of God—Amos is a good example of what Paul wrote in 1 Corinthians 1:26–29. God often bypasses the so-called great people and chooses to call and bless the humble and the weak. Yes, God can also use those who are gifted and who hold high positions in this world, but He is not limited to them. Both Moses (Acts 7:22) and Paul (Acts 26:24) were well educated, but at least seven of our Lord's disciples were common fishermen (John 21:1–3). R. A. Torrey was a brilliant man and a gifted evangelist; he worked closely with evangelist Dwight L. Moody, who had very little education. God used both men in a remarkable way because both gave all they had to the Lord.

¹²Then Amaziah said to Amos:

> "Go, you seer!
> Flee to the land of Judah.
> There eat bread,
> And there prophesy.
> ¹³ But never again prophesy at Bethel,
> For it *is* the king's sanctuary,
> And it *is* the royal residence."

¹⁴Then Amos answered, and said to Amaziah:

> "I *was* no prophet,
> Nor *was* I a son of a prophet,
> But I *was* a sheepbreeder*ⁿ*
> And a tender of sycamore fruit.
> ¹⁵ Then the LORD took me as I followed the
>   flock,
> And the LORD said to me,
> 'Go, prophesy to My people Israel.'
> ¹⁶ Now therefore, hear the word of the LORD:
> You say, 'Do not prophesy against Israel,
> And do not spout against the house of Isaac.'

¹⁷"Therefore thus says the LORD:

> 'Your wife shall be a harlot in the city;
> Your sons and daughters shall fall by the
>   sword;
> Your land shall be divided by *survey* line;
> You shall die in a defiled land;
> And Israel shall surely be led away captive
> From his own land.' "

8 Thus* the Lord GOD showed me: Behold, a basket of summer fruit. ²And He said, "Amos, what do you see?"
So I said, "A basket of summer fruit."
Then the LORD said to me:

> "The end has come upon My people Israel;
> I will not pass by them anymore.
> ³ And the songs of the temple
> Shall be wailing in that day,"
> Says the Lord GOD—
> "Many dead bodies everywhere,
> They shall be thrown out in silence."

> ⁴ Hear this, you who swallow up° the needy,
> And make the poor of the land fail,

⁵Saying:

> "When will the New Moon be past,
> That we may sell grain?
> And the Sabbath,
> That we may trade wheat?
> Making the ephah small and the shekel
>   large,
> Falsifying the scales by deceit,
> ⁶ That we may buy the poor for silver,
> And the needy for a pair of sandals—
> Even sell the bad wheat?"

> ⁷ The LORD has sworn by the pride of Jacob:
> "Surely I will never forget any of their
>   works.
> ⁸ Shall the land not tremble for this,

CHAPTER 8

8:1ff Amos's fourth vision gave one clear message: "Israel is ripe for judgment!" As the farmer cuts off the ripe fruit, so God will cut off Israel. He had been long-suffering with them, but now the day of reckoning had come. The wealthy had sinned against both men and God. They were weary of their religious duties and only endured the Sabbath, waiting until they could start making money again. They changed God's standards so that they might exploit the poor, and they cheapened their products and then raised the prices. No wonder God was angry with them.

Amos told them to expect an earthquake (v. 8; 1:1), an eclipse (v. 9), a funeral (v. 10), and a famine (vv. 11–14). God's Word is our spiritual nourishment (Matt. 4:4; 1 Pet. 2:2), and there can be no substitute. When God's people reject His Word, He sometimes judges them by taking away His Word and leaving them to go hungry as they live on substitutes.

7:14 ⁿCompare 2 Kings 3:4   8:4 °Or *trample on* (compare 2:7)

And everyone mourn who dwells in it?
All of it shall swell like the River,[p]
Heave and subside
Like the River of Egypt.

9 "And it shall come to pass in that day," says
the Lord GOD,
"That I will make the sun go down at noon,
And I will darken the earth in broad
daylight;
10 I will turn your feasts into mourning,
And all your songs into lamentation;
I will bring sackcloth on every waist,
And baldness on every head;
I will make it like mourning for an only *son*,
And its end like a bitter day.

11 "Behold, the days are coming," says the
Lord GOD,
"That I will send a famine on the land,
Not a famine of bread,
Nor a thirst for water,
But of hearing the words of the LORD.
12 They shall wander from sea to sea,
And from north to east;
They shall run to and fro, seeking the word
of the LORD,
But shall not find *it*.

13 "In that day the fair virgins
And strong young men
Shall faint from thirst.
14 Those who swear by the sin[q] of Samaria,
Who say,
'As your god lives, O Dan!'
And, 'As the way of Beersheba lives!'
They shall fall and never rise again."

CHAPTER 9

9:1–4 Judging. Amos saw the Lord at the sanctuary at Bethel, where the people were carrying on their hypocritical worship. He was about to destroy the sanctuary and all the worshipers; nobody would escape. If anyone tried to escape, he would be tracked down and slain. It is a basic principle that judgment begins at the house of the Lord (1 Pet. 4:17; see also Ezek. 9:6).

9 I* saw the Lord standing by the altar, and He said:

"Strike the doorposts, that the thresholds
may shake,
And break them on the heads of them all.
I will slay the last of them with the sword.
He who flees from them shall not get away,
And he who escapes from them shall not
be delivered.

2 "Though they dig into hell,[r]
From there My hand shall take them;
Though they climb up to heaven,
From there I will bring them down;
3 And though they hide themselves on top of
Carmel,
From there I will search and take them;
Though they hide from My sight at the
bottom of the sea,
From there I will command the serpent, and
it shall bite them;
4 Though they go into captivity before their
enemies,
From there I will command the sword,
And it shall slay them.
I will set My eyes on them for harm and
not for good."

8:8 [p]That is, the Nile; some Hebrew manuscripts, Septuagint, Syriac, Targum, and Vulgate read *River;* Masoretic Text reads *the light.*   8:14 [q]Or *Ashima,* a Syrian goddess   9:2 [r]Or *Sheol*

5 The Lord God of hosts,
He who touches the earth and it melts,
And all who dwell there mourn;
All of it shall swell like the River,[s]
And subside like the River of Egypt.
6 He who builds His layers in the sky,
And has founded His strata in the earth;
Who calls for the waters of the sea,
And pours them out on the face of the
earth—
The Lord *is* His name.

7 "*Are* you not like the people of Ethiopia to
Me,
O children of Israel?" says the Lord.
"Did I not bring up Israel from the land of
Egypt,
The Philistines from Caphtor,
And the Syrians from Kir?

8 *"Behold, the eyes of the Lord God *are* on the
sinful kingdom,
And I will destroy it from the face of the
earth;
Yet I will not utterly destroy the house of
Jacob,"
Says the Lord.

9:8–10 Sifting. God would destroy the sanctuary at Bethel, but He would not utterly destroy His people. He would send them among the Gentiles and sift out the true from the false. In His grace, God spares a remnant so that the nation might continue.

9 "For surely I will command,
And will sift the house of Israel among all
nations,
As *grain* is sifted in a sieve;
Yet not the smallest grain shall fall to the
ground.
10 All the sinners of My people shall die by
the sword,
Who say, 'The calamity shall not overtake
nor confront us.'

11 *"On that day I will raise up
The tabernacle[t] of David, which has fallen
down,
And repair its damages;
I will raise up its ruins,
And rebuild it as in the days of old;
12 That they may possess the remnant of
Edom,[u]
And all the Gentiles who are called by My
name,"
Says the Lord who does this thing.

9:11–15 Blessing. The royal dynasty of David was like a tent or booth that had fallen down, but God will raise it, repair it and restore it. His people will return to their land and enjoy once again the blessings of God (Isa. 11). Meanwhile, God is calling out His church from both Jews and Gentiles (Acts 15:6–21), and our task is to share the gospel with every creature.

13 "Behold, the days are coming," says the
Lord,
"When the plowman shall overtake the
reaper,
And the treader of grapes him who sows
seed;
The mountains shall drip with sweet
wine,
And all the hills shall flow *with it.*
14 I will bring back the captives of My people
Israel;
They shall build the waste cities and inhabit
them;
They shall plant vineyards and drink wine
from them;

9:5 [s]That is, the Nile   9:11 [t]Literally *booth,* figure of a deposed dynasty   9:12 [u]Septuagint reads *mankind.*

They shall also make gardens and eat fruit
from them.
15 I will plant them in their land,
And no longer shall they be pulled up
From the land I have given them,"
Says the LORD your God.

OBADIAH

When the Babylonians destroyed Jerusalem, the Edomites rejoiced and helped the enemy instead of helping their brethren (Gen. 25:21–26; Ps. 137:7–9). It was a repetition of the ancient conflict between Esau and Jacob, which symbolizes the battle between the flesh and the Spirit.

The vision of Obadiah.

Thus says the Lord GOD concerning Edom
(We have heard a report from the LORD,
And a messenger has been sent among the
    nations, *saying,*
"Arise, and let us rise up against her for
    battle"):

2 *"Behold, I will make you small among the
    nations;
You shall be greatly despised.
3 The pride of your heart has deceived you,
You who dwell in the clefts of the rock,
Whose habitation is high;
You who say in your heart, 'Who will bring
    me down to the ground?'
4 Though you ascend *as* high as the eagle,
And though you set your nest among the
    stars,
From there I will bring you down," says the
    LORD.

5 "If thieves had come to you,
If robbers by night—
Oh, how you will be cut off!—
Would they not have stolen till they had
    enough?
If grape-gatherers had come to you,
Would they not have left *some* gleanings?

6 "Oh, how Esau shall be searched out!
How his hidden treasures shall be sought
    after!
7 All the men in your confederacy
Shall force you to the border;
The men at peace with you
Shall deceive you *and* prevail against you.
Those who eat your bread shall lay a trap[a]
    for you.
No one is aware of it.

8 "Will I not in that day," says the LORD,
"Even destroy the wise *men* from Edom,
And understanding from the mountains of
    Esau?
9 Then your mighty men, O Teman, shall be
    dismayed,

Vv. 2–16 What were the sins of Edom? *Pride* stands at the top of the list, and God promised to bring them down (vv. 2–4). They were also guilty of *looting* (v. 13), and God said they would be looted (vv. 5–7). They were *violent* (v. 10) and *indifferent* (v. 11), and they *rejoiced* at the plight of the Jews (v. 12; Prov. 24:17–18); but God warned that they would one day be slaughtered (v. 8). What they had done to others would be done to them (v. 15), and there was no escape. (See Jer. 50:29, Matt. 7:12 and Gal. 6:7–8.)

---

7 [a]Or *wound,* or *plot*

"The Other Side"—It is a cruel thing to stand "on the other side" when our brothers and sisters need our help. The priest and the Levite retreated to "the other side" instead of helping the wounded pilgrim (Luke 10:31–32). If it is in our power to help, we must do so (Prov. 24:11–12), and we must not substitute words for deeds (James 2:14–17; 1 John 3:16–19).

To the end that everyone from the
mountains of Esau
May be cut off by slaughter.

10 "For violence against your brother Jacob,
Shame shall cover you,
And you shall be cut off forever.
11 In the day that you stood on the other side—
In the day that strangers carried captive his
forces,
When foreigners entered his gates
And cast lots for Jerusalem—
Even you *were* as one of them.

12 "But you should not have gazed on the day
of your brother
In the day of his captivity;[b]
Nor should you have rejoiced over the
children of Judah
In the day of their destruction;
Nor should you have spoken proudly
In the day of distress.
13 You should not have entered the gate of My
people
In the day of their calamity.
Indeed, you should not have gazed on their
affliction
In the day of their calamity,
Nor laid *hands* on their substance
In the day of their calamity.
14 You should not have stood at the crossroads
To cut off those among them who escaped;
Nor should you have delivered up those
among them who remained
In the day of distress.

15 "For the day of the Lord upon all the nations
is near;
As you have done, it shall be done to you;
Your reprisal shall return upon your own
head.
16 For as you drank on My holy mountain,
So shall all the nations drink continually;
Yes, they shall drink, and swallow,
And they shall be as though they had never
been.

Vv. 17–21 But there is a bright future for
Israel, for they shall "possess their
possessions" (v. 17). Babylon burned the
city of Jerusalem and the temple, but Israel
will be a fire to burn the enemy: "And the
kingdom shall be the Lord's" (v. 21)!

17*"But on Mount Zion there shall be
deliverance,
And there shall be holiness;
The house of Jacob shall possess their
possessions.
18 The house of Jacob shall be a fire,
And the house of Joseph a flame;
But the house of Esau *shall be* stubble;
They shall kindle them and devour them,
And no survivor shall *remain* of the house
of Esau,"
For the Lord has spoken.

19 The South[c] shall possess the mountains of
Esau,
And the Lowland shall possess Philistia.
They shall possess the fields of Ephraim
And the fields of Samaria.
Benjamin *shall possess* Gilead.
20 And the captives of this host of the children
of Israel

---

12 *b*Literally *On the day he became a foreigner* / 19 *c*Hebrew
Negev

Shall possess the land of the Canaanites
As far as Zarephath.
The captives of Jerusalem who are in
  Sepharad
Shall possess the cities of the South.[d]
21 Then saviors[e] shall come to Mount Zion
To judge the mountains of Esau,
And the kingdom shall be the LORD's.

---

20 [d]Hebrew *Negev* 21 [e]Or *deliverers*

JONAH

The prophet Jonah was a real person and not just a character in a parable (2 Kings 14:25; Matt. 12:39–41). God sent him to Nineveh, the capital of the Assyrian Empire, to a people despised by the Jews. Jonah would rather that Nineveh be destroyed than that the city have an opportunity to repent and be spared. The Assyrians were a cruel people who showed no mercy to their enemies, and Jonah wanted them out of the way.

The book emphasizes God's grace both to Nineveh and to Jonah. Though Nineveh was a wicked city, God gave the inhabitants opportunity to be spared. Though Jonah was a rebellious servant, God forgave him, used him, and tenderly sought to help him overcome his anger. One outline of the book is the following: chapter 1—rebellion: Jonah goes down; chapter 2—repentance: Jonah goes up; chapter 3—restoration: Jonah goes to; and chapter 4—resentment: Jonah goes out.

The main character in this book is neither the prophet nor the great fish but *God*, who is mentioned thirty-eight times. The book deals with the important question, "How do you respond to the word and will of God?"

CHAPTER 1

1:1–4 Jonah thought he had a choice. He forgot that the will of God is not an option: it is an obligation and an opportunity. When we run from God's will, we always go down (vv. 3, 5, 15, 17; 2:6). We may end up sacrificing safety for danger and peace for a storm.

1:5–13 The "pagan" sailors reveal more character than does the prophet of God. While Jonah was sleeping, they were crying out to their gods, and they did their best to save him (v. 13). Jonah was a Jew, and the Jews were to be a blessing to the whole world (Gen. 12:1–3). But the man who should have been saving the lost was being saved by the lost!

❝*To fear God is to stand in awe of Him; to be afraid of God is to run away from Him.*❞
—Carroll E. Simcox

1 Now* the word of the LORD came to Jonah the son of Amittai, saying, 2"Arise, go to Nineveh, that great city, and cry out against it; for their wickedness has come up before Me." 3But Jonah arose to flee to Tarshish from the presence of the LORD. He went down to Joppa, and found a ship going to Tarshish; so he paid the fare, and went down into it, to go with them to Tarshish from the presence of the LORD.

4But the LORD sent out a great wind on the sea, and there was a mighty tempest on the sea, so that the ship was about to be broken up.

5*Then the mariners were afraid; and every man cried out to his god, and threw the cargo that was in the ship into the sea, to lighten the load.ᵃ But Jonah had gone down into the lowest parts of the ship, had lain down, and was fast asleep.

6So the captain came to him, and said to him, "What do you mean, sleeper? Arise, call on your God; perhaps your God will consider us, so that we may not perish."

7And they said to one another, "Come, let us cast lots, that we may know for whose cause this trouble *has come* upon us." So they cast lots, and the lot fell on Jonah. 8Then they said to him, "Please tell us! For whose cause *is* this trouble upon us? What is your occupation? And where do you come from? What is your country? And of what people are you?"

9So he said to them, "I *am* a Hebrew; and I fear the LORD, the God of heaven, who made the sea and the dry *land*."

10Then the men were exceedingly afraid, and said to him, "Why have you done this?" For the men knew that he fled from the presence of the LORD, because he had told them. 11Then they said to him, "What shall we do to you that the sea may be calm for us?"—for the sea was growing more tempestuous.

12And he said to them, "Pick me up and throw me into the sea; then the sea will become calm

---

1:5 ᵃLiterally *from upon them*

for you. For I know that this great tempest *is* because of me."

¹³Nevertheless the men rowed hard to return to land, but they could not, for the sea continued to grow more tempestuous against them. ¹⁴*Therefore they cried out to the LORD and said, "We pray, O LORD, please do not let us perish for this man's life, and do not charge us with innocent blood; for You, O LORD, have done as it pleased You." ¹⁵So they picked up Jonah and threw him into the sea, and the sea ceased from its raging. ¹⁶Then the men feared the LORD exceedingly, and offered a sacrifice to the LORD and took vows.

¹⁷Now the LORD had prepared a great fish to swallow Jonah. And Jonah was in the belly of the fish three days and three nights.

2 Then* Jonah prayed to the LORD his God from the fish's belly. ²And he said:

"I cried out to the LORD because of my
    affliction,
And He answered me.

"Out of the belly of Sheol I cried,
And You heard my voice.
3 For You cast me into the deep,
    Into the heart of the seas,
    And the floods surrounded me;
    All Your billows and Your waves passed
      over me.
4 *Then I said, 'I have been cast out of Your
    sight;
    Yet I will look again toward Your holy
      temple.'
5 The waters surrounded me, *even* to my soul;
    The deep closed around me;
    Weeds were wrapped around my head.
6 I went down to the moorings of the
    mountains;
    The earth with its bars *closed* behind me
      forever;
    Yet You have brought up my life from the
      pit,
    O LORD, my God.

7 "When my soul fainted within me,
    I remembered the LORD;
    And my prayer went *up* to You,
    Into Your holy temple.

8 "Those who regard worthless idols
    Forsake their own Mercy.
9 *But I will sacrifice to You
    With the voice of thanksgiving;
    I will pay what I have vowed.
    Salvation *is* of the LORD."

¹⁰So the LORD spoke to the fish, and it vomited Jonah onto dry *land.*

3 Now* the word of the LORD came to Jonah the second time, saying, ²"Arise, go to Nineveh, that great city, and preach to it the message that I tell you." ³So Jonah arose and went to Nineveh, according to the word of the LORD. Now Nineveh was an exceedingly great city, a three-day journey[b] *in* extent. ⁴And Jonah began to enter

3:3 [b]Exact meaning unknown

1:14–17 A believer out of fellowship with God can cause a great deal of trouble. Jonah put the crew in danger and left the Ninevites without a message of hope. God loves us too much to let us run away; therefore, He disciplines us (Heb. 12:1–11), and He keeps working on us until we submit to Him.

CHAPTER 2

2:1 When God first called him, Jonah should have prayed for divine help in carrying out his mission. Then he would have escaped discipline and the need for crying out to God for deliverance. When it was almost too late, the prophet prayed; and God graciously forgave him and rescued him.

2:4, 7 The Old Testament Jew looked toward the temple in Jerusalem when he prayed (vv. 4, 7; Dan. 6:10). Perhaps Jonah claimed the promise of 1 Kings 8:46–53, just as today we claim the promise of 1 John 1:9. God is merciful toward His children and ready to forgive (Ps. 86:5).

2:9 How did Jonah get into all that trouble? He forgot God and neglected prayer (v. 7) and believed lies (v. 8). He learned the hard way that he could not escape God's will. But he was wise enough to run back to God and ask for forgiveness!

CHAPTER 3

3:1ff How gracious God is to give us another opportunity after we have failed Him (Ps. 103:8–14)! God is as much concerned about the worker as He is the work. He could have sent somebody else to preach to Nineveh, but Jonah would have missed out on the lessons he needed to learn. God wants to work *in* us as well as *through* us.

How gracious God is to lost sinners! Why would a holy God give the vicious Ninevites an opportunity to repent? Because He is "not willing that any should perish" (2 Pet. 3:9) but "desires all men to be saved" (1 Tim. 2:4). Do you have a burden to share the gospel with a lost world that does not deserve to be saved? Remember, somebody shared it with you!

How gracious God is to bless the ministry of an imperfect servant! Jonah did not love the people he preached to, yet God used his message to bring the whole city to repentance. There is power in God's Word; it can convict and convert the greatest of sinners.

the city on the first day's walk. Then he cried out and said, "Yet forty days, and Nineveh shall be overthrown!"

⁵So the people of Nineveh believed God, proclaimed a fast, and put on sackcloth, from the greatest to the least of them. ⁶Then word came to the king of Nineveh; and he arose from his throne and laid aside his robe, covered *himself* with sackcloth and sat in ashes. ⁷And he caused *it* to be proclaimed and published throughout Nineveh by the decree of the king and his nobles, saying,

Let neither man nor beast, herd nor flock, taste anything; do not let them eat, or drink water. ⁸But let man and beast be covered with sackcloth, and cry mightily to God; yes, let every one turn from his evil way and from the violence that is in his hands. ⁹Who can tell *if* God will turn and relent, and turn away from His fierce anger, so that we may not perish?

¹⁰Then God saw their works, that they turned from their evil way; and God relented from the disaster that He had said He would bring upon them, and He did not do it.

CHAPTER 4

4:1ff If God wanted only to save the city of Nineveh, the book would have ended at chapter 3. But there was still more work to do, for God wanted to save His servant from himself. Jonah was an angry man (vv. 1, 2, 4, 9) who wanted to see Nineveh destroyed. Like the elder brother, he stayed outside and vented his bitterness (Luke 15:25–32).
The basic problem was that Jonah was not completely yielded to God. His mind knew God's truth, and his will obeyed God's orders; but he did not do the will of God "from the heart" (Eph. 6:6). He obeyed only because he was afraid of what God might do to him. His was not a ministry of love. When we are angry with God, everything in life gets out of perspective, and we say and do selfish things. Things become more important than people, and comfort more important than ministry.
But God is long-suffering and tenderly deals with us to bring us to Himself. *It is essential in Christian service to be happy with the will of God.* Each of us should be able to say, "I delight to do Your will, O my God, and Your law is within my heart" (Ps. 40:8).

4 But* it displeased Jonah exceedingly, and he became angry. ²So he prayed to the LORD, and said, "Ah, LORD, was not this what I said when I was still in my country? Therefore I fled previously to Tarshish; for I know that You *are* a gracious and merciful God, slow to anger and abundant in lovingkindness, One who relents from doing harm. ³Therefore now, O LORD, please take my life from me, for *it is* better for me to die than to live!"

⁴Then the LORD said, "*Is it* right for you to be angry?"

⁵So Jonah went out of the city and sat on the east side of the city. There he made himself a shelter and sat under it in the shade, till he might see what would become of the city. ⁶And the LORD God prepared a plantᶜ and made it come up over Jonah, that it might be shade for his head to deliver him from his misery. So Jonah was very grateful for the plant. ⁷But as morning dawned the next day God prepared a worm, and it *so* damaged the plant that it withered. ⁸And it happened, when the sun arose, that God prepared a vehement east wind; and the sun beat on Jonah's head, so that he grew faint. Then he wished death for himself, and said, "*It is* better for me to die than to live."

⁹Then God said to Jonah, "*Is it* right for you to be angry about the plant?"

And he said, "*It is* right for me to be angry, even to death!"

¹⁰But the LORD said, "You have had pity on the plant for which you have not labored, nor made it grow, which came up in a night and perished in a night. ¹¹And should I not pity Nineveh, that great city, in which are more than one hundred and twenty thousand persons who cannot discern between their right hand and their left—and much livestock?"

4:6 ᶜHebrew *kikayon*, exact identity unknown

MICAH

Micah was a contemporary of Isaiah (Isa. 1:1) and Hosea (Hos. 1:1) and prophesied concerning both Judah and Israel (Samaria). In this book, he gives us three messages, each introduced by a call to hear. He declared the coming judgment (chaps. 1—2), the future kingdom (chaps. 3—5), and God's invitation to the people to turn to the Lord (chaps. 6—7). He hoped that the people of Judah would learn from the sad experience of Israel, but they did not. His is a message of judgment mingled with mercy and hope. Micah's name means "who is like the Lord?" The prophet Jeremiah's life was saved by a quotation from Micah (Jer. 26:18; Mic. 3:12).

1 The word of the LORD that came to Micah of Moresheth in the days of Jotham, Ahaz, *and* Hezekiah, kings of Judah, which he saw concerning Samaria and Jerusalem.

2 *Hear, all you peoples!
   Listen, O earth, and all that is in it!
   Let the Lord GOD be a witness against you,
   The Lord from His holy temple.

3 For behold, the LORD is coming out of His
       place;
   He will come down
   And tread on the high places of the earth.
4 The mountains will melt under Him,
   And the valleys will split
   Like wax before the fire,
   Like waters poured down a steep place.
5 All this is for the transgression of Jacob
   And for the sins of the house of Israel.
   What *is* the transgression of Jacob?
   Is it not Samaria?
   And what *are* the high places of Judah?
   Are they not Jerusalem?

6 "Therefore I will make Samaria a heap of
       ruins in the field,
   Places for planting a vineyard;
   I will pour down her stones into the valley,
   And I will uncover her foundations.
7 All her carved images shall be beaten to
       pieces,
   And all her pay as a harlot shall be burned
       with the fire;
   All her idols I will lay desolate,
   For she gathered *it* from the pay of a harlot,
   And they shall return to the pay of a harlot."

8 *Therefore I will wail and howl,
   I will go stripped and naked;
   I will make a wailing like the jackals
   And a mourning like the ostriches,
9 For her wounds *are* incurable.
   For it has come to Judah;
   It has come to the gate of My people—
   To Jerusalem.

CHAPTER 1

1:2–7 The lawsuit. Micah convenes the court and announces Jehovah's verdict against Israel: judgment is coming! Assyria invaded the northern kingdom in 722 B.C. and made the capital city Samaria a heap of ruins. The nation's idolatry was but harlotry against the Lord, and unfaithfulness must be judged.

1:8–16 The lament. But the Assyrians would also invade Judah, which they did in 701 B.C., and would destroy nearly fifty villages. Although they tried, they could not conquer Jerusalem (Isa. 36—37), for the Lord spared it for David's sake (Isa. 37:35).
The prophet wept over the terrible things that would happen to the people. He did not say, "They are getting what they deserve!" Instead, he mourned like a man at a funeral. Does the certainty of coming judgment cause us to mourn over lost sinners and seek to win them to Christ?

Hebrew Wordplay—In the Hebrew original of Micah 1:10–16, the prophet uses some clever wordplay to get his point across. *Beth Aphrah* means "house of dust." *Shaphir* means "beautiful." *Zaanan* means "going out," and *Beth Ezel* means "house of nearness." *Maroth* means "bitterness," *Lachish* sounds like the word for "a team of horses," *Achzib* means "a lie," and *Mareshah* means "an inheritance." Put these meanings with the prophet's statements about these towns and see what you discover.

10 Tell *it* not in Gath,
   Weep not at all;
   In Beth Aphrah[a]
   Roll yourself in the dust.
11 Pass by in naked shame, you inhabitant of
      Shaphir;
   The inhabitant of Zaanan[b] does not go out.
   Beth Ezel mourns;
   Its place to stand is taken away from you.

12 For the inhabitant of Maroth pined[c] for
      good,
   But disaster came down from the LORD
   To the gate of Jerusalem.
13 O inhabitant of Lachish,
   Harness the chariot to the swift steeds
   (She *was* the beginning of sin to the
      daughter of Zion),
   For the transgressions of Israel were found
      in you.

14 Therefore you shall give presents to
      Moresheth Gath;[d]
   The houses of Achzib[e] *shall be* a lie to the
      kings of Israel.
15 I will yet bring an heir to you, O inhabitant
      of Mareshah;[f]
   The glory of Israel shall come to Adullam.
16 Make yourself bald and cut off your hair,
   Because of your precious children;
   Enlarge your baldness like an eagle,
   For they shall go from you into captivity.

CHAPTER 2

2:1–5 Micah names some of the sins of the people, beginning with *covetousness,* which is idolatry (Col. 3:5). The rich were exploiting the poor and getting away with it. But when the invader comes, nobody's boundary lines would be respected.

2 Woe* to those who devise iniquity,
   And work out evil on their beds!
   At morning light they practice it,
   Because it is in the power of their hand.
2 They covet fields and take *them* by violence,
   Also houses, and seize *them.*
   So they oppress a man and his house,
   A man and his inheritance.

3Therefore thus says the LORD:

   "Behold, against this family I am devising
      disaster,
   From which you cannot remove your necks;
   Nor shall you walk haughtily,
   For this *is* an evil time.
4 In that day *one* shall take up a proverb
      against you,
   And lament with a bitter lamentation,
      saying:
   'We are utterly destroyed!
   He has changed the heritage of my people;
   How He has removed *it* from me!
   To a turncoat He has divided our fields.' "

5 Therefore you will have no one to determine
      boundaries[g] by lot
   In the assembly of the LORD.

2:6–11 Another sin was *rejecting God's Word.* The false prophets tried to silence Micah because he was announcing doom. They wanted a pleasant message about security and strong drink. The "prosperity preachers" are usually popular while those who declare God's Word are often persecuted. But God's Word does good in the lives of those who want to do good and obey the Lord.

6 *"Do not prattle," *you say to those* who
      prophesy.
   So they shall not prophesy to you;[h]

1:10 [a]Literally *House of Dust*   1:11 [b]Literally *Going Out*
1:12 [c]Literally *was sick*   1:14 [d]Literally *Possession of Gath* [e]Literally *Lie*   1:15 [f]Literally *Inheritance*   2:5 [g]Literally one casting a surveyor's line*   2:6 [h]Literally *to these*

They shall not return insult for insult.[l]
7   *You who are* named the house of Jacob:
"Is the Spirit of the LORD restricted?
Are these His doings?
Do not My words do good
To him who walks uprightly?

8   "Lately My people have risen up as an
enemy—
You pull off the robe with the garment
From those who trust *you,* as they pass by,
Like men returned from war.
9   The women of My people you cast out
From their pleasant houses;
From their children
You have taken away My glory forever.

10* "Arise and depart,
For this *is* not *your* rest;
Because it is defiled, it shall destroy,
Yes, with utter destruction.
11 If a man should walk in a false spirit
And speak a lie, *saying,*
'I will prophesy to you of wine and drink,'
Even he would be the prattler of this people.

12* "I will surely assemble all of you, O Jacob,
I will surely gather the remnant of Israel;
I will put them together like sheep of the
fold,[j]
Like a flock in the midst of their pasture;
They shall make a loud noise because of *so
many* people.
13 The one who breaks open will come up
before them;
They will break out,
Pass through the gate,
And go out by it;
Their king will pass before them,
With the LORD at their head."

3 And* I said:

"Hear now, O heads of Jacob,
And you rulers of the house of Israel:
Is it not for you to know justice?
2   You who hate good and love evil;
Who strip the skin from My people,[k]
And the flesh from their bones;
3   Who also eat the flesh of My people,
Flay their skin from them,
Break their bones,
And chop *them* in pieces
Like *meat* for the pot,
Like flesh in the caldron."

4   Then they will cry to the LORD,
But He will not hear them;
He will even hide His face from them at that
time,
Because they have been evil in their deeds.

5   *Thus says the LORD concerning the prophets
Who make my people stray;
Who chant "Peace"
While they chew with their teeth,
But who prepare war against him
Who puts nothing into their mouths:

2:10 They had *defiled the land* with their idolatry and harlotry (Lev. 18:24–30), and now the land would destroy them. Personal sin will always affect society.

2:12, 13 How gracious of God to end with a promise of hope! He will spare a remnant (4:7; 5:7–8; 7:18) and gather them together for His future kingdom. Their King will be their Shepherd!

CHAPTER 3

3:1–4 "Hear now!" introduces Micah's second message, which was directed to the leaders. Because of *their* sins, the nation disobeyed God and eventually had to be judged (Lam. 2:14; 4:13). He used three pictures to describe their sins.
  Hunters. Instead of caring for the people, the leaders treated them like animals and devoured them. But the day would come when those leaders would cry out to God and He would not answer them.

3:5–7 Shepherds. Instead of guiding the flock in God's paths, they led them astray with their message of false peace (v. 11; Jer. 6:14). Their deception would be followed by darkness, and they would have no hope.

---

[l]Vulgate reads *He shall not take shame.*   2:12 [j]Hebrew *Bozrah*   3:2 [k]Literally *them*

3:10, 11 Builders. Instead of building the city on the law of the Lord, they broke the law and built with bloodshed. Why? Because they wanted to get more money (1 Tim. 6:9–10). But everything they built would be torn down, and their money would be useless to them.

A true leader protects the people, guides them in God's will, and serves without thought of personal gain.

CHAPTER 4

4:1–5 In four pictures, Micah presents a vision of the judgment of Israel's enemies and the establishment of the future kingdom. *A city.* Even though Jerusalem would be destroyed by Babylon, one day the city would become the capital of the kingdom. It will be a time of peace when all men will want to learn about the Lord and walk in His ways.

6   "Therefore you shall have night without
     vision,
    And you shall have darkness without
     divination;
    The sun shall go down on the prophets,
    And the day shall be dark for them.
7   So the seers shall be ashamed,
    And the diviners abashed;
    Indeed they shall all cover their lips;
    For *there is* no answer from God."

8   But truly I am full of power by the Spirit
    of the LORD,
    And of justice and might,
    To declare to Jacob his transgression
    And to Israel his sin.
9   Now hear this,
    You heads of the house of Jacob
    And rulers of the house of Israel,
    Who abhor justice
    And pervert all equity,
10 *Who build up Zion with bloodshed
    And Jerusalem with iniquity:
11 Her heads judge for a bribe,
    Her priests teach for pay,
    And her prophets divine for money.
    Yet they lean on the LORD, and say,
    "Is not the LORD among us?
    No harm can come upon us."
12 Therefore because of you
    Zion shall be plowed *like* a field,
    Jerusalem shall become heaps of ruins,
    And the mountain of the temple*l*
    Like the bare hills of the forest.

4   Now* it shall come to pass in the latter days
    That the mountain of the LORD's house
    Shall be established on the top of the
     mountains,
    And shall be exalted above the hills;
    And peoples shall flow to it.
2   Many nations shall come and say,
    "Come, and let us go up to the mountain of
     the LORD,
    To the house of the God of Jacob;
    He will teach us His ways,
    And we shall walk in His paths."
    For out of Zion the law shall go forth,
    And the word of the LORD from Jerusalem.
3   He shall judge between many peoples,
    And rebuke strong nations afar off;
    They shall beat their swords into
     plowshares,
    And their spears into pruning hooks;
    Nation shall not lift up sword against
     nation,
    Neither shall they learn war anymore.*m*

4   But everyone shall sit under his vine and
     under his fig tree,
    And no one shall make *them* afraid;
    For the mouth of the LORD of hosts has
     spoken.
5   For all people walk each in the name of his
     god,
    But we will walk in the name of the LORD
     our God
    Forever and ever.

3:12 *l*Literally *house*   4:3 *m*Compare Isaiah 2:2–4

6 *"In that day," says the LORD,
  "I will assemble the lame,
  I will gather the outcast
  And those whom I have afflicted;
7 I will make the lame a remnant,
  And the outcast a strong nation;
  So the LORD will reign over them in Mount
    Zion
  From now on, even forever.
8 And you, O tower of the flock,
  The stronghold of the daughter of Zion,
  To you shall it come,
  Even the former dominion shall come,
  The kingdom of the daughter of Jerusalem."

9 *Now why do you cry aloud?
  Is there no king in your midst?
  Has your counselor perished?
  For pangs have seized you like a woman
    in labor.
10 Be in pain, and labor to bring forth,
  O daughter of Zion,
  Like a woman in birth pangs.
  For now you shall go forth from the city,
  You shall dwell in the field,
  And to Babylon you shall go.
  There you shall be delivered;
  There the LORD will redeem you
  From the hand of your enemies.

11 *Now also many nations have gathered
    against you,
  Who say, "Let her be defiled,
  And let our eye look upon Zion."
12 But they do not know the thoughts of the
    LORD,
  Nor do they understand His counsel;
  For He will gather them like sheaves to the
    threshing floor.

13 "Arise and thresh, O daughter of Zion;
  For I will make your horn iron,
  And I will make your hooves bronze;
  You shall beat in pieces many peoples;
  I will consecrate their gain to the LORD,
  And their substance to the Lord of the whole
    earth."

5 Now* gather yourself in troops,
  O daughter of troops;
  He has laid siege against us;
  They will strike the judge of Israel with a
    rod on the cheek.
2 "But you, Bethlehem Ephrathah,
  Though you are little among the thousands
    of Judah,
  Yet out of you shall come forth to Me
  The One to be Ruler in Israel,
  Whose goings forth are from of old,
  From everlasting."

3 *Therefore He shall give them up,
  Until the time that she who is in labor has
    given birth;
  Then the remnant of His brethren
  Shall return to the children of Israel.
4 And He shall stand and feed His flock
  In the strength of the LORD,
  In the majesty of the name of the LORD His
    God;
  And they shall abide,
  For now He shall be great

4:6–8 A flock. The Lord will gather His flock (the remnant) and care for the lame and the afflicted. Their Shepherd will be their King, and He will reign in righteousness.

4:9, 10 A birth. As the pregnant woman must deliver the child, so Judah must be taken captive to Babylon. It would be a time of pain, but it would eventually bring blessing. God promised to deliver them and restore them.

4:11–13 A harvest. The day will come when God's people will defeat their enemies who seek to destroy them. It will be like the threshing of grain, and the harvest will be given to the Lord.

CHAPTER 5

5:1, 2 The focus is on Israel's Deliverer, the Lord Jesus Christ.
  Two cities. Micah contrasts great Jerusalem, experiencing the Babylonian siege, and humble Bethlehem, where the Eternal One will step into time to save His people. The future of God's plan of salvation lay in lowly Bethlehem (Luke 2:1–20; see also Isa. 9:6).

5:3, 4 Two births. The birth of Messiah brought hope to Israel, but the nation would not receive Him. He had to give them up (Luke 13:34–35) until the day He returns to restore them (Rom. 9). Their salvation will be the birth of a nation (Isa. 66:8), and there will be peace to the ends of the earth.

5:5–15 Two victories. Messiah will win a victory over His enemies and will make His people victorious (the lion) and fruitful (the dew). But He will also win a victory over His own people and purge them of their sins (vv. 10–15). The things they trusted will then be removed—armaments, fortresses, sorceries, and idols—and they will learn to trust the Lord.

Perhaps God wants to remove some things from your life so you can enjoy His peace.

To the ends of the earth;
5 *And this *One* shall be peace.

When the Assyrian comes into our land,
And when he treads in our palaces,
Then we will raise against him
Seven shepherds and eight princely men.
6 They shall waste with the sword the land
   of Assyria,
And the land of Nimrod at its entrances;
Thus He shall deliver *us* from the Assyrian,
When he comes into our land
And when he treads within our borders.

7 Then the remnant of Jacob
Shall be in the midst of many peoples,
Like dew from the LORD,
Like showers on the grass,
That tarry for no man
Nor wait for the sons of men.
8 And the remnant of Jacob
Shall be among the Gentiles,
In the midst of many peoples,
Like a lion among the beasts of the forest,
Like a young lion among flocks of sheep,
Who, if he passes through,
Both treads down and tears in pieces,
And none can deliver.
9 Your hand shall be lifted against your
   adversaries,
And all your enemies shall be cut off.

10 "And it shall be in that day," says the LORD,
"That I will cut off your horses from your
   midst
And destroy your chariots.
11 I will cut off the cities of your land
And throw down all your strongholds.
12 I will cut off sorceries from your hand,
And you shall have no soothsayers.
13 Your carved images I will also cut off,
And your sacred pillars from your midst;
You shall no more worship the work of your
   hands;
14 I will pluck your wooden images[n] from your
   midst;
Thus I will destroy your cities.
15 And I will execute vengeance in anger and
   fury
On the nations that have not heard."[o]

CHAPTER 6

6:1–5 We are once more in the courtroom. The indictment. God called the mountains to witness His complaint against Israel. What had He done to His people that they should despise His Word and sin against Him? (See Isa. 5.) Had they forgotten all that He did for them? It is good for us to review God's gracious acts toward us and make sure we express gratitude to Him.

6 Hear* now what the LORD says:

"Arise, plead your case before the
   mountains,
And let the hills hear your voice.
2 Hear, O you mountains, the LORD'S
   complaint,
And you strong foundations of the earth;
For the LORD has a complaint against His
   people,
And He will contend with Israel.

5:14 [n]Hebrew *Asherim,* Canaanite deities   5:15 [o]Or *obeyed*

"Sublime Revelation"—Micah 6:8 is not the gospel. We are not saved by obeying these words, but we cannot obey them unless we are saved. Our religious words and deeds (vv. 6–8) mean nothing to God if we lack character wrought by the Holy Spirit as we yield to Him. "All controversy, all resentful intellectualism, all selfish calculation, all vicious political Christianity, must fall before that sublime revelation," wrote Joseph Parker.

3 "O My people, what have I done to you?
    And how have I wearied you?
    Testify against Me.
4 For I brought you up from the land of Egypt,
    I redeemed you from the house of bondage;
    And I sent before you Moses, Aaron, and
    Miriam.
5 O My people, remember now
    What Balak king of Moab counseled,
    And what Balaam the son of Beor answered
    him,
    From Acacia Grove[p] to Gilgal,
    That you may know the righteousness of the
    LORD."

6 *With what shall I come before the LORD,
    And bow myself before the High God?
    Shall I come before Him with burnt
    offerings,
    With calves a year old?
7 Will the LORD be pleased with thousands of
    rams,
    Ten thousand rivers of oil?
    Shall I give my firstborn *for* my
    transgression,
    The fruit of my body *for* the sin of my soul?

8 He has shown you, O man, what *is* good;
    And what does the LORD require of you
    But to do justly,
    To love mercy,
    And to walk humbly with your God?

9 *The LORD's voice cries to the city—
    Wisdom shall see Your name:

    "Hear the rod!
    Who has appointed it?
10 Are there yet the treasures of wickedness
    In the house of the wicked,
    And the short measure *that is* an
    abomination?
11 Shall I count pure *those* with the wicked
    scales,
    And with the bag of deceitful weights?
12 For her rich men are full of violence,
    Her inhabitants have spoken lies,
    And their tongue is deceitful in their mouth.

13 "Therefore I will also make *you* sick by
    striking you,
    By making *you* desolate because of your
    sins.
14 You shall eat, but not be satisfied;
    Hunger[q] *shall be* in your midst.
    You may carry *some* away,[r] but shall not
    save *them*;
    And what you do rescue I will give over to
    the sword.

15 "You shall sow, but not reap;
    You shall tread the olives, but not anoint
    yourselves with oil;
    And *make* sweet wine, but not drink wine.
16 For the statutes of Omri are kept;
    All the works of Ahab's house *are done*;

6:6–8 The confession. All that the people could say was, "Guilty!" The Judge did not want sacrifices; He wanted obedience (Isa. 1:10–18). Verse 8 tells us how we should live as God's forgiven people (Deut. 10:12).

6:9–16 The sentence. They would feel the rod of punishment because of their sins, and their efforts would be cursed. Omri and Ahab were two of the most wicked kings who ever ruled Israel (1 Kings 16:21—22:40), and the nation suffered because they followed their bad examples.

The Judge is the Savior, but He cannot save those who persist in disobeying Him.

6:5 [p]Hebrew *Shittim* (compare Numbers 25:1; Joshua 2:1; 3:1)
6:14 [q]Or *Emptiness* or *Humiliation* [r]Targum and Vulgate read
You shall take hold.

And you walk in their counsels,
That I may make you a desolation,
And your inhabitants a hissing.
Therefore you shall bear the reproach of My
people."[s]

CHAPTER 7

7:1–7 *A faithful God.* The prophet was disgusted because the people were all given over to deception. He couldn't even find one faithful man (1 Kings 19:10; Ps. 12:1; Isa. 57:1). When people fail you, remember that the Lord is always faithful. Make the same three decisions that the prophet made: "I will look, I will wait, I will pray" (v. 7).

7 Woe[*] is me!
For I am like those who gather summer
   fruits,
Like those who glean vintage grapes;
There is no cluster to eat
Of the first-ripe fruit *which* my soul desires.
2 The faithful *man* has perished from the
   earth,
And *there is* no one upright among men.
They all lie in wait for blood;
Every man hunts his brother with a net.

3 That they may successfully do evil with both
   hands—
The prince asks *for gifts,*
The judge *seeks* a bribe,
And the great *man* utters his evil desire;
So they scheme together.
4 The best of them *is* like a brier;
The most upright *is sharper* than a thorn
   hedge;
The day of your watchman and your
   punishment comes;
Now shall be their perplexity.

5 Do not trust in a friend;
Do not put your confidence in a companion;
Guard the doors of your mouth
From her who lies in your bosom.
6 For son dishonors father,
Daughter rises against her mother,
Daughter-in-law against her mother-in-law;
A man's enemies *are* the men of his own
   household.
7 Therefore I will look to the LORD;
I will wait for the God of my salvation;
My God will hear me.

7:8–10 *A righteous God.* God lifts up those who fall and gives light to those who are in the darkness. Even when He must deal with us because of our sins, He does what is best. Be patient, for He will one day defeat your enemies and bring you into blessing.

8 *Do not rejoice over me, my enemy;
When I fall, I will arise;
When I sit in darkness,
The LORD *will be* a light to me.
9 I will bear the indignation of the LORD,
Because I have sinned against Him,
Until He pleads my case

6:16 [s]Following Masoretic Text, Targum, and Vulgate; Septuagint reads *of nations.*

God's Pardon

In wonder lost, with trembling joy,
We take the pardon of our God,
Pardon for sins of deepest dye,
A pardon bought with Jesus' blood.
Who is a pardoning God like Thee?
Or who has grace so rich and free?
             Samuel Davies

And executes justice for me.
He will bring me forth to the light;
I will see His righteousness.
10 Then *she who is* my enemy will see,
And shame will cover her who said to me,
"Where is the LORD your God?"
My eyes will see her;
Now she will be trampled down
Like mud in the streets.

11 *In* the day when your walls are to be built,
In that day the decree shall go far and wide.*t*
12 *In* that day they*u* shall come to you
From Assyria and the fortified cities,*v*
From the fortress*w* to the River,*x*
From sea to sea,
And mountain *to* mountain.
13 Yet the land shall be desolate
Because of those who dwell in it,
And for the fruit of their deeds.

14 *Shepherd Your people with Your staff,
The flock of Your heritage,
Who dwell solitarily *in* a woodland,
In the midst of Carmel;
Let them feed *in* Bashan and Gilead,
As in days of old.

15 "As in the days when you came out of the
land of Egypt,
I will show them*y* wonders."

16 The nations shall see and be ashamed of
all their might;
They shall put *their* hand over *their* mouth;
Their ears shall be deaf.
17 They shall lick the dust like a serpent;
They shall crawl from their holes like
snakes of the earth.
They shall be afraid of the LORD our God,
And shall fear because of You.
18 Who *is* a God like You,
Pardoning iniquity
And passing over the transgression of the
remnant of His heritage?

He does not retain His anger forever,
Because He delights *in* mercy.
19 He will again have compassion on us,
And will subdue our iniquities.

You will cast all our*z* sins
Into the depths of the sea.
20 You will give truth to Jacob
And mercy to Abraham,
Which You have sworn to our fathers
From days of old.

7:14–20 *A pardoning God.* God delights in mercy! When we come to Him and confess our sins, He pardons us, puts our sins underfoot like defeated enemies, and hurls them into the depths of the sea and they are seen no more. (See Ps. 103:12; Isa. 38:17; Jer. 31:34; Acts 3:19.)

7:11 *t*Or *the boundary shall be extended*   7:12 *u*Literally *he,* collective of the captives   *v*Hebrew *arey mazor,* possibly *cities of Egypt*   *w*Hebrew *mazor,* possibly *Egypt*   *x*That is, the Euphrates   7:15 *y*Literally *him,* collective for the captives   7:19 *z*Literally *their*

NAHUM

Jonah was sent to Nineveh, the capital of the Assyrian Empire, to give the people an opportunity to repent. But Nahum was called to announce that their judgment was imminent. The city fell to the Medes and Babylonians in 612 B.C. The prophet Zephaniah also prophesied the fall of Nineveh (Zeph. 2:13–14).

Nahum means "comfort," and his message was certainly a comfort to the Jews who feared and hated the cruel Assyrians' threats to their security. The book focuses on the holy character of God who cannot allow sin to go unpunished. In chapter 1, Nahum *declares* Nineveh's fall; in chapter 2, he *describes* it; and in chapter 3, he *defends* it.

CHAPTER 1

1:2 God is jealous. This means He deserves total obedience and will not permit any rivals. It is the jealousy of the husband over his wife or the mother over her child. He is jealous over His people and for His glory; therefore, He must punish sin.

1:3–6 God is long-suffering. God does not have "temper tantrums." He patiently waits for sinners to hear His Word and repent. See Exodus 34:6, Numbers 14:18 and Romans 9:22.

God is sovereign. He has His way because His way is best and He is totally in control. He commands the forces of nature, and no one can stand before His anger.

1:7–15 God is good. Nineveh will be destroyed by a flood (v. 8) and a fire (v. 10); but God's people will be safe in their refuge, Jehovah God (Ps. 46). Judah had been afflicted by Assyria, but that would now end and the yoke would be taken off (vv. 12–13). Judah would hear the good news from the courier that Nineveh had been destroyed! (See Isa. 40:9; 52:7; Rom. 10:15.)

1 The burden^a against Nineveh. The book of the vision of Nahum the Elkoshite.

2 *God *is* jealous, and the LORD avenges;
The LORD avenges and *is* furious.
The LORD will take vengeance on His adversaries,
And He reserves *wrath* for His enemies;
3 *The LORD *is* slow to anger and great in power,
And will not at all acquit *the wicked.*

The LORD has His way
In the whirlwind and in the storm,
And the clouds *are* the dust of His feet.
4 He rebukes the sea and makes it dry,
And dries up all the rivers.
Bashan and Carmel wither,
And the flower of Lebanon wilts.
5 The mountains quake before Him,
The hills melt,
And the earth heaves^b at His presence,
Yes, the world and all who dwell in it.

6 Who can stand before His indignation?
And who can endure the fierceness of His anger?
His fury is poured out like fire,
And the rocks are thrown down by Him.

7 *The LORD *is* good,
A stronghold in the day of trouble;
And He knows those who trust in Him.
8 But with an overflowing flood
He will make an utter end of its place,
And darkness will pursue His enemies.

9 What do you conspire against the LORD?
He will make an utter end *of it.*
Affliction will not rise up a second time.
10 For while tangled *like* thorns,
And while drunken *like* drunkards,
They shall be devoured like stubble fully dried.
11 From you comes forth *one*
Who plots evil against the LORD,
A wicked counselor.

12 Thus says the LORD:

1:1 ^aOr *oracle*   1:5 ^bTargum reads *burns.*

"Though *they are* safe, and likewise many,
Yet in this manner they will be cut down
When he passes through.
Though I have afflicted you,
I will afflict you no more;
13 For now I will break off his yoke from you,
And burst your bonds apart."

14 The LORD has given a command concerning
    you:
"Your name shall be perpetuated no longer.
Out of the house of your gods
I will cut off the carved image and the
    molded image.
I will dig your grave,
For you are vile."

15 Behold, on the mountains
The feet of him who brings good tidings,
Who proclaims peace!
O Judah, keep your appointed feasts,
Perform your vows.
For the wicked one shall no more pass
    through you;
He is utterly cut off.

2 He* who scatters[c] has come up before
    your face.
Man the fort!
Watch the road!
Strengthen *your* flanks!
Fortify *your* power mightily.

2 For the LORD will restore the excellence of
    Jacob
Like the excellence of Israel,
For the emptiers have emptied them out
And ruined their vine branches.

3 The shields of his mighty men *are* made red,
The valiant men *are* in scarlet.
The chariots *come* with flaming torches
In the day of his preparation,
And the spears are brandished.[d]
4 The chariots rage in the streets,
They jostle one another in the broad roads;
They seem like torches,
They run like lightning.

5 He remembers his nobles;
They stumble in their walk;
They make haste to her walls,
And the defense is prepared.
6 The gates of the rivers are opened,
And the palace is dissolved.
7 It is decreed:[e]
She shall be led away captive,
She shall be brought up;
And her maidservants shall lead *her* as with
    the voice of doves,
Beating their breasts.

8 Though Nineveh of old *was* like a pool of
    water,
Now they flee away.
"Halt! Halt!" *they cry;*
But no one turns back.

CHAPTER 2

2:1ff What a dramatic picture of the
invasion (vv. 1–4), the battle (vv. 5–7), the
victory (vv. 8–10), and the humiliation of
Nineveh before the Lord and her enemies
(vv. 11–13)! It was not the Babylonians and
the Medes who defeated Assyria; it was the
Lord God of Israel (Isa. 10:5–19).

The watchmen on the walls see the
enemy army approaching (v. 1) with their
scarlet uniforms and shields and their swift
chariots (vv. 3–4). The general puts his best
troops on the wall, but they stumble over
one another and cannot move fast enough
(v. 5).

The invaders dam up a river and release
the water, which destroys part of the city
wall and the palace (v. 6; 1:8). The people
start to flee, many are taken captive, and
the city is pillaged (vv. 7–10).

Assyria was identified with the lion, an
image in many of their sculptures (vv. 11–
13). But the Assyrian lion would devour no
longer, for it had been devoured! Assyria
would roar no more and kill no more, but
Judah would be restored and enjoy the
blessing of God (v. 2).

2:1 [c]Vulgate reads *He who destroys.* 2:3 [d]Literally *the
cypresses are shaken;* Septuagint and Syriac read *the horses
rush about;* Vulgate reads *the drivers are stupefied.*
2:7 [e]Hebrew *Huzzab*

9 Take spoil of silver!
 Take spoil of gold!
 There is no end of treasure,
 Or wealth of every desirable prize.
10 She is empty, desolate, and waste!
 The heart melts, and the knees shake;
 Much pain *is* in every side,
 And all their faces are drained of color.[f]

11 Where *is* the dwelling of the lions,
 And the feeding place of the young lions,
 Where the lion walked, the lioness *and*
 lion's cub,
 And no one made *them* afraid?
12 The lion tore in pieces enough for his cubs,
 Killed for his lionesses,
 Filled his caves with prey,
 And his dens with flesh.

13 "Behold, I *am* against you," says the LORD of hosts, "I will burn your[g] chariots in smoke, and the sword shall devour your young lions; I will cut off your prey from the earth, and the voice of your messengers shall be heard no more."

3 Woe to the bloody city!
 It *is* all full of lies *and* robbery.
 Its victim never departs.
2 The noise of a whip
 And the noise of rattling wheels,
 Of galloping horses,
 Of clattering chariots!
3 Horsemen charge with bright sword and
 glittering spear.
 There is a multitude of slain,
 A great number of bodies,
 Countless corpses—
 They stumble over the corpses—
4 *Because of the multitude of harlotries of the
 seductive harlot,
 The mistress of sorceries,
 Who sells nations through her harlotries,
 And families through her sorceries.

5 "Behold, I *am* against you," says the LORD
 of hosts;
 "I will lift your skirts over your face,
 I will show the nations your nakedness,
 And the kingdoms your shame.
6 I will cast abominable filth upon you,
 Make you vile,
 And make you a spectacle.
7 It shall come to pass *that* all who look upon
 you
 Will flee from you, and say,
 'Nineveh is laid waste!
 Who will bemoan her?'
 Where shall I seek comforters for you?"

8 Are you better than No Amon[h]
 That was situated by the River,[i]
 That had the waters around her,
 Whose rampart *was* the sea,
 Whose wall *was* the sea?
9 Ethiopia and Egypt *were* her strength,
 And *it was* boundless;
 Put and Lubim were your[j] helpers.

CHAPTER 3

3:4–7 The harlot. This image frequently occurs in Scripture for those who abandon truth and give themselves wholly to sin to gain wealth and pleasure. The Assyrian goddess of sex and war was Ishtar, a harlot. God would expose Assyria's shame and make her vile.

2:10 [f]Compare Joel 2:6 2:13 [g]Literally *her* 3:8 [h]That is, ancient Thebes; Targum and Vulgate read *populous Alexandria.* [i]Literally *rivers,* that is, the Nile and the surrounding canals 3:9 [j]Septuagint reads *her.*

10 Yet she *was* carried away,
   She went into captivity;
   Her young children also were dashed to
      pieces
   At the head of every street;
   They cast lots for her honorable men,
   And all her great men were bound in chains.
11 *You also will be drunk;
   You will be hidden;
   You also will seek refuge from the enemy.

12 *All your strongholds *are* fig trees with
      ripened figs:
   If they are shaken,
   They fall into the mouth of the eater.
13 Surely, your people in your midst *are*
      women!
   The gates of your land are wide open for
      your enemies;
   Fire shall devour the bars of your *gates.*

14 Draw your water for the siege!
   Fortify your strongholds!
   Go into the clay and tread the mortar!
   Make strong the brick kiln!
15 *There the fire will devour you,
   The sword will cut you off;
   It will eat you up like a locust.

   Make yourself many—like the locust!
   Make yourself many— like the *swarming*
      locusts!
16 You have multiplied your merchants more
      than the stars of heaven.
   The locust plunders and flies away.
17 Your commanders *are* like *swarming*
      locusts,
   And your generals like great grasshoppers,
   Which camp in the hedges on a cold day;
   When the sun rises they flee away,
   And the place where they *are* is not known.

18 *Your shepherds slumber, O king of Assyria;
   Your nobles rest *in the dust.*
   Your people are scattered on the mountains,
   And no one gathers them.
19 *Your injury *has* no healing,
   Your wound is severe.
   All who hear news of you
   Will clap *their* hands over you,
   For upon whom has not your wickedness
      passed continually?

3:11 *The drunkard.* How could drunken
soldiers hope to win a war! The nation had
to drink God's cup of wrath (Jer. 25:15–29).

3:12 *The fig tree.* Ripe figs will fall easily
when the tree is shaken, and these figs
would fall right into the farmer's mouth!
Nineveh's defenses were inadequate, and
the city would fall right into the enemy's
hands.

3:15–17 *The locusts.* Assyria had swarmed
on other nations and stripped them, but now
an army would swarm on them and empty
the city of people and wealth. The great
Assyrian leaders would be like cold locusts
in a stupor; but when the heat came, they
would wake up and try to escape. The
mighty nation was just a swarm of weak
insects!

3:18 *The flock.* The shepherds (leaders)
were dead, and the sheep were scattered.
Nobody would care for them or gather them.

3:19 *The victim.* Wounded and sick, the
nation was about to die; there was no way
to bring healing. Jeremiah used the same
image concerning God's people, but he
promised that God would heal them (Jer.
30:12–17). For Nineveh, there was no
promise of hope.

HABAKKUK

The name *Habakkuk* may come from a Hebrew word that means "to embrace." In his book, he comes to grips with some serious problems and lays hold of God by faith when everything in his life seems to be falling apart.

Habakkuk saw the impending Babylonian invasion, and he wondered that God would use a wicked nation to punish His chosen people. His book describes three stages in Habakkuk's experience—perplexity: faith wavers (chap. 1); perspective: faith watches (chap. 2); and perseverance: faith worships (chap. 3).

The key text is 2:4, "But the just shall live by his faith." It is quoted in Romans 1:17, Galatians 3:11, and Hebrews 10:38. The theme of Romans is "the just" and how to be justified before God. Galatians tells us how the just "shall live," and the emphasis in Hebrews is on living "by faith." It takes three New Testament epistles to explain one Old Testament text!

CHAPTER 1

1:2–4 *An unanswered prayer.* Habakkuk saw the wickedness of God's people in Judah and prayed for God to work, but the Lord didn't seem to hear. The prophet longed to see God bring revival to the land, but his prayer went unanswered—or so he thought.

1:5–11 *An unexpected plan.* God told His servant that his prayers would be answered in a way he never expected. God was going to bring Babylon against Judah and chasten His people. From the human point of view, the invasion of the land and the captivity of the people would seem a tragedy, but it was God's work just the same.

1 The burden*a* which the prophet Habakkuk saw.

2 *O Lord, how long shall I cry,
  And You will not hear?
  Even cry out to You, "Violence!"
  And You will not save.
3 Why do You show me iniquity,
  And cause *me* to see trouble?
  For plundering and violence *are* before me;
  There is strife, and contention arises.
4 Therefore the law is powerless,
  And justice never goes forth.
  For the wicked surround the righteous;
  Therefore perverse judgment proceeds.

5 *"Look among the nations and watch—
  Be utterly astounded!
  For *I will* work a work in your days
  Which you would not believe, though it
    were told *you*.
6 For indeed I am raising up the Chaldeans,
  A bitter and hasty nation
  Which marches through the breadth of the
    earth,
  To possess dwelling places *that are* not
    theirs.
7 They are terrible and dreadful;
  Their judgment and their dignity proceed
    from themselves.
8 Their horses also are swifter than leopards,
  And more fierce than evening wolves.
  Their chargers charge ahead;
  Their cavalry comes from afar;
  They fly as the eagle *that* hastens to eat.

9 "They all come for violence;
  Their faces are set *like* the east wind.
  They gather captives like sand.
10 They scoff at kings,
  And princes are scorned by them.
  They deride every stronghold,
  For they heap up earthen *mounds* and seize
    it.
11 Then *his* mind*b* changes, and he
  transgresses;

1:1 *a*Or *oracle*   1:11 *b*Literally *spirit* or *wind*

He commits offense,
Ascribing this power to his god."

12 *Are You not from everlasting,
O LORD my God, my Holy One?
We shall not die.
O LORD, You have appointed them for
    judgment;
O Rock, You have marked them for
    correction.
13 *You are* of purer eyes than to behold evil,
And cannot look on wickedness.
Why do You look on those who deal
    treacherously,
And hold Your tongue when the wicked
    devours
A *person* more righteous than he?
14 *Why* do You make men like fish of the sea,
Like creeping things *that have* no ruler over
    them?

15 They take up all of them with a hook,
They catch them in their net,
And gather them in their dragnet.
Therefore they rejoice and are glad.
16 Therefore they sacrifice to their net,
And burn incense to their dragnet;
Because by them their share *is* sumptuous
And their food plentiful.
17 Shall they therefore empty their net,
And continue to slay nations without pity?

2 I* will stand my watch
And set myself on the rampart,
And watch to see what He will say to me,
And what I will answer when I am
    corrected.

2 Then the LORD answered me and said:

"Write the vision
And make *it* plain on tablets,
That he may run who reads it.
3 For the vision *is* yet for an appointed
    time;
But at the end it will speak, and it will not
    lie.
Though it tarries, wait for it;
Because it will surely come,
It will not tarry.

4 "Behold the proud,
His soul is not upright in him;
But the just shall live by his faith.

5 "Indeed, because he transgresses by wine,
He is a proud man,
And he does not stay at home.
Because he enlarges his desire as hell,[c]
And he *is* like death, and cannot be satisfied,
He gathers to himself all nations
And heaps up for himself all peoples.

6 "Will not all these take up a proverb against
    him,
And a taunting riddle against him, and say,
'Woe to him who increases
What is not his—how long?'

1:12–17 *An unsolved problem.* Now the prophet has a greater problem: how can a holy God use a wicked nation to punish His chosen people? God seemed to hold His tongue as His servant cried out (v. 13), but soon the answer came. It was not the answer Habakkuk expected, but it finally brought him peace.

It is good to wrestle with God about the questions that perplex you—just be sure to stop talking long enough to listen.

CHAPTER 2

2:1ff Habakkuk needed a right perspective on what God was doing in His world. Although it is good to pray about these things, it is also good to "be still and know that [He is] God" (Ps. 46:10). The Lord emphasized two truths about Himself.

God is just. The five "woes" made it clear that God knew the sins of His people and would deal with them in due time. He hates pride, greed, selfishness, murder, drunkenness, lust, and idolatry.

God is faithful. Three key verses (4, 14, 20) reveal this trait. You can trust Him because His character never changes and His Word never fails (v. 4). It may not seem that way now, but one day His glory will be revealed in all the earth (v. 14). Meanwhile, God is on His throne and has everything under control (v. 20). So, instead of looking around and asking God a lot of questions, *look up* and lay hold of His assurances.

❝*Do not rejoice in earthly reality, rejoice in Christ, rejoice in His word, rejoice in His law. . . . There will be peace and tranquillity in the Christian heart; but only as long as our faith is watchful; if, however, our faith sleeps, we are in danger.*❞

—St. Augustine

2:5 [c]Or *Sheol*

And to him who loads himself with many
pledges"?[d]

7 Will not your creditors[e] rise up suddenly?
Will they not awaken who oppress you?
And you will become their booty.

8 Because you have plundered many nations,
All the remnant of the people shall plunder
you,
Because of men's blood
And the violence of the land *and* the city,
And of all who dwell in it.

9 "Woe to him who covets evil gain for his
house,
That he may set his nest on high,
That he may be delivered from the power
of disaster!

10 You give shameful counsel to your house,
Cutting off many peoples,
And sin *against* your soul.

11 For the stone will cry out from the wall,
And the beam from the timbers will answer
it.

12 "Woe to him who builds a town with
bloodshed,
Who establishes a city by iniquity!

13 Behold, *is it* not of the LORD of hosts
That the peoples labor to feed the fire,[f]
And nations weary themselves in vain?

14 For the earth will be filled
With the knowledge of the glory of the
LORD,
As the waters cover the sea.

15 "Woe to him who gives drink to his neighbor,
Pressing[g] *him to* your bottle,
Even to make *him* drunk,
That you may look on his nakedness!

16 You are filled with shame instead of glory.
You also—drink!
And be exposed as uncircumcised![h]
The cup of the LORD's right hand *will be*
turned against you,
And utter shame will be on your glory.

17 For the violence *done to* Lebanon will cover
you,
And the plunder of beasts *which* made them
afraid,
Because of men's blood
And the violence of the land *and* the city,
And of all who dwell in it.

18 "What profit is the image, that its maker
should carve it,
The molded image, a teacher of lies,
That the maker of its mold should trust in
it,
To make mute idols?

19 Woe to him who says to wood, 'Awake!'
To silent stone, 'Arise! It shall teach!'
Behold, it is overlaid with gold and silver,
Yet in it there is no breath at all.

20 "But the LORD is in His holy temple.
Let all the earth keep silence before Him."

2:6 [d]Syriac and Vulgate read *thick clay.*   2:7 [e]Literally *those
who bite you*   2:13 [f]Literally *for what satisfies fire,* that is,
for what is of no lasting value   2:15 [g]Literally *Attaching* or
Joining   2:16 [h]Dead Sea Scrolls and Septuagint read *And
reel!;* Syriac and Vulgate read *And fall fast asleep!*

3 A prayer of Habakkuk the prophet, on Shigionoth.[i]

2 *O LORD, I have heard Your speech *and* was afraid;
　　O LORD, revive Your work in the midst of the years!
　　In the midst of the years make *it* known;
　　In wrath remember mercy.

3 *God came from Teman,
　　The Holy One from Mount Paran.　　Selah

　　His glory covered the heavens,
　　And the earth was full of His praise.
4 *His* brightness was like the light;
　　He had rays *flashing* from His hand,
　　And there His power *was* hidden.
5 Before Him went pestilence,
　　And fever followed at His feet.

6 He stood and measured the earth;
　　He looked and startled the nations.
　　And the everlasting mountains were scattered,
　　The perpetual hills bowed.
　　His ways *are* everlasting.
7 I saw the tents of Cushan in affliction;
　　The curtains of the land of Midian trembled.

8 O LORD, were *You* displeased with the rivers,
　　Was Your anger against the rivers,
　　Was Your wrath against the sea,
　　That You rode on Your horses,
　　Your chariots of salvation?
9 Your bow was made quite ready;
　　Oaths were sworn over *Your* arrows.[j]
　　　　　　　　　　　　　　Selah

　　You divided the earth with rivers.
10 The mountains saw You *and* trembled;
　　The overflowing of the water passed by.
　　The deep uttered its voice,
　　And lifted its hands on high.

3:1 [i]Exact meaning unknown　3:9 [j]Literally *rods* or *tribes* (compare verse 14)

CHAPTER 3

3:2 *Request.* God said He was at work (1:5) so the prophet asked Him to keep on working (v. 2) but to be merciful to His sinful people. Prayer means reminding God of His promises and claiming them for ourselves.

3:3–15 *Review.* Habakkuk reviewed God's work in the past and recalled His greatness and power. In every era of Jewish history, God was there to work for His people; He would not fail them now. The Babylonian invasion and captivity would be painful experiences, but God would use them for His glory and the good of His people (Rom. 8:28).

Glorious Feet—God wants His people to have *bathed* feet (John 13:1–11) so we can fellowship with Him; *beautiful* feet (Rom. 10:15) so we can share His gospel with others; and *bounding* feet (Hab. 3:19) so we can overcome the obstacles of life.

Divine Guide

Begone unbelief, my Saviour is near,
And for my relief will surely appear;
By prayer let me wrestle and He will perform;
With Christ in the vessel, I smile at the storm.
Though dark be my way, since He is my guide
'Tis mine to obey, 'tis His to provide;
Though cisterns be broken and creatures all fail,
The word He hath spoken shall surely prevail.
　　　　　　　　　　　　　　John Newton

11 The sun and moon stood still in their
    habitation;
  At the light of Your arrows they went,
  At the shining of Your glittering spear.

12 You marched through the land in
    indignation;
  You trampled the nations in anger.

13 You went forth for the salvation of Your
    people,
  For salvation with Your Anointed.
  You struck the head from the house of the
    wicked,
  By laying bare from foundation to neck.
                      Selah

14 You thrust through with his own arrows
  The head of his villages.
  They came out like a whirlwind to scatter
    me;
  Their rejoicing was like feasting on the poor
    in secret.

15 You walked through the sea with Your
    horses,
  Through the heap of great waters.

16 When I heard, my body trembled;
  My lips quivered at *the* voice;
  Rottenness entered my bones;
  And I trembled in myself,
  That I might rest in the day of trouble.
  When he comes up to the people,
  He will invade them with his troops.

3:17–19 *Rejoicing.* Habakkuk started in the deep valley (chap. 1), then went up to the watchtower (chap. 2), but now finds himself on the mountains! Faith always lifts us higher and makes us happier. Even when we cannot rejoice in the economy, we can rejoice in the Lord!

17 *Though the fig tree may not blossom,
  Nor fruit be on the vines;
  Though the labor of the olive may fail,
  And the fields yield no food;
  Though the flock may be cut off from the
    fold,
  And there be no herd in the stalls—

18 Yet I will rejoice in the LORD,
  I will joy in the God of my salvation.

19 The LORD God[k] is my strength;
  He will make my feet like deer's *feet*,
  And He will make me walk on my high hills.

To the Chief Musician. With my stringed instruments.

3:19 [k]Hebrew *YHWH Adonai*

ZEPHANIAH

Zephaniah may be the only Old Testament prophet who had royal blood in his veins. But his kinship with King Josiah didn't prevent his preaching a message of judgment at a time when the king was leading the nation in a religious reformation (2 Kings 22—23). Both Jeremiah and Zephaniah saw that the "reform" was not true revival, for it never got to the hearts of the people. It was only a surface change because the king promoted it and the people went along with whatever was popular.

The prophet's emphasis is on "the day of the LORD," a phrase we have met in Joel and Amos. It applies historically to the invasion of Babylon in 606 B.C., but prophetically it speaks of a future day of wrath in the end times.

Like Habakkuk, Zephaniah saw both the wrath and the mercy of God. He announced that judgment would come to Jerusalem and Judah (chap. 1) and to the gentile nations (chap. 2), but that God would be merciful to a remnant (chap. 3). In wrath, He would remember mercy (Hab. 3:2).

1 The word of the LORD which came to Zephaniah the son of Cushi, the son of Gedaliah, the son of Amariah, the son of Hezekiah, in the days of Josiah the son of Amon, king of Judah.

2 *"I will utterly consume everything
From the face of the land,"
Says the LORD;
3 "I will consume man and beast;
I will consume the birds of the heavens,
The fish of the sea,
And the stumbling blocks[a] along with the wicked.
I will cut off man from the face of the land,"
Says the LORD.

4 "I will stretch out My hand against Judah,
And against all the inhabitants of Jerusalem.
I will cut off every trace of Baal from this place,
The names of the idolatrous priests[b] with the pagan priests—
5 Those who worship the host of heaven on the housetops;
Those who worship and swear oaths by the LORD,
But who also swear by Milcom;[c]
6 Those who have turned back from following the LORD,
And have not sought the LORD, nor inquired of Him."

7 Be silent in the presence of the Lord GOD;
For the day of the LORD is at hand,
For the LORD has prepared a sacrifice;
He has invited[d] His guests.

8 *"And it shall be,
In the day of the LORD's sacrifice,

CHAPTER 1

1:2–7 Preaching a message of judgment at a time of national religious reformation would not be easy; but a true prophet not only sees *farther*, he also sees *deeper*.

I will consume. God's wrath will consume His creation (vv. 2–3) and the hypocrites in the land (vv. 4–6). It will be a sacrificial feast, prepared for Babylon (v. 7; Jer. 46:10; Rev. 19:17–21).

1:8–11 *I will punish.* Starting at the royal palace, the prophet walked through the city and invited the people to lament with him. The merchants would be especially grieved because their ill-gotten wealth would be seized.

That I will punish the princes and the king's
children,
And all such as are clothed with foreign
apparel.
9 In the same day I will punish
All those who leap over the threshold,^e
Who fill their masters' houses with violence
and deceit.

10 "And there shall be on that day," says the
LORD,
"The sound of a mournful cry from the Fish
Gate,
A wailing from the Second Quarter,
And a loud crashing from the hills.
11 Wail, you inhabitants of Maktesh!^f
For all the merchant people are cut down;
All those who handle money are cut off.

12*"And it shall come to pass at that time
That I will search Jerusalem with lamps,
And punish the men
Who are settled in complacency,^g
Who say in their heart,
'The LORD will not do good,
Nor will He do evil.'
13 Therefore their goods shall become booty,
And their houses a desolation;
They shall build houses, but not inhabit
them;
They shall plant vineyards, but not drink
their wine."

14 *The great day of the LORD is near;
It is near and hastens quickly.
The noise of the day of the LORD is
bitter;
There the mighty men shall cry out.
15 That day is a day of wrath,
A day of trouble and distress,
A day of devastation and desolation,
A day of darkness and gloominess,
A day of clouds and thick darkness,
16 A day of trumpet and alarm
Against the fortified cities
And against the high towers.

17 "I will bring distress upon men,
And they shall walk like blind men,
Because they have sinned against the
LORD;
Their blood shall be poured out like dust,
And their flesh like refuse."

18 Neither their silver nor their gold
Shall be able to deliver them
In the day of the LORD's wrath;
But the whole land shall be devoured
By the fire of His jealousy,
For He will make speedy riddance
Of all those who dwell in the land.

2 Gather* yourselves together, yes, gather
together,
O undesirable^h nation,
2 Before the decree is issued,
Or the day passes like chaff,

1:12, 13 I will search. The people of
Jerusalem would try to hide, but the invading
soldiers would find them and slay them. The
complacent would discover that their
theology was all wrong. What a rude
awakening!

1:14–18 I will bring distress. Note the
words that describe this day, among them:
bitter, trouble, devastation, darkness, and
alarm. People will be treated like refuse!
Behind the literal fire that destroyed
Jerusalem was the fire of God's jealous love
over His people (v. 18; Nah. 1:2). Because
of that love, He accepts no rivals and permits
no rebellion.

CHAPTER 2

2:1ff Because of their sins, the nations
around Judah would also feel the wrath of
God. The other prophets had warned them
that judgment was coming (Isa. 14—20; Jer.
46—49; Amos 1—2), but the Gentiles did
not repent. The prophet used several
agricultural images to describe their coming
judgment: like chaff (v. 2), like a tree
uprooted (v. 4), "overrun with weeds" (v. 9),
like a desert (v. 13).
God would punish their mistreatment of
His people (v. 8; Gen. 12:1–3), their pride
(v. 10), and their worship of false gods
(v. 11). God still punishes these sins today.
In His mercy, God called the people to
turn from their sins and seek the Lord (vv.
1–3). The meek ones (God's remnant; 3:12)
would be hidden in God and cared for during
the day of wrath (1 Thess. 1:10; 5:9–10;
Rev. 3:10). Are you among the humble or
the haughty (v. 10)?

1:9 ^eCompare 1 Samuel 5:5   1:11 ^fLiterally *Mortar,* a market
district of Jerusalem   1:12 ^gLiterally *on their lees,* that is,
settled like the dregs of wine   2:1 ^hOr *shameless*

Before the LORD's fierce anger comes upon
    you,
Before the day of the LORD's anger comes
    upon you!
3   Seek the LORD, all you meek of the earth,
Who have upheld His justice.
Seek righteousness, seek humility.
It may be that you will be hidden
In the day of the LORD's anger.

4   For Gaza shall be forsaken,
And Ashkelon desolate;
They shall drive out Ashdod at noonday,
And Ekron shall be uprooted.
5   Woe to the inhabitants of the seacoast,
The nation of the Cherethites!
The word of the LORD *is* against you,
O Canaan, land of the Philistines:
"I will destroy you;
So there shall be no inhabitant."

6   The seacoast shall be pastures,
With shelters[i] for shepherds and folds for
    flocks.
7   The coast shall be for the remnant of the
    house of Judah;
They shall feed *their* flocks there;
In the houses of Ashkelon they shall lie
    down at evening.
For the LORD their God will intervene for
    them,
And return their captives.

8   "I have heard the reproach of Moab,
And the insults of the people of Ammon,
With which they have reproached My
    people,
And made arrogant threats against their
    borders.
9   Therefore, as I live,"
Says the LORD of hosts, the God of Israel,
"Surely Moab shall be like Sodom,
And the people of Ammon like Gomorrah—
Overrun with weeds and saltpits,
And a perpetual desolation.
The residue of My people shall plunder
    them,
And the remnant of My people shall possess
    them."

10 This they shall have for their pride,
Because they have reproached and made
    arrogant threats
Against the people of the LORD of hosts.
11 The LORD *will be* awesome to them,
For He will reduce to nothing all the gods
    of the earth;
People shall worship Him,
Each one from his place,
Indeed all the shores of the nations.

12 "You Ethiopians also,
You shall be slain by My sword."

13 And He will stretch out His hand against
    the north,
Destroy Assyria,
And make Nineveh a desolation,
As dry as the wilderness.

2:6 [i]Literally *excavations,* either underground huts or cisterns

14 The herds shall lie down in her midst,
Every beast of the nation.
Both the pelican and the bittern
Shall lodge on the capitals *of her pillars;*
Their voice shall sing in the windows;
Desolation *shall be* at the threshold;
For He will lay bare the cedar work.

15 This is the rejoicing city
That dwelt securely,
That said in her heart,
"I *am it,* and *there is* none besides me."
How has she become a desolation,
A place for beasts to lie down!
Everyone who passes by her
Shall hiss and shake his fist.

CHAPTER 3

3:1–7 *The rebellious.* The leaders in Jerusalem would not listen to God's servants or heed God's warnings. When God corrected them, they only committed greater sin. The time had come for God to judge them. It does not pay to test the long-suffering of God or tempt Him.

3 Woe* to her who is rebellious and polluted,
To the oppressing city!
2 She has not obeyed *His* voice,
She has not received correction;
She has not trusted in the LORD,
She has not drawn near to her God.

3 Her princes in her midst *are* roaring
lions;
Her judges *are* evening wolves
That leave not a bone till morning.
4 Her prophets are insolent, treacherous
people;
Her priests have polluted the sanctuary,
They have done violence to the law.
5 The LORD *is* righteous in her midst,
He will do no unrighteousness.
Every morning He brings His justice to
light;
He never fails,
But the unjust knows no shame.

6 "I have cut off nations,
Their fortresses are devastated;
I have made their streets desolate,
With none passing by.
Their cities are destroyed;
There is no one, no inhabitant.
7 I said, 'Surely you will fear Me,
You will receive instruction'—
So that her dwelling would not be cut off,
Despite everything for which I punished
her.
But they rose early and corrupted all their
deeds.

8 "Therefore wait for Me," says the LORD,
"Until the day I rise up for plunder;*
My determination *is* to gather the nations
To My assembly of kingdoms,
To pour on them My indignation,
All My fierce anger;
All the earth shall be devoured
With the fire of My jealousy.

3:9–13 *The restored.* The prophet looked ahead to the last days when the people would be regathered and restored to their land. They would call on Him, serve Him, and have nothing to fear.

9 *"For then I will restore to the peoples a pure
language,
That they all may call on the name of the
LORD,
To serve Him with one accord.
10 From beyond the rivers of Ethiopia

3:8 *Septuagint and Syriac read *for witness;* Targum reads *for the day of My revelation for judgment;* Vulgate reads *for the day of My resurrection that is to come.*

My worshipers,
The daughter of My dispersed ones,
Shall bring My offering.
11 In that day you shall not be shamed for any
of your deeds
In which you transgress against Me;
For then I will take away from your midst
Those who rejoice in your pride,
And you shall no longer be haughty
In My holy mountain.
12 I will leave in your midst
A meek and humble people,
And they shall trust in the name of the LORD.
13 The remnant of Israel shall do no
unrighteousness
And speak no lies,
Nor shall a deceitful tongue be found in
their mouth;
For they shall feed *their* flocks and lie down,
And no one shall make *them* afraid."

14 *Sing, O daughter of Zion!
Shout, O Israel!
Be glad and rejoice with all *your* heart,
O daughter of Jerusalem!
15 The LORD has taken away your judgments,
He has cast out your enemy.
The King of Israel, the LORD, *is* in your
midst;
You shall see[k] disaster no more.

16 In that day it shall be said to Jerusalem:
"Do not fear;
Zion, let not your hands be weak.
17 The LORD your God in your midst,
The Mighty One, will save;
He will rejoice over you with gladness,
He will quiet *you* with His love,
He will rejoice over you with singing."

18 "I will gather those who sorrow over the
appointed assembly,
Who are among you,
To whom its reproach *is* a burden.
19 Behold, at that time
I will deal with all who afflict you;
I will save the lame,
And gather those who were driven out;
I will appoint them for praise and fame
In every land where they were put to shame.
20 At that time I will bring you back,
Even at the time I gather you;
For I will give you fame and praise
Among all the peoples of the earth,
When I return your captives before your
eyes,"
Says the LORD.

3:14–17 *The rejoicing.* The people will
rejoice and sing because their discipline is
ended, the enemy has been defeated, and
the Lord is King over Israel. But the Lord
will also sing (v. 17)! Like a loving Father,
He takes His fearful children in His arms
and quiets them with His love. Note the
repeated "I will" promises that God gives.

If we delight in the Lord and obey Him,
He delights in us and shares His best with
us. If we sin, He will chasten us in love. If
we turn to Him in repentance, He will forgive
us and restore our joy and peace: "I will
heal their backsliding, I will love them freely"
(Hos. 14:4).

3:15 [k]Some Hebrew manuscripts, Septuagint, and Bomberg
read *see;* Masoretic Text and Vulgate read *fear.*

HAGGAI

In 538 B.C., about fifty thousand Jews left Babylon and returned to their homeland to rebuild the temple and restore the nation. In 536 B.C., they laid the foundation of the temple; but the work was stopped by their enemies and was not resumed until 520 B.C. under the preaching of Haggai and Zechariah. (Review Ezra 1—6.)

The book is comprised of four messages that Haggai gave during a period of four months. His purpose was to get the workers back on the job and to keep them working until the temple was completed. His first message called them to *be honest* (1:1–15) and put God's house ahead of their own houses. Then he appealed to them to *be strong* (2:1–9), *be clean* (2:10–19), and *be encouraged* (2:20–23).

Whenever God's work is being neglected, the preaching of the Word gets things going again.

CHAPTER 1

1:2–4 Priorities. If Haggai could have used a New Testament text for his sermon, it would have been Matthew 6:33. It is *never* time to sacrifice to do the Lord's work, but it is *always* time to do things for ourselves.

1:5–11 Adversities. When we put God first, we have the promise of His care. But when we put self first, we lose His blessing *and* whatever we spent on ourselves! The people knew God's covenant with Israel. He promised to bless them if they obeyed His Word and to discipline them if they disobeyed (Lev. 26). You never lose when you put God first in your life.

1:12–15 Ministries. God used the Word to arouse the leaders and the people, and they began to rebuild the temple. Accomplishing God's work takes leaders and workers, both stirred by the Lord and walking in the fear of the Lord.

David asked, "If the foundations are destroyed, what can the righteous do?" (Ps. 11:3). *Get to work and lay the foundations again!*

❝*The test of a preacher is that his congregation goes away saying, not 'What a lovely sermon!' but, 'I will do something!'*❞
—Francis de Sales

1 In the second year of King Darius, in the sixth month, on the first day of the month, the word of the LORD came by Haggai the prophet to Zerubbabel the son of Shealtiel, governor of Judah, and to Joshua the son of Jehozadak, the high priest, saying, 2*"Thus speaks the LORD of hosts, saying: 'This people says, "The time has not come, the time that the LORD's house should be built." ' "

3Then the word of the LORD came by Haggai the prophet, saying, 4"Is it time for you yourselves to dwell in your paneled houses, and this temple*a* to *lie* in ruins?" 5*Now therefore, thus says the LORD of hosts: "Consider your ways!

6 "You have sown much, and bring in little;
You eat, but do not have enough;
You drink, but you are not filled with drink;
You clothe yourselves, but no one is warm;
And he who earns wages,
Earns wages *to put* into a bag with holes."

7Thus says the LORD of hosts: "Consider your ways! 8Go up to the mountains and bring wood and build the temple, that I may take pleasure in it and be glorified," says the LORD. 9"You looked for much, but indeed *it came to* little; and when you brought it home, I blew it away. Why?" says the LORD of hosts. "Because of My house that *is in* ruins, while every one of you runs to his own house. 10Therefore the heavens above you withhold the dew, and the earth withholds its fruit. 11For I called for a drought on the land and the mountains, on the grain and the new wine and the oil, on whatever the ground brings forth, on men and livestock, and on all the labor of *your* hands."

12*Then Zerubbabel the son of Shealtiel, and Joshua the son of Jehozadak, the high priest, with all the remnant of the people, obeyed the voice of the LORD their God, and the words of Haggai the prophet, as the LORD their God had sent him; and the people feared the presence of the LORD. 13Then Haggai, the LORD's messenger, spoke the LORD's message to the people, saying, "I *am* with you, says the LORD." 14So the LORD stirred up the spirit of Zerubbabel the son of Shealtiel, governor

1:4 *a*Literally *house,* and so in verse 8

of Judah, and the spirit of Joshua the son of Jeho-zadak, the high priest, and the spirit of all the remnant of the people; and they came and worked on the house of the LORD of hosts, their God, 15on the twenty-fourth day of the sixth month, in the second year of King Darius.

2 In* the seventh *month*, on the twenty-first of the month, the word of the LORD came by Haggai the prophet, saying: 2"Speak now to Zerubba-bel the son of Shealtiel, governor of Judah, and to Joshua the son of Jehozadak, the high priest, and to the remnant of the people, saying: 3'Who is left among you who saw this temple[b] in its for-mer glory? And how do you see it now? In com-parison with it, *is this* not in your eyes as nothing? 4Yet now be strong, Zerubbabel,' says the LORD; 'and be strong, Joshua, son of Jehozadak, the high priest; and be strong, all you people of the land,' says the LORD, 'and work; for I *am* with you,' says the LORD of hosts. 5'*According to* the word that I covenanted with you when you came out of Egypt, so My Spirit remains among you; do not fear!'

6"For thus says the LORD of hosts: 'Once more (it *is* a little while) I will shake heaven and earth, the sea and dry land; 7and I will shake all nations, and they shall come to the Desire of All Nations,[c] and I will fill this temple with glory,' says the LORD of hosts. 8'The silver *is* Mine, and the gold *is* Mine,' says the LORD of hosts. 9'The glory of this latter temple shall be greater than the former,' says the LORD of hosts. 'And in this place I will give peace,' says the LORD of hosts."

10*On the twenty-fourth *day* of the ninth *month*, in the second year of Darius, the word of the LORD came by Haggai the prophet, saying, 11"Thus says the LORD of hosts: 'Now, ask the priests *concern-ing the* law, saying, 12"If one carries holy meat in the fold of his garment, and with the edge he touches bread or stew, wine or oil, or any food, will it become holy?"''"

Then the priests answered and said, "No."

13And Haggai said, "If *one who is* unclean *be-cause* of a dead body touches any of these, will it be unclean?"

So the priests answered and said, "It shall be unclean."

14Then Haggai answered and said, "'So is this people, and so is this nation before Me,' says the LORD, 'and so is every work of their hands; and what they offer there is unclean.

15'And now, carefully consider from this day forward: from before stone was laid upon stone in the temple of the LORD— 16since those *days*, when *one* came to a heap of twenty ephahs, there were *but* ten; when *one* came to the wine vat to draw out fifty baths from the press, there were *but* twenty. 17I struck you with blight and mildew and hail in all the labors of your hands; yet you did not *turn* to Me,' says the LORD. 18'Consider now from this day forward, from the twenty-fourth day of the ninth month, from the day that the foundation of the LORD's temple was laid— consider it: 19Is the seed still in the barn? As yet the vine, the fig tree, the pomegranate, and the olive tree have not yielded *fruit. But* from this day I will bless you.'"

2:3 *b*Literally *house,* and so in verses 7 and 9   2:7 *c*Or *the desire of all nations*

CHAPTER 2

2:1–9 Three messages are presented in this chapter.

Be strong! The times were hard, the people were poor, and the leaders were discouraged. (Was there ever an *easy* building program?) The restored temple would be nothing like the temple of Solomon, and the people were wondering, "Is it really worth it all?" They did not realize that the Lord of glory Himself would minister in this temple! Beware that golden memories do not rob you of present opportunities.

2:10–19 Be clean! The priests could not share holiness, but they could spread sin. The people had been defiled, and God could not bless them; but now they had returned to the Lord, and He promised them His blessing.

❝*Whereas the house of God today is no longer material but spiritual, the material is still a very real symbol of the spiritual. When the Church of God in any place in any locality is careless about the material place of assembly, the place of its worship and its work, it is a sign and evidence that its life is at a low ebb.*❞

—G. Campbell Morgan

2:20–23 *Be encouraged!* This was addressed to their governor who is a type of the Lord Jesus Christ. In the latter days, God will overthrow the gentile powers and restore David's line, to which Zerubbabel belonged (Matt. 1:12). Perhaps the governor thought his work was unimportant because the temple was so ordinary, or because the nation was so small and weak; but he was part of the plan that would lead one day to the coming of the Messiah.

Your part in God's kingdom today is not insignificant or unimportant, no matter how it appears to you. Be encouraged and keep working!

20*And again the word of the LORD came to Haggai on the twenty-fourth day of the month, saying, 21"Speak to Zerubbabel, governor of Judah, saying:

'I will shake heaven and earth.
22 I will overthrow the throne of kingdoms;
    I will destroy the strength of the Gentile
        kingdoms.
    I will overthrow the chariots
    And those who ride in them;
    The horses and their riders shall come
        down,
    Every one by the sword of his brother.

23'In that day,' says the LORD of hosts, 'I will take you, Zerubbabel My servant, the son of Shealtiel,' says the LORD, 'and will make you like a signet *ring*; for I have chosen you,' says the LORD of hosts."

ZECHARIAH

The prophet Zechariah ministered with Haggai as they encouraged the Jewish remnant to rebuild the temple. God gave Zechariah *eight visions* concerning Jerusalem and the Jews (chaps. 1—6) and *two burdens* (oracles) about the nation's future (chaps. 9—14). Chapters 7—8 deal with a question about fasting.

The focus is on Jerusalem, which is named over forty times in the book, and the key text is, "I am zealous for Jerusalem and for Zion with great zeal" (1:14). The city seemed to be forsaken, but God would remember His people and keep His promises. (*Zechariah* means "God remembers.") For God's people, the best is yet to come!

Haggai and Zechariah worked together, yet each ministry was unique. Haggai's book is brief and records no visions; Zechariah wrote a long book containing eight visions. Haggai focused on the present work of the people; Zechariah challenged them to look ahead. Both kinds of ministry were needed then to encourage God's people to work, and both are needed today. Like Ezekiel and Jeremiah, Zechariah was also a priest (1:1; Neh. 12:1—4, 16).

1 In* the eighth month of the second year of Darius, the word of the LORD came to Zechariah the son of Berechiah, the son of Iddo the prophet, saying, 2"The LORD has been very angry with your fathers. 3Therefore say to them, 'Thus says the LORD of hosts: "Return to Me," says the LORD of hosts, "and I will return to you," says the LORD of hosts. 4"Do not be like your fathers, to whom the former prophets preached, saying, 'Thus says the LORD of hosts: "Turn now from your evil ways and your evil deeds." ' But they did not hear nor heed Me," says the LORD.

5 "Your fathers, where *are* they?
   And the prophets, do they live forever?
6 Yet surely My words and My statutes,
   Which I commanded My servants the
      prophets,
   Did they not overtake your fathers?

"So they returned and said:

'Just as the LORD of hosts determined to do
      to us,
   According to our ways and according to our
      deeds,
   So He has dealt with us.' " ' "

7*On the twenty-fourth day of the eleventh month, which is the month Shebat, in the second year of Darius, the word of the LORD came to Zechariah the son of Berechiah, the son of Iddo the prophet: 8I saw by night, and behold, a man riding on a red horse, and it stood among the myrtle trees in the hollow; and behind him *were* horses: red, sorrel, and white. 9Then I said, "My lord, what *are* these?" So the angel who talked with me said to me, "I will show you what they *are.*"

10And the man who stood among the myrtle trees answered and said, "These *are the ones* whom the LORD has sent to walk to and fro throughout the earth."

11So they answered the Angel of the LORD, who stood among the myrtle trees, and said, "We have

CHAPTER 1

1:1–6 God's anger was directed against three targets.

The previous generation. Their sins had helped to bring about the ruin of the nation, but the new generation was committing the same sins. Sin has a way of following us and finally overtaking us, like a wild beast let loose on our trail. It is always time to repent.

1:7–21 ***The complacent nations.*** God's angels patrol His earth and work on behalf of His people (Heb. 1:14). The nations were at peace, but Israel was still in difficulty. When God used the other nations to punish Israel, they were excessively cruel; now God would repay them. Horns are a symbol of power, and God would break the power of the nations.

The feeble remnant, working on the temple, must have been greatly encouraged by God's promise of mercy and help (vv. 14–17). Are you claiming His promises today?

1:12 *The present generation.* During the seventy years of captivity, the nation felt God's anger; but now the time had come for God to show mercy. His discipline had accomplished His purposes; now He would begin to heal and restore His people.

walked to and fro throughout the earth, and behold, all the earth is resting quietly.''

12*Then the Angel of the LORD answered and said, "O LORD of hosts, how long will You not have mercy on Jerusalem and on the cities of Judah, against which You were angry these seventy years?''

13And the LORD answered the angel who talked to me, *with* good *and* comforting words. 14So the angel who spoke with me said to me, "Proclaim, saying, 'Thus says the LORD of hosts:

"I am zealous for Jerusalem
        And for Zion with great zeal.
15   I am exceedingly angry with the nations at
        ease;
        For I was a little angry,
        And they helped—*but* with evil *intent*.''

16"Therefore thus says the LORD:

"I am returning to Jerusalem with mercy;
        My house shall be built in it,'' says the LORD
        of hosts,
    "And a *surveyor's* line shall be stretched out
        over Jerusalem.'' '

17"Again proclaim, saying, 'Thus says the LORD of hosts:

"My cities shall again spread out through
        prosperity;
    The LORD will again comfort Zion,
        And will again choose Jerusalem.'' ' ''

18Then I raised my eyes and looked, and there *were* four horns. 19And I said to the angel who talked with me, "What *are* these?''

So he answered me, "These *are* the horns that have scattered Judah, Israel, and Jerusalem.''

20Then the LORD showed me four craftsmen. 21And I said, "What are these coming to do?''

So he said, "These *are* the horns that scattered Judah, so that no one could lift up his head; but the craftsmen[a] are coming to terrify them, to cast out the horns of the nations that lifted up *their* horn against the land of Judah to scatter it.''

CHAPTER 2

2:1–5 *Promise.* The act of measuring was an indication that God owned the city and had plans for it. No matter how discouraged the people of the Jewish remnant were, they could be sure that their work was not in vain. There was a glorious future for Jerusalem.

2:6, 7 *Proclamation.* Many Jews still in Babylon should have returned to their land. Babylon was destined to fall (Jer. 50—51), but Jerusalem would have a new beginning. Why stay in a condemned city? But some believers today still choose to stay in the world (2 Cor. 6:14–18; Rev. 18:1–8).

2 Then* I raised my eyes and looked, and behold, a man with a measuring line in his hand. 2So I said, "Where are you going?''

And he said to me, "To measure Jerusalem, to see what *is* its width and what *is* its length.''

3And there *was* the angel who talked with me, going out; and another angel was coming out to meet him, 4who said to him, "Run, speak to this young man, saying: 'Jerusalem shall be inhabited *as* towns without walls, because of the multitude of men and livestock in it. 5For I,' says the LORD, 'will be a wall of fire all around her, and I will be the glory in her midst.' ''

6*"Up, up! Flee from the land of the north,'' says the LORD; "for I have spread you abroad like the four winds of heaven,'' says the LORD. 7Up, Zion!

1:21 [a]Literally *these*

Being Silent—God called the Jews to sing, but He told the nations to be silent (2:13). Why? Because He was about to pour out His wrath on them for their sins. It was the lull before the storm. (See Hab. 2:20; Zeph. 1:7.)

Escape, you who dwell with the daughter of Babylon."

8*For thus says the LORD of hosts: "He sent Me after glory, to the nations which plunder you; for he who touches you touches the apple of His eye. 9For surely I will shake My hand against them, and they shall become spoil for their servants. Then you will know that the LORD of hosts has sent Me.

10*"Sing and rejoice, O daughter of Zion! For behold, I am coming and I will dwell in your midst," says the LORD. 11"Many nations shall be joined to the LORD in that day, and they shall become My people. And I will dwell in your midst. Then you will know that the LORD of hosts has sent Me to you. 12And the LORD will take possession of Judah as His inheritance in the Holy Land, and will again choose Jerusalem. 13Be silent, all flesh, before the LORD, for He is aroused from His holy habitation!"

3 Then* he showed me Joshua the high priest standing before the Angel of the LORD, and Satan standing at his right hand to oppose him. 2And the LORD said to Satan, "The LORD rebuke you, Satan! The LORD who has chosen Jerusalem rebuke you! Is this not a brand plucked from the fire?"

3*Now Joshua was clothed with filthy garments, and was standing before the Angel.

4Then He answered and spoke to those who stood before Him, saying, "Take away the filthy garments from him." And to him He said, "See, I have removed your iniquity from you, and I will clothe you with rich robes."

5And I said, "Let them put a clean turban on his head."

So they put a clean turban on his head, and they put the clothes on him. And the Angel of the LORD stood by.

6*Then the Angel of the LORD admonished Joshua, saying, 7"Thus says the LORD of hosts:

'If you will walk in My ways,
And if you will keep My command,
Then you shall also judge My house,
And likewise have charge of My courts;
I will give you places to walk
Among these who stand here.

8 'Hear, O Joshua, the high priest,
You and your companions who sit before you,
For they are a wondrous sign;
For behold, I am bringing forth My Servant the BRANCH.

9 For behold, the stone
That I have laid before Joshua:
Upon the stone are seven eyes.
Behold, I will engrave its inscription,'
Says the LORD of hosts,
'And I will remove the iniquity of that land in one day.

10 In that day,' says the LORD of hosts,
'Everyone will invite his neighbor
Under his vine and under his fig tree.' "

2:8, 9 Protection. The Lord speaks and promises to care for His people. The pupil of the eye is vulnerable and feels pain keenly. God cares for us because we are dear to Him (Deut. 32:10; Ps. 17:8; Prov. 7:2).

2:10–12 Praise. Their sighing would be turned into singing, for the Lord was coming to them and would dwell with them. He will claim His inheritance (Exod. 19:5), and they will know Him and serve Him. The covenant with Abraham (Gen. 12:1–3) will be fulfilled as the gentile nations come to the Lord because of the glory of God in Israel.

CHAPTER 3
When we come to God to be forgiven, what does He do for us?

3:1, 2 He rebukes the enemy. Satan is the accuser (Rev. 12:10), but Christ is the Advocate (1 John 1:9—2:2). We are chosen by God and belong to Him, and the enemy cannot condemn us (Rom. 8:31–39). The Spirit convicts in love to woo us back to God. Satan accuses us in hatred to make us despair of God's help. Be sure to distinguish these two voices.

3:3–5 He removes the iniquity. The dirty garments symbolized the sinfulness of the nation, for the high priest was to keep himself clean before the Lord. God removes our sin and clothes us anew because Jesus died for our sins and lives to intercede for us.

3:6–10 He restores the ministry. God did not set Joshua aside, for the purpose of restoration is ministry. God told him to go back and minister to the people and tell them about the coming Messiah, the BRANCH. Just as Joshua was cleansed and restored, so Israel will be cleansed and restored when Messiah comes to reign (vv. 9–10; 12:10—13:1).

In the Words of Zechariah—In the prophecy of Zechariah, the Lord Jesus Christ is presented as the BRANCH (3:8; 6:12; Isa. 11:1), the Stone (3:9; 10:4; Isa. 28:16), the King (9:9; 14:9, 16–17), and the rejected Shepherd (11:12; 13:7).

CHAPTER 4

4:1–6, 11–14 Zechariah ministered to discouraged people attempting to accomplish a difficult task. If you find yourself ready to quit, consider the assurances God gives His workers. **God provides power.** Oil is symbolic of God's Holy Spirit, and He alone can give us the power to finish His work. Are you depending on Him or on your own strength and expertise? Ponder Ephesians 3:20–21.

4:7 God removes obstacles. Unbelief makes mountains out of molehills, but faith in God makes mountains into plains! The leaders faced all kinds of obstacles, but God would open the way for them. (See Isa. 41:15; Matt. 17:20.)

4:9 God gives promises. God finishes what He starts (Phil. 1:6; Heb. 12:1–2), so we can trust Him even in the midst of opposition. The temple project was delayed for many years, but God eventually helped them finish it.

4:10 God rejoices over our work. To the eyes of men, the temple project was but a small thing (Hag. 2:3); but to the eyes of God, it was a source of great joy. Do your work to please God and let Him be the final judge (1 Cor. 4:5).

CHAPTERS 5—6

5:1–4 Wickedness condemned. The scroll was fifteen feet by thirty feet, so it could easily be seen and read. God condemned the thieves and the liars. (Satan is both; John 8:44.) These sins are violations of the third and the eighth commandments and are still condemned by God (Eph. 4:25–28).

---

4 Now* the angel who talked with me came back and wakened me, as a man who is wakened out of his sleep. 2And he said to me, "What do you see?"

So I said, "I am looking, and there *is* a lampstand of solid gold with a bowl on top of it, and on the *stand* seven lamps with seven pipes to the seven lamps. 3Two olive trees *are* by it, one at the right of the bowl and the other at its left." 4So I answered and spoke to the angel who talked with me, saying, "What *are* these, my lord?"

5Then the angel who talked with me answered and said to me, "Do you not know what these are?"

And I said, "No, my lord."

6So he answered and said to me:

"This *is* the word of the LORD to Zerubbabel:
'Not by might nor by power, but by My Spirit,'
Says the LORD of hosts.
7 *'Who *are* you, O great mountain?
Before Zerubbabel *you shall become* a plain!
And he shall bring forth the capstone
With shouts of "Grace, grace to it!" ' "

8Moreover the word of the LORD came to me, saying:

9 *"The hands of Zerubbabel
Have laid the foundation of this temple;[b]
His hands shall also finish *it*.
Then you will know
That the LORD of hosts has sent Me to you.
10 *For who has despised the day of small things?
For these seven rejoice to see
The plumb line in the hand of Zerubbabel.
They are the eyes of the LORD,
Which scan to and fro throughout the whole earth."

11Then I answered and said to him, "What *are* these two olive trees—at the right of the lampstand and at its left?" 12And I further answered and said to him, "What *are these* two olive branches that *drip* into the receptacles[c] of the two gold pipes from which the golden *oil* drains?"

13Then he answered me and said, "Do you not know what these *are*?"

And I said, "No, my lord."

14So he said, "These *are* the two anointed ones, who stand beside the Lord of the whole earth."

5 Then* I turned and raised my eyes, and saw there a flying scroll.
2And he said to me, "What do you see?"

So I answered, "I see a flying scroll. Its length *is* twenty cubits and its width ten cubits."

3Then he said to me, "This *is* the curse that goes out over the face of the whole earth: 'Every thief

---

4:9 [b]Literally *house*   4:12 [c]Literally *into the hands of*

Small Things—God delights in using small things: Moses' rod (Exod. 4:2), David's sling (1 Sam. 17), a jawbone (Judg. 15:15), a hammer and a tent peg (Judg. 4:17–24), a piece of rope (Josh. 2:15–21), a basket (Acts 9:23–25), loaves and fish (John 6:9), a cup of cold water (Matt. 10:42), and even mud (John 9:6–7).

shall be expelled,' according *to* this side of *the scroll;* and, 'Every perjurer shall be expelled,' according *to* that side of it."

⁴ "I will send out *the curse*," says the LORD of
      hosts;
   "It shall enter the house of the thief
   And the house of the one who swears falsely
      by My name.
   It shall remain in the midst of his house
   And consume it, with its timber and stones."

⁵*Then the angel who talked with me came out and said to me, "Lift your eyes now, and see what this *is* that goes forth."
⁶So I asked, "What *is* it?" And he said, "It *is* a basket*ᵈ* that is going forth."
   He also said, "This *is* their resemblance throughout the earth: ⁷Here *is* a lead disc lifted up, and this *is* a woman sitting inside the basket"; ⁸then he said, "This *is* Wickedness!" And he thrust her down into the basket, and threw the lead cover*ᵉ* over its mouth. ⁹Then I raised my eyes and looked, and there *were* two women, coming with the wind in their wings; for they had wings like the wings of a stork, and they lifted up the basket between earth and heaven.
   ¹⁰So I said to the angel who talked with me, "Where are they carrying the basket?"
   ¹¹And he said to me, "To build a house for it in the land of Shinar;*ᶠ* when it is ready, *the basket* will be set there on its base."

6 Then* I turned and raised my eyes and looked, and behold, four chariots *were* coming from between two mountains, and the mountains *were* mountains of bronze. ²With the first chariot *were* red horses, with the second chariot black horses, ³with the third chariot white horses, and with the fourth chariot dappled horses—strong *steeds.* ⁴Then I answered and said to the angel who talked with me, "What *are* these, my lord?"
   ⁵And the angel answered and said to me, "These *are* four spirits of heaven, who go out from *their* station before the Lord of all the earth. ⁶The one with the black horses is going to the north country, the white are going after them, and the dappled are going toward the south country." ⁷Then the strong *steeds* went out, eager to go, that they might walk to and fro throughout the earth. And He said, "Go, walk to and fro throughout the earth." So they walked to and fro throughout the earth. ⁸And He called to me, and spoke to me, saying, "See, those who go toward the north country have given rest to My Spirit in the north country."
   ⁹*Then the word of the LORD came to me, saying: ¹⁰"Receive *the gift* from the captives—from Heldai, Tobijah, and Jedaiah, who have come from Babylon—and go the same day and enter

5:5–11 *Wickedness confined.* In the end times, there will be a concentration of evil at Babylon, that last expression of the evil world system (Rev. 17—18). The word *wickedness* is feminine in Hebrew, which explains why a woman was used as the illustration.

6:1–8 *Wickedness controlled.* The vision parallels Zechariah 1:7–11 and reminds us that God's angelic servants patrol the earth. The Jews frequently were invaded from the north, but God was keeping those nations at rest so the remnant could build the temple.

6:9–15 *Wickedness conquered.* Three Jews from Babylon came to Jerusalem with gold and silver for the temple. But God told Zechariah to make a crown and put it on Joshua and make him a king-priest! No Jewish priest had ever reigned as king, and no king was permitted to serve as a priest (2 Chron. 26:16–21). All of this was symbolic of the coming Messiah, the King-Priest (Ps. 110:4; Heb. 7:1–3) who would reign from the future glorious temple (Ezek. 40ff.). Just as the three men brought gifts from afar, so the Gentiles would bring gifts to help build the future temple (Isa. 60:4–7).
   As Haggai encouraged the people in their daily work, Zechariah urged them to live "in the future tense" and work because they were a part of God's glorious future. A "blessed hope" is a great motivation for service and faithfulness (Titus 2:11–15).

5:6 *ᵈ*Hebrew *ephah,* a measuring container, and so elsewhere
5:8 *ᵉ*Literally *stone*   5:11 *ᶠ*That is, Babylon

Messianic Titles—"The BRANCH" is an important messianic title, signifying our Lord's coming from the stock of David (Isa. 11:1). As Branch, He is King (Jer. 23:5; 33:15), God's Servant (Zech. 3:8), "the Man whose name is the BRANCH" (Zech. 6:12), and "the Branch of the LORD" (Isa. 4:2). Some see in these four titles a parallel to the four Gospels. Matthew presents the Branch of David, the King; Mark, the Servant; Luke, the Man; and John, "the Branch of the Lord" who is God come in human flesh (John 20:30–31).

the house of Josiah the son of Zephaniah. [11]Take the silver and gold, make an elaborate crown, and set *it* on the head of Joshua the son of Jehozadak, the high priest. [12]Then speak to him, saying, 'Thus says the LORD of hosts, saying:

"Behold, the Man whose name *is* the
    BRANCH!
From His place He shall branch out,
And He shall build the temple of the LORD;
[13] Yes, He shall build the temple of the LORD.
He shall bear the glory,
And shall sit and rule on His throne;
So He shall be a priest on His throne,
And the counsel of peace shall be between
    them both." '

[14]"Now the elaborate crown shall be for a memorial in the temple of the LORD for Helem,[g] Tobijah, Jedaiah, and Hen the son of Zephaniah. [15]Even those from afar shall come and build the temple of the LORD. Then you shall know that the LORD of hosts has sent Me to you. And *this* shall come to pass if you diligently obey the voice of the LORD your God."

7 Now in the fourth year of King Darius it came to pass *that* the word of the LORD came to Zechariah, on the fourth day of the ninth month, Chislev, [2]when *the people*[h] sent Sherezer,[i] with Regem-Melech and his men, *to* the house of God,[j] to pray before the LORD, [3]*and* to ask the priests who *were* in the house of the LORD of hosts, and the prophets, saying, "Should I weep in the fifth month and fast as I have done for so many years?"

[4]Then the word of the LORD of hosts came to me, saying, [5]*"Say to all the people of the land, and to the priests: 'When you fasted and mourned in the fifth and seventh *months* during those seventy years, did you really fast for Me—for Me? [6]When you eat and when you drink, do you not eat and drink *for yourselves?* [7]Should *you* not *have obeyed* the words which the LORD proclaimed through the former prophets when Jerusalem and the cities around it were inhabited and prosperous, and the South[k] and the Lowland were inhabited?' "

[8]Then the word of the LORD came to Zechariah, saying, [9]*"Thus says the LORD of hosts:

'Execute true justice,
Show mercy and compassion
Everyone to his brother.
[10] Do not oppress the widow or the fatherless,
The alien or the poor.
Let none of you plan evil in his heart
Against his brother.'

[11]*But they refused to heed, shrugged their shoulders, and stopped their ears so that they could not hear. [12]Yes, they made their hearts like flint, refusing to hear the law and the words which the LORD of hosts had sent by His Spirit through the former prophets. Thus great wrath came from the LORD of hosts. [13]Therefore it happened, *that*

CHAPTER 7

7:5 While in Babylon, the Jews started a new tradition: fasting on the ninth day of the fifth month to commemorate the destruction of Jerusalem. But a remnant was now rebuilding the city and the temple, and the prophets said that an even greater city and temple were yet to come. Should this fast be continued? There is nothing wrong with traditions that do not involve practices contrary to the Word of God. But it is good to examine these traditions from time to time just to make sure they are meaningful. *Are we doing this unto the Lord?* Or is it just a ceremony that we endure regularly? If the Lord is left out, the tradition lacks both life and heart. (See Rom. 14:1–9.)

7:9, 10 *Does doing this help us serve others?* The fast God wants is not an annual ceremony but a daily way of life. It means showing compassion and mercy and helping the poor and needy. God wants mercy, not sacrifice (Hos. 6:6; Amos 5:21–24; Mic. 6:8; Matt. 15:1–9).

7:11, 12 *Does doing this make us obedient to His Word?* The previous generation carried out their traditions but hardened their hearts to the Word of God. Are we doing the same thing?

6:14 [g]Following Masoretic Text, Targum, and Vulgate; Syriac reads *for Heldai* (compare verse 10); Septuagint reads *for the patient ones.*   7:2 [h]Literally *they* (compare verse 5) [i]Or *Sar-Ezer* [j]Hebrew *Bethel*   7:7 [k]Hebrew *Negev*

just as He proclaimed and they would not hear, so they called out and I would not listen," says the LORD of hosts. 14"But I scattered them with a whirlwind among all the nations which they had not known. Thus the land became desolate after them, so that no one passed through or returned; for they made the pleasant land desolate."

8 Again* the word of the LORD of hosts came, saying, 2"Thus says the LORD of hosts:

'I am zealous for Zion with great zeal;
With great fervor I am zealous for her.'

3"Thus says the LORD:

'I will return to Zion,
And dwell in the midst of Jerusalem.
Jerusalem shall be called the City of Truth,
The Mountain of the LORD of hosts,
The Holy Mountain.'

4"Thus says the LORD of hosts:

'Old men and old women shall again sit
In the streets of Jerusalem,
Each one with his staff in his hand
Because of great age.
5   The streets of the city
Shall be full of boys and girls
Playing in its streets.'

6"Thus says the LORD of hosts:

'If it is marvelous in the eyes of the remnant
of this people in these days,
Will it also be marvelous in My eyes?'
Says the LORD of hosts.

7"Thus says the LORD of hosts:

'Behold, I will save My people from the land
of the east
And from the land of the west;
8   I will bring them *back*,
And they shall dwell in the midst of
Jerusalem.
They shall be My people
And I will be their God,
In truth and righteousness.'

9*"Thus says the LORD of hosts:

'Let your hands be strong,
You who have been hearing in these days
These words by the mouth of the prophets,
Who *spoke* in the day the foundation was
laid
For the house of the LORD of hosts,
That the temple might be built.
10   For before these days
There were no wages for man nor any hire
for beast;
There was no peace from the enemy for
whoever went out or came in;

CHAPTER 8

8:1–8 Zechariah is still answering the question about the fast, but he uses this opportunity to encourage the Jews in their work. "Do not fear!" (vv. 13, 15) is the emphasis of this brief message, and he gave them three promises to encourage them.

God will restore Jerusalem. He looked beyond that present day to the day when Messiah would come, establish His kingdom, and make Jerusalem a city of truth and peace. The old would sit safely in the sunny streets, and the children would play without fear.

8:9–17 *God will prosper your work.* The people had not been faithful to God, so He had withheld His blessing (Hag. 1:1–11); but now He would prosper their labors, bless them, and make them a blessing (1 Cor. 15:58).

Traditions—The only fast God required of the Jews was on the annual Day of Atonement (Lev. 16:29). The four fasts mentioned in Zechariah 8:19 commemorated (in order) the breaching of Jerusalem's walls, the burning of the temple, the assassination of Gedaliah (Jer. 41), and the beginning of the siege of Jerusalem. The nation was adept at developing new religious traditions, but it was not good at obeying the Word of God.

For I set all men, everyone, against his
neighbor.

11But now I *will* not *treat* the remnant of this people as in the former days,' says the LORD of hosts.

12 'For the seed *shall be* prosperous,
The vine shall give its fruit,
The ground shall give her increase,
And the heavens shall give their dew—
I will cause the remnant of this people
To possess all these.
13 And it shall come to pass
That just as you were a curse among the
nations,
O house of Judah and house of Israel,
So I will save you, and you shall be a
blessing.
Do not fear,
Let your hands be strong.'

14"For thus says the LORD of hosts:

'Just as I determined to punish you
When your fathers provoked Me to wrath,'
Says the LORD of hosts,
'And I would not relent,
15 So again in these days
I am determined to do good
To Jerusalem and to the house of Judah.
Do not fear.
16 These *are* the things you shall do:
Speak each man the truth to his neighbor;
Give judgment in your gates for truth,
justice, and peace;
17 Let none of you think evil in your*l* heart
against your neighbor;
And do not love a false oath.
For all these *are things* that I hate,'
Says the LORD."

**8:18–23 God will turn fasting into
feasting.** In the future kingdom, there will
be no need for fasting. The events of the
past will be forgotten in the glory of the
worship of the Lord. Jesus came to bring
us joy, not sorrow (Matt. 9:14–17).

18*Then the word of the LORD of hosts came to
me, saying, 19"Thus says the LORD of hosts:

'The fast of the fourth *month,*
The fast of the fifth,
The fast of the seventh,
And the fast of the tenth,
Shall be joy and gladness and cheerful
feasts
For the house of Judah.
Therefore love truth and peace.'

20"Thus says the LORD of hosts:

'Peoples shall yet come,
Inhabitants of many cities;
21 The inhabitants of one *city* shall go to
another, saying,
"Let us continue to go and pray before the
LORD,
And seek the LORD of hosts.
I myself will go also."
22 Yes, many peoples and strong nations
Shall come to seek the LORD of hosts in
Jerusalem,
And to pray before the LORD.'

23"Thus says the LORD of hosts: 'In those days
ten men from every language of the nations shall

8:17 *l*Literally *his*

grasp the sleeve of a Jewish man, saying, "Let us go with you, for we have heard *that* God *is* with you." ' "

9

The* burden*m* of the word of the LORD
Against the land of Hadrach,
And Damascus its resting place
(For the eyes of men
And all the tribes of Israel
Are on the LORD);
2 Also *against* Hamath, *which* borders on it,
And *against* Tyre and Sidon, though they
are very wise.

3 For Tyre built herself a tower,
Heaped up silver like the dust,
And gold like the mire of the streets.
4 Behold, the LORD will cast her out;
He will destroy her power in the sea,
And she will be devoured by fire.

5 Ashkelon shall see *it* and fear;
Gaza also shall be very sorrowful;
And Ekron, for He dried up her expectation.
The king shall perish from Gaza,
And Ashkelon shall not be inhabited.

6 "A mixed race shall settle in Ashdod,
And I will cut off the pride of the Philistines.
7 I will take away the blood from his mouth,
And the abominations from between his
teeth.
But he who remains, even he *shall be* for
our God,
And shall be like a leader in Judah,
And Ekron like a Jebusite.
8 I will camp around My house
Because of the army,
Because of him who passes by and him who
returns.
No more shall an oppressor pass through
them,
For now I have seen with My eyes.

9 *"Rejoice greatly, O daughter of Zion!
Shout, O daughter of Jerusalem!
Behold, your King is coming to you;
He *is* just and having salvation,
Lowly and riding on a donkey,
A colt, the foal of a donkey.
10 I will cut off the chariot from Ephraim
And the horse from Jerusalem;
The battle bow shall be cut off.
He shall speak peace to the nations;
His dominion *shall be* 'from sea to sea,
And from the River to the ends of the
earth.'*n*

11*"As for you also,
Because of the blood of your covenant,
I will set your prisoners free from the
waterless pit.
12 *Return to the stronghold,
You prisoners of hope.
Even today I declare
That I will restore double to you.
13 For I have bent Judah, My *bow,*
Fitted the bow with Ephraim,

CHAPTERS 9—14

9:1ff Zechariah closes his book by giving two oracles (burdens) that focus on the future history of Israel.

Chapters 9—11 deal primarily with Christ's first coming when He presented Himself to His people (9:9) and was rejected (11:12). Events leading up to His coming include the conquests of Alexander the Great (9:1–8) and conflicts during the time of the Maccabees, 168–134 B.C. (9:14–17). Daniel 8:9–14 also touches on this latter period. Israel under Roman rule is seen in chapter 11.

Chapters 12—14 highlight Messiah's second coming and the establishing of His glorious kingdom on earth. The key phrase is "in that day." Zechariah describes the events that will take place "in that day" when Christ returns to earth. When the nations gather together against Jerusalem, He will come in power and deliver His people. The nation will recognize Him, repent, and be cleansed; and Jesus Christ will reign as King from Jerusalem.

Symbolism appears often in chapters 9—14, and at times the prophet refers to our Lord's first and second advents in succeeding verses; but this is not unusual in prophetic literature (Isa. 9:6, for example). As you read, see Christ in His grace and glory, and rejoice in His promised victory.

CHAPTER 9

9:1–8 The spread of Alexander's kingdom (vv. 1–8) helped to prepare the way for the birth of the Lord Jesus. God controls history and uses it to accomplish His purposes. Events in the news today, depressing as they may seem, are all in the hands of God.

9:9, 10 Verse 9 was fulfilled when Jesus rode into Jerusalem (Matt. 21:1–11); verse 10 will not be fulfilled until He returns and sets up His kingdom. Israel rejected her own King and said (as people do today), "We have no king but Caesar!"

9:11–17 Verses 11–17 focus on the future deliverance of God's people. It will be like releasing prisoners from a pit (v. 11), gathering a scattered flock, putting jewels in a crown, and assembling a conquering army (vv. 16–17). What a glorious day that will be!

9:12 God appeals in verse 12 to the Jews still in Babylon, urging them to return to their people and their land. He promises twice as much blessing to those who will obey Him, so be sure you are in the place of His choosing.

9:1 *m*Or *oracle*   9:10 *n*Psalm 72:8

And raised up your sons, O Zion,
Against your sons, O Greece,
And made you like the sword of a mighty man."

14 Then the LORD will be seen over them,
And His arrow will go forth like lightning.
The Lord GOD will blow the trumpet,
And go with whirlwinds from the south.
15 The LORD of hosts will defend them;
They shall devour and subdue with slingstones.
They shall drink *and* roar as if with wine;
They shall be filled *with blood* like basins,
Like the corners of the altar.
16 The LORD their God will save them in that day,
As the flock of His people.
For they *shall be like* the jewels of a crown,
Lifted like a banner over His land—
17 For how great is its[o] goodness
And how great its[p] beauty!
Grain shall make the young men thrive,
And new wine the young women.

10 Ask* the LORD for rain
In the time of the latter rain.[q]
The LORD will make flashing clouds;
He will give them showers of rain,
Grass in the field for everyone.

2 For the idols[r] speak delusion;
The diviners envision lies,
And tell false dreams;
They comfort in vain.
Therefore *the people* wend their way like sheep;
They are in trouble because *there is* no shepherd.

3 "My anger is kindled against the shepherds,
And I will punish the goatherds.
For the LORD of hosts will visit His flock,
The house of Judah,
And will make them as His royal horse in the battle.
4 From him comes the cornerstone,
From him the tent peg,
From him the battle bow,
From him every ruler[s] together.
5 They shall be like mighty men,
Who tread down *their enemies*
In the mire of the streets in the battle.
They shall fight because the LORD is with them,
And the riders on horses shall be put to shame.

6 "I will strengthen the house of Judah,
And I will save the house of Joseph.
I will bring them back,
Because I have mercy on them.
They shall be as though I had not cast them aside;

9:17 [o]Or *His* [p]Or *His* 10:1 [q]That is, spring rain 10:2 [r]Hebrew *teraphim* 10:4 [s]Or *despot*

CHAPTERS 10—11

10:1ff Chapters 10 and 11 portray Israel as God's flock and their leaders as shepherds.

The faithful Shepherd. The flock was in trouble because it had no shepherd to care for it. But the Lord will return and be the Shepherd. He will rescue the people, strengthen them, and establish them in peace.

God's Strength—When God gives strength to His people, they become victorious. The sheep becomes a war horse (Zech. 10:3), and the worm becomes a threshing machine (Isa. 41:14–16). The feeblest person can be a hero like David (Zech. 12:8) when you go in the strength of the Lord.

For I *am* the LORD their God,
And I will hear them.
7 *Those of* Ephraim shall be like a mighty
        man,
And their heart shall rejoice as if with wine.
Yes, their children shall see *it* and be glad;
Their heart shall rejoice in the LORD.
8 I will whistle for them and gather them,
For I will redeem them;
And they shall increase as they once
        increased.

9 "I will sow them among the peoples,
And they shall remember Me in far
        countries;
They shall live, together with their children,
And they shall return.
10 I will also bring them back from the land
        of Egypt,
And gather them from Assyria.
I will bring them into the land of Gilead and
        Lebanon,
Until no *more room* is found for them.
11 He shall pass through the sea with affliction,
And strike the waves of the sea:
All the depths of the River† shall dry up.
Then the pride of Assyria shall be brought
        down,
And the scepter of Egypt shall depart.

12 "So I will strengthen them in the LORD,
And they shall walk up and down in His
        name,"
Says the LORD.

11

Open* your doors, O Lebanon,
That fire may devour your cedars.
2 Wail, O cypress, for the cedar has fallen,
Because the mighty *trees* are ruined.
Wail, O oaks of Bashan,
For the thick forest has come down.
3 *There is* the sound of wailing shepherds!
For their glory is in ruins.
There is the sound of roaring lions!
For the pride^u of the Jordan is in ruins.

4Thus says the LORD my God, "Feed the flock for slaughter, 5whose owners slaughter them and feel no guilt; those who sell them say, 'Blessed be the LORD, for I am rich'; and their shepherds do not pity them. 6For I will no longer pity the inhabitants of the land," says the LORD. "But indeed I will give everyone into his neighbor's hand and into the hand of his king. They shall attack the land, and I will not deliver *them* from their hand."

7So I fed the flock for slaughter, in particular the poor of the flock.^v I took for myself two staffs: the one I called Beauty,^w and the other I called Bonds;^x and I fed the flock. 8I dismissed the three shepherds in one month. My soul loathed them, and their soul also abhorred me. 9Then I said, "I will not feed you. Let what is dying die, and what is perishing perish. Let those that are left eat each other's flesh." 10And I took my staff, Beauty, and

11:1–14 *The false shepherds.* The leaders were not true to God or their people, and God sent ruin (vv. 1–3). The flock was destined for slaughter (the Roman conquest in A.D. 70), division (the broken rod), and dispersion among the Gentiles. The prophet is a picture of the true Shepherd who cares for the flock, is rejected by the false shepherds, and is sold like a slave (vv. 12–13; Exod. 21:32; Matt. 26:14–16).

10:11 †That is, the Nile   11:3 ^uOr *floodplain, thicket*
11:7 ^vFollowing Masoretic Text, Targum, and Vulgate;
Septuagint reads *for the Canaanites.* ^wOr *Grace,* and so in
verse 10 ^xOr *Unity,* and so in verse 14

11:15–17 The foolish shepherd. This is the last world ruler, Antichrist, whom Israel will accept as their friend. He will agree to protect Israel but then will break his promise (Dan. 9:27). When you reject the true, it is much easier to accept the false (John 5:43). But God will strike the false shepherd and judge him (Rev. 19:11–21).

Jeremiah stated, "It is not in man who walks to direct his steps" (Jer. 10:23). We all need a shepherd, so be sure you follow the right one.

CHAPTERS 12

12:3 The phrase "in that day" used frequently in chapters 12—14 refers to the time of the end when "the day of the LORD" will climax with the return of Jesus Christ to the earth to defeat His enemies, deliver Israel, and establish His kingdom.

Jerusalem will be at the center of world attention. Note the images of Jerusalem that the prophet used: a cup of strong wine that will make the nations drunk (v. 2); a heavy stone that will crush the nations (v. 3); and a firepan and torch that will devour the nations (v. 6). Those who attack Israel will only defeat themselves, for God has covenanted to protect Israel (Gen. 12:1–3).

12:10–14 When the people of Israel see the Messiah (v. 10), they will recognize Him (Matt. 24:30; Rev. 1:7), repent, and be cleansed and forgiven. Their sorrow will exceed the sorrow displayed at the tragic death of godly King Josiah (v. 11; 2 Chron. 35:20–27).

Like God's people Israel, we experience many trials and testings; but the Lord will see us through and share His kingdom and glory with us (Acts 14:22).

cut it in two, that I might break the covenant which I had made with all the peoples. 11So it was broken on that day. Thus the poor^y of the flock, who were watching me, knew that it *was* the word of the LORD. 12Then I said to them, "If it is agreeable to you, give *me* my wages; and if not, refrain." So they weighed out for my wages thirty *pieces* of silver.

13And the LORD said to me, "Throw it to the potter"—that princely price they set on me. So I took the thirty *pieces* of silver and threw them into the house of the LORD for the potter. 14Then I cut in two my other staff, Bonds, that I might break the brotherhood between Judah and Israel.

15*And the LORD said to me, "Next, take for yourself the implements of a foolish shepherd. 16For indeed I will raise up a shepherd in the land *who* will not care for those who are cut off, nor seek the young, nor heal those that are broken, nor feed those that still stand. But he will eat the flesh of the fat and tear their hooves in pieces.

17 "Woe to the worthless shepherd,
Who leaves the flock!
A sword *shall be* against his arm
And against his right eye;
His arm shall completely wither,
And his right eye shall be totally blinded."

12 The burden^z of the word of the LORD against Israel. Thus says the LORD, who stretches out the heavens, lays the foundation of the earth, and forms the spirit of man within him: 2"Behold, I will make Jerusalem a cup of drunkenness to all the surrounding peoples, when they lay siege against Judah and Jerusalem. 3*And it shall happen in that day that I will make Jerusalem a very heavy stone for all peoples; all who would heave it away will surely be cut in pieces, though all nations of the earth are gathered against it. 4In that day," says the LORD, "I will strike every horse with confusion, and its rider with madness; I will open My eyes on the house of Judah, and will strike every horse of the peoples with blindness. 5And the governors of Judah shall say in their heart, 'The inhabitants of Jerusalem *are* my strength in the LORD of hosts, their God.' 6In that day I will make the governors of Judah like a firepan in the woodpile, and like a fiery torch in the sheaves; they shall devour all the surrounding peoples on the right hand and on the left, but Jerusalem shall be inhabited again in her own place—Jerusalem.

7"The LORD will save the tents of Judah first, so that the glory of the house of David and the glory of the inhabitants of Jerusalem shall not become greater than that of Judah. 8In that day the LORD will defend the inhabitants of Jerusalem; the one who is feeble among them in that day shall be like David, and the house of David *shall be* like God, like the Angel of the LORD before them. 9It shall be in that day *that* I will seek to destroy all the nations that come against Jerusalem.

10*"And I will pour on the house of David and on the inhabitants of Jerusalem the Spirit of grace and supplication; then they will look on Me whom they pierced. Yes, they will mourn for Him as one

11:11 ^yFollowing Masoretic Text, Targum, and Vulgate; Septuagint reads *the Canaanites.* 12:1 ^zOr *oracle*

mourns for *his* only *son,* and grieve for Him as one grieves for a firstborn. [11]In that day there shall be a great mourning in Jerusalem, like the mourning at Hadad Rimmon in the plain of Megiddo.[a] [12]And the land shall mourn, every family by itself: the family of the house of David by itself, and their wives by themselves; the family of the house of Nathan by itself, and their wives by themselves; [13]the family of the house of Levi by itself, and their wives by themselves; the family of Shimei by itself, and their wives by themselves; [14]all the families that remain, every family by itself, and their wives by themselves.

13 "In* that day a fountain shall be opened for the house of David and for the inhabitants of Jerusalem, for sin and for uncleanness.

[2]"It shall be in that day," says the LORD of hosts, "*that* I will cut off the names of the idols from the land, and they shall no longer be remembered. I will also cause the prophets and the unclean spirit to depart from the land. [3]It shall come to pass *that* if anyone still prophesies, then his father and mother who begot him will say to him, 'You shall not live, because you have spoken lies in the name of the LORD.' And his father and mother who begot him shall thrust him through when he prophesies.

[4]"And it shall be in that day *that* every prophet will be ashamed of his vision when he prophesies; they will not wear a robe of coarse hair to deceive. [5]But he will say, 'I *am* no prophet, I *am* a farmer; for a man taught me to keep cattle from my youth.' [6]And *one* will say to him, 'What are these wounds between your arms?'[b] Then he will answer, '*Those* with which I was wounded in the house of my friends.'

7 *"Awake, O sword, against My Shepherd,
    Against the Man who is My Companion,"
    Says the LORD of hosts.
    "Strike the Shepherd,
    And the sheep will be scattered;
    Then I will turn My hand against the little
      ones.
8   *And it shall come to pass in all the land,"
    Says the LORD,
    "*That* two-thirds in it shall be cut off *and* die,
    But *one*-third shall be left in it:
9   I will bring the *one*-third through the fire,
    Will refine them as silver is refined,
    And test them as gold is tested.
    They will call on My name,
    And I will answer them.
    I will say, 'This *is* My people';
    And each one will say, 'The LORD *is* my
      God.' "

14 Behold,* the day of the LORD is coming,
    And your spoil will be divided in your midst.
2   For I will gather all the nations to battle
      against Jerusalem;
    The city shall be taken,
    The houses rifled,
    And the women ravished.
    Half of the city shall go into captivity,
    But the remnant of the people shall not be
      cut off from the city.

12:11 [a]Hebrew *Megiddon*   13:6 [b]Or *hands*

CHAPTERS 13

13:1–6 The fountain. The defiled will be cleansed of sin (Jer. 31:31–34), and the deceived will have all their idols and false prophets removed. Verse 6 refers not to Jesus Christ but to a false prophet who has wounded his body in some religious ritual (1 Kings 18:28). He tries to prove that he is not a prophet because he wants to escape judgment.

13:7 The flock. To save His flock, the Good Shepherd must be smitten, and that means suffering and death (Isa. 53:4, 10; Matt. 26:31). The next time you are smitten because of your faith, remember that your Shepherd felt it before you did (Matt. 5:38–42; 10:16–26).

13:8, 9 The furnace. Israel's terrible suffering at the close of the age will be like a refining furnace, separating the true from the false (Isa. 48:10). Suffering in the will of God can be a time of purification when we can bring glory to God (Job 23:10).

CHAPTERS 14

14:1ff The prophet describes the great campaign that we call the Battle of Armageddon (Rev. 14:17–20; 16:14–16), when the nations of the world will gather against Jerusalem.

See the demonstrations of His power! He will make changes in the heavens (vv. 6–7) and the earth (vv. 3–5), and will send a plague that will frighten and destroy the enemy (vv. 12–15). He will cause a river to flow that will restore and refresh the land (Ezek. 47).

Zechariah proclaimed, "And the LORD shall be King over all the earth" (v. 9)! Our prayer "Thy kingdom come" will be answered, and we shall reign with Him (Rev. 5:10; 20:6). The nations will "worship the King" (vv. 16–17), and even ordinary items like harnesses and kitchen pots will be holy to the Lord. No outsiders will be there to defile God's holy temple (v. 21).

The Feast of Tabernacles was Israel's most joyful celebration (Lev. 23:33–44), so the kingdom age will be a time of holiness and happiness in worshiping and serving the Lord.

3 Then the LORD will go forth
And fight against those nations,
As He fights in the day of battle.
4 And in that day His feet will stand on the
Mount of Olives,
Which faces Jerusalem on the east.
And the Mount of Olives shall be split in
two,
From east to west,
Making a very large valley;
Half of the mountain shall move toward the
north
And half of it toward the south.

5 Then you shall flee *through* My mountain
valley,
For the mountain valley shall reach to
Azal.
Yes, you shall flee
As you fled from the earthquake
In the days of Uzziah king of Judah.

Thus the LORD my God will come,
And all the saints with You.[c]

6 It shall come to pass in that day
That there will be no light;
The lights will diminish.
7 It shall be one day
Which is known to the LORD—
Neither day nor night.
But at evening time it shall happen
That it will be light.

8 And in that day it shall be
That living waters shall flow from
Jerusalem,
Half of them toward the eastern sea
And half of them toward the western sea;
In both summer and winter it shall occur.
9 And the LORD shall be King over all the
earth.
In that day it shall be—
"The LORD *is* one,"[d]
And His name one.

10 All the land shall be turned into a plain from
Geba to Rimmon south of Jerusalem. *Jerusalem*[e]
shall be raised up and inhabited in her place from
Benjamin's Gate to the place of the First Gate and
the Corner Gate, and *from* the Tower of Hananel
to the king's winepresses.

11 *The people* shall dwell in it;
And no longer shall there be utter
destruction,
But Jerusalem shall be safely inhabited.

12 And this shall be the plague with which the
LORD will strike all the people who fought against
Jerusalem:

Their flesh shall dissolve while they stand
on their feet,
Their eyes shall dissolve in their sockets,
And their tongues shall dissolve in their
mouths.

14:5 [c]Or *you*; Septuagint, Targum, and Vulgate read *Him*.
14:9 [d]Compare Deuteronomy 6:4   14:10 [e]Literally *She*

13 It shall come to pass in that day
    That a great panic from the LORD will be
        among them.
    Everyone will seize the hand of his
        neighbor,
    And raise his hand against his neighbor's
        hand;
14 Judah also will fight at Jerusalem.
    And the wealth of all the surrounding
        nations
    Shall be gathered together:
    Gold, silver, and apparel in great
        abundance.

15 Such also shall be the plague
    On the horse *and* the mule,
    On the camel and the donkey,
    And on all the cattle that will be in those
        camps.
    So *shall* this plague *be.*

16And it shall come to pass *that* everyone who
is left of all the nations which came against Jerusalem shall go up from year to year to worship
the King, the LORD of hosts, and to keep the Feast
of Tabernacles. 17And it shall be *that* whichever
of the families of the earth do not come up to
Jerusalem to worship the King, the LORD of hosts,
on them there will be no rain. 18If the family of
Egypt will not come up and enter in, they *shall
have* no rain; they shall receive the plague with
which the LORD strikes the nations who do not
come up to keep the Feast of Tabernacles. 19This
shall be the punishment of Egypt and the punishment of all the nations that do not come up to
keep the Feast of Tabernacles.

20In that day "HOLINESS TO THE LORD" shall
be *engraved* on the bells of the horses. The pots
in the LORD's house shall be like the bowls before
the altar. 21Yes, every pot in Jerusalem and Judah
shall be holiness to the LORD of hosts.*f* Everyone
who sacrifices shall come and take them and cook
in them. In that day there shall no longer be a
Canaanite in the house of the LORD of hosts.

14:21 *f*Or *on every pot . . . shall be (engraved) "HOLINESS
TO THE LORD OF HOSTS"*

MALACHI

Ministering about four centuries before Christ, Malachi encountered the same religious situation described in Ezra 9—10 and Nehemiah 8—13. The people were backslidden, the priests were worldly, and the nation was far from God. The name *Malachi* means "my messenger" (2:7; 3:1).

Because the promised kingdom did not come immediately, the Jews questioned God's love (1:2) and justice (2:17) and complained about the way He was treating His chosen people. It was not long before the priests grew careless in their ministry, and the people followed their bad example.

The book may be outlined as follows:
1. God questions their love (1:1–5)
2. God condemns their sins (1:6—2:17)
    a) Despising His name (1:6–14)
    b) Profaning His covenant (2:1–17)
3. God seeks their repentance (3:1—4:6)

We know nothing about Malachi the person; he does not even tell us his father's name as prophets usually do. But after all, he was a messenger; the important thing about a messenger is the message. Malachi was concerned about being faithful, not being famous.

CHAPTER 1

1:2ff Six times the Lord refers to *His name* (vv. 6, 11, 14), which means His character and His reputation. He wants His name to be magnified in all the earth (v. 5). The priests, however, despised His name, and He rebuked them for it. How do we despise the Lord's name?

We show disrespect to His name by questioning His love (vv. 2–5). The times were tough, and the people blamed the situation on God. But their own sins had created their problems (Hag. 1), and God was willing to bless if they were willing to repent.

We despise His name by doing His work in a careless manner (vv. 7–11). They were bored with their blessings, and doing the work of the Lord wearied them.

Along with that, we despise the Lord's name when we offer Him less than our best (vv. 12–14). They offered defective sacrifices, animals that they would never give as gifts to their friends. They even brought sacrifices that were stolen! "I will not take what is yours for the LORD," said David, "nor offer burnt offerings with that which costs me nothing" (1 Chron. 21:24).

Beware when you get bored with your blessings and start taking for granted the privilege of ministry. God may take your privileges away from you.

1 The burden[a] of the word of the LORD to Israel by Malachi.

2 *"I have loved you," says the LORD.
"Yet you say, 'In what way have You loved us?'
Was not Esau Jacob's brother?"
Says the LORD.
"Yet Jacob I have loved;
3   But Esau I have hated,
    And laid waste his mountains and his heritage
    For the jackals of the wilderness."

4   Even though Edom has said,
"We have been impoverished,
But we will return and build the desolate places,"

Thus says the LORD of hosts:

"They may build, but I will throw down;
They shall be called the Territory of Wickedness,
And the people against whom the LORD will have indignation forever.
5   Your eyes shall see,
    And you shall say,
'The LORD is magnified beyond the border of Israel.'

6   "A son honors *his* father,
    And a servant *his* master.
    If then I am the Father,
    Where *is* My honor?
    And if I *am* a Master,

1:1 ᵃOr *oracle*

Where *is* My reverence?
Says the LORD of hosts
To you priests who despise My name.
Yet you say, 'In what way have we despised
    Your name?'

7 "You offer defiled food on My altar,
    But say,
    'In what way have we defiled You?'
    By saying,
    'The table of the LORD is contemptible.'
8 And when you offer the blind as a sacrifice,
    Is it not evil?
    And when you offer the lame and sick,
    Is it not evil?
    Offer it then to your governor!
    Would he be pleased with you?
    Would he accept you favorably?"
    Says the LORD of hosts.

9 "But now entreat God's favor,
    That He may be gracious to us.
    While this is being *done* by your hands,
    Will He accept you favorably?"
    Says the LORD of hosts.
10 "Who *is there* even among you who would
        shut the doors,
    So that you would not kindle fire *on* My
        altar in vain?
    I have no pleasure in you,"
    Says the LORD of hosts,
    "Nor will I accept an offering from your
        hands.
11 For from the rising of the sun, even to its
        going down,
    My name *shall be* great among the Gentiles;
    In every place incense *shall be* offered to
        My name,
    And a pure offering;
    For My name shall be great among the
        nations,"
    Says the LORD of hosts.

12 "But you profane it,
    In that you say,
    'The table of the LORD[b] is defiled;
    And its fruit, its food, *is* contemptible.'
13 You also say,
    'Oh, what a weariness!'
    And you sneer at it,"
    Says the LORD of hosts.
    "And you bring the stolen, the lame, and the
        sick;
    Thus you bring an offering!
    Should I accept this from your hand?"
    Says the LORD.
14 "But cursed *be* the deceiver
    Who has in his flock a male,
    And takes a vow,
    But sacrifices to the Lord what is
        blemished—
    For I *am* a great King,"
    Says the LORD of hosts,
    "And My name *is to be* feared among the
        nations.

2 "And* now, O priests, this commandment
        is for you.
2 If you will not hear,

1:12 [b]Following Bomberg; Masoretic Text reads *Lord.*

CHAPTER 2

2:1–9 The emphasis is on *covenants*
(vv. 4, 5, 8, 10, 14); three are mentioned
specifically.
    The covenant with Levi. God gave the
priesthood to the tribe of Levi and told them
to teach and obey the law of the Lord. But
they corrupted the covenant and disobeyed
His Word, and God had to judge them by
cursing their blessings. Their blessing of the
people would turn out to be a curse (Num.
6:23–27), and Israel would bring trouble
instead of blessing to the world (Deut. 28).

And if you will not take *it* to heart,
To give glory to My name,"
Says the LORD of hosts,
"I will send a curse upon you,
And I will curse your blessings.
Yes, I have cursed them already,
Because you do not take *it* to heart.

3 "Behold, I will rebuke your descendants
And spread refuse on your faces,
The refuse of your solemn feasts;
And *one* will take you away with it.
4 Then you shall know that I have sent this
commandment to you,
That My covenant with Levi may continue,"
Says the LORD of hosts.
5 "My covenant was with him, *one* of life and
peace,
And I gave them to him *that he might* fear
Me;
So he feared Me
And was reverent before My name.
6 The law of truth[c] was in his mouth,
And injustice was not found on his lips.
He walked with Me in peace and equity,
And turned many away from iniquity.

7 "For the lips of a priest should keep
knowledge,
And *people* should seek the law from his
mouth;
For he is the messenger of the LORD of hosts.
8 But you have departed from the way;
You have caused many to stumble at the
law.
You have corrupted the covenant of Levi,"
Says the LORD of hosts.
9 "Therefore I also have made you
contemptible and base
Before all the people,
Because you have not kept My ways
But have shown partiality in the law."

2:10–12 *The covenant with Israel.* This
was made at Sinai when the nation was
"married to Jehovah" (Exod. 19—20). But
His bride was not faithful to Him because
she committed adultery with false gods.
Jeremiah warned about this (Jer. 2), and it
is the underlying theme of the book of
Hosea.

10 *Have we not all one Father?
Has not one God created us?
Why do we deal treacherously with one
another
By profaning the covenant of the fathers?
11 Judah has dealt treacherously,
And an abomination has been committed in
Israel and in Jerusalem,
For Judah has profaned
The LORD's holy *institution* which He loves:
He has married the daughter of a foreign
god.
12 May the LORD cut off from the tents of Jacob
The man who does this, being awake and
aware,[d]

2:6 [c]Or *true instruction*   2:12 [d]Talmud and Vulgate read
teacher and student.

Blessings and Curses—God is able to turn curses into blessings (Neh. 13:2) and blessings into
curses (Mal. 2:1–2). It is painful enough when God *removes* His blessings from us; but when He
turns those blessings into curses, the pain is terrible.
The Extent of Sin—"Have we not all one Father?" (Mal. 2:10) does not mean that everybody is
a child of God and therefore going to heaven. The context is Jewish: God created the nation and
claimed Israel as His firstborn (Isa. 63:16; Exod. 4:22). When the Jewish men divorced their wives
to marry heathen women, they were sinning not only against God but also against their brethren
(1 Thess. 4:1–8).

Yet who brings an offering to the LORD of
hosts!

13 *And this is the second thing you do:
You cover the altar of the LORD with tears,
With weeping and crying;
So He does not regard the offering anymore,
Nor receive *it* with goodwill from your
hands.
14 Yet you say, "For what reason?"
Because the LORD has been witness
Between you and the wife of your youth,
With whom you have dealt treacherously;
Yet she is your companion
And your wife by covenant.
15 But did He not make *them* one,
Having a remnant of the Spirit?
And why one?
He seeks godly offspring.
Therefore take heed to your spirit,
And let none deal treacherously with the
wife of his youth.

16 "For the LORD God of Israel says
That He hates divorce,
For it covers one's garment with violence,"
Says the LORD of hosts.
"Therefore take heed to your spirit,
That you do not deal treacherously."

17 You have wearied the LORD with your
words;
Yet you say,
"In what way have we wearied *Him?*"
In that you say,
"Everyone who does evil
Is good in the sight of the LORD,
And He delights in them,"
Or, "Where *is* the God of justice?"

3 "Behold,* I send My messenger,
And he will prepare the way before Me.
And the Lord, whom you seek,
Will suddenly come to His temple,
Even the Messenger of the covenant,
In whom you delight.
Behold, He is coming,"
Says the LORD of hosts.

2 "But who can endure the day of His coming?
And who can stand when He appears?
For He *is* like a refiner's fire
And like launderers' soap.
3 He will sit as a refiner and a purifier of
silver;
He will purify the sons of Levi,
And purge them as gold and silver,
That they may offer to the LORD
An offering in righteousness.

4 "Then the offering of Judah and Jerusalem
Will be pleasant to the LORD,
As in the days of old,
As in former years.
5 And I will come near you for judgment;
I will be a swift witness
Against sorcerers,
Against adulterers,
Against perjurers,
Against those who exploit wage earners and
widows and orphans,
And against those who turn away an alien—

2:13–16 *The covenant of marriage.* The
men were divorcing their wives and marrying
foreign women (Exod. 34:10–17; Ezra 10),
a sin that led even King Solomon into
idolatry (1 Kings 11). The marriage covenant
involves the husband and the wife *and God,*
and He expects us to be faithful. The
unfaithful husbands could weep and bring
sacrifices (v. 13), but God would not accept
them.

We expect God to be faithful to keep His
word. Why do we think we have the privilege
of not keeping our promises?

CHAPTER 3

3:1–5 *Refining.* As is often done in the
prophetic Scriptures, events from our Lord's
first advent (v. 1) are combined with events
to take place at His second advent (vv. 2–
5). The messenger was John the Baptist
(Matt. 11:7–10) who prepared the way for
the Lord (Isa. 40:3; John 1:23). When Christ
comes as Judge, He will purify Israel,
especially the priests, and will judge the
sinners.

3:6, 7 Returning. God does not change; therefore, He kept His covenant and did not destroy Israel, though she deserved it. The faithfulness of God sustains us (Lam. 3:22–24).

3:8–12 Robbing. Not only did the people bring the Lord defective sacrifices, but they failed to bring tithes and offerings commanded by the Law. Consequently, He cursed their blessings (2:2) and destroyed their crops. *When we rob God, we only rob ourselves.* We cannot keep anything that rightfully belongs to God.

3:16–18 Remembering. There is always a faithful remnant who fears the Lord, obeys Him, ponders His truth, and exercises spiritual discernment. God sees those people and keeps a record of their names. They are His jewels, and they will be spared in the coming day of judgment.

Because they do not fear Me,"
Says the LORD of hosts.

6 *"For I *am* the LORD, I do not change;
Therefore you are not consumed, O sons of Jacob.
7 Yet from the days of your fathers
You have gone away from My ordinances
And have not kept *them.*
Return to Me, and I will return to you,"
Says the LORD of hosts.
"But you said,
'In what way shall we return?'

8 *"Will a man rob God?
Yet you have robbed Me!
But you say,
'In what way have we robbed You?'
In tithes and offerings.
9 You are cursed with a curse,
For you have robbed Me,
Even this whole nation.
10 Bring all the tithes into the storehouse,
That there may be food in My house,
And try Me now in this,"
Says the LORD of hosts,
"If I will not open for you the windows of heaven
And pour out for you *such* blessing
That *there will* not *be room* enough *to receive it.*

11 "And I will rebuke the devourer for your sakes,
So that he will not destroy the fruit of your ground,
Nor shall the vine fail to bear fruit for you in the field,"
Says the LORD of hosts;
12 And all nations will call you blessed,
For you will be a delightful land,"
Says the LORD of hosts.
13 "Your words have been harsh against Me,"
Says the LORD,
"Yet you say,
'What have we spoken against You?'
14 You have said,
'It is useless to serve God;
What profit *is it* that we have kept His ordinance,
And that we have walked as mourners
Before the LORD of hosts?
15 So now we call the proud blessed,
For those who do wickedness are raised up;
They even tempt God and go free.' "

16 *Then those who feared the LORD spoke to one another,
And the LORD listened and heard *them;*
So a book of remembrance was written before Him
For those who fear the LORD
And who meditate on His name.

17 "They shall be Mine," says the LORD of hosts,
"On the day that I make them My jewels.*e*
And I will spare them
As a man spares his own son who serves him."

3:17 *e*Literally *special treasure*

18 Then you shall again discern
Between the righteous and the wicked,
Between one who serves God
And one who does not serve Him.

4 "For* behold, the day is coming,
Burning like an oven,
And all the proud, yes, all who do wickedly
will be stubble.
And the day which is coming shall burn
them up,"
Says the LORD of hosts,
"That will leave them neither root nor
branch.
2 *But to you who fear My name
The Sun of Righteousness shall arise
With healing in His wings;
And you shall go out
And grow fat like stall-fed calves.
3 You shall trample the wicked,
For they shall be ashes under the soles of
your feet
On the day that I do *this*,"
Says the LORD of hosts.

4 *"Remember the Law of Moses, My servant,
Which I commanded him in Horeb for all
Israel,
With the statutes and judgments.
5 Behold, I will send you Elijah the prophet
Before the coming of the great and dreadful
day of the LORD.
6 And he will turn
The hearts of the fathers to the children,
And the hearts of the children to their
fathers,
Lest I come and strike the earth with a
curse."

CHAPTER 4

4:1 Burning. The day of the Lord will be a time of fierce judgment on the earth, and the wicked will be burned like stubble. The fire of God's jealousy will burn (Zeph. 1:18).

4:2 Healing. "Sun of Righteousness" is a title for Jesus Christ (Ps. 84:11). He is to His people what the sun is to our galaxy: the center of all things and the source of life and light (John 1:4). The same Sun that brings burning to the lost will bring blessing to the saved.

4:4–6 Obeying. Malachi pointed back to the Law and commanded Israel to obey and be prepared for what God was going to do. Then he pointed ahead to the ministry of Elijah, which was fulfilled in a spiritual sense in John the Baptist (Luke 1:16–17; Matt. 17:10–13). It may be fulfilled literally if Elijah is one of the two witnesses described in Revelation 11:1–13.

The Old Testament ends with the awesome word *curse*. At the close of the New Testament, the promise is, "And there shall be no more curse" (Rev. 22:3). What made the difference? On the cross, Jesus Christ was made a curse for us (Gal. 3:13).

> **"**Men are not in hell because God is angry with them: they are in wrath and darkness because they have done to the light, which infinitely flows forth from God, as that man does to the light of the sun who puts out his own eyes.**"**
> —William Law

Fire—In Scripture, fire is often associated with judgment, for it is a symbol of the holy wrath of God. Fire consumed God's enemies (2 Kings 1) as well as His servants who disobeyed Him (Lev. 10:1–3). He has reserved the world for a judgment of fire (2 Pet. 3:10), and hell is compared to a lake of fire (Rev. 20:10, 14; 21:8) and a furnace of fire (Matt. 13:42, 50). Jesus often spoke of the fiery judgment that awaits those who do not trust Him (Matt. 5:22; 18:8–9; 25:41; Mark 9:44–48). When He returns to judge the world, He will come "in flaming fire" (2 Thess. 1:8). It behooves us to be ready and to share the Gospel with others.

THE
NEW TESTAMENT

THE FOUR GOSPELS

The word *gospel* means "good news." It is the message that Jesus Christ forgives the sins of all who trust in Him (1 Cor. 15:1–11; Gal. 1:6–9). *Gospel* also refers to the first four books of the New Testament, which present the life and teachings of the Savior. Apart from Jesus Christ—who He is, what He taught, and what He did—there can be no good news for lost sinners (Acts 4:12).

The four Gospels are not biographies in the modern sense of the word nor do they tell us everything about Jesus (John 20:30–31). Led by the Spirit, the authors selected material that helped them accomplish their purpose for writing.

Matthew wrote primarily for the Jews and explained that Jesus Christ is the Messiah who fulfills the Old Testament prophecies. Mark directed his book to the Romans and pictured Jesus as the active Servant of the Lord. Luke wrote for the Greeks and presented Jesus as the perfect and compassionate Son of man. John had the whole world in mind when he wrote and presented Jesus as Son of God and Savior of the world.

The first three Gospels give a somewhat parallel account of the life of Jesus and therefore are called "synoptic Gospels." (The word *synoptic* means "to see together.") John's gospel, written much later, contains material that supplements the accounts by the synoptic writers. Each gospel is unique, and all four are needed to provide a well-rounded view of the life, teachings, and works of Jesus Christ.

MATTHEW

Matthew ("gift of God") was a Jewish tax collector who obeyed Christ's call and became one of the original twelve apostles (Matt. 9:9–13). His given name was Levi (Luke 5:27).

Writing especially for the Jews, Matthew proves that Jesus Christ is the Son of David, the Messiah, the rightful heir to David's throne. At least 129 Old Testament quotations and allusions appear in his gospel, and the word *kingdom* is found over fifty times. Matthew's gospel stands first in the New Testament as the perfect bridge between the old covenant and the new, Israel and the church, prophecy and fulfillment.

The King presented Himself to His people (chaps. 1—10), but the religious leaders resisted Him (chaps. 11—13). The King therefore withdrew from the crowds with His disciples to prepare them for His coming arrest and crucifixion (chaps. 14—20). He was rejected and crucified (chaps. 21—27), but He arose from the dead and commissioned His disciples to take His message to the whole world (chap. 28).

As you read Matthew's gospel, you will be impressed with the authority of Jesus Christ over disease, demons, circumstances, and even death. He has authority over our lives, and we should follow Him in obedience.

CHAPTER 1

1:1 *A special book.* The Old Testament is "the book of the genealogy of Adam" (Gen. 5:1), but the New Testament is "the book of the genealogy of Jesus Christ." In fact, the genealogy of Jesus Christ is the last one given in the Bible, here and in Luke 3:23–28. The important thing is not your *first* birth but your *second* birth (John 3).

1:2–17 *A special providence.* What may be to some readers a boring list of difficult names is actually the record of God's working throughout the ages to bring His Son to earth. God ruled and overruled and fulfilled His great promises. In the same way, He will keep His promises and send Jesus back again.

1 The* book of the genealogy of Jesus Christ, the Son of David, the Son of Abraham:
2*Abraham begot Isaac, Isaac begot Jacob, and Jacob begot Judah and his brothers. 3Judah begot Perez and Zerah by Tamar, Perez begot Hezron, and Hezron begot Ram. 4Ram begot Amminadab, Amminadab begot Nahshon, and Nahshon begot Salmon. 5Salmon begot Boaz by Rahab, Boaz begot Obed by Ruth, Obed begot Jesse, 6and Jesse begot David the king.

David the king begot Solomon by her *who had been the wife*ᵃ of Uriah. 7Solomon begot Rehoboam, Rehoboam begot Abijah, and Abijah begot Asa.ᵇ 8Asa begot Jehoshaphat, Jehoshaphat begot Joram, and Joram begot Uzziah. 9Uzziah begot Jotham, Jotham begot Ahaz, and Ahaz begot Hezekiah. 10Hezekiah begot Manasseh, Manasseh begot Amon,ᶜ and Amon begot Josiah. 11Josiah begot Jeconiah and his brothers about the time they were carried away to Babylon.

12And after they were brought to Babylon, Jeconiah begot Shealtiel, and Shealtiel begot Zerubbabel. 13Zerubbabel begot Abiud, Abiud begot Eliakim, and Eliakim begot Azor. 14Azor begot Zadok, Zadok begot Achim, and Achim begot Eliud. 15Eliud begot Eleazar, Eleazar begot Matthan, and Matthan begot Jacob. 16And Jacob begot Joseph the husband of Mary, of whom was born Jesus who is called Christ.

17So all the generations from Abraham to David *are* fourteen generations, from David until the captivity in Babylon *are* fourteen generations, and

---

1:6 ᵃWords in italic type have been added for clarity. They are not found in the original Greek.   1:7 ᵇNU-Text reads *Asaph.*   1:10 ᶜNU-Text reads *Amos.*

The Virgin Birth—The virgin birth of Jesus Christ is vital to the truth of the gospel (Isa. 7:14). Since Jesus Christ is God, He existed before Mary; therefore, He could not have been conceived as are other babies. He was not only *born,* but He "came into the world" (John 18:37). He is both God and man, the sinless Lamb of God (1 Pet. 1:19). Matthew opens and closes his book with "God with us" (1:23; 28:20).

from the captivity in Babylon until the Christ *are* fourteen generations.

18*Now the birth of Jesus Christ was as follows: After His mother Mary was betrothed to Joseph, before they came together, she was found with child of the Holy Spirit. 19Then Joseph her husband, being a just *man*, and not wanting to make her a public example, was minded to put her away secretly. 20But while he thought about these things, behold, an angel of the Lord appeared to him in a dream, saying, "Joseph, son of David, do not be afraid to take to you Mary your wife, for that which is conceived in her is of the Holy Spirit. 21And she will bring forth a Son, and you shall call His name JESUS, for He will save His people from their sins."

22So all this was done that it might be fulfilled which was spoken by the Lord through the prophet, saying: 23"*Behold, the virgin shall be with child, and bear a Son, and they shall call His name Immanuel,*"*d* which is translated, "God with us."

24Then Joseph, being aroused from sleep, did as the angel of the Lord commanded him and took to him his wife, 25and did not know her till she had brought forth her firstborn Son.*e* And he called His name JESUS.

2 Now* after Jesus was born in Bethlehem of Judea in the days of Herod the king, behold, wise men from the East came to Jerusalem, 2saying, "Where is He who has been born King of the Jews? For we have seen His star in the East and have come to worship Him."

3*When Herod the king heard *this*, he was troubled, and all Jerusalem with him. 4And when he had gathered all the chief priests and scribes of the people together, he inquired of them where the Christ was to be born. 5*So they said to him, "In Bethlehem of Judea, for thus it is written by the prophet:

6   '*But you, Bethlehem, in the land of Judah,*
     Are not the least among the rulers of Judah;
     For out of you shall come a Ruler
     Who will shepherd My people Israel.'"*f*

7Then Herod, when he had secretly called the wise men, determined from them what time the star appeared. 8And he sent them to Bethlehem and said, "Go and search carefully for the young Child, and when you have found *Him*, bring back word to me, that I may come and worship Him also."

9When they heard the king, they departed; and behold, the star which they had seen in the East went before them, till it came and stood over where the young Child was. 10When they saw the star, they rejoiced with exceedingly great joy. 11And when they had come into the house, they saw the young Child with Mary His mother, and

1:18–25 *A special Child.* The birth of Jesus was different from every other birth: He was conceived by the Spirit in Mary's womb and born with a sinless nature. He is "God with us," and He is also God *like us* because He took our nature and entered into human life and experience. What a wonderful Savior!

CHAPTER 2

2:1, 2 What were the responses to His birth?

Creation responded by putting a miraculous star in the heavens to tell the world a King had been born (Num. 24:17).

The Gentiles responded by worshiping Him and bringing Him gifts. Matthew shows early in his book that Jesus came to save Gentiles as well as Jews. The wise men were astrologer-scientists who studied the heavens. The star led them to the Scriptures, and the Scriptures led them to the Savior. (See Ps. 19.) God speaks to us in ways we can understand.

2:3, 4 *Herod* responded with fear and deception. He wanted no new King to threaten his reign.

2:5, 6 *The chief priests and scribes* gave the right information but the wrong response. They were only five miles away from the Messiah, yet they refused to go to see Him! What good is it to understand Bible prophecy if it doesn't make a difference in your life?

1:23 *d*Isaiah 7:14. Words in oblique type in the New Testament are quoted from the Old Testament.   1:25 *e*NU-Text reads *a Son.*   2:6 *f*Micah 5:2

The Magi—The wise men (Magi) were scientists, yet they saw no conflict between science and Scripture or between searching for truth and worshiping the Savior. Devout Christians can worship the Lord with the mind as well as the heart (Matt. 22:37). "Science without religion is lame," said Albert Einstein. "Religion without science is blind."

fell down and worshiped Him. And when they had opened their treasures, they presented gifts to Him: gold, frankincense, and myrrh.

12Then, being divinely warned in a dream that they should not return to Herod, they departed for their own country another way.

13Now when they had departed, behold, an angel of the Lord appeared to Joseph in a dream, saying, "Arise, take the young Child and His mother, flee to Egypt, and stay there until I bring you word; for Herod will seek the young Child to destroy Him."

14When he arose, he took the young Child and His mother by night and departed for Egypt, 15and was there until the death of Herod, that it might be fulfilled which was spoken by the Lord through the prophet, saying, *"Out of Egypt I called My Son."*g

16Then Herod, when he saw that he was deceived by the wise men, was exceedingly angry; and he sent forth and put to death all the male children who were in Bethlehem and in all its districts, from two years old and under, according to the time which he had determined from the wise men. 17Then was fulfilled what was spoken by Jeremiah the prophet, saying:

18 *"A voice was heard in Ramah,*
Lamentation, weeping, and great mourning,
Rachel weeping for her children,
Refusing to be comforted,
*Because they are no more."*h

19Now when Herod was dead, behold, an angel of the Lord appeared in a dream to Joseph in Egypt, 20saying, "Arise, take the young Child and His mother, and go to the land of Israel, for those who sought the young Child's life are dead." 21Then he arose, took the young Child and His mother, and came into the land of Israel.

22But when he heard that Archelaus was reigning over Judea instead of his father Herod, he was afraid to go there. And being warned by God in a dream, he turned aside into the region of Galilee. 23And he came and dwelt in a city called Nazareth, that it might be fulfilled which was spoken by the prophets, "He shall be called a Nazarene."

CHAPTER 3

3:1ff John the Baptist was a model preacher. He was a *road builder* who prepared the way for the Lord (v. 3; Isa. 40:3), and an *axman* who got to the root of sin and exposed it (3:10). He was not intimidated by people, nor was he afraid to preach about judgment (v. 12). He was obedient to his Lord and magnified Him in all things (John 3:30).

Some people heard God's Word and confessed their sins (3:5–6), while others heard it and covered their sins (vv. 7–9; Prov. 28:13). The first group became children of God, but the second group were children of the devil (3:7; John 8:44).

Jesus is the Son of God. The Scriptures (3:3), John the Baptist (v. 11), the Holy Spirit (v. 16), and the Father (v. 17) attested to that truth.

3 In* those days John the Baptist came preaching in the wilderness of Judea, 2and saying, "Repent, for the kingdom of heaven is at hand!" 3For this is he who was spoken of by the prophet Isaiah, saying:

"The voice of one crying in the wilderness:
'Prepare the way of the LORD;
*Make His paths straight.' "*i

4Now John himself was clothed in camel's hair, with a leather belt around his waist; and his food

---

2:15 gHosea 11:1　2:18 hJeremiah 31:15　3:3 iIsaiah 40:3

Significance of Baptism—Jesus was not baptized to confess any sins (v. 5), since He was sinless. His baptism was His presentation to Israel (John 1:31) as well as a picture of His future baptism on the cross when "all the waves and billows" of judgment would go over Him (Matt. 20:22; Ps. 42:7). The baptism of John looked forward to the coming of Messiah (Acts 19:1–7). Christian baptism today looks back to the death, burial, and resurrection of Jesus Christ and witnesses of the believer's identification with Him (Col. 2:12; Acts 10:47–48).

was locusts and wild honey. [5]Then Jerusalem, all Judea, and all the region around the Jordan went out to him [6]and were baptized by him in the Jordan, confessing their sins.

[7]But when he saw many of the Pharisees and Sadducees coming to his baptism, he said to them, "Brood of vipers! Who warned you to flee from the wrath to come? [8]Therefore bear fruits worthy of repentance, [9]and do not think to say to yourselves, 'We have Abraham as *our* father.' For I say to you that God is able to raise up children to Abraham from these stones. [10]And even now the ax is laid to the root of the trees. Therefore every tree which does not bear good fruit is cut down and thrown into the fire. [11]I indeed baptize you with water unto repentance, but He who is coming after me is mightier than I, whose sandals I am not worthy to carry. He will baptize you with the Holy Spirit and fire.[j] [12]His winnowing fan *is* in His hand, and He will thoroughly clean out His threshing floor, and gather His wheat into the barn; but He will burn up the chaff with unquenchable fire."

[13]Then Jesus came from Galilee to John at the Jordan to be baptized by him. [14]And John *tried to* prevent Him, saying, "I need to be baptized by You, and are You coming to me?"

[15]But Jesus answered and said to him, "Permit *it to be so* now, for thus it is fitting for us to fulfill all righteousness." Then he allowed Him.

[16]When He had been baptized, Jesus came up immediately from the water; and behold, the heavens were opened to Him, and He[k] saw the Spirit of God descending like a dove and alighting upon Him. [17]And suddenly a voice *came* from heaven, saying, "This is My beloved Son, in whom I am well pleased."

4 Then Jesus was led up by the Spirit into the wilderness to be tempted by the devil. [2]And when He had fasted forty days and forty nights, afterward He was hungry. [3]Now when the tempter came to Him, he said, "If You are the Son of God, command that these stones become bread."

[4]*But He answered and said, "It is written, '*Man shall not live by bread alone, but by every word that proceeds from the mouth of God.*'"[l]

[5]Then the devil took Him up into the holy city, set Him on the pinnacle of the temple, [6]and said to Him, "If You are the Son of God, throw Yourself down. For it is written:

'He shall give His angels charge over you,'

and,

'In their hands they shall bear you up,
Lest you dash your foot against a stone.'"[m]

[7]Jesus said to him, "It is written again, 'You shall not tempt the LORD your God.'"[n]

[8]Again, the devil took Him up on an exceedingly high mountain, and showed Him all the kingdoms of the world and their glory. [9]And he said to Him, "All these things I will give You if You will fall down and worship me."

[10]Then Jesus said to him, "Away with you,[o]

CHAPTER 4

4:4–11 The Victor. Public ministry is built on private victory. Our Lord was not tempted so that God could examine Him, for the Father had already approved Him (3:17). He was tempted for our sake, that He might personally know temptation and be able to help us when we are tempted (Heb. 2:17–18; 4:15). He overcame the devil by using the same weapons available to us today: the Word of God ("It is written"), the power of the Spirit (4:1; Luke 4:1), and prayer (Luke 3:21; 1 Cor. 10:13).

❝*Let no man think himself to be holy because he is not tempted, for the holiest and highest in life have the most temptations. How much higher the hill is, so much is the wind there greater; so, how much higher the life is, so much the stronger is the temptation of the enemy.*❞

—John Wycliffe

3:11 [j]M-Text omits *and fire.*   3:16 [k]Or *he*   4:4 [l]Deuteronomy 8:3   4:6 [m]Psalm 91:11, 12   4:7 [n]Deuteronomy 6:16   4:10 [o]M-Text reads *Get behind Me.*

4:12–22 The Master. Having defeated "the strong man," Jesus now invaded his house and began to spoil his goods (vv. 24–30). He both obeyed the Word (vv. 15–16; Isa. 9:1–2) and preached it, calling men to become His disciples. Everyone must decide whether to follow Christ or make bargains with the devil (vv. 8–10). What is *your* decision?

4:23–25 The Healer. Our Lord's main ministry was teaching and preaching, but His compassion moved Him to minister to the physical needs of the people. How tragic that most of the people who followed Him wanted His services but not His salvation, the gifts but not the Giver; and these people are with us today.

THE SERMON ON THE MOUNT

5:1ff The Sermon on the Mount was our Lord's "ordination sermon" for His apostles (Luke 6:12ff.). The theme is God's righteousness as contrasted with the hypocritical righteousness of the scribes and Pharisees (5:17–20; Matt. 23). The sermon is not a second Law with new commandments. It goes much deeper than the Law because it deals with internal attitudes as well as outward actions. It presents a picture of the truly righteous person and shows the spiritual principles that control his or her life. Jesus opened the sermon with a description of the truly righteous person (5:1–16). Then He defined what sin is (vv. 21–48) and what real righteousness is in the areas of worship (6:1–18) and wealth (6:19–34). He concluded with warnings against making hypocritical judgments (7:1–12), following false prophets (7:13–20), and failing to obey God's will (7:21–29). You are not saved by trying to obey the Sermon on the Mount any more than you are saved by trying to keep the Ten Commandments. Because they involve inner attitudes, the demands of the Sermon on the Mount are much more difficult than those found in the law of Moses. Only the true believer in Jesus Christ can put the Sermon on the Mount into practice (Rom. 8:1–4).

CHAPTER 5

5:3–12 Citizens. We enter the kingdom through the new birth (John 3:1–16), but we enjoy the kingdom by living for those things that please God the most (6:33). The world (and worldly believers) would disagree with Christ's description of a blessed (happy) person, but the description is true just the same. God majors on character, and so should we.

Satan! For it is written, *'You shall worship the* LORD *your God, and Him only you shall serve.'"*p 11Then the devil left Him, and behold, angels came and ministered to Him.

12*Now when Jesus heard that John had been put in prison, He departed to Galilee. 13And leaving Nazareth, He came and dwelt in Capernaum, which is by the sea, in the regions of Zebulun and Naphtali, 14that it might be fulfilled which was spoken by Isaiah the prophet, saying:

15 *"The land of Zebulun and the land of Naphtali,*
    By the way of the sea, beyond the Jordan, Galilee of the Gentiles:
16   *The people who sat in darkness have seen a great light,*
    *And upon those who sat in the region and shadow of death Light has dawned."*q

17From that time Jesus began to preach and to say, "Repent, for the kingdom of heaven is at hand."

18And Jesus, walking by the Sea of Galilee, saw two brothers, Simon called Peter, and Andrew his brother, casting a net into the sea; for they were fishermen. 19Then He said to them, "Follow Me, and I will make you fishers of men." 20They immediately left *their* nets and followed Him.

21Going on from there, He saw two other brothers, James *the son* of Zebedee, and John his brother, in the boat with Zebedee their father, mending their nets. He called them, 22and immediately they left the boat and their father, and followed Him.

23*And Jesus went about all Galilee, teaching in their synagogues, preaching the gospel of the kingdom, and healing all kinds of sickness and all kinds of disease among the people. 24Then His fame went throughout all Syria; and they brought to Him all sick people who were afflicted with various diseases and torments, and those who were demon-possessed, epileptics, and paralytics; and He healed them. 25Great multitudes followed Him—from Galilee, and *from* Decapolis, Jerusalem, Judea, and beyond the Jordan.

5 And* seeing the multitudes, He went up on a mountain, and when He was seated His disciples came to Him. 2Then He opened His mouth and taught them, saying:

3 *"Blessed *are* the poor in spirit,
    For theirs is the kingdom of heaven.
4   Blessed *are* those who mourn,
    For they shall be comforted.
5   Blessed *are* the meek,
    For they shall inherit the earth.
6   Blessed *are* those who hunger and thirst for righteousness,
    For they shall be filled.
7   Blessed *are* the merciful,
    For they shall obtain mercy.
8   Blessed *are* the pure in heart,
    For they shall see God.
9   Blessed *are* the peacemakers,
    For they shall be called sons of God.

---

pDeuteronomy 6:13   4:16 qIsaiah 9:1, 2

¹⁰ Blessed are those who are persecuted for
righteousness' sake,
For theirs is the kingdom of heaven.

¹¹"Blessed are you when they revile and persecute
you, and say all kinds of evil against you falsely
for My sake. ¹²Rejoice and be exceedingly glad,
for great *is* your reward in heaven, for so they
persecuted the prophets who were before you.

¹³*"You are the salt of the earth; but if the salt
loses its flavor, how shall it be seasoned? It is
then good for nothing but to be thrown out and
trampled underfoot by men.

¹⁴"You are the light of the world. A city that is
set on a hill cannot be hidden. ¹⁵Nor do they light
a lamp and put it under a basket, but on a lampstand, and it gives light to all *who are* in the house.
¹⁶Let your light so shine before men, that they
may see your good works and glorify your Father
in heaven.

¹⁷"Do not think that I came to destroy the Law
or the Prophets. I did not come to destroy but to
fulfill. ¹⁸For assuredly, I say to you, till heaven
and earth pass away, one jot or one tittle will by
no means pass from the law till all is fulfilled.
¹⁹Whoever therefore breaks one of the least of
these commandments, and teaches men so, shall
be called least in the kingdom of heaven; but
whoever does and teaches *them,* he shall be called
great in the kingdom of heaven. ²⁰For I say to
you, that unless your righteousness exceeds *the
righteousness* of the scribes and Pharisees, you
will by no means enter the kingdom of heaven.

²¹*"You have heard that it was said to those of
old, 'You shall not murder,ʳ and whoever murders
will be in danger of the judgment.' ²²But I say to
you that whoever is angry with his brother without a causeˢ shall be in danger of the judgment.
And whoever says to his brother, 'Raca!' shall be
in danger of the council. But whoever says, 'You
fool!' shall be in danger of hell fire. ²³Therefore
if you bring your gift to the altar, and there remember that your brother has something against
you, ²⁴leave your gift there before the altar, and
go your way. First be reconciled to your brother,
and then come and offer your gift. ²⁵Agree with
your adversary quickly, while you are on the
way with him, lest your adversary deliver you to
the judge, the judge hand you over to the officer,
and you be thrown into prison. ²⁶Assuredly, I say
to you, you will by no means get out of there till
you have paid the last penny.

²⁷*"You have heard that it was said to those of
old,ᵗ 'You shall not commit adultery.'ᵘ ²⁸But I say
to you that whoever looks at a woman to lust for
her has already committed adultery with her in
his heart. ²⁹If your right eye causes you to sin,
pluck it out and cast *it* from you; for it is more
profitable for you that one of your members perish, than for your whole body to be cast into hell.
³⁰And if your right hand causes you to sin, cut it
off and cast *it* from you; for it is more profitable
for you that one of your members perish, than
for your whole body to be cast into hell.

³¹"Furthermore it has been said, 'Whoever divorces his wife, let him give her a certificate of

5:13–16 *Salt and light.* Tasteless salt and
hidden light are good for nothing! Salt
arrests decay in our world, and light
banishes darkness. Salt is hidden, but light
is visible. Both are needed in the world, and
both must give of themselves in order to
serve.

❝*In taking revenge, a man is but
even with his enemy; but in passing
it over, he is superior.*❞
—Francis Bacon

5:21–26 *Worshipers.* If you bring anger to
the altar, you cannot worship God, so get
rid of the anger quickly. Angry feelings lead
to angry words and deeds, and the result
could be murder. (See Eph. 4:25–32.)

5:27–30 *Surgeons.* Obviously Jesus is not
suggesting literal surgery, for the real
problem is in the heart (v. 28). This is a vivid
reminder that sin is terrible, and we are
better off "maimed" than whole and going
to hell. Deal drastically with sin!

5:21 ʳExodus 20:13; Deuteronomy 5:17   5:22 ˢNU-Text omits
without a cause.   5:27 ᵗNU-Text and M-Text omit *to those of
old.* ᵘExodus 20:14; Deuteronomy 5:18

5:33–48 Children of the Father. "What do you do more than others?" (v. 47). We must measure ourselves not by others but by the Father (v. 48). This includes our words (vv. 33–37), our responses to injuries (vv. 38–42), and our dealings with our enemies (vv. 43–48).

divorce.' ³²But I say to you that whoever divorces his wife for any reason except sexual immorality^v causes her to commit adultery; and whoever marries a woman who is divorced commits adultery.

³³*"Again you have heard that it was said to those of old, 'You shall not swear falsely, but shall perform your oaths to the Lord.' ³⁴But I say to you, do not swear at all: neither by heaven, for it is God's throne; ³⁵nor by the earth, for it is His footstool; nor by Jerusalem, for it is the city of the great King. ³⁶Nor shall you swear by your head, because you cannot make one hair white or black. ³⁷But let your 'Yes' be 'Yes,' and your 'No,' 'No.' For whatever is more than these is from the evil one.

³⁸"You have heard that it was said, 'An eye for an eye and a tooth for a tooth.'^w ³⁹But I tell you not to resist an evil person. But whoever slaps you on your right cheek, turn the other to him also. ⁴⁰If anyone wants to sue you and take away your tunic, let him have your cloak also. ⁴¹And whoever compels you to go one mile, go with him two. ⁴²Give to him who asks you, and from him who wants to borrow from you do not turn away.

⁴³"You have heard that it was said, 'You shall love your neighbor^x and hate your enemy.' ⁴⁴But I say to you, love your enemies, bless those who curse you, do good to those who hate you, and pray for those who spitefully use you and persecute you,^y ⁴⁵that you may be sons of your Father in heaven; for He makes His sun rise on the evil and on the good, and sends rain on the just and on the unjust. ⁴⁶For if you love those who love you, what reward have you? Do not even the tax collectors do the same? ⁴⁷And if you greet your brethren^z only, what do you do more than others? Do not even the tax collectors^a do so? ⁴⁸Therefore you shall be perfect, just as your Father in heaven is perfect.

CHAPTER 6

6:1–4 Praise. We should give only to please God and receive His praise. If we give to win the praise of others, or to be able to compliment ourselves (v. 3), we get the *immediate* reward—praise—but we lose the *eternal* reward. We cannot get our reward twice, so we must decide which one we want.

6:5–15 Prayer. Our public praying is only as good as our private praying, and our private praying should be secret (vv. 5–6), sincere (vv. 7–8), and systematic (vv. 9–13). The Lord's Prayer is a pattern for us to follow so that we will put God's concerns first and not forget to forgive others.

6 "Take* heed that you do not do your charitable deeds before men, to be seen by them. Otherwise you have no reward from your Father in heaven. ²Therefore, when you do a charitable deed, do not sound a trumpet before you as the hypocrites do in the synagogues and in the streets, that they may have glory from men. Assuredly, I say to you, they have their reward. ³But when you do a charitable deed, do not let your left hand know what your right hand is doing, ⁴that your charitable deed may be in secret; and your Father who sees in secret will Himself reward you openly.^b

⁵*"And when you pray, you shall not be like the hypocrites. For they love to pray standing in the synagogues and on the corners of the streets, that they may be seen by men. Assuredly, I say

5:32 ^vOr fornication   5:38 ^wExodus 21:24; Leviticus 24:20; Deuteronomy 19:21   5:43 ^xCompare Leviticus 19:18
5:44 ^yNU-Text omits three clauses from this verse, leaving, "But I say to you, love your enemies and pray for those who persecute you."   5:47 ^zM-Text reads friends. ^aNU-Text reads Gentiles.   6:4 ^bNU-Text omits openly.

Treasures in Heaven—We lay up treasures in heaven when we consider that all we have belongs to God and we use it to magnify His righteousness and advance His kingdom (Matt. 6:33). It means much more than merely giving offerings to God, although that is important. It means total stewardship of life so that God is in complete control and our one desire is to glorify Him. This is the secret of a unified life (Matt. 6:24) free of worry.

to you, they have their reward. 6But you, when you pray, go into your room, and when you have shut your door, pray to your Father who *is* in the secret *place;* and your Father who sees in secret will reward you openly.*c* 7And when you pray, do not use vain repetitions as the heathen *do.* For they think that they will be heard for their many words.

8"Therefore do not be like them. For your Father knows the things you have need of before you ask Him. 9In this manner, therefore, pray:

> Our Father in heaven,
> Hallowed be Your name.
> 10   Your kingdom come.
> Your will be done
> On earth as *it is* in heaven.
> 11   Give us this day our daily bread.
> 12   And forgive us our debts,
> As we forgive our debtors.
> 13   And do not lead us into temptation,
> But deliver us from the evil one.
> For Yours is the kingdom and the power
> and the glory forever. Amen.*d*

14"For if you forgive men their trespasses, your heavenly Father will also forgive you. 15But if you do not forgive men their trespasses, neither will your Father forgive your trespasses.

16"Moreover, when you fast, do not be like the hypocrites, with a sad countenance. For they disfigure their faces that they may appear to men to be fasting. Assuredly, I say to you, they have their reward. 17But you, when you fast, anoint your head and wash your face, 18so that you do not appear to men to be fasting, but to your Father who *is* in the secret *place;* and your Father who sees in secret will reward you openly.*e*

19*"Do not lay up for yourselves treasures on earth, where moth and rust destroy and where thieves break in and steal; 20but lay up for yourselves treasures in heaven, where neither moth nor rust destroys and where thieves do not break in and steal. 21For where your treasure is, there your heart will be also.

22"The lamp of the body is the eye. If therefore your eye is good, your whole body will be full of light. 23But if your eye is bad, your whole body will be full of darkness. If therefore the light that is in you is darkness, how great *is* that darkness!

24"No one can serve two masters; for either he will hate the one and love the other, or else he will be loyal to the one and despise the other. You cannot serve God and mammon.

25"Therefore I say to you, do not worry about your life, what you will eat or what you will drink; nor about your body, what you will put on. Is not life more than food and the body more than clothing? 26Look at the birds of the air, for they neither sow nor reap nor gather into barns; yet your heavenly Father feeds them. Are you not of more value than they? 27Which of you by worrying can add one cubit to his stature?

28"So why do you worry about clothing? Consider the lilies of the field, how they grow: they neither toil nor spin; 29and yet I say to you that even Solomon in all his glory was not arrayed

6:19–34 Possessions. We need *things* to live (v. 32), and God provides these things for us (v. 33); but acquiring things must not be the main goal of life. You are living for things when they capture your heart (vv. 19–21), divide your mind (vv. 22–23), and control your will (v. 24); and the result of this is *worry.* The solution is to put God first and start living with eternity's values in view.

6:6 *c*NU-Text omits *openly.*   6:13 *d*NU-Text omits *For Yours* through *Amen.*   6:18 *e*NU-Text and M-Text omit *openly.*

like one of these. 30Now if God so clothes the grass of the field, which today is, and tomorrow is thrown into the oven, *will He* not much more *clothe* you, O you of little faith?

31"Therefore do not worry, saying, 'What shall we eat?' or 'What shall we drink?' or 'What shall we wear?' 32For after all these things the Gentiles seek. For your heavenly Father knows that you need all these things. 33But seek first the kingdom of God and His righteousness, and all these things shall be added to you. 34Therefore do not worry about tomorrow, for tomorrow will worry about its own things. Sufficient for the day *is* its own trouble.

CHAPTER 7

7:1–5 *Judges.* One of the easiest ways to cover our sins is to judge others. It is not wrong to exercise discernment (v. 6), but we must start with ourselves. Often we are guilty of the sins we think we see in others (Rom. 2:1–3). We need prayer and love if we are to perform successful "eye surgery" on our brothers and sisters. We must treat them the way we want them to treat us.

7 "Judge* not, that you be not judged. 2For with what judgment you judge, you will be judged; and with the measure you use, it will be measured back to you. 3And why do you look at the speck in your brother's eye, but do not consider the plank in your own eye? 4Or how can you say to your brother, 'Let me remove the speck from your eye'; and look, a plank *is* in your own eye? 5Hypocrite! First remove the plank from your own eye, and then you will see clearly to remove the speck from your brother's eye.

6"Do not give what is holy to the dogs; nor cast your pearls before swine, lest they trample them under their feet, and turn and tear you in pieces.

7"Ask, and it will be given to you; seek, and you will find; knock, and it will be opened to you. 8For everyone who asks receives, and he who seeks finds, and to him who knocks it will be opened. 9Or what man is there among you who, if his son asks for bread, will give him a stone? 10Or if he asks for a fish, will he give him a serpent? 11If you then, being evil, know how to give good gifts to your children, how much more will your Father who is in heaven give good things to those who ask Him! 12Therefore, whatever you want men to do to you, do also to them, for this is the Law and the Prophets.

13*"Enter by the narrow gate; for wide *is* the gate and broad *is* the way that leads to destruction, and there are many who go in by it. 14Because*f* narrow *is* the gate and difficult *is* the way which leads to life, and there are few who find it.

7:13, 14 *Pilgrims.* The gate into real life is narrow, and the way is difficult, so don't try to carry a lot of excess baggage. False teachers make the way easy and popular; if you truly follow Jesus, you pay a price and the way sometimes becomes lonely.

7:15–20 *Trees.* Life produces fruit, and good trees produce good fruit. There was a great deal of profession in the lives of the scribes and Pharisees, but no evidence of spiritual fruit.

15*"Beware of false prophets, who come to you in sheep's clothing, but inwardly they are ravenous wolves. 16You will know them by their fruits. Do men gather grapes from thornbushes or figs from thistles? 17Even so, every good tree bears good fruit, but a bad tree bears bad fruit. 18A good tree cannot bear bad fruit, nor *can* a bad tree bear good fruit. 19Every tree that does not bear good fruit is cut down and thrown into the fire. 20Therefore by their fruits you will know them.

7:21–27 *Builders.* To "build on the rock" means to obey the Word of God. *Saying* is not enough; there must be *doing* (James 1:22–25). If you claim to be a disciple of Jesus Christ, expect to have your profession tested in this life and the next. Fair-weather faith will not pass the test.

21*"Not everyone who says to Me, 'Lord, Lord,' shall enter the kingdom of heaven, but he who does the will of My Father in heaven. 22Many will say to Me in that day, 'Lord, Lord, have we not prophesied in Your name, cast out demons in Your name, and done many wonders in Your name?' 23And then I will declare to them, 'I never knew you; depart from Me, you who practice lawlessness!'

7:14 *f*NU-Text and M-Text read *How . . . !*

²⁴"Therefore whoever hears these sayings of Mine, and does them, I will liken him to a wise man who built his house on the rock: ²⁵and the rain descended, the floods came, and the winds blew and beat on that house; and it did not fall, for it was founded on the rock.

²⁶"But everyone who hears these sayings of Mine, and does not do them, will be like a foolish man who built his house on the sand: ²⁷and the rain descended, the floods came, and the winds blew and beat on that house; and it fell. And great was its fall."

²⁸And so it was, when Jesus had ended these sayings, that the people were astonished at His teaching, ²⁹for He taught them as one having authority, and not as the scribes.

8 When* He had come down from the mountain, great multitudes followed Him. ²*And behold, a leper came and worshiped Him, saying, "Lord, if You are willing, You can make me clean."

³Then Jesus put out *His* hand and touched him, saying, "I am willing; be cleansed." Immediately his leprosy was cleansed.

⁴And Jesus said to him, "See that you tell no one; but go your way, show yourself to the priest, and offer the gift that Moses commanded, as a testimony to them."

⁵Now when Jesus had entered Capernaum, a centurion came to Him, pleading with Him, ⁶saying, "Lord, my servant is lying at home paralyzed, dreadfully tormented."

⁷And Jesus said to him, "I will come and heal him."

⁸The centurion answered and said, "Lord, I am not worthy that You should come under my roof. But only speak a word, and my servant will be healed. ⁹For I also am a man under authority, having soldiers under me. And I say to this *one,* 'Go,' and he goes; and to another, 'Come,' and he comes; and to my servant, 'Do this,' and he does *it.*"

¹⁰When Jesus heard *it,* He marveled, and said to those who followed, "Assuredly, I say to you, I have not found such great faith, not even in Israel! ¹¹And I say to you that many will come from east and west, and sit down with Abraham, Isaac, and Jacob in the kingdom of heaven. ¹²But the sons of the kingdom will be cast out into outer darkness. There will be weeping and gnashing of teeth." ¹³Then Jesus said to the centurion, "Go your way; and as you have believed, *so* let it be done for you." And his servant was healed that same hour.

¹⁴Now when Jesus had come into Peter's house, He saw his wife's mother lying sick with a fever.

CHAPTERS 8—9

8:1ff In chapters 8—9, Matthew assembled several of our Lord's miracles and recorded them as proof that Jesus is the promised Messiah (1 Cor. 1:22; Isa. 35:4–6). In 8:17, he quoted Isaiah 53:4 and applied it to Christ's healing ministry while He was on earth. Some helpful lessons are evident in these miracles.

8:2 *God is concerned with individuals.* Jesus did not minister only to crowds (8:1; 9:36); He had time for individuals. He had compassion on people shunned by others. Peter and John had this same spirit: they ministered to thousands (Acts 2) and also took time for one beggar (Acts 3).

Growing in Your Faith—Some people have "no faith" (Mark 4:40), while others have "little faith" (Matt. 6:30). God wants us to have "great faith" (Matt. 8:10; 15:28). Faith is like a seed that grows if it is planted and cultivated in the heart (Matt. 17:20). The Word of God encourages faith (Rom. 10:17). As you exercise your faith in times of trial and testing, your faith grows and you glorify God (James 1:1–8; 1 Pet. 1:1–9). It is faith, not feeling, that gives the victory (1 John 5:1–5).

Peter and Jesus—The healing of Peter's mother-in-law was the first of several miracles that Jesus performed especially for Peter. On two occasions, He enabled Peter to catch many fish (Luke 5:1–11; John 21:1–8), and He even helped him catch one fish with a coin in its mouth (Matt. 17:24–27). Jesus enabled Peter to walk on the water (Matt. 14:22–33). When Peter cut off the ear of Malchus, Jesus healed it (Luke 22:50–53); and He delivered Peter from prison and death (Acts 12). No wonder Peter wrote, "Casting all your care upon Him, for He cares for you" (1 Pet. 5:7).

8:16 God can meet every need. Nothing is too hard for the Lord (Jer. 32:17). He can heal the sick and afflicted, calm the storm, cast out demons, and even raise the dead. Do you cast *every* care on Him (1 Pet. 5:7)?

8:23 God responds to faith. The centurion had *great* faith (v. 10), while the disciples were guilty of *little* faith (v. 26). The men who brought their friend exercised *cooperative* faith (9:2), while the sick woman had almost *superstitious* faith (9:21). Christ asks you the same question He asked the two blind men: "Do you believe that I am able to do this?" (9:28). What is your reply?

9:1 God's greatest concern is the salvation of sinners. The healing of the sick is a great miracle, and the raising of the dead an even greater one; but the salvation of the lost soul is the greatest miracle of all. Jesus is the Great Physician who came to heal sinners (vv. 12–13), the Bridegroom who invites sinners to the wedding feast (vv. 14–17), and the Good Shepherd who has compassion on the struggling sheep (vv. 35–36).

15So He touched her hand, and the fever left her. And she arose and served them.g
16*When evening had come, they brought to Him many who were demon-possessed. And He cast out the spirits with a word, and healed all who were sick, 17that it might be fulfilled which was spoken by Isaiah the prophet, saying:

> "He Himself took our infirmities
> And bore our sicknesses."h

18And when Jesus saw great multitudes about Him, He gave a command to depart to the other side. 19Then a certain scribe came and said to Him, "Teacher, I will follow You wherever You go."
20And Jesus said to him, "Foxes have holes and birds of the air *have* nests, but the Son of Man has nowhere to lay *His* head."
21Then another of His disciples said to Him, "Lord, let me first go and bury my father."
22But Jesus said to him, "Follow Me, and let the dead bury their own dead."
23*Now when He got into a boat, His disciples followed Him. 24And suddenly a great tempest arose on the sea, so that the boat was covered with the waves. But He was asleep. 25Then His disciples came to *Him* and awoke Him, saying, "Lord, save us! We are perishing!"
26But He said to them, "Why are you fearful, O you of little faith?" Then He arose and rebuked the winds and the sea, and there was a great calm.
27So the men marveled, saying, "Who can this be, that even the winds and the sea obey Him?"
28When He had come to the other side, to the country of the Gergesenes,i there met Him two demon-possessed *men,* coming out of the tombs, exceedingly fierce, so that no one could pass that way. 29And suddenly they cried out, saying, "What have we to do with You, Jesus, You Son of God? Have You come here to torment us before the time?"
30Now a good way off from them there was a herd of many swine feeding. 31So the demons begged Him, saying, "If You cast us out, permit us to go awayj into the herd of swine."
32And He said to them, "Go." So when they had come out, they went into the herd of swine. And suddenly the whole herd of swine ran violently down the steep place into the sea, and perished in the water.
33Then those who kept *them* fled; and they went away into the city and told everything, including what *had happened* to the demon-possessed *men.*
34And behold, the whole city came out to meet Jesus. And when they saw Him, they begged *Him* to depart from their region.

9 So* He got into a boat, crossed over, and came to His own city. 2Then behold, they brought to Him a paralytic lying on a bed. When Jesus saw their faith, He said to the paralytic, "Son, be of good cheer; your sins are forgiven you."
3And at once some of the scribes said within themselves, "This Man blasphemes!"
4But Jesus, knowing their thoughts, said, "Why do you think evil in your hearts? 5For which is

---

8:15 gNU-Text and M-Text read *Him.*   8:17 hIsaiah 53:4
8:28 iNU-Text reads *Gadarenes.*   8:31 jNU-Text reads *send us.*

easier, to say, 'Your sins are forgiven you,' or to say, 'Arise and walk'? [6]But that you may know that the Son of Man has power on earth to forgive sins''—then He said to the paralytic, "Arise, take up your bed, and go to your house." [7]And he arose and departed to his house.

[8]Now when the multitudes saw *it*, they marveled[k] and glorified God, who had given such power to men.

[9]As Jesus passed on from there, He saw a man named Matthew sitting at the tax office. And He said to him, "Follow Me." So he arose and followed Him.

[10]Now it happened, as Jesus sat at the table in the house, *that* behold, many tax collectors and sinners came and sat down with Him and His disciples. [11]And when the Pharisees saw *it*, they said to His disciples, "Why does your Teacher eat with tax collectors and sinners?"

[12]When Jesus heard *that*, He said to them, "Those who are well have no need of a physician, but those who are sick. [13]But go and learn what *this* means: '*I desire mercy and not sacrifice.*'[l] For I did not come to call the righteous, but sinners, to repentance."[m]

[14]Then the disciples of John came to Him, saying, "Why do we and the Pharisees fast often,[n] but Your disciples do not fast?"

[15]And Jesus said to them, "Can the friends of the bridegroom mourn as long as the bridegroom is with them? But the days will come when the bridegroom will be taken away from them, and then they will fast. [16]No one puts a piece of unshrunk cloth on an old garment; for the patch pulls away from the garment, and the tear is made worse. [17]Nor do they put new wine into old wineskins, or else the wineskins break, the wine is spilled, and the wineskins are ruined. But they put new wine into new wineskins, and both are preserved."

[18]While He spoke these things to them, behold, a ruler came and worshiped Him, saying, "My daughter has just died, but come and lay Your hand on her and she will live." [19]So Jesus arose and followed him, and so *did* His disciples.

[20]And suddenly, a woman who had a flow of blood for twelve years came from behind and touched the hem of His garment. [21]For she said to herself, "If only I may touch His garment, I shall be made well." [22]But Jesus turned around, and when He saw her He said, "Be of good cheer, daughter; your faith has made you well." And the woman was made well from that hour.

[23]When Jesus came into the ruler's house, and saw the flute players and the noisy crowd wailing, [24]He said to them, "Make room, for the girl is not dead, but sleeping." And they ridiculed Him. [25]But when the crowd was put outside, He went in and took her by the hand, and the girl arose. [26]And the report of this went out into all that land.

[27]When Jesus departed from there, two blind men followed Him, crying out and saying, "Son of David, have mercy on us!"

[28]And when He had come into the house, the blind men came to Him. And Jesus said to them, "Do you believe that I am able to do this?"

They said to Him, "Yes, Lord."

9:8 [k]NU-Text reads *were afraid.*   9:13 [l]Hosea 6:6 [m]NU-Text omits *to repentance.*   9:14 [n]NU-Text brackets *often* as disputed.

29Then He touched their eyes, saying, "According to your faith let it be to you." 30And their eyes
were opened. And Jesus sternly warned them,
saying, "See *that* no one knows *it*." 31But when
they had departed, they spread the news about
Him in all that country.
32As they went out, behold, they brought to Him
a man, mute and demon-possessed. 33And when
the demon was cast out, the mute spoke. And the
multitudes marveled, saying, "It was never seen
like this in Israel!"
34But the Pharisees said, "He casts out demons
by the ruler of the demons."
35*Then Jesus went about all the cities and villages, teaching in their synagogues, preaching the
gospel of the kingdom, and healing every sickness
and every disease among the people.[o] 36But when
He saw the multitudes, He was moved with compassion for them, because they were weary[p] and
scattered, like sheep having no shepherd. 37Then
He said to His disciples, "The harvest truly *is* plentiful, but the laborers *are* few. 38Therefore pray
the Lord of the harvest to send out laborers into
His harvest."

10 And* when He had called His twelve disciples to *Him*, He gave them power *over* unclean spirits, to cast them out, and to heal all kinds
of sickness and all kinds of disease. 2Now the
names of the twelve apostles are these: first, Simon, who is called Peter, and Andrew his brother;
James the *son* of Zebedee, and John his brother;
3Philip and Bartholomew; Thomas and Matthew
the tax collector; James the *son* of Alphaeus, and
Lebbaeus, whose surname was[q] Thaddaeus;
4Simon the Cananite,[r] and Judas Iscariot, who
also betrayed Him.
5These twelve Jesus sent out and commanded
them, saying: "Do not go into the way of the Gentiles, and do not enter a city of the Samaritans.
6But go rather to the lost sheep of the house of
Israel. 7And as you go, preach, saying, 'The kingdom of heaven is at hand.' 8*Heal the sick, cleanse
the lepers, raise the dead,[s] cast out demons. Freely
you have received, freely give. 9Provide neither
gold nor silver nor copper in your money belts,
10nor bag for *your* journey, nor two tunics, nor
sandals, nor staffs; for a worker is worthy of his
food.
11"Now whatever city or town you enter, inquire who in it is worthy, and stay there till you
go out. 12And when you go into a household, greet
it. 13If the household is worthy, let your peace
come upon it. But if it is not worthy, let your peace
return to you. 14And whoever will not receive you
nor hear your words, when you depart from that
house or city, shake off the dust from your feet.
15Assuredly, I say to you, it will be more tolerable
for the land of Sodom and Gomorrah in the day
of judgment than for that city!
16*"Behold, I send you out as sheep in the midst
of wolves. Therefore be wise as serpents and
harmless as doves. 17But beware of men, for they
will deliver you up to councils and scourge you
in their synagogues. 18You will be brought before

9:35 [o]NU-Text omits *among the people*. 9:36 [p]NU-Text and M-Text read *harassed*. 10:3 [q]NU-Text omits *Lebbaeus, whose surname was*. 10:4 [r]NU-Text reads *Cananaean*. 10:8 [s]NU-Text reads *raise the dead, cleanse the lepers;* M-Text omits *raise the dead*.

9:35 *God calls us to help Him reach the lost.* Peter opened his home and Jesus healed many there (8:14–16), and Matthew used his home to introduce his friends to Jesus (9:9–17). The blind men who were healed spread the news about Jesus to the whole country (9:31). Jesus is seeking disciples (8:18–22) and harvesters (9:37–38) to help Him get the job done.

CHAPTER 10

10:1 If you start to pray for laborers (9:38), beware: you may become an answer to your own prayer! You pray, and then you are sent out!

Some of these instructions applied mainly to the apostles (vv. 5–15) and some to those serving just before the Lord's return (vv. 16–23). However, spiritual principles are here for all God's servants.

Christ calls and equips. If the Lord calls you, He will equip you for the task He wants you to fulfill. It has well been said, "The will of God does not send you where the grace of God cannot keep you."

10:8 *Christ wants us to give freely to others.* The apostles had power to do miracles, but even giving a cup of cold water is service to the Lord (v. 42). Everything we have is a gift from God (John 3:27; 1 Cor. 4:7) and must be shared lovingly with others. We must live by faith and trust Him to provide.

10:16–25 *Christ does not promise an easy life.* It is a wonderful privilege to be an ambassador for the King, but there is a price to pay. We are sheep among wolves (v. 16), sword-bearers (vv. 34–36), and cross-bearers (vv. 37–39). The world hates us because it hates Him (vv. 24–25; Phil. 3:10).

governors and kings for My sake, as a testimony to them and to the Gentiles. 19But when they deliver you up, do not worry about how or what you should speak. For it will be given to you in that hour what you should speak; 20for it is not you who speak, but the Spirit of your Father who speaks in you.

21"Now brother will deliver up brother to death, and a father *his* child; and children will rise up against parents and cause them to be put to death. 22And you will be hated by all for My name's sake. But he who endures to the end will be saved. 23When they persecute you in this city, flee to another. For assuredly, I say to you, you will not have gone through the cities of Israel before the Son of Man comes.

24"A disciple is not above *his* teacher, nor a servant above his master. 25It is enough for a disciple that he be like his teacher, and a servant like his master. If they have called the master of the house Beelzebub,*t* how much more *will they call* those of his household! 26*Therefore do not fear them. For there is nothing covered that will not be revealed, and hidden that will not be known.

27"Whatever I tell you in the dark, speak in the light; and what you hear in the ear, preach on the housetops. 28And do not fear those who kill the body but cannot kill the soul. But rather fear Him who is able to destroy both soul and body in hell. 29Are not two sparrows sold for a copper coin? And not one of them falls to the ground apart from your Father's will. 30But the very hairs of your head are all numbered. 31Do not fear therefore; you are of more value than many sparrows.

32"Therefore whoever confesses Me before men, him I will also confess before My Father who is in heaven. 33But whoever denies Me before men, him I will also deny before My Father who is in heaven.

34"Do not think that I came to bring peace on earth. I did not come to bring peace but a sword. 35For I have come to 'set a man against his father, a daughter against her mother, and a daughter-in-law against her mother-in-law'; 36and 'a man's enemies will be those of his own household.'*u* 37He who loves father or mother more than Me is not worthy of Me. And he who loves son or daughter more than Me is not worthy of Me. 38And he who does not take his cross and follow after Me is not worthy of Me. 39He who finds his life will lose it, and he who loses his life for My sake will find it.

40"He who receives you receives Me, and he who receives Me receives Him who sent Me. 41He who receives a prophet in the name of a prophet shall receive a prophet's reward. And he who receives a righteous man in the name of a righteous man shall receive a righteous man's reward. 42And whoever gives one of these little ones only a cup of cold *water* in the name of a disciple, assuredly, I say to you, he shall by no means lose his reward."

11 Now it came to pass, when Jesus finished commanding His twelve disciples, that He departed from there to teach and to preach in their cities.

10:26–33 *Christ can take away all fear.* If you fear God, you need fear nothing else (vv. 27–31; Ps. 112). You are precious to your Father, and He will care for you. God's servants are immortal until their work is done.

Review the chapter and mark the promises you need to claim today.

10:25 *t*NU-Text and M-Text read *Beelzebul*.   10:36 *u*Micah 7:6

CHAPTER 11

11:2, 3 John the Baptist was perplexed and perhaps discouraged. He had served God faithfully and yet was in prison. His work was ended, and he was not sure that Jesus was ministering in the right way. When you find yourself in a similar situation, do what John did: tell it to Jesus and wait for His word (vv. 4–6; Isa. 35:4–6). Isaiah 50:10 is a great promise to claim in dark days of disappointment.

11:7–15 John's disciples did not hear Jesus praise their leader. John was not a compromiser (a reed) or a celebrity; he was God's greatest prophet. John was in prison because of a cruel king and a crowd that was childish (vv. 16–19) instead of childlike (v. 25).

Leave the judgment to the Lord (vv. 20–24), and wait for Him to fulfill His perfect plan. You may think you have failed, but God will see to it that your work is blessed. In fact, John won people to Jesus long after he was dead and buried (John 10:40–42)! Surrender to Christ's loving yoke and you will experience His perfect rest (11:25–30).

2*And when John had heard in prison about the works of Christ, he sent two of° his disciples 3and said to Him, "Are You the Coming One, or do we look for another?"

4Jesus answered and said to them, "Go and tell John the things which you hear and see: 5The blind see and *the* lame walk; *the* lepers are cleansed and *the* deaf hear; *the* dead are raised up and *the* poor have the gospel preached to them. 6And blessed is he who is not offended because of Me."

7*As they departed, Jesus began to say to the multitudes concerning John: "What did you go out into the wilderness to see? A reed shaken by the wind? 8But what did you go out to see? A man clothed in soft garments? Indeed, those who wear soft *clothing* are in kings' houses. 9But what did you go out to see? A prophet? Yes, I say to you, and more than a prophet. 10For this is *he* of whom it is written:

'Behold, I send My messenger before
　Your face,
Who will prepare Your way before You.'°

11"Assuredly, I say to you, among those born of women there has not risen one greater than John the Baptist; but he who is least in the kingdom of heaven is greater than he. 12And from the days of John the Baptist until now the kingdom of heaven suffers violence, and the violent take it by force. 13For all the prophets and the law prophesied until John. 14And if you are willing to receive *it*, he is Elijah who is to come. 15He who has ears to hear, let him hear!

16"But to what shall I liken this generation? It is like children sitting in the marketplaces and calling to their companions, 17and saying:

'We played the flute for you,
　And you did not dance;
We mourned to you,
　And you did not lament.'

18For John came neither eating nor drinking, and they say, 'He has a demon.' 19The Son of Man came eating and drinking, and they say, 'Look, a glutton and a winebibber, a friend of tax collectors and sinners!' But wisdom is justified by her children."°

20Then He began to rebuke the cities in which most of His mighty works had been done, because they did not repent: 21"Woe to you, Chorazin! Woe to you, Bethsaida! For if the mighty works which were done in you had been done in Tyre and Sidon, they would have repented long ago in sackcloth and ashes. 22But I say to you, it will be more tolerable for Tyre and Sidon in the day of judgment than for you. 23And you, Capernaum, who are exalted to heaven, will be° brought down to Hades; for if the mighty works which were done in you had been done in Sodom, it would have remained until this day. 24But I say to you that it shall be more tolerable for the land of Sodom in the day of judgment than for you."

25At that time Jesus answered and said, "I thank

11:2 °NU-Text reads *by* for *two of.*　11:10 °Malachi 3:1
11:19 °NU-Text reads *works.*　11:23 °NU-Text reads *will you be exalted to heaven? No, you will be.*

You, Father, Lord of heaven and earth, that You have hidden these things from *the* wise and prudent and have revealed them to babes. 26Even so, Father, for so it seemed good in Your sight. 27All things have been delivered to Me by My Father, and no one knows the Son except the Father. Nor does anyone know the Father except the Son, and *the one* to whom the Son wills to reveal *Him.* 28Come to Me, all *you* who labor and are heavy laden, and I will give you rest. 29Take My yoke upon you and learn from Me, for I am gentle and lowly in heart, and you will find rest for your souls. 30For My yoke *is* easy and My burden is light."

12 At that time Jesus went through the grainfields on the Sabbath. And His disciples were hungry, and began to pluck heads of grain and to eat. 2*And when the Pharisees saw *it,* they said to Him, "Look, Your disciples are doing what is not lawful to do on the Sabbath!"

3But He said to them, "Have you not read what David did when he was hungry, he and those who were with him: 4how he entered the house of God and ate the showbread which was not lawful for him to eat, nor for those who were with him, but only for the priests? 5Or have you not read in the law that on the Sabbath the priests in the temple profane the Sabbath, and are blameless? 6Yet I say to you that in this place there is *One* greater than the temple. 7But if you had known what *this* means, *'I desire mercy and not sacrifice,'*z you would not have condemned the guiltless. 8For the Son of Man is Lord even*a* of the Sabbath."

9*Now when He had departed from there, He went into their synagogue. 10And behold, there was a man who had a withered hand. And they asked Him, saying, "Is it lawful to heal on the Sabbath?"—that they might accuse Him.

11Then He said to them, "What man is there among you who has one sheep, and if it falls into a pit on the Sabbath, will not lay hold of it and lift *it* out? 12Of how much more value then is a man than a sheep? Therefore it is lawful to do good on the Sabbath." 13Then He said to the man, "Stretch out your hand." And he stretched *it* out, and it was restored as whole as the other. 14Then the Pharisees went out and plotted against Him, how they might destroy Him.

15But when Jesus knew *it,* He withdrew from there. And great multitudesb followed Him, and He healed them all. 16Yet He warned them not to make Him known, 17that it might be fulfilled which was spoken by Isaiah the prophet, saying:

12:7 zHosea 6:6   12:8 aNU-Text and M-Text omit *even.*
12:15 bNU-Text brackets *multitudes* as disputed.

CHAPTER 12

12:2 *Hostility.* The religious leaders were waiting for an opportunity to attack Jesus, and He deliberately gave it to them. What a tragedy to be burdened by legalism when you could enjoy the true Sabbath rest (11:28–30)! When Jesus is your Lord, all of life becomes a Sabbath and every place is God's temple, even a grain field.

12:9–14 *Hypocrisy.* The Pharisees were concerned about keeping the Sabbath but not about showing love to a man with a handicapping condition. Jesus wants mercy, not sacrifice (v. 7; Hos. 6:6; Mic. 6:6–8). Do you *use* people or *serve* them?

The Unpardonable Sin—The unpardonable sin is committed by people who resist the work of the Spirit and reject His witness concerning Jesus. It is a sin of the heart, not the lips, because what we say comes from the heart (Matt. 12:33–37). When the religious leaders allowed John the Baptist to be arrested and slain, they sinned against God the Father who sent him. When they crucified Christ, they sinned against God the Son. Jesus asked for their forgiveness (Luke 23:34), and God gave them another chance. When they persecuted the apostles and then killed Stephen, they sinned against the Holy Spirit who was working through them (Acts 7:51). That sin against the Spirit brought about the downfall of the nation. God can forgive all sins except the sin of rejecting His Son (John 3:36). God's children cannot commit an unpardonable sin, for all of their sins were forgiven when they trusted Jesus Christ (John 3:18; Rom. 8:1; Col. 2:13).

18 "Behold! My Servant whom I have chosen,
   My Beloved in whom My soul is well
      pleased!
   I will put My Spirit upon Him,
   And He will declare justice to the Gentiles.
19 He will not quarrel nor cry out,
   Nor will anyone hear His voice in the
      streets.
20 A bruised reed He will not break,
   And smoking flax He will not quench,
   Till He sends forth justice to victory;
21 And in His name Gentiles will trust."c

22Then one was brought to Him who was demon-possessed, blind and mute; and He healed him, so that the blind andd mute man both spoke and saw. 23And all the multitudes were amazed and said, "Could this be the Son of David?"
24Now when the Pharisees heard it they said, "This fellow does not cast out demons except by Beelzebub,e the ruler of the demons."
25But Jesus knew their thoughts, and said to them: "Every kingdom divided against itself is brought to desolation, and every city or house divided against itself will not stand. 26If Satan casts out Satan, he is divided against himself. How then will his kingdom stand? 27And if I cast out demons by Beelzebub, by whom do your sons cast them out? Therefore they shall be your judges. 28*But if I cast out demons by the Spirit of God, surely the kingdom of God has come upon you. 29Or how can one enter a strong man's house and plunder his goods, unless he first binds the strong man? And then he will plunder his house. 30He who is not with Me is against Me, and he who does not gather with Me scatters abroad.
31"Therefore I say to you, every sin and blasphemy will be forgiven men, but the blasphemy against the Spirit will not be forgiven men. 32Anyone who speaks a word against the Son of Man, it will be forgiven him; but whoever speaks against the Holy Spirit, it will not be forgiven him, either in this age or in the age to come.
33"Either make the tree good and its fruit good, or else make the tree bad and its fruit bad; for a tree is known by its fruit. 34Brood of vipers! How can you, being evil, speak good things? For out of the abundance of the heart the mouth speaks. 35A good man out of the good treasure of his heartf brings forth good things, and an evil man out of the evil treasure brings forth evil things. 36But I say to you that for every idle word men may speak, they will give account of it in the day of judgment. 37For by your words you will be justified, and by your words you will be condemned."
38Then some of the scribes and Pharisees answered, saying, "Teacher, we want to see a sign from You."
39But He answered and said to them, "An evil and adulterous generation seeks after a sign, and no sign will be given to it except the sign of the prophet Jonah. 40For as Jonah was three days and three nights in the belly of the great fish, so will the Son of Man be three days and three nights in the heart of the earth. 41The men of Nineveh will rise up in the judgment with this generation and condemn it, because they repented at the

12:28–30 Victory. Jesus is the Stronger Man who has invaded Satan's house, overcome him, taken his weapons, and is now claiming his spoils (Eph. 1:15–23; Col. 2:15). Put on the armor and join Him in victory (Eph. 6:10ff.).

12:21 cIsaiah 42:1–4   12:22 dNU-Text omits blind and.
12:24 eNU-Text and M-Text read Beelzebul.   12:35 fNU-Text and M-Text omit of his heart.

preaching of Jonah; and indeed a greater than Jonah *is* here. ⁴²The queen of the South will rise up in the judgment with this generation and condemn it, for she came from the ends of the earth to hear the wisdom of Solomon; and indeed a greater than Solomon *is* here.

⁴³*"When an unclean spirit goes out of a man, he goes through dry places, seeking rest, and finds none. ⁴⁴Then he says, 'I will return to my house from which I came.' And when he comes, he finds *it* empty, swept, and put in order. ⁴⁵Then he goes and takes with him seven other spirits more wicked than himself, and they enter and dwell there; and the last *state* of that man is worse than the first. So shall it also be with this wicked generation."

⁴⁶While He was still talking to the multitudes, behold, His mother and brothers stood outside, seeking to speak with Him. ⁴⁷Then one said to Him, "Look, Your mother and Your brothers are standing outside, seeking to speak with You."

⁴⁸But He answered and said to the one who told Him, "Who is My mother and who are My brothers?" ⁴⁹And He stretched out His hand toward His disciples and said, "Here are My mother and My brothers! ⁵⁰For whoever does the will of My Father in heaven is My brother and sister and mother."

13 On the same day Jesus went out of the house and sat by the sea. ²And great multitudes were gathered together to Him, so that He got into a boat and sat; and the whole multitude stood on the shore.

³*Then He spoke many things to them in parables, saying: "Behold, a sower went out to sow. ⁴And as he sowed, some *seed* fell by the wayside; and the birds came and devoured them. ⁵Some fell on stony places, where they did not have much earth; and they immediately sprang up because they had no depth of earth. ⁶But when the sun was up they were scorched, and because they had no root they withered away. ⁷And some fell among thorns, and the thorns sprang up and choked them. ⁸But others fell on good ground and yielded a crop: some a hundredfold, some sixty, some thirty. ⁹He who has ears to hear, let him hear!"

¹⁰And the disciples came and said to Him, "Why do You speak to them in parables?"

¹¹He answered and said to them, "Because it has been given to you to know the mysteries of the kingdom of heaven, but to them it has not been given. ¹²For whoever has, to him more will be given, and he will have abundance; but whoever does not have, even what he has will be taken away from him. ¹³Therefore I speak to them in parables, because seeing they do not see, and hearing they do not hear, nor do they understand. ¹⁴And in them the prophecy of Isaiah is fulfilled, which says:

> 'Hearing you will hear and shall not
>   understand,

12:43–45 Neutrality. Beware an empty life! It is a standing invitation for Satan to go to work. In the spiritual war being waged today, you cannot be neutral. You are either for Him or against Him.

CHAPTER 13

13:3ff These parables explain how God is at work in the world today. The kingdom of heaven is not the true church, for the kingdom of heaven contains both true and false, saved and lost. The kingdom of heaven is made up of all who profess any kind of allegiance to the King.

God is sowing His Word in human hearts and looking for fruit (vv. 1–9, 18–23). He is sowing His people in the world where they can produce a harvest (vv. 24–30, 36–43). At the end of the age, He will separate the true from the false and the good from the bad.

Is your profession of Christ authentic? Or will you be seen as a counterfeit at the end of the age? (See Matt. 7:21–29.)

Does your heart receive the Word? The seed has life and power and can produce a harvest of blessing in your life. Do you hear it?

Can God "plant you" where He wants you? You are a seed containing His divine life, but a seed must be planted to produce fruit (John 12:23–28).

Do you share with others what He teaches you (51–52)? Truth must not be hoarded; it must be shared so that others can be saved and built up in the faith.

Receive the Truth—The word *parable* comes from a Greek word that means "to throw alongside." Jesus used the familiar to teach the unfamiliar ("things new and old" Matt. 13:52). He did that not to hide the truth but to arouse interest in the truth (Matt. 13:13–15). He wanted to get the people to open their eyes and ears and receive the truth into their sluggish hearts.

And seeing you will see and not perceive;
15 For the hearts of this people have grown dull.
Their ears are hard of hearing,
And their eyes they have closed,
Lest they should see with their eyes and hear with their ears,
Lest they should understand with their hearts and turn,
So that I should[g] heal them.'[h]

16But blessed *are* your eyes for they see, and your ears for they hear; 17for assuredly, I say to you that many prophets and righteous *men* desired to see what you see, and did not see *it*, and to hear what you hear, and did not hear *it*.

18"Therefore hear the parable of the sower: 19When anyone hears the word of the kingdom, and does not understand *it*, then the wicked *one* comes and snatches away what was sown in his heart. This is he who received seed by the wayside. 20But he who received the seed on stony places, this is he who hears the word and immediately receives it with joy; 21yet he has no root in himself, but endures only for a while. For when tribulation or persecution arises because of the word, immediately he stumbles. 22Now he who received seed among the thorns is he who hears the word, and the cares of this world and the deceitfulness of riches choke the word, and he becomes unfruitful. 23But he who received seed on the good ground is he who hears the word and understands *it*, who indeed bears fruit and produces: some a hundredfold, some sixty, some thirty."

24Another parable He put forth to them, saying: "The kingdom of heaven is like a man who sowed good seed in his field; 25but while men slept, his enemy came and sowed tares among the wheat and went his way. 26But when the grain had sprouted and produced a crop, then the tares also appeared. 27So the servants of the owner came and said to him, 'Sir, did you not sow good seed in your field? How then does it have tares?' 28He said to them, 'An enemy has done this.' The servants said to him, 'Do you want us then to go and gather them up?' 29But he said, 'No, lest while you gather up the tares you also uproot the wheat with them. 30Let both grow together until the harvest, and at the time of harvest I will say to the reapers, "First gather together the tares and bind them in bundles to burn them, but gather the wheat into my barn."'"

31Another parable He put forth to them, saying: "The kingdom of heaven is like a mustard seed, which a man took and sowed in his field, 32which indeed is the least of all the seeds; but when it is grown it is greater than the herbs and becomes a tree, so that the birds of the air come and nest in its branches."

33Another parable He spoke to them: "The kingdom of heaven is like leaven, which a woman took and hid in three measures[i] of meal till it was all leavened."

34All these things Jesus spoke to the multitude in parables; and without a parable He did not speak to them, 35that it might be fulfilled which was spoken by the prophet, saying:

13:15 [g]NU-Text and M-Text read *would*. [h]Isaiah 6:9, 10
13:33 [i]Greek *sata*, approximately two pecks in all

*"I will open My mouth in parables;
I will utter things kept secret from the
foundation of the world."[j]*

36Then Jesus sent the multitude away and went
into the house. And His disciples came to Him,
saying, "Explain to us the parable of the tares of
the field."

37He answered and said to them: "He who sows
the good seed is the Son of Man. 38The field is
the world, the good seeds are the sons of the kingdom, but the tares are the sons of the wicked *one.*
39The enemy who sowed them is the devil, the
harvest is the end of the age, and the reapers are
the angels. 40Therefore as the tares are gathered
and burned in the fire, so it will be at the end of
this age. 41The Son of Man will send out His angels, and they will gather out of His kingdom all
things that offend, and those who practice lawlessness, 42and will cast them into the furnace of
fire. There will be wailing and gnashing of teeth.
43Then the righteous will shine forth as the sun
in the kingdom of their Father. He who has ears
to hear, let him hear!

44"Again, the kingdom of heaven is like treasure
hidden in a field, which a man found and hid;
and for joy over it he goes and sells all that he
has and buys that field.

45"Again, the kingdom of heaven is like a merchant seeking beautiful pearls, 46who, when he
had found one pearl of great price, went and sold
all that he had and bought it.

47"Again, the kingdom of heaven is like a dragnet that was cast into the sea and gathered some
of every kind, 48which, when it was full, they drew
to shore; and they sat down and gathered the good
into vessels, but threw the bad away. 49So it will
be at the end of the age. The angels will come
forth, separate the wicked from among the just,
50and cast them into the furnace of fire. There
will be wailing and gnashing of teeth."

51Jesus said to them,[k] "Have you understood
all these things?"

They said to Him, "Yes, Lord."[l]

52Then He said to them, "Therefore every scribe
instructed concerning[m] the kingdom of heaven is
like a householder who brings out of his treasure
things new and old."

53Now it came to pass, when Jesus had finished
these parables, that He departed from there.
54When He had come to His own country, He
taught them in their synagogue, so that they were
astonished and said, "Where did this *Man* get this
wisdom and *these* mighty works? 55Is this not the
carpenter's son? Is not His mother called Mary?
And His brothers James, Joses,[n] Simon, and Judas? 56And His sisters, are they not all with us?
Where then did this *Man* get all these things?"
57So they were offended at Him.

But Jesus said to them, "A prophet is not without honor except in his own country and in his
own house." 58Now He did not do many mighty
works there because of their unbelief.

14 At that time Herod the tetrarch heard the
report about Jesus 2and said to his servants,
"This is John the Baptist; he is risen from the

13:35 [j]Psalm 78:2   13:51 [k]NU-Text omits *Jesus said to
them.* [l]NU-Text omits *Lord.*   13:52 [m]Or *for*   13:55 [n]NU-Text
reads *Joseph.*

❝He is nigh when He seems
absent. He is watching when He
seems blind. He is active when He
seems idle.**❞**

—G. Campbell Morgan

14:12 Tell it to Jesus. The disciples of John the Baptist were stunned, so they shared their grief with Jesus. Life will bring its disappointments, and you must learn how to handle them. Jesus will help you (Ps. 55:22; 1 Peter 5:7).

14:15–21 Bring it to Jesus. The Twelve said, "Send them away!" But Jesus said, "Bring what you have to Me!" Give Him your all, and He will use it to meet the need. He can do the impossible with whatever is wholly given to Him. You can even bring to Him *people* who need His touch (v. 35).

14:28–32 Look to Jesus. Some storms come because of our disobedience, but this one came because they obeyed Jesus. Peter *did* walk on the water; but when distracted by dangers around him, he took his eyes off Jesus. We look to Jesus by faith when we trust His word (Heb. 12:1–3). Beware distractions!

dead, and therefore these powers are at work in him." ³For Herod had laid hold of John and bound him, and put *him* in prison for the sake of Herodias, his brother Philip's wife. ⁴Because John had said to him, "It is not lawful for you to have her." ⁵And although he wanted to put him to death, he feared the multitude, because they counted him as a prophet.

⁶But when Herod's birthday was celebrated, the daughter of Herodias danced before them and pleased Herod. ⁷Therefore he promised with an oath to give her whatever she might ask. ⁸So she, having been prompted by her mother, said, "Give me John the Baptist's head here on a platter."

⁹And the king was sorry; nevertheless, because of the oaths and because of those who sat with him, he commanded *it* to be given to *her.* ¹⁰So he sent and had John beheaded in prison. ¹¹And his head was brought on a platter and given to the girl, and she brought *it* to her mother. ¹²*Then his disciples came and took away the body and buried it, and went and told Jesus.

¹³When Jesus heard *it,* He departed from there by boat to a deserted place by Himself. But when the multitudes heard it, they followed Him on foot from the cities. ¹⁴And when Jesus went out He saw a great multitude; and He was moved with compassion for them, and healed their sick. ¹⁵*When it was evening, His disciples came to Him, saying, "This is a deserted place, and the hour is already late. Send the multitudes away, that they may go into the villages and buy themselves food."

¹⁶But Jesus said to them, "They do not need to go away. You give them something to eat."

¹⁷And they said to Him, "We have here only five loaves and two fish."

¹⁸He said, "Bring them here to Me." ¹⁹Then He commanded the multitudes to sit down on the grass. And He took the five loaves and the two fish, and looking up to heaven, He blessed and broke and gave the loaves to the disciples; and the disciples gave to the multitudes. ²⁰So they all ate and were filled, and they took up twelve baskets full of the fragments that remained. ²¹Now those who had eaten were about five thousand men, besides women and children.

²²Immediately Jesus made His disciples get into the boat and go before Him to the other side, while He sent the multitudes away. ²³And when He had sent the multitudes away, He went up on the mountain by Himself to pray. Now when evening came, He was alone there. ²⁴But the boat was now in the middle of the sea,ᵒ tossed by the waves, for the wind was contrary.

²⁵Now in the fourth watch of the night Jesus went to them, walking on the sea. ²⁶And when the disciples saw Him walking on the sea, they were troubled, saying, "It is a ghost!" And they cried out for fear.

²⁷But immediately Jesus spoke to them, saying, "Be of good cheer! It is I; do not be afraid."

²⁸*And Peter answered Him and said, "Lord, if it is You, command me to come to You on the water."

²⁹So He said, "Come." And when Peter had come down out of the boat, he walked on the wa-

---

14:24 ᵒNU-Text reads *many furlongs away from the land.*

ter to go to Jesus. [30]But when he saw that the wind *was* boisterous,[p] he was afraid; and beginning to sink he cried out, saying, "Lord, save me!" [31]And immediately Jesus stretched out *His* hand and caught him, and said to him, "O you of little faith, why did you doubt?" [32]And when they got into the boat, the wind ceased.

[33]Then those who were in the boat came and[q] worshiped Him, saying, "Truly You are the Son of God."

[34]When they had crossed over, they came to the land of[r] Gennesaret. [35]And when the men of that place recognized Him, they sent out into all that surrounding region, brought to Him all who were sick, [36]and begged Him that they might only touch the hem of His garment. And as many as touched *it* were made perfectly well.

15 Then* the scribes and Pharisees who were from Jerusalem came to Jesus, saying, [2]"Why do Your disciples transgress the tradition of the elders? For they do not wash their hands when they eat bread."

[3]He answered and said to them, "Why do you also transgress the commandment of God because of your tradition? [4]For God commanded, saying, 'Honor your father and your mother';[s] and, 'He who curses father or mother, let him be put to death.'[t] [5]But you say, 'Whoever says to his father or mother, "Whatever profit you might have received from me *is a gift to God*"— [6]then he need not honor his father or mother.'[u] Thus you have made the commandment[v] of God of no effect by your tradition. [7]Hypocrites! Well did Isaiah prophesy about you, saying:

[8]   'These people draw near to Me with their
              mouth,
         And[w] honor Me with their lips,
         But their heart is far from Me.
[9]   And in vain they worship Me,
         Teaching as doctrines the commandments
              of men.' "[x]

[10]When He had called the multitude to *Himself*, He said to them, "Hear and understand: [11]Not what goes into the mouth defiles a man; but what comes out of the mouth, this defiles a man."

[12]Then His disciples came and said to Him, "Do You know that the Pharisees were offended when they heard this saying?"

[13]But He answered and said, "Every plant which My heavenly Father has not planted will be uprooted. [14]Let them alone. They are blind leaders of the blind. And if the blind leads the blind, both will fall into a ditch."

[15]Then Peter answered and said to Him, "Explain this parable to us."

[16]So Jesus said, "Are you also still without understanding? [17]Do you not yet understand that whatever enters the mouth goes into the stomach and is eliminated? [18]But those things which proceed out of the mouth come from the heart, and

---

14:30 [p]NU-Text brackets *that* and *boisterous* as disputed. 14:33 [q]NU-Text omits *came and.* 14:34 [r]NU-Text reads *came to land at.* 15:4 [s]Exodus 20:12; Deuteronomy 5:16 [t]Exodus 21:17 15:6 [u]NU-Text omits *or mother.* [v]NU-Text reads *word.* 15:8 [w]NU-Text omits *draw near to Me with their mouth, And.* 15:9 [x]Isaiah 29:13

CHAPTER 15

15:1–20 Our Lord's disciples never knew what would happen next! You can check your own responses to life's challenges as you consider how they handled three different situations.

Offended people. Jesus rejected the man-made traditions of the scribes and Pharisees because they focused on the outside and ignored the inner person. These men were plants that God did not plant (13:24–30) and blind guides who were leading people astray. "Let them alone!" was our Lord's counsel.

15:21–31 Persistent people. Again, the disciples were wrong. Jesus seemed to ignore the woman, but He wanted only to increase her faith. His delays are not His denials. Jesus was ministering in gentile territory, and the people "glorified the God of Israel" (v. 31).

15:32–33 Hungry people. The disciples had already forgotten the miracle of feeding the five thousand! When you are faced with a crisis, take time to review His past mercies; remind yourself that He does not change.
Try to respond to people today the way Jesus responded. Ask Him for discernment.

CHAPTER 16
16:1–4 Are you guilty of these misunderstandings?
About the times. People believe the weather report but not God's Word! They fail to see what God is doing in His world. Keep your eyes open, and ask God for wisdom to understand His plan.

they defile a man. 19For out of the heart proceed evil thoughts, murders, adulteries, fornications, thefts, false witness, blasphemies. 20These are *the things* which defile a man, but to eat with unwashed hands does not defile a man."

21*Then Jesus went out from there and departed to the region of Tyre and Sidon. 22And behold, a woman of Canaan came from that region and cried out to Him, saying, "Have mercy on me, O Lord, Son of David! My daughter is severely demon-possessed."

23But He answered her not a word.
And His disciples came and urged Him, saying, "Send her away, for she cries out after us."

24But He answered and said, "I was not sent except to the lost sheep of the house of Israel."

25Then she came and worshiped Him, saying, "Lord, help me!"

26But He answered and said, "It is not good to take the children's bread and throw *it* to the little dogs."

27And she said, "Yes, Lord, yet even the little dogs eat the crumbs which fall from their masters' table."

28Then Jesus answered and said to her, "O woman, great *is* your faith! Let it be to you as you desire." And her daughter was healed from that very hour.

29Jesus departed from there, skirted the Sea of Galilee, and went up on the mountain and sat down there. 30Then great multitudes came to Him, having with them *the* lame, blind, mute, maimed, and many others; and they laid them down at Jesus' feet, and He healed them. 31So the multitude marveled when they saw *the* mute speaking, *the* maimed made whole, *the* lame walking, and *the* blind seeing; and they glorified the God of Israel.

32*Now Jesus called His disciples to *Himself* and said, "I have compassion on the multitude, because they have now continued with Me three days and have nothing to eat. And I do not want to send them away hungry, lest they faint on the way."

33Then His disciples said to Him, "Where could we get enough bread in the wilderness to fill such a great multitude?"

34Jesus said to them, "How many loaves do you have?"
And they said, "Seven, and a few little fish."

35So He commanded the multitude to sit down on the ground. 36And He took the seven loaves and the fish and gave thanks, broke *them* and gave *them* to His disciples; and the disciples *gave* to the multitude. 37So they all ate and were filled, and they took up seven large baskets full of the fragments that were left. 38Now those who ate were four thousand men, besides women and children. 39And He sent away the multitude, got into the boat, and came to the region of Magdala.y

16 Then* the Pharisees and Sadducees came, and testing Him asked that He would show them a sign from heaven. 2He answered and said to them, "When it is evening you say, 'It will be fair weather, for the sky is red'; 3and in the morning, 'It will be foul weather today, for the sky is

15:39 yNU-Text reads *Magadan.*

red and threatening.' Hypocrites!ᶻ You know how to discern the face of the sky, but you cannot *discern* the signs of the times. ⁴A wicked and adulterous generation seeks after a sign, and no sign shall be given to it except the sign of the prophetᵃ Jonah." And He left them and departed.

⁵*Now when His disciples had come to the other side, they had forgotten to take bread. ⁶Then Jesus said to them, "Take heed and beware of the leaven of the Pharisees and the Sadducees."

⁷And they reasoned among themselves, saying, "*It is* because we have taken no bread."

⁸But Jesus, being aware of *it,* said to them, "O you of little faith, why do you reason among yourselves because you have brought no bread?ᵇ ⁹Do you not yet understand, or remember the five loaves of the five thousand and how many baskets you took up? ¹⁰Nor the seven loaves of the four thousand and how many large baskets you took up? ¹¹How is it you do not understand that I did not speak to you concerning bread?—*but* to beware of the leaven of the Pharisees and Sadducees." ¹²Then they understood that He did not tell *them* to beware of the leaven of bread, but of the doctrine of the Pharisees and Sadducees.

¹³*When Jesus came into the region of Caesarea Philippi, He asked His disciples, saying, "Who do men say that I, the Son of Man, am?"

¹⁴So they said, "Some *say* John the Baptist, some Elijah, and others Jeremiah or one of the prophets."

¹⁵He said to them, "But who do you say that I am?"

¹⁶Simon Peter answered and said, "You are the Christ, the Son of the living God."

¹⁷Jesus answered and said to him, "Blessed are you, Simon Bar-Jonah, for flesh and blood has not revealed *this* to you, but My Father who is in heaven. ¹⁸And I also say to you that you are Peter, and on this rock I will build My church, and the gates of Hades shall not prevail against it. ¹⁹And I will give you the keys of the kingdom of heaven, and whatever you bind on earth will be bound in heaven, and whatever you loose on earth will be loosedᶜ in heaven."

²⁰Then He commanded His disciples that they should tell no one that He was Jesus the Christ.

²¹*From that time Jesus began to show to His disciples that He must go to Jerusalem, and suffer many things from the elders and chief priests and scribes, and be killed, and be raised the third day. ²²Then Peter took Him aside and began to rebuke Him, saying, "Far be it from You, Lord; this shall not happen to You!"

²³But He turned and said to Peter, "Get behind Me, Satan! You are an offense to Me, for you are not mindful of the things of God, but the things of men."

16:5–12 *About false doctrine.* Jesus compared false doctrine to *yeast.* It appears small and insignificant, but it grows secretly and soon permeates everything (Gal. 5:9). The only remedy is to remove it (1 Cor. 5:6–7).

16:13–20 *About Jesus Christ.* The crowd is confused about Jesus; do not follow it. Instead, let the Father reveal the Savior to you (11:25–27), and confess Him before others. He is the Son of God.

16:21–27 *About discipleship.* In his misguided attempt to keep Jesus from suffering and dying, Peter the stone became Peter the stumbling block. Confessing Christ must lead to following Christ. The world encourages you to pamper yourself, but the Lord calls you to deny yourself. The only way to live is to die to self and follow Christ by faith.

16:3 ᶻNU-Text omits *Hypocrites.* 16:4 ᵃNU-Text omits *the prophet.* 16:8 ᵇNU-Text reads *you have no bread.* 16:19 ᶜOr *will have been bound . . . will have been loosed*

Peter—The name *Peter* means "a stone" (John 1:40–42). All of God's people are "living stones," but Jesus is the Rock (1 Pet. 2:4–8; Acts 4:11–12; Ps. 118:22), and His church is built on Him (1 Cor. 3:11). Whoever confesses faith in Christ becomes a living stone built into the spiritual temple (Eph. 2:19–22). Peter was given not the keys of heaven, for Jesus holds them (Rev. 1:18), but the "keys of the kingdom of heaven" (Matt. 16:19). He had the privilege of opening "the door of faith" (Acts 14:27) to the Jews at Pentecost (Acts 2), the Samaritans (Acts 8:14ff.), and the Gentiles (Acts 10).

24Then Jesus said to His disciples, "If anyone desires to come after Me, let him deny himself, and take up his cross, and follow Me. 25For whoever desires to save his life will lose it, but whoever loses his life for My sake will find it. 26For what profit is it to a man if he gains the whole world, and loses his own soul? Or what will a man give in exchange for his soul? 27For the Son of Man will come in the glory of His Father with His angels, and then He will reward each according to his works. 28Assuredly, I say to you, there are some standing here who shall not taste death till they see the Son of Man coming in His kingdom."

17 Now after six days Jesus took Peter, James, and John his brother, led them up on a high mountain by themselves; 2and He was transfigured before them. His face shone like the sun, and His clothes became as white as the light. 3And behold, Moses and Elijah appeared to them, talking with Him. 4Then Peter answered and said to Jesus, "Lord, it is good for us to be here; if You wish, let usd make here three tabernacles: one for You, one for Moses, and one for Elijah."
5*While he was still speaking, behold, a bright cloud overshadowed them; and suddenly a voice came out of the cloud, saying, "This is My beloved Son, in whom I am well pleased. Hear Him!" 6And when the disciples heard it, they fell on their faces and were greatly afraid. 7But Jesus came and touched them and said, "Arise, and do not be afraid." 8When they had lifted up their eyes, they saw no one but Jesus only.
9Now as they came down from the mountain, Jesus commanded them, saying, "Tell the vision to no one until the Son of Man is risen from the dead."
10And His disciples asked Him, saying, "Why then do the scribes say that Elijah must come first?"
11Jesus answered and said to them, "Indeed, Elijah is coming firste and will restore all things. 12But I say to you that Elijah has come already, and they did not know him but did to him whatever they wished. Likewise the Son of Man is also about to suffer at their hands." 13Then the disciples understood that He spoke to them of John the Baptist.
14And when they had come to the multitude, a man came to Him, kneeling down to Him and saying, 15"Lord, have mercy on my son, for he is an epilepticf and suffers severely; for he often falls into the fire and often into the water. 16So I brought him to Your disciples, but they could not cure him."
17Then Jesus answered and said, "O faithless and perverse generation, how long shall I be with you? How long shall I bear with you? Bring him here to Me." 18And Jesus rebuked the demon, and it came out of him; and the child was cured from that very hour.
19*Then the disciples came to Jesus privately and said, "Why could we not cast it out?"
20So Jesus said to them, "Because of your unbelief;g for assuredly, I say to you, if you have faith as a mustard seed, you will say to this mountain,

---

CHAPTER 17

17:5 Listen to the King! This event was a picture of the coming kingdom (16:27–28) and a proof that Jesus Christ is indeed the Son of the living God. The Law (Moses) and the prophets (Elijah) all converge in Him (Heb. 1:1–2). But the thing Peter remembered most was the emphasis on the unchanging Word of God (2 Pet. 1:16–21). The memory of visions will fade, but the Word endures forever. Hear Him!

17:19, 20 Trust the King! Jesus gave the disciples power to cast out demons (10:1, 8), but their unbelief and lack of prayer (vv. 20–21) robbed them of the power they needed. We cannot stay on the mountain of glory; there are needs to be met in the valley.

17:4 dNU-Text reads I will.   17:11 eNU-Text omits first.
17:15 fLiterally moonstruck   17:20 gNU-Text reads little faith.

'Move from here to there,' and it will move; and nothing will be impossible for you. 21However, this kind does not go out except by prayer and fasting."[h]

22Now while they were staying[i] in Galilee, Jesus said to them, "The Son of Man is about to be betrayed into the hands of men, 23and they will kill Him, and the third day He will be raised up." And they were exceedingly sorrowful.

24When they had come to Capernaum,[j] those who received the *temple* tax came to Peter and said, "Does your Teacher not pay the *temple* tax?"

25He said, "Yes."

And when he had come into the house, Jesus anticipated him, saying, "What do you think, Simon? From whom do the kings of the earth take customs or taxes, from their sons or from strangers?"

26Peter said to Him, "From strangers."

Jesus said to him, "Then the sons are free. 27*Nevertheless, lest we offend them, go to the sea, cast in a hook, and take the fish that comes up first. And when you have opened its mouth, you will find a piece of money;[k] take that and give it to them for Me and you."

18 At* that time the disciples came to Jesus, saying, "Who then is greatest in the kingdom of heaven?"

2Then Jesus called a little child to Him, set him in the midst of them, 3and said, "Assuredly, I say to you, unless you are converted and become as little children, you will by no means enter the kingdom of heaven. 4Therefore whoever humbles himself as this little child is the greatest in the kingdom of heaven. 5Whoever receives one little child like this in My name receives Me.

6"Whoever causes one of these little ones who believe in Me to sin, it would be better for him if a millstone were hung around his neck, and he were drowned in the depth of the sea. 7Woe to the world because of offenses! For offenses must come, but woe to that man by whom the offense comes!

8"If your hand or foot causes you to sin, cut it off and cast *it* from you. It is better for you to enter into life lame or maimed, rather than having two hands or two feet, to be cast into the everlasting fire. 9And if your eye causes you to sin, pluck it out and cast *it* from you. It is better for you to enter into life with one eye, rather than having two eyes, to be cast into hell fire.

10"Take heed that you do not despise one of these little ones, for I say to you that in heaven their angels always see the face of My Father who is in heaven. 11For the Son of Man has come to save that which was lost.[l]

12"What do you think? If a man has a hundred sheep, and one of them goes astray, does he not leave the ninety-nine and go to the mountains to seek the one that is straying? 13And if he should find it, assuredly, I say to you, he rejoices more over that *sheep* than over the ninety-nine that did not go astray. 14Even so it is not the will of your

17:27 Obey the King! The tax was an annual assessment of the Jewish men for the support of the temple (Exod. 30:11–16). Jesus affirmed His kingship by controlling a coin and a fish, but He affirmed His servanthood by submitting to their demands. "Lest we offend them" (17:27) is a good principle when you lay aside your rights, but be careful not to set aside God's truth (15:12–14).

CHAPTER 18

18:1–11 Greatness. A child totally depends on others and must live by faith. An unspoiled child accepts his position in life, enjoys it, and does not try to act like someone older (Ps. 131). "He will be greatest who has the least idea he is great," wrote A. H. McNeile.

The way we treat children (including those who are "children in the faith") indicates how much humility we practice. Do we receive them (18:5) or despise them (v. 10)? Do we imitate them (vv. 3–4) or cause them to stumble by our bad example (vv. 6–9)? It was a *sheep,* not a *lamb,* that went astray (vv. 10–14)!

❝*He who cannot forgive breaks the bridge over which he himself must pass.*❞
—George Herbert

18:15–17 Truthfulness. "Speaking the truth in love" (Eph. 4:15) is the secret of maintaining Christian fellowship. The longer we resist, the more people we involve in the problem (Matt. 5:21–26). Humility and honesty must work together in producing harmony.

18:21–35 Forgiveness. Peter wanted a rule to obey, which shows he was not in the spirit of what Jesus taught (Rom. 12:8–10). The parable is not about salvation but about forgiveness among God's people. We are to forgive others because God has forgiven us (Eph. 4:32; Col. 3:13), *and He has forgiven us at great cost to Himself!* It is possible to *receive* forgiveness but not truly *experience* forgiveness in our hearts; therefore, we have a hard time *sharing* forgiveness with others.
When you have an unforgiving spirit, you put yourself in prison spiritually and emotionally; you pay dearly for the luxury of carrying a grudge. Is it worth it?

CHAPTER 19

19:3–12 Let Jesus heal your marriage. Some practices are lawful but not biblical, so follow the principles given in Scripture. God's original plan was one man for one woman for all of life (Gen. 2:18–25), but He made a concession for Israel and permitted divorce (Deut. 24:1–4). Divorce is not given as the solution to the problem. It takes a change of heart for two people to make a new beginning, and only Jesus can change hearts. Before you run away, run to God and seek His help.

❝*A good marriage is not a contract between two persons but a sacred covenant between three. Too often Christ is never invited to the wedding and finds no room in the home.*❞
—Donald T. Kauffman

Father who is in heaven that one of these little ones should perish.

15*"Moreover if your brother sins against you, go and tell him his fault between him and you alone. If he hears you, you have gained your brother. 16But if he will not hear, take with you one or two more, that *'by the mouth of two or three witnesses every word may be established.'*m 17And if he refuses to hear them, tell *it* to the church. But if he refuses even to hear the church, let him be to you like a heathen and a tax collector.

18"Assuredly, I say to you, whatever you bind on earth will be bound in heaven, and whatever you loose on earth will be loosed in heaven.

19"Again I say*n* to you that if two of you agree on earth concerning anything that they ask, it will be done for them by My Father in heaven. 20For where two or three are gathered together in My name, I am there in the midst of them."

21*Then Peter came to Him and said, "Lord, how often shall my brother sin against me, and I forgive him? Up to seven times?"

22Jesus said to him, "I do not say to you, up to seven times, but up to seventy times seven. 23Therefore the kingdom of heaven is like a certain king who wanted to settle accounts with his servants. 24And when he had begun to settle accounts, one was brought to him who owed him ten thousand talents. 25But as he was not able to pay, his master commanded that he be sold, with his wife and children and all that he had, and that payment be made. 26The servant therefore fell down before him, saying, 'Master, have patience with me, and I will pay you all.' 27Then the master of that servant was moved with compassion, released him, and forgave him the debt.

28"But that servant went out and found one of his fellow servants who owed him a hundred denarii; and he laid hands on him and took *him* by the throat, saying, 'Pay me what you owe!' 29So his fellow servant fell down at his feet*o* and begged him, saying, 'Have patience with me, and I will pay you all.'*p* 30And he would not, but went and threw him into prison till he should pay the debt. 31So when his fellow servants saw what had been done, they were very grieved, and came and told their master all that had been done. 32Then his master, after he had called him, said to him, 'You wicked servant! I forgave you all that debt because you begged me. 33Should you not also have had compassion on your fellow servant, just as I had pity on you?' 34And his master was angry, and delivered him to the torturers until he should pay all that was due to him.

35"So My heavenly Father also will do to you if each of you, from his heart, does not forgive his brother his trespasses."*q*

19 Now it came to pass, when Jesus had finished these sayings, *that* He departed from Galilee and came to the region of Judea beyond the Jordan. 2And great multitudes followed Him, and He healed them there.

3*The Pharisees also came to Him, testing Him,

18:16 *m*Deuteronomy 19:15   18:19 *n*NU-Text and M-Text read *Again, assuredly, I say.*   18:29 *o*NU-Text omits *at his feet.* *p*NU-Text and M-Text omit *all.*   18:35 *q*NU-Text omits *his trespasses.*

and saying to Him, "Is it lawful for a man to divorce his wife for *just* any reason?"

4And He answered and said to them, "Have you not read that He who made*r* *them* at the beginning *'made them male and female,'s* 5and said, *'For this reason a man shall leave his father and mother and be joined to his wife, and the two shall become one flesh'?t* 6So then, they are no longer two but one flesh. Therefore what God has joined together, let not man separate."

7They said to Him, "Why then did Moses command to give a certificate of divorce, and to put her away?"

8He said to them, "Moses, because of the hardness of your hearts, permitted you to divorce your wives, but from the beginning it was not so. 9And I say to you, whoever divorces his wife, except for sexual immorality,*u* and marries another, commits adultery; and whoever marries her who is divorced commits adultery."

10His disciples said to Him, "If such is the case of the man with *his* wife, it is better not to marry."

11But He said to them, "All cannot accept this saying, but only *those* to whom it has been given: 12For there are eunuchs who were born thus from *their* mother's womb, and there are eunuchs who were made eunuchs by men, and there are eunuchs who have made themselves eunuchs for the kingdom of heaven's sake. He who is able to accept *it,* let him accept *it.*"

13*Then little children were brought to Him that He might put *His* hands on them and pray, but the disciples rebuked them. 14But Jesus said, "Let the little children come to Me, and do not forbid them; for of such is the kingdom of heaven." 15And He laid *His* hands on them and departed from there.

16*Now behold, one came and said to Him, "Good*v* Teacher, what good thing shall I do that I may have eternal life?"

17So He said to him, "Why do you call Me good?*w* No one *is* good but One, *that is,* God.*x* But if you want to enter into life, keep the commandments."

18He said to Him, "Which ones?"

Jesus said, *"'You shall not murder,' 'You shall not commit adultery,' 'You shall not steal,' 'You shall not bear false witness,'* 19*'Honor your father and your mother,'y* and, *'You shall love your neighbor as yourself.'"z*

20The young man said to Him, "All these things I have kept from my youth.*a* What do I still lack?"

21Jesus said to him, "If you want to be perfect, go, sell what you have and give to the poor, and you will have treasure in heaven; and come, follow Me."

22But when the young man heard that saying, he went away sorrowful, for he had great possessions.

23Then Jesus said to His disciples, "Assuredly, I say to you that it is hard for a rich man to enter the kingdom of heaven. 24And again I say to you, it is easier for a camel to go through the eye of a

19:13–15 *Let Jesus bless your family.* Children want to come to Jesus (v. 14), but too often adults get in the way. The best parents make it easy for their children to come to Christ, love Him, and receive His blessing.

19:16–30 *Let Jesus have your all.* The wealthy young man had much in his favor, but he thought too highly of himself and was not really honest before God. Money stood between him and salvation, and he would not repent and renounce his false god. You never lose when you give everything to Jesus. He blesses you in this life and in the life to come.

19:4 *r*NU-Text reads *created.* *s*Genesis 1:27; 5:2
19:5 *t*Genesis 2:24   19:9 *u*Or *fornication*   19:16 *v*NU-Text omits *Good.*   19:17 *w*NU-Text reads *Why do you ask Me about what is good?* *x*NU-Text reads *There is One who is good.*   19:19 *y*Exodus 20:12–16; Deuteronomy 5:16–20
*z*Leviticus 19:18   19:20 *a*NU-Text omits *from my youth.*

needle than for a rich man to enter the kingdom of God."

25When His disciples heard *it*, they were greatly astonished, saying, "Who then can be saved?"

26But Jesus looked at *them* and said to them, "With men this is impossible, but with God all things are possible."

27Then Peter answered and said to Him, "See, we have left all and followed You. Therefore what shall we have?"

28So Jesus said to them, "Assuredly I say to you, that in the regeneration, when the Son of Man sits on the throne of His glory, you who have followed Me will also sit on twelve thrones, judging the twelve tribes of Israel. 29And everyone who has left houses or brothers or sisters or father or mother or wife*b* or children or lands, for My name's sake, shall receive a hundredfold, and inherit eternal life. 30But many *who are* first will be last, and the last first.

CHAPTER 20

20:1–16 What shall we have? The parable is not about salvation, for we cannot work for salvation; nor is it about rewards, for we do not all receive the same reward. The story concerns the selfish attitude implicit in Peter's question. The key to the parable is that the first workers hired *demanded a contract and insisted on knowing how much they would get.* The other workers trusted the landowner. If you ask God for a contract, you will only rob yourself, for He is generous with His workers. Be faithful to do your job and avoid watching the other workers, and He will deal with you generously.

20:20–28 What do you wish? Salome remembered His promise (19:28) and claimed it for her two sons. But she forgot what Jesus had just said about the cross (vv. 17–19). She should have known that the only way to glory is through suffering (1 Pet. 5:10). You do not *pray* for a throne; you *pay* for it. Beware selfish prayers: the Lord may answer them. James was the first apostle to be martyred (Acts 12:1–2), and John experienced great trial as a Roman prisoner (Rev. 1:9).

20 "For* the kingdom of heaven is like a landowner who went out early in the morning to hire laborers for his vineyard. 2Now when he had agreed with the laborers for a denarius a day, he sent them into his vineyard. 3And he went out about the third hour and saw others standing idle in the marketplace, 4and said to them, 'You also go into the vineyard, and whatever is right I will give you.' So they went. 5Again he went out about the sixth and the ninth hour, and did likewise. 6And about the eleventh hour he went out and found others standing idle,*c* and said to them, 'Why have you been standing here idle all day?' 7They said to him, 'Because no one hired us.' He said to them, 'You also go into the vineyard, and whatever is right you will receive.'*d*

8"So when evening had come, the owner of the vineyard said to his steward, 'Call the laborers and give them *their* wages, beginning with the last to the first.' 9And when those came who *were* hired about the eleventh hour, they each received a denarius. 10But when the first came, they supposed that they would receive more; and they likewise received each a denarius. 11And when they had received *it*, they complained against the landowner, 12saying, 'These last *men* have worked *only* one hour, and you made them equal to us who have borne the burden and the heat of the day.' 13But he answered one of them and said, 'Friend, I am doing you no wrong. Did you not agree with me for a denarius? 14Take *what is* yours and go your way. I wish to give to this last man *the same* as to you. 15Is it not lawful for me to do what I wish with my own things? Or is your eye evil because I am good?' 16So the last will be first, and the first last. For many are called, but few chosen."*e*

17Now Jesus, going up to Jerusalem, took the twelve disciples aside on the road and said to them, 18"Behold, we are going up to Jerusalem, and the Son of Man will be betrayed to the chief priests and to the scribes; and they will condemn Him to death, 19and deliver Him to the Gentiles to mock and to scourge and to crucify. And the third day He will rise again."

20*Then the mother of Zebedee's sons came to

19:29 *b*NU-Text omits *or wife.*   20:6 *c*NU-Text omits *idle.*
20:7 *d*NU-Text omits the last clause of this verse.
20:16 *e*NU-Text omits the last sentence of this verse.

Him with her sons, kneeling down and asking something from Him.

²¹And He said to her, "What do you wish?"

She said to Him, "Grant that these two sons of mine may sit, one on Your right hand and the other on the left, in Your kingdom."

²²But Jesus answered and said, "You do not know what you ask. Are you able to drink the cup that I am about to drink, and be baptized with the baptism that I am baptized with?"ᶠ

They said to Him, "We are able."

²³So He said to them, "You will indeed drink My cup, and be baptized with the baptism that I am baptized with;ᵍ but to sit on My right hand and on My left is not Mine to give, but it is for those for whom it is prepared by My Father."

²⁴And when the ten heard it, they were greatly displeased with the two brothers. ²⁵But Jesus called them to Himself and said, "You know that the rulers of the Gentiles lord it over them, and those who are great exercise authority over them. ²⁶Yet it shall not be so among you; but whoever desires to become great among you, let him be your servant. ²⁷And whoever desires to be first among you, let him be your slave— ²⁸just as the Son of Man did not come to be served, but to serve, and to give His life a ransom for many."

²⁹Now as they went out of Jericho, a great multitude followed Him. ³⁰*And behold, two blind men sitting by the road, when they heard that Jesus was passing by, cried out, saying, "Have mercy on us, O Lord, Son of David!"

³¹Then the multitude warned them that they should be quiet; but they cried out all the more, saying, "Have mercy on us, O Lord, Son of David!"

³²So Jesus stood still and called them, and said, "What do you want Me to do for you?"

³³They said to Him, "Lord, that our eyes may be opened." ³⁴So Jesus had compassion and touched their eyes. And immediately their eyes received sight, and they followed Him.

21 Now when they drew near Jerusalem, and came to Bethphage,ʰ at the Mount of Olives, then Jesus sent two disciples, ²saying to them, "Go into the village opposite you, and immediately you will find a donkey tied, and a colt with her. Loose them and bring them to Me. ³And if anyone says anything to you, you shall say, 'The Lord has need of them,' and immediately he will send them."

⁴Allⁱ this was done that it might be fulfilled which was spoken by the prophet, saying:

5 *"Tell the daughter of Zion,
   'Behold, your King is coming to you,

20:22 ᶠNU-Text omits and be baptized with the baptism that I am baptized with. 20:23 ᵍNU-Text omits and be baptized with the baptism that I am baptized with. 21:1 ʰM-Text reads Bethsphage. 21:4 ⁱNU-Text omits All.

20:30–34 What do you want Me to do for you? They knew what they wanted, and they trusted Him for it. Do you know what you want when you come to Him in prayer? Do you persist even if others try to discourage you? What a promise we have in Hebrews 4:16!

CHAPTER 21

21:5, 9 The King. The people were blind to their Scriptures (Zech. 9:9). They praised Him with Psalm 118:26 but overlooked verses 22–23, which Jesus quoted later (v. 42). Beware knowing the Bible but not knowing the Lord when He is at work in your midst.

The Last Week—Traditionally, the events during our Lord's last week are as follows: Sunday—He entered Jerusalem as King. Monday—He cleansed the temple and cursed the fig tree. Tuesday—He debated with the Jewish leaders and gave the Olivet Discourse (Matt. 24—25). Wednesday—He rested. Thursday—He had the Last Supper; He was arrested in the Garden. Friday—He was crucified and buried. Saturday—He lay in the tomb. Sunday—He arose from the dead. Keep in mind that the Jewish day begins with sundown, so that their Friday begins Thursday evening.

Lowly, and sitting on a donkey,
A colt, the foal of a donkey.' "[j]

6So the disciples went and did as Jesus commanded them. 7They brought the donkey and the colt, laid their clothes on them, and set *Him*[k] on them. 8And a very great multitude spread their clothes on the road; others cut down branches from the trees and spread *them* on the road. 9Then the multitudes who went before and those who followed cried out, saying:

"Hosanna to the Son of David!
'*Blessed is He who comes in the name of*
the LORD!'[l]
Hosanna in the highest!"

10And when He had come into Jerusalem, all the city was moved, saying, "Who is this?"
11So the multitudes said, "This is Jesus, the prophet from Nazareth of Galilee."
12*Then Jesus went into the temple of God[m] and drove out all those who bought and sold in the temple, and overturned the tables of the money changers and the seats of those who sold doves. 13And He said to them, "It is written, '*My house shall be called a house of prayer,*'[n] but you have made it a '*den of thieves.*' "[o]
14Then *the* blind and *the* lame came to Him in the temple, and He healed them. 15But when the chief priests and scribes saw the wonderful things that He did, and the children crying out in the temple and saying, "Hosanna to the Son of David!" they were indignant 16and said to Him, "Do You hear what these are saying?"

And Jesus said to them, "Yes. Have you never read,

'*Out of the mouth of babes and nursing*
infants
You have perfected praise'? "[p]

17Then He left them and went out of the city to Bethany, and He lodged there.
18Now in the morning, as He returned to the city, He was hungry. 19And seeing a fig tree by the road, He came to it and found nothing on it but leaves, and said to it, "Let no fruit grow on you ever again." Immediately the fig tree withered away.
20And when the disciples saw *it*, they marveled, saying, "How did the fig tree wither away so soon?"
21So Jesus answered and said to them, "Assuredly, I say to you, if you have faith and do not doubt, you will not only do what was done to the fig tree, but also if you say to this mountain, 'Be removed and be cast into the sea,' it will be done. 22And whatever things you ask in prayer, believing, you will receive."
23*Now when He came into the temple, the chief priests and the elders of the people confronted Him as He was teaching, and said, "By what authority are You doing these things? And who gave You this authority?"
24But Jesus answered and said to them, "I also

21:12–22 *The Judge.* Jesus cleansed the temple and cursed the fig tree, two "unusual acts" for Him who came not to judge but to save (Isa. 28:21). Like the temple, Israel was corrupt within; and like the fig tree, it was fruitless without. A church can become a "den of thieves" if that is where we go to cover up our sins (Isa. 56:7; 1:10–20; Jer. 7:11). A person whose life is "nothing but leaves" is in danger of judgment, for Christ seeks fruit (7:15–20).

21:23–40 *The Son.* Jesus has authority because He is the Son of God! The vineyard is Israel (Isa. 5) whose leaders did not respect the Son when He came. The nation rejected the Father when they refused the witness of John, and now they were about to reject the Son.

21:5 [j]Zechariah 9:9   21:7 [k]NU-Text reads *and He sat.*
21:9 [l]Psalm 118:26   21:12 [m]NU-Text omits *of God.*
21:13 [n]Isaiah 56:7 [o]Jeremiah 7:11   21:16 [p]Psalm 8:2

will ask you one thing, which if you tell Me, I likewise will tell you by what authority I do these things: 25The baptism of John—where was it from? From heaven or from men?"

And they reasoned among themselves, saying, "If we say, 'From heaven,' He will say to us, 'Why then did you not believe him?' 26But if we say, 'From men,' we fear the multitude, for all count John as a prophet." 27So they answered Jesus and said, "We do not know."

And He said to them, "Neither will I tell you by what authority I do these things.

28"But what do you think? A man had two sons, and he came to the first and said, 'Son, go, work today in my vineyard.' 29He answered and said, 'I will not,' but afterward he regretted it and went. 30Then he came to the second and said likewise. And he answered and said, 'I go, sir,' but he did not go. 31Which of the two did the will of his father?"

They said to Him, "The first."

Jesus said to them, "Assuredly, I say to you that tax collectors and harlots enter the kingdom of God before you. 32For John came to you in the way of righteousness, and you did not believe him; but tax collectors and harlots believed him; and when you saw it, you did not afterward relent and believe him.

33"Hear another parable: There was a certain landowner who planted a vineyard and set a hedge around it, dug a winepress in it and built a tower. And he leased it to vinedressers and went into a far country. 34Now when vintage-time drew near, he sent his servants to the vinedressers, that they might receive its fruit. 35And the vinedressers took his servants, beat one, killed one, and stoned another. 36Again he sent other servants, more than the first, and they did likewise to them. 37Then last of all he sent his son to them, saying, 'They will respect my son.' 38But when the vinedressers saw the son, they said among themselves, 'This is the heir. Come, let us kill him and seize his inheritance.' 39So they took him and cast him out of the vineyard and killed him.

40"Therefore, when the owner of the vineyard comes, what will he do to those vinedressers?"

41*They said to Him, "He will destroy those wicked men miserably, and lease his vineyard to other vinedressers who will render to him the fruits in their seasons."

42Jesus said to them, "Have you never read in the Scriptures:

'The stone which the builders rejected
Has become the chief cornerstone.
This was the LORD's doing,
And it is marvelous in our eyes'?q

43"Therefore I say to you, the kingdom of God will be taken from you and given to a nation bearing the fruits of it. 44And whoever falls on this stone will be broken; but on whomever it falls, it will grind him to powder."

45Now when the chief priests and Pharisees heard His parables, they perceived that He was speaking of them. 46But when they sought to lay hands on Him, they feared the multitudes, because they took Him for a prophet.

21:41–46 The Stone. The Jewish leaders pronounced their own sentence. Jesus quoted Psalm 118:22–23 to prove that their sins would not hinder His victory (Isa. 8:14–15; Dan. 2:34; Acts 4:11; 1 Pet. 2:9). If only they had become like the children and praised the Lord instead of fighting Him (21:15–16; Ps. 8:2)!

CHAPTER 22

22:1–14 *The Bridegroom.* The rejected Son is resurrected and reigns in glory. He is the Bridegroom who wants everybody to come to His feast. Israel's rejection of the invitation led to the destruction of Jerusalem (v. 7). But the invitation is still open today.

Just be sure not to wear your self-righteousness (Isa. 64:6); let Him provide the garment of His righteousness (Isa. 61:10; 2 Cor. 5:21).

22:15–46 His enemies questioned Jesus, hoping to get Him in trouble with Rome. After Passover, they could have Him arrested and tried. But how can mortal man question God and hope to win (Job 38:1–3)? What arrogance—and what ignorance! Jesus asked the key question: "Who is your Lord?" (22:41–46; Ps. 110). If Jesus Christ is your Lord, the other questions pose no problem. You will be a good citizen (22:15–22; Rom. 13); you will not worry about the hereafter (vv. 23–33); and you will love God and your neighbor (vv. 34–40).

People who like to argue usually lack humility and need to submit to Christ (Phil. 2:1–11). Although it is good to ponder the great questions of life, it is also good to admit our ignorance and to worship Christ "in whom are hidden all the treasures of wisdom and knowledge" (Col. 2:3).

22 And* Jesus answered and spoke to them again by parables and said: 2"The kingdom of heaven is like a certain king who arranged a marriage for his son, 3and sent out his servants to call those who were invited to the wedding; and they were not willing to come. 4Again, he sent out other servants, saying, 'Tell those who are invited, "See, I have prepared my dinner; my oxen and fatted cattle *are* killed, and all things *are* ready. Come to the wedding." ' 5But they made light of it and went their ways, one to his own farm, another to his business. 6And the rest seized his servants, treated *them* spitefully, and killed *them.* 7But when the king heard *about it,* he was furious. And he sent out his armies, destroyed those murderers, and burned up their city. 8Then he said to his servants, 'The wedding is ready, but those who were invited were not worthy. 9Therefore go into the highways, and as many as you find, invite to the wedding.' 10So those servants went out into the highways and gathered together all whom they found, both bad and good. And the wedding *hall* was filled with guests.

11"But when the king came in to see the guests, he saw a man there who did not have on a wedding garment. 12So he said to him, 'Friend, how did you come in here without a wedding garment?' And he was speechless. 13Then the king said to the servants, 'Bind him hand and foot, take him away, and*r* cast *him* into outer darkness; there will be weeping and gnashing of teeth.'

14"For many are called, but few *are* chosen."

15*Then the Pharisees went and plotted how they might entangle Him in *His* talk. 16And they sent to Him their disciples with the Herodians, saying, "Teacher, we know that You are true, and teach the way of God in truth; nor do You care about anyone, for You do not regard the person of men. 17Tell us, therefore, what do You think? Is it lawful to pay taxes to Caesar, or not?"

18But Jesus perceived their wickedness, and said, "Why do you test Me, *you* hypocrites? 19Show Me the tax money."

So they brought Him a denarius.

20And He said to them, "Whose image and inscription *is* this?"

21They said to Him, "Caesar's."

And He said to them, "Render therefore to Caesar the things that are Caesar's, and to God the things that are God's." 22When they had heard *these words,* they marveled, and left Him and went their way.

23The same day the Sadducees, who say there is no resurrection, came to Him and asked Him, 24saying: "Teacher, Moses said that if a man dies, having no children, his brother shall marry his wife and raise up offspring for his brother. 25Now there were with us seven brothers. The first died after he had married, and having no offspring, left his wife to his brother. 26Likewise the second also, and the third, even to the seventh. 27Last of all the woman died also. 28Therefore, in the resurrection, whose wife of the seven will she be? For they all had her."

29Jesus answered and said to them, "You are mistaken, not knowing the Scriptures nor the power of God. 30For in the resurrection they neither marry nor are given in marriage, but are like

---

22:13 *r*NU-Text omits *take him away, and.*

angels of God[s] in heaven. [31]But concerning the resurrection of the dead, have you not read what was spoken to you by God, saying, [32]*I am the God of Abraham, the God of Isaac, and the God of Jacob'?*[t] God is not the God of the dead, but of the living." [33]And when the multitudes heard *this,* they were astonished at His teaching.

[34]But when the Pharisees heard that He had silenced the Sadducees, they gathered together. [35]Then one of them, a lawyer, asked Him a question, testing Him, and saying, [36]"Teacher, which is the great commandment in the law?"

[37]Jesus said to him, " *'You shall love the LORD your God with all your heart, with all your soul, and with all your mind.'*[u] [38]This is *the* first and great commandment. [39]And *the* second is like it: *'You shall love your neighbor as yourself.'*[v] [40]On these two commandments hang all the Law and the Prophets."

[41]While the Pharisees were gathered together, Jesus asked them, [42]saying, "What do you think about the Christ? Whose Son is He?"

They said to Him, *"The Son* of David."

[43]He said to them, "How then does David in the Spirit call Him *'Lord,'* saying:

[44] *'The* LORD *said to my Lord,*
  "Sit at My right hand,
  Till I make Your enemies Your
    footstool"' ?[w]

[45]If David then calls Him *'Lord,'* how is He his Son?" [46]And no one was able to answer Him a word, nor from that day on did anyone dare question Him anymore.

23
Then* Jesus spoke to the multitudes and to His disciples, [2]saying: "The scribes and the Pharisees sit in Moses' seat. [3]Therefore whatever they tell you to observe,[x] *that* observe and do, but do not do according to their works; for they say, and do not do. [4]For they bind heavy burdens, hard to bear, and lay *them* on men's shoulders; but they *themselves* will not move them with one of their fingers. [5]But all their works they do to be seen by men. They make their phylacteries broad and enlarge the borders of their garments. [6]They love the best places at feasts, the best seats in the synagogues, [7]greetings in the marketplaces, and to be called by men, 'Rabbi, Rabbi.' [8]But you, do not be called 'Rabbi'; for One is your Teacher, the Christ,[y] and you are all brethren. [9]Do not call anyone on earth your father; for One is your Father, He who is in heaven. [10]And do not be called teachers; for One is your Teacher, the Christ. [11]But he who is greatest among you shall be your servant. [12]And whoever exalts himself will be humbled, and he who humbles himself will be exalted.

[13]"But woe to you, scribes and Pharisees,

22:30 [s]NU-Text omits *of God.*   22:32 [t]Exodus 3:6, 15
22:37 [u]Deuteronomy 6:5   22:39 [v]Leviticus 19:18
22:44 [w]Psalm 110:1   23:3 [x]NU-Text omits *to observe.*
23:8 [y]NU-Text omits *the Christ.*   23:14 [z]NU-Text omits this verse.

CHAPTER 23

23:1ff The Word of God has authority even if the people who teach it lack integrity (vv. 1–3). Our Lord's standard is that we both *do* and *teach* His truth (vv. 17–20; 1 Thess. 2:10–12). Those who practice hypocrisy erode their character and do untold damage to others. The tragedy is that hypocrisy blinds people (23:16–19, 24, 26) so that they cannot see the Lord, themselves, or other people.

The God of the Pharisees is not the God of the Bible. He is a rigorous Law Giver who pays back those who pay Him. He is not "the God of all grace" (1 Pet. 5:10) or the loving Father who cares for His children (Ps. 103:1–14).

The Pharisees were blind to themselves. *They* were right, and everybody else was wrong. Because they majored on the externals, they never saw the rottenness in their hearts (23:25–28). Because they majored on the minor details, they ignored the great principles of the Word (v. 23).

Hypocrites never see the damage done to others: closing doors of blessing (v. 13); defiling those who touch them (v. 27); giving people a wrong sense of values (vv. 16–22). No wonder Jesus wept! These "woes" were born of anguish, not anger; and perhaps He is weeping over you and me.

Hypocrisy—Failing to reach your goals or to be all that you want to be is not hypocrisy. Pretending that you have "arrived" is hypocrisy. The word *hypocrite* comes from the Greek word for the mask worn by an actor. Hypocrites deliberately play a part so people will think they are more spiritual than they really are. The remedy for hypocrisy is honesty with yourself and with God (1 John 1:5–10).

hypocrites! For you shut up the kingdom of heaven against men; for you neither go in *yourselves,* nor do you allow those who are entering to go in. [14]Woe to you, scribes and Pharisees, hypocrites! For you devour widows' houses, and for a pretense make long prayers. Therefore you will receive greater condemnation.[z]

[15]"Woe to you, scribes and Pharisees, hypocrites! For you travel land and sea to win one proselyte, and when he is won, you make him twice as much a son of hell as yourselves.

[16]"Woe to you, blind guides, who say, 'Whoever swears by the temple, it is nothing; but whoever swears by the gold of the temple, he is obliged *to perform it.*' [17]Fools and blind! For which is greater, the gold or the temple that sanctifies[a] the gold? [18]And, 'Whoever swears by the altar, it is nothing; but whoever swears by the gift that is on it, he is obliged *to perform it.*' [19]Fools and blind! For which is greater, the gift or the altar that sanctifies the gift? [20]Therefore he who swears by the altar, swears by it and by all things on it. [21]He who swears by the temple, swears by it and by Him who dwells[b] in it. [22]And he who swears by heaven, swears by the throne of God and by Him who sits on it.

[23]"Woe to you, scribes and Pharisees, hypocrites! For you pay tithe of mint and anise and cummin, and have neglected the weightier *matters* of the law: justice and mercy and faith. These you ought to have done, without leaving the others undone. [24]Blind guides, who strain out a gnat and swallow a camel!

[25]"Woe to you, scribes and Pharisees, hypocrites! For you cleanse the outside of the cup and dish, but inside they are full of extortion and self-indulgence.[c] [26]Blind Pharisee, first cleanse the inside of the cup and dish, that the outside of them may be clean also.

[27]"Woe to you, scribes and Pharisees, hypocrites! For you are like whitewashed tombs which indeed appear beautiful outwardly, but inside are full of dead *men's* bones and all uncleanness. [28]Even so you also outwardly appear righteous to men, but inside you are full of hypocrisy and lawlessness.

[29]"Woe to you, scribes and Pharisees, hypocrites! Because you build the tombs of the prophets and adorn the monuments of the righteous, [30]and say, 'If we had lived in the days of our fathers, we would not have been partakers with them in the blood of the prophets.' [31]"Therefore you are witnesses against yourselves that you are sons of those who murdered the prophets. [32]Fill up, then, the measure of your fathers' *guilt.* [33]Serpents, brood of vipers! How can you escape the condemnation of hell? [34]Therefore, indeed, I send you prophets, wise men, and scribes: *some* of them you will kill and crucify, and *some* of them you will scourge in your synagogues and persecute from city to city, [35]that on you may come all the righteous blood shed on the earth, from the blood of righteous Abel to the blood of Zechariah, son of Berechiah, whom you murdered between the temple and the altar. [36]Assuredly, I say to you, all these things will come upon this generation.

[37]"O Jerusalem, Jerusalem, the one who kills

23:17 [a]NU-Text reads *sanctified.* 23:21 [b]M-Text reads *dwelt.*
23:25 [c]M-Text reads *unrighteousness.*

the prophets and stones those who are sent to her! How often I wanted to gather your children together, as a hen gathers her chicks under *her* wings, but you were not willing! 38See! Your house is left to you desolate; 39for I say to you, you shall see Me no more till you say, '*Blessed is He who comes in the name of the LORD!*' "d

24 Then* Jesus went out and departed from the temple, and His disciples came up to show Him the buildings of the temple. 2And Jesus said to them, "Do you not see all these things? Assuredly, I say to you, not *one* stone shall be left here upon another, that shall not be thrown down."

3Now as He sat on the Mount of Olives, the disciples came to Him privately, saying, "Tell us, when will these things be? And what *will be* the sign of Your coming, and of the end of the age?"

4*And Jesus answered and said to them: "Take heed that no one deceives you. 5For many will come in My name, saying, 'I am the Christ,' and will deceive many. 6*And you will hear of wars and rumors of wars. See that you are not troubled; for alle *these things* must come to pass, but the end is not yet. 7For nation will rise against nation, and kingdom against kingdom. And there will be famines, pestilences,f and earthquakes in various places. 8All these *are* the beginning of sorrows.

9"Then they will deliver you up to tribulation and kill you, and you will be hated by all nations for My name's sake. 10And then many will be offended, will betray one another, and will hate one another. 11Then many false prophets will rise up and deceive many. 12*And because lawlessness will abound, the love of many will grow cold. 13But he who endures to the end shall be saved. 14And this gospel of the kingdom will be preached in all the world as a witness to all the nations, and then the end will come.

15"Therefore when you see the '*abomination of desolation,*'g spoken of by Daniel the prophet, standing in the holy place" (whoever reads, let him understand), 16"then let those who are in Judea flee to the mountains. 17Let him who is on the housetop not go down to take anything out of his house. 18And let him who is in the field not go back to get his clothes. 19But woe to those who are pregnant and to those who are nursing babies in those days! 20And pray that your flight may not be in winter or on the Sabbath. 21For then there will be great tribulation, such as has not been since the beginning of the world until this time, no, nor ever shall be. 22And unless those days were shortened, no flesh would be saved; but for the elect's sake those days will be shortened.

23"Then if anyone says to you, 'Look, here *is* the Christ!' or 'There!' do not believe *it*. 24For false christs and false prophets will rise and show great signs and wonders to deceive, if possible, even the elect. 25See, I have told you beforehand.

26"Therefore if they say to you, 'Look, He is in the desert!' do not go out; *or* 'Look, *He is* in the inner rooms!' do not believe *it*. 27For as the lightning comes from the east and flashes to the west, so also will the coming of the Son of Man be.

CHAPTER 24

24:1–35 The Olivet Discourse. Our Lord's words about the desolation of the temple (23:37–39) prompted the disciples to ask Him about the future of the city, the temple, and the nation. In 24:1–35, the theme is the Tribulation ("day of the Lord") that will come upon the world in the last days. Jesus explained the events of the first half of the tribulation (vv. 1–14) and the last half (vv. 15–28); and then He announced His return to earth after the Tribulation (vv. 29–35).

In 24:1–35, the emphasis is on *the signs of His coming to the earth* and is directed primarily to Israel (vv. 15–28), telling the people to watch and be ready. But these words have a message for the church today, because "coming events cast their shadows before." We are looking for the Savior and not for signs (Phil. 3:20), because He can come at any time; but as we see these things developing in our world, we are encouraged to expect Him soon.

24:4, 11 When you listen to the news and see the tensions and troubles in today's world, keep in mind the warnings that the Lord gave.

Do not be deceived. People will make grandiose claims and promises and will deceive many. You have the Word of God to enlighten you (Isa. 8:20) and the Holy Spirit to teach you (John 16:13–15), so you should not go astray (1 John 2:18–29).

24:6–8 *Do not be discouraged.* Political and natural disturbances have always been a part of world history, so do not allow them to discourage you. They are "the beginning of sorrows" (v. 8). The word translated "sorrows" means "birth-pangs." The world's troubles are pregnant with possibilities! God is still on the throne!

24:12, 13 *Do not be defeated.* This has to do with faithfulness under testing until the Lord returns. Do not let the lawlessness around you rob you of your fervor (v. 12). A lost world around you needs to hear the gospel (v. 14), so get busy!

23:39 dPsalm 118:26   24:6 eNU-Text omits *all*.
24:7 fNU-Text omits *pestilences*.   24:15 gDaniel 11:31; 12:11

24:34, 35 Do not be doubtful. Religious leaders will come and go, stand and fall; but the Word will not change. Believe it, obey it, and hold to it—no matter what others may say or do. Your Bible is God's light in this dark world (2 Pet. 1:19–21).

24:36—25:46 This part of the Olivet Discourse focuses on the church rather than Israel. The emphasis is not on signs but on the fact that Jesus can return at any time (vv. 36, 44, 50). When He comes, He will reckon with His servants and reward those who have been faithful; it behooves us to be ready.

24:42–44 Do not be distracted. We "watch" when we stay alert and remind ourselves that our Lord may come at any time. When in your heart you delay His coming (v. 48), you start to lose your effectiveness and witness. Keep watching and working!

CHAPTER 25

25:1–13 When Jesus Christ returns, it will be a time of *separation:* the wise will be separated from the foolish, the faithful servants from the unfaithful, the blessed (sheep) from the cursed (goats). The wise virgins had oil and were prepared to meet the Bridegroom. Many people profess to be Christians but do not have the Holy Spirit (Rom. 8:9) and are not born again. They may mingle with the saved, but they are not really one of them; and they will not enter into the marriage feast.

❝*Great services reveal our possibilities; small services our consecration.*❞

—George Morrison

28For wherever the carcass is, there the eagles will be gathered together.

29"Immediately after the tribulation of those days the sun will be darkened, and the moon will not give its light; the stars will fall from heaven, and the powers of the heavens will be shaken. 30Then the sign of the Son of Man will appear in heaven, and then all the tribes of the earth will mourn, and they will see the Son of Man coming on the clouds of heaven with power and great glory. 31And He will send His angels with a great sound of a trumpet, and they will gather together His elect from the four winds, from one end of heaven to the other.

32"Now learn this parable from the fig tree: When its branch has already become tender and puts forth leaves, you know that summer *is* near. 33So you also, when you see all these things, know that it*h* is near—at the doors! 34*Assuredly, I say to you, this generation will by no means pass away till all these things take place. 35Heaven and earth will pass away, but My words will by no means pass away.

36*"But of that day and hour no one knows, not even the angels of heaven,*i* but My Father only. 37But as the days of Noah *were,* so also will the coming of the Son of Man be. 38For as in the days before the flood, they were eating and drinking, marrying and giving in marriage, until the day that Noah entered the ark, 39and did not know until the flood came and took them all away, so also will the coming of the Son of Man be. 40Then two *men* will be in the field: one will be taken and the other left. 41Two *women will be* grinding at the mill: one will be taken and the other left. 42*Watch therefore, for you do not know what hour*j* your Lord is coming. 43But know this, that if the master of the house had known what hour the thief would come, he would have watched and not allowed his house to be broken into. 44Therefore you also be ready, for the Son of Man is coming at an hour you do not expect.

45"Who then is a faithful and wise servant, whom his master made ruler over his household, to give them food in due season? 46Blessed *is* that servant whom his master, when he comes, will find so doing. 47Assuredly, I say to you that he will make him ruler over all his goods. 48But if that evil servant says in his heart, 'My master is delaying his coming,'*k* 49and begins to beat *his* fellowservants, and to eat and drink with the drunkards, 50the master of that servant will come on a day when he is not looking for *him* and at an hour that he is not aware of, 51and will cut him in two and appoint *him* his portion with the hypocrites. There shall be weeping and gnashing of teeth.

25 "Then* the kingdom of heaven shall be likened to ten virgins who took their lamps and went out to meet the bridegroom. 2Now five of them were wise, and five *were* foolish. 3Those who *were* foolish took their lamps and took no oil with them, 4but the wise took oil in their vessels with their lamps. 5But while the bridegroom was delayed, they all slumbered and slept.

6"And at midnight a cry was *heard:* 'Behold, the bridegroom is coming;*l* go out to meet him!'

24:33 *h*Or *He*   24:36 *i*NU-Text adds *nor the Son.*
24:42 *j*NU-Text reads *day.*   24:48 *k*NU-Text omits *his coming.*
25:6 *l*NU-Text omits *is coming.*

7Then all those virgins arose and trimmed their lamps. 8And the foolish said to the wise, 'Give us *some* of your oil, for our lamps are going out.' 9But the wise answered, saying, 'No, lest there should not be enough for us and you; but go rather to those who sell, and buy for yourselves.' 10And while they went to buy, the bridegroom came, and those who were ready went in with him to the wedding; and the door was shut.

11"Afterward the other virgins came also, saying, 'Lord, Lord, open to us!' 12But he answered and said, 'Assuredly, I say to you, I do not know you.'

13"Watch therefore, for you know neither the day nor the hour[m] in which the Son of Man is coming.

14*"For *the kingdom of heaven is* like a man traveling to a far country, *who* called his own servants and delivered his goods to them. 15And to one he gave five talents, to another two, and to another one, to each according to his own ability; and immediately he went on a journey. 16Then he who had received the five talents went and traded with them, and made another five talents. 17And likewise he who *had received* two gained two more also. 18But he who had received one went and dug in the ground, and hid his lord's money. 19After a long time the lord of those servants came and settled accounts with them.

20"So he who had received five talents came and brought five other talents, saying, 'Lord, you delivered to me five talents; look, I have gained five more talents besides them.' 21His lord said to him, 'Well *done,* good and faithful servant; you were faithful over a few things, I will make you ruler over many things. Enter into the joy of your lord.' 22He also who had received two talents came and said, 'Lord, you delivered to me two talents; look, I have gained two more talents besides them.' 23His lord said to him, 'Well *done,* good and faithful servant; you have been faithful over a few things, I will make you ruler over many things. Enter into the joy of your lord.'

24"Then he who had received the one talent came and said, 'Lord, I knew you to be a hard man, reaping where you have not sown, and gathering where you have not scattered seed. 25And I was afraid, and went and hid your talent in the ground. Look, *there* you have *what is* yours.'

26"But his lord answered and said to him, 'You wicked and lazy servant, you knew that I reap where I have not sown, and gather where I have not scattered seed. 27So you ought to have deposited my money with the bankers, and at my coming I would have received back my own with interest. 28So take the talent from him, and give *it* to him who has ten talents.

29'For to everyone who has, more will be given, and he will have abundance; but from him who does not have, even what he has will be taken away. 30And cast the unprofitable servant into the outer darkness. There will be weeping and gnashing of teeth.'

31*"When the Son of Man comes in His glory, and all the holy[n] angels with Him, then He will sit on the throne of His glory. 32All the nations will be gathered before Him, and He will separate them one from another, as a shepherd divides *his*

25:14–30 His coming also means *evaluation.* As we wait for the Lord to return, we must invest our lives and earn dividends for His glory. Christ gives us opportunities that match our abilities, and the one-talent servant is just as important as the five-talent servant. The key is *faithfulness* (1 Cor. 4:2), for God measures us against ourselves and not against the other servants. Are you afraid to step out by faith and take some risks for God?

25:31–46 When Christ returns, it will be a time of *commendation.* We will be surprised to learn about ministries we performed that we thought were insignificant but that He will reward. This parable is not teaching salvation by good works. Christ's sheep know that they are sheep (John 10:14, 27–30), but they do not always realize what their service means to Christ. We will experience some surprises in that day!

25:13 *m*NU-Text omits the rest of this verse.   25:31 *n*NU-Text omits *holy.*

sheep from the goats. 33And He will set the sheep on His right hand, but the goats on the left. 34Then the King will say to those on His right hand, 'Come, you blessed of My Father, inherit the kingdom prepared for you from the foundation of the world: 35for I was hungry and you gave Me food; I was thirsty and you gave Me drink; I was a stranger and you took Me in; 36I *was* naked and you clothed Me; I was sick and you visited Me; I was in prison and you came to Me.'

37"Then the righteous will answer Him, saying, 'Lord, when did we see You hungry and feed *You,* or thirsty and give *You* drink? 38When did we see You a stranger and take *You* in, or naked and clothe *You?* 39Or when did we see You sick, or in prison, and come to You?' 40And the King will answer and say to them, 'Assuredly, I say to you, inasmuch as you did *it* to one of the least of these My brethren, you did *it* to Me.'

41"Then He will also say to those on the left hand, 'Depart from Me, you cursed, into the everlasting fire prepared for the devil and his angels: 42for I was hungry and you gave Me no food; I was thirsty and you gave Me no drink; 43I was a stranger and you did not take Me in, naked and you did not clothe Me, sick and in prison and you did not visit Me.'

44"Then they also will answer Him,º saying, 'Lord, when did we see You hungry or thirsty or a stranger or naked or sick or in prison, and did not minister to You?' 45Then He will answer them, saying, 'Assuredly, I say to you, inasmuch as you did not do *it* to one of the least of these, you did not do *it* to Me.' 46And these will go away into everlasting punishment, but the righteous into eternal life."

CHAPTER 26

26:1ff Life presents us with many opportunities; how we respond to them depends on what we love and what we look for in life.

26:3–5 The Jewish leaders looked for opportunity to destroy Jesus, while at the same time Jesus was anticipating the opportunity to obey His Father and bring Him glory.

26:6–16 Mary used the opportunity she had for expressing her devotion to Christ, but Judas used that same opportunity to criticize her. Nothing given in love to Jesus is ever wasted. Judas was the one who ended up wasting his life!

❝*God's best gifts are not things but opportunities. What we call adversity, God calls opportunity.*❞

26 Now* it came to pass, when Jesus had finished all these sayings, *that* He said to His disciples, 2"You know that after two days is the Passover, and the Son of Man will be delivered up to be crucified."

3*Then the chief priests, the scribes,ᴾ and the elders of the people assembled at the palace of the high priest, who was called Caiaphas, 4and plotted to take Jesus by trickery and kill *Him.* 5But they said, "Not during the feast, lest there be an uproar among the people."

6*And when Jesus was in Bethany at the house of Simon the leper, 7a woman came to Him having an alabaster flask of very costly fragrant oil, and she poured *it* on His head as He sat *at the table.* 8But when His disciples saw *it,* they were indignant, saying, "Why this waste? 9For this fragrant oil might have been sold for much and given to *the* poor."

10But when Jesus was aware of *it,* He said to them, "Why do you trouble the woman? For she has done a good work for Me. 11For you have the poor with you always, but Me you do not have always. 12For in pouring this fragrant oil on My body, she did *it* for My burial. 13Assuredly, I say to you, wherever this gospel is preached in the whole world, what this woman has done will also be told as a memorial to her."

14Then one of the twelve, called Judas Iscariot, went to the chief priests 15and said, "What are you willing to give me if I deliver Him to you?"

25:44 ºNU-Text and M-Text omit *Him.* 26:3 ᴾNU-Text omits *the scribes.*

And they counted out to him thirty pieces of silver. ¹⁶So from that time he sought opportunity to betray Him.

¹⁷Now on the first *day* of the *Feast* of Unleavened Bread the disciples came to Jesus, saying to Him, "Where do You want us to prepare for You to eat the Passover?"

¹⁸And He said, "Go into the city to a certain man, and say to him, 'The Teacher says, "My time is at hand; I will keep the Passover at your house with My disciples." ' "

¹⁹So the disciples did as Jesus had directed them; and they prepared the Passover.

²⁰*When evening had come, He sat down with the twelve. ²¹Now as they were eating, He said, "Assuredly, I say to you, one of you will betray Me."

²²And they were exceedingly sorrowful, and each of them began to say to Him, "Lord, is it I?"

²³He answered and said, "He who dipped *his* hand with Me in the dish will betray Me. ²⁴The Son of Man indeed goes just as it is written of Him, but woe to that man by whom the Son of Man is betrayed! It would have been good for that man if he had not been born."

²⁵Then Judas, who was betraying Him, answered and said, "Rabbi, is it I?"

He said to him, "You have said it."

²⁶And as they were eating, Jesus took bread, blessed^q and broke *it*, and gave *it* to the disciples and said, "Take, eat; this is My body."

²⁷Then He took the cup, and gave thanks, and gave *it* to them, saying, "Drink from it, all of you. ²⁸For this is My blood of the new^r covenant, which is shed for many for the remission of sins. ²⁹But I say to you, I will not drink of this fruit of the vine from now on until that day when I drink it new with you in My Father's kingdom."

³⁰And when they had sung a hymn, they went out to the Mount of Olives.

³¹Then Jesus said to them, "All of you will be made to stumble because of Me this night, for it is written:

'I will strike the Shepherd,
   And the sheep of the flock will be
      scattered.'^s

³²But after I have been raised, I will go before you to Galilee."

³³*Peter answered and said to Him, "Even if all are made to stumble because of You, I will never be made to stumble."

³⁴Jesus said to him, "Assuredly, I say to you that this night, before the rooster crows, you will deny Me three times."

³⁵Peter said to Him, "Even if I have to die with You, I will not deny You!"

And so said all the disciples.

³⁶Then Jesus came with them to a place called Gethsemane, and said to the disciples, "Sit here while I go and pray over there." ³⁷And He took with Him Peter and the two sons of Zebedee, and He began to be sorrowful and deeply distressed. ³⁸Then He said to them, "My soul is exceedingly sorrowful, even to death. Stay here and watch with Me."

26:20–32 Jesus eagerly anticipated the opportunity to be with His disciples, even though He knew one would betray Him, one would deny Him, and all would forsake Him. He sought to help them and prepare them for the trial before them.

26:33–75 Peter missed his opportunities to become strong and be a victor. He boasted when he should have listened (vv. 32–35), slept when he should have prayed (vv. 36–46), fought when he should have surrendered (vv. 47–56), and followed when he should have fled for safety (vv. 57–75; note v. 31). But when the opportunity came for him to repent, he wept.

No matter what others did, Jesus was in complete command and knew how to make the most of every opportunity. "Not as I will, but as You will" is the secret (v. 39). God will give you many opportunities today. Use them wisely!

26:26 ^qM-Text reads *gave thanks for.*   26:28 ^rNU-Text omits *new.*   26:31 ^sZechariah 13:7

39He went a little farther and fell on His face, and prayed, saying, "O My Father, if it is possible, let this cup pass from Me; nevertheless, not as I will, but as You *will*."

40Then He came to the disciples and found them sleeping, and said to Peter, "What! Could you not watch with Me one hour? 41Watch and pray, lest you enter into temptation. The spirit indeed *is* willing, but the flesh *is* weak."

42Again, a second time, He went away and prayed, saying, "O My Father, if this cup cannot pass away from Me unless[t] I drink it, Your will be done." 43And He came and found them asleep again, for their eyes were heavy.

44So He left them, went away again, and prayed the third time, saying the same words. 45Then He came to His disciples and said to them, "Are *you* still sleeping and resting? Behold, the hour is at hand, and the Son of Man is being betrayed into the hands of sinners. 46Rise, let us be going. See, My betrayer is at hand."

47And while He was still speaking, behold, Judas, one of the twelve, with a great multitude with swords and clubs, came from the chief priests and elders of the people.

48Now His betrayer had given them a sign, saying, "Whomever I kiss, He is the One; seize Him." 49Immediately he went up to Jesus and said, "Greetings, Rabbi!" and kissed Him.

50But Jesus said to him, "Friend, why have you come?"

Then they came and laid hands on Jesus and took Him. 51And suddenly, one of those *who were* with Jesus stretched out *his* hand and drew his sword, struck the servant of the high priest, and cut off his ear.

52But Jesus said to him, "Put your sword in its place, for all who take the sword will perish[u] by the sword. 53Or do you think that I cannot now pray to My Father, and He will provide Me with more than twelve legions of angels? 54How then could the Scriptures be fulfilled, that it must happen thus?"

55In that hour Jesus said to the multitudes, "Have you come out, as against a robber, with swords and clubs to take Me? I sat daily with you, teaching in the temple, and you did not seize Me. 56But all this was done that the Scriptures of the prophets might be fulfilled."

Then all the disciples forsook Him and fled.

57And those who had laid hold of Jesus led *Him* away to Caiaphas the high priest, where the scribes and the elders were assembled. 58But Peter followed Him at a distance to the high priest's courtyard. And he went in and sat with the servants to see the end.

59Now the chief priests, the elders,[v] and all the council sought false testimony against Jesus to put Him to death, 60but found none. Even though many false witnesses came forward, they found none.[w] But at last two false witnesses[x] came forward 61and said, "This *fellow* said, 'I am able to destroy the temple of God and to build it in three days.'"

62And the high priest arose and said to Him,

26:42 [t]NU-Text reads *if this may not pass away unless.*
26:52 [u]M-Text reads *die.*   26:59 [v]NU-Text omits *the elders.*
26:60 [w]NU-Text puts a comma after *but found none,* does not capitalize *Even,* and omits *they found none.* [x]NU-Text omits *false witnesses.*

"Do You answer nothing? What *is it* these men testify against You?" [63]But Jesus kept silent. And the high priest answered and said to Him, "I put You under oath by the living God: Tell us if You are the Christ, the Son of God!"

[64]Jesus said to him, "*It is as* you said. Nevertheless, I say to you, hereafter you will see the Son of Man sitting at the right hand of the Power, and coming on the clouds of heaven."

[65]Then the high priest tore his clothes, saying, "He has spoken blasphemy! What further need do we have of witnesses? Look, now you have heard His blasphemy! [66]What do you think?"

They answered and said, "He is deserving of death."

[67]Then they spat in His face and beat Him; and others struck *Him* with the palms of their hands, [68]saying, "Prophesy to us, Christ! Who is the one who struck You?"

[69]Now Peter sat outside in the courtyard. And a servant girl came to him, saying, "You also were with Jesus of Galilee."

[70]But he denied it before *them* all, saying, "I do not know what you are saying."

[71]And when he had gone out to the gateway, another *girl* saw him and said to those *who were* there, "This *fellow* also was with Jesus of Nazareth."

[72]But again he denied with an oath, "I do not know the Man!"

[73]And a little later those who stood by came up and said to Peter, "Surely you also are *one* of them, for your speech betrays you."

[74]Then he began to curse and swear, *saying*, "I do not know the Man!"

Immediately a rooster crowed. [75]And Peter remembered the word of Jesus who had said to him, "Before the rooster crows, you will deny Me three times." So he went out and wept bitterly.

27 When* morning came, all the chief priests and elders of the people plotted against Jesus to put Him to death. [2]And when they had bound Him, they led Him away and delivered Him to Pontius[y] Pilate the governor.

[3]Then Judas, His betrayer, seeing that He had been condemned, was remorseful and brought back the thirty pieces of silver to the chief priests and elders, [4]saying, "I have sinned by betraying innocent blood."

And they said, "What *is that* to us? You see to it!"

[5]Then he threw down the pieces of silver in the temple and departed, and went and hanged himself.

[6]But the chief priests took the silver pieces and said, "It is not lawful to put them into the treasury, because they are the price of blood." [7]And they consulted together and bought with them the potter's field, to bury strangers in. [8]Therefore that field has been called the Field of Blood to this day.

[9]Then was fulfilled what was spoken by Jeremiah the prophet, saying, *"And they took the thirty pieces of silver, the value of Him who was priced, whom they of the children of Israel priced,* [10]*and gave them for the potter's field, as the Lord directed me."*[z]

CHAPTER 27

27:1ff Jesus is the example to follow when you suffer unjustly (1 Pet. 2:18–23).

❝Leave out the cross, and you have killed the religion of Jesus. Atonement by the blood of Jesus is not an arm of Christian truth; it is the heart of it.❞
—Charles Haddon Spurgeon

27:2 [y]NU-Text omits *Pontius.*   27:10 [z]Jeremiah 32:6–9

27:11–14 *He did not reply when accused.* In this, He fulfilled Isaiah 53:7. There is a time to speak and a time to be silent (Eccles. 3:7), and we must exercise discernment. One thing is sure: no matter what He said, they would not have believed Him.

27:20–31 *He did not retaliate when abused.* He had the power to destroy those who mocked Him; in fact, legions of angels would have delivered Him. But it was the Father's will that He suffer as He did, and Jesus was obedient to His Father's will.

27:34 *He did not accept the cup.* The narcotic drink would have helped deaden the pain, but Jesus refused it. He drank the cup of suffering instead.

11*Now Jesus stood before the governor. And the governor asked Him, saying, "Are You the King of the Jews?"

Jesus said to him, "*It is as* you say." 12And while He was being accused by the chief priests and elders, He answered nothing.

13Then Pilate said to Him, "Do You not hear how many things they testify against You?" 14But He answered him not one word, so that the governor marveled greatly.

15Now at the feast the governor was accustomed to releasing to the multitude one prisoner whom they wished. 16And at that time they had a notorious prisoner called Barabbas.*a* 17Therefore, when they had gathered together, Pilate said to them, "Whom do you want me to release to you? Barabbas, or Jesus who is called Christ?" 18For he knew that they had handed Him over because of envy.

19While he was sitting on the judgment seat, his wife sent to him, saying, "Have nothing to do with that just Man, for I have suffered many things today in a dream because of Him."

20*But the chief priests and elders persuaded the multitudes that they should ask for Barabbas and destroy Jesus. 21The governor answered and said to them, "Which of the two do you want me to release to you?"

They said, "Barabbas!"

22Pilate said to them, "What then shall I do with Jesus who is called Christ?"

They all said to him, "Let Him be crucified!"

23Then the governor said, "Why, what evil has He done?"

But they cried out all the more, saying, "Let Him be crucified!"

24When Pilate saw that he could not prevail at all, but rather *that* a tumult was rising, he took water and washed *his* hands before the multitude, saying, "I am innocent of the blood of this just Person.*b* You see *to it.*"

25And all the people answered and said, "His blood *be* on us and on our children."

26Then he released Barabbas to them; and when he had scourged Jesus, he delivered *Him* to be crucified.

27Then the soldiers of the governor took Jesus into the Praetorium and gathered the whole garrison around Him. 28And they stripped Him and put a scarlet robe on Him. 29When they had twisted a crown of thorns, they put *it* on His head, and a reed in His right hand. And they bowed the knee before Him and mocked Him, saying, "Hail, King of the Jews!" 30Then they spat on Him, and took the reed and struck Him on the head. 31And when they had mocked Him, they took the robe off Him, put His *own* clothes on Him, and led Him away to be crucified.

32Now as they came out, they found a man of Cyrene, Simon by name. Him they compelled to bear His cross. 33And when they had come to a place called Golgotha, that is to say, Place of a Skull, 34*they gave Him sour*c* wine mingled with gall to drink. But when He had tasted *it,* He would not drink.

35Then they crucified Him, and divided His garments, casting lots,*d* that it might be fulfilled which was spoken by the prophet:

27:16 *a*NU-Text reads *Jesus Barabbas.*   27:24 *b*NU-Text omits *just.*   27:34 *c*NU-Text omits *sour.*   27:35 *d*NU-Text and M-Text omit the rest of this verse.

"They divided My garments among them,
And for My clothing they cast lots."e

36Sitting down, they kept watch over Him there. 37And they put up over His head the accusation written against Him:

THIS IS JESUS
THE KING OF THE JEWS.

38Then two robbers were crucified with Him, one on the right and another on the left.

39*And those who passed by blasphemed Him, wagging their heads 40and saying, "You who destroy the temple and build *it* in three days, save Yourself! If You are the Son of God, come down from the cross."

41Likewise the chief priests also, mocking with the scribes and elders,f said, 42"He saved others; Himself He cannot save. If He is the King of Israel,g let Him now come down from the cross, and we will believe Him.h 43He trusted in God; let Him deliver Him now if He will have Him; for He said, 'I am the Son of God.'"

44Even the robbers who were crucified with Him reviled Him with the same thing.

45Now from the sixth hour until the ninth hour there was darkness over all the land. 46And about the ninth hour Jesus cried out with a loud voice, saying, "Eli, Eli, lama sabachthani?" that is, *"My God, My God, why have You forsaken Me?"i*

47Some of those who stood there, when they heard *that,* said, "This Man is calling for Elijah!" 48Immediately one of them ran and took a sponge, filled *it* with sour wine and put *it* on a reed, and offered it to Him to drink.

49The rest said, "Let Him alone; let us see if Elijah will come to save Him."

50And Jesus cried out again with a loud voice, and yielded up His spirit.

51Then, behold, the veil of the temple was torn in two from top to bottom; and the earth quaked, and the rocks were split, 52and the graves were opened; and many bodies of the saints who had fallen asleep were raised; 53and coming out of the graves after His resurrection, they went into the holy city and appeared to many.

54So when the centurion and those with him, who were guarding Jesus, saw the earthquake and the things that had happened, they feared greatly, saying, "Truly this was the Son of God!"

55And many women who followed Jesus from Galilee, ministering to Him, were there looking on from afar, 56among whom were Mary Magdalene, Mary the mother of James and Joses,j and the mother of Zebedee's sons.

57Now when evening had come, there came a rich man from Arimathea, named Joseph, who himself had also become a disciple of Jesus. 58This man went to Pilate and asked for the body of Jesus. Then Pilate commanded the body to be given to him. 59When Joseph had taken the body, he wrapped it in a clean linen cloth, 60and laid it in his new tomb which he had hewn out of the rock; and he rolled a large stone against the door

27:39–44 *He did not come down from the cross.* Had He come down from the cross, the people still would not have believed in Him. And if He saved Himself, He could not save others (John 12:23–28). First the suffering, then the glory; first the cross, then the crown. Remember that the next time you are tempted to take the easy way.

ePsalm 22:18   27:41 fM-Text reads *with the scribes, the Pharisees, and the elders.*   27:42 gNU-Text reads *He is the King of Israel!* hNU-Text and M-Text read *we will believe in Him.*   27:46 iPsalm 22:1   27:56 jNU-Text reads *Joseph.*

of the tomb, and departed. [61]And Mary Magdalene was there, and the other Mary, sitting opposite the tomb.

[62]On the next day, which followed the Day of Preparation, the chief priests and Pharisees gathered together to Pilate, [63]saying, "Sir, we remember, while He was still alive, how that deceiver said, 'After three days I will rise.' [64]Therefore command that the tomb be made secure until the third day, lest His disciples come by night[k] and steal Him *away*, and say to the people, 'He has risen from the dead.' So the last deception will be worse than the first."

[65]Pilate said to them, "You have a guard; go your way, make *it* as secure as you know how." [66]So they went and made the tomb secure, sealing the stone and setting the guard.

CHAPTER 28

28:2–5 The message of the empty tomb is, "Do not be afraid!"

He overcomes His enemies. In His death and resurrection, our Lord defeated the world (John 16:33), the flesh (Rom. 6:1–7), the devil (John 12:31), and death itself (1 Cor. 15:50–58). You need not be afraid of life or death, time or eternity (Rev. 1:17–18).

28:6 ***He keeps His promises.*** Because His followers forgot His resurrection promise, they were sorrowing instead of rejoicing. The Lord always keeps His promises, no matter how dark the day may be.

28:7–10 ***He goes before you.*** When the women ran to share the message, they met the Lord; you always meet Him in the path of obedience. The Shepherd goes before the sheep and prepares the way for them (John 10:4). You have a living and victorious Savior who has everything under control. Trust Him!

28 Now after the Sabbath, as the first *day* of the week began to dawn, Mary Magdalene and the other Mary came to see the tomb. [2]*And behold, there was a great earthquake; for an angel of the Lord descended from heaven, and came and rolled back the stone from the door,[l] and sat on it. [3]His countenance was like lightning, and his clothing as white as snow. [4]And the guards shook for fear of him, and became like dead *men.*

[5]But the angel answered and said to the women, "Do not be afraid, for I know that you seek Jesus who was crucified. [6]*He is not here; for He is risen, as He said. Come, see the place where the Lord lay. [7]*And go quickly and tell His disciples that He is risen from the dead, and indeed He is going before you into Galilee; there you will see Him. Behold, I have told you."

[8]So they went out quickly from the tomb with fear and great joy, and ran to bring His disciples word.

[9]And as they went to tell His disciples,[m] behold, Jesus met them, saying, "Rejoice!" So they came and held Him by the feet and worshiped Him. [10]Then Jesus said to them, "Do not be afraid. Go *and* tell My brethren to go to Galilee, and there they will see Me."

[11]Now while they were going, behold, some of the guard came into the city and reported to the chief priests all the things that had happened. [12]When they had assembled with the elders and consulted together, they gave a large sum of money to the soldiers, [13]saying, "Tell them, 'His disciples came *away* at night and stole Him *away* while we slept.' [14]And if this comes to the governor's ears, we will appease him and make you secure." [15]So they took the money and did as they were instructed; and this saying is commonly reported among the Jews until this day.

[16]Then the eleven disciples went away into Galilee, to the mountain which Jesus had appointed for them. [17]When they saw Him, they worshiped Him; but some doubted.

27:64 [k]NU-Text omits *by night*.   28:2 [l]NU-Text omits *from the door*.   28:9 [m]NU-Text omits the first clause of this verse.

The Resurrection—The resurrection of Jesus Christ is a vital part of the gospel message, for a dead Christ can save nobody (1 Cor. 15:1–19). The empty tomb is proof that He is the Son of God (Rom. 1:4); that believers have a future inheritance (1 Pet. 1:3ff.); that we will once again meet Christians who have died (1 Thess. 4:14–18); that our Christian ministry is not in vain (1 Cor. 15:50–58); and that Jesus Christ will one day judge lost sinners (Acts 17:30–31). The early church bore witness of the resurrection of Jesus Christ (Acts 1:22; 4:2, 33), and so should we today.

18*And Jesus came and spoke to them, saying, "All authority has been given to Me in heaven and on earth. 19Go therefore[n] and make disciples of all the nations, baptizing them in the name of the Father and of the Son and of the Holy Spirit, 20teaching them to observe all things that I have commanded you; and lo, I am with you always, *even* to the end of the age." Amen.[o]

28:19 [n]M-Text omits *therefore.*   28:20 [o]NU-Text omits *Amen.*

28:18–20 *He is our Lord.* He has *all* authority; He commands us to take the gospel to *all nations;* and He promises to be with us *always.* What more assurance could we want? We are His ambassadors (2 Cor. 5:20) and should be faithful to Him in *all things.*

MARK

John Mark was the cousin of Barnabas (Col. 4:10; Acts 4:36–37; 11:19–30) and the son of Mary, a leading woman in the Jerusalem church (Acts 12:12). He helped Paul and Barnabas on their first missionary journey (Acts 12:25—13:5) but for some reason did not remain with them (Acts 13:13). That failure caused Paul and Barnabas to separate, but Barnabas gave Mark another chance (Acts 15:36–41). In later years, Mark became one of Paul's associates (Philem. 24); and Paul commended him for his work (2 Tim. 4:11). It all ended well.

First Peter 5:13 suggests that John Mark was converted through Peter's ministry. Many Bible scholars believe that Mark's gospel is a record of Peter's reports of the ministry of Christ, presenting Jesus Christ as the Servant of God (Mark 10:45). Mark often used the word *immediately*, for he describes the work of a Servant who was busy obeying His Father and meeting the needs of people (1:10, 12, 20–21, etc.). Mark wrote with the Romans in mind, an active people who admired accomplishment.

After a brief introduction (1:1–13), the book tells of Christ's ministry in Galilee (1:14—9:50), His journey to Jerusalem (chap. 10), His ministry in Jerusalem, climaxing with His crucifixion (chaps. 11—15), and His resurrection and ascension (chap. 16).

CHAPTER 1

1:2–13 Even a servant must have credentials, and our Lord has the very best. His coming was prophesied by Isaiah (40:3) and Malachi (3:1) and announced by John the Baptist. The Father and the Holy Spirit commended Him (vv. 9–11), and Satan could not defeat Him (vv. 12–13). He is a Servant you can trust.

1 The beginning of the gospel of Jesus Christ, the Son of God. 2*As it is written in the Prophets:[a]

> "Behold, I send My messenger before Your face,
>   Who will prepare Your way before You."[b]
> 3 "The voice of one crying in the wilderness:
>   'Prepare the way of the LORD;
>   Make His paths straight.' "[c]

4John came baptizing in the wilderness and preaching a baptism of repentance for the remission of sins. 5Then all the land of Judea, and those from Jerusalem, went out to him and were all baptized by him in the Jordan River, confessing their sins.

6Now John was clothed with camel's hair and with a leather belt around his waist, and he ate locusts and wild honey. 7And he preached, saying, "There comes One after me who is mightier than I, whose sandal strap I am not worthy to stoop down and loose. 8I indeed baptized you with water, but He will baptize you with the Holy Spirit."

9It came to pass in those days *that* Jesus came from Nazareth of Galilee, and was baptized by John in the Jordan. 10And immediately, coming up from[d] the water, He saw the heavens parting and the Spirit descending upon Him like a dove. 11Then a voice came from heaven, "You are My beloved Son, in whom I am well pleased."

12Immediately the Spirit drove Him into the wilderness. 13And He was there in the wilderness forty days, tempted by Satan, and was with the wild beasts; and the angels ministered to Him.

14Now after John was put in prison, Jesus came to Galilee, preaching the gospel of the kingdom[e] of God, 15and saying, "The time is fulfilled, and

---

1:2 [a]NU-Text reads *Isaiah the prophet.* [b]Malachi 3:1
1:3 [c]Isaiah 40:3   1:10 [d]NU-Text reads *out of.*   1:14 [e]NU-Text omits *of the kingdom.*

the kingdom of God is at hand. Repent, and believe in the gospel."

16*And as He walked by the Sea of Galilee, He saw Simon and Andrew his brother casting a net into the sea; for they were fishermen. 17Then Jesus said to them, "Follow Me, and I will make you become fishers of men." 18They immediately left their nets and followed Him.

19When He had gone a little farther from there, He saw James the *son* of Zebedee, and John his brother, who also *were* in the boat mending their nets. 20And immediately He called them, and they left their father Zebedee in the boat with the hired servants, and went after Him.

21Then they went into Capernaum, and immediately on the Sabbath He entered the synagogue and taught. 22And they were astonished at His teaching, for He taught them as one having authority, and not as the scribes.

23Now there was a man in their synagogue with an unclean spirit. And he cried out, 24saying, "Let *us* alone! What have we to do with You, Jesus of Nazareth? Did You come to destroy us? I know who You are—the Holy One of God!"

25But Jesus rebuked him, saying, "Be quiet, and come out of him!" 26And when the unclean spirit had convulsed him and cried out with a loud voice, he came out of him. 27Then they were all amazed, so that they questioned among themselves, saying, "What is this? What new doctrine *is* this? For with authority*f* He commands even the unclean spirits, and they obey Him." 28And immediately His fame spread throughout all the region around Galilee.

29Now as soon as they had come out of the synagogue, they entered the house of Simon and Andrew, with James and John. 30But Simon's wife's mother lay sick with a fever, and they told Him about her at once. 31So He came and took her by the hand and lifted her up, and immediately the fever left her. And she served them.

32At evening, when the sun had set, they brought to Him all who were sick and those who were demon-possessed. 33And the whole city was gathered together at the door. 34Then He healed many who were sick with various diseases, and cast out many demons; and He did not allow the demons to speak, because they knew Him.

35*Now in the morning, having risen a long while before daylight, He went out and departed to a solitary place; and there He prayed. 36And Simon and those *who were* with Him searched for Him. 37When they found Him, they said to Him, "Everyone is looking for You."

38But He said to them, "Let us go into the next towns, that I may preach there also, because for this purpose I have come forth."

39And He was preaching in their synagogues throughout all Galilee, and casting out demons.

40Now a leper came to Him, imploring Him, kneeling down to Him and saying to Him, "If You are willing, You can make me clean."

41Then Jesus, moved with compassion, stretched out *His* hand and touched him, and said to him, "I am willing; be cleansed." 42As soon as He had spoken, immediately the leprosy left him, and he was cleansed. 43And He strictly warned him and sent him away at once, 44and said to him,

1:16–45 But what can He do? What is His work? He can guide your life and make it a success (vv. 16–20). He can overcome Satan (vv. 21–28) and sickness (vv. 29–34, 40–45) and use you to bring the message of salvation to a lost and needy world (vv. 35–39). You can be a servant of the Servant and share in His wonderful work.

1:35 Where did the Servant get His power? He depended on the Holy Spirit (v. 12) and prayer (v. 35). He did not allow the demands of the work to rob Him of the time He needed to renew His strength. If the holy Son of God needed to pray, how much more do you need to pray! In the Lord's service, you cannot "run on empty." (See Isa. 40:28–31.)

1:27 *f*NU-Text reads *What is this? A new doctrine with authority.*

"See that you say nothing to anyone; but go your way, show yourself to the priest, and offer for your cleansing those things which Moses commanded, as a testimony to them."

45However, he went out and began to proclaim *it* freely, and to spread the matter, so that Jesus could no longer openly enter the city, but was outside in deserted places; and they came to Him from every direction.

2 And again He entered Capernaum after *some* days, and it was heard that He was in the house. 2Immediately^g many gathered together, so that there was no longer room to receive *them*, not even near the door. And He preached the word to them. 3Then they came to Him, bringing a paralytic who was carried by four *men*. 4And when they could not come near Him because of the crowd, they uncovered the roof where He was. So when they had broken through, they let down the bed on which the paralytic was lying.

5*When Jesus saw their faith, He said to the paralytic, "Son, your sins are forgiven you."

6And some of the scribes were sitting there and reasoning in their hearts, 7"Why does this *Man* speak blasphemies like this? Who can forgive sins but God alone?"

8But immediately, when Jesus perceived in His spirit that they reasoned thus within themselves, He said to them, "Why do you reason about these things in your hearts? 9Which is easier, to say to the paralytic, '*Your* sins are forgiven you,' or to say, 'Arise, take up your bed and walk'? 10But that you may know that the Son of Man has power on earth to forgive sins"—He said to the paralytic, 11"I say to you, arise, take up your bed, and go to your house." 12Immediately he arose, took up the bed, and went out in the presence of them all, so that all were amazed and glorified God, saying, "We never saw *anything* like this!"

13Then He went out again by the sea; and all the multitude came to Him, and He taught them. 14*As He passed by, He saw Levi the *son* of Alphaeus sitting at the tax office. And He said to him, "Follow Me." So he arose and followed Him.

15Now it happened, as He was dining in *Levi's* house, that many tax collectors and sinners also sat together with Jesus and His disciples; for there were many, and they followed Him. 16And when the scribes and^h Pharisees saw Him eating with the tax collectors and sinners, they said to His disciples, "How *is* it that He eats and drinks with tax collectors and sinners?"

17When Jesus heard *it*, He said to them, "Those who are well have no need of a physician, but those who are sick. I did not come to call *the* righteous, but sinners, to repentance."^{i}

18The disciples of John and of the Pharisees were fasting. Then they came and said to Him, "Why do the disciples of John and of the Pharisees fast, but Your disciples do not fast?"

CHAPTER 2

2:5–12 Consider the unique ministries of God's Servant, Jesus Christ. **He forgives our sins.** Imagine a servant having such authority! The healing of the body is a great miracle, but it does not last. The forgiveness of sin is God's greatest miracle, for it lasts forever and accomplishes the greatest good. The Servant forgives us *and pays the price for the miracle!*

2:14–22 He fellowships with "sinners." Why? Because they are sick, and He is the only Physician who can heal them. They are hungry and lonely, and He is the Bridegroom who asks them to His wedding feast. Their lives are in tatters, and He wants to give them a new robe of righteousness. Others may be able to patch up life, but He alone can give new life.

2:2 ^{g}NU-Text omits *Immediately*.   2:16 ^{h}NU-Text reads *of the*.
2:17 ^{i}NU-Text omits *to repentance*.

Garments of New Life—Our first parents tried to cover their sins with garments they made (Gen. 3:7), but God would not accept them. Instead, He clothed them with skins (Gen. 3:21); blood had to be shed (Heb. 9:22). Jesus did not come to do a patchwork job on our lives; He came to make us whole. We have been raised from the dead (Eph. 2:1–10); and like Lazarus, we must take off the old garments of death and put on the garments of new life (John 11:44; Col. 3:1ff.).

19And Jesus said to them, "Can the friends of the bridegroom fast while the bridegroom is with them? As long as they have the bridegroom with them they cannot fast. 20But the days will come when the bridegroom will be taken away from them, and then they will fast in those days. 21No one sews a piece of unshrunk cloth on an old garment; or else the new piece pulls away from the old, and the tear is made worse. 22And no one puts new wine into old wineskins; or else the new wine bursts the wineskins, the wine is spilled, and the wineskins are ruined. But new wine must be put into new wineskins."

23*Now it happened that He went through the grainfields on the Sabbath; and as they went His disciples began to pluck the heads of grain. 24And the Pharisees said to Him, "Look, why do they do what is not lawful on the Sabbath?"

25But He said to them, "Have you never read what David did when he was in need and hungry, he and those with him: 26how he went into the house of God *in the days* of Abiathar the high priest, and ate the showbread, which is not lawful to eat except for the priests, and also gave some to those who were with him?"

27And He said to them, "The Sabbath was made for man, and not man for the Sabbath. 28Therefore the Son of Man is also Lord of the Sabbath."

3 And* He entered the synagogue again, and a man was there who had a withered hand. 2So they watched Him closely, whether He would heal him on the Sabbath, so that they might accuse Him. 3And He said to the man who had the withered hand, "Step forward." 4Then He said to them, "Is it lawful on the Sabbath to do good or to do evil, to save life or to kill?" But they kept silent. 5And when He had looked around at them with anger, being grieved by the hardness of their hearts, He said to the man, "Stretch out your hand." And he stretched *it* out, and his hand was restored as whole as the other.*j* 6Then the Pharisees went out and immediately plotted with the Herodians against Him, how they might destroy Him.

7*But Jesus withdrew with His disciples to the sea. And a great multitude from Galilee followed Him, and from Judea 8and Jerusalem and Idumea and beyond the Jordan; and those from Tyre and Sidon, a great multitude, when they heard how many things He was doing, came to Him. 9So He told His disciples that a small boat should be kept ready for Him because of the multitude, lest they should crush Him. 10For He healed many, so that as many as had afflictions pressed about Him to touch Him. 11And the unclean spirits, whenever they saw Him, fell down before Him and cried out, saying, "You are the Son of God." 12But He sternly warned them that they should not make Him known.

13And He went up on the mountain and called to *Him* those He Himself wanted. And they came to Him. 14Then He appointed twelve,*k* that they might be with Him and that He might send them out to preach, 15and to have power to heal sicknesses and*l* to cast out demons: 16Simon,*m* to

2:23–28 *He frees us from bondage.* He is Lord of the Sabbath, the Giver of rest (Matt. 11:28–30). Man's religious traditions can be a terrible yoke of bondage; but when you follow the Lord, you experience freedom and rest.

CHAPTER 3

3:1–6, 20–30 *Some resist the Servant.* The religious leaders were more concerned about protecting their tradition than helping a man with a handicapping condition. In spite of all that Jesus did and said, they hardened their hearts and resisted His ministry, even to the extent of accusing Him of being in league with Satan. In the end, *they* cooperated with the evil one!

3:7–19 *Some assist the Servant.* The crowds were so large that Jesus had to empower His disciples to help Him in ministry. There is a job for everyone, even if only giving Him a little boat to use (v. 9). If you want to assist Him, remember that the most important thing is *being with Him* (v. 14). As He said, "Without Me, you can do nothing" (John 15:5).

3:5 *j*NU-Text omits *as whole as the other.* 3:14 *k*NU-Text adds *whom He also named apostles.* 3:15 *l*NU-Text omits *to heal sicknesses and.* 3:16 *m*NU-Text reads *and He appointed the twelve: Simon . . . .*

whom He gave the name Peter; [17]James the *son* of Zebedee and John the brother of James, to whom He gave the name Boanerges, that is, "Sons of Thunder"; [18]Andrew, Philip, Bartholomew, Matthew, Thomas, James the *son* of Alphaeus, Thaddaeus, Simon the Cananite; [19]and Judas Iscariot, who also betrayed Him. And they went into a house.

[20]Then the multitude came together again, so that they could not so much as eat bread. [21]But when His own people heard *about this,* they went out to lay hold of Him, for they said, "He is out of His mind."

[22]And the scribes who came down from Jerusalem said, "He has Beelzebub," and, "By the ruler of the demons He casts out demons."

[23]So He called them to *Himself* and said to them in parables: "How can Satan cast out Satan? [24]If a kingdom is divided against itself, that kingdom cannot stand. [25]And if a house is divided against itself, that house cannot stand. [26]And if Satan has risen up against himself, and is divided, he cannot stand, but has an end. [27]No one can enter a strong man's house and plunder his goods, unless he first binds the strong man. And then he will plunder his house.

[28]"Assuredly, I say to you, all sins will be forgiven the sons of men, and whatever blasphemies they may utter; [29]but he who blasphemes against the Holy Spirit never has forgiveness, but is subject to eternal condemnation"— [30]because they said, "He has an unclean spirit."

[31]*Then His brothers and His mother came, and standing outside they sent to Him, calling Him. [32]And a multitude was sitting around Him; and they said to Him, "Look, Your mother and Your brothers[n] are outside seeking You."

[33]But He answered them, saying, "Who is My mother, or My brothers?" [34]And He looked around in a circle at those who sat about Him, and said, "Here are My mother and My brothers! [35]For whoever does the will of God is My brother and My sister and mother."

3:31–35 *Some mistrust the Servant.* Mary bore other children after the birth of Jesus, but they did not believe in Him (John 7:1–5). Even His mother seemed to have doubts about her "popular" Son who was arousing the anger of the leaders. But Jesus was doing the will of God, and so should we (v. 35).

CHAPTER 4

4:3–25 *Receiving God's Word.* Even when we read the Bible, we should *hear* the voice of God speaking to our hearts. It must be personal. Never treat the Bible like any other book (1 Thess. 2:13). Jesus warns us to take heed *that* we hear (4:9), *what* we hear (v. 24), and *how* we hear (Luke 8:18). The more of the Word we receive and share, the more God will give to us.

4 And again He began to teach by the sea. And a great multitude was gathered to Him, so that He got into a boat and sat *in it* on the sea; and the whole multitude was on the land facing the sea. [2]Then He taught them many things by parables, and said to them in His teaching:

[3]*"Listen! Behold, a sower went out to sow. [4]And it happened, as he sowed, *that* some *seed* fell by the wayside; and the birds of the air[o] came and devoured it. [5]Some fell on stony ground, where it did not have much earth; and immediately it sprang up because it had no depth of earth. [6]But when the sun was up it was scorched, and because it had no root it withered away. [7]And some *seed* fell among thorns; and the thorns grew up and choked it, and it yielded no crop. [8]But other *seed* fell on good ground and yielded a crop that sprang up, increased and produced: some thirtyfold, some sixty, and some a hundred."

[9]And He said to them,[p] "He who has ears to hear, let him hear!"

[10]But when He was alone, those around Him

3:32 [n]NU-Text and M-Text add *and Your sisters.*
4:4 [o]NU-Text and M-Text omit *of the air.*   4:9 [p]NU-Text and M-Text omit *to them.*

with the twelve asked Him about the parable. ¹¹And He said to them, "To you it has been given to know the mystery of the kingdom of God; but to those who are outside, all things come in parables, ¹²so that

> 'Seeing they may see and not perceive,
> And hearing they may hear and not
>   understand;
> Lest they should turn,
> And their sins be forgiven them.'"�q

¹³And He said to them, "Do you not understand this parable? How then will you understand all the parables? ¹⁴The sower sows the word. ¹⁵And these are the ones by the wayside where the word is sown. When they hear, Satan comes immediately and takes away the word that was sown in their hearts. ¹⁶These likewise are the ones sown on stony ground who, when they hear the word, immediately receive it with gladness; ¹⁷and they have no root in themselves, and so endure only for a time. Afterward, when tribulation or persecution arises for the word's sake, immediately they stumble. ¹⁸Now these are the ones sown among thorns; *they are* the ones who hear the word, ¹⁹and the cares of this world, the deceitfulness of riches, and the desires for other things entering in choke the word, and it becomes unfruitful. ²⁰But these are the ones sown on good ground, those who hear the word, accept *it,* and bear fruit: some thirtyfold, some sixty, and some a hundred."

²¹Also He said to them, "Is a lamp brought to be put under a basket or under a bed? Is it not to be set on a lampstand? ²²For there is nothing hidden which will not be revealed, nor has anything been kept secret but that it should come to light. ²³If anyone has ears to hear, let him hear."

²⁴Then He said to them, "Take heed what you hear. With the same measure you use, it will be measured to you; and to you who hear, more will be given. ²⁵For whoever has, to him more will be given; but whoever does not have, even what he has will be taken away from him."

²⁶*And He said, "The kingdom of God is as if a man should scatter seed on the ground, ²⁷and should sleep by night and rise by day, and the seed should sprout and grow, he himself does not know how. ²⁸For the earth yields crops by itself: first the blade, then the head, after that the full grain in the head. ²⁹But when the grain ripens, immediately he puts in the sickle, because the harvest has come."

³⁰Then He said, "To what shall we liken the kingdom of God? Or with what parable shall we picture it? ³¹*It is* like a mustard seed which, when it is sown on the ground, is smaller than all the seeds on earth; ³²but when it is sown, it grows up and becomes greater than all herbs, and shoots out large branches, so that the birds of the air may nest under its shade."

³³And with many such parables He spoke the word to them as they were able to hear *it.* ³⁴But without a parable He did not speak to them. And when they were alone, He explained all things to His disciples.

4:26–29 *Reaping God's harvest.* It is our job to sow the seed; we cannot make the seed germinate and produce a harvest. Even a busy farmer must sleep and let God work! However, when the harvest is ready, we must be alert and reap it, or the harvest may be lost (John 4:35–38).

4:12 �q Isaiah 6:9, 10

4:35–41 *Relying on God's power.* Our faith in His Word is tested in the storms of life. If the disciples had really trusted His Word (v. 35), they would not have panicked and accused Him of not caring. You can trust His Word, for it will never fail.

CHAPTER 5

5:1–20 *The Servant comes to us.* Jesus went through a storm to get to two demoniacs (Matt. 8:28) who needed his help. The demons begged not to be sent to the pit (5:10), the citizens begged Jesus to leave (v. 17), and one healed man begged to be allowed to go with Jesus (v. 18). The citizens were concerned more with financial profit than with spiritual benefit. Imagine asking Jesus to leave you!

35*On the same day, when evening had come, He said to them, "Let us cross over to the other side." 36Now when they had left the multitude, they took Him along in the boat as He was. And other little boats were also with Him. 37And a great windstorm arose, and the waves beat into the boat, so that it was already filling. 38But He was in the stern, asleep on a pillow. And they awoke Him and said to Him, "Teacher, do You not care that we are perishing?"

39Then He arose and rebuked the wind, and said to the sea, "Peace, be still!" And the wind ceased and there was a great calm. 40But He said to them, "Why are you so fearful? How *is it* that you have no faith?"ʳ 41And they feared exceedingly, and said to one another, "Who can this be, that even the wind and the sea obey Him!"

5 Then* they came to the other side of the sea, to the country of the Gadarenes.ˢ 2And when He had come out of the boat, immediately there met Him out of the tombs a man with an unclean spirit, 3who had *his* dwelling among the tombs; and no one could bind him,ᵗ not even with chains, 4because he had often been bound with shackles and chains. And the chains had been pulled apart by him, and the shackles broken in pieces; neither could anyone tame him. 5And always, night and day, he was in the mountains and in the tombs, crying out and cutting himself with stones.

6When he saw Jesus from afar, he ran and worshiped Him. 7And he cried out with a loud voice and said, "What have I to do with You, Jesus, Son of the Most High God? I implore You by God that You do not torment me."

8For He said to him, "Come out of the man, unclean spirit!" 9Then He asked him, "What *is* your name?"

And he answered, saying, "My name *is* Legion; for we are many." 10Also he begged Him earnestly that He would not send them out of the country.

11Now a large herd of swine was feeding there near the mountains. 12So all the demons begged Him, saying, "Send us to the swine, that we may enter them." 13And at once Jesusᵘ gave them permission. Then the unclean spirits went out and entered the swine (there were about two thousand); and the herd ran violently down the steep place into the sea, and drowned in the sea.

14So those who fed the swine fled, and they told *it* in the city and in the country. And they went out to see what it was that had happened. 15Then they came to Jesus, and saw the one *who had been* demon-possessed and had the legion, sitting and clothed and in his right mind. And they were afraid. 16And those who saw it told them how it happened to him *who had been* demon-possessed, and about the swine. 17Then they began to plead with Him to depart from their region.

18And when He got into the boat, he who had been demon-possessed begged Him that he might be with Him. 19However, Jesus did not permit him, but said to him, "Go home to your friends, and tell them what great things the Lord has done for you, and how He has had compassion on you." 20And he departed and began to proclaim in De-

---

4:40 ʳNU-Text reads *Have you still no faith?* 5:1 ˢNU-Text reads *Gerasenes.* 5:3 ᵗNU-Text adds *anymore.*
5:13 ᵘNU-Text reads *And He gave.*

capolis all that Jesus had done for him; and all marveled.

21*Now when Jesus had crossed over again by boat to the other side, a great multitude gathered to Him; and He was by the sea. 22And behold, one of the rulers of the synagogue came, Jairus by name. And when he saw Him, he fell at His feet 23and begged Him earnestly, saying, "My little daughter lies at the point of death. Come and lay Your hands on her, that she may be healed, and she will live." 24So Jesus went with him, and a great multitude followed Him and thronged Him.

25Now a certain woman had a flow of blood for twelve years, 26and had suffered many things from many physicians. She had spent all that she had and was no better, but rather grew worse. 27When she heard about Jesus, she came behind Him in the crowd and touched His garment. 28For she said, "If only I may touch His clothes, I shall be made well." 29Immediately the fountain of her blood was dried up, and she felt in her body that she was healed of the affliction. 30And Jesus, immediately knowing in Himself that power had gone out of Him, turned around in the crowd and said, "Who touched My clothes?"

31But His disciples said to Him, "You see the multitude thronging You, and You say, 'Who touched Me?'"

32And He looked around to see her who had done this thing. 33But the woman, fearing and trembling, knowing what had happened to her, came and fell down before Him and told Him the whole truth. 34And He said to her, "Daughter, your faith has made you well. Go in peace, and be healed of your affliction."

35*While He was still speaking, some came from the ruler of the synagogue's house who said, "Your daughter is dead. Why trouble the Teacher any further?"

36As soon as Jesus heard the word that was spoken, He said to the ruler of the synagogue, "Do not be afraid; only believe." 37And He permitted no one to follow Him except Peter, James, and John the brother of James. 38Then He came to the house of the ruler of the synagogue, and saw a tumult and those who wept and wailed loudly. 39When He came in, He said to them, "Why make this commotion and weep? The child is not dead, but sleeping."

40And they ridiculed Him. But when He had put them all outside, He took the father and the mother of the child, and those who were with Him, and entered where the child was lying. 41Then He took the child by the hand, and said to her, "Talitha, cumi," which is translated, "Little girl, I say to you, arise." 42Immediately the girl arose and walked, for she was twelve years of age. And they were overcome with great amazement. 43But He commanded them strictly that no one should know it, and said that something should be given her to eat.

6 Then* He went out from there and came to His own country, and His disciples followed Him. 2And when the Sabbath had come, He began to teach in the synagogue. And many hearing Him were astonished, saying, "Where did this Man get these things? And what wisdom is this which is given to Him, that such mighty works are performed by His hands! 3Is this not the carpenter,

5:21–34 We can come to the Servant. All kinds of people came to the feet of Jesus. A well-known synagogue leader and an anonymous sick woman could find help there. Perhaps the woman's faith was a bit superstitious, but the Lord still honored it. If you cannot grasp His hand, touch the hem of His garment. The first step of faith, no matter how weak, will lead to greater blessings.

5:35–43 The Servant will go with us. No situation is so desperate that Jesus cannot work. Disease, delays, and even death are under His control. Jesus goes with you to the place of disappointment and sorrow and meets your needs. No matter how depressing your situation may appear, "Do not be afraid; only believe" (v. 36). The Servant is working for you.

CHAPTER 6

6:1–29 The Servant cannot work. His neighbors were amazed at what Jesus said and did, but Jesus was amazed at their unbelief that would not let Him do more: "According to your faith let it be to you" (Matt. 9:29; Ps. 78:41). Ask God to strengthen your faith so that you can glorify Him (Rom. 4:20–21). Our Lord's response to their unbelief was to send out His disciples to minister. Herod silenced one voice, but he could not silence the Word of God (Col. 4:2–4).

the Son of Mary, and brother of James, Joses, Judas, and Simon? And are not His sisters here with us?" So they were offended at Him.

⁴But Jesus said to them, "A prophet is not without honor except in his own country, among his own relatives, and in his own house." ⁵Now He could do no mighty work there, except that He laid His hands on a few sick people and healed *them.* ⁶And He marveled because of their unbelief. Then He went about the villages in a circuit, teaching.

⁷And He called the twelve to *Himself,* and began to send them out two *by* two, and gave them power over unclean spirits. ⁸He commanded them to take nothing for the journey except a staff— no bag, no bread, no copper in *their* money belts— ⁹but to wear sandals, and not to put on two tunics.

¹⁰Also He said to them, "In whatever place you enter a house, stay there till you depart from that place. ¹¹And whoeverᵛ will not receive you nor hear you, when you depart from there, shake off the dust under your feet as a testimony against them.ʷ Assuredly, I say to you, it will be more tolerable for Sodom and Gomorrah in the day of judgment than for that city!"

¹²So they went out and preached that *people* should repent. ¹³And they cast out many demons, and anointed with oil many who were sick, and healed *them.*

¹⁴Now King Herod heard *of Him,* for His name had become well known. And he said, "John the Baptist is risen from the dead, and therefore these powers are at work in him."

¹⁵Others said, "It is Elijah."

And others said, "It is the Prophet, orˣ like one of the prophets."

¹⁶But when Herod heard, he said, "This is John, whom I beheaded; he has been raised from the dead!" ¹⁷For Herod himself had sent and laid hold of John, and bound him in prison for the sake of Herodias, his brother Philip's wife; for he had married her. ¹⁸Because John had said to Herod, "It is not lawful for you to have your brother's wife."

¹⁹Therefore Herodias held it against him and wanted to kill him, but she could not; ²⁰for Herod feared John, knowing that he *was* a just and holy man, and he protected him. And when he heard him, he did many things, and heard him gladly.

²¹Then an opportune day came when Herod on his birthday gave a feast for his nobles, the high officers, and the chief *men* of Galilee. ²²And when Herodias' daughter herself came in and danced, and pleased Herod and those who sat with him, the king said to the girl, "Ask me whatever you want, and I will give *it* to you." ²³He also swore to her, "Whatever you ask me, I will give you, up to half my kingdom."

²⁴So she went out and said to her mother, "What shall I ask?"

And she said, "The head of John the Baptist!"

²⁵Immediately she came in with haste to the king and asked, saying, "I want you to give me at once the head of John the Baptist on a platter."

²⁶And the king was exceedingly sorry; *yet,* because of the oaths and because of those who sat with him, he did not want to refuse her. ²⁷Immediately the king sent an executioner and com-

---

6:11 ᵛNU-Text reads *whatever place.* ʷNU-Text omits the rest of this verse.   6:15 ˣNU-Text and M-Text omit *or.*

manded his head to be brought. And he went and beheaded him in prison, 28brought his head on a platter, and gave it to the girl; and the girl gave it to her mother. 29When his disciples heard *of it*, they came and took away his corpse and laid it in a tomb.

30*Then the apostles gathered to Jesus and told Him all things, both what they had done and what they had taught. 31And He said to them, "Come aside by yourselves to a deserted place and rest a while." For there were many coming and going, and they did not even have time to eat. 32So they departed to a deserted place in the boat by themselves.

33But the multitudesʸ saw them departing, and many knew Him and ran there on foot from all the cities. They arrived before them and came together to Him. 34And Jesus, when He came out, saw a great multitude and was moved with compassion for them, because they were like sheep not having a shepherd. So He began to teach them many things. 35When the day was now far spent, His disciples came to Him and said, "This is a deserted place, and already the hour *is* late. 36Send them away, that they may go into the surrounding country and villages and buy themselves bread;ᶻ for they have nothing to eat."

37But He answered and said to them, "You give them something to eat."

And they said to Him, "Shall we go and buy two hundred denarii worth of bread and give them *something* to eat?"

38But He said to them, "How many loaves do you have? Go and see."

And when they found out they said, "Five, and two fish."

39Then He commanded them to make them all sit down in groups on the green grass. 40So they sat down in ranks, in hundreds and in fifties. 41And when He had taken the five loaves and the two fish, He looked up to heaven, blessed and broke the loaves, and gave *them* to His disciples to set before them; and the two fish He divided among *them* all. 42So they all ate and were filled. 43And they took up twelve baskets full of fragments and of the fish. 44Now those who had eaten the loaves were aboutᵃ five thousand men.

45*Immediately He made His disciples get into the boat and go before Him to the other side, to Bethsaida, while He sent the multitude away. 46And when He had sent them away, He departed to the mountain to pray. 47Now when evening came, the boat was in the middle of the sea; and He *was* alone on the land. 48Then He saw them straining at rowing, for the wind was against them. Now about the fourth watch of the night He came to them, walking on the sea, and would have passed them by. 49And when they saw Him walking on the sea, they supposed it was a ghost, and cried out; 50for they all saw Him and were troubled. But immediately He talked with them and said, "Be of good cheer! It is I; do not be afraid." 51Then He went up into the boat to them, and the wind ceased. And they were greatly amazed in themselves beyond measure, and marveled. 52For they had not understood

6:30–44 *The Servant cannot rest.* God's servants become weary as they work (John 4:6) and must care for the body. But when you have a compassionate heart, you will not have an idle hand. Our Lord interrupted His vacation to meet the needs of the people. He need not interrupt anything today, because caring for us is His constant ministry (Heb. 7:25).

6:45–52 *The Servant cannot pray.* After such a demanding time of ministry, Jesus had to go apart to pray (v. 46; 1:35). But once again, He was interrupted, this time by the plight of His disciples in the midst of the sea (v. 48). And it was the disciples who were amazed (v. 51)! Jesus intercedes for you and knows your situation. He will come to you, care for you, and lead you into His peace.

6:33 ʸNU-Text and M-Text read *they*.   6:36 ᶻNU-Text reads *something to eat* and omits the rest of this verse.
6:44 ᵃNU-Text and M-Text omit *about*.

about the loaves, because their heart was hardened.

53When they had crossed over, they came to the land of Gennesaret and anchored there. 54And when they came out of the boat, immediately the people recognized Him, 55ran through that whole surrounding region, and began to carry about on beds those who were sick to wherever they heard He was. 56Wherever He entered, into villages, cities, or the country, they laid the sick in the marketplaces, and begged Him that they might just touch the hem of His garment. And as many as touched Him were made well.

CHAPTER 7

7:1–23 Defilement. Unless we are very careful, religious rituals can create serious problems. They may be given as much authority as God's Word (v. 7) and even replace God's Word (v. 9). They may give a false confidence that what you do on the outside will somehow change the inside. But the heart must be changed, and external rituals cannot do that. The heart can be purified only by faith (Acts 15:9).

7 Then* the Pharisees and some of the scribes came together to Him, having come from Jerusalem. 2Now when*b* they saw some of His disciples eat bread with defiled, that is, with unwashed hands, they found fault. 3For the Pharisees and all the Jews do not eat unless they wash *their* hands in a special way, holding the tradition of the elders. 4When they come from the marketplace, they do not eat unless they wash. And there are many other things which they have received and hold, *like* the washing of cups, pitchers, copper vessels, and couches.

5Then the Pharisees and scribes asked Him, "Why do Your disciples not walk according to the tradition of the elders, but eat bread with unwashed hands?"

6He answered and said to them, "Well did Isaiah prophesy of you hypocrites, as it is written:

> 'This people honors Me with their lips,
> But their heart is far from Me.
> 7 And in vain they worship Me,
> Teaching as doctrines the commandments
> of men.'*c*

8For laying aside the commandment of God, you hold the tradition of men*d*—the washing of pitchers and cups, and many other such things you do."

9He said to them, "*All too* well you reject the commandment of God, that you may keep your tradition. 10For Moses said, '*Honor your father and your mother*';*e* and, '*He who curses father or mother, let him be put to death.*'*f* 11But you say, 'If a man says to his father or mother, "Whatever profit you might have received from me *is* Corban"—' (that is, a gift *to* God), 12then you no longer let him do anything for his father or his mother, 13making the word of God of no effect through your tradition which you have handed down. And many such things you do."

14When He had called all the multitude to *Himself,* He said to them, "Hear Me, everyone, and understand: 15There is nothing that enters a man from outside which can defile him; but the things which come out of him, those are the things that defile a man. 16If anyone has ears to hear, let him hear!"*g*

17When He had entered a house away from the crowd, His disciples asked Him concerning the parable. 18So He said to them, "Are you thus with-

---

7:2 *b*NU-Text omits *when* and *they found fault.*   7:7 *c*Isaiah 29:13   7:8 *d*NU-Text omits the rest of this verse. 7:10 *e*Exodus 20:12; Deuteronomy 5:16 *f*Exodus 21:17 7:16 *g*NU-Text omits this verse.

out understanding also? Do you not perceive that whatever enters a man from outside cannot defile him, 19because it does not enter his heart but his stomach, and is eliminated, *thus* purifying all foods?"*h* 20And He said, "What comes out of a man, that defiles a man. 21For from within, out of the heart of men, proceed evil thoughts, adulteries, fornications, murders, 22thefts, covetousness, wickedness, deceit, lewdness, an evil eye, blasphemy, pride, foolishness. 23All these evil things come from within and defile a man."

24*From there He arose and went to the region of Tyre and Sidon.*i* And He entered a house and wanted no one to know *it,* but He could not be hidden. 25For a woman whose young daughter had an unclean spirit heard about Him, and she came and fell at His feet. 26The woman was a Greek, a Syro-Phoenician by birth, and she kept asking Him to cast the demon out of her daughter. 27But Jesus said to her, "Let the children be filled first, for it is not good to take the children's bread and throw *it* to the little dogs."

28And she answered and said to Him, "Yes, Lord, yet even the little dogs under the table eat from the children's crumbs."

29Then He said to her, "For this saying go your way; the demon has gone out of your daughter."

30And when she had come to her house, she found the demon gone out, and her daughter lying on the bed.

31*Again, departing from the region of Tyre and Sidon, He came through the midst of the region of Decapolis to the Sea of Galilee. 32Then they brought to Him one who was deaf and had an impediment in his speech, and they begged Him to put His hand on him. 33And He took him aside from the multitude, and put His fingers in his ears, and He spat and touched his tongue. 34Then, looking up to heaven, He sighed, and said to him, "Ephphatha," that is, "Be opened."

35Immediately his ears were opened, and the impediment of his tongue was loosed, and he spoke plainly. 36Then He commanded them that they should tell no one; but the more He commanded them, the more widely they proclaimed *it.* 37And they were astonished beyond measure, saying, "He has done all things well. He makes both the deaf to hear and the mute to speak."

8 In those days, the multitude being very great and having nothing to eat, Jesus called His disciples *to Him* and said to them, 2"I have compassion on the multitude, because they have now continued with Me three days and have nothing to eat. 3And if I send them away hungry to their own houses, they will faint on the way; for some of them have come from afar."

4*Then His disciples answered Him, "How can one satisfy these people with bread here in the wilderness?"

5He asked them, "How many loaves do you have?"

And they said, "Seven."

6So He commanded the multitude to sit down on the ground. And He took the seven loaves and gave thanks, broke *them* and gave *them* to His

7:24–30 Distance. Jesus healed both the centurion's servant (Matt. 8:1–13) and this woman's demonized daughter *from a distance.* Both were Gentiles, and the Gentiles were "at a distance" spiritually; but Jesus would erase that distance at the cross (Eph. 2:11–22). As you pray for those far from you, or far from the Lord, remember that He can send His Word and do mighty works (Ps. 107:20).

7:31–37 Deliverance. The miracles of healing this deaf man and healing a blind man (8:22–26) are recorded only by Mark. Both were in gentile territory, which would interest his Roman readers; both were performed away from the crowd; and both were performed despite difficulty. The Servant can work at a distance or when we bring people to Him, and He does not fail.

CHAPTER 8

8:4 Defective faith. The disciples didn't know what to do with the hungry crowd, yet they had seen Jesus feed the five thousand (6:30–44). They apparently "soon forgot His works; they did not wait for His counsel" (Ps. 106:13). Each work that He does should encourage you to trust Him to help you solve the next problem. Keep a long memory for His mercies and a short one for your failures.

7:19 *h*NU-Text ends quotation with *eliminated,* setting off the final clause as Mark's comment that Jesus has declared all foods clean.   7:24 *i*NU-Text omits *and Sidon.*

disciples to set before *them;* and they set *them* before the multitude. 7They also had a few small fish; and having blessed them, He said to set them also before *them.* 8So they ate and were filled, and they took up seven large baskets of leftover fragments. 9Now those who had eaten were about four thousand. And He sent them away, 10immediately got into the boat with His disciples, and came to the region of Dalmanutha.

11Then the Pharisees came out and began to dispute with Him, seeking from Him a sign from heaven, testing Him. 12But He sighed deeply in His spirit, and said, "Why does this generation seek a sign? Assuredly, I say to you, no sign shall be given to this generation."

13And He left them, and getting into the boat again, departed to the other side. 14Now the disciples[j] had forgotten to take bread, and they did not have more than one loaf with them in the boat. 15Then He charged them, saying, "Take heed, beware of the leaven of the Pharisees and the leaven of Herod."

16*And they reasoned among themselves, saying, "*It is* because we have no bread."

17But Jesus, being aware of *it,* said to them, "Why do you reason because you have no bread? Do you not yet perceive nor understand? Is your heart still[k] hardened? 18Having eyes, do you not see? And having ears, do you not hear? And do you not remember? 19When I broke the five loaves for the five thousand, how many baskets full of fragments did you take up?"

They said to Him, "Twelve."

20"Also, when I broke the seven for the four thousand, how many large baskets full of fragments did you take up?"

And they said, "Seven."

21So He said to them, "How *is it* you do not understand?"

22*Then He came to Bethsaida; and they brought a blind man to Him, and begged Him to touch him. 23So He took the blind man by the hand and led him out of the town. And when He had spit on his eyes and put His hands on him, He asked him if he saw anything.

24And he looked up and said, "I see men like trees, walking."

25Then He put *His* hands on his eyes again and made him look up. And he was restored and saw everyone clearly. 26Then He sent him away to his house, saying, "Neither go into the town, nor tell anyone in the town."[l]

27Now Jesus and His disciples went out to the towns of Caesarea Philippi; and on the road He asked His disciples, saying to them, "Who do men say that I am?"

28So they answered, "John the Baptist; but some *say,* Elijah; and others, one of the prophets."

29*He said to them, "But who do you say that I am?"

Peter answered and said to Him, "You are the Christ."

30Then He strictly warned them that they should tell no one about Him.

31And He began to teach them that the Son of Man must suffer many things, and be rejected by the elders and chief priests and scribes, and be

---

8:16 Defective understanding. The disciples did not perceive what He meant by the leaven (vv. 13–21). The blindness of the Pharisees does not surprise us (vv. 11–12), but why were His followers so blind? Like Israel of old, the disciples saw His acts but did not understand His ways (Ps. 103:7). Ask God to give you spiritual insight.

8:22–26 Defective sight. This is the only healing miracle recorded that took place in stages. Bethsaida was under judgment (Matt. 11:21–24), so Jesus took the man out of there and told him not to go back. Be careful where you send people whose eyes have been opened to Jesus and His mercy.

8:29–38 Defective devotion. One minute, Peter is inspired from heaven (Matt. 16:17); and the next minute, his tongue is ignited from hell (8:33; James 3:6). Peter saw only shame in the Cross, but Jesus saw glory. Peter saw defeat, but Jesus saw great victory. Never be afraid or ashamed to be His disciple and bear your cross, for Jesus bore it first.

8:14 [j]NU-Text and M-Text read *they.*   8:17 [k]NU-Text omits *still.*   8:26 [l]NU-Text reads *"Do not even go into the town."*

killed, and after three days rise again. 32He spoke this word openly. Then Peter took Him aside and began to rebuke Him. 33But when He had turned around and looked at His disciples, He rebuked Peter, saying, "Get behind Me, Satan! For you are not mindful of the things of God, but the things of men."

34When He had called the people to *Himself,* with His disciples also, He said to them, "Whoever desires to come after Me, let him deny himself, and take up his cross, and follow Me. 35For whoever desires to save his life will lose it, but whoever loses his life for My sake and the gospel's will save it. 36For what will it profit a man if he gains the whole world, and loses his own soul? 37Or what will a man give in exchange for his soul? 38For whoever is ashamed of Me and My words in this adulterous and sinful generation, of him the Son of Man also will be ashamed when He comes in the glory of His Father with the holy angels."

9 And* He said to them, "Assuredly, I say to you that there are some standing here who will not taste death till they see the kingdom of God present with power."

2Now after six days Jesus took Peter, James, and John, and led them up on a high mountain apart by themselves; and He was transfigured before them. 3His clothes became shining, exceedingly white, like snow, such as no launderer on earth can whiten them. 4And Elijah appeared to them with Moses, and they were talking with Jesus. 5Then Peter answered and said to Jesus, "Rabbi, it is good for us to be here; and let us make three tabernacles: one for You, one for Moses, and one for Elijah"— 6because he did not know what to say, for they were greatly afraid.

7And a cloud came and overshadowed them; and a voice came out of the cloud, saying, "This is My beloved Son. Hear Him!" 8Suddenly, when they had looked around, they saw no one anymore, but only Jesus with themselves.

9Now as they came down from the mountain, He commanded them that they should tell no one the things they had seen, till the Son of Man had risen from the dead. 10So they kept this word to themselves, questioning what the rising from the dead meant.

11And they asked Him, saying, "Why do the scribes say that Elijah must come first?" 12Then He answered and told them, "Indeed, Elijah is coming first and restores all things. And how is it written concerning the Son of Man, that He must suffer many things and be treated with contempt? 13But I say to you that Elijah has also come, and they did to him whatever they wished, as it is written of him."

14And when He came to the disciples, He saw a great multitude around them, and scribes disputing with them. 15Immediately, when they saw Him, all the people were greatly amazed, and running to Him, greeted Him. 16And He asked the scribes, "What are you discussing with them?"

17Then one of the crowd answered and said, "Teacher, I brought You my son, who has a mute spirit. 18And wherever it seizes him, it throws him down; he foams at the mouth, gnashes his teeth, and becomes rigid. So I spoke to Your disciples, that they should cast it out, but they could not."

19*He answered him and said, "O faithless generation, how long shall I be with you? How long

---

CHAPTER 9

9:1–13 Consider some paradoxes of the Christian life.

Glory out of suffering. **What happened** on the Mount of Transfiguration was a confirmation of the testimony Peter gave. But it was also a revelation of the glory of the Cross (Gal. 6:14). First the suffering, then the glory. When you read 1 Peter, you discover that Peter learned his lesson well (1:6–8, 11; 4:12–16; 5:1, 10). Satan offers you glory without suffering (Matt. 4:8–10), but it ends up suffering without glory.

9:19–29 ***Victory out of defeat.*** Their failure to deliver the boy grieved the Lord, gave support to the enemy, and robbed God of glory. The nine disciples who were left behind had neglected their spiritual disciplines and lost their power (v. 29; 6:7). When you find yourself defeated, turn to Him for victory and discover where you went wrong.

❝*One reason sin flourishes is that it is treated like a cream puff instead of a rattlesnake!*❞

—Billy Sunday

shall I bear with you? Bring him to Me." [20]Then they brought him to Him. And when he saw Him, immediately the spirit convulsed him, and he fell on the ground and wallowed, foaming at the mouth.

[21]So He asked his father, "How long has this been happening to him?"

And he said, "From childhood. [22]And often he has thrown him both into the fire and into the water to destroy him. But if You can do anything, have compassion on us and help us."

[23]Jesus said to him, "If you can believe,[m] all things *are* possible to him who believes."

[24]Immediately the father of the child cried out and said with tears, "Lord, I believe; help my unbelief!"

[25]When Jesus saw that the people came running together, He rebuked the unclean spirit, saying to it, "Deaf and dumb spirit, I command you, come out of him and enter him no more!" [26]Then *the spirit* cried out, convulsed him greatly, and came out of him. And he became as one dead, so that many said, "He is dead." [27]But Jesus took him by the hand and lifted him up, and he arose.

[28]And when He had come into the house, His disciples asked Him privately, "Why could we not cast it out?"

[29]So He said to them, "This kind can come out by nothing but prayer and fasting."[n]

[30]Then they departed from there and passed through Galilee, and He did not want anyone to know *it.* [31]For He taught His disciples and said to them, "The Son of Man is being betrayed into the hands of men, and they will kill Him. And after He is killed, He will rise the third day." [32]But they did not understand this saying, and were afraid to ask Him.

[33]Then He came to Capernaum. And when He was in the house He asked them, "What was it you disputed among yourselves on the road?" [34]But they kept silent, for on the road they had disputed among themselves who *would be the* greatest. [35]*And He sat down, called the twelve, and said to them, "If anyone desires to be first, he shall be last of all and servant of all." [36]Then He took a little child and set him in the midst of them. And when He had taken him in His arms, He said to them, [37]"Whoever receives one of these little children in My name receives Me; and whoever receives Me, receives not Me but Him who sent Me."

[38]Now John answered Him, saying, "Teacher, we saw someone who does not follow us casting out demons in Your name, and we forbade him because he does not follow us."

[39]But Jesus said, "Do not forbid him, for no one who works a miracle in My name can soon afterward speak evil of Me. [40]For he who is not against us is on our[o] side. [41]For whoever gives you a cup of water to drink in My name, because you belong to Christ, assuredly, I say to you, he will by no means lose his reward.

[42]"But whoever causes one of these little ones who believe in Me to stumble, it would be better for him if a millstone were hung around his neck, and he were thrown into the sea. [43]*If your hand causes you to sin, cut it off. It is better for you to

9:35–41 Greatness out of service. This is a key passage in Mark's gospel because it emphasizes the importance of service. Do not aim for human greatness; aim to be more like Jesus Christ. Do not measure yourself by other servants (vv. 38–41); measure yourself by Him.

9:43–50 Gain out of loss. If you pamper sin in your life, you will lose your "salty" character and not be able to affect others for Christ. Deal drastically with sin as a surgeon does with a cancerous tumor. You gain by losing.

9:23 [m]NU-Text reads " 'If You can!' All things . . . ."
9:29 [n]NU-Text omits and fasting.   9:40 [o]M-Text reads against you is on your side.

enter into life maimed, rather than having two hands, to go to hell, into the fire that shall never be quenched— [44]where

> 'Their worm does not die
> And the fire is not quenched.'[p]

[45]And if your foot causes you to sin, cut it off. It is better for you to enter life lame, rather than having two feet, to be cast into hell, into the fire that shall never be quenched— [46]where

> 'Their worm does not die
> And the fire is not quenched.'[q]

[47]And if your eye causes you to sin, pluck it out. It is better for you to enter the kingdom of God with one eye, rather than having two eyes, to be cast into hell fire— [48]where

> 'Their worm does not die
> And the fire is not quenched.'[r]

[49]"For everyone will be seasoned with fire,[s] and every sacrifice will be seasoned with salt. [50]Salt is good, but if the salt loses its flavor, how will you season it? Have salt in yourselves, and have peace with one another."

10 Then He arose from there and came to the region of Judea by the other side of the Jordan. And multitudes gathered to Him again, and as He was accustomed, He taught them again.

[2]*The Pharisees came and asked Him, "Is it lawful for a man to divorce *his* wife?" testing Him. [3]And He answered and said to them, "What did Moses command you?"

[4]They said, "Moses permitted *a man* to write a certificate of divorce, and to dismiss *her*."

[5]And Jesus answered and said to them, "Because of the hardness of your heart he wrote you this precept. [6]But from the beginning of the creation, God 'made them male and female.'[t] [7]'For this reason a man shall leave his father and mother and be joined to his wife, [8]and the two shall become one flesh';[u] so then they are no longer two, but one flesh. [9]Therefore what God has joined together, let not man separate."

[10]In the house His disciples also asked Him again about the same *matter.* [11]So He said to them, "Whoever divorces his wife and marries another commits adultery against her. [12]And if a woman divorces her husband and marries another, she commits adultery."

[13]Then they brought little children to Him, that He might touch them; but the disciples rebuked those who brought *them.* [14]But when Jesus saw *it,* He was greatly displeased and said to them, "Let the little children come to Me, and do not forbid them; for of such is the kingdom of God. [15]Assuredly, I say to you, whoever does not receive the kingdom of God as a little child will by no means enter it." [16]And He took them up in His arms, laid *His* hands on them, and blessed them.

[17]*Now as He was going out on the road, one

CHAPTER 10

10:2–12 *How far can I go?* The rabbis didn't agree on their interpretation of the divorce law (Deut. 24:1–4), one school being lenient and the other strict. When you live "by permission," you are tempted to follow those who tell you what you want to hear. Our Lord led the Pharisees back to God's original plan and interpreted it for them.

10:17–27 *How much can I keep?* The rich young man was looking for a bargain, the best of both worlds; but he was doomed to failure. Calculation and crucifixion do not agree. At Calvary, there was no bargaining—just Jesus giving His all.

❝*Has He taken over in your heart? Perhaps He resides there, but does He preside there?*❞
—Vance Havner

9:44 [p]NU-Text omits this verse.   9:46 [q]NU-Text omits the last clause of verse 45 and all of verse 46.   9:48 [r]Isaiah 66:24   9:49 [s]NU-Text omits the rest of this verse.   10:6 [t]Genesis 1:27; 5:2   10:8 [u]Genesis 2:24

came running, knelt before Him, and asked Him, "Good Teacher, what shall I do that I may inherit eternal life?"

18So Jesus said to him, "Why do you call Me good? No one *is* good but One, *that is,* God. 19You know the commandments: *'Do not commit adultery,' 'Do not murder,' 'Do not steal,' 'Do not bear false witness,'* 'Do not defraud,' *'Honor your father and your mother.' ''*v

20And he answered and said to Him, "Teacher, all these things I have kept from my youth."

21Then Jesus, looking at him, loved him, and said to him, "One thing you lack: Go your way, sell whatever you have and give to the poor, and you will have treasure in heaven; and come, take up the cross, and follow Me."

22But he was sad at this word, and went away sorrowful, for he had great possessions.

23Then Jesus looked around and said to His disciples, "How hard it is for those who have riches to enter the kingdom of God!" 24And the disciples were astonished at His words. But Jesus answered again and said to them, "Children, how hard it is for those who trust in richesw to enter the kingdom of God! 25It is easier for a camel to go through the eye of a needle than for a rich man to enter the kingdom of God."

26And they were greatly astonished, saying among themselves, "Who then can be saved?"

27But Jesus looked at them and said, "With men *it is* impossible, but not with God; for with God all things are possible."

28*Then Peter began to say to Him, "See, we have left all and followed You."

29So Jesus answered and said, "Assuredly, I say to you, there is no one who has left house or brothers or sisters or father or mother or wifex or children or lands, for My sake and the gospel's, 30who shall not receive a hundredfold now in this time—houses and brothers and sisters and mothers and children and lands, with persecutions—and in the age to come, eternal life. 31But many *who are* first will be last, and the last first."

32Now they were on the road, going up to Jerusalem, and Jesus was going before them; and they were amazed. And as they followed they were afraid. Then He took the twelve aside again and began to tell them the things that would happen to Him: 33"Behold, we are going up to Jerusalem, and the Son of Man will be betrayed to the chief priests and to the scribes; and they will condemn Him to death and deliver Him to the Gentiles; 34and they will mock Him, and scourge Him, and spit on Him, and kill Him. And the third day He will rise again."

35Then James and John, the sons of Zebedee, came to Him, saying, "Teacher, we want You to do for us whatever we ask."

36And He said to them, "What do you want Me to do for you?"

37They said to Him, "Grant us that we may sit, one on Your right hand and the other on Your left, in Your glory."

38But Jesus said to them, "You do not know what you ask. Are you able to drink the cup that

10:28–45 *How much will we get?* Jesus promises to reward all who faithfully follow Him, but He warns against having rewards as your only motive for service. If you are His disciple, expect a cross, a cup, and a baptism, for the servant is not greater than his Lord. The important question is, "How much can we give?"

10:19 vExodus 20:12–16; Deuteronomy 5:16–20
10:24 wNU-Text omits *for those who trust in riches.*
10:29 xNU-Text omits *or wife.*

I drink, and be baptized with the baptism that I am baptized with?"

[39]They said to Him, "We are able."

So Jesus said to them, "You will indeed drink the cup that I drink, and with the baptism I am baptized with you will be baptized; [40]but to sit on My right hand and on My left is not Mine to give, but *it is for those* for whom it is prepared."

[41]And when the ten heard *it*, they began to be greatly displeased with James and John. [42]But Jesus called them to *Himself* and said to them, "You know that those who are considered rulers over the Gentiles lord it over them, and their great ones exercise authority over them. [43]Yet it shall not be so among you; but whoever desires to become great among you shall be your servant. [44]And whoever of you desires to be first shall be slave of all. [45]For even the Son of Man did not come to be served, but to serve, and to give His life a ransom for many."

[46]Now they came to Jericho. As He went out of Jericho with His disciples and a great multitude, blind Bartimaeus, the son of Timaeus, sat by the road begging. [47]And when he heard that it was Jesus of Nazareth, he began to cry out and say, "Jesus, Son of David, have mercy on me!"

[48]Then many warned him to be quiet; but he cried out all the more, "Son of David, have mercy on me!"

[49]So Jesus stood still and commanded him to be called.

Then they called the blind man, saying to him, "Be of good cheer. Rise, He is calling you."

[50]And throwing aside his garment, he rose and came to Jesus.

[51]So Jesus answered and said to him, "What do you want Me to do for you?"

The blind man said to Him, "Rabboni, that I may receive my sight."

[52]Then Jesus said to him, "Go your way; your faith has made you well." And immediately he received his sight and followed Jesus on the road.

11 Now* when they drew near Jerusalem, to Bethphage[y] and Bethany, at the Mount of Olives, He sent two of His disciples; [2]and He said to them, "Go into the village opposite you; and as soon as you have entered it you will find a colt tied, on which no one has sat. Loose it and bring *it*. [3]And if anyone says to you, 'Why are you doing this?' say, 'The Lord has need of it,' and immediately he will send it here."

[4]So they went their way, and found the[z] colt tied by the door outside on the street, and they loosed it. [5]But some of those who stood there said to them, "What are you doing, loosing the colt?"

[6]And they spoke to them just as Jesus had commanded. So they let them go. [7]Then they brought the colt to Jesus and threw their clothes on it, and He sat on it. [8]And many spread their clothes on the road, and others cut down leafy branches from the trees and spread *them* on the road.

11:1 [y]M-Text reads *Bethsphage*. 11:4 [z]NU-Text and M-Text read *a*.

CHAPTER 11

11:1–10 *Honor.* The donkey was a royal animal, and the event was a coronation celebration (1 Kings 1:32–40). It was the only time our Lord permitted a public demonstration in His honor, and He did it to fulfill prophecy (Zech. 9:9) and turn the people's hearts back to the Word of God. They did not listen. What changes would Jesus make if He entered our places of worship today?

On Giving—The Lord watches *how* we give (Mark 12:41–44) and examines the motives of the heart (Matt. 6:1–4). He also sees *how much* we give and measures the *proportion*, not the *portion* (1 Cor. 16:2). An old epitaph reads, "What I gave, I have. What I spent, I had. What I kept, I lost."

9Then those who went before and those who followed cried out, saying:

> "Hosanna!
> '*Blessed is He who comes in the name of the* LORD!'[a]
> 10 Blessed *is* the kingdom of our father David
> That comes in the name of the Lord![b]
> Hosanna in the highest!"

11And Jesus went into Jerusalem and into the temple. So when He had looked around at all things, as the hour was already late, He went out to Bethany with the twelve.

12*Now the next day, when they had come out from Bethany, He was hungry. 13And seeing from afar a fig tree having leaves, He went to see if perhaps He would find something on it. When He came to it, He found nothing but leaves, for it was not the season for figs. 14In response Jesus said to it, "Let no one eat fruit from you ever again."

And His disciples heard *it.*

15*So they came to Jerusalem. Then Jesus went into the temple and began to drive out those who bought and sold in the temple, and overturned the tables of the money changers and the seats of those who sold doves. 16And He would not allow anyone to carry wares through the temple. 17Then He taught, saying to them, "Is it not written, '*My house shall be called a house of prayer for all nations*'?[c] But you have made it a '*den of thieves.*'"[d]

18And the scribes and chief priests heard it and sought how they might destroy Him; for they feared Him, because all the people were astonished at His teaching. 19When evening had come, He went out of the city.

20Now in the morning, as they passed by, they saw the fig tree dried up from the roots. 21And Peter, remembering, said to Him, "Rabbi, look! The fig tree which You cursed has withered away."

22So Jesus answered and said to them, "Have faith in God. 23For assuredly, I say to you, whoever says to this mountain, 'Be removed and be cast into the sea,' and does not doubt in his heart, but believes that those things he says will be done, he will have whatever he says. 24Therefore I say to you, whatever things you ask when you pray, believe that you receive *them,* and you will have *them.*

25"And whenever you stand praying, if you have anything against anyone, forgive him, that your Father in heaven may also forgive you your trespasses. 26But if you do not forgive, neither will your Father in heaven forgive your trespasses."[e]

27*Then they came again to Jerusalem. And as He was walking in the temple, the chief priests, the scribes, and the elders came to Him. 28And they said to Him, "By what authority are You doing these things? And who gave You this authority to do these things?"

29But Jesus answered and said to them, "I also will ask you one question; then answer Me, and I will tell you by what authority I do these things: 30The baptism of John—was it from heaven or from men? Answer Me."

11:12–14, 20–26 *Hunger.* The fig tree pictures Israel, taking up space but not producing fruit (Luke 13:6–9). When we stop bearing fruit, the problem always starts with the roots (v. 20; Matt. 3:10). Jesus reminds us that we must have faith and forgiveness when we pray, or God will not answer.

11:15–17 *Holiness.* The psalmist proclaimed, "Holiness adorns Your house" (Ps. 93:5). But unholiness made the temple a place for thieves to hide! The leaders were not *praying;* they were *preying* and using religion only to make money.

11:27–33 *Honesty.* The leaders had not been honest with John the Baptist, and now they refused to be honest with Jesus. When we obey, God teaches us more (John 7:17); if we disobey, we close the door on God's truth.

11:9 [a]Psalm 118:26   11:10 [b]NU-Text omits *in the name of the Lord.*   11:17 [c]Isaiah 56:7 [d]Jeremiah 7:11   11:26 [e]NU-Text omits this verse.

³¹And they reasoned among themselves, saying, "If we say, 'From heaven,' He will say, 'Why then did you not believe him?' ³²But if we say, 'From men' "—they feared the people, for all counted John to have been a prophet indeed. ³³So they answered and said to Jesus, "We do not know."

And Jesus answered and said to them, "Neither will I tell you by what authority I do these things."

12 Then* He began to speak to them in parables: "A man planted a vineyard and set a hedge around *it*, dug *a place for* the wine vat and built a tower. And he leased it to vinedressers and went into a far country. ²Now at vintage-time he sent a servant to the vinedressers, that he might receive some of the fruit of the vineyard from the vinedressers. ³And they took *him* and beat him and sent *him* away empty-handed. ⁴Again he sent them another servant, and at him they threw stones,ᶠ wounded *him* in the head, and sent *him* away shamefully treated. ⁵And again he sent another, and him they killed; and many others, beating some and killing some. ⁶Therefore still having one son, his beloved, he also sent him to them last, saying, 'They will respect my son.' ⁷But those vinedressers said among themselves, 'This is the heir. Come, let us kill him, and the inheritance will be ours.' ⁸So they took him and killed *him* and cast *him* out of the vineyard.

⁹"Therefore what will the owner of the vineyard do? He will come and destroy the vinedressers, and give the vineyard to others. ¹⁰Have you not even read this Scripture:

> 'The stone which the builders rejected
> Has become the chief cornerstone.
> ¹¹ This was the LORD's doing,
> And it is marvelous in our eyes'?"ᵍ

¹²And they sought to lay hands on Him, but feared the multitude, for they knew He had spoken the parable against them. So they left Him and went away.

¹³Then they sent to Him some of the Pharisees and the Herodians, to catch Him in *His* words. ¹⁴When they had come, they said to Him, "Teacher, we know that You are true, and care about no one; for You do not regard the person of men, but teach the way of God in truth. Is it lawful to pay taxes to Caesar, or not? ¹⁵Shall we pay, or shall we not pay?"

But He, knowing their hypocrisy, said to them, "Why do you test Me? Bring Me a denarius that I may see *it*." ¹⁶So they brought *it*.

And He said to them, "Whose image and inscription *is* this?" They said to Him, "Caesar's."

¹⁷And Jesus answered and said to them, "Render to Caesar the things that are Caesar's, and to God the things that are God's."

And they marveled at Him.

¹⁸Then *some* Sadducees, who say there is no resurrection, came to Him; and they asked Him, saying: ¹⁹"Teacher, Moses wrote to us that if a man's brother dies, and leaves *his* wife behind, and leaves no children, his brother should take his wife and raise up offspring for his brother. ²⁰Now there were seven brothers. The first took

CHAPTER 12

12:1ff Each family chose its Passover lamb on the tenth day of the month and carefully examined it until the fourteenth day to be sure it had no defects (Exod. 12:1–6). During His last week of public ministry, God's Lamb (John 1:29) was examined in various ways, and He passed every test. No guile was found in His mouth (Isa. 53:9).

In His replies, Jesus revealed to them who He was; yet they would not accept the truth. He is the Son sent by the Father (12:1–9) and the Stone rejected by the builders (vv. 10–11; Ps. 118:22–23; Acts 4:11). His enemies were so intent on destroying Jesus that they did not realize they were destroying only themselves.

All political questions (12:13–17) and hypothetical doctrinal questions (vv. 18–27) are chaff compared to the most important question of all: Is Jesus Christ your Lord (vv. 35–37) and do you love Him (vv. 28–34)?

If you were to point out the spiritual people in this chapter, would you indicate the pious scribes (vv. 38–40) or the poor widow (vv. 41–44)? Read Revelation 2:9 and 3:17.

12:4 ᶠNU-Text omits *and at him they threw stones.*
12:11 ᵍPsalm 118:22, 23

a wife; and dying, he left no offspring. 21And the second took her, and he died; nor did he leave any offspring. And the third likewise. 22So the seven had her and left no offspring. Last of all the woman died also. 23Therefore, in the resurrection, when they rise, whose wife will she be? For all seven had her as wife."

24Jesus answered and said to them, "Are you not therefore mistaken, because you do not know the Scriptures nor the power of God? 25For when they rise from the dead, they neither marry nor are given in marriage, but are like angels in heaven. 26But concerning the dead, that they rise, have you not read in the book of Moses, in the *burning* bush *passage,* how God spoke to him, saying, '*I am* the God of Abraham, the God of Isaac, and the God of Jacob' ?*h* 27He is not the God of the dead, but the God of the living. You are therefore greatly mistaken."

28Then one of the scribes came, and having heard them reasoning together, perceiving*i* that He had answered them well, asked Him, "Which is the first commandment of all?"

29Jesus answered him, "The first of all the commandments *is:* '*Hear, O Israel, the* LORD *our God, the* LORD *is one.* 30And you shall love the* LORD *your God with all your heart, with all your soul, with all your mind, and with all your strength.'*j* This *is* the first commandment.*k* 31And the second, like *it, is* this: '*You shall love your neighbor as yourself.'*l* There is no other commandment greater than these."

32So the scribe said to Him, "Well *said,* Teacher. You have spoken the truth, for there is one God, and there is no other but He. 33And to love Him with all the heart, with all the understanding, with all the soul,*m* and with all the strength, and to love one's neighbor as oneself, is more than all the whole burnt offerings and sacrifices."

34Now when Jesus saw that he answered wisely, He said to him, "You are not far from the kingdom of God."

But after that no one dared question Him.

35Then Jesus answered and said, while He taught in the temple, "How *is it* that the scribes say that the Christ is the Son of David? 36For David himself said by the Holy Spirit:

'The LORD said to my Lord,
"Sit at My right hand,
    Till I make Your enemies Your footstool." '*n*

37Therefore David himself calls Him '*Lord*'; how is He *then* his Son?"

And the common people heard Him gladly.

38Then He said to them in His teaching, "Beware of the scribes, who desire to go around in long robes, *love* greetings in the marketplaces, 39the best seats in the synagogues, and the best places at feasts, 40who devour widows' houses, and for a pretense make long prayers. These will receive greater condemnation."

41Now Jesus sat opposite the treasury and saw how the people put money into the treasury. And many *who were* rich put in much. 42Then one poor

---

12:26 *h*Exodus 3:6, 15   12:28 *i*NU-Text reads *seeing.*
12:30 *j*Deuteronomy 6:4, 5   *k*NU-Text omits this sentence.
12:31 *l*Leviticus 19:18   12:33 *m*NU-Text omits *with all the soul.*
12:36 *n*Psalm 110:1

widow came and threw in two mites,*o* which make a quadrans. 43So He called His disciples to *Himself* and said to them, "Assuredly, I say to you that this poor widow has put in more than all those who have given to the treasury; 44for they all put in out of their abundance, but she out of her poverty put in all that she had, her whole livelihood."

13 Then as He went out of the temple, one of His disciples said to Him, "Teacher, see what manner of stones and what buildings *are* here!"

2And Jesus answered and said to him, "Do you see these great buildings? Not *one* stone shall be left upon another, that shall not be thrown down."

3*Now as He sat on the Mount of Olives opposite the temple, Peter, James, John, and Andrew asked Him privately, 4"Tell us, when will these things be? And what *will be* the sign when all these things will be fulfilled?"

5*And Jesus, answering them, began to say: "Take heed that no one deceives you. 6For many will come in My name, saying, 'I am *He*,' and will deceive many. 7But when you hear of wars and rumors of wars, do not be troubled; for *such things* must happen, but the end *is* not yet. 8For nation will rise against nation, and kingdom against kingdom. And there will be earthquakes in various places, and there will be famines and troubles.*p* These *are* the beginnings of sorrows.

9"But watch out for yourselves, for they will deliver you up to councils, and you will be beaten in the synagogues. You will be brought*q* before rulers and kings for My sake, for a testimony to them. 10And the gospel must first be preached to all the nations. 11But when they arrest *you* and deliver you up, do not worry beforehand, or premeditate*r* what you will speak. But whatever is given you in that hour, speak that; for it is not you who speak, but the Holy Spirit. 12Now brother will betray brother to death, and a father *his* child; and children will rise up against parents and cause them to be put to death. 13And you will be hated by all for My name's sake. But he who endures to the end shall be saved.

14"So when you see the *'abomination of desolation,'s* spoken of by Daniel the prophet,*t* standing where it ought not" (let the reader understand), "then let those who are in Judea flee to the mountains. 15Let him who is on the housetop not go down into the house, nor enter to take anything out of his house. 16And let him who is in the field not go back to get his clothes. 17But woe to those who are pregnant and to those who are nursing babies in those days! 18And pray that your flight may not be in winter. 19For *in* those days there will be tribulation, such as has not been since the beginning of the creation which God created until this time, nor ever shall be. 20And unless the Lord had shortened those days, no flesh would be saved; but for the elect's sake, whom He chose, He shortened the days.

21"Then if anyone says to you, 'Look, here *is* the Christ!' or, 'Look, *He is* there!' do not believe it. 22For false christs and false prophets will rise

---

CHAPTER 13

13:3–37 This is Mark's version of the Olivet Discourse (Matt. 24—25), written with gentile readers in mind (13:14). If we are to be ready and faithful in these last days, we must heed the admonitions of Jesus.

13:5 *Take heed that no one deceives you.* Political and geological disruption will give false prophets and false Christs great opportunity to deceive people. Persecution against God's people will either strengthen us or weaken us.

12:42 *o*Greek *lepta*, very small copper coins worth a fraction of a penny   13:8 *p*NU-Text omits *and troubles.*   13:9 *q*NU-Text and M-Text read *will stand.*   13:11 *r*NU-Text omits *or premeditate.*   13:14 *s*Daniel 11:31; 12:11 *t*NU-Text omits *spoken of by Daniel the prophet.*

13:23 Take heed to what Jesus taught.
The Word of God is the only dependable
light in this dark world (2 Pet. 1:19). Jesus
has told us beforehand what to expect and
what to avoid, and we must heed His words.
His Word is dependable and durable, so
trust it.

13:33 Take heed, watch, and pray. During
the tribulation period, various signs will
signal Christ's return to earth; but believers
today are looking for the Savior and not for
signs. "Be alert and keep praying!" is His
admonition. "Do the work I have given you
to do." You want to be found faithful when
He comes, and He could come today.

CHAPTER 14
14:1, 2, 10, 11 Preparation for betrayal.
Judas solved the chief priests' problem by
offering to lead them to Jesus. But how do
you "conveniently" betray the Son of God?
Is it not a *costly* endeavor in every way?

14:3–9 Preparation for burial. Mary's act
of worship brought joy to the heart of Jesus
and malice to the heart of Judas, who
wanted the money she had spent (John
12:6). Other women came to anoint Him
after His burial (16:1), but Mary did it when
He could be encouraged by her love.

14:12–26 Preparation for fellowship. It
meant much to Jesus to spend those hours
with His disciples. He loved them (John
13:1), and their presence encouraged Him.
He took the cup and the bread of the
Passover and transformed them into
memorials of His own blood and body, for
He wanted the disciples to remember Him.

and show signs and wonders to deceive, if possible, even the elect. 23*But take heed; see, I have
told you all things beforehand.

24"But in those days, after that tribulation, the
sun will be darkened, and the moon will not give
its light; 25the stars of heaven will fall, and the
powers in the heavens will be shaken. 26Then they
will see the Son of Man coming in the clouds with
great power and glory. 27And then He will send
His angels, and gather together His elect from the
four winds, from the farthest part of earth to the
farthest part of heaven.

28"Now learn this parable from the fig tree:
When its branch has already become tender, and
puts forth leaves, you know that summer is near.
29So you also, when you see these things happening, know that it*u* is near—at the doors! 30As-
suredly, I say to you, this generation will by no
means pass away till all these things take place.
31Heaven and earth will pass away, but My words
will by no means pass away.

32"But of that day and hour no one knows, not
even the angels in heaven, nor the Son, but only
the Father. 33*Take heed, watch and pray; for you
do not know when the time is. 34*It is* like a man
going to a far country, who left his house and
gave authority to his servants, and to each his
work, and commanded the doorkeeper to watch.
35Watch therefore, for you do not know when the
master of the house is coming—in the evening,
at midnight, at the crowing of the rooster, or in
the morning— 36lest, coming suddenly, he find
you sleeping. 37And what I say to you, I say to
all: Watch!"

14 After* two days it was the Passover and *the
Feast* of Unleavened Bread. And the chief
priests and the scribes sought how they might
take Him by trickery and put *Him* to death.
2But they said, "Not during the feast, lest there
be an uproar of the people."

3*And being in Bethany at the house of Simon
the leper, as He sat at the table, a woman came
having an alabaster flask of very costly oil of
spikenard. Then she broke the flask and poured
it on His head. 4But there were some who were
indignant among themselves, and said, "Why
was this fragrant oil wasted? 5For it might have
been sold for more than three hundred denarii
and given to the poor." And they criticized her
sharply.

6But Jesus said, "Let her alone. Why do you
trouble her? She has done a good work for Me.
7For you have the poor with you always, and
whenever you wish you may do them good; but
Me you do not have always. 8She has done what
she could. She has come beforehand to anoint My
body for burial. 9Assuredly, I say to you, wherever
this gospel is preached in the whole world, what
this woman has done will also be told as a memorial to her."

10Then Judas Iscariot, one of the twelve, went
to the chief priests to betray Him to them. 11And
when they heard *it*, they were glad, and promised
to give him money. So he sought how he might
conveniently betray Him.

12*Now on the first day of Unleavened Bread,
when they killed the Passover *lamb*, His disciples

13:29 *u*Or *He*

said to Him, "Where do You want us to go and prepare, that You may eat the Passover?"

13And He sent out two of His disciples and said to them, "Go into the city, and a man will meet you carrying a pitcher of water; follow him. 14Wherever he goes in, say to the master of the house, 'The Teacher says, "Where is the guest room in which I may eat the Passover with My disciples?" ' 15Then he will show you a large upper room, furnished *and* prepared; there make ready for us."

16So His disciples went out, and came into the city, and found it just as He had said to them; and they prepared the Passover.

17In the evening He came with the twelve. 18Now as they sat and ate, Jesus said, "Assuredly, I say to you, one of you who eats with Me will betray Me."

19And they began to be sorrowful, and to say to Him one by one, "*Is it I?*" And another *said,* "*Is it I?*"v

20He answered and said to them, "*It is* one of the twelve, who dips with Me in the dish. 21The Son of Man indeed goes just as it is written of Him, but woe to that man by whom the Son of Man is betrayed! It would have been good for that man if he had never been born."

22And as they were eating, Jesus took bread, blessed and broke *it,* and gave *it* to them and said, "Take, eat;w this is My body."

23Then He took the cup, and when He had given thanks He gave *it* to them, and they all drank from it. 24And He said to them, "This is My blood of the newx covenant, which is shed for many. 25Assuredly, I say to you, I will no longer drink of the fruit of the vine until that day when I drink it new in the kingdom of God."

26And when they had sung a hymn, they went out to the Mount of Olives.

27*Then Jesus said to them, "All of you will be made to stumble because of Me this night,y for it is written:

> 'I will strike the Shepherd,
>   And the sheep will be scattered.'z

28"But after I have been raised, I will go before you to Galilee."

29Peter said to Him, "Even if all are made to stumble, yet I *will* not *be.*"

30Jesus said to him, "Assuredly, I say to you that today, *even* this night, before the rooster crows twice, you will deny Me three times."

31But he spoke more vehemently, "If I have to die with You, I will not deny You!"

And they all said likewise.

32*Then they came to a place which was named Gethsemane; and He said to His disciples, "Sit here while I pray." 33And He took Peter, James, and John with Him, and He began to be troubled and deeply distressed. 34Then He said to them, "My soul is exceedingly sorrowful, *even* to death. Stay here and watch."

35He went a little farther, and fell on the ground, and prayed that if it were possible, the hour might pass from Him. 36And He said, "Abba, Father, all

14:27–31, 66–72 Preparation for danger. The good fellowship in the Upper Room made the Twelve forget the danger outside, so Jesus gave them warning. Peter was not the only one who boasted and felt self-confident: "And they all said likewise" (v. 31). Heed His warnings; He knows what is coming.

14:32–36 Preparation for death. Jesus' prayers reveal the conflict in His holy soul as He faced bearing the sins of the world on the cross. When you have a Gethsemane experience, pray what He prayed: "Not what I will, but what You will" (v. 36). Peter had a sword (v. 47), but Jesus took a cup. You need not fear the cup the Father has prepared for you. Jesus could submit to the abuse of men (v. 65) because He had already submitted to the will of God.

14:19 vNU-Text omits this sentence.   14:22 wNU-Text omits *eat.*   14:24 xNU-Text omits *new.*   14:27 yNU-Text omits *because of Me this night.* zZechariah 13:7

things *are* possible for You. Take this cup away from Me; nevertheless, not what I will, but what You *will*."

37Then He came and found them sleeping, and said to Peter, "Simon, are you sleeping? Could you not watch one hour? 38Watch and pray, lest you enter into temptation. The spirit indeed *is* willing, but the flesh *is* weak."

39Again He went away and prayed, and spoke the same words. 40And when He returned, He found them asleep again, for their eyes were heavy; and they did not know what to answer Him.

41Then He came the third time and said to them, "Are you still sleeping and resting? It is enough! The hour has come; behold, the Son of Man is being betrayed into the hands of sinners. 42Rise, let us be going. See, My betrayer is at hand."

43And immediately, while He was still speaking, Judas, one of the twelve, with a great multitude with swords and clubs, came from the chief priests and the scribes and the elders. 44Now His betrayer had given them a signal, saying, "Whomever I kiss, He is the One; seize Him and lead *Him* away safely."

45As soon as he had come, immediately he went up to Him and said to Him, "Rabbi, Rabbi!" and kissed Him.

46Then they laid their hands on Him and took Him. 47And one of those who stood by drew his sword and struck the servant of the high priest, and cut off his ear.

48Then Jesus answered and said to them, "Have you come out, as against a robber, with swords and clubs to take Me? 49I was daily with you in the temple teaching, and you did not seize Me. But the Scriptures must be fulfilled."

50Then they all forsook Him and fled.

51Now a certain young man followed Him, having a linen cloth thrown around *his* naked *body*. And the young men laid hold of him, 52and he left the linen cloth and fled from them naked.

53And they led Jesus away to the high priest; and with him were assembled all the chief priests, the elders, and the scribes. 54But Peter followed Him at a distance, right into the courtyard of the high priest. And he sat with the servants and warmed himself at the fire.

55Now the chief priests and all the council sought testimony against Jesus to put Him to death, but found none. 56For many bore false witness against Him, but their testimonies did not agree.

57Then some rose up and bore false witness against Him, saying, 58"We heard Him say, 'I will destroy this temple made with hands, and within three days I will build another made without hands.'" 59But not even then did their testimony agree.

60And the high priest stood up in the midst and asked Jesus, saying, "Do You answer nothing? What *is it* these men testify against You?" 61But He kept silent and answered nothing.

Again the high priest asked Him, saying to Him, "Are You the Christ, the Son of the Blessed?"

62Jesus said, "I am. And you will see the Son of Man sitting at the right hand of the Power, and coming with the clouds of heaven."

63Then the high priest tore his clothes and said, "What further need do we have of witnesses? 64You have heard the blasphemy! What do you think?"

And they all condemned Him to be deserving of death.

65Then some began to spit on Him, and to blindfold Him, and to beat Him, and to say to Him, "Prophesy!" And the officers struck Him with the palms of their hands.a

66Now as Peter was below in the courtyard, one of the servant girls of the high priest came. 67And when she saw Peter warming himself, she looked at him and said, "You also were with Jesus of Nazareth."

68But he denied it, saying, "I neither know nor understand what you are saying." And he went out on the porch, and a rooster crowed.

69And the servant girl saw him again, and began to say to those who stood by, "This is one of them." 70But he denied it again.

And a little later those who stood by said to Peter again, "Surely you are one of them; for you are a Galilean, and your speech shows it."b

71Then he began to curse and swear, "I do not know this Man of whom you speak!"

72A second time the rooster crowed. Then Peter called to mind the word that Jesus had said to him, "Before the rooster crows twice, you will deny Me three times." And when he thought about it, he wept.

15 Immediately,* in the morning, the chief priests held a consultation with the elders and scribes and the whole council; and they bound Jesus, led Him away, and delivered Him to Pilate. 2Then Pilate asked Him, "Are You the King of the Jews?"

He answered and said to him, "It is as you say."

3And the chief priests accused Him of many things, but He answered nothing. 4Then Pilate asked Him again, saying, "Do You answer nothing? See how many things they testify against You!"c 5But Jesus still answered nothing, so that Pilate marveled.

6Now at the feast he was accustomed to releasing one prisoner to them, whomever they requested. 7And there was one named Barabbas, who was chained with his fellow rebels; they had committed murder in the rebellion. 8Then the multitude, crying aloud,d began to ask him to do just as he had always done for them. 9But Pilate answered them, saying, "Do you want me to release to you the King of the Jews?" 10For he knew that the chief priests had handed Him over because of envy.

11But the chief priests stirred up the crowd, so that he should rather release Barabbas to them. 12Pilate answered and said to them again, "What

CHAPTER 15

15:1 When you face the unjust assaults of an evil world, remember Jesus. The world says, "Defend yourself!" but Jesus was silent (vv. 1–5). The world says, "Pamper yourself!" but Jesus refused the drug (v. 23). The world says, "Save yourself!" but Jesus remained on the cross and finished the work the Father gave Him to do (v. 30).

14:65 aNU-Text reads received Him with slaps. 14:70 bNU-Text omits and your speech shows it. 15:4 cNU-Text reads of which they accuse You. 15:8 dNU-Text reads going up.

Simon and the Cross—Simon of Cyrene had probably come to Jerusalem to celebrate Passover (Acts 2:10), and he met the Lamb of God! It seems certain that he was converted and went home to lead his two sons to faith in Christ. These men were known to Mark's Roman readers, so they must have become leaders in the church (Rom. 16:13). The next time your plans are interrupted and you have to carry another cross, remember what Simon did for Jesus—and what Jesus did for Simon.

Jesus Gave Himself—The devil told Jesus, "Serve Yourself!" (Matt. 4:3–4). Peter said, "Pity Yourself!" (Matt. 16:21–23). His unsaved relatives said, "Show Yourself!" (John 7:4). The crowd at Calvary said, "Save Yourself!" But Jesus was deaf to all those appeals and gave Himself.

15:15–25 The chief priests were guilty of *envy* (v. 10), and Pilate was guilty of *compromise* (v. 15). Their sins led to the release of an evil man (v. 15), the embarrassment of an innocent man (v. 21), and the death of a good Man (v. 25); yet envy and compromise are not looked upon as terrible sins today. Should they be? Man was doing his worst, but God was doing His best and fulfilling His Word (vv. 28, 34): "But where sin abounded, grace abounded much more" (Rom. 5:20). And He did it for you and me!

then do you want me to do *with Him* whom you call the King of the Jews?"

13So they cried out again, "Crucify Him!"

14Then Pilate said to them, "Why, what evil has He done?"

But they cried out all the more, "Crucify Him!"

15*So Pilate, wanting to gratify the crowd, released Barabbas to them; and he delivered Jesus, after he had scourged *Him,* to be crucified.

16Then the soldiers led Him away into the hall called Praetorium, and they called together the whole garrison. 17And they clothed Him with purple; and they twisted a crown of thorns, put it on His *head,* 18and began to salute Him, "Hail, King of the Jews!" 19Then they struck Him on the head with a reed and spat on Him; and bowing the knee, they worshiped Him. 20And when they had mocked Him, they took the purple off Him, put His own clothes on Him, and led Him out to crucify Him.

21Then they compelled a certain man, Simon a Cyrenian, the father of Alexander and Rufus, as he was coming out of the country and passing by, to bear His cross. 22And they brought Him to the place Golgotha, which is translated, Place of a Skull. 23Then they gave Him wine mingled with myrrh to drink, but He did not take *it.* 24And when they crucified Him, they divided His garments, casting lots for them to determine what every man should take.

25Now it was the third hour, and they crucified Him. 26And the inscription of His accusation was written above:

THE KING OF THE JEWS.

27With Him they also crucified two robbers, one on His right and the other on His left. 28So the Scripture was fulfilled[e] which says, *"And He was numbered with the transgressors."[f]*

29And those who passed by blasphemed Him, wagging their heads and saying, "Aha! *You* who destroy the temple and build *it* in three days, 30save Yourself, and come down from the cross!"

31Likewise the chief priests also, mocking among themselves with the scribes, said, "He saved others; Himself He cannot save. 32Let the Christ, the King of Israel, descend now from the cross, that we may see and believe."[g] Even those who were crucified with Him reviled Him.

33Now when the sixth hour had come, there was darkness over the whole land until the ninth hour. 34And at the ninth hour Jesus cried out with a loud voice, saying, "Eloi, Eloi, lama sabachthani?" which is translated, *"My God, My God, why have You forsaken Me?"[h]*

35Some of those who stood by, when they heard *that,* said, "Look, He is calling for Elijah!" 36Then someone ran and filled a sponge full of sour wine, put *it* on a reed, and offered *it* to Him to drink, saying, "Let Him alone; let us see if Elijah will come to take Him down."

37And Jesus cried out with a loud voice, and breathed His last.

38Then the veil of the temple was torn in two from top to bottom. 39So when the centurion, who stood opposite Him, saw that He cried out like

15:28 [e]Isaiah 53:12 [f]NU-Text omits this verse.   15:32 [g]M-Text reads *believe Him.*   15:34 [h]Psalm 22:1

this and breathed His last,[i] he said, "Truly this Man was the Son of God!"

40There were also women looking on from afar, among whom were Mary Magdalene, Mary the mother of James the Less and of Joses, and Salome, 41who also followed Him and ministered to Him when He was in Galilee, and many other women who came up with Him to Jerusalem.

42Now when evening had come, because it was the Preparation Day, that is, the day before the Sabbath, 43Joseph of Arimathea, a prominent council member, who was himself waiting for the kingdom of God, coming and taking courage, went in to Pilate and asked for the body of Jesus. 44Pilate marveled that He was already dead; and summoning the centurion, he asked him if He had been dead for some time. 45So when he found out from the centurion, he granted the body to Joseph. 46Then he bought fine linen, took Him down, and wrapped Him in the linen. And he laid Him in a tomb which had been hewn out of the rock, and rolled a stone against the door of the tomb. 47And Mary Magdalene and Mary the mother of Joses observed where He was laid.

16 Now* when the Sabbath was past, Mary Magdalene, Mary the mother of James, and Salome bought spices, that they might come and anoint Him. 2Very early in the morning, on the first day of the week, they came to the tomb when the sun had risen. 3And they said among themselves, "Who will roll away the stone from the door of the tomb for us?" 4But when they looked up, they saw that the stone had been rolled away—for it was very large. 5And entering the tomb, they saw a young man clothed in a long white robe sitting on the right side; and they were alarmed.

6But he said to them, "Do not be alarmed. You seek Jesus of Nazareth, who was crucified. He is risen! He is not here. See the place where they laid Him. 7But go, tell His disciples—and Peter— that He is going before you into Galilee; there you will see Him, as He said to you."

8So they went out quickly[j] and fled from the tomb, for they trembled and were amazed. And they said nothing to anyone, for they were afraid.

9*Now when He rose early on the first day of the week, He appeared first to Mary Magdalene, out of whom He had cast seven demons. 10She went and told those who had been with Him, as they mourned and wept. 11And when they heard that He was alive and had been seen by her, they did not believe.

12After that, He appeared in another form to two of them as they walked and went into the country. 13And they went and told it to the rest, but they did not believe them either.

CHAPTERS 16

16:1–8 He arose. Because they forgot His resurrection promises, the women were in sorrow and worrying about the future: "Who will roll away the stone?" When they learned that Jesus was alive, their first response was fear and not faith; but then they became the first heralds of the Resurrection. The angel had a special word for Peter (v. 7) who was no doubt still grieving his sins. The living Christ gives you something to rejoice in, something to talk about, and something to look forward to. He goes before you!

16:9–18 He appeared. This section summarizes the Lord's resurrection appearances. All to whom He appeared became witnesses of His resurrection (Acts 1:22), just as we should be today (Rom. 6:4; Phil. 3:10).

15:39 [i]NU-Text reads that He thus breathed His last.
16:8 [j]NU-Text and M-Text omit quickly.

Saved Through Faith—Sinners are saved through faith in Christ (Eph. 2:8–9), and they bear witness of their faith through baptism (Mark 16:16; Acts 10:47). Some signs described in Mark 16:17–18 occurred during the apostolic period described in the book of Acts. They were the "credentials" of the apostles (Heb. 2:1–4; Rom. 15:19; 2 Cor. 12:12), so we must not assume that they belong to every believer today. It is foolish to *tempt God* by drinking poison or handling poisonous snakes, but it is not foolish to *trust God* when obedience to His will takes us into dangerous situations. Presumption can kill us, but faith can deliver us.

14Later He appeared to the eleven as they sat at the table; and He rebuked their unbelief and hardness of heart, because they did not believe those who had seen Him after He had risen. 15And He said to them, "Go into all the world and preach the gospel to every creature. 16He who believes and is baptized will be saved; but he who does not believe will be condemned. 17And these signs will follow those who believe: In My name they will cast out demons; they will speak with new tongues; 18they*k* will take up serpents; and if they drink anything deadly, it will by no means hurt them; they will lay hands on the sick, and they will recover."

19*So then, after the Lord had spoken to them, He was received up into heaven, and sat down at the right hand of God. 20And they went out and preached everywhere, the Lord working with *them* and confirming the word through the accompanying signs. Amen.*l*

16:19, 20 *He ascended.* The Servant is the Sovereign at the Father's right hand! He humbled Himself in obedience, and God exalted Him in glory (Phil. 2:5–11). But He is not idle, for He is working with His people as they take the gospel to every nation. What an encouragement to be a witness for your Lord!

16:18 *k*NU-Text reads *and in their hands they will.*
16:20 *l*Verses 9–20 are bracketed in NU-Text as not original. They are lacking in Codex Sinaiticus and Codex Vaticanus, although nearly all other manuscripts of Mark contain them.

LUKE

Luke was a physician, probably a Greek (Col. 4:10–11, 14), the companion of Paul on some of his journeys. (Note the pronouns "we" and "us" in Acts 16:10; 20:5; 21:1; 27:1.) He wrote the gospel of Luke and the book of Acts (Luke 1:1–4; Acts 1:1–3), both of which are records of journeys: Christ's journey to Jerusalem (Luke 9:51) and Paul's journey to Rome.

Dr. Luke wrote with the Greeks in mind and presented Jesus Christ as the perfect Son of man, the compassionate Savior (Luke 19:10). He mentions women, children, and the poor often in his gospel; and *joy* and *rejoicing* are repeated many times. There is also an emphasis on prayer and on God's love for the whole world. Luke addressed both books to Theophilus ("lover of God"), a Roman believer, possibly an official, who needed grounding in the faith.

Luke's approach is simple. He records our Lord's birth and early life (chaps. 1—2); His baptism and temptation (3:1—4:13); His ministry in Galilee (4:14—9:17); His ministry en route to Jerusalem (9:18—19:27); and His final week of ministry in Jerusalem (19:28—24:53).

As you read the gospel of Luke, you will come to love the compassionate Son of man who cares for those in need and wants His message of salvation to be taken to the whole world.

1 Inasmuch as many have taken in hand to set in order a narrative of those things which have been fulfilled[a] among us, 2just as those who from the beginning were eyewitnesses and ministers of the word delivered them to us, 3it seemed good to me also, having had perfect understanding of all things from the very first, to write to you an orderly account, most excellent Theophilus, 4that you may know the certainty of those things in which you were instructed.

5There was in the days of Herod, the king of Judea, a certain priest named Zacharias, of the division of Abijah. His wife *was* of the daughters of Aaron, and her name *was* Elizabeth. 6And they were both righteous before God, walking in all the commandments and ordinances of the Lord blameless. 7But they had no child, because Elizabeth was barren, and they were both well advanced in years.

8*So it was, that while he was serving as priest before God in the order of his division, 9according to the custom of the priesthood, his lot fell to burn incense when he went into the temple of the Lord. 10And the whole multitude of the people was praying outside at the hour of incense. 11Then an angel of the Lord appeared to him, standing on the right side of the altar of incense. 12And when Zacharias saw *him*, he was troubled, and fear fell upon him.

13But the angel said to him, "Do not be afraid, Zacharias, for your prayer is heard; and your wife Elizabeth will bear you a son, and you shall call

1:1 [a]Or *are most surely believed*

CHAPTER 1

1:8–25 Serving. His disappointment at not having a son did not keep Zacharias from serving the Lord. Be faithful; you never know when God's angel may arrive. Zacharias had the faith to keep on praying; but when the answer came, he did not have the faith to accept it. He looked at his limitations rather than God's great power. Unbelief produces silence (Ps. 116:10; 2 Cor. 4:13); faith opens your mouth in praise to God.

Jesus' Greatness—It was said of John the Baptist, "He will be great in the sight of the Lord" (Luke 1:15); but of Jesus it was said, "He will be great" (Luke 1:32). He is the great Prophet (Luke 7:16), the great God and Savior (Titus 2:13), the great High Priest (Heb. 4:14), and the great Shepherd of the sheep (Heb. 13:20).

"Do Not Be Afraid"—The encouraging phrase "Do not be afraid!" is found often in Luke's gospel, for the message of salvation replaces fear with joy. All kinds of people heard it: Zacharias (1:13), Mary (1:30), the shepherds (2:10), Peter (5:10), Jairus (8:50), and the disciples (12:7, 32).

his name John. ¹⁴And you will have joy and gladness, and many will rejoice at his birth. ¹⁵For he will be great in the sight of the Lord, and shall drink neither wine nor strong drink. He will also be filled with the Holy Spirit, even from his mother's womb. ¹⁶And he will turn many of the children of Israel to the Lord their God. ¹⁷He will also go before Him in the spirit and power of Elijah, 'to turn the hearts of the fathers to the children,'ᵇ and the disobedient to the wisdom of the just, to make ready a people prepared for the Lord."

¹⁸And Zacharias said to the angel, "How shall I know this? For I am an old man, and my wife is well advanced in years."

¹⁹And the angel answered and said to him, "I am Gabriel, who stands in the presence of God, and was sent to speak to you and bring you these glad tidings. ²⁰But behold, you will be mute and not able to speak until the day these things take place, because you did not believe my words which will be fulfilled in their own time."

²¹And the people waited for Zacharias, and marveled that he lingered so long in the temple. ²²But when he came out, he could not speak to them; and they perceived that he had seen a vision in the temple, for he beckoned to them and remained speechless.

²³So it was, as soon as the days of his service were completed, that he departed to his own house. ²⁴Now after those days his wife Elizabeth conceived; and she hid herself five months, saying, ²⁵"Thus the Lord has dealt with me, in the days when He looked on me, to take away my reproach among people."

²⁶Now in the sixth month the angel Gabriel was sent by God to a city of Galilee named Nazareth, ²⁷to a virgin betrothed to a man whose name was Joseph, of the house of David. The virgin's name was Mary. ²⁸And having come in, the angel said to her, "Rejoice, highly favored one, the Lord is with you; blessed are you among women!"ᶜ

²⁹But when she saw him,ᵈ she was troubled at his saying, and considered what manner of greeting this was. ³⁰Then the angel said to her, "Do not be afraid, Mary, for you have found favor with God. ³¹And behold, you will conceive in your womb and bring forth a Son, and shall call His name Jesus. ³²He will be great, and will be called the Son of the Highest; and the Lord God will give Him the throne of His father David. ³³And He will reign over the house of Jacob forever, and of His kingdom there will be no end."

³⁴Then Mary said to the angel, "How can this be, since I do not know a man?"

³⁵And the angel answered and said to her, "The Holy Spirit will come upon you, and the power of the Highest will overshadow you; therefore, also, that Holy One who is to be born will be called the Son of God. ³⁶Now indeed, Elizabeth your relative has also conceived a son in her old age; and this is now the sixth month for her who was called barren. ³⁷For with God nothing will be impossible."

³⁸*Then Mary said, "Behold the maidservant of the Lord! Let it be to me according to your word." And the angel departed from her.

³⁹Now Mary arose in those days and went into

1:38 Submitting. What an honor to be chosen to be the mother of the Messiah! Mary humbly submitted to the Lord because she had faith that He would keep His promise. Her decision would bring her sorrow and suffering, but she willingly yielded it. She was "blessed among women" because of the grace of God given to her (vv. 28, 30). All who trust Christ as their Savior are highly graced by the Lord (Eph. 1:6).

1:17 ᵇMalachi 4:5, 6   1:28 ᶜNU-Text omits blessed are you among women.   1:29 ᵈNU-Text omits when she saw him.

the hill country with haste, to a city of Judah, [40]and entered the house of Zacharias and greeted Elizabeth. [41]And it happened, when Elizabeth heard the greeting of Mary, that the babe leaped in her womb; and Elizabeth was filled with the Holy Spirit. [42]Then she spoke out with a loud voice and said, "Blessed *are* you among women, and blessed *is* the fruit of your womb! [43]But why *is* this *granted* to me, that the mother of my Lord should come to me? [44]For indeed, as soon as the voice of your greeting sounded in my ears, the babe leaped in my womb for joy. [45]Blessed *is* she who believed, for there will be a fulfillment of those things which were told her from the Lord."

[46]*And Mary said:

"My soul magnifies the Lord,
[47] And my spirit has rejoiced in God my
      Savior.
[48] For He has regarded the lowly state of His
      maidservant;
      For behold, henceforth all generations will
      call me blessed.
[49] For He who is mighty has done great things
      for me,
      And holy *is* His name.
[50] And His mercy *is* on those who fear Him
      From generation to generation.
[51] He has shown strength with His arm;
      He has scattered *the* proud in the
      imagination of their hearts.
[52] He has put down the mighty from *their*
      thrones,
      And exalted *the* lowly.
[53] He has filled *the* hungry with good things,
      And *the* rich He has sent away empty.
[54] He has helped His servant Israel,
      In remembrance of *His* mercy,
[55] As He spoke to our fathers,
      To Abraham and to his seed forever."

[56]And Mary remained with her about three months, and returned to her house.

[57]Now Elizabeth's full time came for her to be delivered, and she brought forth a son. [58]When her neighbors and relatives heard how the Lord had shown great mercy to her, they rejoiced with her.

[59]So it was, on the eighth day, that they came to circumcise the child; and they would have called him by the name of his father, Zacharias. [60]His mother answered and said, "No; he shall be called John."

[61]But they said to her, "There is no one among your relatives who is called by this name." [62]So they made signs to his father—what he would have him called.

[63]And he asked for a writing tablet, and wrote, saying, "His name is John." So they all marveled. [64]Immediately his mouth was opened and his tongue *loosed,* and he spoke, praising God. [65]Then fear came on all who dwelt around them; and all these sayings were discussed throughout all the hill country of Judea. [66]And all those who heard *them* kept *them* in their hearts, saying, "What kind of child will this be?" And the hand of the Lord was with him.

[67]Now his father Zacharias was filled with the Holy Spirit, and prophesied, saying:

[68] "Blessed *is* the Lord God of Israel,
      For He has visited and redeemed His people,

1:46–55, 67–79 Singing. A pregnant Jewish girl from Nazareth, engaged to marry a poor carpenter, what did Mary have to sing about? She sang about the Lord, what He did for *her* (vv. 46–49), for *all who fear Him* (vv. 50–53), and for *His people Israel* (vv. 54–55). God gives power to the weak, thrones to the lowly, and food to the hungry; but the strong, the rich, and the mighty go away empty.

Zacharias praised God for what He would do for His people, Israel. It was the dawning of a new day (vv. 78–79) because the Messiah was about to be born. God keeps His promises and is faithful to His covenants.

69 And has raised up a horn of salvation for
us
In the house of His servant David,
70 As He spoke by the mouth of His holy
prophets,
Who *have been* since the world began,
71 That we should be saved from our enemies
And from the hand of all who hate us,
72 To perform the mercy *promised* to our
fathers
And to remember His holy covenant,
73 The oath which He swore to our father
Abraham:
74 To grant us that we,
Being delivered from the hand of our
enemies,
Might serve Him without fear,
75 In holiness and righteousness before Him
all the days of our life.

76 "And you, child, will be called the prophet
of the Highest;
For you will go before the face of the Lord
to prepare His ways,
77 To give knowledge of salvation to His
people
By the remission of their sins,
78 Through the tender mercy of our God,
With which the Dayspring from on high has
visited[e] us;
79 To give light to those who sit in darkness
and the shadow of death,
To guide our feet into the way of peace."

80 So the child grew and became strong in spirit,
and was in the deserts till the day of his manifestation to Israel.

CHAPTER 2

2:1 You cannot escape Jesus Christ. His birth affected Caesar's politics (vv. 1–3), the ministry of the angels (vv. 8–15), and the activities of common men (vv. 15–20). In that day, shepherds were looked upon with disdain; but God singled them out to be the first human messengers of Messiah's birth. His coming touched worshipers (vv. 21–38) and even scholars (vv. 39–52).

The angels sang about Him, and He is still the theme of the greatest music. Luke wrote about Him, and He is still the subject of the greatest literature. The shepherds hastened to behold Him, and He is still at the center of the greatest art. Teachers listened to Him and marveled, and He is still the focal point for all truth and wisdom. In His development, Jesus was perfectly balanced (v. 52): intellectually (wisdom), physically (stature), spiritually (in favor with God), and socially (in favor with man); and He is still the greatest example for childhood and youth.

He alone is worthy of our worship! Oh, come! Let us adore Him!

2 And* it came to pass in those days *that* a decree went out from Caesar Augustus that all
the world should be registered. 2This census first
took place while Quirinius was governing Syria.
3So all went to be registered, everyone to his own
city.
4Joseph also went up from Galilee, out of the
city of Nazareth, into Judea, to the city of David,
which is called Bethlehem, because he was of the
house and lineage of David, 5to be registered with
Mary, his betrothed wife,[f] who was with child.
6So it was, that while they were there, the days
were completed for her to be delivered. 7And she
brought forth her firstborn Son, and wrapped Him
in swaddling cloths, and laid Him in a manger,
because there was no room for them in the inn.
8Now there were in the same country shepherds
living out in the fields, keeping watch over their
flock by night. 9And behold,[g] an angel of the Lord
stood before them, and the glory of the Lord shone
around them, and they were greatly afraid.
10Then the angel said to them, "Do not be afraid,
for behold, I bring you good tidings of great joy
which will be to all people. 11For there is born to
you this day in the city of David a Savior, who
is Christ the Lord. 12And this *will be* the sign to
you: You will find a Babe wrapped in swaddling
cloths, lying in a manger."
13And suddenly there was with the angel a mul-

1:78 [e]NU-Text reads *shall visit.*   2:5 [f]NU-Text omits *wife.*
2:9 [g]NU-Text omits *behold.*

titude of the heavenly host praising God and saying:

14 "Glory to God in the highest,
  And on earth peace, goodwill toward
      men!"[h]

15So it was, when the angels had gone away from them into heaven, that the shepherds said to one another, "Let us now go to Bethlehem and see this thing that has come to pass, which the Lord has made known to us." 16And they came with haste and found Mary and Joseph, and the Babe lying in a manger. 17Now when they had seen *Him*, they made widely[i] known the saying which was told them concerning this Child. 18And all those who heard *it* marveled at those things which were told them by the shepherds. 19But Mary kept all these things and pondered *them* in her heart. 20Then the shepherds returned, glorifying and praising God for all the things that they had heard and seen, as it was told them.

21And when eight days were completed for the circumcision of the Child,[j] His name was called JESUS, the name given by the angel before He was conceived in the womb.

22Now when the days of her purification according to the law of Moses were completed, they brought Him to Jerusalem to present *Him* to the Lord 23(as it is written in the law of the Lord, *"Every male who opens the womb shall be called holy to the LORD"*),[k] 24and to offer a sacrifice according to what is said in the law of the Lord, *"A pair of turtledoves or two young pigeons."*[l]

25And behold, there was a man in Jerusalem whose name was Simeon, and this man was just and devout, waiting for the Consolation of Israel, and the Holy Spirit was upon him. 26And it had been revealed to him by the Holy Spirit that he would not see death before he had seen the Lord's Christ. 27So he came by the Spirit into the temple. And when the parents brought in the Child Jesus, to do for Him according to the custom of the law, 28he took Him up in his arms and blessed God and said:

29 "Lord, now You are letting Your servant
          depart in peace,
      According to Your word;
30 For my eyes have seen Your salvation
31 Which You have prepared before the face
          of all peoples,
32 A light to *bring* revelation to the Gentiles,
      And the glory of Your people Israel."

33And Joseph and His mother[m] marveled at those things which were spoken of Him. 34Then Simeon blessed them, and said to Mary His mother, "Behold, this *Child* is destined for the fall and rising of many in Israel, and for a sign which will be spoken against 35(yes, a sword will pierce through your own soul also), that the thoughts of many hearts may be revealed."

36Now there was one, Anna, a prophetess, the daughter of Phanuel, of the tribe of Asher. She was of a great age, and had lived with a husband seven years from her virginity; 37and this woman *was* a widow of about eighty-four years,[n] who did not depart from the temple, but served *God* with fastings and prayers night and day. 38And coming in that instant she gave thanks to the Lord,[o] and spoke of Him to all those who looked for redemption in Jerusalem.

39So when they had performed all things according to the law of the Lord, they returned to Galilee, to their *own* city, Nazareth. 40And the Child grew and became strong in spirit,[p] filled with wisdom; and the grace of God was upon Him.

41His parents went to Jerusalem every year at the Feast of the Passover. 42And when He was twelve years old, they went up to Jerusalem according to the custom of the feast. 43When they had finished the days, as they returned, the Boy Jesus lingered behind in Jerusalem. And Joseph and His mother[q] did not know *it;* 44but supposing Him to have been in the company, they went a day's journey, and sought Him among *their* relatives and acquaintances. 45So when they did not find Him, they returned to Jerusalem, seeking Him. 46Now so it was *that* after three days they found Him in the temple, sitting in the midst of the teachers, both listening to them and asking them questions. 47And all who heard Him were astonished at His understanding and answers. 48So when they saw Him, they were amazed; and His mother said to Him, "Son, why have You done this to us? Look, Your father and I have sought You anxiously."

49And He said to them, "Why did you seek Me? Did you not know that I must be about My Father's business?" 50But they did not understand the statement which He spoke to them.

51Then He went down with them and came to Nazareth, and was subject to them, but His mother kept all these things in her heart. 52And Jesus increased in wisdom and stature, and in favor with God and men.

3 Now in the fifteenth year of the reign of Tiberius Caesar, Pontius Pilate being governor of Judea, Herod being tetrarch of Galilee, his brother Philip tetrarch of Iturea and the region of Trachonitis, and Lysanias tetrarch of Abilene, 2*while Annas and Caiaphas were high priests,[r] the word of God came to John the son of Zacharias in the wilderness. 3And he went into all the region around the Jordan, preaching a baptism of repentance for the remission of sins, 4as it is written in the book of the words of Isaiah the prophet, saying:

> "The voice of one crying in the wilderness:
> 'Prepare the way of the LORD;
> Make His paths straight.
> 5 Every valley shall be filled
> And every mountain and hill brought low;
> The crooked places shall be made straight
> And the rough ways smooth;
> 6 And all flesh shall see the salvation of
> God.' "[s]

CHAPTER 3

3:2–6 Prophecy. God's message did not come to any of the "great leaders" of that day. It came to John the Baptist, the last and the greatest of God's prophets. John's ministry was foretold by the prophet Isaiah (vv. 4–6; Isa. 40:3–5). John was a prophet who was the subject of prophecy!

2:37 [n]NU-Text reads *a widow until she was eighty-four.*
2:38 [o]NU-Text reads *to God.* 2:40 [p]NU-Text omits *in spirit.*
2:43 [q]NU-Text reads *And His parents.* 3:2 [r]NU-Text and M-Text read *in the high priesthood of Annas and Caiaphas.*
3:6 [s]Isaiah 40:3–5

7*Then he said to the multitudes that came out to be baptized by him, "Brood of vipers! Who warned you to flee from the wrath to come? 8Therefore bear fruits worthy of repentance, and do not begin to say to yourselves, 'We have Abraham as *our* father.' For I say to you that God is able to raise up children to Abraham from these stones. 9And even now the ax is laid to the root of the trees. Therefore every tree which does not bear good fruit is cut down and thrown into the fire."

10So the people asked him, saying, "What shall we do then?"

11He answered and said to them, "He who has two tunics, let him give to him who has none; and he who has food, let him do likewise."

12Then tax collectors also came to be baptized, and said to him, "Teacher, what shall we do?"

13And he said to them, "Collect no more than what is appointed for you."

14Likewise the soldiers asked him, saying, "And what shall we do?"

So he said to them, "Do not intimidate anyone or accuse falsely, and be content with your wages."

15Now as the people were in expectation, and all reasoned in their hearts about John, whether he was the Christ *or* not, 16John answered, saying to all, "I indeed baptize you with water; but One mightier than I is coming, whose sandal strap I am not worthy to loose. He will baptize you with the Holy Spirit and fire. 17His winnowing fan *is* in His hand, and He will thoroughly clean out His threshing floor, and gather the wheat into His barn; but the chaff He will burn with unquenchable fire."

18And with many other exhortations he preached to the people. 19But Herod the tetrarch, being rebuked by him concerning Herodias, his brother Philip's wife,*t* and for all the evils which Herod had done, 20also added this, above all, that he shut John up in prison.

21*When all the people were baptized, it came to pass that Jesus also was baptized; and while He prayed, the heaven was opened. 22And the Holy Spirit descended in bodily form like a dove upon Him, and a voice came from heaven which said, "You are My beloved Son; in You I am well pleased."

23*Now Jesus Himself began *His ministry* at about thirty years of age, being (as was supposed) the son of Joseph, *the son* of Heli, 24*the son* of Matthat,*u the son* of Levi, *the son* of Melchi, *the son* of Janna, *the son* of Joseph, 25*the son* of Mattathiah, *the son* of Amos, *the son* of Nahum, *the son* of Esli, *the son* of Naggai, 26*the son* of Maath, *the son* of Mattathiah, *the son* of Semei, *the son* of Joseph, *the son* of Judah, 27*the son* of Joannas, *the son* of Rhesa, *the son* of Zerubbabel, *the son* of Shealtiel, *the son* of Neri, 28*the son* of Melchi, *the son* of Addi, *the son* of Cosam, *the son* of Elmodam, *the son* of Er, 29*the son* of Jose, *the son* of Eliezer, *the son* of Jorim, *the son* of Matthat, *the son* of Levi, 30*the son* of Simeon, *the*

3:7–19 Ministry. John was privileged to prepare the nation for the Messiah and then present Him to them. John preached against sin and told the people to repent. He gave specific instructions to his converts on how to put their faith into practice. He was inspecting fruit (v. 8), getting to the root of sin (v. 9), and warning about wrath to come (vv. 7, 17). Would you accept that kind of ministry?

3:21, 22 Mystery. The Son of God is baptized; the Spirit lights upon Him like a dove; and the Father speaks His approval from heaven. Never forget that all of the holy Trinity is involved in your salvation (Eph. 1:1–14).

3:23–38 History. The genealogy (vv. 23–38) is that of Mary whose father was Heli. Joseph was not the biological father of Jesus, though that was what people assumed (John 1:45; 6:42). The genealogy of Joseph is found in Matthew 1. It was unusual to pay attention to the genealogy of a woman, which shows Dr. Luke's concern for neglected people. Gentile history (v. 1) and Jewish history (vv. 23–38) are in the hands of almighty God, fulfilling His purposes.

3:19 *t*NU-Text reads *his brother's wife*. 3:24 *u*This and several other names in the genealogy are spelled somewhat differently in the NU-Text. Since the New King James Version uses the Old Testament spelling for persons mentioned in the New Testament, these variations, which come from the Greek, have not been footnoted.

son of Judah, *the son* of Joseph, *the son* of Jonan, *the son* of Eliakim, 31*the son* of Melea, *the son* of Menan, *the son* of Mattathah, *the son* of Nathan, *the son* of David, 32*the son* of Jesse, *the son* of Obed, *the son* of Boaz, *the son* of Salmon, *the son* of Nahshon, 33*the son* of Amminadab, *the son* of Ram, *the son* of Hezron, *the son* of Perez, *the son* of Judah, 34*the son* of Jacob, *the son* of Isaac, *the son* of Abraham, *the son* of Terah, *the son* of Nahor, 35*the son* of Serug, *the son* of Reu, *the son* of Peleg, *the son* of Eber, *the son* of Shelah, 36*the son* of Cainan, *the son* of Arphaxad, *the son* of Shem, *the son* of Noah, *the son* of Lamech, 37*the son* of Methuselah, *the son* of Enoch, *the son* of Jared, *the son* of Mahalalel, *the son* of Cainan, 38*the son* of Enosh, *the son* of Seth, *the son* of Adam, *the son* of God.

4 Then* Jesus, being filled with the Holy Spirit, returned from the Jordan and was led by the Spirit intoᵛ the wilderness, 2being tempted for forty days by the devil. And in those days He ate nothing, and afterward, when they had ended, He was hungry.

3And the devil said to Him, "If You are the Son of God, command this stone to become bread."

4But Jesus answered him, saying,ʷ "It is written, *'Man shall not live by bread alone, but by every word of God.'"*ˣ

5Then the devil, taking Him up on a high mountain, showed Himʸ all the kingdoms of the world in a moment of time. 6And the devil said to Him, "All this authority I will give You, and their glory; for *this* has been delivered to me, and I give it to whomever I wish. 7Therefore, if You will worship before me, all will be Yours."

8And Jesus answered and said to him, "Get behind Me, Satan!ᶻ Forᵃ it is written, *'You shall worship the LORD your God, and Him only you shall serve.'"*ᵇ

9Then he brought Him to Jerusalem, set Him on the pinnacle of the temple, and said to Him, "If You are the Son of God, throw Yourself down from here. 10For it is written:

> *'He shall give His angels charge over you,*
> *To keep you,'*

11and,

> *'In their hands they shall bear you up,*
> *Lest you dash your foot against a stone.'"*ᶜ

12And Jesus answered and said to him, "It has been said, *'You shall not tempt the LORD your God.'"*ᵈ

13Now when the devil had ended every temptation, he departed from Him until an opportune time.

14*Then Jesus returned in the power of the Spirit to Galilee, and news of Him went out through all the surrounding region. 15And He taught in their synagogues, being glorified by all.

CHAPTER 4

4:1–13 The Conqueror. You can be filled with the Spirit (v. 1) and obedient to God's will and still experience temptations and trials. Because He faced the enemy and conquered, Jesus can identify with you in your temptations and can help you win the victory (Heb. 2:17–18). It is not a sin to be tempted, for Jesus was tempted; but it is a sin to yield. Satan's promise is, "All will be yours" (v. 7); but in Jesus Christ, you already have all things (1 Cor. 3:21–23), and Satan can give you nothing.

4:14–30 The Preacher. The Spirit not only gives us victory, but He leads us (v. 14) and empowers us for service (v. 18). The text for our Lord's message was Isaiah 61:1–2. It describes what Jesus came to do and what He is still doing in lives today. The people in the synagogue wanted a comforting sermon, not a convicting sermon. When Jesus mentioned God's grace to the Gentiles (vv. 23–27), the people became angry and threw Him out! They forfeited His blessings because they rejected His word.

4:1 ᵛNU-Text reads *in.*   4:4 ʷDeuteronomy 8:3 ˣNU-Text omits *but by every word of God.*   4:5 ʸNU-Text reads *And taking Him up, he showed Him.*   4:8 ᶻNU-Text omits *Get behind Me, Satan.* ᵃNU-Text and M-Text omit *For.* ᵇDeuteronomy 6:13   4:11 ᶜPsalm 91:11, 12   4:12 ᵈDeuteronomy 6:16

¹⁶So He came to Nazareth, where He had been brought up. And as His custom was, He went into the synagogue on the Sabbath day, and stood up to read. ¹⁷And He was handed the book of the prophet Isaiah. And when He had opened the book, He found the place where it was written:

> ¹⁸ "The Spirit of the LORD is upon Me,
> Because He has anointed Me
> To preach the gospel to the poor;
> He has sent Me to heal the brokenhearted,ᵉ
> To proclaim liberty to the captives
> And recovery of sight to the blind,
> To set at liberty those who are oppressed;
> ¹⁹ To proclaim the acceptable year of the
> LORD."ᶠ

²⁰Then He closed the book, and gave *it* back to the attendant and sat down. And the eyes of all who were in the synagogue were fixed on Him. ²¹And He began to say to them, "Today this Scripture is fulfilled in your hearing." ²²So all bore witness to Him, and marveled at the gracious words which proceeded out of His mouth. And they said, "Is this not Joseph's son?"

²³He said to them, "You will surely say this proverb to Me, 'Physician, heal yourself! Whatever we have heard done in Capernaum,ᵍ do also here in Your country.'" ²⁴Then He said, "Assuredly, I say to you, no prophet is accepted in his own country. ²⁵But I tell you truly, many widows were in Israel in the days of Elijah, when the heaven was shut up three years and six months, and there was a great famine throughout all the land; ²⁶but to none of them was Elijah sent except to Zarephath,ʰ in the region of Sidon, to a woman *who was* a widow. ²⁷And many lepers were in Israel in the time of Elisha the prophet, and none of them was cleansed except Naaman the Syrian."

²⁸So all those in the synagogue, when they heard these things, were filled with wrath, ²⁹and rose up and thrust Him out of the city; and they led Him to the brow of the hill on which their city was built, that they might throw Him down over the cliff. ³⁰Then passing through the midst of them, He went His way.

³¹*Then He went down to Capernaum, a city of Galilee, and was teaching them on the Sabbaths. ³²And they were astonished at His teaching, for His word was with authority. ³³Now in the synagogue there was a man who had a spirit of an unclean demon. And he cried out with a loud voice, ³⁴saying, "Let *us* alone! What have we to do with You, Jesus of Nazareth? Did You come to destroy us? I know who You are—the Holy One of God!"

³⁵But Jesus rebuked him, saying, "Be quiet, and come out of him!" And when the demon had thrown him in *their* midst, it came out of him and did not hurt him. ³⁶Then they were all amazed and spoke among themselves, saying, "What a word this *is!* For with authority and power He commands the unclean spirits, and they come out." ³⁷And the report about Him went out into every place in the surrounding region.

4:31–44 *The Healer.* Jesus fulfilled His commission (vv. 18–19) by bringing healing and deliverance to the poor and needy by the authority of His word. Had He not overcome the devil privately, Jesus could not have defeated him publicly. While the preaching of the Word was His major ministry (vv. 42–44), Jesus had compassion on the sick and healed them. We may not have the power to heal, but we can comfort and assist those who are needy; and we can do it in Jesus' name (Matt. 25:34–40).

4:18 ᵉNU-Text omits *to heal the brokenhearted.*   4:19 ᶠIsaiah 61:1, 2   4:23 ᵍHere and elsewhere the NU-Text spelling is *Capharnaum.*   4:26 ʰGreek *Sarepta*

38Now He arose from the synagogue and entered Simon's house. But Simon's wife's mother was sick with a high fever, and they made request of Him concerning her. 39So He stood over her and rebuked the fever, and it left her. And immediately she arose and served them.

40When the sun was setting, all those who had any that were sick with various diseases brought them to Him; and He laid His hands on every one of them and healed them. 41And demons also came out of many, crying out and saying, "You are the Christ,*i* the Son of God!"

And He, rebuking *them,* did not allow them to speak, for they knew that He was the Christ.

42Now when it was day, He departed and went into a deserted place. And the crowd sought Him and came to Him, and tried to keep Him from leaving them; 43but He said to them, "I must preach the kingdom of God to the other cities also, because for this purpose I have been sent." 44And He was preaching in the synagogues of Galilee.*j*

5 So it was, as the multitude pressed about Him to hear the word of God, that He stood by the Lake of Gennesaret, 2and saw two boats standing by the lake; but the fishermen had gone from them and were washing *their* nets. 3Then He got into one of the boats, which was Simon's, and asked him to put out a little from the land. And He sat down and taught the multitudes from the boat.

4*When He had stopped speaking, He said to Simon, "Launch out into the deep and let down your nets for a catch."

5But Simon answered and said to Him, "Master, we have toiled all night and caught nothing; nevertheless at Your word I will let down the net." 6And when they had done this, they caught a great number of fish, and their net was breaking. 7So they signaled to *their* partners in the other boat to come and help them. And they came and filled both the boats, so that they began to sink. 8When Simon Peter saw *it,* he fell down at Jesus' knees, saying, "Depart from me, for I am a sinful man, O Lord!"

9For he and all who were with him were astonished at the catch of fish which they had taken; 10and so also *were* James and John, the sons of Zebedee, who were partners with Simon. And Jesus said to Simon, "Do not be afraid. From now on you will catch men." 11So when they had brought their boats to land, they forsook all and followed Him.

12*And it happened when He was in a certain city, that behold, a man who was full of leprosy saw Jesus; and he fell on *his* face and implored Him, saying, "Lord, if You are willing, You can make me clean."

13Then He put out *His* hand and touched him, saying, "I am willing; be cleansed." Immediately the leprosy left him. 14And He charged him to tell no one, "But go and show yourself to the priest,

CHAPTER 5

5:4–11 *Jesus responds to submission.* If you had fished all night and caught nothing, would you be getting ready to go out fishing again? One reason Jesus called several fishermen to be His disciples was that they never quit! Peter may have thought he knew more about fishing than Jesus did, but he did what Jesus commanded; and the Lord honored his obedient faith. No failure is final if you come to the Lord for a new start.

5:12–14 *Jesus responds to sickness.* Lepers were not to approach people; but the man came to Jesus in desperation, and Jesus healed him. The offering Jesus referred to is described in Leviticus 14 and pictures the salvation work of the Lord. Ponder it.

4:41 *i*NU-Text omits *the Christ.*   4:44 *j*NU-Text reads *Judea.*

"They Forsook All"—Peter and his associates had met the Lord earlier (John 1:35–42), had gone with Him on His ministry through Galilee (Mark 1:16–20), but had returned to their fishing business. They now had the call to leave everything and follow the Lord as His apostles (Luke 5:9–11).

and make an offering for your cleansing, as a testimony to them, just as Moses commanded."

15*However, the report went around concerning Him all the more; and great multitudes came together to hear, and to be healed by Him of their infirmities. 16So He Himself *often* withdrew into the wilderness and prayed.

17*Now it happened on a certain day, as He was teaching, that there were Pharisees and teachers of the law sitting by, who had come out of every town of Galilee, Judea, and Jerusalem. And the power of the Lord was *present* to heal them.[k] 18Then behold, men brought on a bed a man who was paralyzed, whom they sought to bring in and lay before Him. 19And when they could not find how they might bring him in, because of the crowd, they went up on the housetop and let him down with *his* bed through the tiling into the midst before Jesus.

20When He saw their faith, He said to him, "Man, your sins are forgiven you."

21And the scribes and the Pharisees began to reason, saying, "Who is this who speaks blasphemies? Who can forgive sins but God alone?"

22But when Jesus perceived their thoughts, He answered and said to them, "Why are you reasoning in your hearts? 23Which is easier, to say, 'Your sins are forgiven you,' or to say, 'Rise up and walk'? 24But that you may know that the Son of Man has power on earth to forgive sins"—He said to the man who was paralyzed, "I say to you, arise, take up your bed, and go to your house."

25Immediately he rose up before them, took up what he had been lying on, and departed to his own house, glorifying God. 26And they were all amazed, and they glorified God and were filled with fear, saying, "We have seen strange things today!"

27After these things He went out and saw a tax collector named Levi, sitting at the tax office. And He said to him, "Follow Me." 28So he left all, rose up, and followed Him.

29Then Levi gave Him a great feast in his own house. And there were a great number of tax collectors and others who sat down with them. 30And their scribes and the Pharisees[l] complained against His disciples, saying, "Why do You eat and drink with tax collectors and sinners?"

31Jesus answered and said to them, "Those who are well have no need of a physician, but those who are sick. 32I have not come to call *the* righteous, but sinners, to repentance."

33Then they said to Him, "Why do[m] the disciples of John fast often and make prayers, and likewise those of the Pharisees, but Yours eat and drink?"

34And He said to them, "Can you make the friends of the bridegroom fast while the bridegroom is with them? 35But the days will come when the bridegroom will be taken away from them; then they will fast in those days."

36Then He spoke a parable to them: "No one puts a piece from a new garment on an old one;[n] otherwise the new makes a tear, and also the piece that was *taken* out of the new does not match

5:15, 16 *Jesus responds to success.* The crowds sought Him, but Jesus withdrew to pray and commune with the Father. He did not allow popularity to detour Him from the Father's will. Vance Havner said, "Success can feather our nest so comfortably that we forget how to fly."

5:17–39 *Jesus responds to sinners.* He forgave the paralytic, Matthew the publican, and Matthew's friends who trusted Him because He is the "friend of sinners" (Matt. 11:19). He could not forgive the scribes and Pharisees because they would not admit they were sick and in need of new clothes!

5:17 [k]NU-Text reads *present with Him to heal.*   5:30 [l]NU-Text reads *But the Pharisees and their scribes.*   5:33 [m]NU-Text omits *Why do,* making the verse a statement.   5:36 [n]NU-Text reads *No one tears a piece from a new garment and puts it on an old one.*

the old. 37And no one puts new wine into old wineskins; or else the new wine will burst the wineskins and be spilled, and the wineskins will be ruined. 38But new wine must be put into new wineskins, and both are preserved.o 39And no one, having drunk old *wine*, immediatelyp desires new; for he says, 'The old is better.' "q

CHAPTER 6

6:1–11 *True liberty*. People who live only by "Is it lawful?" cannot understand our Lord's principle, "Is it loving?" The scribes and Pharisees had transformed the Sabbath from a day of blessing into a day of bondage, and Jesus deliberately healed on the Sabbath so He could challenge them. It is always right to do good and to meet human need (Mic. 6:8), for love fulfills the law (Rom. 13:8–10).

6 Now* it happened on the second Sabbath after the firstr that He went through the grainfields. And His disciples plucked the heads of grain and ate *them*, rubbing *them* in *their* hands. 2And some of the Pharisees said to them, "Why are you doing what is not lawful to do on the Sabbath?"

3But Jesus answering them said, "Have you not even read this, what David did when he was hungry, he and those who were with him: 4how he went into the house of God, took and ate the showbread, and also gave some to those with him, which is not lawful for any but the priests to eat?" 5And He said to them, "The Son of Man is also Lord of the Sabbath."

6Now it happened on another Sabbath, also, that He entered the synagogue and taught. And a man was there whose right hand was withered. 7So the scribes and Pharisees watched Him closely, whether He would heal on the Sabbath, that they might find an accusation against Him. 8But He knew their thoughts, and said to the man who had the withered hand, "Arise and stand here." And he arose and stood. 9Then Jesus said to them, "I will ask you one thing: Is it lawful on the Sabbath to do good or to do evil, to save life or to destroy?"s 10And when He had looked around at them all, He said to the man,t "Stretch out your hand." And he did so, and his hand was restored as whole as the other.u 11But they were filled with rage, and discussed with one another what they might do to Jesus.

6:12–26 *True values*. In His ordination sermon for the apostles, Jesus emphasized the true spiritual values of life in contrast to the false values of the Pharisees (Matt. 23). Comfortable living is not always Christian living.

12*Now it came to pass in those days that He went out to the mountain to pray, and continued all night in prayer to God. 13And when it was day, He called His disciples to *Himself;* and from them He chose twelve whom He also named apostles: 14Simon, whom He also named Peter, and Andrew his brother; James and John; Philip and Bartholomew; 15Matthew and Thomas; James the *son* of Alphaeus, and Simon called the Zealot; 16Judas *the son* of James, and Judas Iscariot who also became a traitor.

17And He came down with them and stood on a level place with a crowd of His disciples and a great multitude of people from all Judea and Jerusalem, and from the seacoast of Tyre and Sidon, who came to hear Him and be healed of their diseases, 18as well as those who were tormented with unclean spirits. And they were healed. 19And the whole multitude sought to touch Him, for power went out from Him and healed *them* all.

20Then He lifted up His eyes toward His disciples, and said:

"Blessed *are you* poor,
    For yours is the kingdom of God.

5:38 oNU-Text omits *and both are preserved.* 5:39 pNU-Text omits *immediately.* qNU-Text reads *good.* 6:1 rNU-Text reads *on a Sabbath.* 6:9 sM-Text reads *to kill.* 6:10 tNU-Text and M-Text read *to him.* uNU-Text omits *as whole as the other.*

21 Blessed *are you* who hunger now,
    For you shall be filled.
Blessed *are you* who weep now,
    For you shall laugh.
22 Blessed are you when men hate you,
    And when they exclude you,
    And revile *you*, and cast out your name
        as evil,
    For the Son of Man's sake.
23 Rejoice in that day and leap for joy!
    For indeed your reward *is* great in heaven,
    For in like manner their fathers did to the
        prophets.

24 "But woe to you who are rich,
    For you have received your consolation.
25 Woe to you who are full,
    For you shall hunger.
Woe to you who laugh now,
    For you shall mourn and weep.
26 Woe to you^v when all^w men speak well of
    you,
    For so did their fathers to the false
       prophets.

27*"But I say to you who hear: Love your enemies, do good to those who hate you, 28bless those who curse you, and pray for those who spitefully use you. 29To him who strikes you on the *one* cheek, offer the other also. And from him who takes away your cloak, do not withhold *your* tunic either. 30Give to everyone who asks of you. And from him who takes away your goods do not ask *them* back. 31And just as you want men to do to you, you also do to them likewise.

32"But if you love those who love you, what credit is that to you? For even sinners love those who love them. 33And if you do good to those who do good to you, what credit is that to you? For even sinners do the same. 34And if you lend *to those* from whom you hope to receive back, what credit is that to you? For even sinners lend to sinners to receive as much back. 35But love your enemies, do good, and lend, hoping for nothing in return; and your reward will be great, and you will be sons of the Most High. For He is kind to the unthankful and evil. 36Therefore be merciful, just as your Father also is merciful.

37"Judge not, and you shall not be judged. Condemn not, and you shall not be condemned. Forgive, and you will be forgiven. 38Give, and it will be given to you: good measure, pressed down, shaken together, and running over will be put into your bosom. For with the same measure that you use, it will be measured back to you."

39And He spoke a parable to them: "Can the blind lead the blind? Will they not both fall into the ditch? 40A disciple is not above his teacher, but everyone who is perfectly trained will be like his teacher. 41And why do you look at the speck in your brother's eye, but do not perceive the plank in your own eye? 42Or how can you say to your brother, 'Brother, let me remove the speck that *is* in your eye,' when you yourself do not see the plank that *is* in your own eye? Hypocrite! First remove the plank from your own eye, and then you will see clearly to remove the speck that is in your brother's eye.

43"For a good tree does not bear bad fruit, nor

6:27–45 *True love.* Yes, God's people have their enemies, even as Jesus did; and we must be Christlike in the way we treat them. We must be giving and forgiving; and we must pray for them, not that God would destroy them but that He would change them. The best way to conquer an enemy is to make him a friend. Keep your heart right with God (v. 45) and the Lord will produce the good fruit in your life.

does a bad tree bear good fruit. [44]For every tree is known by its own fruit. For *men* do not gather figs from thorns, nor do they gather grapes from a bramble bush. [45]A good man out of the good treasure of his heart brings forth good; and an evil man out of the evil treasure of his heart[x] brings forth evil. For out of the abundance of the heart his mouth speaks.

[46]*"But why do you call Me 'Lord, Lord,' and not do the things which I say? [47]Whoever comes to Me, and hears My sayings and does them, I will show you whom he is like: [48]He is like a man building a house, who dug deep and laid the foundation on the rock. And when the flood arose, the stream beat vehemently against that house, and could not shake it, for it was founded on the rock.[y] [49]But he who heard and did nothing is like a man who built a house on the earth without a foundation, against which the stream beat vehemently; and immediately it fell.[z] And the ruin of that house was great."

6:46–49 *True obedience.* True obedience is not just words but deeds, and it involves hearing the Word and doing it (1 Thess. 2:13). Judas knew the vocabulary, but he did not do the will of God; and when the storm came, his house fell.

CHAPTER 7

7:1–10 *He did not deserve it.* "I am not worthy" was the centurion's confession of humility; and his confession of faith was, "Say the word!" It is great faith when we trust Christ to work just by speaking the Word. We can never deserve His blessings, but we can ask for them in faith.

7 Now* when He concluded all His sayings in the hearing of the people, He entered Capernaum. [2]And a certain centurion's servant, who was dear to him, was sick and ready to die. [3]So when he heard about Jesus, he sent elders of the Jews to Him, pleading with Him to come and heal his servant. [4]And when they came to Jesus, they begged Him earnestly, saying that the one for whom He should do this was deserving, [5]"for he loves our nation, and has built us a synagogue."

[6]Then Jesus went with them. And when He was already not far from the house, the centurion sent friends to Him, saying to Him, "Lord, do not trouble Yourself, for I am not worthy that You should enter under my roof. [7]Therefore I did not even think myself worthy to come to You. But say the word, and my servant will be healed. [8]For I also am a man placed under authority, having soldiers under me. And I say to one, 'Go,' and he goes; and to another, 'Come,' and he comes; and to my servant, 'Do this,' and he does *it.*"

[9]When Jesus heard these things, He marveled at him, and turned around and said to the crowd that followed Him, "I say to you, I have not found such great faith, not even in Israel!" [10]And those who were sent, returning to the house, found the servant well who had been sick.[a]

7:11–17 *She did not expect it.* Nobody knew that Jesus would arrive and break up the funeral! Never despair, because your Lord may surprise you at the last minute and do the impossible for you.

[11]*Now it happened, the day after, *that* He went into a city called Nain; and many of His disciples went with Him, and a large crowd. [12]And when He came near the gate of the city, behold, a dead man was being carried out, the only son of his mother; and she was a widow. And a large crowd from the city was with her. [13]When the Lord saw her, He had compassion on her and said to her, "Do not weep." [14]Then He came and touched the open coffin, and those who carried *him* stood still. And He said, "Young man, I say to you, arise." [15]So he who was dead sat up and began to speak. And He presented him to his mother.

6:45 [x]NU-Text omits *treasure of his heart.*   6:48 [y]NU-Text reads *for it was well built.*   6:49 [z]NU-Text reads *collapsed.* 7:10 [a]NU-Text omits *who had been sick.*

True Rest—Christ's invitation to come to Him for rest (Matt. 11:28–30) precedes Luke 7:36–50. The sinful woman had heard that invitation and had come to Christ, and she found rest. She was ashamed of her past, but she was not ashamed of her Savior or of her tears.

¹⁶Then fear came upon all, and they glorified God, saying, "A great prophet has risen up among us"; and, "God has visited His people." ¹⁷And this report about Him went throughout all Judea and all the surrounding region.

¹⁸*Then the disciples of John reported to him concerning all these things. ¹⁹And John, calling two of his disciples to *him*, sent *them* to Jesus,*ᵇ* saying, "Are You the Coming One, or do we look for another?"

²⁰When the men had come to Him, they said, "John the Baptist has sent us to You, saying, 'Are You the Coming One, or do we look for another?' " ²¹And that very hour He cured many of infirmities, afflictions, and evil spirits; and to many blind He gave sight.

²²Jesus answered and said to them, "Go and tell John the things you have seen and heard: that *the* blind see, *the* lame walk, *the* lepers are cleansed, *the* deaf hear, *the* dead are raised, *the* poor have the gospel preached to them. ²³And blessed is *he* who is not offended because of Me."

²⁴When the messengers of John had departed, He began to speak to the multitudes concerning John: "What did you go out into the wilderness to see? A reed shaken by the wind? ²⁵But what did you go out to see? A man clothed in soft garments? Indeed those who are gorgeously appareled and live in luxury are in kings' courts. ²⁶But what did you go out to see? A prophet? Yes, I say to you, and more than a prophet. ²⁷This is *he* of whom it is written:

'Behold, I send My messenger before Your face,
Who will prepare Your way before You.'*ᶜ*

²⁸For I say to you, among those born of women there is not a greater prophet than John the Baptist;*ᵈ* but he who is least in the kingdom of God is greater than he."

²⁹And when all the people heard *Him*, even the tax collectors justified God, having been baptized with the baptism of John. ³⁰But the Pharisees and lawyers rejected the will of God for themselves, not having been baptized by him.

³¹And the Lord said,*ᵉ* "To what then shall I liken the men of this generation, and what are they like? ³²They are like children sitting in the marketplace and calling to one another, saying:

'We played the flute for you,
And you did not dance;
We mourned to you,
And you did not weep.'

³³For John the Baptist came neither eating bread nor drinking wine, and you say, 'He has a demon.' ³⁴The Son of Man has come eating and drinking, and you say, 'Look, a glutton and a winebibber, a friend of tax collectors and sinners!' ³⁵But wisdom is justified by all her children."

³⁶*Then one of the Pharisees asked Him to eat with him. And He went to the Pharisee's house, and sat down to eat. ³⁷And behold, a woman in the city who was a sinner, when she knew that

7:18–35 *He did not understand it.* When the Lord is not doing what you expect Him to do, tell Him about it and listen to His Word. You may feel that your ministry has failed, but you are not the judge. Let Jesus have the final word.

7:36–50 *She could not hide it.* The sinful woman trusted Christ and He saved her; now she wanted to express her love to Him. True faith cannot be hidden, and true faith shows itself in love and worship. Simon the Pharisee was blind: he could not see himself, the Lord, or the woman. He did not know the debt he owed!

7:19 *ᵇ*NU-Text reads *the Lord.*   7:27 *ᶜ*Malachi 3:1
7:28 *ᵈ*NU-Text reads *there is none greater than John.*
7:31 *ᵉ*NU-Text and M-Text omit *And the Lord said.*

Jesus sat at the table in the Pharisee's house, brought an alabaster flask of fragrant oil, 38and stood at His feet behind *Him* weeping; and she began to wash His feet with her tears, and wiped *them* with the hair of her head; and she kissed His feet and anointed *them* with the fragrant oil. 39Now when the Pharisee who had invited Him saw *this*, he spoke to himself, saying, "This Man, if He were a prophet, would know who and what manner of woman *this is* who is touching Him, for she is a sinner."

40And Jesus answered and said to him, "Simon, I have something to say to you."

So he said, "Teacher, say it."

41"There was a certain creditor who had two debtors. One owed five hundred denarii, and the other fifty. 42And when they had nothing with which to repay, he freely forgave them both. Tell Me, therefore, which of them will love him more?"

43Simon answered and said, "I suppose the *one* whom he forgave more."

And He said to him, "You have rightly judged." 44Then He turned to the woman and said to Simon, "Do you see this woman? I entered your house; you gave Me no water for My feet, but she has washed My feet with her tears and wiped *them* with the hair of her head. 45You gave Me no kiss, but this woman has not ceased to kiss My feet since the time I came in. 46You did not anoint My head with oil, but this woman has anointed My feet with fragrant oil. 47Therefore I say to you, her sins, *which are* many, are forgiven, for she loved much. But to whom little is forgiven, *the same* loves little."

48Then He said to her, "Your sins are forgiven."

49And those who sat at the table with Him began to say to themselves, "Who is this who even forgives sins?"

50Then He said to the woman, "Your faith has saved you. Go in peace."

CHAPTER 8

8:1–25 *A multitude hearing Him.* Jesus was not impressed by the crowds that followed Him, for He knew the spiritual condition of their hearts. The parable of the sower helps us examine our hearts to see how we respond to the Word. But it is not enough to hear the Word (vv. 8, 18); we must also obey it (v. 21) and trust it when the time of testing comes (vv. 22–25).

8 Now* it came to pass, afterward, that He went through every city and village, preaching and bringing the glad tidings of the kingdom of God. And the twelve *were* with Him, 2and certain women who had been healed of evil spirits and infirmities—Mary called Magdalene, out of whom had come seven demons, 3and Joanna the wife of Chuza, Herod's steward, and Susanna, and many others who provided for Him*f* from their substance.

4And when a great multitude had gathered, and they had come to Him from every city, He spoke by a parable: 5"A sower went out to sow his seed. And as he sowed, some fell by the wayside; and it was trampled down, and the birds of the air devoured it. 6Some fell on rock; and as soon as it sprang up, it withered away because it lacked moisture. 7And some fell among thorns, and the thorns sprang up with it and choked it. 8But others fell on good ground, sprang up, and yielded a crop a hundredfold." When He had said these things He cried, "He who has ears to hear, let him hear!"

9Then His disciples asked Him, saying, "What does this parable mean?"

10And He said, "To you it has been given to know the mysteries of the kingdom of God, but to the rest *it is given* in parables, that

---

8:3 *f*NU-Text and M-Text read *them*.

'Seeing they may not see,
And hearing they may not understand.'g

11"Now the parable is this: The seed is the word of God. 12Those by the wayside are the ones who hear; then the devil comes and takes away the word out of their hearts, lest they should believe and be saved. 13But the ones on the rock *are those* who, when they hear, receive the word with joy; and these have no root, who believe for a while and in time of temptation fall away. 14Now the ones *that* fell among thorns are those who, when they have heard, go out and are choked with cares, riches, and pleasures of life, and bring no fruit to maturity. 15But the ones *that* fell on the good ground are those who, having heard the word with a noble and good heart, keep *it* and bear fruit with patience.

16"No one, when he has lit a lamp, covers it with a vessel or puts *it* under a bed, but sets *it* on a lampstand, that those who enter may see the light. 17For nothing is secret that will not be revealed, nor *anything* hidden that will not be known and come to light. 18Therefore take heed how you hear. For whoever has, to him *more* will be given; and whoever does not have, even what he seems to have will be taken from him."

19Then His mother and brothers came to Him, and could not approach Him because of the crowd. 20And it was told Him *by some,* who said, "Your mother and Your brothers are standing outside, desiring to see You."

21But He answered and said to them, "My mother and My brothers are these who hear the word of God and do it."

22Now it happened, on a certain day, that He got into a boat with His disciples. And He said to them, "Let us cross over to the other side of the lake." And they launched out. 23But as they sailed He fell asleep. And a windstorm came down on the lake, and they were filling *with water,* and were in jeopardy. 24And they came to Him and awoke Him, saying, "Master, Master, we are perishing!"

Then He arose and rebuked the wind and the raging of the water. And they ceased, and there was a calm. 25But He said to them, "Where is your faith?"

And they were afraid, and marveled, saying to one another, "Who can this be? For He commands even the winds and water, and they obey Him!"

26*Then they sailed to the country of the Gadarenes,h which is opposite Galilee. 27And when He stepped out on the land, there met Him a certain man from the city who had demons for a long time. And he wore no clothes,i nor did he live in a house but in the tombs. 28When he saw Jesus, he cried out, fell down before Him, and with a loud voice said, "What have I to do with You, Jesus, Son of the Most High God? I beg You, do not torment me!" 29For He had commanded the unclean spirit to come out of the man. For it had often seized him, and he was kept under guard, bound with chains and shackles; and he broke the bonds and was driven by the demon into the wilderness.

8:26–39 *A multitude rejecting Him.* The healing of the Gadarene demoniacs (Matt. 8:28) should have endeared Jesus to the people, but the citizens were concerned more about pigs and money than about people and mercy. The man who begged to go with Jesus was the sanest one of all!

8:10 gIsaiah 6:9   8:26 hNU-Text reads *Gerasenes.*
8:27 iNU-Text reads *who had demons and for a long time wore no clothes.*

30Jesus asked him, saying, "What is your name?"

And he said, "Legion," because many demons had entered him. 31And they begged Him that He would not command them to go out into the abyss.

32Now a herd of many swine was feeding there on the mountain. So they begged Him that He would permit them to enter them. And He permitted them. 33Then the demons went out of the man and entered the swine, and the herd ran violently down the steep place into the lake and drowned.

34When those who fed *them* saw what had happened, they fled and told *it* in the city and in the country. 35Then they went out to see what had happened, and came to Jesus, and found the man from whom the demons had departed, sitting at the feet of Jesus, clothed and in his right mind. And they were afraid. 36They also who had seen *it* told by what means he who had been demon-possessed was healed. 37Then the whole multitude of the surrounding region of the Gadarenes[j] asked Him to depart from them, for they were seized with great fear. And He got into the boat and returned.

38Now the man from whom the demons had departed begged Him that he might be with Him. But Jesus sent him away, saying, 39"Return to your own house, and tell what great things God has done for you." And he went his way and proclaimed throughout the whole city what great things Jesus had done for him.

40*So it was, when Jesus returned, that the multitude welcomed Him, for they were all waiting for Him. 41*And behold, there came a man named Jairus, and he was a ruler of the synagogue. And he fell down at Jesus' feet and begged Him to come to his house, 42for he had an only daughter about twelve years of age, and she was dying.

But as He went, the multitudes thronged Him. 43Now a woman, having a flow of blood for twelve years, who had spent all her livelihood on physicians and could not be healed by any, 44came from behind and touched the border of His garment. And immediately her flow of blood stopped.

45And Jesus said, "Who touched Me?"

When all denied it, Peter and those with him[k] said, "Master, the multitudes throng and press You, and You say, 'Who touched Me?' "[l]

46But Jesus said, "Somebody touched Me, for I perceived power going out from Me." 47Now when the woman saw that she was not hidden, she came trembling; and falling down before Him, she declared to Him in the presence of all the people the reason she had touched Him and how she was healed immediately.

48And He said to her, "Daughter, be of good cheer;[m] your faith has made you well. Go in peace."

49While He was still speaking, someone came from the ruler of the synagogue's *house*, saying to him, "Your daughter is dead. Do not trouble the Teacher."[n]

50But when Jesus heard *it*, He answered him, saying, "Do not be afraid; only believe, and she will be made well." 51When He came into the

8:40 *A multitude welcoming Him.* This was on the other side of the Sea of Galilee, near Capernaum. Why did they welcome Him? Probably not because of their love for Him, but because they had seen many of His miracles and wanted Him to meet their needs. If Jesus were coming today, would you welcome Him? Why?

8:41–56 *A multitude thronging Him.* The people wanted to get next to Jesus so He could help them; but though they thronged Him, they did not have the touch of faith that the poor sick woman had. Being in the crowd is no assurance of receiving the blessing. Sometimes God has to get you away from the crowd before He can meet the need (v. 51).

8:37 [j]NU-Text reads *Gerasenes*.   8:45 [k]NU-Text omits *and those with him*.   [l]NU-Text omits *and You say, 'Who touched Me?'*   8:48 [m]NU-Text omits *be of good cheer*.
8:49 [n]NU-Text adds *anymore*.

house, He permitted no one to go in*o* except Peter, James, and John,*p* and the father and mother of the girl. 52Now all wept and mourned for her; but He said, "Do not weep; she is not dead, but sleeping." 53And they ridiculed Him, knowing that she was dead.

54But He put them all outside,*q* took her by the hand and called, saying, "Little girl, arise." 55Then her spirit returned, and she arose immediately. And He commanded that she be given *something* to eat. 56And her parents were astonished, but He charged them to tell no one what had happened.

9 Then* He called His twelve disciples together and gave them power and authority over all demons, and to cure diseases. 2He sent them to preach the kingdom of God and to heal the sick. 3And He said to them, "Take nothing for the journey, neither staffs nor bag nor bread nor money; and do not have two tunics apiece.

4"Whatever house you enter, stay there, and from there depart. 5And whoever will not receive you, when you go out of that city, shake off the very dust from your feet as a testimony against them."

6So they departed and went through the towns, preaching the gospel and healing everywhere.

7Now Herod the tetrarch heard of all that was done by Him; and he was perplexed, because it was said by some that John had risen from the dead, 8and by some that Elijah had appeared, and by others that one of the old prophets had risen again. 9Herod said, "John I have beheaded, but who is this of whom I hear such things?" So he sought to see Him.

10And the apostles, when they had returned, told Him all that they had done. Then He took them and went aside privately into a deserted place belonging to the city called Bethsaida. 11But when the multitudes knew *it*, they followed Him; and He received them and spoke to them about the kingdom of God, and healed those who had need of healing. 12*When the day began to wear away, the twelve came and said to Him, "Send the multitude away, that they may go into the surrounding towns and country, and lodge and get provisions; for we are in a deserted place here."

13But He said to them, "You give them something to eat."

And they said, "We have no more than five loaves and two fish, unless we go and buy food for all these people." 14For there were about five thousand men.

Then He said to His disciples, "Make them sit down in groups of fifty." 15And they did so, and made them all sit down.

16Then He took the five loaves and the two fish, and looking up to heaven, He blessed and broke *them*, and gave *them* to the disciples to set before the multitude. 17So they all ate and were filled, and twelve baskets of the leftover fragments were taken up by them.

18*And it happened, as He was alone praying, *that* His disciples joined Him, and He asked them, saying, "Who do the crowds say that I am?"

CHAPTER 9

9:1–6 *Christ equips us.* He will never send us out to do a task without first giving us what we need. We are prone to trust what we have, but we should trust in Him alone. If we are in His will, we will have His supply.

9:12–17 *Christ enables us.* How could twelve men feed five thousand people? Only through the enabling of the Lord, for He did the miracle: they only distributed the blessing. Christ is looking for clean empty hands that He can fill.

9:18–36 *Christ encourages us.* If you confess Christ as Son of God and Savior, and take up your cross and follow Him, He will reveal to you His kingdom and His glory. When you experience the glory of God, the demands of discipleship become blessings that carry you along in joyful obedience.

8:51 *o*NU-Text adds *with Him.*   *p*NU-Text and M-Text read *Peter, John, and James.*   8:54 *q*NU-Text omits *put them all outside.*

19So they answered and said, "John the Baptist, but some *say* Elijah; and others *say* that one of the old prophets has risen again."

20He said to them, "But who do you say that I am?"

Peter answered and said, "The Christ of God."

21And He strictly warned and commanded them to tell this to no one, 22saying, "The Son of Man must suffer many things, and be rejected by the elders and chief priests and scribes, and be killed, and be raised the third day."

23Then He said to *them* all, "If anyone desires to come after Me, let him deny himself, and take up his cross daily,*r* and follow Me. 24For whoever desires to save his life will lose it, but whoever loses his life for My sake will save it. 25For what profit is it to a man if he gains the whole world, and is himself destroyed or lost? 26For whoever is ashamed of Me and My words, of him the Son of Man will be ashamed when He comes in His *own* glory, and in *His* Father's, and of the holy angels. 27But I tell you truly, there are some standing here who shall not taste death till they see the kingdom of God."

28Now it came to pass, about eight days after these sayings, that He took Peter, John, and James and went up on the mountain to pray. 29As He prayed, the appearance of His face was altered, and His robe *became* white *and* glistening. 30And behold, two men talked with Him, who were Moses and Elijah, 31who appeared in glory and spoke of His decease which He was about to accomplish at Jerusalem. 32But Peter and those with him were heavy with sleep; and when they were fully awake, they saw His glory and the two men who stood with Him. 33Then it happened, as they were parting from Him, *that* Peter said to Jesus, "Master, it is good for us to be here; and let us make three tabernacles: one for You, one for Moses, and one for Elijah"—not knowing what he said.

34While he was saying this, a cloud came and overshadowed them; and they were fearful as they entered the cloud. 35And a voice came out of the cloud, saying, "This is My beloved Son.*s* Hear Him!" 36When the voice had ceased, Jesus was found alone. But they kept quiet, and told no one in those days any of the things they had seen.

37*Now it happened on the next day, when they had come down from the mountain, that a great multitude met Him. 38Suddenly a man from the multitude cried out, saying, "Teacher, I implore You, look on my son, for he is my only child. 39And behold, a spirit seizes him, and he suddenly cries out; it convulses him so that he foams *at the mouth*; and it departs from him with great difficulty, bruising him. 40So I implored Your disciples to cast it out, but they could not."

41Then Jesus answered and said, "O faithless and perverse generation, how long shall I be with you and bear with you? Bring your son here." 42And as he was still coming, the demon threw him down and convulsed *him*. Then Jesus rebuked the unclean spirit, healed the child, and gave him back to his father.

43And they were all amazed at the majesty of God.

9:37–62 *Christ endures us.* What strange words from the lips of Jesus: "How long shall I be with you and bear with you?" (v. 41). He must bear with our unbelief and failure (vv. 37–42), our spiritual blindness (vv. 43–45), our pride (vv. 46–48), our lack of love (vv. 49–56), and our lack of dedication (vv. 57–62). Is Jesus blessing you—or bearing with you?

9:23 *M-Text omits *daily*.   9:35 *NU-Text reads *This is My Son, the Chosen One.*

But while everyone marveled at all the things which Jesus did, He said to His disciples, 44"Let these words sink down into your ears, for the Son of Man is about to be betrayed into the hands of men." 45But they did not understand this saying, and it was hidden from them so that they did not perceive it; and they were afraid to ask Him about this saying.

46Then a dispute arose among them as to which of them would be greatest. 47And Jesus, perceiving the thought of their heart, took a little child and set him by Him, 48and said to them, "Whoever receives this little child in My name receives Me; and whoever receives Me receives Him who sent Me. For he who is least among you all will be great."

49Now John answered and said, "Master, we saw someone casting out demons in Your name, and we forbade him because he does not follow with us."

50But Jesus said to him, "Do not forbid *him*, for he who is not against us[t] is on our[u] side."

51Now it came to pass, when the time had come for Him to be received up, that He steadfastly set His face to go to Jerusalem, 52and sent messengers before His face. And as they went, they entered a village of the Samaritans, to prepare for Him. 53But they did not receive Him, because His face was *set* for the journey to Jerusalem. 54And when His disciples James and John saw *this*, they said, "Lord, do You want us to command fire to come down from heaven and consume them, just as Elijah did?"[v]

55But He turned and rebuked them,[w] and said, "You do not know what manner of spirit you are of. 56For the Son of Man did not come to destroy men's lives but to save *them*."[x] And they went to another village.

57Now it happened as they journeyed on the road, *that* someone said to Him, "Lord, I will follow You wherever You go."

58And Jesus said to him, "Foxes have holes and birds of the air *have* nests, but the Son of Man has nowhere to lay *His* head."

59Then He said to another, "Follow Me."

But he said, "Lord, let me first go and bury my father."

60Jesus said to him, "Let the dead bury their own dead, but you go and preach the kingdom of God."

61And another also said, "Lord, I will follow You, but let me first go *and* bid them farewell who are at my house."

62But Jesus said to him, "No one, having put his hand to the plow, and looking back, is fit for the kingdom of God."

10

After* these things the Lord appointed seventy others also,[y] and sent them two by two before His face into every city and place where He Himself was about to go. 2Then He said to them, "The harvest truly *is* great, but the laborers *are* few; therefore pray the Lord of the harvest to send out laborers into His harvest. 3Go your way; behold, I send you out as lambs among wolves. 4Carry neither money bag, knapsack, nor

Serving Him

Faithful to my Lord's commands,
I still would choose the better part;
Serve with careful Martha's hands
And loving Mary's heart.

—Charles Wesley

CHAPTER 10

10:1, 2 The chapter asks four questions by way of personal inventory.

What makes you serve? Jesus was not limited to the Twelve; seventy others obeyed Him and helped to reap the harvest. But the laborers are still few, and Luke 9:57–62 tells why. The ministry is difficult and dangerous, but it is also very rewarding. Are you obedient to His call?

9:50 [t]NU-Text reads *you.* [u]NU-Text reads *your.*
9:54 [v]NU-Text omits *just as Elijah did.* 9:55 [w]NU-Text omits the rest of this verse. 9:56 [x]NU-Text omits the first sentence of this verse. 10:1 [y]NU-Text reads *seventy-two others.*

> **"** *Justice seeks out the merits of the case, but pity only regards the need.* **"**
> —Bernard of Clairvaux

sandals; and greet no one along the road. 5But whatever house you enter, first say, 'Peace to this house.' 6And if a son of peace is there, your peace will rest on it; if not, it will return to you. 7And remain in the same house, eating and drinking such things as they give, for the laborer is worthy of his wages. Do not go from house to house. 8Whatever city you enter, and they receive you, eat such things as are set before you. 9And heal the sick there, and say to them, 'The kingdom of God has come near to you.' 10But whatever city you enter, and they do not receive you, go out into its streets and say, 11'The very dust of your city which clings to us*z* we wipe off against you. Nevertheless know this, that the kingdom of God has come near you.' 12But*a* I say to you that it will be more tolerable in that Day for Sodom than for that city.

13"Woe to you, Chorazin! Woe to you, Bethsaida! For if the mighty works which were done in you had been done in Tyre and Sidon, they would have repented long ago, sitting in sackcloth and ashes. 14But it will be more tolerable for Tyre and Sidon at the judgment than for you. 15And you, Capernaum, who are exalted to heaven, will be brought down to Hades.*b* 16He who hears you hears Me, he who rejects you rejects Me, and he who rejects Me rejects Him who sent Me."

17*Then the seventy*c* returned with joy, saying, "Lord, even the demons are subject to us in Your name."

18And He said to them, "I saw Satan fall like lightning from heaven. 19Behold, I give you the authority to trample on serpents and scorpions, and over all the power of the enemy, and nothing shall by any means hurt you. 20Nevertheless do not rejoice in this, that the spirits are subject to you, but rather*d* rejoice because your names are written in heaven."

21In that hour Jesus rejoiced in the Spirit and said, "I thank You, Father, Lord of heaven and earth, that You have hidden these things from *the* wise and prudent and revealed them to babes. Even so, Father, for so it seemed good in Your sight. 22All*e* things have been delivered to Me by My Father, and no one knows who the Son is except the Father, and who the Father is except the Son, and *the one* to whom the Son wills to reveal *Him.*"

23Then He turned to *His* disciples and said privately, "Blessed *are* the eyes which see the things you see; 24for I tell you that many prophets and kings have desired to see what you see, and have not seen *it,* and to hear what you hear, and have not heard *it.*"

25*And behold, a certain lawyer stood up and tested Him, saying, "Teacher, what shall I do to inherit eternal life?"

26He said to him, "What is written in the law? What is your reading *of it?*"

27So he answered and said, "'*You shall love the* LORD *your God with all your heart, with all your soul, with all your strength, and with all your mind,*'*f* and '*your neighbor as yourself.*'"*g*

10:17–24 *What makes you rejoice?* When the disciples rejoiced over their successful ministry, Jesus told them to rejoice because they were the citizens of heaven. After all, their work might not always be successful; but their salvation would never change. Jesus rejoiced because the Father's will was being accomplished in their lives. What brings joy to your heart?

10:25–37 *What makes you pause?* It is not difficult to discuss neighborliness in the abstract, but it costs something to be a real neighbor. Do you pause to help when you see injustice and hurt, or like the priest and the Levite, do you look for an escape? You are never more Christlike than when you feel another's hurt and seek to help.

10:11 *z*NU-Text reads *our feet.*   10:12 *a*NU-Text and M-Text omit *But.*   10:15 *b*NU-Text reads *will you be exalted to heaven? You will be thrust down to Hades!*   10:17 *c*NU-Text reads *seventy-two.*   10:20 *d*NU-Text and M-Text omit *rather.* 10:22 *e*M-Text reads *And turning to the disciples He said, "All . . . . .*   10:27 *f*Deuteronomy 6:5 *g*Leviticus 19:18

28And He said to him, "You have answered rightly; do this and you will live."

29But he, wanting to justify himself, said to Jesus, "And who is my neighbor?"

30Then Jesus answered and said: "A certain *man* went down from Jerusalem to Jericho, and fell among thieves, who stripped him of his clothing, wounded *him,* and departed, leaving *him* half dead. 31Now by chance a certain priest came down that road. And when he saw him, he passed by on the other side. 32Likewise a Levite, when he arrived at the place, came and looked, and passed by on the other side. 33But a certain Samaritan, as he journeyed, came where he was. And when he saw him, he had compassion. 34So he went to *him* and bandaged his wounds, pouring on oil and wine; and he set him on his own animal, brought him to an inn, and took care of him. 35On the next day, when he departed,*h* he took out two denarii, gave *them* to the innkeeper, and said to him, 'Take care of him; and whatever more you spend, when I come again, I will repay you.' 36So which of these three do you think was neighbor to him who fell among the thieves?"

37And he said, "He who showed mercy on him." Then Jesus said to him, "Go and do likewise."

38*Now it happened as they went that He entered a certain village; and a certain woman named Martha welcomed Him into her house. 39And she had a sister called Mary, who also sat at Jesus'*i* feet and heard His word. 40But Martha was distracted with much serving, and she approached Him and said, "Lord, do You not care that my sister has left me to serve alone? Therefore tell her to help me."

41And Jesus*j* answered and said to her, "Martha, Martha, you are worried and troubled about many things. 42But one thing is needed, and Mary has chosen that good part, which will not be taken away from her."

11 Now* it came to pass, as He was praying in a certain place, when He ceased, *that* one of His disciples said to Him, "Lord, teach us to pray, as John also taught his disciples."

2So He said to them, "When you pray, say:

Our Father in heaven,*k*
Hallowed be Your name.
Your kingdom come.*l*
Your will be done
On earth as *it is* in heaven.
3   Give us day by day our daily bread.
4   And forgive us our sins,
For we also forgive everyone who is
     indebted to us.
And do not lead us into temptation,
But deliver us from the evil one."*m*

5And He said to them, "Which of you shall have a friend, and go to him at midnight and say to him, 'Friend, lend me three loaves; 6for a friend of mine has come to me on his journey, and I have nothing to set before him'; 7and he will answer from within and say, 'Do not trouble me;

10:38–42 *What makes you listen?* Here is the basis for all ministry, taking time to sit at the feet of Jesus and hear His Word. It is important to serve the Lord and serve others, but it is even more important to delight your Lord by spending time with Him. Are you so busy serving Him that you have no time to love Him and listen to Him?

CHAPTER 11

11:1–13 *His generosity.* If Jesus, John the Baptist, and the Twelve all needed to pray, how much more do *we* need to pray! We must put God's concerns first (vv. 2–4), because prayer is based on *sonship,* not friendship. God is a loving Father, not a grouchy neighbor; He gives us what we need. He neither slumbers nor sleeps; and He doesn't become irritated when we ask for help (James 1:5).

❝*Prayer is a mighty instrument, not for getting man's will done in Heaven, but for getting God's will done in earth.*❞

—Robert Law

10:35 *h*NU-Text omits *when he departed.* 10:39 *i*NU-Text reads *the Lord's.* 10:41 *j*NU-Text reads *the Lord.* 11:2 *k*NU-Text omits *Our* and *in heaven.* *l*NU-Text omits the rest of this verse. 11:4 *m*NU-Text omits *But deliver us from the evil one.*

the door is now shut, and my children are with me in bed; I cannot rise and give to you'? 8I say to you, though he will not rise and give to him because he is his friend, yet because of his persistence he will rise and give him as many as he needs.

9"So I say to you, ask, and it will be given to you; seek, and you will find; knock, and it will be opened to you. 10For everyone who asks receives, and he who seeks finds, and to him who knocks it will be opened. 11If a son asks for bread[n] from any father among you, will he give him a stone? Or if he asks for a fish, will he give him a serpent instead of a fish? 12Or if he asks for an egg, will he offer him a scorpion? 13If you then, being evil, know how to give good gifts to your children, how much more will your heavenly Father give the Holy Spirit to those who ask Him!"

11:14–36 *His authority.* More dangerous than open hostility (vv. 14–22) is attempted neutrality (vv. 23–26), for an empty life is an opportunity for Satan to move in and take over. The only sign we need is the "sign of Jonah," our Lord's resurrection from the dead (Acts 2:22–36). Jesus has won the victory over the prince of darkness. Obey Satan and you let in darkness rather than light, and soon you will not be able to distinguish between them (Matt. 6:22–23).

14*And He was casting out a demon, and it was mute. So it was, when the demon had gone out, that the mute spoke; and the multitudes marveled. 15But some of them said, "He casts out demons by Beelzebub,[o] the ruler of the demons."

16Others, testing Him, sought from Him a sign from heaven. 17But He, knowing their thoughts, said to them: "Every kingdom divided against itself is brought to desolation, and a house *divided* against a house falls. 18If Satan also is divided against himself, how will his kingdom stand? Because you say I cast out demons by Beelzebub. 19And if I cast out demons by Beelzebub, by whom do your sons cast *them* out? Therefore they will be your judges. 20But if I cast out demons with the finger of God, surely the kingdom of God has come upon you. 21When a strong man, fully armed, guards his own palace, his goods are in peace. 22But when a stronger than he comes upon him and overcomes him, he takes from him all his armor in which he trusted, and divides his spoils. 23He who is not with Me is against Me, and he who does not gather with Me scatters.

24"When an unclean spirit goes out of a man, he goes through dry places, seeking rest; and finding none, he says, 'I will return to my house from which I came.' 25And when he comes, he finds *it* swept and put in order. 26Then he goes and takes with *him* seven other spirits more wicked than himself, and they enter and dwell there; and the last *state* of that man is worse than the first."

27And it happened, as He spoke these things, that a certain woman from the crowd raised her voice and said to Him, "Blessed *is* the womb that bore You, and *the* breasts which nursed You!"

28But He said, "More than that, blessed *are* those who hear the word of God and keep it!"

29And while the crowds were thickly gathered together, He began to say, "This is an evil generation. It seeks a sign, and no sign will be given to it except the sign of Jonah the prophet.[p] 30For as Jonah became a sign to the Ninevites, so also the Son of Man will be to this generation. 31The queen of the South will rise up in the judgment with the men of this generation and condemn them, for she came from the ends of the earth to hear the wisdom of Solomon; and indeed a greater than Solomon *is* here. 32The men of Nineveh will rise up in the judgment with this generation and con-

11:11 [n]NU-Text omits the words from *bread* through *for* in the next sentence.   11:15 [o]NU-Text and M-Text read *Beelzebul.*   11:29 [p]NU-Text omits *the prophet.*

demn it, for they repented at the preaching of
Jonah; and indeed a greater than Jonah *is* here.
33"No one, when he has lit a lamp, puts *it* in a
secret place or under a basket, but on a lampstand, that those who come in may see the light.
34The lamp of the body is the eye. Therefore, when
your eye is good, your whole body also is full of
light. But when *your eye* is bad, your body also
is full of darkness. 35Therefore take heed that the
light which is in you is not darkness. 36If then
your whole body *is* full of light, having no part
dark, *the* whole *body* will be full of light, as when
the bright shining of a lamp gives you light."
37*And as He spoke, a certain Pharisee asked
Him to dine with him. So He went in and sat down
to eat. 38When the Pharisee saw *it*, he marveled
that He had not first washed before dinner.
39Then the Lord said to him, "Now you Pharisees make the outside of the cup and dish clean,
but your inward part is full of greed and wickedness. 40Foolish ones! Did not He who made the
outside make the inside also? 41But rather give
alms of such things as you have; then indeed all
things are clean to you.
42"But woe to you Pharisees! For you tithe mint
and rue and all manner of herbs, and pass by justice and the love of God. These you ought to have
done, without leaving the others undone. 43Woe
to you Pharisees! For you love the best seats in
the synagogues and greetings in the marketplaces. 44Woe to you, scribes and Pharisees, hypocrites![q] For you are like graves which are not seen,
and the men who walk over *them* are not aware
of them."
45Then one of the lawyers answered and said
to Him, "Teacher, by saying these things You reproach us also."
46And He said, "Woe to you also, lawyers! For
you load men with burdens hard to bear, and you
yourselves do not touch the burdens with one of
your fingers. 47Woe to you! For you build the
tombs of the prophets, and your fathers killed
them. 48In fact, you bear witness that you approve
the deeds of your fathers; for they indeed killed
them, and you build their tombs. 49Therefore the
wisdom of God also said, 'I will send them prophets and apostles, and *some* of them they will kill
and persecute,' 50that the blood of all the prophets
which was shed from the foundation of the world
may be required of this generation, 51from the
blood of Abel to the blood of Zechariah who perished between the altar and the temple. Yes, I say
to you, it shall be required of this generation.
52"Woe to you lawyers! For you have taken
away the key of knowledge. You did not enter in
yourselves, and those who were entering in you
hindered."
53And as He said these things to them,[r] the
scribes and the Pharisees began to assail *Him* vehemently, and to cross-examine Him about many
things, 54lying in wait for Him, and seeking to
catch Him in something He might say, that they
might accuse Him.[s]

12 In* the meantime, when an innumerable
multitude of people had gathered together,

11:44 [q]NU-Text omits *scribes and Pharisees, hypocrites.*
11:53 [r]NU-Text reads *And when He left there.*
11:54 [s]NU-Text omits *and seeking* and *that they might accuse Him.*

11:37–54 *His honesty.* He was a guest in the home, but Jesus did not flatter His host or the other guests by avoiding the truth. He exposed their hypocrisy and condemned them for their sins (Matt. 23). They defiled people (v. 44), burdened them (v. 46), and locked the door on them (v. 52), all the while posing as holy men of God. Instead of taking the opportunity of repenting and being forgiven, they opposed Jesus and attacked Him. What fools!

CHAPTER 12

12:1–12 *A fearful heart.* When you fear people, you start to hide things, and this leads to hypocrisy. You fail to confess Christ openly and depend on the Holy Spirit (vv. 8–12), and this silences your witness. When you fear God alone, you need fear no one else; and you can boldly witness for Christ. You are important to God and precious in His sight, so never fear what people can say or do.

so that they trampled one another, He began to say to His disciples first *of all,* "Beware of the leaven of the Pharisees, which is hypocrisy. [2]For there is nothing covered that will not be revealed, nor hidden that will not be known. [3]Therefore whatever you have spoken in the dark will be heard in the light, and what you have spoken in the ear in inner rooms will be proclaimed on the housetops.

[4]"And I say to you, My friends, do not be afraid of those who kill the body, and after that have no more that they can do. [5]But I will show you whom you should fear: Fear Him who, after He has killed, has power to cast into hell; yes, I say to you, fear Him!

[6]"Are not five sparrows sold for two copper coins?[t] And not one of them is forgotten before God. [7]But the very hairs of your head are all numbered. Do not fear therefore; you are of more value than many sparrows.

[8]"Also I say to you, whoever confesses Me before men, him the Son of Man also will confess before the angels of God. [9]But he who denies Me before men will be denied before the angels of God.

[10]"And anyone who speaks a word against the Son of Man, it will be forgiven him; but to him who blasphemes against the Holy Spirit, it will not be forgiven.

[11]"Now when they bring you to the synagogues and magistrates and authorities, do not worry about how or what you should answer, or what you should say. [12]For the Holy Spirit will teach you in that very hour what you ought to say."

[13]Then one from the crowd said to Him, "Teacher, tell my brother to divide the inheritance with me."

[14]But He said to him, "Man, who made Me a judge or an arbitrator over you?" [15]And He said to them, "Take heed and beware of covetousness,[u] for one's life does not consist in the abundance of the things he possesses."

[16]Then He spoke a parable to them, saying: "The ground of a certain rich man yielded plentifully. [17]And he thought within himself, saying, 'What shall I do, since I have no room to store my crops?' [18]So he said, 'I will do this: I will pull down my barns and build greater, and there I will store all my crops and my goods. [19]And I will say to my soul, "Soul, you have many goods laid up for many years; take your ease; eat, drink, *and* be merry." ' [20]But God said to him, 'Fool! This night your soul will be required of you; then whose will those things be which you have provided?'

[21]"So *is* he who lays up treasure for himself, and is not rich toward God."

[22]*Then He said to His disciples, "Therefore I say to you, do not worry about your life, what you will eat; nor about the body, what you will put on. [23]Life is more than food, and the body *is more* than clothing. [24]Consider the ravens, for they neither sow nor reap, which have neither storehouse nor barn; and God feeds them. Of how much more value are you than the birds? [25]And which of you by worrying can add one cubit to his stature? [26]If you then are not able to do *the*

12:13–21 *A greedy heart.* Imagine being so greedy that you would interrupt a sermon to ask for help to get more money! The weeds were certainly growing in that man's heart (Matt. 13:22). We all need a certain amount of money to live, but money is not a guarantee of security. If anything, it creates a *false* confidence that leads to foolishness.

12:22–34 *A divided heart.* The word translated "worry" (v. 22) means "to be pulled apart," and that is what worry does to you. If your heart is centered on Christ and trusting wholly in Him (v. 31), you will have a united heart that fears God alone (Ps. 86:11). If your treasures are heavenly, you need not worry; no enemy can take them!

12:6 [t]Greek *assarion,* a coin of very small value   12:15 [u]NU-Text reads *all covetousness.*

least, why are you anxious for the rest? 27Consider the lilies, how they grow: they neither toil nor spin; and yet I say to you, even Solomon in all his glory was not arrayed like one of these. 28If then God so clothes the grass, which today is in the field and tomorrow is thrown into the oven, how much more *will He clothe* you, O *you* of little faith?

29"And do not seek what you should eat or what you should drink, nor have an anxious mind. 30For all these things the nations of the world seek after, and your Father knows that you need these things. 31But seek the kingdom of God, and all these things^v shall be added to you.

32"Do not fear, little flock, for it is your Father's good pleasure to give you the kingdom. 33Sell what you have and give alms; provide yourselves money bags which do not grow old, a treasure in the heavens that does not fail, where no thief approaches nor moth destroys. 34For where your treasure is, there your heart will be also.

35*"Let your waist be girded and *your* lamps burning; 36and you yourselves be like men who wait for their master, when he will return from the wedding, that when he comes and knocks they may open to him immediately. 37Blessed *are* those servants whom the master, when he comes, will find watching. Assuredly, I say to you that he will gird himself and have them sit down *to eat,* and will come and serve them. 38And if he should come in the second watch, or come in the third watch, and find *them* so, blessed are those servants. 39But know this, that if the master of the house had known what hour the thief would come, he would have watched and^w not allowed his house to be broken into. 40Therefore you also be ready, for the Son of Man is coming at an hour you do not expect."

41Then Peter said to Him, "Lord, do You speak this parable *only* to us, or to all *people?*"

42And the Lord said, "Who then is that faithful and wise steward, whom *his* master will make ruler over his household, to give *them their* portion of food in due season? 43Blessed *is* that servant whom his master will find so doing when he comes. 44Truly, I say to you that he will make him ruler over all that he has. 45But if that servant says in his heart, 'My master is delaying his coming,' and begins to beat the male and female servants, and to eat and drink and be drunk, 46the master of that servant will come on a day when he is not looking for *him,* and at an hour when he is not aware, and will cut him in two and appoint *him* his portion with the unbelievers. 47And that servant who knew his master's will, and did not prepare *himself* or do according to his will, shall be beaten with many *stripes.* 48But he who did not know, yet committed things deserving of stripes, shall be beaten with few. For everyone to whom much is given, from him much will be required; and to whom much has been committed, of him they will ask the more.

49"I came to send fire on the earth, and how I wish it were already kindled! 50But I have a baptism to be baptized with, and how distressed I am till it is accomplished! 51Do *you* suppose that I came to give peace on earth? I tell you, not at all, but rather division. 52For from now on five in

12:35–59 *A cold heart.* We are God's servants, and He expects us to be faithfully doing our work when Jesus Christ returns. But when we stop looking for His coming, loving it (2 Tim. 4:8), and longing for it (Rev. 22:20), our hearts get cold, and we get worldly. The Lord will deal with careless servants when He returns, so we had better be ready.

12:31 ^vNU-Text reads *His kingdom, and these things.*
12:39 ^wNU-Text reads *he would not have allowed.*

one house will be divided: three against two, and two against three. 53Father will be divided against son and son against father, mother against daughter and daughter against mother, mother-in-law against her daughter-in-law and daughter-in-law against her mother-in-law."

54Then He also said to the multitudes, "Whenever *you see* a cloud rising out of the west, immediately you say, 'A shower is coming'; and so it is. 55And when you see the south wind blow, you say, 'There will be hot weather'; and there is. 56Hypocrites! You can discern the face of the sky and of the earth, but how *is it* you do not discern this time?

57"Yes, and why, even of yourselves, do you not judge what is right? 58When you go with your adversary to the magistrate, make every effort along the way to settle with him, lest he drag you to the judge, the judge deliver you to the officer, and the officer throw you into prison. 59I tell you, you shall not depart from there till you have paid the very last mite."

13 There* were present at that season some who told Him about the Galileans whose blood Pilate had mingled with their sacrifices. 2And Jesus answered and said to them, "Do you suppose that these Galileans were worse sinners than all *other* Galileans, because they suffered such things? 3I tell you, no; but unless you repent you will all likewise perish. 4Or those eighteen on whom the tower in Siloam fell and killed them, do you think that they were worse sinners than all *other* men who dwelt in Jerusalem? 5I tell you, no; but unless you repent you will all likewise perish."

6He also spoke this parable: "A certain *man* had a fig tree planted in his vineyard, and he came seeking fruit on it and found none. 7Then he said to the keeper of his vineyard, 'Look, for three years I have come seeking fruit on this fig tree and find none. Cut it down; why does it use up the ground?' 8But he answered and said to him, 'Sir, let it alone this year also, until I dig around it and fertilize *it*. 9And if it bears fruit, *well*. But if not, after thatˣ you can cut it down.' "

10*Now He was teaching in one of the synagogues on the Sabbath. 11And behold, there was a woman who had a spirit of infirmity eighteen years, and was bent over and could in no way raise *herself* up. 12But when Jesus saw her, He called *her* to *Him* and said to her, "Woman, you are loosed from your infirmity." 13And He laid *His* hands on her, and immediately she was made straight, and glorified God.

14But the ruler of the synagogue answered with indignation, because Jesus had healed on the Sabbath; and he said to the crowd, "There are six days on which men ought to work; therefore come and be healed on them, and not on the Sabbath day."

15The Lord then answered him and said, "Hypocrite!ʸ Does not each one of you on the Sabbath loose his ox or donkey from the stall, and lead *it* away to water it? 16So ought not this woman, being a daughter of Abraham, whom Satan has bound—think of it—for eighteen years, be loosed

13:1–9 *Tragedy.* How easy it is to ask questions about others' tragedies and fail to learn the lessons they teach! The big question is not "Why do people die in tragic and seemingly meaningless ways?" but "Why does God keep me alive?" Am I really worth it? Am I bearing fruit or just taking up space?

13:10–17 *Hypocrisy.* The ruler of the synagogue was a hypocrite because he treated animals better than he treated people. Suppose the woman did come to the synagogue on another day. Could he have healed her? Of course not! We wonder how many needy people come to church meetings looking for love and help and go away disappointed.

❝*Yesterday is a canceled check. Tomorrow is a promissory note. Today is the only cash you have, so invest it wisely.*❞

13:9 ˣNU-Text reads *And if it bears fruit after that, well. But if not, you can cut it down.* 13:15 ʸNU-Text and M-Text read *Hypocrites.*

from this bond on the Sabbath?" ¹⁷And when He said these things, all His adversaries were put to shame; and all the multitude rejoiced for all the glorious things that were done by Him.

¹⁸*Then He said, "What is the kingdom of God like? And to what shall I compare it? ¹⁹It is like a mustard seed, which a man took and put in his garden; and it grew and became a large^z tree, and the birds of the air nested in its branches."

²⁰And again He said, "To what shall I liken the kingdom of God? ²¹It is like leaven, which a woman took and hid in three measures^a of meal till it was all leavened."

²²And He went through the cities and villages, teaching, and journeying toward Jerusalem. ²³Then one said to Him, "Lord, are there few who are saved?"

And He said to them, ²⁴"Strive to enter through the narrow gate, for many, I say to you, will seek to enter and will not be able. ²⁵When once the Master of the house has risen up and shut the door, and you begin to stand outside and knock at the door, saying, 'Lord, Lord, open for us,' and He will answer and say to you, 'I do not know you, where you are from,' ²⁶then you will begin to say, 'We ate and drank in Your presence, and You taught in our streets.' ²⁷But He will say, 'I tell you I do not know you, where you are from. Depart from Me, all you workers of iniquity.' ²⁸There will be weeping and gnashing of teeth, when you see Abraham and Isaac and Jacob and all the prophets in the kingdom of God, and yourselves thrust out. ²⁹They will come from the east and the west, from the north and the south, and sit down in the kingdom of God. ³⁰And indeed there are last who will be first, and there are first who will be last."

³¹On that very day^b some Pharisees came, saying to Him, "Get out and depart from here, for Herod wants to kill You."

³²And He said to them, "Go, tell that fox, 'Behold, I cast out demons and perform cures today and tomorrow, and the third *day* I shall be perfected.' ³³Nevertheless I must journey today, tomorrow, and the *day* following; for it cannot be that a prophet should perish outside of Jerusalem.

³⁴O Jerusalem, Jerusalem, the one who kills the prophets and stones those who are sent to her! How often I wanted to gather your children together, as a hen *gathers* her brood under *her* wings, but you were not willing! ³⁵See! Your house is left to you desolate; and assuredly,^{c} I say to you, you shall not see Me until *the time* comes when you say, 'Blessed is He who comes in the name of the LORD!' "^{d}

14 Now* it happened, as He went into the house of one of the rulers of the Pharisees to eat bread on the Sabbath, that they watched Him closely. ²And behold, there was a certain man before Him who had dropsy. ³And Jesus, answering, spoke to the lawyers and Pharisees, saying, "Is it lawful to heal on the Sabbath?"^{e}

⁴But they kept silent. And He took *him* and healed him, and let him go. ⁵Then He answered them, saying, "Which of you, having a donkey^f

13:18–35 Opportunity. God's kingdom is at work in this world, but many people fail to take advantage of their opportunities. Instead of entering the kingdom, some people only ask questions about it. Salvation is not a theory to discuss; it is a miracle to experience. No wonder Jesus wept when He saw sinners passing by their opportunities to be saved! Do not wait for opportunities to come; they are already here.

CHAPTER 14

14:1–14 Do I exploit people? When we eat together, it should be a time of loving fellowship and joyful gratitude to God; but the Pharisees turned tables into traps and exploited people. They used a man with a handicapping condition in trying to catch Jesus; they went to feasts only to receive honors; and they invited to their feasts only people who would return the favor. Hospitality is ministry only if our motive is to help others and glorify God.

13:19 ^{z}NU-Text omits *large*.   13:21 ^{a}Greek *sata*, approximately two pecks in all   13:31 ^{b}NU-Text reads *In that very hour*.   13:35 ^{c}NU-Text and M-Text omit *assuredly*. ^{d}Psalm 118:26   14:3 ^{e}NU-Text adds *or not*. 14:5 ^{f}NU-Text and M-Text read *son*.

or an ox that has fallen into a pit, will not immediately pull him out on the Sabbath day?" 6And they could not answer Him regarding these things.

7So He told a parable to those who were invited, when He noted how they chose the best places, saying to them: 8"When you are invited by anyone to a wedding feast, do not sit down in the best place, lest one more honorable than you be invited by him; 9and he who invited you and him come and say to you, 'Give place to this man,' and then you begin with shame to take the lowest place. 10But when you are invited, go and sit down in the lowest place, so that when he who invited you comes he may say to you, 'Friend, go up higher.' Then you will have glory in the presence of those who sit at the table with you. 11For whoever exalts himself will be humbled, and he who humbles himself will be exalted."

12Then He also said to him who invited Him, "When you give a dinner or a supper, do not ask your friends, your brothers, your relatives, nor rich neighbors, lest they also invite you back, and you be repaid. 13But when you give a feast, invite *the* poor, *the* maimed, *the* lame, *the* blind. 14And you will be blessed, because they cannot repay you; for you shall be repaid at the resurrection of the just."

15*Now when one of those who sat at the table with Him heard these things, he said to Him, "Blessed *is* he who shall eat bread{{g}} in the kingdom of God!"

16Then He said to him, "A certain man gave a great supper and invited many, 17and sent his servant at supper time to say to those who were invited, 'Come, for all things are now ready.' 18But they all with one *accord* began to make excuses. The first said to him, 'I have bought a piece of ground, and I must go and see it. I ask you to have me excused.' 19And another said, 'I have bought five yoke of oxen, and I am going to test them. I ask you to have me excused.' 20Still another said, 'I have married a wife, and therefore I cannot come.' 21So that servant came and reported these things to his master. Then the master of the house, being angry, said to his servant, 'Go out quickly into the streets and lanes of the city, and bring in here *the* poor and *the* maimed and *the* lame and *the* blind.' 22And the servant said, 'Master, it is done as you commanded, and still there is room.' 23Then the master said to the servant, 'Go out into the highways and hedges, and compel *them* to come in, that my house may be filled. 24For I say to you that none of those men who were invited shall taste my supper.'"

25*Now great multitudes went with Him. And He turned and said to them, 26"If anyone comes to Me and does not hate his father and mother, wife and children, brothers and sisters, yes, and his own life also, he cannot be My disciple. 27And whoever does not bear his cross and come after Me cannot be My disciple. 28For which of you, intending to build a tower, does not sit down first and count the cost, whether he has *enough* to finish *it*— 29lest, after he has laid the foundation, and is not able to finish, all who see *it* begin to mock him, 30saying, 'This man began to build and was not able to finish.' 31Or what king, going to make war against another king, does not sit down first and consider whether he is able with

14:15–24 Do I invite people? Salvation is a feast, not a funeral (5:33–39); and God wants His house filled. As His servants, we have the privilege to tell the world, "Come, for all things are now ready!" (v. 17). Even if some reject the invitation, keep sharing it. Those who think they are the least worthy are the ones He wants to have at His feast.

14:25–35 Do I follow people? It is easy to be part of the crowd and follow a popular Jesus, but that is not true discipleship. He calls you away from the crowd to take up your cross and follow Him. When it comes to winning the lost, God wants His house filled; but when it comes to discipleship, Christ thins out the ranks and wants only those who will die to self and live for Him.

14:15 {{g}}M-Text reads *dinner.*

ten thousand to meet him who comes against him with twenty thousand? ³²Or else, while the other is still a great way off, he sends a delegation and asks conditions of peace. ³³So likewise, whoever of you does not forsake all that he has cannot be My disciple.

³⁴"Salt *is* good; but if the salt has lost its flavor, how shall it be seasoned? ³⁵It is neither fit for the land nor for the dunghill, *but* men throw it out. He who has ears to hear, let him hear!'"

15 Then* all the tax collectors and the sinners drew near to Him to hear Him. ²And the Pharisees and scribes complained, saying, "This Man receives sinners and eats with them." ³So He spoke this parable to them, saying:

⁴"What man of you, having a hundred sheep, if he loses one of them, does not leave the ninety-nine in the wilderness, and go after the one which is lost until he finds it? ⁵And when he has found *it,* he lays *it* on his shoulders, rejoicing. ⁶And when he comes home, he calls together *his* friends and neighbors, saying to them, 'Rejoice with me, for I have found my sheep which was lost!' ⁷I say to you that likewise there will be more joy in heaven over one sinner who repents than over ninety-nine just persons who need no repentance.

⁸"Or what woman, having ten silver coins,^h if she loses one coin, does not light a lamp, sweep the house, and search carefully until she finds *it*? ⁹And when she has found *it,* she calls *her* friends and neighbors together, saying, 'Rejoice with me, for I have found the piece which I lost!' ¹⁰Likewise, I say to you, there is joy in the presence of the angels of God over one sinner who repents."

¹¹Then He said: "A certain man had two sons. ¹²And the younger of them said to *his* father, 'Father, give me the portion of goods that falls *to me.*' So he divided to them *his* livelihood. ¹³And not many days after, the younger son gathered all together, journeyed to a far country, and there wasted his possessions with prodigal living. ¹⁴But when he had spent all, there arose a severe famine in that land, and he began to be in want. ¹⁵Then he went and joined himself to a citizen of that country, and he sent him into his fields to feed swine. ¹⁶And he would gladly have filled his stomach with the pods that the swine ate, and no one gave him *anything.*

¹⁷"But when he came to himself, he said, 'How many of my father's hired servants have bread enough and to spare, and I perish with hunger! ¹⁸I will arise and go to my father, and will say to him, "Father, I have sinned against heaven and before you, ¹⁹and I am no longer worthy to be called your son. Make me like one of your hired servants."'

²⁰"And he arose and came to his father. But when he was still a great way off, his father saw him and had compassion, and ran and fell on his neck and kissed him. ²¹And the son said to him, 'Father, I have sinned against heaven and in your sight, and am no longer worthy to be called your son.'

²²"But the father said to his servants, 'Bringⁱ out the best robe and put *it* on him, and put a

---

CHAPTER 15

15:1ff These parables are Christ's defense of His ministry, explaining why He fellowshiped with sinners and even ate with them.

He saw what they were. They were sheep that had gone astray and needed a shepherd to bring them home. They were lost coins, stamped with the image of God, needing to get back into circulation again. They were disobedient sons who were wasting their inheritance and needed to come home to the Father.

He saw how they got that way. Sheep are foolish animals and naturally go astray, but the spiritual shepherds in Israel had not faithfully ministered to them (Jer. 23; Ezek. 34). The woman lost the coin because of carelessness, and the son was lost because of his willfulness. The father did not search for the boy but let him learn his lessons the hard way and discover how good it was back home. (See Rom. 2:4.)

He saw what they could be. Jesus always saw the potential in people. The sheep could be brought back to the flock and bring joy to the shepherd; the coin could be found; and the son could return home and lovingly serve his father. There is hope for every sinner because Jesus welcomes everyone.

15:8 ^hGreek *drachma,* a valuable coin often worn in a ten-piece garland by married women   15:22 ⁱNU-Text reads *Quickly bring.*

ring on his hand and sandals on *his* feet. 23And bring the fatted calf here and kill *it*, and let us eat and be merry; 24for this my son was dead and is alive again; he was lost and is found.' And they began to be merry.

25"Now his older son was in the field. And as he came and drew near to the house, he heard music and dancing. 26So he called one of the servants and asked what these things meant. 27And he said to him, 'Your brother has come, and because he has received him safe and sound, your father has killed the fatted calf.'

28"But he was angry and would not go in. Therefore his father came out and pleaded with him. 29So he answered and said to *his* father, 'Lo, these many years I have been serving you; I never transgressed your commandment at any time; and yet you never gave me a young goat, that I might make merry with my friends. 30But as soon as this son of yours came, who has devoured your livelihood with harlots, you killed the fatted calf for him.'

31"And he said to him, 'Son, you are always with me, and all that I have is yours. 32It was right that we should make merry and be glad, for your brother was dead and is alive again, and was lost and is found.'"

16 He* also said to His disciples: "There was a certain rich man who had a steward, and an accusation was brought to him that this man was wasting his goods. 2*So he called him and said to him, 'What is this I hear about you? Give an account of your stewardship, for you can no longer be steward.'

3"Then the steward said within himself, 'What shall I do? For my master is taking the stewardship away from me. I cannot dig; I am ashamed to beg. 4I have resolved what to do, that when I am put out of the stewardship, they may receive me into their houses.'

5"So he called every one of his master's debtors to *him*, and said to the first, 'How much do you owe my master?' 6And he said, 'A hundred measures*j* of oil.' So he said to him, 'Take your bill, and sit down quickly and write fifty.' 7Then he said to another, 'And how much do you owe?' So he said, 'A hundred measures*k* of wheat.' And he said to him, 'Take your bill, and write eighty.' 8So the master commended the unjust steward because he had dealt shrewdly. For the sons of this world are more shrewd in their generation than the sons of light.

9"And I say to you, make friends for yourselves by unrighteous mammon, that when you fail,*l* they may receive you into an everlasting home. 10*He who *is* faithful in *what is* least is faithful also in much; and he who is unjust in *what is* least is unjust also in much. 11Therefore if you have not been faithful in the unrighteous mammon, who will commit to your trust the true *riches*? 12And if you have not been faithful in what is another man's, who will give you what is your own?

13"No servant can serve two masters; for either he will hate the one and love the other, or else

---

CHAPTER 16

16:1 The subject is money, and the object is to teach us the proper place of money in life.

We can waste money. Stewards should use wealth for their masters' good and not for their own pleasure (1 Cor. 4:2). God wants us to *enjoy* His gifts (1 Tim. 6:17), but He also wants us to *employ* them wisely.

16:2–9 *We can serve God with money.* The man had a rude awakening: he had to give an account of his stewardship (Rom. 14:10–12; 2 Cor. 5:10). Then he learned to be wise and to invest wealth in people and in the future. We do not "buy" friends, but we can make friends for the Lord by the wise use of money. Will people welcome you to heaven because your stewardship made it possible for them to hear the gospel and be saved?

16:10–18 *We can try to serve God and money.* The Pharisees tried it but it cannot be done. How can you serve both righteousness and unrighteousness, what is greatest and what is least, what God honors and what He abominates? The world measures people by how much they get, but God measures them by how much they give.

❝*Make all you can, save all you can, give all you can.*❞
—John Wesley

❝*Money is a wonderful servant, a terrible master, and an abominable god.*❞

16:6 *j*Greek *batos*, eight or nine gallons each (Old Testament *bath*) 16:7 *k*Greek *koros*, ten or twelve bushels each (Old Testament *kor*) 16:9 *l*NU-Text reads *it fails.*

he will be loyal to the one and despise the other. You cannot serve God and mammon.''

14Now the Pharisees, who were lovers of money, also heard all these things, and they derided Him. 15And He said to them, "You are those who justify yourselves before men, but God knows your hearts. For what is highly esteemed among men is an abomination in the sight of God.

16"The law and the prophets *were* until John. Since that time the kingdom of God has been preached, and everyone is pressing into it. 17And it is easier for heaven and earth to pass away than for one tittle of the law to fail.

18"Whoever divorces his wife and marries another commits adultery; and whoever marries her who is divorced from *her* husband commits adultery.

19*"There was a certain rich man who was clothed in purple and fine linen and fared sumptuously every day. 20But there was a certain beggar named Lazarus, full of sores, who was laid at his gate, 21desiring to be fed with the crumbs which fell^m from the rich man's table. Moreover the dogs came and licked his sores. 22So it was that the beggar died, and was carried by the angels to Abraham's bosom. The rich man also died and was buried. 23And being in torments in Hades, he lifted up his eyes and saw Abraham afar off, and Lazarus in his bosom.

24"Then he cried and said, 'Father Abraham, have mercy on me, and send Lazarus that he may dip the tip of his finger in water and cool my tongue; for I am tormented in this flame.' 25But Abraham said, 'Son, remember that in your lifetime you received your good things, and likewise Lazarus evil things; but now he is comforted and you are tormented. 26And besides all this, between us and you there is a great gulf fixed, so that those who want to pass from here to you cannot, nor can those from there pass to us.'

27"Then he said, 'I beg you therefore, father, that you would send him to my father's house, 28for I have five brothers, that he may testify to them, lest they also come to this place of torment.' 29Abraham said to him, 'They have Moses and the prophets; let them hear them.' 30And he said, 'No, father Abraham; but if one goes to them from the dead, they will repent.' 31But he said to him, 'If they do not hear Moses and the prophets, neither will they be persuaded though one rise from the dead.' ''

17 Then* He said to the disciples, "It is impossible that no offenses should come, but woe *to him* through whom they do come! 2It would be better for him if a millstone were hung around his neck, and he were thrown into the sea, than that he should offend one of these little ones. 3Take heed to yourselves. If your brother sins against you,^n rebuke him; and if he repents, forgive him. 4And if he sins against you seven times in a day, and seven times in a day returns to you,^o saying, 'I repent,' you shall forgive him.''

5*And the apostles said to the Lord, "Increase our faith.''

6So the Lord said, "If you have faith as a mustard seed, you can say to this mulberry tree, 'Be

16:19–31 *We can let money be our god.* The rich man did not go to Hades because he was rich; he went there because riches were his god. Abraham was a wealthy man, and yet he was in paradise. Money can help send people to heaven (v. 9), or it can help send people to hell.

CHAPTER 17

17:1–4 Faith is like a seed: it seems small and weak, but it has life in it; and if it is cultivated, it will grow and release power. We need faith for many areas of life.

Faith to forgive. When people sin repeatedly, giving up on them is easy; but we must forgive them and trust God to work in their lives. We must be stepping stones and not stumbling blocks.

17:5–10 *Faith to serve.* It takes faith to do your duty, whether tending a field or a flock or preparing a meal. It takes faith to do the extraordinary, like moving a mountain.

16:21 ^mNU-Text reads *with what fell.*   17:3 ^nNU-Text omits *against you.*   17:4 ^oM-Text omits *to you.*

pulled up by the roots and be planted in the sea,'
and it would obey you. 7And which of you, having
a servant plowing or tending sheep, will say to
him when he has come in from the field, 'Come
at once and sit down to eat'? 8But will he not
rather say to him, 'Prepare something for my supper, and gird yourself and serve me till I have
eaten and drunk, and afterward you will eat and
drink'? 9Does he thank that servant because he
did the things that were commanded him? I think
not.[p] 10So likewise you, when you have done all
those things which you are commanded, say, 'We
are unprofitable servants. We have done what
was our duty to do.'"

17:11–19 *Faith to pray.* The ten men believed that Jesus could help them, and He did. The Samaritan not only brought joy to Christ's heart but received salvation from His hand: "Your faith has saved you!" When God answers your prayers, be sure to tell Him "thank You!"

11*Now it happened as He went to Jerusalem
that He passed through the midst of Samaria and
Galilee. 12Then as He entered a certain village,
there met Him ten men who were lepers, who
stood afar off. 13And they lifted up *their* voices
and said, "Jesus, Master, have mercy on us!"
14So when He saw *them*, He said to them, "Go,
show yourselves to the priests." And so it was
that as they went, they were cleansed.
15And one of them, when he saw that he was
healed, returned, and with a loud voice glorified
God, 16and fell down on *his* face at His feet, giving
Him thanks. And he was a Samaritan.
17So Jesus answered and said, "Were there not
ten cleansed? But where *are* the nine? 18Were
there not any found who returned to give glory
to God except this foreigner?" 19And He said to
him, "Arise, go your way. Your faith has made
you well."

17:20–37 *Faith to be ready when He comes.* The important thing is not to set dates but to be ready when He comes, for true faith leads to faithfulness. To *look around* at the increase in sin will discourage you, and to *look back* (as did Lot's wife, Gen. 19:28) may destroy you, so *look up* and eagerly expect the Lord's return today!

20*Now when He was asked by the Pharisees
when the kingdom of God would come, He answered them and said, "The kingdom of God does
not come with observation; 21nor will they say,
'See here!' or 'See there!'[q] For indeed, the kingdom of God is within you."
22Then He said to the disciples, "The days will
come when you will desire to see one of the days
of the Son of Man, and you will not see *it*.
23And they will say to you, 'Look here!' or 'Look
there!'[r] Do not go after *them* or follow *them*.
24For as the lightning that flashes out of one *part*
under heaven shines to the other *part* under
heaven, so also the Son of Man will be in His
day. 25But first He must suffer many things and
be rejected by this generation. 26And as it was in
the days of Noah, so it will be also in the days of
the Son of Man: 27They ate, they drank, they married wives, they were given in marriage, until the
day that Noah entered the ark, and the flood came
and destroyed them all. 28Likewise as it was also
in the days of Lot: They ate, they drank, they
bought, they sold, they planted, they built;
29but on the day that Lot went out of Sodom it
rained fire and brimstone from heaven and destroyed *them* all. 30Even so will it be in the day
when the Son of Man is revealed.
31"In that day, he who is on the housetop, and
his goods *are* in the house, let him not come down
to take them away. And likewise the one who is
in the field, let him not turn back. 32Remember
Lot's wife. 33Whoever seeks to save his life will
lose it, and whoever loses his life will preserve
it. 34I tell you, in that night there will be two *men*

17:9 [p]NU-Text ends verse with *commanded;* M-Text omits *him.* 17:21 [q]NU-Text reverses *here* and *there.*
17:23 [r]NU-Text reverses *here* and *there.*

in one bed: the one will be taken and the other will be left. 35Two *women* will be grinding together: the one will be taken and the other left. 36Two *men* will be in the field: the one will be taken and the other left."s

37And they answered and said to Him, "Where, Lord?"

So He said to them, "Wherever the body is, there the eagles will be gathered together."

18 Then* He spoke a parable to them, that men always ought to pray and not lose heart, 2saying: "There was in a certain city a judge who did not fear God nor regard man. 3Now there was a widow in that city; and she came to him, saying, 'Get justice for me from my adversary.' 4And he would not for a while; but afterward he said within himself, 'Though I do not fear God nor regard man, 5yet because this widow troubles me I will avenge her, lest by her continual coming she weary me.'"

6Then the Lord said, "Hear what the unjust judge said. 7And shall God not avenge His own elect who cry out day and night to Him, though He bears long with them? 8I tell you that He will avenge them speedily. Nevertheless, when the Son of Man comes, will He really find faith on the earth?"

9*Also He spoke this parable to some who trusted in themselves that they were righteous, and despised others: 10"Two men went up to the temple to pray, one a Pharisee and the other a tax collector. 11The Pharisee stood and prayed thus with himself, 'God, I thank You that I am not like other men—extortioners, unjust, adulterers, or even as this tax collector. 12I fast twice a week; I give tithes of all that I possess.' 13And the tax collector, standing afar off, would not so much as raise *his* eyes to heaven, but beat his breast, saying, 'God, be merciful to me a sinner!' 14I tell you, this man went down to his house justified *rather* than the other; for everyone who exalts himself will be humbled, and he who humbles himself will be exalted."

15Then they also brought infants to Him that He might touch them; but when the disciples saw *it,* they rebuked them. 16But Jesus called them to *Him* and said, "Let the little children come to Me, and do not forbid them; for of such is the kingdom of God. 17Assuredly, I say to you, whoever does not receive the kingdom of God as a little child will by no means enter it."

18*Now a certain ruler asked Him, saying, "Good Teacher, what shall I do to inherit eternal life?"

19So Jesus said to him, "Why do you call Me good? No one *is* good but One, *that is,* God. 20You know the commandments: 'Do not commit adultery,' 'Do not murder,' 'Do not steal,' 'Do not bear false witness,' 'Honor your father and your mother.'"t

21And he said, "All these things I have kept from my youth."

22So when Jesus heard these things, He said to him, "You still lack one thing. Sell all that you have and distribute to the poor, and you will have treasure in heaven; and come, follow Me."

CHAPTER 18

18:1–8 Confident prayer. If an unjust judge helps a poor widow, how much more will a loving Father meet the needs of His children? We have open access into His treasury (Rom. 5:2) and can claim His gracious promises (Luke 11:9–10), so we ought to pray with faith and confidence. No need to argue—just come!

18:9–17 Arrogant prayer. True prayer should humble us and make us love others more. We should be like children coming to a Father and not like attorneys bringing an indictment. If prayer doesn't bless the one praying, it isn't likely to help anybody else.

18:18–27 Ignorant prayer. Although the young man had many good qualities, one of them was not spiritual understanding. He did not really see himself, Jesus, or the peril he was in because of his riches. The publican went away justified (v. 14) while the young man went away sorrowful (v. 23). What happens at the close of your prayers?

❝*The revelation of our spiritual standing is what we ask in prayer; sometimes what we ask is an insult to God; we ask with our eyes on the possibilities or on ourselves, not on Jesus Christ.*❞
—Oswald Chambers

17:36 sNU-Text and M-Text omit verse 36.   18:20 tExodus 20:12–16; Deuteronomy 5:16–20

23But when he heard this, he became very sorrowful, for he was very rich.

24And when Jesus saw that he became very sorrowful, He said, "How hard it is for those who have riches to enter the kingdom of God! 25For it is easier for a camel to go through the eye of a needle than for a rich man to enter the kingdom of God."

26And those who heard it said, "Who then can be saved?"

27But He said, "The things which are impossible with men are possible with God."

28Then Peter said, "See, we have left all[u] and followed You."

29So He said to them, "Assuredly, I say to you, there is no one who has left house or parents or brothers or wife or children, for the sake of the kingdom of God, 30who shall not receive many times more in this present time, and in the age to come eternal life."

31Then He took the twelve aside and said to them, "Behold, we are going up to Jerusalem, and all things that are written by the prophets concerning the Son of Man will be accomplished. 32For He will be delivered to the Gentiles and will be mocked and insulted and spit upon. 33They will scourge *Him* and kill Him. And the third day He will rise again."

34But they understood none of these things; this saying was hidden from them, and they did not know the things which were spoken.

35*Then it happened, as He was coming near Jericho, that a certain blind man sat by the road begging. 36And hearing a multitude passing by, he asked what it meant. 37So they told him that Jesus of Nazareth was passing by. 38And he cried out, saying, "Jesus, Son of David, have mercy on me!"

39Then those who went before warned him that he should be quiet; but he cried out all the more, "Son of David, have mercy on me!"

40So Jesus stood still and commanded him to be brought to Him. And when he had come near, He asked him, 41saying, "What do you want Me to do for you?"

He said, "Lord, that I may receive my sight."

42Then Jesus said to him, "Receive your sight; your faith has made you well." 43And immediately he received his sight, and followed Him, glorifying God. And all the people, when they saw *it*, gave praise to God.

18:35–43 Persistent prayer. The blind man was not to be stopped! He had his great opportunity, and he would not let it pass. Our Lord stopped, looked, listened—and healed! Jesus is not too busy to hear you. Just be sure you are in earnest when you pray.

CHAPTER 19

19:1–10 The day of salvation. Verse 10 is illustrated in the experience of Zacchaeus: Jesus *came* to him, *sought* him, and *saved* him. Though He was surrounded by a great crowd of people, Jesus took time for individuals, and He even saw a man in a tree! He is still the seeking Savior, but now He uses *your* eyes and lips.

19 Then* *Jesus* entered and passed through Jericho. 2Now behold, *there was* a man named Zacchaeus who was a chief tax collector, and he was rich. 3And he sought to see who Jesus was, but could not because of the crowd, for he was of short stature. 4So he ran ahead and climbed up into a sycamore tree to see Him, for He was going to pass that *way.* 5And when Jesus came to the place, He looked up and saw him,[v] and said to him, "Zacchaeus, make haste and come down, for today I must stay at your house." 6So he made haste and came down, and received Him joyfully. 7But when they saw *it*, they all com-

18:28 [u]NU-Text reads *our own.*   19:5 [v]NU-Text omits *and saw him.*

God Seeks . . . —What is God looking for? He is seeking the lost (Luke 19:10), worshipers (John 4:23), fruit in our lives (Luke 13:7), and faithful servants (Ezek. 22:30). Has He found you?

plained, saying, "He has gone to be a guest with a man who is a sinner."

8Then Zacchaeus stood and said to the Lord, "Look, Lord, I give half of my goods to the poor; and if I have taken anything from anyone by false accusation, I restore fourfold."

9And Jesus said to him, "Today salvation has come to this house, because he also is a son of Abraham; 10for the Son of Man has come to seek and to save that which was lost."

11*Now as they heard these things, He spoke another parable, because He was near Jerusalem and because they thought the kingdom of God would appear immediately. 12Therefore He said: "A certain nobleman went into a far country to receive for himself a kingdom and to return. 13So he called ten of his servants, delivered to them ten minas,w and said to them, 'Do business till I come.' 14But his citizens hated him, and sent a delegation after him, saying, 'We will not have this man to reign over us.'

15"And so it was that when he returned, having received the kingdom, he then commanded these servants, to whom he had given the money, to be called to him, that he might know how much every man had gained by trading. 16Then came the first, saying, 'Master, your mina has earned ten minas.' 17And he said to him, 'Well done, good servant; because you were faithful in a very little, have authority over ten cities.' 18And the second came, saying, 'Master, your mina has earned five minas.' 19Likewise he said to him, 'You also be over five cities.'

20"Then another came, saying, 'Master, here is your mina, which I have kept put away in a handkerchief. 21For I feared you, because you are an austere man. You collect what you did not deposit, and reap what you did not sow.' 22And he said to him, 'Out of your own mouth I will judge you, you wicked servant. You knew that I was an austere man, collecting what I did not deposit and reaping what I did not sow. 23Why then did you not put my money in the bank, that at my coming I might have collected it with interest?'

24"And he said to those who stood by, 'Take the mina from him, and give it to him who has ten minas.' 25(But they said to him, 'Master, he has ten minas.') 26'For I say to you, that to everyone who has will be given; and from him who does not have, even what he has will be taken away from him. 27But bring here those enemies of mine, who did not want me to reign over them, and slay them before me.' "

28*When He had said this, He went on ahead, going up to Jerusalem. 29And it came to pass, when He drew near to Bethphagex and Bethany, at the mountain called Olivet, that He sent two of His disciples, 30saying, "Go into the village opposite you, where as you enter you will find a colt tied, on which no one has ever sat. Loose it and bring it here. 31And if anyone asks you, 'Why are you loosing it?' thus you shall say to him, 'Because the Lord has need of it.' "

32So those who were sent went their way and found it just as He had said to them. 33But as they were loosing the colt, the owners of it said to them, "Why are you loosing the colt?"

19:11–27 *The day of evaluation.* There are three possible relationships with the King. You can reject His rule and be an enemy, but that leads to judgment. You can accept His rule and be unfaithful, but that leads to loss of reward. Or you can accept His rule, do His will faithfully, and receive His reward. You are not to *protect* what He gives you but to *invest* it for His glory.

19:28–43 *The day of visitation.* What a tragedy that the Jewish nation did not know their own King when He came to them! But when He comes again, "will He really find faith on the earth" (18:8)? Our Lord wept, for He saw the terrible judgment that was coming to the city and the people.

19:13 *ᵂThe mina* (Greek *mna,* Hebrew *minah*) was worth about three months' salary.   19:29 ˣM-Text reads *Bethsphage.*

34And they said, "The Lord has need of him."
35Then they brought him to Jesus. And they threw
their own clothes on the colt, and they set Jesus
on him. 36And as He went, *many* spread their
clothes on the road.

37Then, as He was now drawing near the descent of the Mount of Olives, the whole multitude
of the disciples began to rejoice and praise God
with a loud voice for all the mighty works they
had seen, 38saying:

" '*Blessed is the King who comes in the name
    of the LORD!*'y
Peace in heaven and glory in the highest!"

39And some of the Pharisees called to Him from
the crowd, "Teacher, rebuke Your disciples."
40But He answered and said to them, "I tell you
that if these should keep silent, the stones would
immediately cry out."

41Now as He drew near, He saw the city and
wept over it, 42saying, "If you had known, even
you, especially in this your day, the things *that
make* for your peace! But now they are hidden
from your eyes. 43For days will come upon you
when your enemies will build an embankment
around you, surround you and close you in on
every side, 44and level you, and your children
within you, to the ground; and they will not leave
in you one stone upon another, because you did
not know the time of your visitation."

45Then He went into the temple and began to
drive out those who bought and sold in it,z
46saying to them, "It is written, '*My house is*a a
house of prayer,'b but you have made it a '*den of
thieves.*'"c

47And He was teaching daily in the temple. But
the chief priests, the scribes, and the leaders of
the people sought to destroy Him, 48and were unable to do anything; for all the people were very
attentive to hear Him.

CHAPTER 20

20:1–8 In spite of their evasive and
hypocritical reply, the leaders *could not
escape the past* (vv. 1–8). They had
rejected the ministry of John the Baptist, and
that led to their refusal to trust Jesus Christ.
You may forget your decisions, but they will
not forget you. You may even try to bury
them, but they will be resurrected to accuse
you.

20:9–19 Nor could they *escape future
judgment* They would reject the Son and
the Stone, and that would bring about their
ruin. Christ either saves you or judges you;
there is no middle ground.

66*Truth is incontrovertible. Panic
may resent it; ignorance may deride
it; malice may distort it; but
there it is.* 99
— Sir Winston Churchill

20 Now* it happened on one of those days, as
He taught the people in the temple and
preached the gospel, *that* the chief priests and
the scribes, together with the elders, confronted
Him 2and spoke to Him, saying, "Tell us, by what
authority are You doing these things? Or who is
he who gave You this authority?"

3But He answered and said to them, "I also will
ask you one thing, and answer Me: 4The baptism
of John—was it from heaven or from men?"

5And they reasoned among themselves, saying,
"If we say, 'From heaven,' He will say, 'Why thend
did you not believe him?' 6But if we say, 'From
men,' all the people will stone us, for they are
persuaded that John was a prophet." 7So they answered that they did not know where *it was* from.

8And Jesus said to them, "Neither will I tell you
by what authority I do these things."

9*Then He began to tell the people this parable:
"A certain man planted a vineyard, leased it to
vinedressers, and went into a far country for a
long time. 10Now at vintage-time he sent a servant
to the vinedressers, that they might give him some
of the fruit of the vineyard. But the vinedressers

19:38 yPsalm 118:26   19:45 zNU-Text reads *those who were
selling.*   19:46 aNU-Text reads *shall be.* bIsaiah
56:7 cJeremiah 7:11   20:5 dNU-Text and M-Text omit *then.*

beat him and sent *him* away empty-handed.
11Again he sent another servant; and they beat
him also, treated *him* shamefully, and sent *him*
away empty-handed. 12And again he sent a third;
and they wounded him also and cast *him* out.

13"Then the owner of the vineyard said, 'What
shall I do? I will send my beloved son. Probably
they will respect *him* when they see him.' 14But
when the vinedressers saw him, they reasoned
among themselves, saying, 'This is the heir. Come,
let us kill him, that the inheritance may be ours.'
15So they cast him out of the vineyard and killed
him. Therefore what will the owner of the vineyard do to them? 16He will come and destroy those
vinedressers and give the vineyard to others."

And when they heard *it* they said, "Certainly
not!"

17Then He looked at them and said, "What then
is this that is written:

> 'The stone which the builders rejected
> Has become the chief cornerstone'?e

18Whoever falls on that stone will be broken; but
on whomever it falls, it will grind him to powder."

19And the chief priests and the scribes that very
hour sought to lay hands on Him, but they feared
the peoplef—for they knew He had spoken this
parable against them.

20*So they watched *Him*, and sent spies who
pretended to be righteous, that they might seize
on His words, in order to deliver Him to the power
and the authority of the governor.

21Then they asked Him, saying, "Teacher, we
know that You say and teach rightly, and You
do not show personal favoritism, but teach the
way of God in truth: 22Is it lawful for us to pay
taxes to Caesar or not?"

23But He perceived their craftiness, and said to
them, "Why do you test Me?g 24Show Me a denarius. Whose image and inscription does it have?"

They answered and said, "Caesar's."

25And He said to them, "Render therefore to
Caesar the things that are Caesar's, and to God
the things that are God's."

26But they could not catch Him in His words
in the presence of the people. And they marveled
at His answer and kept silent.

27Then some of the Sadducees, who deny that
there is a resurrection, came to *Him* and asked
Him, 28saying: "Teacher, Moses wrote to us *that*
if a man's brother dies, having a wife, and he dies
without children, his brother should take his wife
and raise up offspring for his brother. 29Now there
were seven brothers. And the first took a wife,
and died without children. 30And the secondh took
her as wife, and he died childless. 31Then the third
took her, and in like manner the seven also; and
they left no children,i and died. 32Last of all the
woman died also. 33Therefore, in the resurrection,
whose wife does she become? For all seven had
her as wife."

34Jesus answered and said to them, "The sons
of this age marry and are given in marriage.
35But those who are counted worthy to attain that

20:20–47 The leaders even failed to
escape present responsibility. In asking
Jesus trick questions, they hoped He would
say something they could accuse; but His
answers only exposed their folly and
increased their guilt. They were fighting a
losing battle and would not surrender.

20:17 ePsalm 118:22   20:19 fM-Text reads *but they were
afraid.*   20:23 gNU-Text omits *Why do you test Me?*
20:30 hNU-Text ends verse 30 here.   20:31 iNU-Text and
M-Text read *the seven also left no children.*

age, and the resurrection from the dead, neither marry nor are given in marriage; 36nor can they die anymore, for they are equal to the angels and are sons of God, being sons of the resurrection. 37But even Moses showed in the *burning* bush *passage* that the dead are raised, when he called the Lord *'the God of Abraham, the God of Isaac, and the God of Jacob.'*[j] 38For He is not the God of the dead but of the living, for all live to Him."

39Then some of the scribes answered and said, "Teacher, You have spoken well." 40But after that they dared not question Him anymore.

41And He said to them, "How can they say that the Christ is the Son of David? 42Now David himself said in the Book of Psalms:

> 'The LORD said to my Lord,
> "Sit at My right hand,
> 43   Till I make Your enemies Your footstool." '[k]

44Therefore David calls Him *'Lord'*; how is He then his Son?"

45Then, in the hearing of all the people, He said to His disciples, 46"Beware of the scribes, who desire to go around in long robes, love greetings in the marketplaces, the best seats in the synagogues, and the best places at feasts, 47who devour widows' houses, and for a pretense make long prayers. These will receive greater condemnation."

CHAPTER 21

21:1–4 Maintaining the temple. Many of the religious leaders were corrupt, but the temple was still the place where God put His name and where sincere people could worship Him. Jesus did not criticize the people for supporting the temple ministry (Matt. 23:1–3), but He did notice *what* they gave. The *proportion*, not the portion, is important. Those who give "the widow's mite" give their all, not their least.

21:5–36 Destroying the temple. This is Luke's version of the Olivet Discourse found also in Matthew 24—25 and Mark 13. He is the only gospel writer who deals with our Lord's prediction of the fall of Jerusalem, which occurred in A.D. 70 (vv. 20–24). The rest of his report describes events in the last days before the return of Jesus Christ to earth. It will be a time of testing and testimony, oppression and opportunity, vengeance and victory.

21 And* He looked up and saw the rich putting their gifts into the treasury, 2and He saw also a certain poor widow putting in two mites. 3So He said, "Truly I say to you that this poor widow has put in more than all; 4for all these out of their abundance have put in offerings for God,[l] but she out of her poverty put in all the livelihood that she had."

5*Then, as some spoke of the temple, how it was adorned with beautiful stones and donations, He said, 6"These things which you see—the days will come in which not *one* stone shall be left upon another that shall not be thrown down."

7So they asked Him, saying, "Teacher, but when will these things be? And what sign *will there be* when these things are about to take place?"

8And He said: "Take heed that you not be deceived. For many will come in My name, saying, 'I am *He*,' and, 'The time has drawn near.' Therefore[m] do not go after them. 9But when you hear of wars and commotions, do not be terrified; for these things must come to pass first, but the end *will not come* immediately."

10Then He said to them, "Nation will rise against nation, and kingdom against kingdom. 11And there will be great earthquakes in various places, and famines and pestilences; and there will be fearful sights and great signs from heaven. 12But before all these things, they will lay their hands on you and persecute *you*, delivering *you* up to the synagogues and prisons. You will be brought before kings and rulers for My name's sake. 13But it will turn out for you as an occasion for testimony. 14Therefore settle *it* in your hearts not to meditate beforehand on what you will answer; 15for I will give you a mouth and wisdom

---

20:37 [j]Exodus 3:6, 15   20:43 [k]Psalm 110:1   21:4 [l]NU-Text omits *for God*.   21:8 [m]NU-Text omits *Therefore*.

which all your adversaries will not be able to contradict or resist. 16You will be betrayed even by parents and brothers, relatives and friends; and they will put *some* of you to death. 17And you will be hated by all for My name's sake. 18But not a hair of your head shall be lost. 19By your patience possess your souls.

20"But when you see Jerusalem surrounded by armies, then know that its desolation is near. 21Then let those who are in Judea flee to the mountains, let those who are in the midst of her depart, and let not those who are in the country enter her. 22For these are the days of vengeance, that all things which are written may be fulfilled. 23But woe to those who are pregnant and to those who are nursing babies in those days! For there will be great distress in the land and wrath upon this people. 24And they will fall by the edge of the sword, and be led away captive into all nations. And Jerusalem will be trampled by Gentiles until the times of the Gentiles are fulfilled.

25"And there will be signs in the sun, in the moon, and in the stars; and on the earth distress of nations, with perplexity, the sea and the waves roaring; 26men's hearts failing them from fear and the expectation of those things which are coming on the earth, for the powers of the heavens will be shaken. 27Then they will see the Son of Man coming in a cloud with power and great glory. 28Now when these things begin to happen, look up and lift up your heads, because your redemption draws near."

29Then He spoke to them a parable: "Look at the fig tree, and all the trees. 30When they are already budding, you see and know for yourselves that summer is now near. 31So you also, when you see these things happening, know that the kingdom of God is near. 32Assuredly, I say to you, this generation will by no means pass away till all things take place. 33Heaven and earth will pass away, but My words will by no means pass away.

34"But take heed to yourselves, lest your hearts be weighed down with carousing, drunkenness, and cares of this life, and that Day come on you unexpectedly. 35For it will come as a snare on all those who dwell on the face of the whole earth. 36Watch therefore, and pray always that you may be counted worthy[n] to escape all these things that will come to pass, and to stand before the Son of Man."

37*And in the daytime He was teaching in the temple, but at night He went out and stayed on the mountain called Olivet. 38Then early in the morning all the people came to Him in the temple to hear Him.

22 Now* the Feast of Unleavened Bread drew near, which is called Passover. 2And the chief priests and the scribes sought how they might kill Him, for they feared the people.

3Then Satan entered Judas, surnamed Iscariot, who was numbered among the twelve. 4So he went his way and conferred with the chief priests and captains, how he might betray Him to them. 5And they were glad, and agreed to give him money. 6So he promised and sought opportunity to betray Him to them in the absence of the multitude.

21:37, 38 Ministering in the temple. As a boy of twelve, Jesus discussed the Word in the temple (2:41–50); and He spent the last week before His death teaching the Word in His Father's house. He was hated by the religious leaders, and the temple was a den of thieves; but needy people were there, and Jesus taught them. He was quick to seize the opportunity, and the people were glad to hear Him.

CHAPTER 22

22:1–6 Satan in the temple. Judas was energized by Satan when he made his agreement with the religious leaders. Satan is a liar and murderer (John 8:44), and he helped Judas with his deception. But Satan deceived Judas as well, and the former disciple ended up a suicide. It is dangerous to make deals with the devil.

21:36 [n]NU-Text reads *may have strength.*

7Then came the Day of Unleavened Bread,
when the Passover must be killed. 8And He sent
Peter and John, saying, "Go and prepare the Passover for us, that we may eat."
9So they said to Him, "Where do You want us
to prepare?"
10And He said to them, "Behold, when you have
entered the city, a man will meet you carrying a
pitcher of water; follow him into the house which
he enters. 11Then you shall say to the master of
the house, 'The Teacher says to you, "Where is
the guest room where I may eat the Passover with
My disciples?" ' 12Then he will show you a large,
furnished upper room; there make ready."
13So they went and found it just as He had said
to them, and they prepared the Passover.
14When the hour had come, He sat down, and
the twelve[o] apostles with Him. 15Then He said to
them, "With *fervent* desire I have desired to eat
this Passover with you before I suffer; 16for I say
to you, I will no longer eat of it until it is fulfilled
in the kingdom of God."
17Then He took the cup, and gave thanks, and
said, "Take this and divide *it* among yourselves;
18for I say to you,[p] I will not drink of the fruit of
the vine until the kingdom of God comes."
19And He took bread, gave thanks and broke
it, and gave *it* to them, saying, "This is My body
which is given for you; do this in remembrance
of Me."
20Likewise He also *took* the cup after supper,
saying, "This cup *is* the new covenant in My
blood, which is shed for you. 21But behold, the
hand of My betrayer *is* with Me on the table.
22And truly the Son of Man goes as it has been
determined, but woe to that man by whom He is
betrayed!"
23Then they began to question among themselves, which of them it was who would do this
thing.

22:24–38 ***Satan in the Upper Room.*** Satan already controlled Judas, but he had to ask for permission to tempt Peter (Job 1:12; 2:6). Satan is not all-powerful and must obey the limits set by the Lord (1 Cor. 10:13). The apostles had experienced some great blessings that evening, but danger was very near. Be on your guard when you have had a rich spiritual experience, for Satan is about to attack. And especially beware when you are trying to decide who is the greatest!

24*Now there was also a dispute among them,
as to which of them should be considered the
greatest. 25And He said to them, "The kings of
the Gentiles exercise lordship over them, and
those who exercise authority over them are called
'benefactors.' 26But not so *among* you; on the contrary, he who is greatest among you, let him be
as the younger, and he who governs as he who
serves. 27For who *is* greater, he who sits at the
table, or he who serves? *Is* it not he who sits at
the table? Yet I am among you as the One who
serves.
28"But you are those who have continued with
Me in My trials. 29And I bestow upon you a kingdom, just as My Father bestowed *one* upon Me,
30that you may eat and drink at My table in My
kingdom, and sit on thrones judging the twelve
tribes of Israel."
31And the Lord said,[q] "Simon, Simon! Indeed,
Satan has asked for you, that he may sift *you* as
wheat. 32But I have prayed for you, that your faith
should not fail; and when you have returned to
Me, strengthen your brethren."
33But he said to Him, "Lord, I am ready to go
with You, both to prison and to death."
34Then He said, "I tell you, Peter, the rooster
shall not crow this day before you will deny three
times that you know Me."

22:14 [o]NU-Text omits *twelve.* 22:18 [p]NU-Text adds *from now on.* 22:31 [q]NU-Text omits *And the Lord said.*

35And He said to them, "When I sent you without money bag, knapsack, and sandals, did you lack anything?"

So they said, "Nothing."

36Then He said to them, "But now, he who has a money bag, let him take *it*, and likewise a knapsack; and he who has no sword, let him sell his garment and buy one. 37For I say to you that this which is written must still be accomplished in Me: 'And He was numbered with the transgressors.'*r* For the things concerning Me have an end."

38So they said, "Lord, look, here *are* two swords."

And He said to them, "It is enough."

39*Coming out, He went to the Mount of Olives, as He was accustomed, and His disciples also followed Him. 40When He came to the place, He said to them, "Pray that you may not enter into temptation."

41And He was withdrawn from them about a stone's throw, and He knelt down and prayed, 42saying, "Father, if it is Your will, take this cup away from Me; nevertheless not My will, but Yours, be done." 43Then an angel appeared to Him from heaven, strengthening Him. 44And being in agony, He prayed more earnestly. Then His sweat became like great drops of blood falling down to the ground.*s*

45When He rose up from prayer, and had come to His disciples, He found them sleeping from sorrow. 46Then He said to them, "Why do you sleep? Rise and pray, lest you enter into temptation."

47And while He was still speaking, behold, a multitude; and he who was called Judas, one of the twelve, went before them and drew near to Jesus to kiss Him. 48But Jesus said to him, "Judas, are you betraying the Son of Man with a kiss?"

49When those around Him saw what was going to happen, they said to Him, "Lord, shall we strike with the sword?" 50And one of them struck the servant of the high priest and cut off his right ear.

51But Jesus answered and said, "Permit even this." And He touched his ear and healed him.

52Then Jesus said to the chief priests, captains of the temple, and the elders who had come to Him, "Have you come out, as against a robber, with swords and clubs? 53When I was with you daily in the temple, you did not try to seize Me. But this is your hour, and the power of darkness."

54*Having arrested Him, they led *Him* and brought Him into the high priest's house. But Peter followed at a distance. 55Now when they had kindled a fire in the midst of the courtyard and sat down together, Peter sat among them. 56And a certain servant girl, seeing him as he sat by the fire, looked intently at him and said, "This man was also with Him."

57But he denied Him,*t* saying, "Woman, I do not know Him."

58And after a little while another saw him and said, "You also are of them."

But Peter said, "Man, I am not!"

59Then after about an hour had passed, another

22:39–53 *Satan in the Garden.* Jesus said to those who had come to arrest Him, "But this is your hour, and the power of darkness" (v. 53). Because He had prayed and was yielded to the Father's will, Jesus was prepared for the arrest, but the disciples were not. If ever the work of Christ appeared to be ruined, it was in the garden; *but that was when Jesus was doing His very best in the Father's will.*

22:54–71 *Satan in the courts.* Satan was in the courtyard to sift Peter and in the council chamber to lead the men astray. His victory over Peter was only temporary, for the apostle wept, repented, and was restored. His victory over the religious leaders was complete, for he blinded their eyes to the truth (2 Cor. 4:3–6) and they condemned their own Messiah.

confidently affirmed, saying, "Surely this *fellow* also was with Him, for he is a Galilean."

60But Peter said, "Man, I do not know what you are saying!"

Immediately, while he was still speaking, the rooster[u] crowed. 61And the Lord turned and looked at Peter. Then Peter remembered the word of the Lord, how He had said to him, "Before the rooster crows,[v] you will deny Me three times." 62So Peter went out and wept bitterly.

63Now the men who held Jesus mocked Him and beat Him. 64And having blindfolded Him, they struck Him on the face and asked Him,[w] saying, "Prophesy! Who is the one who struck You?" 65And many other things they blasphemously spoke against Him.

66As soon as it was day, the elders of the people, both chief priests and scribes, came together and led Him into their council, saying, 67"If You are the Christ, tell us."

But He said to them, "If I tell you, you will by no means believe. 68And if I also ask *you*, you will by no means answer Me or let *Me* go.[x] 69Hereafter the Son of Man will sit on the right hand of the power of God."

70Then they all said, "Are You then the Son of God?"

So He said to them, "You *rightly* say that I am."

71And they said, "What further testimony do we need? For we have heard it ourselves from His own mouth."

CHAPTER 23

23:1–25 *Pilate* wanted to get rid of Jesus as quickly and as easily as possible, but you cannot avoid making serious decisions about Him. Pilate ended up condemning an innocent Man, releasing a guilty man, and making friends with a wicked man. What a record for a Roman ruler whose responsibility it was to uphold the law and give people justice!

23:8, 9 *Herod* wanted to see Jesus do a miracle! The evil king would make the Son of God into a court entertainer. Jesus performed no miracle; He spoke no word. Herod had silenced God's voice, and there was nothing left for him but divine judgment.

23 Then[*] the whole multitude of them arose and led Him to Pilate. 2And they began to accuse Him, saying, "We found this *fellow* perverting the[y] nation, and forbidding to pay taxes to Caesar, saying that He Himself is Christ, a King."

3Then Pilate asked Him, saying, "Are You the King of the Jews?"

He answered him and said, "*It is as* you say." 4So Pilate said to the chief priests and the crowd, "I find no fault in this Man."

5But they were the more fierce, saying, "He stirs up the people, teaching throughout all Judea, beginning from Galilee to this place."

6When Pilate heard of Galilee,[z] he asked if the Man were a Galilean. 7And as soon as he knew that He belonged to Herod's jurisdiction, he sent Him to Herod, who was also in Jerusalem at that time. 8*Now when Herod saw Jesus, he was exceedingly glad; for he had desired for a long *time* to see Him, because he had heard many things about Him, and he hoped to see some miracle done by Him. 9Then he questioned Him with many words, but He answered him nothing. 10And the chief priests and scribes stood and vehemently accused Him. 11Then Herod, with his men of war, treated Him with contempt and mocked *Him,* arrayed Him in a gorgeous robe, and sent Him back to Pilate. 12That very day Pilate and Herod became friends with each other, for previously they had been at enmity with each other.

22:60 [u]NU-Text and M-Text read *a rooster.*   22:61 [v]NU-Text adds *today.*   22:64 [w]NU-Text reads *And having blindfolded Him, they asked Him.*   22:68 [x]NU-Text omits *also* and *Me or let Me go.*   23:2 [y]NU-Text reads *our.*   23:6 [z]NU-Text omits *of Galilee.*

13Then Pilate, when he had called together the chief priests, the rulers, and the people, 14said to them, "You have brought this Man to me, as one who misleads the people. And indeed, having examined *Him* in your presence, I have found no fault in this Man concerning those things of which you accuse Him; 15no, neither did Herod, for I sent you back to him;*a* and indeed nothing deserving of death has been done by Him. 16I will therefore chastise Him and release *Him*" 17(for it was necessary for him to release one to them at the feast).*b*

18*And they all cried out at once, saying, "Away with this *Man*, and release to us Barabbas"— 19who had been thrown into prison for a certain rebellion made in the city, and for murder.

20Pilate, therefore, wishing to release Jesus, again called out to them. 21But they shouted, saying, "Crucify *Him*, crucify Him!"

22Then he said to them the third time, "Why, what evil has He done? I have found no reason for death in Him. I will therefore chastise Him and let *Him* go."

23But they were insistent, demanding with loud voices that He be crucified. And the voices of these men and of the chief priests prevailed.*c* 24So Pilate gave sentence that it should be as they requested. 25And he released to them*d* the one they requested, who for rebellion and murder had been thrown into prison; but he delivered Jesus to their will.

26Now as they led Him away, they laid hold of a certain man, Simon a Cyrenian, who was coming from the country, and on him they laid the cross that he might bear *it* after Jesus.

27And a great multitude of the people followed Him, and women who also mourned and lamented Him. 28But Jesus, turning to them, said, "Daughters of Jerusalem, do not weep for Me, but weep for yourselves and for your children. 29For indeed the days are coming in which they will say, 'Blessed *are* the barren, wombs that never bore, and breasts which never nursed!' 30Then they will begin *'to say to the mountains, "Fall on us!" and to the hills, "Cover us!" '*e* 31For if they do these things in the green wood, what will be done in the dry?"

32There were also two others, criminals, led with Him to be put to death. 33And when they had come to the place called Calvary, there they crucified Him, and the criminals, one on the right hand and the other on the left. 34*Then Jesus said, "Father, forgive them, for they do not know what they do."*f*

And they divided His garments and cast lots. 35And the people stood looking on. But even the rulers with them sneered, saying, "He saved others; let Him save Himself if He is the Christ, the chosen of God."

36The soldiers also mocked Him, coming and offering Him sour wine, 37and saying, "If You are the King of the Jews, save Yourself."

38And an inscription also was written over Him in letters of Greek, Latin, and Hebrew:*g*

23:18, 19, 25 *Barabbas* deserved to die but was set free because Jesus took his place. Did Barabbas go to Calvary and look at the Man who died for him? Probably not. He was glad to be free from the sentence of death so he could return to his old ways. He was free but still in the bondage of sin.

23:34 *And for those people—and many more*—Jesus prayed, "Father, forgive them, for they do not know what they do." What grace!

23:15 *a*NU-Text reads *for he sent Him back to us.*
23:17 *b*NU-Text omits verse 17.   23:23 *c*NU-Text omits *and of the chief priests.*   23:25 *d*NU-Text and M-Text omit *to them.*
23:30 *e*Hosea 10:8   23:34 *f*NU-Text brackets the first sentence as a later addition.   23:38 *g*NU-Text omits *written* and *in letters of Greek, Latin, and Hebrew.*

THIS IS THE KING OF THE JEWS.

39Then one of the criminals who were hanged blasphemed Him, saying, "If You are the Christ,[h] save Yourself and us."

40*But the other, answering, rebuked him, saying, "Do you not even fear God, seeing you are under the same condemnation? 41And we indeed justly, for we receive the due reward of our deeds; but this Man has done nothing wrong." 42Then he said to Jesus, "Lord,[i] remember me when You come into Your kingdom."

43And Jesus said to him, "Assuredly, I say to you, today you will be with Me in Paradise."

44Now it was[j] about the sixth hour, and there was darkness over all the earth until the ninth hour. 45Then the sun was darkened,[k] and the veil of the temple was torn in two. 46And when Jesus had cried out with a loud voice, He said, "Father, 'into Your hands I commit My spirit.' "[l] Having said this, He breathed His last.

47So when the centurion saw what had happened, he glorified God, saying, "Certainly this was a righteous Man!"

48And the whole crowd who came together to that sight, seeing what had been done, beat their breasts and returned. 49But all His acquaintances, and the women who followed Him from Galilee, stood at a distance, watching these things.

50*Now behold, there was a man named Joseph, a council member, a good and just man. 51He had not consented to their decision and deed. He was from Arimathea, a city of the Jews, who himself was also waiting[m] for the kingdom of God. 52This man went to Pilate and asked for the body of Jesus. 53Then he took it down, wrapped it in linen, and laid it in a tomb that was hewn out of the rock, where no one had ever lain before. 54That day was the Preparation, and the Sabbath drew near.

55And the women who had come with Him from Galilee followed after, and they observed the tomb and how His body was laid. 56Then they returned and prepared spices and fragrant oils. And they rested on the Sabbath according to the commandment.

24 Now* on the first day of the week, very early in the morning, they, and certain other women with them,[n] came to the tomb bringing the spices which they had prepared. 2But they found the stone rolled away from the tomb. 3Then they went in and did not find the body of the Lord Jesus. 4And it happened, as they were greatly[o] perplexed about this, that behold, two men stood by them in shining garments. 5Then, as they were afraid and bowed their faces to the earth, they said to them, "Why do you seek the living among the dead? 6He is not here, but is risen! Remember how He spoke to you when He was still in Galilee, 7saying, 'The Son of Man must be delivered into the hands of sinful men, and be crucified, and the third day rise again.' "

8And they remembered His words. 9Then they

23:40–43 *The thief* exercised great faith when he asked Jesus to remember him, for Jesus did not look like He was able to save anybody.

23:50–53 *Joseph* exercised great courage when he openly took our Lord's body from the cross. He defiled himself for Passover week, but it made no difference: he had met the Lamb of God, and that was all that mattered.

CHAPTER 24

24:1–12 *Forgetting His word.* The stone was rolled away, the body of Jesus was gone, and the women were perplexed. Why? Because they had forgotten His word. Today, angels do not come to remind us of His word; the Holy Spirit has that ministry (John 14:26). Yield to the Spirit and let Him remind you of the promises that will encourage your heart.

23:39 [h]NU-Text reads *Are You not the Christ?*
23:42 [i]NU-Text reads *And he said, "Jesus, remember me.*
23:44 [j]NU-Text adds *already.*   23:45 [k]NU-Text reads *obscured.*   23:46 [l]Psalm 31:5   23:51 [m]NU-Text reads *who was waiting.*   24:1 [n]NU-Text omits *and certain other women with them.*   24:4 [o]NU-Text omits *greatly.*

returned from the tomb and told all these things
to the eleven and to all the rest. 10It was Mary
Magdalene, Joanna, Mary *the mother* of James,
and the other *women* with them, who told these
things to the apostles. 11And their words seemed
to them like idle tales, and they did not believe
them. 12But Peter arose and ran to the tomb; and
stooping down, he saw the linen cloths lying[p] by
themselves; and he departed, marveling to himself
at what had happened.
13*Now behold, two of them were traveling that
same day to a village called Emmaus, which was
seven miles[q] from Jerusalem. 14And they talked
together of all these things which had happened.
15So it was, while they conversed and reasoned,
that Jesus Himself drew near and went with them.
16But their eyes were restrained, so that they did
not know Him.
17And He said to them, "What kind of conversation *is* this that you have with one another as you
walk and are sad?"[r]
18Then the one whose name was Cleopas answered and said to Him, "Are You the only
stranger in Jerusalem, and have You not known
the things which happened there in these days?"
19And He said to them, "What things?"
So they said to Him, "The things concerning
Jesus of Nazareth, who was a Prophet mighty in
deed and word before God and all the people,
20and how the chief priests and our rulers delivered Him to be condemned to death, and crucified
Him. 21But we were hoping that it was He who
was going to redeem Israel. Indeed, besides all
this, today is the third day since these things happened. 22Yes, and certain women of our company,
who arrived at the tomb early, astonished us.
23When they did not find His body, they came
saying that they had also seen a vision of angels
who said He was alive. 24And certain of those *who
were* with us went to the tomb and found *it* just
as the women had said; but Him they did not see."
25Then He said to them, "O foolish ones, and
slow of heart to believe in all that the prophets
have spoken! 26Ought not the Christ to have suffered these things and to enter into His glory?"
27And beginning at Moses and all the Prophets,
He expounded to them in all the Scriptures the
things concerning Himself.
28Then they drew near to the village where they
were going, and He indicated that He would have
gone farther. 29But they constrained Him, saying,
"Abide with us, for it is toward evening, and the
day is far spent." And He went in to stay with
them.
30Now it came to pass, as He sat at the table
with them, that He took bread, blessed and broke
it, and gave it to them. 31Then their eyes were
opened and they knew Him; and He vanished
from their sight.
32And they said to one another, "Did not our
heart burn within us while He talked with us on
the road, and while He opened the Scriptures to
us?" 33So they rose up that very hour and returned
to Jerusalem, and found the eleven and those *who
were* with them gathered together, 34saying, "The
Lord is risen indeed, and has appeared to Simon!" 35And they told about the things *that had*

24:12 [p]NU-Text omits *lying*. 24:13 [q]Literally *sixty stadia*
24:17 [r]NU-Text reads *as you walk? And they stood still, looking sad.*

24:13–35 *Learning the Word.* Those two men could have walked and talked for days and never gotten rid of their disappointment. Why? Because they lacked the key that unlocks the Old Testament: Messiah must suffer and die before entering His glory. Their hearts burned as they heard Him teach the Scriptures; and soon, the mourners became missionaries and shared the good news with others. Do you allow the Holy Spirit to teach you (John 16:13–15)?

24:36–45 Receiving the Word. Their hearts were troubled, frightened, and doubtful; yet the Lord lovingly reassured them with His word. We today cannot see or feel His body, but we have the Holy Spirit to make Him real to us from the Scriptures. When your heart is troubled or frightened, see Jesus in the Word (John 14:1–6). When your faith is weak, see Jesus in the Word (Rom. 10:17). The first step toward peace is receiving the Word.

24:46–53 Sharing the Word. God opens our eyes (v. 31) and opens our understanding (v. 45) so that when He opens the Scriptures to us (vv. 27, 32), we may open our mouths and tell others about Him (v. 48). Jesus gives us the commission, the power, and the message. There is no reason to be silent! When we experience joyful worship (vv. 52–53), we will have little problem giving the world a joyful witness.

happened on the road, and how He was known to them in the breaking of bread. 36*Now as they said these things, Jesus Himself stood in the midst of them, and said to them, "Peace to you." 37But they were terrified and frightened, and supposed they had seen a spirit. 38And He said to them, "Why are you troubled? And why do doubts arise in your hearts? 39Behold My hands and My feet, that it is I Myself. Handle Me and see, for a spirit does not have flesh and bones as you see I have." 40When He had said this, He showed them His hands and His feet.*s* 41But while they still did not believe for joy, and marveled, He said to them, "Have you any food here?" 42So they gave Him a piece of a broiled fish and some honeycomb.*t* 43And He took *it* and ate in their presence.

44Then He said to them, "These *are* the words which I spoke to you while I was still with you, that all things must be fulfilled which were written in the Law of Moses and *the* Prophets and *the* Psalms concerning Me." 45And He opened their understanding, that they might comprehend the Scriptures.

46*Then He said to them, "Thus it is written, and thus it was necessary for the Christ to suffer and to rise*u* from the dead the third day, 47and that repentance and remission of sins should be preached in His name to all nations, beginning at Jerusalem. 48And you are witnesses of these things. 49Behold, I send the Promise of My Father upon you; but tarry in the city of Jerusalem*v* until you are endued with power from on high."

50And He led them out as far as Bethany, and He lifted up His hands and blessed them. 51Now it came to pass, while He blessed them, that He was parted from them and carried up into heaven. 52And they worshiped Him, and returned to Jerusalem with great joy, 53and were continually in the temple praising and*w* blessing God. Amen.*x*

24:40 *s*Some printed New Testaments omit this verse. It is found in nearly all Greek manuscripts. 24:42 *t*NU-Text omits *and some honeycomb.* 24:46 *u*NU-Text reads *written, that the Christ should suffer and rise.* 24:49 *v*NU-Text omits *of Jerusalem.* 24:53 *w*NU-Text omits *praising and.* *x*NU-Text omits *Amen.*

JOHN

John had two purposes in mind when he wrote his gospel: to prove that Jesus Christ is the Son of God, and to invite people to believe in Him and be saved (20:30–31). His evidence for the deity of Jesus Christ is threefold: (1) the miracles He performed; (2) the words He spoke; and (3) the testimony of witnesses who knew Him.

As you read the gospel of John, you will hear Jesus speak (7:46), see Him act in power, and watch people respond to what He says and does. Seven witnesses declare that He is the Son of God: John the Baptist (1:34), Nathanael (1:49), Peter (6:69), a man who had been blind (9:35–38), Martha (11:27), Thomas (20:28), and the apostle John (20:31). Jesus also declared His deity (5:25; 10:36).

Matthew wrote for the Jews, Mark for the Romans, and Luke for the Greeks. However, John had the whole world in mind when he wrote and frequently used the word *world*. But he alludes to the Old Testament over one hundred times, showing that he was mindful of his Jewish readers.

The invitation in the synoptic Gospels is, "Come and hear!" But in the Gospel of John, the invitation is also, "Come and see!" There are sixty-seven references in the book to seeing and fifty-eight to hearing. His *works* and His *words* prove that Jesus is indeed the Son of God.

After the introduction (1:1–18), John describes the ministry of Christ to His people (1:19—12:50), to His disciples (chaps. 13—17), and then to the whole world (chaps. 18—21). In the first section, He is the Miracle Worker; in the second, the Teacher; and in the third, the Victor. Of course, throughout the book, Jesus is seen as Savior and Lord.

1 In* the beginning was the Word, and the Word was with God, and the Word was God. ²He was in the beginning with God. ³All things were made through Him, and without Him nothing was made that was made. ⁴In Him was life, and the life was the light of men. ⁵And the light shines in the darkness, and the darkness did not comprehend[a] it.

⁶There was a man sent from God, whose name *was* John. ⁷This man came for a witness, to bear witness of the Light, that all through him might believe. ⁸He was not that Light, but *was sent* to bear witness of that Light. ⁹That was the true Light which gives light to every man coming into the world.[b]

¹⁰He was in the world, and the world was made through Him, and the world did not know Him. ¹¹He came to His own,[c] and His own[d] did not receive Him. ¹²But as many as received Him, to them He gave the right to become children of God, to those who believe in His name: ¹³who were born, not of blood, nor of the will of the flesh, nor of the will of man, but of God. ¹⁴And the Word became flesh and dwelt among us, and we beheld His glory, the glory as of the only begotten of the Father, full of grace and truth.

1:5 [a]Or *overcome*   1:9 [b]Or *That was the true Light which, coming into the world, gives light to every man.*   1:11 [c]That is, His own things or domain   [d]That is, His own people

---

CHAPTER 1

1:1–14 *The Creator came.* Compare this passage with Genesis 1 and note the emphasis on *light* and *life.* Moses wrote about the old creation, but John wrote about the new creation (2 Cor. 5:17). Jesus is the creative Word and the living Word who reveals the Father to us. In His many miracles, Jesus showed His power as Creator. He is a faithful Creator, and you can trust your life to Him (1 Pet. 4:19).

Images of Jesus—John pictures our Lord's death as the slaying of the lamb (1:29), the destroying of a temple (2:19), the lifting up of a serpent (3:14), the voluntary death of a shepherd (10:11–18), and the planting of a seed (12:20–25).

1:15–34 *The Savior came.* He came with grace and truth, not law and judgment. He revealed the Father and gave the Holy Spirit to those who trusted Him. He is the Lamb of God who alone can take away sins. The blood of lambs *covered* the sins of *the Jews,* but the blood of Christ *takes away* the sins of *the whole world* (v. 29; 4:42).

15*John bore witness of Him and cried out, saying, "This was He of whom I said, 'He who comes after me is preferred before me, for He was before me.'"

16And[e] of His fullness we have all received, and grace for grace. 17For the law was given through Moses, *but* grace and truth came through Jesus Christ. 18No one has seen God at any time. The only begotten Son,[f] who is in the bosom of the Father, He has declared *Him.*

19Now this is the testimony of John, when the Jews sent priests and Levites from Jerusalem to ask him, "Who are you?"

20He confessed, and did not deny, but confessed, "I am not the Christ."

21And they asked him, "What then? Are you Elijah?"

He said, "I am not."

"Are you the Prophet?"

And he answered, "No."

22Then they said to him, "Who are you, that we may give an answer to those who sent us? What do you say about yourself?"

23He said: "I *am*

    'The voice of one crying in the wilderness:
    "*Make straight the way of the LORD*," '[g]

as the prophet Isaiah said."

24Now those who were sent were from the Pharisees. 25And they asked him, saying, "Why then do you baptize if you are not the Christ, nor Elijah, nor the Prophet?"

26John answered them, saying, "I baptize with water, but there stands One among you whom you do not know. 27It is He who, coming after me, is preferred before me, whose sandal strap I am not worthy to loose."

28These things were done in Bethabara[h] beyond the Jordan, where John was baptizing.

29The next day John saw Jesus coming toward him, and said, "Behold! The Lamb of God who takes away the sin of the world! 30This is He of whom I said, 'After me comes a Man who is preferred before me, for He was before me.' 31I did not know Him; but that He should be revealed to Israel, therefore I came baptizing with water."

32And John bore witness, saying, "I saw the Spirit descending from heaven like a dove, and He remained upon Him. 33I did not know Him, but He who sent me to baptize with water said to me, 'Upon whom you see the Spirit descending, and remaining on Him, this is He who baptizes with the Holy Spirit.' 34And I have seen and testified that this is the Son of God."

1:35–51 *The Master came.* Jesus called a few men to follow Him, and He transformed their lives and used them to transform the lives of others. Simon's new name (Peter, meaning "a stone") symbolized a new beginning in his life. He became a part of the new creation, sharing in the fullness of grace (v. 16). Jesus calls each one individually and uses different approaches, but the same Master calls. Have you heeded His call?

35*Again, the next day, John stood with two of his disciples. 36And looking at Jesus as He walked, he said, "Behold the Lamb of God!"

37The two disciples heard him speak, and they followed Jesus. 38Then Jesus turned, and seeing them following, said to them, "What do you seek?"

They said to Him, "Rabbi" (which is to say, when translated, Teacher), "where are You staying?"

39He said to them, "Come and see." They came

1:16 [e]NU-Text reads *For.* 1:18 [f]NU-Text reads *only begotten God.* 1:23 [g]Isaiah 40:3 1:28 [h]NU-Text and M-Text read *Bethany.*

and saw where He was staying, and remained with Him that day (now it was about the tenth hour).

⁴⁰One of the two who heard John *speak,* and followed Him, was Andrew, Simon Peter's brother. ⁴¹He first found his own brother Simon, and said to him, "We have found the Messiah" (which is translated, the Christ). ⁴²And he brought him to Jesus.

Now when Jesus looked at him, He said, "You are Simon the son of Jonah.ⁱ You shall be called Cephas" (which is translated, A Stone).

⁴³The following day Jesus wanted to go to Galilee, and He found Philip and said to him, "Follow Me." ⁴⁴Now Philip was from Bethsaida, the city of Andrew and Peter. ⁴⁵Philip found Nathanael and said to him, "We have found Him of whom Moses in the law, and also the prophets, wrote—Jesus of Nazareth, the son of Joseph."

⁴⁶And Nathanael said to him, "Can anything good come out of Nazareth?"

Philip said to him, "Come and see."

⁴⁷Jesus saw Nathanael coming toward Him, and said of him, "Behold, an Israelite indeed, in whom is no deceit!"

⁴⁸Nathanael said to Him, "How do You know me?"

Jesus answered and said to him, "Before Philip called you, when you were under the fig tree, I saw you."

⁴⁹*Nathanael answered and said to Him, "Rabbi, You are the Son of God! You are the King of Israel!"

⁵⁰Jesus answered and said to him, "Because I said to you, 'I saw you under the fig tree,' do you believe? You will see greater things than these." ⁵¹And He said to him, "Most assuredly, I say to you, hereafterʲ you shall see heaven open, and the angels of God ascending and descending upon the Son of Man."

2 On* the third day there was a wedding in Cana of Galilee, and the mother of Jesus was there. ²Now both Jesus and His disciples were invited to the wedding. ³And when they ran out of wine, the mother of Jesus said to Him, "They have no wine."

⁴Jesus said to her, "Woman, what does your concern have to do with Me? My hour has not yet come."

⁵His mother said to the servants, "Whatever He says to you, do *it.*"

⁶Now there were set there six waterpots of stone, according to the manner of purification of the Jews, containing twenty or thirty gallons apiece. ⁷Jesus said to them, "Fill the waterpots

---

1:42 ⁱNU-Text reads *John.*   1:51 ʲNU-Text omits *hereafter.*

1:49 The King came. Jesus came to His own creation and everything in creation obeyed Him; but His own people did not receive Him (v. 11; 12:37–41). During His trial before Pilate, His kingship was the paramount issue (18:33—19:22); and it is still the issue today. Who is the king of *your* life?

CHAPTER 2

Look at Jesus!

2:1–11 He is joyous. A Jewish wedding is a joyful event, and Jesus was very much at home there. He was "a man of sorrows" (Isa. 53:3), but He also experienced great joy (Luke 10:21); and He can share the joys and sorrows (chap. 11) of our lives. The joy the world offers will eventually fail, but the joy He supplies goes on forever. Be sure to invite Him, and be sure to obey what He says.

Understanding Divine Truths—In his gospel, John points out that unsaved people did not understand what Jesus taught. When He used symbolic language to illustrate a spiritual truth, they took it literally. That was true when He spoke about the temple (2:18–22), the new birth (3:1–9), living water (4:7–15), and eating His flesh and drinking His blood (6:51–52). Apart from the Spirit, you cannot understand His Word (1 Cor. 2:6–16).

Miraculous Works—Out of the many miracles Jesus performed, John selected seven to reveal His glory and prove His deity: turning water into wine (2:1–11); healing the nobleman's son (4:46–54); healing the man sick for thirty-eight years (chap. 5); feeding the five thousand (6:1–14); walking on the stormy sea (6:15–21); restoring sight to a man born blind (chap. 9); and raising Lazarus from the dead (chap. 11). The catch of fish (chap. 21), was performed after His resurrection.

with water." And they filled them up to the brim. 8And He said to them, "Draw *some* out now, and take *it* to the master of the feast." And they took *it*. 9When the master of the feast had tasted the water that was made wine, and did not know where it came from (but the servants who had drawn the water knew), the master of the feast called the bridegroom. 10And he said to him, "Every man at the beginning sets out the good wine, and when the *guests* have well drunk, then the inferior. You have kept the good wine until now!"

11This beginning of signs Jesus did in Cana of Galilee, and manifested His glory; and His disciples believed in Him.

12After this He went down to Capernaum, He, His mother, His brothers, and His disciples; and they did not stay there many days.

13*Now the Passover of the Jews was at hand, and Jesus went up to Jerusalem. 14And He found in the temple those who sold oxen and sheep and doves, and the money changers doing business. 15When He had made a whip of cords, He drove them all out of the temple, with the sheep and the oxen, and poured out the changers' money and overturned the tables. 16And He said to those who sold doves, "Take these things away! Do not make My Father's house a house of merchandise!" 17Then His disciples remembered that it was written, *"Zeal for Your house has eaten^k Me up."^l*

18*So the Jews answered and said to Him, "What sign do You show to us, since You do these things?"

19Jesus answered and said to them, "Destroy this temple, and in three days I will raise it up."

20Then the Jews said, "It has taken forty-six years to build this temple, and will You raise it up in three days?"

21But He was speaking of the temple of His body. 22Therefore, when He had risen from the dead, His disciples remembered that He had said this to them;^m and they believed the Scripture and the word which Jesus had said.

23Now when He was in Jerusalem at the Passover, during the feast, many believed in His name when they saw the signs which He did. 24But Jesus did not commit Himself to them, because He knew all *men*, 25and had no need that anyone should testify of man, for He knew what was in man.

3 There* was a man of the Pharisees named Nicodemus, a ruler of the Jews. 2This man came to Jesus by night and said to Him, "Rabbi, we know that You are a teacher come from God; for no one can do these signs that You do unless God is with him."

3Jesus answered and said to him, "Most assuredly, I say to you, unless one is born again, he cannot see the kingdom of God."

4Nicodemus said to Him, "How can a man be born when he is old? Can he enter a second time into his mother's womb and be born?"

2:13–17 He is righteous. The other gospels record His cleansing of the temple at the close of His ministry, but John tells us He started His ministry by cleansing the temple. Judgment begins at the house of God (1 Pet. 4:17). The temple was then "a house of merchandise" (2:16); three years later, it was a "den of thieves" (Matt. 21:13). Outward reformation without inward renewal is a temporary thing.

2:18–22 He is victorious. The Jews repeatedly asked Him for a sign (1 Cor. 1:22) and then rejected the evidence He provided (12:37–41). His resurrection was the greatest proof of His deity (Matt. 12:38–40), but the Jews did not understand what He was talking about (8:42–45). They would destroy the temple by crucifying Him, but He would triumph over them in His resurrection.

CHAPTER 3

3:1–8 A birth from above. In our first birth, we are "born of the flesh" and "born of water"; but in our second birth, we are "born from above [again]" and "born of the Spirit." Our first birth leads to death, but our second birth brings eternal life. The new birth is a new beginning that results in "newness of life" (Rom. 6:4).

2:17 ^kNU-Text and M-Text read *will eat*. ^lPsalm 69:9
2:22 ^mNU-Text and M-Text omit *to them*.

Nicodemus—Nicodemus came to Jesus by night, but he finally came out into the light and identified with the Lord Jesus (19:38–42). Nicodemus gave Jesus an honest hearing (7:45–52), examined the Word, and became a believer.

5Jesus answered, "Most assuredly, I say to you, unless one is born of water and the Spirit, he cannot enter the kingdom of God. 6That which is born of the flesh is flesh, and that which is born of the Spirit is spirit. 7Do not marvel that I said to you, 'You must be born again.' 8The wind blows where it wishes, and you hear the sound of it, but cannot tell where it comes from and where it goes. So is everyone who is born of the Spirit."

9Nicodemus answered and said to Him, "How can these things be?"

10Jesus answered and said to him, "Are you the teacher of Israel, and do not know these things? 11Most assuredly, I say to you, We speak what We know and testify what We have seen, and you do not receive Our witness. 12If I have told you earthly things and you do not believe, how will you believe if I tell you heavenly things? 13*No one has ascended to heaven but He who came down from heaven, *that is,* the Son of Man who is in heaven.[n] 14And as Moses lifted up the serpent in the wilderness, even so must the Son of Man be lifted up, 15that whoever believes in Him should not perish but[o] have eternal life. 16For God so loved the world that He gave His only begotten Son, that whoever believes in Him should not perish but have everlasting life. 17For God did not send His Son into the world to condemn the world, but that the world through Him might be saved.

18"He who believes in Him is not condemned; but he who does not believe is condemned already, because he has not believed in the name of the only begotten Son of God. 19And this is the condemnation, that the light has come into the world, and men loved darkness rather than light, because their deeds were evil. 20For everyone practicing evil hates the light and does not come to the light, lest his deeds should be exposed. 21But he who does the truth comes to the light, that his deeds may be clearly seen, that they have been done in God."

22After these things Jesus and His disciples came into the land of Judea, and there He remained with them and baptized. 23Now John also was baptizing in Aenon near Salim, because there was much water there. And they came and were baptized. 24For John had not yet been thrown into prison.

25Then there arose a dispute between *some* of John's disciples and the Jews about purification. 26And they came to John and said to him, "Rabbi, He who was with you beyond the Jordan, to whom you have testified—behold, He is baptizing, and all are coming to Him!"

27*John answered and said, "A man can receive nothing unless it has been given to him from heaven. 28You yourselves bear me witness, that I said, 'I am not the Christ,' but, 'I have been sent before Him.' 29He who has the bride is the bridegroom; but the friend of the bridegroom, who stands and hears him, rejoices greatly because of the bridegroom's voice. Therefore this joy of mine is fulfilled. 30He must increase, but I *must* decrease. 31He who comes from above is above all; he who is of the earth is earthly and speaks of the earth. He who comes from heaven is above all. 32And what He has seen and heard, that He testifies; and no one receives His testimony.

3:13–21 *A Savior from above.* Jesus is the Son of God come down from heaven. He is the serpent Moses wrote about (Num. 21:4–9); He is the Father's love gift (3:16); He is the Light in a dark world (v. 19). Like the serpent, He was lifted up, and He died on a cross for the sins of the world. All who look to Him by faith receive eternal life.

3:27–36 *A witness from above.* John's ministry was given to him from heaven (v. 27). His task was to bear witness to Jesus (1:6–8). Jesus is the Word, and John was only a voice proclaiming the Word (1:23). Jesus is the Bridegroom, but John was only the best man. John did no miracles, but his witness was used to win people to Christ, even after he was dead (10:40–42). Can you honestly say, "He must increase, but I must decrease" (3:30)?

3:13 [n]NU-Text omits *who is in heaven.* 3:15 [o]NU-Text omits *not perish but.*

33He who has received His testimony has certified that God is true. 34For He whom God has sent speaks the words of God, for God does not give the Spirit by measure. 35The Father loves the Son, and has given all things into His hand. 36He who believes in the Son has everlasting life; and he who does not believe the Son shall not see life, but the wrath of God abides on him.''

4 Therefore, when the Lord knew that the Pharisees had heard that Jesus made and baptized more disciples than John 2(though Jesus Himself did not baptize, but His disciples), 3He left Judea and departed again to Galilee. 4But He needed to go through Samaria.

5So He came to a city of Samaria which is called Sychar, near the plot of ground that Jacob gave to his son Joseph. 6Now Jacob's well was there. Jesus therefore, being wearied from *His* journey, sat thus by the well. It was about the sixth hour.

7*A woman of Samaria came to draw water. Jesus said to her, "Give Me a drink." 8For His disciples had gone away into the city to buy food.

9Then the woman of Samaria said to Him, "How is it that You, being a Jew, ask a drink from me, a Samaritan woman?" For Jews have no dealings with Samaritans.

10Jesus answered and said to her, "If you knew the gift of God, and who it is who says to you, 'Give Me a drink,' you would have asked Him, and He would have given you living water."

11The woman said to Him, "Sir, You have nothing to draw with, and the well is deep. Where then do You get that living water? 12Are You greater than our father Jacob, who gave us the well, and drank from it himself, as well as his sons and his livestock?"

13Jesus answered and said to her, "Whoever drinks of this water will thirst again, 14but whoever drinks of the water that I shall give him will never thirst. But the water that I shall give him will become in him a fountain of water springing up into everlasting life."

15The woman said to Him, "Sir, give me this water, that I may not thirst, nor come here to draw."

16Jesus said to her, "Go, call your husband, and come here."

17The woman answered and said, "I have no husband."

Jesus said to her, "You have well said, 'I have no husband,' 18for you have had five husbands, and the one whom you now have is not your husband; in that you spoke truly."

19The woman said to Him, "Sir, I perceive that You are a prophet. 20Our fathers worshiped on this mountain, and you *Jews* say that in Jerusalem is the place where one ought to worship."

21Jesus said to her, "Woman, believe Me, the hour is coming when you will neither on this mountain, nor in Jerusalem, worship the Father. 22You worship what you do not know; we know what we worship, for salvation is of the Jews. 23But the hour is coming, and now is, when the true worshipers will worship the Father in spirit and truth; for the Father is seeking such to worship Him. 24God *is* Spirit, and those who worship Him must worship in spirit and truth."

25The woman said to Him, "I know that Messiah is coming" (who is called Christ). "When He comes, He will tell us all things."

CHAPTER 4

4:7–26 *Thirst.* Because Jesus was truly human, He experienced weariness, hunger, and thirst, but His deepest desire was for the salvation of the sinful woman. He forgot His physical needs and concentrated on her spiritual needs. Patiently He revealed Himself to her: "a Jew" (v. 9), "greater than Jacob" (v. 12), "a prophet" (v. 19), "Messiah" (vv. 25, 29). She believed in Him, and her life was so changed that she immediately shared the good news with others (20:30–31).

26Jesus said to her, "I who speak to you am *He*."

27And at this *point* His disciples came, and they marveled that He talked with a woman; yet no one said, "What do You seek?" or, "Why are You talking with her?"

28The woman then left her waterpot, went her way into the city, and said to the men, 29"Come, see a Man who told me all things that I ever did. Could this be the Christ?" 30Then they went out of the city and came to Him.

31*In the meantime His disciples urged Him, saying, "Rabbi, eat."

32But He said to them, "I have food to eat of which you do not know."

33Therefore the disciples said to one another, "Has anyone brought Him *anything* to eat?"

34Jesus said to them, "My food is to do the will of Him who sent Me, and to finish His work. 35Do you not say, 'There are still four months and *then* comes the harvest'? Behold, I say to you, lift up your eyes and look at the fields, for they are already white for harvest! 36And he who reaps receives wages, and gathers fruit for eternal life, that both he who sows and he who reaps may rejoice together. 37For in this the saying is true: 'One sows and another reaps.' 38I sent you to reap that for which you have not labored; others have labored, and you have entered into their labors."

39And many of the Samaritans of that city believed in Him because of the word of the woman who testified, "He told me all that I *ever* did." 40So when the Samaritans had come to Him, they urged Him to stay with them; and He stayed there two days. 41And many more believed because of His own word.

42Then they said to the woman, "Now we believe, not because of what you said, for we ourselves have heard *Him* and we know that this is indeed the Christ,p the Savior of the world."

43Now after the two days He departed from there and went to Galilee. 44For Jesus Himself testified that a prophet has no honor in his own country. 45So when He came to Galilee, the Galileans received Him, having seen all the things He did in Jerusalem at the feast; for they also had gone to the feast.

46*So Jesus came again to Cana of Galilee where He had made the water wine. And there was a certain nobleman whose son was sick at Capernaum. 47When he heard that Jesus had come out of Judea into Galilee, he went to Him and implored Him to come down and heal his son, for he was at the point of death. 48Then Jesus said to him, "Unless you *people* see signs and wonders, you will by no means believe."

49The nobleman said to Him, "Sir, come down before my child dies!"

50Jesus said to him, "Go your way; your son lives." So the man believed the word that Jesus spoke to him, and he went his way. 51And as he was now going down, his servants met him and told *him*, saying, "Your son lives!"

52Then he inquired of them the hour when he got better. And they said to him, "Yesterday at the seventh hour the fever left him." 53So the father knew that *it was* at the same hour in which

4:31–38 Hunger. The will of God should be food that nourishes us, not medicine that upsets us. The disciples were satisfied with material food, but Jesus wanted the satisfying spiritual food from God. The will of God gives us the strength we need to do our job in the great harvest all around us.

4:46–54 Health. Salvation is to the inner person what health is to the body. The boy would have died had Jesus not intervened and given him health. The father *heard* (v. 47), *believed* (v. 50), and *knew* (v. 53), which is a normal Christian experience.

Jesus won the woman; the woman won many Samaritans; and the father won his whole household. Are you busy in the harvest?

4:42 PNU-Text omits *the Christ*.

Jesus said to him, "Your son lives." And he himself believed, and his whole household.

54This again is the second sign Jesus did when He had come out of Judea into Galilee.

5 After* this there was a feast of the Jews, and Jesus went up to Jerusalem. 2Now there is in Jerusalem by the Sheep Gate a pool, which is called in Hebrew, Bethesda,q having five porches. 3In these lay a great multitude of sick people, blind, lame, paralyzed, waiting for the moving of the water. 4For an angel went down at a certain time into the pool and stirred up the water; then whoever stepped in first, after the stirring of the water, was made well of whatever disease he had.r 5Now a certain man was there who had an infirmity thirty-eight years. 6When Jesus saw him lying there, and knew that he already had been in that condition a long time, He said to him, "Do you want to be made well?"

7The sick man answered Him, "Sir, I have no man to put me into the pool when the water is stirred up; but while I am coming, another steps down before me."

8Jesus said to him, "Rise, take up your bed and walk." 9And immediately the man was made well, took up his bed, and walked.

And that day was the Sabbath. 10The Jews therefore said to him who was cured, "It is the Sabbath; it is not lawful for you to carry your bed."

11He answered them, "He who made me well said to me, 'Take up your bed and walk.' "

12Then they asked him, "Who is the Man who said to you, 'Take up your bed and walk'?" 13But the one who was healed did not know who it was, for Jesus had withdrawn, a multitude being in that place. 14Afterward Jesus found him in the temple, and said to him, "See, you have been made well. Sin no more, lest a worse thing come upon you."

15The man departed and told the Jews that it was Jesus who had made him well. 16For this reason the Jews persecuted Jesus, and sought to kill Him,s because He had done these things on the Sabbath. 17But Jesus answered them, "My Father has been working until now, and I have been working."

18Therefore the Jews sought all the more to kill Him, because He not only broke the Sabbath, but also said that God was His Father, making Himself equal with God. 19Then Jesus answered and said to them, "Most assuredly, I say to you, the Son can do nothing of Himself, but what He sees the Father do; for whatever He does, the Son also does in like manner. 20For the Father loves the Son, and shows Him all things that He Himself does; and He will show Him greater works than these, that you may marvel. 21For as the Father raises the dead and gives life to them, even so the Son gives life to whom He will. 22*For the Father judges no one, but has committed all judgment to the Son, 23*that all should honor the Son just as they honor the Father. He who does not honor the Son does not honor the Father who sent Him.

24"Most assuredly, I say to you, he who hears

CHAPTER 5

5:1–21 Works. The Father "broke" His Sabbath rest to help two sinners (Gen. 3:8ff.), and Jesus followed His example. In the world of nature, the Father is healing bodies, multiplying food, turning water into wine, and so forth; but He takes longer to do those things. Our Lord's miracles are the Father's works done instantly. Whether instantly or gradually, they are wonderful works of God.

5:22, 24–30 Wrath. Today, Jesus is the Savior; tomorrow, He will be the Judge (Rev. 20:11–15). Even death cannot keep lost sinners from the judgment, for He will raise them from the dead. There is no escape, except faith in Jesus Christ (5:24).

5:23 Worship. If you worship God the Father, you must also worship the Son; and if you dishonor the Son, you dishonor the Father. Those who claim to worship God but ignore the Son are not even worshiping God! They are only fooling themselves.

5:2 qNU-Text reads Bethzatha.　5:4 rNU-Text omits waiting for the moving of the water at the end of verse 3, and all of verse 4.　5:16 sNU-Text omits and sought to kill Him.

My word and believes in Him who sent Me has everlasting life, and shall not come into judgment, but has passed from death into life. 25Most assuredly, I say to you, the hour is coming, and now is, when the dead will hear the voice of the Son of God; and those who hear will live. 26For as the Father has life in Himself, so He has granted the Son to have life in Himself, 27and has given Him authority to execute judgment also, because He is the Son of Man. 28Do not marvel at this; for the hour is coming in which all who are in the graves will hear His voice 29and come forth—those who have done good, to the resurrection of life, and those who have done evil, to the resurrection of condemnation. 30I can of Myself do nothing. As I hear, I judge; and My judgment is righteous, because I do not seek My own will but the will of the Father who sent Me.

31*"If I bear witness of Myself, My witness is not true. 32There is another who bears witness of Me, and I know that the witness which He witnesses of Me is true. 33You have sent to John, and he has borne witness to the truth. 34Yet I do not receive testimony from man, but I say these things that you may be saved. 35He was the burning and shining lamp, and you were willing for a time to rejoice in his light. 36But I have a greater witness than John's; for the works which the Father has given Me to finish—the very works that I do—bear witness of Me, that the Father has sent Me. 37And the Father Himself, who sent Me, has testified of Me. You have neither heard His voice at any time, nor seen His form. 38But you do not have His word abiding in you, because whom He sent, Him you do not believe. 39You search the Scriptures, for in them you think you have eternal life; and these are they which testify of Me. 40But you are not willing to come to Me that you may have life.

41"I do not receive honor from men. 42But I know you, that you do not have the love of God in you. 43I have come in My Father's name, and you do not receive Me; if another comes in his own name, him you will receive. 44How can you believe, who receive honor from one another, and do not seek the honor that *comes* from the only God? 45Do not think that I shall accuse you to the Father; there is *one* who accuses you—Moses, in whom you trust. 46For if you believed Moses, you would believe Me; for he wrote about Me. 47But if you do not believe his writings, how will you believe My words?"

6 After* these things Jesus went over the Sea of Galilee, which is *the Sea* of Tiberias. 2Then a great multitude followed Him, because they saw His signs which He performed on those who were diseased. 3And Jesus went up on the mountain, and there He sat with His disciples.

4Now the Passover, a feast of the Jews, was near. 5Then Jesus lifted up *His* eyes, and seeing a great multitude coming toward Him, He said to Philip, "Where shall we buy bread, that these may eat?" 6But this He said to test him, for He Himself knew what He would do.

7Philip answered Him, "Two hundred denarii worth of bread is not sufficient for them, that every one of them may have a little."

8One of His disciples, Andrew, Simon Peter's brother, said to Him, 9"There is a lad here who has five barley loaves and two small fish, but what are they among so many?"

5:31–47 Witness. How can anyone deny that Jesus is the Son of God when so many witnesses affirm that He is: John the Baptist (vv. 31–35), the miracles (v. 36), the Father (v. 37; Mark 1:11), and the Scriptures (5:38–39)? But when people believe in Him, they have the witness within themselves (vv. 39–47; 1 John 5:9–13).

CHAPTER 6

6:1–14 The disciples faced three tests because of the great crowds that followed Jesus.

Feeding the multitude. Philip thought the answer was money, but Andrew saw the answer in a lad with a lunch. When you face a seemingly unsolvable problem, claim the promise of verse 6, give what you have to Jesus, and let Him tell you what to do.

10Then Jesus said, "Make the people sit down." Now there was much grass in the place. So the men sat down, in number about five thousand. 11And Jesus took the loaves, and when He had given thanks He distributed *them* to the disciples, and the disciples[t] to those sitting down; and likewise of the fish, as much as they wanted. 12So when they were filled, He said to His disciples, "Gather up the fragments that remain, so that nothing is lost." 13Therefore they gathered *them* up, and filled twelve baskets with the fragments of the five barley loaves which were left over by those who had eaten. 14Then those men, when they had seen the sign that Jesus did, said, "This is truly the Prophet who is to come into the world."

15*Therefore when Jesus perceived that they were about to come and take Him by force to make Him king, He departed again to the mountain by Himself alone.

16Now when evening came, His disciples went down to the sea, 17got into the boat, and went over the sea toward Capernaum. And it was already dark, and Jesus had not come to them. 18Then the sea arose because a great wind was blowing. 19So when they had rowed about three or four miles,[u] they saw Jesus walking on the sea and drawing near the boat; and they were afraid. 20But He said to them, "It is I; do not be afraid." 21Then they willingly received Him into the boat, and immediately the boat was at the land where they were going.

22*On the following day, when the people who were standing on the other side of the sea saw that there was no other boat there, except that one which His disciples had entered,[v] and that Jesus had not entered the boat with His disciples, but His disciples had gone away alone— 23however, other boats came from Tiberias, near the place where they ate bread after the Lord had given thanks— 24when the people therefore saw that Jesus was not there, nor His disciples, they also got into boats and came to Capernaum, seeking Jesus. 25And when they found Him on the other side of the sea, they said to Him, "Rabbi, when did You come here?"

26Jesus answered them and said, "Most assuredly, I say to you, you seek Me, not because you saw the signs, but because you ate of the loaves and were filled. 27Do not labor for the food which perishes, but for the food which endures to everlasting life, which the Son of Man will give you, because God the Father has set His seal on Him."

28Then they said to Him, "What shall we do, that we may work the works of God?"

29Jesus answered and said to them, "This is the work of God, that you believe in Him whom He sent."

30Therefore they said to Him, "What sign will You perform then, that we may see it and believe You? What work will You do? 31Our fathers ate the manna in the desert; as it is written, '*He gave them bread from heaven to eat.*'[w]

32Then Jesus said to them, "Most assuredly, I say to you, Moses did not give you the bread from

6:15–21 Leaving the multitude. This incident occurred at the high point of our Lord's popularity. The disciples (especially Judas) would have welcomed a kingdom, so Jesus sent them away into a storm. They went from popularity to peril, but they were safer in the storm than with the multitude; and Jesus came to them and met their needs (Isa. 43:2). Can you obey His will even when you disagree with Him?

6:22–71 Losing the multitude. People want the Lord to meet their physical needs but not their spiritual needs. The manna (Exod. 16) came only to the Jews and *sustained* physical life, but Jesus came for the whole world and *gives* eternal life. Just as you take food into your body, so you take Christ into your life; and He becomes one with you. The disciples had opportunity to follow the crowd, but they remained with Jesus.

6:11 [t]NU-Text omits *to the disciples, and the disciples.*
6:19 [u]Literally *twenty-five or thirty stadia*   6:22 [v]NU-Text omits *that* and *which His disciples had entered.*   6:31 [w]Exodus 16:4; Nehemiah 9:15; Psalm 78:24

heaven, but My Father gives you the true bread from heaven. 33For the bread of God is He who comes down from heaven and gives life to the world."

34Then they said to Him, "Lord, give us this bread always."

35And Jesus said to them, "I am the bread of life. He who comes to Me shall never hunger, and he who believes in Me shall never thirst. 36But I said to you that you have seen Me and yet do not believe. 37All that the Father gives Me will come to Me, and the one who comes to Me I will by no means cast out. 38For I have come down from heaven, not to do My own will, but the will of Him who sent Me. 39This is the will of the Father who sent Me, that of all He has given Me I should lose nothing, but should raise it up at the last day. 40And this is the will of Him who sent Me, that everyone who sees the Son and believes in Him may have everlasting life; and I will raise him up at the last day."

41The Jews then complained about Him, because He said, "I am the bread which came down from heaven." 42And they said, "Is not this Jesus, the son of Joseph, whose father and mother we know? How is it then that He says, 'I have come down from heaven'?"

43Jesus therefore answered and said to them, "Do not murmur among yourselves. 44No one can come to Me unless the Father who sent Me draws him; and I will raise him up at the last day. 45It is written in the prophets, 'And they shall all be taught by God.'x Therefore everyone who has heard and learnedy from the Father comes to Me. 46Not that anyone has seen the Father, except He who is from God; He has seen the Father. 47Most assuredly, I say to you, he who believes in Mez has everlasting life. 48I am the bread of life. 49Your fathers ate the manna in the wilderness, and are dead. 50This is the bread which comes down from heaven, that one may eat of it and not die. 51I am the living bread which came down from heaven. If anyone eats of this bread, he will live forever; and the bread that I shall give is My flesh, which I shall give for the life of the world."

52The Jews therefore quarreled among themselves, saying, "How can this Man give us His flesh to eat?"

53Then Jesus said to them, "Most assuredly, I say to you, unless you eat the flesh of the Son of Man and drink His blood, you have no life in you. 54Whoever eats My flesh and drinks My blood has eternal life, and I will raise him up at the last day. 55For My flesh is food indeed,a and My blood is drink indeed. 56He who eats My flesh and drinks My blood abides in Me, and I in him. 57As the living Father sent Me, and I live because of the Father, so he who feeds on Me will live because of Me. 58This is the bread which came down from heaven—not as your fathers ate the manna, and are dead. He who eats this bread will live forever."

59These things He said in the synagogue as He taught in Capernaum.

60Therefore many of His disciples, when they heard this, said, "This is a hard saying; who can understand it?"

6:45 xIsaiah 54:13 yM-Text reads hears and has learned.
6:47 zNU-Text omits in Me.   6:55 aNU-Text reads true food and true drink.

61When Jesus knew in Himself that His disciples complained about this, He said to them, "Does this offend you? 62*What* then if you should see the Son of Man ascend where He was before? 63It is the Spirit who gives life; the flesh profits nothing. The words that I speak to you are spirit, and *they* are life. 64But there are some of you who do not believe." For Jesus knew from the beginning who they were who did not believe, and who would betray Him. 65And He said, "Therefore I have said to you that no one can come to Me unless it has been granted to him by My Father."

66From that *time* many of His disciples went back and walked with Him no more. 67Then Jesus said to the twelve, "Do you also want to go away?"

68But Simon Peter answered Him, "Lord, to whom shall we go? You have the words of eternal life. 69Also we have come to believe and know that You are the Christ, the Son of the living God."*b*

70Jesus answered them, "Did I not choose you, the twelve, and one of you is a devil?" 71He spoke of Judas Iscariot, *the son* of Simon, for it was he who would betray Him, being one of the twelve.

CHAPTER 7

7:2–10 *How the world thinks.* Because He was doing the Father's will, Jesus lived on a divine timetable (v. 30; 2:4; 8:20; 13:1), and so should we (Ps. 31:14–15). The world does not understand this and will give you advice contrary to God's will. Live on God's schedule and you will always have God's help.

7:11–44 *How the world decides.* This discussion reveals the confusion and unbelief of the people. Some were for Him because of His miracles, while others opposed Him because He broke the Sabbath laws. Some waited to see what their leaders would do (v. 26), and their leaders wanted to kill Him. They were judging by appearances (v. 24) and going astray.

7 After these things Jesus walked in Galilee; for He did not want to walk in Judea, because the Jews*c* sought to kill Him. 2*Now the Jews' Feast of Tabernacles was at hand. 3His brothers therefore said to Him, "Depart from here and go into Judea, that Your disciples also may see the works that You are doing. 4For no one does anything in secret while he himself seeks to be known openly. If You do these things, show Yourself to the world." 5For even His brothers did not believe in Him.

6Then Jesus said to them, "My time has not yet come, but your time is always ready. 7The world cannot hate you, but it hates Me because I testify of it that its works are evil. 8You go up to this feast. I am not yet*d* going up to this feast, for My time has not yet fully come." 9When He had said these things to them, He remained in Galilee.

10But when His brothers had gone up, then He also went up to the feast, not openly, but as it were in secret. 11*Then the Jews sought Him at the feast, and said, "Where is He?" 12And there was much complaining among the people concerning Him. Some said, "He is good"; others said, "No, on the contrary, He deceives the people." 13However, no one spoke openly of Him for fear of the Jews.

14Now about the middle of the feast Jesus went up into the temple and taught. 15And the Jews marveled, saying, "How does this Man know letters, having never studied?"

16Jesus*e* answered them and said, "My doctrine is not Mine, but His who sent Me. 17If anyone wills to do His will, he shall know concerning the doctrine, whether it is from God or *whether* I speak on My own *authority*. 18He who speaks from himself seeks his own glory; but He who seeks the

6:69 *b*NU-Text reads *You are the Holy One of God.*
7:1 *c*That is, the ruling authorities 7:8 *d*NU-Text omits *yet.*
7:16 *e*NU-Text and M-Text read *So Jesus.*

Life—*Life* is a key theme in John's gospel; he uses the word nearly fifty times. Jesus is the life (14:6), the light of life (1:4; 8:12), and the bread of life (6:48); and He gives the water of life (7:37–39). Jesus laid down His life so that we might have life (10:14–18, 27–30).

glory of the One who sent Him is true, and no unrighteousness is in Him. [19]Did not Moses give you the law, yet none of you keeps the law? Why do you seek to kill Me?"

[20]The people answered and said, "You have a demon. Who is seeking to kill You?"

[21]Jesus answered and said to them, "I did one work, and you all marvel. [22]Moses therefore gave you circumcision (not that it is from Moses, but from the fathers), and you circumcise a man on the Sabbath. [23]If a man receives circumcision on the Sabbath, so that the law of Moses should not be broken, are you angry with Me because I made a man completely well on the Sabbath? [24]Do not judge according to appearance, but judge with righteous judgment."

[25]Now some of them from Jerusalem said, "Is this not He whom they seek to kill? [26]But look! He speaks boldly, and they say nothing to Him. Do the rulers know indeed that this is truly[f] the Christ? [27]However, we know where this Man is from; but when the Christ comes, no one knows where He is from."

[28]Then Jesus cried out, as He taught in the temple, saying, "You both know Me, and you know where I am from; and I have not come of Myself, but He who sent Me is true, whom you do not know. [29]But[g] I know Him, for I am from Him, and He sent Me."

[30]Therefore they sought to take Him; but no one laid a hand on Him, because His hour had not yet come. [31]And many of the people believed in Him, and said, "When the Christ comes, will He do more signs than these which this *Man* has done?"

[32]The Pharisees heard the crowd murmuring these things concerning Him, and the Pharisees and the chief priests sent officers to take Him. [33]Then Jesus said to them,[h] "I shall be with you a little while longer, and *then* I go to Him who sent Me. [34]You will seek Me and not find *Me*, and where I am you cannot come."

[35]Then the Jews said among themselves, "Where does He intend to go that we shall not find Him? Does He intend to go to the Dispersion among the Greeks and teach the Greeks? [36]What is this thing that He said, 'You will seek Me and not find Me, and where I am you cannot come'?"

[37]*On the last day, that great *day* of the feast, Jesus stood and cried out, saying, "If anyone thirsts, let him come to Me and drink. [38]He who believes in Me, as the Scripture has said, out of his heart will flow rivers of living water." [39]But this He spoke concerning the Spirit, whom those believing[i] in Him would receive; for the Holy[j] Spirit was not yet *given*, because Jesus was not yet glorified.

[40]Therefore many[k] from the crowd, when they heard this saying, said, "Truly this is the Prophet." [41]Others said, "This is the Christ."

But some said, "Will the Christ come out of Galilee? [42]Has not the Scripture said that the Christ comes from the seed of David and from the town of Bethlehem, where David was?" [43]So there was

7:37–39 *What the world needs.* One ritual during the Feast of Tabernacles was the pouring out of water in the temple. It was a reminder that God gave Israel water in the wilderness. Water for drinking pictures the Holy Spirit who is given to those who trust Christ. The world is thirsty and can find its thirst quenched only by coming to Christ.

7:26 [f]NU-Text omits *truly*.   7:29 [g]NU-Text and M-Text omit *But*.   7:33 [h]NU-Text and M-Text omit *to them*.   7:39 [i]NU-Text reads *who believed*. [j]NU-Text omits *Holy*.   7:40 [k]NU-Text reads *some*.

a division among the people because of Him. 44Now some of them wanted to take Him, but no one laid hands on Him.

45Then the officers came to the chief priests and Pharisees, who said to them, "Why have you not brought Him?"

46The officers answered, "No man ever spoke like this Man!"

47Then the Pharisees answered them, "Are you also deceived? 48Have any of the rulers or the Pharisees believed in Him? 49But this crowd that does not know the law is accursed."

50Nicodemus (he who came to Jesus by night,l being one of them) said to them, 51"Does our law judge a man before it hears him and knows what he is doing?"

52They answered and said to him, "Are you also from Galilee? Search and look, for no prophet has arisenm out of Galilee."

53And everyone went to his *own* house.n

8 But Jesus went to the Mount of Olives. 2Now earlyo in the morning He came again into the temple, and all the people came to Him; and He sat down and taught them. 3*Then the scribes and Pharisees brought to Him a woman caught in adultery. And when they had set her in the midst, 4they said to Him, "Teacher, this woman was caughtp in adultery, in the very act. 5Now Moses, in the law, commandedq us that such should be stoned.r But what do You say?"s 6This they said, testing Him, that they might have *something* of which to accuse Him. But Jesus stooped down and wrote on the ground with *His* finger, as though He did not hear.t

7So when they continued asking Him, He raised Himself upu and said to them, "He who is without sin among you, let him throw a stone at her first." 8And again He stooped down and wrote on the ground. 9Then those who heard *it*, being convicted by *their* conscience,v went out one by one, beginning with the oldest *even* to the last. And Jesus was left alone, and the woman standing in the midst. 10When Jesus had raised Himself up and saw no one but the woman, He said to her,w "Woman, where are those accusers of yours?x Has no one condemned you?"

11She said, "No one, Lord."

And Jesus said to her, "Neither do I condemn you; go andy sin no more."

CHAPTER 8

8:3–11 *Condemnation.* The woman was guilty, but where was the man? Both of them deserved to die (Lev. 20:10). It was a trap and Jesus knew it, but He ended up trapping the trappers. Did He write on the ground to remind them that He had written the Law (Exod. 31:18) or to refer them to Jeremiah 17:13 (see Luke 10:20)? Here is our wonderful assurance: "There is therefore now no condemnation to those who are in Christ Jesus" (Rom. 8:1).

7:50 lNU-Text reads *before.* 7:52 mNU-Text reads *is to rise.* 7:53 nThe words *And everyone* through *sin no more* (8:11) are bracketed by NU-Text as not original. They are present in over 900 manuscripts. 8:2 oM-Text reads *very early.* 8:4 pM-Text reads *we found this woman.* 8:5 qM-Text reads *in our law Moses commanded.* rNU-Text and M-Text read *to stone such.* sM-Text adds *about her.* 8:6 tNU-Text and M-Text omit *as though He did not hear.* 8:7 uM-Text reads *He looked up.* 8:9 vNU-Text and M-Text omit *being convicted by their conscience.* 8:10 wNU-Text omits *and saw no one but the woman;* M-Text reads *He saw her and said.* xNU-Text and M-Text omit *of yours.* 8:11 yNU-Text and M-Text add *from now on.*

Whose Child Are You?—There is no record that Jesus ever called the publicans and sinners "children of the devil." He reserved that title for the hypocritical Pharisees. By nature, we are all "children of wrath"; and by choice, we become "children of disobedience" (Eph. 2:1–3). When you receive Jesus Christ, you become a child of God (John 1:12–13). But if you reject Christ and have a false righteousness (Rom. 9:30—10:13), you are in danger of becoming a "child of the devil," for Satan is an imitator (2 Cor. 11:13–15). If Satan becomes your father, hell will be your home.

12*Then Jesus spoke to them again, saying, "I am the light of the world. He who follows Me shall not walk in darkness, but have the light of life."

13The Pharisees therefore said to Him, "You bear witness of Yourself; Your witness is not true."

14Jesus answered and said to them, "Even if I bear witness of Myself, My witness is true, for I know where I came from and where I am going; but you do not know where I come from and where I am going. 15You judge according to the flesh; I judge no one. 16And yet if I do judge, My judgment is true; for I am not alone, but I *am* with the Father who sent Me. 17It is also written in your law that the testimony of two men is true. 18I am One who bears witness of Myself, and the Father who sent Me bears witness of Me."

19Then they said to Him, "Where is Your Father?"

Jesus answered, "You know neither Me nor My Father. If you had known Me, you would have known My Father also."

20These words Jesus spoke in the treasury, as He taught in the temple; and no one laid hands on Him, for His hour had not yet come.

21Then Jesus said to them again, "I am going away, and you will seek Me, and will die in your sin. Where I go you cannot come."

22So the Jews said, "Will He kill Himself, because He says, 'Where I go you cannot come'?"

23And He said to them, "You are from beneath; I am from above. You are of this world; I am not of this world. 24Therefore I said to you that you will die in your sins; for if you do not believe that I am *He,* you will die in your sins."

25Then they said to Him, "Who are You?"

And Jesus said to them, "Just what I have been saying to you from the beginning. 26I have many things to say and to judge concerning you, but He who sent Me is true; and I speak to the world those things which I heard from Him."

27They did not understand that He spoke to them of the Father.

28Then Jesus said to them, "When you lift up the Son of Man, then you will know that I am *He,* and *that* I do nothing of Myself; but as My Father taught Me, I speak these things. 29And He who sent Me is with Me. The Father has not left Me alone, for I always do those things that please Him." 30*As He spoke these words, many believed in Him.

31Then Jesus said to those Jews who believed Him, "If you abide in My word, you are My disciples indeed. 32And you shall know the truth, and the truth shall make you free."

33They answered Him, "We are Abraham's descendants, and have never been in bondage to anyone. How *can* You say, 'You will be made free'?"

34Jesus answered them, "Most assuredly, I say to you, whoever commits sin is a slave of sin. 35And a slave does not abide in the house forever, *but* a son abides forever. 36Therefore if the Son makes you free, you shall be free indeed.

37"I know that you are Abraham's descendants, but you seek to kill Me, because My word has no place in you. 38I speak what I have seen with My Father, and you do what you have seen with[z] your father."

8:12–29 *Illumination.* The religious leaders did not know where they were going or where He was going because they were in the dark spiritually. They had the light of the Law (v. 5; Prov. 6:23) and of conscience (8:9), but they did not have the light of life. Consequently, they did not know the Father or understand what Jesus taught them.

8:30–36 *Liberation.* The people were in bondage to Rome and to the Law of Moses, yet they said they were free! In verse 35, Jesus may have been referring to Isaac and Ishmael (Gen. 21:8–21), since the Jews had mentioned Abraham (8:33). The Son makes you free (v. 36), so trust Him and follow Him. His truth makes you free (v. 32), so study it, believe it, and obey it. Satan imposes slavery that seems like freedom (2 Pet. 2:19); Jesus gives you a yoke that sets you free (Matt. 11:28–30).

8:38 [z]NU-Text reads *heard from.*

³⁹They answered and said to Him, "Abraham is our father."

Jesus said to them, "If you were Abraham's children, you would do the works of Abraham. ⁴⁰But now you seek to kill Me, a Man who has told you the truth which I heard from God. Abraham did not do this. ⁴¹You do the deeds of your father."

Then they said to Him, "We were not born of fornication; we have one Father—God."

⁴²Jesus said to them, "If God were your Father, you would love Me, for I proceeded forth and came from God; nor have I come of Myself, but He sent Me. ⁴³Why do you not understand My speech? Because you are not able to listen to My word. ⁴⁴You are of *your* father the devil, and the desires of your father you want to do. He was a murderer from the beginning, and does not stand in the truth, because there is no truth in him. When he speaks a lie, he speaks from his own *resources,* for he is a liar and the father of it. ⁴⁵But because I tell the truth, you do not believe Me. ⁴⁶Which of you convicts Me of sin? And if I tell the truth, why do you not believe Me? ⁴⁷He who is of God hears God's words; therefore you do not hear, because you are not of God."

⁴⁸Then the Jews answered and said to Him, "Do we not say rightly that You are a Samaritan and have a demon?"

⁴⁹Jesus answered, "I do not have a demon; but I honor My Father, and you dishonor Me. ⁵⁰And I do not seek My *own* glory; there is One who seeks and judges. ⁵¹Most assuredly, I say to you, if anyone keeps My word he shall never see death."

⁵²Then the Jews said to Him, "Now we know that You have a demon! Abraham is dead, and the prophets; and You say, 'If anyone keeps My word he shall never taste death.' ⁵³Are You greater than our father Abraham, who is dead? And the prophets are dead. Who do You make Yourself out to be?"

⁵⁴Jesus answered, "If I honor Myself, My honor is nothing. It is My Father who honors Me, of whom you say that He is your^a God. ⁵⁵Yet you have not known Him, but I know Him. And if I say, 'I do not know Him,' I shall be a liar like you; but I do know Him and keep His word. ⁵⁶Your father Abraham rejoiced to see My day, and he saw *it* and was glad."

⁵⁷Then the Jews said to Him, "You are not yet fifty years old, and have You seen Abraham?"

⁵⁸Jesus said to them, "Most assuredly, I say to you, before Abraham was, I AM."

⁵⁹Then they took up stones to throw at Him; but Jesus hid Himself and went out of the temple,^b going through the midst of them, and so passed by.

CHAPTER 9

9:1–12 *Irritation.* By putting clay on the man's eyes, Jesus encouraged him to obey and wash on the Sabbath. Sometimes the Lord irritates us before He illuminates us.

His power is so great that He can use common things like dirt and water to produce a miracle. The man could hear but not see, and the Word produced faith (Rom. 10:17).

9 Now* as *Jesus* passed by, He saw a man who was blind from birth. ²And His disciples asked Him, saying, "Rabbi, who sinned, this man or his parents, that he was born blind?"

³Jesus answered, "Neither this man nor his parents sinned, but that the works of God should be revealed in him. ⁴I^c must work the works of Him who sent Me while it is day; *the* night is coming

---

8:54 ^aNU-Text and M-Text read *our.*   8:59 ^bNU-Text omits the rest of this verse.   9:4 ^cNU-Text reads *We.*

when no one can work. 5As long as I am in the world, I am the light of the world."

6When He had said these things, He spat on the ground and made clay with the saliva; and He anointed the eyes of the blind man with the clay. 7And He said to him, "Go, wash in the pool of Siloam" (which is translated, Sent). So he went and washed, and came back seeing.

8Therefore the neighbors and those who previously had seen that he was blindd said, "Is not this he who sat and begged?"

9Some said, "This is he." Others said, "He is like him."e

He said, "I am he."

10Therefore they said to him, "How were your eyes opened?"

11He answered and said, "A Man called Jesus made clay and anointed my eyes and said to me, 'Go to the pool off Siloam and wash.' So I went and washed, and I received sight."

12Then they said to him, "Where is He?"

He said, "I do not know."

13*They brought him who formerly was blind to the Pharisees. 14Now it was a Sabbath when Jesus made the clay and opened his eyes. 15Then the Pharisees also asked him again how he had received his sight. He said to them, "He put clay on my eyes, and I washed, and I see."

16Therefore some of the Pharisees said, "This Man is not from God, because He does not keep the Sabbath."

Others said, "How can a man who is a sinner do such signs?" And there was a division among them.

17They said to the blind man again, "What do you say about Him because He opened your eyes?"

He said, "He is a prophet."

18But the Jews did not believe concerning him, that he had been blind and received his sight, until they called the parents of him who had received his sight. 19And they asked them, saying, "Is this your son, who you say was born blind? How then does he now see?"

20His parents answered them and said, "We know that this is our son, and that he was born blind; 21but by what means he now sees we do not know, or who opened his eyes we do not know. He is of age; ask him. He will speak for himself." 22His parents said these things because they feared the Jews, for the Jews had agreed already that if anyone confessed that He was Christ, he would be put out of the synagogue. 23Therefore his parents said, "He is of age; ask him."

24So they again called the man who was blind, and said to him, "Give God the glory! We know that this Man is a sinner."

25He answered and said, "Whether He is a sinner or not I do not know. One thing I know: that though I was blind, now I see."

26Then they said to him again, "What did He do to you? How did He open your eyes?"

27He answered them, "I told you already, and you did not listen. Why do you want to hear it again? Do you also want to become His disciples?"

9:13–34 Interrogation. The man was questioned by the neighbors (v. 10) and by the Pharisees (vv. 15, 19, 26). Instead of seeking the truth and the freedom it brings (8:32), the Pharisees denied the truth and ended up in worse bondage. If we ask questions sincerely, with a willingness to obey, the Lord will lead us to the truth (7:17). If we are not honest with God, He will never show us His light.

9:8 dNU-Text reads a beggar.   9:9 eNU-Text reads "No, but he is like him."   9:11 fNU-Text omits the pool of.

28Then they reviled him and said, "You are His disciple, but we are Moses' disciples. 29We know that God spoke to Moses; *as for* this *fellow,* we do not know where He is from."

30The man answered and said to them, "Why, this is a marvelous thing, that you do not know where He is from; yet He has opened my eyes! 31Now we know that God does not hear sinners; but if anyone is a worshiper of God and does His will, He hears him. 32Since the world began it has been unheard of that anyone opened the eyes of one who was born blind. 33If this Man were not from God, He could do nothing."

34They answered and said to him, "You were completely born in sins, and are you teaching us?" And they cast him out.

35*Jesus heard that they had cast him out; and when He had found him, He said to him, "Do you believe in the Son of God?"*g*

36He answered and said, "Who is He, Lord, that I may believe in Him?"

37And Jesus said to him, "You have both seen Him and it is He who is talking with you."

38Then he said, "Lord, I believe!" And he worshiped Him.

39And Jesus said, "For judgment I have come into this world, that those who do not see may see, and that those who see may be made blind."

40Then *some* of the Pharisees who were with Him heard these words, and said to Him, "Are we blind also?"

41Jesus said to them, "If you were blind, you would have no sin; but now you say, 'We see.' Therefore your sin remains.

9:35–41 Identification. The Pharisees were false shepherds who threw the man out, but Jesus the Good Shepherd took him in! The man knew that He was "a Man called Jesus" (v. 11), "a prophet" (v. 17), and "a Man of God" (v. 33); but he needed to learn that He is "the Son of God" (v. 35). He believed and was saved. Beware a spiritual experience that comes short of true salvation.

CHAPTER 10

10:1–30 God's people are His flock (Ps. 100:3; Acts 20:28), and they must beware strangers (10:5), thieves (vv. 1, 10), and hirelings (v. 12). Jesus is the Good Shepherd who knows His sheep (vv. 14–15) and speaks to them (v. 27), so He is not like the strangers. He protects the sheep (vv. 28–29), so He is not like the thieves; and He gives His life for the sheep, so He is not like the hirelings who run away from danger (vv. 11–13).

When you trust the Good Shepherd, He leads you out of the wrong fold and into the right flock (vv. 3–4, 16). He goes before you and leads you by His Word (v. 4), and He leads you in and out to find spiritual nourishment (v. 9).

There are many churches but only "one flock and one shepherd" (v. 16). Is the Lord using you to bring the "other sheep" to Him?

10 "Most* assuredly, I say to you, he who does not enter the sheepfold by the door, but climbs up some other way, the same is a thief and a robber. 2But he who enters by the door is the shepherd of the sheep. 3To him the doorkeeper opens, and the sheep hear his voice; and he calls his own sheep by name and leads them out. 4And when he brings out his own sheep, he goes before them; and the sheep follow him, for they know his voice. 5Yet they will by no means follow a stranger, but will flee from him, for they do not know the voice of strangers." 6Jesus used this illustration, but they did not understand the things which He spoke to them.

7Then Jesus said to them again, "Most assuredly, I say to you, I am the door of the sheep. 8All who *ever* came before Me*h* are thieves and robbers, but the sheep did not hear them. 9I am the door. If anyone enters by Me, he will be saved, and will go in and out and find pasture. 10The thief does not come except to steal, and to kill, and to destroy. I have come that they may have life, and that they may have *it* more abundantly. 11"I am the good shepherd. The good shepherd gives His life for the sheep. 12But a hireling, *he*

9:35 *g*NU-Text reads *Son of Man.*   10:8 *h*M-Text omits *before Me.*

In the Good Shepherd's Flock—Why does the Lord compare His people to sheep? They are prone to wander (Isa. 53:6) and need a shepherd to guide them. Sheep are clean animals (1 Pet. 2:25; 2 Pet. 2:20–22) and were used for sacrifices (Rom. 8:36; 12:1). They flock together (Acts 4:32) and are useful because they produce milk, lambs, and wool. The Good Shepherd knows His sheep intimately and calls them by name. He protects them and provides for them (Ps. 23). How wonderful to be one of His sheep!

who is not the shepherd, one who does not own the sheep, sees the wolf coming and leaves the sheep and flees; and the wolf catches the sheep and scatters them. 13The hireling flees because he is a hireling and does not care about the sheep. 14I am the good shepherd; and I know My *sheep*, and am known by My own. 15As the Father knows Me, even so I know the Father; and I lay down My life for the sheep. 16And other sheep I have which are not of this fold; them also I must bring, and they will hear My voice; and there will be one flock *and* one shepherd.

17"Therefore My Father loves Me, because I lay down My life that I may take it again. 18No one takes it from Me, but I lay it down of Myself. I have power to lay it down, and I have power to take it again. This command I have received from My Father."

19Therefore there was a division again among the Jews because of these sayings. 20And many of them said, "He has a demon and is mad. Why do you listen to Him?"

21Others said, "These are not the words of one who has a demon. Can a demon open the eyes of the blind?"

22Now it was the Feast of Dedication in Jerusalem, and it was winter. 23And Jesus walked in the temple, in Solomon's porch. 24Then the Jews surrounded Him and said to Him, "How long do You keep us in doubt? If You are the Christ, tell us plainly."

25Jesus answered them, "I told you, and you do not believe. The works that I do in My Father's name, they bear witness of Me. 26But you do not believe, because you are not of My sheep, as I said to you.*i* 27My sheep hear My voice, and I know them, and they follow Me. 28And I give them eternal life, and they shall never perish; neither shall anyone snatch them out of My hand. 29My Father, who has given *them* to Me, is greater than all; and no one is able to snatch *them* out of My Father's hand. 30I and *My* Father are one."

31Then the Jews took up stones again to stone Him. 32Jesus answered them, "Many good works I have shown you from My Father. For which of those works do you stone Me?"

33The Jews answered Him, saying, "For a good work we do not stone You, but for blasphemy, and because You, being a Man, make Yourself God."

34Jesus answered them, "Is it not written in your law, *'I said, "You are gods"'?j* 35If He called them gods, to whom the word of God came (and the Scripture cannot be broken), 36do you say of Him whom the Father sanctified and sent into the world, 'You are blaspheming,' because I said, 'I am the Son of God'? 37If I do not do the works of My Father, do not believe Me; 38but if I do, though you do not believe Me, believe the works, that you may know and believe*k* that the Father *is* in Me, and I in Him." 39Therefore they sought again to seize Him, but He escaped out of their hand.

40And He went away again beyond the Jordan to the place where John was baptizing at first, and there He stayed. 41Then many came to Him and said, "John performed no sign, but all the

10:26 *i*NU-Text omits *as I said to you.*   10:34 *j*Psalm 82:6
10:38 *k*NU-Text reads *understand.*

things that John spoke about this Man were true." [42]And many believed in Him there.

CHAPTER 11

11:1–3 This experience was difficult for the Bethany family, but look at it in the light of God's love (vv. 3, 5, 36).
Love hears. The sisters sent their message to the Lord because they knew He was concerned about them. God's love keeps His ears open to our cries (Ps. 34:12–16).

11:4–6 Love waits. We think that love must act immediately, but sometimes delay brings a greater blessing. "God's delays are not God's denials." Jesus gave them a promise to encourage them while they waited (v. 4). The promise seemed to have failed, but Jesus knew what He was doing.

11:7–16 Love risks. It was dangerous for Jesus to return to Judea, but He went just the same. The raising of Lazarus helped to precipitate the plans that led to His death (vv. 45–57).

11:17–32 Love comforts. Jesus came to the sisters, listened to them, and assured them with His word. He cannot really help us until we move from "Lord, if . . ." (vv. 21, 32) to "Yes, Lord, I believe" (v. 27).

❝*If God is at work week by week raising men from the dead, there will always be people coming to see how it is done. You cannot find an empty church that has conversion for its leading feature. Do you want to know how to fill empty chapels? Here is the answer: Get your Lazarus.*❞

—Samuel Chadwick, Methodist evangelist and educator (1860–1932)

---

11 Now* a certain *man* was sick, Lazarus of Bethany, the town of Mary and her sister Martha. [2]It was *that* Mary who anointed the Lord with fragrant oil and wiped His feet with her hair, whose brother Lazarus was sick. [3]Therefore the sisters sent to Him, saying, "Lord, behold, he whom You love is sick."

[4]*When Jesus heard *that,* He said, "This sickness is not unto death, but for the glory of God, that the Son of God may be glorified through it."

[5]Now Jesus loved Martha and her sister and Lazarus. [6]So, when He heard that he was sick, He stayed two more days in the place where He was. [7]*Then after this He said to *the* disciples, "Let us go to Judea again."

[8]*The* disciples said to Him, "Rabbi, lately the Jews sought to stone You, and are You going there again?"

[9]Jesus answered, "Are there not twelve hours in the day? If anyone walks in the day, he does not stumble, because he sees the light of this world. [10]But if one walks in the night, he stumbles, because the light is not in him." [11]These things He said, and after that He said to them, "Our friend Lazarus sleeps, but I go that I may wake him up."

[12]Then His disciples said, "Lord, if he sleeps he will get well." [13]However, Jesus spoke of his death, but they thought that He was speaking about taking rest in sleep.

[14]Then Jesus said to them plainly, "Lazarus is dead. [15]And I am glad for your sakes that I was not there, that you may believe. Nevertheless let us go to him."

[16]Then Thomas, who is called the Twin, said to his fellow disciples, "Let us also go, that we may die with Him."

[17]*So when Jesus came, He found that he had already been in the tomb four days. [18]Now Bethany was near Jerusalem, about two miles[l] away. [19]And many of the Jews had joined the women around Martha and Mary, to comfort them concerning their brother.

[20]Now Martha, as soon as she heard that Jesus was coming, went and met Him, but Mary was sitting in the house. [21]Now Martha said to Jesus, "Lord, if You had been here, my brother would not have died. [22]But even now I know that whatever You ask of God, God will give You."

[23]Jesus said to her, "Your brother will rise again."

[24]Martha said to Him, "I know that he will rise again in the resurrection at the last day."

[25]Jesus said to her, "I am the resurrection and the life. He who believes in Me, though he may die, he shall live. [26]And whoever lives and believes in Me shall never die. Do you believe this?"

[27]She said to Him, "Yes, Lord, I believe that You are the Christ, the Son of God, who is to come into the world."

[28]And when she had said these things, she went her way and secretly called Mary her sister, saying, "The Teacher has come and is calling for you." [29]As soon as she heard *that,* she arose quickly and came to Him. [30]Now Jesus had not yet come into the town, but was[m] in the place

---

11:18 [l]Literally *fifteen stadia*   11:30 [m]NU-Text adds *still.*

where Martha met Him. [31]Then the Jews who were with her in the house, and comforting her, when they saw that Mary rose up quickly and went out, followed her, saying, "She is going to the tomb to weep there."[n]

[32]Then, when Mary came where Jesus was, and saw Him, she fell down at His feet, saying to Him, "Lord, if You had been here, my brother would not have died."

[33]*Therefore, when Jesus saw her weeping, and the Jews who came with her weeping, He groaned in the spirit and was troubled. [34]And He said, "Where have you laid him?"

They said to Him, "Lord, come and see."

[35]Jesus wept. [36]Then the Jews said, "See how He loved him!"

[37]And some of them said, "Could not this Man, who opened the eyes of the blind, also have kept this man from dying?"

[38]*Then Jesus, again groaning in Himself, came to the tomb. It was a cave, and a stone lay against it. [39]Jesus said, "Take away the stone."

Martha, the sister of him who was dead, said to Him, "Lord, by this time there is a stench, for he has been *dead* four days."

[40]Jesus said to her, "Did I not say to you that if you would believe you would see the glory of God?" [41]Then they took away the stone *from the place* where the dead man was lying.[o] And Jesus lifted up *His* eyes and said, "Father, I thank You that You have heard Me. [42]And I know that You always hear Me, but because of the people who are standing by I said *this*, that they may believe that You sent Me." [43]Now when He had said these things, He cried with a loud voice, "Lazarus, come forth!" [44]And he who had died came out bound hand and foot with graveclothes, and his face was wrapped with a cloth. Jesus said to them, "Loose him, and let him go."

[45]Then many of the Jews who had come to Mary, and had seen the things Jesus did, believed in Him. [46]But some of them went away to the Pharisees and told them the things Jesus did. [47]Then the chief priests and the Pharisees gathered a council and said, "What shall we do? For this Man works many signs. [48]If we let Him alone like this, everyone will believe in Him, and the Romans will come and take away both our place and nation."

[49]And one of them, Caiaphas, being high priest that year, said to them, "You know nothing at all, [50]nor do you consider that it is expedient for us[p] that one man should die for the people, and not that the whole nation should perish." [51]Now this he did not say on his own *authority*; but being high priest that year he prophesied that Jesus would die for the nation, [52]and not for that nation only, but also that He would gather together in one the children of God who were scattered abroad.

[53]Then, from that day on, they plotted to put Him to death. [54]Therefore Jesus no longer walked openly among the Jews, but went from there into the country near the wilderness, to a city called Ephraim, and there remained with His disciples.

[55]And the Passover of the Jews was near, and

11:33–36 *Love weeps.* Jesus identifies with our sorrows (Heb. 4:15–16). He knew He would raise Lazarus from the dead, but He still wept with the sisters and their friends.

11:38–44 *Love serves.* We today are not able to raise the dead, but we can serve others as they go through the valley (Rom. 12:15). A loving heart will always find a way to bear others' burdens (Gal. 6:2).

11:31 [n]NU-Text reads *supposing that she was going to the tomb to weep there.*   11:41 [o]NU-Text omits *from the place where the dead man was lying.*   11:50 [p]NU-Text reads *you.*

CHAPTER 12

12:3–8 Fragrance. What would your plans be if you knew you had only six days to live? Jesus took time to visit dear friends and fellowship with them. Mary's adoration not only revealed her love, but it brought joy to His heart, exposed Judas's sin, and gave the church an example to follow. Are the places where you go filled with Christ's fragrance because of you (2 Cor. 2:15–16)?

12:12–19 Festival. Jesus took advantage of the large Passover crowd to present Himself as King (Zech. 9:9). He was forcing the Jewish leaders to act, for it was the Father's will that Jesus die on Passover. The crowd did not stay with Him. It is easier to shout in a parade than stand at a cross.

many went from the country up to Jerusalem before the Passover, to purify themselves. 56Then they sought Jesus, and spoke among themselves as they stood in the temple, "What do you think—that He will not come to the feast?" 57Now both the chief priests and the Pharisees had given a command, that if anyone knew where He was, he should report it, that they might seize Him.

12 Then, six days before the Passover, Jesus came to Bethany, where Lazarus was who had been dead,q whom He had raised from the dead. 2There they made Him a supper; and Martha served, but Lazarus was one of those who sat at the table with Him. 3*Then Mary took a pound of very costly oil of spikenard, anointed the feet of Jesus, and wiped His feet with her hair. And the house was filled with the fragrance of the oil.

4But one of His disciples, Judas Iscariot, Simon's son, who would betray Him, said, 5"Why was this fragrant oil not sold for three hundred denariir and given to the poor?" 6This he said, not that he cared for the poor, but because he was a thief, and had the money box; and he used to take what was put in it.

7But Jesus said, "Let her alone; she has kepts this for the day of My burial. 8For the poor you have with you always, but Me you do not have always."

9Now a great many of the Jews knew that He was there; and they came, not for Jesus' sake only, but that they might also see Lazarus, whom He had raised from the dead. 10But the chief priests plotted to put Lazarus to death also, 11because on account of him many of the Jews went away and believed in Jesus.

12*The next day a great multitude that had come to the feast, when they heard that Jesus was coming to Jerusalem, 13took branches of palm trees and went out to meet Him, and cried out:

"Hosanna!
'Blessed is He who comes in the name of the LORD!'t
The King of Israel!"

14Then Jesus, when He had found a young donkey, sat on it; as it is written:

15 "Fear not, daughter of Zion;
Behold, your King is coming,
Sitting on a donkey's colt."u

16His disciples did not understand these things at first; but when Jesus was glorified, then they remembered that these things were written about Him and that they had done these things to Him.

17Therefore the people, who were with Him when He called Lazarus out of his tomb and raised him from the dead, bore witness. 18For this reason the people also met Him, because they heard that He had done this sign. 19The Pharisees therefore said among themselves, "You see that you are accomplishing nothing. Look, the world has gone after Him!"

20Now there were certain Greeks among those

12:1 qNU-Text omits who had been dead.   12:5 rAbout one year's wages for a worker   12:7 sNU-Text reads that she may keep.   12:13 tPsalm 118:26   12:15 uZechariah 9:9

who came up to worship at the feast. 21Then they came to Philip, who was from Bethsaida of Galilee, and asked him, saying, "Sir, we wish to see Jesus."

22Philip came and told Andrew, and in turn Andrew and Philip told Jesus.

23*But Jesus answered them, saying, "The hour has come that the Son of Man should be glorified. 24Most assuredly, I say to you, unless a grain of wheat falls into the ground and dies, it remains alone; but if it dies, it produces much grain. 25He who loves his life will lose it, and he who hates his life in this world will keep it for eternal life. 26If anyone serves Me, let him follow Me; and where I am, there My servant will be also. If anyone serves Me, him My Father will honor.

27"Now My soul is troubled, and what shall I say? 'Father, save Me from this hour'? But for this purpose I came to this hour. 28Father, glorify Your name."

Then a voice came from heaven, *saying*, "I have both glorified *it* and will glorify *it* again."

29Therefore the people who stood by and heard *it* said that it had thundered. Others said, "An angel has spoken to Him."

30Jesus answered and said, "This voice did not come because of Me, but for your sake. 31Now is the judgment of this world; now the ruler of this world will be cast out. 32And I, if I am lifted up from the earth, will draw all *peoples* to Myself." 33This He said, signifying by what death He would die.

34The people answered Him, "We have heard from the law that the Christ remains forever; and how *can* You say, 'The Son of Man must be lifted up'? Who is this Son of Man?"

35Then Jesus said to them, "A little while longer the light is with you. Walk while you have the light, lest darkness overtake you; he who walks in darkness does not know where he is going. 36While you have the light, believe in the light, that you may become sons of light." These things Jesus spoke, and departed, and was hidden from them.

37*But although He had done so many signs before them, they did not believe in Him, 38that the word of Isaiah the prophet might be fulfilled, which he spoke:

"Lord, who has believed our report?
    And to whom has the arm of the LORD been
    revealed?"v

39Therefore they could not believe, because Isaiah said again:

40 "He has blinded their eyes and hardened
    their hearts,
    Lest they should see with their eyes,
    Lest they should understand with their
        hearts and turn,
    So that I should heal them." w

41These things Isaiah said whenx he saw His glory and spoke of Him.

42Nevertheless even among the rulers many believed in Him, but because of the Pharisees they did not confess Him, lest they should be put out

12:23–33 Fruitfulness. Jesus looked upon His death as an opportunity to glorify God (vv. 23, 28). Do you take that attitude when you face a time of trial? He saw Himself as a seed that would die and produce fruit and as a conqueror who would defeat Satan (v. 31; Col. 2:14–15). The Cross would open the way of salvation for both Jews and Gentiles (12:32).

12:37–50 Faithlessness. In His words and works, Jesus showed Israel the light, but they chose to walk in darkness. The praise of men meant more to them than the praise of God (5:44). Be careful what you do with His words because you will hear them again when you see the Savior (12:48).

12:38 vIsaiah 53:1   12:40 wIsaiah 6:10   12:41 xNU-Text reads *because*.

of the synagogue; [43]for they loved the praise of men more than the praise of God.

[44]Then Jesus cried out and said, "He who believes in Me, believes not in Me but in Him who sent Me. [45]And he who sees Me sees Him who sent Me. [46]I have come as a light into the world, that whoever believes in Me should not abide in darkness. [47]And if anyone hears My words and does not believe,[y] I do not judge him; for I did not come to judge the world but to save the world. [48]He who rejects Me, and does not receive My words, has that which judges him—the word that I have spoken will judge him in the last day. [49]For I have not spoken on My own authority; but the Father who sent Me gave Me a command, what I should say and what I should speak. [50]And I know that His command is everlasting life. Therefore, whatever I speak, just as the Father has told Me, so I speak."

CHAPTER 13

13:1–11 What Jesus knew. Because of what Jesus knew, He did what He did: He washed the disciples' feet. Jesus knew where He came from and where He was going. He knew that the Father had given Him all things (3:35). If you have all things in your hand, you will have no problem picking up a towel (1 Cor. 3:21–23). Jesus taught them a lesson in fellowship and in keeping themselves clean before the Lord (1 John 1:5—2:1).

13:12–20 What the disciples knew. Jesus taught them a second lesson: true happiness comes from humble service. Jesus gave them an example that we must follow today (Phil. 2:1–11). Alas, soon after this lesson, the disciples began to argue over who was the greatest (Luke 22:24–30).

13 Now* before the Feast of the Passover, when Jesus knew that His hour had come that He should depart from this world to the Father, having loved His own who were in the world, He loved them to the end. [2]And supper being ended,[z] the devil having already put it into the heart of Judas Iscariot, Simon's son, to betray Him, [3]Jesus, knowing that the Father had given all things into His hands, and that He had come from God and was going to God, [4]rose from supper and laid aside His garments, took a towel and girded Himself. [5]After that, He poured water into a basin and began to wash the disciples' feet, and to wipe them with the towel with which He was girded. [6]Then He came to Simon Peter. And Peter said to Him, "Lord, are You washing my feet?"

[7]Jesus answered and said to him, "What I am doing you do not understand now, but you will know after this."

[8]Peter said to Him, "You shall never wash my feet!"

Jesus answered him, "If I do not wash you, you have no part with Me."

[9]Simon Peter said to Him, "Lord, not my feet only, but also my hands and my head!"

[10]Jesus said to him, "He who is bathed needs only to wash his feet, but is completely clean; and you are clean, but not all of you." [11]For He knew who would betray Him; therefore He said, "You are not all clean."

[12]*So when He had washed their feet, taken His garments, and sat down again, He said to them, "Do you know what I have done to you? [13]You call Me Teacher and Lord, and you say well, for so I am. [14]If I then, your Lord and Teacher, have washed your feet, you also ought to wash one another's feet. [15]For I have given you an example, that you should do as I have done to you. [16]Most assuredly, I say to you, a servant is not greater than his master; nor is he who is sent greater than he who sent him. [17]If you know these things, blessed are you if you do them.

[18]"I do not speak concerning all of you. I know whom I have chosen; but that the Scripture may be fulfilled, 'He who eats bread with Me[a] has lifted up his heel against Me.'[b] [19]Now I tell you before

---

12:47 [y]NU-Text reads keep them.   13:2 [z]NU-Text reads And during supper.   13:18 [a]NU-Text reads My bread. [b]Psalm 41:9

it comes, that when it does come to pass, you may believe that I am *He*. 20Most assuredly, I say to you, he who receives whomever I send receives Me; and he who receives Me receives Him who sent Me."

21*When Jesus had said these things, He was troubled in spirit, and testified and said, "Most assuredly, I say to you, one of you will betray Me." 22Then the disciples looked at one another, perplexed about whom He spoke.

23Now there was leaning on Jesus' bosom one of His disciples, whom Jesus loved. 24Simon Peter therefore motioned to him to ask who it was of whom He spoke.

25Then, leaning backc on Jesus' breast, he said to Him, "Lord, who is it?"

26Jesus answered, "It is he to whom I shall give a piece of bread when I have dipped *it*." And having dipped the bread, He gave *it* to Judas Iscariot, *the son* of Simon. 27Now after the piece of bread, Satan entered him. Then Jesus said to him, "What you do, do quickly." 28But no one at the table knew for what reason He said this to him. 29For some thought, because Judas had the money box, that Jesus had said to him, "Buy *those things* we need for the feast," or that he should give something to the poor.

30Having received the piece of bread, he then went out immediately. And it was night.

31So, when he had gone out, Jesus said, "Now the Son of Man is glorified, and God is glorified in Him. 32If God is glorified in Him, God will also glorify Him in Himself, and glorify Him immediately. 33Little children, I shall be with you a little while longer. You will seek Me; and as I said to the Jews, 'Where I am going, you cannot come,' so now I say to you. 34*A new commandment I give to you, that you love one another; as I have loved you, that you also love one another. 35By this all will know that you are My disciples, if you have love for one another."

36Simon Peter said to Him, "Lord, where are You going?"

Jesus answered him, "Where I am going you cannot follow Me now, but you shall follow Me afterward."

37Peter said to Him, "Lord, why can I not follow You now? I will lay down my life for Your sake."

38Jesus answered him, "Will you lay down your life for My sake? Most assuredly, I say to you, the rooster shall not crow till you have denied Me three times."

14 "Let* not your heart be troubled; you believe in God, believe also in Me. 2In My Father's house are many mansions;d if *it were* not so, I would have told you. I go to prepare a place for you.e 3And if I go and prepare a place for you, I will come again and receive you to Myself; that

13:21–30 *What Judas knew.* Jesus did not reveal Judas's secret; in fact, He treated him just like the others and they detected nothing amiss. What love that Jesus should not only protect the man who betrayed Him but even wash his feet! Jesus with the towel is the perfect example of humility; Judas with the bread is a perfect example of hypocrisy and treachery.

13:34, 35 *What the world must know.* The distinguishing mark of true disciples is their love for one another (1 John 2:7–11), and it is the kind of love that the world can see. He commands us to love, and He gives us the power to obey (Rom. 5:5).

CHAPTER 14

14:1–6 No wonder the disciples were troubled (vv. 1, 27): Jesus was going to leave them, one of them would betray Him, and Peter would deny Him. Jesus encouraged them by telling them about Himself and the Father.

Jesus takes us to the Father. We have a home in heaven when life is over, and we shall meet Jesus and the Father. James M. Gray wrote, "Who could mind the journey when the road leads home?" Blessed assurance!

13:25 cNU-Text and M-Text add *thus*.   14:2 dLiterally *dwellings* eNU-Text adds a word which would cause the text to read either *if it were not so, would I have told you that I go to prepare a place for you?* or *if it were not so I would have told you; for I go to prepare a place for you.*

The Holy Spirit—The Holy Spirit is the Father's gift to you, a gift that will never be taken back (John 14:16). The Spirit is a person, like the Father and the Son, and is God; and He dwells in God's people (14:17). He enables you to witness for Christ (15:26–27; Acts 1:8) and through your witness convicts the lost (16:7–11). He will teach you the Word (14:26) and use it in your life to glorify Christ (16:12–15).

14:7–11 Jesus reveals the Father. In what He said (7:16) and did (5:19) during His earthly ministry, Jesus revealed the Father: "I and My Father are one" (10:30). How can we not love the Father when He is like Jesus?

14:12–18 Jesus glorifies the Father. He does it through His people as they do God's works and keep His commandments. Apart from the power of the Holy Spirit and prayer, we could never glorify the Lord.

14:19–31 Jesus and the Father dwell with us. It is one thing for us to go to heaven and quite something else for heaven to come to us! There is a deeper fellowship with the Son and the Father for those who love Him, seek Him, and obey Him. We experience His peace as we commune with the Father and the Son in love. Jesus is the way to the Father; He reveals the truth about the Father; and He shares the life of the Father with us. Why should our hearts be troubled?

where I am, *there* you may be also. 4And where I go you know, and the way you know."

5Thomas said to Him, "Lord, we do not know where You are going, and how can we know the way?"

6Jesus said to him, "I am the way, the truth, and the life. No one comes to the Father except through Me.

7*"If you had known Me, you would have known My Father also; and from now on you know Him and have seen Him."

8Philip said to Him, "Lord, show us the Father, and it is sufficient for us."

9Jesus said to him, "Have I been with you so long, and yet you have not known Me, Philip? He who has seen Me has seen the Father; so how can you say, 'Show us the Father'? 10Do you not believe that I am in the Father, and the Father in Me? The words that I speak to you I do not speak on My own *authority;* but the Father who dwells in Me does the works. 11Believe Me that I *am* in the Father and the Father in Me, or else believe Me for the sake of the works themselves.

12*"Most assuredly, I say to you, he who believes in Me, the works that I do he will do also; and greater *works* than these he will do, because I go to My Father. 13And whatever you ask in My name, that I will do, that the Father may be glorified in the Son. 14If you ask^f anything in My name, I will do *it.*

15"If you love Me, keep^g My commandments. 16And I will pray the Father, and He will give you another Helper, that He may abide with you forever— 17the Spirit of truth, whom the world cannot receive, because it neither sees Him nor knows Him; but you know Him, for He dwells with you and will be in you. 18I will not leave you orphans; I will come to you.

19*"A little while longer and the world will see Me no more, but you will see Me. Because I live, you will live also. 20At that day you will know that I *am* in My Father, and you in Me, and I in you. 21He who has My commandments and keeps them, it is he who loves Me. And he who loves Me will be loved by My Father, and I will love him and manifest Myself to him."

22Judas (not Iscariot) said to Him, "Lord, how is it that You will manifest Yourself to us, and not to the world?"

23Jesus answered and said to him, "If anyone loves Me, he will keep My word; and My Father will love him, and We will come to him and make Our home with him. 24He who does not love Me does not keep My words; and the word which you hear is not Mine but the Father's who sent Me.

25"These things I have spoken to you while being present with you. 26But the Helper, the Holy Spirit, whom the Father will send in My name, He will teach you all things, and bring to your remembrance all things that I said to you. 27Peace I leave with you, My peace I give to you; not as the world gives do I give to you. Let not your heart be troubled, neither let it be afraid. 28You have heard Me say to you, 'I am going away and coming *back* to you.' If you loved Me, you would rejoice because I said,^{h} 'I am going to the Father,' for My Father is greater than I.

29"And now I have told you before it comes,

14:14 ^{f}NU-Text adds *Me.* 14:15 ^{g}NU-Text reads *you will keep.* 14:28 ^{h}NU-Text omits *I said.*

that when it does come to pass, you may believe. [30]I will no longer talk much with you, for the ruler of this world is coming, and he has nothing in Me. [31]But that the world may know that I love the Father, and as the Father gave Me commandment, so I do. Arise, let us go from here.

15 "I* am the true vine, and My Father is the vinedresser. [2]Every branch in Me that does not bear fruit He takes away;[i] and every *branch* that bears fruit He prunes, that it may bear more fruit. [3]You are already clean because of the word which I have spoken to you. [4]Abide in Me, and I in you. As the branch cannot bear fruit of itself, unless it abides in the vine, neither can you, unless you abide in Me.

[5]"I am the vine, you *are* the branches. He who abides in Me, and I in him, bears much fruit; for without Me you can do nothing. [6]If anyone does not abide in Me, he is cast out as a branch and is withered; and they gather them and throw *them* into the fire, and they are burned. [7]If you abide in Me, and My words abide in you, you will[j] ask what you desire, and it shall be done for you. [8]By this My Father is glorified, that you bear much fruit; so you will be My disciples.

[9]*"As the Father loved Me, I also have loved you; abide in My love. [10]If you keep My commandments, you will abide in My love, just as I have kept My Father's commandments and abide in His love.

[11]"These things I have spoken to you, that My joy may remain in you, and *that* your joy may be full. [12]This is My commandment, that you love one another as I have loved you. [13]Greater love has no one than this, than to lay down one's life for his friends. [14]You are My friends if you do whatever I command you. [15]No longer do I call you servants, for a servant does not know what his master is doing; but I have called you friends, for all things that I heard from My Father I have made known to you. [16]You did not choose Me, but I chose you and appointed you that you should go and bear fruit, and *that* your fruit should remain, that whatever you ask the Father in My name He may give you. [17]These things I command you, that you love one another.

[18]*"If the world hates you, you know that it hated Me before *it hated* you. [19]If you were of the world, the world would love its own. Yet because you are not of the world, but I chose you out of the world, therefore the world hates you. [20]Remember the word that I said to you, 'A servant is not greater than his master.' If they persecuted Me, they will also persecute you. If they kept My word, they will keep yours also. [21]But all these things they will do to you for My name's sake, because they do not know Him who sent Me. [22]If I had not come and spoken to them, they would have no sin, but now they have no excuse for their sin. [23]He who hates Me hates My Father also. [24]If I had not done among them the works which no one else did, they would have no sin; but now they have seen and also hated both Me and My Father. [25]But *this happened* that the word might be fulfilled which is written in their law, 'They hated Me without a cause.'[k]

[26]"But when the Helper comes, whom I shall

CHAPTER 15

15:1-8 *His life.* A branch is good for only one thing—bearing fruit. It may be weak in itself, but it has a living relationship with the vine and can be productive. To abide in Christ means to be in communion with Him so that our lives please Him. We know that we are abiding when the Father prunes us, cutting away the good so that we can produce the best. We glorify God with fruit, more fruit, much fruit.

15:9-17 *His love.* Abiding depends on obeying, and obeying depends on loving. Love and joy go together and make it easy for us to obey His will. We should love Him, love His will, and love one another. Note the "fruit of the Spirit": love (v. 10), joy (v. 11), and peace (14:27; Gal. 5:22).

15:18-27 *His name.* We enjoy the love of Christ and of the brethren, but we also must endure the hatred of the world for His name's sake. The more we are like Christ, the more the world system will oppose us. Depend on the Spirit's power and you will be a fruitful, faithful Christian (vv. 26-27).

15:2 [i]Or *lifts up*   15:7 [j]NU-Text omits *you will.*   15:25 [k]Psalm 69:4

CHAPTER 16

16:1–15 The world's opposition. The Lord warned them about the opposition that would come. Do not be surprised when you are persecuted by religious people (v. 2), for this has been going on ever since Cain killed Abel (Gen. 4; Luke 11:47–51). The Spirit helps us witness to the world and glorify Christ before the world (Acts 4:8ff.), so depend on Him.

16:16–24 The world's joy. When Jesus was arrested, crucified, and buried, the world system rejoiced because their Enemy was out of the way. But today He is alive, and we have every reason to rejoice! The Lord does not *replace* our sorrow with joy; He *transforms* our sorrow into joy. The same baby that gives the mother pain also gives her joy. The world's joy does not last, but the believer's joy is forever (Ps. 16:11).

send to you from the Father, the Spirit of truth who proceeds from the Father, He will testify of Me. 27And you also will bear witness, because you have been with Me from the beginning.

16 "These* things I have spoken to you, that you should not be made to stumble. 2They will put you out of the synagogues; yes, the time is coming that whoever kills you will think that he offers God service. 3And these things they will do to you[l] because they have not known the Father nor Me. 4But these things I have told you, that when the[m] time comes, you may remember that I told you of them.

"And these things I did not say to you at the beginning, because I was with you. 5"But now I go away to Him who sent Me, and none of you asks Me, 'Where are You going?' 6But because I have said these things to you, sorrow has filled your heart. 7Nevertheless I tell you the truth. It is to your advantage that I go away; for if I do not go away, the Helper will not come to you; but if I depart, I will send Him to you. 8And when He has come, He will convict the world of sin, and of righteousness, and of judgment: 9of sin, because they do not believe in Me; 10of righteousness, because I go to My Father and you see Me no more; 11of judgment, because the ruler of this world is judged.

12"I still have many things to say to you, but you cannot bear *them* now. 13However, when He, the Spirit of truth, has come, He will guide you into all truth; for He will not speak on His own *authority*, but whatever He hears He will speak; and He will tell you things to come. 14He will glorify Me, for He will take of what is Mine and declare *it* to you. 15All things that the Father has are Mine. Therefore I said that He will take of Mine and declare *it* to you.[n]

16*"A little while, and you will not see Me; and again a little while, and you will see Me, because I go to the Father."

17Then *some* of His disciples said among themselves, "What is this that He says to us, 'A little while, and you will not see Me; and again a little while, and you will see Me'; and, 'because I go to the Father'?" 18They said therefore, "What is this that He says, 'A little while'? We do not know what He is saying."

19Now Jesus knew that they desired to ask Him, and He said to them, "Are you inquiring among yourselves about what I said, 'A little while, and you will not see Me; and again a little while, and you will see Me'? 20Most assuredly, I say to you that you will weep and lament, but the world will rejoice; and you will be sorrowful, but your sorrow will be turned into joy. 21A woman, when she is in labor, has sorrow because her hour has come; but as soon as she has given birth to the child, she no longer remembers the anguish, for joy that a human being has been born into the world. 22Therefore you now have sorrow; but I will see you again and your heart will rejoice, and your joy no one will take from you.

23"And in that day you will ask Me nothing. Most assuredly, I say to you, whatever you ask

---

16:3 [l]NU-Text and M-Text omit *to you.* 16:4 [m]NU-Text reads *their.* 16:15 [n]NU-Text and M-Text read *He takes of Mine and will declare it to you.*

the Father in My name He will give you. 24Until
now you have asked nothing in My name. Ask,
and you will receive, that your joy may be full.
25"These things I have spoken to you in figurative language; but the time is coming when I will
no longer speak to you in figurative language, but
I will tell you plainly about the Father. 26In that
day you will ask in My name, and I do not say
to you that I shall pray the Father for you;
27for the Father Himself loves you, because you
have loved Me, and have believed that I came
forth from God. 28I came forth from the Father
and have come into the world. Again, I leave the
world and go to the Father."
29His disciples said to Him, "See, now You are
speaking plainly, and using no figure of speech!
30Now we are sure that You know all things, and
have no need that anyone should question You.
By this we believe that You came forth from God."
31Jesus answered them, "Do you now believe?
32Indeed the hour is coming, yes, has now come,
that you will be scattered, each to his own, and
will leave Me alone. And yet I am not alone, because the Father is with Me. 33*These things I have
spoken to you, that in Me you may have peace.
In the world you will[o] have tribulation; but be of
good cheer, I have overcome the world."

17 Jesus spoke these words, lifted up His eyes
to heaven, and said: "Father, the hour has
come. Glorify Your Son, that Your Son also may
glorify You, 2as You have given Him authority
over all flesh, that He should[p] give eternal life to
as many as You have given Him. 3And this is eternal life, that they may know You, the only true
God, and Jesus Christ whom You have sent.
4I have glorified You on the earth. I have finished
the work which You have given Me to do. 5And
now, O Father, glorify Me together with Yourself,
with the glory which I had with You before the
world was.
6"I have manifested Your name to the men
whom You have given Me out of the world. They
were Yours, You gave them to Me, and they have
kept Your word. 7Now they have known that all
things which You have given Me are from You.
8For I have given to them the words which You
have given Me; and they have received *them,* and
have known surely that I came forth from You;
and they have believed that You sent Me.
9"I pray for them. I do not pray for the world
but for those whom You have given Me, for they
are Yours. 10And all Mine are Yours, and Yours
are Mine, and I am glorified in them. 11Now I am
no longer in the world, but these are in the world,
and I come to You. Holy Father, keep through
Your name those whom You have given Me,[q] that
they may be one as We *are.* 12While I was with
them in the world,[r] I kept them in Your name.
Those whom You gave Me I have kept;[s] and none

16:33 [o]NU-Text and M-Text omit *will.* 17:2 [p]M-Text reads *shall.* 17:11 [q]NU-Text and M-Text read *keep them through Your name which You have given Me.* 17:12 [r]NU-Text omits *in the world.* [s]NU-Text reads *in Your name which You gave Me. And I guarded them;* (or *it;*).

16:33 ***The world's defeat.*** In the next few hours, the disciples would watch their world fall apart; and yet Jesus assured them that He was the winner. "I have overcome the world" is a fact, not a promise, and it applies to us today. We are overcomers through Him (1 John 5:1–5).

CHAPTER 17

17:1ff In this, his high priestly prayer, Jesus prayed for Himself (vv. 1–5), His disciples (vv. 6–19), and all of His church (vv. 20–26).

The prayer reveals our Lord's spiritual priorities: glorifying the Father (v. 1), the unity of the church (vv. 21–23), the sanctity of the church (v. 17), and the winning of a lost world (vv. 18–19). Are these priorities in your life?

It also reveals the gifts He has given His people: eternal life (vv. 2–3), the Word (vv. 8, 14), and His glory (v. 22). But note that believers are the Father's gift to Him (vv. 2, 6, 9, 11–12), just as Jesus is the Father's love gift to us (3:16). It is all of grace!

The word *world* appears nineteen times in this prayer, for this prayer tells us how to "overcome the world" (16:33). We must seek God's glory first (vv. 1–5), experience His joy (v. 13), be sanctified by the Word (v. 17), seek to win the lost (vv. 18–19), and encourage the unity of God's people (vv. 20–23).

Glory is another key word. Christ laid aside His glory to come to earth (v. 5b), glorified God on earth (v. 4), and was glorified when He returned to heaven (v. 5a). Christ is glorified in His church (v. 10) and has shared His glory with the church (vv. 22, 24). We already have the glory; we are just waiting for it to be fully revealed (Rom. 8:18–21, 30).

The Scottish Reformer John Knox had this prayer read to him daily during his last illness. But you would benefit by starting now to read it and meditate on it. What a treasury of truth it is!

Judas the Lost—Judas was not a saved man, even though he was one of the Twelve. He never believed in Jesus (6:66–71) and therefore was never washed from his sins (13:11). He was not chosen by Christ (13:18) and therefore not kept (17:12). Judas is a frightening example of how near one can get to the kingdom and still be lost.

of them is lost except the son of perdition, that the Scripture might be fulfilled. 13But now I come to You, and these things I speak in the world, that they may have My joy fulfilled in themselves. 14I have given them Your word; and the world has hated them because they are not of the world, just as I am not of the world. 15I do not pray that You should take them out of the world, but that You should keep them from the evil one. 16They are not of the world, just as I am not of the world. 17Sanctify them by Your truth. Your word is truth. 18As You sent Me into the world, I also have sent them into the world. 19And for their sakes I sanctify Myself, that they also may be sanctified by the truth.

20"I do not pray for these alone, but also for those who willᶠ believe in Me through their word; 21that they all may be one, as You, Father, *are* in Me, and I in You; that they also may be one in Us, that the world may believe that You sent Me. 22And the glory which You gave Me I have given them, that they may be one just as We are one: 23I in them, and You in Me; that they may be made perfect in one, and that the world may know that You have sent Me, and have loved them as You have loved Me.

24"Father, I desire that they also whom You gave Me may be with Me where I am, that they may behold My glory which You have given Me; for You loved Me before the foundation of the world. 25O righteous Father! The world has not known You, but I have known You; and these have known that You sent Me. 26And I have declared to them Your name, and will declare *it,* that the love with which You loved Me may be in them, and I in them."

18 When* Jesus had spoken these words, He went out with His disciples over the Brook Kidron, where there was a garden, which He and His disciples entered. 2And Judas, who betrayed Him, also knew the place; for Jesus often met there with His disciples. 3Then Judas, having received a detachment *of troops,* and officers from the chief priests and Pharisees, came there with lanterns, torches, and weapons. 4Jesus therefore, knowing all things that would come upon Him, went forward and said to them, "Whom are you seeking?"

5They answered Him, "Jesus of Nazareth."

Jesus said to them, "I am *He.*" And Judas, who betrayed Him, also stood with them. 6Now when He said to them, "I am *He,*" they drew back and fell to the ground.

7Then He asked them again, "Whom are you seeking?"

And they said, "Jesus of Nazareth."

8Jesus answered, "I have told you that I am *He.* Therefore, if you seek Me, let these go their way," 9that the saying might be fulfilled which He spoke, "Of those whom You gave Me I have lost none."

10Then Simon Peter, having a sword, drew it and struck the high priest's servant, and cut off his right ear. The servant's name was Malchus.

11So Jesus said to Peter, "Put your sword into the sheath. Shall I not drink the cup which My Father has given Me?"

12Then the detachment *of troops* and the captain and the officers of the Jews arrested Jesus

CHAPTER 18

18:1ff Judas depended on the strength of numbers, Peter on the strength of his arm, Annas and Caiaphas on the strength of their position, but Jesus on the strength of love and devotion to the Father. Jesus had a cup in His hand (Luke 22:42), not a sword, but that cup was His scepter. He was in complete control.

On the other hand, Peter fought when he should have yielded and followed when he should have fled. Yielding and fleeing looked like defeat, but they were the Father's will; and Peter should have obeyed. While Jesus was giving His witness to the high priest, Peter was denying the Lord. Which was the successful witness, Peter or Jesus?

As a Roman governor, Pilate was worried about the threat of another kingdom. Verse 36 is certainly a rebuke to believers who follow the example of Peter. At Pentecost, Peter wielded the sword of the Spirit and won a victory.

17:20 ᶠNU-Text and M-Text omit *will.*

and bound Him. [13]And they led Him away to Annas first, for he was the father-in-law of Caiaphas who was high priest that year. [14]Now it was Caiaphas who advised the Jews that it was expedient that one man should die for the people.

[15]And Simon Peter followed Jesus, and so *did* another[u] disciple. Now that disciple was known to the high priest, and went with Jesus into the courtyard of the high priest. [16]But Peter stood at the door outside. Then the other disciple, who was known to the high priest, went out and spoke to her who kept the door, and brought Peter in. [17]Then the servant girl who kept the door said to Peter, "You are not also *one* of this Man's disciples, are you?"

He said, "I am not."

[18]Now the servants and officers who had made a fire of coals stood there, for it was cold, and they warmed themselves. And Peter stood with them and warmed himself.

[19]The high priest then asked Jesus about His disciples and His doctrine.

[20]Jesus answered him, "I spoke openly to the world. I always taught in synagogues and in the temple, where the Jews always meet,[v] and in secret I have said nothing. [21]Why do you ask Me? Ask those who have heard Me what I said to them. Indeed they know what I said."

[22]And when He had said these things, one of the officers who stood by struck Jesus with the palm of his hand, saying, "Do You answer the high priest like that?"

[23]Jesus answered him, "If I have spoken evil, bear witness of the evil; but if well, why do you strike Me?"

[24]Then Annas sent Him bound to Caiaphas the high priest.

[25]Now Simon Peter stood and warmed himself. Therefore they said to him, "You are not also *one* of His disciples, are you?"

He denied *it* and said, "I am not!"

[26]One of the servants of the high priest, a relative *of him* whose ear Peter cut off, said, "Did I not see you in the garden with Him?" [27]Peter then denied again; and immediately a rooster crowed.

[28]Then they led Jesus from Caiaphas to the Praetorium, and it was early morning. But they themselves did not go into the Praetorium, lest they should be defiled, but that they might eat the Passover. [29]Pilate then went out to them and said, "What accusation do you bring against this Man?"

[30]They answered and said to him, "If He were not an evildoer, we would not have delivered Him up to you."

[31]Then Pilate said to them, "You take Him and judge Him according to your law."

Therefore the Jews said to him, "It is not lawful for us to put anyone to death," [32]that the saying of Jesus might be fulfilled which He spoke, signifying by what death He would die.

[33]Then Pilate entered the Praetorium again, called Jesus, and said to Him, "Are You the King of the Jews?"

[34]Jesus answered him, "Are you speaking for yourself about this, or did others tell you this concerning Me?"

18:15 [u]M-Text reads *the other.*   18:20 [v]NU-Text reads *where all the Jews meet.*

35Pilate answered, "Am I a Jew? Your own nation and the chief priests have delivered You to me. What have You done?"

36Jesus answered, "My kingdom is not of this world. If My kingdom were of this world, My servants would fight, so that I should not be delivered to the Jews; but now My kingdom is not from here."

37Pilate therefore said to Him, "Are You a king then?"

Jesus answered, "You say *rightly* that I am a king. For this cause I was born, and for this cause I have come into the world, that I should bear witness to the truth. Everyone who is of the truth hears My voice."

38Pilate said to Him, "What is truth?" And when he had said this, he went out again to the Jews, and said to them, "I find no fault in Him at all.

39"But you have a custom that I should release someone to you at the Passover. Do you therefore want me to release to you the King of the Jews?"

40Then they all cried again, saying, "Not this Man, but Barabbas!" Now Barabbas was a robber.

19 So then Pilate took Jesus and scourged *Him.* 2*And the soldiers twisted a crown of thorns and put *it* on His head, and they put on Him a purple robe. 3Then they said,w "Hail, King of the Jews!" And they struck Him with their hands.

4Pilate then went out again, and said to them, "Behold, I am bringing Him out to you, that you may know that I find no fault in Him."

5Then Jesus came out, wearing the crown of thorns and the purple robe. And *Pilate* said to them, "Behold the Man!"

6Therefore, when the chief priests and officers saw Him, they cried out, saying, "Crucify *Him,* crucify *Him!*"

Pilate said to them, "You take Him and crucify *Him,* for I find no fault in Him."

7The Jews answered him, "We have a law, and according to ourx law He ought to die, because He made Himself the Son of God."

8Therefore, when Pilate heard that saying, he was the more afraid, 9and went again into the Praetorium, and said to Jesus, "Where are You from?" But Jesus gave him no answer.

10Then Pilate said to Him, "Are You not speaking to me? Do You not know that I have power to crucify You, and power to release You?"

11Jesus answered, "You could have no power at all against Me unless it had been given you from above. Therefore the one who delivered Me to you has the greater sin."

12From then on Pilate sought to release Him, but the Jews cried out, saying, "If you let this Man go, you are not Caesar's friend. Whoever makes himself a king speaks against Caesar."

13When Pilate therefore heard that saying, he brought Jesus out and sat down in the judgment seat in a place that is called *The* Pavement, but in Hebrew, Gabbatha. 14Now it was the Prepara-

---

CHAPTER 19

19:2–5 *The crown.* Jesus and Pilate had been talking about a kingdom, so it was only right that the King have a crown. It was meant for mockery, but it preached a message, for Jesus was wearing the consequences of Adam's sins (Gen. 3:17–19). But a crown is a sign of victory. He has overcome!

19:3 wNU-Text reads *And they came up to Him and said.*
19:7 xNU-Text reads *the law.*

Our Final Payment—The Greek word translated "It is finished!" was a familiar word in that day. Bankers used it when the final payment had been made on a debt. Jesus completely paid the debt we owed, and it will be remembered against us no more forever. Hallelujah, what a Savior!

tion Day of the Passover, and about the sixth hour. And he said to the Jews, "Behold your King!"

15But they cried out, "Away with *Him,* away with *Him!* Crucify Him!"

Pilate said to them, "Shall I crucify your King?"

The chief priests answered, "We have no king but Caesar!"

16Then he delivered Him to them to be crucified. Then they took Jesus and led *Him* away.ʸ

17*And He, bearing His cross, went out to a place called *the Place* of a Skull, which is called in Hebrew, Golgotha, 18where they crucified Him, and two others with Him, one on either side, and Jesus in the center. 19Now Pilate wrote a title and put *it* on the cross. And the writing was:

JESUS OF NAZARETH,
THE KING OF THE JEWS.

20Then many of the Jews read this title, for the place where Jesus was crucified was near the city; and it was written in Hebrew, Greek, *and* Latin.
21Therefore the chief priests of the Jews said to Pilate, "Do not write, 'The King of the Jews,' but, 'He said, "I am the King of the Jews."' "
22Pilate answered, "What I have written, I have written."
23Then the soldiers, when they had crucified Jesus, took His garments and made four parts, to each soldier a part, and also the tunic. Now the tunic was without seam, woven from the top in one piece. 24They said therefore among themselves, "Let us not tear it, but cast lots for it, whose it shall be," that the Scripture might be fulfilled which says:

"They divided My garments among them,
And for My clothing they cast lots."ᶻ

Therefore the soldiers did these things.
25Now there stood by the cross of Jesus His mother, and His mother's sister, Mary the *wife* of Clopas, and Mary Magdalene. 26When Jesus therefore saw His mother, and the disciple whom He loved standing by, He said to His mother, "Woman, behold your son!" 27Then He said to the disciple, "Behold your mother!" And from that hour that disciple took her to his own *home.*
28After this, Jesus, knowingᵃ that all things were now accomplished, that the Scripture might be fulfilled, said, "I thirst!" 29Now a vessel full of sour wine was sitting there; and they filled a sponge with sour wine, put *it* on hyssop, and put *it* to His mouth. 30*So when Jesus had received the sour wine, He said, "It is finished!" And bowing His head, He gave up His spirit.
31Therefore, because it was the Preparation *Day,* that the bodies should not remain on the cross on the Sabbath (for that Sabbath was a high day), the Jews asked Pilate that their legs might be broken, and *that* they might be taken away. 32Then the soldiers came and broke the legs of the first and of the other who was crucified with Him. 33But when they came to Jesus and saw that He was already dead, they did not break His legs. 34But one of the soldiers pierced His side with a spear, and immediately blood and water came out.

19:17 *The cross.* Jesus started out bearing His own cross, but then Simon was drafted to carry it for Him (Mark 15:21). We are not told why, although tradition says that Jesus fell and could not carry it. Considering all He had been through, that is not difficult to believe. Criminals carried the cross as a sign of guilt, *and Jesus was not guilty!*

19:30 *The conquest.* "It is finished!" was the cry of a conqueror. Jesus accomplished what all of the old covenant sacrifices could not do (Heb. 10:1–18). The prophecies and types were fulfilled and the sacrifice for sins made once and for all forever. It was not a martyr that Joseph and Nicodemus put into the tomb; it was a victor.

35And he who has seen has testified, and his testimony is true; and he knows that he is telling the truth, so that you may believe. 36For these things were done that the Scripture should be fulfilled, *"Not one of His bones shall be broken."*[b] 37And again another Scripture says, *"They shall look on Him whom they pierced."*[c]

38After this, Joseph of Arimathea, being a disciple of Jesus, but secretly, for fear of the Jews, asked Pilate that he might take away the body of Jesus; and Pilate gave *him* permission. So he came and took the body of Jesus. 39And Nicodemus, who at first came to Jesus by night, also came, bringing a mixture of myrrh and aloes, about a hundred pounds. 40Then they took the body of Jesus, and bound it in strips of linen with the spices, as the custom of the Jews is to bury. 41Now in the place where He was crucified there was a garden, and in the garden a new tomb in which no one had yet been laid. 42So there they laid Jesus, because of the Jews' Preparation *Day*, for the tomb was nearby.

CHAPTER 20

20:1–10 Confusion. Mary jumped to conclusions and soon had Peter and John on the run. They were busy, but they had nothing to say and were accomplishing little. They saw the evidence for the Resurrection, but it did not change their lives. They needed a meeting with the living Christ.

20:11–18 Love. Unbelief blinds our eyes to the Lord's presence. When He speaks His word to us, faith and love are rekindled. Mary was changed from a mourner to a missionary when she met the living Lord.

20 Now* the first *day* of the week Mary Magdalene went to the tomb early, while it was still dark, and saw *that* the stone had been taken away from the tomb. 2Then she ran and came to Simon Peter, and to the other disciple, whom Jesus loved, and said to them, "They have taken away the Lord out of the tomb, and we do not know where they have laid Him."

3Peter therefore went out, and the other disciple, and were going to the tomb. 4So they both ran together, and the other disciple outran Peter and came to the tomb first. 5And he, stooping down and looking in, saw the linen cloths lying *there;* yet he did not go in. 6Then Simon Peter came, following him, and went into the tomb; and he saw the linen cloths lying *there,* 7and the handkerchief that had been around His head, not lying with the linen cloths, but folded together in a place by itself. 8Then the other disciple, who came to the tomb first, went in also; and he saw and believed. 9For as yet they did not know the Scripture, that He must rise again from the dead. 10Then the disciples went away again to their own homes.

11*But Mary stood outside by the tomb weeping, and as she wept she stooped down *and looked* into the tomb. 12And she saw two angels in white sitting, one at the head and the other at the feet, where the body of Jesus had lain. 13Then they said to her, "Woman, why are you weeping?"

She said to them, "Because they have taken away my Lord, and I do not know where they have laid Him."

14Now when she had said this, she turned around and saw Jesus standing *there,* and did not know that it was Jesus. 15Jesus said to her, "Woman, why are you weeping? Whom are you seeking?"

She, supposing Him to be the gardener, said to Him, "Sir, if You have carried Him away, tell me where You have laid Him, and I will take Him away."

16Jesus said to her, "Mary!"

She turned and said to Him,[d] "Rabboni!" (which is to say, Teacher).

19:36 [b]Exodus 12:46; Numbers 9:12; Psalm 34:20
19:37 [c]Zechariah 12:10   20:16 [d]NU-Text adds *in Hebrew.*

¹⁷Jesus said to her, "Do not cling to Me, for I have not yet ascended to My Father; but go to My brethren and say to them, 'I am ascending to My Father and your Father, and *to* My God and your God.'"

¹⁸Mary Magdalene came and told the disciples that she had seen the Lord,ᵉ and *that* He had spoken these things to her.

¹⁹*Then, the same day at evening, being the first *day* of the week, when the doors were shut where the disciples were assembled,ᶠ for fear of the Jews, Jesus came and stood in the midst, and said to them, "Peace *be* with you." ²⁰When He had said this, He showed them *His* hands and His side. Then the disciples were glad when they saw the Lord.

²¹So Jesus said to them again, "Peace to you! As the Father has sent Me, I also send you." ²²And when He had said this, He breathed on *them,* and said to them, "Receive the Holy Spirit. ²³If you forgive the sins of any, they are forgiven them; if you retain the *sins* of any, they are retained."

²⁴*Now Thomas, called the Twin, one of the twelve, was not with them when Jesus came. ²⁵The other disciples therefore said to him, "We have seen the Lord."

So he said to them, "Unless I see in His hands the print of the nails, and put my finger into the print of the nails, and put my hand into His side, I will not believe."

²⁶And after eight days His disciples were again inside, and Thomas with them. Jesus came, the doors being shut, and stood in the midst, and said, "Peace to you!" ²⁷Then He said to Thomas, "Reach your finger here, and look at My hands; and reach your hand *here,* and put *it* into My side. Do not be unbelieving, but believing."

²⁸And Thomas answered and said to Him, "My Lord and my God!"

²⁹Jesus said to him, "Thomas,ᵍ because you have seen Me, you have believed. Blessed *are* those who have not seen and yet have believed."

³⁰And truly Jesus did many other signs in the presence of His disciples, which are not written in this book; ³¹but these are written that you may believe that Jesus is the Christ, the Son of God, and that believing you may have life in His name.

21

After* these things Jesus showed Himself again to the disciples at the Sea of Tiberias, and in this way He showed *Himself:* ²Simon Peter, Thomas called the Twin, Nathanael of Cana in Galilee, the *sons* of Zebedee, and two others of His disciples were together. ³Simon Peter said to them, "I am going fishing."

They said to him, "We are going with you also." They went out and immediatelyʰ got into the boat, and that night they caught nothing. ⁴But when the morning had now come, Jesus stood on the shore; yet the disciples did not know that it was Jesus. ⁵*Then Jesus said to them, "Children, have you any food?"

They answered Him, "No."

⁶And He said to them, "Cast the net on the right side of the boat, and you will find *some.*" So they

20:19–23 *Peace.* Locked doors will not give you peace, nor will they keep out your loving Savior. He comes with the message of peace based on His sacrifice on the cross (v. 20; Rom. 5:1).

20:24–31 *Faith.* The Lord tenderly deals with our doubts and unbelief. We today cannot see Him or feel His wounds, but we have the Word of God to assure us (vv. 9, 30–31). When your faith falters, do not ask for signs. Open His Word and let Him reassure you.

CHAPTER 21

21:1–4 *Jesus the Stranger.* When Peter returned to the old life, he took six other men with him. Their work was in vain (15:5) because the Lord was not with them. How kind He is to come to us when we have disobeyed Him and have failed in our work!

21:5–8 *Jesus the Master.* When Jesus takes charge, failure is turned into success; and the difference was only the width of the ship! You never know how close you are to victory, so admit your failure and obey what He tells you to do. He never fails.

21:9–14 Jesus the Host. It took six men to drag the net (v. 8), but Peter did it alone when Jesus gave the orders (v. 11). We should always remember that "God's commandment is God's enablement." Did the fire of coals remind Peter of his denials (18:18ff.)? Did the miraculous catch of fish remind him of his call to service (Luke 5:1–11)? How kind of Jesus to feed Peter before dealing with him about his sins!

21:15–17 Jesus the Shepherd. The most important thing in ministry is loving Christ, for all ministry flows from that. Peter the fisherman was also to be a shepherd and care for the lambs and sheep.

21:18–22 Jesus the Lord. By saying, "Follow Me," Jesus reinstated Peter as an apostle. But Peter turned around and took his eyes off the Lord (Matt. 14:30), and Jesus had to rebuke him. The next time you are tempted to meddle in somebody else's ministry, ponder Christ's words: "What is that to you? You follow Me!" (18:22). Peter followed the Lord right into the excitement of the book of Acts!

cast, and now they were not able to draw it in because of the multitude of fish.

7Therefore that disciple whom Jesus loved said to Peter, "It is the Lord!" Now when Simon Peter heard that it was the Lord, he put on *his* outer garment (for he had removed it), and plunged into the sea. 8But the other disciples came in the little boat (for they were not far from land, but about two hundred cubits), dragging the net with fish. 9*Then, as soon as they had come to land, they saw a fire of coals there, and fish laid on it, and bread. 10Jesus said to them, "Bring some of the fish which you have just caught."

11Simon Peter went up and dragged the net to land, full of large fish, one hundred and fifty-three; and although there were so many, the net was not broken. 12Jesus said to them, "Come *and* eat breakfast." Yet none of the disciples dared ask Him, "Who are You?"—knowing that it was the Lord. 13Jesus then came and took the bread and gave it to them, and likewise the fish.

14This *is* now the third time Jesus showed Himself to His disciples after He was raised from the dead.

15So when they had eaten breakfast, Jesus said to Simon Peter, "Simon, *son* of Jonah,ⁱ do you love Me more than these?"

He said to Him, "Yes, Lord; You know that I love You."

He said to him, "Feed My lambs."

16He said to him again a second time, "Simon, *son* of Jonah,ʲ do you love Me?"

He said to Him, "Yes, Lord; You know that I love You."

He said to him, "Tend My sheep."

17He said to him the third time, "Simon, *son* of Jonah,ᵏ do you love Me?" Peter was grieved because He said to him the third time, "Do you love Me?"

And he said to Him, "Lord, You know all things; You know that I love You."

Jesus said to him, "Feed My sheep. 18*Most assuredly, I say to you, when you were younger, you girded yourself and walked where you wished; but when you are old, you will stretch out your hands, and another will gird you and carry *you* where you do not wish." 19This He spoke, signifying by what death he would glorify God. And when He had spoken this, He said to him, "Follow Me."

20Then Peter, turning around, saw the disciple whom Jesus loved following, who also had leaned on His breast at the supper, and said, "Lord, who is the one who betrays You?" 21Peter, seeing him, said to Jesus, "But Lord, what *about* this man?"

22Jesus said to him, "If I will that he remain till I come, what *is that* to you? You follow Me."

23Then this saying went out among the brethren that this disciple would not die. Yet Jesus did not say to him that he would not die, but, "If I will that he remain till I come, what *is that* to you?"

24This is the disciple who testifies of these things, and wrote these things; and we know that his testimony is true.

25And there are also many other things that Jesus did, which if they were written one by one, I suppose that even the world itself could not contain the books that would be written. Amen.

21:15 ⁱNU-Text reads John.   21:16 ʲNU-Text reads John.
21:17 ᵏNU-Text reads John.

ACTS

Perhaps a better title is "The Acts of the Holy Spirit through the Church." This story tells how God's people obeyed the Lord's commission to take the gospel to the whole world. Luke wrote it as a companion volume to his gospel (1:1–3; Luke 1:1–4), and it describes what Jesus *continued to do and teach* after He returned to heaven.

Peter's ministry dominates the first part of the book (chaps. 1—12), and then Luke focuses on Paul's ministry (chaps. 13—28). These two men had parallel experiences of both trial and ministry. Peter used the "keys" (Matt. 16:19) to open the door of faith to the Jews (chap. 2), the Samaritans (chap. 8), and the Gentiles (chap. 10); Paul took the good news to the Gentiles in the Roman Empire.

Acts 1:8 outlines the book, for the gospel went from Jerusalem (chaps. 1—7) to Judea and Samaria (chaps. 8—9) and then to the ends of the earth (chaps. 10—28). The book of Acts describes a transition from ministry to Jews to ministry to the Gentiles and explains how the gospel got from Jerusalem to Rome.

This book is for every Christian who wants to experience the power of the Holy Spirit and be a witness for Jesus Christ "to the end of the earth" (1:8). Ask God what part He wants you to play in taking the gospel to the whole world, starting right where you are. "Lord, what do You want me to do?" (9:6).

1 The* former account I made, O Theophilus, of all that Jesus began both to do and teach, ²until the day in which He was taken up, after He through the Holy Spirit had given commandments to the apostles whom He had chosen, ³to whom He also presented Himself alive after His suffering by many infallible proofs, being seen by them during forty days and speaking of the things pertaining to the kingdom of God.

⁴*And being assembled together with *them,* He commanded them not to depart from Jerusalem, but to wait for the Promise of the Father, "which," *He said,* "you have heard from Me; ⁵for John truly baptized with water, but you shall be baptized with the Holy Spirit not many days from now." ⁶Therefore, when they had come together, they asked Him, saying, "Lord, will You at this time restore the kingdom to Israel?" ⁷And He said to them, "It is not for you to know times or seasons which the Father has put in His own authority. ⁸But you shall receive power when the Holy Spirit has come upon you; and you shall be witnesses to Me*ᵃ* in Jerusalem, and in all Judea and Samaria, and to the end of the earth."

⁹*Now when He had spoken these things, while they watched, He was taken up, and a cloud received Him out of their sight. ¹⁰And while they looked steadfastly toward heaven as He went up, behold, two men stood by them in white apparel,

---

1:8 ᵃNU-Text reads *My witnesses.*

CHAPTER 1

1:1–3 One hundred and twenty ordinary people (v. 15) hardly constitute an imposing army; but in a few days, they would make an impact that is being felt even today. The same resources God gave them are still available to us.

A living Lord. Christ is the Head of the church (Eph. 1:22; 4:15) and supplies life to His body, giving dynamic and direction to His people. What He began to do and teach, the church continues as He guides and empowers through His Spirit.

1:4–8 *The power of the Spirit.* God's power is available to God's people who want to do His will and be His witnesses. You do not have to be an apostle to have the power of the Spirit in your life (Eph. 5:18).

1:9–11 *The promise of His return.* He is the Lord of history, working out His purposes in this world. The church may lose some battles, but we will win the war!

Trust God's Guidance—If we are faithful to read God's Word, study it, meditate on it, and obey it, God will guide us when we have decisions to make. The Holy Spirit teaches us (John 14:26; 16:13–14) and directs us when we pray and seek the Lord's will. The Holy Spirit uses truth, not ignorance; so the more facts we have, the better. We should use our common sense but not lean on it (Prov. 3:5–6), for we walk by faith and not by sight. If we sincerely move in the wrong direction, the Lord will show us (Acts 16:6–10; Phil. 3:15), so we need not fear. It is good for believers to read the Word and pray together as they seek the mind of the Lord.

11who also said, "Men of Galilee, why do you stand gazing up into heaven? This *same* Jesus, who was taken up from you into heaven, will so come in like manner as you saw Him go into heaven."

12*Then they returned to Jerusalem from the mount called Olivet, which is near Jerusalem, a Sabbath day's journey. 13And when they had entered, they went up into the upper room where they were staying: Peter, James, John, and Andrew; Philip and Thomas; Bartholomew and Matthew; James *the son* of Alphaeus and Simon the Zealot; and Judas *the son* of James. 14These all continued with one accord in prayer and supplication,b with the women and Mary the mother of Jesus, and with His brothers.

15*And in those days Peter stood up in the midst of the disciplesc (altogether the number of names was about a hundred and twenty), and said, 16"Men *and* brethren, this Scripture had to be fulfilled, which the Holy Spirit spoke before by the mouth of David concerning Judas, who became a guide to those who arrested Jesus; 17for he was numbered with us and obtained a part in this ministry."

18(Now this man purchased a field with the wages of iniquity; and falling headlong, he burst open in the middle and all his entrails gushed out. 19And it became known to all those dwelling in Jerusalem; so that field is called in their own language, Akel Dama, that is, Field of Blood.)

20"For it is written in the Book of Psalms:

'Let his dwelling place be desolate,
And let no one live in it';d

and,

'Lete another take his office.'f

21"Therefore, of these men who have accompanied us all the time that the Lord Jesus went in and out among us, 22beginning from the baptism of John to that day when He was taken up from us, one of these must become a witness with us of His resurrection."

23And they proposed two: Joseph called Barsabas, who was surnamed Justus, and Matthias. 24And they prayed and said, "You, O Lord, who know the hearts of all, show which of these two You have chosen 25to take part in this ministry and apostleship from which Judas by transgression fell, that he might go to his own place." 26And they cast their lots, and the lot fell on Matthias. And he was numbered with the eleven apostles.

2 When* the Day of Pentecost had fully come, they were all with one accordg in one place.

1:12–14, 24–26 The power of prayer. God shares His power with us as we pray and ask Him for His help. Throughout Acts, notice Luke's emphasis on prayer. The first church was a praying church.

1:15–23 The guidance of Scripture. His Word is still our lamp and light (Ps. 119:105), and we must obey what it says. God guides His people when they are willing to follow.

CHAPTER 2

2:1–4 The Spirit came, not because the believers prayed but because the day of Pentecost had come, the day appointed for the "birthday of the church" (Lev. 23:15–21). He baptized the believers into one body (1 Cor. 12:13) so that they had a living connection with their Head exalted in heaven. Luke 2 describes the birth of the Lord's *physical* body and Acts 2 the birth of His *spiritual* body.

1:14 bNU-Text omits *and supplication.* 1:15 cNU-Text reads *brethren.* 1:20 dPsalm 69:25 ePsalm 109:8 fGreek *episkopen,* position of overseer 2:1 gNU-Text reads *together.*

The Gift of Tongues—The believers praised God in "other tongues," that is, known languages understood by the people present (Acts 2:6–11). The apostles worshiped and praised God in tongues (v. 11) but preached the gospel in Aramaic, a tongue the Jews could understand. During the transition in ministry from Jews to Gentiles, each time Peter used the "keys," the gift of tongues was evident: among the Jews (2:1–4), the Samaritans (8:14ff.), and the Gentiles (10:44–48). Not all believers speak in tongues (1 Cor. 12:30), and it is not identified as one of the most important gifts (1 Cor. 12:7–11).

2And suddenly there came a sound from heaven, as of a rushing mighty wind, and it filled the whole house where they were sitting. 3Then there appeared to them divided tongues, as of fire, and *one* sat upon each of them. 4*And they were all filled with the Holy Spirit and began to speak with other tongues, as the Spirit gave them utterance.

5And there were dwelling in Jerusalem Jews, devout men, from every nation under heaven. 6And when this sound occurred, the multitude came together, and were confused, because everyone heard them speak in his own language. 7Then they were all amazed and marveled, saying to one another, "Look, are not all these who speak Galileans? 8And how *is it that* we hear, each in our own language in which we were born? 9Parthians and Medes and Elamites, those dwelling in Mesopotamia, Judea and Cappadocia, Pontus and Asia, 10Phrygia and Pamphylia, Egypt and the parts of Libya adjoining Cyrene, visitors from Rome, both Jews and proselytes, 11Cretans and Arabs—we hear them speaking in our own tongues the wonderful works of God." 12So they were all amazed and perplexed, saying to one another, "Whatever could this mean?"

13Others mocking said, "They are full of new wine."

14But Peter, standing up with the eleven, raised his voice and said to them, "Men of Judea and all who dwell in Jerusalem, let this be known to you, and heed my words. 15For these are not drunk, as you suppose, since it is *only* the third hour of the day. 16But this is what was spoken by the prophet Joel:

17 'And it shall come to pass in the last days,
        says God,
    That I will pour out of My Spirit on all flesh;
    Your sons and your daughters shall
        prophesy,
    Your young men shall see visions,
    Your old men shall dream dreams.
18 And on My menservants and on My
        maidservants
    I will pour out My Spirit in those days;
    And they shall prophesy.
19 I will show wonders in heaven above
    And signs in the earth beneath:
    Blood and fire and vapor of smoke.
20 The sun shall be turned into darkness,
    And the moon into blood,
    Before the coming of the great and awesome
        day of the LORD.
21 And it shall come to pass
    That whoever calls on the name of the LORD
    Shall be saved.'h

22"Men of Israel, hear these words: Jesus of Nazareth, a Man attested by God to you by miracles, wonders, and signs which God did through Him in your midst, as you yourselves also know— 23Him, being delivered by the determined purpose and foreknowledge of God, you have takeni by lawless hands, have crucified, and put to death; 24whom God raised up, having loosed the pains of death, because it was not possible that He should be held by it. 25For David says concerning Him:

2:4–40 The Spirit also filled the believers and empowered them for witness. He gave Peter insight into the Word and the ability to show men Christ in the Word. The Spirit used the witness of the church to convict the lost, just as Jesus said He would do (16:7–10).

2:21 hJoel 2:28–32   2:23 iNU-Text omits *have taken.*

'I foresaw the LORD always before my face,
For He is at my right hand, that I may not
  be shaken.
26 Therefore my heart rejoiced, and my tongue
  was glad;
Moreover my flesh also will rest in hope.
27 For You will not leave my soul in Hades,
Nor will You allow Your Holy One to see
  corruption.
28 You have made known to me the ways of
  life;
You will make me full of joy in Your
  presence.'[i]

29"Men *and* brethren, let *me* speak freely to you of the patriarch David, that he is both dead and buried, and his tomb is with us to this day. 30Therefore, being a prophet, and knowing that God had sworn with an oath to him that of the fruit of his body, according to the flesh, He would raise up the Christ to sit on his throne,[k] 31he, foreseeing this, spoke concerning the resurrection of the Christ, that His soul was not left in Hades, nor did His flesh see corruption. 32This Jesus God has raised up, of which we are all witnesses. 33Therefore being exalted to the right hand of God, and having received from the Father the promise of the Holy Spirit, He poured out this which you now see and hear. 34"For David did not ascend into the heavens, but he says himself:

'The LORD said to my Lord,
  "Sit at My right hand,
35 Till I make Your enemies Your footstool." '[l]

36"Therefore let all the house of Israel know assuredly that God has made this Jesus, whom you crucified, both Lord and Christ."

37Now when they heard *this*, they were cut to the heart, and said to Peter and the rest of the apostles, "Men *and* brethren, what shall we do?" 38Then Peter said to them, "Repent, and let every one of you be baptized in the name of Jesus Christ for the remission of sins; and you shall receive the gift of the Holy Spirit. 39For the promise is to you and to your children, and to all who are afar off, as many as the Lord our God will call."

40And with many other words he testified and exhorted them, saying, "Be saved from this perverse generation." 41*Then those who gladly[m] received his word were baptized; and that day about three thousand souls were added *to them.* 42And they continued steadfastly in the apostles' doctrine and fellowship, in the breaking of bread, and in prayers. 43Then fear came upon every soul, and many wonders and signs were done through the apostles. 44Now all who believed were together, and had all things in common, 45and sold their possessions and goods, and divided them among all, as anyone had need.

46So continuing daily with one accord in the temple, and breaking bread from house to house, they ate their food with gladness and simplicity of heart, 47praising God and having favor with

2:41–47 But the same Holy Spirit assisted the believers in their church fellowship. The original group was outnumbered by the new believers, but there was still harmony in the church family. They worshiped daily and witnessed daily, and "the Lord added to the church daily" (v. 47). Is your experience with the Lord a *daily* one?

2:28 [i]Psalm 16:8–11   2:30 [k]NU-Text omits *according to the flesh, He would raise up the Christ* and completes the verse with *He would seat one on his throne.*   2:35 [l]Psalm 110:1   2:41 [m]NU-Text omits *gladly.*

all the people. And the Lord added to the church[n] daily those who were being saved.

3 Now* Peter and John went up together to the temple at the hour of prayer, the ninth *hour.* [2]And a certain man lame from his mother's womb was carried, whom they laid daily at the gate of the temple which is called Beautiful, to ask alms from those who entered the temple; [3]who, seeing Peter and John about to go into the temple, asked for alms. [4]And fixing his eyes on him, with John, Peter said, "Look at us." [5]So he gave them his attention, expecting to receive something from them. [6]Then Peter said, "Silver and gold I do not have, but what I do have I give you: In the name of Jesus Christ of Nazareth, rise up and walk." [7]And he took him by the right hand and lifted *him* up, and immediately his feet and ankle bones received strength. [8]So he, leaping up, stood and walked and entered the temple with them—walking, leaping, and praising God. [9]And all the people saw him walking and praising God. [10]Then they knew that it was he who sat begging alms at the Beautiful Gate of the temple; and they were filled with wonder and amazement at what had happened to him.

[11]Now as the lame man who was healed held on to Peter and John, all the people ran together to them in the porch which is called Solomon's, greatly amazed. [12]So when Peter saw *it,* he responded to the people: "Men of Israel, why do you marvel at this? Or why look so intently at us, as though by our own power or godliness we had made this man walk? [13]The God of Abraham, Isaac, and Jacob, the God of our fathers, glorified His Servant Jesus, whom you delivered up and denied in the presence of Pilate, when he was determined to let *Him* go. [14]But you denied the Holy One and the Just, and asked for a murderer to be granted to you, [15]and killed the Prince of life, whom God raised from the dead, of which we are witnesses. [16]And His name, through faith in His name, has made this man strong, whom you see and know. Yes, the faith which *comes* through Him has given him this perfect soundness in the presence of you all.

[17]"Yet now, brethren, I know that you did *it* in ignorance, as *did* also your rulers. [18]But those things which God foretold by the mouth of all His prophets, that the Christ would suffer, He has thus fulfilled. [19]Repent therefore and be converted, that your sins may be blotted out, so that times of refreshing may come from the presence of the Lord, [20]and that He may send Jesus Christ, who was preached to you before,[o] [21]whom heaven must receive until the times of restoration of all things, which God has spoken by the mouth of all His holy prophets since the world began. [22]For Moses truly said to the fathers, 'The LORD your God will raise up for you a Prophet like me from your brethren. Him you shall hear in all things, whatever He says to you. [23]And it shall be that every soul who will not hear that Prophet shall be utterly destroyed from among the people.'[p] [24]Yes, and all the prophets, from Samuel and those who follow, as many as have spoken,

CHAPTER 3

3:1ff *Priorities.* Peter and John were not so caught up with large crowds that they had no time for individuals. Nor were they so busy in ministry that they could not pray. They had learned their lessons well from the Lord Jesus (Mark 1:35; Luke 8:40ff.).

Power. The emphasis in chapters 3—4 is on the name of Jesus (3:6, 13, 16, 20, 26; 4:2, 7, 10, 12, 17—18), the name above every name (Phil. 2:9—11). Faith in the name of Jesus releases power so that lives are changed. To pray or minister in His name means to ask or act on His authority (Matt. 28:18—20) so that He alone gets the glory.

Proclamation. At Pentecost, the sound of a rushing wind drew the crowd (2:2, 6); but here the witness of a changed life brought the people together. Thus, Peter had the opportunity to preach, and two thousand people were converted. Reach out to the individual (v. 7) and God will give you opportunities for a bigger harvest (John 4:28ff.).

❝*It's the individual touch that tells. He [Jesus] doesn't love in the mass, but in ones.*❞
—Amy Carmichael

2:47 [n]NU-Text omits *to the church.* 3:20 [o]NU-Text and M-Text read *Christ Jesus, who was ordained for you before.* 3:23 [p]Deuteronomy 18:15, 18, 19

have also foretold*q* these days. 25You are sons of the prophets, and of the covenant which God made with our fathers, saying to Abraham, *'And in your seed all the families of the earth shall be blessed.'r* 26To you first, God, having raised up His Servant Jesus, sent Him to bless you, in turning away every one *of you* from your iniquities."

4 Now* as they spoke to the people, the priests, the captain of the temple, and the Sadducees came upon them, 2being greatly disturbed that they taught the people and preached in Jesus the resurrection from the dead. 3And they laid hands on them, and put *them* in custody until the next day, for it was already evening. 4However, many of those who heard the word believed; and the number of the men came to be about five thousand.

5And it came to pass, on the next day, that their rulers, elders, and scribes, 6as well as Annas the high priest, Caiaphas, John, and Alexander, and as many as were of the family of the high priest, were gathered together at Jerusalem. 7And when they had set them in the midst, they asked, "By what power or by what name have you done this?"

8Then Peter, filled with the Holy Spirit, said to them, "Rulers of the people and elders of Israel: 9If we this day are judged for a good deed *done* to a helpless man, by what means he has been made well, 10let it be known to you all, and to all the people of Israel, that by the name of Jesus Christ of Nazareth, whom you crucified, whom God raised from the dead, by Him this man stands here before you whole. 11This is the *'stone which was rejected by you builders, which has become the chief cornerstone.'s* 12Nor is there salvation in any other, for there is no other name under heaven given among men by which we must be saved."

13Now when they saw the boldness of Peter and John, and perceived that they were uneducated and untrained men, they marveled. And they realized that they had been with Jesus. 14And seeing the man who had been healed standing with them, they could say nothing against it. 15But when they had commanded them to go aside out of the council, they conferred among themselves, 16saying, "What shall we do to these men? For, indeed, that a notable miracle has been done through them *is* evident to all who dwell in Jerusalem, and we cannot deny *it.* 17But so that it spreads no further among the people, let us severely threaten them, that from now on they speak to no man in this name."

18So they called them and commanded them not to speak at all nor teach in the name of Jesus. 19But Peter and John answered and said to them, "Whether it is right in the sight of God to listen to you more than to God, you judge. 20For we cannot but speak the things which we have seen and heard." 21So when they had further threatened them, they let them go, finding no way of punishing them, because of the people, since they all glorified God for what had been done. 22For the man was over forty years old on whom this miracle of healing had been performed.

23And being let go, they went to their own *com-*

CHAPTER 4

4:1ff In his sermon at Pentecost, Peter proved from the Scriptures that Jesus was alive; but now he proved it by the miraculous change in the beggar's life. The man was healed through the power of the name of Jesus. The Sadducees did not believe in resurrection (23:6–8), so they wanted to put a stop to the ministry of the apostles. This was the beginning of the official persecution of Christians.

What do you do when they tell you to stop sharing the gospel? What did the apostles do? Certainly they recalled the words of Jesus Christ (Matt. 10:16–26) and depended on the Holy Spirit to help them. Furthermore, they were so filled with their message and with love for Christ that they could not stop telling people about Him!

They depended on prayer (vv. 23–31) and directed their prayer to a sovereign God who made everything and can do anything. They based their petitions on Psalm 2, a marvelous psalm to read when you are being attacked.

When you are "let go," where do you go (v. 23)? When you are in trouble, to whom do you turn?

3:24 *q*NU-Text and M-Text read *proclaimed.* 3:25 *r*Genesis 22:18; 26:4; 28:14 4:11 *s*Psalm 118:22

panions and reported all that the chief priests and elders had said to them. ²⁴So when they heard that, they raised their voice to God with one accord and said: "Lord, You *are* God, who made heaven and earth and the sea, and all that is in them, ²⁵who by the mouth of Your servant David^t have said:

'Why did the nations rage,
And the people plot vain things?
26 The kings of the earth took their stand,
And the rulers were gathered together
Against the LORD and against His Christ.'^u

²⁷"For truly against Your holy Servant Jesus, whom You anointed, both Herod and Pontius Pilate, with the Gentiles and the people of Israel, were gathered together ²⁸to do whatever Your hand and Your purpose determined before to be done. ²⁹Now, Lord, look on their threats, and grant to Your servants that with all boldness they may speak Your word, ³⁰by stretching out Your hand to heal, and that signs and wonders may be done through the name of Your holy Servant Jesus."

³¹And when they had prayed, the place where they were assembled together was shaken; and they were all filled with the Holy Spirit, and they spoke the word of God with boldness.

³²Now the multitude of those who believed were of one heart and one soul; neither did anyone say that any of the things he possessed was his own, but they had all things in common. ³³And with great power the apostles gave witness to the resurrection of the Lord Jesus. And great grace was upon them all. ³⁴Nor was there anyone among them who lacked; for all who were possessors of lands or houses sold them, and brought the proceeds of the things that were sold, ³⁵and laid *them* at the apostles' feet; and they distributed to each as anyone had need.

³⁶And Joses,^v who was also named Barnabas by the apostles (which is translated Son of Encouragement), a Levite of the country of Cyprus, ³⁷having land, sold *it*, and brought the money and laid *it* at the apostles' feet.

5 But* a certain man named Ananias, with Sapphira his wife, sold a possession. ²And he kept back *part* of the proceeds, his wife also being aware *of it*, and brought a certain part and laid *it* at the apostles' feet. ³But Peter said, "Ananias, why has Satan filled your heart to lie to the Holy Spirit and keep back *part* of the price of the land for yourself? ⁴While it remained, was it not your own? And after it was sold, was it not in your own control? Why have you conceived this thing in your heart? You have not lied to men but to God."

⁵Then Ananias, hearing these words, fell down and breathed his last. So great fear came upon all those who heard these things. ⁶And the young men arose and wrapped him up, carried *him* out, and buried *him*.

⁷Now it was about three hours later when his wife came in, not knowing what had happened.

"We make our decisions, and then our decisions turn around and make us.**"**
—F. W. Boreham

CHAPTER 5
5:1–11 Pretending. Barnabas's gift (4:36–37) exposed the sin of Ananias and Sapphira, just as Mary's gift exposed Judas's sin (John 12). The couple lied to the Spirit, to the church, and to Peter; and it cost them their lives. Their sin was not in taking money from God but in pretending to be something they were not.

"There is no more miserable human being than one in whom nothing is habitual but indecision.**"**
—William James

5:12–16 Obeying. Dealing with sin in the church often results in new power for the church. Can you imagine a church so spiritual that people were afraid to join with them? Even Peter's shadow had power!

5:17–32 Opposing. Because the Sadducees could not tolerate evidences of resurrection power, they arrested the apostles again and told them to be quiet. "We ought to obey God rather than men" (v. 29) is the only position to hold when you have the Word of God on your side. Be sure it is conviction and not just opinion.

8And Peter answered her, "Tell me whether you sold the land for so much?"

She said, "Yes, for so much."

9Then Peter said to her, "How is it that you have agreed together to test the Spirit of the Lord? Look, the feet of those who have buried your husband *are* at the door, and they will carry you out." 10Then immediately she fell down at his feet and breathed her last. And the young men came in and found her dead, and carrying *her* out, buried *her* by her husband. 11So great fear came upon all the church and upon all who heard these things.

12*And through the hands of the apostles many signs and wonders were done among the people. And they were all with one accord in Solomon's Porch. 13Yet none of the rest dared join them, but the people esteemed them highly. 14And believers were increasingly added to the Lord, multitudes of both men and women, 15so that they brought the sick out into the streets and laid *them* on beds and couches, that at least the shadow of Peter passing by might fall on some of them. 16Also a multitude gathered from the surrounding cities to Jerusalem, bringing sick people and those who were tormented by unclean spirits, and they were all healed.

17*Then the high priest rose up, and all those who *were* with him (which is the sect of the Sadducees), and they were filled with indignation, 18and laid their hands on the apostles and put them in the common prison. 19But at night an angel of the Lord opened the prison doors and brought them out, and said, 20"Go, stand in the temple and speak to the people all the words of this life."

21And when they heard *that*, they entered the temple early in the morning and taught. But the high priest and those with him came and called the council together, with all the elders of the children of Israel, and sent to the prison to have them brought.

22But when the officers came and did not find them in the prison, they returned and reported, 23saying, "Indeed we found the prison shut securely, and the guards standing outsidew before the doors; but when we opened them, we found no one inside!" 24Now when the high priest,x the captain of the temple, and the chief priests heard these things, they wondered what the outcome would be. 25So one came and told them, saying,y "Look, the men whom you put in prison are standing in the temple and teaching the people!"

26Then the captain went with the officers and brought them without violence, for they feared the people, lest they should be stoned. 27And when they had brought them, they set *them* before the council. And the high priest asked them, 28saying, "Did we not strictly command you not to teach in this name? And look, you have filled Jerusalem with your doctrine, and intend to bring this Man's blood on us!"

29But Peter and the *other* apostles answered and said: "We ought to obey God rather than men. 30The God of our fathers raised up Jesus whom you murdered by hanging on a tree. 31Him God has exalted to His right hand *to be* Prince and Savior, to give repentance to Israel and forgive-

---

5:23 wNU-Text and M-Text omit *outside*.   5:24 xNU-Text omits *the high priest*.   5:25 yNU-Text and M-Text omit *saying*.

ness of sins. ³²And we are His witnesses to these things, and *so* also *is* the Holy Spirit whom God has given to those who obey Him."

³³*When they heard *this*, they were furious and plotted to kill them. ³⁴Then one in the council stood up, a Pharisee named Gamaliel, a teacher of the law held in respect by all the people, and commanded them to put the apostles outside for a little while. ³⁵And he said to them: "Men of Israel, take heed to yourselves what you intend to do regarding these men. ³⁶For some time ago Theudas rose up, claiming to be somebody. A number of men, about four hundred, joined him. He was slain, and all who obeyed him were scattered and came to nothing. ³⁷After this man, Judas of Galilee rose up in the days of the census, and drew away many people after him. He also perished, and all who obeyed him were dispersed. ³⁸And now I say to you, keep away from these men and let them alone; for if this plan or this work is of men, it will come to nothing; ³⁹but if it is of God, you cannot overthrow it—lest you even be found to fight against God."

⁴⁰And they agreed with him, and when they had called for the apostles and beaten *them*, they commanded that they should not speak in the name of Jesus, and let them go. ⁴¹So they departed from the presence of the council, rejoicing that they were counted worthy to suffer shame for Hisᶻ name. ⁴²And daily in the temple, and in every house, they did not cease teaching and preaching Jesus *as* the Christ.

6 Now* in those days, when *the number of* the disciples was multiplying, there arose a complaint against the Hebrews by the Hellenists,ᵃ because their widows were neglected in the daily distribution. ²Then the twelve summoned the multitude of the disciples and said, "It is not desirable that we should leave the word of God and serve tables. ³Therefore, brethren, seek out from among you seven men of *good* reputation, full of the Holy Spirit and wisdom, whom we may appoint over this business; ⁴but we will give ourselves continually to prayer and to the ministry of the word."

⁵And the saying pleased the whole multitude. And they chose Stephen, a man full of faith and the Holy Spirit, and Philip, Prochorus, Nicanor, Timon, Parmenas, and Nicolas, a proselyte from Antioch, ⁶whom they set before the apostles; and when they had prayed, they laid hands on them.

⁷Then the word of God spread, and the number of the disciples multiplied greatly in Jerusalem, and a great many of the priests were obedient to the faith.

⁸*And Stephen, full of faithᵇ and power, did great wonders and signs among the people. ⁹*Then there arose some from what is called the Synagogue of the Freedmen (Cyrenians, Alexandrians, and those from Cilicia and Asia), disputing with Stephen. ¹⁰And they were not able to resist

---

5:41 ᶻNU-Text reads *the name;* M-Text reads *the name of Jesus.* 6:1 ᵃThat is, Greek-speaking Jews 6:8 ᵇNU-Text reads *grace.*

5:33–39 Hesitating. Gamaliel advised neutrality, which means avoiding the truth and letting Satan move in (Matt. 12:30, 43–45). With all the evidence they had seen, the council's neutrality was actually dishonesty. If you followed Gamaliel's advice in any area of life—science, cooking, finance—it would lead to paralysis and then death.

❝*There are many of us that are willing to do great things for the Lord; but few of us are willing to do little things.*❞

—D. L. Moody

CHAPTER 6

6:1–7 When you yield yourself to do God's will, you never know what challenges you will face.

Serving tables. No ministry is unimportant for a Christlike servant, for Jesus said, "I am among you as the One who serves" (Luke 22:27). In serving tables, the men released the apostles for their ministry of prayer and the Word; and the result was an increase in conversions (v. 7). People filled with the Spirit see no small jobs or big places. They see only their Master and the opportunity to glorify Him.

6:8 Doing wonders. From serving tables to doing miracles! Stephen reached out to the lost and sought to win them to Christ. If you are faithful with a few things, the Lord may give you many things (Matt. 25:21).

6:9–15 Facing enemies. The unbelievers treated Stephen the way the Sanhedrin treated Jesus: they arrested him on trumped-up charges and hired false witnesses to testify. Stephen experienced "the fellowship of His sufferings" (Phil. 3:10), and so will you if your witness hits home (Matt. 5:11–12). They said Stephen was opposing Moses, but he had a shining face just like Moses (Exod. 34)!

Tradition or Truth?—They accused Stephen of being unorthodox in his beliefs (Acts 6:13); but yesterday's orthodoxy had become today's heresy, and the council was behind the times! The Law had been nailed to the cross (Col. 2:14), and the veil of the temple had been torn in two. Within a few years, both the city and the temple would be gone, and Hosea 3:4 would be fulfilled. Are you following man's tradition or God's truth?

CHAPTER 7

7:2ff The main thrust of Stephen's message is that Israel always resisted the truth and rejected the deliverers God sent to them. They opposed Moses and repeatedly wanted to return to Egypt. They opposed Joseph, and he later became their redeemer! They rejected the many prophets God sent to warn them and call them back to His way. Finally, they rejected their own Messiah and crucified Him.

Israel's history reveals the patience of God and the hardness of man's heart. But it also reveals a ray of hope: Israel rejected their deliverers the first time *but accepted them the second time.* That was true of Moses and Joseph, and it will be true of Jesus when He returns (Zech. 12:10).

Stephen's death was the third murder in Israel's history and a turning point in God's dealings with the nation. They had rejected the Father when they allowed John the Baptist to be slain; they had rejected the Son when they asked for Jesus to be crucified; and now they had rejected the Holy Spirit. There could be no more forgiveness (Matt. 12:31–32). The line had been crossed, and the gospel moved out to Judea and Samaria.

the wisdom and the Spirit by which he spoke. 11Then they secretly induced men to say, "We have heard him speak blasphemous words against Moses and God." 12And they stirred up the people, the elders, and the scribes; and they came upon *him,* seized him, and brought *him* to the council. 13They also set up false witnesses who said, "This man does not cease to speak blasphemousᶜ words against this holy place and the law; 14for we have heard him say that this Jesus of Nazareth will destroy this place and change the customs which Moses delivered to us." 15And all who sat in the council, looking steadfastly at him, saw his face as the face of an angel.

7 Then the high priest said, "Are these things so?"

2*And he said, "Brethren and fathers, listen: The God of glory appeared to our father Abraham when he was in Mesopotamia, before he dwelt in Haran, 3and said to him, *'Get out of your country and from your relatives, and come to a land that I will show you.'*ᵈ 4Then he came out of the land of the Chaldeans and dwelt in Haran. And from there, when his father was dead, He moved him to this land in which you now dwell. 5And God gave him no inheritance in it, not even *enough* to set his foot on. But even when *Abraham* had no child, He promised to give it to him for a possession, and to his descendants after him. 6But God spoke in this way: that his descendants would dwell in a foreign land, and that they would bring them into bondage and oppress *them* four hundred years. 7'And the nation to whom they will be in bondage I will judge,'ᵉ said God, 'and after that they shall come out and serve Me in this place.'ᶠ 8Then He gave him the covenant of circumcision; and so *Abraham* begot Isaac and circumcised him on the eighth day; and Isaac *begot* Jacob, and Jacob *begot* the twelve patriarchs.

9"And the patriarchs, becoming envious, sold Joseph into Egypt. But God was with him 10and delivered him out of all his troubles, and gave him favor and wisdom in the presence of Pharaoh, king of Egypt; and he made him governor over Egypt and all his house. 11Now a famine and great trouble came over all the land of Egypt and Canaan, and our fathers found no sustenance. 12But when Jacob heard that there was grain in Egypt, he sent out our fathers first. 13And the second *time* Joseph was made known to his brothers, and Joseph's family became known to the Pharaoh. 14Then Joseph sent and called his father Jacob and all his relatives to *him,* seventy-fiveᵍ people. 15So Jacob went down to Egypt; and he died, he and our fathers. 16And they were carried back to Shechem and laid in the tomb that Abraham bought for a sum of money from the sons of Hamor, *the father* of Shechem.

17"But when the time of the promise drew near which God had sworn to Abraham, the people grew and multiplied in Egypt 18till another king arose who did not know Joseph. 19This man dealt

---

6:13 ᶜNU-Text omits *blasphemous.*   7:3 ᵈGenesis 12:1
7:7 ᵉGenesis 15:14 ᶠExodus 3:12   7:14 ᵍOr *seventy* (compare Exodus 1:5)

Stephen—The name *Stephen* means "a crown," and he won the crown of life because he was faithful unto death (Rev. 2:10).

treacherously with our people, and oppressed our forefathers, making them expose their babies, so that they might not live. 20At this time Moses was born, and was well pleasing to God; and he was brought up in his father's house for three months. 21But when he was set out, Pharaoh's daughter took him away and brought him up as her own son. 22And Moses was learned in all the wisdom of the Egyptians, and was mighty in words and deeds.

23"Now when he was forty years old, it came into his heart to visit his brethren, the children of Israel. 24And seeing one of *them* suffer wrong, he defended and avenged him who was oppressed, and struck down the Egyptian. 25For he supposed that his brethren would have understood that God would deliver them by his hand, but they did not understand. 26And the next day he appeared to two of them as they were fighting, and *tried* to reconcile them, saying, 'Men, you are brethren; why do you wrong one another?' 27But he who did his neighbor wrong pushed him away, saying, *'Who made you a ruler and a judge over us? 28Do you want to kill me as you did the Egyptian yesterday?'*[h] 29Then, at this saying, Moses fled and became a dweller in the land of Midian, where he had two sons.

30"And when forty years had passed, an Angel of the Lord[i] appeared to him in a flame of fire in a bush, in the wilderness of Mount Sinai. 31When Moses saw *it,* he marveled at the sight; and as he drew near to observe, the voice of the Lord came to him, 32saying, *'I am the God of your fathers—the God of Abraham, the God of Isaac, and the God of Jacob.'*[j] And Moses trembled and dared not look. 33'Then the LORD said to him, *"Take your sandals off your feet, for the place where you stand is holy ground. 34I have surely seen the oppression of My people who are in Egypt; I have heard their groaning and have come down to deliver them. And now come, I will send you to Egypt."'*[k]

35"This Moses whom they rejected, saying, *'Who made you a ruler and a judge?'*[l] is the one God sent *to be* a ruler and a deliverer by the hand of the Angel who appeared to him in the bush. 36He brought them out, after he had shown wonders and signs in the land of Egypt, and in the Red Sea, and in the wilderness forty years.

37"This is that Moses who said to the children of Israel,[m] *'The LORD your God will raise up for you a Prophet like me from your brethren. Him you shall hear.'*[n]

38"This is he who was in the congregation in the wilderness with the Angel who spoke to him on Mount Sinai, and *with* our fathers, the one who received the living oracles to give to us, 39whom our fathers would not obey, but rejected. And in their hearts they turned back to Egypt, 40saying to Aaron, *'Make us gods to go before us; as for this Moses who brought us out of the land of Egypt, we do not know what has become of him.'*[o] 41And they made a calf in those days, offered sacrifices to the idol, and rejoiced in the works of their own hands. 42Then God turned and gave

---

7:28 [h]Exodus 2:14   7:30 [i]NU-Text omits *of the Lord.*
7:32 [j]Exodus 3:6, 15   7:34 [k]Exodus 3:5, 7, 8, 10
7:35 [l]Exodus 2:14   7:37 [m]Deuteronomy 18:15 [n]NU-Text and M-Text omit *Him you shall hear.*   7:40 [o]Exodus 32:1, 23

them up to worship the host of heaven, as it is written in the book of the Prophets:

> 'Did you offer Me slaughtered animals and
>   sacrifices during forty years in the
>   wilderness,
>   O house of Israel?
> 43 You also took up the tabernacle of Moloch,
>   And the star of your god Remphan,
>   Images which you made to worship;
>   And I will carry you away beyond
>   Babylon.'ᵖ

44"Our fathers had the tabernacle of witness in the wilderness, as He appointed, instructing Moses to make it according to the pattern that he had seen, 45which our fathers, having received it in turn, also brought with Joshua into the land possessed by the Gentiles, whom God drove out before the face of our fathers until the days of David, 46who found favor before God and asked to find a dwelling for the God of Jacob. 47But Solomon built Him a house.

48"However, the Most High does not dwell in temples made with hands, as the prophet says:

> 49 'Heaven is My throne,
>   And earth is My footstool.
>   What house will you build for Me? says the
>   LORD,
>   Or what is the place of My rest?
> 50 Has My hand not made all these things?'q

51"You stiff-necked and uncircumcised in heart and ears! You always resist the Holy Spirit; as your fathers did, so do you. 52Which of the prophets did your fathers not persecute? And they killed those who foretold the coming of the Just One, of whom you now have become the betrayers and murderers, 53who have received the law by the direction of angels and have not kept it."

54When they heard these things they were cut to the heart, and they gnashed at him with their teeth. 55But he, being full of the Holy Spirit, gazed into heaven and saw the glory of God, and Jesus standing at the right hand of God, 56and said, "Look! I see the heavens opened and the Son of Man standing at the right hand of God!"

57Then they cried out with a loud voice, stopped their ears, and ran at him with one accord; 58and they cast him out of the city and stoned him. And the witnesses laid down their clothes at the feet of a young man named Saul. 59And they stoned Stephen as he was calling on God and saying, "Lord Jesus, receive my spirit." 60Then he knelt down and cried out with a loud voice, "Lord, do not charge them with this sin." And when he had said this, he fell asleep.

8 Now* Saul was consenting to his death. At that time a great persecution arose against the church which was at Jerusalem; and they were all scattered throughout the regions of Judea and Samaria, except the apostles. 2And devout men carried Stephen to his burial, and made great lamentation over him.

3As for Saul, he made havoc of the church, entering every house, and dragging off men and women, committing them to prison.

*❝I live for souls and for eternity,
I want to win some soul to Christ.
If you want this and work for it,
eternity alone can tell the result.❞*
—D. L. Moody

CHAPTER 8

8:1 The death of Stephen seemed to be a defeat for the church, but it resulted in some great victories for the Lord. Wherever the believers went, they shared the gospel and many trusted the Savior (vv. 1–7; 11:19). Stephen's witness made a tremendous impression on Saul and was instrumental in his conversion (22:20). Never give up when the enemy seems to be winning. It may be your finest hour of victory.

7:43 ᵖAmos 5:25–27   7:50 qIsaiah 66:1, 2

4Therefore those who were scattered went everywhere preaching the word. 5*Then Philip went down to the[r] city of Samaria and preached Christ to them. 6And the multitudes with one accord heeded the things spoken by Philip, hearing and seeing the miracles which he did. 7For unclean spirits, crying with a loud voice, came out of many who were possessed; and many who were paralyzed and lame were healed. 8And there was great joy in that city.

9But there was a certain man called Simon, who previously practiced sorcery in the city and astonished the people of Samaria, claiming that he was someone great, 10to whom they all gave heed, from the least to the greatest, saying, "This man is the great power of God." 11And they heeded him because he had astonished them with his sorceries for a long time. 12But when they believed Philip as he preached the things concerning the kingdom of God and the name of Jesus Christ, both men and women were baptized. 13Then Simon himself also believed; and when he was baptized he continued with Philip, and was amazed, seeing the miracles and signs which were done.

14Now when the apostles who were at Jerusalem heard that Samaria had received the word of God, they sent Peter and John to them, 15who, when they had come down, prayed for them that they might receive the Holy Spirit. 16For as yet He had fallen upon none of them. They had only been baptized in the name of the Lord Jesus. 17Then they laid hands on them, and they received the Holy Spirit.

18And when Simon saw that through the laying on of the apostles' hands the Holy Spirit was given, he offered them money, 19saying, "Give me this power also, that anyone on whom I lay hands may receive the Holy Spirit."

20But Peter said to him, "Your money perish with you, because you thought that the gift of God could be purchased with money! 21You have neither part nor portion in this matter, for your heart is not right in the sight of God. 22Repent therefore of this your wickedness, and pray God if perhaps the thought of your heart may be forgiven you. 23For I see that you are poisoned by bitterness and bound by iniquity."

24Then Simon answered and said, "Pray to the Lord for me, that none of the things which you have spoken may come upon me."

25So when they had testified and preached the word of the Lord, they returned to Jerusalem, preaching the gospel in many villages of the Samaritans.

26*Now an angel of the Lord spoke to Philip, saying, "Arise and go toward the south along the road which goes down from Jerusalem to Gaza." This is desert. 27So he arose and went. And behold, a man of Ethiopia, a eunuch of great authority under Candace the queen of the Ethiopians, who had charge of all her treasury, and had come to Jerusalem to worship, 28was returning. And sitting in his chariot, he was reading Isaiah the prophet. 29Then the Spirit said to Philip, "Go near and overtake this chariot."

30So Philip ran to him, and heard him reading the prophet Isaiah, and said, "Do you understand what you are reading?"

8:5–25 Like Stephen, Philip was a deacon who was also an evangelist; and God led him to witness in Samaria to people hostile to the Jews (John 4:9). The coming of Peter and John and the giving of the Holy Spirit linked the Samaritan believers to the saints in Jerusalem and the ancient division was healed. The way to turn enemies into friends is to make them brothers and sisters in Christ.

In times of great blessing, wherever God sows true seed, the devil sows a counterfeit (Matt. 13:24–30, 36–43). Like Peter, we must be alert and exercise discernment.

8:26–40 Philip left a great harvest to talk to one man, but that is the mark of a true servant of the Lord. We must go where God sends us, do what God tells us, and leave the results with Him.

31And he said, "How can I, unless someone guides me?" And he asked Philip to come up and sit with him. 32The place in the Scripture which he read was this:

> "He was led as a sheep to the slaughter;
> And as a lamb before its shearer is silent,
> So He opened not His mouth.
> 33   In His humiliation His justice was taken away,
> And who will declare His generation?
> For His life is taken from the earth."s

34So the eunuch answered Philip and said, "I ask you, of whom does the prophet say this, of himself or of some other man?" 35Then Philip opened his mouth, and beginning at this Scripture, preached Jesus to him. 36Now as they went down the road, they came to some water. And the eunuch said, "See, here is water. What hinders me from being baptized?"

37Then Philip said, "If you believe with all your heart, you may."

And he answered and said, "I believe that Jesus Christ is the Son of God."t

38So he commanded the chariot to stand still. And both Philip and the eunuch went down into the water, and he baptized him. 39Now when they came up out of the water, the Spirit of the Lord caught Philip away, so that the eunuch saw him no more; and he went on his way rejoicing. 40But Philip was found at Azotus. And passing through, he preached in all the cities till he came to Caesarea.

9 Then Saul, still breathing threats and murder against the disciples of the Lord, went to the high priest 2and asked letters from him to the synagogues of Damascus, so that if he found any who were of the Way, whether men or women, he might bring them bound to Jerusalem.

3As he journeyed he came near Damascus, and suddenly a light shone around him from heaven. 4Then he fell to the ground, and heard a voice saying to him, "Saul, Saul, why are you persecuting Me?"

5And he said, "Who are You, Lord?"

Then the Lord said, "I am Jesus, whom you are persecuting.u It is hard for you to kick against the goads."

6So he, trembling and astonished, said, "Lord, what do You want me to do?"

Then the Lord said to him, "Arise and go into the city, and you will be told what you must do."

7And the men who journeyed with him stood speechless, hearing a voice but seeing no one. 8Then Saul arose from the ground, and when his eyes were opened he saw no one. But they led him by the hand and brought him into Damascus. 9And he was three days without sight, and neither ate nor drank.

10*Now there was a certain disciple at Damascus named Ananias; and to him the Lord said in a vision, "Ananias."

And he said, "Here I am, Lord."

CHAPTER 9

9:10–30 The conversion of Saul of Tarsus was a turning point in the church's history, and God used several people to touch his life. We remember Paul and are prone to forget the people who helped him get started.

The witness of Stephen was significant (22:20) as were the testimonies and prayers of persons Saul persecuted (Matt. 5:44). Ananias baptized him and encouraged him, and the disciples at Damascus saved his life. When the church in Jerusalem feared to welcome Saul into their fellowship, Barnabas ("son of encouragement") built the bridge. Barnabas later enlisted Saul to serve in the Antioch church (11:25–26) and traveled with him in evangelistic ministry among the Gentiles (13:1–3).

You may not be called to a prominent work as Saul was, but you can do the job God has called you to do and be an encouragement to others. We do not know the names of the brave men who smuggled Saul out of Damascus (v. 25), but holding the ropes was an important job!

8:33 sIsaiah 53:7, 8   8:37 tNU-Text and M-Text omit this verse. It is found in Western texts, including the Latin tradition. 9:5 uNU-Text and M-Text omit the last sentence of verse 5 and begin verse 6 with But arise and go.

11So the Lord *said* to him, "Arise and go to the street called Straight, and inquire at the house of Judas for *one* called Saul of Tarsus, for behold, he is praying. 12And in a vision he has seen a man named Ananias coming in and putting *his* hand on him, so that he might receive his sight."

13Then Ananias answered, "Lord, I have heard from many about this man, how much harm he has done to Your saints in Jerusalem. 14And here he has authority from the chief priests to bind all who call on Your name."

15But the Lord said to him, "Go, for he is a chosen vessel of Mine to bear My name before Gentiles, kings, and the children of Israel. 16For I will show him how many things he must suffer for My name's sake."

17And Ananias went his way and entered the house; and laying his hands on him he said, "Brother Saul, the Lord Jesus,ᵛ who appeared to you on the road as you came, has sent me that you may receive your sight and be filled with the Holy Spirit." 18Immediately there fell from his eyes *something* like scales, and he received his sight at once; and he arose and was baptized.

19So when he had received food, he was strengthened. Then Saul spent some days with the disciples at Damascus.

20Immediately he preached the Christʷ in the synagogues, that He is the Son of God.

21Then all who heard were amazed, and said, "Is this not he who destroyed those who called on this name in Jerusalem, and has come here for that purpose, so that he might bring them bound to the chief priests?"

22But Saul increased all the more in strength, and confounded the Jews who dwelt in Damascus, proving that this *Jesus* is the Christ.

23Now after many days were past, the Jews plotted to kill him. 24But their plot became known to Saul. And they watched the gates day and night, to kill him. 25Then the disciples took him by night and let *him* down through the wall in a large basket.

26And when Saul had come to Jerusalem, he tried to join the disciples; but they were all afraid of him, and did not believe that he was a disciple. 27But Barnabas took him and brought *him* to the apostles. And he declared to them how he had seen the Lord on the road, and that He had spoken to him, and how he had preached boldly at Damascus in the name of Jesus. 28So he was with them at Jerusalem, coming in and going out. 29And he spoke boldly in the name of the Lord Jesus and disputed against the Hellenists, but they attempted to kill him. 30When the brethren found out, they brought him down to Caesarea and sent him out to Tarsus.

31Then the churchesˣ throughout all Judea, Galilee, and Samaria had peace and were edified. And walking in the fear of the Lord and in the comfort of the Holy Spirit, they were multiplied.

32Now it came to pass, as Peter went through all *parts of the country,* that he also came down to the saints who dwelt in Lydda. 33There he found a certain man named Aeneas, who had been bedridden eight years and was paralyzed. 34And Peter said to him, "Aeneas, Jesus the Christ heals

9:17 ᵛM-Text omits *Jesus.*   9:20 ʷNU-Text reads *Jesus.*
9:31 ˣNU-Text reads *church . . . was edified.*

CHAPTER 10

10:1ff Peter uses the "keys" for the third and last time as he opens the door of faith to the Gentiles. How wonderful is the providence of God! Paul, the apostle to the Gentiles, was being prepared for his life's work; and Peter was about to break down the ancient barriers between Jews and Gentiles: "Known to God from eternity are all His works" (15:18).
But God had to prepare both Peter and Cornelius. He spoke to Cornelius while he was praying and to Peter while he was relaxing. Be alert to the voice of God; you never know when He may have a word for you.

❝*You can say 'Lord,' and you can say 'Not so,' but you cannot say, 'Not so, Lord.'* ❞
—W. Graham Scroggie

10:14 "Not so, Lord! For I have never . . ." is the response that leads to defeat. God was about to do a new thing, and Peter wanted to hold on to the old. He calls Him Lord but refuses to obey Him! Yet God tenderly instructed Peter, and the apostle surrendered to His will.

you. Arise and make your bed." Then he arose immediately. 35So all who dwelt at Lydda and Sharon saw him and turned to the Lord.

36At Joppa there was a certain disciple named Tabitha, which is translated Dorcas. This woman was full of good works and charitable deeds which she did. 37But it happened in those days that she became sick and died. When they had washed her, they laid *her* in an upper room. 38And since Lydda was near Joppa, and the disciples had heard that Peter was there, they sent two men to him, imploring *him* not to delay in coming to them. 39Then Peter arose and went with them. When he had come, they brought *him* to the upper room. And all the widows stood by him weeping, showing the tunics and garments which Dorcas had made while she was with them. 40But Peter put them all out, and knelt down and prayed. And turning to the body he said, "Tabitha, arise." And she opened her eyes, and when she saw Peter she sat up. 41Then he gave her *his* hand and lifted her up; and when he had called the saints and widows, he presented her alive. 42And it became known throughout all Joppa, and many believed on the Lord. 43So it was that he stayed many days in Joppa with Simon, a tanner.

10 There* was a certain man in Caesarea called Cornelius, a centurion of what was called the Italian Regiment, 2a devout *man* and one who feared God with all his household, who gave alms generously to the people, and prayed to God always. 3About the ninth hour of the day he saw clearly in a vision an angel of God coming in and saying to him, "Cornelius!"

4And when he observed him, he was afraid, and said, "What is it, lord?"

So he said to him, "Your prayers and your alms have come up for a memorial before God. 5Now send men to Joppa, and send for Simon whose surname is Peter. 6He is lodging with Simon, a tanner, whose house is by the sea.ʸ He will tell you what you must do." 7And when the angel who spoke to him had departed, Cornelius called two of his household servants and a devout soldier from among those who waited on him continually. 8So when he had explained all *these* things to them, he sent them to Joppa.

9The next day, as they went on their journey and drew near the city, Peter went up on the housetop to pray, about the sixth hour. 10Then he became very hungry and wanted to eat; but while they made ready, he fell into a trance 11and saw heaven opened and an object like a great sheet bound at the four corners, descending to him and let down to the earth. 12In it were all kinds of four-footed animals of the earth, wild beasts, creeping things, and birds of the air. 13And a voice came to him, "Rise, Peter; kill and eat."

14*But Peter said, "Not so, Lord! For I have never eaten anything common or unclean."

15And a voice *spoke* to him again the second time, "What God has cleansed you must not call common." 16This was done three times. And the object was taken up into heaven again.

17Now while Peter wondered within himself what this vision which he had seen meant, behold,

10:6 ʸNU-Text and M-Text omit the last sentence of this verse.

the men who had been sent from Cornelius had made inquiry for Simon's house, and stood before the gate. 18And they called and asked whether Simon, whose surname was Peter, was lodging there.

19While Peter thought about the vision, the Spirit said to him, "Behold, three men are seeking you. 20Arise therefore, go down and go with them, doubting nothing; for I have sent them."

21Then Peter went down to the men who had been sent to him from Cornelius,[z] and said, "Yes, I am he whom you seek. For what reason have you come?"

22And they said, "Cornelius the centurion, a just man, one who fears God and has a good reputation among all the nation of the Jews, was divinely instructed by a holy angel to summon you to his house, and to hear words from you." 23Then he invited them in and lodged them.

On the next day Peter went away with them, and some brethren from Joppa accompanied him.

24And the following day they entered Caesarea. Now Cornelius was waiting for them, and had called together his relatives and close friends. 25As Peter was coming in, Cornelius met him and fell down at his feet and worshiped him. 26But Peter lifted him up, saying, "Stand up; I myself am also a man." 27And as he talked with him, he went in and found many who had come together. 28Then he said to them, "You know how unlawful it is for a Jewish man to keep company with or go to one of another nation. But God has shown me that I should not call any man common or unclean. 29Therefore I came without objection as soon as I was sent for. I ask, then, for what reason have you sent for me?"

30So Cornelius said, "Four days ago I was fasting until this hour; and at the ninth hour[a] I prayed in my house, and behold, a man stood before me in bright clothing, 31and said, 'Cornelius, your prayer has been heard, and your alms are remembered in the sight of God. 32Send therefore to Joppa and call Simon here, whose surname is Peter. He is lodging in the house of Simon, a tanner, by the sea.[b] When he comes, he will speak to you.' 33So I sent to you immediately, and you have done well to come. Now therefore, we are all present before God, to hear all the things commanded you by God."

34Then Peter opened his mouth and said: "In truth I perceive that God shows no partiality. 35But in every nation whoever fears Him and works righteousness is accepted by Him. 36The word which God sent to the children of Israel, preaching peace through Jesus Christ—He is Lord of all— 37that word you know, which was proclaimed throughout all Judea, and began from Galilee after the baptism which John preached: 38how God anointed Jesus of Nazareth with the Holy Spirit and with power, who went about doing good and healing all who were oppressed by the devil, for God was with Him. 39And we are witnesses of all things which He did both in the land of the Jews and in Jerusalem, whom they[c] killed by hanging on a tree. 40Him God raised up

---

10:21 [z]NU-Text and M-Text omit who had been sent to him from Cornelius.   10:30 [a]NU-Text reads Four days ago to this hour, at the ninth hour.   10:32 [b]NU-Text omits the last sentence of this verse.   10:39 [c]NU-Text and M-Text add also.

on the third day, and showed Him openly, [41]not to all the people, but to witnesses chosen before by God, *even* to us who ate and drank with Him after He arose from the dead. [42]And He commanded us to preach to the people, and to testify that it is He who was ordained by God *to be* Judge of the living and the dead. [43]To Him all the prophets witness that, through His name, whoever believes in Him will receive remission of sins."

[44]*While Peter was still speaking these words, the Holy Spirit fell upon all those who heard the word. [45]And those of the circumcision who believed were astonished, as many as came with Peter, because the gift of the Holy Spirit had been poured out on the Gentiles also. [46]For they heard them speak with tongues and magnify God.

Then Peter answered, [47]"Can anyone forbid water, that these should not be baptized who have received the Holy Spirit just as we *have?*" [48]And he commanded them to be baptized in the name of the Lord. Then they asked him to stay a few days.

10:44 Peter did not get to finish his sermon. When he said, "Whosoever believes in Him will receive remission of sins" (v. 43), they believed and were saved. What a great way to stop a sermon!

CHAPTER 11

11:1ff *Some people make things happen.* Peter was available to the Lord, and God used him to officially bring gentile believers into the church. The wall between Jews and Gentiles had been broken down (Eph. 2:11ff.)! The news was astounding to the Jewish believers, for they thought the Gentiles must first become Jewish proselytes before they could become Christians. Thank God that Peter was the kind of person who makes things happen! *Some people hear that things happen.* This category may include most of us, but how do you respond when you hear that God has done something new? Do you sincerely try to get the facts, or do you depend on hearsay? We are to "test all things; hold fast what is good" (1 Thess. 5:22). *Some people oppose things happening.* The legalistic members of the Jerusalem assembly attacked Peter for eating with the Gentiles, so he explained how God had led. He proved from Scripture (v. 16; 1:5) that what happened was the will of God, and his explanation silenced his critics for the time. However, the legalistic element in the church would rise again (chap. 15) and seek to limit the freedom of the gospel. *Some people help other people make things happen.* Barnabas enlisted Saul (vv. 25–26) and put him to work in the Antioch church, which led to their going together to the Gentiles with the message of salvation. Barnabas lived up to his name of "son of encouragement."

11 Now* the apostles and brethren who were in Judea heard that the Gentiles had also received the word of God. [2]And when Peter came up to Jerusalem, those of the circumcision contended with him, [3]saying, "You went in to uncircumcised men and ate with them!"

[4]But Peter explained *it* to them in order from the beginning, saying: [5]"I was in the city of Joppa praying; and in a trance I saw a vision, an object descending like a great sheet, let down from heaven by four corners; and it came to me. [6]When I observed it intently and considered, I saw four-footed animals of the earth, wild beasts, creeping things, and birds of the air. [7]And I heard a voice saying to me, 'Rise, Peter; kill and eat.' [8]But I said, 'Not so, Lord! For nothing common or unclean has at any time entered my mouth.' [9]But the voice answered me again from heaven, 'What God has cleansed you must not call common.' [10]Now this was done three times, and all were drawn up again into heaven. [11]At that very moment, three men stood before the house where I was, having been sent to me from Caesarea. [12]Then the Spirit told me to go with them, doubting nothing. Moreover these six brethren accompanied me, and we entered the man's house. [13]And he told us how he had seen an angel standing in his house, who said to him, 'Send men to Joppa, and call for Simon whose surname is Peter, [14]who will tell you words by which you and all your household will be saved.' [15]And as I began to speak, the Holy Spirit fell upon them, as upon us at the beginning. [16]Then I remembered the word of the Lord, how He said, 'John indeed baptized with water, but you shall be baptized with the Holy Spirit.' [17]If therefore God gave them the same gift as *He gave* us when we believed on the Lord Jesus Christ, who was I that I could withstand God?"

[18]When they heard these things they became silent; and they glorified God, saying, "Then God has also granted to the Gentiles repentance to life."

[19]Now those who were scattered after the persecution that arose over Stephen traveled as far as

He Worked for the Great Physician—John Calvin's physician told him to stop working or he would die, and Calvin replied, "Would you have my Master come and find me loitering?"

Phoenicia, Cyprus, and Antioch, preaching the word to no one but the Jews only. 20But some of them were men from Cyprus and Cyrene, who, when they had come to Antioch, spoke to the Hellenists, preaching the Lord Jesus. 21And the hand of the Lord was with them, and a great number believed and turned to the Lord.

22Then news of these things came to the ears of the church in Jerusalem, and they sent out Barnabas to go as far as Antioch. 23When he came and had seen the grace of God, he was glad, and encouraged them all that with purpose of heart they should continue with the Lord. 24For he was a good man, full of the Holy Spirit and of faith. And a great many people were added to the Lord.

25Then Barnabas departed for Tarsus to seek Saul. 26And when he had found him, he brought him to Antioch. So it was that for a whole year they assembled with the church and taught a great many people. And the disciples were first called Christians in Antioch.

27And in these days prophets came from Jerusalem to Antioch. 28Then one of them, named Agabus, stood up and showed by the Spirit that there was going to be a great famine throughout all the world, which also happened in the days of Claudius Caesar. 29Then the disciples, each according to his ability, determined to send relief to the brethren dwelling in Judea. 30This they also did, and sent it to the elders by the hands of Barnabas and Saul.

12 Now* about that time Herod the king stretched out *his* hand to harass some from the church. 2Then he killed James the brother of John with the sword. 3And because he saw that it pleased the Jews, he proceeded further to seize Peter also. Now it was *during* the Days of Unleavened Bread. 4So when he had arrested him, he put *him* in prison, and delivered *him* to four squads of soldiers to keep him, intending to bring him before the people after Passover.

5Peter was therefore kept in prison, but constantd prayer was offered to God for him by the church. 6And when Herod was about to bring him out, that night Peter was sleeping, bound with two chains between two soldiers; and the guards before the door were keeping the prison. 7Now behold, an angel of the Lord stood by *him,* and a light shone in the prison; and he struck Peter on the side and raised him up, saying, "Arise quickly!" And his chains fell off *his* hands. 8Then the angel said to him, "Gird yourself and tie on your sandals"; and so he did. And he said to him, "Put on your garment and follow me." 9So he went out and followed him, and did not know that what was done by the angel was real, but thought he was seeing a vision. 10When they were past the first and the second guard posts, they came to the iron gate that leads to the city, which opened to them of its own accord; and they went out and went down one street, and immediately the angel departed from him.

11And when Peter had come to himself, he said, "Now I know for certain that the Lord has sent His angel, and has delivered me from the hand of Herod and *from* all the expectation of the Jewish people."

CHAPTER 12

12:1ff The will of the Lord is always wise and good, but it is not always predictable. God spared Peter but allowed James to be killed. He did not deliver Peter from prison until the last minute. He allowed Herod to slay James, but He did not permit the king to act like a god. Is that how *you* would have done it?

Some Christians are like Job's friends: they think they always know exactly what God is doing, will do, and wants done; but they may be wrong. Whenever you are tempted to "play God" in somebody's life, ponder Isaiah 55:8–9.

12:5 dNU-Text reads *constantly* (or *earnestly*).

12:12–15 It is always right to pray, even if your faith is so weak you are surprised when the answer comes! Keep knocking—God opens doors.

12*So, when he had considered *this,* he came to the house of Mary, the mother of John whose surname was Mark, where many were gathered together praying. 13And as Peter knocked at the door of the gate, a girl named Rhoda came to answer. 14When she recognized Peter's voice, because of *her* gladness she did not open the gate, but ran in and announced that Peter stood before the gate. 15But they said to her, "You are beside yourself!" Yet she kept insisting that it was so. So they said, "It is his angel."

16Now Peter continued knocking; and when they opened *the door* and saw him, they were astonished. 17But motioning to them with his hand to keep silent, he declared to them how the Lord had brought him out of the prison. And he said, "Go, tell these things to James and to the brethren." And he departed and went to another place.

18Then, as soon as it was day, there was no small stir among the soldiers about what had become of Peter. 19But when Herod had searched for him and not found him, he examined the guards and commanded that *they* should be put to death.

And he went down from Judea to Caesarea, and stayed *there.*

20Now Herod had been very angry with the people of Tyre and Sidon; but they came to him with one accord, and having made Blastus the king's personal aide their friend, they asked for peace, because their country was supplied with food by the king's *country.*

21So on a set day Herod, arrayed in royal apparel, sat on his throne and gave an oration to them. 22And the people kept shouting, "The voice of a god and not of a man!" 23Then immediately an angel of the Lord struck him, because he did not give glory to God. And he was eaten by worms and died.

24But the word of God grew and multiplied.

25And Barnabas and Saul returned from*e* Jerusalem when they had fulfilled *their* ministry, and they also took with them John whose surname was Mark.

CHAPTER 13

13:1–3 *Opportunities come to people busy serving the Lord.* God calls people who take time to worship and minister to the Lord. If you want God's guidance, get busy where you are, and He will show you the next step.

13 Now* in the church that was at Antioch there were certain prophets and teachers: Barnabas, Simeon who was called Niger, Lucius of Cyrene, Manaen who had been brought up with Herod the tetrarch, and Saul. 2As they ministered to the Lord and fasted, the Holy Spirit said, "Now separate to Me Barnabas and Saul for the work to which I have called them." 3Then, having fasted and prayed, and laid hands on them, they sent *them* away.

4So, being sent out by the Holy Spirit, they went down to Seleucia, and from there they sailed to Cyprus. 5And when they arrived in Salamis, they preached the word of God in the synagogues of the Jews. They also had John as *their* assistant.

6*Now when they had gone through the island*f* to Paphos, they found a certain sorcerer, a false

13:6–12, 45, 50 *Opportunities usually produce opposition* (1 Cor. 16:9). Here is another example of the parable of the tares (Matt. 13:24–30, 36–43): God sowed the good seed (Paul and Barnabas),and Satan sowed a counterfeit.

12:25 *e*NU-Text and M-Text read *to.*   13:6 *f*NU-Text reads *the whole island.*

His Word Endures Forever—Note the emphasis in Acts 13 on the Word of God (vv. 5, 7, 15, 26, 44, 46, 48–49). In his preaching, Paul quoted from 1 Samuel, Isaiah, Habakkuk, and Psalms. He preached salvation by faith in Jesus Christ whom God raised from the dead (vv. 38–39). Our words do not last, but the Word of the Lord endures forever.

prophet, a Jew whose name *was* Bar-Jesus, [7]who was with the proconsul, Sergius Paulus, an intelligent man. This man called for Barnabas and Saul and sought to hear the word of God. [8]But Elymas the sorcerer (for so his name is translated) withstood them, seeking to turn the proconsul away from the faith. [9]Then Saul, who also *is called* Paul, filled with the Holy Spirit, looked intently at him [10]and said, "O full of all deceit and all fraud, *you* son of the devil, *you* enemy of all righteousness, will you not cease perverting the straight ways of the Lord? [11]And now, indeed, the hand of the Lord *is* upon you, and you shall be blind, not seeing the sun for a time."

And immediately a dark mist fell on him, and he went around seeking someone to lead him by the hand. [12]Then the proconsul believed, when he saw what had been done, being astonished at the teaching of the Lord.

[13]*Now when Paul and his party set sail from Paphos, they came to Perga in Pamphylia; and John, departing from them, returned to Jerusalem. [14]But when they departed from Perga, they came to Antioch in Pisidia, and went into the synagogue on the Sabbath day and sat down. [15]And after the reading of the Law and the Prophets, the rulers of the synagogue sent to them, saying, "Men *and* brethren, if you have any word of exhortation for the people, say on."

[16]Then Paul stood up, and motioning with *his* hand said, "Men of Israel, and you who fear God, listen: [17]The God of this people Israel[g] chose our fathers, and exalted the people when they dwelt as strangers in the land of Egypt, and with an uplifted arm He brought them out of it. [18]Now for a time of about forty years He put up with their ways in the wilderness. [19]And when He had destroyed seven nations in the land of Canaan, He distributed their land to them by allotment.

[20]"After that He gave *them* judges for about four hundred and fifty years, until Samuel the prophet. [21]And afterward they asked for a king; so God gave them Saul the son of Kish, a man of the tribe of Benjamin, for forty years. [22]And when He had removed him, He raised up for them David as king, to whom also He gave testimony and said, 'I have found David[h] the *son* of Jesse, *a man after My own heart,* who will do all My will.'[i] [23]From this man's seed, according to *the* promise, God raised up for Israel a Savior—Jesus—[j] [24]after John had first preached, before His coming, the baptism of repentance to all the people of Israel. [25]And as John was finishing his course, he said, 'Who do you think I am? I am not *He.* But behold, there comes One after me, the sandals of whose feet I am not worthy to loose.'

[26]"Men *and* brethren, sons of the family of Abraham, and those among you who fear God, to you the word of this salvation has been sent. [27]For those who dwell in Jerusalem, and their rulers, because they did not know Him, nor even the voices of the Prophets which are read every Sabbath, have fulfilled *them* in condemning Him. [28]And though they found no cause for death *in* Him, they asked Pilate that He should be put to

13:13 *Opportunities reveal character.* Paul and Barnabas kept going, but John Mark returned home. We do not know why, nor should we pass judgment (1 Cor. 10:12). Barnabas reclaimed John Mark (15:36–41) and Paul eventually accepted him (2 Tim. 4:11).

Opportunities develop leadership. The trip began with "Barnabas and Saul" (v. 2), but it became "Paul and his party" (v. 13). Barnabas rejoiced to see Paul being used so mightily of God (Rom. 12:9–11). It was a team effort, and the vital thing was the glory of God.

13:17 [g]M-Text omits *Israel.*   13:22 [h]Psalm 89:20 [i]1 Samuel 13:14   13:23 [j]M-Text reads *for Israel salvation.*

death. 29Now when they had fulfilled all that was written concerning Him, they took *Him* down from the tree and laid *Him* in a tomb. 30But God raised Him from the dead. 31He was seen for many days by those who came up with Him from Galilee to Jerusalem, who are His witnesses to the people. 32And we declare to you glad tidings—that promise which was made to the fathers. 33God has fulfilled this for us their children, in that He has raised up Jesus. As it is also written in the second Psalm:

> *'You are My Son,*
> *Today I have begotten You.'*k

34And that He raised Him from the dead, no more to return to corruption, He has spoken thus:

> *'I will give you the sure mercies of David.'*l

35Therefore He also says in another *Psalm:*

> *'You will not allow Your Holy One to see*
> *corruption.'*m

36"For David, after he had served his own generation by the will of God, fell asleep, was buried with his fathers, and saw corruption; 37but He whom God raised up saw no corruption. 38Therefore let it be known to you, brethren, that through this Man is preached to you the forgiveness of sins; 39and by Him everyone who believes is justified from all things from which you could not be justified by the law of Moses. 40Beware therefore, lest what has been spoken in the prophets come upon you:

> 41 *'Behold, you despisers,*
> *Marvel and perish!*
> *For I work a work in your days,*
> *A work which you will by no means believe,*
> *Though one were to declare it to you.'"*n

42So when the Jews went out of the synagogue,o the Gentiles begged that these words might be preached to them the next Sabbath. 43Now when the congregation had broken up, many of the Jews and devout proselytes followed Paul and Barnabas, who, speaking to them, persuaded them to continue in the grace of God.

44On the next Sabbath almost the whole city came together to hear the word of God. 45But when the Jews saw the multitudes, they were filled with envy; and contradicting and blaspheming, they opposed the things spoken by Paul. 46Then Paul and Barnabas grew bold and said, "It was necessary that the word of God should be spoken to you first; but since you reject it, and judge yourselves unworthy of everlasting life, behold, we turn to the Gentiles. 47For so the Lord has commanded us:

> *'I have set you as a light to the Gentiles,*
> *That you should be for salvation to the ends*
> *of the earth.'"*p

13:33 kPsalm 2:7   13:34 lIsaiah 55:3   13:35 mPsalm 16:10
13:41 nHabakkuk 1:5   13:42 oOr *And when they went out of the synagogue of the Jews;* NU-Text reads *And when they went out of the synagogue, they begged.*   13:47 pIsaiah 49:6

⁴⁸Now when the Gentiles heard this, they were glad and glorified the word of the Lord. And as many as had been appointed to eternal life believed.

⁴⁹And the word of the Lord was being spread throughout all the region. ⁵⁰But the Jews stirred up the devout and prominent women and the chief men of the city, raised up persecution against Paul and Barnabas, and expelled them from their region. ⁵¹But they shook off the dust from their feet against them, and came to Iconium. ⁵²And the disciples were filled with joy and with the Holy Spirit.

14 Now* it happened in Iconium that they went together to the synagogue of the Jews, and so spoke that a great multitude both of the Jews and of the Greeks believed. ²But the unbelieving Jews stirred up the Gentiles and poisoned their minds against the brethren. ³Therefore they stayed there a long time, speaking boldly in the Lord, who was bearing witness to the word of His grace, granting signs and wonders to be done by their hands.

⁴But the multitude of the city was divided: part sided with the Jews, and part with the apostles. ⁵And when a violent attempt was made by both the Gentiles and Jews, with their rulers, to abuse and stone them, ⁶they became aware of it and fled to Lystra and Derbe, cities of Lycaonia, and to the surrounding region. ⁷And they were preaching the gospel there.

⁸And in Lystra a certain man without strength in his feet was sitting, a cripple from his mother's womb, who had never walked. ⁹*This* man heard Paul speaking. Paul, observing him intently and seeing that he had faith to be healed, ¹⁰said with a loud voice, "Stand up straight on your feet!" And he leaped and walked. ¹¹Now when the people saw what Paul had done, they raised their voices, saying in the Lycaonian *language,* "The gods have come down to us in the likeness of men!" ¹²And Barnabas they called Zeus, and Paul, Hermes, because he was the chief speaker. ¹³Then the priest of Zeus, whose temple was in front of their city, brought oxen and garlands to the gates, intending to sacrifice with the multitudes.

¹⁴But when the apostles Barnabas and Paul heard this, they tore their clothes and ran in among the multitude, crying out ¹⁵and saying, "Men, why are you doing these things? We also are men with the same nature as you, and preach to you that you should turn from these useless things to the living God, who made the heaven, the earth, the sea, and all things that are in them, ¹⁶who in bygone generations allowed all nations to walk in their own ways. ¹⁷Nevertheless He did not leave Himself without witness, in that He did good, gave us rain from heaven and fruitful seasons, filling our hearts with food and gladness." ¹⁸And with these sayings they could scarcely restrain the multitudes from sacrificing to them.

¹⁹Then Jews from Antioch and Iconium came there; and having persuaded the multitudes, they stoned Paul *and* dragged *him* out of the city, supposing him to be dead. ²⁰However, when the disciples gathered around him, he rose up and went into the city. And the next day he departed with Barnabas to Derbe.

²¹And when they had preached the gospel to that city and made many disciples, they returned

CHAPTER 14

14:1ff Paul was a man on the move but not a man easily moved because of difficulties. "But none of these things move me" was his testimony of faith (20:24), and he lived it.

When he and Barnabas were expelled from Antioch in Pisidia, they shook off the dust of their feet and went to Iconium (13:50–52; Luke 10:11). When the people there tried to stone them, they went to Lystra where they were treated like gods! (That was a greater danger than persecution.) Crowds are fickle: they changed their minds and stoned Paul, but he just got up and went to Derbe.

That was not all. Paul and Barnabas had the courage to retrace their steps so they could help and encourage the new Christians! And when they returned home, they told the church what the Lord had done, not what they had suffered.

Paul and Barnabas put Christ first, others second, and themselves last. They had a job to do, and they were determined by God's grace to do it. How much does it take to move you out of the will of God?

❝*The will to persevere is often the difference between failure and success.*❞

—David Sarnoff

to Lystra, Iconium, and Antioch, [22]strengthening the souls of the disciples, exhorting *them* to continue in the faith, and *saying*, "We must through many tribulations enter the kingdom of God." [23]So when they had appointed elders in every church, and prayed with fasting, they commended them to the Lord in whom they had believed. [24]And after they had passed through Pisidia, they came to Pamphylia. [25]Now when they had preached the word in Perga, they went down to Attalia. [26]From there they sailed to Antioch, where they had been commended to the grace of God for the work which they had completed.

[27]Now when they had come and gathered the church together, they reported all that God had done with them, and that He had opened the door of faith to the Gentiles. [28]So they stayed there a long time with the disciples.

CHAPTER 15

15:1–29 When God opens a door (14:27), the enemy has somebody handy to try to close it. In this case, the legalists from Judea visited the Antioch church and taught that Gentiles must become Jews before they can be Christians. Their teaching was a denial of salvation by grace through faith (10:43; Eph. 2:8–9).

It was difficult for the orthodox Jews to see that their glorious religious system, given by God, had been fulfilled in Christ and was now out-of-date. (That is why the book of Hebrews was written.) Rather than abandon it, they tried to blend the old religion with the new (Matt. 9:14–17).

When sincere Christians disagree, they must get together, see what God is doing in His church, and find out what the Word has to say about it. Peter, Paul, and Barnabas told what God was doing among the Gentiles, and James related it to the Word (Amos 9:11–12).

In the decision, there was no compromise doctrinally, but there was consideration practically. In the decree, the church asked the Gentiles not to deliberately offend the Jews. You will find the expansion of this principle, the basic principle of love, in Romans 14—15 and 1 Corinthians 8—10.

15 And* certain *men* came down from Judea and taught the brethren, "Unless you are circumcised according to the custom of Moses, you cannot be saved." [2]Therefore, when Paul and Barnabas had no small dissension and dispute with them, they determined that Paul and Barnabas and certain others of them should go up to Jerusalem, to the apostles and elders, about this question.

[3]So, being sent on their way by the church, they passed through Phoenicia and Samaria, describing the conversion of the Gentiles; and they caused great joy to all the brethren. [4]And when they had come to Jerusalem, they were received by the church and the apostles and the elders; and they reported all things that God had done with them. [5]But some of the sect of the Pharisees who believed rose up, saying, "It is necessary to circumcise them, and to command *them* to keep the law of Moses."

[6]Now the apostles and elders came together to consider this matter. [7]And when there had been much dispute, Peter rose up and said to them: "Men and brethren, you know that a good while ago God chose among us, that by my mouth the Gentiles should hear the word of the gospel and believe. [8]So God, who knows the heart, acknowledged them by giving them the Holy Spirit, just as *He did* to us, [9]and made no distinction between us and them, purifying their hearts by faith. [10]Now therefore, why do you test God by putting a yoke on the neck of the disciples which neither our fathers nor we were able to bear? [11]But we believe that through the grace of the Lord Jesus Christ[q] we shall be saved in the same manner as they."

[12]Then all the multitude kept silent and listened to Barnabas and Paul declaring how many miracles and wonders God had worked through them among the Gentiles. [13]And after they had become silent, James answered, saying, "Men *and* brethren, listen to me: [14]Simon has declared how God at the first visited the Gentiles to take out of them a people for His name. [15]And with this the words of the prophets agree, just as it is written:

[16]   'After this I will return
         And will rebuild the tabernacle of David,
            which has fallen down;

15:11 [q]NU-Text and M-Text omit *Christ*.

> I will rebuild its ruins,
> And I will set it up;

17 So that the rest of mankind may seek the
> Lord,
> Even all the Gentiles who are called by My
> name,
> Says the Lord who does all these things.'

18"Known to God from eternity are all His works.*s* 19Therefore I judge that we should not trouble those from among the Gentiles who are turning to God, 20but that we write to them to abstain from things polluted by idols, *from* sexual immorality,*t* *from* things strangled, and *from* blood. 21For Moses has had throughout many generations those who preach him in every city, being read in the synagogues every Sabbath."

22Then it pleased the apostles and elders, with the whole church, to send chosen men of their own company to Antioch with Paul and Barnabas, *namely,* Judas who was also named Barsabas,*u* and Silas, leading men among the brethren. 23They wrote this *letter* by them:

The apostles, the elders, and the brethren,

To the brethren who are of the Gentiles in Antioch, Syria, and Cilicia:

Greetings.

24 Since we have heard that some who went out from us have troubled you with words, unsettling your souls, saying, "*You must be circumcised and keep the law*"*v*—to whom we gave no *such* commandment— 25it seemed good to us, being assembled with one accord, to send chosen men to you with our beloved Barnabas and Paul, 26men who have risked their lives for the name of our Lord Jesus Christ. 27We have therefore sent Judas and Silas, who will also report the same things by word of mouth. 28For it seemed good to the Holy Spirit, and to us, to lay upon you no greater burden than these necessary things: 29that you abstain from things offered to idols, from blood, from things strangled, and from sexual immorality.*w* If you keep yourselves from these, you will do well.

Farewell.

30So when they were sent off, they came to Antioch; and when they had gathered the multitude together, they delivered the letter. 31When they had read it, they rejoiced over its encouragement. 32Now Judas and Silas, themselves being prophets also, exhorted and strengthened the brethren with many words. 33And after they had stayed *there* for a time, they were sent back with greetings from the brethren to the apostles.*x* 34However, it seemed good to Silas to remain

---

15:17 *r*Amos 9:11, 12   15:18 *s*NU-Text (combining with verse 17) reads *Says the Lord, who makes these things known from eternity (of old).*   15:20 *t*Or *fornication*   15:22 *u*NU-Text and M-Text read *Barsabbas.*   15:24 *v*NU-Text omits *saying, "You must be circumcised and keep the law."*   15:29 *w*Or *fornication*   15:33 *x*NU-Text reads *to those who had sent them.*

CHAPTER 16

16:1–5 Paul wrote, "But in all things we commend ourselves as ministers of God: in much patience" (2 Cor. 6:4). See the patience of Paul . . .

In waiting for a helper. Timothy replaced John Mark and became a true son in the faith to Paul. God has the right person ready at the right time, so be patient.

16:6–10 In seeking God's will. He was an apostle, yet he did not always know the direction God wanted him to take. He took steps, God closed doors, so he waited; and then God showed him the way.

16:11–15 In ministering the Word. They waited "some days" before seeking a place to witness, and God had hearts all prepared.

❝*Patience is power. With time and patience, the mulberry leaf becomes silk.*❞
—Chinese Proverb

16:16–18 In bearing annoyance. Paul put up with the demonic promotion as long as he could and then cast out the demon. Paul knew that his action would create problems for him, and it did.

there.ʸ ³⁵Paul and Barnabas also remained in Antioch, teaching and preaching the word of the Lord, with many others also.

³⁶Then after some days Paul said to Barnabas, "Let us now go back and visit our brethren in every city where we have preached the word of the Lord, *and see* how they are doing." ³⁷Now Barnabas was determined to take with them John called Mark. ³⁸But Paul insisted that they should not take with them the one who had departed from them in Pamphylia, and had not gone with them to the work. ³⁹Then the contention became so sharp that they parted from one another. And so Barnabas took Mark and sailed to Cyprus; ⁴⁰but Paul chose Silas and departed, being commended by the brethren to the grace of God. ⁴¹And he went through Syria and Cilicia, strengthening the churches.

16 Then* he came to Derbe and Lystra. And behold, a certain disciple was there, named Timothy, *the* son of a certain Jewish woman who believed, but his father *was* Greek. ²He was well spoken of by the brethren who were at Lystra and Iconium. ³Paul wanted to have him go on with him. And he took *him* and circumcised him because of the Jews who were in that region, for they all knew that his father was Greek. ⁴And as they went through the cities, they delivered to them the decrees to keep, which were determined by the apostles and elders at Jerusalem. ⁵So the churches were strengthened in the faith, and increased in number daily.

⁶*Now when they had gone through Phrygia and the region of Galatia, they were forbidden by the Holy Spirit to preach the word in Asia. ⁷After they had come to Mysia, they tried to go into Bithynia, but the Spiritᶻ did not permit them. ⁸So passing by Mysia, they came down to Troas. ⁹And a vision appeared to Paul in the night. A man of Macedonia stood and pleaded with him, saying, "Come over to Macedonia and help us." ¹⁰Now after he had seen the vision, immediately we sought to go to Macedonia, concluding that the Lord had called us to preach the gospel to them.

¹¹*Therefore, sailing from Troas, we ran a straight course to Samothrace, and the next *day* came to Neapolis, ¹²and from there to Philippi, which is the foremost city of that part of Macedonia, a colony. And we were staying in that city for some days. ¹³And on the Sabbath day we went out of the city to the riverside, where prayer was customarily made; and we sat down and spoke to the women who met *there.* ¹⁴Now a certain woman named Lydia heard *us.* She was a seller of purple from the city of Thyatira, who worshiped God. The Lord opened her heart to heed the things spoken by Paul. ¹⁵And when she and her household were baptized, she begged *us,* saying, "If you have judged me to be faithful to the Lord, come to my house and stay." So she persuaded us.

¹⁶*Now it happened, as we went to prayer, that a certain slave girl possessed with a spirit of divination met us, who brought her masters much profit by fortune-telling. ¹⁷This girl followed Paul

---

15:34 ʸNU-Text and M-Text omit this verse.   16:7 ᶻNU-Text adds *of Jesus.*

and us, and cried out, saying, "These men are the servants of the Most High God, who proclaim to us the way of salvation." 18And this she did for many days.

But Paul, greatly annoyed, turned and said to the spirit, "I command you in the name of Jesus Christ to come out of her." And he came out that very hour. 19*But when her masters saw that their hope of profit was gone, they seized Paul and Silas and dragged *them* into the marketplace to the authorities.

20And they brought them to the magistrates, and said, "These men, being Jews, exceedingly trouble our city; 21and they teach customs which are not lawful for us, being Romans, to receive or observe." 22Then the multitude rose up together against them; and the magistrates tore off their clothes and commanded *them* to be beaten with rods. 23And when they had laid many stripes on them, they threw *them* into prison, commanding the jailer to keep them securely. 24Having received such a charge, he put them into the inner prison and fastened their feet in the stocks.

25But at midnight Paul and Silas were praying and singing hymns to God, and the prisoners were listening to them. 26*Suddenly there was a great earthquake, so that the foundations of the prison were shaken; and immediately all the doors were opened and everyone's chains were loosed. 27And the keeper of the prison, awaking from sleep and seeing the prison doors open, supposing the prisoners had fled, drew his sword and was about to kill himself. 28But Paul called with a loud voice, saying, "Do yourself no harm, for we are all here."

29Then he called for a light, ran in, and fell down trembling before Paul and Silas. 30And he brought them out and said, "Sirs, what must I do to be saved?"

31So they said, "Believe on the Lord Jesus Christ, and you will be saved, you and your household." 32Then they spoke the word of the Lord to him and to all who were in his house. 33And he took them the same hour of the night and washed *their* stripes. And immediately he and all his family were baptized. 34Now when he had brought them into his house, he set food before them; and he rejoiced, having believed in God with all his household.

35And when it was day, the magistrates sent the officers, saying, "Let those men go."

36So the keeper of the prison reported these words to Paul, saying, "The magistrates have sent to let you go. Now therefore depart, and go in peace."

37But Paul said to them, "They have beaten us openly, uncondemned Romans, *and* have thrown *us* into prison. And now do they put us out secretly? No indeed! Let them come themselves and get us out."

38And the officers told these words to the magistrates, and they were afraid when they heard that they were Romans. 39Then they came and pleaded with them and brought *them* out, and asked *them* to depart from the city. 40So they went out of the prison and entered *the house of* Lydia; and when they had seen the brethren, they encouraged them and departed.

17 Now* when they had passed through Amphipolis and Apollonia, they came to Thessalonica, where there was a synagogue of the

16:19–25 *In enduring suffering.* Paul did not use his Roman citizenship to protect himself from pain (22:22–29), but later he used it to protect the new church (vv. 35–40). When you hurt, ask God to give you songs in the night (Ps. 42:8).

16:26–34 *In winning a lost soul.* Paul had his eyes on the keeper of the prison and in kindness won him to Christ. How much are we willing to suffer to win someone to the Lord, especially someone who has hurt us?

CHAPTER 17

17:1–9 *Rejecting the new.* The Jews in Thessalonica were not interested in the new faith or the "new king" that Paul preached, but the Gentile "God seekers" accepted the gospel and were saved. Read 1 Thessalonians 1 to see the change they experienced.

Jews. 2Then Paul, as his custom was, went in to them, and for three Sabbaths reasoned with them from the Scriptures, 3explaining and demonstrating that the Christ had to suffer and rise again from the dead, and *saying,* "This Jesus whom I preach to you is the Christ." 4And some of them were persuaded; and a great multitude of the devout Greeks, and not a few of the leading women, joined Paul and Silas.

5But the Jews who were not persuaded, becoming envious,*a* took some of the evil men from the marketplace, and gathering a mob, set all the city in an uproar and attacked the house of Jason, and sought to bring them out to the people. 6But when they did not find them, they dragged Jason and some brethren to the rulers of the city, crying out, "These who have turned the world upside down have come here too. 7Jason has harbored them, and these are all acting contrary to the decrees of Caesar, saying there is another king—Jesus." 8And they troubled the crowd and the rulers of the city when they heard these things. 9So when they had taken security from Jason and the rest, they let them go.

10*Then the brethren immediately sent Paul and Silas away by night to Berea. When they arrived, they went into the synagogue of the Jews. 11These were more fair-minded than those in Thessalonica, in that they received the word with all readiness, and searched the Scriptures daily *to find out* whether these things were so. 12Therefore many of them believed, and also not a few of the Greeks, prominent women as well as men. 13But when the Jews from Thessalonica learned that the word of God was preached by Paul at Berea, they came there also and stirred up the crowds. 14Then immediately the brethren sent Paul away, to go to the sea; but both Silas and Timothy remained there. 15So those who conducted Paul brought him to Athens; and receiving a command for Silas and Timothy to come to him with all speed, they departed.

16Now while Paul waited for them at Athens, his spirit was provoked within him when he saw that the city was given over to idols. 17Therefore he reasoned in the synagogue with the Jews and with the *Gentile* worshipers, and in the marketplace daily with those who happened to be there. 18Then*b* certain Epicurean and Stoic philosophers encountered him. And some said, "What does this babbler want to say?"

Others said, "He seems to be a proclaimer of foreign gods," because he preached to them Jesus and the resurrection.

19*And they took him and brought him to the Areopagus, saying, "May we know what this new doctrine *is* of which you speak? 20For you are bringing some strange things to our ears. Therefore we want to know what these things mean." 21For all the Athenians and the foreigners who were there spent their time in nothing else but either to tell or to hear some new thing.

22Then Paul stood in the midst of the Areopagus and said, "Men of Athens, I perceive that in all things you are very religious; 23for as I was passing through and considering the objects of your

17:10–12 *Investigating the new.* The next town was just the opposite! The Jews in Berea took time to examine the evidence and study the Scriptures. There are fair-minded people in every nation, and God knows who they are.

17:19–34 *Looking for the new.* The people in Athens "spent their time in nothing else but either to tell or to hear some new thing" (v. 21). How like our world today! The quest for novelty overshadows the search for reality. Paul's sermon was a masterpiece of tact and teaching, and a few people were converted. Paul offered them "newness of life" through the Resurrection (Rom. 6:4), and most of the listeners rejected it.

17:5 *a*NU-Text omits *who were not persuaded;* M-Text omits *becoming envious.*   17:18 *b*NU-Text and M-Text add *also.*

worship, I even found an altar with this inscription:

TO THE UNKNOWN GOD.

Therefore, the One whom you worship without knowing, Him I proclaim to you: 24God, who made the world and everything in it, since He is Lord of heaven and earth, does not dwell in temples made with hands. 25Nor is He worshiped with men's hands, as though He needed anything, since He gives to all life, breath, and all things. 26And He has made from one blood[c] every nation of men to dwell on all the face of the earth, and has determined their preappointed times and the boundaries of their dwellings, 27so that they should seek the Lord, in the hope that they might grope for Him and find Him, though He is not far from each one of us; 28for in Him we live and move and have our being, as also some of your own poets have said, 'For we are also His offspring.' 29Therefore, since we are the offspring of God, we ought not to think that the Divine Nature is like gold or silver or stone, something shaped by art and man's devising. 30Truly, these times of ignorance God overlooked, but now commands all men everywhere to repent, 31because He has appointed a day on which He will judge the world in righteousness by the Man whom He has ordained. He has given assurance of this to all by raising Him from the dead."

32And when they heard of the resurrection of the dead, some mocked, while others said, "We will hear you again on this *matter.*" 33So Paul departed from among them. 34However, some men joined him and believed, among them Dionysius the Areopagite, a woman named Damaris, and others with them.

18 After these things Paul departed from Athens and went to Corinth. 2And he found a certain Jew named Aquila, born in Pontus, who had recently come from Italy with his wife Priscilla (because Claudius had commanded all the Jews to depart from Rome); and he came to them. 3*So, because he was of the same trade, he stayed with them and worked; for by occupation they were tentmakers. 4And he reasoned in the synagogue every Sabbath, and persuaded both Jews and Greeks.

5When Silas and Timothy had come from Macedonia, Paul was compelled by the Spirit, and testified to the Jews *that* Jesus *is* the Christ. 6*But

---

17:26 cNU-Text omits *blood.*

18:3 *The tentmaker.* All Jewish rabbis had a trade because they did not charge their pupils for their lessons. Paul worked hard to support himself and his associates in their ministry. He also worked so that the unsaved could not accuse him of preaching the gospel just to make money (1 Cor. 9). What sacrifices do we make today to further the gospel?

18:6 *The watchman.* The image is from Ezekiel 3:16–21. As a faithful watchman, Paul warned sinners of the wrath to come, so his hands were free from their blood.

He Is with Us—"I am with you" is a promise God gave to Isaac (Gen. 26:24), Jacob (Gen. 28:15), the Jewish remnant returning from Babylon (Isa. 41:10; 43:5), Jeremiah (Jer. 1:8, 19; 15:20), and the Jews rebuilding the temple (Hag. 1:13; 2:4); and Jesus gave it to us (Matt. 28:20). He said, "I will never leave you nor forsake you" (Heb. 13:5).

A Godly Couple—Aquila and Priscilla, husband and wife, appear several times in apostolic history and were important workers in the early church. They are always mentioned together because they were a team. Being Jews, they were expelled from Rome; as a result, they met Paul in Corinth and opened their home to him. Paul left them in Ephesus where they helped Apollos better understand the gospel (Acts 18:18–28). They returned to Rome where they had a church in their home (Rom. 16:3–5). We do not know how they risked their lives for Paul; but their actions show how much they loved him. They were with Paul in Ephesus when he wrote 1 Corinthians (1 Cor. 16:8, 19), so perhaps it had something to do with the riot described in Acts 19. In his last epistle, Paul sent loving greetings to them (2 Tim. 4:19). Every pastor is grateful to God for couples like Priscilla and Aquila whose hearts, hands, and homes are completely given to the Lord.

18:7–10 *The evangelist.* Paul moved next door to the synagogue and kept witnessing! He was not one to run away from either the battlefield or the harvestfield. The Lord promised, "I am with you" (v. 10), a promise He gave to many people and still gives to us today (Isa. 41:10; Matt. 28:20).

18:11–23 *The builder.* Paul did not just win souls; he also built a local church by teaching the converts the Word of God (1 Cor. 3:9–23). In fact, he followed the commission of Matthew 28:18–20. After reporting to his home base in Antioch, Paul revisited some churches to build them up in the faith.

when they opposed him and blasphemed, he shook *his* garments and said to them, "Your blood *be* upon your *own* heads; I *am* clean. From now on I will go to the Gentiles." 7*And he departed from there and entered the house of a certain *man* named Justus,[d] *one* who worshiped God, whose house was next door to the synagogue. 8Then Crispus, the ruler of the synagogue, believed on the Lord with all his household. And many of the Corinthians, hearing, believed and were baptized.

9Now the Lord spoke to Paul in the night by a vision, "Do not be afraid, but speak, and do not keep silent; 10for I am with you, and no one will attack you to hurt you; for I have many people in this city." 11*And he continued *there* a year and six months, teaching the word of God among them.

12When Gallio was proconsul of Achaia, the Jews with one accord rose up against Paul and brought him to the judgment seat, 13saying, "This *fellow* persuades men to worship God contrary to the law."

14And when Paul was about to open *his* mouth, Gallio said to the Jews, "If it were a matter of wrongdoing or wicked crimes, O Jews, there would be reason why I should bear with you. 15But if it is a question of words and names and your own law, look *to it* yourselves; for I do not want to be a judge of such *matters.*" 16And he drove them from the judgment seat. 17Then all the Greeks[e] took Sosthenes, the ruler of the synagogue, and beat *him* before the judgment seat. But Gallio took no notice of these things.

18So Paul still remained a good while. Then he took leave of the brethren and sailed for Syria, and Priscilla and Aquila *were* with him. He had *his* hair cut off at Cenchrea, for he had taken a vow. 19And he came to Ephesus, and left them there; but he himself entered the synagogue and reasoned with the Jews. 20When they asked *him* to stay a longer time with them, he did not consent, 21but took leave of them, saying, "I must by all means keep this coming feast in Jerusalem;[f] but I will return again to you, God willing." And he sailed from Ephesus.

22And when he had landed at Caesarea, and gone up and greeted the church, he went down to Antioch. 23After he had spent some time *there*, he departed and went over the region of Galatia and Phrygia in order, strengthening all the disciples.

24Now a certain Jew named Apollos, born at Alexandria, an eloquent man *and* mighty in the Scriptures, came to Ephesus. 25This man had been instructed in the way of the Lord; and being fervent in spirit, he spoke and taught accurately the things of the Lord, though he knew only the baptism of John. 26So he began to speak boldly in the synagogue. When Aquila and Priscilla heard him, they took him aside and explained to him the way of God more accurately. 27And when he desired to cross to Achaia, the brethren wrote, exhorting the disciples to receive him; and when he arrived, he greatly helped those who had believed through grace; 28for he vigorously refuted the Jews publicly, showing from the Scriptures that Jesus is the Christ.

18:7 [d]NU-Text reads *Titius Justus.* 18:17 [e]NU-Text reads *they all.* 18:21 [f]NU-Text omits *I must* through *Jerusalem.*

19

And* it happened, while Apollos was at Corinth, that Paul, having passed through the upper regions, came to Ephesus. And finding some disciples 2he said to them, "Did you receive the Holy Spirit when you believed?"

So they said to him, "We have not so much as heard whether there is a Holy Spirit."

3And he said to them, "Into what then were you baptized?"

So they said, "Into John's baptism."

4Then Paul said, "John indeed baptized with a baptism of repentance, saying to the people that they should believe on Him who would come after him, that is, on Christ Jesus."

5When they heard this, they were baptized in the name of the Lord Jesus. 6And when Paul had laid hands on them, the Holy Spirit came upon them, and they spoke with tongues and prophesied. 7Now the men were about twelve in all.

8And he went into the synagogue and spoke boldly for three months, reasoning and persuading concerning the things of the kingdom of God. 9But when some were hardened and did not believe, but spoke evil of the Way before the multitude, he departed from them and withdrew the disciples, reasoning daily in the school of Tyrannus. 10And this continued for two years, so that all who dwelt in Asia heard the word of the Lord Jesus, both Jews and Greeks.

11Now God worked unusual miracles by the hands of Paul, 12so that even handkerchiefs or aprons were brought from his body to the sick, and the diseases left them and the evil spirits went out of them. 13*Then some of the itinerant Jewish exorcists took it upon themselves to call the name of the Lord Jesus over those who had evil spirits, saying, "Weg exorcise you by the Jesus whom Paul preaches." 14Also there were seven sons of Sceva, a Jewish chief priest, who did so.

15And the evil spirit answered and said, "Jesus I know, and Paul I know; but who are you?"

16Then the man in whom the evil spirit was leaped on them, overpoweredh them, and prevailed against them,i so that they fled out of that house naked and wounded. 17This became known both to all Jews and Greeks dwelling in Ephesus; and fear fell on them all, and the name of the Lord Jesus was magnified. 18And many who had believed came confessing and telling their deeds. 19Also, many of those who had practiced magic brought their books together and burned them in the sight of all. And they counted up the value of them, and it totaled fifty thousand pieces of silver. 20So the word of the Lord grew mightily and prevailed.

21When these things were accomplished, Paul purposed in the Spirit, when he had passed through Macedonia and Achaia, to go to Jerusalem, saying, "After I have been there, I must also see Rome." 22So he sent into Macedonia two of those who ministered to him, Timothy and Erastus, but he himself stayed in Asia for a time.

23*And about that time there arose a great commotion about the Way. 24For a certain man named Demetrius, a silversmith, who made silver shrines of Diana,j brought no small profit to the craftsmen. 25He called them together with the workers

---

19:13 gNU-Text reads I.   19:16 hM-Text reads and they overpowered. iNU-Text reads both of them.   19:24 jGreek Artemis

CHAPTER 19

19:1–7 We read in this chapter that "the word of the Lord grew mightily and prevailed" (v. 20). When does this happen? **When we confirm our faith.** When you believe in Jesus Christ, you receive the gift of the Holy Spirit (Acts 10:43–48; Rom. 8:9). Many people think they are converted but do not have the Spirit's witness within (1 John 5:9–13). Paul could not build a church on men with an inadequate spiritual experience, nor can we today. We must be honest with God.

19:13–20 **When we confess our sins.** The devil is a great imitator, but in this case, his attempt was a humiliating failure. The Lord used it for good, because the believers became convicted about their secret sins and confessed them. Then the Spirit could work in mighty power, and the Word increased!

19:23–41 **When we confront the enemy.** Paul did not openly attack their idolatry by picketing the temple of Diana or petitioning the city government. He simply shared the Word, and lives were changed. Of course, the real issue was money, not religion. Paul was wise not to go into the theater, although we admire him for his courage. But the riot only called attention to the gospel and gave the believers more opportunity to witness. Circumstances that look like obstacles are really opportunities when you let God work.

of similar occupation, and said: "Men, you know that we have our prosperity by this trade. 26Moreover you see and hear that not only at Ephesus, but throughout almost all Asia, this Paul has persuaded and turned away many people, saying that they are not gods which are made with hands. 27So not only is this trade of ours in danger of falling into disrepute, but also the temple of the great goddess Diana may be despised and her magnificence destroyed,^{k} whom all Asia and the world worship."

28Now when they heard *this,* they were full of wrath and cried out, saying, "Great *is* Diana of the Ephesians!" 29So the whole city was filled with confusion, and rushed into the theater with one accord, having seized Gaius and Aristarchus, Macedonians, Paul's travel companions. 30And when Paul wanted to go in to the people, the disciples would not allow him. 31Then some of the officials of Asia, who were his friends, sent to him pleading that he would not venture into the theater. 32Some therefore cried one thing and some another, for the assembly was confused, and most of them did not know why they had come together. 33And they drew Alexander out of the multitude, the Jews putting him forward. And Alexander motioned with his hand, and wanted to make his defense to the people. 34But when they found out that he was a Jew, all with one voice cried out for about two hours, "Great *is* Diana of the Ephesians!"

35And when the city clerk had quieted the crowd, he said: "Men of Ephesus, what man is there who does not know that the city of the Ephesians is temple guardian of the great goddess Diana, and of the *image* which fell down from Zeus? 36Therefore, since these things cannot be denied, you ought to be quiet and do nothing rashly. 37For you have brought these men here who are neither robbers of temples nor blasphemers of your^l goddess. 38Therefore, if Demetrius and his fellow craftsmen have a case against anyone, the courts are open and there are proconsuls. Let them bring charges against one another. 39But if you have any other inquiry to make, it shall be determined in the lawful assembly. 40For we are in danger of being called in question for today's uproar, there being no reason which we may give to account for this disorderly gathering." 41And when he had said these things, he dismissed the assembly.

20 After* the uproar had ceased, Paul called the disciples to *himself,* embraced *them,* and departed to go to Macedonia. 2Now when he had gone over that region and encouraged them with many words, he came to Greece 3and stayed three months. And when the Jews plotted against him as he was about to sail to Syria, he decided to return through Macedonia. 4And Sopater of Berea accompanied him to Asia—also Aristarchus and Secundus of the Thessalonians, and Gaius of

CHAPTER 20

20:1–16 The uproars usually cease, so be patient; but be sure to get ready for the next battle.

Paul was going to Jerusalem. Along the way, he met with dear friends, ministered the Word, and even enjoyed a quiet voyage and a refreshing walk (v. 13). God's servants need to get away from people and have time alone to think, meditate, and pray. Paul knew he was facing danger in Jerusalem (vv. 22–23), and he wanted to be prepared spiritually.

19:27 ^{k}NU-Text reads *she be deposed from her magnificence.* 19:37 ^{l}NU-Text reads *our.*

Paul's Roles—As Paul reviewed his ministry in Acts 20:24–26, he saw himself as an *accountant* ("I count"), a *runner* ("I may finish my race"), a *steward* ("the ministry which I received"), a *witness* ("to testify"), a *herald* ("preaching the kingdom"), and a *watchman* ("innocent of the blood"). What a responsibility it is to be a servant of God!

Derbe, and Timothy, and Tychicus and Trophimus of Asia. ⁵These men, going ahead, waited for us at Troas. ⁶But we sailed away from Philippi after the Days of Unleavened Bread, and in five days joined them at Troas, where we stayed seven days.

⁷Now on the first *day* of the week, when the disciples came together to break bread, Paul, ready to depart the next day, spoke to them and continued his message until midnight. ⁸There were many lamps in the upper room where they*ᵐ* were gathered together. ⁹And in a window sat a certain young man named Eutychus, who was sinking into a deep sleep. He was overcome by sleep; and as Paul continued speaking, he fell down from the third story and was taken up dead. ¹⁰But Paul went down, fell on him, and embracing *him* said, "Do not trouble yourselves, for his life is in him." ¹¹Now when he had come up, had broken bread and eaten, and talked a long while, even till daybreak, he departed. ¹²And they brought the young man in alive, and they were not a little comforted.

¹³Then we went ahead to the ship and sailed to Assos, there intending to take Paul on board; for so he had given orders, intending himself to go on foot. ¹⁴And when he met us at Assos, we took him on board and came to Mitylene. ¹⁵We sailed from there, and the next *day* came opposite Chios. The following *day* we arrived at Samos and stayed at Trogyllium. The next *day* we came to Miletus. ¹⁶For Paul had decided to sail past Ephesus, so that he would not have to spend time in Asia; for he was hurrying to be at Jerusalem, if possible, on the Day of Pentecost.

¹⁷*From Miletus he sent to Ephesus and called for the elders of the church. ¹⁸And when they had come to him, he said to them: "You know, from the first day that I came to Asia, in what manner I always lived among you, ¹⁹serving the Lord with all humility, with many tears and trials which happened to me by the plotting of the Jews; ²⁰how I kept back nothing that was helpful, but proclaimed it to you, and taught you publicly and from house to house, ²¹testifying to Jews, and also to Greeks, repentance toward God and faith toward our Lord Jesus Christ. ²²And see, now I go bound in the spirit to Jerusalem, not knowing the things that will happen to me there, ²³except that the Holy Spirit testifies in every city, saying that chains and tribulations await me. ²⁴But none of these things move me; nor do I count my life dear to myself,ⁿ so that I may finish my race with joy, and the ministry which I received from the Lord Jesus, to testify to the gospel of the grace of God.

²⁵"And indeed, now I know that you all, among whom I have gone preaching the kingdom of God, will see my face no more. ²⁶Therefore I testify to you this day that I *am* innocent of the blood of all *men*. ²⁷For I have not shunned to declare to you the whole counsel of God. ²⁸Therefore take heed to yourselves and to all the flock, among which the Holy Spirit has made you overseers, to shepherd the church of Godᵒ which He purchased with His own blood. ²⁹For I know this, that after my departure savage wolves will come in

20:17–38 In his farewell message to the elders, Paul reviewed his past ministry (vv. 18–21), shared his present concerns (vv. 22–24), and revealed future dangers (vv. 28–31). If you want to catch the heart of Paul, consider his statements: "Serving the Lord . . . I kept back nothing . . . that I may finish my race with joy. . . . It is more blessed to give than to receive."

One day, life will end, and we will have to give our farewell speech. Can we look back without regret and look ahead without fear? Will we finish our race with joy even while others are weeping?

20:8 ᵐNU-Text and M-Text read *we*. 20:24 ⁿNU-Text reads *But I do not count my life of any value or dear to myself.* 20:28 ᵒM-Text reads *of the Lord and God.*

among you, not sparing the flock. ³⁰Also from among yourselves men will rise up, speaking perverse things, to draw away the disciples after themselves. ³¹Therefore watch, and remember that for three years I did not cease to warn everyone night and day with tears.

³²"So now, brethren, I commend you to God and to the word of His grace, which is able to build you up and give you an inheritance among all those who are sanctified. ³³I have coveted no one's silver or gold or apparel. ³⁴Yes,ᵖ you yourselves know that these hands have provided for my necessities, and for those who were with me. ³⁵I have shown you in every way, by laboring like this, that you must support the weak. And remember the words of the Lord Jesus, that He said, 'It is more blessed to give than to receive.' "

³⁶And when he had said these things, he knelt down and prayed with them all. ³⁷Then they all wept freely, and fell on Paul's neck and kissed him, ³⁸sorrowing most of all for the words which he spoke, that they would see his face no more. And they accompanied him to the ship.

CHAPTER 21

21:1–14 The traveler. This farewell journey brought both joy and sorrow to Paul, but life is like that. He knew what lay ahead of him but kept going (Luke 9:51). Years before, the Lord had told him to get out of Jerusalem (22:18). Was he wrong in going back?

21 Now* it came to pass, that when we had departed from them and set sail, running a straight course we came to Cos, the following *day* to Rhodes, and from there to Patara. ²And finding a ship sailing over to Phoenicia, we went aboard and set sail. ³When we had sighted Cyprus, we passed it on the left, sailed to Syria, and landed at Tyre; for there the ship was to unload her cargo. ⁴And finding disciples,q we stayed there seven days. They told Paul through the Spirit not to go up to Jerusalem. ⁵When we had come to the end of those days, we departed and went on our way; and they all accompanied us, with wives and children, till *we were* out of the city. And we knelt down on the shore and prayed. ⁶When we had taken our leave of one another, we boarded the ship, and they returned home.

⁷And when we had finished *our* voyage from Tyre, we came to Ptolemais, greeted the brethren, and stayed with them one day. ⁸On the next *day* we who were Paul's companionsr departed and came to Caesarea, and entered the house of Philip the evangelist, who was *one* of the seven, and stayed with him. ⁹Now this man had four virgin daughters who prophesied. ¹⁰And as we stayed many days, a certain prophet named Agabus came down from Judea. ¹¹When he had come to us, he took Paul's belt, bound his *own* hands and feet, and said, "Thus says the Holy Spirit, 'So shall the Jews at Jerusalem bind the man who owns this belt, and deliver *him* into the hands of the Gentiles.' "

¹²Now when we heard these things, both we and those from that place pleaded with him not to go up to Jerusalem. ¹³Then Paul answered, "What do you mean by weeping and breaking my heart? For I am ready not only to be bound, but also to die at Jerusalem for the name of the Lord Jesus."

¹⁴So when he would not be persuaded, we ceased, saying, "The will of the Lord be done."

¹⁵And after those days we packed and went up to Jerusalem. ¹⁶Also some of the disciples from

---

20:34 ᵖNU-Text and M-Text omit *Yes.*   21:4 qNU-Text reads *the disciples.*   21:8 rNU-Text omits *who were Paul's companions.*

Caesarea went with us and brought with them a certain Mnason of Cyprus, an early disciple, with whom we were to lodge.

17And when we had come to Jerusalem, the brethren received us gladly. 18*On the following *day* Paul went in with us to James, and all the elders were present. 19When he had greeted them, he told in detail those things which God had done among the Gentiles through his ministry. 20And when they heard *it,* they glorified the Lord. And they said to him, "You see, brother, how many myriads of Jews there are who have believed, and they are all zealous for the law; 21but they have been informed about you that you teach all the Jews who are among the Gentiles to forsake Moses, saying that they ought not to circumcise *their* children nor to walk according to the customs. 22What then? The assembly must certainly meet, for they will[s] hear that you have come. 23Therefore do what we tell you: We have four men who have taken a vow. 24Take them and be purified with them, and pay their expenses so that they may shave *their* heads, and that all may know that those things of which they were informed concerning you are nothing, but *that* you yourself also walk orderly and keep the law. 25But concerning the Gentiles who believe, we have written *and* decided that they should observe no such thing,[t] except that they should keep themselves from *things* offered to idols, from blood, from things strangled, and from sexual immorality."

26Then Paul took the men, and the next day, having been purified with them, entered the temple to announce the expiration of the days of purification, at which time an offering should be made for each one of them.

27*Now when the seven days were almost ended, the Jews from Asia, seeing him in the temple, stirred up the whole crowd and laid hands on him, 28crying out, "Men of Israel, help! This is the man who teaches all *men* everywhere against the people, the law, and this place; and furthermore he also brought Greeks into the temple and has defiled this holy place." 29(For they had previously[u] seen Trophimus the Ephesian with him in the city, whom they supposed that Paul had brought into the temple.)

30And all the city was disturbed; and the people ran together, seized Paul, and dragged him out of the temple; and immediately the doors were shut. 31Now as they were seeking to kill him, news came to the commander of the garrison that all Jerusalem was in an uproar. 32He immediately took soldiers and centurions, and ran down to them. And when they saw the commander and the soldiers, they stopped beating Paul. 33Then the commander came near and took him, and commanded *him* to be bound with two chains; and he asked who he was and what he had done. 34And some among the multitude cried one thing and some another.

So when he could not ascertain the truth because of the tumult, he commanded him to be taken into the barracks. 35When he reached the stairs, he had to be carried by the soldiers because

21:18–26 *The peacemaker.* Paul moved from "the will of the Lord be done" (v. 14) to "do what we tell you" (v. 23). So anxious was Paul to bring unity to the Jews and Gentiles in the church that he agreed to the plan. Was he following "wisdom from above" or "earthly wisdom" (James 3:13–18)? Not every decision we make turns out to bring peace.

21:27–36 *The prisoner.* The plan almost worked; on the last day, however, trouble started (v. 27). Of course, their charges were absurd; yet the mob lives on "suppose" and not fact. Paul had been careful not to cause any unrest in the city (24:10–13), but his efforts had been in vain. He would spend the next five years as a prisoner of Rome.

Sometimes our plans and good intentions seem to bring only trouble. But God is still in control! He used Paul's trials to accomplish His purposes so that His servant got to Rome (23:11). He can do the same for His people today. Walk by faith!

21:22 [s]NU-Text reads *What then is to be done? They will certainly.* 21:25 [t]NU-Text omits *that they should observe no such thing, except.* 21:29 [u]M-Text omits *previously.*

of the violence of the mob. 36For the multitude of the people followed after, crying out, "Away with him!"

37Then as Paul was about to be led into the barracks, he said to the commander, "May I speak to you?"

He replied, "Can you speak Greek? 38Are you not the Egyptian who some time ago stirred up a rebellion and led the four thousand assassins out into the wilderness?"

39But Paul said, "I am a Jew from Tarsus, in Cilicia, a citizen of no mean city; and I implore you, permit me to speak to the people."

40So when he had given him permission, Paul stood on the stairs and motioned with his hand to the people. And when there was a great silence, he spoke to *them* in the Hebrew language, saying,

CHAPTER 22

22:1–16 The *starting point* of Paul's defense was his identification with the Jews (vv. 1–16; 1 Cor. 9:19–23). His birth, training, and early ministry as a rabbi were strictly orthodox. He associated his conversion with Ananias, "a devout man according to the law" (v. 12). He was very tactful, but it takes tact to have contact.

❝*God is the master of the scenes; we must not choose what part we shall act; it concerns us only to be careful that we do it well, always saying, 'If this please God, let it be as it is.'*❞

—Jeremy Taylor

22 "Brethren* and fathers, hear my defense before you now." 2And when they heard that he spoke to them in the Hebrew language, they kept all the more silent.

Then he said: 3"I am indeed a Jew, born in Tarsus of Cilicia, but brought up in this city at the feet of Gamaliel, taught according to the strictness of our fathers' law, and was zealous toward God as you all are today. 4I persecuted this Way to the death, binding and delivering into prisons both men and women, 5as also the high priest bears me witness, and all the council of the elders, from whom I also received letters to the brethren, and went to Damascus to bring in chains even those who were there to Jerusalem to be punished.

6"Now it happened, as I journeyed and came near Damascus at about noon, suddenly a great light from heaven shone around me. 7And I fell to the ground and heard a voice saying to me, 'Saul, Saul, why are you persecuting Me?' 8So I answered, 'Who are You, Lord?' And He said to me, 'I am Jesus of Nazareth, whom you are persecuting.'

9"And those who were with me indeed saw the light and were afraid,ᵛ but they did not hear the voice of Him who spoke to me. 10So I said, 'What shall I do, Lord?' And the Lord said to me, 'Arise and go into Damascus, and there you will be told all things which are appointed for you to do.' 11And since I could not see for the glory of that light, being led by the hand of those who were with me, I came into Damascus.

12"Then a certain Ananias, a devout man according to the law, having a good testimony with all the Jews who dwelt *there*, 13came to me; and he stood and said to me, 'Brother Saul, receive your sight.' And at that same hour I looked up at him. 14Then he said, 'The God of our fathers has chosen you that you should know His will, and see the Just One, and hear the voice of His mouth. 15For you will be His witness to all men of what you have seen and heard. 16And now why are you waiting? Arise and be baptized, and wash away your sins, calling on the name of the Lord.'

17"Now it happened, when I returned to Jerusalem and was praying in the temple, that I was in

---

22:9 ᵛNU-Text omits *and were afraid.*

Don't Delay—Actually, Felix was the prisoner, and Paul was the prosecutor. Felix knew he was guilty; but instead of accepting Christ, he delayed. The convenient time to be saved is *now* (2 Cor. 6:1–2; see also Isa. 55:6–7).

a trance [18]and saw Him saying to me, 'Make haste and get out of Jerusalem quickly, for they will not receive your testimony concerning Me.' [19]So I said, 'Lord, they know that in every synagogue I imprisoned and beat those who believe on You. [20]And when the blood of Your martyr Stephen was shed, I also was standing by consenting to his death,[w] and guarding the clothes of those who were killing him.' [21]*Then He said to me, 'Depart, for I will send you far from here to the Gentiles.' "

[22]And they listened to him until this word, and then they raised their voices and said, "Away with such a fellow from the earth, for he is not fit to live!" [23]*Then, as they cried out and tore off their clothes and threw dust into the air, [24]the commander ordered him to be brought into the barracks, and said that he should be examined under scourging, so that he might know why they shouted so against him. [25]And as they bound him with thongs, Paul said to the centurion who stood by, "Is it lawful for you to scourge a man who is a Roman, and uncondemned?"

[26]When the centurion heard that, he went and told the commander, saying, "Take care what you do, for this man is a Roman."

[27]Then the commander came and said to him, "Tell me, are you a Roman?"

He said, "Yes."

[28]The commander answered, "With a large sum I obtained this citizenship."

And Paul said, "But I was born a citizen."

[29]Then immediately those who were about to examine him withdrew from him; and the commander was also afraid after he found out that he was a Roman, and because he had bound him.

[30]The next day, because he wanted to know for certain why he was accused by the Jews, he released him from his bonds, and commanded the chief priests and all their council to appear, and brought Paul down and set him before them.

23 Then* Paul, looking earnestly at the council, said, "Men and brethren, I have lived in all good conscience before God until this day." [2]And the high priest Ananias commanded those who stood by him to strike him on the mouth. [3]Then Paul said to him, "God will strike you, you whitewashed wall! For you sit to judge me according to the law, and do you command me to be struck contrary to the law?"

[4]And those who stood by said, "Do you revile God's high priest?"

[5]Then Paul said, "I did not know, brethren, that he was the high priest; for it is written, 'You shall not speak evil of a ruler of your people.' "[x]

[6]*But when Paul perceived that one part were Sadducees and the other Pharisees, he cried out in the council, "Men and brethren, I am a Pharisee, the son of a Pharisee; concerning the hope and resurrection of the dead I am being judged!"

[7]And when he had said this, a dissension arose between the Pharisees and the Sadducees; and the assembly was divided. [8]For Sadducees say that there is no resurrection—and no angel or spirit; but the Pharisees confess both. [9]Then there arose a loud outcry. And the scribes of the Pharisees' party arose and protested, saying, "We find

22:21 The turning point of Paul's defense was his use of the word Gentiles (v. 17). Had he not used that word, Paul might have been set free; but the whole burden of his life was to reach the Gentiles (Eph. 3:1–13). Paul was arrested because of religious bigotry; his people did not realize that God was doing a new thing in the world.

22:23–29 The finishing point was the threat of a scourging, which Paul avoided by asserting his Roman citizenship (vv. 22–29). From then on, it would be one hearing after another and a delay of two years in Caesarea. But God was working out His will in His time, and Paul was willing to wait.

CHAPTER 23

23:1–5 Paul was in danger. If the Romans did not imprison him, the Jews would kill him (22:22). What means did God use to help Paul?

Integrity. Paul had nothing to hide, and his conscience was clear. Ananias was out of line when he had Paul slapped; but Paul showed respect for the office, not the man.

23:6–10 Strategy. This did not set Paul free, but it did divide the enemy camp and get the Romans to protect their prisoner better.

22:20 ʷNU-Text omits to his death.   23:5 ˣExodus 22:28

23:11 Advocacy. Paul had the best lawyer available! Christ had assured him when he was in Corinth (18:9–11), and He would assure him again (27:21–25; 2 Tim. 4:16–18). Paul knew that "if God is for us, who can be against us?" (Rom. 8:31).

23:12–22 Opportunity. Paul's nephew lived in the city, and by the providence of God, he discovered the Jewish plot. Only the Lord could have worked that out. We never know what friend or relative God will use to help us.

23:23–35 Authority. Paul had the protection of 472 Roman soldiers, and the whole authority of the government was behind him. The Romans did not give Paul a fair hearing, but God still used them to protect Paul and get him to Rome.

no evil in this man; but if a spirit or an angel has spoken to him, let us not fight against God." [y]

10Now when there arose a great dissension, the commander, fearing lest Paul might be pulled to pieces by them, commanded the soldiers to go down and take him by force from among them, and bring *him* into the barracks.

11*But the following night the Lord stood by him and said, "Be of good cheer, Paul; for as you have testified for Me in Jerusalem, so you must also bear witness at Rome."

12*And when it was day, some of the Jews banded together and bound themselves under an oath, saying that they would neither eat nor drink till they had killed Paul. 13Now there were more than forty who had formed this conspiracy. 14They came to the chief priests and elders, and said, "We have bound ourselves under a great oath that we will eat nothing until we have killed Paul. 15Now you, therefore, together with the council, suggest to the commander that he be brought down to you tomorrow,[z] as though you were going to make further inquiries concerning him; but we are ready to kill him before he comes near."

16So when Paul's sister's son heard of their ambush, he went and entered the barracks and told Paul. 17Then Paul called one of the centurions to *him* and said, "Take this young man to the commander, for he has something to tell him." 18So he took him and brought *him* to the commander and said, "Paul the prisoner called me to *him* and asked *me* to bring this young man to you. He has something to say to you."

19Then the commander took him by the hand, went aside, and asked privately, "What is it that you have to tell me?"

20And he said, "The Jews have agreed to ask that you bring Paul down to the council tomorrow, as though they were going to inquire more fully about him. 21But do not yield to them, for more than forty of them lie in wait for him, men who have bound themselves by an oath that they will neither eat nor drink till they have killed him; and now they are ready, waiting for the promise from you."

22So the commander let the young man depart, and commanded *him,* "Tell no one that you have revealed these things to me."

23*And he called for two centurions, saying, "Prepare two hundred soldiers, seventy horsemen, and two hundred spearmen to go to Caesarea at the third hour of the night; 24and provide mounts to set Paul on, and bring *him* safely to Felix the governor." 25He wrote a letter in the following manner:

26   Claudius Lysias,

      To the most excellent governor Felix:

      Greetings.

27   This man was seized by the Jews and was about to be killed by them. Coming with the troops I rescued him, having learned that

---

23:9 [y]NU-Text omits last clause and reads *what if a spirit or an angel has spoken to him?*   23:15 [z]NU-Text omits *tomorrow.*

he was a Roman. 28And when I wanted to know the reason they accused him, I brought him before their council. 29I found out that he was accused concerning questions of their law, but had nothing charged against him deserving of death or chains. 30And when it was told me that the Jews lay in wait for the man,*a* I sent him immediately to you, and also commanded his accusers to state before you the charges against him.

Farewell.

31Then the soldiers, as they were commanded, took Paul and brought *him* by night to Antipatris. 32The next day they left the horsemen to go on with him, and returned to the barracks. 33When they came to Caesarea and had delivered the letter to the governor, they also presented Paul to him. 34And when the governor had read *it*, he asked what province he was from. And when he understood that *he was* from Cilicia, 35he said, "I will hear you when your accusers also have come." And he commanded him to be kept in Herod's Praetorium.

24 Now after five days Ananias the high priest came down with the elders and a certain orator *named* Tertullus. These gave evidence to the governor against Paul. 2*And when he was called upon, Tertullus began his accusation, saying: "Seeing that through you we enjoy great peace, and prosperity is being brought to this nation by your foresight, 3we accept *it* always and in all places, most noble Felix, with all thankfulness. 4Nevertheless, not to be tedious to you any further, I beg you to hear, by your courtesy, a few words from us. 5*For we have found this man a plague, a creator of dissension among all the Jews throughout the world, and a ringleader of the sect of the Nazarenes. 6He even tried to profane the temple, and we seized him,*b* and wanted to judge him according to our law. 7But the commander Lysias came by and with great violence took *him* out of our hands, 8commanding his accusers to come to you. By examining him yourself you may ascertain all these things of which we accuse him." 9And the Jews also assented,*c* maintaining that these things were so.

10*Then Paul, after the governor had nodded to him to speak, answered: "Inasmuch as I know that you have been for many years a judge of this nation, I do the more cheerfully answer for myself, 11because you may ascertain that it is no more than twelve days since I went up to Jerusalem to worship. 12And they neither found me in the temple disputing with anyone nor inciting the crowd, either in the synagogues or in the city. 13Nor can they prove the things of which they now accuse me. 14But this I confess to you, that according to the Way which they call a sect, so I worship the God of my fathers, believing all things which are written in the Law and in the

CHAPTER 24

24:2–4 How do the unsaved go about opposing the Lord's servants and their work?

Tertullus started with *flattery,* knowing that many people in high places are susceptible to it (12:20–24). Flattery appeals to our pride. If we did not flatter ourselves, others could not successfully flatter us. We really *want* to believe what they say!

24:5–8 Then Tertullus used *slander.* Napoleon said, "He who knows how to flatter also knows how to slander." As his last weapon, the lawyer called on *false witnesses* (v. 9) who together supported Tertullus's lies about Paul.

24:10–27 Paul's defense was threefold: his life, his faith and his service to his nation. Although his enemies could not prove their accusations, Paul did not go free. *The safest place for Paul was in that prison,* for God had work for him to do in Rome.

You may not understand why God permits lies to triumph, but leave it all in His hands. He is in control, and the final judgment rests with Him.

23:30 *a*NU-Text reads *there would be a plot against the man.*
24:6 *b*NU-Text ends the sentence here and omits the rest of verse 6, all of verse 7, and the first clause of verse 8.
24:9 *c*NU-Text and M-Text read *joined the attack.*

Prophets. 15I have hope in God, which they themselves also accept, that there will be a resurrection of *the* dead,[d] both of *the* just and *the* unjust. 16This *being* so, I myself always strive to have a conscience without offense toward God and men.

17"Now after many years I came to bring alms and offerings to my nation, 18in the midst of which some Jews from Asia found me purified in the temple, neither with a mob nor with tumult. 19They ought to have been here before you to object if they had anything against me. 20Or else let those who are *here* themselves say if they found any wrongdoing[e] in me while I stood before the council, 21unless *it is* for this one statement which I cried out, standing among them, 'Concerning the resurrection of the dead I am being judged by you this day.' "

22But when Felix heard these things, having more accurate knowledge of *the* Way, he adjourned the proceedings and said, "When Lysias the commander comes down, I will make a decision on your case." 23So he commanded the centurion to keep Paul and to let *him* have liberty, and told him not to forbid any of his friends to provide for or visit him.

24And after some days, when Felix came with his wife Drusilla, who was Jewish, he sent for Paul and heard him concerning the faith in Christ. 25Now as he reasoned about righteousness, self-control, and the judgment to come, Felix was afraid and answered, "Go away for now; when I have a convenient time I will call for you." 26Meanwhile he also hoped that money would be given him by Paul, that he might release him.[f] Therefore he sent for him more often and conversed with him.

27But after two years Porcius Festus succeeded Felix; and Felix, wanting to do the Jews a favor, left Paul bound.

CHAPTER 25

25:1ff Festus tried to use Paul as a political pawn to win favor with the Jews (vv. 3, 9). If he had succeeded and sent Paul to Jerusalem, the apostle would have been killed. Paul did the wise thing: he used his rights as a Roman citizen and appealed to Caesar. There are times when believers must use the law to protect themselves and the ministry.

But now Festus had a problem. How could he send Paul to Caesar when he had no charges against him that could be proved? God's people sometimes are treated like the guilty even though they are innocent. Remember Joseph, David, Daniel, and Jeremiah, not to mention our Lord Jesus Christ.

In all that happened, God was fulfilling His promise to Paul that he would witness before rulers (9:15) and finally get to Rome (23:11). Being a prisoner and enduring the hearings were difficult for Paul, but he used his opportunities wisely. He believed Jesus' words: "But it will turn out for you as an occasion for testimony" (Luke 21:13).

25 Now* when Festus had come to the province, after three days he went up from Caesarea to Jerusalem. 2Then the high priest[g] and the chief men of the Jews informed him against Paul; and they petitioned him, 3asking a favor against him, that he would summon him to Jerusalem—while *they* lay in ambush along the road to kill him. 4But Festus answered that Paul should be kept at Caesarea, and that he himself was going *there* shortly. 5"Therefore," he said, "let those who have authority among you go down with *me* and accuse this man, to see if there is any fault in him."

6And when he had remained among them more than ten days, he went down to Caesarea. And the next day, sitting on the judgment seat, he commanded Paul to be brought. 7When he had come, the Jews who had come down from Jerusalem stood about and laid many serious complaints against Paul, which they could not prove, 8while he answered for himself, "Neither against the law of the Jews, nor against the temple, nor against Caesar have I offended in anything at all."

9But Festus, wanting to do the Jews a favor, answered Paul and said, "Are you willing to go

---

24:15 [d]NU-Text omits *of the dead.*   24:20 [e]NU-Text and M-Text read *say what wrongdoing they found.*
24:26 [f]NU-Text omits *that he might release him.*
25:2 [g]NU-Text reads *chief priests.*

up to Jerusalem and there be judged before me concerning these things?"

10So Paul said, "I stand at Caesar's judgment seat, where I ought to be judged. To the Jews I have done no wrong, as you very well know. 11For if I am an offender, or have committed anything deserving of death, I do not object to dying; but if there is nothing in these things of which these men accuse me, no one can deliver me to them. I appeal to Caesar."

12Then Festus, when he had conferred with the council, answered, "You have appealed to Caesar? To Caesar you shall go!"

13And after some days King Agrippa and Bernice came to Caesarea to greet Festus. 14When they had been there many days, Festus laid Paul's case before the king, saying: "There is a certain man left a prisoner by Felix, 15about whom the chief priests and the elders of the Jews informed me, when I was in Jerusalem, asking for a judgment against him. 16To them I answered, 'It is not the custom of the Romans to deliver any man to destruction*h* before the accused meets the accusers face to face, and has opportunity to answer for himself concerning the charge against him.' 17Therefore when they had come together, without any delay, the next day I sat on the judgment seat and commanded the man to be brought in. 18When the accusers stood up, they brought no accusation against him of such things as I supposed, 19but had some questions against him about their own religion and about a certain Jesus, who had died, whom Paul affirmed to be alive. 20And because I was uncertain of such questions, I asked whether he was willing to go to Jerusalem and there be judged concerning these matters. 21But when Paul appealed to be reserved for the decision of Augustus, I commanded him to be kept till I could send him to Caesar."

22Then Agrippa said to Festus, "I also would like to hear the man myself."

"Tomorrow," he said, "you shall hear him."

23So the next day, when Agrippa and Bernice had come with great pomp, and had entered the auditorium with the commanders and the prominent men of the city, at Festus' command Paul was brought in. 24And Festus said: "King Agrippa and all the men who are here present with us, you see this man about whom the whole assembly of the Jews petitioned me, both at Jerusalem and here, crying out that he was not fit to live any longer. 25But when I found that he had committed nothing deserving of death, and that he himself had appealed to Augustus, I decided to send him. 26I have nothing certain to write to my lord concerning him. Therefore I have brought him out before you, and especially before you, King Agrippa, so that after the examination has taken place I may have something to write. 27For it seems to me unreasonable to send a prisoner and not to specify the charges against him."

26

Then Agrippa said to Paul, "You are permitted to speak for yourself."

So Paul stretched out his hand and answered for himself: 2"I think myself happy, King Agrippa, because today I shall answer for myself before you concerning all the things of which I am

Almost persuaded to be a Christian is like the man who was almost pardoned, but he was hanged; like the man who was almost rescued, but he was burned in the house. A man that is almost saved is damned.

—Charles Spurgeon

25:16 *h*NU-Text omits *to destruction*, although it is implied.

CHAPTER 26

26:6–16 Paul saw the light. Instead of defending himself, Paul used the opportunity to present the gospel to King Agrippa and others with him (1 Pet. 3:13–17). When Paul met Jesus on the road to Damascus, he made some important and life-changing discoveries: his religion was out-of-date; his zeal for God was only hurting God; Jesus was alive; and Jesus had a job for Paul to do. Talk about a rude awakening!

26:17–23 The Gentiles need the light. Paul's great learning and zeal would be devoted to the spread of the gospel among the Gentiles (vv. 17–18). Lost sinners are in spiritual darkness and only Christ can give them light.

26:24–28 Agrippa rejected the light. He tried to discredit the message by accusing Paul of being mad, and he tried to minimize his own conviction by his nonchalant reply (v. 28). He turned his back on the light; he was "almost" when he might have been "altogether."

accused by the Jews, 3especially because you are expert in all customs and questions which have to do with the Jews. Therefore I beg you to hear me patiently.

4"My manner of life from my youth, which was spent from the beginning among my own nation at Jerusalem, all the Jews know. 5They knew me from the first, if they were willing to testify, that according to the strictest sect of our religion I lived a Pharisee. 6*And now I stand and am judged for the hope of the promise made by God to our fathers. 7To this *promise* our twelve tribes, earnestly serving *God* night and day, hope to attain. For this hope's sake, King Agrippa, I am accused by the Jews. 8Why should it be thought incredible by you that God raises the dead?

9"Indeed, I myself thought I must do many things contrary to the name of Jesus of Nazareth. 10This I also did in Jerusalem, and many of the saints I shut up in prison, having received authority from the chief priests; and when they were put to death, I cast my vote against *them*. 11And I punished them often in every synagogue and compelled *them* to blaspheme; and being exceedingly enraged against them, I persecuted *them* even to foreign cities.

12"While thus occupied, as I journeyed to Damascus with authority and commission from the chief priests, 13at midday, O king, along the road I saw a light from heaven, brighter than the sun, shining around me and those who journeyed with me. 14And when we all had fallen to the ground, I heard a voice speaking to me and saying in the Hebrew language, 'Saul, Saul, why are you persecuting Me? *It is* hard for you to kick against the goads.' 15So I said, 'Who are You, Lord?' And He said, 'I am Jesus, whom you are persecuting. 16But rise and stand on your feet; for I have appeared to you for this purpose, to make you a minister and a witness both of the things which you have seen and of the things which I will yet reveal to you. 17*I will deliver you from the *Jewish* people, as well as *from* the Gentiles, to whom I now[f] send you, 18to open their eyes, *in order to* turn *them* from darkness to light, and *from* the power of Satan to God, that they may receive forgiveness of sins and an inheritance among those who are sanctified by faith in Me.'

19"Therefore, King Agrippa, I was not disobedient to the heavenly vision, 20but declared first to those in Damascus and in Jerusalem, and throughout all the region of Judea, and *then* to the Gentiles, that they should repent, turn to God, and do works befitting repentance. 21For these reasons the Jews seized me in the temple and tried to kill *me*. 22Therefore, having obtained help from God, to this day I stand, witnessing both to small and great, saying no other things than those which the prophets and Moses said would come— 23that the Christ would suffer, that He would be the first to rise from the dead, and would proclaim light to the *Jewish* people and to the Gentiles."

24*Now as he thus made his defense, Festus said with a loud voice, "Paul, you are beside yourself! Much learning is driving you mad!"

25But he said, "I am not mad, most noble Festus, but speak the words of truth and reason. 26For the king, before whom I also speak freely, knows

---

26:17 [f]NU-Text and M-Text omit *now*.

these things; for I am convinced that none of these things escapes his attention, since this thing was not done in a corner. 27King Agrippa, do you believe the prophets? I know that you do believe."

28Then Agrippa said to Paul, "You almost persuade me to become a Christian."

29And Paul said, "I would to God that not only you, but also all who hear me today, might become both almost and altogether such as I am, except for these chains."

30When he had said these things, the king stood up, as well as the governor and Bernice and those who sat with them; 31and when they had gone aside, they talked among themselves, saying, "This man is doing nothing deserving of death or chains."

32Then Agrippa said to Festus, "This man might have been set free if he had not appealed to Caesar."

27 And when it was decided that we should sail to Italy, they delivered Paul and some other prisoners to one named Julius, a centurion of the Augustan Regiment. 2So, entering a ship of Adramyttium, we put to sea, meaning to sail along the coasts of Asia. Aristarchus, a Macedonian of Thessalonica, was with us. 3And the next day we landed at Sidon. And Julius treated Paul kindly and gave him liberty to go to his friends and receive care. 4When we had put to sea from there, we sailed under the shelter of Cyprus, because the winds were contrary. 5And when we had sailed over the sea which is off Cilicia and Pamphylia, we came to Myra, a city of Lycia. 6There the centurion found an Alexandrian ship sailing to Italy, and he put us on board.

7When we had sailed slowly many days, and arrived with difficulty off Cnidus, the wind not permitting us to proceed, we sailed under the shelter of Crete off Salmone. 8Passing it with difficulty, we came to a place called Fair Havens, near the city of Lasea.

9*Now when much time had been spent, and sailing was now dangerous because the Fast was already over, Paul advised them, 10saying, "Men, I perceive that this voyage will end with disaster and much loss, not only of the cargo and ship, but also our lives." 11Nevertheless the centurion was more persuaded by the helmsman and the owner of the ship than by the things spoken by Paul. 12And because the harbor was not suitable to winter in, the majority advised to set sail from there also, if by any means they could reach Phoenix, a harbor of Crete opening toward the southwest and northwest, and winter there.

13When the south wind blew softly, supposing that they had obtained their desire, putting out to sea, they sailed close by Crete. 14But not long after, a tempestuous head wind arose, called Euroclydon.j 15So when the ship was caught, and could not head into the wind, we let her drive. 16And running under the shelter of an island called Clauda,k we secured the skiff with difficulty. 17When they had taken it on board, they used cables to undergird the ship; and fearing lest they should run aground on the Syrtisl Sands, they struck sail and so were driven. 18And because we

CHAPTER 27

27:9–13 *Rejecting Paul's counsel.* What did a Jewish tentmaker know about sailing a ship? So, the advice of the experts (v. 11) and the vote of the majority (v. 12) carried the day. When you are impatient (v. 7) and uncomfortable (v. 12), and when the golden opportunity seems to come along (v. 13), beware! A storm may be brewing!

27:14 jNU-Text reads Euraquilon.   27:16 kNU-Text reads Cauda.   27:17 lM-Text reads Syrtes.

were exceedingly tempest-tossed, the next *day* they lightened the ship. [19]On the third *day* we threw the ship's tackle overboard with our own hands. [20]Now when neither sun nor stars appeared for many days, and no small tempest beat on *us*, all hope that we would be saved was finally given up.

[21]*But after long abstinence from food, then Paul stood in the midst of them and said, "Men, you should have listened to me, and not have sailed from Crete and incurred this disaster and loss. [22]And now I urge you to take heart, for there will be no loss of life among you, but only of the ship. [23]For there stood by me this night an angel of the God to whom I belong and whom I serve, [24]saying, 'Do not be afraid, Paul; you must be brought before Caesar; and indeed God has granted you all those who sail with you.' [25]Therefore take heart, men, for I believe God that it will be just as it was told me. [26]However, we must run aground on a certain island."

[27]Now when the fourteenth night had come, as we were driven up and down in the Adriatic *Sea*, about midnight the sailors sensed that they were drawing near some land. [28]And they took soundings and found *it* to be twenty fathoms; and when they had gone a little farther, they took soundings again and found *it* to be fifteen fathoms. [29]Then, fearing lest we should run aground on the rocks, they dropped four anchors from the stern, and prayed for day to come. [30]And as the sailors were seeking to escape from the ship, when they had let down the skiff into the sea, under pretense of putting out anchors from the prow, [31]Paul said to the centurion and the soldiers, "Unless these men stay in the ship, you cannot be saved." [32]Then the soldiers cut away the ropes of the skiff and let it fall off.

[33]And as day was about to dawn, Paul implored *them* all to take food, saying, "Today is the fourteenth day you have waited and continued without food, and eaten nothing. [34]Therefore I urge you to take nourishment, for this is for your survival, since not a hair will fall from the head of any of you." [35]*And when he had said these things, he took bread and gave thanks to God in the presence of them all; and when he had broken *it* he began to eat. [36]Then they were all encouraged, and also took food themselves. [37]And in all we were two hundred and seventy-six persons on the ship. [38]So when they had eaten enough, they lightened the ship and threw out the wheat into the sea.

[39]When it was day, they did not recognize the land; but they observed a bay with a beach, onto which they planned to run the ship if possible. [40]And they let go the anchors and left *them* in the sea, meanwhile loosing the rudder ropes; and they hoisted the mainsail to the wind and made for shore. [41]But striking a place where two seas met, they ran the ship aground; and the prow stuck fast and remained immovable, but the stern was being broken up by the violence of the waves.

[42]And the soldiers' plan was to kill the prisoners, lest any of them should swim away and escape. [43]But the centurion, wanting to save Paul, kept them from *their* purpose, and commanded that those who could swim should jump *overboard* first and get to land, [44]and the rest, some on boards and some on *parts* of the ship. And so it was that they all escaped safely to land.

27:21–26, 33, 34 *Hearing Paul's encouragement.* Paul was right to say, "I told you so!" But he followed it with a word of promise from the Lord and a word of encouragement from his believing heart. At a time like that, people needed promises, not preaching.

27:35–37 *Following Paul's example.* Paul publicly gave thanks and directed their hearts to God, which encouraged everybody. The weary passengers needed strength for what lay ahead, and that meant taking time to eat. Paul was practical as well as perceptive.

Although Paul started the voyage as a prisoner and passenger, he ended it as the captain of the ship. The ship was lost; but by the grace of God, Paul's presence saved all the passengers. Can the Lord depend on you to sail by faith when you face the storms? Can others depend on you?

28

Now* when they had escaped, they then found out that the island was called Malta. ²And the natives showed us unusual kindness; for they kindled a fire and made us all welcome, because of the rain that was falling and because of the cold. ³*But when Paul had gathered a bundle of sticks and laid *them* on the fire, a viper came out because of the heat, and fastened on his hand. ⁴So when the natives saw the creature hanging from his hand, they said to one another, "No doubt this man is a murderer, whom, though he has escaped the sea, yet justice does not allow to live." ⁵But he shook off the creature into the fire and suffered no harm. ⁶However, they were expecting that he would swell up or suddenly fall down dead. But after they had looked for a long time and saw no harm come to him, they changed their minds and said that he was a god.

⁷In that region there was an estate of the leading citizen of the island, whose name was Publius, who received us and entertained us courteously for three days. ⁸And it happened that the father of Publius lay sick of a fever and dysentery. Paul went in to him and prayed, and he laid his hands on him and healed him. ⁹So when this was done, the rest of those on the island who had diseases also came and were healed. ¹⁰They also honored us in many ways; and when we departed, they provided such things as were necessary.

¹¹After three months we sailed in an Alexandrian ship whose figurehead was the Twin Brothers, which had wintered at the island. ¹²And landing at Syracuse, we stayed three days. ¹³From there we circled round and reached Rhegium. And after one day the south wind blew; and the next day we came to Puteoli, ¹⁴where we found brethren, and were invited to stay with them seven days. And so we went toward Rome. ¹⁵*And from there, when the brethren heard about us, they came to meet us as far as Appii Forum and Three Inns. When Paul saw them, he thanked God and took courage.

¹⁶Now when we came to Rome, the centurion delivered the prisoners to the captain of the guard; but Paul was permitted to dwell by himself with the soldier who guarded him.

¹⁷*And it came to pass after three days that Paul called the leaders of the Jews together. So when they had come together, he said to them: "Men *and* brethren, though I have done nothing against our people or the customs of our fathers, yet I was delivered as a prisoner from Jerusalem into the hands of the Romans, ¹⁸who, when they had examined me, wanted to let *me* go, because there was no cause for putting me to death. ¹⁹But when the Jews^m spoke against *it*, I was compelled to appeal to Caesar, not that I had anything of which to accuse my nation. ²⁰For this reason therefore I have called for you, to see *you* and speak with *you*, because for the hope of Israel I am bound with this chain."

²¹Then they said to him, "We neither received letters from Judea concerning you, nor have any

---

28:19 ᵐThat is, the ruling authorities

CHAPTER 28

28:1, 2, 7–10 Does anything in this chapter surprise you?

That the natives were kind? The natives may have been superstitious, but even unsaved people can show concern for those in need. The pagan sailors worked hard to save Jonah before they threw him into the sea (Jon. 1:11–16).

28:3 *That Paul picked up sticks?* If you had saved 276 people from drowning, would you feel it necessary to do menial labor like picking up sticks? Certainly the grateful passengers would have relieved Paul of the task! But Paul was a servant, and he did the job that needed to be done (Phil. 2:1–11).

That Paul was bitten? Had he not already been through enough suffering? When Satan cannot win as the lion (1 Pet. 5:8), then he comes as the serpent (2 Cor. 11:3). We must constantly be on guard and trust the Lord to care for us (Mark 16:18).

28:15 *That Paul welcomed encouragement?* Even an apostle needs to be encouraged at times, and the saints who met Paul did just that. The group at Appii Forum traveled about ten miles farther than the other group. How far would you go to encourage a fellow believer?

28:17–31 *That the Jewish leaders rejected the Word?* God's chosen people should have known the Scriptures; yet when it was time to decide, the group was divided. But Paul kept witnessing and let God bless the Word as He pleased.

Paul's Last Years—Paul was a prisoner in Rome from 61 to 63, and during that time wrote Ephesians, Philippians, Colossians, and Philemon. From 63 to 65, he was free to minister, and he wrote 1 Timothy and Titus. Paul was imprisoned again in 66, wrote 2 Timothy, and was martyred at Rome in late 66 or early 67.

of the brethren who came reported or spoken any evil of you. 22But we desire to hear from you what you think; for concerning this sect, we know that it is spoken against everywhere."

23So when they had appointed him a day, many came to him at *his* lodging, to whom he explained and solemnly testified of the kingdom of God, persuading them concerning Jesus from both the Law of Moses and the Prophets, from morning till evening. 24And some were persuaded by the things which were spoken, and some disbelieved. 25So when they did not agree among themselves, they departed after Paul had said one word: "The Holy Spirit spoke rightly through Isaiah the prophet to our[n] fathers, 26saying,

'Go to this people and say:
"Hearing you will hear, and shall not
     understand;
And seeing you will see, and not perceive;
27   For the hearts of this people have grown
     dull.
Their ears are hard of hearing,
And their eyes they have closed,
Lest they should see with their eyes and
     hear with their ears,
Lest they should understand with their
     hearts and turn,
So that I should heal them." '[o]

28"Therefore let it be known to you that the salvation of God has been sent to the Gentiles, and they will hear it!" 29And when he had said these words, the Jews departed and had a great dispute among themselves.[p]

30Then Paul dwelt two whole years in his own rented house, and received all who came to him, 31preaching the kingdom of God and teaching the things which concern the Lord Jesus Christ with all confidence, no one forbidding him.

28:25 [n]NU-Text reads *your.*   28:27 [o]Isaiah 6:9, 10
28:29 [p]NU-Text omits this verse.

ROMANS

Paul was on his third missionary journey when he wrote the epistle to the Romans, probably from Corinth. He had long planned to visit the believers in Rome, many of whom he knew (chap. 16), and this letter prepared the way. In the letter, he answers the false accusations made about him (3:8; 6:1) and explains why he had not visited Rome sooner (15:23–29). He also gives the grandest presentation of Christian doctrine found anywhere in Scripture.

Romans is one of three books written to explain Habakkuk 2:4: "The just shall live by his faith" (Rom. 1:17; Gal. 3:11; Heb. 10:38). The basic theme is "the just," what it means to be justified (declared righteous by God) and to live a righteous life. *Righteousness* is used in one form or another over forty times.

The book easily falls into three parts: God's righteousness and salvation (chaps. 1—8), God's righteousness and Israel (chaps. 9—11), and God's righteousness and practical Christian living (chaps. 12—16). Romans 1:16–17 is a key statement.

Romans is a closely knit argument that defends the righteousness of God. You can summarize the argument by noting the verses containing "therefore" (3:20, 28; 5:1; 8:1; 12:1).

Justification is God's gracious act by which He *declares* the believing sinner righteous in Jesus Christ because of the work of Christ on the cross. When you believe, Christ's righteousness is *imputed*, that is, "put to your account." Sanctification is God's work in the believer whereby He *imparts* His righteousness and develops holy character and conduct. A righteous standing before God leads to a holy life before men. We are not saved by works or by faith plus works; we are saved by a faith that works (James 2:14–26).

1 Paul,* a bondservant of Jesus Christ, called to be an apostle, separated to the gospel of God 2which He promised before through His prophets in the Holy Scriptures, 3concerning His Son Jesus Christ our Lord, who was born of the seed of David according to the flesh, 4and declared to be the Son of God with power according to the Spirit of holiness, by the resurrection from the dead. 5Through Him we have received grace and apostleship for obedience to the faith among all nations for His name, 6among whom you also are the called of Jesus Christ;

7To all who are in Rome, beloved of God, called to be saints:

Grace to you and peace from God our Father and the Lord Jesus Christ.

8First, I thank my God through Jesus Christ for you all, that your faith is spoken of throughout the whole world. 9For God is my witness, whom I serve with my spirit in the gospel of His Son, that without ceasing I make mention of you always in my prayers, 10making request if, by some means, now at last I may find a way in the will of God to come to you. 11For I long to see you, that I may impart to you some spiritual gift, so that you may be established— 12that is, that I may be encouraged together with you by the mutual faith both of you and me.

CHAPTER 1

1:1–17 The gospel of God. God has good news! It is *promised* in the Old Testament and centered in Jesus Christ. He came to earth a Jew, died, and arose again; and He saves all who will trust in Him. He alone *purchased* salvation, and this message must be *preached* to the whole world. Why? Because the gospel alone is "the *power* of God to salvation" (v. 16, italics added).

Paul was gripped by the gospel; his whole life was controlled by it. Called to be an apostle (v. 1), he felt himself a debtor to the whole world (v. 14). Through His church, God is calling people to Jesus Christ (vv. 5–7). Has the gospel gripped you?

❝*Religions are man's search for God; the Gospel is God's search for man. There are many religions, but one Gospel.*❞

—E. Stanley Jones

Spiritual Debts—God's people are free from the debt of sin, but they are debtors to witness to a lost world (Rom. 1:14), obey the Holy Spirit (8:13), love all people (13:8), encourage their weaker brothers and sisters (15:1), and help the people of Israel (15:25–27). Are you paying your spiritual debts?

13Now I do not want you to be unaware, brethren, that I often planned to come to you (but was hindered until now), that I might have some fruit among you also, just as among the other Gentiles. 14I am a debtor both to Greeks and to barbarians, both to wise and to unwise. 15So, as much as is in me, *I am* ready to preach the gospel to you who are in Rome also.

16For I am not ashamed of the gospel of Christ,[a] for it is the power of God to salvation for everyone who believes, for the Jew first and also for the Greek. 17For in it the righteousness of God is revealed from faith to faith; as it is written, *"The just shall live by faith."*[b]

18*For the wrath of God is revealed from heaven against all ungodliness and unrighteousness of men, who suppress the truth in unrighteousness, 19because what may be known of God is manifest in them, for God has shown *it* to them. 20For since the creation of the world His invisible *attributes* are clearly seen, being understood by the things that are made, *even* His eternal power and Godhead, so that they are without excuse, 21because, although they knew God, they did not glorify *Him* as God, nor were thankful, but became futile in their thoughts, and their foolish hearts were darkened. 22Professing to be wise, they became fools, 23and changed the glory of the incorruptible God into an image made like corruptible man—and birds and four-footed animals and creeping things.

24Therefore God also gave them up to uncleanness, in the lusts of their hearts, to dishonor their bodies among themselves, 25who exchanged the truth of God for the lie, and worshiped and served the creature rather than the Creator, who is blessed forever. Amen.

26For this reason God gave them up to vile passions. For even their women exchanged the natural use for what is against nature. 27Likewise also the men, leaving the natural use of the woman, burned in their lust for one another, men with men committing what is shameful, and receiving in themselves the penalty of their error which was due.

28And even as they did not like to retain God in *their* knowledge, God gave them over to a debased mind, to do those things which are not fitting; 29being filled with all unrighteousness, sexual immorality,[c] wickedness, covetousness, maliciousness; full of envy, murder, strife, deceit, evil-mindedness; *they are* whisperers, 30backbiters, haters of God, violent, proud, boasters, inventors of evil things, disobedient to parents, 31undiscerning, untrustworthy, unloving, unforgiving,[d] unmerciful; 32who, knowing the righteous judgment of God, that those who practice such things are deserving of death, not only do the same but also approve of those who practice them.

CHAPTER 2

2 Therefore* you are inexcusable, O man, whoever you are who judge, for in whatever you judge another you condemn yourself; for you who judge practice the same things. 2But we know that the judgment of God is according to truth against

---

1:18–32 The wrath of God. Paul's main theme is the righteousness of God, but he presents it against the dark background of the judgment of God, *which is going on right now.* Men know God from creation and conscience (vv. 19–20) but refuse to honor Him as God. They live for the creature, not the Creator, and make themselves into gods (v. 25; Gen. 3:4–5). So, God gave them up (vv. 24, 26, 28) and let them suffer the consequences. *The greatest judgment God can inflict on us is to let us have our own way.*

But the same God who delivered up sinners to judgment *delivered up His own Son for lost sinners* (8:32)! That is the gospel. Do you believe it? Are you sharing it?

❝*How rarely we weigh our neighbor in the same balance in which we weigh ourselves.*❞
—Thomas à Kempis

2:1–3 If you know Jesus Christ as your Savior, your sins have already been judged on the cross (John 5:24; Rom. 8:1). But are you ready for the judgment seat of Christ where your works will be judged (Rom. 14:10–12; 2 Cor. 5:10)? Ask yourself the following questions.
Do I judge myself or others? How easy it is to cover up my own failures by criticizing others (Matt. 7:1–5)!

1:16 [a]NU-Text omits *of Christ.*   1:17 [b]Habakkuk 2:4
1:29 [c]NU-Text omits *sexual immorality.*   1:31 [d]NU-Text omits *unforgiving.*

those who practice such things. 3And do you think this, O man, you who judge those practicing such things, and doing the same, that you will escape the judgment of God? 4*Or do you despise the riches of His goodness, forbearance, and longsuffering, not knowing that the goodness of God leads you to repentance? 5*But in accordance with your hardness and your impenitent heart you are treasuring up for yourself wrath in the day of wrath and revelation of the righteous judgment of God, 6who *"will render to each one according to his deeds":e* 7eternal life to those who by patient continuance in doing good seek for glory, honor, and immortality; 8but to those who are selfseeking and do not obey the truth, but obey unrighteousness—indignation and wrath, 9tribulation and anguish, on every soul of man who does evil, of the Jew first and also of the Greek; 10but glory, honor, and peace to everyone who works what is good, to the Jew first and also to the Greek. 11For there is no partiality with God.

12*For as many as have sinned without law will also perish without law, and as many as have sinned in the law will be judged by the law 13(for not the hearers of the law *are* just in the sight of God, but the doers of the law will be justified; 14for when Gentiles, who do not have the law, by nature do the things in the law, these, although not having the law, are a law to themselves, 15who show the work of the law written in their hearts, their conscience also bearing witness, and between themselves *their* thoughts accusing or else excusing *them*) 16in the day when God will judge the secrets of men by Jesus Christ, according to my gospel.

17*Indeedf you are called a Jew, and rest on the law, and make your boast in God, 18and know *His* will, and approve the things that are excellent, being instructed out of the law, 19and are confident that you yourself are a guide to the blind, a light to those who are in darkness, 20an instructor of the foolish, a teacher of babes, having the form of knowledge and truth in the law. 21You, therefore, who teach another, do you not teach yourself? You who preach that a man should not steal, do you steal? 22You who say, "Do not commit adultery," do you commit adultery? You who abhor idols, do you rob temples? 23You who make your boast in the law, do you dishonor God through breaking the law? 24For *"the name of God is blasphemed among the Gentiles because of you,"g* as it is written.

25For circumcision is indeed profitable if you keep the law; but if you are a breaker of the law, your circumcision has become uncircumcision. 26Therefore, if an uncircumcised man keeps the righteous requirements of the law, will not his uncircumcision be counted as circumcision? 27And will not the physically uncircumcised, if he fulfills the law, judge you who, *even with your* written *code* and circumcision, *are* a transgressor of the law? 28For he is not a Jew who *is one* outwardly, nor *is* circumcision that which *is* outward in the flesh; 29but *he is* a Jew who *is one* inwardly; and circumcision *is that* of the heart, in the Spirit, not in the letter; whose praise *is* not from men but from God.

2:4 *Am I grateful for God's goodness?* It is not the badness of man but the goodness of God that brings us to repentance (Luke 15:17–19). Do I take God's many blessings for granted?

2:5–11 *Is my faith proved by works?* Paul was not teaching salvation by works but works that prove salvation. Do I obey God's truth and persist in holy living? Do I have a hard heart or a tender heart?

2:12–16, 25–29 *Am I hiding behind religion?* The Jews boasted of their law, but it could not save them. External rituals do not guarantee internal changes. God searches the heart. What does He see in my heart?

2:17–24 *Do I practice what I profess?* Do I tell others what is right but then do what is wrong? Do I expect more of others than I do of myself?

God judges honestly (v. 2) and without partiality (v. 11), and no secret is hidden from Him (v. 16). Are you prepared?

2:6 ePsalm 62:12; Proverbs 24:12   2:17 fNU-Text reads *But if.*   2:24 gIsaiah 52:5; Ezekiel 36:22

3 What advantage then has the Jew, or what *is* the profit of circumcision? [2]Much in every way! Chiefly because to them were committed the oracles of God. [3]For what if some did not believe? Will their unbelief make the faithfulness of God without effect? [4]Certainly not! Indeed, let God be true but every man a liar. As it is written:

> "That You may be justified in Your words,
> And may overcome when You are judged."[h]

[5]But if our unrighteousness demonstrates the righteousness of God, what shall we say? *Is* God unjust who inflicts wrath? (I speak as a man.) [6]Certainly not! For then how will God judge the world?

[7]For if the truth of God has increased through my lie to His glory, why am I also still judged as a sinner? [8]And *why* not *say,* "Let us do evil that good may come"?—as we are slanderously reported and as some affirm that we say. Their condemnation is just.

[9]*What then? Are we better *than they?* Not at all. For we have previously charged both Jews and Greeks that they are all under sin.

[10]As it is written:

> "There is none righteous, no, not one;
> [11]   There is none who understands;
>   There is none who seeks after God.
> [12]   They have all turned aside;
>   They have together become unprofitable;
>   There is none who does good, no, not one."[i]
> [13] "Their throat is an open tomb;
>   With their tongues they have practiced deceit";[j]
>   "The poison of asps is under their lips";[k]
> [14] "Whose mouth is full of cursing and bitterness."[l]
> [15] "Their feet are swift to shed blood;
> [16]   Destruction and misery are in their ways;
> [17]   And the way of peace they have not known."[m]
> [18] "There is no fear of God before their eyes."[n]

[19]Now we know that whatever the law says, it says to those who are under the law, that every mouth may be stopped, and all the world may become guilty before God. [20]*Therefore by the deeds of the law no flesh will be justified in His sight, for by the law is the knowledge of sin.

[21]*But now the righteousness of God apart from the law is revealed, being witnessed by the Law and the Prophets, [22]even the righteousness of God, through faith in Jesus Christ, to all and on all[o] who believe. For there is no difference; [23]for all have sinned and fall short of the glory of God, [24]being justified freely by His grace through the redemption that is in Christ Jesus, [25]whom God set forth *as* a propitiation by His blood, through faith, to demonstrate His righteousness, because in His forbearance God had passed over the sins that were previously committed, [26]to demonstrate at the present time His righ-

---

CHAPTER 3

3:9–19 Paul, the attorney, summarizes his case.

All are condemned. Both Jews and Gentiles (religious and irreligious) are guilty before God, and one is no better than the other (v. 9). Paul quotes from Psalms and Isaiah to show that, from head to foot, we are all lost sinners. Do you want to argue about this? Then your mouth has not been stopped! God cannot save you until you say, "Guilty!" and shut your mouth.

3:20 *We cannot save ourselves.* The law is a mirror that reveals our sin; only the blood of Christ can wash away our sin. It is good to do good works, but good works are not good enough to save us (Eph. 2:8–9).

3:21–31 *God's salvation is lawful.* But how can a *holy* God forgive *guilty* people? Is that lawful? If our judges did that, society would fall apart. But God the Law Giver and Judge obeyed His own law, died for us, and paid the penalty for our sins. The Judge is now the Savior!

Have you shut your mouth, trusted Jesus Christ, and heard God say, "Not guilty"?

3:4 [h]Psalm 51:4   3:12 [i]Psalms 14:1–3; 53:1–3; Ecclesiastes 7:20   3:13 [j]Psalm 5:9 [k]Psalm 140:3   3:14 [l]Psalm 10:7   3:17 [m]Isaiah 59:7, 8   3:18 [n]Psalm 36:1   3:22 [o]NU-Text omits *and on all.*

teousness, that He might be just and the justifier of the one who has faith in Jesus.

27Where *is* boasting then? It is excluded. By what law? Of works? No, but by the law of faith. 28Therefore we conclude that a man is justified by faith apart from the deeds of the law. 29Or *is* He the God of the Jews only? *Is He* not also the God of the Gentiles? Yes, of the Gentiles also, 30since *there is* one God who will justify the circumcised by faith and the uncircumcised through faith. 31Do we then make void the law through faith? Certainly not! On the contrary, we establish the law.

4 What* then shall we say that Abraham our father has found according to the flesh?P 2For if Abraham was justified by works, he has *something* to boast about, but not before God. 3For what does the Scripture say? *"Abraham believed God, and it was accounted to him for righteousness."q* 4Now to him who works, the wages are not counted as grace but as debt.

5*But to him who does not work but believes on Him who justifies the ungodly, his faith is accounted for righteousness, 6just as David also describes the blessedness of the man to whom God imputes righteousness apart from works:

7   *"Blessed are those whose lawless deeds are forgiven,*
    And whose sins are covered;
8   *Blessed is the man to whom the LORD shall not impute sin."r*

9*Does* this blessedness then *come* upon the circumcised *only,* or upon the uncircumcised also? For we say that faith was accounted to Abraham for righteousness. 10How then was it accounted? While he was circumcised, or uncircumcised? Not while circumcised, but uncircumcised. 11And he received the sign of circumcision, a seal of the righteousness of the faith which *he had while still* uncircumcised, that he might be the father of all those who believe, though they are uncircumcised, that righteousness might be imputed to them also, 12and the father of circumcision to those who not only *are* of the circumcision, but who also walk in the steps of the faith which our father Abraham *had while still* uncircumcised.

13*For the promise that he would be the heir of the world *was* not to Abraham or to his seed through the law, but through the righteousness of faith. 14For if those who are of the law *are* heirs, faith is made void and the promise made of no effect, 15because the law brings about wrath; for where there is no law *there is* no transgression.

16Therefore it *is* of faith that it *might be* according to grace, so that the promise might be sure to all the seed, not only to those who are of the law, but also to those who are of the faith of Abraham, who is the father of us all 17(as it is written,

4:1 POr *Abraham our (fore)father according to the flesh has found?*   4:3 qGenesis 15:6   4:8 rPsalm 32:1, 2

CHAPTER 4
4:1–4, 9–12 *How was Abraham saved?* Not by works, but by faith (Gen. 15:6). Salvation is not like wages that you earn or works that you can boast about. Abraham was not saved by keeping the law because the law had not been given, nor was he saved by obeying a religious ritual. It was all by God's grace!

4:5–8 *How was David saved?* David wrote Psalm 32 after his great sin with Bathsheba (2 Sam. 11). Can God forgive a man who commits adultery, deceit, and murder? Yes! When David repented and turned to God, he was forgiven, even though the Lord allowed David to feel the bitter consequences of his sins (2 Sam. 12). God justifies *the ungodly,* not the righteous (v. 5; Matt. 9:9–13).

4:13–25 *How can you be saved?* Simply by believing God's promise as Abraham did. *Faith* and *promise* go together just as *law* and *works* go together. Abraham is the father of the Jewish nation physically, but he is the "father" of all believers spiritually (v. 16; Matt. 3:7–9). At Calvary, our sins were put on Christ's account; when you trust Christ, God puts Christ's righteousness on your account (2 Cor. 5:21). What can be more blessed than to know that your sins are forgiven?

Our Sins Are Covered—Because he preached salvation by grace alone, Paul was accused of promoting sin (Rom. 3:5–8), but the accusation was false. Persons who experience the grace of God in forgiveness have no desire to sin; and if they do sin, they confess it to the Lord (1 John 1:5—2:1). They are tempted (1 Cor. 10:13), and sometimes they fall; but they do not stay down (Ps. 37:23–24). Read all of Psalm 32 to see what God does for His own.

"I have made you a father of many nations"[s]) in the presence of Him whom he believed—God, who gives life to the dead and calls those things which do not exist as though they did; [18]who, contrary to hope, in hope believed, so that he became the father of many nations, according to what was spoken, "So shall your descendants be."[t] [19]And not being weak in faith, he did not consider his own body, already dead (since he was about a hundred years old), and the deadness of Sarah's womb. [20]He did not waver at the promise of God through unbelief, but was strengthened in faith, giving glory to God, [21]and being fully convinced that what He had promised He was also able to perform. [22]And therefore "it was accounted to him for righteousness."[u]

[23]Now it was not written for his sake alone that it was imputed to him, [24]but also for us. It shall be imputed to us who believe in Him who raised up Jesus our Lord from the dead, [25]who was delivered up because of our offenses, and was raised because of our justification.

CHAPTER 5

5:1–5 In chapter 4, Paul went back to Abraham and David to explain how God declares believing sinners righteous; now he goes all the way back to Adam. Adam's sin passed sin and death on to the whole human race, but Christ's obedience gives righteousness and life to all who trust Him. In our first birth, we became condemned children of Adam; but in our second birth, we are the forgiven children of God. Note the blessings of justification.

Riches. Peace, access into God's grace, joy, hope, love, the Holy Spirit—what riches we have in Christ! And trials work *for* us, not *against* us, and develop Christian character. How rich we are!

5:6–11 Reconciliation. We are at peace with God and need not be afraid. If He did so much for us when we were enemies, think what He will do for us now that we are His children!

5:12–21 Reigning. When we belonged to the old creation under Adam, death and sin reigned; now that we are in Christ in the new creation (2 Cor. 5:17), grace is reigning, *and we are reigning in life* (v. 17). You can live like a king by the grace of God!

5 Therefore,* having been justified by faith, we have[v] peace with God through our Lord Jesus Christ, [2]through whom also we have access by faith into this grace in which we stand, and rejoice in hope of the glory of God. [3]And not only that, but we also glory in tribulations, knowing that tribulation produces perseverance; [4]and perseverance, character; and character, hope. [5]Now hope does not disappoint, because the love of God has been poured out in our hearts by the Holy Spirit who was given to us.

[6]*For when we were still without strength, in due time Christ died for the ungodly. [7]For scarcely for a righteous man will one die; yet perhaps for a good man someone would even dare to die. [8]But God demonstrates His own love toward us, in that while we were still sinners, Christ died for us. [9]Much more then, having now been justified by His blood, we shall be saved from wrath through Him. [10]For if when we were enemies we were reconciled to God through the death of His Son, much more, having been reconciled, we shall be saved by His life. [11]And not only that, but we also rejoice in God through our Lord Jesus Christ, through whom we have now received the reconciliation.

[12]*Therefore, just as through one man sin entered the world, and death through sin, and thus death spread to all men, because all sinned— [13](For until the law sin was in the world, but sin is not imputed when there is no law. [14]Nevertheless death reigned from Adam to Moses, even over those who had not sinned according to the likeness of the transgression of Adam, who is a type of Him who was to come. [15]But the free gift *is* not like the offense. For if by the one man's offense many died, much more the grace of God and the gift by the grace of the one Man, Jesus Christ, abounded to many. [16]And the gift *is* not like *that which came* through the one who sinned. For the judgment *which came* from one *offense resulted* in condemnation, but the free gift *which came* from many offenses *resulted* in justification. [17]For if by the one man's offense death reigned through the one, much more those

4:17 [s]Genesis 17:5   4:18 [t]Genesis 15:5   4:22 [u]Genesis 15:6
5:1 [v]Another ancient reading is, *let us have peace.*

who receive abundance of grace and of the gift of righteousness will reign in life through the One, Jesus Christ.)

18Therefore, as through one man's offense *judgment* came to all men, resulting in condemnation, even so through one Man's righteous act *the free gift* came to all men, resulting in justification of life. 19For as by one man's disobedience many were made sinners, so also by one Man's obedience many will be made righteous.

20Moreover the law entered that the offense might abound. But where sin abounded, grace abounded much more, 21so that as sin reigned in death, even so grace might reign through righteousness to eternal life through Jesus Christ our Lord.

6 What* shall we say then? Shall we continue in sin that grace may abound? 2Certainly not! How shall we who died to sin live any longer in it? 3Or do you not know that as many of us as were baptized into Christ Jesus were baptized into His death? 4Therefore we were buried with Him through baptism into death, that just as Christ was raised from the dead by the glory of the Father, even so we also should walk in newness of life.

5For if we have been united together in the likeness of His death, certainly we also shall be *in the likeness* of *His* resurrection, 6knowing this, that our old man was crucified with *Him*, that the body of sin might be done away with, that we should no longer be slaves of sin. 7For he who has died has been freed from sin. 8Now if we died with Christ, we believe that we shall also live with Him, 9knowing that Christ, having been raised from the dead, dies no more. Death no longer has dominion over Him. 10For *the death* that He died, He died to sin once for all; but *the life* that He lives, He lives to God. 11Likewise you also, reckon yourselves to be dead indeed to sin, but alive to God in Christ Jesus our Lord.

12*Therefore do not let sin reign in your mortal body, that you should obey it in its lusts. 13And do not present your members *as* instruments of unrighteousness to sin, but present yourselves to God as being alive from the dead, and your members *as* instruments of righteousness to God. 14For sin shall not have dominion over you, for you are not under law but under grace.

15What then? Shall we sin because we are not under law but under grace? Certainly not! 16Do you not know that to whom you present yourselves slaves to obey, you are that one's slaves whom you obey, whether of sin *leading* to death, or of obedience *leading* to righteousness? 17But God be thanked that *though* you were slaves of sin, yet you obeyed from the heart that form of doctrine to which you were delivered. 18And having been set free from sin, you became slaves of righteousness. 19I speak in human *terms* because of the weakness of your flesh. For just as you presented your members *as* slaves of uncleanness, and of lawlessness *leading* to *more* lawlessness, so now present your members *as* slaves *of* righteousness for holiness.

20For when you were slaves of sin, you were

CHAPTER 6

6:1–11 Being a Christian is *a matter of life or death.* Persons who do not understand the grace of God argue, "If God is gracious, then we should sin more so we receive more grace." Those who trust Christ are identified with Him by the Spirit in His death, burial, and resurrection, as pictured in baptism. The old life is buried! We can reckon it dead (v. 11) and walk in newness of resurrection life.

6:12–22 Being a Christian is *a matter of bondage or freedom.* Who is your master, Jesus Christ or the old life? You are not under the authority of Moses (v. 15), but that does not mean you have freedom to break God's moral law (8:1–5). Yield yourself to the Lord; He is the most wonderful Master, and the "salary" He pays lasts forever.

"Alive to God"—The most vivid illustration of Romans 6 is Lazarus (John 11). Jesus raised him from the dead and then said, "Loose him, and let him go" (John 11:44). Lazarus left the grave, got rid of the graveclothes, and began a new life (Col. 3:1ff.). God's people are both "dead" and "alive" (v. 11) and by faith must live accordingly.

6:23 Being a Christian is *a matter of rewards or wages.* We quote this verse as we witness to the lost, and rightly so; but Paul wrote it originally to believers. Although God forgives the sins of His children, He may not stop the painful consequences of sin. The pleasures of sin are never compensated for by the wages of sin. Sinning is not worth it!

CHAPTER 7

7:1ff Believers are not under the law, but that does not give them license to become outlaws. They have a new life (6:1–11) and a new Master (6:12–23), and they also have a new love: they are *married to Christ* (vv. 1–6). If a marriage must be based on laws instead of love, it is going to make for an unhappy home.

If the law cannot change us or control us, what good is it? Its purpose is to reveal sin, and it does its job well (v. 7). Paul learned that the law even aroused evil desires in him (v. 8). If something as holy as God's law (v. 12) can arouse sinful desires, what wicked sinners we must be!

Law brings out the worst in us, but love brings out the best in us. The Holy Spirit within us helps us to do what God wants us to do (Rom. 8:1–5) and to be what God wants us to be (Gal. 5:22–23). Keep your love relationship with the Lord alive and exciting, and you will have righteousness instead of wretchedness.

free in regard to righteousness. 21What fruit did you have then in the things of which you are now ashamed? For the end of those things *is* death. 22But now having been set free from sin, and having become slaves of God, you have your fruit to holiness, and the end, everlasting life. 23*For the wages of sin *is* death, but the gift of God *is* eternal life in Christ Jesus our Lord.

7 Or* do you not know, brethren (for I speak to those who know the law), that the law has dominion over a man as long as he lives? 2For the woman who has a husband is bound by the law to *her* husband as long as he lives. But if the husband dies, she is released from the law of *her* husband. 3So then if, while *her* husband lives, she marries another man, she will be called an adulteress; but if her husband dies, she is free from that law, so that she is no adulteress, though she has married another man. 4Therefore, my brethren, you also have become dead to the law through the body of Christ, that you may be married to another—to Him who was raised from the dead, that we should bear fruit to God. 5For when we were in the flesh, the sinful passions which were aroused by the law were at work in our members to bear fruit to death. 6But now we have been delivered from the law, having died to what we were held by, so that we should serve in the newness of the Spirit and not *in* the oldness of the letter.

7What shall we say then? *Is* the law sin? Certainly not! On the contrary, I would not have known sin except through the law. For I would not have known covetousness unless the law had said, *"You shall not covet."*w 8But sin, taking opportunity by the commandment, produced in me all *manner of evil* desire. For apart from the law sin *was* dead. 9I was alive once without the law, but when the commandment came, sin revived and I died. 10And the commandment, which *was* to *bring* life, I found to *bring* death. 11For sin, taking occasion by the commandment, deceived me, and by it killed *me.* 12Therefore the law *is* holy, and the commandment holy and just and good.

13Has then what is good become death to me? Certainly not! But sin, that it might appear sin, was producing death in me through what is good, so that sin through the commandment might become exceedingly sinful. 14For we know that the law is spiritual, but I am carnal, sold under sin. 15For what I am doing, I do not understand. For what I will to do, that I do not practice; but what I hate, that I do. 16If, then, I do what I will not to do, I agree with the law that *it is* good. 17But now, *it is* no longer I who do it, but sin that dwells in me. 18For I know that in me (that is, in my flesh) nothing good dwells; for to will is present with me, but *how* to perform what is good I do not find. 19For the good that I will *to do,* I do not do; but the evil I will not *to do,* that I practice. 20Now if I do what I will not *to do,* it

---

7:7 wExodus 20:17; Deuteronomy 5:21

A Yielded Life—Romans 7:21–25 does not suggest that you live a divided life because that is impossible. You must choose your Master (6:15–23) and be true to your Husband, Jesus Christ (7:1–6). "The mind" refers to the new nature from God and "the body of death" the old nature from Adam. We cannot serve God with an old nature that is sinful (7:18), but the Holy Spirit enables us to do His will as we yield to Him. The human body is not sinful, but human nature is.

is no longer I who do it, but sin that dwells in me. 21I find then a law, that evil is present with me, the one who wills to do good. 22For I delight in the law of God according to the inward man. 23But I see another law in my members, warring against the law of my mind, and bringing me into captivity to the law of sin which is in my members. 24O wretched man that I am! Who will deliver me from this body of death? 25I thank God—through Jesus Christ our Lord!

So then, with the mind I myself serve the law of God, but with the flesh the law of sin.

8 There* is therefore now no condemnation to those who are in Christ Jesus,ˣ who do not walk according to the flesh, but according to the Spirit. 2For the law of the Spirit of life in Christ Jesus has made me free from the law of sin and death. 3For what the law could not do in that it was weak through the flesh, God did by sending His own Son in the likeness of sinful flesh, on account of sin: He condemned sin in the flesh, 4that the righteous requirement of the law might be fulfilled in us who do not walk according to the flesh but according to the Spirit. 5For those who live according to the flesh set their minds on the things of the flesh, but those who live according to the Spirit, the things of the Spirit. 6For to be carnally minded is death, but to be spiritually minded is life and peace. 7Because the carnal mind is enmity against God; for it is not subject to the law of God, nor indeed can be. 8So then, those who are in the flesh cannot please God.

9But you are not in the flesh but in the Spirit, if indeed the Spirit of God dwells in you. Now if anyone does not have the Spirit of Christ, he is not His. 10And if Christ is in you, the body is dead because of sin, but the Spirit is life because of righteousness. 11But if the Spirit of Him who raised Jesus from the dead dwells in you, He who raised Christ from the dead will also give life to your mortal bodies through His Spirit who dwells in you.

12*Therefore, brethren, we are debtors—not to the flesh, to live according to the flesh. 13For if you live according to the flesh you will die; but if by the Spirit you put to death the deeds of the body, you will live. 14For as many as are led by the Spirit of God, these are sons of God. 15For you did not receive the spirit of bondage again to fear, but you received the Spirit of adoption by whom we cry out, "Abba, Father." 16The Spirit Himself bears witness with our spirit that we are children of God, 17and if children, then heirs—heirs of God and joint heirs with Christ, if indeed we suffer with Him, that we may also be glorified together.

18*For I consider that the sufferings of this present time are not worthy to be compared with the glory which shall be revealed in us. 19For the earnest expectation of the creation eagerly waits for the revealing of the sons of God. 20For the creation was subjected to futility, not willingly, but because of Him who subjected it in hope; 21because the creation itself also will be delivered from the bondage of corruption into the glorious liberty of the children of God. 22For we know that the whole creation groans and labors with birth pangs

CHAPTER 8

8:1–11 Paul asked, "Who will deliver me from this body of death?" (7:24). This chapter gives the answer: the Holy Spirit of God. The blessings He brings make us "more than conquerors" (v. 37)!

Life. When God saved you, He gave you a new life, not a new law; as you yield to that life, you obey His law. Keep your mind centered on the things of the Lord (Col. 3:1–4) and seek to please God in all things. Let the Spirit live His life in you.

8:12–17 Liberty. We enter God's family by the new birth, not by adoption (John 3); but adoption gives us an adult standing in His family. He deals with us as mature sons and daughters and not as "little children." We can talk ("Abba, Father" [v. 15]), walk, and use our inheritance right now. We are free, but we are still debtors to the Lord (v. 12).

8:18–25 Hope. We are not frustrated by the suffering we experience or see in our world because we have hope. When Jesus returns, we will enter into glorious liberty! The Spirit is the beginning of the harvest and assures us that the best is yet to come.

❝*The Holy Spirit longs to reveal to you the deeper things of God. He longs to love through you. He longs to work through you. Through the blessed Holy Spirit you may have: strength for every duty, wisdom for every problem, comfort in every sorrow, joy in His overflowing service.*❞
—T. J. Bach

8:1 ˣNU-Text omits the rest of this verse.

8:26–30 *Guidance.* God's purpose is to make His children like His Son, and He will succeed. The Spirit intercedes for us and guides us as we pray, and the circumstances of life work for our good, no matter how painful they may be.

8:31–39 *Love.* The Spirit of God makes the love of God real to us (5:5; John 14:23–27). The Father is for us (vv. 31–32), the Son is for us (v. 34), and the Spirit is for us (vv. 26–27). Nothing can separate us from His love. Is there any reason why we should not be "more than conquerors"?

CHAPTER 9

9:1ff In a part of the Bible that emphasizes the sovereignty of God, We see Paul sorrowing (9:1–3), praying (10:1), and worshiping (11:33–36). He did not feel that God's sovereignty in any way destroyed man's responsibility. The God who ordains the end (saving the lost) also ordains the means to the end, the prayers and witness of His people. They go together. God is not obligated to save anybody, for all deserve to be condemned. Even Israel was chosen only because of His grace and love (Deut. 7:6–8). Therefore, nobody can criticize God or say He is unfair. That He is merciful to sinners should make us rejoice! Israel's rejection of Christ did not ruin God's plan, for He went to the Gentiles (Acts 10:1ff.; 15:14) who gladly received the good news. However, God has a remnant among the Jews (vv. 27–29), and believing Jews and Gentiles are one in the church (Eph. 2:11–22). His mercy endures forever!

together until now. 23Not only *that*, but we also who have the firstfruits of the Spirit, even we ourselves groan within ourselves, eagerly waiting for the adoption, the redemption of our body. 24For we were saved in this hope, but hope that is seen is not hope; for why does one still hope for what he sees? 25But if we hope for what we do not see, we eagerly wait for *it* with perseverance. 26*Likewise the Spirit also helps in our weaknesses. For we do not know what we should pray for as we ought, but the Spirit Himself makes intercession for usʸ with groanings which cannot be uttered. 27Now He who searches the hearts knows what the mind of the Spirit *is*, because He makes intercession for the saints according to *the will of* God.

28And we know that all things work together for good to those who love God, to those who are the called according to *His* purpose. 29For whom He foreknew, He also predestined *to be* conformed to the image of His Son, that He might be the firstborn among many brethren. 30Moreover whom He predestined, these He also called; whom He called, these He also justified; and whom He justified, these He also glorified.

31*What then shall we say to these things? If God *is* for us, who *can* be against us? 32He who did not spare His own Son, but delivered Him up for us all, how shall He not with Him also freely give us all things? 33Who shall bring a charge against God's elect? *It is* God who justifies. 34Who *is* he who condemns? *It is* Christ who died, and furthermore is also risen, who is even at the right hand of God, who also makes intercession for us. 35Who shall separate us from the love of Christ? *Shall* tribulation, or distress, or persecution, or famine, or nakedness, or peril, or sword? 36As it is written:

> "For Your sake we are killed all day long;
> We are accounted as sheep for the
> slaughter."ᶻ

37Yet in all these things we are more than conquerors through Him who loved us. 38For I am persuaded that neither death nor life, nor angels nor principalities nor powers, nor things present nor things to come, 39nor height nor depth, nor any other created thing, shall be able to separate us from the love of God which is in Christ Jesus our Lord.

9 I* tell the truth in Christ, I am not lying, my conscience also bearing me witness in the Holy Spirit, 2that I have great sorrow and continual grief in my heart. 3For I could wish that I myself were accursed from Christ for my brethren, my countrymenᵃ according to the flesh, 4who are Israelites, to whom *pertain* the adoption, the glory, the covenants, the giving of the law, the service *of God*, and the promises; 5of whom *are* the fathers and from whom, according to the flesh,

---

8:26 ʸNU-Text omits *for us.* 8:36 ᶻPsalm 44:22 9:3 ᵃOr *relatives*

God's People—In Romans 9—11, Paul's discussion of Israel is not an interruption but an illustration of his theme. He explains Israel's past election (chap. 9), present rejection (chap. 10), and future reception (chap. 11); and he proves that God has been righteous in all His dealings with Israel. God has not failed to work out His divine purposes for the Jews, nor will He fail to work out His purposes for His church.

Christ *came*, who is over all, *the* eternally blessed God. Amen.

6But it is not that the word of God has taken no effect. For they *are* not all Israel who *are* of Israel, 7nor *are they* all children because they are the seed of Abraham; but, *"In Isaac your seed shall be called."*b 8That is, those who *are* the children of the flesh, these *are* not the children of God; but the children of the promise are counted as the seed. 9For this *is* the word of promise: *"At this time I will come and Sarah shall have a son."*c

10And not only *this*, but when Rebecca also had conceived by one man, *even* by our father Isaac 11(for *the children* not yet being born, nor having done any good or evil, that the purpose of God according to election might stand, not of works but of Him who calls), 12it was said to her, *"The older shall serve the younger."*d 13As it is written, *"Jacob I have loved, but Esau I have hated."*e

14What shall we say then? *Is there* unrighteousness with God? Certainly not! 15For He says to Moses, *"I will have mercy on whomever I will have mercy, and I will have compassion on whomever I will have compassion."*f 16So then *it is* not of him who wills, nor of him who runs, but of God who shows mercy. 17For the Scripture says to the Pharaoh, *"For this very purpose I have raised you up, that I may show My power in you, and that My name may be declared in all the earth."*g 18Therefore He has mercy on whom He wills, and whom He wills He hardens.

19You will say to me then, "Why does He still find fault? For who has resisted His will?" 20But indeed, O man, who are you to reply against God? Will the thing formed say to him who formed *it*, "Why have you made me like this?" 21Does not the potter have power over the clay, from the same lump to make one vessel for honor and another for dishonor?

22What if God, wanting to show *His* wrath and to make His power known, endured with much longsuffering the vessels of wrath prepared for destruction, 23and that He might make known the riches of His glory on the vessels of mercy, which He had prepared beforehand for glory, 24*even* us whom He called, not of the Jews only, but also of the Gentiles?

25As He says also in Hosea:

"I will call them My people, who were not
    My people,
And her beloved, who was not beloved."h
26 "And it shall come to pass in the place where
    it was said to them,
'You are not My people,'
There they shall be called sons of the living
    God."i

27Isaiah also cries out concerning Israel:j

"Though the number of the children of Israel
    be as the sand of the sea,
The remnant will be saved.
28 For He will finish the work and cut it short
    in righteousness,

9:7 bGenesis 21:12   9:9 cGenesis 18:10, 14   9:12 dGenesis 25:23   9:13 eMalachi 1:2, 3   9:15 fExodus 33:19
9:17 gExodus 9:16   9:25 hHosea 2:23   9:26 iHosea 1:10
9:27 jIsaiah 10:22, 23

*Because the LORD will make a short work
upon the earth.''k*

29And as Isaiah said before:

*"Unless the LORD of Sabaothl had left us a
seed,
We would have become like Sodom,
And we would have been made like
Gomorrah.''m*

30What shall we say then? That Gentiles, who
did not pursue righteousness, have attained to
righteousness, even the righteousness of faith;
31but Israel, pursuing the law of righteousness,
has not attained to the law of righteousness.n
32Why? Because *they did* not *seek it* by faith, but
as it were, by the works of the law.o For they stumbled at that stumbling stone. 33As it is written:

*"Behold, I lay in Zion a stumbling stone and
rock of offense,
And whoever believes on Him will not be
put to shame.''p*

CHAPTER 10

10:1ff Why did Israel stumble over Christ
and reject Him? Because they did not
understand the kind of righteousness God
wanted or how to get it. Like the Pharisees
(and many people today), they thought only
of righteous *works* and could not
comprehend a righteousness that comes by
faith (v. 13; Joel 2:32; Acts 2:21).

The missionary heart of Paul comes out
in verses 14–17. Salvation is by faith, and
faith comes "by hearing . . . the word of God"
(v. 17). But unbelieving sinners (including
Israel) cannot hear unless we tell them. God
needs people with beautiful feet (Isa. 52:7)
to carry the gospel to the lost.

Despite Paul's broken heart (v. 1) and
God's outstretched hands (v. 21; Isa. 65:2),
Israel did not believe; but the Gentiles did
believe and God saved them! When you feel
discouraged in your witnessing, remember
Paul; continue caring, praying, and sharing
the good news. Keep those feet beautiful!

10 Brethren, *my heart's desire and prayer to
God for Israelq is that they may be saved.
2For I bear them witness that they have a zeal
for God, but not according to knowledge. 3For
they being ignorant of God's righteousness, and
seeking to establish their own righteousness, have
not submitted to the righteousness of God.
4For Christ *is* the end of the law for righteousness
to everyone who believes.
5For Moses writes about the righteousness
which is of the law, *"The man who does those
things shall live by them.''r* 6But the righteousness
of faith speaks in this way, *"Do not say in your
heart, 'Who will ascend into heaven?' ''s* (that is,
to bring Christ down *from above*) 7or, " *'Who will
descend into the abyss?' ''t* (that is, to bring Christ
up from the dead). 8But what does it say? *"The
word is near you, in your mouth and in your
heart''u* (that is, the word of faith which we
preach): 9that if you confess with your mouth the
Lord Jesus and believe in your heart that God
has raised Him from the dead, you will be saved.
10For with the heart one believes unto righteousness, and with the mouth confession is made unto
salvation. 11For the Scripture says, *"Whoever believes on Him will not be put to shame.''v* 12For
there is no distinction between Jew and Greek,
for the same Lord over all is rich to all who call
upon Him. 13For *"whoever calls on the name of
the LORD shall be saved.''w*
14How then shall they call on Him in whom they
have not believed? And how shall they believe

9:28 kNU-Text reads *For the* LORD *will finish the work and
cut it short upon the earth.*   9:29 lLiterally, in Hebrew,
Hosts mIsaiah 1:9   9:31 nNU-Text omits *of righteousness.*
9:32 oNU-Text reads *by works.*   9:33 pIsaiah 8:14; 28:16
10:1 qNU-Text reads *them.*   10:5 rLeviticus 18:5
10:6 sDeuteronomy 30:12   10:7 tDeuteronomy 30:13
10:8 uDeuteronomy 30:14   10:11 vIsaiah 28:16   10:13 wJoel
2:32

God's Part and Our Part—Charles Spurgeon was asked how he reconciled divine sovereignty
and human responsibility, and he replied, "I never try to reconcile friends." Augustine said that we
must pray as though it all depended on God and work as though it all depended on us. That biblical
balance makes for blessing.

in Him of whom they have not heard? And how shall they hear without a preacher? 15And how shall they preach unless they are sent? As it is written:

> "How beautiful are the feet of those who
> preach the gospel of peace,ˣ
> Who bring glad tidings of good things!"ʸ

16But they have not all obeyed the gospel. For Isaiah says, "LORD, who has believed our report?"ᶻ 17So then faith comes by hearing, and hearing by the word of God.

18But I say, have they not heard? Yes indeed:

> "Their sound has gone out to all the earth,
> And their words to the ends of the world."ᵃ

19But I say, did Israel not know? First Moses says:

> "I will provoke you to jealousy by those who
> are not a nation,
> I will move you to anger by a foolish
> nation."ᵇ

20But Isaiah is very bold and says:

> "I was found by those who did not seek Me;
> I was made manifest to those who did not
> ask for Me."ᶜ

21But to Israel he says:

> "All day long I have stretched out My hands
> To a disobedient and contrary people."ᵈ

11 I *say then, has God cast away His people? Certainly not! For I also am an Israelite, of the seed of Abraham, of the tribe of Benjamin. 2God has not cast away His people whom He foreknew. Or do you not know what the Scripture says of Elijah, how he pleads with God against Israel, saying, 3"LORD, they have killed Your prophets and torn down Your altars, and I alone am left, and they seek my life"?ᵉ 4But what does the divine response say to him? "I have reserved for Myself seven thousand men who have not bowed the knee to Baal."ᶠ 5Even so then, at this present time there is a remnant according to the election of grace. 6And if by grace, then it is no longer of works; otherwise grace is no longer grace.ᵍ But if it is of works, it is no longer grace; otherwise work is no longer work.

7What then? Israel has not obtained what it seeks; but the elect have obtained it, and the rest were blinded. 8Just as it is written:

> "God has given them a spirit of stupor,
> Eyes that they should not see
> And ears that they should not hear,
> To this very day."ʰ

9And David says:

***

❝Fate says the thing is and must be, so it is decreed. But the true doctrine is—God has appointed this and that, not because it must be, but because it is best that it should be. Fate is blind, but the destiny of Scripture is full of eyes. Fate is stern and adamantine, and has no tears for human sorrow. But the arrangements of providence are kind and good.**❞**

—Charles Spurgeon

***

CHAPTER 11

11:1ff The theology of Romans 9—11 magnifies God's grace and extols His sovereignty. Never lose the wonder of your salvation or of the greatness of God. No matter how deep the valley or difficult the battle, a vision of God's greatness puts joy in your heart and strength in your soul. God knows what He is doing even if you do not understand it fully.

There is a future for Israel; Paul is proof of that (v. 1; 1 Tim. 1:16), and so is Israel's past history (vv. 2–10). God has always had a believing remnant in Israel, no matter how dark the day. When you become discouraged about the future of the church and feel that you may be the only faithful Christian left, read 1 Kings 19 and focus on God's greatness.

We cannot explain all the purposes and plans of God, but we can worship and praise Him for who He is (vv. 33–36). The end result of all Bible study is worship, and the end result of all worship is service to the God we love.

***

10:15 ˣNU-Text omits *preach the gospel of peace, Who.* ʸIsaiah 52:7; Nahum 1:15   10:16 ᶻIsaiah 53:1   10:18 ᵃPsalm 19:4   10:19 ᵇDeuteronomy 32:21   10:20 ᶜIsaiah 65:1   10:21 ᵈIsaiah 65:2   11:3 ᵉ1 Kings 19:10, 14   11:4 ᶠ1 Kings 19:18   11:6 ᵍNU-Text omits the rest of this verse.   11:8 ʰDeuteronomy 29:4; Isaiah 29:10

> "Let their table become a snare and a trap,
> A stumbling block and a recompense to
> them.
> 10 Let their eyes be darkened, so that they do
> not see,
> And bow down their back always."[l]

11I say then, have they stumbled that they should fall? Certainly not! But through their fall, to provoke them to jealousy, salvation *has come* to the Gentiles. 12Now if their fall *is* riches for the world, and their failure riches for the Gentiles, how much more their fullness!

13For I speak to you Gentiles; inasmuch as I am an apostle to the Gentiles, I magnify my ministry, 14if by any means I may provoke to jealousy *those who are* my flesh and save some of them. 15For if their being cast away *is* the reconciling of the world, what *will* their acceptance *be* but life from the dead?

16For if the firstfruit *is* holy, the lump *is* also *holy;* and if the root *is* holy, so *are* the branches. 17And if some of the branches were broken off, and you, being a wild olive tree, were grafted in among them, and with them became a partaker of the root and fatness of the olive tree, 18do not boast against the branches. But if you do boast, *remember that* you do not support the root, but the root supports you.

19You will say then, "Branches were broken off that I might be grafted in." 20Well *said.* Because of unbelief they were broken off, and you stand by faith. Do not be haughty, but fear. 21For if God did not spare the natural branches, He may not spare you either. 22Therefore consider the goodness and severity of God: on those who fell, severity; but toward you, goodness,[j] if you continue in *His* goodness. Otherwise you also will be cut off. 23And they also, if they do not continue in unbelief, will be grafted in, for God is able to graft them in again. 24For if you were cut out of the olive tree which is wild by nature, and were grafted contrary to nature into a cultivated olive tree, how much more will these, who *are* natural *branches,* be grafted into their own olive tree?

25For I do not desire, brethren, that you should be ignorant of this mystery, lest you should be wise in your own opinion, that blindness in part has happened to Israel until the fullness of the Gentiles has come in. 26And so all Israel will be saved,[k] as it is written:

> "The Deliverer will come out of Zion,
> And He will turn away ungodliness from
> Jacob;
> 27 For this is My covenant with them,
> When I take away their sins."[l]

28Concerning the gospel *they are* enemies for your sake, but concerning the election *they are* beloved for the sake of the fathers. 29For the gifts and the calling of God *are* irrevocable. 30For as you were once disobedient to God, yet have now obtained mercy through their disobedience, 31even so these also have now been disobedient, that through the mercy shown you they also may obtain mercy. 32For God has committed them all

---

11:10 [l]Psalm 69:22, 23   11:22 [j]NU-Text adds *of God.*
11:26 [k]Or *delivered*   11:27 [l]Isaiah 59:20, 21

to disobedience, that He might have mercy on all. 33Oh, the depth of the riches both of the wisdom and knowledge of God! How unsearchable *are* His judgments and His ways past finding out!

34 *"For who has known the mind of the LORD?*
  *Or who has become His counselor?"*m
35 *"Or who has first given to Him*
  *And it shall be repaid to him?"*n

36For of Him and through Him and to Him *are* all things, to whom *be* glory forever. Amen.

12 I* beseech you therefore, brethren, by the mercies of God, that you present your bodies a living sacrifice, holy, acceptable to God, *which is* your reasonable service. 2And do not be conformed to this world, but be transformed by the renewing of your mind, that you may prove what *is* that good and acceptable and perfect will of God.

3*For I say, through the grace given to me, to everyone who is among you, not to think *of himself* more highly than he ought to think, but to think soberly, as God has dealt to each one a measure of faith. 4*For as we have many members in one body, but all the members do not have the same function, 5so we, *being* many, are one body in Christ, and individually members of one another. 6Having then gifts differing according to the grace that is given to us, *let us use them:* if prophecy, *let us prophesy* in proportion to our faith; 7or ministry, *let us use it* in *our* ministering; he who teaches, in teaching; 8he who exhorts, in exhortation; he who gives, with liberality; he who leads, with diligence; he who shows mercy, with cheerfulness.

9*Let* love *be* without hypocrisy. Abhor what is evil. Cling to what is good. 10Be kindly affectionate to one another with brotherly love, in honor giving preference to one another; 11not lagging in diligence, fervent in spirit, serving the Lord; 12rejoicing in hope, patient in tribulation, continuing steadfastly in prayer; 13distributing to the needs of the saints, given to hospitality.

14Bless those who persecute you; bless and do not curse. 15Rejoice with those who rejoice, and weep with those who weep. 16Be of the same mind toward one another. Do not set your mind on high things, but associate with the humble. Do not be wise in your own opinion.

17*Repay no one evil for evil. Have regard for good things in the sight of all men. 18If it is possible, as much as depends on you, live peaceably with all men. 19Beloved, do not avenge yourselves, but *rather* give place to wrath; for it is written, *"Vengeance is Mine, I will repay,"*o says the Lord. 20Therefore

  "If your enemy is hungry, feed him;
    If he is thirsty, give him a drink;
    For in so doing you will heap coals of fire
      *on his head."*p

21Do not be overcome by evil, but overcome evil with good.

CHAPTER 12

12:1–2 The biblical pattern is to relate doctrine and duty, for what you believe must determine how you behave. In these closing chapters, Paul discusses your relationship with the Lord (12:1–2), yourself (12:3), the church (12:4–16), your enemies (12:17–21), government (chap. 13), and believers who disagree (chaps. 14—15).
  Transformation. The Spirit of God transforms your life by renewing your mind (2 Cor. 3:18), but He cannot do this unless you give Him your body. When you give yourself to God in spiritual worship, you become a living sacrifice to the glory of God.

12:3 *Evaluation.* To think more highly of yourself, *or less highly,* is sin, so have a proper estimate of who you are and what God has given you (Gal. 6:3–5).

12:4–16 *Cooperation.* You are part of the body of Christ with a ministry to fulfill, so do your part lovingly and joyfully.

12:17–21 *Vindication.* If yours is a godly life, you are bound to have enemies (Matt. 5:10–12; 2 Tim. 3:12); but leave all judgment to the Lord. If you let the Lord have His way, He will use your enemies to build you and make you more like Christ.

11:34 *m*Isaiah 40:13; Jeremiah 23:18   11:35 *n*Job 41:11
12:19 *o*Deuteronomy 32:35   12:20 *p*Proverbs 25:21, 22

CHAPTER 13

13:1–7 Believers are citizens of heaven, but we must not minimize our responsibilities on earth. We must be exemplary citizens so that the Lord will be glorified (1 Pet. 2:11–17).

Law. God has established human government because people are sinners and must be controlled. Governmental authority comes from God, so you must respect the office even if you cannot respect the officer.

The fear of punishment is not the highest motivation for obedience, but it is better than having chaos.

13:8–10 ***Love.*** Love for God and for your neighbor is the highest motive for obedience. Love does what is right and just and seeks the best for others. By nature, we do not have this kind of love (Titus 3:3); the Lord gives it to us (Rom. 5:5).

13:11–14 ***Light.*** Christian citizens live in the light of the Lord's return. Paul admonishes, "Wake up—dress up—clean up—look up!" Are you heeding it?

CHAPTER 14

14:1–9 Your love may be tested more by Christians who disagree with you than by unbelievers who persecute you. It takes a diamond to cut a diamond. What should you do when your brother or sister disagrees with you about how God's people ought to live?

Acceptance. Not all believers are mature, and love demands that the mature members of the family defer to the immature. Love protects people and gives them a chance to grow up. People may be difficult, but we must accept them in love for the Lord's sake.

> *Whatever makes men good Christians makes them good citizens.*
>
> —Daniel Webster

13 Let* every soul be subject to the governing
authorities. For there is no authority except
from God, and the authorities that exist are appointed by God. 2Therefore whoever resists the
authority resists the ordinance of God, and those
who resist will bring judgment on themselves.
3For rulers are not a terror to good works, but to
evil. Do you want to be unafraid of the authority?
Do what is good, and you will have praise from
the same. 4For he is God's minister to you for
good. But if you do evil, be afraid; for he does
not bear the sword in vain; for he is God's minister, an avenger to *execute* wrath on him who
practices evil. 5Therefore *you* must be subject, not
only because of wrath but also for conscience'
sake. 6For because of this you also pay taxes, for
they are God's ministers attending continually to
this very thing. 7Render therefore to all their due:
taxes to whom taxes *are due,* customs to whom
customs, fear to whom fear, honor to whom
honor.

8*Owe no one anything except to love one another, for he who loves another has fulfilled the
law. 9For the commandments, *"You shall not commit adultery," "You shall not murder," "You shall
not steal," "You shall not bear false witness,"*[q]
"You shall not covet,"[r] and if *there is* any other
commandment, are *all* summed up in this saying,
namely, *"You shall love your neighbor as yourself."*[s] 10Love does no harm to a neighbor; therefore love *is* the fulfillment of the law.

11*And *do* this, knowing the time, that now *it
is* high time to awake out of sleep; for now our
salvation *is* nearer than when we *first* believed.
12The night is far spent, the day is at hand. Therefore let us cast off the works of darkness, and let
us put on the armor of light. 13Let us walk properly, as in the day, not in revelry and drunkenness, not in lewdness and lust, not in strife and
envy. 14But put on the Lord Jesus Christ, and
make no provision for the flesh, to *fulfill its* lusts.

14 Receive* one who is weak in the faith, *but*
not to disputes over doubtful things.
2For one believes he may eat all things, but he
who is weak eats *only* vegetables. 3Let not him
who eats despise him who does not eat, and let
not him who does not eat judge him who eats;
for God has received him. 4Who are you to judge
another's servant? To his own master he stands
or falls. Indeed, he will be made to stand, for God
is able to make him stand.

5One person esteems *one* day above another;
another esteems every day *alike.* Let each be fully
convinced in his own mind. 6He who observes the
day, observes *it* to the Lord;[t] and he who does
not observe the day, to the Lord he does not observe *it.* He who eats, eats to the Lord, for he
gives God thanks; and he who does not eat, to
the Lord he does not eat, and gives God thanks.
7For none of us lives to himself, and no one dies

13:9 [q]NU-Text omits *"You shall not bear false witness."* [r]Exodus 20:13–15, 17; Deuteronomy 5:17–19, 21 [s]Leviticus 19:18 14:6 [t]NU-Text omits the rest of this sentence.

Gaining Strength—The weak Christian does not yet understand and practice freedom in Jesus Christ. Jewish believers, raised under the law of Moses, had a difficult time adjusting to their new life. Conscience becomes strong as we accept what God says about us in the Word and act on it by faith. However, it takes time for conscience to develop, and we must be patient with one another.

to himself. 8For if we live, we live to the Lord; and if we die, we die to the Lord. Therefore, whether we live or die, we are the Lord's. 9For to this end Christ died and rose[u] and lived again, that He might be Lord of both the dead and the living. 10*But why do you judge your brother? Or why do you show contempt for your brother? For we shall all stand before the judgment seat of Christ.[v] 11For it is written:

> "As I live, says the LORD,
> Every knee shall bow to Me,
> And every tongue shall confess to God."[w]

12So then each of us shall give account of himself to God. 13*Therefore let us not judge one another anymore, but rather resolve this, not to put a stumbling block or a cause to fall in *our* brother's way.

14I know and am convinced by the Lord Jesus that *there is* nothing unclean of itself; but to him who considers anything to be unclean, to him *it is* unclean. 15Yet if your brother is grieved because of *your* food, you are no longer walking in love. Do not destroy with your food the one for whom Christ died. 16Therefore do not let your good be spoken of as evil; 17for the kingdom of God is not eating and drinking, but righteousness and peace and joy in the Holy Spirit. 18For he who serves Christ in these things[x] *is* acceptable to God and approved by men.

19Therefore let us pursue the things *which make* for peace and the things by which one may edify another. 20Do not destroy the work of God for the sake of food. All things indeed *are* pure, but *it is* evil for the man who eats with offense. 21It is good neither to eat meat nor drink wine nor *do anything* by which your brother stumbles or is offended or is made weak.[y] 22Do you have faith?[z] Have *it* to yourself before God. Happy *is* he who does not condemn himself in what he approves. 23But he who doubts is condemned if he eats, because *he does* not *eat* from faith; for whatever *is* not from faith is sin.[a]

15 We* then who are strong ought to bear with the scruples of the weak, and not to please ourselves. 2Let each of us please *his* neighbor for *his* good, leading to edification. 3For even Christ did not please Himself; but as it is written, *"The reproaches of those who reproached You fell on Me."*[b] 4For whatever things were written before were written for our learning, that we through the patience and comfort of the Scriptures might have hope. 5Now may the God of patience and comfort grant you to be like-minded toward one another, according to Christ Jesus, 6that you may with one mind *and* one mouth glorify the God and Father of our Lord Jesus Christ.

7*Therefore receive one another, just as Christ also received us,[c] to the glory of God. 8Now I say that Jesus Christ has become a servant to the circumcision for the truth of God, to confirm the promises *made* to the fathers, 9and that the

14:10–12 Accountability. We have no right to judge and condemn one another because the Judge is the Lord. Each believer will have enough to do in keeping his own account right without interfering with others' accounts!

14:13–23 Ambition. Our desire must not be to get everybody to agree with us; our desire must be to pursue peace, not cause others to stumble, and help others to mature in Christ. What starts as *grieving* (v. 15) can become *offending* (v. 21), *making weak* (v. 21), and *causing others to stumble and fall* (vv. 13, 21). The result might be *destroying* a brother's or sister's faith (vv. 15, 20). Is destroying another just to have your own way worth it?

CHAPTER 15

15:1–6 A debt to the weak. The strong must bear the weak and help them grow, and that takes love and patience. If we live to please ourselves, we will not follow the example of Christ who lived to please the Father and help others.

> ❝To consider persons and events and situations only in the light of their effect upon myself is to live on the doorstep of hell.❞
> —Thomas Merton

15:7–21 A debt to the lost. God saved the Jews so that they might reach the Gentiles and lead them in praising the Lord. God has saved us so that we might win others. We have a debt to pay (1:14).

14:9 [u]NU-Text omits *and rose.*   14:10 [v]NU-Text reads *of God.*
14:11 [w]Isaiah 45:23   14:18 [x]NU-Text reads *this.*
14:21 [y]NU-Text omits *or is offended or is made weak.*
14:22 [z]NU-Text reads *The faith which you have—have.*
14:23 [a]M-Text puts Romans 16:25–27 here.   15:3 [b]Psalm 69:9   15:7 [c]NU-Text and M-Text read *you.*

Gentiles might glorify God for *His* mercy, as it is written:

> "For this reason I will confess to You among
>   the Gentiles,
> And sing to Your name."[d]

10And again he says:

> "Rejoice, O Gentiles, with His people!"[e]

11And again:

> "Praise the LORD, all you Gentiles!
> Laud Him, all you peoples!"[f]

12And again, Isaiah says:

> "There shall be a root of Jesse;
> And He who shall rise to reign over the
>   Gentiles,
> In Him the Gentiles shall hope."[g]

13Now may the God of hope fill you with all joy and peace in believing, that you may abound in hope by the power of the Holy Spirit.

14Now I myself am confident concerning you, my brethren, that you also are full of goodness, filled with all knowledge, able also to admonish one another.[h] 15Nevertheless, brethren, I have written more boldly to you on *some* points, as reminding you, because of the grace given to me by God, 16that I might be a minister of Jesus Christ to the Gentiles, ministering the gospel of God, that the offering of the Gentiles might be acceptable, sanctified by the Holy Spirit. 17Therefore I have reason to glory in Christ Jesus in the things *which pertain* to God. 18For I will not dare to speak of any of those things which Christ has not accomplished through me, in word and deed, to make the Gentiles obedient— 19in mighty signs and wonders, by the power of the Spirit of God, so that from Jerusalem and round about to Illyricum I have fully preached the gospel of Christ. 20And so I have made it my aim to preach the gospel, not where Christ was named, lest I should build on another man's foundation, 21but as it is written:

> "To whom He was not announced, they shall
>   see;
> And those who have not heard shall
>   understand."[i]

22*For this reason I also have been much hindered from coming to you. 23But now no longer having a place in these parts, and having a great desire these many years to come to you, 24whenever I journey to Spain, I shall come to you.[j] For I hope to see you on my journey, and to be helped on my way there by you, if first I may enjoy your *company* for a while. 25But now I am going to Jerusalem to minister to the saints. 26For it pleased those from Macedonia and Achaia to make a certain contribution for the poor among the saints who are in Jerusalem. 27It pleased them

15:22–23 *A debt to Israel.* The Gentiles are indebted to the Jews (John 4:22). And that debt is paid by praying for them (Ps. 122:6), witnessing to them in love, and sharing our material gifts to assist them.

15:9 [d]2 Samuel 22:50; Psalm 18:49   15:10 [e]Deuteronomy 32:43   15:11 [f]Psalm 117:1   15:12 [g]Isaiah 11:10   15:14 [h]M-Text reads *others.*   15:21 [i]Isaiah 52:15   15:24 [j]NU-Text omits *I shall come to you* (and joins *Spain* with the next sentence).

indeed, and they are their debtors. For if the Gentiles have been partakers of their spiritual things, their duty is also to minister to them in material things. 28Therefore, when I have performed this and have sealed to them this fruit, I shall go by way of you to Spain. 29But I know that when I come to you, I shall come in the fullness of the blessing of the gospel[k] of Christ.

30Now I beg you, brethren, through the Lord Jesus Christ, and through the love of the Spirit, that you strive together with me in prayers to God for me, 31that I may be delivered from those in Judea who do not believe, and that my service for Jerusalem may be acceptable to the saints, 32that I may come to you with joy by the will of God, and may be refreshed together with you. 33Now the God of peace be with you all. Amen.

16 I* commend to you Phoebe our sister, who is a servant of the church in Cenchrea, 2that you may receive her in the Lord in a manner worthy of the saints, and assist her in whatever business she has need of you; for indeed she has been a helper of many and of myself also.

3Greet Priscilla and Aquila, my fellow workers in Christ Jesus, 4who risked their own necks for my life, to whom not only I give thanks, but also all the churches of the Gentiles. 5Likewise greet the church that is in their house.

Greet my beloved Epaenetus, who is the first-fruits of Achaia[l] to Christ. 6Greet Mary, who labored much for us. 7Greet Andronicus and Junia, my countrymen and my fellow prisoners, who are of note among the apostles, who also were in Christ before me.

8Greet Amplias, my beloved in the Lord. 9Greet Urbanus, our fellow worker in Christ, and Stachys, my beloved. 10Greet Apelles, approved in Christ. Greet those who are of the household of Aristobulus. 11Greet Herodion, my countryman.[m] Greet those who are of the household of Narcissus who are in the Lord.

12Greet Tryphena and Tryphosa, who have labored in the Lord. Greet the beloved Persis, who labored much in the Lord. 13Greet Rufus, chosen in the Lord, and his mother and mine. 14Greet Asyncritus, Phlegon, Hermas, Patrobas, Hermes, and the brethren who are with them. 15Greet Philologus and Julia, Nereus and his sister, and Olympas, and all the saints who are with them.

16Greet one another with a holy kiss. The[n] churches of Christ greet you.

17Now I urge you, brethren, note those who cause divisions and offenses, contrary to the doctrine which you learned, and avoid them. 18For those who are such do not serve our Lord Jesus[o] Christ, but their own belly, and by smooth words and flattering speech deceive the hearts of the simple. 19For your obedience has become known to all. Therefore I am glad on your behalf; but I want you to be wise in what is good, and simple concerning evil. 20And the God of peace will crush Satan under your feet shortly.

The grace of our Lord Jesus Christ be with you. Amen.

21Timothy, my fellow worker, and Lucius, Jason, and Sosipater, my countrymen, greet you.

CHAPTER 16

16:1ff We are prone to honor Paul and forget the many ordinary people who helped make his ministry possible. Paul was the human author of the epistle to the Romans, but Tertius wrote it down (v. 22), Gaius gave Paul a place to live and work (v. 23), and Phoebe carried the completed letter to Rome. Nobody in God's family is unimportant to Him, and no ministry is insignificant. Find the work He wants you to do and faithfully do it.

There is a "hidden romance of history" that is not recorded in the Bible. When and how did Priscilla and Aquila risk their lives to save Paul (vv. 3–4)? When were Andronicus and Junia in prison with Paul (v. 7)? How was Rufus's mother a mother to Paul (v. 13)? Who were the troublemakers about whom Paul warned the Roman believers (vv. 17–18)? Perhaps one day in heaven we will be given the answers!

Meanwhile, the important thing is that we are obedient to the Lord (v. 19) and lead others into "obedience to the faith" (v. 26). The God of patience and comfort (15:5), the God of hope (15:13), and the God of peace (16:20) will establish you and enable you (16:25).

❝The service we render for others is really the rent we pay for our room on this earth.❞
—Wilfred Grenfell

15:29 [k]NU-Text omits of the gospel.   16:5 [l]NU-Text reads Asia.   16:11 [m]Or relative   16:16 [n]NU-Text reads All the churches.   16:18 [o]NU-Text and M-Text omit Jesus.

22I, Tertius, who wrote *this* epistle, greet you in the Lord.

23Gaius, my host and *the host* of the whole church, greets you. Erastus, the treasurer of the city, greets you, and Quartus, a brother. 24The grace of our Lord Jesus Christ *be* with you all. Amen.*p*

25Now to Him who is able to establish you according to my gospel and the preaching of Jesus Christ, according to the revelation of the mystery kept secret since the world began 26but now made manifest, and by the prophetic Scriptures made known to all nations, according to the commandment of the everlasting God, for obedience to the faith— 27to God, alone wise, *be* glory through Jesus Christ forever. Amen.*q*

16:24 *p*NU-Text omits this verse.　16:27 *q*M-Text puts Romans 16:25–27 after Romans 14:23.

1 CORINTHIANS

Corinth, the capital of Achaia, was perhaps the richest and most important city in Greece. It was also the most corrupt. A center for trade, Corinth was invaded by all kinds of religions and philosophies. Paul founded the Corinthian church during his second missionary journey (Acts 18) and ministered there a year and a half.

After he left, serious problems developed in the church, and Paul wrote the members a stern letter that was not successful (1 Cor. 5:9). He heard that the church was divided (1:11), and then a delegation from the church arrived in Ephesus with a letter asking Paul's help regarding specific questions. First Corinthians was his response.

Paul dealt with sin in the church (chaps. 1—6), and then he answered the questions they asked (chaps. 7—16; note the repeated phrase, "Now concerning . . ."). He discussed marriage (chap. 7), idolatry (chaps. 8—10), public worship (chap. 11), spiritual gifts (chaps. 12—14), the Resurrection (chap. 15), and the special offering he was taking for the Jews (chap. 16).

Paul had planted a church in the city, but the city had gotten into the church; and that explained why there were so many problems. The believers in Corinth needed to heed Romans 12:2, and so do we today.

1 Paul, called *to be* an apostle of Jesus Christ through the will of God, and Sosthenes *our* brother,

2*To the church of God which is at Corinth, to those who are sanctified in Christ Jesus, called *to be* saints, with all who in every place call on the name of Jesus Christ our Lord, both theirs and ours:

3Grace to you and peace from God our Father and the Lord Jesus Christ.

4I thank my God always concerning you for the grace of God which was given to you by Christ Jesus, 5that you were enriched in everything by Him in all utterance and all knowledge, 6even as the testimony of Christ was confirmed in you, 7so that you come short in no gift, eagerly waiting for the revelation of our Lord Jesus Christ, 8who will also confirm you to the end, *that you may be* blameless in the day of our Lord Jesus Christ. 9God *is* faithful, by whom you were called into the fellowship of His Son, Jesus Christ our Lord.

10*Now I plead with you, brethren, by the name of our Lord Jesus Christ, that you all speak the same thing, and *that* there be no divisions among you, but *that* you be perfectly joined together in the same mind and in the same judgment. 11For it has been declared to me concerning you, my brethren, by those of Chloe's *household,* that there are contentions among you. 12Now I say this, that each of you says, "I am of Paul," or "I am of Apollos," or "I am of Cephas," or "I am of Christ." 13Is Christ divided? Was Paul crucified for you? Or were you baptized in the name of Paul?

14I thank God that I baptized none of you except Crispus and Gaius, 15lest anyone should say that I had baptized in my own name. 16Yes, I also baptized the household of Stephanas. Besides, I do not know whether I baptized any other. 17*For

CHAPTER 1

1:2–9, 24–29 Even though believers are "all one in Christ Jesus" (Gal. 3:28), the local church often suffers from division. Why?

For one thing, we forget the calling we have in Christ (1:2, 9, 24–29). It is only by God's grace that we have been called, and this fact should humble us and encourage us to love one another (John 15:17).

1:10–16 Another factor is our tendency to follow human leaders and develop a fan club mentality. Christ died for us and lives to bless us, and He must have the preeminence.

1:17–31 A third factor is dependence on human wisdom and philosophies, of which there were many in Corinth. The world's wisdom had crept into the church, and it did not mix with the wisdom of God (Isa. 8:20). Various theologies are the attempts of scholars to interpret the Word of God, but they are not the Word. Never allow them to be a cause of division.

Christ did not send me to baptize, but to preach the gospel, not with wisdom of words, lest the cross of Christ should be made of no effect.

18For the message of the cross is foolishness to those who are perishing, but to us who are being saved it is the power of God. 19For it is written:

> "I will destroy the wisdom of the wise,
> And bring to nothing the understanding of
>   the prudent."a

20Where is the wise? Where is the scribe? Where is the disputer of this age? Has not God made foolish the wisdom of this world? 21For since, in the wisdom of God, the world through wisdom did not know God, it pleased God through the foolishness of the message preached to save those who believe. 22For Jews request a sign, and Greeks seek after wisdom; 23but we preach Christ crucified, to the Jews a stumbling block and to the Greeksb foolishness, 24but to those who are called, both Jews and Greeks, Christ the power of God and the wisdom of God. 25Because the foolishness of God is wiser than men, and the weakness of God is stronger than men.

26For you see your calling, brethren, that not many wise according to the flesh, not many mighty, not many noble, are called. 27But God has chosen the foolish things of the world to put to shame the wise, and God has chosen the weak things of the world to put to shame the things which are mighty; 28and the base things of the world and the things which are despised God has chosen, and the things which are not, to bring to nothing the things that are, 29that no flesh should glory in His presence. 30But of Him you are in Christ Jesus, who became for us wisdom from God—and righteousness and sanctification and redemption— 31that, as it is written, "He who glories, let him glory in the LORD."c

CHAPTER 2

2:1–5 Power. Paul did not imitate the itinerant teachers in Corinth who depended on their eloquence and intellectual brilliance. Paul's faith was in God, not in himself (Zech. 4:6). He wanted sinners to trust in Christ's power. You may think you lack ability to serve God, but God can turn your weakness into strength. The gospel still works (Rom. 1:16)!

2:6–16 Wisdom. The Jews asked for demonstrations of power and the Greeks looked for wisdom, both of which are available in Jesus Christ (1:24). A deeper wisdom of God is available for those who are mature (Heb. 5:12–14). Allow the Spirit of God to teach you about the Son of God from the Word of God, and grow up in Him. Wisdom and power go together. They need each other, and they keep the Christian life balanced.

2 And* I, brethren, when I came to you, did not come with excellence of speech or of wisdom declaring to you the testimonyd of God. 2For I determined not to know anything among you except Jesus Christ and Him crucified. 3I was with you in weakness, in fear, and in much trembling. 4And my speech and my preaching were not with persuasive words of humane wisdom, but in demonstration of the Spirit and of power, 5that your faith should not be in the wisdom of men but in the power of God.

6*However, we speak wisdom among those who are mature, yet not the wisdom of this age, nor of the rulers of this age, who are coming to nothing. 7But we speak the wisdom of God in a mystery, the hidden wisdom which God ordained before the ages for our glory, 8which none of the rulers of this age knew; for had they known, they would not have crucified the Lord of glory.

9But as it is written:

> "Eye has not seen, nor ear heard,
> Nor have entered into the heart of man
> The things which God has prepared for
>   those who love Him."f

1:19 aIsaiah 29:14   1:23 bNU-Text reads Gentiles.
1:31 cJeremiah 9:24   2:1 dNU-Text reads mystery.
2:4 eNU-Text omits human.   2:9 fIsaiah 64:4

¹⁰But God has revealed *them* to us through His Spirit. For the Spirit searches all things, yes, the deep things of God. ¹¹For what man knows the things of a man except the spirit of the man which is in him? Even so no one knows the things of God except the Spirit of God. ¹²Now we have received, not the spirit of the world, but the Spirit who is from God, that we might know the things that have been freely given to us by God.

¹³These things we also speak, not in words which man's wisdom teaches but which the Holy^g Spirit teaches, comparing spiritual things with spiritual. ¹⁴But the natural man does not receive the things of the Spirit of God, for they are foolishness to him; nor can he know *them,* because they are spiritually discerned. ¹⁵But he who is spiritual judges all things, yet he himself is *rightly* judged by no one. ¹⁶For *"who has known the mind of the L*ORD *that he may instruct Him?"*^h But we have the mind of Christ.

3 And* I, brethren, could not speak to you as to spiritual *people* but as to carnal, as to babes in Christ. ²I fed you with milk and not with solid food; for until now you were not able *to receive it,* and even now you are still not able; ³for you are still carnal. For where *there are* envy, strife, and divisions among you, are you not carnal and behaving like *mere* men? ⁴For when one says, "I am of Paul," and another, "I *am* of Apollos," are you not carnal?

⁵*Who then is Paul, and who *is* Apollos, but ministers through whom you believed, as the Lord gave to each one? ⁶I planted, Apollos watered, but God gave the increase. ⁷So then neither he who plants is anything, nor he who waters, but God who gives the increase. ⁸Now he who plants and he who waters are one, and each one will receive his own reward according to his own labor.

⁹For we are God's fellow workers; you are God's field, *you are* God's building. ¹⁰*According to the grace of God which was given to me, as a wise master builder I have laid the foundation, and another builds on it. But let each one take heed how he builds on it. ¹¹For no other foundation can anyone lay than that which is laid, which is Jesus Christ. ¹²Now if anyone builds on this foundation *with* gold, silver, precious stones, wood, hay, straw, ¹³each one's work will become clear; for the Day will declare it, because it will be revealed by fire; and the fire will test each one's work, of what sort it is. ¹⁴If anyone's work which he has built on *it* endures, he will receive a reward. ¹⁵If anyone's work is burned, he will suffer loss; but he himself will be saved, yet so as through fire.

¹⁶Do you not know that you are the temple of God and *that* the Spirit of God dwells in you? ¹⁷If anyone defiles the temple of God, God will destroy him. For the temple of God is holy, which *temple* you are.

¹⁸*Let no one deceive himself. If anyone among you seems to be wise in this age, let him become a fool that he may become wise. ¹⁹For the wisdom of this world is foolishness with God. For it is written, *"He catches the wise in their own craftiness"*;ⁱ ²⁰and again, *"The L*ORD *knows the thoughts of the wise, that they are futile."*^j

CHAPTER 3

3:1–4 *Maturing.* We never outgrow the nourishing milk of the Word (1 Pet. 2:2), but we cannot grow strong unless we also have the "solid food" (Heb. 5:12–14; Matt. 4:4). You grow by eating and exercising (1 Tim. 4:6–8), and it takes both. Age is no guarantee of spiritual maturity.

3:5–9 *Harvesting.* Everybody has a place in the Lord's harvest, and all are doing His work (John 4:34–38). There must be no competing or comparing, for the Lord alone recognizes the work and gives the reward. It makes no difference who the servant is so long as Jesus Christ is Lord of the harvest.

3:10–17 *Building.* Paul writes about the local church and the materials we put into it as we minister (Prov. 2:1–5; 3:13–15). Substituting man's wisdom for God's Word means building with perishable materials that will burn up at the judgment seat of Christ.

❝*If you lack knowledge, go to school. If you lack wisdom, get on your knees! Knowledge is not wisdom. Wisdom is the proper use of knowledge.*❞

—Vance Havner

3:18–23 *Glorifying God.* Because the Corinthian believers gloried in human teachers (1:12) and human wisdom, they robbed God of the glory that rightly belonged to Him. "Let no one boast in men" is a command, not a suggestion.

2:13 ^gNU-Text omits *Holy.* 2:16 ^hIsaiah 40:13   3:19 ⁱJob 5:13   3:20 ^jPsalm 94:11

CHAPTER 4

4:1–5 Life is *a stewardship,* so be faithful. We judge ourselves, and others judge us; but the Final Judge is the Lord. Live to please Him alone.

4:6–8 Life is *a gift,* so be humble. Your abilities and blessings came from God; you cannot take credit for them. They are God's gift to you, and your use of them is your gift to God. It is sinful to contrast various Christian workers (1:12) because only God knows their hearts.

4:9–13 Life is *a battle,* so be courageous. If the apostles were the greatest Christians who ever lived, and they were filth and the scum of the earth, where did that leave the boasting Corinthians?

4:14–21 Life is *a school,* so be teachable. Paul saw himself as a father in the Lord who had to instruct and discipline his children. Our Father in heaven uses many hands and voices to teach us, and we must be willing pupils as we go through life.

CHAPTER 5

5:1–7 *Separation.* The background of the chapter is the Passover Feast (Exod. 12). The presence of the immoral man should have turned the feast into a funeral (v. 2), but the church was boasting about the sinner instead of weeping over him. Tolerating known sin in the church is like putting leaven into the Passover Feast: it does not belong.

21Therefore let no one boast in men. For all things are yours: 22whether Paul or Apollos or Cephas, or the world or life or death, or things present or things to come—all are yours. 23And you *are* Christ's, and Christ *is* God's.

4 Let* a man so consider us, as servants of Christ and stewards of the mysteries of God. 2Moreover it is required in stewards that one be found faithful. 3But with me it is a very small thing that I should be judged by you or by a human court.*k* In fact, I do not even judge myself. 4For I know of nothing against myself, yet I am not justified by this; but He who judges me is the Lord. 5Therefore judge nothing before the time, until the Lord comes, who will both bring to light the hidden things of darkness and reveal the counsels of the hearts. Then each one's praise will come from God.

6*Now these things, brethren, I have figuratively transferred to myself and Apollos for your sakes, that you may learn in us not to think beyond what is written, that none of you may be puffed up on behalf of one against the other. 7For who makes you differ *from another?* And what do you have that you did not receive? Now if you did indeed receive *it,* why do you boast as if you had not received *it?*

8You are already full! You are already rich! You have reigned as kings without us—and indeed I could wish you did reign, that we also might reign with you! 9*For I think that God has displayed us, the apostles, last, as men condemned to death; for we have been made a spectacle to the world, both to angels and to men. 10We *are* fools for Christ's sake, but you *are* wise in Christ! We *are* weak, but you *are* strong! You *are* distinguished, but we *are* dishonored! 11To the present hour we both hunger and thirst, and we are poorly clothed, and beaten, and homeless. 12And we labor, working with our own hands. Being reviled, we bless; being persecuted, we endure; 13being defamed, we entreat. We have been made as the filth of the world, the offscouring of all things until now.

14*I do not write these things to shame you, but as my beloved children I warn you. 15For though you might have ten thousand instructors in Christ, yet *you* do not *have* many fathers; for in Christ Jesus I have begotten you through the gospel. 16Therefore I urge you, imitate me. 17For this reason I have sent Timothy to you, who is my beloved and faithful son in the Lord, who will remind you of my ways in Christ, as I teach everywhere in every church.

18Now some are puffed up, as though I were not coming to you. 19But I will come to you shortly, if the Lord wills, and I will know, not the word of those who are puffed up, but the power. 20For the kingdom of God *is* not in word but in power. 21What do you want? Shall I come to you with a rod, or in love and a spirit of gentleness?

5 It* is actually reported *that there is* sexual immorality among you, and such sexual immor-

4:3 *k*Literally *day*

Share in Fellowship—The phrase "deliver such a one to Satan" (1 Cor. 5:5) suggests that there is spiritual safety within the fellowship of the local church. To be disciplined and dismissed from fellowship makes us vulnerable to Satan's attacks. Far better to confess our sins, be forgiven, and be restored to fellowship.

ality as is not even named[l] among the Gentiles—
that a man has his father's wife! [2]And you are
puffed up, and have not rather mourned, that he
who has done this deed might be taken away from
among you. [3]For I indeed, as absent in body but
present in spirit, have already judged (as though
I were present) him who has so done this deed.
[4]In the name of our Lord Jesus Christ, when you
are gathered together, along with my spirit, with
the power of our Lord Jesus Christ, [5]deliver such
a one to Satan for the destruction of the flesh,
that his spirit may be saved in the day of the Lord
Jesus.[m]

[6]Your glorying is not good. Do you not know
that a little leaven leavens the whole lump?
[7]Therefore purge out the old leaven, that you may
be a new lump, since you truly are unleavened.
For indeed Christ, our Passover, was sacrificed
for us.[n] [8]*Therefore let us keep the feast, not with
old leaven, nor with the leaven of malice and
wickedness, but with the unleavened bread of sincerity and truth.

[9]*I wrote to you in my epistle not to keep company with sexually immoral people. [10]Yet I certainly did not mean with the sexually immoral
people of this world, or with the covetous, or extortioners, or idolaters, since then you would need
to go out of the world. [11]But now I have written
to you not to keep company with anyone named
a brother, who is sexually immoral, or covetous,
or an idolater, or a reviler, or a drunkard, or an
extortioner—not even to eat with such a person.

[12]For what have I to do with judging those also
who are outside? Do you not judge those who are
inside? [13]But those who are outside God judges.
Therefore "put away from yourselves the evil
person."[o]

6 Dare* any of you, having a matter against another, go to law before the unrighteous, and
not before the saints? [2]Do you not know that the
saints will judge the world? And if the world will
be judged by you, are you unworthy to judge the
smallest matters? [3]Do you not know that we shall
judge angels? How much more, things that pertain
to this life? [4]If then you have judgments concerning things pertaining to this life, do you appoint
those who are least esteemed by the church to
judge? [5]I say this to your shame. Is it so, that there
is not a wise man among you, not even one, who
will be able to judge between his brethren?
[6]But brother goes to law against brother, and that
before unbelievers!

[7]*Now therefore, it is already an utter failure
for you that you go to law against one another.
Why do you not rather accept wrong? Why do
you not rather let yourselves be cheated? [8]No, you
yourselves do wrong and cheat, and you do these
things to your brethren! [9]Do you not know that
the unrighteous will not inherit the kingdom of
God? Do not be deceived. Neither fornicators, nor
idolaters, nor adulterers, nor homosexuals,[p] nor

5:8 Celebration. Paul saw the Christian life
as "keeping the feast" (v. 8), that is, feeding
on Christ, being ready to move, and being
sure we are not defiled by sin (leaven,
yeast). The Lamb has set us free, and we
are on our way to our promised inheritance!

5:9–13 Isolation. Sin in the life of the
believer is far worse than sin in the life of
an unbeliever. We cannot isolate ourselves
from the world, but we can separate
ourselves from disobedient believers so that
God can discipline them.

CHAPTER 6

6:1–6 Not only were the Corinthian
believers compromising with the world, but
they were also losing their testimony before
the world by taking each other to court
before pagan judges. Paul repeatedly
asked, "Do you not know?" (vv. 2, 3, 15,
16, 19). They were ignorant of some basic
truths of the Christian life.
   We will judge angels. If God entrusts that
great a responsibility to His people, can't He
help us with our petty decisions today?

6:7–12 We have been changed. We are
not what we once were, so why should we
live as we once lived? It is a matter not of
"What is lawful?" but of "What is helpful?"

5:1 [l]NU-Text omits named.   5:5 [m]NU-Text omits Jesus.
5:7 [n]NU-Text omits for us.   5:13 [o]Deuteronomy 17:7; 19:19;
22:21, 24; 24:7   6:9 [p]That is, catamites

Flee These Temptations—"Flee sexual immorality" (1 Cor. 6:18) reminds us of Joseph when he
fled from Potiphar's wife (Gen. 39). "Flee also youthful lusts" (2 Tim. 2:22) is a parallel admonition.
When it comes to the devil, resist him and he will flee from you (James 4:7); but when it comes to
temptations of the flesh, you do the fleeing!

6:13–20 We belong to the Lord. He made the human body, He dwells in believers by His Spirit, and He purchased us at the Cross. The believer's body belongs to God and must be used to glorify Him.

7:1–9 Marriage is *a gift,* and not everybody has the same gift. Some people have more self-control than others. People remain unmarried for different reasons (Matt. 19:11–12), and each one must know the will of God.

7:10–16 Marriage is *a ministry.* He addressed people who had been converted after marriage and who wondered if they should remain with their unsaved spouses. "Yes," said Paul, "because you might win them to Christ." But even Christian spouses can have a wonderful ministry to each other as they grow in the Lord and love each other (Eph. 5:22ff.).

❝*Success in marriage involves much more than finding the right mate. It also requires being the right mate.*❞

sodomites, 10nor thieves, nor covetous, nor drunkards, nor revilers, nor extortioners will inherit the kingdom of God. 11And such were some of you. But you were washed, but you were sanctified, but you were justified in the name of the Lord Jesus and by the Spirit of our God.

12All things are lawful for me, but all things are not helpful. All things are lawful for me, but I will not be brought under the power of any. 13*Foods for the stomach and the stomach for foods; but God will destroy both it and them. Now the body *is* not for sexual immorality but for the Lord, and the Lord for the body. 14And God both raised up the Lord and will also raise us up by His power.

15Do you not know that your bodies are members of Christ? Shall I then take the members of Christ and make *them* members of a harlot? Certainly not! 16Or do you not know that he who is joined to a harlot is one body *with her?* For *"the two,"* He says, *"shall become one flesh."*q 17But he who is joined to the Lord is one spirit *with Him.*

18Flee sexual immorality. Every sin that a man does is outside the body, but he who commits sexual immorality sins against his own body. 19Or do you not know that your body is the temple of the Holy Spirit *who is* in you, whom you have from God, and you are not your own? 20For you were bought at a price; therefore glorify God in your bodyr and in your spirit, which are God's.

7 Now* concerning the things of which you wrote to me:

It is good for a man not to touch a woman. 2Nevertheless, because of sexual immorality, let each man have his own wife, and let each woman have her own husband. 3Let the husband render to his wife the affection due her, and likewise also the wife to her husband. 4The wife does not have authority over her own body, but the husband *does.* And likewise the husband does not have authority over his own body, but the wife *does.* 5Do not deprive one another except with consent for a time, that you may give yourselves to fasting and prayer; and come together again so that Satan does not tempt you because of your lack of self-control. 6But I say this as a concession, not as a commandment. 7For I wish that all men were even as I myself. But each one has his own gift from God, one in this manner and another in that.

8But I say to the unmarried and to the widows: It is good for them if they remain even as I am; 9but if they cannot exercise self-control, let them marry. For it is better to marry than to burn *with passion.*

10*Now to the married I command, *yet* not I but the Lord: A wife is not to depart from *her* husband. 11But even if she does depart, let her remain unmarried or be reconciled to *her* husband. And a husband is not to divorce *his* wife.

12But to the rest I, not the Lord, say: If any brother has a wife who does not believe, and she is willing to live with him, let him not divorce her. 13And a woman who has a husband who does not believe, if he is willing to live with her, let her not divorce him. 14For the unbelieving husband is sanctified by the wife, and the unbelieving

---

6:16 qGenesis 2:24   6:20 rNU-Text ends the verse at *body.*

wife is sanctified by the husband; otherwise your children would be unclean, but now they are holy. [15]But if the unbeliever departs, let him depart; a brother or a sister is not under bondage in such *cases*. But God has called us to peace. [16]For how do you know, O wife, whether you will save *your* husband? Or how do you know, O husband, whether you will save *your* wife?

[17]*But as God has distributed to each one, as the Lord has called each one, so let him walk. And so I ordain in all the churches. [18]Was anyone called while circumcised? Let him not become uncircumcised. Was anyone called while uncircumcised? Let him not be circumcised. [19]Circumcision is nothing and uncircumcision is nothing, but keeping the commandments of God *is what matters*. [20]Let each one remain in the same calling in which he was called. [21]Were you called *while* a slave? Do not be concerned about it; but if you can be made free, rather use *it*. [22]For he who is called in the Lord *while* a slave is the Lord's freedman. Likewise he who is called *while* free is Christ's slave. [23]You were bought at a price; do not become slaves of men. [24]Brethren, let each one remain with God in that *state* in which he was called.

[25]*Now concerning virgins: I have no commandment from the Lord; yet I give judgment as one whom the Lord in His mercy *has made* trustworthy. [26]I suppose therefore that this is good because of the present distress—that *it is* good for a man to remain as he is: [27]Are you bound to a wife? Do not seek to be loosed. Are you loosed from a wife? Do not seek a wife. [28]But even if you do marry, you have not sinned; and if a virgin marries, she has not sinned. Nevertheless such will have trouble in the flesh, but I would spare you.

[29]But this I say, brethren, the time *is* short, so that from now on even those who have wives should be as though they had none, [30]those who weep as though they did not weep, those who rejoice as though they did not rejoice, those who buy as though they did not possess, [31]and those who use this world as not misusing *it*. For the form of this world is passing away.

[32]But I want you to be without care. He who is unmarried cares for the things of the Lord—how he may please the Lord. [33]But he who is married cares about the things of the world—how he may please *his* wife. [34]There is[s] a difference between a wife and a virgin. The unmarried woman cares about the things of the Lord, that she may be holy both in body and in spirit. But she who is married cares about the things of the world—how she may please *her* husband. [35]And this I say for your own profit, not that I may put a leash on you, but for what is proper, and that you may serve the Lord without distraction.

[36]But if any man thinks he is behaving improperly toward his virgin, if she is past the flower of youth, and thus it must be, let him do what he wishes. He does not sin; let them marry. [37]Nevertheless he who stands steadfast in his heart, having no necessity, but has power over his own will, and has so determined in his heart that he will keep his virgin,[t] does well. [38]So then he who gives her[u] in marriage does well, but he

7:17–24 Marriage is *a calling*. When you become a Christian, that does not annul what you were before you trusted Christ. Jews are still Jews, slaves are still slaves, and married people are still married. But now, with the Lord's help, you can fulfill that calling in a greater way.

7:25–40 Marriage is *a challenge*. Paul does not deny the blessings of marriage, but he does remind us of the burdens that marriage brings, especially when the times are tough. Building a Christian home is a great ministry, but nobody should enter into it lightly or carelessly.

7:34 [s]M-Text adds *also*. 7:37 [t]Or *virgin daughter* 7:38 [u]NU-Text reads *his own virgin*.

CHAPTER 8

8:1ff *Life is controlled by conscience.*
Conscience is the judge within that
commends us for doing right and condemns
us for doing wrong (Rom. 2:14–15). If we
sin against conscience, we do terrible
damage to the inner person.
*Conscience is strengthened by
knowledge.* As we grow in spiritual
understanding, a weak conscience becomes
stronger, and we appreciate our freedom in
Christ more and more. The weak believer
must not run ahead of his conscience, and
the strong believer must never force him to
do so.

Knowledge must be balanced by love.
Your spiritual knowledge can be either a
weapon to hurt people or a tool to build
people. If your knowledge puffs you up, it
will tear others down. Love knows when and
how to yield to others without compromising
the truth. Review Romans 14—15.

CHAPTER 9

9:1ff We do not have the right to give up
our freedom, for that was purchased by
Christ (Gal. 5:1); *but we do have the
freedom to give up our rights.* For the sake
of winning the lost (9:12), Paul gave up his
right to receive financial support, and he
begged the Corinthians to give up their rights
for the sake of the saved.
Christian ministry is like fighting a war,
caring for a vineyard, tending a flock, and
cultivating a field (vv. 7–11). Meditate on
these images, and see what they teach you
about serving the Lord.
Ministry is a stewardship (v. 17), and the
servant must be faithful (4:2). Ministers of
Christ are also like runners who must keep
the rules or be disqualified (9:24–27).
Verses 19–23 call for courtesy and
wisdom in witness, not for compromise. "I
have become all things to all men" does not
mean Paul had no personal convictions. It
means he used his convictions to build
bridges, not walls. If he seemed
inconsistent, it was only because people did
not look deep enough. *His one great desire
was to win the lost,* and that governed his
every decision.

❝*Knowledge is proud that he has
learned so much; Wisdom is humble
that he knows no more.*❞
—William Cowper

who does not give *her* in marriage does better.
39A wife is bound by law as long as her husband
lives; but if her husband dies, she is at liberty to
be married to whom she wishes, only in the Lord.
40But she is happier if she remains as she is, according to my judgment—and I think I also have
the Spirit of God.

8 Now* concerning things offered to idols: We
know that we all have knowledge. Knowledge
puffs up, but love edifies. 2And if anyone thinks
that he knows anything, he knows nothing yet
as he ought to know. 3But if anyone loves God,
this one is known by Him.
4Therefore concerning the eating of things offered to idols, we know that an idol *is* nothing in
the world, and that *there is* no other God but one.
5For even if there are so-called gods, whether in
heaven or on earth (as there are many gods and
many lords), 6yet for us *there is* one God, the Father, of whom *are* all things, and we for Him; and
one Lord Jesus Christ, through whom *are* all
things, and through whom we *live.*
7However, *there is* not in everyone that knowledge; for some, with consciousness of the idol,
until now eat *it* as a thing offered to an idol; and
their conscience, being weak, is defiled. 8But food
does not commend us to God; for neither if we
eat are we the better, nor if we do not eat are we
the worse.
9But beware lest somehow this liberty of yours
become a stumbling block to those who are weak.
10For if anyone sees you who have knowledge eating in an idol's temple, will not the conscience of
him who is weak be emboldened to eat those
things offered to idols? 11And because of your
knowledge shall the weak brother perish, for
whom Christ died? 12But when you thus sin
against the brethren, and wound their weak conscience, you sin against Christ. 13Therefore, if
food makes my brother stumble, I will never again
eat meat, lest I make my brother stumble.

9 Am* I not an apostle? Am I not free? Have I
not seen Jesus Christ our Lord? Are you not
my work in the Lord? 2If I am not an apostle to
others, yet doubtless I am to you. For you are the
seal of my apostleship in the Lord.
3My defense to those who examine me is this:
4Do we have no right to eat and drink? 5Do we
have no right to take along a believing wife, as
do also the other apostles, the brothers of the
Lord, and Cephas? 6Or *is it* only Barnabas and I
who have no right to refrain from working?
7Who ever goes to war at his own expense? Who
plants a vineyard and does not eat of its fruit?
Or who tends a flock and does not drink of the
milk of the flock?
8Do I say these things as a *mere* man? Or does
not the law say the same also? 9For it is written
in the law of Moses, *"You shall not muzzle an
ox while it treads out the grain."*ᵛ Is it oxen God
is concerned about? 10Or does He say *it* altogether
for our *sakes?* For our sakes, no doubt, *this* is
written, that he who plows should plow in hope,
and he who threshes in hope should be partaker
of his hope. 11If we have sown spiritual things
for you, *is it* a great thing if we reap your material

9:9 ᵛDeuteronomy 25:4

things? 12If others are partakers of *this* right over you, *are* we not even more?

Nevertheless we have not used this right, but endure all things lest we hinder the gospel of Christ. 13Do you not know that those who minister the holy things eat *of the things* of the temple, and those who serve at the altar partake of *the offerings of* the altar? 14Even so the Lord has commanded that those who preach the gospel should live from the gospel.

15But I have used none of these things, nor have I written these things that it should be done so to me; for it *would be* better for me to die than that anyone should make my boasting void. 16For if I preach the gospel, I have nothing to boast of, for necessity is laid upon me; yes, woe is me if I do not preach the gospel! 17For if I do this willingly, I have a reward; but if against my will, I have been entrusted with a stewardship. 18What is my reward then? That when I preach the gospel, I may present the gospel of Christ*w* without charge, that I may not abuse my authority in the gospel.

19For though I am free from all *men,* I have made myself a servant to all, that I might win the more; 20and to the Jews I became as a Jew, that I might win Jews; to those *who are* under the law, as under the law,*x* that I might win those *who are* under the law; 21to those *who are* without law, as without law (not being without law toward God,*y* but under law toward Christ*z*), that I might win those *who are* without law; 22to the weak I became as*a* weak, that I might win the weak. I have become all things to all *men,* that I might by all means save some. 23Now this I do for the gospel's sake, that I may be partaker of it with you.

24Do you not know that those who run in a race all run, but one receives the prize? Run in such a way that you may obtain *it.* 25And everyone who competes *for the prize* is temperate in all things. Now they *do it* to obtain a perishable crown, but we *for* an imperishable *crown.* 26Therefore I run thus: not with uncertainty. Thus I fight: not as *one who* beats the air. 27But I discipline my body and bring *it* into subjection, lest, when I have preached to others, I myself should become disqualified.

10 Moreover,* brethren, I do not want you to be unaware that all our fathers were under the cloud, all passed through the sea, 2all were baptized into Moses in the cloud and in the sea, 3all ate the same spiritual food, 4and all drank the same spiritual drink. For they drank of that spiritual Rock that followed them, and that Rock was Christ. 5But with most of them God was not well pleased, for *their bodies* were scattered in the wilderness.

6*Now these things became our examples, to the intent that we should not lust after evil things as they also lusted. 7And do not become idolaters as *were* some of them. As it is written, *"The people sat down to eat and drink, and rose up to play."b* 8Nor let us commit sexual immorality, as some of them did, and in one day twenty-three thousand

---

9:18 *w*NU-Text omits *of Christ.*   9:20 *x*NU-Text adds *though not being myself under the law.*   9:21 *y*NU-Text reads *God's law.* *z*NU-Text reads *Christ's law.*   9:22 *a*NU-Text omits *as.* 10:7 *b*Exodus 32:6

" *Tact is the art of making a point without making an enemy.* **"**
—Howard W. Newton

" *When you flee from temptation, be sure you do not leave a forwarding address behind.* **"**

CHAPTER 10

10:1–5 If you insist on using your rights, you may cause a weaker believer to stumble; *and you may also bring trouble on yourself.* When you face difficult decisions, take these factors into consideration.

God's blessing. The parallel to God's people today is obvious. We have been redeemed from the world, identified with Jesus Christ, and nourished by spiritual food and drink. But these blessings are no guarantee that we will be successful.

10:6–12 God's judgment. When Israel sinned, God disciplined them; and He will do the same to His people today. Do you practice and tolerate in your life any of the sins named here? God gives His children freedom, but the freedom to sin is not included.

fell; [9]nor let us tempt Christ, as some of them also tempted, and were destroyed by serpents; [10]nor complain, as some of them also complained, and were destroyed by the destroyer. [11]Now all[c] these things happened to them as examples, and they were written for our admonition, upon whom the ends of the ages have come.

[12]Therefore let him who thinks he stands take heed lest he fall. [13]*No temptation has overtaken you except such as is common to man; but God *is* faithful, who will not allow you to be tempted beyond what you are able, but with the temptation will also make the way of escape, that you may be able to bear *it.*

10:13–22 *God's promise.* God knows how much we can take and always provides the way of escape. Sometimes the smartest thing to do is to flee (v. 14; 6:18). Always look for the open door and the blessing on the other side.

[14]Therefore, my beloved, flee from idolatry. [15]I speak as to wise men; judge for yourselves what I say. [16]The cup of blessing which we bless, is it not the communion of the blood of Christ? The bread which we break, is it not the communion of the body of Christ? [17]For we, *though* many, are one bread *and* one body; for we all partake of that one bread.

[18]Observe Israel after the flesh: Are not those who eat of the sacrifices partakers of the altar? [19]What am I saying then? That an idol is anything, or what is offered to idols is anything? [20]Rather, that the things which the Gentiles sacrifice they sacrifice to demons and not to God, and I do not want you to have fellowship with demons. [21]You cannot drink the cup of the Lord and the cup of demons; you cannot partake of the Lord's table and of the table of demons. [22]Or do we provoke the Lord to jealousy? Are we stronger than He?

10:23–33 *God's glory.* Two extremes must be avoided: practicing license in the name of Christian freedom, and being so fussy that we cannot live in a real world and make rational decisions. When you seek to edify others and glorify the Lord, you will know what to do.

[23]*All things are lawful for me,[d] but not all things are helpful; all things are lawful for me,[e] but not all things edify. [24]Let no one seek his own, but each one the other's *well-being.*

[25]Eat whatever is sold in the meat market, asking no questions for conscience' sake; [26]for *"the earth is the LORD's, and all its fullness."[f]*

[27]If any of those who do not believe invites you *to dinner,* and you desire to go, eat whatever is set before you, asking no question for conscience' sake. [28]But if anyone says to you, "This was offered to idols," do not eat it for the sake of the one who told you, and for conscience' sake;[g] for *"the earth is the LORD's, and all its fullness."[h]* [29]"Conscience," I say, not your own, but that of the other. For why is my liberty judged by another *man's* conscience? [30]But if I partake with thanks, why am I evil spoken of for *the food* over which I give thanks?

[31]Therefore, whether you eat or drink, or whatever you do, do all to the glory of God. [32]Give no offense, either to the Jews or to the Greeks or to the church of God, [33]just as I also please all *men* in all *things,* not seeking my own profit, but the *profit* of many, that they may be saved.

CHAPTER 11

11:3–16 Some matters discussed in this chapter may have only local significance, but the spiritual principles apply to us today. When it comes to sharing in public worship, we must ask ourselves serious questions. ***Do I dishonor authority?*** We must be careful not to dishonor the Lord, no matter what the cultural standards may be. God has established headship in creation and in the church, and we must respect it.

11 Imitate me, just as I also *imitate* Christ. [2]Now I praise you, brethren, that you remember me in all things and keep the traditions just as I delivered *them* to you. [3]*But I want you to know that the head of every man is Christ, the head of woman *is* man, and the head of Christ *is* God. [4]Every man praying or prophesying, having

---

10:11 [c]NU-Text omits *all.*   10:23 [d]NU-Text omits *for me.*
[e]NU-Text omits *for me.*   10:26 [f]Psalm 24:1   10:28 [g]NU-Text omits the rest of this verse.   [h]Psalm 24:1

his head covered, dishonors his head. 5But every woman who prays or prophesies with *her* head uncovered dishonors her head, for that is one and the same as if her head were shaved. 6For if a woman is not covered, let her also be shorn. But if it is shameful for a woman to be shorn or shaved, let her be covered. 7For a man indeed ought not to cover *his* head, since he is the image and glory of God; but woman is the glory of man. 8For man is not from woman, but woman from man. 9Nor was man created for the woman, but woman for the man. 10For this reason the woman ought to have *a symbol of* authority on *her* head, because of the angels. 11Nevertheless, neither *is* man independent of woman, nor woman independent of man, in the Lord. 12For as woman *came* from man, even so man also *comes* through woman; but all things are from God.

13Judge among yourselves. Is it proper for a woman to pray to God with her head uncovered? 14Does not even nature itself teach you that if a man has long hair, it is a dishonor to him? 15But if a woman has long hair, it is a glory to her; for *her* hair is given to her[i] for a covering. 16But if anyone seems to be contentious, we have no such custom, nor *do* the churches of God.

17*Now in giving these instructions I do not praise *you*, since you come together not for the better but for the worse. 18For first of all, when you come together as a church, I hear that there are divisions among you, and in part I believe it. 19For there must also be factions among you, that those who are approved may be recognized among you. 20Therefore when you come together in one place, it is not to eat the Lord's Supper. 21For in eating, each one takes his own supper ahead of *others*; and one is hungry and another is drunk. 22What! Do you not have houses to eat and drink in? Or do you despise the church of God and shame those who have nothing? What shall I say to you? Shall I praise you in this? I do not praise *you*.

23*For I received from the Lord that which I also delivered to you: that the Lord Jesus on the *same* night in which He was betrayed took bread; 24and when He had given thanks, He broke *it* and said, "Take, eat;[j] this is My body which is broken[k] for you; do this in remembrance of Me." 25In the same manner *He* also *took* the cup after supper, saying, "This cup is the new covenant in My blood. This do, as often as you drink *it*, in remembrance of Me."

26For as often as you eat this bread and drink this cup, you proclaim the Lord's death till He comes.

27Therefore whoever eats this bread or drinks *this* cup of the Lord in an unworthy manner will be guilty of the body and blood[l] of the Lord. 28But let a man examine himself, and so let him eat of the bread and drink of the cup. 29For he who eats and drinks in an unworthy manner[m] eats and drinks judgment to himself, not discerning the Lord's[n] body. 30For this reason many *are* weak and sick among you, and many sleep. 31For if we would judge ourselves, we would not be judged. 32But when we are judged, we are chastened by

11:17–22 *Do I despise the church?* We are one in Christ and in love must honor one another. By the way they ate their love feast, the rich embarrassed the poor and brought shame to the church.

11:23–34 *Do I discern the body?* When we meet to celebrate the Communion service, we must examine ourselves and not one another; and we must be honest with the Lord as we confess our sins. We discern His body in the bread, but we also discern it in the members of the church who eat with us. The Lord's Supper is a family feast. While it must be personal, it must not become so individual that it becomes selfish. It should be a means of promoting the unity of the church.

11:15 [i]M-Text omits *to her.*   11:24 [j]NU-Text omits *Take, eat.* [k]NU-Text omits *broken.*   11:27 [l]NU-Text and M-Text read *the blood.*   11:29 [m]NU-Text omits *in an unworthy manner.* [n]NU-Text omits *Lord's.*

the Lord, that we may not be condemned with the world. ³³Therefore, my brethren, when you come together to eat, wait for one another. ³⁴But if anyone is hungry, let him eat at home, lest you come together for judgment. And the rest I will set in order when I come.

CHAPTER 12

12:1–11 The Corinthian believers were especially gifted by God (1:4–7), but some of them were creating problems by using their spiritual gifts in unspiritual ways. Paul reminded those people of three basic truths. *There is one Lord.* The Spirit glorifies Christ (John 16:14), not Himself. The Spirit gives us gifts so that we can serve Christ and His church "for the profit of all" (12:7) and not for our own selfish enjoyment. Have you discovered what the Spirit has given you? Have you thanked God for it, and are you using your gift(s) under Christ's lordship?

12:12–31 *There is one body.* As members of the same body, we belong to one another, and we need one another. The believers you think you can do without may be the ones you need the most! We must minister to one another and care for one another as one body.

❝*None understand better the nature of real distinction than those who have entered into unity.*❞
—Johannes Tauler

12:25 *There is one danger.* When a part of your physical body declares independence from the other parts, it starts to die and you have to visit the doctor. Division in the local church brings weakness and pain (1:10–17) because no Christian can go it alone and be successful. Do you thank God for fellow Christians and seek to care for them?

12 Now* concerning spiritual *gifts*, brethren, I do not want you to be ignorant: ²You know that^o you were Gentiles, carried away to these dumb idols, however you were led. ³Therefore I make known to you that no one speaking by the Spirit of God calls Jesus accursed, and no one can say that Jesus is Lord except by the Holy Spirit.

⁴There are diversities of gifts, but the same Spirit. ⁵There are differences of ministries, but the same Lord. ⁶And there are diversities of activities, but it is the same God who works all in all. ⁷But the manifestation of the Spirit is given to each one for the profit *of all:* ⁸for to one is given the word of wisdom through the Spirit, to another the word of knowledge through the same Spirit, ⁹to another faith by the same Spirit, to another gifts of healings by the same^p Spirit, ¹⁰to another the working of miracles, to another prophecy, to another discerning of spirits, to another *different* kinds of tongues, to another the interpretation of tongues. ¹¹But one and the same Spirit works all these things, distributing to each one individually as He wills.

¹²*For as the body is one and has many members, but all the members of that one body, being many, are one body, so also *is* Christ. ¹³For by one Spirit we were all baptized into one body—whether Jews or Greeks, whether slaves or free—and have all been made to drink into^q one Spirit. ¹⁴For in fact the body is not one member but many.

¹⁵If the foot should say, "Because I am not a hand, I am not of the body," is it therefore not of the body? ¹⁶And if the ear should say, "Because I am not an eye, I am not of the body," is it therefore not of the body? ¹⁷If the whole body *were* an eye, where *would be* the hearing? If the whole *were* hearing, where *would be* the smelling? ¹⁸But now God has set the members, each one of them, in the body just as He pleased. ¹⁹And if they *were* all one member, where *would* the body *be?*

²⁰But now indeed *there are* many members, yet one body. ²¹And the eye cannot say to the hand, "I have no need of you"; nor again the head to the feet, "I have no need of you." ²²No, much rather, those members of the body which seem to be weaker are necessary. ²³And those *members* of the body which we think to be less honorable, on these we bestow greater honor; and our unpresentable *parts* have greater modesty, ²⁴but our presentable *parts* have no need. But God composed the body, having given greater honor to that *part* which lacks it, ²⁵*that there should be no schism in the body, but *that* the members should have the same care for one another. ²⁶And if one member suffers, all the members suffer with *it;* or if one member is honored, all the members rejoice with *it.*

²⁷Now you are the body of Christ, and members

12:2 ^oNU-Text and M-Text add *when.* 12:9 ^pNU-Text reads *one.* 12:13 ^qNU-Text omits *into.*

individually. 28And God has appointed these in the church: first apostles, second prophets, third teachers, after that miracles, then gifts of healings, helps, administrations, varieties of tongues. 29*Are* all apostles? *Are* all prophets? *Are* all teachers? *Are* all workers of miracles? 30Do all have gifts of healings? Do all speak with tongues? Do all interpret? 31But earnestly desire the best[r] gifts. And yet I show you a more excellent way.

13 Though* I speak with the tongues of men and of angels, but have not love, I have become sounding brass or a clanging cymbal. 2And though I have *the gift of* prophecy, and understand all mysteries and all knowledge, and though I have all faith, so that I could remove mountains, but have not love, I am nothing. 3And though I bestow all my goods to feed *the poor,* and though I give my body to be burned,[s] but have not love, it profits me nothing.

4*Love suffers long *and* is kind; love does not envy; love does not parade itself, is not puffed up; 5does not behave rudely, does not seek its own, is not provoked, thinks no evil; 6does not rejoice in iniquity, but rejoices in the truth; 7bears all things, believes all things, hopes all things, endures all things.

8*Love never fails. But whether *there are* prophecies, they will fail; whether *there are* tongues, they will cease; whether *there is* knowledge, it will vanish away. 9For we know in part and we prophesy in part. 10But when that which is perfect has come, then that which is in part will be done away.

11When I was a child, I spoke as a child, I understood as a child, I thought as a child; but when I became a man, I put away childish things. 12For now we see in a mirror, dimly, but then face to face. Now I know in part, but then I shall know just as I also am known.

13And now abide faith, hope, love, these three; but the greatest of these *is* love.

14 Pursue* love, and desire spiritual *gifts,* but especially that you may prophesy. 2For he who speaks in a tongue does not speak to men but to God, for no one understands *him;* however, in the spirit he speaks mysteries. 3But he who prophesies speaks edification and exhortation and comfort to men. 4He who speaks in a tongue edifies himself, but he who prophesies edifies the church. 5I wish you all spoke with tongues, but even more that you prophesied; for[t] he who prophesies *is* greater than he who speaks with tongues, unless indeed he interprets, that the church may receive edification.

6But now, brethren, if I come to you speaking with tongues, what shall I profit you unless I speak to you either by revelation, by knowledge, by prophesying, or by teaching? 7Even things without life, whether flute or harp, when they make a sound, unless they make a distinction in the sounds, how will it be known what is piped or played? 8For if the trumpet makes an uncertain sound, who will prepare for battle? 9So likewise you, unless you utter by the tongue words easy to understand, how will it be known what is spoken? For you will be speaking into the air.

CHAPTER 13

13:1–3 This so-called hymn to love was Paul's prescription for solving the sickness in the church body in Corinth. The believers had spiritual gifts, but they lacked spiritual graces and needed to be reminded why love is so important in the Christian life.

Love puts *quality into service* (vv. 1–3). When you have love, your words and actions amount to something and help other people.

13:4–7 Love also puts *maturity into character* (vv. 4–7). The Corinthians were impatient with each other, suing each other, tolerating sin in the church, and creating problems because they did not have love. Whatever qualities you may have, they are nothing without love.

13:8–13 Love puts *eternity into life.* Love lasts, and what love does will last. Love is the greatest and does the greatest because "God is love" (1 John 4:8).

"*God hates the great things in which love is not the motive power; but He delights in the little things that are prompted by a feeling of love.*"

—D. L. Moody

CHAPTER 14

14:1ff Why go to church? God's people assemble for one purpose: to worship God. They worship Him by their praying and singing (v. 15), teaching and preaching (v. 3). Worship should result in glory to God, blessing for God's people (v. 3), and fear and conviction for sinners (vv. 23–25).

But for these things to happen, Jesus Christ must be Lord of our lives, and we must yield to the Holy Spirit. If we come to church to display our spirituality, we will not only miss the blessing ourselves but also cause others to miss the blessing. We come to honor Him.

A key word in this chapter is *edification* (vv. 3–5, 12, 17, 26), which means "building up." A worship service should lift up the Lord and build up the saints, not puff up the participants.

12:31 [r]NU-Text reads *greater.*   13:3 [s]NU-Text reads *so I may boast.*   14:5 [t]NU-Text reads *and.*

10There are, it may be, so many kinds of languages in the world, and none of them *is* without significance. 11Therefore, if I do not know the meaning of the language, I shall be a foreigner to him who speaks, and he who speaks *will be* a foreigner to me. 12Even so you, since you are zealous for spiritual *gifts, let it be* for the edification of the church *that* you seek to excel.

13Therefore let him who speaks in a tongue pray that he may interpret. 14For if I pray in a tongue, my spirit prays, but my understanding is unfruitful. 15What is *the conclusion* then? I will pray with the spirit, and I will also pray with the understanding. I will sing with the spirit, and I will also sing with the understanding. 16Otherwise, if you bless with the spirit, how will he who occupies the place of the uninformed say "Amen" at your giving of thanks, since he does not understand what you say? 17For you indeed give thanks well, but the other is not edified.

18I thank my God I speak with tongues more than you all; 19yet in the church I would rather speak five words with my understanding, that I may teach others also, than ten thousand words in a tongue.

20Brethren, do not be children in understanding; however, in malice be babes, but in understanding be mature.

21In the law it is written:

> "With men of other tongues and other lips
> I will speak to this people;
> And yet, for all that, they will not hear Me,"u

says the Lord.

22Therefore tongues are for a sign, not to those who believe but to unbelievers; but prophesying is not for unbelievers but for those who believe. 23Therefore if the whole church comes together in one place, and all speak with tongues, and there come in *those who are* uninformed or unbelievers, will they not say that you are out of your mind? 24But if all prophesy, and an unbeliever or an uninformed person comes in, he is convinced by all, he is convicted by all. 25And thusv the secrets of his heart are revealed; and so, falling down on *his* face, he will worship God and report that God is truly among you.

26How is it then, brethren? Whenever you come together, each of you has a psalm, has a teaching, has a tongue, has a revelation, has an interpretation. Let all things be done for edification. 27If anyone speaks in a tongue, *let there be* two or at the most three, *each* in turn, and let one interpret. 28But if there is no interpreter, let him keep silent in church, and let him speak to himself and to God. 29Let two or three prophets speak, and let the others judge. 30But if *anything* is revealed to another who sits by, let the first keep silent. 31For you can all prophesy one by one, that all may learn and all may be encouraged. 32And the spirits of the prophets are subject to the prophets. 33For God is not *the author* of confusion but of peace, as in all the churches of the saints.

34Let yourw women keep silent in the churches, for they are not permitted to speak; but *they are* to be submissive, as the law also says. 35And if

---

14:21 uIsaiah 28:11, 12　　14:25 vNU-Text omits *And thus*.
14:34 wNU-Text omits *your*.

they want to learn something, let them ask their own husbands at home; for it is shameful for women to speak in church.

36Or did the word of God come *originally* from you? Or *was it* you only that it reached? 37If anyone thinks himself to be a prophet or spiritual, let him acknowledge that the things which I write to you are the commandments of the Lord. 38But if anyone is ignorant, let him be ignorant. x

39Therefore, brethren, desire earnestly to prophesy, and do not forbid to speak with tongues. 40Let all things be done decently and in order.

15 Moreover,* brethren, I declare to you the gospel which I preached to you, which also you received and in which you stand, 2by which also you are saved, if you hold fast that word which I preached to you—unless you believed in vain.

3For I delivered to you first of all that which I also received: that Christ died for our sins according to the Scriptures, 4and that He was buried, and that He rose again the third day according to the Scriptures, 5and that He was seen by Cephas, then by the twelve. 6After that He was seen by over five hundred brethren at once, of whom the greater part remain to the present, but some have fallen asleep. 7After that He was seen by James, then by all the apostles. 8Then last of all He was seen by me also, as by one born out of due time.

9For I am the least of the apostles, who am not worthy to be called an apostle, because I persecuted the church of God. 10But by the grace of God I am what I am, and His grace toward me was not in vain; but I labored more abundantly than they all, yet not I, but the grace of God which *was* with me. 11Therefore, whether *it was* I or they, so we preach and so you believed.

12Now if Christ is preached that He has been raised from the dead, how do some among you say that there is no resurrection of the dead? 13But if there is no resurrection of the dead, then Christ is not risen. 14And if Christ is not risen, then our preaching *is* empty and your faith *is* also empty. 15Yes, and we are found false witnesses of God, because we have testified of God that He raised up Christ, whom He did not raise up—if in fact the dead do not rise. 16For if *the* dead do not rise, then Christ is not risen. 17And if Christ is not risen, your faith *is* futile; you are still in your sins! 18Then also those who have fallen asleep in Christ have perished. 19If in this life only we have hope in Christ, we are of all men the most pitiable.

20*But now Christ is risen from the dead, *and* has become the firstfruits of those who have fallen asleep. 21For since by man *came* death, by Man also *came* the resurrection of the dead. 22For as in Adam all die, even so in Christ all shall be made alive. 23But each one in his own order: Christ the firstfruits, afterward those *who are* Christ's at His coming. 24Then *comes* the end, when He delivers the kingdom to God the Father, when He puts an end to all rule and all authority and power. 25For He must reign till He has put all enemies under His feet. 26The last enemy *that* will be

CHAPTER 15

15:1–8 *We have a living Lord.* Jesus is alive, and the gospel message is true! Witnesses who saw Him have passed along their testimony to us. When you trust Him, you receive resurrection life, eternal life (John 5:24); death can hold you no more.

❝*In God's world, for those who are in earnest, there is no failure. No work truly done, no word earnestly spoken, no sacrifice freely made, was ever made in vain.*❞
—F. W. Robertson

15:20–49 *We have a living hope.* Jesus Christ will come again, and the dead in Christ will be raised. We will have glorified bodies like Christ's body (1 John 3:1–3). Keep in mind that resurrection is not reconstruction. God does not reassemble the original body that has turned to dust. Like flowers and fruit from the planted seed, the glorified body is related to the "planted" body but different from it.

14:38 xNU-Text reads *if anyone does not recognize this, he is not recognized.*

destroyed is death. 27For "He has put all things under His feet."y But when He says "all things are put under Him," it is evident that He who put all things under Him is excepted. 28Now when all things are made subject to Him, then the Son Himself will also be subject to Him who put all things under Him, that God may be all in all.

29Otherwise, what will they do who are baptized for the dead, if the dead do not rise at all? Why then are they baptized for the dead? 30And why do we stand in jeopardy every hour? 31I affirm, by the boasting in you which I have in Christ Jesus our Lord, I die daily. 32If, in the manner of men, I have fought with beasts at Ephesus, what advantage is it to me? If the dead do not rise, "Let us eat and drink, for tomorrow we die!"z 33Do not be deceived: "Evil company corrupts good habits." 34Awake to righteousness, and do not sin; for some do not have the knowledge of God. I speak this to your shame.

35But someone will say, "How are the dead raised up? And with what body do they come?" 36Foolish one, what you sow is not made alive unless it dies. 37And what you sow, you do not sow that body that shall be, but mere grain—perhaps wheat or some other grain. 38But God gives it a body as He pleases, and to each seed its own body.

39All flesh is not the same flesh, but there is one kind of flesha of men, another flesh of animals, another of fish, and another of birds.

40There are also celestial bodies and terrestrial bodies; but the glory of the celestial is one, and the glory of the terrestrial is another. 41There is one glory of the sun, another glory of the moon, and another glory of the stars; for one star differs from another star in glory.

42So also is the resurrection of the dead. The body is sown in corruption, it is raised in incorruption. 43It is sown in dishonor, it is raised in glory. It is sown in weakness, it is raised in power. 44It is sown a natural body, it is raised a spiritual body. There is a natural body, and there is a spiritual body. 45And so it is written, "The first man Adam became a living being."b The last Adam became a life-giving spirit.

46However, the spiritual is not first, but the natural, and afterward the spiritual. 47The first man was of the earth, made of dust; the second Man is the Lordc from heaven. 48As was the man of dust, so also are those who are made of dust; and as is the heavenly Man, so also are those who are heavenly. 49And as we have borne the image of the man of dust, we shall also beard the image of the heavenly Man.

50*Now this I say, brethren, that flesh and blood cannot inherit the kingdom of God; nor does corruption inherit incorruption. 51Behold, I tell you a mystery: We shall not all sleep, but we shall all be changed— 52in a moment, in the twinkling of an eye, at the last trumpet. For the trumpet will sound, and the dead will be raised incorruptible, and we shall be changed. 53For this corruptible must put on incorruption, and this mortal must put on immortality. 54So when this corruptible has put on incorruption, and this mortal has put on immortality, then shall be brought to pass the say-

15:50–58 We have a living dynamic. We have no reason to give up because Jesus has conquered sin and death! If you really believe in the resurrection and return of Jesus, verse 58 will characterize your life. The best is yet to come, so let us give Him our best now.

15:27 yPsalm 8:6   15:32 zIsaiah 22:13   15:39 aNU-Text and M-Text omit of flesh.   15:45 bGenesis 2:7   15:47 cNU-Text omits the Lord.   15:49 dM-Text reads let us also bear.

ing that is written: *"Death is swallowed up in victory."*[e]

55 *"O Death, where is your sting?*[f]
    O Hades, where is your victory?"[g]

56The sting of death *is* sin, and the strength of sin *is* the law. 57But thanks *be* to God, who gives us the victory through our Lord Jesus Christ. 58Therefore, my beloved brethren, be steadfast, immovable, always abounding in the work of the Lord, knowing that your labor is not in vain in the Lord.

16 Now* concerning the collection for the saints, as I have given orders to the churches of Galatia, so you must do also: 2On the first *day* of the week let each one of you lay something aside, storing up as he may prosper, that there be no collections when I come. 3And when I come, whomever you approve by *your* letters I will send to bear your gift to Jerusalem. 4But if it is fitting that I go also, they will go with me.

5*Now I will come to you when I pass through Macedonia (for I am passing through Macedonia). 6And it may be that I will remain, or even spend the winter with you, that you may send me on my journey, wherever I go. 7For I do not wish to see you now on the way; but I hope to stay a while with you, if the Lord permits.

8But I will tarry in Ephesus until Pentecost. 9For a great and effective door has opened to me, and *there are* many adversaries.

10And if Timothy comes, see that he may be with you without fear; for he does the work of the Lord, as I also *do.* 11Therefore let no one despise him. But send him on his journey in peace, that he may come to me; for I am waiting for him with the brethren.

12Now concerning *our* brother Apollos, I strongly urged him to come to you with the brethren, but he was quite unwilling to come at this time; however, he will come when he has a convenient time.

13*Watch, stand fast in the faith, be brave, be strong. 14Let all *that* you do be done with love.

15I urge you, brethren—you know the household of Stephanas, that it is the firstfruits of Achaia, and *that* they have devoted themselves to the ministry of the saints— 16that you also submit to such, and to everyone who works and labors with *us.*

17I am glad about the coming of Stephanas, Fortunatus, and Achaicus, for what was lacking on your part they supplied. 18For they refreshed my spirit and yours. Therefore acknowledge such men.

19The churches of Asia greet you. Aquila and Priscilla greet you heartily in the Lord, with the

CHAPTER 16

16:1–4 Love for the needy. These instructions concern the offering Paul was taking up from the churches to help the needy believers in Judea (Rom. 15:25–27). The principles involved may be applied to Christian giving in general: our giving should be voluntary, in proportion to God's blessing, systematic, and handled honestly.

16:5–12 Love for leaders. We have the privilege of encouraging God's work as we pray for His servants. Even men like Paul, Timothy, and Apollos needed the help and encouragement of God's people. Are you praying for leaders?

16:13–18 Love for the church. Love, steadfastness, and submission make for a strong church. When you have people who are devoted to the work of the Lord, people who refresh you in the Lord, God is going to bless. What a joy to be a part of a church family that ministers in love!

15:54 eIsaiah 25:8   15:55 fHosea 13:14 gNU-Text reads *O Death, where is your victory? O Death, where is your sting?*

How Do You Pray?—"O Lord, come!" (1 Cor. 16:22) is in Aramaic *marana tha,* often seen as *maranatha.* In the Lord's Prayer, we pray, "Your kingdom come" (Matt. 6:10); and the apostle John prayed, "Even so, come, Lord Jesus!" (Rev. 22:20). We should long for His coming, not just because we want to escape the trials of life but because we love Him and want to see Him face-to-face.

16:22 *Love for Christ*. "O Lord, come!" is a prayer that reveals Paul's daily anticipation of the return of the Lord. When he made his plans (vv. 5–8), he included the blessed hope. Do you love Him and love His appearing (2 Tim. 4:8)?

church that is in their house. [20]All the brethren greet you.

Greet one another with a holy kiss.

[21]The salutation with my own hand—Paul's.

[22]*If anyone does not love the Lord Jesus Christ, let him be accursed.[h] O Lord, come![i]

[23]The grace of our Lord Jesus Christ *be* with you. [24]My love *be* with you all in Christ Jesus. Amen.

16:22 [h]Greek *anathema* [i]Aramaic *Maranatha*

2 CORINTHIANS

The problems in the Corinthian church grew worse, and Paul had to make a painful visit to Corinth to confront the people causing the trouble (2 Cor. 2:1ff.). He then wrote a severe letter and sent it with Titus (2 Cor. 2:4–9; 7:8–12). After some delays, he and Titus finally met; and in response to the good news Titus brought from Corinth, Paul wrote this letter.

First, Paul described his ministry and explained why he had changed his plans (chaps. 1—7). It was a plea for *reconciliation*. Then he detailed the plans for taking up the love offering for the church in Judea (chaps. 8—9). It was a plea for *cooperation*. Because a group in the church questioned his authority, Paul concluded his letter defending his apostleship (chaps. 10—13). It was a plea for *appreciation* and obedience to the Word.

One key word in 2 Corinthians is *comfort* (encouragement), used in one form or another twenty-nine times. Yet there are many references to suffering, too. In this very personal letter Paul opens his heart and shares his deepest joys and sorrows. After all, Christians are human and must be honest in expressing their feelings.

1 Paul, an apostle of Jesus Christ by the will of God, and Timothy *our* brother,

To the church of God which is at Corinth, with all the saints who are in all Achaia:

2Grace to you and peace from God our Father and the Lord Jesus Christ. 3Blessed *be* the God and Father of our Lord Jesus Christ, the Father of mercies and God of all comfort, 4*who comforts us in all our tribulation, that we may be able to comfort those who are in any trouble, with the comfort with which we ourselves are comforted by God. 5For as the sufferings of Christ abound in us, so our consolation also abounds through Christ. 6Now if we are afflicted, *it is* for your consolation and salvation, which is effective for enduring the same sufferings which we also suffer. Or if we are comforted, *it is* for your consolation and salvation. 7And our hope for you *is* steadfast, because we know that as you are partakers of the sufferings, so also *you will partake* of the consolation.

8For we do not want you to be ignorant, brethren, of our trouble which came to us in Asia: that we were burdened beyond measure, above strength, so that we despaired even of life. 9Yes, we had the sentence of death in ourselves, that we should not trust in ourselves but in God who raises the dead, 10who delivered us from so great a death, and does[a] deliver us; in whom we trust that He will still deliver *us*, 11you also helping together in prayer for us, that thanks may be given by many persons on our[b] behalf for the gift *granted* to us through many.

12For our boasting is this: the testimony of our

CHAPTER 1

1:4 *Christians need comfort.* While trying to help the church, Paul experienced suffering so intense that he was almost ready to give up (vv. 8–9). God does not shelter His people from trials, not even gifted apostles who are doing His will. "Be kind," said John Watson, "for everyone you meet is fighting a battle."

Christians receive comfort. Your God is the "God of all comfort" (v. 3), and He will give you the grace you need when you need it. Sufferings are not accidents; they are divine appointments, and your Father is in complete control. You will find comfort in praying, in claiming the promises of the Word (vv. 18–20), and in having deeper fellowship with the Lord.

Christians share comfort. God's comfort is not *given;* it is *loaned,* and you are expected to pass it on to others. The pain you experience now will help you encourage others in their trials. When you suffer, avoid self-pity, for self-pity will make you a reservoir instead of a channel. If you fail to share God's comfort with others, your experience in the furnace will be wasted; and it is a tragic thing to waste your sufferings.

1:10 [a]NU-Text reads *shall.*   1:11 [b]M-Text reads *your behalf.*

Blessed Be the Lord—What do 2 Corinthians 1:3, Ephesians 1:3, and 1 Peter 1:3 have in common? All three are doxologies, praising the Lord for what He does for His people. They deal with past, present, and future blessings in the Christian life. In your sufferings, take time to praise the Lord. It is good medicine for a hurting heart.

> **"***God does not comfort us to make us comfortable, but to make us comforters.***"**
>
> —John Henry Jowett

conscience that we conducted ourselves in the world in simplicity and godly sincerity, not with fleshly wisdom but by the grace of God, and more abundantly toward you. 13For we are not writing any other things to you than what you read or understand. Now I trust you will understand, even to the end 14(as also you have understood us in part), that we are your boast as you also *are* ours, in the day of the Lord Jesus.

15And in this confidence I intended to come to you before, that you might have a second benefit— 16to pass by way of you to Macedonia, to come again from Macedonia to you, and be helped by you on my way to Judea. 17Therefore, when I was planning this, did I do it lightly? Or the things I plan, do I plan according to the flesh, that with me there should be Yes, Yes, and No, No? 18But *as* God *is* faithful, our word to you was not Yes and No. 19For the Son of God, Jesus Christ, who was preached among you by us—by me, Silvanus, and Timothy—was not Yes and No, but in Him was Yes. 20For all the promises of God in Him *are* Yes, and in Him Amen, to the glory of God through us. 21Now He who establishes us with you in Christ and has anointed us *is* God, 22who also has sealed us and given us the Spirit in our hearts as a guarantee.

23Moreover I call God as witness against my soul, that to spare you I came no more to Corinth. 24Not that we have dominion over your faith, but are fellow workers for your joy; for by faith you stand.

CHAPTER 2

2:1–5 *Feelings.* From a heart of love touched with pain, Paul wrote a severe letter to the church, hoping to correct the problem. It brought grief to his dear friends, and that brought grief to Paul; but they disciplined the man who had caused the trouble. Paul was not afraid to share his feelings with others. When you are out of touch with your feelings, you are out of touch with reality.

2:6–11 *Forgiveness.* When sinners truly repent, we should forgive them and reaffirm our love to them. Otherwise, they might become discouraged and give Satan an opportunity to accuse and attack (Rev. 12:10). Love does not condone sin, but it does cover sin when God has washed it away (James 5:20).

2:12–17 *Fragrance.* Paul described a Roman Triumph, the official parade given to a victorious general when he returned to Rome. The incense carried by the priests meant life to the Roman soldiers but death to the prisoners who would end up in the arena with the wild beasts. Christ has conquered, and we are privileged to march in His triumphal procession!

2 But* I determined this within myself, that I would not come again to you in sorrow. 2For if I make you sorrowful, then who is he who makes me glad but the one who is made sorrowful by me?

3And I wrote this very thing to you, lest, when I came, I should have sorrow over those from whom I ought to have joy, having confidence in you all that my joy is *the joy* of you all. 4For out of much affliction and anguish of heart I wrote to you, with many tears, not that you should be grieved, but that you might know the love which I have so abundantly for you.

5But if anyone has caused grief, he has not grieved me, but all of you to some extent—not to be too severe. 6*This punishment which *was inflicted* by the majority *is* sufficient for such a man, 7so that, on the contrary, you *ought* rather to forgive and comfort *him,* lest perhaps such a one be swallowed up with too much sorrow. 8Therefore I urge you to reaffirm *your* love to him. 9For to this end I also wrote, that I might put you to the test, whether you are obedient in all things. 10Now whom you forgive anything, I also *forgive.* For if indeed I have forgiven anything, I have forgiven that onec for your sakes in the presence of Christ, 11lest Satan should take advantage of us; for we are not ignorant of his devices.

12*Furthermore, when I came to Troas to *preach* Christ's gospel, and a door was opened to me by the Lord, 13I had no rest in my spirit, because I did not find Titus my brother; but taking my leave of them, I departed for Macedonia.

14Now thanks *be* to God who always leads us

2:10 cNU-Text reads *For indeed, what I have forgiven, if I have forgiven anything, I did it.*

in triumph in Christ, and through us diffuses the fragrance of His knowledge in every place. 15For we are to God the fragrance of Christ among those who are being saved and among those who are perishing. 16To the one *we are* the aroma of death *leading* to death, and to the other the aroma of life *leading* to life. And who *is* sufficient for these things? 17For we are not, as so many,d peddling the word of God; but as of sincerity, but as from God, we speak in the sight of God in Christ.

3 Do* we begin again to commend ourselves? Or do we need, as some *others,* epistles of commendation to you or *letters* of commendation from you? 2You are our epistle written in our hearts, known and read by all men; 3clearly *you are* an epistle of Christ, ministered by us, written not with ink but by the Spirit of the living God, not on tablets of stone but on tablets of flesh, *that is,* of the heart.

4*And we have such trust through Christ toward God. 5Not that we are sufficient of ourselves to think of anything as *being* from ourselves, but our sufficiency *is* from God, 6who also made us sufficient as ministers of the new covenant, not of the letter but of the Spirit;e for the letter kills, but the Spirit gives life.

7*But if the ministry of death, written *and* engraved on stones, was glorious, so that the children of Israel could not look steadily at the face of Moses because of the glory of his countenance, which *glory* was passing away, 8how will the ministry of the Spirit not be more glorious? 9For if the ministry of condemnation *had* glory, the ministry of righteousness exceeds much more in glory. 10For even what was made glorious had no glory in this respect, because of the glory that excels. 11For if what is passing away *was* glorious, what remains *is* much more glorious.

12Therefore, since we have such hope, we use great boldness of speech— 13unlike Moses, *who* put a veil over his face so that the children of Israel could not look steadily at the end of what was passing away. 14But their minds were blinded. For until this day the same veil remains unlifted in the reading of the Old Testament, because the *veil* is taken away in Christ. 15But even to this day, when Moses is read, a veil lies on their heart. 16Nevertheless when one turns to the Lord, the veil is taken away. 17*Now the Lord is the Spirit; and where the Spirit of the Lord *is,* there *is* liberty. 18But we all, with unveiled face, beholding as in a mirror the glory of the Lord, are being transformed into the same image from glory to glory, just as by the Spirit of the Lord.

4 Therefore,* since we have this ministry, as we have received mercy, we do not lose heart. 2But we have renounced the hidden things of shame, not walking in craftiness nor handling the word of God deceitfully, but by manifestation of the truth commending ourselves to every man's conscience in the sight of God. 3But even if our gospel is veiled, it is veiled to those who are perishing, 4whose minds the god of this age has blinded, who do not believe, lest the light of the gospel of the glory of Christ, who is the image of God, should shine on them. 5For we do not

CHAPTER 3

3:1–3 The legalists who caused trouble in both Antioch and Jerusalem (Acts 15) had come to Corinth and enticed some of the believers into living by the law of Moses. Paul refuted their position by showing the wonders of the new covenant ministry. The background is Exodus 34:29–35.

It changes hearts. The law only reveals sin; it cannot renew the inner person. The Spirit wants to write a new version of His Word on your heart. Will you let Him?

3:4–6 *It gives life.* The law kills, but grace gives life and sustains that life. God's children have a living relationship with Him through the Spirit of life (Rom. 8:2).

3:7–16 *It gets more and more glorious.* The glory of the law is gone: the temple, the priesthood, the ceremonies, and the awesome revelations of God's power. But the glory of God's grace remains and grows more glorious (v. 18; Prov. 4:18).

3:17, 18 *It brings freedom.* The law brings bondage (Acts 15:10), but grace gives glorious freedom that makes us more and more like Jesus Christ. Each day, you can have your own personal transfiguration as you worship the Lord and yield to the Spirit.

❝*Lord, Thou knowest better than I know that I am growing older. Keep me from getting too talkative and thinking I must say something on every subject and on every occasion. Release me from craving to straighten out everybody's affairs. Teach me the glorious lesson that occasionally it is possible that I may be mistaken. Make me thoughtful, but not moody; helpful, but not bossy; Thou knowest, Lord, that what I want is a few friends at the end.*❞

CHAPTER 4

4:1–6 *The glory of salvation.* Unlike the legalists who had invaded the church, Paul had nothing to hide. The Jewish religious system veiled the gospel, but Paul sought to reveal the gospel. The image is taken from Genesis 1:1–3 and transferred from the old creation to the new creation (2 Cor. 5:17).

2:17 dM-Text reads *the rest.*   3:6 eOr *spirit*

4:7–12 The glory of service. Paul paid a price for his ministry, but the legalists went about collecting honors (3:1). We are vessels; the treasure of the gospel life within is important. As vessels, we must be clean and available for His use (2 Tim. 2:20–21).

4:13–18 The glory of suffering. Jesus suffered and turned that suffering into glory; by faith, we can do the same thing. It is not wrong to care for the outward person, so long as you recognize that it is perishing. Concentrate on the inner person. It is the invisible that is imperishable. The best is yet to come!

CHAPTER 5

5:1 We know. This building is our new body that we will receive when we see the Lord (Phil. 3:20–21) because God saves the whole person (1 Cor. 15:42–58).

5:2–4 We groan. Creation is groaning and God's people also groan (Rom. 8:18–23), yearning for the Lord Jesus to come again. We do not want to die and leave our "houses"; we want these bodies to be "clothed with" the glory of God from heaven (1 John 3:1–2). Paul longed to see Jesus come in his lifetime.

5:5–8 We are confident. God's Word gives us the truth about death and beyond, and God's Spirit guarantees that God's children will go to heaven. We claim this by faith and walk with confidence, and what peace it gives!

5:9–21 We aim to please Him. Paul's spiritual motivations for service include the judgment seat of Christ (vv. 9–11), the love of Christ (vv. 12–16), the power of the gospel (v. 17), and the commission of the Lord (vv. 18–21). What motivates you to do His will?

preach ourselves, but Christ Jesus the Lord, and ourselves your bondservants for Jesus' sake. 6For it is the God who commanded light to shine out of darkness, who has shone in our hearts to *give* the light of the knowledge of the glory of God in the face of Jesus Christ.

7*But we have this treasure in earthen vessels, that the excellence of the power may be of God and not of us. 8*We are* hard-pressed on every side, yet not crushed; *we are* perplexed, but not in despair; 9persecuted, but not forsaken; struck down, but not destroyed— 10always carrying about in the body the dying of the Lord Jesus, that the life of Jesus also may be manifested in our body. 11For we who live are always delivered to death for Jesus' sake, that the life of Jesus also may be manifested in our mortal flesh. 12So then death is working in us, but life in you.

13*And since we have the same spirit of faith, according to what is written, *"I believed and therefore I spoke,"* we also believe and therefore speak, 14knowing that He who raised up the Lord Jesus will also raise us up with Jesus, and will present *us* with you. 15For all things *are* for your sakes, that grace, having spread through the many, may cause thanksgiving to abound to the glory of God.

16Therefore we do not lose heart. Even though our outward man is perishing, yet the inward *man* is being renewed day by day. 17For our light affliction, which is but for a moment, is working for us a far more exceeding *and* eternal weight of glory, 18while we do not look at the things which are seen, but at the things which are not seen. For the things which are seen *are* temporary, but the things which are not seen *are* eternal.

5 For* we know that if our earthly house, *this* tent, is destroyed, we have a building from God, a house not made with hands, eternal in the heavens. 2*For in this we groan, earnestly desiring to be clothed with our habitation which is from heaven, 3if indeed, having been clothed, we shall not be found naked. 4For we who are in *this* tent groan, being burdened, not because we want to be unclothed, but further clothed, that mortality may be swallowed up by life. 5*Now He who has prepared us for this very thing *is* God, who also has given us the Spirit as a guarantee.

6So *we are* always confident, knowing that while we are at home in the body we are absent from the Lord. 7For we walk by faith, not by sight. 8We are confident, yes, well pleased rather to be absent from the body and to be present with the Lord.

9*Therefore we make it our aim, whether present or absent, to be well pleasing to Him. 10For we must all appear before the judgment seat of Christ, that each one may receive the things *done* in the body, according to what he has done, whether good or bad. 11Knowing, therefore, the terror of the Lord, we persuade men; but we are well known to God, and I also trust are well known in your consciences.

12For we do not commend ourselves again to you, but give you opportunity to boast on our behalf, that you may have *an answer* for those who boast in appearance and not in heart. 13For if we

---

4:13 *Psalm 116:10

are beside ourselves, *it is* for God; or if we are of sound mind, *it is* for you. ¹⁴For the love of Christ compels us, because we judge thus: that if One died for all, then all died; ¹⁵and He died for all, that those who live should live no longer for themselves, but for Him who died for them and rose again.

¹⁶Therefore, from now on, we regard no one according to the flesh. Even though we have known Christ according to the flesh, yet now we know *Him thus* no longer. ¹⁷Therefore, if anyone *is* in Christ, *he is* a new creation; old things have passed away; behold, all things have become new. ¹⁸Now all things *are* of God, who has reconciled us to Himself through Jesus Christ, and has given us the ministry of reconciliation, ¹⁹that is, that God was in Christ reconciling the world to Himself, not imputing their trespasses to them, and has committed to us the word of reconciliation.

²⁰Now then, we are ambassadors for Christ, as though God were pleading through us: we implore *you* on Christ's behalf, be reconciled to God. ²¹For He made Him who knew no sin *to be* sin for us, that we might become the righteousness of God in Him.

6 We* then, *as* workers together *with Him* also plead with *you* not to receive the grace of God in vain. ²For He says:

> "In an acceptable time I have heard you,
> And in the day of salvation I have helped
> you."ᵍ

Behold, now *is* the accepted time; behold, now *is* the day of salvation.

³*We give no offense in anything, that our ministry may not be blamed. ⁴But in all *things* we commend ourselves as ministers of God: in much patience, in tribulations, in needs, in distresses, ⁵in stripes, in imprisonments, in tumults, in labors, in sleeplessness, in fastings; ⁶by purity, by knowledge, by longsuffering, by kindness, by the Holy Spirit, by sincere love, ⁷by the word of truth, by the power of God, by the armor of righteousness on the right hand and on the left, ⁸by honor and dishonor, by evil report and good report; as deceivers, and *yet* true; ⁹as unknown, and *yet* well known; as dying, and behold we live; as chastened, and *yet* not killed; ¹⁰as sorrowful, yet always rejoicing; as poor, yet making many rich; as having nothing, and *yet* possessing all things.

¹¹O Corinthians! We have spoken openly to you, our heart is wide open. ¹²You are not restricted by us, but you are restricted by your *own* affections. ¹³Now in return for the same (I speak as to children), you also be open.

¹⁴*Do not be unequally yoked together with unbelievers. For what fellowship has righteousness with lawlessness? And what communion has light with darkness? ¹⁵And what accord has Christ with Belial? Or what part has a believer with an unbeliever? ¹⁶And what agreement has the temple of God with idols? For youʰ are the temple of the living God. As God has said:

> "I will dwell in them
> And walk among them.

CHAPTER 6

6:1, 2 Acceptance. Often those in the church who cause problems are people who have never truly been born again. They may think they are saved, but they are not. *Now* is the time to accept God's grace. Tomorrow may be too late.

6:3–13 Appreciation. It is easy to forget the sacrifices others have made so we can know the Lord. Paul never spoke about his sufferings unless his words helped to protect the ministry (11:16ff.). Do you take your church fellowship for granted? Have you thanked those who came before you and made it possible?

6:14–18 Agreement. Believers in the church were compromising with the world and not walking in a separated way (Ps. 1:1). God longs to have a closer fellowship with us, but He will not share the yoke with the world.

6:2 ᵍIsaiah 49:8   6:16 ʰNU-Text reads *we.*

I will be their God,
And they shall be My people."[i]

17Therefore

"Come out from among them
And be separate, says the Lord.
Do not touch what is unclean,
And I will receive you."[j]
18 *"I will be a Father to you,*
And you shall be My sons and daughters,
Says the LORD *Almighty."[k]*

CHAPTER 7

7:1 Cleansing. It is one thing to ask God to cleanse you (Ps. 51:2, 7) and quite something else to cleanse yourself and put away the things that defile (Isa. 1:16). Separation sometimes demands surgery.

7:2–7 Comforting. The same people who give you joy can also cause you sorrow. When Titus reported that the church had disciplined the offender, the apostle was overjoyed. Have you ever been an answer to somebody's prayers as Titus was?

7:8–11 Clearing. If we are serious about repentance, we will do everything we can to clear things up. Remorse and regret do not go far enough; there must be repentance followed by restitution.

7:12–16 Caring. Both Paul and Titus cared about the believers in Corinth, and this love finally won the day. You take a risk when you love others, for they may hurt you; but it is worth the risk to be like Jesus Christ and live a life of love.

7 Therefore,* having these promises, beloved, let us cleanse ourselves from all filthiness of the flesh and spirit, perfecting holiness in the fear of God.

2*Open *your hearts* to us. We have wronged no one, we have corrupted no one, we have cheated no one. 3I do not say *this* to condemn; for I have said before that you are in our hearts, to die together and to live together. 4Great *is* my boldness of speech toward you, great *is* my boasting on your behalf. I am filled with comfort. I am exceedingly joyful in all our tribulation.

5For indeed, when we came to Macedonia, our bodies had no rest, but we were troubled on every side. Outside *were* conflicts, inside *were* fears. 6Nevertheless God, who comforts the downcast, comforted us by the coming of Titus, 7and not only by his coming, but also by the consolation with which he was comforted in you, when he told us of your earnest desire, your mourning, your zeal for me, so that I rejoiced even more.

8*For even if I made you sorry with my letter, I do not regret it; though I did regret it. For I perceive that the same epistle made you sorry, though only for a while. 9Now I rejoice, not that you were made sorry, but that your sorrow led to repentance. For you were made sorry in a godly manner, that you might suffer loss from us in nothing. 10For godly sorrow produces repentance *leading* to salvation, not to be regretted; but the sorrow of the world produces death. 11For observe this very thing, that you sorrowed in a godly manner: What diligence it produced in you, *what* clearing *of yourselves, what* indignation, *what* fear, *what* vehement desire, *what* zeal, *what* vindication! In all *things* you proved yourselves to be clear in this matter. 12*Therefore, although I wrote to you, I *did* not *do it* for the sake of him who had done the wrong, nor for the sake of him who suffered wrong, but that our care for you in the sight of God might appear to you.

13Therefore we have been comforted in your comfort. And we rejoiced exceedingly more for the joy of Titus, because his spirit has been refreshed by you all. 14For if in anything I have boasted to him about you, I am not ashamed. But as we spoke all things to you in truth, even so our boasting to Titus was found true. 15And his affections are greater for you as he remembers the obedience of you all, how with fear and trem-

---

6:16 [i]Leviticus 26:12; Jeremiah 32:38; Ezekiel 37:27
6:17 [j]Isaiah 52:11; Ezekiel 20:34, 41   6:18 [k]2 Samuel 7:14

True Repentance—*Regret* involves the mind primarily, and *remorse* involves the emotions. But *repentance* includes a change of mind, a hatred for sin, and a willingness to make things right. If the will is not touched, conviction has not gone deep enough.

bling you received him. [16]Therefore I rejoice that I have confidence in you in everything.

8 Moreover,* brethren, we make known to you the grace of God bestowed on the churches of Macedonia: [2]that in a great trial of affliction the abundance of their joy and their deep poverty abounded in the riches of their liberality. [3]For I bear witness that according to *their* ability, yes, and beyond *their* ability, *they were* freely willing, [4]imploring us with much urgency that we would receive[l] the gift and the fellowship of the ministering to the saints. [5]And not *only* as we had hoped, but they first gave themselves to the Lord, and *then* to us by the will of God. [6]So we urged Titus, that as he had begun, so he would also complete this grace in you as well. [7]But as you abound in everything—in faith, in speech, in knowledge, in all diligence, and in your love for us—*see* that you abound in this grace also.

[8]*I speak not by commandment, but I am testing the sincerity of your love by the diligence of others. [9]For you know the grace of our Lord Jesus Christ, that though He was rich, yet for your sakes He became poor, that you through His poverty might become rich.

[10]*And in this I give advice: It is to your advantage not only to be doing what you began and were desiring to do a year ago; [11]but now you also must complete the doing *of it;* that as *there was* a readiness to desire *it,* so *there* also *may be* a completion out of what *you* have. [12]For if there is first a willing mind, *it is* accepted according to what one has, *and* not according to what he does not have.

[13]For *I do* not *mean* that others should be eased and you burdened; [14]but by an equality, *that* now at this time your abundance *may supply* their lack, that their abundance also may supply your lack— that there may be equality. [15]As it is written, *"He who gathered much had nothing left over, and he who gathered little had no lack."*[m]

[16]*But thanks *be* to God who puts[n] the same earnest care for you into the heart of Titus. [17]For he not only accepted the exhortation, but being more diligent, he went to you of his own accord. [18]And we have sent with him the brother whose praise *is* in the gospel throughout all the churches, [19]and not only *that,* but who was also chosen by the churches to travel with us with this gift, which is administered by us to the glory of the Lord Himself and *to show* your ready mind, [20]avoiding this: that anyone should blame us in this lavish gift which is administered by us— [21]providing honorable things, not only in the sight of the Lord, but also in the sight of men. [22]And we have sent with them our brother whom we have often proved diligent in many things, but now much more diligent, because of the great confidence which *we have* in you. [23]If *anyone inquires* about Titus, *he is* my partner and fellow worker concerning you. Or if our brethren *are inquired* about, *they are* messengers of the churches, the glory of Christ. [24]Therefore show to them, and[o] before the churches the proof of your love and of our boasting on your behalf.

CHAPTERS 8—9

8:1–7 Chapters 8—9 focus on the offering Paul was taking for the needy believers in Judea. The Corinthian church had agreed to share in the collection but had been remiss in doing so. Paul reminded them of their promise and at the same time explained some principles of Christian giving.

It begins with surrender to the Lord. You cannot give your substance until you first give yourself (v. 5; Rom. 12:1–2). When you belong to the Lord, you start looking for opportunities to give instead of excuses not to give.

8:8, 9 It is motivated by grace. Jesus was rich in heaven but became poor on earth (even to death on a cross!) that we might share His eternal riches. It was all by grace because *giving is a grace.* Law *commands,* but grace *consents* and does so joyfully.

8:10–15 It requires faith. The example of the manna (Exod. 16) shows that God always provides what we need. Paul also used the image of sowing to encourage generous giving (9:6). God's promises can be trusted.

8:16–24 It also requires faithfulness. Those who handle the Lord's money should be dedicated and faithful, making certain that everything is honest and honorable.

8:4 [l]NU-Text and M-Text omit *that we would receive,* thus changing text to *urgency for the favor and fellowship . . . .*
8:15 [m]Exodus 16:18   8:16 [n]NU-Text reads *has put.*
8:24 [o]NU-Text and M-Text omit *and.*

9:1–5 *It is a testimony to others.* A year before, the zeal of the Corinthians had stirred others to give: now Paul had to stir up the Corinthians! We must not give to be praised by people (Matt. 6:1–4), but we must also be good examples before others. If we make promises, we should keep them.

9:6–15 *It must be done gladly.* If you want spiritual enrichment from your giving (9:11), you must practice enjoyment and be glad for opportunities to give. Look at God's promises to faithful givers! How can you lose?

❝*For the Macedonian Christians, giving was not a chore but a challenge, not a burden but a blessing. Giving was not something to be avoided but a privilege to be desired.*❞

—George Sweeting

CHAPTER 10

10:1 Satan seeks to blind minds to God's light (4:3–6), fortify minds against God's truth (10:1–6), and seduce minds from God's love (11:1–4). Paul gives some practical counsel for victory in spiritual warfare.

Be Christlike. Boldness must be balanced with meekness, for God's power is experienced in humility. Satan is our enemy, not people held by his power.

10:2–6 *Use spiritual weapons.* Paul may have had in mind Joshua's victory at Jericho (Josh. 6) when the walls came down because of Israel's faith. Read Ephesians 6:1–20, and be sure you are wearing the whole armor.

10:7–11 *Keep your eyes on the Lord.* That the Corinthians accused Paul of inconsistency gave Satan opportunity to work in their lives.

9 Now* concerning the ministering to the saints, it is superfluous for me to write to you; 2for I know your willingness, about which I boast of you to the Macedonians, that Achaia was ready a year ago; and your zeal has stirred up the majority. 3Yet I have sent the brethren, lest our boasting of you should be in vain in this respect, that, as I said, you may be ready; 4lest if *some* Macedonians come with me and find you unprepared, we (not to mention you!) should be ashamed of this confident boasting.p 5Therefore I thought it necessary to exhort the brethren to go to you ahead of time, and prepare your generous gift beforehand, which *you had* previously promised, that it may be ready as *a matter of* generosity and not as a grudging obligation.

6*But this *I say:* He who sows sparingly will also reap sparingly, and he who sows bountifully will also reap bountifully. 7So *let* each one *give* as he purposes in his heart, not grudgingly or of necessity; for God loves a cheerful giver. 8And God *is* able to make all grace abound toward you, that you, always having all sufficiency in all *things,* may have an abundance for every good work. 9As it is written:

"He has dispersed abroad,
He has given to the poor;
His righteousness endures forever."q

10Now mayr He who supplies seed to the sower, and bread for food, supply and multiply the seed you have *sown* and increase the fruits of your righteousness, 11while *you are* enriched in everything for all liberality, which causes thanksgiving through us to God. 12For the administration of this service not only supplies the needs of the saints, but also is abounding through many thanksgivings to God, 13while, through the proof of this ministry, they glorify God for the obedience of your confession to the gospel of Christ, and for *your* liberal sharing with them and all *men,* 14and by their prayer for you, who long for you because of the exceeding grace of God in you. 15Thanks *be* to God for His indescribable gift!

10 Now* I, Paul, myself am pleading with you by the meekness and gentleness of Christ—who in presence *am* lowly among you, but being absent am bold toward you. 2*But I beg *you* that when I am present I may not be bold with that confidence by which I intend to be bold against some, who think of us as if we walked according to the flesh. 3For though we walk in the flesh, we do not war according to the flesh. 4For the weapons of our warfare *are* not carnal but mighty in God for pulling down strongholds, 5casting down arguments and every high thing that exalts itself against the knowledge of God, bringing every thought into captivity to the obedience of Christ, 6and being ready to punish all disobedience when your obedience is fulfilled.

7*Do you look at things according to the outward appearance? If anyone is convinced in himself that he is Christ's, let him again consider this in himself, that just as he *is* Christ's, even so we *are* Christ's.s 8For even if I should boast somewhat

---

9:4 PNU-Text reads *this confidence.*   9:9 QPsalm 112:9
9:10 rNU-Text reads *Now He who supplies . . .*
will supply . . . .   10:7 sNU-Text reads *even as we are.*

more about our authority, which the Lord gave us[t] for edification and not for your destruction, I shall not be ashamed— 9lest I seem to terrify you by letters. 10"For *his* letters," they say, "*are* weighty and powerful, but *his* bodily presence *is* weak, and *his* speech contemptible." 11Let such a person consider this, that what we are in word by letters when we are absent, such *we will* also *be* in deed when we are present.

12*For we dare not class ourselves or compare ourselves with those who commend themselves. But they, measuring themselves by themselves, and comparing themselves among themselves, are not wise. 13We, however, will not boast beyond measure, but within the limits of the sphere which God appointed us—a sphere which especially includes you. 14For we are not overextending ourselves (as though *our authority* did not extend to you), for it was to you that we came with the gospel of Christ; 15not boasting of things beyond measure, *that is,* in other men's labors, but having hope, *that* as your faith is increased, we shall be greatly enlarged by you in our sphere, 16to preach the gospel in the *regions* beyond you, *and* not to boast in another man's sphere of accomplishment.

17*But *"he who glories, let him glory in the* LORD."[u] 18For not he who commends himself is approved, but whom the Lord commends.

11 Oh,* that you would bear with me in a little folly—and indeed you do bear with me. 2For I am jealous for you with godly jealousy. For I have betrothed you to one husband, that I may present *you as* a chaste virgin to Christ. 3But I fear, lest somehow, as the serpent deceived Eve by his craftiness, so your minds may be corrupted from the simplicity[v] that is in Christ. 4For if he who comes preaches another Jesus whom we have not preached, or *if* you receive a different spirit which you have not received, or a different gospel which you have not accepted—you may well put up with it!

5*For I consider that I am not at all inferior to the most eminent apostles. 6Even though *I am* untrained in speech, yet *I am* not in knowledge. But we have been thoroughly manifested[w] among you in all things.

7Did I commit sin in humbling myself that you might be exalted, because I preached the gospel of God to you free of charge? 8I robbed other churches, taking wages *from them* to minister to you. 9And when I was present with you, and in need, I was a burden to no one, for what I lacked the brethren who came from Macedonia supplied. And in everything I kept myself from being burdensome to you, and so I will keep *myself.* 10As the truth of Christ is in me, no one shall stop me from this boasting in the regions of Achaia. 11Why? Because I do not love you? God knows!

12But what I do, I will also continue to do, that I may cut off the opportunity from those who desire an opportunity to be regarded just as we are in the things of which they boast. 13For such *are* false apostles, deceitful workers, transforming themselves into apostles of Christ. 14And no wonder! For Satan himself transforms himself into an angel of light. 15Therefore *it is* no great thing if

10:12–16 *Accept the sphere of service God gives you.* Every Christian soldier has a place to fill; if we are all following His orders, the church will win the battle.

10:17, 18 *Seek God's glory alone.* How can we boast in victories that God alone can give? Paul quoted Jeremiah 9:24 to remind us where the glory belongs.

CHAPTER 11

11:1–4 Paul compares himself to a father with obligations to his spiritual children. *Protection.* Spiritual leaders must protect the church from false teachers who are like suitors trying to seduce the church from devotion to Christ. Beware losing your love for Christ and for those who helped you trust the Savior.

11:5–12 *Provision.* Paul had the right to receive financial support at Corinth, but he laid it aside and sacrificed for them in love. They did not appreciate it! But do you appreciate the sacrifices others make for you? Are you willing to sacrifice for others even when they do not thank you?

❝*The principle of sacrifice is that we choose to do or to suffer what apart from our love we should not choose to do or to suffer. When love is returned, this sacrifice is the most joyful thing in the world, and heaven is the life of joyful sacrifice. But in a selfish world it must be painful, and the pain is the source of triumph.*❞

—William Temple

10:8 [t]NU-Text omits *us.*   10:17 [u]Jeremiah 9:24
11:3 [v]NU-Text adds *and purity.*   11:6 [w]NU-Text omits *been.*

11:16–33 *Suffering.* Paul mentioned his sufferings only to defend the gospel and the authority of his ministry. The false teachers bragged about their triumphs, but Paul boasted about his trials.

his ministers also transform themselves into ministers of righteousness, whose end will be according to their works.

16*I say again, let no one think me a fool. If otherwise, at least receive me as a fool, that I also may boast a little. 17What I speak, I speak not according to the Lord, but as it were, foolishly, in this confidence of boasting. 18Seeing that many boast according to the flesh, I also will boast. 19For you put up with fools gladly, since you *yourselves* are wise! 20For you put up with it if one brings you into bondage, if one devours *you*, if one takes *from you*, if one exalts himself, if one strikes you on the face. 21To *our* shame I say that we were too weak for that! But in whatever anyone is bold—I speak foolishly—I am bold also.

22Are they Hebrews? So *am* I. Are they Israelites? So *am* I. Are they the seed of Abraham? So *am* I. 23Are they ministers of Christ?—I speak as a fool—I *am* more: in labors more abundant, in stripes above measure, in prisons more frequently, in deaths often. 24From the Jews five times I received forty *stripes* minus one. 25Three times I was beaten with rods; once I was stoned; three times I was shipwrecked; a night and a day I have been in the deep; 26in journeys often, *in* perils of waters, *in* perils of robbers, *in* perils of *my own* countrymen, *in* perils of the Gentiles, *in* perils in the city, *in* perils in the wilderness, *in* perils in the sea, *in* perils among false brethren; 27in weariness and toil, in sleeplessness often, in hunger and thirst, in fastings often, in cold and nakedness— 28besides the other things, what comes upon me daily: my deep concern for all the churches. 29Who is weak, and I am not weak? Who is made to stumble, and I do not burn *with indignation?*

30If I must boast, I will boast in the things which concern my infirmity. 31The God and Father of our Lord Jesus Christ, who is blessed forever, knows that I am not lying. 32In Damascus the governor, under Aretas the king, was guarding the city of the Damascenes with a garrison, desiring to arrest me; 33but I was let down in a basket through a window in the wall, and escaped from his hands.

CHAPTER 12

12:7 *Permission.* Just as God permitted Satan to test Job (Job 1—2) and Peter (Luke 22:31–34), so He permitted Satan to attack Paul. God wanted to keep Paul humble after his exciting visit to heaven. In the loving will of God, suffering has a purpose that can be fulfilled in no other way. Accept it, and it will become a heavenly blessing; fight it, and it will become a heavy burden.

❝We must form our estimate of men less from their achievements and failures and more from their sufferings.❞

—Dietrich Bonhoeffer

12 It is doubtless^x not profitable for me to boast. I will come to visions and revelations of the Lord: 2I know a man in Christ who fourteen years ago—whether in the body I do not know, or whether out of the body I do not know, God knows—such a one was caught up to the third heaven. 3And I know such a man—whether in the body or out of the body I do not know, God knows— 4how he was caught up into Paradise and heard inexpressible words, which it is not lawful for a man to utter. 5Of such a one I will boast; yet of myself I will not boast, except in my infirmities. 6For though I might desire to boast, I will not be a fool; for I will speak the truth. But I refrain, lest anyone should think of me above what he sees me *to be* or hears from me.

7*And lest I should be exalted above measure by the abundance of the revelations, a thorn in the flesh was given to me, a messenger of Satan to buffet me, lest I be exalted above measure.

12:1 xNU-Text reads *necessary, though not profitable, to boast.*

8*Concerning this thing I pleaded with the Lord three times that it might depart from me. 9And He said to me, "My grace is sufficient for you, for My strength is made perfect in weakness." Therefore most gladly I will rather boast in my infirmities, that the power of Christ may rest upon me. 10Therefore I take pleasure in infirmities, in reproaches, in needs, in persecutions, in distresses, for Christ's sake. For when I am weak, then I am strong.

11*I have become a fool in boasting;y you have compelled me. For I ought to have been commended by you; for in nothing was I behind the most eminent apostles, though I am nothing. 12Truly the signs of an apostle were accomplished among you with all perseverance, in signs and wonders and mighty deeds. 13For what is it in which you were inferior to other churches, except that I myself was not burdensome to you? Forgive me this wrong!

14Now for the third time I am ready to come to you. And I will not be burdensome to you; for I do not seek yours, but you. For the children ought not to lay up for the parents, but the parents for the children. 15And I will very gladly spend and be spent for your souls; though the more abundantly I love you, the less I am loved.

16But be that as it may, I did not burden you. Nevertheless, being crafty, I caught you by cunning! 17Did I take advantage of you by any of those whom I sent to you? 18I urged Titus, and sent our brother with him. Did Titus take advantage of you? Did we not walk in the same spirit? Did we not walk in the same steps?

19Again, do you thinkz that we excuse ourselves to you? We speak before God in Christ. But we do all things, beloved, for your edification. 20For I fear lest, when I come, I shall not find you such as I wish, and that I shall be found by you such as you do not wish; lest there be contentions, jealousies, outbursts of wrath, selfish ambitions, backbitings, whisperings, conceits, tumults; 21lest, when I come again, my God will humble me among you, and I shall mourn for many who have sinned before and have not repented of the uncleanness, fornication, and lewdness which they have practiced.

13 This* will be the third time I am coming to you. "By the mouth of two or three witnesses every word shall be established."a 2I have told you before, and foretell as if I were present the second time, and now being absent I writeb to those who have sinned before, and to all the rest, that if I come again I will not spare— 3since you seek a proof of Christ speaking in me, who is not weak toward you, but mighty in you. 4For though He was crucified in weakness, yet He lives by the power of God. For we also are weak in Him, but we shall live with Him by the power of God toward you.

12:11 yNU-Text omits in boasting.   12:19 zNU-Text reads You have been thinking for a long time . . . .   13:1 aDeuteronomy 19:15   13:2 bNU-Text omits I write.

12:8:10 Prayer. Like our Lord in Gethsemane (Matt. 26:44), Paul prayed three times for God to deliver him; but the Lord did not answer that prayer as Paul wanted. However, God did meet the need and gave His servant the grace he required. Paul did not simply make the best of it—he made the most of it! Grace can do that for you.

12:11–21 Perplexity. Paul was concerned more about the sins of the saints than about his own physical problems. Like a loving father, he wanted to go to Corinth and enjoy his dear children, but they were forcing him to discipline them. Yet, even discipline is an evidence of love (Heb. 12).

CHAPTER 13

13:1–4 As Paul planned his trip to Corinth, he envisioned the different kinds of people he would meet there.

The disobedient. Why would God's people want to disobey Him (12:20) and create problems for Paul and grief for the Lord, not to speak of problems for their church? Disobedient children must be dealt with, and Paul intended to be a faithful and loving father.

Solutions—Every local church problem can be solved by being humble and honest and by drawing on the spiritual resources listed in 2 Corinthians 13:14. Do you avail yourself of these riches? Are you a part of the problem or a part of the answer?

13:5 *The disqualified.* Some church members have never been born again, and that is why they create problems. Paul urges us to examine our hearts to be sure we are in the faith.

13:11, 12 *The devoted.* These are the true brothers and sisters in the Lord, the set-apart ones (saints), the people who love one another and promote the peace and purity of the church. They are the mature ones in the fellowship who encourage spiritual growth.
To which group do you belong?

5*Examine yourselves *as to* whether you are in the faith. Test yourselves. Do you not know yourselves, that Jesus Christ is in you?—unless indeed you are disqualified. 6But I trust that you will know that we are not disqualified. 7Now Ic pray to God that you do no evil, not that we should appear approved, but that you should do what is honorable, though we may seem disqualified. 8For we can do nothing against the truth, but for the truth. 9For we are glad when we are weak and you are strong. And this also we pray, that you may be made complete. 10Therefore I write these things being absent, lest being present I should use sharpness, according to the authority which the Lord has given me for edification and not for destruction.

11*Finally, brethren, farewell. Become complete. Be of good comfort, be of one mind, live in peace; and the God of love and peace will be with you.
12Greet one another with a holy kiss.
13All the saints greet you.
14The grace of the Lord Jesus Christ, and the love of God, and the communion of the Holy Spirit *be* with you all. Amen.

13:7 cNU-Text reads *we.*

GALATIANS

The churches Paul founded in the Roman province of Galatia (Acts 13—14) were invaded by false teachers like those Paul had refuted in the Jerusalem Council (Acts 15). We call these people "Judaizers" because they tried to bring Christians into bondage to the law of Moses.

Paul wrote this letter to magnify God's grace in salvation and to explain the freedom of God's people because of that grace (Gal. 5:1). It opens with a *personal affirmation* (chaps. 1—2) as Paul explains how God delivered him from bondage through faith in Jesus Christ. He then gives a *doctrinal explanation* and shows the relationship between law and grace (chaps. 3—4). He closes with a *practical application* that tells you how to enjoy grace and freedom in your daily life (chaps. 5—6).

Christian freedom is the liberty to become all that you can in Jesus Christ; it is not the license to do whatever you please. The worst bondage you can experience is living for yourself and yielding to the desires of the old nature (Rom. 6). "We have freedom to do good or evil," wrote St. Francis de Sales, "yet to make choice of evil, is not to use, but to abuse our freedom." Christ did not free us to be our own; He freed us to be His and His alone.

1 Paul,* an apostle (not from men nor through man, but through Jesus Christ and God the Father who raised Him from the dead), ²and all the brethren who are with me,

To the churches of Galatia:

³Grace to you and peace from God the Father and our Lord Jesus Christ, ⁴who gave Himself for our sins, that He might deliver us from this present evil age, according to the will of our God and Father, ⁵to whom *be* glory forever and ever. Amen.

⁶*I marvel that you are turning away so soon from Him who called you in the grace of Christ, to a different gospel, ⁷which is not another; but there are some who trouble you and want to pervert the gospel of Christ. ⁸But even if we, or an angel from heaven, preach any other gospel to you than what we have preached to you, let him be accursed. ⁹As we have said before, so now I say again, if anyone preaches any other gospel to you than what you have received, let him be accursed.

¹⁰For do I now persuade men, or God? Or do I seek to please men? For if I still pleased men, I would not be a bondservant of Christ.

¹¹But I make known to you, brethren, that the gospel which was preached by me is not according to man. ¹²For I neither received it from man, nor was I taught *it*, but *it came* through the revelation of Jesus Christ.

¹³For you have heard of my former conduct in Judaism, how I persecuted the church of God beyond measure and *tried to* destroy it. ¹⁴And I advanced in Judaism beyond many of my contemporaries in my own nation, being more exceedingly zealous for the traditions of my fathers.

¹⁵But when it pleased God, who separated me from my mother's womb and called *me* through His grace, ¹⁶to reveal His Son in me, that I might preach Him among the Gentiles, I did not immediately confer with flesh and blood, ¹⁷nor did I go

CHAPTER 1

1:1–5 To Paul, the gospel was much more than a message he preached: it was a miracle he had experienced. The gospel is "the power of God to salvation" (Rom. 1:16) and it brings freedom. Christ died "that He might deliver us" (1:4). When Paul trusted Christ, he became a free man. The shackles of sin and legalistic religion were broken!

1:6–17 But the gospel was also a treasure that Paul guarded (vv. 6–17). Paul did not invent the gospel or learn it from others; God gave it to him (1 Cor. 15:1–11). *There is no other gospel.* To add to this message, take from it, or substitute another message is to destroy it. No wonder Paul attacked those who attacked the gospel; when you lose the gospel, you lose everything.

> ❝*The gospel is neither a discussion nor a debate. It is an announcement.*❞
>
> —Paul S. Rees

1:18–24 The gospel is a tie that binds God's people together (vv. 18–24). Saul the enemy became Paul the brother, and he was able to fellowship with people he once had persecuted. Christians may disagree on minor matters of interpretation and organization, but they agree on the message of the gospel.

CHAPTER 2

2:1–5 *The runner.* Paul saw himself as a man running a race, and he was sure he was on the right track and headed for the right goal. The Judaizers were trying to move the church into bondage and get them on a detour (5:7; Acts 15).

2:6–10 *The steward.* God has committed the gospel to His people, and we must guard it and share it with others. God is not looking for popular celebrities; He is looking for faithful stewards (1 Cor. 4:1–2).

❝*Whitefield and Wesley might preach the gospel better than I do, but they cannot preach a better gospel.*❞
—Charles Spurgeon

2:11–14 *The watchman.* Paul was not afraid to confront the apostle Peter when Peter moved away from the truth of the gospel. "Eternal vigilance is the price of liberty!" said Wendell Phillips, and that applies to our spiritual liberty as well.

2:15–21 *The destroyer.* Jesus destroyed the law by fulfilling it (Matt. 5:17–20). His death tore the temple veil (Luke 23:44–45) and removed the wall between Jews and Gentiles (Eph. 2:14–18). To go back to Moses is to rebuild what Jesus tore down and say that He did not really save us when we trusted Him.

up to Jerusalem to those *who were* apostles before me; but I went to Arabia, and returned again to Damascus. 18*Then after three years I went up to Jerusalem to see Peter,[a] and remained with him fifteen days. 19But I saw none of the other apostles except James, the Lord's brother. 20(Now *concerning* the things which I write to you, indeed, before God, I do not lie.) 21Afterward I went into the regions of Syria and Cilicia. 22And I was unknown by face to the churches of Judea which *were* in Christ. 23But they were hearing only, "He who formerly persecuted us now preaches the faith which he once *tried to* destroy." 24And they glorified God in me.

2 Then* after fourteen years I went up again to Jerusalem with Barnabas, and also took Titus with *me.* 2And I went up by revelation, and communicated to them that gospel which I preach among the Gentiles, but privately to those who were of reputation, lest by any means I might run, or had run, in vain. 3Yet not even Titus who *was* with me, being a Greek, was compelled to be circumcised. 4And *this occurred* because of false brethren secretly brought in (who came in by stealth to spy out our liberty which we have in Christ Jesus, that they might bring us into bondage), 5to whom we did not yield submission even for an hour, that the truth of the gospel might continue with you.

6*But from those who seemed to be something—whatever they were, it makes no difference to me; God shows personal favoritism to no man—for those who seemed *to be something* added nothing to me. 7But on the contrary, when they saw that the gospel for the uncircumcised had been committed to me, as *the gospel* for the circumcised *was* to Peter 8(for He who worked effectively in Peter for the apostleship to the circumcised also worked effectively in me toward the Gentiles), 9and when James, Cephas, and John, who seemed to be pillars, perceived the grace that had been given to me, they gave me and Barnabas the right hand of fellowship, that we *should go* to the Gentiles and they to the circumcised. 10*They desired* only that we should remember the poor, the very thing which I also was eager to do.

11*Now when Peter[b] had come to Antioch, I withstood him to his face, because he was to be blamed; 12for before certain men came from James, he would eat with the Gentiles; but when they came, he withdrew and separated himself, fearing those who were of the circumcision. 13And the rest of the Jews also played the hypocrite with him, so that even Barnabas was carried away with their hypocrisy.

14But when I saw that they were not straightforward about the truth of the gospel, I said to Peter before *them* all, "If you, being a Jew, live in the manner of Gentiles and not as the Jews, why do you[c] compel Gentiles to live as Jews?[d] 15*We *who are* Jews by nature, and not sinners of the Gentiles, 16knowing that a man is not justified by the works of the law but by faith in Jesus Christ, even we have believed in Christ Jesus, that we might

---

1:18 [a]NU-Text reads *Cephas.*   2:11 [b]NU-Text reads *Cephas.*
2:14 [c]NU-Text reads *how can you.* [d]Some interpreters stop the quotation here.

be justified by faith in Christ and not by the works of the law; for by the works of the law no flesh shall be justified.

17"But if, while we seek to be justified by Christ, we ourselves also are found sinners, is Christ therefore a minister of sin? Certainly not! 18For if I build again those things which I destroyed, I make myself a transgressor. 19For I through the law died to the law that I might live to God. 20I have been crucified with Christ; it is no longer I who live, but Christ lives in me; and the life which I now live in the flesh I live by faith in the Son of God, who loved me and gave Himself for me. 21I do not set aside the grace of God; for if righteousness comes through the law, then Christ died in vain."

3 O* foolish Galatians! Who has bewitched you that you should not obey the truth,e before whose eyes Jesus Christ was clearly portrayed among you' as crucified? 2This only I want to learn from you: Did you receive the Spirit by the works of the law, or by the hearing of faith? 3Are you so foolish? Having begun in the Spirit, are you now being made perfect by the flesh? 4Have you suffered so many things in vain—if indeed it was in vain?

5Therefore He who supplies the Spirit to you and works miracles among you, does He do it by the works of the law, or by the hearing of faith?— 6just as Abraham "believed God, and it was accounted to him for righteousness."g 7Therefore know that only those who are of faith are sons of Abraham. 8And the Scripture, foreseeing that God would justify the Gentiles by faith, preached the gospel to Abraham beforehand, saying, "In you all the nations shall be blessed."h 9So then those who are of faith are blessed with believing Abraham.

10For as many as are of the works of the law are under the curse; for it is written, "Cursed is everyone who does not continue in all things which are written in the book of the law, to do them."i 11But that no one is justified by the law in the sight of God is evident, for "the just shall live by faith."j 12Yet the law is not of faith, but "the man who does them shall live by them."k

13Christ has redeemed us from the curse of the law, having become a curse for us (for it is written, "Cursed is everyone who hangs on a tree"l), 14that the blessing of Abraham might come upon the Gentiles in Christ Jesus, that we might receive the promise of the Spirit through faith.

15*Brethren, I speak in the manner of men: Though it is only a man's covenant, yet if it is confirmed, no one annuls or adds to it. 16Now to Abraham and his Seed were the promises made. He does not say, "And to seeds," as of many, but as of one, "And to your Seed,"m who is Christ. 17And this I say, that the law, which was four hundred and thirty years later, cannot annul the covenant that was confirmed before by God in Christ,n that it should make the promise of no effect. 18For if the inheritance is of the law, it is no

CHAPTER 3

3:1–14 Examination. It does us good to examine ourselves to make sure our spiritual experience is valid (2 Cor. 13:5). Do you have the Spirit living within? (See Rom. 8:9.) If you began in the Spirit (which is the only way to begin), are you trying to continue in the power of the flesh? Like Abraham, were you saved by faith; and are you now, like Abraham, walking by faith?

3:15–25 Explanation. The Judaizers wanted the Galatians to go back to Moses, but that was not far enough. We must go back to Abraham where the promise started. The law did not annul the promise; the law was given to reveal sin and prepare the way for Christ to come and fulfill the promise. The law is a tutor, not a savior; a mirror, not a cleanser.

3:1 eNU-Text omits that you should not obey the truth. fNU-Text omits among you. 3:6 gGenesis 15:6 3:8 hGenesis 12:3; 18:18; 22:18; 26:4; 28:14 3:10 iDeuteronomy 27:26 3:11 jHabakkuk 2:4 3:12 kLeviticus 18:5 3:13 lDeuteronomy 21:23 3:16 mGenesis 12:7; 13:15; 24:7 3:17 nNU-Text omits in Christ.

longer of promise; but God gave *it* to Abraham by promise.

19What purpose then *does* the law *serve?* It was added because of transgressions, till the Seed should come to whom the promise was made; *and it was* appointed through angels by the hand of a mediator. 20Now a mediator does not *mediate* for one *only,* but God is one.

21*Is* the law then against the promises of God? Certainly not! For if there had been a law given which could have given life, truly righteousness would have been by the law. 22But the Scripture has confined all under sin, that the promise by faith in Jesus Christ might be given to those who believe. 23But before faith came, we were kept under guard by the law, kept for the faith which would afterward be revealed. 24Therefore the law was our tutor *to bring us* to Christ, that we might be justified by faith. 25But after faith has come, we are no longer under a tutor.

26*For you are all sons of God through faith in Christ Jesus. 27For as many of you as were baptized into Christ have put on Christ. 28There is neither Jew nor Greek, there is neither slave nor free, there is neither male nor female; for you are all one in Christ Jesus. 29And if you *are* Christ's, then you are Abraham's seed, and heirs according to the promise.

4 Now* I say *that* the heir, as long as he is a child, does not differ at all from a slave, though he is master of all, 2but is under guardians and stewards until the time appointed by the father. 3Even so we, when we were children, were in bondage under the elements of the world. 4But when the fullness of the time had come, God sent forth His Son, born° of a woman, born under the law, 5to redeem those who were under the law, that we might receive the adoption as sons. 6And because you are sons, God has sent forth the Spirit of His Son into your hearts, crying out, "Abba, Father!" 7Therefore you are no longer a slave but a son, and if a son, then an heir of° God through Christ.

8But then, indeed, when you did not know God, you served those which by nature are not gods. 9But now after you have known God, or rather are known by God, how *is it that* you turn again to the weak and beggarly elements, to which you desire again to be in bondage? 10You observe days and months and seasons and years. 11I am afraid for you, lest I have labored for you in vain.

12Brethren, I urge you to become like me, for I *became* like you. You have not injured me at all. 13You know that because of physical infirmity I preached the gospel to you at the first. 14And my trial which was in my flesh you did not despise or reject, but you received me as an angel of God,

---

3:26–29 *Exhortation.* Beware! A false gospel robs you of salvation and of membership in the family of God where all believers are one in Christ. It robs you of your spiritual riches as an heir of the promise. Are you rejoicing in the freedom you have in Christ?

CHAPTER 4
4:1ff Are you a child of God through faith in Jesus Christ? Then you are also an heir, and all of Christ's riches are yours (Eph. 1:3)! A child must wait until maturity to inherit the family wealth, but God's children can have His wealth now (Phil. 4:19).

Are you a child of God through faith in Jesus Christ? Then you are free! A child is in bondage and must be guarded by adults, but a grown son or daughter enjoys freedom. To live under Law is to be a slave, and God wants His children to enjoy their freedom in Christ.

Are you a child of God through faith in Jesus Christ? Then you can become like Him as you yield to the Spirit (4:19; 2 Cor. 3:18).

Are you a child of God through faith in Jesus Christ? Then your citizenship is secure in heaven because you are a child of promise (4:21–31; Gen. 16). You were born free!

4:4 °Or *made*   4:7 PNU-Text reads *through God* and omits *through Christ.*

Freedom in Christ—An allegory is a narrative in which people and events teach deeper lessons. John Bunyan's *Pilgrim's Progress* is a classic example. Paul used Genesis 16 to illustrate your freedom in Christ. Hagar is the law, while Sarah stands for God's grace. Ishmael was born after the flesh (your first birth), while Isaac was born by the power of God (the new birth). Abraham represents faith, so Isaac was born "by grace [Sarah] . . . through faith [Abraham]" (Eph. 2:8). The Judaizers wanted to bring Hagar back again, but she was sent away because law and grace cannot coexist. Like Hagar, the law was a servant that had a temporary ministry. Once the Son arrived, that ministry was fulfilled.

even as Christ Jesus. 15What*q* then was the blessing you *enjoyed?* For I bear you witness that, if possible, you would have plucked out your own eyes and given them to me. 16Have I therefore become your enemy because I tell you the truth?

17They zealously court you, *but* for no good; yes, they want to exclude you, that you may be zealous for them. 18But it is good to be zealous in a good thing always, and not only when I am present with you. 19My little children, for whom I labor in birth again until Christ is formed in you, 20I would like to be present with you now and to change my tone; for I have doubts about you.

21Tell me, you who desire to be under the law, do you not hear the law? 22For it is written that Abraham had two sons: the one by a bondwoman, the other by a freewoman. 23But he *who was* of the bondwoman was born according to the flesh, and he of the freewoman through promise, 24which things are symbolic. For these are the*r* two covenants: the one from Mount Sinai which gives birth to bondage, which is Hagar— 25for this Hagar is Mount Sinai in Arabia, and corresponds to Jerusalem which now is, and is in bondage with her children— 26but the Jerusalem above is free, which is the mother of us all. 27For it is written:

"Rejoice, O barren,
    You who do not bear!
Break forth and shout,
    You who are not in labor!
For the desolate has many more children
    Than she who has a husband.""*s*

28Now we, brethren, as Isaac *was,* are children of promise. 29But, as he who was born according to the flesh then persecuted him *who was* born according to the Spirit, even so *it is* now. 30Nevertheless what does the Scripture say? *"Cast out the bondwoman and her son, for the son of the bondwoman shall not be heir with the son of the freewoman."*t 31So then, brethren, we are not children of the bondwoman but of the free.

5 Stand* fast therefore in the liberty by which Christ has made us free,*u* and do not be entangled again with a yoke of bondage. 2Indeed I, Paul, say to you that if you become circumcised, Christ will profit you nothing. 3And I testify again to every man who becomes circumcised that he is a debtor to keep the whole law. 4*You have become estranged from Christ, you who *attempt to* be justified by law; you have fallen from grace. 5For we through the Spirit eagerly wait for the hope of righteousness by faith. 6For in Christ Jesus neither circumcision nor uncircumcision avails anything, but faith working through love.

7*You ran well. Who hindered you from obeying the truth? 8This persuasion does not *come* from Him who calls you. 9*A little leaven leavens the whole lump. 10I have confidence in you, in the Lord, that you will have no other mind; but he who troubles you shall bear his judgment, whoever he is.

11And I, brethren, if I still preach circumcision,

> **Every time we say, 'I believe in the Holy Spirit,' we mean that we believe there is a living God able and willing to enter human personality and change it.**
> —J. B. Phillips

CHAPTER 5

5:1 *Are you standing free?* Your freedom in Christ is a costly thing, for it cost Jesus His life. In Him, you stand free; the yoke of the law has been removed (Acts 15:6–11).

5:4 *Are you falling?* To fall from grace does not mean to lose one's salvation. It means to move out of the sphere of grace into the sphere of law. It means to substitute regulations for a personal relationship with the Lord.

5:7 *Are you running on course?* Or has false teaching gotten you on a detour?

5:9 *Are you being leavened?* Jesus used leaven to picture sin (Matt. 16:6–12). Like yeast, false teaching is introduced quietly, it grows secretly, and soon it affects every part of your life.

4:15 *q*NU-Text reads *Where.*   4:24 *r*NU-Text and M-Text omit *the.*   4:27 *s*Isaiah 54:1   4:30 *t*Genesis 21:10   5:1 *u*NU-Text reads *For freedom Christ has made us free; stand fast therefore.*

5:13, 14 *Are you serving others?* Freedom brings with it the responsibility to serve. Love motivates us to fulfill the law of God (Rom. 13:8–14).

5:16–26 *Are you walking in the Spirit?* Life, not law, changes behavior; and as you yield to the Spirit, Christ's life is manifest in the fruit of the Spirit.
Law works by compulsion from without, but grace works by compassion from within.

CHAPTER 6

6:1, 2 *See others humbly.* Your response to another's fall reveals your own walk, whether it is spiritual or not. Pride will make it impossible for you to help the fallen, but humility will bring blessing to you and to them.

6:3–5 *See yourself honestly.* Do you use somebody's fall to make yourself look better? Or do you know yourself, accept yourself, and seek to please God alone?

6:6–10 *See your leaders appreciatively.* When you give to others whose ministry blesses you, you are sowing seed that will bear fruit. When you use your resources for sinful purposes, you sow to the flesh and will reap a sad harvest.

6:12–18 *See the Cross clearly.* The false teachers wanted the world's praise, so they avoided the Cross; but the true believer will glory in the Cross, even if it means suffering the world's enmity.

why do I still suffer persecution? Then the offense of the cross has ceased. 12I could wish that those who trouble you would even cut themselves off! 13*For you, brethren, have been called to liberty; only do not *use* liberty as an opportunity for the flesh, but through love serve one another. 14For all the law is fulfilled in one word, *even* in this: "*You shall love your neighbor as yourself.*"ᵛ 15But if you bite and devour one another, beware lest you be consumed by one another!

16*I say then: Walk in the Spirit, and you shall not fulfill the lust of the flesh. 17For the flesh lusts against the Spirit, and the Spirit against the flesh; and these are contrary to one another, so that you do not do the things that you wish. 18But if you are led by the Spirit, you are not under the law.

19Now the works of the flesh are evident, which are: adultery,ʷ fornication, uncleanness, lewdness, 20idolatry, sorcery, hatred, contentions, jealousies, outbursts of wrath, selfish ambitions, dissensions, heresies, 21envy, murders,ˣ drunkenness, revelries, and the like; of which I tell you beforehand, just as I also told *you* in time past, that those who practice such things will not inherit the kingdom of God.

22But the fruit of the Spirit is love, joy, peace, longsuffering, kindness, goodness, faithfulness, 23gentleness, self-control. Against such there is no law. 24And those *who are* Christ's have crucified the flesh with its passions and desires. 25If we live in the Spirit, let us also walk in the Spirit. 26Let us not become conceited, provoking one another, envying one another.

6 Brethren,* if a man is overtaken in any trespass, you who *are* spiritual restore such a one in a spirit of gentleness, considering yourself lest you also be tempted. 2Bear one another's burdens, and so fulfill the law of Christ. 3*For if anyone thinks himself to be something, when he is nothing, he deceives himself. 4But let each one examine his own work, and then he will have rejoicing in himself alone, and not in another. 5For each one shall bear his own load.

6*Let him who is taught the word share in all good things with him who teaches.

7Do not be deceived, God is not mocked; for whatever a man sows, that he will also reap. 8For he who sows to his flesh will of the flesh reap corruption, but he who sows to the Spirit will of the Spirit reap everlasting life. 9And let us not grow weary while doing good, for in due season we shall reap if we do not lose heart. 10Therefore, as we have opportunity, let us do good to all, especially to those who are of the household of faith.

11See with what large letters I have written to you with my own hand! 12*As many as desire to make a good showing in the flesh, these *would* compel you to be circumcised, only that they may not suffer persecution for the cross of Christ. 13For not even those who are circumcised keep the law, but they desire to have you circumcised

---

5:14 ᵛLeviticus 19:18   5:19 ʷNU-Text omits *adultery*.
5:21 ˣNU-Text omits *murders*.

Faithfully Restore Them—The word translated "restore" in Galatians 6:1 also means "to set a broken bone." How gentle and loving we must be when we seek to help fallen brothers or sisters, for what we do will affect them and the body of Christ.

that they may boast in your flesh. 14But God forbid that I should boast except in the cross of our Lord Jesus Christ, by whom*y* the world has been crucified to me, and I to the world. 15For in Christ Jesus neither circumcision nor uncircumcision avails anything, but a new creation.

16And as many as walk according to this rule, peace and mercy *be* upon them, and upon the Israel of God.

17From now on let no one trouble me, for I bear in my body the marks of the Lord Jesus.

18Brethren, the grace of our Lord Jesus Christ *be* with your spirit. Amen.

6:14 *y* Or *by which* (the cross)

EPHESIANS

On his second missionary journey, Paul visited Ephesus and left Aquila and Priscilla there (Acts 18:19–21). He returned to Ephesus two years later and ministered for three years, reaching the whole province of Asia with the gospel (Acts 19). Some years later when Paul was a prisoner in Rome (3:1; 4:1; 6:20), he wrote this letter to the believers in Ephesus.

One major theme of Ephesians is that God is at work in this world, through His church, putting things together (1:10). In the first three chapters, Paul explains this as a work of redemption (chap. 1), resurrection (2:1–10), and reconciliation (2:11—3:21). In chapters 4—6, Paul states the responsibilities of believers in the light of God's great purpose. Note the emphasis on the word *walk*.

Ephesus was an important city and boasted of being custodian of the temple of Diana, one of the seven wonders of the ancient world. The city was devoted to idolatry, which explains why Paul had so much to say about defeating the devil (6:10ff.).

The Ephesian letter shows the balance in the Christian life between doctrine (chaps. 1—3) and duty (chaps. 4—6), divine sovereignty and human responsibility. We do not obey God so that He will give us His grace; we obey Him in response to grace already given.

CHAPTER 1

1:1ff Salvation is of God. Man does not save himself, for "salvation is of the LORD" (Jon. 2:9). You receive spiritual blessings from the Father (1:1–6), the Son (vv. 7–12), and the Spirit (vv. 13–14); and in Jesus Christ, you have all you need for life and service.

Salvation is all of grace. Paul emphasizes this point throughout the letter, especially in 2:1–10. Grace is God's favor bestowed on people who do not and cannot deserve it.

Salvation is for God's glory. God saves sinners not to solve their problems but to bring glory to Himself (1:6, 12, 14; 3:21). The church will glorify Him for all eternity!

Salvation reveals God's greatness (15–23). Ask God to open your spiritual eyes to see the greatness of His power. Jesus is alive and has conquered every enemy! You may draw on His power to meet every need in life.

1 Paul,* an apostle of Jesus Christ by the will of God,

To the saints who are in Ephesus, and faithful in Christ Jesus:

2Grace to you and peace from God our Father and the Lord Jesus Christ.

3Blessed *be* the God and Father of our Lord Jesus Christ, who has blessed us with every spiritual blessing in the heavenly *places* in Christ, 4just as He chose us in Him before the foundation of the world, that we should be holy and without blame before Him in love, 5having predestined us to adoption as sons by Jesus Christ to Himself, according to the good pleasure of His will, 6to the praise of the glory of His grace, by which He made us accepted in the Beloved.

7In Him we have redemption through His blood, the forgiveness of sins, according to the riches of His grace 8which He made to abound toward us in all wisdom and prudence, 9having made known to us the mystery of His will, according to His good pleasure which He purposed in Himself, 10that in the dispensation of the fullness of the times He might gather together in one all things in Christ, both*a* which are in heaven and which are on earth—in Him. 11In Him also we have obtained an inheritance, being predestined according to the purpose of Him who works all things according to the counsel of His will, 12that we who first trusted in Christ should be to the praise of His glory.

13In Him you also *trusted,* after you heard the

1:10 *a*NU-Text and M-Text omit *both.*

Praying in His Will—The two prayers in Ephesians complement each other. Ephesians 1:15–23 focuses on knowing what God has done for you in Christ, while 3:14–21 emphasizes experiencing His blessings. The first is for *enlightenment;* the second is for *enablement.* For other prison prayers of Paul, see Philippians 1:9–11 and Colossians 1:9–12. You may use these prayers for yourself and know that you are praying in the will of God.

word of truth, the gospel of your salvation; in whom also, having believed, you were sealed with the Holy Spirit of promise, [14]who[b] is the guarantee of our inheritance until the redemption of the purchased possession, to the praise of His glory.

[15]Therefore I also, after I heard of your faith in the Lord Jesus and your love for all the saints, [16]do not cease to give thanks for you, making mention of you in my prayers: [17]that the God of our Lord Jesus Christ, the Father of glory, may give to you the spirit of wisdom and revelation in the knowledge of Him, [18]the eyes of your understanding[c] being enlightened; that you may know what is the hope of His calling, what are the riches of the glory of His inheritance in the saints, [19]and what is the exceeding greatness of His power toward us who believe, according to the working of His mighty power [20]which He worked in Christ when He raised Him from the dead and seated Him at His right hand in the heavenly places, [21]far above all principality and power and might and dominion, and every name that is named, not only in this age but also in that which is to come.

[22]And He put all things under His feet, and gave Him to be head over all things to the church, [23]which is His body, the fullness of Him who fills all in all.

2 And* you He made alive, who were dead in trespasses and sins, [2]in which you once walked according to the course of this world, according to the prince of the power of the air, the spirit who now works in the sons of disobedience, [3]among whom also we all once conducted ourselves in the lusts of our flesh, fulfilling the desires of the flesh and of the mind, and were by nature children of wrath, just as the others.

[4]But God, who is rich in mercy, because of His great love with which He loved us, [5]even when we were dead in trespasses, made us alive together with Christ (by grace you have been saved), [6]and raised us up together, and made us sit together in the heavenly places in Christ Jesus, [7]that in the ages to come He might show the exceeding riches of His grace in His kindness toward us in Christ Jesus. [8]For by grace you have been saved through faith, and that not of yourselves; it is the gift of God, [9]not of works, lest anyone should boast. [10]For we are His workmanship, created in Christ Jesus for good works, which God prepared beforehand that we should walk in them.

[11]Therefore remember that you, once Gentiles in the flesh—who are called Uncircumcision by what is called the Circumcision made in the flesh by hands— [12]that at that time you were without Christ, being aliens from the commonwealth of Israel and strangers from the covenants of promise, having no hope and without God in the world. [13]But now in Christ Jesus you who once were far off have been brought near by the blood of Christ.

[14]For He Himself is our peace, who has made both one, and has broken down the middle wall of separation, [15]having abolished in His flesh the enmity, that is, the law of commandments contained in ordinances, so as to create in Himself

CHAPTER 2

2:1ff *From death to life.* Lost sinners are not simply sick people needing help; they are dead people needing life. The Son of God died that we might receive life through faith in Him (John 5:24).

From bondage to freedom. Lost sinners are in bondage to the world, the flesh, and the devil (2:1–3) and cannot free themselves. In Christ, you have true freedom (John 12:31–32; Gal. 1:4; 5:24). Now God is working in you and through you to accomplish His great purposes (2:10).

From the tomb to the throne. God did not give you life and leave you in the cemetery. He lifted you up to sit on the throne with His victorious Son!

From separation to reconciliation. In Jesus Christ, believing Jews and Gentiles are now one; the barriers have been removed. Believers are members of one body, citizens of one holy nation, and living stones in one temple (1 Pet. 2:1–10).

All of this is of God, His marvelous love (2:4), and His grace and kindness (v. 7). No wonder Paul opened this letter with a doxology (1:3)!

1:14 [b]NU-Text reads which. 1:18 [c]NU-Text and M-Text read hearts.

CHAPTER 3

3:1, 14 *A purpose.* "For this reason" refers to what Paul wrote at the end of chapter 2, the building of the church. That was the purpose behind his praying and his ministering. Jesus said, "I will build My church" (Matt. 16:18), but He uses people to help get the job done. Is the building of the church your motivation to pray and serve?

3:2–13 *A parenthesis.* The word *Gentiles* (v. 1) put Paul in prison (Acts 22:21). God gave him a special commission to evangelize the Gentiles and to explain to both Jews and Gentiles God's "mystery" (sacred secret): in Christ, believing Jews and Gentiles are one and share the same spiritual riches. As He builds His church in this world, God is putting things together. Are you helping Him?

3:14–21 *A prayer.* This prayer is for spiritual vision, to see and lay hold of the greatness of God's love and power. God wants you to be concerned about "the whole building" (2:21), "the whole family" (3:15), "the whole body" (4:16), and "all the saints" (v. 18). Is narrowness in your life leading to shallowness and weakness?

CHAPTER 4

4:1–13 To "give place to the devil" (v. 27) is to allow unconfessed sin in your life that gives Satan an opportunity to take over. Some sins to avoid are discussed here. ***Disunity.*** Believers are "all one in Christ Jesus" (Gal. 3:28), but we must endeavor to make that spiritual unity a practical reality in our daily lives. Satan uses people who like to have their own way.

one new man *from* the two, *thus* making peace, ¹⁶and that He might reconcile them both to God in one body through the cross, thereby putting to death the enmity. ¹⁷And He came and preached peace to you who were afar off and to those who were near. ¹⁸For through Him we both have access by one Spirit to the Father.

¹⁹Now, therefore, you are no longer strangers and foreigners, but fellow citizens with the saints and members of the household of God, ²⁰having been built on the foundation of the apostles and prophets, Jesus Christ Himself being the chief corner*stone,* ²¹in whom the whole building, being fitted together, grows into a holy temple in the Lord, ²²in whom you also are being built together for a dwelling place of God in the Spirit.

3 For* this reason I, Paul, the prisoner of Christ Jesus for you Gentiles— ²*if indeed you have heard of the dispensation of the grace of God which was given to me for you, ³how that by revelation He made known to me the mystery (as I have briefly written already, ⁴by which, when you read, you may understand my knowledge in the mystery of Christ), ⁵which in other ages was not made known to the sons of men, as it has now been revealed by the Spirit to His holy apostles and prophets: ⁶that the Gentiles should be fellow heirs, of the same body, and partakers of His promise in Christ through the gospel, ⁷of which I became a minister according to the gift of the grace of God given to me by the effective working of His power.

⁸To me, who am less than the least of all the saints, this grace was given, that I should preach among the Gentiles the unsearchable riches of Christ, ⁹and to make all see what *is* the fellowship^d of the mystery, which from the beginning of the ages has been hidden in God who created all things through Jesus Christ;^e ¹⁰to the intent that now the manifold wisdom of God might be made known by the church to the principalities and powers in the heavenly *places,* ¹¹according to the eternal purpose which He accomplished in Christ Jesus our Lord, ¹²in whom we have boldness and access with confidence through faith in Him. ¹³Therefore I ask that you do not lose heart at my tribulations for you, which is your glory.

¹⁴*For this reason I bow my knees to the Father of our Lord Jesus Christ,^f ¹⁵from whom the whole family in heaven and earth is named, ¹⁶that He would grant you, according to the riches of His glory, to be strengthened with might through His Spirit in the inner man, ¹⁷that Christ may dwell in your hearts through faith; that you, being rooted and grounded in love, ¹⁸may be able to comprehend with all the saints what *is* the width and length and depth and height— ¹⁹to know the love of Christ which passes knowledge; that you may be filled with all the fullness of God.

²⁰Now to Him who is able to do exceedingly abundantly above all that we ask or think, according to the power that works in us, ²¹to Him *be* glory in the church by Christ Jesus to all generations, forever and ever. Amen.

4 I,* therefore, the prisoner of the Lord, beseech you to walk worthy of the calling with which

---

3:9 ^dNU-Text and M-Text read *stewardship* (dispensation). ^eNU-Text omits *through Jesus Christ.*
3:14 ^fNU-Text omits *of our Lord Jesus Christ.*

you were called, [2]with all lowliness and gentleness, with longsuffering, bearing with one another in love, [3]endeavoring to keep the unity of the Spirit in the bond of peace. [4]*There is* one body and one Spirit, just as you were called in one hope of your calling; [5]one Lord, one faith, one baptism; [6]one God and Father of all, who *is* above all, and through all, and in you[g] all.

[7]But to each one of us grace was given according to the measure of Christ's gift. [8]Therefore He says:

"When He ascended on high,
He led captivity captive,
And gave gifts to men."[h]

[9](Now this, *"He ascended"*—what does it mean but that He also first[i] descended into the lower parts of the earth? [10]He who descended is also the One who ascended far above all the heavens, that He might fill all things.) [11]And He Himself gave some *to be* apostles, some prophets, some evangelists, and some pastors and teachers, [12]for the equipping of the saints for the work of ministry, for the edifying of the body of Christ, [13]till we all come to the unity of the faith and of the knowledge of the Son of God, to a perfect man, to the measure of the stature of the fullness of Christ; [14]*that we should no longer be children, tossed to and fro and carried about with every wind of doctrine, by the trickery of men, in the cunning craftiness of deceitful plotting, [15]but, speaking the truth in love, may grow up in all things into Him who is the head—Christ— [16]from whom the whole body, joined and knit together by what every joint supplies, according to the effective working by which every part does its share, causes growth of the body for the edifying of itself in love.

[17]*This I say, therefore, and testify in the Lord, that you should no longer walk as the rest of[j] the Gentiles walk, in the futility of their mind, [18]having their understanding darkened, being alienated from the life of God, because of the ignorance that is in them, because of the blindness of their heart; [19]who, being past feeling, have given themselves over to lewdness, to work all uncleanness with greediness.

[20]But you have not so learned Christ, [21]if indeed you have heard Him and have been taught by Him, as the truth is in Jesus: [22]that you put off, concerning your former conduct, the old man which grows corrupt according to the deceitful lusts, [23]and be renewed in the spirit of your mind, [24]and that you put on the new man which was created according to God, in true righteousness and holiness.

[25]Therefore, putting away lying, *"Let each one of you speak truth with his neighbor,"*[k] for we are members of one another. [26]*"Be angry, and do not sin":*[l] do not let the sun go down on your wrath, [27]nor give place to the devil. [28]Let him who stole steal no longer, but rather let him labor, working with *his* hands what is good, that he may have something to give him who has need. [29]Let no corrupt word proceed out of your mouth, but what is good for necessary edification, that

4:14–16 Immaturity. Spiritual birth must lead to spiritual growth as we become more like Jesus Christ (1 Pet. 1:22—2:3). If we are maturing in Christ, we will show it by being able to speak the truth in love. Satan is a liar and a murderer (John 8:44) and has a difficult time being successful when believers practice truth and love.

4:17–32 Impurity. You have been set free from the old life, so why live in those old sins anymore? Anything evil from the old life that is brought into the new life will give the devil a beachhead. Paul names such things as lying, losing your temper, stealing, corrupt speech, bitterness, and an unforgiving spirit. These sins invite Satan into your life, and they hurt you, harm the church, and grieve the Spirit of God. Is it worth it?

4:6 [g]NU-Text omits *you;* M-Text reads *us.*   4:8 [h]Psalm 68:18
4:9 [i]NU-Text omits *first.*   4:17 [j]NU-Text omits *the rest of.*
4:25 [k]Zechariah 8:16   4:26 [l]Psalm 4:4

CHAPTER 5

5:1–7 As he encourages us to live godly lives, Paul takes us to *the temple* and reminds us of the sacrifice Jesus made for us. If we walk in love, our lives will be living sacrifices (Rom. 12:1–2; Phil. 2:17), fragrant to the Lord (John 12:1–8). Sin is ugly and a stench in God's nostrils (Isa. 3:24).

5:8–14 Then Paul goes to *the field* and reminds us that walking in the light produces spiritual fruit (Gal. 5:22–23). If we walk in the light, we cannot have fellowship with the darkness (2 Cor. 6:14–18).

5:15–17 He takes us to *the marketplace* and exhorts us to be like good merchants who know how to buy up an opportunity. When you walk in wisdom, you use your time wisely.

5:18–21 Then we follow him to *the banqueting hall* and learn to walk in the Spirit (Gal. 5:16–26) and be joyful, thankful, and submissive to one another.

5:22–33 Paul's last visit is to *the home* where he uses marriage as a picture of the relationship between Christ and the church. Christ *loved* us and died for us, but today He *loves* us and cares for us. This intimate life is pictured in the Song of Solomon and can be a reality for all who will yield to Him.

❝ *Stand up, stand up for Jesus,*
Stand in His strength alone;
The arm of flesh will fail you,
You dare not trust your own.
Put on the gospel armor,
Each piece put on with prayer;
Where duty calls or danger,
Be never wanting there. ❞

—George Duffield

---

it may impart grace to the hearers. 30And do not grieve the Holy Spirit of God, by whom you were sealed for the day of redemption. 31Let all bitterness, wrath, anger, clamor, and evil speaking be put away from you, with all malice. 32And be kind to one another, tenderhearted, forgiving one another, even as God in Christ forgave you.

5 Therefore* be imitators of God as dear children. 2And walk in love, as Christ also has loved us and given Himself for us, an offering and a sacrifice to God for a sweet-smelling aroma.

3But fornication and all uncleanness or covetousness, let it not even be named among you, as is fitting for saints; 4neither filthiness, nor foolish talking, nor coarse jesting, which are not fitting, but rather giving of thanks. 5For this you know,^{m} that no fornicator, unclean person, nor covetous man, who is an idolater, has any inheritance in the kingdom of Christ and God. 6Let no one deceive you with empty words, for because of these things the wrath of God comes upon the sons of disobedience. 7Therefore do not be partakers with them.

8*For you were once darkness, but now you are light in the Lord. Walk as children of light 9(for the fruit of the Spirit^n is in all goodness, righteousness, and truth), 10finding out what is acceptable to the Lord. 11And have no fellowship with the unfruitful works of darkness, but rather expose *them*. 12For it is shameful even to speak of those things which are done by them in secret. 13But all things that are exposed are made manifest by the light, for whatever makes manifest is light. 14Therefore He says:

"Awake, you who sleep,
Arise from the dead,
And Christ will give you light."

15*See then that you walk circumspectly, not as fools but as wise, 16redeeming the time, because the days are evil. 17Therefore do not be unwise, but understand what the will of the Lord *is*. 18*And do not be drunk with wine, in which is dissipation; but be filled with the Spirit, 19speaking to one another in psalms and hymns and spiritual songs, singing and making melody in your heart to the Lord, 20giving thanks always for all things to God the Father in the name of our Lord Jesus Christ, 21submitting to one another in the fear of God.^{o} 22*Wives, submit to your own husbands, as to the Lord. 23For the husband is head of the wife, as also Christ is head of the church; and He is the Savior of the body. 24Therefore, just as the church is subject to Christ, so *let* the wives *be* to their own husbands in everything.

25Husbands, love your wives, just as Christ also

5:5 ^{m}NU-Text reads *For know this.*   5:9 ^{n}NU-Text reads *light.*
5:21 ^{o}NU-Text reads *Christ.*

Under the Spirit's Influence—To be "filled with" means "to be controlled by" (Luke 4:28; 5:26). On the day of Pentecost, the believers were filled with the Holy Spirit and were accused of being drunk (Acts 2:13). Just as a drunk is influenced by alcohol, so a believer should be controlled by the Spirit. However, there are important differences. The drunk loses self-control, but the Spirit gives the believer self-control (Gal. 5:23). The drunk has an artificial happiness that does not last, while the Spirit-filled believer has a deep joy in the Lord. Drunken people do stupid things that hurt others and bring them embarrassment, but Spirit-filled believers help others and live to the glory of God.

loved the church and gave Himself for her,
26that He might sanctify and cleanse her with the
washing of water by the word, 27that He might
present her to Himself a glorious church, not having spot or wrinkle or any such thing, but that
she should be holy and without blemish. 28So husbands ought to love their own wives as their own
bodies; he who loves his wife loves himself.
29For no one ever hated his own flesh, but nourishes and cherishes it, just as the Lord *does* the
church. 30For we are members of His body,[p] of
His flesh and of His bones. 31*"For this reason a
man shall leave his father and mother and be
joined to his wife, and the two shall become one
flesh."*[q] 32This is a great mystery, but I speak concerning Christ and the church. 33Nevertheless let
each one of you in particular so love his own wife
as himself, and let the wife *see* that she respects
her husband.

6 Children,* obey your parents in the Lord, for
this is right. 2*"Honor your father and mother,"*
which is the first commandment with promise:
3*"that it may be well with you and you may live
long on the earth."*[r]
4And you, fathers, do not provoke your children
to wrath, but bring them up in the training and
admonition of the Lord.
5Bondservants, be obedient to those who are
your masters according to the flesh, with fear and
trembling, in sincerity of heart, as to Christ;
6not with eyeservice, as men-pleasers, but as
bondservants of Christ, doing the will of God from
the heart, 7with goodwill doing service, as to the
Lord, and not to men, 8knowing that whatever
good anyone does, he will receive the same from
the Lord, whether *he is* a slave or free.
9And you, masters, do the same things to them,
giving up threatening, knowing that your own
Master also[s] is in heaven, and there is no partiality
with Him.
10Finally, my brethren, be strong in the Lord
and in the power of His might. 11Put on the whole
armor of God, that you may be able to stand
against the wiles of the devil. 12For we do not
wrestle against flesh and blood, but against principalities, against powers, against the rulers of the
darkness of this age,[t] against spiritual *hosts* of
wickedness in the heavenly *places.* 13Therefore
take up the whole armor of God, that you may
be able to withstand in the evil day, and having
done all, to stand.
14Stand therefore, having girded your waist
with truth, having put on the breastplate of righteousness, 15and having shod your feet with the
preparation of the gospel of peace; 16above all,
taking the shield of faith with which you will be
able to quench all the fiery darts of the wicked
one. 17And take the helmet of salvation, and the
sword of the Spirit, which is the word of God;
18praying always with all prayer and supplication
in the Spirit, being watchful to this end with all
perseverance and supplication for all the saints—
19and for me, that utterance may be given to me,
that I may open my mouth boldly to make known
the mystery of the gospel, 20for which I am an

5:30 [p]NU-Text omits the rest of this verse. 5:31 [q]Genesis 2:24 6:3 [r]Deuteronomy 5:16 6:9 [s]NU-Text reads *He who is both their Master and yours.* 6:12 [t]NU-Text reads *rulers of this darkness.*

CHAPTER 6

6:1ff Spirit-filled Christians will manifest Christlikeness in the home (vv. 1–4), on the job (vv. 5–9), and on the battlefield (vv. 10–20). If we do not learn to obey at home, we are not likely to be obedient on the job or in the army of the Lord. Likewise, if we have not learned to *take* orders, we will not be too successful at *giving* orders, either as parents or as employers.

The danger in the home is parents who are *authoritarian* but do not exercise loving spiritual *authority.* The danger on the job is the employee who is a clock-watcher and does not obey from the heart, and the "boss" who forgets that he is second in command and must one day give an account to the Lord.

The danger on the battlefield is that we do not take the enemy seriously and therefore fail to put on all of the armor. By faith, you put on the armor through prayer, which must be done at the beginning of every day. Never underestimate the strategy and strength of the devil.

ambassador in chains; that in it I may speak boldly, as I ought to speak.

21But that you also may know my affairs *and* how I am doing, Tychicus, a beloved brother and faithful minister in the Lord, will make all things known to you; 22whom I have sent to you for this very purpose, that you may know our affairs, and *that* he may comfort your hearts.

23Peace to the brethren, and love with faith, from God the Father and the Lord Jesus Christ. 24Grace *be* with all those who love our Lord Jesus Christ in sincerity. Amen.

PHILIPPIANS

Founded on Paul's second missionary journey (Acts 16), the church at Philippi was a source of real joy to him. Hearing that Paul was a prisoner in Rome, the Philippian believers sent a special love offering; and in this letter, Paul wrote to express his thanks. He also wrote to explain why Epaphroditus, their messenger, had been delayed and to encourage the believers to work together to bring unity to the church.

The overriding theme of the letter is Jesus Christ and the ministry of the gospel. Christ is the message of our ministry (chap. 1) as well as the model (chap. 2), the motive (chap. 3), and the means (chap. 4). The theme of joy is also woven throughout the letter. Despite his difficult circumstances, Paul rejoiced in the Lord and urged his readers to do so. After all, the joy of the Lord is the strength of Christian service (Neh. 8:10).

1 Paul* and Timothy, bondservants of Jesus Christ,

To all the saints in Christ Jesus who are in Philippi, with the bishops^a and deacons:

2Grace to you and peace from God our Father and the Lord Jesus Christ.

3I thank my God upon every remembrance of you, 4always in every prayer of mine making request for you all with joy, 5for your fellowship in the gospel from the first day until now, 6being confident of this very thing, that He who has begun a good work in you will complete *it* until the day of Jesus Christ; 7just as it is right for me to think this of you all, because I have you in my heart, inasmuch as both in my chains and in the defense and confirmation of the gospel, you all are partakers with me of grace. 8For God is my witness, how greatly I long for you all with the affection of Jesus Christ.

9And this I pray, that your love may abound still more and more in knowledge and all discernment, 10that you may approve the things that are excellent, that you may be sincere and without offense till the day of Christ, 11being filled with the fruits of righteousness which *are* by Jesus Christ, to the glory and praise of God.

12*But I want you to know, brethren, that the things *which happened* to me have actually turned out for the furtherance of the gospel, 13so that it has become evident to the whole palace guard, and to all the rest, that my chains are in Christ; 14and most of the brethren in the Lord, having become confident by my chains, are much more bold to speak the word without fear.

15Some indeed preach Christ even from envy and strife, and some also from goodwill: 16The former^b preach Christ from selfish ambition, not sincerely, supposing to add affliction to my

CHAPTER 1

1:1–11 Paul wrote, "For to me, to live is Christ" (v. 21). But he did more than *write* that statement; he *lived* it. Jesus Christ is mentioned eighteen times in this chapter and is seen involved in many aspects of Paul's life.

His friends. Paul loved the saints in Philippi; he thought about them, prayed for them, and longed to see them. Christ made this fellowship possible.

1:12–18 His circumstances. He was a prisoner not of Rome but of Jesus Christ, and his chains were "in Christ" (v. 13). Paul was practicing Romans 8:28—and it worked! Do you think first of Christ when circumstances are difficult?

1:1 ^aLiterally *overseers*   1:16 ^bNU-Text reverses the contents of verses 16 and 17.

Alive to Christ—"Life is what we are alive to," wrote Maltbie Babcock. Sports fans may be weary, but if they hear of an athletic event taking place, they come alive and want to attend. Hungry people are alive to the mention of food, and avid shoppers come alive at the announcement of a sale. So Christians are alive to all pertaining to Jesus Christ, for Christ is their very life.

1:19–26 *His future.* Paul's life was in danger; if he lost the trial, he could be killed as an enemy of Rome. But when Christ is your life, death is not your enemy; and you have the assurance of being with Christ when life ends.

1:27–30 *His enemies.* When you suffer, you suffer for Christ's sake; and you need not fear your enemies. The vital thing is that God's people unite in Christ and oppose the enemy, not one another!

CHAPTER 2

2:1–11 *Look out.* Christ is the model for Christian life and service because He thought first of others, not of Himself. Do you look out for the interests of others, or do you think only of yourself? Do you have the servant attitude of Jesus Christ, willing to sacrifice for others? Will you empty yourself that others might be filled?

2:12–16 *Work out.* As you yield to the Lord, He works in and you work out; in this way, you fulfill His plan for your life (Eph. 2:10). God cannot shine *through* you until He works *in* you, so let Him have His way. You are a light in a dark world, a runner holding forth the living Word to a dead world.

❝*I used to think that God's gifts were on shelves one above the other, and that the taller we grew in Christian character the more easily we could reach them. I now find that God's gifts are on shelves one beneath the other and that it is not a question of growing taller but of stooping lower.* ❞

—F. B. Meyer

chains; [17]but the latter out of love, knowing that I am appointed for the defense of the gospel. [18]What then? Only *that* in every way, whether in pretense or in truth, Christ is preached; and in this I rejoice, yes, and will rejoice.

[19]*For I know that this will turn out for my deliverance through your prayer and the supply of the Spirit of Jesus Christ, [20]according to my earnest expectation and hope that in nothing I shall be ashamed, but with all boldness, as always, so now also Christ will be magnified in my body, whether by life or by death. [21]For to me, to live *is* Christ, and to die *is* gain. [22]But if *I* live on in the flesh, this *will mean* fruit from *my* labor; yet what I shall choose I cannot tell. [23]For[c] I am hard-pressed between the two, having a desire to depart and be with Christ, *which is* far better. [24]Nevertheless to remain in the flesh *is* more needful for you. [25]And being confident of this, I know that I shall remain and continue with you all for your progress and joy of faith, [26]that your rejoicing for me may be more abundant in Jesus Christ by my coming to you again.

[27]*Only let your conduct be worthy of the gospel of Christ, so that whether I come and see you or am absent, I may hear of your affairs, that you stand fast in one spirit, with one mind striving together for the faith of the gospel, [28]and not in any way terrified by your adversaries, which is to them a proof of perdition, but to you of salvation,[d] and that from God. [29]For to you it has been granted on behalf of Christ, not only to believe in Him, but also to suffer for His sake, [30]having the same conflict which you saw in me and now hear *is* in me.

2 Therefore* if *there is* any consolation in Christ, if any comfort of love, if any fellowship of the Spirit, if any affection and mercy, [2]fulfill my joy by being like-minded, having the same love, *being* of one accord, of one mind. [3]*Let* nothing *be done* through selfish ambition or conceit, but in lowliness of mind let each esteem others better than himself. [4]Let each of you look out not only for his own interests, but also for the interests of others.

[5]Let this mind be in you which was also in Christ Jesus, [6]who, being in the form of God, did not consider it robbery to be equal with God, [7]but made Himself of no reputation, taking the form of a bondservant, *and* coming in the likeness of men. [8]And being found in appearance as a man, He humbled Himself and became obedient to *the point of* death, even the death of the cross. [9]Therefore God also has highly exalted Him and given Him the name which is above every name, [10]that at the name of Jesus every knee should bow, of those in heaven, and of those on earth, and of those under the earth, [11]and *that* every tongue should confess that Jesus Christ *is* Lord, to the glory of God the Father.

[12]*Therefore, my beloved, as you have always obeyed, not as in my presence only, but now much more in my absence, work out your own salvation with fear and trembling; [13]for it is God who works in you both to will and to do for *His* good pleasure.

[14]Do all things without complaining and

1:23 [c]NU-Text and M-Text read *But.*   1:28 [d]NU-Text reads *of your salvation.*

disputing, 15that you may become blameless and harmless, children of God without fault in the midst of a crooked and perverse generation, among whom you shine as lights in the world, 16holding fast the word of life, so that I may rejoice in the day of Christ that I have not run in vain or labored in vain.

17*Yes, and if I am being poured out *as a drink offering* on the sacrifice and service of your faith, I am glad and rejoice with you all. 18For the same reason you also be glad and rejoice with me.

19But I trust in the Lord Jesus to send Timothy to you shortly, that I also may be encouraged when I know your state. 20For I have no one likeminded, who will sincerely care for your state. 21For all seek their own, not the things which are of Christ Jesus. 22But you know his proven character, that as a son with *his* father he served with me in the gospel. 23Therefore I hope to send him at once, as soon as I see how it goes with me. 24But I trust in the Lord that I myself shall also come shortly.

25Yet I considered it necessary to send to you Epaphroditus, my brother, fellow worker, and fellow soldier, but your messenger and the one who ministered to my need; 26since he was longing for you all, and was distressed because you had heard that he was sick. 27For indeed he was sick almost unto death; but God had mercy on him, and not only on him but on me also, lest I should have sorrow upon sorrow. 28Therefore I sent him the more eagerly, that when you see him again you may rejoice, and I may be less sorrowful. 29Receive him therefore with all gladness, and hold such men in esteem; 30because for the work of Christ he came close to death, not regarding his life, to supply what was lacking in your service toward me.

3 Finally,* my brethren, rejoice in the Lord. For me to write the same things to you *is* not tedious, but for you *it is* safe.

2Beware of dogs, beware of evil workers, beware of the mutilation! 3For we are the circumcision, who worship God in the Spirit,e rejoice in Christ Jesus, and have no confidence in the flesh, 4though I also might have confidence in the flesh. If anyone else thinks he may have confidence in the flesh, I more so: 5circumcised the eighth day, of the stock of Israel, *of* the tribe of Benjamin, a Hebrew of the Hebrews; concerning the law, a Pharisee; 6concerning zeal, persecuting the church; concerning the righteousness which is in the law, blameless.

7*But what things were gain to me, these I have counted loss for Christ. 8Yet indeed I also count all things loss for the excellence of the knowledge of Christ Jesus my Lord, for whom I have suffered the loss of all things, and count them as rubbish, that I may gain Christ 9and be found in Him, not having my own righteousness, which *is* from the law, but that which *is* through faith in Christ, the righteousness which is from God by faith; 10that I may know Him and the power of His resurrection, and the fellowship of His sufferings, being conformed to His death, 11if, by any means, I may attain to the resurrection from the dead.

12*Not that I have already attained, or am

2:17–30 *Poured out*. The image is that of the drink offering, poured out on the altar (Num. 15:1–10). Paul was willing to pour out his very life for the sake of the Lord and the church, and to do it *joyfully*. Timothy and Epaphroditus had the same attitude of service and sacrifice, giving themselves for others.

CHAPTER 3

3:1 *Rejoicing*. If you cannot rejoice in your circumstances, you can always rejoice in the Lord who controls your circumstances. Fix your attention on Him. He may not change your situation, but He will change you; and that is even better.

3:7–11 *Counting*. What is important to you? Do you feel you have made sacrifices to follow the Lord? Paul did not feel he had lost anything worthwhile by trusting Christ. Instead, he gained everything really worth having.

3:12–16 *Reaching*. Christians are like runners who refuse to look around or look back but keep running with their eyes on the goal. To look back at past successes or failures, or to look around to see what others are doing or saying, is to invite defeat. Heed Hebrews 12:1–2.

3:3 eNU-Text and M-Text read *who worship in the Spirit of God.*

already perfected; but I press on, that I may lay hold of that for which Christ Jesus has also laid hold of me. 13Brethren, I do not count myself to have apprehended; but one thing *I do*, forgetting those things which are behind and reaching forward to those things which are ahead, 14I press toward the goal for the prize of the upward call of God in Christ Jesus.

15Therefore let us, as many as are mature, have this mind; and if in anything you think otherwise, God will reveal even this to you. 16Nevertheless, to *the degree* that we have already attained, let us walk by the same rule,*f* let us be of the same mind.

17Brethren, join in following my example, and note those who so walk, as you have us for a pattern. 18*For many walk, of whom I have told you often, and now tell you even weeping, *that they are* the enemies of the cross of Christ: 19whose end *is* destruction, whose god *is their* belly, and *whose* glory *is* in their shame—who set their mind on earthly things. 20*For our citizenship is in heaven, from which we also eagerly wait for the Savior, the Lord Jesus Christ, 21who will transform our lowly body that it may be conformed to His glorious body, according to the working by which He is able even to subdue all things to Himself.

4 Therefore,* my beloved and longed-for brethren, my joy and crown, so stand fast in the Lord, beloved.

2I implore Euodia and I implore Syntyche to be of the same mind in the Lord. 3And*g* I urge you also, true companion, help these women who labored with me in the gospel, with Clement also, and the rest of my fellow workers, whose names *are* in the Book of Life.

4Rejoice in the Lord always. Again I will say, rejoice!

5Let your gentleness be known to all men. The Lord *is* at hand.

6Be anxious for nothing, but in everything by prayer and supplication, with thanksgiving, let your requests be made known to God; 7and the peace of God, which surpasses all understanding, will guard your hearts and minds through Christ Jesus.

8Finally, brethren, whatever things are true, whatever things *are* noble, whatever things *are* just, whatever things *are* pure, whatever things *are* lovely, whatever things *are* of good report, if *there is* any virtue and if *there is* anything praiseworthy—meditate on these things. 9The things which you learned and received and heard and saw in me, these do, and the God of peace will be with you.

10But I rejoiced in the Lord greatly that now at last your care for me has flourished again; though you surely did care, but you lacked opportunity. 11Not that I speak in regard to need, for I have learned in whatever state I am, to be content: 12I know how to be abased, and I know how to

---

3:18, 19 *Weeping.* This is the only mention of tears in a letter devoted to joy. Paul wept over professed Christians who lived to please themselves. Instead of having the mind of Christ, they thought like the world, and these people are with us today.

3:20, 21 *Looking.* Paul looked up and eagerly anticipated the return of the Lord. Christ had taken care of his past (v. 13), and He would also take care of his future. And as for Paul's present, his confidence was knowing that "He is able!" (v. 21).

CHAPTER 4

4:1ff The message of our ministry is the gospel of Christ (chap. 1). The model for our ministry is the example of Christ (chap. 2). The motive for our ministry is the reward of Christ (chap. 3). The means of our ministry is the provision of Christ (chap. 4). He provides unity when we disagree with our fellow Christians (vv. 1–5), and peace when we are prone to worry (vv. 6–9). If we pray as we ought to pray and think as we ought to think, the peace of God will guard us, and the God of peace will go with us.

He provides the power we need for life and service (vv. 10–13) and the material needs we have as well (vv. 14–20). Paul did not have a wealthy organization giving him support, but he did have a great God who enabled generous friends to meet his needs. Paul saw their gift as a fragrant sacrifice to the Lord (v. 18), and he rejoiced in the Lord for what they did.

3:16 *f*NU-Text omits *rule* and the rest of the verse.
4:3 *g*NU-Text and M-Text read *Yes.*

Reach Your Potential—Charles W. Koller affirmed that through Christ you can be what you ought to be (Phil. 4:11), do what you ought to do (v. 13), and have what you ought to have (v. 19), all to the glory of God.

abound. Everywhere and in all things I have learned both to be full and to be hungry, both to abound and to suffer need. [13]I can do all things through Christ[h] who strengthens me.

[14]Nevertheless you have done well that you shared in my distress. [15]Now you Philippians know also that in the beginning of the gospel, when I departed from Macedonia, no church shared with me concerning giving and receiving but you only. [16]For even in Thessalonica you sent *aid* once and again for my necessities. [17]Not that I seek the gift, but I seek the fruit that abounds to your account. [18]Indeed I have all and abound. I am full, having received from Epaphroditus the things *sent* from you, a sweet-smelling aroma, an acceptable sacrifice, well pleasing to God. [19]And my God shall supply all your need according to His riches in glory by Christ Jesus. [20]Now to our God and Father *be* glory forever and ever. Amen.

[21]Greet every saint in Christ Jesus. The brethren who are with me greet you. [22]All the saints greet you, but especially those who are of Caesar's household.

[23]The grace of our Lord Jesus Christ be with you all.[i] Amen.

4:13 [h]NU-Text reads *Him who.*   4:23 [i]NU-Text reads *your spirit.*

COLOSSIANS

Epaphras, one of Paul's converts, founded the church in Colosse (1:7; 4:12–13); Paul had never been there personally (2:1). While imprisoned in Rome, Paul heard that false doctrines were being introduced in the church, so he wrote this letter to warn the believers and to establish them in the faith.

The key theme is the preeminence of Christ (1:18) because the false teachers made Christ one of several emanations from God. They mixed Christian truth with their doctrines of Jewish legalism and Oriental mysticism. Colossians is the perfect answer to the so-called New Age movement today, for Paul affirms that in Jesus Christ believers are complete and have the fullness of God available to them (2:9–10).

Chapters 1—2 are doctrinal and present Jesus Christ as the preeminent Creator, Savior, and Lord. Chapters 3—4 are practical and show how the believer works out the preeminence of Christ in daily living. Because the epistles to the Ephesians and Colossians were written about the same time, you will see parallels; but Ephesians emphasizes the body (the church), while Colossians emphasizes the Head of the body (Jesus Christ). The letters complement each other.

1 Paul, an apostle of Jesus Christ by the will of God, and Timothy our brother,

2To the saints and faithful brethren in Christ *who are* in Colosse:

Grace to you and peace from God our Father and the Lord Jesus Christ.*a*
3We give thanks to the God and Father of our Lord Jesus Christ, praying always for you, 4since we heard of your faith in Christ Jesus and of your love for all the saints; 5*because of the hope which is laid up for you in heaven, of which you heard before in the word of the truth of the gospel, 6which has come to you, as *it has* also in all the world, and is bringing forth fruit,*b* as *it is* also among you since the day you heard and knew the grace of God in truth; 7as you also learned from Epaphras, our dear fellow servant, who is a faithful minister of Christ on your behalf, 8who also declared to us your love in the Spirit.

9For this reason we also, since the day we heard it, do not cease to pray for you, and to ask that you may be filled with the knowledge of His will in all wisdom and spiritual understanding; 10that you may walk worthy of the Lord, fully pleasing *Him*, being fruitful in every good work and increasing in the knowledge of God; 11strengthened with all might, according to His glorious power, for all patience and longsuffering with

CHAPTER 1

1:5 *The hope before you.* These people were going to heaven! They had heard the Word and trusted the Savior, and they had given evidence of their faith by their love for God and God's people. God qualified them (v. 12); they did not save themselves.

1:2 *a*NU-Text omits *and the Lord Jesus Christ.* 1:6 *b*NU-Text and M-Text add *and growing.*

Firstborn—"Firstborn over all creation" (Col. 1:15) does not mean Jesus was a created being and not eternal God, nor does "firstborn from the dead" (v. 18) mean He was the first one raised from the dead. *Firstborn* is a term of honor and means "the highest, of first rank and importance." Jesus was prior to all creation (John 1:1–3) and is the highest in creation. He is the highest of all who were raised from the dead (Rev. 1:17–18).

Thanksgiving—Note the emphasis on *thanksgiving* in Colossians (1:3, 12; 2:7; 3:17; 4:2). The more wonderful we see Jesus to be, the more we will be grateful to God for Him and His blessings.

joy; 12giving thanks to the Father who has qualified us to be partakers of the inheritance of the saints in the light. 13He has delivered us from the power of darkness and conveyed *us* into the kingdom of the Son of His love, 14in whom we have redemption through His blood,c the forgiveness of sins.

15He is the image of the invisible God, the firstborn over all creation. 16For by Him all things were created that are in heaven and that are on earth, visible and invisible, whether thrones or dominions or principalities or powers. All things were created through Him and for Him. 17And He is before all things, and in Him all things consist. 18And He is the head of the body, the church, who is the beginning, the firstborn from the dead, that in all things He may have the preeminence.

19For it pleased *the Father that* in Him all the fullness should dwell, 20and by Him to reconcile all things to Himself, by Him, whether things on earth or things in heaven, having made peace through the blood of His cross.

21And you, who once were alienated and enemies in your mind by wicked works, yet now He has reconciled 22in the body of His flesh through death, to present you holy, and blameless, and above reproach in His sight— 23*if indeed you continue in the faith, grounded and steadfast, and are not moved away from the hope of the gospel which you heard, which was preached to every creature under heaven, of which I, Paul, became a minister.

24I now rejoice in my sufferings for you, and fill up in my flesh what is lacking in the afflictions of Christ, for the sake of His body, which is the church, 25of which I became a minister according to the stewardship from God which was given to me for you, to fulfill the word of God, 26the mystery which has been hidden from ages and from generations, but now has been revealed to His saints. 27*To them God willed to make known what are the riches of the glory of this mystery among the Gentiles: whichd is Christ in you, the hope of glory. 28Him we preach, warning every man and teaching every man in all wisdom, that we may present every man perfect in Christ Jesus. 29To this *end* I also labor, striving according to His working which works in me mightily.

2 For* I want you to know what a great conflict I have for you and those in Laodicea, and *for* as many as have not seen my face in the flesh, 2that their hearts may be encouraged, being knit together in love, and *attaining* to all riches of the full assurance of understanding, to the knowledge of the mystery of God, both of the Father ande of Christ, 3in whom are hidden all the treasures of wisdom and knowledge.

4*Now this I say lest anyone should deceive you with persuasive words. 5For though I am absent in the flesh, yet I am with you in spirit, rejoicing to see your *good* order and the steadfastness of your faith in Christ.

6As you therefore have received Christ Jesus the Lord, so walk in Him, 7rooted and built up in Him and established in the faith, as you have been taught, abounding in itf with thanksgiving.

1:23 *The hope beneath you.* Hope is a foundation on which you stand when all around you is shaking. The city of Colosse was located in an earthquake area, so Paul's admonition was especially meaningful to them (v. 23). The false teachers wanted the saints to shift their foundation, but Paul pointed the church to Jesus Christ: Savior (vv. 13–14), eternal God (v. 15), Creator (vv. 16–17), and Head of the church (v. 18). What a perfect foundation for your hope!

1:27 *The hope within you.* Heaven is more than a destination; it is a motivation because Christ lives within. It is a living hope (1 Pet. 1:3) that affects how we think and act all day long. Because Christ is within us, we need not fear what is ahead.

CHAPTER 2

2:1 Paul wrote to the Colossians, "You must never allow anyone to come between you and Christ. In Him is all wisdom and knowledge (v. 3) and all the fullness of God (v. 9), and you are complete in Him (v. 10). Why accept a substitute?"

2:4 *Let no one deceive you.* Religious systems seem so inviting, and their leaders are so persuasive. But if you follow them, you will substitute man's ideas for God's truth.

❝*The greatest philosophy ever produced does not come within a thousand leagues of the fathomless profundity of our Lord's statements, e.g., 'Learn of Me, for I am meek and lowly in heart.'* ❞

—Oswald Chambers

1:14 cNU-Text and M-Text omit *through His blood.*
1:27 dM-Text reads *who.*   2:2 eNU-Text omits *both of the Father and.*   2:7 fNU-Text omits *in it.*

2:8 *Let no one cheat you.* Here the thief is man-made philosophy and tradition, pleasing to the world but rejected by the Lord. If you have all fullness in Christ, why substitute man's empty philosophies?

2:16 *Let no one judge you.* Legalism is the robber here (v. 21), stealing your liberty in Christ and making you live by religious regulations instead of by God's grace.

2:18 *Let no one defraud you.* Here the culprit is religious mysticism that replaces spiritual nourishment from Christ with empty (but exciting) religious experiences. You have in Christ all that you need. Beware substitutes!

CHAPTER 3

3:1–7 Having laid the doctrinal foundation, Paul now makes the personal application, for truth is something to *live* as well as to *learn.*

Put to death. In Christ, you have died to the old life and been raised to a new life (Rom. 6:1–14; Eph. 2:1–10), so make the new life the focus of your attention. Set your mind on it; seek to experience all that you have in Christ.

3:8, 9 *Put off.* Like Lazarus (John 11:44), you must get rid of the graveclothes that belong to the old life. By faith, put off the old sins that bound you; Christ has set you free.

8*Beware lest anyone cheat you through philosophy and empty deceit, according to the tradition of men, according to the basic principles of the world, and not according to Christ. 9For in Him dwells all the fullness of the Godhead bodily; 10and you are complete in Him, who is the head of all principality and power.

11In Him you were also circumcised with the circumcision made without hands, by putting off the body of the sinsg of the flesh, by the circumcision of Christ, 12buried with Him in baptism, in which you also were raised with *Him* through faith in the working of God, who raised Him from the dead. 13And you, being dead in your trespasses and the uncircumcision of your flesh, He has made alive together with Him, having forgiven you all trespasses, 14having wiped out the handwriting of requirements that was against us, which was contrary to us. And He has taken it out of the way, having nailed it to the cross. 15Having disarmed principalities and powers, He made a public spectacle of them, triumphing over them in it.

16*So let no one judge you in food or in drink, or regarding a festival or a new moon or sabbaths, 17which are a shadow of things to come, but the substance is of Christ. 18*Let no one cheat you of your reward, taking delight in *false* humility and worship of angels, intruding into those things which he has noth seen, vainly puffed up by his fleshly mind, 19and not holding fast to the Head, from whom all the body, nourished and knit together by joints and ligaments, grows with the increase *that is* from God.

20Therefore,i if you died with Christ from the basic principles of the world, why, as *though* living in the world, do you subject yourselves to regulations— 21"Do not touch, do not taste, do not handle," 22which all concern things which perish with the using—according to the commandments and doctrines of men? 23These things indeed have an appearance of wisdom in self-imposed religion, *false* humility, and neglect of the body, *but are* of no value against the indulgence of the flesh.

3 If* then you were raised with Christ, seek those things which are above, where Christ is, sitting at the right hand of God. 2Set your mind on things above, not on things on the earth. 3For you died, and your life is hidden with Christ in God. 4When Christ *who is* our life appears, then you also will appear with Him in glory.

5Therefore put to death your members which are on the earth: fornication, uncleanness, passion, evil desire, and covetousness, which is idolatry. 6Because of these things the wrath of God is coming upon the sons of disobedience, 7in which you yourselves once walked when you lived in them.

8*But now you yourselves are to put off all these: anger, wrath, malice, blasphemy, filthy lan-

---

2:11 gNU-Text omits *of the sins.*   2:18 hNU-Text omits *not.*
2:20 iNU-Text and M-Text omit *Therefore.*

Filled with the Word—Colossians 3:16—4:1 parallels Ephesians 5:18—6:9, except that the emphasis here is on being filled with the *Word* of God. When the Word controls your life, you will be joyful (3:16), thankful (3:17), and submissive (3:18—4:1), and these are the same characteristics of the Spirit-filled Christian as explained in Ephesians 5:18—6:9. To be filled with the Spirit of God means to be controlled by the Word of God.

guage out of your mouth. 9Do not lie to one another, since you have put off the old man with his deeds, 10*and have put on the new *man* who is renewed in knowledge according to the image of Him who created him, 11where there is neither Greek nor Jew, circumcised nor uncircumcised, barbarian, Scythian, slave *nor* free, but Christ *is* all in all.

12Therefore, as *the* elect of God, holy and beloved, put on tender mercies, kindness, humility, meekness, longsuffering; 13bearing with one another, and forgiving one another, if anyone has a complaint against another; even as Christ forgave you, so you also *must do.* 14But above all these things put on love, which is the bond of perfection. 15And let the peace of God rule in your hearts, to which also you were called in one body; and be thankful. 16Let the word of Christ dwell in you richly in all wisdom, teaching and admonishing one another in psalms and hymns and spiritual songs, singing with grace in your hearts to the Lord. 17And *whatever* you do in word or deed, *do* all in the name of the Lord Jesus, giving thanks to God the Father through Him.

18Wives, submit to your own husbands, as is fitting in the Lord.

19Husbands, love your wives and do not be bitter toward them.

20Children, obey your parents in all things, for this is well pleasing to the Lord.

21Fathers, do not provoke your children, lest they become discouraged.

22Bondservants, obey in all things your masters according to the flesh, not with eyeservice, as men-pleasers, but in sincerity of heart, fearing God. 23And whatever you do, do it heartily, as to the Lord and not to men, 24knowing that from the Lord you will receive the reward of the inheritance; for*j* you serve the Lord Christ. 25But he who does wrong will be repaid for what he has done, and there is no partiality.

4 Masters, give your bondservants what is just and fair, knowing that you also have a Master in heaven.

2*Continue earnestly in prayer, being vigilant in it with thanksgiving; 3meanwhile praying also for us, that God would open to us a door for the word, to speak the mystery of Christ, for which I am also in chains, 4that I may make it manifest, as I ought to speak.

5*Walk in wisdom toward those *who are* outside, redeeming the time. 6Let your speech always *be* with grace, seasoned with salt, that you may know how you ought to answer each one.

7*Tychicus, a beloved brother, faithful minister, and fellow servant in the Lord, will tell you all the news about me. 8I am sending him to you for this very purpose, that he*k* may know your circumstances and comfort your hearts, 9with Onesimus, a faithful and beloved brother, who is one

---

3:24 *j*NU-Text omits *for.*   4:8 *k*NU-Text reads *you may know our circumstances and he may.*

3:10–25 *Put on.* God wants you to wear the graceclothes, not the graveclothes! If your focus is on things heavenly, you will obey God in things on earth, especially in your relationships with others.

CHAPTER 4

4:2–4, 12, 13 *Praying.* Prayer involves a persevering will, an alert mind, and a grateful heart; and our requests should be specific and related to the ministry of the Word. Paul asked not for an open prison door but for an open door of ministry (1 Cor. 16:9; 2 Cor. 2:12; Rev. 3:7–8).

4:5, 6 *Witnessing.* The unsaved are outside the family of God, and it is our task to bring them in. Effective witness involves walking wisely, being alert to every opportunity, and being careful in what we say and how we say it (1 Pet. 3:15–17).

4:7–9 *Informing.* Paul did not hesitate to share his needs with others, because he depended on their prayer support (Rom. 15:30; Eph. 6:19; Phil. 1:19; 1 Thess. 5:25; Philem. 22). Do you pray for Christian leaders in places of importance? They need it!

Servants of the Lord—Years before, Paul had refused to serve with John Mark (Acts 15:36–41) because Mark had left the work (Acts 13:5–13); but now Paul and John Mark were friends and colaborers. Luke had been a part of Paul's team since their ministry at Philippi (Acts 16:10). Alas, Demas would eventually forsake Paul and the Lord (Philem. 24; 2 Tim. 4:10). Do you pray for the men and women who serve with Christian leaders, that they might be faithful to the Lord?

4:10–18 Serving. Paul names six men who were working at his side and encouraging him in the Lord. Even an apostle cannot get the job done alone, and how grateful he was for the saints serving faithfully in Colosse!

of you. They will make known to you all things which *are happening* here.

10*Aristarchus my fellow prisoner greets you, with Mark the cousin of Barnabas (about whom you received instructions: if he comes to you, welcome him), 11and Jesus who is called Justus. These *are my* only fellow workers for the kingdom of God who are of the circumcision; they have proved to be a comfort to me.

12Epaphras, who is *one* of you, a bondservant of Christ, greets you, always laboring fervently for you in prayers, that you may stand perfect and complete[l] in all the will of God. 13For I bear him witness that he has a great zeal[m] for you, and those who are in Laodicea, and those in Hierapolis. 14Luke the beloved physician and Demas greet you. 15Greet the brethren who are in Laodicea, and Nymphas and the church that *is* in his[n] house.

16Now when this epistle is read among you, see that it is read also in the church of the Laodiceans, and that you likewise read the epistle from Laodicea. 17And say to Archippus, "Take heed to the ministry which you have received in the Lord, that you may fulfill it."

18This salutation by my own hand—Paul. Remember my chains. Grace *be* with you. Amen.

4:12 [l]NU-Text reads *fully assured.*   4:13 [m]NU-Text reads *concern.*   4:15 [n]NU-Text reads *Nympha . . . her house.*

THE THESSALONIAN EPISTLES

Acts 17:1–15 records the founding of the church in Thessalonica. Paul ministered there a short time, possibly only a month; but the Lord did a great work, and the witness of the church was known far and wide.

Paul had to leave the city and was not able to return, so he sent Timothy to see how things were going. Paul wrote the first letter from Corinth (Acts 18:5) in response to Timothy's report (3:6). He wanted to encourage the saints in their Christian walk and assure them of his love and concern.

The second letter was written a few months later to encourage the church to be steadfast in the midst of persecution. Some of the people thought the "day of the Lord" had come, so Paul dealt with that theme as well. Both letters emphasize the coming of Christ and the practical effect it should have on our lives.

1 THESSALONIANS

CHAPTER 1

1:2–4 Paul's description of the believers in Thessalonica suggests that they typify an ideal congregation. Ask yourself these questions. *Are others thankful for me?* Paul was grateful for their faith, hope, and love, and that these Christian qualities revealed themselves in work, labor, and patience. Can others tell that we belong to God? Are they thankful for our spiritual growth?

1:5–7 *Is God's power seen in my life?* This comes when you receive the Word of God by faith and allow the Spirit of God to minister to your heart. It also involves suffering for the Lord and letting Him give you His joy.

1:8–10 *Do I make it easier for others to talk about Jesus?* Some believers are such poor examples as Christians that their lives give unbelievers an excuse for rejecting Christ. But the Thessalonian Christians made it easy for Paul to preach the gospel! Their testimony had gone before him and met him wherever he went.

CHAPTER 2

2:1–6 *Faithfulness.* Paul's sufferings in Philippi might have made him hesitate to minister in Thessalonica, but he was a steward who wanted to be faithful to the Lord. His message and motive were pure, and God blessed his ministry. It is better to be approved by God and suffer than to be applauded by men and prosper. When you feel like quitting, keep going (1 Cor. 4:2).

2:7–9 *Gentleness.* Young believers need a spiritual parent to lovingly nurture them in the Lord. Paul's ministry was motivated by love, not by pride or the desire for material gain.

---

1 Paul, Silvanus, and Timothy,

To the church of the Thessalonians in God the Father and the Lord Jesus Christ:

Grace to you and peace from God our Father and the Lord Jesus Christ.[a]

2*We give thanks to God always for you all, making mention of you in our prayers, 3remembering without ceasing your work of faith, labor of love, and patience of hope in our Lord Jesus Christ in the sight of our God and Father, 4knowing, beloved brethren, your election by God. 5*For our gospel did not come to you in word only, but also in power, and in the Holy Spirit and in much assurance, as you know what kind of men we were among you for your sake.

6And you became followers of us and of the Lord, having received the word in much affliction, with joy of the Holy Spirit, 7so that you became examples to all in Macedonia and Achaia who believe. 8*For from you the word of the Lord has sounded forth, not only in Macedonia and Achaia, but also in every place. Your faith toward God has gone out, so that we do not need to say anything. 9For they themselves declare concerning us what manner of entry we had to you, and how you turned to God from idols to serve the living and true God, 10and to wait for His Son from heaven, whom He raised from the dead, *even* Jesus who delivers us from the wrath to come.

2 For* you yourselves know, brethren, that our coming to you was not in vain. 2But even[b] after we had suffered before and were spitefully treated at Philippi, as you know, we were bold in our God to speak to you the gospel of God in much conflict. 3For our exhortation *did* not *come* from error or uncleanness, nor *was it* in deceit.

4But as we have been approved by God to be entrusted with the gospel, even so we speak, not as pleasing men, but God who tests our hearts. 5For neither at any time did we use flattering words, as you know, nor a cloak for covetousness—God *is* witness. 6Nor did we seek glory from men, either from you or from others, when we might have made demands as apostles of Christ. 7*But we were gentle among you, just as a nursing *mother* cherishes her own children. 8So, affectionately longing for you, we were well pleased to impart to you not only the gospel of God, but also our own lives, because you had become dear to us. 9For you remember, brethren, our labor and toil; for laboring night and day, that we might

---

1:1 [a]NU-Text omits *from God our Father and the Lord Jesus Christ.* 2:2 [b]NU-Text and M-Text omit *even.*

Jesus' Return—Every chapter in 1 Thessalonians ends with a reference to the return of Jesus Christ, and that truth is applied to daily living. An eager looking for His return is an evidence of salvation (1:9–10), a motivation for soul winning (2:17–20), and an encouragement for holy living (3:11–13). This truth is a comfort in sorrow (4:18) and a stimulus to have more confidence in the Lord (5:23–24).

not be a burden to any of you, we preached to you the gospel of God.

10*You *are* witnesses, and God *also*, how devoutly and justly and blamelessly we behaved ourselves among you who believe; 11as you know how we exhorted, and comforted, and charged[c] every one of you, as a father *does* his own children, 12that you would walk worthy of God who calls you into His own kingdom and glory.

13*For this reason we also thank God without ceasing, because when you received the word of God which you heard from us, you welcomed *it* not *as* the word of men, but as it is in truth, the word of God, which also effectively works in you who believe. 14For you, brethren, became imitators of the churches of God which are in Judea in Christ Jesus. For you also suffered the same things from your own countrymen, just as they *did* from the Judeans, 15who killed both the Lord Jesus and their own prophets, and have persecuted us; and they do not please God and are contrary to all men, 16forbidding us to speak to the Gentiles that they may be saved, so as always to fill up *the measure of* their sins; but wrath has come upon them to the uttermost.

17*But we, brethren, having been taken away from you for a short time in presence, not in heart, endeavored more eagerly to see your face with great desire. 18Therefore we wanted to come to you—even I, Paul, time and again—but Satan hindered us. 19For what *is* our hope, or joy, or crown of rejoicing? *Is it* not even you in the presence of our Lord Jesus Christ at His coming? 20For you are our glory and joy.

3 Therefore,* when we could no longer endure it, we thought it good to be left in Athens alone, 2and sent Timothy, our brother and minister of God, and our fellow laborer in the gospel of Christ, to establish you and encourage you concerning your faith, 3that no one should be shaken by these afflictions; for you yourselves know that we are appointed to this. 4For, in fact, we told you before when we were with you that we would suffer tribulation, just as it happened, and you know. 5For this reason, when I could no longer endure it, I sent to know your faith, lest by some means the tempter had tempted you, and our labor might be in vain.

6But now that Timothy has come to us from you, and brought us good news of your faith and love, and that you always have good remembrance of us, greatly desiring to see us, as we also *to see* you— 7therefore, brethren, in all our affliction and distress we were comforted concerning you by your faith. 8For now we live, if you stand fast in the Lord.

9For what thanks can we render to God for you, for all the joy with which we rejoice for your sake before our God, 10night and day praying exceedingly that we may see your face and perfect what is lacking in your faith?

11Now may our God and Father Himself, and our Lord Jesus Christ, direct our way to you. 12And may the Lord make you increase and abound in love to one another and to all, just as we *do* to you, 13so that He may establish your hearts blameless in holiness before our God and

2:10–12 *Blamelessness.* How important it is to be good examples before young believers! Children do what we do, not what we say. Does your example as a Christian make it easier for others to grow?

2:13–16 *Eagerness.* These people had an appetite for the Word of God, and that helped them to grow (Jer. 15:16; 1 Pet. 2:2). When they heard God's Word, they eagerly welcomed it and put it to work immediately.

2:17–20 *Hopefulness.* Paul hoped to visit his beloved friends again; but even if they did not meet on earth, he would meet them at the coming of the Lord. When Jesus comes, will you rejoice in His presence because of people you have influenced for Christ?

CHAPTER 3

3:1ff What should you do when people you love need your help, but you cannot go to them? The new believers in Thessalonica desperately needed Paul's ministry, but he was not able to return to help them. So, he did what he could.

First, he sent Timothy to minister to the church. If you cannot go, try to get somebody qualified to go in your place.

Then, he prayed for them (v. 10) because prayer is not limited by time or place. Your prayers for your loved ones will do more good than you realize, so keep praying.

Paul encouraged them by writing them at least two letters. His great concern was not their comfort or safety but their faith (vv. 2, 5–7, 10), their love (v. 12), and their obedience to the Lord (v. 13). Perhaps today you could write a letter or send a card to someone who needs your encouragement.

2:11 [c]NU-Text and M-Text read *implored.*

CHAPTER 4

4:1–8 "More and more" should be the desire of the dedicated Christian (vv. 1, 10). **More holiness.** Your body belongs to God, and His will is that you use it for holy purposes. Christ purchased your body (1 Cor. 6:18–20), the Spirit dwells in your body (4:8), and the Father has called you to holy living (v. 7). Disobey and the penalties are great!

4:9, 10 More love. You are taught to love by the Father (1 John 4:19), the Son (John 13:34), and the Spirit (Rom. 5:5). Love is one mark of the true believer (1 John 3:14).

4:11, 12 More quietness. Because they expected the Lord to return any day, some believers had quit their jobs and become idlers and meddlers (2 Thess. 3:6–15). What kind of testimony would this be to the lost?

4:13–18 More hope. Christians sorrow because God made us to weep; but it is not the hopeless sorrow of the world. Jesus is coming again, and that means reunion and eternal rejoicing!

❝*I have noticed this, that when a man is full of the Holy Ghost, he is the very last man to be complaining of other people. He loves everybody too tenderly. He loves even a cold church, and is anxious to lift them up and bring them to a kinder feeling and sympathy.*❞

—D. L. Moody

CHAPTER 5

5:1–11 False peace. The "day of the Lord" is that time when God will pour out His wrath on the world. God's people have been saved from wrath, so they need not worry (v. 9; 1:10); but the lost world will be caught at a time when they think they are secure. To be ready for Christ's coming, God's people must be sober and live in the light.

Father at the coming of our Lord Jesus Christ with all His saints.

4 Finally* then, brethren, we urge and exhort in the Lord Jesus that you should abound more and more, just as you received from us how you ought to walk and to please God; 2for you know what commandments we gave you through the Lord Jesus.

3For this is the will of God, your sanctification: that you should abstain from sexual immorality; 4that each of you should know how to possess his own vessel in sanctification and honor, 5not in passion of lust, like the Gentiles who do not know God; 6that no one should take advantage of and defraud his brother in this matter, because the Lord *is* the avenger of all such, as we also forewarned you and testified. 7For God did not call us to uncleanness, but in holiness. 8Therefore he who rejects *this* does not reject man, but God, who has also given[d] us His Holy Spirit.

9*But concerning brotherly love you have no need that I should write to you, for you yourselves are taught by God to love one another; 10and indeed you do so toward all the brethren who are in all Macedonia. But we urge you, brethren, that you increase more and more; 11*that you also aspire to lead a quiet life, to mind your own business, and to work with your own hands, as we commanded you, 12that you may walk properly toward those who are outside, and *that* you may lack nothing.

13*But I do not want you to be ignorant, brethren, concerning those who have fallen asleep, lest you sorrow as others who have no hope. 14For if we believe that Jesus died and rose again, even so God will bring with Him those who sleep in Jesus.[e]

15For this we say to you by the word of the Lord, that we who are alive *and* remain until the coming of the Lord will by no means precede those who are asleep. 16For the Lord Himself will descend from heaven with a shout, with the voice of an archangel, and with the trumpet of God. And the dead in Christ will rise first. 17Then we who are alive *and* remain shall be caught up together with them in the clouds to meet the Lord in the air. And thus we shall always be with the Lord. 18Therefore comfort one another with these words.

5 But* concerning the times and the seasons, brethren, you have no need that I should write to you. 2For you yourselves know perfectly that the day of the Lord so comes as a thief in the night. 3For when they say, "Peace and safety!" then sudden destruction comes upon them, as labor pains upon a pregnant woman. And they shall not escape. 4But you, brethren, are not in dark-

---

4:8 dNU-Text reads *who also gives.* 4:14 eOr *those who through Jesus sleep*

Welcome the Spirit's Ministry—"Do not quench the Spirit" (1 Thess. 5:19) is an admonition to Christians not to resist and reject the ministry of the Spirit. The image is that of fire (Isa. 34:4; Acts 2:3; Rev. 4:5). Just as fire brings light, heat, and cleansing, so the Spirit enlightens, enables, and purifies His people. Paul reminded Timothy to "stir up the gift of God" (2 Tim. 1:6), which means "get the fire burning again." Are you allowing the fire to go out on the altar of your life (Lev. 6:9, 12)?

ness, so that this Day should overtake you as a thief. 5You are all sons of light and sons of the day. We are not of the night nor of darkness. 6Therefore let us not sleep, as others *do*, but let us watch and be sober. 7For those who sleep, sleep at night, and those who get drunk are drunk at night. 8But let us who are of the day be sober, putting on the breastplate of faith and love, and *as* a helmet the hope of salvation. 9For God did not appoint us to wrath, but to obtain salvation through our Lord Jesus Christ, 10who died for us, that whether we wake or sleep, we should live together with Him.

11Therefore comfort each other and edify one another, just as you also are doing.

12*And we urge you, brethren, to recognize those who labor among you, and are over you in the Lord and admonish you, 13and to esteem them very highly in love for their work's sake. Be at peace among yourselves.

14Now we exhort you, brethren, warn those who are unruly, comfort the fainthearted, uphold the weak, be patient with all. 15See that no one renders evil for evil to anyone, but always pursue what is good both for yourselves and for all.

16Rejoice always, 17pray without ceasing, 18in everything give thanks; for this is the will of God in Christ Jesus for you.

19Do not quench the Spirit. 20Do not despise prophecies. 21Test all things; hold fast what is good. 22Abstain from every form of evil.

23*Now may the God of peace Himself sanctify you completely; and may your whole spirit, soul, and body be preserved blameless at the coming of our Lord Jesus Christ. 24He who calls you *is* faithful, who also will do *it*.

25Brethren, pray for us.

26Greet all the brethren with a holy kiss.

27I charge you by the Lord that this epistle be read to all the holy*f* brethren.

28The grace of our Lord Jesus Christ *be* with you. Amen.

5:27 *f*NU-Text omits *holy*.

5:12–22 *Family peace.* The local church fellowship should reflect God's peace; and it will if God's people obey authority, minister to one another, and submit to the Spirit of God. Verse 21 emphasizes the positive and verse 22 the negative, and both are important.

5:23, 24 *Faithful peace.* Holiness and peace go together (Isa. 32:17), for the God who quiets the heart also cleanses the heart (James 3:17). A disturbed heart is sometimes evidence of unconfessed sin. God is faithful; let Him bring purity and peace to your heart.

2 THESSALONIANS

CHAPTER 1

1:1ff Along with persecutions on the outside, the church was facing problems on the inside. Some people were suffering great trials for their faith. Others had quit working and were idlers. Still others were harboring the wrong idea that they were experiencing the "day of the Lord." Paul wrote this letter to encourage the suffering (chap. 1), enlighten the confused (chap. 2), and warn the careless (chap. 3).

In times of trial, the essential thing is your faith (v. 3). God will see you through, so trust His promises. Remember that others are watching you and you can encourage them (v. 4). You may be tempted to fight back, but leave that to the Lord (vv. 5–9).

The lost will be eternally separated from God's glory (v. 9), while the saved will bring glory to the Lord (v. 10). Meanwhile, be sure that God is glorified by your life today (vv. 11–12).

❝*No pain, no palm; no thorns, no throne; no gall, no glory; no cross, no crown.*❞

—William Penn

CHAPTER 2

2:1ff. Satan wants to shake the saints and make them lose their confidence, and one of his chief weapons is deception. Someone claimed to have a letter from Paul saying that the day of the Lord was present, and others said they had messages through the Spirit (1 Thess. 5:21). The believers forgot what Paul had taught them (2:5), so they were trapped by the lies of the enemy.

The "times and seasons" of God's prophetic plan are in God's hands (Acts 1:6–8), and He has everything in control. A sequence of events is sketched here to assure us that the church is destined for salvation and not judgment (2:13; 1 Thess. 1:10; 5:9). The Spirit of God in this world is keeping God's program on schedule. Beware "prophets" who contradict what God has already said in His Word (2:15). If you stand on the Word, you will not fall for the devil's lies. God's people can face the future with assurance, hope, and comfort because of the unfailing grace of God (vv. 13–17).

1 Paul,* Silvanus, and Timothy,

To the church of the Thessalonians in God our Father and the Lord Jesus Christ:

2 Grace to you and peace from God our Father and the Lord Jesus Christ.

3 We are bound to thank God always for you, brethren, as it is fitting, because your faith grows exceedingly, and the love of every one of you all abounds toward each other, 4 so that we ourselves boast of you among the churches of God for your patience and faith in all your persecutions and tribulations that you endure, 5 which is manifest evidence of the righteous judgment of God, that you may be counted worthy of the kingdom of God, for which you also suffer; 6 since it is a righteous thing with God to repay with tribulation those who trouble you, 7 and to give you who are troubled rest with us when the Lord Jesus is revealed from heaven with His mighty angels, 8 in flaming fire taking vengeance on those who do not know God, and on those who do not obey the gospel of our Lord Jesus Christ. 9 These shall be punished with everlasting destruction from the presence of the Lord and from the glory of His power, 10 when He comes, in that Day, to be glorified in His saints and to be admired among all those who believe,ᵃ because our testimony among you was believed.

11 Therefore we also pray always for you that our God would count you worthy of this calling, and fulfill all the good pleasure of His goodness and the work of faith with power, 12 that the name of our Lord Jesus Christ may be glorified in you, and you in Him, according to the grace of our God and the Lord Jesus Christ.

2 Now,* brethren, concerning the coming of our Lord Jesus Christ and our gathering together to Him, we ask you, 2 not to be soon shaken in mind or troubled, either by spirit or by word or by letter, as if from us, as though the day of Christᵇ had come. 3 Let no one deceive you by any means; for that Day will not come unless the falling away comes first, and the man of sinᶜ is revealed, the son of perdition, 4 who opposes and exalts himself above all that is called God or that is worshiped, so that he sits as Godᵈ in the temple of God, showing himself that he is God.

5 Do you not remember that when I was still with you I told you these things? 6 And now you know what is restraining, that he may be revealed in his own time. 7 For the mystery of lawlessness is already at work; only Heᵉ who now restrains will do so until Heᶠ is taken out of the way. 8 And then the lawless one will be revealed, whom the Lord will consume with the breath of His mouth and destroy with the brightness of His coming. 9 The coming of the lawless one is according to the working of Satan, with all power, signs, and

---

1:10 ᵃNU-Text and M-Text read *have believed.*   2:2 ᵇNU-Text reads *the Lord.*   2:3 ᶜNU-Text reads *lawlessness.*
2:4 ᵈNU-Text omits *as God.*   2:7 ᵉOr *he* ᶠOr *he*

lying wonders, [10]and with all unrighteous deception among those who perish, because they did not receive the love of the truth, that they might be saved. [11]And for this reason God will send them strong delusion, that they should believe the lie, [12]that they all may be condemned who did not believe the truth but had pleasure in unrighteousness.

[13]But we are bound to give thanks to God always for you, brethren beloved by the Lord, because God from the beginning chose you for salvation through sanctification by the Spirit and belief in the truth, [14]to which He called you by our gospel, for the obtaining of the glory of our Lord Jesus Christ. [15]Therefore, brethren, stand fast and hold the traditions which you were taught, whether by word or our epistle.

[16]Now may our Lord Jesus Christ Himself, and our God and Father, who has loved us and given us everlasting consolation and good hope by grace, [17]comfort your hearts and establish you in every good word and work.

3 Finally,* brethren, pray for us, that the word of the Lord may run *swiftly* and be glorified, just as *it is* with you, [2]and that we may be delivered from unreasonable and wicked men; for not all have faith. [3]*But the Lord is faithful, who will establish you and guard *you* from the evil one. [4]And we have confidence in the Lord concerning you, both that you do and will do the things we command you.

[5]Now may the Lord direct your hearts into the love of God and into the patience of Christ.

[6]*But we command you, brethren, in the name of our Lord Jesus Christ, that you withdraw from every brother who walks disorderly and not according to the tradition which he[g] received from us. [7]For you yourselves know how you ought to follow us, for we were not disorderly among you; [8]nor did we eat anyone's bread free of charge, but worked with labor and toil night and day, that we might not be a burden to any of you, [9]not because we do not have authority, but to make ourselves an example of how you should follow us. [10]For even when we were with you, we commanded you this: If anyone will not work, neither shall he eat. [11]For we hear that there are some who walk among you in a disorderly manner, not working at all, but are busybodies. [12]Now those who are such we command and exhort through our Lord Jesus Christ that they work in quietness and eat their own bread.

[13]But *as for* you, brethren, do not grow weary *in* doing good. [14]And if anyone does not obey our word in this epistle, note that person and do not keep company with him, that he may be ashamed. [15]Yet do not count *him* as an enemy, but admonish *him* as a brother.

[16]Now may the Lord of peace Himself give you peace always in every way. The Lord *be* with you all.

[17]The salutation of Paul with my own hand, which is a sign in every epistle; so I write.

[18]The grace of our Lord Jesus Christ *be* with you all. Amen.

3:6 [g]NU-Text and M-Text read *they.*

3:1, 2 Conflict. Anyone who seeks to live for the Lord will have enemies (2 Tim. 3:12). The weapon we use is prayer, and the purpose for which we pray is the sharing of the Word of God (Col. 4:2–3). Not everybody in the church at Thessalonica was devoted to the Lord, but Paul still asked for their prayers.

3:3–5 Confidence. God's faithfulness to us is the basis for our faithfulness to Him. If we love Him, we will keep His Word, and we will be patient in times of trial.

3:6–15 Command. The word *command* (vv. 4, 6, 10, 12) means "a military order." Some of the Christian soldiers in the church were breaking rank and disobeying orders, and Paul had to admonish them. Those who cannot work must be cared for by others, but those who *will not* work must be disciplined. Never let the bad example of others keep you from being a good example.

> **❝**Work is not primarily a thing one does to live, but the thing one lives to do. It is, or should be, the full expression of the worker's faculties, the thing in which he finds spiritual, mental and bodily satisfaction, and the medium in which he offers himself to God.**❞**
>
> —Dorothy L. Sayers

1 TIMOTHY

Paul's trial in Rome came out in his favor, and he was released. It is likely he went to Colosse to visit Philemon (Philem. 22). He may have written 1 Timothy from Colosse or from Philippi.

The child of a mixed marriage (Acts 16:1), Timothy was raised in a godly home (2 Tim. 1:5; 3:15) and came to know Christ through Paul's ministry (1 Tim. 1:2). Paul added him to his team at Lystra (Acts 16:1–3) and made him one of his special assistants (Phil. 2:19–22). Timothy eventually was sent to pastor the church in Ephesus (1 Tim. 1:3).

First Timothy is a ministerial letter, telling pastors and people how they should conduct themselves in the local assembly (3:15). Paul stresses preaching the truth (chaps. 1, 4), praying (chap. 2), and appointing qualified leaders (chap. 3). He closes by giving counsel on how to minister to various kinds of people in the church (chaps. 5—6).

CHAPTER 1

1:3–11 The work in Ephesus was not easy, and Timothy wanted a new assignment; but Paul urged him to stay where he was and get the job done (1:3). The next time you want to abandon your assigned place, consider the arguments Paul gave Timothy for staying where he was.
For the work's sake. What Paul warned the Ephesian elders about had come true: false teachers were in the church (Acts 20:28–30). The pastor's job is to warn them and teach the people the truth. If he abandoned the flock, Timothy would be a hireling and not a shepherd (John 10:12–13).

1:12–17 For the Lord's sake. Jesus died to save sinners, and He lives to equip and enable His servants to do the work of the ministry. The same God who empowered Paul could empower Timothy—and can empower us today. God is faithful!

1 Paul, an apostle of Jesus Christ, by the commandment of God our Savior and the Lord Jesus Christ, our hope,

2To Timothy, a true son in the faith:

Grace, mercy, *and* peace from God our Father and Jesus Christ our Lord.
3*As I urged you when I went into Macedonia— remain in Ephesus that you may charge some that they teach no other doctrine, 4nor give heed to fables and endless genealogies, which cause disputes rather than godly edification which is in faith. 5Now the purpose of the commandment is love from a pure heart, *from* a good conscience, and *from* sincere faith, 6from which some, having strayed, have turned aside to idle talk, 7desiring to be teachers of the law, understanding neither what they say nor the things which they affirm.

8But we know that the law *is* good if one uses it lawfully, 9knowing this: that the law is not made for a righteous person, but for *the* lawless and insubordinate, for *the* ungodly and for sinners, for *the* unholy and profane, for murderers of fathers and murderers of mothers, for manslayers, 10for fornicators, for sodomites, for kidnappers, for liars, for perjurers, and if there is any other thing that is contrary to sound doctrine, 11according to the glorious gospel of the blessed God which was committed to my trust.
12*And I thank Christ Jesus our Lord who has enabled me, because He counted me faithful, putting *me* into the ministry, 13although I was formerly a blasphemer, a persecutor, and an insolent man; but I obtained mercy because I did *it* ignorantly in unbelief. 14And the grace of our Lord was exceedingly abundant, with faith and love which are in Christ Jesus. 15This *is* a faithful saying and worthy of all acceptance, that Christ Jesus came into the world to save sinners, of whom I am chief. 16However, for this reason I obtained mercy, that in me first Jesus Christ might show all longsuffering, as a pattern to those who are going to believe on Him for everlasting life. 17Now to the King eternal, immortal, invisible, to

Responsibility—Someone defined *responsibility* as "our response to God's ability."

God who alone is wise,[a] be honor and glory forever and ever. Amen.

18*This charge I commit to you, son Timothy, according to the prophecies previously made concerning you, that by them you may wage the good warfare, 19having faith and a good conscience, which some having rejected, concerning the faith have suffered shipwreck, 20of whom are Hymenaeus and Alexander, whom I delivered to Satan that they may learn not to blaspheme.

2 Therefore* I exhort first of all that supplications, prayers, intercessions, and giving of thanks be made for all men, 2for kings and all who are in authority, that we may lead a quiet and peaceable life in all godliness and reverence. 3For this is good and acceptable in the sight of God our Savior, 4who desires all men to be saved and to come to the knowledge of the truth. 5For there is one God and one Mediator between God and men, the Man Christ Jesus, 6who gave Himself a ransom for all, to be testified in due time, 7for which I was appointed a preacher and an apostle—I am speaking the truth in Christ[b] and not lying—a teacher of the Gentiles in faith and truth.

8*I desire therefore that the men pray everywhere, lifting up holy hands, without wrath and doubting; 9in like manner also, that the women adorn themselves in modest apparel, with propriety and moderation, not with braided hair or gold or pearls or costly clothing, 10but, which is proper for women professing godliness, with good works. 11Let a woman learn in silence with all submission. 12And I do not permit a woman to teach or to have authority over a man, but to be in silence. 13For Adam was formed first, then Eve. 14And Adam was not deceived, but the woman being deceived, fell into transgression. 15Nevertheless she will be saved in childbearing if they continue in faith, love, and holiness, with self-control.

3 This* is a faithful saying: If a man desires the position of a bishop,[c] he desires a good work. 2A bishop then must be blameless, the husband of one wife, temperate, sober-minded, of good behavior, hospitable, able to teach; 3not given to wine, not violent, not greedy for money,[d] but gentle, not quarrelsome, not covetous; 4one who rules his own house well, having his children in submission with all reverence 5(for if a man does not know how to rule his own house, how will he take care of the church of God?); 6not a novice, lest being puffed up with pride he fall into the same condemnation as the devil. 7Moreover he must have a good testimony among those who are outside, lest he fall into reproach and the snare of the devil.

8*Likewise deacons must be reverent, not double-tongued, not given to much wine, not greedy for money, 9holding the mystery of the faith with a pure conscience. 10But let these also first be tested; then let them serve as deacons, being found blameless. 11Likewise, their wives must be reverent, not slanderers, temperate, faithful in all

1:18–20 For our own sake. God had equipped Timothy, called him, and given him a solemn charge. There was a battle to fight, and he dare not run away. If we flee the post of duty, we rob ourselves of opportunities to grow, to serve, and to glorify God.

When the winds of adversity blow, set your sails in the right direction, and let Christ handle the rudder. Otherwise, you may be shipwrecked.

CHAPTER 2

2:1 What is the most vital ministry of the local church? According to Paul, it is prayer. Prayer moves the hand that governs the world. We must pray for government leaders, that the doors of ministry will be kept open and souls will be won to Christ. Because God's people do not pray for people in authority, wars close mission fields, officials do not grant needed visas, and the work of the Lord suffers.

2:8–15 Paul reminds Christian men that Christian women are important to the Lord and to the work of the church. The gospel brought freedom to women in the Roman Empire, but some of them did not know how to handle it and went to extremes asserting their liberty. Hence, the reminder about the spiritual leadership of the men in the church.

Modesty, true spiritual beauty (1 Pet. 3:1–6), godliness, and good works—these will characterize the woman God blesses.

CHAPTER 3

3:1–7 Being a leader of God's people is a serious task, and no one should accept an office who is not qualified and willing to use that office to help the church.

Watching. The title bishop means "overseer" and describes the work of the elder (Acts 20:17, 28). God's people are like sheep; they need shepherds to watch over them, protect them, and lead them. Pray for your spiritual leaders that they might more and more be what God wants them to be.

❝A good woman is the best thing on earth. Women were last at the cross and first at the open tomb. The church owes a debt to her faithful women which she can never estimate, to say nothing of the debt we owe in our homes to godly wives and mothers.❞

—Vance Havner

> **❝***It is in willing submission, rather than grudging capitulation, that the woman in the church (whether married or single) and the wife in the home find their fulfillment.***❞**
> —Elisabeth Elliot

3:8–13 Working. The word *deacon* means "servant." The deacons assist the elders in carrying out the work of the church (Acts 6:1–7). As with the elders, the deacons should be qualified spiritually and set the right example in their homes.

3:15, 16 Worshiping. The church is much more than a group of like-minded people who assemble from time to time. The living God is in their midst (Matt. 18:20), and the truth of God has been deposited with them! They worship the Son of God who alone is worthy of praise! Yes, it is a serious thing to be a part of a local church. Do you take it seriously?

CHAPTER 4

4:1–5 Watch yourself. Satan is at work spreading false doctrine, and his ministers are already in the church (2 Cor. 11:13–15). God's servants must preach the truth and fight the devil's lies. Declaring war may not make us popular, but it will keep us faithful.

4:6–11 Exercise yourself. If believers would put as much effort into the spiritual life as they do their recreation and hobbies, what a difference it would make! Physical exercise is important, but spiritual exercise is even more essential. Both discipline and devotion are needed to make a winning athlete and an effective Christian.

4:12–16 Give yourself. It takes real effort to grow in the Christian life and to be successful in Christian service. God asks for our wholehearted surrender, no matter what the cost. Ponder these admonitions that Paul wrote to Timothy and see how they apply in your life.

CHAPTER 5

5:1ff What causes problems in churches? Often, it is people not getting along with each *(continued)*

things. 12Let deacons be the husbands of one wife, ruling *their* children and their own houses well. 13For those who have served well as deacons obtain for themselves a good standing and great boldness in the faith which is in Christ Jesus.

14These things I write to you, though I hope to come to you shortly; 15*but if I am delayed, *I write* so that you may know how you ought to conduct yourself in the house of God, which is the church of the living God, the pillar and ground of the truth. 16And without controversy great is the mystery of godliness:

> Gode was manifested in the flesh,
> Justified in the Spirit,
> Seen by angels,
> Preached among the Gentiles,
> Believed on in the world,
> Received up in glory.

4 Now* the Spirit expressly says that in latter times some will depart from the faith, giving heed to deceiving spirits and doctrines of demons, 2speaking lies in hypocrisy, having their own conscience seared with a hot iron, 3forbidding to marry, *and commanding* to abstain from foods which God created to be received with thanksgiving by those who believe and know the truth. 4For every creature of God *is* good, and nothing is to be refused if it is received with thanksgiving; 5for it is sanctified by the word of God and prayer.

6*If you instruct the brethren in these things, you will be a good minister of Jesus Christ, nourished in the words of faith and of the good doctrine which you have carefully followed. 7But reject profane and old wives' fables, and exercise yourself toward godliness. 8For bodily exercise profits a little, but godliness is profitable for all things, having promise of the life that now is and of that which is to come. 9This *is* a faithful saying and worthy of all acceptance. 10For to this *end* we both labor and suffer reproach,f because we trust in the living God, who is *the* Savior of all men, especially of those who believe. 11These things command and teach.

12*Let no one despise your youth, but be an example to the believers in word, in conduct, in love, in spirit,g in faith, in purity. 13Till I come, give attention to reading, to exhortation, to doctrine. 14Do not neglect the gift that is in you, which was given to you by prophecy with the laying on of the hands of the eldership. 15Meditate on these things; give yourself entirely to them, that your progress may be evident to all. 16Take heed to yourself and to the doctrine. Continue in them, for in doing this you will save both yourself and those who hear you.

5 Do* not rebuke an older man, but exhort *him* as a father, younger men as brothers, 2older

---

3:16 eNU-Text reads *Who.* 4:10 fNU-Text reads *we labor and strive.* 4:12 gNU-Text omits *in spirit.*

Advance!—The word translated "progress" in 1 Timothy 4:15 means "pioneer advance." As we walk with the Lord and serve Him, we must move into new territory and not stay the same spiritually. There are new truths to learn, new battles to fight, and new victories to win. "Restlessness is discontent," said Thomas Alva Edison, "and discontent is the first necessity of progress. Show me a thoroughly satisfied man and I will show you a failure."

women as mothers, younger women as sisters, with all purity.

3Honor widows who are really widows. 4But if any widow has children or grandchildren, let them first learn to show piety at home and to repay their parents; for this is good and*h* acceptable before God. 5Now she who is really a widow, and left alone, trusts in God and continues in supplications and prayers night and day. 6But she who lives in pleasure is dead while she lives. 7And these things command, that they may be blameless. 8But if anyone does not provide for his own, and especially for those of his household, he has denied the faith and is worse than an unbeliever.

9Do not let a widow under sixty years old be taken into the number, *and not unless* she has been the wife of one man, 10well reported for good works: if she has brought up children, if she has lodged strangers, if she has washed the saints' feet, if she has relieved the afflicted, if she has diligently followed every good work.

11But refuse *the* younger widows; for when they have begun to grow wanton against Christ, they desire to marry, 12having condemnation because they have cast off their first faith. 13And besides they learn *to be* idle, wandering about from house to house, and not only idle but also gossips and busybodies, saying things which they ought not. 14Therefore I desire that *the* younger *widows* marry, bear children, manage the house, give no opportunity to the adversary to speak reproachfully. 15For some have already turned aside after Satan. 16If any believing man or*i* woman has widows, let them relieve them, and do not let the church be burdened, that it may relieve those who are really widows.

17Let the elders who rule well be counted worthy of double honor, especially those who labor in the word and doctrine. 18For the Scripture says, "You shall not muzzle an ox while it treads out the grain,"*j* and, "The laborer *is* worthy of his wages."*k* 19Do not receive an accusation against an elder except from two or three witnesses. 20Those who are sinning rebuke in the presence of all, that the rest also may fear.

21I charge *you* before God and the Lord Jesus Christ and the elect angels that you observe these things without prejudice, doing nothing with partiality. 22Do not lay hands on anyone hastily, nor share in other people's sins; keep yourself pure.

23No longer drink only water, but use a little wine for your stomach's sake and your frequent infirmities.

24Some men's sins are clearly evident, preceding *them* to judgment, but those of some *men* follow later. 25Likewise, the good works *of some* are clearly evident, and those that are otherwise cannot be hidden.

6 Let* as many bondservants as are under the yoke count their own masters worthy of all honor, so that the name of God and *His* doctrine

---

5:4 *h*NU-Text and M-Text omit *good and.*   5:16 *i*NU-Text omits *man or.*   5:18 *j*Deuteronomy 25:4 *k*Luke 10:7

(continued from previous page) other. Brothers and sisters do not always dwell together in unity (Ps. 133).

Paul suggests that we treat other people the way we would treat members of our own family (vv. 1–2). If the older people complain about things, deal with them as you would your father or mother, and accept the younger believers as brothers and sisters. This is simply a call to love others as God loves you.

Not everybody who asks for help should receive it (vv. 3–16). Charity should begin at home (vv. 4, 16), and church leaders must exercise discernment lest they create more problems than they solve.

Sometimes trouble comes because we believe reports that cannot be verified (v. 19), or we show partiality (v. 21), or we make decisions before getting the facts (v. 22). Not every church member has a character as good as his or her reputation (vv. 24–25), so take care!

CHAPTER 6

6:1, 2 Watch your motives. Be obedient so you do not bring reproach on the Word (v. 1; Titus 2:10) or show disrespect for persons in authority over you (v. 2). Never take advantage of fellow believers; rather, do all you can to help them.

Proper Conduct—First Timothy tells you how to "conduct yourself in the house of God" (3:15). This involves exercising yourself (4:7), giving yourself (4:15), taking heed to yourself (4:16), saving yourself (4:16), keeping yourself pure (5:22), and withdrawing yourself from troublemakers (6:5). Are you taking care of yourself as the Lord directs?

6:3–5 *Watch your attitudes.* Do you enjoy arguing about the Bible? Then search your heart to see if any of these sinful attitudes are hiding there. You can never debate people into the kingdom or into a more sanctified life.

6:6–10, 17–19 *Watch your values.* Are you content with the necessities of life, or must God give you luxuries? God wants you to enjoy His gifts (v. 17) and employ them for the good of others; but beware when your heart is set on getting rich (Prov. 15:27; Eccles. 5:10).

6:11–16 *Watch your testimony.* Know the things you should flee, follow, and fight, and do not confuse them. When you think it too difficult to stand up for the Lord, remember how He stood up for you.

6:20, 21 *Watch your stewardship.* You have a deposit of spiritual truth to guard and invest (1:18; 2 Tim. 1:14; 2:2), and the enemy wants to take it from you. Beware those who want to give you "new knowledge" beyond what God says in His Word.

may not be blasphemed. 2And those who have believing masters, let them not despise *them* because they are brethren, but rather serve *them* because those who are benefited are believers and beloved. Teach and exhort these things.

3*If anyone teaches otherwise and does not consent to wholesome words, *even* the words of our Lord Jesus Christ, and to the doctrine which accords with godliness, 4he is proud, knowing nothing, but is obsessed with disputes and arguments over words, from which come envy, strife, reviling, evil suspicions, 5useless wranglings*l* of men of corrupt minds and destitute of the truth, who suppose that godliness is a *means of* gain. From such withdraw yourself.*m*

6*Now godliness with contentment is great gain. 7For we brought nothing into *this* world, *and it is certain*n we can carry nothing out. 8And having food and clothing, with these we shall be content. 9But those who desire to be rich fall into temptation and a snare, and *into* many foolish and harmful lusts which drown men in destruction and perdition. 10For the love of money is a root of all *kinds of* evil, for which some have strayed from the faith in their greediness, and pierced themselves through with many sorrows.

11*But you, O man of God, flee these things and pursue righteousness, godliness, faith, love, patience, gentleness. 12Fight the good fight of faith, lay hold on eternal life, to which you were also called and have confessed the good confession in the presence of many witnesses. 13I urge you in the sight of God who gives life to all things, and *before* Christ Jesus who witnessed the good confession before Pontius Pilate, 14that you keep *this* commandment without spot, blameless until our Lord Jesus Christ's appearing, 15which He will manifest in His own time, *He who is* the blessed and only Potentate, the King of kings and Lord of lords, 16who alone has immortality, dwelling in unapproachable light, whom no man has seen or can see, to whom *be* honor and everlasting power. Amen.

17Command those who are rich in this present age not to be haughty, nor to trust in uncertain riches but in the living God, who gives us richly all things to enjoy. 18*Let them* do good, that they be rich in good works, ready to give, willing to share, 19storing up for themselves a good foundation for the time to come, that they may lay hold on eternal life.

20*O Timothy! Guard what was committed to your trust, avoiding the profane *and* idle babblings and contradictions of what is falsely called knowledge— 21by professing it some have strayed concerning the faith.

Grace *be* with you. Amen.

6:5 *l*NU-Text and M-Text read *constant friction.* *m*NU-Text omits this sentence.   6:7 *n*NU-Text omits *and it is certain.*

2 TIMOTHY

Paul's freedom did not last long. He was arrested again, taken to Rome for trial, and eventually executed. He wrote this letter to his beloved son in the faith to encourage him to remain strong in the Lord (chaps. 1—2), to explain the perilous times (chap. 3), and to urge him to come to Rome as soon as possible (chap. 4). This very personal letter focuses on faithfulness in the ministry.

It was a difficult time for Paul. Not only was he facing trial and almost certain death, but he was abandoned by the believers who should have stood with him (1:15; 4:16). His statement in 4:6–8 is one of the greatest confessions of faith in the Bible.

We are now in those perilous times that Paul wrote about centuries ago. This letter teaches us how to live and serve successfully in them.

1 Paul, an apostle of Jesus Christ*a* by the will of God, according to the promise of life which is in Christ Jesus,

2To Timothy, a beloved son:

Grace, mercy, *and* peace from God the Father and Christ Jesus our Lord.
3I thank God, whom I serve with a pure conscience, as *my* forefathers *did*, as without ceasing I remember you in my prayers night and day, 4*greatly desiring to see you, being mindful of your tears, that I may be filled with joy, 5when I call to remembrance the genuine faith that is in you, which dwelt first in your grandmother Lois and your mother Eunice, and I am persuaded is in you also. 6*Therefore I remind you to stir up the gift of God which is in you through the laying on of my hands. 7*For God has not given us a spirit of fear, but of power and of love and of a sound mind.
8*Therefore do not be ashamed of the testimony of our Lord, nor of me His prisoner, but share with me in the sufferings for the gospel according to the power of God, 9who has saved us and called *us* with a holy calling, not according to our works, but according to His own purpose and grace which was given to us in Christ Jesus before time began, 10but has now been revealed by the appearing of our Savior Jesus Christ, *who* has abolished death and brought life and immortality to light through the gospel, 11to which I was appointed a preacher, an apostle, and a teacher of the Gentiles.*b* 12For this reason I also suffer these things; nevertheless I am not ashamed, for I know whom I have believed and am persuaded that He is able to keep what I have committed to Him until that Day.
13*Hold fast the pattern of sound words which you have heard from me, in faith and love which are in Christ Jesus. 14That good thing which was committed to you, keep by the Holy Spirit who dwells in us.
15This you know, that all those in Asia have turned away from me, among whom are Phygellus and Hermogenes. 16The Lord grant mercy to

CHAPTER 1

1:4 Perhaps some of the "enemies" that attacked Timothy are attacking you and making you want to give up.

Self-pity. Timothy was having a hard time in Ephesus and wanted to leave (1 Tim. 1:3). Perhaps that caused his tears. When you start feeling sorry for yourself, remember that others are praying for you and that God still honors your faith.

1:6 Neglect. Timothy had neglected his spiritual life (1 Tim. 4:14), and the flame was low on the altar of his heart. No wonder he needed to exercise himself (1 Tim. 4:7–8)!

1:7 Timidity. Fear in this verse means "cowardice" or "timidity." Timothy was not enthusiastic in his witness or ministry. The Holy Spirit can give us the resources we need to get the job done.

1:8, 12, 16 Shame. Paul was not ashamed of the gospel (Rom. 1:16) or of the Lord. His friend Onesiphorus was not ashamed of being identified with Paul (v. 16). Timothy should not be ashamed of either the Lord or Paul (v. 8).

1:13, 14 Carelessness. Paul committed the message to Timothy, and Timothy's responsibility was to guard it (1 Tim. 6:20) and share it with others (2 Tim. 2:2). Again, the Spirit of God enables us to be faithful.

1:1 *a*NU-Text and M-Text read *Christ Jesus.* 1:11 *b*NU-Text omits *of the Gentiles.*

CHAPTER 2

2:1ff God's grace strengthens us and enables us to be faithful teachers (v. 2), soldiers (vv. 3–4), athletes (v. 5), farmers (v. 6), workers (v. 15), vessels (vv. 20–23), and servants (vv. 24–26). The world looks on us as evildoers; but we are God's elect, willing to live and die for Jesus Christ (vv. 8–13).

God's grace enables us to overcome our three great enemies: the world (v. 4), the flesh (v. 22), and the devil (v. 26).

God's grace enables us to endure hardship (vv. 3, 10) as we fight the Lord's battles, so that we do not deny the Lord (vv. 11–13). It helps us do work of which we are not ashamed (v. 15) and deal with problem people of whom we are not afraid (vv. 23–26).

the household of Onesiphorus, for he often refreshed me, and was not ashamed of my chain; [17]but when he arrived in Rome, he sought me out very zealously and found *me*. [18]The Lord grant to him that he may find mercy from the Lord in that Day—and you know very well how many ways he ministered *to me*[c] at Ephesus.

2 You* therefore, my son, be strong in the grace that is in Christ Jesus. [2]And the things that you have heard from me among many witnesses, commit these to faithful men who will be able to teach others also. [3]You therefore must endure[d] hardship as a good soldier of Jesus Christ. [4]No one engaged in warfare entangles himself with the affairs of *this* life, that he may please him who enlisted him as a soldier. [5]And also if anyone competes in athletics, he is not crowned unless he competes according to the rules. [6]The hardworking farmer must be first to partake of the crops. [7]Consider what I say, and may[e] the Lord give you understanding in all things.

[8]Remember that Jesus Christ, of the seed of David, was raised from the dead according to my gospel, [9]for which I suffer trouble as an evildoer, *even* to the point of chains; but the word of God is not chained. [10]Therefore I endure all things for the sake of the elect, that they also may obtain the salvation which is in Christ Jesus with eternal glory.

[11]*This is* a faithful saying:

> For if we died with *Him*,
>   We shall also live with *Him*.
> [12] If we endure,
>   We shall also reign with *Him*.
> If we deny *Him*,
>   He also will deny us.
> [13] If we are faithless,
>   He remains faithful;
>   He cannot deny Himself.

[14]Remind *them* of these things, charging *them* before the Lord not to strive about words to no profit, to the ruin of the hearers. [15]Be diligent to present yourself approved to God, a worker who does not need to be ashamed, rightly dividing the word of truth. [16]But shun profane *and* idle babblings, for they will increase to more ungodliness. [17]And their message will spread like cancer. Hymenaeus and Philetus are of this sort, [18]who have strayed concerning the truth, saying that the resurrection is already past; and they overthrow the faith of some. [19]Nevertheless the solid foundation of God stands, having this seal: "The Lord knows those who are His," and, "Let everyone who names the name of Christ[f] depart from iniquity."

[20]But in a great house there are not only vessels of gold and silver, but also of wood and clay, some for honor and some for dishonor. [21]Therefore if anyone cleanses himself from the latter, he will be a vessel for honor, sanctified and useful for the Master, prepared for every good work. [22]Flee also youthful lusts; but pursue righteousness, faith, love, peace with those who call on the Lord

❝Grace is but glory begun, and glory is but grace perfected.**❞**
—Jonathan Edwards

1:18 *cTo me* is from the Vulgate and a few Greek manuscripts.
2:3 *d*NU-Text reads *You must share.*   2:7 *e*NU-Text reads *the Lord will give you.*   2:19 *f*NU-Text and M-Text read *the Lord.*

out of a pure heart. ²³But avoid foolish and ignorant disputes, knowing that they generate strife. ²⁴And a servant of the Lord must not quarrel but be gentle to all, able to teach, patient, ²⁵in humility correcting those who are in opposition, if God perhaps will grant them repentance, so that they may know the truth, ²⁶and *that* they may come to their senses *and escape* the snare of the devil, having been taken captive by him to *do* his will.

3 But* know this, that in the last days perilous times will come: ²For men will be lovers of themselves, lovers of money, boasters, proud, blasphemers, disobedient to parents, unthankful, unholy, ³unloving, unforgiving, slanderers, without self-control, brutal, despisers of good, ⁴traitors, headstrong, haughty, lovers of pleasure rather than lovers of God, ⁵having a form of godliness but denying its power. And from such people turn away! ⁶For of this sort are those who creep into households and make captives of gullible women loaded down with sins, led away by various lusts, ⁷always learning and never able to come to the knowledge of the truth. ⁸Now as Jannes and Jambres resisted Moses, so do these also resist the truth: men of corrupt minds, disapproved concerning the faith; ⁹but they will progress no further, for their folly will be manifest to all, as theirs also was.

¹⁰*But you have carefully followed my doctrine, manner of life, purpose, faith, longsuffering, love, perseverance, ¹¹persecutions, afflictions, which happened to me at Antioch, at Iconium, at Lystra—what persecutions I endured. And out of *them* all the Lord delivered me. ¹²Yes, and all who desire to live godly in Christ Jesus will suffer persecution. ¹³But evil men and impostors will grow worse and worse, deceiving and being deceived. ¹⁴But you must continue in the things which you have learned and been assured of, knowing from whom you have learned *them,* ¹⁵*and that from childhood you have known the Holy Scriptures, which are able to make you wise for salvation through faith which is in Christ Jesus. ¹⁶All Scripture *is* given by inspiration of God, and *is* profitable for doctrine, for reproof, for correction, for instruction in righteousness, ¹⁷that the man of God may be complete, thoroughly equipped for every good work.

4 I* charge *you* therefore before God and the Lord Jesus Christ, who will judge the living and the dead at*ᵍ* His appearing and His kingdom:

4:1 *ᵍ*NU-Text omits *therefore* and reads *and by* for *at.*

CHAPTER 3

3:1–9 *Perilous* in verse 1 means "difficult," "hard to deal with," or "dangerous." It is the same Greek word used to describe the demoniac in Matthew 8:28 and translated "exceedingly fierce." How do we live for Christ in such terrible times?

Expect them. The person who is looking for a soon-coming paradise on earth is destined for disappointment. To expect these perilous times is to become not a pessimist but a realist. Note the emphasis on the wrong kind of love (vv. 2, 4).

3:10–12 *Follow the right examples.* We tend to emulate the people we admire, so be careful about the heroes you select. Modern-day Christian celebrities may not exemplify the life-style God wants us to have.

3:15–17 *Stay with the Bible.* Believe God's Word will save you (v. 15), mature you from childhood to adulthood (vv. 15, 17), and equip you to serve the Lord (v. 17). Satanic deception is rampant today and has infected the church (v. 13), and the only weapon that defeats the deceivers is God's inspired Word.

CHAPTER 4

4:1, 2 *Christ is coming!* In view of this, we must know our task and be faithful to do it. Review 2 Corinthians 5:9–11, and read 1 John 2:28—3:2.

Watch for Counterfeits!—Jannes and Jambres (v. 8) were magicians in Pharaoh's court who imitated the miracles that Moses performed (Exod. 7:8–13). Satan is an imitator who produces counterfeit Christians (vv. 5, 13; 2 Cor. 11:13–15) who infiltrate the church and create divisions. God's people need discernment in these difficult days.

Respond to Opportunities—Paul's plea, "Come before winter" (2 Tim. 4:21), is a reminder to us that opportunities do not wait forever. Once the winter season began, Timothy could not travel easily to Rome and see his beloved friend for the last time. "Before winter or never!" said Dr. Clarence Macartney in his famous sermon "Come Before Winter." He continued, "There are some things which will never be done unless they are done 'before winter.'" Are there opportunities you are neglecting today that may soon vanish forever? Are there people you should contact and decisions you should make? Today is yours; tomorrow may be too late. Come before winter!

4:3, 4 *Apostasy is coming!* Indeed, it is now here. Many professed Christians have no "ear" for the Word of God. They prefer religious entertainment and sermons that will tickle their ears instead of cut their hearts.

4:6–8 *Departure is coming!* Paul saw his approaching death as the offering of a sacrifice to God (v. 6; Phil. 2:17), the ending of a difficult race (v. 7), and the gaining of a glorious crown (v. 8; Rev. 2:10). This is the victor's crown given to winners at the Greek Olympic Games.

4:9–21 *Help is coming!* Paul was greatly disappointed when the people he had ministered to turned away from him and were ashamed of his bonds. He asked Timothy to come as soon as possible and to bring Mark with him. But best of all, the Lord came to Paul and encouraged him! No matter what His people may do, Jesus will never leave you or forsake you (Acts 18:9–11; Heb. 13:5–6).

2Preach the word! Be ready in season *and* out of season. Convince, rebuke, exhort, with all long-suffering and teaching. 3*For the time will come when they will not endure sound doctrine, but according to their own desires, *because* they have itching ears, they will heap up for themselves teachers; 4and they will turn *their* ears away from the truth, and be turned aside to fables. 5But you be watchful in all things, endure afflictions, do the work of an evangelist, fulfill your ministry.

6*For I am already being poured out as a drink offering, and the time of my departure is at hand. 7I have fought the good fight, I have finished the race, I have kept the faith. 8Finally, there is laid up for me the crown of righteousness, which the Lord, the righteous Judge, will give to me on that Day, and not to me only but also to all who have loved His appearing.

9*Be diligent to come to me quickly; 10for Demas has forsaken me, having loved this present world, and has departed for Thessalonica—Crescens for Galatia, Titus for Dalmatia. 11Only Luke is with me. Get Mark and bring him with you, for he is useful to me for ministry. 12And Tychicus I have sent to Ephesus. 13Bring the cloak that I left with Carpus at Troas when you come—and the books, especially the parchments.

14Alexander the coppersmith did me much harm. May the Lord repay him according to his works. 15You also must beware of him, for he has greatly resisted our words.

16At my first defense no one stood with me, but all forsook me. May it not be charged against them.

17But the Lord stood with me and strengthened me, so that the message might be preached fully through me, and *that* all the Gentiles might hear. Also I was delivered out of the mouth of the lion. 18And the Lord will deliver me from every evil work and preserve *me* for His heavenly kingdom. To Him *be* glory forever and ever. Amen!

19Greet Prisca and Aquila, and the household of Onesiphorus. 20Erastus stayed in Corinth, but Trophimus I have left in Miletus sick.

21Do your utmost to come before winter.

Eubulus greets you, as well as Pudens, Linus, Claudia, and all the brethren.

22The Lord Jesus Christ[h] be with your spirit. Grace be with you. Amen.

4:22 [h]NU-Text omits *Jesus Christ*.

TITUS

Titus was a Greek (Gal. 2:3) whom Paul won to Christ (Titus 1:4) and enlisted in service. Like Timothy, he became one of Paul's special assistants, sent to the churches to represent the apostle. He was serving in Crete when this letter was written. Paul wrote it, probably from Corinth, after his release from prison.

The letter emphasizes good works (1:16; 2:7, 14; 3:1, 8, 14). We are not saved by good works (3:5), but good works are one evidence of salvation. Apparently the saints on Crete were better at professing the faith than practicing it.

After his greeting (1:1–4), Paul gives the qualifications (1:5–9) and duties (1:10–16) of elders and urges Titus to organize the local churches and deal with the false teachers. He then tells Titus how to minister to various kinds of people in the church (2:1—3:11) and closes the letter with personal information (3:12–14) and a farewell (3:15).

1 Paul,* a bondservant of God and an apostle of Jesus Christ, according to the faith of God's elect and the acknowledgment of the truth which accords with godliness, ²in hope of eternal life which God, who cannot lie, promised before time began, ³but has in due time manifested His word through preaching, which was committed to me according to the commandment of God our Savior;

⁴To Titus, a true son in *our* common faith:

Grace, mercy, *and* peace from God the Father and the Lord Jesus Christ*ᵃ* our Savior.

⁵*For this reason I left you in Crete, that you should set in order the things that are lacking, and appoint elders in every city as I commanded you— ⁶if a man is blameless, the husband of one wife, having faithful children not accused of dissipation or insubordination. ⁷For a bishop*ᵇ* must be blameless, as a steward of God, not self-willed, not quick-tempered, not given to wine, not violent, not greedy for money, ⁸but hospitable, a lover of what is good, sober-minded, just, holy, self-controlled, ⁹holding fast the faithful word as he has been taught, that he may be able, by sound doctrine, both to exhort and convict those who contradict.

¹⁰*For there are many insubordinate, both idle talkers and deceivers, especially those of the circumcision, ¹¹whose mouths must be stopped, who subvert whole households, teaching things which they ought not, for the sake of dishonest gain. ¹²One of them, a prophet of their own, said, "Cretans *are* always liars, evil beasts, lazy gluttons." ¹³This testimony is true. Therefore rebuke them sharply, that they may be sound in the faith, ¹⁴not giving heed to Jewish fables and commandments of men who turn from the truth. ¹⁵To the pure all things are pure, but to those who are

---

1:4 ᵃNU-Text reads and Christ Jesus. 1:7 ᵇLiterally overseer

CHAPTER 1

1:1–4 Titus wanted another assignment from Paul because he was having a hard time ministering in Crete. When you feel like quitting, follow the counsel Paul gave to Titus.

Focus on the privileges of ministry. God declares His truth through dedicated people, and it is a joy to share the Word with others. The angels in heaven would love to change places with us, so we should never cease to marvel that God would use us!

1:5–9 *Obey the Word.* Sometimes there are problems because unqualified people get into places of leadership or because places of leadership have not been filled. The Greek word translated "set in order" is a medical term that means "to set a broken bone." The church body suffers when we avoid facing and solving serious problems.

1:10–16 *Face the enemy.* Perhaps like Timothy (2 Tim. 1:7), Titus was too timid to confront the enemy; but it had to be done. "Sound doctrine" (v. 9) means "healthy doctrine," teaching that contributes to the spiritual health of the church. Just as a physician must attack infection and disease, so local church leaders must attack false doctrine.

A Pure Mind—"To the pure all things are pure" (Titus 1:15) concerns false teaching about dietary laws (1 Tim. 4:2–5). It does not mean that a "pure mind" remains pure after beholding what is impure. When God's truth enlightens your conscience, you will know right from wrong and will avoid that which is evil. A defiled conscience is like a dirty window: no light can enter (Matt. 6:22–23).

defiled and unbelieving nothing is pure; but even their mind and conscience are defiled. [16]They profess to know God, but in works they deny Him, being abominable, disobedient, and disqualified for every good work.

CHAPTER 2

2:1–10 Living. Whether we are young or old, married or single, we are all needed in the local church; and God has a job for us to do. One test of spiritual fellowship is its ability to accept and minister to a variety of people. How we live either blasphemes the Word (v. 5) or beautifies it (v. 10), and those who minister should set the example (vv. 7–8).

2:11, 12 Learning. God's grace not only saves us but also teaches us how to live the Christian life. Those who use God's grace as an excuse for sin have never experienced its saving power (Rom. 6:1; Jude 4). The same grace that redeems us also renews us so that we want to obey His Word (v. 14).

2:13, 14 Looking. What starts with grace will lead to glory! The return of Jesus Christ for His people is more than a blessed hope; it is a joyful hope (Rom. 5:2; 12:12), a unifying hope (Eph. 4:4), a living hope (1 Pet. 1:3), a stabilizing hope (Heb. 6:19), and a purifying hope (1 John 3:3).

CHAPTER 3

3:1, 2 We all need frequent reminders! **Remember what you should do.** Christians are citizens of earth as well as citizens of heaven, and they should be the kind of people described in these two brief verses.

3:3 Remember what you were. God has forgotten our sins, and we should, too; but it does us good to remember what it was like to be a lost sinner. (See Deut. 5:15; 15:15; 24:18, 22; 1 Pet. 4:1–4.)

3:4–7 Remember what God did for you. Did you deserve to hear the gospel and receive the gift of eternal life? No, it all happened because of God's kindness, love, and grace. "He saved us"—we did not save *(continued)*

66I never begin my work in the morning without thinking that perhaps He may interrupt my work and begin His own. I am not looking for death, I am looking for Him.**99**

—G. Campbell Morgan

2 But* as for you, speak the things which are proper for sound doctrine: [2]that the older men be sober, reverent, temperate, sound in faith, in love, in patience; [3]the older women likewise, that they be reverent in behavior, not slanderers, not given to much wine, teachers of good things— [4]that they admonish the young women to love their husbands, to love their children, [5]to be discreet, chaste, homemakers, good, obedient to their own husbands, that the word of God may not be blasphemed.

[6]Likewise, exhort the young men to be soberminded, [7]in all things showing yourself *to be* a pattern of good works; in doctrine *showing* integrity, reverence, incorruptibility,[c] [8]sound speech that cannot be condemned, that one who is an opponent may be ashamed, having nothing evil to say of you.[d]

[9]*Exhort* bondservants to be obedient to their own masters, to be well pleasing in all *things,* not answering back, [10]not pilfering, but showing all good fidelity, that they may adorn the doctrine of God our Savior in all things.

[11]*For the grace of God that brings salvation has appeared to all men, [12]teaching us that, denying ungodliness and worldly lusts, we should live soberly, righteously, and godly in the present age, [13]*looking for the blessed hope and glorious appearing of our great God and Savior Jesus Christ, [14]who gave Himself for us, that He might redeem us from every lawless deed and purify for Himself *His* own special people, zealous for good works.

[15]Speak these things, exhort, and rebuke with all authority. Let no one despise you.

3 Remind* them to be subject to rulers and authorities, to obey, to be ready for every good work, [2]to speak evil of no one, to be peaceable, gentle, showing all humility to all men. [3]*For we ourselves were also once foolish, disobedient, deceived, serving various lusts and pleasures, living in malice and envy, hateful and hating one another. [4]*But when the kindness and the love of God our Savior toward man appeared, [5]not by works of righteousness which we have done, but according to His mercy He saved us, through the washing of regeneration and renewing of the Holy Spirit, [6]whom He poured out on us abundantly through Jesus Christ our Savior, [7]that having been justified by His grace we should become heirs according to the hope of eternal life. [8]*This is a faithful saying, and these things I want you to affirm constantly, that those who have believed in God should be careful to maintain good works. These things are good and profitable to men. [9]But avoid foolish disputes, genealogies, contentions, and strivings about the law; for they are unprofitable and useless. [10]Reject a divisive man after the first and second admonition, [11]knowing

2:7 [c]NU-Text omits *incorruptibility.*   2:8 [d]NU-Text and M-Text read *us.*

that such a person is warped and sinning, being self-condemned.

¹²When I send Artemas to you, or Tychicus, be diligent to come to me at Nicopolis, for I have decided to spend the winter there. ¹³Send Zenas the lawyer and Apollos on their journey with haste, that they may lack nothing. ¹⁴And let our *people* also learn to maintain good works, to *meet* urgent needs, that they may not be unfruitful.

¹⁵All who *are* with me greet you. Greet those who love us in the faith.

Grace *be* with you all. Amen.

(continued from previous page)
ourselves. He has washed away our sins; we stand justified in His sight; and we face the future confidently because we are the heirs of God.

3:8–11 *Remember what God expects of you.* A major theme in this letter is *good works* (1:16; 2:7, 14; 3:1, 8, 14). People who are busy for the Lord do not have time for useless arguments.

PHILEMON

Vv. 1ff *Providence.* While a prisoner in Rome, Paul met Onesimus ("unprofitable" [v. 11]), a runaway slave who belonged to Philemon, a friend Paul had led to Christ (v. 19). Paul won Onesimus to Christ and sent him back to his master in Colosse (Col. 4:7–9). The providence of God is amazing, that Paul and Onesimus should meet in the great city of Rome! Perhaps Philemon's prayers brought the men together (v. 22). Philemon certainly saw Romans 8:28 in action!

Friendship. Paul has so much good to say about Philemon. He was a beloved friend, a man of faith and love, a refreshing Christian, a praying man, a man who obeyed God's will. Can your friends say these things about you?

Reconciliation. According to Roman law, Onesimus could have been executed for his crimes. But he had become a brother in Christ, and Philemon had to forgive him and take him back. True reconciliation is not cheap; there is a price to pay. Paul knew this and was willing to pay the price himself. Can God use you as a reconciler? Are you willing to pay the price?

Paul,* a prisoner of Christ Jesus, and Timothy *our* brother,

To Philemon our beloved *friend* and fellow laborer, 2to the beloved[a] Apphia, Archippus our fellow soldier, and to the church in your house:

3Grace to you and peace from God our Father and the Lord Jesus Christ.

4I thank my God, making mention of you always in my prayers, 5hearing of your love and faith which you have toward the Lord Jesus and toward all the saints, 6that the sharing of your faith may become effective by the acknowledgment of every good thing which is in you[b] in Christ Jesus. 7For we have[c] great joy[d] and consolation in your love, because the hearts of the saints have been refreshed by you, brother.

8Therefore, though I might be very bold in Christ to command you what is fitting, 9yet for love's sake I rather appeal *to you*—being such a one as Paul, the aged, and now also a prisoner of Jesus Christ— 10I appeal to you for my son Onesimus, whom I have begotten *while* in my chains, 11who once was unprofitable to you, but now is profitable to you and to me.

12I am sending him back.[e] You therefore receive him, that is, my own heart, 13whom I wished to keep with me, that on your behalf he might minister to me in my chains for the gospel. 14But without your consent I wanted to do nothing, that your good deed might not be by compulsion, as it were, but voluntary.

15For perhaps he departed for a while for this *purpose,* that you might receive him forever, 16no longer as a slave but more than a slave—a beloved brother, especially to me but how much more to you, both in the flesh and in the Lord.

17If then you count me as a partner, receive him as *you would* me. 18But if he has wronged you or owes anything, put that on my account. 19I, Paul, am writing with my own hand. I will repay—not to mention to you that you owe me even your own self besides. 20Yes, brother, let me have joy from you in the Lord; refresh my heart in the Lord.

21Having confidence in your obedience, I write to you, knowing that you will do even more than I say. 22But, meanwhile, also prepare a guest room for me, for I trust that through your prayers I shall be granted to you.

23Epaphras, my fellow prisoner in Christ Jesus, greets you, 24as *do* Mark, Aristarchus, Demas, Luke, my fellow laborers.

25The grace of our Lord Jesus Christ *be* with your spirit. Amen.

---

2 [a]NU-Text reads *to our sister Apphia.* 6 [b]NU-Text and M-Text read *us.* 7 [c]NU-Text reads *had.* [d]M-Text reads *thanksgiving.* 12 [e]NU-Text reads *back to you in person, that is, my own heart.*

Accepted and Redeemed—Two statements in Paul's letter to Philemon remind us of what Jesus did for us. "Receive him [Onesimus] as you would me" (v. 17) reminds us that we are "accepted in the Beloved" (Eph. 1:6). "Put that on my account" (v. 18) reminds us that Jesus paid the price for our redemption (Rom. 4:1–8; 2 Cor. 5:21).

HEBREWS

The author of Hebrews is unknown to us, but the theme of the book is clear: "Let us go on to perfection [spiritual maturity]" (6:1). The epistle was written to Jewish believers who were tempted to abandon the fullness of Christ and go back to the emptiness of a religious system soon to be destroyed.

Lost people are still "in Egypt" and need to be redeemed through faith in Christ. Those who are redeemed are privileged to enter their spiritual inheritance ("Canaan") and enjoy His "rest" (4:11; Matt. 11:28–30). Entering Canaan is not a type of going to heaven. It is a picture of conquering the enemy and claiming your spiritual inheritance by faith.

But too many believers, like Israel in the Old Testament, are wandering in the wilderness of unbelief and yearning to go back to the old life. The message of Hebrews is especially for them: "Let us go on to maturity!"

Hebrews is one of three New Testament letters written to explain Habakkuk 2:4, "The just shall live by his faith." (See Rom. 1:17; Gal. 3:11; Heb. 10:38.) The emphasis in Hebrews is on "by faith." God has spoken through His Son, and we must respond to that Word. Our response determines the kind of life we live and how much of our spiritual inheritance we claim. We are not only *saved* by faith, but we must *live* by faith.

One key word in Hebrews is *better*. Christ is better than the angels (chaps. 1—2) and better than Moses and Aaron (chaps. 3—6). He has a better priesthood (chap. 7), covenant (chap. 8), sanctuary (chap. 9), and sacrifice (chap. 10); and He gives His people a better life (chaps. 11—13), a life of faith.

As you meditate on this profound letter, ask yourself, Am I looking back and craving the old life, or am I pressing on by faith to claim my inheritance in Christ? Am I wandering in a wilderness of unbelief or resting in His finished work and faithful Word?

1 God,* who at various times and in various ways spoke in time past to the fathers by the prophets, ²has in these last days spoken to us by *His* Son, whom He has appointed heir of all things, through whom also He made the worlds; ³who being the brightness of *His* glory and the express image of His person, and upholding all things by the word of His power, when He had by Himself[a] purged our[b] sins, sat down at the right hand of the Majesty on high, ⁴having become so much better than the angels, as He has by inheritance obtained a more excellent name than they.

⁵For to which of the angels did He ever say:

"You are My Son,
Today I have begotten You"?[c]

And again:

1:3 [a]NU-Text omits *by Himself*. [b]NU-Text omits *our*.
1:5 [c]Psalm 2:7

CHAPTER 1

1:1–3 "God has spoken to us!" What a tremendous statement, and what a great responsibility it brings to you if you have heard His voice through His Word: "See that you do not refuse Him who speaks" (12:25). What you do with the Word of God *(continued)*

❝*Other men had the threads of truth; but Christ took the threads, and wove them into a glorious robe, put it on, and came forth clothed with every truth of God.*❞

—Charles Haddon Spurgeon

Angels—Jesus is greater than the angels because He is the eternal Son of God Whom the angels worship and serve. Angels serve God's people (Heb. 1:14), even though we may not recognize them (Heb. 13:2; Gen. 18). Angels give special care to children (Matt. 18:10) and intervene in the lives of God's servants when they need special help (Acts 5:17–21; 12:1–10). When believers die, the angels escort them to glory (Luke 16:22); and when Christ returns, angels will accompany Him (Matt. 25:31). We must not worship angels (Rev. 22:9) or pray to them; but we can trust God to send them when we need them most.

(continued from previous page)
determines what you will enjoy of God's will and claim of your inheritance.

Jesus Christ is the Father's last word. In Him, divine revelation is *seen* and *heard* in its fullness; and in Him, God's revelation is complete. When we see Him, we see the Father (John 14:1–11). Through Christ, we understand where everything came from, where it is going, what keeps it going, and why it is here.

We also understand what He has done for us. *He died for us!* Today He is enthroned in glory, ministering to us and for us (13:20–21). He wants to mature us and teach us how to walk by faith. One day He will defeat all His enemies and bring in His righteous kingdom.

With a Savior like that, why look for a substitute?

CHAPTER 2

2:1–4 *Hear Him.* This is the first of five solemn admonitions to believers to pay attention to what God says in His Word. During Old Testament times, God dealt with those who disobeyed His Word. In these last days, we have a greater obligation to obey because we have the complete Scriptures
(continued)

> "I will be to Him a Father,
>   And He shall be to Me a Son"?[d]

6But when He again brings the firstborn into the world, He says:

> "Let all the angels of God worship Him."[e]

7And of the angels He says:

> "Who makes His angels spirits
>   And His ministers a flame of fire."[f]

8But to the Son He says:

> "Your throne, O God, is forever and ever;
>   A scepter of righteousness is the scepter of Your kingdom.
> 9   You have loved righteousness and hated lawlessness;
>   Therefore God, Your God, has anointed You
>   With the oil of gladness more than Your companions."[g]

10And:

> "You, LORD, in the beginning laid the foundation of the earth,
>   And the heavens are the work of Your hands.
> 11   They will perish, but You remain;
>   And they will all grow old like a garment;
> 12   Like a cloak You will fold them up,
>   And they will be changed.
>   But You are the same,
>   And Your years will not fail."[h]

13But to which of the angels has He ever said:

> "Sit at My right hand,
>   Till I make Your enemies Your footstool"?[i]

14Are they not all ministering spirits sent forth to minister for those who will inherit salvation?

2 Therefore* we must give the more earnest heed to the things we have heard, lest we drift away. 2For if the word spoken through angels proved steadfast, and every transgression and disobedience received a just reward, 3how shall we escape if we neglect so great a salvation, which at the first began to be spoken by the Lord, and was confirmed to us by those who heard *Him*, 4God also bearing witness both with signs and wonders, with various miracles, and gifts of the Holy Spirit, according to His own will?

---

[d]2 Samuel 7:14 1:6 [e]Deuteronomy 32:43 (Septuagint, Dead Sea Scrolls); Psalm 97:7 1:7 [f]Psalm 104:4 1:9 [g]Psalm 45:6, 7 1:12 [h]Psalm 102:25–27 1:13 [i]Psalm 110:1

A Sensitive Heart—Hebrews is a book of exhortations (13:22). The word means "encouragement" and is a title for the Holy Spirit, the "Comforter, Helper" (John 14:16, 26). The writer encourages us not to neglect the Word (2:1–4), harden our hearts to the Word (3:7–19), become deaf to the Word (5:11–14), defy the Word (10:26–39) or disobey the Word deliberately (12:14–19). God deals in love with His people when they will not listen and obey (12:3ff.), so it pays to have a heart sensitive to God's voice.

Secure in the Promise—Ponder these verses: "We wish to see Jesus" (John 12:21), "We see Jesus" (Heb. 2:9), and "We shall see Him [Jesus]" (1 John 3:2). The first is the plea of the sinner; the second is the privilege of the saint; the third is the promise of the Scripture.

5*For He has not put the world to come, of which we speak, in subjection to angels. 6But one testified in a certain place, saying:

> "What is man that You are mindful of him,
>   Or the son of man that You take care of
>   him?
> 7   You have made him a little lower than the
>   angels;
>   You have crowned him with glory and
>   honor,ʲ
>   And set him over the works of Your hands.
> 8   You have put all things in subjection under
>   his feet."ᵏ

For in that He put all in subjection under him, He left nothing *that is* not put under him. But now we do not yet see all things put under him. 9But we see Jesus, who was made a little lower than the angels, for the suffering of death crowned with glory and honor, that He, by the grace of God, might taste death for everyone.

10*For it was fitting for Him, for whom *are* all things and by whom *are* all things, in bringing many sons to glory, to make the captain of their salvation perfect through sufferings. 11For both He who sanctifies and those who are being sanctified *are* all of one, for which reason He is not ashamed to call them brethren, 12saying:

> "I will declare Your name to My brethren;
>   In the midst of the assembly I will sing
>   praise to You."ˡ

13And again:

> "I will put My trust in Him."ᵐ

And again:

> "Here am I and the children whom God has
>   given Me."ⁿ

14Inasmuch then as the children have partaken of flesh and blood, He Himself likewise shared in the same, that through death He might destroy him who had the power of death, that is, the devil, 15and release those who through fear of death were all their lifetime subject to bondage. 16For indeed He does not give aid to angels, but He does give aid to the seed of Abraham. 17Therefore, in all things He had to be made like *His* brethren, that He might be a merciful and faithful High Priest in things *pertaining* to God, to make propitiation for the sins of the people. 18For in that He Himself has suffered, being tempted, He is able to aid those who are tempted.

3 Therefore,* holy brethren, partakers of the heavenly calling, consider the Apostle and High Priest of our confession, Christ Jesus,

---

2:7 ʲNU-Text and M-Text omit the rest of verse 7.   2:8 ᵏPsalm 8:4–6   2:12 ˡPsalm 22:22   2:13 ᵐ2 Samuel 22:3; Isaiah 8:17 ⁿIsaiah 8:18

(continued from previous page)
and the full revelation of God in Jesus Christ. Are you serious about what God says to you?

2:5–9 *See Him.* There is a "world to come," and how you live today will help to determine your place in the future kingdom of Christ (1:13; 10:13; 12:28). Today, we see man fallen in Adam; but by faith, we see Christ and His victory. Because He is glorified, we shall be glorified in Him!

2:10–18 *Trust Him.* Persons who trust Christ are God's children (v. 13) on their way to glory (v. 10). The Redeemer has defeated death and the devil, and He understands how His people feel as they face the temptations and trials of life. When you come to Him by faith, you come to a sympathetic High Priest who can meet your every need. Trust Him!

CHAPTER 3
3:1–6 *Consider Him.* Hebrews focuses on Jesus Christ. The writer wants us to "see" Him (2:9), "consider" Him (3:1), and keep our eyes of faith fixed on Him (12:1–2). Whenever you are tempted to look at your circumstances or at yourself, look to Jesus by faith and rejoice in His faithfulness.

Are You Hearing?—People with hard hearts know the truth but resist it and refuse to obey it. They know that God chastens disobedient children, but they almost defy God to act. They think they can sin and get away with it. The first step toward a hard heart is neglect of the Word of God (Heb. 2:1–4), not taking it seriously. It is either "hearing" or "hardening." Take your choice (Ps. 95).

2who was faithful to Him who appointed Him, as
Moses also *was faithful* in all His house. 3For this
One has been counted worthy of more glory than
Moses, inasmuch as He who built the house has
more honor than the house. 4For every house is
built by someone, but He who built all things *is*
God. 5And Moses indeed *was* faithful in all His
house as a servant, for a testimony of those things
which would be spoken *afterward,* 6but Christ as
a Son over His own house, whose house we are
if we hold fast the confidence and the rejoicing
of the hope firm to the end.[o]
7*Therefore, as the Holy Spirit says:

"Today, if you will hear His voice,
8 *Do not harden your hearts as in the*
rebellion,
In the day of trial in the wilderness,
9 *Where your fathers tested Me, tried Me,*
And saw My works forty years.
10 *Therefore I was angry with that generation,*
And said, 'They always go astray in their
heart,
And they have not known My ways.'
11 *So I swore in My wrath,*
'They shall not enter My rest.' "[p]

12Beware, brethren, lest there be in any of you
an evil heart of unbelief in departing from the
living God; 13but exhort one another daily, while
it is called *"Today,"* lest any of you be hardened
through the deceitfulness of sin. 14For we have
become partakers of Christ if we hold the beginning of our confidence steadfast to the end,
15while it is said:

"Today, if you will hear His voice,
Do not harden your hearts as in the
rebellion."[q]

16*For who, having heard, rebelled? Indeed, *was*
it not all who came out of Egypt, *led* by Moses?
17Now with whom was He angry forty years? *Was*
it not with those who sinned, whose corpses fell
in the wilderness? 18And to whom did He swear
that they would not enter His rest, but to those
who did not obey? 19So we see that they could
not enter in because of unbelief.

4 Therefore,* since a promise remains of entering His rest, let us fear lest any of you seem
to have come short of it. 2For indeed the gospel
was preached to us as well as to them; but the
word which they heard did not profit them,[r] not
being mixed with faith in those who heard *it.*
3For we who have believed do enter that rest, as
He has said:

"So I swore in My wrath,
'They shall not enter My rest,' "[s]

3:7–15 ***Obey Him.*** The writer uses the failure of Israel as a warning against a hard heart. How does a believer's heart become hard? By refusing His words, despising His works, and being ignorant of His ways. Sin is deceitful. You think you are getting away with it, but all the while it is hardening your heart and robbing you of blessing.

3:16–19 ***Believe Him.*** Here is another exhortation to faith. The fact that the Jews were delivered from Egypt was no guarantee they would claim their inheritance. Because of their unbelief, they failed to enter the land (Num. 13). An "evil heart of unbelief" (v. 12) will rob you of what God has planned for you in your Christian life, so pay attention to God's Word. As Paul wrote, "Faith comes by hearing, and hearing by the word of God" (Rom. 10:17).

CHAPTER 4

4:1–10 ***His rest.*** Three different "rests" are in view: God's Sabbath rest after creation (v. 4; Gen. 2:2); Israel's rest of victory in Canaan (v. 3; Josh. 21:44); and the believer's rest of faith today (vv. 1, 9–10). Israel was delivered from Egypt, but a whole generation failed to enter Canaan and claim their promised inheritance. Why? Because of their unbelief. "Let us fear!" (v. 1).

3:6 [o]NU-Text omits *firm to the end.* 3:11 [p]Psalm 95:7–11
3:15 [q]Psalm 95:7, 8 4:2 [r]NU-Text and M-Text read *profit them, since they were not united by faith with those who heeded it.* 4:3 [s]Psalm 95:11

A Throne of Grace—To the unsaved, God's throne is a throne of judgment (Rev. 20:11–15); but to God's children, it is a throne of grace. When you are tempted, you can come to your great High Priest for mercy and grace. If you sin, you can come to your Advocate for forgiveness (1 John 1:9—2:2). The way is always open.

although the works were finished from the foundation of the world. [4]For He has spoken in a certain place of the seventh *day* in this way: *"And God rested on the seventh day from all His works";*[t] [5]and again in this *place: "They shall not enter My rest."*[u]

[6]Since therefore it remains that some *must* enter it, and those to whom it was first preached did not enter because of disobedience, [7]again He designates a certain day, saying in David, *"Today,"* after such a long time, as it has been said:

"Today, if you will hear His voice,
Do not harden your hearts."[v]

[8]For if Joshua had given them rest, then He would not afterward have spoken of another day. [9]There remains therefore a rest for the people of God. [10]For he who has entered His rest has himself also ceased from his works as God *did* from His.

[11]*Let us therefore be diligent to enter that rest, lest anyone fall according to the same example of disobedience. [12]For the word of God *is* living and powerful, and sharper than any two-edged sword, piercing even to the division of soul and spirit, and of joints and marrow, and is a discerner of the thoughts and intents of the heart. [13]And there is no creature hidden from His sight, but all things *are* naked and open to the eyes of Him to whom we *must give* account.

[14]*Seeing then that we have a great High Priest who has passed through the heavens, Jesus the Son of God, let us hold fast *our* confession. [15]For we do not have a High Priest who cannot sympathize with our weaknesses, but was in all *points* tempted as *we are,* yet without sin. [16]Let us therefore come boldly to the throne of grace, that we may obtain mercy and find grace to help in time of need.

5 For* every high priest taken from among men is appointed for men in things *pertaining* to God, that he may offer both gifts and sacrifices for sins, [2]He can have compassion on those who are ignorant and going astray, since he himself is also subject to weakness. [3]Because of this he is required as for the people, so also for himself, to offer *sacrifices* for sins. [4]And no man takes this honor to himself, but he who is called by God, just as Aaron *was.*

[5]So also Christ did not glorify Himself to become High Priest, *but it* was He who said to Him:

"You are My Son,
Today I have begotten You."[w]

[6]As He also *says* in another *place:*

"You are a priest forever
According to the order of Melchizedek";[x]

4:11–13 His sight. God sees the heart and uses His sword to help us see our true spiritual condition (Jer. 17:9). Spend time daily reading the Word and meditating on it, always applying its truths to your heart. One day you will give account to God of what you have done with His Word, so be faithful.

4:14–16 His throne. You cannot claim your inheritance in your own power or wisdom. But you have a great High Priest who can give you the mercy and the grace you need just when you need them. He lives to intercede for you (7:25) and to help you do His will (13:20–21).

CHAPTER 5

5:1–6 Selected. Just as the Jewish high priest was appointed by God, so our great High Priest was appointed by the Father (Ps. 110:4); and He alone is worthy to serve. Never allow anybody to come between you and God, for Christ is the only mediator (1 Tim. 2:5). "The order of Melchizedek" refers to Genesis 14:18–24. Being from the tribe of Judah, Jesus could not serve as priest on earth; but He can serve as priest in heaven. He is there ministering for you today.

4:4 [t]Genesis 2:2　4:5 [u]Psalm 95:11　4:7 [v]Psalm 95:7, 8
5:5 [w]Psalm 2:7　5:6 [x]Psalm 110:4

Mature in Christ—Mature believers understand the heavenly priesthood of Jesus Christ and know how to come to the throne of grace for help. They are skillful in using God's truth in their personal lives, and they can also teach others. Do you qualify?

5:7–10 Perfected. Jesus had to prepare for His priestly ministry by experiencing the trials His people experience as they walk by faith (4:15). Because of the life that He lived and the death that He died, He is able to identify with your needs and give you grace to see you through. He understands!

5:11–14 Neglected. The "milk" of the Word represents the "first principles" of the Christian life, that is, what Jesus Christ did for us when He was on earth. The "meat" of the Word is the teaching about what Jesus is now doing for us in heaven, His ministry as High Priest. How sad it is when Christians neglect God's Word and stop growing in grace.

CHAPTER 6

6:1–8 The impossible. The ABC's of the Christian life are important, but they must be a launching pad and not a parking lot, for the challenge is, "Let us go on to maturity." If we get sluggish (v. 12) and dull (5:11) toward the Word, we may fall by the wayside (v. 6; Gal. 6:1) and stop being fruitful. As long as disobedient believers are bringing shame to Christ, it is impossible to bring them to repentance, and God must deal with them.

6:9–12 The improbable. But the writer did not believe that his readers were in that condition. Although they had a long way to go in their Christian experience, the fruit was there. Diligence, faith, and patience are required to live the Christian life. Maturity is not automatic.

6:13–20 The immutable. The chapter ends with one of the greatest statements on security found anywhere in Scripture. God's promise and God's oath assure us that we are His, and God's character backs up His words. Instead of drifting (2:1), we are anchored heavenward where Jesus ministers in the very presence of God, and that anchor will not fail. We are anchored so we can make progress!

7*who, in the days of His flesh, when He had offered up prayers and supplications, with vehement cries and tears to Him who was able to save Him from death, and was heard because of His godly fear, 8though He was a Son, yet He learned obedience by the things which He suffered. 9And having been perfected, He became the author of eternal salvation to all who obey Him, 10called by God as High Priest *"according to the order of Melchizedek,"* 11*of whom we have much to say, and hard to explain, since you have become dull of hearing.

12For though by this time you ought to be teachers, you need *someone* to teach you again the first principles of the oracles of God; and you have come to need milk and not solid food. 13For everyone who partakes *only* of milk *is* unskilled in the word of righteousness, for he is a babe. 14But solid food belongs to those who are of full age, *that is,* those who by reason of use have their senses exercised to discern both good and evil.

6 Therefore,* leaving the discussion of the elementary *principles* of Christ, let us go on to perfection, not laying again the foundation of repentance from dead works and of faith toward God, 2of the doctrine of baptisms, of laying on of hands, of resurrection of the dead, and of eternal judgment. 3And this we will^y do if God permits. 4For *it is* impossible for those who were once enlightened, and have tasted the heavenly gift, and have become partakers of the Holy Spirit, 5and have tasted the good word of God and the powers of the age to come, 6if they fall away,^z to renew them again to repentance, since they crucify again for themselves the Son of God, and put *Him* to an open shame.

7For the earth which drinks in the rain that often comes upon it, and bears herbs useful for those by whom it is cultivated, receives blessing from God; 8but if it bears thorns and briers, *it is* rejected and near to being cursed, whose end *is* to be burned.

9*But, beloved, we are confident of better things concerning you, yes, things that accompany salvation, though we speak in this manner. 10For God *is* not unjust to forget your work and labor of^a love which you have shown toward His name, *in that* you have ministered to the saints, and do minister. 11And we desire that each one of you show the same diligence to the full assurance of hope until the end, 12that you do not become sluggish, but imitate those who through faith and patience inherit the promises.

13*For when God made a promise to Abraham, because He could swear by no one greater, He swore by Himself, 14saying, *"Surely blessing I will bless you, and multiplying I will multiply you."*^b 15And so, after he had patiently endured, he obtained the promise. 16For men indeed swear by the greater, and an oath for confirmation *is* for them an end of all dispute. 17Thus God, determining to show more abundantly to the heirs of promise the immutability of His counsel, confirmed *it* by an oath, 18that by two immutable things, in which it *is* impossible for God to lie, we might^c have strong consolation, who have fled for refuge to lay hold of the hope set before *us.*

6:3 ^yM-Text reads *let us do.*   6:6 ^zOr *and have fallen away*
6:10 ^aNU-Text omits *labor of.*   6:14 ^bGenesis 22:17
6:18 ^cM-Text omits *might.*

19This *hope* we have as an anchor of the soul, both sure and steadfast, and which enters the Presence *behind* the veil, 20where the forerunner has entered for us, *even* Jesus, having become High Priest forever according to the order of Melchizedek.

7 For* this Melchizedek, king of Salem, priest of the Most High God, who met Abraham returning from the slaughter of the kings and blessed him, 2to whom also Abraham gave a tenth part of all, first being translated "king of righteousness," and then also king of Salem, meaning "king of peace," 3without father, without mother, without genealogy, having neither beginning of days nor end of life, but made like the Son of God, remains a priest continually.

4Now consider how great this man *was,* to whom even the patriarch Abraham gave a tenth of the spoils. 5And indeed those who are of the sons of Levi, who receive the priesthood, have a commandment to receive tithes from the people according to the law, that is, from their brethren, though they have come from the loins of Abraham; 6but he whose genealogy is not derived from them received tithes from Abraham and blessed him who had the promises. 7Now beyond all contradiction the lesser is blessed by the better. 8Here mortal men receive tithes, but there he *receives them,* of whom it is witnessed that he lives. 9Even Levi, who receives tithes, paid tithes through Abraham, so to speak, 10for he was still in the loins of his father when Melchizedek met him.

11Therefore, if perfection were through the Levitical priesthood (for under it the people received the law), what further need *was there* that another priest should rise according to the order of Melchizedek, and not be called according to the order of Aaron? 12For the priesthood being changed, of necessity there is also a change of the law. 13For He of whom these things are spoken belongs to another tribe, from which no man has officiated at the altar.

14For *it is* evident that our Lord arose from Judah, of which tribe Moses spoke nothing concerning priesthood.*d* 15And it is yet far more evident if, in the likeness of Melchizedek, there arises another priest 16who has come, not according to the law of a fleshly commandment, but according to the power of an endless life. 17For He testifies:*e*

> "You are a priest forever
> According to the order of Melchizedek."*f*

18For on the one hand there is an annulling of the former commandment because of its weakness and unprofitableness, 19for the law made nothing perfect; on the other hand, *there is the* bringing in of a better hope, through which we draw near to God.

20And inasmuch as He *was* not *made priest* without an oath 21(for they have become priests without an oath, but He with an oath by Him who said to Him:

> "The Lord has sworn
> And will not relent,

CHAPTER 7

7:1ff With this chapter, the writer begins to explain the better priesthood of Christ; and he begins with the *better order,* the order of Melchizedek (Gen. 14).

Jesus Christ is both King and Priest, and His throne is a throne of grace (4:16). As King, He can control circumstances around you; as Priest, He can change attitudes within you. You will experience righteousness and peace as you yield to Him (v. 2; Pss. 72:7; 85:9–10; Isa. 32:17).

Because He is a Priest forever, He saves forever (vv. 23–25). "To the uttermost" means "completely," "perfectly." You are secure as long as He lives, and He lives eternally. You can live by the power of His endless life!

A perfect salvation should lead to a life of growing maturity. An earthly priesthood can make nothing perfect (v. 11), nor can the law of God (v. 19) or the sacrifices (10:1–2); but Jesus can lead you into spiritual maturity as you walk by faith (13:20–21). He invites you to come to His throne, and He understands you better than you understand yourself.

7:14 *d*NU-Text reads *priests.*   7:17 *e*NU-Text reads *it is testified.* *f*Psalm 110:4

'You are a priest forever[g]
According to the order of Melchizedek' "),[h]

22by so much more Jesus has become a surety of a better covenant.

23Also there were many priests, because they were prevented by death from continuing. 24But He, because He continues forever, has an unchangeable priesthood. 25Therefore He is also able to save to the uttermost those who come to God through Him, since He always lives to make intercession for them.

26For such a High Priest was fitting for us, who is holy, harmless, undefiled, separate from sinners, and has become higher than the heavens; 27who does not need daily, as those high priests, to offer up sacrifices, first for His own sins and then for the people's, for this He did once for all when He offered up Himself. 28For the law appoints as high priests men who have weakness, but the word of the oath, which came after the law, appoints the Son who has been perfected forever.

8 Now* this is the main point of the things we are saying: We have such a High Priest, who is seated at the right hand of the throne of the Majesty in the heavens, 2*a Minister of the sanctuary and of the true tabernacle which the Lord erected, and not man.

3For every high priest is appointed to offer both gifts and sacrifices. Therefore it is necessary that this One also have something to offer. 4For if He were on earth, He would not be a priest, since there are priests who offer the gifts according to the law; 5who serve the copy and shadow of the heavenly things, as Moses was divinely instructed when he was about to make the tabernacle. For He said, "See that you make all things according to the pattern shown you on the mountain."[i] 6But now He has obtained a more excellent ministry, inasmuch as He is also Mediator of a better covenant, which was established on better promises.

7*For if that first covenant had been faultless, then no place would have been sought for a second. 8Because finding fault with them, He says: "Behold, the days are coming, says the Lord, when I will make a new covenant with the house of Israel and with the house of Judah— 9not according to the covenant that I made with their fathers in the day when I took them by the hand to lead them out of the land of Egypt; because they did not continue in My covenant, and I disregarded them, says the Lord. 10For this is the covenant that I will make with the house of Israel after those days, says the Lord: I will put My laws in their mind and write them on their hearts; and I will be their God, and they shall be My people. 11None of them shall teach his neighbor, and none his brother, saying, 'Know the Lord,' for all shall know Me, from the least of them to the greatest of them. 12For I will be merciful to their unrighteousness, and their sins and their lawless deeds[j] I will remember no more."[k]

13In that He says, "A new covenant," He has made the first obsolete. Now what is becoming obsolete and growing old is ready to vanish away.

CHAPTER 8

8:1 Finality. There were no chairs in the Jewish tabernacle or temple because the priests' work was never finished. But Jesus finished the work of redemption (John 19:30) and sat down on the throne (10:11–14). Rejoice!

8:2–6 Reality. The Jewish priests in the temple ministered with copies and shadows, but Christ in heaven ministers in the original sanctuary from which the things on earth were copied. When you trust Christ, you enter a life of reality, and you are forever finished with substitutes. Rejoice!

8:7–13 Maturity. The law of Moses was given to the children of Israel as a tutor to help them grow up and be prepared for their Messiah's coming (Gal. 4:1–7). They were like children; God had to take them by the hand and lead them. But the new covenant, with its heavenly priesthood, leads us to spiritual maturity: God puts His Word in our hearts and transforms our character (2 Cor. 3:1–3, 18). Rejoice and be exceedingly glad!

7:21 [g]NU-Text ends the quotation here. [h]Psalm 110:4
8:5 [i]Exodus 25:40   8:12 [j]NU-Text omits and their lawless deeds. [k]Jeremiah 31:31–34

9 Then* indeed, even the first *covenant* had ordinances of divine service and the earthly sanctuary. ²For a tabernacle was prepared: the first *part*, in which *was* the lampstand, the table, and the showbread, which is called the sanctuary; ³and behind the second veil, the part of the tabernacle which is called the Holiest of All, ⁴which had the golden censer and the ark of the covenant overlaid on all sides with gold, in which *were* the golden pot that had the manna, Aaron's rod that budded, and the tablets of the covenant; ⁵and above it were the cherubim of glory overshadowing the mercy seat. Of these things we cannot now speak in detail.

⁶Now when these things had been thus prepared, the priests always went into the first part of the tabernacle, performing *the services*. ⁷But into the second part the high priest *went* alone once a year, not without blood, which he offered for himself and *for* the people's sins *committed* in ignorance; ⁸the Holy Spirit indicating this, that the way into the Holiest of All was not yet made manifest while the first tabernacle was still standing. ⁹It *was* symbolic for the present time in which both gifts and sacrifices are offered which cannot make him who performed the service perfect in regard to the conscience—¹⁰*concerned* only with foods and drinks, various washings, and fleshly ordinances imposed until the time of reformation.

¹¹But Christ came *as* High Priest of the good things to come,ᶦ with the greater and more perfect tabernacle not made with hands, that is, not of this creation. ¹²*Not with the blood of goats and calves, but with His own blood He entered the Most Holy Place once for all, having obtained eternal redemption. ¹³For if the blood of bulls and goats and the ashes of a heifer, sprinkling the unclean, sanctifies for the purifying of the flesh, ¹⁴how much more shall the blood of Christ, who through the eternal Spirit offered Himself without spot to God, cleanse your conscience from dead works to serve the living God? ¹⁵And for this reason He is the Mediator of the new covenant, by means of death, for the redemption of the transgressions under the first covenant, that those who are called may receive the promise of the eternal inheritance.

¹⁶*For where there *is* a testament, there must also of necessity be the death of the testator. ¹⁷For a testament *is* in force after men are dead, since it has no power at all while the testator lives. ¹⁸Therefore not even the first *covenant* was dedicated without blood. ¹⁹For when Moses had spoken every precept to all the people according to the law, he took the blood of calves and goats, with water, scarlet wool, and hyssop, and sprinkled both the book itself and all the people, ²⁰saying, *"This is the blood of the covenant which God has commanded you."*ᵐ ²¹Then likewise he sprinkled with blood both the tabernacle and all the vessels of the ministry. ²²And according to the law almost all things are purified with blood,

CHAPTER 9

9:1–11 *A better sanctuary.* In every way, the present heavenly sanctuary is better than any sanctuary on earth, including the temple in Jerusalem. In the earthly temple, the furnishings were only symbols, the work was never finished, and the ministry could never change the human heart. We should be grateful for the price Jesus paid to make His heavenly ministry possible.

9:12–15 *A better service.* The Jewish high priest could deal only with externals, but Jesus deals with the heart and conscience. He can purify us and perfect us (13:20–21) so that we can serve God acceptably. Do you come to Him daily and ask for His ministry?

9:16–28 *A better sacrifice.* The blood that purchased your eternal redemption came not from unwilling animals but from the Son of God who willingly laid down His life for you (John 10:14–18). The spotless Lamb of God had to die only once; the sacrifice need not be repeated. Have you trusted that blood to save you?

9:11 ᶦNU-Text reads *that have come.*   9:20 ᵐExodus 24:8

Jesus' Appearings—Hebrews 9:24–28 mentions three "appearings" of Jesus Christ: a *past* appearing (v. 26) for our salvation, a *present* appearing (v. 24) for our sanctification, and a *future* appearing for our glorification (v. 28).

and without shedding of blood there is no remission.

23Therefore *it was* necessary that the copies of the things in the heavens should be purified with these, but the heavenly things themselves with better sacrifices than these. 24For Christ has not entered the holy places made with hands, *which are* copies of the true, but into heaven itself, now to appear in the presence of God for us; 25not that He should offer Himself often, as the high priest enters the Most Holy Place every year with blood of another— 26He then would have had to suffer often since the foundation of the world; but now, once at the end of the ages, He has appeared to put away sin by the sacrifice of Himself. 27And as it is appointed for men to die once, but after this the judgment, 28so Christ was offered once to bear the sins of many. To those who eagerly wait for Him He will appear a second time, apart from sin, for salvation.

CHAPTER 10

10:1–18 *Forgiveness.* The sacrifices under the Old Covenant brought a *reminder* of sin, not a *remission* of sin. The blood of God's Son took care of sin once and for all. Because there is no more offering for sin, there is also no more remembrance of sin (v. 17; Jer. 31:34), and we can rejoice that we have a righteous standing before God.

10 For* the law, having a shadow of the good things to come, *and* not the very image of the things, can never with these same sacrifices, which they offer continually year by year, make those who approach perfect. 2For then would they not have ceased to be offered? For the worshipers, once purified, would have had no more consciousness of sins. 3But in those *sacrifices there is* a reminder of sins every year. 4For *it is* not possible that the blood of bulls and goats could take away sins.

5Therefore, when He came into the world, He said:

"Sacrifice and offering You did not desire,
But a body You have prepared for Me.
6   In burnt offerings and sacrifices for sin
You had no pleasure.
7   Then I said, 'Behold, I have come—
In the volume of the book it is written of
Me—
To do Your will, O God.' "n

8Previously saying, "Sacrifice and offering, burnt offerings, and offerings for sin You did not desire, nor had pleasure in them" (which are offered according to the law), 9then He said, "Behold, I have come to do Your will, O God."o He takes away the first that He may establish the second. 10By that will we have been sanctified through the offering of the body of Jesus Christ once *for all.*

11And every priest stands ministering daily and offering repeatedly the same sacrifices, which can never take away sins. 12But this Man, after He had offered one sacrifice for sins forever, sat down at the right hand of God, 13from that time waiting till His enemies are made His footstool. 14For by one offering He has perfected forever those who are being sanctified.

15But the Holy Spirit also witnesses to us; for after He had said before,

16"This is the covenant that I will make with them after those days, says the LORD: I will put My laws into their hearts, and in their minds I will write them,"p 17then He adds, "Their sins and their lawless deeds I will remember no more."q

10:7 nPsalm 40:6–8   10:9 oNU-Text and M-Text omit O God.
10:16 pJeremiah 31:33   10:17 qJeremiah 31:34

18Now where there is remission of these, *there is* no longer an offering for sin.

19*Therefore, brethren, having boldness to enter the Holiest by the blood of Jesus, 20by a new and living way which He consecrated for us, through the veil, that is, His flesh, 21and *having* a High Priest over the house of God, 22let us draw near with a true heart in full assurance of faith, having our hearts sprinkled from an evil conscience and our bodies washed with pure water. 23Let us hold fast the confession of *our* hope without wavering, for He who promised *is* faithful. 24And let us consider one another in order to stir up love and good works, 25not forsaking the assembling of ourselves together, as *is* the manner of some, but exhorting *one another,* and so much the more as you see the Day approaching.

26*For if we sin willfully after we have received the knowledge of the truth, there no longer remains a sacrifice for sins, 27but a certain fearful expectation of judgment, and fiery indignation which will devour the adversaries. 28Anyone who has rejected Moses' law dies without mercy on the testimony of two or three witnesses. 29Of how much worse punishment, do you suppose, will he be thought worthy who has trampled the Son of God underfoot, counted the blood of the covenant by which he was sanctified a common thing, and insulted the Spirit of grace? 30For we know Him who said, *"Vengeance is Mine, I will repay,"*r says the Lord.s And again, *"The LORD will judge His people."*t 31It is a fearful thing to fall into the hands of the living God.

32But recall the former days in which, after you were illuminated, you endured a great struggle with sufferings: 33partly while you were made a spectacle both by reproaches and tribulations, and partly while you became companions of those who were so treated; 34for you had compassion on meu in my chains, and joyfully accepted the plundering of your goods, knowing that you have a better and an enduring possession for yourselves in heaven.v 35Therefore do not cast away your confidence, which has great reward. 36For you have need of endurance, so that after you have done the will of God, you may receive the promise:

37 *"For yet a little while,*
     And Hew who is coming will come and will
       not tarry.
38 *Now thex just shall live by faith;*
     But if anyone draws back,
     *My soul has no pleasure in him."*y

39But we are not of those who draw back to perdition, but of those who believe to the saving of the soul.

11 Now* faith is the substance of things hoped for, the evidence of things not seen. 2For by it the elders obtained a *good* testimony.

3By faith we understand that the worlds were framed by the word of God, so that the things

10:19–25 Faithfulness. The same Savior who died for you now lives for you and invites you to come into His presence to worship and to share your needs. The Old Testament high priest could go behind the veil only once a year, but we can come into God's presence any time. Be sure that you are cleansed and prepared to meet Him. You can trust Him: "He who promised is faithful" (v. 23).

10:26–39 Fearfulness. The privilege of entering His presence brings with it the responsibility of obeying His precepts. This exhortation applies to those who repeatedly defy God's will and disgrace God's name. God deals with His children; He will not have them acting like rebels. The chapter closes on a note of encouragement. God warns us so that we will not be presumptuous, but He comforts us so that we will not be discouraged. The hard heart needs the warning; the broken heart needs the comfort.

CHAPTER 11

11:1ff Faith is confidence in God that leads to obedience to God. True faith is based on what God says and is demonstrated in what we do. People with faith *do* things for God, and God does things for them.

Faith is not a luxury; it is a necessity. It is for common people and not just great leaders. We need faith for worshiping (v. 4) as well as for working (v. 7), walking (vv. 8–9), waiting (vv. 10–12), and warring (vv. 30–34). In any area of life where you ignore faith, you will sin (Rom. 14:23).

The phrase "still others" (v. 36) reminds us that we can live by faith and appear to be defeated. Not everybody who trusted God was delivered or protected (vv. 36–40). But the important thing is not God's deliverance; it is God's approval (v. 39). Faith in God gives you the ability to endure when others are giving up.

Where does this faith come from? Read Romans 10:17 and 15:4.

10:30 rDeuteronomy 32:35 sNU-Text omits *says the Lord.* tDeuteronomy 32:36 10:34 uNU-Text reads *the prisoners* instead of *me in my chains.* vNU-Text omits *in heaven.* 10:37 wOr *that which* 10:38 xNU-Text reads *My just one.* yHabakkuk 2:3, 4

❝*Faith makes all things possible; love makes all things easy.* **❞**
               —D. L. Moody

which are seen were not made of things which are visible.

4By faith Abel offered to God a more excellent sacrifice than Cain, through which he obtained witness that he was righteous, God testifying of his gifts; and through it he being dead still speaks.

5By faith Enoch was taken away so that he did not see death, *"and was not found, because God had taken him";*z for before he was taken he had this testimony, that he pleased God. 6But without faith *it is* impossible to please *Him,* for he who comes to God must believe that He is, and *that* He is a rewarder of those who diligently seek Him.

7By faith Noah, being divinely warned of things not yet seen, moved with godly fear, prepared an ark for the saving of his household, by which he condemned the world and became heir of the righteousness which is according to faith.

8By faith Abraham obeyed when he was called to go out to the place which he would receive as an inheritance. And he went out, not knowing where he was going. 9By faith he dwelt in the land of promise as *in* a foreign country, dwelling in tents with Isaac and Jacob, the heirs with him of the same promise; 10for he waited for the city which has foundations, whose builder and maker *is* God.

11By faith Sarah herself also received strength to conceive seed, and she bore a childa when she was past the age, because she judged Him faithful who had promised. 12Therefore from one man, and him as good as dead, were born *as many* as the stars of the sky in multitude—innumerable as the sand which is by the seashore.

13These all died in faith, not having received the promises, but having seen them afar off were assured of them,b embraced *them* and confessed that they were strangers and pilgrims on the earth. 14For those who say such things declare plainly that they seek a homeland. 15And truly if they had called to mind that *country* from which they had come out, they would have had opportunity to return. 16But now they desire a better, that is, a heavenly *country.* Therefore God is not ashamed to be called their God, for He has prepared a city for them.

17By faith Abraham, when he was tested, offered up Isaac, and he who had received the promises offered up his only begotten *son,* 18of whom it was said, *"In Isaac your seed shall be called,"*c 19concluding that God *was* able to raise *him* up, even from the dead, from which he also received him in a figurative sense.

20By faith Isaac blessed Jacob and Esau concerning things to come.

21By faith Jacob, when he was dying, blessed each of the sons of Joseph, and worshiped, *leaning* on the top of his staff.

22By faith Joseph, when he was dying, made

11:5 zGenesis 5:24 11:11 aNU-Text omits *she bore a child.*
11:13 bNU-Text and M-Text omit *were assured of them.*
11:18 cGenesis 21:12

Steady in the Faith—The great theologian John Calvin defined *faith* as "a steady and certain knowledge of the Divine benevolence towards us, which, being founded on the truth of the gratuitous promise in Christ, is both revealed to our minds, and confirmed to our hearts, by the Holy Spirit." Note that faith is founded on divine truth (God's promise) and is witnessed to by the Spirit in the heart. It has both objective and subjective aspects, and both are essential.

mention of the departure of the children of Israel, and gave instructions concerning his bones. 23By faith Moses, when he was born, was hidden three months by his parents, because they saw *he was* a beautiful child; and they were not afraid of the king's command.

24By faith Moses, when he became of age, refused to be called the son of Pharaoh's daughter, 25choosing rather to suffer affliction with the people of God than to enjoy the passing pleasures of sin, 26esteeming the reproach of Christ greater riches than the treasures in*d* Egypt; for he looked to the reward.

27By faith he forsook Egypt, not fearing the wrath of the king; for he endured as seeing Him who is invisible. 28By faith he kept the Passover and the sprinkling of blood, lest he who destroyed the firstborn should touch them.

29By faith they passed through the Red Sea as by dry *land, whereas* the Egyptians, attempting *to do* so, were drowned.

30By faith the walls of Jericho fell down after they were encircled for seven days. 31By faith the harlot Rahab did not perish with those who did not believe, when she had received the spies with peace.

32And what more shall I say? For the time would fail me to tell of Gideon and Barak and Samson and Jephthah, also *of* David and Samuel and the prophets: 33who through faith subdued kingdoms, worked righteousness, obtained promises, stopped the mouths of lions, 34quenched the violence of fire, escaped the edge of the sword, out of weakness were made strong, became valiant in battle, turned to flight the armies of the aliens. 35Women received their dead raised to life again.

Others were tortured, not accepting deliverance, that they might obtain a better resurrection. 36Still others had trial of mockings and scourgings, yes, and of chains and imprisonment. 37They were stoned, they were sawn in two, were tempted,*e* were slain with the sword. They wandered about in sheepskins and goatskins, being destitute, afflicted, tormented— 38of whom the world was not worthy. They wandered in deserts and mountains, *in* dens and caves of the earth.

39And all these, having obtained a good testimony through faith, did not receive the promise, 40God having provided something better for us, that they should not be made perfect apart from us.

12 Therefore* we also, since we are surrounded by so great a cloud of witnesses, let us lay aside every weight, and the sin which so easily ensnares *us,* and let us run with endurance the race that is set before us, 2looking unto Jesus, the author and finisher of *our* faith, who for the joy that was set before Him endured the cross, despising the shame, and has sat down at the right hand of the throne of God.

3For consider Him who endured such hostility from sinners against Himself, lest you become weary and discouraged in your souls. 4You have not yet resisted to bloodshed, striving against sin. 5*And you have forgotten the exhortation which speaks to you as to sons:

11:26 *d*NU-Text and M-Text read *of.* 11:37 *e*NU-Text omits *were tempted.*

❝You can judge the quality of their faith from the way they behave. Discipline is an index to doctrine.**❞**

—Tertullian

❝We cry too often to be delivered from the punishment, instead of the sin that lies behind it. We are anxious to escape from the things that cause us pain rather than from the things that cause God pain.**❞**

—G. Campbell Morgan

CHAPTER 12

12:1–4 *Runners.* The people listed in chapter 11 are the "cloud" that witnesses to us, "God can be trusted! Put your faith in His Word and keep running the race!" When you read the Old Testament, your faith should grow, for the account shows what God did in and through people who dared to trust His promises (Rom. 15:4). When you read the Gospels, you see the greatest example of endurance in Jesus Christ.

12:5–11 *Children.* "Chastening" refers to child training, helping the child prepare for adulthood. It does not necessarily mean punishment for disobedience, although that sometimes might be included. The successful runner must exercise discipline and submit to training. Never fear the chastening hand of the Lord; it is controlled by a loving heart. God's goal is your maturity.

"My son, do not despise the chastening of
the LORD,
Nor be discouraged when you are rebuked
by Him;
6 For whom the LORD loves He chastens,
And scourges every son whom He
receives."ᶠ

7Ifᵍ you endure chastening, God deals with you as with sons; for what son is there whom a father does not chasten? 8But if you are without chastening, of which all have become partakers, then you are illegitimate and not sons. 9Furthermore, we have had human fathers who corrected us, and we paid them respect. Shall we not much more readily be in subjection to the Father of spirits and live? 10For they indeed for a few days chastened us as seemed best to them, but He for our profit, that we may be partakers of His holiness. 11Now no chastening seems to be joyful for the present, but painful; nevertheless, afterward it yields the peaceable fruit of righteousness to those who have been trained by it.

12Therefore strengthen the hands which hang down, and the feeble knees, 13and make straight paths for your feet, so that what is lame may not be dislocated, but rather be healed.

14Pursue peace with all people, and holiness, without which no one will see the Lord: 15looking carefully lest anyone fall short of the grace of God; lest any root of bitterness springing up cause trouble, and by this many become defiled; 16lest there be any fornicator or profane person like Esau, who for one morsel of food sold his birthright. 17For you know that afterward, when he wanted to inherit the blessing, he was rejected, for he found no place for repentance, though he sought it diligently with tears.

18*For you have not come to the mountain thatʰ may be touched and that burned with fire, and to blackness and darknessⁱ and tempest, 19and the sound of a trumpet and the voice of words, so that those who heard it begged that the word should not be spoken to them anymore. 20(For they could not endure what was commanded: "And if so much as a beast touches the mountain, it shall be stonedʲ or shot with an arrow."ᵏ 21And so terrifying was the sight that Moses said, "I am exceedingly afraid and trembling."ˡ)

22But you have come to Mount Zion and to the city of the living God, the heavenly Jerusalem, to an innumerable company of angels, 23to the general assembly and church of the firstborn who are registered in heaven, to God the Judge of all, to the spirits of just men made perfect, 24to Jesus the Mediator of the new covenant, and to the blood of sprinkling that speaks better things than that of Abel.

25See that you do not refuse Him who speaks. For if they did not escape who refused Him who spoke on earth, much more shall we not escape if we turn away from Him who speaks from heaven, 26whose voice then shook the earth; but now He has promised, saying, "Yet once more I

12:18–29 Citizens. The people of Israel had a frightening experience of law at Sinai (Exod. 19), but our experience at Mount Zion is one of grace and glory. We are citizens of the heavenly city and will one day fellowship with patriarchs and angels—and God! But this does not mean we can ignore His solemn voice to us. If God is shaking things in your life, listen to His Word. You will discover the things that cannot be shaken, and you will run the race to the end.

12:6 ᶠProverbs 3:11, 12   12:7 ᵍNU-Text and M-Text read It is for discipline that you endure; God . . . .   12:18 ʰNU-Text reads to that which. ⁱNU-Text reads gloom.   12:20 ʲNU-Text and M-Text omit the rest of this verse. ᵏExodus 19:12, 13   12:21 ˡDeuteronomy 9:19

shake*m* not only the earth, but also heaven."*n*
27Now this, "Yet once more," indicates the removal of those things that are being shaken, as of things that are made, that the things which cannot be shaken may remain.

28Therefore, since we are receiving a kingdom which cannot be shaken, let us have grace, by which we may*o* serve God acceptably with reverence and godly fear. 29For our God is a consuming fire.

13 Let brotherly love continue. 2Do not forget to entertain strangers, for by so *doing* some have unwittingly entertained angels. 3Remember the prisoners as if chained with them—those who are mistreated—since you yourselves are in the body also.

4Marriage is honorable among all, and the bed undefiled; but fornicators and adulterers God will judge.

5Let your conduct be without covetousness; be content with such things as you have. For He Himself has said, "I will never leave you nor forsake you."*p* 6So we may boldly say:

"The LORD is my helper;
I will not fear.
What can man do to me?"*q*

7*Remember those who rule over you, who have spoken the word of God to you, whose faith follow, considering the outcome of their conduct. 8Jesus Christ is the same yesterday, today, and forever. 9Do not be carried about*r* with various and strange doctrines. For it is good that the heart be established by grace, not with foods which have not profited those who have been occupied with them.

10We have an altar from which those who serve the tabernacle have no right to eat. 11For the bodies of those animals, whose blood is brought into the sanctuary by the high priest for sin, are burned outside the camp. 12Therefore Jesus also, that He might sanctify the people with His own blood, suffered outside the gate. 13Therefore let us go forth to Him, outside the camp, bearing His reproach. 14For here we have no continuing city, but we seek the one to come. 15Therefore by Him let us continually offer the sacrifice of praise to God, that is, the fruit of our lips, giving thanks to His name. 16But do not forget to do good and to share, for with such sacrifices God is well pleased.

17*Obey those who rule over you, and be submissive, for they watch out for your souls, as those who must give account. Let them do so with joy and not with grief, for that would be unprofitable for you.

18*Pray for us; for we are confident that we have a good conscience, in all things desiring to live honorably. 19But I especially urge you to do this, that I may be restored to you the sooner.

20Now may the God of peace who brought up our Lord Jesus from the dead, that great Shepherd of the sheep, through the blood of the everlasting covenant, 21make you complete in every good

CHAPTER 13

13:7, 8 Lest we get the idea that we can run the race successfully alone, the writer closes his letter by reminding us to follow our spiritual leaders. If we do, we will love the brothers and sisters (v. 1), help strangers (v. 2) and prisoners (v. 3), live above lust (v. 4) and covetousness (vv. 5–6), and not be led astray by false doctrines (v. 9).

Remember them. This may refer to leaders now dead, but their ministry goes on. Remember what they taught you, how they lived, and what they lived for. Church leaders may come and go, but Jesus is the same; and they must fix our eyes on Him.

13:17 Obey them. If they are faithful to care for your soul and teach you the Word, you have the responsibility to obey. A spiritual leader is not a dictator who drives you from behind. He is a shepherd who goes before and leads the way.

13:18, 19 Pray for them. When you come to the throne of grace, ask God to make His shepherds faithful and fruitful. Pray that the Great Shepherd will use them to "make you complete in every good work" (vv. 20–21).

12:26 *m*NU-Text reads will shake. *n*Haggai 2:6   12:28 *o*M-Text omits may.   13:5 *p*Deuteronomy 31:6, 8; Joshua 1:5   13:6 *q*Psalm 118:6   13:9 *r*NU-Text and M-Text read away.

work to do His will, working in you[s] what is well pleasing in His sight, through Jesus Christ, to whom *be* glory forever and ever. Amen.

22And I appeal to you, brethren, bear with the word of exhortation, for I have written to you in few words. 23Know that *our* brother Timothy has been set free, with whom I shall see you if he comes shortly.

24*Greet all those who rule over you, and all the saints. Those from Italy greet you.

25Grace *be* with you all. Amen.

13:24 *Greet them.* You should know your leaders personally and be on good terms with them. Let nothing come between you that could create problems in the fellowship (12:14—15).

13:21 [s]NU-Text and M-Text read *us.*

JAMES

The man who wrote this letter was the half brother of our Lord (Mark 6:3) and the leader of the church in Jerusalem (Acts 1:14; 12:17; 1 Cor. 15:7). He was a devout Jew and wrote to Jewish believers scattered throughout the Roman world. They were troubled by trials and testings as well as by problems in their assemblies; and James wrote to help them mature in their faith (1:4; 2:22; 3:2).

The epistle of James is a practical book that discusses living the faith. It contains echoes of the Sermon on the Mount and the book of Proverbs, both of which are practical.

If we truly practice our faith, it will be seen in how we face trials (chap. 1), in the way we treat people (chap. 2), in what we say (chap. 3), in how we deal with sin in our lives (chap. 4), and in our prayer life (chap. 5).

1 James, a bondservant of God and of the Lord Jesus Christ,

To the twelve tribes which are scattered abroad:

Greetings.

2*My brethren, count it all joy when you fall into various trials, 3knowing that the testing of your faith produces patience. 4But let patience have *its* perfect work, that you may be perfect and complete, lacking nothing. 5If any of you lacks wisdom, let him ask of God, who gives to all liberally and without reproach, and it will be given to him. 6But let him ask in faith, with no doubting, for he who doubts is like a wave of the sea driven and tossed by the wind. 7For let not that man suppose that he will receive anything from the Lord; 8*he is* a double-minded man, unstable in all his ways.

9Let the lowly brother glory in his exaltation, 10but the rich in his humiliation, because as a flower of the field he will pass away. 11For no sooner has the sun risen with a burning heat than it withers the grass; its flower falls, and its beautiful appearance perishes. So the rich man also will fade away in his pursuits.

12*Blessed *is* the man who endures temptation; for when he has been approved, he will receive the crown of life which the Lord has promised to those who love Him. 13Let no one say when he is tempted, "I am tempted by God"; for God cannot be tempted by evil, nor does He Himself tempt anyone. 14But each one is tempted when he is drawn away by his own desires and enticed. 15Then, when desire has conceived, it gives birth to sin; and sin, when it is full-grown, brings forth death.

16Do not be deceived, my beloved brethren. 17Every good gift and every perfect gift is from above, and comes down from the Father of lights, with whom there is no variation or shadow of turning. 18Of His own will He brought us forth by the word of truth, that we might be a kind of firstfruits of His creatures.

CHAPTER 1

1:2–8 Note some essentials for mature living.

The wisdom of God. You need wisdom in trials so you will not waste your suffering and miss the spiritual growth that should result. When you trust God, trials work for you and not against you; but be sure your heart is wholly yielded to Him. If your heart and mind are divided, trials will tear you apart.

1:12–18 **The goodness of God.** When you realize how good God is to you, you will have no interest in the temptations the enemy puts before you. When you are tempted, count your blessings; and you will soon have strength to say no.

> **"**He is already half false who speculates on truth and does not do it. Truth is given, not to be contemplated, but to be done.**"**
> —F. W. Robertson

Word Pictures—In his letter, James relies on many illustrations from nature. In chapter 1, he compares doubt to the waves of the sea (v. 6), riches to fading flowers (vv. 9–10), and sin to pregnancy (vv. 13–15; Ps. 7:14), weeds (v. 21), and dirt (v. 27). As you continue to read, notice how James uses pictures to make truth vivid and memorable.

1:21–25 The Word of God. The Word gives us spiritual birth (v. 18; 1 Pet. 1:22–23). It is like seed planted in the heart that produces spiritual fruit (v. 21). It is a mirror that helps us examine ourselves (vv. 23–25) and cleanse our lives. We must *do* the Word of God, not just read it or study it; the blessing is in the *doing*.

CHAPTER 2

2:1–13 If you have true saving faith, you will practice *impartiality* and see people in terms of character and not clothing. You will not cater to the rich or ignore the poor, but you will love each person for the sake of Jesus Christ. Christian love simply means treating others the way the Lord treats you and doing it in the power of the Spirit.

2:14–26 True saving faith is also seen in *activity*. Faith is not something you only talk about; it is something that motivates your life so that you think of others and serve them. Abraham was saved by faith (Gen. 15:6), but he proved that faith by obeying God and offering his son (Gen. 22). Rahab was saved by trusting God (Heb. 11:31), but she showed the reality of her faith by protecting the spies (Josh. 2; 6:17–27). James and Paul do not contradict each other (Rom. 4:1–5; 5:1); they complement each other. We are justified (declared righteous) before God by faith, but we are justified before men by works. God can see our faith, but men can see only our works.

19So then,[a] my beloved brethren, let every man be swift to hear, slow to speak, slow to wrath; 20for the wrath of man does not produce the righteousness of God.

21*Therefore lay aside all filthiness and overflow of wickedness, and receive with meekness the implanted word, which is able to save your souls.

22But be doers of the word, and not hearers only, deceiving yourselves. 23For if anyone is a hearer of the word and not a doer, he is like a man observing his natural face in a mirror; 24for he observes himself, goes away, and immediately forgets what kind of man he was. 25But he who looks into the perfect law of liberty and continues *in it*, and is not a forgetful hearer but a doer of the work, this one will be blessed in what he does.

26If anyone among you[b] thinks he is religious, and does not bridle his tongue but deceives his own heart, this one's religion *is* useless. 27Pure and undefiled religion before God and the Father is this: to visit orphans and widows in their trouble, *and* to keep oneself unspotted from the world.

2 My* brethren, do not hold the faith of our Lord Jesus Christ, *the Lord* of glory, with partiality. 2For if there should come into your assembly a man with gold rings, in fine apparel, and there should also come in a poor man in filthy clothes, 3and you pay attention to the one wearing the fine clothes and say to him, "You sit here in a good place," and say to the poor man, "You stand there," or, "Sit here at my footstool," 4have you not shown partiality among yourselves, and become judges with evil thoughts?

5Listen, my beloved brethren: Has God not chosen the poor of this world *to be* rich in faith and heirs of the kingdom which He promised to those who love Him? 6But you have dishonored the poor man. Do not the rich oppress you and drag you into the courts? 7Do they not blaspheme that noble name by which you are called?

8If you really fulfill *the* royal law according to the Scripture, *"You shall love your neighbor as yourself,"*[c] you do well; 9but if you show partiality, you commit sin, and are convicted by the law as transgressors. 10For whoever shall keep the whole law, and yet stumble in one *point*, he is guilty of all. 11For He who said, *"Do not commit adultery,"*[d] also said, *"Do not murder."*[e] Now if you do not commit adultery, but you do murder, you have become a transgressor of the law. 12So speak and so do as those who will be judged by the law of liberty. 13For judgment is without mercy to the one who has shown no mercy. Mercy triumphs over judgment.

14*What *does it* profit, my brethren, if someone says he has faith but does not have works? Can faith save him? 15If a brother or sister is naked and destitute of daily food, 16and one of you says to them, "Depart in peace, be warmed and filled," but you do not give them the things which are needed for the body, what *does it* profit? 17Thus also faith by itself, if it does not have works, is dead.

18But someone will say, "You have faith, and I

1:19 [a]NU-Text reads *Know this* or *This you know.*   1:26 [b]NU-Text omits *among you.*   2:8 [c]Leviticus 19:18   2:11 [d]Exodus 20:14; Deuteronomy 5:18 [e]Exodus 20:13; Deuteronomy 5:17

have works." Show me your faith without your[f] works, and I will show you my faith by my[g] works. 19You believe that there is one God. You do well. Even the demons believe—and tremble! 20But do you want to know, O foolish man, that faith without works is dead?[h] 21Was not Abraham our father justified by works when he offered Isaac his son on the altar? 22Do you see that faith was working together with his works, and by works faith was made perfect? 23And the Scripture was fulfilled which says, *"Abraham believed God, and it was accounted to him for righteousness."[i]* And he was called the friend of God. 24You see then that a man is justified by works, and not by faith only.

25Likewise, was not Rahab the harlot also justified by works when she received the messengers and sent *them* out another way? 26For as the body without the spirit is dead, so faith without works is dead also.

3 My* brethren, let not many of you become teachers, knowing that we shall receive a stricter judgment. 2For we all stumble in many things. If anyone does not stumble in word, he *is* a perfect man, able also to bridle the whole body. 3Indeed,[j] we put bits in horses' mouths that they may obey us, and we turn their whole body. 4Look also at ships: although they are so large and are driven by fierce winds, they are turned by a very small rudder wherever the pilot desires. 5*Even so the tongue is a little member and boasts great things.

See how great a forest a little fire kindles! 6And the tongue *is* a fire, a world of iniquity. The tongue is so set among our members that it defiles the whole body, and sets on fire the course of nature; and it is set on fire by hell. 7For every kind of beast and bird, of reptile and creature of the sea, is tamed and has been tamed by mankind. 8But no man can tame the tongue. *It is* an unruly evil, full of deadly poison. 9With it we bless our God and Father, and with it we curse men, who have been made in the similitude of God. 10Out of the same mouth proceed blessing and cursing. My brethren, these things ought not to be so. 11Does a spring send forth fresh *water* and bitter from the same opening? 12Can a fig tree, my brethren, bear olives, or a grapevine bear figs? Thus no spring yields both salt water and fresh.[k]

13*Who *is* wise and understanding among you? Let him show by good conduct *that* his works *are done* in the meekness of wisdom. 14But if you have bitter envy and self-seeking in your hearts, do not boast and lie against the truth. 15This wisdom does not descend from above, but *is* earthly, sensual, demonic. 16For where envy and self-seeking *exist,* confusion and every evil thing *are* there. 17But the wisdom that is from above is first pure, then peaceable, gentle, willing to yield, full of mercy and good fruits, without partiality and without hypocrisy. 18Now the fruit of righteousness is sown in peace by those who make peace.

4 Where* do wars and fights *come* from among you? Do *they* not *come* from your desires for

---

2:18 [f]NU-Text omits *your.* [g]NU-Text omits *my.* 2:20 [h]NU-Text reads *useless.* 2:23 [i]Genesis 15:6 3:3 [j]NU-Text reads *Now if.* 3:12 [k]NU-Text reads *Neither can a salty spring produce fresh water.*

❝*Of your unspoken words, you are the master; of your spoken words, the servant; of your written words, the slave.*❞

—Quaker Proverb

CHAPTER 3

3:1–4 The believers James wrote to were having problems with their tongues (1:26; 2:12; 4:1, 11–12). Of course, the tongue is not the problem; it is the *heart* (v. 14; Matt. 12:35–37). But before you say anything, ask yourself some questions.

Who is in control? If your tongue is under God's control, you will take what you say seriously (v. 1), and your whole body will be under His discipline (v. 2). Just as a horse needs a rider holding the reins, and a ship needs a pilot at the rudder, so your tongue needs a master; and God is the only one who can do the job. Psalm 141:1–4 is a good prayer if you need help in this area.

3:5–12 What will the consequences be? Are you starting a fire that may get out of control and do a lot of damage? Are you turning loose a dangerous beast or poisoning a refreshing spring? Once your words are spoken, you cannot take them back, so look ahead.

3:13–18 What are my motives? Is there bitterness in your heart or envy? Are you speaking from God's wisdom or the wisdom of the world? Are you a peacemaker or a troublemaker? If your heart is right before God (Heb. 4:12), He will use your words to produce the right kind of fruit.

CHAPTER 4

4:1–3 Of the early church, it was said, "Behold how they love one another!" Today, people might say, "Behold how they compete with one another!" Why is it sometimes so difficult for God's people to get along?

Selfishness. The wars among us are caused by the wars within us. We want to please ourselves, even if it hurts somebody else. If we are not careful, even our prayers can become selfish!

4:4, 5 *Worldliness.* Because Abraham was separated from sin, he was the friend of God (2:23); but Lot was the friend of the world (Gen. 13:1–13). Ponder 1 John 2:15–17.

4:6–10 *Pride.* Satan knows how to use pride to defeat you as he defeated Eve (Gen. 3:1–6). Are you laughing when you should be weeping over your sins? Are you resisting the devil or resisting the Lord?

❝*A whole new generation of Christians has come up believing that it is possible to 'accept' Christ without forsaking the world.*❞
—A. W. Tozer

❝*It is right for the church to be in the world; it is wrong for the world to be in the church. A boat in water is good; that is what boats are for. However, water inside the boat causes it to sink.*❞
—Harold Lindsell

4:11, 12 *Criticism.* One of the easiest ways to hide our sins is to expose the sins of others. Gossip and slander grieve the Spirit and divide the family. God called us to be witnesses, not judges!

4:13–17 *Boasting.* Life is short and the future unknown, so do the will of God today. When you make plans, always say, "If the Lord wills" (Prov. 27:1).

CHAPTER 5

5:1–6 In these last days, before the coming of the Lord, what does God want in our lives?
Priorities. To live only to get wealth is to rob yourself of true riches (1 Tim. 6:6–10, 17–19). It is to worry instead of worship (Matt. 6:19–34). God knows you have needs, and He will meet them if you practice Matthew 6:33.

5:7–12 *Patience.* If you have sown the right seed, you will eventually reap a harvest of blessing, so be patient. If others have exploited you, be patient; the Judge is at the door. If you are going through trials, be patient; God is still on the throne.

pleasure that war in your members? 2You lust and do not have. You murder and covet and cannot obtain. You fight and war. Yet[l] you do not have because you do not ask. 3You ask and do not receive, because you ask amiss, that you may spend *it* on your pleasures. 4*Adulterers and[m] adulteresses! Do you not know that friendship with the world is enmity with God? Whoever therefore wants to be a friend of the world makes himself an enemy of God. 5Or do you think that the Scripture says in vain, "The Spirit who dwells in us yearns jealously"? 6*But He gives more grace. Therefore He says:

"God resists the proud,
But gives grace to the humble."[n]

7Therefore submit to God. Resist the devil and he will flee from you. 8Draw near to God and He will draw near to you. Cleanse *your* hands, *you* sinners; and purify *your* hearts, *you* doubleminded. 9Lament and mourn and weep! Let your laughter be turned to mourning and *your* joy to gloom. 10Humble yourselves in the sight of the Lord, and He will lift you up.
11*Do not speak evil of one another, brethren. He who speaks evil of a brother and judges his brother, speaks evil of the law and judges the law. But if you judge the law, you are not a doer of the law but a judge. 12There is one Lawgiver,[o] who is able to save and to destroy. Who[p] are you to judge another?[q]
13*Come now, you who say, "Today or tomorrow we will[r] go to such and such a city, spend a year there, buy and sell, and make a profit"; 14whereas you do not know what *will happen* tomorrow. For what *is* your life? It is even a vapor that appears for a little time and then vanishes away. 15Instead you *ought* to say, "If the Lord wills, we shall live and do this or that." 16But now you boast in your arrogance. All such boasting is evil.
17Therefore, to him who knows to do good and does not do *it*, to him it is sin.

5 Come* now, *you* rich, weep and howl for your miseries that are coming upon *you!* 2Your riches are corrupted, and your garments are moth-eaten. 3Your gold and silver are corroded, and their corrosion will be a witness against you and will eat your flesh like fire. You have heaped up treasure in the last days. 4Indeed the wages of the laborers who mowed your fields, which you kept back by fraud, cry out; and the cries of the reapers have reached the ears of the Lord of Sabaoth.[s] 5You have lived on the earth in pleasure and luxury; you have fattened your hearts as[t] in a day of slaughter. 6You have condemned, you have murdered the just; he does not resist you.

7*Therefore be patient, brethren, until the coming of the Lord. See *how* the farmer waits for the precious fruit of the earth, waiting patiently for it until it receives the early and latter rain.

4:2 [l]NU-Text and M-Text omit *Yet.*   4:4 [m]NU-Text omits *Adulterers and.*   4:6 [n]Proverbs 3:34   4:12 [o]NU-Text adds *and Judge.* [p]NU-Text and M-Text read *But who.* [q]NU-Text reads *a neighbor.*   4:13 [r]M-Text reads *let us.*   5:4 [s]Literally, in Hebrew, *Hosts*   5:5 [t]NU-Text omits *as.*

⁸You also be patient. Establish your hearts, for the coming of the Lord is at hand.

⁹Do not grumble against one another, brethren, lest you be condemned.ᵘ Behold, the Judge is standing at the door! ¹⁰My brethren, take the prophets, who spoke in the name of the Lord, as an example of suffering and patience. ¹¹Indeed we count them blessed who endure. You have heard of the perseverance of Job and seen the end *intended by* the Lord—that the Lord is very compassionate and merciful.

¹²But above all, my brethren, do not swear, either by heaven or by earth or with any other oath. But let your "Yes" be "Yes," and *your* "No," "No," lest you fall into judgment.ᵛ

¹³*Is anyone among you suffering? Let him pray. Is anyone cheerful? Let him sing psalms. ¹⁴Is anyone among you sick? Let him call for the elders of the church, and let them pray over him, anointing him with oil in the name of the Lord. ¹⁵And the prayer of faith will save the sick, and the Lord will raise him up. And if he has committed sins, he will be forgiven. ¹⁶Confess *your* trespassesʷ to one another, and pray for one another, that you may be healed. The effective, fervent prayer of a righteous man avails much. ¹⁷Elijah was a man with a nature like ours, and he prayed earnestly that it would not rain; and it did not rain on the land for three years and six months. ¹⁸And he prayed again, and the heaven gave rain, and the earth produced its fruit.

¹⁹*Brethren, if anyone among you wanders from the truth, and someone turns him back, ²⁰let him know that he who turns a sinner from the error of his way will save a soulˣ from death and cover a multitude of sins.

5:9 ᵘNU-Text and M-Text read *judged.*   5:12 ᵛM-Text reads *hypocrisy.*   5:16 ʷNU-Text reads *Therefore confess your sins.*   5:20 ˣNU-Text reads *his soul.*

5:13–18 *Prayer.* Many kinds of prayer are named here: prayer for the sick, prayer for forgiveness, prayer for the nation, even prayer about the weather. There is no need that prayer cannot meet and no problem that prayer cannot solve.

5:19, 20 *Personal concern.* Once again, James emphasizes ministry to individuals (1:27; 2:1–4, 14–16). Can you detect when a fellow believer starts to stray? Are you truly concerned? Will you try to help? Will you wait too long?

1 PETER

The apostle Peter was chosen to be the first to take the gospel to the Gentiles (Acts 10; 15:7), but his ministry was primarily to the Jews (Gal. 2:1–10). He wrote these two letters to believers scattered in five areas of the Roman Empire, two of which Paul had not been allowed to enter (Acts 16:7). In writing these letters, Peter fulfilled the commission given him in Luke 22:32 and John 21:15–17.

The theme of the first letter is *the grace of God* (5:12), and Peter tells us how to live as aliens in a hostile world. The theme of the second letter is *spiritual knowledge* (he uses *knowledge* seven times in the letter), and he warns us about false teachers.

Peter opens his first epistle by reminding his readers of what God's grace has done for them in saving them (1:1—2:10). He then points out that God's grace helps them in various relationships of life (2:11—3:12) and in the coming time of persecution (3:13—5:14). Peter sums up the themes of both letters in his benediction in 2 Peter 3:18: "But grow in the grace [1 Pet.] and knowledge [2 Pet.] of our Lord and Savior Jesus Christ." That is the only way to succeed in these last days.

CHAPTER 1

1:1, 2, 15 *Salvation is a calling.* We are chosen by the Father, who gives us the new birth (v. 3). We are set apart by the Spirit, who gave the Word and enables God's servants to declare it (vv. 10–12), and gives sinners the faith to believe the promise (v. 22). We have been purchased by the blood of God's Son (vv. 18–21), who died for us, rose again, and is coming for us to give us our inheritance (vv. 3–4, 13). No wonder Peter opened his letter with a song of praise! (See Eph. 1:3–14.)

1:3, 23 *Salvation is a birth.* This is the spiritual birth Jesus tried to explain to Nicodemus (John 3). When you put your *faith* in Jesus Christ (vv. 5, 7, 9, 21), you are born from above. You receive *hope* (vv. 3–4, 13, 21) and *love* for Christ (v. 8) and His people (v. 22). Because we are God's children, we want to obey Him (vv. 14–16).

1 Peter,* an apostle of Jesus Christ,
To the pilgrims of the Dispersion in Pontus, Galatia, Cappadocia, Asia, and Bithynia, ²elect according to the foreknowledge of God the Father, in sanctification of the Spirit, for obedience and sprinkling of the blood of Jesus Christ:

Grace to you and peace be multiplied.

³*Blessed *be* the God and Father of our Lord Jesus Christ, who according to His abundant mercy has begotten us again to a living hope through the resurrection of Jesus Christ from the dead, ⁴to an inheritance incorruptible and undefiled and that does not fade away, reserved in heaven for you, ⁵who are kept by the power of God through faith for salvation ready to be revealed in the last time.

⁶In this you greatly rejoice, though now for a little while, if need be, you have been grieved by various trials, ⁷that the genuineness of your faith, *being* much more precious than gold that perishes, though it is tested by fire, may be found to praise, honor, and glory at the revelation of Jesus Christ, ⁸whom having not seen*ᵃ* you love. Though now you do not see *Him,* yet believing, you rejoice with joy inexpressible and full of glory, ⁹receiving the end of your faith—the salvation of *your* souls.

¹⁰Of this salvation the prophets have inquired and searched carefully, who prophesied of the grace *that would come* to you, ¹¹searching what, or what manner of time, the Spirit of Christ who was in them was indicating when He testified beforehand the sufferings of Christ and the glories that would follow. ¹²To them it was revealed that, not to themselves, but to us*ᵇ* they were ministering the things which now have been reported to

---

1:8 *ᵃ*M-Text reads *known.*　1:12 *ᵇ*NU-Text and M-Text read *you.*

Living Hope—Men's hopes are dead hopes. Like cut flowers, they bloom awhile and then fade and die (1 Pet. 1:24–25). The Christian's hope is fresh and fruitful because it is a "living hope" (v. 3), purchased by the living Christ (v. 3) and promised in the living Word (v. 23).

you through those who have preached the gospel to you by the Holy Spirit sent from heaven— things which angels desire to look into.

13Therefore gird up the loins of your mind, be sober, and rest *your* hope fully upon the grace that is to be brought to you at the revelation of Jesus Christ; 14as obedient children, not conforming yourselves to the former lusts, *as* in your ignorance; 15but as He who called you *is* holy, you also be holy in all *your* conduct, 16because it is written, *"Be holy, for I am holy."*c

17*And if you call on the Father, who without partiality judges according to each one's work, conduct yourselves throughout the time of your stay *here* in fear; 18knowing that you were not redeemed with corruptible things, *like* silver or gold, from your aimless conduct *received* by tradition from your fathers, 19but with the precious blood of Christ, as of a lamb without blemish and without spot. 20He indeed was foreordained before the foundation of the world, but was manifest in these last times for you 21who through Him believe in God, who raised Him from the dead and gave Him glory, so that your faith and hope are in God.

22Since you have purified your souls in obeying the truth through the Spiritd in sincere love of the brethren, love one another fervently with a pure heart, 23having been born again, not of corruptible seed but incorruptible, through the word of God which lives and abides forever,e 24because

> *"All flesh is as grass,*
> *And all the glory of man*f *as the flower of*
>   *the grass.*
> *The grass withers,*
> *And its flower falls away,*
> 25 *But the word of the Lord endures forever."*g

Now this is the word which by the gospel was preached to you.

2 Therefore,* laying aside all malice, all deceit, hypocrisy, envy, and all evil speaking, 2as newborn babes, desire the pure milk of the word, that you may grow thereby,h 3if indeed you have tasted that the Lord *is* gracious.

4*Coming to Him *as to* a living stone, rejected indeed by men, but chosen by God *and* precious, 5you also, as living stones, are being built up a spiritual house, a holy priesthood, to offer up spiritual sacrifices acceptable to God through Jesus Christ. 6Therefore it is also contained in the Scripture,

> *"Behold, I lay in Zion*
> *A chief cornerstone, elect, precious,*
> *And he who believes on Him will by no*
>   *means be put to shame."*i

7Therefore, to you who believe, *He is* precious; but to those who are disobedient,j

> *"The stone which the builders rejected*
> *Has become the chief cornerstone,"*k

1:17–21 *Salvation is a redemption.* The apostle is referring to the Passover Feast (Exod. 12). Jesus is the Lamb slain for us, and His blood was sprinkled to shelter us (v. 2). The Jews in Egypt had to be ready to depart, and we must have the same attitude (v. 13). When Jesus comes again, we will make our exodus from this world!

And all of this was "for you" (vv. 4, 10, 12, 13, 20, 25). Are you praising Him?

CHAPTER 2

2:1–3 *Growing.* Just as a baby has an appetite for the mother's milk, so the child of God has an appetite for the Father's Word. If you lose that appetite and stop growing, check to see if any of the sins listed in verse 1 are infecting your life.

2:4–8 *Building.* God is building a temple out of living stones (Eph. 2:19–22), and we are privileged to be part of it. We are built on Jesus Christ, so there is no way the temple can be destroyed.

1:16 cLeviticus 11:44, 45; 19:2; 20:7   1:22 dNU-Text omits *through the Spirit.*   1:23 eNU-Text omits *forever.*
1:24 fNU-Text reads *all its glory.*   1:25 gIsaiah 40:6–8
2:2 hNU-Text adds *up to salvation.*   2:6 iIsaiah 28:16
2:7 jNU-Text reads *to those who disbelieve.* kPsalm 118:22

[8]and

*"A stone of stumbling
And a rock of offense."[l]*

They stumble, being disobedient to the word, to which they also were appointed.

[9]*But you *are* a chosen generation, a royal priesthood, a holy nation, His own special people, that you may proclaim the praises of Him who called you out of darkness into His marvelous light; [10]who once *were* not a people but *are* now the people of God, who had not obtained mercy but now have obtained mercy.

[11]*Beloved, I beg *you* as sojourners and pilgrims, abstain from fleshly lusts which war against the soul, [12]having your conduct honorable among the Gentiles, that when they speak against you as evildoers, they may, by *your* good works which they observe, glorify God in the day of visitation.

[13]*Therefore submit yourselves to every ordinance of man for the Lord's sake, whether to the king as supreme, [14]or to governors, as to those who are sent by him for the punishment of evildoers and *for the* praise of those who do good. [15]For this is the will of God, that by doing good you may put to silence the ignorance of foolish men— [16]as free, yet not using liberty as a cloak for vice, but as bondservants of God. [17]Honor all *people.* Love the brotherhood. Fear God. Honor the king.

[18]Servants, *be* submissive to *your* masters with all fear, not only to the good and gentle, but also to the harsh. [19]For this *is* commendable, if because of conscience toward God one endures grief, suffering wrongfully. [20]For what credit *is it* if, when you are beaten for your faults, you take it patiently? But when you do good and suffer, if you take it patiently, this *is* commendable before God. [21]For to this you were called, because Christ also suffered for us,[m] leaving us[n] an example, that you should follow His steps:

[22] *"Who committed no sin,
Nor was deceit found in His mouth";[o]*

[23]who, when He was reviled, did not revile in return; when He suffered, He did not threaten, but committed *Himself* to Him who judges righteously; [24]who Himself bore our sins in His own body on the tree, that we, having died to sins, might live for righteousness—by whose stripes you were healed. [25]For you were like sheep going astray, but have now returned to the Shepherd and Overseer[p] of your souls.

3 Wives,* likewise, *be* submissive to your own husbands, that even if some do not obey the word, they, without a word, may be won by the conduct of their wives, [2]when they observe your chaste conduct *accompanied* by fear. [3]Do not let

---

2:9, 10 Sacrificing. Each believer is a priest before God and can bring sacrifices to the Lord through Jesus Christ. As we worship the Lord, we proclaim His virtues to a lost world. That is what God called Israel to do (Exod. 19:1–9), and they failed. Are we also failing?

2:11, 12 Abstaining. As strangers whose citizenship is in heaven, we are carefully watched by the world; and we must live to glorify God. It may be difficult today, but it will be worth it when Jesus returns.

2:13–25 Submitting. Peter's counsel is that Christians be good citizens and employees so that God will be glorified. (See Jeremiah's advice to the captives [Jer. 29].) The example for us to follow is Jesus Christ who submitted even to death.

CHAPTER 3

3:1–7 Peter compared believers to sheep (2:25), and sheep are gentle animals. He then called for Christians to practice gentleness in several areas of life.
In the home. Christian wives with unsaved husbands should seek to win them to the Lord with true spiritual beauty and not with artificial glamour or nagging. External glamour may fade, but a meek and quiet spirit is incorruptible. Husbands should live as though their wives were priceless porcelain vases and treat them with gentle love.

❝*Nothing is so strong as gentleness, and nothing so gentle as real strength.*❞
—Francis de Sales

2:8 [l]Isaiah 8:14   2:21 [m]NU-Text reads *you.* [n]NU-Text and M-Text read *you.*   2:22 [o]Isaiah 53:9   2:25 [p]Greek *Episkopos*

A Godly Life—The Christians who received Peter's letter were being slandered by others (2:12, 15, 23; 3:9, 16; 4:4, 14). Peter told them that the best weapon against slander was a godly life that nobody could criticize. H. A. Ironside said, "If what they say about you is true, mend your ways. If it isn't true, forget it, and go on and serve the Lord."

your adornment be *merely* outward—arranging the hair, wearing gold, or putting on *fine* apparel— [4]rather *let it be* the hidden person of the heart, with the incorruptible *beauty* of a gentle and quiet spirit, which is very precious in the sight of God. [5]For in this manner, in former times, the holy women who trusted in God also adorned themselves, being submissive to their own husbands, [6]as Sarah obeyed Abraham, calling him lord, whose daughters you are if you do good and are not afraid with any terror.

[7]Husbands, likewise, dwell with *them* with understanding, giving honor to the wife, as to the weaker vessel, and as *being* heirs together of the grace of life, that your prayers may not be hindered.

[8]*Finally, all *of you* be of one mind, having compassion for one another; love as brothers, *be* tenderhearted, *be* courteous;[q] [9]not returning evil for evil or reviling for reviling, but on the contrary blessing, knowing that you were called to this, that you may inherit a blessing. [10]For

"He who would love life
And see good days,
Let him refrain his tongue from evil,
And his lips from speaking deceit.
[11] Let him turn away from evil and do good;
Let him seek peace and pursue it.
[12] For the eyes of the LORD are on the righteous,
And His ears are open to their prayers;
But the face of the LORD is against those who do evil."[r]

[13]*And who *is* he who will harm you if you become followers of what is good? [14]But even if you should suffer for righteousness' sake, *you are* blessed. *"And do not be afraid of their threats, nor be troubled."*[s] [15]But sanctify the Lord God[t] in your hearts, and always *be* ready to *give* a defense to everyone who asks you a reason for the hope that is in you, with meekness and fear; [16]having a good conscience, that when they defame you as evildoers, those who revile your good conduct in Christ may be ashamed. [17]For *it is* better, if it is the will of God, to suffer for doing good than for doing evil.

[18]For Christ also suffered once for sins, the just for the unjust, that He might bring us[u] to God, being put to death in the flesh but made alive by the Spirit, [19]by whom also He went and preached to the spirits in prison, [20]who formerly were disobedient, when once the Divine longsuffering waited[v] in the days of Noah, while *the* ark was being prepared, in which a few, that is, eight souls, were saved through water. [21]There is also an antitype which now saves us—baptism (not the removal of the filth of the flesh, but the answer of a good conscience toward God), through the resurrection of Jesus Christ, [22]who has gone into heaven and is at the right hand of God, angels and authorities and powers having been made subject to Him.

3:8–12 *In the church.* Imagine having to remind Christians to show one another love and courtesy! But as James 4 shows, not every local assembly is a place of peace.

3:13–18 *In the world.* Anybody can suffer for doing wrong, but Christians must learn to suffer for doing what is right. Of course, Jesus is the example for us to follow (v. 18; 2:18–25). We witness not by making noise and fighting back but by showing meekness and fear (v. 15). A gentle witness can make a big difference in a violent world.

3:8 [q]NU-Text reads *humble.*   3:12 [r]Psalm 34:12–16
3:14 [s]Isaiah 8:12   3:15 [t]NU-Text reads *Christ as Lord.*
3:18 [u]NU-Text and M-Text read *you.*   3:20 [v]NU-Text and M-Text read *when the longsuffering of God waited patiently.*

4:1–6 *Do not be controlled by the past.* People who have been born again through faith in Christ (1:23) should not allow the old life to control them. The past has been buried, and they are new creatures in Christ. Furthermore, life is too short to waste it on godless living, especially when you realize that one day we will all stand before God.

4:7–11 *Be serious about the present.* No matter how difficult life may be, there is a job to do; and we must be faithful. Take time to pray. Show love to the saints. Use your gifts and talents to serve others. The Lord who gave you the ability will also give you the strength to use it for His glory.

4:12–19 *Be prepared for the future.* A "fiery trial" was about to come to the church. Peter told his readers to expect it, use it as an opportunity to witness for Christ, and in all things seek to glorify God. The trial came under the Roman emperor Nero who accused the Christians of burning Rome. The church today faces persecution. Are you prepared?

CHAPTER 5

5:1–4 Even apart from the end-times suffering that the church will experience, believers must face their three great enemies.
The world. Christian leaders are tempted to act like the world and "lord it over" God's people (Matt. 20:20–28). But leaders are shepherds, and sheep must be *led*, not *driven.* Our service must be willing and humble; we must be eager to help others.

4 Therefore,* since Christ suffered for us[w] in the flesh, arm yourselves also with the same mind, for he who has suffered in the flesh has ceased from sin, 2that he no longer should live the rest of *his* time in the flesh for the lusts of men, but for the will of God. 3For we *have spent* enough of our past lifetime[x] in doing the will of the Gentiles—when we walked in lewdness, lusts, drunkenness, revelries, drinking parties, and abominable idolatries. 4In regard to these, they think it strange that you do not run with *them* in the same flood of dissipation, speaking evil of *you.* 5They will give an account to Him who is ready to judge the living and the dead. 6For this reason the gospel was preached also to those who are dead, that they might be judged according to men in the flesh, but live according to God in the spirit.

7*But the end of all things is at hand; therefore be serious and watchful in your prayers. 8And above all things have fervent love for one another, for *"love will cover a multitude of sins."*[y] 9Be hospitable to one another without grumbling. 10As each one has received a gift, minister it to one another, as good stewards of the manifold grace of God. 11If anyone speaks, *let him speak* as the oracles of God. If anyone ministers, *let him do it* as with the ability which God supplies, that in all things God may be glorified through Jesus Christ, to whom belong the glory and the dominion forever and ever. Amen.

12*Beloved, do not think it strange concerning the fiery trial which is to try you, as though some strange thing happened to you; 13but rejoice to the extent that you partake of Christ's sufferings, that when His glory is revealed, you may also be glad with exceeding joy. 14If you are reproached for the name of Christ, blessed *are you,* for the Spirit of glory and of God rests upon you.[z] On their part He is blasphemed, but on your part He is glorified. 15But let none of you suffer as a murderer, a thief, an evildoer, or as a busybody in other people's matters. 16Yet if *anyone suffers* as a Christian, let him not be ashamed, but let him glorify God in this matter.[a]

17For the time *has come* for judgment to begin at the house of God; and if *it begins* with us first, what will *be* the end of those who do not obey the gospel of God? 18Now

"If the righteous one is scarcely saved,
Where will the ungodly and the sinner appear?"[b]

19Therefore let those who suffer according to the will of God commit their souls *to Him* in doing good, as to a faithful Creator.

5 The* elders who are among you I exhort, I who am a fellow elder and a witness of the sufferings of Christ, and also a partaker of the glory that will be revealed: 2Shepherd the flock

4:1 [w]NU-Text omits *for us.* 4:3 [x]NU-Text reads *time.* 4:8 [y]Proverbs 10:12 4:14 [z]NU-Text omits the rest of this verse. 4:16 [a]NU-Text reads *name.* 4:18 [b]Proverbs 11:31

Persecution—Peter said that judgment begins at the house (church) of God (1 Pet. 4:17). The first purpose of persecution is to purify the church so that it will be able to witness to the lost. But it is also a warning to the lost. If God judges His own children for their sins, how much more will He judge lost sinners! (See Prov. 11:31; Ezek. 9.)

of God which is among you, serving as overseers, not by compulsion but willingly,[c] not for dishonest gain but eagerly; ³nor as being lords over those entrusted to you, but being examples to the flock; ⁴and when the Chief Shepherd appears, you will receive the crown of glory that does not fade away.

⁵*Likewise you younger people, submit yourselves to *your* elders. Yes, all of *you* be submissive to one another, and be clothed with humility, for

> "God resists the proud,
> But gives grace to the humble."[d]

⁶Therefore humble yourselves under the mighty hand of God, that He may exalt you in due time, ⁷casting all your care upon Him, for He cares for you.

⁸*Be sober, be vigilant; because[e] your adversary the devil walks about like a roaring lion, seeking whom he may devour. ⁹Resist him, steadfast in the faith, knowing that the same sufferings are experienced by your brotherhood in the world. ¹⁰But may[f] the God of all grace, who called us[g] to His eternal glory by Christ Jesus, after you have suffered a while, perfect, establish, strengthen, and settle *you*. ¹¹To Him *be* the glory and the dominion forever and ever. Amen.

¹²By Silvanus, our faithful brother as I consider him, I have written to you briefly, exhorting and testifying that this is the true grace of God in which you stand.

¹³She who is in Babylon, elect together with *you*, greets you; and *so does* Mark my son. ¹⁴Greet one another with a kiss of love.

Peace to you all who are in Christ Jesus. Amen.

5:5–7 The flesh. By nature, we do not want to submit to others. The phrase "clothed with humility" reminds us of our Savior when He wore a towel and washed Peter's feet (John 13:1–11). If we are submitted to the Lord, we will submit to His people. Humility leads to honor; pride leads to shame.

5:8–11 The devil. The devil is an adversary, not a friend; he is a roaring lion, not a playful pet. He wants to devour you, and you had better be on guard. Peter thought he was well able to defeat the enemy, so he did not heed the Lord's warning (Luke 22:31–34). The results were failure and shame. You can resist Satan by faith if you are wearing the armor and trusting the Spirit (Eph. 6:10–20).

5:2 [c]NU-Text adds *according to God.*   5:5 [d]Proverbs 3:34
5:8 [e]NU-Text and M-Text omit *because.*   5:10 [f]NU-Text reads *But the God of all grace . . . will perfect, establish, strengthen, and settle you.* [g]NU-Text and M-Text read *you.*

2 PETER

When he wrote 2 Peter, the apostle was conscious that death was near (1:13–14) and that the church was in danger, for false teachers were creeping in. He urged the believers to hold to the precious Word and grow spiritually (chap. 1), to identify and shun false teachers (chap. 2), and to keep the promise of Christ's return uppermost in their hearts (chap. 3). He stressed *spiritual knowledge* that comes from God's Word.

CHAPTER 1

1:3–11 *Power for the present.* When you trusted Christ, He gave you all that you need for life and godliness. All you have to do is to appropriate what you need from His resources. His Word feeds the divine nature within, and you can grow in knowledge and in grace. This is not automatic; you must be diligent to use the means of grace that God has provided.

1:12–18 *Assurance from the past.* Peter would be martyred soon (John 21:18), so he took occasion to remind his readers that they could trust the Word of God. Although Peter's experience on the Mount of Transfiguration was wonderful (Matt. 17:1–13), experiences are not a substitute for the unchanging Word of God.

1:19–21 *Hope for the future.* The Word is a light in this dark world, pointing to the return of the Lord. "Private interpretation" means that no prophecy should be isolated from the rest of Scripture or interpreted apart from the leading of the Spirit who gave it to us. The Spirit wrote one Book, and it must be understood as a whole. Believers may differ on individual matters of prophecy, but they all agree on the "one hope" (Eph. 4:4)—Jesus is coming again!

1 Simon Peter, a bondservant and apostle of Jesus Christ,

To those who have obtained like precious faith with us by the righteousness of our God and Savior Jesus Christ:

2Grace and peace be multiplied to you in the knowledge of God and of Jesus our Lord, 3*as His divine power has given to us all things that *pertain* to life and godliness, through the knowledge of Him who called us by glory and virtue, 4by which have been given to us exceedingly great and precious promises, that through these you may be partakers of the divine nature, having escaped the corruption *that is* in the world through lust.

5But also for this very reason, giving all diligence, add to your faith virtue, to virtue knowledge, 6to knowledge self-control, to self-control perseverance, to perseverance godliness, 7to godliness brotherly kindness, and to brotherly kindness love. 8For if these things are yours and abound, *you will be* neither barren nor unfruitful in the knowledge of our Lord Jesus Christ. 9For he who lacks these things is shortsighted, even to blindness, and has forgotten that he was cleansed from his old sins.

10Therefore, brethren, be even more diligent to make your call and election sure, for if you do these things you will never stumble; 11for so an entrance will be supplied to you abundantly into the everlasting kingdom of our Lord and Savior Jesus Christ.

12*For this reason I will not be negligent to remind you always of these things, though you know and are established in the present truth. 13Yes, I think it is right, as long as I am in this tent, to stir you up by reminding you, 14knowing that shortly I *must* put off my tent, just as our Lord Jesus Christ showed me. 15Moreover I will be careful to ensure that you always have a reminder of these things after my decease.

16For we did not follow cunningly devised fables when we made known to you the power and coming of our Lord Jesus Christ, but were eyewitnesses of His majesty. 17For He received from God the Father honor and glory when such a voice came to Him from the Excellent Glory: "This is My beloved Son, in whom I am well pleased." 18And we heard this voice which came from heaven when we were with Him on the holy mountain.

19*And so we have the prophetic word confirmed,[a] which you do well to heed as a light that

---

1:19 [a]Or *We also have the more sure prophetic word.*

shines in a dark place, until the day dawns and the morning star rises in your hearts; [20]knowing this first, that no prophecy of Scripture is of any private interpretation,[b] [21]for prophecy never came by the will of man, but holy men of God[c] spoke *as they were* moved by the Holy Spirit.

2 But[*] there were also false prophets among the people, even as there will be false teachers among you, who will secretly bring in destructive heresies, even denying the Lord who bought them, *and* bring on themselves swift destruction. [2]And many will follow their destructive ways, because of whom the way of truth will be blasphemed. [3]By covetousness they will exploit you with deceptive words; for a long time their judgment has not been idle, and their destruction does[d] not slumber.

[4]For if God did not spare the angels who sinned, but cast *them* down to hell and delivered *them* into chains of darkness, to be reserved for judgment; [5]and did not spare the ancient world, but saved Noah, *one of* eight *people*, a preacher of righteousness, bringing in the flood on the world of the ungodly; [6]and turning the cities of Sodom and Gomorrah into ashes, condemned *them* to destruction, making *them* an example to those who afterward would live ungodly; [7]and delivered righteous Lot, *who was* oppressed by the filthy conduct of the wicked [8](for that righteous man, dwelling among them, tormented *his* righteous soul from day to day by seeing and hearing *their* lawless deeds)— [9]then the Lord knows how to deliver the godly out of temptations and to reserve the unjust under punishment for the day of judgment, [10]and especially those who walk according to the flesh in the lust of uncleanness and despise authority. *They are* presumptuous, self-willed. They are not afraid to speak evil of dignitaries, [11]whereas angels, who are greater in power and might, do not bring a reviling accusation against them before the Lord.

[12]But these, like natural brute beasts made to be caught and destroyed, speak evil of the things they do not understand, and will utterly perish in their own corruption, [13]and will receive the wages of unrighteousness, *as* those who count it pleasure to carouse in the daytime. *They are* spots and blemishes, carousing in their own deceptions while they feast with you, [14]having eyes full of adultery and that cannot cease from sin, enticing unstable souls. *They have* a heart trained in covetous practices, *and are* accursed children. [15]They have forsaken the right way and gone astray, following the way of Balaam the *son* of Beor, who loved the wages of unrighteousness; [16]but he was rebuked for his iniquity: a dumb donkey speaking with a man's voice restrained the madness of the prophet.

[17]These are wells without water, clouds[e] carried by a tempest, for whom is reserved the blackness of darkness forever.[f]

[18]For when they speak great swelling *words* of emptiness, they allure through the lusts of the flesh, through lewdness, the ones who have actually escaped[g] from those who live in error.

CHAPTER 2

2:1ff The description of the false teachers is clear enough to help you detect them and vivid enough to make you want to avoid them. It is not enough to reject their false teachings. You must also reject their way of life and the hypocrisy behind it.

Their tool is deception, so you must know God's Word and exercise discernment when you hear their impressive language (v. 18) and alluring promises (v. 19). They fellowship with you only to find out what they can get from you (vv. 12–14), and then they will leave you in worse shape than they found you. They are deceptive and destructive, so beware!

Their purpose is personal pleasure and financial gain, and their destiny is judgment. Like Balaam (Num. 22—24), they cause others to sin by using religion for personal gain. They are not God's sheep; they are pigs and dogs in sheep's clothing (Prov. 26:11; Matt. 7:15) and eventually go back to their natural habits. True sheep keep themselves clean because they follow the Shepherd (John 10:27–28).

1:20 [b]Or *origin*   1:21 [c]NU-Text reads *but men spoke from God.*   2:3 [d]M-Text reads *will not.*   2:17 [e]NU-Text reads *and mists.*   [f]NU-Text omits *forever.*   2:18 [g]NU-Text reads *are barely escaping.*

CHAPTER 3

3:3ff When false teachers cannot accomplish their devious purposes with lies, they start to scoff and ridicule the Word of God. They want you to forget that the very Word they deride is in control of God's universe. God created everything by His Word, and His Word holds it together (Col. 1:16–17; Heb. 1:1–2). His Word caused the Flood (Gen. 6—9), and His Word will one day bring a judgment of fire to the ungodly world (vv. 7–10).

Whoever robs you of God's Word robs you of your future. People who have no future hope have no motivation for life today. No wonder Peter closes with "Beloved, be diligent!" (v. 14) and "Beloved, beware!" (v. 17). We live in dangerous days, but the opportunities have never been greater. God is patiently waiting for the lost to trust Christ (v. 15), but he needs you to share the gospel with them.

[19]While they promise them liberty, they themselves are slaves of corruption; for by whom a person is overcome, by him also he is brought into bondage. [20]For if, after they have escaped the pollutions of the world through the knowledge of the Lord and Savior Jesus Christ, they are again entangled in them and overcome, the latter end is worse for them than the beginning. [21]For it would have been better for them not to have known the way of righteousness, than having known *it*, to turn from the holy commandment delivered to them. [22]But it has happened to them according to the true proverb: *"A dog returns to his own vomit,"*[h] and, "a sow, having washed, to her wallowing in the mire."

3 Beloved, I now write to you this second epistle (in *both of* which I stir up your pure minds by way of reminder), [2]that you may be mindful of the words which were spoken before by the holy prophets, and of the commandment of us,[i] the apostles of the Lord and Savior, [3]*knowing this first: that scoffers will come in the last days, walking according to their own lusts, [4]and saying, "Where is the promise of His coming? For since the fathers fell asleep, all things continue as *they were* from the beginning of creation." [5]For this they willfully forget: that by the word of God the heavens were of old, and the earth standing out of water and in the water, [6]by which the world *that* then existed perished, being flooded with water. [7]But the heavens and the earth *which* are now preserved by the same word, are reserved for fire until the day of judgment and perdition of ungodly men.

[8]But, beloved, do not forget this one thing, that with the Lord one day *is* as a thousand years, and a thousand years as one day. [9]The Lord is not slack concerning *His* promise, as some count slackness, but is longsuffering toward us,[j] not willing that any should perish but that all should come to repentance.

[10]But the day of the Lord will come as a thief in the night, in which the heavens will pass away with a great noise, and the elements will melt with fervent heat; both the earth and the works that are in it will be burned up.[k] [11]Therefore, since all these things will be dissolved, what manner *of persons* ought you to be in holy conduct and godliness, [12]looking for and hastening the coming of the day of God, because of which the heavens will be dissolved, being on fire, and the elements will melt with fervent heat? [13]Nevertheless we, according to His promise, look for new heavens and a new earth in which righteousness dwells.

2:22 [h]Proverbs 26:11   3:2 [i]NU-Text and M-Text read *commandment of the apostles of your Lord and Savior* or *commandment of your apostles of the Lord and Savior.* 3:9 [j]NU-Text reads *you.*   3:10 [k]NU-Text reads *laid bare* (literally *found*).

"The Dreadful Day!" —"The darkness grows thicker around us, and godly servants of the Most High become rarer and more rare. Impiety and licentiousness are rampant throughout the world, and we live like pigs, like wild beasts, devoid of all reason. But a voice will soon be heard thundering forth: 'Behold, the bridegroom cometh!' God will not be able to bear this wicked world much longer, but will come, with the dreadful day, and chastise the scorners of his Word." Does that sound like a statement by one of our contemporary prophetic preachers? It was said by Martin Luther, who lived from 1483 to 1546. If Luther felt that the Lord's return was near in his day, what should we think today!

¹⁴Therefore, beloved, looking forward to these things, be diligent to be found by Him in peace, without spot and blameless; ¹⁵and consider *that* the longsuffering of our Lord *is* salvation—as also our beloved brother Paul, according to the wisdom given to him, has written to you, ¹⁶as also in all his epistles, speaking in them of these things, in which are some things hard to understand, which untaught and unstable *people* twist to their own destruction, as *they do* also the rest of the Scriptures.

¹⁷You therefore, beloved, since you know *this* beforehand, beware lest you also fall from your own steadfastness, being led away with the error of the wicked; ¹⁸but grow in the grace and knowledge of our Lord and Savior Jesus Christ.

To Him *be* the glory both now and forever. Amen.

1 JOHN

The apostle wrote this letter to his dear "little children" (the phrase is used nine times) to help them find assurance of personal salvation (5:13). When you are sure of your salvation, you can have fellowship with God and God's people (1:3), experience joy (1:4), and have victory over sin (2:1–2). John also wrote to warn believers about false teachers (2:26–27; 4:1–6). Both Peter and John were concerned about purity of doctrine in the church; and we should be, too.

Chapters 1—2 focus on *fellowship* and contrast *saying* and *doing*. It is easy to talk the Christian life, but God wants the walk. John emphasizes *sonship* in chapters 3—5 (the phrase "born of God" is used several times) and gives three marks of the true child of God: doing God's will (chap. 3), loving the brethren (chap. 4), and believing the truth (chap. 5).

"God is light" (1:5), and His children should walk in the light. "God is love" (4:8, 16), and His children should walk in love. "The Spirit is truth" (5:6), and God's children should believe and obey the truth.

CHAPTER 1

1:1–3 God wants you to have a *living fellowship* with Him and His children. In Jesus Christ, He has revealed what true life really is. Even though you cannot see Him and touch Him as the apostles did centuries ago, He can still be real to you as His Holy Spirit opens the Word to your heart.

1:4 He wants you to have a *joyful fellowship*. It is not the fellowship of a slave with a master but that of a child with a parent. God delights in His children (Ps. 18:19) and longs to share His love with them (John 14:19–24). When you are happy in the will of God, you are ready to live for Him and serve Him.

1:5–10 He wants you to have an *honest fellowship*. This means "walking in the light" and dealing honestly with sin. Salvation is a matter of life or death, but fellowship is a matter of light or darkness. If you lie to God, to others, and to yourselves, you will lose your fellowship with God and your character. A godly character does not develop in the darkness.

CHAPTER 2

2:1, 2 In Jesus Christ, you have *an Advocate*, representing you before God's throne (Zech. 3). When you sin, confess it to Him, and receive His faithful forgiveness.

2:3–6 In Him, you also have *an example*, and you should "walk just as He walked." Ask the indwelling Holy Spirit to make you more like Jesus Christ, and saturate yourself with His life as you read the Gospels.

1 That* which was from the beginning, which we have heard, which we have seen with our eyes, which we have looked upon, and our hands have handled, concerning the Word of life— 2the life was manifested, and we have seen, and bear witness, and declare to you that eternal life which was with the Father and was manifested to us— 3that which we have seen and heard we declare to you, that you also may have fellowship with us; and truly our fellowship *is* with the Father and with His Son Jesus Christ. 4*And these things we write to you that youra joy may be full.

5*This is the message which we have heard from Him and declare to you, that God is light and in Him is no darkness at all. 6If we say that we have fellowship with Him, and walk in darkness, we lie and do not practice the truth. 7But if we walk in the light as He is in the light, we have fellowship with one another, and the blood of Jesus Christ His Son cleanses us from all sin.

8If we say that we have no sin, we deceive ourselves, and the truth is not in us. 9If we confess our sins, He is faithful and just to forgive us *our* sins and to cleanse us from all unrighteousness. 10If we say that we have not sinned, we make Him a liar, and His word is not in us.

2 My* little children, these things I write to you, so that you may not sin. And if anyone sins, we have an Advocate with the Father, Jesus Christ the righteous. 2And He Himself is the propitiation for our sins, and not for ours only but also for the whole world.

3*Now by this we know that we know Him, if we keep His commandments. 4He who says, "I know Him," and does not keep His commandments, is a liar, and the truth is not in him. 5But whoever keeps His word, truly the love of

---

1:4 aNU-Text and M-Text read *our.*

His Life Was Manifested—*Manifest* is one of John's favorite words. Jesus was manifested that He might reveal God's life (1 John 1:2), take away our sins (3:5), destroy the devil's works (3:8), and disclose God's love for sinners (4:9).

God is perfected in him. By this we know that we are in Him. 6He who says he abides in Him ought himself also to walk just as He walked.

7*Brethren,b I write no new commandment to you, but an old commandment which you have had from the beginning. The old commandment is the word which you heard from the beginning.c 8Again, a new commandment I write to you, which thing is true in Him and in you, because the darkness is passing away, and the true light is already shining.

9He who says he is in the light, and hates his brother, is in darkness until now. 10He who loves his brother abides in the light, and there is no cause for stumbling in him. 11But he who hates his brother is in darkness and walks in darkness, and does not know where he is going, because the darkness has blinded his eyes.

12* I write to you, little children,
Because your sins are forgiven you for His name's sake.
13 I write to you, fathers,
Because you have known Him who is from the beginning.
I write to you, young men,
Because you have overcome the wicked one.
I write to you, little children,
Because you have known the Father.
14 I have written to you, fathers,
Because you have known Him who is from the beginning.
I have written to you, young men,
Because you are strong, and the word of God abides in you,
And you have overcome the wicked one.

15*Do not love the world or the things in the world. If anyone loves the world, the love of the Father is not in him. 16For all that is in the world—the lust of the flesh, the lust of the eyes, and the pride of life—is not of the Father but is of the world. 17And the world is passing away, and the lust of it; but he who does the will of God abides forever.

18Little children, it is the last hour; and as you have heard that thed Antichrist is coming, even now many antichrists have come, by which we know that it is the last hour. 19They went out from us, but they were not of us; for if they had been of us, they would have continued with us; but they went out that they might be made manifest, that none of them were of us.

20But you have an anointing from the Holy One, and you know all things.e 21I have not written to you because you do not know the truth, but because you know it, and that no lie is of the truth. 22Who is a liar but he who denies that Jesus is the Christ? He is antichrist who denies the Father and the Son. 23Whoever denies the Son does not have the Father either; he who acknowledges the Son has the Father also.

24Therefore let that abide in you which you heard from the beginning. If what you heard from the beginning abides in you, you also will abide

2:7–11 From Jesus Christ, you have *a commandment* to love God's people. The Father gave this commandment to Israel (Lev. 19:18) and the Son to His disciples (John 13:34), and the Spirit enables us to obey it (Rom. 5:5).

2:12–14 Because of Jesus Christ, you have *a family.* The members are at different stages of spiritual development, but all can receive the Word and grow. How wonderful it is when the "little children" become young men and then fathers!

2:15–27 You also have *some enemies,* the world and the false teachers. Christians who love the world lose the enjoyment of the Father's love and the desire to do His will. We overcome the world with God's love and the liars with God's truth (vv. 24–27).

❝*Some Christians try to go to heaven alone, in solitude. But believers are not compared to bears or lions or other animals that wander alone. Those who belong to Christ are sheep in this respect, that they love to get together. Sheep go in flocks, and so do God's people.*❞
—Charles Haddon Spurgeon

2:7 bNU-Text reads *Beloved.* cNU-Text omits *from the beginning.*   2:18 dNU-Text omits *the.*   2:20 eNU-Text reads *you all know.*

2:28, 29 You have *a wonderful hope,* the coming of Jesus Christ. Abide in Him so you will not be ashamed when He comes.

CHAPTER 3

3:1–3 Deliberate sin is a serious thing. When you deliberately sin, you grieve the heart of the Father who loves you and has a wonderful future planned for you.

3:4–8 You also grieve the Savior who died for you and delivered you from the power of Satan.

3:9–15 Deliberate sin grieves the Holy Spirit who lives in you and gave you new birth. You have a new nature and a new Father; therefore, you should live a new life. To John, lack of love is the same as hatred; and hatred is the moral equivalent of murder (Matt. 5:21–26).

3:16–24 Deliberate sin also grieves God's people, because we cannot minister to them as we should if we are not walking in love and in the light. Strive to have a heart that is right before God and men (Acts 24:16). Ask God to use you to be an encouragement and help to others (James 2). Love is more than a matter of words (v. 18).

in the Son and in the Father. 25And this is the promise that He has promised us—eternal life.

26These things I have written to you concerning those who *try to* deceive you. 27But the anointing which you have received from Him abides in you, and you do not need that anyone teach you; but as the same anointing teaches you concerning all things, and is true, and is not a lie, and just as it has taught you, you will*ᶦ* abide in Him.

28*And now, little children, abide in Him, that when*ᵍ* He appears, we may have confidence and not be ashamed before Him at His coming. 29If you know that He is righteous, you know that everyone who practices righteousness is born of Him.

3 Behold* what manner of love the Father has bestowed on us, that we should be called children of God!*ʰ* Therefore the world does not know us,*ᶦ* because it did not know Him. 2Beloved, now we are children of God; and it has not yet been revealed what we shall be, but we know that when He is revealed, we shall be like Him, for we shall see Him as He is. 3And everyone who has this hope in Him purifies himself, just as He is pure.

4*Whoever commits sin also commits lawlessness, and sin is lawlessness. 5And you know that He was manifested to take away our sins, and in Him there is no sin. 6Whoever abides in Him does not sin. Whoever sins has neither seen Him nor known Him.

7Little children, let no one deceive you. He who practices righteousness is righteous, just as He is righteous. 8He who sins is of the devil, for the devil has sinned from the beginning. For this purpose the Son of God was manifested, that He might destroy the works of the devil. 9*Whoever has been born of God does not sin, for His seed remains in him; and he cannot sin, because he has been born of God.

10In this the children of God and the children of the devil are manifest: Whoever does not practice righteousness is not of God, nor *is* he who does not love his brother. 11For this is the message that you heard from the beginning, that we should love one another, 12not as Cain *who* was of the wicked one and murdered his brother. And why did he murder him? Because his works were evil and his brother's righteous.

13Do not marvel, my brethren, if the world hates you. 14We know that we have passed from death to life, because we love the brethren. He who does not love *his* brother*ʲ* abides in death. 15Whoever hates his brother is a murderer, and you know that, no murderer has eternal life abiding in him.

16*By this we know love, because He laid down His life for us. And we also ought to lay down *our* lives for the brethren. 17But whoever has this world's goods, and sees his brother in need, and shuts up his heart from him, how does the love of God abide in him?

18My little children, let us not love in word or in tongue, but in deed and in truth. 19And by this we know*ᵏ* that we are of the truth, and shall assure our hearts before Him. 20For if our heart con-

---

2:27 *ᶦ*NU-Text reads *you abide.*   2:28 *ᵍ*NU-Text reads *if.*
3:1 *ʰ*NU-Text adds *And we are.* *ᶦ*M-Text reads *you.*
3:14 *ʲ*NU-Text omits *his brother.*   3:19 *ᵏ*NU-Text reads *we shall know.*

demns us, God is greater than our heart, and knows all things. 21Beloved, if our heart does not condemn us, we have confidence toward God. 22And whatever we ask we receive from Him, because we keep His commandments and do those things that are pleasing in His sight. 23And this is His commandment: that we should believe on the name of His Son Jesus Christ and love one another, as He gave us*l* commandment.

24Now he who keeps His commandments abides in Him, and He in him. And by this we know that He abides in us, by the Spirit whom He has given us.

4 Beloved, do not believe every spirit, but test the spirits, whether they are of God; because many false prophets have gone out into the world. 2By this you know the Spirit of God: Every spirit that confesses that Jesus Christ has come in the flesh is of God, 3and every spirit that does not confess that*m* Jesus Christ has come in the flesh is not of God. And this is the *spirit* of the Antichrist, which you have heard was coming, and is now already in the world.

4You are of God, little children, and have overcome them, because He who is in you is greater than he who is in the world. 5They are of the world. Therefore they speak *as* of the world, and the world hears them. 6We are of God. He who knows God hears us; he who is not of God does not hear us. By this we know the spirit of truth and the spirit of error.

7*Beloved, let us love one another, for love is of God; and everyone who loves is born of God and knows God. 8He who does not love does not know God, for God is love. 9In this the love of God was manifested toward us, that God has sent His only begotten Son into the world, that we might live through Him. 10In this is love, not that we loved God, but that He loved us and sent His Son *to be* the propitiation for our sins. 11Beloved, if God so loved us, we also ought to love one another.

12*No one has seen God at any time. If we love one another, God abides in us, and His love has been perfected in us. 13By this we know that we abide in Him, and He in us, because He has given us of His Spirit. 14And we have seen and testify that the Father has sent the Son *as* Savior of the world. 15Whoever confesses that Jesus is the Son of God, God abides in him, and he in God. 16And we have known and believed the love that God has for us. God is love, and he who abides in love abides in God, and God in him.

17*Love has been perfected among us in this: that we may have boldness in the day of judgment; because as He is, so are we in this world. 18There is no fear in love; but perfect love casts out fear, because fear involves torment. But he who fears has not been made perfect in love. 19We love Him*n* because He first loved us. 20If someone says, "I love God," and hates his brother, he is a liar; for he who does not love his brother whom he has seen, how can*o* he love God whom he has not seen? 21And this commandment we have from Him: that he who loves God *must* love his brother also.

CHAPTER 4
4:7–21 Love is evidence of salvation. If you are born of God through faith in Jesus Christ, you have His nature within (2 Pet. 1:4). Since "God is love" (vv. 8, 16), His children who have His nature should also manifest His love. The children should be like the Father!

4:12–14 Our love for others makes God's love real and visible to them so we can better witness to them about Christ. It also makes God real and personal to us. Merely reading in the Bible about God's love is not enough. Seek to *experience* that love in your heart by sharing it with others.

4:17–19 Just as truth is victorious over lies (vv. 1–6), love is victorious over fear. As you mature in your love for God, you realize that you have nothing to fear, for your Father has everything under control. You trust those you love, and faith and love will give victory over fear.

3:23 *l*M-Text omits *us*.   4:3 *m*NU-Text omits *that* and *Christ has come in the flesh*.   4:19 *n*NU-Text omits *Him*.
4:20 *o*NU-Text reads *he cannot*.

CHAPTER 5

5:1–3 When you are born of God, you are born to love. You will love the Father who gave you life and the Son who gave His life for you. You will also love His children, for you all belong to the same family.

5:4, 5 When you are born of God, you are born to win. Your first birth made you a sinner and a loser, but your second birth makes you a conqueror. The world wants to entice you (2:15–17) and the devil wants to seduce you (Gen. 3:6), but Christ will give you the victory you need if you trust Him.

5:6–13 When you are born of God, you are born to assurance, and you can know that you have eternal life.

5:14–17 When you are born of God, you are born to talk to your Father in prayer and receive from Him what you need.

5:18–21 When you are born of God, you are born secure, and the evil one cannot harm you. You do not keep yourself saved, for the Father does that (John 10:27–30); but you keep yourself from the clutches of the wicked one. As you abide in Christ, you experience His love and care.

5 Whoever* believes that Jesus is the Christ is born of God, and everyone who loves Him who begot also loves him who is begotten of Him. 2By this we know that we love the children of God, when we love God and keep His commandments. 3For this is the love of God, that we keep His commandments. And His commandments are not burdensome. 4*For whatever is born of God overcomes the world. And this is the victory that has overcome the world—our*p* faith. 5Who is he who overcomes the world, but he who believes that Jesus is the Son of God?

6*This is He who came by water and blood—Jesus Christ; not only by water, but by water and blood. And it is the Spirit who bears witness, because the Spirit is truth. 7For there are three that bear witness in heaven: the Father, the Word, and the Holy Spirit; and these three are one. 8And there are three that bear witness on earth:*q* the Spirit, the water, and the blood; and these three agree as one.

9If we receive the witness of men, the witness of God is greater; for this is the witness of God which*r* He has testified of His Son. 10He who believes in the Son of God has the witness in himself; he who does not believe God has made Him a liar, because he has not believed the testimony that God has given of His Son. 11And this is the testimony: that God has given us eternal life, and this life is in His Son. 12He who has the Son has life; he who does not have the Son of God does not have life. 13These things I have written to you who believe in the name of the Son of God, that you may know that you have eternal life,*s* and that you may *continue to* believe in the name of the Son of God.

14*Now this is the confidence that we have in Him, that if we ask anything according to His will, He hears us. 15And if we know that He hears us, whatever we ask, we know that we have the petitions that we have asked of Him.

16If anyone sees his brother sinning a sin *which does* not *lead* to death, he will ask, and He will give him life for those who commit sin not *leading* to death. There is sin *leading* to death. I do not say that he should pray about that. 17All unrighteousness is sin, and there is sin not *leading* to death.

18*We know that whoever is born of God does not sin; but he who has been born of God keeps himself,*t* and the wicked one does not touch him.

19We know that we are of God, and the whole world lies *under the sway of* the wicked one.

20And we know that the Son of God has come and has given us an understanding, that we may know Him who is true; and we are in Him who is true, in His Son Jesus Christ. This is the true God and eternal life.

21Little children, keep yourselves from idols. Amen.

5:4 *p*M-Text reads *your.*   5:8 *q*NU-Text and M-Text omit the words from *in heaven* (verse 7) through *on earth* (verse 8). Only four or five very late manuscripts contain these words in Greek.   5:9 *r*NU-Text reads *God, that.*   5:13 *s*NU-Text omits the rest of this verse.   5:18 *t*NU-Text reads *him.*

2 JOHN

John wrote this letter to an anonymous Christian woman whose home was open for God's people to meet for fellowship and worship. The emphasis is on truth and love, and John points out three dangers believers must avoid.

The Elder,

To the elect lady and her children, whom I love in truth, and not only I, but also all those who have known the truth, 2because of the truth which abides in us and will be with us forever:

3Grace, mercy, *and* peace will be with you*a* from God the Father and from the Lord Jesus Christ, the Son of the Father, in truth and love.

4*I rejoiced greatly that I have found *some* of your children walking in truth, as we received commandment from the Father. 5And now I plead with you, lady, not as though I wrote a new commandment to you, but that which we have had from the beginning: that we love one another. 6This is love, that we walk according to His commandments. This is the commandment, that as you have heard from the beginning, you should walk in it.

7*For many deceivers have gone out into the world who do not confess Jesus Christ *as* coming in the flesh. This is a deceiver and an antichrist. 8Look to yourselves, that we*b* do not lose those things we worked for, but *that* we*c* may receive a full reward.

9*Whoever transgresses*d* and does not abide in the doctrine of Christ does not have God. He who abides in the doctrine of Christ has both the Father and the Son. 10If anyone comes to you and does not bring this doctrine, do not receive him into your house nor greet him; 11for he who greets him shares in his evil deeds.

12Having many things to write to you, I did not wish *to do so* with paper and ink; but I hope to come to you and speak face to face, that our joy may be full.

13The children of your elect sister greet you. Amen.

---

3 *a*NU-Text and M-Text read *us*.   8 *b*NU-Text reads *you*.   *c*NU-Text reads *you*.   9 *d*NU-Text reads *goes ahead*.

Vv. 4–6 *Knowing the truth but not practicing it.* We must walk in truth and walk according to His commandments. The Word of God is meant for *doing* and not just *knowing.* "If we say" (1 John 1:6, 8, 10) but do not obey, we are hypocrites.

Vv. 7, 8, 10, 11 *Practicing truth but not defending it.* The enemy is busy, and we must oppose him. Love must be balanced by truth (Eph. 4:15), or you will start supporting lies in the name of love (Phil. 1:9–11). It is easy to lose what you have gained by making friends with the wrong people.

V. 9 *Going beyond the truth.* The word *transgress* means "to go beyond." When you go beyond God's Word, you are going too far. It is not progress but regress. Beware anybody who has something to add to your Bible.

❝*Truth is always strong, no matter how weak it looks, and falsehood is always weak, no matter how strong it looks.*❞

—Phillips Brooks

3 JOHN

John wrote this letter to his friend Gaius to encourage him in a difficult situation in his local church. Again, he concentrated on making God's truth a vital part of life.

Vv. 3, 4 *Walking in truth.* People could see the truth in Gaius because he loved it and walked in obedience to it, and that brought great joy to John. Every Christian parent can echo verse 4 and even make it a prayer.

Vv. 5–8 *Working for truth.* When you assist and encourage God's servants, you become a fellow worker with them in spreading the truth. Christian hospitality was important in those days and ought to be revived today.

Vv. 9, 10 *Welcoming the truth.* Can you imagine Diotrephes rejecting a message from the apostle John! He was so "separated" that he did not even receive John's friends. When we welcome God's people, we welcome God's truth.

Vv. 11, 12 *Witnessing for the truth.* Not all church members are like Diotrephes; there are people like Demetrius who love the truth and live it. They are the ones who make the local church healthy (v. 2).

T he Elder,

To the beloved Gaius, whom I love in truth:

2Beloved, I pray that you may prosper in all things and be in health, just as your soul prospers. 3*For I rejoiced greatly when brethren came and testified of the truth *that is* in you, just as you walk in the truth. 4I have no greater joy than to hear that my children walk in truth.*a*

5*Beloved, you do faithfully whatever you do for the brethren and*b* for strangers, 6who have borne witness of your love before the church. *If* you send them forward on their journey in a manner worthy of God, you will do well, 7because they went forth for His name's sake, taking nothing from the Gentiles. 8We therefore ought to receive*c* such, that we may become fellow workers for the truth.

9*I wrote to the church, but Diotrephes, who loves to have the preeminence among them, does not receive us. 10Therefore, if I come, I will call to mind his deeds which he does, prating against us with malicious words. And not content with that, he himself does not receive the brethren, and forbids those who wish to, putting *them* out of the church.

11*Beloved, do not imitate what is evil, but what is good. He who does good is of God, but*d* he who does evil has not seen God.

12Demetrius has a *good* testimony from all, and from the truth itself. And we also bear witness, and you know that our testimony is true.

13I had many things to write, but I do not wish to write to you with pen and ink; 14but I hope to see you shortly, and we shall speak face to face.

Peace to you. Our friends greet you. Greet the friends by name.

---

4 *a*NU-Text reads *the truth.*   5 *b*NU-Text adds *especially.*
8 *c*NU-Text reads *support.*   11 *d*NU-Text and M-Text omit *but.*

JUDE

Jude, like James, was a half brother of the Lord Jesus (Mark 6:3). His letter focuses on false teachers and echoes Peter's warnings in 2 Peter 2.

Jude, a bondservant of Jesus Christ, and brother of James,

To those who are called, sanctified[a] by God the Father, and preserved in Jesus Christ:

2Mercy, peace, and love be multiplied to you. 3Beloved, while I was very diligent to write to you concerning our common salvation, I found it necessary to write to you exhorting you to contend earnestly for the faith which was once for all delivered to the saints. 4*For certain men have crept in unnoticed, who long ago were marked out for this condemnation, ungodly men, who turn the grace of our God into lewdness and deny the only Lord God[b] and our Lord Jesus Christ.

5*But I want to remind you, though you once knew this, that the Lord, having saved the people out of the land of Egypt, afterward destroyed those who did not believe. 6And the angels who did not keep their proper domain, but left their own abode, He has reserved in everlasting chains under darkness for the judgment of the great day; 7as Sodom and Gomorrah, and the cities around them in a similar manner to these, having given themselves over to sexual immorality and gone after strange flesh, are set forth as an example, suffering the vengeance of eternal fire.

8Likewise also these dreamers defile the flesh, reject authority, and speak evil of dignitaries. 9Yet Michael the archangel, in contending with the devil, when he disputed about the body of Moses, dared not bring against him a reviling accusation, but said, "The Lord rebuke you!" 10But these speak evil of whatever they do not know; and whatever they know naturally, like brute beasts, in these things they corrupt themselves. 11Woe to them! For they have gone in the way of Cain, have run greedily in the error of Balaam for profit, and perished in the rebellion of Korah.

12*These are spots in your love feasts, while they feast with you without fear, serving only themselves. They are clouds without water, carried about[c] by the winds; late autumn trees without fruit, twice dead, pulled up by the roots; 13raging waves of the sea, foaming up their own shame; wandering stars for whom is reserved the blackness of darkness forever.

14Now Enoch, the seventh from Adam, prophesied about these men also, saying, "Behold, the Lord comes with ten thousands of His saints,

V. 4 Who they are. Jude wanted to write about salvation, but the Lord directed him to write about invasion instead. False teachers were creeping into the church and going undetected. These are unsaved people (v. 19), ungodly people, and unprincipled people who use grace as an excuse for sin.

Vv. 5–11 What they do. Like the Jews in the wilderness, the fallen angels, and the evil cities of the plain, they reject the authority of God. Their words are defiant and defiling. Like Cain (Gen. 4), they have no saving faith, but they do have religion. Like Balaam (Num. 22—24), they use religion as a way to make money; and like Korah (Num. 16), they defy the Word of God and the authority of God's chosen servants.

Vv. 12–16 What they are. False teachers promise much but produce little, like rainless clouds and fruitless trees. Enoch had the best word for them: ungodly.

1 aNU-Text reads beloved. 4 bNU-Text omits God.
12 cNU-Text and M-Text read along.

Seek Wisdom—In trying to minister to people, we must be careful and exercise discernment lest they do us more harm than we do good (Jude 22–23). Concerning the Pharisees, Jesus said to His disciples, "Let them alone" (Matt. 15:14). God told the prophet Hosea, "Ephraim is joined to idols, let him alone" (Hos. 4:17). And Paul told Timothy to withdraw himself from certain troublemakers (1 Tim. 6:3–5). Ask God for wisdom as you seek to help persons wandering from the faith.

15to execute judgment on all, to convict all who are ungodly among them of all their ungodly deeds which they have committed in an ungodly way, and of all the harsh things which ungodly sinners have spoken against Him."

16These are grumblers, complainers, walking according to their own lusts; and they mouth great swelling *words*, flattering people to gain advantage. 17*But you, beloved, remember the words which were spoken before by the apostles of our Lord Jesus Christ: 18how they told you that there would be mockers in the last time who would walk according to their own ungodly lusts. 19These are sensual persons, who cause divisions, not having the Spirit.

20But you, beloved, building yourselves up on your most holy faith, praying in the Holy Spirit, 21keep yourselves in the love of God, looking for the mercy of our Lord Jesus Christ unto eternal life.

22And on some have compassion, making a distinction;*d* 23but others save with fear, pulling *them* out of the fire,*e* hating even the garment defiled by the flesh.

24 Now to Him who is able to keep you*f* from
   stumbling,
   And to present *you* faultless
   Before the presence of His glory with
      exceeding joy,
25 To God our Savior,*g*
   Who alone is wise,*h*
   Be glory and majesty,
   Dominion and power,*i*
   Both now and forever.
   Amen.

22 *d*NU-Text reads *who are doubting* (or *making distinctions*). 23 *e*NU-Text adds *and on some have mercy with fear* and omits *with fear* in first clause.   24 *f*M-Text reads *them.* 25 *g*NU-Text reads *To the only God our Savior.* *h*NU-Text omits *Who . . . is wise* and adds *Through Jesus Christ our Lord.* *i*NU-Text adds *Before all time.*

Vv. 17–25 *What we must do.* Remember the Word and build yourself up in your Christian faith. True believers are "preserved in Jesus Christ" (v. 1), and they prove this by keeping themselves in God's love (v. 21). Therefore, God can keep them from falling (vv. 24–25).

THE REVELATION OF JESUS CHRIST

John was a Roman prisoner on the Isle of Patmos when God gave him this revelation of Jesus Christ. The book reveals Jesus Christ the Priest-King (chap. 1), the Judge of the churches (chaps. 2—3), the Creator (chap. 4), the Redeemer (chap. 5), the Lord of history (chaps. 6—18), the Conqueror (chaps. 19—20), and the Bridegroom (chaps. 21—22). The key name for Christ in this book is *the Lamb*. John never lets you forget that Jesus died for the sins of the world (John 1:29).

Another key word is *throne*, used over forty times. The Revelation describes the conflict between the throne of the Lamb in heaven and the throne of Satan on earth. As John writes, he depicts worship in heaven and warfare on earth; and the Lord is the victor. No matter how dark the day or how strong the forces of evil, the Lamb of God wins the victory.

The key verse is 1:19. John was told to write "the things which you have seen [chap. 1], and the things which are [chaps. 2—3], and the things which will take place after this [chaps. 4—22]."

Revelation 6—19 parallels Matthew 24 and Mark 13 in describing the day of the Lord or the Tribulation. The first part is described in chapters 6—9; the middle in chapters 10—14; and the last part ("the great tribulation") in chapters 15—19. While good and godly people disagree on the details of interpreting John's numbers and symbols, most agree that the last days will be marked by the increase of evil, the rise of a world government and world ruler, the attempt of Satan to destroy God's people, the pouring out of God's wrath on a rebellious world, and the return of Jesus Christ to deliver His own and establish His kingdom.

As you read, do not get lost in details, but try to see the big picture. And keep in mind that John wrote this book to encourage believers who were going through persecution. Every generation of Christians has had its Antichrist and Babylon, and the hope of the Lord's return has kept the saints going when the going was tough.

Revelation is the climax of the Bible, the fulfillment of what God started in Genesis. Many symbols in Genesis are found in this fascinating book: light and darkness, stars, Babylon, the bride, a garden, a tree of life, a serpent, and so on. He is "the Alpha and the Omega" (1:8). What He starts, He finishes.

1 The* Revelation of Jesus Christ, which God gave Him to show His servants—things which must shortly take place. And He sent and signified *it* by His angel to His servant John, [2]who bore witness to the word of God, and to the testimony of Jesus Christ, to all things that he saw. [3]Blessed *is* he who reads and those who hear the words of this prophecy, and keep those things which are written in it; for the time *is* near.

[4]John, to the seven churches which are in Asia:

Grace to you and peace from Him who is and who was and who is to come, and from the seven

CHAPTER 1

1:1–8 This book is first of all the revelation of Jesus Christ, not just the revelation of future events. Before John describes end-time events, he describes the Lord Jesus and reminds you of who He is and what He has done.

According to verse 5, He is the faithful witness (the Prophet), the firstborn from the dead (the Priest), and the ruler over the kings of the earth (the King). He is also the Savior (vv. 5b–6) who has made His people
(continued)

A Blessed Book—You will find seven "beatitudes" in Revelation: 1:3; 14:13; 16:15; 19:9; 20:6; 22:7, 14. It is indeed a book with a blessing!

Let Your Light Shine—In the Old Testament tabernacle, there was one lampstand with seven branches; but here John saw seven lampstands (Rev. 1:12), symbolizing the seven churches addressed in chapters 2—3 (v. 20). Each local assembly of believers should shine for the Lord (Matt. 5:16) by holding fast the Word of life and proclaiming it in a dark world (Phil. 2:14–16).

(continued from previous page)
a kingdom of priests (Exod. 19:1–6; 1 Pet. 2:1–10). Never forget that Jesus shed His blood for you, and that His blood cleanses (1:5; 7:14), redeems (5:9), and overcomes (12:11).

1:17 When John was in the Upper Room, he leaned on Jesus' bosom (John 13:23); but when he saw the glorified Christ, he fell at His feet as a dead man (2 Cor. 5:16). Like John, we must begin with worship if God's revelations in this book are to have any meaning to us.

1:18 One day "there shall be no more death" (21:4) because Jesus has conquered death. When you know Him as Savior and Lord, you need not fear the future; He has the keys in His hand.

CHAPTER 2

2:1–7 Judgment begins at "the house of God" (1 Pet. 4:17), so Jesus deals with the seven churches before He deals with the lost world. These churches illustrate the good and the bad in churches everywhere and in every age. If you were looking for a church to join, which of these seven would you select and why?
(continued)

Spirits who are before His throne, [5]and from Jesus Christ, the faithful witness, the firstborn from the dead, and the ruler over the kings of the earth.

To Him who loved us and washed[a] us from our sins in His own blood, [6]and has made us kings[b] and priests to His God and Father, to Him *be* glory and dominion forever and ever. Amen.

[7]Behold, He is coming with clouds, and every eye will see Him, even they who pierced Him. And all the tribes of the earth will mourn because of Him. Even so, Amen.

[8]"I am the Alpha and the Omega, *the* Beginning and *the* End,"[c] says the Lord,[d] "who is and who was and who is to come, the Almighty."

[9]I, John, both[e] your brother and companion in the tribulation and kingdom and patience of Jesus Christ, was on the island that is called Patmos for the word of God and for the testimony of Jesus Christ. [10]I was in the Spirit on the Lord's Day, and I heard behind me a loud voice, as of a trumpet, [11]saying, "I am the Alpha and the Omega, the First and the Last," and,[f] "What you see, write in a book and send *it* to the seven churches which are in Asia:[g] to Ephesus, to Smyrna, to Pergamos, to Thyatira, to Sardis, to Philadelphia, and to Laodicea."

[12]Then I turned to see the voice that spoke with me. And having turned I saw seven golden lampstands, [13]and in the midst of the seven lampstands *One* like the Son of Man, clothed with a garment down to the feet and girded about the chest with a golden band. [14]His head and hair *were* white like wool, as white as snow, and His eyes like a flame of fire; [15]His feet *were* like fine brass, as if refined in a furnace, and His voice as the sound of many waters; [16]He had in His right hand seven stars, out of His mouth went a sharp two-edged sword, and His countenance *was* like the sun shining in its strength. [17]And when I saw Him, I fell at His feet as dead. But He laid His right hand on me, saying to me,[h] "Do not be afraid; I am the First and the Last. [18]I *am* He who lives, and was dead, and behold, I am alive forevermore. Amen. And I have the keys of Hades and of Death. [19]Write[i] the things which you have seen, and the things which are, and the things which will take place after this. [20]The mystery of the seven stars which you saw in My right hand, and the seven golden lampstands: The seven stars are the angels of the seven churches, and the seven lampstands which you saw[j] are the seven churches.

2 "To[*] the angel of the church of Ephesus write, 'These things says He who holds the seven stars in His right hand, who walks in the midst of the seven golden lampstands: [2]"I know your works, your labor, your patience, and that you cannot bear those who are evil. And you have

---

1:5 [a]NU-Text reads *loves us and freed;* M-Text reads *loves us and washed.*   1:6 [b]NU-Text and M-Text read *a kingdom.* 1:8 [c]NU-Text and M-Text omit *the Beginning and the End.* [d]NU-Text and M-Text add *God.*   1:9 [e]NU-Text and M-Text omit *both.*   1:11 [f]NU-Text and M-Text omit *I am* through third *and.* [g]NU-Text and M-Text omit *which are in Asia.*   1:17 [h]NU-Text and M-Text omit *to me.*   1:19 [i]NU-Text and M-Text read *Therefore, write.*   1:20 [j]NU-Text and M-Text omit *which you saw.*

tested those who say they are apostles and are not, and have found them liars; 3and you have persevered and have patience, and have labored for My name's sake and have not become weary. 4Nevertheless I have *this* against you, that you have left your first love. 5Remember therefore from where you have fallen; repent and do the first works, or else I will come to you quickly and remove your lampstand from its place—unless you repent. 6But this you have, that you hate the deeds of the Nicolaitans, which I also hate.

7"He who has an ear, let him hear what the Spirit says to the churches. To him who overcomes I will give to eat from the tree of life, which is in the midst of the Paradise of God." '

8*"And to the angel of the church in Smyrna write,

'These things says the First and the Last, who was dead, and came to life: 9"I know your works, tribulation, and poverty (but you are rich); and *I know* the blasphemy of those who say they are Jews and are not, but *are* a synagogue of Satan. 10Do not fear any of those things which you are about to suffer. Indeed, the devil is about to throw *some* of you into prison, that you may be tested, and you will have tribulation ten days. Be faithful until death, and I will give you the crown of life.

11"He who has an ear, let him hear what the Spirit says to the churches. He who overcomes shall not be hurt by the second death." '

12*"And to the angel of the church in Pergamos write,

'These things says He who has the sharp two-edged sword: 13"I know your works, and where you dwell, where Satan's throne *is.* And you hold fast to My name, and did not deny My faith even in the days in which Antipas *was* My faithful martyr, who was killed among you, where Satan dwells. 14But I have a few things against you, because you have there those who hold the doctrine of Balaam, who taught Balak to put a stumbling block before the children of Israel, to eat things sacrificed to idols, and to commit sexual immorality. 15Thus you also have those who hold the doctrine of the Nicolaitans, which thing I hate.*k* 16Repent, or else I will come to you quickly and will fight against them with the sword of My mouth.

17"He who has an ear, let him hear what the Spirit says to the churches. To him who overcomes I will give some of the hidden manna to eat. And I will give him a white stone, and on the stone a new name written which no one knows except him who receives *it*." '

18*"And to the angel of the church in Thyatira write,

'These things says the Son of God, who has eyes like a flame of fire, and His feet like fine brass: 19I know your works, love, service, faith,*l* and your patience; and *as* for your works, the last *are* more than the first. 20Nevertheless I have a few things

---

2:15 *k*NU-Text and M-Text read *likewise* for *which thing I hate.*
2:19 *l*NU-Text and M-Text read *faith, service.*

(continued from previous page)

Ephesus. There is so much good in this church that we are surprised to discover they had left (not lost) their first love. The honeymoon was over (Jer. 2:2)! No amount of separation, sacrifice, or service can make up for your lack of love toward the Lord. The word *Nicolaitans* means "conquer the people." Apparently a group in the church lorded it over the people and promoted a separation of "clergy" and "laity." (See Matt. 21:20–27; 23:1–12.)

2:8–11 Smyrna. The name *Smyrna* comes from "myrrh," which is a bitter herb, a suitable name for a church facing persecution. Would the believers be *fearful* or *faithful* (v. 10)? Suffering can enrich us, even if we think we are poor; and what people think is wealth might turn out to be poverty (3:17)! What difference does it make if people slander you so long as you have the Lord's approval?

2:12–17 Pergamos. These believers held to the faith even when it might have cost them their lives. But they were too tolerant of false doctrine and were in danger of having the Lord declare war on the church. Balaam convinced Israel to compromise with their unbelieving neighbors, disobey the Lord, and indulge in immorality (Num. 22—24). Being willing to die for the faith is no substitute for living the faith.

2:18–29 Thyatira. Verse 19 gives you the impression that all is well in the church, but keep reading! Like the saints in Pergamos, the believers in Thyatira tolerated sin in the church. Idolatry and immorality usually go together, and Jezebel personifies both (1 Kings 16:29–34; 21; 2 Kings 9:30–37). Not everybody in the fellowship was guilty of sin, and the Lord did not warn them. Instead, He encouraged them to hold to the truth and be faithful.

To the Overcomers—Each of these messages to the churches ends with a promise to the overcomers. These overcomers are not an elite group in the church but true believers who have trusted Christ (1 John 5:1–5). No matter how unspiritual an assembly may become, Christ will always honor those who belong to Him if they are faithful to His Word. The promises to the overcomers follow Old Testament history, from the Garden of Eden (Rev. 2:7) to the kingdom throne (3:21).

against you, because you allow[m] that woman[n] Jezebel, who calls herself a prophetess, to teach and seduce[o] My servants to commit sexual immorality and eat things sacrificed to idols. 21And I gave her time to repent of her sexual immorality, and she did not repent.[p] 22Indeed I will cast her into a sickbed, and those who commit adultery with her into great tribulation, unless they repent of their[q] deeds. 23I will kill her children with death, and all the churches shall know that I am He who searches the minds and hearts. And I will give to each one of you according to your works.

24"Now to you I say, and[r] to the rest in Thyatira, as many as do not have this doctrine, who have not known the depths of Satan, as they say, I will[s] put on you no other burden. 25But hold fast what you have till I come. 26And he who overcomes, and keeps My works until the end, to him I will give power over the nations—

27   'He shall rule them with a rod of iron;
      They shall be dashed to pieces like the
      potter's vessels'[t]—

as I also have received from My Father; 28and I will give him the morning star. 29"He who has an ear, let him hear what the Spirit says to the churches." '

3 "And* to the angel of the church in Sardis write,
'These things says He who has the seven Spirits of God and the seven stars: "I know your works, that you have a name that you are alive, but you are dead. 2Be watchful, and strengthen the things which remain, that are ready to die, for I have not found your works perfect before God.[u] 3Remember therefore how you have received and heard; hold fast and repent. Therefore if you will not watch, I will come upon you as a thief, and you will not know what hour I will come upon you. 4You[v] have a few names even in Sardis who have not defiled their garments; and they shall walk with Me in white, for they are worthy. 5He who overcomes shall be clothed in white garments, and I will not blot out his name from the Book of Life; but I will confess his name before My Father and before His angels.

6"He who has an ear, let him hear what the Spirit says to the churches." '

7*"And to the angel of the church in Philadelphia write,
'These things says He who is holy, He who is true, "He who has the key of David, He who opens and no one shuts, and shuts and no one opens":[w] 8I know your works. See, I have set before you an open door, and no one can shut it;[x] for you have a little strength, have kept My word, and have not denied My name. 9Indeed I will make

CHAPTER 3

3:1–6 Sardis. This church had a great reputation, but close examination showed that its ministry did not live up to its name. In fact, the church was ready to die! What was the cause? Many of the people were defiling themselves by compromising with sin (2 Cor. 6:14–18; James 1:27). The "Book of Life" contains the names of all living persons; and when a person dies without Christ, the name is blotted out. Believers have their names in the Lamb's Book of Life and can never be blotted out.

3:7–13 Philadelphia. The name means "brotherly love," and Jesus had a special love for these people (v. 9). Weak as they were, they were given an open door of service; and the Lord urged them to take advantage of it. When God opens a door for you, nobody can shut it; but you can ignore or neglect it.

2:20 [m]NU-Text and M-Text read *I have against you that you tolerate.* [n]M-Text reads *your wife Jezebel.* [o]NU-Text and M-Text read *and teaches and seduces.*   2:21 [p]NU-Text and M-Text read *time to repent, and she does not want to repent of her sexual immorality.*   2:22 [q]NU-Text and M-Text read *her.*   2:24 [r]NU-Text and M-Text omit *and.* [s]NU-Text and M-Text omit *will.*   2:27 [t]Psalm 2:9   3:2 [u]NU-Text and M-Text read *My God.*   3:4 [v]NU-Text and M-Text read *Nevertheless you have a few names in Sardis.*   3:7 [w]Isaiah 22:22   3:8 [x]NU-Text and M-Text read *which no one can shut.*

those of the synagogue of Satan, who say they are Jews and are not, but lie—indeed I will make them come and worship before your feet, and to know that I have loved you. [10]Because you have kept My command to persevere, I also will keep you from the hour of trial which shall come upon the whole world, to test those who dwell on the earth. [11]Behold,[y] I am coming quickly! Hold fast what you have, that no one may take your crown. [12]He who overcomes, I will make him a pillar in the temple of My God, and he shall go out no more. I will write on him the name of My God and the name of the city of My God, the New Jerusalem, which comes down out of heaven from My God. And *I will write on him My new name.* [13]"He who has an ear, let him hear what the Spirit says to the churches." '

[14]"And to the angel of the church of the Laodiceans[z] write,

'These things says the Amen, the Faithful and True Witness, the Beginning of the creation of God: [15]"I know your works, that you are neither cold nor hot. I could wish you were cold or hot. [16]So then, because you are lukewarm, and neither cold nor hot,[a] I will vomit you out of My mouth. [17]Because you say, 'I am rich, have become wealthy, and have need of nothing'—and do not know that you are wretched, miserable, poor, blind, and naked— [18]I counsel you to buy from Me gold refined in the fire, that you may be rich; and white garments, that you may be clothed, *that* the shame of your nakedness may not be revealed; and anoint your eyes with eye salve, that you may see. [19]As many as I love, I rebuke and chasten. Therefore be zealous and repent. [20]Behold, I stand at the door and knock. If anyone hears My voice and opens the door, I will come in to him and dine with him, and he with Me. [21]To him who overcomes I will grant to sit with Me on My throne, as I also overcame and sat down with My Father on His throne. [22]"He who has an ear, let him hear what the Spirit says to the churches." ' "

4 After* these things I looked, and behold, a door *standing* open in heaven. And the first voice which I heard *was* like a trumpet speaking with me, saying, "Come up here, and I will show you things which must take place after this." [2]*Immediately I was in the Spirit; and behold, a throne set in heaven, and One sat on the throne. [3]*And He who sat there was[b] like a jasper and a sardius stone in appearance; and *there was* a rainbow around the throne, in appearance like an emerald. [4]Around the throne *were* twenty-four thrones, and on the thrones I saw twenty-four elders sitting, clothed in white robes; and they had crowns[c] of gold on their heads. [5]And from the throne proceeded lightnings, thunderings, and voices.[d] Seven lamps of fire *were* burning before the throne, which are the[e] seven Spirits of God. [6]*Before the throne *there was*[f] a sea of glass,

3:14–22 Laodicea. This church did not know how bad off it was! It was a working church, but its service was lukewarm. The members lacked spiritual enthusiasm. It was a wealthy church, but it was really poor—and did not know its own sad condition. Worst of all, the Lord was *outside the church trying to get in!* If only one member would yield to Him, the church could be changed.

God's people must be open and honest with the Lord and humbly submit to His spiritual diagnosis. No church or Christian is so far gone that He cannot bring renewal, but we must be willing to repent and return to Him.

❝*The more I study nature, the more I am amazed at the Creator.*❞

—Louis Pasteur

❝*Thus does the world forget You, its Creator, and falls in love with what You have created instead of with You.*❞

—Augustine

CHAPTER 4

4:1 A door. God will one day open the door, the trumpet will sound, and God's people will be called to heaven (1 Thess. 4:13–18). Meanwhile, we must take advantage of the open door of service that He gives us (3:8).

4:2–5 A throne. Revelation is the book of the throne. John saw God the Father on the throne and was so overwhelmed that he had to refer to precious stones to describe what he beheld. Satan may have his throne on earth (2:13), but God's throne in heaven rules over all and will not be defeated.

4:3 A rainbow. This emerald rainbow was *around* the throne, a complete circle and not just an arc. It pictures the grace of God (Gen. 9:11–17). On earth, we see the rainbow *after* the storm; but John saw it *before* the storm of judgment came. God gives His people His gracious promise, and they need not fear the coming storm (3:10; 1 Thess. 1:10; 5:8).

4:6–11 A choir. The living creatures represent creation praising the Creator (Gen. 1:28–31), and the elders represent God's people worshiping Him. When you lose the wonder of the Creator, you cease

(continued)

3:11 [y]NU-Text and M-Text omit *Behold.*   3:14 [z]NU-Text and M-Text read *in Laodicea.*   3:16 [a]NU-Text and M-Text read *hot nor cold.*   4:3 [b]M-Text omits *And He who sat there was* (which makes the description in verse 3 modify the throne rather than God).   4:4 [c]NU-Text and M-Text read *robes, with crowns.*   4:5 [d]NU-Text and M-Text read *voices, and thunderings.* [e]M-Text omits *the.*   4:6 [f]NU-Text and M-Text add *something like.*

(continued from previous page)
to become a good steward of the creation (11:18). All of creation praises the Lord while sinful man praises himself and ignores his Creator.

CHAPTER 5

5:1 *The scroll* represents the title deed to creation, for Jesus Christ alone is the rightful Heir (Ps. 2:8; Heb. 1:2). Satan offered Him the whole world in return for one act of worship (Matt. 4:8–10), but Jesus won the right to receive the scroll when He gave Himself on the cross. Have you placed the scroll of your life in His hands?

5:5, 6 *The Lamb* is Jesus Christ who was slain as a sacrifice for sin (1 Pet. 1:18–20); He is both Lamb (John 1:29) and Lion (Gen. 49:8–10), the Savior and the Sovereign. He is also the Root of David, for He existed before David and brought David's kingly line into being. As Lamb, Jesus offers salvation; as Lion, He judges those who reject Him. Marvel at the many aspects of His person and work!

5:8 *The incense* represents prayer (Ps. 141:1–3). For centuries, God's people have been praying, "Thy kingdom come"; and those prayers are about to be answered. Saints on earth do not pray to or through the saints now in heaven; our praying is to the Father and through the Son. But the prayers of God's people play a vital part in God's governing of the world.

5:9–14 *The worship.* He is worthy of our worship, not only because He is Creator (chap. 4) but even more because He is our Redeemer. See how the circle of praise grows until every creature worships Him. Heaven is a place of worship, so begin to get ready now to join in the praise!

❝*If the veil of the world's machinery were lifted off, how much we would find is done in answer to the prayers of God's children.*❞
—Robert Murray M'Cheyne

like crystal. And in the midst of the throne, and around the throne, *were* four living creatures full of eyes in front and in back. 7The first living creature *was* like a lion, the second living creature like a calf, the third living creature had a face like a man, and the fourth living creature *was* like a flying eagle. 8*The* four living creatures, each having six wings, were full of eyes around and within. And they do not rest day or night, saying:

"Holy, holy, holy,*g*
Lord God Almighty,
Who was and is and is to come!"

9Whenever the living creatures give glory and honor and thanks to Him who sits on the throne, who lives forever and ever, 10the twenty-four elders fall down before Him who sits on the throne and worship Him who lives forever and ever, and cast their crowns before the throne, saying:

11 "You are worthy, O Lord,*h*
To receive glory and honor and power;
For You created all things,
And by Your will they exist*i* and were created."

5 And* I saw in the right *hand* of Him who sat on the throne a scroll written inside and on the back, sealed with seven seals. 2Then I saw a strong angel proclaiming with a loud voice, "Who is worthy to open the scroll and to loose its seals?" 3And no one in heaven or on the earth or under the earth was able to open the scroll, or to look at it.

4So I wept much, because no one was found worthy to open and read*j* the scroll, or to look at it. 5*But one of the elders said to me, "Do not weep. Behold, the Lion of the tribe of Judah, the Root of David, has prevailed to open the scroll and to loose*k* its seven seals."

6And I looked, and behold,*l* in the midst of the throne and of the four living creatures, and in the midst of the elders, stood a Lamb as though it had been slain, having seven horns and seven eyes, which are the seven Spirits of God sent out into all the earth. 7Then He came and took the scroll out of the right hand of Him who sat on the throne.

8*Now when He had taken the scroll, the four living creatures and the twenty-four elders fell down before the Lamb, each having a harp, and golden bowls full of incense, which are the prayers of the saints. 9*And they sang a new song, saying:

"You are worthy to take the scroll,
And to open its seals;
For You were slain,
And have redeemed us to God by Your blood
Out of every tribe and tongue and people and nation,

4:8 *g*M-Text has *holy* nine times.   4:11 *h*NU-Text and M-Text read *our Lord and God.* *i*NU-Text and M-Text read *existed.* 5:4 *j*NU-Text and M-Text omit *and read.* 5:5 *k*NU-Text and M-Text omit *to loose.* 5:6 *l*NU-Text and M-Text read *I saw in the midst . . . a Lamb standing.*

10 And have made us[m] kings[n] and priests to
    our God;
    And we[o] shall reign on the earth."

11Then I looked, and I heard the voice of many
angels around the throne, the living creatures, and
the elders; and the number of them was ten thousand times ten thousand, and thousands of thousands, 12saying with a loud voice:

"Worthy is the Lamb who was slain
    To receive power and riches and wisdom,
    And strength and honor and glory and
        blessing!"

13And every creature which is in heaven and
on the earth and under the earth and such as are
in the sea, and all that are in them, I heard saying:

"Blessing and honor and glory and power
    Be to Him who sits on the throne,
    And to the Lamb, forever and ever!"[p]

14Then the four living creatures said, "Amen!"
And the twenty-four[q] elders fell down and worshiped Him who lives forever and ever.[r]

6 Now* I saw when the Lamb opened one of
  the seals;[s] and I heard one of the four living
creatures saying with a voice like thunder, "Come
and see." 2And I looked, and behold, a white
horse. He who sat on it had a bow; and a crown
was given to him, and he went out conquering
and to conquer.
3*When He opened the second seal, I heard the
second living creature saying, "Come and see."[t]
4Another horse, fiery red, went out. And it was
granted to the one who sat on it to take peace
from the earth, and that people should kill one
another; and there was given to him a great
sword.
5When He opened the third seal, I heard the
third living creature say, "Come and see." So I
looked, and behold, a black horse, and he who
sat on it had a pair of scales in his hand. 6And I
heard a voice in the midst of the four living creatures saying, "A quart[u] of wheat for a denarius,[v]
and three quarts of barley for a denarius; and do
not harm the oil and the wine."
7When He opened the fourth seal, I heard the
voice of the fourth living creature saying, "Come
and see." 8So I looked, and behold, a pale horse.
And the name of him who sat on it was Death,
and Hades followed with him. And power was
given to them over a fourth of the earth, to kill

CHAPTER 6

6:1, 2 The world ruler (Antichrist) begins his
conquest of the nations by peacefully taking
control. He has a weapon but no
ammunition; and men are saying, "Peace
and safety!" (1 Thess. 5:1–3). Satan usually
declares peace before he declares war, so
beware his offers.

6:3–17 Soon the world is at war (vv. 3–4),
and suffering results from famine and
plagues (vv. 5–8) and cosmic disturbances
(vv. 12–17). Jesus said these things would
happen (Matt. 24:4–13).

●●*Love makes the whole difference
between an execution and a
martyrdom.*●●

—Evelyn Underhill

5:10 [m]NU-Text and M-Text read *them.* [n]NU-Text reads *a
kingdom.* [o]NU-Text and M-Text read *they.* 5:13 [p]M-Text
adds *Amen.* 5:14 [q]NU-Text and M-Text omit *twenty-
four.* [r]NU-Text and M-Text omit *Him who lives forever and
ever.* 6:1 [s]NU-Text and M-Text read *seven seals.*
6:3 [t]NU-Text and M-Text omit *and see.* 6:6 [u]Greek *choinix;*
that is, approximately one quart [v]This was approximately one
day's wage for a worker.

Conterfeit Christ—There are two important riders in Revelation: Antichrist at the opening of the
book (6:1–2) and Christ at the close (19:11–16). The prefix *anti* in Greek means "instead of" as well
as "against." The world ruler is a counterfeit Christ, energized by the master counterfeiter, Satan
(2 Cor. 11:13–15). John does not use the term *Antichrist;* instead, he calls him "the beast" (chap.
13). The world would not receive the true Christ, but it will receive the false Christ (John 5:43).

6:9–11 The martyrs are seen "under the altar" because that is where the blood was placed (Lev. 4:7; 17:11). Death for Jesus' sake is not waste; it is sacrifice and worship. They pray not for personal vengeance but for God's glorification and vindication. When it appears that God is not working as you think He should, be patient and let Him do His will in His time.

CHAPTER 7

7:1ff When the storm starts to get worse, John sees two groups of people and takes courage. Why? Because he realizes that God is at work even in the midst of tribulation.

God has His servants who will proclaim His message and honor His name (vv. 1–8). We are not told what these sealed Jews will do, but we assume they will point people to the Lord. Times of tribulation give opportunities for witness (Matt. 24:14).

Apparently the 144,000 Jews will be sealed at the beginning of the Tribulation; and at the end, a great multitude of saved Gentiles will be seen (vv. 9–17). The day of the Lord will bring judgment and destruction, and it will also result in the saving of people. In wrath, God remembers mercy (Hab. 3:2). When you experience trials, ask God to use you to win others to the Savior even in the midst of troubles. Trials do not last forever. One day, you will come out of tribulation and experience the gracious comforts of God. Wait and be faithful, and He will see you through.

❝*We make a great mistake if we connect with our conception of heaven the thought of rest from work. Rest from toil, from weariness, from exhaustion—yes; rest from work, from productiveness, from service—no. 'They serve God day and night.'* ❞
—B. F. Westcott

with sword, with hunger, with death, and by the beasts of the earth.

9*When He opened the fifth seal, I saw under the altar the souls of those who had been slain for the word of God and for the testimony which they held. 10And they cried with a loud voice, saying, "How long, O Lord, holy and true, until You judge and avenge our blood on those who dwell on the earth?" 11Then a white robe was given to each of them; and it was said to them that they should rest a little while longer, until both *the number of* their fellow servants and their brethren, who would be killed as they *were*, was completed.

12I looked when He opened the sixth seal, and behold,ʷ there was a great earthquake; and the sun became black as sackcloth of hair, and the moonˣ became like blood. 13And the stars of heaven fell to the earth, as a fig tree drops its late figs when it is shaken by a mighty wind. 14Then the sky receded as a scroll when it is rolled up, and every mountain and island was moved out of its place. 15And the kings of the earth, the great men, the rich men, the commanders,ʸ the mighty men, every slave and every free man, hid themselves in the caves and in the rocks of the mountains, 16and said to the mountains and rocks, "Fall on us and hide us from the face of Him who sits on the throne and from the wrath of the Lamb! 17For the great day of His wrath has come, and who is able to stand?"

7 After* these things I saw four angels standing at the four corners of the earth, holding the four winds of the earth, that the wind should not blow on the earth, on the sea, or on any tree. 2Then I saw another angel ascending from the east, having the seal of the living God. And he cried with a loud voice to the four angels to whom it was granted to harm the earth and the sea, 3saying, "Do not harm the earth, the sea, or the trees till we have sealed the servants of our God on their foreheads." 4And I heard the number of those who were sealed. One hundred *and* forty-four thousand of all the tribes of the children of Israel *were* sealed:

5　of the tribe of Judah twelve thousand *were* sealed;ᶻ
　　of the tribe of Reuben twelve thousand *were* sealed;
　　of the tribe of Gad twelve thousand *were* sealed;
6　of the tribe of Asher twelve thousand *were* sealed;
　　of the tribe of Naphtali twelve thousand *were* sealed;
　　of the tribe of Manasseh twelve thousand *were* sealed;
7　of the tribe of Simeon twelve thousand *were* sealed;
　　of the tribe of Levi twelve thousand *were* sealed;

6:12 ʷNU-Text and M-Text omit *behold.* ˣNU-Text and M-Text read *the whole moon.*   6:15 ʸNU-Text and M-Text read *the commanders, the rich men.*   7:5 ᶻIn NU-Text and M-Text *were sealed* is stated only in verses 5a and 8c; the words are understood in the remainder of the passage.

of the tribe of Issachar twelve thousand
  were sealed;
8   of the tribe of Zebulun twelve thousand
    were sealed;
of the tribe of Joseph twelve thousand *were*
  sealed;
of the tribe of Benjamin twelve thousand
  were sealed.

9After these things I looked, and behold, a great multitude which no one could number, of all nations, tribes, peoples, and tongues, standing before the throne and before the Lamb, clothed with white robes, with palm branches in their hands, 10and crying out with a loud voice, saying, "Salvation *belongs* to our God who sits on the throne, and to the Lamb!" 11All the angels stood around the throne and the elders and the four living creatures, and fell on their faces before the throne and worshiped God, 12saying:

"Amen! Blessing and glory and wisdom,
Thanksgiving and honor and power and
  might,
Be to our God forever and ever.
Amen."

13Then one of the elders answered, saying to me, "Who are these arrayed in white robes, and where did they come from?"
14And I said to him, "Sir,*a* you know."
So he said to me, "These are the ones who come out of the great tribulation, and washed their robes and made them white in the blood of the Lamb. 15Therefore they are before the throne of God, and serve Him day and night in His temple. And He who sits on the throne will dwell among them. 16They shall neither hunger anymore nor thirst anymore; the sun shall not strike them, nor any heat; 17for the Lamb who is in the midst of the throne will shepherd them and lead them to living fountains of waters.*b* And God will wipe away every tear from their eyes."

8 When* He opened the seventh seal, there was silence in heaven for about half an hour. 2And I saw the seven angels who stand before God, and to them were given seven trumpets. 3Then another angel, having a golden censer, came and stood at the altar. He was given much incense, that he should offer *it* with the prayers of all the saints upon the golden altar which was before the throne. 4And the smoke of the incense, with the prayers of the saints, ascended before God from the angel's hand. 5*Then the angel took the censer, filled it with fire from the altar, and threw *it* to the earth. And there were noises, thunderings, lightnings, and an earthquake.
6So the seven angels who had the seven trumpets prepared themselves to sound.
7The first angel sounded: And hail and fire followed, mingled with blood, and they were thrown to the earth.*c* And a third of the trees were burned up, and all green grass was burned up.
8Then the second angel sounded: And *something* like a great mountain burning with fire was

CHAPTERS 8—9

8:1–4 *Incense at the altar.* The silence in heaven is the lull before the storm (Hab. 2:20; Zeph. 1:7). Even the heavenly hosts stop their worship as they contemplate the awesome judgments about to fall. But those judgments are the answer to the saints' prayers (5:8), "Thy kingdom come!" Do not stop praying!

8:5—9:12 *Fire from the altar.* The world will not come to the altar for forgiveness (9:21), so the altar sends forth judgment. Heaven and earth are struck as the trumpets sound, and the bottomless pit belches out demonic creatures to torment mankind. Rather than repent, people will try to commit suicide; but they will not be able to die (9:6). They will continue in their sins: occult practices, murder, immorality, and thievery (9:20–21), all of which sound very contemporary.

7:14 *a*NU-Text and M-Text read *My lord.*   7:17 *b*NU-Text and M-Text read *to fountains of the waters of life.*   8:7 *c*NU-Text and M-Text add *and a third of the earth was burned up.*

thrown into the sea, and a third of the sea became blood. 9And a third of the living creatures in the sea died, and a third of the ships were destroyed.

10Then the third angel sounded: And a great star fell from heaven, burning like a torch, and it fell on a third of the rivers and on the springs of water. 11The name of the star is Wormwood. A third of the waters became wormwood, and many men died from the water, because it was made bitter.

12Then the fourth angel sounded: And a third of the sun was struck, a third of the moon, and a third of the stars, so that a third of them were darkened. A third of the day did not shine, and likewise the night.

13And I looked, and I heard an angel^d flying through the midst of heaven, saying with a loud voice, "Woe, woe, woe to the inhabitants of the earth, because of the remaining blasts of the trumpet of the three angels who are about to sound!"

9 Then the fifth angel sounded: And I saw a star fallen from heaven to the earth. To him was given the key to the bottomless pit. 2And he opened the bottomless pit, and smoke arose out of the pit like the smoke of a great furnace. So the sun and the air were darkened because of the smoke of the pit. 3Then out of the smoke locusts came upon the earth. And to them was given power, as the scorpions of the earth have power. 4They were commanded not to harm the grass of the earth, or any green thing, or any tree, but only those men who do not have the seal of God on their foreheads. 5And they were not given *authority* to kill them, but to torment them *for* five months. Their torment *was* like the torment of a scorpion when it strikes a man. 6In those days men will seek death and will not find it; they will desire to die, and death will flee from them.

7The shape of the locusts was like horses prepared for battle. On their heads were crowns of something like gold, and their faces *were* like the faces of men. 8They had hair like women's hair, and their teeth were like lions' *teeth.* 9And they had breastplates like breastplates of iron, and the sound of their wings *was* like the sound of chariots with many horses running into battle. 10They had tails like scorpions, and there were stings in their tails. Their power *was* to hurt men five months. 11And they had as king over them the angel of the bottomless pit, whose name in Hebrew *is* Abaddon, but in Greek he has the name Apollyon.

12One woe is past. Behold, still two more woes are coming after these things.

13*Then the sixth angel sounded: And I heard a voice from the four horns of the golden altar which is before God, 14saying to the sixth angel who had the trumpet, "Release the four angels who are bound at the great river Euphrates." 15So the four angels, who had been prepared for the hour and day and month and year, were released to kill a third of mankind. 16Now the number of the army of the horsemen *was* two hundred million; I heard the number of them. 17And thus I saw the horses in the vision: those who sat on them had breastplates of fiery red, hyacinth blue, and sulfur yellow; and the heads of the horses

9:13–19 *A voice from the altar.* God has His legions ready to be released at the right time, and torment will be replaced by death. Men have wanted to die, so God will send His servants to do the job. One-third of mankind will be killed (9:15), which means that half of the world's population is now dead (6:8)! The world must make a choice: life or death (Deut. 30:19). Are you offering them the gift of life in Jesus Christ?

8:13 ^dNU-Text and M-Text read *eagle.*

were like the heads of lions; and out of their mouths came fire, smoke, and brimstone. 18By these three *plagues* a third of mankind was killed—by the fire and the smoke and the brimstone which came out of their mouths. 19For their power[e] is in their mouth and in their tails; for their tails *are* like serpents, having heads; and with them they do harm.

20But the rest of mankind, who were not killed by these plagues, did not repent of the works of their hands, that they should not worship demons, and idols of gold, silver, brass, stone, and wood, which can neither see nor hear nor walk. 21And they did not repent of their murders or their sorceries[f] or their sexual immorality or their thefts.

10 I saw still another mighty angel coming down from heaven, clothed with a cloud. And a rainbow *was* on his head, his face *was* like the sun, and his feet like pillars of fire. 2He had a little book open in his hand. And he set his right foot on the sea and *his* left *foot* on the land, 3*and cried with a loud voice, as *when* a lion roars. When he cried out, seven thunders uttered their voices. 4Now when the seven thunders uttered their voices,[g] I was about to write; but I heard a voice from heaven saying to me,[h] "Seal up the things which the seven thunders uttered, and do not write them."

5*The angel whom I saw standing on the sea and on the land raised up his hand[i] to heaven 6and swore by Him who lives forever and ever, who created heaven and the things that are in it, the earth and the things that are in it, and the sea and the things that are in it, that there should be delay no longer, 7but in the days of the sounding of the seventh angel, when he is about to sound, the mystery of God would be finished, as He declared to His servants the prophets.

8*Then the voice which I heard from heaven spoke to me again and said, "Go, take the little book which is open in the hand of the angel who stands on the sea and on the earth."

9So I went to the angel and said to him, "Give me the little book."

And he said to me, "Take and eat it; and it will make your stomach bitter, but it will be as sweet as honey in your mouth."

10Then I took the little book out of the angel's hand and ate it, and it was as sweet as honey in my mouth. But when I had eaten it, my stomach became bitter. 11And he[j] said to me, "You must prophesy again about many peoples, nations, tongues, and kings."

11 Then* I was given a reed like a measuring rod. And the angel stood,[k] saying, "Rise and measure the temple of God, the altar, and those who worship there. 2But leave out the court which is outside the temple, and do not measure it, for it has been given to the Gentiles. And they will tread the holy city underfoot *for* forty-two months. 3*And I will give power to my two witnesses, and

CHAPTER 10

10:3, 4 *The voice of the thunders.* We do not know what the angel shouted or what the seven thunders uttered (Ps. 29). God has given sufficient truth in His Word for salvation and godly living, so we must not crave to know the hidden things (Deut. 29:29). The purpose of Scripture is to save sinners and sanctify character, not satisfy curiosity.

10:5–7 *The voice of the angel.* The angel said, "There will be delay no longer!" What joy this statement will bring to the martyrs (and others) who ask, "How long?" (6:9–11). God has His times (Eccles. 3:1–8) and will accomplish His purposes on schedule. Our responsibility is to be faithful and not inquisitive (Acts 1:6–8).

10:8–11 *The voice of the apostle.* God still needed John to declare His message to the people. No angel could take his place. But to share God's message, we must take the Word, receive it inwardly like food, and let it become part of us (Jer. 15:16; Ezek. 3:1–11; 1 Thess. 2:13). The Word is sweet when you read it (Ps. 119:103) but bitter when it goes deeper and you digest it.

CHAPTER 11

11:1 To measure something is to claim it for yourself, as when the new owner of a house measures it for carpets, drapes, and so forth. John claims the temple in Jerusalem for the Lord even though in a short time the Antichrist will take it over (2 Thess. 2:3–4). God may seem to lose some battles, but He will finally win the war. We walk by faith.

11:3–12 We do not know who the two witnesses are, but they encourage us to be faithful to the Lord in difficult times. God protects them and then permits them to be slain (Acts 12:1–10). God's servants are immortal until their work is done. But Satan's victory is short, for God takes the two men to heaven. Satan's victory is defeat, but God's seeming defeat is victory.

❝*If you conscientiously undertake to walk in the truth revealed, you too will know something of its bitterness. . . . We need the bitter as well as the sweet; and every soul who has walked in the truth, as God has revealed it to him, has found, at last, the blessedness of obedience.*❞

—H. A. Ironside

9:19 [e]NU-Text and M-Text read *the power of the horses.* 9:21 [f]NU-Text and M-Text read *drugs.* 10:4 [g]NU-Text and M-Text read *sounded.* [h]NU-Text and M-Text omit *to me.* 10:5 [i]NU-Text and M-Text read *right hand.* 10:11 [j]NU-Text and M-Text read *they.* 11:1 [k]NU-Text and M-Text omit *And the angel stood.*

&&*No doctrine in the whole Word of God has more excited the hatred of mankind than the truth of the absolute sovereignty of God. The fact that 'the Lord reigneth' is indisputable, and it is this fact that arouses the utmost opposition in the unrenewed human heart.***&&*
—Charles Haddon Spurgeon

11:10–19 No matter what the enemy may do to the temple on earth, he cannot touch the temple in heaven (v. 19). The rejoicing of evil men soon becomes lamentation (vv. 10–14), while the hosts of heaven proclaim the sovereign reign of Jesus Christ (vv. 15–18). Let the nations rage (Ps. 2): Jesus Christ will reign forever and ever!

they will prophesy one thousand two hundred and sixty days, clothed in sackcloth.''

4These are the two olive trees and the two lampstands standing before the God*l* of the earth. 5And if anyone wants to harm them, fire proceeds from their mouth and devours their enemies. And if anyone wants to harm them, he must be killed in this manner. 6These have power to shut heaven, so that no rain falls in the days of their prophecy; and they have power over waters to turn them to blood, and to strike the earth with all plagues, as often as they desire.

7When they finish their testimony, the beast that ascends out of the bottomless pit will make war against them, overcome them, and kill them. 8And their dead bodies *will lie* in the street of the great city which spiritually is called Sodom and Egypt, where also our*m* Lord was crucified. 9Then *those* from the peoples, tribes, tongues, and nations will see their dead bodies three-and-a-half days, and not allow*n* their dead bodies to be put into graves. 10*And those who dwell on the earth will rejoice over them, make merry, and send gifts to one another, because these two prophets tormented those who dwell on the earth.

11Now after the three-and-a-half days the breath of life from God entered them, and they stood on their feet, and great fear fell on those who saw them. 12And they*o* heard a loud voice from heaven saying to them, "Come up here." And they ascended to heaven in a cloud, and their enemies saw them. 13In the same hour there was a great earthquake, and a tenth of the city fell. In the earthquake seven thousand people were killed, and the rest were afraid and gave glory to the God of heaven.

14The second woe is past. Behold, the third woe is coming quickly.

15Then the seventh angel sounded: And there were loud voices in heaven, saying, "The kingdoms*p* of this world have become *the kingdoms of our Lord and of His Christ, and He shall reign forever and ever!*" 16And the twenty-four elders who sat before God on their thrones fell on their faces and worshiped God, 17saying:

> "We give You thanks, O Lord God Almighty,
> The One who is and who was and who is to come,*q*
> Because You have taken Your great power and reigned.
> 18 The nations were angry, and Your wrath has come,
> And the time of the dead, that they should be judged,
> And that You should reward Your servants the prophets and the saints,
> And those who fear Your name, small and great,
> And should destroy those who destroy the earth."

19Then the temple of God was opened in heaven, and the ark of His covenant*r* was seen

---

11:4 *l*NU-Text and M-Text read *Lord.*   11:8 *m*NU-Text and M-Text read *their.*   11:9 *n*NU-Text and M-Text read *nations see . . . and will not allow.*   11:12 *o*M-Text reads *I.* 11:15 *p*NU-Text and M-Text read *kingdom . . . has become.* 11:17 *q*NU-Text and M-Text omit *and who is to come.* 11:19 *r*M-Text reads *the covenant of the Lord.*

in His temple. And there were lightnings, noises, thunderings, an earthquake, and great hail.

12 Now* a great sign appeared in heaven: a woman clothed with the sun, with the moon under her feet, and on her head a garland of twelve stars. 2Then being with child, she cried out in labor and in pain to give birth.

3And another sign appeared in heaven: behold, a great, fiery red dragon having seven heads and ten horns, and seven diadems on his heads. 4His tail drew a third of the stars of heaven and threw them to the earth. And the dragon stood before the woman who was ready to give birth, to devour her Child as soon as it was born. 5She bore a male Child who was to rule all nations with a rod of iron. And her Child was caught up to God and His throne. 6Then the woman fled into the wilderness, where she has a place prepared by God, that they should feed her there one thousand two hundred and sixty days.

7*And war broke out in heaven: Michael and his angels fought with the dragon; and the dragon and his angels fought, 8but they did not prevail, nor was a place found for thems in heaven any longer. 9So the great dragon was cast out, that serpent of old, called the Devil and Satan, who deceives the whole world; he was cast to the earth, and his angels were cast out with him.

10*Then I heard a loud voice saying in heaven, "Now salvation, and strength, and the kingdom of our God, and the power of His Christ have come, for the accuser of our brethren, who accused them before our God day and night, has been cast down. 11And they overcame him by the blood of the Lamb and by the word of their testimony, and they did not love their lives to the death. 12*Therefore rejoice, O heavens, and you who dwell in them! Woe to the inhabitants of the earth and the sea! For the devil has come down to you, having great wrath, because he knows that he has a short time."

13Now when the dragon saw that he had been cast to the earth, he persecuted the woman who gave birth to the male *Child*. 14But the woman was given two wings of a great eagle, that she might fly into the wilderness to her place, where she is nourished for a time and times and half a time, from the presence of the serpent. 15So the serpent spewed water out of his mouth like a flood after the woman, that he might cause her to be carried away by the flood. 16But the earth helped the woman, and the earth opened its mouth and swallowed up the flood which the dragon had spewed out of his mouth. 17And the dragon was enraged with the woman, and he went to make war with the rest of her offspring, who keep the commandments of God and have the testimony of Jesus Christ.t

13 Then* Iu stood on the sand of the sea. And I saw a beast rising up out of the sea, having seven heads and ten horns,v and on his horns ten crowns, and on his heads a blasphemous name. 2Now the beast which I saw was like a leopard, his feet were like *the feet of* a bear, and his mouth

CHAPTER 12

12:1–6 *The Murderer.* The Child is Jesus Christ, and the woman represents Israel who brought the Savior into the world. The dragon is Satan who tried to keep Jesus from being born and attempted to kill Him after He was born. Satan wants to rule this world, and he will not submit to the King (v. 5; Ps. 2:9).

12:7–9 *The Deceiver.* This is a picture of the fall of Satan (Isa. 14:12–17). He was able to deceive one-third of the angels into following him (v. 4), and now he deceives the world into worshiping him.

12:10, 11 *The Accuser.* Satan has access to God's throne where he accuses God's people (Job 1—2; Zech. 3). The Lamb overcomes him because of His victory at Calvary (Rom. 8:31–34; 1 John 2:1–2) and because of the power of the Word (Eph. 6:17).

12:12–17 *The Persecutor.* The war may be over in heaven, but it is getting more intense here on earth. Satan is angry and seeks to destroy the Jews and make war with anyone who trusts the Lord. God is able to shelter His people in spite of Satan's attacks, but be sure you wear the armor (Eph. 6:10–18) and trust the blood of Jesus.

CHAPTER 13

13:1–4 *Worship.* The beast from the sea is Satan's final and greatest masterpiece—Antichrist, who towers above all the tyrants and dictators of world history. This man accepts the offer that Satan gave to Jesus (v. 2; Matt. 4:8–10). The world worships him as a god, but heaven sees him as a beast (Dan. 7). The counterfeit Christ is now on the scene!

> ❝*I'm not afraid of the devil. The devil can handle me—he's got judo I never heard of. But he can't handle the One to whom I'm joined; he can't handle the One to whom I'm united; he can't handle the One whose nature dwells in my nature.*❞
>
> —A. W. Tozer

12:8 sM-Text reads *him.*   12:17 tNU-Text and M-Text omit *Christ.*   13:1 uNU-Text reads *he.* vNU-Text and M-Text read *ten horns and seven heads.*

13:5–10 Warfare. The Beast fights God by speaking blasphemous words (Dan. 7:8, 11, 20, 25) and by persecuting the saints (v. 7; Dan. 7:25). It may seem strange that God should permit His people to be defeated, yet this is part of His plan (Heb. 11:35–40). In every age, God's people have had to battle some satanic beast.

13:11–18 Wealth. The Beast's "prime minister" leads the world to worship the Beast by controlling all the wealth. It was a matter of life or death! When you combine political power with economic power and all religion, you have a formula for controlling the whole world. But the lost world worships money and power, so the task will not be too difficult.

like the mouth of a lion. The dragon gave him his power, his throne, and great authority. 3And I saw one of his heads as if it had been mortally wounded, and his deadly wound was healed. And all the world marveled and followed the beast. 4So they worshiped the dragon who gave authority to the beast; and they worshiped the beast, saying, "Who is like the beast? Who is able to make war with him?"

5*And he was given a mouth speaking great things and blasphemies, and he was given authority to continuew for forty-two months. 6Then he opened his mouth in blasphemy against God, to blaspheme His name, His tabernacle, and those who dwell in heaven. 7It was granted to him to make war with the saints and to overcome them. And authority was given him over every tribe,x tongue, and nation. 8All who dwell on the earth will worship him, whose names have not been written in the Book of Life of the Lamb slain from the foundation of the world.

9If anyone has an ear, let him hear. 10He who leads into captivity shall go into captivity; he who kills with the sword must be killed with the sword. Here is the patience and the faith of the saints.

11*Then I saw another beast coming up out of the earth, and he had two horns like a lamb and spoke like a dragon. 12And he exercises all the authority of the first beast in his presence, and causes the earth and those who dwell in it to worship the first beast, whose deadly wound was healed. 13He performs great signs, so that he even makes fire come down from heaven on the earth in the sight of men. 14And he deceives thosey who dwell on the earth by those signs which he was granted to do in the sight of the beast, telling those who dwell on the earth to make an image to the beast who was wounded by the sword and lived. 15He was granted power to give breath to the image of the beast, that the image of the beast should both speak and cause as many as would not worship the image of the beast to be killed. 16He causes all, both small and great, rich and poor, free and slave, to receive a mark on their right hand or on their foreheads, 17and that no one may buy or sell except one who has the mark orz the name of the beast, or the number of his name.

18Here is wisdom. Let him who has understanding calculate the number of the beast, for it is the number of a man: His number is 666.

13:5 wM-Text reads make war.　13:7 xNU-Text and M-Text add and people.　13:14 yM-Text reads my own people.　13:17 zNU-Text and M-Text omit or.

Which Riches Are Yours

Since all the riches of this world
May be gifts from the Devil and earthly kings,
I should suspect that I worshiped the Devil
If I thanked God for worldly things.
The countless gold of a merry heart,
The rubies and pearls of a loving eye,
The indolent never can bring to the mart,
Nor the cunning hoard up in his treasury.

　　　　　　　　　　　　William Blake

14 Then I looked, and behold, a[a] Lamb standing on Mount Zion, and with Him one hundred *and* forty-four thousand, having[b] His Father's name written on their foreheads. [2]And I heard a voice from heaven, like the voice of many waters, and like the voice of loud thunder. And I heard the sound of harpists playing their harps. [3]They sang as it were a new song before the throne, before the four living creatures, and the elders; and no one could learn that song except the hundred *and* forty-four thousand who were redeemed from the earth. [4]*These are the ones who were not defiled with women, for they are virgins. These are the ones who follow the Lamb wherever He goes. These were redeemed[c] from *among* men, *being* firstfruits to God and to the Lamb. [5]And in their mouth was found no deceit,[d] for they are without fault before the throne of God.[e]

[6]Then I saw another angel flying in the midst of heaven, having the everlasting gospel to preach to those who dwell on the earth—to every nation, tribe, tongue, and people— [7]saying with a loud voice, "Fear God and give glory to Him, for the hour of His judgment has come; and worship Him who made heaven and earth, the sea and springs of water."

[8]*And another angel followed, saying, "Babylon[f] is fallen, is fallen, that great city, because she has made all nations drink of the wine of the wrath of her fornication."

[9]Then a third angel followed them, saying with a loud voice, "If anyone worships the beast and his image, and receives *his* mark on his forehead or on his hand, [10]he himself shall also drink of the wine of the wrath of God, which is poured out full strength into the cup of His indignation. He shall be tormented with fire and brimstone in the presence of the holy angels and in the presence of the Lamb. [11]And the smoke of their torment ascends forever and ever; and they have no rest day or night, who worship the beast and his image, and whoever receives the mark of his name."

[12]Here is the patience of the saints; here *are* those[g] who keep the commandments of God and the faith of Jesus.

[13]Then I heard a voice from heaven saying to me,[h] "Write: 'Blessed *are* the dead who die in the Lord from now on.'"

"Yes," says the Spirit, "that they may rest from their labors, and their works follow them."

[14]*Then I looked, and behold, a white cloud, and on the cloud sat *One* like the Son of Man, having on His head a golden crown, and in His hand a sharp sickle. [15]And another angel came out of the temple, crying with a loud voice to Him who sat on the cloud, "Thrust in Your sickle and reap, for the time has come for You[i] to reap, for the harvest of the earth is ripe." [16]So He who sat on the cloud thrust in His sickle on the earth, and the earth was reaped.

CHAPTER 14

14:4 John used agricultural images to tell us that the time was ripe for judgment.

Firstfruits. God takes the best for Himself before the harvest begins. We met the 144,000 in chapter 7, God's sealed servants who come through the Tribulation and sing the praises of the Lamb. The description in verse 4 should be taken in a spiritual sense: they did not commit fornication by worshiping the Beast or his image (Exod. 34:15; James 4:4).

14:8, 10 *Wine.* The "cup of wrath" is an image borrowed from Jeremiah 25:15ff. God pours out His wrath on those who follow the Beast and reject God's truth. Although verse 13 may be applied to all believers who die, it will have a special meaning to the martyrs of that evil day.

14:14–20 *Reaping.* God is allowing the seeds of sin to grow and produce a harvest (vv. 14–16). One day, the world will reap what it has sown. John also uses the grape harvest to illustrate the coming judgment (vv. 17–20). The "vine of the earth" is ripening, and one day God will apply the sickle. Meanwhile, the branches in the True Vine (John 15:1–8) should be bearing more and more fruit.

14:1 [a]NU-Text and M-Text read *the.* [b]NU-Text and M-Text add *His name and.* 14:4 [c]M-Text adds *by Jesus.* 14:5 [d]NU-Text and M-Text read *falsehood.* [e]NU-Text and M-Text omit *before the throne of God.* 14:8 [f]NU-Text reads *Babylon the great is fallen, is fallen, which has made;* M-Text reads *Babylon the great is fallen. She has made.* 14:12 [g]NU-Text and M-Text omit *here are those.* 14:13 [h]NU-Text and M-Text omit *to me.* 14:15 [i]NU-Text and M-Text omit *for You.*

¹⁷Then another angel came out of the temple which is in heaven, he also having a sharp sickle. ¹⁸And another angel came out from the altar, who had power over fire, and he cried with a loud cry to him who had the sharp sickle, saying, "Thrust in your sharp sickle and gather the clusters of the vine of the earth, for her grapes are fully ripe." ¹⁹So the angel thrust his sickle into the earth and gathered the vine of the earth, and threw *it* into the great winepress of the wrath of God. ²⁰And the winepress was trampled outside the city, and blood came out of the winepress, up to the horses' bridles, for one thousand six hundred furlongs.

CHAPTER 15

15:1, 6, 7 John reaches back into the Old Testament to teach us about God's judgment and grace.
The seven angels have bowls of wrath, plagues to pour on a wicked world. They remind us of the plagues God sent to Egypt in the days of Moses (Exod. 7—12). Note in chapter 16 how the plagues parallel those God sent to Egypt.

15:2–4 God delivered Israel from Egypt, and they sang a song of victory at the Red Sea (Exod. 15). John saw the tribulation victors singing by the heavenly sea of glass. Moses and the Lamb come together in the song of triumph.

15:8 The heavenly tabernacle is filled with smoke, just as the glory of God filled both the tabernacle (Exod. 40:34–38) and the temple (1 Kings 8:10–11). But the glory then was a mark of God's presence and blessing. The glory John saw was an announcement that God's wrath was about to be poured out on a wicked world.
Sinners will not learn from the past, but believers can be encouraged by the past.
The God of Moses and Israel is still defending His people. There is a new song for you to sing.

CHAPTER 16

16:1–7 No matter what the unbelieving world may say, God's judgments are righteous. Sinners reap what they sow. Because "righteousness and justice are the foundation of His throne" (Ps. 97:2), nobody can accuse God of being unfair.

15 Then* I saw another sign in heaven, great and marvelous: seven angels having the seven last plagues, for in them the wrath of God is complete.
²*And I saw *something* like a sea of glass mingled with fire, and those who have the victory over the beast, over his image and over his mark^j *and* over the number of his name, standing on the sea of glass, having harps of God. ³They sing the song of Moses, the servant of God, and the song of the Lamb, saying:

> "Great and marvelous *are* Your works,
> Lord God Almighty!
> Just and true *are* Your ways,
> O King of the saints!^k
> 4 Who shall not fear You, O Lord, and glorify Your name?
> For *You* alone *are* holy.
> For all nations shall come and worship before You,
> For Your judgments have been manifested."

⁵After these things I looked, and behold,^l the temple of the tabernacle of the testimony in heaven was opened. ⁶And out of the temple came the seven angels having the seven plagues, clothed in pure bright linen, and having their chests girded with golden bands. ⁷Then one of the four living creatures gave to the seven angels seven golden bowls full of the wrath of God who lives forever and ever. ⁸*The temple was filled with smoke from the glory of God and from His power, and no one was able to enter the temple till the seven plagues of the seven angels were completed.

16 Then* I heard a loud voice from the temple saying to the seven angels, "Go and pour out the bowls^m of the wrath of God on the earth."
²So the first went and poured out his bowl upon the earth, and a foul and loathsome sore came upon the men who had the mark of the beast and those who worshiped his image.

❝*In righteousness God reveals chiefly His love of holiness; in justice, chiefly his hatred of sin . . . Neither justice nor righteousness . . . is a matter of arbitrary will. They are revelations of the inmost nature of God.***❞**
—Augustus Hopkins Strong

15:2 ^jNU-Text and M-Text omit *over his mark.*   15:3 ^kNU-Text and M-Text read *nations.*   15:5 ^lNU-Text and M-Text omit *behold.*   16:1 ^mNU-Text and M-Text read *seven bowls.*

The Battlefield—*Armageddon* (Rev. 16:16) is Hebrew for "the hill of Megiddo"; and *Megiddo* means "place of slaughter." It is the plain in the Holy Land where Barak defeated the Canaanites (Judg. 5:19) and Gideon the Midianites (Judg. 7). King Saul fought his last battle there (1 Sam. 31). One of the greatest natural battlefields in the world, it is where the Antichrist will gather the world's armies to fight against Jesus Christ (Isa. 24; Joel 3; Zech. 12—14). Revelation 19:11–21 records the outcome.

3Then the second angel poured out his bowl on
the sea, and it became blood as of a dead *man;*
and every living creature in the sea died.
4Then the third angel poured out his bowl on
the rivers and springs of water, and they became
blood. 5And I heard the angel of the waters saying:

"You are righteous, O Lord,[n]
The One who is and who was and who is
to be,[o]
Because You have judged these things.
6 For they have shed the blood of saints and
prophets,
And You have given them blood to drink.
For[p] it is their just due."

7And I heard another from[q] the altar saying,
"Even so, Lord God Almighty, true and righteous
are Your judgments."
8*Then the fourth angel poured out his bowl on
the sun, and power was given to him to scorch
men with fire. 9And men were scorched with great
heat, and they blasphemed the name of God who
has power over these plagues; and they did not
repent and give Him glory.
10Then the fifth angel poured out his bowl on
the throne of the beast, and his kingdom became
full of darkness; and they gnawed their tongues
because of the pain. 11They blasphemed the God
of heaven because of their pains and their sores,
and did not repent of their deeds.
12Then the sixth angel poured out his bowl on
the great river Euphrates, and its water was dried
up, so that the way of the kings from the east
might be prepared. 13And I saw three unclean
spirits like frogs *coming* out of the mouth of the
dragon, out of the mouth of the beast, and out of
the mouth of the false prophet. 14For they are spirits of demons, performing signs, *which* go out to
the kings of the earth and[r] of the whole world,
to gather them to the battle of that great day of
God Almighty.
15*"Behold, I am coming as a thief. Blessed *is*
he who watches, and keeps his garments, lest he
walk naked and they see his shame."
16And they gathered them together to the place
called in Hebrew, Armageddon.[s]
17*Then the seventh angel poured out his bowl
into the air, and a loud voice came out of the temple of heaven, from the throne, saying, "It is
done!" 18And there were noises and thunderings
and lightnings; and there was a great earthquake,
such a mighty and great earthquake as had not
occurred since men were on the earth. 19Now the
great city was divided into three parts, and the
cities of the nations fell. And great Babylon was
remembered before God, to give her the cup of
the wine of the fierceness of His wrath. 20Then
every island fled away, and the mountains were
not found. 21And great hail from heaven fell upon
men, *each hailstone* about the weight of a talent.
Men blasphemed God because of the plague of
the hail, since that plague was exceedingly great.

16:8–11 God's judgments do not change men's hearts. God judges sinners not to reveal His grace but to uphold His holiness. Sinners in the last days will be like Pharaoh in the days of Moses; they will harden their hearts more as God's judgments increase.

16:15 Against the dark background of judgment shines the promise of God. Christ is coming soon, and we must watch eagerly and walk carefully (3:1–6) so that we will be ready to meet Him (1 John 2:28).

16:17–21 God's judgment will one day be finished. God's long-suffering will finally end, and His wrath will be revealed. What holds Him back today? Read 2 Peter 3:9, 15 for the answer.

16:5 [n]NU-Text and M-Text omit *O Lord.* [o]NU-Text and M-Text read *who was, the Holy One.* 16:6 [p]NU-Text and M-Text omit *For.* 16:7 [q]NU-Text and M-Text omit *another from.*
16:14 [r]NU-Text and M-Text omit *of the earth and.*
16:16 [s]M-Text reads *Megiddo.*

CHAPTER 17

17:1ff Each person must identify with either the harlot or the bride (21:9); there can be no compromise. The woman represents the ultimate in godless world religion. She is joined with government (carried by the Beast) and corrupts everything she touches. The bride is the true church of Jesus Christ, cleansed by His blood and destined for glory.

Participating in false religion is like committing adultery: you are unfaithful to the one to whom you pledged your love (Isa. 57:3; Jer. 3:8–9; Hos. 2:4). The harlot was popular for a time, but then her "lovers" turned on her and destroyed her (v.6). The Antichrist will use a world church to get himself into power and then establish his own religion (13:11–15).

Though Christians must be good citizens and seek to influence government for the Lord, the church must not marry political systems. The systems will only use the church to promote their own plans and then abandon it. Christ's kingdom is not of this world (John 18:33–38), and the enemy is spiritual (Eph. 6:10 ff.). We must use spiritual weapons (2 Cor. 10:3–6) to fight spiritual enemies.

CHAPTER 18

18:1ff The harlot and the bride are each identified with a city: the harlot with Babylon and the bride with heavenly Jerusalem (21:9ff.). The heavenly city will be the bride's home for eternity, but Babylon will be destroyed by God. The world's economy will be ruined.

John certainly had Rome in mind when he wrote this chapter, but his imagery means much more. Babylon symbolizes the whole godless world system that caters to the appetites of sinful men and women (1 John 2:15–17). True believers have nothing in common with the harlot and her city and should be separated from them (v. 4; Jer. 50:8; 51:6; 2 Cor. 6:14–18). In every age, the church has had to identify its Babylon and separate from it.

When God judges sinners, earth laments and heaven rejoices (v. 20). Most people are concerned primarily with satisfying their physical desires; they are not concerned about things spiritual or eternal. They live for the temporary and the immediate, not the eternal.

17 Then* one of the seven angels who had the seven bowls came and talked with me, saying to me,[t] "Come, I will show you the judgment of the great harlot who sits on many waters, [2]with whom the kings of the earth committed fornication, and the inhabitants of the earth were made drunk with the wine of her fornication." [3]So he carried me away in the Spirit into the wilderness. And I saw a woman sitting on a scarlet beast *which was* full of names of blasphemy, having seven heads and ten horns. [4]The woman was arrayed in purple and scarlet, and adorned with gold and precious stones and pearls, having in her hand a golden cup full of abominations and the filthiness of her fornication.[u] [5]And on her forehead a name *was* written:

MYSTERY, BABYLON THE GREAT, THE MOTHER OF HARLOTS AND OF THE ABOMINATIONS OF THE EARTH.

[6]I saw the woman, drunk with the blood of the saints and with the blood of the martyrs of Jesus. And when I saw her, I marveled with great amazement.

[7]But the angel said to me, "Why did you marvel? I will tell you the mystery of the woman and of the beast that carries her, which has the seven heads and the ten horns. [8]The beast that you saw was, and is not, and will ascend out of the bottomless pit and go to perdition. And those who dwell on the earth will marvel, whose names are not written in the Book of Life from the foundation of the world, when they see the beast that was, and is not, and yet is.[v]

[9]"Here *is* the mind which has wisdom: The seven heads are seven mountains on which the woman sits. [10]There are also seven kings. Five have fallen, one is, *and* the other has not yet come. And when he comes, he must continue a short time. [11]The beast that was, and is not, is himself also the eighth, and is of the seven, and is going to perdition.

[12]"The ten horns which you saw are ten kings who have received no kingdom as yet, but they receive authority for one hour as kings with the beast. [13]These are of one mind, and they will give their power and authority to the beast. [14]These will make war with the Lamb, and the Lamb will overcome them, for He is Lord of lords and King of kings; and those *who are* with Him *are* called, chosen, and faithful."

[15]Then he said to me, "The waters which you saw, where the harlot sits, are peoples, multitudes, nations, and tongues. [16]And the ten horns which you saw on[w] the beast, these will hate the harlot, make her desolate and naked, eat her flesh and burn her with fire. [17]For God has put it into their hearts to fulfill His purpose, to be of one mind, and to give their kingdom to the beast, until the words of God are fulfilled. [18]And the woman whom you saw is that great city which reigns over the kings of the earth."

18 After* these things I saw another angel coming down from heaven, having great authority, and the earth was illuminated with his

17:1 [t]NU-Text and M-Text omit *to me.*   17:4 [u]M-Text reads *the filthiness of the fornication of the earth.*   17:8 [v]NU-Text and M-Text read *and shall be present.*   17:16 [w]NU-Text and M-Text read *saw, and the beast.*

glory. 2And he cried mightily[x] with a loud voice, saying, "Babylon the great is fallen, is fallen, and has become a dwelling place of demons, a prison for every foul spirit, and a cage for every unclean and hated bird! 3For all the nations have drunk of the wine of the wrath of her fornication, the kings of the earth have committed fornication with her, and the merchants of the earth have become rich through the abundance of her luxury."

4And I heard another voice from heaven saying, "Come out of her, my people, lest you share in her sins, and lest you receive of her plagues. 5For her sins have reached[y] to heaven, and God has remembered her iniquities. 6Render to her just as she rendered to you,[z] and repay her double according to her works; in the cup which she has mixed, mix double for her. 7In the measure that she glorified herself and lived luxuriously, in the same measure give her torment and sorrow; for she says in her heart, 'I sit as queen, and am no widow, and will not see sorrow.' 8Therefore her plagues will come in one day—death and mourning and famine. And she will be utterly burned with fire, for strong is the Lord God who judges[a] her.

9"The kings of the earth who committed fornication and lived luxuriously with her will weep and lament for her, when they see the smoke of her burning, 10standing at a distance for fear of her torment, saying, 'Alas, alas, that great city Babylon, that mighty city! For in one hour your judgment has come.'

11"And the merchants of the earth will weep and mourn over her, for no one buys their merchandise anymore: 12merchandise of gold and silver, precious stones and pearls, fine linen and purple, silk and scarlet, every kind of citron wood, every kind of object of ivory, every kind of object of most precious wood, bronze, iron, and marble; 13and cinnamon and incense, fragrant oil and frankincense, wine and oil, fine flour and wheat, cattle and sheep, horses and chariots, and bodies and souls of men. 14The fruit that your soul longed for has gone from you, and all the things which are rich and splendid have gone from you,[b] and you shall find them no more at all. 15The merchants of these things, who became rich by her, will stand at a distance for fear of her torment, weeping and wailing, 16and saying, 'Alas, alas, that great city that was clothed in fine linen, purple, and scarlet, and adorned with gold and precious stones and pearls! 17For in one hour such great riches came to nothing.' Every shipmaster, all who travel by ship, sailors, and as many as trade on the sea, stood at a distance 18and cried out when they saw the smoke of her burning, saying, 'What is like this great city?'

19"They threw dust on their heads and cried out, weeping and wailing, and saying, 'Alas, alas, that great city, in which all who had ships on the sea became rich by her wealth! For in one hour she is made desolate.'

20"Rejoice over her, O heaven, and you holy apostles[c] and prophets, for God has avenged you on her!"

❝In our well-intentioned identification with the world, we do not mold it—it molds us. We are not to be isolated but insulated, moving in the midst of evil but untouched by it.**❞**
—Vance Havner

18:2 [x]NU-Text and M-Text omit mightily. 18:5 [y]NU-Text and M-Text read have been heaped up. 18:6 [z]NU-Text and M-Text omit to you. 18:8 [a]NU-Text and M-Text read has judged. 18:14 [b]NU-Text and M-Text read been lost to you. 18:20 [c]NU-Text and M-Text read saints and apostles.

19:1–6 Celebration. Sinners cry "Alas!" but saints shout "Hallelujah!" at the fall of the godless world system called Babylon. Sin has been judged, God's servants have been vindicated, God has been glorified, and Christ is about to usher in His kingdom. Even as you anticipate these victories, by faith you can shout "Hallelujah!"

19:7–9, 17–21 Proclamation. Two contrasting suppers are named in this chapter: the marriage supper of the Lamb (v. 9), which brings blessing, and the "supper of the great God" (vv. 17–21), which brings judgment. The bride makes herself ready at the judgment seat of Christ where her "spots and wrinkles" are taken away (Eph. 5:25–27) and she receives rewards for faithful service. In contrast, the godless armies of earth are defeated by the Lord and become food for the birds. This is the battle of Armageddon mentioned in Revelation 16:16.

19:11–16 Revelation. The conquering Christ comes with His armies and defeats all His enemies! Contrast this with His ride into Jerusalem on Palm Sunday (Matt. 21:1–11), and review the Father's promises in Psalm 2. Also contrast it with the ride of the Antichrist (6:1–2). It encourages us to know that our Savior is *today* King of kings and Lord of lords, and that the future is secure because He is reigning.

The Coming Kingdom

❝ *His kingdom is coming!*
Oh, tell me the story!
God's banner exalted shall be;
The earth shall be filled with
His wonder and glory,
As waters that cover
the sea. ❞

—Anonymous

21Then a mighty angel took up a stone like a great millstone and threw *it* into the sea, saying, "Thus with violence the great city Babylon shall be thrown down, and shall not be found anymore. 22The sound of harpists, musicians, flutists, and trumpeters shall not be heard in you anymore. No craftsman of any craft shall be found in you anymore, and the sound of a millstone shall not be heard in you anymore. 23The light of a lamp shall not shine in you anymore, and the voice of bridegroom and bride shall not be heard in you anymore. For your merchants were the great men of the earth, for by your sorcery all the nations were deceived. 24And in her was found the blood of prophets and saints, and of all who were slain on the earth."

19 After* these things I heard[d] a loud voice of a great multitude in heaven, saying, "Alleluia! Salvation and glory and honor and power *belong* to the Lord[e] our God! 2For true and righteous *are* His judgments, because He has judged the great harlot who corrupted the earth with her fornication; and He has avenged on her the blood of His servants *shed* by her." 3Again they said, "Alleluia! Her smoke rises up forever and ever!" 4And the twenty-four elders and the four living creatures fell down and worshiped God who sat on the throne, saying, "Amen! Alleluia!" 5Then a voice came from the throne, saying, "Praise our God, all you His servants and those who fear Him, both[f] small and great!"

6And I heard, as it were, the voice of a great multitude, as the sound of many waters and as the sound of mighty thunderings, saying, "Alleluia! For the[g] Lord God Omnipotent reigns! 7*Let us be glad and rejoice and give Him glory, for the marriage of the Lamb has come, and His wife has made herself ready." 8And to her it was granted to be arrayed in fine linen, clean and bright, for the fine linen is the righteous acts of the saints.

9Then he said to me, "Write: 'Blessed *are* those who are called to the marriage supper of the Lamb!'" And he said to me, "These are the true sayings of God." 10And I fell at his feet to worship him. But he said to me, "See *that you do* not *do that!* I am your fellow servant, and of your brethren who have the testimony of Jesus. Worship God! For the testimony of Jesus is the spirit of prophecy."

11*Now I saw heaven opened, and behold, a white horse. And He who sat on him *was* called Faithful and True, and in righteousness He judges and makes war. 12His eyes *were* like a flame of fire, and on His head *were* many crowns. He had[h] a name written that no one knew except Himself. 13He *was* clothed with a robe dipped in blood, and His name is called The Word of God. 14And the armies in heaven, clothed in fine linen, white and clean,[i] followed Him on white horses. 15Now out of His mouth goes a sharp[j] sword, that with it He should strike the nations. And He Himself will rule them with a rod of iron. He Himself treads the winepress of the fierceness and wrath

---

19:1 [d]NU-Text and M-Text add *something like.* [e]NU-Text and M-Text omit *the Lord.* 19:5 [f]NU-Text and M-Text omit *both.* 19:6 [g]NU-Text and M-Text read *our.* 19:12 [h]M-Text adds *names written, and.* 19:14 [i]NU-Text and M-Text read *pure white linen.* 19:15 [j]M-Text adds *two-edged.*

of Almighty God. ¹⁶And He has on *His* robe and
on His thigh a name written:

KING OF KINGS AND LORD OF LORDS.

¹⁷Then I saw an angel standing in the sun; and
he cried with a loud voice, saying to all the birds
that fly in the midst of heaven, "Come and gather
together for the supper of the great God,ᵏ ¹⁸that
you may eat the flesh of kings, the flesh of captains, the flesh of mighty men, the flesh of horses
and of those who sit on them, and the flesh of
all *people,* free*ˡ* and slave, both small and great."
¹⁹And I saw the beast, the kings of the earth,
and their armies, gathered together to make war
against Him who sat on the horse and against
His army. ²⁰Then the beast was captured, and
with him the false prophet who worked signs in
his presence, by which he deceived those who received the mark of the beast and those who worshiped his image. These two were cast alive into
the lake of fire burning with brimstone. ²¹And the
rest were killed with the sword which proceeded
from the mouth of Him who sat on the horse. And
all the birds were filled with their flesh.

20 Then* I saw an angel coming down from
heaven, having the key to the bottomless
pit and a great chain in his hand. ²He laid hold
of the dragon, that serpent of old, who is *the* Devil
and Satan, and bound him for a thousand years;
³and he cast him into the bottomless pit, and shut
him up, and set a seal on him, so that he should
deceive the nations no more till the thousand
years were finished. But after these things he must
be released for a little while.

⁴*And I saw thrones, and they sat on them, and
judgment was committed to them. Then *I saw* the
souls of those who had been beheaded for their
witness to Jesus and for the word of God, who
had not worshiped the beast or his image, and
had not received *his* mark on their foreheads or
on their hands. And they lived and reigned with
Christ for aᵐ thousand years. ⁵But the rest of the
dead did not live again until the thousand years
were finished. This *is* the first resurrection.
⁶Blessed and holy *is* he who has part in the first
resurrection. Over such the second death has no
power, but they shall be priests of God and of
Christ, and shall reign with Him a thousand
years.

⁷Now when the thousand years have expired,
Satan will be released from his prison ⁸and will
go out to deceive the nations which are in the
four corners of the earth, Gog and Magog, to
gather them together to battle, whose number *is*
as the sand of the sea. ⁹They went up on the
breadth of the earth and surrounded the camp of
the saints and the beloved city. And fire came
down from God out of heaven and devoured them.
¹⁰The devil, who deceived them, was cast into the
lake of fire and brimstone whereⁿ the beast and
the false prophet *are.* And they will be tormented
day and night forever and ever.

¹¹*Then I saw a great white throne and Him
who sat on it, from whose face the earth and the
heaven fled away. And there was found no place
for them. ¹²And I saw the dead, small and great,

19:17 ᵏNU-Text and M-Text read *the great supper of God.*
19:18 ˡNU-Text and M-Text read *both free.* 20:4 ᵐM-Text
reads *the.* 20:10 ⁿNU-Text and M-Text add *also.*

CHAPTER 20

20:1–3, 7–10 *The lost throne.* Since
Satan's rebellion (Isa. 14:12–15), God has
permitted him to work on this earth, but He
has always kept him in control (Job 1—2).
Satan will exchange his throne for a
bottomless pit, and his final destiny will be
the lake of fire where he will spend eternity
with the Beast and the false prophet (v. 10;
19:20)—and with those who choose to follow
Satan instead of Jesus Christ (Matt. 25:41).

20:4–6 *The kingdom thrones.* The first
resurrection takes place before Jesus
ushers in His kingdom and involves only
those who have trusted Christ (John 5:24–
29; 1 Thess. 4:13–18). They will reign with
Him (Matt. 19:28) and have responsibilities
commensurate with their faithful service
while living on earth (Matt. 25:14–30).

20:11–15 *The great white throne.* This
judgment involves only the lost and follows
the second resurrection, the resurrection to
condemnation. Sinners who rejected Christ
will face Him (John 5:22) and hear Him say,
"Depart from Me!" (Matt. 7:23; 25:41). This
solemn scene ought to move us to pray for
the lost and witness to them, and thank the
Lord for His grace in saving us!

standing before God,[o] and books were opened. And another book was opened, which is *the Book of Life*. And the dead were judged according to their works, by the things which were written in the books. [13]The sea gave up the dead who were in it, and Death and Hades delivered up the dead who were in them. And they were judged, each one according to his works. [14]Then Death and Hades were cast into the lake of fire. This is the second death.[p] [15]And anyone not found written in the Book of Life was cast into the lake of fire.

CHAPTER 21

21:1ff For those who believe in Jesus Christ, the future means "all things new" (v. 5); but for those who reject Him, it means the same old sins for all eternity (vv. 8, 27; 22:11, 15).

Human history begins with a garden (Gen. 2:8–17) and ends with a city that is like a garden. However, the most important thing about the heavenly city is not the absence of sin but the presence of God in all His glory (vv. 3, 11, 23), for His presence makes "all things new."

He is the temple (v. 22) and the light (v. 23); and His presence means there is no more sin, pain, death, sorrow, or crying (v. 4), and no more curse (22:3; Gen. 3:9–19). Heaven is so wonderful that the only way John can describe it is to tell us what will *not* be there! Its beauties and blessings are beyond human words to describe or explain.

Why did Jesus give John this preview of eternal glory? *To encourage His people who go through testing and persecution.* "I go to prepare a place for you" (John 14:1–6) is the best medicine for a broken heart and the best foundation for wavering feet.

❝*The hope of heaven under troubles is like the wind and sails to the soul.*❞
—Samuel Rutherford

❝*No man ought to look for anything in heaven but what one way or another he has some experience in this life.*❞
—John Owen

21 Now* I saw a new heaven and a new earth, for the first heaven and the first earth had passed away. Also there was no more sea. [2]Then I, John,[q] saw the holy city, New Jerusalem, coming down out of heaven from God, prepared as a bride adorned for her husband. [3]And I heard a loud voice from heaven saying, "Behold, the tabernacle of God *is* with men, and He will dwell with them, and they shall be His people. God Himself will be with them *and be* their God. [4]And God will wipe away every tear from their eyes; there shall be no more death, nor sorrow, nor crying. There shall be no more pain, for the former things have passed away."

[5]Then He who sat on the throne said, "Behold, I make all things new." And He said to me,[r] "Write, for these words are true and faithful."

[6]And He said to me, "It is done![s] I am the Alpha and the Omega, the Beginning and the End. I will give of the fountain of the water of life freely to him who thirsts. [7]He who overcomes shall inherit all things,[t] and I will be his God and he shall be My son. [8]But the cowardly, unbelieving,[u] abominable, murderers, sexually immoral, sorcerers, idolaters, and all liars shall have their part in the lake which burns with fire and brimstone, which is the second death."

[9]Then one of the seven angels who had the seven bowls filled with the seven last plagues came to me[v] and talked with me, saying, "Come, I will show you the bride, the Lamb's wife."[w] [10]And he carried me away in the Spirit to a great and high mountain, and showed me the great city, the holy[x] Jerusalem, descending out of heaven from God, [11]having the glory of God. Her light *was* like a most precious stone, like a jasper stone, clear as crystal. [12]Also she had a great and high wall with twelve gates, and twelve angels at the gates, and names written on them, which are *the names* of the twelve tribes of the children of Israel: [13]three gates on the east, three gates on the north, three gates on the south, and three gates on the west.

[14]Now the wall of the city had twelve foundations, and on them were the names[y] of the twelve apostles of the Lamb. [15]And he who talked with me had a gold reed to measure the city, its gates, and its wall. [16]The city is laid out as a square; its

20:12 [o]NU-Text and M-Text read *the throne.* 20:14 [p]NU-Text and M-Text add *the lake of fire.* 21:2 [q]NU-Text and M-Text omit *John.* 21:5 [r]NU-Text and M-Text omit *to me.* 21:6 [s]M-Text omits *It is done.* 21:7 [t]M-Text reads *overcomes, I shall give him these things.* 21:8 [u]M-Text adds *and sinners.* 21:9 [v]NU-Text and M-Text omit *to me.* [w]M-Text reads *I will show you the woman, the Lamb's bride.* 21:10 [x]NU-Text and M-Text omit *the great* and read *the holy city, Jerusalem.* 21:14 [y]NU-Text and M-Text read *twelve names.*

length is as great as its breadth. And he measured the city with the reed: twelve thousand furlongs. Its length, breadth, and height are equal. 17Then he measured its wall: one hundred *and* forty-four cubits, *according* to the measure of a man, that is, of an angel. 18The construction of its wall was *of* jasper; and the city *was* pure gold, like clear glass. 19The foundations of the wall of the city *were* adorned with all kinds of precious stones: the first foundation *was* jasper, the second sapphire, the third chalcedony, the fourth emerald, 20the fifth sardonyx, the sixth sardius, the seventh chrysolite, the eighth beryl, the ninth topaz, the tenth chrysoprase, the eleventh jacinth, and the twelfth amethyst. 21The twelve gates *were* twelve pearls: each individual gate was of one pearl. And the street of the city *was* pure gold, like transparent glass.

22But I saw no temple in it, for the Lord God Almighty and the Lamb are its temple. 23The city had no need of the sun or of the moon to shine in it,z for the glorya of God illuminated it. The Lamb *is* its light. 24And the nations of those who are savedb shall walk in its light, and the kings of the earth bring their glory and honor into it.c 25Its gates shall not be shut at all by day (there shall be no night there). 26And they shall bring the glory and the honor of the nations into it.d 27But there shall by no means enter it anything that defiles, or causese an abomination or a lie, but only those who are written in the Lamb's Book of Life.

22 And* he showed me a puref river of water of life, clear as crystal, proceeding from the throne of God and of the Lamb. 2In the middle of its street, and on either side of the river, *was* the tree of life, which bore twelve fruits, each *tree* yielding its fruit every month. The leaves of the tree *were* for the healing of the nations. 3And there shall be no more curse, but the throne of God and of the Lamb shall be in it, and His servants shall serve Him. 4They shall see His face, and His name *shall be* on their foreheads. 5There shall be no night there: They need no lamp nor light of the sun, for the Lord God gives them light. And they shall reign forever and ever.

6Then he said to me, "These words *are* faithful and true." And the Lord God of the holyg prophets sent His angel to show His servants the things which must shortly take place.

7"Behold, I am coming quickly! Blessed *is* he who keeps the words of the prophecy of this book."

8Now I, John, saw and heardh these things. And when I heard and saw, I fell down to worship before the feet of the angel who showed me these things.

9Then he said to me, "See *that you do* not *do that.* Fori I am your fellow servant, and of your brethren the prophets, and of those who keep the

CHAPTER 22

22:1ff How do you respond to the promise of the Lord's return? John's last chapter can help you take inventory.

Are you treasuring His Word and obeying it (v. 7)? This is *His* message to you (v. 16), and it must not be altered (vv. 18–19). There is a special blessing for the obedient (v. 14).

Are you doing the work He has called you to do (v. 12)? He promises to reward faithful servants (Luke 12:35–48).

Do you really *want* Jesus to return today (v. 20)? Do you "love His appearing" (2 Tim. 4:8)? If Jesus were to come today, would you be disappointed and your plans be upset?

Are you urging lost sinners to trust Him and be ready for His coming (v. 17)? The Holy Spirit works through the church to bring lost people to the Savior. The people described in 21:8 and 22:11 can be saved (1 Cor. 6:9–11) and become new creatures ready for the new heaven and earth (2 Cor. 5:17). Will you tell them?

21:23 zNU-Text and M-Text omit *in it.* aM-Text reads *the very glory.* 21:24 bNU-Text and M-Text omit *of those who are saved.* cM-Text reads *the glory and honor of the nations to Him.* 21:26 dM-Text adds *that they may enter in.* 21:27 eNU-Text and M-Text read *anything profane, nor one who causes.* 22:1 fNU-Text and M-Text omit *pure.* 22:6 gNU-Text and M-Text read *spirits of the prophets.* 22:8 hNU-Text and M-Text read *am the one who heard and saw.* 22:9 iNU-Text and M-Text omit *For.*

words of this book. Worship God." [10]And he said to me, "Do not seal the words of the prophecy of this book, for the time is at hand. [11]He who is unjust, let him be unjust still; he who is filthy, let him be filthy still; he who is righteous, let him be righteous[j] still; he who is holy, let him be holy still."

[12]"And behold, I am coming quickly, and My reward is with Me, to give to every one according to his work. [13]I am the Alpha and the Omega, the Beginning and the End, the First and the Last."[k]

[14]Blessed are those who do His command-ments,[l] that they may have the right to the tree of life, and may enter through the gates into the city. [15]But[m] outside are dogs and sorcerers and sexually immoral and murderers and idolaters, and whoever loves and practices a lie.

[16]"I, Jesus, have sent My angel to testify to you these things in the churches. I am the Root and the Offspring of David, the Bright and Morning Star."

[17]And the Spirit and the bride say, "Come!" And let him who hears say, "Come!" And let him who thirsts come. Whoever desires, let him take the water of life freely.

[18]For[n] I testify to everyone who hears the words of the prophecy of this book: If anyone adds to these things, God will add[o] to him the plagues that are written in this book; [19]and if anyone takes away from the words of the book of this prophecy, God shall take away[p] his part from the Book[q] of Life, from the holy city, and from the things which are written in this book.

[20]He who testifies to these things says, "Surely I am coming quickly."

Amen. Even so, come, Lord Jesus!

[21]The grace of our Lord Jesus Christ be with you all.[r] Amen.

22:11 [j]NU-Text and M-Text read do right.   22:13 [k]NU-Text and M-Text read the First and the Last, the Beginning and the End.   22:14 [l]NU-Text reads wash their robes.
22:15 [m]NU-Text and M-Text omit But.   22:18 [n]NU-Text and M-Text omit For.   [o]M-Text reads may God add.
22:19 [p]M-Text reads may God take away.   [q]NU-Text and M-Text read tree of life.   22:21 [r]NU-Text reads with all; M-Text reads with all the saints.

Amazing Grace

Amazing grace! How sweet the
  sound,
That saved a wretch like me!
I once was lost, but now am found;
Was blind, but now I see!

When we've been there ten
  thousand years,
Bright shining as the sun,
We've no less days to sing God's
  praise
Than when we'd first begun.

—John Newton

REDISCOVERING THE TRANSFORMING POWER OF WORSHIP

If you and I are to make any real progress in a pilgrimage toward rediscovering the transforming power of worship, we must decide what we mean by *worship* and *transformation*. Let's begin with *worship* and then consider *transformation*.

I realize that definitions can *create* problems as well as *solve* them. The English novelist Samuel Butler wrote that a definition is "the enclosing of a wilderness of idea within a wall of words." My favorite example of that is Samuel Johnson's famous definition of *network:* "Any thing reticulated or decussated, at equal distances, with interstices between the intersections." Talk about wilderness!

The Problem of Definitions

However, we must face the fact that some things are very difficult to define. A devoted husband and wife might have to struggle to define the love they feel so deeply, and a gifted artist may not be able to define "beauty." Even the great theologian St. Augustine had his troubles. "What, then, is time?" he asked. "If no one asks of me, I know; if I wish to explain to him who asks, I know not."

We must be careful, too, that our definition is not so high a wall that we find ourselves in an intellectional and emotional prison. Good definitions must set limits, but they must also leave room for expansion. It is all right to put up walls so long as you include a door and a few windows. This may have been what Erasmus meant when he wrote, "Every definition is dangerous."

We must also keep in mind that good definitions must relate to experience. They must not be merely intellectually constructed to satisfy the lexicographer! After all, the Bible does not give us many definitions, but it does major on demonstrations and descriptions. The Bible is not a dictionary or an encyclopedia. Rather, it is a *Who's Who* of people who knew God, trusted Him, and got things accomplished. The cast of characters found in Scripture would agree with Thomas à Kempis: "I had rather feel compunction, than understand the definition thereof." Experience is important to understanding.

As you probably know, our English word *worship* simply means "worth-ship." We worship that which is worthy. "You are worthy, O Lord, to receive glory and honor and power" (Rev. 4:11). "Worthy is the Lamb who was slain" (Rev. 5:12). Man is not worthy of worship, and certainly the idols that man makes are not worthy. Only God is worthy of our worship. What a person worships is a good indication of what is really valuable to him.

Four different Hebrew words are translated "worship" in the Authorized Version, but the one used most often is *shāchāh,* which means "to bow down, to do homage." It is first used in Genesis 18:2 where Abraham bowed down to the three visitors, one of whom (he discovered) was the Lord from heaven.

The key Greek word is *proskuneō,* which literally means "to kiss toward." It conveys the idea of showing reverence or doing obeisance, to God (John 4:21–24), man (Matt. 18:26), or even Satan (Rev. 13:4). Another important Greek word is *latreuō,* which basically means "to serve, minister" (see Matt. 4:10, Heb. 9:9 and 14, and Rev. 22:3 for examples). A related word is *leitourgos,* which means "a priestly minister" and gives us our English word *liturgy.*

When you consider all of the words used for worship in both the Old and New Testaments, and when you put the meanings together, you find that worship involves both attitudes (awe, reverence, respect) and actions (bowing, praising, serving). It is both a subjective experience and an objective activity. Worship is not an unexpressed feeling, nor is it an empty formality. True worship is balanced and involves the mind, the emotions, and the will. It must be intelligent; it must reach deep within and be motivated by love; and it must lead to obedient actions that glorify God.

Evelyn Underhill has defined *worship* as "the total adoring response of man to the one Eternal God self-revealed in time." I like that phrase "adoring response." It reminds me that worship is personal and passionate, not formal and cold; and that it is our response to the living God, voluntarily offered to Him as He has offered Himself to us.

In His conversation with the woman of Samaria, Jesus made it clear that there was both true worship and false worship, ignorant worship and intelligent worship (John 4:19–24). What passes for Christian worship, even in some of our churches, may not be acceptable to God at all. The Pharisees thought they were practicing exemplary worship, but Jesus thought otherwise: "These people draw near to Me with their mouth, and honor Me with their lips, but their heart is far from Me. And in vain they worship Me, teaching as doctrines the commandmends of men" (Matt. 15:8, 9).

But what concerns us is that we agree on the meaning of *worship.* One of my favorite definitions comes from William Temple, Archbishop of Canterbury (1942–44). I want to quote the entire paragraph from his *Readings in St. John's Gospel,* First Series.

Both for perplexity and for dulled conscience the remedy is the same; sincere and spiritual worship. For worship is the submission of all our nature to God. It is the quickening of conscience by His holiness;

the nourishment of mind with His truth; the purifying of imagination by His beauty; the opening of the heart to His love; the surrender of will to His purpose—and all of this gathered up in adoration, the most selfless emotion of which our nature is capable and therefore the chief remedy for that self-centeredness which is our original sin and the source of all actual sin. Yes—worship in spirit and truth is the way to the solution of perplexity and to the liberation from sin.

To Temple, worship is the response of all that man is to all that God is and does. We do not worship God for what we get out of it, but because He is worthy of worship. "Whoever seeks God as a means toward desired ends will not find God," wrote A. W. Tozer. "God will not be used." If you worship because it pays, it won't pay. Of course, this runs contrary to much of the popular preaching and teaching today that promises health, wealth, content-ment, and a problem-free life to all who will "turn themselves over to God." Those who proclaim this pernicious doctrine would be brokenhearted if their own children loved them only for what they could get out of them.

Alfred North Whitehead could hardly be called an evangelical believer, yet he made a profound statement about worship that needs to be heeded today: "The worship of God is not a rule of safety—it is an adventure of the spirit, a flight after the unattainable." "My soul thirsts for God, for the living God," wrote the psalmist. "When shall I come and appear before God?" (Ps. 42:2). Think of the danger-ous experiences David went through in order to give us the psalms! Isaiah's vision of God's glorious throne eventually cost him his life, and Paul's experiences in the heavenlies brought him prison and death. True worship is not cheap entertainment.

Nor is it escape. I confess that I sometimes feel anguish within when I hear someone pray, "Oh Lord, thank You that we can come apart from the world to worship You, that we can leave our cares and burdens outside as we enter Your house." I may be wrong, but I carry my cares and burdens with me into the worship service, because it is there that I can get the right perspective to deal with them successfully. "When I thought how to understand this," Asaph wrote about his problem. "It was too painful for me—until I went into the sanctuary of God" (Ps. 73:16, 17). "He did not merely forget his problem for the time being," wrote D. Martyn Lloyd-Jones; "he found a solution."

"God is our refuge *and strength* (Ps. 46:1, italics mine). God "hides" us so that He might help us. We are not refugees who are looking for escape; rather, we are wounded and weary soldiers who need rest and rehabilitation so we can go back into the battle. People who worship for "escape" do not know what true worship is, and they are wasting their time. True worship should lead to personal enrichment and enablement, the kind of spiritual strength that helps the believer carry the burdens and fight the battles of life.

Worship as escape becomes a selfish experience. Granted, all of us at one time or another have identified with David's groan, "Oh, that I had wings like a dove! I would fly away and be at rest" (Ps. 55:6). But I trust our identification with this selfish attitude has been only momentary, for if it becomes a settled way of life it leads to immaturity and unreality. It turns God into a celestial Physician Whose only task is to bind our wounds, and it robs us of the growth that can come when we discover the excitement of relating worship to daily life.

Subjective and Objective Aspects

True worship has both its objective and subjective aspects, and we must maintain this balance. Jesus may have had this in mind when He said, "God is Spirit, and those who worship Him must worship in spirit and truth" (John 4:24). "In spirit" (note that the s is not capitalized) refers to the subjective side of worship; "in truth" refers to the objective side. If we do not submit to some kind of objective revelation, some Word from God, then our worship is ignorant and probably false. On the other hand, if we know the truth but merely go through the outward motions of worship, our worship will be hypocritical and empty. "When thou prayest," wrote John Bunyan, "rather let thy heart be without words, than thy words without heart." Paul called this formal worship "having a form of godliness but denying its power" (2 Tim. 3:5).

The important thing is that we keep the right balance. There is today such an emphasis on Bible knowledge that we are in danger of ignoring, or even opposing, personal spiritual experience. While we must not base our theology on experience, neither must we debase our theology by divorcing it from experience. If true worship is the response of the *whole* person to God, then we dare not neglect the emotions. We permit people to express their emotions at weddings, funerals, and athletic events, but not at a worship service. The important thing today seems to be that you mark your Bible and write outlines in your notebook, but whatever else you do, keep your emotions hidden!

This attitude, I am sure, is an overreaction to some of the extremes that Christians have seen in certain segments of the modern charismatic movement. While I personally deplore religious emotionalism, as opposed to true emotion, I must admit that I tend to agree with Bishop Handley Moule who said that he would rather tone down a fanatic than resurrect a corpse. It would be better not to have either extreme, of course; but if I have to make a choice, give me the fanatic.

The objective truth found in God's Word is important, but so is the subjective experience of that truth. In our quest to maintain our orthodoxy we have forgotten that the very word *orthodox* means "right praise" as well as "right opinion." We defend the faith and then descend into formalism, proud that our doctrine is correct but ignorant of the fact that our worship is dull and lifeless. Like the church at Laodicea, we are neither cold nor hot, but disgustingly lukewarm (Rev. 3:14–22). Campbell Morgan had this to say about the "formalists" in the church:

> He [Christ] does not ask that outward form be given up, or helpful rite abandoned. He will not suggest the setting aside of any form or ceremony that in itself is helpful. He has no criticism for these things. He permits the music and the methods, always providing that they are expressive of the deeper fact of life. These things He hates when they become the grave-clothes wrapped about death. The true ideal of worship is that of man communing with God.

Once we understand the subjective and objective aspects of worship, we are better prepared to deal with some of the problems that worship seems to create. For one thing, we can better understand why different Christian communions express their worship in different ways. After all, if there is one God and one Bible, why should we not all worship in the same way? The answer is simply that we are all different and live in different cultural contexts.

Objective truth never changes, but our understanding of it deepens and our experience of it should become more and more meaningful. Divine revelation is one thing; human realization is something quite different. The Holy Spirit does not violate a believer's personality, but rather uses it to express praise to God. No two Christians have the identical worship experience even though they participate in the same service, at the same time, in the same sanctuary. For that matter, no two congregations, even in the same fellowship, express the same worship while following the same liturgy. Christian worship is both individual and corporate, personal and congregational. Led by the Spirit, we have the right, even the responsibility, to express our praise to God in the manner that best reflects our individual personalities and cultures. If all of us would keep this in mind, it might encourage a deeper appreciation for one another's form of worship.

The Element of Mystery

Before we try to tie all of this together, one more aspect of worship must be mentioned; and that is the fear of the Lord. If we major only on our "adoring response," we may find ourselves out of balance. After all, God's love for us is a *holy* love; and we must beware of trying to get chummy with God. I know, the apostle John leaned on the bosom of Jesus in the Upper Room; but he fell at the feet of Jesus when he beheld Him in His sovereign glory (Rev. 1:17). The old saints and mystics reveled in their experience of His love, but they also remembered that their God was "a consuming fire" (Heb. 12:29). As the Lord drew near to them, they kept in mind that He had not abdicated His throne but was still "high and lifted up." A. W. Tozer is right: "No one can know the true grace of God who has not first known the fear of God."

Phillips Brooks once said that familiarity breeds contempt only with contemptible people or contemptible things. There is an undue familiarity with God that only proves that the worshiper does not really know God at all. True worship must always involve *mystery*. There are many things we cannot explain but that we can experience.

Mystery and humility go together, and there can be no real worship without humility. God reveals Himself but He rarely explains Himself. Christians do not live on explanations; they live on promises, and on deepening relationships. The unpardonable sin in the ministry today is for a man to admit, "I do not know—but it should never be so. God deliberately keeps some things secret so that you and I will stay humble and learn to trust Him even when we do not understand what He is doing.

In our desire to explain everything and avoid whatever we cannot explain, we have almost robbed worship of the dimension of mystery. We no longer cry out with Paul, "Oh, the depth of the riches both of the wisdom and knowledge of God! How unsearchable are His judgments and His ways past finding out!" (Rom. 11:33). Paul prayed that we might "know the love of Christ which passes knowledge" (Eph. 3:19), a paradox indeed—a mystery if there ever was one.

"But you are promoting *mysticism!*" some orthodox saint may shout. "Mysticism is dangerous!" But that depends, my friend, on what kind of mysticism it is. A mystic is simply someone who believes that there is a real spiritual world behind the physical world that we see; and a Christian mystic sees Jesus Christ as Lord of both the seen and the unseen. Discussing what happened to the believers at Pentecost, Campbell Morgan wrote: "This is mysticism. Christianity is mysticism."

Christian worship must be intelligent, but there are some things that we cannot explain. Christian worship must be based solidly on objective truth, but it must include subjective experience; and that is where Christian mysticism enters in. God is a Person, and our relationship to Him must be personal. Just as a devoted husband and wife, or parent and child, will experience what they cannot easily define or explain, so the devoted saint of God, thirsty for spiritual reality, will enjoy an experience of God that transcends the academic. Even the biblical writers had to resort to divinely inspired signs and symbols in order to express the inexpressible.

Certainly the spirits must be tried and experience tested by truth, or what we think is spiritual experience might turn out to be the flesh or the demonic. But the sincere Christian who knows his Bible and is yielded to the Spirit is not likely to be duped, especially if he keeps in touch with God's people in the church. The saints have a way of keeping us in balance.

A Working Definition

No definition is final, so accept this one for the time being, and we can refine it as we go along:

Worship is the believer's response of all that he is—mind, emotions, will, and body—to all that God is and says and does. This response has its mystical side in subjective experience, and its practical side in objective obedience to God's revealed truth. It is a loving response that is balanced by the fear of the Lord, and it is a deepening response as the believer comes to know God better.

And what should be the result of all this?

Transformation

We worship God because He is worthy and not because we as worshipers get something out of it. If we look upon worship only as a means of getting something from God, rather than giving something to God, then we make God our servant instead of our Lord, and the elements of worship become a cheap formula for selfish gratification. We then become like those backslidden priests that the prophet Malachi denounced, men who said, "It is useless to serve God; what profit is it that we have kept His ordinance, and that we have walked as mourners before the LORD of hosts?" (Mal. 3:14).

Worshiping God with a wrong motive can be as deadening as worshiping the wrong God with a sincere motive. Both are wrong, but certainly the enlightened Christian faces a greater judgment than the sincere pagan. After all, we *know* the God we worship! We live in His world; we bear His image; and as believers, we even belong to His family. We have His revelation in His Word and the personal instruction of His Spirit. The believer who has a pragmatic approach to worship has certainly forgotten all of this and has turned God into a celestial Servant Who rewards him for his faithful worship.

We worship God because He is worthy and because He has commanded us to worship Him. However, this is not to say that there are no personal benefits from worshiping God, because there are. God has ordained that everything we *are* and *do* shall flow out of worship as "blessed by-products" of our fellowship with God. True spiritual worship ought to contribute something powerful and lasting to our personalities, our relationships, our service, and our total lives as Christians.

According to Albert W. Palmer, worship "means a release of energy. It puts into life something which steps it up to a higher voltage. Through worship man comes to God at first hand, has an immediate experience with God, and goes forth transformed and stimulated to new levels of endeavor."

Transformed. That is the word we are interested in. If true worship is anything, it is a transforming experience. We need to understand this word and then discover what kind of transformation takes place in the life of the person who worships God "in spirit and truth."

Metamorphosis *vs.* Masquerade

When I was a lad in grade school, our class spent several weeks watching a cocoon and hoping that a beautiful butterfly would emerge. We were studying metamorphosis, that marvelous process of nature that changes tadpoles into frogs and caterpillars into moths or butterflies. Little did I know that one day I would meet that word *metamorphosis* in a seminary Greek class.

The Greek word *metamorphoumai* (the passive form of *metamorphoō*) means "to be changed into another form," but this change *comes from within.* In other words, the change on the outside is the normal and natural expression of the nature on the inside. You would never produce a butterfly by pinning wings on a worm! The changes must come from within.

There is another Greek word that describes changes on the outside that do *not* come from within. It is *metaschēmatizomai* and it is usually translated "fashioned" or "conformed." (A related word is *suschēmatizomai.*) When a Christian conforms to this world and fashions his life after the pattern of unbelievers, he is changing the outside, *but the changes is not coming from the inside.* It is not metamorphosis; it is *masquerade.*

There is a striking illustration of this difference given by Paul in 2 Corinthians 11:13—"For such are false apostles, deceitful workers, transforming themselves into apostles of Christ." These false teachers adopted the disguise of true apostles of Christ, but in reality they were the ministers of Satan. Their outward change was a masquerade, not a metamorphosis. The outward image did not agree with the inward nature. They were only pretending.

Our Lord's transfiguration illustrates the meaning of *metamorphoumai:* "and He was transfigured before them. His face shone like the sun, and His clothes became as white as the light" (Matt. 17:2). What did the disciples see? The glory of God that was within Him, radiating in shadowless splendor! The apostle John wrote: "And we beheld His glory, the glory as of the only begotten of the Father, full of grace and truth" (John 1:14). And Peter testified, "We . . . were eyewitnesses of His majesty" (2 Pet. 1:16).

Our Lord's transfiguration was not a masquerade. The angels did not shine spotlights on Him: The glory came from within. He was transformed on the outside by revealing the glory that was on the inside.

It is this kind of experience to which you and I are called by God. He wants to transform us. He also wants to work through us to transform the people and circumstances that make up our lives.

Every Christian is either a "conformer" or a "transformer." We are either fashioning our lives by pressure from without, or we are transforming our lives by power from within. The difference is—worship.

Living as a Sacrifice

Now we are ready to consider two texts—Romans 12:1, 2 and 2 Corinthians 3:18—because both of them explain what this spiritual metamorphosis is and how we can begin to experience it.

> I beseech you therefore, brethren, by the mercies of God, that you present your bodies a living sacrifice, holy, acceptable to God, which is your reasonable service [spiritual worship]. And do not be conformed to this world, but be transformed [*metamorphoumai*] by the renewing of your mind, that you may prove what is that good and acceptable and perfect will of God.

Paul is contrasting two ways of life, that of the believer who is being transformed by God, and that of the believer who is being conformed to the world. It is the contrast between metamorphosis and masquerade. As I said earlier, the "transformer" lives by power from within, but the "conformer" lives by pressure from without. The paraphrase by J. B. Phillips brings this out beautifully: "Don't let the world around you squeeze you into its own mould, but let God remake you so that your whole attitude of mind is changed."

The image here is that of the priest offering a sacrifice on the altar. The Greek word translated "present" is the technical term for the offering of a sacrifice. The difference, of course, is that you and I are to be *living* sacrifices and not corpses. We are to be like Jesus Christ Who today bears on His body the marks of Calvary. He is a living sacrifice.

While I want to avoid formulas that smack of technique, I cannot help but see in this text three gifts that God wants me to present to Him in order that I may worship Him and experience His transforming powers.

To begin with, *God wants my body*. The Greek verb indicates that this is to be a once-for-all presentation, as I give my body to God to be used for His service. However, this does not prevent me from reaffirming this dedication daily when I set aside time to worship the Lord. Israel had its "continual burnt offering," morning and evening (Exod. 29:38–42), and this may be a good pattern for us to follow today.

It is unfortunate that an overdose of the wrong kind of Greek philosophy has infected Christian theology and given people the idea that the body is sinful. Or that worship is an experience so "spiritual" that it denies the body or the use of anything material. The human body is neutral; it can be an instrument of sin or of holiness. "And do not present your members as instruments of unrighteousness to sin," Paul admonished the Romans, "but present yourselves to God as being alive from the dead [living sacrifices!], and your members as instruments of righteousness to God" (Rom. 6:13).

The body of the Christian is God's temple (1 Cor. 6:19, 20) and God's tool (Rom. 6:13). God lives in the believer's body! God can use that body to accomplish His work and glorify His name. Paul prayed that Christ might be magnified in his body (Phil. 1:20). "Let your light so shine before men, that they may see your good works and glorify your Father in heaven" (Matt. 5:16). Worship must not stop with a personal mystical experience. It must lead to a practical ministry experience, something we do with our bodies, that brings help to others and honor to God. "The best public worship," wrote Bishop J. C. Ryle, "is that which produces the best private Christianity.

The second gift God asks for is *my mind*. Since we are made in the image of God, we have intelligence, emotion, and will. To be sure, all three suffer from the terrible effects of man's fall; but God can renew them and use them for His glory. A balanced Christian life involves more than duty (the will) and delight (the emotions); it also involves discernment (the mind). Passionate action without intelligence is fanaticism. We are to love God with the mind as well as the heart (Luke 10:27).

Christians should think the way God thinks and not the way the world thinks. The believer's mind ought to be so saturated with divine truth that it can determine the divine perspective on every question, issue, or decision. A renewed mind is a mind alert to the world's false philosophies and Satan's subtle strategy. A renewed mind directs the believer to offer intelligent worship to the Lord. "All Christian worship," says Dr. John Stott, "public and private, should be an intelligent response to God's self-revelation in his words and works recorded in Scripture."

It is the Word of God, taught by the Spirit of God, that renews the mind. This Word may come through preaching and teaching, through personal witness in word or song, or through study and meditation; but it always comes (if we are receptive) with that power to renew us. This is why the believer must spend time daily with the Bible, reading and meditating; and why the Word must be an important part of public worship.

God asks for my body, my mind, and *my will*. For the most part, my mind controls my body, and my will controls my mind. I usually think about what I *want* to think about. Christianity is basically a religion centering on man's will, not man's feelings. Christian love is not a feeling; it is an act of the will. Otherwise, Jesus could not *command* us to love one another. I am not denying that there is a wonderful emotional dimension to Christian love; I am only emphasizing that Christian love is primarily what we *do*, not what we *feel*. This makes the will very important in Christian living.

Three times our Lord prayed in Gethsemane, "O My Father, if it is possible, let this cup pass from me; nevertheless, not as I will, but as You will" (Matt. 26:39).

God does not have three wills—one good, another acceptable, and yet another perfect—because a perfect God can only will for us that which is perfect. The will of God is not like the merchandise in a mail-order catalog, labeled "Good," "Better," and "Best" and if you want "Best," you have to pay more for it. God has one will for your life; anything else is simply not what He willed, even though He may permit it. We prove *by experience* (that is the meaning of the Greek verb) that God's will is good, pleasing to Him, and complete in every aspect. We want nothing more, nothing less, nothing else.

God expects body, mind, and will to be yielded to Him and to be used by the Spirit as we worship Him. He also wants us to worship Him in love from a heart that is caught up in Him and His beauty. But more about this later. We must now turn to the second key "transformation" text, 2 Corinthians 3:18.

Radiating the Glory of God

Before we examine the text, we must understand some of the background. Paul is contrasting the ministry of grace with the ministry of law under the old covenant. The law of Moses was written on stones, but God's Word in the new covenant is written on the human heart by the Spirit of God. It is a ministry of internal change, not external compulsion. Furthermore, the old covenant was a ministry of death; but the new covenant ministry of grace brings life. Under law, the people were in bondage; but under grace, they enjoy spiritual liberty.

But Paul's greatest emphasis is on the contrast between the glory of the old covenant and the glory of the new covenant. There certainly was glory under the Law: God revealed His glory at Mount Sinai, and then His glory dwelt in the holy of holies in the tabernacle. When Moses worshiped God on the top of the mount, he picked up some of that glory so that his face shone when he returned to the camp (see Exod. 34:29–35). Moses was not *radiating* glory from within; he was only *reflecting* glory that had been seen on the mount.

And that glory faded away! It was temporary. Moses had to put a veil over his face so that the people could not see the fading glory (2 Cor. 3:13). The glory of the law was temporary, but the glory of the new covenant is both permanent and increasing. It is getting more and more glorious! Instead of veiling our faces, we want the world to see what the grace of God can do in the life of the Christian. We have nothing to hide!

But we all, with unveiled face, beholding as in a mirror the glory of the Lord, are being transformed [*metamorphoumai*] into the same image from glory to glory, just as by the Spirit of the Lord. (2 Cor. 3:18)

The mirror is a symbol of God's Word (James 1:23–25) in which we see God's Son. As we worship Him and behold His glory, we are transformed by His Spirit to share in His own image and glory. Instead of hiding a fading glory, we reveal an increasing glory that causes others to see Christ and honor Him. "But the path of the just is like the shining sun, that shines ever brighter unto the perfect day" (Prov. 4:18).

We become like the god that we worship (Ps. 115:8). As we worship the true God, in spirit and truth, we are transformed to become more like Him. What we are and what we do are both determined by what we worship.

Paul's instruction in Romans 12:1, 2 involves a crisis, but 2 Corinthians 3:18 speaks about a process. The two go together; for as we yield body, mind, and will to the Lord, and as we meditate on His Word, the Spirit of God transforms us into "living sacrifices" who have "renewed minds," people who radiate the glory of God. We become transformers, not conformers.

However, a warning is needed here: we must not put the emphasis on our own spiritual condition but on the glory of God. There are "religious hypochondriacs" who are so wrapped up in the techniques of spiritual living that they become unbalanced and unspiritual. "Those Christians whose chief concern is their own spiritual condition," wrote Washington Gladden, "are a very poor sort of Christians. A self-conscious holiness is a contradiction in terms." These people perform so many spiritual dissections that they have no strength left to serve the Lord! And they get so concerned about themselves that they neglect ministering to their fellow Christians. It is a false holiness that reveals none of the glory of God.

A Call to Transformation

What we have been discussing seems to be very exciting: beholding God's glory in the Word, seeing God's Son in the Word, being transformed by the Spirit, radiating God's glory in our daily lives, and becoming more like Jesus Christ. Why would any Christian believer not want this kind of worship experience?

For one thing, this kind of experience demands devotion and discipline, and many believers are not interested in discipline. Paul admonished young Timothy to exercise himself to godliness (1 Tim. 4:7, 8), suggesting that the believer needs the same kind of discipline that makes an athlete successful. If each of us devoted himself or herself to spiritual things with the same kind of intensity and discipline that the Olympic contender shows, we would be much better Christians than we now are!

But there is another reason why some believers steer away from this kind of worship experience: the consequences may be dangerous. Each of us must honestly answer the question, "Am I willing to pay the price, in my own home and church, so that I might have a worship experience that will please God and accomplish His purposes in my life?" It is not likely that many of us will become martyrs, but we may find ourselves suffering in other ways. It is my feeling that many Christians do not want a transforming experience of worship. So, when a transformed believer shows up among them, they are immediately threatened by his presence—and this can lead to some difficult situations in homes and churches. *"Transformers" do not create problems; they reveal them.*

Transformers are participants, but most Christians want to be spectators. Most Christians are content to attend church, give their money, and allow a professional staff to "lead in worship" and provide religious entertainment Sunday by Sunday.

Transformers patiently wait for the Spirit to change them and make them more like the Savior, but most church members want immediate results that can be categorized and computed. The transformer looks for *fruit* while the conformer calculates *results*.

Transformers quietly resist the "celebrityism" that marks the church today, while many professed believers are so taken up with "famous Christians" that their dedication to them almost becomes cultic. A believer with a renewed mind is happy to hear God's Word from any sincere servant of God, known or unknown; but other Christians insist on listening to the "leading expositors of the day," who are often media superstars.

Transformers trust God to work as they worship, pray and sow the seed of the Word, but conformers run from seminar to seminar, seeking to discover new techniques for getting God's work done in this world. They often follow the latest fads without asking where these fads originated or on what biblical principles they are founded.

Transformers have a different set of values from that of their conforming friends. They are not impressed by budgets and buildings, but they do look for fruit that glorifies God. To them, it is more important to care for the needy than to build another building or start a new "ministry" that is really not needed. Transformers would rather see a growing fellowship divide and start a new church where one is needed than unite to build a larger sanctuary.

Transformers are not concerned about getting the approval of the world or being popular with the world's leaders. They are content to live to please the Lord and serve others. If they are noticed, they get embarrassed; if they are unnoticed, they rejoice. So-called Christian celebrities do not interest them, particularly those of the "Hollywood" variety who sing in nightclubs on Saturday night and then in a church service on Sunday morning.

Now you understand why I warned you: if you decide you want to pursue a meaningful worship experience, *do not expect the encouragement.* True worship examines us deeply; our motives and our values are scrutinized by God. In worship, God is calling us to wholeness; but first He must reveal our brokenness and our blemishes. He is calling us to spiritual health, but first He must expose our "wounds and bruises and putrefying sores" (Isa. 1:6); and we cannot ask for a second opinion.

In short, the most dangerous thing we can do is to return to spiritual worship. It would mean the end of the personality cults that have invaded the church. It would also mean the end of the "Christian consumerism" that has so twisted our sense of spiritual values. I have no doubt that the church that returned to true worship would lose people—"important" people—and probably have to make drastic cuts in the budget.

But then—*something would happen!*

A beautiful new sense of spiritual reality would result, with people glorifying God instead of praising men. There would be a new unity among God's people, no matter what label they might wear; and the divisive spirit of competition would gradually vanish. Nobody would be going around asking, "Who is the greatest in the kingdom of heaven?"

Some organizations and "ministries" would go out of business and new ministries would appear. Congregations would start to make better use of their facilities, and money that would have been spent on brick and mortar would be invested in serving people in the name of Jesus. Small, struggling churches would merge and assist each other, and the watching world would see new demonstrations of love and harmony.

There would be new power in prayer and worship and a new attention to the Word. Families would pray together and do so joyfully. Marriages would be mended. Satan would be defeated in his attempts to destroy God's people and God's church.

This is not to suggest that all our problems would be solved and the kingdom would be established. No, we would face a whole new set of problems; but they would be caused by the expansion of spiritual ministry and not the expression of carnal Christians. Most of the problems in the church today are not caused by spiritual growth and development. They are caused by carnal, worldly people—including church leaders—who stand in the way of spiritual growth. Ministers and church officers must spend so much time running around to put out brush fires that they have no time left for the work of the ministry itself.

And we have accepted this sick situation as normal!

Why? Because we have so long been away from the bright light of true worship that we can no longer see clearly to evaluate our own situation. Our measurements for ministry and for spiritual success are so unbiblical that we are leading one another astray and not knowing it. We are like the pilot who announced from the cockpit, "Folks, we are lost, but we are making very good time!"

The goal of worship is Christlikeness in our character and conduct. The more we become like Christ, the more we will be treated by others the way He was treated:

They crucified Him because He said He would put an end to the building program and tear down the temple.

They crucified Him because He opposed the religious merchandising that was going on in the temple.

Then they stoned Stephen—another man with a shining face—because he dared to say that God did not live in the temple but would one day destroy it.

God's call to true worship, to an experience of transformation, is a call to dangerous and costly Christian living.

It is a call to wonder, to witness, and to warfare.

Will you heed the call?

GRACIOUS FATHER,

We did not realize when we started this journey that there would be a price to pay.

We confess that we are comfortable as conformers.

We are not sure we really want to be transformers!

Father, do a beautiful work in our lives so that others will want this same work in their lives.

Give us patience. Give us humility. Keep us from judging others in our fellowship.

Remind us that You look with favor on those who are poor, and of a contrite spirit, who tremble at Your word (Isa. 66:2).

Father, we are about to consider the wonder of worship. Our minds and hearts are so jaded by a multitude of shallow, counterfeit experiences, that we have lost that thrilling sense of wonder.

Restore to us, O God, the wonder of it all!

In the Name of Him Whose Name is Wonderful,

AMEN.

Read Your Bible Through in a Year

A systematic division of the books of the Bible, primarily for reading.

JANUARY

Date	MORNING MATT.	EVENING GEN.
1	1	1, 2, 3
2	2	4, 5, 6
3	3	7, 8, 9
4	4	10, 11, 12
5	5: 1–26	13, 14, 15
6	5:27–48	16, 17
7	6: 1–18	18, 19
8	6:19–34	20, 21, 22
9	7	23, 24
10	8: 1–17	25, 26
11	8:18–34	27, 28
12	9: 1–17	29, 30
13	9:18–38	31, 32
14	10: 1–20	33, 34, 35
15	10:21–42	36, 37, 38
16	11	39, 40
17	12: 1–23	41, 42
18	12:24–50	43, 44, 45
19	13: 1–30	46, 47, 48
20	13:31–58	49, 50
		EX.
21	14: 1–21	1, 2, 3
22	14:22–36	4, 5, 6
23	15: 1–20	7, 8
24	15:21–39	9, 10, 11
25	16	12, 13
26	17	14, 15
27	18: 1–20	16, 17, 18
28	18:21–35	19, 20
29	19	21, 22
30	20: 1–16	23, 24
31	20:17–34	25, 26

FEBRUARY

Date	MORNING MATT.	EVENING EX.
1	21: 1–22	27, 28
2	21:23–46	29, 30
3	22: 1–22	31, 32, 33
4	22:23–46	34, 35
5	23: 1–22	36, 37, 38
6	23:23–39	39, 40
		LEV.
7	24: 1–28	1, 2, 3
8	24:29–51	4, 5
9	25: 1–30	6, 7
10	25:31–46	8, 9, 10
11	26: 1–25	11, 12
12	26:26–50	13
13	26:51–75	14
14	27: 1–26	15, 16
15	27:27–50	17, 18
16	27:51–66	19, 20
17	28	21, 22
	MARK	
18	1: 1–22	23, 24
19	1:23–45	25
20	2	26, 27
		NUM.
21	3: 1–19	1, 2
22	3:20–35	3, 4
23	4: 1–20	5, 6
24	4:21–41	7, 8
25	5: 1–20	9, 10, 11
26	5:21–43	12, 13, 14
27	6: 1–29	15, 16
28	6:30–56	17, 18, 19
29	7: 1–13	20, 21, 22

MARCH

Date	MORNING MARK	EVENING NUM.
1	7:14–37	23, 24, 25
2	8: 1–21	26, 27
3	8:22–38	28, 29, 30
4	9: 1–29	31, 32, 33
5	9:30–50	34, 35, 36
		DEUT.
6	10: 1–31	1, 2
7	10:32–52	3, 4
8	11: 1–18	5, 6, 7
9	11:19–33	8, 9, 10
10	12: 1–27	11, 12, 13
11	12:28–44	14, 15, 16
12	13: 1–20	17, 18, 19
13	13:21–37	20, 21, 22
14	14: 1–26	23, 24, 25
15	14:27–53	26, 27
16	14:54–72	28, 29
17	15: 1–25	30, 31
18	15:26–47	32, 33, 34
		JOSH.
19	16	1, 2, 3
	LUKE	
20	1: 1–20	4, 5, 6
21	1:21–38	7, 8, 9
22	1:39–56	10, 11, 12
23	1:57–80	13, 14, 15
24	2: 1–24	16, 17, 18
25	2:25–52	19, 20, 21
26	3	22, 23, 24
		JUDG.
27	4: 1–30	1, 2, 3
28	4:31–44	4, 5, 6
29	5: 1–16	7, 8
30	5:17–39	9, 10
31	6: 1–26	11, 12

APRIL

Date	MORNING LUKE	EVENING JUDG.
1	6:27–49	13, 14, 15
2	7: 1–30	16, 17, 18
3	7:31–50	19, 20, 21
		RUTH
4	8: 1–25	1, 2, 3, 4
		1 SAM.
5	8:26–56	1, 2, 3
6	9: 1–17	4, 5, 6
7	9:18–36	7, 8, 9
8	9:37–62	10, 11, 12
9	10: 1–24	13, 14
10	10:25–42	15, 16
11	11: 1–28	17, 18
12	11:29–54	19, 20, 21
13	12: 1–31	22, 23, 24
14	12:32–59	25, 26
15	13: 1–22	27, 28, 29
16	13:23–35	30, 31
		2 SAM.
17	14: 1–24	1, 2
18	14:25–35	3, 4, 5
19	15: 1–10	6, 7, 8
20	15:11–32	9, 10, 11
21	16	12, 13
22	17: 1–19	14, 15
23	17:20–37	16, 17, 18
24	18: 1–23	19, 20
25	18:24–43	21, 22
26	19: 1–27	23, 24
		1 KIN.
27	19:28–48	1, 2
28	20: 1–26	3, 4, 5
29	20:27–47	6, 7
30	21: 1–19	8, 9

MAY

Date	MORNING LUKE	EVENING 1 KIN.
1	21:20–38	10, 11
2	22: 1–20	12, 13
3	22:21–46	14, 15
4	22:47–71	16, 17, 18
5	23: 1–25	19, 20
6	23:26–56	21, 22
		2 KIN.
7	24: 1–35	1, 2, 3
8	24:36–53	4, 5, 6
	JOHN	
9	1: 1–28	7, 8, 9
10	1:29–51	10, 11, 12
11	2	13, 14
12	3: 1–18	15, 16
13	3:19–38	17, 18
14	4: 1–30	19, 20, 21
15	4:31–54	22, 23
16	5: 1–24	24, 25
		1 CHR.
17	5:25–47	1, 2, 3
18	6: 1–21	4, 5, 6
19	6:22–44	7, 8, 9
20	6:45–71	10, 11, 12
21	7: 1–27	13, 14, 15
22	7:28–53	16, 17, 18
23	8: 1–27	19, 20, 21
24	8:28–59	22, 23, 24
25	9: 1–23	25, 26, 27
26	9:24–41	28, 29
		2 CHR.
27	10: 1–23	1, 2, 3
28	10:24–42	4, 5, 6
29	11: 1–29	7, 8, 9
30	11:30–57	10, 11, 12
31	12: 1–26	13, 14

JUNE

Date	MORNING JOHN	EVENING 2 CHR.
1	12:27–50	15, 16
2	13: 1–20	17, 18
3	13:21–38	19, 20
4	14	21, 22
5	15	23, 24
6	16	25, 26, 27
7	17	28, 29
8	18: 1–18	30, 31
9	18:19–40	32, 33
10	19: 1–22	34, 35, 36
		EZRA
11	19:23–42	1, 2
12	20	3, 4, 5
13	21	6, 7, 8
	ACTS	
14	1	9, 10
		NEH.
15	2: 1–21	1, 2, 3
16	2:22–47	4, 5, 6
17	3	7, 8, 9
18	4: 1–22	10, 11
19	4:23–37	12, 13
		ESTH.
20	5: 1–21	1, 2
21	5:22–42	3, 4, 5
22	6	6, 7, 8
23	7: 1–21	9, 10
		JOB
24	7:22–43	1, 2
25	7:44–60	3, 4
26	8: 1–25	5, 6, 7
27	8:26–40	8, 9, 10
28	9: 1–21	11, 12, 13
29	9:22–43	14, 15, 16
30	10: 1–23	17, 18, 19

JULY

Date	MORNING ACTS	EVENING JOB
1	10:24–48	20, 21
2	11	22, 23, 24
3	12	25, 26, 27
4	13: 1–25	28, 29
5	13:26–52	30, 31
6	14	32, 33
7	15: 1–21	34, 35
8	15:22–41	36, 37
9	16: 1–21	38, 39, 40
10	16:22–40	41, 42
		PS.
11	17: 1–15	1, 2, 3
12	17:16–34	4, 5, 6
13	18	7, 8, 9
14	19: 1–20	10, 11, 12
15	19:21–41	13, 14, 15
16	20: 1–16	16, 17
17	20:17–38	18, 19
18	21: 1–17	20, 21, 22
19	21:18–40	23, 24, 25
20	22	26, 27, 28
21	23: 1–15	29, 30
22	23:16–35	31, 32
23	24	33, 34
24	25	35, 36
25	26	37, 38, 39
26	27: 1–26	40, 41, 42
27	27:27–44	43, 44, 45
28	28	46, 47, 48
	ROM.	
29	1	49, 50
30	2	51, 52, 53
31	3	54, 55, 56

AUGUST

Date	MORNING ROM.	EVENING PS.
1	4	57, 58, 59
2	5	60, 61, 62
3	6	63, 64, 65
4	7	66, 67
5	8: 1–21	68, 69
6	8:22–39	70, 71
7	9: 1–15	72, 73
8	9:16–33	74, 75, 76
9	10	77, 78
10	11: 1–18	79, 80
11	11:19–36	81, 82, 83
12	12	84, 85, 86
13	13	87, 88
14	14	89, 90
15	15: 1–13	91, 92, 93
16	15:14–33	94, 95, 96
17	16	97, 98, 99
	1 COR.	
18	1	100, 101, 102
19	2	103, 104
20	3	105, 106
21	4	107, 108, 109
22	5	110, 111, 112
23	6	113, 114, 115
24	7: 1–19	116, 117, 118
25	7:20–40	119: 1–88
26	8	119: 89–176
27	9	120, 121, 122
28	10: 1–18	123, 124, 125
29	10:19–33	126, 127, 128
30	11: 1–16	129, 130, 131
31	11:17–34	132, 133, 134

SEPTEMBER

Date	MORNING 1 COR.	EVENING PS.
1	12	135, 136
2	13	137, 138, 139
3	14: 1–20	140, 141, 142
4	14:21–40	143, 144, 145
5	15: 1–28	146, 147
6	15:29–58	148, 149, 150
		PROV.
7	16	1, 2
	2 COR.	
8	1	3, 4, 5
9	2	6, 7
10	3	8, 9
11	4	10, 11, 12
12	5	13, 14, 15
13	6	16, 17, 18
14	7	19, 20, 21
15	8	22, 23, 24
16	9	25, 26
17	10	27, 28, 29
18	11: 1–15	30, 31
		ECCL.
19	11:16–33	1, 2, 3
20	12	4, 5, 6
21	13	7, 8, 9
	GAL.	
22	1	10, 11, 12
		SONG
23	2	1, 2, 3
24	3	4, 5
25	4	6, 7, 8
		IS.
26	5	1, 2
27	6	3, 4
	EPH.	
28	1	5, 6
29	2	7, 8
30	3	9, 10

OCTOBER

Date	MORNING EPH.	EVENING IS.
1	4	11, 12, 13
2	5: 1–16	14, 15, 16
3	5:17–33	17, 18, 19
4	6	20, 21, 22
	PHIL.	
5	1	23, 24, 25
6	2	26, 27
7	3	28, 29
8	4	30, 31
	COL.	
9	1	32, 33
10	2	34, 35, 36
11	3	37, 38
12	4	39, 40
	1 THESS.	
13	1	41, 42
14	2	43, 44
15	3	45, 46
16	4	47, 48, 49
17	5	50, 51, 52
	2 THESS.	
18	1	53, 54, 55
19	2	56, 57, 58
20	3	59, 60, 61
	1 TIM.	
21	1	62, 63, 64
22	2	65, 66
		JER.
23	3	1, 2
24	4	3, 4, 5
25	5	6, 7, 8
26	6	9, 10, 11
	2 TIM.	
27	1	12, 13, 14
28	2	15, 16, 17
29	3	18, 19
30	4	20, 21
	TITUS	
31	1	22, 23

NOVEMBER

Date	MORNING TITUS	EVENING JER.
1	2	24, 25, 26
2	3	27, 28, 29
3	PHILEM.	30, 31
	HEB.	
4	1	32, 33
5	2	34, 35, 36
6	3	37, 38, 39
7	4	40, 41, 42
8	5	43, 44, 45
9	6	46, 47
10	7	48, 49
11	8	50
12	9	51, 52
		LAM.
13	10: 1–18	1, 2
14	10:19–39	3, 4, 5
		EZEK.
15	11: 1–19	1, 2
16	11:20–40	3, 4
17	12	5, 6, 7
18	13	8, 9, 10
	JAMES	
19	1	11, 12, 13
20	2	14, 15
21	3	16, 17
22	4	18, 19
23	5	20, 21
	1 PET.	
24	1	22, 23
25	2	24, 25, 26
26	3	27, 28, 29
27	4	30, 31, 32
28	5	33, 34
	2 PET.	
29	1	35, 36
30	2	37, 38, 39

DECEMBER

Date	MORNING 2 PET.	EVENING EZEK.
1	3	40, 41
	1 JOHN	
2	1	42, 43, 44
3	2	45, 46
4	3	47, 48
		DAN.
5	4	1, 2
6	5	3, 4
7	2 JOHN	5, 6, 7
8	3 JOHN	8, 9, 10
9	JUDE	11, 12
	REV.	
10	1	1, 2, 3, 4
11	2	5, 6, 7, 8
12	3	9, 10, 11
13	4	12, 13, 14
14	5	JOEL
		AMOS
15	6	1, 2, 3
16	7	4, 5, 6
17	8	7, 8, 9
18	9	OBAD.
19	10	JON.
		MIC.
20	11	1, 2, 3
21	12	4, 5
22	13	6, 7
23	14	NAH.
24	15	HAB.
25	16	ZEPH.
26	17	HAG.
		ZECH.
27	18	1, 2, 3, 4
28	19	5, 6, 7, 8
29	20	9, 10, 11, 12
30	21	13, 14
31	22	MAL.

HARMONY OF THE GOSPELS

Date	Event	Location	Matthew	Mark	Luke	John	Related References
	Luke's Introduction Pre-fleshly state of Christ Genealogy of Jesus Christ		1:1–17		1:1–4 3:23–38	1:1–18	Acts 1:1 Heb. 1:1–14 Ruth 4:18–22 1 Chr. 1:1–4

BIRTH, INFANCY, AND ADOLESCENCE OF JESUS AND JOHN THE BAPTIST IN 17 EVENTS

Date	Event	Location	Matthew	Mark	Luke	John	Related References
7 B.C.	(1) Announcement of Birth of John	Jerusalem (Temple)			1:5–25		Num. 6:3
7 or 6 B.C.	(2) Announcement of Birth of Jesus to the Virgin	Nazareth			1:26–38		Is. 7:14
c. 5 B.C.	(3) Song of Elizabeth to Mary	⎰Hill Country ⎱of Judea			1:39–45		
	(4) Mary's Song of Praise				1:46–56		Ps. 103:17
5 B.C.	(5) Birth, Infancy, and Purpose for Future of John the Baptist	Judea			1:57–80		Mal. 3:1
	(6) Announcement of Jesus' Birth to Joseph	Nazareth	1:18–25				Is. 9:6, 7
5–4 B.C.	(7) Birth of Jesus Christ	Bethlehem	1:24, 25		2:1–7		Is. 7:14
	(8) Proclamation by the Angels	⎰Near ⎱Bethlehem			2:8–14		1 Tim. 3:16
	(9) The Visit of Homage by Shepherds	Bethlehem			2:15–20		
	(10) Jesus' Circumcision	Bethlehem			2:21		Lev. 12:3
4 B.C.	(11) First Temple Visit with Acknowledgments by Simeon and Anna	Jerusalem			2:22–38		Ex. 13:2 Lev. 12
	(12) Visit of the Wise Men	⎰Jerusalem & ⎱Bethlehem	2:1–12				Num. 24:17
	(13) Flight into Egypt and Massacre of Innocents	⎰Bethlehem, ⎰Jerusalem & ⎱Egypt	2:13–18				Jer. 31:15
	(14) From Egypt to Nazareth with Jesus		2:19–23		2:39		
Afterward A.D. 7–8	(15) Childhood of Jesus	Nazareth			2:40, 51		
	(16) Jesus, 12 Years Old, Visits the Temple	Jerusalem			2:41–50		Deut. 16:1–8
Afterward	(17) 18-Year Account of Jesus' Adolescence and Adulthood	Nazareth			2:51, 52		1 Sam. 2:26

TRUTHS ABOUT JOHN THE BAPTIST

Date	Event	Location	Matthew	Mark	Luke	John	Related References
c. A.D. 25–27	John's Ministry Begins Man and Message His Picture of Jesus His Courage	Judean Wilderness	3:1 3:2–12 3:11, 12 14:4–12	1:1–4 1:2–8 1:7, 8	3:1, 2 3:3–14 3:15–18 3:19, 20	1:19–28 1:26, 27	Mal. 3:1 Is. 40:3 Acts 2:38

BEGINNING OF JESUS' MINISTRY IN 12 EVENTS

Date	Event	Location	Matthew	Mark	Luke	John	Related References
c. A.D. 27	(1) Jesus Baptized	Jordan River	3:13–17	1:9–11	3:21–23	1:29–34	Ps. 2:7
	(2) Jesus Tempted	Wilderness	4:1–11	1:12, 13	4:1–13		Ps. 91:11
	(3) Calls First Disciples	Beyond Jordan				1:35–51	
	(4) The First Miracle	Cana in Galilee				2:1–11	
	(5) First Stay in Capernaum	(Capernaum is "His" city)				2:12	
A.D. 27	(6) First Cleansing of the Temple	Jerusalem				2:13–22	Ps. 69:9
	(7) Received at Jerusalem	Judea				2:23–25	
	(8) Teaches Nicodemus about Second Birth	Judea				3:1–21	Num. 21:8, 9
	(9) Co-Ministry with John	Judea				3:22–30	

Date	Event	Location	Matthew	Mark	Luke	John	Related References
A.D. 27	(10) Leaves for Galilee	Judea	4:12	1:14	4:14	4:1–4	
	(11) Samaritan Woman at Jacob's Well	Samaria				4:5–42	Josh. 24:32
	(12) Returns to Galilee			1:15	4:15	4:43–45	

A.D. 27–29 THE GALILEAN MINISTRY OF JESUS IN 55 EVENTS

Date	Event	Location	Matthew	Mark	Luke	John	Related References
A.D. 27	(1) Healing of the Nobleman's Son	Cana				4:46–54	
	(2) Rejected at Nazareth	Nazareth			4:16–30		Is. 61:1, 2
	(3) Moved to Capernaum	Capernaum	4:13–17				Is. 9:1, 2
	(4) Four Become Fishers of Men	Sea of Galilee	4:18–22	1:16–20	5:1–11		Ps. 33:9
	(5) Demoniac Healed on the Sabbath Day	Capernaum		1:21–28	4:31–37		
c. A.D. 27	(6) Peter's Mother-in-Law Cured, Plus Others	Capernaum	8:14–17	1:29–34	4:38–41		Is. 53:4
	(7) First Preaching Tour of Galilee	Galilee	4:23–25	1:35–39	4:42–44		
	(8) Leper Healed and Response Recorded	Galilee	8:1–4	1:40–45	5:12–16		Lev. 13:49
	(9) Paralytic Healed	Capernaum	9:1–8	2:1–12	5:17–26		Rom. 3:23
	(10) Matthew's Call and Reception Held	Capernaum	9:9–13	2:13–17	5:27–32		Hos. 6:6
A.D. 28	(11) Disciples Defended via a Parable	Capernaum	9:14–17	2:18–22	5:33–39		
	(12) Goes to Jerusalem for Second Passover; Heals Lame Man	Jerusalem				5:1–47	Ex. 20:10
	(13) Plucked Grain Precipitates Sabbath Controversy	En Route to Galilee	12:1–8	2:23–28	6:1–5		Deut. 5:14
	(14) Withered Hand Healed Causes Another Sabbath Controversy	Galilee	12:9–14	3:1–6	6:6–11		
	(15) Multitudes Healed	Sea of Galilee	12:15–21	3:7–12	6:17–19		
	(16) Twelve Apostles Selected After a Night of Prayer	Near Capernaum		3:13–19	6:12–16		
	(17) Sermon on the Mt.	Near Capernaum	5:1—7:29		6:20–49		
	(18) Centurion's Servant Healed	Capernaum	8:5–13		7:1–10		Is. 49:12, 13
	(19) Raises Widow's Son from Dead	Nain			7:11–17		Job 19:25
	(20) Jesus Allays John's Doubts	Galilee	11:2–19		7:18–35		Mal. 3:1
	(21) Woes Upon the Privileged		11:20–30				Gen. 19:24
	(22) A Sinful Woman Anoints Jesus	Simon's House, Capernaum			7:36–50		
	(23) Another Tour of Galilee	Galilee			8:1–3		
	(24) Jesus Accused of Blasphemy	Capernaum	12:22–37	3:20–30	11:14–23		
	(25) Jesus' Answer to a Demand for a Sign	Capernaum	12:38–45		11:24–26, 29–36		
	(26) Mother, Brothers Seek Audience	Capernaum	12:46–50	3:31–35	8:19–21		
	(27) Famous Parables of Sower, Seed, Tares, Mustard Seed, Leaven, Treasure, Pearl, Dragnet, Lamp Told	By Sea of Galilee	13:1–52	4:1–34	8:4–18		Joel 3:13
	(28) Sea Made Serene	Sea of Galilee	8:23–27	4:35–41	8:22–25		
	(29) Gadarene Demoniac Healed	E. Shore of Galilee	8:28–34	5:1–20	8:26–39		
	(30) Jairus' Daughter Raised and Woman with Hemorrhage Healed		9:18–26	5:21–43	8:40–56		
	(31) Two Blind Men's Sight Restored		9:27–31				

Date	Event	Location	Matthew	Mark	Luke	John	Related References
A.D. 28	(32) Mute Demoniac Healed		9:32–34				
	(33) Nazareth's Second Rejection of Christ	Nazareth	13:53–58	6:1–6			
	(34) Twelve Sent Out		9:35—11:1	6:6–13	9:1–6		1 Cor. 9:14
	(35) Fearful Herod Beheads John	Galilee	14:1–12	6:14–29	9:7–9		
Spring A.D. 29	(36) Return of 12, Jesus Withdraws, 5000 Fed	Near Bethsaida	14:13–21	6:30–44	9:10–17	6:1–14	
	(37) Walks on the Water	Sea of Galilee	14:22–33	6:45–52		6:15–21	
	(38) Sick of Gennesaret Healed	Gennesaret	14:34–36	6:53–56			
	(39) Peak of Popularity Passes in Galilee	Capernaum				6:22–71 7:1	Is. 54:13
A.D. 29	(40) Traditions Attacked		15:1–20	7:1–23			Ex. 21:17
	(41) Aborted Retirement in Phoenicia: Syro-Phoenician Healed	Phoenicia	15:21–28	7:24–30			
	(42) Afflicted Healed	Decapolis	15:29–31	7:31–37			
	(43) 4000 Fed	Decapolis	15:32–39	8:1–9			
	(44) Pharisees Increase Attack	Magdala	16:1–4	8:10–13			
	(45) Disciples' Carelessness Condemned; Blind Man Healed		16:5–12	8:14–26			Jer. 5:21
	(46) Peter Confesses Jesus Is the Christ	Near Caesarea Philippi	16:13–20	8:27–30	9:18–21		
	(47) Jesus Foretells His Death	Caesarea Philippi	16:21–26	8:31–37	9:22–25		
	(48) Kingdom Promised		16:27, 28	9:1	9:26, 27		Prov. 24:12
	(49) The Transfiguration	Mountain Unnamed	17:1–13	9:2–13	9:28–36		Is. 42:1
	(50) Epileptic Healed	Mt. of Transfiguration	17:14–21	9:14–29	9:37–42		
	(51) Again Tells of Death, Resurrection	Galilee	17:22, 23	9:30–32	9:43–45		
	(52) Taxes Paid	Capernaum	17:24–27				Ex. 30:11–15
	(53) Disciples Contend About Greatness; Jesus Defines; also Patience, Loyalty, Forgiveness	Capernaum	18:1–35	9:33–50	9:46–62		
	(54) Jesus Rejects Brothers' Advice	Galilee				7:2–9	
c. Sept. A.D. 29	(55) Galilee Departure and Samaritan Rejection		19:1		9:51–56	7:10	

A.D. 29–30   LAST JUDEAN AND PEREAN MINISTRY OF JESUS IN 42 EVENTS

Date	Event	Location	Matthew	Mark	Luke	John	Related References
Oct. A.D. 29	(1) Feast of Tabernacles	Jerusalem				7:2, 11–52	
	(2) Forgiveness of Adulteress	Jerusalem				7:53—8:11	Lev. 20:10
A.D. 29	(3) Christ—the Light of the World	Jerusalem				8:12–20	
	(4) Pharisees Can't Meet the Prophecy Thus Try to Destroy the Prophet	Jerusalem—Temple				8:12–59	Is. 6:9
	(5) Man Born Blind Healed; Following Consequences	Jerusalem				9:1–41	
	(6) Parable of the Good Shepherd	Jerusalem				10:1–21	
	(7) The Service of the Seventy	Probably Judea			10:1–24		
	(8) Lawyer Hears the Story of the Good Samaritan	Judea (?)			10:25–37		
	(9) The Hospitality of Martha and Mary	Bethany			10:38–42		
	(10) Another Lesson on Prayer	Judea (?)			11:1–13		

Date	Event	Location	Matthew	Mark	Luke	John	Related References
A.D. 29	(11) Accused of Connection with Beelzebub				11:14–36		
	(12) Judgment Against Lawyers and Pharisees				11:37–54		Mic. 6:8
	(13) Jesus Deals with Hypocrisy, Covetousness, Worry, and Alertness				12:1–59		Mic. 7:6
	(14) Repent or Perish				13:1–5		
	(15) Barren Fig Tree				13:6–9		
	(16) Crippled Woman Healed on Sabbath				13:10–17		Deut. 5:12–15
	(17) Parables of Mustard Seed and Leaven	{Probably {Perea			13:18–21		
Winter A.D. 29	(18) Feast of Dedication	Jerusalem				10:22–39	Ps. 82:6
	(19) Withdrawal Beyond Jordan					10:40–42	
	(20) Begins Teaching Return to Jerusalem with Special Words About Herod	Perea			13:22–35		Ps. 6:8
	(21) Meal with a Pharisee Ruler Occasions Healing Man with Dropsy; Parables of Ox, Best Places, and Great Supper				14:1–24		
	(22) Demands of Discipleship	Perea			14:25–35		
	(23) Parables of Lost Sheep, Coin, Son				15:1–32		1 Pet. 2:25
	(24) Parables of Unjust Steward, Rich Man and Lazarus				16:1–31		
	(25) Lessons on Service, Faith, Influence				17:1–10		
	(26) Resurrection of Lazarus	{Perea to {Bethany				11:1–44	
	(27) Reaction to It: Withdrawal of Jesus					11:45–54	
A.D. 30	(28) Begins Last Journey to Jerusalem via Samaria & Galilee	{Samaria, {Galilee			17:11		
	(29) Heals Ten Lepers				17:12–19		Lev. 13:45, 46
	(30) Lessons on the Coming Kingdom				17:20–37		Gen. 6—7
	(31) Parables: Persistent Widow, Pharisee and Tax Collector				18:1–14		
	(32) Doctrine on Divorce		19:1–12	10:1–12			Deut. 24:1–4 Gen. 2:23–25
	(33) Jesus Blesses Children: Objections	Perea	19:13–15	10:13–16	18:15–17		Ps. 131:2
	(34) Rich Young Ruler	Perea	19:16–30	10:17–31	18:18–30		Ex. 20:1–17
	(35) Laborers of the 11th Hour		20:1–16				
	(36) Foretells Death and Resurrection	{Near {Jordan	20:17–19	10:32–34	18:31–34		Ps. 22
	(37) Ambition of James and John		20:20–28	10:35–45			
	(38) Blind Bartimaeus Healed	Jericho		10:46–52	18:35–43		
	(39) Interview with Zacchaeus	Jericho			19:1–10		
	(40) Parable: the Minas	Jericho			19:11–27		
	(41) Returns to Home of Mary and Martha	Bethany				{11:55— {12:1	
	(42) Plot to Kill Lazarus	Bethany				12:9–11	

Spring A.D. 30

JESUS' FINAL WEEK OF WORK AT JERUSALEM IN 41 EVENTS

Date	Event	Location	Matthew	Mark	Luke	John	Related References
Sunday	(1) Triumphal Entry	Bethany, Jerusalem, Bethany	21:1–9	11:1–11	19:28–44	12:12–19	Zech. 9:9

Date	Event	Location	Matthew	Mark	Luke	John	Related References
Monday	(2) Fig Tree Cursed and Temple Cleansed	Bethany to Jerusalem	21:10–19	11:12–18	19:45–48		Jer. 7:11
	(3) The Attraction of Sacrifice	Jerusalem				12:20–50	Is. 6:10
Tuesday	(4) Withered Fig Tree Testifies	Bethany to Jerusalem	21:20–22	11:19–26			
	(5) Sanhedrin Challenges Jesus. Answered by Parables: Two Sons, Wicked Vinedressers and Marriage Feast	Jerusalem	21:23— 22:14	11:27— 12:12	20:1–19		Is. 5:1, 2
	(6) Tribute to Caesar	Jerusalem	22:15–22	12:13–17	20:20–26		
	(7) Sadducees Question the Resurrection	Jerusalem	22:23–33	12:18–27	20:27–40		Ex. 3:6
	(8) Pharisees Question Commandments	Jerusalem	22:34–40	12:28–34			
	(9) Jesus and David	Jerusalem	22:41–46	12:35–37	20:41–44		Ps. 110:1
	(10) Jesus' Last Sermon	Jerusalem	23:1–39	12:38–40	20:45–47		
	(11) Widow's Mite	Jerusalem		12:41–44	21:1–4		Lev. 27:30
	(12) Jesus Tells of the Future	Mt. Olives	24:1–51	13:1–37	21:5–36		Dan. 12:1
	(13) Parables: Ten Virgins, Talents. The Day of Judgment	Mt. Olives	25:1–46				Zech. 14:5
	(14) Jesus Tells Date of Crucifixion		26:1–5	14:1, 2	22:1, 2		
	(15) Anointing by Mary at Simon's Feast	Bethany	26:6–13	14:3–9		12:2–8	
	(16) Judas Contracts the Betrayal		26:14–16	14:10, 11	22:3–6		Zech. 11:12
Thursday	(17) Preparation for the Passover	Jerusalem	26:17–19	14:12–16	22:7–13		Ex. 12:14–28
Thursday P.M.	(18) Passover Eaten, Jealousy Rebuked	Jerusalem	26:20	14:17	22:14–16, 24–30		
	(19) Feet Washed	Upper Room				13:1–20	
	(20) Judas Revealed, Defects	Upper Room	26:21–25	14:18–21	22:21–23	13:21–30	Ps. 41:9
	(21) Jesus Warns About Further Desertion; Cries of Loyalty	Upper Room	26:31–35	14:27–31	22:31–38	13:31–38	Zech. 13:7
	(22) Institution of the Lord's Supper	Upper Room	26:26–29	14:22–25	22:17–20		1 Cor. 11:23–34
	(23) Last Speech to the Apostles and Intercessory Prayer	Jerusalem				14:1— 17:26	Ps. 35:19
Thursday-Friday	(24) The Grief of Gethsemane	Mt. Olives	26:30, 36–46	14:26, 32–42	22:39–46	18:1	Ps. 42:6
Friday	(25) Betrayal, Arrest, Desertion	Gethsemane	26:47–56	14:43–52	22:47–53	18:2–12	
	(26) First Examined by Annas	Jerusalem				18:12–14, 19–23	
	(27) Trial by Caiaphas and Council; Following Indignities	Jerusalem	26:57, 59–68	14:53, 55–65	22:54, 63–65	18:24	Lev. 24:16
	(28) Peter's Triple Denial	Jerusalem	26:58, 69–75	14:54, 66–72	22:54–62	18:15–18, 25–27	
	(29) Condemnation by the Council	Jerusalem	27:1	15:1	22:66–71		Ps. 110:1
	(30) Suicide of Judas	Jerusalem	27:3–10				Acts 1:18, 19
	(31) First Appearance Before Pilate	Jerusalem	27:2, 11–14	15:1–5	23:1–7	18:28–38	
	(32) Jesus Before Herod	Jerusalem			23:6–12		
	(33) Second Appearance Before Pilate	Jerusalem	27:15–26	15:6–15	23:13–25	18:39— 19:16	Deut. 21:6–9
	(34) Mockery by Roman Soldiers	Jerusalem	27:27–30	15:16–19			
	(35) Led to Golgotha	Jerusalem	27:31–34	15:20–23	23:26–33	19:16, 17	Ps. 69:21
	(36) 6 Events of First 3 Hours on Cross	Calvary	27:35–44	15:24–32	23:33–43	19:18–27	Ps. 22:18
	(37) Last 3 Hours on Cross	Calvary	27:45–50	15:33–37	23:44–46	19:28–30	Ps. 22:1
	(38) Events Attending Jesus' Death		27:51–56	15:38–41	23:45, 47–49		
Friday-Saturday	(39) Burial of Jesus	Jerusalem	27:57–60	15:42–46	23:50–54	19:31–37	Ex. 12:46
	(40) Tomb Sealed	Jerusalem	27:61–66		23:55, 56		Ex. 20:8–11
	(41) Women Watch	Jerusalem		15:47			

Date	Event	Location	Matthew	Mark	Luke	John	Related References
A.D. 30	**THE RESURRECTION THROUGH THE ASCENSION IN 12 EVENTS**						
Dawn of First Day (Sunday, "Lord's Day")	(1) Women Visit the Tomb	Near Jerusalem	28:1–10	16:1–8	24:1–11		
	(2) Peter and John See the Empty Tomb				24:12	20:1–10	
	(3) Jesus' Appearance to Mary Magdalene	Jerusalem		16:9–11		20:11–18	
	(4) Jesus' Appearance to the Other Women	Jerusalem	28:9, 10				
	(5) Guards' Report of the Resurrection		28:11–15				
Sunday Afternoon	(6) Jesus' Appearance to Two Disciples on Way to Emmaus			16:12, 13	24:13–35		1 Cor. 15:5
Late Sunday	(7) Jesus' Appearance to Ten Disciples Without Thomas	Jerusalem		16:14	24:36–43	20:19–25	
One Week Later	(8) Appearance to Disciples with Thomas	Jerusalem				20:26–31	
During 40 Days until Ascension	(9) Jesus' Appearance to Seven Disciples by Sea of Galilee	Galilee				21:1–25	
	(10) Appearance to 500	Mt. in Galilee					1 Cor. 15:6
	(11) Great Commission		28:16–20	16:15–18	24:44–49		
	(12) The Ascension	Mt. Olivet		16:19, 20	24:50–53		Acts 1:4–11

TEACHINGS AND ILLUSTRATIONS OF CHRIST

Subject	Reference	Subject	Reference	Subject	Reference
Gentleness	Matt. 5:5	Integrity	Luke 16:10	Murder	Matt. 15:19
Giving	Luke 6:38	Intercession	John 17:9	Mysteries	
Gladness	Luke 15:32	Investment	Matt. 6:19, 20	of Heaven	Matt. 13:11
Glorifying God	Matt. 5:16	**Jealousy**	Luke 15:25–30	**Narrow way**	Matt. 7:13, 14
Gluttony	Luke 21:34	John the Baptist	Luke 7:24–28	Neglect	Luke 12:47
God	Matt. 19:17, 26	Jonah	Matt. 12:39–41	Neighbor	Matt. 19:19
Godlessness	John 5:42, 44	Joy	Matt. 25:21	Neutrality	Matt. 12:30
Golden Rule	Matt. 7:12		Luke 15:7, 10	New birth	John 3:3, 5–8
Gospel	Luke 4:18	Judge not	Matt. 7:1, 2	Noah	Luke 17:26, 27
Grace	2 Cor. 12:9	Judgment	Matt. 11:24	**Oath**	Matt. 5:33–37
Greatness	Matt. 5:19	Judgment day	Matt. 25:31–46	Obedience	Matt. 12:50
Grumble	John 6:43	Justice	John 5:30	Offering	Matt. 5:25
Guidance	John 16:13	Justification,		Offerings	Luke 21:3, 4
Hairs numbered	Matt. 10:30	self	Luke 16:15	Opportunity	Matt. 5:25
Hand of God	John 10:27–29	**Killing**	Matt. 5:21, 22	**Parables**	Mark 4:11, 12
Happiness	Matt. 5:12	Kindness	Luke 10:30–35	Paradise	Luke 23:43
	John 13:16, 17	Kingdom	Luke 7:28	Pardoning	Luke 6:37
Harlots	Matt. 21:31		John 18:36	Parents	Matt. 10:21
Harvest	Matt. 9:37, 38	Kiss	Luke 7:45	Patriotism	Matt. 22:21
Hatred	John 15:18, 19	Knowledge	John 8:31, 32	Peace	Mark 9:50
Healing	Matt. 10:7, 8	**Labor**	Matt. 20:1–14	Peacemakers	Matt. 5:9
	Mark 2:17	Laughter	Luke 6:21	Penitence	Luke 18:13
Heart	Matt. 13:19	Law	Luke 16:16	Perception	John 8:43
Heaven	Luke 16:17	Lawsuit	Matt. 5:25, 40	Perfection	Matt. 5:48
	John 3:13	Lawyers	Luke 11:46	Persecution	Matt. 24:9
Hell	Matt. 5:22	Leaven	Matt. 16:6	Perseverance	Matt. 10:22
	Matt. 10:28		Luke 13:20, 21	Pharisaism	Matt. 23:2–33
Helper	John 14:16	Lending	Luke 6:34, 35	Pharisee and	
	John 15:26	Lepers	Matt. 10:7, 8	tax collector	Luke 18:10–14
Helpless	John 6:44	Levite	Luke 10:30–32	Pharisees	Matt. 5:20
Hireling	John 10:11–13	Liars	John 8:44, 45	Philanthropy	Luke 11:41
Holy Spirit	John 14:26	Liberality	Luke 6:30, 38	Physician	Matt. 9:12
Home	Mark 5:19	Liberty	Luke 4:18	Piety	John 1:47
Honesty	Luke 8:15	Life	Matt. 6:25	Pleasing God	John 8:29
	Mark 10:19		John 5:40	Pleasures	Luke 8:14
Honor of men	Matt. 6:2	Light	Luke 11:33	Poison	Mark 16:17, 18
Honor			John 8:12	Poll tax	Matt. 22:19–21
of parents	Matt. 15:3–6	Living water	John 4:10	Polygamy	Matt. 19:8, 9
Hospitality	Luke 14:12–14	Log	Luke 6:41, 42	Poor	Mark 14:7
Humility	John 13:14	Loneliness	John 16:32	Power	Matt. 6:13
	Matt. 11:29	Lord's Supper	Matt. 26:26–29	Prayer	Matt. 7:7–11
Hunger,		Loss of soul	Matt. 16:25, 26		Matt. 6:9–13
spiritual	Luke 6:21	Lost		Preaching	Mark 16:15, 16
	Matt. 5:6	opportunity	Matt. 25:7–12	Procrastination	Matt. 25:3
Hypocrisy	Matt. 6:5	Love	Matt. 22:37–40	Profit and loss	Matt. 16:26
	Luke 6:42	Lukewarmness	Matt. 26:40, 41	Prophets	Matt. 10:41
Ignorance	Matt. 22:29	Lunatic	Matt. 17:14, 15		Matt. 7:15
Immortality	Matt. 25:46	Lust	Mark 4:18, 19	Proselyte	Luke 23:15
	John 11:25, 26	**Magistrates**	Luke 12:11, 58	Protection	Luke 18:3
Impartiality		Mammon	Matt. 6:24	Providence	Matt. 6:25–33
of God	Matt. 5:45	Marriage	Matt. 19:4–6	Prudence	Matt. 10:16–20
Inconsistency	Matt. 7:3–5		Mark 12:25	Punishment	Matt. 21:41
	Luke 6:41, 42	Martyrdom	John 16:1–3	Purity	Matt. 5:8
Indecision	Luke 9:62	Mary's choice	Luke 10:41, 42	**Ransom**	Matt. 20:28
Indifference	Matt. 24:12	Memorial	Matt. 26:13	Reaping	John 4:35–38
Industry	John 4:36	Mercy	Matt. 5:7	Receiving	
Infidelity	John 3:18		Luke 16:24	Christ	Mark 9:37
Influence	Matt. 5:13	Minister	Luke 10:2	Reconciliation	Matt. 5:23, 24
Ingratitude	Luke 17:17, 18	Miracles	Matt. 12:28	Regeneration	Matt. 19:28
Innocence	Matt. 10:16	Money lender,		Rejecting	
Insincerity	Luke 16:15	creditor	Luke 7:41, 42	Christ	John 3:18
Inspiration	Luke 12:12	Moses	Matt. 19:8	Rejoicing	Luke 10:20
Instability	Matt. 7:26, 27	Moses' Law	John 7:19	Release	Luke 4:18
Instruction	John 6:45	Mother	Matt. 10:37	Religion	Mark 7:6–8
Insufficiency	Mark 10:21	Mourn	Matt. 5:4		Matt. 25:34–36

Subject	Reference	Subject	Reference	Subject	Reference
Repentance	Matt. 11:21	Self-sacrifice	Matt. 16:25	Teaching	Matt. 28:19, 20
	Luke 13:28	Serpents	Matt. 23:33		John 13:13–15
Reproof	Matt. 11:21–23		John 3:14	Temperance	Luke 21:34
Resignation	Matt. 26:39	Service	Luke 22:27	Temptations	Matt. 4:1–11
Responsibility	Luke 12:47, 48	Sheep	Luke 15:4–7		Luke 8:13
Rest	Matt. 26:45	Shepherd	John 10:1–18	Thieves	Matt. 6:19
	Matt. 11:28–30	Sickness	Matt. 10:8		John 10:1, 8
Resurrection	John 6:40	Signs	John 4:48	Timidness	Mark 4:40
Retaliation	Matt. 5:39–44		Luke 11:16	Tithes	Luke 18:11, 12
Retribution	Matt. 23:34, 35	Silence	Matt. 17:9	Traditions	Mark 7:9, 13
Reward	Matt. 10:42	Sin	John 8:34	Transgres-	
Riches	Mark 4:19		Matt. 26:28	sions	Matt. 15:2
Righteousness	Matt. 5:6, 20	Sincerity	Matt. 5:13–16	Treasures	Matt. 6:19–21
	John 16:10	Skepticism	John 20:27, 29	Tribulation	Matt. 24:9
Robbers	Luke 10:30	Slaves	Matt. 18:23		John 16:33
	John 10:1		John 15:15	Truth	John 14:6
Robbery	Matt. 23:25	Sleep	Mark 4:26, 27	Unbelievers	Luke 12:46
Sabbath	Matt. 12:5–8		Mark 13:35, 36	Uncharitable-	
Sackcloth	Matt. 11:21	Slothfulness	Matt. 25:26–30	ness	John 7:24
Sacrifice	Matt. 12:7	Son of Man	Luke 9:22	Unchastity	Matt. 5:31, 32
Sacrilege	Matt. 21:13	Sorrow	Matt. 19:22	Uncleanness	Matt. 23:27
Sadducees	Matt. 16:6		John 16:6	Unity	John 17:20, 21
Salt	Matt. 5:13	Soul	Matt. 10:28	Unpardonable	
	Mark 9:50		Luke 12:19, 20	sin	Matt. 12:31, 32
Salvation	Luke 19:19	Soul winners	Matt. 4:19	Vengeance	Matt. 5:39, 40
	John 4:22	Sowing	Mark 4:14	Vine	John 15:1, 4, 5
Samaritan	Luke 10:30–35	Speech	John 8:43	Visions	Matt. 17:9
Sanctification	John 17:17	Spirit	Matt. 26:41	Walks of Life	John 12:35
Satan	Matt. 4:10		Mark 5:8		John 8:12
	Mark 4:15	Statement	Matt. 5:37	War	Matt. 24:26
Scripture	Matt. 21:42	Steadfastness	Matt. 10:22	Watchfulness	Matt. 24:42, 44
	Luke 4:21	Stealing	Matt. 19:18		Luke 12:37–40
Secrecy	Luke 12:2, 3	Steward	Luke 12:42, 43	Wedding	Luke 14:8–10
Security	Luke 6:47, 48		Luke 16:1–8	Widow	Mark 12:43, 44
Seduction	Mark 13:22	Stewardship	Luke 19:13–27	Wine	Luke 5:37–39
Seeking the		Stomach	Matt. 15:17	Wisdom	Luke 21:15
kingdom	Matt. 6:19, 20	Strife	Luke 22:24	Witness	John 8:14
Self-		Stubborn-		Witness, false	Matt. 19:18
condemnation	Matt. 23:29–32	ness	John 5:40	Witnessing	Acts 1:8
	Luke 19:20–24	Stumbling		Wives	Luke 14:20, 26
Self-control	Matt. 5:21	block	Matt. 23:13	Worker	Matt. 10:10
Self-deception	Luke 12:16–21	Submission	Matt. 26:39, 42	Worldliness	Luke 21:34
Self-denial	Matt. 16:24–26	Suffering	Matt. 26:38	Worm	Mark 9:43–48
Self-exaltation	Matt. 23:12	Supper,		Worries	
Self-		The Lord's	Luke 22:14–20	of the world	Matt. 13:22
examination	Matt. 7:3–5	Swearing	Matt. 23:16–22	Worship	Matt. 4:10
Selfishness	Luke 6:32–35	Talents	Matt. 18:24	Yoke	Matt. 11:28, 29
Self-		Taxes	Matt. 22:19–21	Zacchaeus	Luke 19:5
righteousness	Matt. 23:23–27	Tax collectors	Matt. 5:46, 47	Zeal	John 2:17

PROPHECIES OF THE MESSIAH FULFILLED IN JESUS CHRIST

Presented Here in Their Order of Fulfillment

PROPHETIC SCRIPTURE	SUBJECT	FULFILLED
Gen. 3:15 "And I will put enmity between you and the woman, and between your seed and her Seed; He shall bruise your head, and you shall bruise His heel."	**seed of a woman**	**Gal. 4:4** "But when the fullness of the time had come, God sent forth His Son, born of a woman, born under the law,"
Gen. 12:3 "I will bless those who bless you, and I will curse him who curses you; And in you all the families of the earth shall be blessed."	**descendant of Abraham**	**Matt. 1:1** "The book of the genealogy of Jesus Christ, the Son of David, the Son of Abraham;"
Gen. 17:19 "Then God said, 'No, Sarah your wife shall bear you a son, and you shall call his name Isaac; I will establish My covenant with him for an everlasting covenant, *and* with his descendants after him.'"	**descendant of Isaac**	**Luke 3:34** "*the son* of Jacob, *the son* of Isaac, *the son* of Abraham, *the son* of Terah, *the son* of Nahor,"
Num. 24:17 "I see Him, but not now; I behold Him, but not near; a Star shall come out of Jacob; a Scepter shall rise out of Israel, and batter the brow of Moab, and destroy all the sons of tumult."	**descendant of Jacob**	**Matt. 1:2** "Abraham begot Isaac, Isaac begot Jacob, and Jacob begot Judah and his brothers."
Gen. 49:10 "The scepter shall not depart from Judah, nor a lawgiver from between his feet, until Shiloh comes; and to Him *shall be* the obedience of the people."	**from the tribe of Judah**	**Luke 3:33** "*the son* of Amminadab, *the son* of Ram, *the son* of Hezron, *the son* of Perez, *the son* of Judah."
Is. 9:7 "Of the increase of *His* government and peace *there will be* no end, upon the throne of David and over His kingdom, to order it and establish it with judgment and justice from that time forward, even forever. The zeal of the LORD of hosts will perform this."	**heir to the throne of David**	**Luke 1:32, 33** "He will be great, and will be called the Son of the Highest; and the Lord God will give Him the throne of His father David. And He will reign over the house of Jacob forever, and of His kingdom there will be no end."
Ps. 45:6, 7, p. 651; 102:25-27 "Your throne, O God, *is* forever and ever; a scepter of righteousness *is* the scepter of Your kingdom. You love righteousness and hate wickedness; therefore God, Your God, has anointed You with the oil of gladness more than Your companions." "Of old You laid the foundation of the earth, and the heavens *are* the work of Your hands. They will perish, but You will endure; yes, all of them will grow old like a garment; like a cloak You will change them, and they will be changed. But You *are* the same, and Your years will have no end."	**anointed and eternal**	**Heb. 1:8-12** "But to the Son *He says:* 'Your throne, O God, is forever and ever; a scepter of righteousness is the scepter of Your kingdom. You have loved righteousness and hated lawlessness; therefore God, Your God, has anointed You with the oil of gladness more than Your companions.' And: 'You, LORD, in the beginning laid the foundation of the earth, and the heavens are the work of Your hands; they will perish, but You remain; and they will all grow old like a garment; like a cloak You will fold them up, and they will be changed. But You are the same, and Your years will not fail.'"

PROPHETIC SCRIPTURE	SUBJECT	FULFILLED
Mic. 5:2 "But you, Bethlehem, Ephrathah, *though* you are little among the thousands of Judah, *yet* out of you shall come forth to Me the One to be ruler in Israel, whose goings forth *have been* from of old, from everlasting."	born in Bethlehem	*Luke 2:4, 5, 7* "And Joseph also went up from Galilee, out of the city of Nazareth, into Judea, to the city of David, which is called Bethlehem, because he was of the house and lineage of David, to be registered with Mary, his betrothed wife, who was with child. . . . And she brought forth her first-born Son, and wrapped Him in swaddling cloths, and laid Him in a manger, because there was no room for them in the inn."
Dan. 9:25 "Know therefore and understand, *that* from the going forth of the command to restore and build Jerusalem until Messiah the Prince, *there shall be* seven weeks and sixty-two weeks; the street shall be built again, and the wall, even in troublesome times."	time for His birth	*Luke 2:1, 2* "And it came to pass in those days *that* a decree went out from Caesar Augustus that all the world should be registered. This census first took place while Quirinius was governing Syria."
Is. 7:14 "Therefore the Lord Himself will give you a sign: Behold, the virgin shall conceive and bear a Son, and shall call His name Immanuel."	to be born of a virgin	*Luke 1:26, 27, 30, 31* "Now in the sixth month the angel Gabriel was sent by God to a city of Galilee named Nazareth, to a virgin betrothed to a man whose name was Joseph, of the house of David. The virgin's name *was* Mary. . . . Then the angel said to her, 'Do not be afraid, Mary, for you have found favor with God. And behold, you will conceive in your womb and bring forth a Son, and shall call His name JESUS.'"
Jer. 31:15 "Thus says the LORD: 'A voice was heard in Ramah, lamentation *and* bitter weeping, Rachel weeping for her children, refusing to be comforted for her children, because they *are* no more.'"	slaughter of children	*Matt. 2:16–18* "Then Herod, when he saw that he was deceived by the wise men, was exceedingly angry; and he sent forth and put to death all the male children who were in Bethlehem and in all its districts, from two years old and under, according to the time which he had determined from the wise men. Then was fulfilled what was spoken by Jeremiah the prophet, saying: 'A *voice was heard in Ramah, lamentation, weeping, and great mourning, Rachel weeping for her children, refusing to be comforted, because they were no more.*'"
Hos. 11:1 "When Israel *was* a child, I loved him, and out of Egypt I called My son."	flight to Egypt	*Matt. 2:14, 15* "When he arose, he took the young Child and His mother by night and departed for Egypt, and was there until the death of Herod, that it might be fulfilled which was spoken by the Lord through the prophet, saying, '*Out of Egypt I called My Son.*'"
Is. 40:3–5 "The voice of one crying in the wilderness: 'Prepare the way of the LORD; make straight in the desert a highway for our God. Every valley shall be exalted, and every mountain and hill shall be made low; the crooked places shall be made straight, and the rough places smooth; the glory of the LORD shall be revealed, and all flesh shall see *it* together; for the mouth of the LORD has spoken.'"	the way prepared	*Luke 3:3–6* "And he went into all the region around the Jordan, preaching a baptism of repentance for the remission of sins, as it is written in the book of the words of Isaiah the prophet, saying: '*The voice of one crying in the wilderness: "Prepare the way of the LORD, make His paths straight. Every valley shall be filled and every mountain and hill brought low; and the crooked places shall be made straight and the rough ways made smooth; and all flesh shall see the salvation of God."*'"

PROPHETIC SCRIPTURE	SUBJECT	FULFILLED
Mal 3:1 "'Behold, I send My messenger, and he will prepare the way before Me. And the Lord, whom you seek, will suddenly come to His temple, even the messenger of the covenant, in whom you delight. Behold, He is coming,' says the LORD of hosts."	preceded by a forerunner	**Luke 7:24, 27** "When the messengers of John had departed, He began to speak to the multitudes concerning John: 'What did you go out into the wilderness to see? A reed shaken by the wind?. . . This is *he* of whom it is written: *"Behold, I send My messenger before Your face, who will prepare Your way before You."*'"
Mal. 4:5, 6 "Behold I will send you Elijah the prophet before the coming of the great and dreadful day of the LORD. And he will turn the hearts of the fathers to the children, and the hearts of the children to their fathers, lest I come and strike the earth with a curse."	preceded by Elijah	**Matt. 11:13, 14** "For all the prophets and the law prophesied until John. And if you are willing to receive *it*, he is Elijah who is to come."
Ps. 2:7 "I will declare the decree: the LORD has said to Me, "You *are* My Son, today I have begotten You."	declared the Son of God	**Matt. 3:17** "And suddenly a voice *came* from heaven, saying, 'This is My beloved Son, in whom I am well pleased.'"
Is. 9:1, 2 "Nevertheless the gloom *will* not *be* upon her who *is* distressed, as when at first He lightly esteemed the land of Zebulun and the land of Naphtali, and afterward more heavily oppressed *her*, *by* the way of the sea, beyond the Jordan, in Galilee of the Gentiles. The people who walked in darkness have seen a great light; those who dwelt in the land of the shadow of death, upon them a light has shined."	Galilean ministry	**Matt. 4:13–16** "And leaving Nazareth, He came and dwelt in Capernaum, which is by the sea, in the regions of Zebulun and Naphtali, that it might be fulfilled which was spoken by Isaiah the prophet, saying: *The land of Zebulun and the land of Naphtali, the way of the sea, beyond the Jordan, Galilee of the Gentiles: The people who sat in darkness saw a great light, and upon those who sat in the region and shadow of death light has dawned.*'"
Ps. 78:2–4 "I will open my mouth in a parable; I will utter dark sayings of old, which we have heard and known, and our fathers have told us. We will not hide *them* from their children, telling to the generation to come the praises of the LORD, and His strength and His wonderful works that He has done."	speaks in parables	**Matt. 13:34, 35** "All these things Jesus spoke to the multitude in parables; and without a parable He did not speak to them that it might be fulfilled which was spoken by the prophet, saying: *'I will open My mouth in parables; I will utter things which have been kept secret from the foundation of the world.'*"
Deut. 18:15 "The LORD your God will raise up for you a Prophet like me from your midst, from your brethren. Him you shall hear."	a prophet	**Acts 3:20, 22** "And that He may send Jesus Christ, who was preached to you before, . . . For Moses truly said to the fathers, *'The LORD your God will raise up for you a Prophet like me from your brethren. Him you shall hear in all things, whatever He says to you.'*"
Is. 61:1, 2 "The Spirit of the Lord GOD *is* upon Me, because the LORD has anointed Me to preach good tidings to the poor; He has sent Me to heal the brokenhearted, to proclaim liberty to the captives, and the opening of the prison to *those who are* bound; to proclaim the acceptable year of the LORD, and the day of vengeance of our God; to comfort all who mourn."	to bind up the brokenhearted	**Luke 4:18, 19** "*The Spirit of the LORD is upon Me, because He has anointed Me to preach the gospel to the poor. He has sent Me to heal the brokenhearted, to preach deliverance to the captives and recovery of sight to the blind, to set at liberty those who are oppressed, to preach the acceptable year of the LORD.*"
Is. 53:3 "He is despised and rejected by men, a man of sorrows and acquainted with grief. And we hid, as it were, *our* faces from Him; He was despised, and we did not esteem Him."	rejected by His own people, the Jews	**John 1:11** "He came to His own, and His own did not receive Him." **Luke 23:18** "And they all cried out at once, saying, 'Away with this *Man*, and release to us Barabbas'"——

PROPHETIC SCRIPTURE	SUBJECT	FULFILLED
Ps. 110:4 "The LORD has sworn and will not relent, 'You *are* a priest forever according to the order of Melchizedek.'"	priest after order of Melchizedek	**Heb. 5:5, 6** "So also Christ did not glorify Himself to become High Priest, *but it* was He who said to Him: *'You are My Son, today I have begotten You.'* As *He* also *says* in another place: *'You are a priest forever according to the order of Melchizedek.'*"
Zech. 9:9 "Rejoice greatly, O daughter of Zion! Shout, O daughter of Jerusalem! Behold, your King is coming to you; He *is* just and having salvation, lowly and riding on a donkey, a colt, the foal of a donkey."	triumphal entry	**Mark 11:7, 9, 11** "Then they brought the colt to Jesus and threw their garments on it, and He sat on it. . . . Then those who went before and those who followed cried out, saying: 'Hosanna! *Blessed is He who comes in the name of the LORD!'* . . . And Jesus went into Jerusalem and into the temple. So when He had looked around at all things, as the hour was already late, He went out to Bethany with the twelve."
Ps. 8:2 "Out of the mouth of babes and infants You have ordained strength, because of Your enemies, that You may silence the enemy and the avenger."	adored by infants	**Matt. 21:15, 16** "But when the chief priests and scribes saw the wonderful things that He did, and the children crying out in the temple and saying, 'Hosanna to the Son of David!' they were indignant and said to Him, 'Do You hear what these are saying?' And Jesus said to them, 'Yes. Have you never read, *"Out of the mouth of babes and nursing infants You have perfected praise"?*'"
Is. 53:1 "Who has believed our report? And to whom has the arm of the LORD been revealed?"	not believed	**John 12:37, 38** "But although He had done so many signs before them, they did not believe in Him, that the word of Isaiah the prophet might be fulfilled, which he spoke: *'Lord, who has believed our report? And to whom has the arm of the LORD been revealed?'*"
Ps. 41:9 "Even my own familiar friend in whom I trusted, who ate my bread, has lifted up *his* heel against me."	betrayed by a close friend	**Luke 22:47, 48** "And while He was still speaking, behold, a multitude; and he who was called Judas, one of the twelve, went before them and drew near to Jesus to kiss Him. But Jesus said to him, 'Judas, are you betraying the Son of Man with a kiss?'"
Zech. 11:12 "Then I said to them, 'If it is agreeable to you, give *me* my wages; and if not, refrain.' So they weighed out for my wages thirty *pieces* of silver."	betrayed for thirty pieces of silver	**Matt. 26:14, 15** "Then one of the twelve, called Judas Iscariot, went to the chief priests and said, 'What are you willing to give me if I deliver Him to you?' And they counted out to him thirty pieces of silver."
Ps. 35:11 "Fierce witnesses rise up; they ask me *things* that I do not know."	accused by false witnesses	**Mark 14:57, 58** "And some rose up and bore false witness against Him, saying, 'We heard Him say, "I will destroy this temple that *is* made with hands, and within three days I will build another made without hands."'"
Is. 53:7 "He was oppressed and He was afflicted, yet He opened not His mouth; He was led as a lamb to the slaughter, and as a sheep before its shearers is silent, so He opened not His mouth."	silent to accusations	**Mark 15:4, 5** "Then Pilate asked Him again, saying, 'Do You answer nothing? See how many things they testify against You!' But Jesus still answered nothing, so that Pilate marveled."

PROPHETIC SCRIPTURE	SUBJECT	FULFILLED
Is. 50:6 "I gave My back to those who struck *Me*, and My cheeks to those who plucked out the beard; I did not hide My face from shame and spitting."	**spat on and struck**	**Matt. 26:67** "Then they spat in His face and beat Him; and others struck *Him* with the palms of their hands,"
Ps. 35:19 "Let them not rejoice over me who are wrongfully my enemies; nor let them wink with the eye who hate me without a cause."	**hated without reason**	**John 15:24** "If I had not done among them the works which no one else did, they would have no sin; but now they have seen and also hated both Me and My Father. But *this happened* that the word might be fulfilled which is written in their law, 'They hated Me without a cause.'"
Is. 53:5 "But He *was* wounded for our transgressions, *He was* bruised for our iniquities; the chastisement for our peace *was* upon Him, and by His stripes we are healed."	**vicarious sacrifice**	**Rom. 5:6, 8** "For when we were still without strength, in due time Christ died for the ungodly. . . . But God demonstrates His own love toward us, in that while we were still sinners, Christ died for us."
Is. 53:12 "Therefore I will divide Him a portion with the great, and He shall divide the spoil with the strong, because He poured out His soul unto death, and He was numbered with the transgressors, and He bore the sin of many, and made intercession for the transgressors."	**crucified with malefactors**	**Mark 15:27, 28** "With Him they also crucified two robbers, one on His right and the other on His left. So the Scripture was fulfilled which says, 'And He was numbered with the transgressors.'"
Zech. 12:10 "And I will pour on the house of David and on the inhabitants of Jerusalem the Spirit of grace and supplication; then they will look on Me whom they have pierced; they will mourn for Him as one mourns for *his* only *son*, and grieve for Him as one grieves for a firstborn."	**pierced through hands and feet**	**John 20:27** "Then He said to Thomas, 'Reach your finger here, and look at My hands; and reach your hand *here*, and put *it* into My side. Do not be unbelieving, but believing.'"
Ps. 22:7, 8 "All those who see Me laugh Me to scorn; they shoot out the lip, they shake the head, *saying*, 'He trusted in the LORD, let Him rescue Him; let Him deliver Him, since He delights in Him!'"	**sneered and mocked**	**Luke 23:35** "And the people stood looking on. But even the rulers with them sneered, saying, 'He saved others; let Him save Himself if He is the Christ, the chosen of God.'"
Ps. 69:9 "Because zeal for Your house has eaten me up, and the reproaches of those who reproach You have fallen on me."	**was reproached**	**Rom. 15:3,** "For even Christ did not please Himself; but as it is written, 'The reproaches of those who reproached You fell on Me.'"
Ps. 109:4 "In return for my love they are my accusers, but I *give myself to* prayer."	**prayer for His enemies**	**Luke 23:34** "Then Jesus said, 'Father, forgive them, for they do not know what they do.' And they divided His garments and cast lots."
Ps. 22:17, 18 "I can count all My bones. They look *and* stare at Me. They divide My garments among them, and for My clothing they cast lots."	**soldiers gambled for His clothing**	**Matt. 27:35, 36** "Then they crucified Him, and divided His garments, casting lots, that it might be fulfilled which was spoken by the prophet: 'They divided My garments among them, and for My clothing they cast lots.' Sitting down, they kept watch over Him there."
Ps. 22:1 "My God, My God, why have You forsaken Me? *Why are You so* far from helping Me, *and from* the words of My groaning?"	**forsaken by God**	**Matt. 27:46** "And about the ninth hour Jesus cried out with a loud voice, saying, 'Eli, Eli, lama sabachthani?' that is, 'My God, My God, why have You forsaken Me?'"

PROPHETIC SCRIPTURE	SUBJECT	FULFILLED
Ps. 34:20 "He guards all his bones; not one of them is broken."	**no bones broken**	*John 19:32, 33, 36* "Then the soldiers came and broke the legs of the first and of the other who was crucified with Him. But when they came to Jesus and saw that He was already dead, they did not break His legs. . . . For these things were done that the Scripture should be fulfilled, 'Not one of His bones shall be broken.'"
Zech. 12:10 "And I will pour on the house of David and on the inhabitants of Jerusalem the Spirit of grace and supplication; then they will look on Me whom they have pierced; they will mourn for Him as one mourns for *his* only *son*, and grieve for Him as one grieves for a firstborn."	**His side pierced**	*John 19:34* "But one of the soldiers pierced His side with a spear, and immediately blood and water came out."
Is. 53:9 "And they made His grave with the wicked—but with the rich at His death, because He had done no violence, nor *was any* deceit in His mouth."	**buried with the rich**	*Matt. 27:57-60* "Now when evening had come, there came a rich man from Arimathea, named Joseph, who himself had also become a disciple of Jesus. This man went to Pilate and asked for the body of Jesus. Then Pilate commanded the body to be given to him. And when Joseph had taken the body, he wrapped it in a clean linen cloth, and laid it in his new tomb which he had hewn out of the rock; and he rolled a large stone against the door of the tomb, and departed."
Ps. 16:10 "For You will not leave my soul in Sheol, nor will You allow Your Holy One to see corruption." *Ps. 49:15* "But God will redeem my soul from the power of the grave, for He shall receive me. Selah"	**to be resurrected**	*Mark 16:6, 7* "But he said to them, 'Do not be alarmed. You seek Jesus of Nazareth, who was crucified. He is risen! He is not here. See the place where they laid Him. But go and tell His disciples—and Peter—that He is going before you into Galilee; there you will see Him, as He said to you.'"
Ps. 68:18 "You have ascended on high, You have led captivity captive; You have received gifts among men; even *among* the rebellious, that the LORD God might dwell *there*."	**His ascension to God's right hand**	*Mark 16:19* "So then after the Lord had spoken to them, He was received up into heaven, and sat down at the right hand of God." *1 Cor. 15:4* "And that He was buried, and that He rose again the third day according to the Scriptures." *Eph. 4:8* "Therefore He says: 'When He ascended on high, He led captivity captive, and gave gifts to men.'"